Constitutional Law

Aspen Casebook Series

Constitutional Law

Eighth Edition

Geoffrey R. Stone
Edward H. Levi Distinguished Service Professor of Law
University of Chicago Law School

Louis Michael Seidman
Carmack Waterhouse Professor of Constitutional Law
Georgetown University Law Center

Cass R. Sunstein
Felix Frankfurter Professor of Law
Harvard Law School

Mark V. Tushnet
William Nelson Cromwell Professor of Law
Harvard Law School

Pamela S. Karlan
Kenneth & Harle Montgomery Professor of Public Interest Law
Stanford Law School

Wolters Kluwer

Published by Wolters Kluwer in New York.

Wolters Kluwer Legal & Regulatory U.S. serves customers worldwide with CCH, Aspen Publishers, and Kluwer Law International products. (www.WKLegaledu.com)

To contact Customer Service, e-mail customer.service@wolterskluwer.com, call 1-800-234-1660, fax 1-800-901-9075, or mail correspondence to:

Wolters Kluwer
Attn: Order Department
PO Box 990
Frederick, MD 21705

Printed in the United States of America.

1 2 3 4 5 6 7 8 9 0

ISBN 978-1-4548-7667-0

Library of Congress Cataloging-in-Publication Data

Names: Stone, Geoffrey R., author. | Seidman, Louis Michael, author. |
  Sunstein, Cass R., author. | Tushnet, Mark V., 1945- author. | Karlan,
  Pamela S., author.
Title: Constitutional law / Geoffrey R. Stone, Edward H. Levi Distinguished
  Service Professor of Law University of Chicago Law School; Louis Michael
  Seidman, Carmack Waterhouse Professor of Constitutional Law, Georgetown
  University Law Center; Cass R. Sunstein, Felix Frankfurter Professor of
  Law, Harvard Law School; Mark V. Tushnet William Nelson Cromwell Professor
  of Law, Harvard Law School; Pamela S. Karlan, Kenneth & Harle Montgomery
  Professor of Public Interest Law, Stanford Law School.
Description: Eighth edition. | New York : Wolters Kluwer Legal & Regulatory
  U.S., [2017] | Series: Aspen casebook series | Includes index.
Identifiers: LCCN 2017049100 | ISBN 9781454876670
Subjects: LCSH: Constitutional law — United States. | LCGFT: Casebooks.
Classification: LCC KF4550 .C5936 2017 | DDC 342.73 — dc23
LC record available at https://lccn.loc.gov/2017049100

About Wolters Kluwer Legal & Regulatory U.S.

Wolters Kluwer Legal & Regulatory U.S. delivers expert content and solutions in the areas of law, corporate compliance, health compliance, reimbursement, and legal education. Its practical solutions help customers successfully navigate the demands of a changing environment to drive their daily activities, enhance decision quality and inspire confident outcomes.

Serving customers worldwide, its legal and regulatory portfolio includes products under the Aspen Publishers, CCH Incorporated, Kluwer Law International, ftwilliam.com and MediRegs names. They are regarded as exceptional and trusted resources for general legal and practice-specific knowledge, compliance and risk management, dynamic workflow solutions, and expert commentary.

For our families

Summary of Contents

I

The Constitution and the Supreme Court   1

II

Federalism at Work: Congress

and the National Economy   175

VII

Freedom of Expression   1009

VIII

The Constitution and Religion   1431

IX

State Action   1529

Contents

II

Federalism at Work: Congress and the National Economy

III

The Scope of Congress's Powers: Taxing and Spending, War Powers, Individual Rights, and State Autonomy

IV

The Distribution of National Powers   377

V

Equality and the Constitution   465

VI

Implied Fundamental Rights   719

VII

Freedom of Expression   1009

Contents

VIII

The Constitution and Religion   1431

IX

State Action — 1529

Preface to the Eighth Edition

After observing that every new edition of a constitutional law casebook addresses numerous issues that the Supreme Court had not dealt with in detail before — and implicitly observing that issues that once concerned the Court fall off the docket for years — the Preface to the Seventh Edition of this casebook referred to an "American tendency to constitutionalize political controversy" and noted:

> [The] Justices present themselves and the results they reach as above politics. Their interpretive techniques, doctrinal tests, and rhetorical tropes are designed to separate — or, at least to create the appearance of separation — between constitutional analysis and political disputation. A student cannot become proficient in constitutional law without mastering these tools and taking them seriously on their own terms. [Constitutional] law is an insider's game, and the opinions of the Justices establish the rules by which it is played. It follows that teachers must explain these rules, and students must master them.
>
> But no thoughtful student of constitutional law can remain solely an insider. It would be odd indeed if the Court's regular engagement with intensely controversial issues remained altogether uncontaminated by political passions. Even the most casual outside observer cannot help but notice that the Justices often divide according to familiar, if no doubt overly simple, political categories.

Yet, we continued,

> [The] familiar law/politics divide is itself too simple. The bifurcation obscures the different senses in which the terms "law" and "politics" are used. Constitutional law is not ordinary law, and constitutional politics is not ordinary politics. Constitutional law is inevitably embedded in the history and culture of the period in which it is made. Constitutional politics is not about — or at least not just about — partisan division, but also about the deepest questions of political theory.

We continue to offer the perspectives we described then in this Eighth Edition. As before, we present recent developments in constitutional law with what we hope is an appropriate emphasis — taking some developments as perhaps portending substantial change in the universe of constitutional doctrine and others as having more modest effects on doctrine. Examples include the apparent stabilization of doctrine dealing with central features of gay rights (while leaving other issues open, particularly those dealing with transgendered people and with whether and if so how constitutional law does and should deal with accommodating religious and other objectors to antidiscrimination law), and the continuing recasting of freedom of expression in libertarian and corporate-favoring terms. In contrast, after a flurry of interest the Court has stepped back from developing dormant commence clause doctrine, and we have accordingly somewhat reduced our treatment of that area.

The results of the 2016 election have already inserted new issues, or revived old ones, in discussions of constitutional law. For the second time in five presidential elections since 2000, for example, the Electoral College system produced a president who received fewer votes than his principal opponent (although campaign strategies shaped by the Electoral College system undoubtedly affect raw vote total). The first months of the Trump administration have led to reflections upon the relative role of law and norms in stabilizing the U.S. constitutional system, to a degree perhaps not matched since the political turmoil that accompanied Franklin D. Roosevelt's Court-packing proposal in 1937. As of the time we write this Preface, the Supreme Court has barely begun to address these issues, in part because of the actions the Senate took with respect to the nominations of Merrick Garland and Neil Gorsuch to the Supreme Court — actions that, themselves, pushed questions about political norms to the fore.

We live in deeply unsettled times, and the future is even more unknowable than usual. It is at least possible that over the lifetime of this Edition, crucial issues of constitutional stability will take center stage. If that happens, our hope for this Edition is that it gives teachers of constitutional law the raw materials to foster intelligent discussion of a constitutional crisis. Whether it happens or not, teachers will have to decide for themselves how to incorporate discussions of our new and evolving situation into their courses. We have tried to write a book that is provocative but not tendentious, that suggests avenues for discussion but does not insist on a particular resolution.

Near the conclusion of the prior Preface, we wrote, "Our aim for this book is to teach students about both the inside and the outside of constitutional law. [We] have tried to ask questions of our students that, for one reason or another, the Justices have failed to ask of themselves." As before, and now more than ever, "We are guided by the firm conviction that thinking clearly about constitutional law — both what it is and what it might be — is vital for law students and, indeed, for citizens generally."

G.R.S.
L.M.S.
C.R.S.
M.V.T.
P.S.K.

October 2017

Acknowledgments

We owe special thanks to Charles Barzun, who provided detailed and insightful comments on the previous edition. We gratefully acknowledge Derreck Brown, Joshua Davis, Sean Donahue, Jeremy Friedman, Troy Froebe, Katherine Goodman, Eric Holt, Lance Jolley, Ruth Kwon, Katya Lexin, Brian Polovoy, Christy Mallory, Barbara Roth, Zinta Saulkalns, Nancy Selbst, Jacqueline Shapiro, Peter Skagestad, Rebecca Smith, Kathleen Tenoever, Elise Tillinghast, Kathryne Young (and others acknowledged in earlier editions) for their diligent research and editorial assistance; Sandra Leone, and the members of the Georgetown University Law Center Faculty Support Service for their invaluable secretarial assistance.

Excerpts from the following books and articles appear with the kind permission of the copyright holders:

Ackerman, Bruce. Beyond *Carolene Products*. 98 Harvard Law Review 713 (1985). Copyright © 1985 by the Harvard Law Review Association.

Bator, Paul. Congressional Power over the Jurisdiction of the Federal Courts. 27 Villanova Law Review 1030 (1982). Reprinted with permission.

Bernstein, David. Roots of the "Underclass": The Decline of Laissez-Faire Jurisprudence and the Rise of Racist Labor Legislation. 43 American University Law Review 85 (1993). Reprinted with permission.

Bickel, Alexander. The Least Dangerous Branch. Copyright © Yale University Press. Reprinted with permission.

Black, Charles Lund. Structure and Relationship in Constitutional Law (1969). Reprinted with permission of the Trustees of Princeton University.

Bollinger, Lee. Images of a Free Press. Copyright © 1991 University of Chicago Press. Reprinted with permission.

Bollinger, Lee, and Stone, Geoffrey. Eternally Vigilant: Free Speech in the Modern Era. Copyright © 2002. Used with permission of The University of Chicago Press.

Bork, Robert. Neutral Principles and Some First Amendment Problems. 47 Indiana Law Journal 1 (1971). Reprinted with permission.

Carter, Stephen L. Parents, Religion, and Schools: Reflections on *Pierce*, 70 Years Later. 27 Seton Hall Law Review 1194 (1997). Reprinted with permission.

Case, Mary Anne. Of Richard Epstein and Other Radical Feminists. 18 Harvard Journal of Law and Public Policy 369 (1995). Reprinted with permission.

Clark, Lorenne. "Liberalism and Pornography." Originally appearing in In Search of the Feminist Perspective: The Changing Potency of Women (Resources for Feminist Research Special Publication # 5, Toronto, Spring 1975). Reprinted with permission.

Collins, Ronald, and David Skover. The Death of Discourse (1996). Copyright © 1996 by Perseus Books. Reprinted with permission of the authors.

Currie, David. The Constitution in the Supreme Court: Limitations on State Power. 51 University of Chicago Law Review 329 (1983). Reprinted with permission.

_____. The Constitution in the Supreme Court: The Powers of the Federal Courts, 1801-1835. 49 University of Chicago Law Review 646 (1982). Reprinted with permission.

Ely, John Hart. Democracy and Distrust. Copyright © 1980 by the President and Fellows of Harvard College. Reprinted with permission of Harvard University Press.

_____. Flag Desecration: A Case Study in the Roles of Categorization and Balancing in First Amendment Analysis. 88 Harvard Law Review 1482 (1975). Copyright © 1975 by The Harvard Law Review.

_____. The Constitutionality of Reverse Racial Discrimination. 41 University of Chicago Law Review 723 (1974). Reprinted with permission.

_____. The Wages of Crying Wolf: A Comment on Roe v. Wade. Reprinted by permission of The Yale Law Journal Company and William S. Hein Company from The Yale Law Journal Company and William S. Hein Company from The Yale Law Journal, Vol. 82, pages 920-949.

Franklin, Cary. The Anti-Stereotyping Principle in Constitutional Law. 85 N.Y.U.L. Rev. 83, 86-90 (2010). Reprinted with permission of the author.

Garrett, Elizabeth. Institutional Lessons from the 2000 Presidential Election. 29 Florida State University Law Review 975 (2001). Copyright © 2001 by the Florida State University Law Review. Reprinted with permission.

Ginsburg, Ruth. Sexual Equality under the Fourteenth and Equal Rights Amendments. 1979 Washington University Law Quarterly 161. Reprinted with permission of the Washington University Law Quarterly and the author.

Graber, Mark. Old Wine in New Bottles: The Constitutional Status of Unconstitutional Speech. 48 Vanderbilt Law Review 349 (1995). Permission granted by Vanderbilt Law Review.

Heymann, Philip, and Douglas Barzelay. The Forest and the Trees: _Roe v. Wade_ and Its Critics. 53 Boston University Law Review 765 (1973). Reprinted with permission.

Hundt, Reed. The Public's Airwaves: What Does the Public Interest Require of Television Broadcasters? 45 Duke Law Journal 1080 (1996). Reprinted with permission.

Kaczorowski, Robert. The Politics of Judicial Interpretation: The Federal Courts and the Department of Justice and Civil Rights (1985). Reprinted with permission of Oceana Publications.

Kagan, Elena. The Changing Faces of First Amendment Neutrality. 1992 Supreme Court Review 29. Copyright © by The University of Chicago Press. Reprinted with permission of the University of Chicago Press.

Acknowledgments

Karlan, Pamela. Easing the Spring: Strict Scrutiny and Affirmative Action after the Redistricting Cases. 43 William and Mary Law Review 1569 (2000). Copyright © 2000 by the William and Mary Law Review. Reprinted with permission.

_____. Two Section Twos and Two Section Fives: Voting Rights and Remedies after *Flores*. 39 William and Mary Law Review 725 (1998). Copyright © by William and Mary Law Review. Reprinted with permission.

Krieger, Linda. Civil Rights Perestroika: Intergroup Relations after Affirmative Action. 86 California Law Review, 1251, 1264, 1267, 1279, 1283, 1331-32. Copyright © by the California Law Review. By permission of the University of California, Berkeley.

Lawrence, Michael A. Toward a More Coherent Dormant Commerce Clause: A Proposed Unitary Framework. 21 Harvard Journal of Law and Public Policy 395 (1998). Reprinted with permission.

Laycock, Douglas. The Underlying Unity of Separation and Neutrality. 46 Emory Law Journal 49 (1997). Reprinted with permission.

Lempert, Richard, The Force of Irony: On the Morality of Affirmative Action and United Steelworkers v. Weber. 95 Ethics 86 (1984). Copyright © by The University of Chicago Press. Reprinted with permission of the University of Chicago Press.

Marcus, Maeva. Truman and the Steel Seizure Case: The Limits of Presidential Power. Copyright © 1977 by Columbia University Press. Reprinted with permission of the author.

Michelman, Frank. Welfare Rights in a Constitutional Democracy. 1979 Washington University Law Quarterly 659 (1979). Reprinted with permission.

_____. "Formal and Associational Aims in Procedural Due Process" in NOMOS: Due Process (1977). Reprinted with permission of the New York University Press.

Nagel, Thomas. How Useful Is Judicial Review in Free Speech Cases? 69 Cornell Law Review 302 (1984). Reprinted with permission.

Post, Robert. Foreword: Fashioning the Legal Constitution: Culture, Courts, and Law. 117 Harvard Law Review 4 (2003). Copyright © 2003 by The Harvard Law Review Association. Reprinted with permission of The Harvard Law Review Association and the author.

_____. Racist Speech, Democracy, and the First Amendment. 32 William and Mary Law Review 267 (1991). Reprinted with permission.

Powell, John A. As Justice Requires/Permits: The Delimitation of Harmful Speech in a Democratic Society. 16 Journal of Law and Inequality 1261 (1998). Reprinted with permission.

Rapaczynski, Andrzej. From Sovereignty to Process: The Jurisprudence of Federalism after Garcia. 1985 Supreme Court Review 341. Copyright © The University of Chicago Press. Reprinted with permission of the University of Chicago Press.

Robinson, Donald. Slavery in the Structure of American Politics, 1765-1820 (1971). Copyright © 1971. Reprinted with permission.

Rosberg, Gerald. The Protection of Aliens from Discriminatory Treatment by the National Government. 1977 Supreme Court Review 275. Copyright © by The University of Chicago Press. Reprinted with permission of The University of Chicago Press.

Rubenfeld, Jed. The First Amendment's Purpose. 53 Stanford Law Review 767 (2001). Reprinted with permission.

Seidman, Louis Michael. Confusion at the Border: *Cruzan*, "The Right to Die," and the Public/Private Distinction. 1991 The Supreme Court Review 47. Copyright © by The University of Chicago. Reprinted with permission.

Siegan, Bernard. Economic Liberties and the Constitution. Copyright © 1980. Reprinted with permission of the author.

Siegel, Neil S. The Virtue of Judicial Statesmanship. 86 Tex. L. Rev. 959, 1009-13 (2008). Reprinted with permission.

Stevens, John Paul. The Life Span of a Judge-Made Rule. 58 New York University Law Review 1 (1983). Copyright © 1983 by the New York University Law Review. Reprinted with permission.

Stone, Geoffrey. Restrictions of Speech because of Its Content: The Peculiar Case of Subject Matter Restrictions. 46 University of Chicago Law Review 81 (1978). Reprinted with permission.

Strauss, David. Persuasion, Autonomy, and Freedom of Expression. 91 Columbia Law Review 334 (1991). Copyright © 1991 by the Directors of the Columbia Law Review Association, Inc. Reprinted with permission.

_____. Corruption, Equality, and Campaign Finance Reform. 94 Columbia Law Review 1369 (1994). Copyright © 1994 by the Directors of the Columbia Law Review Association. Reprinted with permission.

Sunstein, Cass. Republic.Com. Copyright © 2001 by Princeton University Press. Reprinted with permission.

_____. Homosexuality and the Constitution. 70 Indiana Law Journal 1 (1994). Reprinted with permission.

_____. Democracy and the Problem of Free Speech, Copyright © 1993 by Cass R. Sunstein. Reprinted with permission.

_____. Free Speech Now. 59 University of Chicago Law Review 255 (1992). Reprinted with permission.

Thompson, Judith Jarvis. A Defense of Abortion. 1 Phil. & Pub. Aff. 47, 48-49, 55-59 (1971). Reprinted with permission.

Tribe, Laurence. Constitutional Choices. Copyright © 1985 by the President and Fellows of Harvard College. Reprinted with permission of Harvard University Press.

_____. American Constitutional Law, Second Edition (1988). Reprinted by permission of Foundation Press, New York, New York.

_____. American Constitutional Law, First Edition (1978). Reprinted by permission of Foundation Press, New York, New York.

Editorial Notice

Throughout this book additions to quoted material are indicated by brackets, and deletions are indicated either by brackets or ellipses. Citations and footnotes are sometimes omitted without notice.

The Constitution of
the United States

We the People of the United States, in Order to form a more perfect Union, establish Justice, insure domestic Tranquility, provide for the common defence, promote the general Welfare, and secure the Blessings of Liberty to ourselves and our Posterity, do ordain and establish this Constitution for the United States of America.

ARTICLE I

Section 1. All legislative Powers herein granted shall be vested in a Congress of the United States which shall consist of a Senate and House of Representatives.

Section 2. [1] The House of Representatives shall be composed of Members chosen every second Year by the People of the several States, and the Electors in each State shall have the Qualifications requisite for Electors of the most numerous Branch of the State Legislature.

[2] No Person shall be a Representative who shall not have attained to the Age of twenty five Years, and been seven Years a Citizen of the United States, and who shall not, when elected, be an Inhabitant of that State in which he shall be chosen.

[3] Representatives and direct Taxes shall be apportioned among the several States which may be included within this Union, according to their respective Numbers, which shall be determined by adding to the whole Number of free Persons, including those bound to Service for a Term of Years, and excluding Indians not taxed, three fifths of all other Persons. The actual Enumeration shall be made within three Years after the first Meeting of the Congress of the United States, and within every subsequent Term of ten Years, in such Manner as they shall by Law direct. The Number of Representatives shall not exceed one for every thirty Thousand, but each State shall have at Least One Representative; and until such enumeration shall be made, the State of New Hampshire shall be entitled to chuse three, Massachusetts eight, Rhode Island and Providence Plantations one, Connecticut five, New York six, New Jersey four, Pennsylvania eight, Delaware one, Maryland six, Virginia ten, North Carolina five, South Carolina five, and Georgia three.

[4] When vacancies happen in the Representation from any State, the Executive Authority thereof shall issue Writs of Election to fill such Vacancies.

[5] The House of Representatives shall chuse their Speaker and other Officers; and shall have the sole Power of Impeachment.

Section 3. [1] The Senate of the United States shall be composed of two Senators from each State, chosen by the Legislature thereof, for six Years; and each Senator shall have one Vote.

[2] Immediately after they shall be assembled in Consequence of the first Election, they shall be divided as equally as may be into three Classes. The Seats of the Senators of the first Class shall be vacated at the Expiration of the second Year, of the second Class at the Expiration of the fourth Year, and of the third Class at the Expiration of the sixth Year, so that one third may be chosen every second Year; and if Vacancies happen by Resignation, or otherwise, during the Recess of the Legislature of any State, the Executive thereof may make temporary Appointments until the next Meeting of the Legislature, which shall then fill such Vacancies.

[3] No Person shall be a Senator who shall not have attained to the Age of thirty Years, and been nine Years a Citizen of the United States, and who shall not, when elected, be an Inhabitant of that State for which he shall be chosen.

[4] The Vice President of the United States shall be President of the Senate, but shall have no Vote, unless they be equally divided.

[5] The Senate shall chuse their other Officers, and also a President pro tempore, in the absence of the Vice President, or when he shall exercise the Office of President of the United States.

[6] The Senate shall have the sole Power to try all Impeachments. When sitting for that Purpose, they shall be on Oath or Affirmation. When the President of the United States is tried, the Chief Justice shall preside: And no Person shall be convicted without the Concurrence of two thirds of the Members present.

[7] Judgment in Cases of Impeachment shall not extend further than to removal from Office, and disqualification to hold and enjoy any Office of honor, Trust or Profit under the United States: but the Party convicted shall nevertheless be liable and subject to Indictment, Trial, Judgment and Punishment, according to Law.

Section 4. [1] The Times, Places and Manner of holding Elections for Senators and Representatives, shall be prescribed in each State by the Legislature thereof; but the Congress may at any time by Law make or alter such Regulations, except as to the Place of chusing Senators.

[2] The Congress shall assemble at least once in every Year, and such Meeting shall be on the first Monday in December, unless they shall by Law appoint a different Day.

Section 5. [1] Each House shall be the judge of the Elections, Returns and Qualifications of its own Members, and a Majority of each shall constitute a Quorum to do Business; but a smaller Number may adjourn from day to day, and may be authorized to compel the Attendance of absent Members, in such Manner, and under such Penalties as each House may provide.

[2] Each House may determine the Rules of its Proceedings, punish its Members for disorderly Behavior, and, with the Concurrence of two thirds, expel a Member.

[3] Each House shall keep a Journal of its Proceedings, and from time to time publish the same, excepting such Parts as may in their Judgment require Secrecy;

and the Yeas and Nays of the Members of either House on any question shall, at the Desire of one fifth of those Present, be entered on the Journal.

[4] Neither House, during the Session of Congress, shall, without the Consent of the other, adjourn for more than three days, nor to any other Place than that in which the two Houses shall be sitting.

Section 6. [1] The Senators and Representatives shall receive a Compensation for their Services, to be ascertained by Law, and paid out of the Treasury of the United States. They shall in all Cases, except Treason, Felony and Breach of the Peace, be privileged from Arrest during their Attendance at the Session of their respective Houses, and in going to and returning from the same; and for any Speech or Debate in either House, they shall not be questioned in any other Place.

[2] No Senator or Representative shall, during the Time for which he was elected, be appointed to any civil Office under the Authority of the United States, which shall have been created, or the Emoluments whereof shall have been encreased during such time; and no Person holding any Office under the United States, shall be a Member of either House during his Continuance in Office.

Section 7. [1] All Bills for raising Revenue shall originate in the House of Representatives; but the Senate may propose or concur with Amendments as on other Bills.

[2] Every Bill which shall have passed the House of Representatives and the Senate, shall, before it becomes a Law, be presented to the President of the United States; If he approve he shall sign it, but if not he shall return it, with his Objections to that House in which it shall have originated, who shall enter the Objections at large on their Journal, and proceed to reconsider it. If after such Reconsideration two thirds of that House shall agree to pass the Bill, it shall be sent, together with the Objections, to the other House, by which it shall likewise be reconsidered, and if approved by two thirds of that House, it shall become a Law. But in all such Cases the Votes of both Houses shall be determined by Yeas and Nays, and the Names of the Persons voting for and against the Bill shall be entered on the Journal of each House respectively. If any Bill shall not be returned by the President within ten Days (Sundays excepted) after it shall have been presented to him, the Same shall be a Law, in like Manner as if he had signed it, unless the Congress by their Adjournment prevents its Return, in which Case it shall not be a Law.

[3] Every Order, Resolution, or Vote to Which the Concurrence of the Senate and House of Representatives may be necessary (except on a question of Adjournment) shall be presented to the President of the United States; and before the Same shall take Effect, shall be approved by him, or being disapproved by him, shall be repassed by two thirds of the Senate and House of Representatives, according to the Rules and Limitations prescribed in the Case of a Bill.

Section 8. [1] The Congress shall have Power To lay and collect Taxes, Duties, Imposts and Excises, to pay the Debts and provide for the common Defence and general Welfare of the United States; but all Duties, Imposts and Excises shall be uniform throughout the United States;

[2] To borrow money on the credit of the United States;

[3] To regulate Commerce with foreign Nations, and among the several States, and with the Indian Tribes;

[4] To establish an uniform Rule of Naturalization, and uniform Laws on the subject of Bankruptcies throughout the United States;

[5] To coin Money, regulate the value thereof, and of foreign Coin, and fix the Standard of Weights and Measures;

[6] To provide for the Punishment of counterfeiting the Securities and current Coin of the United States;

[7] To establish Post Offices and post Roads;

[8] To promote the Progress of Science and useful Arts, by securing for limited Times to Authors and Inventors the exclusive Right to their respective Writings and Discoveries;

[9] To constitute Tribunals inferior to the supreme Court;

[10] To define and punish Piracies and Felonies committed on the high Seas, and Offenses against the Law of Nations;

[11] To declare War, grant Letters of Marque and Reprisal, and make Rules concerning Captures on Land and Water;

[12] To raise and support Armies, but no Appropriation of Money to that Use shall be for a longer Term than two Years;

[13] To provide and maintain a Navy;

[14] To make Rules for the Government and Regulation of the land and naval Forces;

[15] To provide for calling forth the Militia to execute the Laws of the Union, suppress Insurrections and repel Invasions;

[16] To provide for organizing, arming, and disciplining the Militia, and for governing such Part of them as may be employed in the Service of the United States, reserving to the States respectively, the Appointment of the Officers, and the Authority of training the Militia according to the discipline prescribed by Congress;

[17] To exercise exclusive Legislation in all Cases whatsoever, over such District (not exceeding ten Miles square) as may, by Cession of particular States, and the Acceptance of Congress, become the Seat of the Government of the United States, and to exercise like Authority over all Places purchased by the Consent of the Legislature of the State in which the Same shall be, for the Erection of Forts, Magazines, Arsenals, dock-Yards, and other needful Buildings; — And

[18] To make all Laws which shall be necessary and proper for carrying into Execution the foregoing Powers, and all other Powers vested by this Constitution in the Government of the United States, or in any Department or Officer thereof.

Section 9. [1] The Migration or Importation of such Persons as any of the States now existing shall think proper to admit, shall not be prohibited by the Congress prior to the Year one thousand eight hundred and eight, but a Tax or duty may be imposed on such Importation, not exceeding ten dollars for each Person.

[2] The privilege of the Writ of Habeas Corpus shall not be suspended, unless when in Cases of Rebellion or Invasion the public Safety may require it.

[3] No Bill of Attainder or ex post facto Law shall be passed.

[4] No Capitation, or other direct, Tax shall be laid, unless in Proportion to the Census or Enumeration herein before directed to be taken.

[5] No Tax or Duty shall be laid on Articles exported from any State.

[6] No Preference shall be given by any Regulation of Commerce or Revenue to the Ports of one State over those of another: nor shall Vessels bound to, or from, one State, be obliged to enter, clear, or pay Duties in another.

[7] No Money shall be drawn from the Treasury, but in Consequence of Appropriations made by Law; and a regular Statement and Account of the

Receipts and Expenditures of all public Money shall be published from time to time.

[8] No Title of Nobility shall be granted by the United States: And no Person holding any Office of Profit or Trust under them, shall, without the Consent of the Congress, accept of any present, Emolument, Office, or Title, of any kind whatever, from any King, Prince, or foreign State.

Section 10. [1] No State shall enter into any Treaty, Alliance, or Confederation; grant Letters of Marque and Reprisal; coin Money; emit Bills of Credit; make any Thing but gold and silver Coin a Tender in Payment of Debts; pass any Bill of Attainder, ex post facto Law, or Law impairing the Obligation of Contracts, or grant any Title of Nobility.

[2] No State shall, without the Consent of the Congress, lay any Imposts or Duties on Imports or Exports, except what may be absolutely necessary for executing its inspection Laws: and the net Produce of all Duties and Imposts, laid by any State on Imports or Exports, shall be for the Use of the Treasury of the United States; and all such Laws shall be subject to the Revision and Controul of the Congress.

[3] No State shall, without the Consent of Congress, lay any Duty of Tonnage, keep Troops, or Ships of War in time of Peace, enter into any Agreement or Compact with another State, or with a foreign Power, or engage in War, unless actually invaded, or in such imminent Danger as will not admit of delay.

ARTICLE II

Section 1. [1] The executive Power shall be vested in a President of the United States of America. He shall hold his Office during the Term of four Years, and, together with the Vice President, chosen for the same Term, be elected, as follows:

[2] Each State shall appoint, in such Manner as the Legislature thereof may direct, a Number of Electors, equal to the whole Number of Senators and Representatives to which the State may be entitled in the Congress: but no Senator or Representative, or Person holding an Office of Trust or Profit under the United States, shall be appointed an Elector.

[3] The Electors shall meet in their respective States, and vote by Ballot for two Persons, of whom one at least shall not be an Inhabitant of the same State with themselves. And they shall make a List of all the Persons voted for, and of the Number of Votes for each; which List they shall sign and certify, and transmit sealed to the Seat of the Government of the United States, directed to the President of the Senate. The President of the Senate shall, in the Presence of the Senate and House of Representatives, open all the Certificates, and the Votes shall then be counted. The Person having the greatest Number of Votes shall be the President, if such Number be a Majority of the whole Number of Electors appointed; and if there be more than one who have such Majority, and have an equal Number of Votes, then the House of Representatives shall immediately chuse by Ballot one of them for President; and if no Person have a Majority, then from the five highest on the List the said House shall in like Manner chuse the President. But in chusing the President, the Votes shall be taken by States, the Representation from each State having one Vote, a quorum for this Purpose shall consist of a Member or Members from two thirds of the States, and a Majority of all the States shall be necessary to a Choice. In every Case, after the Choice of the

President, the Person having the greatest Number of Votes of the Electors shall be the Vice President. But if there should remain two or more who have equal Votes, the Senate shall chuse from them by Ballot the Vice President.

[4] The Congress may determine the Time of chusing the Electors, and the Day on which they shall give their Votes; which Day shall be the same throughout the United States.

[5] No person except a natural born Citizen, or a Citizen of the United States, at the time of the Adoption of this Constitution, shall be eligible to the Office of President; neither shall any Person be eligible to that Office who shall not have attained to the Age of thirty-five Years, and been fourteen Years a Resident within the United States.

[6] In case of the removal of the President from Office, or of his Death, Resignation or Inability to discharge the Powers and Duties of the said Office, the Same shall devolve on the Vice President, and the Congress may by Law provide for the Case of Removal, Death, Resignation or Inability, both of the President and Vice President, declaring what Officer shall then act as President, and such Officer shall act accordingly, until the Disability be removed, or a President shall be elected.

[7] The President shall, at stated Times, receive for his Services, a Compensation, which shall neither be increased nor diminished during the Period for which he shall have been elected, and he shall not receive within that Period any other Emolument from the United States, or any of them.

[8] Before he enter on the Execution of his Office, he shall take the following Oath or Affirmation: "I do solemnly swear (or affirm) that I will faithfully execute the Office of President of the United States, and will to the best of my Ability, preserve, protect and defend the Constitution of the United States."

Section 2. [1] The President shall be Commander in Chief of the Army and Navy of the United States, and of the Militia of the several States, when called into the actual Service of the United States; he may require the Opinion, in writing, of the principal Officer in each of the executive Departments, upon any subject relating to the Duties of their respective Offices, and he shall have Power to grant Reprieves and Pardons for Offenses against the United States, except in Cases of Impeachment.

[2] He shall have Power, by and with the Advice and Consent of the Senate, to make Treaties, provided two thirds of the Senators present concur; and he shall nominate, and by and with the Advice and Consent of the Senate, shall appoint Ambassadors, other public Ministers and Consuls, Judges of the supreme Court, and all other Officers of the United States, whose Appointments are not herein otherwise provided for, and which shall be established by Law: but the Congress may by Law vest the Appointment of such inferior Officers, as they think proper, in the President alone, to the Courts of Law, or in the Heads of Departments.

[3] The President shall have Power to fill up all Vacancies that may happen during the Recess of the Senate, by granting Commissions which shall expire at the End of their next Session.

Section 3. He shall from time to time give to the Congress Information of the State of the Union, and recommend to their Consideration such Measures as he shall judge necessary and expedient; he may, on extraordinary occasions, convene both Houses, or either of them, and in Case of Disagreement between them, with Respect to the time of Adjournment, he may adjourn them to such Time as he shall think proper; he shall receive Ambassadors and other public Ministers;

he shall take Care that the Laws be faithfully executed, and shall Commission all the Officers of the United States.

Section 4. The President, Vice President and all civil Officers of the United States, shall be removed from Office on Impeachment for, and Conviction of, Treason, Bribery, or other high Crimes and Misdemeanors.

ARTICLE III

Section 1. The judicial Power of the United States, shall be vested in one supreme Court, and in such inferior Courts as the Congress may from time to time ordain and establish. The Judges, both of the supreme and inferior Courts, shall hold their Offices during good Behaviour, and shall, at stated Times, receive for their Services, a Compensation, which shall not be diminished during their Continuance in Office.

Section 2. [1] The Judicial Power shall extend to all Cases, in Law and Equity, arising under this Constitution, the Laws of the United States, and Treaties made, or which shall be made, under their Authority; — to all Cases affecting Ambassadors, other public Ministers and Consuls; — to all Cases of admiralty and maritime Jurisdiction; — to Controversies to which the United States shall be a Party; — to Controversies between two or more States; — between a State and Citizens of another State; — between Citizens of different States; — between Citizens of the same State claiming Lands under Grants of different States, and between a State, or the Citizens thereof, and foreign States, Citizens or Subjects.

[2] In all Cases affecting Ambassadors, other public Ministers and Consuls, and those in which a State shall be a Party, the supreme Court shall have original Jurisdiction. In all the other Cases before mentioned, the supreme Court shall have appellate Jurisdiction, both as to Law and Fact, with such Exceptions, and under such Regulations as the Congress shall make.

[3] The trial of all Crimes, except in Cases of Impeachment, shall be by jury; and such Trial shall be held in the State where the said Crimes shall have been committed; but when not committed within any State, the Trial shall be at such Place or Places as the Congress may by Law have directed.

Section 3. [1] Treason against the United States, shall consist only in levying War against them, or in adhering to their Enemies, giving them Aid and Comfort. No person shall be convicted of Treason unless on the Testimony of two Witnesses to the same overt Act, or on Confession in open Court.

[2] The Congress shall have Power to declare the Punishment of Treason, but no Attainder of Treason shall work Corruption of Blood, or Forfeiture except during the Life of the Person attainted.

ARTICLE IV

Section 1. Full Faith and Credit shall be given in each State to the public Acts, Records, and judicial Proceedings of every other State. And the Congress may by general Laws prescribe the Manner in which such Acts, Records and Proceedings shall be proved, and the Effect thereof.

Section 2. [1] The Citizens of each State shall be entitled to all Privileges and Immunities of Citizens in the several States.

[2] A Person charged in any State with Treason, Felony, or other Crime, who shall flee from Justice, and be found in another State, shall on demand of the executive Authority of the State from which he fled, be delivered up, to be removed to the State having Jurisdiction of the Crime.

[3] No Person held to Service or Labour in one State, under the Laws thereof, escaping into another, shall, in Consequence of any Law or Regulation therein, be discharged from such Service or Labour, but shall be delivered up on Claim of the Party to whom such Service or Labour may be due.

Section 3. [1] New States may be admitted by the Congress into this Union; but no new State shall be formed or erected within the Jurisdiction of any other State; nor any State be formed by the Junction of two or more States, or Parts of States, without the Consent of the Legislatures of the States concerned as well as of the Congress.

[2] The Congress shall have Power to dispose of and make all needful Rules and Regulations respecting the Territory or other Property belonging to the United States; and nothing in this Constitution shall be so construed as to Prejudice any Claims of the United States, or of any particular State.

Section 4. The United States shall guarantee to every State in this Union a Republican Form of Government, and shall protect each of them against Invasion; and on Application of the Legislature, or of the Executive (when the Legislature cannot be convened) against domestic Violence.

ARTICLE V

The Congress, whenever two thirds of both Houses shall deem it necessary, shall propose Amendments to this Constitution, or, on the Application of the Legislatures of two thirds of the several States, shall call a Convention for proposing Amendments, which, in either Case, shall be valid to all Intents and Purposes, as part of this Constitution, when ratified by the Legislatures of three fourths of the several States, or by Conventions in three fourths thereof, as the one or the other Mode of Ratification may be proposed by the Congress; Provided that no Amendment which may be made prior to the Year One thousand eight hundred and eight shall in any Manner affect the first and fourth Clauses in the Ninth Section of the first Article; and that no State, without its Consent, shall be deprived of its equal Suffrage in the Senate.

ARTICLE VI

[1] All Debts contracted and Engagements entered into, before the Adoption of this Constitution, shall be as valid against the United States under this Constitution, as under the Confederation.

[2] This Constitution, and the Laws of the United States which shall be made in Pursuance thereof; and all Treaties made, or which shall be made, under the Authority of the United States, shall be the supreme Law of the Land; and the Judges in every State shall be bound thereby, any Thing in the Constitution or Laws of any State to the Contrary notwithstanding.

[3] The Senators and Representatives before mentioned, and the Members of the several State Legislatures, and all executive and judicial Officers, both of the United States and of the several States, shall be bound by Oath or Affirmation, to

support this Constitution; but no religious Test shall ever be required as a Qualification to any Office or public Trust under the United States.

Article VII

The Ratification of the Conventions of nine States shall be sufficient for the Establishment of this Constitution between the States so ratifying the Same.

Done in Convention by the Unanimous Consent of the States present the Seventeenth Day of September in the Year of our Lord one thousand seven hundred and Eighty seven and of the Independence of the United States of America the Twelfth.

ARTICLES IN ADDITION TO, AND AMENDMENT OF, THE CONSTITUTION OF THE UNITED STATES OF AMERICA, PROPOSED BY CONGRESS, AND RATIFIED BY THE LEGISLATURES OF THE SEVERAL STATES, PURSUANT TO THE FIFTH ARTICLE OF THE ORIGINAL CONSTITUTION

Amendment I [1791]

Congress shall make no law respecting an establishment of religion, or prohibiting the free exercise thereof; or abridging the freedom of speech, or of the press; or the right of the people peaceably to assemble, and to petition the Government for a redress of grievances.

Amendment II [1791]

A well regulated Militia, being necessary to the security of a free State, the right of the people to keep and bear Arms, shall not be infringed.

Amendment III [1791]

No Soldier shall, in time of peace be quartered in any house, without the consent of the Owner, nor in time of war, but in a manner to be prescribed by law.

Amendment IV [1791]

The right of the people to be secure in their persons, houses, papers, and effects, against unreasonable searches and seizures, shall not be violated, and no Warrants shall issue, but upon probable cause, supported by Oath or affirmation, and particularly describing the place to be searched, and the persons or things to be seized.

Amendment V [1791]

No person shall be held to answer for a capital, or otherwise infamous crime, unless on a presentment or indictment of a Grand Jury, except in cases arising in the land or naval forces, or in the Militia, when in actual service in time of War or public danger; nor shall any person be subject for the same offence to be twice put in jeopardy of life or limb; nor shall be compelled in any criminal case to be a witness against himself, nor be deprived of life, liberty, or property, without due process of law; nor shall private property be taken for public use, without just compensation.

AMENDMENT VI [1791]

In all criminal prosecutions, the accused shall enjoy the right to a speedy and public trial, by an impartial jury of the State and district wherein the crime shall have been committed, which district shall have been previously ascertained by law, and to be informed of the nature and cause of the accusation; to be confronted with the witnesses against him; to have compulsory process for obtaining witnesses in his favor, and to have the Assistance of Counsel for his defence.

AMENDMENT VII [1791]

In Suits at common law, where the value in controversy shall exceed twenty dollars, the right of trial by jury shall be preserved, and no fact tried by a jury, shall be otherwise re-examined in any Court of the United States, than according to the rules of the common law.

AMENDMENT VIII [1791]

Excessive bail shall not be required, nor excessive fines imposed, nor cruel and unusual punishments inflicted.

AMENDMENT IX [1791]

The enumeration in the Constitution, of certain rights, shall not be construed to deny or disparage others retained by the people.

AMENDMENT X [1791]

The powers not delegated to the United States by the Constitution, nor prohibited by it to the States, are reserved to the States respectively, or to the people.

AMENDMENT XI [1798]

The Judicial power of the United States shall not be construed to extend to any suit in law or equity, commenced or prosecuted against one of the United States by Citizens of another State, or by Citizens or Subjects of any Foreign State.

AMENDMENT XII [1804]

The Electors shall meet in their respective states and vote by ballot for President and Vice-President, one of whom, at least, shall not be an inhabitant of the same state with themselves; they shall name in their ballots the person voted for as President, and in distinct ballots the person voted for as Vice-President, and they shall make distinct lists of all persons voted for as President, and of all persons voted for as Vice-President, and of the number of votes for each, which lists they shall sign and certify, and transmit sealed to the seat of the government of the

United States, directed to the President of the Senate; — The President of the Senate shall, in the presence of the Senate and House of Representatives, open all the certificates and the votes shall then be counted; — The person having the greatest number of votes for President, shall be the President, if such number be a majority of the whole number of Electors appointed; and if no person have such majority, then from the persons having the highest numbers not exceeding three on the list of those voted for as President, the House of Representatives shall choose immediately, by ballot, the President. But in choosing the President, the votes shall be taken by states, the representation from each state having one vote; a quorum for this purpose shall consist of a member or members from two-thirds of the states, and a majority of all the states shall be necessary to a choice. And if the House of Representatives shall not choose a President whenever the right of choice shall devolve upon them, before the fourth day of March next following, then the Vice-President shall act as President, as in the case of the death or other constitutional disability of the President. — The person having the greatest number of votes as Vice-President, shall be the Vice-President, if such number be a majority of the whole number of Electors appointed, and if no person have a majority, then from the two highest numbers on the list, the Senate shall choose the Vice-President; a quorum for the purpose shall consist of two-thirds of the whole number of Senators, and a majority of the whole number shall be necessary to a choice. But no person constitutionally ineligible to the office of President shall be eligible to that of Vice-President of the United States.

Amendment XIII [1865]

Section 1. Neither slavery nor involuntary servitude, except as a punishment for crime whereof the party shall have been duly convicted, shall exist within the United States, or any place subject to their jurisdiction.

Section 2. Congress shall have power to enforce this article by appropriate legislation.

Amendment XIV [1868]

Section 1. All persons born or naturalized in the United States, and subject to the jurisdiction thereof, are citizens of the United States and of the State wherein they reside. No State shall make or enforce any law which shall abridge the privileges or immunities of citizens of the United States; nor shall any State deprive any person of life, liberty, or property, without due process of law; nor deny to any person within its jurisdiction the equal protection of the laws.

Section 2. Representatives shall be apportioned among the several States according to their respective numbers, counting the whole number of persons in each State, excluding Indians not taxed. But when the right to vote at any election for the choice of electors for President and Vice President of the United States, Representatives in Congress, the Executive and Judicial officers of a State, or the members of the Legislature thereof, is denied to any of the male inhabitants of such State, being twenty-one years of age, and citizens of the United States, or in any way abridged, except for participation in rebellion, or other crime, the basis of representation therein shall be reduced in the proportion which the number of such male citizens shall bear to the whole number of male citizens twenty-one years of age in such State.

Section 3. No person shall be a Senator or Representative in Congress, or elector of President and Vice President, or hold any office, civil or military, under the United States, or under any State, who, having previously taken an oath, as a member of Congress, or as an officer of the United States, or as a member of any State legislature, or as an executive or judicial officer of any State, to support the Constitution of the United States, shall have engaged in insurrection or rebellion against the same, or given aid or comfort to the enemies thereof. But Congress may by a vote of two-thirds of each House, remove such disability.

Section 4. The validity of the public debt of the United States, authorized by law, including debts incurred for payment of pensions and bounties for services in suppressing insurrection or rebellion, shall not be questioned. But neither the United States nor any State shall assume or pay any debt or obligation incurred in aid of insurrection or rebellion against the United States, or any claim for the loss of emancipation of any slave; but all such debts, obligations and claims shall be held illegal and void.

Section 5. The Congress shall have power to enforce, by appropriate legislation, the provisions of this article.

AMENDMENT **XV** [1870]

Section 1. The right of citizens of the United States to vote shall not be denied or abridged by the United States or by any State on account of race, color, or previous condition of servitude.

Section 2. The Congress shall have power to enforce this article by appropriate legislation.

AMENDMENT **XVI** [1913]

The Congress shall have power to lay and collect taxes on incomes, from whatever source derived, without apportionment among the several States, and without regard to any census or enumeration.

AMENDMENT **XVII** [1913]

[1] The Senate of the United States shall be composed of two Senators from each State, elected by the people thereof, for six years, and each Senator shall have one vote. The electors in each State shall have the qualifications requisite for electors of the most numerous branch of the State legislatures.

[2] When vacancies happen in the representation of any State in the Senate, the executive authority of such State shall issue writs of election to fill such vacancies: *Provided*, That the legislature of any State may empower the executive thereof to make temporary appointments until the people fill the vacancies by election as the legislature may direct.

[3] This amendment shall not be so construed as to affect the election or term of any Senator chosen before it becomes valid as part of the Constitution.

AMENDMENT **XVIII** [1919]

Section 1. After one year from the ratification of this article the manufacture, sale, or transportation of intoxicating liquors within, the importation thereof into, or the exportation thereof from the United States and all territory subject to the jurisdiction thereof for beverage purposes is hereby prohibited.

Section 2. The Congress and the several States shall have concurrent power to enforce this article by appropriate legislation.

Section 3. This article shall be inoperative unless it shall have been ratified as an amendment to the Constitution by the legislatures of the several States, as provided in the Constitution, within seven years from the date of the submission hereof to the States by the Congress.

Amendment **XIX** [1920]

[1] The right of citizens of the United States to vote shall not be denied or abridged by the United States or by any State on account of sex.

[2] Congress shall have power to enforce this article by appropriate legislation.

Amendment **XX** [1933]

Section 1. The terms of the President and Vice President shall end at noon on the 20th day of January, and the terms of Senators and Representatives at noon on the 3d day of January, of the years in which such terms would have ended if this article had not been ratified; and the terms of their successors shall then begin.

Section 2. The Congress shall assemble at least once in every year, and such meeting shall begin at noon on the 3d day of January, unless they shall by law appoint a different day.

Section 3. If, at the time fixed for the beginning of the term of the President, the President elect shall have died, the Vice President elect shall become President. If a President shall not have been chosen before the time fixed for the beginning of his term, or if the President elect shall have failed to qualify, then the Vice President elect shall act as President until a President shall have qualified; and the Congress may by law provide for the case wherein neither a President elect nor a Vice President elect shall have qualified, declaring who shall then act as President, or the manner in which one who is to act shall be selected, and such person shall act accordingly until a President or Vice President shall have qualified.

Section 4. The Congress may by law provide for the case of the death of any of the persons from whom the House of Representatives may choose a President whenever the right of choice shall have devolved upon them, and for the case of the death of any of the persons from whom the Senate may choose a Vice President whenever the right of choice shall have devolved upon them.

Section 5. Sections 1 and 2 shall take effect on the 15th day of October following the ratification of this article.

Section 6. This article shall be inoperative unless it shall have been ratified as an amendment to the Constitution by the legislatures of three-fourths of the several States within seven years from the date of its submission.

Amendment **XXI** [1933]

Section 1. The eighteenth article of amendment to the Constitution of the United States is hereby repealed.

Section 2. The transportation or importation into any State, Territory, or possession of the United States for delivery or use therein of intoxicating liquors, in violation of the laws thereof, is hereby prohibited.

Section 3. This article shall be inoperative unless it shall have been ratified as an amendment to the Constitution by conventions in the several States, as provided in the Constitution, within seven years from the date of the submission hereof to the States by the Congress.

AMENDMENT **XXII** [1951]

Section 1. No person shall be elected to the office of the President more than twice, and no person who has held the office of President, or acted as President, for more than two years of a term to which some other person was elected President shall be elected to the office of the President more than once. But this Article shall not apply to any person holding the office of President when this Article was proposed by the Congress, and shall not prevent any person who may be holding the office of President, or acting as President, during the term within which the Article becomes operative from holding the office of President or acting as President during the remainder of such term.

Section 2. This article shall be inoperative unless it shall have been ratified as an amendment to the Constitution by the legislatures of three-fourths of the several States within seven years from the date of its submission to the States by the Congress.

AMENDMENT **XXIII** [1961]

Section 1. The District constituting the seat of Government of the United States shall appoint in such manner as the Congress may direct: A number of electors of President and Vice President equal to the whole number of Senators and Representatives in Congress to which the District would be entitled if it were a State, but in no event more than the least populous State; they shall be in addition to those appointed by the States, but they shall be considered, for the purposes of the election of President and Vice President, to be electors appointed by a State; and they shall meet in the District and perform such duties as provided by the twelfth article of amendment.

Section 2. The Congress shall have power to enforce this article by appropriate legislation.

AMENDMENT **XXIV** [1964]

Section 1. The right of citizens of the United States to vote in any primary or other election for President or Vice President, for electors for President or Vice President, or for Senator or Representative in Congress, shall not be denied or abridged by the United States or any State by reason of failure to pay any poll tax or other tax.

Section 2. The Congress shall have power to enforce this article by appropriate legislation.

Amendment XXV [1967]

Section 1. In case of the removal of the President from office or of his death or resignation, the Vice President shall become President.

Section 2. Whenever there is a vacancy in the office of the Vice President, the President shall nominate a Vice President who shall take office upon confirmation by a majority vote of both Houses of Congress.

Section 3. Whenever the President transmits to the President pro tempore of the Senate and the Speaker of the House of Representatives his written declaration that he is unable to discharge the powers and duties of his office, and until he transmits to them a written declaration to the contrary, such powers and duties shall be discharged by the Vice President as Acting President.

Section 4. Whenever the Vice President and a Majority of either the principal officers of the executive departments or of such other body as Congress may by law provide, transmit to the President pro tempore of the Senate and the Speaker of the House of Representatives their written declaration that the President is unable to discharge the powers and duties of his office, the Vice President shall immediately assume the powers and duties of the office as Acting President.

Thereafter, when the President transmits to the President pro tempore of the Senate and the Speaker of the House of Representatives his written declaration that no inability exists, he shall resume the powers and duties of his office unless the Vice President and a majority of either the principal officers of the executive department or of such other body as Congress may by law provide, transmit within four days to the President pro tempore of the Senate and the Speaker of the House of Representatives their written declaration that the President is unable to discharge the powers and duties of his office. Thereupon Congress shall decide the issue, assembling within forty-eight hours for that purpose if not in session. If the Congress, within twenty-one days after receipt of the latter written declaration, or, if Congress is not in session, within twenty-one days after Congress is required to assemble, determines by two-thirds vote of both Houses that the President is unable to discharge the powers and duties of his office, the Vice President shall continue to discharge the same as Acting President; otherwise, the President shall resume the powers and duties of his office.

Amendment XXVI [1971]

Section 1. The right of citizens of the United States, who are eighteen years of age or older, to vote shall not be denied or abridged by the United States or by any State on account of age.

Section 2. The Congress shall have power to enforce this article by appropriate legislation.

Amendment XXVII [1992]

No law varying the Compensation for the services of the Senators and Representatives shall take effect, unless an election of Representatives shall have intervened.

Biographical Notes on Selected U.S. Supreme Court Justices

The brief sketches that follow are designed to offer at least some sense of the background, personality, and intellectual style of the justices who have had the greatest impact on modern constitutional law. Because they are no substitute for serious biography, we have frequently suggested additional sources for further investigation. On less significant justices, see Currie, The Most Insignificant Justice: A Preliminary Inquiry, 50 U. Chi. L. Rev. 466 (1983); Easterbrook, The Most Insignificant Justice: Further Evidence, 50 U. Chi. L. Rev. 481 (1983).

SAMUEL A. ALITO, JR. (1950–): The son of two school teachers (his father went on to become New Jersey's first Director of the Office of Legislative Services), Justice Alito graduated from Princeton and then from Yale Law School where he served as an editor of the Yale Law Journal. He served as an assistant to the United States Solicitor General and Deputy Assistant to the Attorney General before becoming the United States Attorney for the District of New Jersey. He developed the reputation of a tough but fair prosecutor and was known especially for his efforts directed against drug trafficking and organized crime. Before his Supreme Court appointment in 2006, he served for sixteen years as a judge on the United States Court of Appeals for the Third Circuit.

HUGO L. BLACK (1886–1971): In 1937, President Roosevelt chose Hugo Black to fill the first available vacancy on the Court. A southern progressive who had defended the rights of labor organizers and investigated police brutality before coming to Washington, Black served in the U.S. Senate for ten years prior to his appointment. As a senator, he strongly defended New Deal programs, including Roosevelt's "Court-packing" plan. Shortly after his confirmation he became the subject of controversy when it was revealed that he had belonged to the Ku Klux Klan for two years in the 1920s. The controversy subsided after Black, in a dramatic radio address, admitted his prior membership, but added that he had resigned many years before and would comment no further. As a justice, Black was known for his insistence on what he claimed to be literal enforcement of constitutional guarantees, especially the first amendment guarantee of free speech. Although frequently characterized as an "activist" because of his willingness to subject to intensive review legislation that arguably violated express constitutional provisions, Black himself thought that literalism was necessary to confine judicial power. Thus, his insistence that the fourteenth amendment incorporated and made applicable to the states the guarantees of the first eight amendments was premised in part on his belief that any other approach would leave justices free to read their own values into the Constitution. See Adamson v. California, 332 U.S. 46 (1947). Consistent with this view, in cases such as Griswold v. Connecticut, 381 U.S. 479 (1965), Black rejected the notion that the Constitution contained general guarantees of "privacy" or "natural rights" beyond those expressly articulated in the text. See R. Newman, Hugo Black: A Biography (1994); G. Dunne, Hugo Black and the Judicial Revolution (1977).

HARRY A. BLACKMUN (1908–1999): Harry Blackmun was President Nixon's third choice to fill the seat vacated when Abe Fortas resigned in 1970. After failing to secure confirmation of Clement Haynsworth of South Carolina and G. Harrold Carswell of Florida, Nixon announced that the Senate "as it is presently constituted" would not confirm a southerner and turned to Blackmun, a judge on the Eighth Circuit Court of Appeals. A boyhood friend of Chief Justice Burger, Blackmun was quickly dubbed "the Minnesota Twin" by the press. During his early years on the Court, he regularly voted with the chief justice. Later he distanced himself from the Court's conservative bloc and increasingly joined Justices Marshall and Brennan in dissent. Blackmun is best known for his majority opinion in Roe v. Wade, 410 U.S. 113 (1973), upholding the constitutional right of women to decide for themselves whether to have an abortion. It has been suggested that the opinion was influenced by Blackmun's experience before joining the Court as house counsel for the Mayo Clinic, where he frequently advised doctors and defended their right to make medical judgments.

JOSEPH P. BRADLEY (1813–1892): The oldest of eleven children, Joseph Bradley was raised in poverty on a small farm. As a lawyer, he specialized in corporate and commercial law and represented several railroads. A Whig before the Civil War, Bradley was an avid supporter of the Union cause and became identified with the radical wing of the Republican Party in the postwar period. His appointment to the Court by President Grant in 1870 was later the subject of controversy because it made possible the reversal of the Court's earlier decision involving the validity of the Civil War legal tender acts. Compare Hepburn v. Griswold, 75 U.S. (8 Wall.) 603 (1870) with The Legal Tender Cases, 79 U.S. (12 Wall.) 457 (1871). As a justice, Bradley supported the power of Congress to regulate the interstate movement of goods, even if the regulation limited state authority. His dissent in The Slaughter-House Cases, 83 U.S. (16 Wall.) 36 (1873), also showed a willingness to read the newly enacted fourteenth amendment as an important expansion of federal authority. In 1877, Bradley was a last-minute substitute on the electoral commission established to resolve the disputed presidential election of 1876. With the commission deadlocked seven to seven, Bradley cast the deciding vote to make Rutherford B. Hayes the President. See G. White, The American Judicial Tradition ch. 4 (1976); Fairman, Mr. Justice Bradley, in A. Dunham and P. Kurland, Mr. Justice 65–93 (1956).

LOUIS D. BRANDEIS (1856–1941): The son of Jewish immigrants from Bohemia, Louis Brandeis successfully practiced law in Boston for forty years before his nomination to the Court. Although he became wealthy from his practice, Brandeis preferred to live simply and set a ceiling on personal expenditures of one-fifth of his income. Even after his appointment to the Court, he provided financial support for the work of his proteges, one of whom was Felix Frankfurter. He devoted himself to a host of public causes. He defended municipal control of Boston's subway system, opposed monopolistic practices of the New Haven Railroad, arbitrated labor disputes in New York's garment industry, and argued in support of the constitutionality of state maximum hour and minimum wage statutes. His nomination to the Court by President Wilson in 1916 sparked heated opposition, including protests from seven ex-presidents of the American Bar Association. During his long tenure on the Court, Brandeis insisted on respect for jurisdictional and procedural limitations on the Court's power. His distrust of large and powerful institutions, and of dogmatic adherence to the received wisdom, led him to support the constitutional authority of the states to experiment with unconventional social and economic theories. He also frequently dissented from the Court's conservative majority when it blocked efforts of the federal government to intervene in the economy. Some of his most eloquent opinions, however, were written in defense of limits on governmental power when civil liberties were at issue. His famous concurring opinion in Whitney v. California, 274 U.S. 357 (1927), argued for freedom of expression on the ground that "it is hazardous to discourage thought, hope and imagination; that fear breeds repression; that repression breeds hate; that hate menaces stable government; that the path of safety lies in the opportunity to discuss freely supposed grievances and proposed remedies; and that the fitting remedy for evil counsels is good ones." And in Olmstead v. United States, 277 U.S. 438 (1928), Brandeis dissented from the Court's refusal to condemn wiretapping, noting that "[o]ur Government is the potent, the omnipresent teacher. For good or for ill, it teaches the whole people by its example." See L. Paper, Brandeis (1983); M. Urofsky, Louis B. Brandeis and the Progressive Tradition (1981).

WILLIAM J. BRENNAN, JR. (1906–1997): After graduating from Harvard Law School, William Brennan returned to his native Newark, where he joined a prominent law firm and specialized in labor law. As his practice grew, Brennan, a devoted family man, resented the demands it made on his time and accepted an appointment on the New Jersey Superior Court in order to lessen his workload. Brennan attracted attention as an efficient and fair-minded judge and was elevated to the New Jersey Supreme Court in 1952. President Eisenhower appointed him to the Supreme Court in 1956. The appointment was criticized at the time as "political" on the ground that the nomination of a Catholic Democrat on the eve of the 1956 presidential election was intended to win votes. Once on the Court, Justice Brennan firmly established himself as a leader of the "liberal" wing. He authored important opinions in the areas of free expression, criminal procedure, and reapportionment. Often credited with providing critical behind-the-scenes leadership during the Warren Court years, Brennan continued to play a significant role — although more often as a dissenter lamenting what he believed to be the evisceration of Warren Court precedents — as the ideological complexion of the Court shifted in the 1970s and 1980s. Brennan's own spirit is perhaps best captured in his celebration in New York Times v. Sullivan, 376 U.S. 255 (1964), of "our profound national commitment to the principle that debate on public issues should be uninhibited, robust, and wide-open."

STEPHEN G. BREYER (1938–): Prior to his appointment to the Supreme Court, Stephen Breyer had compiled a distinguished record as a legal academic and in all three branches of the federal government. Educated at Oxford and Harvard Law School, he served as law clerk to Justice Arthur Goldberg and in the Justice Department before returning to Harvard to teach. During leaves of absence, he worked for Watergate Special Counsel Archibald Cox and served as chief counsel to the Senate Judiciary Committee. In 1980, President Carter named him to the U.S. Court of Appeals. As chief judge of the First Circuit, Breyer gained a reputation for his ability to forge consensus and to write opinions that were clear, concise, and trenchant. An expert on administrative law and an author of important works about risk assessment, Breyer has most often voted with the Court's "liberal" bloc, although his interest in government regulation of the new technologies has sometimes led him to reject first amendment challenges to such regulation. He is known for his pragmatism, his erudition, and his willingness to rethink old ideas.

WARREN E. BURGER (1907–1995): The son of financially hard-pressed parents, Warren Burger attended college and law school at night while selling life insurance during the day. After graduation, he entered private practice and assisted Harold Stassen in his unsuccessful bid for the Republican presidential nomination in 1948. In 1953, he came to Washington to serve as assistant attorney general for the Civil Division of the Justice Department. While in that post, he attracted public attention by defending the government's dismissal of John F. Peters for disloyalty after Solicitor General Sobeloff refused to argue the case on grounds of conscience. Shortly thereafter President Eisenhower appointed him to the U.S. Court of Appeals for the District of Columbia Circuit. His tenure on that court was marked by sharp clashes with the court's liberal majority, especially over criminal justice issues. In 1969, President Nixon named Burger chief justice to replace Earl Warren. A strong advocate of "strict construction" and a "plain meaning" approach to statutory and constitutional interpretation, Burger firmly identified himself with the Court's conservative wing and often voted to limit Warren Court decisions. But he also authored important opinions upholding the right of trial judges to order busing as a remedy for school segregation, interpreting federal civil rights statutes as imposing an "effects" test for employment discrimination, and upholding the right of the press to remain free of prior restraints in covering criminal trials. Burger wrote for a unanimous Court in United States v. Nixon, 418 U.S. 683 (1974), upholding the subpoena for the Watergate tapes, which a few days later resulted in President Nixon's resignation. The Court's legacy under his leadership is much disputed, with some seeing continuity with the Warren Court years and others claiming that he began a period of substantial retrenchment. See E. Maltz, The Chief Justiceship of Warren Burger, 1969–1989 (2000).

BENJAMIN N. CARDOZO (1870–1938): The son of a Tammany Hall judge who was implicated in the Boss Tweed scandal and resigned, rather than face impeachment, Benjamin Cardozo began his judicial career by narrowly defeating a Tammany candidate for a position on the New York Supreme Court. Shortly thereafter he was appointed to the New York Court of Appeals, where he served for eighteen years, during the last six of which he was chief judge. Cardozo is probably best remembered for his skill as a state common law judge. He was responsible for making the New York Court of Appeals the most respected state court in the country, and his judicial writings and lectures were immensely influential. Upon Justice Holmes's retirement, President Hoover was inundated with requests that Cardozo be elevated to the Supreme Court. But there were already two New Yorkers and one Jew serving on the Court, and Hoover resisted. Only when Justice Stone offered to resign to make way for Cardozo did the President relent. Cardozo was a bachelor who had very few friends and lived for most of his life with his unmarried sister. Called "the hermit philosopher" by some, Cardozo was remembered by others for "the strangely compelling power of [his] reticent, sensitive almost mystical personality." See R. Posner, Cardozo, A Study in Reputation (1990); G. Hellman, Benjamin N. Cardozo (1940).

WILLIAM O. DOUGLAS (1898–1980): Widely regarded as one of the most brilliant, eccentric, and independent persons to serve on the Court, William Douglas sat as an associate justice for thirty-six years, seven months — longer than any other justice. Born in poverty in Minnesota, he spent his early years in Yakima, Washington. Although financially hard pressed, he managed to go east to study law at Columbia Law School, where he taught before joining the Yale faculty in 1929. President Roosevelt named him to the newly created Securities and Exchange Commission in 1934, and Douglas became its chairman in 1937. Roosevelt nominated him to be an associate justice in 1939. Douglas's early opinions gave little hint of the controversy that would surround him in later years. Indeed, Roosevelt came close to choosing him as his running mate in 1944 — a decision that would have made him President on Roosevelt's death a year later. In subsequent years, however, Douglas's controversial statements both on and off the bench, his strong support for unpopular political causes, and his unconventional lifestyle (he was married four times) stirred up a whirlwind of political opposition. Congress twice began impeachment proceedings against him, although neither effort came close to success. A prodigiously rapid worker, Douglas often ridiculed his colleagues for complaining about the Court's workload. By his own account, he once assisted a colleague who had fallen behind in his work by ghostwriting a majority opinion that responded to his own dissent. He often finished his work for the term early and retreated to his nearly inaccessible summer home in Yakima, to which lawyers were forced to trek when emergency matters arose. Critics claimed that his opinions showed the signs of haste; admirers emphasized the forceful, direct manner in which he cut through legal doctrine to reach the core issue in a case. His opinions were marked by a fierce commitment to individual rights and distrust of government power. See B. Murphy, Wild Bill: The Legend and Life of William O. Douglas (2003); W. Douglas, The Court Years 1939–1975 (1980); W. Douglas, Go East Young Man (1974); V. Countryman, Douglas of the Supreme Court (1959).

STEPHEN J. FIELD (1816–1899): In 1863, Congress authorized an additional seat on the Court in part to assure a majority sympathetic to the Union cause in the Civil War. President Lincoln named Stephen Field, a Democrat who had nonetheless staunchly opposed secession, to fill the seat. Field was part of an illustrious family: His brothers included a well-known politician and lawyer, a widely read author, and a famous entrepreneur; he served for the last seven years of his tenure on the Court with his nephew, Justice Brewer; Anita Whitney, the left-wing activist who gained notoriety in Whitney v. California, 274 U.S. 357 (1927), was his niece. Justice Field himself was personally involved in a landmark Supreme Court case. When his personal bodyguard killed former Chief Justice Terry of the California Supreme Court, allegedly while defending Justice Field's life, the ensuing litigation ended in In re Neagle, 135 U.S. 1 (1890). In light of the circumstances surrounding his appointment, it was ironic that, once on the Court, Field tended to defend the South in particular and state sovereignty in general against extension of federal power during the Reconstruction period. In the period before substantive due process secured majority support on the Court, Field sought to provide constitutional protection for business enterprises. His dissenting opinion in The Slaughter-House Cases, 83 U.S. (16 Wall.) 36 (1873), for example, read the fourteenth amendment as providing significant protection to property rights and was an important precursor of Lochner v. New York, 198 U.S. 45 (1905). By the time of his retirement in 1897, Field had surpassed John Marshall's record for length of service. See P. Kens, Justice Stephen Field: Shaping Liberty from the Gold Rush to the Gilded Age (1997); C. Swisher, Stephen J. Field: Craftsman of the Law (1930).

ABE FORTAS (1910–1984): Founder of the Washington law firm Arnold, Fortas, and Porter, Abe Fortas provided behind-the-scenes advice to Democratic politicians for years before his appointment to the Court in 1965. As a young man, Fortas held a series of jobs in the Roosevelt administration, including undersecretary of the interior under Harold Ickes. After entering private practice, Fortas found time to defend victims of McCarthyism and to litigate several important civil rights cases, including Gideon v. Wainwright, 372 U.S. 335 (1963). In 1948, Fortas successfully represented Congressman Lyndon Johnson when his forty-eight-vote victory in the Democratic senatorial primary was challenged. (The election earned Johnson the nickname "Landslide Lyndon.") Fortas became one of Johnson's close friends, and when Justice Goldberg resigned to become United Nations ambassador, Johnson appointed him to the Court. In 1968, when Chief Justice Warren indicated that he intended to retire, Johnson chose Fortas as Warren's successor. The nomination had long-term consequences that neither man could have foreseen. Republicans and conservative Democrats charged Johnson with "cronyism" and ultimately forced him to withdraw the nomination, but not before it was revealed that Fortas had received $15,000 to teach a course at a local university while on the bench. The next year Life magazine revealed that Fortas had accepted and then returned $20,000 from a charitable foundation controlled by the family of an indicted stock manipulator. Although denying any wrongdoing, Fortas resigned from the Court. As a consequence, President Nixon was able to fill two vacancies early in his term, thereby helping to fulfill his campaign promise to "roll back" the Warren Court revolution. See L. Kalman, Abe Fortas: A Biography (1990); B. Murphy, Fortas: The Rise and Ruin of a Supreme Court Justice (1988).

FELIX FRANKFURTER (1882–1965): An immigrant from Austria, Felix Frankfurter grew up in poverty on New York's lower east side. Before his appointment to the Court by President Roosevelt in 1939, he taught at the Harvard Law School, helped found The New Republic, served in a variety of public positions, and provided important, informal advice to Roosevelt in formulating the New Deal. Frankfurter's scholarly writings contributed significantly to understanding of administrative law, labor law, and the relationship between federal and state courts. As a justice, Frankfurter's career was marked by a preoccupation with problems of judicial legitimacy and self-restraint. He frequently clashed with Justices Douglas and Black, also Roosevelt appointees, over the "preferred position" of the first amendment and the incorporation doctrine. His concern over the countermajoritarian aspect of judicial review led him to argue for deference to legislative judgment in such landmark cases as Dennis v. United States, 341 U.S. 494 (1951), and Baker v. Carr, 369 U.S. 186 (1962). See Hirsch, The Enigma of Felix Frankfurter (1981); J. Lash, From the Diaries of Felix Frankfurter (1974); P. Kurland, Felix Frankfurter on the Supreme Court (1970); L. Baker, Felix Frankfurter (1969).

RUTH BADER GINSBURG (1933–): When Ruth Bader Ginsburg graduated from law school, one of her mentors suggested to Justice Felix Frankfurter that he take her on as a law clerk. Despite Ginsburg's brilliant law school record (earned while caring for an infant daughter), Justice Frankfurter told her sponsor that he just was not ready to hire a woman. Thirty-three years after this rebuff, Ginsburg assumed her seat on the Supreme Court. In the intervening years, Ginsburg gained fame as the first tenured woman professor at Columbia Law School; as the director of the Women's Rights Project of the American Civil Liberties Union, where she won many pioneering victories in the legal battle against gender discrimination; and as a judge on the U.S. Court of Appeals for the District of Columbia Circuit. She has been called "the Thurgood Marshall of gender equality law" and is said to be "as responsible as any one person for legal advances that women made under the Equal Protection Clause." A strong defender of abortion rights, she has nonetheless criticized Roe v. Wade for rejecting a narrower approach to the abortion question that might have "served to reduce rather than to fuel controversy." On the bench, she has often sided with her "liberal" colleagues. She authored a strong dissent in Bush v. Gore and wrote for a divided Court that invalidated the Virginia Military Institute's policy excluding women students.

NEIL MCGILL GORSUCH (1967–): After the sudden death of Justice Antonin Scalia in 2016, President Obama nominated Merrick Garland, the well-regarded chief judge of the United States Court of Appeals for the District of Columbia Circuit, to take Justice Scalia's seat. Senate Republicans announced that they would not hold hearings or a vote on the nomination or confirm any other nominee until after the presidential election, and Judge Garland's nomination expired. When Donald Trump assumed office, he quickly nominated Neil Gorsuch to assume the seat, and Gorsuch was confirmed by a 54-45 vote. Gorsuch came to the Court after a distinguished legal career. A classmate of Barack Obama's at Harvard Law School, he also received a Ph.D. from Oxford University, where he wrote a dissertation, opposing the legalization of assisted suicide and euthanasia, that was later published in book form. He then went on to clerk for Justices Kennedy and White on the United States Supreme Court. (When he joined Justice Kennedy on the Court he became the only justice in history to serve with the justice he had clerked for). After a stint in private practice, Gorsuch was appointed to the United States Court of Appeals for the Tenth Circuit by George W. Bush. Gorsuch developed a reputation as a facile writer and a strong conservative. He is especially identified with defense of the right of religious objectors to an exemption from otherwise applicable law and with vigorous judicial review of administrative decisions.

JOHN MARSHALL HARLAN (1833–1911): Although a slaveholder and a member of the southern aristocracy, John Harlan remained loyal to the Union during the Civil War and commanded a regiment of Kentucky volunteers in the Union forces. At a critical moment in the deadlocked Republican convention of 1876, Harlan threw the support of the Kentucky delegation behind Rutherford B. Hayes, who rewarded him a year later with an appointment to the Court. Before his appointment, Harlan opposed the postwar amendments ending slavery and guaranteeing equal rights for blacks. (He opposed Lincoln and supported Democrat John McClellan in the 1864 presidential election.) Once on the Court, however, he advocated a broad reading of these amendments. His famous dissenting opinions in The Civil Rights Cases, 109 U.S. 3 (1883), and Plessy v. Ferguson, 163 U.S. 537 (1896), argued for Congress's power to defend the newly freed slaves from "private" discrimination and against the constitutionality of state-mandated separation of the races. It was in Plessy that Harlan declared that "[o]ur Constitution is color blind" and rightly predicted that "the judgment this day rendered will, in time, prove to be quite as pernicious as the decision . . . in the Dred Scott case." Well known for his distinctive personal style, Harlan often delivered his opinions extemporaneously in the fashion of an old-time Kentucky stump speech. Justice Holmes described him as "the last of the tobacco-spitting judges." See F. Latham, The Great Dissenter: John Marshall Harlan (1970).

JOHN MARSHALL HARLAN (1899–1971): The grandson of the first Justice Harlan, John Harlan was appointed to the Court by President Eisenhower in 1955. Before his appointment, Harlan spent a quarter of a century in practice with a prominent Wall Street law firm, served as chief counsel to the New York State Crime Commission, and sat briefly on the U.S. Court of Appeals for the Second Circuit. On the Court, Justice Harlan became the intellectual leader of the "conservative" wing, often dissenting from "activist" decisions during the stewardship of Chief Justice Warren. He defended the values of federalism and never accepted the incorporation of the bill of rights against the states. Nor was he ever reconciled to the Court's broad reading of the equal protection clause, especially when strict scrutiny was utilized to defend "fundamental" values. There was also a strong libertarian strain in Justice Harlan's opinions, however. His belief in federalism and rejection of "judicial activism" did not prevent him from finding, for example, that the due process clause precluded the states from restricting the use of contraceptives by married couples. He also wrote for the Court in a series of important first amendment decisions, narrowly construing federal statutes prohibiting subversive advocacy and defending the right of a Vietnam War protestor to wear a jacket inscribed with the message "Fuck the Draft." It was in the latter case that Harlan proclaimed that "one man's vulgarity is another's lyric." During his tenure, Harlan was widely respected, even by opponents of his philosophy, for his thoroughness, candor, and civility. Although he often disagreed publicly with Justice Black, they were close friends in private. They were hospitalized together during their final illnesses and died within a short period of each other. See T. Yarbrough, John Marshall Harlan: Great Dissenter of the Warren Court (1992); D. Shapiro, The Evolution of a Judicial Philosophy: Selected Opinions and Papers of Justice John M. Harlan (1969).

OLIVER WENDELL HOLMES, JR. (1841–1935): Oliver Wendell Holmes, the son of a famous poet and essayist, survived three wounds in the

Civil War. He had already enjoyed a distinguished career as a practitioner, author, professor, and justice on the Supreme Judicial Court of Massachusetts before his appointment to the Supreme Court by President Roosevelt in 1902. Holmes, then sixty-two years old, seemed to be at the close of his career. A life-long Republican, he was expected to be a loyal supporter of the President on the bench. Few could have anticipated that he would serve on the Court for twenty-nine years, that his tenure would be marked by a fierce independence, and that he would exercise virtually unparalleled influence over modern constitutional theory. Holmes is perhaps best remembered for his formulation of the "clear and present danger test" for subversive advocacy and his rejection of substantive due process as a limitation on state social and economic legislation. His judicial philosophy was marked by skepticism, particularism, and pragmatism. He doubted that general propositions decided particular cases or that broad value judgments could be objectively defended. He thought that the law was necessarily unconcerned with the thought processes of those it regulated, and that it had no independent existence apart from what people did in response to what judges said. For twenty-five years, he walked daily the two and one-half miles from his home to the Court, never missing a session. He finally retired at ninety years of age and died two days before his ninety-fourth birthday. See A. Alschuler, Law without Values: The Life, Work and Legacy of Justice Holmes (2000); G. White, Justice Oliver Wendell Holmes: Law and the Inner Self (1993); M. Howe, Justice Oliver Wendell Holmes: The Proving Years (1963); M. Howe, Justice Oliver Wendell Holmes: The Shaping Years (1957).

CHARLES EVANS HUGHES (1862–1948): After defeating William Randolph Hearst for the governorship of New York, Charles Evans Hughes served as governor for one term and part of another until 1910, when President Taft appointed him to the Court. In 1916, Hughes resigned to run for the presidency on the Republican and Progressive tickets against Woodrow Wilson. On election eve, he went to bed thinking that he was President, but when the final returns were counted, he had lost by a scant twenty-three electoral votes. Hughes returned to New York law practice until President Harding appointed him secretary of state. In 1930, President Hoover returned Hughes to the Court, this time as chief justice. Hughes served as chief justice during the tumultuous eleven-year period when the Court blocked much of President Roosevelt's New Deal, then survived a direct attack on its independence, and finally reconciled itself to the fundamental changes wrought by Roosevelt's program. Throughout this period, Hughes occupied a centrist position. Although closely identified with the conservative New York bar, he often joined the liberals on the Court who dissented from invalidation of social and economic legislation. But he also defended the institutional independence of the Court when it was attacked by President Roosevelt. At a crucial point in the "Court-packing" controversy, Hughes sent a letter to Senator Wheeler arguing that the Court was current in its work, and that the addition of new justices would create serious inefficiencies. Upon his retirement in 1941, Justice Frankfurter likened his leadership ability to that of "Toscanini lead[ing] an orchestra." See M. Pusey, Charles Evans Hughes (1951).

ROBERT H. JACKSON (1892–1954): A skillful advocate and brilliant legal stylist, Robert Jackson rose quickly in the early Roosevelt administration, eventually becoming one of President Roosevelt's closest advisors. After serving as counsel to the Internal Revenue Bureau, where he won a $750,000 judgment against former Treasury Secretary Andrew W. Mellon, Jackson served successively as assistant attorney general, solicitor general, and attorney general. President Roosevelt named him to the Supreme Court in 1941 to fill the seat vacated by Justice Stone when Stone was appointed chief justice. Jackson is perhaps best remembered for his graceful prose and his subtle and original efforts to articulate a coherent theory of separation of powers in his opinions in such cases as Youngstown Sheet & Tube Co. v. Sawyer, 342 U.S. 579 (1952), and Korematsu v. United States, 323 U.S. 214 (1944). In 1945, while still on the Court, Jackson served as the chief U.S. prosecutor at the Nuremberg war crimes trial. This exposure to German fascism may have influenced Jackson's subsequent approach to constitutional interpretation. Many of his later first amendment opinions, for example, were preoccupied with the attempt to draw a bright line between protected freedom of conscience and unprotected speech that threatened the public peace and order. Jackson's willingness to permit government regulation of subversive or abusive advocacy in cases such as Dennis v. United States, 341 U.S. 494 (1951), and Terminiello v. Chicago, 337 U.S. 1 (1949), brought him into sharp conflict with Justices Black and Douglas — conflict that was exacerbated by deteriorating personal relationships. When Chief Justice Stone died, it was reported that several justices threatened to resign if Jackson was elevated to the chief justiceship. Jackson never became chief justice, but remained on the Court until his death in 1954. See E. Gerhart, America's Advocate: Robert H. Jackson (1958); G. White, The American Judicial Tradition ch. 11 (1976).

ELENA KAGAN (1960–): Named to the Supreme Court by Barack Obama in 2010, Elena Kagan is the first person nominated to the Court without judicial experience in almost forty years. After graduating magna cum laude from Harvard Law School, she clerked for Justice Thurgood Marshall, who nicknamed her "shorty" because of her 5'3" height. She then embarked on a distinguished academic career, first at the University of Chicago Law School and then at Harvard Law School, where she eventually became the first woman dean. For four years she served President Clinton as Associate White House Counsel, Deputy Assistant to the President for Domestic Policy, and Deputy Director of the Domestic Policy Council. In 2009, President Obama named her Solicitor General of the United States. Kagan is known for her powerful intellect, effective writing style, and puckish sense of humor.

ANTHONY M. KENNEDY (1936–): President Reagan's effort to fill the seat vacated by the retirement of Justice Powell, who was widely viewed as a "swing vote" on a number of important issues, sparked an extraordinary controversy about the future direction of the Supreme Court. His first nominee, Robert Bork, was defeated on the Senate floor after a long and bitter debate that pitted "originalists" against those who would treat the Constitution as incorporating values not directly derived from the text. His second nominee, Douglas Ginsburg, was forced to withdraw from consideration after it was revealed that he had used marijuana. In the wake of these events, the Senate greeted with relief the nomination of Anthony Kennedy, a relatively colorless and nonideological conservative. After graduating from Harvard Law School in 1961, Kennedy worked as a lawyer and lobbyist in California until his appointment to the Ninth Circuit by President Ford in 1975. Since joining the Supreme Court, he has most often voted with the "conservative" bloc. He criticized his colleagues for "trivializing constitutional adjudication" by engaging in a "jurisprudence of minutiae" in its enforcement of the establishment clause and for moving "from 'separate but equal' to 'unequal but benign'" in upholding an affirmative action plan. However, he joined some of his liberal colleagues when he twice cast the deciding vote to uphold the first amendment right of protestors to burn the American flag and disappointed some of his conservative supporters when he coauthored a joint opinion with Justices Souter and O'Connor declining to overrule Roe v. Wade and wrote for the Court to invalidate state-sponsored prayers at public school events. He is best known for a series of opinions supporting the constitutional rights of gay men and lesbians, culminating in Obergefell v. Hodges, 135 S. Ct. 2584 (2015), which invalidated prohibitions on same-sex marriage.

JOHN MARSHALL (1755–1835): A century and a half after his death, John Marshall remains perhaps the most important single figure in American constitutional history. Born in a log cabin on the Virginia frontier, he served in the Continental Army during the Revolutionary War. After only the briefest formal instruction, he began the practice of law, specializing in the defense of Virginians against British creditors. Before entering public life, Marshall himself was constantly hounded by creditors. He wrote his five-volume biography of George Washington in an unsuccessful effort to raise money to pay off his debts. In 1799, Marshall entered the House of Representatives, and the following year he became secretary of state in the Adams administration. During his brief tenure, he signed and sealed, but failed to deliver, the famous commission naming William Marbury justice of the peace for the District of Columbia. In 1800, Adams appointed Marshall chief justice after John Jay, the Court's first chief justice, declined reappointment to the position. Marshall served for thirty-four years, participated in more than one thousand decisions, and wrote over five hundred opinions. He is best remembered for establishing the Court's power to declare congressional statutes unconstitutional in Marbury v. Madison, 5 U.S. (1 Cranch) 137 (1803), although his contemporaries found the portion of Marbury asserting judicial control over presidential appointees much more controversial. But in some ways his refusal to invalidate a statute enacted pursuant to Congress's powers in McCulloch v. Maryland, 17 U.S. (4 Wheat.) 316 (1819), and his willingness to strike down state statutes interfering with federal powers or individual rights in such cases as McCulloch, Gibbons v. Ogden, 22 U.S. (9 Wheat.) 1 (1824), and Fletcher v. Peck, 10 U.S. (6 Cranch) 87 (1810), were even more influential on modern constitutional theory. In 1807, Marshall presided over the treason trial of former Vice President Aaron Burr. In the course of that trial, he signed the famous subpoena directing President Jefferson to produce various documents relevant to the trial — a precedent much cited over a century and a half later when Richard Nixon asserted "executive privilege" to resist a judicial subpoena. See L. Baker, John Marshall: A Life in the Law (1974); A. Beveridge, The Life of John Marshall (1916).

THURGOOD MARSHALL (1908–1993): The son of a primary school teacher and a club steward, Thurgood Marshall became the first African American to serve on the Court when he was appointed by President Johnson in 1967. But Marshall had already made an enduring mark on American legal history decades before his judicial career began. After graduating first in his class from Howard Law School, Marshall began his long involvement with the National Association for the Advancement of Colored People. For two decades, he traveled across the country coordinating the NAACP's attack on segregation in housing, employment, voting, public accommodations, and, especially, education. His most famous victory during this period came in Brown v. Board of Education, 347 U.S. 483 (1954), where he successfully argued that segregated public education violated the equal protection clause. In 1961, President Kennedy nominated him to serve on the U.S. Court of Appeals for the Second Circuit. Although southern senators blocked his confirmation for a year, he finally assumed his seat, where he served until 1965, when President Johnson appointed him solicitor general. As a justice, Marshall was known primarily for his unstinting defense of racial and other minorities, his liberal interpretation of free speech and press guarantees, his "multi-tiered" theory of equal protection analysis, and his fervent opposition to capital punishment. See J. Williams, Thurgood Marshall: An American Revolutionary (1998); M. Tushnet, Making Constitutional Law: Thurgood Marshall and the Supreme Court 1961–1991 (1997); M. Tushnet, Making Civil Rights Law: Thurgood Marshall and the Supreme Court, 1931–1961 (1994).

JAMES C. McREYNOLDS (1862–1946): Although remembered today primarily as one of the "four horsemen of reaction" who helped block Franklin Roosevelt's New Deal, James McReynolds first came to public attention as a vigorous "trust buster" in the Theodore Roosevelt and Wilson administrations. In the year that he served as Wilson's attorney general, he angered many members of Congress and of the administration with his arrogance and ill-temper. President Wilson named him to the Court in 1914 largely to quiet the controversy. His judicial career was marked by an unyielding commitment to strict constructionism and conservative principles. His personal manner continued to alienate many of his colleagues. After The Gold Clause Cases were decided in 1935, he proclaimed, "Shame and humiliation are on us now. Moral and financial chaos may confidently be expected." Chief Justice Taft remarked that McReynolds "has a continual grouch" and "seems to delight in making others uncomfortable." Widely accused of anti-Semitism, McReynolds conspicuously failed to sign the letter of affection and regret drafted by his brethren on Justice Brandeis's retirement from the Court.

SANDRA DAY O'CONNOR (1930–): The first woman ever to serve on the Court, Sandra Day O'Connor was appointed by President Reagan in 1981. O'Connor was a classmate of Justice Rehnquist at the Stanford Law School, where she was an editor of the Stanford Law Review. Despite her outstanding academic achievements, O'Connor found it difficult to locate a job on graduation. When she applied to the firm in which future Attorney General William French Smith was a partner, she was offered the position of secretary. After briefly serving as deputy county attorney for San Mateo County in California, she worked as a civilian attorney for the army while her husband served his tour of duty. She then spent eight years as a mother, homemaker, and volunteer while her three children grew up. When she resumed her legal career, she became an assistant attorney general in Arizona. In 1970, she was elected to the Arizona senate and eventually became majority leader. She then served on the Superior Court for Maricopa County and the Arizona Court of Appeals. Perhaps more often than any other justice in the Court's history, Justice O'Connor cast the deciding vote in important cases. She showed a preference for a balancing approach to constitutional law and case-by-case particularism — a stance that created conflict with Justice Scalia, who favored a rule-based approach. She initially urged her colleagues to reconsider the Court's analysis of the abortion question in Roe v. Wade, but later surprised many by coauthoring an important opinion preserving Roe's central holding at a time when many thought it would be overruled. She wrote for a five-to-four majority to permit universities to utilize affirmative action programs to help achieve racial diversity and authored the majority opinion holding that the executive could not indefinitely hold "enemy combatants" without providing a procedure under which they could challenge their detention. Widely respected for her incisive and informed questioning at oral argument, O'Connor was known for her deference to the political branches of government, for her defense of federalism, and for her original approach to the problem of church-state relations. See S. O'Connor, Lazy B: Growing up on a Cattle Ranch in the American Southwest (2002); Comment, The Emerging Jurisprudence of Justice O'Connor, 52 U. Chi. L. Rev. 389 (1985).

LEWIS F. POWELL, JR. (1907–1998): Following his graduation from Harvard Law School, Lewis Powell returned to his native Virginia, where he joined one of Richmond's most prestigious law firms. As president of the Richmond school board during a period of intense controversy concerning school desegregation, Powell gained a reputation as a racial moderate. Despite intense pressure from those advocating "massive resistance," he insisted on keeping the schools open. Powell was elected president of the American Bar Association in 1964. In that capacity, he worked to establish a legal services program within the Office of Economic Opportunity and spoke out against civil disobedience and "parental permissiveness." In 1971, President Nixon fulfilled his promise to name a southerner to the Court by selecting Powell to fill the vacancy created by the resignation of Justice Black. A few years after his appointment, Powell seemed to speak for the South in his concurring opinion in Keyes v. School District, 413 U.S. 189 (1973), in which he argued that there was no significant legal distinction between northern and southern school segregation. Over time, Powell gained the reputation as an ad hoc "balancer," often casting the critical "swing vote" in important decisions. In Regents of the University of California v. Bakke, 438 U.S. 265 (1978), Trimble v. Gordon, 430 U.S. 762 (1977), and Branzburg v. Hayes, 408 U.S. 665 (1972), for example, he controlled the disposition even though he was the only justice adopting his particular view of affirmative action, the rights of nonmarital children, and press rights, respectively. See J. Jeffries, Justice Lewis F. Powell, Jr. (1994).

WILLIAM H. REHNQUIST (1924–2005): After graduating from Stanford Law School, William Rehnquist came to Washington in 1952 to clerk for Associate Justice Robert Jackson. During his clerkship, he wrote a controversial memorandum for Justice Jackson supporting the constitutionality of "separate but equal" education for blacks. When the memorandum surfaced years later during Rehnquist's confirmation hearings, he explained that it represented Jackson's views and not his own. Following his clerkship, Rehnquist moved to Phoenix, Arizona, where he became involved in Republican politics. A strong supporter of Barry Goldwater, Rehnquist headed the Justice Department's Office of Legal Counsel in the Nixon administration. President Nixon named him to the Court in 1971, and President Reagan named him chief justice in 1986. Chief Justice Rehnquist was known for his commitment to judicial restraint and majoritarianism. His opinions in the areas of equal protection, due process, and free speech consistently reflected a narrow construction of constitutional rights. For example, he would have limited strict scrutiny under the equal protection clause to cases involving racial discrimination. Unlike conservative justices of an earlier era, however, Rehnquist maintained the same deferential stance when reviewing state legislation arguably interfering with private markets and the free flow of commerce. See, e.g., his opinion for the Court in Posadas de Puerto Rico Associates v. Tourism Co. of Puerto Rico, 478 U.S. 328 (1986), and his dissenting opinion in Kassel v. Consolidated Freightways Corp., 450 U.S. 662 (1981). Nonetheless, Rehnquist supported judicial intervention to protect the prerogatives of the states from federal interference and to place constitutional limits on affirmative action programs arguably discriminating in favor of racial minorities. See Shapiro, Mr. Justice Rehnquist: A Preliminary View, 90 Harv. L. Rev. 293 (1976).

JOHN G. ROBERTS, JR. (1955–): Originally nominated by President George W. Bush to replace Justice O'Connor, John Roberts was renominated for the position of Chief Justice of the United States following the death of Chief Justice Rehnquist. Upon his confirmation in 2005, he became the third youngest chief justice in American history and the first justice to replace the justice for whom he had clerked. After graduating magna cum laude from Harvard Law School, Roberts served as a special assistant to the Attorney General, Associate Counsel to the President, and the Principal Deputy Solicitor General. He is one of the most experienced and successful Supreme Court advocates ever to have been appointed to the Court. While in government service, he argued thirty-nine cases before the Supreme Court, winning twenty-five of them. Upon leaving government, he became head of the appellate practice of a major Washington law firm, in which capacity he argued fourteen additional cases before the Court. In 2003, he became a judge on the United States Court of Appeals for the District of Columbia Circuit. Since becoming chief justice, he has spoken repeatedly in favor of having the Court decide cases narrowly and uniting behind a single majority opinion. He angered and disappointed many conservatives when he cast the decisive vote in National Federation of Independent Business v. Sebelius, 132 S. Ct. 2566 (2012) to uphold the "individual mandate" in the Affordable Care Act.

ANTONIN SCALIA (1936–2016): The son of an Italian immigrant, Antonin Scalia was the first Italian American to be appointed to the Supreme Court. A former law professor and assistant attorney general, he earned a reputation as an intelligent, hardworking, and dedicated conservative while serving as a judge on the U.S. Court of Appeals for the District of Columbia Circuit. When elevated to the Supreme Court, Justice Scalia became a hero for many conservatives, although his unwillingness to compromise and sharply worded opinions limited his ability to assemble majorities on the Couort. He was known for his spirited defense of originalism and opposition to constitutional balancing tests. This posture most often led him to "conservative" outcomes, especially with regard to gay rights, abortion, affirmative action, and gun rights. The same posture occasionally led him to vote with the Court's "liberals," however, especially on free speech and search and seizure questions. In a concurring opinion concerning the status of "enemy combatants," he went further than the majority by insisting that the Constitution did not grant the President authority to hold

American citizens without trial. Some commentators considered him the Court's most accomplished stylist, while others decried the effect of his sharply worded opinions on civility in constitutional discourse.

SONIA SOTOMAYOR (1954–): Justice Sotomayor is the daughter of a factory worker with a third grade education who died when she was nine and a nurse who raised her as a single mother. She grew up in a public housing project in the South Bronx. After graduating valedictorian of her high school class, she enrolled at Princeton, where she graduated summa cum laude and Yale Law School, where she was an editor of the Yale Law Journal. She served as a prosecutor and in private practice until she was appointed to the United States District Court by George H.W. Bush. In 1995, she issued a ruling that effectively ended the Major League Baseball strike, a decision that, according to a reporter for the Philadelphia Inquirer, caused her to join "the ranks of Joe DiMaggio, Willie Mays, Jackie Robinson, and Ted Williams." In 1998, President Bill Clinton appointed her to the United States Court of Appeals for the Second Circuit, where she served as the first Latina on that court. Nominated by Barack Obama, she joined the Supreme Court in 2009. Since her elevation, Justice Sotomayor has generally voted with the Court's liberal wing. She has become known for her probing questions at oral argument and her mastery of the record in complex cases. See Sonia Sotomayor, *My Beloved World* (2013).

DAVID HACKETT SOUTER (1939–): Prior to his nomination to the Supreme Court by the first President Bush, David Souter was a virtual unknown. In his long career as a justice on the New Hampshire Supreme Court, a judge on the New Hampshire trial court, and New Hampshire's attorney general, he seldom had occasion to express his views on contentious constitutional issues such as abortion and affirmative action. Indeed, some critics suggested that President Bush, mindful of the searing controversy surrounding the nomination of Judge Bork, selected Souter principally because he lacked a "paper trail." But although Souter had little experience in constitutional adjudication, he came to the Court with solid intellectual credentials. A Rhodes Scholar and graduate of the Harvard Law School, he was praised by liberals and conservatives alike for his intelligence and fair-mindedness. The counsel for the New Hampshire State Democratic Party and president of the New Hampshire Bar Association characterized him as "an enormous intellectual" and "about 135 pounds — and about 120 pounds of brain." Before his appointment, Justice Souter lived by himself in a ramshackle New Hampshire farmhouse laden with stacks of books. Friends said that he liked to work seven days a week, taking time out to hike and listen to classical music. As a justice, Souter was known for careful, lawyerlike opinions and his moderate, nonideological stance toward controversial constitutional issues.

JOHN PAUL STEVENS (1920–): A graduate of Northwestern Law School, John Paul Stevens clerked for Justice Wiley B. Rutledge before joining a Chicago law firm specializing in antitrust work. He taught part-time at the University of Chicago and Northwestern Law Schools until his appointment to the Seventh Circuit Court of Appeals in 1970. Although a registered Republican, Justice Stevens was never active in partisan politics. President Ford elevated him to the Supreme Court in 1975. Stevens was known for his independence and an unwillingness to be bound by rigid formulas. He rejected the position that equal protection analysis can be reduced to various "tiers" of review, for example, arguing that various factors must be weighed under the same standard in every case to ensure that the state has met its obligation to govern impartially. And in free speech cases Stevens staked out his own theory that fits comfortably within neither the traditional "liberal" nor the traditional "conservative" ideology. See, e.g., Smith v. United States, 431 U.S. 291 (1977); Young v. American Mini Theatres, 427 U.S. 50 (1976).

POTTER STEWART (1915–1985): Son of the Republican mayor of Cincinnati, Potter Stewart became active in Ohio Republican politics at an early age. He was twice elected to the city council and served one term as vice mayor before President Eisenhower appointed him to the Sixth Circuit Court of Appeals in 1954. In 1958, Eisenhower elevated him to the Supreme Court, where he served until his retirement in 1981. Although his political background was conservative, Stewart occupied a centrist position on the Court. He frequently voted with the liberal justices on first amendment issues (an orientation perhaps influenced by his experience as editor of a student newspaper while at Yale), but with conservative justices on equal protection issues. On many questions, his position simply could not be predicted in advance, and he had little difficulty in changing his mind about views he had expressed in earlier opinions. Perhaps his most famous opinion was a concurrence in Jacobellis v. Ohio, 378 U.S. 184 (1964), in which he said of "hard core" pornography, "I shall not today attempt further to define the kinds of material I understand to be embraced within that shorthand description; and perhaps I could never succeed in intelligibly doing so. But I know it when I see it, and the motion picture involved in this case is not that." Although sometimes ridiculed, this statement in some ways summarized Stewart's judicial philosophy, which tended to be particularistic, intuitive, and pragmatic.

HARLAN FISKE STONE (1872–1946): For twenty-five years, Harlan Fiske Stone practiced law with a Wall Street law firm and served as a professor and the dean of Columbia Law School. In 1924, President Coolidge appointed Stone, his old friend and classmate, to head a Department of Justice demoralized by the Teapot Dome scandal. A year later Coolidge appointed Stone to the Court. Although a Republican and moderate conservative, Stone sided with the wing of the Court willing to uphold New Deal programs during the great controversy that engulfed the Court in the early 1930s. In 1941, President Roosevelt elevated Stone to chief justice, an appointment that Archibald MacLeish called "the perfect word spoken at the perfect moment." Justice Stone's footnote 4 in United States v. Carolene Products, 304 U.S. 144 (1938), is doubtless the most famous footnote in constitutional law and has formed the basis of much of modern constitutional theory. During his twenty-one years on the bench, Stone occupied every seat from junior associate justice to senior associate justice to chief justice He died "with his boots on" — stricken while reading a dissenting opinion from the bench in 1946. See A. Mason, Harlan Fiske Stone: A Pillar of the Law (1956); G. White, The American Judicial Tradition ch. 10 (1976); Dunham, Mr. Chief Justice Stone, in A. Dunham and P. Kurland, Mr. Justice 229–251 (1956).

JOSEPH STORY (1779–1845): Joseph Story was only thirty-two years old and had had no judicial experience when James Madison appointed him to the Court in 1811. Although a Republican, Story had strong nationalist sympathies and sided with John Marshall throughout much of his judicial career. His opinion in Martin v. Hunter's Lessee, 14 U.S. (1 Wheat.) 304 (1816), established the finality of the Court's constitutional authority against the states. His nationalist inclinations were also reflected in Swift v. Tyson, 41 U.S. (16 Pet.) 1 (1842), which upheld the power of federal courts to create a national commercial law. As a circuit justice, Story was said to absorb "jurisdiction as a sponge took up water," and some claimed that, "if a bucket of water were brought into his court with a corn cob floating in it, he would at once extend the admiralty jurisdiction of the United States over it." A serious scholar, Story was elected to the Harvard Board of Overseers and played a key role in the founding of Harvard Law School. His Commentaries on the Constitution, published in 1833, was a classic of its time. On Marshall's death in 1835, Story hoped to be nominated chief justice, but Andrew Jackson, who had called him "the most dangerous man in America," named Roger Taney instead. Story was frequently in dissent during the nine years he sat on the Taney Court. See, e.g., Charles River Bridge v. Warren Bridge, 36 U.S. (11 Pet.) 420 (1837). Frustrated by the direction of the Court, which he saw as undermining the Marshall Court's conception of the Constitution, he planned to resign in 1845, but fell ill and died before he could complete his unfinished business. See G. Dunne, Justice Joseph Story and the Rise of the Supreme Court (1970); K. Neumyer, Supreme Court Justice Joseph Story: Statesman of the Old Republic (1984).

GEORGE SUTHERLAND (1862–1942): A friend and close advisor to President Harding, George Sutherland was appointed to the Court in 1922. Before his appointment, he served in the U.S. Senate for twelve years, where he developed a reputation as an authority on constitutional questions and a conservative who nonetheless occasionally supported progressive causes. While on the Court, he was the intellectual leader of the conservative wing. He strongly objected to what he considered the evisceration of the contract clause and vigorously opposed the constitutionality of minimum wage laws. See Home Building & Loan Association v. Blaisdell, 290 U.S. 398 (1934); Adkins v. Children's Hospital, 261 U.S. 525 (1923). But his concern for the rights of individuals and broad reading of the due process clause also led him to write for the majority in Powell v. Alabama, 287 U.S. 45 (1932), which reversed the conviction of the "Scottsboro Boys" and began the process of applying constitutionally based rules of criminal procedure to the states. See H. Arkes, The Return of George Sutherland: Restoring Jurisprudence of Natural Rights (1994); J. Paschal, Mr. Justice Sutherland: A Man against the State (1951).

WILLIAM HOWARD TAFT (1857–1930): The only person to serve as both President and chief justice, William Howard Taft's career was marked by genial conservatism and a commitment to the institutional independence of each branch of the federal government. Taft served as secretary of war in Theodore Roosevelt's administration and became one of Roosevelt's closest advisors. With support from Roosevelt, he was elected President in 1908. Soon after his inauguration, however, he and Roosevelt split, and he lost his bid for reelection in 1912, when Roosevelt splintered the Republican vote by running as a third-party candidate. After leaving the presidency, Taft taught constitutional law at Yale University and served for a year as president of the American Bar Association. Along with several other former ABA presidents, Taft fought to block Louis Brandeis's nomination to the Court in 1916. President Harding named Taft chief justice in 1921. Taft was responsible for passage of the Judiciary Act of 1925, which gave the Supreme Court effective control over its own appellate jurisdiction and for the appropriation of funds for construction of the present Supreme Court building. See A. Mason, William Howard Taft: Chief Justice (1964).

ROGER B. TANEY (1777–1864): Prior to his appointment as chief justice by President Jackson in 1835, Roger Taney served as Jackson's attorney general and secretary of the treasury. While serving in Jackson's cabinet, he became enmeshed in the controversy surrounding the second Bank of the United States. As attorney general, Taney drafted Jackson's message vetoing the bank's recharter, and when the secretary of the treasury refused to withdraw federal funds from the Bank, Jackson named Taney to the post so that he could do so. But when Jackson submitted Taney's name to the Senate for confirmation, he was defeated and forced to withdraw. Senate Whigs, who feared that Taney was too radical, again blocked his nomination as associate justice in 1835. Shortly thereafter, however, he was successfully nominated to replace John Marshall as chief justice. Taney's career on the Court is overshadowed by his opinion in Scott v. Sandford, 60 U.S. (19 How.) 393 (1857), widely viewed as one of the great legal and moral blunders in the Court's history. The rest of his tenure, however, was marked by the cautious and careful use of judicial power. Contrary to the expectations of his contemporaries, he did not support the wholesale abandonment of the Marshall legacy. Instead, he steered a middle course between the extreme nationalism and extreme localism of his colleagues. But as the nation approached civil war, the ground in the middle became increasingly unstable, and Taney's one spasmodic effort to end the nation's agony over slavery by imposing a constitutional solution in Dred Scott ended in a tragedy that permanently marred his reputation. See C. Swisher, Roger B. Taney (1935); G. White, The American Judicial Tradition ch. 3 (1976).

CLARENCE THOMAS (1948–): Born into grinding poverty in segregated coastal Georgia, Clarence Thomas became the second African American and one of the youngest justices to join the Court when he was appointed by President Bush in 1991. He was confirmed by the Senate to fill the seat vacated by the retirement of Thurgood Marshall after extraordinary confirmation hearings that opened with a moving account of his personal saga and closed with charges of sexual harassment leveled against him by Anita Hill, who had worked with him at the Department of Education and the Equal Employment Opportunity Commission. A graduate of Yale Law School, he served as assistant secretary for civil rights at the Department of Education and chair of the Equal Employment Opportunity Commission in the Reagan administration. During his controversial seven-year stewardship of the EEOC, Thomas's fierce opposition to affirmative action antagonized liberals and members of the civil rights community. In 1989, President Bush appointed Thomas to the U.S. Court of Appeals for the District of Columbia Circuit, where he served for fifteen months before his elevation to the Supreme Court. Known as a staunch conservative, Thomas's extrajudicial writings suggest an interest in natural law as a basis for constitutional adjudication. Since joining the Court, he has written a series of distinctive dissents and concurrences, often demonstrating a willingness to reject settled precedent in favor of his understanding of the constitutional text. On racial issues, he strongly opposes what he considers liberal condescension in the form of affirmative action and the assumption that majority black institutions are necessarily inferior. See K. Foskett, Judging Thomas: The Life and Times of Clarence Thomas (2004); A. Thomas, Clarence Thomas: A Biography (2001).

WILLIS VAN DEVANTER (1859–1941): A lawyer's lawyer, William Van Devanter invariably sided with the conservative wing of the Court, but, unlike some of his colleagues, never resorted to divisive ideological rhetoric. Instead, he relied on his mastery of technical doctrine to become a "master of formulas that decided cases without creating precedents." Van Devanter, who was active in Republican politics in Wyoming, came to Washington during the McKinley administration and was named to the Eighth Circuit Court of Appeals by Theodore Roosevelt. When President Taft nominated him to serve as an associate justice, William Jennings Bryan complained that he was "the judge that held that two railroads running parallel to each other for two thousand miles were not competing lines, one of the roads being that of Union Pacific," one of Van Devanter's former clients. It has been said that Van Devanter came to the Court "fully equipped with a lawyer's understanding of federal jurisdiction, a frontiersman's knowledge of Indian affairs, and a native hostility to governmental regulation." His years on the Court were marked by a concern for technical jurisdictional questions and opposition to government intervention in all forms. His retirement in June 1937 gave Franklin Roosevelt his first appointment and helped defuse the crisis created by the Court's opposition to the New Deal.

EARL WARREN (1891–1974): Both vilified and canonized during and since his tenure, Earl Warren presided as chief justice over one of the most tumultuous and portentous periods in the Court's history. The emotions that he aroused are hard to reconcile with his political stance, which was, essentially, centrist and pragmatic. As Republican attorney general and governor of California, he denounced "communistic radicals" and supported the wartime order to forcibly evacuate Japanese Americans. (The Court subsequently upheld the constitutionality of the evacuation in Korematsu v. United States, 323 U.S. 214 (1944).) In his later years as governor, however, he developed a reputation as a progressive and proposed state programs for prepaid medical insurance and liberal welfare benefits. In 1948, he ran for Vice President on the ticket headed by Thomas Dewey. In 1952, he mounted his own presidential effort. At the Republican convention, however, he threw his support behind Dwight Eisenhower. President Eisenhower repaid Warren by nominating him as chief justice in 1953 — a nomination Eisenhower later called "the biggest damn-fool mistake I ever made." Perhaps Warren's greatest accomplishment on the Court was his painstaking and successful effort to maintain a united front as the Court overturned the separate but equal doctrine in Brown v. Board of Education, 347 U.S. 873 (1954), and then confronted southern violence and intransigence. Warren himself believed that his opinion in Reynolds v. Sims, 377 U.S. 533 (1964), establishing the one person, one vote formula, was of greater significance. In the end, however, it may have been his opinions in the field of criminal procedure — especially Miranda v. Arizona, 384 U.S. 436 (1966) — that attracted the most controversy. This controversy tended to obscure the fact that there was a strong conservative and moralistic tone to many of Warren's opinions. He opposed constitutional protection for "pornographic" literature, for example, and dissented in Shapiro v. Thompson, 394 U.S. 618 (1969), when the Court invalidated durational residency requirements for welfare recipients. Warren was distrustful of complex doctrinal argument. His opinions were thus marked by a confident, intuitively grounded insistence on fair play and fundamental justice. See B. Schwartz, Superchief (1983); E. Warren, The Memoirs of Earl Warren (1977); G. White, Earl Warren (1982).

BYRON R. WHITE (1917–1992): An outstanding scholar-athlete, Byron "Whizzer" White was first in his class at the University of Colorado, a Rhodes Scholar, and a professional football player with the Detroit Lions before beginning his legal career. White served in the navy during World War II and graduated from Yale Law School magna cum laude. After serving as law clerk to Chief Justice Fred Vinson, he returned to his native Colorado where he practiced with a prominent Denver law firm for fourteen years. A long-time friend of John F. Kennedy, White headed Kennedy's preconvention presidential campaign in Colorado in 1960 and subsequently became chairman of National Citizens for Kennedy. After the election, President Kennedy named him deputy attorney general and in 1962 elevated him to the Court. As a justice, White was known as a strong advocate of school desegregation and a defender of the rights of minorities. Although more ready than his colleagues to find legislation lacking in a "rational basis" when challenged under "low-level" equal protection review, he also criticized his colleagues for too aggressive use of substantive due process analysis. For example, joined only by Justice Rehnquist, White dissented in Roe v. Wade, 410 U. S. 113 (1973), which held that women have a constitutionally protected liberty interest in securing abortions. In Bowers v. Hardwick, 478 U.S. 186 (1986), he wrote for the Court to reject a claim that "the federal Constitution confers a fundamental right upon homosexuals to engage in sodomy," noting that "to claim that a right to engage in such conduct is 'deeply rooted in this Nation's history and tradition' or 'implicit in the concept of ordered liberty' is, at best, facetious." See D. Hutchinson, The Man Who Was Whizzer White: A Portrait of Justice Byron R. White (1998).

The Supreme Court since 1789

Administration	Chief Justice	2	3	4	5	6	7	8	9	Major Cases
Washington	John Jay	John Rutledge	William Cushing	James Wilson	John Blair	James Iredell				
(1790)		Thomas Johnson								
		William Paterson								
(1795)	John Rutledge / Oliver Ellsworth				Samuel Chase					
				Bushrod Washington						
J. Adams						Alfred Moore				
(1800)	John Marshall (Adams)									
Jefferson						William Johnson				Marbury v. Madison (1803)
		H. Brockholst Livingston								
							Thomas Todd			

1789
1790
1795
1800
1805

McCulloch v. Maryland (1819)

Gibbons v. Ogden (1824)

Barron v. Baltimore (1833)

Robert Trimble

John McLean

Gabriel Duvall

Henry Baldwin

Joseph Story

Smith Thompson

Madison

Monroe

J. Q. Adams

Jackson

1810

1815

1820

1825

1830

Year	Administration	Chief Justice	2	3	4	5	6	7	8	9	Major Cases
1835		Roger B. Taney									
	Van Buren					Philip P. Barbour	James M. Wayne		John Catron	John McKinley	
1840	W. Harrison Tyler					Peter V. Daniel (Van Buren)					
			Samuel Nelson (Tyler)								
1845	Polk			Levi Woodbury	Robert C. Grier						
1850	Taylor Fillmore			Benjamin R. Curtis							
1855	Pierce									John A. Campbell	

Dred Scott v. Sandford (1857)

Slaughter-House Cases (1873)

David Davis

John M. Harlan

10
Stephen J. Field

Noah H. Swayne

Joseph P. Bradley

Samuel F. Miller

William Strong

Nathan Clifford

Ward Hunt

Salmon P. Chase

Morrison R. Waite

Buchanan

Lincoln

A. Johnson

Grant

Hayes

1860

1865**

1870

1875

Administration	Chief Justice	2	3	4	5	6	7	8	9	Major Cases
Garfield / Arthur			Horace Gray (Arthur)	William B. Woods			Stanley Matthews (Garfield)			
		Samuel Blatchford								Civil Rights Cases (1883)
Cleveland										
B. Harrison	Melville W. Fuller			Lucius Q. C. Lamar	Henry B. Brown	George Shiras	David J. Brewer			
				Howell E. Jackson (Harrison)						
Cleveland		Edward D. White		Rufus W. Peckham						
McKinley								Joseph McKenna		Plessy v. Ferguson (1896)

Years (left axis): 1880, 1885, 1890, 1895

Lochner v. N.Y. (1905)

Schenk v. U.S. (1919)

Mahlon Pitney

Charles E. Hughes

John H. Clarke

William R. Day

William H. Moody

Joseph R. Lamar

Louis D. Brandeis

Horace H. Lurton

James C. McReynolds

Oliver W. Holmes

Willis Van Devanter

Edward D. White

William H. Taft

T. Roosevelt

Taft

Wilson

Harding

1900

1905

1910

1915

1920

	Administration	Chief Justice	2	3	4	5	6	7	8	9	Major Cases
1925	Coolidge						Pierce Butler	George Sutherland		Edward T. Sanford (Harding)	
1930	Hoover	Charles E. Hughes		Benjamin N. Cardozo					Harlan F. Stone	Owen J. Roberts	
1935	F. D. Roosevelt		Hugo L. Black	Felix Frankfurter		William O. Douglas	Frank Murphy	Stanley F. Reed			Schechter Poultry v. U.S. (1935)
											West Coast Hotel v. Parrish (1937)
1940											U.S. v. Carolene Prods. (1938)

Dennis v. U.S. (1951)

Youngstown Sheet v. Sawyer (1952)

Brown v. Bd. Of Ed. (1954)

Harold H. Burton

Potter Stewart

Robert H. Jackson

John M. Harlan

Charles E. Whittaker

Byron R. White

Tom C. Clark

James F. Byrnes

Wiley B. Rutledge

Sherman Minton

William J. Brennan

Arthur J. Goldberg

Harlan F. Stone

Fred M. Vinson

Earl Warren

Truman

Eisenhower

Kennedy

1945   1950   1955   1960

Year	Administration	Chief Justice	2	3	4	5	6	7	8	9	Major Cases
	L. B. Johnson										N.Y. Times v. Sullivan (1964)
1965											
	Nixon	Warren E. Burger		Abe Fortas							Brandenburg v. Ohio (1969)
1970			Lewis F. Powell	Harry A. Blackmun							N.Y. Times v. U.S. (1971)
							Thurgood Marshall				
									William H. Rehnquist		Roe v. Wade (1973)
											U.S. v. Nixon (1974)
	Ford					John Paul Stevens					
1975											
	Carter										Washington v. Davis (1976)
											U. Cal. v. Bakke (1978)
1980	Reagan									Sandra Day O'Conor	

City of Richmond v. J.A. Croson Co. (1989)

Planned Parenthood of S.E. Pa. v. Casey (1992)

United States v. Lopez (1995)
Adarand Constr. v. Pena (1995)
United States v. Virginia (1996)
City of Boerne v. Flores (1997)

Grutter v. Bollinger (2003)

Antonin Scalia

Ruth Bader Ginsburg

Clarence Thomas

David H. Souter

Stephen G. Breyer

Anthony M. Kennedy

William H. Rehnquist

G. H. W. Bush

Clinton

G. W. Bush

1985
1990
1995
2000
2001
2002

	Administration	Chief Justice	2	3	4	5	6	7	8	9	Major Cases
2003											Lawrence v. Texas (2003)
–											Hamdi v. Rumsfeld (2004)
2005		John G. Roberts, Jr.									Hamdan v. Rumsfeld (2006)
–										Samuel A. Alito, Jr.	Gonzales v. Carhart (2007)
–											District of Columbia v. Heller (2008)
–											Boumediene v. Bush (2008)
2009	Obama				Sonia Sotomayor						
2010						Elena Kagan					Citizens United v. Federal Election Commission (2010)
–											
–											
2012											National Federation of Independent Business v. Sebelius (2012)
2015											Obergefell v. Hodges (2015)
–											
2017	Donald J. Trump								Neil Gorsuch		

*In 1863 Congress established a tenth seat, to which Stephen J. Field was appointed.
**In 1866 Congress reduced the size of the Court to six justices. Consequently, the seats of Justices Catron and Wayne remained unfilled after their deaths in 1865 and 1867. Congress restored the Court to nine seats in 1869.

Constitutional Law

I

The Constitution and the
Supreme Court

This chapter deals with the creation of the American Constitution and with the role of the Supreme Court in interpreting the Constitution. We have two central concerns: (1) What was the founding all about? (2) What is the power of the Supreme Court, and when it is interpreting the Constitution, what does it do, exactly? We begin with history.

A. THE ORIGINS OF THE U.S. CONSTITUTION

The Declaration of Independence was signed in 1776. Here are its most famous words:

> We hold these truths to be self-evident, that all men are created equal, that they are endowed by their Creator with certain unalienable Rights, that among these are Life, Liberty and the pursuit of Happiness. — That to secure these rights, Governments are instituted among Men, deriving their just powers from the consent of the governed, — That whenever any Form of Government becomes destructive of these ends, it is the Right of the People to alter or to abolish it, and to institute new Government, laying its foundation on such principles and organizing its powers in such form, as to them shall seem most likely to effect their Safety and Happiness.

Hostilities with England substantially ceased in 1781 after the Yorktown campaign; the American Revolution was formally completed in 1783 with the signing of a final peace treaty with England. In February of 1781, the thirteen colonies ratified the Articles of Confederation, under which they lived for seven years. The Constitution was written in 1787 and ratified in 1789. Two years later the bill of rights was added.

Why did the states find it necessary to adopt a new Constitution? What were the problems for which the Constitution was supposed a remedy? Did the Constitution embody the principles of the American Revolution, or did it betray those

1

principles? Views about the Constitution and its framers span a wide range. Many Americans since have seen the framers as intellectual giants, equipped with extraordinary foresight, vision, and faith in individual rights and self-rule, who were able to rise above the squabbles of the day, or somewhat to take advantage of them, in order to institute into law principles that are timeless or at least enduring. See C. Bowen, Miracle at Philadelphia (1986); J. Fiske, The Critical Period of American History (1888). To those who think this way, the framers, and especially Alexander Hamilton and James Madison (but others too), were able to combine deep theoretical insights with practical sense, allowing them to produce new understandings of political institutions, of self-government, and of individual rights.

To skeptics, much of the Constitution is best understood as a series of ad hoc compromises, designed to rescue an immensely difficult situation and to resolve very specific issues over which the young country was divided. The compromises worked — or at least were made to work — but compromises they were. (Two examples are the maintenance of slavery and the immense power of small states.) See M. Farrand, The Framing of the Constitution of the United States (1913). A third strand in American historical thought treats the Constitution as a product, at least in part, of elitist conservatives who, far from trusting the people and believing in self-rule, intended to protect private property, and the position of the relatively well-to-do, from the workings of democratic politics. See W. Holton, Unruly Americans and the Origins of the Constitution (2007); C. Beard, An Economic Interpretation of the Constitution of the United States (1913). This third view could be given sympathetic or less sympathetic treatments.

There are, of course, numerous variations on these general approaches. For discussion, see M. Klarman. The Framers' Coup (2016); G. Wood, The Creation of the American Republic, 1776–1787 (1969); G. Wood, ed., The Confederation and the Constitution (1978); G. Wood, The Radicalism of the American Revolution (1993); R. Horwitz, ed., The Moral Foundations of the American Republic (2d ed. 1979); J. G. A. Pocock, The Machiavellian Moment (1975); Kloppenberg, The Virtues of Liberalism: Christianity, Republicanism and Ethics in Early American Political Discourse, 74 J. Am. Hist. 9 (1987).

To understand the Constitution and the surrounding debates on its purposes and effects, it is useful to have some understanding of the Articles of Confederation, which the Constitution replaced. The Articles were adopted in order to ensure some unification of the states regarding common foreign and domestic problems, but the overriding understanding was that the states would remain sovereign. The Articles begin without any kind of poetry:

> To all to whom these Presents shall come, we the undersigned Delegates of the States affixed to our Names send greeting.
>   Articles of Confederation and perpetual Union between the states of New Hampshire, Massachusetts-bay Rhode Island and Providence Plantations, Connecticut, New York, New Jersey, Pennsylvania, Delaware, Maryland, Virginia, North Carolina, South Carolina and Georgia.

Notice that the Articles are formed by the states and their delegates — not by We the People. (Compare, if you would, the soaring start of the Constitution that followed the Articles, produced just sixteen years later.) The very first article of the Articles did give an enduring name to the Confederacy: "the United States of America." But the second more or less took it back, announcing that "each state retains its sovereignty, freedom, and independence, and every Power, Jurisdiction, and right, which is not by this confederation expressly delegated to the United States, in Congress assembled."

To be sure, a number of powers were conferred on "the United States in Congress assembled." These powers included "the sole and exclusive right and power of determining on peace and war"; the authority to resolve disputes between the states; the power to regulate "the alloy and value of coin struck by their own authority, or by that of the respective states"; and the authority to control dealings with Indian tribes, to establish or regulate post offices, and to appoint naval and other offices in federal service. But at least by modern standards, there were conspicuous gaps. Two of the most important powers of the modern national government were missing altogether: the power to tax and the power to regulate commerce. Moreover, two of the three branches of the national government were absent. There was no executive authority. (One reason was deep distrust of the idea of anything like a king.) There was no general national judicial authority; the only relevant provision authorized Congress to establish a national appellate tribunal to decide maritime cases. Of course, there was no bill of rights (though it should be noted that the absence of a bill of rights was not in any way the impetus behind the Constitution, and indeed the federalists thought, at the time of ratification, that a bill of rights did not belong in the Constitution at all).

As experience under the Articles of Confederation accumulated, many leading political figures became deeply dissatisfied with the performance of the government it created. In fact, the situation appeared to be disastrous. Among the complaints were that states refused to provide money owed to the federal government, refused to comply with treaties entered into by the United States, interfered with the commerce of other states, forgave debts, and issued inflated paper currency. These grievances came in the context of economic decline, which produced a general sense of unease. Just a decade after the American Revolution, the nation's high ideals and aspirations appeared doomed. James Madison wrote that people "unanimously agree that the existing Confederacy is tottering to its foundation," and added, "It is not possible that a government can last long under these circumstances." James Madison to Edmund Randolph, February 25, 1787, in *Founders Online*, National Archives, http://founders.archives.gov/documents/Madison/01-09-02-0154.

In April 1787, preparing for the Constitutional Convention, Madison wrote himself a memorandum that describes the situation from the point of view of those advocating substantial changes:

1.   FAILURE OF THE STATES TO COMPLY WITH THE CONSTITUTIONAL REQUISITIONS. This evil has been so fully experienced both during the war and since the peace, results so naturally from the number and independent authority of the States and has been so uniformly exemplified in every similar Confederacy, that it may be considered as not less radically and permanently inherent in than it is fatal to the object of the present system.

2. ENCROACHMENTS BY THE STATES ON THE FEDERAL AUTHORITY. Examples of this are numerous and repetitions may be foreseen in almost every case where any favorite object of a State shall present a temptation. Among these examples are the wars and treaties of Georgia with the Indians. The unlicensed compacts between Virginia and Maryland, and between Pennsylvania & New Jersey — the troops raised and to be kept up by Massachusetts.

3. VIOLATIONS OF THE LAW OF NATIONS AND OF TREATIES. From the number of Legislatures, the sphere of life from which most of their members are taken, and the circumstances under which their legislative business is carried on, irregularities of this kind must frequently happen. Accordingly not a year has passed without instances of them in some one or other of the States. The Treaty of Peace — the treaty with France — the treaty with Holland have each been violated. [See the complaints to Congress on these subjects.] The causes of these irregularities must necessarily produce frequent violations of the law of nations in other respects.

As yet foreign powers have not been rigorous in animadverting on us. This moderation, however cannot be mistaken for a permanent partiality to our faults, or a permanent security against those disputes with other nations, which being among the greatest of public calamities, it ought to be least in the power of any part of the community to bring on the whole.

4. TRESPASSES OF THE STATES ON THE RIGHTS OF EACH OTHER. These are alarming symptoms, and may be daily apprehended as we are admonished by daily experience. See the law of Virginia restricting foreign vessels to certain ports — of Maryland in favor of vessels belonging to her own citizens — of New York in favor of the same.

Paper money, instalments of debts, occlusion of Courts, making property a legal tender, may likewise be deemed aggressions on the rights of other States. As the Citizens of every State aggregately taken stand more or less in the relation of Creditors or debtors, to the Citizens of every other State, Acts of the debtor State in favor of debtors, affect the Creditor State, in the same manner as they do its own citizens who are relatively creditors towards other citizens. This remark may be extended to foreign nations. If the exclusive regulation of the value and alloy of coin was properly delegated to the federal authority, the policy of it equally requires a controul on the States in the cases above mentioned. It must have been meant 1. to preserve uniformity in the circulating medium throughout the nation. 2. to prevent those frauds on the citizens of other States, and the subjects of foreign powers, which might disturb the tranquility at home, or involve the Union in foreign contests.

The practice of many States in restricting the commercial intercourse with other States, and putting their productions and manufacturers on the same footing with those of foreign nations, though not contrary to the federal articles, is certainly adverse to the spirit of the Union, and tends to beget retaliating regulations, not less expensive and vexatious in themselves than they are destructive of the general harmony.

5. WANT OF CONCERT IN MATTERS WHERE COMMON INTEREST REQUIRES IT. This defect is strongly illustrated in the state of our commercial affairs. How much has the national dignity, interest, and revenue, suffered from this cause? Instances of inferior moment are the want of uniformity in the laws concerning naturalization & literary property; of provision for national seminaries, for grants of incorporation for national purposes, for canals and other works of general utility, which may at present be defeated by the perverseness of particular States whose concurrence is necessary.

6. WANT OF GUARANTY TO THE STATES OF THEIR CONSTITUTIONS & LAWS AGAINST INTERNAL VIOLENCE. The confederation is silent on this point and therefore by the second article the hands of the federal authority are tied. According to Republican Theory, Right and power being both vested in the majority, are held to be synonimous. According to fact and experience a minority may in an appeal to force, be an over-match for the majority. 1. if the minority happen to include all such as possess the skill and habits of military life, & such as possess the great pecuniary resources, one-third only may conquer the remaining two-thirds. 2. one-third of those who participate in the choice of the rulers, may be rendered a majority by the accession of those whose poverty excludes

them from a right of suffrage, and who for obvious reasons will be more likely to join the standard of sedition than that of the established Government. 3. where slavery exists the republican Theory becomes still more fallacious.

7. WANT OF SANCTION TO THE LAWS, AND OF COERCION IN THE GOVERNMENT OF THE CONFEDERACY. A sanction is essential to the idea of law, as coercion is to that of Government. The federal system being destitute of both, wants the great vital principles of a Political Constitution. Under the form of such a constitution, it is in fact nothing more than a treaty of amity of commerce and of alliance, between independent and Sovereign States. From what cause could so fatal an omission have happened in the articles of Confederation? from a mistaken confidence that the justice, the good faith, the honor, the sound policy, of the several legislative assemblies would render superfluous any appeal to the ordinary motives by which the laws secure the obedience of individuals: a confidence which does honor to the enthusiastic virtue of the compilers, as much as the inexperience of the crisis apologizes for their errors. The time which has since elapsed has had the double effect, of increasing the light and tempering the warmth, with which the arduous work may be revised. It is no longer doubted that a unanimous and punctual obedience of 13 independent bodies, to the acts of the federal Government ought not to be calculated on. Even during the war, when external danger supplied in some degree the defect of legal & coercive sanctions, how imperfectly did the States fulfill their obligations to the Union? In time of peace, we see already what is to be expected. How indeed could it be otherwise? In the first place, Every general act of the Union must necessarily bear unequally hard on some particular member or members of it, secondly the partiality of the members to their own interests and rights, a partiality which will be fostered by the courtiers of popularity, will naturally exaggerate the inequality where it exists, and even suspect it where it has no existence, thirdly a distrust of the voluntary compliance of each other may prevent the compliance of any, although it should be the latent disposition of all. Here are causes & pretexts which will never fail to render federal measures abortive. If the laws of the States were merely recommendatory to their citizens, or if they were to be rejudged by County authorities, what security, what probability would exist, that they would be carried into execution? Is the security or probability greater in favor of the acts of Congress which depending for their execution on the will of the State legislatures, which are tho' nominally authoritative, in fact recommendatory only?

8. WANT OF RATIFICATION BY THE PEOPLE OF THE ARTICLES OF CONFEDERATION. In some of the States the Confederation is recognized by, and forms a part of the Constitution. In others however it has received no other sanction than that of the legislative authority. [As] far as the union of the States is to be regarded as a league of sovereign powers, and not as a political Constitution by virtue of which they are become one sovereign power, so far it seems to follow from the doctrine of compacts, that a breach of any of the articles of the Confederation by any of the parties to it, absolves the other parties from their respective Obligations, and gives them a right if they chuse to exert it, of dissolving the Union altogether.

9. MULTIPLICITY OF LAWS IN THE SEVERAL STATES. In developing the evils which viciate the political system of the U.S., it is proper to include those which are found within the States individually, as well as those which directly affect the States collectively, since the former class have an indirect influence on the general malady and must not be overlooked in forming a compleat remedy. Among the evils then of our situation may well be ranked the multiplicity of laws from which no State is exempt. As far as laws are necessary to mark with precision the duties of those who are to obey them, and to take from those who are to administer them a discretion which might be abused, their number is the price of liberty. As far as laws exceed this limit, they are a nuisance; a nuisance of the most pestilent kind. Try the Codes of the several States by this test, and what a luxuriancy of legislation

do they present. The short period of independency has filled as many pages as the
century which preceded it. Every year, almost every session, adds a new volume.
This may be the effect in part, but it can only be in part, of the situation in which the
revolution has placed us. A review of the several Codes will shew that every
necessary and useful part of the least voluminous of them might be compressed
into one tenth of the compass, and at the same time be rendered ten fold as
perspicuous. . . .

11. INJUSTICE OF THE LAWS OF THE STATES. [Injustice] betrays a defect
still more alarming: more alarming not merely because it is a greater evil in itself;
but because it brings more into question the fundamental principle of republican
Government, that the majority who rule in such governments are the safest Guardians both of public Good and private rights. . . .

In 1786, state representatives met in Annapolis to discuss problems that had
arisen under the Articles; they adopted a resolution to hold a convention in
Philadelphia to remedy those problems. But the nation's charge to the framers
was much narrower than the ultimate product would suggest. The framers,
chosen by state legislatures, were instructed "to meet at Philadelphia [to] take
into consideration the situation of the United States, to devise such further provisions as shall appear to them necessary to render the constitution of the federal
government adequate to the exigencies of the Union." The limited character of
this charge proved a serious embarrassment to the framers, whose product
reflected their view that it was necessary to provide not "further provisions"
but an entirely new governing document whose character was not clearly proportionate to the weaknesses of the Articles.

There is therefore a sense in which the Constitution was itself an unlawful act.
As noted above, the Convention disregarded the amending procedure set out in
the Articles, which required approval by all thirteen state legislatures. The Constitution was instead sent to Congress, with a request that it be sent in turn to state
legislatures. The state legislatures would then send it to popularly elected state
ratifying conventions.

The Constitution changed the framework set up by the Articles of Confederation in a number of ways. Among the most important changes were the creation
of an executive branch; the grant to Congress of the powers to tax and to regulate
commerce; and the creation of a federal judiciary, including the Supreme Court
and, if Congress chose, lower federal courts. The tenth amendment, added two
years later, was a pale echo of the first provisions of the Articles of Confederation,
deleting the word "expressly," and it was countered by the clause granting Congress the authority to make "all laws necessary and proper" to effectuate the
enumerated powers of the federal government.

Was there an underlying theory that justified this expansion of federal power?
Many historians think so. They insist that the delegates to the Convention were
responding to serious flaws under the Articles of Confederation, and that they
created a document that reflected on a novel theory of self-government. Others
contend that the new Constitution was an effort to solve distinctly practical
problems, and that it is not best seen as a theoretical project. Still others claim
that many of the delegates were motivated largely by interest-group politics
advanced under the cloak of high political theory. State legislators had favored
the interests of farmers and taxpayers against the interests of creditors and the
commercial class. The latter group responded by attempting to change the
structure of government so as to disadvantage the former group. See generally

W. Holton, Unruly Americans and the Origins of the Constitution (2007). For a valuable perspective, see Klarman, The Framers' Coup, supra.

Whatever one's conclusion on these issues, there can be no doubt that the struggle over the design of the founding document, and also over its ratification, produced an outpouring of fresh thinking. As you read the material that follows, consider the extent to which the tinking of the framers and ratifiers should influence contemporary constitutional interpretation.

One of the central disputes at the Convention was disagreement over the implications of classical republican theory, fueled by the recent memory of the American Revolution. Republican theorists placed a premium on the idea of self-government. The colonists were particularly influenced by the French theorist Montesquieu, who famously divided governments into three kinds: "a republican government is that in which the body, or only a part of the people, is possessed of the supreme power; monarchy, that in which a single person governs by fixed and established laws; a despotic government, that in which a single person directs everything by his own will and caprice." Montesquieu, The Spirit of Laws 8 (1906). In the period that preceded the Revolution, the colonists were seized by republican thinking, which repudiated the whole idea of a monarchy, and which ended up as a challenge to hierarchies of many different kinds. See G. Wood, The Radicalism of the American Revolution (rev. ed. 1998).

In the long history of republican thought, many theorists stressed the importance of civic virtue — the willingness of citizens to subordinate their private interests to the general good. Politics thus consisted of self-rule, but it was self-rule of a particular sort. Self-rule was a matter not of pursuing self-interest, or of aggregating "preferences," but instead of selecting the values that ought to control public and private life. Dialogue and discussion among the citizenry were critical features in the governmental process. In a republic, political participation should be active and frequent and not limited to voting or other similar statements of preference. Civil society was to operate as a sort of teacher, inculcating virtue, and not merely as a regulator of private conduct. The model for government was the town meeting, a metaphor that played an explicit role in the conception of politics put forth primarily by the proposed Constitution's opponents. Consider in this regard Thomas Jefferson's suggestion that the Constitution should be amended in every generation, partly in order to promote general attention to public affairs; this suggestion was a natural one for those who saw frequent participation and virtue as important ingredients in democratic self-government. See Letter to Samuel Kercheval, July 12, 1816, in The Portable Thomas Jefferson 557–558 (M. Peterson ed., 1975).

For republican theorists, one of government's tasks was to ensure the flourishing of the necessary public-spiritedness. Many believed in small republics and hence a high degree of decentralization; only in small communities would it be possible to find and develop the unselfishness and devotion to the public good on which genuine freedom depends. The Articles of Confederation promote such decentralization. "Brutus," writing in opposition to the proposed Constitution, emphasized the need for homogeneity: "In a republic, the manners, sentiments, and interests of the people should be similar. If this be not the case, there will be a constant clashing of opinions; and the representatives of one part will be continually striving against those of the other." 2 The Complete Antifederalist 369 (H. Storing ed., 1980).

The Constitution's opponents, referred to as "antifederalists," were especially hostile to a dramatic expansion in the size and power of the national government.

They thought that it threatened liberty itself, and that it endangered the princi-ples for which the Revolution had been fought. A powerful national government would threaten liberty; it could be a return to monarchy. It would undermine the spirit of civic virtue, creating heterogeneity and distance from the sphere of power, both of which would undermine deliberative processes and the citizens' willingness to subordinate their private interests to the public good. Closely connected to this view was the antifederalists' desire to avoid extreme disparities in wealth, education, and power.

It should not be difficult to see why the antifederalists would have had at best an ambivalent attitude toward a system in which decisions were made by repre-sentatives of the people rather than by the people themselves — certainly if the representatives were not close to the people. According to one strand of republican thought, all decisions should be made in small communities or even during a face-to-face process of deliberation and debate. Such a process would inculcate civic virtue in the public at large, virtue from which the process itself would simultaneously benefit.

The antifederalists did not go so far. By 1787, all agreed that representation was necessary at both the state and the national levels. The size of both governments made it impossible to conduct political affairs on the model of the town meeting. The proposed Constitution's opponents believed that it would prevent citizens from having effective control over their representatives and deprive them of an opportunity to participate in public affairs. It would thus pose a severe threat to the underlying principle of civic virtue. Rule by remote national leaders would attenuate the scheme of representation, rupturing the alliance of interests between the rulers and the ruled. It would create a class of quasi-aristocrats, charging them with the task of directing a huge national government. The anti-federalists foresaw a system in which the people would be effectively excluded from the world of public affairs and in which national leaders, only weakly accountable, would have enormous discretion to make law and policy.

The antifederalists were also skeptical of the emerging interest in commercial development that played a prominent role in the decision to abandon the Articles of Confederation. In the antifederalists' view, commerce was a threat to the principles underlying the Revolution, for it gave rise to ambition and avarice and thus to the dissolution of communal bonds. Montesquieu, an important source for federalists and antifederalists alike, had said that "in countries where the people are actuated only by the spirit of commerce, they make a traffic of all the humane, all the moral virtues; the most trifling things, those which humanity would demand, are there done, or there given, only for money." Mon-tesquieu, The Spirit of Laws bk. XX, ch. ii (spec. ed. 1984) (1751).

In sum, the antifederalists attacked the proposed Constitution on the ground that it was inconsistent with the underlying principles of republicanism. The removal of the people from the political process, the creation of a powerful, remote, and liberty-threatening national government, and the new emphasis on commerce — all of these threatened to undermine the purposes for which the Revolution had been fought.

The antifederalist objections to the proposed Constitution provoked a theo-retical justification that amounted in many respects to a new conception of politics — in Gordon Wood's words, a "political theory worthy of a prominent place in the history of Western thought." G. Wood, The Creation of the American Republic, 1776–1787, at 615 (1969). That conception consisted of a reformulation of the principles of republicanism — a reformulation that attempted to synthesize elements of traditional republicanism with an emerging theory that welcomed rather than feared heterogeneity, and that understood the reality that the spirit of faction could not be eliminated.

Much of that reformulation can be found in The Federalist Papers — essays attempting to defend the proposed Constitution to the country against antifederalist attack. The Federalist Papers were published under the name "Publius," but they were in fact written by James Madison, Alexander Hamilton, and John Jay. Although the papers are rightly consulted as a means of understanding the theory underlying the Constitution, and the understandings of its drafters, it is important to keep in mind that the essays were designed to persuade the ambivalent. Nonetheless, The Federalist Papers count among the classic works in the theory of democracy and constitutionalism.

The Federalist No. 10 (Madison)

(1787)

TO THE PEOPLE OF THE STATE OF NEW YORK:

Among the numerous advantages promised by a well-constructed Union, none deserves to be more accurately developed than its tendency to break and control the violence of faction. The friend of popular governments never finds himself so much alarmed for their character and fate, as when he contemplates their propensity to this dangerous vice. [The] instability, injustice, and confusion introduced into the public councils, have, in truth, been the mortal diseases under which popular governments have everywhere perished; as they continue to be the favorite and fruitful topics from which the adversaries to liberty derive their most specious declamations. [Complaints] are everywhere heard from our most considerate and virtuous citizens, equally the friends of public and private faith, and of public and personal liberty, that our governments are too unstable, that the public good is disregarded in the conflicts of rival parties, and that measures are too often decided, not according to the rules of justice and the rights of the minor party, but by the superior force of an interested and overbearing majority. However anxiously we may wish that these complaints had no foundation, the evidence of known facts will not permit us to deny that they are in some degree true. [The] distresses under which we labor [must] be chiefly, if not wholly, effects of the unsteadiness and injustice with which a factious spirit has tainted our public administrations.

By a faction, I understand a number of citizens, whether amounting to a majority or minority of the whole, who are united and actuated by some common impulse of passion, or of interest, adverse to the rights of other citizens, or to the permanent and aggregate interests of the community.

There are two methods of curing the mischiefs of faction: the one, by removing its causes; the other, by controlling its effects.

There are again two methods of removing the causes of faction: the one, by destroying the liberty which is essential to its existence; the other, by giving to every citizen the same opinions, the same passions, and the same interests.

It could never be more truly said than of the first remedy, that it was worse than the disease. Liberty is to faction what air is to fire, an aliment without which it instantly expires. But it could not be less folly to abolish liberty, which is essential to political life, because it nourishes faction, than it would be to wish the annihilation of air, which is essential to animal life, because it imparts to fire its destructive agency.

The second expedient is as impracticable as the first would be unwise. As long as the reason of man continues fallible, and he is at liberty to exercise it, different opinions will be formed. As long as the connection subsists between his reason and his self-love, his opinions and his passions will have a reciprocal influence on each other; and the former will be objects to which the latter will attach themselves. The diversity in the faculties of men, from which the rights of property originate, is not less an insuperable obstacle to a uniformity of interests. The protection of these faculties is the first object of government. From the protection of different and unequal faculties of acquiring property, the possession of different degrees and kinds of property immediately results; and from the influence of these on the sentiments and views of the respective proprietors, ensues a division of the society into different interests and parties.

The latent causes of faction are thus sown in the nature of man; and we see them everywhere brought into different degrees of activity, according to the different circumstances of civil society. A zeal for different opinions, concerning religion, concerning government, and many other points, as well of speculation as of practice; an attachment to different leaders ambitiously contending for preeminence and power; or to persons of other descriptions whose fortunes have been interesting to the human passions, have, in turn, divided mankind into parties, inflamed them with mutual animosity, and rendered them much more disposed to vex and oppress each other than to co-operate for their common good. So strong is this propensity of mankind to fall into mutual animosities, that where no substantial occasion presents itself, the most frivolous and fanciful distinctions have been sufficient to kindle their unfriendly passions and excite their most violent conflicts. But the most common and durable source of factions has been the various and unequal distribution of property. Those who hold and those who are without property have ever formed distinct interests in society. Those who are creditors, and those who are debtors, fall under a like discrimination. A landed interest, a manufacturing interest, a mercantile interest, a moneyed interest, with many lesser interests, grow up of necessity in civilized nations, and divide them into different classes, actuated by different sentiments and views. The regulation of these various and interfering interests forms the principal task of modern legislation, and involves the spirit of party and faction in the necessary and ordinary operations of the government.

No man is allowed to be a judge in his own cause, because his interest would certainly bias his judgment, and, not improbably, corrupt his integrity. With equal, nay with greater reason, a body of men are unfit to be both judges and parties at the same time; yet what are many of the most important acts of legislation, but so many judicial determinations, not indeed concerning the rights of single persons, but concerning the rights of large bodies of citizens? And what are the different classes of legislators but advocates and parties to the causes which they determine? Is a law proposed concerning private debts? It is a question to which the creditors are parties on one side and the debtors on the other. Justice ought to hold the balance between them. Yet the parties are, and must be, themselves, the judges; and the most numerous party, or, in other words, the most powerful faction must be expected to prevail. Shall domestic manufacturers be encouraged, and in what degree, by restrictions on foreign manufacturers? are questions which would be differently decided by the landed and the manufacturing classes, and probably by neither with a sole regard to justice and the public good.

It is in vain to say that enlightened statesmen will be able to adjust these clashing interests, and render them all subservient to the public good. Enlightened statesmen will not always be at the helm. . . .

The inference to which we are brought is, that the causes of faction cannot be removed, and that relief is only to be sought in the means of controlling its effects.

If a faction consists of less than a majority, relief is supplied by the republican principle, which enables the majority to defeat its sinister views by regular vote. It may clog the administration, it may convulse the society; but it will be unable to execute and mask its violence under the forms of the Constitution. When a majority is included in a faction, the form of popular government, on the other hand, enables it to sacrifice to its ruling passion or interest both the public good and the rights of other citizens. To secure the public good and private rights against the danger of such a faction, and at the same time to preserve the spirit and the form of popular government, is then the great object to which our inquiries are directed. Let me add that it is the great desideratum by which this form of government can be rescued from the opprobrium under which it has so long labored, and be recommended to the esteem and adoption of mankind.

By what means is this object attainable? Evidently by one of two only. Either the existence of the same passion or interest in a majority at the same time must be prevented, or the majority, having such coexistent passion or interest, must be rendered, by their number and local situation, unable to concert and carry into effect schemes of oppression. If the impulse and the opportunity be suffered to coincide, we well know that neither moral nor religious motives can be relied on as an adequate control. They are not found to be such on the injustice and violence of individuals, and lose their efficacy in proportion to the number combined together, that is, in proportion as their efficacy becomes needful.

From this view of the subject it may be concluded that a pure democracy, by which I mean a society consisting of a small number of citizens, who assemble and administer the government in person, can admit of no cure for the mischiefs of faction. A common passion or interest will, in almost every case, be felt by a majority of the whole; a communication and concert result from the form of government itself; and there is nothing to check the inducements to sacrifice the weaker party or an obnoxious individual. Hence it is that such democracies have ever been spectacles of turbulence and contention; have ever been found incompatible with personal security or the rights of property; and have in general been as short in their lives as they have been violent in their deaths. Theoretic politicians, who have patronized this species of government, have erroneously supposed that by reducing mankind to a perfect equality in their political rights, they would, at the same time, be perfectly equalized and assimilated in their possessions, their opinions, and their passions.

A republic, by which I mean a government in which the scheme of representation takes place, opens a different prospect, and promises the cure for which we are seeking. . . .

The two great points of difference between a democracy and a republic are: first, the delegation of the government, in the latter, to a small number of citizens elected by the rest; secondly, the greater number of citizens, and greater sphere of country, over which the latter may be extended.

The effect of the first difference is, on the one hand, to refine and enlarge the public views, by passing them through the medium of a chosen body of citizens, whose wisdom may best discern the true interest of their country, and whose patriotism and love of justice will be least likely to sacrifice it to temporary or partial considerations. Under such a regulation, it may well happen that the public voice, pronounced by the representatives of the people, will be more consonant to the public good than if pronounced by the people themselves, convened for the purpose. On the other hand, the effect may be inverted. Men of factious tempers, of local prejudices, or of sinister designs, may, by intrigue, by corruption, or by other means, first obtain the suffrages, and then betray the interests, of the people. The question resulting is, whether small or extensive republics are more favorable to the election of proper guardians of the public weal; and it is clearly decided in favor of the latter by two obvious considerations:

In the first place, it is to be remarked that, however small the republic may be, the representatives must be raised to a certain number, in order to guard against the cabals of a few; and that, however large it may be, they must be limited to a certain number, in order to guard against the confusion of a multitude. Hence, the number of representatives in the two cases not being in proportion to that of the two constituents, and being proportionally greater in the small republic, it follows that, if the proportion of fit characters be not less in the large than in the small republic, the former will present a greater option, and consequently a greater probability of a fit choice.

In the next place, as each representative will be chosen by a greater number of citizens in the large than in the small republic, it will be more difficult for unworthy candidates to practice with success the vicious arts by which elections are too often carried; and the suffrages of the people being more free, will be more likely to center in men who possess the most attractive merit and the most diffusive and established characters.

It must be confessed that in this, as in most other cases, there is a mean, on both sides of which inconveniences will be found to lie. By enlarging too much the number of electors, you render the representative too little acquainted with all their local circumstances and lesser interests as by reducing it too much, you render him unduly attached to these, and too little fit to comprehend and pursue great and national objects. The federal Constitution forms a happy combination in this respect; the great and aggregate interests being referred to the national, the local and particular to the State legislatures.

The other point of difference is, the greater number of citizens and extent of territory which may be brought within the compass of republican than of democratic government; and it is this circumstance principally which renders factious combinations less to be dreaded in the former than in the latter. The smaller the society, the fewer probably will be the distinct parties and interests composing it; the fewer the distinct parties and interests, the more frequently will a majority be found of the same party; and the smaller the number of individuals composing a majority, and the smaller the compass within which they are placed, the more easily will they concert and execute their plans of oppression. Extend the sphere, and you take in a greater variety of parties and interests; you make it less probable that a majority of the whole will have a common motive to invade the rights of other citizens; or if such a common motive exists, it will be more difficult for all who feel it to discover their own strength, and to act in unison with each other. Besides other impediments, it may be remarked that, where there is a consciousness of unjust or dishonorable purposes, communication is always checked by distrust in proportion to the number whose concurrence is necessary.

Hence, it clearly appears, that the same advantage which a republic has over a democracy, in controlling the effects of faction, is enjoyed by a large over a small republic, — is enjoyed by the Union over the States composing it. Does the advantage consist in the substitution of representatives whose enlightened views and virtuous sentiments render them superior to local prejudices and to schemes of injustice? It will not be denied that the representation of the Union will be most likely to possess these requisite endowments. Does it consist in the greater security afforded by a greater variety of parties, against the event of any one party being able to outnumber and oppress the rest? In an equal degree does the increased variety of parties comprised within the Union, increase this security. Does it, in fine, consist in the greater obstacles opposed to the concert and accomplishment of the secret wishes of an unjust and interested majority? Here, again, the extent of the Union gives it the most palpable advantage.

The influence of factious leaders may kindle a flame within their particular States, but will be unable to spread a general conflagration through the other States. A religious sect may degenerate into a political faction in a part of the Confederacy; but the variety of sects dispersed over the entire face of it must secure the national councils against any danger from that source. A rage for paper money, for an abolition of debts, for an equal division of property, or for any other improper or wicked project, will be less apt to pervade the whole body of the Union than a particular member of it; in the same proportion as such a malady is more likely to taint a particular county or district, than an entire State.

In the extent and proper structure of the Union, therefore, we behold a republican remedy for the diseases most incident to republican government. And according to the degree of pleasure and pride we feel in being republicans, ought to be our zeal in cherishing the spirit and supporting the character of Federalists.

Publius

Note: *Madisonian Republicanism*

As The Federalist No. 10 reveals Madison agreed with the antifederalists that a primary problem of governance was control of factions. The antifederalists rooted the problem of faction in that of corruption, understood broadly as the capture of public institutions by private interests. Their solution rested in the effort to control the factional spirit and the power of representatives. In their view, the civic virtue of the citizenry and of its representatives would work as a safeguard against factional tyranny.

The Federalist No. 10 turned the antifederalist understanding on its head. For Madison, and for many other federalists, factions were an inevitable product of liberty, which would produce inequality in the ownership of property. Therefore, the problem could not be solved by the traditional republican means of education and inculcation of virtue. Moreover, the problem of faction was likely to be most, not least, severe in a small republic. It was in a small republic that a self-interested private group would be most likely to be able to seize political power in order to distribute wealth or opportunities in its favor. Indeed, in the view of the federalists, this was precisely what had happened in the years since the

Revolution. In that period, factions had usurped the processes of state government, putting both liberty and property at risk.

Consider in this regard Madison's rejection of Jefferson's proposal of frequent constitutional amendment on the ground that such a proposal would produce "the most violent struggle between the parties interested in reviving and those interested in reforming the antecedent state of property." M. Meyers, ed., The Mind of the Founder 232 (1969). For Jefferson, by contrast, turbulence is "productive of good. It prevents the degeneracy of government, and nourishes a general attention to the public affairs. I hold that a little rebellion now and then is a good thing." Letter to Madison, Jan. 30, 1787, in The Portable Thomas Jefferson 416–417 (M. Peterson ed., 1975). For Madison, ongoing processes of self-government produced not the promise of genuine self-determination but instead the danger of factional warfare.

Madison believed that self-interest was an inevitable force in political behavior. The federalists did not, however, suppose that self-interest was all there was to human beings. "The supposition of universal venality in human nature is little less an error in political reasoning than the supposition of universal rectitude," wrote Hamilton in The Federalist No. 76. And in No. 55, Madison made the same point, claiming that "[as] there is a degree of depravity in mankind which requires a certain degree of circumspection and distrust, so there are other qualities in human nature, which justify a certain portion of esteem and confidence." In any case, the specter of faction was sufficient to justify rejection of the anti-federalist understanding that in a small republic the problem of faction could be overcome. But it was in developing a solution that Madison, Hamilton, and their colleagues were particularly original. The solution began with the insight that in a direct democracy the problem posed by factions is especially acute, for a "common passion or interest will, in almost every case, be felt by a majority of the whole" and there will be no protection for the minority. But safeguards would be found in a large republic. There, the diversity of interests would reduce the risk that a common desire would be felt by sufficient numbers of people to oppress minorities. In this respect, the likelihood of factional tyranny contained a built-in check in a large republic.

On this view, heterogeneity — Brutus's fear — was a positive good. It would work against factionalism and parochialism. At the same time "differences of opinion, and the jarrings of parties [would] . . . promote deliberation and circumspection; and serve to check the excesses of the majority." The Federalist No. 70. Differences and disagreement were not harmful to a deliberative republic. On the contrary, they were indispensable to its successful operation.

Nor were these the only virtues of size. The other feature of the large republic was that the principle of representation would serve in that setting as a substantial solution to the problem of faction. The central phrase here is Madison's suggestion that that principle would "refine and enlarge the public views, by passing them through the medium of a chosen body of citizens, whose wisdom may best discern the true interest of their country, and whose patriotism and love of justice will be least likely to sacrifice it to temporary or partial considerations." This is so in part because in a large republic the dangers produced by undue attachment to local interests would be reduced.

This conception of representation appears throughout The Federalist Papers and indeed throughout the work of both Madison and Hamilton. In No. 57, Madison urges that "the aim of every political constitution is, or ought to be, first to obtain for rulers men who possess most wisdom to discern, and most virtue to pursue, the common good of society; and in the next place, to take the most effectual precautions for keeping them virtuous while they continue to hold the public trust." Elsewhere he suggests that "wisdom" and "virtue" will characterize national representatives. Where the antifederalists accepted representation as a necessary evil, Madison regarded it as an opportunity for achieving governance by officials devoted to a public good distinct from the struggle of private interests.

For these reasons, Madison favored long length of service and large election districts — precisely what the antifederalists most feared. In the Madisonian account, representatives were to have the time and temperament to engage in a form of collective reasoning. They were not to be mere "transmission belts" for the will of the various constituencies, much less to be a mechanism for aggregating interests. The hope, in short, was for a genuinely national politics. The representatives of the people — not the people themselves — would be free to engage in the process of discussion and debate from which the common good would emerge. Consider the fact that the first Congress rejected a right to instruct, by which constituents would be authorized to give binding instructions to representatives. Those who opposed this right contended that it would be inconsistent with the point of the legislative meeting: public-spirited deliberation among people with different points of view.

Even if The Federalist No. 10 is taken to set out some central themes in the new Constitution, it is far from the entire story. The Constitution embodies a set of structural provisions designed to bring about public-spirited representation, to provide safeguards in the event that it is absent, and to ensure an important measure of popular control. The various systems of representation in the different branches of the national government were designed to promote deliberation in government and to control possible abuses. Recognizing that sovereignty lay in the people, the framers designed a system in which no branch could speak authoritatively for the people themselves. On this view, the Constitution's structural provisions can be seen as a kind of bill of rights, designed to protect against tyranny. Many of the framers, including Hamilton, saw the structural provisions in exactly that way.

Bicameralism — the division of Congress into the House and the Senate, with two-year and six-year terms, respectively — was intended to ensure that some representatives would be relatively isolated from the people and that others would be relatively close to them. The fact that the houses of the legislature were divided in this way would combine political accountability (on the part of the House) with a degree of independence (on the part of the Senate), enabling the Senate to serve a kind of "cooling" function. Indirect election of representatives played a far more important role at the time of ratification than it does today. Only the House of Representatives was to be directly elected. The original Constitution provided that Senators would be chosen by state legislatures, and envisioned an electoral college whose members would deliberate over the choice of the president. These features provided additional insulation from political pressure and factional tyranny.

Perhaps most important, the system of checks and balances was designed with the recognition that even national representatives may be prone to the influence of "interests" that is inconsistent with the public welfare. In The Federalist No. 10 itself, Madison recognizes that "[enlightened] statesmen will not always be at the helm." The Federalist No. 51 is the most celebrated elaboration of this point.

The Federalist No. 51 (Madison)
(1788)

In order to lay a due foundation for that separate and distinct exercise of the different powers of government, which to a certain extent is admitted on all hands to be essential to the preservation of liberty, it is evident that each department should have a will of its own; and consequently should be so constituted that the members of each should have as little agency as possible in the appointment of the members of the others. Were this principle rigorously adhered to, it would require that all the appointments for the supreme executive, legislative, and judiciary magistracies should be drawn from the same fountain of authority, the people, through channels having no communication whatever with one another. [Some] difficulties, and some additional expense would attend the execution of it. Some deviations, therefore, from the principle must be admitted. In the constitution of the judiciary department in particular, it might be inexpedient to insist rigorously on the principle: first, because peculiar qualifications being essential in the members, the primary consideration ought to be to select that mode of choice which best secures these qualifications; secondly, because the permanent tenure by which the appointments are held in that department, must soon destroy all sense of dependence on the authority conferring them.

It is equally evident, that the members of each department should be as little dependent as possible on those of the others, for the emoluments annexed to their offices. Were the executive magistrate, or the judges, not independent of the legislature in this particular, their independence in every other would be merely nominal.

But the great security against a gradual concentration of the several powers in the same department, consists in giving to those who administer each department the necessary constitutional means and personal motives to resist encroachments of the others. The provision for defence must in this, as in all other cases, be made commensurate to the danger of attack. Ambition must be made to counteract ambition. The interest of the man must be connected with the constitutional rights of the place. It may be a reflection on human nature, that such devices should be necessary to control the abuses of government. But what is government itself, but the greatest of all reflections on human nature? If men were angels, no government would be necessary. If angels were to govern men, neither external nor internal controls on government would be necessary. In framing a government which is to be administered by men over men, the great difficulty lies in this: you must first enable the government to control the governed; and in the next place oblige it to control itself. A dependence on the people is, no doubt, the primary control on the government; but experience has taught mankind the necessity of auxiliary precautions.

This policy of supplying, by opposite and rival interests, the defect of better motives, might be traced through the whole system of human affairs, private as well as public. We see it particularly displayed in all the subordinate distributions of power, where the constant aim is to divide and arrange the several offices in such a manner as that each may be a check on the other — that the private interest of every individual may be a sentinel over the public rights. These inventions of prudence cannot be less requisite in the distribution of the supreme powers of the State.

But it is not possible to give to each department an equal power of self-defence. In republican government, the legislative authority necessarily predominates. The remedy for this inconveniency is to divide the legislature into different branches; and to render them, by different modes of election and different principles of action, as little connected with each other as the nature of their common functions and their common dependence on the society will admit. It may even be necessary to guard against dangerous encroachments by still further precautions. As the weight of the legislative authority requires that it should be thus divided, the weakness of the executive may require, on the other hand, that it should be fortified. An absolute negative on the legislature appears, at first view, to be the natural defence with which the executive magistrate should be armed. But perhaps it would be neither altogether safe nor alone sufficient. On ordinary occasions it might not be exerted with the requisite firmness, and on extraordinary occasions it might be perfidiously abused. May not this defect of an absolute negative be supplied by some qualified connection between this weaker department and the weaker branch of the stronger department, by which the latter may be led to support the constitutional rights of the former, without being too much detached from the rights of its own department?

There are, moreover, two considerations particularly applicable to the federal system of America, which place that system in a very interesting point of view.

First. In a single republic, all the power surrendered by the people is submitted to the administration of a single government; and the usurpations are guarded against by a division of the government into distinct and separate departments. In the compound republic of America, the power surrendered by the people is first divided between two distinct governments, and then the portion allotted to each subdivided among distinct and separate departments. Hence a double security arises to the rights of the people. The different governments will control each other, at the same time that each will be controlled by itself.

Second. It is of great importance in a republic not only to guard the society against the oppression of its rulers, but to guard one part of the society against the injustice of the other part. Different interests necessarily exist in different classes of citizens. If a majority be united by a common interest, the rights of the minority will be insecure. There are but two methods of providing against this evil: the one by creating a will in the community independent of the majority — that is, of the society itself; the other, by comprehending in the society so many separate descriptions of citizens as will render an unjust combination of a majority of the whole very improbable, if not impracticable. The first method [is] but a precarious security; because a power independent of the society may as well espouse the unjust views of the major, as the rightful interests of the minor party, and may possibly be turned against both parties. The second method will be exemplified in the federal republic of the United States. Whilst all authority in it will be derived from and dependent on the society, the society itself will be broken into so many parts, interests and classes of citizens, that the rights of individuals, or of the minority, will be in little danger from interested combinations of the majority. In a free government the security for civil rights must be the same as that for religious rights. It consists in the one case in the multiplicity of interests, and in the other in the multiplicity of sects. The degree of security in both cases will depend on the number of interests and sects; and this may be presumed to depend on the extent of country and number of people comprehended under the same government. This view of the subject must particularly recommend a proper federal system to all the sincere and considerate friends of republican government, since it shows that in exact proportion as the territory of the Union may be formed into more circumscribed Confederacies, or States, oppressive combinations of a majority will be facilitated; the best security, under the republican forms, for the rights of every class of citizens, will be diminished; and consequently the stability and independence of some members of the government, the only other security, must be proportionally increased.

[In] a society under the forms of which the stronger faction can readily unite and oppress the weaker, anarchy may as truly be said to reign as in a state of nature, where the weaker individual is not secured against the violence of the stronger; and as, in the latter state, even the stronger individuals are prompted, by the uncertainty of their condition, to submit to a government which may protect the weak as well as themselves; so, in the former state, will the more powerful factions or parties be gradually induced, by a like motive, to wish for a government which will protect all parties, the weaker as well as the more powerful. It can be little doubted that if the State of Rhode Island was separated from the Confederacy and left to itself, the insecurity of rights under the popular form of government, within such narrow limits would be displayed by such reiterated oppressions of factious majorities that some power altogether independent of the people would soon be called for by the voice of the very factions whose misrule had proved the necessity of it. In the extended republic of the United States, and among the great variety of interests, parties, and sects which it embraces, a coalition of a majority of the whole society could seldom take place on any other principles than those of justice and the general good; whilst there being thus less danger to a minor from the will of a major party, there must be less pretext, also, to provide for the security of the former, by introducing into the government a will not dependent on the latter, or, in other words, a will independent of the society itself. It is no less certain than it is important, notwithstanding the contrary opinions which have been entertained, that the larger the society, provided it lie within a practical sphere, the more duly capable it will be of self-government. And happily for the republican cause, the practicable sphere may be carried to a very great extent, by a judicious modification and mixture of the federal principle.

Publius

Note: *Madisonian Republicanism and Checks and Balances*

The system of checks and balances within the federal structure was intended to prevent both factionalism and self-interested representation. If a segment of rulers was influenced by interests that diverged from those of the people, other national officials would have both the incentive and the means to resist. The result is an additional protection against tyranny. We might also think of the system as one in which the sovereign people can pursue a strategy of divide and conquer. Rather than undemocratically limiting majority will, the distribution of national powers might be seen, at least in part, as a way of maximizing the power of the public by fragmenting the power of the governors. See, on this and related questions, Sunstein, Constitutionalism after the New Deal, 101 Harv. L. Rev. 421, 430–437 (1989). Of course, this view is controversial. The fragmentation allows the status quo to remain undisturbed, and many have argued that this effect insulates existing practices, including distributions of wealth, from democratic control.

This was a particular theme in the New Deal period, when President Franklin Delano Roosevelt succeeded in concentrating power — including lawmaking and law interpreting power — in the executive branch. See id.; 2 B. Ackerman, We the People: Transformations (1998).

The federal system, too, would act as an important safeguard. The "different governments will control each other" and ensure stalemate rather than action at the behest of particular private interests. The jealousy of state governments, and the attachment of the citizenry to local interests, would provide additional protection against the aggrandizement of power in national institutions. The federal system would allow flexibility, experimentation, accountability, and diversity and permit a measure of self-determination through the classically republican institution of small governmental units. At the same time, the power of individual citizens to move from one state to another would operate as a check on governmental tyranny. The right of "exit" would deter local oppression, as people could vote with their feet.

The result is a complex system of checks: National representation, bicameralism, indirect election, distribution of powers, and the federal-state relationship would operate in concert to counteract the effects of faction in spite of the inevitability of the factional spirit. And the Constitution itself, enforced by disinterested judges and adopted at a moment in which that spirit had perhaps been temporarily extinguished, would prevent majorities or minorities from usurping government power to distribute wealth or opportunities in their favor.

The protection of property rights and contractual liberty were principal interests of the framers, and one of their principal targets was debtor-relief legislation. Some of the framers saw a close practical relationship between the desire to protect private property (along with other forms of private liberty) from governmental intrusion and devices to guard against the dangers posed by faction. For the framers, the problem of faction lay partly in the danger that a self-interested group would obtain governmental power in order to put rights of property at risk. The experience under the Articles of Confederation, in which popular majorities had operated as factions in state legislatures, confirmed the existence of this danger.

In this respect, the federalists may be contrasted with their antifederalist opponents, whose generally weaker objections to laws redistributing property coexisted easily with their preference for decentralized democracy. Indeed, many of the antifederalists approved of debtor-relief laws and saw economic equality as indispensable to a republic. As "Centinel" wrote, a "republican, or free government, can only exist where the body of the people are virtuous, and where property is pretty equally divided; in such a government the people are the sovereign and their sense or opinion is the criterion of every public measure; for when this ceases to be the case, the nature of the government is changed, and an aristocracy, monarchy, or despotism will rise on its ruin." The Antifederalist 16 (H. Storing ed., M. Dry abr. 1985). Moreover, the federalists' hospitable view toward lengthy deliberation and government inaction may be associated with a desire to protect property rights. Inaction, of course, preserves the existing distribution of wealth.

The picture that emerges is in an important sense one of a government that was intended to engage in deliberation. But politics was to be deliberative in a special sense. Representatives were to be accountable to the public; their deliberative task was not disembodied. The framers were thus careful to create political checks designed to ensure that representatives would not stray too far from the desires of their constituents. The result was a kind of hybrid conception of representation, in which legislators were neither to respond blindly to constituent pressures nor to undertake their deliberations in a vacuum. (Note also the restrictions on who would do the deliberating: The framers appeared comfortable with many limits on the franchise; women and slaves, among others, could not vote.)

Where does judicial review fit into this framework? Notice that the Constitution does not explicitly authorize judicial review, but at least in some form it appears to have been widely anticipated — a kind of background understanding. As part of doing their duty, and speaking for the law of the land, judges would strike down legislation that violated the founding document. See P. Hamburger, Law and Judicial Duty (2008). To that extent, the Court would enforce the lines of division set down in the Constitution to ensure that the areas marked off from politics would not be subject to political revision. The boundaries set in the Constitution, and thus by "We the People," were to be unrevisable by electoral majorities — a safeguard that would buttress the other institutional checks. In this sense, judicial review would ensure the supremacy of the Constitution, embodying the will of the sovereign public, against temporary majorities. This idea responded to the distinction drawn by the framers between "law" — the realm of judgment — and "politics" — the realm of will, or personal preference. See The Federalist No. 78, infra. The existence of a realm of "law" immune from "politics" fit securely within a system intended to protect both the public good and private rights from perceived majoritarian excesses.

Note finally, and importantly, that this entire framework reflects a new conception of sovereignty, which lay with the people, not with any king, and not with any branch or set of rulers. Recall that one of the most important contributions of the new Constitution consisted in the rejection of the monarchical legacy in favor of this new understanding of where sovereignty could be found.

Note: *Madisonian Republicanism and Contemporary Constitutionalism*

The foregoing materials raise a large set of questions; we will be exploring them at many places in this book. Here are a few problems that might be kept in mind at the outset.

1. *The complexity of history versus the simplifications of theory.* The account that we have offered — of a particular understanding of Madisonian republicanism — is an attempt to reconstruct the founders' views, but any such attempt is bound to be controversial. Some people think that an account of the kind offered here gives too little emphasis to the framers' belief in individual rights, operating as checks against politics — even deliberative politics. Others think that the framers offered a highly complex set of ideas not reducible to any single "account." Still others think that deliberation was a theme in the founding generation but not an entirely central one; in their view, the framers were well aware of the importance of interest groups, and they did not place a great premium on political deliberation. For discussions, see M. Klarman, supra; W. Bessette, The Mild Voice of Reason (1994).

2. *Republican theory and judicial review.* What does republicanism, Madisonian or otherwise, have to offer to people currently assessing American constitutional law? In the light of history, how should we think about current

politics, and about associated constitutional issues, for example, those involving campaign finance restrictions and access to the ballot? With respect to judicial review, republican thought might argue in favor of a deferential rather than an aggressive judicial role. If democratic self-determination is the end, a powerful judiciary hardly seems the means. But consider the view that under modern circumstances the Supreme Court provides one of the few sites where true deliberation over the public good remains possible. See generally Michelman, Foreword: Traces of Self-Government, 100 Harv. L. Rev. 4 (1986).

3. *Problems with deliberation and direct democracy.* Contrary to Madison's view, many people have argued in favor of a larger role for popular referenda, in which decisions are made on particular issues not by representatives but instead by popular vote. It might be urged that the process of referendum is far more democratic than the process of decision by representative bodies. In recent years, popular referenda in the states have both grown out of and produced constitutional confrontations. Uses of the Internet and discussions of "electronic town meetings" have heightened interest in more direct forms of democracy; modern technologies make direct popular input far more feasible. On referenda generally, see S. Tierney, Constitutional Referendums (rev. ed. 2014); T. Cronin, Direct Democracy (1989); D. Magleby, Direct Legislation (1991); Charlow, Judicial Review, Equal Protection and the Problem with Plebiscites, 79 Cornell L. Rev. 527 (1994); Eule, Judicial Review of Direct Democracy, 99 Yale L.J. 1503 (1990).

4. *Adapting or living with an old constitution.* In some ways, the original constitutional commitments have been severely qualified in the nineteenth and twentieth centuries. For example, the national government engages in many tasks originally thought to be within the province of the states — a phenomenon that can be attributed in large part to the Civil War and Franklin Roosevelt's New Deal, which saw a huge expansion in federal power. The system of checks and balances has been altered by the grant of broad adjudicatory and policymaking power to the President and regulatory agencies. The American conception of constitutional rights has come to include rights of political participation, of freedom of expression, of antidiscrimination on the basis of race and sex, and of "privacy" that were either unanticipated by the founders or are far broader than what they expected. On some of these issues, see T. Lowi, The Personal President (1985).

5. *"Constitutional moments" revisited.* Consider Bruce Ackerman's argument that we have a "dualist democracy" where constitutional change occurs at "constitutional moments" involving popular mobilization. 1 B. Ackerman, We the People: Foundations (1991), argues that there have been three such moments: the founding period, the Civil War era, and the New Deal period. In his view, much of the work of the Supreme Court can be understood as efforts to synthesize the commitments of these three different republics. Ackerman's arguments are controversial, but as we will see, both the Civil War period and the New Deal did help inaugurate major changes in constitutional law, not all of which can be explained by changes in the Constitution's text. See also M. Tushnet, The New Constitutional Order (2003), for an argument that the constitutional arrangements that prevailed in the United States from the 1930s to the 1990s have ended. Tushnet suggests that the nation's new constitutional order is characterized by divided government, ideologically organized parties, and subdued constitutional ambition.

Note: Why (and How) Does the Constitution Bind?

1. *Popular sovereignty.* Why is the Constitution binding? One reason might be that it is a reflection of popular sovereignty. The first three words of the document claim that it is legitimate because it is the work of "We the People." Can popular sovereignty make the text of a new constitution binding?

The American constitutional text was widely debated in what amounted to a national symposium on constitutional theory and ratified by popularly elected state conventions. For the definitive account, see P. Maier, Ratification: The People Debate the Constitution, 1787–1788 (2010). Do these facts create a duty to obey the Constitution?

Although the ratification process was relatively democratic by the standards of the time, African Americans, American Indians, women, and most people who did not own property were excluded from the process. Even aside from these deficiencies,

> the ratification project lacked democratic legitimacy in several ways. [Behind] the closed doors of the Philadelphia convention, some Founders referred to democracy in disparaging terms — "the worst . . . of all political evils," according to Elbridge Gerry. Madison opposed a second convention specifically on the ground that the People, at least at that moment, were neither well enough informed nor sufficiently dispassionate to participate responsibly in making a constitution. In Massachusetts, Federalists were horrified at the idea that the state ratifying convention should be adjourned in order to enable delegates to consult their constituents. In Congress, some Federalists were so distrustful of the People that they preferred to close the House galleries before debating possible amendments to the Constitution.

Klarman, Book Review, 125 Harv. L. Rev. 544, 571 (2011).

2. *The dead hand problem.* Even if the Constitution was supported by mobilized popular majorities in the late eighteenth century, no one alive today voted to ratify it. Why should the "dead hand" of the framers control people alive today? Consider in this regard Thomas Jefferson's insistence that "[the] earth belongs in usufruct to the living; the dead have neither powers nor rights over it," and that "one generation is to another as one independent nation to another." Letter from Thomas Jefferson to James Madison (Sept. 6, 1789), in 6 The Works of Thomas Jefferson 3-4, 8-9 (1904).

Sometimes constitutions are justified on the theory that one aspect of freedom is the ability of a people to bind itself in the future. According to ancient myth, Ulysses had his men bind him to the mast so that he could listen to the song of the Sirens without succumbing. So, too, perhaps constitution makers, fearful of their own future weakness, bind themselves to behave in certain ways. Perhaps the ability to make these decisions is part of what it means for a people to be free and to exist as a continuing entity. See generally J. Elster, Ulysses Unbound: Studies in Rationality, Precommitment, and Constraints (2000).

Consider the extent to which the United States "commitments over time" have involved resistance to, as well as embrace of, constitutional obligation. For example, some of our most revered Presidents have exhibited at best an ambivalent attitude toward constitutional obligation. Thomas Jefferson negotiated the Louisiana Purchase despite his belief that he lacked the constitutional power to do so. Explaining his actions years after he left office, Jefferson wrote that "[a] strict observance of the written laws is doubtless one of the high duties of a good citizen, but it is not the highest. The laws of necessity, of self-preservation, of saving our country when in danger, are of higher obligation." Letter from Thomas Jefferson to John B. Colvin (Sept. 20, 1810), in 11 The Works of Thomas Jefferson 146 (1905). Abraham Lincoln defended the constitutionality of many (but, importantly not all) of his actions at the beginning of the Civil War, but he also made clear that he thought those actions were justified even if they violated the Constitution. See Abraham Lincoln, Special Session Message (July 4, 1861), in 7 A Compilation of the Messages and Papers of the Presidents 3226 (1917) ("Are all the laws, but one, to go unexecuted, and the government itself go to pieces, lest that one be violated?"). See also Barron and Lederman, The Commander in Chief at the Lowest Ebb, 121 Harv. L. Rev. 689, 997–1008 (2008).

Franklin Roosevelt believed that the Constitution was "a layman's document, not a lawyer's contract," Roosevelt, Address on Constitution Day, Washington, DC (Sept. 19, 1937), in 1 The Public Papers and Addresses of Franklin D. Roosevelt 359 (1941), and in his first inaugural address provided clear hints that he was prepared to go beyond commonly understood limits on executive authority if necessary to meet the emergency created by the Great Depression. See Franklin D. Roosevelt, First Inaugural Address, available at http://www.bartleby.com/124/pres49.html ("It is to be hoped that the normal balance of executive and legislative authority may be wholly adequate to meet the unprecedented task before us. But it may be that an unprecedented demand and need for undelayed action may call for temporary departure from that normal balance of public procedure.").

3. *A quick dead hand solution.* Consider a simple answer to the dead hand question: Ideas about democracy and legitimacy are a distraction, and a dead end. We have to ask about human welfare. That is an admittedly large idea, but we might be able to make progress in terms of human welfare without getting into deep philosophical waters. The fact is that if we take the Constitution as binding, we are a lot better off in terms of welfare. What would we do without it?

4. *The problem of constitutional mistake (or worse).* If a constitution contained only provisions that the people of the United States today thought wise, the problem of constitutional obligation would never arise. The people would then follow constitutional commands because of an independent judgment that they would reach even if there were no constitution. The problem of obedience becomes acute only when constitutional commands depart from these independent judgments.

For an example illustrating the problem, consider the fact that the Constitution, as originally drafted, had many provisions that protected the rights of slave holders at the expense of enslaved individuals. Article I, section 2, clause 3 inflated the representation of slave states in Congress by counting three-fifths of all slaves as persons for purposes of congressional apportionment. Article I, section 9, clause 1 prohibited Congress from outlawing the slave trade until 1808. Article IV, section 2, clause 3 required free states to return enslaved persons who had escaped to their territory. Citing these provisions, Supreme Court Justice Thurgood Marshall once wrote that he did not "find the wisdom, foresight, and sense of justice exhibited by the framers particularly profound. To the contrary, the government they devised was defective from the [start]." Marshall, Commentary: Reflections on the Bicentennial of the United States Constitution, 101 Harv. L. Rev. 1, 2 (1987). Why should anyone have felt obligated to obey provisions in the original Constitution that protected slavery?

Of course, the modern, amended Constitution outlaws, rather than protects slavery. See U.S. Const. amend. XIII. Still, even as amended, the Constitution contains provisions that many think anachronistic, foolish, or morally questionable. See generally S. Levinson, Our Undemocratic Constitution: Where the Constitution Goes Wrong (and How We the People Can Correct It) (2006).

For example, article II, section 1, clause 5 requires the President to be a "natural born Citizen" of the United States. Suppose a substantial majority of the people of the United States believe that a particular naturalized citizen would make the best President. Why should the text of the Constitution prevent the election of this person? Consider the following possibilities:

5. *Amendments and supermajorities.* Perhaps the Constitution is entitled to respect because if the people disapprove of specific constitutional commands, they can change them through the amendment process. Note, though, that the requirements to amend the United States Constitution are extraordinarily arduous. Article V provides that amendments can be proposed by two-thirds of both Houses of Congress or by application for a constitutional convention proposed by two-thirds of the states. In either event, proposed amendments must be approved by three-fourths of the states. What makes the requirements of article V legitimate?

Does the very difficulty of amendment, as well as the supermajority requirements for initial ratification, provide a built-in guarantee that constitutional provisions are wise? Consider McGinnis and Rappaport, Originalism and the Good Constitution, 98 Geo. L.J. 1693, 1696 (2010):

> [Supermajority] rule helps assure the bipartisan consensus that facilitates the widespread allegiance of citizens and guarantees rights for minorities. [Supermajority rule also] improves the erratic judgment of legislators about entrenchment by restricting the agenda of proposals and creating a veil of ignorance that promotes disinterested decision making.

Notice, though, that supermajority requirements can also give a relatively small group veto power over the entire constitution and therefore create the potential of constitutionalizing narrow, special interest provisions. For example, as noted above, delegates to the constitutional convention from slave states made clear that they would not vote for the new constitution unless slavery was granted constitutional protection.

6. *The good (enough) constitution.* Back to well-being: Is constitutional obligation justified on the ground that, for the most part, the Constitution is substantively sound and that it is worth putting up with its suboptimal features given the risk of chaos or tyranny if it were ignored? One's reaction to this suggestion depends on how deficient one thinks the Constitution is, on the one hand, and on how great one thinks the risk of chaos or tyranny would be if provisions were ignored, on the other. In this regard, skeptics might want to consider:

a. the fact that the Constitution as currently written allows for the election of a President who loses the popular vote and gives wildly disproportionate representation to small states in the Senate;

b. the fact that we have in the past ignored some clear constitutional provisions without obvious adverse consequences. For example, article I, section 3, clause 2 provides that all senators, except for the first set of senators, are to serve for six years, yet ever since Vermont was admitted as the first new state in 1791, one senator from new states has always served less than six years so as to provide for the staggered election of senators.

7. *Modern acquiescence.* The framers of the Constitution have no actual power over us. If the Constitution is obeyed today, it is because of the consent of living people who could disregard it if they chose to do so. Can constitutional obligation be grounded on modern acquiescence? See Dorf, The Undead Constitution, 125 Harv. L. Rev. 2011, 2015–2016 (2012) ("The Constitution is not law today simply because its provisions were adopted by the People in 1789, 1791, 1868, and so forth. The Constitution is law today because it continues to be accepted today.") But if the Constitution's legitimacy rests on this ground, "[how] do we know [it] is accepted today? Is the absence of a revolution sufficient to legitimate the Constitution?" Id. at 2016. Moreover, if the acquiescence is founded on the belief that there is an obligation to obey, but the obligation to obey rests on acquiescence, the argument is circular. If modern acquiescence is the basis for obligation, does it follow that particular provisions of the Constitution should not be enforced when public opinion (measured how?) opposes enforcement?

8. *The relevance of the question.* For better or worse, constitutional obligation is generally taken to be an axiom of our system. See, e.g., Monaghan, Our Perfect Constitution, 56 N.Y.U. L. Rev. 353, 383–384 (1981) ("The authoritative status of the written constitution is a legitimate matter of debate for political theorists interested in the nature of political obligation. [For] purposes of legal reasoning, the binding quality of the constitutional text is itself incapable of and not in need of further demonstration.").

Note, however, recent polling data showing that 76 percent of the American people think that justices of the Supreme Court at least sometimes decide cases because of their personal or political views rather than because of legal analysis. See Results of New York Times/CBS Poll, available at http://www.nytimes.com/interactive/2012/06/08/us/politics/08scotus-poll-documents.html?ref = politics.

Moreover, although justices on the Supreme Court, presidents, and members of Congress rarely or never question constitutional obligation, constitutional law is dominated by debate about what the Constitution consists of and how it should be interpreted. Contending sides in this debate regularly make claims that various forms of constitutional interpretation are inconsistent with true obligation.

B.   THE BASIC FRAMEWORK

Marbury v. Madison

5 U.S. (1 Cranch) 137 (1803)

[William Marbury had been appointed a justice of the peace by the defeated incumbent Federalist President, John Adams, in the closing stages of the Adams administration. The Federalist-controlled Senate confirmed the appointments of Adams's last-minute appointees, including Marbury, on March 3, 1801. The formal commissions had not been delivered when Thomas Jefferson, the Republican President, assumed office several days later. Jefferson refused to deliver the commissions of the justices appointed by Adams. Marbury and others sought a writ of mandamus to compel Madison, Jefferson's Secretary of State (replacing John Marshall, Adams's Secretary of State), to deliver the commissions. (The underlying controversy is set out in more detail in a historical note that follows the opinion.)]

Opinion of the Court [by MARSHALL, CHIEF JUSTICE].

At the last term on the affidavits then read and filed with the clerk, a rule was granted in this case, requiring the secretary of state to show cause why a mandamus should not issue, directing him to deliver to William Marbury his commission as a justice of the peace for the county of Washington, in the district of Columbia.

No cause has been shown, and the present motion is for a mandamus. The peculiar delicacy of this case, the novelty of some of its circumstances, and the real difficulty attending the points which occur in it, require a complete exposition of the principles on which the opinion to be given by the court is founded.

In the order in which the court has viewed this subject, the following questions have been considered and decided.

1st. Has the applicant a right to the commission he demands?

2dly. If he has a right, and that right has been violated, do the laws of his country afford him a remedy?

3dly. If they do afford him a remedy, is it a mandamus issuing from this court?

The first object of inquiry is,

1st. Has the applicant a right to the commission he demands?

His right originates in an act of congress passed in February, 1801, concerning the district of Columbia. . . .

In order to determine whether he is entitled to this commission, it becomes necessary to inquire whether he has been appointed to the office. For if he has been appointed, the law continues him in office for five years, and he is entitled to the possession of those evidences of office, which, being completed, became his property.

The last act to be done by the president is the signature of the commission: he has then acted on the advice and consent of the senate to his own nomination. The time for deliberation has then passed. . . .

It is, [decidedly] the opinion of the court, that when a commission has been signed by the president, the appointment is made; and that the commission is complete, when the seal of the United States has been affixed to it by the secretary of state.

Where an officer is removable at the will of the executive, the circumstance which completes his appointment is of no concern; because the act is at any time revocable; and the commission may be arrested, if still in the office. But when the officer is not removable at the will of the executive, the appointment is not revocable, and cannot be annulled: it has conferred legal rights which cannot be resumed. [To] withhold his commission, therefore, is an act deemed by the court not warranted by law, but violative of a vested legal right.

2. This brings us to the second inquiry; which is: If he has a right, and that right has been violated, do the laws of his country afford him a remedy? The very

essence of civil liberty certainly consists in the right of every individual to claim the protection of the laws, whenever he receives an injury. One of the first duties of government is to afford that protection. In Great Britain, the king himself is sued in the respectful form of a petition, and he never fails to comply with the judgment of his court.

The government of the United States has been emphatically termed a government of laws, and not of men. It will certainly cease to deserve this high appellation, if the laws furnish no remedy for the violation of a vested legal right. If this obloquy is to be cast on the jurisprudence of our country, it must arise from the peculiar character of the case.

It behooves us, then, to inquire whether there be in its composition any ingredient which shall exempt it from legal investigation, or exclude the injured party from legal redress. . . .

Is it in the nature of the transaction? Is the act of delivering or withholding a commission to be considered as a mere political act, belonging to the executive department alone, for the performance of which entire confidence is placed by our constitution in the supreme executive; and for any misconduct respecting which, the injured individual has no remedy? That there may be such cases is not to be questioned; but that every act of duty, to be performed in any of the great departments of government, constitutes such a case, is not to be admitted.

It follows, then, that the question, whether the legality of an act of the head of a department be examinable in a court of justice or not, must always depend on the nature of that act. If some acts be examinable, and others not, there must be some rule of law to guide the court in the exercise of its jurisdiction. In some instances, there may be difficulty in applying the rule to particular cases; but there cannot, it is believed, be much difficulty in laying down the rule.

By the constitution of the United States, the president is invested with certain important political powers, in the exercise of which he is to use his own discretion, and is accountable only to his country in his political character, and to his own conscience. To aid him in the performance of these duties, he is authorized to appoint certain officers, who act by his authority, and in conformity with his orders. In such cases, their acts are his acts; and whatever opinion may be entertained of the manner in which executive discretion may be used, still there exists, and can exist, no power to control that discretion. The subjects are political: they respect the nation, not individual rights, and being entrusted to the executive, the decision of the executive is conclusive. The application of this remark will be perceived, by adverting to the act of congress for establishing the department of foreign affairs. This officer, as his duties were prescribed by that act, is to conform precisely to the will of the president: he is the mere organ by whom that will is communicated. The acts of such an officer, as an officer, can never be examinable by the courts. But when the legislature proceeds to impose on that officer other duties; when he is directed peremptorily to perform certain acts; when the rights of individuals are dependent on the performance of those acts; he is so far the officer of the law; is amenable to the laws for his conduct; and cannot, at his discretion, sport away the vested rights of others.

The conclusion from this reasoning is, that where the heads of departments are the political or confidential agents of the executive, merely to execute the will of the president, or rather to act in cases in which the executive possesses a constitutional or legal discretion, nothing can be more perfectly clear, than that their acts are only politically examinable. But where a specific duty is assigned by law, and individual rights depend upon the performance of that duty, it seems equally clear, that the individual who considers himself injured, has a right to resort to the laws of his country for a remedy.

The question whether a right has vested or not, is, in its nature, judicial, and must be tried by the judicial authority. If, for example, Mr. Marbury had taken the oaths of a magistrate, and proceeded to act as one; in consequence of which, a suit has been instituted against him, in which his defence had depended on his being a magistrate, the validity of his appointment must have been determined by judicial authority. So, if he conceives that, by virtue of his appointment, he has a legal right either to the commission which has been made out for him, or to a copy of that commission, it is equally a question examinable in a court, and the decision of the court upon it must depend on the opinion entertained of his appointment. That question has been discussed, and the opinion is, that the latest point of time which can be taken as that at which the appointment was complete, and evidenced, was when, after the signature of the president, the seal of the United States was affixed to the commission.

It is, then, the opinion of the Court: 1st. That by signing the commission of Mr. Marbury, the President of the United States appointed him a justice of peace [and] that the appointment conferred on him a legal right to the office for the space of five years. 2d. That, having this legal title to the office, he has a consequent right to the commission; a refusal to deliver which is a plain violation of that right, for which the laws of his country afford him a remedy.

3. It remains to be inquired whether he is entitled to the remedy for which he applies? This depends on — 1st. The nature of the writ applied for; and 2d. The power of this court.

1st. The nature of the writ. . . . [To] render the mandamus a proper remedy, the officer to whom it is to be directed, must be one to whom, on legal principles, such writ may be directed; and the person applying for it must be without any other specific and legal remedy.

1. With respect to the officer to whom it would be directed. The intimate political relation subsisting between the president of the United States and the heads of departments, necessarily renders any legal investigation of the acts of one of those high officers peculiarly irksome, as well as delicate; and excites some hesitation with respect to the propriety of entering into such investigation. Impressions are often received, without much reflection or examination, and it is not wonderful, that in such a case as this, the assertion, by an individual, of his legal claims in a court of justice, to which claims it is the duty of that court to attend, should at first view be considered by some, as an attempt to intrude into the cabinet, and to intermeddle with the prerogatives of the executive.

It is scarcely necessary for the court to disclaim all pretensions to such a jurisdiction. An extravagance, so absurd and excessive, could not have been entertained for a moment. The province of the court is, solely, to decide on the rights of individuals, not to inquire how the executive, or executive officers, perform duties in which they have a discretion. Questions in their nature political, or which are, by the constitution and laws, submitted to the executive, can never be made in this court.

But, if this be not such a question; if, so far from being an intrusion into the secrets of the cabinet, it respects a paper which, according to law, is upon record, and to a copy of which the law gives a right, on the payment of ten cents; if it be no intermeddling with a subject over which the executive can be considered as having exercised any control; what is there, in the exalted station of the officer, which shall bar a citizen from asserting, in a court of justice, his legal rights, or shall forbid a court to listen to the claim, or to issue a mandamus, directing the performance of a duty, not depending on executive discretion, but on particular acts of congress, and the general principles of law? [Where the head of a department] is directed by law to do a certain act affecting the absolute rights of individuals, [it] is not perceived on what grounds the courts of the country are [excused] from the duty of giving judgment. . . . [This,] then, is a plain case for a mandamus, either to deliver the commission, or a copy of it from the record; and it only remains to be inquired,

Whether it can issue from this court.

The act to establish the judicial courts of the United States authorizes the supreme court "to issue writs of mandamus, in cases warranted by the principles and usages of law, to any courts appointed, or persons holding, office, under the authority of the United States."[*]

The secretary of state, being a person holding an office under the authority of the United States, is precisely within the letter of the description; and if this court is not authorized to issue a writ of mandamus to such an officer, it must be because the law is unconstitutional, and therefore absolutely incapable of conferring the authority, and assigning the duties which its words purport to confer and assign.

The constitution vests the whole judicial power of the United States in one supreme court, and such inferior courts as congress shall, from time to time, ordain and establish. This power is expressly extended to all cases arising under the laws of the United States; and, consequently, in some form, may be exercised over the present case; because the right claimed is given by a law of the United States.

In the distribution of this power it is declared that "the supreme court shall have original jurisdiction in all cases affecting ambassadors, other public ministers and consuls, and those in which a state shall be a party. In all other cases, the supreme court shall have appellate jurisdiction."

It has been insisted, at the bar, that as the original grant of jurisdiction, to the supreme and inferior courts, is general, and the clause, assigning original jurisdiction to the supreme court, contains no negative or restrictive words, the power remains to the legislature, to assign original jurisdiction to that court in other cases than those specified in the article which has been recited; provided those cases belong to the judicial power of the United States.

---

* [The full text of Section 13 of the Judiciary Act of 1789, 1 Stat. 73, reads:

And be it further enacted, That the Supreme Court shall have exclusive jurisdiction of all controversies of a civil nature, where a state is a party, except between a state and its citizens; and except also between a state and citizens of other states, or aliens, in which latter case it shall have original but not exclusive jurisdiction. And shall have exclusively all such jurisdiction of suits or proceedings against ambassadors, or other public ministers, or their domestics, or domestic servants, as a court of law can have or exercise consistently with the law of nations; and original, but not exclusive jurisdiction of all suits brought by ambassadors, or other public ministers, or in which a consul, or vice consul, shall be a party. And the trial of issues of fact in the Supreme Court, in all actions at law against citizens of the United States, shall be by jury. The Supreme Court shall also have appellate jurisdiction from the circuit courts and courts of the several states, in the cases herein after specially provided for; and shall have power to issue writs of prohibition to the district courts, when proceeding as courts of admiralty and maritime jurisdiction, and writs of mandamus, in cases warranted by the principles and usages of law, to any courts appointed, or persons holding office, under the authority of the United States.]

If it had been intended to leave it in the discretion of the legislature to apportion the judicial power between the supreme and inferior courts according to the will of that body, it would certainly have been useless to have proceeded further than to have defined the judicial power, and the tribunals in which it should be vested. The subsequent part of the section is mere surplusage, is entirely without meaning, if such is to be the construction. If congress remains at liberty to give this court appellate jurisdiction, where the constitution has declared their jurisdiction shall be original; and original jurisdiction where the constitution has declared it shall be appellate; the distribution of jurisdiction, made in the constitution, is form without substance.

Affirmative words are often, in their operation, negative of other objects than those affirmed; and in this case, a negative or exclusive sense must be given to them, or they have no operation at all.

It cannot be presumed that any clause in the constitution is intended to be without effect; and, therefore, such a construction is inadmissible, unless the words require it. . . . When an instrument organizing fundamentally a judicial system, divides it into one supreme, and so many inferior courts as the legislature may ordain and establish; then enumerates its powers, and proceeds so far to distribute them, as to define the jurisdiction of the supreme court by declaring the cases in which it shall take original jurisdiction, and that in others it shall take appellate jurisdiction; the plain import of the words seems to be, that in one class of cases its jurisdiction is original, and not appellate; in the other it is appellate, and not original. If any other construction would render the clause inoperative, that is an additional reason for rejecting such other construction, and for adhering to their obvious meaning.

To enable this court, then, to issue a mandamus, it must be shown to be an exercise of appellate jurisdiction, or to be necessary to enable them to exercise appellate jurisdiction.

It has been stated at the bar that the appellate jurisdiction may be exercised in a variety of forms, and that if it be the will of the legislature that a mandamus should be used for that purpose, that will must be obeyed. This is true, yet the jurisdiction must be appellate, not original.

It is the essential criterion of appellate jurisdiction, that it revises and corrects the proceedings in a cause already instituted, and does not create that cause. Although, therefore, a mandamus may be directed to courts, yet to issue such a writ to an officer for the delivery of a paper, is in effect the same as to sustain an original action for that paper, and, therefore, seems not to belong to appellate, but to original jurisdiction. Neither is it necessary in such a case as this, to enable the court to exercise its appellate jurisdiction.

The authority, therefore, given to the supreme court, by the act establishing the judicial courts of the United States, to issue writs of mandamus to public officers, appears not to be warranted by the constitution; and it becomes necessary to inquire whether a jurisdiction so conferred can be exercised.

The question, whether an act, repugnant to the constitution, can become the law of the land, is a question deeply interesting to the United States; but, happily, not of an intricacy proportioned to its interest. It seems only necessary to recognize certain principles, supposed to have been long and well established, to decide it.

That the people have an original right to establish, for their future government, such principles as, in their opinion, shall most conduce to their own happiness is the basis on which the whole American fabric has been erected. The exercise of this original right is a very great exertion; nor can it, nor ought it, to be frequently repeated. The principles, therefore, so established, are deemed fundamental. And as the authority from which they proceed is supreme, and can seldom act, they are designed to be permanent.

This original and supreme will organizes the government, and assigns to different departments their respective powers. It may either stop here, or establish certain limits not to be transcended by those departments.

The government of the United States is of the latter description. The powers of the legislature are defined and limited; and that those limits may not be mistaken, or forgotten, the constitution is written. To what purpose are powers limited, and to what purpose is that limitation committed to writing, if these limits may, at any time, be passed by those intended to be restrained? The distinction between a government with limited and unlimited powers is abolished, if those limits do not confine the persons on whom they are imposed, and if acts prohibited and acts allowed, are of equal obligation. It is a proposition too plain to be contested, that the constitution controls any legislative act repugnant to it; or, that the legislature may alter the constitution by an ordinary act.

Between these alternatives there is no middle ground. The constitution is either a superior paramount law, unchangeable by ordinary means, or it is on a level with ordinary legislative acts, and, like other acts, is alterable when the legislature shall please to alter it.

If the former part of the alternative be true, then a legislative act contrary to the constitution is not law: if the latter part be true, then written constitutions are absurd attempts, on the part of the people, to limit a power in its own nature illimitable.

Certainly all those who have framed written constitutions contemplate them as forming the fundamental and paramount law of the nation, and, consequently, the theory of every such government must be, that an act of the legislature, repugnant to the constitution, is void.

This theory is essentially attached to a written constitution, and, is consequently, to be considered, by this court, as one of the fundamental principles of our society. It is not therefore to be lost sight of in the further consideration of this subject.

If an act of the legislature, repugnant to the constitution, is void, does it, notwithstanding its invalidity, bind the courts, and oblige them to give it effect? Or, in other words, though it be not law, does it constitute a rule as operative as if it was a law? This would be to overthrow in fact what was established in theory; and would seem, at first view, an absurdity too gross to be insisted on. It shall, however, receive a more attentive consideration.

It is emphatically the province and duty of the judicial department to say what the law is. Those who apply the rule to particular cases, must of necessity expound and interpret that rule. If two laws conflict with each other, the courts must decide on the operation of each.

So if a law be in opposition to the constitution; if both the law and the constitution apply to a particular case, so that the court must either decide that case conformably to the law, disregarding the constitution; or conformably to the constitution, disregarding the law; the court must determine which of these conflicting rules governs the case. This is of the very essence of judicial duty. If, then, the courts are to regard the constitution, and the constitution is superior to any ordinary act of the legislature, the constitution, and not such ordinary act, must govern the case to which they both apply.

Those, then, who controvert the principle that the constitution is to be considered, in court, as a paramount law, are reduced to the necessity of maintaining that courts must close their eyes on the constitution, and see only the law.

This doctrine would subvert the very foundation of all written constitutions. It would declare that an act which, according to the principles and theory of our government, is entirely void, is yet, in practice, completely obligatory. It would declare that if the legislature shall do what is expressly forbidden, such act, notwithstanding the express prohibition, is in reality effectual. It would be giving to the legislature a practical and real omnipotence, with the same breath which professes to restrict their powers within narrow limits. It is prescribing limits, and declaring that those limits may be passed at pleasure.

That it thus reduces to nothing what we have deemed the greatest improvement on political institutions, a written constitution, would of itself be sufficient, in America, where written constitutions have been viewed with so much reverence, for rejecting the construction. But the peculiar expressions of the constitution of the United States furnish additional arguments in favor of its rejection.

The judicial power of the United States is extended to all cases arising under the constitution.

Could it be the intention of those who gave this power, to say that in using it the constitution should not be looked into? That a case arising under the constitution should be decided without examining the instrument under which it arises?

This is too extravagant to be maintained.

In some cases, then, the constitution must be looked into by the judges. And if they can open it at all, what part of it are they forbidden to read or to obey?

There are many other parts of the constitution which serve to illustrate this subject.

It is declared that "no tax or duty shall be laid on articles exported from any state." Suppose a duty on the export of cotton, of tobacco, or of flour; and a suit instituted to recover it. Ought judgment to be rendered in such a case? Ought the judges to close their eyes on the constitution, and only see the law?

The constitution declares "that no bill of attainder or ex post facto law shall be passed."

If, however, such a bill should be passed, and a person should be prosecuted under it; must the court condemn to death those victims whom the constitution endeavors to preserve?

"No person," says the constitution, "shall be convicted of treason unless on the testimony of two witnesses to the same overt act, or on confession in open court."

Here the language of the constitution is addressed especially to the courts. It prescribes, directly for them, a rule of evidence not to be departed from. If the legislature should change that rule, and declare one witness, or a confession out of court, sufficient for conviction, must the constitutional principle yield to the legislative act?

From these, and many other selections which might be made, it is apparent, that the framers of the constitution contemplated that instrument as a rule for the government of courts, as well as of the legislature.

Why otherwise does it direct the judges to take an oath to support it? This oath certainly applies in an especial manner, to their conduct in their official character. How immoral to impose it on them, if they were to be used as the instruments, and the knowing instruments, for violating what they swear to support!

The oath of office, too, imposed by the legislature, is completely demonstrative of the legislative opinion on this subject. It is in these words: "I do solemnly swear that I will administer justice without respect to persons, and do equal right to the poor and to the rich; and that I will faithfully and impartially discharge all the duties incumbent on me as, according to the best of my abilities and understanding, agreeably to the constitution and laws of the United States."

Why does a judge swear to discharge his duties agreeably to the constitution of the United States, if that constitution forms no rule for his government? if it is closed upon him, and cannot be inspected by him? If such be the real state of things, this is worse than solemn mockery. To prescribe, or to take this oath, becomes equally a crime.

It is also not entirely unworthy of observation, that in declaring what shall be the supreme law of the land, the constitution itself is first mentioned; and not the laws of the United States generally, but those only which shall be made in pursuance of the constitution, have that rank.

Thus, the particular phraseology of the constitution of the United States confirms and strengthens the principle, supposed to be essential to all written constitutions, that a law repugnant to the constitution is void; and that courts, as well as other departments, are bound by that instrument.

The rule must be discharged.

Note: *Marbury v. Madison*

1. *Background.* The *Marbury* case was decided against a complex background and was in some respects the culmination of a lengthy political battle. The Federalist President, John Adams, had been defeated by the Republican candidate, Thomas Jefferson, who was to take office on March 4, 1801. The Federalist Congress responded by, among other things, attempting to retain control of the federal judiciary. On February 16, 1801, that Congress enacted the Circuit Court Act, creating sixteen new circuit judges and eliminating the circuit-riding duties of the Supreme Court. Congress also decreased the size of the Supreme Court in order to deny the incoming President Jefferson the power to appoint a successor to Justice Cushing. Two weeks later Congress enacted another statute creating forty-two positions for justices of the peace in the District of Columbia. President Adams nominated the authorized judges, who were confirmed on March 2 and 3, just one day before President Jefferson was to assume office.

At this point, John Marshall, then Secretary of State under President Adams — who had appointed Marbury and the other petitioners in the *Marbury* case — became involved in the circumstances that gave rise to the case. Although Marshall took his oath of office as Chief Justice on February 4, 1801, he continued to serve as Secretary of State at least until March 3 of that year. President Adams and Acting Secretary of State Marshall had signed the commissions of the petitioners in the *Marbury* case by March 3, but the commissions had not been delivered by the time Adams and Marshall left the executive branch. Adams's successor, Thomas Jefferson, thereafter refused to deliver the commissions, claiming that they were nullities. (Should Marshall have disqualified himself from *Marbury*?) In the next year — before *Marbury* was decided — the Circuit Court Act was repealed by the Republican Congress; the statute creating justices of the peace was left intact. But Congress also abolished the June and December terms of the Court, leaving the Court adjourned from December 1801 until February 1803 — and thus abolishing the 1802 term. The reason for Congress's actions was to avoid a constitutional challenge to the repeal of the Circuit Court Act.

A footnote: Six days after *Marbury* was decided, the Court upheld the repeal. Stuart v. Laird, 5 U.S. (1 Cranch) 299 (1803). The history is illuminatingly discussed in O'Fallon, *Marbury*, 44 Stan. L. Rev. 219 (1992).

2. *Method, antecedents.* What does the opinion in Marbury v. Madison indicate about opinion-writing method? What are the sources of the decision? What in the Constitution supports judicial review?

a. Chief Justice Marshall does not begin the opinion in *Marbury* with the question of jurisdiction, although a court's jurisdiction is usually the first problem to be examined. Why did Chief Justice Marshall fail to deal first with the jurisdictional issue?

b. The actual holding of *Marbury* is that the Supreme Court lacks power to direct the President to deliver Marbury's commission. This conclusion allowed the Court to avoid the problem of ordering President Jefferson to deliver commissions to President Adams's appointees. There was, of course, no assurance that President Jefferson would have complied with such a decree. The existence of judicial review was therefore established in a case in which the Court concluded that it had no power to do anything to remedy official illegality. Consider in this regard the suggestion that the "decision is a masterwork of indirection, a brilliant example of Chief Justice Marshall's capacity to sidestep danger while seeming to court it, to advance in one direction while his opponents are looking in another." R. McCloskey, The American Supreme Court 40 (1960).

What is the basis for Chief Justice Marshall's conclusion that the Court lacked jurisdiction? Consider the following rejoinders to his reasoning: (1) The categories of original and appellate jurisdiction are not mutually exclusive. The Constitution sets up a provisional allocation, which Congress can alter if it wishes. The power to alter is recognized in the "exceptions" clause. It is therefore constitutional for Congress to grant to the Court original jurisdiction over cases over which it had appellate jurisdiction under the Constitution's provisional allocation. (2) The Constitution defines an irreducible minimum of original jurisdiction but permits Congress to expand original jurisdiction if it chooses to do so. Is either of these views less persuasive, as a textual matter, than Chief Justice Marshall's?

Note in this regard that the reasoning of *Marbury* has been rejected insofar as it suggests that Congress may not give the lower courts jurisdiction over cases falling within the original jurisdiction of the Supreme Court. See, e.g., Illinois v. Milwaukee, 406 U.S. 91 (1972).

c. Chief Justice Marshall acknowledges that, "where the heads of departments are the political or confidential agents of the executive, merely to execute the will of the president, or rather to act in cases in which the executive possesses a constitutional or legal discretion, nothing can be more perfectly clear, than that their acts are only politically examinable." This acknowledgment created the category of cases involving "political questions," which are not subject to judicial review. See section E infra. What falls in this category? In Chief Justice Marshall's view, is there any case of official illegality that is not judicially cognizable? On one view, the answer is no. Political questions, as Chief Justice Marshall understands them, are questions in which there is no constitutional obstacle to the acts in question. Note also the contrast drawn by Chief Justice Marshall between cases involving "individual rights" and cases involving "discretion." What is the relationship between those two categories of cases?

d. The most important holding in the case is that the Supreme Court has the power to declare acts of Congress unconstitutional — that is, that it has the power of judicial review. It is striking to many modern readers that Chief Justice Marshall's principal arguments rely not on the text of the Constitution but instead on its structure and on the consequences of a conclusion that judicial review was unavailable.

Consider the following view:

> [The] issue of judicial review was by no means new. The Privy Council had occasionally applied the ultra vires principle to set aside legislative acts contravening municipal or colonial charters. State courts had set aside state statutes under constitutions no more explicit about judicial review than the federal. The Supreme Court itself had measured a state law against a state constitution in Cooper v. Telfair, 4 U.S. (4 Dall.) 14 (1800), and had struck down another under the supremacy clause in Ware v. Hylton, 3 U.S. (3 Dall.) 199 (1796); in both cases the power of judicial review was expressly affirmed. Even Acts of Congress had been struck down by federal circuit courts, and the Supreme Court, while purporting to reserve the question of its power to do so, had reviewed the constitutionality of a federal statute in Hylton v. United States, 3 U.S. (3 Dall.) 171 (1796). Justice James Iredell had explicitly asserted this power both in Chisholm v. Georgia, 2 U.S. (2 Dall.) 419 (1793) and in Calder v. Bull, 3 U.S. (3 Dall.) 386 (1798), and Chase had acknowledged it in [Cooper]. In the Convention, moreover, both proponents and opponents of the proposed Council of Revision had recognized that the courts would review the validity of congressional legislation, and Alexander Hamilton had proclaimed the same doctrine in The Federalist. Yet though Marshall's principal arguments echoed those of Hamilton, he made no mention of any of this material, writing as if the question had never arisen before.

Currie, The Constitution in the Supreme Court: The Powers of the Federal Courts, 1801–1835, 49 U. Chi. L. Rev. 646, 655–656 (1982). For a comprehensive account, see P. Hamburger, Law and Judicial Duty (2008). In what ways was the issue in *Ware* and *Cooper* different from that in *Marbury*? Consider the proposition that Marshall's arguments for judicial review supported what has been called "departmentalism." According to one version of departmentalism, each branch has the power to determine for itself, and finally, the constitutionality of legislation affecting its own functions. How expansive would judicial review be under this version of departmentalism?

3. *The justifications for judicial review.* Consider the various arguments for judicial review.

a. *Written Constitution.* Chief Justice Marshall's first argument is that judicial review is a necessary inference from the fact of a written Constitution. "The distinction between a government with limited and unlimited powers is abolished, if those limits do not confine the persons on whom they are imposed, and if acts prohibited and acts allowed, are of equal obligation." But this argument seems to confound two different issues. (1) Is the Constitution binding on the national government? (2) Are the courts authorized to enforce their interpretation of the Constitution against that of other branches of the national government? Even if the answer to the first question is "yes," that answer does not dictate an answer to the second question. Many countries have had written constitutions without having judicial review. Would it be plausible to respond that the

Constitution would be ineffective or merely hortatory if it were not subject to judicial enforcement?

Consider in this regard The Federalist No. 78, infra; and note that in Eastern Europe, emerging from communism, and South Africa, emerging from apartheid, nations have chosen both a written constitution and judicial review of one sort or another. Indeed, judicial review has been seen as a central part of the new constitutional orders. Consider also Currie, supra, at 657: "Surely the Framers were reasonable people, and surely they could not have meant to appoint the fox as guardian of the henhouse." But on the facts of *Marbury*, who was the fox? Note also that in some nations, certain constitutional provisions, such as those involving social and economic guarantees and environmental protection, are expressly made nonjusticiable.

b. *Notions of judicial role.* Chief Justice Marshall claims that the ordinary role of the courts is to interpret the law. That role, he claims, requires judges to construe the Constitution in the ordinary course of conducting judicial business. But it might be responded that constitutional interpretation — when it takes the form of invalidation of the outcomes reached by the more political branches — is special because of its highly intrusive and largely final character. Should this difference mean that the ordinary interpretive task is no longer appropriate? For an emphatic negative answer, grounded in history, see P. Hamburger, supra.

c. *Supremacy clause.* The supremacy clause provides that the "Constitution, and the Laws of the United States which shall be made in Pursuance thereof . . . shall be the supreme Law of the Land." Does this establish the existence of judicial review?

> Assuming that an act repugnant to the Constitution is not a law "in pursuance thereof" and thus must not be given effect as the supreme law of the land, who according to the Constitution, is to make the determination as to whether any given law is in fact repugnant to the Constitution itself? [Chief Justice Marshall] never confronts this question. His substitute question, whether a law repugnant to the Constitution still binds the courts, assumes that such repugnance has appropriately been determined by those granted such power under the Constitution. It is clear, however, that the supremacy clause itself cannot be the clear textual basis for a claim by the judiciary that this prerogative to determine repugnancy belongs to it.

Van Alstyne, A Critical Guide to Marbury v. Madison, 1969 Duke L.J. 1, 22.

Note also that Chief Justice Marshall gains rhetorical force for his position by referring to clauses that in his view have a "plain" meaning opposed to acts of Congress. But one might doubt whether constitutional provisions are likely to have such meanings in many cases on which Congress and Court will differ. In any event, consider the possibility that the use of these hypothetical cases is misleading in light of the more open-ended character of most constitutional interpretation — of which *Marbury* itself is an example.

d. *Grant of jurisdiction.* The Constitution extends the judicial power of the United States to all cases arising under the Constitution. Chief Justice Marshall argues that the grant of jurisdiction would be meaningless if the courts did not have authority to examine the constitutionality of acts of Congress. Consider A. Bickel, The Least Dangerous Branch 6 (1962):

> If it were impossible to conceive a case "arising under the Constitution" which would not require the Court to pass on the constitutionality of congressional

legislation, then [Marshall might be correct, for without judicial review] this clause [would be] quite senseless. But there are such cases which may call into question the constitutional validity of judicial, administrative, or military actions without attacking legislative or even presidential acts as well, or which call upon the Court, under appropriate statutory authorization, to apply the Constitution to acts of the states. Any reading but his own was for Marshall "too extravagant to be maintained." His own, although out of line with the general scheme of Article III, may be possible; but it is optional. This is the strongest bit of textual evidence in support of Marshall's view, but it is merely a hint.

e. *Judges' oath*. Chief Justice Marshall relies on the fact that judges take an oath to uphold the Constitution. But consider the fact that the

> oath to support the Constitution is not peculiar to the judges, but is taken indiscriminately by every officer of the government, and is designed rather as a test of the political principles of the man, than to bind the officer in the discharge of his duty. [But] granting it to relate to the official conduct of the judge, as well as every other officer, and not to his political principles, still it must be understood in reference to supporting the constitution, only as far as that may be involved in his official duty; and consequently, if his official duty does not comprehend an inquiry into the authority of the legislature, neither does his oath.

Eakin v. Raub, 12 Serg. & Rawle 330, 353 (Pa. 1825). In short, the oath requires judges to support the Constitution; however, if the Constitution assigns ultimate interpretive power to the legislature, or to the President, then judicial review is not contemplated by the Constitution but is in violation of it. Does this suggest that the "oath" argument is a makeweight?

Perhaps these various arguments appear more forceful in combination than they appear when separated. One might claim that while none is independently decisive, the various arguments together suggest that judicial review is a part of the constitutional structure.

4. *The view of the framers and the ratifiers*. The relevant documents at the time of the framing, and before, indicate that judicial review was generally contemplated. See also A. Bickel, supra, at 15–16:

> [It] is as clear as such matters can be that the Framers of the Constitution specifically, if tacitly, expected that the federal courts would assume a power — of whatever exact dimensions — to pass on the constitutionality of actions of the Congress and the President, as well as of the several states. Moreover, not even a colorable showing of decisive historical evidence to the contrary can be made. Nor can it be maintained that the language of the Constitution is compellingly the other way. At worst it may be said that the intentions of the Framers cannot be ascertained with finality.

Consider Hamilton's views in The Federalist No. 78:

> There is no position which depends on clearer principles, than that every act of a delegated authority, contrary to the tenor of the commission under which it is exercised, is void. No legislative act, therefore, contrary to the Constitution, can be valid. To deny this, would be to affirm, that the deputy is greater than his principal; that the servant is above his master; that the representatives of the people are superior to the people themselves; that men acting by virtue of powers, may do not only what their powers do not authorize, but what they forbid.

If it be said that the legislative body are themselves the constitutional judges of their own powers, and that the construction they put upon them is conclusive upon the other departments, it may be answered, that this cannot be the natural presumption, where it is not to be collected from any particular provisions in the Constitution. It is not otherwise to be supposed, that the Constitution could intend to enable the representatives of the people to substitute their will to that of their constituents. It is far more rational to suppose, that the courts were designed to be an intermediate body between the people and the legislature, in order, among other things, to keep the latter within the limits assigned to their authority. The interpretation of the laws is the proper and peculiar province of the courts. A constitution is, in fact, and must be regarded by the judges, as a fundamental law. It therefore belongs to them to ascertain its meaning, as well as the meaning of any particular act proceeding from the legislative body. If there should happen to be an irreconcilable variance between the two, that which has the superior obligation and validity ought, of course, to be preferred; or, in other words, the Constitution ought to be preferred to the statute, the intention of the people to the intention of their agents.

Nor does this conclusion by any means suppose a superiority of the judicial to the legislative power. It only supposes that the power of the people is superior to both; and that where the will of the legislature, declared in its statutes, stands in opposition to that of the people, declared in the Constitution, the judges ought to be governed by the latter rather than the former. They ought to regulate their decisions by the fundamental laws, rather than by those which are not fundamental. . . .

It can be of no weight to say that the courts, on the pretence of a repugnancy, may substitute their own pleasure to the constitutional intentions of the legislature. This might as well happen in the case of two contradictory statutes; or it might as well happen in every adjudication upon any single statute. The courts must declare the sense of the law; and if they should be disposed to exercise WILL instead of JUDGMENT, the consequence would equally be the substitution of their pleasure to that of the legislative body. The observation, if it prove any thing, would prove that there ought to be no judges distinct from that body.

How, if at all, do Hamilton's justifications for judicial review differ from Chief Justice Marshall's?

For a detailed treatment of some relevant historical issues, see Kramer, Foreword: We the Court, 115 Harv. L. Rev. 4 (2001). Kramer urges that for the framers the "Constitution was not ordinary law, not peculiarly the stuff of courts and judges." Instead it was "a special form of popular law, law made by the people to bind their governors." Id. at 10. For many members of the revolutionary generation, constitutional principles were subject to "popular enforcement," id. at 40, that is, public insistence on compliance with the Constitution, rather than judicial activity. "It was the legislature's delegated responsibility to decide whether a proposed law was constitutionally authorized, subject to oversight by the people. Courts simply had nothing to do with it, and they were acting as interlopers if they tried to second-guess the legislature's decision." Id. at 49. Kramer traces the controversial early growth of the practice of judicial review, with many seeing it as an "act of resistance." Id. at 54. At the founding, a "handful of participants saw a role for judicial review, though few of these imagined it as a powerful or important device, and none seemed anxious to emphasize it. Others were opposed. . . . The vast majority of participants were still thinking in terms of popular constitutionalism and so focused on traditional political means of enforcing the new charter; the notion of judicial review simply never crossed their minds." Id. at 66.

In Kramer's account, constitutional limits would be enforced not through courts, but as a result of republican institutions and the citizenry's own commitment to its founding document. Kramer raises serious doubts about the account in Marbury v. Madison and in particular about judicial supremacy in the interpretation of the Constitution. He suggests that for some of the framers, judicial review was "a substitute for popular resistance" and to be used "only when the unconstitutionality of a law was clear beyond dispute." See also L. Kramer, The People Themselves (2004), for an expanded version of this argument.

Note, however, that many and probably most historians and historically minded lawyers disagree, and believe that Marbury v. Madison had it essentially right. See P. Hamburger, supra; R. Clinton, Marbury v. Madison and Judicial Review (1989). For valuable historical treatments, see W. Nelson, Marbury v. Madison: The Origins and Legacy of Judicial Review (2000); B. Ackerman, The Failure of the Founding Fathers: Jefferson, Marshall, and the Rise of Presidential Democracy (2007).

Martin v. Hunter's Lessee

14 U.S. (1 Wheat.) 304 (1816)

[This case arose out of a dispute over the ownership of land in Virginia. Hunter claimed the land pursuant to a grant from the state of Virginia in 1789, which confiscated lands owned by British subjects. Martin, a British subject, claimed that the attempted confiscation was ineffective under anticonfiscation clauses of treaties between the United States and England.

[The Virginia trial court held in favor of Martin; the Virginia Court of Appeals reversed, concluding that the state's title to the land had vested before the relevant treaties, and alternatively that Martin's claim was defeated by a 1796 Act of Compromise between the state and Martin's uncle, from whom Martin's claim derived. The Supreme Court of the United States reversed the Virginia Court of Appeals, neglecting to mention the Act of Compromise, but claiming that Virginia had not perfected its title before the relevant treaties. Fairfax's Devisee v. Hunter's Lessee, 7 Cranch 603 (1813). The Supreme Court remanded the case to the Virginia Court of Appeals with instructions to enter judgment for the appellant. But on remand the Virginia court declined. The court said that section 25 of the Judiciary Act was unconstitutional insofar as it extended the appellate jurisdiction of the Supreme Court to the Virginia court.

[In its opinion, the court emphasized that the act placed the courts of one sovereign — Virginia — under the direct control of another, an arrangement incompatible with the notion of sovereignty. "It must have been foreseen that controversies would sometimes arise as to the boundaries of the two jurisdictions. Yet the constitution has provided no umpire, has erected no tribunal by which they shall be settled. The omission proceeded, probably, from the belief, that such a tribunal would produce evils greater than those of the occasional collisions which it would be designed to remedy."

[The excerpts here deal only with the question of whether the Supreme Court has appellate jurisdiction over constitutional decisions by state courts.]

Mr. Justice Story delivered the opinion of the Court. . . .

[The] appellate power is not limited by the terms of the third article to any particular courts. The words are, "the judicial power (which includes appellate power) shall extend to all cases," &c., and "in all other cases before mentioned the supreme court shall have appellate jurisdiction." It is the case, then, and not the court, that gives the jurisdiction. If the judicial power extends to the case, it will be in vain to search in the letter of the constitution for any qualification as to the tribunal where it depends. [If] the text be clear and distinct, no restriction upon its plain and obvious import ought to be admitted, unless the inference be irresistible.

If the constitution meant to limit the appellate jurisdiction to cases pending in the courts of the United States, it would necessarily follow that the jurisdiction of these courts would, in all the cases enumerated in the constitution, be exclusive of state tribunals. How otherwise could the jurisdiction extend to all cases arising under the constitution, laws, and treaties of the United States, or to all cases of admiralty and maritime jurisdiction? If some of these cases might be entertained by state tribunals, and no appellate jurisdiction as to them should exist, then the appellate power would not extend to all, but to some cases. If state tribunals might exercise concurrent jurisdiction over all or some of the other classes of cases in the constitution without control, then the appellate jurisdiction of the United States might, as to such cases, have no real existence, contrary to the manifest intent of the constitution. [This] construction would abridge the jurisdiction of such court far more than has been ever contemplated in any act of congress. . . .

[It] is plain that the framers of the constitution did contemplate that cases within the judicial cognizance of the United States not only might but would arise in the state courts, in the exercise of their ordinary jurisdiction. With this view the sixth article declares, that "this constitution, and the laws of the United States, which shall be made in pursuance thereof, and all treaties made, or which shall be made, under the authority of the United States, shall be the supreme law of the land, and the judges in every state shall be bound thereby, any thing in the constitution or laws of any state to the contrary notwithstanding." It is obvious that this obligation is imperative upon the state judges in their official, and not merely in their private, capacities. From the very nature of their judicial duties they would be called upon to pronounce the law applicable to the case in judgment. They were not to decide merely according to the laws or constitution of the state, but according to the constitution, laws and treaties of the United States — "the supreme law of the land."

A moment's consideration will show us the necessity and propriety of this provision in cases where the jurisdiction of the state courts is unquestionable. Suppose a contract for the payment of money is made between citizens of the same state, and performance thereof is sought in the courts of that state; no person can doubt that the jurisdiction completely and exclusively attaches, in the first instance, to such courts. Suppose at the trial the defendant sets up in his defence a tender under a state law, making paper money a good tender, or a state law, impairing the obligation of such contract, which law, if binding, would defeat the suit. The constitution of the United States has declared that no state shall make any thing but gold or silver coin a tender in payment of debts, or pass a law impairing the obligation of contracts. If congress shall not have passed a law providing for the removal of such a suit to the courts of the United States, must not the state court proceed to hear and determine it? [Suppose] an indictment for a crime in a state court, and the defendant should allege in his defence that the crime was created by an ex post facto act of the state, must not the state court, in the exercise of a jurisdiction which has already rightfully attached, have a right to pronounce on the validity and sufficiency of the defence? It would be extremely difficult, upon any legal principles, to give a negative answer to these inquiries. Innumerable instances of the same sort might be stated, in illustration of the position; and unless the state courts could sustain jurisdiction in such cases, this clause of the sixth article would be without meaning or effect, and public mischiefs, of a most enormous magnitude, would inevitably ensue.

It must, therefore, be conceded that the constitution not only contemplated, but meant to provide for cases within the scope of the judicial power of the United States, which might yet depend before state tribunals. It was foreseen that in the exercise of their ordinary jurisdiction, state courts would incidentally take cognizance of cases arising under the constitution, the laws, and treaties of the United States. Yet to all these cases the judicial power, by the very terms of the constitution, is to extend. It cannot extend by original jurisdiction if that was already rightfully and exclusively attached in the state courts, which (as has been already shown) may occur; it must, therefore, extend by appellate jurisdiction, or not at all. It would seem to follow that the appellate power of the United States must, in such cases, extend to state tribunals; and if in such cases, there is no reason why it should not equally attach upon all others within the purview of the constitution.

It has been argued that such an appellate jurisdiction over state courts is inconsistent with the genius of our governments, and the spirit of the constitution. That the latter was never designed to act upon state sovereignties, but only upon the people, and that if the power exists, it will materially impair the sovereignty of the states, and the independence of their courts. . . .

It is a mistake that the constitution was not designed to operate upon states, in their corporate capacities. It is crowded with provisions which restrain or annul the sovereignty of the states in some of the highest branches of their prerogatives. The tenth section of the first article contains a long list of disabilities and prohibitions imposed upon the states. Surely, when such essential portions of state sovereignty are taken away, or prohibited to be exercised, it cannot be correctly asserted that the constitution does not act upon the states. The language of the constitution is also imperative upon the states as to the performance of many duties. It is imperative upon the state legislatures to make laws prescribing the time, places, and manner of holding elections for senators and representatives, and for electors of president and vice-president. And in these, as well as some other cases, congress have a right to revise, amend, or supercede the laws which may be passed by state legislatures. When, therefore, the states are stripped of some of the highest attributes of sovereignty, and the same are given to the United States; when the legislatures of the states are, in some respects, under the control of congress, and in every case are, under the constitution, bound by the paramount authority of the United States; it is certainly difficult to support the argument that the appellate power over the decisions of state courts is contrary to the genius of our institutions. The courts of the United States can, without question, revise the proceedings of the executive and legislative authorities of the states, and if they are found to be contrary to the constitution, may declare them to be of no legal validity. Surely the exercise of the same right over judicial tribunals is not a higher or more dangerous act of sovereign power.

Nor can such a right be deemed to impair the independence of state judges. It is assuming the very ground in controversy to assert that they possess an absolute independence of the United States. In respect to the powers granted to the United States, they are not independent; they are expressly bound to obedience by the letter of the constitution; and if they should unintentionally transcend their authority, or misconstrue the constitution, there is no more reason for giving their judgments an absolute and irresistible force, than for giving it to the acts of the other co-ordinate departments of state sovereignty.

The argument urged from the possibility of the abuse of the revising power, is equally unsatisfactory. It is always a doubtful course, to argue against the use or existence of a power, from the possibility of its abuse. It is still more difficult, by such an argument, to ingraft upon a general power a restriction which is not to be found in the terms in which it is given. From the very nature of things, the absolute right of decision, in the last resort, must rest somewhere — wherever it may be vested it is susceptible of abuse. In all questions of jurisdiction the inferior, or appellate court, must pronounce the final judgment; and common sense, as well as legal reasoning, has conferred it upon the latter.

It is further argued, that no great public mischief can result from a construction which shall limit the appellate power of the United States to cases in their own courts: first, because state judges are bound by an oath to support the constitution of the United States, and must be presumed to be men of learning and integrity; and, secondly, because congress must have an unquestionable right to remove all cases within the scope of the judicial power from the state courts to the courts of the United States, at any time before final judgment, though not after final judgment. As to the first reason — admitting that the judges of the state courts are, and always will be, of as much learning, integrity, and wisdom, as those of the courts of the United States, (which we very cheerfully admit,) it does not aid the argument. It is manifest that the constitution has proceeded upon a theory of its own, and given or withheld powers according to the judgment of the American people, by whom it was adopted. [The] constitution has presumed (whether rightly or wrongly we do not inquire) that state attachments, state prejudices, state jealousies, and state interests, might sometimes obstruct, or control, or be supposed to obstruct or control, the regular administration of justice. Hence, in controversies between states; between citizens of different states; between citizens claiming grants under different states; between a state and its citizens, or foreigners, and between citizens and foreigners, it enables the parties, under the authority of congress, to have the controversies heard, tried, and determined before the national tribunals. No other reason than that which has been stated can be assigned, why some, at least, of those cases should not have been left to the cognizance of the state courts. In respect to the other enumerated cases — the cases arising under the constitution, laws, and treaties of the United States, cases affecting ambassadors and other public ministers, and cases of admiralty and maritime jurisdiction — reasons of a higher and more extensive nature, touching the safety, peace, and sovereignty of the nation, might well justify a grant of exclusive jurisdiction.

This is not all. A motive of another kind, perfectly compatible with the most sincere respect for state tribunals, might induce the grant of appellate power over their decisions. That motive is the importance, and even necessity of uniformity of decisions throughout the whole United States, upon all subjects within the purview of the constitution. Judges of equal learning and integrity, in different states, might differently interpret a statute, or a treaty of the United States, or even the constitution itself: If there were no revising authority to control these jarring and discordant judgments, and harmonize them into uniformity, the laws, the treaties, and the constitution of the United States would be different in different states, and might, perhaps, never have precisely the same construction, obligation, or efficacy, in any two states. The public mischiefs that would attend such a state of things would be truly deplorable; and it cannot be believed that they could have escaped the enlightened convention which formed the constitution. What, indeed, might then have been only prophecy, has now become fact; and the appellate jurisdiction must continue to be the only adequate remedy for such evils.

There is an additional consideration, which is entitled to great weight. The constitution of the United States was designed for the common and equal benefit of all the people of the United States. The judicial power was granted for the same benign and salutary purposes. It was not to be exercised exclusively for the benefit of parties who might be plaintiffs, and would elect the national forum, but also for the protection of defendants who might be entitled to try their rights, or assert their privileges, before the same forum. Yet, if the construction contended for be correct, it will follow, that as the plaintiff may always elect the state court, the defendant may be deprived of all the security which the constitution intended in aid of his rights. Such a state of things can, in no respect, be considered as giving equal rights. . . .

On the whole, the court are of opinion, that the appellate power of the United States does extend to cases pending in the state courts; and that the 25th section of the judiciary act, which authorizes the exercise of this jurisdiction in the specified cases, by a writ of error, is supported by the letter and spirit of the constitution. We find no clause in that instrument which limits this power; and we dare not interpose a limitation where the people have not been disposed to create one. . . .

[Reversed.]

Note: Supreme Court Review of State Courts and State Laws

1. *Supreme Court review of state court decisions — underlying concerns.* In what ways does the issue in *Martin* differ from that in *Marbury*? Why is it important to have Supreme Court jurisdiction over the state courts? Justice Story's opinion stresses that, if there were "no revising authority," the federal system would make possible "jarring and discordant judgment." The appellate jurisdiction of the Supreme Court is, in this view, necessary to ensure the uniformity of federal law. But that raises the question why federal law must be uniform. As a general rule, legal requirements may vary from one state to another. What would be the evil in having disparate interpretations of the federal Constitution?

The Virginia judges in *Martin* made two arguments for their conclusion. First, they claimed not that the Constitution did not bind state judges, but that one sovereign could not control another; the risk of centralization thus outweighed the risk of disharmony. Second, they contended that other devices were available in order to minimize that latter risk and to bring about uniformity. Congress could, for example, allow removal to federal court of all cases involving a federal question. The position of the Virginia judges was that Congress had to take action to eliminate the risk of lack of uniformity through creating lower federal courts and expanding removal jurisdiction. The Court's view, by contrast, is that the more direct mechanism of control — appellate jurisdiction — is constitutionally permissible.

In addition to the uniformity point, note the possibility that Supreme Court review is necessary because of state hostility to, or lack of sufficient sympathy for, federal rights. The argument here is that state judges will be less likely to react sympathetically to federal claims — either because they lack the tenure and salary protections of article III, and are thus more susceptible to political influence, or because they have a natural alliance with the legislative and executive parts of state government. Perhaps, in short, state judges are insufficiently independent of the forces against which constitutional guarantees are supposed to run. Neuborne, The Myth of Parity, 90 Harv. L. Rev. 1105, 1127–1128 (1977), speaks of the difference between federal district judges and state trial judges, but the arguments are applicable to appellate judges as well:

> Federal district judges [are] as insulated from majoritarian pressures as is function- ally possible, precisely to insure their ability to enforce the Constitution without fear of reprisal. State trial judges, on the other hand, generally are elected for a fixed term, rendering them vulnerable to majoritarian pressure when deciding constitutional cases. [This] insulation factor, I suggest, explains the historical pref- erence for federal enforcement of controversial constitutional norms.

This view has often played an important role in constitutional history. But one might ask whether it might not be the federal judges who are likely to be biased.

Another justification for Supreme Court review of state court decisions stresses the comparative expertise of the federal courts in dealing with federal constitutional questions. Neuborne, supra, at 1120, suggests that "federal trial courts tend to be better equipped to analyze complex, often conflicting lines of authority and more likely to produce competently written, persuasive opinions than are state trial courts." Why should this be the case?

2. *Supreme Court review of state laws — constitutional basis. Martin* involved Supreme Court review of state court decisions, not of state laws; but elements of the Court's reasoning are applicable to the latter problem. Do the arguments, textual and otherwise, for the power of judicial review of state laws carry more force than those for judicial review of federal laws? Consider Justice Holmes's view: "I do not think the United States would come to an end if we lost our power to declare an Act of Congress void. I do think the Union would be imperiled if we could not make that declaration as to the laws of the several States." O. W. Holmes, Collected Legal Papers 295–296 (1920).

3. *Justice Story and article III.* In *Martin,* Justice Story interpreted article III to require that the whole judicial power of the United States should be at all times vested, either in an original or appellate form, in some courts created under its authority. If it were accepted, this conclusion would have dramatic practical consequences. It means that, at any time, some federal court must have the power to decide any case to which the federal judicial power extends. On what does Justice Story base his conclusion?

Consider Currie, The Constitution in the Supreme Court: The Powers of the Federal Courts, 1801–1835, 49 U. Chi. L. Rev. 646, 685–686 (1982), suggesting that Story's conclusion

> was contrary to Supreme Court precedent [as] well as to consistent congressional practice. [The] strongest argument against giving a natural reading to the ostensibly unlimited discretion of Congress to limit federal jurisdiction is *Marbury*'s principle that the courts were intended to enforce constitutional limits on legislative power.

Country would be in ruins w/ ths extn Clock.

Story's interpretation poorly comports with that principle, for it outlaws such minor caseload adjustments as the jurisdictional amount while allowing Congress to evade any substantial check by vesting sole power over important constitutional questions in a single lower court selected for the complaisance of its judges.

4. *Cohens v. Virginia.* In Cohens v. Virginia, 19 U.S. (6 Wheat.) 264 (1821), the Court reaffirmed *Martin* in the context of review of state criminal proceedings. The case involved defendants who had been convicted of the unlawful sale of lottery tickets in Virginia. They defended on the ground that an act of Congress authorized the local government of the District of Columbia to establish a lottery. The Court, per Chief Justice Marshall, affirmed, concluding that the congressional statute did not authorize the sale outside the territorial boundaries of the District of Columbia. But the importance of the case lies in the holding that the Supreme Court could exercise jurisdiction over decisions of the state courts in criminal cases and in cases in which the state was a party. As to the fact that the state was a party, Chief Justice Marshall noted that "the judicial power, as originally given, extends to all cases arising under the constitution or a law of the United States, whoever may be the party." The language of article III, Chief Justice Marshall claimed, referred to "all" federal question cases. The same reasoning applied to the claim that the fact that a criminal case was involved made *Cohens* different from *Martin*.

5. *Federal supremacy reaffirmed.* In James v. City of Boise, 136 S. Ct. 685 (2016), the Supreme Court reaffirmed that its interpretations of federal law are supreme and binding on state courts. In Hughes v. Rowe, 449 U.S. 5 (1980) (per curiam), the Supreme Court had interpreted 42 U.S.C. §1988 to permit a prevailing defendant in a civil rights suit to recover fees only if "the plaintiff's action was frivolous, unreasonable, or without foundation." The Idaho Supreme Court concluded that it was not bound by the Court's interpretation, reasoning that "[although] the Supreme Court may have the authority to limit the discretion of lower federal courts, it does not have the authority to limit the discretion of state courts where such limitation is not contained in the statute." The Idaho Supreme Court proceeded to award attorney's fees under section 1988 without first determining whether the plaintiff's action was frivolous, unreasonable, or without foundation. In reversing, the Supreme Court stated:

"It is this Court's responsibility to say what a [federal] statute means, and once the Court has spoken, it is the duty of other courts to respect that understanding of the governing rule of law. (citations omitted). . . . As Justice Story explained 200 years ago, if state courts were permitted to disregard this Court's rulings on federal law, 'the laws, the treaties, and the constitution of the United States would be different in different states, and might, perhaps, never have precisely the same construction, obligation, or efficacy, in any two states. The public mischiefs that would attend such a state of things would be truly deplorable.' Martin v. Hunter's Lessee, 14 U.S. (1 Wheat) 304, 348 (1816)."

Note: *Judicial Exclusivity in Constitutional Interpretation?*

In Cooper v. Aaron, 358 U.S. 1 (1958), Arkansas had failed to comply with a district court order requiring desegregation. The school board's petition for certiorari described the situation: "[the] legislative, executive, and judicial departments of the state government opposed the desegregation of Little Rock schools by enacting laws, calling out troops, making statements vilifying federal law and federal courts, and failing to utilize state law enforcement agencies and judicial processes to maintain public peace."

The state argued that desegregation would lead to undue violence and disorder and that those consequences justified disobedience of the decree. The Court rejected that argument on the ground that "law and order are not here to be preserved by depriving the Negro children of their constitutional rights." But the Court went on to meet the view that "the Governor and Legislature [are] not bound by our holding in the *Brown* case":

> Article VI of the Constitution makes the Constitution the "supreme Law of the Land." In 1803, Chief Justice Marshall, speaking for a unanimous Court, referring to the Constitution as "the fundamental and paramount law of the nation," declared in the notable case of Marbury v. Madison [that] "It is emphatically the province and duty of the judicial department to say what the law is." This decision declared the basic principle that the federal judiciary is supreme in the exposition of the law of the Constitution, and that principle has ever since been respected by this Court and the Country as a permanent and indispensable feature of our constitutional system. It follows that the interpretation of the Fourteenth Amendment enunciated by this Court in the *Brown* case is the supreme law of the land, and Art. VI of the Constitution makes it of binding effect on the States "any Thing in the Constitution or Laws of any State to the Contrary notwithstanding." Every state legislator and executive and judicial officer is solemnly committed by oath taken pursuant to Art. VI, cl. 3, "to support this Constitution."

Cooper might well be thought to go beyond *Marbury*. *Marbury* established that in the course of deciding cases, courts must look to the Constitution as an enforceable source of law. When there is a conflict between the Constitution and a statute, and when the conflict is relevant to the resolution of a justiciable controversy, the courts must allow the Constitution, as they interpret it, to prevail. But this principle might not establish any special judicial authority to interpret the Constitution. On one view, *Marbury* means only that every branch of government, acting within its sphere, is authorized to interpret the Constitution.

Cooper v. Aaron suggests that the courts should see themselves as having been entrusted with a special and distinctive role as ultimate guardians of the meaning of the Constitution, and that other government officials must not interpret the Constitution for themselves but instead must look to the courts' interpretation and take it as authoritative. The result would be that judicial rulings are authoritative, even if there is no decree against the relevant officials in a litigated case. Perhaps more generally such a view would suggest that Presidents, members of Congress, and others should not think independently about what the Constitution requires, but should instead ask how the Supreme Court would be likely to decide.

If the passage from *Cooper* should be so understood, does it go too far in establishing "judicial supremacy"? What are the practical differences between *Cooper* and the narrower interpretation of *Marbury*?

1. *The view from the presidency.* Consider in this regard the responsibility of political actors, including most prominently the President, in circumstances in which (a) they believe that a statute is unconstitutional in the face of a court's conclusion that it is constitutional, or in the expectation that the court will uphold it, and (b) they believe that the statute or measure is constitutional in

the face of a judicial conclusion that it is unconstitutional, or in the expectation that the court will invalidate it. The two circumstances might seem very different.

Consider the view that in the first situation, political officials can legitimately make their own judgments about what the Constitution means, and act on the basis of those judgments. More particularly: Suppose that the Supreme Court has upheld or would uphold a statute that the President believes unconstitutional. (It might be an environmental statute, regulating private property owners and attacked as a "taking" of property, or it might be a restriction on commercial advertising, or it might be discrimination against transgender persons.) The Constitution imposes on all branches of government, not just the courts, a duty to comply with the Constitution. A necessary inference is that the President and members of Congress must make their own judgments on constitutional issues.

This responsibility might seem especially insistent in light of the fact that moral issues frequently become constitutional issues. If the courts' duty is exclusive, politics becomes drained of morality, and political actors will be making decisions on the basis of expediency alone. Thus, for example, if the President or a member of Congress believes that a statute is unconstitutional, he or she must ignore it, even if the Court would uphold it. The Constitution plainly speaks to all public officials, and it is simply too important to be left entirely to the justices. See the veto message of Andrew Jackson, 1832, on an act to recharter the Bank of the United States, 2 Messages and Papers of the Presidents 576, 581–582 (J. Richardson ed., 1900) (vetoing on constitutional grounds a measure that had been upheld by the Court: "[The] opinion of the judges has no more authority over Congress than the opinion of Congress has over the judges, and on that point the President is independent of both").

In support of this general conclusion, consider the views expressed by Jefferson, Letter to Abigail Adams, Sept. 11, 1804, in 8 The Writings of Thomas Jefferson 310 (M. Ford ed., 1897):

> You seem to think it devolved on the judges to decide on the validity of the sedition law. But nothing in the Constitution has given them a right to decide for the Executive, any more than to the Executive to decide for them. Both magistracies are equally independent in the sphere of action assigned to them. The judges, believing the law constitutional, had a right to pass a sentence of fine and imprisonment, because that power was placed in their hands by the Constitution. But the Executive, believing the law to be unconstitutional, was bound to remit the execution of it; because that power has been confided to him by the Constitution. That instrument meant that its coordinate branches should be checks on each other. But the opinion which gives to the judges the right to decide what laws are constitutional, and what not, not only for themselves in their sphere of action, but for the Legislature and Executive also, would make the judiciary a despotic branch.

The second situation might be a lot harder. Suppose the President, or some other public official, believes that the Supreme Court has wrongly invalidated a statute. Examples include decisions invalidating laws restricting abortions, laws forbidding the President from engaging in certain actions designed to reduce the risk of a terrorist attack, or laws requiring states to recognize same-sex marriage. What is the President's duty in the face of such laws? May he sign or propose legislation that would run afoul of the Court's decision? May he attempt to get the Court to overrule its decision through such acts and through repetitive and insistent litigation? May he campaign against the Court? See Lincoln's First

Inaugural Address, Mar. 4, 1861, in 6 Messages and Papers of the Presidents 5 (J. Richardson ed., 1900):

> I do not forget the position assumed by some that constitutional questions are to be decided by the Supreme Court; nor do I deny that such decisions must be binding, in any case, upon the parties to a suit, as to the object of that suit, while they are also entitled to a very high respect and consideration in all parallel cases by all other departments of the government. And, while it is obviously possible that such decision may be erroneous in any given case, still the evil effect following it, being limited to that particular case, with the chance that it may be overruled and never become a precedent for other cases, can better be borne than could the evils of a different practice. At the same time, the candid citizen must confess that if the policy of the government, upon vital questions affecting the whole people, is to be irrevocably fixed by decisions of the Supreme Court, the instant they are made, in ordinary litigation between parties in personal actions, the people will have ceased to be their own rulers, having to that extent practically resigned the government into the hands of that eminent tribunal. Nor is there in this view any assault upon the court or the judges. It is a duty from which they may not shrink to decide cases properly brought before them, and it is no fault of theirs if others seek to turn their decisions to political purposes.

Other Presidents, including Franklin Roosevelt and Richard Nixon, have expressed similar views. Can this position be distinguished from the refusal of Governor Faubus of Arkansas to comply with the decision in Brown v. Board of Education? See if you can draw a distinction that does not speak of the moral or legal correctness of *Brown*.

Consider the views of President Reagan's Attorney General Edwin Meese in The Law of the Constitution, 61 Tul. L. Rev. 979 (1987):

> [There] is [a] necessary distinction between the Constitution and constitutional law. The two are not synonymous. . . .
>
> Obviously [a Supreme Court decision] does have binding quality: It binds the parties in a case and also the executive branch for whatever enforcement is necessary. But such a decision does not establish a "supreme Law of the Land" that is binding on all persons and parts of government, henceforth and forevermore. . . .
>
> To confuse the Constitution with judicial pronouncements allows no standard by which to criticize and to seek the overruling of [cases] such as *Dred Scott*, and Plessy v. Ferguson. To do otherwise, as Lincoln said, is to submit to government by judiciary. But such a state could never be consistent with the principles of our Constitution. Indeed, it would be utterly inconsistent with the very idea of the rule of law to which we, as a people, have always subscribed.

2. *"Underenforced" constitutional norms.* It might be argued that the Constitution sometimes invalidates official action, even if the Supreme Court declines so to hold. There is, in this view, a difference between what the Constitution requires and what the Court says it requires. The Court might decide that, because of the need to defer to other branches of government or because of other limitations on its own competence, some measure does not violate the Constitution; but such a holding might not bind other officials in the process of deciding whether a proposed course of action is constitutional, since those officials are not constrained by principles of deference.

See Sager, Fair Measure: The Status of Underenforced Constitutional Norms, 91 Harv. L. Rev. 1212, 1220–1221, 1227 (1978):

> Conventional analysis does not distinguish between fully enforced and underenforced constitutional norms; as a general matter, the scope of a constitutional norm is considered to be coterminous with the scope of its judicial enforcement. [Where] a federal judicial construct is found not to extend to certain official behavior because of institutional concerns rather than analytical perceptions, it seems strange to regard the resulting decision as a statement about the meaning of the constitutional norm in question. After all, what the members of the federal tribunal have actually determined is that there are good reasons for stopping short of exhausting the content of the constitutional concept with which they are dealing; the limited judicial construct which they have fashioned or accepted is occasioned by this determination and does not derive from a judgment about the scope of the constitutional concept itself.
>
> [The] most direct consequence of adopting this revised view is the perception that government officials have a legal obligation to obey an underenforced constitutional norm which extends beyond its interpretation by the federal judiciary to the full dimensions of the concept which the norm embodies. This obligation to obey constitutional norms at their underenforced margins requires governmental officials to fashion their own conceptions of these norms and measure their conduct by reference to these conceptions. Public officials cannot consider themselves free to act at what they perceive or ought to perceive to be peril to constitutional norms merely because the federal judiciary is unable to enforce these norms at their margins.

On this view, branches of government other than courts act properly when they interpret the Constitution more expansively than does the Court. Perhaps, then, political branches are within their rights if they conclude (for example) that the death penalty is unconstitutional, that affirmative action programs are unconstitutional, that environmental statutes violate the takings clause, or that government must fund abortions — even if the Supreme Court disagrees.

3. *Settlement.* Consider the position that the view of judicial supremacy suggested in Cooper v. Aaron can be defended simply as a way of ensuring settlement of questions that badly need to be settled. See Alexander and Schauer, On Extrajudicial Constitutional Interpretation, 110 Harv. L. Rev. 1377 (1997). In this argument, "good institutional design requires norms that compel decision-makers to defer to the judgments of others with which they disagree." Id. at 1387. But it might be asked whether it is possible, or desirable, for the Supreme Court to have the power to "settle" constitutional questions.

C.   THE SOURCES OF JUDICIAL DECISIONS: TEXT, ORIGINAL MEANING, STRUCTURE, MORALITY

This section explores several sources of constitutional doctrine that have, in one or another form, played an important role in constitutional adjudication: the text; the original meaning; structure; and natural law and natural rights, sometimes understood in the modern era as moral or philosophical argument about rights.

Of course, these are hardly the only sources of constitutional doctrine. At various times, the Supreme Court has also considered tradition, the meaning of its own prior precedent, public policy, contemporary mores, and international norms in resolving constitutional disputes. The use of all of these sources of law is discussed at much greater length throughout this book.

1.   Text and Original Meaning

For purposes of exposition, we are putting text and original meaning in the same section, but as we shall emphasize, the two can be, and often are, separated. Almost everyone agrees that the text of the Constitution is binding. (We will raise some questions about this view, but in general, it is true.) It is more controversial to say that the original meaning of the text is binding. In the following opinion, the text is understood to mean what (in the Court's view) it originally meant:

DISTRICT OF COLUMBIA v. HELLER, 554 U.S. 570 (2008). The second amendment provides: "A well regulated Militia, being necessary to the security of a free State, the right of the people to keep and bear Arms shall not be infringed." The issue in this case was whether a District of Columbia statute, which prohibited possession of usable handguns in a home, violated the amendment. In a five-to-four decision, the Court, per Justice Scalia, held that the statute was unconstitutional.

The Court's opinion begins by distinguishing between an "individual right" view of the amendment, which protects the right of individuals to bear arms, especially for self-defense, and a "collective right" view, which protects the right only in connection with militia service. The Court endorses the first view.

The Court's argument for this position begins by carefully focusing on the language of the second clause of the amendment, which it refers to as the "operative clause." Justice Scalia points out that the phrase "right of the people" or a very similar phrase is used three other times in the Constitution (in the first, fourth, and ninth amendments) and that on each occasion it refers to an individual right and to all members of the political community, not just to a subset like members of a militia.

Turning to the phrase "keep and bear arms," Justice Scalia consults eighteenth-century dictionaries to determine that "arms" referred to all weapons, not just those specifically designed for military use or employed in a military capacity. On the other hand, "arms" was not limited to weapons in existence at the time the second amendment was adopted. "We do not interpret constitutional rights that way. Just as the First Amendment protects modern forms of communications, and the Fourth Amendment applies to modern forms of search, the Second Amendment extends, prima facie, to all instruments that constitute bearable arms, even those that were not in existence at the time of the founding."

Examination of eighteenth-century sources also established that the words "keep" and "bear" were unconnected to the possession of arms for military purposes. According to the Court,

> [the] phrase "bear Arms" also had at the time of the founding an idiomatic meaning that was significantly different from its natural meaning: "to serve as a soldier, do military service, fight" or "to wage war." But it *unequivocally* bore that idiomatic

meaning only when followed by the preposition "against," which was in turn followed by the target of the hostilities.

The Court's conclusion was reinforced by English legal history, which the Court found relevant because the second amendment codified a preexisting right. The right guaranteed by William and Mary in the Declaration of Right was an individual right not related to militias; Blackstone had understood the right as "having the use of arms for self-preservation and defence."

Having established the meaning of the "operative clause," the Court turned its attention to the "prefatory clause" ("A well regulated Militia, being necessary to the security of a free State"). The Court interpreted the word "Militia" to mean "all males physically capable of acting in concert for the common defense." It found that "'Well-regulated' implies nothing more than the imposition of proper discipline and training." Such a militia might be "necessary to the security of a free State" because it could counter invasion or insurrection and render large standing armies unnecessary and because "able-bodied men of a nation [trained] in arms and organized [are] better able to resist tyranny."

The Court then turned to the relationship between the prefatory and operative clauses. The Court concluded that

> [history] showed that the way tyrants had eliminated a militia consisting of all the able-bodied men was not by banning the militia but simply by taking away the people's arms and enabling a select militia or standing army to suppress political opponents. . . .
>
> It is therefore entirely sensible that the Second Amendment's prefatory clause announces the purpose for which the right was codified: to prevent elimination of the militia. The prefatory clause does not suggest that preserving the militia was the only reason Americans valued the ancient right; they most undoubtedly thought it was even more important for self-defense and hunting. But the threat that the new Federal Government would destroy the citizens' militia by taking away their arms was the reason that right — unlike some other English rights — was codified in a written Constitution.

Finally, the Court examined postratification commentary and case law. In the Court's view this material was relevant because it helped "to determine *the public understanding* of a legal text in the period after its enactment or ratification. That sort of inquiry is a critical tool of constitutional interpretation." The Court concluded that "virtually all interpreters of the Second Amendment in the century after its enactment interpreted the amendment as we do."

It did not follow that the right to bear arms was unlimited, however.

> From Blackstone through the 19th-century cases, commentators and courts routinely explained that the right was not a right to keep and carry any weapon whatsoever in any manner whatsoever and for whatever purpose. For example, the majority of the 19th-century courts to consider the question held that the prohibitions on carrying concealed weapons were lawful under the Second Amendment or state analogues. Although we do not undertake an exhaustive historical analysis today of the full scope of the Second Amendment, nothing in our opinion should be taken to cast doubt on longstanding prohibitions on possession of firearms by felons and the mentally ill, or laws forbidding the carrying of firearms in sensitive places such as schools and government buildings or laws imposing conditions and qualifications on the commercial sale of arms.

The Court added that "another important limitation on the right" was that it was limited to those weapons "in common use at the time." And in a footnote, the Court noted that "[we] identify these presumptively lawful regulatory measures only as examples; our list does not purport to be exhaustive."

Turning to the constitutionality of the particular District of Columbia statute at issue, the Court rejected what it characterized as an "interest balancing" approach advocated by Justice Breyer in his dissenting opinion.

> We know of no other enumerated constitutional right whose core protection has been subjected to a freestanding "interest-balancing" approach. The very enumeration of the right takes out of the hands of government — even the Third Branch of Government — the power to decide on a case-by-case basis whether the right is *really worth* insisting upon. A constitutional guarantee subject to future judges' assessments of its usefulness is no constitutional guarantee at all. Constitutional rights are enshrined with the scope they were understood to have when the people adopted them, whether or not future legislatures or (yes) even future judges think that scope too broad. . . .
>
> We are aware of the problem of handgun violence in this country, and we take seriously the concerns raised by the many *amici* who believe that prohibition of handgun ownership is a solution. The Constitution leaves the District of Columbia a variety of tools for combating that problem, including some measures regulating handguns. But the enshrinement of constitutional rights necessarily takes certain policy choices off the table.

In a dissenting opinion joined by Justices Souter, Ginsburg, and Breyer, Justice Stevens characterized the question presented as whether the second amendment protects the right to possess and use guns for nonmilitary purposes such as hunting and self-defense. Examining the same language that the Court parsed, he concluded that it did not protect these uses. In his view, the prefatory clause's omission of any statement of purpose related to hunting or personal self-defense was especially striking in light of the fact that other contemporary statements of similar rights mentioned this purpose. Justice Stevens argued that other portions of the Constitution referred to "the people" in their collective capacity, and that the Court, itself, did not hold that all individual people (for example, convicted felons or the mentally ill) had the right to bear arms. In contemporary discourse, the words "bear arms" meant "to serve as a soldier, do military service, fight." The word "keep" referred to "the requirement that militia members store their arms at their homes, ready to be used for service when necessary." Justice Stevens concluded by arguing that

> [today's decision] will surely give rise to a far more active judicial role in making vitally important national policy decisions than was envisioned at any time in the 18th, 19th, or 20th centuries.
>
> The Court properly disclaims any interest in evaluating the wisdom of the specific policy choice challenged in this case, but it fails to pay heed to a far more important policy choice — the choice made by the Framers themselves. The Court would have us believe that over 200 years ago, the Framers made a choice to limit the tools available to elected officials wishing to regulate civilian uses of weapons, and to authorize this Court to use the common-law processes of case-by-case judicial lawmaking to define the contours of acceptable gun control policy. Absent compelling evidence that is nowhere to be found in the Court's opinion, I could not possibly conclude that the Framers made such a choice.

In a separate dissenting opinion, joined by Justices Stevens, Souter, and Ginsburg, Justice Breyer argued that

> the protection the Amendment provides is not absolute. The Amendment permits government to regulate the interests that it serves. Thus, irrespective of what those interests are — whether they do or do not include an independent interest in self-defense — the majority view cannot be correct unless it can show that the District's regulation is unreasonable or inappropriate in Second Amendment terms. This the majority cannot do. . . .
>
> [Any] self-defense interest at the time of the Framing could not have focused exclusively upon urban-crime related dangers. Two hundred years ago, most Americans, many living on the frontier, would likely have thought of self-defense primarily in terms of outbreaks of fighting with Indian tribes, rebellions such as Shays' Rebellion, marauders, and crime-related dangers to travelers on the roads, on footbaths, or along waterways. . . .
>
> The majority derides my approach as "judge empowering." I take this criticism seriously, but I do not think it accurate. . . .
>
> The majority's methodology is, in my view, substantially less transparent than mine. . . .
>
> Given the purposes for which the Framers enacted the Second Amendment, how should it be applied to modern-day circumstances that they could not have anticipated? Assume for argument's sake that the Framers did intend the Amendment to offer a degree of self-defense protection. Does that mean that the Framers also intended to guarantee the right to possess a loaded gun near swimming pools, parks, and playgrounds? That they would not have cared about the children who might pick up a loaded gun on their parents' bedside table? That they (who certainly showed concern for the risk of fire) would have lacked concern for the risk of accidental deaths or suicides that readily accessible loaded handguns in urban areas might bring? Unless we believe that they intended future generations to ignore such matters, answering questions such as the questions in this case requires judgment — judicial judgment exercised within a framework for constitutional analysis that guides that judgment and which makes its exercise transparent. One cannot answer those questions by combining inclusive historical research with judicial *ipse dixit*.

Note: Text and "Original Public Meaning"

1. *The role of text.* Consider the following view: "Whatever else you might think, you should agree with one proposition: *The text of the Constitution is binding.*" On this view, judges have a duty of fidelity above all to the Constitution's words. If the Second Amendment question is difficult, it is because judges cannot be sure what the words mean, just by reading them. Actually that happens a lot. The First Amendment protects "the freedom of speech," but it is not clear, in the abstract, whether it forbids restrictions on commercial advertising, on libel, on hate speech, and on campaign finance regulation. Consider, then, the following view: "Of course the text is binding, but it leaves so many hard questions unresolved!"

2. *The original meaning.* Contemporary "originalists" usually argue that the Constitution's meaning is settled by asking about its "original public meaning." See A. Scalia, A Matter of Interpretation (1998); Solum, Originalist Methodology, 84 U. Chi. L. Rev. 269 (2017). If we are speaking about a provision ratified in 1787, the question is: What was the public meaning of that provision, at the time that it was ratified?

While that is the dominant view, some people think that we should investigate not the original public meaning, but the intentions of those who wrote and/or ratified constitutional provisions. The two views about originalism will often lead in the same direction, but they are importantly different. If you ask about original public meaning, you are asking about something that seems objective, whereas if you ask about original intentions, you are asking about what is inside people's minds. And if you ask about original meaning, you will focus on what We the People, the Constitution's ratifiers, thought — not on what the Constitution's drafters thought.

Note that if you investigate the original meaning, you might find concrete answers to concrete questions. Perhaps the original meaning of the Second Amendment was that individuals have a right to possess firearms. Perhaps the original meaning of the First Amendment was that commercial advertising can be regulated. But if you investigate the original meaning, you might find instead that some provisions were originally meant to be broad concepts whose specific meaning is not meant to be frozen in time. In that case, judges might be licensed to decide on specific meanings. If so, originalism would leave important gaps. The central point is that for originalists, the initial question is always historical.

3. *The authority of the original meaning.* You might ask why, exactly, the original meaning is binding. Here are three kinds of answers: (1) If the Constitution is law, it just follows that the text, as originally understood, is binding. That's what it means for something to be law. (2) If judges are interpreting the Constitution, they must ask about the original meaning. That's what it means to interpret a text. If the judges do not focus on the original meaning, they are not engaged in interpretation at all. (3) Originalism is justified on pragmatic grounds. It promotes stability; it ensures that the meaning of the Constitution does not change over time. It reduces the discretion of judges, which can be a real threat to self-rule. It ensures that We the People are ultimately in charge. As Justice Antonin Scalia put it, "If you somehow adopt a philosophy that the Constitution itself is not static, but rather, it morphs from age to age to say whatever it ought to say — which is probably whatever the people would want it to say — you've eliminated the whole purpose of a constitution. And that's essentially what the 'living constitution' leaves you with." All Things Considered, "Scalia Vigorously Defends a 'Dead' Constitution," NPR, April 28, 2008.

4. *The Second Amendment.* Both the majority and Justice Stevens's dissent are preoccupied with the task of determining how the language of the second amendment would have been understood in the late eighteenth century. What are we to make of the fact that the justices, all presumably acting in good faith and working with the same historical materials, read the text differently? That the different readings correlate with the widely perceived split between the "conservative" and "liberal" justices? It might, be a problem, for originalism, that when originalist judges seem to be affected by their political predilections. See F. Cross, The Failed Promise of Originalism (2013). How much of a problem is that?

5. *Original meaning and historical change.* If constitutional interpretation consists of uncovering the meaning that people would have attached to words at the time the words were written, how are we to make sense of changed circumstances? Consider, in this regard, the Court's assertion that second amendment protection is not limited to weapons that the framers knew about. Did the "original public meaning" of "arms" as used in the second amendment include rifles, machine guns, and automatic pistols, none of which had been invented in the eighteenth century? If not, are these weapons nonetheless covered because

the framers, if they had thought about the matter, would have included these weapons in their definition of arms? How do we know that? If the text allows us to take account of weapons that did not exist at the time of framing, then what about other circumstances that did not exist, like widespread urbanization or increases in gun violence?

6. *Original public meaning and discretion.* The Court insists that its approach precludes considerations of policy and that "[a] constitutional guarantee subject to future judges' assessments of its usefulness is no constitutional guarantee at all." Yet the Court strongly implies that the second amendment right does not extend to the carrying of concealed weapons, the possession of weapons by felons or the mentally ill, or the possession of weapons in "sensitive places." Does the original public meaning of the text support these limitations? If not, and if the Court's assessment of the "usefulness" of a constitutional guarantee has no role in constitutional interpretation, where do the limitations come from?

7. *Justice Breyer's approach.* According to Justice Breyer, interpreting the second amendment requires the exercise of "judicial judgment [within] a framework of constitutional analysis that guides that judgment and which makes its exercise transparent." Is "judicial judgment" different from the sort of public policy judgments that a legislator would make? How, precisely, are these judgments constrained by "a framework of constitutional analysis"? If the justices are in fact deciding cases by reference to their personal value preferences, are these decisions made legitimate by the fact that justices are doing so transparently?

8. *Stun guns.* In Caetano v. Massachusetts, 136 S. Ct. 1027 (2016), the Court disapproved of three reasons given by a lower court to justify the state's categorical ban on stun guns.

> The [Massachusetts] court offered three explanations to support its holding that the Second Amendment does not extend to stun guns. First, the court explained that stun guns are not protected because they "were not in common use at the time of the Second Amendment's enactment." This is inconsistent with *Heller*'s clear statement that the Second Amendment "extends . . . to . . . arms . . . that were not in existence at the time of the founding." *District of Columbia v. Heller*, 554 U.S. 570, 582 (2008).
>
> The court next asked whether stun guns are "dangerous per se at common law and unusual," in an attempt to apply one "important limitation on the right to keep and carry arms," *Heller*, 554 U.S. at 627; *see id.* (referring to "the historical tradition of prohibiting the carrying of 'dangerous and unusual weapons'"). In so doing, the court concluded that stun guns are "unusual" because they are "a thoroughly modern invention." . . . By equating "unusual" with "in common use at the time of the Second Amendment's enactment," the court's second explanation is the same as the first; it is inconsistent with *Heller* for the same reason.
>
> Finally, the court used "a contemporary lens" and found "nothing in the record to suggest that [stun guns] are readily adaptable to use in the military." . . . But *Heller* rejected the proposition "that only those weapons useful in warfare are protected." 554 U.S. at 624-25.
>
> For these three reasons, the explanation the Massachusetts court offered for upholding the law contradicts this Court's precedent. . . .

With a more elaborate opinion, Justice Alito (joined by Justice Thomas) concurred in the judgment. The reasoning of the Massachusetts Supreme Judicial Court, he wrote, "defies our decision in *Heller*, which rejected as 'bordering on the frivolous' the argument 'that only those arms in existence in the 18th century are protected by the Second Amendment.' 554 U.S. at 582. . . . [T]he pertinent Second Amendment inquiry is whether stun guns are commonly possessed by law-abiding citizens for lawful purposes *today*. . . . While less popular than handguns, stun guns are widely owned and accepted as a legitimate means of self-defense across the country. Massachusetts' categorical ban of such weapons therefore violates the Second Amendment."

Justice Alito further emphasized that the Second Amendment "vindicates the 'basic right' of 'individual self-defense,'" and noted that the defendant had acquired the stun gun in order to defend herself against a violent ex-boyfriend. He concluded that "[t]he decision below [does] a grave disservice to vulnerable individuals like Caetano who must defend themselves because the State will not. . . . The Supreme Judicial Court suggested that Caetano could have simply gotten a firearm to defend herself. . . . But the right to bear other weapons is 'no answer' to a ban on the possession of protected arms. *Heller*, 554 U.S. at 629. Moreover, a weapon is an effective means of self-defense only if one is prepared to use it, and it is presumptuous to tell Caetano she should have been ready to shoot the father of her two young children if she wanted to protect herself. Courts should not be in the business of demanding that citizens use *more* force for self-defense than they are comfortable wielding."

2. *Structure*

McCulloch v. Maryland

17 U.S. (4 Wheat.) 316 (1819)

[This was an action brought by John James, for himself and the state of Maryland, against James McCulloch, cashier of a branch of the Bank of the United States. James alleged that McCulloch had failed to pay a state tax assessed against the bank. The court below held for the plaintiff. For background, see the Note following the opinion.]

Mr. Chief Justice Marshall delivered the opinion of the Court.

In the case now to be determined, the defendant, a sovereign State, denies the obligation of a law enacted by the legislature of the Union, and the plaintiff, on his part, contests the validity of an act which has been passed by the legislature of that State. The constitution of our country, in its most interesting and vital parts, is to be considered; the conflicting powers of the government of the Union and of its members, as marked in that constitution, are to be discussed; and an opinion given, which may essentially influence the great operations of the government. No tribunal can approach such a question without a deep sense of its importance, and of the awful responsibility involved in its decision. But it must be decided peacefully, or remain a source of hostile legislation, perhaps of hostility of a still more serious nature; and if it is to be so decided, by this tribunal alone can the decision be made. On the Supreme Court of the United States has the constitution of our country devolved this important duty.

The first question made in the cause is, has Congress power to incorporate a bank?

It has been truly said, that this can scarcely be considered as an open question, entirely unprejudiced by the former proceedings of the nation respecting it. The principle now contested was introduced at a very early period of our history, has been recognized by many successive legislatures, and has been acted upon by the judicial department, in cases of peculiar delicacy, as a law of undoubted obligation.

It will not be denied, that a bold and daring usurpation might be resisted, after an acquiescence still longer and more complete than this. But it is conceived that a doubtful question [ought] to receive a considerable impression from that practice. An exposition of the constitution, deliberately established by legislative acts, on the faith of which an immense property has been advanced, ought not to be lightly disregarded.

The power now contested was exercised by the first Congress elected under the present constitution. The bill for incorporating the bank of the United States did not steal upon an unsuspecting legislature, and pass unobserved. Its principle was completely understood, and was opposed with equal zeal and ability. After being resisted, first in the fair and open field of debate, and afterwards in the executive cabinet, with as much persevering talent as any measure has ever experienced, and being supported by arguments which convinced minds as pure and as intelligent as this country can boast, it became a law. The original act was permitted to expire; but a short experience of the embarrassments to which the refusal to revive it exposed the government, convinced those who were most prejudiced against the measure of its necessity, and induced the passage of the present law. It would require no ordinary share of intrepidity to assert that a measure adopted under these circumstances was a bold and plain usurpation, to which the constitution gave no countenance.

These observations belong to the cause; but they are not made under the impression that, were the question entirely new, the law would be found irreconcilable with the constitution.

In discussing this question, the counsel for the State of Maryland have deemed it of some importance, in the construction of the constitution, to consider that instrument not as emanating from the people, but as the act of sovereign and independent States. The powers of the general government, it has been said, are delegated by the States, who alone are truly sovereign; and must be exercised in subordination to the States, who alone possess supreme dominion.

It would be difficult to sustain this proposition. The Convention which framed the constitution was indeed elected by the State legislatures. But the instrument, when it came from their hands, was a mere proposal, without obligation, or pretensions to it. It was reported to the then existing Congress of the United States, with a request that it might "be submitted to a Convention of Delegates, chosen in each State by the people thereof, under the recommendation of its Legislature, for their assent and ratification." This mode of proceeding was adopted; and by the Convention, by Congress, and by the State Legislatures, the instrument was submitted to the people. They acted upon it in the only manner in which they can act safely, effectively, and wisely, on such a subject, by assembling in Convention. It is true, they assembled in their several States — and where else should they have assembled? No political dreamer was ever wild enough to think of breaking down the lines which separate the States, and of compounding the American people into one common mass. Of consequence, when they act, they act in their States. But the measures they adopt do not, on that account, cease to be the measures of the people themselves, or become the measures of the State governments.

From these Conventions the constitution derives its whole authority. The government proceeds directly from the people; is "ordained and established" in the name of the people; and is declared to be ordained, "in order to form a more perfect union, establish justice, ensure domestic tranquillity, and secure the blessings of liberty to themselves and to their posterity." The assent of the States, in their sovereign capacity, is implied in calling a Convention, and thus submitting that instrument to the people. But the people were at perfect liberty to accept or reject it; and their act was final. It required not the affirmance, and could not be negatived, by the State governments. The constitution, when thus adopted, was of complete obligation, and bound the State sovereignties. . . .

The government of the Union, then, (whatever may be the influence of this fact on the case), is emphatically, and truly, a government of the people. In form and in substance it emanates from them. Its powers are granted by them, and are to be exercised directly on them, and for their benefit.

This government is acknowledged by all to be one of enumerated powers. The principle that it can exercise only the powers granted to it [is] now universally admitted. But the question respecting the extent of the powers actually granted, is perpetually arising, and will probably continue to arise, as long as our system shall exist.

In discussing these questions, the conflicting powers of the general and State governments must be brought into view, and the supremacy of their respective laws, when they are in opposition, must be settled.

If any one proposition could command the universal assent of mankind, we might expect it would be this — that the government of the Union, though limited in its powers, is supreme within its sphere of action. This would seem to result necessarily from its nature. It is the government of all; its powers are delegated by all; it represents all, and acts for all. Though any one State may be willing to control its operations, no State is willing to allow others to control them. The nation, on those subjects on which it can act, must necessarily bind its component parts. But this question is not left to mere reason: the people have, in express terms, decided it, by saying, "this constitution, and the laws of the United States, which shall be made in pursuance thereof," "shall be the supreme law of the land," and by requiring that the members of the State legislatures, and the officers of the executive and judicial departments of the States, shall take the oath of fidelity to it. . . .

Among the enumerated powers, we do not find that of establishing a bank or creating a corporation. But there is no phrase in the instrument which, like the articles of confederation, excludes incidental or implied powers; and which requires that every thing granted shall be expressly and minutely described. Even the 10th amendment, which was framed for the purpose of quieting the excessive jealousies which had been excited, omits the word "expressly," and declares only that the powers "not delegated to the United States, nor prohibited to the States, are reserved to the States or to the people" thus leaving the question, whether the particular power which may become the subject of contest has been delegated to the one government, or prohibited to the other, to depend on a fair construction of the whole instrument. The men who drew and adopted this amendment had experienced the embarrassments resulting from the insertion of this word in the articles of confederation, and probably omitted it to avoid those embarrassments. A constitution, to contain an accurate detail of all the subdivisions of which its great powers will admit, and of all the means by which they may be carried into execution, would partake of the prolixity of a legal code, and could scarcely be embraced by the human mind. It would probably never be understood by the public. Its nature, therefore, requires, that only its great outlines should be marked, its important objects designated, and the minor ingredients which compose those objects be deduced from the nature of the objects themselves. That this idea was entertained by the framers of the American constitution, is not only to be inferred from the nature of the instrument, but from the language. Why else were some of the limitations, found in the ninth section of the 1st article, introduced? It is also, in some degree, warranted by their having omitted to use any restrictive term which might prevent its receiving a fair and just interpretation. In considering this question, then, we must never forget, that it is a constitution we are expounding.

Although, among the enumerated powers of government, we do not find the word "bank" or "incorporation," we find the great powers to lay and collect taxes; to borrow money; to regulate commerce; to declare and conduct a war; and to raise and support armies and navies. The sword and the purse, all the external relations, and no inconsiderable portion of the industry of the nation, are entrusted to its government. It can never be pretended that these vast powers draw after them others of inferior importance, merely because they are inferior. Such an idea can never be advanced. But it may with great reason be contended, that a government, entrusted with such ample powers, on the due execution of which the happiness and prosperity of the nation so vitally depends, must also be entrusted with ample means for their execution. The power being given, it is the interest of the nation to facilitate its execution. It can never be their interest, and cannot be presumed to have been their intention, to clog and embarrass its execution by withholding the most appropriate means. Throughout this vast republic, from the St. Croix to the Gulf of Mexico, from the Atlantic to the Pacific, revenue is to be collected and expended, armies are to be marched and supported. The exigencies of the nation may require that the treasure raised in the north should be transported to the south, that raised in the east conveyed to the west, or that this order should be reversed. Is that construction of the constitution to be preferred which would render these operations difficult, hazardous, and expensive? Can we adopt that construction, (unless the words imperiously require it,) which would impute to the framers of that instrument, when granting these powers for the public good, the intention of impeding their exercise by withholding a choice of means? . . .

It is not denied, that the powers given to the government imply the ordinary means of execution. That, for example, of raising revenue, and applying it to national purposes, is admitted to imply the power of conveying money from place to place, as the exigencies of the nation may require, and of employing the usual means of conveyance. . . .

But the constitution of the United States has not left the right of Congress to employ the necessary means, for the execution of the powers conferred on the government, to general reasoning. To its enumeration of powers is added that of making "all laws which shall be necessary and proper, for carrying into execution the foregoing powers, and all other powers vested by this constitution, in the government of the United States, or in any department thereof." The counsel for the State of Maryland have urged various arguments, to prove that this clause, though in terms a grant of power, is not so in effect; but is really restrictive of the general right, which might otherwise be implied, of selecting means for executing the enumerated powers. . . .

[The] argument on which most reliance is placed, is drawn from the peculiar language of this clause. Congress is not empowered by it to make all laws, which may have relation to the powers conferred on the government, but such only as may be "necessary and proper" for carrying them into execution. The word "necessary" is considered as controlling the whole sentence, and as limiting the right to pass laws for the execution of the granted powers, to such as are indispensable, and without which the power would be nugatory. That it excludes the choice of means, and leaves to Congress, in each case, that only which is most direct and simple. Is it true, that this is the sense in which the word "necessary" is always used? Does it always import an absolute physical necessity, so strong, that one thing, to which another may be termed necessary, cannot exist without that other? We think it does not. If reference be had to its use, in the common affairs of the world, or in approved authors, we find that it frequently imports no more than that one thing is convenient, or useful, or essential to another. To employ the means necessary to an end, is generally understood as employing any means calculated to produce the end, and not as being confined to those single means, without which the end would be entirely unattainable. Such is the character of human language, that no word conveys to the mind, in all situations, one single definite idea; and nothing is more common than to use words in a figurative sense. Almost all compositions contain words, which, taken in their rigorous sense, would convey a meaning different from that which is obviously intended. It is essential to just construction, that many words which import something excessive, should be understood in a more mitigated sense — in that sense which common usage justifies. The word "necessary" is of this description. It has not a fixed character peculiar to itself. It admits of all degrees of comparison; and is often connected with other words, which increase or diminish the impression the mind receives of the urgency it imports. A thing may be necessary, very necessary, absolutely or indispensably necessary. To no mind would the same idea be conveyed, by these several phrases. This comment on the word is well illustrated, by the passage cited at the bar, from the 10th section of the 1st article of the constitution. It is, we think, impossible to compare the sentence which prohibits a State from laying "imposts, or duties on imports or exports, except what may be absolutely necessary for executing its inspection laws," with that which authorizes Congress "to make all laws which shall be necessary and proper for carrying into execution" the powers of the general government, without feeling a conviction that the convention understood itself to change materially the meaning of the word "necessary," by prefixing the word "absolutely." This word, then, like others, is used in various senses; and, in its construction, the subject, the context, the intention of the person using them, are all to be taken into view.

Let this be done in the case under consideration. The subject is the execution of those great powers on which the welfare of a nation essentially depends. It must have been the intention of those who gave these powers, to insure, as far as human prudence could insure, their beneficial execution. This could not be done by confiding the choice of means to such narrow limits as not to leave it in the power of Congress to adopt any which might be appropriate, and which were conducive to the end. This provision is made in a constitution intended to endure for ages to come, and, consequently, to be adapted to the various crises of human affairs. To have prescribed the means by which government should, in all future time, execute its powers, would have been to change, entirely, the character of the instrument, and give it the properties of a legal code. It would have been an unwise attempt to provide, by immutable rules, for exigencies which, if foreseen at all, must have been seen dimly, and which can be best provided for as they occur. To have declared that the best means shall not be used, but those alone without which the power given would be nugatory, would have been to deprive the legislature of the capacity to avail itself of experience, to exercise its reason, and to accommodate its legislation to circumstances. If we apply this principle of construction to any of the powers of the government, we shall find it so pernicious in its operation that we shall be compelled to discard it. . . .

So, with respect to the whole penal code of the United States: whence arises the power to punish in cases not prescribed by the constitution? All admit that the government may, legitimately, punish any violation of its laws; and yet, this is not among the enumerated powers of Congress. The right to enforce the observance of law, by punishing its infraction, might be denied with the more plausibility, because it is expressly given in some cases. Congress is empowered "to provide for the punishment of counterfeiting the securities and current coin of the United States," and "to define and punish piracies and felonies committed on the high seas, and offenses against the law of nations." The several powers of Congress may exist, in a very imperfect state to be sure, but they may exist and be carried into execution, although no punishment should be inflicted in cases where the right to punish is not expressly given.

Take, for example, the power "to establish post offices and post roads." This power is executed by the single act of making the establishment. But, from this has been inferred the power and duty of carrying the mail along the post road, from one post office to another. And, from this implied power, has again been inferred the right to punish those who steal letters from the post office, or rob the mail. It may be said, with some plausibility, that the right to carry the mail, and to punish those who rob it, is not indispensably necessary to the establishment of a post office and post road. This right is indeed essential to the beneficial exercise of the power, but not indispensably necessary to its existence. So, of the punishment of the crimes of stealing or falsifying a record or process of a Court of the United States, or of perjury in such Court. To punish these offenses is certainly conducive to the due administration of justice. But courts may exist, and may decide the causes brought before them, though such crimes escape punishment.

The baneful influence of this narrow construction in all the operations of the government, and the absolute impracticability of maintaining it without rendering the government incompetent to its great objects, might be illustrated by numerous examples drawn from the constitution, and from our laws. . . .

In ascertaining the sense in which the word "necessary" is used in this clause of the constitution, we may derive some aid from that with which it is associated. Congress shall have power "to make all laws which shall be necessary and proper to carry into execution" the powers of the government. If the word "necessary" was used in that strict and rigorous sense for which the counsel for the State of Maryland contend, it would be an extraordinary departure from the usual course of the human mind, as exhibited in composition, to add a word, the only possible effect of which is to qualify that strict and rigorous meaning; to present to the mind the idea of some choice of means of legislation not straitened and compressed within the narrow limits for which gentlemen contend.

But the argument which most conclusively demonstrates the error of the construction contended for by the counsel for the State of Maryland, is founded on the intention of the Convention, as manifested in the whole clause. To waste time and argument in proving that, without it, Congress might carry its powers into execution, would be not much less idle than to hold a lighted taper to the sun. As little can it be required to prove, that in the absence of this clause, Congress would have some choice of means. That it might employ those which, in its judgment, would most advantageously effect the object to be accomplished. That any means adapted to the end, any means which tended directly to the execution of the constitutional powers of the government, were in themselves constitutional. This clause, as construed by the State of Maryland, would abridge, and almost annihilate this useful and necessary right of the legislature to select its means. That this could not be intended, is, we should think, had it not been already controverted, too apparent for controversy. We think so for the following reasons:

1st. The clause is placed among the powers of Congress, not among the limitations on those powers.

2nd. Its terms purport to enlarge, not to diminish the powers vested in the government. It purports to be an additional power, not a restriction on those already granted. No reason has been, or can be assigned for thus concealing an intention to narrow the discretion of the national legislature under words which purport to enlarge it. . . .

The result of the most careful and attentive consideration bestowed upon this clause is, that if it does not enlarge, it cannot be construed to restrain the powers of Congress, or to impair the right of the legislature to exercise its best judgment in the selection of measures to carry into execution the constitutional powers of the government. If no other motive for its insertion can be suggested, a sufficient one is found in the desire to remove all doubts respecting the right to legislate on that vast mass of incidental powers which must be involved in the constitution, if that instrument be not a splendid bauble.

We admit, as all must admit, that the powers of the government are limited, and that its limits are not to be transcended. But we think the sound construction of the constitution must allow to the national legislature that discretion, with respect to the means by which the powers it confers are to be carried into execution, which will enable that body to perform the high duties assigned to it, in the manner most beneficial to the people. Let the end be legitimate, let it be within the scope of the constitution, and all means which are appropriate, which are plainly adapted to that end, which are not prohibited, but consist with the letter and spirit of the constitution, are constitutional. . . .

If a corporation may be employed indiscriminately with other means to carry into execution the powers of the government, no particular reason can be assigned for excluding the use of a bank, if required for its fiscal operations. To use one, must be within the discretion of Congress, if it be an appropriate mode of executing the powers of government. That it is a convenient, a useful, and essential instrument in the prosecution of its fiscal operations, is not now a subject of controversy. All those who have been concerned in the administration of our finances, have concurred in representing its importance and necessity; and so strongly have they been felt, that statesmen of the first class, whose previous opinions against it had been confirmed by every circumstance which can fix the human judgment, have yielded those opinions to the exigencies of the nation. Under the confederation, Congress, justifying the measure by its necessity, transcended perhaps its powers to obtain the advantage of a bank; and our own legislation attests the universal conviction of the utility of this measure. The time has passed away when it can be necessary to enter into any discussion in order to prove the importance of this instrument, as a means to effect the legitimate objects of the government.

But, were its necessity less apparent, none can deny its being an appropriate measure; and if it is, the degree of its necessity, as has been very justly observed, is to be discussed in another place. Should Congress, in the execution of its powers, adopt measures which are prohibited by the constitution; or should Congress, under the pretext of executing its powers, pass laws for the accomplishment of objects not entrusted to the government; it would become the painful duty of this tribunal, should a case requiring such a decision come before it, to say that such an act was not the law of the land. But where the law is not prohibited, and is really calculated to effect any of the objects entrusted to the government, to undertake here to inquire into the degree of its necessity, would be to pass the line which circumscribes the judicial department, and to tread on legislative ground. This court disclaims all pretensions to such a power. . . .

It being the opinion of the Court, that the act incorporating the bank is constitutional; and that the power of establishing a branch in the State of Maryland might be properly exercised by the bank itself, we proceed to inquire —

2. Whether the State of Maryland may, without violating the constitution, tax that branch?

That the power of taxation is one of vital importance; that it is retained by the States; that it is not abridged by the grant of a similar power to the government of the Union; that it is to be concurrently exercised by the two governments: are truths which have never been denied. But, such is the paramount character of the constitution, that its capacity to withdraw any subject from the action of even this power, is admitted. The States are expressly forbidden to lay any duties on imports or exports, except what may be absolutely necessary for executing their inspection laws. If the obligation of this prohibition must be conceded — if it may restrain a State from the exercise of its taxing power on imports and exports; the same paramount character would seem, to restrain, as it certainly may restrain, a State from such other exercise of this power, as is in its nature incompatible with, and repugnant to, the constitutional laws of the Union. A law, absolutely repugnant to another, as entirely repeals that other as if express terms of repeal were used.

On this ground the counsel for the bank place its claim to be exempted from the power of a State to tax its operations. There is no express provision for the case, but the claim has been sustained on a principle which so entirely pervades the constitution, is so intermixed with the materials which compose it, so interwoven with its web, so blended with its texture, as to be incapable of being separated from it, without rendering it into shreds.

This great principle is that the constitution and the laws made in pursuance thereof are supreme; that they control the constitution and laws of the respective States, and cannot be controlled by them. From this, which may be almost termed an axiom, other propositions are deduced as corollaries, on the truth or error of which, and on their application to this case, the cause has been supposed to depend. These are, 1st. that a power to create implies a power to preserve. 2nd. That a power to destroy, if wielded by a different hand, is hostile to, and incompatible with these powers to create and to preserve. 3d. That where this repugnancy exists, that authority which is supreme must control, not yield to that over which it is supreme. . . .

That the power of taxing it by the States may be exercised so as to destroy it, is too obvious to be denied. But taxation is said to be an absolute power, which acknowledges no other limits than those expressly prescribed in the constitution, and like sovereign power of every other description, is trusted to the discretion of those who use it. But the very terms of this argument admit that the sovereignty of the State, in the article of taxation itself, is subordinate to, and may be controlled by the constitution of the United States. How far it has been controlled by that instrument must be a question of construction. In making this construction, no principle not declared, can be admissible, which would defeat the legitimate operations of a supreme government. It is of the very essence of supremacy to remove all obstacles to its action within its own sphere, and so to modify every power vested in subordinate governments, as to exempt its own operations from their own influence. This effect need not be stated in terms. It is so involved in the declaration of supremacy, so necessarily implied in it, that the expression of it could not make it more certain. We must, therefore, keep it in view while construing the constitution.

The argument on the part of the State of Maryland, is, not that the States may directly resist a law of Congress, but that they may exercise their acknowledged powers upon it, and that the constitution leaves them this right in the confidence that they will not abuse it.

Before we proceed to examine this argument, and to subject it to the test of the constitution, we must be permitted to bestow a few considerations on the nature and extent of this original right of taxation, which is acknowledged to remain with the States. It is admitted that the power of taxing the people and their property is essential to the very existence of government, and may be legitimately exercised on the objects to which it is applicable, to the utmost extent to which the government may choose to carry it. The only security against the abuse of this power, is found in the structure of the government itself. In imposing a tax the legislature acts upon its constituents. This is in general a sufficient security against erroneous and oppressive taxation.

The people of a State, therefore, give to their government a right of taxing themselves and their property, and as the exigencies of government cannot be limited, they prescribe no limits to the exercise of this right, resting confidently on the interest of the legislator, and on the influence of the constituents over their representative, to guard them against its abuse. But the means employed by the government of the Union have no such security, nor is the right of a State to tax them sustained by the same theory. Those means are not given by the people of a particular State, not given by the constituents of the legislature, which claim the right to tax them, but by the people of all the States. They are given by all for the benefit of all — and upon theory, should be subjected to that government only which belongs to all. . . .

We find, then, on just theory, a total failure of this original right to tax the means employed by the government of the Union, for the execution of its powers. The right never existed, and the question whether it has been surrendered, cannot arise.

But, waiving this theory for the present, let us resume the inquiry, whether this power can be exercised by the respective States, consistently with a fair construction of the constitution?

That the power to tax involves the power to destroy; that the power to destroy may defeat and render useless the power to create; that there is a plain repugnance, in conferring on one government a power to control the constitutional measures of another, which other, with respect to those very measures, is declared to be supreme over that which exerts the control, are propositions not to be

MD thinks they can ignore con. law

denied. But all inconsistencies are to be reconciled by the magic of the word CONFIDENCE. Taxation, it is said, does not necessarily and unavoidably destroy. To carry it to the excess of destruction would be an abuse, to presume which, would banish that confidence which is essential to all government.

But is this a case of confidence? Would the people of any one State trust those of another with a power to control the most insignificant operations of their State government? We know they would not. Why, then, should we suppose that the people of any one State should be willing to trust those of another with a power to control the operations of a government to which they have confided their most important and most valuable interests? In the legislature of the Union alone, are all represented. The legislature of the Union alone, therefore, can be trusted by the people with the power of controlling measures which concern all, in the confidence that it will not be abused. This, then, is not a case of confidence, and we must consider it as it really is. . . .

If we apply the principle for which the State of Maryland contends, to the constitution generally, we shall find it capable of changing totally the character of that instrument. We shall find it capable of arresting all the measures of the government, and of prostrating it at the foot of the States. [If] the states may tax one instrument, [they] may tax any and every other instrument. [The] American people [did] not design to make their government dependent on the states. . . .

It has also been insisted, that, as the power of taxation in the general and State governments is acknowledged to be concurrent, every argument which would sustain the right of the general government to tax banks chartered by the States, will equally sustain the right of the States to tax banks chartered by the general government.

But the two cases are not on the same reason. The people of all the States have created the general government, and have conferred upon it the general power of taxation. The people of all the States, and the States themselves, are represented in Congress, and, by their representatives, exercise this power. When they tax the chartered institutions of the States, they tax their constituents; and these taxes must be uniform. But, when a State taxes the operations of the government of the United States, it acts upon institutions created, not by their own constituents, but by people over whom they claim no control. It acts upon the measures of a government created by others as well as themselves, for the benefit of others in common with themselves. The difference is that which always exists, and always must exist, between the action of the whole on a part, and the action of a part on the whole — between the laws of a government declared to be supreme, and those of a government which, when in opposition to those laws, is not supreme.

But if the full application of this argument could be admitted, it might bring into question the right of Congress to tax the State banks, and could not prove the right of the States to tax the Bank of the United States. . . .

[We] conclude that the states have no power, by taxation or otherwise, to retard, impede, burden, or in any manner control, the operations of the constitutional laws enacted by Congress. . . .

This opinion does not deprive the States of any resources which they originally possessed. It does not extend to a tax paid by the real property of the bank, in common with the other real property within the State, nor to a tax imposed on the interest which the citizens of Maryland may hold in this institution, in common with other property of the same description throughout the State.

[Reversed.]

Note: *Constitutional Methodology and Interpretation*
in McCulloch

McCulloch resolves several important questions, relating both to the judicial role and to the allocation of powers as between the federal government and the states.

1. *Background.* The first Bank of the United States was created in 1790, shortly after ratification of the Constitution, to furnish loans to the federal government and to help collect taxes. The constitutional issue was sharply debated. Madison, a member of the House of Representatives, spoke against the bank, claiming that Congress had no constitutional authority to create it. Hamilton, Secretary of the Treasury, was one of its staunchest supporters and indeed drafted the plan for the bank. Jefferson also opposed the first bank on constitutional grounds, invoking the tenth amendment and venturing as well that "the Constitution allows only the means which are necessary, not merely 'convenient,' for effecting the enumerated powers. If such a latitude of construction be allowed to this phrase as to give any non-enumerated power [to Congress,] it would swallow up all the delegated powers, and reduce the whole to one power." Opinion on the Constitutionality of the Bill for Establishing a National Bank, in 19 Papers of Thomas Jefferson 275, 279–280 (J. Boyd ed., 1974).

In 1811, the bank's charter lapsed, and Congress did not renew it. The private business and banking communities vigorously opposed renewal. In 1815, however, Congress created a second Bank of the United States, responding to a period of considerable economic turmoil following the War of 1812. At this stage, there was little discussion of the constitutional question. Jefferson himself supported the bank, partly in response to political pressures and perceived practical necessities, and Madison wrote that the issue had been settled in favor of its constitutionality. But many states objected to the creation of a second bank and imposed taxes of the sort at issue in *McCulloch.* To what extent, if any, do you think the decision in *McCulloch* was or should have been different in 1819 from what it would have been had the issue arisen in 1791?

2. *Methods of constitutional interpretation.* Note Chief Justice Marshall's remarks on the distinctive character of constitutions and of constitutional interpretation.

Chief Justice Marshall's suggestion that "it is a constitution we are expounding" has been called, by no less an authority than Justice Frankfurter, "the single most important utterance in the literature of constitutional law — most important because most comprehensive and most comprehending." Frankfurter, John Marshall and the Judicial Function, 69 Harv. L. Rev. 217, 219 (1955). But the statement and the interpretive strategies to which it has led are not universally admired. Compare, for example, Justice Frankfurter's suggestion that "precisely because 'it is a constitution we are expounding,' we ought not to take liberties with it." National Mutual Insurance Co. v. Tidewater Transfer Co., 337 U.S. 581, 647 (1949) (Frankfurter, J., dissenting). See also Kurland, Curia Regis: Some Comments on the Divine Right of Kings and Courts to Say What the Law Is, 23 Ariz. L. Rev. 582, 591 (1981), suggesting that, whenever a judge quotes this passage, "you can be sure that the court will be throwing the constitutional text, its history, and its structure to the winds in reaching its conclusion."

Consider the following possible interpretations of Chief Justice Marshall's position: (a) The power-granting provisions of the Constitution should be broadly construed. Those provisions are meant to endure over time. They should be interpreted flexibly as new and unforeseen problems arise. But to say this is emphatically not to say that courts ought to have a license, often or ever, to expand national authority beyond what the Constitution authorizes — or to strike down legislative action on grounds of changed circumstances. (b) All provisions of the Constitution, including those granting powers and those creating rights, should be broadly construed. Constitutions simply do not contain specific answers to all questions for all times. (c) The meaning of the Constitution changes with changing circumstances, in accordance with changing social norms and needs. Judges need not adhere to the original meaning of the text, but must interpret the document flexibly in light of contemporary necessities.

3. *Structural approaches to constitutional interpretation.* In the view of some, the approach in *McCulloch* is distinctive in large part because of Chief Justice Marshall's willingness to rely on the "structures and relationships" set up by the Constitution, and not only the text, in resolving constitutional questions.

> I am inclined to think well of the method of reasoning from structure and relation. I think well of it, above all, because to succeed it has to make sense — current, practical sense. The textual-explication method, operating on general language, [contains] within itself no guarantee that it will make sense, for a court may always present itself or even see itself as being bound by the stated intent, however non-sensical, of somebody else. [With structural approaches] we can and must begin to argue at once about the practicalities and proprieties of the thing, without getting out dictionaries whose entries will not really respond to the question we are putting. [We] will have to deal with policy and not with grammar.

C. Black, Structure and Relationship in Constitutional Law 22–23 (1969). Consider this objection: Black's position means that the Constitution should be interpreted to mean whatever the judges think it should mean. Once judges are asking about "the practicalities and proprieties," they can do whatever they want. Does a structural approach leave more or less interpretive freedom than a textual approach? Compare Amar, Intratextualism, 112 Harv. L. Rev. 747 (1999), which argues that textualism can impose more than usual discipline if judges look at how constitutional terms are used in different contexts. In support of that view, a narrow version of structural interpretation might see if we can learn about the meaning of a disputed phrase by inquiring into its meaning in a different part of the Constitution. Most obviously, the word "treason," in the impeachment clause, might be construed by looking at the specific definition of "treason" that the Constitution elsewhere provides. Perhaps we could make a lot of progress, in hard cases, by an approach of this kind.

4. *The necessary and proper clause; implied powers.*

a. What, if anything, does the necessary and proper clause add, in the Court's view, to the constitutional powers granted to the Congress? Does the *McCulloch* decision recognize implied powers at all? Perhaps it merely recognizes that a power naturally includes the appropriate means for achieving the intended end. Would that be a better understanding of the opinion?

b. The Court's construction of the necessary and proper clause resolved an extraordinarily important interpretive question that had divided, among others, Thomas Jefferson and Alexander Hamilton. On what does Chief Justice Marshall base his acceptance of the Hamilton position? Note the pertinence of the suggestion that that "provision is made in a constitution intended to endure for ages to come, and, consequently, to be adapted to the various crises of human affairs."

c. Even with the Court's interpretation of the necessary and proper clause, it remains to explain how the creation of a national bank is "necessary and proper" to the exercise of one of Congress's enumerated powers. What enumerated powers are helpful here? Consider Currie, The Constitution in the Supreme Court: State and National Powers, 1801–1835, 49 U. Chi. L. Rev. 887, 932–933 (1982), noting that Chief Justice Marshall "mentioned in passing various enumerated powers to which the creation of a bank might be incidental. [What] is striking is that he made no serious effort to demonstrate how the bank was necessary and proper, or even conducive, to any one of them." But consider the implications of Chief Justice Marshall's reference to the extended territory of the United States. Is Hamilton's explanation persuasive in this regard?

d. What limitations does Chief Justice Marshall recognize on congressional power? The key sentence here, frequently quoted by the Supreme Court throughout its history, is this: "Let the end be legitimate, let it be within the scope of the Constitution, and all means which are appropriate, which are plainly adapted to that end, which are not prohibited, but consist with the letter and spirit of the Constitution, are constitutional." The Court adds that if Congress enacts a law "for the accomplishment of objects not entrusted to the national government," and if Congress has acted under the "pretext" of using its enumerated powers, the law will be invalidated. Does this mean that the Court will scrutinize the motivations of legislators? (The benefits and disadvantages of motivation-centered inquiries are explored in Chapters 3 and 5 infra.) What else might it mean? See Barnett, Necessary and Proper, 44 UCLA L. Rev. 745 (1997).

5. *The tenth amendment.* The second principal provision interpreted in *McCulloch* is the tenth amendment. How does Chief Justice Marshall construe this provision? Does the tenth amendment add anything of substance to the Constitution in Chief Justice Marshall's view? Perhaps it does not, but the tenth amendment might nonetheless have important civic purposes, by reminding everyone of the limited nature of the federal government. Note that in the Articles of Confederation the word "expressly" preceded the limitation analogous to the tenth amendment. How much support does the deletion of that word add to Chief Justice Marshall's construction?

6. *Representation reinforcement.* Chief Justice Marshall finds an implicit prohibition on state taxation of the national bank. What constitutional provision does the tax violate?

Chief Justice Marshall's analysis of the problem is largely an inquiry not into the constitutional text and history but into the operations of representative government. "In imposing a tax the legislature acts upon its constituents. This is in general a sufficient security against erroneous and oppressive taxation." And in "the legislature of the Union alone, are all represented." The claim here is that the power to elect representatives will act as a safeguard against the abuse of political power by elected officials. The judicial role is defined by reference to the understanding that the political process itself will ensure against improper conduct. Does Chief Justice Marshall overlook the possibility that constituents, or subgroups thereof, might not have sufficient political power to prevent oppression?

Chief Justice Marshall also indicates that the ordinary presumption — that the processes of representation are an effective safeguard against abuse — disappears when a state imposes taxes on a national instrumentality because in so doing, the state is harming people who are not represented in the state legislature. Judicial intervention is justified in order to make up for the absence of political remedies for those burdened by legislative action. But if citizens generally are oppressed by state taxation of national banks, doesn't Congress have the power to enact a law to outlaw state taxation? Why is judicial intervention necessary or appropriate? Consider the possibility that the immunity is conferred by the statute creating the bank, interpreted in light of the concerns about representation.

Note, by contrast, Chief Justice Marshall's suggestion that, while the federal government has an (implicit) immunity from state taxation, states may not be immune from federal taxation.

How does Chief Justice Marshall's theory of representation operate differently here? For further discussion of intergovernmental immunity, see Chapter 2 infra.

McCulloch might be understood as the foundation for the notion of "representation-reinforcement" as a justification of and guide for judicial action — an occasionally prominent theme in constitutional law. The central idea is that the judicial role is to make up for defects in the ordinary operation of representative government; the source of judicial decision is a breakdown in political processes. See generally J. Ely, Democracy and Distrust (1980). How does this approach differ from that in *Marbury*? The problem of representation-reinforcement is taken up in Chapters 2, 3, and 5 infra.

3. Natural Law and Natural Rights

CALDER v. BULL, 3 U.S. (3 DALL.) 386 (1798). The Connecticut legislature ordered a new trial in a will contest, setting aside a judicial decree. The Court unanimously held that the legislature's action was not an "ex post facto Law" forbidden the states by article I, section 10. Although Justices Chase and Iredell agreed on the "ex post facto" issue, they disagreed over the appropriate role of "natural law" in constitutional interpretation. Justice Chase wrote:

"I cannot subscribe to the omnipotence of a state legislature, or that it is absolute and without control; although its authority should not be expressly restrained by the constitution, or fundamental law of the state. The people of the United States erected their constitutions or forms of government, to establish justice, to promote the general welfare, to secure the blessings of liberty, and to protect their persons and property from violence. The purposes for which men enter into society will determine the nature and terms of the social compact; and as they are the foundation of the legislative power, they will decide what are the proper objects of it. The nature, and ends of legislative power will limit the exercise of it. This fundamental principle flows from the very nature of our free republican governments. [There] are acts which the federal, or state legislature cannot do, without exceeding their authority. There are certain vital principles in our free republican governments, which will determine and overrule an apparent and flagrant abuse of legislative power. [An] act of the legislature (for I cannot call it a law), contrary to the great first principles in the social compact, cannot be considered a rightful exercise of legislative authority. [A] law that punishes a citizen for an innocent [action;] a law that destroys or impairs the lawful private contracts of citizens; a law that makes a man a judge in his own cause; or a law that takes property from A. and gives it to B.: it is against all reason and justice, for a people to entrust a legislature with such powers; and therefore, it cannot be presumed that they have done it. The genius, the nature and the spirit of our state governments, amount to a prohibition of such acts of legislation; and the general principles of law and reason forbid them. [To] maintain that our federal, or state legislature possesses such powers, if they had not been expressly restrained, would, in my opinion, be a political heresy, altogether inadmissible in our free republican governments." (Chase upheld the legislature's action, however, on the ground that it impaired no vested right.)

Justice Iredell replied: "[Some] speculative jurists have held, that a legislative act against natural justice must, in itself, be void; but I cannot think that, under such a government any court of justice would possess a power to declare it so. [It] has been the policy of all the American states, [and] of the people of the United States, [to] define with precision the objects of the legislative power, and to restrain its exercise within marked and settled boundaries. If any act of congress, or of the legislature of a state, violates those constitutional provisions, it is unquestionably void. [If,] on the other hand, the legislature of the Union, or the legislature of any member of the Union, shall pass a law, within the general scope of their constitutional power, the court cannot pronounce it to be void, merely because it is, in their judgment, contrary to the principles of natural justice. The ideas of natural justice are regulated by no fixed standard: the ablest and the purest men have differed upon the subject; and all that the court could properly say, in such an event, would be, that the legislature (possessed of an equal right of opinion) had passed an act which, in the opinion of the judges, was inconsistent with the abstract principles of natural justice. [If] the legislature pursue the authority delegated to them, their acts are valid. [In such circumstances,] they exercise the discretion vested in them by the people, to whom alone they are responsible for the faithful discharge of their trust."

Note: Natural Law, Moral Argument, and the Supreme Court

In one form or another, the dispute between Justice Chase and Justice Iredell has proved fundamental to constitutional law.

1. *The original understanding.* Marbury v. Madison rested in part on the understanding that a written Constitution necessarily contemplated judicial enforcement of its terms. Otherwise, the restrictions imposed by the Constitution would be meaningless. We have seen that the argument is in some respects vulnerable. But Justice Chase goes further. His position is that there is an "unwritten" Constitution, consisting of principles of natural law, which is enforceable as against the states even though it cannot be found in the Constitution.

Justice Iredell's response is that the very fact of a written Constitution is authority against the position that courts may call on principles of natural justice. But does Justice Chase's position itself show that at least some of the framers and ratifiers believed in the existence of a natural law supplement to the Constitution's explicit prohibitions? Sherry, The Founders' Unwritten Constitution, 54 U. Chi. L. Rev. 1127 (1987), contains an extended argument for that view, with multiple references. See also Grey, Do We Have an Unwritten Constitution?, 27 Stan. L. Rev. 703 (1975); Grey, Origins of the Unwritten Constitution, 30 Stan. L. Rev. 843 (1978), suggesting that the framers believed that judges would enforce a category of natural law constraints on state and federal legislation. But see J. Ely, Democracy and Distrust (1980), for a skeptical view. For provocative treatments, emphasizing the centrality of liberty, see R. Barnett,

Restoring the Lost Constitution (rev. ed. 2013); Barnett, Our Republican Constitution (2016).

    2. *Judges as political philosophers?* What would be the advantages and disadvantages of recognizing judicial authority of the sort claimed by Justice Chase? Think, for example, of the following questions: (1) Are maximum hour laws unconstitutional? (2) Are rent control laws unconstitutional? (3) Must states recognize same-sex marriage? (4) Does the first amendment protect pornography? (5) What are the limits of the federal government's power to look at people's email and social media postings? (6) Can the national government ban people from majority-Muslim nations from getting visas? Consider M. Perry, The Courts, the Constitution, and Human Rights 100–101 (1982):

> In any recent generation, certain political issues have been widely perceived to be fundamental moral issues as well — issues that challenge and unsettle conventional ways of understanding the moral universe and that serve as occasions for forging alternative ways of understanding. . . . Our electorally accountable policymaking institutions are not well suited to deal with such issues in a way that is faithful to the notion of moral evolution. [Those] institutions, when finally they confront such issues at all, tend simply to rely on established moral conventions and to refuse to see in such issues occasions for moral revaluation and possible moral growth. [Executive] and especially legislative officials tend to deal with fundamental political-moral problems, at least highly controversial ones, by reflexive reference to the established moral conventions of the greater part of their particular constituencies.

See also A. Bickel, The Least Dangerous Branch (1962); R. Dworkin, Freedom's Law (1997); Dworkin, The Forum of Principle, 56 N.Y.U. L. Rev. 469 (1981); Wellington, Common Law Rules and Constitutional Double Standards: Some Notes on Adjudication, 83 Yale L.J. 221 (1973).

    But don't executive and legislative officials think about what morality requires? Aren't they subject to their constituents, who certainly think about that issue? Perry's view may depend on an unduly skeptical view of the political process. In its most extreme form, this view treats politics as an unprincipled power struggle among self-interested groups, or factions. This view has played a prominent role in modern political and economic theory. See Stigler, The Theory of Economic Regulation, 2 Bell. J.L. & Mgmt. Sci. 3 (1971); R. Dahl, A Preface to Democratic Theory (1956). In this view, Justice Chase's classic violation of natural law — taking from A to give to B — is a frequent occurrence. If the skeptical view is accepted, an active judicial role in deciding moral issues might seem attractive. At the very least, it might seem to make sense to embrace an active judicial role in preventing any situation in which legislators steal from A to give to B. (But how do we know that A deserved what he had in the first place?)

    Consider the possibility that Perry's view says too little about the role of morality in politics, and is rooted as well in an unduly optimistic view of judicial decisionmaking. Whether representatives in fact respond mechanically to political pressures is a sharply disputed question. A. Maass, Congress and the Common Good (1983), suggests that members of Congress often engage in some form of deliberation about what the public good requires. See also S. Kelman, Making Public Policy (1985). If representative processes embody a large measure of deliberation — as Madison anticipated — the comparative advantage claimed for courts may not exist at all. Indeed, the comparative advantage may not exist if citizens themselves deliberate and if representatives respond to them. Many of the largest advances in American conceptions of rights have come from the democratic process, not the courts; consider the Americans with Disabilities Act.

Are justices likely to know what the right answers are? What makes judges so good at thinking well about difficult moral issues? One might respond to a natural law court in the same way as did Judge Learned Hand: "For myself it would be most irksome to be ruled by a bevy of nine Platonic Guardians, even if I knew how to choose them, which I assuredly do not." L. Hand, The Bill of Rights 73 (1958). Consider also Hand's claim that "[a] society so riven that the spirit of moderation is gone, no court can save; a society where that spirit flourishes, no court need save; and in a society which evades its responsibilities by thrusting upon the courts the nurture of that spirit, that spirit in the end will perish." L. Hand, The Contribution of an Independent Judiciary to Civilization (1944), in The Spirit of Liberty 155, 164 (I. Dilliard ed., 1960).

See also A. Cox, The Role of the Supreme Court in American Government 116 (1976): "I should be no less irked than Judge Hand if the Supreme Court were to void an ordinance adopted in the open Town Meeting in the New England town in which I live — a meeting in which all citizens can participate — but I should have little such feeling about a statute enacted by the Massachusetts legislature in the normal political pattern, and none about a law made in that pattern by the Congress of the United States." Does this view undervalue the fact that state and federal laws are at least in some sense the product of representative processes? For an emphasis on what the author, himself an influential judge, sees as the unmistakably political nature of Supreme Court decisions, see R. Posner, How Judges Think (2008).

3. *The ninth amendment.* The ninth amendment provides, "The enumeration in the Constitution, of certain rights, shall not be construed to deny or disparage others retained by the people." Does the amendment provide a textual grounding for the enforcement of natural rights that are not, themselves, enumerated in the text? Consider the following views:

a. Testimony of Robert Bork, Nomination of Robert H. Bork to Be Associate Justice of the Supreme Court of the United States: Hearings Before the S. Comm. on the Judiciary, 100th Cong., 249 (1987): "I do not think you can use the ninth amendment unless you know something of what it means. For example, if you had an amendment that says 'Congress shall make no' and then there is an ink blot and you cannot read the rest of it and that is the only copy you have, I do not think the court can make up what might be under the ink blot."

b. Barnett, The Ninth Amendment: It Means What It Says, 81 Tex. L. Rev. 1, 1 (2006): "[The] evidence establishes that the Ninth Amendment actually meant at the time of its enactment what it appears now to say: the unenumerated (natural) rights that people possessed prior to the formation of government, and which they retain afterwards, should be treated in the same manner as those (natural) rights that were enumerated in the Bill of Rights.

c. Seidman, Our Unsettled Ninth Amendment: An Essay on Unenumerated Rights and the Impossibility of Textualism, 98 Cal. L. Rev. 2129 (2010): "Because of the Ninth Amendment, the Constitution does not 'deny' or 'disparage [natural] rights, but neither does it embrace or imply them. The Amendment puts off to another day a final reckoning of the extent to which we are bound by constitutional text."

d. McConnell, The Ninth Amendment in Light of Text and History, 2010 Cato S. Ct. Rev. 13, 23 "[The] rights retained by the people are indeed individual natural rights, but those rights enjoy precisely the same status, and are protected in the same way, as before the Bill of Rights was added to the Constitution. They are not relinquished, denied, or disparaged. Nor do natural rights become 'constitutional rights.' They are simply what all retained rights were before the enactment of the Bill of Rights: a guide to equitable interpretation and a rationale for narrow construction of statutes that might be thought to infringe them, but not superior to explicit positive law."

For further discussion of the ninth amendment, see Chapter 6, section F1, infra.

D. POLITICAL CONTROL OVER THE SUPREME COURT

This section examines how the Court's authority is subject to external political control.

Note: Amendment, Appointment, Impeachment, and the Election Returns

1. *Constitutional amendment.* The most straightforward way for the people to respond to a Supreme Court decision with which they disagree is to amend the Constitution. But an amendment is exceedingly difficult to obtain. Under article V, the amending process may begin only if two-thirds of both Houses propose an amendment or if the legislatures of two-thirds of the states call for a constitutional convention. No amendment may be adopted until it is ratified by three-fourths of the states. These requirements were a deliberate effort to make it difficult to amend the Constitution. Why were constitutional amendments to be discouraged? And is discouraging them a good idea?

Consider in this regard Jefferson's view that the Constitution should be rewritten by the people every generation, on the theory that without frequent constitution-making there would be too little participation in and concern for the affairs of government. See Letter to Samuel Kercheval, July 12, 1816, in The Portable Thomas Jefferson 552, 558–561 (M. Peterson ed., 1975). Note in particular the view that

> [some] men look at constitutions with sanctimonious reverence, and deem them like the ark of the covenant, too sacred to be touched. They ascribe to the men of the preceding age a wisdom more than human, and suppose what they did to be beyond amendment. I knew that age well. [It] was very like the present, but without the experience of the present. [Let] us [not] weakly believe that one generation is not as capable as another of taking care of itself, and of ordering its own affairs. . . . The dead have no rights.

Id. at 558–559. See generally H. Arendt, On Revolution (1965), for discussion of Jefferson's preference for citizen participation in affairs of government and for frequent constitutional revision.

Madison rejected such proposals on the ground that they would produce "the most violent struggle between the parties interested in reviving and those interested in reforming the antecedent state of property." Letter to Thomas Jefferson, Feb. 4, 1790, in The Mind of the Founder 232 (M. Meyers ed., 1969). Compare The Federalist Nos. 10 and 51, section A, supra. Jefferson's contrary view was that even turbulence "is productive of good. It prevents the degeneracy of government, and nourishes a general attention to the public affairs. I hold that a little rebellion now and then is a good thing." Letter to Madison, Jan. 30, 1787, in The Portable Thomas Jefferson, supra, at 416–417. Under this view, frequent revision of basic institutional arrangements might be welcomed.

But as Madison's view suggests, the stability of the Constitution is often taken to be one of its great virtues. Consider in this regard the discussion of the separation of the realm of law and the realm of politics in The Federalist No. 78 and in *Marbury* itself. If frequent constitutional amendments were permitted, that distinction would be much less crisp; the effect of insulating certain decisions from politics would be undermined. Would that be a good or a bad thing? See generally Citizens for the Constitution, "Great and Extraordinary Occasions": Developing Guidelines for Constitutional Change (1999); S. Holmes, Passions and Constraint (1995); S. Levinson, ed., Responding to Imperfection (1995).

Note also that many states make it possible to amend their state constitutions through simple referendum. As a result, state constitutions are frequently altered. Thus, the Alabama Constitution has been amended over 700 times; the New York Constitution, over 200 times; the California Constitution, over 500 times; and the Texas Constitution, over 300 times. Under such regimes, the public is frequently involved in the process of constitutional decisionmaking — in such areas as budget deficits, permissible tax levels, environmental protection, and discrimination on the basis of race and sexual orientation. Consider the fact that constitutional amendments have frequently been on the national agenda in the last two decades. Might systems that allow frequent amendment operate as a salutary check on judicial review, or do they erase the advantages of ensuring that an insulated body will decide constitutional issues? Note also that many other nations, especially those emerging from communism, make it relatively easy to amend the Constitution.

There are now over two dozen amendments to the federal Constitution. Four of them represent successful efforts to overturn decisions by the Supreme Court. See U.S. Const. amends. XI (limiting jurisdiction of federal courts to hear suits brought against states), XIV (deeming Americans of African descent citizens of the United States), XVI (expanding power of Congress to tax), XXVI (setting voting age). Numerous other amendments have been offered but thus far without success. They have dealt with, for example, gay marriage, child labor, abortion, school desegregation, school prayer, flag burning, the line-item veto, and a balanced budget. Proposed constitutional amendments were especially popular in the 1970s, 1980s, and 1990s. Consider also the lengthy history of the proposed equal rights amendment, discussed in Chapter 5 infra, which would have provided that equality under the law may not be denied on the basis of sex. See J. Mansbridge, Why We Lost the ERA (1986). For what issues is constitutional amendment desirable?

Where does an individual rights provision fit in this framework? Consider the efforts in the wake of Texas v. Johnson, Chapter 7 infra, to amend the Constitution to protect the American flag against desecration. Many constitutional scholars argued vigorously that it would be especially risky to allow a constitutional amendment to counteract a Supreme Court decision protecting individual rights. Might there be a Jeffersonian response to this concern?

Even if efforts at amendment are unsuccessful, perhaps they should be welcomed because of the effect that they have on the public and the Court itself. Consider the possibility that amendment efforts, like political pressures generally, exercise some influence over Supreme Court decisions. The effort to amend the Constitution might be a salutary part of an ongoing conversation among the Court, other branches, and the public at large.

If a constitutional convention were called, would its authority be limited to particular issues or would it have general authority to amend the constitution as it chooses? See Special Constitutional Convention Study Committee, American Bar Association, Amendment of the Constitution by the Convention Method under Article V (1974). Should a court decide the issue? See the materials on the political question doctrine, section F infra.

On the amending process generally, see S. Levinson, ed., Responding to Imperfection (1995); C. Vose, Constitutional Change: Amendment Politics and Supreme Court Litigation Since 1900 (1972); Corwin and Ramsey, The Constitutional Law of Constitutional Amendment, 26 Notre Dame Law. 165 (1951); Dellinger, The Legitimacy of Constitutional Change: Rethinking the Amendment Process, 97 Harv. L. Rev. 386 (1983); Symposium on the Article V Convention Process, 66 Mich. L. Rev. 837 (1968). For an excellent overview, see D. Kyvig, Explicit and Authentic Acts: Amending the U.S. Constitution 1776–1995 (1996). For recommendations, see Citizens for the Constitution, "Great and Extraordinary Occasions": Developing Guidelines for Constitutional Change (1999).

Note also that many nations allow constitutional amendment through a process that is far less arduous than the American one, and also that some constitutions allow legislatures to "overrule" decisions of the highest court. Consider in this regard article 33 of the Canadian Constitution Act of 1982, which allows Parliament to declare expressly that a particular statute shall stand despite its conflict with many (not all) of the enumerated rights of the citizen.

2. *The power to appoint.* Members of the Supreme Court are appointed by the President, subject to the advice and consent of the Senate. As a result, the President has an opportunity to put justices on the Court who share his views. The appointing power has been important in controlling the direction of the Supreme Court. President Roosevelt responded to the efforts of the Court to invalidate aspects of the New Deal by appointing, among others, Justices Black, Douglas, Frankfurter, and Jackson. All of them turned out to be generally sympathetic to government regulation of the economy, although there developed sharp disputes over the scope of judicial protection of individual rights. After election campaigns marked by an emphasis on obtaining "strict constructionists" on the Court, President Nixon appointed Chief Justice Burger and Justices Blackmun, Powell, and Rehnquist. Those appointments led to a more conservative Court and brought about some significant changes of direction, albeit of disputed scope. See V. Blasi, ed., The Burger Court: The Counterrevolution That Wasn't (1983).

President Reagan's appointees — Chief Justice Rehnquist and Justices O'Connor, Scalia, and Kennedy — generally moved the Court in directions favored by President Reagan, although on several issues of individual autonomy — for example, abortion and gay rights — the cohort of Reagan-appointed justices has been divided. Similarly, President Clinton's appointees — Justices Ginsburg and Breyer — have generally resisted the Court's more conservative turn. President George W. Bush's appointees — Chief Justice Roberts and Justice Alito — have not disappointed the expectations of the Bush White House, and Justices

Sotomayor and Kagan have generally been the liberal voices that the Obama administration expected them to be. Early evidence strongly suggests that Justice Gorsuch will be the conservative member sought by President Trump.

The overall picture, then, is that Supreme Court appointees vote in ways that broadly fit with the hopes and expectations of appointing Presidents, at least over the past century or so. But Presidents have sometimes been surprised to find that their appointees' performance on the bench was more "liberal" or more "conservative" than expected. President Eisenhower, for example, appointed Earl Warren as Chief Justice, relying in part on Warren's conservative, law-and-order reputation as governor of California. Eisenhower later claimed that the appointment was one of the worst mistakes he had ever made. Eisenhower also appointed Justice Brennan, whose record turned out to be quite different from what had been expected. Some of the votes of Justices O'Connor, Kennedy, and Souter were a disappointment to many supporters of Presidents Reagan and Bush; consider their failure to vote to overrule Roe v. Wade, discussed in Chapter 6 infra.

Events of this sort indicate that the appointments process is not a guarantee of political control; justices do not move in lockstep with the President who appointed them. But the record strongly suggests that presidential control can shift the Court significantly, and that the appointments process makes it unlikely that Supreme Court justices will diverge too sharply or for too long from the desires of those with political power. For detailed treatments, showing the complexities here, see generally L. Epstein and J. Siegel, Advice and Consent (2007); Epstein et al., Ideological Drift among Supreme Court Justices, 101 Nw. U. L. Rev. 1483 (2007); H. Abraham, Justices and Presidents (1985); J. Schmidhauser, Judges and Justices (1979). Note, however, that ideology is far from the only consideration in the appointments process. Region, race, gender, and religion of the appointee will sometimes play a role in the President's decision. For general discussion, see id. at 41–82.

The appointment decision is not the President's alone. Early Senates often exercised an active role, and the Senate has regularly failed to confirm lower court judges. See generally L. Tribe, God Save This Honorable Court (1985). Consider the view that "the role of the Senate as well as interest groups cannot be overlooked. Particularly in periods in which a President lacked party or ideological support in the Senate, the influence of senatorial confirmation assumed far-reaching importance. Approximately one-fifth of the presidential nominations for Supreme Court appointments have been dealt with negatively by the Senate." Id. at 91. The Senate's power to advise and consent may affect the composition of the Court in two ways. First, it may lead the President to avoid highly controversial appointees. Second, the Senate may refuse to confirm presidential appointees — for reasons of incompetence, venality, or ideology.

Since 1900, Supreme Court nominees have been explicitly rejected, by vote, on only four occasions — President Reagan's appointment of Judge Robert Bork, President Nixon's appointments of Judges Clement Haynesworth and Harold Carswell, and President Hoover's appointment of Judge John Parker. Some cases are more ambiguous. A Republican-led Senate refused to hold hearings for President Obama's nominee, Merrick Garland. George W. Bush's nomination of White House Counsel Harriet Miers was withdrawn in the face of strong, conservative opposition. President Reagan's nominee Judge Douglas Ginsburg withdrew after reports that he had smoked marijuana.

Is an aggressive role from the Senate desirable? Should the Senate disapprove Supreme Court nominees who are perceived to be too "conservative" or too "liberal"?

Consider, as a starting point, the extraordinary public debate in 1987 over President Reagan's nomination of Judge Robert Bork. Judge Bork had been known as a distinguished lawyer, professor, and judge; he was also one of the most outspoken critics of what he saw as unjustified judicial activism on the part of the Supreme Court under Chief Justices Warren and Burger. An especially controversial article, Bork, Neutral Principles and Some First Amendment Problems, 47 Ind. L.J. 1 (1971), was taken by many readers as a broadside attack on the Supreme Court's decisions in such areas as privacy, voting rights, and discrimination. This Indiana Law Journal article — and other writings by Judge Bork — provided the focus for a heated and lengthy confirmation process in which the Senate Judiciary Committee heard testimony from Judge Bork himself and from numerous lawyers and law professors. There was intense lobbying on both sides; the lobbying efforts included national advertisements, in newspapers and journals as well as on television and radio, predicting the consequences of Judge Bork's confirmation. See generally Bork's own account in The Tempting of America (1989) and The Bork Nomination: Essays and Reports, 9 Cardozo L. Rev. 1 (1987).

Judge Bork's nomination was defeated by the largest margin of any Supreme Court nominee in American history. What, if any, implications does the defeat have for constitutional interpretation? It is possible to think that the nation in some sense rejected Judge Bork's views; it is also possible to think that his defeat was a result of an intense and in many ways misleading lobbying effort — producing a new word, "Borking," said to involve an all-out, often personal campaign against a public figure.

Does the experience with Judge Bork suggest that an aggressive senatorial role in the confirmation process is valuable? What does it suggest about the idea that the appointments process weakens the countermajoritarian difficulty? For varying views on these and related questions, see Essays on the Supreme Court Appointment Process, 101 Harv. L. Rev. 1146 (1988); S. Carter, The Confirmation Mess (1993), deploring the role of caricature and "soundbite politics." Many people believe that the defeat of the Bork nomination has contributed to general caution on the part of Presidents, ensuring that they will not appoint controversial candidates, and that they will avoid nominees with a contestable "paper trail."

Return to the Senate's failure to hold hearings on Merrick Garland, President Obama's choice and a widely admired judge, purportedly on the grounds that the President should not be able to seat a new Supreme Court justice in a final year. Is that a good principle? Or is the real principle this: In the modern era, there is a real possibility that Republicans or Democrats, or both, will use every device they have, and every argument they can make, to defeat nominees who won't vote as they like?

3. *Impeachment.* Justices of the Supreme Court "hold their Offices during good Behavior." U.S. Const. art. III, §1. They may "be removed from Office on Impeachment for, and Conviction of, Treason, Bribery, or other high Crimes and Misdemeanors." Under what circumstances may federal judges be impeached? See, for general discussion, Chapter 4 infra; R. Berger, Impeachment (1970), C. Sunstein, Impeachment: A Citizen's Guide (2017). In the context of judges, here's a big question: What, exactly, counts as high crime and misdemeanor?

No Supreme Court justice has been removed from office in the nation's history, although Justice Abe Fortas was forced to resign after revelation of financial improprieties; Justice Samuel Chase was impeached but not convicted. Members of the lower federal courts have been impeached and removed from office, and there have been efforts to impeach Supreme Court justices. See K. Hall, The Politics of Justice (1979). The most celebrated example involved Justice Douglas. A resolution calling for an investigation referred, among other things, to Justice William O. Douglas's having married four times; to the fact that one of his former wives was "a cocktail waitress"; to his votes in favor of defendants in cases involving "subversive questions"; to his traveling to Peking; and to various "left-wing" statements in his book, Points of Rebellion. See 116 Cong. Rec. H12,111–12,114 (daily ed. Apr. 16, 1970). An impeachment resolution was introduced against him in part on the basis of articles published in Playboy magazine, in which Justice Douglas, among other things, expressed some sympathy for rebellious groups in the 1960s. In the course of the proceedings, then-Representative Gerald Ford argued that the grounds for impeachment were "whatever a majority of the House of Representatives considers them to be at a given moment in history." 116 Cong. Rec. H3113–3114 (daily ed. Apr. 15, 1970).

Notwithstanding the latter suggestion, the device of impeachment has not been used as a means of obtaining political control over the Supreme Court. This phenomenon may be attributable in part to the prestige of an independent judiciary, in part to general acceptance of Marbury v. Madison, and in part to legal doubts about the wisdom and legality of using the impeachment mechanisms for this purpose. On the latter question, see Chapter 4 infra.

4. *Life tenure.* Under the Constitution, federal judges are appointed for life. This provision is obviously associated with the goal of promoting judicial independence. But there are other ways to promote independence. Some states and some nations impose an age ceiling on judges, requiring retirement at age sixty-five or seventy. The "independent regulatory commissions," including for example the Federal Trade Commission, allow members to serve for multiyear terms, and they can be removed for "neglect of duty, malfeasance, or inefficiency in office." If you were starting a constitutional order from scratch — in, say, South Africa, Romania, or Poland — what sort of design would you favor?

5. *Controlling sitting judges; informal mechanisms and self-imposed limits.* To what extent is the Supreme Court subject to informal mechanisms of control? Mr. Dooley — the pen name and principal character of Finley Peter Dunne, who wrote around the turn of the twentieth century — explained in a now-celebrated statement that "[no] matter whether th' constitution follows th' flag or not, th' supreme court follows th' ilection returns." F. P. Dunne, The Supreme Court's Decisions, in Mr. Dooley's Opinions 26 (1900). This statement is not literally true, but there can be little doubt that the Court has exhibited reluctance to make decisions that depart too sharply from what it perceives as a political consensus. Many of the Court's most controversial decisions — involving, say, school segregation, women's rights, the individual right to have guns — actually fit with, and did not contradict, widespread social convictions. See C. Sunstein, A Constitution of Many Minds (2009).

Why is this? On one view, the appointment process is a big part of the picture; because justices are selected by Presidents, and must be confirmed by the Senate, there is a link between their views and the views of the citizenry. Perhaps inescapably, people's views about the meaning of the Constitution are affected by their deepest convictions, and so it appears, whether you are appointed by

President Clinton, Bush, Obama, or Trump. But there is another point: Justices also live in society, and for that reason, their beliefs may well be affected by what society thinks or is perceived to think. The Court's decisions striking down racial segregation and sex discrimination, vindicating the individual right to have guns, and requiring states to recognize same-sex marriage can easily be seen as examples.

Some have suggested that the Court has, or perceives itself as having, a limited amount of "political capital," and it tends to budget its expenditure of that capital in the number and kinds of controversial decisions it renders. See J. Choper, Judicial Review and the National Political Process (1981); A. Bickel, The Least Dangerous Branch (1962). The Court's perception of its limited political capital may sometimes manifest itself in sensitivity to the views of elected officials and private citizens. Thus, for example, the end of the *Lochner* period — in which the Court struggled against government regulation of the economy, see Chapter 6 infra — may be understood in part as a response to popular pressures, though the problem of identifying "cause and effect" is formidable. See C. Vose, supra. There are few occasions in the nation's history in which the Court has persisted in a course to which the country is sharply opposed. See A. Bickel, supra.

On the other hand, the Court's decisions may themselves help to shape a national consensus (is that a good or a bad thing?), and it is undoubtedly true that on occasion the Court has been willing to insist on a course of action notwithstanding considerable public disagreement. Consider in this regard the school prayer controversy, Chapter 8 infra; the problem of school desegregation, Chapter 5 infra; and the abortion controversy, Chapter 6 infra.

There is helpful but sparse empirical work on the effect of popular opinion on Supreme Court decisions, perhaps because of the difficulties in tracing causation. For a valuable collection, see Public Opinion and Constitutional Controversy (N. Persily et al. eds. 2008). It does seem clear that the Court is sometimes sensitive to the perceived mood of the country, and that it is generally unwilling to continue for long periods on courses that face intense popular disagreement. A provocative, important, and controversial discussion is G. Rosenberg, The Hollow Hope (rev. ed. 2008), which discusses what the author claims to be the surprisingly limited effectiveness of the Supreme Court in producing social change, even in the area of race relations, and which suggests that the Court's lack of political authority is connected with its lack of effectiveness.

Ex parte McCardle

74 U.S. (7 Wall.) 506 (1869)

[McCardle published articles in a newspaper in Mississippi, which was then under the control of the national army pursuant to the Reconstruction plan adopted by Congress after the Civil War. He was arrested under charges of libel; disturbing the peace; inciting insurrection, disorder, and violence; and impeding reconstruction. McCardle sought habeas corpus from a federal court in Mississippi, claiming that Congress lacked constitutional authority to establish a system of military government in the states. The case was in this sense a fundamental challenge to Congress's reconstruction power. After losing in the trial court, McCardle appealed, invoking a habeas corpus act enacted in 1867. Congress feared that the case would be a vehicle for invalidating the reconstruction plan. Congress therefore enacted — while the case was pending, and over presidential veto on constitutional grounds — a statute that repealed the provision of the 1867 habeas corpus act that McCardle had invoked.]

THE CHIEF JUSTICE [CHASE] delivered the opinion of the court.

The first question necessarily is that of jurisdiction; for, if the act of March, 1868, takes away the jurisdiction defined by the act of February, 1867, it is useless, if not improper, to enter into any discussion of other questions.

It is quite true, as was argued by the counsel for the petitioner, that the appellate jurisdiction of this court is not derived from acts of Congress. It is, strictly speaking, conferred by the Constitution. But it is conferred "with such exceptions and under such regulations as Congress shall make." It is unnecessary to consider whether, if Congress had made no exceptions and no regulations, this court might not have exercised general appellate jurisdiction under rules prescribed by itself. For among the earliest acts of the first Congress, at its first session, was the act of September 24th, 1789, to establish the judicial courts of the United States. That act provided for the organization of this court, and prescribed regulations for the exercise of its jurisdiction. . . .

The principle that the affirmation of appellate jurisdiction implies the negation of all such jurisdiction not affirmed having been thus established, it was an almost necessary consequence that acts of Congress, providing for the exercise of jurisdiction, should come to be spoken of as acts granting jurisdiction, and not as acts making exceptions to the constitutional grant of it.

The exception to appellate jurisdiction in the case before us, however, is not an inference from the affirmation of other appellate jurisdiction. It is made in terms. The provision of the act of 1867, affirming the appellate jurisdiction of this court in cases of habeas corpus is expressly repealed. It is hardly possible to imagine a plainer instance of positive exception. We are not at liberty to inquire into the motives of the legislature. We can only examine into its power under the Constitution; and the power to make exceptions to the appellate jurisdiction of this court is given by express words.

What, then, is the effect of the repealing act upon the case before us? We cannot doubt as to this. Without jurisdiction the court cannot proceed at all in any cause. Jurisdiction is power to declare the law, and when it ceases to exist, the only function remaining to the court is that of announcing the fact and dismissing the cause. And this is not less clear upon authority than upon principle.

Counsel seem to have supposed, if effect be given to the repealing act in question, that the whole appellate power of the court, in cases of habeas corpus, is denied. But this is an error. The act of 1868 does not except from that jurisdiction any cases but appeals from Circuit Courts under the act of 1867. It does not affect the jurisdiction which was previously exercised.

The appeal of the petitioner in this case must be dismissed for want of jurisdiction.

Note: Political Control over Jurisdiction of Article III Courts

Does Ex parte McCardle stand for the proposition that Congress has plenary power over the appellate jurisdiction of the Supreme Court? In Ex parte Yerger, 75 U.S. (8 Wall.) 85 (1869), the Court converted into a holding the last paragraph of the McCardle opinion. In Yerger, the Court asserted appellate jurisdiction over a habeas corpus proceeding brought by a petitioner in military detention. The source of jurisdiction was certiorari based on pre-1867 legislation. The language of Ex parte McCardle suggests that there are no constitutional constraints on Congress's power over the appellate jurisdiction of the Supreme Court; but its holding might be read more narrowly in light of the conclusion, noted in *McCardle* itself and made clear in *Yerger*, that there was an alternative means of obtaining Supreme Court review.

The question of congressional power over the appellate jurisdiction of the Supreme Court has occasionally assumed considerable importance, with proposals to prevent the Supreme Court from hearing cases involving (among other things) school prayer, reapportionment, school desegregation, and abortion. No such proposal has passed Congress. But there has been substantial debate about the constitutionality of the proposals, versions of which have been introduced at numerous stages in the history of the nation. Consider the following proposal:

> The Supreme Court shall not have jurisdiction to review, by appeal, writ of certiorari, or otherwise, any case arising out of any State statute, ordinance, rule, regulation, or any part thereof, or arising out of any act interpreting, applying, or enforcing a State statute, ordinance, rule, or regulation, which relates to voluntary prayers in public schools and public buildings.

Would this proposal be constitutional? If one thought that Supreme Court decisions restricting school prayer should be overruled, why might one think that this proposal would be counterproductive?

1. *Restricting jurisdiction and the separation of powers.* If plenary power to restrict jurisdiction existed, Congress could immunize state and federal laws from Supreme Court review. Congress could, for example, enact a law and provide that the Supreme Court could not assess its constitutionality. Indeed, Congress could for all practical purposes cut the Supreme Court out of the constitutional scheme — for example, by depriving the Court of jurisdiction in all federal question cases. At first glance, such a power might seem to be a striking intrusion on the separation of powers system.

Would it be possible to argue that the power to restrict jurisdiction is not such an intrusion at all but is instead a means of making it tolerable to have judicial review in a system of representative government? See C. Black, Decision According to Law (1981). Under this view, the availability of the power to limit jurisdiction is an important check on the Supreme Court, discouraging it from straying too far from "popular will," as expressed in legislative and executive enactments, and allowing the legislature to retain ultimate control over the Court. At the same time, the existence of an unexercised, but broad, exceptions power gives reason to find public acquiescence in or ratification of Supreme Court decisions. But perhaps such arguments attribute too much to legislative inaction.

In any event, the nature and limits of the exceptions power remain shrouded in uncertainty. The remainder of this Note outlines some of the competing views.

2. *The plenary power argument.* To some, the exceptions clause grants Congress plenary power over the appellate jurisdiction of the Supreme Court. Congress may make exceptions whenever and for whatever reasons it chooses. This view draws support from the literal language of the Constitution. The text itself contains no limits on congressional power to make "exceptions" to the appellate jurisdiction of the Supreme Court. The only limits in this view are those that

derive from the political process. The plenary power argument obtains support from *McCardle* and from numerous dicta in early cases. See Van Alstyne, A Critical Guide to Ex parte McCardle, 15 Ariz. L. Rev. 229 (1973).

3. *Separation of powers constraints: the "essential functions" hypothesis.* One argument against recognition of a plenary power under the exceptions clause is based on the proposition that Congress cannot "destroy the essential role of the Supreme Court in the constitutional plan." Hart, The Power of Congress to Limit the Jurisdiction of Federal Courts: An Exercise in Dialectic, 66 Harv. L. Rev. 1362, 1365 (1953). The argument is largely a structural one. The framers and ratifiers, it is claimed, intended the Court to perform an important function in the separation of powers scheme: to ensure that Congress, the President, and the states are kept within constitutional limits. (Consider The Federalist No. 78 and Martin v. Hunter's Lessee.) If Congress had power to remove the Court's jurisdiction, it could insulate its own laws, or those of the states, from constitutional attack, effectively writing the Court out of the constitutional system. Such a power, it is sometimes claimed, is not consistent with the intended function of courts in the constitutional order. See Ratner, Congressional Power over the Appellate Jurisdiction of the Supreme Court, 109 U. Pa. L. Rev. 157 (1960).

Can this view be reconciled with the language of the exceptions clause? Proponents suggest that the use of the term "exceptions" itself contemplates a narrow power, one that is consistent with the general view that the Court would exercise jurisdiction in all or most federal question cases. See Ratner, supra; Sager, Foreword: Constitutional Limitations on Congress' Authority to Regulate the Jurisdiction of the Federal Courts, 95 Harv. L. Rev. 17 (1981). On this view, the extent of Congress's power may not be subject to precise limits, but it is clear that Congress cannot deprive the Court of jurisdiction in (all or some?) constitutional cases. See also R. Berger, Congress vs. the Supreme Court (1969) (suggesting that the exceptions power is limited to issues of fact).

Is this position supported or undermined by Marbury v. Madison? Consider Wechsler, The Courts and the Constitution, 65 Colum. L. Rev. 1001, 1005–1006 (1965):

> The plan of the Constitution for the courts [was] quite simply that the Congress would decide from time to time how far the federal judicial institution should be used within the limits of the federal judicial power. [Federal] courts, including the Supreme Court, do not pass on constitutional questions because there is a special function vested in them to enforce the Constitution or police the other agencies of government. They do so rather for the reason that they must decide a litigated case that is otherwise within their jurisdiction and in doing so must give effect to the supreme law of the land. That is, at least, what Marbury v. Madison was all about.

Is this a proper reading of *Marbury*? Consider the following view: *Marbury* and The Federalist No. 78 rest on the broader ground that the Supreme Court was accorded a distinctive role as the guarantor of the supremacy of the federal Constitution as against the states and the federal legislature. Recognition of an unlimited power to make exceptions would be inconsistent with the intended role of the Supreme Court in the separation of powers scheme, generating precisely the evils that led Hamilton to support the existence of judicial review. Compare Cooper v. Aaron, supra.

Does it matter whether the exceptions power is used to insulate federal or state laws from judicial review? Would the dangers be different in the two different cases? See Sager, supra, at 55:

> To remove or permit the removal from the entire federal judiciary, including the Supreme Court, of the constitutional review of state conduct would be to alter the balance of federal authority fundamentally and dangerously. In an observation intended to defuse rather than ignite the sense of crisis that surrounded the Court in 1913, Justice Holmes uttered his famous words on the matter of Supreme Court jurisdiction: "I do not think the United States would come to an end if we lost our power to declare an Act of Congress void. I do think the Union would be imperiled if we could not make that declaration as to the laws of the several States." [The] case for regarding federal judicial supervision of the states as essential to the scheme of the Constitution is a strong one.

Even if it is accepted that there is an "essential functions" limitation on jurisdictional restrictions, the question remains whether particular provisions are inconsistent with the Court's "essential function." Would the bill reprinted above, eliminating federal court jurisdiction in school prayer cases, destroy the Supreme Court's "essential role"? Consider the fact that the Court would retain jurisdiction in all other cases raising constitutional questions.

4. *Independent constitutional barriers.* There is little doubt that other constitutional provisions, like the equal protection component of the due process clause, limit Congress's power under the exceptions clause. For example, Congress could not constitutionally provide that Republicans, but no one else, may have access to the Supreme Court. Such a provision would violate the first amendment and thus would be independently unconstitutional.

How far does this rationale extend? Does it justify a conclusion that selective withdrawals of jurisdiction — for example, busing, abortion, or school prayer — are unconstitutional? See Tribe, Jurisdictional Gerrymandering: Zoning Disfavored Rights out of the Federal Courts, 16 Harv. C.R.-C.L. L. Rev. 129 (1981). Consider Bator, Congressional Power over the Jurisdiction of the Federal Courts, 27 Vill. L. Rev. 1030, 1036–1037 (1982):

> Neither the equal protection clause nor any other clause of the Constitution requires equal jurisdiction treatment for different subject-matters of litigation. [A] somewhat narrower argument is that if it is shown that Congress' motive in requiring a certain category of case to be brought in the exclusive original jurisdiction of the state courts is "hostility" to the substantive constitutional right in question, it can be struck down. I do not understand how such a rule could be administered. What would be an adequate indication of hostility? [The] state courts, equally with the federal, are charged with the task of enforcing and protecting federal constitutional rights.

5. *The relevance of United States v. Klein.* Consider in this regard United States v. Klein, 80 U.S. (13 Wall.) 128 (1872). Klein had sued for indemnification of property taken during the Civil War. It was a necessary predicate for relief that the claimant show that he was not a supporter of the rebellion against the national government, and the courts had held that a presidential pardon was evidence that the claimant had not in fact participated.

A statute, enacted while the United States' appeal was pending from a decision awarding indemnification to Klein, provided that a presidential pardon was to be used as evidence that the person pardoned had participated in a rebellion. The statute added that courts should dismiss suits involving such claimants for want of jurisdiction. The Court invalidated the statute on the ground that dismissal would allow Congress to "prescribe rules of decision to the Judicial Department of the government in cases pending before it." According to the Court, this was inconsistent with the separation of powers. The Court added that the statute would be permissible under the exceptions clause if it were a denial of "the right to appeal in a particular class of cases." The problem here was that it was "a means to an end," that is, denial "to pardons granted by the President of the effect which this court had adjudged them to have."

Perhaps *Klein* is different from *McCardle* because it involved not merely a withdrawal of jurisdiction but also an effort "to bind the Court to decide [the] case in accordance with a rule of law [that is] independently unconstitutional." See P. Bator, P. Mishkin, D. Shapiro, and H. Wechsler, Hart & Wechsler's The Federal Courts and the Federal System 316 (2d ed. 1973).

Note also Justice Douglas's contention that "[there] is a serious question whether the *McCardle* case could command a majority view today." Glidden Co. v. Zdanok, 370 U.S. 530, 605 (1962) (dissenting opinion).

6. *The lower federal courts.* The power of Congress over the jurisdiction of the lower federal courts raises somewhat different issues. It is generally agreed that article III imposes on Congress no obligation to create lower federal courts at all. See Sheldon v. Sill, 49 U.S. (8 How.) 441 (1850). If Congress need not create lower federal courts, a natural inference might be that Congress has plenary power over the sorts of issues that lower courts might hear. This is a classic "lesser included" argument: The authority to create the lower courts necessarily includes the power to restrict the lower courts to certain specified issues.

The argument is also, however,

> based on the fact that this reading is the only one consistent with the understanding which animated the compromise adopted by the Framers. The essence of that compromise was an agreement that the question whether access to the lower courts was necessary to assure the effectiveness of federal law [should] be left a matter of political and legislative judgment, to be made from time to time in the light of particular circumstances. It would make nonsense of that notion to hold that the only power to be exercised is the all-or-nothing power to decide whether none or all of the cases to which the federal judicial power extends need the haven of a lower court.

Bator, supra, at 1031.

Are there any limits on Congress's power over the lower federal courts? Suppose, for example, that Congress bars the lower federal courts from hearing cases involving abortion, school prayer, or desegregation — as numerous bills introduced in the late 1970s and 1980s threatened to do. Consider the following possibilities.

a. Eisenberg, in Congressional Authority to Restrict Lower Federal Court Jurisdiction, 83 Yale L.J. 498, 532–533 (1974), relies on the expansion of the caseload of the lower federal courts and their important role in protecting federal rights to argue:

> The inability of the Supreme Court to do justice in every case within the Article III grant of jurisdiction has broad implications. It means that Congress cannot deny

lower federal courts jurisdiction on the ground that Supreme Court review of state court judgments provides an adequate vindication for federal rights. [The] lower federal courts are thus indispensable if the judiciary is to be a co-equal branch and if the "judicial Power of the United States" is to remain the power to protect rights guaranteed by the Constitution and its amendments. Abolition of the lower federal courts is no longer constitutionally permissible.

b. The "independent constitutional constraints" on congressional limits on the jurisdiction of the Supreme Court apply as well to limits on the jurisdiction of the lower courts. Here, the same considerations apply as discussed above.

c. Note also the position of Justice Story in Martin v. Hunter's Lessee, supra, to the effect that at any time some federal court must have jurisdiction over any case to which the article III power extends. This view, however, has been rejected in modern practice. Note, for example, that diversity jurisdiction extends only to cases in which the amount in controversy is over $75,000 and that Congress has never granted the Supreme Court appellate jurisdiction over diversity cases brought in state courts.

For a careful elaboration on these questions of a position similar to that of Justice Story, see Amar, A Neo-Federalist View of Article III: Separating the Two Tiers of Federal Jurisdiction, 65 B.U. L. Rev. 205 (1985).

Note: The Power of Reprisal — General Thoughts

What conclusions do these various mechanisms of control — constitutional amendment, appointment, impeachment, popular opinion, and jurisdictional limits — suggest? Do Congress and the President have enough, or too much, authority over the Court?

Consider the following views: (1) In light of the various mechanisms of control, the countermajoritarian difficulty said to be produced by the existence of judicial review is much less severe than it appears at first glance. The various safeguards make it much less troublesome that interpretation is often or inevitably discretionary; there is usually a political corrective, even in the short run. (2) The mechanisms of control make the courts so dependent on the political branches that justifications for *Marbury* that rely on the political insulation of the judges ultimately break down. It turns out that the judges are not insulated at all. They are emphatically political actors. (3) The various mechanisms are insufficient to eliminate and even to reduce the countermajoritarian difficulty. It remains the case that the power of judicial review permits unelected judges to have what is in effect the final say on issues of public importance. The fact that the judges are subject to some control through other means does not respond to the basic problem.

Consider, finally, the question of efficacy. Sometimes Supreme Court decisions have less fundamental consequences for the real world than its advocates and its critics think. For example, only about 2 percent of black children in the South attended desegregated schools ten years after the Supreme Court's decision in Brown v. Board of Education. Especially when the Court is attempting to engage in large-scale social reform, its efforts are likely to be disappointing. Frequently lawyers and law students assume that society will simply follow Supreme Court decisions, but difficulties of implementation severely complicate this assumption. It may be that these difficulties provide an additional argument against an active judicial role in social reform. For elaborations of this theme, see G. Rosenberg, The Hollow Hope (rev. ed. 2008); D. Horowitz, The Courts and Social Policy (1979).

E.   "CASE OR CONTROVERSY" REQUIREMENTS AND THE PASSIVE VIRTUES

A number of devices require or permit federal courts not to resolve certain cases. Most of these devices are, in whole or in part, an inference from article III, section 2, providing that the "Judicial Power shall extend" to enumerated "Cases" and "Controversies." This provision, it is often said, forbids the courts from invalidating legislative or executive action "merely" because it is unconstitutional. The courts may rule only in the context of a constitutional case.

This principle has a number of concrete implications. In general, it means that courts may not issue "advisory opinions"; may not decide "political questions"; must have before them someone with "standing," or with some kind of personal stake in the controversy; and may not decide issues that are either "premature" or "moot." What purposes are served by the "case or controversy" requirement? There are several candidates.

First, the requirement might promote democratic self-government by ensuring a measure of judicial restraint. By limiting the occasions for judicial intervention into legislative or executive processes, the case or controversy requirement reduces the presence of the federal judiciary in American life — and so too friction between the branches produced by judicial review. This rationale is often tied to a concern with the countermajoritarian difficulty. The questions raised by this rationale are whether judicial restraint, thus understood, is desirable, and, if so, whether the case or controversy requirement is a sensible way to promote such restraint. Note in particular that judicial restraint is promoted by these devices not by requiring a deferential approach to the merits but by preventing the courts from reaching the merits at all.

Second, the case or controversy requirement might ensure that constitutional issues will be resolved only in the context of concrete disputes rather than in response to problems that may be hypothetical, abstract, or speculative. This consequence, it is sometimes said, distinguishes legislative and judicial decision-making and promotes sound constitutional conclusions. Notice, however, that even if a decision comes in a concrete setting, the decision's effects extend far more broadly. When the Supreme Court held that Jane Roe had a right to an abortion in Roe v. Wade or that Linda Brown had the right to attend a nonsegregated school in Brown v. Board of Education, no one thinks that the Court's primary focus was on the particular cases before it.

Third, the case or controversy requirement is said to promote the ends of individual autonomy and self-determination, by ensuring that constitutional decisions are rendered at the behest of those actually injured rather than at the behest of bystanders attempting to disrupt mutually advantageous accommodations or to impose their own views of public policy on government. Consider, for example, the fact that people can object to racial discrimination or environmental harm only if they have been subject to those injuries. Outsiders with an ideological interest are barred. This rationale is sometimes accompanied by a suggestion that case or controversy limitations ensure real adversity between the parties and thus ensure against collusive litigation. But note that sometimes the fact that a lawsuit has not resulted stems from ignorance, poverty, or alienation rather than from satisfaction with the status quo.

Consider also A. Bickel, The Least Dangerous Branch 115–116 (1962):

> One of the chief faculties of the judiciary, which is lacking in the legislature and which fits the courts for the function of evolving and applying constitutional principles, is that the judgment of courts can come later, after the hopes and prophecies expressed in legislation have been tested in the actual workings of our society; the judgment of courts may be had in concrete cases that exemplify the actual consequences of legislative or executive actions. [It] may be added that the opportunity to relate a legislative policy to the flesh-and-blood facts of an actual case [to] observe and describe in being what the legislature may or may not have foreseen as probable — this opportunity as much as, or more than, anything else enables the Court to appeal to the nation's second thought. Moreover, [these requirements] create a time lag between legislation and adjudication. [Hence] it cushions the clash between the Court and any given legislative majority.

In Bickel's view, the "passive virtues" of inaction operate as a necessary means of mediating between the two (competing) ideas at work in U.S. government: electoral accountability and governance according to principle. The "passive virtues" operate to ensure that the latter idea does not swallow up the former, by permitting the Court to defer to the political process without resolving the issue either way. But see Gunther, The Subtle Vices of the Passive Virtues, 64 Colum. L. Rev. 1 (1964), objecting that an "unprincipled" approach to justiciability issues is unacceptable and will ultimately undermine the Court's role. Note also that some of the various justiciability doctrines are largely a creation not of the founding period but of the twentieth century — in particular, of efforts by Justices Brandeis, Frankfurter, and others seeking to immunize what they considered to be progressive government, and especially administrative agencies, from judicial review. The fact that some justiciability constraints are mostly traceable to this period, rather than to the founding, might have significant implications for current approaches to those constraints. But see Woolhandler and Nelson, Does History Defeat Standing Doctrine?, 102 Mich. L. Rev. 689 (2004) (arguing that during the eighteenth and nineteenth centuries, American courts imposed various limitations on the standing of private individuals that were "influenced by . . . ideas about the proper role of the judiciary, its relationship to the political branches of the state and federal governments, and the legitimate allocations of public and private power").

1. Advisory Opinions

One justiciability doctrine is unquestionably traceable to the early period. Under the first President, the Supreme Court said that it was constitutionally forbidden to issue "advisory opinions" — opinions on the constitutionality of legislative or executive actions that did not grow out of a case or controversy. President Washington, through Secretary of State Thomas Jefferson, asked the justices whether he might request their views about legal questions growing out of a war, in which the United States was neutral, between England and France. The justices responded:

> The three departments of the government [being] in certain respects checks upon each other, and our being judges of a court in the last resort, are considerations which accord strong arguments against the propriety of our extrajudicially deciding the questions alluded to, especially as the power given by the Constitution to the President, of calling on the heads of departments for opinions, seems to have been purposely as well as expressly united to the executive departments. We exceedingly regret every event that may cause embarrassment to your administration, but we derive consolation from the reflection that your judgment will discern what is right.

Is the Court's conclusion a natural or an inevitable interpretation of article III? Suppose that a President asked the Chief Justice to provide him with advice about a policy matter in an unofficial capacity. Would it be unconstitutional for the Chief Justice to respond? Is not the clear implication of the justice's response to President Jefferson that any opinion the justices offered would be in their unofficial capacity? Note in this regard that Chief Justice Earl Warren served as head of the commission that investigated the assassination of President Kennedy and that by statute the Chief Justice serves on the Board of Regents of the Smithsonian Institute. The Chief Justice also regularly testifies before Congress and makes recommendations regarding matters relating to the federal judiciary. Surely these activities are constitutional? Some state supreme courts, including the Supreme Judicial Court of Massachusetts, are authorized to issue advisory opinions; many courts in Eastern Europe have been given this power in the aftermath of communism.

Note also that the Office of Legal Counsel of the Department of Justice has, at least for the executive branch, assumed an advice-giving role, informing the President and other members of the executive branch of its views about the constitutionality of proposed courses of action. See 28 U.S.C. §§511-513 (authorizing the Attorney General to give his advice and opinion on questions of law to the President and to heads of executive departments). The Office of Legal Counsel has made public a wide variety of legal opinions issued since 1977. Perhaps, however, advisory bodies of this kind end up having close collegial relations with those to whom they give advice. Note, for example, that the assistant attorney general in charge of the Office of Legal Counsel is a political appointee. As a result, the judgments of that office might suffer from an absence of independence — an issue that received considerable attention in connection with the war on terror and the administration of George W. Bush. See J. Goldsmith, The Terror Presidency (2007). See also B. Ackerman, The Decline and Fall of the American Republic 146 (2010) (calling for creation of a "Supreme Executive Tribunal" of nine presidentially nominated, Senate-confirmed "judges for the executive branch.").

Some of the gains provided by advisory opinions are furnished by the declaratory judgment procedure, which enables a party under certain circumstances to obtain a declaration of its rights and obligations before engaging in contemplated conduct. Why is that procedure constitutional? See Nashville, Cincinnati & St. Louis Railway v. Wallace, 288 U.S. 249 (1933).

2. Standing

Lujan v. Defenders of Wildlife
504 U.S. 555 (1992)

JUSTICE SCALIA delivered the opinion of the Court with respect to Parts I, II, III-A, and IV, and an opinion with respect to Part III-B in which [CHIEF JUSTICE REHN-QUIST], JUSTICE WHITE, and JUSTICE THOMAS join.

This case involves a challenge to a rule promulgated by the Secretary of the Interior interpreting §7 of the Endangered Species Act of 1973 (ESA), in such fashion as to render it applicable only to actions within the United States or on the high seas. The preliminary issue, and the only one we reach, is whether the respondents here, plaintiffs below, have standing to seek judicial review of the rule.

I

The ESA seeks to protect species of animals against threats to their continuing existence caused by man. The ESA instructs the Secretary of the Interior to promulgate by regulation a list of those species which are either endangered or threatened under enumerated criteria, and to define the critical habitat of these species. Section 7(a)(2) of the Act then provides, in pertinent part:

> Each Federal agency shall, in consultation with and with the assistance of the Secretary [of the Interior], insure that any action authorized, funded, or carried out by such agency . . . is not likely to jeopardize the continued existence of any endangered species or threatened species or result in the destruction or adverse modification of habitat of such species which is determined by the Secretary, after consultation as appropriate with affected States, to be critical.

In 1978, the Fish and Wildlife Service (FWS) and the National Marine Fisheries Service (NMFS), on behalf of the Secretary of the Interior and the Secretary of Commerce respectively, promulgated a joint regulation stating that the obligations imposed by §7(a)(2) extend to actions taken in foreign nations. The next year, however, the Interior Department began to reexamine its position. A revised joint regulation, reinterpreting §7(a)(2) to require consultation only for actions taken in the United States or on the high seas, was proposed in 1983, and promulgated in 1986.

Shortly thereafter, respondents, organizations dedicated to wildlife conservation and other environmental causes, filed this action against the Secretary of the Interior, seeking a declaratory judgment that the new regulation is in error as to the geographic scope of §7(a)(2), and an injunction requiring the Secretary to promulgate a new regulation restoring the initial interpretation. . . .

II

Over the years, our cases have established that the irreducible constitutional minimum of standing contains three elements: First, the plaintiff must have suffered an "injury in fact" — an invasion of a legally-protected interest which is (a) concrete and particularized, and (b) "actual or imminent, not 'conjectural' or 'hypothetical.'" Second, there must be a causal connection between the injury and the conduct complained of — the injury has to be "fairly . . . traceable to the challenged action of the defendant, and not . . . the result [of] the independent action of some third party not before the court." Third, it must be "likely," as opposed to merely "speculative," that the injury will be "redressed by a favorable decision."

The party invoking federal jurisdiction bears the burden of establishing these elements. [At] the pleading stage, general factual allegations of injury resulting from the defendant's conduct may suffice, for on a motion to dismiss we "presume that general allegations embrace those specific facts that are necessary to support the claim." In response to a summary judgment motion, however, the plaintiff can no longer rest on such "mere allegations," but must "set forth" by affidavit or other evidence "specific facts," Fed. Rule Civ. Proc. 56(e), which for purposes of the summary judgment motion will be taken to be true. And at the final stage, those facts (if controverted) must be "supported adequately by the evidence adduced at trial." When the suit is one challenging the legality of government action or inaction, the nature and extent of facts that must be averred (at the summary judgment stage) or proved (at the trial stage) in order to establish standing depends considerably upon whether the plaintiff is himself an object of the action (or forgone action) at issue. If he is, there is ordinarily little question that the action or inaction has caused him injury, and that a judgment preventing or requiring the action will redress it. When, however, as in this case, a plaintiff's asserted injury arises from the government's allegedly unlawful regulation (or lack of regulation) of someone else, much more is needed. In that circumstance, causation and redressability ordinarily hinge on the response of the regulated (or regulable) third party to the government action or inaction — and perhaps on the response of others as well. The existence of one or more of the essential elements of standing "depends on the unfettered choices made by independent actors not before the courts and whose exercise of broad and legitimate discretion the courts cannot presume either to control or to predict," ASARCO Inc. v. Kadish, 490 U.S. 605, 615 (1989) (opinion of Kennedy, J.); and it becomes the burden of the plaintiff to adduce facts showing that those choices have been or will be made in such manner as to produce causation and permit redressability of injury. Thus, when the plaintiff is not himself the object of the government action or inaction he challenges, standing is not precluded, but it is ordinarily "substantially more difficult" to establish. . . .

III

A

Respondents' claim to injury is that the lack of consultation with respect to certain funded activities abroad "increases the rate of extinction of endangered and threatened species." Of course, the desire to use or observe an animal species, even for purely aesthetic purposes, is undeniably a cognizable interest for purpose of standing. . . .

[With] respect to this aspect of the case, the Court of Appeals focused on the affidavits of two Defenders' members — Joyce Kelly and Amy Skilbred. Ms. Kelly stated that she traveled to Egypt in 1986 and "observed the traditional habitat of the endangered Nile crocodile there and intends to do so again, and hopes to observe the crocodile directly," and that she "will suffer harm in fact as a result of [the] American . . . role . . . in overseeing the rehabilitation of the Aswan High Dam on the Nile . . . and [in] developing . . . Egypt's . . . Master Water Plan." Ms. Skilbred averred that she traveled to Sri Lanka in 1981 and "observed the habitat" of "endangered species such as the Asian elephant and the leopard" at what is now the site of the Mahaweli Project funded by the Agency for International Development (AID), although she "was unable to see any of the endangered species"; "this development project," she continued, "will seriously reduce endangered, threatened, and endemic species habitat including areas that I visited . . . [, which] may severely shorten the future of these species"; that threat, she concluded, harmed her because she "intends to return to Sri Lanka in the future and hopes to be more fortunate in spotting at least the endangered elephant and leopard." When Ms. Skilbred was asked at a subsequent deposition if and when she had any plans to return to Sri Lanka, she reiterated that "I intend to go back to Sri Lanka," but confessed that she had no current plans: "I don't know when. There is a civil war going on right now. I don't know. Not next year, I will say. In the future."

We shall assume for the sake of argument that these affidavits contain facts showing that certain agency-funded projects threaten listed species — though that is questionable. They plainly contain no facts, however, showing how damage to the species will produce "imminent" injury to Mss. Kelly and Skilbred. That the women "had visited" the areas of the projects before the projects commenced proves nothing. [Such] "some day" intentions — without any description of concrete plans, or indeed even any specification of when the some day will be — do not support a finding of the "actual or imminent" injury that our cases require.

Besides relying upon the Kelly and Skilbred affidavits, respondents propose a series of novel standing theories. The first, inelegantly styled "ecosystem nexus," proposes that any person who uses any part of a "contiguous ecosystem" adversely affected by a funded activity has standing even if the activity is located a great distance away. This approach, as the Court of Appeals correctly observed, is inconsistent with our opinion in [Lujan v. National Wildlife Federation, 497 U.S. 871, 887–889 (1990)], which held that a plaintiff claiming injury from environmental damage must use the area affected by the challenged activity and not an area roughly "in the vicinity" of it. It makes no difference that the general-purpose section of the ESA states that the Act was intended in part "to provide a means whereby the ecosystems upon which endangered species and threatened species depend may be conserved," 16 U.S.C. §1531(b). To say that the Act protects ecosystems is not to say that the Act creates (if it were possible) rights of action in persons who have not been injured in fact, that is, persons who use portions of an ecosystem not perceptibly affected by the unlawful action in question.

Respondents' other theories are called, alas, the "animal nexus" approach, whereby anyone who has an interest in studying or seeing the endangered animals anywhere on the globe has standing; and the "vocational nexus" approach, under which anyone with a professional interest in such animals can sue. Under these theories, anyone who goes to see Asian elephants in the Bronx Zoo, and anyone who is a keeper of Asian elephants in the Bronx Zoo, has standing to sue because the Director of AID did not consult with the Secretary regarding the AID-funded project in Sri Lanka. This is beyond all reason. Standing is not "an ingenious academic exercise in the conceivable," United States v. Students

[margin handwritten note: preceding case]

Challenging Regulatory Agency Procedures (SCRAP), 412 U.S. 669, 688 (1973), but as we have said requires, at the summary judgment stage, a factual showing of perceptible harm. It is clear that the person who observes or works with a particular animal threatened by a federal decision is facing perceptible harm, since the very subject of his interest will no longer exist. It is even plausible — though it goes to the outermost limit of plausibility — to think that a person who observes or works with animals of a particular species in the very area of the world where that species is threatened by a federal decision is facing such harm, since some animals that might have been the subject of his interest will no longer exist, see Japan Whaling Assn. v. American Cetacean Soc., 478 U.S. 221, 231, n.4 (1986). It goes beyond the limit, however, and into pure speculation and fantasy, to say that anyone who observes or works with an endangered species, anywhere in the world, is appreciably harmed by a single project affecting some portion of that species with which he has no more specific connection. . . .

Scalia's issue w/ injury

B

The most obvious problem in the present case is redressability. Since the agencies funding the projects were not parties to the case, the District Court could accord relief only against the Secretary: He could be ordered to revise his regulation to require consultation for foreign projects. But this would not remedy respondents' alleged injury unless the funding agencies were bound by the Secretary's regulation, which is very much an open question. . . .

Respondents assert that this legal uncertainty did not affect redressability (and hence standing) because the District Court itself could resolve the issue of the Secretary's authority as a necessary part of its standing inquiry. Assuming that it is appropriate to resolve an issue of law such as this in connection with a threshold standing inquiry, resolution by the District Court would not have remedied respondents' alleged injury anyway, because it would not have been binding upon the agencies. They were not parties to the suit, and there is no reason they should be obliged to honor an incidental legal determination the suit produced. . . .

Why redressability is an issue

A further impediment to redressability is the fact that the agencies generally supply only a fraction of the funding for a foreign project. AID, for example, has provided less than 10% of the funding for the Mahaweli Project. Respondents have produced nothing to indicate that the projects they have named will either be suspended, or do less harm to listed species, if that fraction is eliminated. As in [Simon v. Eastern Kentucky Welfare Rights Organization, 426 U.S. 26 (1976)], it is entirely conjectural whether the nonagency activity that affects respondents will be altered or affected by the agency activity they seek to achieve. There is no standing.

IV

The Court of Appeals found that respondents had standing for an additional reason: because they had suffered a "procedural injury." The so-called "citizen-suit" provision of the ESA provides, in pertinent part, that "any person may commence a civil suit on his own behalf (A) to enjoin any person, including the United States and any other governmental instrumentality or agency . . . who is alleged to be in violation of any provision of this chapter." The court held that, because §7(a)(2) requires interagency consultation, the citizen-suit provision creates a "procedural right" to consultation in all "persons" — so that anyone can file suit in federal court to challenge the Secretary's (or presumably any other official's) failure to follow the assertedly correct consultative procedure, notwithstanding their inability to allege any discrete injury flowing from that failure. To understand the remarkable nature of this holding one must be clear about what it does not rest upon: This is not a case where plaintiffs are seeking to enforce a procedural requirement the disregard of which could impair a separate concrete interest of theirs (e.g., the procedural requirement for a hearing prior to denial of their license application, or the procedural requirement for an environmental impact statement before a federal facility is constructed next door to them).[7] Nor is it simply a case where concrete injury has been suffered by many persons, as in mass fraud or mass tort situations. Nor, finally, is it the unusual case in which Congress has created a concrete private interest in the outcome of a suit against a private party for the government's benefit, by providing a cash bounty for the victorious plaintiff. Rather, the court held that the injury-in-fact requirement had been satisfied by congressional conferral upon all persons of an abstract, self-contained, noninstrumental "right" to have the Executive observe the procedures required by law. We reject this view.

We have consistently held that a plaintiff raising only a generally available grievance about government — claiming only harm to his and every citizen's interest in proper application of the Constitution and laws, and seeking relief that no more directly and tangibly benefits him than it does the public at large — does not state an Article III case or controversy. . . .

To be sure, our generalized-grievance cases have typically involved Government violation of procedures assertedly ordained by the Constitution rather than the Congress. But there is absolutely no basis for making the Article III inquiry turn on the source of the asserted right. Whether the courts were to act on their own, or at the invitation of Congress, in ignoring the concrete injury requirement described in our cases, they would be discarding a principle fundamental to the separate and distinct constitutional role of the Third Branch — one of the essential elements that identifies those "Cases" and "Controversies" that are the business of the courts rather than of the political branches. "The province of the court," as Chief Justice Marshall said in Marbury v. Madison, 1 Cranch 137, 170 (1803), "is, solely, to decide on the rights of individuals." Vindicating the public interest (including the public interest in government observance of the Constitution and laws) is the function of Congress and the Chief Executive.

---

7. There is this much truth to the assertion that "procedural rights" are special: The person who has been accorded a procedural right to protect his concrete interests can assert that right without meeting all the normal standards for redressability and immediacy. Thus, under our case law, one living adjacent to the site for proposed construction of a federally licensed dam has standing to challenge the licensing agency's failure to prepare an Environmental Impact Statement, even though he cannot establish with any certainty that the Statement will cause the license to be withheld or altered, and even though the dam will not be completed for many years. (That is why we do not rely, in the present case, upon the Government's argument that, even if the other agencies were obliged to consult with the Secretary, they might not have followed his advice.) What respondents' "procedural right" argument seeks, however, is quite different from this: standing for persons who have no concrete interests affected — persons who live (and propose to live) at the other end of the country from the dam.

The question presented here is whether the public interest in proper administration of the laws (specifically, in agencies' observance of a particular, statutorily
prescribed procedure) can be converted into an individual right by a statute that
denominates it as such, and that permits all citizens (or, for that matter, a subclass
of citizens who suffer no distinctive concrete harm) to sue. If the concrete injury
requirement has the separation-of-powers significance we have always said, the
answer must be obvious: To permit Congress to convert the undifferentiated
public interest in executive officers' compliance with the law into an "individual
right" vindicable in the courts is to permit Congress to transfer from the President
to the courts the Chief Executive's most important constitutional duty, to "take
Care that the Laws be faithfully executed," Art. II, §3. It would enable the courts,
with the permission of Congress, "to assume a position of authority over the
governmental acts of another and co-equal department," Frothingham v. Mellon,
262 U.S., at 489, and to become "'virtually continuing monitors of the wisdom
and soundness of Executive action.'" [Allen v. Wright,] 468 U.S., at 760 (quoting
Laird v. Tatum, 408 U.S. 1, 15 (1972)). We have always rejected that vision of
our role:

> When Congress passes an Act empowering administrative agencies to carry on
> governmental activities, the power of those agencies is circumscribed by the author-
> ity granted. This permits the courts to participate in law enforcement entrusted to
> administrative bodies only to the extent necessary to protect justiciable individual
> rights against administrative action fairly beyond the granted powers. . . . This is
> very far from assuming that the courts are charged more than administrators or
> legislators with the protection of the rights of the people. Congress and the
> Executive supervise the acts of administrative agents. . . . But under Article III,
> Congress established courts to adjudicate cases and controversies as to claims of
> infringement of individual rights whether by unlawful action of private persons or
> by the exertion of unauthorized administrative power.

Stark v. Wickard, 321 U.S. 288, 309–310 (1944). "Individual rights," within the
meaning of this passage, do not mean public rights that have been legislatively
pronounced to belong to each individual who forms part of the public. See also
[Sierra Club v. Morton, 405 U.S. 727, 740–741 n.16 (1972)].

Nothing in this contradicts the principle that "the . . . injury required by Art.
III may exist solely by virtue of 'statutes creating legal rights, the invasion of which
creates standing.'" [Warth v. Seldin, 422 U.S. 490, 500 (1975) (quoting Linda R.
S. v. Richard D., 410 U.S. 614, 617 n.3 (1973)).] Both of the cases used by Linda
R. S. as an illustration of that principle involved Congress's elevating to the status
of legally cognizable injuries concrete, de facto injuries that were previously
inadequate in law (namely, injury to an individual's personal interest in living
in a racially integrated community, see Trafficante v. Metropolitan Life Ins. Co.,
409 U.S. 205, 208–212 (1972), and injury to a company's interest in marketing its
product free from competition, see Hardin v. Kentucky Utilities Co., 390 U.S. 1,
6 (1968)). As we said in *Sierra Club*, "[Statutory] broadening [of] the categories of
injury that may be alleged in support of standing is a different matter from
abandoning the requirement that the party seeking review must himself have
suffered an injury." 405 U.S., at 738. Whether or not the principle set forth in
Warth can be extended beyond that distinction, it is clear that in suits against the
government, at least, the concrete injury requirement must remain.

We hold that respondents lack standing to bring this action.

JUSTICE KENNEDY, with whom JUSTICE SOUTER joins, concurring in part and concurring in the judgment. . . .

While it may seem trivial to require that Mss. Kelly and Skilbred acquire airline tickets to the project sites or announce a date certain upon which they will return, this is not a case where it is reasonable to assume that the affiants will be using the sites on a regular basis, nor do the affiants claim to have visited the sites since the projects commenced. [I] am not willing to foreclose the possibility, however, that in different circumstances a nexus theory similar to those proffered here might support a claim to standing. See Japan Whaling Assn. v. American Cetacean Soc., 478 U.S. 221, 231, n.4 (1986) ("respondents . . . undoubtedly have alleged a sufficient 'injury in fact' in that the whale watching and studying of their members will be adversely affected by continued whale harvesting").

In light of the conclusion that respondents have not demonstrated a concrete injury here sufficient to support standing under our precedents, I would not reach the issue of redressability. . . .

I also join [the] Court's opinion with the following observations. As government programs and policies become more complex and far-reaching, we must be sensitive to the articulation of new rights of action that do not have clear analogs in our common-law tradition. [In] my view, Congress has the power to define injuries and articulate chains of causation that will give rise to a case or controversy where none existed before, and I do not read the Court's opinion to suggest a contrary view. In exercising this power, however, Congress must at the very least identify the injury it seeks to vindicate and relate the injury to the class of persons entitled to bring suit. The citizen-suit provision of the Endangered Species Act does not meet these minimal requirements, because while the statute purports to confer a right on "any person . . . to enjoin . . . the United States and any other governmental instrumentality or agency . . . who is alleged to be in violation of any provision of this chapter," it does not of its own force establish that there is an injury in "any person" by virtue of any "violation."

JUSTICE STEVENS, concurring in the judgment. . . .

In my opinion a person who has visited the critical habitat of an endangered species has a professional interest in preserving the species and its habitat, and intends to revisit them in the future has standing to challenge agency action that threatens their destruction. [We] have no license to demean the importance of the interest that particular individuals may have in observing any species or its habitat, whether those individuals are motivated by aesthetic enjoyment, an interest in professional research, or an economic interest in preservation of the species. Indeed, this Court has often held that injuries to such interests are sufficient to confer standing, and the Court reiterates that holding today.

The Court nevertheless concludes that respondents have not suffered "injury in fact" because they have not shown that the harm to the endangered species will produce "imminent" injury to them. I disagree. An injury to an individual's interest in studying or enjoying a species and its natural habitat occurs when someone (whether it be the government or a private party) takes action that harms that species and habitat. . . .

The plurality also concludes that respondents' injuries are not redressable in this litigation for two reasons. First, respondents have sought only a declaratory judgment that the Secretary of the Interior's regulation interpreting §7(a)(2) to require consultation only for agency actions in the United States or on the high seas is invalid and an injunction requiring him to promulgate a new regulation requiring consultation for agency actions abroad as well. But, the plurality opines, even if respondents succeed and a new regulation is promulgated, there is no guarantee that federal agencies that are not parties to this case will actually consult with the Secretary. Furthermore, the plurality continues, respondents have not demonstrated that federal agencies can influence the behavior of the foreign governments where the affected projects are located. Thus, even if the agencies consult with the Secretary and terminate funding for foreign projects, the foreign governments might nonetheless pursue the projects and jeopardize the endangered species. Neither of these reasons is persuasive.

We must presume that if this Court holds that §7(a)(2) requires consultation, all affected agencies would abide by that interpretation and engage in the requisite consultations. Certainly the Executive Branch cannot be heard to argue that an authoritative construction of the governing statute by this Court may simply be ignored by any agency head. Moreover, if Congress has required consultation between agencies, we must presume that such consultation will have a serious purpose that is likely to produce tangible results. . . .

Although I believe that respondents have standing, I nevertheless concur in the judgment of reversal because I am persuaded that the Government is correct in its submission that §7(a)(2) does not apply to activities in foreign countries. . . .

JUSTICE BLACKMUN, with whom JUSTICE O'CONNOR joins, dissenting. . . .

[By] requiring a "description of concrete plans" or "specification of when the some day [for a return visit] will be" the Court, in my view, demands what is likely an empty formality. No substantial barriers prevent Kelly or Skilbred from simply purchasing plane tickets to return to the Aswan and Mahaweli projects. . . .

The Court also rejects respondents' claim of vocational or professional injury. The Court says that it is "beyond all reason" that a zoo "keeper" of Asian elephants would have standing to contest his government's participation in the eradication of all the Asian elephants in another part of the world. I am unable to see how the distant location of the destruction necessarily (for purposes of ruling at summary judgment) mitigates the harm to the elephant keeper. If there is no more access to a future supply of the animal that sustains a keeper's livelihood, surely there is harm.

I have difficulty imagining this Court applying its rigid principles of geographic formalism anywhere outside the context of environmental claims. As I understand it, environmental plaintiffs are under no special constitutional standing disabilities. . . .

I find myself unable to agree with the plurality's analysis of redressability, based as it is on its invitation of executive lawlessness, ignorance of principles of collateral estoppel, unfounded assumptions about causation, and erroneous conclusions about what the record does not say. In my view, respondents have satisfactorily shown a genuine issue of fact as to whether their injury would likely be redressed by a decision in their favor. . . .

The Court expresses concern that allowing judicial enforcement of "agencies' observance of a particular, statutorily prescribed procedure" would "transfer from the President to the courts the Chief Executive's most important constitutional duty, to 'take Care that the Laws be faithfully executed,' Art. II, sec. 3." In fact, the principal effect of foreclosing judicial enforcement of such procedures is to transfer power into the hands of the Executive at the expense — not of the courts — but of Congress, from which that power originates and emanates. . . .

[There] may be factual circumstances in which a congressionally imposed procedural requirement is so insubstantially connected to the prevention of a substantive harm that it cannot be said to work any conceivable injury to an individual litigant. But, as a general matter, the courts owe substantial deference to Congress' substantive purpose in imposing a certain procedural requirement. In all events, "our separation-of-powers analysis does not turn on the labeling of an activity as 'substantive' as opposed to 'procedural.'" There is no room for a per se rule or presumption excluding injuries labeled "procedural" in nature.

In conclusion, I cannot join the Court on what amounts to a slash-and-burn expedition through the law of environmental standing. In my view, "the very essence of civil liberty certainly consists in the right of every individual to claim the protection of the laws, whenever he receives an injury." Marbury v. Madison, 1 Cranch 137, 163 (1803).

I dissent.

Massachusetts v. EPA

549 U.S. 497 (2007)

JUSTICE STEVENS delivered the opinion of the Court.

A well-documented rise in global temperatures has coincided with a significant increase in the concentration of carbon dioxide in the atmosphere. Respected scientists believe the two trends are related. For when carbon dioxide is released into the atmosphere, it acts like the ceiling of a greenhouse, trapping solar energy and retarding the escape of reflected heat. It is therefore a species — the most important species — of a "greenhouse gas."

Calling global warming "the most pressing environmental challenge of our time," a group of States, local governments, and private organizations, alleged in a petition for certiorari that the Environmental Protection Agency (EPA) has abdicated its responsibility under the Clean Air Act to regulate the emissions of four greenhouse gases, including carbon dioxide. Specifically, petitioners asked us to answer two questions concerning the meaning of §202(a)(1) of the Act: whether EPA has the statutory authority to regulate greenhouse gas emissions from new motor vehicles; and if so, whether its stated reasons for refusing to do so are consistent with the statute. . . .

I

Section 202(a)(1) of the Clean Air Act, provides:

> The [EPA] Administrator shall by regulation prescribe (and from time to time revise) in accordance with the provisions of this section, standards applicable to the emission of any air pollutant from any class or classes of new motor vehicles or new motor vehicle engines, which in his judgment cause, or contribute to, air pollution which may reasonably be anticipated to endanger public health or welfare. . . .

The Act defines "air pollutant" to include "any air pollution agent or combination of such agents, including any physical, chemical, biological, radioactive . . . substance or matter which is emitted into or otherwise enters the ambient air." §7602(g). "Welfare" is also defined broadly: among other things, it includes "effects on . . . weather . . . and climate." §7602(h). . . .

IV

Article III of the Constitution limits federal-court jurisdiction to "Cases" and "Controversies." . . .

The parties' dispute turns on the proper construction of a congressional statute, a question eminently suitable to resolution in federal court. Congress has moreover authorized this type of challenge to EPA action. That authorization is of critical importance to the standing inquiry: "Congress has the power to define injuries and articulate chains of causation that will give rise to a case or controversy where none existed before." *Lujan*, 504 U.S., at 580 (Kennedy, J., concurring in part and concurring in judgment). "In exercising this power, however, Congress must at the very least identify the injury it seeks to vindicate and relate the injury to the class of persons entitled to bring suit." We will not, therefore, "entertain citizen suits to vindicate the public's nonconcrete interest in the proper administration of the laws."

EPA maintains that because greenhouse gas emissions inflict widespread harm, the doctrine of standing presents an insuperable jurisdictional obstacle. We do not agree. . . .

To ensure the proper adversarial presentation, *Lujan* holds that a litigant must demonstrate that it has suffered a concrete and particularized injury that is either actual or imminent, that the injury is fairly traceable to the defendant, and that it is likely that a favorable decision will redress that injury. However, a litigant to whom Congress has "accorded a procedural right to protect his concrete interests," — here, the right to challenge agency action unlawfully withheld, §7607(b)(1) — "can assert that right without meeting all the normal standards for redressability and immediacy." When a litigant is vested with a procedural right, that litigant has standing if there is some possibility that the requested relief will prompt the injury-causing party to reconsider the decision that allegedly harmed the litigant.

Only one of the petitioners needs to have standing to permit us to consider the petition for review. We stress here [the] special position and interest of Massachusetts. It is of considerable relevance that the party seeking review here is a sovereign State and not, as it was in *Lujan*, a private individual.

Well before the creation of the modern administrative state, we recognized that States are not normal litigants for the purposes of invoking federal jurisdiction. As Justice Holmes explained in Georgia v. Tennessee Copper Co., 206 U.S. 230, 237 (1907), a case in which Georgia sought to protect its citizens from air pollution originating outside its borders:

> The case has been argued largely as if it were one between two private parties; but it is not. The very elements that would be relied upon in a suit between fellow-citizens as a ground for equitable relief are wanting here. The State owns very little of the territory alleged to be affected, and the damage to it capable of estimate in money, possibly, at least, is small. This is a suit by a State for an injury to it in its capacity of *quasi*-sovereign. In that capacity the State has an interest independent of and behind the titles of its citizens, in all the earth and air within its domain. It has

the last word as to whether its mountains shall be stripped of their forests and its inhabitants shall breathe pure air.

Just as Georgia's "independent interest . . . in all the earth and air within its domain" supported federal jurisdiction a century ago, so too does Massachusetts' well-founded desire to preserve its sovereign territory today. That Massachusetts does in fact own a great deal of the "territory alleged to be affected" only reinforces the conclusion that its stake in the outcome of this case is sufficiently concrete to warrant the exercise of federal judicial power. [Given][its] procedural right and Massachusetts' stake in protecting its quasi-sovereign interests, the Commonwealth is entitled to special solicitude in our standing analysis.

With that in mind, it is clear that petitioners' submissions as they pertain to Massachusetts have satisfied the most demanding standards of the adversarial process. EPA's steadfast refusal to regulate greenhouse gas emissions presents a risk of harm to Massachusetts that is both "actual" and "imminent." [*Lujan*, 504 U.S., at 560 (internal quotation marks omitted).]

There is, moreover, a "substantial likelihood that the judicial relief requested" will prompt EPA to take steps to reduce that risk.

The Injury

The harms associated with climate change are serious and well recognized. Indeed, the NRC Report itself — which EPA regards as an "objective and independent assessment of the relevant science," — identifies a number of environmental changes that have already inflicted significant harms, including "the global retreat of mountain glaciers, reduction in snow-cover extent, the earlier spring melting of rivers and lakes, [and] the accelerated rate of rise of sea levels during the 20th century relative to the past few thousand years. . . ." NRC Report 16.

Petitioners allege that this only hints at the environmental damage yet to come. According to the climate scientist Michael MacCracken, "qualified scientific experts involved in climate change research" have reached a "strong consensus" that global warming threatens (among other things) a precipitate rise in sea levels by the end of the century, "severe and irreversible changes to natural ecosystems," a "significant reduction in water storage in winter snow-pack in mountainous regions with direct and important economic consequences," and an increase in the spread of disease. He also observes that rising ocean temperatures may contribute to the ferocity of hurricanes.

That these climate-change risks are "widely shared" does not minimize Massachusetts' interest in the outcome of this litigation. See Federal Election Comm'n v. Akins, 524 U.S. 11, 24 (1998) ("[W]here a harm is concrete, though widely shared, the Court has found 'injury in fact'"). According to petitioners' unchallenged affidavits, global sea levels rose somewhere between 10 and 20 centimeters over the 20th century as a result of global warming. These rising seas have already begun to swallow Massachusetts' coastal land. Because the Commonwealth "owns a substantial portion of the state's coastal property," it has alleged a particularized injury in its capacity as a landowner. The severity of that injury will only increase over the course of the next century: If sea levels continue to rise as predicted, one Massachusetts official believes that a significant fraction of coastal property will be "either permanently lost through inundation or temporarily lost through periodic storm surge and flooding events."

Remediation costs alone, petitioners allege, could run well into the hundreds of millions of dollars.

Causation

EPA does not dispute the existence of a causal connection between man-made greenhouse gas emissions and global warming. At a minimum, therefore, EPA's refusal to regulate such emissions "contributes" to Massachusetts' injuries.

EPA nevertheless maintains that its decision not to regulate greenhouse gas emissions from new motor vehicles contributes so insignificantly to petitioners' injuries that the agency cannot be haled into federal court to answer for them. For the same reason, EPA does not believe that any realistic possibility exists that the relief petitioners seek would mitigate global climate change and remedy their injuries. That is especially so because predicted increases in greenhouse gas emissions from developing nations, particularly China and India, are likely to offset any marginal domestic decrease.

But EPA overstates its case. Its argument rests on the erroneous assumption that a small incremental step, because it is incremental, can never be attacked in a federal judicial forum. Yet accepting that premise would doom most challenges to regulatory action. Agencies, like legislatures, do not generally resolve massive problems in one fell regulatory swoop. They instead whittle away at them over time, refining their preferred approach as circumstances change and as they develop a more-nuanced understanding of how best to proceed. That a first step might be tentative does not by itself support the notion that federal courts lack jurisdiction to determine whether that step conforms to law.

And reducing domestic automobile emissions is hardly a tentative step. Even leaving aside the other greenhouse gases, the United States transportation sector emits an enormous quantity of carbon dioxide into the atmosphere — according to the MacCracken affidavit, more than 1.7 billion metric tons in 1999 alone. That accounts for more than 6% of worldwide carbon dioxide emissions. To put this in perspective: Considering just emissions from the transportation sector, which represent less than one-third of this country's total carbon dioxide emissions, the United States would still rank as the third-largest emitter of carbon dioxide in the world, outpaced only by the European Union and China. Judged by any standard, U.S. motor-vehicle emissions make a meaningful contribution to greenhouse gas concentrations and hence, according to petitioners, to global warming.

The Remedy

While it may be true that regulating motor-vehicle emissions will not by itself *reverse* global warming, it by no means follows that we lack jurisdiction to decide whether EPA has a duty to take steps to *slow* or *reduce* it. Because of the enormity of the potential consequences associated with man-made climate change, the fact that the effectiveness of a remedy might be delayed during the (relatively short) time it takes for a new motor-vehicle fleet to replace an older one is essentially irrelevant. Nor is it dispositive that developing countries such as China and India are poised to increase greenhouse gas emissions substantially over the next century: A reduction in domestic emissions would slow the pace of global emissions increases, no matter what happens elsewhere.

We moreover attach considerable significance to EPA's "agree[ment] with the President that 'we must address the issue of global climate change,'" (quoting remarks announcing Clear Skies and Global Climate Initiatives, 2002 Public

Papers of George W. Bush, Vol. 1, Feb. 14, p. 227 (2004)), and to EPA's ardent support for various voluntary emission-reduction programs. . . .

In sum — at least according to petitioners' uncontested affidavits — the rise in sea levels associated with global warming has already harmed and will continue to harm Massachusetts. The risk of catastrophic harm, though remote, is nevertheless real. That risk would be reduced to some extent if petitioners received the relief they seek. We therefore hold that petitioners have standing to challenge the EPA's denial of their rulemaking petition. . . .

[On the merits, the Court ruled that the EPA does have statutory authority to regulate greenhouse gases and that it would be required on remand to ground any decision not to take regulatory action in the text of the relevant statute.]

VIII

The judgment of the Court of Appeals is reversed, and the case is remanded for further proceedings consistent with this opinion.

It is so ordered.

CHIEF JUSTICE ROBERTS, with whom JUSTICE SCALIA, JUSTICE THOMAS, and JUSTICE ALITO join, dissenting.

Global warming may be a "crisis," even "the most pressing environmental problem of our time." Indeed, it may ultimately affect nearly everyone on the planet in some potentially adverse way, and it may be that governments have done too little to address it. It is not a problem, however, that has escaped the attention of policymakers in the Executive and Legislative Branches of our Government, who continue to consider regulatory, legislative, and treaty-based means of addressing global climate change.

Apparently dissatisfied with the pace of progress on this issue in the elected branches, petitioners have come to the courts claiming broad-ranging injury, and attempting to tie that injury to the Government's alleged failure to comply with a rather narrow statutory provision. I would reject these challenges as nonjusticiable. . . .

Dissent sees it as petitioners circumventing the policymaking process.

I . . .

[Petitioners] bear the burden of alleging an injury that is fairly traceable to the Environmental Protection Agency's failure to promulgate new motor vehicle greenhouse gas emission standards, and that is likely to be redressed by the prospective issuance of such standards.

Before determining whether petitioners can meet this familiar test, however, the Court changes the rules. It asserts that "States are not normal litigants for the purposes of invoking federal jurisdiction," and that given "Massachusetts' stake in protecting its quasi-sovereign interests, the Commonwealth is entitled to *special solicitude* in our standing analysis."

Relaxing Article III standing requirements because asserted injuries are pressed by a State, however, has no basis in our jurisprudence, and support for any such "special solicitude" is conspicuously absent from the Court's opinion. [The] Court has to go back a full century in an attempt to justify its novel standing rule, but even there it comes up short. The Court's analysis hinges on Georgia v.

Tennessee Copper Co., 206 U.S. 230 (1907) — a case that did indeed draw a distinction between a State and private litigants, but solely with respect to available remedies. The case had nothing to do with Article III standing. . . .

In contrast to the present case, there was no question in *Tennessee Copper* about Article III injury. There was certainly no suggestion that the State could show standing where the private parties could not; there was no dispute, after all, that the private landowners had "an action at law." *Tennessee Copper* has since stood for nothing more than a State's right, in an original jurisdiction action, to sue in a representative capacity as *parens patriae*. Nothing about a State's ability to sue in that capacity dilutes the bedrock requirement of showing injury, causation, and redressability to satisfy Article III.

[Far] from being a substitute for Article III injury, *parens patriae* actions raise an additional hurdle for a state litigant: the articulation of a "quasi-sovereign interest" "*apart* from the interests of particular private parties." Just as an association suing on behalf of its members must show not only that it represents the members but that at least one satisfies Article III requirements, so too a State asserting quasi-sovereign interests as *parens patriae* must still show that its citizens satisfy Article III. Focusing on Massachusetts's interests as quasi-sovereign makes the required showing here harder, not easier. . . .

II

It is not at all clear how the Court's "special solicitude" for Massachusetts plays out in the standing analysis, except as an implicit concession that petitioners cannot establish standing on traditional terms. But the status of Massachusetts as a State cannot compensate for petitioners' failure to demonstrate injury in fact, causation, and redressability.

[If] petitioners rely on loss of land as the Article III injury, . . . they must ground the rest of the standing analysis in that specific injury. . . . The very concept of global warming seems inconsistent with this particularization requirement. Global warming is a phenomenon "harmful to humanity at large," 415 F.3d, at 60 (Sentelle, J., dissenting in part and concurring in judgment), and the redress petitioners seek is focused no more on them than on the public generally — it is literally to change the atmosphere around the world.

If petitioners' particularized injury is loss of coastal land, it is also that injury that must be "actual or imminent, not conjectural or hypothetical."

As to "actual" injury, the Court observes that "global sea levels rose somewhere between 10 and 20 centimeters over the 20th century as a result of global warming" and that [these] rising seas have already begun to swallow Massachusetts' coastal land. But none of petitioners' declarations supports that connection. One declaration states that "a rise in sea level due to climate change is occurring on the coast of Massachusetts, in the metropolitan Boston area," but there is no elaboration. And the declarant goes on to identify a "significan[t]" *non*-global-warming cause of Boston's rising sea level: land subsidence. Thus, aside from a single conclusory statement, there is nothing in petitioners' 43 standing declarations and accompanying exhibits to support an inference of actual loss of Massachusetts coastal land from 20th century global sea level increases. It is pure conjecture.

The Court's attempts to identify "imminent" or "certainly impending" loss of Massachusetts coastal land fares no better. One of petitioners' declarants predicts global warming will cause sea level to rise by 20 to 70 centimeters *by the year 2100*. Another uses a computer modeling program to map the Commonwealth's coastal land and its current elevation, and calculates that the high-end estimate of sea level rise would result in the loss of significant state-owned coastal land. But the computer modeling program has a conceded average error of about 30 centimeters and a maximum observed error of 70 centimeters. As an initial matter, if it is possible that the model underrepresents the elevation of coastal land to an extent equal to or in excess of the projected sea level rise, it is difficult to put much stock in the predicted loss of land. But even placing that problem to the side, accepting a century-long time horizon and a series of compounded estimates renders requirements of imminence and immediacy utterly toothless. . . .

III

Petitioners' reliance on Massachusetts's loss of coastal land as their injury in fact for standing purposes creates insurmountable problems for them with respect to causation and redressability. To establish standing, petitioners must show a causal connection between that specific injury and the lack of new motor vehicle greenhouse gas emission standards, and that the promulgation of such standards would likely redress that injury. . . . And importantly, when a party is challenging the Government's allegedly unlawful regulation, or lack of regulation, of a third party, satisfying the causation and redressability requirements becomes "substantially more difficult."

Petitioners view the relationship between their injuries and EPA's failure to promulgate new motor vehicle greenhouse gas emission standards as simple and direct: Domestic motor vehicles emit carbon dioxide and other greenhouse gases. Worldwide emissions of greenhouse gases contribute to global warming and therefore also to petitioners' alleged injuries. Without the new vehicle standards, greenhouse gas emissions — and therefore global warming and its attendant harms — have been higher than they otherwise would have been; once EPA changes course, the trend will be reversed.

The Court ignores the complexities of global warming, and does so by now disregarding the "particularized" injury it relied on in step one, and using the dire nature of global warming itself as a bootstrap for finding causation and redressability. First, it is important to recognize the extent of the emissions at issue here. Because local greenhouse gas emissions disperse throughout the atmosphere and remain there for anywhere from 50 to 200 years, it is global emissions data that are relevant. According to one of petitioners' declarations, domestic motor vehicles contribute about 6 percent of global carbon dioxide emissions and 4 percent of global greenhouse gas emissions. The amount of global emissions at issue here is smaller still; §202(a)(1) of the Clean Air Act covers only *new* motor vehicles and *new* motor vehicle engines, so petitioners' desired emission standards might reduce only a fraction of 4 percent of global emissions.

This gets us only to the relevant greenhouse gas emissions; linking them to global warming and ultimately to petitioners' alleged injuries next requires consideration of further complexities. As EPA explained in its denial of petitioners' request for rulemaking, predicting future climate change necessarily involves a complex web of economic and physical factors including: our ability to predict future global anthropogenic emissions of [greenhouse gases] and aerosols; the fate of these emissions once they enter the atmosphere (e.g., what percentage are absorbed by vegetation or are taken up by the oceans); the impact of those emissions that remain in the atmosphere on the radiative properties of the atmosphere; changes in critically important climate feedbacks (e.g., changes in cloud cover and ocean circulation); changes in temperature characteristics (e.g., average temperatures, shifts in daytime and evening temperatures); changes in other climatic parameters (e.g., shifts in precipitation, storms); and ultimately the impact of such changes on human health and welfare (e.g., increases or decreases in agricultural productivity, human health impacts).

Petitioners are never able to trace their alleged injuries back through this complex web to the fractional amount of global emissions that might have been limited with EPA standards. In light of the bit-part domestic new motor vehicle greenhouse gas emissions have played in what petitioners describe as a 150-year global phenomenon, and the myriad additional factors bearing on petitioners' alleged injury — the loss of Massachusetts coastal land — the connection is far too speculative to establish causation.

IV

Redressability is even more problematic. To the tenuous link between petitioners' alleged injury and the indeterminate fractional domestic emissions at issue here, add the fact that petitioners cannot meaningfully predict what will come of the 80 percent of global greenhouse gas emissions that originate outside the United States. As the Court acknowledges, "developing countries such as China and India are poised to increase greenhouse gas emissions substantially over the next century," so the domestic emissions at issue here may become an increasingly marginal portion of global emissions, and any decreases produced by petitioners' desired standards are likely to be overwhelmed many times over by emissions increases elsewhere in the world.

Petitioners offer declarations attempting to address this uncertainty, contending that "[if] the U.S. takes steps to reduce motor vehicle emissions, other countries are very likely to take similar actions regarding their own motor vehicles using technology developed in response to the U.S. program." In other words, do not worry that other countries will contribute far more to global warming than will U.S. automobile emissions; someone is bound to invent something, and places like the People's Republic of China or India will surely require use of the new technology, regardless of cost. The Court previously has explained that when the existence of an element of standing "depends on the unfettered choices made by independent actors not before the courts and whose exercise of broad and legitimate discretion the courts cannot presume either to control or to predict," a party must present facts supporting an assertion that the actor will proceed in such a manner. The declarations' conclusory (not to say fanciful) statements do not even come close.

No matter, the Court reasons, because *any* decrease in domestic emissions will "slow the pace of global emissions increases, no matter what happens elsewhere." Every little bit helps, so Massachusetts can sue over any little bit.

The Court's sleight-of-hand is in failing to link up the different elements of the three-part standing test. What must be *likely* to be redressed is the particular injury in fact. The injury the Court looks to is the asserted loss of land. The Court contends that regulating domestic motor vehicle emissions will reduce carbon dioxide in the atmosphere, *and therefore* redress Massachusetts' injury. But even if regulation *does* reduce emissions — to some indeterminate degree, given events elsewhere in the world, the Court never explains why that makes it *likely* that the injury in fact — the loss of land — will be redressed. Schoolchildren know that a kingdom might be lost "all for the want of a horseshoe nail," but "likely" redressability is a different matter. The realities make it pure conjecture to suppose that EPA regulation of new automobile emissions will *likely* prevent the loss of Massachusetts coastal land.

V

Petitioners' difficulty in demonstrating causation and redressability is not surprising given the evident mismatch between the source of their alleged injury — catastrophic global warming — and the narrow subject matter of the Clean Air Act provision at issue in this suit. The mismatch suggests that petitioners' true goal for this litigation may be more symbolic than anything else. The constitutional role of the courts, however, is to decide concrete cases — not to serve as a convenient forum for policy debates.

[The] good news is that the Court's "special solicitude" for Massachusetts limits the future applicability of the diluted standing requirements applied in this case. The bad news is that the Court's self-professed relaxation of those Article III requirements has caused us to transgress "the proper — and properly limited — role of the courts in a democratic society."

I respectfully dissent.

Clapper v. Amnesty International USA

133 S. Ct. 1138 (2013)

JUSTICE ALITO delivered the opinion of the Court.

Section 702 of the Foreign Intelligence Surveillance Act of 1978, 50 U.S.C. §1881a (2006 ed., Supp. V), allows the Attorney General and the Director of National Intelligence to acquire foreign intelligence information by jointly authorizing the surveillance of individuals who are not "United States persons" and are reasonably believed to be located outside the United States. Before doing so, the Attorney General and the Director of National Intelligence normally must obtain the Foreign Intelligence Surveillance Court's approval. Respondents are United States persons whose work, they allege, requires them to engage in sensitive international communications with individuals who they believe are likely targets of surveillance under §1881a. Respondents seek a declaration that §1881a is unconstitutional, as well as an injunction against §1881a-authorized surveillance. The question before us is whether respondents have Article III standing to seek this prospective relief.

Respondents assert that they can establish injury in fact because there is an objectively reasonable likelihood that their communications will be acquired under §1881a at some point in the future. But respondents' theory of *future* injury is too speculative to satisfy the well-established requirement that threatened injury must be "certainly impending." And even if respondents could demonstrate that the threatened injury is certainly impending, they still would not be able to establish that this injury is fairly traceable to §1881a. As an alternative argument, respondents contend that they are suffering *present* injury because the risk of §1881a-authorized surveillance already has forced them to take costly and burdensome measures to protect the confidentiality of their international communications. But respondents cannot manufacture standing by choosing to make expenditures based on hypothetical future harm that is not certainly impending. We therefore hold that respondents lack Article III standing.

I

A . . .

The present case involves a constitutional challenge to §1881a. Surveillance under §1881a is subject to statutory conditions, judicial authorization, congressional supervision, and compliance with the Fourth Amendment. Section 1881a provides that, upon the issuance of an order from the Foreign Intelligence Surveillance Court [FISC], "the Attorney General and the Director of National Intelligence may authorize jointly, for a period of up to 1 year . . . , the targeting of persons reasonably believed to be located outside the United States to acquire foreign intelligence information." Surveillance under §1881a may not be intentionally targeted at any person known to be in the United States or any U.S. person reasonably believed to be located abroad. Additionally, acquisitions under §1881a must comport with the Fourth Amendment. Moreover, surveillance under §1881a is subject to congressional oversight and several types of Executive Branch review.

Section 1881a mandates that the Government obtain the Foreign Intelligence Surveillance Court's approval of "targeting" procedures, "minimization" procedures, and a governmental certification regarding proposed surveillance. Among other things, the Government's certification must attest that (1) procedures are in place "that have been approved, have been submitted for approval, or will be submitted with the certification for approval by the [FISC] that are reasonably designed" to ensure that an acquisition is "limited to targeting persons reasonably believed to be located outside" the United States; (2) minimization procedures adequately restrict the acquisition, retention, and dissemination of nonpublic information about unconsenting U.S. persons, as appropriate; (3) guidelines have been adopted to ensure compliance with targeting limits and the Fourth Amendment; and (4) the procedures and guidelines referred to above comport with the Fourth Amendment.

The Foreign Intelligence Surveillance Court's role includes determining whether the Government's certification contains the required elements. . . .

B

Respondents are attorneys and human rights, labor, legal, and media organizations whose work allegedly requires them to engage in sensitive and sometimes privileged telephone and e-mail communications with colleagues, clients, sources, and other individuals located abroad. [Respondents] claim that they communicate by telephone and e-mail with people the Government "believes or believed to be associated with terrorist organizations," "people located in geographic areas that are a special focus" of the Government's counterterrorism or diplomatic efforts, and activists who oppose governments that are supported by the United States Government.

Respondents claim that §1881a compromises their ability to locate witnesses, cultivate sources, obtain information, and communicate confidential information to their clients. Respondents also assert that they "have ceased engaging" in certain telephone and e-mail conversations. According to respondents, the threat of surveillance will compel them to travel abroad in order to have in-person conversations. In addition, respondents declare that they have undertaken "costly and burdensome measures" to protect the confidentiality of sensitive communications. . . .

III

A

Respondents assert that they can establish injury in fact that is fairly traceable to §1881a because there is an objectively reasonable likelihood that their communications with their foreign contacts will be intercepted under §1881a at some point in the future. This argument fails. . . .

[Respondents'] argument rests on their highly speculative fear that: (1) the Government will decide to target the communications of non-U.S. persons with whom they communicate; (2) in doing so, the Government will choose to invoke its authority under §1881a rather than utilizing another method of surveillance; (3) the Article III judges who serve on the Foreign Intelligence Surveillance Court will conclude that the Government's proposed surveillance procedures satisfy §1881a's many safeguards and are consistent with the Fourth Amendment; (4) the Government will succeed in intercepting the communications of respondents' contacts; and (5) respondents will be parties to the particular communications that the Government intercepts. . . .

[Respondents'] theory of standing, which relies on a highly attenuated chain of possibilities, does not satisfy the requirement that threatened injury must be certainly impending. Moreover, even if respondents could demonstrate injury in fact, the second link in the above-described chain of contingencies — which amounts to mere speculation about whether surveillance would be under §1881a or some other authority — shows that respondents cannot satisfy the requirement that any injury in fact must be fairly traceable to §1881a.

First, it is speculative whether the Government will imminently target communications to which respondents are parties. Section 1881a expressly provides that respondents, who are U.S. persons, cannot be targeted for surveillance under §1881a. . . .

Accordingly, respondents' theory necessarily rests on their assertion that the Government will target *other individuals* — namely, their foreign contacts.

Yet respondents have no actual knowledge of the Government's §1881a targeting practices. Instead, respondents merely speculate and make assumptions about whether their communications with their foreign contacts will be acquired under §1881a. For example, journalist Christopher Hedges states: "I have no choice but to *assume* that any of my international communications *may* be subject to government surveillance, and I have to make decisions . . . in light of that *assumption*." Similarly, attorney Scott McKay asserts that, "[b]ecause of the [FISA Amendments Act], we now have to *assume* that every one of our international communications *may* be monitored by the government." . . .

[Because] §1881a at most *authorizes* — but does not *mandate* or *direct* — the surveillance that respondents fear, respondents' allegations are necessarily conjectural. Simply put, respondents can only speculate as to how the Attorney General and the Director of National Intelligence will exercise their discretion in determining which communications to target.

Second, even if respondents could demonstrate that the targeting of their foreign contacts is imminent, respondents can only speculate as to whether the Government will seek to use §1881 authorized surveillance (rather than other methods) to do so. The Government has numerous other methods of conducting surveillance, none of which is challenged here. Even after the enactment of the FISA Amendments Act, for example, the Government may still conduct electronic surveillance of persons abroad under the older provisions of FISA so long as it satisfies the applicable requirements, including a demonstration of probable cause to believe that the person is a foreign power or agent of a foreign power. The Government may also obtain information from the intelligence services of foreign nations. . . . Even if respondents could demonstrate that their foreign contacts will imminently be targeted — indeed, even if they could show that interception of their own communications will imminently occur — they would still need to show that their injury is fairly traceable to §1881a. But, because respondents can only speculate as to whether any (asserted) interception would be under §1881a or some other authority, they cannot satisfy the "fairly traceable" requirement.

Third, even if respondents could show that the Government will seek the Foreign Intelligence Surveillance Court's authorization to acquire the communications of respondents' foreign contacts under §1881a, respondents can only speculate as to whether that court will authorize such surveillance. . . .

We decline to abandon our usual reluctance to endorse standing theories that rest on speculation about the decisions of independent actors. In sum, respondents' speculative chain of possibilities does not establish that injury based on potential future surveillance is certainly impending or is fairly traceable to §1881a.

B

Respondents' alternative argument — namely, that they can establish standing based on the measures that they have undertaken to avoid §1881a-authorized surveillance — fares no better. Respondents assert that they are suffering ongoing injuries that are fairly traceable to §1881a because the risk of surveillance under §1881a requires them to take costly and burdensome measures to protect the confidentiality of their communications. Respondents claim, for instance, that the threat of surveillance sometimes compels them to avoid certain e-mail and phone conversations, to "tal[k] in generalities rather than specifics," or to travel so that they can have in-person conversations. . . .

Respondents' contention that they have standing because they incurred certain costs as a reasonable reaction to a risk of harm is unavailing — because the harm respondents seek to avoid is not certainly impending. In other words, respondents cannot manufacture standing merely by inflicting harm on themselves based on their fears of hypothetical future harm that is not certainly impending. Any ongoing injuries that respondents are suffering are not fairly traceable to §1881a.

If the law were otherwise, an enterprising plaintiff would be able to secure a lower standard for Article III standing simply by making an expenditure based on a nonparanoid fear. . . .

Thus, allowing respondents to bring this action based on costs they incurred in response to a speculative threat would be tantamount to accepting a repackaged version of respondents' first failed theory of standing.

Another reason that respondents' present injuries are not fairly traceable to §1881a is that even before §1881a was enacted, they had a similar incentive to engage in many of the countermeasures that they are now taking. . . .

IV

A

Respondents incorrectly maintain that "[t]he kinds of injuries incurred here — injuries incurred because of [respondents'] reasonable efforts to avoid greater injuries that are otherwise likely to flow from the conduct they challenge — are the same kinds of injuries that this Court held to support standing in cases such as" Laidlaw [and] Meese v. Keene, 481 U.S. 465 (1987). . . .
[Each] of these cases was very different from the present case.

In Laidlaw, plaintiffs' standing was based on "the proposition that a company's continuous and pervasive illegal discharges of pollutants into a river would cause nearby residents to curtail their recreational use of that waterway and would subject them to other economic and aesthetic harms." Because the unlawful discharges of pollutants were "concededly ongoing," the only issue was whether "nearby residents" — who were members of the organizational plaintiffs — acted reasonably in refraining from using the polluted area. Laidlaw is therefore quite unlike the present case, in which it is not "concede[d]" that respondents would be subject to unlawful surveillance but for their decision to take preventive measures. Laidlaw would resemble this case only if (1) it were undisputed that the Government was using §1881a-authorized surveillance to acquire respondents' communications and (2) the sole dispute concerned the reasonableness of respondents' preventive measures.

In Keene, the plaintiff challenged the constitutionality of the Government's decision to label three films as "political propaganda." The Court held that the plaintiff, who was an attorney and a state legislator, had standing because he demonstrated, through "detailed affidavits," that he "could not exhibit the films without incurring a risk of injury to his reputation and of an impairment of his political career." Unlike the present case, Keene involved "more than a 'subjective chill'" based on speculation about potential governmental action; the plaintiff in that case was unquestionably regulated by the relevant statute, and the films that he wished to exhibit had already been labeled as "political propaganda." . . .

B

Respondents also suggest that they should be held to have standing because otherwise the constitutionality of §1881a could not be challenged. It would be wrong, they maintain, to "insulate the government's surveillance activities from meaningful judicial review." Respondents' suggestion is both legally and factually incorrect. First, "'[t]he assumption that if respondents have no standing to sue, no one would have standing, is not a reason to find standing.'"

Second, our holding today by no means insulates §1881a from judicial review. As described above, Congress created a comprehensive scheme in which the Foreign Intelligence Surveillance Court evaluates the Government's certifications, targeting procedures, and minimization procedures — including assessing whether the targeting and minimization procedures comport with the Fourth Amendment. Any dissatisfaction that respondents may have about the Foreign Intelligence Surveillance Court's rulings — or the congressional delineation of that court's role — is irrelevant to our standing analysis.

Additionally, if the Government intends to use or disclose information obtained or derived from a §1881a acquisition in judicial or administrative proceedings, it must provide advance notice of its intent, and the affected person may challenge the lawfulness of the acquisition. . . .

Finally, any electronic communications service provider that the Government directs to assist in §1881a surveillance may challenge the lawfulness of that directive before the FISC. Indeed, at the behest of a service provider, the Foreign Intelligence Surveillance Court of Review previously analyzed the constitutionality of electronic surveillance directives issued pursuant to a now-expired set of FISA amendments.

* * *

We hold that respondents lack Article III standing because they cannot demonstrate that the future injury they purportedly fear is certainly impending and because they cannot manufacture standing by incurring costs in anticipation of non-imminent harm. We therefore reverse the judgment of the Second Circuit and remand the case for further proceedings consistent with this opinion.

It is so ordered.

JUSTICE BREYER, with whom JUSTICE GINSBURG, JUSTICE SOTOMAYOR, and JUSTICE KAGAN join, dissenting.

I . . .

No one here denies that the Government's interception of a private telephone or e-mail conversation amounts to an injury that is "concrete and particularized." Moreover, the plaintiffs, respondents here, seek as relief a judgment declaring unconstitutional (and enjoining enforcement of) a statutory provision authorizing those interceptions; and, such a judgment would redress the injury by preventing it. Thus, the basic question is whether the injury, *i.e.*, the interception, is "actual or imminent."

II

A . . .

The addition of §1881a in 2008 changed [prior] law in three important ways. First, it eliminated the requirement that the Government describe to the court each specific target and identify each facility at which its surveillance would be

directed, thus permitting surveillance on a programmatic, not necessarily individualized, basis. Second, it eliminated the requirement that a target be a "foreign power or an agent of a foreign power." Third, it diminished the court's
authority to insist upon, and eliminated its authority to supervise, instance-
specific privacy-intrusion minimization procedures (though the Government
still must use court-approved general minimization procedures). Thus, using
the authority of §1881a, the Government can obtain court approval for its surveillance of electronic communications between places within the United States
and targets in foreign territories by showing the court (1) that "a significant
purpose of the acquisition is to obtain foreign intelligence information," and
(2) that it will use general targeting and privacy-intrusion minimization procedures of a kind that the court had previously approved.

B . . .

Plaintiff Scott McKay [says] in an affidavit (1) that he is a lawyer; (2) that he
represented "Mr. Sami Omar Al-Hussayen, who was acquitted in June 2004 on
terrorism charges"; (3) that he continues to represent "Mr. Al-Hussayen, who, in
addition to facing criminal charges after September 11, was named as a
defendant in several civil cases"; (4) that he represents Khalid Sheik Mohammed,
a detainee, "before the Military Commissions at Guantanamo Bay, Cuba"; (5)
that in representing these clients he "communicate[s] by telephone and email
with people outside the United States, including Mr. Al-Hussayen himself,"
"experts, investigators, attorneys, family members . . . and others who are located
abroad"; and (6) that prior to 2008 "the U.S. government had intercepted some
10,000 telephone calls and 20,000 e-mail communications involving [his client]
Al-Hussayen." . . .

[Another] plaintiff, Joanne Mariner, says in her affidavit (1) that she is a human
rights researcher, (2) that "some of the work [she] do[es] involves trying to track
down people who were rendered by the CIA to countries in which they were
tortured"; (3) that many of those people "the CIA has said are (or were) associated
with terrorist organizations"; and (4) that, to do this research, she "communicate[s] by telephone and e-mail with . . . former detainees, lawyers for detainees,
relatives of detainees, political activists, journalists, and fixers" "all over the world,
including in Jordan, Egypt, Pakistan, Afghanistan, [and] the Gaza Strip." . . .

III

Several considerations, based upon the record along with commonsense inferences, convince me that there is a very high likelihood that Government, *acting
under the authority of* §1881a, will intercept at least some of the communications
just described. First, the plaintiffs have engaged, and continue to engage, in
electronic communications of a kind that the 2008 amendment, but not the
prior Act, authorizes the Government to intercept. These communications
include discussions with family members of those detained at Guantanamo,
friends and acquaintances of those persons, and investigators, experts, and others
with knowledge of circumstances related to terrorist activities. These persons are
foreigners located outside the United States. They are not "foreign power[s]" or
"agent[s] of . . . foreign power[s]." And the plaintiffs state that they exchange with
these persons "foreign intelligence information," defined to include information

that "relates to" "international terrorism" and "the national defense or the security of the United States."

Second, the plaintiffs have a strong *motive* to engage in, and the Government has a strong *motive* to listen to, conversations of the kind described. A lawyer representing a client normally seeks to learn the circumstances surrounding the crime (or the civil wrong) of which the client is accused. A fair reading of the affidavit of Scott McKay, for example, taken together with elementary considerations of a lawyer's obligation to his client, indicates that McKay will engage in conversations that concern what suspected foreign terrorists, such as his client, have done; in conversations that concern his clients' families, colleagues, and contacts; in conversations that concern what those persons (or those connected to them) have said and done, at least in relation to terrorist activities; in conversations that concern the political, social, and commercial environments in which the suspected terrorists have lived and worked; and so forth. Journalists and human rights workers have strong similar motives to conduct conversations of this kind.

At the same time, the Government has a strong motive to conduct surveillance of conversations that contain material of this kind. The Government, after all, seeks to learn as much as it can reasonably learn about suspected terrorists (such as those detained at Guantanamo), as well as about their contacts and activities, along with those of friends and family members. And the Government is motivated to do so, not simply by the desire to help convict those whom the Government believes guilty, but also by the critical, overriding need to protect America from terrorism.

Third, the Government's *past behavior* shows that it has sought, and hence will in all likelihood continue to seek, information about alleged terrorists and detainees through means that include surveillance of electronic communications. As just pointed out, plaintiff Scott McKay states that the Government (under the authority of the pre-2008 law) "intercepted some 10,000 telephone calls and 20,000 e-mail communications involving [his client] Mr. Al-Hussayen."

Fourth, the Government has the *capacity* to conduct electronic surveillance of the kind at issue. To some degree this capacity rests upon technology available to the Government. [This] capacity also includes the Government's authority to obtain the kind of information here at issue from private carriers such as AT&T and Verizon. We are further told by *amici* that the Government is expanding that capacity.

Of course, to exercise this capacity the Government must have intelligence court authorization. But the Government rarely files requests that fail to meet the statutory criteria. As the intelligence court itself has stated, its review under §1881a is "narrowly circumscribed." There is no reason to believe that the communications described would all fail to meet the conditions necessary for approval. Moreover, compared with prior law, §1881a simplifies and thus expedites the approval process, making it more likely that the Government will use §1881a to obtain the necessary approval.

The upshot is that (1) similarity of content, (2) strong motives, (3) prior behavior, and (4) capacity all point to a very strong likelihood that the Government will intercept at least some of the plaintiffs' communications, including some that the 2008 amendment, §1881a, but not the pre-2008 Act, authorizes the Government to intercept. . . .

Consequently, we need only assume that the Government is doing its job (to find out about, and combat, terrorism) in order to conclude that there is a high

probability that the Government will intercept at least some electronic communication to which at least some of the plaintiffs are parties. The majority is wrong
when it describes the harm threatened plaintiffs as "speculative."

IV

A

The majority more plausibly says that the plaintiffs have failed to show that the
threatened harm is *"certainly impending."* But [*certainty*] is not, and never has
been, the touchstone of standing. The future is inherently uncertain. Yet federal
courts frequently entertain actions for injunctions and for declaratory relief
aimed at preventing future activities that are reasonably likely or highly likely,
but not absolutely certain, to take place. And that degree of certainty is all that is
needed to support standing here.

The Court's use of the term "certainly impending" is not to the contrary. . . .

Taken together the case law uses the word "certainly" as if it emphasizes, rather
than literally defines, the immediately following term "impending."

B

1

More important, the Court's holdings in standing cases show that standing
exists here. The Court has often *found* standing where the occurrence of the
relevant injury was far *less* certain than here. Consider a few, fairly typical, cases.
Consider *Pennell.* A city ordinance forbade landlords to raise the rent charged to
a tenant by more than 8 percent where doing so would work an unreasonably
severe hardship on that tenant. A group of landlords sought a judgment declaring
the ordinance unconstitutional. The Court held that, to have standing, the landlords had to demonstrate a *"'realistic danger of sustaining a direct injury* as a result
of the statute's operation.'" It found that the landlords had done so by showing a
likelihood of enforcement and a "probability," that the ordinance would make
the landlords charge lower rents — even though the landlords had not shown (1)
that they intended to raise the relevant rents to the point of causing unreasonably
severe hardship; (2) that the tenants would challenge those increases; or (3) that
the city's hearing examiners and arbitrators would find against the landlords.
Here, even more so than in *Pennell,* there is a *"realistic danger"* that the relevant
harm will occur. . . .

How could the law be otherwise? Suppose that a federal court faced a claim by
homeowners that (allegedly) unlawful dam-building practices created a high risk
that their homes would be flooded. Would the court deny them standing on the
ground that the risk of flood was only 60, rather than 90, percent?

Would federal courts deny standing to a plaintiff in a diversity action who
claims an anticipatory breach of contract where the future breach depends on
probabilities? The defendant, say, has threatened to load wheat onto a ship bound
for India despite a promise to send the wheat to the United States. No one can
know for certain that this will happen. Perhaps the defendant will change his
mind; perhaps the ship will turn and head for the United States. Yet, despite the
uncertainty, the Constitution does not prohibit a federal court from hearing such
a claim. . . .

Neither do ordinary declaratory judgment actions always involve the degree of certainty upon which the Court insists here. See, *e.g.*, . . . Aetna Life Ins. Co. v. Haworth, 300 U.S. 227, 239–244 (1937).

2

In some standing cases, the Court has found that a reasonable probability of *future* injury comes accompanied with *present* injury that takes the form of reasonable efforts to mitigate the threatened effects of the future injury or to prevent it from occurring. . . .

Virtually identical circumstances are present here. Plaintiff McKay, for example, points out that, when he communicates abroad about, or in the interests of, a client (*e.g.*, a client accused of terrorism), he must "make an assessment" whether his "client's interests would be compromised" should the Government "acquire the communications." If so, he must either forgo the communication or travel abroad. . . .

4

In sum [the] word "certainly" in the phrase "certainly impending" does not refer to absolute certainty. As our case law demonstrates, what the Constitution requires is something more akin to "reasonable probability" or "high probability." The use of some such standard is all that is necessary here to ensure the actual concrete injury that the Constitution demands. The considerations set forth in Parts II and III, *supra*, make clear that the standard is readily met in this case.

* * *

While I express no view on the merits of the plaintiffs' constitutional claims, I do believe that at least some of the plaintiffs have standing to make those claims. I dissent, with respect, from the majority's contrary conclusion.

Note: The Law of Standing

1. *Underlying concerns.* What functions are served by standing limitations? Consider the following possibilities.

(a) They ensure that the courts will decide cases that are concrete rather than abstract or hypothetical. To what extent is this so? Was the dispute in *Lujan* abstract or hypothetical?

(b) They promote judicial restraint by limiting the occasions for judicial intervention into the political process. But are standing limitations a good means of limiting such intrusions? Maybe they are, if the consequence of such limitations is to ensure that, if citizens generally or as a whole have a complaint, they have to go to the political process, not to the federal courts.

(c) They ensure that decisions will be made at the behest of those directly affected rather than on behalf of outsiders with a purely ideological interest in the controversy. This factor will simultaneously promote vigorous advocacy. Was there a danger of insufficiently vigorous advocacy in *Lujan*, Massachusetts v. EPA, or *Clapper*? Note that sometimes those directly affected will fail to sue for reasons other than contentment with the status quo. Note also that one needs a theory with which to decide who is "directly affected" and who is an "outsider." And note the potential preclusive effects that litigation by a relatively uninterested party might have, especially given devices such as class actions.

(d) Standing doctrines are an important part of the separation of powers system. They ensure that courts will not hear cases simply because they want to; they require a concrete stake and thus give the executive and legislative branches a range of breathing space. For discussion of some of these considerations, see Scalia, The Doctrine of Standing as an Essential Element of the Separation of Powers, 17 Suffolk U. L. Rev. 881 (1983); Sunstein, Standing and the Privatization of Public Law, 88 Colum. L. Rev. 1432 (1988).

(e) Standing doctrines ensure that people can bring suit only if some source of law has given them a cause of action. People cannot sue simply because they are unhappy, dissatisfied, or outraged. They must be able to point to some source of law that entitles them to have access to federal court.

2. *The constitutional and prudential components of standing doctrine.* The Court has divided standing requirements into several parts. Our focus is on article III, which is now taken to require (a) an injury in fact that (b) is due to the defendant's behavior and (c) is likely to be redressed by a decree in the plaintiff's favor. For many years, the Court has also said that prudential requirements, not based on article III and subject to congressional override, require that the plaintiff's injury (a) be arguably within the zone of interests protected or regulated by the statutory or constitutional provision at issue and (b) not be too generalized, that is, be particular and not shared by all or almost all citizens. See Federal Election Commission v. Akins, 524 U.S. 11 (1998). Prudential requirements are "judicially self-imposed limits on the exercise of federal jurisdiction," *Allen,* 468 U.S. at 751, while the article III–based components of standing are binding constraints on judicial power.

More recently, however, the Court has said that the zone of interests test is not prudential but is instead a reading of the Administrative Procedure Act, and also that the ban on generalized injuries is an Article III requirement. See Lexmark International, Inc. v. Static Control Components, Inc., 134 S. Ct. 1377 (2014). We will return to this suggestion.

3. *Standing — what are injuries, in fact?* A significant part of standing doctrine focuses on what sorts of injuries can confer standing.

a. *Injury in fact.* Standing limitations, in their current form, are actually relatively new. The injury in fact requirement evolved from the earlier requirement of a "legal injury." A "legal injury" pointed to different considerations from those embodied in the requirement of "injury in fact." To show a legal injury, one had to show that some law entitled one to relief; this showing could be made by identifying an injury to an interest that was protected at common law, or that entitled the plaintiff to redress under a relevant statute. On this view, the question whether there was standing was essentially the question whether there was a cause of action. Without a cause of action, there was no "case" and no "controversy." Someone would have "standing" if she had a claim to relief under a statute. In this sense, the questions of standing, cause of action, and the merits were fused. Some of current doctrine reflects the view that people need a cause of action in order to bring suit; but the law is not adequately captured in that phrase.

In the early days of standing doctrine — the first decades of the twentieth century — a common law interest was often treated as a necessary basis for standing. Standing limits, like other justiciability doctrines, were elaborated by justices allied with the progressive movement or the New Deal — most notably Justices Brandeis and Frankfurter, defenders of the regulatory state — who sought to develop devices immunizing government from judicial review. See, e.g., Joint Anti-Fascist Refugee Committee v. McGrath, 341 U.S. 123, 154–155 (1951) (Frankfurter, J., concurring); Alabama Power Co. v. Ickes, 302 U.S. 464, 479–480 (1938); Ashwander v. Tennessee Valley Authority, 297 U.S. 288, 341–345 (1936) (Brandeis, J., concurring); Fairchild v. Hughes, 258 U.S. 126, 129–130 (1922).

Although these justices were hardly critical of government intervention into the economy, the consequence of the new standing requirements was a body of doctrine that was in fact rooted in a sharp split between the public and private spheres. Usually one had to show at least a common law interest to obtain standing. Beneficiaries of government action — consumers, public interest groups, victims of discrimination — were denied standing. Judicial intervention could be invoked by those trying to fend off government activity but not by those trying to obtain government protection. Invasion of private property rights was the usual basis for obtaining review. This understanding was an amalgam of common law and statutory interpretation. For the most part it was not thought to be constitutional in nature. For a detailed discussion of the relevant history, along with an evaluation of standing limits, see Winter, The Metaphor of Standing and the Problem of Self-Governance, 40 Stan. L. Rev. 1371 (1988). For a contrary view, see Woolhandler and Nelson, Does History Defeat Standing Doctrine?, 102 Mich. L. Rev. 689 (2004).

In the 1960s and 1970s, however, courts emphasized that people invoking statutory interests also suffered "legal injury." On this view, the fact that an interest protected by statute was at stake gave rise to an inference that Congress had intended to allow someone invoking that interest to bring suit. For example, people who listened to the radio could challenge decisions of the Federal Communications Commission, and people who enjoyed the environment could challenge the building of a power plant near a river. See Office of Communication of the United Church of Christ v. FCC, 359 F.2d 994 (D.C. Cir. 1966); Scenic Hudson Preservation Conference v. FPC, 354 F.2d 608 (2d Cir. 1965). Notably, this broadening of standing was done under the rubric of statutory interpretation. It continued the original idea that whether someone had standing depended on whether Congress had conferred on that person a right to relief. Thus far, no "injury in fact" was required, and article III was implicated only insofar as courts treated a congressional grant of a right to relief as a necessary condition for standing.

The real roots of modern standing law can be found not in the founding period, and not even during the New Deal, but instead in Association of Data Processing Services Organizations v. Camp, 397 U.S. 150 (1970). In that case, the Court boldly altered previous law by abandoning the legal interest test altogether in favor of a new inquiry into whether there was injury in fact. It is noteworthy that the injury in fact requirement seemed to be an interpretation of the Administrative Procedure Act, not an interpretation of the Constitution, though the Court was ambiguous on that point. It is also noteworthy that the Court clearly intended to broaden, rather than to narrow, standing. It emphasized that the injury in fact requirement is relatively lenient. According to the Court, it may include a wide variety of economic, aesthetic, environmental, and other harms.

The consequence of *Data Processing* is that beneficiaries of government regulation, not merely those trying to fend off government action, can have standing to sue. But even under *Data Processing*, a merely ideological interest — or an interest in bringing about compliance with the law — is insufficient. But what is the line between an "injury in fact" and a "mere" ideological injury? Might not that line turn on whether Congress has created a right to relief?

Standing was denied on injury in fact grounds in Sierra Club v. Morton, 405 U.S. 727 (1972). The case involved an effort by an organization with "a special interest in the conservation and sound maintenance of the national parks" to challenge construction of a recreation area in a national forest. In the plaintiffs' view, the construction would have violated federal law. The Court denied standing, saying that the fact that an aesthetic, conservational, or recreational harm would be sufficient did not mean that the Court would abandon "the requirement that the party seeking review must have himself suffered an injury." In this case, the "Sierra Club failed to allege that it or its members" used the site in question.

What is the purpose of denying standing in *Sierra Club*? Would the Sierra Club have been an ineffective or a half-hearted advocate? Was there no case or controversy? Consider the view that the Sierra Club was litigating the rights of others who had a more direct stake in the controversy and the idea that those others, and not an intermeddling bystander, should have an exclusive right to raise the underlying legal issues.

Sierra Club might also be contrasted with United States v. SCRAP, 412 U.S. 669 (1973), in which the Court held that environmental groups could challenge the Interstate Commerce Commission's failure to suspend a surcharge on railroad freight rates as unlawful under the Interstate Commerce Commission Act. The plaintiffs claimed that their members "used the forests, streams, mountains, and other resources in the Washington metropolitan area for camping, hiking, fishing, and sightseeing." According to the Court, the Constitution was satisfied by the

> attenuated line of causation to the eventual injury of which the [plaintiffs] complained — a general rate increase would allegedly cause increased use of nonrecyclable commodities as compared to recyclable goods, thus resulting in the need to use more natural resources to produce such goods, some of which resources might be taken from the Washington area, and resulting in more refuse that might be discarded in national parks in the Washington area.

It is not at all clear, however, that SCRAP could command a majority today, as Massachusetts v. EPA reveals. The Court distinguished SCRAP in Summers v. Earth Island Institute, 555 U.S. 488 (2009). Plaintiffs, a group of environmental organizations, challenged the failure of the United States Forest Service to enforce regulations requiring it to establish notice, comment, and appeal procedures for proposed actions implementing land and resource management plans. The Court held that an affidavit submitted by a member of one of the organizations that he "has visited many National Forests and plans to visit several unnamed National Forests in the future" was insufficient to establish standing because it failed

> to allege that *any* particular timber sale or other project claimed to be unlawfully subject to regulations will impede a specific and concrete plan of [the affiant's] to enjoy the National Forests. The National Forests occupy more than 190 million acres, an area larger than Texas. There may be a chance, but it is hardly a likelihood, that [affiant's] wanderings will bring him to a parcel about to be affected by a project unlawfully subject to the regulations. Indeed, without further specification, it is impossible to tell *which* projects are in respondents' view unlawfully subject to regulations.

Compare Justice Breyer's dissenting opinion, joined by Justices Stevens, Souter, and Ginsburg. He observed that the plaintiff organizations had "hundreds of thousands of members who use forests regularly across the nation." The members' activities led him to this analogy: "To know, virtually for certain, that snow will fall in New England this winter is not to know the name of each particular town where it is bound to arrive. The law of standing does not require the latter kind of specificity."

b. *Injuries to third parties.* The notion that a plaintiff may not litigate the rights of third parties is closely related to the "injury in fact" requirement. The plaintiff must litigate on the basis of an injury to him or her; it is up to third parties to litigate their own rights. See, e.g., Tileston v. Ullman, 318 U.S. 44 (1943) (doctor may not challenge statute on ground that it would deprive patients of their lives without due process). See generally Monaghan, Third Party Standing, 84 Colum. L. Rev. 567 (1984); Brilmayer, The Jurisprudence of Article III: Perspectives on the "Case or Controversy" Requirement, 93 Harv. L. Rev. 297 (1979).

c. *Procedural violations.* To what extent can procedural violations count as injury in fact to establish constitutional standing? Consider Spokeo, Inc. v. Robins, 136 S. Ct. 1540 (2016).

The Fair Credit Reporting Act of 1970 requires consumer reporting agencies to "follow reasonable procedures to assure maximum possible accuracy of" consumer reports, and imposes liability on "[a]ny person who willfully fails to comply with any requirement [of the Act] with respect to any" individual. 15 U.S.C. §§1681e(b), 1681n(a). Robins brought a class action alleging that Spokeo's online "people search engine" generated a profile of him that contained inaccurate information and thus violated the FCRA's requirements. The District Court dismissed, finding that Robins had not satisfied article III's injury-in-fact test. The Court of Appeals for the Ninth Circuit reversed, concluding that Robins had established injury in fact because "Spokeo violated *his* statutory rights" and because his "personal interests in the handling of his credit information [were] *individualized.*"

Writing for the Court, Justice Alito elaborated on the meaning of the injury-in-fact test's particularization and concreteness requirements, finding that the Ninth Circuit's standing analysis was "incomplete" because it failed to address the question "whether the particular procedural violations alleged in [the] case [entailed] a degree of risk sufficient to meet the concreteness requirement."

> For an injury to be "particularized," it "must affect the plaintiff in a personal and individual way." [Particularization] is necessary to establish injury in fact, but it is not sufficient. An injury in fact must also be "concrete." Under the Ninth Circuit's analysis, however, that independent requirement was elided. [The] Ninth Circuit concluded that Robins' complaint alleges "concrete, *de facto*" injuries for essentially two reasons. [First], the court noted that Robins "alleges that Spokeo violated *his* statutory rights, not just the statutory rights of other people." [Second], the court wrote that "Robins's personal interests in the handling of his credit information are *individualized rather than collective.*" [Both] of these observations concern particularization, not concreteness. We have made it clear time and time again that an injury in fact must be both concrete *and* particularized. . . .
>
> A "concrete" injury must be "*de facto*"; that is, it must actually exist. [When] we have used the adjective "concrete," we have meant to convey the usual meaning of the term — "real," and not "abstract." [Concreteness], therefore, is quite different from particularization. ["Concrete"] is not, however, necessarily synonymous with "tangible." Although tangible injuries are perhaps easier to recognize, we have

confirmed in many of our previous cases that intangible injuries can nevertheless be concrete. . . .

In determining whether an intangible harm constitutes injury in fact, both history and the judgment of Congress play important roles. Because the doctrine of standing derives from the case-or-controversy requirement, and because that requirement in turn is grounded in historical practice, it is instructive to consider whether an alleged intangible harm has a close relationship to a harm that has traditionally been regarded as providing a basis for a lawsuit in English or American courts. *See Vermont Agency of Natural Resources v. United States* ex rel. *Stevens*, 529 U.S. 765, 775–777 (2000). In addition, because Congress is well positioned to identify intangible harms that meet minimum Article III requirements, its judgment is also instructive and important. Thus, we said in *Lujan* that Congress may "elevat[e] to the status of legally cognizable injuries concrete, *de facto* injuries that were previously inadequate in law." [Similarly], Justice Kennedy's concurrence in that case explained that "Congress has the power to define injuries and articulate chains of causation that will give rise to a case or controversy where none existed before." . . .

Congress' role in identifying and elevating intangible harms does not mean that a plaintiff automatically satisfies the injury-in-fact requirement whenever a statute grants a person a statutory right and purports to authorize that person to sue to vindicate that right. Article III standing requires a concrete injury even in the context of a statutory violation. For that reason, Robins could not, for example, allege a bare procedural violation, divorced from any concrete harm, and satisfy the injury-in-fact requirement of Article III. *See Summers v. Earth Island Institute*, 555 U.S. 488, 496 (2009) ("[D]eprivation of a procedural right without some concrete interest that is affected by the deprivation . . . is insufficient to create Article III standing"); *see also Lujan, supra*, at 572.

This does not mean, however, that the risk of real harm cannot satisfy the requirement of concreteness. *See, e.g., Clapper v. Amnesty Int'l USA*, 568 U.S. —(2013). For example, the law has long permitted recovery by certain tort victims even if their harms may be difficult to prove or measure. [Just] as the common law permitted suit in such instances, the violation of a procedural right granted by statute can be sufficient in some circumstances to constitute injury in fact. In other words, a plaintiff in such a case need not allege any *additional* harm beyond the one Congress has identified. *See Federal Election Comm'n v. Akins*, 524 U.S. 11, 20–25 (1998) (confirming that a group of voters' "inability to obtain information" that Congress had decided to make public is a sufficient injury in fact to satisfy Article III); *Public Citizen v. Department of Justice*, 491 U.S. 440, 449 (1989) (holding that two advocacy organizations' failure to obtain information subject to disclosure under the Federal Advisory Committee Act "constitutes a sufficiently distinct injury to provide standing to sue").

The Court concluded that although "Congress plainly sought to curb the dissemination of false information by adopting procedures designed to decrease that risk," Robins "[could not] satisfy the demands of article III by alleging a bare procedural violation." It reasoned:

A violation of one of the FCRA's procedural requirements may result in no harm. For example, even if a consumer reporting agency fails to provide the required notice to a user of the agency's consumer information, that information regardless may be entirely accurate. In addition, not all inaccuracies cause harm or present any material risk of harm. An example that comes readily to mind is an incorrect zip code. It is difficult to imagine how the dissemination of an incorrect zip code, without more, could work any concrete harm.

Justice Thomas concurred in the judgment and wrote a separate opinion "to explain how, in [his] view, the injury-in-fact requirement applies to different types of rights." He stated:

> The judicial power of common-law courts was historically limited depending on the nature of the plaintiff's suit. Common-law courts more readily entertained suits from private plaintiffs who alleged a violation of their own rights, in contrast to private plaintiffs who asserted claims vindicating public rights. . . . Historically, common-law courts possessed broad power to adjudicate suits involving the alleged violation of private rights, even when plaintiffs alleged only the violation of those rights and nothing more. [Generally], only the government had the authority to vindicate a harm borne by the public at large, such as the violation of the criminal laws, and [e]ven in limited cases where private plaintiffs could bring a claim for the violation of public rights, they had to allege that the violation caused them "some extraordinary damage, beyond the rest of the [community]. . . .

Noting that this distinction underlies modern standing doctrine, Justice Thomas explained:

> Congress can create new private rights and authorize private plaintiffs to sue based simply on the violation of those private rights. [A] plaintiff seeking to vindicate a statutorily created private right need not allege actual harm beyond the invasion of that private right. . . . A plaintiff seeking to vindicate a public right embodied in a federal statute, however, must demonstrate that the violation of that public right has caused him a concrete, individual harm distinct from the general population. [Thus], Congress cannot authorize private plaintiffs to enforce *public* rights in their own names, absent some showing that the plaintiff has suffered a concrete harm particular to him.

Justice Thomas concluded:

> The Fair Credit Reporting Act creates a series of regulatory duties. Robins has no standing to sue Spokeo, in his own name, for violations of the duties that Spokeo owes to the public collectively, absent some showing that he has suffered concrete and particular harm. [But] a remand is required because one claim in Robins' complaint rests on a statutory provision that could arguably establish a private cause of action to vindicate the violation of a privately held right. Section 1681e(b) requires Spokeo to "follow reasonable procedures to assure maximum possible accuracy of the information *concerning the individual about whom the report relates.*" §1681e(b) (emphasis added). If Congress has created a private duty owed personally to Robins to protect *his* information, then the violation of the legal duty suffices for Article III injury in fact. If that provision, however, vests any and all consumers with the power to police the "reasonable procedures" of Spokeo, without more, then Robins has no standing to sue for its violation absent an allegation that he has suffered individualized harm. On remand, the Court of Appeals can consider the nature of this claim.

Justice Ginsburg wrote a dissenting opinion (joined by Justice Sotomayor) in which she argued that Robins' injury was sufficiently "concrete." She wrote:

> Robins would not qualify, the Court observes, if he alleged a "bare" procedural violation [one] that results in no harm, for example, "an incorrect zip code." Far from an incorrect zip code, Robins complains of misinformation about his

education, family situation, and economic status, inaccurate representations that could affect his fortune in the job market. The FCRA's procedural requirements aimed to prevent such harm. [I] therefore see no utility in returning this case to the Ninth Circuit to underscore what Robins' complaint already conveys concretely: Spokeo's misinformation "cause[s] actual harm to [his] employment prospects."

d. *Threatened injury.* The "injury in fact" requirement is usually met by those who can show a sufficient threat of future injury. As *Clapper* holds, this threat must be real and immediate rather than "merely" speculative or hypothetical. The refusal to recognize speculative or hypothetical harms plays an important role in suits seeking injunctive relief. Consider City of Los Angeles v. Lyons, 461 U.S. 95 (1983), an action brought against the Los Angeles police department and city officials, seeking injunctive relief to prevent the use of "chokeholds" in arrests. Lyons, the plaintiff, had in fact been the victim of a chokehold; he also brought an action for damages. But the Court said that the fact that he was also seeking damages did not mean he could obtain an injunction when he was not "likely to suffer future injury from the use of chokeholds by police officers." To show such a likelihood, he would have "to make the incredible assertion either, (1) that all police officers in Los Angeles always choke any citizen with whom they happen to have an encounter whether for the purpose of arrest, issuing a citation or for questioning or, (2) that the City ordered or authorized police officers to act in such a manner." Assume the practice at issue in *Lyons* is unconstitutional. Would anyone have standing to enjoin it?

e. *Widely diffused harms.* Should the Court refuse to decide cases in which the harm caused by government action is widely diffused — in the sense that many or all citizens feel it equally? Consider in this regard Schlesinger v. Reservists to Stop the War, 418 U.S. 208 (1974), which involved a claim, made by an association of present and former members of the Reserves, that the Reserve membership of certain members of Congress violated the incompatibility clause. That clause provides that "no Person holding any Office under the United States, shall be a member of either House during his Continuance in Office." The Court said:

> The only interest [is one] shared by all citizens. [The] claimed nonobservance [of that Clause], standing alone, would adversely affect only the generalized interest of all citizens in constitutional governance, and that is an abstract injury. . . .
>
>   To permit a complainant who has no concrete injury to require a court to rule on important constitutional issues in the abstract would create the potential for abuse of the judicial process, distort the role of the Judiciary in its relationship to the Executive and the Legislature and open the Judiciary to an arguable charge of "government by injunction."

The Court added that the plaintiffs did not meet the requirements of Flast v. Cohen, infra. Justices Douglas, Brennan, and Marshall dissented.

Consider also United States v. Richardson, 418 U.S. 166 (1974), an effort by a taxpayer to challenge the Central Intelligence Agency Act of 1949, which provides that Central Intelligence Agency expenditures may not be made public. According to the plaintiff, the act violated article I, section 9, clause 7 of the Constitution, which provides that "a regular statement of Account of the Receipts and Expenditures of all public Money shall be published from time to time." The Court responded that the plaintiff's claim was only "a generalized grievance" that was "common to all members of the public. While we can hardly dispute that this respondent has a genuine interest in the use of funds and that his interest may be prompted by his status as a taxpayer, he has not alleged that, as a taxpayer, he is in danger of suffering any particular concrete injury as a result of the operation of this statute." The Court added:

> It can be argued that if respondent is not permitted to litigate this issue, no one can do so. In a very real sense, the absence of any particular individual or class to litigate these claims gives support to the argument that the subject matter is committed to the surveillance of Congress, and ultimately to the political process. Any other conclusion would mean that the Founding Fathers intended to set up something in the nature of an Athenian democracy or a New England town meeting to oversee the conduct of the National Government by means of lawsuits in federal courts. The Constitution created a representative Government with the representatives directly responsible to their constituents at stated periods of two, four, and six years; that the Constitution does not afford a judicial remedy does not, of course, completely disable the citizen who is not satisfied with the "ground rules" established by the Congress for reporting expenditures of the Executive Branch. Lack of standing within the narrow confines of Art. III jurisdiction does not impair the right to assert his views in the political forum or at the polls. Slow, cumbersome, and unresponsive though the traditional electoral process may be thought at times, our system provides for changing members of the political branches when dissatisfied citizens convince a sufficient number of their fellow electors that elected representatives are delinquent in performing duties committed to them.

In an influential concurring opinion, Justice Powell added:

> The power recognized in [*Marbury*] is a potent one. Its prudent use seems to me incompatible with unlimited notions of taxpayer and citizen standing. [Due] to what many have regarded as the unresponsiveness of the Federal Government to recognized needs or serious inequities in our society, recourse to the federal courts has attained an unprecedented popularity in recent decades. Those courts have often acted as a major instrument of social reform. But this has not always been the case, as experiences under the New Deal illustrate. The public reaction to the substantive due process holdings of the federal courts during that period requires no elaboration, and it is not unusual for history to repeat itself.
>
> Quite apart from this possibility, we risk a progressive impairment of the effectiveness of the federal courts if their limited resources are diverted increasingly from their historic role to the resolution of public-interest suits brought by litigants who cannot distinguish themselves from all taxpayers or all citizens. The irreplaceable value of the power articulated by Mr. Chief Justice Marshall lies in the protection it has afforded the constitutional rights and liberties of individual citizens and minority groups against oppressive or discriminatory government action. It is this role, not some amorphous general supervision of the operations of government, that has maintained public esteem for the federal courts and has permitted the peaceful coexistence of the countermajoritarian implications of judicial review and the democratic principles upon which our Federal Government in the final analysis rests.
>
> The considerations outlined above underlie, I believe, the traditional hostility of the Court to federal taxpayer or citizen standing where the plaintiff has nothing at stake other than his interest as a taxpayer or citizen. It merits noting how often and how unequivocally the Court has expressed its antipathy to efforts to convert the Judiciary into an open forum for the resolution of political or ideological disputes about the performance of government.

The problem of widely diffused injuries is associated with that of taxpayer standing. The Court has rarely recognized such standing, but did so in Flast v. Cohen, 392 U.S. 83 (1968), which involved a taxpayer challenge to aid to religious schools. The Court said that taxpayer standing would be permitted in *Flast* because there was "a logical nexus between the status asserted and the claim thought to be adjudicated." According to the Court,

> the nexus demanded of federal taxpayers has two aspects to it. First, the taxpayer must establish a logical link between that status and the type of legislative enactment attacked. [It] will not be sufficient to allege an incidental expenditure of tax funds in the administration of an essentially regulatory measure. Secondly, the taxpayer must establish a nexus between that status and the precise nature of the constitutional infringement alleged. Under this requirement, the taxpayer must show that the challenged enactment exceeds specific constitutional limitations imposed upon the exercise of the congressional taxing and spending powers.

The Court held that the requirement was satisfied in the case of a taxpayer challenging an expenditure of public funds as violative of the establishment clause.

In other cases, the Court has denied taxpayer standing. See Frothingham v. Mellon, 262 U.S. 447 (1923) (refusing to allow taxpayer to enjoin under the tenth amendment expenditures made to reduce maternal and infant mortality under federal statute), and Valley Forge Christian College v. Americans United, 454 U.S. 464 (1982), in which the Court refused to permit a taxpayer to challenge under the establishment clause a conveyance of property formerly used as a military hospital to the Valley Forge Christian College. In *Valley Forge*, the Court emphasized that the plaintiffs challenged a property transfer, not an expenditure of funds.

In Hein v. Freedom from Religion Foundation, 551 U.S. 587 (2007), the Court essentially confined *Flast* to its facts. *Hein* involved a challenge to President Bush's Faith-Based and Community Initiatives Program. Taxpayers complained that the executive branch had used public money to fund conferences with the purpose and effect of promoting religion. They contended that the resulting expenditures violated the establishment clause. Justice Alito, writing for himself, Chief Justice Roberts, and Justice Kennedy, said that *Flast* meant only that taxpayers could challenge an explicit congressional decision to use taxpayer funds for arguably religious purposes. If the executive branch used a general appropriation to promote religion, taxpayers could not bring suit. Justice Scalia, writing for himself and Justice Thomas, contended that *Flast* was an anomaly and should be overruled. Justice Souter, joined by Justices Stevens, Ginsburg, and Breyer, contended that for purposes of standing, there was no relevant distinction between a specific congressional appropriation and the executive's use of taxpayer funds for religious purposes.

In DaimlerChrysler Corp. v. Cuno, 547 U.S. 332 (2006), the Supreme Court held that municipal taxpayers in Toledo, Ohio, lacked standing to challenge a state tax credit offered to DaimlerChrysler as an incentive for it to expand its operations in the city. The taxpayers alleged that the tax breaks, which they asserted violated the commerce clause, would increase their own tax burdens. The Court held that "affording state taxpayers standing to press such challenges simply because their tax burden gives them an interest in the state treasury would interpose the federal courts as 'virtually continuing monitors of the wisdom and soundness' of state fiscal administration, contrary to the more modest role Article III envisions for federal courts."

Compare Federal Election Commission v. Akins, 524 U.S. 11 (1998). At issue there was an effort by interested citizens to require the Federal Election Commission (FEC) to classify the American Israel Public Affairs Committee (AIPAC) as a "political committee," and thus to require AIPAC to make disclosures to the public about its membership, contributions, and expenditures. The FEC contended that because the plaintiffs could not distinguish themselves from all other citizens, standing should be denied. The Court held that the ban on generalized grievances was prudential, and not rooted in article III, and hence that standing was available here because Congress had expressly given a cause of action to "any person." The Court said that the injury in fact "consists of their inability to obtain information [that], on respondents' view of the law, the statute requires that AIPAC make public."

The Court acknowledged that it had "sometimes determined that where large numbers of Americans suffer alike, the political process, rather than the judicial process, may provide the more appropriate remedy for a widely shared grievance." In those cases, however, the injury was "not only widely shared, but [also] of an abstract and indefinite nature." Here, the injury was "concrete, though widely shared," and hence sufficient for standing. The Court distinguished United States v. Richardson, supra, on the ground that in *Akins* there was a statute that "does seek to protect individuals such as respondents from the kind of harm they say they have suffered." Justice Scalia dissented, joined by Justices O'Connor and Thomas.

Consider the following views. (1) *Richardson, Schlesinger, Valley Forge*, and *Hein* were rightly decided, and *Flast* and *Akins* wrongly. If a harm is shared by the plaintiff in common with all other citizens or taxpayers, the appropriate forum is the legislature, not the court. The mechanisms of political accountability are a sufficient guaranty. And if those mechanisms fail, the problem must not be severe in any event. The Constitution requires more than able litigants and a legal question. (2) Constitutional requirements are not meant to vary with popular opinion; they operate largely as constraints on outcomes, even if they accurately reflect popular opinion. *Richardson, Schlesinger, Valley Forge*, and *Hein* were incorrectly decided because they render constitutional constraints unenforceable. If the plaintiffs in those cases do not have standing, no one ever will. (3) The real standing question is whether any law creates a cause of action. When a constitutional provision benefits all citizens, courts should not infer from it a cause of action on behalf of any citizen in particular. *Flast* is a sensible exception because of the distinctive character of the establishment clause, a guarantee against the expenditure of taxpayer funds for religion.

Why, under *Akins*, is the "generalized injury" requirement prudential, rather than constitutional, in nature?

4. *Nexus*. The nexus requirement has two prongs. The plaintiff must show that (1) the allegedly unlawful conduct has caused his or her "injury in fact" and (2) the injury is likely to be redressed by a favorable decision. In practice, these two prongs almost always amount to the same thing.

The nexus requirement has been an important limitation in standing cases. One of the key cases is Linda R. S. v. Richard D., 410 U.S. 614 (1972), which involved an action by an unwed mother to enjoin discriminatory application of a Texas criminal statute that penalized any parent who failed to support his children. The plaintiff contended that judicial interpretation had excluded unwed fathers from prosecution and sought to require a prosecutor to initiate criminal proceedings against the father of her child for failure to provide child support. The Court denied standing, asserting that, because prosecution might lead only to the father's incarceration, the "prospect that prosecution will [result] in payment of support can, at best, be termed only speculative." *Linda R. S.* took place in an unusual setting, for criminal prosecutors have usually been held to have unreviewable discretion whether to bring enforcement actions. Should the decision have been based on standing grounds? Consider Easterbrook, Foreword: The Court and the Economic System, 98 Harv. L. Rev. 4, 40 (1984): "[It] is hard to take seriously the claim that enforcement of legal rules does not affect bystanders. [I] suffer an injury if the police announce that they will no longer enforce [the rule against murder] in my neighborhood. [A] plaintiff need not show a sure gain from winning in order to prove that some probability of gain is better than none, and thus he suffers injury in fact." Consider also the view that the plaintiff's claim in *Linda R. S.* was of unequal treatment, and if the injury is one of inequality under the law, there is no problem of redressability.

Another case in the same vein as *Linda R. S.* is Simon v. Eastern Kentucky Welfare Rights Organization (EKWRO), 426 U.S. 26 (1976). Several indigents and organizations brought suit challenging an Internal Revenue Service Revenue ruling that granted favorable tax treatment to certain nonprofit hospitals that limited aid to indigents for emergency room services. According to the plaintiffs, the ruling was unlawful because it reduced the amount of services necessary to qualify as charitable corporations. The consequence, plaintiffs claimed, was that the indigents would have less in the way of medical services available to them.

The Court, in an opinion by Justice Powell, held that there was no standing. In the Court's view, the plaintiffs' contention that the new ruling "encouraged" denial of services to indigents was inadequate.

> It is purely speculative whether the denials of service specified in the complaint fairly can be traced to the Service's "encouragement" or instead result from decisions made by hospitals without regard to their tax implications. [It] is equally speculative whether the desired exercise of the court's remedial powers in this suit would result in the availability [of] such services. So far as the complaint sheds light, it is just as plausible that the hospitals to which plaintiffs may apply for service would elect to forego favorable tax treatment to avoid the undetermined financial drain of an increase in the level of uncompensated services.

Justice Brennan, joined by Justice Marshall, dissented. Justice Brennan claimed that the relevant injury was to the "opportunity and ability" to receive free medical services, that that interest was not too diffuse to support standing, and that the further requirement imposed by the Court served no purpose. Under what circumstances should a plaintiff have standing to bring suit against the government for "encouraging" harmful activity? Should the intervening conduct of third parties — hospitals in Simon v. Eastern Kentucky Welfare Rights Organization and schools in Allen v. Wright — play a role in the standing inquiry?

Compare Duke Power Co. v. Carolina Environmental Study Group, 438 U.S. 59 (1978). In that case, the plaintiffs — forty people who lived near planned power plants, an environmental group, and a labor organization — sought to challenge the Price-Anderson Act, which limited aggregate liability for a single nuclear power plant accident to $560 million. Plaintiffs claimed that the plant

would produce environmental and aesthetic injuries. The Court found a sufficiently concrete injury: "It is enough that several of the 'immediate' impacts were
found to harm appellees. Certainly the environmental and aesthetic consequences of the thermal pollution of the two lakes in the vicinity of the disputed
power plants is the type of harmful effect which has been deemed adequate in
prior cases to satisfy the 'injury in fact' standard."

Note also Regents of the University of California v. Bakke, 438 U.S. 265
(1978), where plaintiff challenged an affirmative action program established
by the University of California at Davis without alleging that, if the program
were not in place, he would have been admitted to the medical school. The
Court responded:

> The constitutional element of standing is plaintiff's demonstration of any injury to
> himself that is likely to be redressed by favorable decision of his claim. The trial
> court found such an injury, apart from failure to be admitted, in the University's
> decision not to permit Bakke to compete for all 100 places in the class, simply
> because of his race. Hence the constitutional requirements of Art. III were met. The
> question of Bakke's admission vel non is merely one of relief.

If the Court is correct on this point, is *EKWRO* wrongly decided? Compare with
Lujan the striking decision in Northeastern Florida Chapter of Associated
General Contractors v. Jacksonville, 508 U.S. 656 (1993). Jacksonville enacted
an ordinance requiring that 10 percent of the money spent on city contracts be
"set aside" for minority business enterprises. A contractors' association, consisting
mostly of members who would not qualify as minority enterprises, brought suit,
claiming that the set-aside violated the equal protection clause. The lower court
denied standing on the ground that no member of the association had demonstrated that, "but for the program, any AGC member would have bid successfully
for any of these contracts." There was therefore no injury in fact.

The Supreme Court responded:

> When the government erects a barrier that makes it more difficult for members of
> one group to obtain a benefit than it is for members of another group, a member of
> the former group seeking to challenge the barrier need not allege that he would
> have obtained the benefit but for the barrier in order to establish standing. The
> "injury in fact" in an equal protection case of this variety is the denial of equal
> treatment resulting from the imposition of the barrier, not the ultimate inability to
> obtain the benefit. And in the context of a challenge to a set-aside program, the
> "injury in fact" is the inability to compete on an equal footing in the bidding
> process, not the loss of a contract. To establish standing, therefore, a party chal-
> lenging a set-aside program like Jacksonville's need only demonstrate that it is able
> and ready to bid on contracts and that a discriminatory policy prevents it from doing
> so on an equal basis.

In an intriguing footnote, the Court added, "It follows from our definition of
'injury in fact' that petitioner has sufficiently alleged both that the city's ordinance is the 'cause' of its injury and that a judicial decree directly to the city to
discontinue its program would 'redress' the injury."

What is the purpose of the "nexus" or "causation" requirement? Is that requirement merely one of pleading — or does it establish a threshold requirement of
proof on the plaintiff's part? One possibility is that the requirement operates as a
safeguard against advisory opinions. If the plaintiff is unable to show that the

requested relief would remedy his injury, it becomes necessary to ask why the court should become involved at all. Is this a persuasive justification for the results in *Linda R. S.* and *EKWRO?* What level of certainty should be necessary in order to justify judicial relief?

A divided Court built on *Northeastern Florida Chapter* in Gratz v. Bollinger, 539 U.S. 244 (2003). Patrick Hamacher, a plaintiff in the case, objected to an affirmative action program used by the University of Michigan in undergraduate admissions. The problem was that although Hamacher said that he intended to apply for admission as a transfer student, he had not actually made any such application. Dissenting, Justice Stevens urged that because Hamacher had not yet applied, his claim of injury was conjectural and hypothetical. The Court disagreed. It said that for standing, it was enough that Hamacher claimed that "he was 'able and ready' to apply as a transfer student" if the university stopped using race in undergraduate admissions. This claim of intent supported standing "to seek prospective relief with respect to the University's continued use of race in undergraduate admissions."

Consider the view that whether an injury is speculative depends on how it is characterized. If the injury in *Bakke* and *Gratz* is characterized as a denial of admission, standing should be denied; if it is characterized as an opportunity to compete, standing should be available. So, too, in *EKWRO*, standing should be denied if the injury is described as a refusal to grant medical care; but if it is described as a denial of the opportunity to receive such care in a system undistorted by unlawful tax incentives, standing should be granted. When should an injury be treated as a harm to an "opportunity," and when should it be treated as a narrower and more discrete, common law–like one? For discussion, see Sunstein, What's Standing after *Lujan?* Of Citizen Suits, "Injuries," and Article III, 91 Mich. L. Rev. 163 (1992); Fallon, Of Justiciability, Remedies, and Public Law Litigation: Notes on the Jurisprudence of Lyons, 59 N.Y.U. L. Rev. 1 (1984); Nichol, Causation as a Standing Requirement: The Unprincipled Use of Judicial Restraint, 69 Ky. L. Rev. 185 (1980–1981).

In this regard, it is useful to compare Steel Company v. Citizens for a Better Environment, 523 U.S. 83 (1998), with Friends of the Earth v. Laidlaw Environmental Services, 528 U.S. 167 (2000). In *Steel Company*, the plaintiffs, an environmental organization, sued a company that had released discharges of toxic pollutants in excess of those allowed by its permit. After the suit was filed, the company agreed to comply with its duties under its permit. The plaintiffs nonetheless continued the suit, attempting to ensure that the company would pay civil penalties to the U.S. Treasury. The Court held that plaintiffs lacked standing because they could not meet the redressability requirement. There was no showing that the payment of civil penalties to the Treasury would benefit the plaintiffs at all.

In *Laidlaw*, the plaintiffs contended that they used certain areas for swimming and recreational activity, and that these areas had been polluted by the defendants' unlawful discharges. The plaintiffs sought civil damages, partly to "encourage defendants to discontinue current violations and deter them from committing future ones." The Court distinguished *Steel Company* on the ground that "in that case there was no allegation in the complaint of any continuing or imminent violation." Here, by contrast, the violations were "ongoing at the time of the complaint" and "could continue into the future if undeterred." See also Federal Election Commission v. Akins, supra, where the Court rejected the claim that standing should be denied on the ground that "even had the FEC agreed with respondent's view of the law, it would still have decided in the exercise of its discretion not to require AIPAC to produce the information." The Court said: "Agencies often have discretion about whether or not to take a particular action. Yet those adversely affected by a discretionary agency decision generally have standing to complain that the agency based its decision upon an improper legal ground." Consider the view that this holding is inconsistent with the views of the plurality on the issue of redressability in *Lujan*. Is there a way to reconcile the two?

An emerging issue involves the status of "probabilistic injuries." Suppose that, because of an agency's action, someone faces a 1 in 10,000 risk of dying from contaminated food or from air pollution. Should courts conclude that the injury is "too speculative"? Or is the (small) probability of injury enough? Note that many people would be willing to pay some amount of money (say, $50) to eliminate a risk of 1 in 10,000. If a loss of $50 is enough for standing, why not a risk that is its equivalent? But what about a risk of 1 in 100,000? 1 in 1,000,000? The Court has yet to answer these questions.

5. *Congressional power and citizens' suits.* Does *Lujan* mean that Congress is completely without constitutional power to grant standing to citizens as such? If so, what is the source of this conclusion in article III or the relevant history? Consider the view that citizen standing was fairly common in England and the colonies at the time of the framing. See Berger, Standing to Sue in Public Actions: Is It a Constitutional Requirement?, 78 Yale L.J. 816 (1969); Jaffe, Standing in Public Actions, 74 Harv. L. Rev. 1265, 1274 (1961); Sunstein, What's Standing after *Lujan*?, supra. Is *Lujan* an "originalist" opinion? Should it have been?

Compare the following cases after *Lujan*.

(a) The plaintiffs obtain a plane ticket to go to the relevant nations. The implication of *Lujan* is that the injury in fact requirement would be met in that event — but four justices indicated that there would continue to be a problem of redressability.

(b) Congress tries to grant standing to citizens to enforce the environmental law against both private defendants and government officials — but unlike in *Lujan*, it also says that every victorious plaintiff receives a $200 bounty. In Vermont Agency of Natural Resources v. United States, 529 U.S. 765 (2000), the Court held that Congress has the power to create "qui tam" actions, by which citizens can sue to obtain damages on behalf of the United States, to recover damages done to the United States. In a qui tam action, the plaintiff receives money as a kind of bounty. In upholding this action, the Court emphasized the long history of support for its validity. The Court also said that the qui tam action should be understood to create an assignment from the United States to the plaintiff as "assignee," recovering money not as a stranger but as a result of the assignment. But is a simple bounty the same as a qui tam action, in which there is a suit on behalf of the United States?

Recall Federal Election Commission v. Akins, supra, where the Court upheld a legislative grant of standing to "any person" to bring suit to compel disclosure of information from political committees. The Court held that Congress could create an "injury in fact," in the form of deprivation of legally required information, and allow every citizen in the nation to bring suit to redress that injury. Is it sensible to say that the difference between *Akins* and *Lujan* is that in the latter case, unlike the former, there was no injury in fact? (For discussion of the tension between the two cases, see Sunstein, Informational Regulation and

Informational Standing: *Akins* and Beyond, 147 U. Pa. L. Rev. 613 (1999).) Suppose that you have answered "yes" to the question just asked. Now suppose that Congress amends the Endangered Species Act to create a "property interest," on the part of each American, in the continued existence of some or all endangered species — and that Congress then gives each American a right to bring suit against any action, or failure to act, that threatens to infringe that "property interest." Is the case more like *Lujan* or more like *Akins*?

Finally, suppose that members of Congress bring suit to object to a statute that, in their view, intrudes on their powers as representatives. How can they show injury in fact? See Raines v. Byrd, 521 U.S. 811 (1997), where six members brought suit to challenge the Line Item Veto Act, which, in their view, violated the separation of powers. (The Court subsequently agreed; see Clinton v. New York, 524 U.S. 417 (1998).) The Court held that no "personal injury" had been established, a judgment informed by the suggestion that "our standing inquiry has been especially rigorous when reaching the merits of the dispute would force us to decide whether an action taken by one of the other two branches was unconstitutional." In this case, the plaintiffs "have not alleged that they voted for a specific bill, that there were sufficient votes to pass the bill, and that the bill was nonetheless deemed defeated." In this way the Court distinguished Coleman v. Miller, 307 U.S. 433 (1939), where, by a five-to-four vote, standing had been granted to twenty of Kansas's state senators, complaining that the child labor amendment had been unlawfully adopted. The Coleman plaintiffs claimed that with a twenty-twenty split, the amendment would not have been ratified, but that a procedural irregularity, in the form of a tie-breaking vote by the Lieutenant Governor, produced a false and unlawful claim of ratification. "There is a vast difference between the level of vote nullification at issue in *Coleman* and the abstract dilution of institutional legislative power that is alleged here." What, then, must members of Congress show in order to have standing?

The Court distinguished *Raines* and relied on *Coleman* to uphold the standing of the Arizona Legislature in Arizona State Legislature v. Arizona Independent Redistricting Commn., 135 S. Ct. 2652 (2015). At issue was a proposition adopted by Arizona voters through the initiative process that vested redistricting decisions in an independent redistricting commission. The Arizona legislature brought suit, alleging that the proposition violated article I, §4, cl. 1 of the Constitution, which provides that "[the] Times, Places and Manner of holding Elections for Senators and Representatives, shall be prescribed in each state by the Legislature [thereof]." The Arizona legislature maintained that by depriving it of the power to engage in redistricting, the proposition violated its rights. In an opinion by Justice Ginsburg, the Court held that the Legislature had standing to raise this claim. The Court noted that in *Raines* it was significant that the plaintiffs had not been authorized to represent their respective houses of Congress. In contrast, "the Arizona legislature was an institutional plaintiff, asserting an institutional injury, and it commenced this action after authorizing votes in both chambers." Because the proposition would nullify votes by the Legislature on redistricting plans, the Legislature had standing to raise the claim. Justice Scalia, joined by Justice Thomas, dissented on the standing question.

6. Perry *and* Windsor. The Court divided five-to-four on standing questions in two important cases involving same-sex marriage. The facts of United States v. Windsor, 133 S. Ct. 2675 (2013), were as follows. New York recognized the marriage of Edith Windsor and Thea Spyer, who wed in Ontario, Canada, in 2007. Spyer died in 2009, leaving her estate to Windsor, who sought to claim the

federal estate tax exemption for surviving spouses. She was barred from doing so by section 3 of the federal Defense of Marriage Act (DOMA), which defines "marriage" and "spouse" as excluding same-sex partners. Windsor paid $363,053 in estate taxes and sought a refund, which the Internal Revenue Service denied. Windsor brought suit, objecting that DOMA is inconsistent with the Fifth Amendment.

While the case was pending, the Attorney General notified the Speaker of the House of Representatives that the Department of Justice would no longer defend the constitutionality of section 3. In response, the Bipartisan Legal Advisory Group (BLAG) of the House of Representatives sought to intervene in the litigation to defend the constitutionality of section 3. The district court allowed intervention and ruled in Windsor's favor, ordering the Treasury to refund her tax with interest. The court of appeals affirmed. Although the United States agreed with the court's conclusion, it did not comply with the judgment, but instead sought certiorari in the Supreme Court.

In an opinion by Justice Kennedy (joined by Justices Breyer, Ginsburg, Sotomayor, and Kagan), the Court held that there was no standing problem:

> In this case the United States retains a stake sufficient to support Article III jurisdiction on appeal and in proceedings before this Court. The judgment in question orders the United States to pay Windsor the refund she seeks. An order directing the Treasury to pay money is "a real and immediate economic injury," indeed as real and immediate as an order directing an individual to pay a tax. That the Executive may welcome this order to pay the refund if it is accompanied by the constitutional ruling it wants does not eliminate the injury to the national Treasury if payment is made, or to the taxpayer if it is not. The judgment orders the United States to pay money that it would not disburse but for the court's order. The Government of the United States has a valid legal argument that it is injured even if the Executive disagrees with §3 of DOMA, which results in Windsor's liability for the tax. Windsor's ongoing claim for funds that the United States refuses to pay thus establishes a controversy sufficient for Article III jurisdiction. It would be a different case if the Executive had taken the further step of paying Windsor the refund to which she was entitled under the District Court's ruling.

The Court acknowledged that "[a] party who receives all that he has sought generally is not aggrieved by the judgment affording the relief and cannot appeal from it." But it said that this rule "does not have its source in the jurisdictional limitations of Art. III. In an appropriate case, appeal may be permitted [at] the behest of the party who has prevailed on the merits, so long as that party retains a stake in the appeal satisfying the requirements of Art. III."

The Court also noted that there was a risk that the case lacked "concrete adversariness," because the executive branch was in agreement with Windsor. It concluded, however, that this problem involved not article III but prudential considerations, and that those considerations were not sufficient to justify a refusal to rule on the merits:

> In the case now before the Court the attorneys for BLAG present a substantial argument for the constitutionality of §3 of DOMA. BLAG's sharp adversarial presentation of the issues satisfies the prudential concerns that otherwise might counsel against hearing an appeal from a decision with which the principal parties agree. Were this Court to hold that prudential rules require it to dismiss the case, and, in consequence, that the Court of Appeals erred in failing to dismiss it as well,

extensive litigation would ensue. The district courts in 94 districts throughout the Nation would be without precedential guidance not only in tax refund suits but also in cases involving the whole of DOMA's sweep involving over 1,000 federal statutes and a myriad of federal regulations. For instance, the opinion of the Court of Appeals for the First Circuit, addressing the validity of DOMA in a case involving regulations of the Department of Health and Human Services, likely would be vacated with instructions to dismiss, its ruling and guidance also then erased. Rights and privileges of hundreds of thousands of persons would be adversely affected, pending a case in which all prudential concerns about justiciability are absent. [In] these unusual and urgent circumstances, the very term "prudential" counsels that it is a proper exercise of the Court's responsibility to take jurisdiction. For these reasons, the prudential and Article III requirements are met here; and, as a consequence, the Court need not decide whether BLAG would have standing to challenge the District Court's ruling and its affirmance in the Court of Appeals on BLAG's own authority.

Justice Scalia (joined by Chief Justice Roberts and Justice Thomas) dissented. He wrote that "the plaintiff and the Government agree entirely on what should happen in this lawsuit. They agree that the court below got it right; and they agreed in the court below that the court below that one got it right as well. What, then, are we *doing* here?" He added:

What the petitioner United States asks us to do in the case before us is exactly what the respondent Windsor asks us to do: not to provide relief from the judgment below but to say that that judgment was correct. And the same was true in the Court of Appeals: Neither party sought to undo the judgment for Windsor, and so that court should have dismissed the appeal (just as we should dismiss) for lack of jurisdiction. Since both parties agreed with the judgment of the District Court for the Southern District of New York, the suit should have ended there. The further proceedings have been a contrivance, having no object in mind except to elevate a District Court judgment that has no precedential effect in other courts, to one that has precedential effect throughout the Second Circuit, and then (in this Court) precedential effect throughout the United States.

In a separate dissenting opinion, Justice Alito essentially agreed with Justice Scalia with respect to the United States, but concluded that "the House of Representatives, which has authorized BLAG to represent its interests in this matter," suffered injury in fact, because the adverse decision had injured its ability to legislate. "In the narrow category of cases in which a court strikes down an Act of Congress and the Executive declines to defend the Act, Congress both has standing to defend the undefended statute and is a proper party to do so."

Having disposed of the standing issue, the Court reached the merits and held that DOMA was unconstitutional.

In Hollingsworth v. Perry, 133 S. Ct. 2652 (2013), the merits involved the constitutionality of a ballot initiative known as Proposition 8, which amended the California Constitution to define marriage as a union between a man and a woman. Same-sex couples, seeking to marry, filed suit in federal court, challenging Proposition 8 under the fourteenth amendment. After California officials (the named defendants) refused to defend the law, the district court allowed the initiative's official proponents to intervene to defend it. After a trial, the court declared Proposition 8 unconstitutional, and enjoined public officials from enforcing it. Those officials elected not to appeal, but the proponents did so.

The court of appeals certified to the California Supreme Court the question whether official proponents of a ballot initiative have authority to assert the State's interest in defending the constitutionality of the initiative when public officials refuse to do so. The California Supreme Court answered that they did.

Notwithstanding that answer, the Court concluded that the requirements of article III were not met. Chief Justice Roberts (joined by Justices Scalia, Ginsburg, Breyer, and Kagan) explained that the proponents of the law had only a generalized grievance and no "direct stake" in the case. "Their only interest in having the District Court order reversed was to vindicate the constitutional validity of a generally applicable California law." To be sure, the proponents of a ballot proposition have a particular interest under California law, "but only when it comes to the process of enacting the law." After enactment, they "have no 'personal stake' in defending its enforcement that is distinguishable from the general interest of every citizen of California."

The Court acknowledged the proponents' argument that "even if they have no cognizable interest in appealing the District Court's judgment, the State of California does, and they may assert that interest on the State's behalf." But the Court responded that it is "a 'fundamental restriction on our authority' that '[i]n the ordinary course, a litigant must assert his or her own legal rights and interests, and cannot rest a claim to relief on the legal rights or interests of third parties.'" Exceptions to that presumption could not be found here. To the argument that California itself recognized a right here, the Court said that "no matter its reasons, the fact that a State thinks a private party should have standing to seek relief for a generalized grievance cannot override our settled law to the contrary. [We] have never before upheld the standing of a private party to defend the constitutionality of a state statute when state officials have chosen not to. We decline to do so for the first time here."

In dissent, Justice Kennedy (writing for himself and for Justices Thomas, Alito, and Sotomayor) emphasized that "[under] California law, a proponent has the authority to appear in court and assert the State's interest in defending an enacted initiative when the public officials charged with that duty refuse to do so." In his view, that authority is akin to a property right, one that gives rise to injury in fact. "Proponents' authority under state law is not a contrivance. It is not a fictional construct. It is the product of the California Constitution and the California Elections Code." As a matter of state law, the purpose of the initiative process "is undermined if the very officials the initiative process seeks to circumvent are the only parties who can defend an enacted initiative when it is challenged in a legal proceeding."

Is the Court's majority saying that a state lacks the constitutional power to create a legal right to defend the outcome of a referendum? If so, how is its decision consistent with *Akins*? Is *Windsor* consistent with *Perry*?

ELK GROVE UNIFIED SCHOOL DISTRICT v. NEWDOW, 542 U.S. 1 (2004). The plaintiff, Newdow, was the father of a girl who attended elementary school in the Elk Grove Unified School District. Pursuant to state law, every day her teacher led the children in a group recitation of the Pledge of Allegiance. The plaintiff argued that because the pledge contains the words "under God," it constituted religious indoctrination in violation of the first amendment. The court of appeals agreed.

The Supreme Court, however, reversed the court of appeals, holding that Newdow lacked standing. Justice Stevens delivered the opinion of the Court.

"Our standing jurisprudence contains two strands: Article III standing, which enforces the Constitution's case or controversy requirement; and prudential standing, which embodies 'judicially self-imposed limits on the exercise of federal jurisdiction.' Although we have not exhaustively defined the prudential dimensions of the standing doctrine, we have explained that prudential standing encompasses 'the general prohibition on a litigant's raising another person's legal rights, the rule barring adjudication of generalized grievances more appropriately addressed in the representative branches, and the requirement that a plaintiff's complaint fall within the zone of interests protected by the law invoked.'"

He concluded that as a matter of prudence, the Court should decline to adjudicate Newdow's claim:

"[One] of the principal areas in which this Court has customarily declined to intervene is the realm of domestic relations. Long ago we observed that 'the whole subject of the domestic relations of husband and wife, parent and child, belongs to the laws of the States and not to the laws of the United States.' In re Burrus, 136 U.S. 586 (1890). [So] strong is our deference to state law in this area that we have recognized a 'domestic relations exception' that 'divests the federal courts of power to issue divorce, alimony, and child custody decrees.' Ankenbrandt v. Richards, 504 U.S. 6 (1992). We have also acknowledged that it might be appropriate for the federal courts to decline to hear a case involving 'elements of the domestic relationship.' [Thus,] while rare instances arise in which it is necessary to answer a substantial federal question that transcends or exists apart from the family law issue, in general it is appropriate for the federal courts to leave delicate issues of domestic relations to the state courts." In this case, it turned out that although Newdow and Banning (the child's mother) shared legal custody of their daughter, a state-court custody order provided that Banning "makes the final decisions if the two . . . disagree. . . . Newdow's rights, as in many cases touching upon family relations, cannot be viewed in isolation. This case concerns not merely Newdow's interest in inculcating his child with his views on religion, but also the rights of the child's mother as a parent generally and under the Superior Court orders specifically. And most important, it implicates the interests of a young child who finds herself at the center of a highly public debate over her custody, the propriety of a widespread national ritual, and the meaning of our Constitution.

"The interests of the affected persons in this case are in many respects antagonistic. Of course, legal disharmony in family relations is not uncommon, and in many instances that disharmony poses no bar to federal-court adjudication of proper federal questions. What makes this case different is that Newdow's standing derives entirely from his relationship with his daughter, but he lacks the right to litigate as her next friend. [The] interests of this parent and this child are not parallel and, indeed, are potentially in conflict." The Court concluded that although, as a matter of state law, Newdow had a "cognizable right to influence his daughter's religious upbringing," that right had not been impaired by the school board's actions, since "[the] California cases simply do not stand for the proposition that Newdow has a right to dictate to others what they may and may not say to his child respecting religion. . . . The cases speak not at all to the problem of a parent seeking to reach outside the private parent-child sphere to restrain the acts of a third party. A next friend surely could exercise such a right, but the Superior Court's order has deprived Newdow of that status. . . . In our view, it is improper for the federal courts to entertain a claim by a plaintiff whose standing to sue is founded on family law rights that are in dispute when prosecution of the lawsuit may have an adverse effect on the person who is the source of the plaintiff's claimed standing. When hard questions of domestic relations are sure to affect the outcome, the prudent course is for the federal court to stay its hand rather than reach out to resolve a weighty question of federal constitutional law. There is a vast difference between Newdow's right to communicate with his child — which both California law and the First Amendment recognize — and his claimed right to shield his daughter from influences to which she is exposed in school despite the terms of the custody order. We conclude that, having been deprived under California law of the right to sue as next friend, Newdow lacks prudential standing to bring this suit in federal court." In a footnote, the Court rejected Newdow's other asserted bases for standing: that he "at times has himself attended — and will in the future attend — class with his daughter"; that he "has considered teaching elementary school students in [the School District]"; that he "has attended and will continue to attend" school board meetings at which the Pledge is "routinely recited"; and that the school district used tax dollars to implement its pledge policy: "Even if these arguments suffice to establish Article III standing, they do not respond to our prudential concerns. As for taxpayer standing, Newdow does not reside in or pay taxes to the School District; he alleges that he pays taxes to the District only 'indirectly' through his child support payments to Banning. That allegation does not amount to the 'direct dollars-and-cents injury' that our strict taxpayer-standing doctrine requires. Doremus v. Board of Ed. of Hawthorne, 342 U.S. 429 (1952)."

Chief Justice Rehnquist, joined by Justices O'Connor and Thomas, argued that Newdow did have standing: "[Here] is the Court's new prudential standing principle: 'It is improper for the federal courts to entertain a claim by a plaintiff whose standing to sue is founded on family law rights that are in dispute when prosecution of the lawsuit may have an adverse effect on the person who is the source of the plaintiff's claimed standing.' . . .

"The Court does not take issue with the fact that, under California law, respondent retains a right to influence his daughter's religious upbringing and to expose her to his views. But it relies on Banning's view of the merits of this case to diminish respondent's interest, stating that the respondent 'wishes to forestall his daughter's exposure to religious ideas that her mother, who wields a form of veto power, endorses, and to use his parental status to challenge the influences to which his daughter may be exposed in school when he and Banning disagree.' As alleged by respondent and as recognized by the Court of Appeals, respondent wishes to enjoin the School District from endorsing a form of religion inconsistent with his own views because he has a right to expose his daughter to those views without the State's placing its imprimatur on a particular religion. Under the Court of Appeals' construction of California law, Banning's 'veto power' does not override respondent's right to challenge the pledge ceremony. . . .

"Respondent asserts that the School District's pledge ceremony infringes his right under California law to expose his daughter to his religious views. While she is intimately associated with the source of respondent's standing (the father-daughter relationship and respondent's rights thereunder), the daughter is not the source of respondent's standing; instead it is their relationship that provides respondent his standing, which is clear once respondent's interest is properly described. . . .

"Although the Court may have succeeded in confining this novel principle almost narrowly enough to be, like the proverbial excursion ticket — good for this day only — our doctrine of prudential standing should be governed by general principles, rather than ad hoc improvisations."

Note: Prudential Standing

1. *Prudential standing and injury in fact.* Even when article III's standing requirements are met, courts nonetheless sometimes decline to hear a case for "prudential" reasons connected to standing. That is, although there is undeniably an injury in fact, caused by the defendant, and likely to be redressed by a favorable ruling, courts sometimes decline to allow a particular plaintiff to raise the claim. Why doesn't Newdow, as biological father, have a legally protected interest, under the establishment clause, sufficient to permit him to challenge the pledge? Would the standing issue be different if the relevant public school were attempting to indoctrinate his child in a particular religion?

2. *Prudential concerns and the political process.* Consider the following view: The Court worked very hard to avoid deciding this case. It did so because the underlying issue seemed genuinely difficult to some of the justices, and because a ruling in favor of Newdow, while not implausible on the merits, would have been a political catastrophe for the Court. This was a case in which the Court attempted to display the passive virtues to avoid a contestable constitutional ruling that would undoubtedly have divided the nation, especially but not only if the Court had accepted Newdow's argument.

In thinking about the prudence of the Court's decision in *Newdow*, consider that while the case was pending, Congress passed, and the President signed into law, Pub. L. 107-293, "reaffirm[ing] the reference to one Nation under God in the Pledge of Allegiance." And in the fall of 2004, following the Court's decision, the House of Representatives passed H.R. 2028, which would have created a new jurisdictional statute, 28 U.S.C. §1632, providing in pertinent part that "No court created by Act of Congress shall have any jurisdiction, and the Supreme Court shall have no appellate jurisdiction, to hear or decide any question pertaining to the interpretation of, or the validity under the Constitution of, the Pledge of Allegiance . . . or its recitation."

3. *The abandonment of prudential limits?* The Court offered a new account of the foundations of the prudential requirements in Lexmark International v. Static Control Components, 134 S. Ct. 1377 (2014). Static Control Components contended that Lexmark had violated the Lanham Act by engaging in certain false and misleading conduct. In particular, Static Control Components claimed that Lexmark falsely advised companies that it was illegal to use Static Control's products to refurbish cartridges used for printing. Lexmark responded that courts should use "prudential standing" doctrines, and especially the zone-of-interests test, to deny standing to Static Control Components.

The Court unanimously disagreed. In an opinion by Justice Scalia, the Court said that the zone-of-interests test should be understood as posing an issue of statutory construction:

> Whether a plaintiff comes within "the 'zone of interests'" is an issue that requires us to determine, using traditional tools of statutory interpretation, whether a legislatively conferred cause of action encompasses a particular plaintiff's claim. As Judge Silberman of the D.C. Circuit recently observed, "'prudential standing' is a misnomer" as applied to the zone-of-interests analysis, which asks whether "this

particular class of persons ha[s] a right to sue under this substantive statute." [In] sum, the question this case presents is whether Static Control falls within the class of plaintiffs whom Congress has authorized to sue under [the Lanham Act]. In other words, we ask whether Static Control has a cause of action under the statute. That question requires us to determine the meaning of the congressionally enacted provision creating a cause of action. In doing so, we apply traditional principles of statutory interpretation.

In a potentially important footnote, the Court added:

> The zone-of-interests test is not the only concept that we have previously clas-sified as an aspect of "prudential standing" but for which, upon closer inspection, we have found that label inapt. Take, for example, our reluctance to entertain generalized grievances — i.e., suits "claiming only harm to [the plaintiff's] and every citizen's interest in proper application of the Constitution and laws, and seeking relief that no more directly and tangibly benefits him than it does the public at large." Lujan v. Defenders of Wildlife, 504 U.S. 555, 573–574 (1992). While we have at times grounded our reluctance to entertain such suits in the "counsels of prudence" (albeit counsels "close[ly] relat[ed] to the policies reflected in" Article III), Valley Forge Christian College v. Americans United for Separation of Church and State, Inc., 454 U.S. 464, 475 (1982), we have since held that such suits do not present constitutional "cases" or "controversies." They are barred for constitutional reasons, not "prudential" ones.

On the merits, the Court concluded that Static Control did indeed have a right to sue, because the zone-of-interests test is "an appropriate tool for determining who may invoke the cause of action," because that test is not meant to be espe-cially demanding, and because that "lenient approach is an appropriate means of preserving the flexibility of the APA's omnibus judicial-review provision, which permits suit for violations of numerous statutes of varying character that do not themselves include causes of action for judicial review." Under the Lanham Act, a plaintiff must allege an injury to a commercial interest in reputation or sales. Under that test, standing was available here:

> To begin, Static Control's alleged injuries — lost sales and damage to its business reputation — are injuries to precisely the sorts of commercial interests the Act protects. . . . There is no doubt that it is within the zone of interests protected by the statute.
> Static Control also sufficiently alleged that its injuries were proximately caused by Lexmark's misrepresentations. . . . [A]lthough diversion of sales to a direct com-petitor may be the paradigmatic direct injury from false advertising, it is not the only type of injury cognizable under [the Lanham Act].
> First, Static Control alleged that Lexmark disparaged its business and products by asserting that Static Control's business was illegal. When a defendant harms a plaintiff's reputation by casting aspersions on its business, the plaintiff's injury flows directly from the audience's belief in the disparaging statements. As we have observed, a defendant who "'seeks to promote his own interests by telling a known falsehood to or about the plaintiff or his product'" may be said to have proximately caused the plaintiff's harm.
> In addition, Static Control adequately alleged proximate causation by alleging that it designed, manufactured, and sold microchips that both (1) were necessary for, and (2) had no other use than, refurbishing Lexmark toner cartridges. [To] invoke the Lanham Act's cause of action for false advertising, a plaintiff must plead

(and ultimately prove) an injury to a commercial interest in sales or business reputation proximately caused by the defendant's misrepresentations. Static Control has adequately pleaded both elements.

Query: How, exactly, does the Court's formulation of the zone-of-interests test change preexisting law?

4. *Concluding thoughts.* Consider the following view: Standing doctrine went wrong in *Data Processing.* The real question is whether Congress has created a cause of action, not whether there is an "injury in fact" or adequate causation. The existence of an injury in fact is necessary only when Congress has said that people with an injury in fact have standing — as, arguably, Congress did in the Administrative Procedure Act. But what article III requires is a congressional grant of a right to bring suit, not an "injury in fact." It follows that there are few or perhaps no limits on Congress's power to confer standing. It also follows that the Court has both denied standing where it should be allowed and granted it where it should be denied. In any case, the Court has failed to ask the relevant question. That question is not always easy to answer, but it is the right one. It is also the one that prevailed at the time of the framing.

This view is set out in Fletcher, The Structure of Standing, 98 Yale L.J. 221, 229 (1988): "The essence of a true standing question is the following: Does the plaintiff have a legal right to judicial enforcement of an enforceable legal duty? This question should be seen as a question of substantive law, answerable by reference to the statutory or constitutional provision whose protection is invoked." Fletcher goes on to suggest that this question would call for a reexamination of all of current standing law. He also urges that, where a constitutional violation is at issue, the question is whether the constitutional provision confers on the plaintiff a right to relief. Similar views are expressed in Albert, Standing to Challenge Administrative Action: An Inadequate Surrogate for Claims for Relief, 83 Yale L.J. 425 (1974); Currie, Misunderstanding Standing, 1981 Sup. Ct. Rev. 41; Sunstein, What's Standing after *Lujan*?, supra. If Fletcher's view were to prevail, how would the cases in this section come out?

3. *Political Questions*

Baker v. Carr
369 U.S. 186 (1962)

[Voters in Tennessee brought suit challenging a provision enacted in 1901 that apportioned the members of the state General Assembly among the state's ninety-five counties. Under the 1901 standard, representation had been allocated among counties in accordance with the number of qualified voters in each county. But substantial population growth and redistribution over the ensuing years meant that by 1961 legislative districts contained dramatically different numbers of people. The plaintiffs claimed that their voting power was unconstitutionally diluted by the continued use of the 1901 apportionment.]

MR. JUSTICE BRENNAN delivered the opinion of the Court.

[We] hold that this challenge to an apportionment presents no nonjusticiable "political question." . . .

Of course the mere fact that the suit seeks protection of a political right does not mean it presents a political question. Such an objection "is little more than a play upon words." Rather, it is argued that apportionment cases, whatever the actual wording of the complaint, can involve no federal constitutional right except one resting on the guaranty of a republican form of government, and that complaints based on that clause have been held to present political questions which are nonjusticiable.

Our discussion [requires] review of a number of political question cases, in order to expose the attributes of the doctrine — attributes which, in various settings, diverge, combine, appear, and disappear in seeming disorderliness.

We have said that "In determining whether a question falls within [the political question] category, the appropriateness under our system of government of attributing finality to the action of the political departments and also the lack of satisfactory criteria for a judicial determination are dominant considerations." The nonjusticiability of a political question is primarily a function of the separation of powers. Much confusion results from the capacity of the "political question" label to obscure the need for case-by-case inquiry. Deciding whether a matter has in any measure been committed by the Constitution to another branch of government, or whether the action of that branch exceeds whatever authority has been committed, is itself a delicate exercise in constitutional interpretation, and is a responsibility of this Court as ultimate interpreter of the Constitution. . . .

It is apparent that several formulations which vary slightly according to the settings in which the questions arise may describe a political question, although each has one or more elements which identify it as essentially a function of the separation of powers. Prominent on the surface of any case held to involve a political question is found a textually demonstrable constitutional commitment of the issue to a coordinate political department; or a lack of judicially discoverable and manageable standards for resolving it; or the impossibility of deciding without an initial policy determination of a kind clearly for nonjudicial discretion; or the impossibility of a court's undertaking independent resolution without expressing lack of the respect due coordinate branches of government; or an unusual need for unquestioning adherence to a political decision already made; or the potentiality of embarrassment from multifarious pronouncements by various departments on one question.

Unless one of these formulations is inextricable from the case at bar, there should be no dismissal for nonjusticiability on the ground of a political question's presence. The doctrine of which we treat is one of "political questions," not one of "political cases." . . .

But it is argued that this case shares the characteristics of decisions . . . concerning the Constitution's guaranty [of] a republican form of government. [Guaranty] Clause claims involve those elements which define a "political question," and for that reason and no other, they are nonjusticiable. In particular, [the] nonjusticiability of such claims has nothing to do with their touching upon matters of state governmental organization.

Luther v. Borden, [7 How. 1 (1849)], though in form simply an action for damages for trespass was, as Daniel Webster said in opening the argument for the defense, "an unusual case." The defendants, admitting an otherwise tortious breaking and entering, sought to justify their action on the ground that they were agents of the established lawful government of Rhode Island, which State was then under martial law to defend itself from active insurrection; that the plaintiff was engaged in that insurrection; and that they entered under orders to arrest the plaintiff. The case arose "out of the unfortunate political differences which agitated the people of Rhode Island in 1841 and 1842," [and] which had resulted in a situation wherein two groups laid competing claims to recognition as the lawful government. The plaintiff's right to recover depended upon which of the two groups was entitled to such recognition; but the lower court's refusal to receive evidence or hear argument on that issue, its charge to the jury that the earlier established or "charter" government was lawful, and the verdict for the defendants, were affirmed upon appeal to this Court.

Chief Justice Taney's opinion for the Court reasoned as follows: (1) If a court were to hold the defendants' acts unjustified because the charter government had no legal existence during the period in question, it would follow that all of that government's actions — laws enacted, taxes collected, salaries paid, accounts settled, sentences passed — were of no effect; and that "the officers who carried their decisions into operation [were] answerable as trespassers, if not in some cases as criminals." [A] decision for the plaintiff would inevitably have produced some significant measure of chaos. . . .

(2) No state court had recognized as a judicial responsibility settlement of the issue of the locus of state governmental authority. Indeed, the courts of Rhode Island had in several cases held that "it rested with the political power to decide whether the charter government had been displaced or not," and that that department had acknowledged no change.

(3) Since "[t]he question relates, altogether, to the constitution and laws of [the] . . . State," the courts of the United States had to follow the state courts' decisions unless there was a federal constitutional ground for overturning them.

(4) No provision of the Constitution could be or had been invoked for this purpose except Art. IV, §4, the Guaranty Clause. Having already noted the absence of standards whereby the choice between governments could be made by a court acting independently, Chief Justice Taney now found further textual and practical reasons for concluding that, if any department of the United States was empowered by the Guaranty Clause to resolve the issue, it was not the judiciary:

> Under this article of the Constitution it rests with Congress to decide what government is the established one in a State. . . .
>
> [After] the President has acted and called out the militia, is a Circuit Court of the United States authorized to inquire whether his decision was right? . . . If the judicial power extends so far, the guarantee contained in the Constitution of the United States is a guarantee of anarchy, and not of order. . . .

Clearly, several factors were thought by the Court in *Luther* to make the question there "political": the commitment to the other branches of the decision as to which is the lawful state government; the unambiguous action by the President, in recognizing the charter government as the lawful authority; the need for finality in the executive's decision; and the lack of criteria by which a court could determine which form of government was republican.

But the only significance that *Luther* could have for our immediate purposes is in its holding that the Guaranty Clause is not a repository of judicially manageable standards which a court could utilize independently in order to identify a State's lawful government.

We come, finally, to the ultimate inquiry whether our precedents as to what constitutes a nonjusticiable "political question" bring the case before us under the umbrella of that doctrine. A natural beginning is to note whether any of the common characteristics which we have been able to identify and label descriptively are present. We find none: The question here is the consistency of state action with the Federal Constitution. We have no question decided, or to be decided, by a political branch of government coequal with this Court. Nor do we risk embarrassment of our government abroad, or grave disturbance at home if we take issue with Tennessee as to the constitutionality of her action here challenged. Nor need the appellants, in order to succeed in this action, ask the Court to enter upon policy determinations for which judicially manageable standards are lacking. Judicial standards under the Equal Protection Clause are well developed and familiar, and it has been open to courts since the enactment of the Fourteenth Amendment to determine, if on the particular facts they must, that a discrimination reflects no policy, but simply arbitrary and capricious action.

This case does, in one sense, involve the allocation of political power within a State, and the appellants might conceivably have added a claim under the Guaranty Clause. Of course, as we have seen, any reliance on that clause would be futile. But because any reliance on the Guaranty Clause could not have succeeded it does not follow that appellants may not be heard on the equal protection claim which in fact they tender. True, it must be clear that the Fourteenth Amendment claim is not so enmeshed with those political question elements which render Guaranty Clause claims nonjusticiable as actually to present a political question itself. But we have found that not to be the case here.

[Reversed and remanded.]

MR. JUSTICE FRANKFURTER, whom MR. JUSTICE HARLAN joins, dissenting. The Court today reverses a uniform course of decision established by a dozen cases, including one by which the very claim now sustained was unanimously rejected only five years ago. The impressive body of rulings thus cast aside reflected the equally uniform course of our political history regarding the relationship between population and legislative representation — a wholly different matter from denial of the franchise to individuals because of race, color, religion or sex. [Disregard] of inherent limits in the effective exercise of the Court's "judicial Power" not only presages the futility of judicial intervention in the essentially political conflict of forces by which the relation between population and representation has time out of mind been and now is determined. It may well impair the Court's position as the ultimate organ of "the supreme Law of the Land" in that vast range of legal problems, often strongly entangled in popular feeling, on which this Court must pronounce. The Court's authority — possessed of neither the purse nor the sword — ultimately rests on sustained public confidence in its moral sanction. Such feeling must be nourished by the Court's complete detachment, in fact and in appearance, from political entanglements and by abstention from injecting itself into the clash of political forces in political settlements. . . .

[There should be] a frank acknowledgment that there is not under our Constitution a judicial remedy for every political mischief, for every undesirable exercise of legislative power. [Appeal] must be to an informed, civically militant electorate. In a democratic society like ours, relief must come through an aroused popular conscience that sears the conscience of the people's representatives. In any event there is nothing judicially more unseemly nor more self-defeating than for this Court to make in terrorem pronouncements, to indulge in merely empty rhetoric, sounding a word of promise to the ear, sure to be disappointing to the hope.

[From] its earliest opinions this Court has consistently recognized a class of controversies which do not lend themselves to judicial standards and judicial remedies. . . .

1. The cases concerning war or foreign affairs, for example, are usually explained by the necessity of the country's speaking with one voice in such matters. While this concern alone undoubtedly accounts for many of the decisions, others do not fit the pattern. It would hardly embarrass the conduct of war were this Court to determine, in connection with private transactions between litigants, the date upon which war is to be deemed terminated. But the Court has refused to do so. [A] controlling factor in such cases is that [there] exists no standard ascertainable [by] reference to which a political decision affecting the question at issue between the parties can be judged. . . .

2. The Court has been particularly unwilling to intervene in matters concerning the structure and organization of the political institutions of the States. The abstention from judicial entry into such areas has been greater even than that which marks the Court's ordinary approach to issues of state power challenged under broad federal guarantees. . . .

3. The cases involving Negro disfranchisement are no exception to the principle of avoiding federal judicial intervention into matters of state government in the absence of an explicit and clear constitutional imperative. For here the controlling command of Supreme Law is plain and unequivocal. An end of discrimination against the Negro was the compelling motive of the Civil War Amendments. . . .

4. The Court has refused to exercise its jurisdiction to pass on "abstract questions of political power, of sovereignty, of government." [The] "political question" doctrine, in this aspect, reflects the policies underlying the requirement of "standing": that the litigant who would challenge official action must claim infringement of an interest particular and personal to himself, as distinguished from a cause of dissatisfaction with the general frame and functioning of government — a complaint that the political institutions are awry. . . . [Courts] are not fit instruments of decision where what is essentially at stake is the composition of those large contests of policy traditionally fought out in non-judicial forums, by which governments and the actions of governments are made and unmade. . . .

5. The influence of these converging considerations — the caution not to undertake decision where standards meet for judicial judgment are lacking, the reluctance to interfere with matters of state government in the absence of an unquestionable and effectively enforceable mandate, the unwillingness to make courts arbiters of the broad issues of political organization historically committed to other institutions and for whose adjustment the judicial process is ill-adapted — has been decisive of the settled line of cases, reaching back more than a century, which holds that Art. IV, §4, of the Constitution, guaranteeing to the States "a Republican Form of Government," is not enforceable through the courts. . . .

The present case involves all of the elements that have made the Guarantee Clause cases nonjusticiable. It is, in effect, a Guarantee Clause claim masquerading under a different label. . . .

[Appellants] invoke the right to vote[, but] they are permitted to vote and their votes are counted. [Their] complaint is simply that the representatives are not sufficiently numerous or powerful. [It] will add a virulent source of friction and tension in Federal-state relations to embroil the Federal judiciary in [apportionment battles]. . . .

[Concurring opinions by Justices Douglas, Clark, and Stewart are omitted here. Justice Clark stressed that Tennessee's apportionment scheme was "a crazy quilt." A dissenting opinion by Justice Harlan, arguing that no federal constitutional right was at stake, is also omitted.]

Note: The Bases for Finding a Political Question

Baker identifies a variety of bases for finding an issue nonjusticiable. Do these various reasons for finding a case nonjusticiable add up to a coherent "political question" doctrine?

1. A *"textually demonstrable commitment"* of the issue to one of the political branches. In Marbury v. Madison, 5 U.S. (1 Cranch) 137, 166 (1803), Chief Justice Marshall wrote that in cases where "the executive possesses a constitutional or legal discretion, nothing can be more perfectly clear than that [his] acts are only politically examinable." Does this state a doctrine of nonjusticiability or is it instead actually a judgment on the merits?

Consider an application of this strand of the political question doctrine. In Nixon v. United States, 506 U.S. 224 (1993), Nixon, a former district court judge who was convicted at a criminal trial of making false statements before a federal grand jury, sought judicial review of his subsequent removal from office. He claimed that the Senate had failed to "try" him within the meaning of the impeachment clause of article I, section 3, which provides that the Senate "shall have the sole Power to try all Impeachments." Upon receiving articles of impeachment from the House, the Senate referred the matter to a committee, which reported to the full body. Although the committee presented the Senate with a transcript of the proceedings and Nixon was permitted to make a personal appeal to the Senate, the full body did not receive any of the evidence.

Chief Justice Rehnquist's opinion for the Court held that Nixon's challenge presented a nonjusticiable political question. Nixon had argued that the word "try" required that he receive the kind of process normally accorded in a criminal trial. But the Court disagreed:

The word "try," both in 1787 and later, has considerably broader meanings than those to which petitioner would limit it. [Based] on the variety of definitions, [we] cannot say that the Framers used the word [as] an implied limitation on the method by which the Senate might proceed in trying impeachments. . . .

The conclusion that the use of the word "try" [lacks] sufficient precision to afford any judicially manageable standard of review of the Senate's actions is fortified by the existence of the three very specific requirements that the Constitution does impose on the Senate when trying impeachments: the members must be under oath, a two-thirds vote is required to convict, and the Chief Justice presides when the President is tried. These limitations are quite precise, and their nature suggests that the Framers did not intend to impose additional limitations on the form of the Senate proceedings by the use of the word ["try"].

Given the fact that the impeachment clause also accorded the Senate "sole" power to try impeachments, the Court concluded that "the Senate alone shall have authority to determine whether an individual should be acquitted or convicted."

> In addition to the textual commitment argument, we are persuaded that the lack of finality and the difficulty of fashioning relief counsel against justiciability. [Opening] the door of judicial review to the procedures used by the Senate in trying impeachments would "expose the political life of the country to months, or perhaps years, of chaos." This lack of finality would manifest itself most dramatically if the President were impeached. The legitimacy of any successor, and hence his effectiveness, would be impaired severely, not merely while the judicial process was running its course, but during any retrial that a differently constituted Senate might conduct if its first judgment of conviction were invalidated. Equally uncertain is the question of what relief a court may give other than simply setting aside the judgment of conviction. Could it order the reinstatement of a convicted federal judge, or order Congress to create an additional judgeship if the seat had been filled in the interim? . . .

Justice Souter concurred in the judgment, reserving the question whether courts might intervene in impeachment proceedings under some circumstances:

> One can . . . envision different and unusual circumstances that might justify a more searching review of impeachment proceedings. If the Senate were to act in a manner seriously threatening the integrity of its results, convicting, say, upon a coin-toss, or upon a summary determination that an officer of the United States was simply "a bad guy," judicial interference might well be appropriate. In such circumstances, the Senate's action might be so far beyond the scope of its constitutional authority, and the consequent impact on the Republic so great, as to merit a judicial response despite the prudential concerns that would ordinarily counsel silence.

By contrast, Justice White, joined by Justice Blackmun, concurred in the judgment, but because they thought, on the merits, that Nixon's challenge to the procedures used to try him lacked merit.

Justice Stevens also concurred in the decision.

Consider the view that invocation of political question doctrine in cases such as *Nixon* "does no work not already done by substantive provisions of constitutional law." Seidman, The Secret Life of the Political Question Doctrine, 37 J. Marshall L. Rev. 441, 444 (2004). On this view,

> It should be obvious that [the Court's] holding amounts to a determination that Nixon's constitutional rights were not violated. Like many constitutional provisions, the impeachment clause affords Congress discretion — in this case, discretion in its choice of methods by which an impeached official is "tried." Because the Senate's conduct fell within this zone of discretion, Nixon had no ground for complaint. Had the Senate's conduct fallen outside the zone of discretion, it would have "transgressed identifiable textual limits." This transgression, in turn, would have meant that there were "judicially discoverable and manageable standards" — viz., the textual limits. Moreover, the textual limits themselves would have demonstrated that there was no textual commitment permitting the Senate to use this method of trying impeachments. Thus, Nixon's case posed a political

question only because he lost. If he had had a valid claim on the merits, the political question doctrine would not have shielded it from judicial vindication.

Id. at 446–447. See also Henkin, Is There a Political Question Doctrine?, 85 Yale L.J. 597 (1976).

Consider also whether prudential concerns, rather than textual commitment, are driving the Court's analysis. Does the Court's reference to the possible implications of judicial review of a presidential impeachment shed light on this issue? Article II, section 4 provides that the President "shall be removed from Office on Impeachment for, and Conviction of, Treason, Bribery, or other high Crimes and Misdemeanors." Suppose that the House were to impeach, and the Senate were to convict, a President because Congress disagrees with a policy choice the President has made, or because, to use Justice Souter's phraseology, it decides, for partisan reasons, that the President is "a bad guy."

In 1998, the House of Representatives impeached President Clinton. Both of the articles of impeachment arose out of the President's involvement as a defendant in a lawsuit alleging he had sexually harassed a state employee when he was governor of Arkansas. The articles of impeachment charged that he had lied during the lawsuit and during a subsequent grand jury investigation and had obstructed justice. Suppose that President Clinton had objected, in court, that the impeachment was unconstitutional, because not telling the truth in a civil deposition involving his conduct prior to becoming President did not amount to a high crime or misdemeanor within the meaning of the Constitution. Would his claim have been justiciable? Would permitting litigation of that question pose serious dangers to the operation of the government?

President Clinton was acquitted by the Senate. Suppose in a future case that the President were to be convicted on the basis of articles of impeachment that the Court believed did not set out a high crime or misdemeanor. Could the Court order a President to be reinstated?

Contrast *Nixon* with Powell v. McCormack, 395 U.S. 486 (1969). *Powell* involved a House resolution that forbade Adam Clayton Powell from taking his seat in the House of Representatives because of a finding that Powell had, among other things, "wrongfully diverted House funds for the use of others and himself" and had "made false reports on expenditures of foreign currency to the Committee on House Administration." Noting that he satisfied the age, citizenship, and residence requirements of article I, section 2, clause 2, Powell sued various members and officers of the House, including Speaker John McCormack, seeking a declaration that his exclusion was unconstitutional.

Article I, section 5, clause 1 states that "each House shall be the Judge of the ... Qualifications of its own Members." Faced with a claim that the qualifications clause revealed a textually demonstrable commitment to the House of ·the power to set qualifications for membership and to judge whether those qualifications had been met, the Court explained that:

> [if] examination of §5 disclosed that the Constitution gives the House judicially unreviewable power to set qualifications for membership and to judge whether prospective members meet those qualifications, further review of the House determination might well be barred by the political question doctrine. On the other hand, if the Constitution gives the House power to judge only whether elected members possess the three standing qualifications set forth in the Constitution,

further consideration would be necessary to determine whether any of the other formulations of the political question doctrine are inextricable from the case at bar.

In other words, whether there is a "textually demonstrable constitutional commitment of the issue to a coordinate political department" of government and what is the scope of such commitment are questions we must resolve for the first time in this case. . . .

Our examination of the relevant historical materials leads us to the conclusion that [Powell is] correct and that the Constitution leaves the House without authority to exclude any person, duly elected by his constituents, who meets all the requirements for membership expressly prescribed in the Constitution.

[Respondents'] alternate contention is that the case presents a political question because judicial resolution of petitioners' claim would produce a "potentially embarrassing confrontation between coordinate branches" of the Federal Government. But, as our interpretation of Art. I, §5, discloses, a determination of petitioner Powell's right to sit would require no more than an interpretation of the Constitution. Such a determination falls within the traditional role accorded courts to interpret the law, and does not involve a "lack of the respect due [a] coordinate [branch] of government," nor does it involve an "initial policy determination of a kind clearly for nonjudicial discretion." [Baker v. Carr.]

2. *The political question doctrine and foreign affairs.* A substantial number of "political question" cases have been connected in some way to foreign affairs, and even when the Court does review a claim of unconstitutionality in that context, it is often quite deferential to the President and Congress. How might this phenomenon be justified? Is it a textual argument, in that some of the very few specified powers of the executive under article II involve the conduct of foreign affairs, or is the argument more functional? Perhaps it is because the costs of error on the part of the Court are unusually high, and because the courts' expertise and accountability are low. Or is there something distinctive about foreign affairs that makes it more important for the nation to speak with one voice?

Consider in this regard Goldwater v. Carter, 444 U.S. 996 (1979). At the end of the Chinese Revolution, both the Republic of China (ROC), headquartered in Taiwan, and the People's Republic of China (PRC), which controlled the mainland, claimed to be the sole legitimate government of China. The United States sided with the ROC, and in 1954 signed a mutual defense treaty, which was approved by the Senate in 1955. Article X of the treaty provided that it would remain in force "indefinitely," but gave either party the ability to terminate the treaty "one year after notice has been given to the other Party." In the 1970s, the United States began to pursue normalization of relations with the PRC. The PRC pressed the United States to withdraw its various support for the ROC, including the mutual defense treaty.

In September 1978 Congress passed and the President signed an act containing a provision stating that "[it] is the sense of the Congress that there should be prior consultation between the Congress and the executive branch on any proposed policy changes affecting the continuation in force of the Mutual Defense Treaty of 1954." Nonetheless, on December 15, 1978, President Carter announced that the United States would recognize the PRC as the sole government of China, would withdraw recognition from the ROC, and would terminate the mutual defense treaty at the end of the one-year notice period.

Several senators and representatives (along with one former senator) brought suit, arguing that the President could not terminate the treaty without the advice and consent of the Senate or the approval of both houses of Congress. The plaintiffs argued that the President's unilateral notice of termination "violated their legislative right to be consulted and to vote on the termination and also impaired the effectiveness of prior votes approving the 1954 Mutual Defense Treaty." The district court found that the current legislators had standing and that the case did not present a nonjusticiable political question. Reaching the merits, it granted summary judgment to the plaintiffs. The court of appeals agreed that the legislators had standing — because the President's action had deprived the senators of the right to vote on the question whether the treaty should be terminated — but held on the merits that the President was entitled to terminate the treaty without congressional approval.

The Supreme Court summarily vacated the judgment of the court of appeals and remanded the case with directions to dismiss the complaint. Justice Rehnquist, joined by Chief Justice Burger, and Justices Stewart and Stevens, wrote an opinion concurring in the judgment:

> I am of the view that the basic question presented by the petitioners in this case is "political" and therefore nonjusticiable because it involves the authority of the President in the conduct of our country's foreign relations and the extent to which the Senate or the Congress is authorized to negate the action of the President. . . .
>
> Here, while the Constitution is express as to the manner in which the Senate shall participate in the ratification of a treaty, it is silent as to that body's participation in the abrogation of a treaty. [I]n] light of the absence of any constitutional provision governing the termination of a treaty, and the fact that different termination procedures may be appropriate for different treaties the instant case in my view also "must surely be controlled by political standards." I think that the justifications for concluding that the question here is political in nature are [especially] compelling . . . because it involves foreign relations — specifically a treaty commitment to use military force in the defense of a foreign government if attacked.
>
> [Here we] are asked to settle a dispute between coequal branches of our Government, each of which has resources available to protect and assert its interests, resources not available to private litigants outside the judicial forum. Moreover, [the] effect of this action, as far as we can tell, is "entirely external to the United States, and [falls] within the category of foreign affairs." Finally, as already noted, the situation presented here is closely akin to that presented in *Coleman*, where the Constitution spoke only to the procedure for ratification of an amendment, not to its rejection.

Justice Powell wrote a separate concurring opinion:

> Although I agree with the result reached by the Court, I would dismiss the complaint as not ripe for judicial review. . . .
>
> Prudential considerations persuade me that a dispute between Congress and the President is not ready for judicial review unless and until each branch has taken action asserting its constitutional authority. . . . The Judicial Branch should not decide issues affecting the allocation of power between the President and Congress until the political branches reach a constitutional impasse. Otherwise, we would encourage small groups or even individual Members of Congress to seek judicial resolution of issues before the normal political process has the opportunity to resolve the conflict.
>
> In this case, a few Members of Congress claim that the President's action in terminating the treaty with Taiwan has deprived them of their constitutional role with respect to a change in the supreme law of the land. Congress has taken no

official action. In the present posture of this case, we do not know whether there ever will be an actual confrontation between the Legislative and Executive Branches. Although the Senate has considered a resolution declaring that Senate approval is necessary for the termination of any mutual defense treaty . . . no final vote has been taken on the resolution. It cannot be said that either the Senate or the House has rejected the President's claim. If the Congress chooses not to confront the President, it is not our task to do so.

In response to Justice Rehnquist's assertion that the case involved a nonjusticiable political question, Justice Powell replied:

[No] constitutional provision explicitly confers upon the President the power to terminate treaties. Further, Art. II, §2, of the Constitution authorizes the President to make treaties with the advice and consent of the Senate. Article VI provides that treaties shall be a part of the supreme law of the land. These provisions add support to the view that the text of the Constitution does not unquestionably commit the power to terminate treaties to the President alone.

[There] is no "lack of judicially discoverable and manageable standards for resolving" this case; nor is a decision impossible "without an initial policy determination of a kind clearly for nonjudicial discretion." We are asked to decide whether the President may terminate a treaty under the Constitution without congressional approval. Resolution of the question may not be easy, but it only requires us to apply normal principles of interpretation to the constitutional provisions at issue. The present case involves neither review of the President's activities as Commander in Chief nor impermissible interference in the field of foreign affairs. [This] case "touches" foreign relations, but the question presented to us concerns only the constitutional division of power between Congress and the President.

[Interpretation] of the Constitution does not imply lack of respect for a coordinate branch. If the President and the Congress had reached irreconcilable positions, final disposition of the question presented by this case would eliminate, rather than create, multiple constitutional interpretations. The specter of the Federal Government brought to a halt because of the mutual intransigence of the President and the Congress would require this Court to provide a resolution pursuant to our duty "to say what the law is."

Justice Brennan would have affirmed the court of appeals' decision on the merits:

In stating that this case presents a nonjusticiable "political question," Mr. Justice Rehnquist, in my view, profoundly misapprehends the political-question principle as it applies to matters of foreign relations. Properly understood, the political-question doctrine restrains courts from reviewing an exercise of foreign policy judgment by the coordinate political branch to which authority to make that judgment has been "constitutional[ly] commit[ted]." But the doctrine does not pertain when a court is faced with the antecedent question whether a particular branch has been constitutionally designated as the repository of political decisionmaking power. The issue of decisionmaking authority must be resolved as a matter of constitutional law, not political discretion; accordingly, it falls within the competence of the courts.

The constitutional question raised here is prudently answered in narrow terms. Abrogation of the defense treaty with Taiwan was a necessary incident to Executive recognition of the Peking Government, because the defense treaty was predicated upon the now-abandoned view that the Taiwan Government was the only legitimate political authority in China. Our cases firmly establish that the Constitution commits to the President alone the power to recognize, and withdraw recognition

from, foreign regimes. That mandate being clear, our judicial inquiry into the
treaty rupture can go no further.

Justices Blackmun and White believed that the case should have been set for
plenary consideration, after full briefing and oral argument. Justice Marshall
concurred in the judgment without explanation.

Compare *Goldwater* to Zivotofsky ex rel. Zivotofsky v. Clinton, 566 U.S. 189
(2012). A federal statute provides that Americans born in Jerusalem may have
"Israel" listed as their place of birth on their passports. The United States has
never recognized Jerusalem as Israel's capital, and the executive branch has
consistently claimed that the statute unconstitutionally infringes on the executive
power over foreign affairs and to determine the terms on which recognition is
given to foreign states. Instead of complying with the statute, the State Department directs that passports refer to "Jerusalem" as the place of birth. Zivotofsky
sued to enforce his statutory rights, but the court of appeals held that the suit was
barred by the political question doctrine.

In an eight-to-one decision written by Chief Justice Roberts, the Supreme
Court reversed:

> The lower courts ruled that this case involves a political question because deciding
> Zivotofsky's claim would force the Judicial Branch to interfere with the President's
> exercise of constitutional power committed to him alone. The District Court
> understood Zivotofsky to ask the courts to "decide the political status of Jerusalem."
> [This] misunderstands the issue presented. Zivotofsky does not ask the courts to
> determine whether Jerusalem is the capital of Israel. He instead seeks to determine
> whether he may vindicate his statutory right [to] choose to have Israel recorded on
> his passport as his place of birth. . . .
>   The federal courts are not being asked to supplant a foreign policy decision of the
> political branches with the courts' own unmoored determination of what United
> States policy toward Jerusalem should be. Instead, Zivotofsky requests that the
> courts enforce a specific statutory right. . . .
>   [The] only real question for the courts is whether the statute is
> constitutional. . . .
>   [Determining] the constitutionality of [the statute] involves deciding whether
> the statute impermissibly intrudes upon Presidential powers under the Constitu-
> tion. If so, the law must be invalidated and Zivotofsky's case should be dismissed for
> failure to state a claim. If, on the other hand, the statute does not trench on the
> President's powers, then the Secretary must be ordered to issue Zivotofsky a passport
> that complies with [the statute]. Either way, the political question doctrine is not
> implicated.

The Court remanded the case to the court of appeals to rule in the first instance
on the constitutionality of the statute.

Does the Court's reasoning successfully distinguish *Nixon*? Just as the issue in
Zivotofsky was not the political status of Jerusalem, so, too, the issue in *Nixon* was
not whether Judge Nixon should be impeached. Are the cases different because
Zivotofsky relied on a statute, whereas *Nixon* relied on a provision in the Constitution? Consider in this regard Justice Sotomayor's opinion in *Zivotofsky* concurring in part and concurring in the judgment:

> [If] Congress passed a statute [purporting] to award financial relief to those improp-
> erly "tried" of impeachment offenses[, adjudication of] claims under such a statute

would require a court to resolve the very same issue we found nonjusticiable in *Nixon*. Such examples are atypical, but they suffice to show that the foreclosure altogether of political question analysis in statutory cases is unwarranted.

Consider also Justice Breyer's dissent:

Four sets of prudential considerations, taken together, lead me to [the conclusion that a court should not decide the case].

First, the issue before us arises in the field of foreign affairs. . . .

Second, if the courts must answer the constitutional question before us, they may well have to evaluate the foreign policy implications of foreign policy decisions. . . .

Third, the countervailing interest in obtaining judicial resolution of the constitutional determination are not particularly strong ones. Zivotofsky does not assert the kind of interest, e.g., an interest in property or bodily integrity, which courts have traditionally sought to protect. [Nor], importantly, does he assert an interest in vindicating a basic right of the kind that the Constitution grants individuals. . . .

Fourth, insofar as the controversy reflects different foreign policy views among the political branches of Government, those branches have nonjudicial methods of working out their differences.

Justice Alito filed a separate opinion concurring in the judgment.

Consider the following case: The President initiates a war in circumstances in which he is not constitutionally authorized to do so. (On the question of presidential warmaking authority, see Chapter 4, section C1, infra.) If a declaration or injunction is sought, is judicial review available? Some of these issues arose in the context of the Vietnam War. See Mora v. McNamara, 389 U.S. 934 (1967) (Stewart, J., dissenting from denial of certiorari in case involving legality of Vietnam War); Orlando v. Laird, 443 F.2d 1039 (2d Cir. 1971) (finding some issues raised by Vietnam War to be justiciable). See generally Tigar, The "Political Question" Doctrine and Foreign Relations, 17 UCLA L. Rev. 1135 (1970); Velvel, The War in Viet Nam: Unconstitutional, Justiciable, and Jurisdictionally Attackable, 16 Kan. L. Rev. 449 (1968).

Are political safeguards sufficient in this context? See J. Ely, War and Responsibility: Constitutional Lessons of Vietnam and Its Aftermath 55–56 (1993) (arguing that the Court's first duty is "to try to fashion manageable standards" for deciding whether the President's use of military force complies with constitutional restrictions).

3. *Justiciable standards.* The primary ground on which the Court has found a case to involve a nonjusticiable political question is that there are no "judicially cognizable standards" by which to assess the claim of unconstitutionality. This understanding means that, in order to say whether there is a political question, the court has to examine both the relevant constitutional provision and the plaintiff's legal claim: Does the former set out criteria by which a court can assess the latter? If it does not, the question is labeled "political." Note also that in cases in which there are no legal standards for assessing a claim of unconstitutionality, there is no tension between the political question doctrine and Marbury v. Madison. The Court retains the authority to "say what the law is." The reason the case is nonjusticiable is that the law does not say anything that is relevant to the particular dispute.

For an example of the Court's treatment of this branch of the political question doctrine, see Caperton v. A.T. Massey Coal Co., 556 U.S. 868 (2009), where the Court, in an opinion by Justice Kennedy, held that the due process clause required a state supreme court justice to recuse himself from a case involving an individual who had spent roughly $3 million in support of the justice's election. The Court found that the applicable standard was whether

> there is a serious risk of actual bias — based on objective and reasonable perceptions — [that] a person with a personal stake in a particular case had a significant and disproportionate influence in placing the judge on the case by raising funds or directing the judge's election campaign when the case was pending or imminent. The inquiry centers on the contribution's relative size in comparison to the total amount of money contributed to the campaign, the total amount spent in the election, and the apparent effect such contribution had on the outcome of the election. . . .
>   It is true that extreme cases often test the bounds of established legal principles, and sometimes no administrable standard may be available to address the perceived wrong. But it is also true that extreme cases are more likely to cross constitutional limits, requiring this Court's intervention and formulation of objective standards.

In a dissenting opinion, Chief Justice Roberts asserted that "the standard the majority articulates [fails] to provide clear, workable guidance for future cases," and provided a numbered list of forty questions he claimed the Court's opinion left open, such as "How much money is too much money?," "Must the judge recuse in cases involving individuals or groups who spent large amounts of money trying unsuccessfully to defeat him?," and "If causation is a pertinent factor, how do we know whether the contribution or expenditure had any effect on the outcome of the election?" He concluded: "The Court's inability to formulate a 'judicially discernible and manageable standard' strongly counsels against the recognition of a novel constitutional right."

Compare the Court's treatment of the justiciable standards problem in *Caperton* with its treatment of the same issue regarding political gerrymandering, discussed at pages 138–141, infra.

4. *Constitutional amendments.* Assume there is some irregularity in the process by which a constitutional amendment is ratified. Should a court declare the amendment ineffective? The principal case here is Coleman v. Miller, 307 U.S. 433 (1939), which involved a child labor amendment to the Constitution proposed by Congress in 1924. Initially, in 1925, the Kansas Legislature rejected the amendment, but in 1937, the state revisited the issue and voted to ratify the amendment. The senators who had voted against ratification brought suit, claiming that because of the passage of time since approval by Congress, the amendment had lost its vitality.

The Court, in an opinion by Chief Justice Hughes, concluded that the case was not justiciable:

> Where are to be found the criteria for such a judicial determination? None are to be found in the Constitution itself. In their endeavor to answer this question petitioners' counsel have suggested that at least two years should be allowed; that six years would not seem to be unreasonably long. [To] this list of variables, counsel add that "the nature and extent of publicity and the activity of the public and of legislatures of the several States in relation to any particular proposal should be taken into consideration." This statement is pertinent, but there are additional

matters to be examined and weighed. [In] short, the question of a reasonable time in many cases would involve, as this case does involve, an appraisal of a great variety of relevant conditions, political, social and economic, which can hardly be said to be within the appropriate range of evidence receivable in a court of justice. [These] conditions are appropriate for the consideration of the political departments of the Government.

Several separate opinions were filed. Justice Black, joined by Justices Roberts, Frankfurter, and Douglas, expressed a somewhat broader view. He wrote that the

Constitution grants Congress exclusive power to control submission of constitutional amendments. [In] the exercise of that power, Congress, of course, is governed by the Constitution. However, whether submission, intervening procedure, or Congressional determination of ratification conforms to the commands of the Constitution, calls for decisions by a "political department" of questions of a type which this Court has frequently designated "political."

Justice Frankfurter expressed the view that the state senators had no standing to bring suit. Justice Butler dissented. In his view, "[article] V impliedly requires amendments submitted to be ratified within a reasonable time after proposal," and "more than a reasonable time had elapsed" in this case. To what extent should *Coleman* be read to immunize the amendment process from judicial supervision?

Consider the history of the twenty-seventh amendment, which requires that congressional pay raises take effect only after an election has intervened. The amendment had been among the first proposed by James Madison and sent to the states for ratification by the first Congress. Five states ratified the amendment in 1789–1791 and one in 1873. From 1978 on, ratifications gradually accumulated, and the Michigan legislature became the thirty-eighth state to ratify the amendment on May 7, 1992, over two hundred years after it was proposed.

Is the amendment now part of the Constitution? A federal statute provides that the National Archivist must certify the receipt of a sufficient number of ratifications, after which a constitutional amendment becomes "valid." If the Archivist refused to so certify on the ground that there was insufficient indication of contemporaneous consensus on the amendment, who would have standing to challenge that refusal? If the Archivist did so certify, who might have standing to challenge that decision and to make the ensuing claim that the amendment was unlawfully included in the Constitution? In any event, is certification necessary under the Constitution?

Suppose no one — member of the public or member of Congress — has standing to raise the question whether the amendment was part of the Constitution and the Supreme Court never answers that question. Is it meaningful to say that the amendment is (or is not) part of the Constitution in the same way that the third amendment, or the guaranty clause, is? Suppose Congress adopts the practice of deferring the effective date of pay raises, consistent with the amendment. Does that strengthen or weaken the claim that the amendment is part of the Constitution?

The Office of Legal Counsel in the Department of Justice issued an opinion concluding that the amendment was ratified pursuant to article V and is accordingly now part of the Constitution and that the Archivist was required to publish the amendment along with a certification that the amendment was now part of the Constitution. See http://www.usdoj.gov/olc/congress.17.htm.

In thinking through these questions, consider Dellinger, The Legitimacy of Constitutional Change: Rethinking the Amendment Process, 97 Harv. L. Rev. 386, 397–398, 411 (1983), which labels *Coleman* an "aberration" and contends that

[the] assumption that judicial review is precluded by the existence of the exclusive power of the promulgating Congress to determine the validity of ratifications is, in my view, wholly unwarranted. Neither the text of the Constitution nor prior congressional practice nor judicial precedent supports this bestowal of exclusive power on Congress. [Whether] or not judicial review of Article V issues would materially advance larger goals of the amendment process, such review is justified as an initial matter by the same considerations that have made judicial review an accepted part of the Constitution since Marbury v. Madison.

Dellinger stresses the increased certainty that would result from some judicial supervision of the amendment process.

Compare Tribe, A Constitution We Are Amending: In Defense of a Restrained Judicial Role, 97 Harv. L. Rev. 433, 435–446 (1983). Tribe identifies

the danger [of] having the Supreme Court closely "oversee the very constitutional process used to reverse its decision." [The] resort to amendment — to constitutional politics as opposed to constitutional law — should be taken as a sign that the legal system has come to a point of discontinuity, a point at which something less radical than revolution but distinctly more radical than ordinary legal evolution is called for. To say that at such a moment in history we should necessarily conduct our legal business as usual, seeking certainty and harmony rather than tolerating discord, is to miss the very essence of the event at hand.

5. *Miscellaneous cases.* In many cases, of course, the Court has reached the merits of a constitutional controversy notwithstanding the implications for foreign affairs, the high stakes, or the fact of interbranch disagreement. In INS v. Chadha, 462 U.S. 919 (1983), the Court rejected a political question challenge to its power to consider the legality of the "legislative veto" — a device, opposed by every President from Woodrow Wilson to Ronald Reagan, by which one House of Congress might "veto" executive action by a majority vote. The Court observed that the controversy "may, in a sense, be termed 'political.' But the presence of constitutional issues with significant political overtones does not automatically invoke the political question doctrine. Resolution of litigation challenging the constitutional authority of one of the three branches cannot be evaded by courts because the issues have political implications in the sense urged by Congress."

See also Dames & Moore v. Regan, 453 U.S. 654 (1981) (reaching merits of dispute over legality of President Carter's executive agreement for the release of U.S. hostages in Iran); United States v. Nixon, 418 U.S. 683 (1974) (ordering President Nixon to turn over Watergate tapes); Youngstown Sheet & Tube Co. v. Sawyer, 343 U.S. 579 (1952) (invalidating President Truman's seizure of the steel mills despite President's claim that national emergency required seizure); United States v. Curtiss-Wright Export Corp., 299 U.S. 304 (1936) (reaching merits of congressional delegation of power to President to prohibit sale of arms to countries engaged in armed conflict). In Supreme Court cases involving the war on terror, no serious political question argument has even been raised. See, e.g., Hamdan v. Rumsfeld, 548 U.S. 557 (2006).

6. *The peculiar case of the "Republican Form of Government" clause.* Section 4 of article IV of the Constitution provides that "[the] United States shall guarantee to every State in this Union a Republican Form of Government." Several times this provision has been invoked by private litigants, but as Baker v. Carr suggests, the Supreme Court appears to have definitively determined that the question is not justiciable.

The key case is Luther v. Borden, 7 How. 1 (1849), an action for trespass. *Luther* grew out of the Dorr Rebellion in Rhode Island and a conflict between various people claiming authority to act for the government of Rhode Island. The defendants claimed that the acts charged as a trespass were done under the authority of the charter government during a period of martial law. The plaintiffs claimed that the charter government was unlawful. The case thus turned on which of the two groups was entitled to recognition as the lawful government.

The Court responded:

[It] rests with congress to decide what government is the established one in a State. For, as the United States guarantee to each State a republican government, congress must necessarily decide what government is established in the State before it can determine whether it is republican or not. And when the senators and representatives of a State are admitted into the councils of the Union, the authority of the government under which they are appointed, as well as its republican character, is recognized by the proper constitutional authority. And its decision is binding on every other department of the government, and could not be questioned in a judicial tribunal. It is true that the contest in this case did not last long enough to bring the matter to this issue; and as no senators or representatives were elected under the authority of the government of which Mr. Dorr was the head, congress was not called upon to decide the controversy. Yet the right to decide is placed there, and not in the courts.

Recall the Court's explanation of *Luther* in Baker v. Carr. Is the explanation faithful to the opinion in *Luther*?

In Pacific Telephone Co. v. Oregon, 223 U.S. 118 (1912), plaintiffs challenged a citizen initiatives provision in the Oregon constitution, which permitted citizens to have issues placed on the ballot for a popular vote. Any proposal approved in that way would become law. The law at issue in *Pacific Telephone* taxed certain telephone and telegraph companies at a particular rate. According to those companies, direct democracy through the initiative procedure violated the republican form of government clause.

The Court responded by referring to "the inconceivable expansion of the judicial power" that would result from adjudicating that claim, and refused to decide whether the initiative process was consistent with republican government. Note that the republican form of government clause is addressed to the "United States," not only to Congress. Suppose a state set up a monarchy. Would the guarantee clause be unavailable? For discussion, see W. Wiecek, The Guarantee Clause of the United States Constitution (1947); Bonfield, The Guarantee Clause of Article IV, Section 4: A Study in Constitutional Desuetude, 46 Minn. L. Rev. 513 (1962); Note, A Niche for the Guarantee Clause, 94 Harv. L. Rev. 681 (1981). For an argument that the guarantee clause, rather than the equal protection clause, would have provided a better basis for the Court's holding in *Baker*, see McConnell, The Redistricting Cases: Original Mistakes and Current Consequences, 24 Harv. J.L. & Pub. Poly. 103–114 (2000).

Note: The Development of Standards for Reviewing Political Fairness

In *Baker*, the Court rejected the argument that no judicially administrable standards were available to evaluate the constitutionality of malapportioned districts. Two years after *Baker* in Reynolds v. Sims, 377 U.S. 533 (1964), the Court announced the standard it would use: a one person, one vote test that required equality of population across districts. Consider the following defense of the standard:

> Justice Frankfurter used to say that reapportionment was a "political thicket" that the courts should avoid. The critics love to quote him, but in truth the meaning of the point is blurred. Sometimes it has meant that there can be no administrable standard. [That] is nothing short of silly. For the very standard the Court chose [is] certainly administrable. In fact administrability is its long suit, and the more troublesome question is what else it has to recommend it.

J. Ely, Democracy and Distrust 120–121 (1980). According to Ely, one person, one vote might initially seem an extraordinarily intrusive judicial intervention into the apportionment process — imposing nationwide a rigid mathematical test plucked from nowhere in the constitutional text. But any more nuanced rule, he concluded, would ultimately be more intrusive, or at least more subject to judicial value imposition, because it would require "difficult and unseemly inquiries into the power alignments prevalent in the various states whose plans came before it." Id. at 124.

Shortly after announcing the one person, one vote rule, the Court acknowledged the possibility that even if a redistricting plan complied with one person, one vote, "[it] might well be that, designedly or otherwise," a particular "apportionment scheme, under the circumstances of a particular case, would operate to minimize or cancel out the voting strength of racial or political elements of the voting population." Fortson v. Dorsey, 379 U.S. 433, 439 (1965). During the 1970s and 1980s, the Court developed a jurisprudence identifying the circumstances under which a plan unconstitutionally diluted a racial minority group's voting strength.

In Davis v. Bandemer, 478 U.S. 109 (1986), the Supreme Court held that claims of partisan gerrymandering were also justiciable. Justice White delivered the Court's opinion with respect to the political question issue: "Disposition of this question does not involve us in a matter more properly decided by a coequal branch of our Government. There is no risk of foreign or domestic disturbance, and in light of our cases since *Baker* we are not persuaded that there are no judicially discernible and manageable standards by which political gerrymander cases are to be decided." Justice White acknowledged that "the type of claim that was presented in Baker v. Carr was subsequently resolved in this Court by the formulation of the 'one person, one vote' rule. See, e.g., Reynolds v. Sims, 377 U.S. at 557–561. The mere fact, however, that we may not now similarly perceive a likely arithmetic presumption in the instant context does not compel a conclusion that the claims presented here are nonjusticiable." Justice O'Connor, writing in dissent for herself, Chief Justice Burger, and Justice Rehnquist, would have held claims of unconstitutional political gerrymandering nonjusticiable.

The six justices in *Bandemer* who agreed that political gerrymandering claims were justiciable split into two camps with respect to the substantive standard to be applied to such claims, with Justice White (now writing for himself and three other justices) adopting a relatively stringent standard that required plaintiffs to show that "the electoral system is arranged in a manner that will consistently degrade [a] group of voters' influence on the political process as a whole," while Justice Powell, writing for himself and Justice Stevens, proposed a more plaintiff-friendly standard that looked at factors such as the nature of the procedures by which the challenged redistricting was accomplished and the intent behind the redistricting; the shapes of the districts and their conformity with political subdivision boundaries and other "neutral" geographic criteria; and the lack of any nonpartisan explanation for the district boundaries. (The substantive standard for proving claims of unconstitutional political gerrymandering is covered in more detail in Chapter 6 infra.) Following *Bandemer*, although a significant number of political gerrymandering cases were brought, they were uniformly unsuccessful, essentially because it was impossible to meet *Bandemer*'s "consistent degradation" test.

Two decades later, the Court twice revisited the justiciability of political gerrymandering without resolving the issue.

VIETH v. JUBELIRER, 541 U.S. 267 (2004). This case involved an overt political gerrymander of Pennsylvania's congressional districts following the 2000 census. The case produced five separate opinions. Justice Scalia, writing for himself, Chief Justice Rehnquist, and Justices O'Connor and Thomas, announced the judgment of the Court. He would have held the plaintiffs' claims nonjusticiable. At one point in his opinion, Justice Scalia seemed to be pointing to a demonstrable textual commitment of the question to another branch, observing that "[it] is significant that the Framers provided a remedy for such practices in the Constitution. Article 1, §4, while leaving in state legislatures the initial power to draw districts for federal elections, permitted Congress to 'make or alter' those districts if it wished." But the bulk of his opinion was devoted to arguing that there was no judicially manageable standard for addressing claims of political gerrymandering:

"Eighteen years of judicial effort with virtually nothing to show for it justify us in revisiting the question whether the standard promised by *Bandemer* exists. As the following discussion reveals, no judicially discernible and manageable standards for adjudicating political gerrymandering claims have emerged. Lacking them, we must conclude that political gerrymandering claims are nonjusticiable and that *Bandemer* was wrongly decided.

"We begin our review of possible standards with that proposed by Justice White's plurality opinion in *Bandemer* because, as the narrowest ground for our decision in that case, it has been the standard employed by the lower courts. . . .

"In the lower courts, the legacy of the plurality's test is one long record of puzzlement and consternation. . . . The test has been criticized for its indeterminacy by a host of academic commentators. . . .

"[The standard proposed by Justice Powell in *Bandemer*] is essentially a totality-of-the-circumstances analysis, where all conceivable factors, none of which is dispositive, are weighed with an eye to ascertaining whether the particular gerrymander has gone too far — or, in Justice Powell's terminology, whether it is not 'fair.' Fairness' does not seem to us a judicially manageable standard. . . . Some criterion more solid and more demonstrably met than that seems to us necessary to enable the state legislatures to discern the limits of their districting discretion, to meaningfully constrain the discretion of the courts, and to win public acceptance for the courts' intrusion into a process that is the very foundation of democratic decisionmaking."

Justice Scalia also dismissed the standards proposed by the three dissenting opinions in *Vieth*, "prefac[ing]" his rejection "with the observation that the mere fact that these four dissenters come up with three different standards — all of them different from the two proposed in *Bandemer* and the one proposed here by appellants — goes a long way to establishing that there is no constitutionally discernible standard. . . .

"Much of [Justice Stevens's] dissent is addressed to the incompatibility of severe partisan gerrymanders with democratic principles. We do not disagree with that judgment, any more than we disagree with the judgment that it would be unconstitutional for the Senate to employ, in impeachment proceedings, procedures that are incompatible with its obligation to 'try' impeachments. The issue we have discussed is not whether severe partisan gerrymanders violate the Constitution, but whether it is for the courts to say when a violation has occurred, and to design a remedy."

With respect to the tests proposed by Justice Souter (joined by Justice Ginsburg) and Justice Breyer, Justice Scalia argued that the tests failed to provide determinate answers because they were based on substantive notions of fairness or unjustified entrenchment of the incumbent party.

Justice Kennedy concurred in the judgment. While he agreed with the plurality that the plaintiffs' complaint should have been dismissed, he "would not foreclose all possibility of judicial relief if some limited and precise rationale were found to correct an established violation of the Constitution in some redistricting cases":

"That no such standard has emerged in this case should not be taken to prove that none will emerge in the future. Where important rights are involved, the impossibility of full analytical satisfaction is reason to err on the side of caution. Allegations of unconstitutional bias in apportionment are most serious claims, for we have long believed that 'the right to vote' is one of 'those political processes ordinarily to be relied upon to protect minorities.' United States v. Carolene Products Co., 304 U.S. 144, 153, n.4 (1938). . . .

"The plurality says that 18 years, in effect, prove the negative. . . . [By] the timeline of the law 18 years is rather a short period. In addition, the rapid evolution of technologies in the apportionment field suggests yet unexplored possibilities. . . . [These] new technologies may produce new methods of analysis that make more evident the precise nature of the burdens gerrymanders impose on the representational rights of voters and parties. That would facilitate court efforts to identify and remedy the burdens, with judicial intervention limited by the derived standards.

"If suitable standards with which to measure the burden a gerrymander imposes on representational rights did emerge, hindsight would show that the Court prematurely abandoned the field. That is a risk the Court should not take. . . ."

There were three separate dissents in *Vieth*. Justice Stevens's dissent took issue with the plurality's claim that no judicially manageable standards existed:

"The plurality candidly acknowledges that legislatures can fashion standards to remedy political gerrymandering that are perfectly manageable and, indeed, that the legislatures in Iowa and elsewhere have done so. If a violation of the Constitution is found, a court could impose a remedy patterned after such a statute.

Thus, the problem, in the plurality's view, is not that there is no judicially manageable standard to fix an unconstitutional partisan gerrymander, but rather that the Judiciary lacks the ability to determine when a state legislature has violated its duty to govern impartially.

"Quite obviously, however, several standards for identifying impermissible partisan influence are available to judges who have the will to enforce them. . . . What is clear is that it is not the unavailability of judicially manageable standards that drives today's decision. It is, instead, a failure of judicial will to condemn even the most blatant violations of a state legislature's fundamental duty to govern impartially."

Justice Souter, joined by Justice Ginsburg, recognized that political fairness "cannot possibly be described with the hard edge of one person, one vote," but proposed a "fresh start" involving a new five-part test for identifying cases of unconstitutional partisanship. "The enquiries I am proposing are not, to be sure, as hard-edged as I wish they could be, but neither do they have a degree of subjectivity inconsistent with the judicial function." Similarly, Justice Breyer's dissent set out "a set of circumstances in which the use of purely political districting criteria could conflict with constitutionally mandated democratic requirements," and for which courts could devise a workable test.

Two years later, in League of United Latin Am. Citizens v. Perry, 548 U.S. 399 (2006), the Court once again found itself unable to generate a controlling opinion. The case involved a challenge to Texas's mid-decade congressional redistricting, a redistricting undertaken with the express purpose of favoring Republican candidates. Justice Scalia, joined by Justice Thomas, reiterated his position in Vieth that political gerrymanders are nonjusticiable. Justice Kennedy did not "revisit the justiciability holding" in Vieth, but found that appellants had failed to "offer the Court a manageable, reliable measure of fairness for determining whether a partisan gerrymander violates the Constitution." In particular, he rejected their claim that the decision to conduct a mid-decade redistricting rendered the plan unconstitutional.

Chief Justice Roberts, joined by Justice Alito — both of whom had joined the Court after the decision in Vieth — agreed with Justice Kennedy's conclusion that the challengers "ha[d] not provided 'a reliable standard for identifying unconstitutional political gerrymanders,'" and asserted, somewhat surprisingly, that "[t]he question whether any such standard exists — that is, whether a challenge to a political gerrymander presents a justiciable case or controversy — has not been argued in these cases." He therefore took "no position on that question, which has divided the Court," and joined the Court's disposition of the political gerrymandering claims "without specifying whether appellants have failed to state a claim on which relief can be granted, or have failed to present a justiciable controversy."

The other four justices all reiterated their view that claims of unconstitutional political gerrymandering are justiciable. Justices Stevens and Breyer would have reached the merits of the challengers' claims and struck down the plan. In light of the Court's continued division, Justice Souter, joined by Justice Ginsburg, "[saw] nothing to be gained by working through these cases on the standard I would have applied in [Vieth,] because here as in Vieth we have no majority for any single criterion of impermissible gerrymander." He would "therefore [have] treat[ed] the broad issue of gerrymander much as the subject of an improvident grant of certiorari."

Bush v. Gore

531 U.S. 98 (2000)

PER CURIAM:

[Following an agonizingly close presidential election in Florida, the Florida Supreme Court ordered a manual recount of undervotes — ballots on which no vote had been registered during the machine count — in all counties that had not yet completed a recount. In addition, it ordered that additional votes recovered during prior but untimely manual recounts in several other counties be included in the vote total.]

II . . .

B

The individual citizen has no federal constitutional right to vote for electors for the President of the United States unless and until the state legislature chooses a statewide election as the means to implement its power to appoint members of the Electoral College. U.S. Const., Art. II, §1. This is the source for the statement in McPherson v. Blacker, 146 U.S. 1, 35 (1892), that the State legislature's power to select the manner for appointing electors is plenary; it may, if it so chooses, select the electors itself, which indeed was the manner used by State legislatures in several States for many years after the Framing of our Constitution. History has now favored the voter, and in each of the several States the citizens themselves vote for Presidential electors. When the state legislature vests the right to vote for President in its people, the right to vote as the legislature has prescribed is fundamental; and one source of its fundamental nature lies in the equal weight accorded to each vote and the equal dignity owed to each voter. . . .

The right to vote is protected in more than the initial allocation of the franchise. Equal protection applies as well to the manner of its exercise. Having once granted the right to vote on equal terms, the State may not, by later arbitrary and disparate treatment, value one person's vote over that of another. See, e.g., Harper v. Virginia Bd. of Elections, 383 U.S. 663, 665 (1966) ("[Once] the franchise is granted to the electorate, lines may not be drawn which are inconsistent with the Equal Protection Clause of the Fourteenth Amendment"). It must be remembered that "the right of suffrage can be denied by a debasement or dilution of the weight of a citizen's vote just as effectively as by wholly prohibiting the free exercise of the franchise." Reynolds v. Sims, 377 U.S. 533, 555 (1964). . . .

Much of the controversy seems to revolve around ballot cards designed to be perforated by a stylus but which, either through error or deliberate omission, have not been perforated with sufficient precision for a machine to count them. In some cases a piece of the card — a chad — is hanging, say by two corners. In other cases there is no separation at all, just an indentation.

The Florida Supreme Court has ordered that the intent of the voter be discerned from such ballots. For purposes of resolving the equal protection challenge, it is not necessary to decide whether the Florida Supreme Court had the authority under the legislative scheme for resolving election disputes to define what a legal vote is and to mandate a manual recount implementing that definition. The recount mechanisms implemented in response to the decisions of the Florida Supreme Court do not satisfy the minimum requirement for non-arbitrary treatment of voters necessary to secure the fundamental right. Florida's basic command for the count of legally cast votes is to consider the "intent of the voter." This is unobjectionable as an abstract proposition and a starting principle. The problem inheres in the absence of specific standards to ensure its equal application. The formulation of uniform rules to determine intent based on these recurring circumstances is practicable and, we conclude, necessary. . . .

The State Supreme Court ratified this uneven treatment. It mandated that the recount totals from [several] counties [be] included in the certified total [even though] each of the counties used varying standards to determine what was a legal vote. Broward County used a more forgiving standard than Palm Beach County, and uncovered almost three times as many new votes, a result markedly disproportionate to the difference in population between the counties. . . .

The recount process, in its features here described, is inconsistent with the minimum procedures necessary to protect the fundamental right of each voter in the special instance of a statewide recount under the authority of a single state judicial officer. Our consideration is limited to the present circumstances, for the problem of equal protection in election processes generally presents many complexities.

The question before the Court is not whether local entities, in the exercise of their expertise, may develop different systems for implementing elections. Instead, we are presented with a situation where a state court with the power to assure uniformity has ordered a statewide recount with minimal procedural safeguards. When a court orders a statewide remedy, there must be at least some assurance that the rudimentary requirements of equal treatment and fundamental fairness are satisfied. . . .

Upon due consideration of the difficulties identified to this point, it is obvious that the recount cannot be conducted in compliance with the requirements of equal protection and due process without substantial additional work. It would require not only the adoption (after opportunity for argument) of adequate statewide standards for determining what is a legal vote, and practicable procedures to implement them, but also orderly judicial review of any disputed matters that might arise. . . .

The Supreme Court of Florida has said that the legislature intended the State's electors to "participat[e] fully in the federal electoral process," as provided in 3 U.S.C. §5.[1] That statute, in turn, requires that any controversy or contest that is designed to lead to a conclusive selection of electors be

---

1. [This provision is part of a complex scheme dealing with congressional procedures for the counting of electoral votes, enacted in the wake of the disputed presidential election of 1876. The statute provides that

[if] any State shall have provided, by laws enacted prior to the day fixed for the appointment of the electors, for its final determination of any controversy or contest concerning the appointment of [electors] by judicial or other [methods], and such determination shall have been made at least six days before the time fixed for the meeting of the electors, such determination made pursuant to such law so existing on said day, and made at least six days prior to said time of meeting of the electors, shall be [conclusive].

— Eds.].

completed by December 12. That date is upon us, and there is no recount procedure in place under the State Supreme Court's order that comports with minimal constitutional standards. Because it is evident that any recount seeking to meet the December 12 date will be unconstitutional for the reasons we have discussed, we reverse the judgment of the Supreme Court of Florida ordering a recount to proceed. . . .

None are more conscious of the vital limits on judicial authority than are the members of this Court, and none stand more in admiration of the Constitution's design to leave the selection of the President to the people, through their legislatures, and to the political sphere. When contending parties invoke the process of the courts, however, it becomes our unsought responsibility to resolve the federal and constitutional issues the judicial system has been forced to confront.

The judgment of the Supreme Court of Florida is reversed, and the case is remanded for further proceedings not inconsistent with this opinion.

CHIEF JUSTICE REHNQUIST, with whom JUSTICE SCALIA and JUSTICE THOMAS join, concurring.

We join the per curiam opinion. We write separately because we believe there are additional grounds that require us to reverse the Florida Supreme Court's decision.

I

We deal here not with an ordinary election, but with an election for the President of the United States. . . .

[In] Anderson v. Celebrezze, 460 U.S. 780, 794–795 (1983), we said: "In the context of a Presidential election, state-imposed restrictions implicate a uniquely important national interest. For the President and the Vice President of the United States are the only elected officials who represent all the voters in the Nation." In most cases, comity and respect for federalism compel us to defer to the decisions of state courts on issues of state law. That practice reflects our understanding that the decisions of state courts are definitive pronouncements of the will of the States as sovereigns. Of course, in ordinary cases, the distribution of powers among the branches of a State's government raises no questions of federal constitutional law, subject to the requirement that the government be republican in character. See U.S. Const., Art. IV, §4. But there are a few exceptional cases in which the Constitution imposes a duty or confers a power on a particular branch of a State's government. This is one of them. Article II, §1, cl. 2, provides that "each State shall appoint, in such Manner as the *Legislature* thereof may direct," electors for President and Vice President. (Emphasis added.) Thus, the text of the election law itself, and not just its interpretation by the courts of the States, takes on independent significance. . . .

In any election but a Presidential election, the Florida Supreme Court can give as little or as much deference to Florida's executives as it chooses, so far as Article II is concerned, and this Court will have no cause to question the court's actions. But, with respect to a Presidential election, the court must be both mindful of the legislature's role under Article II in choosing the manner of appointing electors and deferential to those bodies expressly empowered by the legislature to carry out its constitutional mandate. . . .

III

The scope and nature of the remedy ordered by the Florida Supreme Court jeopardizes the "legislative wish" to take advantage of the safe harbor provided by 3 U.S.C. §5. December 12, 2000, is the last date for a final determination of the Florida electors that will satisfy §5. Yet in the late afternoon of December 8th — four days before this deadline — the Supreme Court of Florida ordered recounts of tens of thousands of so-called "undervotes" spread through 64 of the State's 67 counties. This was done in a search for elusive — perhaps delusive — certainty as to the exact count of 6 million votes. But no one claims that these ballots have not previously been tabulated; they were initially read by voting machines at the time of the election, and thereafter reread by virtue of Florida's automatic recount provision. No one claims there was any fraud in the election. The Supreme Court of Florida ordered this additional recount under the provision of the election code giving the circuit judge the authority to provide relief that is "appropriate under such circumstances." Fla. Stat. §102.168(8) (2000).

Surely when the Florida Legislature empowered the courts of the State to grant "appropriate" relief, it must have meant relief that would have become final by the cut-off date of 3 U.S.C. §5. In light of the inevitable legal challenges and ensuing appeals to the Supreme Court of Florida and petitions for certiorari to this Court, the entire recounting process could not possibly be completed by that date. . . .

Given all these factors, and in light of the legislative intent identified by the Florida Supreme Court to bring Florida within the "safe harbor" provision of 3 U.S.C. §5, the remedy prescribed by the Supreme Court of Florida cannot be deemed an "appropriate" one as of December 8. It significantly departed from the statutory framework in place on November 7, and authorized open-ended further proceedings which could not be completed by December 12, thereby preventing a final determination by that date.

For these reasons, in addition to those given in the per curiam, we would reverse.

Justice Stevens, with whom Justice Ginsburg and Justice Breyer join, dissenting.

The Constitution assigns to the States the primary responsibility for determining the manner of selecting the Presidential electors. See Art. II, §1, cl. 2. When questions arise about the meaning of state laws, including election laws, it is our settled practice to accept the opinions of the highest courts of the States as providing the final answers. On rare occasions, however, either federal statutes or the Federal Constitution may require federal judicial intervention in state elections. This is not such an occasion.

The federal questions that ultimately emerged in this case are not substantial. Article II provides that "[e]ach State shall appoint, in such Manner as the Legislature thereof may direct, a Number of Electors." It does not create state legislatures out of whole cloth, but rather takes them as they come — as creatures born of, and constrained by, their state constitutions. [The] legislative power in Florida is subject to judicial review pursuant to Article V of the Florida Constitution, and nothing in Article II of the Federal Constitution frees the state legislature from the constraints in the state constitution that created it. [The] Florida

Supreme Court's exercise of appellate jurisdiction therefore was wholly consistent with, and indeed contemplated by, the grant of authority in Article II. . . .

Admittedly, the use of differing substandards for determining voter intent in different counties employing similar voting systems may raise serious concerns. Those concerns are alleviated — if not eliminated — by the fact that a single impartial magistrate will ultimately adjudicate all objections arising from the recount process. . . .

What must underlie petitioners' entire federal assault on the Florida election procedures is an unstated lack of confidence in the impartiality and capacity of the state judges who would make the critical decisions if the vote count were to proceed. Otherwise, their position is wholly without merit. The endorsement of that position by the majority of this Court can only lend credence to the most cynical appraisal of the work of judges throughout the land. It is confidence in the men and women who administer the judicial system that is the true backbone of the rule of law. Time will one day heal the wound to that confidence that will be inflicted by today's decision. One thing, however, is certain. Although we may never know with complete certainty the identity of the winner of this year's Presidential election, the identity of the loser is perfectly clear. It is the Nation's confidence in the judge as an impartial guardian of the rule of law.

I respectfully dissent.

JUSTICE SOUTER, with whom JUSTICE BREYER joins, [dissenting]. . . .

Petitioners have raised an equal protection claim (or, alternatively, a due process claim), in the charge that unjustifiably disparate standards are applied in different electoral jurisdictions to otherwise identical facts. It is true that the Equal Protection Clause does not forbid the use of a variety of voting mechanisms within a jurisdiction, even though different mechanisms will have different levels of effectiveness in recording voters' intentions; local variety can be justified by concerns about cost, the potential value of innovation, and so on. But evidence in the record here suggests that a different order of disparity obtains under rules for determining a voter's intent that have been applied (and could continue to be applied) to identical types of ballots used in identical brands of machines and exhibiting identical physical characteristics (such as "hanging" or "dimpled" chads). I can conceive of no legitimate state interest served by these differing treatments of the expressions of voters' fundamental rights. The differences appear wholly arbitrary.

In deciding what to do about this, we should take account of the fact that electoral votes are due to be cast in six days. I would therefore remand the case to the courts of Florida with instructions to establish uniform standards for evaluating the several types of ballots that have prompted differing treatments, to be applied within and among counties when passing on such identical ballots in any further recounting (or successive recounting) that the courts might order.

Unlike the majority, I see no warrant for this Court to assume that Florida could not possibly comply with this requirement before the date set for the meeting of electors, December 18. . . .

I respectfully dissent.

JUSTICE GINSBURG, with whom JUSTICE STEVENS joins, and with whom JUSTICE SOUTER and JUSTICE BREYER join as to Part I, dissenting.

I . . .

The Chief Justice says that Article II, by providing that state legislatures shall direct the manner of appointing electors, authorizes federal superintendence over the relationship between state courts and state legislatures, and licenses a departure from the usual deference we give to state court interpretations of state law. The Framers of our Constitution, however, understood that in a republican government, the judiciary would construe the legislature's enactments. See U.S. Const., Art. III; The Federalist No. 78 (A. Hamilton). In light of the constitutional guarantee to States of a "Republican Form of Government," U.S. Const., Art. IV, §4, Article II can hardly be read to invite this Court to disrupt a State's republican regime. Yet the Chief Justice today would reach out to do just that. By holding that Article II requires our revision of a state court's construction of state laws in order to protect one organ of the State from another, The Chief Justice contradicts the basic principle that a State may organize itself as it sees fit. See, e.g., Gregory v. Ashcroft, 501 U.S. 452, 460 (1991) ("Through the structure of its government, and the character of those who exercise government authority, a State defines itself as a sovereign."); Highland Farms Dairy v. Agnew, 300 U.S. 608, 612 (1937) ("How power shall be distributed by a state among its governmental organs is commonly, if not always, a question for the state itself."). Article II does not call for the scrutiny undertaken by this Court. . . .

II . . .

I cannot agree that the recount adopted by the Florida court, flawed as it may be, would yield a result any less fair or precise than the certification that preceded that recount. . . .

I dissent.

JUSTICE BREYER . . . dissenting. . . .

II

[This portion of Justice Breyer's opinion was joined by Justices Stevens, Ginsburg, and Souter.] Despite the reminder that this case involves "an election for the President of the United States," (Rehnquist, C.J., concurring), no preeminent legal concern, or practical concern related to legal questions, required this Court to hear this case, let alone to issue a stay that stopped Florida's recount process in its tracks. With one exception, petitioners' claims do not ask us to vindicate a constitutional provision designed to protect a basic human right. See, e.g., Brown v. Board of Education, 347 U.S. 483 (1954). Petitioners invoke fundamental fairness, namely, the need for procedural fairness, including finality. But with the one "equal protection" exception, they rely upon law that focuses, not upon that basic need, but upon the constitutional allocation of power. . . .

Of course, the selection of the President is of fundamental national importance. But that importance is political, not legal. And this Court should resist the temptation unnecessarily to resolve tangential legal disputes, where doing so threatens to determine the outcome of the election.

The Constitution and federal statutes themselves make clear that restraint is appropriate. They set forth a road map of how to resolve disputes about electors, even after an election as close as this one. That road map foresees resolution of electoral disputes by state courts. See 3 U.S.C. §5. [But] it nowhere provides for involvement by the United States Supreme Court.

To the contrary, the Twelfth Amendment commits to Congress the authority and responsibility to count electoral votes. A federal statute, the Electoral Count Act, enacted after the close 1876 Hayes-Tilden Presidential election, specifies that, after States have tried to resolve disputes (through "judicial" or other means), Congress is the body primarily authorized to resolve remaining disputes. See Electoral Count Act of 1887, 24 Stat. 373, 3 U.S.C. §§5, 6, and 15.

The legislative history of the Act makes clear its intent to commit the power to resolve such disputes to Congress, rather than the courts:

> "The two Houses are, by the Constitution, authorized to make the count of electoral votes. They can only count legal votes, and in doing so must determine, from the best evidence to be had, what are legal votes. . . . The power to determine rests with the two Houses, and there is no other constitutional tribunal." H. Rep. No. 1638, 49th Cong., 1st Sess., 2 (1886) (report submitted by Rep. Caldwell, Select Committee on the Election of President and Vice-President). . . .

Given this detailed, comprehensive scheme for counting electoral votes, there is no reason to believe that federal law either foresees or requires resolution of such a political issue by this Court. Nor, for that matter, is there any reason to think that the Constitution's Framers would have reached a different conclusion. Madison, at least, believed that allowing the judiciary to choose the presidential electors "was out of the question." Madison, July 25, 1787 (reprinted in 5 Elliot's Debates on the Federal Constitution 363 (2d ed. 1876)).

The decision by both the Constitution's Framers and the 1886 Congress to minimize this Court's role in resolving close federal presidential elections is as wise as it is clear. However awkward or difficult it may be for Congress to resolve difficult electoral disputes, Congress, being a political body, expresses the people's will far more accurately than does an unelected Court. And the people's will is what elections are about. . . .

[The history of the disputed election of 1876, including] the participation in the work of the electoral commission by five Justices, including Justice Bradley, did not lend that process legitimacy. Nor did it assure the public that the process had worked fairly, guided by the law. Rather, it simply embroiled Members of the Court in partisan conflict, thereby undermining respect for the judicial process. And the Congress that later enacted the Electoral Count Act knew it.

This history may help to explain why I think it not only legally wrong, but also most unfortunate, for the Court simply to have terminated the Florida recount. Those who caution judicial restraint in resolving political disputes have described the quintessential case for that restraint as a case marked, among other things, by the "strangeness of the issue," its "intractability to principled resolution," its "sheer momentousness, . . . which tends to unbalance judicial judgment," and "the inner vulnerability, the self-doubt of an institution which is electorally irresponsible and has no earth to draw strength from [citing A. Bickel, The Least Dangerous Branch 184 (1962)]." Those characteristics mark this case. . . .

I fear that in order to bring this agonizingly long election process to a definitive conclusion, we have not adequately attended to that necessary "check upon our own exercise of power," "our own sense of self-restraint." United States v. Butler, 297 U.S. 1, 79 (1936) (Stone, J., dissenting). Justice Brandeis once said of the Court, "The most important thing we do is not doing." Bickel, supra, at 71. What it does today, the Court should have left undone. I would repair the damage done as best we now can, by permitting the Florida recount to continue under uniform standards.

I respectfully dissent.

Note: Political Questions and Partisan Issues

1. *Reconciling Bush v. Gore and* Vieth. Note the diametrically opposite lineups of the Court in these cases. The five justices who thought the Florida recount procedure violated the equal protection clause are the same five justices who professed an inability to discern a judicially manageable standard for assessing political fairness in the redistricting process. Are these positions consistent?

In *Vieth*, Justice Scalia states that article I, section 4 "provide[s] a remedy for [unfair redistricting] practices" by authorizing "Congress to 'make or alter' those districts if it wished." If this is arguably a textual commitment of constitutional oversight over redistricting to Congress, is the twelfth amendment a similar commitment of resolution of disputes over presidential elections to Congress?

2. *Standing and the political question doctrine.* The Court's opinion in Bush v. Gore implicates many of the considerations raised in the prior sections' discussions of standing and political questions. On the issue of standing, consider the following: If the injury identified in the per curiam is the exclusion of valid undervotes in some counties because those counties are using a more stringent standard for assessing voter intent and the exclusion of valid overvotes by an incomplete recount process, who has standing to raise these claims?

Does George W. Bush have standing? Why? Bush was not himself a registered voter in Florida who could claim a violation of his equal protection rights.

In this respect, consider Tribe, EroG v. HsuB and Its Disguises: Freeing Bush v. Gore from Its Hall of Mirrors, 115 Harv. L. Rev. 170, 229–231 (2001):

> [I]t is hardly credible — indeed, it borders on the fantastic — to argue that Bush himself lacked standing to press an equal protection claim in the Florida lawsuit. . . . [H]e surely had third-party standing. His injury was obvious: the Florida Supreme Court was in essence [replacing the certification he had received with] . . . a recount to be conducted by a process he regarded as an unconstitutional roulette game rigged in favor of his opponent. . . . Bush potentially had standing on this theory to represent at least those who had voted for him and whose votes stood to be devalued during a recount. More generally, he shared with all the voters a sufficiently common interest in protecting the integrity of the vote count to ensure his standing as third-party plaintiff. . . . Because of the significant obstacles any individual voter would face in seeking to ensure a fair count, Bush not only had standing but was particularly well placed to assert voters' equal protection rights — even though his ultimate goal was to have some of their votes excluded.

Is "insuring the integrity of the vote count" the kind of "shared individuated right" as to which the Court has traditionally denied standing? Consider in this regard Karlan, Nothing Personal: The Evolution of the Newest Equal Protection from Shaw v. Reno to Bush v. Gore, 79 N.C. L. Rev. 1345, 1357–1360, 1363–1364 (2001):

> One striking thing about the Supreme Court's opinion in Bush v. Gore is that it doesn't distinguish [among the different potential claims of injury in fact]. But its general tone seems to focus largely on the claims of individual excluded voters, rather than on voters whose preferred candidate was potentially disadvantaged by the recount the Florida Supreme Court ordered. Perhaps this was a tactical decision by the majority, which sought to avoid having its decision appear partisan: to say that the injury was suffered only by Republican voters whose overall voting strength was diluted by the recount standard would have made explicit that this was a case about partisan outcomes rather than abstract principles. . . .
>
> [George W. Bush] is an especially unlikely candidate for third-party standing. It is hard to see George W. Bush as the champion of a claim by undervoters in overwhelmingly Democratic Palm Beach County that they are being denied equal protection because their votes would have been included under the more liberal Broward County standard. Indeed, Bush's third-party complaint . . . alleged, among other things, that the standard used in Broward County was partisan, inconsistent, and unfair. The relief he sought was a declaration that "the illegal votes counted in Broward County under the new rules established after the election should be excluded under the Due Process Clause. . . ." Nothing in that proposed remedy vindicates the rights of excluded voters in Palm Beach County or elsewhere. . . .
>
> The equal protection right of individual voters to participate can really be vindicated only by expanding the scope of the prescribed recount. The only equal protection right that can be vindicated by abolishing recounts altogether is a group-based aggregation interest that depends on the partisan composition of the unrecovered pool, precisely the issue the Supreme Court seemed to want to avoid by couching its discussion in individualistic, atomistic terms. . . .
>
> Whatever interest the Supreme Court's decision vindicated, it was not the interest of an identifiable individual voter. Rather it was a perceived systemic interest in having recounts conducted according to a uniform standard or not at all. . . .

Is Bush an appropriate plaintiff to raise this more systemic claim? Would he be an appropriate plaintiff to raise the article II claim?

3. *The twelfth amendment as a "textual commitment" to the political branches?* On the subject of the political question doctrine, consider whether article II and the twelfth amendment represent a textual commitment of the question of who is entitled to a state's electoral votes to Congress. Is this an implication of Justice Breyer's dissent? Does this explain the per curiam's decision to rely on the equal protection clause in light of *Baker*'s assurance that the equal protection clause provides judicially enforceable standards for overseeing the political process? See Karlan, Equal Protection: Bush v. Gore and the Making of a Precedent, in The Unfinished Election of 2000 (J. Rakove ed., 2001).

For an extensive discussion of the evolution of the political question doctrine and its relevance to Bush v. Gore, see Issacharoff, Political Judgments, in The Vote: Bush, Gore & the Supreme Court 55 (C. Sunstein and R. Epstein eds. 2001). Issacharoff argues that the overall structure of the Electoral Count Act of 1887 — the source for 3 U.S.C. §5 — commits the questions raised in the Florida process to political actors. He quotes Senator John Sherman — coincidentally both one of the sponsors of the act and one of the prime movers behind the equal protection clause — arguing on the floor of the Senate against Supreme Court involvement in presidential election controversies:

> Another plan which has been proposed in the debates at different times and I think also in the constitutional convention, was to allow questions of this kind to be certified at once to the Supreme Court for its decisions in case of a division between the two Houses. If the House should be one way and the Senate the other, then it was proposed to let the case be referred directly to the prompt and summary decision of the Supreme Court. But there is a feeling in this country that we ought not to mingle our great judicial tribunal with political questions, and therefore this proposition has not met with much favor. It would be a very grave fault indeed and a very serious objection to refer a political question in which the people of the country were aroused, about which their feelings were excited, to this great tribunal, which after all has to sit upon the life and property of all the people of the United States. It would tend to bring that court into public odium of one or the other of the two great parties. Therefore that plan may probably be rejected as an unwise provision. I believe, however, that it is the provision made in other countries.

17 Cong. Rec. 817–818 (1886) (Sen. Sherman). Issacharoff argues that had the Electoral Count Act been followed more faithfully, the relevant players in the dispute would have been Florida's governor and its legislature and the newly elected members of Congress. He observes:

> No doubt, this scenario would look to many modern observers like a pure power grab, a partisan circumvention of orderly legal processes. But why is it either surprising or alarming that an electoral deadlock should be resolved by political officials and bodies elected by the same voters? [In] the heated rhetorical battle of Election 2000, no charge was bandied about with greater derision than the claim that one or another group of partisans was engaged in partisanship. But it was, after all, a partisan election that was at stake. It hardly seems an affront to democratic self-governance to channel the ultimate resolution of a true electoral deadlock into other democratically-elected branches of government.

4. *Questions of institutional respect and institutional competence.* On the more general question of what Bush v. Gore shows about the Supreme Court's role in the constitutional order, consider Garrett, Institutional Lessons from the 2000 Presidential Election, 29 Fla. St. U. L. Rev. 975, 975–976, 979–980, 982–983 (2001):

> [T]he Bush-Gore election concretely illustrates that institutional design is a crucial consideration in determining which part of the government is best suited to render particular decisions. When institutions must become involved in majoritarian political decisions such as the selection of a President, it may be better to rely largely on the political branches than on the judiciary for several reasons. This allocation of decisionmaking authority is preferable because of the greater democratic credentials of Congress. . . . In addition, there is a less-often recognized advantage of institutional design enjoyed by the legislature. . . . [T]he legislature can adopt procedural frameworks to shape decisionmaking and restrain partisan opportunism before a particular controversy arises. In the case of the 2000 election, the United States Congress actually had a framework in place. . . . [The Electoral Count Act long antedated the Bush-Gore election and] would have ensured that

decisions were made transparently so voters could have held politicians accountable both for their ultimate decision and for the manner in which they reached it.

In contrast, . . . the Supreme Court's early intervention into the 2000 election reveals the greater possibility for strategic behavior when an institution acts ex post with relatively full information about how its decisions will affect particular and concrete interests. The presidential election thus provides on the federal level both an example of ex ante rules — the Electoral Count Act — and an example of ex post decisionmaking — the judicial interventions into the political process. While the former contained gaps because its drafters did not foresee all the problems that could arise in a presidential election, the latter provided substantial leeway for opportunistic behavior designed to advance the Justices' preferences. . . .

Although the Constitution's equal protection guarantee was adopted long before the presidential dispute in 2000, it is so open-textured and vague that virtually all the specification occurs when it is applied to particular cases. As an ex ante framework, it is essentially all gap to be filled in the future. Not only did the Court articulate its specification of equal protection for the first time in this case, but it also explicitly limited the doctrine's applicability to the case before it, evading the protection against self-interested decisionmaking that generality in rules can provide. . . .

Others have defended the Supreme Court's repeated intervention into the election contest as a courageous move to save the country from crisis — courageous because the Justices adopted an aggressive role at some risk to the reputations of their institution and themselves. Such fears of a political disaster are overstated, and they reflect an elitist distrust of the relatively messy arena of politics. Congress would not have discharged its responsibility to determine any election contest without some amount of heated rhetoric, opportunistic behavior, and partisan wrangling. However, Congress had the ability to apply [the Electoral Count Act] in a transparent and accountable way.

Consider also Barkow, More Supreme than Court? The Fall of the Political Question Doctrine and the Rise of Judicial Supremacy, 102 Colum. L. Rev. 237, 295-297 (2002):

The Court was well aware that its decision essentially would determine the outcome of the 2000 presidential election. Never before in our nation's history has the Court held that it had the power to issue such a ruling. . . .

Nor was the Court applying "judicially discoverable and manageable standards" in determining whether the state court overstepped its bounds. Rather, the Article II question required the Court to address fundamental questions of state allocation of authority with no constitutional benchmarks or precedent to guide it. The Article II question presented the same type of anterior question of governance found to be so problematic in the Guarantee Clause cases and described by the *Baker* Court as involving a "policy determination of a kind clearly for nonjudicial discretion."

Taking the decision away from the political process left little room for deliberation or protest. The Court itself obviously recognized the importance of the case and the need for the public to have some access to the proceedings. The Court permitted an unprecedented same day audio rebroadcast of the oral argument, an acknowledgement that there was a special need for transparency. The Court was injecting itself into the democratic process in a way that it had not done before, and therefore special public access seemed necessary. But the public never heard the Court's deliberations as it would have if Congress had resolved the controversy. The people were left with nothing more than rushed opinions — and no formal outlet to express their disagreement or to demand answers. Because the Supreme Court Justices hold their terms for life, the people cannot express their discontent or satisfaction at the ballot box. At most, and unfortunately, the only political outlet is the next Supreme Court confirmation hearing.

With respect to the pragmatic defense of the Court's decision — that it avoided the "constitutional trainwreck" that would have occurred had the election been thrown into the House of Representatives — see R. Posner, Breaking the Deadlock: The 2000 Election, the Constitution, and the Courts 137–145 (2001). Consider Sunstein, Order without Law, 68 U. Chi. L. Rev. 757, 758–759 (2001):

> The Court's decision in Bush v. Gore did have two fundamental virtues. First, it produced a prompt and decisive conclusion to the chaotic post-election period of 2000. Indeed, it probably did so in a way that carried more simplicity and authority than anything that might have been expected from the United States Congress. The Court might even have avoided a genuine constitutional crisis. Second, the Court's equal protection holding carries considerable appeal. On its face, that holding has the potential to create the most expansive, and perhaps sensible, protection for voting rights since the Court's one-person, one-vote decisions of mid-century. . . .
>
> The Court's decision also had two large vices. First, the Court effectively resolved the presidential election not unanimously, but by a 5-4 vote, with the majority consisting entirely of the Court's most conservative justices. Second, the Court's rationale was not only exceedingly ambitious but also embarrassingly weak. However appealing, its equal protection holding had no basis in precedent or in history. It also raises a host of puzzles for the future, which the Court appeared to try to resolve with its minimalist cry of "here, but nowhere else." . . .
>
> From the standpoint of constitutional order, the Court might well have done the nation a service. From the standpoint of legal reasoning, the Court's decision was very bad. In short, the Court's decision produced order without law. . . .

5. *The merits of the Court's decision.* The Court's decision has been subjected to voluminous scholarly and popular discussion. In general, the scholarship has been scathing in its treatment of the per curiam's equal protection analysis. For representative examples, see Klarman, Bush v. Gore through the Lens of Constitutional History, 89 Cal. L. Rev. 1721 (2001); Sunstein, Order without Law, supra; Seidman, What's So Bad about Bush v. Gore: An Essay on Our Unsettled Election, 47 Wayne St. L. Rev. 953 (2001). Much of the criticism focuses not on the abstract equal protection question of whether a vote should have the same likelihood of being included regardless of where the vote was cast — a sort of "equal protection for ballots" — but on the question of remedy: Did stopping the manual recount actually protect any voter's equal protection interest? For a defense of the equal protection holding, see Lund, The Unbearable Rightness of Bush v. Gore, 23 Cardozo L. Rev. 1219 (2002).

Most defenders of the outcome of Bush v. Gore have defended the case either on the grounds advanced in the Chief Justice's concurrence or on more pragmatic grounds — in Judge Richard Posner's phrase, that it averted a "constitutional trainwreck." For representative samples of this scholarship, see Epstein, "In Such Manner as the Legislature Thereof May Direct": The Outcome in Bush v. Gore Defended, in The Vote, supra; R. Posner, Breaking the Deadlock: The 2000 Election, the Constitution, and the Courts (2001).

4. *Questions of Timing — Ripeness and Mootness*

Additional justiciability barriers involve the timing of judicial review. The doctrine of ripeness bars courts from deciding cases that are premature — too speculative or remote to warrant judicial intervention. A classic example would be a case brought to challenge a criminal statute before a prosecution is initiated, in circumstances in which the mere existence of the statute is not alleged to produce actual harm. The doctrine of mootness prevents courts from hearing cases when changed circumstances deprive the plaintiff of a stake in the action. A classic example would be a case brought by a plaintiff challenging a statute prohibiting her from obtaining employment where the plaintiff has been given the job before the appeal. A case is not ripe when it is brought too soon; it is moot when it is brought too late.

Ripeness. Laird v. Tatum, 408 U.S. 1 (1972), involved a class action brought for injunctive relief against alleged "surveillance of lawful citizen political activity" by the U.S. Army. According to the plaintiffs, the army had collected information about political activities that had some potential for civil disorder; plaintiffs also claimed that they were targets of the surveillance, and that, as a result, they were "chilled" from engaging in constitutionally protected activity. The Court held that the plaintiffs did not present "a case for resolution by the courts." According to the Court, a "chilling effect" was insufficient if it arose "merely from the individual's knowledge that a government agency was engaged in certain activities or from the individual's concomitant fear that, armed with the fruits of those activities, the agency might in the future take some other and additional action detrimental to that individual." The Court said that the plaintiffs' "approach would have the federal courts as virtually continuing monitors of the wisdom and soundness of Executive action; such a role is appropriate for the Congress rather than the judiciary, absent actual present or immediately threatened injury resulting from unlawful governmental action." Justice Douglas, joined by Justice Marshall, dissented. What was the timing problem in *Tatum*? When might these litigants be able to challenge the surveillance?

Compare with *Tatum* the decision in Adler v. Board of Education, 342 U.S. 485 (1952), which involved a challenge to a state law disqualifying from employment in public schools anyone who was a member of assorted "subversive organizations." The plaintiffs seeking a declaratory judgment included parents and teachers of school children. The Court reached the merits without discussion, notwithstanding a dissent on ripeness grounds by Justice Frankfurter, who invoked United Public Workers v. Mitchell, 330 U.S. 75 (1947). In *Mitchell*, federal civil service employees sought a declaratory judgment against the Hatch Act, which prohibits federal employees from participating in the management of political campaigns. The Court said that the plaintiffs' affidavits

> declare a desire to act contrary to the rule against political activity but not that the rule has been violated. [Appellants] seem clearly to seek advisory opinions upon broad claims. [Appellants] want to engage in "political management and political campaigns," [but] such generality of objection is really an attack on the political expediency of the Hatch Act, not a presentation of legal issues. It is beyond the competence of courts to render such a decision.

Did *Mitchell* in fact involve a legal question? Why was the threat of prosecution in *Mitchell* (or *Tatum*) insufficient to justify judicial relief? Was the abstract character of the dispute a real problem?

See also Socialist Labor Party v. Gilligan, 406 U.S. 583 (1972) (refusing to hear challenge to a statute requiring party members to pledge that they were not engaged in "an attempt to overthrow the government by force"; Court notes that the pleadings did not allege that party members have ever refused in the past or will now refuse to sign the oath, which has been in existence since 1941); Poe v. Ullman, 367 U.S. 497 (1961) (refusing to hear challenge to Connecticut prohibition on use of contraceptive devices on ground that there was no allegation that state threatened prosecution).

Mootness. DeFunis v. Odegaard, 416 U.S. 312 (1974), involved a challenge to a preferential admissions program adopted by the University of Washington Law School. By the time the case reached the Court, DeFunis was in his third year of law school as a result of a decision below ordering his admission. According to the law school, his registration would not be cancelled regardless of the Supreme Court's decision. The Court noted that voluntary cessation of allegedly unlawful conduct does not make the case moot; if it did, the defendant would be "free to return to his old ways." Here, however, mootness "depends not at all upon a 'voluntary cessation' of the admissions practices that were the subject of this litigation. It depends, instead, upon the simple fact that DeFunis is now in the final quarter of the final year of his course of study, and the settled and unchallenged policy of the Law School to permit him to complete the term for which he is now enrolled." The lower court found the case moot.

Compare Roe v. Wade, 410 U.S. 113 (1973), involving a challenge to abortion statutes. Roe herself was no longer pregnant by the time the case came to the Supreme Court. The Court nonetheless held that it was not moot, relying on an established exception for cases that are "capable of repetition, yet evading review." If the termination of a pregnancy, the Court said, "makes a case moot, pregnancy litigation seldom will survive much beyond the trial stage, and appellate review will be effectively denied."

F.   THE JURISDICTION OF THE SUPREME COURT

Note: *Jurisdiction, Certiorari, and the U.S. Supreme Court*

1. *Jurisdiction in general.* For constitutional purposes, the jurisdiction of the Supreme Court is set out in article III. But Congress has never granted litigants access to the Court in all cases for which article III provides authorization. The governing provisions are set out in 28 U.S.C. §§1251–1257.

These provisions furnish two principal routes to the Supreme Court. The first, abandoned in 1988 except for rare cases, is through an appeal; the second is through certiorari.

It is generally said that the Supreme Court's appellate jurisdiction is "mandatory." If a party who has lost below seeks review, the Court must hear any case that falls within its appellate jurisdiction. Today, the two largest classes of cases falling within the Court's mandatory jurisdiction concern judicial regulation of the political process. Title 28 U.S.C. §2284(a) provides, in pertinent part, that "[a] district court of three judges shall be convened when otherwise required by Act of Congress, or when an action is filed challenging the constitutionality of the apportionment of congressional districts or the apportionment of any statewide legislative body." Similarly, section 5 of the Voting Rights Act of 1965, 42 U.S.C. §1973c, also requires the use of three-judge district courts and direct appellate review in cases involving a particularly stringent remedial statute that forbids certain jurisdictions from changing their election laws without prior federal approval. 28 U.S.C. §1253 provides that "[except] as otherwise provided by law, any party may appeal to the Supreme Court from an order granting or denying, after notice and hearing, an interlocutory or permanent injunction in any civil action, suit or proceeding required by any Act of Congress to be heard and determined by a district court of three judges." Consider why Congress retained the three-judge court, direct mandatory appeal process for these cases. Is the decision connected to a desire to resolve cases touching on fundamental questions of state self-government quickly? See Solimine, The Three-Judge District Court in Voting-Rights Litigation, 30 U. Mich. J.L. Reform 79 (1996).

Certiorari jurisdiction, by contrast, is discretionary. The Court may deny certiorari for a range of reasons other than its agreement with the decision below — the unimportance of the issue, the unusual character of the particular facts, the desire to see the issue "percolate" in the lower courts, the controversial character of the problem, or the wish to allow the political process time to consider the problem before an authoritative resolution is obtained. For a classic discussion of the denial of certiorari as an exercise of the Court's "passive virtues," see A. Bickel, The Least Dangerous Branch 115–116 (1965).

2. *The certiorari process.* Litigants seeking certiorari must file a petition for certiorari, setting out the reasons the case deserves plenary consideration. Supreme Court Rule 10, "although neither controlling nor fully measuring the Court's discretion, indicate[s] the character of the reasons" the Court considers:

> (a) a United States court of appeals has entered a decision in conflict with the decision of another United States court of appeals on the same important matter; has decided an important federal question in a way that conflicts with a decision by a state court of last resort; or has so far departed from the accepted and usual course of judicial proceedings, or sanctioned such a departure by a lower court, as to call for an exercise of this Court's supervisory power;
>
> (b) a state court of last resort has decided an important federal question in a way that conflicts with the decision of another state court of last resort or of a United States court of appeals;
>
> (c) a state court or a United States court of appeals has decided an important question of federal law that has not been, but should be, settled by this Court, or has decided an important federal question in a way that conflicts with relevant decisions of this Court.

Rules of the Supreme Court, http://www.supremecourtus.gov/ctrules/ctrules.html (2007). After the petitioner files its petition, the respondents are entitled to file a brief in opposition, explaining why the Court should not consider the case.

Roughly 8,000 petitions for certiorari are filed with the Court each year. The manner of screening cases varies among the justices. For discussions of these practices over time, see, e.g., Caldeira and Wright, The Discuss List: Agenda Building and the Supreme Court, 24 Law & Soc. Rev. 807, 811–812 (1990).

Most of the justices now on the Court participate in a "cert pool," in which one law clerk is assigned responsibility for writing a memorandum circulated to many of the chambers. Some members of the Court supplement the pool by having their own clerks prepare an additional memorandum. Two members of the Court do not participate in the pool, but instead rely on their own clerks. Prior justices sometimes handled the petition review entirely by themselves.

Normally, the Court provides no reason for its denial of a petition for certiorari, although justices who voted to hear the case will on occasion dissent from the denial of certiorari, explaining why they thought the petition should have been granted.

Far less often, justices who voted to deny the petition for certiorari will explain their reasons. See, e.g., Padilla v. Hanft, 547 U.S. 1062 (2006) (giving prudential reasons for voting to deny the petition); McCray v. New York, 461 U.S. 961 (1983) (urging lower courts to continue addressing the question presented).

Until sometime in the 1930s, the justices apparently discussed all petitions for certiorari. Since then, however, the Court has discussed as an institution only those petitions that at least one justice asks to have put on a "discuss list." See Caldeira and Wright, supra, at 812. The vast majority of all petitions are placed instead on a "dead list" and are denied without further discussion.

The general rule is that a denial of certiorari does not have any precedential value. See Teague v. Lane, 489 U.S. 288, 296 (1989). Why might the Court be careful to ensure the perpetuation of that rule?

The Court normally agrees to give plenary consideration to any case that at least four justices wish to hear. For a discussion of the history of the so-called Rule of Four, see Revesz and Karlan, Nonmajority Rules and the Supreme Court, 136 U. Pa. L. Rev. 1067, 1069–1071 (1988). For an evaluation of the rule, consider Justice Stevens's observations. Justice Stevens notes that in recent years somewhere between a quarter and a third of the Court's cases have been granted by the votes of only four justices:

> Mere numbers, however, provide an inadequate measure of the significance of the cases that were heard because of the rule. For I am sure that some Court opinions in cases that were granted by only four votes have made a valuable contribution to the development of our jurisprudence. My experience has persuaded me, however, that such cases are exceptionally rare. I am convinced that a careful study of all of the cases that have been granted on the basis of only four votes would indicate that in a surprisingly large number the law would have fared just as well if the decision of the court of appeals or the state court had been allowed to stand. . . .
>
> The Rule of Four is sometimes justified by the suggestion that if four justices of the Supreme Court consider a case important enough to warrant full briefing and argument on the merits, that should be sufficient evidence of the significance of the question presented. But a countervailing argument has at least equal force. Every case that is granted on the basis of four votes is a case that five members of the Court thought should not be granted. For the most significant work of the Court, it is assumed that the collective judgment of its majority is more reliable than the views of the minority. Arguably, therefore, deference to the minority's desire to add additional cases to the argument docket may rest on an assumption that whether the Court hears a few more or a few less cases in any term is not a matter of first importance.
>
> History and logic both support the conclusion that the Rule of Four must inevitably enlarge the size of the Court's argument docket and cause it to hear a substantial number of cases that a majority of the Court deems unworthy of review.

Stevens, The Life Span of a Judge-Made Rule, 58 N.Y.U. L. Rev. 1, 17–20 (1983). At the time Justice Stevens wrote, the Court was hearing roughly 150 cases a year. In recent years, in part as a result of the 1988 change to its jurisdiction, but in part as a result of the justices' voting behavior at the certiorari stage, the Court has dramatically decreased the number of cases it hears, giving plenary consideration to roughly eighty cases each term. See Cordray and Cordray, The Calendar of the Justices: How the Supreme Court's Timing Affects Its Decisionmaking, 36 Ariz. St. L.J. 183, 201 (2004); O'Brien, Join-3 Votes, the Rule of Four, the Cert. Pool, and the Supreme Court's Shrinking Plenary Docket, 13 J.L. & Pol. 779 (1997). For a now-classic, if outdated, account of the Supreme Court's workload, see Hart, The Time Chart of the Justices, 73 Harv. L. Rev. 84 (1959). For general discussion of the caseload problem of the federal courts, see R. Posner, Federal Courts: Crisis and Reform (1985); for the caseload in the Supreme Court, see the annual Supreme Court issues of the Harvard Law Review.

For comprehensive discussion of the Court's policies and of practice before the Court, see S. Bloch, V. Jackson, and T. Krattenmaker, Inside the Supreme Court: The Institution and Its Procedures (2d ed. 2008); E. Gressman, K. Geller, S. Shapiro, T. Bishop, and E. Hartnett, Supreme Court Practice (9th ed. 2007).

II

Federalism at Work: Congress and the National Economy

Article I, section 8 lists a number of legislative powers given to Congress. Enumeration is one technique by which the Constitution creates, or confirms the existence of, federalism. Over the course of U.S. history, one of the enumerated powers most important for defining the contours of federalism has been the power to "regulate Commerce with foreign Nations, and among the several States, and with the Indian Tribes." This chapter uses the power to regulate interstate commerce as the vehicle for examining fundamentals about federalism — the allocation of governing power between the nation and the states. Those fundamentals include (1) what, if any, are the limits on the power to regulate interstate commerce; (2) what are the mechanisms by which any such limits are enforced; and (3) in particular, what is the role of the courts in enforcing such limits?

The chapter begins with an overview of the values of federalism and the techniques for implementing it. Section B presents some doctrinal fundamentals through three classic cases, each of which articulates a different view of the limits, if any, on congressional power and of the mechanisms for enforcing such limits. Section C then examines the historical development of commerce clause doctrine, deepening the presentation of the doctrinal frameworks the Supreme Court has used. Section D concludes by examining the limits the commerce clause places on state legislation affecting interstate commerce, in the absence of express congressional legislation (the so-called dormant commerce clause).

A. THE VALUES OF FEDERALISM AND SOME TECHNIQUES FOR IMPLEMENTING THEM

Note: A Government of Enumerated Powers

1. *The origins of enumeration.* The experience of the new American nation prior to the framing of the Constitution made it clear to the framers that the primary defect in the Articles of Confederation was the failure to give sufficient

power to the national government. The framers therefore wanted to increase the power of the new government as compared to the old. This raised two problems: (1) The framers believed that states ought to remain as significant units of government, and that the national government ought to exercise its power only on distinctively national subjects, while states would exercise control over most matters of general government. (2) Power granted to the national government might be improvidently used, so as to suppress liberty and choke economic development. The framers sought to respond to those concerns by enumerating the powers granted to the national government.

The framers regarded it as significant that, whereas the prior government was a federation created by the states, the new one was created by "the People." The contemporary significance of this choice was discussed in U.S. Term Limits v. Thornton, 514 U.S. 779 (1995). In arguing that states could not impose term limits on members of Congress, Justice Stevens wrote:

> Prior to the adoption of the Constitution, the States had joined together under the Articles of Confederation. In that system, "the States retained most of their sovereignty, like independent nations bound together only by treaties." Wesberry v. Sanders, 376 U.S. 1, 9 (1964). After the Constitutional Convention convened, the Framers [adopted] "[a] plan not merely to amend the Articles of Confederation but to create an entirely new National [Government]." In adopting that plan, the Framers envisioned a uniform national system, rejecting the notion that the Nation was a collection of States, and instead creating a direct link between the National Government and the people of the United States. In that National Government, representatives owe primary allegiance not to the people of a State, but to the people of the Nation. [The] Congress of the United States, therefore, is not a confederation of nations in which separate sovereigns are represented by appointed delegates, but is instead a body composed of representatives of the people.

Justice Kennedy, concurring, added:

> The Framers split the atom of sovereignty. It was the genius of their idea that our citizens would have two political capacities, one state and one federal, each protected from incursion by the other. [A] distinctive character of the National Government [is] that it owes its existence to the act of the whole people who created it. [There] can be no doubt [that] there exists [a] relationship between the people of the Nation and their National Government, with which the States may not interfere.

Justice Thomas, in dissent, responded, "Our system of government rests on one overriding principle: all power stems from the consent of the people. [The] ultimate source of the Constitution's authority is the consent of the people of each individual State, not the consent of the undifferentiated people of the Nation as a whole." Do these different conceptions of the relations among individuals, states, and the nation imply different conceptions of the scope of national power? Of the scope of state power?

2. *How enumeration limits powers: explicit limitations as an alternative.* In The Federalist No. 84, Hamilton argued that the enumeration of national powers made unnecessary a bill of rights, which would explicitly limit Congress's powers:

> It has been several times truly remarked that bills of rights are, in their origin, stipulations between kings and their subjects, abridgments of prerogative in favor

of privilege, reservations of rights not surrendered to the prince. [Here,] in strictness, the people surrender nothing; and as they retain everything they have no need of particular reservations. . . .

I go further and affirm that bills of rights [are] not only unnecessary in the proposed Constitution but would even be dangerous. They would contain various exceptions to powers not granted; and, on this very account, would afford a colorable pretext to claim more than were granted. For why declare that things shall not be done which there is no power to do? Why, for instance, should it be said that the liberty of the press shall not be restrained, when no power is given by which restrictions may be imposed? I will not contend that such a provision would confer a regulating power; but it is evident that it would furnish, to men disposed to usurp, a plausible pretense for claiming that power. They might urge with a semblance of reason that the Constitution ought not to be charged with the absurdity of providing against the abuse of an authority which was not given, and that the provision against restraining the liberty of the press afforded a clear implication that a power to prescribe proper regulations concerning it was intended to be vested in the national government. . . .

On the subject of the liberty of the press, [I] infer that its security, whatever fine declarations may be inserted in any constitution respecting it, must altogether depend on public opinion, and on the general spirit of the people and of the government.* And here, after all, [must] we seek for the only solid basis of all our rights.

As you study the materials that follow, consider whether Hamilton was right.

Note: The Values of Federalism

What values are served by a system that distributes governmental authority between state and nation, that is, by federalism? For an overview of contemporary issues, see D. L. Shapiro, Federalism: A Dialogue (1995).

1. *Efficiency.* Given wide variations in the circumstances obtaining in different areas of the country, it is likely that different solutions to specific problems will be appropriate in different areas. But a national government can respond to problems created for one state or region by activities elsewhere. Economic integration means that economic problems in one area can be addressed with assistance from other areas, and it allows all regions to gain the benefits of goods such as defense, transportation, and communications, which are more efficiently provided on larger scales.

2. *Promoting individual choice.* A national government can enforce the values shared by a majority in the nation as a whole, even against those who are a majority in one or a few states. Consider these observations by James Madison, from The Federalist No. 46:

---

* To show that there is a power in the Constitution by which the liberty of the press may be affected, recourse has been had to the power of taxation. It is said that duties may be laid upon the publications so high as to amount to a prohibition. I know not by what logic it could be maintained that the declarations in the State constitutions, in favor of the freedom of the press, would be a constitutional impediment to the imposition of duties upon publications by the State legislatures. [And] if duties of any kind may be laid without a violation of that liberty, it is evident that the extent must depend on legislative discretion, regulated by public opinion; so that, after all, general declarations respecting the liberty of the press will give it no greater security than it will have without them. [It] would be quite as significant to declare that government ought to be free, that taxes ought not to be excessive, etc., as that the liberty of the press ought not to be restrained.

[The] federal and State governments are in fact but different agents and trustees of the people, constituted with different powers and designed for different purposes. [The] ultimate authority, wherever the derivative may be found, resides in the people alone, and [it] will not depend merely on the comparative ambition or address of the different governments whether either, or which of them, will be able to enlarge its sphere of jurisdiction at the expense of the other. . . .

If, therefore, [the] people should in future become more partial to the federal than to the State governments, the change can only result from such manifest and irresistible proofs of a better administration as will overcome all their antecedent propensities. And in that case, the people ought not surely to be precluded from giving most of their confidence where they may discover it to be most due; but even in that case the State governments could have little to apprehend, because it is only within a certain sphere that the federal power can, in the nature of things, be advantageously administered. . . .

In contrast, disabling the national government from acting on some subjects while allowing states to act in varying ways allows people to move from one area to another in order to select the kind of government policies they prefer.

Prichard, Securing the Canadian Economic Union: Federalism and Internal Barriers to Trade, in Federalism and the Canadian Economic Union 17–18 (M. Trebilcock et al. eds., 1983), suggests that the political process is likely to favor decentralization:

First, interest groups that may be minorities nationally are more likely to be majorities locally. Second, [the] greater the homogeneity of interests on a geographical basis, the more often minorities become majorities as decentralization increases. Third, decentralization of functions in a hierarchical way disaggregates policy packages and allows a citizen to cast different votes on different components of policy because they are vested in different levels of government in the jurisdictional hierarchy. Fourth, decentralization, by creating a diversity of jurisdictions, allows a better matching of preferences and policies because voters can choose that jurisdiction which offers the most preferred policy package. That is, citizens may "vote with their feet," searching out the jurisdiction offering the most attractive set of policies. Simultaneously, the threat of exit by voters from a jurisdiction forces the decentralized governments to reflect the policy preferences of their existing or potential constituents as the jurisdictions compete for voters. Fifth, given the greater homogeneity of tastes as boundaries contract, decentralization reduces the likelihood of policy compromises being adopted that create minimum winning coalitions but do not accurately reflect the interests of any particular interest group. . . .

A sixth advantage of decentralization is the reduction of "signalling" and other "transactions costs" for expressing citizen preferences [such as] participation in efforts to influence the actions of lobbies and large pressure groups [and] voting or the act of giving one's support to or withholding it from a candidate of a political party or, in very special cases, a policy.

The origin of this approach is Tiebout, A Pure Theory of Local Expenditures, 64 J. Pol. Econ. 416 (1956). Note that this view of federalism may overestimate the ease with which voters may relocate. For elaboration and critique, see A. Hirschman, Exit, Voice, and Loyalty (1970); D. Mueller, Public Choice 125–147 (1979).

3. *Encouraging experimentation.* Justice Brandeis, dissenting in New State Ice Co. v. Liebmann, 285 U.S. 262 (1932), wrote:

To stay experimentation in things social and economic is a grave responsibility. Denial of the right to experiment may be fraught with serious consequences to the Nation. It is one of the happy incidents of the federal system that a single courageous State may, if its citizens choose, serve as a laboratory; and try novel social and economic experiments without risk to the rest of the country. This Court has the power to prevent an experiment. [But] in the exercise of this high power, we must ever be on our guard, lest we erect our prejudices into legal principles. If we would guide by the light of reason, we must let our minds be bold.

Note that experiments on the local level can teach the people of the whole nation that particular innovations are valuable enough to be adopted throughout the nation.

A national government with plenary power might choose to exercise that power in ways that encourage experimentation, efficiency, and choice. It could divide the nation into administrative regions and give revocable grants of autonomy to the regions with respect to certain subjects. It could create a system in which national laws were applicable unless national administrators waived them to allow states to pursue their own paths. What values of federalism would be impaired by such a system? Do national lawmakers have incentives to set up such a system?

4. *Promoting democracy*. State and local governments provide the opportunity for people to participate directly in the activities of governments that have significant effects on their lives. This participation would make them the active citizens valued in one version of democratic theory rather than the passive subjects of a remote national government. Does federalism serve this value today?

5. *Preventing tyranny*. Consider Rapaczynski, From Sovereignty to Process: The Jurisprudence of Federalism after *Garcia*, 1985 Sup. Ct. Rev. 341, at 341, 385–386, 388–389:

> [Although] the states are more easily captured by relatively undifferentiated majoritarian interests intent on suppressing small minorities, the federal government may be a more likely subject of capture by a set of special minoritarian interests, precisely because the majority interest of the national constituency is so large, diffuse, and enormously difficult to organize. . . .
>
> [Should] the federal government ever be captured by an authoritarian movement [the] resulting oppression would almost certainly be much more severe and durable than that of which any state would be capable. [It] is precisely because the states are governmental bodies that break the national authorities' monopoly on coercion that they constitute the most fundamental bastion against a successful conversion of the federal government into a vehicle of the worst kind of oppression.

6. *Protecting liberty*. As the Court stated in Bond v. United States, 564 U.S. 211 (2011):

> Federalism secures the freedom of the individual. It allows States to respond, through the enactment of positive law, to the initiative of those who seek a voice in shaping the destiny of their own times without having to rely solely upon the political processes that control a remote central power. [Federalism] also protects the liberty of all persons within a State by ensuring that laws enacted in excess of delegated governmental power cannot direct or control their actions. By denying any one government complete jurisdiction over all the concerns of public life, federalism protects the liberty of the individual from arbitrary power. When government acts in excess of its lawful powers, that liberty is at stake.

Note two themes. (a) State-level *legislation* can affirmatively promote freedom. (b) Legislation "in excess of delegated power" threatens liberty. How can that be so with respect to national-level legislation of a sort that states could permissibly adopt without violating (state- or national-level) protections of liberty?

7. *A skeptical view of federalism's values.* Feeley and Rubin, Federalism: Political Identity and Tragic Compromise 15, 16 (2009), argue that federalism "serves as a means of modulating, or varying, political identity. [If] people's political identity is associated with some region that has been subsumed into a larger polity, federalism provides a means by which the disjunction between their political identity and their territorial mode of governance can be reduced. [Federalism] will only be appealing to people if the region itself [relates] to their sense of political identity." On this understanding, is federalism an appropriate form of governance for the United States?

Feeley and Rubin distinguish federalism from decentralization and local democracy. Decentralization "is a managerial strategy by which a centralized regime can achieve the results it desires in a more effective manner." Id. at 20. "[Federalism] does not necessarily increase participation; it simply authorizes a set of specified political subunits to decide for themselves how much participation is desirable. Some might choose to encourage participation, but others might choose to suppress it." National policymakers could "achiev[e] the same goal [by] hiring community organizers, funding local organizations, and requiring approvals for government decisions from different sectors of the population," and "[in] a truly federal regime, some states might opt for elections, while others might not." Id. at 22, 23.

On the argument that federalism promotes economic efficiency, Feeley and Rubin argue that "[federalism] allows a multiplicity of norms, not simply a multiplicity of rules. In a truly federal system, some subunits might not be interested in economic efficiency; [they] might be primarily motivated by the desire to preserve an agrarian lifestyle, to protect the environment, or to encourage individual spirituality. [They] might lose out in the competition for factories and corporate executives [but] rather than perceiving their losses as a chastening lesson [they] might perceive them as a necessary cost or as a positive advantage." Id. at 24.

Calabresi & Fish, Federalism and Moral Disagreement, 101 Minn. L. Rev. 1 (2016), argue that "states form federalist unions when they want to align for economic and security reasons in spite of fundamental moral disagreements. [But] such federalist compromises are frequently unstable, because one part of a union will sometimes seek to impose its strong moral views on the whole." Among the possible responses to this instability are secession and compromise and de-escalation. "Embracing moral federalism might entail a kind of epistemic humility, recognizing that one's own moral view may not be the correct one, or even adopting a principle that even correct moral views should not be imposed on the unwilling." But, they conclude, "[One] cannot help but ask: When is nationalizing [moral issues] worth the risk? And when is not taking the risk itself moral?" Frame the questions Calabresi and Fish raise with reference to (a) racial discrimination, (b) abortion, (c) LGBTQ rights, and (d) accommodations of antidiscrimination laws to religious beliefs.

For a collection of essays on secession, see Levinson ed., Nullification and Secession in Modern Constitutional Law (2016).

8. *Doctrinal implications.* Assuming that a political system should advance the values of federalism, do the ones listed above provide guidance on the content of a judicially enforced doctrine of federalism?

9. *The forms of federalism.* In considering the material in this chapter, keep in mind that there are a number of ways to distribute power in a federal system.

a. Neither state nor nation may have power to act. The first amendment, applicable to the states through the fourteenth amendment, exemplifies this situation: If some regulation violates the first amendment, neither state governments nor Congress may adopt it (although sometimes the substantive standards applicable to analyze the constitutional question will vary depending on whether the enacting body is a state government or Congress).

b. The national government may be given exclusive power to regulate in some area. Article I, section 10 itemizes a number of activities in which states may not engage even though Congress is given power in article I, section 8 to do so: States may not, but Congress may, "coin Money," for example.

c. State governments may have exclusive power to regulate in some area. The central controversies in this chapter involve two related questions about this category: Are there any subjects in the category, and, if so, what subjects may the states, but not Congress, regulate?

d. State and national governments may have concurrent power to regulate in some area. The supremacy clause, article VI, paragraph 2, establishes that, where the nation and the states have concurrent power that Congress chooses to exercise, the national legislation prevails over conflicting state legislation. Section D examines such questions as these: Has Congress chosen to exercise its concurrent power? Does state legislation conflict with national statutes? Does Congress's failure to exercise its power authorize — or prohibit — state legislation in the area?

10. *Cooperative federalism.* A substantial literature on cooperative federalism is summarized in Ryan, Negotiating Federalism and the Structural Constitution: Navigating the Separation of Powers Both Vertically and Horizontally, 115 Colum. L. Rev. Sidebar 4 (April 2015). Cooperative federalism takes many forms, but all involve sustained interactions in the development, implementation, and enforcement of policy nominally determined by the national government. Cooperative federalism is sometimes suggested as a way of avoiding the problems associated with a constitutional federalism whose defining characteristic is the allocation of powers between the nation and the states. Are there any constitutional objections to truly cooperative federalism? Note that sometimes states may object that their cooperation has been coerced.

B.   DOCTRINAL FUNDAMENTALS: FEDERALISM AND JUDICIAL REVIEW

Gibbons v. Ogden

22 U.S. (9 Wheat.) 1 (1824)

[The New York legislature enacted a statute granting Robert Fulton and Robert Livingston the exclusive right to operate steamboats in New York waters. The statute was designed to encourage investment in the development of the then-novel technology of steamboats. Fulton and Livingston licensed Ogden to operate a ferry between New York City and Elizabethtown Point in New Jersey. Gibbons began operating a competing ferry service that, because it necessarily entered New York waters, violated the grant to Fulton and Livingston and the license to Ogden. Gibbons's ferries were, however, licensed as "vessels [in] the coasting trade" under a statute enacted by Congress in 1793. Ogden obtained an injunction against Gibbons from the New York courts.]

MR. CHIEF JUSTICE MARSHALL delivered the opinion of the Court. . . .

[The] subject to be regulated is commerce; and our constitution being [one] of enumeration, and not of definition, to ascertain the extent of the power, it becomes necessary to settle the meaning of the word. The counsel for the appellee would limit it to traffic, to buying and selling, or the interchange of commodities, and do not admit that it comprehends navigation. This would restrict a general term, applicable to many objects, to one of its significations. Commerce, undoubtedly, is traffic, but it is something more: it is intercourse. It describes the commercial intercourse between nations, and parts of nations, in all its branches, and is regulated by prescribing rules for carrying on that intercourse. . . .

[All] America understands [the] word "commerce," to comprehend navigation. [The] power over commerce, including navigation, was one of the primary objects for which the people of American adopted their government. . . .

The subject to which the power is next applied, is to commerce "among the several States." The word "among" means intermingled with. A thing which is among others, is intermingled with them. Commerce among the States, cannot stop at the external boundary line of each State, but may be introduced into the interior.

It is not intended to say that these words comprehend that commerce, which is completely internal, which is carried on between man and man in a State, or between different parts of the same State, and which does not extend to or affect other States. Such a power would be inconvenient, and is certainly unnecessary.

Comprehensive as the word "among" is, it may very properly be restricted to that commerce which concerns more States than one. The phrase is not one which would probably have been selected to indicate the completely interior traffic of a State. [The] enumeration presupposes something not enumerated; and that something, if we regard the language or the subject of the sentence, must be the exclusively internal commerce of a State. The genius and character of the whole government seem to be, that its action is to be applied to all the external concerns of the nation, and to those internal concerns which affect the States generally; but not to those which are completely within a particular State, which do not affect other States, and with which it is not necessary to interfere, for the purpose of executing some of the general powers of the government. The completely internal commerce of a State, then, may be considered as reserved for the State itself.

But, in regulating commerce with foreign nations, the power of Congress does not stop at the jurisdictional lines of the several States. It would be a very useless power, if it could not pass those lines. [The] deep streams which penetrate our country in every direction, pass through the interior of almost every State in the Union, and furnish the means of exercising this right. If Congress has the power to regulate it, that power must be exercised whenever the subject exists. . . .

This principle is [still] more clear when applied to commerce "among the several States." They either join each other, in which case they are separated by a mathematical line, or they are remote from each other, in which case other States lie between them. What is commerce "among" them; and how is it to be conducted? Can a trading expedition between two adjoining States, commence and terminate outside of each? And if the trading intercourse be between two States remote from each other, must it not commence in one, terminate in the other, and probably pass through a third? Commerce among the States must, of necessity, be commerce with the States. [The] power of Congress, then, whatever it may be, must be exercised within the territorial jurisdiction of the several States. . . .

[What] is this power?

It is the power [to] prescribe the rule by which commerce is to be governed. This power, like all others vested in Congress, is complete in itself, may be exercised to its utmost extent, and acknowledges no limitations, other than are prescribed in the constitution. [If,] as has always been understood, the sovereignty of Congress, though limited to specified objects, is plenary as to those objects, the power over commerce with foreign nations, and among the several States, is vested in Congress as absolutely as it would be in a single government, having in its constitution the same restrictions on the exercise of the power as are found in the constitution of the United States. The wisdom and the discretion of Congress, their identity with the people, and the influence which their constituents possess at elections, are, in this, as in many other instances, as that, for example, of declaring war, the sole restraints on which they have relied, to secure them from its abuse. They are the restraints on which the people must often rely solely, in all representative governments.

[Ogden argued that state laws requiring inspections of cargo demonstrated that the power to regulate commerce was not exclusively in Congress.] That inspection laws may have a remote and considerable influence on commerce, will not be denied; but that a power to regulate commerce is the source from which the right to pass them is derived, cannot be admitted. The object of inspection laws, is to improve the quality of articles produced by the labour of a country; to fit them for exportation; or, it may be, for domestic use. They act upon the subject before it becomes an article of foreign commerce, or of commerce among the States, and prepare it for that purpose. They form a portion of that immense mass of legislation, which embraces everything within the territory of a State, not surrendered to the general government: all which can be most advantageously exercised by the States themselves. Inspection laws, quarantine laws, health laws of every description, as well as laws for regulating the internal commerce of a State, and those which respect turnpike roads, ferries, &c., are component parts of this mass.

No direct general power over these objects is granted to Congress; and, consequently, they remain subject to State legislation. If the legislative power of the Union can reach them, it must be for national purposes; it must be where the power is expressly given for a special purpose, or is clearly incidental to some power which is expressly given. . . .

Powerful and ingenious minds, taking, as postulates, that the powers expressly granted to the government of the Union, are to be contracted by construction, into the narrowest possible compass, and that the original powers of the States are retained, if any possible construction will retain them, may, by a course of well digested, but refined and metaphysical reasoning, founded on these premises, explain away the constitution of our country, and leave it, a magnificent structure, indeed, to look at, but totally unfit for use. They may so entangle and perplex the understanding, as to obscure principles, which were before thought quite plain, and induce doubts where, if the mind were to pursue its own course, none would be perceived. In such a case, it is peculiarly necessary to recur to safe and fundamental principles to sustain those principles, and when sustained, to make them the tests of the arguments to be examined.

[The Court interpreted the 1793 statute to authorize the entry of Gibbons's ferries into New York waters. The New York monopoly was therefore invalid under the supremacy clause, and the injunction was accordingly dissolved.]

Note: Gibbons v. Ogden

1. *The purposes of the commerce clause.* What were the purposes for which Congress was given the power to regulate interstate commerce? Consider the description of the problems under the Articles of Confederation from Justice Johnson's concurring opinion in *Gibbons*: "For a century the States had submitted, with murmurs, to the commercial restrictions imposed by the parent State; and now, finding themselves in the unlimited possession of those powers over their own commerce, which they had so long been deprived of, and so earnestly coveted, that selfish principle which, well controlled, is so salutary, and which, unrestricted, is so unjust and tyrannical, guided by inexperience and jealousy, began to show itself in iniquitous laws and impolitic measures, from which grew up a conflict of commercial regulations, destructive to the harmony of the States, and fatal to their commercial interests abroad." Does this history justify interpreting the commerce clause to do more than authorize Congress to override state laws obstructing the free flow of trade across state and national borders? On this view, does the commerce clause authorize Congress to enact regulations that it regards as appropriate to the development of the national economy?

2. *Limiting the commerce clause.* The commerce clause could be limited in two ways: (a) "Internal" limits: The clause might define a specific subject matter, such that Congress could not "regulate" anything but "interstate and foreign commerce." Doctrine would define "regulate" and "commerce among the several States." This subject matter limit protects the values of federalism. (b) "External" limits: The clause might allow Congress to do anything reasonably regarded as regulation of anything reasonably regarded as interstate or foreign commerce, but other provisions of the Constitution, such as the first amendment, might bar the exercise of a power concededly granted. Recall here Chief Justice Marshall's statement in *McCulloch*, Chapter 1 supra:

> Let the end be legitimate, let it be within the scope of the constitution, and all means which are appropriate, which are plainly adapted to that end, which are not prohibited, but consist with the letter and spirit of the constitution, are constitutional. [Should] Congress, in the execution of its powers, adopt measures which are prohibited by the constitution; or should Congress, under the pretext of executing its powers, pass laws for the accomplishment of objects not entrusted to the government; it would become the painful duty of this tribunal, should a case requiring such a decision come before it, to say that such an act was not the law of the land. But where the law is not prohibited, and is really calculated to effect any of the objects entrusted to the government, to undertake here to inquire into the degree of its necessity, would be to pass the line which circumscribes the judicial department, and to tread on legislative ground.

Does this imply that the courts will enforce both internal and external limits? The distinction between internal and external limits is closely tied to resolution of questions about judicial enforcement of limits on Congress's powers: It is usually conceded that the courts can enforce external limits such as the first amendment. But judicial enforcement of federalism-based limits is more controversial. Consider the implications of the claim that, although limits such as the first amendment are relatively clear, there are no equivalently clear provisions available for the courts to rely on in enforcing federalism-based limits on Congress's power.

3. *Internal limits.* What "internal" limits might be found in the commerce clause? Chief Justice Marshall considers three:

a. "Commerce." Is there a plausible theory under which the operation of a ferry, or navigation, is not commerce? Note that, when discussing state inspection laws, Chief Justice Marshall suggests that they act on the subject "before it becomes an article of" interstate commerce. Does this indicate a retreat from the broad definition earlier in the opinion? This phrase occurs when Chief Justice Marshall is considering whether the national power is exclusive. Does the difference in context explain or justify a difference in definition?

b. "Among the several States." Chief Justice Marshall says that the clause does not extend to "that commerce which is completely internal [and] which does not [affect] other States." Later he adds that Congress may lack power only if, in addition to these conditions being satisfied, it was "unnecessary" to regulate commerce. Note the conjunctive form of the statements. Was there such commerce in 1824? Can any commercial activity today satisfy all three requirements? Are the courts in a good position to determine whether congressional regulation of some (arguably or clearly) intrastate commerce is necessary? Whether that intrastate commerce affects other states? Why would giving power to Congress to regulate "completely internal" commerce be "inconvenient"?

c. "Regulate." How does Chief Justice Marshall define "regulation"? According to his definition, must a statute, in order to qualify as a "regulation," be directed at commercial goals?

Hammer v. Dagenhart (The Child Labor Case)

247 U.S. 251 (1918)

[In 1916, Congress responded to a decade-long lobbying effort by enacting the Child Labor Act. The act prohibited the transportation in interstate commerce of goods produced in factories employing children under age fourteen or employing fourteen- to sixteen-year-olds for more than eight hours a day, or six days a week, or at night. Two children, one under age fourteen and the other under age sixteen, were employed in a cotton mill in North Carolina. Their father secured an injunction against the enforcement of the act on grounds of its unconstitutionality.]

MR. JUSTICE DAY delivered the opinion of the Court. . . .

[The] thing intended to be accomplished by this statute is the denial of the facilities of interstate commerce to those manufacturers in the States who employ children within the prohibited ages. The act in its effect does not regulate transportation among the States, but aims to standardize the ages at which children may be employed in mining and manufacturing within the States. The goods shipped are of themselves harmless. [When] offered for shipment, and before transportation begins, the labor of their production is over, and the mere fact that they were intended for interstate commerce transportation does not make their production subject to federal control under the commerce power. . . .

It is further contended that the authority of Congress may be exerted to control interstate commerce in the shipment of child-made goods because of the effect of the circulation of such goods in other States where the evil of this class of labor has been recognized by local legislation, and the right to thus employ child labor has been more rigorously restrained than in the State of production. In other words, that the unfair competition, thus engendered, may be controlled by closing the channels of interstate commerce to manufacturers in those States where the local laws do not meet what Congress deems to be the more just standard of other States.

There is no power vested in Congress to require the States to exercise their police power so as to prevent possible unfair competition. Many causes may cooperate to give one State, by reason of local laws or conditions, an economic advantage over others. The Commerce Clause was not intended to give to Congress a general authority to equalize such conditions. . . .

[To] sustain this statute would not be in our judgment a recognition of the lawful exertion of congressional authority over interstate commerce, but would sanction an invasion by the federal power of the control of a matter purely local in its character, and over which no authority has been delegated to Congress in conferring the power to regulate commerce among the States. . . .

In our view the necessary effect of this act is, by means of a prohibition against the movement in interstate commerce of ordinary commercial commodities, to regulate the hours of labor of children in factories and mines within the States, a purely state authority. Thus the act in a twofold sense is repugnant to the Constitution. It not only transcends the authority delegated to Congress over commerce but also exerts a power as to a purely local matter to which the federal authority does not extend. The far reaching result of upholding the act cannot be more plainly indicated than by pointing out that if Congress can thus regulate matters entrusted to local authority by prohibition of the movement of commodities in interstate commerce, all freedom of commerce will be at an end, and the power of the States over local matters may be eliminated, and thus our system of government be practically destroyed.

MR. JUSTICE HOLMES, dissenting. . . .

[If] an act is within the powers specifically conferred upon Congress, it seems to me that it is not made any less constitutional because of the indirect effects that it may have, however obvious it may be that it will have those effects, and that we are not at liberty upon such grounds to hold it void. . . .

[The] statute in question is within the power expressly given to Congress if considered only as to its immediate effects and [if] invalid it is so only upon some collateral ground. The statute confines itself to prohibiting the carriage of certain goods in interstate or foreign commerce. Congress is given power to regulate such commerce in unqualified terms. . . .

[The] question then is narrowed to whether the exercise of its otherwise constitutional power by Congress can be pronounced unconstitutional because of its possible reaction upon the conduct of the States in a matter upon which I have admitted that they are free from direct control. . . .

[The] manufacture of oleomargarine is as much a matter of state regulation as the manufacture of cotton cloth. Congress levied a tax upon the compound when colored so as to resemble butter that was so great as obviously to prohibit the manufacture and sale. In a very elaborate discussion the present Chief Justice excluded any inquiry into the purpose of an act which apart from that purpose was within the power of Congress. McCray v. United States, 195 U.S. 27. . . .

The notion that prohibition is any less prohibition when applied to things now thought evil I do not understand. But if there is any matter upon which civilized countries have agreed, [it] is the evil of premature and excessive child labor. I should have thought that if we were to introduce our own moral conceptions where in my opinion they do not belong, this was preeminently a case for upholding the exercise of all its powers by the United States. . . .

The act does not meddle with anything belonging to the States. They may regulate their internal affairs and their domestic commerce as they like. But when they seek to send their products across the state line they are no longer within their rights. [The] national welfare as understood by Congress may require a different attitude within its sphere from that of some self-seeking State. It seems to me entirely constitutional for Congress to enforce its understanding by all the means at its command.

MR. JUSTICE MCKENNA, MR. JUSTICE BRANDEIS, and MR. JUSTICE CLARKE concur in this opinion.

Wickard v. Filburn

317 U.S. 111 (1942)

[Under the Agricultural Adjustment Act, the Secretary of Agriculture set a quota for wheat production, after finding that the total supply of wheat would substantially exceed a normal year's domestic consumption and export needs. The 1941 quota was approved in a referendum of wheat growers, required by the act, by 81 to 19 percent. Under the quota, each wheat grower was given an allotment. Filburn had a dairy farm in Montgomery County, Ohio, on which he also raised small amounts of wheat for his livestock, for making flour at home, for seed purposes, and for sale. His 1941 allotment was 222 bushels, but he harvested 461 bushels. Under the act, he was penalized $117. Filburn sued the Secretary of Agriculture to enjoin enforcement of the penalty. The lower court issued the injunction.]

MR. JUSTICE JACKSON delivered the opinion of the Court. . . .

It is urged that under the Commerce Clause, [Congress] does not possess the power it has in this instance sought to exercise. The question would merit little consideration [except] for that fact that this Act extends federal regulation to production not intended in any part for commerce but wholly for consumption on the farm. [Marketing] quotas not only embrace all that may be sold without penalty but also what may be consumed on the premises. . . .

Appellee says that this is a regulation of production and consumption of wheat. Such activities are, he urges, [local] in character, and their effects upon interstate commerce are at most "indirect." . . .

[Questions] of the power of Congress are not to be decided by reference to any formula which would give controlling force to nomenclature such as "production" and "indirect" and foreclose consideration of the actual effects of the activity in question upon interstate commerce.

At the beginning Chief Justice Marshall described the federal commerce power with a breadth never yet exceeded. [Gibbons v. Ogden.] He made emphatic the embracing and penetrating nature of this power by warning that effective restraints on its exercise must proceed from political rather than from judicial processes. . . .

The Court's recognition of the relevance of the economic effects in the application of the Commerce Clause [has] made the mechanical application of legal formulas no longer feasible. Once an economic measure of the reach of the power granted to Congress in the Commerce Clause is accepted, questions of federal power cannot be decided simply by finding the activity in question to be "production," nor can consideration of its economic effects be foreclosed by calling them "indirect." . . .

Whether the subject of the regulation in question was "production," "consumption," or "marketing" is, therefore, not material for purposes of deciding the question of federal power before us. [But] even if appellee's activity be local and though it may not be regarded as commerce, it may still, whatever its nature, be reached by Congress if it exerts a substantial economic effect on interstate commerce, and this irrespective of whether such effect is what might at some earlier time have been defined as "direct" or "indirect." The parties have stipulated a summary of the economics of the wheat industry. . . .

The wheat industry has been a problem industry for some years. Largely as a result of increased foreign production and import restrictions, annual exports of wheat and flour from the United States during the ten-year period ending in 1940 averaged less than 10 per cent of total production, while during the 1920's they averaged more than 25 per cent. The decline in the export trade has left a large surplus in production which, in connection with an abnormally large supply of wheat, [caused] congestion in a number of markets; tied up railroad cars; and caused elevators in some instances to turn away grains, and railroads to institute embargoes to prevent further congestion. . . .

The effect of consumption of home-grown wheat on interstate commerce is due to the fact that it constitutes the most variable factor in the disappearance of the wheat crop. Consumption on the farm where grown appears to vary in an amount greater than 20 per cent of average production. The total amount of wheat consumed as food varies but relatively little, and use as seed is relatively constant.

The maintenance by government regulation of a price for wheat undoubtedly can be accomplished as effectively by sustaining or increasing the demand as by limiting the supply. The effect of the statute before us is to restrict the amount which may be produced for market and the extent as well to which one may forestall resort to the market by producing to meet his own needs. That appellee's own contribution to the demand for wheat may be trivial by itself is not enough to remove him from the scope of federal regulation where, as here, his contribution, taken together with that of many others similarly situated, is far from trivial.

[A] factor of such volume and variability as home-consumed wheat would have a substantial influence on price and market conditions. This may arise because being in marketable condition such wheat overhangs the market and, if induced by rising prices, tends to flow into the market and check price increases. But if we assume that it is never marketed, it supplies a need of the man who grew it which would otherwise be reflected by purchases in the open market. Home-grown wheat in this sense competes with wheat in commerce. The stimulation of commerce is a use of the regulatory function quite as definitely as prohibitions or restrictions thereon. This record leaves us in no doubt that Congress may properly have considered that wheat consumed on the farm where grown, if wholly outside the scheme of regulation, would have a substantial effect in defeating and obstructing its purpose to stimulate trade therein at increased prices. . . .

[Reversed.]

Note: *Political Constraints versus Judicial Enforcement*

The Constitution's enumeration of congressional powers, including the power to regulate commerce among the states, allocates power between the nation and the states. Is that allocation to be enforced by the courts or through political checks on Congress? Note that both the courts and the political process are imperfect. Courts may invalidate laws that are consistent with the proper allocation, and Congress may enact laws inconsistent with the proper allocation despite the political constraints. Note also that the courts have the opportunity to review only laws Congress has enacted.

1. *Madison's argument.* In The Federalist No. 45 and No. 46, Madison suggests that members of Congress will be so imbued with respect for local governments that they will rarely exercise even broad grants of power improvidently. From The Federalist No. 45:

The State governments will have the advantage of the federal government, whether we compare them in respect to the immediate dependence of the one on the other; to the weight of personal influence which each side will possess; to the powers respectively vested in them; to the predilection and probable support of the people; to the disposition and faculty of resisting and frustrating the measures of each other.

The State governments may be regarded as constituent and essential parts of the federal government; whilst the latter is nowise essential to the operation or organization of the former. Without the intervention of the State legislatures, the President of the United States cannot be elected at all. They must in all cases have a great share in his appointment. [The] Senate will be elected absolutely and exclusively by the State legislatures. Even the House of Representatives, though drawn immediately from the people, will be chosen very much under the influence of that class of men whose influence over the people obtains for themselves an election into the State legislatures. Thus, each of the principal branches of the federal government will owe its existence more or less to the favor of the State governments, and must consequently feel a dependence, which is much more likely to beget a disposition too obsequious than too overbearing towards them. On the other side, the component parts of the State governments will in no instance be indebted for their appointment to the direct agency of the federal government, and very little, if at all, to the local influence of its members.

The number of individuals employed under the Constitution of the United States will be much smaller than the number employed under the particular States.

There will consequently be less of personal influence on the side of the former than of the latter. . . .

The powers delegated by the proposed Constitution to the federal government are few and defined. Those which are to remain in the State governments are numerous and indefinite. The former will be exercised principally on external objects, as war, peace, negotiation, and foreign commerce; with which last the power of taxation will, for the most part, be connected. The powers reserved to the several States will extend to all the objects which, in the ordinary course of affairs, concern the lives, liberties, and properties of the people, and the internal order, improvement, and prosperity of the State.

The operations of the federal government will be most extensive and important in times of war and danger; those of the State governments in times of peace and security. As the former periods will probably bear a small proportion to the latter, the State governments will here enjoy another advantage over the federal government. The more adequate, indeed, the federal powers may be rendered to the national defense, the less frequent will be those scenes of danger which might favor their ascendancy over the governments of the particular States. . . .

From The Federalist No. 46:

Many considerations [seem] to place it beyond doubt that the first and most natural attachment of the people will be to the governments of their respective States. Into the administration of these a greater number of individuals will expect to rise. From the gift of these a greater number of offices and emoluments will flow. By the superintending care of these, all the more domestic and personal interests of the people will be regulated and provided for. With the affairs of these, the people will be more familiarly and minutely conversant. And with the members of these will a greater proportion of the people have the ties of personal acquaintance and friendship, and of family and party attachments; on the side of these, therefore, the popular bias may well be expected most strongly to incline. . . .

[The] prepossessions, which the members themselves will carry into the federal government, will generally be favorable to the States; whilst it will rarely happen that the members of the State governments will carry into the public councils a bias in favor of the general government. A local spirit will infallibly prevail much more in the members of Congress than a national spirit will prevail in the legislatures of the particular States. Everyone knows that a great proportion of the errors committed by the State legislatures proceeds from the disposition of the members to sacrifice the comprehensive and permanent interest of the State to the particular and separate views of the counties or districts in which they reside. And if they do not sufficiently enlarge their policy to embrace the collective welfare of their particular State, how can it be imagined that they will make the aggregate prosperity of the Union, and the dignity and respectability of its government, the objects of their affections and consultations? [Measures] will too often be decided according to their probable effect, not on the national prosperity and happiness, but on the prejudices, interests, and pursuits of the governments and people of the individual States. [The] new federal government [will] partake sufficiently of the spirit of both to be disinclined to invade the rights of the individual States, or the prerogatives of their governments. The motives on the part of the State governments to augment their prerogatives by defalcations from the federal government will be overruled by no reciprocal predispositions in the members.

Were it admitted, however, that the federal government may feel an equal disposition with the State governments to extend its power beyond the due limits, the latter would still have the advantage in the means of defeating such encroachments. If an act of a particular State, though unfriendly to the national government, be generally popular in that State, and should not too grossly violate the oaths of the

State officers, it is executed [immediately]. The opposition of the federal government, or the interposition of federal officers, would but inflame the zeal of all parties on the side of the State, and the evil could not be prevented or repaired, if at all, without the employment of means which must always be resorted to with reluctance and difficulty. On the other hand, should an unwarrantable measure of the federal government be unpopular in particular States, which would seldom fail to be the case, or even a warrantable measure be so, which may sometimes be the case, the means of opposition to it are powerful and at hand. The disquietude of the people; their repugnance and, perhaps, refusal to co-operate with the officers of the Union; the frowns of the executive magistracy of the State; the embarrassments created by legislative devices, which would often be added on such occasions, would oppose, in any State, difficulties not to be despised; would form, in a large State, very serious impediments; and where the sentiments of several adjoining States happened to be in unison, would present obstructions which the federal government would hardly be willing to encounter.

But ambitious encroachments of the federal government on the authority of the State governments would not excite the opposition of a single State, or of a few States only. They would be signals of general alarm. Every government would espouse the common cause. A correspondence would be opened. Plans of resistance would be concerted. One spirit would animate and conduct the whole. . . .

Do Madison's reasons seem persuasive under modern conditions?

2. *Wechsler's argument.* Herbert Wechsler updated Madison's argument in The Political Safeguards of Federalism, in H. Wechsler, Principles, Politics, and Fundamental Law 49–82 (1961; first published in 1954). To Wechsler, "Madison's analysis has never lost its thrust," despite "the rise of national parties [and] the shift to popular election of the Senate." Wechsler began by noting that "national action has [always] been regarded as exceptional in our polity. [Those] who would advocate [the] exercise [of national power] must [answer] the preliminary question why the matter should not be left to the states." Wechsler augmented Madison's argument by invoking more modern political devices that led the Senate "to function as the guardian of state interests as such," including seniority and the filibuster. As to the House, he relied on "the states' control of voters' qualifications [and] of districting." Even though the President must "balance the localism and the separatism of the Congress by presenting programs that reflect the needs of the entire nation," that office is influenced by localism as well. The allocation of votes in the electoral college affects the allocation of time in presidential campaigns; party rules allocate convention votes based on some localist considerations. To build a winning coalition, a presidential candidate must appeal to groups that "approach balance-of-power status in important states"; some of these groups may promote "local values." For Wechsler, the size of the present national government is attributable "mainly to the magnitude of unavoidable responsibility under the circumstances of our time." Wechsler drew the following conclusion:

[Judicial review was intended to maintain] national supremacy against nullification or usurpation by the individual states. [The] Court is on weakest ground when it opposes its interpretation of the Constitution to that of Congress in the interest of the states, whose representatives control the legislative process and, by hypothesis, have broadly acquiesced in sanctioning the challenged Act of Congress. Federal intervention as against the states is thus primarily a matter for congressional determination in our system as it now stands.

See also J. Choper, Judicial Review and the National Political Process 171–259 (1980).

3. *The New Nationalism/Federalism*. For a collection of essays on federalism and nationalism, see Feature, Federalism as the New Nationalism, 123 Yale L.J. 1888 (2014). The essays draw upon an account of the way in which state and local governments actually interact with the national government. Evoking older notions of states as laboratories of experimentation, the authors note that many issues are initially crystallized into policies at the local and state levels, generating support for their expansion elsewhere, including at the national level. In addition, many national programs are — by national choice — administered by state and local officials. This gives them the opportunity both to communicate with executive and legislative officials on the national level about how the program works, and to implement the programs — within parameters set, sometimes loosely, by national legislation — in locally distinctive ways. (The latter possibility is enhanced by the inclusion of provisions authorizing national officials to waive some requirements of the national statute.) These opportunities, in turn, can contribute to reshaping the national statute in practice and by prompting formal amendments. NFIB v. Sebelius, below, places some limits on the extent to which the national government can require that states participate in national programs, which in turn gives state officials bargaining leverage in shaping the national programs. In addition, political parties dominant at the national level might not be dominant in all states, which creates loci of potential resistance to national policies.

These arguments differ from Wechsler's by relying not on the Constitution's structural features but on an analysis of contemporary political realities.

To what extent should understandings of the Constitution or constitutional doctrine be shaped by such an analysis? For a discussion, see Pildes, Romanticizing Democracy, Political Fragmentation, and the Decline of American Government, 124 Yale L. J. 804 (2014). Note that (a) those political realities change from time to time, (b) accurately describing them can be controversial, and (c) the normative implications of even agreed upon descriptions may be controversial. Consider the possibility that such realities might be relevant to understanding the Constitution but not to the development of constitutional doctrine.

4. *Some views from the justices*. In Garcia v. San Antonio Metropolitan Transit Authority, 469 U.S. 528 (1985), writing for a majority upholding the constitutionality of the application of federal wage and hour laws to state and local employees, Justice Blackmun wrote:

> [The] principal means chosen by the Framers to ensure the role of the States in the federal system lies in the structure of the Federal Government itself. It is no novelty to observe that the composition of the Federal Government was designed in large part to protect the States from overreaching by Congress.[11] . . .
>   The extent to which the structure of the Federal Government itself was relied on to insulate the interests of the States is evident in the views of the Framers. [Citing The Federalist No. 46.] [The] Framers chose to rely on a federal system in which special restraints on federal power over the States inhered principally in the workings of the National Government itself, rather than in discrete limitations on the objects of federal authority. State sovereign interests [are] more properly protected by procedural safeguards inherent in the structure of the federal system than by judicially created limitations on federal power.

11. See, e.g., [Choper; Wechsler, supra].

The effectiveness of the federal political process in preserving the States' interests is apparent even today in the course of federal legislation. . . .

[At] the same time that the States have exercised their influence to obtain federal support, they have been able to exempt themselves from a wide variety of obligations imposed by Congress under the Commerce Clause. For example, [the] National Labor Relations Act, [the] Occupational Safety and Health Act, the Employee Retirement Insurance Security Act, and the Sherman Act all contain express or implied exemptions for States and their subdivisions. The fact that some federal statutes such as the FLSA [Fair Labor Standards Act] extend general obligations to the States cannot obscure the extent to which the political position of the States in the federal system has served to minimize the burdens that the States bear under the Commerce Clause.

We realize that changes in the structure of the Federal Government have taken place since 1789, not the least of which has been the substitution of popular election of Senators by the adoption of the Seventeenth Amendment in 1913, and that these changes may work to alter the influence of the States in the federal political process. Nonetheless, against this background, we are convinced that the fundamental limitation that the constitutional scheme imposes on the Commerce Clause to protect the "States as States" is one of process rather than one of result.

Justice Powell responded:

Members of Congress are elected from the various States, but once in office they are members of the federal government.[8] Although the States participate in the Electoral College, this is hardly a reason to view the President as a representative of the States' interest against federal encroachment. We noted recently "the hydraulic pressure inherent within each of the separate Branches to exceed the outer limits of its power. . . ." Immigration and Naturalization Service v. Chadha, 462 U.S. 919, 951 (1983). The Court offers no reason to think that this pressure will not operate when Congress seeks to invoke its powers under the Commerce Clause, notwithstanding the electoral role of the States.[9] The Court apparently thinks that the States' success at obtaining federal funds for various projects and exemptions from the obligations of some federal statutes is indicative of the "effectiveness of the federal political process in preserving the States' interests. . . ." But such political success is not relevant to the question whether the political processes

8. One can hardly imagine this Court saying that because Congress is composed of individuals, individual rights guaranteed by the Bill of Rights are amply protected by the political process. Yet, the position adopted today is indistinguishable in principle. The Tenth Amendment also is an essential part of the Bill of Rights.

9. At one time in our history, the view that the structure of the federal government sufficed to protect the States might have had a somewhat more practical, although not a more logical, basis. Professor Wechsler, whose seminal article in 1954 proposed the view adopted by the Court today, predicated his argument on assumptions that simply do not accord with current reality. Professor Wechsler wrote: "National action has . . . always been regarded as exceptional in our polity. . . ." Not only is the premise of this view clearly at odds with the proliferation of national legislation over the past 30 years, but "a variety of structural and political changes in this century have combined to make Congress particularly insensitive to state and local values." Advisory Commission on Intergovernmental Relations [ACIR], Regulatory Federalism: Policy, Process, Impact and Reform 50 (1984). The adoption of the Seventeenth Amendment (providing for direct election of senators), the weakening of political parties on the local level, and the rise of national media, among other things, have made Congress increasingly less representative of State and local interests, and more likely to be responsive to the demands of various national constituencies. [Thus,] even if one were to ignore the numerous problems with the Court's position in terms of constitutional theory, there would remain serious questions as to its factual premises.

are the proper means of enforcing constitutional limitations.[11] The fact that Congress generally does not transgress constitutional limits on its power to reach State activities does not make judicial review any less necessary to rectify the cases in which it does do so.[12] The States' role in our system of government is a matter of constitutional law, not of legislative grace. . . .

More troubling than the logical infirmities in the Court's reasoning is the result of its holding, i.e., that federal political officials, invoking the Commerce Clause, are the sole judges of the limits of their own power. This result is inconsistent with the fundamental principles of our constitutional system. At least since Marbury v. Madison it has been the settled province of the federal judiciary "to say what the law is" with respect to the constitutionality of acts of Congress. In rejecting the role of the judiciary in protecting the States from federal overreaching, the Court's opinion offers no explanation for ignoring the teaching of the most famous case in our history.[13]

Note that Justice Blackmun asserted that the political process had in fact protected state interests to a satisfactory degree. The state in *Garcia* contended that, whatever might be true about congressional protection of state interests in other contexts, here the congressional process had failed to do so. What response, if any, could Justice Blackmun offer to that argument? To Justice Powell's reliance on *Marbury*? To Justice Powell's note about individual rights?

Consider this suggestion, from Regan, How to Think about the Federal Commerce Power and Incidentally Rewrite United States v. Lopez, 94 Mich. L. Rev. 554, 557, 560–561 (1995):

[In] thinking about whether the federal government has the power to do something or other, we should ask what special reason there is for the federal government to have that power. What reason is there to think the states are incapable or untrustworthy? [Is there] any reason why the regulation under consideration should come from the federal government[?]

Should this be supplemented by another question: "What reason is there to think that the courts are better able than Congress to determine whether the states are incapable or untrustworthy?"

5. *The seventeenth amendment and other constitutional changes.* The seventeenth amendment replaced election of senators by state legislators with direct

---

11. Apparently in an effort to reassure the States, the Court identifies several major statutes that thus far have not been made applicable to State governments. [The] Court does not suggest that this restraint will continue after its decision here. Indeed, it is unlikely that special interest groups will fail to accept the Court's open invitation to urge Congress to extend these and other statutes to apply to the States and their local subdivisions.

12. This Court has never before abdicated responsibility for assessing the constitutionality of challenged action on the ground that affected parties theoretically are able to look out for their own interests through the electoral process. [A] much stronger argument as to inherent structural protections could have been made in either Buckley v. Valeo, 424 U.S. 1 (1976), or Myers v. United States, 272 U.S. 52 (1926), than can be made here. In these cases, the President signed legislation that limited his authority with respect to certain appointments and thus arguably "it was no concern of this Court that the law violated the Constitution." 426 U.S., at 841–842 n.12. The Court nevertheless held the laws unconstitutional because they infringed on presidential authority, the President's consent notwithstanding. . . .

13. [The] Court does not explain how leaving the States virtually at the mercy of the federal government, without recourse to judicial review, will enhance their opportunities to experiment and serve as "laboratories."

election. Justice Souter, dissenting in United States v. Morrison, 529 U.S. 598 (2000), argued that the seventeenth amendment, along with the Reconstruction amendments, fundamentally altered the assumptions about the division of power between states and nation. Consider the following argument: In 1789 the framers believed (a) that they were creating a government of limited powers and (b) that the grant of power to Congress to regulate commerce among the several states did not give Congress the power to regulate everything. These two beliefs were compatible in 1789. Belief (b) is no longer accurate, given transformations in the economy, but it is important to maintain the compatibility between the contemporary facts and the overall Constitution. The seventeenth amendment demonstrates that the underlying theory of the Constitution has changed in a way that makes it possible to reject belief (a) and make the Constitution compatible with contemporary reality. How does this argument differ from the "political safeguards" one?

6. *The significance of unfunded mandates.* The Unfunded Mandates Reform Act of 1995, 2 U.S.C. §1501ff (1995), establishes a procedure for consideration of bills that would impose unfunded mandates on state and local governments. Such mandates prescribe rules, compliance with which is costly, but do not authorize the expenditure of federal funds to offset those costs. The act applies to mandates of $50 million or more; it exempts mandates that enforce constitutional rights or antidiscrimination statutory rights. It structures the internal procedures of the House and Senate, with the effect that each House must take a separate and recorded vote on whether to impose an unfunded mandate.

7. *A procedural perspective.* Justice Breyer, dissenting in United States v. Morrison, 529 U.S. 598 (2000), found it significant, and perhaps dispositive of a constitutional challenge, that Congress "followed procedures that help to protect the federalism values at stake. It provided adequate notice to the States of its intent to legislate. [In] response, attorneys general in [thirty-eight] States supported congressional legislation." Further, Congress compiled "a 'mountain of data'" supporting its legislation. The resulting statutes "focused [upon] documented deficiencies in state legal systems," and Congress "tailored the law to prevent its use in certain areas. [The] law [seems] to represent an instance, not of state/federal conflict, but of state/federal efforts to [cooperate]." The majority responded that Congress's data and findings were irrelevant because they were predicated on a theory of the commerce clause that the Court rejected. Is there a relation between Justice Breyer's procedural emphasis and the idea of political enforcement?

8. *Some objections.* Does the Madisonian argument, as updated to take account of present political practices, meet the objection that modern conditions have altered the political forces on which the argument relies? Consider the impact of increasing mobility among the population (and among people with political ambitions). Note that, in the past, service in state and local government may have been the best method to gain exposure to congressional-district and statewide constituencies, and consider the extent to which candidates may today gain similar exposure by other methods. Is the party system so strong as to overcome localist biases? The power of special interest groups? The power of single-issue lobbies? What is the impact of decisions requiring that states district strictly according to population? Consider the objection that judicial review may sometimes eliminate legislation enacted by Congress that serves the interest of several regions at the expense of the interests of another region, and in this connection consider the implications of the Civil War and its outcome.

9. *The Constitution as structure.* Arguments like Madison's rely on the incentives political actors have as the primary guarantee that legislation will respect constitutional norms. Proponents of term limits believe that altering the incentives legislators have will affect outcomes. The twenty-seventh amendment has a similar purpose. Consider (a) whether designing appropriate incentives for legislators is a more effective guarantee that the Constitution's norms will be respected than is judicial review, and (b) the extent to which the Constitution relies on such incentives.

C.   THE EVOLUTION OF COMMERCE CLAUSE DOCTRINE: THE LESSONS(?) OF HISTORY

Until the late nineteenth century, Congress rarely exercised its power to regulate interstate commerce. It acted to promote economic growth by establishing, for part of the era, the Bank of the United States; by transferring public lands to private owners; and by securing the nation's borders and its trade against foreign attack. The slavery controversy limited the opportunities for a consensus to form in favor of extensive exercise of the commerce power.

The Civil War and its aftermath inaugurated an era in which Congress began to act more vigorously. The economy became obviously interconnected; problems were no longer localized, so it became difficult to imagine a purely internal commerce that affected no other states. During the Reconstruction era, supporters of the Union saw that the rights of freed slaves and their friends in the South were not adequately protected by state governments. They concluded that national intervention was appropriate and developed theories of federalism that justified broad exercises of national power. Finally, the mobilization of the northern economy to fight the Civil War showed that national power could be used efficiently, rather than wastefully, and the experience of the Civil War demonstrated that national power could indeed be used to promote liberty.

These factors combined to make Congress more willing to exercise its power to regulate interstate commerce. The Interstate Commerce Act of 1887 and the Sherman Antitrust Act of 1890 illustrate the commencement of the new era. Congress's earlier interventions in the economy, such as its disposal of public lands, had not created constituencies that strongly objected to the interventions. But the new regulatory mode of action automatically generated such constituencies in the groups newly burdened by regulation. When these groups objected to national legislation on the ground that only the states could regulate their activities, they could provide relatively concrete examples of how in their view the national legislation threatened liberty and impaired the incentives needed to promote economic growth.

This section opens by examining a number of doctrinal devices that the Supreme Court developed to deal with federalism-based objections to national legislation, and then turns to the abandonment and revival of such doctrines. The legislation subject to review takes two forms. Sometimes Congress imposes regulation on the industry, and sometimes it prohibits the shipment across state lines of goods that failed to meet specified conditions. Do the doctrinal tests differ depending on the form of the legislation? Should they?

Note also that congressional legislation only sometimes was designed to promote commercial goals directly. (Did those goals always include the promotion of the free flow of goods?) At other times, Congress acted to promote social goals, which were viewed as valuable wholly apart from their relation to economic development. Are such uses of the power to regulate interstate commerce appropriate? Are they constitutional? Did the doctrinal tests differ depending on the goal of the legislation? Should they? Is it possible to sustain the distinction between commercial and social goals?

The cases invoked two general approaches. Under the formal approach, the Court examined the statute and the regulated activity to determine whether certain objective criteria are satisfied. For example, upholding regulation triggered by the fact that goods cross state lines is a formal approach that ignores actual economic effects and actual legislative motivation. In contrast, the realist approach attempted to determine the actual economic impact of the regulation or the actual motivation of Congress. Both formalism and realism were used to invalidate legislation and to uphold it. Can you discern any pattern to the results? Do the availability and use of competing approaches to yield varying results illuminate the question of whether courts should enforce limits on Congress's power in the name of federalism?

UNITED STATES v. E. C. KNIGHT CO., 156 U.S. 1 (1895). The United States invoked the Sherman Act to set aside the acquisition by the American Sugar Refining Company of four competing refineries. The acquisition left only one independent refinery in operation, which produced 2 percent of the sugar refined in the country. The Supreme Court, through Chief Justice Fuller, held that the Sherman Act did not reach this monopoly because the Constitution did not allow Congress to regulate "manufacturing." The government argued "that the power to control the manufacture of refined sugar is a monopoly over a necessary of life, to the enjoyment of which by a large part of the population of the United States interstate commerce is indispensable, and that, therefore, the general government may repress such monopoly directly and set aside the instruments which have created it." Chief Justice Fuller responded, "[This] argument cannot be confined to necessaries of life merely, and must include all articles of general consumption. Doubtless the power to control the manufacture of a given thing involves in a certain sense the control of its disposition, but this is a secondary and not the primary sense; and although the exercise of that power may result in bringing the operation of commerce into play, it does not control it, and affects it only incidentally and indirectly. Commerce succeeds to manufacture, and is not a part of it. [The] fact that an article is manufactured for export to another State does not of itself make it an article of interstate commerce, and the intent of the manufacturer does not determine the time when the article or product passes from the control of the State and belongs to commerce." Justice Harlan dissented. Agreeing that it was important to preserve "the just authority of the States," he insisted that it was equally important to preserve national authority, whose "destruction [would] be fatal to the peace and wellbeing of the American people." To him, a monopoly that "obstructs freedom in buying and selling articles" to be sold out of state "affects, not incidentally, but directly, the people of all the States. [When] manufacture ends, that which has been manufactured becomes a subject of commerce; [buying] and selling succeed manufacture, come into existence after the process of manufacture is completed, precede transportation, and are as much commercial intercourse, where articles are bought to be carried from one State to another, as is the manual transportation of such articles after they have been so purchased. [Whatever] improperly obstructs the free course of interstate intercourse and trade, as involved in the buying and selling of articles to be carried from one State to another, may be reached by Congress. . . .

"[In] my judgment, the general government is not placed by the Constitution in such a condition of helplessness that it must fold its arms and remain inactive while capital combines, under the name of a corporation, to destroy competition, not in one State only, but throughout the entire country, in the buying and selling of articles — especially the necessaries of life — that go into commerce among the States. The doctrine of the autonomy of the States cannot properly be invoked to justify a denial of power in the national government to meet such an emergency. . . .

"[To] the general government has been committed the control of commercial intercourse among the States, to the end that it may be free at all times from any restraints except such as Congress may impose or permit for the benefit of the whole country. The common government of all the people is the only one that can adequately deal with a matter which directly and injuriously affects the entire commerce of the country, which concerns equally all the people of the Union, and which, it must be confessed, cannot be adequately controlled by any one State. Its authority should not be so weakened by construction that it cannot reach and eradicate evils that, beyond all question, tend to defeat an object which that government is entitled, by the Constitution, to accomplish."

HOUSTON, EAST & WEST TEXAS RAILWAY v. UNITED STATES (The Shreveport Rate Cases), 234 U.S. 342 (1914). The railway operated lines between Texas and Louisiana. Shipments from Dallas to Marshall, Texas, a distance of 150 miles, cost 37 cents; shipments from Shreveport, Louisiana, to Marshall (42 miles), cost 56 cents. The Interstate Commerce Commission set a maximum rate for shipments from Shreveport to Texas and ordered the railway to charge no higher rates per mile for shipments to Marshall from Shreveport or Dallas in order to eliminate the "discrimination" against Shreveport. The Supreme Court, in an opinion by Justice Hughes, held that the commission could set rates for the intrastate Dallas-to-Marshall route.

Congress's "authority, extending to these interstate carriers as instruments of interstate commerce, necessarily embraces the right to control their operations in all matters having such a close and substantial relation to interstate traffic that the control is essential or appropriate to the security of that traffic, to the efficiency of the interstate service, and to the maintenance of conditions under which interstate commerce may be conducted upon fair terms and without molestation or hindrance. [Wherever] the interstate and intrastate transactions of carriers are so related that the government of the one involves the control of the other, it is Congress, and not the State, that is entitled to prescribe the final and dominant rule, for otherwise Congress would be denied the exercise of its constitutional authority and the State, and not the Nation, would be supreme within the national field. . . .

"Congress in the exercise of its paramount power may prevent the common instrumentalities of interstate and intrastate commercial intercourse from being used in their intrastate operations to the injury of interstate commerce. This is not to say that Congress possesses the authority to regulate the internal commerce of a State, as such, but that it does possess the power to foster and protect interstate commerce, and to take all measures necessary or appropriate to that end, although intrastate transactions of interstate carriers may thereby be controlled."

Justices Lurton and Pitney dissented.

Note: Direct, Indirect, and Stream of Commerce Tests

1. *Intent and Congress's power.* Suppose the government proved that American Sugar intended by its near-monopoly to restrict interstate commerce and not merely production. On Chief Justice Fuller's analysis, would Congress then have power to regulate? Coronado Coal Co. v. United Mine Workers, 268 U.S. 295 (1925), applied the Sherman Act to a strike against mine operators. Carter v. Carter Coal Co., infra, distinguished *Coronado* from *E. C. Knight*: "The acts of the persons involved were local in character, but the intent was to restrain interstate commerce, and the means employed were calculated to carry that intent into effect. Interstate commerce was the direct object of attack; and the restraint of such commerce was the necessary consequence of the acts and the immediate end in view." Reducing the supply of a good is "ordinarily an indirect and remote obstruction" of interstate commerce, but "when the intent [is] to restrain or control the supply" in interstate commerce, the Sherman Act is violated.

2. *The formalist approach.* Chief Justice Fuller appears to have some temporal sequence in mind as the basis for his exclusion of categories of activities from the scope of the power of Congress to regulate interstate commerce: Certain activities, which are not commerce, precede it (manufacturing), and presumably other activities, which are also not commerce, succeed it (retail sales?). Does Chief Justice Fuller explain why the relevant temporal line is drawn to exclude manufacturing, rather than at an earlier point, such as acquisition of raw materials?

3. *National power where states cannot effectively act.* The monopolist in *E. C. Knight* conceded that New Jersey could prohibit locally chartered corporations from acquiring monopolies. Note that, so long as a single state is willing to allow its corporations to acquire monopolies — for example, in exchange for an annual tax that is less than the monopolistic profits — the practical consequence of American Sugar's position is to make it impossible to have effective antimonopoly legislation for manufacturing. Does the inability of any single state or group of states to control manufacturing monopolies justify finding power in Congress to do so?

4. *"Stream of commerce."* Stafford v. Wallace, 258 U.S. 495 (1922), involved the Packers and Stockyards Act of 1921, which authorized the Secretary of Commerce to regulate rates and prescribe standards for the operation of stockyards where livestock was kept for sale or shipment in interstate commerce. Chief Justice Taft's opinion for the Court upholding the act said that the "only question [is] whether the business done in the stockyards between the receipt of the live stock in the yards and the shipment of them therefrom is a part of interstate commerce. [The] stockyards are but a throat through which the current flows, and the transactions which occur therein are only incident to this current from the West to the East, and from one State to another. Such transactions can not be separated from the movement to which they contribute and necessarily take on its character." Is the metaphor of a "current" or "stream of commerce" helpful? How do you know when a stream begins and ends? Why doesn't *Stafford* involve two

streams of commerce, one ending with the arrival of the cattle at the stockyards and the other beginning with their departure?

5. *Consistent precedents?* As Congress began to regulate the national economy more extensively, the Supreme Court generally focused on practical reality and found that Congress had exercised its power in accordance with the Constitution. In addition to the principal cases, see Southern Railway v. United States, 222 U.S. 20 (1911) (upholding Federal Safety Appliance Act as applied to railroad cars with defective couplers because, although the cars were used in intrastate traffic, the act applied to cars "used on any railroad engaged in interstate commerce"). Even *E. C. Knight* had limited effects. Swift & Co. v. United States, 196 U.S. 375 (1905), sustained the application of the Sherman Act to meat dealers, invoking the "current of commerce" metaphor and calling interstate commerce "not a technical legal conception, but a practical one." Cushman, Formalism and Realism in Commerce Clause Jurisprudence, 67 U. Chi. L. Rev. 1089 (2000), argues that the Court during this period applied the tests available to it in a principled way. According to Cushman, the Supreme Court confined state regulatory power to businesses affected with a public interest. With respect to the "stream of commerce" test, only those "local" enterprises "affected with a public interest" could be located in a stream of interstate commerce, and with respect to Shreveport, that case "recognized federal power to regulate the intrastate rates charged by an interstate business affected with a public interest. So long as the power of Congress to regulate interstate rates remained confined to businesses affected with a public interest, its derivative power to regulate intrastate rates would remain similarly confined." Id. at 1129, 1131.

In Champion v. Ames, presented next, a version of formalism leads to upholding a statute, whereas in Hammer v. Dagenhart, supra, a version of realism led to invalidating a statute. Are these versions sufficiently similar to the ones you have already examined to justify treating "formalism" and "realism" as unifying themes?

CHAMPION v. AMES (The Lottery Case), 188 U.S. 321 (1903). The Federal Lottery Act of 1895 prohibited the interstate transportation of foreign lottery tickets. Champion was indicted for shipping a box of Paraguayan lottery tickets from Texas to California. In an opinion by Justice Harlan, the Supreme Court rejected his challenge to the constitutionality of the act. Justice Harlan's opinion stated, "[Undoubtedly,] the carrying from one State to another by independent carriers of things or commodities that are ordinary subjects of traffic, and which have in themselves a recognized value in money, constitutes interstate commerce." Harlan continued, "[It] is said that the statute in question does not regulate the carrying of lottery tickets from State to State, but by punishing those who cause them to be so carried Congress in effect prohibits such carrying. [If] lottery traffic, carried on through interstate commerce, is a matter of which Congress may take cognizance and over which its power may be exerted, [may] not Congress, for the protection of the people of all the States, [devise] such means, within the scope of the Constitution, and not prohibited by it, as will drive that traffic out of commerce among the States? . . .

"[It] must not be forgotten that the power of Congress to regulate commerce among the States is plenary, is complete in itself, and is subject to no limitations except such as may be found in the Constitution. [What] clause can be cited which, in any degree, countenances the suggestion that one may, of right, carry or cause to be carried from one State to another that which will harm the public morals? [Surely] it will not be said to be a part of any one's liberty, as recognized by the supreme law of the land, that he shall be allowed to introduce into commerce among the States an element that will be confessedly injurious to the public morals." According to Justice Harlan, "Congress [does] not assume to interfere with traffic or commerce in lottery tickets carried on exclusively within the limits of any State, but has in view only commerce of that kind among the several States. It has not assumed to interfere with the completely internal affairs of any State, and has only legislated in respect of a matter which concerns the people of the United States. As a State may, for the purpose of guarding the morals of its own people, forbid all sales of lottery tickets within its limits, so Congress, for the purpose of guarding the people of the United States against the 'widespread pestilence of lotteries' and to protect the commerce which concerns all the States, may prohibit the carrying of lottery tickets from one State to another. In legislating upon the subject of the traffic in lottery tickets, as carried on through interstate commerce, Congress only supplemented the action of those States — perhaps all of them — which, for the protection of the public morals, prohibit the drawing of lotteries, as well as the sale or circulation of lottery tickets, within their respective limits. It said, in effect, that it would not permit the declared policy of the States, which sought to protect their people against the mischiefs of the lottery business, to be overthrown or disregarded by the agency of interstate commerce."

[handwritten margin note: Congress's perspective]

The opinion concluded, "It is said, however, that if, in order to suppress lotteries carried on through interstate commerce, Congress may exclude lottery tickets from such commerce, that principle leads necessarily to the conclusion that Congress may arbitrarily exclude from commerce among the States any article, commodity or thing, of whatever kind or nature, or however useful or valuable, which it may choose, no matter with what motive, to declare shall not be carried from one State to another. [The] present case does not require the court to declare the full extent of the power that Congress may exercise in the regulation of commerce among the States. We may, however, repeat, in this connection, what the court has heretofore said, that the power of Congress to regulate commerce among the States, although plenary, cannot be deemed arbitrary, since it is subject to such limitations or restrictions as are prescribed by the Constitution. This power, therefore, may not be exercised so as to infringe rights secured or protected by that instrument. It would not be difficult to imagine legislation that would be justly liable to such an objection as that stated, and be hostile to the objects for the accomplishment of which Congress was invested with the general power to regulate commerce among the several States. But, as often said, the possible abuse of a power is not an argument against its existence. There is probably no governmental power that may not be exerted to the injury of the public. If what is done by Congress is manifestly in excess of the powers granted to it, then upon the courts will rest the duty of adjudging that its action is neither legal nor binding upon the people. But if what Congress does is within the limits of its power, and is simply unwise or injurious, the remedy is that suggested by Chief Justice Marshall in Gibbons v. Ogden [quoting the 'wisdom and discretion' passage]."

Chief Justice Fuller, joined by Justices Brewer, Shiras, and Peckham, dissented, arguing that the Court's analysis gave Congress a "general police power" because it amounted to saying "that everything is an article of commerce the moment it is taken to be transported from place to place, and of interstate commerce if from State to State.

[handwritten margin note: Dissent]

"An invitation to dine, or to take a drive, or a note of introduction, all become articles of commerce under the ruling in this case, by being deposited with an express company for transportation. This in effect breaks down all the differences between that which is, and that which is not, an article of commerce, and the necessary consequence is to take from the States all jurisdiction over the subject so far as interstate communication is concerned. It is a long step in the direction of wiping out all traces of state lines, and the creation of a centralized Government."

Note: Prohibiting Interstate Transportation — Proper Regulation or Improper Pretext?

1. *Enforcement of limits again.* Does Justice Harlan define any judicially enforceable limits on Congress's power to regulate by means of prohibiting interstate shipment? Note the concluding citation to Gibbons v. Ogden. What reasons does he suggest for Congress's action? Can its reason for prohibiting the shipment of lottery tickets be distinguished from the usual reasons for exercising a general police power?

2. *Regulation or pretext?* Under the majority's holding, is there anything left to the "pretext" limitation stated by Chief Justice Marshall in *McCulloch*? Should it make a difference that *Champion* involves a regulation whose apparent purpose is not obviously "commercial"? Is there a "commercial" argument for the statute in *Champion*?

If the statute's purpose were to promote moral or social goals, would the use of the commerce power be a pretext of the sort Chief Justice Marshall disapproved in *McCulloch*? Consider that applying a "pretext" test requires a definition of the proper purposes for which a power may be exercised. Did Chief Justice Marshall in *Gibbons* say or assume that the commerce power was limited to commercial purposes? If it is not limited to commercial purposes, how might a "pretext" test be applied?

3. *Concluding remarks.* Does the Court's record from the 1880s to the 1920s on the issues considered here reflect (a) a principled effort to develop a coherent body of law in an area where determining appropriate doctrine is difficult; (b) an unprincipled effort to uphold laws that enough justices thought wise and to strike down those they thought unwise; (c) an effort to ensure that Congress attend to considerations of federalism by developing a doctrinal repertoire that allowed the Court occasionally to hold a statute unconstitutional?

Whatever the Court's intentions, by 1930 it had at hand a group of precedents that gave it substantial flexibility in assessing the constitutionality of Congress's efforts to regulate the economy. Over the following decade, those precedents were applied and then abandoned.

Note: The New Deal Crisis

As soon as Franklin D. Roosevelt took office in 1933, he proposed — and Congress quickly enacted — a series of statutes designed to ameliorate the consequences of the ongoing economic crisis and to stabilize the economy so that such a severe crisis could not recur. It was possible to find analogues in the past for each specific item of legislation, yet their sheer numbers, the swiftness with which they were enacted, and the sense of national crisis joined to make the New Deal legislation unprecedented in an important sense.

Much of the legislation interfered with what many had come to regard as the prerogatives of private property and, incidentally, the proper domain of the states. The New Deal statutes were sure to generate challenges to their constitutionality. Supporters of the statutes, and those who attacked them, could draw on a complex, well developed, and not entirely coherent body of law regarding the extent of Congress's power to regulate interstate commerce. (In addition, a similarly complex and not entirely coherent body of law existed regarding external limits — notably the due process clause — on Congress's power.) In 1934 and 1935, the first challenges reached the Supreme Court. A useful discussion of the overall litigation is P. Irons, The New Deal Lawyers (1982). The Court's first signals were mixed. By five-to-four votes, the Court rejected challenges to state legislation designed to alleviate the effects of the Depression in Home Building & Loan Association v. Blaisdell, 290 U.S. 398 (1934) (obligation of contracts clause), and Nebbia v. New York, 291 U.S. 502 (1934) (due process clause). It also upheld the Roosevelt administration's repudiation of contractual duties to repay debts in gold, Norman v. Baltimore & Ohio Railroad, 294 U.S. 240 (1935). But the Court invalidated a portion of the National Industrial Recovery Act of 1933, holding that the act excessively delegated power to the President, Panama Refining Co. v. Ryan, 293 U.S. 388 (1935).

Railroad Retirement Board v. Alton Railroad Co., 295 U.S. 330 (1935), foreshadowed what was to come. There, the Court invalidated the Railroad Retirement Act of 1934. Justice Roberts's opinion for a five-person majority held that, though Congress had power to regulate the safety of railroad operation, it lacked power to establish a compulsory retirement and pension plan. Such a plan was not "related to efficiency of transportation" and was too "remote from any regulation of commerce as such." Three weeks later the Court decided the *Schechter* case, invalidating the National Industrial Recovery Act of 1933, in many ways the conceptual centerpiece of the New Deal recovery program.

A. L. A. SCHECHTER POULTRY CORP. v. UNITED STATES, 295 U.S. 495 (1935). The National Industrial Recovery Act authorized the President to approve "codes of fair competition" developed by boards from various industries. President Roosevelt approved a Live Poultry Code applicable in metropolitan New York, the largest live poultry market in the country. The code established a forty-hour work week and a minimum wage of 50 cents per hour; it prohibited child labor and established the right of employees to organize and bargain collectively. The code also regulated a variety of trade practices.

Virtually all of the live poultry sold in New York was shipped by railroad from other states. After arrival, the poultry was assigned to commission sales agents, who sold the poultry to slaughterhouse operators such as the Schechters. They bought poultry for slaughter and resale. The poultry was shipped by truck from the rail terminals to the Schechters' slaughterhouse in Brooklyn and from there, within twenty-four hours, to butchers who sold directly to consumers. The Schechters were convicted of violating the wage and hour provisions of the code, as well as a trade practice requirement that purchasers buy an entire "run" of a coop, including sick poultry. The Supreme Court struck down the statute.

Chief Justice Hughes's opinion for the Court began by addressing the relation between the Constitution and "the grave national crisis with which Congress was confronted. Undoubtedly, the conditions to which power is addressed are always to be considered when the exercise of power is challenged. Extraordinary conditions may call for extraordinary remedies. But [extraordinary] conditions do not create or enlarge constitutional power. The Constitution established a national government with powers deemed to be adequate, [but] these powers of the national government are limited by the constitutional grants. Those who act under these grants are not at liberty to transcend the imposed limits because they believe that more or different power is necessary. Such assertions of extra-constitutional authority were anticipated and precluded by the explicit terms of the Tenth Amendment." Turning to the application of the Live Poultry Code to intrastate transactions, Chief Justice Hughes first asked whether these transactions were "in" interstate commerce. "Much is made of the fact that almost all the poultry coming to New York is sent there from other States. But [when] defendants had made their purchases, [the] poultry was trucked to their slaughterhouses in Brooklyn for local disposition. The interstate transactions in relation to that poultry then ended. Defendants held the poultry at their slaughterhouse markets for slaughter and local sale to retail dealers and butchers who in turn sold directly to consumers. Neither the slaughtering nor the sales by defendants were transactions in interstate commerce.

"The undisputed facts thus afford no warrant for the argument that the poultry handled by defendants at their slaughterhouse markets was in a 'current' or 'flow' of interstate commerce and was thus subject to congressional regulation. The mere fact that there may be a constant flow of commodities into a State does not mean that the flow continues after the property has arrived and has become commingled with the mass of property within the State and is there held solely for local disposition and use. So far as the poultry here in question is concerned, the flow in interstate commerce had ceased. [Hence], decisions which deal with a stream of interstate commerce — where goods come to rest within a State temporarily and are later to go forward in interstate commerce — [are] not applicable here."

Next Chief Justice Hughes asked whether the transactions "directly 'affect' interstate commerce. [In] determining how far the federal government may go in controlling intrastate transactions upon the ground that they 'affect' interstate commerce, there is a necessary and well-established distinction between direct and indirect effects. [Direct] effects are illustrated by [the] effect of failure to use prescribed safety appliances on railroads which are the highways of both interstate and intrastate commerce, [and] the fixing of rates for intrastate transportation which unjustly discriminate against interstate commerce. But where the effect of intrastate transactions upon interstate commerce is merely indirect, such transactions remain within the domain of state power. If the commerce clause were construed to reach all enterprises and transactions which could be said to have an indirect effect upon interstate commerce, the federal authority would embrace practically all the activities of the people and the authority of the State over its domestic concerns would exist only by sufferance of the federal government. Indeed, on such a theory, even the development of the State's commercial facilities would be subject to federal control." The wages and hours provisions "are imposed in order to govern the details of defendants' management of their local business. The persons employed in slaughtering and selling in local trade are not employed in interstate commerce. Their hours and wages have no direct relation to interstate commerce. [This] appears from an examination of the considerations urged by the Government with respect to conditions in the poultry trade. Thus, the Government argues that hours and wages affect prices; that slaughterhouse men sell at a small margin above operating costs; that labor represents 50 to 60 per cent of these costs; that a slaughterhouse operator paying lower wages or reducing his cost by exacting long hours of work, translates his saving into lower prices; that this results in demands for a cheaper grade of goods; and that the cutting of prices brings about a demoralization of the price structure. [The] argument of the Government proves too much. If the federal government may determine the wages and hours of employees in the internal commerce of a State, because of their relation to cost and prices and their indirect effect upon interstate commerce, it would seem that a similar control might be exerted over other elements of cost, also affecting prices. . . ."

The opinion concluded, "It is not the province of the Court to consider the economic advantages or disadvantages of [a] centralized system. It is sufficient to say that the Federal Constitution does not provide for it. Our growth and development have called for wide use of the commerce power of the federal government in its control over the expanded activities of interstate commerce, and in protecting that commerce from burdens, interferences, and conspiracies to restrain and monopolize it. But the authority of the federal government may not be pushed to such an extreme as to destroy the distinction, which the commerce clause itself establishes, between commerce 'among the several States' and the internal concerns of a State. [Stress] is laid upon the great importance of maintaining wage distributions which would provide the necessary stimulus in starting 'the cumulative forces making for expanding commercial activity.' Without in any way disparaging this motive, it is enough to say that the recuperative efforts of the federal government must be made in a manner consistent with the authority granted by the Constitution."

Justice Cardozo, joined by Justice Stone, concurred: "[There] is a view of causation that would obliterate the distinction between what is national and what is local in the activities of commerce. Motion at the outer rim is communicated perceptibly, though minutely, to recording instruments at the center. A society such as ours 'is an elastic medium which transmits all tremors throughout its territory; the only question is of their size.' Per Learned Hand, J., in the court below. The law is not indifferent to considerations of degree. Activities local in their immediacy do not become interstate and national because of distant repercussions. What is near and what is distant may at times be uncertain. There is no penumbra of uncertainty obscuring judgment here. To find immediacy or directness here is to find it almost everywhere. If centripetal forces are to be isolated to the exclusion of the forces that oppose and counteract them, there will be an end to our federal system."

CARTER v. CARTER COAL CO., 298 U.S. 238 (1936). The Bituminous Coal Conservation Act of 1935 was intended to stabilize the industry during a period of sustained industrial crisis. The first section of the act contained a long recitation of the importance of coal to the national economy, the need for "just and rational relations" between labor and management, and the existence of inefficient practices that "directly affect[ed] interstate commerce." The act established a system of local coal boards to set minimum prices, with variations for particular mines as each board thought appropriate. The boards were to administer a code that allowed employees to bargain collectively. Once a sufficient number of collective bargaining agreements had been negotiated, their wage and hour terms would bind all mine operators in the area. A stockholder in Carter Coal sued to enjoin the company from complying with the code. The Court, in an opinion by Justice Sutherland, invalidated the statute's labor provisions. Holding that those provisions were not severable from the price-fixing provisions, the Court did not discuss the price-fixing provisions separately.

Justice Sutherland said that "the recitals contained in [the first section of] the act plainly suggest that its makers were of opinion that its constitutionality could be sustained under some general federal power, thought to exist, apart from the specific grants of the Constitution. [These] affirmations [do] not constitute an exertion of the will of Congress which is legislation, but a recital of considerations which in the opinion of that body existed and justified the expression of its will in the present act. Nevertheless, this preamble may not be disregarded. On the contrary it is important, because it makes clear, except for the pure assumption that the conditions described 'directly' affect interstate commerce, that the powers which Congress undertook to exercise are not specific but of the most general character — namely, to protect the general public interest and the health and comfort of the people, to conserve privately-owned coal, maintain just relations between producers and employees and others, and promote the general welfare, by controlling nation-wide production and distribution of coal. These, it may be conceded, are objects of great worth; but are they ends, the attainment of which has been committed by the Constitution to the federal government?" Justice Sutherland continued, "The ruling and firmly established principle is that the powers which the general government may exercise are only those specifically enumerated in the Constitution, and such implied powers as are necessary and proper to carry into effect the enumerated powers. Whether the end sought to be attained by an act of Congress is legitimate is wholly a matter of constitutional power and not at all of legislative discretion. [The] distinction between these two things — power and discretion — is not only very plain but very important. Thus, it may be said that to a constitutional end many ways are open; but to an end not within the terms of the Constitution, all ways are closed.

"[Every] journey to a forbidden end begins with the first step; and the danger of such a step by the federal government in the direction of taking over the powers of the states is that the end of the journey may find the states so despoiled of their powers, or — what may amount to the same thing — so relieved of the responsibilities which possession of the powers necessarily enjoins, as to reduce them to little more than geographical subdivisions of the national domain. . . ."

For Justice Sutherland, "[the] word 'commerce' is the equivalent of the phrase 'intercourse for the purposes of trade.' Plainly, the incidents leading up to and culminating in the mining of coal do not constitute such intercourse. The employment of men, the fixing of their wages, hours of labor and working conditions, the bargaining in respect of these things — whether carried on separately or collectively — each and all constitute intercourse for the purposes of production, not of trade. [Extraction] of coal from the mine is the aim and the completed result of local activities. Commerce in the coal mined is not brought into being by force of these activities, but by negotiations, agreements, and circumstances entirely apart from production. Mining brings the subject matter of commerce into existence. Commerce disposes of it." Citing *Schechter*, Justice Sutherland continued, "Everything which moves in interstate commerce has had a local origin. Without local production somewhere, interstate commerce, as now carried on, would practically disappear. Nevertheless, the local character of mining, of manufacturing and of crop growing is a fact, and remains a fact, whatever may be done with the products." In discussing the "direct/indirect" test, Justice Sutherland wrote, "Whether the effect of a given activity or condition is direct or indirect is not always easy to determine. The word 'direct' implies that the activity or condition invoked or blamed shall operate proximately — not mediately, remotely, or collaterally — to produce the effect. [The] distinction between a direct and an indirect effect turns, not upon the magnitude of either the cause or the effect, but entirely upon the manner in which the effect has been brought about. If the production by one man of a single ton of coal intended for interstate sale and shipment, and actually so sold and shipped, affects interstate commerce indirectly, the effect does not become direct by multiplying the tonnage, or increasing the number of men employed, or adding to the expense or complexities of the business, or by all combined. It is quite true that rules of law are sometimes qualified by considerations of degree, as the government argues. But the matter of degree has no bearing upon the question here, since that question is not — What is the extent of the local activity or condition, or the extent of the effect produced upon interstate commerce? but — What is the relation between the activity or condition and the effect?

"Much stress is put upon the evils which come from the struggle between employers and employees over the matter of wages, working conditions, the right of collective bargaining, etc., and the resulting strikes, curtailment and irregularity of production and effect on prices; and it is insisted that interstate commerce is greatly affected thereby. But, [the] conclusive answer is that the evils are all local evils over which the federal government has no legislative control. [Working] conditions are obviously local conditions. The employees are not engaged in or about commerce, but exclusively in producing a commodity. And the controversies and evils, which it is the object of the act to regulate and minimize, are local controversies and evils affecting local work undertaken to accomplish that local result. Such effect as they may have upon commerce, however extensive it may be, is secondary and indirect. An increase in the greatness of the effect adds to its importance. It does not alter its character." Justice Sutherland argued that "[the] only perceptible difference between [Schechter] and this [case] is that [there] the federal power was asserted with respect to commodities which had come to rest after their interstate transportation; while here, the case deals with commodities at rest before interstate commerce has begun. That difference is without significance. The federal regulatory power ceases when interstate commercial intercourse ends; and, correlatively, the power does not attach until interstate commercial intercourse begins."

Justice Cardozo, joined by Justices Brandeis and Stone, would have upheld the price-fixing provisions, finding the labor provisions severable and the challenge to them premature. "Regulation of prices being an exercise of the commerce power in respect of interstate transactions, the question remains whether it comes within that power as applied to intrastate sales where interstate prices are directly or intimately affected. [Sometimes] it is said that the relation must be 'direct' to bring that power into play. In many circumstances such a description will be sufficiently precise to meet the needs of the occasion. But a great principle of constitutional law is not susceptible of comprehensive statement in an adjective. The underlying thought is merely this, that 'the law is not indifferent to considerations of degree.' [Schechter, concurring opinion.] It cannot be indifferent to them without an expansion of the commerce clause that would absorb or imperil the reserved powers of the states. At times, as in the case cited, the waves of causation will have radiated so far that their undulatory motion, if discernible at all, will be too faint or obscure, too broken by crosscurrents, to be heeded by the law. [Always] the setting of the facts is to be viewed if one would know the closeness of the tie. Perhaps, if one group of adjectives is to be chosen in preference to another, 'intimate' and 'remote' will be found to be as good as any. At all events, 'direct' and 'indirect,' even if accepted as sufficient, must not be read too narrowly. A survey of the cases shows that the words have been interpreted with suppleness of adaptation and flexibility of meaning. The power is as broad as the need that evokes it."

Justice Cardozo then discussed the distinction between direct and indirect effects on commerce, in light of the Shreveport Rate Cases. "What the cases really mean is that the causal relation in such circumstances is so close and intimate and obvious as to permit it to be called direct without subjecting the word to an unfair or excessive strain. There is a like immediacy here. Within rulings the most orthodox, the prices for intrastate sales of coal have so inescapable a relation to those for interstate sales that a system of regulation for transactions of the one class is necessary to give adequate protection to the system of regulation adopted for the other. . . ." According to Justice Cardozo, "Congress was not condemned to inaction in the face of price wars and wage wars so pregnant with disaster. Commerce had been choked and burdened; its normal flow had been diverted from one state to another; there had been bankruptcy and waste and ruin alike for capital and for labor. [There] is testimony [even] by the assailants of the statute [that] only through a system of regulated prices can the industry be stabilized and set upon the road of orderly and peaceful progress. [After] making every allowance for difference of opinion as to the most efficient cure, the student of the subject is confronted with the indisputable truth that there were ills to be corrected, and ills that had a direct relation to the maintenance of commerce among the states without friction or diversion. An evil existing, and also the power to correct it, the lawmakers were at liberty to use their own discretion in the selection of the means." Chief Justice Hughes agreed that the labor provisions were unconstitutional but wrote separately to say that the price-fixing provisions were severable.

Note: New Deal Legislation and Commerce Clause Tests in the 1930s

1. Schechter's *significance*. At the start of the New Deal, the NIRA was a popular and apparently successful program, less because the codes of fair competition established a sensible regime for developing macroeconomic policy than because the evidence of concerted national action gave the public confidence that something was being done. Over the next two years, however, the regulatory apparatus became much less popular. The codes had done little to stabilize, much less restore, production, and opponents fearing congressional control of the economy obtained injunctions against some codes, which further weakened the program. The act was due to expire a few weeks after *Schechter* was decided, and there had been no effort to extend its life even before the decision. The decision in *Schechter* was thus less important for its precise holding than for the approaches it articulated toward Congress's powers.

What values of federalism are served by limiting Congress's power in *Schechter*?

2. *"Current of commerce."* Why were the chickens not still part of a flow of interstate commerce? Does the Court explain why the flow ended at the slaughterhouses and not, for example, at the butcher's final sale? Or even further at the disposition of the chickens' bones at the garbage dump?

3. *"Direct effects."* Justice Sutherland invokes the *E. C. Knight* approach to directness, treating it as a logical category defined in terms of a beginning and an end to interstate commerce. Justice Cardozo treats directness as he would the tort law concept of proximate cause, in which directness is determined with reference to the purposes sought to be achieved by the test. According to Justice Cardozo, what are those purposes? Could Justice Sutherland have used Justice Cardozo's test to hold the Bituminous Coal Act unconstitutional? Is Cardozo's effort to distinguish *Schechter* and *Carter* persuasive?

4. *The New Deal response to the Court.* Because *Schechter* dealt with an activity near the retailing end of the spectrum of economic activity, supporters of the New Deal thought that their program could survive in areas closer to the center of the economy. The Bituminous Coal Conservation Act of 1935 was enacted after *Schechter*. It was invalidated in Carter v. Carter Coal Co. The National Labor Relations Act became effective after *Schechter*, and supporters of the New Deal believed that the Court might hold it unconstitutional. See also United States v. Butler, 297 U.S. 1 (1936), Chapter 3 infra (holding Agricultural Adjustment Act of 1933 unconstitutional as beyond the scope of the spending power); Morehead v. New York ex rel. Tipaldo, 298 U.S. 587 (1936) (invalidating state minimum wage law for women as violating due process).

These decisions, coupled with Roosevelt's massive victory in the 1936 elections, led Roosevelt to propose changes in the structure of the Supreme Court. Seizing on the fact that six justices were over seventy years old in 1937, Roosevelt proposed that one additional justice, up to a total of fifteen, be appointed for each justice over seventy who did not resign or retire. His message to Congress argued that older justices were unable to fulfill their responsibilities, thus increasing the workload of the younger justices. Yet it was widely understood that the real point of the proposal was to increase the number of justices who would find New Deal legislation constitutional, and that the workload argument was essentially a makeweight.

The proposal encountered substantial opposition: It was attacked as disingenuous and contrary to the spirit of the Constitution. (Was it the latter?) During the debate over the proposal, Justice Van Devanter retired. In addition, the Court upheld a state minimum wage statute in West Coast Hotel Co. v. Parrish, 300 U.S. 379 (1937). Justice Roberts, who had voted with the five-person majority in *Morehead*, now voted to uphold a similar statute. The Court had taken a preliminary vote in *West Coast Hotel* before Roosevelt submitted his "Court-packing" plan. A later memorandum by Justice Roberts explained that he had joined the majority in *Morehead* only because those seeking to uphold the minimum wage statute sought to distinguish prior cases, instead of urging that they be overruled. When in *West Coast Hotel* the argument for overruling was made, Justice Roberts agreed with it. Note his position in National Labor Relations Board (NLRB) v. Jones & Laughlin Steel Co., infra, decided while the Senate was debating the Court-packing plan. Roberts's position was widely characterized as "the switch in time that saved Nine." The Senate Judiciary Committee on June 14, after *Jones & Laughlin* and *West Coast Hotel*, emphatically rejected Roosevelt's proposal. The majority leader of the Senate, Joseph Robinson, exerted a great deal of personal pressure on other senators and appeared to have accumulated enough votes to secure passage of a slightly modified Court-packing bill by early July. However, Robinson died of a heart attack before the vote was taken, and the plan was rejected in the Senate in mid-July. See Leuchtenberg, The Origins of Franklin D. Roosevelt's "Court-Packing" Plan, 1966 Sup. Ct. Rev. 347.

Was the New Deal position on national powers completely vindicated by the cases that follow, and by Wickard v. Filburn, section B supra? Should *Schechter* and *Carter* be understood as aberrational deviations from well established prior law? Should the New Deal cases be so understood? For a vigorous challenge to the post–New Deal expansion of the commerce power, see Epstein, The Proper Scope of the Commerce Power, 73 Va. L. Rev. 1387 (1987).

NLRB v. Jones & Laughlin Steel Corp.
301 U.S. 1 (1937)

[The National Labor Relations Act established a comprehensive system for regulating labor/management relations. It established the right of employees to organize and bargain collectively and created a board to supervise elections and to enforce the act's prohibition of such unfair labor practices as discrimination against union members. The act contained the following "findings":

> The denial by employers of the right of employees to organize and the refusal by employers to accept the procedure of collective bargaining lead to strikes and other forms of industrial strife or unrest, which have the intent or the necessary effect of burdening or obstructing commerce by (a) impairing the efficiency, safety, or operation of the instrumentalities of commerce; (b) occurring in the current of commerce; (c) materially affecting, restraining, or controlling the flow of raw materials or manufactured or processed goods from or into the channels of commerce, or the prices of such materials or goods in commerce; or (d) causing diminution of employment and wages in such volume as substantially to impair or disrupt the market for goods flowing from or into the channels of commerce.
>
> The inequality of bargaining power between employees who do not possess full freedom of association or actual liberty of contract, and employers who are organized in the corporate or other forms of ownership association substantially burdens and affects the flow of commerce, and tends to aggravate recurrent business depressions, by depressing wage rates and the purchasing power of wage earners in industry and by preventing the stabilization of competitive wage rates and working conditions within and between industries.
>
> Experience has proved that protection by law of the right of employees to organize and bargain collectively safeguards commerce from injury, impairment, or interruption, and promotes the flow of commerce by removing certain recognized sources of industrial strife and unrest, by encouraging practices fundamental to the friendly adjustment of industrial disputes arising out of differences as to wages, hours, or other working conditions, and by restoring equality of bargaining power between employers and employees.
>
> It is hereby declared to be the policy of the United States to eliminate the causes of certain substantial obstructions to the free flow of commerce and to mitigate and eliminate these obstructions when they have occurred by encouraging the practice and procedure of collective bargaining and by protecting the exercise by workers of full freedom of association, self-organization, and designation of representatives of

their own choosing, for the purpose of negotiating the terms and conditions of their employment or other mutual aid or protection.

[The National Labor Relations Board charged Jones & Laughlin with the unfair labor practice of firing employees because they sought to organize a union. The court of appeals held the act unconstitutional.]

Mr. Chief Justice Hughes delivered the opinion of the Court. . . .

The facts as to the nature and scope of the business of the Jones & Laughlin Steel Corporation have been found by the Labor Board, and, so far as they are essential to the determination of this controversy, they are not in dispute. The Labor Board has found: the corporation is engaged in the business of manufacturing iron and steel in plants situated in Pittsburgh and nearby Aliquippa, Pennsylvania. It manufactures and distributes a widely diversified line of steel and pig iron, being the fourth largest producer of steel in the United States. With its subsidiaries — nineteen in number — it is a completely integrated enterprise, owning and operating ore, coal and limestone properties, lake and river transportation facilities and terminal railroads located at its manufacturing plants. It owns or controls mines in Michigan and Minnesota. It operates four ore steamships on the Great Lakes, used in the transportation of ore to its factories. It owns coal mines in Pennsylvania. It operates towboats and steam barges used in carrying coal to its factories. It owns limestone properties in various places in Pennsylvania and West Virginia. It owns the Monongahela connecting railroad which connects the plants of the Pittsburgh works and forms an interconnection with the Pennsylvania, New York Central and Baltimore and Ohio Railroad systems. It owns the Aliquippa and Southern Railroad Company which connects the Aliquippa works with the Pittsburgh and Lake Erie part of the New York Central system. Much of its product is shipped to its warehouses in Chicago, Detroit, Cincinnati and Memphis, — to the last two places by means of its own barges and transportation equipment. In Long Island City, New York, and in New Orleans it operates structural steel fabricating shops in connection with the warehousing of semi-finished materials sent from its works. Through one of its wholly-owned subsidiaries it owns, leases and operates stores, warehouses and yards for the distribution of equipment and supplies for drilling and operating oil and gas wells and for pipe lines, refineries and pumping stations. It has sales offices in twenty cities in the United States and a wholly-owned subsidiary which is devoted exclusively to distributing its product in Canada. Approximately 75 percent of its product is shipped out of Pennsylvania.

Summarizing these operations, the Labor Board concluded that the works in Pittsburgh and Aliquippa "might be likened to the heart of a self-contained, highly integrated body. They draw in the raw materials from Michigan, Minnesota, West Virginia, Pennsylvania in part through arteries and by means controlled by the respondent; they transform the materials and then pump them out to all parts of the nation through the vast mechanism which the respondent has elaborated." . . .

Respondent points to evidence that the Aliquippa plant, in which the discharged men were employed, contains complete facilities for the production of finished and semi-finished iron and steel products from raw materials. [The] iron ore which is procured from mines in Minnesota and Michigan and transported to respondent's plant is stored in stock piles for future use, the amount of ore in storage varying with the season but usually being enough to maintain operations from nine to ten months. . . .

First. The Scope of the Act

[It] is a familiar principle that acts which directly burden or obstruct interstate or foreign commerce, or its free flow, are within the reach of the congressional power. Acts having that effect are not rendered immune because they grow out of labor disputes. It is the effect upon commerce, not the source of the injury, which is the criterion. Whether or not particular action does affect commerce in such a close and intimate fashion as to be subject to federal control [is] left by the statute to be determined as individual cases arise. We are thus to inquire whether in the instant case the constitutional boundary has been passed.

Second. The Unfair Labor Practices in Question . . .

[In] its present application, the statute goes no further than to safeguard the right of employees to self-organization and to select representatives of their own choosing for collective bargaining or other mutual protection without restraint or coercion by their employer.

That is a fundamental right. Employees have as clear a right to organize and select their representatives for lawful purposes as the respondent has to organize its business and select its own officers and agents. Discrimination and coercion to prevent the free exercise of the right of employees to self-organization and representation is a proper subject for condemnation by competent legislative authority. . . .

Third. The Application of the Act to Employees Engaged in Production. The Principle Involved

Respondent says that whatever may be said of employees engaged in interstate commerce, the industrial relations and activities in the manufacturing department of respondent's enterprise are not subject to federal regulation. The argument rests upon the proposition that manufacturing in itself is not commerce. [Schechter; Carter v. Carter Coal Co.] The Government distinguishes these cases. The various parts of respondent's enterprise are described as interdependent. [It] is urged that these activities constitute a "stream" or "flow" of commerce, of which the Aliquippa manufacturing plant is the focal point, and that industrial strife at that point would cripple the entire movement. Reference is made to [Stafford v. Wallace]. . . .

We do not find it necessary to determine whether these features of defendant's business dispose of the asserted analogy to the "stream of commerce" cases. The instances in which that metaphor has been used are but particular, and not exclusive, illustrations of the protective power which the Government invokes in support of the present Act. The congressional authority to protect interstate commerce from burdens and obstructions is not limited to transactions which can be deemed to be an essential part of a "flow" of interstate or foreign commerce. Burdens and obstructions may be due to injurious action springing from other sources. [Although] activities may be intrastate in character when separately considered, if they have such a close and substantial relation to interstate commerce that their control is essential or appropriate to protect that commerce from burdens and obstructions, Congress cannot be denied the power to exercise that control. [*Schechter*.] Undoubtedly the scope of this power must be considered in the light of our dual system of government and may not be extended so as to embrace effects upon interstate commerce so indirect and remote that to embrace them, in view of our complex society, would effectually obliterate the distinction between what is national and what is local and create a completely centralized government. The question is necessarily one of degree. . . .

It is thus apparent that the fact that the employees here concerned were engaged in production is not determinative. The question remains as to the effect upon interstate commerce of the labor practice involved. In the *Schechter* case, we found that the effect there was so remote as to be beyond the federal power. To find "immediacy or directness" there was to find it "almost everywhere," a result inconsistent with the maintenance of our federal system. In the *Carter* case, the Court was of the opinion that the provisions of the statute relating to production were invalid upon several grounds — that there was improper delegation of legislative power, and that the requirements not only went beyond any sustainable measure of protection of interstate commerce, but were also inconsistent with due process. These cases are not controlling here.

Fourth. Effects of the Unfair Labor Practice in Respondent's Enterprise

Giving full weight to respondent's contention with respect to a break in the complete continuity of the "stream of commerce" by reason of respondent's manufacturing operations, the fact remains that the stoppage of those operations by industrial strife would have a most serious effect upon interstate commerce. In view of respondent's far-flung activities, it is idle to say that the effect would be indirect or remote. It is obvious that it would be immediate and might be catastrophic. We are asked to shut our eyes to the plainest facts of our national life and to deal with the question of direct and indirect effects in an intellectual vacuum. [When] industries organize themselves on a national scale, making their relation to interstate commerce the dominant factor in their activities, how can it be maintained that their industrial labor relations constitute a forbidden field into which Congress may not enter when it is necessary to protect interstate commerce from the paralyzing consequences of industrial war? We have often said that interstate commerce itself is a practical conception. It is equally true that interferences with that commerce must be appraised by a judgment that does not ignore actual experience.

Experience has abundantly demonstrated that the recognition of the right of employees to self-organization and to have representatives of their own choosing for the purpose of collective bargaining is often an essential condition of industrial peace. Refusal to confer and negotiate has been one of the most prolific causes of strife. . . .

[Reversed.]

[Justices McReynolds, Van Devanter, Sutherland, and Butler dissented.]

UNITED STATES v. DARBY, 312 U.S. 100 (1941). Darby was charged with violating the Fair Labor Standards Act of 1938. The act prohibited the shipment in interstate commerce of goods manufactured by employees who were paid less than a prescribed minimum wage or who worked more than a prescribed maximum number of hours and prohibited the employment of workers in production "for interstate commerce" at other than the prescribed wages and hours. The district court sustained Darby's objections to the constitutionality of the act. The Supreme Court reversed, in an opinion by Justice Stone.

The opinion said that the act's purpose was "to exclude from interstate commerce goods produced for the commerce and to prevent their production for interstate commerce, under conditions detrimental to the maintenance of the minimum standards of living necessary for health and general well-being; and to prevent the use of interstate commerce as the means of competition in the distribution of goods so produced, and as the means of spreading and perpetuating such substandard labor conditions among the workers of the several states."

Justice Stone's analysis began with this statement: "While manufacture is not of itself interstate commerce, the shipment of manufactured goods interstate is such commerce and the prohibition of such shipment by Congress is indubitably a regulation of the commerce." Responding to the argument that "while the prohibition is nominally a regulation of the commerce its motive or purpose is regulation of wages and hours of persons engaged in manufacture, the control of which has been reserved to the states and upon which Georgia and some of the states of destination have placed no restriction," Justice Stone wrote, "[Congress,] following its own conception of public policy concerning the restrictions which may appropriately be imposed on interstate commerce, is free to exclude from the commerce articles whose use in the states for which they are destined it may conceive to be injurious to the public health, morals, or welfare, even though the state has not sought to regulate their use. [Lottery Case.]

"Such regulation is not a forbidden invasion of state power merely because either its motive or its consequence is to restrict the use of articles of commerce within the states of destination; and is not prohibited unless by other Constitutional provisions. It is no objection to the assertion of the power to regulate interstate commerce that its exercise is attended by the same incidents which attend the exercise of the police power of the states."

Justice Stone continued, "The motive and purpose of the present regulation are plainly to make effective the Congressional conception of public policy that interstate commerce should not be made the instrument of competition in the distribution of goods produced under substandard labor conditions, which competition is injurious to the commerce and to the states from and to which the commerce flows. The motive and purpose of a regulation of interstate commerce are matters for the legislative judgment upon the exercise of which the Constitution places no restriction and over which the courts are given no control. [Whatever] their motive and purpose, regulations of commerce which do not infringe some constitutional prohibition are within the plenary power conferred on Congress by the Commerce Clause. Subject only to that limitation, [we] conclude that the prohibition of the shipment interstate of goods produced under the forbidden substandard labor conditions is within the constitutional authority of Congress."

According to Justice Stone, only Hammer v. Dagenhart was inconsistent with this analysis, and that case "has not been followed. [The] conclusion is inescapable that Hammer v. Dagenhart was a departure from the principles which have prevailed in the interpretation of the Commerce Clause both before and since the decision and that such vitality, as a precedent, as it then had has long since been exhausted. It should be and now is overruled."

The Court upheld the wage and hour requirements as applied to employees producing goods for interstate commerce, defining that category to include employees working on goods that the employer intends or expects to be sent to out-of-state customers. According to Justice Stone, Congress's power "extends to those activities intrastate which so affect interstate commerce [as] to make regulation of them appropriate means to the attainment of a legitimate end, the exercise of the granted power of Congress to regulate interstate commerce. [Congress], having by the present Act adopted the policy of excluding from interstate commerce all goods produced for the commerce which do not conform to the specified labor standards, it may choose the means reasonably adapted to the attainment of the permitted end, even though they involve control of intrastate activities."

According to the Court, these provisions were also "sustainable independently" of the ban on interstate shipment. "[The] evils aimed at by the Act are the spread of substandard labor conditions through the use of the facilities of interstate commerce for competition by the goods so produced with those produced under the prescribed or better labor conditions; and the consequent dislocation of the commerce itself caused by the impairment or destruction of local businesses by competition made effective through interstate commerce. The Act is thus directed at the suppression of a method or kind of competition in interstate commerce which it has in effect condemned as '[unfair.]'"

The opinion also said, "Our conclusion is unaffected by the Tenth Amendment. [The] amendment states but a truism that all is retained which has not been surrendered. There is nothing in the history of its adoption to suggest that it was more than declaratory of the relationship between the national and state governments as it had been established by the Constitution before the amendment or that its purpose was other than to allay fears that the new national government might seek to exercise powers not granted, and that the states might not be able to exercise fully their reserved powers."

[handwritten margin note: Court Don't Give a Fuck about 10th amendment]

Note: The New Deal Legacy

1. *Two perspectives on* Jones & Laughlin. Consider these interpretations of *Jones & Laughlin.* (a) Chief Justice Hughes's description of Jones & Laughlin's operations shows that the Court chose the "economic" or "pragmatic" approach, focusing on actual economic realities, to determining whether an activity affects interstate commerce. Recall that in Wickard v. Filburn, the Court focused on the national market in wheat, while in *Jones & Laughlin*, it focused on Jones & Laughlin's own steel plants. (b) The NLRA regulated labor relations and strikes that interrupted the productions of goods and services, and thereby directly affected interstate commerce, whereas the NRA's production codes regulated production practices, whose effects on interstate commerce were only indirect. *Jones & Laughlin*'s language supports both interpretations; the case has generally been taken to embody the first.

2. *The "formalist" approach. Darby* is divided into two parts. Are the analyses the same in both?

a. *Prohibiting interstate shipment*. Congress prohibited the shipment in inter-state commerce of certain goods. Does this intrude on state policies in a way distinguishable from the statutes in the Lottery Case? Note that the Court refuses to use Congress's "motive and purpose" as a basis for its constitutional analysis. Can that be reconciled with the "pretext" language of *McCulloch*? Can a "pretext" test ever be applied without the courts' exercising "control" over motive and purpose?

Consider the suggestion in Friedman & Lakier, "To Regulate," Not "To Pro-hibit": Limiting the Commerce Power, 2012 Sup. Ct. Rev. 255, 261-262 (2013):

> [In light of] Framing-era understandings of the proper division between the national and state government [and] modern economic analysis of the values of federalism, [the] only conceivable justification for allowing Congress to ban mar-kets [is] to control the spillover costs of state diversity. [This] rationale standing alone is insufficient justification to allow Congress to prohibit commerce. [But Congress] would still be able to ban goods when doing so serves [interstate] markets. [Because "in-service" laws do] not work to shut interstate commerce down, but instead typically help enforce rules by which interstate commerce operates, they do not represent prohibition of commerce. [Congress] would also have the power to adopt "helper" statutes [that] lend federal enforcement authority to states that have chosen through their own democratic processes to ban certain goods.

b. *Regulating directly*. Congress directly regulated the wages and hours of employees producing goods for interstate commerce. The Court in *Darby* jus-tifies the direct regulation as a necessary and proper means of enforcing the ban on interstate shipment. Are there any limitations to the use of this technique? Does this approach eliminate all distinctions between direct regulation and a prohibition on interstate shipment, on the theory that direct regulation will always be a necessary and proper method of ensuring that the prohibition will not be violated?

c. *Unfair competition*. The Court justifies the direct regulation on an "independent" ground, that of eliminating unfair competition. In what sense is the competition "unfair"? Note that, absent the federal statute, paying sub-"minimum" wages was lawful in some states. Paying such wages is "unfair" only in that some states choose to require employers located there to pay higher wages.

3. *Later developments*. Perez v. United States, 402 U.S. 146 (1971), upheld a federal criminal statute prohibiting "extortionate credit transactions" — loan-sharking enforced by threats of violence. Justice Douglas's opinion for the Court recited the findings Congress had made after a series of hearings, although the statute itself resulted from a floor amendment. With regard to the findings, Justice Douglas wrote, "We have mentioned in detail the economic, financial, and social setting of the problem as revealed to Congress. We do so not to infer that Congress need make particularized findings in order to legislate. We relate the history of the Act in detail to answer the impassioned plea of petitioner that all that is involved in loan sharking is a traditionally local activity." The Court relied on *Darby* to uphold the statute. There, Justice Douglas said, "*a class of activities* was held properly regulated by Congress without proof that the particular intra-state activity against which a sanction was laid had an effect on commerce. [Petitioner] is clearly *a member of the class* which engages in 'extortionate credit transactions' as defined by Congress and the description of that class has the required definiteness. [Where] the class of activities is regulated and that class

is within the reach of federal power, the courts have no power 'to excise, as trivial, individual instances' of the class. Maryland v. Wirtz, 392 U.S. 183, 193." Justice Stewart dissented, saying that he could not "discern any rational distinction between loan sharking and other local crime." For him, it was "not enough to say that loan sharking is a national problem, for all crime is a national problem. It is not enough to say that some loan sharking has interstate characteristics, for any crime may have an interstate setting. And the circumstance that loan sharking has an adverse impact on interstate business is not a distinguishing attribute, for interstate business suffers from almost all criminal activity, be it shoplifting or violence in the streets."

4. *Federalism and statutory interpretation.* In *Wickard*, Justice Jackson said that considerations of federalism might affect the courts' construction of a statute: "That an activity is of local character may help in a doubtful case to determine whether Congress intended to reach it." Why? What is a "doubtful case"? In United States v. Bass, 404 U.S. 336 (1971), the Court held that, under the following statute, a defendant could not be convicted for possessing a gun without proof that the gun had been possessed "in commerce or affecting commerce": "Any person who — (1) has been convicted [of] a felony [and] who receives, possesses, or transports in commerce or affecting commerce [any] fire arm shall be fined not more than $10,000 or imprisoned for not more than two years, or both." It found the statute ambiguous on the question of whether the "in commerce or affecting commerce" phrase modified "transports" only, or "receives [or] possesses" as well. Justice Blackmun disagreed: "The structure of the vital language and its punctuation make it refer to one who receives, to one who possesses, and to one who transports in commerce. If one wished to say that he would welcome a cat, would welcome a dog, or would welcome a cow that jumps over the moon, he would likely say 'I would like to have a cat, a dog, or a cow that jumps over the moon.' So it is here."

HEART OF ATLANTA MOTEL v. UNITED STATES, 379 U.S. 241 (1964). Title II of the 1964 Civil Rights Act provides that "all persons shall be entitled to the full and equal enjoyment of the goods, services, . . . and accommodations of any place of public accommodation . . . without discrimination or segregation on the ground of race, color, religion, or national origin." The statute defines places of public accommodation as those whose "operations affect commerce." It declares that hotels and motels that provide rooms for transient guests affect commerce per se. A restaurant is covered if it serves or offers to serve interstate travelers or if "a substantial portion of the food which it serves . . . has moved in commerce." The Heart of Atlanta Motel sought a declaratory judgment that Title II was unconstitutional. The motel, located in downtown Atlanta, had 216 rooms. It advertised in national magazines and on billboards. About 75 percent of its registered guests were from out of state.

The Court upheld the statute as a valid exercise of the power to regulate interstate commerce. The Court relied on evidence elicited in congressional hearings "of the burdens that discrimination by race or color places upon interstate commerce. This testimony included the fact that our people have become increasingly mobile with millions of people of all races traveling from State to State; that Negroes in particular have been the subject of discrimination in transient accommodations, having to travel great distances to secure the same; that often they have been unable to obtain accommodations and have had to call upon friends to put them up overnight; and that these conditions had become so acute as to require the listing of available lodging for Negroes in a special guide book which was itself 'dramatic testimony to the difficulties' Negroes encounter in travel." The evidence "indicated a qualitative as well as quantitative effect on interstate travel by Negroes. The former was the obvious impairment of the Negro traveler's pleasure and convenience that resulted when he continually was uncertain of finding lodging. As for the latter, there was evidence that this uncertainty stemming from racial discrimination had the effect of discouraging travel on the part of a substantial portion of the Negro community."

The Court acknowledged that "[in] framing Title II of this Act Congress was also dealing with what it considered a moral problem. But that fact does not detract from the overwhelming evidence of the disruptive effect that racial discrimination has had on commercial intercourse. It was this burden which empowered Congress to enact appropriate legislation, and, given this basis for the exercise of its power, Congress was not restricted by the fact that the particular obstruction to interstate commerce with which it was dealing was also deemed a moral and social wrong." Further, it did not matter that the motel was "of a purely local character" because "the power of Congress to promote interstate commerce also includes the power to regulate the local incidents thereof, including local activities in both the States of origin and destination, which might have a substantial and harmful effect upon that commerce. One need only examine the evidence [to] see that Congress may [prohibit] racial discrimination by motels serving travelers, however 'local' their operations may appear." Justice Clark's opinion for the Court concluded, "How obstructions in commerce may be removed — what means are to be employed — is within the sound and exclusive discretion of the Congress. It is subject only to one caveat — that the means chosen by it must be reasonably adapted to the end permitted by the Constitution. We cannot say that its choice here was not so adapted. The Constitution requires no more."

KATZENBACH v. McCLUNG, 379 U.S. 294 (1964). This was a companion case to *Heart of Atlanta Motel*. It involved Ollie's Barbecue, a family-owned restaurant in Birmingham, Alabama, with a seating capacity of 220 customers. "It is located on a state highway 11 blocks from an interstate one and a somewhat greater distance from railroad and bus stations. The restaurant caters to a family and white-collar trade with a take-out service for Negroes. It employs 36 persons, two-thirds of whom are Negroes." The restaurant bought about $150,000 worth of food, of which about $70,000 worth was meat bought from a local supplier who purchased it out of state. The restaurant challenged the constitutionality of applying Title II of the 1964 Civil Rights Act to it.

Justice Clark's opinion for the Court relied on congressional testimony "that discrimination in restaurants had a direct and highly restrictive effect upon interstate travel by Negroes. This resulted, it was said, because discriminatory practices prevent Negroes from buying prepared food served on the premises while on a trip, except in isolated and unkempt restaurants and under most unsatisfactory and often unpleasant conditions. This obviously discourages travel and obstructs interstate commerce for one can hardly travel without eating. Likewise, it was said, that discrimination deterred professional, as well as skilled, people from moving into areas where such practices occurred and thereby caused industry to be reluctant to establish there."

This was sufficient to support "the conclusion that established restaurants in such areas sold less interstate goods because of the discrimination, that interstate travel was obstructed directly by it, that business in general suffered and that many new businesses refrained from establishing there as a result of it." The Court agreed that "viewed in isolation, the volume of food purchased by Ollie's Barbecue from sources supplied from out of state was insignificant when compared with the total foodstuffs moving in commerce." The restaurant argued that the Constitution required "a case-by-case determination — judicial or administrative — that racial discrimination in a particular restaurant affects commerce." The Court disagreed. "Here, as [in *Darby*] Congress has determined for itself that refusals of service to Negroes have imposed burdens both upon the interstate flow of food and upon the movement of products generally. Of course, the mere fact that Congress has said when particular activity shall be deemed to affect commerce does not preclude further examination by this Court. But where we find that the legislators, in light of the facts and testimony before them, have a rational basis for finding a chosen regulatory scheme necessary to the protection of commerce, our investigation is at an end. The only remaining question — one answered in the affirmative by the court below — is whether the particular restaurant either serves or offers to serve interstate travelers or serves food a substantial portion of which has moved in interstate commerce." Congress, the Court said, "had a rational basis for finding that racial discrimination in restaurants had a direct and adverse effect on the free flow of interstate commerce. Insofar as the sections of the Act here relevant are concerned, Congress prohibited discrimination only in those establishments having a close tie to interstate commerce, i.e., those, like the McClungs', serving food that has come from out of the State. We think in so doing that Congress acted well within its power to protect and foster commerce in extending the coverage of Title II only to those restaurants offering to serve interstate travelers or serving food, a substantial portion of which has moved in interstate commerce."

Justice Black's concurring opinion applied to both *Heart of Atlanta Motel* and *Katzenbach v. McClung*. "[I] recognize that every remote, possible, speculative effect on commerce should not be accepted as an adequate constitutional ground to uproot and throw into the discard all our traditional distinctions between what is purely local, and therefore controlled by state laws, and what affects the national interest and is therefore subject to control by federal laws. I recognize too that some isolated and remote lunchroom which sells only to local people and buys almost all its supplies in the locality may possibly be beyond the reach of the power of Congress to regulate commerce, just as such an establishment is not covered by the present Act. But in deciding the constitutional power of Congress in cases like the two before us we do not consider the effect on interstate commerce of only one isolated, individual, local event, without regard to the fact that this single local event when added to many others of a similar nature may impose a burden on interstate commerce by reducing its volume or distorting its flow. There are approximately 20,000,000 Negroes in our country. Many of them are able to, and do, travel among the States in automobiles. Certainly it would seriously discourage such travel by them if, as evidence before the Congress indicated has been true in the past, they should in the future continue to be unable to find a decent place along their way in which to lodge or eat. And the flow of interstate commerce may be impeded or distorted substantially if local sellers of interstate food are permitted to exclude all Negro consumers. Measuring, as this Court has so often held is required, by the aggregate effect of a great number of such acts of discrimination, I am of the opinion that Congress has constitutional power under the Commerce and Necessary and Proper Clauses to protect interstate commerce from the injuries bound to befall it from these discriminatory practices."

Note: Federalism and Congressional Motivation

1. *Commerce clause versus (?) fourteenth amendment motivations.* The central issues arising from these cases involve the tension between the evident motivation behind the enactment of the statute — an antidiscrimination, moral motivation — and the use of the commerce power. Those issues arose because the Civil Rights Cases, 109 U.S. 3 (1883), held unconstitutional the Civil Rights Act of 1875, which relied on section 5 of the fourteenth amendment to prohibit discrimination in "inns, public conveyances, . . . theaters, and other places of public amusement." In *Heart of Atlanta Motel*, the Court's opinion observed, "the fact that certain kinds of businesses may not in 1875 have been sufficiently involved in interstate commerce to warrant bringing them within the ambit of the commerce power is not necessarily dispositive of the same question today. Our populace had not reached its present mobility, nor were facilities, goods and services circulating as readily in interstate commerce as they are today. Although the principles which we apply today are those first formulated by Chief Justice Marshall in Gibbons v. Ogden, the conditions of transportation and commerce have changed dramatically, and we must apply those principles to the present state of commerce. The sheer increase in volume of interstate traffic alone would give discriminatory practices which inhibit travel a far larger impact upon the Nation's commerce than such practices had on the economy of another day." Justice Douglas, concurring, wrote, "A decision based on the Fourteenth Amendment would have a more settling effect, making unnecessary litigation over whether a particular restaurant or inn is within the commerce definitions of the Act or whether a particular customer is an interstate traveler."

Should Congress have relied on the fourteenth amendment instead of the commerce clause? Suppose a member of Congress believed that the 1964 Civil Rights Act actually served the equality goals of the fourteenth amendment and (a) believed that the Civil Rights Cases had been wrongly decided or (b) believed that the Supreme Court in 1964 would have overruled the Civil Rights Cases or (c) was uncertain about the Court's position in 1964. How, if at all, would these views affect the design of the statute? Should they affect the member's vote on the statute in the form actually presented?

2. *The scope of the rationale.* Must there be a connection between the activities found to "affect" commerce and the regulations Congress imposes? Consider in this connection the role played in the analysis by the food Ollie's Barbecue purchased. Do the food purchases demonstrate that the restaurant's actions "affect" interstate commerce? Could Congress require that the restaurant comply with regulations for the disposal by its carry-out customers of their trash? Regulations regarding the maintenance of its lawn and parking lot? Alternatively, is the activity that affects commerce the discrimination? Is racial discrimination in the sale of services a commercial activity?

United States v. Lopez

514 U.S. 549 (1995)

CHIEF JUSTICE REHNQUIST delivered the opinion of the Court.

In the Gun-Free School Zones Act of 1990, Congress made it a federal offense "for any individual knowingly to possess a firearm at a place that the individual

Can't
have guns in school zone

knows, or has reasonable cause to believe, is a school zone." 18 U.S.C. §922(q)(1)(A). The Act neither regulates a commercial activity nor contains a requirement that the possession be connected in any way to interstate commerce. We hold that the Act exceeds the authority of Congress "to regulate Commerce . . . among the several States. . . ." . . .

Jones & Laughlin Steel, Darby, and Wickard ushered in an era of Commerce Clause jurisprudence that greatly expanded the previously defined authority of Congress under that Clause. In part, this was a recognition of the great changes that had occurred in the way business was carried on in this country. Enterprises that had once been local or at most regional in nature had become national in scope. But the doctrinal change also reflected a view that earlier Commerce Clause cases artificially had constrained the authority of Congress to regulate interstate commerce.

But even these modern-era precedents which have expanded congressional power under the Commerce Clause confirm that this power is subject to outer limits. . . .

[We] have identified three broad categories of activity that Congress may regulate under its commerce power. First, Congress may regulate the use of the channels of interstate commerce. Second, Congress is empowered to regulate and protect the instrumentalities of interstate commerce, or persons or things in interstate commerce, even though the threat may come only from intrastate activities. Finally, Congress' commerce authority includes the power to regulate those activities having a substantial relation to interstate commerce, [Jones & Laughlin Steel], i.e., those activities that substantially affect interstate commerce.

Within this final category, [our] case law has not been clear whether an activity must "affect" or "substantially affect" interstate commerce in order to be within Congress' power to regulate it under the Commerce Clause. We conclude, consistent with the great weight of our case law, that the proper test requires an analysis of whether the regulated activity "substantially affects" interstate commerce. . . .

[If] §922(q) is to be sustained, it must be under the third category as a regulation of an activity that substantially affects interstate commerce.

First, we have upheld a wide variety of congressional Acts regulating intrastate economic activity where we have concluded that the activity substantially affected interstate commerce. [Where] economic activity substantially affects interstate commerce, legislation regulating that activity will be sustained. . . .

Section 922(q) is a criminal statute that by its terms has nothing to do with "commerce" or any sort of economic enterprise, however broadly one might define those terms. Section 922(q) is not an essential part of a larger regulation of economic activity, in which the regulatory scheme could be undercut unless the intrastate activity were regulated. . . .

Second, §922(q) contains no jurisdictional element which would ensure, through case-by-case inquiry, that the firearm possession in question affects interstate commerce. . . .

The Government's essential contention [is] that we may determine here that §922(q) is valid because possession of a firearm in a local school zone does indeed substantially affect interstate commerce. The Government argues that possession of a firearm in a school zone may result in violent crime and that violent crime can be expected to affect the functioning of the national economy in two ways. First, the costs of violent crime are substantial, and, through the mechanism of insurance, those costs are spread throughout the population. Second, violent crime reduces the willingness of individuals to travel to areas within the country that are perceived to be unsafe. Cf. [*Heart of Atlanta Motel*]. The Government also argues that the presence of guns in schools poses a substantial threat to the educational process by threatening the learning environment. A handicapped educational process, in turn, will result in a less productive citizenry. That, in turn, would have an adverse effect on the Nation's economic well-being. As a result, the Government argues that Congress could rationally have concluded that §922(q) substantially affects interstate commerce.

We pause to consider the implications of the Government's arguments. The Government admits, under its "costs of crime" reasoning, that Congress could regulate not only all violent crime, but all activities that might lead to violent crime, regardless of how tenuously they relate to interstate commerce. Similarly, under the Government's "national productivity" reasoning, Congress could regulate any activity that it found was related to the economic productivity of individual citizens: family law (including marriage, divorce, and child custody), for example. . . .

Justice Breyer [reasons] that (1) gun-related violence is a serious problem; (2) that problem, in turn, has an adverse effect on classroom learning; and (3) that adverse effect on classroom learning, in turn, represents a substantial threat to trade and commerce. This analysis would be equally applicable, if not more so, to subjects such as family law and direct regulation of education.

For instance, if Congress can, pursuant to its Commerce Clause power, regulate activities that adversely affect the learning environment, then, a fortiori, it also can regulate the educational process directly. Congress could determine that a school's curriculum has a "significant" effect on the extent of classroom learning. As a result, Congress could mandate a federal curriculum for local elementary and secondary schools because what is taught in local schools has a significant "effect on classroom learning," and that, in turn, has a substantial effect on interstate commerce. [Justice] Breyer's rationale lacks any real limits because, depending on the level of generality, any activity can be looked upon as commercial. Under the dissent's rationale, Congress could just as easily look at child rearing as "falling on the commercial side of the line" because it provides a "valuable service — namely, to equip [children] with the skills they need to survive in life and, more specifically, in the workplace." We do not doubt that Congress has authority under the Commerce Clause to regulate numerous commercial activities that substantially affect interstate commerce and also affect the educational process. That authority, though broad, does not include the authority to regulate each and every aspect of local schools. . . .

These are not precise formulations, and in the nature of things they cannot be. But we think they point the way to a correct decision of this case. The possession of a gun in a local school zone is in no sense an economic activity that might, through repetition elsewhere, substantially affect any sort of interstate commerce. Respondent was a local student at a local school; there is no indication that he had recently moved in interstate commerce, and there is no requirement that his possession of the firearm have any concrete tie to interstate commerce.

To uphold the Government's contentions here, we would have to pile inference upon inference in a manner that would bid fair to convert congressional authority under the Commerce Clause to a general police power of the sort retained by the States. Admittedly, some of our prior cases have taken long steps down that road, giving great deference to congressional action. The broad language in these opinions has suggested the possibility of additional expansion, but we decline here to proceed any further. To do so would require us to conclude that the Constitution's enumeration of powers does not presuppose some thing not enumerated, cf. Gibbons v. Ogden, and that there never will be a distinction between what is truly national and what is truly local. This we are unwilling to do.

For the foregoing reasons the judgment of the Court of Appeals is affirmed.

JUSTICE KENNEDY, with whom JUSTICE O'CONNOR joins, concurring.

The history of the judicial struggle to interpret the Commerce Clause during the transition from the economic system the Founders knew to the single, national market still emergent in our own era counsels great restraint before the Court determines that the Clause is insufficient to support an exercise of the national power. That history gives me some pause about today's decision, but I join the Court's opinion with these observations on what I conceive to be its necessary though limited holding. . . .

The theory that two governments accord more liberty than one requires for its realization two distinct and discernable lines of political accountability: one between the citizens and the Federal Government; the second between the citizens and the States. If, as Madison expected, the federal and state governments are to control each other, see The Federalist No. 51, and hold each other in check by competing for the affections of the people, see The Federalist No. 46, those citizens must have some means of knowing which of the two governments to hold accountable for the failure to perform a given function. [Were] the Federal Government to take over the regulation of entire areas of traditional state concern, areas having nothing to do with the regulation of commercial activities, the boundaries between the spheres of federal and state authority would blur and political responsibility would become illusory. The resultant inability to hold either branch of the government answerable to the citizens is more dangerous even than devolving too much authority to the remote central power. . . .

The statute before us upsets the federal balance to a degree that renders it an unconstitutional assertion of the commerce power, and our intervention is required. [In] a sense any conduct in this interdependent world of ours has an ultimate commercial origin or consequence, but we have not yet said the commerce power may reach so far. If Congress attempts that extension, then at the least we must inquire whether the exercise of national power seeks to intrude upon an area of traditional state concern.

An interference of these dimensions occurs here, for it is well established that education is a traditional concern of the States. The proximity to schools, including of course schools owned and operated by the States or their subdivisions, is the very premise for making the conduct criminal. In these circumstances, we have a particular duty to insure that the federal-state balance is not destroyed. . . .

Education normally State concern [handwritten marginal note]

If a State or municipality determines that harsh criminal sanctions are necessary and wise to deter students from carrying guns on school premises, the reserved powers of the States are sufficient to enact those measures. Indeed, over 40 States already have criminal laws outlawing the possession of firearms on or near school grounds.

Other, more practicable means to rid the schools of guns may be thought by the citizens of some States to be preferable for the safety and welfare of the schools those States are charged with maintaining. These might include inducements to inform on violators where the information leads to arrests or confiscation of the guns, programs to encourage the voluntary surrender of guns with some provision for amnesty, penalties imposed on parents or guardians for failure to supervise the child, laws providing for suspension or expulsion of gun-toting students, or programs for expulsion with assignment to special facilities.

The statute now before us forecloses the States from experimenting and exercising their own judgment in an area to which States lay claim by right of history and expertise, and it does so by regulating an activity beyond the realm of commerce in the ordinary and usual sense of that term. . . .

This is not a case where the etiquette of federalism has been violated by a formal command from the National Government directing the State to enact a certain policy, cf. New York v. United States, 505 U.S. 144 (1992), or to organize its governmental functions in a certain way. While the intrusion on state sovereignty may not be as severe in this instance as in some of our recent Tenth Amendment cases, the intrusion is nonetheless significant. Absent a stronger connection or identification with commercial concerns that are central to the Commerce Clause, that interference contradicts the federal balance the Framers designed and that this Court is obliged to enforce.

For these reasons, I join in the opinion and judgment of the Court.

JUSTICE THOMAS, concurring. . . .

At the time the original Constitution was ratified, "commerce" consisted of selling, buying, and bartering, as well as transporting for these purposes. . . . As one would expect, the term "commerce" was used in contradistinction to productive activities such as manufacturing and agriculture. Alexander Hamilton, for example, repeatedly treated commerce, agriculture, and manufacturing as three separate endeavors. See, e.g., The Federalist No. 36, at 224 (referring to "agriculture, commerce, manufactures"). . . .

[Interjecting] a modern sense of commerce into the Constitution generates significant textual and structural problems. For example, one cannot replace "commerce" with a different type of enterprise, such as manufacturing. When a manufacturer produces a car, assembly cannot take place "with a foreign nation" or "with the Indian Tribes." Parts may come from different States or other nations and hence may have been in the flow of commerce at one time, but manufacturing takes place at a discrete site. Agriculture and manufacturing involve the production of goods; commerce encompasses traffic in such articles. . . .

Put simply, much if not all of Art. I, §8 (including portions of the Commerce Clause itself) would be surplusage if Congress had been given authority over matters that substantially affect interstate commerce. An interpretation of cl. 3 that makes the rest of §8 superfluous simply cannot be correct. Yet this Court's Commerce Clause jurisprudence has endorsed just such an interpretation: the power we have accorded Congress has swallowed Art. I, §8. . . .

[The] substantial effects test suffers from the further flaw that it appears to grant Congress a police power over the Nation [because] of its "aggregation principle." Under so-called "class of activities" statutes, Congress can regulate whole categories of activities that are not themselves either "interstate" or "commerce." In applying the effects test, we ask whether the class of activities as a whole substantially affects interstate commerce, not whether any specific activity within the class has such effects when considered in isolation.

The aggregation principle is clever, but has no stopping point. Suppose all would agree that gun possession within 1,000 feet of a school does not substantially affect commerce, but that possession of weapons generally [does]. Under our substantial effects doctrine, even though Congress cannot single out gun possession, it can prohibit weapon possession generally. But one always can draw the circle broadly enough to cover an activity that, when taken in isolation, would not have substantial effects on commerce. . . .

JUSTICE STEVENS, dissenting. . . .

Guns are both articles of commerce and articles that can be used to restrain commerce. [The] market for the possession of handguns by school-age children is, distressingly, substantial. Whether or not the national interest in eliminating that market would have justified federal legislation in 1789, it surely does today.

JUSTICE SOUTER, dissenting.

In reviewing congressional legislation under the Commerce Clause, we defer to what is often a merely implicit congressional judgment that its regulation addresses a subject substantially affecting interstate commerce "if there is any rational basis for such a finding."

The practice of deferring to rationally based legislative judgments "is a paradigm of judicial restraint." FCC v. Beach Communications, Inc., 508 U.S. 307, 314 (1993). In judicial review under the Commerce Clause, it reflects our respect for the institutional competence of the Congress on a subject expressly assigned to it by the Constitution and our appreciation of the legitimacy that comes from Congress's political accountability in dealing with matters open to a wide range of possible choices. . . .

[Justice Souter reviewed the history of the Court's commerce clause doctrine.]

There is today [a] backward glance at [the] old pitfalls, as the Court treats deference under the rationality rule as subject to gradation according to the commercial or noncommercial nature of the immediate subject of the challenged regulation. The distinction between what is patently commercial and what is not looks much like the old distinction between what directly affects commerce and what touches it only indirectly. And the act of calibrating the level of deference by drawing a line between what is patently commercial and what is less purely so will probably resemble the process of deciding how much interference with contractual freedom was fatal. Thus, it seems fair to ask whether the step taken by the Court today does anything but portend a return to the untenable jurisprudence from which the Court extricated itself almost 60 years ago. The answer is not reassuring. . . .

Because Justice Breyer's opinion demonstrates beyond any doubt that the Act in question passes the rationality review that the Court continues to espouse, today's decision may be seen as only a misstep, its reasoning and its suggestions not quite in gear with the prevailing standard, but hardly an epochal case. I would not argue otherwise, but I would raise a caveat. Not every epochal case has come in epochal trappings. *Jones & Laughlin* did not reject the direct-indirect standard in so many words; it just said the relation of the regulated subject matter to commerce was direct enough. But we know what happened.

I respectfully dissent.

JUSTICE BREYER, with whom JUSTICE STEVENS, JUSTICE SOUTER, and JUSTICE GINSBURG join, dissenting. . . .

I . . .

[The] Constitution requires us to judge the connection between a regulated activity and interstate commerce, not directly, but at one remove. Courts must give Congress a degree of leeway in determining the existence of a significant factual connection between the regulated activity and interstate commerce — both because the Constitution delegates the commerce power directly to Congress and because the determination requires an empirical judgment of a kind that a legislature is more likely than a court to make with accuracy. The traditional words "rational basis" capture this leeway. . . .

II . . .

[Could] Congress rationally have found that "violent crime in school zones," through its effect on the "quality of education," significantly (or substantially) affects "interstate" or "foreign commerce"? As long as one views the commerce connection, not as a "technical legal conception," but as "a practical one," Swift & Co. v. United States, 196 U.S. 375, 398 (1905) (Holmes, J.), the answer to this question must be yes. Numerous reports and studies — generated both inside and outside government — make clear that Congress could reasonably have found the empirical connection that its law, implicitly or explicitly, asserts. (See Appendix for a sample of the documentation. . . .)

For one thing, reports, hearings, and other readily available literature make clear that the problem of guns in and around schools is widespread and extremely serious. [Based] on reports such as these, Congress obviously could have thought that guns and learning are mutually exclusive. . . .

Having found that guns in schools significantly undermine the quality of education in our Nation's classrooms, Congress could also have found, given the effect of education upon interstate and foreign commerce, that gun-related violence in and around schools is a commercial, as well as a human, problem. Education, although far more than a matter of economics, has long been inextricably intertwined with the Nation's economy. . . .

Finally, there is evidence that, today more than ever, many firms base their location decisions upon the presence, or absence, of a work force with a basic education. . . .

The economic links I have just sketched seem fairly obvious. Why then is it not equally obvious, in light of those links, that a widespread, serious, and substantial physical threat to teaching and learning also substantially threatens the commerce to which that teaching and learning is inextricably tied? That is to say, guns in the hands of six percent of inner-city high school students and gun-related violence throughout a city's schools must threaten the trade and commerce that those schools support. The only question, then, is whether the latter threat is (to use the majority's terminology) "substantial." And, the evidence of (1) the extent of the gun-related violence problem, (2) the extent of the resulting negative effect on classroom learning, and (3) the extent of the consequent negative commercial effects, when taken together, indicate a threat to trade and commerce that is "substantial." At the very least, Congress could rationally have concluded that the links are "substantial." . . .

To hold this statute constitutional is not to "obliterate" the "distinction of what is national and what is local"; nor is it to hold that the Commerce Clause permits the Federal Government to "regulate any activity that it found was related to the economic productivity of individual citizens," to regulate "marriage, divorce, and child custody," or to regulate any and all aspects of education. For one thing, this statute is aimed at curbing a particularly acute threat to the educational process — the possession (and use) of life-threatening firearms in, or near, the classroom. The empirical evidence that I have discussed above unmistakably documents the special way in which guns and education are incompatible. [For] another thing, the immediacy of the connection between education and the national economic well-being is documented by scholars and accepted by society at large in a way and to a degree that may not hold true for other social institutions. It must surely be the rare case, then, that a statute strikes at conduct that (when considered in the abstract) seems so removed from commerce, but which (practically speaking) has so significant an impact upon commerce. . . .

IV

In sum, to find this legislation within the scope of the Commerce Clause would [interpret] the Clause as this Court has traditionally interpreted it, with the exception of one wrong turn subsequently corrected. Upholding this legislation would do no more than simply recognize that Congress had a "rational basis" for finding a significant connection between guns in or near schools and (through their effect on education) the interstate and foreign commerce they threaten. For these reasons, I would reverse the judgment of the Court of Appeals.

Respectfully, I dissent.

[The Appendix, listing over 160 sources, is omitted.]

UNITED STATES v. MORRISON, 529 U.S. 598 (2000). The Court held the civil remedy provision of the Violence Against Women Act unconstitutional. The statute, enacted in 1994, provided a damage remedy for the victim against any person "who commits a crime of violence motivated by gender." The statute contains detailed findings, backed up by a substantial legislative history, that "gender-motivated violence affects interstate commerce 'by deterring potential victims from traveling interstate, from engaging in employment in interstate business, and from transacting with business, and in places involved in interstate commerce.'"

Chief Justice Rehnquist, writing for the same justices who formed the majority in *Lopez*, wrote that "[gender]-motivated crimes of violence are not [economic] activity. While we need not adopt a categorical rule against aggregating the effects of any noneconomic activity in order to decide these cases, thus far in our Nation's history our cases have upheld Commerce Clause regulation of intrastate activity only where that activity is economic in nature." Congress's findings "are substantially weakened by the fact that they rely so heavily on a method of reasoning that we have already rejected as unworkable if we are to maintain the Constitution's enumeration of powers. [Given] these findings, [the] concern we expressed in *Lopez* that Congress might use the Commerce Clause to completely obliterate the Constitution's distinction between national and local authority seems well-founded. The reasoning [seeks] to follow the but-for causal chain from the initial occurrence of violent crime (the suppression of which has always been the prime object of the States' police power) to every attenuated effect upon interstate commerce. If accepted, petitioners' reasoning would allow Congress to regulate any crime as long as the nationwide, aggregated impact of that crime has substantial effects on employment, production, transit, or consumption." He concluded, "The Constitution requires a distinction between what is truly national and what is truly local. In recognizing this fact we preserve one of the few principles that has been consistent since the Clause was adopted."

Justice Souter, writing for the four dissenters, observed: "If we now ask why the formalistic economic/noneconomic distinction might matter today, after its rejection in *Wickard*, the answer is not that the majority fails to see causal connections in an integrated economic world. The answer is that in the minds of the majority there is a new animating theory that makes categorical formalism seem useful again. Just as the old formalism had value in the service of an economic conception, the new one is useful in serving a conception of federalism. It is the instrument by which assertions of national power are to be limited in favor of preserving a supposedly discernible, proper sphere of state autonomy to legislate or refrain from legislating as the individual States see fit. The legitimacy of the Court's current emphasis on the noncommercial nature of regulated activity, then, does not turn on any logic serving the text of the Commerce Clause or on the realism of the majority's view of the national economy."

Justice Souter's opinion concluded, "[The] practice of such ad hoc review cannot preserve the distinction between the judicial and the legislative, and this Court, in any event, lacks the institutional capacity to maintain such a regime for very long. [The] facts that cannot be ignored today are the facts of integrated national commerce and a political relationship between States and Nation much affected by their respective treasuries and constitutional modifications adopted by the people. The federalism of some earlier time is no more adequate to account for those facts today than the theory of laissez-faire was able to govern the national economy 70 years ago."

Justice Breyer also wrote a dissent. He asked, "Does the local street corner mugger engage in 'economic' activity or 'noneconomic' activity when he mugs for money? Would evidence that desire for economic domination underlies many brutal crimes against women save the present statute? [The] Court itself would permit Congress to aggregate, hence regulate, 'noneconomic' activity taking place at economic establishments. [Can] Congress simply rewrite the present law and limit its application to restaurants, hotels, perhaps universities, and other places of public accommodation? [Can] Congress save the present law by including it, or much of it, in a broader 'Safe Transport' or 'Workplace Safety' act? More important, why should we give critical constitutional importance to the economic, or noneconomic, nature of an interstate-commerce-affecting cause? If chemical emanations through indirect environmental change cause identical, severe commercial harm outside a State, why should it matter whether local factories or home fireplaces release them?" He noted, "[In] a world where most everyday products or their component parts cross interstate boundaries, Congress will frequently find it possible to redraft a statute using language that ties the regulation to the interstate movement of some relevant object, thereby regulating local criminal activity or, for that matter, family affairs. Although this possibility does not give the Federal Government the power to regulate everything, it means that any substantive limitation will apply randomly in terms of the interests the majority seeks to protect. How much would be gained, for example, were Congress to reenact the present law in the form of 'An Act Forbidding Violence Against Women Perpetrated at Public

Accommodations or by Those Who Have Moved in, or through the Use of Items that Have Moved in, Interstate Commerce'? Complex Commerce Clause rules creating fine distinctions that achieve only random results do little to further the important federalist interests that called them into being."

Note: Federalism after the New Deal

1. *The values of federalism.* Which values of federalism, if any, does *Lopez* promote? Consider Justice Kennedy's discussion of alternative modes of regulation. Are any of them incompatible with the federal statute? Does the fact that forty states prohibit guns in schools demonstrate the value of states as laboratories of social experimentation? Why could not Congress conclude on the basis of those experiments that such a criminal prohibition was sound enough policy to be imposed nationwide?

Congress reenacted the Gun Free School Zones Act, modifying the statute to make it a criminal offense to possess a weapon near a school if the weapon has been transported in interstate commerce. (The statute has the same designation, 18 U.S.C. §922(q).) Is the new statute constitutional under *Lopez*? If so, what values of federalism does *Lopez* serve? If not, are the criminal statutes Justice Breyer describes unconstitutional?

Consider Shane, Federalism's "Old Deal": What's Right and Wrong with Conservative Judicial Activism, 45 Vill. L. Rev. 201, 221 (2000):

> Compare [a] national anti-prostitution statute with a hypothetical federal law purporting to mandate compulsory education in some East Asian language as a prerequisite to high school graduation. The first regulates economic activity and the second not. Yet, the second law is obviously grounded in economic motivations that probably do not animate the first. There is no reason consistent with the Commerce Clause why Congress' commerce-driven compulsion of Asian language education should be more suspect than its morally driven regulation of prostitution.

Consider these observations about why some matters ought to be left exclusively to state control:

> [State] sovereignty over family law preserves the constitutional ideal of citizenship by promoting the development of civic virtue [in] maturing children. Federalism [destroys] the federal government's power to mold the moral character of future citizens in its own uniform image. [The] communitarian nature of family law requires a level of political engagement and a sense of community identity that lie beyond the reach of national politics. [As] the bonds of community thin out, the danger that shared values will degenerate into governmentally dictated values increases. By situating communitarian politics at the state level, [localism] ensures that the civic participation, political dialogue, and shared values essential to family law will develop within the states' smaller, relatively more accessible political locales. Second, state sovereignty over family law serves to diffuse governmental power over the formation of individual values and moral aspirations. [Localism] promotes diversity [in] the name of preserving citizen choice in matters of family life.

Dailey, Federalism and Families, 143 U. Pa. L. Rev. 1787, 1820, 1871–1872 (1995). To what extent can a parallel argument be made as to education? Consumer protection laws?

2. *The doctrine.* Is the Court correct in saying that the dissent fails to indicate limits on congressional power? Under the dissent's theory, could Congress prescribe the curriculum to be followed in all public schools? Under the dissent's theory, could Congress require that no divorces be granted when the married couple has children under the age of ten, unless a state court finds that the divorce will have no adverse consequences for the psychological well-being of the children?

3. *Wickard* revisited. Gonzales v. Raich, 545 U.S. 1 (2005), upheld the constitutionality of a comprehensive federal ban on the private cultivation and use of marijuana, as applied to marijuana grown at a person's home and intended solely for use by that person or a person for whom the grower was a caretaker, legal under state law, as a medical treatment. Justice Stevens, writing for the Court, cited *Wickard* for the proposition that "Congress can regulate purely intrastate activity that is not itself 'commercial,' in that it is not produced for sale, if it concludes that failure to regulate that class of activity would undercut the regulation of the interstate market in that commodity." Congress "had a rational basis for concluding [that] the high demand in the interstate market will draw such marijuana into that market."

The marijuana growers pointed to three factual differences between their case and *Wickard:* The statute in *Wickard* exempted small farming operations, *Wickard* "involved a 'quintessential economic activity' — a commercial farm — whereas respondents do not sell marijuana," and the record in *Wickard* "made it clear that the aggregate production of wheat for use on farms had a significant impact on market prices." The Court concluded that these distinctions were irrelevant. The statutory exemption was a matter of policy discretion that had not affected the substance of *Wickard*'s analysis; the Court did not treat the activity on which Wickard premised his challenge, "the cultivation of wheat for home consumption," as "part of his commercial farming operation," and Congress had made findings that production of marijuana for local use had a significant impact on the national market.

Justice Scalia concurred in the judgment, with a separate opinion emphasizing that the congressional prohibition was constitutionally permissible as a necessary and proper means of executing the power to regulate interstate commerce in marijuana. "The regulation of an intrastate activity may be essential to a comprehensive regulation of interstate commerce even though the intrastate activity does not itself 'substantially affect' interstate commerce."

Justice O'Connor wrote a dissent, joined by Chief Justice Rehnquist and in large part by Justice Thomas, who also wrote a separate dissent. Justice O'Connor concluded that "[there] is simply no evidence that homegrown medicinal marijuana users constitute, in the aggregate, a sizable enough class to have a discernable, let alone substantial, impact on the national illicit drug market — or otherwise to threaten the [overall regulatory] regime." On the commerce clause issue, Justice Thomas's dissent restated his position in *Lopez.*

After *Raich,* might the civil remedy provision of the Violence Against Women Act be upheld as an integral part of a larger scheme for regulating safety at educational institutions, places of public accommodations, and workplaces? Note that Justice Breyer in *Morrison* suggested an analysis along those lines, arguing that the *Morrison* decision simply counseled Congress to draft its statutes more carefully. How should the Court address a constitutional challenge to a provision enacted "on its own," but which could be understood *either* as part of a larger scheme assembled statute-by-statute *or* as a free-standing statute?

4. *The necessary and proper clause and congressional power.* United States v. Comstock, 560 U.S. 126 (2010), upheld the constitutionality of a federal statute authorizing the civil commitment of mentally ill, sexually dangerous federal prisoners after the dates they would otherwise be released, finding the statute supported by the necessary and proper clause. Justice Breyer's opinion for the Court "base[d] this conclusion on five considerations, taken together." (1) "[In] determining whether the Necessary and Proper Clause grants Congress the legislative authority to enact a particular federal statute, we look to see whether the statute constitutes a means that is rationally related to the implementation of a constitutionally enumerated power." (2) "[T]he civil-commitment statute before us constitutes a modest addition to a set of federal prison-related mental-health statutes that have existed for many decades. A history of involvement [can] be 'helpful in reviewing the substance of a congressional statutory scheme,'" (3) "[The] Federal Government is the custodian of its prisoners. As federal custodian, it has the constitutional power to act in order to protect nearby (and other) communities from the danger federal prisoners may pose." (4) "[The] statute properly accounts for state interests. [It] requires *accommodation* of state interests," by requiring that relevant state authorities be informed of the civil commitment and requiring the release from federal custody of those for whom a state is willing to accept responsibility. (5) "[The] links between [the statute] and an enumerated Article I power are not too attenuated. Neither is the statutory provision too sweeping in its scope."

Justice Kennedy concurred in the result, observing that "[t]he terms 'rationally related' and 'rational basis' must be employed with care, particularly if either is to be used as a stand-alone test." Justice Alito also concurred in the result, finding that the statute "is a necessary and proper means of carrying into execution the enumerated powers that support the federal criminal statutes under which the affected prisoners were convicted."

Justice Thomas, joined by Justice Scalia, dissented. "Must each of the five considerations exist before the Court sustains future federal legislation as proper exercises of Congress' Necessary and Proper Clause authority? What if the facts of a given case support a finding of only four considerations? Or three? And if three or four will suffice, *which* three or four are imperative?"

For additional discussion of the necessary and proper clause, see United States v. Kebodeaux, 133 S. Ct. 2496 (2013).

5. *Statutory interpretation as an "alternative"?* The Chemical Weapons Convention Implementation Act prohibits the use of "any chemical weapon." The statute defines a chemical weapon as "[a] toxic chemical," and defines a toxic chemical as "any chemical which through its chemical action on life processes can cause death, temporary incapacitation or permanent harm to humans or animals. The term includes all such chemicals[.]" In Bond v. United States, 134 S. Ct. 2077 (2014), a defendant was prosecuted under the Act for spreading two chemicals on the car handles and mailbox of a woman who had become pregnant after intercourse with the defendant's husband. The chemicals "are toxic to humans and, in high enough doses, potentially lethal." The defendant challenged the constitutionality of the Act. Chief Justice Roberts for a six-person majority did not address the constitutional claims, but held that the Act did not apply to the defendant's actions. (For a discussion of the constitutional arguments, see page 359, infra.) The majority "doubt[ed] that a treaty about *chemical weapons* has anything to do with Bond's conduct." The statute "must be read consistent with principles of [federalism]," which make it "appropriate to refer to

basic principles of federalism [to] resolve ambiguity in a federal statute. In this case, the ambiguity derives from the improbably broad reach of the key statutory definition given the term — 'chemical weapon' — being defined; the deeply serious consequences of adopting such a boundless reading; and the lack of any apparent need to do so in light of the context from which the statute arose — a treaty about chemical warfare and terrorism." Justices Scalia, Thomas, and Alito each filed separate opinions concurring in the result. Each of them found that the statute covered the alleged conduct, but that it was unconstitutional.

6. *"Cuing" Congress.* Why did Congress enact the statute in *Lopez?* Consider the possibility that members of Congress were attempting primarily to claim credit for addressing a problem their constituents cared about, without concern for actually reducing crime. The existence of state statutes addressing the problem suggests little need for a national statute. Could Congress have thought that local enforcement efforts would be inadequate? Should a court be concerned about these issues?

P. Bobbitt, Constitutional Fate 191, 195 (1982), describes a "cuing" function of constitutional decisions. Such decisions remind members of Congress that they must "[judge] their own actions to see if they conform to the limits and restraints placed on them by the Constitution." Was *Lopez* an exercise of this cuing function? Was it an appropriate case for exercising it? Given *Lopez*, was *Morrison?* Can a decision justified as an exercise of the cuing function properly generate doctrine that the courts should enforce in subsequent cases?

7. *The commerce clause after Reconstruction.* Should the Court attempt to develop an interpretation of the commerce clause that takes account of subsequent *constitutional* developments? Consider the argument of Jackson, Holistic Interpretation: Fitzpatrick v. Bitzer and Our Bifurcated Constitution, 53 Stan. L. Rev. 1259 (2001), for a "holistic" interpretation of the Constitution, in which the adoption of the fourteenth amendment (and others) properly should affect the interpretation of the commerce clause. Jackson proposes that

> where the special concern or "central value" of the Fourteenth and subsequent equality-oriented Amendments is at stake — a concern [with] overcoming barriers to full participation in public life, both economic and political, by groups traditionally disadvantaged by a history of government-sponsored discrimination — the federal government's powers across the Constitution should be interpreted in light of the now basic constitutional commitment to equality of treatment for all members of the polity.

Id. at 1301–1302. Jackson suggests that this may provide the "articulable limit" the Court seeks on theories that require long chains of causation between the regulated subject and a substantial effect on interstate commerce.

Should we treat the Constitution as an integrated document even though portions were adopted at different times, in the absence of evidence that those who inserted the later portions intended to affect the interpretation of what had been adopted before? Jackson argues that "a sensible reconciliation of constitutionalism (in the sense of precommitment) with democracy is to give greater weight to the constitutional views [of] more contemporary supermajorities as compared with ratifiers who lived many more generations removed." Id. at 1290.

8. *The New Deal legacy in light of* Lopez. Consider the argument that the text and the original understanding conflict in *Lopez:*

There is little doubt that the scope of the powers now exercised by Congress far exceeds that imagined by the framers. They struggled over whether the commerce power included the power to build roads; they wouldn't have struggled over its power to reach the possession of guns near schools. But [the] language of the Constitution [plainly] supports this expanse of federal power. [As] commerce today seems plainly to reach practically every activity of social life, it would seem to follow that Congress has the power to reach, through regulation, practically every activity of social life.

Lessig, Translating Federalism: United States v. Lopez, 1995 Sup. Ct. Rev. 125, 129–130. Can the original balance between state and nation be restored through interpreting the commerce power?

National Federation of Independent Business v. Sebelius

567 U.S. 519 (2012)

CHIEF JUSTICE ROBERTS announced the judgment of the Court and delivered the opinion of the Court with respect to Parts I [and] II.

[Although five justices — the Chief Justice and the joint dissenters — held in the portions of the opinion printed here that the individual mandate could not be justified as an exercise of Congress's power to regulate interstate commerce, a different majority — the Chief Justice and the four justices who dissented on the commerce clause issue — held that the individual mandate was a constitutionally permissible exercise of Congress's power to impose taxes. For the opinions discussing that issue, see Chapter 3, section A1, infra.]

Today we resolve constitutional challenges to two provisions of the Patient Protection and Affordable Care Act of 2010: the individual mandate, which requires individuals to purchase a health insurance policy providing a minimum level of coverage; and the Medicaid expansion, which gives funds to the States on the condition that they provide specified health care to all citizens whose income falls below a certain threshold. [The portions of the Chief Justice's opinion dealing with the Medicaid expansion are excerpted infra, page 319.] We do not consider whether the Act embodies sound policies. That judgment is entrusted to the Nation's elected leaders. We ask only whether Congress has the power under the Constitution to enact the challenged provisions.

In our federal system, the National Government possesses only limited powers; the States and the people retain the remainder. Nearly two centuries ago, Chief Justice Marshall observed that "the question respecting the extent of the powers actually granted" to the Federal Government "is perpetually arising, and will probably continue to arise, as long as our system shall exist." [*McCulloch*]. In this case we must again determine whether the Constitution grants Congress powers it now asserts, but which many States and individuals believe it does not possess. Resolving this controversy requires us to examine both the limits of the Government's power, and our own limited role in policing those boundaries. . . .

. . . [Because] the police power is controlled by 50 different States instead of one national sovereign, the facets of governing that touch on citizens' daily lives are normally administered by smaller governments closer to the governed. The Framers thus ensured that powers which "in the ordinary course of affairs,

concern the lives, liberties, and properties of the people" were held by governments more local and more accountable than a distant federal bureaucracy. The
Federalist No. 45. The independent power of the States also serves as a check on
the power of the Federal Government: "By denying any one government
complete jurisdiction over all the concerns of public life, federalism protects
the liberty of the individual from arbitrary power." Bond v. United States, 564
U.S. 211 (2011).

This case concerns two powers that the Constitution does grant the Federal
Government, but which must be read carefully to avoid creating a general federal
authority akin to the police power. The Constitution authorizes Congress to
"regulate Commerce with foreign Nations, and among the several States, and
with the Indian Tribes." . . .

The reach of the Federal Government's enumerated powers is broader still
because the Constitution authorizes Congress to "make all Laws which shall be
necessary and proper for carrying into Execution the foregoing Powers." We have
long read this provision to give Congress great latitude in exercising its powers:
"Let the end be legitimate, let it be within the scope of the constitution, and all
means which are appropriate, which are plainly adapted to that end, which are
not prohibited, but consist with the letter and spirit of the constitution, are
constitutional." [*McCulloch*].

Our permissive reading of these powers is explained in part by a general ret-
icence to invalidate the acts of the Nation's elected leaders. "Proper respect for a
coordinate branch of the government" requires that we strike down an Act of
Congress only if "the lack of constitutional authority to pass [the] act in question
is clearly demonstrated." United States v. Harris, 106 U.S. 629 (1883). Members
of this Court are vested with the authority to interpret the law; we possess neither
the expertise nor the prerogative to make policy judgments. Those decisions are
entrusted to our Nation's elected leaders, who can be thrown out of office if the
people disagree with them. It is not our job to protect the people from the
consequences of their political choices.

Our deference in matters of policy cannot, however, become abdication in
matters of law. "The powers of the legislature are defined and limited; and that
those limits may not be mistaken, or forgotten, the constitution is written." [*Marbury*]. Our respect for Congress's policy judgments thus can never extend so far as
to disavow restraints on federal power that the Constitution carefully
constructed. . . .

I

In 2010, Congress enacted the Patient Protection and Affordable Care Act. [This]
case concerns constitutional challenges to two key provisions, commonly referred
to as the individual mandate. . . .

The individual mandate requires most Americans to maintain "minimum
essential" health insurance coverage. [Editors' summary: Individuals who do
not receive coverage through their employers or through government programs
and do not purchase coverage from a private insurance company must make a
"shared responsibility payment" to the federal government. The payment is based
on household income subject to a statutory cap; the payment was estimated at
around $700.] . . .

[handwritten margin note: basis for striking down act]

III . . .

A

The Government's first argument is that the individual mandate is a valid exercise of Congress's power under the Commerce Clause and the Necessary and Proper Clause. According to the Government, the health care market is characterized by a significant cost-shifting problem. Everyone will eventually need health care at a time and to an extent they cannot predict, but if they do not have insurance, they often will not be able to pay for it. Because state and federal laws nonetheless require hospitals to provide a certain degree of care to individuals without regard to their ability to pay, hospitals end up receiving compensation for only a portion of the services they provide. To recoup the losses, hospitals pass on the cost to insurers through higher rates, and insurers, in turn, pass on the cost to policy holders in the form of higher premiums. Congress estimated that the cost of uncompensated care raises family health insurance premiums, on average, by over $1,000 per year.

In the Affordable Care Act, Congress addressed the problem of those who cannot obtain insurance coverage because of preexisting conditions or other health issues. It did so through the Act's "guaranteed-issue" and "community-rating" provisions. These provisions together prohibit insurance companies from denying coverage to those with such conditions or charging unhealthy individuals higher premiums than healthy individuals.

The guaranteed-issue and community-rating reforms do not, however, address the issue of healthy individuals who choose not to purchase insurance to cover potential health care needs. In fact, the reforms sharply exacerbate that problem, by providing an incentive for individuals to delay purchasing health insurance until they become sick, relying on the promise of guaranteed and affordable coverage. The reforms also threaten to impose massive new costs on insurers, who are required to accept unhealthy individuals but prohibited from charging them rates necessary to pay for their coverage. This will lead insurers to significantly increase premiums on everyone.

The individual mandate was Congress's solution to these problems. By requiring that individuals purchase health insurance, the mandate prevents cost-shifting by those who would otherwise go without it. In addition, the mandate forces into the insurance risk pool more healthy individuals, whose premiums on average will be higher than their health care expenses. This allows insurers to subsidize the costs of covering the unhealthy individuals the reforms require them to accept. . . .

   1

The Government contends that the individual mandate is within Congress's power because the failure to purchase insurance "has a substantial and deleterious effect on interstate commerce" by creating the cost-shifting problem. . . .

Given its expansive scope, it is no surprise that Congress has employed the commerce power in a wide variety of ways to address the pressing needs of the time. But Congress has never attempted to rely on that power to compel individuals not engaged in commerce to purchase an unwanted product.[3] Legislative

_____

3. The examples of other congressional mandates cited by Justice Ginsburg are not to the contrary. Each of those mandates — to report for jury duty, to register for the draft, to purchase

novelty is not necessarily fatal; there is a first time for everything. But sometimes "the most telling indication of [a] severe constitutional problem . . . is the lack of historical precedent" for Congress's action. Free Enterprise Fund v. Public Company Accounting Oversight Bd., 130 S. Ct. 3138 (2010). At the very least, we should "pause to consider the implications of the Government's arguments" when confronted with such new conceptions of federal power. [Lopez].

The Constitution grants Congress the power to "regulate *Commerce*" (emphasis added). The power to *regulate* commerce presupposes the existence of commercial activity to be regulated. If the power to "regulate" something included the power to create it, many of the provisions in the Constitution would be superfluous [citing Art. I, §8, cl. 5, the power to "coin Money" and to "regulate the Value thereof," and the powers to "raise and support" armies and make rules for them]. [The] language of the Constitution reflects the natural understanding that the power to regulate assumes there is already something to be regulated.[4]

Our precedent also reflects this understanding. As expansive as our cases construing the scope of the commerce power have been, they all have one thing in common: They uniformly describe the power as reaching "activity." It is nearly impossible to avoid the word when quoting them. See, e.g., [Lopez; Perez; Wickard; NLRB v. Jones & Laughlin Steel Corp.].

The individual mandate, however, does not regulate existing commercial activity. It instead compels individuals to become active in commerce by purchasing a product, on the ground that their failure to do so affects interstate commerce. Construing the Commerce Clause to permit Congress to regulate individuals precisely because they are doing nothing would open a new and potentially vast domain to congressional authority. Every day individuals do not do an infinite number of things. In some cases they decide not to do something; in others they simply fail to do it. Allowing Congress to justify federal regulation by pointing to the effect of inaction on commerce would bring countless decisions an individual could potentially make within the scope of federal regulation, and — under the Government's theory — empower Congress to make those decisions for him. . . .

Wickard has long been regarded as "perhaps the most far reaching example of Commerce Clause authority over intrastate activity," [Lopez], but the Government's theory in this case would go much further. Under Wickard it is within Congress's power to regulate the market for wheat by supporting its price. But price can be supported by increasing demand as well as by decreasing supply. The aggregated decisions of some consumers not to purchase wheat have a substantial effect on the price of wheat, just as decisions not to purchase health insurance have on the price of insurance. Congress can therefore command that those not buying wheat do so, just as it argues here that it may command that those not buying health insurance do so. The farmer in Wickard was at least

---

firearms in anticipation of militia service, to exchange gold currency for paper currency, and to file a tax return — are based on constitutional provisions other than the Commerce Clause.

4. Justice Ginsburg suggests that "at the time the Constitution was framed, to 'regulate' meant, among other things, to require action." But to reach this conclusion, the case cited by Justice Ginsburg relied on a dictionary in which "[t]o order; to command" was the fifth-alternative definition of "to direct," which was itself the second-alternative definition of "to regulate." It is unlikely that the Framers had such an obscure meaning in mind when they used the word "regulate." Far more commonly, "[t]o regulate" meant "[t]o adjust by rule or method," which presupposes something to adjust.

actively engaged in the production of wheat, and the Government could regulate that activity because of its effect on commerce. The Government's theory here would effectively override that limitation, by establishing that individuals may be regulated under the Commerce Clause whenever enough of them are not doing something the Government would have them do.

Indeed, the Government's logic would justify a mandatory purchase to solve almost any problem. To consider a different example in the health care market, many Americans do not eat a balanced diet. [The] failure of that group to have a healthy diet increases health care costs, to a greater extent than the failure of the uninsured to purchase insurance. Those increased costs are borne in part by other Americans who must pay more, just as the uninsured shift costs to the insured. Congress addressed the insurance problem by ordering everyone to buy insurance. Under the Government's theory, Congress could address the diet problem by ordering everyone to buy vegetables.

People, for reasons of their own, often fail to do things that would be good for them or good for society. Those failures — joined with the similar failures of others — can readily have a substantial effect on interstate commerce. Under the Government's logic, that authorizes Congress to use its commerce power to compel citizens to act as the Government would have them act.

That is not the country the Framers of our Constitution envisioned. James Madison explained that the Commerce Clause was "an addition which few oppose and from which no apprehensions are entertained." The Federalist No. 45. While Congress's authority under the Commerce Clause has of course expanded with the growth of the national economy, our cases have "always recognized that the power to regulate commerce, though broad indeed, has limits." Maryland v. Wirtz, 392 U.S. 183 (1968). The Government's theory would erode those limits, permitting Congress to reach beyond the natural extent of its authority, "everywhere extending the sphere of its activity and drawing all power into its impetuous vortex." The Federalist No. 48. Congress already enjoys vast power to regulate much of what we do. Accepting the Government's theory would give Congress the same license to regulate what we do not do, fundamentally changing the relation between the citizen and the Federal Government.

To an economist, perhaps, there is no difference between activity and inactivity; both have measurable economic effects on commerce. But the distinction between doing something and doing nothing would not have been lost on the Framers, who were "practical statesmen," not metaphysical philosophers. [The] Framers gave Congress the power to *regulate* commerce, not to *compel* it, and for over 200 years both our decisions and Congress's actions have reflected this understanding. There is no reason to depart from that understanding now.

The Government sees things differently. It argues that because sickness and injury are unpredictable but unavoidable, "the uninsured as a class are active in the market for health care, which they regularly seek and obtain." The individual mandate "merely regulates how individuals finance and pay for that active participation — requiring that they do so through insurance, rather than through attempted self-insurance with the back-stop of shifting costs to others."

The Government repeats the phrase "active in the market for health care" throughout its brief, but that concept has no constitutional significance. An individual who bought a car two years ago and may buy another in the future is not "active in the car market" in any pertinent sense. The phrase "active in the market" cannot obscure the fact that most of those regulated by the individual mandate are not currently engaged in any commercial activity involving health

[handwritten margin note: this would force individuals to act as the gov. would want them to do.]

care, and that fact is fatal to the Government's effort to "regulate the uninsured as a class." Our precedents recognize Congress's power to regulate "class[es] of activities," [*Raich*], (emphasis added), not classes of *individuals*, apart from any activity in which they are engaged.

The individual mandate's regulation of the uninsured as a class is, in fact, particularly divorced from any link to existing commercial activity. The mandate primarily affects healthy, often young adults who are less likely to need significant health care and have other priorities for spending their money. It is precisely because these individuals, as an actuarial class, incur relatively low health care costs that the mandate helps counter the effect of forcing insurance companies to cover others who impose greater costs than their premiums are allowed to reflect. If the individual mandate is targeted at a class, it is a class whose commercial inactivity rather than activity is its defining feature.

The Government, however, claims that this does not matter. The Government regards it as sufficient to trigger Congress's authority that almost all those who are uninsured will, at some unknown point in the future, engage in a health care transaction. Asserting that "[t]here is no temporal limitation in the Commerce Clause," the Government argues that because "[e]veryone subject to this regulation is in or will be in the health care market," they can be "regulated in advance." . . .

Everyone will likely participate in the markets for food, clothing, transportation, shelter, or energy; that does not authorize Congress to direct them to purchase particular products in those or other markets today. The Commerce Clause is not a general license to regulate an individual from cradle to grave, simply because he will predictably engage in particular transactions. Any police power to regulate individuals as such, as opposed to their activities, remains vested in the States. . . .

2

The Government next contends that Congress has the power under the Necessary and Proper Clause to enact the individual mandate because the mandate is an "integral part of a comprehensive scheme of economic regulation" — the guaranteed-issue and community-rating insurance reforms. Under this argument, it is not necessary to consider the effect that an individual's inactivity may have on interstate commerce; it is enough that Congress regulate commercial activity in a way that requires regulation of inactivity to be effective. The power to "make all Laws which shall be necessary and proper for carrying into Execution" the powers enumerated in the Constitution vests Congress with authority to enact provisions "incidental to the [enumerated] power, and conducive to its beneficial exercise" [*McCulloch*]. Although the Clause gives Congress authority to "legislate on that vast mass of incidental powers which must be involved in the constitution," it does not license the exercise of any "great substantive and independent power[s]" beyond those specifically enumerated. Instead, the Clause is "merely a declaration, for the removal of all uncertainty, that the means of carrying into execution those [powers] otherwise granted are included in the grant" (VI Writings of James Madison 383 (G. Hunt ed. 1906)).

As our jurisprudence under the Necessary and Proper Clause has developed, we have been very deferential to Congress's determination that a regulation is "necessary." We have thus upheld laws that are "'convenient, or useful' or 'conducive' to the authority's 'beneficial exercise.'" [*Comstock*]. But we have also carried out our responsibility to declare unconstitutional those laws that undermine the structure of government established by the Constitution. Such laws, which are not "consist[ent] with the letter and spirit of the constitution," *McCulloch*, are not "proper [means] for carrying into Execution" Congress's enumerated powers. Rather, they are, "in the words of The Federalist, 'merely acts of usurpation' which 'deserve to be treated as such.'" [*Printz*].

Applying these principles, the individual mandate cannot be sustained under the Necessary and Proper Clause as an essential component of the insurance reforms. Each of our prior cases upholding laws under that Clause involved exercises of authority derivative of, and in service to, a granted power. [The] individual mandate, by contrast, vests Congress with the extraordinary ability to create the necessary predicate to the exercise of an enumerated power.

This is in no way an authority that is "narrow in scope" [*Comstock*], or "incidental" to the exercise of the commerce power [*McCulloch*]. Rather, such a conception of the Necessary and Proper Clause would work a substantial expansion of federal authority. No longer would Congress be limited to regulating under the Commerce Clause those who by some preexisting activity bring themselves within the sphere of federal regulation. Instead, Congress could reach beyond the natural limit of its authority and draw within its regulatory scope those who otherwise would be outside of it. Even if the individual mandate is "necessary" to the Act's insurance reforms, such an expansion of federal power is not a "proper" means for making those reforms effective. . . .

* * *

The Framers created a Federal Government of limited powers, and assigned to this Court the duty of enforcing those limits. The Court does so today. But the Court does not express any opinion on the wisdom of the Affordable Care Act. Under the Constitution, that judgment is reserved to the people.

The judgment of the Court of Appeals for the Eleventh Circuit is affirmed in part and reversed in part.

It is so ordered.

JUSTICE GINSBURG, with whom JUSTICE SOTOMAYOR joins, and with whom JUSTICE BREYER and JUSTICE KAGAN join as to Parts I, II, III, and IV, concurring in part, concurring in the judgment in part, and dissenting in part. . . .

I

The provision of health care is today a concern of national dimension, just as the provision of old-age and survivors' benefits was in the 1930's. In the Social Security Act, Congress installed a federal system to provide monthly benefits to retired wage earners and, eventually, to their survivors. Beyond question, Congress could have adopted a similar scheme for health care. Congress chose, instead, to preserve a central role for private insurers and state governments. According to the Chief Justice, the Commerce Clause does not permit that preservation. This rigid reading of the Clause makes scant sense and is stunningly retrogressive.

Since 1937, our precedent has recognized Congress' large authority to set the Nation's course in the economic and social welfare realm. The Chief Justice's crabbed reading of the Commerce Clause harks back to the era in which the Court routinely thwarted Congress' efforts to regulate the national economy in the interest of those who labor to sustain it.

It is a reading that should not have staying power. . . .

B

The large number of individuals without health insurance, Congress found, heavily burdens the national health-care market. [The] cost of emergency care or treatment for a serious illness generally exceeds what an individual can afford to pay on her own. Unlike markets for most products, however, the inability to pay for care does not mean that an uninsured individual will receive no care. Federal and state law, as well as professional obligations and embedded social norms, require hospitals and physicians to provide care when it is most needed, regardless of the patient's ability to pay.

As a consequence, medical-care providers deliver significant amounts of care to the uninsured for which the providers receive no payment. . . .

Health-care providers do not absorb these bad debts. Instead, they raise their prices, passing along the cost of uncompensated care to those who do pay reliably: the government and private insurance companies. In response, private insurers increase their premiums, shifting the cost of the elevated bills from providers onto those who carry insurance. The net result: Those with health insurance subsidize the medical care of those without it. As economists would describe what happens, the uninsured "free ride" on those who pay for health insurance. . . .

[Insurance] companies and health-care providers know that some percentage of healthy, uninsured people will suffer sickness or injury each year and will receive medical care despite their inability to pay. In anticipation of this uncompensated care, health-care companies raise their prices, and insurers their premiums. In other words, because any uninsured person may need medical care at any moment and because health-care companies must account for that risk, every uninsured person impacts the market price of medical care and medical insurance. . . .

this affects interstate commerce

C

States cannot resolve the problem of the uninsured on their own. Like Social Security benefits, a universal health-care system, if adopted by an individual State, would be "bait to the needy and dependent elsewhere, encouraging them to migrate and seek a haven of repose." Helvering v. Davis, 301 U.S. 619 (1937). An influx of unhealthy individuals into a State with universal health care would result in increased spending on medical services. To cover the increased costs, a State would have to raise taxes, and private health-insurance companies would have to increase premiums. Higher taxes and increased insurance costs would, in turn, encourage businesses and healthy individuals to leave the State.

States that undertake health-care reforms on their own thus risk "placing themselves in a position of economic disadvantage as compared with neighbors or competitors." [*Davis*]. Facing that risk, individual States are unlikely to take the initiative in addressing the problem of the uninsured, even though solving that problem is in all States' best interests. Congress' intervention was needed to overcome this collective-action impasse.

D

Aware that a national solution was required, Congress could have taken over the health-insurance market by establishing a tax-and-spend federal program like

Social Security. Such a program, commonly referred to as a single-payer system (where the sole payer is the Federal Government), would have left little, if any, room for private enterprise or the States. Instead of going this route, Congress enacted the ACA, a solution that retains a robust role for private insurers and state governments. To make its chosen approach work, however, Congress had to use some new tools, including a requirement that most individuals obtain private health insurance coverage. [By] employing these tools, Congress was able to achieve a practical, altogether reasonable, solution. . . .

The minimum coverage provision serves a further purpose vital to Congress' plan to reduce the number of uninsured. Congress knew that encouraging individuals to purchase insurance would not suffice to solve the problem, because most of the uninsured are not uninsured by choice. Of particular concern to Congress were people who, though desperately in need of insurance, often cannot acquire it: persons who suffer from preexisting medical conditions.

Before the ACA's enactment, private insurance companies took an applicant's medical history into account when setting insurance rates or deciding whether to insure an individual. Because individuals with preexisting medical conditions cost insurance companies significantly more than those without such conditions, insurers routinely refused to insure these individuals, charged them substantially higher premiums, or offered only limited coverage that did not include the preexisting illness.

To ensure that individuals with medical histories have access to affordable insurance, Congress devised a three-part solution. First, Congress imposed a "guaranteed issue" requirement, which bars insurers from denying coverage to any person on account of that person's medical condition or history. Second, Congress required insurers to use "community rating" to price their insurance policies. Community rating, in effect, bars insurance companies from charging higher premiums to those with preexisting conditions.

But these two provisions, Congress comprehended, could not work effectively unless individuals were given a powerful incentive to obtain insurance. . . .

Congress comprehended that guaranteed-issue and community-rating laws alone will not work. When insurance companies are required to insure the sick at affordable prices, individuals can wait until they become ill to buy insurance. Pretty soon, those in need of immediate medical care — i.e., those who cost insurers the most — become the insurance companies' main customers. This "adverse selection" problem leaves insurers with two choices: They can either raise premiums dramatically to cover their ever-increasing costs or they can exit the market. In the seven States that tried guaranteed-issue and community-rating requirements without a minimum coverage provision, that is precisely what insurance companies did.

Massachusetts, Congress was told, cracked the adverse selection problem. By requiring most residents to obtain insurance, the Commonwealth ensured that insurers would not be left with only the sick as customers. As a result, federal lawmakers observed, Massachusetts succeeded where other States had failed. In coupling the minimum coverage provision with guaranteed-issue and community-rating prescriptions, Congress followed Massachusetts' lead.

* * *

In sum, Congress passed the minimum coverage provision as a key component of the ACA to address an economic and social problem that has plagued the Nation for decades: the large number of U.S. residents who are unable or unwilling to obtain health insurance. Whatever one thinks of the policy decision

Congress made, it was Congress' prerogative to make it. Reviewed with appropriate deference, the minimum coverage provision, allied to the guaranteed-issue and community-rating prescriptions, should survive measurement under the Commerce and Necessary and Proper Clauses.

II . . .

B

Consistent with the Framers' intent, we have repeatedly emphasized that Congress' authority under the Commerce Clause is dependent upon "practical" considerations, including "actual experience." [*Jones & Laughlin*; *Wickard*]. We afford Congress the leeway "to undertake to solve national problems directly and realistically." American Power & Light Co. v. SEC, 329 U.S. 90 (1946).

Until today, this Court's pragmatic approach to judging whether Congress validly exercised its commerce power was guided by two familiar principles. First, Congress has the power to regulate economic activities "that substantially affect interstate commerce." [*Raich*]. This capacious power extends even to local activities that, viewed in the aggregate, have a substantial impact on interstate commerce.

Second, we owe a large measure of respect to Congress when it frames and enacts economic and social legislation. See [*Raich*]. When appraising such legislation, we ask only (1) whether Congress had a "rational basis" for concluding that the regulated activity substantially affects interstate commerce, and (2) whether there is a "reasonable connection between the regulatory means selected and the asserted ends." [*Hodel*]. In answering these questions, we presume the statute under review is constitutional and may strike it down only on a "plain showing" that Congress acted irrationally. [*Morrison*].

C

Straightforward application of these principles would require the Court to hold that the minimum coverage provision is proper Commerce Clause legislation. Beyond dispute, Congress had a rational basis for concluding that the uninsured, as a class, substantially affect interstate commerce. Those without insurance consume billions of dollars of health-care products and services each year. . . .

The minimum coverage provision, furthermore, bears a "reasonable connection" to Congress' goal of protecting the health-care market from the disruption caused by individuals who fail to obtain insurance. By requiring those who do not carry insurance to pay a toll, the minimum coverage provision gives individuals a strong incentive to insure. This incentive, Congress had good reason to believe, would reduce the number of uninsured and, correspondingly, mitigate the adverse impact the uninsured have on the national health-care market.

Congress also acted reasonably in requiring uninsured individuals, whether sick or healthy, either to obtain insurance or to pay the specified penalty. As earlier observed, because every person is at risk of needing care at any moment, all those who lack insurance, regardless of their current health status, adversely affect the price of health care and health insurance. Moreover, an insurance-purchase requirement limited to those in need of immediate care simply could not work. Insurance companies would either charge these individuals prohibitively expensive premiums, or, if community-rating regulations were in place, close up shop. . . .

D . . .

1

a . . .

[Everyone] will, at some point, consume health-care products and services. Thus, if the Chief Justice is correct that an insurance-purchase requirement can be applied only to those who "actively" consume health care, the minimum coverage provision fits the bill.

The Chief Justice does not dispute that all U.S. residents participate in the market for health services over the course of their lives. But, the Chief Justice insists, the uninsured cannot be considered active in the market for health care, because "[t]he proximity and degree of connection between the [uninsured today] and [their] subsequent commercial activity is too lacking."

This argument has multiple flaws. First, more than 60% of those without insurance visit a hospital or doctor's office each year. Nearly 90% will within five years. An uninsured's consumption of health care is thus quite proximate: It is virtually certain to occur in the next five years and more likely than not to occur this year.

Equally evident, Congress has no way of separating those uninsured individuals who will need emergency medical care today (surely their consumption of medical care is sufficiently imminent) from those who will not need medical services for years to come. No one knows when an emergency will occur, yet emergencies involving the uninsured arise daily. To capture individuals who unexpectedly will obtain medical care in the very near future, then, Congress needed to include individuals who will not go to a doctor anytime soon. Congress, our decisions instruct, has authority to cast its net that wide.[5]

Second, it is Congress' role, not the Court's, to delineate the boundaries of the market the Legislature seeks to regulate. The Chief Justice defines the health-care market as including only those transactions that will occur either in the next instant or within some (unspecified) proximity to the next instant. But Congress could reasonably have viewed the market from a long-term perspective, encompassing all transactions virtually certain to occur over the next decade, not just those occurring here and now. . . .

Our decisions [acknowledge] Congress' authority, under the Commerce Clause, to direct the conduct of an individual today (the farmer in *Wickard,* stopped from growing excess wheat; the plaintiff in *Raich,* ordered to cease cultivating marijuana) because of a prophesied future transaction (the eventual sale of that wheat or marijuana in the interstate market). Congress' actions are even more rational in this case, where the future activity (the consumption of medical

---

5. Echoing the Chief Justice, the joint dissenters urge that the minimum coverage provision impermissibly regulates young people who "have no intention of purchasing [medical care]" and are too far "removed from the [health-care] market." This criticism ignores the reality that a healthy young person may be a day away from needing health care. A victim of an accident or unforeseen illness will consume extensive medical care immediately, though scarcely expecting to do so.

care) is certain to occur, the sole uncertainty being the time the activity will take place.

Maintaining that the uninsured are not active in the health-care market, the Chief Justice draws an analogy to the car market. An individual "is not 'active in the car market,'" the Chief Justice observes, simply because he or she may someday buy a car. The analogy is inapt. The inevitable yet unpredictable need for medical care and the guarantee that emergency care will be provided when required are conditions nonexistent in other markets. That is so of the market for cars, and of the market for broccoli as well. Although an individual might buy a car or a crown of broccoli one day, there is no certainty she will ever do so. And if she eventually wants a car or has a craving for broccoli, she will be obliged to pay at the counter before receiving the vehicle or nourishment. She will get no free ride or food, at the expense of another consumer forced to pay an inflated price. Upholding the minimum coverage provision on the ground that all are participants or will be participants in the health-care market would therefore carry no implication that Congress may justify under the Commerce Clause a mandate to buy other products and services.

Nor is it accurate to say that the minimum coverage provision "compel[s] individuals . . . to purchase an unwanted product" or "suite of products." If unwanted today, medical service secured by insurance may be desperately needed tomorrow. Virtually everyone, I reiterate, consumes health care at some point in his or her life. Health insurance is a means of paying for this care, nothing more. In requiring individuals to obtain insurance, Congress is therefore not mandating the purchase of a discrete, unwanted product. Rather, Congress is merely defining the terms on which individuals pay for an interstate good they consume: Persons subject to the mandate must now pay for medical care in advance (instead of at the point of service) and through insurance (instead of out of pocket). Establishing payment terms for goods in or affecting interstate commerce is quintessential economic regulation well within Congress' domain.

The Chief Justice also calls the minimum coverage provision an illegitimate effort to make young, healthy individuals subsidize insurance premiums paid by the less hale and hardy. This complaint, too, is spurious. Under the current health-care system, healthy persons who lack insurance receive a benefit for which they do not pay: They are assured that, if they need it, emergency medical care will be available, although they cannot afford it. Those who have insurance bear the cost of this guarantee. By requiring the healthy uninsured to obtain insurance or pay a penalty structured as a tax, the minimum coverage provision ends the free ride these individuals currently enjoy.

In the fullness of time, moreover, today's young and healthy will become society's old and infirm. Viewed over a lifespan, the costs and benefits even out: The young who pay more than their fair share currently will pay less than their fair share when they become senior citizens. And even if, as undoubtedly will be the case, some individuals, over their lifespans, will pay more for health insurance than they receive in health services, they have little to complain about, for that is how insurance works. Every insured person receives protection against a catastrophic loss, even though only a subset of the covered class will ultimately need that protection.

b

In any event, the Chief Justice's limitation of the commerce power to the regulation of those actively engaged in commerce finds no home in the text of the Constitution or our decisions. . . .

[In] separating the power to regulate from the power to bring the subject of the regulation into existence, the Chief Justice asserts, "[t]he language of the Constitution reflects the natural understanding that the power to regulate assumes there is already something to be regulated."

This argument is difficult to fathom. Requiring individuals to obtain insurance unquestionably regulates the interstate health-insurance and health-care markets, both of them in existence well before the enactment of the ACA. Thus, the "something to be regulated" was surely there when Congress created the minimum coverage provision. . . .

In concluding that the Commerce Clause does not permit Congress to regulate commercial "inactivity," and therefore does not allow Congress to adopt the practical solution it devised for the health-care problem, the Chief Justice views the Clause as a "technical legal conception," precisely what our case law tells us not to do. [*Wickard*]. This Court's former endeavors to impose categorical limits on the commerce power have not fared well. . . .

These line-drawing exercises were untenable, and the Court long ago abandoned them. "[Q]uestions of the power of Congress [under the Commerce Clause]," we held in *Wickard*, "are not to be decided by reference to any formula which would give controlling force to nomenclature such as 'production' and 'indirect' and foreclose consideration of the actual effects of the activity in question upon interstate commerce." Failing to learn from this history, the Chief Justice plows ahead with his formalistic distinction between those who are "active in commerce," and those who are not.

It is not hard to show the difficulty courts (and Congress) would encounter in distinguishing statutes that regulate "activity" from those that regulate "inactivity." [An] individual who opts not to purchase insurance from a private insurer can be seen as actively selecting another form of insurance: self-insurance. The minimum coverage provision could therefore be described as regulating activists in the self-insurance market.[7] *Wickard* is another example. Did the statute there at issue target activity (the growing of too much wheat) or inactivity (the farmer's failure to purchase wheat in the marketplace)? If anything, the Court's analysis suggested the latter. . . .

2

Underlying the Chief Justice's view that the Commerce Clause must be confined to the regulation of active participants in a commercial market is a fear that the commerce power would otherwise know no limits. The joint dissenters express a similar apprehension. This concern is unfounded.

First, the Chief Justice could certainly uphold the individual mandate without giving Congress *carte blanche* to enact any and all purchase mandates. As several times noted, the unique attributes of the health-care market render everyone

---

7. The Chief Justice's characterization of individuals who choose not to purchase private insurance as "doing nothing," is similarly questionable. A person who self-insures opts against prepayment for a product the person will in time consume. When aggregated, exercise of that option has a substantial impact on the health-care market.

active in that market and give rise to a significant free-riding problem that does not occur in other markets.

Nor would the commerce power be unbridled, absent the Chief Justice's "activity" limitation. Congress would remain unable to regulate noneconomic conduct that has only an attenuated effect on interstate commerce and is traditionally left to state law. . . .

An individual's decision to self-insure, I have explained, is an economic act with the requisite connection to interstate commerce. Other choices individuals make are unlikely to fit the same or similar description. As an example of the type of regulation he fears, the Chief Justice cites a Government mandate to purchase green vegetables. One could call this concern "the broccoli horrible." . . .

Consider the chain of inferences the Court would have to accept to conclude that a vegetable-purchase mandate was likely to have a substantial effect on the health-care costs borne by lithe Americans. The Court would have to believe that individuals forced to buy vegetables would then eat them (instead of throwing or giving them away), would prepare the vegetables in a healthy way (steamed or raw, not deep-fried), would cut back on unhealthy foods, and would not allow other factors (such as lack of exercise or little sleep) to trump the improved diet.[9] Such "pil[ing of] inference upon inference" is just what the Court refused to do in *Lopez* and *Morrison*. . . .

Supplementing these legal restraints is a formidable check on congressional power: the democratic process. As the controversy surrounding the passage of the Affordable Care Act attests, purchase mandates are likely to engender political resistance. This prospect is borne out by the behavior of state legislators. Despite their possession of unquestioned authority to impose mandates, state governments have rarely done so.

When contemplated in its extreme, almost any power looks dangerous. The commerce power, hypothetically, would enable Congress to prohibit the purchase and home production of all meat, fish, and dairy goods, effectively compelling Americans to eat only vegetables. Yet no one would offer the "hypothetical and unreal possibilit[y]," Pullman Co. v. Knott, 235 U.S. 23 (1914), of a vegetarian state as a credible reason to deny Congress the authority ever to ban the possession and sale of goods. The Chief Justice accepts just such specious logic when he cites the broccoli horrible as a reason to deny Congress the power to pass the individual mandate.

3

To bolster his argument that the minimum coverage provision is not valid Commerce Clause legislation, the Chief Justice emphasizes the provision's novelty. While an insurance-purchase mandate may be novel, the Chief Justice's argument certainly is not. "[I]n almost every instance of the exercise of the [commerce] power differences are asserted from previous exercises of it and made a ground of attack." Hoke v. United States, 227 U.S. 308 (1913). For

---

9. The failure to purchase vegetables in the Chief Justice's hypothetical, then, is not what leads to higher health-care costs for others; rather, it is the failure of individuals to maintain a healthy diet, and the resulting obesity, that creates the cost-shifting problem. Requiring individuals to purchase vegetables is thus several steps removed from solving the problem. The failure to obtain health insurance, by contrast, is the immediate cause of the cost-shifting Congress sought to address through the ACA. Requiring individuals to obtain insurance attacks the source of the problem directly, in a single step.

decades, the Court has declined to override legislation because of its novelty, and for good reason. As our national economy grows and changes, we have recognized, Congress must adapt to the changing "economic and financial realities." Hindering Congress' ability to do so is shortsighted; if history is any guide, today's constriction of the Commerce Clause will not endure.

III

A . . .

The Necessary and Proper Clause "empowers Congress to enact laws in effectuation of its [commerce] powe[r] that are not within its authority to enact in isolation." [*Raich*] (Scalia, J., concurring in judgment). . . .

Recall that one of Congress' goals in enacting the Affordable Care Act was to eliminate the insurance industry's practice of charging higher prices or denying coverage to individuals with preexisting medical conditions. The commerce power allows Congress to ban this practice, a point no one disputes.

Congress knew, however, that simply barring insurance companies from relying on an applicant's medical history would not work in practice. Without the individual mandate, Congress learned, guaranteed-issue and community-rating requirements would trigger an adverse-selection death-spiral in the health-insurance market: Insurance premiums would skyrocket, the number of uninsured would increase, and insurance companies would exit the market. When complemented by an insurance mandate, on the other hand, guaranteed issue and community rating would work as intended, increasing access to insurance and reducing uncompensated care. The minimum coverage provision is thus an "essential par[t] of a larger regulation of economic activity"; without the provision, "the regulatory scheme [w]ould be undercut." [*Raich*]. Put differently, the minimum coverage provision, together with the guaranteed-issue and community-rating requirements, is "'reasonably adapted' to the attainment of a legitimate end under the commerce power": the elimination of pricing and sales practices that take an applicant's medical history into account.

B . . .

In failing to explain why the individual mandate threatens our constitutional order, the Chief Justice disserves future courts. . . .

It is more than exaggeration to suggest that the minimum coverage provision improperly intrudes on "essential attributes of state sovereignty." First, the Affordable Care Act does not operate "in [an] are[a] such as criminal law enforcement or education where States historically have been sovereign." [*Lopez*]. [The] Federal Government plays a lead role in the health-care sector, both as a direct payer and as a regulator.

Second, [the] minimum coverage provision, along with other provisions of the ACA, addresses the very sort of interstate problem that made the commerce power essential in our federal system. The crisis created by the large number of U.S. residents who lack health insurance is one of national dimension that States are "separately incompetent" to handle. Far from trampling on States' sovereignty, the ACA attempts a federal solution for the very reason that the

States, acting separately, cannot meet the need. Notably, the ACA serves the general welfare of the people of the United States while retaining a prominent role for the States.[11] . . .

JUSTICE SCALIA, JUSTICE KENNEDY, JUSTICE THOMAS, and JUSTICE ALITO, dissenting. . . .

[Whatever] may be the conceptual limits upon the Commerce Clause, [they] cannot be such as will enable the Federal Government to regulate all private conduct and to compel the States to function as administrators of federal programs.

That clear principle carries the day here. The striking case of Wickard v. Filburn [always] has been regarded as the ne plus ultra of expansive Commerce Clause jurisprudence. To go beyond that, and to say the *failure* to grow wheat (which is not an economic activity, or any activity at all) nonetheless affects commerce and therefore can be federally regulated, is to make mere breathing in and out the basis for federal prescription and to extend federal power to virtually all human activity. . . .

I

THE INDIVIDUAL MANDATE

. . . If [the individual mandate] "regulates" anything, it is the *failure* to maintain minimum essential coverage. One might argue that it regulates that failure by requiring it to be accompanied by payment of a penalty. But that failure — that abstention from commerce — is not "Commerce." To be sure, *purchasing* insurance *is* "Commerce"; but one does not regulate commerce that does not exist by compelling its existence.

In Gibbons v. Ogden, Chief Justice Marshall wrote that the power to regulate commerce is the power "to prescribe the rule by which commerce is to be governed." That understanding is consistent with the original meaning of "regulate" at the time of the Constitution's ratification, when "to regulate" meant "[t]o adjust by rule, method or established mode," 2 N. Webster, An American Dictionary of the English Language (1828); "[t]o adjust by rule or method," 2 S. Johnson, A Dictionary of the English Language (7th ed. 1785); "[t]o adjust, to direct according to rule," 2 J. Ash, New and Complete Dictionary of the English Language (1775); "to put in order, set to rights, govern or keep in order," T. Dyche & W. Pardon, A New General English Dictionary (16th ed. 1777). It can

---

11. In a separate argument, the joint dissenters contend that the minimum coverage provision is not necessary and proper because it was not the "only . . . way" Congress could have made the guaranteed-issue and community-rating reforms work. . . .
Neither a surcharge on those who purchase insurance nor the denial of a tax credit to those who do not would solve the problem created by guaranteed-issue and community-rating requirements. Neither would prompt the purchase of insurance before sickness or injury occurred.
But even assuming there were "practicable" alternatives to the minimum coverage provision, "we long ago rejected the view that the Necessary and Proper Clause demands that an Act of Congress be 'absolutely necessary' to the exercise of an enumerated power." Jinks v. Richland County, 538 U.S. 456 (2003). Rather, the statutory provision at issue need only be "conducive" and "[reasonably] adapted" to the goal Congress seeks to achieve. The minimum coverage provision meets this requirement.

mean to direct the manner of something but not to direct that something come into being. There is no instance in which this Court or Congress (or anyone else, to our knowledge) has used "regulate" in that peculiar fashion. . . .

We do not doubt that the buying and selling of health insurance contracts is commerce generally subject to federal regulation. But when Congress provides that (nearly) all citizens must buy an insurance contract, it goes beyond "adjust[ing] by rule or method," or "direct[ing] according to rule"; it directs the creation of commerce. . . .

A . . .

The Government presents the Individual Mandate as a unique feature of a complicated regulatory scheme governing many parties with countervailing incentives that must be carefully balanced. Congress has imposed an extensive set of regulations on the health insurance industry, and compliance with those regulations will likely cost the industry a great deal. If the industry does not respond by increasing premiums, it is not likely to survive. And if the industry does increase premiums, then there is a serious risk that its products — insurance plans — will become economically undesirable for many and prohibitively expensive for the rest.

This is not a dilemma unique to regulation of the health-insurance industry. Government regulation typically imposes costs on the regulated industry — especially regulation that prohibits economic behavior in which most market participants are already engaging, such as "piecing out" the market by selling the product to different classes of people at different prices (in the present context, providing much lower insurance rates to young and healthy buyers). And many industries so regulated face the reality that, without an artificial increase in demand, they cannot continue on. When Congress is regulating these industries directly, it enjoys the broad power to enact "'all appropriate legislation'" to "'protec[t]'" and "'advanc[e]'" commerce, [NLRB v. Jones & Laughlin Steel Corp.]. Thus, Congress might protect the imperiled industry by prohibiting low-cost competition, or by according it preferential tax treatment, or even by granting it a direct subsidy.

Here, however, Congress has impressed into service third parties, healthy individuals who could be but are not customers of the relevant industry, to offset the undesirable consequences of the regulation. Congress' desire to force these individuals to purchase insurance is motivated by the fact that they are further removed from the market than unhealthy individuals with pre-existing conditions, because they are less likely to need extensive care in the near future. If Congress can reach out and command even those furthest removed from an interstate market to participate in the market, then the Commerce Clause becomes a font of unlimited power, or in Hamilton's words, "the hideous monster whose devouring jaws . . . spare neither sex nor age, nor high nor low, nor sacred nor profane." The Federalist No. 33.

At the outer edge of the commerce power, this Court has insisted on careful scrutiny of regulations that do not act directly on an interstate market or its participants. . . . [The] lesson of these cases is that the Commerce Clause, even when supplemented by the Necessary and Proper Clause, is not carte blanche for doing whatever will help achieve the ends Congress seeks by the regulation of commerce. . . .

With the present statute, [there] are many ways other than this unprecedented Individual Mandate by which the regulatory scheme's goals of reducing insurance premiums and ensuring the profitability of insurers could be achieved. For instance, those who did not purchase insurance could be subjected to a surcharge when they do enter the health insurance system. Or they could be denied a full income tax credit given to those who do purchase the insurance. . . .

B

The Government's second theory in support of the Individual Mandate is that §5000A is valid because it is actually a "regulat[ion of] activities having a substantial relation to interstate commerce, . . . i.e., . . . activities that substantially affect interstate commerce." This argument takes a few different forms, but the basic idea is that §5000A regulates "the way in which individuals finance their participation in the health-*care* market." That is, the provision directs the manner in which individuals purchase health care services and related goods (directing that they be purchased through insurance) and is therefore a straightforward exercise of the commerce power.

The primary problem with this argument is that §5000A does not apply only to persons who purchase all, or most, or even any, of the health care services or goods that the mandated insurance covers. Indeed, the main objection many have to the Mandate is that they have no intention of purchasing most or even any of such goods or services and thus no need to buy insurance for those purchases. The Government responds that the health-care market involves "essentially universal participation." The principal difficulty with this response is that it is, in the only relevant sense, not true. It is true enough that everyone consumes "health care," if the term is taken to include the purchase of a bottle of aspirin. But the health care "market" that is the object of the Individual Mandate not only includes but principally consists of goods and services that the young people primarily affected by the Mandate do not purchase. They are quite simply not participants in that market, and cannot be made so (and thereby subjected to regulation) by the simple device of defining participants to include all those who will, later in their lifetime, probably purchase the goods or services covered by the mandated insurance. Such a definition of market participants is unprecedented, and were it to be a premise for the exercise of national power, it would have no principled limits.

In a variation on this attempted exercise of federal power, the Government points out that Congress in this Act has purported to regulate "economic and financial decision[s] to forego [sic] health insurance coverage and [to] attempt to self-insure," since those decisions have "a substantial and deleterious effect on interstate commerce." But as the discussion above makes clear, the decision to forgo participation in an interstate market is not itself commercial activity (or indeed any activity at all) within Congress' power to regulate. It is true that, at the end of the day, it is inevitable that each American will affect commerce and become a part of it, even if not by choice. But if every person comes within the Commerce Clause power of Congress to regulate by the simple reason that he will one day engage in commerce, the idea of a limited Government power is at an end.

Wickard v. Filburn has been regarded as the most expansive assertion of the commerce power in our history. A close second is Perez v. United States. [Both] of those cases, however, involved commercial *activity*. To go beyond that, and to say that the failure to grow wheat or the refusal to make loans affects commerce, so that growing and lending can be federally compelled, is to extend federal power to virtually everything. All of us consume food, and when we do so the Federal Government can prescribe what its quality must be and even how much we must pay. But the mere fact that we all consume food and are thus, sooner or later, participants in the "market" for food, does not empower the Government to say when and what we will buy. That is essentially what this Act seeks to do with respect to the purchase of health care. It exceeds federal power.

C

A few respectful responses to Justice Ginsburg's dissent on the issue of the Mandate are in order. That dissent duly recites the test of Commerce Clause power that our opinions have applied, but disregards the premise the test contains. It is true enough that Congress needs only a "'rational basis' for concluding that the *regulated activity* substantially affects interstate commerce" (emphasis added). But it must be *activity* affecting commerce that is regulated, and not merely the failure to engage in commerce. [Ultimately] the dissent is driven to saying that there is really no difference between action and inaction, a proposition that has never recommended itself, neither to the law nor to common sense. To say, for example, that the inaction here consists of activity in "the self-insurance market" seems to us wordplay. By parity of reasoning the failure to buy a car can be called participation in the non-private-car-transportation market. Commerce becomes everything. . . .

The dissent's exposition of the wonderful things the Federal Government has achieved through exercise of its assigned powers, such as "the provision of old-age and survivors' benefits" in the Social Security Act, is quite beside the point. The issue here is whether the federal government can impose the Individual Mandate through the Commerce Clause. And the relevant history is not that Congress has achieved wide and wonderful results through the proper exercise of its assigned powers in the past, but that it has never before used the Commerce Clause to compel entry into commerce. The dissent treats the Constitution as though it is an enumeration of those problems that the Federal Government can address — among which, it finds, is "the Nation's course in the economic and social welfare realm," and more specifically "the problem of the uninsured." The Constitution is not that. It enumerates not federally soluble problems, but federally available powers. The Federal Government can address whatever problems it wants but can bring to their solution only those powers that the Constitution confers, among which is the power to regulate commerce. None of our cases say anything else. Article I contains no whatever-it-takes-to-solve-a-national-problem power.

The dissent dismisses the conclusion that the power to compel entry into the health-insurance market would include the power to compel entry into the new-car or broccoli markets. [The] differences [identified in the dissent] make a very good argument by the dissent's own lights, since they show that the failure to purchase health insurance, unlike the failure to purchase cars or broccoli, creates a national, social-welfare problem that is (in the dissent's view) included among the unenumerated "problems" that the Constitution authorizes the Federal Government to solve. But those differences do not show that the failure to enter the health-insurance market, unlike the failure to buy cars and broccoli, is an activity that Congress can "regulate." (Of course one day the failure of some of the public to purchase American cars may endanger the existence of domestic automobile manufacturers; or the failure of some to eat broccoli may be found to deprive them of a newly discovered cancer-fighting chemical which only that food contains, producing health-care costs that are a burden on the rest of us — in which case, under the theory of Justice Ginsburg's dissent, moving against those inactivities will also come within the Federal Government's unenumerated problem-solving powers.) . . .

V

[Having concluded that the individual-mandate provision was unconstitutional, the dissenters considered whether the Act's other provisions were severable from the mandate (and the Medicaid expansion). They concluded that they were inseverable.]

For the reasons here stated, we would find the Act invalid in its entirety. We respectfully dissent.

JUSTICE THOMAS, dissenting.

[The] joint dissent and the Chief Justice correctly apply our precedents to conclude that the Individual Mandate is beyond the power granted to Congress under the Commerce Clause and the Necessary and Proper Clause. [I] adhere to my view that "the very notion of a 'substantial effects' test under the Commerce Clause is inconsistent with the original understanding of Congress' powers and with this Court's early Commerce Clause cases." [*Morrison*]. [The] Court's continued use of that test "has encouraged the Federal Government to persist in its view that the Commerce Clause has virtually no limits." [*Morrison*]. The Government's unprecedented claim in this suit that it may regulate not only economic activity but also inactivity that substantially affects interstate commerce is a case in point.

Note: Activity and Inactivity

1. *Labeling the opinions.* Note that the joint opinion of Justices Scalia, Kennedy, Thomas, and Alito is referred to by all the Justices as a "dissent," even though its authors' positions on the constitutionality of the individual mandate (and the Medicaid expansion, infra page 319) are needed to constitute a majority holding on those two issues.

2. *The economics of health insurance.* The government argued that the market for health insurance differed from the market for broccoli or automobiles because of the problems of moral hazard and adverse selection. Consider the case of a healthy young person who does not currently need health care. She then becomes ill or injured in an accident. With guaranteed issue and community rating, she can immediately purchase health insurance to cover the costs of her health care. Those costs will almost inevitably be larger than the regulated cost of health-care insurance. The adverse selection problem is that only those currently needing health care will purchase health insurance, thereby driving the cost of insurance up; the moral hazard problem is that the person who buys insurance only when health care is needed similarly drives the cost of insurance up. Most economists would assert that the markets for broccoli and automobiles do not

have those characteristics. If they are right, should that affect the constitutional analysis?

3. *The characterization issue.* If Congress lacks the power to regulate "inactivity," everything turns on the characterization of the regulatory target as "action" or "inaction." The Chief Justice and the joint dissent reject the characterization of the regulatory target as "participating in the self-insurance market." Are there other possible characterizations? Consider characterizing the target as "voluntarily participating in activities that expose a person to the risk of illness or injury." Could "refusing to provide restaurant service to African Americans" be characterized as inaction rather than action? On what basis can the choice of characterizations be made?

4. *Activity and inactivity.* What rationales do the Chief Justice and the joint dissent offer for supplementing the distinction between commercial and non-commercial activity with the distinction between activity and inactivity? Recall as well the older distinction between direct and indirect regulations of commerce.

5. *"Proximity" and the commerce clause.* Justice Ginsburg quotes the Chief Justice's discussion of the proximity between a failure to act and subsequent action. Is that discussion persuasive? Is "proximity" a temporal or a conceptual category? Consider Justice Ginsburg's response to the "broccoli" hypothetical. Should her analysis be cast in terms of the commerce clause or as a general requirement that government action be reasonable? With respect to both proximity and reasonableness, are courts well positioned to make such determinations?

6. *The "antinovelty" principle.* Relying on *NFIB* and *Printz* (discussed in Section III-C below), Katyal & Schmidt, Active Avoidance: The Modern Supreme Court and Legal Change, 128 Harv. L. Rev. 2109, 2139-2149 (2015), discuss the emergence of an "antinovelty" doctrine, according to which "a law without historical precedent is constitutionally suspect." What grounds might there be for such a doctrine? If the exercise of the asserted power is "attractive" in principle, perhaps the fact that Congress in the past refrained from seeking to justify statutes with reference to the power might be taken as evidence of a congressional understanding that the Constitution did not in fact confer the power on it. Yet, if the problem Congress addresses is itself novel, why should novelty in the exercise of an enumerated power count against constitutionality, in a Constitution designed to endure for ages to come, as McCulloch v. Maryland put it? Katyal and Schmidt argue that the antinovelty principle is inconsistent with the presumption of constitutionality because it places the burden on the government to justify the exercise of congressional power. Id. at 2139-2140. Note that whether an exercise of power counts as novel will depend on the specificity with which the exercise is described.

(In United States v. Windsor, 133 S. Ct. 2675 (2013), Justice Kennedy's opinion for the Court observed that the Defense of Marriage Act, held unconstitutional on equal protection grounds, was "an unusual deviation from the usual tradition of recognizing and accepting state definitions of marriage[, which] is strong evidence of a law having the purpose and effect of disapproval of that class." That "purpose and effect" were what rendered the statute unconstitutional as a violation of equality. *Windsor* is excerpted at greater length in Chapter 6.)

7. *Why search for limits?* Rosen & Schmidt, Why Broccoli?: Limiting Principles and Popular Constitutionalism in the Health Care Case, 61 UCLA L. Rev. 66, 70, 71 (2013), argue that "a survey of constitutional history shows that when confronted with novel constitutional questions, the Court almost always declines

to provide limiting principles that define the metes and bounds of the constitutional power or right at issue. Instead, [it] typically answers the question in a narrow [fashion] that analyzes [the] constitutionality of only the governmental action that is before the Court. Indeed, the Court typically avoids any attempt at identifying a limiting principle until it has considered the constitutional question many times, and not infrequently it declines to *ever* identify a limiting principle." Rosen and Schmidt connect the case to ideas about popular constitutionalism, and argue that the *NFIB* Court sought a limiting principle even though the constitutional question was novel because "popular constitutional demands [structured] public expectations about the stakes of the ACA challenge to such a degree that it would have been notable had the Court chosen not to go beyond the facts of the case to engage with the limits of congressional power."

For a collection of essays on *NFIB*, see Persily, Metzger, & Morrison, eds., The Health Care Case: The Supreme Court's Decision and Its Implications (2013).

Note: Observations on Court-Imposed Limitations on Congress's Powers

Over its history, the Court has sporadically attempted to enforce federalism-based limitations on Congress's power. It has repeatedly abandoned those efforts after a time, only to revive them a while later. What accounts for this pattern? Consider the proposition that the Court has from time to time forgotten what the Constitution means. But did it forget during the periods of enforcement or of nonenforcement of such limits?

D.   STATE REGULATION OF INTERSTATE COMMERCE

Since the early years of constitutional adjudication, the Supreme Court has asserted the authority to invalidate state and local laws that the Court finds to interfere improperly with interstate and foreign commerce. When it invalidates state laws for this reason, it says that the commerce clause has been violated (even though the commerce clause, by its terms, is only a grant of power to Congress, not a restriction on state power). This chapter deals with two major problems: (1) What is the *source* of the Court's authority in this area (the primary subject of section Dl), and (2) what are the *criteria* for determining when a state or local law improperly interferes with interstate commerce (the primary subject of the remainder of the section)?

1.   The Fundamental Framework

Note: The Classical View

1. *The vices of "protectionism."* The framers were concerned that states would erect barriers to trade in order to protect the economic activities of local residents.

Protectionism may impede economic development by making it more difficult for goods and capital to move to places where they are more valued. It also may impair the development of a sense of national unity. These two vices of protectionism may have different implications for the constitutional scheme. Regardless of the reasons for their creation, barriers to trade impede economic development. But they need not impair national unity if out-of-state residents understand that the barriers were created to further important local goals unrelated to the suppression of free trade.

The materials that follow address several aspects of the vices of protectionism: (a) Whatever free trade norms the Constitution embodies, which branch — Congress or the courts — should enforce them? (b) How can protectionist legislation be identified? Some statutes apply one rule to economic activity originating locally and another to activity originating elsewhere. Are all such statutes protectionist? Other statutes have a disparate impact on local and out-of-state trade. When should they be characterized as protectionist? Will the degree of the disparate impact matter? Still other statutes erect barriers to trade without regard to where the activity originates. Should such statutes ever be considered protectionist or otherwise constitutionally suspect?

2. *Exclusive congressional power?* In Gibbons v. Ogden, section B supra, Chief Justice Marshall found "great force" in an argument made in Justice Johnson's concurrence, that Congress's power to regulate interstate commerce was exclusive — that is, that the Constitution necessarily withdrew that power from the states. Under this view, the states lacked power to enact laws that regulated interstate commerce, and the courts could invalidate any such laws on the ground that they exceeded the states' authority in our federal system.

The exclusive power argument was troublesome for practical reasons because if Congress's power were exclusive, the states could not act, even if Congress has failed to act. (Note that the acceptability of the "exclusive power" argument may turn on the scope one gives to the affirmative grant of power to Congress.) If *some* regulation is thought appropriate, the "exclusive power" argument may go too far in insisting that the regulation always derive from Congress.

Difficulties with the breadth of the "exclusive power" argument led the Court to develop a number of doctrines designed to limit it.

a. *Purpose.* In *Gibbons,* Justice Johnson coupled his "exclusive power" argument with the contention that Congress was granted the power to regulate interstate commerce only to achieve commercial ends. It followed that the states lacked power only insofar as they sought to achieve similar ends, such as the protection of local enterprises from out-of-state competition, but not insofar as they exercised their general "police" powers, those designed to promote the health and safety of their citizens. This limitation requires the Court to distinguish between statutes designed to serve commercial goals and those designed to serve police power ones; determining the legislature's purpose in light of the impact of its actions may be quite difficult.

b. *Direct/indirect.* DiSanto v. Pennsylvania, 273 U.S. 34 (1927), invalidated a licensing statute for those wishing to sell tickets for transportation to or from foreign countries. The state argued that the statute was designed to prevent exploitation of recent immigrants who wished to purchase tickets for relatives still in Europe; before the licensing scheme was adopted, some ticket agents had required the immigrants to make payments into an account with the agents, who would not purchase the tickets until full payment had been made. The majority, noting that

"Congress has complete and paramount authority to regulate foreign commerce and [to] protect the public against [frauds,]" stated that a "statute which by its necessary operation directly interferes with or burdens foreign commerce is a prohibited regulation and invalid, regardless of the purpose with which it was passed. Such legislation cannot be sustained as an exertion of the police power of the State to prevent possible fraud." Justice Stone's dissent called the "direct/indirect" test "too mechanical, too uncertain in its application, and too remote from actualities to be of value." For a modern application of the directness test, see Brown-Forman Distillers Corp. v. New York State Liquor Authority, 476 U.S. 573 (1986).

c. *Inherently local/national.* Cooley v. Board of Port Wardens, 53 U.S. (12 How.) 299 (1852), involved a Pennsylvania law, adopted in 1803, requiring all ships entering or leaving the port of Philadelphia to use a local pilot or pay a fine into a fund to support retired pilots and their dependents. The Court agreed that the regulation of pilots was a regulation of interstate commerce, even though pilots stayed with the ships for only brief periods. It upheld the statute:

> [The] power to regulate commerce, embraces a vast field, containing not only many, but exceedingly various subjects, quite unlike in their nature; some imperatively demanding a single uniform rule, operating equally on the commerce of the United States in every port; and some, like the subject now in question, as imperatively demanding that diversity, which alone can meet the local necessities of navigation.
>
> Either absolutely to affirm, or to deny that the nature of this power requires exclusive legislation by Congress, is to lose sight of the nature of the subjects of this power, and to assert concerning all of them, what is really applicable but to a part. Whatever subjects of this power are in their nature national, or admit only of one uniform system [may] justly be said to be of such a nature as to require exclusive legislation by Congress. That this cannot be affirmed of laws for the regulation of [pilotage] is clear.

As you study the modern cases, note the extent to which intuitions or express judgments about (a) the "national versus local" nature of the problem, (b) the "commercial versus police powers" purposes of the regulation, and (c) the directness of the effect on interstate commerce appear to influence outcomes and doctrinal formulations. Eventually the Court abandoned the classical framework, although it retains some vestigial force.

Note: The Modern View

1. *General theories.* The modern law of the commerce clause, in its negative or dormant aspect considered in this section, rests on at least three theories, which sometimes conflict in particular cases.

a. *A purely political theory.* Some state statutes are incompatible with the ideal of a unified nation. In particular, "protectionist" statutes — those that aim at (or achieve?) the promotion of in-state interests at the expense of out-of-state interests — demonstrate that the enacting state does not take seriously the proposition that all the states are partners in a single national enterprise. If the statute says expressly that local interests will be treated differently from out-of-state interests, it signals clearly the state's indifference to its national obligations. What if the statute does not draw such an express line, but the inference of indifference is strong in light of the differential impact of the statute on in-state and out-of-state interests?

b. A *purely economic theory.* Protectionist legislation, as well as some other laws, interferes with the efficient disposition of resources throughout the country. By excluding some commerce from a state, these statutes may lead to a lower level of economic performance than would be possible in the absence of the statutes.

c. A *mixed political and economic theory.* Protectionist legislation, and some other laws, result from the operation of a political process that can be understood as "distorted" in ways that lead to the enactment of economically inefficient statutes. In particular, consider this observation by Justice Stone in South Carolina State Highway Department v. Barnwell Brothers, 303 U.S. 177 (1938):

> State regulations affecting interstate commerce, whose purpose or effect is to gain for those within the state an advantage at the expense of those without, or to burden those out of the state without any corresponding advantage to those within, have been thought to impinge upon the constitutional prohibition even though Congress has not acted.
>
> Underlying the stated rule has been the thought, often expressed in judicial opinion, that when the regulation is of such a character that its burden falls principally upon those without the state, legislative action is not likely to be subjected to those political restraints which are normally exerted on legislation where it affects adversely some interests within the state. See [*Cooley*].

Under modern conditions, where interest groups often exercise political power through campaign contributions or advertising, how cogent is the distinction between "in-state" and "out-of-state" political interests? In what sense is a corporation with shareholders throughout the nation and the world a "local" interest in the state in which it operates or is incorporated?

d. *Consider the possibility of a fourth approach,* **formalism.** One could apply the preceding approaches directly and ask whether a statute is protectionist or results from a distorted political process. A formalist may argue against directly applying the approaches, and might conclude that statutes using geographical terms should be viewed with great suspicion, not because every such statute is protectionist or expresses a state's willingness to separate itself from the rest of the nation, but because *most* such statutes do so. Legislatures directed never to use geographical terms will adopt fewer protectionist or otherwise troublesome statutes than legislatures whose actions are tested against some more complicated standards.

2. *The relevance of preemption and consent.* In Exxon Corp. v. Governor of Maryland, 437 U.S. 117 (1978), discussed more fully in section D3 infra, the Court rejected a commerce clause challenge to a statute prohibiting gasoline producers and refiners from operating retail gas stations in the state. Suppose the major gasoline producers such as Exxon continue to object to the burdens the statute places on them. The major producers might seek congressional action to preempt Maryland's law. Once Congress acts, its statutes prevail over conflicting state laws by reason of the supremacy clause.

Suppose the Court had held that the Maryland statute violated the commerce clause. Could the local retailers who supported the statute have it reinstated by persuading Congress to act on their behalf?

a. *Early formulations of congressional power to consent or preempt.* In 1827, the Supreme Court held that states could not exercise their power to tax items of interstate commerce so long as the items remained in their original packages. Brown v. Maryland, 25 U.S. (12 Wheat.) 419 (1827), limited in Michelin Tire Corp. v. Wages, 423 U.S. 276 (1976). In 1873, Iowa passed a statute prohibiting the sale of beer. In Leisy v. Hardin, 135 U.S. 100 (1890), the Leisys brewed beer in Illinois and shipped it to Iowa, where they sought to sell it in the original kegs. When Hardin, the town marshal, seized the kegs, the Leisys sued for their return. They argued that, although Iowa had the power to regulate liquor consumption, the original package doctrine barred it from regulating the sale of beer in its original kegs. A divided Supreme Court agreed.

Supporters of prohibition accepted the Court's suggestion that they seek congressional permission for state prohibition laws. In August 1890, a few months after *Leisy*, Congress enacted the Wilson Act, which stated that liquor imported into a state "shall upon arrival [be] subject to" local laws as if it had been locally produced, "and shall not be exempt therefrom by reason of being [in] original packages." In re Rahrer, 140 U.S. 545 (1891), held that the Wilson Act was a constitutional exercise of Congress's exclusive power to regulate interstate commerce and that Rahrer's conviction for selling liquor in its original package contrary to Kansas law did not violate the Constitution. According to the Court,

> Congress could [in] the exercise of the discretion reposed in it, concluding that the common interests did not require entire freedom in the traffic in ardent spirits enact the law in question. In so doing Congress [has] taken its own course and made its own regulation, applying to these subjects of interstate commerce one common rule, whose uniformity is not affected by variations in state laws in dealing with such property.

b. *Congressional silence and inertia.* Taken together, the doctrines of preemption and consent mean that a judicial decision on a commerce clause challenge need not be final. If the challenge is rejected, those who oppose state regulation may secure federal legislation preempting it. If the challenge is sustained, those who support state regulation may secure federal legislation permitting it. Under these circumstances, why should the courts intervene rather than letting the burdens of regulation lie where they fall and allowing the political process to adjust the balance between burdens and benefits?

Concurring in Duckworth v. Arkansas, 314 U.S. 390 (1941), Justice Jackson said:

> [These] restraints are individually too petty, too diversified, and too local to get the attention of a Congress hard pressed with more urgent matters. [The] sluggishness of government, the multitude of matters that clamor for attention, and the relative ease with which men are persuaded to postpone troublesome decisions, all make inertia one of the most decisive powers in determining the course of our affairs and frequently gives [sic] to the established order of things a longevity and vitality much beyond its merits.

Thus, he concluded, the courts should intervene because of congressional inertia. If the restraints are indeed petty, in what sense could they unduly burden interstate commerce? Should the assumption be instead that restraints serious enough to violate the Constitution ought to be of such economic significance as to attract congressional attention? How can we distinguish congressional inaction due to inertia from inaction due to a considered judgment that on balance the state regulation does not unduly burden interstate commerce? Why should inaction with respect to statutes that *regulate* be treated differently from inaction that takes the form of *failing* to regulate? Note Powell, The Still Small Voice of the Commerce Clause, in 3 Selected Essays on Constitutional Law 932 (1938):

> If congress keeps silent about the interstate commerce that is not national in character, [then] congress is silently silent, and the states may regulate. But if congress keeps silent about the kind of commerce that is national in character, [then] congress is silently vocal and says that the commerce must be free from state regulation.

For discussions of congressional silence, see Bikle, The Silence of Congress, 41 Harv. L. Rev. 200 (1927); Tribe, Toward a Syntax of the Unsaid: Construing the Sounds of Congressional and Constitutional Silence, 57 Ind. L.J. 515 (1982).

Note that securing congressional action is costly. If the costs of mobilizing Congress to act exceed the burdens a regulation places on interstate commerce, Congress's failure to act may reflect a rational calculation of the costs and benefits of political action. Judicial intervention might be justified if it is less expensive than the burdens on interstate commerce and the cost of mobilizing Congress.

c. *Allocating the burden of inertia.* Under the modern view, the fundamental issue in this area is who should bear the burden of overcoming congressional inertia. Note that Justice Jackson's justification for judicial intervention concludes with a reference to the "merits" of the status quo. What are the criteria for determining the "merits" in this setting?

(1) *Substantive preference for free trade.* H. P. Hood & Sons v. DuMond, 336 U.S. 525 (1949) (Jackson, J.):

> While the Constitution vests in Congress the power to regulate commerce among the states, it does not say what the states may or may not do in the absence of congressional action. [This] Court has advanced the solidarity and prosperity of this Nation by the meaning it has given to these great silences of the Constitution. . . .
>
> [The] principle that our economic unit is the Nation, which alone has the gamut of powers necessary to control the economy, including the vital power of erecting customs barriers against foreign competition, has as its corollary that the states are not separable economic units. . . .

Justice Jackson's description of the political and economic benefits of free trade reflects the preconstitutional history of interstate commercial rivalries and the modern economic theory of free trade.

(2) *Minimizing costs.* Obtaining congressional preemption or consent requires interest groups to invest time and effort in the political process. If the burden of overcoming inertia is placed on the group *less* likely to succeed in that effort, it may be discouraged from the investment. If that occurs, the courts will have arrived at the outcome that Congress would have, and at a lower cost. How accurately can the courts determine who is less likely to succeed? What if the loser in the courts is not discouraged?

Consider the extent to which the distinction in *Cooley* between national and local subject matters and that in *Gibbons* between commercial and police power regulations assist in determining who should bear the burden of overcoming congressional inertia.

3. *A preliminary overview.* It may help in understanding the material that follows to have a summary of the Court's overall doctrine in mind. Lawrence, Toward a More Coherent Dormant Commerce Clause: A Proposed Unitary Framework, 21 Harv. J.L. & Pub. Poly. 395, 416–417 (1998), proposes the following analysis: If the statute is facially discriminatory, it is "virtually *per se* invalid. The State has the heavy burden of proving that the measure is virtually certain to achieve its legitimate purpose and that the purpose cannot be served as well by available *less* discriminatory means." Statutes with discriminatory purposes are analyzed similarly; challengers must establish the impermissible purpose. If the statutes are applied even-handedly to both in-state and out-of-state commerce, they are constitutional unless the challenger shows that the statute's burden on interstate commerce "is clearly excessive in relation to state benefits." Lawrence concludes the analysis of categories with the following:

> Where a measure imposes a burden *mostly*, although not exclusively, on out-of-state interests, the State has the burden of justifying that the measure is likely to achieve its legitimate purpose; the challenger then has the burden of either rebutting the State's justification or of showing that the purpose can be served as well by available nondiscriminatory [alternatives]. Where the measure imposes a burden *exclusively* on out-of-state interests, the State has the burden of proving that the measure is *highly* likely to achieve its legitimate purpose *and* that the purpose cannot be served as well by available nondiscriminatory alternatives.

2. Protection against Discrimination

Note: General Considerations

1. *Cost-benefit analysis.* The costs of economic regulation are not always paid by those who receive its benefits. The distribution of costs and benefits across different groups means that the mere adoption of a regulation need not establish that its benefits to the entire society exceed its costs. Further, the distribution of costs and benefits across different groups affects the political forces supporting and opposing adoption or repeal of regulations. Under what conditions might regulations be adopted when their total social costs exceed their total social benefits?

If benefits will be conferred on a relatively small group, each member can agree to finance lobbying efforts to secure the legislation (on the condition that every other member also contribute). (Why is the condition important?) Each will expect to recover his or her investment in political activity from the benefits to be gained by the legislation. If the regulation also imposes costs on a broad group, those who bear the costs will find it difficult to organize in opposition. The costs imposed on each member of the group are likely to be smaller than the amount each would have to invest in an effective lobbying effort. Further, there is a free-rider problem: Each member of the group may hang back, expecting that others will engage in lobbying that, if successful, would benefit the free rider at no cost to him- or herself. This theory is developed in detail in M. Olson, The Logic of Collective Action (1965). Consider the extent to which a theory like Olson's may underlie the discrimination cases that follow and the "undue burden" cases in section D3 infra.

2. *"Exporting" costs.* Regulations may be adopted when the beneficiaries within the jurisdiction adopting it outweigh in political power those within the jurisdiction who will bear (some of) its costs. They may do so because of numbers or because of the organizational factors discussed by Olson. Total social costs may still exceed total social benefits, but if the local beneficiaries can export enough costs so that the local benefits exceed the local costs, the regulation may be adopted. Is this the "thought" Stone described in *Barnwell Brothers?*

Note that in every case some local residents — those who prefer doing business with out-of-staters — will be worse off. In the simplest case, the benefits to local residents exceed the costs to local residents. Even though some local residents (and therefore voters) will bear some costs, the "gross state product" will be greater after the regulation is adopted than before. The local beneficiaries may then use some of their new profits to subsidize the local cost-bearers, reducing the political opposition to the adoption of the regulation. Consider in this connection Dean Milk Co. v. Madison, infra. Under what circumstances can a state export the costs of regulation? This is the subject of a branch of economics called incidence analysis. Should the courts rely on what economists have to say on this question?

City of Philadelphia v. New Jersey
437 U.S. 617 (1978)

MR. JUSTICE STEWART delivered the opinion of the Court.

A New Jersey law prohibits the importation of most "solid or liquid waste which originated or was collected outside the territorial limits of the State." In this case we are required to decide whether this statutory prohibition violates the Commerce Clause of the United States Constitution. . . .

[Private landfill operators challenged the statute on preemption and constitutional grounds. The state supreme court found that the statute "advanced vital health and environmental objectives with no economic discrimination against, and with little burden upon, interstate commerce." It also found no preemption.]

We agree with the New Jersey court that the state law has not been preempted by federal legislation.[4] The dispositive question, therefore, is whether the law is constitutionally permissible in light of the Commerce Clause of the Constitution.

II . . .

[All] objects of interstate trade merit Commerce Clause protection; none is excluded by definition at the outset. Hence, we reject the state court's suggestion

---

4. [From] our review of this federal legislation, we find no "clear and manifest purpose of Congress," Rice v. Santa Fe Elevator Corp., 331 U.S. 218, 230, to preempt the entire field of interstate waste management or transportation, either by express statutory command, or by implicit legislative design. To the contrary, Congress expressly has provided that "the collection and disposal of solid wastes should continue to be primarily the function of State, regional, and local agencies. . . ." 42 U.S.C. §6901(a)(4) (1976 ed.). Similarly, [the statute] is not preempted because of a square conflict with particular provisions of federal law or because of general incompatibility with basic federal objectives. . . .

that the banning of "valueless" out-of-state wastes by [the statute] implicates no constitutional protection. Just as Congress has power to regulate the interstate movement of these wastes, States are not free from constitutional scrutiny when they restrict that movement.

III . . .

The opinions of the Court through the years have reflected an alertness to the evils of "economic isolation" and protectionism, while at the same time recognizing that incidental burdens on interstate commerce may be unavoidable when a State legislates to safeguard the health and safety of its people. Thus, where simple economic protectionism is effected by state legislation, a virtually per se rule of invalidity has been erected. See, e.g., [H. P. Hood & Sons]. The clearest example of such legislation is a law that overtly blocks the flow of interstate commerce at a State's borders. But where other legislative objectives are credibly advanced and there is no patent discrimination against interstate trade, the Court has adopted a much more flexible approach, the general contours of which were outlined in Pike v. Bruce Church, Inc., 397 U.S. 137, 142:

> Where the statute regulates evenhandedly to effectuate a legitimate local public interest, and its effects on interstate commerce are only incidental, it will be upheld unless the burden imposed on such commerce is clearly excessive in relation to the putative local benefits. . . . If a legitimate local purpose is found, then the question becomes one of degree. And the extent of the burden that will be tolerated will of course depend on the nature of the local interest involved, and on whether it could be promoted as well with a lesser impact on interstate activities.

The crucial inquiry, therefore, must be directed to determining whether [the statute] is basically a protectionist measure, or whether it can fairly be viewed as a law directed to legitimate local concerns, with effects upon interstate commerce that are only incidental.

B . . .

[The] evil of protectionism can reside in legislative means as well as legislative ends. Thus, it does not matter whether the ultimate aim of [the statute] is to reduce the waste disposal costs of New Jersey residents or to save remaining open lands from pollution, for we assume New Jersey has every right to protect its residents' pocketbooks as well as their environment. And it may be assumed as well that New Jersey may pursue those ends by slowing the flow of all waste into the State's remaining landfills, even though interstate commerce may incidentally be affected. But whatever New Jersey's ultimate purpose, it may not be accomplished by discriminating against articles of commerce from outside the State unless there is some reason, apart from their origin, to treat them differently. Both on its face and in its plain effect, [the statute] violates this principle of nondiscrimination. . . .

The New Jersey law at issue in this case falls squarely within the area that the Commerce Clause puts off limits to state regulation. On its face, it imposes on out-of-state commercial interests the full burden of conserving the state's remaining landfill space. [What] is crucial is the attempt by one State to isolate itself from a problem common to many by erecting a barrier against the movement of interstate trade. . . .

Today, cities in Pennsylvania and New York find it expedient or necessary to send their waste into New Jersey for disposal, and New Jersey claims the right to close its borders to such traffic. Tomorrow, cities in New Jersey may find it expedient or necessary to send their waste into Pennsylvania or New York for disposal, and those States might then claim the right to close their borders. The Commerce Clause will protect New Jersey in the future, just as it protects her neighbors now, from efforts by one State to isolate itself in the stream of interstate commerce from a problem shared by all. The judgment is reversed.

[A dissenting opinion by Mr. Justice Rehnquist, with whom [Chief Justice Burger] joined, is omitted.]

Note: Facial/Intentional Discrimination

1. *Winners and losers.* Who gains the benefits and who bears the costs of New Jersey's statute? There are four groups to consider: out-of-state waste producers, out-of-state landfill operators, in-state waste producers, and in-state landfill operators. (Into which category do in-state environmentalists fall?) (a) *Costs:* The statute reduces the supply of landfill available to out-of-state waste producers and may therefore increase the price they must pay for disposal. It reduces the demand for New Jersey landfills and may therefore decrease the profits of in-state landfill operators. (b) *Benefits:* The statute benefits in-state waste producers by reducing demand and decreasing prices and by improving their environment; it benefits out-of-state landfill operators by increasing demand and raising profits. Out-of-state waste producers might benefit from increased costs that encourage each of them to reduce the amount of waste each produces, which might benefit them in the aggregate. Note that from the point of view of cost exporting, New Jersey does not care whether the benefits to out-of-state landfill operators exceed the costs to out-of-state waste producers. Its sole concern is that the decreased prices paid by New Jersey waste producers exceed the profits New Jersey operators lose by being unable to accept out-of-state waste. Is it likely that the local benefits exceed the local costs? (What is the relevance, if any, of the fact that New Jersey landfill operators are among the plaintiffs in the case?)

Consider the proposition that this Note's focus on a detailed analysis of economic effects is misguided because the Court (a) properly uses facial discrimination as a rough indication that out-of-state burdens exceed local benefits and (b) refrains from looking at economic effects in more detail because it lacks the expertise to do so (in contrast to Congress, which may displace the Court's judgment if it chooses). If the courts cannot do a full cost-benefit analysis, should they refrain from invalidating state laws on commerce clause grounds? Consider also the proposition that the focus on economic effects and their relation to interest-group politics is misguided because interest-group politics are irrelevant to a proper interpretation of the Constitution.

2. *Issues of distribution.* The welfare of the Northeast might be increased by making New Jersey a little less polluted and Pennsylvania a little more. Pennsylvania's failure to regulate waste production can be considered *its* attempt to export costs to New Jersey. Should the Court take such issues into consideration?

3. *Intent.* Is it fair to say that the Court infers from a statute's use of distinctions between in-state and out-of-state economic actors an intent to benefit local

interests and harm out-of-state ones? Does the use of a local/out-of-state distinction justify a presumption of intent to export costs?

4. *The relevance of retaliation.* City of Philadelphia v. New Jersey concludes by invoking fears of retaliatory responses by other states. Why should that be a matter of concern? Retaliation would increase the costs borne by local residents, thus eliminating the export of costs and reducing the incentive to adopt the regulation. Note, however, that retaliation may not be completely effective, so that it inflicts some pure economic losses on the states involved with neither an economic nor a distributive justification, and that retaliation, at least until the trade barriers are lowered, is likely to alter the patterns of investment as resources shift to take account of the costs imposed by retaliatory regulations in one sector of the economy but not in another.

Consider Sporhase v. Nebraska, 458 U.S. 941 (1982): A Nebraska statute prohibited the withdrawal of groundwater from any well within Nebraska intended for use in another state that fails to grant reciprocal rights to withdraw and transport groundwater to Nebraska. Colorado does not grant reciprocal rights. Owners of contiguous land on the Nebraska/Colorado border claimed that the statute unconstitutionally barred them from transferring groundwater from a Nebraska well to the Colorado land. The Supreme Court agreed. It found the reciprocity requirement not "narrowly tailored" to serve conservation goals. Citing A&P Tea Co. v. Cottrell, 424 U.S. 366 (1976), it noted that the reciprocity requirement could not be justified "as a response to another State's unreasonable burden on commerce." Why not?

Cottrell defended its position that retaliation was not permitted, even if it was intended to provide an incentive to eliminate trade barriers, on the ground that the state's proper remedy for trade barriers was a challenge in court, not retaliation. (Suppose a state desires to "retaliate" against another state's *failure* to regulate.) Retaliation is common in the international sphere. It is dealt with by the negotiation of bilateral and multilateral trade agreements. Have the states already negotiated such an agreement, calling it the commerce clause rather than a trade treaty?

5. *Permissible discrimination.* In Maine v. Taylor, 477 U.S. 131 (1986), the Court upheld the constitutionality of a Maine statute that prohibited the importation of live baitfish. Writing for eight justices, Justice Blackmun noted that the statute affirmatively discriminated against interstate transactions and therefore could be upheld only if it survived "the strictest scrutiny." The burden was on the state to show that the statute served a legitimate local purpose, and that the purpose could not be served as well by an available nondiscriminatory means. In this case, however, the Court held that, in light of the trial court's findings of fact, both branches of this test had been satisfied. Evidence before the trial court indicated that Maine's population of wild fish might be placed at risk by parasites prevalent in out-of-state baitfish but not common in wild fish in Maine. Moreover, nonnative species inadvertently included in shipments of live baitfish could disturb Maine's aquatic ecology to an unpredictable extent by competing with, or preying on, native species. Finally, there was no satisfactory way to inspect imported baitfish for parasites and commingled species.

The Supreme Court held that these findings were sufficient to sustain the statute. Although importation of the baitfish might not adversely affect the environment, "Maine has a legitimate interest in guarding against imperfectly understood environmental risks, despite the possibility that they may ultimately prove to be negligible." Moreover, the mere "abstract possibility" of developing an acceptable testing procedure did not constitute an available nondiscriminatory alternative. Nor was there convincing evidence that the statute was the product of a protectionist intent. The state's justification was not undermined "by the fact that other States may not have enacted similar bans" because "Maine's fisheries are unique and unusually fragile." Nor was it relevant "that fish can swim directly into Maine from New Hampshire" because "impediments to complete success [cannot] be [grounds] for preventing a state from using its best efforts to limit [an environmental] risk."

C & A Carbone, Inc. v. Clarkstown

511 U.S. 383 (1994)

JUSTICE KENNEDY delivered the opinion of the Court. . . .

[Clarkstown, New York, subsidized a private "waste transfer station" to collect solid waste, separate recyclable from nonrecyclable items, and dispose of the waste, by guaranteeing a minimum flow of waste to the station, which would then collect a fee that exceeded the disposal cost of unsorted solid waste in the private market. To assure the guaranteed flow, Clarkstown enacted a "flow control ordinance," requiring that all solid waste within the town be deposited at the station. Carbone was a private recycler with a sorting facility in Clarkstown. It collected waste from elsewhere in New York and New Jersey, carried it to its facility, and sorted it into recyclable and nonrecyclable items. The flow control ordinance required Carbone to take the nonrecyclable material to the transfer station and pay the fee. Without the ordinance, Carbone would have shipped the nonrecyclable materials to out-of-state destinations at a lower cost than the fee the transfer station charged. The Supreme Court upheld Carbone's challenge to the constitutionality of the flow control ordinance.]

While the immediate effect of the ordinance is to direct local transport of solid waste to a designated site within the local jurisdiction, its economic effects are interstate in reach. The Carbone facility in Clarkstown receives and processes waste from places other than Clarkstown, including from out of State. By requiring Carbone to send the nonrecyclable portion of this waste to the [transfer] station at an additional cost, the flow control ordinance drives up the cost for out-of-state interests to dispose of their solid waste. Furthermore, even as to waste originant in Clarkstown, the ordinance prevents everyone except the favored local operator from performing the initial processing step. The ordinance thus deprives out-of-state businesses of access to a local market. These economic effects are more than enough to bring the Clarkstown ordinance within the purview of the Commerce Clause. . . .

Clarkstown protests that its ordinance does not discriminate because it does not differentiate solid waste on the basis of its geographic origin. All solid waste, regardless of origin, must be processed at the designated transfer station before it leaves the town. Unlike the statute in *Philadelphia*, says the town, the ordinance erects no barrier to the import or export of any solid waste but requires only that the waste be channeled through the designated facility. [As] the town itself points out, what makes garbage a profitable business is not its own worth but the fact that its possessor must pay to get rid of it. In other words, the article of commerce is not so much the solid waste itself, but rather the service of processing and disposing of it.

With respect to this stream of commerce, the flow control ordinance discriminates, for it allows only the favored operator to process waste that is within the limits of the town. The ordinance is no less discriminatory because in-state or in-town processors are also covered by the prohibition. In Dean Milk Co. v. Madison, 340 U.S. 349 (1951), we struck down a city ordinance that required all milk sold in the city to be pasteurized within five miles of the city lines. We found it "immaterial that Wisconsin milk from outside the Madison area is subjected to the same proscription as that moving in interstate commerce." Id., at 354, n.4.

In this light, the flow control ordinance is just one more instance of local processing requirements that we long have held invalid. The essential vice in laws of this sort is that they bar the import of the processing service. . . .

Discrimination against interstate commerce in favor of local business or investment is per se invalid, save in a narrow class of cases in which the municipality can demonstrate, under rigorous scrutiny, that it has no other means to advance a legitimate local interest. A number of amici [suggest] that as landfill space diminishes and environmental cleanup costs escalate, measures like flow control become necessary to ensure the safe handling and proper treatment of solid waste.

The teaching of our cases is that these arguments must be rejected absent the clearest showing that the unobstructed flow of interstate commerce itself is unable to solve the local problem. . . .

The flow control ordinance does serve a central purpose that a nonprotectionist regulation would not: It ensures that the town-sponsored facility will be profitable, so that the local contractor can build it and Clarkstown can buy it back at nominal cost in five years. In other words, [the] flow control ordinance is a financing measure. By itself, of course, revenue generation is not a local interest that can justify discrimination against interstate commerce. Otherwise States could impose discriminatory taxes against solid waste originating outside the State.

Clarkstown maintains that special financing is necessary to ensure the long-term survival of the designated facility. If so, the town may subsidize the facility through general taxes or municipal bonds. New Energy Co. of Indiana v. Limbach, 486 U.S. 269, 278 (1988). But having elected to use the open market to earn revenues for its project, the town may not employ discriminatory regulation to give that project an advantage over rival businesses from out of State. . . .

State and local governments may not use their regulatory power to favor local enterprise by prohibiting patronage of out-of-state competitors or their facilities. We reverse the judgment and remand the case for proceedings not inconsistent with this decision.

Justice O'Connor, concurring in the judgment.

Local Law 9 [lacks] an important feature common to the regulations at issue in [prior] cases — namely, discrimination on the basis of geographic origin. [In] Dean Milk, [the] city of Madison drew a line around its perimeter and required that all milk sold in the City be pasteurized only by dairies located inside the line. This type of geographic distinction, which confers an economic advantage on local interests in general, is common to all the local processing cases cited by the majority. And the Court has, I believe, correctly concluded that these arrangements are protectionist either in purpose or practical effect, and thus amount to virtually per se discrimination.

[The] garbage sorting monopoly is achieved at the expense of all competitors, be they local or nonlocal. That the ordinance does not discriminate on the basis of geographic origin is vividly illustrated by the identity of the plaintiff in this very action: petitioner is a local recycler, physically located in Clarkstown, that desires to process waste itself, and thus bypass the town's designated transfer facility. Because in-town processors — like petitioner — and out-of-town processors are treated equally, I cannot agree that Local Law 9 "discriminates" against interstate commerce. Rather, Local Law 9 "discriminates" evenhandedly against all potential participants in the waste processing business, while benefiting only the chosen operator of the transfer facility.

I believe this distinction has more doctrinal significance than the majority acknowledges. [The] existence of substantial in-state interests harmed by a regulation is "a powerful safeguard" against legislative discrimination. The Court generally defers to health and safety regulations because "their burden usually falls on local economic interests as well as other States' economic interests, thus insuring that a State's own political processes will serve as a check against unduly burdensome regulations." Raymond Motor Transportation, Inc. v. Rice, 434 U.S. 429, 444, n.18 (1978). Thus, while there is no bright line separating those enactments which are virtually per se invalid and those which are not, the fact that in-town competitors of the transfer facility are equally burdened by Local Law 9 leads me to conclude that Local Law 9 does not discriminate against interstate commerce.

[Justice O'Connor concluded that the ordinance imposed "an excessive burden on interstate trade when considered in relation to the local benefits conferred." See section D3 infra.]

JUSTICE SOUTER, with whom [CHIEF JUSTICE REHNQUIST] and JUSTICE BLACKMUN join, dissenting.

[The] exclusion worked by Clarkstown's Local Law 9 bestows no benefit on a class of local private actors, but instead directly aids the government in satisfying a traditional governmental responsibility. The law does not differentiate between all local and all out-of-town providers of a service, but instead between the one entity responsible for ensuring that the job gets done and all other enterprises, regardless of their location. The ordinance thus falls outside that class of tariff or protectionist measures that the Commerce Clause has traditionally been thought to bar States from enacting against each other. . . .

II . . .

The outstanding feature of the statutes [in] the local processing cases is their distinction between two classes of private economic actors according to location, favoring [milk] pasteurizers within five miles of the center of Madison, and so on. Since nothing in these local processing laws prevented a proliferation of local businesses within the State or town, the out-of-town processors were not excluded as part and parcel of a general exclusion of private firms from the market, but as a result of discrimination among such firms according to geography alone. It was because of that discrimination in favor of local businesses, preferred at the expense of their out-of-town or out-of-state competitors, that the Court struck down those local processing laws as classic examples of [economic] protectionism. . . .

[Local] Law 9's exclusion of outside capital is part of a broader exclusion of private capital, not a discrimination against out-of-state investors as such. Thus, while these differences may underscore the ordinance's anticompetitive effect, they substantially mitigate any protectionist effect, for subjecting out-of-town investors and facilities to the same constraints as local ones is not economic protectionism. . . .

III

[The] monopolistic character of Local Law 9's effects is not itself suspicious for purposes of the Commerce Clause. [The] dormant Commerce Clause does not "protect the particular structure or methods of operation in any . . . market." Exxon Corp. v. Governor of Md., 437 U.S. 117, 127 (1978). The only right to compete that it protects is the right to compete on terms independent of one's location.

While the monopolistic nature of the burden may be disregarded, any geographically discriminatory elements must be assessed with care. We have already observed that there is no geographically based selection among private firms, and it is clear from the face of the ordinance that nothing hinges on the source of trash that enters Clarkstown or upon the destination of the processed waste that leaves the transfer station. There is, to be sure, an incidental local economic benefit, for the need to process Clarkstown's trash in Clarkstown will create local jobs. But this local boon is mitigated by another feature of the ordinance, in that it finances whatever benefits it confers on the town from the pockets of the very citizens who passed it into law. On the reasonable assumption that no one can avoid producing some trash, every resident of Clarkstown must bear a portion of the burden Local Law 9 imposes to support the municipal monopoly, an uncharacteristic feature of statutes claimed to violate the Commerce Clause. . . .

This skepticism that protectionism is afoot here is confirmed again when we examine the governmental interests apparently served by the local law. [The] State and its municipalities need prompt, sanitary trash processing, which is imperative whether or not the private market sees fit to serve this need at an affordable price and to continue doing so dependably into the future. The state and local governments also have a substantial interest in the flow-control feature to minimize the risk of financing this service, for [a] "put or pay" contract of the type Clarkstown signed will be a significant inducement to accept municipal responsibility to guarantee efficiency and sanitation in trash processing. Waste disposal with minimal environmental damage requires serious capital investment, and there are limits on any municipality's ability to incur debt or to finance facilities out of tax revenues.

Moreover, flow control offers an additional benefit that could not be gained by financing through a subsidy derived from general tax revenues, in spreading the cost of the facility among all Clarkstown residents who generate trash. [It] is far from clear that the alternative to flow control (i.e., subsidies from general tax revenues or municipal bonds) would be less disruptive of interstate commerce than flow control, since a subsidized competitor can effectively squelch competition by underbidding it. . . .

Note: Geographic Discrimination

1. *Facial discrimination?* In what sense do *Carbone* and *Dean Milk* involve facial discrimination against out-of-state interests, given that in-state interests of the same type are equally adversely affected? Consider this definition: Facial discrimination occurs when a statute regulating transactions between private parties uses some geographical terminology whose effect is to confer some advantage on at least one in-state enterprise and to impose some burden on at least one out-of-state enterprise. On what theory of the dormant commerce clause should the (mere) use of geographic terminology matter so much?

2. *The Scope of* Carbone. United Haulers Association v. Oneida-Herkimer Solid Waste Management Authority, 550 U.S. 330 (2007), involved "flow control" ordinances like that in *Carbone*, but in *United Haulers* the facility to which solid waste was required to be sent was owned by a public agency. This was sufficient to distinguish the case from *Carbone*.

> Unlike private enterprise, government is vested with the responsibility of protecting the health, safety, and welfare of its citizens. These important responsibilities set state and local government apart from a typical private business.
>   Given these differences, it does not make sense to regard laws favoring local government and laws favoring private industry with equal skepticism. [Laws] favoring local government [may] be directed toward any number of legitimate goals unrelated to protectionism.
>   [The] contrary approach [would] lead to unprecedented and unbounded interference by the courts with state and local government. The dormant Commerce Clause is not a roving license for federal courts to decide what activities are appropriate for state and local government to undertake, and what activities must be the province of private market competition. [It] is not the province of the Commerce Clause to control the decision of the voters on whether government or the private sector should provide waste management services.

Chief Justice Roberts's opinion observed that "the most palpable harm imposed by the ordinances — more expensive trash removal — is likely to fall upon the very people who voted for the laws. [There] is no reason to [hand] local businesses a victory they could not obtain through the political process." (Writing for a plurality, Chief Justice Roberts also found that the ordinances did not impose an excessive burden that was disproportionate to its benefits. Justice Scalia did not join this portion of the opinion.)

Justice Thomas concurred in the judgment, stating that, although he had joined *Carbone*, he "no longer believe[d] it was correctly decided," because the "negative Commerce Clause has no basis in the Constitution [and] has proved unworkable in practice." Justice Alito, joined by Justices Stevens and Kennedy, dissented, arguing that the case was indistinguishable from *Carbone*.

3. *Reasonable alternatives and the relevance of harms to in-state producers.* Dean Milk Co. v. Madison, 340 U.S. 349 (1951), invalidated an ordinance adopted by the Madison City Council that prohibited the sale of milk in the city unless it had been bottled at an approved plant within five miles of the city. The "avowed purpose," ensuring by inspection of bottling plants that milk was bottled under sanitary conditions, was acceptable. But the "practical effect" was to prevent the sale in Madison of wholesome milk produced in Illinois and in parts of Wisconsin. The Court held that

[in] thus erecting an economic barrier protecting a major local industry against competition from without the State, Madison plainly discriminates against interstate commerce. This it cannot do, even in the exercise of its unquestioned power to protect the health and safety of its people, if reasonable nondiscriminatory alternatives, adequate to serve legitimate local interests, are available.

The Court concluded that two alternatives existed: Madison could send its inspectors to Illinois and charge the reasonable costs of inspection to the importing producers, or it could rely on inspections by federal authorities complying with the regulatory standards in the Madison ordinance, which itself adopted the provisions of a model ordinance recommended by a federal agency. "To permit Madison to adopt a regulation not essential for the protection of local health interests and placing a discriminatory burden on interstate commerce would invite a multiplication of preferential trade areas destructive of the very purpose of the Commerce Clause." Is the doctrinal formulation in *Dean Milk* the same as that in *Carbone*? Do the cases pose the same problem?

4. *The relevance of conflict.* In Bibb v. Navajo Freight Lines, 359 U.S. 520 (1959), Justice Douglas wrote the Court's opinion invalidating an Illinois law requiring that trucks in the state use curved mudguards to prevent spatter and promote safety. Straight mudflaps were legal in forty-five other states; curved mudflaps were illegal in Arkansas and were required in no other state. The trial court found that curved mudflaps have "no" safety advantages over straight ones and introduce "hazards previously unknown to those using the highways" by increasing the heat around the tires and thereby reducing the effectiveness of the trucks' brakes. However, the Court said, "If we had here only a question whether the cost of adjusting an interstate operation to these new local safety regulations [unduly] burdened interstate commerce, we would have to sustain the law. [The] same result would obtain if we had to resolve the much discussed issues of safety." The case was different, though, because of the impossibility of using a single truck whose mudflaps complied with both Illinois and Arkansas law. Further, the Illinois law "seriously [interfered] with" interlining, the practice of having one carrier bring a trailer to a depot and another take it to its destination without unloading and reloading. The case was "one of those cases — few in number — where local safety measures that are nondiscriminatory place an unconstitutional burden on interstate commerce." In what sense do the Arkansas and Illinois regulations conflict other than that complying with both would increase costs enormously by requiring unloading and reloading? Why is it a problem for Illinois, rather than for Arkansas, that a shipper could not use a single trailer that complied with both states' regulations?

Note these observations from Justice O'Connor's opinion in *Carbone*:

[The] practical effect of [Local Law 9] must be evaluated not only by considering the consequences of the statute itself, but also by considering how the challenged statute may interact with the legitimate regulatory regimes of the other States and what effect would arise if not one, but many or every, [jurisdiction] adopted similar legislation. [Wyoming v. Oklahoma.] This is not a hypothetical inquiry. Over 20 states have enacted statutes authorizing local governments to adopt flow control laws. If the localities in these States impose the type of restriction on the movement of waste that Clarkstown has adopted, the free movement of solid waste in the stream of commerce will be severely impaired. Indeed, pervasive flow control would result in the type of balkanization the Clause is primarily intended to prevent. See [*H. P. Hood & Sons*].

Given that many jurisdictions are contemplating or enacting flow control, the potential for conflicts is high. For example, in the State of New Jersey, just south of Clarkstown, local waste may be removed from the State for the sorting of recyclables "as long as the residual solid waste is returned to New Jersey." Under Local Law 9, however, if petitioners bring waste from New Jersey for recycling at their Clarkstown operation, the residual waste may not be returned to New Jersey, but must be transported to Clarkstown's transfer facility. As a consequence, operations like petitioners' cannot comply with the requirements of both jurisdictions. Non-discriminatory state or local laws which actually conflict with the enactments of other States are constitutionally infirm if they burden interstate commerce. The increasing number of flow control regimes virtually ensures some inconsistency between jurisdictions, with the effect of eliminating the movement of waste between jurisdictions.

5. *Are the regulated subjects "the same"?* General Motors Corp. v. Tracy, 519 U.S. 278 (1997), discussed a question the Court said often "remained dormant" in dormant commerce clause cases: whether the subjects treated differently were "substantially similar." The question matters because

> the difference in products may mean that the different entities serve different markets and would continue to do so even if the supposedly discriminatory burden were removed. If in fact that should be the case, eliminating the tax or other regulatory differential would not serve the dormant Commerce Clause's fundamental objective of preserving a national market for competition undisturbed by preferential advantages conferred by a State upon its residents or resident competitors.

The Court then engaged in a detailed analysis of the market for natural gas products. Can an argument be developed in each of the cases in this section that the subjects were not substantially similar because they served different markets?

West Lynn Creamery, Inc. v. Healy

512 U.S. 186 (1994)

JUSTICE STEVENS delivered the opinion of the Court.

[Massachusetts taxed all milk sales in the state. The taxes, collected on sales of milk produced both in the state and outside it, went to a subsidy fund whose proceeds were then distributed to Massachusetts milk producers. An out-of-state producer challenged the combined nondiscriminatory-tax-plus-local-subsidy program. The Court found the program unconstitutional.]

The paradigmatic example of a law discriminating against interstate commerce is the protective tariff or customs duty, which taxes goods imported from other States, but does not tax similar products produced in-state. A tariff is an attractive measure because it simultaneously raises revenue and benefits local producers by burdening their out-of-state competitors. Nevertheless, it violates the principle of the unitary national market by handicapping out-of-state competitors, thus artificially encouraging in-state production even when the same goods could be produced at lower cost in other States. . . .

[Massachusetts'] pricing order is clearly unconstitutional. Its avowed purpose and its undisputed effect are to enable higher cost Massachusetts dairy farmers to compete with lower cost dairy farmers in other States. The "premium payments" are effectively a tax which makes milk produced out of State more expensive. Although the tax also applies to milk produced in Massachusetts, its effect on Massachusetts producers is entirely (indeed more than) offset by the subsidy provided exclusively to Massachusetts dairy farmers. Like an ordinary tariff, the tax is thus effectively imposed only on out-of-state products. The pricing order thus allows Massachusetts dairy farmers who produce at higher cost to sell at or below the price charged by lower cost out-of-state producers. . . .

[Respondent] argues that the payments to Massachusetts dairy farmers from the Dairy Equalization Fund are valid, because subsidies are constitutional exercises of state power, and that the order premium which provides money for the Fund is valid, because it is a nondiscriminatory tax. Therefore the pricing order is constitutional, because it is merely the combination of two independently lawful regulations. In effect, respondent argues, if the State may impose a valid tax on dealers, it is free to use the proceeds of the tax as it chooses; and if it may independently subsidize its farmers, it is free to finance the subsidy by means of any legitimate tax. . . .

[Respondent] errs in assuming that the constitutionality of the pricing order follows logically from the constitutionality of its component parts. By conjoining a tax and a subsidy, Massachusetts has created a program more dangerous to interstate commerce than either part alone. [When] a nondiscriminatory tax is coupled with a subsidy to one of the groups hurt by the tax, a state's political processes can no longer be relied upon to prevent legislative abuse, because one of the in-state interests which would otherwise lobby against the tax has been mollified by the subsidy. So, in this case, one would ordinarily have expected at least three groups to lobby against the order premium, which, as a tax, raises the price (and hence lowers demand) for milk: dairy farmers, milk dealers, and consumers. But because the tax was coupled with a subsidy, one of the most powerful of these groups, Massachusetts dairy farmers, instead of exerting their influence against the tax, were in fact its primary supporters. . . .

[Respondent] ignores the fact that Massachusetts dairy farmers are part of an integrated interstate market. [The] purpose and effect of the pricing order are to divert market share to Massachusetts dairy farmers. This diversion necessarily injures the dairy farmers in neighboring States. [The] obvious impact of the order on out-of-state production demonstrates that it is simply wrong to assume that the pricing order burdens only Massachusetts consumers and dealers.

JUSTICE SCALIA, with whom JUSTICE THOMAS joins, concurring in the judgment. . . .

There are at least four possible devices that would enable a State to produce the economic effect that Massachusetts has produced here: (1) a discriminatory tax upon the industry, imposing a higher liability on out-of-state members than on their in-state competitors; (2) a tax upon the industry that is nondiscriminatory in its assessment, but that has an "exemption" [for] in-state members; (3) a nondiscriminatory tax upon the industry, the revenues from which are placed into a segregated fund, which fund is disbursed as "rebates" [to] in-state members of the industry; [and] (4) [a] subsidy for the in-state members of the industry, funded from the State's general revenues. It is long settled that the first of these methodologies is unconstitutional under the negative Commerce Clause. The second of them, "exemption" from [a] "neutral" tax, is no different in principle from the first, and has likewise been held invalid. The fourth methodology, application of

essentially
a tariff?
new creal?

City says they
don't
observe
thus not
invalid

#3
our
dilemma →

a state subsidy from general revenues, is so far removed from what we have hitherto held to be unconstitutional, that prohibiting it must be regarded as an extension of our negative-Commerce-Clause jurisprudence and therefore, to me, unacceptable. . . .

The issue before us in the present case is whether the third of these methodologies must fall. Although the question is close, I conclude it would not be a principled point at which to disembark from the negative-Commerce-Clause train. The only difference between methodology (2) [and] methodology (3) [is] that the money is taken and returned rather than simply left with the favored in state taxpayer in the first place. The difference between (3) and (4), on the other hand, is the difference between assisting in-state industry through discriminatory taxation, and assisting in-state industry by other means.

I would therefore allow a State to subsidize its domestic industry so long as it does so from nondiscriminatory taxes that go into the State's general revenue fund. Perhaps [that] line comports with an important economic reality: a State is less likely to maintain a subsidy when its citizens perceive that the money (in the general fund) is available for any number of competing, non-protectionist, purposes. That is not, however, the basis for my position. [I] draw the line where I do because it is a clear, rational line at the limits of our extant negative-Commerce-Clause jurisprudence.

CHIEF JUSTICE REHNQUIST, with whom JUSTICE BLACKMUN joins, dissenting. . . .

[There] are still at least two strong interest groups opposed to the milk order — consumers and milk dealers. More importantly, nothing in the dormant Commerce Clause suggests that the fate of state regulation should turn upon the particular lawful manner in which the state subsidy is enacted or promulgated. Analysis of interest group participation in the political process may serve many useful purposes, but serving as a basis for interpreting the dormant Commerce Clause is not one of them. . . .

Note: The Alternative of Subsidies

1. *Tax incentives as subsidies.* Camps Newfound/Owatonna, Inc. v. Town of Harrison, 520 U.S. 564 (1997), held unconstitutional a tax statute that exempted property owned by local charitable organizations but denied the exemption to organizations operated principally for nonresidents. The Court first concluded that the statute would violate the commerce clause if it were targeted at profit-making organizations because it encouraged them "to limit their out-of-state clientele" in a way that would lead to economic balkanization. It was "functionally [an] export tariff that targets out-of-state customers by taxing the businesses that principally serve them." Relying on New Energy Co. of Indiana v. Limbach, cited in *Carbone*, the Court then rejected the argument that the tax exemption amounted to a permissible "discriminatory subsidy." Even if such subsidies were constitutional, discriminatory tax exemptions were not.

2. *The politics of subsidies.* Why are subsidies from general revenues permissible but ones from industry-specific taxes impermissible? Note that an annual appropriation in the form of a direct subsidy might be more visible politically than the indirect subsidy through regulation. Justice Stevens's opinion suggests that the courts should carefully examine legislation that shifts one interest group from one side of an issue to another. Is there any economic regulation that does

not have that effect? Coenen, Business Subsidies and the Dormant Commerce Clause, 107 Yale L.J. 965, 985–992 (1998), enumerates a number of functional distinctions between direct subsidies and tax breaks:

> [A] state's imposition of costs on its citizens is more visible when the state awards outright subsidies than when it doles out tax relief. [The] extent of cost [is] more readily perceptible when the state's support of local industry takes the form of a monetary subsidy [because] the total amount of subsidy payments can be determined through the easy means of tallying total payments [whereas] tax expenditures are made [passively]. [Tax] credits, exemptions, and the like are resistant to repeal because legislatures typically enact them as presumptively permanent features of state tax codes. In contrast, because subsidies involve the direct expenditure of funds, they routinely show up — and are subject to recurring reevaluation — as expense items in perennially controversial state budget bills.

Are Justices Scalia and Rehnquist correct in asserting that consideration of the politics of subsidies is irrelevant to constitutional analysis?

Note: Other Doctrines Concerning Discrimination

1. *The market-participant doctrine.* The Supreme Court has held that states may discriminate when they act as participants in the market, but not when they act as regulators.

a. *The contours of the doctrine.* Hughes v. Alexandria Scrap Corp., 426 U.S. 794 (1976), upheld a Maryland program designed to reduce the number of abandoned cars in the state. It purchased junked cars, paying a "bounty" for those with Maryland license plates and imposing more stringent documentation requirements on out-of-state processors of junked cars than on in-state processors. The Court said that "nothing in the purposes animating the Commerce Clause prohibits a State [from] participating in the market and exercising the right to favor its own citizens over others." See also Reeves, Inc. v. Stake, 447 U.S. 429 (1980) (upholding a state policy restricting the sale of cement produced in a state-owned plant to state residents).

What is the distinction between regulation and market participation? South-Central Timber Development v. Wunnicke, 467 U.S. 82 (1984), held unconstitutional Alaska's inclusion of a requirement that purchasers of state-owned timber process it within the state before it was shipped out of state. According to a plurality opinion by Justice White, Alaska could not impose "downstream" conditions in the timber-processing market as a result of its ownership of the timber itself. The opinion summarized "[the] limit of the market-participant doctrine" as "[allowing] a State to impose burdens on commerce within the market in which it is a participant, but [to] go no further. The State may not impose conditions [that] have a substantial regulatory effect outside of that particular market."

b. *Is the **economic** effect of discriminatory market participation different from that of discriminatory regulation?* According to Justice Blackmun's opinion for the Court in Reeves v. Stake, when states act in the marketplace, they resemble private businesses and should be free to exercise a similar discretion to choose the parties with whom they deal. Note that private businesses are constrained to some extent by competition and the profit motive to purchase from the cheapest seller and sell to the buyer willing to pay most. States in contrast may buy and sell without that constraint, using their power to tax as the mechanism to force some taxpayers to subsidize "uneconomic" transactions. See generally Wells and Hellerstein, The Governmental-Proprietary Distinction in Constitutional Law, 66 Va. L. Rev. 1073 (1980).

c. *Can the market-participant doctrine be defended as allowing states to capture the benefits of their tax expenditures?* Consider L. Tribe, Constitutional Choices 145 (1985): The doctrine is justified by

> the sense of fairness in allowing a community to retain the public benefits created by its own public investment. [The] broader theme that underlies each case seems to be *creation* of commerce: whatever the state's ultimate goal, the state is approaching that goal by channeling its resources into commerce rather than by placing restrictions on commerce already in existence.

In *Reeves,* the public expenditure is the outlay for cement production. How does that differ from the state's expenditures for the general provision of social order in Philadelphia v. New Jersey? The expenditures differ in the specificity with which they affect particular transactions, but is that relevant to any constitutionally significant matters?

Consider that we have now seen four types of subsidy: via regulation, via targeted tax breaks, via participation in the market, and via direct appropriations from general revenues. Only the first two are subject to close commerce clause scrutiny. Recall the suggestion that direct appropriations have more political visibility than do regulatory subsidies. Which does a market-participation subsidy more closely resemble?

Do the same considerations that justify the market-participant doctrine justify *United Haulers* and *Davis?* (Why are those cases *not* market-participant cases?)

2. *The privileges and immunities clause of article IV.* Article IV provides, "The citizens of each State shall be entitled to all the Privileges and Immunities of Citizens in the several States."

a. *The contours of the doctrine.* United Building & Construction Trades Council v. Mayor of Camden, 465 U.S. 208 (1984), involved a New Jersey statute authorizing cities to adopt affirmative action plans. Camden passed an ordinance requiring that at least 40 percent of the employees of contractors and subcontractors on city projects be Camden residents. After holding that the privilege and immunities clause was applicable even though the ordinance excluded citizens of New Jersey (those living outside of Camden) as well as citizens from Pennsylvania and other states, Justice Rehnquist's opinion for the Court described the clause's primary purpose: "to help fuse into one Nation a collection of independent, sovereign States. It was designed to insure to a citizen of State A who ventures into State B the same privileges which the citizens of State B enjoy." The clause applied when a privilege or immunity was burdened. The Court held that an out-of-state resident's interest in employment on public works contracts was "'fundamental' to the promotion of interstate harmony" and therefore protected by the clause. The Court remanded the case for consideration of whether the infringement of a right protected by the clause was constitutionally permissible. The clause "does not preclude discrimination against citizens of other States where there is a 'substantial reason' for the difference in treatment. '[T]he inquiry in each case must be concerned with whether such reasons do exist and whether the degree of discrimination bears a close relation to them.'" As part of any justification offered for the discriminatory law, nonresidents must somehow be shown to "constitute a peculiar source of the evil at which the statute is aimed." Preference for residents might be justified as a necessary means of counteracting "[spiralling] unemployment, a sharp decline in population, and a dramatic reduction in the number of businesses located in the city [which] have eroded property values and depleted the city's tax base."

See also Supreme Court of New Hampshire v. Piper, 470 U.S. 274 (1985) (holding that a rule limiting bar admission to local residents violated the privileges and immunities clause).

b. *The doctrine's history.* In Corfield v. Coryell, 6 F. Cas. 546 (C.C.E.D. Pa. 1823) (No. 3230), Justice Bushrod Washington stated that the clause protected interests

> which are fundamental; which belong, of right, to the citizens of all free governments. [These] may [all be] comprehended under the following general heads: Protection by the government, the enjoyment of life and liberty, with the right to acquire and possess property of every kind, and to pursue and obtain happiness and safety; subject nevertheless to such restraints as the government may prescribe for the general good of the whole.

Corfield held that a New Jersey statute forbidding nonresidents from gathering clams from state waters did not violate the clause because the clams were the property of the state. (What result under modern commerce clause doctrine?) See generally Varat, State "Citizenship" and Interstate Equality, 48 U. Chi. L. Rev. 487 (1981). (The fourteenth amendment also contains a privileges *or* immunities clause, which has been held to prohibit state infringements of the privileges of national citizenship. See Chapter 6, infra.)

c. *What does article IV, section 2 add to the commerce clause?* Suppose Camden had imposed the residency requirement on all businesses located in Camden or supplying goods to the city. What result under the commerce clause? In many ways, the modern function of article IV, section 2 appears to be that of carving out an exception to the market-participant exception to the commerce clause. Note, however, that corporations are not "citizens" within the meaning of the privileges and immunities clause. Paul v. Virginia, 75 U.S. (8 Wall.) 168 (1868). Is the test formulated by the Court in *Camden* different from the undue burden test under the commerce clause? Note, however, that Camden's ordinance is discriminatory. What commerce clause test would apply to it?

d. Justice Blackmun's dissent in *Camden* argued that New Jersey residents excluded from jobs in Camden could adequately represent the interests of out-of-state citizens. Justice Rehnquist replied that the ordinance was enacted pursuant to a state law authorizing every city to adopt similar programs. This, he said, made it "hard to see how New Jersey residents living outside Camden will protect the interests of out-of-state citizens." Is this problem different from that in *Dean Milk?*

e. *For a recent discussion of the privileges and immunities clause and the dormant commerce clause,* see McBurney v. Young, 133 S. Ct. 1709 (2013), holding that a Virginia freedom of information statute limiting its use to state citizens is constitutional. According to the Court, statutory access to state-held information is not a "fundamental" right protected by the privileges and immunities clause, the distinction was not drawn to provide economic protection to citizens engaged in businesses using state-held information, and Virginia provided reasonable alternative methods by which out-of-state citizens could get access to information about judicial and other public proceedings. Questioning whether the statute triggered dormant commerce clause scrutiny (because the statute did not prohibit access to an interstate market or unduly burden such access), the Court held that the market-participant doctrine permitted the distinction because the state had created the market for information subject to the freedom of information act.

3. *The equal protection clause.* Consider Metropolitan Life Insurance Co. v. Ward, 470 U.S. 869 (1985). Paul v. Virginia, supra, held that insurance contracts were not in interstate commerce. As a result, states developed extensive and sometimes burdensome systems for regulating insurance. In 1944, the Court rejected *Paul* in United States v. South-Eastern Underwriters Association, 322 U.S. 533. Congress responded by passing the McCarran-Ferguson Act, which declared it to be national policy that "the continued regulation and taxation by the several States of the business of insurance is in the public interest, and that silence on the part of Congress shall not be construed to impose any barrier to the regulation or taxation of such business by the several States." Alabama placed a 1 percent tax on the gross receipts of local insurance companies, while requiring that out-of-state companies pay a tax of 3 to 4 percent, which could be lowered by 1 percent if the companies invested substantially in Alabama. The equal protection clause allows such discrimination if it is a rational means to accomplish a "legitimate state purpose." The Court, dividing five to four, held that the state's purpose of "encouraging the formation of new insurance companies in Alabama" was an impermissible one. It was "purely and completely discriminatory" for Alabama "to [erect] barriers to foreign companies [in] order to improve its domestic insurers' ability to compete at home." This is "the very sort of parochial discrimination that the Equal Protection Clause was intended to prevent." The McCarran-Ferguson Act was irrelevant because it lifted commerce clause restrictions but not equal protection ones:

> Under Commerce Clause analysis, the State's interest, if legitimate, is weighed against the burden the state law would impose on interstate commerce. In the equal protection context, however, if the State's purpose is found to be legitimate, the state law stands as long as the burden it imposes is found to be rationally related to that purpose, a relationship that is not difficult to establish. The two [provisions] perform different functions — [one] protects interstate commerce, and the other protects persons from unconstitutional discrimination.

The Court conceded that "the *effect* of the discrimination in this case is similar to the type of burden with which the Commerce Clause would also be concerned," but said that "acceptance of [the] contention that promotion of domestic industry is always a legitimate state purpose under equal protection analysis would eviscerate the Equal Protection Clause in this context."

Justice O'Connor's long dissent was joined by Justices Brennan, Marshall, and Rehnquist. She said that "it is obviously legitimate for a State to seek to promote local business."

Why is encouraging entry by exempting out-of-state companies from regulation different from doing so by differential taxation? Note that in *Metropolitan Life,* if the state's policy succeeds, local insurers will face greater competition. What result in *Metropolitan Life* under the commerce clause? Is the Court's distinction between the purposes of the two clauses persuasive where, as in *Metropolitan Life,* the commerce clause challenge rests on facial discrimination? Would the Court "weigh" the competing interests in a commerce clause challenge to Alabama's statute? What is the effect of the McCarran-Ferguson Act after *Metropolitan Life*?

Note: Concluding Observations

The various doctrines concerning discrimination are not entirely consistent. The market-participant doctrine exempts states from judicial supervision pursuant to ordinary commerce clause analysis; the privileges and immunities clause reimposes that scrutiny in cases involving individuals (perhaps under a somewhat less rigorous standard); and the equal protection clause may reimpose it in cases involving corporations (again perhaps under a somewhat less rigorous standard). Why has the Court constructed the doctrine in this complex way?

Consider the possibility that the Court finds itself caught between the implications of two intuitions. The dormant commerce clause may imply that states may never favor their own citizens. Yet, basic ideas of federalism suggest that one of the points of having state governments is to allow state citizens control over their governors precisely in order to secure benefits to themselves that they do not have to distribute to outsiders. Does the fundamental difficulty stem from attempting to implement the "thought" that the Constitution endorses some vision of a governmental process in which the preferences of citizens are perfectly aggregated, in a federal system where, because people are simultaneously citizens of state and nation, it is always unclear whose preferences ought to be perfectly aggregated?

3.   Facially Neutral Statutes with Significant Effects on Interstate Commerce

Two related issues arise in connection with statutes that are facially neutral but have significant effects on interstate commerce. First, is a particular statute facially neutral but adopted with the intent of discriminating against out-of-state commerce? How can the courts identify statutes adopted with such intent? Note in the materials that follow repeated suggestions that patterns of exemptions, and statements by sponsors, support the inference that the statute at issue was adopted with a discriminatory purpose. The cases also suggest that facially neutral statutes adopted with discriminatory purposes should be analyzed according to the principles used in analyzing facially discriminatory statutes.

Second, what standard is used to assess the constitutionality of facially neutral statutes, not adopted with a discriminatory intent, that have significant effects on interstate commerce? Some formulations suggest that the courts should balance the in-state benefits and the out-of-state effects; others suggest that facially neutral statutes with significant effects on interstate commerce are constitutional unless the in-state benefits are trivial or nonexistent. Which of the approaches are consistent with which of the general theories of the dormant commerce clause?

Two cases from the New Deal era set the stage for more recent developments. In South Carolina Highway Department v. Barnwell Brothers, 303 U.S. 177 (1938), the Court upheld a state law prohibiting the use of large trucks on the state's highways. The trial court had found that trucks defined as large under the state statute could be used without damage to those highways. According to then-Justice Stone, "few subjects of state regulation are so peculiarly of local concern as is the use of state highways." In the absence of congressional action, the test was "whether the state legislature [has] acted within its province, and whether the means of regulation chosen are reasonably adapted to the end sought." In "resolving the second [inquiry], the courts do not sit as Legislatures [to weigh] all the conflicting interests. [Fairly] debatable questions as to [a regulation's] reasonableness, wisdom and propriety are not for the determination of courts, but for the legislative body." The court must decide "upon the whole record whether it is possible to say that the legislative choice is without rational basis."

In Southern Pacific Co. v. Arizona, 325 U.S. 761 (1945), the Court, again through Chief Justice Stone, found unconstitutional a 1912 statute limiting train lengths to fourteen passenger or seventy freight cars. The "matters for ultimate determination" were "the nature and extent of the burden which the state regulation, [adopted] as a safety measure, imposes on interstate commerce, and whether the relative weights of the state and national interests are such as to make inapplicable the rule [that] the free flow of interstate commerce [in] matters requiring uniformity of regulation" is protected by the commerce clause. The Court reviewed "detailed findings of fact" made in a long trial below. Breaking up and remaking long trains at the state's borders delayed traffic. The Court held that

> [enforcement] of the law in Arizona [must] inevitably result in an impairment of efficient railroad operation because the railroads are subjected to regulation which is not uniform in its application. [Either trains are broken up and reconstituted, or] the carrier [must] conform to the lowest train limit restriction of any of the states through which its trains pass, whose laws thus control the carriers' operations both within and without the regulating state.

The Court then turned to the safety benefits of the law:

> The decisive question is whether in the circumstances the total effect of the law as a safety measure in reducing accidents and casualties is so slight or problematical as not to outweigh the national interest in keeping interstate commerce free from interferences which seriously impede it and subject it to local regulation which does not have a uniform effect on the interstate train journey which it interrupts.

Longer trains cause accidents by "slack action," the movement of one car before it transmits its momentum to the next one to which it is loosely coupled. But the evidence showed that, in states leaving train lengths unregulated, the accident rate on long trains was the same as that on Arizona's shorter trains. Further, because the regulation meant that more trains had to be used, there were more grade-crossing collisions and collisions between trains in the course of switching tracks. The Court found that the regulation,

> viewed as a safety measure, affords at most slight and dubious advantage, if any, over unregulated train lengths, because it results in an increase in the number of trains and train operations and the consequent increases in train accidents of a character generally more severe than those due to slack action.

Justice Black's dissenting opinion described the Arizona statute as the product of a long-standing political struggle between railroads and railroad workers, conducted in state legislatures and in Congress. He called the trial in *Southern Pacific* "extraordinary" in that the issue was "whether the law was unconstitutional [because] the legislature had been guilty of misjudging the facts concerning the degree of the danger of long trains." He continued, "the evil [the Court] finds in a lack of uniformity is that it (1) delays interstate commerce, (2) increases its cost and (3) impairs its efficiency. All three of these boil down to the same thing, and that is that running shorter trains would increase the cost of railroad operations. [The] conclusion that a requirement for long trains will 'burden interstate commerce' is a mere euphemism for the statement that a requirement for long trains will increase the cost of railroad operations." Justice Black criticized the Court for "requiring that money costs outweigh human values" in the name of "an 'economical national railroad system.'"

HUNT v. WASHINGTON STATE APPLE ADVERTISING COMMISSION, 432 U.S. 333 (1977). North Carolina enacted a statute requiring all closed containers of apples sold or shipped into the state to bear "no grade other than the applicable U.S. grade or standard." Washington, the country's largest producer of apples, requires that apples be tested and graded under a system of grades superior to the standards adopted by the U.S. Department of Agriculture. North Carolina agreed that the statute placed substantial financial burdens on Washington apple producers, who could comply with North Carolina law only by altering the containers used to pack apples, by repacking those that were shipped to North Carolina, or by discontinuing use of preprinted containers with the Washington grades entirely. North Carolina defended its regulation as a measure designed to protect against fraud in apple marketing. The Court held the regulation unconstitutional. Chief Justice Burger wrote:

> The challenged statute has the practical effect of not only burdening interstate sales of Washington apples, but also discriminating against them. This discrimination takes various forms. The first [is] the statute's consequence of raising the costs of doing business in the North Carolina market for Washington apple growers and dealers, while leaving those of their North Carolina counterparts unaffected. [This] disparate effect results from the fact that North Carolina apple producers, unlike their Washington competitors, were not forced to alter their marketing practices in order to comply with the statute. They were still free to market their wares under the USDA grade or none at all as they had done prior to the statute's enactment. Obviously, the increased costs imposed by the statute would tend to shield the local apple industry from the competition of Washington apple growers and dealers who are already at a competitive disadvantage because of their great distance from the North Carolina market.
>
> Second, the statute has the effect of stripping away from the Washington apple industry the competitive and economic advantages it has earned for itself through its expensive inspection and grading system. [The] Washington apple-grading system has gained nationwide acceptance in the apple trade. [Apple] brokers and dealers located both inside and outside of North Carolina [state] their preference [for] apples graded under the Washington [system] because of [its] greater consistency, its emphasis on color, and its supporting mandatory inspections. Once again, the statute had no similar impact on the North Carolina apple industry and thus operated to its benefit.

Third, by prohibiting Washington growers and dealers from marketing apples under their State's grades, the statute has a leveling effect which insidiously operates to the advantage of local apple producers. [The] Washington State grades are equal or superior to the USDA grades in all corresponding categories. Hence, with free market forces at work, Washington sellers would normally enjoy a distinct market advantage vis-à-vis local producers in those categories where the Washington grade is superior. However, because of the statute's operation, Washington apples which would otherwise qualify for and be sold under the superior Washington grades will now have to be marketed under their inferior USDA counterparts. Such "down-grading" offers the North Carolina apple industry the very sort of protection against competing out-of-state products that the Commerce Clause was designed to prohibit. . . .

The several States unquestionably possess a substantial interest in protecting their citizens from confusion and deception in the marketing of foodstuffs, but the challenged statute does remarkably little to further that laudable goal at least with respect to Washington apples and grades. The statute [permits] the marketing of closed containers of apples under no grades at all. Such a result can hardly be thought to eliminate the problems of deception and confusion created by the multiplicity of differing state grades; indeed, it magnifies them by depriving pur-chasers of all information concerning the quality of the contents of closed apple containers. [In] addition, it appears that nondiscriminatory alternatives to the out-right ban of Washington State grades are readily available. For example, North Carolina could effectuate its goal by permitting out-of-state growers to utilize state grades only if they also marked their shipments with the applicable USDA label. . . .

Note: Inferring Intent from Effect

Should the courts infer a discriminatory or anticommercial purpose from neutral criteria that have the effect of distinguishing in-state and out-of-state producers? How precisely must the neutral criteria target out-of-state producers to justify that inference? Consider these comments in the Court's opinion in *Hunt*:

Despite the statute's facial neutrality, the Commission suggests that its discrimina-tory impact on interstate commerce was not an unintended byproduct and there are some indications in the record to that effect. The most glaring is the response of the North Carolina Agriculture Commissioner to the Commission's request for an exemption following the statute's passage in which he indicated that before he could support such an exemption, he would "want to have the sentiment from our apple producers *since they were mainly responsible for this legislation being passed. . . .*" [However], we need not ascribe an economic protection motive to the North Carolina Legislature to resolve this case; we conclude that the chal-lenged statute cannot stand insofar as it prohibits the display of Washington State grades even if enacted for the declared purpose of protecting consumers from deception and fraud in the marketplace.

How important should be the presence or absence of evidence like that taken from the state's Agriculture Commissioner?

Consider Minnesota v. Clover Leaf Creamery Co., 449 U.S. 456 (1981). Minnesota prohibited the sale of milk in plastic disposable containers but allowed its sale in paper nonreturnable cartons. The Supreme Court accepted the argument that the statute served its stated purposes of promoting conserva-tion, easing waste disposal problems, and conserving energy. The state's trial court had found that the "actual basis" of the statute "was to promote the economic interests of certain segments of the local dairy and pulpwood industries at the expense of the economic interests of other segments of the dairy industry and the plastics industry." It also had found that banning the use of plastic bottles would not in fact promote conservation or save energy because paper containers are "a more environmentally harmful product." The Supreme Court responded:

> Minnesota's statute does not effect "simple protectionism," but "regulates even-handedly" by prohibiting all milk retailers from selling their products in plastic, nonreturnable milk containers, without regard to whether the milk, the containers, or the sellers are from outside the State. This statute is therefore unlike statutes discriminating against interstate commerce, which we have consistently struck down. E.g., [*Hughes*; Philadelphia v. New Jersey; *Hunt*]. . . .
>
> [Within] Minnesota, business will presumably shift from manufacturers of plastic nonreturnable containers to producers of paperboard cartons, refillable bottles, and plastic pouches, but there is no reason to suspect that the gainers will be Minnesota firms, or the losers out-of-state firms. Indeed, two of the three dairies, the sole milk retailer, and the sole milk container producer challenging the statute in this litigation are Minnesota firms.[17]
>
> Pulpwood producers are the only Minnesota industry likely to benefit significantly from the Act at the expense of out-of-state firms. Respondents point out that plastic resin, the raw material used for making plastic nonreturnable milk jugs, is produced entirely by non-Minnesota firms, while pulpwood, used for making paperboard, is a major Minnesota product. Nevertheless, it is clear that respondents exaggerate the degree of burden on out-of-state interests, both because plastics will continue to be used in the production of plastic pouches, plastic returnable bottles, and paperboard itself, and because out-of-state pulpwood producers will presumably absorb some of the business generated by the Act. . . .

Is this analysis of the issue of intent persuasive? Is the problem addressed here different from that in *Hunt*? In Philadelphia v. New Jersey?

Exxon Corp. v. Governor of Maryland

437 U.S. 117 (1978)

Mr. Justice Stevens delivered the opinion of the Court.

A Maryland statute provides that a producer or refiner of petroleum products [may] not operate any retail service station within the State. . . .

[All] of the gasoline sold by Exxon in Maryland is transported into the State from refineries located elsewhere. Although Exxon sells the bulk of this gas to wholesalers and independent retailers, it also sells directly to the consuming public through 36 company-operated stations. Exxon uses these stations to test innovative marketing concepts or products. . . .

[Approximately] 3,800 retail service stations in Maryland sell over 20 different brands of gasoline. However, no petroleum products are produced or refined in Maryland, and the number of stations actually operated by a refiner or an affiliate is relatively small, representing about 5% of the total number of Maryland retailers. . . .

---

17. The existence of major in-state interests adversely affected by the Act is a powerful safeguard against legislative abuse. [*Barnwell Bros.*]

Plainly, the Maryland statute does not discriminate against interstate goods, nor does it favor local producers and refiners. Since Maryland's entire gasoline supply flows in interstate commerce and since there are no local producers or refiners, such claims of disparate treatment between interstate and local commerce would be meritless. Appellants, however, focus on the retail market, arguing that the effect of the statute is to protect in-state independent dealers from out-of-state competition. They contend that the divestiture provisions "create a protected enclave for Maryland independent dealers. . . ." As support for this proposition, they rely on the fact that the burden of the divestiture requirements falls solely on interstate companies. . . .

As the record shows, there are several major interstate marketers of petroleum that own and operate their own retail gasoline stations. These interstate dealers, who compete directly with the Maryland independent dealers, are not affected by the Act because they do not refine or produce gasoline. In fact, the Act creates no barriers whatsoever against interstate independent dealers; it does not prohibit the flow of interstate goods, place added costs upon them, or distinguish between in-state and out-of-state companies in the retail market. [While] the refiners will no longer enjoy their same status in the Maryland market, in-state independent dealers will have no competitive advantage over out-of-state dealers. The fact that the burden of a state regulation falls on some interstate companies does not, by itself, establish a claim of discrimination against interstate commerce.[16]

The crux of appellants' claim is that, regardless of whether the State has interfered with the movement of goods in interstate commerce, it has interfered "with the natural functioning of the interstate market either through prohibition or through burdensome regulation." Hughes v. Alexandria Scrap Corp., 426 U.S. 794, 806. Appellants then claim that the statute "will surely change the market structure by weakening the independent refiners. . . ." We cannot, however, accept appellants' underlying notion that the Commerce Clause protects the particular structure or methods of operation in a retail market. As indicated by the Court in *Hughes*, the Clause protects the interstate market, not particular interstate firms, from prohibitive or burdensome regulations. It may be true that the consuming public will be injured by the loss of the high-volume, low-priced stations operated by the independent refiners, but again that argument relates to the wisdom of the statute, not to its burden on commerce.

[The Court also rejected a preemption argument made by Exxon.]

The judgment is affirmed.

So ordered.

MR. JUSTICE POWELL took no part in the consideration or decision of these cases.

16. If the effect of a state regulation is to cause local goods to constitute a larger share, and goods with an out-of-state source to constitute a smaller share, of the total sales in the market — as in [*Dean Milk*] — the regulation may have a discriminatory effect on interstate commerce. But the Maryland statute has no impact on the relative proportions of local and out-of-state goods sold in Maryland and, indeed, no demonstrable effect whatsoever on the interstate flow of goods. The sales by independent retailers are just as much a part of the flow of interstate commerce as the sales made by the refiner-operated stations.

MR. JUSTICE BLACKMUN, [dissenting as to the commerce clause issue].

[The] divestiture provisions preclude out-of-state competitors from retailing gasoline within Maryland. The effect is to protect in-state retail service station dealers from the competition of the out-of-state businesses. This protectionist discrimination is not justified by any legitimate state interest that cannot be vindicated by more evenhanded regulation. . . .

I . . .

B . . .

No facial inequality exists. [But] given the structure of the retail gasoline market in Maryland, the effect [is] to exclude a class of predominantly out-of-state gasoline retailers while providing protection from competition to a class of nonintegrated retailers that is overwhelmingly composed of local businessman. [Of] the class of stations statutorily insulated from the competition of the out-of-state integrated firms [more] than 99% were operated by local business interests. Of the class of enterprises excluded entirely from participation in the retail gasoline market, 95% were out-of-state firms, operating 98% of the stations in the class. . . .

[The] ban [will] preclude the majors from enhancing brand recognition and consumer acceptance through retail outlets with company-controlled standards. Their ability directly to monitor consumer preferences and reactions will be diminished. And their opportunity for experimentation with retail marketing techniques will be curtailed. In short, the divestiture provisions [will] inflict significant economic hardship on Maryland's major brand companies, all of which are out-of-state firms.

Similar hardship is not imposed upon the local service station dealers by the divestiture provisions. Indeed, rather than restricting their ability to compete, the Maryland Act effectively and perhaps intentionally improves their competitive position by insulating them from competition by out-of-state integrated producers and refiners. [The] foundation of the discrimination in this case is that the local dealers may continue to enter retail transactions and to compete for retail profits while the statute will deny similar opportunities to the class composed almost entirely of out-of-state businesses. . . .

The State's showing may be so meager because any legitimate interest in competition can be vindicated with more evenhanded regulation. [To] the extent that the State's interest in competition is nothing more than a desire to protect particular competitors — less efficient local businessmen — from the legal competition of more efficient out-of-state firms, the interest is illegitimate under the Commerce Clause. . . . [8]

8. There is support in the record for the inference that the Maryland Legislature passed the divestiture provisions in response to the pleas of local gasoline dealers for protection against the competition of both the price marketers and the major oil companies. [The] executive director of the Greater Washington/Maryland Service Station Association [testified] before the [Maryland] Senate:

> . . . Now beset by the critical gasoline supply situation, the squeeze by his landlord-supplier and the shrinking service [market], the dealer is now faced with an even more serious threat.
>   That is the sinister threat of the major oil companies to complete their takeover to the retail-marketing of gasoline, not just to be in competition with their own branded dealers, but to squeeze them out and convert their stations to company operation. . . .

II . . .

To accept the argument of the Court, that is, that discrimination must be universal to offend the Commerce Clause, naively will foster protectionist discrimination against interstate commerce.[13] In the future, States will be able to insulate in-state interests from competition by identifying the most potent segments of out-of-state business, banning them, and permitting less effective out-of-state actors to remain. The record shows that the Court permits Maryland to effect just such discrimination in this case. The State bans the most powerful out-of-state firms from retailing gasoline within its boundaries. It then insulates the forced divestiture of 199 service stations from constitutional attack by permitting out-of-state firms [to] continue to operate 34 gasoline stations. . . .

[Merely] demonstrating a burden on some out-of-state actors does not prove unconstitutional discrimination. But when the burden is significant, when it falls on the most numerous and effective group of out-of-state competitors, when a similar burden does not fall on the class of protected in-state businessmen, and when the State cannot justify the resulting disparity by showing that its legislative interests cannot be vindicated by more evenhanded regulation, unconstitutional discrimination exists. . . .

[The state] Court of Appeals reasoned that [the statute] did not discriminate against the class of out-of-state refiners and producers because the wholesale flow of petroleum products into the State was not restricted. [The] Maryland statute has not effected discrimination with regard to the wholesaling or interstate transport of petroleum. The discrimination exists with regard to retailing. The fact that gasoline will continue to flow into the State does not permit the State to deny out-of-state firms the opportunity to retail it once it arrives. . . .

Note: *Facially Neutral Statutes with (Merely?) Disproportionate Effects for Commercial or Social Purposes*

1. *Gerrymandering or mere facial neutrality?* Is the inference of anticommercial intent weaker in *Exxon* than in *Hunt*? Note footnote 8 in Justice Blackmun's opinion in *Exxon*. Does *Exxon* involve anticommercial intent but no significant anticommercial impact? Consider whether the cases make a statute's use of express or strongly implied discrimination conclusive. Is such formalism justified on the grounds that form is strongly, though not perfectly, correlated with cost exporting, and that the gains from allowing courts to look beyond form are outweighed by the costs in encouraging complex litigation?

Are the legislators of Maryland about to let this octopus loose and unrestricted in the state of Maryland, among our small businessmen to devour them? We sincerely hope not. . . .

13. [Footnote] 16 of the Court's opinion suggests that unconstitutional discrimination does not exist unless there is an effect on the quantity of out-of-state goods entering a State. This is too narrow a view of the Commerce Clause. [Interstate] commerce consists of far more than mere production of goods. It also consists of transactions — of repeated buying and selling of both goods and services. By focusing exclusively on the quantity of goods, the Court limits the protection of the Clause to producers and handlers of goods before they enter a discriminating State. In our complex national economy, commercial transactions continue after the goods enter a State. The Court today permits a State to impose protectionist discrimination upon these latter transactions to the detriment of out-of-state participants. [Relocated footnote. — Eds.]

2. *Commerce — gasoline or retailing?* The Court argues in *Exxon* that interstate commerce in gasoline will be unaffected by the statute because all it can do is force Maryland consumers to switch from cheaper brands of gasoline originating out of state to more expensive brands also originating out of state. Justice Blackmun argues that the courts should confine their attention to the subject regulated — here, retailing. Why? Consider the implications of the following argument: In a strongly interconnected economy, local regulations can do no more than alter the patterns of interstate trade; they cannot reduce it. Isn't this the lesson of Wickard v. Filburn and Katzenbach v. McClung, supra? States may succeed in protecting particular local industries, but they cannot protect their entire economies. Thus, local regulations serve only distributional goals, altering the relative wealth of in-state and out-of-state producers and of consumers. What, if anything, is there in the materials presented here that suggests that the Constitution is concerned with these goals?

3. *Cost-benefit analysis.* Who bears the costs and gains the benefits of Maryland's statutes? How substantial are the higher prices that Maryland consumers are likely to face? Consider L. Tribe, American Constitutional Law 417 (2d ed. 1988):

> Behind the Court's analysis in *Exxon* stands an important doctrinal theme: the negative implications of the commerce clause derive principally from a *political* theory of union, not from an *economic* theory of free trade. The function of the clause is to ensure national solidarity, not economic efficiency. Although the Court's commerce clause opinions have often employed the language of economics, the decisions have not interpreted the Constitution as establishing the inviolability of the free market. More particularly, the constitutional vice of economic protectionism is not implicated by a regulation which makes impossible the economies of scale that a fully open market permits.

How is national solidarity promoted other than by economic integration? By prohibiting states from enacting statutes designed to hurt other states' interests? By prohibiting states from adopting statutes whose terms indicate willingness to go it alone?

4. *The problem of sales and compensating use taxes.* Henneford v. Silas Mason Co., 300 U.S. 577 (1937), involved Washington's sales and use taxes. The state adopted a 2 percent tax. To avoid losing business to retailers in other states, it also adopted a 2 percent "compensating use tax," levied on the price of goods purchased elsewhere for the "privilege of using" them in Washington. Justice Cardozo's opinion for the Court, upholding the compensating use tax, described it as designed to promote equality.

A modern discussion of compensating use taxes is Oregon Waste Systems v. Department of Environmental Quality, 511 U.S. 93 (1994). Oregon charged a fee of $0.85 per ton on the disposal of waste generated in Oregon and a fee of $2.25 on the disposal in Oregon of waste generated outside the state. The Court held that the differential was discriminatory and triggered the "virtually per se rule of invalidity." Treating the differential as a compensatory use tax, the Court, in an opinion by Justice Thomas, clarified the doctrine by stressing that the fact that a tax or fee is "compensatory" is "merely a specific way of justifying a facially discriminatory tax." Compensating use taxes must be imposed on "substantially equivalent events." This implied that the state could not justify a specific tax like the one at issue here by pointing to "general taxation, such as income taxes," that in-state generators pay, but out-of-state generators do not.

Note that compensating use taxes are not facially neutral. The Court treated Henneford v. Silas Mason as still good law because sale and use are "substantially equivalent taxable events." Chief Justice Rehnquist's dissent in *Oregon Waste Systems* claimed that out-of-state commerce gained a competitive advantage from the Court's rule that it will not consider whether general taxes in Oregon offset the difference between the higher fees charged those who dispose of out-of-state waste and those who dispose of in-state waste: Only Oregon businesses "will have to pay the 'nondisposal' fees associated with solid waste: landfill siting, landfill clean-up, insurance to cover environmental accidents, and transportation improvement costs associated with out-of-state waste being transported into the State." Could the courts administer a rule examining general taxes to see if they offset the difference?

Kassel v. Consolidated Freightways Corp.

450 U.S. 662 (1981)

JUSTICE POWELL announced the judgment of the Court and delivered an opinion, in which JUSTICE WHITE, JUSTICE BLACKMUN, and JUSTICE STEVENS joined.

The question is whether an Iowa statute that prohibits the use of certain large trucks within the State unconstitutionally burdens interstate commerce.

I . . .

[Consolidated, one of the nation's largest common carriers, used two types of trucks: the "semi," 55 feet long, and the "double," a 65-foot-long combination of a tractor and two trailers. It operated on Interstate Routes 80 and 35, major transportation corridors through Iowa.] Unlike all other States in the West and Midwest, Iowa generally prohibits the use of 65-foot doubles within its borders. Instead, most truck combinations are restricted to 55 feet in length. Doubles, mobile homes, trucks carrying vehicles such as tractors and other farm equipment, and singles hauling livestock, are permitted to be as long as 60 feet. Not withstanding these restrictions, Iowa's statute permits cities abutting the state line by local ordinance to adopt the length limitations of the adjoining State. Where a city has exercised this option, otherwise oversized trucks are permitted within the city limits and in nearby commercial zones.

Iowa also provides for two other relevant exemptions. An Iowa truck manufacturer may obtain a permit to ship trucks that are as large as 70 feet. Permits also are available to move oversized mobile homes, provided that the unit is to be moved from a point within Iowa or delivered for an Iowa resident.[7] . . .

In a 14-day trial, both sides adduced evidence on safety, and on the burden on interstate commerce imposed by Iowa's law. On the question of safety, the

---

7. The parochial restrictions in the mobile home provision were enacted after Governor Ray vetoed a bill that would have permitted the interstate shipment of all mobile homes through Iowa. Governor Ray commented, in his veto message: "This bill . . . would make Iowa a bridge state as these oversized units are moved into Iowa after being manufactured in another state and sold in a third. None of this activity would be of particular economic benefit to Iowa."

District Court found that the "evidence clearly establishes that the twin is as safe as the semi." For that reason,

> there is no valid safety reason for barring twins from Iowa's highways because of their configuration. . . .
> Twins and semis have different characteristics. Twins are more maneuverable, are less sensitive to wind, and create less splash and spray. However, they are more likely than semis to jackknife or upset. They can be backed only for a short distance. The negative characteristics are not such that they render the twin less safe than semis overall. Semis are more stable but are more likely to "rear end" another vehicle. . . .

safety concerns

III

[We] conclude that the Iowa truck-length limitations unconstitutionally burden interstate commerce. [The] State failed to present any persuasive evidence that 65-foot doubles are less safe than 55-foot singles. Moreover, Iowa's law is now out of step with the laws of all other Midwestern and Western States. Iowa thus substantially burdens the interstate flow of goods by truck. In the absence of congressional action to set uniform standards, some burdens associated with state safety regulations must be tolerated. But where, as here, the State's safety interest has been found to be illusory, and its regulations impair significantly the federal interest in efficient and safe interstate transportation, the state law cannot be harmonized with the Commerce Clause.[12]

A . . .

[The] District Court found that the "evidence clearly establishes that the twin is as safe as the semi." The record supports this finding. . . .

B

Consolidated's answer

Consolidated, meanwhile, demonstrated that Iowa's law substantially burdens interstate commerce. Trucking companies that wish to continue to use 65-foot doubles must route them around Iowa or detach the trailers of the doubles and ship them through separately. Alternatively, trucking companies must use the smaller 55-foot singles or 60-foot doubles permitted under Iowa law. Each of these options engenders inefficiency and added expense. The record shows that Iowa's law added about $12.6 million each year to the costs of trucking companies. Consolidated alone incurred about $2 million per year in increased costs.

In addition to increasing the costs of the trucking companies (and, indirectly, of the service to consumers), Iowa's law may aggravate, rather than ameliorate, the problem of highway accidents. Fifty-five-foot singles carry less freight than 65-foot doubles. Either more small trucks must be used to carry the same quantity of goods through Iowa, or the same number of larger trucks must drive longer distances to bypass Iowa. In either case, [the] restriction requires more highway miles to be driven to transport the same quantity of goods. Other things being equal, accidents are proportional to distance traveled. Thus, if 65-foot doubles are

---

12. It is highly relevant that [the] state statute contains exemptions that weaken the deference traditionally accorded to a state safety regulation.

as safe as 55-foot singles, Iowa's law tends to *increase* the number of accidents, and to shift the incidence of them from Iowa to other States.[18]

IV

Perhaps recognizing the weakness of the evidence supporting its safety argument, and the substantial burden on commerce that its regulations create, Iowa urges the Court simply to "defer" to the safety judgment of the State. It argues that the length of trucks is generally, although perhaps imprecisely, related to safety. The task of drawing a line is one that Iowa contends should be left to its legislature.

The Court normally does accord "special deference" to state highway safety regulations. [Raymond Motor Transportation, Inc. v. Rice, 434 U.S. 429.] This traditional deference "derives in part from the assumption that where such regulations do not discriminate on their face against interstate commerce, their burden usually falls on local economic interests as well as other States' economic interests, thus insuring that a State's own political processes will serve as a check against unduly burdensome regulations." Less deference to the legislative judgment is due, however, where the local regulation bears disproportionately on out-of-state residents and businesses. Such a disproportionate burden is apparent here. Iowa's scheme, although generally banning large doubles from the State, nevertheless has several exemptions that secure to Iowans many of the benefits of large trucks while shunting to neighboring States many of the costs associated with their use.

At the time of trial there were two particularly significant exemptions. First, singles hauling livestock or farm vehicles were permitted to be as long as 60 feet. [This] provision undoubtedly was helpful to local interests. Second, cities abutting other States were permitted to enact local ordinances adopting the larger length limitation of the neighboring State. This exemption offered the benefits of longer trucks to individuals and businesses in important border cities without burdening Iowa's highways with interstate through traffic.

The origin of the "border cities exemption" also suggests that Iowa's statute may not have been designed to ban dangerous trucks, but rather to discourage interstate truck traffic. In 1974, the legislature passed a bill that would have permitted 65-foot doubles in the State. Governor Ray vetoed the bill. He said:

> I find sympathy with those who are doing business in our state and whose enterprises could gain from increased cargo carrying ability by trucks. However, with this bill, the Legislature has pursued a course that would benefit only a few Iowa-based companies while providing a great advantage for out-of-state trucking firms and competitors at the expense of our Iowa citizens.

After the veto, the "border cities exemption" was immediately enacted and signed by the Governor.

It is thus far from clear that Iowa was motivated primarily by a judgment that 65-foot doubles are less safe than 55-foot singles. Rather, Iowa seems to have

---

18. The District Court [noted] that Iowa's law causes "more accidents, more injuries, more fatalities and more fuel consumption." Appellant Kassel conceded as much at trial. Kassel explained, however, that most of these additional accidents occur in States other than Iowa because truck traffic is deflected around the State. He noted: "Our primary concern is the citizens of Iowa and our own highway system we operate in this state."

hoped to limit the use of its highways by deflecting some through traffic. [A] State cannot constitutionally promote its own parochial interests by requiring safe vehicles to detour around it.

V . . .

Because Iowa has imposed this burden without any significant countervailing safety interest, its statute violates the Commerce Clause. The judgment of the Court of Appeals is affirmed.

    It is so ordered.

    JUSTICE BRENNAN, with whom JUSTICE MARSHALL joins, concurring in the judgment. . . .

    Though my Brother Powell recognizes that the State's actual purpose in maintaining the truck-length regulation was "to limit the use of its highways by deflecting some through traffic," he fails to recognize that this purpose, being *protectionist* in nature, is *impermissible* under the Commerce Clause. . . . Iowa may not shunt off its fair share of the burden of maintaining interstate truck routes, nor may it create increased hazards on the highways of neighboring States in order to decrease the hazards on Iowa highways. Such an attempt has all the hallmarks of the "simple . . . protectionism" this Court has condemned in the economic area. [Philadelphia v. New Jersey.] . . .

    I therefore concur in the judgment.

    JUSTICE REHNQUIST, with whom [CHIEF JUSTICE BURGER] and JUSTICE STEWART join, dissenting. . . .

I . . .

[Iowa's] action in limiting the length of trucks which may travel on its highway is in no sense unusual. Every State in the Union regulates the length of vehicles permitted to use the public roads. Nor is Iowa a renegade in having the length limits which operate to exclude the 65-foot doubles favored by Consolidated. These trucks are prohibited in other areas of the country as well, some 17 States and the District of Columbia, including all of New England and most of the Southeast. . . .

II . . .

A determination that a state law is a rational safety measure does not end the Commerce Clause inquiry. A "sensitive consideration" of the safety purpose in relation to the burden on commerce is required. [*Raymond.*] When engaging in such a consideration the Court does not directly compare safety benefits to commerce costs and strike down the legislation if the latter can be said in some vague sense to "outweigh" the former. . . .

    The purpose of the "sensitive consideration" [is] rather to determine if the asserted safety justification, although rational, is merely a pretext for discrimination against interstate commerce. We will conclude that it is if the safety benefits from the regulation are demonstrably trivial while the burden on commerce is great. . . .

III

Iowa defends its statute as a highway safety regulation. There can be no doubt that the challenged statute is a valid highway safety regulation and thus entitled to the strongest presumption of validity against Commerce Clause challenges. As noted, all 50 States regulate the length of trucks which may use their highways. . . .

Iowa adduced evidence supporting the relation between vehicle length and highway safety. The evidence indicated that longer vehicles take greater time to pass, thereby increasing the risks of accidents, particularly during the inclement weather not uncommon in Iowa. The 65-foot vehicle exposes a passing driver to visibility-impairing splash and spray during bad weather for a longer period than do the shorter trucks permitted in Iowa. . . .

The answering of the relevant question is not appreciably advanced by comparing trucks slightly over the length limit with those at the length limit. It is emphatically not our task to balance any incremental safety benefits from prohibiting 65-foot doubles as opposed to 60-foot doubles against the burden on interstate commerce. Lines drawn for safety purposes will rarely pass muster if the question is whether a slight increment can be permitted without sacrificing safety. [The] question is rather whether it can be said that the benefits flowing to Iowa from a rational truck-length limitation are "slight or problematical." See [Bibb]. The particular line chosen by Iowa — 60 feet — is relevant only to the question whether the limit is a rational one. Once a court determines that it is, it considers the overall safety benefits *from the regulation* against burdens on interstate commerce, and not any marginal benefits from the scheme the State established as opposed to that the plaintiffs desire.

The difficulties with the contrary approach are patent. While it may be clear that there are substantial safety benefits from a 55-foot truck as compared to a 105-foot truck, these benefits may not be discernible in 5-foot jumps. Appellee's approach would permit what could not be accomplished in one lawsuit to be done in 10 separate suits, each challenging an additional five feet. . . .

[Striking] down Iowa's law because Consolidated has made a voluntary business decision to employ 65-foot doubles, a decision based on the actions of other state legislatures, would essentially be compelling Iowa to yield to the policy choices of neighboring States. Under our constitutional scheme, however, there is only one legislative body which can preempt the rational policy determination of the Iowa Legislature and that is Congress. Forcing Iowa to yield to the policy choices of neighboring States perverts the primary purpose of the Commerce Clause, that of vesting power to regulate interstate commerce in Congress, where all the States are represented. . . .

Both the plurality and concurring opinions attach great significance to the Governor's veto of a bill passed by the Iowa Legislature permitting 65-foot doubles. [The] law which the Court strikes down today was not passed to achieve the protectionist goals the plurality and the concurrence ascribe to the Governor. Iowa's 60-foot length limit was established in 1963, at a time when very few States permitted 65-foot doubles. Striking down legislation on the basis of asserted legislative motives is dubious enough, but the plurality and concurrence strike down the legislation involved in this case because of asserted impermissible motives for *not* enacting *other* legislation, motives which could not possibly have been present when the legislation under challenge here was considered and passed. Such action is, so far as I am aware, unprecedented in this Court's history.

Furthermore, the effort in both the plurality and concurring opinions to portray the legislation involved here as protectionist is in error. Whenever a State enacts more stringent safety measures than its neighbors, in an area which affects commerce, the safety law will have the incidental effect of deflecting interstate commerce to the neighboring States. Indeed, the safety and protectionist motives cannot be separated: The whole purpose of safety regulation of vehicles is to *protect* the State from unsafe vehicles. If a neighboring State chooses *not* to protect its citizens from the danger discerned by the enacting State, that is its business, but the enacting State should not be penalized when the vehicles it considers unsafe travel through the neighboring State. . . .

Note: Facially Neutral Statutes with (Merely?) Disproportionate Effects for Police Power Purposes

1. *Discrimination?* Did Iowa discriminate against interstate commerce? Are any of the in-staters who benefit from the statute competitors of out-of-staters who bear its costs? Are there nondiscriminatory explanations for the exceptions in the statute? (Is the "farm vehicles" exemption relevant at all?) Justice Rehnquist argues that the existence of an undue burden triggers inquiry into whether the regulation is a pretext for discrimination but does not in itself establish a commerce clause violation. Is that an accurate characterization of the cases you have read?

Is the evidence of discriminatory intent more persuasive in *Kassel* than in *Exxon?* Is the social purpose of the statute in *Exxon,* to preserve corner gas stations from absorption into the major oil producers, more substantial than the social purpose of the statute in *Kassel?* Is the statute in *Exxon* more likely to accomplish its purposes than the statute in *Kassel?* Regan, The Supreme Court and State Protectionism: Making Sense of the Dormant Commerce Clause, 84 Mich. L. Rev. 1091, 1185 (1986), argues that the Supreme Court should protect the national transportation network from state legislation that places excessive burdens on it because in such cases "there is a national interest in the existence of an effective transportation network linking the states." Should *Kassel* be treated as a transportation case in this sense? Should *Exxon?*

2. *Economic isolationism?* If Iowa's statute is treated as nondiscriminatory, what benefits does it provide? Does it enhance safety in Iowa? In the region? Justice Brennan says that Iowa must bear its "fair share" of safety problems in the region. Suppose Iowa provides so little maintenance on its highways that shippers choose to send their trucks on routes through Missouri. Would Iowa's policy violate the commerce clause? If not, how might Justice Brennan distinguish that policy from the prohibition on sixty-five-foot trucks?

3. *"Obstructing" commerce.* In Buck v. Kuykendall, 267 U.S. 307 (1925), Buck, a citizen of Washington, wished to operate an "auto stage" line between Portland, Oregon, and Seattle, Washington. After obtaining a license from Oregon, he applied to the Washington authorities for a certificate that would allow him to begin operations. The certificate was denied on the ground that the route was already adequately served by railroads and four other auto stage lines. The Court held that the denial violated the commerce clause. The purpose was "the prohibition of competition." Its

effect was "not merely to burden [interstate commerce], but to obstruct it." The Court also noted that the prohibition "[defeated] the purpose of Congress" in legislation providing federal aid for highway construction.

Aside from preemption, why should Washington be barred from limiting competition in transportation? Who bears the burdens and gains the benefits of Washington's statute? Assuming that the statute protects existing carriers from competition, is it protectionist in the sense of promoting local carriers at the expense of out-of-state ones? Does the case rest on the proposition that the Constitution embodies a substantive preference for free trade sufficient to place the burden of overcoming congressional inertia on those who support regulations that have significant, though nondiscriminatory, effects on interstate commerce?

4. *Judicial capacity.* Consider Justice Souter's observation in Department of Revenue of Kentucky v. Davis, 553 U.S. 328 (2008), about the limited capacity of the courts to engage in "cost-benefit analysis":

> What is most significant about these cost-benefit questions is not even the difficulty of answering them or the inevitable uncertainty of the predictions that might be made in trying to come up with answers, but the unsuitability of the judicial process and judicial forums for making whatever predictions and reaching whatever answers are possible at all. While it is not our business to suggest that the current system be reconsidered, if it is to be placed in question a congressional forum has two advantages. Congress has some hope of acquiring more complete information than adversary trials may produce, and an elected legislature is the preferable institution for incurring the economic risks of any alteration in the way things have traditionally been done.

5. *Congressional intervention.* Do *Southern Pacific* and *Kassel* turn on implicit decisions that, under *Cooley*, the regulation of train and truck lengths is an inherently national subject? Who should bear the burden of persuading Congress that length regulation is desirable or undesirable?

In 1981, Congress enacted the Economic Recovery Tax Act, which substantially reduced individual income tax rates. In 1982, it enacted the Surface Transportation Act. One provision of the act recaptured some of the revenue lost in 1981 by increasing the excise tax on trucks and the tax on gasoline and diesel fuel. Trucking interests opposed these increased taxes but withdrew their opposition in exchange for another provision in the act eliminating the restrictions states placed on the use of doubles on interstate highways, to take effect in 1984. Although the increased tax on gasoline went into effect relatively quickly, collection of the excise tax on trucks was deferred until 1985 because of technical difficulties in defining truck weights. A 1984 amendment to the act allows the Secretary of Transportation, rather than the states, to invoke safety reasons for excluding doubles from some portions of the interstate system. Governors may petition the Secretary for such an exclusion and must demonstrate that the safety reasons are genuine. In addition, the Secretary may, with the permission of a state's governor, open primary noninterstate highways to doubles. Is this congressional action relevant to the constitutional issues discussed in the cases?

Note: Taxation of Interstate Commerce

Consider Commonwealth Edison Co. v. Montana, 453 U.S. 609 (1981). In 1975, Montana imposed a tax on the severance of coal. The rate of 30 percent of the contract sales price was substantially higher than the rate of similar severance taxes in most other states. The proceeds of the tax were to be put into a permanent trust fund from which appropriations of principal could be made only by a three-fourths vote of both houses of the state legislature. The tax produced almost 20 percent of the state's revenue. Montana has 25 percent of the nation's coal reserves and over 50 percent of its low-sulfur coal reserves. Low-sulfur coal can be burned to produce electricity while complying with environmental regulations in plants that do not require extensive modification. Approximately 90 percent of the coal is shipped out of state.

The Court rejected a commerce clause challenge to the tax. It applied a four-part test as stated in Complete Auto Transit v. Brady, 430 U.S. 274 (1977): The tax must be "applied to an activity with a substantial nexus with the taxing State, [must be] fairly apportioned, [must] not discriminate against interstate commerce, and [must be] fairly related to services provided by the State." On the discrimination issue, the Court said:

> [The] Montana tax is computed at the same rate regardless of the final destination of the coal, and there is no suggestion here that tax is administered in a manner that departs from this evenhanded formula. We are not, therefore, confronted here with the type of differential tax treatment of interstate and intrastate commerce that the Court has found in other "discrimination" cases. [Philadelphia v. New Jersey.]
>
> Instead, the gravamen of appellants' claim is that a state tax must be considered discriminatory for purposes of the Commerce Clause if the tax burden is borne primarily by out-of-state consumers. . . .
>
> [There] is no real discrimination in this case; the tax burden is borne according to the amount of coal consumed and not according to any distinction between in-state and out-of-state consumers. Rather, appellants assume that the Commerce Clause gives residents of one State a right of access at reasonable prices to resources located in another State that is richly endowed with such resources, without regard to whether and on what terms residents of the resource-rich State have access to resources. We are not convinced that the Commerce Clause, of its own force, gives the residents of one State the right to control in this fashion the terms of resource development and depletion in a sister State.[8] Cf. [Philadelphia v. New Jersey].[18]

8. Nor do we share appellants' apparent view that the Commerce Clause injects principles of antitrust law into the relations between the States by reference to such imprecise standards as whether one State is "exploiting" its "monopoly" position with respect to a natural resource when the flow of commerce among them is not otherwise impeded. The threshold questions whether a State enjoys a "monopoly" position and whether the tax burden is shifted out of state, rather than borne by in-state producers and consumers, would require complex factual inquiries about such issues as elasticity of demand for the product and alternative sources of supply. Moreover, under this approach, the constitutionality of a state tax could well turn on whether the in-state producer is able, through sales contracts or otherwise, to shift the burden of the tax forward to its out-of-state customers. . . .

18. The controversy over the Montana tax has not escaped the attention of the Congress. Several bills were introduced during the 96th Congress to limit the rate of state severance taxes. Similar bills have been introduced in the 97th Congress.

The Court also rejected a preemption argument. Justice White began his concurring opinion by calling the case "very troublesome," but concluded:

> Congress has the power to protect interstate commerce from intolerable or even undesirable burdens. It is also very much aware of the Nation's energy needs, of the Montana tax, and of the trend in the energy-rich States to aggrandize their position and perhaps lessen the tax burdens on their own citizens by imposing unusually high taxes on mineral extraction. But Congress is so far content to let the matter rest.

Complete Auto Transit shows that the stated tests in cases challenging taxes as undue burdens on interstate commerce differ from the stated tests in cases challenging regulations. Should they? The doctrines applying the commerce clause to state taxes are extremely complex, but *Complete Auto Transit* and *Commonwealth Edison* suggest that doctrines regarding taxes and regulations are in the process of converging. Did Justice White properly allocate the burden of securing congressional action?

Comptroller of the Treasury of Maryland v. Wynne, 135 S. Ct. 1787 (2015), held unconstitutional portions of Maryland's income tax statute because it *might* lead to double taxation. Compare this with the Court's concern for conflicts among state regulations in *Bibb* and similar cases.

In connection with inferences from Congress's failure to act, consider the implications of the following sequence of cases. National Bellas Hess, Inc. v. Department of Revenue, 386 U.S. 753 (1967), held unconstitutional attempts by states to collect use taxes not from purchasers but from out-of-state mail-order sellers who had neither outlets nor sales representatives in the state. The Court held that the states violated the due process clause of the fourteenth amendment in attempting to tax entities that had insufficient connections with them. It also held that requiring the sellers to collect the use taxes imposed an unconstitutional burden on interstate commerce. Note that the due process holding probably (why only probably?) barred Congress from enacting a statute allowing states to require mail-order sellers to collect use taxes.

In Quill Corp. v. North Dakota, 504 U.S. 298 (1992), the Supreme Court revisited this issue. It overruled the due process holding of *National Bellas Hess* but reaffirmed the commerce clause holding. Five justices joined an opinion by Justice Stevens that justified the result on the ground that it developed a "bright-line rule" to

> demarcat[e] a discrete realm of commercial activity that is free from interstate taxation. [Like] other bright-line tests, the *Bellas Hess* rule appears artificial at the edges. [This] artificiality, however, is more than offset by the benefits of a clear rule. Such a rule firmly establishes the boundaries of legitimate state authority to impose a duty to collect sales and use taxes and reduces litigation concerning those taxes.

Justice Scalia, joined by Justices Kennedy and Thomas, concurred in the result, relying entirely on stare decisis considerations regarding the commerce clause holding.

Justice Stevens's opinion concluded by pointing out that the issue was "not only one that Congress may be better qualified to resolve, but also one that Congress has the ultimate power to resolve." It also noted that congressional inaction might have been "dictated" by the due process holding in *National Bellas Hess,* "but today we have put that problem to rest. Accordingly, Congress is now free to decide whether, when, and to what extent the States may burden interstate mail-order concerns with a duty to collect use taxes."

E.   PREEMPTION

Arizona v. United States

567 U.S. 387 (2012)

JUSTICE KENNEDY delivered the opinion of the Court.

[Arizona's S.B. 1070 contained several provisions whose enforcement the United States sought to enjoin on the ground that they were preempted by federal immigration law. Section 3 made failure to comply with federal alien-registration requirements a state misdemeanor. Section 5 made it a misdemeanor for an unauthorized alien to seek or engage in work in Arizona. (The U.S. government sought to enjoin the enforcement of several other provisions of S.B. 1070; the Court's analysis of those provisions is omitted.)] . . .

II

A

The Government of the United States has broad, undoubted power over the subject of immigration and the status of aliens. . . .

[Immigration] policy can affect trade, investment, tourism, and diplomatic relations for the entire Nation, as well as the perceptions and expectations of aliens in this country who seek the full protection of its laws. Perceived mistreatment of aliens in the United States may lead to harmful reciprocal treatment of American citizens abroad. . . .

Federal governance of immigration and alien status is extensive and complex. . . .

Discretion in the enforcement of immigration law embraces immediate human concerns. Unauthorized workers trying to support their families, for example, likely pose less danger than alien smugglers or aliens who commit a serious crime. The equities of an individual case may turn on many factors, including whether the alien has children born in the United States, long ties to the community, or a record of distinguished military service. Some discretionary decisions involve policy choices that bear on this Nation's international relations. Returning an alien to his own country may be deemed inappropriate even where he has committed a removable offense or fails to meet the criteria for admission. The foreign state may be mired in civil war, complicit in political persecution, or enduring conditions that create a real risk that the alien or his family will be harmed upon return. The dynamic nature of relations with other countries requires the Executive Branch to ensure that enforcement policies are consistent with this Nation's foreign policy with respect to these and other realities. . . .

B

The pervasiveness of federal regulation does not diminish the importance of immigration policy to the States. Arizona bears many of the consequences of unlawful immigration. Hundreds of thousands of deportable aliens are apprehended in Arizona each year. . . .

Statistics alone do not capture the full extent of Arizona's concerns. Accounts in the record suggest there is an "epidemic of crime, safety risks, serious property damage, and environmental problems" associated with the influx of illegal migration across private land near the Mexican border. . . .

These concerns are the background for the formal legal analysis that follows. The issue is whether, under preemption principles, federal law permits Arizona to implement the state-law provisions in dispute.

III

Federalism, central to the constitutional design, adopts the principle that both the National and State Governments have elements of sovereignty the other is bound to respect. From the existence of two sovereigns follows the possibility that laws can be in conflict or at cross-purposes. The Supremacy Clause provides a clear rule that federal law "shall be the supreme Law of the Land; and the Judges in every State shall be bound thereby, any Thing in the Constitution or Laws of any State to the Contrary notwithstanding." Art. VI, cl. 2. Under this principle, Congress has the power to preempt state law. There is no doubt that Congress may withdraw specified powers from the States by enacting a statute containing an express preemption provision.

State law must also give way to federal law in at least two other circumstances. First, the States are precluded from regulating conduct in a field that Congress, acting within its proper authority, has determined must be regulated by its exclusive governance. The intent to displace state law altogether can be inferred from a framework of regulation "so pervasive . . . that Congress left no room for the States to supplement it" or where there is a "federal interest . . . so dominant that the federal system will be assumed to preclude enforcement of state laws on the same subject." Rice v. Santa Fe Elevator Corp., 331 U.S. 218, 230 (1947).

Second, state laws are preempted when they conflict with federal law. This includes cases where "compliance with both federal and state regulations is a physical impossibility," Florida Lime & Avocado Growers, Inc. v. Paul, 373 U.S. 132, 142–143 (1963), and those instances where the challenged state law "stands as an obstacle to the accomplishment and execution of the full purposes and objectives of Congress," Hines [v. Davidowitz], 312 U.S. [52], 67 (1941). In preemption analysis, courts should assume that "the historic police powers of the States" are not superseded "unless that was the clear and manifest purpose of Congress." [Rice]. . . .

IV

A

Section 3

Section 3 [adds] a state-law penalty for conduct proscribed by federal law. . . .

The framework enacted by Congress leads to the conclusion [that] the Federal Government has occupied the field of alien registration. [Where] Congress occupies an entire field, as it has in the field of alien registration, even complementary state regulation is impermissible. Field preemption reflects a congressional decision to foreclose any state regulation in the area, even if it is parallel to federal standards. . . .

B

Section 5(C)

Unlike §3, which replicates federal statutory requirements, §5(C) enacts a state criminal prohibition where no federal counterpart exists. The provision makes it a state misdemeanor for "an unauthorized alien to knowingly apply for work, solicit work in a public place or perform work as an employee or independent contractor" in Arizona. . . .

[Congress] enacted [the Immigration Reform and Control Act] as a comprehensive framework for "combating the employment of illegal aliens." The law makes it illegal for employers to knowingly hire, recruit, refer, or continue to employ unauthorized workers. It also requires every employer to verify the employment authorization status of prospective employees. These requirements are enforced through criminal penalties and an escalating series of civil penalties tied to the number of times an employer has violated the provisions.

This comprehensive framework does not impose federal criminal sanctions on the employee side (*i.e.*, penalties on aliens who seek or engage in unauthorized work). Under federal law some civil penalties are imposed instead. With certain exceptions, aliens who accept unlawful employment are not eligible to have their status adjusted to that of a lawful permanent resident. Aliens also may be removed from the country for having engaged in unauthorized work. . . .

IRCA's express preemption provision, which in most instances bars States from imposing penalties on employers of unauthorized aliens, is silent about whether additional penalties may be imposed against the employees themselves. But the existence of an "express pre-emption provisio[n] does *not* bar the ordinary working of conflict pre-emption principles" or impose a "special burden" that would make it more difficult to establish the preemption of laws falling outside the clause. Geier v. American Honda Motor Co., 529 U.S. 861, 869–872 (2000).

The ordinary principles of preemption include the well-settled proposition that a state law is preempted where it "stands as an obstacle to the accomplishment and execution of the full purposes and objectives of Congress." [*Hines*]. Under §5(C) of S.B. 1070, Arizona law would interfere with the careful balance struck by Congress with respect to unauthorized employment of aliens. Although §5(C) attempts to achieve one of the same goals as federal law — the deterrence of unlawful employment — it involves a conflict in the method of enforcement. The Court has recognized that a "[c]onflict in technique can be fully as disruptive to the system Congress enacted as conflict in overt policy." Motor Coach Employees v. Lockridge, 403 U.S. 274, 287 (1971). The correct instruction to draw from the text, structure, and history of IRCA is that Congress decided it would be inappropriate to impose criminal penalties on aliens who seek or engage in unauthorized employment. It follows that a state law to the contrary is an obstacle to the regulatory system Congress chose. . . .

[The Court's analysis of the other challenged sections of S.B. 1070 is omitted].

V . . .

The National Government has significant power to regulate immigration. With power comes responsibility, and the sound exercise of national power over immigration depends on the Nation's meeting its responsibility to base its laws on a political will informed by searching, thoughtful, rational civic discourse. Arizona may have understandable frustrations with the problems caused by illegal immigration while that process continues, but the State may not pursue policies that undermine federal law.

* * *

The judgment of the Court of Appeals for the Ninth Circuit is affirmed in part and reversed in part. . . .

JUSTICE KAGAN took no part in the consideration or decision of this case.

JUSTICE SCALIA, dissenting in [relevant] part.
The United States is an indivisible "Union of sovereign States." Hinderlider v. La Plata River & Cherry Creek Ditch Co., 304 U.S. 92, 104 (1938). Today's opinion, approving virtually all of the Ninth Circuit's injunction against enforcement of the four challenged provisions of Arizona's law, deprives States of what most would consider the defining characteristic of sovereignty: the power to exclude from the sovereign's territory people who have no right to be there. Neither the Constitution itself nor even any law passed by Congress supports this result. I dissent. . . .

II . . .

[I] accept as a given that State regulation is excluded by the Constitution when (1) it has been prohibited by a valid federal law, or (2) it conflicts with federal regulation — when, for example, it admits those whom federal regulation would exclude, or excludes those whom federal regulation would admit.
Possibility (1) need not be considered here: there is no federal law prohibiting the States' sovereign power to exclude (assuming federal authority to enact such a law). The mere existence of federal action in the immigration area — and the so-called field preemption arising from that action, upon which the Court's opinion so heavily relies — cannot be regarded as such a prohibition. We are not talking here about a federal law prohibiting the States from regulating bubble-gum advertising, or even the construction of nuclear plants. We are talking about a federal law going to the *core* of state sovereignty: the power to exclude. . . .
Nor can federal power over illegal immigration be deemed exclusive because of what the Court's opinion solicitously calls "foreign countries['] concern[s] about the status, safety, and security of their nationals in the United States." [Even] in its international relations, the Federal Government must live with the inconvenient fact that it is a Union of independent States, who have their own sovereign powers. [Though] it may upset foreign powers — and even when the Federal Government desperately wants to avoid upsetting foreign powers — the States have the right to protect their borders against foreign nationals. . . .

JUSTICE THOMAS, dissenting in [relevant] part. . . .

[There] is no conflict between the "ordinary meanin[g]" of the relevant federal laws and that of the four provisions of Arizona law at issue here. . . .

Despite the lack of any conflict between the ordinary meaning of the Arizona law and that of the federal laws at issue here, the Court holds that various provisions of the Arizona law are pre-empted because they "stan[d] as an obstacle to the accomplishment and execution of the full purposes and objectives of Congress." [*Hines*]. [The] "purposes and objectives" theory of implied pre-emption is inconsistent with the Constitution because it invites courts to engage in freewheeling speculation about congressional purpose that roams well beyond statutory text. Under the Supremacy Clause, pre-emptive effect is to be given to congressionally enacted laws, not to judicially divined legislative purposes. Thus, even assuming the existence of some tension between Arizona's law and the supposed "purposes and objectives" of Congress, I would not hold that any of the provisions of the Arizona law at issue here are pre-empted on that basis.

JUSTICE ALITO, dissenting in [relevant] part. . . .

Not only is there little evidence that Congress intended to pre-empt state laws like §5(C), there is some evidence that Congress intended the opposite result. In making it unlawful for employers to hire unauthorized aliens, Congress made it clear that "any State or local law imposing civil or criminal sanctions (other than through licensing and similar laws)" upon employers was pre-empted, [8 U.S.C.] §1324a(h)(2). Noticeably absent is any similar directive pre-empting state or local laws targeting aliens who seek or obtain unauthorized employment. Given that Congress expressly pre-empted certain state and local laws pertaining to employers but remained silent about laws pertaining to employees, one could infer that Congress intended to preserve state and local authority to regulate the employee side of the equation. At the very least, it raises serious doubts about whether Congress intended to pre-empt such authority.

The Court dismisses any inferences that might be drawn from the express pre-emption provision. But even though the existence of that provision "does *not* bar the ordinary working of conflict pre-emption principles" or impose a "'special burden'" against pre-emption, Geier v. American Honda Motor Co., 529 U.S. 861, 869–870 (2000), it is still probative of congressional intent. . . .

The Court infers from Congress' decision not to impose *federal* criminal penalties that Congress intended to pre-empt *state* criminal penalties. But given that the express pre-emption provision covers only state and local laws regulating *employers*, one could just as well infer that Congress did not intend to pre-empt state or local laws aimed at alien *employees* who unlawfully seek or obtain work. Surely Congress' decision not to extend its express pre-emption provision to state or local laws like §5(C) is more probative of its intent on the subject of pre-emption than its decision not to impose federal criminal penalties for unauthorized work. In any event, the point I wish to emphasize is that inferences can be drawn either way. There are no necessary inferences that point decisively for or against pre-emption. Therefore, if we take seriously that state employment regulation is a traditional state concern and can be pre-empted only on a showing of "clear and manifest" congressional intent as required by *De Canas*, then §5(C) must survive.

Notes: Preemption

Should Congress alone deal with state regulations that assertedly interfere with interstate commerce? According to the Court, "[The] question whether a certain state action is preempted by federal law is one of congressional intent. 'The purpose of Congress is the ultimate touch stone.'" Gade v. National Solid Wastes Management Association, 505 U.S. 88 (1992), citing Allis-Chalmers Corp. v. Lueck, 471 U.S. 202, 206 (1985).

The Court has distinguished three types of preemption. (1) Express preemption: Here a statute contains a provision specifically referring to preemption and indicating which state laws the national statute supplants. Note, however, that the courts will often be called on to interpret the precise scope of the express preemption provision, and that in doing so they may invoke more general concerns. (2) Field preemption: Here the scheme of federal regulation is "so pervasive as to make reasonable the inference that Congress left no room for the States to supplement it," Rice v. Santa Fe Elevator Corp., 331 U.S. 218, 230 (1947). (3) Conflict preemption: Here "compliance with both federal and state regulations is a physical impossibility," Florida Lime & Avocado Growers, Inc. v. Paul, 373 U.S. 132, 142–143 (1963), or state law "stands as an obstacle to the accomplishment and execution of the full purposes and objectives of Congress," Hines v. Davidowitz, 312 U.S. 52, 67 (1941). Arizona v. United States deals with the latter two forms of preemption, with Justice Alito's opinion addressing some issues arising from express preemption provisions.

1. *The statute-specificity of preemption.* Preemption decisions are often tied closely to the language and purposes of particular statutes. Compare these pairs of cases: (a)(1) Medtronic, Inc. v. Lohr, 518 U.S. 470 (1996), held that the preemption provision of the Medical Device Amendments of 1976 — which provides, "no State . . . may establish . . . any requirement which is different from, or in addition to, any requirement applicable" under the MDA to devices intended for human use "which relates to the safety or effectiveness of the device" — did not preempt state tort law claims of negligent design, negligent manufacturing, and failure to warn, as applied to a device that had received a form of fast-track approval by the Food and Drug Administration. (2) Riegel v. Medtronic, Inc., 552 U.S. 312 (2008), held that the MDA's preemption provision did preempt similar claims with respect to a device that had received a full-scale premarket approval.

(b)(1) Geier v. American Honda Motor Co., 529 U.S. 861 (2000), involved a preemption provision's savings clause, which stated that "compliance with" a federal safety standard did not preempt common law liability. The Court held that, though the savings clause applied only to state statutory regulations, ordinary conflict preemption principles barred the Geiers from pursuing their claim that Honda had negligently failed to equip their car with airbags. The applicable federal regulations, according to the Court, provided car makers with a range of choices for passive restraints during a phase-in period covering the Geiers' claims. (2) Williamson v. Mazda Motor, 562 U.S. 323 (2011), involved the same statute and held that ordinary conflict preemption principles did not require preemption of a claim that a car maker had negligently designed its minivan with lap belts rather than lap-and-shoulder belts for rear seats. The federal regulations, according to the Court, gave manufacturers a completely free choice among designs.

(c)(1) Wyeth v. Levine, 555 U.S. 555 (2009), held that federal law did not preempt claims for failure to warn about risks associated with a specific method of administering a federally regulated drug. (2) PLIVA v. Mensing, 564 U.S. 604 (2011), held that federal law preempted claims against the manufacturer of a generic drug for failure to warn about risks. The labels the generic-drug maker used copied those approved by the FDA for the patented drug, and the makers of generic drugs were prohibited from altering their labels on their own.

Understanding and evaluating these decisions requires close attention to details associated with each statute, its purposes, and its accompanying regulations.

2. *Conflict and express preemption.* Consider *Gade*, supra. Illinois enacted two laws dealing with the licensing of workers who handle solid waste, for the stated purpose of "promot[ing] job safety" and "protect[ing] life, limb, and property." The laws required workers to take forty hours of approved training in Illinois, pass a written examination, and complete an annual refresher course. Federal regulations under the Occupational Safety and Health Act required that the workers receive a minimum of forty hours of instruction off-site and a minimum of three days of field experience under the supervision of a trained supervisor. A sharply divided Court held that the federal regulations preempted the state laws. Justice O'Connor's opinion for the Court found the state laws impliedly preempted "as in conflict with the full purposes and objectives of the OSH Act," which indicated that "Congress intended to subject employers and employees to only one set of regulations." Justice Kennedy, in an opinion concurring in the judgment, would have found express preemption because Congress intended to displace state regulations even when, as he believed was true in *Gade*, there was no actual conflict between the state laws and the federal regulations. Justice Souter, joined by Justices Blackmun, Stevens, and Thomas, dissented. He relied on the "rule" that "traditional police powers of the State survive until Congress has made a purpose to preempt them clear."

Is the purpose of the state regulation in *Gade* workplace safety or safety of state citizens, including but not limited to workers? On what basis might the Court select the former characterization over the latter? Would the choice affect the result of the preemption analysis? Consider the proposition that dormant commerce clause concerns strongly influence the choice: National uniformity in workplace safety regulation is extremely important, whereas the varying social policies states might choose to pursue justify refraining from the broader characterization of the field.

3. *Federalism and preemption.* Individual justices' general attitudes about federalism may influence their decisions. Preemption decisions may be influenced by the same considerations that enter into dormant commerce clause decisions. For example, finding that federal statutes "occupy the field" in some area may not be significantly different from finding that the area is inherently national under *Cooley*. What result in *Gade* under the commerce clause?

4. A *"presumption against preemption"*? Rice v. Santa Fe Elevator Corp. states that there is a "presumption against preemption." If congressional intent is the touchstone, what is the source of that presumption? Should the presumption be invoked not only to determine field, conflict, or obstacle preemption, but also to interpret express preemption provisions? Justice Scalia has argued that it should not, and that express preemption provisions should be interpreted using "ordinary principles of statutory construction." Cipollone v. Liggett Group, 505 U.S. 504,

545 (1992). What is the argument *for* invoking the presumption in construing an express preemption provision?

The Court sometimes invokes and sometimes ignores the supposed presumption against preemption. For a discussion, see Young, "The Ordinary Diet of the Law": The Presumption against Preemption in the Roberts Court, 2012 Sup. Ct. Rev. 253.

5. *Characterizing preemption.* Each of the three types of preemption raises questions of characterization, in two directions: (1) What subjects did Congress expressly preempt, or what is the field that Congress has occupied? *Geier* involves a related question: What is the scope of a statutory savings clause? (2) Is the state regulation in question one that falls within the domain that Congress expressly preempted or occupied? What concerns influence the Court's approach to the characterization questions? Frequently the concerns that underlie dormant commerce clause analysis — national uniformity, interference with interstate commerce, preservation of a proper sphere for local regulation — affect the Court's decisions. For an overview of contemporary issues in preemption law, see Nelson, Preemption, 86 Va. L. Rev. 225 (2000).

6. *Field preemption.* Note the consequences of finding field preemption when there is no federal regulation of the specific matter state law attempts to regulate, as with work *by* undocumented immigrants in Arizona v. United States: There is no federal regulation with which the state law conflicts (otherwise preemption by conflict would occur); finding preemption therefore means that the matter is left unregulated by both federal and state law. Does that justify a strong presumption against preemption of this sort? What if a system of nonregulation makes social or economic sense? See Farmers Educational & Cooperative Union v. WDAY, Inc., 360 U.S. 525 (1959), holding that the Federal Communications Act, which required broadcasters to carry some political speeches without censoring them, occupied the field and therefore immunized broadcasters from liability under state libel laws.

7. *Preemption in the service of other interests.* Note the Court's discussion of the foreign-affairs implications of Arizona's regulation. Crosby v. National Foreign Trade Council, 530 U.S. 363 (2000), relied on a statute delegating broad power to the President to devise a strategy for imposing economic sanctions on Burma to induce it to improve its human rights performance as the basis for finding preempted a Massachusetts statute barring the state government's departments from buying goods or services from companies doing business with Burma. The state statute, the Court held, stood as an obstacle to the accomplishment of the federal statute's purposes, and was inconsistent with Congress's purpose of ensuring that the President would have flexibility in devising strategies for inducing Burma to improve its performance. See also Pennsylvania v. Nelson, 350 U.S. 497 (1956), which held that the federal Smith Act, prohibiting the knowing advocacy of the overthrow of the national government by force and violence, preempted the Pennsylvania Sedition Act. In contemporaneous decisions, the Court was influenced by first amendment concerns to construe the Smith Act fairly narrowly.

For an argument that Arizona v. United States exemplifies a distinctive form of "plenary power preemption," see Abrams, Plenary Power Preemption, 99 Va. L. Rev. 601 (2013). What subjects might be covered by such a doctrine, in addition to immigration/alienage and foreign affairs? In what sense is national power over such subjects "plenary" while national power over interstate commerce is not? How might "plenary power preemption" differ from "field preemption"?

8. *An overview.* Consider the following argument: The courts will consider issues about the scope of preemption only when there are reasonable arguments supporting competing characterizations of what Congress sought to accomplish in expressly preempting, occupying the field, or enacting regulations with which the state laws are said to conflict. No matter how detailed the statutory scheme, it will be applied (or at least litigated) in situations that Congress did not anticipate. The courts will therefore be called on to fill gaps. In dormant commerce clause cases, the courts may say, "Leave the problem to Congress." In preemption cases, however, Congress has acted, and saying "Leave it to Congress" amounts to imposing on Congress a requirement of explicitness, usually in cases where it is relatively easy to find that Congress had not acted explicitly enough to displace state regulation.

Note: Concluding Observations

Consider Justice Scalia's assessment of the law in this area, as expressed in his opinion dissenting in relevant part in Tyler Pipe Industries, Inc. v. Washington State Department of Revenue, 483 U.S. 232 (1987), where the Court held unconstitutional some provisions of Washington's system of taxing goods in interstate commerce. Justice Scalia argued that

> to the extent that we have gone beyond guarding against rank discrimination against citizens of other States — which is regulated not by the Commerce Clause but by the Privileges and Immunities Clause — the Court for over a century has engaged in an enterprise that it has been unable to justify by textual support or even coherent nontextual theory, that it was almost certainly not intended to undertake, and that it has not undertaken very well.

He noted that "preemption of state legislation would automatically follow [if] the grant of power to Congress to regulate interstate commerce were exclusive," but added that

> the language of the Commerce Clause gives no indication of exclusivity. Nor can one assume generally that Congress' Article I powers are exclusive. [Furthermore], there is no correlative denial of power over commerce to the States [as] there is [with] the power to coin money or make treaties. [The] exclusivity rationale is infinitely less attractive today than it was in 1847. Now that we know interstate commerce embraces such activities as growing wheat for home consumption [*Wickard*] and local loan sharking [Perez v. United States, section C supra], it is more difficult to imagine what state activity would survive an exclusive Commerce Clause than to imagine what would be precluded.

Justice Scalia argued that the Court could not distinguish, as *Cooley* attempted to, among the subjects of the commerce power because the Constitution treats commerce "as a unitary subject," or between preempting state laws "*intended* to regulate commerce (as opposed to those intended, for example, to promote health)," because the distinction was "metaphysical, [not] useful as a practical technique for marking out the powers of separate sovereigns." He called "least plausible" the theory that in enforcing the negative Commerce Clause the Court is not applying a constitutional command at all, but is merely interpreting the will of Congress, whose silence in certain fields of interstate commerce (but not in others) is to be taken as a prohibition of regulation. There is no conceivable reason why congressional inaction under the Commerce Clause should be deemed to have the same preemptive effect elsewhere accorded only to congressional action. There, as elsewhere, "Congress' silence is just that — silence."

Are there plausible answers to this criticism? Consider whether the law in this area might be justified as articulating a series of canons of construction to be applied to whatever federal legislation there is that regulates the subject matter of the state laws at issue.

III

The Scope of Congress's Powers: Taxing and Spending, War Powers, Individual Rights, and State Autonomy

The previous chapter explored the scope of Congress's power under the commerce clause, the dimensions of judicially enforceable limits on that power in the name of federalism, and the justifications for those limits. As we saw, for many years the commerce clause functioned almost as a plenary grant of power, at least insofar as Congress was seeking to regulate behavior that had some connection to economic activity. In fact, as the discussion of the commerce clause decisions upholding the validity of the Civil Rights Act of 1964, in Chapter 2, section C, supra, suggested, sometimes the commerce clause served as a mechanism for addressing problems that might at first blush have seemed more appropriately addressed by other constitutional provisions.

This pattern of pragmatic reliance on a variety of enumerated powers to circumvent potential judicial limitations on the scope of national regulation plays out with respect to a number of other specific powers as well. This chapter considers some of the most significant and often litigated powers. Section A considers Congress's deployment of its taxing and spending powers to influence behavior that it lacks the power to regulate directly, as well as examining briefly Congress's use of its war power to regulate domestic parties. (The distribution of warmaking authority between Congress and the president is taken up in Chapter 4.) Section B then considers Congress's powers under the enforcement clauses of the Reconstruction amendments. Section C looks at Congress's use of the treaty power to regulate domestic conduct. Finally, section D considers the question of whether the tenth amendment places any independent limitations on congressional power. With respect to each of the powers, consider the following questions, versions of which will be raised throughout: Is the scope of this power broader than, narrower than, or simply equivalent to, the scope of the commerce power? Are the political constraints on Congress different with respect to this provision, so that judicial review is either more or less appropriate than it is in commerce clause–based cases?

A.   REGULATION THROUGH TAXING, SPENDING, AND THE WAR POWER

The first clause of article I, section 8, gives Congress "Power to lay and collect Taxes" — the taxing power — and to "pay the Debts and provide for the common Defence and general Welfare of the United States" — referred to as the spending power. Can these powers be exercised only in the service of pursuing goals enumerated elsewhere in the Constitution — a view taken by James Madison — or can they serve as a more sweeping basis for national regulation?

1.   The Taxing Power

In Hammer v. Dagenhart, 247 U.S. 251 (1918), discussed in Chapter 2, section B, supra, the Supreme Court struck down the Child Labor Act, which prohibited the transportation in interstate commerce of goods produced in factories employing young children. The Court held that the Act was not at its core a regulation of interstate commerce but was instead an attempt to usurp the states' police power over working conditions. Congress responded by enacting the Child Labor Tax Act. The statute required that anyone who employed child labor, defined as it had been in the statute invalidated in *Hammer,* pay an excise tax equivalent to 10 percent of the entire net profits of the mine or factory. The clear effect of the tax would be to make child labor so economically unattractive that employers would decline to hire child workers.

Congress's strategy was seemingly based on the fact that in a series of then-recent cases, the Court had upheld various provisions of the Narcotic Drug Act of 1914 (often called the Harrison Act) that had also used the taxing power as a lever for attacking a moral issue. The Harrison Act required individuals connected with the production, importation, and distribution of opium- or coca leaf–based products to register with the Internal Revenue Service, pay a special tax, keep various records, and distribute such drugs only to persons who made orders on forms issued by the Commissioner of Internal Revenue. Section 2 of the Act made it a federal crime not to comply with the Act's various requirements. In United States v. Doremus, 249 U.S. 86 (1919), the Court upheld the indictment of a doctor under the Act for selling heroin to "a person popularly known as a 'dope fiend' . . . for the purpose of gratifying his appetite for the drug as an habitual user thereof." Justice Day's opinion for the Court rejected the argument that the Harrison Act exceeded Congress's power:

> The only limitation upon the power of Congress to levy excise taxes of the character now under consideration is geographical uniformity throughout the United States. [Subject] to such limitation Congress may select the subjects of taxation, and may exercise the power conferred at its discretion. Of course Congress may not in the exercise of federal power exert authority wholly reserved to the States. [And] from an early day the court has held that the fact that other motives may impel the exercise of federal taxing power does not authorize the courts to inquire into that subject. If the legislation enacted has some reasonable relation to the exercise of the taxing authority conferred by the Constitution, it cannot be invalidated because of the supposed motives which induced it. . . .
>
> The act may not be declared unconstitutional because its effect may be to accomplish another purpose as well as the raising of revenue. If the legislation is within the taxing authority of Congress — that is sufficient to sustain it.

[In an earlier decision construing the Harrison Act], we said: "It may be assumed that the statute has a moral end as well as revenue in view, but we are of opinion that the District Court, in treating those ends as to be reached only through a revenue measure and within the limits of a revenue measure, was right." United States v. Jin Fuey Moy, 241 U.S. 394, 402. Considering the full power of Congress over excise taxation the decisive question here is: Have the provisions in question any relation to the raising of revenue? That Congress might levy an excise tax upon such dealers, and others who are named in §1 of the act, cannot be successfully disputed. The provisions of §2, to which we have referred, aim to confine sales to registered dealers and to those dispensing the drugs as physicians, and to those who come to dealers with legitimate prescriptions of physicians. Congress, with full power over the subject, short of arbitrary and unreasonable action which is not to be assumed, inserted these provisions in an act specifically providing for the raising of revenue. Considered of themselves, we think they tend to keep the traffic above-board and subject to inspection by those authorized to collect the revenue. They tend to diminish the opportunity of unauthorized persons to obtain the drugs and sell them clandestinely without paying the tax imposed by the federal law. . . .

But in Bailey v. Drexel Furniture Co., 259 U.S. 20 (1922), the Supreme Court struck down the Child Labor Act. It posed the issue in this way: "Does this law impose a tax with only that incidental restraint and regulation which a tax must inevitably involve? Or does it regulate by the use of the so-called tax as a penalty?" The "detailed and specified course of conduct in business" set out in the act demonstrated its purpose, as did provisions authorizing inspection of factories and mines by the Department of Labor, "whose normal function is the advancement and protection of the welfare of workers. In the light of these features of the act, a court must be blind not to see that the so-called tax is imposed to stop the employment of children within the age limits prescribed. Its prohibitory and regulatory effect and purpose are palpable. All others can see and understand this. How can we properly shut our minds to it?"
The Court continued:

Grant the validity of this law, and all that Congress would need to do, hereafter, in seeking to take over to its control any one of the great number of subjects of public interest, jurisdiction of which the States have never parted with, and which are reserved to them by the Tenth Amendment, would be to enact a detailed measure of complete regulation of the subject and enforce it by a so-called tax upon departures from it. To give such magic to the word "tax" would be to break down all constitutional limitation of the powers of Congress and completely wipe out the sovereignty of the States.
[Where] the sovereign enacting the law has power to impose both tax and penalty the difference between revenue production and mere regulation may be immaterial, but not so when one sovereign can impose a tax only, and the power of regulation rests in another. . . . Although Congress does not invalidate the contract of employment or expressly declare that the employment within the mentioned ages is illegal, it does exhibit its intent practically to achieve the latter result by adopting the criteria of wrongdoing and imposing its principal consequence on those who transgress its standard.

The *Bailey* Court distinguished *Doremus* this way:

The court [in *Doremus*] said that the act could not be declared invalid just because another motive than taxation, not shown on the face of the act, might have contributed to its passage. This case does not militate against the conclusion we have reached in respect of the law now before us. The court, there, made manifest its view that the provisions of the so-called taxing act must be naturally and reasonably adapted to the collection of the tax and not solely to the achievement of some other purpose plainly within state power.

Are you persuaded that *Doremus* is distinguishable from *Bailey*?

Is the distinction between a penalty and a tax cogent? Does it turn on Congress's motive? Recall from the discussion of the commerce power in Chapter 2 that a "pretext" analysis requires a prior determination of the proper purposes for which a power may be exercised. Are the purposes of the power to tax more clearly defined than those of the power to regulate interstate commerce?

Many taxes serve both revenue-raising and regulatory purposes. Is it helpful to say that taxes must raise nontrivial amounts of revenue, even if they have a substantial regulatory effect? Rejecting a challenge to the federal occupational tax levied on people in the business of accepting bets in United States v. Kahriger, 345 U.S. 22 (1953), the Court listed cases in which it had upheld taxes on colored oleomargarine, McCray v. United States, 195 U.S. 27 (1904); on narcotics, United States v. Doremus, discussed supra; and on firearms, Sonzinsky v. United States, 300 U.S. 506 (1937). A footnote added:

> One of the indicia which appellee offers to support his contention that the wagering tax is not a proper revenue measure is that the tax amount collected under it was $4,371,869, as compared with an expected amount of $400,000,000 a year. The figure of $4,371,869, however, is relatively large when it is compared with the $3,501 collected under the tax on adulterated and process or renovated butter and filled cheese, the $914,910 collected under the tax on narcotics, including marihuana and special taxes, and the $28,911 collected under the tax on firearms, transfer and occupational taxes.

(The Court later held that the occupational tax violated the self-incrimination clause of the fifth amendment. Marchetti v. United States, 390 U.S. 39 (1968).)

National Federation of Independent Business v. Sebelius

567 U.S. 519 (2012)

CHIEF JUSTICE ROBERTS announced the judgment of the Court and delivered the opinion of the Court with respect to Par[t][III-C], [and] an opinion with respect to Par[t][III-B].

[A key provision of the Affordable Care Act of 2010 is the so-called individual mandate, which requires most Americans to maintain "minimum essential" health insurance coverage. Beginning in 2014, individuals who do not comply with the mandate must make a "[s]hared responsibility payment" to the Federal Government. The Act provides that this "penalty" will be paid to the Internal Revenue Service with an individual's taxes, and "shall be assessed and collected in the same manner" as tax penalties.]

III . . .

B . . .

The Government's tax power argument asks us to [read] the mandate not as ordering individuals to buy insurance, but rather as imposing a tax on those who do not buy that product.

The text of a statute can sometimes have more than one possible meaning. . . .

The most straightforward reading of the mandate is that it commands individuals to purchase insurance. After all, it states that individuals "shall" maintain health insurance. [Under] our precedent, it is therefore necessary to ask whether the Government's alternative reading of the statute — that it only imposes a tax on those without insurance — is a reasonable one.

Under the mandate, if an individual does not maintain health insurance, the only consequence is that he must make an additional payment to the IRS when he pays his taxes. That, according to the Government, means the mandate can be regarded as establishing a condition — not owning health insurance — that triggers a tax — the required payment to the IRS. Under that theory, the mandate is not a legal command to buy insurance. Rather, it makes going without insurance just another thing the Government taxes, like buying gasoline or earning income. And if the mandate is in effect just a tax hike on certain taxpayers who do not have health insurance, it may be within Congress's constitutional power to tax.

. . . [The] Government asks us to interpret the mandate as imposing a tax, if it would otherwise violate the Constitution. Granting the Act the full measure of deference owed to federal statutes, it can be so read, for the reasons set forth below.

C

The exaction the Affordable Care Act imposes on those without health insurance looks like a tax in many respects. The "[s]hared responsibility payment," as the statute entitles it, is paid into the Treasury by "taxpayer[s]" when they file their tax returns. It does not apply to individuals who do not pay federal income taxes because their household income is less than the filing threshold in the Internal Revenue Code. For taxpayers who do owe the payment, its amount is determined by such familiar factors as taxable income, number of dependents, and joint filing status. The requirement to pay is found in the Internal Revenue Code and enforced by the IRS, which — as we previously explained — must assess and collect it "in the same manner as taxes." This process yields the essential feature of any tax: it produces at least some revenue for the Government. [United States v. Kahriger.] Indeed, the payment is expected to raise about $4 billion per year by 2017. . . .

Our cases confirm this functional approach. For example, in [Bailey v.] Drexel Furniture Co., we focused on three practical characteristics of the so-called tax on employing child laborers that convinced us the "tax" was actually a penalty. First, the tax imposed an exceedingly heavy burden — 10 percent of a company's net income — on those who employed children, no matter how small their infraction. Second, it imposed that exaction only on those who knowingly employed underage laborers. Such scienter requirements are typical of punitive statutes, because Congress often wishes to punish only those who intentionally break the law. Third, this "tax" was enforced in part by the Department of Labor, an agency responsible for punishing violations of labor laws, not collecting revenue. The same analysis here suggests that the shared responsibility payment may for constitutional purposes be considered a tax, not a penalty: First, for most Americans the amount due will be far less than the price of insurance, and, by statute, it can never be more. It may often be a reasonable financial decision to make the payment rather than purchase insurance, unlike the "prohibitory" financial punishment in *Drexel Furniture*. Second, the individual mandate contains no scienter requirement. Third, the payment is collected solely by the IRS through the normal means of taxation — except that the Service is not allowed to use those means most suggestive of a punitive sanction, such as criminal prosecution. The reasons the Court in *Drexel Furniture* held that what was called a "tax" there was a penalty support the conclusion that what is called a "penalty" here may be viewed as a tax.

None of this is to say that the payment is not intended to affect individual conduct. Although the payment will raise considerable revenue, it is plainly designed to expand health insurance coverage. But taxes that seek to influence conduct are nothing new. Some of our earliest federal taxes sought to deter the purchase of imported manufactured goods in order to foster the growth of domestic industry. Today, federal and state taxes can compose more than half the retail price of cigarettes, not just to raise more money, but to encourage people to quit smoking. And we have upheld such obviously regulatory measures as taxes on selling marijuana and sawed-off shotguns. Indeed, "[e]very tax is in some measure regulatory. . . . That §5000A seeks to shape decisions about whether to buy health insurance does not mean that it cannot be a valid exercise of the taxing power. . . .

. . . [It] is estimated that four million people each year will choose to pay the IRS rather than buy insurance. We would expect Congress to be troubled by that prospect if such conduct were unlawful. That Congress apparently regards such extensive failure to comply with the mandate as tolerable suggests that Congress did not think it was creating four million outlaws. It suggests instead that the shared responsibility payment merely imposes a tax citizens may lawfully choose to pay in lieu of buying health insurance.

The joint dissenters argue that we cannot uphold §5000A as a tax because Congress did not "frame" it as such. In effect, they contend that even if the Constitution permits Congress to do exactly what we interpret this statute to do, the law must be struck down because Congress used the wrong labels. An example may help illustrate why labels should not control here. Suppose Congress enacted a statute providing that every taxpayer who owns a house without energy efficient windows must pay $50 to the IRS. The amount due is adjusted based on factors such as taxable income and joint filing status, and is paid along with the taxpayer's income tax return. Those whose income is below the filing threshold need not pay. The required payment is not called a "tax," a "penalty," or anything else. No one would doubt that this law imposed a tax, and was within Congress's power to tax. That conclusion should not change simply because Congress used the word "penalty" to describe the payment. Interpreting such a law to be a tax would hardly "[i]mpos[e] a tax through judicial legislation." Rather, it would give practical effect to the Legislature's enactment. . . .

There may, however, be a more fundamental objection to a tax on those who lack health insurance. Even if only a tax, the payment under §5000A(b) remains a burden that the Federal Government imposes for an omission, not an act. If it is troubling to interpret the Commerce Clause as authorizing Congress to regulate those who abstain from commerce, perhaps it should be similarly troubling to permit Congress to impose a tax for not doing something.

Three considerations allay this concern. First, and most importantly, it is abundantly clear the Constitution does not guarantee that individuals may avoid taxation through inactivity. A capitation, after all, is a tax that everyone must pay simply for existing, and capitations are expressly contemplated by the Constitution. The Court today holds that our Constitution protects us from federal regulation under the Commerce Clause so long as we abstain from the regulated activity. But from its creation, the Constitution has made no such promise with respect to taxes. . . .

Congress's use of the Taxing Clause to encourage buying something is, by contrast [to its use of the commerce power], not new. Tax incentives already promote, for example, purchasing homes and professional educations. Sustaining the mandate as a tax depends only on whether Congress *has* properly exercised its taxing power to encourage purchasing health insurance, not whether it *can*. Upholding the individual mandate under the Taxing Clause thus does not recognize any new federal power. It determines that Congress has used an existing one.

Second, Congress's ability to use its taxing power to influence conduct is not without limits. A few of our cases policed these limits aggressively, invalidating punitive exactions obviously designed to regulate behavior otherwise regarded at the time as beyond federal authority. . . .

We have already explained that the shared responsibility payment's practical characteristics pass muster as a tax under our narrowest interpretations of the taxing power. Because the tax at hand is within even those strict limits, we need not here decide the precise point at which an exaction becomes so punitive that the taxing power does not authorize it. It remains true, however, that the "power to tax is not the power to destroy while this Court sits" [Panhandle Oil Co. v. Mississippi ex rel. Knox, 277 U.S. 218 (1928) (Holmes, J., dissenting)].

Third, although the breadth of Congress's power to tax is greater than its power to regulate commerce, the taxing power does not give Congress the same degree of control over individual behavior. Once we recognize that Congress may regulate a particular decision under the Commerce Clause, the Federal Government can bring its full weight to bear. Congress may simply command individuals to do as it directs. An individual who disobeys may be subjected to criminal sanctions. Those sanctions can include not only fines and imprisonment, but all the attendant consequences of being branded a criminal: deprivation of otherwise protected civil rights, such as the right to bear arms or vote in elections; loss of employment opportunities; social stigma; and severe disabilities in other controversies, such as custody or immigration disputes.

By contrast, Congress's authority under the taxing power is limited to requiring an individual to pay money into the Federal Treasury, no more. If a tax is properly paid, the Government has no power to compel or punish individuals subject to it. We do not make light of the severe burden that taxation — especially taxation motivated by a regulatory purpose — can impose. But imposition of a tax nonetheless leaves an individual with a lawful choice to do or not do a certain act, so long as he is willing to pay a tax levied on that choice.

The Affordable Care Act's requirement that certain individuals pay a financial penalty for not obtaining health insurance may reasonably be characterized as a tax. Because the Constitution permits such a tax, it is not our role to forbid it, or to pass upon its wisdom or fairness. . . .

———————

Justices Scalia, Kennedy, Thomas, and Alito dissented. They argued that the statutory provision could not fairly be understood to impose a tax, and therefore they did not reach the question whether the statute was a constitutionally permissible exercise of the taxing power. They observed that the question of whether the sanction, if it were a tax, was a direct one (thereby running afoul of article I, section 3) had not been adequately briefed or argued.

2.   *The Spending Power*

United States v. Butler

297 U.S. 1 (1936)

ensure products sold at fair price

[The Agricultural Adjustment Act of 1933 was designed to stabilize production in agriculture by assuring farmers that their products would be sold at a fair price. The act imposed a tax on processors of agricultural commodities such as cotton. The proceeds of the tax were to be used to subsidize farmers who agreed to restrict their production.]

MR. JUSTICE ROBERTS delivered the opinion of the Court. . . .

There should be no misunderstanding as to the function of this court in such a case. It is sometimes said that the court assumes a power to overrule or control the action of the people's representatives. This is a misconception. The Constitution is the supreme law of the land ordained and established by the people. All legislation must conform to the principles it lays down. When an act of Congress is appropriately challenged in the courts as not conforming to the constitutional mandate the judicial branch of the Government has only one duty, — to lay the article of the Constitution which is invoked beside the statute which is challenged and to decide whether the latter squares with the former. All the court does, or can do, is to announce its considered judgment upon the question. The only power it has, if such it may be called, is the power of judgment. This court neither approves nor condemns any legislative policy. Its delicate and difficult office is to ascertain and declare whether the legislation is in accordance with, or in contravention of, the provisions of the Constitution; and, having done that, its duty ends.

The question is not what power the Federal Government ought to have but what powers in fact have been given by the people. [The] federal union is a government of delegated powers. It has only such as are expressly conferred upon it and such as are reasonably to be implied from those granted. . . .

The clause thought to authorize the legislation [confers] upon the Congress power "to lay and collect Taxes, Duties, Imposts and Excises, to pay the Debts and provide for the common Defence and general Welfare of the United States. . . ." It is not contended that this provision grants power to regulate agricultural production upon the theory that such legislation would promote the general welfare. . . . The view that the clause grants power to provide for the general welfare, independently of the taxing power, has never been authoritatively accepted. . . .

Nevertheless the Government asserts that warrant is found in this clause for the adoption of the Agricultural Adjustment Act. The argument is that Congress may appropriate and authorize the spending of moneys for the "general welfare"; that the phrase should be liberally construed to cover anything conducive to national welfare; that decision as to what will promote such welfare rests with Congress alone, and the courts may not review its determination; and finally that the appropriation under attack was in fact for the general welfare of the United States. . . .

Since the foundation of the Nation sharp differences of opinion have persisted as to the true interpretation of the phrase. Madison asserted it amounted to no more than a reference to the other powers enumerated in the subsequent clauses of the same section; that, as the United States is a government of limited and enumerated powers, the grant of power to tax and spend for the general national welfare must be confined to the enumerated legislative fields committed to the Congress. In this view the phrase is mere tautology, for taxation and appropriation are or may be necessary incidents of the exercise of any of the enumerated legislative powers. Hamilton, on the other hand, maintained the clause confers a power separate and distinct from those later enumerated, is not restricted in meaning by the grant of them, and Congress consequently has a substantive power to tax and to appropriate, limited only by the requirement that it shall be exercised to provide for the general welfare of the United States. [We] conclude that the reading advocated by [Hamilton] is the correct one. While, therefore, the power to tax is not unlimited, its confines are set in the clause which confers it, and not in those of §8 which bestow and define the legislative powers of the Congress. It results that the power of Congress to authorize expenditure of public moneys for public purposes is not limited by the direct grants of legislative power found in the Constitution.

But the adoption of the broader construction leaves the power to spend subject to limitations. . . .

We are not now required to ascertain the scope of the phrase "general welfare of the United States" or to determine whether an appropriation in aid of agriculture falls within it. Wholly apart from that question, another principle embedded in our Constitution prohibits the enforcement of the Agricultural Adjustment Act. The act invades the reserved rights of the states. It is a statutory plan to regulate and control agricultural production, a matter beyond the powers delegated to the federal government. The tax, the appropriation of the funds raised, and the direction for their disbursement, are but parts of the plan. They are but means to an unconstitutional end. . . .

At best [the act] is a scheme for purchasing with federal funds submission to federal regulation of a subject reserved to the states. . . .

Congress has no power to enforce its commands on the farmer to the ends sought by the Agricultural Adjustment Act. It must follow that it may not indirectly accomplish those ends by taxing and spending to purchase compliance. The Constitution and the entire plan of our government negative any such use of the power to tax and to spend as the act undertakes to authorize. It does not help to declare that local conditions throughout the nation have created a situation of national concern; for this is but to say that whenever there is a widespread similarity of local conditions, Congress may ignore constitutional limitations upon its own powers and usurp those reserved to the states. If, in lieu of compulsory regulation of subjects within the states' reserved jurisdiction, which is prohibited, the Congress could invoke the taxing and spending power as a means to accomplish the same end, clause 1 of §8 of Article I would become the instrument for total subversion of the governmental powers reserved to the individual states.

If the act before us is a proper exercise of the federal taxing power, evidently the regulation of all industry throughout the United States may be accomplished by similar exercises of the same power. It would be possible to exact money from one branch of an industry and pay it to another branch in every field of activity which lies within the province of the states. The mere threat of such a procedure might well induce the surrender of rights and the compliance with federal regulation as the price of continuance in business. A few instances will illustrate the thought.

Let us suppose Congress should determine that the farmer, the miner or some other producer of raw materials is receiving too much for his products, with consequent depression of the processing industry and idleness of its employees. Though, by confession, there is no power vested in Congress to compel by statute a lowering of the prices of the raw material, the same result might be accomplished, if the questioned act be valid, by taxing the producer upon his output and appropriating the proceeds to the processors, either with or without conditions imposed as the consideration for payment of the subsidy. . . .

Suppose that there are too many garment workers in the large cities; that this results in dislocation of the economic balance. Upon the principle contended for an excise might be laid on the manufacture of all garments manufactured and the proceeds paid to those manufacturers who agree to remove their plants to cities having not more than a hundred thousand population. Thus, through the asserted power of taxation, the federal government, against the will of individual states, might completely redistribute the industrial population. . . .

These illustrations are given, not to suggest that any of the purposes mentioned are unworthy, but to demonstrate the scope of the principle for which the Government contends; to test the principle by its applications; to point out that, by the exercise of the asserted power, Congress would, in effect, under the pretext of exercising the taxing power, in reality accomplish prohibited ends. It cannot be said that they envisage improbable legislation. The supposed cases are no more improbable than would the present act have been deemed a few years ago. . . .
[Affirmed.]

Mr. Justice Stone, dissenting. . . .
The power of courts to declare a statute unconstitutional is subject to two guiding principles of decision which ought never to be absent from judicial consciousness. One is that courts are concerned only with the power to enact statutes, not with their wisdom. The other is that while unconstitutional exercise of power by the executive and legislative branches of the government is subject to judicial restraint, the only check upon our own exercise of power is our own sense of self-restraint. For the removal of unwise laws from the statute books appeal lies not to the courts but to the ballot and to the processes of democratic government. . . .
[The] suggestion of coercion finds no support in the record or in any data showing the actual operation of the Act. Threat of loss, not hope of gain, is the essence of economic coercion. Members of a long depressed industry have undoubtedly been tempted to curtail acreage by the hope of resulting better prices and by the proffered opportunity to obtain needed ready money. . . .
It is upon the contention that state power is infringed by purchased regulation of agricultural production that chief reliance is placed. It is insisted that, while

the Constitution gives to Congress, in specific and unambiguous terms, the power to tax and spend, the power is subject to limitations which do not find their origin in any express provision of the Constitution and to which other expressly delegated powers are not subject.

The Constitution requires that public funds shall be spent for a defined purpose, the promotion of the general welfare. Their expenditure usually involves payment on terms which will insure use by the selected recipients within the limits of the constitutional purpose. Expenditures would fail of their purpose and thus lose their constitutional sanction if the terms of payment were not such that by their influence on the action of the recipients the permitted end would be attained. The power of Congress to spend is inseparable from persuasion to action over which Congress has no legislative control. Congress may not command that the science of agriculture be taught in state universities. But if it would aid the teaching of that science by grants to state institutions, it is appropriate [that] the grant be on the condition [that] it be used for the intended purpose. . . .

The limitation now sanctioned must lead to absurd consequences. The government may give seeds to farmers, but may not condition the gift upon their being planted in places where they are most needed or even planted at all. The government may give money to the unemployed, but may not ask that those who get it shall give labor in return, or even use it to support their families. It may give money to sufferers from earthquake, fire, tornado, pestilence or flood, but may not impose conditions — health precautions designed to prevent the spread of disease, or induce the movement of population to safer or more sanitary areas. All that, because it is purchased regulation infringing state powers, must be left for the states, who are unable or unwilling to supply the necessary relief. [If] the expenditure is for a national public purpose, that purpose will not be thwarted because payment is on condition which will advance that purpose. The action which Congress induces by payments of money to promote the general welfare, but which it does not command or coerce, is but an incident to a specifically granted power, but a permissible means to a legitimate end. If appropriation in aid of a program of curtailment of agricultural production is constitutional, and it is not denied that it is, payment to farmers on condition that they reduce their crop acreage is constitutional. It is not any the less so because the farmer at his own option promises to fulfill the condition.

That the governmental power of the purse is a great one is not now for the first time announced. . . .

The suggestion that it must now be curtailed by judicial fiat because it may be abused by unwise use hardly rises to the dignity of argument. [The] power to tax and spend is not without constitutional restraints. One restriction is that the purpose must be truly national. Another is that it may not be used to coerce action left to state control. Another is the conscience and patriotism of Congress and the Executive. "It must be remembered that legislators are the ultimate guardians of the liberties and welfare of the people in quite as great a degree as the courts." Justice Holmes, in Missouri, Kansas & Texas Ry. Co. v. May, 194 U.S. 267, 270.

A tortured construction of the Constitution is not to be justified by recourse to extreme examples of reckless congressional spending which might occur if courts could not prevent — expenditures which, even if they could be thought to effect any national purpose, would be possible only by action of a legislature lost to all sense of public responsibility. Such suppositions are addressed to the mind accustomed to believe that it is the business of courts to sit in judgment on the wisdom of legislative action. Courts are not the only agency of government that must be assumed to have capacity to govern. Congress and the courts both unhappily may falter or be mistaken in the performance of their constitutional duty. But interpretation of our great charter of government which proceeds on any assumption that the responsibility for the preservation of our institutions is the exclusive concern of any one of the three branches of government, or that it alone can save them from destruction is far more likely, in the long run, "to obliterate the constituent members" of "an indestructible union of indestructible states" than the frank recognition that language, even of a constitution, may mean what it says: that the power to tax and spend includes the power to relieve a nationwide economic maladjustment by conditional gifts of money.

MR. JUSTICE BRANDEIS and MR. JUSTICE CARDOZO join in this opinion.

Note: The Spending Power and the New Deal Court

1. *Consistency within* Butler. Having adopted the Hamiltonian position on the scope of the spending power, is the Court consistent in finding the act unconstitutional? Does Justice Roberts take the position that there are no judicially enforceable *internal* limitations on the spending power — the courts will not determine whether an expenditure promotes the "general welfare" — but that there are judicially enforceable federalism-based *external* limitations on that power? What are those limits? Note Justice Stone's invocation of the legislature's "sense of public responsibility."

2. *Consistency with later decisions.* In Steward Machine Co. v. Davis, 301 U.S. 548 (1937), the Supreme Court upheld the validity of the federal unemployment compensation system. Under that system, employers paid a federal excise tax based on their employees' wages. If the employer also paid into a state unemployment fund that had been certified by the Secretary of the Treasury as meeting certain "minimum criteria" designed to assure financial stability and accountability, the employer received a credit for that amount, reducing its federal excise tax liability by up to 90 percent.

This system, the Court concluded, did not "[involve] the coercion of the States in contravention of the Tenth Amendment or of restrictions implicit in our federal form of government." In his opinion for the Court, Justice Cardozo emphasized the problems caused by the Great Depression: Despite unprecedented levels of unemployment, many states had held back from adopting unemployment insurance "through alarm lest in laying such a toll upon their industries, they would place themselves in a position of economic disadvantage as compared with neighbors or competitors."

The Court emphasized that a "wide range of judgment is given to the several states as to the particular type of statute to be spread upon their books." And it found that Congress had acted permissibly in deciding to offer the credit only to taxpayers in states that had adopted a form of unemployment insurance approved by the federal government. Giving the federal credit without regard to the contents of a state plan would be "manifestly futile in the absence of some assurance that the [state] law leading to the credit" actually addressed the problems that concerned Congress.

And the Court denied that anyone was coerced by the statute:

Who then is coerced through the operation of this statute? Not the taxpayer. He pays in fulfillment of the mandate of the local legislature. Not the state. Even now she does not offer a suggestion that in passing the unemployment law she was affected by duress. For all that appears, she is satisfied with her choice, and would be sorely disappointed if it were now to be annulled. The difficulty with the petitioner's contention is that it confuses motive with coercion.

In particular, the Court refused to say that Alabama, where Steward Machine Co. was located, "was acting, not of her unfettered will, but under the strain of a persuasion equivalent to undue influence, when she chose to have relief administered under laws of her own making, by agents of her own selection, instead of under federal laws, administered by federal officers, with all the ensuing evils, at least to many minds, of federal patronage and power. . . . We think the choice must stand. . . ."

And the Court distinguished United States v. Butler, emphasizing that here, "[t]he proceeds of the tax in controversy are not earmarked for a special group" and "[t]he unemployment compensation law which is a condition of the credit has had the approval of the state and could not be a law without it."

Justices McReynolds, Sutherland, Van Devanter, and Butler dissented. Is *Steward Machine Co.* consistent with *Butler*? Consider the proposition that the unemployment system is more objectionable than the Agricultural Adjustment Act because the former "coerces" the states directly while the latter does so only indirectly by allowing contracts between the United States and private parties that have the effect of undermining local policy. Note that the states are "coerced" into participating by a provision that affects the taxes paid by private parties, who thus have an incentive to locate in participating states and to pressure states through the political process to participate.

3. *Coercion and states' rights.* Why is the state not coerced into participating in the unemployment system by fear that businesses will relocate to states that have qualifying unemployment systems? In *Butler*, Justice Stone said that "Threat of loss, not hope of gain, is the essence of economic coercion." Which one is operating in *Steward Machine Co.*?

The difficulty of the questions turns on identifying a baseline set of "entitlements" held by states — here, the set of activities in which the states and not the national government can engage. For a comprehensive discussion, see Kreimer, Allocational Sanctions: The Problem of Negative Rights in a Positive State, 132 U. Pa. L. Rev. 1293 (1984). For additional discussion, see Chapter 9 infra.

National Federation of Independent Business v. Sebelius

567 U.S. 519 (2012)

CHIEF JUSTICE ROBERTS announced the judgment of the Court and delivered [an] opinion with respect to Part IV, in which JUSTICE BREYER and JUSTICE KAGAN join.

I . . .

Enacted in 1965, Medicaid offers federal funding to States to assist pregnant women, children, needy families, the blind, the elderly, and the disabled in obtaining medical care. In order to receive that funding, States must comply with federal criteria governing matters such as who receives care and what services are provided at what cost. By 1982 every State had chosen to participate in Medicaid. Federal funds received through the Medicaid program have become a substantial part of state budgets, now constituting over 10 percent of most States' total revenue.

The Affordable Care Act expands the scope of the Medicaid program and increases the number of individuals the States must cover. [If] a State does not comply with the Act's new coverage requirements, it may lose not only the federal funding for those requirements, but all of its federal Medicaid funds. . . .

IV

A

The States . . . contend that the Medicaid expansion exceeds Congress's authority under the Spending Clause. They claim that Congress is coercing the States to adopt the changes it wants by threatening to withhold all of a State's Medicaid grants, unless the State accepts the new expanded funding and complies with the conditions that come with it. This, they argue, violates the basic principle that the "Federal Government may not compel the States to enact or administer a federal regulatory program."

There is no doubt that the Act dramatically increases state obligations under Medicaid. The current Medicaid program requires States to cover only certain discrete categories of needy individuals — pregnant women, children, needy families, the blind, the elderly, and the disabled. There is no mandatory coverage for most childless adults, and the States typically do not offer any such coverage. The States also enjoy considerable flexibility with respect to the coverage levels for parents of needy families. On average States cover only those unemployed parents who make less than 37 percent of the federal poverty level, and only those employed parents who make less than 63 percent of the poverty line.

The Medicaid provisions of the Affordable Care Act, in contrast, require States to expand their Medicaid programs by 2014 to cover all individuals under the age of 65 with incomes below 133 percent of the federal poverty line. The Act also establishes a new "[e]ssential health benefits" package, which States must provide to all new Medicaid recipients — a level sufficient to satisfy a recipient's obligations under the individual mandate. The Affordable Care Act provides that the Federal Government will pay 100 percent of the costs of covering these newly eligible individuals through 2016. In the following years, the federal payment level gradually decreases, to a minimum of 90 percent. In light of the expansion in coverage mandated by the Act, the Federal Government estimates that its Medicaid spending will increase by approximately $100 billion per year, nearly 40 percent above current levels. . . .

[Our] cases have recognized limits on Congress's power under the Spending Clause to secure state compliance with federal objectives. [The] legitimacy of Congress's exercise of the spending power "thus rests on whether the State voluntarily and knowingly accepts the terms of the 'contract.'" Respecting this limitation is critical to ensuring that Spending Clause legislation does not undermine the status of the States as independent sovereigns in our federal system.

That system "rests on what might at first seem a counterintuitive insight, that 'freedom is enhanced by the creation of two governments, not one.'" For this reason, "the Constitution has never been understood to confer upon Congress the ability to require the States to govern according to Congress' instructions." Otherwise the two-government system established by the Framers would give way to a system that vests power in one central government, and individual liberty would suffer.

That insight has led [us] to scrutinize Spending Clause legislation to ensure that Congress is not using financial inducements to exert a "power akin to undue influence." Congress may use its spending power to create incentives for States to act in accordance with federal policies. But when "pressure turns into compulsion," the legislation runs contrary to our system of federalism. "[T]he Constitution simply does not give Congress the authority to require the States to regulate." That is true whether Congress directly commands a State to regulate or indirectly coerces a State to adopt a federal regulatory system as its own.

Permitting the Federal Government to force the States to implement a federal program would threaten the political accountability key to our federal system. [Spending] Clause programs do not pose this danger when a State has a legitimate choice whether to accept the federal conditions in exchange for federal funds. In such a situation, state officials can fairly be held politically accountable for choosing to accept or refuse the federal offer. But when the State has no choice, the Federal Government can achieve its objectives without accountability. . . . Indeed, this danger is heightened when Congress acts under the Spending Clause, because Congress can use that power to implement federal policy it could not impose directly under its enumerated powers.

We addressed such concerns in *Steward Machine*. [We] acknowledged the danger that the Federal Government might employ its taxing power to exert a "power akin to undue influence" upon the States. But we observed that Congress adopted the challenged tax and abatement program to channel money to the States that would otherwise have gone into the Federal Treasury for use in providing national unemployment services. Congress was willing to direct businesses to instead pay the money into state programs only on the condition that the money be used for the same purposes. Predicating tax abatement on a State's adoption of a particular type of unemployment legislation was therefore a means to "safeguard [the Federal Government's] own treasury." We held that "[i]n such circumstances, if in no others, inducement or persuasion does not go beyond the bounds of power." . . .

[In] the typical case we look to the States to defend their prerogatives by adopting "the simple expedient of not yielding" to federal blandishments when they do not want to embrace the federal policies as their own. The States are separate and independent sovereigns. Sometimes they have to act like it.

The States, however, argue that the Medicaid expansion is far from the typical case. They object that Congress has "crossed the line distinguishing encouragement from coercion" in the way it has structured the funding: Instead of simply refusing to grant the new funds to States that will not accept the new conditions, Congress has also threatened to withhold those States' existing Medicaid funds. The States claim that this threat serves no purpose other than to force unwilling States to sign up for the dramatic expansion in health care coverage effected by the Act.

Given the nature of the threat and the programs at issue here, we must agree. [Conditions] that do not [govern] the use of the funds, however, cannot be justified on that basis. When, for example, such conditions take the form of threats to terminate other significant independent grants, the conditions are properly viewed as a means of pressuring the States to accept policy changes.

In South Dakota v. Dole, we considered a challenge to a federal law that threatened to withhold five percent of a State's federal highway funds if the State did not raise its drinking age to 21. The Court found that the condition was "directly related to one of the main purposes for which highway funds are expended — safe interstate travel." At the same time, the condition was not a restriction on how the highway funds — set aside for specific highway improvement and maintenance efforts — were to be used.

We accordingly asked whether "the financial inducement offered by Congress" was "so coercive as to pass the point at which 'pressure turns into compulsion.'" By "financial inducement" the Court meant the threat of losing five percent of highway funds; no new money was offered to the States to raise their drinking ages. We found that the inducement was not impermissibly coercive, because Congress was offering only "relatively mild encouragement to the States." We observed that "all South Dakota would lose if she adheres to her chosen course as to a suitable minimum drinking age is 5%" of her highway funds. [Whether] to accept the drinking age change "remain[ed] the prerogative of the States not merely in theory but in fact."

In this case, the financial "inducement" Congress has chosen is much more than "relatively mild encouragement" — it is a gun to the head. [A] State that opts out of the Affordable Care Act's expansion in health care coverage [stands] to lose not merely "a relatively small percentage" of its existing Medicaid funding, but all of it. [It] is easy to see how the *Dole* Court could conclude that the threatened loss of less than half of one percent of South Dakota's budget left that State with a "prerogative" to reject Congress's desired policy, "not merely in theory but in fact." The threatened loss of over 10 percent of a State's overall budget, in contrast, is economic dragooning that leaves the States with no real option but to acquiesce in the Medicaid expansion.[12]

Justice Ginsburg claims that *Dole* is distinguishable because here "Congress has not threatened to withhold funds earmarked for any other program." But that begs the question: The States contend that the expansion is in reality a new program and that Congress is forcing them to accept it by threatening the funds for the existing Medicaid program. We cannot agree that existing Medicaid and the expansion dictated by the Affordable Care Act are all one program simply because "Congress styled" them as such. If the expansion is not properly viewed as a modification of the existing Medicaid program, Congress's decision to so title it is irrelevant.

Here, the Government claims that the Medicaid expansion is properly viewed merely as a modification of the existing program because the States agreed that Congress could change the terms of Medicaid when they signed on in the first place. The Government observes that the Social Security Act, which includes the original Medicaid provisions, contains a clause expressly reserving "[t]he right to alter, amend, or repeal any provision" of that statute. So it does. But "if Congress intends to impose a condition on the grant of federal moneys, it must do so

---

12. Justice Ginsburg observes that state Medicaid spending will increase by only 0.8 percent after the expansion. [The] size of the new financial burden imposed on a State is irrelevant in analyzing whether the State has been coerced into accepting that burden. "Your money or your life" is a coercive proposition, whether you have a single dollar in your pocket or $500.

unambiguously." A State confronted with statutory language reserving the right to "alter" or "amend" the pertinent provisions of the Social Security Act might reasonably assume that Congress was entitled to make adjustments to the Medicaid program as it developed. Congress has in fact done so, sometimes conditioning only the new funding, other times both old and new.

The Medicaid expansion [accomplishes] a shift in kind, not merely degree. The original program was designed to cover medical services for four particular categories of the needy: the disabled, the blind, the elderly, and needy families with dependent children. Previous amendments to Medicaid eligibility merely altered and expanded the boundaries of these categories. Under the Affordable Care Act, Medicaid is transformed into a program to meet the health care needs of the entire nonelderly population with income below 133 percent of the poverty level. It is no longer a program to care for the neediest among us, but rather an element of a comprehensive national plan to provide universal health insurance coverage.[14] . . .

As we have explained, "[t]hough Congress' power to legislate under the spending power is broad, it does not include surprising participating States with postacceptance or 'retroactive' conditions." A State could hardly anticipate that Congress's reservation of the right to "alter" or "amend" the Medicaid program included the power to transform it so dramatically.

Justice Ginsburg claims that in fact this expansion is no different from the previous changes to Medicaid, such that "a State would be hard put to complain that it lacked fair notice." But the prior change she discusses — presumably the most dramatic alteration she could find — does not come close to working the transformation the expansion accomplishes. . . .

The Court in *Steward Machine* did not attempt to "fix the outermost line" where persuasion gives way to coercion. The Court found it "[e]nough for present purposes that wherever the line may be, this statute is within it." We have no need to fix a line either. It is enough for today that wherever that line may be, this statute is surely beyond it. Congress may not simply "conscript state [agencies] into the national bureaucratic army," and that is what it is attempting to do with the Medicaid expansion. . . .

B . . .

[The] Court today limits the financial pressure the Secretary may apply to induce States to accept the terms of the Medicaid expansion. As a practical matter, that means States may now choose to reject the expansion; that is the whole point. But that does not mean all or even any will. Some States may indeed decline to participate, either because they are unsure they will be able to afford their share of the new funding obligations, or because they are unwilling to commit the administrative resources necessary to support the expansion. Other States, however, may voluntarily sign up, finding the idea of expanding Medicaid

14. Justice Ginsburg suggests that the States can have no objection to the Medicaid expansion, because "Congress could have repealed Medicaid [and,] [t]hereafter, . . . could have enacted Medicaid II, a new program combining the pre-2010 coverage with the expanded coverage required by the ACA." But it would certainly not be that easy. Practical constraints would plainly inhibit, if not preclude, the Federal Government from repealing the existing program and putting every feature of Medicaid on the table for political reconsideration. Such a massive undertaking would hardly be "ritualistic." . . .

coverage attractive, particularly given the level of federal funding the Act offers at the outset.

We have no way of knowing how many States will accept the terms of the expansion, but we do not believe Congress would have wanted the whole Act to fall, simply because some may choose not to participate. . . . [Confident] that Congress would not have intended anything different, we conclude that the rest of the Act need not fall in light of our constitutional holding. . . .

JUSTICE SCALIA, JUSTICE KENNEDY, JUSTICE THOMAS, and JUSTICE ALITO, dissenting. . . .

IV . . .

D . . .

2

The Federal Government's argument in this case at best pays lip service to the anticoercion principle. The Federal Government suggests that it is sufficient if States are "free, as a matter of law, to turn down" federal funds. . . .

This argument ignores reality. When a heavy federal tax is levied to support a federal program that offers large grants to the States, States may, as a practical matter, be unable to refuse to participate in the federal program and to substitute a state alternative. Even if a State believes that the federal program is ineffective and inefficient, withdrawal would likely force the State to impose a huge tax increase on its residents, and this new state tax would come on top of the federal taxes already paid by residents to support subsidies to participating States.[13]

Acceptance of the Federal Government's interpretation of the anticoercion rule would permit Congress to dictate policy in areas traditionally governed primarily at the state or local level. Suppose, for example, that Congress enacted legislation offering each State a grant equal to the State's entire annual expenditures for primary and secondary education. Suppose also that this funding came with conditions governing such things as school curriculum, the hiring and tenure of teachers, the drawing of school districts, the length and hours of the school day, the school calendar, a dress code for students, and rules for student discipline. As a matter of law, a State could turn down that offer, but if it did so, its residents would not only be required to pay the federal taxes needed to support this expensive new program, but they would also be forced to pay an equivalent amount in state taxes. And if the State gave in to the federal law, the State and its subdivisions would surrender their traditional authority in the field of education. . . .

E . . .

2

[In] crafting the ACA, Congress clearly expressed its informed view that no State could possibly refuse the offer that the ACA extends. . . .

---

13. Justice Ginsburg argues that "[a] State . . . has no claim on the money its residents pay in federal taxes." This is true as a formal matter. [But] unless Justice Ginsburg thinks that there is no limit to the amount of money that can be squeezed out of taxpayers, heavy federal taxation diminishes the practical ability of States to collect their own taxes.

If Congress had thought that States might actually refuse to go along with the expansion of Medicaid, Congress would surely have devised a backup scheme so that the most vulnerable groups in our society, those previously eligible for Medicaid, would not be left out in the cold. But nowhere in the over 900-page Act is such a scheme to be found. . . .

These features of the ACA convey an unmistakable message: Congress never dreamed that any State would refuse to go along with the expansion of Medicaid. Congress well understood that refusal was not a practical option.

The Federal Government does not dispute the inference that Congress anticipated 100% state participation, but it argues that this assumption was based on the fact that ACA's offer was an "exceedingly generous" gift. As the Federal Government sees things, Congress is like the generous benefactor who offers $1 million with few strings attached to 50 randomly selected individuals. Just as this benefactor might assume that all of these 50 individuals would snap up his offer, so Congress assumed that every State would gratefully accept the federal funds (and conditions) to go with the expansion of Medicaid.

This characterization of the ACA's offer raises obvious questions. If that offer is "exceedingly generous," as the Federal Government maintains, why have more than half the States brought this lawsuit, contending that the offer is coercive? And why did Congress find it necessary to threaten that any State refusing to accept this "exceedingly generous" gift would risk losing all Medicaid funds? Congress could have made just the new funding provided under the ACA contingent on acceptance of the terms of the Medicaid Expansion. . . .

[The joint dissent concluded that the penalty for not participating in the Medicaid expansion could not be severed from the entire scheme of Medicaid expansion, and therefore that the entire expansion, including the option for states to participate, had to fall.]

JUSTICE GINSBURG, with whom JUSTICE SOTOMAYOR joins, [dissenting] in part. . . .

V . . .

Medicaid, as amended by the ACA [is] not two spending programs; it is a single program with a constant aim — to enable poor persons to receive basic health care when they need it. Given past expansions, plus express statutory warning that Congress may change the requirements participating States must meet, there can be no tenable claim that the ACA fails for lack of notice. Moreover, States have no entitlement to receive any Medicaid funds; they enjoy only the opportunity to accept funds on Congress' terms. Future Congresses are not bound by their predecessors' dispositions; they have authority to spend federal revenue as they see fit. The Federal Government, therefore, is not, as The Chief Justice charges, threatening States with the loss of "existing" funds from one spending program in order to induce them to opt into another program. Congress is simply requiring States to do what States have long been required to do to receive Medicaid funding: comply with the conditions Congress prescribes for participation. . . . [17]

17. The Chief Justice and the joint dissenters perceive in cooperative federalism a "threa[t]" to "political accountability." By that, they mean voter confusion: Citizens upset by unpopular government action, they posit, may ascribe to state officials blame more appropriately laid at Congress' door. But no such confusion is apparent in this case: Medicaid's status as a federally funded, state-administered program is hardly hidden from view. [Relocated footnote. — EDS.]

B . . .

Yes, there are federalism-based limits on the use of Congress' conditional spending power. . . .

This case does not present the concerns that led the Court in *Dole* even to consider the prospect of coercion. In *Dole*, . . . in view of the Twenty-First Amendment, it was an open question whether Congress could directly impose a national minimum drinking age.

The ACA, in contrast, relates solely to the federally funded Medicaid program; if States choose not to comply, Congress has not threatened to withhold funds earmarked for any other program. Nor does the ACA use Medicaid funding to induce States to take action Congress itself could not undertake. The Federal Government undoubtedly could operate its own health-care program for poor persons, just as it operates Medicare for seniors' health care.

That is what makes this such a simple case, and the Court's decision so unsettling. . . .

C . . .

1

The starting premise on which The Chief Justice's coercion analysis rests is that the ACA did not really "extend" Medicaid; instead, Congress created an entirely new program to co-exist with the old. The Chief Justice calls the ACA new, but in truth, it simply reaches more of America's poor than Congress originally covered. . . .

Congress has broad authority to construct or adjust spending programs to meet its contemporary understanding of "the general Welfare." Courts owe a large measure of respect to Congress' characterization of the grant programs it establishes. Even if courts were inclined to second-guess Congress' conception of the character of its legislation, how would reviewing judges divine whether an Act of Congress, purporting to amend a law, is in reality not an amendment, but a new creation? At what point does an extension become so large that it "transforms" the basic law? Endeavoring to show that Congress created a new program, the Chief Justice. . . . asserts that, in covering those earning no more than 133% of the federal poverty line, the Medicaid expansion, unlike pre-ACA Medicaid, does not "care for the neediest among us." What makes that so? Single adults earning no more than $14,856 per year — 133% of the current federal poverty level — surely rank among the Nation's poor. . . .

Consider also that Congress could have repealed Medicaid. Thereafter, Congress could have enacted Medicaid II, a new program combining the pre-2010 coverage with the expanded coverage required by the ACA. By what right does a court stop Congress from building up without first tearing down?

2

The Chief Justice finds the Medicaid expansion vulnerable because it took participating States by surprise. "A State could hardly anticipate that Congres[s]" would endeavor to "transform [the Medicaid program] so dramatically," he states. For the notion that States must be able to foresee, when they sign up, alterations

Congress might make later on, The Chief Justice cites only one case: [*Pennhurst*]. . . .

[*Pennhurst's*] rule demands that conditions on federal funds be unambiguously clear at the time a State receives and uses the money — not at the time, perhaps years earlier, when Congress passed the law establishing the program.

In any event, from the start, the Medicaid Act put States on notice that the program could be changed: "The right to alter, amend, or repeal any provision of [Medicaid]," the statute has read since 1965, "is hereby reserved to the Congress." The "effect of these few simple words" has long been settled. By reserving the right to "alter, amend, [or] repeal" a spending program, Congress "has given special notice of its intention to retain . . . full and complete power to make such alterations and amendments . . . as come within the just scope of legislative power." . . .

The Chief Justice nevertheless would rewrite §1304 to countenance only the "right to alter somewhat," or "amend, but not too much." Congress, however, did not so qualify §1304. Indeed, Congress retained discretion to "repeal" Medicaid, wiping it out entirely. . . .

3

The Chief Justice ultimately asks whether "the financial inducement offered by Congress . . . pass[ed] the point at which pressure turns into compulsion." The financial inducement Congress employed here, he concludes, crosses that threshold: The threatened withholding of "existing Medicaid funds" is "a gun to the head" that forces States to acquiesce.[24]

The Chief Justice sees no need to "fix the outermost line" [*Steward Machine*] "where persuasion gives way to coercion." Neither do the joint dissenters.[25] Notably, the decision on which they rely, *Steward Machine*, found the statute at issue inside the line, "wherever the line may be."

When future Spending Clause challenges arrive, as they likely will in the wake of today's decision, how will litigants and judges assess whether "a State has a legitimate choice whether to accept the federal conditions in exchange for federal funds"? Are courts to measure the number of dollars the Federal Government might withhold for noncompliance? The portion of the State's budget at stake? And which State's — or States' — budget is determinative: the lead plaintiff, all challenging States (26 in this case, many with quite different fiscal situations), or some national median? Does it matter that Florida, unlike most States, imposes no state income tax, and therefore might be able to replace foregone

24. The joint dissenters, for their part, would make this the entire inquiry. "[I]f States really have no choice other than to accept the package," they assert, "the offer is coercive." The Chief Justice recognizes Congress' authority to construct a single federal program and "condition the receipt of funds on the States' complying with restrictions on the use of those funds." For the joint dissenters, however, all that matters, it appears, is whether States can resist the temptation of a given federal grant. On this logic, any federal spending program, sufficiently large and well-funded, would be unconstitutional. . . .

Speculations of this genre are characteristic of the joint dissent. The joint dissenters are long on conjecture and short on real-world examples.

25. The joint dissenters also rely heavily on Congress' perceived intent to coerce the States. We should not lightly ascribe to Congress an intent to violate the Constitution (at least as my colleagues read it). This is particularly true when the ACA could just as well be comprehended as demonstrating Congress' mere expectation, in light of the uniformity of past participation and the generosity of the federal contribution, that States would not withdraw.

federal funds with new state revenue?[26] Or that the coercion state officials in fact fear is punishment at the ballot box for turning down a politically popular federal grant?

The coercion inquiry, therefore, appears to involve political judgments that defy judicial calculation. . . .

At bottom, my colleagues' position is that the States' reliance on federal funds limits Congress' authority to alter its spending programs. This gets things backwards: Congress, not the States, is tasked with spending federal money in service of the general welfare. And each successive Congress is empowered to appropriate funds as it sees fit. When the 110th Congress reached a conclusion about Medicaid funds that differed from its predecessors' view, it abridged no State's right to "existing," or "pre-existing," funds. For, in fact, there are no such funds. There is only money States anticipate receiving from future Congresses. . . .

[I] would [hold] that the Medicaid expansion is within Congress' spending power.

Note: Conditional Spending, Coercion, and the Political Process

1. *The* Dole *framework.* In South Dakota v. Dole, 483 U.S. 203 (1987), the Supreme Court faced a challenge to a federal statute that directed the Secretary of Transportation to withhold a portion of federal highway funds from states that did not prohibit the purchase of alcohol by people under the age of twenty-one. Congress used this technique because of uncertainty about its power to impose a national minimum drinking age directly, in light of the twenty-first amendment, which had been treated as giving the states especially broad control over regulations of alcoholic beverages. Although much of Chief Justice Rehnquist's opinion for the Court discussed whether the twenty-first amendment provided an independent limitation on Congress's power to spend, the opinion also contained some general observations about the scope of the conditional spending power:

> The spending power is of course not unlimited, but is instead subject to several general restrictions. [First,] the exercise of the spending power must be in pursuit of "the general welfare." [*Butler.*] In considering whether a particular expenditure is intended to serve general public purposes, courts should defer substantially to the judgment of Congress. Second, [if] Congress desires to condition the States' receipt of federal funds, it "must do so [unambiguously."] Third, our cases have suggested (without significant elaboration) that conditions on federal grants might be illegitimate if they are unrelated "to the federal interest in particular national projects or

---

26. Federal taxation of a State's citizens, according to the joint dissenters, may diminish a State's ability to raise new revenue. This, in turn, could limit a State's capacity to replace a federal program with an "equivalent" state-funded analog. But it cannot be true that "the amount of the federal taxes extracted from the taxpayers of a State to pay for the program in question is relevant in determining whether there is impermissible coercion." When the United States Government taxes United States citizens, it taxes them "in their individual capacities" as "the people of America" — not as residents of a particular State. . . .

A State therefore has no claim on the money its residents pay in federal taxes, and federal "spending programs need not help people in all states in the same measure." In 2004, for example, New Jersey received 55 cents in federal spending for every dollar its residents paid to the Federal Government in taxes, while Mississippi received $1.77 per tax dollar paid. Thus no constitutional problem was created when Arizona declined for 16 years to participate in Medicaid, even though its residents' tax dollars financed Medicaid programs in every other State.

programs." Finally, [other] constitutional provisions may provide an independent bar to the conditional grant of federal funds.

The twenty-one-year-old drinking age condition satisfied all of these requirements. It served the general welfare because different drinking ages in different states created incentives for young people "to combine their desire to drink with their ability to drive."

The Court agreed with the suggestion in *Steward Machine Co.* that at some point "pressure turns into coercion." But here, because

> all South Dakota would lose if she adheres to her chosen course as to a suitable minimum drinking age is 5% of the funds otherwise obtainable under specified highway grant programs, the argument as to coercion is shown to be more rhetoric than fact. [Here] Congress has offered relatively mild encouragement to the States to enact higher minimum drinking ages than they would otherwise choose. [But] the enactment of such laws remains the prerogative of the States not merely in theory but in fact.

Justice O'Connor's dissenting opinion argued that the minimum drinking age "is not sufficiently related to interstate highway construction to justify" the condition placed on funds "appropriated for that purpose":

> When Congress appropriates money to build a highway, it is entitled to insist that the highway be a safe one. But it is not entitled to insist as a condition of the use of highway funds that the State impose or change regulations in other areas of the State's social and economic life because of an attenuated or tangential relationship to highway use or safety. [If] the rule were otherwise, the Congress could effectively regulate almost any area of a State's social, political, or economic life on the theory that use of the interstate transportation system is somehow enhanced.

Prior to *NFIB*, courts had generally used the *Dole* framework to analyze the constitutionality of conditional spending statutes. Consider the following observations about Chief Justice Roberts' opinion:

> The *Dole* test provides the Court with multiple avenues through which it may invalidate a statute as exceeding the powers granted under the Spending Clause. Chief Justice Roberts did not recite the *Dole* test in his opinion, relying instead solely on an assessment of whether the federal law is coercive. In order to achieve consensus, this approach requires agreement on a single, vague, and highly normatively charged standard.

Greene, Maximinimalism, 38 Cardozo L. Rev. 623, 643 (2016).

2. *Distinguishing conditions from coercion.* What are the criteria for determining when a conditional offer becomes coercion? For additional discussion, see Chapter 9, section E, infra. Does the application of those criteria, whatever they might be, "involve political [as distinct from legal] judgments," as Justice Ginsburg asserts? Would it be constitutionally permissible for Congress to reduce existing Medicaid expenditures by 5 percent in states that did not expand the program fully? By 10 percent?

3. *Repeal and reenact?* Note the Chief Justice's response to Justice Ginsburg's "repeal and reenact" hypothetical. What precisely are the "practical considerations" that would stand in the way of that course? Note that the argument must

refer to the time of the Act's initial adoption, not to the time when Congress might be required to reconsider its initial decisions in light of a judicial holding of unconstitutionality. (Why might the practical considerations be different at those two times?)

Bagenstos, The Anti-Leveraging Principle and the Spending Clause After NFIB, 101 Geo. L.J. 861 (2013), suggests that the Chief Justice's opinion rests on an "anti-leveraging principle": that "[w]hen Congress takes an entrenched federal program that provides large sums to the states and tells states that they can continue to participate in that program only if they *also* agree to participate in a separate and independent program, the condition is unconstitutionally coercive." When Congress does not repeal a prior program, it must, however, provide a "separate enticement" if it wishes for states to participate in a new program. "It may be harder for Congress to get states to agree to participate in both programs, but that is a far cry from a rule that would require Congress to continue spending in a way that [clashes] with its current understanding of the general welfare."

4. *States' rights limitations on conditional spending.* What limitations does the Court suggest? Is it helpful to say that the issues are ones of degree and fact? What sort of facts?

Note that over time, the Court's interpretation of the spending power has seemed to dovetail with its treatment of the commerce power: In eras where the commerce power was relatively circumscribed, the Court seemed more willing to impose limits on the spending power as well, while in eras where the commerce power was treated as close to plenary, the Court also deferred to congressional use of the spending power.

Must the conditions imposed be related to the activity receiving the federal subsidy? Note that the Court's precise formulation in *Steward Machine Co.* is "unrelated to the fiscal need [or] to any other end legitimately national." Is the latter anything more than the Hamiltonian position on the scope of the spending power? Could Congress require that state universities whose students receive federally guaranteed loans (a) not discriminate on the basis of race and gender in their admissions policies; (b) not discriminate on the basis of race and gender in faculty employment; (c) conduct research for federal agencies on the development of nuclear power? Could Congress require that states accepting federal funds for elementary and secondary education ban the possession of guns near schools? That such states suspend students who bring guns to schools? Note that a number of federal statutes — for example, title VI of the Civil Rights Act of 1964 — regulate recipients of federal funds.

5. *Avoiding the race to the bottom.* Consider the following argument in support of national legislation such as the statute at issue in *Steward Machine*: Every state desires to alleviate the burdens of unemployment by adopting some sort of unemployment system. But any state that does so runs the risk that a neighboring state will not, or will adopt a somewhat different system. If the neighboring state has no unemployment system, or has one financed more favorably to employers, the state that adopts the less favorable system runs the risk that employers will relocate. In order to assure that no risk of "unfair competition" of this sort — sometimes called a "race to the bottom" — can occur, coordinated action on the national level is necessary. For a development of this account, see Cooter and Siegel, Collective Action Federalism: A General Theory of Article I, Section 8, 63 Stan. L. Rev. 115 (2010).

Note the following points about this argument: (a) Mechanisms of voluntary coordination exist, as the Court discussed in Carter v. Carter Coal Co. (b) Can we distinguish between failure of a state legislature to act because it fears unfair competition from a neighboring state and failure to act because it believes that unemployment compensation systems are unsound as a matter of policy? Is it sufficient to answer that that is the kind of judgment we leave to Congress? (c) Note that five states, including New York and California, had adopted unemployment compensation systems before Congress acted. Does that cast doubt on the argument that states failed to act out of fear of unfair competition? Would those states have feared such competition any less than other states did? (d) Is there a race to the bottom problem in connection with the provision of health care insurance? Cooter and Siegel, supra, suggest that there is: States that attempt to implement a program like the Affordable Care Act will find themselves attracting people with preexisting conditions, making their programs unsustainable.

6. *Statutory interpretation as a limiting technique.* The questions just discussed can be avoided by construing ambiguous statutes so as not to impose the problematic obligations on the states. As Justice Rehnquist wrote in South Dakota v. Dole, Congress must state "unambiguously" the conditions it imposes on states that accept federal funds. See Arlington Central School District Board of Education v. Murphy, 548 U.S. 291 (2006) (noting that "[in] a Spending Clause case, the key is . . . what the States are clearly told regarding the conditions that go along with the acceptance of those funds").

3.   The "War" Power

Article I, section 8 articulates a range of congressional powers related to war: for example, the power to "declare War," to "provide for the common Defence," to "raise and support Armies" and to "provide and maintain a Navy," to "make Rules for the Government and Regulation of the land and naval Forces," and the like. How do these express war powers interact with the necessary and proper clause in delineating the scope of congressional power during wartime?

(The general question whether during times of war constitutional constraints on civil rights or civil liberties are (or should be) relaxed is dealt with more extensively in Chapter 4, section D; Chapter 5, section C; and Chapter 7, section B, infra.)

The Supreme Court has observed that "[the] war power of the national government is 'the power to wage war successfully.'" See Charles Evans Hughes, War Powers under the Constitution, 42 A.B.A. Rep. 232, 238. It extends to every matter and activity so related to war as substantially to affect its conduct and progress. The power is not restricted to the winning of victories in the field and the repulse of enemy forces. It embraces every phase of the national defense. . . ." Hirabayashi v. United States, 320 U.S. 81, 93 (1943). At the same time, the Court has also observed that "[the] phrase 'war power' cannot be invoked as a talismanic incantation to support any exercise of congressional power which can be brought within its ambit," United States v. Robel, 389 U.S. 258, 263 (1968), and that "[even] the war power does not remove constitutional limitations safeguarding essential liberties," Home Building & Loan Association v. Blaisdell, 290 U.S. 398, 426 (1934).

In Woods v. Cloyd W. Miller Co., 333 U.S. 138 (1948), the Supreme Court upheld the constitutionality of the Housing and Rent Act of 1947, which froze rents at their wartime levels. It concluded that "the war power sustains this legislation." Even though the President had declared hostilities terminated on

December 31, 1946, before the statute was enacted, "the war power does not necessarily end with the cessation of hostilities." When Congress acted, there was a

> deficit in housing which in considerable measure was caused by the heavy demo-bilization of veterans and by the cessation or reduction in residential construction during the period of hostilities due to the allocation of building materials to military projects. Since the war effort contributed heavily to that deficit, Congress has the power even after the cessation of hostilities to act to control the forces that a short supply of the needed article created. . . .
>   We recognize the force of the argument that the effects of war under modern conditions may be felt in the economy for years and years, and that if the war power can be used in days of peace to treat all the wounds which war inflicts on our society, it may not only swallow up all other powers of Congress but largely oblit-erate the Ninth and Tenth Amendments as well. There are no such implications in today's decision. We deal here with the consequences of a housing deficit greatly intensified during the period of hostilities by the war effort. Any power, of course, can be abused. But we cannot assume that Congress is not alert to its constitutional responsibilities. And the question whether the war power has been properly employed in cases such as this is open to judicial inquiry.
>   The question of the constitutionality of action taken by Congress does not depend on recitals of the power which it undertakes to exercise. Here it is plain from the legislative history that Congress was invoking its war power to cope with a current condition of which the war was a direct and immediate cause.

Justice Jackson's concurring opinion expressed "misgivings" about "this vague, undefined and indefinable 'war power'":

> No one will question that this power is the most dangerous one to free government in the whole catalogue of powers. It is usually invoked in haste and excitement when calm legislative consideration of constitutional limitation is difficult. It is executed in a time of patriotic fervor that makes moderation unpopular. And, worst of all, it is interpreted by judges under the influence of the same passions and pressures. Always, [the] Government urges hasty decision to forestall some emergency or serve some purposes and pleads that paralysis will result if its claims to power are denied or their confirmation delayed.
>   Particularly when the war power is invoked to do things to the liberties of people, or to their property or economy that only indirectly affect conduct of the war and do not relate to the management of the war itself, the constitutional basis should be scrutinized with care.

Nonetheless, he concluded that "the present state of war [was not] merely technical," and that the statute was constitutional.

What is "the war power" on which the Court relies? Justice Jackson suggests that the political constraints on congressional action are loosened in all areas when the war powers are invoked. Is he correct?

Note: Individual Rights and the War Power

A common view is that congressional legislation during wartime tends to constrict individual rights and liberties. But see Posner and Vermeule, Accom-modating Emergencies, 56 Stan. L. Rev. 605 (2003) (suggesting this view is somewhat exaggerated). Does the consensus depend on how individual rights and liberties are defined? For example, did the statute at issue in *Woods* constrict or expand rights? From whose perspective ought this to be measured?

1. *Voting rights.* Consider the expansion of the franchise during World War II. From the end of Reconstruction through the mid-twentieth century, black citizens were disenfranchised throughout much of the South. Southern congressmen blocked virtually every attempt to enact legislation protecting or expanding the right to vote because of their fear that such legislation would enfranchise black voters.

One of the primary disenfranchising devices was the poll tax, particularly in states such as Virginia, Arkansas, and Texas. In 1942, President Roosevelt proposed, and Congress passed, "An act to provide for a method of voting, in time of war, by members of the land and naval forces absent from the place of their residence," Pub. L. No. 77-712, 56 Stat. 753. Section 2 of the act provided that "[no] person in military service in time of war shall be required, as a condition of voting in any election for President, Vice President, . . . or for Senator or Member of the House of Representatives, to pay any poll tax. . . ." A few years earlier, the Supreme Court had upheld Texas's poll tax against a constitutional attack. See Breedlove v. Suttles, 302 U.S. 277 (1937). (*Breedlove* was subsequently overruled by Harper v. Virginia State Board of Elections, 383 U.S. 663 (1966), discussed in Chapter 6, section E, infra.) The act also overrode state laws regarding absentee voting by providing a more uniform federal absentee voting process for members of the armed forces.

The act's supporters sought to circumvent *Breedlove* by relying on the war power. According to an oral history that discussed the act:

> We had to argue that the war power, which previously had been held, for example, to permit Congress to put a moratorium on the foreclosure of mortgages representing the obligations of service personnel, sustained the power of Congress to protect the rights of military personnel to vote — that the war power included a power to prevent or remedy dislocation produced by the legitimate exercise of national powers in the fighting of the war, and that the same principle operated to permit Congress in its wisdom to prevent service personnel from being required by state law to lose the benefit of the franchise conferred by state law.

Silber and Miller, Toward "Neutral Principles" in the Law: Selections from the Oral History of Herbert Wechsler, 93 Colum. L. Rev. 854, 880 (1993) (quoting Wechsler, who participated in drafting the act).

> Although the 1942 act and its 1944 successor did not explicitly address racial discrimination, southern legislators correctly saw them as the "opening wedge for congressional intrusion in the electoral process, with its ultimate implications for breaking down the disenfranchisement of blacks." Id. at 879. For a more general argument that the right to vote is a striking counterexample to the common argument that civil liberties are legislatively constricted during wartime, see Karlan, Ballots and Bullets: The Exceptional History of the Right to Vote, 71 U. Cin. L. Rev. 1345 (2003).

2. *The first amendment.* To what extent does the first amendment constrain Congress's use of its spending and war powers? Rumsfeld v. FAIR, 547 U.S. 47 (2006), upheld the Solomon Amendment, 10 U.S.C. §983(b)(1), which withholds federal funds from institutions of higher education that deny military

recruiters the same access to campuses and students that they provide to other employers. Before the Court reached the question whether the first amendment limited Congress's power, it addressed the antecedent question of Congress's general power to obtain access for military recruiters in the first place. In a unanimous opinion by Chief Justice Roberts, the Court identified two complementary sources of congressional power:

> The Constitution grants Congress the power to "provide for the common Defence," "[t]o raise and support Armies," and "[t]o provide and maintain a Navy." Art. I, §8, cls. 1, 12–13. Congress' power in this area "is broad and sweeping," and there is no dispute in this case that it includes the authority to require campus access for military recruiters. . . .
>
> Although Congress has broad authority to legislate on matters of military recruiting, it nonetheless chose to secure campus access for military recruiters indirectly, through its Spending Clause power. The Solomon Amendment gives universities a choice: Either allow military recruiters the same access to students afforded any other recruiter or forgo certain federal funds. Congress' decision to proceed indirectly does not reduce the deference given to Congress in the area of military affairs. Congress' choice to promote its goal by creating a funding condition deserves at least as deferential treatment as if Congress had imposed a mandate on universities.
>
> Congress' power to regulate military recruiting under the Solomon Amendment is arguably greater because universities are free to decline the federal funds. . . .

Given contemporary realities in higher education, are institutions actually free to decline federal funds? What are *NFIB*'s implications for the analysis of this question?

B.   CONGRESS'S ENFORCEMENT POWER UNDER THE RECONSTRUCTION AMENDMENTS

The thirteenth, fourteenth, and fifteenth amendments, passed following the Civil War, introduced a distinctive structure into the Constitution. The first section of each amendment contains a prohibitory provision and each amendment also contains a separate section providing, in virtually identical language, that "Congress shall have power to enforce" the provision "by appropriate legislation."

What power do the enforcement clauses give to Congress? Does the textual reference to Congress imply that the relationship between judicial and congressional interpretations of the Reconstruction amendments should differ from the relationship that obtains with respect to other constitutional provisions, such as the commerce clause? Does the fact that the thirteenth and fourteenth amendments were at least in significant part a direct, congressionally generated repudiation of the Supreme Court's pre–Civil War decision in Dred Scott v. Sandford, and were intended to overrule the Court's interpretation, shed light on the express allocation of enforcement power to Congress?

In most of this section, we consider issues that have arisen with respect to Congress's enforcement power under section 5 of the fourteenth amendment, since that amendment has served as the basis for the most legislation and has generated the most judicial and scholarly attention. We return at the conclusion, however, to some questions regarding interpretation of the other enforcement clauses.

Note: Possible Interpretations of the Section 5 Power

Standing alone, section 1 of the fourteenth amendment, among other things, forbids states from denying persons within their jurisdiction due process of law or the equal protection of the laws. (The contours of these prohibitions are examined in depth in other parts of this book, particularly Chapters 5 through 8, infra.) Under the most modest interpretation, section 5 gives Congress the power to provide causes of action allowing those individuals whose rights to equal protection or due process are violated to *bring* a lawsuit, rather than simply to assert their fourteenth amendment rights as a defense. What more might section 5 authorize?

1. *Complex remedies.* Section 5 might authorize Congress to create remedies that courts would have difficulty developing on their own in the ordinary course of case-by-case adjudication. Consider in this connection South Carolina v. Katzenbach, 383 U.S. 301 (1966): After an extensive investigation into racial discrimination in voting practices, Congress enacted the Voting Rights Act of 1965, which gave the Attorney General and the Director of the Census unreviewable authority to make factual determinations about whether a jurisdiction had used a literacy test or other "device" and the level of voter registration or turnout. Once those findings were made, the use of "tests or devices" was suspended in jurisdictions with low levels of participation. In addition, the state or subdivision could not adopt any new standards or procedures with respect to voting without prior submission of the standards to federal authorities (the so-called preclearance process). The jurisdiction's changes would be approved only if either the Department of Justice or a special three-judge federal court concluded that the changes had neither a racially discriminatory purpose nor a racially discriminatory effect. Shortly after their passage, the Court upheld these provisions as permissible exercises of Congress's power under section 2 of the fifteenth amendment "to enforce . . . by appropriate legislation" the right guaranteed by section 1 of that amendment. (The cases have not distinguished between the enforcement powers granted Congress by the fourteenth amendment and those granted by the fifteenth.) Decades later, the Court struck down the formula for deciding which jurisdictions were required to preclear their voting changes. See Shelby County v. Holder, 133 S. Ct. 2612 (2013), discussed later in this section. (In the interim, the Court upheld a temporary nationwide ban on literacy tests and similar devices, see Oregon v. Mitchell, 400 U.S. 112 (1970), that was later made permanent, see 52 U.S.C. §10501.)

2. *Preventive or "prophylactic" remedies.* Congress might have the power to forestall the occurrence of acts that would violate rights that the courts have found or would find protected by the Constitution. Note that the "remedy" here occurs before the "violation" does. See City of Rome v. United States, 446 U.S. 156 (1980). The city challenged the application of the preclearance provisions on the ground, among others, that the fifteenth amendment prohibited only purposeful discrimination. The Voting Rights Act required rejecting proposed changes that had discriminatory effects, even if they had no discriminatory purpose. The Attorney General had found that the city's proposed changes had a discriminatory effect, but not that they were motivated by a discriminatory purpose. Under those circumstances, the city argued, Congress's power to enforce the fifteenth amendment did not extend to forbidding its proposed changes. The Court, through Justice Marshall, rejected the city's argument. It assumed   that   the   fifteenth   amendment   prohibited   only   intentional

discrimination. But "Congress could rationally have concluded that, because electoral changes by jurisdictions with a demonstrable history of intentional racial discrimination in voting create the risk of purposeful discrimination, it was proper to prohibit changes that have a discriminatory impact."

Is the "risk" that at some time in the future, the city will adopt purposefully discriminatory changes? If so, why won't addressing those changes when they occur be adequate to vindicate the fifteenth amendment? Or is the "risk" that neither the Attorney General nor the courts will be able accurately to determine in every instance whether a change had a discriminatory purpose? How substantial must either of these risks be? Is it enough that Congress found them substantial, or must the Court agree, based on its independent analysis of the situation? Justice Rehnquist's dissent, joined by Justice Stewart, argued that, having established that it had no discriminatory purpose, the city would not violate the Constitution in adopting its new rules, and that Congress therefore lacked power to "remedy" a nonexistent violation by requiring preclearance of the changes.

KATZENBACH v. MORGAN, 384 U.S. 641 (1966). Lassiter v. Northampton Election Board, 360 U.S. 45 (1959), held that a fairly administered English-language literacy requirement for prospective voters did not violate the substantive guarantees of the fourteenth and fifteenth amendments. In 1965, as part of the Voting Rights Act, Congress enacted section 4(e), which provided, in pertinent part:

> (1) Congress hereby declares that to secure the rights under the fourteenth amendment of persons educated in American-flag schools in which the predominant classroom language was other than English, it is necessary to prohibit the States from conditioning the right to vote of such persons on ability to read, write, understand, or interpret any matter in the English language. . . .
>
> (2) No person who demonstrates that he has successfully completed the sixth primary grade in a public school in, or a private school accredited by, any State or territory, the District of Columbia, or the Commonwealth of Puerto Rico in which the predominant classroom language was other than English, shall be denied the right to vote in any Federal, State, or local election because of his inability to read, write, understand, or interpret any matter in the English language. . . .

This provision was designed to enfranchise several hundred thousand people who had migrated to New York from Puerto Rico by overriding a New York statute requiring that voters be literate in English.

Justice Brennan, writing for the Court, rejected the argument that section 4(e) could be sustained only after a judicial decision that English-language literacy requirements violate the Equal Protection Clause itself. Such a construction of the enforcement power would "depreciate both congressional resourcefulness and congressional responsibility for implementing the Amendment. It would confine the legislative power in this context to the insignificant role of abrogating only those state laws that the judicial branch was prepared to adjudge unconstitutional, or of merely informing the judgment of the judiciary by particularizing the 'majestic generalities' of §1 of the Amendment."

The Court explained that Section 4(e) "may be viewed as a measure to secure for the Puerto Rican community residing in New York nondiscriminatory treatment by government — both in the imposition of voting qualifications and the provision or administration of governmental services, such as public schools,

[handwritten margin note: pretty much anti-discrimination laws for not knowing english]

public housing and law enforcement. [The] practical effect of §4(e) is to prohibit New York from denying the right to vote to large segments of its Puerto Rican community. [This] enhanced political power will be helpful in gaining nondiscriminatory treatment in public services for the entire Puerto Rican community. [It] was well within congressional authority to say that this need of the Puerto Rican minority for the vote warranted federal intrusion upon any state interests served by the English literacy requirement. It was for Congress [to] assess and weigh the various conflicting considerations — the risk or pervasiveness of the discrimination in governmental services, the effectiveness of eliminating the state restriction on the right to vote as a means of dealing with the evil, the adequacy or availability of alternative remedies, and the nature and significance of the state interests that would be affected by the nullification of the English literacy requirement. [It] is not for us to review the congressional resolution of these factors. It is enough that we be able to perceive a basis upon which the Congress might resolve the conflict as it did."

The Court then considered "whether §4(e) was merely legislation aimed at the elimination of an invidious discrimination in establishing voter qualifications. We are told that New York's English literacy requirement originated in the desire to provide an incentive for non-English speaking immigrants to learn the English language and in order to assure the intelligent exercise of the franchise. Yet Congress might well have questioned, in light of the many exemptions provided and some evidence suggesting that prejudice played a prominent role in the enactment of the requirement whether these were actually the interests being served. Congress might have also questioned whether denial of a right deemed so precious and fundamental in our society was a necessary or appropriate means of encouraging persons to learn English, or of furthering the goal of an intelligent exercise of the franchise. Finally, Congress might well have concluded that as a means of furthering the intelligent exercise of the franchise, an ability to read or understand Spanish is as effective as ability to read English for those to whom Spanish-language newspapers and Spanish-language radio and television programs are available to inform them of election issues and governmental affairs. Since Congress undertook to legislate so as to preclude the enforcement of the state law, and did so in the context of a general appraisal of literacy requirements for voting, to which it brought a specially informed legislative competence, it was Congress' prerogative to weigh these competing considerations. Here again, it is enough that we perceive a basis upon which Congress might predicate a judgment that the application of New York's English literacy requirement to deny the right to vote to a person with a sixth grade education in Puerto Rican schools in which the language of instruction was other than English constituted an invidious discrimination in violation of the Equal Protection Clause."

Justice Harlan, joined by Justice Stewart, dissented. He interpreted the decision as adopting a test of rationality: "[Was] Congress acting rationally in declaring that the New York statute is irrational?" For him, it was "a judicial question whether the condition with which Congress has thus sought to deal is in truth an infringement of the Constitution, something that is the necessary prerequisite to bringing the §5 power into play at all. [Were] the rule otherwise, Congress would be able to qualify this Court's constitutional decisions under the Fourteenth and Fifteenth Amendments [by] resorting to congressional power under the Necessary and Proper Clause. [In] effect the Court reads §5 of the Fourteenth Amendment as giving Congress the power to define the *substantive* scope of the Amendment. If that indeed be the true reach of §5, then I do not see why Congress should not be able as well to exercise its §5 'discretion' by enacting statutes so as in effect to dilute equal protection and due process decisions of this Court. In all such cases there is room for reasonable men to differ as to whether or not a denial of equal protection or due process has occurred, and the final decision is one of judgment. Until today this judgment has always been one for the judiciary to resolve." He acknowledged that "[decisions] on questions of equal protection and due process are based not on abstract logic, but on empirical foundations. To the extent 'legislative facts' are relevant to a judicial determination, Congress is well equipped to investigate them, and such determinations are of course entitled to due respect." But he found "no [factual] data" showing that "Spanish-speaking citizens are fully as capable of making informed decisions in a New York election as are English-speaking citizens. Nor was there any showing [to] support the Court's alternative argument that §4(e) should be viewed as but a remedial measure designed to cure or assure against unconstitutional discrimination of other varieties." He concluded, "To deny the effectiveness of this congressional enactment is not of course to disparage Congress' exertion of authority in the field of civil rights; it is simply to recognize that the Legislative Branch like the other branches of federal authority is subject to the governmental boundaries set by the Constitution. To hold, on this record, that §4(e) overrides the New York literacy requirement seems to me tantamount to allowing the Fourteenth Amendment to swallow the State's constitutionally ordained primary authority in this field. For if Congress by what, as here, amounts to mere *ipse dixit* can set that otherwise permissible requirement partially at naught I see no reason why it could not also substitute its judgment for that of the States in other fields of their exclusive primary competence as well."

Note: The Scope of Section 5

What interpretation of section 5 does *Morgan* adopt? The Court mentions a preventive or prophylactic rationale, but some of its language suggests broader interpretations.

1. *Remedies for arguable violations.* The interpretations of section 5 authorizing complex or preventive remedies rest on the proposition that somewhere in the situation lurks a constitutional violation that the courts would themselves declare to be a violation. Karlan, Two Section Twos and Two Section Fives: Voting Rights and Remedies after *Flores*, 39 Wm. & Mary L. Rev. 725, 728–729 (1998), suggests, after reviewing *Morgan* and several later cases upholding congressional expansion of the ban on literacy tests, that

> [the] cases . . . offer three models of congressionally corrigible invidious discrimination: the internal, the external, and the prospective. . . .
>
> First, under the internal model, literacy tests themselves might be the source of invidious discrimination; that is, the unconstitutional discrimination might occur within the electoral system. Congress and the Court had substantial evidence that literacy tests were administered in deliberately discriminatory ways for the purpose of excluding black citizens who possessed the same abilities as white individuals who were permitted to register. Under this view, Congress could ban literacy tests because the available evidence gave it "reason to believe that many of the laws affected by the congressional enactment have a significant likelihood of being unconstitutional." The congressional ban might — and in fact did — reach some

literacy tests that could not be proven to be purposefully discriminatory. But [the] Constitution does not require a perfect fit.

Second, in the external model, purposeful governmental discrimination outside the electoral system might play out within the electoral system, where it would be observed in the disparate impact of otherwise acceptable policies. For example, the inability of minority voters to pass even a fairly administered literacy test might be "the direct consequence of previous governmental discrimination in education." Under this view, Congress could ban literacy tests to reach and remedy the effects of that impermissible prior discrimination. . . .

Third, under the prospective model, literacy tests might be seen as enabling future invidious action. For example, if literacy tests eliminate a disproportionate number of minority citizens from the electorate, then their diminished voting power might leave minorities vulnerable to discrimination in a wide range of government programs by officials who would be relieved of any practical need to be responsive to the minority's concerns. Under this expansive view, Congress might ban literacy tests "as a remedial measure to deal with . . . discrimination in the provision of public services."

2. *Substantive interpretations.* Is Congress better situated than the Court to determine whether a particular practice denies rights conferred by the fourteenth amendment? On what bases might we rest an independent power in Congress to interpret the Constitution in ways that the Court would (might?) not?

a. *Fact-finding ability.* Is Congress better situated than the courts to engage in fact-finding about equality on the ground? Consider Colker and Brudney, Dissing Congress, 100 Mich. L. Rev. 80, 117 (2001), who point to the distinctive "skill and sophistication that Congress brings to the information-gathering process. Congress educates itself not just through structured record evidence" — as courts do — "but through a range of informal contacts — including local meetings with constituents, ex parte contacts between members (or staff) and lobbyists, and exchanges with executive branch representatives. This institutional virtue, the capacity to gather and evaluate information in both structured and informal settings, contributes to a distinctive Section 5 role for Congress."

b. *Reasonable alternative interpretations of "liberty."* Consider the possibility that (1) with respect to some constitutional guarantees, there is a (broad or narrow) range of permissible interpretations; and (2) the courts are sometimes constrained by their institutional characteristics — for example, by limits on their ability to define rules with sufficient clarity — to adopt only one interpretation within that range. Congress, lacking the same kinds of institutional characteristics, might adopt another interpretation yet still remain within the range of permissible interpretations. Note that some "expansions" of one constitutional "right" might contract other constitutional "rights." In *Morgan* itself, the plaintiffs who challenged section 4(e) were registered voters in New York who claimed that the statute's expansion of the franchise diluted the weight of their votes. Is Section 4(e) an expansion or a dilution of constitutional rights?

Carter, The *Morgan* "Power" and the Forced Reconsideration of Constitutional Decisions, 53 U. Chi. L. Rev. 819, 824 (1986), argues that *Morgan* is "best understood as a tool that permits the Congress to use its power to enact ordinary legislation to engage the Court in a dialogue about our fundamental rights, thereby 'forcing' the Justices to take a fresh look at their own judgments."

City of Boerne v. Flores

521 U.S. 507 (1997)

JUSTICE KENNEDY delivered the opinion of the Court.

A decision by local zoning authorities to deny a church a building permit was challenged under the Religious Freedom Restoration Act of 1993 (RFRA). The case calls into question the authority of Congress to enact RFRA. We conclude the statute exceeds Congress' power. . . .

II

Congress enacted RFRA in direct response to the Court's decision in Employment Div., Dept. of Human Resources of Ore. v. Smith, 494 U.S. 872 (1990) [Chapter 8 infra]. There we considered a Free Exercise Clause claim brought by members of the Native American Church who were denied unemployment benefits when they lost their jobs because they had used peyote. Their practice was to ingest peyote for sacramental purposes, and they challenged an Oregon statute of general applicability which made use of the drug criminal. In evaluating the claim, we declined to apply the balancing test set forth in Sherbert v. Verner, 374 U.S. 398 (1963). [We] stated:

> Government's ability to enforce generally applicable prohibitions of socially harmful conduct . . . cannot depend on measuring the effects of a governmental action on a religious objector's spiritual development. To make an individual's obligation to obey such a law contingent upon the law's coincidence with his religious beliefs, except where the State's interest is "compelling" . . . contradicts both constitutional tradition and common sense. . . .

[These] points of constitutional interpretation were debated by Members of Congress in hearings and floor debates. Many criticized the Court's reasoning, and this disagreement resulted in the passage of RFRA. . . .

RFRA prohibits "government" from "substantially burdening" a person's exercise of religion even if the burden results from a rule of general applicability unless the government can demonstrate the burden "(1) is in furtherance of a compelling governmental interest; and (2) is the least restrictive means of furthering that compelling governmental interest." The Act's mandate applies to any "branch, department, agency, instrumentality, and official (or other person acting under color of law) of the United States," as well as to any "State, or . . . subdivision of a State." . . .

III

A . . .

[In] defense of the Act respondent contends [that] RFRA is permissible enforcement legislation. Congress, it is said, is only protecting by legislation one of the liberties guaranteed by the Fourteenth Amendment's Due Process Clause, the free exercise of religion, beyond what is necessary under *Smith*. It is said the congressional decision to dispense with proof of deliberate or overt discrimination and instead concentrate on a law's effects accords with the settled understanding that §5 includes the power to enact legislation designed to prevent as well as remedy constitutional violations. It is further contended that Congress' §5 power is not limited to remedial or preventive legislation. . . .

[Legislation] which deters or remedies constitutional violations can fall within the sweep of Congress' enforcement power even if in the process it prohibits conduct which is not itself unconstitutional and intrudes into "legislative spheres of autonomy previously reserved to the States." Fitzpatrick v. Bitzer, 427 U.S. 445, 455 (1976). . . .

[In] assessing the breadth of §5's enforcement power, we begin with its text. Congress has been given the power "to enforce" the "provisions of this article." [Congress'] power to enforce the Free Exercise Clause follows from our holding in Cantwell v. Connecticut, 310 U.S. 296, 303 (1940), that the "fundamental concept of liberty embodied in [the fourteenth amendment's due process clause] embraces the liberties guaranteed by the First Amendment."

Congress' power under §5, however, extends only to "enforcing" the provisions of the Fourteenth Amendment. The Court has described this power as "remedial" [South Carolina v. Katzenbach]. The design of the Amendment and the text of §5 are inconsistent with the suggestion that Congress has the power to decree the substance of the Fourteenth Amendment's restrictions on the States. Legislation which alters the meaning of the Free Exercise Clause cannot be said to be enforcing the Clause. Congress does not enforce a constitutional right by changing what the right is. It has been given the power "to enforce," not the power to determine what constitutes a constitutional violation. Were it not so, what Congress would be enforcing would no longer be, in any meaningful sense, the "provisions of [the Fourteenth Amendment]."

While the line between measures that remedy or prevent unconstitutional actions and measures that make a substantive change in the governing law is not easy to discern, and Congress must have wide latitude in determining where it lies, the distinction exists and must be observed. There must be a congruence and proportionality between the injury to be prevented or remedied and the means adopted to that end. Lacking such a connection, legislation may become substantive in operation and effect. . . .

Any suggestion that Congress has a substantive, non-remedial power under the Fourteenth Amendment is not supported by our case law. . . .

There is language in our opinion in Katzenbach v. Morgan which could be interpreted as acknowledging a power in Congress to enact legislation that expands the rights contained in §1 of the Fourteenth Amendment. This is not a necessary interpretation, however, or even the best one. . . .

If Congress could define its own powers by altering the Fourteenth Amendment's meaning, no longer would the Constitution be "superior paramount law, unchangeable by ordinary means." It would be "on a level with ordinary legislative acts, and, like other acts, . . . alterable when the legislature shall please to alter it." [Marbury.] . . .

B

Respondent contends that RFRA is a proper exercise of Congress' remedial or preventive power. The Act, it is said, is a reasonable means of protecting the free exercise of religion as defined by Smith. It prevents and remedies laws which are enacted with the unconstitutional object of targeting religious beliefs and practices. To avoid the difficulty of proving such violations, it is said, Congress can simply invalidate any law which imposes a substantial burden on a religious practice unless it is justified by a compelling interest and is the least restrictive means of accomplishing that interest. If Congress can prohibit laws with discriminatory effects in order to prevent racial discrimination in violation of the Equal Protection Clause, then it can do the same, respondent argues, to promote religious liberty.

While preventive rules are sometimes appropriate remedial measures, there must be a congruence between the means used and the ends to be achieved. The appropriateness of remedial measures must be considered in light of the evil presented. Strong measures appropriate to address one harm may be an unwarranted response to another, lesser one. . . .

[RFRA] cannot be considered remedial, preventive legislation, if those terms are to have any meaning. RFRA is so out of proportion to a supposed remedial or preventive object that it cannot be understood as responsive to, or designed to prevent, unconstitutional behavior. It appears, instead, to attempt a substantive change in constitutional protections. Preventive measures prohibiting certain types of laws may be appropriate when there is reason to believe that many of the laws affected by the congressional enactment have a significant likelihood of being unconstitutional. . . .

[Justice Stevens concurred in the Court's opinion, and noted as well that he believed that RFRA violated the establishment clause of the first amendment. Justice O'Connor dissented, saying that in her view *Smith* was wrongly decided and should be overruled, but she agreed with the Court's analysis of Congress's power under section 5. Justice Breyer joined her discussion of *Smith* but did not "find it necessary" to consider the question of congressional power under section 5. Justice Souter also dissented, saying that the Court should have dismissed the writ of certiorari as improperly granted.]

Note: The Roles of Court and Congress

1. *"Changing" or "defining" constitutional rights.* The Court argues that "Congress does not enforce a constitutional right by changing what the right is." Consider the theory of judicial supremacy implicit in that phrase:

> Congress was not seeking to change the Free Exercise Clause. It was attempting to correct what it considered to be the Supreme Court's misinterpretation, which is not the same thing. The Court stated: "If Congress could define its own powers by altering the Fourteenth Amendment's meaning, no longer would the Constitution be 'superior paramount law, unchangeable by ordinary means.'" But no one — not Congress, not the parties . . . — thought Congress could "alter[] the Fourteenth Amendment's meaning." The question is which body's good faith interpretation of the Amendment — Congress's or the Supreme Court's — is entitled to legal force in this context.

McConnell, Comment, Institutions and Interpretation: A Critique of City of Boerne v. Flores, 111 Harv. L. Rev. 153, 173–174 (1997).

Should Congress have the power to (conclusively) define a right in a reasonable manner inconsistent with a prior judicial determination of what the right is? Would that allow Congress to dilute constitutional protections? Can that question be answered without a broader theory of the relation between Court and Congress in defining constitutional rights? For an argument against judicial supremacy, see M. Tushnet, Taking the Constitution Away from the Courts (1999).

Is the problem in *Boerne* that Congress acted too swiftly and in direct contradiction of a recent Supreme Court decision? What would Congress have to do to establish that a more focused statute, imposing the statutory standard for zoning decisions, for example, was appropriately "congruent" and "proportional"?

Boerne involved Congress enforcing rights defined in the first amendment (but made applicable to the states through the fourteenth amendment's due process clause. See Chapter 6, section C.) Should a different analysis apply when Congress is enforcing principles of equality? Consider the following view:

> In interpretations and enforcements of the Fourteenth Amendment, there appears to be broad agreement between the Court, Congress, and agencies that the Equal Protection Clause advances an antidiscrimination principle broadly defined. But there is considerable disagreement on the standards and rules for implementing this principle. . . . [T]he Court has determined that the poor, the elderly, and the disabled are entitled to neither heightened protection from laws that discriminate against them nor any special accommodation. But Congress through statutes such as the ESEA, Civil Rights Act, ADA, and ADEA and agencies through interpretations of these statutes have provided heightened protections and special accommodations to these groups.
>
> Judicial supremacy would seem to demand judicial invalidation of these congressional and agency Constitution-based determinations because they deviate from those of the Court. But unlike the religious liberty rules, the difference between the equal protection determinations about which classes are entitled to protection and how much protection they are entitled to has not been based on a substantive disagreement between the political branches and the Court about what the Constitution substantively requires. . . . Rather, judicial considerations about the appropriate role for itself as an unelected, unaccountable institution in a democracy demand judicial noninterference when groups are deemed capable of defending themselves in the political process. This institutional logic suggests that more democratic institutions — Congress and administrative agencies — should be given leeway to diverge from the Court's doctrine by enforcing equal protection principles in ways that provide protections to groups left unprotected by the Court.

Ross, Administering Suspect Classes, 66 Duke L.J. 1807, 1844–45 (2017).

2. *The "congruence and proportionality" test.* Consider these observations by Justice Scalia in Tennessee v. Lane, 541 U.S. 509 (2004):

> I joined the Court's opinion in *Boerne* with some misgiving. . . .
>
> I yield to the lessons of experience. The "congruence and proportionality" standard, like all such flabby tests, is a standing invitation to judicial arbitrariness and policy-driven decisionmaking. Worse still, it casts this Court in the role of Congress's taskmaster. Under it, the courts (and ultimately this Court) must regularly check Congress's homework to make sure that it has identified sufficient constitutional violations to make its remedy congruent and proportional. As a general matter, we are ill advised to adopt or adhere to constitutional rules that bring us into constant conflict with a coequal branch of Government. And when conflict is unavoidable, we should not come to do battle with the United States Congress armed only with a test ("congruence and proportionality") that has no demonstrable basis in the text of the Constitution and cannot objectively be shown to have been met or failed. . . .

I would replace "congruence and proportionality" with another test. [One] does not, within any normal meaning of the term, "enforce" a prohibition by issuing a still broader prohibition directed to the same end. One does not, for example, "enforce" a 55-mile-per-hour speed limit by imposing a 45-mile-per-hour speed limit — even though that is indeed directed to the same end of automotive safety and will undoubtedly result in many fewer violations of the 55-mile-per-hour limit. And one does not "enforce" the right of access to the courts at issue in this case, by requiring that disabled persons be provided access to all of the "services, programs, or activities" furnished or conducted by the State. [So-called] "prophylactic legislation" is reinforcement rather than enforcement. . . .

Justice Scalia would restrict congressional power under section 5 to creating causes of action for vindicating fourteenth amendment rights, where courts rather than Congress would define the contours of the rights, and to a few ancillary provisions designed to enable effective litigation of constitutional cases. Consider whether this conforms to the original understanding of the power granted Congress in section 5.

3. *Changing times and prophylactic rules.* Suppose that Congress has before it sufficient evidence to justify adoption of a remedy under section 5 that is proportional to and congruent with constitutional violations but goes beyond providing a remedy for such violations only. Citing cases upholding the Voting Rights Act of 1965, *Boerne* asserts that such prophylactic rules are constitutional. What if, after time passes, the number of direct constitutional violations drops, either because of widespread compliance with the congressional statute or because of changing social norms? Can a statute constitutionally valid when adopted later become disproportionate or incongruent and therefore unconstitutional?

The Supreme Court addressed this question in Shelby County v. Holder, 133 S. Ct. 2612 (2013). Section 4 of the Voting Rights Act provided a "coverage formula" that determined which states were subject to the act's preclearance requirement, which forbid them from making changes in their voting laws without first proving (either to a federal court in Washington, D.C., or to the Department of Justice) that the change would have neither a discriminatory purpose nor a discriminatory effect. The original formula looked at whether the jurisdiction used literacy tests or similar devices as a prerequisite to voting and whether registration or turnout in the 1964 election was significantly below the national average. The formula was amended in 1970 and 1975 to cover jurisdictions with low participation in either or both the 1968 or 1972 election. In 1982 and 2006, Congress extended section 5's preclearance requirement without changing the coverage formula.

Chief Justice Roberts's opinion for the Court held that the coverage formula of section 4 was unconstitutional and could no longer be used to subject jurisdictions to the preclearance regime of section 5. The Court emphasized the burdens on covered jurisdictions, which were required to "beseech the Federal Government for permission to implement laws that they would otherwise have the right to enact and execute on their own." It characterized that burden as particularly severe because of its departure from the normal situation in which states are free to implement their laws until those laws are successfully challenged and because, "despite the tradition of equal sovereignty, the Act applies to only nine States (and several additional counties)."

The Court then declared that "the Act imposes current burdens and must be justified by current needs." While the VRA's "departures from the basic features of our system of government" may have been justified by the pervasive discrimination that existed in 1965, they were no longer justified: "Nearly 50 years later, things have changed dramatically":

> When upholding the constitutionality of the coverage formula in 1966, we concluded that it was "rational in both practice and theory." The formula looked to cause (discriminatory tests) and effect (low voter registration and turnout), and tailored the remedy (preclearance) to those jurisdictions exhibiting both. . . .
>
> Coverage today is based on decades-old data and eradicated practices. The formula captures States by reference to literacy tests and low voter registration and turnout in the 1960s and early 1970s. But such tests have been banned nationwide for over 40 years. And voter registration and turnout numbers in the covered States have risen dramatically in the years since. Racial disparity in those numbers was compelling evidence justifying the preclearance remedy and the coverage formula. There is no longer such a disparity.
>
> In 1965, the States could be divided into two groups: those with a recent history of voting tests and low voter registration and turnout, and those without those characteristics. Congress based its coverage formula on that distinction. Today the Nation is no longer divided along those lines, yet the Voting Rights Act continues to treat it as if it were.

Justice Ginsburg, joined by Justices Breyer, Sotomayor, and Kagan, dissented. Their view was that Congress, rather than the Court, should decide whether the coverage formula remains appropriate:

> It is well established that Congress' judgment regarding exercise of its power to enforce the Fourteenth and Fifteenth Amendments warrants substantial deference. The VRA addresses the combination of race discrimination and the right to vote, which is "preservative of all rights." When confronting the most constitutionally invidious form of discrimination, and the most fundamental right in our democratic system, Congress' power to act is at its height.
>
> The basis for this deference is firmly rooted in both constitutional text and precedent. The Fifteenth Amendment, which targets precisely and only racial discrimination in voting rights, states that, in this domain, "Congress shall have power to enforce this article by appropriate legislation." . . .
>
> It cannot tenably be maintained that the VRA, an Act of Congress adopted to shield the right to vote from racial discrimination, is inconsistent with the letter or spirit of the Fifteenth Amendment, or any provision of the Constitution read in light of the Civil War Amendments. Nowhere in today's opinion [is] there clear recognition of the transformative effect the Fifteenth Amendment aimed to achieve. . . .
>
> The stated purpose of the Civil War Amendments was to arm Congress with the power and authority to protect all persons within the Nation from violations of their rights by the States. In exercising that power, then, Congress may use "all means which are appropriate, which are plainly adapted" to the constitutional ends declared by these Amendments. [McCulloch.] So when Congress acts to enforce the right to vote free from racial discrimination, we ask not whether Congress has chosen the means most wise, but whether Congress has rationally selected means appropriate to a legitimate end. . . .
>
> For three reasons, legislation reauthorizing an existing statute is especially likely to satisfy the minimal requirements of the rational-basis test. First, when reauthorization is at issue, Congress has already assembled a legislative record justifying the

initial legislation. Congress is entitled to consider that preexisting record as well as
the record before it at the time of the vote on reauthorization. . . .

Second, the very fact that reauthorization is necessary arises because Congress
has built a temporal limitation into the Act. . . .

Third, a reviewing court should expect the record supporting reauthorization to
be less stark than the record originally made. Demand for a record of violations
equivalent to the one earlier made would expose Congress to a catch-22. If the
statute was working, there would be less evidence of discrimination, so opponents
might argue that Congress should not be allowed to renew the statute. In contrast, if
the statute was not working, there would be plenty of evidence of discrimination,
but scant reason to renew a failed regulatory regime.

Note: The Interaction of Congressional Enforcement Power and the Eleventh Amendment

The Supreme Court has limited congressional power not only by its construction of the Constitution's grants of substantive power but also by limiting
Congress's power to create judicial remedies for enforcing federal
constitutional and statutory rights. It has relied principally on the eleventh
amendment, which provides, "The judicial power of the United States shall
not be construed to extend to any suit in law or equity, commenced or prosecuted against one of the United States by Citizens of another State, or by
Citizens or Subjects of any Foreign State." The amendment was adopted in
response to the Supreme Court's ruling in Chisholm v. Georgia, 2 U.S. (2
Dall.) 419 (1793), which involved a suit by a South Carolina citizen seeking to
recover a debt owed for materials supplied to Georgia during the Revolutionary
War. The Court upheld federal jurisdiction by a four-to-one vote. Congress
submitted the proposed eleventh amendment to the states within three weeks of
the decision in Chisholm, and the required three-quarters of the states ratified it
within a year, although the official proclamation of ratification did not occur
until 1797.

The amendment's text refers only to suits against states brought by citizens of
other states or foreign nations. In Hans v. Louisiana, 134 U.S. 1 (1890), however,
the Court held that the eleventh amendment also barred suits by citizens against
their own state. As the Court later explained, Hans adopts the view that states'
immunity from suit was a presupposition of the constitutional order, not
displaced by the mere adoption of the Constitution.

Does Congress have the power to abrogate the states' immunity from suit? For
a period the Court held that the Constitution's grants of power to Congress, in
article I, section 8 and elsewhere, gave Congress the power to displace state
immunity. See, e.g., Pennsylvania v. Union Gas, 491 U.S. 1 (1989).

But in Seminole Tribe of Florida v. Florida, 517 U.S. 44 (1996), the Court
rejected those decisions and held that state sovereign immunity could not be
displaced by an exercise of the powers granted Congress in 1789. Alden v. Maine,
527 U.S. 706 (1999), held that Congress also could not require state courts to
entertain suits by individuals seeking damages for violation of a federal statute,
where the state courts refused to do so on the basis of state sovereign immunity
rules that did not themselves discriminate against national claims. The decision
cannot be explained as relying on the text of the eleventh amendment, which
refers only to the judicial power of the United States. The Court instead relied on
a broader principle of sovereign immunity, of which the eleventh amendment is
an illustration.

The Court has held, however, that section 5 of the fourteenth amendment does give Congress the power to displace state immunity when it develops remedies for violations of rights protected by section 1 of that amendment. In the Court's view, not only does the fourteenth amendment come later in time than the eleventh, but it also expresses a view of the relation between the states and the nation in which state sovereign immunity must yield to congressional judgments. Fitzpatrick v. Bitzer, 427 U.S. 445 (1976).

In general, as Chapter 2 showed, during the twentieth century, Congress used its article I powers, particularly its commerce clause powers, even when it was pursuing principles of equality more expressly reflected in the fourteenth amendment. But *Seminole Tribe*'s holding that "[even] when the Constitution vests in Congress complete law-making authority over a particular area, the Eleventh Amendment prevents congressional authorization of suits by private parties against unconsenting States" creates

> a wedge between Congress's essentially plenary power to regulate state economic activity and its ability to enforce its regulations by making damages remedies available. [The] juxtaposition of *Seminole Tribe* and *Alden* on the one hand with *Fitzpatrick* on the other, inevitably places pressure on the question of which source of congressional authority undergirds a statute.

Karlan, Disarming the Private Attorney General, 2003 U. Ill. L. Rev. 183, 189. That issue has been confronted in a series of cases.

In Kimel v. Florida Board of Regents, 528 U.S. 62 (2000), the Court held that Congress lacked power under section 5 to authorize a damages remedy under the Age Discrimination in Employment Act (ADEA) for state employees. Although the Court had earlier held, in EEOC v. Wyoming, 460 U.S. 226 (1983), that extension of the ADEA to state employers constituted a valid exercise of Congress's commerce power, the Court concluded in *Kimel* that the ADEA did not also constitute "appropriate legislation" under section 5. Justice O'Connor's opinion for the Court held that the requirements the ADEA imposed on state governments were "disproportionate to any unconstitutional conduct that conceivably could be targeted by the Act," given that as a matter of constitutional law, states were entitled to treat workers differently based on their age as long as the difference in treatment was not irrational. The ADEA, through its "broad restriction on the use of age as a discriminating factor, prohibits substantially more state employment decisions and practices than would likely be held unconstitutional under the applicable equal protection, rational basis standard." The Court also pointed to the legislative history of the ADEA and found that "Congress had virtually no reason to believe that state and local governments were unconstitutionally discriminating against their employees on the basis of age. Congress' failure to uncover any significant pattern of unconstitutional discrimination here confirms that Congress had no reason to believe that broad prophylactic legislation was necessary in this field."

Similarly, in Florida Prepaid Postsecondary Education Expense Board v. College Savings Bank, 527 U.S. 627 (1999), the Supreme Court rejected congressional attempts to abrogate states' sovereign immunity under the Patent and Plant Variety Protection Remedy Clarification Act, because the Court held that the act did not constitute legislation enacted to enforce the guarantees of the due process clause of the fourteenth amendment. Although patents were a species of property, Congress lacked a legislative record showing that states engaged in pervasive unconstitutional patent infringement (the due process clause requiring proof not just of infringement but also that states refused to provide any remedy).

BOARD OF TRUSTEES v. GARRETT, 531 U.S. 356 (2001). Title I of the Americans with Disabilities Act of 1990 (ADA) prohibits certain employers, including state governments, from discriminating against otherwise qualified individuals with disabilities. Among other things, the ADA requires employers to make "reasonable accommodations" for disabled workers, including making physical facilities accessible to and usable by individuals with disabilities and restructuring job requirements or schedules to enable individuals with disabilities to perform the job. Garrett, a registered nurse, was employed as a nursing director at the University of Alabama in Birmingham Hospital. While she was undergoing treatment for cancer, her supervisor required her to give up her high-level position and to transfer to another, lower-paying position. She filed suit seeking money damages.

Chief Justice Rehnquist wrote for a divided Court rejecting her claim. Relying on City of Cleburne v. Cleburne Living Center, 473 U.S. 432 (1985), the Chief Justice wrote that legislation that treats people with disabilities differently from people without disabilities must satisfy "only the minimum 'rational-basis' review applicable to general social and economic legislation. The legislative record of the ADA [fails] to show that Congress did in fact identify a pattern of irrational state discrimination in employment against the disabled." Moreover, "the rights and remedies created by the ADA against the States would raise the same sort of concerns as to congruence and proportionality as were found in City of Boerne. [The] accommodation duty far exceeds what is constitutionally required."

Justice Kennedy, joined by Justice O'Connor, concurred. Justice Breyer's dissent was joined by Justices Stevens, Souter, and Ginsburg. He described the Court as "[reviewing] the congressional record as if it were an administrative agency record." For the dissenters, "[the] powerful evidence of discriminatory treatment throughout society in general, including discrimination by private persons and local governments, implicates state governments as well, for state agencies form part of that same larger society. There is no particular reason to believe that they are immune from the 'stereotypic assumptions' and pattern of 'purposeful unequal treatment' that Congress found prevalent." The dissenters also emphasized differences between the judicial and legislative processes: There was "no reason to require Congress, seeking to determine facts relevant to the exercise of its §5 authority, to adopt rules or presumptions that reflect a court's institutional limitations. Unlike courts, Congress can readily gather facts from across the Nation, assess the magnitude of a problem, and more easily find an appropriate remedy. Unlike courts, Congress directly reflects public attitudes and beliefs, enabling Congress better to understand where, and to what extent, refusals to accommodate a disability amount to behavior that is callous or unreasonable to the point of lacking constitutional justification. Unlike judges, Members of Congress can directly obtain information from constituents who have first-hand experience with discrimination and related issues. Moreover, unlike judges, Members of Congress are elected. To apply a rule designed to restrict courts as if it restricted Congress' legislative power is to stand the underlying principle — a principle of judicial restraint — on its head."

Note: Congressional Power to Abrogate States' Sovereign Immunity

1. *Introduction: Does the eleventh amendment matter?* The eleventh amendment bars suits against nonconsenting states. On its face, therefore, it might seem to bar a huge amount of litigation and to preclude enforcement of federal law against the states. But as the Court notes repeatedly in cases such as *Alden* and *Garrett,* the eleventh amendment leaves open a variety of enforcement devices:

> The constitutional privilege of a State to assert its sovereign immunity [does] not confer upon the State a concomitant right to disregard the Constitution or valid federal law. The States and their officers are bound by obligations imposed by the Constitution and by federal statutes that comport with the constitutional design. We are unwilling to assume the States will refuse to honor the Constitution or obey the binding laws of the United States. . . .
>
> Sovereign immunity, moreover, does not bar all judicial review of state compliance with the Constitution and valid federal law. . . .
>
> Sovereign immunity bars suits only in the absence of consent. Many States, on their own initiative, have enacted statutes consenting to a wide variety of suits. . . . - Nor, subject to constitutional limitations, does the Federal Government lack the authority or means to seek the States' voluntary consent to private suits. Cf. South Dakota v. Dole, 483 U.S. 203 (1987).
>
> The States have consented, moreover, to some suits pursuant to the plan of the Convention or to subsequent constitutional amendments. In ratifying the Constitution, the States consented to suits brought by other States or by the Federal Government. [Suits] brought by the United States itself require the exercise of political responsibility for each suit prosecuted against a State, a control which is absent from a broad delegation to private persons to sue nonconsenting States. . . .
>
> Nor does sovereign immunity bar all suits against state officers [for] injunctive or declaratory relief.

Alden v. Maine, 527 U.S. 706, 754–757 (1999). Does the Court's reference to *Dole* suggest that Congress could use its spending clause power to induce states to waive their sovereign immunity, for example by conditioning a grant of federal funds to any state agency on the agency's agreement to waive immunity for claims by employees under the ADEA?

Perhaps the most significant way around the eleventh amendment, at least with respect to constitutional claims and a significant number of federal statutory claims, involves suits against state officers under 42 U.S.C. §1983:

> The Eleventh Amendment almost never matters. More precisely, it matters in ways more indirect and attenuated than is usually acknowledged. Most discussions proceed on the (often unstated) assumption that Eleventh Amendment immunity, when applicable, categorically forbids actions against states. That is formally true but substantively misleading. In almost every case where action against a state is barred by the Eleventh Amendment, suit against a state officer is permitted under [42 U.S.C. §1983.] Very generally, a suit against a state officer is functionally a suit against the state, for the state defends the action and pays any adverse judgment. So far as can be assessed, this is true not occasionally and haphazardly but pervasively and dependably. In most jurisdictions, the state's readiness to defend and indemnify constitutional tort claims is a policy rather than a statutory requirement, but it is nonetheless routine. . . .

Jeffries, In Praise of the Eleventh Amendment and Section 1983, 84 Va. L. Rev. 47, 49–50 (1998).

Jeffries notes that liability under section 1983 normally requires a showing of some degree of fault — because of the doctrine of qualified immunity — but states that "[unlike] most others who have studied the matter, I believe that a constitutional tort regime based on fault is wise policy. To that extent, I find the law of the Eleventh Amendment and Section 1983 fundamentally sound, despite rococo doctrine and occasional nuttiness. . . ." Id. at 53–54. In particular, Jeffries argues that the limitation on damages remedies actually "facilitate[s] the creation of new rights by reducing the costs of innovation." Id. at 79.

Is the major function of the eleventh amendment itself, then, largely formal? Consider the Court's explanation in *Alden*:

> Although the Constitution grants broad powers to Congress, our federalism requires that Congress treat the States in a manner consistent with their status as residuary sovereigns and joint participants in the governance of the Nation. [The] founding generation thought it "neither becoming nor convenient that the several States of the Union, invested with that large residuum of sovereignty which had not been delegated to the United States, should be summoned as defendants to answer the complaints of private persons." The principle of sovereign immunity preserved by constitutional design "thus accords the States the respect owed them as members of the federation."

527 U.S. at 748–749.

The alternatives to private damages remedies are not, however, a complete substitute. For example, they may provide less deterrence of violations in the first place, since there may be little incentive for the state government to comply unless it is sued. And some decisions may not be particularly susceptible to prospective relief. Finally, centralized enforcement, in which only the federal government can seek damages, is likely — perhaps more for budgetary and resource reasons than directly for the reasons of political accountability identified in *Alden* — to lead to underenforcement. See generally Karlan, Disarming the Private Attorney General, 2003 U. Ill. L. Rev. 183.

2. *The interaction of rights and remedies.* To what extent is the Court's deference to Congress on remedial issues a function of prior judicial decisions setting out the nature of the fourteenth amendment's restrictions on the state?

In Nevada Department of Human Resources v. Hibbs, 538 U.S. 721 (2003), the Court upheld the abrogation of state sovereign immunity under the Family and Medical Leave Act of 1993 (FMLA), which gave eligible employees the right to take up to twelve work weeks of unpaid leave annually to take care of ailing spouses, children, or parents. The FMLA created a private damages remedy "against any employer (including a public agency)" that violated an employee's rights.

Chief Justice Rehnquist's opinion for the Court began by noting that FMLA was intended to combat gender-based discrimination in the workplace. In prior cases, the Court had subjected purposeful gender discrimination to heightened scrutiny (as opposed to the more deferential rationality review applicable to distinctions based on classifications such as disability). The fact that gender-based distinctions were more likely than other differences in treatment to violate the equal protection clause means that it should be "easier for Congress to show a pattern of state constitutional violations" that would justify a sweeping remedy.

The Chief Justice saw significant evidence in the record before Congress of gender-based distinctions in employee leave policies. In light of this danger of unconstitutional behavior, the Court concluded that the family-care leave provisions of the FMLA were congruent and proportional:

> By creating an across-the-board, routine employment benefit for all eligible employees, Congress sought to ensure that family-care leave would no longer be stigmatized as an inordinate drain on the workplace caused by female employees, and that employers could not evade leave obligations simply by hiring men. By setting a minimum standard of family leave for all eligible employees, irrespective of gender, the FMLA attacks the formerly state-sanctioned stereotype that only women are responsible for family caregiving, thereby reducing employers' incentives to engage in discrimination by basing hiring and promotion decisions on stereotypes. . . .
> [I]n light of the evidence before Congress, a statute [that] simply mandated gender equality in the administration of leave benefits, would not have achieved Congress' remedial object. Such a law would allow States to provide for no family leave at all. Where "two-thirds of the nonprofessional caregivers for older, chronically ill, or disabled persons are working women," and state practices continue to reinforce the stereotype of women as caregivers, such a policy would exclude far more women than men from the workplace.

Justices Kennedy, Scalia, and Thomas dissented.
   The Court suggested reconciling *Garrett* and *Hibbs* on the ground that prior judicial opinions treated discrimination on the basis of disability and discrimination on the basis of sex quite differently.
   In Coleman v. Maryland Court of Appeals, 566 U.S. 30 (2012), however, the Court held that Congress could not validly overcome state sovereign immunity with respect to the self-care provisions of the FMLA. (*Hibbs* had involved the family leave provision.) Writing for himself, the Chief Justice, and Justices Alito and Thomas, Justice Kennedy concluded that the self-care provision did not respond to unconstitutional sex discrimination by state employers. Justice Scalia concurred in the judgment, reiterating his view that "outside of the context of racial discrimination (which is different for *stare decisis* reasons), I would limit Congress's §5 power to the regulation of conduct that *itself* violates the Fourteenth Amendment."
   Justice Ginsburg, joined by Justices Breyer, Sotomayor, and Kagan, dissented. Justices Ginsburg and Breyer repeated their view that Congress can abrogate state sovereign immunity pursuant to its article I powers (such as the commerce power). But Justice Ginsburg also argued that, taken in its historical context, the self-care provision of the FMLA should be understood as a response to substantial evidence of unconstitutional sex discrimination. She thus disagreed with the plurality's characterization of the legislative record. She wrote that the self-care provision had its genesis in a concern that women were being singled out for adverse employment consequences because of employers' views that they were likely to become pregnant and to leave the workforce. She located the FMLA within a broader debate between "equal-treatment" feminists, who did not want a pregnancy-leave–specific bill because it would undercut their broader arguments, and "equal-opportunity" feminists, who were concerned that women were being uniquely disadvantaged by the failure to provide pregnancy leave. "In view of this history, it is impossible to conclude that 'nothing in particular about self-care leave . . . connects it to gender discrimination.'"

Congress [had] good reason to conclude that the self-care provision — which men no doubt would use — would counter employers' impressions that the FMLA would otherwise install female leave. Providing for self-care would thus reduce employers' corresponding incentive to discriminate against women in hiring and promotion. In other words, "[t]he availability of self-care leave to men serves to blunt the force of stereotypes of women as primary caregivers by increasing the odds that men and women will invoke the FMLA's leave provisions in near-equal numbers. . . .

3. *The enforcement power and the countermajoritarian difficulty.* Consider McConnell, Institutions and Interpretation: A Critique of City of Boerne v. Flores, 111 Harv. L. Rev. 153, 156 (1997):

> [W]hen Congress interprets the [Constitution] for purposes of carrying out its enforcement authority under Section Five, it is not bound by the institutional constraints that in many cases lead the courts to adopt a less intrusive interpretation from among the textually and historically plausible meanings of the clause in question. Because these institutional constraints are predicated on the need to protect the discretionary judgments of representative institutions from uncabined judicial interference, there is no reason for Congress — the representatives of the people — to abide by them. Congress need not be concerned that its interpretations [will] trench upon democratic prerogatives, because its actions are the expression of the democratic will of the people.

See also Colker and Brudney, Dissing Congress, 100 Mich. L. Rev. 80, 111 (2001). Colker and Brudney point out that much of the legislation the Court has struck down was enacted long before *Boerne* articulated a retreat from the generally deferential standard laid out in *Morgan.*

> The Court's approach represents a serious challenge to the way Congress legislates. The Court is in effect directing Congress to hold focused hearings and to gather comprehensive evidence that will provide ample support for the existence of a national problem addressable under Congress's enumerated powers. The Court's new heightened review of the legislative record has transformed Congress's role from a coequal branch warranting judicial deference to an entity charged with extensive factfinding responsibilities.

4. *The level at which rights are specified.* In cases such as *Kimel, Florida Prepaid, Garrett,* and *Hibbs,* the Court treated the statute before it as a whole. Tennessee v. Lane, 541 U.S. 509 (2004), took a different approach. *Lane* concerned congressional abrogation of state sovereign immunity under title II of the Americans with Disabilities Act, which prohibits discrimination and requires reasonable accommodation with respect to public services, programs, or activities. (Recall that *Garrett* concerned title I of the ADA, which dealt with employment, both public and private.) The respondent was a paraplegic, who used a wheelchair. He sued the state of Tennessee under title II, claiming that he had been denied access to the state court system by reason of his disability. He alleged that he was compelled to appear to answer a set of criminal charges on the second floor of a county courthouse that had no elevator. At his first appearance, he crawled up two flights of stairs to get to the courtroom. When he returned to the courthouse for a hearing, he refused to crawl again or to be carried by officers to the courtroom; he consequently was arrested and jailed for failure to appear.

The state of Tennessee moved to dismiss the suit on the ground that it was barred by the eleventh amendment.

Justice Stevens's opinion for the Court noted that title II — unlike title I, which dealt only with employment, which is not itself an independently recognized constitutional right — "seeks to enforce a variety of other basic constitutional guarantees, infringements of which are subject to more searching judicial review." He explained that "Congress enacted Title II against a backdrop of pervasive unequal treatment in the administration of state services and programs, including systematic deprivations of fundamental rights." In light of this persistent pattern of discrimination against individuals with disabilities, the Court concluded that title II was appropriate, at least insofar as it was applied to cases alleging denial of access to state judicial proceedings:

> Title II — unlike [the] other statutes we have reviewed for validity under §5 — reaches a wide array of official conduct in an effort to enforce an equally wide array of constitutional guarantees. Petitioner urges us both to examine the broad range of Title II's applications all at once, and to treat that breadth as a mark of the law's invalidity. [But] nothing in our case law requires us to consider Title II, with its wide variety of applications, as an undifferentiated whole. . . .

Chief Justice Rehnquist, joined by Justices Kennedy and Thomas, dissented, emphasizing that Lane was not bringing suit for a denial of his constitutional rights.

Justice Scalia's dissent is quoted above.

In United States v. Georgia, 546 U.S. 151 (2006), the Court refined its analysis of congressional power under section 5. Goodman, an inmate in a Georgia prison, sued various state defendants challenging the conditions of his confinement. He sought money damages under Title II of the ADA, claiming that the state's failure to accommodate his disabilities — he was a paraplegic and was often left for hours at a time in his wheelchair in a cell where he could neither turn around nor reach the toilet facilities — violated the ADA. In a unanimous opinion written by Justice Scalia, the Court noted that "insofar as Title II creates a private cause of action for damages against the States for conduct that *actually* violates the Fourteenth Amendment, Title II validly abrogates state sovereign immunity." If sovereign immunity is designed to relieve states of the burdens of suit, as well as to protect them from liability, is this distinction coherent?

Note: *Congressional Power to Regulate "Private" Action for Civil Rights Purposes*

1. *The thirteenth amendment.* Section 1 of the thirteenth amendment provides that "[neither] slavery nor involuntary servitude . . . shall exist within the United States. . . ." Like section 5 of the fourteenth amendment, section 2 of the thirteenth amendment authorizes Congress "to enforce this article by appropriate legislation."

From its inception, the thirteenth amendment was understood to apply to private as well as governmental action. See The Civil Rights Cases, 109 U.S. 3 (1883). (The Civil Rights Cases are examined in greater detail in Chapter 9, section A, infra.) Thus, the Court repeatedly upheld federal prosecutions of private individuals under statutes that criminalized various forms of forced labor, see, e.g., Bailey v. Alabama, 219 U.S. 219 (1911), because, as The Civil Rights Cases explained, "[under] the Thirteenth Amendment, [federal] legislation, so far as necessary or proper to eradicate all forms and incidents of slavery and involuntary servitude, may be direct and primary, operating upon the acts of individuals, whether sanctioned by State legislation or not." 109 U.S. at 23. For discussion of these issues, see generally G. Rutherglen, Civil Rights in the Shadow of Slavery: The Constitution, Common Law, and the Civil Rights Act of 1866 (2012).

How far beyond targeting slavery and involuntary servitude does Congress's enforcement power extend? The Civil Rights Cases had explained that the enforcement clause gave Congress "power to pass all laws necessary and proper for abolishing all badges and incidents of slavery in the United States."

In Jones v. Alfred H. Mayer Co., 392 U.S. 409 (1968), the Court relied on that principle in interpreting a Reconstruction era civil rights statute, 42 U.S.C. §1982, to apply to private conduct. The plaintiffs alleged that Mayer, the developer of a large suburban housing complex, had refused to sell them a house solely because one of them was black. They claimed that this violated section 1982, which provides: "All citizens [shall] have the same right, in every State and Territory, as is enjoyed by white citizens thereof, to inherit, purchase, lease, sell, hold, and convey real and personal property." The Court, through Justice Stewart, held that the statute barred private racial discrimination in the sale of property — and not merely racially discriminatory laws relating to the ownership and use of property — and that, "thus construed, [it] is a valid exercise of the power of Congress to enforce the Thirteenth Amendment." Quoting the "badges and incidents" language from The Civil Rights Cases, the Court declared that "[surely] Congress has the power rationally to determine what are the badges and the incidents of slavery." It was not "irrational" for Congress to conclude that private restraints on the ability of blacks to engage in otherwise normal market transactions were one such badge.

Is the role that the Court gave Congress in Jones in interpreting the scope of the thirteenth amendment consistent with the Court's more recent decisions in Boerne and its progeny?

In Memphis v. Greene, 451 U.S. 100 (1981), by contrast, the Court held that section 1982 could not support the plaintiffs' challenge to a city's decision to close a street that ran from a predominantly black neighborhood through a predominantly white neighborhood because the disparate impact of the street closure did not constitute a badge or incident of slavery.

2. *The fourteenth amendment.* The fourteenth amendment provides that "no state shall [deny] to any person [the] equal protection of the laws." The reference to "states" has generated a large body of doctrine regarding the so-called state action doctrine, discussed in detail in Chapter 9 infra. For present purposes, the doctrine means that, for the fourteenth amendment to be implicated (and therefore for Congress to have power to enforce its protections), there must be either a sufficient degree of state involvement with the action or a failure by the state to act in circumstances where the Constitution affirmatively requires action.

United States v. Morrison, 529 U.S. 598 (2000), held that the civil remedy provision of the Violence Against Women Act was not a constitutionally permissible exercise of Congress's power under section 5. The statute provided a federal cause of action against a person "who commits a crime of violence motivated by gender and thus deprives another of the right" to be free from such crimes. The private plaintiff in *Morrison*, a student at a state university, sued, among other people, two other students at the university claiming that they had raped her.

The statute's defenders relied on evidence that states had failed to adequately investigate and prosecute gender-related crimes. The Court rejected this argument:

> [The] remedy is simply not "corrective in its character, adapted to counteract and redress the operation of such prohibited state laws or proceedings of state officers." Civil Rights Cases, 109 U.S. at 18. [Section] 13981 is not aimed at proscribing discrimination by officials which the Fourteenth Amendment might not itself proscribe; it is directed not at any State or state actor, but at individuals who have committed criminal acts motivated by gender bias.

Justice Breyer's dissent asked, "[Given] the relation between remedy and violation — the creation of a federal remedy to substitute for constitutionally inadequate state remedies — where is the lack of 'congruence'?"

In this light, consider Rutherglen, Custom and Usage as Action under Color of State Law: An Essay on the Forgotten Terms of Section 1983, 89 Va. L. Rev. 925 (2003). Rutherglen argues for deference to Congress in determining what counts as state action:

> According to the majority in *Morrison*, the Violence Against Women Act failed [the proportionality and congruence] test because it enacted prohibitions directed mainly against private individuals, not against state actors. The rights granted by Section 1 are good only against state action, and thus legislation under Section 5 must be similarly limited. An examination of custom as a source of state law, however, would have turned this conclusion on its head. The combination of official inaction in enforcing laws that prohibited violence against women, and the underlying pattern of such violence itself, gave rise to the customs necessary to support a congressional finding of state action. Congress has resources available to it that a court does not when trying to determine whether there has been state action in violation of Section 1. The hearings and extensive documentation of the intertwined patterns of official neglect and private violence, recounted in the dissenting opinions to show an effect on commerce, could not easily have been made by a court. . . .

Id. at 972–973.

3. *Problems of statutory interpretation.* The statutes discussed here are the legacy of Reconstruction, a period when concepts of civil rights and federalism were different from our own. The Court has been criticized and praised for infusing these old statutes with contemporary content. See, e.g., Casper, Jones v. Mayer: Clio, Bemused and Confused Muse, 1968 Sup. Ct. Rev. 89; Kohl, The Civil Rights Act of 1866, Its Hour Come Round at Last, 55 Va. L. Rev. 272 (1969). For a somewhat less skeptical view, see Rutherglen, The Improbable History of Section 1981: Clio Still Bemused and Confused, 2003 Sup. Ct. Rev. 303. If the language of the statutes is fairly susceptible to the Court's interpretations, should it matter that its adopters had a narrower understanding of civil rights? What if their understanding was confused (on our terms or theirs)?

Modern civil rights statutes cover many of the acts also covered by the Reconstruction statutes under the Court's interpretations. The Civil Rights Act of 1968, for example, makes unlawful the activity at issue in Jones v. Mayer. The act is broader than the 1866 act in some ways, by covering other forms of discrimination and providing additional forms of remedial assistance to a complainant, and is narrower in others, by containing some exemptions. Is it appropriate to revive old statutes when Congress has recently addressed the general problem in a different way? Does the fact that the Court revives old statutes at roughly the same time that Congress is enacting new statutes suggest that the Court is more heavily influenced by contemporary understandings than by the intentions of the drafters of the older statute being interpreted?

C. THE TREATY POWER

Article II, section 2 gives the president "Power, by and with the Advice and Consent of the Senate, to make Treaties, provided two thirds of the Senators present concur." Treaties, like legislation enacted by Congress, can serve as "the supreme Law of the Land." Art. VI, section 2. Many treaty agreements are aimed at activities that take place within national borders. As with the taxing and spending powers discussed earlier in this chapter, the question has arisen to what extent the federal government can reach activities not otherwise within its enumerated powers by exercising the treaty power.

Missouri v. Holland
252 U.S. 416 (1920)

MR. JUSTICE HOLMES delivered the opinion of the court.

This is a bill in equity brought by the State of Missouri to prevent a game warden of the United States from attempting to enforce the Migratory Bird Treaty Act of 1918 and the regulations made by the Secretary of Agriculture in pursuance of the same. The ground of the bill is that the statute is an unconstitutional interference with the rights reserved to the States by the Tenth Amendment, and that the acts of the defendant done and threatened under that authority invade the sovereign right of the State and contravene its will manifested in statutes. . . .

On December 8, 1916, a treaty between the United States and Great Britain was proclaimed by the President. It recited that many species of birds in their annual migrations traversed certain parts of the United States and of Canada, that they were of great value as a source of food and in destroying insects injurious to vegetation, but were in danger of extermination through lack of adequate protection. It therefore provided for specified close seasons [and] agreed that the two powers would take or propose to their law-making bodies the necessary measures for carrying the treaty out. [The act] prohibited the killing, capturing or selling any of the migratory birds included in the terms of the treaty except as permitted by regulations [to] be made by the Secretary of Agriculture. . . .

[It] is not enough to refer to the Tenth Amendment, reserving the powers not delegated to the United States, because by Article II, §2, the power to make treaties is delegated expressly, and by Article VI treaties made under the authority of the United States [are] declared the supreme law of the land. If the treaty is valid there can be no dispute about the validity of the statute under Article I, §8, as a necessary and proper means to execute the powers of the Government. . . .

C. The Treaty Power

It is said that a treaty cannot be valid if it infringes the Constitution, that there are limits, therefore, to the treaty-making power, and that one such limit is that what an act of Congress could not do unaided, in derogation of the powers reserved to the States, a treaty cannot do. An earlier act of Congress that attempted by itself and not in pursuance of a treaty to regulate the killing of migratory birds within the States had been held bad in the District Court. . . .

Whether the [cases] were decided rightly or not they cannot be accepted as a test of the treaty power. Acts of Congress are the supreme law of the land only when made in pursuance of the Constitution, while treaties are declared to be so when made under the authority of the United States. It is open to question whether the authority of the United States means more than the formal acts prescribed to make the convention. We do not mean to imply that there are no qualifications to the treaty-making power; but they must be ascertained in a different way. It is obvious that there may be matters of the sharpest exigency for the national well being that an act of Congress could not deal with but that a treaty followed by such an act could, and it is not lightly to be assumed that, in matters requiring national action, "a power which must belong to and some where reside in every civilized government" is not to be found. [When] we are dealing with words that also are a constituent act, like the Constitution of the United States, we must realize that they have called into life a being the development of which could not have been foreseen completely by the most gifted of its begetters. It was enough for them to realize or to hope that they had created an organism; it has taken a century and has cost their successors much sweat and blood to prove that they created a nation. The case before us must be considered in the light of our whole experience and not merely in that of what was said a hundred years ago. The treaty in question does not contravene any prohibitory words to be found in the Constitution. The only question is whether it is forbidden by some invisible radiation from the general terms of the Tenth Amendment. We must consider what this country has become in deciding what that Amendment has reserved. . . .

Here a national interest of very nearly the first magnitude is involved. It can be protected only by national action in concert with that of another power. The subject matter is only transitorily within the State and has no permanent habitat therein. But for the treaty and the statute there soon might be no birds for any powers to deal with. We see nothing in the Constitution that compels the Government to sit by while a food supply is cut off and the protectors of our forests and our crops are destroyed. It is not sufficient to rely upon the States. The reliance is vain, and were it otherwise, the question is whether the United States is forbidden to act. We are of opinion that the treaty and statute must be upheld.

Decree affirmed.

Mr. Justice Van Devanter and Mr. Justice Pitney dissent.

Note: Limits on the Treaty Power

1. *The treaty power as a source of domestic regulatory power.* Bradley, The Treaty Power and American Federalism, 97 Mich. L. Rev. 390 (1998), argues for "subject[ing] the treaty power to the same federalism restrictions that apply to Congress's legislative powers. [The] treaty power would not confer any additional regulatory powers on the federal government, just the power to bind the United

States on the international plane." Justice Holmes's formulation appears to imply that the treaty power authorizes the national government to bind the nation to take actions that it is otherwise not constitutionally authorized to take. Note that the domain covered by treaties has expanded beyond relations between nations as such to include economic relations (which might be covered by Congress's power to regulate foreign commerce) and human rights. Does this development make it more necessary to devise judicial doctrines limiting the ability of the national government to enact laws under the treaty power?

Can courts determine what are "matters requiring national action" by treaty followed by legislation rather than by legislation alone? How likely is the President to negotiate and the Senate to ratify a treaty on a matter not requiring national action in Holmes's sense?

2. *Self-executing treaties.* The 1916 Migratory Bird Treaty with Great Britain provided that each signatory "would take or propose to [its] law-making bodies the necessary measures for carrying the treaty out." In contemporary terms, this means the treaty was not "self-executing": It required domestic implementing legislation. The Migratory Bird Act at issue in *Holland* was thus entitled "An Act to give effect to the convention." Would different issues arise had the treaty been "self-executing," that is, not requiring additional legislation as a matter of U.S. law to create obligations on Americans that could be enforced in domestic courts? In thinking about this question and its relationship to questions of federalism, consider the Supreme Court's decision in Medellin v. Texas, 552 U.S. 491 (2008).

Medellin, a Mexican national who had lived in the United States since his early childhood, was arrested, charged, and convicted of capital murder and sentenced to death. A central piece of evidence in the state's case was his detailed confession. Medellin gave the confession after being provided with his *Miranda* warnings, but without being informed of his rights under Article 36(1)(b) of the Vienna Convention on Consular Relations (to which the United States is a signatory) to notify the Mexican consulate of his detention. The United States had also ratified an optional protocol to the Vienna Convention providing that any disputes under the Convention would "lie within the compulsory jurisdiction of the International Court of Justice." Finally, as a member of the United Nations, the United States had undertaken, pursuant to Article 94 of the United Nations Charter, "to comply with the decision of the [ICJ] in any case to which it is a party."

The question before the Court in *Medellin* was whether Medellin could enforce, in Texas's courts, a judgment by the ICJ in a case brought against the United States by the Government of Mexico, that the United States was obligated to provide reconsideration of the convictions and sentences of Mexican nationals who had been denied their Vienna Convention rights.

The Supreme Court held that he could not. It found that the United States had not entered into any "self-executing treaty" obligation, and that the judgment issued by the ICJ did "not automatically constitute federal law enforceable in U.S. courts":

> This Court has long recognized the distinction between treaties that automatically have effect as domestic law, and those that — while they constitute international law commitments — do not by themselves function as binding federal law. [While] treaties "may comprise international commitments . . . they are not domestic law unless Congress has either enacted implementing statutes or the treaty itself conveys an intention that it be 'self executing and is ratified on these terms.'" . . .

Our conclusion [that the Vienna Convention is not self-executing] is further supported by general principles of interpretation. [Given] that ICJ judgments may interfere with state procedural rules, one would expect the ratifying parties to the relevant treaties to have clearly stated their intent to give those judgments domestic effect, if they had so intended. . . .

That the judgment of an international tribunal might not automatically become domestic law hardly means the underlying treaty is "useless." Such judgments would still constitute international obligations, the proper subject of political and diplomatic negotiations. . . .

Justice Stevens concurred in the judgment. While he agreed with the majority that the relevant treaties were best read to "contemplat[e] future action by the political branches" and thus to leave "the choice of whether to comply with ICJ judgments, and in what manner, 'to the political, not the judicial department,'" he urged Texas nonetheless to take the treaty obligations into account.

Justice Breyer, joined by Justices Souter and Ginsburg, dissented. They emphasized the wide range of self-executing treaties to which the U.S. was a signatory and would have found the relevant treaty provisions here to have been self-executing. They saw the ICJ's judgment as particularly "well suited to direct judicial enforcement. [Courts] frequently work with criminal procedure and related prejudice. Legislatures do not. Judicial standards are readily available for working in this technical area. Legislative standards are not readily available. Judges typically determine such matters, deciding, for example, whether further hearings are necessary, after reviewing a record in an individual case. Congress does not normally legislate in respect to individual cases." And they emphasized that the President favored enforcement of the judgment.

3. *Constitutional limits on the power to implement treaties.* Bond v. United States, 134 S. Ct. 2077 (2014), involved a federal statute implementing the International Convention on the Prohibition of the Development, Production, Storage, Stockpiling, and Use of Chemical Weapons, a treaty ratified in 1997. A majority of the Court held that the statute did not apply to the defendant's actions. (She had sought revenge against her husband's paramour by spreading two chemicals that met the statute's definition of "chemical weapons" on surfaces the paramour was likely to touch.)

Chief Justice Roberts's opinion for the Court resolved the case on statutory grounds. "Because our constitutional structure leaves local criminal activity primarily to the States, we have generally declined to read federal law as intruding on that responsibility, unless Congress has clearly indicated that the law should have such reach. The Chemical Weapons Convention Implementation Act contains no such clear indication, and we accordingly conclude that it does not cover the unremarkable local offense at issue here." To the contrary, the Court had "doubts that a treaty about *chemical weapons* has anything to do with Bond's conduct. The Convention, a product of years of worldwide study, analysis, and multinational negotiation, arose in response to war crimes and acts of terrorism. There is no reason to think the sovereign nations that ratified the Convention were interested in anything like Bond's common law assault."

By contrast, Justice Scalia, concurring in the judgment, would have held the statute unconstitutional because its only textual foundation was the necessary and proper clause. That clause gave Congress the power to make laws necessary and proper for carrying into execution the "Power [to] make Treaties." It did not grant to Congress a "power to execute the treaties themselves." In his view, the combination of the treaty power with the necessary and proper clause gave Congress the power to "appropriate[ ] money for hiring treaty negotiators, [or to pay] for a bevy of spies to monitor the treaty-related deliberations of other potential signatories. [A] power to help the President *make* treaties is not a power to *implement* treaties already made. [To] legislate compliance with the United States' treaty obligations, Congress must rely upon its independent [Article] I, §8, powers." Justice Thomas joined this part of Justice Scalia's opinion.

Justice Thomas, joined by Justice Scalia and in substantial part by Justice Alito, also concurred in the result, "suggest[ing] that the Treaty Power is [a] limited federal power," which "can be used to arrange intercourse with other nations, but not to regulate purely domestic affairs." He did not offer a definition of "intercourse with other nations," but used the term to refer to treaties "dealing with conditions of commerce, with mutual defense, with belligerent relations, with rights of passage [etc.]." He quoted Madison: "The Federal Government's powers [will] be exercised principally on external objects, as war, peace, negotiation, and foreign commerce — the traditional subjects of treaty-making." He acknowledged that "the Federal Government needed the ability to respond to unforeseeable varieties of intercourse with other nations," but, again quoting Madison, any exercise of the Treaty Power "'must be consistent with the object of the delegation,' which is 'the regulation of intercourse with foreign nations.'"

4. *The scope of Missouri v. Holland as applied to separation of powers and individual rights.* Does Missouri v. Holland deal only with federalism-based limitations on national power?

a. In the early 1950s, a coalition of conservative Republicans and southern Democrats sponsored the Bricker Amendment, which would have added to the Constitution provisions stating that (1) "a provision of a treaty which conflicts with this Constitution shall not be of any force or effect" and (2) "a treaty shall become effective as internal law [only] through legislation which would be valid in the absence of treaty." Was the first provision necessary in light of Missouri v. Holland? What effects would the second provision have had? The southern Democrats who supported the Bricker Amendment did so out of concern that provisions of the United Nations Charter and associated treaties would make unlawful aspects of the existing system of race discrimination. In light of *Heart of Atlanta* and *McClung*, would the Bricker Amendment have had any effects in this area? The Bricker Amendment fell short of adoption by the Senate in 1954 by a vote of sixty in favor, thirty-one opposed.

b. Consider Reid v. Covert, 354 U.S. 1 (1957): Mrs. Covert, a civilian residing with her serviceman husband on a military base in England, was convicted by a military tribunal of killing him. The Supreme Court held that a civilian in her position could not be tried in the military courts. The plurality emphasized that all of Congress's powers, including its power to regulate the armed forces, were limited by the bill of rights, including its requirement of trial by jury. The plurality also discussed the effects of treaties and executive agreements on congressional power:

> [No] agreement with a foreign nation can confer power on the Congress, or on any other branch of Government, which is free from the restraints of the Constitution. . . .
>
> [The] reason treaties were not limited to those made in "pursuance" of the Constitution was so that agreements made by the United States under the Articles

of Confederation, including the important peace treaties which concluded the Revolutionary War, would remain in effect. It would be manifestly contrary to the objectives of those who created the Constitution, as well as those who were responsible for the Bill of Rights — let alone alien to our entire constitutional history and tradition — to construe Article VI as permitting the United States to exercise power under an international agreement without observing constitutional prohibitions. In effect, such construction would permit amendment of that document in a manner not sanctioned by Article V. The prohibitions of the Constitution were designed to apply to all branches of the National Government and they cannot be nullified by the Executive or by the Executive and the Senate combined. . . .

There is nothing in Missouri v. Holland which is contrary to the position taken here. There the Court carefully noted that the treaty involved was not inconsistent with any specific provision of the Constitution. The Court was concerned with the Tenth Amendment which reserves to the States or the people all power not delegated to the National Government. To the extent that the United States can validly make treaties, the people and the States have delegated their power to the National Government and the Tenth Amendment is no barrier.

D.   THE TENTH AMENDMENT AS A FEDERALISM-BASED LIMITATION ON CONGRESSIONAL POWER

The tenth amendment provides that "[the] powers not delegated to the United States by the Constitution, nor prohibited by it to the States, are reserved to the States respectively, or to the people." In New York v. United States, 505 U.S. 144 (1992), discussed later in this section, Justice O'Connor's opinion for the Court explained that the question "whether particular sovereign powers have been granted by the Constitution to the Federal Government or have been retained by the States . . . can be viewed in either of two ways":

In some cases the Court has inquired whether an Act of Congress is authorized by one of the powers delegated to Congress in Article I of the Constitution. In other cases the Court has sought to determine whether an Act of Congress invades the province of state sovereignty reserved by the Tenth Amendment. . . . [T]he two inquiries [can be] mirror images of each other. If a power is delegated to Congress in the Constitution, the Tenth Amendment expressly disclaims any reservation of that power to the States; if a power is an attribute of state sovereignty reserved by the Tenth Amendment, it is necessarily a power the Constitution has not conferred on Congress.

It is in this sense that the Tenth Amendment "states but a truism that all is retained which has not been surrendered." [United States v. Darby] As Justice Story put it, "[t]his amendment is a mere affirmation of what, upon any just reasoning, is a necessary rule of interpreting the constitution. Being an instrument of limited and enumerated powers, it follows irresistibly, that what is not conferred, is withheld, and belongs to the state authorities." 3 J. Story, Commentaries on the Constitution of the United States 752 (1833).

Does the tenth amendment simply reiterate that the national government's powers are limited — to those "delegated to the United States by the Constitution" — or does it articulate some independent constraint on Congress's exercise of its enumerated powers?

Note: *The Modern Revival of Tenth Amendment–Based*
        Restraints on Federal Regulation of State and Local
        Governments

Given the modern expansive definition of "commerce," much of the activity of
state and local governments — particularly in areas such as employment and
contracting for goods and services — constitutes "commerce." Frequently,
when Congress regulates interstate commerce, it includes, either expressly or
implicitly, state and local governments as well as private parties within the
scope of a particular statute. (In the cases discussed in the preceding section
in which the Court held that Congress could not enforce various statutes such
as title I of the ADA or the ADEA by authorizing private damages actions against
states, the Court did not question whether Congress could *regulate* the state
activities in question as long as it enforced its regulation in some other way.)

The Court struggled to define what limits, if any, the tenth amendment
imposes on congressional regulation of state and local governments. The starting
point in the Court's effort was National League of Cities v. Usery, 426 U.S. 833
(1976). There, the Court held that the commerce clause did not empower Congress to enforce the minimum wage and overtime provisions of the Fair Labor
Standards Act (FLSA) against the states "in areas of traditional governmental
functions." The Court agreed that the wages and hours of state employees
affected interstate commerce but found the application of the statute to state
and local employees unconstitutional.

Over the next decade, the Court attempted to identify the contours of the protection afforded state and local governments by *National League of Cities*. It issued
a series of decisions, some of them upholding the constitutionality of federal
regulation of state activities and some of them striking down such regulation.

**GARCIA v. SAN ANTONIO METROPOLITAN TRANSIT
AUTHORITY, 469 U.S. 528 (1985).** The Court overruled *National League
of Cities*, concluding that the "traditional governmental functions" test was
"unworkable." According to Justice Blackmun's majority opinion, "[the] problem
is that [no] distinction [that] purports to separate out important governmental
functions can be faithful to the role of federalism in a democratic society. The
essence of our federal system is that within the realm of authority left open to
them under the Constitution, the States must be equally free to engage in any
activity that their citizens choose for the common weal, no matter how unorthodox or unnecessary anyone else — including the judiciary — deems state involvement to be. Any rule of state immunity that looks to the 'traditional,' 'integral,' or
'necessary' nature of governmental functions inevitably invites an unelected
federal judiciary to make decisions about which state policies it favors and
which ones it dislikes." The Court therefore "reject[ed], as unsound in principle
and unworkable in practice, a rule of state immunity from federal regulation that
turns on a judicial appraisal of whether a particular governmental function is
'integral' or 'traditional.' Any such rule leads to inconsistent results at the same
time that it disserves principles of democratic self-governance, and it breeds
inconsistency precisely because it is divorced from those principles."

Conceding that there are "limits on the Federal Government's power to
interfere with state functions," the Court examined "the manner in which the
Constitution insulates States from the reach of Congress' power under the
Commerce Clause." It was unlikely "that courts ultimately can identify

principled constitutional limitations on the scope of Congress' Commerce Clause powers over the States merely by relying on *a priori* definitions of state sovereignty." The states retained sovereign authority, but "only to the extent that the Constitution has not divested them of their original powers and transferred those powers to the Federal Government. [The] principal means chosen by the Framers to ensure the role of the States in the federal system lies in the structure of the Federal Government itself. [State] sovereign interests, then, are more properly protected by procedural safeguards inherent in the structure of the federal system than by judicially created limitations on federal power."

Chief Justice Burger and Justices Powell, Rehnquist, and O'Connor dissented. Justice Powell's dissent said, "The Framers recognized that the most effective democracy occurs at local levels of government, where people with first hand knowledge of local problems have more ready access to public officials responsible for dealing with them. This is as true today as it was when the Constitution was adopted. 'Participation is likely to be more frequent, and exercised at more different stages of a governmental activity at the local level, or in regional organizations, than at the state and federal levels.'"

Justice Powell referred to the recent "rise of numerous special interest groups that engage in sophisticated lobbying, and make substantial campaign contributions to some members of Congress. These groups are thought to have significant influence in the shaping and enactment of certain types of legislation. Contrary to the Court's view, a 'political process' that functions in this way is unlikely to safeguard the sovereign rights of States and localities." In contrast to the Court's observation that "the standard approved in *National League of Cities* 'disserves principles of democratic self government,'" Justice Powell observed:

"[The] Court looks myopically only to persons elected to positions in the federal government. It disregards entirely the far more effective role of democratic self-government at the state and local levels. One must compare realistically the operation of the state and local governments with that of the federal government. Federal legislation is drafted primarily by the staffs of the congressional committees. In view of the hundreds of bills introduced at each session of Congress and the complexity of many of them, it is virtually impossible for even the most conscientious legislators to be truly familiar with many of the statutes enacted. Federal departments and agencies customarily are authorized to write regulations. Often these are more important than the text of the statutes. As is true of the original legislation, these are drafted largely by staff personnel. The administration and enforcement of federal laws and regulations necessarily are largely in the hands of staff and civil service employees. These employees may have little or no knowledge of the States and localities that will be affected by the statutes and regulations for which they are responsible. In any case, they hardly are as accessible and responsive as those who occupy analogous positions in State and local governments."

Justice O'Connor's dissent stated, "There is more to federalism than the nature of the constraints that can be imposed on the States in 'the realm of authority left open to them by the Constitution.' The central issue of federalism, of course, is whether any realm is left open to the States by the Constitution — whether any area remains in which a State may act free of federal interference. 'The issue . . . is whether the federal system has any *legal* substance, any core of constitutional right that courts will enforce.' C. Black, Perspectives in Constitutional Law 30 (1963). The true 'essence' of federalism is that the States *as States* have legitimate interests which the National Government is bound to respect even though its laws are supreme. If federalism so conceived and so carefully cultivated by the Framers of our Constitution is to remain meaningful, this Court cannot abdicate its constitutional responsibility to oversee the Federal Government's compliance with its duty to respect the legitimate interests of the States." She also said, "[With] the abandonment of *National League of Cities*, all that stands between the remaining essentials of state sovereignty and Congress is the latter's underdeveloped capacity for self-restraint."

Note: From Garcia *to* New York v. United States

1. *The aftermath in Congress.* Nine months after the Court's decision in *Garcia*, Congress enacted the Fair Labor Standards Amendments of 1985. Under the original Fair Labor Standards Act, private employers must pay overtime to employees who work more than a stated number of hours at a rate of one and one-half times their regular pay. The amendments allow public employers to substitute compensatory time off for the overtime pay, again at the rate of one and one-half hours compensatory time for each hour of overtime. Compensatory time off is limited to 480 hours for public safety employees and employees in seasonal work and to 240 hours for other public employees; after that, public employers must pay for overtime. Does the adoption of the amendments demonstrate that *Garcia* was correctly decided? Does it show that the Court unnecessarily forced Congress to act so as to maintain the proper system of federal regulation of state employment practices?

2. Garcia *applied.* A 1982 tax reform statute removed the exemption from federal taxes of income from certain state bonds. In South Carolina v. Baker, 485 U.S. 505 (1988), the Supreme Court upheld the statute. "*Garcia* holds that the limits [on Congress's power] are structural, not substantive — i.e., that States must find their protection from congressional regulation through the national political process, not through judicially defined spheres of unregulable state activity. [Although] *Garcia* left open the possibility that some extraordinary defects in the national political process might render congressional regulation of state activities invalid, [South] Carolina has not even alleged that it was deprived of any right to participate in the national political process or that it was singled out in a way that left it politically isolated and powerless."

Justice O'Connor dissented. Chief Justice Rehnquist concurred in the result.

3. *The aftermath in the Court.* In Gregory v. Ashcroft, 501 U.S. 452 (1991), the Court held that the Age Discrimination in Employment Act (ADEA) did not apply to a state's mandatory retirement provisions affecting appointed state judges. The ADEA bars employers, including state governments, from adopting mandatory retirement policies, but as to state employers, it exempts "appointees on a policymaking level." In interpreting this provision, the Court noted that the state's retirement provision "is a decision of the most fundamental sort for a sovereign entity" and required that Congress's intention to displace state decisions in this area be clearly stated.

NEW YORK v. UNITED STATES, 505 U.S. 144 (1992). The Low-Level Radioactive Waste Policy Amendments Act of 1986 was Congress's effort to deal with the problem posed by the accumulation of low-level nuclear waste from such uses as smoke detectors and construction materials at nuclear power plants. A great deal of such waste is generated each year, and it must be isolated from humans. States were reluctant to develop facilities for locally generated waste, and much was shipped out of state. By 1979 only one facility in South Carolina was accepting the waste. The statute authorized South Carolina (and any other state that had a disposal facility) to impose a surcharge for accepting waste from out of state, until 1992, after which it could exclude outside waste. The statute gave states three "incentives" to develop local facilities: First, some of the surcharge was transferred to the United States, which would disburse these funds to states that reached various milestones with respect to the disposal of this waste. Second, the statute authorized South Carolina eventually to close its facility to outside waste. Finally, if a state did not provide for disposal of waste generated within its borders by 1996, the statute provided that the state had to "take title" to the waste. The state would then be subject to direct federal regulation, as an owner of nuclear waste.

Justice O'Connor wrote the Court's opinion. She began by observing, "Congress exercises its conferred powers subject to the limitations contained in the Constitution. Thus, for example, under the Commerce Clause Congress may regulate publishers engaged in interstate commerce, but Congress is constrained in the exercise of that power by the First Amendment. The Tenth Amendment likewise restrains the power of Congress, but this limit is not derived from the text of the Tenth Amendment itself, which [is] essentially a tautology. Instead, the Tenth Amendment confirms that the power of the Federal Government is subject to limits that may, in a given instance, reserve power to the States. The Tenth Amendment thus directs us to determine [whether] an incident of state sovereignty is protected by a limitation on an Article I power."

The Court upheld the first two incentives. With respect to the first, it held that Congress had the power to authorize states to impose a surcharge on out-of-state waste as part of its commerce power; Congress could then collect some of that surcharge using its taxing power, and disburse it to cooperative states as an exercise of its spending power. With respect to the second incentive, Congress's commerce power similarly allowed it to preempt the interstate movement of the regulated waste out of states that lacked compliant facilities.

But the Court struck down the "take title" provision. "Congress may not simply "commandeer the legislative processes of the States by directly compelling them to enact and enforce a federal regulatory program." The reasons for barring direct commandeering included these:

[Where] the Federal Government compels States to regulate, the accountability of both state and federal officials is diminished. If the citizens of New York, for example, do not consider that making provision for the disposal of radioactive waste is in their best interest, they may elect state officials who share their view. That view can always be pre-empted under the Supremacy Clause if it is contrary to the national view, but in such a case it is the Federal Government that makes the decision in full view of the public, and it will be federal officials that suffer the consequences if the decision turns out to be detrimental or unpopular. But where the Federal Government directs the States to regulate, it may be state officials who will bear the brunt of public disapproval, while the federal officials who devised the regulatory program may remain insulated from the electoral ramifications of their decision. Accountability is thus diminished when, due to federal coercion, elected state officials cannot regulate in accordance with the views of the local electorate in matters not pre-empted by federal regulation.

The "take title" provision "offers States, as an alternative to regulating pursuant to Congress' direction, the option of taking title to and possession of the low level radioactive waste generated within their borders and becoming liable for all damages waste generators suffer as a result of the States' failure to do so promptly. In this provision, Congress has crossed the line distinguishing encouragement from coercion." According to Justice O'Connor, the provision "offers state governments a 'choice' of either accepting ownership of waste or regulating according to the instructions of Congress. [On] one hand, the Constitution would not permit Congress simply to transfer radioactive waste from generators to state governments. Such a forced transfer, standing alone, would in principle be no different than a congressionally compelled subsidy from state governments to radioactive waste producers. The same is true of the provision requiring the States to become liable for the generators' damages. Standing alone, this provision would be indistinguishable from an Act of Congress directing the States to assume the liabilities of certain state residents. Either type of federal action would 'commandeer' state governments into the service of federal regulatory purposes, and would for this reason be inconsistent with the Constitution's division of authority between federal and state governments. On the other hand, the second alternative held out to state governments — regulating pursuant to Congress direction — would, standing alone, present a simple command to state governments to implement legislation enacted by Congress. As we have seen, the Constitution does not empower Congress to subject state governments to this type of instruction."

Responding to the argument that New York officials actively supported the enactment of the statute the state was now challenging as "a bargain among the sited and unsited States, a compromise to which New York was a willing participant and from which New York has reaped much benefit," Justice O'Connor wrote, "The Constitution does not protect the sovereignty of States for the benefit of the States or state governments as abstract political entities, or even for the benefit of the public officials governing the States. To the contrary, the Constitution divides authority between federal and state governments for the protection of individuals. [Where] Congress exceeds its authority relative to the States, therefore, the departure from the constitutional plan cannot be ratified by the 'consent' of state officials."

Justice White, joined by Justices Blackmun and Stevens, dissented, describing the statute as "very much the product of cooperative federalism, in which the States bargained among themselves to achieve compromises for Congress to sanction." For the dissenters, "[the] ultimate irony of the decision today is that in its formalistically rigid obeisance to 'federalism,' the Court gives Congress fewer incentives to defer to the wishes of state officials in achieving local solutions to local problems. This legislation was a classic example of Congress acting as arbiter among the States in their attempts to accept responsibility for managing a problem of grave import." Justice Stevens concurred in part and dissented in part.

PRINTZ v. UNITED STATES, 521 U.S. 898 (1997). The Brady Act required the Attorney General to establish a national instant background check system for weapons purchases by November 1998. Until then, gun dealers were required to send a form identifying a purchaser to the "chief law enforcement officer" (CLEO) of a prospective purchaser's residence, unless the purchaser already had a permit or unless the state already had an instant background check system. The dealer then had to wait five days to complete the sale. When the CLEO received the form, the CLEO had to "make a reasonable effort to ascertain . . . whether receipt or possession would be in violation of the law," as when the purchaser was a convicted felon. Two CLEOs from Montana and Arizona challenged the Brady Act, which the Supreme Court, in an opinion by Justice Scalia, held to be unconstitutional.

The Court agreed with the sheriffs' contention that "compelled enlistment of state executive officers for the administration of federal programs is, until very recent years at least, unprecedented." Contrary examples, the Court found, involved state judges subject to the supremacy clause and accustomed to enforcing the law of other sovereigns, and statutes requesting states to allow their officials to enforce national law. Turning to "the structure of the Constitution," the Court observed, "The power of the Federal Government would be augmented immeasurably if it were able to impress into its service — and at no cost to itself — the police officers of the 50 States." In addition, in tension with article II's requirement that the President "take Care that the Laws be faithfully executed," the Brady Act "transfers this responsibility to thousands of CLEOs in the 50 States, who are left to implement the program without meaningful Presidential control." Relying on *New York*, the Court concluded that the Brady Act was not a "proper" method of implementing a delegated power.

Finally, the Court held that the reasons given in *New York* for denying Congress the power to commandeer state legislatures were applicable as well to attempts to commandeer state executive officials:

> [The] Government also maintains that requiring state officers to perform discrete, ministerial tasks specified by Congress does not violate the principle of *New York* because it does not diminish the accountability of state or federal officials. This argument fails even on its own terms. By forcing state governments to absorb the financial burden of implementing a federal regulatory program, Members of Congress can take credit for "solving" problems without having to ask their constituents to pay for the solutions with higher federal taxes. And even when the States are not forced to absorb the costs of implementing a federal program, they are still put in the position of taking the blame for its burdensomeness and for its defects. Under the present law, for example, it will be the CLEO and not some federal official who stands between the gun purchaser and immediate possession of his gun. And it will likely be the CLEO, not some federal official, who will be blamed for any error (even one in the designated federal database) that causes a purchaser to be mistakenly rejected.

The Court rejected the argument that the Brady Act's constitutionality should be determined by balancing its purposes against the "minimal and only temporary burden" it placed on state officials: "[Where] it is the whole object of the law to direct the functioning of the state executive, [such] a 'balancing' analysis is inappropriate. It is the very principle of separate state sovereignty that such a law offends, and no comparative assessment of the various interests can overcome that fundamental defect."

Justice Stevens, joined by Justices Souter, Ginsburg, and Breyer, dissented: "When Congress exercises the powers delegated to it by the Constitution, it may impose affirmative obligations on executive and judicial officers of state and local governments as well as ordinary citizens. This conclusion is firmly supported by the text of the Constitution, the early history of the Nation, decisions of this Court, and a correct understanding of the basic structure of the Federal Government." He argued that "[under] the Articles of Confederation the National

Government had the power to issue commands to the several sovereign states, but it had no authority to govern individuals directly," but "[that] method of governing proved to be unacceptable [because] it was cumbersome and inefficient. [The] historical materials strongly suggest that the Founders intended to enhance the capacity of the federal government by empowering it — as a part of the new authority to make demands directly on individual citizens — to act through local officials. Hamilton made clear that the new Constitution, 'by extending the authority of the federal head to the individual citizens of the several States, will enable the government to employ the ordinary magistracy of each, in the execution of its laws.' The Federalist No. 27, at 180. Hamilton's meaning was unambiguous; the federal government was to have the power to demand that local officials implement national policy programs."

Justice Stevens disagreed with the Court's assessment of early practice, finding that Congress sometimes had required state officials to enforce national law. Relying on *Garcia*, he argued: "Given the fact that the Members of Congress are elected by the people of the several States, with each State receiving an equivalent number of Senators in order to ensure that even the smallest States have a powerful voice in the legislature, it is quite unrealistic to assume that they will ignore the sovereignty concerns of their constituents. It is far more reasonable to presume that their decisions to impose modest burdens on state officials from time to time reflect a considered judgment that the people in each of the States will benefit therefrom." And he pointed to Congress's passage of the Unfunded Mandates Reform Act as evidence that the states' concerns were being adequately addressed.

A footnote argued that the "concern" about Congress requiring state officials to "'take the blame' for failed programs" was "vastly overstated [because] to the extent that a particular action proves politically unpopular, we may be confident that elected officials charged with implementing it will be quite clear to their constituents where the source of the misfortune lies. [They] will inform disgruntled constituents who have been denied permission to purchase a handgun about the origins of the Brady Act requirements. The Court's suggestion that voters will be confused over who is to 'blame' for the statute reflects a gross lack of confidence in the electorate that is at war with the basic assumptions underlying any democratic government." In addition, Justice Stevens argued, "the majority's rule seems more likely to damage than to preserve the safeguards against tyranny provided by the existence of vital state governments. By limiting the ability of the Federal Government to enlist state officials in the implementation of its programs, the Court creates incentives for the National Government to aggrandize itself. In the name of State's rights, the majority would have the Federal Government create vast national bureaucracies to implement its policies."

Justice Souter's separate dissent focused on his interpretation of several passages in The Federalist Papers.

Note: The "Anticommandeering" Principle

1. *The scope of the decisions: Judicial, legislative, and executive officials.* The Court does not repudiate decisions like Testa v. Katt, 330 U.S. 386 (1947), which require state courts to hear claims arising under federal law to the same extent that they hear state law-based claims. Why do courts fall outside the anticommandeering principle? Note that state executive and legislative officials are

required to take an oath to support the Constitution. Does the supremacy clause bind state judges in a stronger way? Is political responsibility less diffused when state judges enforce national law? In this light, consider also Medellin v. Texas, 552 U.S. 491 (2008), discussed earlier in this chapter. There, the Court refused to require that Texas state courts hear a claim they had concluded was procedurally defaulted, despite the President's directive that they do so. Although the Supreme Court itself did not discuss the anticommandeering doctrine in reaching its conclusion, the presiding judge on the Texas Court of Criminal Appeals emphasized this rationale in his concurrence explaining why the Texas court declined to follow the President's request. See Ex parte Medellin, 206 S.W.2d 584 (Tex. Crim. App. 2006).

2. *Preemption and conditional spending statutes.* Preemption, discussed in Chapter 2, section D, supra, is a command from Congress that states forbear from regulating in some area where they otherwise would. Why is that less offensive than a command that they affirmatively regulate? Siegel, Commandeering and Its Alternatives: A Federalism Perspective, 59 Vand. L. Rev. 1629, 1634–1635 (2006), argues that the anticommandeering decisions "vindicate federalism values [by] requiring the federal government to internalize more of the costs of federal regulation [but undermine] federalism values when the (clearly constitutional) alternative of preemption is reasonably available." He proposes that commandeering should be presumptively unconstitutional "when preemption is not a feasible alternative in the short run, the federal mandate is unfunded and expensive, and the federal government makes little effective effort to alleviate reasonable accountability concerns," but should be constitutional "when preemption constitutes a feasible alternative in the short run and such preemption would reduce state regulatory [control], the federal mandate is fully funded or relatively [inexpensive], and the federal government takes effective measures to maintain lines of accountability." Applying these principles, Siegel concludes that the statute in New York v. United States should have been upheld because preemption there "was reasonably available (and indeed had already been threatened)," and that *Printz* is a closer case. Does this approach provide standards that courts can in practice apply in a principled manner?

3. *Commandeering and the war on terror.* Consider the implications of these decisions for efforts by the national government to gain assistance from (sometimes reluctant) state and local governments in identifying and interrogating people in connection with investigations of alleged terrorist activities. Do the following observations justify the application of these decisions in that context?

> [Federalism], in particular the autonomy protected by the anti-commandeering doctrine, can protect constitutional rights better than the direct assertion of claims based on those rights. State and local government officials exert pressure on the federal government that works differently from constitutional rights. Claims of autonomy [can] arise out of strong interpretations of constitutional rights. These interpretations may be drastically overstated or naively idealistic and, consequently, quite unlikely to move courts to rein in the federal government as it pursues national security. But state and local government autonomy can exert pressure on the federal government to moderate its efforts and take care not to offend constitutional rights, even rights that the courts would not now be willing to enforce. To carry out its programs, the national government will need to inspire the confidence of the vast numbers of police and other personnel employed at the state and, especially, local government level.

Because state and local government autonomy can work as a safeguard for the rights of the people, the anti-commandeering doctrine should remain in place, in full force, unmodified by any sort of emergency exception. [It] is true that this autonomy deprives the national government of a means to carry out programs that may be vitally important. But in cases of the "direst emergency and peril," the great majority of persons employed at the state and local level of government can be expected to respond without objection. Where there are pockets of non-compliance, the federal government can send in its own personnel, including the military. The different levels of government will exert pressure on each other. State and local government will tend to resist only when the emergency is not dire and when the actions of the federal government offend local beliefs, often idealistic beliefs about constitutional rights. The federal government will want to win compliance and will take steps to inspire cooperation, such as offering ample funding and framing demands that take account of ideas about individual rights. Remove the anti-commandeering doctrine, or temper it with an emergency exception, and this beneficial interaction is lost.

Althouse, The Vigor of Anti-Commandeering Doctrine in Times of Terror, 69 Brook. L. Rev. 1231, 1274–1275 (2004).

Consider also the views expressed in Young, Welcome to the Dark Side: Liberals Rediscover Federalism in the Wake of the War on Terror, 69 Brook. L. Rev. 1277, 1311 (2004):

Federalism is about dividing power; nothing much depends on what the power in question is being used for. It is also about providing institutional space for a diversity of political views. As such, it should surprise no one that a commitment to state and local autonomy would take on the hue of political opposition to the prevailing orthodoxy at the center, whatever that orthodoxy happens to be. Relatively few people are likely to embrace federalism for its own [sake]. Rather, support for state autonomy vis-à-vis national power on both Left and Right has ebbed and flowed throughout our history, according to the dynamics of whatever political issue is most salient at any given time.

4. *The tenth amendment and individual rights.* Bond v. United States, 564 U.S. 211 (2011), held that an individual had standing to raise tenth amendment objections to a statute enacted to implement the Chemical Weapons Convention. The statute criminalizes knowing possession or use of any chemical that "can cause death, temporary incapacitation or permanent harm to humans or animals" where not intended for a "peaceful purpose." Bond was indicted under this statute when she placed a caustic substance on various objects her husband's paramour was likely to touch, causing burns to the other woman's hand. Justice Kennedy's opinion stated,

The Framers concluded that allocation of powers between the National Government and the States enhances freedom, first by protecting the integrity of the governments themselves, and second by protecting the people, from whom all governmental powers are derived.

Federalism has more than one dynamic. It is true that the federal structure serves to grant and delimit the prerogatives and responsibilities of the States and the National Government vis-à-vis one another. The allocation of powers in our federal system preserves the integrity, dignity, and residual sovereignty of the States. The federal balance is, in part, an end in itself, to ensure that States function as political entities in their own right.

But that is not its exclusive sphere of operation. Federalism is more than an exercise in setting the boundary between different institutions of government for their own integrity. "State sovereignty is not just an end in itself: 'Rather, federalism secures to citizens the liberties that derive from the diffusion of sovereign power.'" New York v. United States, 505 U.S. 144, 181 (1992). . . .

Federalism secures the freedom of the individual. It allows States to respond, through the enactment of positive law, to the initiative of those who seek a voice in shaping the destiny of their own times without having to rely solely upon the political processes that control a remote central power. True, of course, these objects cannot be vindicated by the Judiciary in the absence of a proper case or controversy; but the individual liberty secured by federalism is not simply derivative of the rights of the States.

Federalism also protects the liberty of all persons within a State by ensuring that laws enacted in excess of delegated governmental power cannot direct or control their actions. . . .

The limitations that federalism entails are not therefore a matter of rights belonging only to the States. States are not the sole intended beneficiaries of federalism. An individual has a direct interest in objecting to laws that upset the constitutional balance between the National Government and the States when the enforcement of those laws causes injury that is concrete, particular, and redressable. Fidelity to principles of federalism is not for the States alone to vindicate.

Ultimately, in Bond v. United States, 134 S. Ct. 2077 (2014), the Court held that Bond's actions were not covered by the statute. That decision is discussed at pages ◆ ◆-◆ ◆, supra.

5. *The tenth amendment and statutory interpretation.* In Gonzales v. Oregon, 546 U.S. 243 (2006), the Supreme Court was faced with a challenge to the Attorney General's interpretation of the federal Controlled Substances Act (CSA), which regulates the distribution of various drugs. After Oregon passed a Death with Dignity Act that exempted physicians from civil or criminal liability for prescribing lethal doses of various drugs to terminally ill patients under defined circumstances, the Attorney General issued an Interpretive Rule declaring that using controlled substances to assist suicide is not a legitimate medical practice and that dispensing or prescribing them for this purpose would be unlawful under the CSA and would subject physicians to loss of their prescribing privileges.

By a six-to-three vote, the Court rejected the Attorney General's position. The Court did not question whether Congress would have the ability, using its commerce power, to forbid physician-assisted suicide. Rather, the question was whether the Attorney General's interpretation of the CSA to forbid physician-assisted suicide was a permissible interpretation of the Act. Much of Justice Kennedy's opinion for the Court was taken up with conventional administrative law analysis. But his opinion also relied on the traditional role of the states in regulating medical practice as an interpretive aid:

The structure and operation of the CSA presume and rely upon a functioning medical profession regulated under the States' police powers. The Attorney General can register a physician to dispense controlled substances "if the applicant is authorized to dispense . . . controlled substances under the laws of the State in which he practices." 21 U.S.C. §823(f). When considering whether to revoke a physician's registration, the Attorney General looks not just to violations of federal drug laws; but he "shall" also consider "the recommendation of the appropriate state licensing board or professional disciplinary authority" and the registrant's compliance with state and local drug laws. The very definition of a "practitioner" eligible to prescribe includes physicians "licensed, registered, or otherwise permitted, by the United States or the jurisdiction in which he practices" to dispense controlled substances. §802(21). Further cautioning against the conclusion that the CSA effectively displaces the States' general regulation of medical practice is the Act's pre-emption provision, which indicates that, absent a positive conflict, none of the Act's provisions should be "construed as indicating an intent on the part of the Congress to occupy the field in which that provision operates . . . to the exclusion of any State law on the same subject matter which would otherwise be within the authority of the State." . . .

Chief Justice Roberts and Justices Scalia and Thomas dissented. After explaining why he thought the Attorney General's interpretation of the CSA was justifiable, Justice Scalia, joined by the other two dissenters, remarked:

> The Court's decision today is perhaps driven by a feeling that the subject of assisted suicide is none of the Federal Government's business. It is easy to sympathize with that position. The prohibition or deterrence of assisted suicide is certainly not among the enumerated powers conferred on the United States by the Constitution, and it is within the realm of public morality (*bonos mores*) traditionally addressed by the so-called police power of the States. But then, neither is prohibiting the recreational use of drugs or discouraging drug addiction among the enumerated powers. From an early time in our national history, the Federal Government has used its enumerated powers, such as its power to regulate interstate commerce, for the purpose of protecting public morality — for example, by banning the interstate shipment of lottery tickets, or the interstate transport of women for immoral purposes. Unless we are to repudiate a long and well-established principle of our jurisprudence, using the federal commerce power to prevent assisted suicide is unquestionably permissible. The question before us is not whether Congress *can* do this, or even whether Congress *should* do this; but simply whether Congress *has* done this in the CSA. I think there is no doubt that it has.

6. *The tenth amendment and state power.* Does the tenth amendment have any implications for the scope of state power? In U.S. Term Limits v. Thornton, 514 U.S. 779 (1995), Justice Stevens's opinion for the Court argued that the tenth amendment "could only 'reserve' that which existed before. As Justice Story recognized, 'the states can exercise no powers whatsoever, which exclusively spring out of the existence of the national government, which the constitution does not delegate to them. . . . No state can say, that it has reserved, what it never possessed.'"
    Justice Thomas's dissent, which was joined by Chief Justice Rehnquist and Justices O'Connor and Scalia, responded:

> As far as the Federal Constitution is concerned, [the] States can exercise all powers that the Constitution does not withhold from them. The Federal Government and the States thus face different default rules: where the Constitution is silent about the exercise of a particular power — that is, where the Constitution does not speak either expressly or by necessary implication — the Federal Government lacks that power and the States enjoy it.

Justice Thomas continued:

> The majority's essential logic is that the state governments could not "reserve" any powers that they did not control at the time the Constitution was drafted. But it was

not the state governments that were doing the reserving. The Constitution derives its authority instead from the consent of the people of the States. Given the fundamental principle that all governmental powers stem from the people of the States, it would simply be incoherent to assert that the people of the States could not reserve any powers that they had not previously controlled.

7. *The tenth amendment and areas of traditional state control.* In United States v. Comstock, 560 U.S. 126 (2010), the Court addressed the constitutionality of a federal statute that authorized the civil commitment of mentally ill, sexually dangerous federal prisoners beyond the release date for their criminal sentence. Writing for the Court, Justice Breyer rejected the argument that the federal statute impermissibly invades a traditional province of state sovereignty:

> [T]he Tenth Amendment's text is clear: "The powers *not delegated to the United States* by the Constitution, nor prohibited by it to the States, are reserved to the States respectively, or to the people." (Emphasis added.) The powers "delegated to the United States by the Constitution" include those specifically enumerated powers listed in Article I along with the implementation authority granted by the Necessary and Proper Clause. Virtually by definition, these powers are not powers that the Constitution "reserved to the States."

Justice Breyer rejected Justice Thomas's claim in dissent that the statute improperly limited states' powers to deal with potentially dangerous individuals:

> To the contrary, it requires *accommodation* of state interests: The Attorney General must inform the State in which the federal prisoner "is domiciled or was tried" that he is detaining someone with respect to whom those States may wish to assert their authority, and he must encourage those States to assume custody of the individual. He must also immediately "release" that person "to the appropriate official of" either State "if such State will assume [such] responsibility." And either State has the right, at any time, to assert its authority over the individual, which will prompt the individual's immediate transfer to State custody. Once such a transfer occurs, the state can determine whether to continue detaining the individual.

In his concurrence in the judgment, Justice Kennedy expressed concern with the Court's tenth amendment analysis:

> I had thought it a basic principle that the powers reserved to the States consist of the whole, undefined residuum of power remaining after taking account of powers granted to the National Government. The Constitution delegates limited powers to the National Government and then reserves the remainder for the States (or the people), not the other way around, as the Court's analysis suggests. And the powers reserved to the States are so broad that they remain undefined. Residual power, sometimes referred to (perhaps imperfectly) as the police power, belongs to the States and the States alone.
>   It is correct in one sense to say that if the National Government has the power to act under the Necessary and Proper Clause then that power is not one reserved to the States. But the precepts of federalism embodied in the Constitution inform which powers are properly exercised by the National Government in the first place. It is of fundamental importance to consider whether essential attributes of state sovereignty are compromised by the assertion of federal power under the Necessary and Proper Clause; if so, that is a factor suggesting that the power is not one properly within the reach of federal power.

The opinion of the Court should not be interpreted to hold that the only, or even the principal, constraints on the exercise of congressional power are the Constitution's express prohibitions. The Court's discussion of the Tenth Amendment invites the inference that restrictions flowing from the federal system are of no import when defining the limits of the National Government's power, as it proceeds by first asking whether the power is within the National Government's reach, and if so it discards federalism concerns entirely.

These remarks explain why the Court ignores important limitations stemming from federalism principles. Those principles are essential to an understanding of the function and province of the States in our constitutional structure.

In dissent, Justice Thomas, joined by Justice Scalia, disagreed with the Court's conclusion that the statutory requirement that the Attorney General offer the states the right to take custody of soon-to-be-released federal inmates satisfied the tenth amendment:

This right of first refusal is mere window dressing. More importantly, it is an altogether hollow assurance that §4248 preserves the principle of dual sovereignty. [For] once it is determined that Congress has the authority to provide for the civil detention of sexually dangerous persons, Congress "is acting within the powers granted it under the Constitution," and "may impose its will on the States." Section 4248's right of first refusal is thus not a matter of constitutional necessity, but an act of legislative grace.

8. *The role of comparative law.* Justice Breyer's separate dissent in *Printz* noted:

At least some other countries, facing the same basic problem, have found that local control is better maintained through application of a principle that is the direct opposite of the principle the majority derives from the silence of our Constitution. The federal systems of Switzerland, Germany, and the European Union [all] provide that constituent states, not federal bureaucracies, will themselves implement many of the laws, rules, regulations, or decrees enacted by the central "federal" body. They do so in part because they believe that such a system interferes less, not more, with the independent authority of the "state," member nation, or other subsidiary government, and helps to safeguard individual liberty as well.

Justice Scalia's opinion for the Court responded, "We think such comparative analysis inappropriate to the task of interpreting a constitution, though it was of course quite relevant to the task of writing one." Justice Breyer replied:

[W]e are interpreting our own Constitution, not those of other nations, and there may be relevant political and structural differences between their systems and our own. But their experience may nonetheless cast an empirical light on the consequences of different solutions to a common legal problem — in this case the problem of reconciling central authority with the need to preserve the liberty-enhancing autonomy of a smaller constituent governmental entity. And that experience here offers empirical confirmation of the implied answer to a question Justice Stevens asks: Why, or how, would what the majority sees as a constitutional alternative — the creation of a new federal gun-law bureaucracy, or the expansion of an existing federal bureaucracy — better promote either state sovereignty or individual liberty?

Consider the following argument: In the absence of controlling constitutional text, courts appropriately make considerations of policy one factor in determining the Constitution's meaning. Examining constitutional experience elsewhere may illuminate the relevant policy considerations. Alternatively, in the absence of controlling constitutional text, courts should interpret the Constitution in a manner consistent with its basic structure. But structural considerations often fail to determine precisely which of many possible structures is most consistent with the U.S. Constitution. Examining constitutional experience elsewhere may illuminate the choice among alternative reasonable specifications of the U.S. Constitution's structure. Are the Court's and Justice Breyer's discussions of comparative constitutional law consistent with either of these arguments?

Note: Concluding Observations on Congress's Powers

Consider this summary:

[The] historic progression of the various models of federalism [reflects] a pendulum-like attempt to achieve the proper balance between underlying federalism values, each model perhaps overcompensating for the excesses of its predecessor. After the Great Depression crippled the capacity of state and local governments to cope with unprecedented levels of social and economic despair, the Supreme Court adopted a model of federalism that exalted the problem-solving value at the expense of the check-and-balance value to approve pragmatic New Deal legislative programs. [Cooperative] federalism [recovers] some of the balance through a partnership-based approach to regulation in areas of interjurisdictional overlap, allowing state and federal governments to take responsibility for interlocking components of a collaborative regulatory regime. [Cooperative] federalism has [been] criticized as an overly pragmatic model that insufficiently protects antityranny values. [The] New Federalism reestablishes the supremacy of the check-and-balance value over all others in order to bolster the line between state and federal authority against pressures [that] would blur the boundary. [But] the New Federalism's focus on preserving bright-line boundaries [renders] it unable to effectively mediate the competition between federalism values, contributing to a governmental ethos that obstructs even desirable regulatory activity in the interjurisdictional gray area (such as federal initiative that might have been taken in the aftermath of Hurricane Katrina). [In] this ironic respect, the New Federalism simply does what New Deal federalism did in the opposite direction — shortchanging the problem-solving value in the name of the check-and-balance value, which it mistakes for federalism generally.

Ryan, Federalism and the Tug of War Within: Seeking Checks and Balances in the Interjurisdictional Gray Area, 66 Md. L. Rev. 503, 511–512 (2007).

IV

The Distribution of National Powers

A. INTRODUCTION

The Constitution disperses authority not only between the national government and the states but also among the legislative, executive, and judicial branches. This chapter explores the purposes and effects of the distribution of national power.

The Federalist No. 47 (Madison)

(1787)

One of the principal objections inculcated by the more respectable adversaries to the Constitution is its supposed violation of the political maxim that the legislative, executive, and judiciary departments ought to be separate and distinct. . . .

The oracle who is always consulted and cited on this subject, is the celebrated Montesquieu. . . .

[Montesquieu] did not mean that these departments ought to have no partial agency in, or no *control* over, the acts of each other. His meaning, [can] amount to no more than this, that where the *whole* power of one department is exercised by the same hands which possess the *whole* power of another department, the fundamental principles of a free constitution are subverted. . . .

If we look into the constitutions of the several States we find that, [there] is not a single instance in which the several departments of power have been kept absolutely separate and distinct. . . .

The Federalist No. 48 (Madison)

(1787)

It was shown in the last paper that the political apothegm there examined does not require that the legislative, executive, and judiciary departments should be wholly unconnected with each other. I shall undertake, in the next place, to show that unless these departments be so far connected and blended as to give to each a constitutional control over the others, the degree of separation which the maxim requires, as essential to a free government, can never in practice be duly maintained. . . .

Will it be sufficient to mark, with precision, the boundaries of these departments in the constitution of the government, and to trust to these parchment barriers against the encroaching spirit of power? This is the security which appears to have been principally relied on by the compilers of most of the American constitutions. But experience assures us that the efficacy of the provision has been greatly overrated; and that some more adequate defense is indispensably necessary for the more feeble against the more powerful members of the government. The legislative department is everywhere extending the sphere of its activity and drawing all power into its impetuous vortex. . . .

In a government where numerous and extensive prerogatives are placed in the hands of an hereditary monarch, the executive department is very justly regarded as the source of danger, and watched with all the jealousy which a zeal for liberty ought to inspire. In a democracy, where a multitude of people exercise in person the legislative functions and are continually exposed, by their incapacity for regular deliberation and concerted measures, to the ambitious intrigues of their executive magistrates, tyranny may well be apprehended, on some favorable emergency, to start up in the same quarter. But in a representative republic where the executive magistracy is carefully limited, both in the extent and the duration of its power; and where the legislative power is exercised by an assembly, which is inspired by a supposed influence over the people with an intrepid confidence in its own strength; which is sufficiently numerous to feel all the passions which actuate a multitude, yet not so numerous as to be incapable of pursuing the objects of its passions by means which reason prescribes; it is against the enterprising ambition of this department that the people ought to indulge all their jealousy and exhaust all their precautions.

Note: The Theory of Separation and Checks and Balances

1. *The purposes of separation and checks.* Throughout American history the distribution of national powers has been said to serve two distinct purposes. The first is efficiency. In this view, a division of labor among the various branches makes government more efficient, especially because of the concentration of executive power in the President, who can act with dispatch. The second purpose is the prevention of tyranny. The separation of powers diffuses governmental power, diminishing the likelihood that any one branch (or any one individual) will be able to use governmental power against the citizenry. Consider the extent to which these two purposes are in tension with each other.

2. *The constitutional distribution of powers: contemporary criticism.* The constitutional distribution of national powers has come under sharp attack. See, e.g., T. Lowi, The End of Liberalism (2d ed. 1980); Cutler and Johnson, Regulation and the Political Process, 84 Yale L.J. 1395 (1975). Consider, for example, the argument that preoccupation with the balance of power between institutions of government has distracted us from concern about the balance of power between *interest groups* like the poor and the rich or residents of urban and rural areas. See Levinson, Foreword, Looking for Power in Public Law, 130 Harv. L. Rev. 31 (2016). Other critics have argued that the powerful checks created by

separation of powers have led to inefficiency and stalemate. A related attack is that the separation of powers scheme, instead of solving the problem of factions, aggravates it by allowing well-organized private groups to block necessary regulation. In these circumstances, it is sometimes urged that constitutional doctrine should be altered to recognize a greater role for the President. See W. Howell & T. Moe, Relic: How Our Constitution Undermines Effective Government and Why We Need a More Powerful Presidency (2016). But see Nzelibe and Stephenson, Complementary Constraints: Separation of Powers, Rational Voting, and Constitutional Design, 123 Harv. L. Rev. 617 (2010) (raising doubts that separation of powers causes "gridlock").

Conversely, some critics argue that power is now concentrated in the executive branch and that it is thus necessary to restore Congress to its original status of preeminence. It is sometimes suggested that the growth of an enormous national bureaucracy, operating for the most part within the executive branch, has fundamentally altered the original constitutional framework and requires some sort of response if the original constitutional concerns are to be satisfied.

Compare E. Posner and A. Vermeule, The Executive Unbound: After the Madisonian Republic 3–4 (2011):

> We live in a regime of executive-centered government, in an age after the separation of powers and the legally constrained executive is now a historical curiosity. . . .
> [The] major constraints on the executive, especially in crises, do not arise from law or from the separation-of-powers framework [but] from politics and public opinion. [De] facto political constraints [have] grown up and, to some degree, [substituted] for legal constraints on the executive. As the bonds of law have loosened, the bonds of politics have tightened their grip.

Consider the possibility that law-based and separation of powers rhetoric plays a role in the political struggle over executive power.

3. *The Problem of Enforcement.* Assuming that separation of powers should be preserved, how should the separation be enforced? Consider Seidman, The Secret History of American Constitutional Skepticism: A Recovery and Preliminary Evaluation, 16 U. Pa. J. Const. L. 1. 25–26 (2014):

> [Madison] never successfully resolved the "parchment barriers" problem. . . .
> [He] started out by saying that the new government with its structure of overlapping powers will protect liberty and the public interest. He recognized that these good outcomes were dependent upon this structure remaining intact and asked how the structural rules could be enforced. But his answer leads to a circle: The structural provisions, he says, will be enforced by the structural provisions.

In contrast, Alexander Hamilton argued that an independent judiciary, with "no influence over either the sword or the purse" possessed of "neither FORCE nor WILL" and the "least dangerous branch" would enforce the separation. How can an institution with neither force nor will provide effective enforcement? Consider Seidman, supra:

> [Hamilton's] argument is the source of an enduring puzzle. The judiciary had to be independent, Hamilton argued, if it was to resist pressure from the other branches of government and from the public to trample on constitutional rights. But unless

we assume that judges are angels, this very independence meant that the judges would be free to defy rather than enforce the Constitution.

Compare J. Choper, Judicial Review and the National Political Process 263, 269, 275 (1982):

The federal judiciary should not decide constitutional questions concerning the respective powers of Congress and the President vis-à-vis one another; rather, the ultimate constitutional issues [should] be held nonjusticiable, their final resolution to be remitted to the interplay of the national political process. [The] important message [to] be gleaned from [the] founders' thinking is that the checks on legislative autocracy that they contemplated exist independently of judicial supervision of the constitutionally mandated separation of powers between the President and Congress.

Does this argument disregard the possibility that a judicial role is necessary to prevent a stalemate between the branches and to avert potential constitutional crises? Does it overemphasize the usefulness of nonjudicial techniques in reaching accommodation?

B.   CASE STUDY: PRESIDENTIAL SEIZURE

Youngstown Sheet & Tube Co. v. Sawyer (The Steel Seizure Case)

343 U.S. 579 (1952)

MR. JUSTICE BLACK delivered the opinion of the Court.

We are asked to decide whether President Truman was acting within his constitutional power when he issued an order directing the Secretary of Commerce to take possession of and operate most of the Nation's steel mills. The mill owners argue that the President's order amounts to lawmaking, a legislative function which the Constitution has expressly confided to the Congress and not to the President. The Government's position is that the order was made on findings of the President that his action was necessary to avert a national catastrophe which would inevitably result from a stoppage of steel production, and that in meeting this grave emergency the President was acting within the aggregate of his constitutional powers as the Nation's Chief Executive and the Commander in Chief of the Armed Forces of the United States. The issue emerges here from the following series of events:

In the latter part of 1951, a dispute arose between the steel companies and their employees over terms and conditions that should be included in new collective bargaining agreements. [On] April 4, 1952, the Union gave notice of a nationwide strike called to begin at 12:01 A.M. April 9. The indispensability of steel as a component of substantially all weapons and other war materials led the President to believe that the proposed work stoppage would immediately jeopardize our national defense and that governmental seizure of the steel mills was necessary in order to assure the continued availability of steel. Reciting these considerations for his action, the President, a few hours before the strike was to begin, issued Executive Order 10340. [The] order directed the Secretary of Commerce to take possession of most of the steel mills and keep them running. [The] next morning the President sent a message to Congress reporting his action.

[Twelve] days later he sent a second message. [Congress] has taken no action. . . .

[The Court noted that the companies had obeyed the order under protest and brought suit against the Secretary of Commerce in district court. On April 30, that court issued a temporary restraining order prohibiting the Secretary from continuing the seizure and possession of the plants. On the same day, the district court's order was stayed by the court of appeals. The Supreme Court granted certiorari on May 3 and heard argument on May 12; the decision was announced on June 2.]

TRO on Sec.

Sup Ct. granted certiorari

The President's power, if any, to issue the order must stem either from an act of Congress or from the Constitution itself. There is no statute that expressly authorizes the President to take possession of property as he did here. Nor is there any act of Congress to which our attention has been directed from which such a power can fairly be implied. [There] are two statutes which do authorize the President to take both personal and real property under certain conditions. However, the Government admits that these conditions were not met and that the President's order was not rooted in either of the statutes. The Government refers to the seizure provisions of one of these statutes as "much too cumbersome, involved, and time-consuming for the crisis which was at hand."

Gov admits they don't meet the exceptions

Moreover, the use of the seizure technique to solve labor disputes in order to prevent work stoppages was not only unauthorized by any congressional enactment; prior to this controversy, Congress had refused to adopt that method of settling labor disputes. When the Taft-Hartley Act was under consideration in 1947, Congress rejected an amendment which would have authorized such governmental seizures in cases of emergency. . . .

It is clear that if the President had authority to issue the order he did, it must be found in some provision of the Constitution. . . .

The order cannot properly be sustained as an exercise of the President's military power as Commander in Chief of the Armed Forces. [Even] though "theater of war" be an expanding concept, we cannot with faithfulness to our constitutional system hold that the Commander in Chief of the Armed Forces has the ultimate power as such to take possession of private property in order to keep labor disputes from stopping production. This is a job for the Nation's lawmakers, not for its military authorities.

does not fall under "theater of war"

Nor can the seizure order be sustained because of the several constitutional provisions that grant executive power to the President. In the framework of our Constitution, the President's power to see that the laws are faithfully executed refutes the idea that he is to be a lawmaker. The Constitution limits his functions in the lawmaking process to the recommending of laws he thinks wise and the vetoing of laws he thinks bad. And the Constitution is neither silent nor equivocal about who shall make laws which the President is to execute. The first section of the first article says that "All legislative Powers herein granted shall be vested in a Congress of the United States. . . ." . . .

The President's order does not direct that a congressional policy be executed in a manner prescribed by Congress — it directs that a presidential policy be executed in a manner prescribed by the President. . . .

It is said that other Presidents without congressional authority have taken possession of private business enterprises in order to settle labor disputes. But even if this be true, Congress has not thereby lost its exclusive constitutional authority to make laws necessary and proper to carry out the powers vested by the Constitution "in the Government of the United States, or any Department or Officer thereof."

The Founders of this Nation entrusted the lawmaking power to the Congress alone in both good and bad times. It would do no good to recall the historical events, the fears of power and the hopes for freedom that lay behind their choice. Such a review would but confirm our holding that this seizure order cannot stand.

The judgment of the District Court is affirmed.

MR. JUSTICE FRANKFURTER, concurring.

[We] must [put] to one side consideration of what powers the President would have had if there had been no legislation whatever bearing on the authority asserted by the seizure, or if the seizure had been only for a short, explicitly temporary period, to be terminated automatically unless Congressional approval were given. . . .

The question before the Court comes in this setting. Congress has frequently — at least 16 times since 1916 — specifically provided for executive seizure of production, transportation, communications, or storage facilities. In every case it has qualified this grant of power with limitations and safeguards. This body of enactments demonstrates that Congress deemed seizure so drastic a power as to require that it be carefully circumscribed whenever the President was vested with this extraordinary authority. . . .

[Nothing] can be plainer than that Congress made a conscious choice of policy in a field full of perplexity and peculiarly within legislative responsibility for choice. In formulating legislation for dealing with industrial conflicts, Congress could not more clearly and emphatically have withheld authority than it did in [the Taft-Hartley Act of] 1947. . . .

It cannot be contended that the President would have had power to issue this order had Congress explicitly negated such authority in formal legislation. Congress has expressed its will to withhold this power from the President as though it had said so in so many words. . . .

[Deeply] embedded traditional ways of conducting government cannot supplant the Constitution or legislation, but they give meaning to the words of a text or supply them. It is an inadmissibly narrow conception of American constitutional law to confine it to the words of the Constitution and to disregard the gloss which life has written upon them. In short, a systematic, unbroken, executive practice, long pursued to the knowledge of the Congress and never before questioned, engaged in by Presidents who have also sworn to uphold the Constitution, making as it were such exercise of power part of the structure of our government, may be treated as a gloss on "executive Power" vested in the President by §1 of Art. II. . . .

[The] list of executive assertions of the power of seizure in circumstances comparable to the present reduces to three in the six-month period from June to December of 1941. [Without] passing on their validity, as we are not called upon to do, it suffices to say that these three isolated instances do not add up, either in number, scope, duration or contemporaneous legal justification, to the necessary kind of executive construction of the Constitution. [Nor] do they come to us sanctioned by long-continued acquiescence of Congress giving decisive weight to a construction by the Executive of its powers. [No] doubt a government with distributed authority, subject to be challenged in the courts of law, at least long enough to consider and adjudicate the challenge, labors under restrictions from which other governments are free. It has not been our tradition to envy such governments. In any event our government was designed to have such restrictions. The price was deemed not too high in view of the safeguards which these restrictions afford. . . .

[Justice Frankfurter added a lengthy historical appendix to his opinion.]

MR. JUSTICE JACKSON, concurring in the judgment and opinion of the Court.

[A] judge, like an executive adviser, may be surprised at the poverty of really useful and unambiguous authority applicable to concrete problems of executive power as they actually present themselves. Just what our forefathers did envision, or would have envisioned had they foreseen modern conditions, must be divined from materials almost as enigmatic as the dreams Joseph was called upon to interpret for Pharaoh. A century and a half of partisan debate and scholarly speculation yields no net result but only supplies more or less apt quotations from respected sources on each side of any question. They largely cancel each other. And court decisions are indecisive because of the judicial practice of dealing with the largest questions in the most narrow way.

The actual art of governing under our Constitution does not and cannot conform to judicial definitions of the power of any of its branches based on isolated clauses or even single Articles torn from context. While the Constitution diffuses power the better to secure liberty, it also contemplates that practice will integrate the dispersed powers into a workable government. It enjoins upon its branches separateness but interdependence, autonomy but reciprocity. Presidential powers are not fixed but fluctuate, depending upon their disjunction or conjunction with those of Congress. We may well begin by a somewhat over-simplified grouping of practical situations in which a President may doubt, or others may challenge, his powers, and by distinguishing roughly the legal consequences of this factor of relativity.

1. When the President acts pursuant to an express or implied authorization of Congress, his authority is at its maximum, for it includes all that he possesses in his own right plus all that Congress can delegate. In these circumstances, and in these only, may he be said (for what it may be worth) to personify the federal sovereignty. If his act is held unconstitutional under these circumstances, it usually means that the Federal Government as an undivided whole lacks power. A seizure executed by the President pursuant to an Act of Congress would be supported by the strongest of presumptions and the widest latitude of judicial interpretation, and the burden of persuasion would rest heavily upon any who might attack it.

2. When the President acts in absence of either a congressional grant or denial of authority, he can only rely upon his own independent powers, but there is a zone of twilight in which he and Congress may have concurrent authority, or in which its distribution is uncertain. Therefore, congressional inertia, indifference or quiescence may sometimes, at least as a practical matter, enable, if not invite, measures on independent presidential responsibility. In this area, any actual test of power is likely to depend on the imperatives of events and contemporary imponderables rather than on abstract theories of law.

3. When the President takes measures incompatible with the expressed or implied will of Congress, his power is at its lowest ebb, for then he can rely only upon his own constitutional powers minus any constitutional powers of Congress over the matter. Courts can sustain exclusive presidential control in

such a case only by disabling the Congress from acting upon the subject. Presidential claim to a power at once so conclusive and preclusive must be scrutinized with caution, for what is at stake is the equilibrium established by our constitutional system.

Into which of these classifications does this executive seizure of the steel industry fit? It is eliminated from the first by admission, for it is conceded that no congressional authorization exists for this seizure. . . .

Can it then be defended under flexible tests available to the second category? It seems clearly eliminated from that class because Congress has not left seizure of private property an open field but has covered it by three statutory policies inconsistent with this seizure. . . .

This leaves the current seizure to be justified only by the severe tests under the third grouping, where it can be supported only by any remainder of executive power after subtraction of such powers as Congress may have over the subject. In short, we can sustain the President only by holding that seizure of such strikebound industries is within his domain and beyond control by Congress. . . .

The Solicitor General seeks the power of seizure in three clauses of the Executive Article, the first reading, "The executive Power shall be vested in a President of the United States of America." [I] quote the interpretation which his brief puts upon it: "In our view, this clause constitutes a grant of all the executive powers of which the Government is capable." If that be true, it is difficult to see why the forefathers bothered to add several specific items, including some trifling ones.

The example of such unlimited executive power that must have most impressed the forefathers was the prerogative exercised by George III, and the description of its evils in the Declaration of Independence leads me to doubt that they were creating their new Executive in his image. [And] if we seek instruction from our own times, we can match it only from the executive powers in those governments we disparagingly describe as totalitarian. . . .

The clause on which the Government next relies is that "The President shall be Commander in Chief of the Army and Navy of the United States. . . ." These cryptic words [undoubtedly put] the Nation's armed forces under presidential command. Hence, this loose appellation is sometimes advanced as support for any presidential action, internal or external, involving use of force, the idea being that it vests power to do anything, anywhere, that can be done with an army or navy. . . .

I cannot foresee all that it might entail if the Court should indorse this argument. Nothing in our Constitution is plainer than that declaration of a war is entrusted only to Congress. Of course, a state of war may in fact exist without a formal declaration. But no doctrine that the Court could promulgate would seem to me more sinister and alarming than that a President whose conduct of foreign affairs is so largely uncontrolled, and often even is unknown, can vastly enlarge his mastery over the internal affairs of the country by his own commitment of the Nation's armed forces to some foreign venture. I do not, however, find it necessary or appropriate to consider the legal status of the Korean enterprise to discountenance argument based on it.

Assuming that we are in a war *de facto*, whether it is or is not a war *de jure*, does that empower the Commander in Chief to seize industries he thinks necessary to supply our army? The Constitution expressly places in Congress power "to raise and *support* Armies" and "to *provide* and *maintain* a Navy." (Emphasis supplied.) This certainly lays upon Congress primary responsibility for supplying the armed forces. Congress alone controls the raising of revenues and their appropriation and may determine in what manner and by what means they shall be spent for military and naval procurement. . . .

There are indications that the Constitution did not contemplate that the title Commander in Chief *of the Army and Navy* will constitute him also Commander in Chief of the country, its industries and its inhabitants. He has no monopoly of "war powers," whatever they are. . . .

The third clause in which the Solicitor General finds seizure powers is that "he shall take Care that the Laws be faithfully executed. . . ." That authority must be matched against words of the Fifth Amendment that "No person shall be . . . deprived of life, liberty or property, without due process of law. . . ." One gives a governmental authority that reaches so far as there is law, the other gives a private right that authority shall go no farther. These signify about all there is of the principle that ours is a government of laws, not of men, and that we submit ourselves to rulers only if under rules.

The Solicitor General lastly grounds support of the seizure upon nebulous, inherent powers never expressly granted but said to have accrued to the office from the customs and claims of preceding administrations. The plea is for a resulting power to deal with a crisis or an emergency according to the necessities of the case, the unarticulated assumption being that necessity knows no law. . . .

The appeal [that] we declare the existence of inherent powers ex necessitate to meet an emergency asks us to do what many think would be wise, although it is something the forefathers omitted. They knew what emergencies were, knew the pressures they engender for authoritative action, knew, too, how they afford a ready pretext for usurpation. We may also suspect that they suspected that emergency powers would tend to kindle emergencies. Aside from suspension of the privilege of the writ of habeas corpus in time of rebellion or invasion, when the public safety may require it, they made no express provision for exercise of extraordinary authority because of a crisis. I do not think we rightfully may so amend their work and, if we could, I am not convinced it would be wise to do so, although many modern nations have forthrightly recognized that war and economic crises may upset the normal balance between liberty and authority. Their experience with emergency powers may not be irrelevant to the argument here that we should say that the Executive, of his own volition, can invest himself with undefined emergency powers.

Germany, after the First World War, framed the Weimar Constitution, designed to secure her liberties in the Western tradition. However, the President of the Republic, without concurrence of the Reichstag, was empowered temporarily to suspend any or all individual rights if public safety and order were seriously disturbed or endangered. This proved a temptation to every government, whatever its shade of opinion, and in 13 years suspension of rights was invoked on more than 250 occasions. Finally, Hitler persuaded President Von Hindenberg to suspend all such rights, and they were never restored.

The French Republic provided for a very different kind of emergency government known as the "state of siege." It differed from the German emergency dictatorship, particularly in that emergency powers could not be assumed at will by the Executive but could only be granted as a parliamentary measure. And it did not, as in Germany, result in a suspension or abrogation of law but was a legal institution governed by special legal rules and terminable by parliamentary authority.

Great Britain also has fought both World Wars under a sort of temporary dictatorship created by legislation. As Parliament is not bound by written constitutional limitations, it established a crisis government simply by delegation to its Ministers of a larger measure than usual of its own unlimited power, which is exercised under its supervision by Ministers whom it may dismiss. This has been called the "highwater mark in the voluntary surrender of liberty," but, as Churchill put it, "Parliament stands custodian of these surrendered liberties, and its most sacred duty will be to restore them in their fullness when victory has crowned our exertions and our perseverance." Thus, parliamentary control made emergency powers compatible with freedom.

This contemporary foreign experience may be inconclusive as to the wisdom of lodging emergency powers somewhere in a modern government. But it suggests that emergency powers are consistent with free government only when their control is lodged elsewhere than in the Executive who exercises them. That is the safeguard that would be nullified by our adoption of the "'inherent powers'" formula. . . .

Such power either has no beginning or it has no end. If it exists, it need submit to no legal restraint. I am not alarmed that it would plunge us straightway into dictatorship, but it is at least a step in that wrong direction.

As to whether there is imperative necessity for such powers, it is relevant to note the gap that exists between the President's paper powers and his real powers. The Constitution does not disclose the measure of the actual controls wielded by the modern presidential office. That instrument must be understood as an Eighteenth-Century sketch of a government hoped for, not as a blueprint of the Government that is. Vast accretions of federal power, eroded from that reserved by the States, have magnified the scope of presidential activity. Subtle shifts take place in the centers of real power that do not show in the face of the Constitution.

Executive power has the advantage of concentration in a single head in whose choice the whole Nation has a part, making him the focus of public hopes and expectations. In drama, magnitude and finality his decisions so far overshadow any others that almost alone he fills the public eye and ear. No other personality in public life can begin to compete with him in access to the public mind through modern methods of communications. By his prestige as head of state and his influence upon public opinion he exerts a leverage upon those who are supposed to check and balance his power which often cancels their effectiveness.

Moreover, rise of the party system has made a significant extraconstitutional supplement to real executive power. No appraisal of his necessities is realistic which overlooks that he heads a political system as well as a legal system. Party loyalties and interests, sometimes more binding than law, extend his effective control into branches of government other than his own and he often may win, as a political leader, what he cannot command under the Constitution. . . .

But I have no illusion that any decision by this Court can keep power in the hands of Congress if it is not wise and timely in meeting its problems. A crisis that challenges the President equally, or perhaps primarily, challenges Congress. If not good law, there was worldly wisdom in the maxim attributed to Napoleon that "The tools belong to the man who can use them." We may say that power to legislate for emergencies belongs in the hands of Congress, but only Congress itself can prevent power from slipping through its fingers.

The essence of our free Government is "leave to live by no man's leave, underneath the law" — to be governed by those impersonal forces which we call law. Our Government is fashioned to fulfill this concept so far as humanly possible. [The] executive action we have here originates in the individual will of the President and represents an exercise of authority without law. No one, perhaps not even the President, knows the limits of the power he may seek to exert in this instance and the parties affected cannot learn the limit of their rights. We do not know today what powers over labor or property would be claimed to flow from Government possession if we should legalize it, what rights to compensation would be claimed or recognized, or on what contingency it would end. With all its defects, delays and inconveniences, men have discovered no technique for long preserving free government except that the Executive be under the law, and that the law be made by parliamentary deliberations.

Such institutions may be destined to pass away. But it is the duty of the Court to be last, not first, to give them up.

MR. JUSTICE DOUGLAS, concurring. . . .

The branch of government that has the power to pay compensation for a seizure is the only one able to authorize a seizure or make lawful one that the President has effected. That seems to me to be the necessary result of the condemnation provision in the Fifth Amendment. It squares with the theory of checks and balances expounded by Mr. Justice Black in the opinion of the Court in which I join.

If we sanctioned the present exercise of power by the President, we would be expanding Article II of the Constitution and rewriting it to suit the political conveniences of the present emergency. . . .

We pay a price for our system of checks and balances, for the distribution of power among the three branches of government. It is a price that today may seem exorbitant to many. Today a kindly President uses the seizure power to effect a wage increase and to keep the steel furnaces in production. Yet tomorrow another President might use the same power to prevent a wage increase, to curb trade-unionists, to regiment labor as oppressively as industry thinks it has been regimented by this seizure.

[The concurring opinions of Justices Burton and Clark are omitted.]

MR. CHIEF JUSTICE VINSON, with whom MR. JUSTICE REED and MR. JUSTICE MINTON join, dissenting.

One is not here called upon even to consider the possibility of executive seizure of a farm, a corner grocery store or even a single industrial plant. Such considerations arise only when one ignores the central fact of this case — that the Nation's entire basic steel production would have shut down completely if there had been no Government seizure. Even ignoring for the moment whatever confidential information the President may possess as "the Nation's organ for foreign affairs," the uncontroverted affidavits in this record amply support the finding that "a work stoppage would immediately jeopardize and imperil our national defense."

Plaintiffs do not remotely suggest any basis for rejecting the President's finding that any stoppage of steel production would immediately place the Nation in peril. [Under the plaintiffs'] view, the President is left powerless at the very moment when the need for action may be most pressing and when no one, other than he, is immediately capable of action. Under this view, he is left powerless because a power not expressly given to Congress is nevertheless found to rest exclusively with Congress. [But the] whole of the "executive Power" is vested in the President. . . .

A review of executive action demonstrates that our Presidents have on many occasions exhibited the leadership contemplated by the Framers when they made the President Commander in Chief, and imposed upon him the trust to "take Care that the Laws be faithfully executed." With or without explicit statutory authorization, Presidents have at such times dealt with national emergencies by acting promptly and resolutely to enforce legislative programs, at least to save those programs until Congress could act. Congress and the courts have responded to such executive initiative with consistent approval. . . .

Much of the argument in this case has been directed at straw men. We do not now have before us the case of a President acting solely on the basis of his own notions of the public welfare. Nor is there any question of unlimited executive power in this case. The President himself closed the door to any such claim when he sent his Message to Congress stating his purpose to abide by any action of Congress, whether approving or disapproving his seizure action. Here, the President immediately made sure that Congress was fully informed of the temporary action he had taken only to preserve the legislative programs from destruction until Congress could act.

The absence of a specific statute authorizing seizure of the steel mills as a mode of executing the laws — both the military procurement program and the anti-inflation program — has not until today been thought to prevent the President from executing the laws. Unlike an administrative commission confined to the enforcement of the statute under which it was created, or the head of a department when administering a particular statute, the President is a constitutional officer charged with taking care that a "mass of legislation" be executed. Flexibility as to mode of execution to meet critical situations is a matter of practical necessity. . . .

The broad executive power granted by Article II to an officer on duty 365 days a year cannot, it is said, be invoked to avert disaster. Instead, the President must confine himself to sending a message to Congress recommending action. Under this messenger-boy concept of the Office, the President cannot even act to preserve legislative programs from destruction so that Congress will have something left to act upon. There is no judicial finding that the executive action was unwarranted because there was in fact no basis for the President's finding of the existence of an emergency for, under this view, the gravity of the emergency and the immediacy of the threatened disaster are considered irrelevant as a matter of law. . . .

Note: Youngstown *and the Power of the President*

1. *Background.* The Steel Seizure Case was decided against a complex background. At the end of 1950, U.S. steel producers and the steelworkers' union had agreed on a wage increase. Shortly thereafter, however, the Economic Stabilization Agency effectively froze all price and wage increases, thus preventing implementation of the agreement. In these circumstances, the steel workers threatened a strike in December 1951. Because the President feared that a strike would endanger the Korean War effort, he prevailed on the union to postpone the strike while his Wage Stabilization Board — made up of representatives of steel producers, workers, and the general public — studied the problem. The board recommended certain staggered wage increases and union benefits, but the

proposals were rejected by the industry. The steelworkers' union set a strike date of April 9, 1952.

By this time, President Truman's popularity, which had soared at the start of the Korean War, had fallen drastically. Despite the decline in his popularity, Truman refused to waver on his plans in Korea or — more particularly — in his refusal to impose any labor injunctions that might be available to him through the Taft-Hartley Act (a measure that had been enacted over his veto). Truman had had a long and close political alliance with organized labor. In order to preserve steel production, Truman issued an executive order transferring control over the industry to the government.

The *Youngstown* decision was reached only two months after Truman executed the seizure — a rapid timetable for which the Court has been criticized, especially in light of the importance of the issues. Consider the implications of the following events, as related by a historian of the dispute:

> By midafternoon [shortly before public announcement that the Supreme Court had granted certiorari in the case, the parties] apparently arrived at a satisfactory settlement, and all that remained to be done was for [the negotiators] to check with other members of their respective groups. The bargaining session recessed to allow them time to do so. During the recess, however, word of the Supreme Court's [decision granting certiorari and prohibiting the government from changing wages or working conditions during the pendency of the suit] flashed across the White House news ticker, and when the bargaining session reconvened, the attitudes of the negotiators had changed dramatically. . . .
>
> Unquestionably, the Supreme Court's [order] radically affected the collective bargaining at the White House. [No] longer under pressure to resolve the dispute, for the threat of a government-imposed wage increase had been removed, the industry saw no reason to make concessions in order to arrive at a settlement when it had nothing to lose by waiting for the Supreme Court to decide the case.

[handwritten margin note: granting of cert. changed political climate]

M. Marcus, Truman and the Steel Seizure Case: The Limits of Presidential Power 147–148 (1977).

Although Supreme Court intervention may have caused a problem that would not otherwise have existed, it is also clear in hindsight that the Truman administration greatly exaggerated the seriousness of the problem. After the Court's ruling on June 2, the union struck for fifty-three days. In fact, no steel shortage materialized, and the strike had no discernible impact on the war effort. Industry owners eventually negotiated an agreement similar to the Wage Stabilization Board's recommendations. For discussion, see M. Marcus, supra; A. Westin, The Anatomy of a Constitutional Case (1958); Corwin, The Steel Seizure Case: A Judicial Brick without Straw, 53 Colum. L. Rev. 53 (1953); Kauper, The Steel Seizure Case: Congress, the President, and the Supreme Court, 51 Mich. L. Rev. 141 (1952).

2. *Implied and emergency powers.* Does the President have any implied or emergency powers after *Youngstown*? The existence of implied or emergency presidential powers has been sharply disputed throughout the nation's history. Note that article I refers to "legislative powers herein granted," whereas article II refers to "executive power" without a "herein granted" qualification. In Alexander Hamilton's view, the "different modes of expression in regard to the two powers confirm the inference that the authority vested in the President is not limited to the specific cases of executive power delineated in Article II." 7 Works of Alexander Hamilton 80 (1851).

This line of reasoning led to the conclusion, reached by Theodore Roosevelt and adhered to by many subsequent Presidents, that the President "was a steward of the people bound actively and affirmatively to do all he could for the people [unless] such action was forbidden by the Constitution or by the law." T. Roosevelt, Autobiography 372 (1914). Contrast with this the view of President Taft and others that the President may exercise only those powers traceable to a constitutional grant of authority. Does *Youngstown* resolve this dispute?

For a detailed historical analysis of implied presidential power, see Monaghan, The Protective Power of the Presidency, 93 Colum. L. Rev. 1 (1993).

Note: The Relevance of Foreign Law

Justice Jackson wrote that the experience of other countries with emergency power "may not be irrelevant" to the issue confronted by the *Youngstown* Court. How likely is it that the constitutional structures he cites caused the different political outcomes in Germany, France, and the United Kingdom? Why should foreign experience under different constitutional systems have any bearing on how the text of the American Constitution is interpreted? For a modern description of how various constitutions have dealt with the problem of emergency power, see F. Aolain and O. Gross, Law in Times of Crisis: Emergency Powers in Theory and Practice 35–66 (2006).

1. *The controversy among the justices.* In recent years, members of the Court have clashed over the relevance of non-U.S. law to domestic constitutional interpretation. Consider, for example, the views of Justices Kennedy and Scalia, expressed in Roper v. Simmons, 543 U.S. 551 (2005), a case concerning the constitutionality of the juvenile death penalty. Writing for the Court, Justice Kennedy stated that

> [our] determination that the death penalty is disproportionate punishment for offenders under 18 finds confirmation in the stark reality that the United States is the only country in the world that continues to give official sanction to the juvenile death penalty. This reality does not become controlling, for the task of interpreting the Eighth Amendment remains our responsibility. . . .
>
> Not the least of the reasons we honor the Constitution, [is] because we know it to be our own. It does not lessen our fidelity to the Constitution or our pride in its origins to acknowledge that the express affirmation of certain fundamental rights by other nations and peoples simply underscores the centrality of those same rights within our own heritage of freedom.

In a dissenting opinion, Justice Scalia replied:

> [The] basic premise of the Court's argument — that American law should conform to the laws of the rest of the world — ought to be rejected out of hand. In fact the Court itself does not believe it. In many significant respects the laws of most other countries differ from our law — including not only such explicit provisions of our Constitution as the right to jury trial and grand jury indictment, but even many interpretations of the Constitution prescribed by this Court itself. . . .
>
> The Court should either profess its willingness to reconsider all these matters in light of the views of foreigners, or else it should cease putting forth foreigners' views as part of the reasoned basis of its decisions. To invoke alien law when it agrees with

one's own thinking, and ignore it otherwise, is not reasoned decisionmaking, but sophistry.

Is the argument for or against the use of non-U.S. law in the context of the juvenile death penalty the same as it is in the context of emergency power?

2. *The assumptions behind the argument.* Does willingness to use non-U.S. law imply views about the nature of constitutional interpretation? About the abilities and trustworthiness of judges? About the underlying similarity of different cultures and political systems? Consider the following views.

a. "The legitimacy of constitutional comparativism should be determined by constitutional theory. [If] a judge interprets the Constitution based on a theory of original intent, then contemporary global practices will be of little service. If a judge espouses a theory that the Constitution embodies natural law principles, then evidence of universal norms may buttress that conception. If a judge grounds his or her decisionmaking on a theory of deference to the legislature, then comparative experiences that offer competing conceptions of 'the good' will be of little relevance. If a judge is a constitutional pragmatist, real-world consequences at home and abroad may be deemed appropriate to cast an empirical light on proposed solutions to common problems." Alford, In Search of a Theory for Constitutional Comparativism, 52 UCLA L. Rev. 639, 641 (2005).

b. "[To] the extent constitutional systems perform similar functions, similar concerns may arise about the consequences of interpretive choices. If more than one interpretation of the Constitution is plausible from domestic legal sources, approaches taken in other countries may provide helpful empirical information in deciding what interpretation will work best here." Jackson, Constitutional Comparisons: Convergence, Resistance, Engagement, 116 Harv. L. Rev. 109, 116 (2005).

c. "In foreign law you can find anything you want. If you don't find it in the decisions of France or Italy, it's in the decisions of Somalia or Japan or Indonesia or wherever. As somebody said in another context, looking at foreign law for support is like looking out over a crowd and picking out your friends. You can find them, they're there. And that actually expands the discretion of the judge. It allows the judge to incorporate his or her own personal preferences, cloak them with the authority of precedent because they're finding precedent in foreign law, and use that to determine the meaning of the Constitution. I think that's a misuse of precedent, not a correct use of precedent." Confirmation Hearing on the Nomination of John G. Roberts, Jr. to Be Chief Justice of the United States Before the S. Comm. on the Judiciary, 109th Cong. 200-01 (statement of Judge John Roberts) (2005).

d. "[Foreign] decisions emerge from complex social, political, cultural, and historical backgrounds of which Supreme Court Justices, like other American judges and lawyers, are largely ignorant. . . . To cite foreign decisions as precedents is indeed to flirt with the idea of universal natural law, or, what amounts to almost the same thing, to suppose fantastically that the world's judges constitute a single, elite community of wisdom and conscience." Posner, Foreword: A Political Court, 119 Harv. L. Rev. 31, 86 (2005).

e. "There is, of course, a learning curve with respect to any form of knowledge, from microeconomics to history to non-U.S. law. In my opinion the curve is not that steep, but even if it is, the scholarly infrastructure is developing to enable judges to learn about non-U.S. law and its uses, just as they have learned microeconomics." Tushnet, When Is Knowing Less Better than Knowing More?

Unpacking the Controversy over Supreme Court Reference to Non-U.S. Law, 90 Minn. L. Rev. 1275, 1298 (2006). Compare Tushnet, The Inevitable Globalization of Constitutional Law, 49 Va. J. Intl. L. 985, 988 (2009) (arguing that "because the globalization of domestic constitutional law is inevitable, notions of separation of powers — or of legislative supremacy qualified by the existence of judicial review — will need to accommodate themselves to that globalization").

C.   FOREIGN AFFAIRS

The Constitution vests in Congress the power to declare war, to "raise and support Armies" and to "provide and maintain a Navy," to "regulate Commerce with foreign Nations," and to "define and punish [Offenses] against the Law of Nations." The Senate is empowered to advise and consent on the making of treaties. The President is given the "executive" power and made the "Commander in Chief of the Army and Navy." He is also empowered to "make Treaties," to "appoint Ambassadors [and] other public Ministers" (although only "by and with the Advice and Consent of the Senate"), and to "receive Ambassadors and other Public Ministers." How useful are these textual provisions in resolving twenty-first century conflicts over the role of the Congress and the President in foreign affairs?

1.   Executive Authority

United States v. Curtiss-Wright Export Corp.
299 U.S. 304 (1936)

MR. JUSTICE SUTHERLAND delivered the opinion of the Court.
   [An] indictment was returned in the court below, the first count of which charges that appellees [conspired] to sell in the United States certain arms of war, namely fifteen machine guns, to Bolivia, a country then engaged in armed conflict in the Chaco, in violation of the Joint Resolution of Congress approved May 28, 1934, and the provisions of a proclamation issued on the same day by the President [pursuant] to authority conferred by §1 of the resolution. [The joint resolution authorized the President to prohibit the sale of arms if he found that such a prohibition would contribute to establishment of peace in the region. The lower court held that the joint resolution was an unconstitutional delegation of legislative power to the President.]
   Whether, if the Joint Resolution had related solely to internal affairs it would be open to the challenge that it constituted an unlawful delegation of legislative power to the Executive, we find it unnecessary to determine. [Curtiss-Wright was decided one year after the Court invalidated the National Industrial Recovery Act on the ground that it impermissibly delegated a legislative function to the President. See A. L. A. Schechter Poultry Corp. v. United States, Chapter 2, section C, supra, and section D2, infra.] The whole aim of the resolution is to affect a situation entirely external to the United States, and falling within the category of foreign affairs. [Assuming] (but not deciding) that the challenged delegation, if it were confined to internal affairs, would be invalid, may it nevertheless be

sustained on the ground that its exclusive aim is to afford a remedy for a hurtful condition within foreign territory?

It will contribute to the elucidation of the question if we first consider the differences between the powers of the federal government in respect of foreign or external affairs and those in respect of domestic or internal affairs. . . .

The two classes of powers are different, both in respect of their origin and their nature. The broad statement that the federal government can exercise no powers except those specifically enumerated in the Constitution, and such implied powers as are necessary and proper to carry into effect the enumerated powers, is categorically true only in respect of our internal affairs. In that field, the primary purpose of the Constitution was to carve from the general mass of legislative powers *then possessed by the states* such portions as it was thought desirable to vest in the federal government, leaving those not included in the enumeration still in the states. [That] this doctrine applies only to powers which the states had, is self evident. And since the states severally never possessed international powers, such powers could not have been carved from the mass of state powers but obviously were transmitted to the United States from some other source. . . .

As a result of the separation from Great Britain by the colonies acting as a unit, the powers of external sovereignty passed from the Crown not to the colonies severally, but to the colonies in their collective and corporate capacity as the United States of America. [Rulers] come and go; governments end and forms of government change; but sovereignty survives. A political society cannot endure without a supreme will somewhere. Sovereignty is never held in suspense. When, therefore, the external sovereignty of Great Britain in respect of the colonies ceased, it immediately passed to the Union. . . .

It results that the investment of the federal government with the powers of external sovereignty did not depend upon the affirmative grants of the Constitution. The powers to declare and wage war, to conclude peace, to make treaties, to maintain diplomatic relations with other sovereignties, if they had never been mentioned in the Constitution, would have vested in the federal government as necessary concomitants of nationality. . . .

[In] this vast external realm, with its important, complicated, delicate and manifold problems, the President alone has the power to speak or listen as a representative of the nation. He *makes* treaties with the advice and consent of the Senate; but he alone negotiates. Into the field of negotiation the Senate cannot intrude; and Congress itself is powerless to invade it. . . .

It is important to bear in mind that we are here dealing not alone with an authority vested in the President by an exertion of legislative power, but with such an authority plus the very delicate, plenary and exclusive power of the President as the sole organ of the federal government in the field of international relations — a power which does not require as a basis for its exercise an act of Congress. [It] is quite apparent that if, in the maintenance of our international relations, embarrassment — perhaps serious embarrassment — is to be avoided and success for our aims achieved, congressional legislation [must] often accord to the President a degree of discretion and freedom from statutory restriction which would not be admissible were domestic affairs alone involved. Moreover, he, not Congress, has the better opportunity of knowing the conditions which prevail in foreign countries, and especially is this true in time of war. He has his confidential sources of information. He has his agents in the form of diplomatic, consular and other officials. Secrecy in respect of information gathered by them may be highly necessary, and the premature disclosure of it productive of harmful results. . . .

In the light of the foregoing observations, it is evident that this court should not be in haste to apply a general rule which will have the effect of condemning legislation like that under review as constituting an unlawful delegation of legislative power. The principles which justify such legislation find overwhelming support in the unbroken legislative practice which has prevailed almost from the inception of the national government to the present day. . . .

[Reversed.]

MR. JUSTICE MCREYNOLDS dissented without opinion.

Dames & Moore v. Regan

453 U.S. 654 (1981)

JUSTICE REHNQUIST delivered the opinion of the Court.

[In 1979, American embassy personnel were seized and held hostage in revolutionary Iran. In response to the resulting crisis, President Carter, acting pursuant to the International Emergency Economic Powers Act, declared a national emergency and blocked the removal or transfer of all property belonging to Iran. Shortly thereafter, the Treasury Department issued a regulation nullifying "any attachment, judgment, decree, lien, execution, garnishment, or other judicial process" with respect to Iranian property.

[After these orders had gone into effect, Dames & Moore filed a suit in United States District Court against the Government of Iran, alleging breach of contract. The district court issued orders of attachment directed against property of the defendant.

[On January 20, 1981, the Americans held hostage were released pursuant to an executive agreement that provided, inter alia, that all litigation "between the Government of each party and the nationals of the other" would be resolved through binding arbitration. The agreement called for the establishment of an Iran-United States Claims Tribunal, which would arbitrate any claims not settled within six months. Awards of the tribunal were to be "final and binding." Moreover, the United States agreed to terminate all legal proceedings in American courts involving such claims and to "bring about the transfer" of all Iranian assets held in the United States by American banks to a security account in the Bank of England, to the account of the Algerian Central Bank, and to use these sums to satisfy awards rendered against Iran by the Claims Tribunal.

[After taking office, President Reagan issued an executive order ratifying the terms of the agreement, suspending all "claims which may be presented to the [Tribunal]," and providing that these claims "shall have no legal effect in any action now pending in any court of the United States." The lower court upheld the executive actions at issue.]

The parties and the lower courts [have] all agreed that much relevant analysis is contained in [*Youngstown*]. . . .

Although we have in the past found and do today find Justice Jackson's classification of executive actions into three general categories analytically useful, [Justice] Jackson himself recognized that his three categories represented "a somewhat over-simplified grouping," and it is doubtless the case that executive action in any particular instance falls, not neatly in one of three pigeonholes, but rather at some point along a spectrum running from explicit congressional authorization to explicit congressional prohibition. This is particularly true as respects cases such as the one before us, involving responses to international crises the nature of which Congress can hardly have been expected to anticipate in any detail. . . .

Because the President's action in nullifying the attachments and ordering the transfer of the assets was taken pursuant to specific congressional authorization, [in §203 of the International Emergency Economic Powers Act (IEEPA)] it is "supported by the strongest of presumptions and the widest latitude of judicial interpretation, and the burden of persuasion would rest heavily upon any who might attack it." *Youngstown*, 343 U.S., at 637 (Jackson, J., concurring). Under the circumstances of this case, we cannot say that petitioner has sustained that heavy burden. A contrary ruling would mean that the Federal Government as a whole lacked the power exercised by the President, and that we are not prepared to say.

Although we have concluded that the IEEPA constitutes specific congressional authorization to the President to nullify the attachments and order the transfer of Iranian assets, there remains the question of the President's authority to suspend claims pending in American courts. Such claims have, of course, an existence apart from the attachments which accompanied them. In terminating these claims [the] President purported to act under authority of both the IEEPA and [the] so-called "Hostage Act." We conclude that neither the IEEPA nor the Hostage Act constitutes specific authorization of the President's action suspending claims. This is not to say, [however,] that these statutory provisions are entirely irrelevant to the question of the validity of the President's action. We think both statutes highly relevant in the looser sense of indicating congressional acceptance of a broad scope for executive action in circumstances such as those presented in this case. [The] IEEPA delegates broad authority to the President to act in times of national emergency with respect to property of a foreign country. The Hostage Act similarly indicates congressional willingness that the President have broad discretion when responding to the hostile acts of foreign sovereigns. . . .

[We] cannot ignore the general tenor of Congress' legislation in this area in trying to determine whether the President is acting alone or at least with the acceptance of Congress. [Congress] cannot anticipate and legislate with regard to every possible action the President may find it necessary to take or every possible situation in which he might act. Such failure of Congress specifically to delegate authority does not, "especially . . . in the areas of foreign policy and national security," imply "congressional disapproval" of action taken by the Executive. On the contrary, the enactment of legislation closely related to the question of the President's authority in a particular case which evinces legislative intent to accord the President broad discretion may be considered to "invite" "measures on independent presidential responsibility." *Youngstown* (Jackson, J., concurring). At least this is so where there is no contrary indication of legislative intent and when, as here, there is a history of congressional acquiescence in conduct of the sort engaged in by the President. It is to that history which we now turn.

Not infrequently in affairs between nations, outstanding claims by Nationals of one country against the government of another country are "sources of friction" between the two sovereigns. To resolve these difficulties, nations have often entered into agreements settling the claims of their respective nations.

[Under] such agreements, the President has agreed to renounce or extinguish claims of United States nationals against foreign governments in return for lump-sum payments or the establishment of arbitration procedures. . . .

Crucial to our decision today is the conclusion that Congress has implicitly approved the practice of claim settlement by executive agreement. This is best demonstrated by Congress' enactment of the International Claims Settlement Act of 1949. . . .

Over the years Congress has frequently amended the International Claims Settlement Act to provide for particular problems arising out of settlement agreements, thus demonstrating Congress' continuing acceptance of the President's claim settlement authority. . . .

In light of all of the foregoing — the inferences to be drawn from the character of the legislation Congress has enacted in the area such as the IEEPA and the Hostage Act, and from the history of acquiescence in executive claims settlement — we conclude that the President was authorized to suspend pending claims. [As] Justice Frankfurter pointed out in *Youngstown*, "a systematic, unbroken, executive practice, long pursued to the knowledge of the Congress and never before questioned . . . may be treated as a gloss on 'Executive Power' vested in the President by §1 of Art. II." Past practice does not, by itself, create power, but "long-continued practice, known to and acquiesced in by Congress, would raise a presumption that the [action] had been [taken] in pursuance of its consent. . . ." United States v. Midwest Oil Co., 236 U.S. 459, 474 (1915). . . .

Just as importantly, Congress has not disapproved of the action taken here. Though Congress has held hearings on the Iranian Agreement itself, Congress has not enacted legislation, or even passed a resolution, indicating its displeasure with the Agreement. Quite the contrary, the relevant Senate Committee has stated that the establishment of the Tribunal is "of vital importance to the United States." We are thus clearly not confronted with a situation in which Congress has in some way resisted the exercise of Presidential authority.

Finally, we re-emphasize the narrowness of our decision. We do not decide that the President possesses plenary power to settle claims, even as against foreign governmental entities. [But] where, as here, the settlement of claims has been determined to be a necessary incident to the resolution of a major foreign policy dispute between our country and another, and where, as here, we can conclude that Congress acquiesced in the President's action, we are not prepared to say that the President lacks the power to settle such claims.

[Affirmed.]

[A concurring opinion by Justice Powell is omitted.]

MEDELLIN v. TEXAS, 552 U.S. 491 1346 (2008). The United States is a signatory of the Vienna Convention on Consular Relations. The Convention obligates signatories to inform detained foreign nationals of the right to request assistance from the consul of their states. At the time that this case arose, the United States was also a signatory of an Optional Protocol providing that the International Court of Justice (ICJ) would have jurisdiction to resolve disputes arising out of the interpretation or application of the Convention.

Medellin, a citizen of Mexico, was convicted of murder in state court and sentenced to death. In his application for state postconviction relief, he claimed that he had not been informed of his consular rights in violation of the Convention. Both the state and federal courts rejected his request for relief on the ground that he had failed to raise the claim earlier.

Meanwhile, the ICJ rendered a decision involving Medellin and fifty other foreign nationals held in the United States, all of whom claimed that they had not been informed of their consular rights. The ICJ held that the United States was obligated to provide, "by means of its own choosing, review and reconsideration of the convictions and sentences" of the affected parties without regard to state procedural default rules.

The Supreme Court granted certiorari to review the lower court decision denying Medellin's claim. While the case was pending, President Bush issued a Memorandum to the United States Attorney General, which provided that he had "determined pursuant to the authority vested in me as President by the Constitution and laws of the United States of America, that the United States will discharge its international obligations under the decision of the [ICJ] by having State courts give effect to the decision." Medellin then filed a second application for postconviction relief in state court, and the U.S. Supreme Court dismissed the petition for certiorari as improvidently granted in order to allow the state proceedings to go forward. When the state again denied relief, the Supreme Court granted certiorari for a second time.

Chief Justice Roberts delivered the opinion of the Court. In the first part of his opinion, excerpted in Chapter 3, the Court held that the Convention was not "self-executing" and, therefore was not binding on state and federal courts as a matter of domestic law. In the second portion of the opinion, the Court turned to the legal effect of the President's memorandum.

"The United States maintains that the President's constitutional role 'uniquely qualifies' him to resolve the sensitive foreign policy decisions that bear on compliance with an ICJ decision and 'to do so expeditiously.' [We] do not question these propositions. [In] this case, the President seeks to vindicate United States interests in ensuring the reciprocal observance of the Vienna Convention, protecting relations with foreign governments and demonstrating commitment to the role of international law. These interests are plainly compelling.

"Such considerations, however, do not allow us to set aside first principles. The President's authority to act, as with the exercise of any governmental power, 'must stem either from an act of Congress or from the Constitution itself.' [*Youngstown; Dames & Moore*]. . . .

"The President has an array of political and diplomatic means available to enforce international obligations, but unilaterally converting a non-self-executing treaty into a self-executing one is not among them. The responsibility for transforming an international obligation arising from a non-self-executing treaty into domestic law falls to Congress. . . .

"Once a treaty is ratified without provisions clearly according it domestic effect, [whether] the treaty will ever have such effect is governed by the fundamental constitutional principle that "'[t]he power to make the necessary laws is in Congress; the power to execute in the President'" [Hamdan v. Rumsfeld, excerpted at page 411, infra, quoting Ex parte Milligan, 4 Wall. 2, 139 (1866).] . . .

"A non-self-executing treaty, by definition, is one that was ratified with the understanding that it is not to have domestic effect of its own force. That understanding precludes the assertion that Congress has implicitly authorized the President 'acting on his own' to achieve precisely the same result. . . .

"When the President asserts the power to 'enforce' a non-self-executing treaty by unilaterally creating domestic law, he acts in conflict with the implicit understanding of the ratifying Senate. His assertion of authority, insofar as it is based on the pertinent non-self-executing treaties, is therefore within Justice Jackson's third category, not the first or even the second. . . .

"The United States nonetheless maintains that the President's Memorandum should be given effect as domestic law because 'this case involves a valid Presidential action in the context of Congressional "acquiescence."' Under the *Youngstown* tripartite framework, congressional acquiescence is pertinent when the President's action falls within the second [category]. Here, however, as we have explained, the President's effort to accord domestic effect to the [ICJ] judgment does not meet that prerequisite.

"In any event, even if we were persuaded that congressional acquiescence could support the President's asserted authority to create domestic law pursuant to a non-self-executing treaty, such acquiescence does not exist here. . . .

"We [turn] to the United States' claim that 'independent of the United States' treaty obligations' the Memorandum is a valid exercise of the President's foreign affairs authority to resolve claims disputes with foreign nations. [The Court cites *Dames & Moore* among other cases.]

"The claims-settlement cases involve a narrow set of circumstances: the making of executive agreements to settle civil claims between American citizens and foreign governments or foreign nationals. They are based on the view that 'a systematic, unbroken, executive practice, long pursued to the knowledge of the Congress and never before questioned,' can 'raise a presumption that the [action] had been [taken] pursuant to its consent.' [*Dames & Moore*]. . . .

"The President's Memorandum is not supported by a 'particularly longstanding practice' of congressional acquiescence, but rather is what the United States itself has described as 'unprecedented action.' Indeed, the Government has not identified a single instance in which the President as attempted (or Congress has acquiesced in) a Presidential directive issued to state courts, much less one that reaches deep into the heart of the State's police powers and compels state courts to reopen final criminal judgments and set aside neutrally applicable state laws. . . .

"Medellin argues that the President's Memorandum is a valid exercise of his 'Take Care' power. [This] authority allows the President to execute the laws, not make them. For the reasons we have stated, the [ICJ] judgment is not domestic law; accordingly, the President cannot rely on his Take Care powers here."

Justice Stevens concurred in the judgment. Justice Breyer, joined by Justices Souter and Ginsburg, dissented.

ZIVOTOFSKY EX REL. ZIVOTOFSKY v. KERRY, 135 S. Ct. 2076 (2015). For many years, Presidents of both parties have refused to recognize Israeli sovereignty over Jerusalem and have instead insisted that the status of Jerusalem should be determined by negotiations between the Israelis and Palestinians. The Foreign Relations Authorization Act for the 2003 fiscal year provided that "[for] purposes of the registration of birth, certification of nationality, or issuance of a passport of a United States citizen, born in the city of Jerusalem, the Secretary shall, upon the request of the citizen or the citizen's legal guardian, record the place of birth as Israel." Although President George W. Bush signed the Act into law, he issued a signing statement stating that if the measure was construed as mandatory, it impermissibly interfered with the President's constitutional authority in the field of international affairs.

Petitioner was born to United States citizens living in Jerusalem, and his mother requested that his passport and the consular report of his birth list his place of birth as Jerusalem, Israel. The State Department refused to comply with the request, and petitioner brought this action. The trial court dismissed the case on the ground that it constituted a nonjusticiable political question, but the Supreme Court reversed. (This aspect of the litigation is discussed at page 148). On remand, the Court of Appeals held that the statute was unconstitutional, and the Supreme Court affirmed.

Justice Kennedy wrote the opinion for the Court. He began his analysis by asserting that petitioner had waived his argument that the consular report of birth abroad should be treated differently from the passport. Accordingly, the opinion addressed only the passport issue. With regard to that issue, the Court noted that under Justice Jackson's tripartite analysis in *Youngstown*, the President was acting in contravention of the views of Congress and that his power was therefore "at its lowest ebb" and his claim must be "scrutinized with caution."

Nonetheless, the Court held that the passport requirement implicated the power to recognize a foreign government and that this power belonged to the President. Although the power was not expressly mentioned in the Constitution, it was a "logical and proper inference" from the power to "receive Ambassadors and other public Ministers" which is granted in article II. This inference was reinforced by the article II powers to make treaties and appoint ambassadors with the advice and consent of the Senate.

"Beyond that, the President himself has the power to open diplomatic channels simply by engaging in direct diplomacy with foreign heads of state and their ministers. The Constitution thus assigns the President means to effect recognition on his own initiative. Congress, by contrast, has no constitutional power that would enable it to initiate diplomatic relations with a foreign nation. Because these specific Clauses confer the recognition power on the President, the Court need not consider whether or to what extent the Vesting Clause, which provides that the 'executive Power' shall be vested in the President, provides further support for the President's action here."

Having found that the President had the recognition power, the Court then proceeded to determine whether the power was exclusive. It held that it was. "The various ways in which the President may unilaterally effect recognition — and the lack of any similar power vested in Congress — suggest that [the power is exclusive]. So, too, do functional considerations. Put simply, the Nation must have a single policy regarding which governments are legitimate in the eyes of the United States and which are not."

The Court then discussed the historical practice, finding that Presidents since the founding had exercised unilateral power to recognize new states and that the Court had endorsed the practice.

In the Court's view, it remained "true [that] many decisions affecting foreign relations — including decisions that may determine the course of our relations with recognized countries — require congressional action. . . .

"If Congress disagrees with the President's recognition policy, there may be consequences. Formal recognition may seem a hollow act if it is not accompanied by the dispatch of an ambassador, the easing of trade restrictions, and the conclusion of treaties. And those decisions require action by the Senate or the whole Congress.

"In practice, then, the President's recognition determination is just one part of a political process that may require Congress to make laws. The President's exclusive recognition power encompasses the authority to acknowledge, in a formal sense, the legitimacy of other states and governments, including their territorial bounds. Albeit limited, the exclusive recognition power is essential to the conduct of Presidential duties."

Finally, the Court held that the passport requirement contained in the Act infringed on the President's recognition power. "If Congress may not pass a law, speaking in its own voice, that effects formal recognition, then it follows that it may not force the President himself to contradict his earlier statement. That congressional command would not only prevent the Nation from speaking with one voice but also prevent the Executive itself from doing so in conducting foreign relations.

"Although the statement required by [the Act] would not itself constitute a formal act of recognition, it is a mandate that the Executive contradict his prior recognition determination in an official document issued by the Secretary of State. As a result, it is unconstitutional."

Justice Breyer wrote a concurring opinion. Justice Thomas wrote an opinion concurring in part and dissenting in part. Justice Scalia, joined by Chief Justice Roberts and Justice Alito, dissented.

Note: The President and Foreign Affairs

1. Curtiss-Wright. The *Curtiss-Wright* case involved a delegation from Congress to the President. The case therefore falls within Justice Jackson's first category, where the President acts with congressional approval. However, in language that was arguably unnecessary to the decision, the Court asserts that the President is "the sole organ of the federal government in the field of international relations." Does this mean that the President's order would have been upheld even if the case had fallen within Jackson's third category, where the President acts in violation of a statute?

The Court makes reference to both text and history, but it relies as well on arguments from function. Only the President, the Court asserts, can "[know] the conditions which prevail in foreign countries," has "confidential sources of information," and can maintain secrecy. Exclusive presidential authority is essential if "embarrassment — perhaps serious embarrassment — is to be avoided and success for our aims achieved." Is this argument independent from controversial political judgments about the appropriate role of the United States in the world?

2. Dames & Moore. Can the result in *Dames & Moore* be reconciled with that in *Youngstown*? Is the Court's reliance on congressional silence consistent with the constitutional requirement that statutes be enacted by both Houses of Congress and subject to a presidential veto? Consider the implications of INS v. Chadha, page 438, infra, striking down the one-House "legislative veto" on the ground that it violated the presentment and bicameralism clauses of the Constitution.

3. Medellin. Is the Court's decision in *Medellin* consistent with the Court's statement in *Curtiss-Wright* that the President is "the sole organ of the federal government in the field of international relations"? Note the Court's statement that the President's effort to give domestic effect to the Treaty was in Justice Jackson's third category, where he acts in the teeth of a congressional prohibition. If Congress had done nothing at all and never ratified the treaty, he would presumably be within the second category. Why should presidential action be more vulnerable to constitutional attack when the President acts to

enforce a treaty than when he acts without any congressional authority at all? According to the Court, was the President attempting to enforce the treaty?

4. *Zivotofsky.* This is a rare case where the Court upholds the President's authority when his actions conflict with a federal statute. According to Justice Jackson's *Youngstown* concurrence, "[presidential] claim to a power at once so conclusive and preclusive must be scrutinized with caution, for what is at stake is the equilibrium established by our constitutional system." Did the *Zivotofsky* court scrutinize the President's claim with appropriate caution? Was the President's "conclusive and preclusive" claim in *Zivotofsky* more convincing than in *Medellin* and in *Youngstown* itself?

Note: The Allocation of Warmaking Authority

The Constitution is notoriously ambiguous on the allocation of warmaking power as between the President and the Congress. The President is made commander in chief of the armed forces, and there is no doubt that the framers intended the President to play the principal role as the representative of the United States in relations with other nations. On the other hand, Congress is expressly empowered to "declare war." How should these provisions be reconciled?

1. *The original understanding.* Some guidance was provided during the Constitutional Convention:

"To make war."

Mr. Pinkney opposed the vesting this power in the Legislature. Its proceedings were too slow. It wd. meet but once a year. The Hs. of Reps. would be too numerous for such deliberations. The Senate would be the best depositary, being more acquainted with foreign affairs, and most capable of proper resolutions. If the States are equally represented in Senate, so as to give no advantage to large States, the power will notwithstanding be safe, as the small have their all at stake in such cases as well as the large States. It would be singular for one authority to make war, and another peace.

Mr. Butler. The Objections agst the Legislature lie in a great degree against the Senate. He was for vesting the power in the President, who will have all the requisite qualities, and will not make war but when the Nation will support it.

Mr. M[adison] and Mr. Gerry moved to insert "*declare*," striking out "*make*" war; leaving to the Executive the power to repel sudden attacks.

Mr. Sharman thought it stood very well. The Executive shd. be able to repel and not to commence war. "Make" better than "declare" the latter narrowing the power too much.

Mr. Gerry never expected to hear in a republic a motion to empower the Executive alone to declare war.

Mr. Ellsworth. There is a material difference between the cases of making *war*, and making *peace*. It shd. be more easy to get out of war, than into it. War also is a simple and overt declaration, peace attended with intricate & secret negotiations.

Mr. Mason was agst giving the power of war to the Executive, because not [safely] to be trusted with it; or to the Senate, because not so constructed as to be entitled to it. He was for clogging rather than facilitating war; but for facilitating peace. He preferred "*declare*" to "*make*."

On the Motion to insert *declare* — in place *of Make,* [it was agreed to].

2. *The meaning of "war" and of "sudden attack."* This colloquy seems to indicate a constitutional judgment that the President should be able to act to "repel sudden attacks." But in other contexts, he could not initiate "war" without a congressional declaration. How much weight should such a colloquy have?

3. *Judicial construction.* Although the existence and scope of the President's power to use the armed forces have been controversial throughout our history, the courts have rarely addressed the issue. The Supreme Court's most extensive discussion appears in The Prize Cases, 67 U.S. (2 Black) 635 (1863). At issue was the lawfulness of President Lincoln's proclamation establishing a blockade of southern ports after the secession of the southern states. The Court, in an opinion by Justice Grier, upheld the blockade. Justice Grier began his analysis by arguing that a state of war existed between the northern and southern states: "As a civil war is never publicly proclaimed, [its] actual existence is a fact in our domestic history which the Court is bound to notice and to know." Although Congress had the exclusive power to declare a national or foreign war, it could not

> declare war against a State, or any number of States, by virtue of any clause in the Constitution. The Constitution confers on the President the whole Executive power. [He] has no power to initiate or declare a war either against a foreign nation or a domestic State. But by [Acts] of Congress, [he] is authorized to [call] out the militia and use the military and naval forces of the United States in case of invasion by foreign nations, and to suppress insurrection against the government of a State or of the United States.
>
> If a war be made by invasion of a foreign nation, the President is not only authorized but bound to resist force by force. He does not initiate the war, but is bound to accept the challenge without waiting for any special legislative authority. And whether the hostile party be a foreign invader, or States organized in rebellion, it is none the less a war, although the declaration of it be *"unilateral."*

Note: The "War on Terror" and the Second Gulf War

1. *The "war on terror."* On September 18, 2001, Congress enacted a joint resolution granting the President authority to

> use all necessary and appropriate force against those nations, organizations, or persons he determines planned, authorized, committed, or aided the terrorist attacks that occurred on September 11, 2001, or harbored such organizations or persons, in order to prevent any future acts of international terrorism against the United States by such nations, organizations or persons.

Joint Resolution of Congress Authorizing the Use of Force, Pub. L. No. 107-40, 115 Stat. 224 (2001).

Is the Resolution the constitutional equivalent of a declaration of war? If so, why did Congress fail to adopt an official declaration of war? Compare Turner, The War on Terrorism and the Modern Relevance of the Congressional Power to "Declare War," 25 Harv. J.L. & Pub. Poly. 519, 521 (2002) (quoting Senate Foreign Relations Committee Chairman Joseph Biden as stating that the resolution was "the constitutional equivalent of a declaration of war"), with Katyal and Tribe, Waging War, Deciding Guilt: Trying the Military Tribunals, 111 Yale L.J. 1259, 1285 (2002) (quoting Representative Conyers as stating that "[by] not declaring war the resolution preserves our precious civil liberties" and that "[this] is important because declarations of war trigger broad statutes that not only criminalize interference with troops and recruitment but also authorize the President to apprehend 'alien enemies'").

If the Resolution is equivalent to a declaration of war, against whom is the war being waged? Traditionally, wars are ended by treaties, subject to ratification by the Senate. Is there some comparable event that will demarcate the end of the war against terrorism?

Notice that the Resolution authorizes military action only with respect to those involved in the September 11 attacks. Does the President have constitutional authority to conduct a broader "war" against alleged terrorists not associated with those attacks? Are military actions against ISIS, which broke from Al Qaeda and considers itself a rival to Al Qaeda, justified under the Resolution?

2. *The Second Gulf War.* On October 16, 2002, Congress enacted the following resolution:

> (a) AUTHORIZATION. The President is authorized to use the Armed Forces of the United States as he determines to be necessary and appropriate in order to —
>
>> (1) defend the national security of the United States against the continuing threat posed by Iraq; and
>>
>> (2) enforce all relevant United Nations Security Council resolutions regarding Iraq.
>
> (b) PRESIDENTIAL DETERMINATION. In connection with the exercise of the authority granted in subsection (a) to use force the President shall, prior to such exercise or as soon thereafter as may be feasible, but no later than 48 hours after exercising such authority, make available to the Speaker of the House of Representatives and the President pro tempore of the Senate his determination that —
>
>> (1) reliance by the United States on further diplomatic or other peaceful means alone either (A) will not adequately protect the national security of the United States against the continuing threat posed by Iraq or (B) is not likely to lead to enforcement of all relevant United Nations Security Council resolutions regarding Iraq; and
>>
>> (2) acting pursuant to this joint resolution is consistent with the United States and other countries continuing to take the necessary actions against international terrorist and terrorist organizations, including those nations, organizations, or persons who planned, authorized, committed or aided the terrorist attacks that occurred on September 11, 2001. . . .

Authorization for Use of Military Force against Iraq Resolution of 2002, Pub. L. No. 107-243, 116 Stat. 1498 (2002).

Months later, acting pursuant to this authority, the President committed American military forces to Iraq. Does a congressional authorization for military action at some point in the indefinite future constitute a declaration of war within the meaning of article I, section 8? Consider in this regard the material on the nondelegation doctrine, section D2, infra, and the implications of United States v. Curtiss-Wright Corp., supra.

The decision in *Hamdi* presented next marks the Court's first response to assertions of presidential authority to wage war in the new environment created by the attacks of September 11.

Hamdi v. Rumsfeld

542 U.S. 507 (2004)

JUSTICE O'CONNOR announced the judgment of the Court and delivered an opinion, in which [CHIEF JUSTICE REHNQUIST], JUSTICE KENNEDY, and JUSTICE BREYER join.

At this difficult time in our Nation's history, we are called upon to consider the legality of the Government's detention of a United States citizen on United States soil as an "enemy combatant" and to address the process that is constitutionally owed to one who seeks to challenge his classification as such. The United States Court of Appeals for the Fourth Circuit held that petitioner's detention was legally authorized and that he was entitled to no further opportunity to challenge his enemy-combatant label. We now vacate and remand. We hold that although Congress authorized the detention of combatants in the narrow circumstances alleged here, due process demands that a citizen held in the United States as an enemy combatant be given a meaningful opportunity to contest the factual basis for that detention before a neutral decisionmaker.

I ...

This case arises out of the detention of [Yaser Esam Hamdi, an American citizen] whom the Government alleges took up arms with the [Taliban]. [In 2001, he was seized in Afghanistan by the Northern Alliance and turned over to the U.S. military. In April 2002, he was transferred to a military brig in Charleston, South Carolina.] The Government contends that Hamdi is an "enemy combatant," and that this status justifies holding him in the United States indefinitely — without formal charges or proceedings — unless and until it makes the determination that access to counsel or further process is warranted. ...

[This action was a habeas corpus petition brought by Hamdi's father, who asserted that Hamdi went to Afghanistan to do relief work, that he had been in the country for less than two months before September 11, 2001, that he had not received military training, and that he was trapped in Afghanistan when the military campaign began.] In response to the petition, the Government filed a declaration written by Michael Mobbs, a Special Advisor to the Undersecretary of Defense. ...

Mobbs [set] forth what remains the sole evidentiary support that the Government has provided to the courts for Hamdi's detention. The declaration states that Hamdi "traveled to Afghanistan" in July or August 2001, and that he thereafter "affiliated with a Taliban military unit and received weapons training." It asserts that Hamdi "remained with his Taliban unit following the attacks of September 11" and that, during the time when Northern Alliance forces were "engaged in battle with the Taliban," "Hamdi's Taliban unit surrendered" to those forces, after which he "surrendered his Kalishnikov assault rifle" to them. The Mobbs Declaration also states that, because al Qaeda and the Taliban "were and are hostile forces engaged in armed conflict with the armed forces of the United States," "individuals associated with" those groups "were and continue to be enemy combatants." Mobbs states that Hamdi was labeled an enemy combatant "[b]ased upon his interviews and in light of his association with the Taliban." According to the declaration, a series of "U.S. military screening team[s]" determined that Hamdi met "the criteria for enemy combatants," and "a subsequent interview of Hamdi has confirmed that he surrendered and gave his firearm to Northern Alliance forces, which supports his classification as an enemy combatant." . . .

II

The threshold question before us is whether the Executive has the authority to detain citizens who qualify as "enemy combatants." [For] purposes of this case, ["enemy] combatant" [is defined as] an individual who, [the government] alleges, was "'part of or supporting forces hostile to the United States or coalition partners'" in Afghanistan and who "'engaged in an armed conflict against the United States'" there. We therefore answer only the narrow question before us: whether the detention of citizens falling within that definition is authorized.

The Government maintains that no explicit congressional authorization is required, because the Executive possesses plenary authority to detain pursuant to Article II of the Constitution. We do not reach the question whether Article II provides such authority, however, because we agree with the Government's alternative position, that Congress has in fact authorized Hamdi's detention, through the [Authorization of Use of Military Force Resolution (AUMF)]. [The Resolution is reproduced above.]

Our analysis on that point, set forth below, substantially overlaps with our analysis of Hamdi's principal argument for the illegality of his detention. He posits that his detention is forbidden by 18 U.S.C. §4001(a). Section 4001(a) states that "[n]o citizen shall be imprisoned or otherwise detained by the United States except pursuant to an Act of Congress." [For] the reasons that follow, we conclude that the AUMF is explicit congressional authorization for the detention of individuals in the narrow category we describe (assuming, without deciding, that such authorization is required), and that the AUMF satisfied §4001(a)'s requirement that a detention be "pursuant to an Act of Congress" (assuming, without deciding, that §4001(a) applies to military detentions).

The AUMF authorizes the President to use "all necessary and appropriate force" against "nations, organizations, or persons" associated with the September 11, 2001, terrorist attacks. There can be no doubt that individuals who fought against the United States in Afghanistan as part of the Taliban, an organization known to have supported the al Qaeda terrorist network responsible for those attacks, are individuals Congress sought to target in passing the AUMF. We conclude that detention of individuals falling into the limited category we are considering, for the duration of the particular conflict in which they were captured, is so fundamental and accepted an incident to war as to be an exercise of the "necessary and appropriate force" Congress has authorized the President to use.

The capture and detention of lawful combatants and the capture, detention, and trial of unlawful combatants, by "universal agreement and practice," are "important [incidents] of war." Ex parte Quirin, 317 U.S., at 28. The purpose of detention is to prevent captured individuals from returning to the field of battle and taking up arms once again. . . .

Hamdi objects, nevertheless, that Congress has not authorized the *indefinite* detention to which he is now subject. [We] take Hamdi's objection to be not to the lack of certainty regarding the date on which the conflict will end, but to the substantial prospect of perpetual detention. [As] the Government concedes, "given its unconventional nature, the current conflict is unlikely to end with a formal cease-fire agreement." The prospect Hamdi raises is therefore not far-fetched. If the Government does not consider this unconventional war won for two generations, and if it maintains during that time that Hamdi might, if released, rejoin forces fighting against the United States, then the position it has taken throughout the litigation of this case suggests that Hamdi's detention could last for the rest of his life. . . .

Hamdi contends that the AUMF does not authorize indefinite or perpetual detention. Certainly, we agree that indefinite detention for the purpose of interrogation is not authorized. Further, we understand Congress' grant of authority for the use of "necessary and appropriate force" to include the authority to detain for the duration of the relevant conflict, and our understanding is based on longstanding law-of-war principles. If the practical circumstances of a given conflict are entirely unlike those of the conflicts that informed the development of the law of war, that understanding may unravel. But that is not the situation we face as of this date. Active combat operations against Taliban fighters apparently are ongoing in Afghanistan. If the record establishes that United States troops are still involved in active combat in Afghanistan, those detentions are part of the exercise of "necessary and appropriate force," and therefore are authorized by the AUMF. . . .

III

Even in cases in which the detention of enemy combatants is legally authorized, there remains the question of what process is constitutionally due to a citizen who disputes his enemy-combatant status. . . .

C

[The Government argues that] further factual exploration is unwarranted and inappropriate in light of the extraordinary constitutional interests at stake. Under the Government's most extreme rendition of this argument, "[r]espect for separation of powers and the limited institutional capabilities of courts in matters of military decision-making in connection with an ongoing conflict" ought to eliminate entirely any individual process, restricting the courts to investigating only whether legal authorization exists for the broader detention scheme. At most, the Government argues, courts should review its determination that a citizen is an enemy combatant under a very deferential "some evidence" standard. Under this review, a court would assume the accuracy of the Government's articulated basis for Hamdi's detention, as set forth in the Mobbs Declaration, and assess only whether that articulated basis was a legitimate one. . . .

Striking the proper constitutional balance here is of great importance to the Nation during this period of ongoing combat. But it is equally vital that our calculus not give short shrift to the values that this country holds dear or to the privilege that is American citizenship. It is during our most challenging and uncertain moments that our Nation's commitment to due process is most severely tested; and it is in those times that we must preserve our commitment at home to the principles for which we fight abroad. . . .

1. notice of factual basis
2. right to rebut

We [hold] that a citizen-detainee seeking to challenge his classification as an enemy combatant must receive notice of the factual basis for his classification, and a fair opportunity to rebut the Government's factual assertions before a neutral decisionmaker.

At the same time, the exigencies of the circumstances may demand that, aside from these core elements, enemy combatant proceedings may be tailored to alleviate their uncommon potential to burden the Executive at a time of ongoing military conflict. Hearsay, for example, may need to be accepted as the most reliable available evidence from the Government in such a proceeding. Likewise, the Constitution would not be offended by a presumption in favor of the Government's evidence, so long as that presumption remained a rebuttable one and fair opportunity for rebuttal were provided. Thus, once the Government puts forth credible evidence that the habeas petitioner meets the enemy-combatant criteria, the onus could shift to the petitioner to rebut that evidence with more persuasive evidence that he falls outside the criteria. A burden-shifting scheme of this sort would meet the goal of ensuring that the errant tourist, embedded journalist, or local aid worker has a chance to prove military error while giving due regard to the Executive once it has put forth meaningful support for its conclusion that the detainee is in fact an enemy combatant. . . .

We think it unlikely that this basic process will have the dire impact on the central functions of warmaking that the Government forecasts. The parties agree that initial captures on the battlefield need not receive the process we have discussed here; that process is due only when the determination is made to continue to hold those who have been seized. [While] we accord the greatest respect and consideration to the judgments of military authorities in matters relating to the actual prosecution of a war, and recognize that the scope of that discretion necessarily is wide, it does not infringe on the core role of the military for the courts to exercise their own time-honored and constitutionally mandated roles of reviewing and resolving claims like those presented here. . . .

D

In so holding, we necessarily reject the Government's assertion that separation of powers principles mandate a heavily circumscribed role for the courts in such circumstances. Indeed, the position that the courts must forgo any examination of the individual case and focus exclusively on the legality of the broader detention scheme cannot be mandated by any reasonable view of separation of powers, as this approach serves only to *condense* power into a single branch of government. We have long since made clear that a state of war is not a blank check for the President when it comes to the rights of the Nation's citizens. *Youngstown Sheet & Tube.* Whatever power the United States Constitution envisions for the Executive in its exchanges with other nations or with enemy organizations in times of conflict, it most assuredly envisions a role for all three branches when individual liberties are at stake. . . .

There remains the possibility that the standards we have articulated could be met by an appropriately authorized and properly constituted military tribunal. [In] the absence of such process, however, a court that receives a petition for a writ of habeas corpus from an alleged enemy combatant must itself ensure that the minimum requirements of due process are achieved. [We] anticipate that a District Court would proceed with the caution that we have indicated is necessary in this setting, engaging in a factfinding process that is both prudent and incremental. . . .

IV

Hamdi asks us to hold that the Fourth Circuit also erred by denying him immediate access to counsel upon his detention and by disposing of the case without permitting him to meet with an attorney. Since our grant of certiorari in this case, Hamdi has been appointed counsel, with whom he has met for consultation purposes on several occasions, and with whom he is now being granted unmonitored meetings. He unquestionably has the right to access to counsel in connection with the proceedings on remand. No further consideration of this issue is necessary at this stage of the case. . . .

The judgment of the United States Court of Appeals for the Fourth Circuit is vacated, and the case is remanded for further proceedings.

JUSTICE SOUTER, with whom JUSTICE GINSBURG joins, concurring in part, dissenting in part, and concurring in the judgment. . . .

The plurality rejects [the Government's position] on the exercise of habeas jurisdiction and so far I agree with its opinion. The plurality does, however, accept the Government's position that if Hamdi's designation as an enemy combatant is correct, his detention (at least as to some period) is authorized by an Act of Congress as required by §4001(a), that is, by the [AUMF]. Here, I disagree and respectfully dissent. The Government has failed to demonstrate that the Force Resolution authorizes the detention complained of here even on the facts the Government claims. If the Government raises nothing further than the record now shows, the Non-Detention Act entitles Hamdi to be released. . . .

III

Under [the] principle of reading §4001(a) robustly to require a clear statement of authorization to detain, none of the Government's arguments suffices to justify Hamdi's detention. . . .

D

Since the Government has given no reason either to deflect the application of §4001(a) or to hold it to be satisfied, I need to go no further; the Government hints of a constitutional challenge to the statute, but it presents none here. I will, however, stray across the line between statutory and constitutional territory just far enough to note the weakness of the Government's mixed claim of inherent, extrastatutory authority under a combination of Article II of the Constitution and the usages of war. [It] is instructive to recall Justice Jackson's observation that the President is not Commander in Chief of the country, only of the military. Youngstown Sheet & Tube Co. v. Sawyer, (concurring opinion); see also id., (Presidential authority is "at its lowest ebb" where the President acts contrary to congressional will).

There may be room for one qualification to Justice Jackson's statement, however: in a moment of genuine emergency, when the Government must act with no time for deliberation, the Executive may be able to detain a citizen if there is reason to fear he is an imminent threat to the safety of the Nation and its people (though I doubt there is any want of statutory authority). This case, however, does not present that question, because an emergency power of necessity must at least be limited by the emergency; Hamdi has been locked up for over two years.

Whether insisting on the careful scrutiny of emergency claims or on a vigorous reading of §4001(a), we are heirs to a tradition given voice 800 years ago by Magna Carta, which, on the barons' insistence, confined executive power by "the law of the land." . . .

JUSTICE SCALIA, with whom JUSTICE STEVENS joins, dissenting. . . .

Where the Government accuses a citizen of waging war against it, our constitutional tradition has been to prosecute him in federal court for treason or some other crime. Where the exigencies of war prevent that, the Constitution's Suspension Clause, Art. I, §9, cl. 2, allows Congress to relax the usual protections temporarily [by suspending the writ of habeas corpus]. Absent suspension, however, the Executive's assertion of military exigency has not been thought sufficient to permit detention without charge. No one contends that the congressional Authorization for Use of Military Force, on which the Government relies to justify its actions here, is an implementation of the Suspension Clause. Accordingly, I would reverse the decision below. . . .

Several limitations give my views in this matter a relatively narrow compass. They apply only to citizens, accused of being enemy combatants, who are detained within the territorial jurisdiction of a federal court. This is not likely to be a numerous group; currently we know of only two, Hamdi and Jose Padilla. Where the citizen is captured outside and held outside the United States, the constitutional requirements may be different. Moreover, even within the United States, the accused citizen-enemy combatant may lawfully be detained once prosecution is in progress or in contemplation. The Government has been notably successful in securing conviction, and hence long-term custody or execution, of those who have waged war against the state.

I frankly do not know whether these tools are sufficient to meet the Government's security needs, including the need to obtain intelligence through interrogation. It is far beyond my competence, or the Court's competence, to determine that. But it is not beyond Congress's. If the situation demands it, the Executive can ask Congress to authorize suspension of the writ — which can be made subject to whatever conditions Congress deems appropriate, including even the procedural novelties invented by the plurality today. . . .

Many think it not only inevitable but entirely proper that liberty give way to security in times of national crisis — that, at the extremes of military exigency, *inter arma silent leges*. Whatever the general merits of the view that war silences law or modulates its voice, that view has no place in the interpretation and application of a Constitution designed precisely to confront war and, in a manner that accords with democratic principles, to accommodate it. Because the Court has proceeded to meet the current emergency in a manner the Constitution does not envision, I respectfully dissent.

JUSTICE THOMAS, dissenting.

The Executive Branch, acting pursuant to the powers vested in the President by the Constitution and with explicit congressional approval, has determined that

Yaser Hamdi is an enemy combatant and should be detained. This detention falls squarely within the Federal Government's war powers, and we lack the expertise and capacity to second-guess that decision. [The] plurality utterly fails to account for the Government's compelling interests and for our own institutional inability to weigh competing concerns correctly. I respectfully dissent. . . .

Justice Scalia apparently does not disagree that the Federal Government has all power necessary to protect the Nation. [I] do not see how suspension would make constitutional otherwise unconstitutional detentions ordered by the President. It simply removes a remedy. Justice Scalia's position might therefore require one or both of the political branches to act unconstitutionally in order to protect the Nation. But the power to protect the Nation must be the power to do so lawfully. . . .

IV . . .

[The] plurality's dismissive treatment of the Government's asserted interests arises from its apparent belief that enemy-combatant determinations are not part of "the actual prosecution of a war," or one of the "central functions of warmaking." This seems wrong: Taking *and holding* enemy combatants is a quintessential aspect of the prosecution of war. Moreover, this highlights serious difficulties in applying the plurality's balancing approach here. First, in the war context, we know neither the strength of the Government's interests nor the costs of imposing additional process.

Second, it is at least difficult to explain why the result should be different for other military operations that the plurality would ostensibly recognize as "central functions of warmaking." [Because] a decision to bomb a particular target might extinguish *life* interests, the plurality's analysis seems to require notice to potential targets. . . .

For these reasons, I would affirm the judgment of the Court of Appeals.

Note: *The Interplay between the President, Congress, and the Court with Regard to the "War on Terror"*

As you read the material below, consider the extent to which the interplay between the President, Congress, and the Court with respect to policies for dealing with the "war on terror" has served constitutional values. Has the interchange made policy more transparent and responsive to public opinion? Has it adequately protected individual rights? Are the various branches performing the functions imagined for them by the framers? Are they sufficiently respectful of the expertise and constitutional responsibilities of the other branches?

1. *The President acts.* In 2001, President Bush signed an executive order establishing military tribunals with jurisdiction to try anyone who is not an American citizen and who the President determined there was reason to believe was a member of al Qaeda, or had "engaged in, aided or abetted, or conspired to commit, acts of international terrorism, or acts in preparation therefor," or who had knowingly harbored such individuals. The order provided for conviction and sentencing upon concurrence of two-thirds of the members of the tribunal with review of the final decision vested solely in the President or the Secretary of

Defense. The order further provided that defendants before the tribunal "shall not be privileged to seek any remedy or maintain any proceeding [in any] court of the United States or any State thereof."

2. *The Court responds.* In Hamdan v. Rumsfeld, 548 U.S. 557 (2006), the Supreme Court held that the military commission system was illegal because it violated both the Uniform Code of Military Justice (UCMJ) and the Geneva Conventions. Writing for the Court, Justice Stevens concluded that it was unnecessary to decide whether without the sanction of Congress, the President could constitutionally convene military commissions because Congress had in fact authorized such commissions in Article 21 of the UCMJ. The Court rejected the President's argument that the Authorization for Military Force, reproduced at page 402, supra, in any way expanded this authority. Moreover, the authority was expressly conditioned on the requirement that the system comply with the laws of war. The military commission convened to adjudicate Hamdan's case was therefore illegal for numerous, separate reasons.

a. The commissions authorized by the President suffered from various procedural deficiencies. The presiding officer could exclude the accused and his civilian counsel from some portions of the proceedings and did not have to allow the defendant to examine all of the evidence introduced against him. The admission of testimonial hearsay and evidence obtained from coercion was permitted. A defendant could be convicted by a two-thirds vote (except in the case of a death penalty), with review by a three-member panel of military officers appointed by the Secretary of Defense, only one of member of which need have experience as a judge. Final review was by the Secretary of Defense and the President. These proceedings differed sharply from procedures required by the UCMJ for ordinary courts martial and therefore, in the Court's view, violated Article 36 of the UCMJ, which required that "[all] rules and regulations made under this article shall be uniform insofar as practicable."

b. The procedures violated Common Article 3 of the Geneva Conventions, as incorporated in the UCMJ's provision requiring that military commissions comply with the laws of war. Common Article 3 requires that trials be before "a regularly constituted court affording all the judicial guarantees which are recognized as indispensable by civilized peoples." In the majority's view, the "regularly constituted [courts] to which this provision refers are the ordinary courts-martial established by statute."

c. Writing only for a plurality of the Court consisting of himself and Justices Souter, Ginsburg, and Breyer, Justice Stevens concluded that conspiracy, the offense with which Hamdan was charged, was not an offense punishable under the laws of war, and none of the overt acts he performed in furtherance of the alleged conspiracy violated the laws of war.

d. Writing for the same plurality, Justice Stevens concluded that the exclusion of the defendant from portions of his own trial and the refusal to allow him to see some evidence against him meant that he had not been provided "judicial guarantees which are recognized as indispensable by civilized people" as required by Common Article 3.

Justice Breyer, joined by Justices Kennedy, Souter, and Ginsburg, wrote a concurring opinion. Justice Kennedy, joined in part by Justices Souter, Ginsburg, and Breyer, also concurred. Justice Alito, joined by Justice Scalia and by Justice Thomas in part, dissented. Chief Justice Roberts, who had participated on the appellate panel that decided the case below, did not participate.

A footnote in the opinion of the Court stated the following:

> Whether or not the President has independent power, absent congressional authorization, to convene military commissions, he may not disregard limitations that Congress has, in proper exercise of its own war powers, placed on his powers. See [*Youngstown*, Jackson, J., concurring)]. The Government does not argue otherwise.

In light of the Government's failure to "argue otherwise," were there any constitutional issues before the Court in *Hamdan*?

3. *Congress acts.* Congress responded to *Hamdi* and *Hamdan* by enacting the Detainee Treatment Act, 119 Stat. 2739 and the Military Commissions Act, 120 Stat. 2600. The Detainee Treatment Act granted exclusive jurisdiction to the United States Court of Appeals for the District of Columbia Circuit to review decisions made by the Combatant Status Review Tribunal, which the President established to provide the review to alleged enemy combatants in the wake of *Hamdi*. The act limited the court's review to whether the status determination was consistent with procedures established by the Secretary of Defense and "to the extent that the Constitution and laws of the United States are applicable, whether the use of such standards and procedures to make the determination are consistent with the Constitution and laws of the United States." The Military Commissions Act gave congressional imprimatur to military commissions to try enemy combatants for war crimes in the wake of *Hamdan*. It also vested the same United States Court of Appeals with exclusive jurisdiction to review judgments of the military tribunals. Review was restricted to "matters of law," and gave the court limited jurisdiction to consider "whether the final decision was consistent with the standards and procedures specified in this chapter" and "to the extent applicable, the Constitution and the laws of the United States."

4. *The Court responds.* In Boumediene v. Bush, 553 U.S. 723 (2008), a five-to-four decision written by Justice Kennedy, the Supreme Court held that the Detainee Treatment Act unconstitutionally restricted the writ of habeas corpus and that the limited review in the United States Court of Appeals provided for in the Act was not an adequate substitute for habeas. Some of the Court's language suggested that the due process rights for detainees outlined in *Hamdi* might not provide sufficient protection.

> [The] privilege of habeas corpus entitles the prisoner to a meaningful opportunity to demonstrate that he is being held pursuant to "the erroneous application or interpretation" of relevant law. And the habeas court must have the power to order the conditional release of an [individual]. But, depending on the circumstances, more may be required. . . .
>
> Petitioners identify what they see as myriad deficiencies in the [Combatant Status Review Tribunals (CSRTs)]. The most relevant for our purposes are the constraints upon the detainee's ability to rebut the factual basis for the Government's assertion that he is an enemy combatant. [The] detainee has limited means to find or present evidence to challenge the Government's case against him. He does not have the assistance of counsel and may not be aware of the most critical allegations that the Government relied upon to order his detention. [The] detainee can confront witnesses that testify during the CSRT proceeding. But given that there are in effect no limits on the admission of hearsay evidence [the] detainee's opportunity to question witnesses is likely to be more theoretical than real. . . .

The Government defends the CSRT process, arguing that it was designed to conform to the procedures suggested by the plurality in *Hamdi*. Setting aside the fact that the relevant language in *Hamdi* did not garner a majority of the Court, it does not control the matter at hand. None of the parties in *Hamdi* argued that there had been a suspension of the writ. . . .

Even if we were to assume that the CSRTs satisfy due process standards, it would not end our inquiry. . . .

For the writ of habeas corpus, or its substitute, to function as an effective and proper remedy in this context, the court that conducts the habeas proceeding must have the means to correct errors that occurred during the CSRT proceedings. This includes some authority to assess the sufficiency of the Government's evidence against the detainee. It also must have the authority to admit and consider relevant exculpatory evidence that was not introduced during the earlier proceedings.

Chief Justice Roberts wrote a dissenting opinion, which was joined by Justices Scalia, Thomas, and Alito. Justice Scalia also wrote a dissenting opinion, which was joined by Chief Justice Roberts and Justices Thomas and Alito.

In the wake of *Boumediene*, the United States Court of Appeals for the District of Columbia Circuit has repeatedly reversed district court decisions granting detainees habeas corpus. See Latif v. Obama, 677 F.3d 1175 (D.C. Cir. 2012); Almerfide v. Obama, 654 F.3d 1 (D.C. Cir. 2011); Uthman v. Obama, 637 F.3d 400 (D.C. Cir. 2011); Al-Adahir v. Obama, 613 F.3d 1102 (D.C. Cir. 2010); Hatim v. Gates, 632 F.3d 720 (D.C. Cir. 2011). The Court of Appeals held that government reports were entitled to a presumption that they were accurate, *Latif*, supra; that detention could be based upon hearsay evidence, Al-Bihani v. Obama, 590 F.3d 866 (D.C. Cir. 2010); and that, at most, the government need establish its case by only a preponderance of the evidence, *Al-Bihani*, supra. The Supreme Court has declined to review any of these decisions.

Note: Some Unanswered Questions

1. *Torture.* Does the President's commander in chief power allow him to override statutes or treaty obligations prohibiting torture if he determines that doing so is necessary to win the war on terror? In a memorandum prepared for the Counsel to the President, the Justice Department's Office of Legal Counsel reached the following conclusions:

Even if an interrogation method arguably were to violate [the federal statute implementing the United Nations Convention against Torture and Other Cruel, Inhuman or Degrading Treatment or Punishment], the statute would be unconstitutional if it impermissibly encroached on the President's constitutional power to conduct a military campaign. As Commander-in-Chief, the President has the constitutional authority to order interrogations of enemy combatants to gain intelligence information concerning the military plans of the enemy. The demands of the Commander-in-Chief power are especially pronounced in the middle of a war in which the nation has already suffered a direct attack. In such a case, the information gained from interrogations may prevent future attacks by foreign enemies. Any effort to apply [the statute] in a manner that interferes with the President's direction of such core war matters as the detention and interrogation of enemy combatants thus would be unconstitutional.

In a memorandum signed on February 7, 2002, President Bush stated that he

> accept[ed] the legal conclusion of the Attorney General and the Department of
> Justice that I have the authority under the Constitution to suspend [Geneva Con-
> vention provisions dealing with the treatment of prisoners] as between the United
> States and Afghanistan, but I decline to exercise that authority at this time. [I]
> reserve the right to exercise this authority in this or future conflicts. [Our] values
> as a Nation [call] for us to treat detainees humanely, including those who are not
> legally entitled to such treatment. [As] a matter of policy, the United States Armed
> Forces shall continue to treat detainees humanely and, to the extent appropriate
> and consistent with military necessity, in a manner consistent with the principles of
> Geneva.

After the Office of Legal Counsel memorandum became public in spring
2004, the President disavowed its conclusions.

In 2006, Congress enacted 42 U.S.C. §2000dd (the "McCain amendment"),
which, in relevant part, provides as follows:

> (a) No individual in the custody or under the physical control of the
> United States Government, regardless of nationality or physical location,
> shall be subject to cruel, inhuman, or degrading treatment or punishment. . . .
>
> (d) In this section, the term "cruel, inhuman, or degrading treatment or
> punishment" means the cruel, unusual, and inhumane treatment or punish-
> ment prohibited by the Fifth, Eighth, and Fourteenth Amendments to the
> Constitution of the United States, as defined in the United States Reservations,
> Declarations and Understandings to the United Nations Convention Against
> Torture and Other Forms of Cruel, Inhuman or Degrading Treatment or
> Punishment done at New York, December 10, 1984.

President Bush signed the measure into law, but made the following statement:

> The executive branch shall construe Title X in Division A of the Act, relating to
> detainees, in a manner consistent with the constitutional authority of the President
> to supervise the unitary executive branch and as Commander in Chief and con-
> sistent with the constitutional limitations on the judicial power, which will assist in
> achieving the shared objective of the Congress and the President, evidenced in
> Title X, of protecting the American people from further terrorist attacks.

President's Statement on Signing of H.R. 2863, the Department of Defense,
Emergency Supplemental Appropriations to Address Hurricanes in the Gulf of
Mexico, and Pandemic Influenza Act, 2006.

Is the President constitutionally obligated to obey the McCain amendment? In
addition to the provisions discussed in *Hamdan*, Common Article 3 of the
Geneva Conventions prohibits cruel treatment, torture, and "outrages upon
personal dignity, in particular, humiliating and degrading treatment." What
effect, if any, does *Hamdan*'s treatment of Common Article 3 have on the President's power with respect to the interrogation of "enemy combatants"?

On his second day in office, President Obama issued Executive Order 13,491,
which provided that

> [consistent] with the requirements of the Federal torture statute, [the McCain
> amendment], the Convention Against Torture, Common Article 3, and other
> laws regulating the treatment and interrogation of individuals detained in any
> armed conflict, [individuals in custody or control of the United States in armed

conflicts] shall in all circumstances be treated humanely and shall not be subjected to violence to life and person (including murder of all kinds, mutilation, cruel treatment, and torture), nor to outrages upon personal dignity (including humiliating and degrading treatment), whenever such individuals are in the custody or under the effective control of an officer, employee, or other agent of the United States Government or detained within a facility owned, operated, or controlled by a department or agency of the United States.

2. *Wiretapping.* In 2006, press reports revealed that the National Security Agency engaged in warrantless intercepts of telephone communications between individuals in the United States and individuals located outside the United States in circumstances where at least one participant in the conversation was suspected of terrorist activity. These intercepts appeared to violate the provisions of the Foreign Intelligence Surveillance Act, 50 U.S.C. §§1801 et seq. (FISA), which set out detailed procedures for obtaining warrants for such searches. The President nonetheless insisted that they were legally permissible because they came within his powers as commander in chief. Relying upon *Hamdi*, he also insisted that the general terms of the AUMF authorized the intercepts, just as the AUMF authorized the detention of "enemy combatants." Do these arguments survive *Hamdan?*

In 2008, Congress passed legislation that amended FISA in ways that expanded the authority of the President to order wiretapping where one portion of the conversation occurred outside the United States and provided statutory authorization for the program. President Bush continued to insist, however, that he had inherent authority to engage in wiretapping not provided for in the legislation.

3. *The relevance of constitutional law.* Suppose that the President determined that Hamdi's continued detention was essential to national security. Is it plausible that he would obey a judicial order to release him? Should he obey such an order? Consider Justice Thomas's argument in *Hamdi* that, even if Congress were to suspend the writ of habeas corpus, the President would nonetheless be under a (not judicially enforceable) obligation to obey constitutional commands. If this argument is correct, does it follow that when Justice Scalia claims that national security can be protected by suspension of the writ, he is counseling constitutional disobedience?

In Korematsu v. United States (excerpted in Chapter 5, section C1, infra), Justice Jackson dissented from the Court's judgment upholding the conviction of a defendant who had disobeyed the order excluding Japanese Americans from the West Coast during World War II. Unlike the other dissenters, however, Justice Jackson did not argue that the exclusion should not have taken place. Jackson wrote that it would be

impracticable and dangerous idealism to expect or insist that each specific military command in an area of probable operations will conform to conventional tests of constitutionality. When an area is so beset that it must be put under military control at all, the paramount consideration is that its measures be successful rather than legal.

For Justice Jackson, the crucial question was not whether the exclusion should have taken place, but whether the courts should endorse the exclusion:

I should hold that a civil court cannot be made to enforce an order which violates constitutional limitations even if it is a reasonable exercise of military authority.

The courts can exercise only the judicial power, can apply only law, and must abide by the Constitution, or they cease to be civil courts and become instruments of military policy.

Note also Justice Jackson's distinction in *Youngstown* between the President's "paper powers" and "real powers." How would Justice Jackson have voted in *Hamdi?*

2.   Legislative Authority

To what extent does the Constitution permit Congress to control presidential conduct of foreign affairs?

Note: The War Powers Resolution

In the waning days of the Vietnam War, Congress enacted the War Powers Resolution, 50 U.S.C. §§1541–1548, which was designed to halt the perceived atrophying of Congress's power to declare war.

1. *The resolution.* In an opening statement of "Purpose and Policy," the resolution declares that the President's power to introduce the armed forces into hostilities or into situations where immediate involvement in hostilities is likely is limited to situations where there has been a declaration of war, a specific statutory authorization, or a national emergency created by an attack on the United States.

The resolution then requires the President "in every possible instance" to consult with Congress before introducing U.S. troops into hostilities and, after introduction, to consult regularly with Congress until the troops have been removed. If there is no declaration of war, the President is required to submit to Congress a report within forty-eight hours whenever troops are introduced into hostilities.

Within sixty days after the report is submitted, the President must terminate use of armed forces unless Congress has declared war or enacted a specific authorization for the use of force, extended the sixty-day period, or is physically unable to meet. The President is permitted to extend the initial sixty-day period for an additional thirty days if he certifies that unavoidable military necessity requires the continued use of the armed forces in the course of bringing about a prompt removal of the forces.

Moreover, at any time that the armed forces are engaged in hostilities outside the territory of the United States without a declaration of war or specific statutory authorization, the President is obligated to remove the forces if so directed by a concurrent resolution. (Consider whether this provision is constitutional in light of INS v. Chadha, page 438, infra.)

Finally, the resolution provides that it is not "intended to alter the constitutional authority of the Congress or of the President or the provisions of existing treaties" and that it "shall [not] be construed as granting any authority to the President [which] [he] would not have had in the absence of [the Resolution]."

2. *The constitutional issue.* Consider, in the light of the preceding materials, the constitutionality of the War Powers Resolution. Which provisions are most troublesome? Consider also the following views:

a. The War Powers Resolution is an unconstitutional infringement on the powers of the President. The Constitution gives the President the authority to introduce armed forces into hostilities without a congressional declaration of war. Moreover, at least in cases of an effort to "repel sudden attacks" on the United States and its allies, the resolution is far too broad. It allows a congressional role in areas in which such a role is constitutionally proscribed.

b. The War Powers Resolution is constitutional. It merely restores the constitutional balance that had been upset by a long period of congressional inactivity before its passage. In essence, the resolution allows Congress to ensure that there is no undeclared war. Indeed, to the extent that it suffers from any constitutional defect, it is in yielding undue power to the President — for the resolution seems to allow the President to wage war without a declaration in far too many circumstances.

c. The final part of the resolution makes the preceding provisions effectively meaningless. It restores the constitutional status quo and remits individuals deciding on the distribution of the war powers — in the executive, legislative, and judicial branches — to the Constitution itself. Why was this section included?

For a comprehensive historical study of the power of Congress to control presidential warmaking, see Barron and Lederman, The Commander in Chief at the Lowest Ebb — Framing the Problem, Doctrine, and Original Understanding, 121 Harv. L. Rev. 689 (2008), and Barron and Lederman, The Commander in Chief at the Lowest Ebb — A Constitutional History, 121 Harv. L. Rev. 941 (2008). The authors conclude that throughout our history Congress has regularly "interfered with the command of the forces and the conduct of campaigns" and that "[several] of our most esteemed Presidents — Washington, Lincoln, and both Roosevelts, among others — never invoked the sort of preclusive claims of authority that some modern Presidents appear to [embrace]."

See also Prakash, Unleashing the Dogs of War: What the Constitution Means by "Declare War," 93 Cornell L. Rev. 45, 50, 120–121 (2007).

3. *Libya.* After conflict broke out between the rebels and the Libyan regime, the United Nations Security Council adopted a resolution authorizing "member States . . . to take all necessary measures . . . to protect civilians and civilian populated areas under threat of attack" and to establish a "no-fly zone" in Libya.

Two days later, on March 19, 2011, the United States, in conjunction with its NATO allies, began air strikes in Libya. Within 48 hours of the beginning of the air strikes, President Obama sent a letter to the Speaker of the House and President pro tempore of the Senate "as part of my efforts to keep Congress fully informed, consistent with the War Powers Resolution." The letter stated that U.S. military forces had begun air strikes for purpose of preparing a no-fly zone and that "[United] States forces are conducting a limited and well-defined mission in support of international efforts to protect civilians and prevent a humanitarian disaster."

On April 1, 2011, the Justice Department's Office of Legal Counsel (OLC) released a memorandum determining that the President had constitutional authority to use military force in Libya without prior congressional approval. Relying on prior OLC opinions in the Clinton administration, particularly those opinions on the unilateral presidential deployments to Haiti (1994) and Bosnia (1995), the memorandum asserted that the President's legal authority to direct military force in Libya turned on two questions: first, whether the United States operations in Libya would serve sufficiently important national interests to permit the President's action as Commander in Chief and Chief Executive and pursuant to his authority to conduct U.S. foreign relations; and second, whether the military operations that the President anticipated ordering would be sufficiently extensive in "nature, scope, and duration" to constitute a "war requiring prior, specific congressional approval under the Declaration of War Clause."

According to the memorandum, this understanding of presidential power "reflects not only the express assignment of powers and responsibilities to the President and Congress in the Constitution, but also [the] "'historical gloss' placed on the Constitution by two centuries of practice."

As to the first question OLC concluded that "the combination of at least two national interests that the President reasonably determined were at stake here" — preserving stability in the Middle East and "supporting the [United Nations Security Council's] credibility and effectiveness" — provided a sufficient basis for the President's exercise of his constitutional authority to order the use of military force.

Turning to the second question, the memorandum acknowledged that presidential authority to deploy military force even in the service of such national security interests might be limited if the engagement constituted a "war" within the meaning of the Declaration of War clause — such as in Vietnam, the first and second Gulf Wars, and, presumably, Korea. (In this way, the opinion differed from the view OLC had articulated in the George W. Bush administration, which was that the President is authorized to initiate actions of this sort without congressional approval.) The memorandum nonetheless concluded that

> the historical practice of presidential military action without congressional approval precludes any suggestion that Congress's authority to declare war covers every military [engagement]. This standard generally will be satisfied only by prolonged and substantial military engagements, typically involving exposure of U.S. military personnel to significant risk over a substantial period.

On April 4, 2011, the United States transferred responsibility for the military operations to NATO, and U.S. involvement assumed a supporting role that included logistical and search and rescue assistance, suppression and destruction of Libyan air defenses, and strikes by unmanned aerial vehicles against particular targets. Although the 60-day period specified in the War Powers Resolution appeared to expire on May 20, 2011, and although Congress failed to pass a measure authorizing U.S. involvement, the involvement continued. At first, the Obama administration offered no defense of its refusal to end the operation in compliance with the Resolution, but on June 15, 2011, the administration sent a letter to congressional leaders. The letter asserted that

> [the] current U.S. military operations [are] consistent with the War Powers Resolution and do not under that law require further congressional authorization, because U.S. military operations are distinct from the kind of "hostilities" contemplated by the Resolution's 60-day termination provision. U.S. forces are playing a constrained and supporting role in a multination coalition, whose operations are both legitimated by and limited to the terms of a United Nations Security Council resolution that authorizes the use of force solely to protect civilians and civilian populated areas under attack or threat of attack and to enforce a no-fly zone and an

arms embargo. U.S. operations do not involve sustained fighting or active exchanges of fire with hostile forces, nor do they involve the presence of U.S. ground troops, U.S. casualties or a serious threat thereof, or any significant chance of escalation into a conflict characterized by those factors.

Was the Libyan operation constitutional in the absence of congressional authorization? Was it in compliance with the War Powers Resolution? Why is the fact that the United States is playing a "supporting role" and that the operations are pursuant to a Security Council resolution relevant to the question whether there are "hostilities"? Does the memorandum mean that "hostilities" do not exist so long as the United States does not use ground troops and attacks a foe that is unable to respond?

4. *Alternative approaches.* Most commentators have agreed that the War Powers Resolution has been ineffective in constraining executive discretion. See, e.g., H. Koh, The National Security Constitution 39–40 (1990).

Could a revised, more carefully drafted War Powers Resolution more effectively ensure a congressional role in warmaking?

Note: *Congressional Control over Agreements with Foreign States — Treaties, Executive Agreements, and Congressional-Executive Agreements*

What role should Congress play when the question is the making of peace rather than war?

1. *Treaties.* Article II, section 2 of the Constitution grants to the President the power "by and with the Advice and Consent of the Senate, to make Treaties, provided two thirds of the Senators present concur," and article VI, section 6 makes "all Treaties made, or which shall be made, under the Authority of the United States" the supreme law of the land. Do these provisions authorize the President, acting with the acquiescence of two-thirds of the Senate and the agreement of a foreign country, to countermand otherwise applicable statutes? See, e.g., Whitney v. Robertson, 124 U.S. 190 (1888):

> By the Constitution, a treaty is placed on the same footing, and made of like obligation, with an act of legislation. Both are declared by that instrument to be the supreme law of the land, and no supreme efficacy is given to either over the other. [If] the two are inconsistent, the one last in date will control the other, provided always the stipulation of the treaty on the subject is self-executing.

Notice that, at least with regard to domestic law, a later act of Congress can also repeal a treaty, although the repeal may violate international law. See, e.g., The Head Money Cases, 112 U.S. 580, 599 (1884). Does it follow that the President can also countermand a treaty if he is exercising executive power under article II? For a discussion of the Bush administration's position on its legal obligation to obey treaties on torture and treatments of war prisoners, see page 411, supra. For a discussion of the limits of a President's power to enforce a treaty through executive order without congressional authorization, see pages 356–361, supra. For a discussion of the impact of treaties on state law, see Chapter 3C, supra.

2. *Executive agreements.* If a President lacks the support of two-thirds of the Senate, may he make domestic law without the acquiescence of either House by entering into an executive agreement with another country? Since the beginning of the country, Presidents have entered into thousands of such agreements. Although there is no express constitutional authority for this practice, the Constitution seems indirectly to recognize the possibility of nontreaty international agreements in article I, section 10, which prohibits states from entering into treaties but authorizes them to enter into an "Agreement or Compact with [a] foreign Power" with the consent of Congress.

Are there constitutional limits on the scope of such agreements when entered into by the President? Consider American Insurance Association v. Garamendi, 539 U.S. 396 (2003). In a five-to-four decision the Court, per Justice Souter, invalidated a California statute that required insurers doing business in the state to disclose details of insurance policies issued to persons in Europe that were in effect between 1920 and 1945. The statute was enacted to assist Holocaust victims and their descendants in their efforts to collect the proceeds of insurance policies that were either unpaid by the companies or seized by the Nazi government. The Court held that the state law was preempted by an executive agreement between the United States and Germany. Although the executive agreement did not expressly deal with California's disclosure requirement, the Court held that the agreement's approach, which emphasized voluntary cooperation and settlement of claims through a special fund established by the German government, conflicted with the statute.

With regard to the constitutional power of the President to reach binding executive agreements with foreign states, the Court said the following:

> [Our] cases have recognized that the President has authority to make "executive agreements" with other countries, requiring no ratification by the Senate or approval by Congress. [This] power [has] been exercised since the early years of the Republic. See [*Dames & Moore*]. [Making] executive agreements to settle claims of American nationals against foreign governments is a particularly long-standing [practice]. Given the fact that the practice goes back over 200 years to the first Presidential administration, and has received congressional acquiescence throughout its history, the conclusion "[t]hat the President's control of foreign relations includes the settlement of claims is indisputable."

Into which of Justice Jackson's three categories does the German-American executive agreement fall? Is the result in *Garamendi* consistent with the Court's holding in *Medellín*, page 400, supra, that the President may not enforce the terms of a treaty without congressional approval? Recall that in *Dames & Moore*, the Court stated that it was "crucial" to its decision that "Congress [had] implicitly approved the practice of claim settlement by executive agreement" through the International Claims Settlement Act. Given *Garamendi*, is this fact still "crucial"?

Would a federal statute that specifically disapproved of the executive agreement relied upon in *Garamendi* be constitutional? The *Garamendi* petitioner argued that Congress had authorized state laws of the sort California had enacted, but the Court held that it "need [not] consider the possible significance for preemption doctrine of tension between an Act of Congress and Presidential foreign policy, cf. generally [*Youngstown* (Jackson, J., concurring)]" because the federal statute did not grant such authorization, and given the President's independent authority in the areas of foreign policy and national security, congressional silence should not be equated with congressional disapproval.

D.   DOMESTIC AFFAIRS

1.   *Executive Authority*

Article II, section 1 of the Constitution vests "the executive power" in the President of the United States, and article II, section 3 provides that the President "shall take Care that the Laws be faithfully executed." To what extent do these powers free the President from legislative and judicial control when he purports to be executing the laws?

United States v. Nixon
418 U.S. 683 (1974)

MR. CHIEF JUSTICE BURGER delivered the opinion of the Court.

[On June 17, 1972, employees of the reelection committee for President Nixon broke into the Democratic National Committee headquarters at the Watergate Hotel in Washington, D.C. In February of the next year, a Senate Select Committee on the Watergate affair was set up by a unanimous vote of the Senate. The committee was charged with investigating the alleged illegal break-in and the question of White House involvement. In late May, under considerable public pressure, President Nixon appointed Archibald Cox as special prosecutor to investigate, among other things, any participation by the White House in the Watergate affair. The President himself was implicated by former White House counsel John Dean in testimony before the Senate in June, and in July one member of the House introduced an impeachment resolution. On February 6, 1974, the House formally authorized the Judiciary Committee to begin impeachment hearings. The hearings were ongoing at the time that the following decision was rendered.]

WH counsel implicated Nixon

This litigation presents for review the denial of a motion, filed in the District Court on behalf of [President Nixon] in the case of United States v. Mitchell, to quash a third-party subpoena duces tecum issued by the [District Court] pursuant to Fed. Rule Crim. Proc. 17(c). The subpoena directed the President to produce certain tape recordings and documents relating to his conversations with aides and advisers.

On March 1, 1974, a grand jury of the United States District Court for the District of Columbia returned an indictment charging seven named individuals with various offenses, including conspiracy to defraud the United States and to obstruct justice. Although he was not designated as such in the indictment, the grand jury named the President, among others, as an unindicted coconspirator. On April 18, 1974, upon motion of the Special Prosecutor, [a] subpoena duces tecum was issued [to] the President by the United States District Court [requiring] the production, in advance of the September 9 trial date, of certain tapes, memoranda, papers, transcripts, or other writings relating to certain precisely identified meetings between the President and others. [On] April 30, the

DC indicted aides

Nixon uncharged conspirator

President publicly released edited transcripts of 43 conversations; portions of 20 conversations subject to subpoena in the present case were included. On May 1, 1974, the President's counsel filed a "special appearance" and a motion to quash the subpoena [on grounds] of privilege.

On May 20, 1974, the District Court denied the motion to [quash]. [The President sought review in the court of appeals, but the Supreme Court granted review before judgment.]

In the District Court, the President's counsel argued that the Court lacked jurisdiction to issue the subpoena because the matter was an intra-branch dispute between a subordinate and superior officer of the Executive Branch and hence not subject to judicial resolution. [Since] the Executive Branch has exclusive authority and absolute discretion to decide whether to prosecute a case, [it] is contended that a President's decision is final in determining what evidence is to be used in a given criminal case. . . .

[The] Attorney General has delegated the authority to represent the United States in these particular matters to a Special Prosecutor with unique authority and tenure. The regulation gives the Special Prosecutor explicit power to contest the invocation of executive privilege in the process of seeking evidence deemed relevant to the performance of these specially delegated duties. . . .

[It] is theoretically possible for the Attorney General to amend or revoke the regulation defining the Special Prosecutor's authority. But he has not done so. So long as this regulation remains in force the Executive Branch is bound by it, and indeed the United States as the sovereign composed of the three branches is bound to respect and to enforce it. . . .

[The Court held that the subpoena met the requirements of Fed. R. Crim. Proc. 17(c), including relevance, specificity, and admissibility.]

[We] turn to the claim that the subpoena should be quashed because it demands "confidential conversations between a President and his close advisors that it would be inconsistent with the public interest to produce." [The] first contention is a broad claim that the separation of powers doctrine precludes judicial review of a President's claim of privilege. The second contention is that if he does not prevail on the claim of absolute privilege, the court should hold as a matter of constitutional law that the privilege prevails over the subpoena duces tecum.

In the performance of assigned constitutional duties each branch of the Government must initially interpret the Constitution, and the interpretation of its powers by any branch is due great respect from the others. The President's counsel [reads] the Constitution as providing an absolute privilege of confidentiality for all Presidential communications. Many decisions of this Court, however, have unequivocally reaffirmed the holding of [Marbury that] "[i]t is emphatically the province and duty of the judicial department to say what the law is." . . .

No holding of the Court has defined the scope of judicial power specifically relating to the enforcement of a subpoena for confidential Presidential communications for use in a criminal prosecution, but other exercises of power by the Executive Branch and the Legislative Branch have been found invalid as in conflict with the Constitution. Powell v. McCormack, 395 U.S. 486 (1969); [Youngstown].

[Notwithstanding] the deference each branch must accord the others, the "judicial Power of the United States" vested in the federal courts [can] no more be shared with the Executive Branch than the Chief Executive, for example, can share with the Judiciary the veto power. [Any] other conclusion would be contrary to the basic concept of separation of powers and the checks and balances that flow from the scheme of a tripartite government. [We] therefore reaffirm that it is the province and duty of this Court "to say what the law is" with respect to the claim of privilege presented in this case.

[In support of his claim of privilege, President Nixon argued that there was a valid need to protect the confidentiality of communications between high government officials, and that the privilege was implicit in the doctrine of separation of powers. The Court recognized the legitimacy of the President's interest in confidentiality.]

However, neither the doctrine of separation of powers, nor the need for confidentiality of high-level communications, without more, can sustain an absolute, unqualified Presidential privilege of immunity from judicial process under all circumstances. The President's need for complete candor and objectivity from advisers calls for great deference from the courts. However, when the privilege depends solely on the broad, undifferentiated claim of public interest in the confidentiality of such conversations, a confrontation with other values arises. Absent a claim of need to protect military, diplomatic, or sensitive national security secrets, we find it difficult to accept the argument that even the very important interest in confidentiality of Presidential communications is significantly diminished by production of such material for in camera inspection with all the protection that a district court will be obliged to provide....

The expectation of a President to the confidentiality of his conversations and correspondence, like the claim of confidentiality of judicial deliberations, for example, has all the values to which we accord deference for the privacy of all citizens and, added to those values, is the necessity for protection of the public interest in candid, objective, and even blunt or harsh opinions in Presidential decisionmaking. [The] privilege is fundamental to the operation of Government and inextricably rooted in the separation of powers under the Constitution....

But this presumptive privilege must be considered in light of our historic commitment to the rule of law. This is nowhere more profoundly manifest than in our view that "the twofold aim [of criminal justice] is that guilt shall not escape or innocence suffer." We have elected to employ an adversary system of criminal justice in which the parties contest all issues before a court of law. The need to develop all relevant facts in the adversary system is both fundamental and comprehensive....

[Evidentiary privileges] are designed to protect weighty and legitimate competing interests. Thus, the Fifth Amendment to the Constitution provides that no man "shall be compelled in any criminal case to be a witness against himself." And, generally, an attorney or a priest may not be required to disclose what has been revealed in professional confidence. These and other interests are recognized in law by privileges against forced disclosure. [Whatever] their origins, these exceptions to the demand for every man's evidence are not lightly created nor expansively construed, for they are in derogation of the search for truth.

In this case the President challenges a subpoena served on him as a third party requiring the production of materials for use in a criminal prosecution; he does so on the claim that he has a privilege against disclosure of confidential communications. He does not place his claim of privilege on the ground they are military or diplomatic secrets. As to these areas of Art. II duties the courts have traditionally shown the utmost deference to Presidential responsibilities.

[No] case of the Court, however, has extended this high degree of deference to a President's generalized interest in confidentiality. Nowhere in the Constitution [is] there any explicit reference to a privilege of confidentiality, yet to the extent this interest relates to the effective discharge of a President's powers, it is constitutionally based.

The right to the production of all evidence at a criminal trial similarly has constitutional dimensions. The Sixth Amendment explicitly confers upon every defendant in a criminal trial the right "to be confronted with the witnesses against him" and "to have compulsory process for obtaining witnesses in his favor." Moreover, the Fifth Amendment also guarantees that no person shall be deprived of liberty without due process of law. . . .

balancing b/ween 6th + 5th amends.

In this case we must weigh the importance of the general privilege of confidentiality of Presidential communications in performance of the President's responsibilities against the inroads of such a privilege on the fair administration of criminal justice.[19] The interest in preserving confidentiality is weighty indeed and entitled to great respect. However, we cannot conclude that advisers will be moved to temper the candor of their remarks by the infrequent occasions of disclosure because of the possibility that such conversations will be called for in the context of a criminal prosecution.

On the other hand, the allowance of the privilege to withhold evidence that is demonstrably relevant in a criminal trial would cut deeply into the guarantee of due process of law and gravely impair the basic function of the courts. . . .

[If] a President concludes that compliance with a subpoena would be injurious to the public interest he may properly, as was done here, invoke a claim of privilege on the return of the subpoena. Upon receiving a claim of privilege from the Chief Executive, it became the further duty of the District Court to treat the subpoenaed material as presumptively privileged and to require the Special Prosecutor to demonstrate that the Presidential material was "essential to the justice of the [pending criminal] case." [We] are unable to conclude that the District Court erred in ordering the inspection. Accordingly we affirm the order of the District Court that subpoenaed materials be transmitted to that court. We now turn to the important question of the District Court's responsibilities in conducting the in camera examination of Presidential materials or communications delivered under the compulsion of the subpoena duces tecum. . . .

[Statements] that meet the test of admissibility and relevance must be isolated; all other material must be excised. At this stage the District Court is not limited to representations of the Special Prosecutor as to the evidence sought by the subpoena; the material will be available to the District Court. It is elementary that in camera inspection of evidence is always a procedure calling for scrupulous protection against any release or publication of material not found by the court, at that stage, probably admissible in evidence and relevant to the issues of the trial for which it is sought. That being true of an ordinary situation, it is obvious that the District Court has a very heavy responsibility to see to it that Presidential

19. We are not here concerned with the balance between the President's generalized interest in confidentiality and the need for relevant evidence in civil litigation, nor with that between the confidentiality interest and congressional demands for information, nor with the President's interest in preserving state secrets. We address only the conflict between the President's assertion of a generalized privilege of confidentiality and the constitutional need for relevant evidence in criminal trials.

conversations, which are either not relevant or not admissible, are accorded that high degree of respect due the President of the United States. . . .
[Affirmed.]

Affirmed DC

MR. JUSTICE REHNQUIST took no part in the consideration or decision of these cases.

Note: *Executive Privilege and Presidential Immunity*

The Court rejected three analytically separate claims made by President Nixon: that the President was immune from judicial process while in office; that he, alone, should determine the scope of executive privilege; and that, even if the scope of the privilege should be decided by the court, his invocation of the privilege was appropriate.

1. *Immunity from judicial process.* The Court held that nothing in the Constitution precludes a subpoena directed against the President. Consider whether the immunity argument has more force in the following alternative settings:

a. *Immunity from injunctive relief.* In Mississippi v. Johnson, 71 U.S. (4 Wall.) 475 (1867), the Court refused to hear a suit attempting to enjoin the President's enforcement of the Reconstruction laws. The Court concluded that courts did not have power to issue an injunction against the President. The Court referred in particular to the difficulties of enforcement and to the alternative route of impeachment. Does *Johnson* survive United States v. Nixon? Note also that, although President Truman was not the named defendant in *Youngstown*, his order was in fact the subject of the Court's injunction.

b. *Damages for misconduct while in office.* In Nixon v. Fitzgerald, 457 U.S. 731 (1982), Fitzgerald brought an action against President Nixon on the ground that he had been discharged from a government position because he had exercised his right to freedom of speech. The Court held, by a five-to-four vote, that the President was immune from an action for damages. The opinion was written by Justice Powell. According to the Court, "[The] President occupies a unique position in the constitutional scheme. [Because] of the singular importance of the President's duties, diversion of his energies by concern with private lawsuits would raise unique risks to the effective functioning of government." The Court referred to "the sheer prominence of the President's office," which would make him "an easily identifiable target for suits for civil damages. Cognizance of this personal vulnerability frequently could distract a President from his public duties, to the detriment not only of the President and his office but also the Nation that the Presidency was designed to serve."

The Court also responded to the suggestion that absolute immunity would "leave the Nation without sufficient protection against misconduct on the part of the Chief Executive." A number of safeguards were already in place: The remedy of impeachment, "constant scrutiny by the press," "vigilant oversight by Congress," "a desire to earn re-election, the need to maintain prestige as an element of Presidential influence, and a President's traditional concern for his historical stature" would all play a role. The Court left open, however, the question whether Congress might constitutionally subject the President to liability for damages.

Notice that Nixon v. Fitzgerald was not brought until after President Nixon had left office. Given its timing, how could such a suit have "[risked] the effective function of government" or "[distracted] a President from his public duties"?

In Harlow v. Fitzgerald, 457 U.S. 800 (1982), the Court declined to extend presidential immunity to presidential aides. Lower-level officials do, however, enjoy "qualified immunity." These officials can be held liable for damages only if they violate law that was "clearly established" at the time of the violation. Id. at 818.

For an interesting application of the qualified immunity doctrine, see Ashcroft v. Al-Kidd, 131 S. Ct. 2074 (2011). In his complaint, al-Kidd alleged that in the aftermath of the World Trade Center attack, then–Attorney General Ashcroft authorized the pretextual use of the material witness statute. The statute authorizes the detention of individuals when their testimony is required for a criminal prosecution and when detention is necessary to ensure their availability at trial. Al-Kidd alleged that the statute was used to detain him because the government suspected him of involvement in terrorist activities but lacked probable cause justifying arrest for any offense. A native-born American citizen, he was detained as he checked in for a flight to Saudi Arabia based upon a material witness warrant. The affidavit filed in support of the warrant asserted that his testimony was "crucial" to the prosecution of another individual and that without his detention, the testimony would be lost. The affidavit did not mention that al-Kidd's parents, wife, and children were all citizens and residents of the United States and stated that he had purchased a one-way ticket, when in fact the ticket was round-trip. Al-Kidd remained in federal custody for sixteen days and on supervised release for fourteen months. He was never called as a witness and never charged with any offense.

In a six-to-three decision, the Court, in an opinion by Justice Scalia, held that on the merits, al-Kidd had failed to allege a fourth amendment violation because the subjective motive of government officials was irrelevant to the lawfulness of arrests and detentions. The Court then went on to hold that, assuming arguendo that the fourth amendment had been violated, Ashcroft was nonetheless entitled to qualified immunity. The Court pointed out that "[at] the time of al-Kidd's arrest, not a single judicial opinion had held pretext could render an objectively reasonable arrest pursuant to a material-witness warrant unconstitutional." While a district court opinion had suggested that such warrants were illegitimate in "footnoted dictum devoid of supporting citation [a] district judge's ipse dixit [falls] far short of what is necessary absent controlling authority." Nor was it sufficient to find clearly established law "lurking in the broad 'history and purposes of the Fourth Amendment.' We have repeatedly told courts [not] to define clearly established law at a high level of generality." In short, "[when] properly applied, [qualified immunity] protects 'all but the plainly incompetent or those who knowingly violate the law.' Ashcroft deserves neither [label]."

In a concurring opinion, Justice Kennedy argued that "[the] fact that the Attorney General holds a high office in the Government must inform what law is clearly established for the purposes of this case." He pointed out that an "official with responsibilities in many jurisdictions may face ambiguous and sometimes inconsistent sources of decisional law." National office holders should therefore "be given some deference for qualified immunity purposes, at least if they implement policies consistent with the governing law of the jurisdiction where the action is taken."

Justice Ginsburg, joined by Justices Breyer and Sotomayor, and Justice Sotomayor, joined by Justices Ginsburg and Breyer, filed opinions concurring in the judgment. See also Ziglar v. Abbasi, 582 U.S. ___ (2017) (upholding qualified immunity for officials who allegedly conspired to mistreat undocumented individuals held after the World Trade Center bombings).

c. *Damages for claims unrelated to service in office.* Compare Nixon v. Fitzgerald with Clinton v. Jones, 520 U.S. 681 (1997). *Jones* differed from *Fitzgerald* in two respects. First, it arose out of alleged misconduct occurring before the President's term began and unrelated to his conduct while in office. Second, the suit was brought during the President's term of office.

Jones alleged that in 1991, while Clinton was governor of Arkansas, he enticed her to a hotel room where he made "abhorrent" sexual advances toward her. She claimed that this conduct violated federal and state law and sought monetary damages. In response, President Clinton did not claim immunity from suit but did argue that the litigation should be delayed until the conclusion of his presidential term. In a unanimous decision, the Supreme Court, per Justice Stevens, rejected this claim. The Court held that *Fitzgerald* was distinguishable because it had involved official conduct. Such immunity

> serves the public interest in enabling [officials] to perform their designated functions effectively without fear that a particular decision may give rise to personal liability. . . . But we have never suggested that the President, or any other official, has an immunity that extends beyond the scope of any action taken in an official capacity.

The Court also rejected Clinton's contention that permitting the suit would risk violation of separation of powers principles:

> Respondent is merely asking the courts to exercise their core Article III jurisdiction to decide cases and controversies. Whatever the outcome of this case, there is no possibility that the decision will curtail the scope of the official powers of the Executive Branch. The litigation of questions that relate entirely to the unofficial conduct of the individual who happens to be the President poses no perceptible risk of misallocation of either judicial power or executive power.

President Clinton claimed that defense of civil litigation would impose an unacceptable burden on his time and energy, thereby impairing his effective performance in office. In the Court's view, however, "if properly managed by the District Court, [it is highly unlikely that defense of the suit would] occupy any substantial amount of petitioner's time." Moreover, "[the] fact that a federal court's exercise of its traditional Article III jurisdiction may significantly burden the time and attention of the Chief Executive is not sufficient to establish a violation of the Constitution." The Court relied on *Youngstown* and United States v. Nixon in support of this proposition, pointing out that in both cases sitting presidents were required to respond to judicial process despite the "serious impact" of the litigation on the President's ability to perform his functions.

The Court also rejected the argument that permitting such litigation would generate a large volume of "politically motivated harassing and frivolous litigation":

> Most frivolous and vexatious litigation is terminated at the pleading stage or on summary judgment, with little if any personal involvement by the defendant. Moreover, the availability of sanctions provides a significant deterrent to litigation directed at the President in his unofficial capacity for purposes of political gain

or harassment. History indicates that the likelihood that a significant number of such cases will be filed is remote. Although scheduling problems may arise, there is no reason to assume that the District Courts will be either unable to accommodate the President's needs or unfaithful to the tradition — especially in matters involving national security — of giving "the utmost deference to Presidential responsibilities."

2. *Exclusive presidential authority to determine the scope of the privilege.* President Nixon argued that even if the Court could entertain an action against him, the President alone should determine the scope of executive privilege. Does allowing the President to determine the scope of his own power entail an inherent contraction? Wasn't the Court determining the scope of *its* own power when it upheld the subpoena?

3. *The scope of the privilege.* Even if the Court should have the final word concerning the scope of the privilege, it might have decided that its scope included the conversations that President Nixon wanted to protect. Did the Court strike the right balance?

Compare United States v. Nixon to Cheney v. United States District Court, 542 U.S. 367 (2004). The case arose out of an effort by two public interest organizations to gain disclosure of the activities of the National Energy Policy Development Group, commonly known as the Energy Policy Task Force. Shortly after assuming office, President George W. Bush established the Task Force and made Vice President Cheney its chair. Plaintiffs relied upon the Federal Advisory Committee Act (FACA), which imposes disclosure requirements on committees and boards established by the President unless the committee is composed wholly of government employees. The President appointed only federal employees to the Task Force, but the plaintiffs alleged that private lobbyists regularly attended meetings and were de facto members.

The trial court permitted plaintiffs to engage in discovery in order to support their theory. Vice President Cheney sought a writ of mandamus in the court of appeals to prevent the discovery, but that court refused to issue the writ. Relying on *Nixon*, the appellate court held that the executive branch must make particularized claims of executive privilege if it wished to resist disclosure.

In an opinion written by Justice Kennedy, the Supreme Court disapproved this decision and remanded the case to the court of appeals. Justice Kennedy distinguished *Nixon* on several grounds. In his view,

> [the] need for information for use in civil cases, while far from negligible, does not share the urgency or significance of the criminal subpoena requests in *Nixon*. [Moreover, the] observation in *Nixon* that production of confidential information would not disrupt the functioning of the Executive Branch cannot be applied in a mechanistic fashion to civil litigation. In the criminal justice system, there are various constraints, albeit imperfect, to filter out insubstantial legal claims. [In] contrast, there are no analogous checks in the civil discovery process here.

Finally, the Court noted that "the narrow subpoena orders in United States v. Nixon stand on an altogether different footing from the overly broad discovery requests approved by the District Court in this case."

The Court went on to hold that specific invocation of executive privilege was not required in this context:

Executive privilege is an extraordinary assertion of [power]. Once [it] is asserted, coequal branches of the Government are set on a collision course. The Judiciary is forced into the difficult task of balancing the need for information in a judicial proceeding and the Executive's Article II prerogatives. This inquiry places courts in the awkward position of evaluating the Executive's claims of confidentiality and autonomy, and pushes to the fore difficult questions of separation of powers and checks and balances.

The Court held that, instead of requiring invocation of the privilege, the lower court should have asked whether permitting the discovery "constituted an unwarranted impairment of another branch in the performance of its constitutional duties." The Court remanded the case so that the court of appeals could make this determination. Justice Stevens filed a concurring opinion, and Justice Thomas, joined by Justice Scalia, filed an opinion concurring in part and dissenting in part. Justice Ginsburg, joined by Justice Souter, dissented.

Note: The Politics of Impeachment

The cases involving Nixon and Clinton each generated a political response that threatened the President's ability to remain in office. In reviewing the material set out below, consider whether the Court played a constructive role in framing the political issues, or whether the issues might better have been left entirely to the political process.

1. *The Nixon resignation.* On July 27, 1974, two days after the Supreme Court handed down its decision in *Nixon*, the House Judiciary Committee adopted an article of impeachment, charging the President with obstruction of justice with respect to the Watergate break-in and other activities. On July 29, it adopted a second article involving abuse of power by misusing executive agencies and violating constitutional rights of the citizenry. On July 30, it adopted a third article, charging the President with willful disobedience of subpoenas issued by the Judiciary Committee. On August 6, twelve days after the Supreme Court decision, President Nixon decided to make the transcript of the tapes available to the public. Three days thereafter, on August 9, he resigned. On August 20, the Judiciary Committee filed its impeachment report with the House, which took no further action.

In light of the ongoing impeachment investigation, did the *Nixon* decision improperly substitute a legal for a political judgment?

Note in this regard the implications of the Court's observations concerning the justiciability of the suit. If President Nixon had ordered the Attorney General to rescind the regulations governing the special prosecutor and then ordered the prosecutor not to seek production of the tapes, what result would have followed? What reasons might President Nixon have had for not pursuing this course?

2. *The Clinton impeachment.* After the Supreme Court rejected President Clinton's argument that the *Jones* suit should be postponed until he left office, the plaintiff commenced pretrial discovery. In deposition testimony, on January 17, 1998, President Clinton denied having a "sexual affair," a "sexual relationship," or "sexual relations" with former White House intern Monica Lewinsky. At the time of his testimony, Clinton was unaware that a day earlier, the Special Division of the United States Court of Appeals for the District of Columbia Circuit had expanded the jurisdiction of Independent Counsel Kenneth Starr

to investigate "whether Monica Lewinsky or others suborned perjury, obstructed justice, intimidated witnesses, or otherwise violated federal law" in conjunction with an affidavit prepared for the *Jones* litigation. On January 27, 1998, the Office of Independent Counsel opened a grand jury inquiry into the Lewinsky affair. Six months later, Lewinsky entered an immunity agreement with the Independent Counsel. On the next day, President Clinton testified before the grand jury via closed circuit television. Although insisting that his testimony at the *Jones* deposition was accurate, he acknowledged "inappropriate contact" with Lewinsky.

On September 9, 1998, Independent Counsel Starr, acting pursuant to the Independent Counsel Act, notified the House of Representatives that he had "substantial and credible information [that] may constitute grounds for impeachment." After hearings marked by rancorous argument and partisan division, the House Judiciary Committee approved four articles of impeachment, alleging that Clinton had perjured himself before the grand jury, that he had obstructed justice by inducing others to lie in order to conceal his affair with Lewinsky, that he had perjured himself in his *Jones* deposition, and that he had abused his power by providing legalistic answers to questions put to him by the House Judiciary Committee. Three months later, the House approved two of the articles, those alleging perjury before the grand jury and obstruction of justice. On February 12, 1999, the Senate voted by margins of fifty-five to forty-five and fifty to fifty to acquit Clinton of both charges. All of the relevant votes were highly partisan, with Democrats overwhelmingly voting against impeachment and conviction, and Republicans voting overwhelmingly in favor.

In light of these events, reconsider the Court's conclusion in *Jones* that "if properly managed by the District Court, it appears to us highly unlikely [that the suit would] occupy any substantial amount of petitioner's time." Do subsequent events demonstrate that the burden of defending civil lawsuits inevitably hampers the President in the performance of his duties and that such lawsuits are bound to be politicized, or instead that President Clinton's response to this lawsuit led to an appropriate inquiry into his fitness for office and that the inquiry did no serious harm to the country?

Note: The "Law" of Impeachment

Article II, section 4 of the Constitution provides that "[the] President, Vice President and all civil Officers of the United States, shall be removed from Office on Impeachment for, and Conviction of, Treason, Bribery, or other high Crimes and Misdemeanors." Article I, section 2 provides that "The House of Representatives shall [have] the sole Power of Impeachment." Article I, section 3 provides as follows:

> The Senate shall have the sole Power to try all Impeachments. When sitting for that Purpose, they shall be on Oath or Affirmation. When the President of the United States is tried, the Chief Justice shall preside: And no Person shall be convicted without the Concurrence of two thirds of the Members present.
>
> Judgment in Cases of Impeachment shall not extend further than to remove from Office, and disqualification to hold and enjoy any Office of honor, Trust or Profit under the United States: but the Party convicted shall nevertheless be liable and subject to Indictment, Trial, Judgment and Punishment, according to Law.

In light of these provisions, consider the following legal issues raised by *Nixon* and *Jones*.

1. *"High Crimes and Misdemeanors."* What kinds of offenses are encompassed by the phrase "high Crimes and Misdemeanors"? For example, was President Clinton's allegedly false testimony in a civil lawsuit unrelated to his official duties covered? Was President Nixon's alleged malfeasance an impeachable offense even if it did not violate the criminal law?

Early proposals at the Constitutional Convention limited the grounds for impeachment to neglect of duty or misuse of official power. At a later point, it was proposed that the grounds for impeachment of the President be limited to "treason or bribery." George Mason opposed this limitation and moved to add "maladministration" to the list. James Madison responded that "[so] vague a term will be equivalent to a tenure during the pleasure of the Senate." Mason thereupon withdrew his motion, and substituted "bribery and other high crimes or misdemeanors against the State." This motion carried. At a later point, the Convention agreed to replace the word "State" with the words "United States." The Committee of Style and Arrangement thereupon eliminated the words "against the United States," apparently because it thought the phrase redundant. In light of this history consider the following views:

a. Dwight, Trial by Impeachment, 6 Am. L. Reg. (N.S.) 257, 264 (1867):
"The decided weight of authority is, that no impeachment will lie except for a true crime [or] a breach of the common or statute law, which [would] be the subject of indictment."

b. R. Berger, Impeachment 62–63, 67, 90 (1973):

"[High] crimes and misdemeanors" appear to be words of art confined to impeachments, without roots in the ordinary criminal law and which, so far as I could discover, had no relation to whether an indictment would lie in the particular circumstances. . . . [But the framers intended] to preclude resort to impeachment of the President for petty misconduct.

c. Testimony of Professor Laurence Tribe before the Subcommittee on the Constitution of the House Judiciary Committee investigating the impeachment of President Clinton:

What distinguishes certain offenses as "high Crimes and Misdemeanors" must be *not* the fact that serious crimes are involved but the fact that those offenses are similar [to] treason and bribery. But that in turn means that [high] crimes and misdemeanors [must] refer to major offenses against our very system of government, or serious abuses of the governmental power with which a public official has been entrusted [or] grave wrongs in pursuit of governmental [power]. . . .
[It] apparently did not occur to the framers or ratifiers that some sufficiently monstrous but purely private crimes against individuals might require impeachment and removal from office in order to safeguard the government and the people it serves.

d. Testimony of Professor Richard Parker before the same body:

[It] is not clear why substantial presidential misconduct should be *presumed* non-impeachable just because it "arose from" a realm of "private" life. . . .
[In] terms of constitutional principle, [this claim makes] no sense. The reason is that the phrase, "other high Crimes and Misdemeanors," must be understood in

light of "Bribery," one of its referents. Acts of bribery — as is well known — tend to arise from the "private" lives of actors. The fact that bribery may arise from private greed (or need) does not presumptively immunize it from impeachment. Why, then, should public acts be presumptively immunized solely on the ground that they arose from private lust?

e. Remarks of then-Congressman Gerald Ford, proposing the impeachment of Justice William O. Douglas in a speech on the House floor in 1970:

> What, then, is an impeachable offense? The only honest answer is that an impeachable offense is whatever a majority of the House of Representatives considers it to be at a given moment in history; conviction results from whatever offense or offenses two-thirds of the other body considers to be sufficiently serious to require removal of the accused from office.

2. *Punishment other than impeachment.* Can a sitting President be indicted for criminal offenses? Although article II makes clear that criminal penalties do not attach to a judgment of impeachment and that such a judgment does not bar subsequent prosecution, the Constitution is silent as to whether such a prosecution can be undertaken while the President is in office. Consider what, if any, bearing *Jones* has on this question. Independent Counsel serving during the Nixon and Clinton administrations actively considered indicting the President, but in both cases they rejected this course (although President Nixon was named as an unindicted coconspirator by the Watergate grand jury).

3. *Law versus politics.* During the latter stages of the Watergate episode, President Nixon's popularity approached historic lows. In contrast, throughout the impeachment proceedings against President Clinton, his personal popularity was extraordinarily high, and large majorities of those polled opposed impeachment. Should a conscientious member of Congress take these facts into account? Should it matter to such a member whether the impeachment resolutions achieved bipartisan support? Whether the President is, or is perceived to be, doing a good job? Are questions about presidential impeachment appropriately resolved as a matter of constitutional principle, as a matter of ordinary politics, or as some mixture of the two?

Consider in this regard Klarman, Constitutional Fetishism and the Clinton Impeachment Debate, 85 Va. L. Rev. 631, 631, 656–657 (1999):

> One striking feature of the impeachment debate was the certitude with which politicians and academics espoused a wide variety of constitutional interpretations, notwithstanding the thinness of the constitutional law governing impeachment. Extraordinary claims were made on both sides of the aisle about what the United States Constitution requires and prohibits regarding various impeachment issues about which the traditional sources of constitutional law — text, original intent, and precedent — rather plainly have little to say. . . .
> In the face of legal indeterminacy, it seems natural that political factors will determine constitutional interpretations. . . .

For comprehensive discussions of the law of impeachment, see M. Gerhardt, The Federal Impeachment Process: A Constitutional and Historic Analysis (1996); R. Berger, Impeachment: The Constitutional Problems (1973). For general discussions of the legal issues raised by the Clinton impeachment, compare Sunstein, Impeaching the President, 147 U. Pa. L. Rev. 279 (1998) (concluding that impeachment was unconstitutional), with R. Posner, The Trial and Impeachment of William Jefferson Clinton (1999) (concluding that impeachment was constitutionally permissible).

2. Legislative Authority

Much of the debate about legislative authority centers around disagreement concerning "formal," as opposed to "functional," theories of constitutional interpretation. See generally Strauss, Formal and Functional Approaches to Separation-of-Powers Questions: A Foolish Inconsistency?, 72 Cornell L. Rev. 488 (1972). Formalists believe that separation of powers doctrine is governed by relatively clear rules that demarcate separate spheres of governmental authority. In contrast, functionalists believe in a more fluid approach that prohibits "aggrandizement of power" or "undue mingling of functions," but that allows some overlap and is more receptive to changing the boundaries so as to deal with changing situations.

The underlying dispute has both a historical and an interpretive dimension. Some formalists defend their position on originalist grounds; see, e.g., Calabresi and Prakash, The President's Power to Execute the Law, 104 Yale L.J. 541 (1994). Some functionalists have used originalism to criticize formalism; see, e.g., Casper, An Essay on Separation of Powers: Some Early Versions and Practices, 30 Wm. & Mary L. Rev. 211 (1989). Other functionalists concede that formalism may be defensible on originalist grounds but defend functionalist decisions as the best way to make sense of the constitutional structure under modern circumstances, in which the President's power threatens to undermine the constitutional structure. See, e.g., Justice White's dissenting opinions in INS v. Chadha and Bowsher v. Synar, page 438 and page 448, infra, respectively; Greene, Checks and Balances in an Era of Presidential Lawmaking, 61 U. Chi. L. Rev. 123 (1994). Further, some defenders of formalism have argued that the Court has a good reason to proceed in a formalist way so as to ensure against various problems presented by modern legislative initiatives, even if formalism is not defensible historically. See Lessig and Sunstein, The President and the Administration, 94 Colum. L. Rev. 1 (1994). See also Manning, Separation of Powers as Ordinary Interpretation, 124 Harv. L. Rev. 1939 (2011) (arguing that "the Constitution adopts no freestanding principle of separation of powers" but instead contains "many particular decisions about how to allocate and condition the exercise of federal power").

As you read the material that follows, consider whether a formalist approach or a functionalist approach makes the best sense of the cases. For an argument that a combination of the two approaches best protects constitutional values, see Huq & Michaels, The Cycles of Separation of Powers Jurisprudence, 126 Yale L.J. 346, 353 (2016).

Note: The Nondelegation Doctrine and "Quasi-Constitutional" Statutes

1. *Introduction.* Conventionally, Congress affects public policy by passing statutes that the executive is bound to administer. Justice Black's opinion for

the Court in *Youngstown*, for example, reflects the view that only Congress can pass laws.

But the conventional understanding — that the legislature is the exclusive lawmaker — no longer reflects reality. In every industrialized nation, administrative agencies, which are generally part of the executive branch, have been granted considerable lawmaking power. Congress has given such agencies regulatory authority, but often it offers them little guidance for the task. It has, for example, told agencies to regulate "unreasonable risks" to consumers and to promote "the public interest" in broadcasting regulation. The process of giving content to these vague standards — a process undertaken by the executive — can only be understood as one of lawmaking.

Under current doctrine, there are very few, if any, constitutional restraints on Congress's power to delegate. But this was not always the case. Early on the Court made clear that article I, by vesting legislative power in Congress, imposed constraints on the national legislature's authority to delegate that power to others. For example, the Court stated that the applicable test was whether Congress has laid "down by legislative act an intelligible principle to which the person or body authorized to take action is directed to conform." J. W. Hampton, Jr. & Co. v. United States, 276 U.S. 394, 409 (1928).

2. Panama Refining *and* Schechter. The issues raised by the nondelegation doctrine came to a head in two cases involving legislation designed to ease the Depression during President Roosevelt's famous first "one hundred days." The National Industrial Recovery Act of 1933 (NIRA) attempted to permit representatives of labor and management in each industry to meet and to design codes of "fair competition." The goal was to help stabilize wages and prices in order to stop the precipitous decline of both, thus restoring the confidence of industry and stabilizing the economy.

The act's declaration of policy referred to Congress's desire to promote cooperative action among trade groups, to maintain united action on the part of management and labor, to eliminate unfair competitive practices, to increase purchasing power and thus consumption of industrial and agricultural products, and to avoid undue restriction of production (except as may be temporarily required). The President was supposed to approve such codes if he made several findings, including (a) that there were "no inequitable restrictions on admission to membership" and (b) that the codes were not designed to promote monopoly or to oppress small enterprises.

In the first case decided under the NIRA, Panama Refining Co. v. Ryan, 293 U.S. 388 (1935), the Court invalidated a provision of the NIRA authorizing the President to prohibit, as part of a petroleum code, the transportation in interstate commerce of oil produced in violation of state-imposed production quotas. The Court emphasized that the statute did not supply standards that would tell the President when to exercise that power. In the Court's view, the NIRA authorized the President to prohibit transportation of "hot oil" whenever he chose.

The second case, A. L. A. Schechter Poultry Corp. v. United States, 295 U.S. 495 (1935), involved the "live poultry code," which contained maximum hour and minimum wage provisions and prohibited various practices said to be "unfair methods of competition." The code identified such practices in provisions that, among other things, (a) barred the sale of unfit chickens and (b) stated that buyers could not be allowed to select particular chickens, but instead must "accept the run of any half coop, coop, or coops." Schechter Poultry was prosecuted for violating both of these provisions. It sought to invalidate the statute authorizing creation of the code on the ground that it was an impermissible delegation of legislative authority. The Court, unanimous on the point, said:

> What is meant by "fair competition" as the term is used in the Act? . . .
>
> The Government urges that the codes will "consist of rules of competition deemed fair for each industry by representative members of that industry — by the persons most vitally concerned and most familiar with its problems." [But] would it be seriously contended that Congress could delegate its legislative authority to trade or industrial associations or groups so as to empower them to enact the laws they deem to be wise and beneficent for the rehabilitation and expansion of their trade or industries? Could trade or industrial associations or groups be constituted legislative bodies for that purpose because such associations or groups are familiar with the problem of their enterprises? [Such] a delegation of legislative power is unknown to our law and is utterly inconsistent with the constitutional prerogatives and duties of Congress.

The Court also held that the NIRA was unconstitutional because it exceeded Congress's power under the commerce clause. This portion of the Court's opinion is discussed in Chapter 2 supra.

3. *The purported demise of the nondelegation doctrine.* The nondelegation doctrine has all but disappeared as a constraint on the delegation of authority to administrative agencies. Indeed, *Panama Refining* and *Schechter* are the only two decisions in the nation's history that have invalidated federal statutes on nondelegation grounds. Statutes authorizing regulation of "unreasonable risks" or administrative action "in the public interest" appear immune from attack. See, for an example of the modern approach, Amalgamated Meat Cutters v. Connally, 337 F. Supp. 737 (D.D.C. 1971). In that case, the court upheld a statute authorizing the President to impose wage and price controls on the ground that implicit standards of "broad fairness and avoidance of gross inequity" were sufficient. The court referred in particular to the temporary character of the delegation, to the fact that the President could not discriminate unreasonably among industries, and to an implicit requirement that the President come up with standards to limit his own discretion. See also Whitman v. American Truckers Association, Inc., 531 U.S. 457 (2001) (rejecting a nondelegation attack on Clean Air Act); Loving v. United States, 517 U.S. 748 (1996) (rejecting a nondelegation challenge to presidential regulations defining the aggravating and mitigating circumstances determining whether a court martial can impose the death penalty); Touby v. United States, 500 U.S. 160 (1991) (rejecting a nondelegation challenge to certain aspects of the Controlled Substances Act).

4. *Nondelegation redux?* Note, however, that *Schechter* itself has never been formally overruled. In recent years, some academic commentary, with some support from the Court, has suggested that a revival of the nondelegation doctrine may be desirable. Consider, for example, the following:

a. Department of Transportation v. Association of American Railroads, 135 S. Ct. 1225 (2015) (Thomas, J., concurring):

> We have held that the Constitution categorically forbids Congress to delegate its legislative power to any other body, but it has become increasingly clear to me that the test we have applied to distinguish legislative from executive power largely abdicates our duty to enforce that prohibition. Implicitly recognizing that the power to fashion legally binding rules is legislative, we have nevertheless classified

rulemaking as executive (or judicial) power when the authorizing statute sets out "an intelligible principle" to guide the rulemaker's discretion. Although the Court may never have intended the boundless standard the "intelligible principle" test has become, it is evident that it does not adequately reinforce the Constitution's allocation of legislative power. I would return to the original understanding of the federal legislative power and require that the Federal Government create generally applicable rules of private conduct only through the constitutionally prescribed legislative process.

b. D. Schoenbrod, Power without Responsibility 10, 21 (1993):

[Delegation] allows legislators to claim credit for benefits which a regulatory statute promises yet escape the blame for the burdens it will impose, because they do not issue the laws needed to achieve those benefits. The public inevitably must suffer regulatory burdens to realize regulatory benefits, but the laws will come from an agency that legislators can then criticize for imposing excessive burdens on their constituents. . . .

[The Supreme Court] has left the decision of whether to delegate largely up to Congress and the president, in part out of a belief that legislators' concern for their own power will keep Congress from delegating too much. This belief is simplistic. Legislators enhance their power by delegating: they retain the ability to influence events by pressuring agencies, while they shed responsibility for the exercise of power by avoiding public votes on hard choices.

See also Lawson, Delegation and Original Meaning, 88 Va. L. Rev. 327 (2002). Compare Posner and Vermeule, Interring the Nondelegation Doctrine, 69 U. Chi. L. Rev. 1721, 1722–1723 (2002) (arguing that the nondelegation rule "lacks any foundation in constitutional text and structure, in standard originalist sources, or in sound economic and political theory").

c. On rare occasions, the doctrine has been invoked as an aid to statutory construction: The fear of a broad delegation may provide a reason to construe administrative authority narrowly. See Industrial Union Department v. American Petroleum Institute, 448 U.S. 607 (1980) (plurality opinion) (narrowing authority of OSHA to regulate toxic substances in the workplace); National Cable Television Association v. United States, 415 U.S. 336 (1974) (narrowly construing fee-setting authority of federal agencies). See also Reynolds v. United States, 565 U.S. 432 (2012) (Scalia, J., dissenting) (arguing that a statute should be read so as to avoid an interpretation that "[left] it to the Attorney General to decide — with no statutory standard whatever governing his discretion — whether a criminal statute will or will not apply to certain individuals. That seems to me sailing close to the wind with regard to the principle that legislative powers are nondelegable.")

For an argument in favor of "nondelegation canons" pursuant to which courts interpret statutes so as to bar delegations in certain, specified areas in the absence of a clear statement from Congress, see Sunstein, Nondelegation Canons, 67 U. Chi. L. Rev. 315 (2000). But compare Whitman v. American Trucking Association, Inc., supra:

We have never suggested that an agency can cure an unlawful delegation of legislative power by adopting in its discretion a limiting construction of the statute. [The] idea that an agency can cure an unconstitutionally standardless delegation of power by declining to exercise some of that power seems to us internally contradictory. The very choice of which portion of the power to exercise [would] *itself be* an exercise of the forbidden legislative authority.

d. Consider the implications of Clinton v. City of New York, 524 U.S. 417 (1998). In a six-to-three decision, the Court, per Justice Stevens, invalidated the "Line Item Veto Act," which authorized the President to "cancel in whole" any items of new spending or any "limited tax benefit." A so-called lock-box provision required that savings resulting from cancelled items be used to reduce the budget deficit. In identifying items for cancellation, the President was directed to consider the legislative history, purposes, and other relevant information about the cancelled items. In addition, before cancelling an item, the statute required the President to find that the cancellation will reduce the budget deficit, not impair essential government functions, and not harm the national interest.

Writing for the Court, Justice Stevens reasoned that the statute authorized the President to amend previously enacted legislation by repealing a portion of it, and that there was "no provision in the Constitution that authorizes the President to enact, to amend, or to repeal statutes." Toward the end of its opinion, the Court noted the following:

> We have been favored with extensive debate about the scope of Congress' power to delegate law-making authority, or its functional equivalent, to the President. The excellent briefs filed by the parties and their amici curiae have provided us with valuable historical information that illuminates the delegation issue but does not really bear on the narrow issue that is dispositive of these cases. Thus, because we conclude that the Act's cancellation provisions violate Article I, §7, of the Constitution [specifying how a bill becomes a law], we find it unnecessary to consider the District Court's alternative holding that the Act "impermissibly disrupts the balance of powers among the three branches of government."

Was the line item veto functionally distinguishable from a delegation of law-making authority to the President? Despite the Court's disclaimer, how can the result in the case be understood absent a prohibition on such delegations? Consider in this connection Justice Scalia's dissenting opinion:

> [Had] the Line Item Veto Act authorized the President to "decline to spend" any item of spending contained in the Balanced Budget Act of 1997, there is not the slightest doubt that authorization would have been constitutional. What the Line Item Veto Act does instead — authorizing the President to "cancel" an item of spending — is technically different. But the technical difference does not relate to the technicalities of the Presentment Clause, which have been fully complied with; and the doctrine of unconstitutional delegation, which is at issue here, is preeminently not a doctrine of technicalities. The title of the Line Item Veto Act [has] succeeded in faking out the Supreme Court.

5. *Structural statutes.* If the nondelegation doctrine is not revived, and if it proves impossible for Congress to set forth clear standards to govern decisions by administrative agencies, are there alternative means by which Congress might establish its original position as lawmaker?

Congress has sporadically attempted to reassert its authority by enacting structural or "quasi-constitutional" statutes. Although consisting of ordinary legislation, these measures attempt to structure future legislative and executive decisions in much the way that a constitution would. For example, Congress has attempted to control administrative agencies by creating a legislative veto, which would allow one or both Houses of Congress to invalidate decisions made by administrative agencies. It has structured prosecutorial decisions when wrong-doing is alleged against high executive officials by mandating the appointment of an Independent Counsel. It has attempted to control future spending decisions by enacting various balanced budget provisions, by structuring executive decisions regarding spending of appropriated funds, and by limiting its own ability to foist unfunded mandates on the states. And it has attempted to control the President's use of the armed forces by enacting a War Powers Resolution.

How should the Supreme Court respond to these experiments in governance? On one view, structural statutes unconstitutionally expand Congress's powers. Advocates of this view insist that the framers bound us to a particular structure of government, and that Congress cannot bind us to a new structure without amending the Constitution. On the opposing view, structural statutes do no more than reestablish Congress's original powers in a modern environment that the framers could not have imagined. Advocates of this view maintain that structural statutes preserve the original balance between Congress and the President in a regulatory context where broad delegations to the executive are a fact of life. As you read the cases that follow, consider which view is more persuasive.

INS v. Chadha

462 U.S. 919 (1983)

CHIEF JUSTICE BURGER delivered the opinion of the Court.

Chadha is an East Indian who was born in Kenya and holds a British passport. He was lawfully admitted to the United States in 1966 on a nonimmigrant student visa. His visa expired on June 30, 1972. On October 11, 1973, the District Director of the Immigration and Naturalization Service ordered Chadha to show cause why he should not be deported for having "remained in the United States for a longer time than permitted." [After a hearing, an immigration judge ordered] that Chadha's deportation be suspended. The immigration judge found that Chadha met the requirements of [the statute]: he had resided continuously in the United States for over seven years, was of good moral character, and would suffer "extreme hardship" if deported.

Pursuant to [the statute the] immigration judge suspended Chadha's deportation and a report of the suspension was transmitted to Congress.

Once the Attorney General's recommendation for suspension of Chadha's deportation was conveyed to Congress, Congress had the power under [the statute to] veto the Attorney General's determination that Chadha should not be deported. . . .

On December 12, 1975, Representative Eilberg, Chairman of the Judiciary Subcommittee on Immigration, Citizenship, and International Law, introduced a resolution opposing "the granting of permanent residence in the United States to [six] aliens," including Chadha. [The] resolution was passed without debate or recorded vote. Since the House action was pursuant to [the statute] the resolution was not treated as an Article I legislative act; it was not submitted to the Senate or presented to the President for his action.

After the House veto of the Attorney General's decision to allow Chadha to remain in the United States, the immigration judge reopened the deportation proceedings and [Chadha] was ordered deported pursuant to the House action. . . .

[handwritten: Can congress do this?]

We turn now to the question whether action of one House of Congress under [the statute] violates strictures of the Constitution. [The] fact that a given law or procedure is efficient, convenient, and useful in facilitating functions of the government, standing alone, will not save it if it is contrary to the Constitution. Convenience and efficiency are not the primary objectives — or the hallmarks — of democratic government and our inquiry is sharpened rather than blunted by the fact that Congressional veto provisions are appearing with increasing frequency in statutes which delegate authority to executive and independent agencies:

> Since 1932, when the first veto provision was enacted into law, 295 congressional veto-type procedures have been inserted in 196 different [statutes]. Abourezk, The Congressional Veto: A contemporary Response to Executive Encroachment on Legislative Prerogatives, 52 Ind. L. Rev. 323,324 (1977). . . .

Explicit and unambiguous provisions of the Constitution prescribe and define the respective functions of the Congress and of the Executive in the legislative process. [Article] I provides:

> All legislative Powers herein granted shall be vested in a Congress of the United States, which shall consist of a Senate *and* a House of Representatives.

Art. I, §1. (Emphasis added).

> Every Bill which shall have passed the House of Representatives and the Senate, *shall*, before it becomes a Law, be presented to the President of the United States; . . .

Art. I, §7, cl. 2. (Emphasis added).

> Every Order, Resolution, or Vote to which the Concurrence of the Senate and House of Representatives may be necessary (except on a question of Adjournment) *shall be* presented to the President of the United States; and before the Same shall take Effect, *shall be* approved by him, or being disapproved by him, *shall be* repassed by two thirds of the Senate and House of Representatives, according to the Rules and Limitations prescribed in the Case of a Bill.

Art. I, §7, cl. 3. (Emphasis added).

These provisions of Art. I are integral parts of the constitutional design for the separation of powers. . . .

[When] the Executive acts, it presumptively acts in an executive or administrative capacity as defined in Art. II. And when, as here, one House of Congress purports to act, it is presumptively acting within its assigned sphere. Beginning with this presumption, we must nevertheless establish that the challenged action under [the statute] is of the kind to which the procedural requirements of Art. I, §7 apply. Not every action taken by either House is subject to the bicameralism and presentment requirements of Art. I. [Whether] actions taken by either House are, in law and fact, an exercise of legislative power depends not on their form but upon "whether they contain matter which is properly to be regarded as legislative in its character and effect." . . .

[handwritten right margin: not every action is subject to bicameralism]

Examination of the action taken here by one House [reveals] that it was essentially legislative in purpose and effect. In purporting to exercise power defined in Art. I, §8, cl. 4 to "establish an uniform Rule of Naturalization," the House took action that had the purpose and effect of altering the legal rights, duties and relations of persons, including the Attorney General, Executive Branch officials and Chadha, all outside the legislative branch. [The] one-House veto operated in this case to overrule the Attorney General and mandate Chadha's deportation; absent the House action, Chadha would remain in the United States. Congress has *acted* and its action has altered Chadha's status.

The legislative character of the one-House veto in this case is confirmed by the character of the Congressional action it supplants. Neither the House of Representatives nor the Senate contends that, absent the veto provision, [either] of them, or both of them acting together, could effectively require the Attorney General to deport an alien once the Attorney General, in the exercise of legislatively delegated authority, had determined the alien should remain in the United States. Without the challenged provision, [this] could have been achieved, if at all, only by legislation requiring deportation. . . .

The nature of the decision implemented by the one-House veto in this case further manifests its legislative character. After long experience with the clumsy, time consuming private bill procedure, Congress made a deliberate choice to delegate to the Executive Branch, [the] authority to allow deportable aliens to remain in this country in certain specified circumstances. It is not disputed that this choice to delegate authority is precisely the kind of decision that can be implemented only in accordance with the procedures set out in Art. I. Disagreement with the Attorney General's decision on Chadha's deportation — that is, Congress' decision to deport Chadha — no less than Congress' original choice to delegate to the Attorney General the authority to make that decision, involves determinations of policy that Congress can implement in only one way, bicameral passage followed by presentment to the President. Congress must abide by its delegation of authority until that delegation is legislatively altered or revoked.

Finally, we see that when the Framers intended to authorize either House of Congress to act alone and outside of its prescribed bicameral legislative role, they narrowly and precisely defined the procedure for such action. There are but four provisions in the Constitution, explicit and unambiguous, by which one House may act alone with the unreviewable force of law, not subject to the President's veto.

[The Court referred to the House's power to initiate impeachments, the Senate's power to conduct trials following impeachment, the Senate's power over presidential appointments, and the Senate's power to ratify treaties.]

[These provisions give] further support for the conclusion that Congressional authority is not to be implied. . . .

The choices we discern as having been made in the Constitutional Convention impose burdens on governmental processes that often seem clumsy, inefficient, even unworkable, but those hard choices were consciously made by men who had lived under a form of government that permitted arbitrary governmental acts to go unchecked. There is no support in the Constitution or decisions of this Court for the proposition that the cumbersomeness and delays often encountered in complying with explicit Constitutional standards may be avoided, either by the Congress or by the President. See [*Youngstown*]. With all the obvious flaws of delay, untidiness, and potential for abuse, we have not yet found a better way to preserve freedom than by making the exercise of power subject to the carefully crafted restraints spelled out in the Constitution.

We hold that the Congressional veto provision [is unconstitutional]. Accordingly, the judgment of the Court of Appeals is affirmed.

JUSTICE POWELL, concurring in the judgment. . . .

On its face, the House's action appears clearly adjudicatory. The House did not enact a general rule; rather it made its own determination that six specific persons did not comply with certain statutory criteria. It thus undertook the type of decision that traditionally has been left to other branches.

The impropriety of the House's assumption of this function is confirmed by the fact that its action raises the very danger the Framers sought to avoid — the exercise of unchecked power. In deciding whether Chadha deserves to be deported, Congress is not subject to any internal constraints that prevent it from arbitrarily depriving him of the right to remain in this country. Unlike the judiciary or an administrative agency, Congress is not bound by established substantive rules. Nor is it subject to the procedural safeguards, such as the right to counsel and a hearing before an impartial tribunal, that are present when a court or an agency adjudicates individual rights. The only effective constraint on Congress' power is political, but Congress is most accountable politically when it prescribes rules of general applicability. When it decides rights of specific persons, those rights are subject to "the tyranny of a shifting majority."

[In] my view, when Congress undertook to apply its rules to Chadha, it exceeded the scope of its constitutionally prescribed authority. I would not reach the broader question whether legislative vetoes are invalid under the Presentment Clauses.

JUSTICE WHITE, dissenting. . . .

Today the Court not only invalidates §244(c)(2) of the Immigration and Nationality Act, but also sounds the death knell for nearly 200 other statutory provisions in which Congress has reserved a "legislative veto." For this reason, the Court's decision is of surpassing importance. And it is for this reason that the Court would have been well-advised to decide the case, if possible, on the narrower grounds of separation of powers, leaving for full consideration the constitutionality of other congressional review statutes operating on such varied matters as war powers and agency rulemaking, some of which concern the independent regulatory agencies.

The prominence of the legislative veto mechanism in our contemporary political system and its importance to Congress can hardly be overstated. It has become a central means by which Congress secures the accountability of executive and independent agencies. Without the legislative veto, Congress is faced with a Hobson's choice: either to refrain from delegating the necessary authority, leaving itself with a hopeless task of writing laws with the requisite specificity to cover endless special circumstances across the entire policy landscape, or in the alternative, to abdicate its lawmaking function to the executive branch and independent agencies. To choose the former leaves major national problems unresolved; to opt for the latter risks unaccountable policymaking by those not elected to fill that role. . . .

[Justice White summarized the history of the legislative veto, noting that it was a response to "the sprawling government structure" created after the Depression; that it "balanced delegations of statutory authority in new areas"; and that it played an important role in disputes in the 1970s over impoundment, war, and national emergency powers.]

Even this brief review suffices to demonstrate that the legislative veto [is an] important if not indispensable political invention that allows the President and Congress to resolve major constitutional and policy differences, assures the accountability of independent regulatory agencies, and preserves Congress' control over lawmaking. . . .

The history of the legislative veto also makes clear that it has not been a sword with which Congress has struck out to aggrandize itself at the expense of the other branches — the concerns of Madison and Hamilton. Rather, the veto has been a means of defense, a reservation of ultimate authority necessary if Congress is to fulfill its designated role under Article I as the nation's lawmaker. While the President has often objected to particular legislative vetoes, generally those left in the hands of congressional committees, the Executive has more often agreed to legislative review as the price for a broad delegation of authority. To be sure, the President may have preferred unrestricted power, but that could be precisely why Congress thought it essential to retain a check on the exercise of delegated authority. . . .

[The] Constitution does not directly authorize or prohibit the legislative veto. Thus, our task should be to determine whether the legislative veto is consistent with the purposes of Art. I and the principles of Separation of Powers. [We] should not find the lack of a specific constitutional authorization for the legislative veto surprising, and I would not infer disapproval of the mechanism from its absence. From the summer of 1787 to the present the government of the United States has become an endeavor far beyond the contemplation of the Framers. Only within the last half century has the complexity and size of the Federal Government's responsibilities grown so greatly that the Congress must rely on the legislative veto as the most effective if not the only means to insure their role as the nation's lawmakers. But the wisdom of the Framers was to anticipate that the nation would grow and new problems of governance would require different solutions. Accordingly, our Federal Government was intentionally chartered with the flexibility to respond to contemporary needs without losing sight of fundamental democratic principles. . . .

[The presentment and bicameralism requirements do] not [answer] the constitutional question before us. The power to exercise a legislative veto is not the power to write new law without bicameral approval or presidential consideration. The veto must be authorized by statute and may only negative what an Executive department or independent agency has proposed. On its face, the legislative veto no more allows one House of Congress to make law than does the presidential veto confer such power upon the President. Accordingly, the Court properly recognizes that it "must establish that the challenged action [is] of the kind to which the procedural requirements of Art. I, §7 apply." . . .

The terms of the Presentment Clauses suggest only that bills and their equivalent are subject to the requirements of bicameral passage and presentment to the President.

Although the Clause does not specify the actions for which the concurrence of both Houses is "necessary," the proceedings at the Philadelphia Convention suggest its purpose was to prevent Congress from circumventing the presentation requirement in the making of new legislation. . . .

When the Convention did turn its attention to the scope of Congress' lawmaking power, the Framers were expansive. The Necessary and Proper Clause,

Art. I, §18, cl. 18, vests Congress with the power "to make all laws which shall be necessary and proper for carrying into Execution the foregoing Powers [the enumerated powers of §8], and all other Powers vested by this Constitution in the government of the United States, or in any Department or Officer thereof." It is long-settled that Congress may "exercise its best judgment in the selection of measures, to carry into execution the constitutional powers of the government," and "avail itself of experience, to exercise its reason, and to accommodate its legislation to circumstances." [*McCulloch.*]

The Court heeded this counsel in approving the modern administrative state. The Court's holding today that all legislative type action must be enacted through the lawmaking process ignores that legislative authority is routinely delegated to the Executive Branch, to the independent regulatory agencies, and to private individuals and groups. . . .

This Court's decisions sanctioning such delegations make clear that Article I does not require all action with the effect of legislation to be passed as a law. . . .

If Congress may delegate lawmaking power to independent and executive agencies, it is most difficult to understand Article I as forbidding Congress from also reserving a check on Legislative power for itself. . . .

The Court also takes no account of perhaps the most relevant consideration: However resolutions of disapproval under [the statute] are formally characterized, in reality, a departure from the status quo occurs only upon the concurrence of opinion among the House, Senate, and President. Reservations of legislative authority to be exercised by Congress should be upheld if the exercise of such reserved authority is consistent with the distribution of and limits upon legislative power that Article I provides. . . .

[Justice White argued that the veto "did not alter the division of actual authority between Congress and the executive," since a change in the alien's legal status could occur only with the concurrence of the President and both Houses. Thus, the purposes of the presentment and bicameralism requirements were satisfied.] . . .

[The Court's decision] reflects a profoundly different conception of the Constitution than that held by the Courts which sanctioned the modern administrative state. Today's decision strikes down in one fell swoop provisions in more laws enacted by Congress than the Court has cumulatively invalidated in its history. I fear it will now be more difficult "to insure that the fundamental policy decisions in our society will be made not by an appointed official but by the body immediately responsible to the people," Arizona v. California, 373 U.S. 546, 625 (1963) (Harlan, J., dissenting). I must dissent.

[Justice Rehnquist dissented on the ground that the legislative veto provision was not severable.]

Note: *The Legislative Veto*

1. Chadha *in context: legislative control of the bureaucracy.* The legislative veto is one of a number of means by which Congress has attempted to control administrative agencies to which Congress has delegated substantial discretionary authority. For example, congressional committees or subcommittees might hold oversight hearings, in which they call executive officials before them and question the officials about past and future conduct. Such hearings may produce considerable publicity and lead to pressure for changes in executive policy. A

more formal mechanism is the appropriations rider — an attachment to an authorization of expenditure of federal funds that prohibits the agency from engaging in certain courses of conduct. Similarly, Congress may decrease or increase an agency's budget, in the annual appropriations process, in order to express its views on the mission of the agency and on whether more or less enforcement is desirable. Alternatively, Congress may enact "sunset" legislation, providing that agency authority will terminate after a certain period unless Congress reenacts the substantive statute. Of course, Congress may also enact a measure repealing the agency's authority or rewrite the statute so as to limit authority. In light of all these clearly constitutional alternatives to the legislative veto mechanism, does the Court's decision accomplish anything of significance? Consider the view that easy circumvention is a necessary cost of respect for formal rules. The very rigidity that formalism prizes means that the rules lack the suppleness necessary to respond to evasive maneuvers. Yet without this rigidity, constitutional commands are reduced to nothing more than shifting and controversial policy judgments that cannot be separated from appropriately contestable views about the merits of political disputes.

Consider the Congressional Review Act (CRA), enacted as section 251 of the Contract with America Advancement Act, P.L. 104-121 (1996). The CRA requires agencies to notify Congress upon promulgation of new rules. Congress is then empowered to use expedited procedures to pass a joint resolution overruling the regulation if it does so within sixty legislative days. If it does so, the agency may not reissue the rule unless specifically authorized by statute enacted after the date of the joint resolution. Prior to 2017, the CRA was successfully invoked only once, but after President Trump assumed office, Congress used the procedure fourteen times to invalidate Obama-era rules.

Compare the Regulations from the Executive in Need of Scrutiny Act (the REINS Act), passed by the House of Representatives in 2017, which provides that a regulation with an annual effect on the economy of $100 million or more could not take effect without congressional approval. The Senate has not passed the Act. If it were enacted how would it differ from the CRA? Would it be constitutional? Compare Statement of Rep. John Conyers, Jr., Ranking Member, H. Comm. on the Judiciary, REINS Act — Promoting Jobs and Expanding Freedom by Reducing Needless Regulations: Hearings Before the Subcomm. on Courts, Commercial & Admin. Law of the H. Comm. on the Judiciary, 112th Cong. 8 (2011) (arguing that the Act would violate Chadha because if an agency promulgated a rule, either House of Congress acting alone could block it by not passing a resolution of approval), with Siegel, The REINS Act and the Struggle to Control Agency Rulemaking, 16 N.Y.U. J. Legis. & Pub. Pol'y 131, 185 (2013) (arguing that the Act is "a bad idea" because Congress lacks the time and expertise to decide these questions but that it is "perfectly constitutional" because it "merely reclaim[s] the power that Congress has ceded over time").

2. *The reach of* Chadha. Should the *Chadha* decision apply to *all* legislative vetoes? The case itself involved, as Justice Powell emphasized, an "adjudicatory" proceeding involving a single person. But in Process Gas Consumers Group v. Consumers Energy Council of America, 463 U.S. 1216 (1983), the Court summarily affirmed, on the authority of *Chadha*, a decision invalidating a legislative veto as applied to certain Federal Energy Regulatory Commission regulations of natural gas pricing. See also United States Senate v. FTC, 463 U.S. 1216 (1983) (summarily affirming decision invalidating legislative veto as applied to rulemaking by the FTC). But see Fisher, CRS Report for Congress, Legislative Vetoes

after Chadha (2005) (concluding that "more than 400 new legislative vetoes (usually of the committee variety) have been enacted since *Chadha*. In addition, legislative vetoes of an informal and nonstatutory nature continue to affect executive-legislative relations. Practice in this area has been determined more by pragmatic agreements hammered out between the elected branches than by doctrines fashioned and announced by the Supreme Court.").

Note: *Where Do Administrative Agencies "Fit" in the Separation of Powers Scheme?*

1. *Introduction.* Article II vests the executive power in the President, not in subordinate officials. This decision was based on a rejection of the notion of a "plural executive." See The Federalist No. 70; E. Corwin, The President — Office and Powers 3–30 (1957).

But the Constitution does not explicitly resolve the question whether Congress may immunize subordinate officials from presidential control. Suppose, for example, Congress provides that the Environmental Protection Agency, or the Civil Rights Commission, should do its work free from interference by the President. Would such a statute be constitutional under the necessary and proper clause? Would such a statute be inconsistent with the framers' decision to create a unitary executive and to vest all of the executive power in one person — the President? Compare Calabresi and Rhodes, The Structural Constitution: Unitary Executive, Plural Judiciary, 105 Harv. L. Rev. 1153 (1992), and Calabresi and Prakash, The President's Power to Execute the Law, 104 Yale L.J. 541 (1994), with Lessig and Sunstein, The President and the Administration, 94 Colum. L. Rev. 1 (1994), and Froomkin, The Imperial Presidency's New Vestments, 88 Nw. U. L. Rev. 1346 (1994). See generally Strauss, The Place of Agencies in Government: Separation of Powers and the Fourth Branch, 84 Colum. L. Rev. 452 (1984). The question is important, especially in an era in which lawmaking authority has been concentrated in executive officials.

2. *Myers and presidential supremacy.* Myers v. United States, 272 U.S. 52 (1926), involved a statute that provided that postmasters "shall be appointed and may be removed by the President and with the advice and consent of the Senate." President Wilson attempted to remove Myers, a postmaster appointed for a four-year term in Portland, Oregon, before the expiration of his term. The Court, in an opinion by Chief Justice (and former President) Taft, held that the removal was lawful because the attempted limitation on the President's removal power was unconstitutional under article II. The Court relied on several conclusions: (a) The act of removal is itself executive in nature and must therefore be performed by the President; (b) under the "take Care" clause, it is the President, not his subordinates, who must take care that the laws be faithfully executed; and (c) article II vests executive power in the President, not subordinate officials.

Justice Holmes, joined by Justices Brandeis and McReynolds, dissented:

> We have to deal with an office that owes its existence to Congress and that Congress may abolish tomorrow. [With] such power over its own creation, I have no more trouble in believing that Congress has power to prescribe a term of life for it free from any interference than I have in accepting the undoubted power of Congress to decree its end.

Under *Myers*, are the civil services statutes — immunizing lower-level federal officials from power to discharge "at will" — constitutionally acceptable? If so, is it because such officials are not "Officers of the United States," see Buckley v. Valeo, infra? Consider the view that *Myers* is satisfied so long as the official in charge of the basic chain of command is subject to presidential control.

Myers derives considerable support from the vesting of executive power in the President and from the basic decision to have a unitary, rather than plural, executive branch. But the historical support for the decision is ambiguous. There is evidence that at least some of the founders distinguished between "executive" and "administrative" authority, and that they believed that Congress should share in the power to remove some of those we now treat as executive officials. See Lessig and Sunstein, supra; Casper, The American Constitutional Tradition of Shared and Separated Powers: An Essay in Separation of Powers, 30 Wm. & Mary L. Rev. 211 (1989); Grundstein, Presidential Power, Administration and Administrative Law, 18 Geo. Wash. L. Rev. 285 (1950).

3. Humphrey's Executor, Wiener, *and the rise of "independent" agencies.* Humphrey's Executor v. United States, 295 U.S. 602 (1935), involved a statute providing that members of the Federal Trade Commission could be "removed by the President for inefficiency, neglect of duty, or malfeasance in office." The history of the statute indicated that the legislative goal was to entrust regulatory decisions to a body of nonpartisan "experts," insulated from political pressures. President Roosevelt removed Humphrey from office, contending not that removal was justified by one of the statutory conditions, but that the limitation of the removal power was unconstitutional under *Myers*. In short, President Roosevelt urged that any subordinate official served, by virtue of article II as interpreted in *Myers*, at the pleasure of the President. A unanimous Court disagreed, distinguishing and confining the reach of *Myers*:

> The office of a postmaster is so essentially unlike the office now involved that the decision in the *Myers* case cannot be accepted as controlling our decision here. A postmaster is an executive officer restricted to the performance of executive functions. . . .
>
> The Federal Trade Commission is an administrative body created by Congress to carry into effect legislative policies embodied in the statute in accordance with the legislative standard therein prescribed, and to perform other specified duties as a legislative or as a judicial aid. Such a body cannot in any proper sense be characterized as an arm or an eye of the executive. Its duties are performed without executive leave and, in the contemplation of the statute, must be free from executive control. [The] Commission acts in part quasi-legislatively and in part quasi-judicially. . . .

See also Wiener v. United States, 357 U.S. 349 (1958) (concluding that, even though the statute creating the War Claims Commission was silent on the question of removal, the commission's adjudicatory nature implied a limitation on the President's power to remove).

Humphrey's Executor and *Wiener* recognize a congressional power to create "independent" agencies — governmental entities that are free from presidential removal power and, to some uncertain degree, presidential power to supervise and control the decisions of their officers. The Federal Trade Commission, the Federal Energy Regulatory Commission, and the Federal Communications Commission are examples of independent agencies.

4. *Buckley v. Valeo.* The Federal Election Campaign Act created an eight-member Federal Election Commission to oversee federal elections. Two members of the commission were appointed by the President pro tempore of the Senate, two by the Speaker of the House, and two by the President. The Secretary of the Senate and the Clerk of the House also served as ex officio, nonvoting members. The commission was authorized to investigate, to maintain records, to make rules governing federal elections, and to impose sanctions on those who violated the Act and the commission's own regulations. In Buckley v. Valeo, 424 U.S. 1 (1976), the Court unanimously held that vesting a commission whose members were appointed in this manner with some of these functions violated the appointments clause of article II of the Constitution. The clause provides:

> [The President] shall nominate, and by and with the Advice and Consent of the Senate, shall appoint Ambassadors, other public Ministers and Consuls, Judges of the supreme Court, and all other Officers of the United States, whose Appointments are not herein otherwise provided for, and which shall be established by Law: but the Congress may by Law vest the Appointment of such inferior Officers, as they think proper, in the President alone, in the Courts of Law, or in the Heads of Departments.

The Court began its analysis by holding that "any appointee exercising significant authority pursuant to the laws of the United States is an 'Officer of the United States' and must, therefore, be appointed in the manner prescribed by [the appointments clause]." Four of the six members of the commission were not appointed by the President, and, although the Constitution permitted appointments by "Heads of Departments," this phrase, "used as it is in conjunction with the phrase 'Courts or Law,' suggests that the Departments referred to are themselves in the Executive Branch or at least have some connection with that branch."

It did not follow from this conclusion that the commission was entirely powerless, according to the Court. "Insofar as the powers confided in the Commission are essentially of an investigative and informative nature, falling in the same general category as those powers which Congress might delegate to one of its own committees, there can be no question that the Commission as presently constituted may exercise them."

However, with regard to the more substantial powers exercised by the Commission, the Court reached a different conclusion:

> The Commission's enforcement power, exemplified by its discretionary power to seek judicial relief, is authority that cannot possibly be regarded as merely in aid of the legislative function of Congress. [It] is to the President, and not to the Congress, that the Constitution entrusts the responsibility to "take Care that the Laws be faithfully executed."

Similarly, it was unconstitutional to vest in a commission so appointed rulemaking power and power to render advisory opinions or to determine the eligibility for funds:

> These functions, exercised free from day-to-day supervision of either Congress or the Executive Branch [are] of kinds usually performed by independent regulatory

agencies or by some department in the Executive Branch under the direction of an Act of Congress. [While] the President may not insist that such functions be delegated to an appointee of his removable at will [(*Humphrey's Executor*)], none of them operates merely in aid of congressional authority to legislate or is sufficiently removed from the administration and enforcement of public law to allow it to be performed by the present Commission.

5. *Limiting executive discretion.* What implications do *Chadha, Myers, Humphrey's Executor,* and *Buckley* hold for other techniques designed to limit executive discretion? Should it matter whether Congress attempts to arrogate to itself control of executive agencies or whether it merely attempts to make the agencies independent of presidential control? Consider the following.

Bowsher v. Synar

478 U.S. 714 (1986)

[This case concerned constitutional questions raised by the Gramm-Rudman-Hollings Act, which mandated "automatic" across-the-board spending reductions in the federal budget under certain circumstances. Opponents of the act challenged the role of the Comptroller General in effecting these cuts. The Comptroller General is the head of the General Accounting Office. The Budget and Accounting Act of 1921 vests him with the authority to investigate all matters relating to the receipt and disbursement of public funds. He is nominated by the President from a list of three individuals recommended by the Speaker of the House of Representatives and the President pro tempore of the Senate. He can be removed only by impeachment or by a joint resolution of Congress (subject to presidential veto) on the basis of permanent disability, inefficiency, neglect of duty, malfeasance, commission of a felony, or conduct involving moral turpitude.

[The Gramm-Rudman-Hollings Act provided that each year the directors of the Office of Management and Budget (OMB) and the Congressional Budget Office (CBO) would estimate the amount of the federal deficit for the next fiscal year. If the deficit exceeded statutory targets, the directors were required to calculate independently, on a program-by-program basis, the budget reductions necessary to meet the target, and to report the results to the Comptroller General. The Comptroller General was thereupon directed to prepare a report to the President. The act required him to exercise independent judgment in evaluating the estimates. Upon receipt of the Comptroller General's report, the President was required to issue a sequestration order, mandating any spending reductions specified by the Comptroller General, which, after a specified period, became final unless Congress legislated other spending reductions to obviate the need for the order. A "fallback" provision of the act provided that, if these procedures were declared unconstitutional, Congress would consider a joint resolution (subject to presidential veto) embodying the reports of the OMB and CBO. Upon its enactment, the joint resolution would then be treated as the equivalent of the Comptroller General's report.

[The Supreme Court, in a seven-to-two decision, held that the Gramm-Rudman-Hollings Act was unconstitutional.]

CHIEF JUSTICE BURGER delivered the opinion of the Court. . . .

The Constitution does not contemplate an active role for Congress in the supervision of officers charged with the execution of the laws it enacts. [The] Constitution explicitly provides for removal of Officers of the United States by Congress only upon impeachment by the House of Representatives and conviction by the Senate. . . .

To permit an officer controlled by Congress to execute the laws would be, in essence, to permit a congressional veto. Congress could simply remove, or threaten to remove, an officer for executing the laws in any fashion found to be unsatisfactory by Congress. . . .

Appellants urge that the Comptroller General performs his duties independently and is not subservient to Congress. [This] contention does not bear close scrutiny. . . .

The [Budget and Accounting Act of 1921] permits removal for "inefficiency," "neglect of duty" or "malfeasance." These terms are very broad and, as interpreted by Congress, could sustain removal of a Comptroller General for any number of actual or perceived transgressions of the legislative will. . . .

Against this background, we see no escape from the conclusion that, because Congress had retained removal authority over the Comptroller General, he may not be entrusted with executive powers. The remaining question is whether the Comptroller General has been assigned such powers in the [Gramm-Rudman-Hollings] Act. . . .

[We] view these functions as plainly entailing execution of the law in constitutional terms. Interpreting a law enacted by Congress to implement the legislative mandate is the very essence of "execution" of the law. Under [the statute], the Comptroller General must exercise judgment concerning facts that affect the application of the Act. He must also interpret the provisions of the Act to determine precisely what budgetary calculations are required. Decisions of that kind are typically made by officers charged with executing a statute. . . .

JUSTICE STEVENS, with whom JUSTICE MARSHALL joins, concurring in the judgment. . . .

I agree with the Court that the [act] contains a constitutional infirmity so severe that the flawed provision may not stand. I disagree with the Court, however, on the reasons why the Constitution prohibits the Comptroller General from exercising the powers assigned to him by [the] Act. It is not the dormant, carefully circumscribed congressional removal power that represents the primary constitutional evil. Nor do I agree with the conclusion of both the majority and the dissent that the analysis depends on labeling of the functions assigned to the Comptroller General as "executive powers." Rather, I am convinced that the Comptroller General must be characterized as an agent of Congress because of his longstanding statutory responsibilities; that the powers assigned to him under the [act] require him to make policy that will bind the Nation; and that, when Congress or a component or agent of Congress, seeks to make policy that will bind the Nation, it must follow the procedures mandated by Article I of the Constitution — through passage by both Houses and presentment to the President. . . .

In short, even though it is well settled that Congress may delegate legislative power to independent agencies or to the Executive, and thereby divest itself of a portion of its lawmaking power, when it elects to exercise such power itself, it may not authorize a lesser representative of the Legislative Branch to act on its behalf. It is for this reason that I believe [the reporting provisions] of the Act are unconstitutional. . . .

JUSTICE WHITE, dissenting. . . .

I have no quarrel with the proposition that the powers exercised by the Comptroller under the Act may be characterized as "executive" in that they involve the interpretation and carrying out of the Act's mandate. I can also accept the general proposition that although Congress has considerable authority in designating the officers who are to execute legislation, the constitutional scheme of separated powers does prevent Congress from reserving an executive role for itself or for its "agents." I cannot accept, however, that the exercise of authority by an officer removable for cause by a joint resolution of Congress is analogous to the impermissible execution of the law by Congress itself, nor would I hold that the congressional role in the removal process renders the Comptroller an "agent" of the Congress. . . .

The Court overlooks or deliberately ignores the decisive difference between the congressional removal provision and the legislative veto struck down in *Chadha*: [Congress] may remove the Comptroller only through a joint resolution, which by definition must be passed by both Houses and signed by the President. In other words, a removal of the Comptroller under the statute *satisfies the requirements of bicameralism and presentment laid down in Chadha.* . . .

That such action may represent a more or less successful attempt by Congress to "control" the actions of an officer of the United States surely does not in itself indicate that it is unconstitutional, for no one would dispute that Congress has the power to "control" administration through legislation imposing duties or substantive restraints on executive officers, through legislation increasing or decreasing the funds made available to such officers or through legislation actually abolishing a particular office.

[Justice Blackmun also wrote a dissenting opinion.]

Morrison v. Olson

487 U.S. 654 (1988)

CHIEF JUSTICE REHNQUIST delivered the opinion of the Court. . . .

This case presents us with a challenge to the independent counsel provisions of the Ethics in Government Act of 1978. We hold today that these provisions of the Act do not violate the Appointments Clause of the Constitution, Art. II, §2, cl. 2, or the limitations of Article III, nor do they impermissibly interfere with the President's authority under Article II in violation of the constitutional principle of separation of powers.

I

IC appointed by Pres.

Act allows for independent counsel to prosecute high gov. officials

Briefly stated, Title VI of the Ethics of Government Act allows for the appointment of an "independent counsel" to investigate and, if appropriate, prosecute certain high-ranking government officials for violations of federal criminal laws. The Act requires the Attorney General, upon receipt of information that he determines is "sufficient to constitute grounds to investigate whether any person [covered by the act] may have violated any Federal criminal law," to conduct a preliminary investigation of the matter. When the Attorney General has completed this investigation, or 90 days has elapsed, he is required to report to a special court (the Special Division) created by the Act "for the purpose of appointing independent counsels." If the Attorney General determines that "there are no reasonable grounds to believe that further investigation is warranted," then he must notify the Special Division of this result. In such a case, "the division of the court shall have no power to appoint an independent counsel." If, however, the Attorney General has determined that there are "reasonable grounds to believe that further investigation or prosecution is warranted," then he "shall apply to the division of the court for the appointment of an independent counsel." The Attorney General's application to the court "shall contain sufficient information to assist the [court] in selecting an independent counsel and in defining that independent counsel's prosecutorial jurisdiction." Upon receiving this application, the Special Division "shall appoint an appropriate independent counsel and shall define that independent counsel's prosecutorial jurisdiction." . . .

[The act provided that the independent counsel can be removed from office only by impeachment or by personal action of the Attorney General for good cause, physical disability, mental incapacity, "or any other condition that substantially impairs the performance of such independent counsel's duties." It also provided that the counsel can be "terminated" if the Special Division finds that "the investigation of all matters within the prosecutorial jurisdiction of such independent counsel [has] been completed or so substantially completed that it would be appropriate for the Department of Justice to complete such investigations and prosecutions."]

A divided Court of Appeals [invalidated the act]. We now reverse. . . .

III

[The Court quotes the appointments clause of article II, reproduced on page 447 supra.]

Several factors lead to [the] conclusion [that appellant is an "inferior officer."]

[The Court relies on the fact that the special prosecutor could be removed by the Attorney General, that she was authorized to perform only certain limited duties, and that her office was limited in jurisdiction and tenure.]

This does not, however, end our inquiry under the Appointments Clause. Appellees argue that even if appellant is an "inferior" officer, the Clause does not empower Congress to place the power to appoint such an officer outside the Executive Branch. [The Court rejects the argument that there was an "incongruity" between the functions normally performed by courts and the duty of the Special Division to appoint a prosecutor and that other powers vested in the Special Division violated Article III of the Constitution.][12] . . .

_____

12. Indeed, in light of judicial experience with prosecutors in criminal cases, it could be said that courts are especially well qualified to appoint prosecutors. This is not a case in which judges are given power to appoint an officer in an area in which they have no special knowledge or expertise, as in, for example, a statute authorizing the courts to appoint officials in the Department of Agriculture or the Federal Energy Regulatory Commission.

V

We now turn to consider whether the Act is invalid under the constitutional principle of separation of powers. Two related issues must be addressed: The first is whether the provision of the Act restricting the Attorney General's power to remove the independent counsel to only those instances in which he can show "good cause," taken by itself, impermissibly interferes with the President's exercise of his constitutionally appointed functions. The second is whether, taken as a whole, the Act violates the separation of powers by reducing the President's ability to control the prosecutorial powers wielded by the independent counsel.

A

We held in *Bowsher* that "Congress cannot reserve for itself the power of removal of an officer charged with the execution of the laws except by impeachment." A primary antecedent for this ruling was our 1925 decision in [*Myers*]. . . .

Unlike both *Bowsher* and *Myers*, this case does not involve an attempt by Congress itself to gain a role in the removal of executive officials other than its established powers of impeachment and conviction. The Act instead puts the removal power squarely in the hands of the Executive Branch; an independent counsel may be removed from office, "only by the personal action of the Attorney General, and only for good cause." There is no requirement of congressional approval of the Attorney General's removal decision, though the decision is subject to judicial review. In our view, the removal provisions of the Act make this case more analogous to Humphrey's Executor v. United States, and Wiener v. United States, than to *Myers* or *Bowsher*. . . .

Appellees contend that *Humphrey's Executor* and *Wiener* are distinguishable from this case because they did not involve officials who performed a "core executive function." They argue that our decision in *Humphrey's Executor* rests on a distinction between "purely executive" officials and officials who exercise "quasi-legislative" and "quasi-judicial" powers. . . .

We undoubtedly did rely on the terms "quasi-legislative" and "quasi-judicial" to distinguish the officials involved in *Humphrey's Executor* and *Wiener* from those in *Myers*, but our present considered view is that the determination of whether the Constitution allows Congress to impose a "good cause"–type restriction on the President's power to remove an official cannot be made to turn on whether or not that official is classified as "purely executive." The analysis contained in our removal cases is designed not to define rigid categories of those officials who may or may not be removed at will by the President, but to ensure that Congress does not interfere with the President's exercise of the "executive power" and his constitutionally appointed duty to "take care that the laws be faithfully executed" under Article II. . . .

We do not mean to suggest that an analysis of the functions served by the officials at issue is irrelevant. But the real question is whether the removal restrictions are of such a nature that they impede the President's ability to perform his constitutional duty, and the functions of the officials in question must be analyzed in that light.

Considering for the moment the "good cause" removal provision in isolation from the other parts of the Act at issue in this case, we cannot say that the imposition of a "good cause" standard for removal by itself unduly trammels on executive authority. . . .

Although the counsel exercises no small amount of discretion and judgment in deciding how to carry out her duties under the Act, we simply do not see how the President's need to control the exercise of that discretion is so central to the functioning of the Executive Branch as to require as a matter of constitutional law that the counsel be terminable at will by the President.

Nor do we think that the "good cause" removal provision at issue here impermissibly burdens the President's power to control or supervise the independent counsel, as an executive official, in the execution of her duties under the Act. [Because] the independent counsel may be terminated for "good cause," the Executive, through the Attorney General, retains ample authority to assure that the counsel is competently performing her statutory responsibilities in a manner that comports with the provisions of the Act. Although we need not decide in this case exactly what is encompassed with the term "good cause" under the Act, the legislative history of the removal provision also makes clear that the Attorney General may remove an independent counsel for "misconduct." . . .

We do not think that this limitation as it presently stands sufficiently deprives the President of control over the independent counsel to interfere impermissibly with his constitutional obligation to ensure the faithful execution of the laws.

B

The final question to be addressed is whether the Act, taken as a whole, violates the principle of separation of powers by unduly interfering with the role of the Executive Branch. . . .

[We] have never held that the Constitution requires that the three Branches of Government "operate with absolute independence." . . .

We observe first that this case does not involve an attempt by Congress to increase its own powers at the expense of the Executive Branch. Unlike some of our previous cases, most recently Bowsher v. Synar, this case simply does not pose a "dange[r] of congressional usurpation of Executive Branch functions," [see] also [Chadha]. . . .

Similarly, we do not think that the Act works any *judicial* usurpation of properly executive functions. . . .

Finally, we do not think that the Act "impermissibly undermine[s]" the powers of the Executive Branch, or "disrupts the proper balance between the coordinate branches [by] prevent[ing] the Executive Branch from accomplishing its constitutionally assigned functions." It is undeniable that the Act reduces the amount of control or supervision that the Attorney General and, through him, the President exercises over the investigation and prosecution of a certain class of alleged criminal activity. . . .

Nonetheless, the Act does give the Attorney General several means of supervising or controlling the prosecutorial powers that may be wielded by an independent counsel. . . .

The decision of the Court of Appeals is therefore reversed. . . .

Justice Scalia, dissenting. . . .

II

If to describe this case is not to decide it, the concept of a government of separate and coordinate powers no longer has meaning. . . .

Art. II, §1, cl. 1 of the Constitution provides: "The executive Power shall be vested in a President of the United States." [This] does not mean *some of* the executive power, but *all of* the executive power. It seems to me, therefore, that the decision of the Court of Appeals invalidating the present statute must be upheld on fundamental separation-of-powers principles if the following two questions are answered affirmatively: (1) Is the conduct of a criminal prosecution (and of an investigation to decide whether to prosecute) the exercise of purely executive power? (2) Does the statute deprive the President of the United States of exclusive control over the exercise of that power? Surprising to say, the Court appears to concede an affirmative answer to both questions, but seeks to avoid the inevitable conclusion that since the statute vests some purely executive power in a person who is not the President of the United States it is void.

The Court concedes that "[t]here is no real dispute that the functions performed by the independent counsel are 'executive,'" though it qualifies that concession by adding "in the sense that they are 'law enforcement' functions that typically have been undertaken by officials within the Executive Branch." The qualifier adds nothing but atmosphere. In what *other* sense can one identify "the executive Power" that is supposed to be vested in the President (unless it includes everything the Executive Branch is given to do) *except* by reference to what has always and everywhere — if conducted by Government at all — been conducted never by the legislature, never by the courts, and always by the executive. There is no possible doubt that the independent counsel's functions fit this description. . . .

As for the second question, whether the statute before us deprives the President of exclusive control over that quintessentially executive activity, the Court does not, and could not possibly, assert that it does not. That is indeed the whole object of the statute. Instead, the Court points out that the President, through his Attorney General, has at least *some* control. That concession is alone enough to invalidate the statute, but I cannot refrain from pointing out that the Court greatly exaggerates the extent of that "some" presidential control. . . .

The utter incompatibility of the Court's approach with our constitutional traditions can be made more clear, perhaps, by applying it to the powers of the other two Branches. Is it conceivable that if Congress passed a statute depriving itself of less than full and entire control over some insignificant area of legislation, we would inquire whether the matter was "so central to the functioning of the Legislative Branch" as really to require complete control, or whether the statute gives Congress "sufficient control over the surrogate legislator to ensure that Congress is able to perform its constitutionally assigned duties"? Of course we would have none of that. Once we determined that a purely legislative power was at issue we would require it to be exercised, wholly and entirely, by Congress. Or to bring the point closer to home, consider a statute giving to non–Article III judges just a tiny bit of purely judicial power in a relatively insignificant field, with substantial control, though not total control, in the courts — perhaps "clear error" review, which would be a fair judicial equivalent of the Attorney General's "for cause" removal power here. Is there any doubt that we would not pause to inquire whether the matter was "so *central* to the functioning of the Judicial Branch" as really to require complete control, or whether we retained "*sufficient* control over the matters to be decided that we are able to perform our constitutionally assigned duties"? We would say that our "constitutionally assigned duties" include *complete* control over all exercises of the judicial power — or, as the plurality opinion said in Northern Pipeline Construction Co. v. Marathon Pipe Line Co. [458 U.S. 50, 58–59 (1982)], that "[t]he inexorable command of [article III] is clear and definite: The judicial power of the United States must be exercised by courts having the attributes prescribed in Art. III." We should say here that the President's constitutionally assigned duties include *complete* control over investigation and prosecution of violations of the law, and that the inexorable command of Article II is clear and definite: the executive power must be vested in the President of the United States.

Is it unthinkable that the President should have such exclusive power, even when alleged crimes by him or his close associates are at issue? No more so than that Congress should have the exclusive power of legislation, even when what is at issue is its own exemption from the burdens of certain laws. No more so than that this Court should have the exclusive power to pronounce the final decision on justiciable cases and controversies, even those pertaining to the constitutionality of a statute reducing the salaries of the Justices. A system of separate and coordinate powers necessarily involves an acceptance of exclusive power that can theoretically be abused. . . .

The Court has, nonetheless, replaced the clear constitutional prescription that the executive power belongs to the President with a "balancing test." What are the standards to determine how the balance is to be struck, that is, how much removal of presidential power is too much? Many countries of the world get along with an Executive that is much weaker than ours — in fact, entirely dependent upon the continued support of the legislature. Once we depart from the text of the Constitution, just where short of that do we stop? The most amazing feature of the Court's opinion is that it does not even purport to give an answer. It simply *announces*, with no analysis, that the ability to control the decision whether to investigate and prosecute the President's closest advisors, and indeed the President himself, is not "so central to the functioning of the Executive Branch" as to be constitutionally required to be within the President's control. . . .

Besides weakening the Presidency by reducing the zeal of his staff, it must also be obvious that the institution of the independent counsel enfeebles him more directly in his constant confrontations with Congress, by eroding his public support. Nothing is so politically effective as the ability to charge that one's opponent and his associates are not merely wrong-headed, naive, ineffective, but, in all probability, "crooks." And nothing so effectively gives an appearance of validity to such charges as a Justice Department investigation and, even better, prosecution. The present statute provides ample means for that sort of attack, assuring that massive and lengthy investigations will occur, not merely when the Justice Department in the application of its usual standards believes they are called for, but whenever it cannot be said that there are "no reasonable grounds to believe" they are called for. . . .

IV

Since our 1935 decision in [*Humphrey's Executor*] — which was considered by many at the time the product of an activist, anti–New Deal court bent on reducing the power of President Franklin Roosevelt — it has been established that the line of permissible restriction upon removal of principal officers lies at the point at which the powers exercised by those officers are no longer purely executive. . . .

By contrast, "our present considered view" is simply that *any* Executive officer's removal can be restricted, so long as the President remains "able to accomplish his constitutional role." There are now no lines. If the removal of a prosecutor, the virtual embodiment of the power to "take care that the laws be faithfully executed," can be restricted, what officer's removal cannot? This is an open invitation for Congress to experiment. What about a special Assistant Secretary of State, with responsibility for one very narrow area of foreign policy, who would not only have to be confirmed by the Senate but could also be removed only pursuant to certain carefully designed restrictions? Could this possibly render the President "[un]able to accomplish his constitutional role"? Or a special Assistant Secretary of Defense for Procurement? The possibilities are endless, and the Court does not understand what the separation of powers, what "[a]mbition . . . counteracting ambition," Federalist No. 51, p. 322 (Madison), is all about, if it does not expect Congress to try them. As far as I can discern from the Court's opinion, it is now open season upon the President's removal power for all executive officers, with not even the superficially principled restriction of *Humphrey's Executor* as cover. The Court essentially says to the President "Trust us. We will make sure that you are able to accomplish your constitutional role." I think the Constitution gives the President — and the people — more protection than that.

V

The purpose of the separation and equilibration of powers in general, and of the unitary Executive in particular, was not merely to assure effective government but to preserve individual freedom. Those who hold or have held offices covered by the Ethics in Government Act are entitled to that protection as much as the rest of us, and I conclude my discussion by considering the effect of the Act upon the fairness of the process they receive.

Only someone who has worked in the field of law enforcement can fully appreciate the vast power and the immense discretion that are placed in the hands of a prosecutor with respect to the objects of his investigation. . . .

Under our system of government, the primary check against prosecutorial abuse is a political one. The prosecutors who exercise this awesome discretion are selected and can be removed by a President, whom the people have trusted enough to elect. Moreover, when crimes are not investigated and prosecuted fairly, nonselectively, with a reasonable sense of proportion, the President pays the cost in political damage to his administration. . . .

That is the system of justice the rest of us are entitled to, but what of that select class consisting of present or former high-level executive-branch officials? If an allegation is made against them of any violation of any federal criminal law (except Class B or C misdemeanors or infractions) the Attorney General must give it his attention. That in itself is not objectionable. But if, after a 90-day investigation without the benefit of normal investigatory tools, the Attorney General is unable to say that there are "no reasonable grounds to believe" that further investigation is warranted, a process is set in motion that is *not* in the full control of persons "dependent on the people," and whose flaws cannot be blamed on the President. An independent counsel is selected, and the scope of her authority prescribed, by a panel of judges. What if they are politically partisan, as judges have been known to be, and select a prosecutor antagonistic to the administration, or even to the particular individual who has been selected for this special treatment? There is no remedy for that, not even a political one. . . .

It is, in other words, an additional advantage of the unitary Executive that it can achieve a more uniform application of the law. Perhaps that is not always achieved, but the mechanism to achieve it is there. The mini-Executive that is the independent counsel, however, operating in an area where so little is law and so much is discretion, is intentionally cut off from the unifying influence of the Justice Department, and from the perspective that multiple responsibilities provide. What would normally be regarded as a technical violation (there are no rules defining such things), may in her small world assume the proportions of an indictable offense. . . .

The ad hoc approach to constitutional adjudication has real attraction, even apart from its work-saving potential. It is guaranteed to produce a result, in every case, that will make a majority of the Court happy with the law. The law is, by definition, precisely what the majority thinks, taking all things into account, it *ought* to be. I prefer to rely upon the judgment of the wise men who constructed our system, and of the people who approved it, and of two centuries of history that have shown it to be sound. Like it or not, that judgment says, quite plainly, that "[t]he executive Power shall be vested in a President of the United States."

Note: *Congressional Control over Administrative Officials*

1. Chadha *and* Bowsher. Although both *Chadha* and *Bowsher* invalidated innovative schemes designed to preserve congressional control of delegated authority, the two decisions utilize different approaches. In *Chadha*, the Court treats Congress's decision regarding Chadha's immigration status as an exercise of legislative authority and finds it invalid because it failed to comport with the presentment and bicameral requirements for the enactment of statutes. A difficulty with this approach is that in the absence of the legislative veto, Chadha's immigration status would be determined by the Immigration and Naturalization Service. Yet the Service's decision also fails to comport with the bicameralism requirement.

Bowsher avoids this difficulty by reversing the analysis. The constitutional defect in the Gramm-Rudman-Hollings Act was not that Congress was legislating, but that it was *not* legislating. The Court treats the Comptroller General's budget-cutting authority as an exercise of *executive* power and holds that Congress had unconstitutionally trenched on executive authority by vesting this authority in an officer under legislative control. Is this approach more satisfactory? If the Comptroller General's budget-cutting authority is executive, why is the "fallback" provision, under which Congress itself would enact the budget cuts, constitutional?

2. Morrison *and* Bowsher. Can *Bowsher* and *Morrison* be reconciled? The Court appears to distinguish between statutory schemes designed to assert congressional control over administrative officials (prohibited in *Myers*, *Chadha*, and *Bowsher*) and statutory schemes designed to protect administrative officials from executive control (permitted in *Humphrey's Executor* and *Morrison*). According to this view, Congress may make some executive officers independent, but it may

not itself control them. Notice that this distinction privileges arrangements that shield administrative officers from accountability to either of the popularly elected branches of government. Doesn't this turn the traditional concern about delegated power on its head?

3. Mistretta *and the "twilight" area.* Consider in this connection the implications of Mistretta v. United States, 488 U.S. 361 (1989). The United States Sentencing Commission has seven members appointed by the President, of whom three must be federal judges; the statute creating the commission states that it is "an independent commission located in the judicial branch." The commission was created in response to concern that sentences for similar offenses and of similar offenders in the federal system varied too substantially to promote the goals of equitable sentencing. Its role is to create mandatory sentencing guidelines specifying rather narrow ranges of permissible sentences for different offenses, taking some account of the different circumstances under which different people commit crimes.

The Court, in an opinion by Justice Blackmun, rejected a variety of separation of powers challenges to the commission. Relying on the "intelligible principle" test derived from prior nondelegation cases, the Court found that the Congress had given the commission sufficiently detailed guidance as to the purposes its guidelines were to serve and the considerations the commission was to take into account. Addressing more general separation of powers concerns, the Court cited Justice Jackson's opinion in *Youngstown* for "the pragmatic, flexible view of differentiated governmental power to which we are heir." In particular, the Court acknowledged a "twilight" area in which the functions of the various branches merge. Thus, although courts may not generally exercise executive and administrative duties of a nonjudicial nature, some forms of judicial rulemaking are permissible: "[Consistent] with separation of powers, Congress may delegate nonadjudicatory functions that do not trench upon the prerogatives of another branch and that are appropriate to the central mission of the Judiciary." For example, Congress had appropriately delegated to the courts the power to develop rules of procedure. In the Court's view, the development of sentencing guidelines also fell within this category.

In a dissenting opinion, Justice Scalia argued that "[the] decisions made by the Commission are far from technical, but are heavily laden [with] value judgments and policy assessments." He therefore expressed some sympathy for the position that the commission's mandate violated the nondelegation doctrine, but acknowledged that the doctrine "is not [readily] enforceable by the courts." However,

> [precisely] because the scope of delegation is largely uncontrollable by the courts, we must be particularly rigorous in preserving the Constitution's structural restrictions that deter excessive delegation. The major one [is] that the power to make law cannot be exercised by anyone other than Congress, except in conjunction with the lawful exercise of executive or judicial power. [Until Morrison v. Olson,] it could have been said that Congress could delegate lawmaking authority only at the expense of increasing the power of either the President or the courts. [Thus,] the need for delegation would have to be important enough to induce Congress to aggrandize its primary competitor for political power, and the recipient of the policymaking authority, while not Congress itself, would at least be politically accountable. . . .
>
> [I] anticipate that Congress will find delegation of its lawmaking powers much more attractive in the future. If rulemaking can be entirely unrelated to the exercise

of judicial or executive powers, I foresee all manner of "expert" bodies, insulated from the political process, to which Congress will delegate various portions of its lawmaking responsibility. . . .

I think the Court errs [not] so much because it mistakes the degree of commingling [of the branches of government], but because it fails to recognize that this case is not about commingling, but about the creation of a new branch altogether, a sort of junior-varsity Congress.

4. *Double insulation.* In Free Enterprise Fund v. Public Company Accounting Oversight Board, 561 U.S. 477 (2010), the Court distinguished *Morrison* and *Humphrey's Executor* and held that it was unconstitutional to insulate an inferior officer from removal by a principal officer when the principal officer was also protected from removal by the President. The Sarbanes-Oxley Act of 2002, 116 Stat. 745, created the Public Company Accounting Oversight Board, composed of five members appointed by the Securities and Exchange Commission. The Board was granted broad authority to oversee the accounting industry, and the Commission could remove Board members only for "good cause shown." The Court assumed for purposes of the case that members of the Commission could be removed by the President only for "inefficiency, neglect of duty, or malfeasance in office."

The Court, in a five-to-four decision written by Chief Justice Roberts, noted that it had previously upheld restrictions on a President's removal power. "In those cases, however, only one level of protected tenure separated the President from an officer exercising executive power. It was the President — or a subordinate he could remove at will — who decided whether the officer's conduct merited removal under the good-cause standard." Here in contrast, decisions about whether good cause existed to remove Board members were vested "in other tenured officers — the Commissioners — none of whom is subject to the President's direct control. The result is a Board that is not accountable to the President, and a President who is not responsible for the Board." In the Court's view,

[the] added layer of tenure protection makes a difference. Without a layer of insulation between the Commission and the Board, the Commission could remove a Board member at any time, and therefore would be fully responsible for what the Board does. The President could then hold the Commission to account for its supervision of the Board, to the same extent that he may hold the Commission to account for everything else that it does.

Does subjecting Board members to at-will removal by the Commission solve the problem that the Court identifies? Compare Justice Breyer's dissenting opinion, joined by Justices Stevens, Ginsburg, and Sotomayor:

[So] long as the President is *legitimately* foreclosed from removing the *Commissioners* except for cause (as the majority assumes), nullifying the Commission's power to remove Board members only for cause will not resolve the problem the Court has identified: The President will *still* be "powerless to intervene" by removing the Board members if the Commission reasonably decides not to do so.

Many statutes establish "partisan balance requirements" for administrative agencies. These provisions require the President to appoint some members of the other party to important positions within the agency. Suppose that you were a lawyer tasked with attacking the constitutionality of these requirements. How might you use *Free Enterprise Fund* to mount such an attack? See generally Krotoszynski, Hodge, & Wintermyer, Partisan Balance Requirements in the Age of New Formalism, 90 Notre Dame L. Rev. 941 (2015).

5. *Recess appointments.* Article II, section 2, clause 2 of the Constitution requires the advice and consent of the Senate for most presidential appointments, but article II, section 2, clause 3 provides that "[the] President shall have the Power to fill up all Vacancies that may happen during the Recess of the Senate, by granting Commissions which shall expire at the End of [Congress's] next session." In National Labor Relations Board v. Noel Canning, 34 S. Ct. 2550 (2014), the Supreme Court for the first time adjudicated a case concerning the scope of this power.

The case arose amidst intense political controversy over the use of the Senate filibuster to block presidential appointments (sometimes because of opposition to the existence of the agency in question rather than because of opposition to the particular nominee) and over the President's attempt to circumvent filibusters by making recess appointments. When the Senate delayed the confirmation of three members of the National Labor Relations Board, President Obama used his putative recess appointments power to place them on the Board. He made the appointments after the Senate adopted a resolution providing that it would take a series of brief recesses beginning on December 17, 2011. The resolution provided that the Senate would hold "pro forma" sessions every Tuesday and Friday until it returned to ordinary business on January 23, 2012. President Obama made the appointments on January 4, between the January 3 and January 6 pro forma sessions.

Noel Canning, which had been found by the Board to have violated the labor laws, claimed that the Board lacked a quorum to act because three of the Board's five members had been illegally appointed.

The Court of Appeals agreed with Noel Canning that the appointments were illegal because, in its view, the words "the recess of the Senate" referred only to Congress's annual inter-session recess, not to its more frequent intra-session recesses, and because the words "vacancies that may happen during the recess" referred only to vacancies that come into existence during the recess, not to vacancies that occur earlier but that remain unfilled during a recess.

By a vote of five-to-four, the Court, per Justice Breyer, rejected both of these arguments. It nonetheless held that the appointments were illegal. The Court reasoned that the pro forma sessions brought to a close the recesses between them. This meant that the appointments occurred during a three-day recess, and the Court held that a "recess of [less] than 10 days is presumptively too short to fall within the Clause. We add the word 'presumptively' to leave open the possibility that some very unusual circumstance — a national catastrophe, for instance, that renders the Senate unavailable but calls for an urgent response — could demand the exercise of the recess-appointment power during a shorter break."

In reaching these conclusions, the Court emphasized its view that the recess appointments power was not meant to "[offer] the President the authority routinely to avoid the need for Senate confirmation." It also emphasized the role of historical practice in interpreting the scope of the power. "We recognize, of course, that the separation of powers can serve to safeguard individual liberty and that it is the 'duty of the judicial department' — in a separation-of-power case as in any other — 'to say what the law is' [quoting Marbury v. Madison]. But it is equally true that the longstanding 'practice of government' [quoting McCulloch v. Maryland] can inform our determination of 'what the law is.'" With regard to the second point, the Court noted that

> Presidents have made recess appointments since the beginning of the Republic. Their frequency suggests that the Senate and President have recognized that recess appointments can be both necessary and appropriate in certain circumstances. We have not previously interpreted the Clause, and, when doing so for the first time in more than 200 years, we must hesitate to upset the compromises and working arrangements that the elected branches of Government themselves have reached.

The Court then turned its attention to whether the clause permitted intra-session as well as inter-session recesses. Finding the term "the recess" ambiguous, the Court relied on its purpose, which, it held, "[demands] the broader interpretation" because "[the] Senate is equally away during both an inter-session and an intra-session recess, and its capacity to participate in the appointments process has nothing to do with the words it uses to signal its departure." In addition, the Court cited a record of frequent intra-session appointments from the post–Civil War period to the present and opinions by the President's legal advisors supporting these appointments.

> The upshot is that restricting the Clause to inter-session recesses would frustrate its purpose. It would make the President's recess-appointment power dependent on a formalistic distinction of Senate procedure. Moreover, the President has consistently and frequently interpreted the word "recess" to apply to intra-session recesses, and has acted on that interpretation. The Senate as a body has done nothing to deny the validity of this practice for at least three-quarters of a century. And three-quarters of a century of settled practice is long enough to entitle a practice to "great weight in a proper interpretation of the constitutional provision."

The Court then considered the second ground on which the lower court had invalidated the appointment — that the vacancy had not "happened" during the recess because it did not initially occur while the Senate was in recess. Once again, the Court found that the language itself was ambiguous, but that its purpose suggested a broader interpretation. The Court reasoned that the President might not have time to fill a vacancy before the Senate went into recess and that, if the office was an important one, the inability to fill the post while the Senate was not in session could have serious adverse consequences. The Court again found that historical practice for more than 200 years supported this interpretation. While recognizing that the interpretation might be thought to allow the President to routinely avoid the confirmation process by making all appointments during recesses, the Court pointed out that this course of conduct had disadvantages, including the fact that the appointee can only serve for a limited term and her provisional status might make her less effective. "Moreover, the Senate, like the President, has institutional 'resources,' including political resources 'available to protect and assert its interests.'"

Finally, the Court turned to the issue of how to treat the "pro forma" sessions. The government argued that these sessions were periods of recess because the Senate did virtually no business during them and was therefore in recess as a functional matter. The Court disagreed:

[The] Senate is in session when it says it is, provided that, under its own rules, it retains the capacity to transact Senate business. The Senate met that standard here.

The standard we apply is consistent with the Constitution's broad delegation of authority to the Senate to determine how and when to conduct its business. The Constitution explicitly empowers the Senate to "determine the Rules of its Proceedings." Art. I, §5, cl. 2. . . .

In addition the Constitution provides the Senate with extensive control over its schedule. . . .

We generally take at face value the Senate's own report of its actions.

Since pro forma sessions interrupted the recess, the Court was forced to decide whether the period between these sessions was long enough to trigger the recess appointments power. It concluded that it was not:

The Recess Appointments Clause seeks to permit the Executive Branch to function smoothly when Congress is unavailable. And though Congress has taken short breaks for almost 200 years, and there have been many thousands of recess appointments in that time, we have not found a single example of a recess appointment made during an intra-session recess that was shorter than 10 days. . . . The lack of examples suggests that the recess appointment power is not needed in that context.

Justice Scalia, in an opinion joined by Chief Justice Roberts and Justices Thomas and Alito, concurred in the judgment. He would have held that the recess appointments power arises only during the annual intermission between two formal legislative sessions and that the recess must first occur during that period. He accused the majority of justifying its "atextual results on an adverse-possession theory of executive authority."

Justice Scalia emphasized that because "separation of power exists for the protection of individual liberty," it was irrelevant that the Senate had approved of or not objected to the encroachment. "Plainly [a] self-aggrandizing practice adopted by one branch well after the founding, often challenged, and never before blessed by this Court [does] not relieve us of our duty to interpret the Constitution in light of its text, structure, and original understanding."

Moreover, Justice Scalia's review of the historical record convinced him that prior practice was "at best ambiguous."

The real tragedy of today's decision is not simply the abolition of the Constitution's limits on the recess-appointment power and the substitution of a novel framework invented by this Court. It is the damage done to our separation-of-powers jurisprudence more generally. [We] should [take] every opportunity to affirm the primacy of the Constitution's enduring principles over the politics of the moment. Our failure to do so today will resonate well beyond the particular dispute at hand. Sad, but true: The Court's embrace of the adverse-possession theory of executive power [will] be cited in diverse contexts, including those presently unimagined, and will have the effect of aggrandizing the Presidency beyond its constitutional bounds and undermining respect for the separation of powers.

6. *Congressional control over administrative agencies after* Chadha *and* Bowsher. Recall that in Buckley v. Valeo, page 447, supra, the Court upheld the Federal Campaign Act insofar as the powers that it delegated to the Federal Election Commission were "essentially of an investigative and informative nature, falling in the same general category as those which Congress might

delegate to one of its own committees." Does this holding survive *Chadha*? Would it survive the approach outlined in Justice Stevens's concurring opinion in *Bowsher*?

Consider in this connection Metropolitan Washington Airports Authority v. Citizens for Abatement of Aircraft Noise, 501 U.S. 252 (1991). When Congress transferred operation of Washington, D.C., airports from the federal government to a new airport authority, it conditioned the transfer on the creation of a board of review with power to veto major decisions made by the authority. The board of review consisted of nine members of Congress, to be chosen by the authority's board of directors from lists provided by the Speaker of the House and the President pro tempore of the Senate. In a six-to-three decision, the Court, per Justice Stevens, held that the statute was unconstitutional. The Court observed that it need not decide whether the power exercised by the board of review was legislative or executive in nature: "If the power is executive, the Constitution does not permit an agent of Congress to exercise it. If the power is legislative, Congress must exercise it in conformity with the bicameralism and presentment requirements of Art. I, §7. [See *Chadha*]."

Note: *Distribution of National Powers — Final Thoughts*

Do the preceding materials suggest that the distribution of national powers has served its intended function? Has it limited factional control over governmental processes? Has it served as an important safeguard of liberty? Or has it created so many "checks" that (1) democratic processes are unable to bring about substantial reform or (2) the government is prevented from taking necessary action?

The preceding materials raise institutional issues as well. To what extent has judicial review contributed to the development of the present distribution of national powers? What has been the effect of structural legislation such as the War Powers Resolution? Consider the possibility that the written Constitution has played only a small role. Do the materials support the suggestion that the process of bargaining between Congress and the executive branch is a sufficient safeguard against abuse? What constitutes abuse in this context?

V

Equality and the Constitution

This chapter explores the Supreme Court's struggle to define and apply the Constitution's requirements of equal treatment. Section A explores the origins of the equal protection clause of the fourteenth amendment in the national experience with race, slavery, and its aftermath. The remaining sections focus more directly on constitutional doctrine. The modern Supreme Court's treatment of equal protection claims has used a means-ends methodology in which judges ask whether the classification the government is using is sufficiently related to the goals it is pursuing. Section B explores the meaning of "equality" in the default context: "rational basis" review of "ordinary" social or economic classifications. Section C focuses on the paradigmatic example of "heightened scrutiny": searching judicial review of classifications based on race. Section D turns to a different form of heightened scrutiny used in cases involving classifications based on gender. Section E considers the question of heightened scrutiny for classifications based on sexual orientation. Finally, Section F explores the claims for heightened scrutiny of other "disadvantaged" groups, such as aliens and the poor.

A. SLAVERY, JIM CROW, AND THE EQUAL PROTECTION PRINCIPLE

Although the Declaration of Independence contained the ringing phrase that "We hold these truths to be self-evident, that all men are created equal," there was no straightforward general guarantee of equality in the original Constitution.* The equal protection clause of the fourteenth amendment has become the primary source of constitutional requirements of equal treatment. Although the equal protection clause is quite general in its language — "nor shall any State . . . deny to any person within its jurisdiction the equal protection of the laws" — its genesis reflects a particular concern: the desire, after the Civil War, to

---

* The Court was later to hold, in Bolling v. Sharpe, 347 U.S. 497 (1954), that the due process clause of the fifth amendment contains an equality principle. See page [490] infra.

protect newly freed African-American slaves from continued discrimination by southern state governments.

In one form or another, controversy about the legal status of African Americans has been central to U.S. law and politics since the founding of the Republic. As you read through this material, consider the extent to which judicial decisions have shaped that controversy and the extent to which they have been shaped by it. At each stage, could the Court have acted differently? Was its power meaningfully constrained by the language and history of the Constitution? By the constellation of social and political forces at the time? By the strategy of individual litigants? By the other branches of government? Does the Supreme Court ultimately have the power to impose its own version of racial justice? Or are its decisions largely the product of broad historical forces over which it exercises little control?

1. Slavery and the Constitution

Although the word "slavery" nowhere appears in the original Constitution, three provisions recognized and arguably legitimated the practice. Article I, section 2, clause 3 required apportionment of seats in the House of Representatives on the basis of the "whole number of free Persons" in each state, minus the number of "Indians not taxed," plus "three fifths of all other Persons." Article I, section 9, clause 1 prohibited Congress from outlawing the "Importation of such Persons as any of the States now existing shall think proper" until 1808. Article IV, section 2, clause 3 required states to "[deliver] up" any "Person held to Service or Labour in one State" who had escaped into their territory.

Do these provisions make the Constitution a pro-slavery document? Consider D. Robinson, Slavery in the Structure of American Politics 1765–1820, at 209, 210, 244–246 (1971):

> In the drama that produced the Constitution, Southern delegates were unmistakably prominent players. James Madison, the man whose leadership during the Convention earned him the title "Father of the Constitution," was a Southerner, a slave-owning Virginian. [John] Rutledge, certainly a leading nationalist and chairman of the important Committee of Detail, which provided the first definition of legislative powers under the Constitution, was one of the wealthiest and best-established planters at the Convention, and deliberately represented the most candid slave owners. [George] Washington [was] an exceedingly rich man, whose fortune arose largely from the labor of slaves in and around Mount Vernon, Virginia. In fact, of the fifteen delegates whom Clinton Rossiter has termed either "principals" or "influentials," seven were planters. . . .
>
> The South's enthusiastic participation in the nationalizing thrust of 1787 carried one portentous qualification: the national government could be as powerful as the vision of a great national empire demanded, *provided that it keep its hands off slavery*. . . .
>
> The framers [dealt] with slavery by seeking, so far as possible, to take it out of the national political arena. They were unable in 1787 to settle the issue, one way or the other. They could not establish straightforward Constitutional guarantees against emancipation, as the South Carolinians desired, because many Northerners, and perhaps some Southerners, would not permit it. Nor could they give Congress power to regulate slavery in any way, much less abolish it, because Southerners refused to yield control over the institution. Realizing that it was utterly beyond their power to fashion a national consensus on slavery, or to "govern" the issue in

[handwritten marginalia:] evidence of slavery

the absence of one, they had contented themselves with measures aimed at preventing friction over slavery between the states and sections. . . .

There is no evidence that any framer thought the Constitution contained power to abolish slavery. They all knew how the Deep Southerners felt, and however much some of them may have regretted the hold that slavery had on the South, they were all fully sympathetic with the determination of the Deep Southerners to resist abolition in the present circumstances. . . .

But there was no guarantee that powers of emancipation were forever denied to the federal government.

The evidence there permits the conclusion that the future, with respect to possible public action against slavery, was left open on purpose. [The] framers, as of 1787, agreed unanimously to place the institution of slavery, as it existed within the South, not "on the course of ultimate extinction," as Lincoln argued, but beyond national regulation.

In light of the provisions in the Constitution protecting slavery, should it have been ratified? Consider the views of Justice Thurgood Marshall:

I [do not] find the wisdom, foresight, and sense of justice exhibited by the framers particularly profound. To the contrary, the government they devised was defective from the start, requiring several amendments, a civil war, and momentous social transformation to attain the system of constitutional government, and its respect for the individual freedoms and human rights we hold as fundamental today.

Marshall, Commentary: Reflections on the Bicentennial of the United States Constitution, 101 Harv. L. Rev. 1, 2 (1987). Abolitionist William Lloyd Garrison went further, terming the original Constitution "an agreement with Death and a covenant with Hell." Witness to America 132 (S. Ambrose and D. Brinkley eds., 1999).

Compare Levinson, 1787: The Constitution in Perspective — Pledging Faith in the Civil Religion; Or, Would You Sign the Constitution?, 29 Wm. & Mary L. Rev. 113, 133 (1987):

[The] central problem with "disunionist" thinking [is] that it focuses more on the immorality of collaboration with slavery [than] on the question of how one most quickly can bring slavery to an end. We know that with ratification chattel slavery ended by 1865. Is there good reason to believe that it would have ended earlier had the Constitution not been ratified and balkanization followed? I suspect not. But the important point is surely this: Can one who believes that the ratification of the Constitution *did* enhance the prospects (and actuality) of chattel slavery sign the Constitution? What precisely is the value of the Constitution and of the concomitant nation that would justify even an extra week's slavery? What precisely is the omelet that justified breaking those particular eggs?

State v. Post

20 N.J.L. 368 (Supreme Court of New Jersey 1845)

NEVIUS, J.

This proceeding is designed to present for our adjudication the question, whether slavery can exist within the limits of this state under its present constitution and laws; and it derives signal and solemn importance from its bearing upon a class of human beings, still claimed to be lawfully held in slavery, and upon the interest of those communities where most of that class are still found. . . .

In 1804, the legislature adopted a plan for the gradual abolition of slavery, and passed an act declaring, "That every child born of a slave, after the 4th of July of that year, should be free, but remain the servant of the owner of the mother [until] he or she should arrive at a specified age." [Under] the operation of [the statute] and the benign spirit of the age, which inclined men to manumit their slaves, slavery has become nearly extinct in this state and must soon pass entirely away. [According] to the last census [the number of slaves] was reduced to 674; of whom [349 were] over the age of fifty-five years. Those who yet survive and have not been manumitted, remain still the slaves of their masters; but have a legal claim upon the latter for maintenance, in the case of their inability to support themselves, unless by the provisions of the new constitution, framed and adopted in 1844, slavery is abolished. If such be the case, it will follow as a legal consequence, that masters too, are absolved from the obligation of maintenance. [These] consequences, while they can have no legitimate influence upon the decision of the question, nevertheless give it more than ordinary importance, and call for our most serious and anxious consideration.

[Abolitionists argued that slavery was made illegal in New Jersey by a provision in the state's 1844 constitution declaring that "all men are by nature free and independent, and have certain natural and unalienable rights, among which are those of enjoying and defending life and liberty, acquiring, possessing and protecting property, and of pursuing and obtaining safety and happiness."]

If the [New Jersey constitutional] convention intended to say that all men, in a state of civil or political society, were free and independent and entitled to the exercise and enjoyment of the rights mentioned, the expression must be understood in a modified sense according to the nature, the condition and laws of the society to which they belong. . . .

[Had] the convention intended to abolish slavery and domestic relations, well known to exist in this state and to be established by law, and to divest the master of his right of property in his slave and the slave of his right to protection and support from the master, no one can doubt but that it would have adopted some clear and definite provision to effect it, and not have left so important and grave a question, involving such extensive consequences, to depend upon the doubtful construction of an indefinite abstract political proposition. . . .

The declaration of independence, the basis of our free government, declares that all men are created free and equal, and the constitution of the United States proclaims that the people have formed it to secure the blessings of liberty to themselves and their posterity; yet by the express language of the latter instrument, the relation of master and slave is recognized; showing that the framers of that constitution did not deem their general declaration in favor of liberty, incompatible with its other provisions; and it has never been judicially determined that slavery, in the United States, was thereby abrogated. On the contrary it has been often adjudged, both by the State and Federal courts, that slavery still exists; that the master's right of property in the slave has not been affected either by the declaration of independence, or the constitution of the United States. [It] was argued before us, that, under the declaration of rights in the constitution of Massachusetts, which contains the same language, it has been judicially held, that slavery was no more. And we are referred to [Commonwealth v. Aves], 18 Pick. R. 193. [In *Aves*], Chief Justice Shaw declares "that slavery is contrary to natural right, to the principles of justice and humanity, and repugnant to the constitution." I am unwilling to yield to any one, in high respect for the supreme judicial tribunal of that enlightened state; but [I] do not find the reason or argument, which satisfies my mind of the soundness of its conclusion. [How] far the humane spirit of abolitionism, which prevailed in that state, the fewness or worthlessness of that species of property, the feebleness of the defence made by masters, or the collateral mode in which the question was presented, or the fact that slavery had only been tolerated, but never actually established by law, may have influenced the opinion of the court, [I] will not undertake to determine. By this remark I mean to cast no imputation upon the judicial intelligence or integrity of that court; but judges must be more than men, if they can always escape the influence of a strong popular opinion of society upon great questions of state policy and human benevolence, which have been long agitated and much discussed; and it is no matter of surprise that Chief Justice Shaw, entertaining the opinions he did upon this question of slavery, should have found it repugnant to the spirit of their constitution. . . .

Note: The Constitutionality of Slavery

1. *The context of* Post. *Post* was a test case brought in the form of a habeas corpus action demanding the release of three individuals. Two of them were a husband and wife who had been born before enactment of the 1804 statute and purchased as slaves by Post in 1836; the other person was a minor, born to a slave, who was being held in servitude until he reached the age of 25. Abolitionists argued that the 1844 New Jersey constitutional provision quoted by Justice Nevius freed them immediately.

2. Post *and the problem of judicial power.* For the nation's entire history, courts have oscillated between attempts to impose a judicial solution to the problem of racial justice and attempts to leave the matter to the political process. In *Post*, the Court chose the latter course. Is the decision an example of moral cowardice or of fidelity to law?

Was the Court bound to reach the result it did by the words of the provision in question? By the intent of the framers? Where else might it have looked for guidance? See Chapter 1, section C, supra.

Justice Nevius says judges must be "more than men" to ignore "strong popular opinion." How likely is it that a court would construe the Constitution in a manner most people violently opposed? That it would succeed in enforcing such a construction in the long run?

Of course, in a southern state in 1845, a judicial decision abolishing slavery would have been revolutionary. If a southern judge had written such a decision, what do you suppose the result would have been? In this light, consider the frequently harsh treatment of southern judges over a century later who enforced the requirement that schools be desegregated.

3. *Constitutional attacks on slavery. Post* typifies judicial analysis of slavery prior to the Civil War. Although abolitionist lawyers won isolated victories, even judges strongly opposed to slavery usually ruled against them. See generally R. Cover, Justice Accused (1975); L. Levy, The Law of the Commonwealth and Chief Justice Shaw (1957).

Although *Post* dealt exclusively with *state* constitutional issues, Alvan Stewart, the abolitionist lawyer who argued *Post*, relied on the federal Constitution as well. See J. TenBroek, The Antislavery Origins of the Fourteenth Amendment 43–45

(1951). See also E. Foner, Free Soil, Free Labor, Free Men: The Ideology of the Republican Party before the Civil War 76–77 (1970). Stewart claimed that slavery deprived slaves of life, liberty, and property in violation of the due process clause of the fifth amendment, that it deprived New Jersey of a republican form of government in violation of article IV, that it violated the preamble of the Constitution, and that it violated the Treaty of Ghent, which outlawed the slave trade. See Ernst, Legal Positivism, Abolitionist Litigation, and the New Jersey Slave Case of 1845, 4 Law & Hist. Rev. 337, 350–351 (1986). The Court apparently thought these arguments too flimsy to merit a response. Are the arguments tenable?

4. *Judicial support for slavery.* Far from combating the evils of slavery, judicial review in the pre–Civil War period quite frequently overturned political decisions intended to *limit* slavery.

Most of the federal litigation centered on the fugitive slave clause, article IV, section 2, which required the return of escaped slaves. In Prigg v. Pennsylvania, 41 U.S. (16 Pet.) 539 (1842), the Court, in an opinion by Justice Story, struck down a Pennsylvania statute that made it a crime to forcibly remove blacks from the state for the purpose of causing them to be enslaved. The Court explained that article IV, section 2 "contemplates the existence of a positive, unqualified right on the part of the owner of the slave, which no state law or regulation can in any way qualify, regulate, control, or restrain." The Court therefore held the statute invalid as applied to an escaped slave because "any state law or state regulation, which interrupts, limits, delays, or postpones the right of the owner to the immediate possession of the slave, and the immediate command of his service and labor, operates, pro tanto, a discharge of the slave therefrom." The Court further held that article IV, section 2 vested Congress with the power to assist owners in securing the return of escaped slaves, that Congress had exercised that power by enacting the Fugitive Slave Act of 1793, that this national power was exclusive, and that any state laws regulating the means by which slaves were to be delivered up were unconstitutional.

Prigg's immediate effect was pro-slavery, but its legacy was ambiguous. The decision left intact the power of both free states and the national government to limit the growth of slavery by freeing slaves brought into free areas. Moreover, by nationalizing the rendition question the Court relieved free states of this distasteful obligation and intensified the political struggle over the future of slavery on a national level. See 5 C. Swisher, History of the Supreme Court of the United States: The Taney Period 1836–64, at 546 (1974).

During the 1830s, 1840s, and 1850s, controversies over slavery erupted repeatedly, both in the streets as pro-slavery and anti-slavery forces fought pitched battles in the territories and within the political process. For a particularly gripping account of congressional attempts to avoid discussion altogether, see W. Miller, Arguing About Slavery: The Great Battle in the United States Congress (1996). Under these circumstances, could the Court actually resolve the controversy?

Dred Scott v. Sandford

60 U.S. (19 How.) 393 (1857)

Mr. Chief Justice Taney delivered the opinion of the Court. . . .

[Dred Scott, admittedly once a slave but claiming now to be a citizen of Missouri, brought an action for trespass in federal court against John F. A.

Sanford — whose name was apparently misspelled in the official case reports — a citizen of New York. Federal jurisdiction was premised on diversity of citizenship. In 1834, Scott's former owner had taken him from Missouri to Illinois, where they resided for two years before moving to Minnesota, then part of the Louisiana Territory. In 1838, they returned to Missouri, and Scott was sold as a slave to Sanford. Although slavery was legal in Missouri, it was prohibited in Illinois by the state constitution and in the Louisiana Territory by the federal statute embodying the Missouri Compromise — the Act of March 6, 1820, 3 Stat. 545. Scott argued that these provisions made him a free man. In response, Sanford contended that the court lacked diversity jurisdiction over Scott's claim because, as a black man, Scott could not be a citizen of Missouri; moreover, he argued that Scott's time in Illinois and Minnesota could not deprive his owner of his property interest in Scott when he returned to Missouri.]

I

[The Court first addressed the question whether Scott was a citizen of Missouri for diversity purposes.]

The words "people of the United States" and "citizens" are synonymous terms, and mean the same thing. They both describe the political body who, according to our republican institutions, form the sovereignty, and who hold the power and conduct the Government through their representatives. They are what we familiarly call the "sovereign people," and every citizen is one of this people, and a constituent member of this sovereignty. The question before us is, whether the class of persons described in the plea in abatement compose a portion of this people, and are constituent members of this sovereignty? We think they are not, and that they are not included, and were not intended to be included, under the word "citizens" in the Constitution, and can therefore claim none of the rights and privileges which that instrument provides for and secures to citizens of the United States. On the contrary, they were at that time considered as a subordinate and inferior class of beings, who had been subjugated by the dominant race, and, whether emancipated or not, yet remained subject to their authority, and had no rights or privileges but such as those who held the power and the Government might choose to grant them.

It is not the province of the court to decide upon the justice or injustice, the policy or impolicy, of these laws. The decision of that question belonged to the political or law-making power; to those who formed the sovereignty and framed the Constitution. The duty of the court is, to interpret the instrument they have framed, with the best lights we can obtain on the subject, and to administer it as we find it, according to its true intent and meaning when it was adopted. . . .

In the opinion of the court, the legislation and histories of the times, and the language used in the Declaration of Independence, show, that neither the class of persons who had been imported as slaves, nor their descendants, whether they had become free or not, were then acknowledged as a part of the people, nor intended to be included in the general words used in that memorable instrument.

It is difficult at this day to realize the state of public opinion in relation to that unfortunate race, which prevailed in the civilized and enlightened portions of the world at the time of the Declaration of Independence, and when the Constitution

of the United States was framed and adopted. But the public history of every
European nation displays it in a manner too plain to be mistaken.

They had for more than a century before been regarded as beings of an inferior
order, and altogether unfit to associate with the white race, either in social or
political relations; and so far inferior, that they had no rights which the white man
was bound to respect; and that the negro might justly and lawfully be reduced to
slavery for his benefit. He was bought and sold, and treated as an ordinary article
of merchandise and traffic, whenever a profit could be made by it. This opinion
was at that time fixed and universal in the civilized portion of the white race. It
was regarded as an axiom in morals as well as in politics, which no one thought of
disputing, or supposed to be open to dispute; and men in every grade and position
in society daily and habitually acted upon it in their private pursuits, as well as in
matters of public concern, without doubting for a moment the correctness of this
opinion. . . .

[Upon] a full and careful consideration of the subject, the court is of opinion,
that, upon the facts stated in the plea in abatement, Dred Scott was not a citizen
of Missouri within the meaning of the Constitution of the United States, and not
entitled as such to sue in its courts; and, consequently, that the Circuit Court had
no jurisdiction of the case, and that the judgment on the plea in abatement is
erroneous. . . .

II . . .

[The Court then discussed whether Scott remained a slave after his sojourn in the
Louisiana Territory and Illinois.]

The act of Congress, upon which the plaintiff relies, declares that slavery
and involuntary servitude, except as a punishment for crime, shall be forever
prohibited in all that part of the [Louisiana Purchase that includes what is now
Minnesota.] And the difficulty which meets us at the threshold of this part of the
inquiry is, whether Congress was authorized to pass this law under any of the
powers granted to it by the Constitution; for if the authority is not given by that
instrument, it is the duty of this court to declare it void and inoperative, and
incapable of conferring freedom upon any one who is held as a slave under the
laws of any one of the States. . . .

[The] power of Congress over the person or property of a citizen can never be a
mere discretionary power under our Constitution and form of Government. The
powers of the Government and the rights and privileges of the citizen are regulated and plainly defined by the Constitution itself. [An] act of Congress which
deprives a citizen of the United States of his liberty or property, merely because
he came himself or brought his property into a particular Territory of the United
States, and who had committed no offence against the laws, could hardly be
dignified with the name of due process of law. . . .

[The] right of property in a slave is distinctly and expressly affirmed in the
Constitution. The right to traffic in it, like an ordinary article of merchandise and
property, was guaranteed to the citizens of the United States, in every State that
might desire it, for twenty years. And the Government in express terms is pledged
to protect it in all future time, if the slave escapes from his owner. This is done in
plain words — too plain to be misunderstood. And no word can be found in the
Constitution which gives Congress a greater power over slave property, or which
entitles property of that kind to less protection than property of any other

description. The only power conferred is the power coupled with the duty of guarding and protecting the owner in his rights.

Upon these considerations, it is the opinion of the court that the act of Congress which prohibited a citizen from holding and owning property of this kind in the territory of the United States [described in the 1820 Act], is not warranted by the Constitution, and is therefore void; and that neither Dred Scott himself, nor any of his family, were made free by being carried into this territory; even if they had been carried there by the owner, with the intention of becoming a permanent resident.

[Finally, the Court addressed Scott's contention that he had been made free by his visit to Illinois, a free state. The Court held that his status on his return to Missouri was to be determined by Missouri law, rather than Illinois law, and that under that law he remained a slave.]

[Justices Wayne, Daniel, Campbell, Crier, Nelson, and Catron each wrote separate concurring opinions. Justices McLean and Curtis dissented.]

Note: Dred Scott *and the Power of Judicial Review*

1. *The meaning of* Dred Scott. After *Dred Scott,* were free blacks in northern states citizens of those states for federal constitutional purposes? Short of amending the Constitution, was there anything that either those states or the federal government could do to make them citizens? If Scott and his owner had remained in the Louisiana Territory, could Congress have prohibited the owner from holding Scott as a slave?

2. *Chief Justice Taney's opinion and the problem of judicial review.* It is frequently noted that the Supreme Court first asserted the power to invalidate acts of Congress in Marbury v. Madison. Less often mentioned is the fact that the Court's second assertion of this power came fifty-four years later in Scott v. Sandford. What lessons does *Dred Scott* teach about judicial review? For an argument that *Dred Scott* was actually not so major a departure from prior practice, see Graber, The New Fiction: *Dred Scott* and the Language of Judicial Authority, 82 Chi.-Kent L. Rev. 177 (2007).

It is generally acknowledged that *Dred Scott* is one of the great disasters in the history of the Supreme Court. But what precisely is wrong with Chief Justice Taney's opinion? Consider the following possibilities:

a. *The Court unnecessarily and unwisely reached out to decide an issue not properly presented.* The first part of Chief Justice Taney's opinion held that Scott was not a citizen of Missouri, and that the court below therefore lacked jurisdiction. Given that holding, was it proper for the Court then to decide the questions addressed in the second part of the opinion? Why was it necessary to address the constitutionality of congressional power to enact the Missouri Compromise?

Did Chief Justice Taney have to read the diversity clause as establishing federal standards for state citizenship? Why wasn't it sufficient to hold that Scott, even if free, was not a citizen of Missouri under Missouri law?

b. *The Court's decision is racist in its premises and morally obtuse in its result.* Whatever else may be true, can it be doubted that the framers viewed slaves as a form of property? Is the problem with *Dred Scott* that the Court was too "active" in reading the contemporary moral attitudes of the justices into the constitutional text or that it was too "passive" in rigidly saddling the country with outdated moral attitudes?

c. *The Court unwisely assumed that it could finally resolve a divisive political issue by taking it "out of politics."* Consider R. Burt, The Constitution in Conflict 193 (1992):

> [*Dred Scott* inflamed] northern fears and [emboldened] southern leaders to escalate their demands for national legitimation of slavery. The Court had already set this course in *Prigg;* by shutting off all possible meliorist interventions in the fugitive slave rendition process, [the] Court drove the abolitionist lawyers out of public institutions [and] into the streets. . . .

Modern constitutional doctrines are sometimes justified on the ground that they remove highly divisive questions from the political process. For example, the abortion decisions and expansive readings of the first amendment religion clauses are sometimes defended on the ground that the underlying questions are inappropriate for political resolution. What are the characteristics of such questions? Was the future and spread of slavery such a question?

d. *The problem was not that the Court attempted to impose a solution to the slavery problem, but that it attempted to impose the wrong solution.* The decision failed to solve the problem and exacerbated sectional tensions. Should Supreme Court decisions be judged by whether they "work" in this sense? Should justices consider whether their decisions will be "accepted"? Whether they will produce "wise" social policy?

e. *The revisionist view.* Is the condemnation of *Dred Scott* largely a problem of hindsight? To be sure, the decision was widely criticized at the time. But some scholars have recently suggested that while the result in *Dred Scott* is certainly unpalatable in light of modern views of slavery and race, the decision was "well within the mainstream of antebellum constitutional thought." M. Graber, *Dred Scott* and the Problem of Constitutional Evil 28 (2006). Graber continues:

> [All] forms of constitutional logic are capable of yielding evil results. Institutional arguments yield evil results whenever elected officials and popular majorities support evil laws. Historical arguments yield evil results whenever constitutional framers and ratifiers constitutionalize evil practices. Aspirational arguments yield evil results whenever constitutional framers have evil constitutional values.

Id. at 83. See also Finkelman, The *Dred Scott* Case, Slavery and the Politics of Law, 20 Hamline L. Rev. 1 (1996). For recent discussion of *Dred Scott* and its role in constitutional interpretation, see Symposium, 150th Anniversary of the *Dred Scott* Decision, 82 Chi.-Kent L. Rev. 3 (2007).

2.   Reconstruction and Retreat

The Civil War and its aftermath saw a major realignment in the constitutional understanding of the relationship between the federal and state governments and in the role of the federal government with respect to individual rights. Prior to the Civil War, "the United States" was treated as a plural noun. In *Dred Scott*, for example, the Court referred to a federal statute passed during the War of 1812 that referred to "the war in which the United States are engaged." After the Civil War, by contrast, "the United States" became a singular noun. See James M. McPherson, Battle Cry of Freedom: The Civil War Era 859 (1988). Similarly, the original Constitution rested on the view that the most serious threat to individual liberty came from the federal government, and that the states could be relied on to "afford complete security against invasions of the public liberty by the national authorities." The Federalist No. 28 (Hamilton). But by the close of the Civil War, it was clear that the southern states could not be depended on to protect the rights of the newly freed slaves, and it could hardly be maintained that the main threat to those rights came from the federal government. Under the pressure of this reality, a shift occurred: Instead of viewing the Constitution as a protection from federal power, at least some people came to see constitutional rights as a basis for the *assertion* of federal power to protect individuals against *state* interference.

Note: The Work of the Reconstruction Congress

The Reconstruction Congress laid the groundwork for the expansion of federal authority by enacting three constitutional amendments, each of which conferred additional substantive power on Congress. On December 31, 1865, the thirteenth amendment became part of the Constitution. The amendment ratified and extended President Lincoln's Emancipation Proclamation by prohibiting slavery and involuntary servitude throughout the United States. In addition, section 2 of the amendment granted Congress the power "to enforce this article by appropriate legislation."

The formal eradication of slavery was insufficient to change the real status of southern blacks. The bonds of slavery were quickly replaced by "Black Codes" in many southern states, which prohibited African Americans from exercising basic civil rights like owning property, pursuing ordinary occupations, or giving testimony in court and which created punishments for ill-defined crimes such as vagrancy or breaking an employment contract that threatened to return large numbers of freedmen to conditions virtually identical to slavery.

Congress attempted to make the thirteenth amendment effective against the challenge posed by the Black Codes through enactment of the Civil Rights Act of 1866. Passed over President Johnson's veto, the act declared that "all persons born in the United States and not subject to any foreign power, excluding Indians not taxed," were citizens of the United States. Such citizens were granted the same right to make and enforce contracts, sue, give evidence, acquire property, and "to full and equal benefit of all laws and proceedings for the security of person and property as is enjoyed by white citizens." Moreover, all citizens were to be "subject to like punishment, pains, and penalties, and to none other, any law, statute, ordinance, regulation or custom to the contrary notwithstanding." For discussion of the 1866 act, see G. Rutherglen, Civil Rights in the Shadow of Slavery: The Constitution, Common Law, and the Civil Rights Act of 1866 (2012).

Even before the civil rights bill was passed, however, doubt arose about Congress's power to enact such a law. Thus, in February 1866, Congressman Bingham introduced the first version of what was to become the fourteenth amendment. It stated that "[the] Congress shall have the power to make all laws which shall be necessary and proper to secure to the citizens of each State all privileges and immunities of citizens in the several States, and to all persons in the several States equal protection in the rights of life, liberty, and property." Cong. Globe, 39th Cong., 1st Sess. 813, 1034 (1866).

On April 30, 1866, after extensive debate, the Joint Committee on Reconstruction reported a new proposal that provided that "[no] state shall make or enforce any law which shall abridge the privileges or immunities of citizens of the United States, nor shall any State deprive any person of life, liberty, or property without due process of law; nor deny any person within its jurisdiction the equal protection of the laws." These substantive prohibitions were coupled with another grant of power to Congress to enforce them "by appropriate legislation." The amendment was adopted by the House in this form. When the amendment reached the Senate, the first sentence of section 1 — making all persons born or naturalized in the United States and subject to the jurisdiction thereof citizens of the United States and of the state wherein they reside, and overruling the Supreme Court's interpretation in *Dred Scott* — was added. (The amendment also contained several other provisions — for example, one superseding the notorious "three fifths clause" for apportioning congressional seats among the states.) For a comprehensive treatment of the drafting history of the fourteenth amendment, see W. Nelson, The Fourteenth Amendment: From Political Principle to Judicial Doctrine (1988). The amendment was ratified on July 28, 1868.

Two years later, on March 30, 1870, Congress added the last of the Reconstruction amendments. It prohibited both the United States and any state from denying or abridging the right to vote on account of race, color, or previous condition of servitude and also contained an enforcement clause.

In thinking about the meaning of the amendments generally, and their effect on constitutional interpretation more generally, note the Reconstruction Congress's reaction to *Dred Scott*. Did the amendments alter the balance of power between the judiciary and the political branches? As previously noted, the primary impetus for passage of the fourteenth amendment was the need to provide a basis for federal *legislative* action against the states. But was the amendment intended as well to be a basis for federal *judicial* power? Consider the following view:

> In the political context of the day, Democratic opponents of the expansion of civil rights were the champions of the judiciary. It is doubtful that the Republicans who drafted and adopted the Amendment would be greatly impressed with the "primary authority" of the institution that had so recently produced Dred Scott v. Sandford[.] Indeed, John Bingham, principal author of the Fourteenth Amendment, advocated taming the Court's power of judicial review by requiring a two-thirds majority of the Court to strike down congressional legislation, and goaded his fellow members of Congress to vote for the proposal by reminding them of the "horrid blasphemy" of *Dred Scott.*

McConnell, Comment, Institutions and Interpretation: A Critique of City of Boerne v. Flores, 111 Harv. L. Rev. 153, 182 (1997).

Note: *The Judicial Reaction*

1. *The Slaughter-House Cases and the reassertion of federalism constraints.* The Supreme Court's first opportunity to assess the impact of the Reconstruction amendments came in The Slaughter-House Cases, 83 U.S. (16 Wall.) 36 (1873), in which the Court rejected a thirteenth and fourteenth amendment attack on a Louisiana statute granting to a single company a monopoly over

operating a slaughterhouse within an area including the city of New Orleans. (These cases are dealt with at greater length in Chapter 6, section B, infra.) Justice Miller's opinion for the Court begins with a ringing declaration that "the one pervading purpose" of the amendments was "[the] freedom of the slave race, the security and firm establishment of that freedom, and the protection of the newly-made freeman and citizen from the oppressions of those who had formerly exercised unlimited dominion over him." The Court emphasized that it did not follow from this purpose that the framers of the amendments intended to transfer general responsibility for protection of civil rights from the states to the federal government. Such a broad reading of the amendments would "degrade the State governments" and "radically [change] the whole theory of the relations of the State and Federal governments to each other and both of these governments to the people." Thus, the privileges and immunities clause of the fourteenth amendment did not provide general federal protection for citizens against state regulation. Rather, it protected only a few rights, "which owe their existence to the Federal government, its National character, its Constitution, or its laws." Nor was the due process clause implicated by the Louisiana statute. As for petitioners' equal protection clause arguments, the Court "[doubted] very much whether any action of a State not directed by way of discrimination against the negroes as a class, or on account of their race, will ever be held to come within the purview of this provision."

2. *Federalism and protection of the newly freed slaves.* The Slaughter-House Cases suggest a two-tiered approach to the fourteenth amendment: When the rights of newly freed slaves are at stake, the amendment must be read expansively to provide comprehensive federal protection. But when racial discrimination is not at issue, the protections are narrower, and a state resident's primary recourse for protection of his rights remains to his own state government.

This approach is consistent with the history of the fourteenth amendment, which was unquestionably written primarily to protect the newly freed slaves. Note, however, that the language of the amendment provides no basis for the distinction. Was the Court correct in emphasizing the history rather than the language?

In some measure, the Court's treatment of the fourteenth amendment in the wake of *Slaughter-House* conformed to the two-tiered approach and, indeed, remnants of it remain today. Thus, on the one hand, the Court has continued to be quite deferential to political outcomes when "ordinary social and economic legislation" is challenged under the fourteenth amendment. On the other hand, the Court quickly established that federal protection was available when the states singled out blacks for discriminatory treatment. See, e.g., Strauder v. West Virginia, 100 U.S. 303 (1879) (reversing the murder conviction of a black man tried before a jury from which members of his race were excluded by law); see also Ex parte Virginia, 100 U.S. 339 (1880).

3. *Judicial invalidation of civil rights legislation.* Within a few years, the Court's narrow interpretation of the Reconstruction amendments started to undermine federal efforts to protect newly freed slaves.

The first intimations of difficulty came in United States v. Reese, 92 U.S. 214 (1875), which involved a federal criminal prosecution against two Kentucky elections inspectors who were charged with violating the 1870 Enforcement Act when they denied a black man the right to vote. Because the relevant sections were not expressly limited to actions that were racially motivated, the Court held that they exceeded Congress's power under the fifteenth amendment, and that the prosecution could not proceed. See also Virginia v. Rives, 100 U.S. 313 (1879).

The Court further restricted the scope of Reconstruction legislation in United States v. Cruikshank, 92 U.S. 542 (1875). The case grew out of the Grant Parish massacre, which has been called "perhaps the bloodiest racial conflict in Louisiana history." R. Kaczorowski, The Politics of Judicial Interpretation: The Federal Courts, Department of Justice and Civil Rights, 1866–1876, at 175 (1985). Following the state election of 1872 both conservatives and Republicans claimed victory. The Republicans gained control of the parish courthouse and were attacked by a "veritable army" of "old time Ku Klux Klan." According to federal investigators sent to the scene, "[at] least 60 freedmen were killed after they had surrendered, and their bodies were mutilated and left to rot in the parching sun." Although ninety-seven defendants were indicted under the Enforcement Act of 1870, only nine defendants were brought to trial, and only three of those were convicted. The Supreme Court reversed the convictions. It rejected the government's argument that the criminal conspiracy section of the 1870 Act was applicable to the lynching of two black men because the lynching interfered with their right of peaceable assembly. Since there was no claim that the victims had assembled to petition the federal government, the prosecution had not alleged that the rights of national citizenship were violated, and punishment therefore exceeded Congress's power under the fourteenth amendment. Nor could the prosecution proceed on the theory that the due process rights of blacks were violated, since "the fourteenth amendment prohibits a State from depriving any person of life, liberty, or property, without due process of law; but this adds nothing to the rights of one citizen as against another." See generally C. Lane, The Day Freedom Died: The Colfax Massacre, The Supreme Court, and the Betrayal of Reconstruction (2008).

In United States v. Harris, 106 U.S. 629 (1883), the Court reached a similar result with respect to the criminal conspiracy sections of the Ku Klux Klan Act of 1871. The Court held that, because the fourteenth amendment did not reach purely private conduct, Congress lacked the power to punish members of a lynch mob who had seized prisoners held by a state deputy sheriff.

But the most damaging judicial attack on Reconstruction legislation came in The Civil Rights Cases, 109 U.S. 3 (1883), where the Court invalidated the public accommodation sections of the 1875 Civil Rights Act. (The Civil Rights Cases are excerpted more fully in Chapter 9, section A, infra.) The Court, in an opinion by Justice Bradley, denied that either the thirteenth or the fourteenth amendment conferred on Congress the power to prohibit private discrimination in public accommodations. The Court's discussion of the fourteenth amendment is usually treated as establishing the requirement of "state action" for a fourteenth amendment violation — a requirement examined in greater detail in Chapter 9. The Court held that "[the] first section of the Fourteenth Amendment [is] prohibitory . . . upon the States. [It] is State action of a particular character that is prohibited. Individual invasion of individual rights is not the subject matter of the amendment." For additional discussion of the Civil Rights Cases, see Rutherglen, State Action, Private Action, and the Thirteenth Amendment, 94 Va. L. Rev. 1367, 1386–1389 (2008).

The Court acknowledged that laws enacted under the thirteenth amendment "may be primary and direct in [character]; for the thirteenth amendment is not a mere prohibition of State laws establishing or upholding slavery, but an absolute declaration that slavery or involuntary servitude shall not exist in any part of the

United States." The Court also agreed that Congress was empowered under the amendment "to pass all laws necessary and proper for abolishing all badges and incidents of slavery in the United States." But the crucial question was whether the discriminatory refusal to serve a black person in a public accommodation was such a badge or incident. The Court thought that accepting this position "would be running the slavery argument into the ground." A refusal of service "has nothing to do with slavery or involuntary servitude. [If] it is violative of any right of the party, his redress is to be sought under the laws of the State; or if those laws are adverse to his rights and do not protect him, his remedy will be found in the corrective legislation which Congress has adopted, or may adopt, for counteracting the effect of State laws, or State action, prohibited by the Fourteenth Amendment."

Was the Reconstruction Court concerned primarily with what the rights of blacks should be, with the source of interference with those rights, or with which organ of government should have the power to vindicate them? In cases where racial discrimination affected federal rights, the Court upheld Reconstruction legislation. Thus, in Ex parte Yarbrough, 110 U.S. 651 (1884), the Court sustained a conviction of a private individual under the Ku Klux Klan Act of 1871 for using violence against blacks voting in a *congressional* election. Similarly, in Logan v. United States, 144 U.S. 263 (1892), the Court held that Congress had the power to punish conspiracies to injure persons in custody of a U.S. marshal. It is at least possible to argue from these cases that the justices were authentically concerned about the expansion of federal power. But what about the expansion of federal *judicial* power that The Civil Rights Cases represented? Was that expansion consistent with the approach of The Slaughter-House Cases? With the intent of the framers of the Reconstruction amendments? Consider McConnell, supra, who suggests that the Reconstruction amendments contained congressional enforcement clauses precisely because the framers thought Congress better positioned than the judiciary to protect the substantive rights the amendments conveyed. In the context of the 1880s, was it meaningful to speak of the rights of blacks without an expansion of federal power? To the extent that it was, because black men remained active politically within those states, did Court decisions that undermined blacks' ability to participate in the political process undermine equality? See J. Kousser, The Shaping of Southern Politics: Suffrage Restrictions and the Establishment of the One-Party South, 1880–1910 (1974); R. Vallely, The Two Reconstructions: The Struggle for Black Enfranchisement (2004).

At the same time that the Court was dismantling much of the Reconstruction legislation, the political coalition behind Reconstruction was also collapsing. The first turning point is usually said to have come with the disputed election of 1876. In return for accepting Hayes's election, Democratic leaders were promised the withdrawal of federal troops from the South and the inclusion of southern Democrats in the cabinet. The post-Reconstruction status of blacks was not, however, a foregone conclusion. As C. Vann Woodward writes in his classic study,

> Southern white people themselves [were not] so united on that subject at first as has been generally assumed. The determination of the Negro's "place" took shape gradually under the influence of economic and political conflicts among divided white people — conflicts that were eventually resolved in part at the expense of the Negro.

C. Woodward, The Strange Career of Jim Crow 6–7 (1957). See also Kousser, supra; Vallely, supra.

Plessy v. Ferguson

163 U.S. 537 (1896)

MR. JUSTICE BROWN [delivered] the opinion of the court.

[A Louisiana statute enacted in 1890 required railroad companies to provide "equal but separate accommodations for the white and colored races," with the provision that "nothing in this act shall be construed as applying to nurses attending children of the other race." A passenger using facilities intended for a different race was made criminally liable. Plessy, who claimed to be seven-eighths Caucasian, was prosecuted under the statute when he failed to leave the coach reserved for whites. The state supreme court upheld the constitutionality of the statute.]

The object of the [fourteenth] amendment was undoubtedly to enforce the absolute equality of the two races before the law, but, in the nature of things, it could not have been intended to abolish distinctions based upon color, or to enforce social, as distinguished from political, equality, or a commingling of the two races upon terms unsatisfactory to either. Laws permitting, and even requiring, their separation, in places where they are liable to be brought into contact, do not necessarily imply the inferiority of either race to the other, and have been generally, if not universally, recognized as within the competency of the state legislatures in the exercise of their police power. The most common instance of this is connected with the establishment of separate schools for white and colored children, which have been held to be a valid exercise of the legislative power even by courts of states where the political rights of the colored race have been longest and most earnestly enforced. . . .

[Counsel for Plessy suggests] that the same argument that will justify the state legislature in requiring railways to provide separate accommodations for the two races will also authorize them to require separate cars to be provided for people whose hair is of a certain color, or who are aliens, or who belong to certain nationalities, or to enact laws requiring colored people to walk upon one side of the street, and white people upon the other, or requiring white men's houses to be painted white, and colored men's black, or their vehicles or business signs to be of different colors, upon the theory that one side of the street is as good as the other, or that a house or vehicle of one color is as good as one of another color. The reply to all this is that every exercise of the police power must be reasonable, and extend only to such laws as are enacted in good faith for the promotion of the public good, and not for the annoyance or oppression of a particular class. . . .

So far, then, as a conflict with the fourteenth amendment is concerned, the case reduces itself to the question whether the statute of Louisiana is a reasonable regulation, and with respect to this there must necessarily be a large discretion on the part of the legislature. In determining the question of reasonableness, it is at liberty to act with reference to the established usages, customs, and traditions of the people, and with a view to the promotion of their comfort, and the preservation of the public peace and good order. Gauged by this standard, we cannot say that a law which authorizes or even requires the separation of the two races in public conveyances is unreasonable, or more obnoxious to the fourteenth amendment than the acts of congress requiring separate schools for colored children in the District of Columbia, the constitutionality of which does not seem to have been questioned, or the corresponding acts of state legislatures.

We consider the underlying fallacy of the plaintiff's argument to consist in the assumption that the enforced separation of the two races stamps the colored race with a badge of inferiority. If this be so, it is not by reason of anything found in the act, but solely because the colored race chooses to put that construction upon it. The argument necessarily assumes that if, as has been more than once the case, and is not unlikely to be so again, the colored race should become the dominant power in the state legislature, and should enact a law in precisely similar terms, it would thereby relegate the white race to an inferior position. We imagine that the white race, at least, would not acquiesce in this assumption. The argument also assumes that social prejudices may be overcome by legislation, and that equal rights cannot be secured to the negro except by an enforced commingling of the two races. We cannot accept this proposition. If the two races are to meet upon terms of social equality, it must be the result of natural affinities, a mutual appreciation of each other's merits, and a voluntary consent of individuals. [Legislation] is powerless to eradicate racial instincts, or to abolish distinctions based upon physical differences, and the attempt to do so can only result in accentuating the difficulties of the present situation. If the civil and political rights of both races be equal, one cannot be inferior to the other civilly or politically. If one race be inferior to the other socially, the constitution of the United States cannot put them upon the same plane. . . .

MR. JUSTICE HARLAN, dissenting. . . .

In respect of civil rights, common to all citizens, the constitution of the United States does not, I think, permit any public authority to know the race of those entitled to be protected in the enjoyment of such rights. Every true man has pride of race, and under appropriate circumstances, when the rights of others, his equals before the law, are not to be affected, it is his privilege to express such pride and to take such action based upon it as to him seems proper. But I deny that any legislative body or judicial tribunal may have regard to the race of citizens when the civil rights of those citizens are involved. Indeed, such legislation as that here in question is inconsistent not only with that equality of rights which pertains to citizenship, national and state, but with the personal liberty enjoyed by every one within the United States. . . .

It was said in argument that the statute of Louisiana does not discriminate against either race, but prescribes a rule applicable alike to white and colored citizens. But this argument does not meet the difficulty. Every one knows that the statute in question had its origin in the purpose, not so much to exclude white persons from railroad cars occupied by blacks, as to exclude colored people from coaches occupied by or assigned to white persons. . . .

[If] a state can prescribe, as a rule of civil conduct, that whites and blacks shall not travel as passengers in the same railroad coach, why may it not so regulate the use of the streets of its cities and towns as to compel white citizens to keep on one side of a street and black citizens to keep on the other? Why may it not, upon like grounds, punish whites and blacks who ride together in street cars or in open vehicles on a public road or street? . . .

The answer given at the argument to these questions was that regulations of the kind they suggest would be unreasonable, and could not, therefore, stand before the law. Is it meant that the determination of questions of legislative power depends upon the inquiry whether the statute whose validity is questioned is, in the judgment of the courts, a reasonable one, taking all the circumstances into consideration? A statute may be unreasonable merely because a sound public policy forbade its enactment. But I do not understand that the courts have anything to do with the policy or expediency of legislation. . . .

The white race deems itself to be the dominant race in this country. And so it is, in prestige, in achievements, in education, in wealth, and in power. So, I doubt not, it will continue to be for all time, if it remains true to its great heritage, and holds fast to the principles of constitutional liberty. But in view of the constitution, in the eye of the law, there is in this country no superior, dominant, ruling class of citizens. There is no caste here. Our constitution is colorblind, and neither knows nor tolerates classes among citizens. In respect of civil rights, all citizens are equal before the law. The humblest is the peer of the most powerful. The law regards man as man, and takes no account of his surroundings or of his color when his civil rights as guaranteed by the supreme law of the land are involved. . . .

In my opinion, the judgment this day rendered will, in time, prove to be quite as pernicious as the decision made by this tribunal in the *Dred Scott* case. [The] present decision, it may well be apprehended, will not only stimulate aggressions, more or less brutal and irritating, upon the admitted rights of colored citizens, but will encourage the belief that it is possible, by means of state enactments, to defeat the beneficent purposes which the people of the United States had in view when they adopted the recent amendments of the constitution. [Sixty] millions of whites are in no danger from the presence here of eight millions of blacks. The destinies of the two races, in this country, are indissolubly linked together, and the interests of both require that the common government of all shall not permit the seeds of race hate to be planted under the sanction of law. What can more certainly arouse race hate, what more certainly create and perpetuate a feeling of distrust between these races, than state enactments which, in fact, proceed on the ground that colored citizens are so inferior and degraded that they cannot be allowed to sit in public coaches occupied by white citizens? That, as all will admit, is the real meaning of such legislation as was enacted in Louisiana.

There is a race so different from our own that we do not permit those belonging to it to become citizens of the United States. [I] allude to the Chinese race. But by the statute in question, a Chinaman can ride in the same passenger coach with white citizens of the United States, while citizens of the black race in Louisiana, many of whom, perhaps, risked their lives for the preservation of the Union, who are entitled by law, to participate in the political control of the State and nation, who are not excluded, by law or by reason of their race, from public stations of any kind, and who have all the legal rights that belong to white citizens, are yet declared to be criminals, liable to imprisonment, if they ride in a public coach occupied by citizens of the white race. It is scarcely just to say that a colored citizen should not object to occupying a public coach assigned to his own race. [He] ought never to cease objecting to the proposition, that citizens of the white and black races can be adjudged criminals because they sit [in] the same public coach on a public highway.

Note: *Separate but Equal*

1. *Equality of separate facilities.* Although Plessy v. Ferguson is often said to have inaugurated the "separate but equal" doctrine, notice that *Plessy* itself does not require the equality of separate facilities.

Three years after *Plessy* the Court squarely addressed that issue in *Cumming v. Board of Education*, 175 U.S. 528 (1899). Petitioners, black taxpayers and parents, challenged their tax assessment on the ground that the money was utilized to support a high school open only to white students. The school board had initially operated a separate black high school, but the facility had been closed to free funds for the education of black primary school students. In an opinion by Justice Harlan, who had dissented in *Plessy* and The Civil Rights Cases, the Court rejected the challenge. The basis for and scope of the Court's holding are not altogether clear. The Court thought it significant that

> the substantial relief asked is an injunction that would either impair the efficiency of the high school provided for white children or compel the Board to close it. But if that were done, the result would only be to take from white children educational privileges enjoyed by them, without giving to colored children additional opportunities for the education furnished in high schools. [If,] in some appropriate proceeding instituted directly for that purpose, the plaintiffs had sought to compel the Board of Education, out of funds in its hands or under its control, to establish and maintain a high school for colored children, and if it appeared that the Board's refusal to maintain such a school was in fact an abuse of its discretion and in hostility to the colored population because of their race, different questions might have arisen in the state court.

The Court made clear, however, that local authorities were to be accorded substantial discretion in allocating funds between white and black facilities, and that "any interference on the part of Federal authority with the management of such schools cannot be justified except in the case of a clear and unmistakable disregard of rights secured by the supreme law of the land."

Compare *Plessy* and *Cumming* with McCabe v. Atchison, Topeka & Santa Fe Railway, 235 U.S. 151 (1914). An Oklahoma statute required railroads to provide separate but equal coach facilities. The statute also authorized railroads to haul sleeping cars, dining cars, and chair cars to be used exclusively by one race but not the other. It did not require the railroad to provide these facilities for both white and black passengers. Five black individuals sued a number of railroads seeking an injunction restraining the railroads from denying them service on the basis of race. The state justified the provision governing sleeping, dining, and chair cars on the ground that the minimal black demand for these facilities made it impractical to haul separate cars for this purpose. The Court found this argument "without merit" because

> [it] makes the constitutional right depend upon the number of persons who may be discriminated against, whereas the essence of the constitutional right is that it is a personal one. Whether or not particular facilities shall be provided may doubtless be conditioned upon there being a reasonable demand therefor, but if facilities are provided, substantial equality of treatment of persons traveling under like conditions cannot be refused. It is the individual who is entitled to the equal protection of the laws, and if he is denied by a common carrier, acting in the matter under the authority of a state law, a facility of convenience in the course of his journey which under substantially the same circumstances is furnished to another traveler, he may properly complain that his constitutional privilege has been invaded.

Can *McCabe* be reconciled with *Cumming*? With *Plessy*?

2. *The state interest in separate facilities.* Note that *Plessy* does not approve all statutes mandating separate treatment. Only those that are "reasonable" are permissible. What state interest made racial separation "reasonable" in *Plessy*? Is respect for majority preferences alone a sufficient justification for separation?

Compare *Plessy* with Berea College v. Kentucky, 211 U.S. 45 (1908). The college, a private institution, was convicted under a statute making it a crime to operate a school "where persons of the white and negro races are both received as pupils for instruction." The Court affirmed the conviction, but on the ground that the college was a corporation that did not have all the rights of individuals. In light *of Plessy*, why did the Court think it necessary to qualify its holding in this way? If an individual had been prosecuted under the same statute, what result?

In Buchanan v. Warley, 245 U.S. 60 (1917), the Court held that a statute prohibiting whites from occupying a residence in a block where the majority of houses were occupied by blacks, and vice versa, violated the fourteenth amendment. The challenge to the statute arose in the context of a suit by a white seller to enforce specifically a contract with a black purchaser, who claimed that the law barred him from occupying the residence. The Court acknowledged that "there exists a serious and difficult problem arising from a feeling of race hostility which the law is powerless to control, and to which it must give a measure of consideration." But the Court believed that "such legislation must have its limitations," and that these legitimate objectives could not "be accomplished by laws or ordinances which deny rights created or protected by the Federal Constitution." The Court distinguished *Plessy* and *Berea College*: "In each instance the complaining person was afforded the opportunity to ride, or to attend institutions of learning, or afforded the thing of whatever nature to which in the particular case he was entitled. The most that was done was to require him as a member of a class to conform with reasonable rules in regard to separation of races. In none of them was he denied the right to use, control, or dispose of his property, as in this case."

Does this distinction make sense? Is there a general principle that explains the results in *Plessy, Cumming, McCabe, Berea College*, and *Buchanan*?

3.   *The Attack on Jim Crow*

As the previous section indicates, the framers of the Reconstruction amendments almost certainly intended that the rights of newly freed slaves would be protected by federal *legislative* action authorized by the new sources of congressional power contained in those amendments. This intent was frustrated by the Court's adherence to an older version of federalism and by the collapse of the political consensus supporting civil rights legislation.

One ironic consequence of the Court's invalidation of Reconstruction legislation was that, when meaningful reform finally came, it was the courts, rather than Congress, that provided the impetus for change. From 1938, when the NAACP won its first Supreme Court victory in a school desegregation case, until the 1960s, when a political consensus favoring civil rights again emerged, the courts stood largely alone in articulating and enforcing the law of race discrimination. What difference might it have made that the protection of blacks was left to judicial interpretations of the Constitution rather than to legislative action?

Note: *The Road to* Brown

1. *The NAACP's decision to attack school segregation.* In 1922, Charles Garland used his inheritance to create the American Fund for Public Service and a committee formed to administer the Fund recommended that the fund finance a campaign for black equality. The Fund gave a grant of $100,000 to the NAACP, along with a memorandum setting out a legal strategy for attacking unequal, segregated schools in the South. See R. Kluger, Simple Justice 132–133 (1976). Using those funds, the NAACP launched a multi-pronged litigation campaign, "attack[ing] what might be called targets of opportunity. [If] the military metaphor referring to a litigation campaign is helpful, the campaign was conducted on a terrain that repeatedly required changes in maneuvers." M. Tushnet, Segregated Schools and Legal Strategy: The NAACP's Campaign against Segregated Education, 1925–1950, at 145–146 (1987). For more on the NAACP's litigation strategy leading up to *Brown*, including a discussion of litigation as a means of social reform, see M. Tushnet, Some Legacies of Brown v. Board of Education, 90 Va. L. Rev. 1693 (2004). Although the NAACP's campaign was neither systematic nor invariably successful, it slowly remade the law.

2. *The higher education cases.* Between 1938 and 1950, the Supreme Court decided a series of cases involving black plaintiffs who challenged their exclusion from state institutions of higher education. In Missouri ex rel. Gaines v. Canada, 305 U.S. 337 (1938), the Court held that Missouri's practice of maintaining an all-white state law school, while agreeing to pay black residents' tuition at institutions in neighboring states, violated the equal protection clause. Writing for the Court, Chief Justice Hughes stated that

> [the] basic consideration is not as to what sort of opportunities other States provide, or whether they are as good as those in Missouri, but as to what opportunities Missouri itself furnishes to white students and denies to negroes solely upon the ground of color. [The] white resident is afforded legal education within the State; the negro resident having the same qualification is refused it there and must go outside the State to obtain it. That is a denial of the equality of legal right to the enjoyment of the privilege which the state has set up, and the provision for the payment of tuition fees in another State does not remove the discrimination.

In Sipuel v. Board of Regents, 332 U.S. 631 (1948), the Court unanimously reaffirmed *Gaines* and held that Oklahoma was required to provide the plaintiff with a legal education and to "provide it as soon as it does for applicants of any other group." On remand, the trial court gave the state the option of either admitting Sipuel or immediately establishing a separate black law school. Sipuel sought mandamus in the Supreme Court, claiming that this disposition was inconsistent with the Court's mandate, since the hastily established black school could not possibly provide an equal education. In Fisher v. Hurst, 333 U.S. 147 (1948), the Court, over two dissents, denied relief. The Court noted that "the petition for certiorari in [*Sipuel*] did not present the issue whether a state might not satisfy the equal protection clause of the Fourteenth Amendment by establishing a separate school for Negroes." For an account of the Court's deliberations over *Sipuel* and *Fisher*, see Hutchinson, Unanimity and Desegregation: Decisionmaking in the Supreme Court, 1948–1958, 68 Geo. L.J. 1, 6–9 (1979).

In Sweatt v. Painter, 339 U.S. 629 (1950), the Court did what it had declined to do in *Fisher* — order the admission of a black student to a white school. Sweatt was denied admission to the University of Texas Law School on the ground that a parallel black school, opened after the litigation commenced, was a substantially equal facility. The Court held that the facility was not in fact equal, and that Sweatt therefore could not be denied admission to the white school. In reaching this conclusion, the Court was aided by the obvious inequality between the two schools in objectively measurable factors like size of library and number of full-time faculty. But the Court did not limit its examination to these factors:

> What is more important, the University of Texas Law School possesses to a far greater degree those qualities which are incapable of objective measurement but which make for greatness in a law school. Such qualities, to name but a few, include reputation of the faculty, experience of the administration, position and influence of the alumni, standing in the community, traditions and prestige. It is difficult to believe that one who had a free choice between these law schools would consider the question close.
>
> Moreover, although the law is a highly learned profession, we are well aware that it is an intensely practical one. The law school, the proving ground for legal learning and practice, cannot be effective in isolation from the individuals and institutions with which the law interacts. Few students and no one who has practiced law would choose to study in an academic vacuum, removed from the interplay of ideas and the exchange of views with which the law is concerned. The law school to which Texas is willing to admit petitioner excludes from its student body members of the racial groups which number 85% of the population of the State and include most of the lawyers, witnesses, jurors, judges and other officials with whom petitioner will inevitably be dealing when he becomes a member of the Texas Bar. With such a substantial and significant segment of society excluded, we cannot conclude that the education offered petitioner is substantially equal to that which he would receive if admitted to the University of Texas Law School.

The Court further elaborated on this theme in McLaurin v. Oklahoma State Regents, 339 U.S. 637 (1950), decided the same day as *Sweatt*. In *McLaurin*, the state, under the pressure of litigation, admitted petitioner to the previously all-white University of Oklahoma Department of Education. However, McLaurin was made to sit in a special classroom seat reserved for blacks, could not eat with other students in the cafeteria, and was given a special table in the library. Although McLaurin could not claim that the physical facilities provided him were unequal, the Court held the restrictions unconstitutional because they "[impaired] and [inhibited] his ability to study, to engage in discussions and exchange views with other students, and, in general, to learn his profession."

What notion of equality do the higher education cases embody? Do they represent an implicit repudiation of *Cumming* and *Plessy*?

3. *The broader context.* Consider the extent to which external events, rather than the internal logic of legal doctrine, explain these legal developments. Between 1938 and 1954, the United States fought and won a world war against an overtly racist regime in Germany; African Americans moved into northern cities in increasing numbers, where they became a much more potent political interest group; America became embroiled in a "cold war" in which racist policies in the South were used to discredit the United States in the underdeveloped world; and the first African-American baseball player joined the Brooklyn Dodgers. For extensive discussions of the relationship between these social,

economic, and political changes and the development of legal doctrine see M. Dudziak, Cold War Civil Rights: Race and the Image of American Democracy (2000); M. Klarman, From Jim Crow to Civil Rights: The Supreme Court and the Struggle for Racial Equality (2004).

4. *Challenges to segregation within public schools.* Consider why the NAACP chose to launch its attack by challenging racial exclusion at the graduate school level. Was this primarily because it was easier to show inequality from a state's complete failure to provide black students with any opportunities at all? Or did it reflect a less legally oriented strategic calculation that courts, or the public, would be less resistant to desegregation at the graduate school level?

By 1950, the NAACP had resolved to launch a frontal attack against racial segregation in public schools. A short time earlier, a group of Mexican-American parents had challenged several California school districts' long-standing policy of assigning Mexican-American students to different schools than Anglo students. In *Mendez v. Westminister School District,* 64 F. Supp. 544 (S.D. Cal. 1946), a district court struck down the school systems' assignment policy as a violation of the fourteenth amendment. Although the court did not view the segregation as "racial" per se, it referred to a series of Supreme Court decisions involving race discrimination in public schools, including *Cumming, Gaines,* and Gong Lum v. Rice, 275 U.S. 78 (1927) (where the Supreme Court had upheld a Mississippi school district's decision to send a Chinese-American student to the "colored" rather than the "white" high school). It concluded:

> "The equal protection of the laws" pertaining to the public school system in California is not provided by furnishing in separate schools the same technical facilities, text books and courses of instruction to children of Mexican ancestry that are available to the other public school children regardless of their ancestry. A paramount requisite in the American system of public education is social equality. It must be open to all children by unified school association regardless of lineage. . . .
>
> The evidence clearly shows that Spanish-speaking children are retarded in learning English by lack of exposure to its use because of segregation, and that commingling of the entire student body instills and develops a common cultural attitude among the school children which is imperative for the perpetuation of American institutions and ideals. It is also established by the record that the methods of segregation prevalent in the defendant school districts foster antagonisms in the children and suggest inferiority among them where none exists.

The court of appeals affirmed. 161 F.2d 774 (9th Cir. 1947). Although the school districts had argued that *Gong Lum* and *Plessy* justified their policies, and several *amici* (including the NAACP), had suggested, in the court's words, that "we should strike out independently on the whole question of segregation, on the ground that recent world stirring events have set men to the reexamination of concepts considered fixed," the court resolved the case in the plaintiffs' favor on the grounds that California law did not affirmatively authorize the segregation of Mexican-American students. (At the time the *Mendez* plaintiffs had brought suit, state law did authorize the creation of separate schools for students of Native American, Chinese, Japanese, and Mongolian ancestry.)

While *Mendez* was pending, the California legislature enacted legislation repealing the state's existing school segregation statute. Shortly after the decision was affirmed, the bill was signed into law by then-Governor Earl Warren, who seven years later wrote the U.S. Supreme Court's opinion in *Brown.*

Brown v. Board of Education of Topeka (*Brown I*)
347 U.S. 483 (1954)

MR. CHIEF JUSTICE WARREN delivered the opinion of the Court. . . .

In each of [these] cases, minors of the Negro race, through their legal representatives, seek the aid of the courts in obtaining admission to the public schools of their community on a nonsegregated basis. In each instance, they had been denied admission to schools attended by white children under laws requiring or permitting segregation according to race. This segregation was alleged to deprive the plaintiffs of the equal protection of the laws under the Fourteenth Amendment. . . .

Reargument was largely devoted to the circumstances surrounding the adoption of the Fourteenth Amendment in 1868. It covered exhaustively consideration of the Amendment in Congress, ratification by the states, then existing practices in racial segregation, and the views of proponents and opponents of the Amendment. This discussion and our own investigation convince us that, although these sources cast some light, it is not enough to resolve the problem with which we are faced. At best, they are inconclusive. The most avid proponents of the post-War Amendments undoubtedly intended them to remove all legal distinctions among "all persons born or naturalized in the United States." Their opponents, just as certainly, were antagonistic to both the letter and the spirit of the Amendments and wished them to have the most limited effect. What others in Congress and the state legislatures had in mind cannot be determined with any degree of certainty.

An additional reason for the inconclusive nature of the Amendment's history, with respect to segregated schools, is the status of public education at that time. In the South, the movement toward free common schools, supported by general taxation, had not yet taken hold. Education of white children was largely in the hands of private groups. Education of Negroes was almost nonexistent, and practically all of the race were illiterate. In fact, any education of Negroes was forbidden by law in some states. Today, in contrast, many Negroes have achieved outstanding success in the arts and sciences as well as in the business and professional world. It is true that public school education at the time of the Amendment had advanced further in the North, but the effect of the Amendment on Northern States was generally ignored in the congressional debates. Even in the North, the conditions of public education did not approximate those existing today. The curriculum was usually rudimentary; ungraded schools were common in rural areas; the school term was but three months a year in many states; and compulsory school attendance was virtually unknown. As a consequence, it is not surprising that there should be so little in the history of the Fourteenth Amendment relating to its intended effect on public education. . . .

In approaching this problem, we cannot turn the clock back to 1868 when the Amendment was adopted, or even to 1896 when [*Plessy*] was written. We must consider public education in the light of its full development and its present place in American life throughout the Nation. Only in this way can it be determined if segregation in public schools deprives these plaintiffs of the equal protection of the laws.

Today, education is perhaps the most important function of state and local governments. Compulsory school attendance laws and the great expenditures for education both demonstrate our recognition of the importance of education to our democratic society. It is required in the performance of our most basic public responsibilities, even service in the armed forces. It is the very foundation of good citizenship. Today it is a principal instrument in awakening the child to cultural values, in preparing him for later professional training, and in helping him to adjust normally to his environment. In these days, it is doubtful that any child may reasonably be expected to succeed in life if he is denied the opportunity of an education. Such an opportunity, where the state has undertaken to provide it, is a right which must be made available to all on equal terms.

We come then to the question presented: Does segregation of children in public schools solely on the basis of race, even though the physical facilities and other "tangible" factors may be equal, deprive the children of the minority group of equal educational opportunities? We believe that it does.

In [*Sweatt*], in finding that a segregated law school for Negroes could not provide them equal educational opportunities, this Court relied in large part on "those qualities which are incapable of objective measurement but which make for greatness in a law school." In [*McLaurin*], the Court, in requiring that a Negro admitted to a white graduate school be treated like all other students, again resorted to intangible considerations: ". . . his ability to study, to engage in discussions and exchange views with other students, and, in general, to learn his profession." Such considerations apply with added force to children in grade and high schools. To separate them from others of similar age and qualifications solely because of their race generates a feeling of inferiority as to their status in the community that may affect their hearts and minds in a way unlikely ever to be undone. The effect of this separation on their educational opportunities was well stated by a finding in the Kansas case by a court which nevertheless felt compelled to rule against the Negro plaintiffs:

> Segregation of white and colored children in public schools has a detrimental effect upon the colored children. The impact is greater when it has the sanction of the law; for the policy of separating the races is usually interpreted as denoting the inferiority of the Negro group. A sense of inferiority affects the motivation of a child to learn. Segregation with the sanction of law, therefore, has a tendency to [retard] the educational and mental development of Negro children and to deprive them of some of the benefits they would receive in a racial[ly] integrated school system.

Whatever may have been the extent of psychological knowledge at the time of [*Plessy*], this finding is amply supported by modern authority.[11] Any language in [*Plessy*] contrary to this finding is rejected.

We conclude that in the field of public education the doctrine of "separate but equal" has no place. Separate educational facilities are inherently unequal. Therefore, we hold that the plaintiffs and others similarly situated for whom the actions have been brought are, by reason of the segregation complained of, deprived of the equal protection of the laws guaranteed by the Fourteenth Amendment.

11. K. B. Clark, Effect of Prejudice and Discrimination on Personality Development (Midcentury White House Conference on Children and Youth, 1950); Witmer & Kotinsky, Personality in the Making (1952), c. VI; Deutscher & Chein, The Psychological Effects of Enforced Segregation: A Survey of Social Science Opinion, 26 J. Psychol. 259 (1948); Chein, What Are the Psychological Effects of Segregation under Conditions of Equal Facilities?, 3 Int. J. Opinion & Attitude Res. 229 (1949); Brameld, Educational Costs, in Discrimination and National Welfare (MacIver ed., 1949), 44–48; Frazier, The Negro in the United States (1949), 674–681. And see generally Myrdal, An American Dilemma (1944).

Note: *Justifications and Explanations for* Brown

1. *The Court's justifications.* Did *Brown* adequately explain why segregation denied minority students equal educational opportunity even when "tangible" factors were equalized? Consider the following arguments that the Court advanced:

a. *The legislative history of the equal protection clause is consistent with outlawing segregated education.* Note that the Court does not assert that the framers of the fourteenth amendment specifically intended to outlaw segregated education. Is such an assertion plausible? In 1868, eight northern states permitted segregated schools, and five additional northern states excluded black children entirely from public education. See R. Kluger, Simple Justice 633–634 (1976). The Reconstruction Congress itself permitted the District of Columbia schools to remain segregated, see Frank and Munro, The Original Understanding of "Equal Protection of the Laws," 1972 Wash. U. L.Q. 421, 460–462, and even the spectators in the gallery listening to the senators debate the fourteenth amendment were segregated by race. See R. Berger, Government by Judiciary: The Transformation of the Fourteenth Amendment 123–125 (1977). Moreover, the sponsors of the Civil Rights Act of 1866, which the fourteenth amendment was intended to constitutionalize, specifically disclaimed any intent to interfere with segregated education. See Statement of James Wilson, Cong. Globe, 39th Cong., 1st Sess. 1117–1118 (1866). See generally Bickel, The Original Understanding and the Segregation Decision, 69 Harv. L. Rev. 1, 11–40 (1955).

For an unusual dissenting view of the original understanding, see McConnell, Originalism and the Desegregation Decisions, 81 Va. L. Rev. 947 (1995). McConnell relies heavily on the ultimately unsuccessful efforts of Republicans in the Reconstruction Congress to include schools within the scope of the 1875 Civil Rights Act, which broadly prohibited segregation in public accommodations, to argue that the framers intended to prohibit school segregation.

Even if McConnell is wrong about the framers' specific intent, might it nonetheless be argued that the equal protection clause represented "a compromise permitting [Moderates and Radicals] to go to the country with language which they could, where necessary, defend against damaging alarms raised by the opposition, but which at the same time was sufficiently elastic to permit reasonable future advances"? Bickel, supra, at 61. If, as Bickel maintains, the legislative history "left the way open to, in fact invited, a decision based on the moral and material state of the nation in 1954, not 1866," id. at 65, does not the burden remain on the defenders of *Brown* to explain why segregation in 1954 denied equality?

In Bolling v. Sharpe, 347 U.S. 497 (1954), decided on the same day as *Brown*, the Court unanimously held school segregation in the District of Columbia unconstitutional. Since the fourteenth amendment applies only to the states, the Court could not rely on the equal protection clause. But although equal protection and due process are not "interchangeable phrases," the Court held that "discrimination may be so unjustifiable as to be violative of [the due process clause of the fifth amendment]." Moreover, "[in] view of our decision that the Constitution prohibits the States from maintaining racially segregated public schools, it would be unthinkable that the same Constitution would impose a lesser duty on the Federal Government."

Does the legislative history of the fifth and fourteenth amendments really make this result "unthinkable"? When the fifth amendment was adopted, most blacks in the United States were slaves, and the Constitution itself implicitly acknowledged that fact. Does *Bolling* suggest that the fourteenth amendment somehow modified the fifth amendment? The framers of the fourteenth amendment chose to make the equal protection guarantee applicable solely to the states. This decision presumably reflected the view that institutional safeguards on the federal level made a constitutional guarantee of equality unnecessary. Does the Court care what those who wrote the fifth and fourteenth amendments meant by them? Should it?

See also the discussion of original intent in constitutional interpretation in Chapter 1, section B, supra, and in Chapter 6, section A, infra.

b. *"Today, education is perhaps the most important function of state and local governments."* Does this observation, even if correct, in any way advance the argument that segregated education is per se unconstitutional? Is *Brown* supported by the deep-seated view of U.S. public schools as a "secular, nationalizing, assimilationist agent [charged] with the task of Americanization, of melding backgrounds, and creating one nation"? A. Bickel, The Supreme Court and the Idea of Progress 121–122 (1970).

In a series of terse per curiam opinions handed down in the years immediately after *Brown*, the Court held segregation to be unconstitutional in a wide variety of other public facilities. See, e.g., Gayle v. Browder, 352 U.S. 903 (1956) (buses); Holmes v. City of Atlanta, 350 U.S. 879 (1955) (municipal golf courses); Mayor of Baltimore v. Dawson, 350 U.S. 877 (1955) (public beaches and bathhouses). In light of these decisions, is it possible to maintain that *Brown* rested on the special status of public education? *[handwritten margin note: on var/o effect of Brown]*

c. *"To separate [minority children] from others of similar age and qualifications solely because of their race generates a feeling of inferiority as to their status in the community that may affect their hearts and minds in a way unlikely ever to be undone."* Is stigma alone a sufficient injury to constitute a denial of equal protection? In *Bolling*, the Court observed that "[segregation] in public education is not reasonably related to any proper governmental objective, and thus it imposes on Negro children [a] burden that constitutes an arbitrary deprivation of their liberty."

Consider Black, The Lawfulness of the Segregation Decisions, 69 Yale L.J. 421, 424–426 (1960): "[Segregation was] set up and continued for the very purpose of keeping [blacks] in an inferior station. [This purpose was a] matter of common notoriety [not] so much for judicial notice as for background knowledge of educated men who live in the world." What accounts for the change from the Court's view in *Plessy* that any stigma was solely a subjective perception beyond the law's concern?

d. *"Segregation with the sanction of law [has] a tendency to [retard] the educational and mental development of Negro children."* *Brown*'s reliance on empirical social science data to support this conclusion has been the subject of continuing controversy. See, e.g., Cahn, Jurisprudence, 30 N.Y.U. L. Rev. 150 (1955); Van den Haag, Social Science Testimony in the Desegregation Cases — A Reply to Professor Kenneth Clark, 6 Vill. L. Rev. 69 (1960). See generally Symposium, The Courts, Social Science and School Desegregation, 39 Law & Contemp. Probs. 1 (Winter/Spring 1975). Indeed, it appears that "[virtually] everyone who has examined the question now agrees that the Court erred [in relying upon the social science data]. The proffered evidence was methodologically unsound." Yudof, School Desegregation: Legal Realism, Reasoned Elaboration, and Social Science Research in the Supreme Court, 42 Law & Contemp. Probs. 57, 70 (1978).

The conflict over the reliability of the data has tended to obscure more fundamental questions. Even if it could be demonstrated unambiguously that blacks perform better in an integrated than a segregated environment, why should that fact be constitutionally determinative? Does the Constitution require the arrangement that maximizes the achievement of black students?

Consider Justice Thomas's comments on the social science arguments for *Brown* in his concurring opinion in Missouri v. Jenkins, 515 U.S. 70 (1995):

> Segregation was not unconstitutional because it might have caused psychological feelings of inferiority. Public school systems that separated blacks and provided them with superior education resources — making blacks "feel" superior to whites sent to lesser schools — would violate the Fourteenth Amendment, whether or not the white students felt stigmatized, just as do school systems in which the positions of the races are reversed. Psychological injury or benefit is irrelevant to the question whether state actors have engaged in intentional discrimination — the critical inquiry for ascertaining violations of the Equal Protection Clause. The judiciary is fully competent to make independent determinations concerning the existence of state action without the unnecessary and misleading assistance of the social sciences.
>
> Regardless of the relative quality of the schools, segregation violated the Constitution because the State classified students based on their race. . . .
>
> "Racial isolation" itself is not a harm; only state-enforced segregation is. After all, if separation itself is a harm, and if integration therefore is the only way that blacks can receive a proper education, then there must be something inferior about blacks. Under this theory, segregation injures blacks because blacks, when left on their own, cannot achieve. To my way of thinking, that conclusion is the result of a jurisprudence based on a theory of black inferiority.

2. *Alternative perspectives.* One of the most widely cited pieces of constitutional law scholarship is Wechsler, Toward Neutral Principles of Constitutional Law, 73 Harv. L. Rev. 1 (1959). Wechsler's starting point is that courts function solely as an illegitimate "naked power organ" when they decide cases based solely on the identity of the parties before them. Judicial decisionmaking must rest on "neutral principles." Wechsler criticized the Supreme Court's decision in *Brown* for treating the problem as one of "discrimination":

> For me, assuming equal facilities, the problem is not one of discrimination at all. Its human and its constitutional dimensions lie entirely elsewhere, in the denial by the state of freedom to associate, a denial that impinges in the same way on any groups or races that may be involved. I think, and I hope not without foundation, that the Southern white also pays heavily for segregation, not only in the sense of guilt he must carry but also in the benefits he is denied. In the days when I was joined with Charles H. Houston in a litigation in the Supreme Court, before the present building was constructed, he did not suffer more than I in knowing that we had to go to Union Station to lunch together during the recess.

Id. at 34. Wechsler saw the "challenge" of *Brown* as discerning a neutral principle that required preferring the claim of black children who wished to associate with white children over the preference of segregationists who wished not to associate with blacks. For responses to Wechsler, see, e.g., Pollak, Racial Discrimination and Judicial Integrity: A Reply to Professor Wechsler, 108 U. Pa. L. Rev. 1 (1959); Black, The Lawfulness of the Segregation Decisions, supra. Consider the response in J. Ely, Democracy and Distrust 55 (1980): "[T]here are neutral principles of every hue. (How about 'No racial segregation, ever?')."

Consider how Wechsler's position relates to another influential critique of *Brown*. Bell, Brown v. Board of Education and the Interest-Convergence Dilemma, 93 Harv. L. Rev. 518, 524–525 (1980):

> [The] decision in *Brown* . . . cannot be understood without some consideration of the decision's value to whites [able] to see the economic and political advantages at home and abroad that would follow the abandonment of segregation. [*Brown* provided] immediate credibility to America's struggle with Communist countries to win the hearts and minds of emerging third world people [and] offered much needed reassurance to American blacks. [Moreover,] there were whites who realized that the South could make the transition from a rural, plantation society to the sunbelt with all its potential and profit only when it ended its struggle to remain divided by state-sponsored segregation.

If desegregation was really in the interest of the white majority, why did it have to be judicially imposed? To what extent does *Brown* reflect the views of a national elite, as opposed to a regional majority? See M. Dudziak, Cold War Civil Rights: Race and the Image of American Democracy (2000) (suggesting that the Cold War imperative played a major role in changing judicial attitudes); M. Klarman, supra; M. Tushnet, supra.

Finally, consider the following argument: Most critics of *Brown* have treated the decision as an unjustified assertion of judicial power. But *Brown* can be viewed instead as a product of the institutional *weakness* of the judiciary. Prior to *Brown*, the Court had committed itself to the position that separate educational facilities had to be equalized, and that the courts were duty bound to decide whether such equality actually existed. Might such a doctrine, by requiring the courts to evaluate the level of "equality" in thousands of segregated school systems throughout the country, have produced an even more serious judicial intrusion on the political branches than *Brown*? Compare J. Ely, Democracy and Distrust: A Theory of Judicial Review 124 (1980) (suggesting that considerations of administrability and fear of becoming embroiled in complex factual determinations about equality may underlie other seemingly expansive Warren Court decisions). Note that, even if you believe that segregated schools as they existed in the southern states in 1954 violated the equal protection clause, it does not follow that *Brown* was correctly decided. The hard question is why desegregation was the constitutionally required alternative to a judicially mandated regime of real equality.

Would black students have been better off had the *Brown* Court strongly enforced material equality, rather than mandating the end of de jure segregation? See D. Bell, Silent Covenants: Brown v. Board of Education and the Unfulfilled Hopes for Racial Reform (2004).

Consider the view that the decision to push for desegregation reflected the conclusion that a requirement of material equality in separate schools would never be enforced:

> The NAACP pushed for integration because it sought to force white-controlled state and local governments to provide a quality education and equal educational opportunity to black schoolchildren. The NAACP had tried for many years to push for educational rights through equalization suits. Equalization suits tried to enforce Plessy v. Ferguson's formula of "separate but equal" by requiring school districts to

provide black schoolchildren with educational opportunities and resources as good as those enjoyed by students in all-white schools. [Many] years of frustrating efforts demonstrated that the mandate of equal educational resources was too easy for state governments to evade. Thus, the NAACP sought to integrate the public schools in part on the theory that "green follows white." It believed that the white establishment would expend monetary resources and ensure quality education for black schoolchildren only if blacks were attending the same schools as the children of white parents. Integration would force whites to take into account the social costs that black children suffered from inferior educational opportunities by linking the fates of white and black schoolchildren together.

Balkin, What *Brown* Teaches Us about Constitutional Theory, 90 Va. L. Rev. 1537, 1570–1571 (2004).

3. *The meaning of* Brown. What precisely did *Brown* require southern school systems to do? Could that question be answered before the ambiguity as to *Brown's* reasoning was resolved? For example, if *Brown* was premised on the stigma associated with state-enforced segregation, then presumably a simple declaration that race would no longer be considered in school assignments would be sufficient. But if *Brown* meant that educational equality could be achieved only if blacks and whites attended school together, something more might be required. Finally, if *Brown* required that black and white children receive equal educations or that educational systems had to be structured to produce equal educational outcomes, the remedy might be more complex still.

The initial *Brown* opinion did not answer the remedy question. Instead, the Court restored the case to the docket for reargument. As you read the opinion that follows, think about whether the Court answered or avoided the substantive questions that remained after *Brown I.*

Brown v. Board of Education of Topeka (*Brown II*)
349 U.S. 294 (1955)

MR. CHIEF JUSTICE WARREN delivered the opinion of the Court.

These cases were decided on May 17, 1954. The opinions of that date, declaring the fundamental principle that racial discrimination in public education is unconstitutional, are incorporated herein by reference. All provisions of federal, state, or local law requiring or permitting such discrimination must yield to this principle. There remains for consideration the manner in which relief is to be accorded.

Because these cases arose under different local conditions and their disposition will involve a variety of local problems, we requested further argument on the question of relief. In view of the nationwide importance of the decision, we invited the Attorney General of the United States, and the Attorneys General of all states requiring or permitting racial discrimination in public education to present their views on that question. . . .

Full implementation of these constitutional principles may require solution of varied local school problems. School authorities have the primary responsibility for elucidating, assessing, and solving these problems; courts will have to consider whether the action of school authorities constitutes good faith implementation of the governing constitutional principles. Because of their proximity to local conditions and the possible need for further hearings, the courts which originally heard these cases can best perform this judicial appraisal. Accordingly, we believe it appropriate to remand the cases to those courts.

In fashioning and effectuating the decrees, the courts will be guided by equitable principles. Traditionally equity has been characterized by a practical flexibility in shaping its remedies and by a facility for adjusting and reconciling public and private needs. These cases call for the exercise of these traditional attributes of equity power. At stake is the personal interest of the plaintiffs in admission to public schools as soon as practicable on a nondiscriminatory basis. To effectuate this interest may call for elimination of a variety of obstacles in making the transition to school systems operated in accordance with the constitutional principles set forth in our May 17, 1954, decision. Courts of equity may properly take into account the public interest in the elimination of such obstacles in a systematic and effective manner. But it should go without saying that the vitality of these constitutional principles cannot be allowed to yield simply because of disagreement with them.

While giving weight to these public and private considerations, the courts will require that the defendants make a prompt and reasonable start toward full compliance with our May 17, 1954, ruling. Once such a start has been made, the courts may find that additional time is necessary to carry out the ruling in an effective manner. The burden rests upon the defendants to establish that such time is necessary in the public interest and is consistent with good faith compliance at the earliest practicable date. To that end, the courts may consider problems related to administration, arising from the physical condition of the school plant, the school transportation system, personnel, revision of school districts and attendance areas into compact units to achieve a system of determining admission to the public schools on a nonracial basis, and revision of local laws and regulations which may be necessary in solving the foregoing problems. They will also consider the adequacy of any plans the defendants may propose to meet these problems and to effectuate a transition to a racially nondiscriminatory school system. During this period of transition, the courts will retain jurisdiction of these cases.

The judgments below, except that in the Delaware case, are accordingly reversed and the cases are remanded to the District Courts to take such proceedings and enter such orders and decrees consistent with this opinion as are necessary and proper to admit to public schools on a racially non-discriminatory basis with all deliberate speed the parties to these cases. The judgment in the Delaware case — ordering the immediate admission of the plaintiffs to schools previously attended only by white children — is affirmed on the basis of the principles stated in our May 17, 1954, opinion, but the case is remanded to the Supreme Court of Delaware for such further proceedings as that Court may deem necessary in light of this opinion.

Note: "All Deliberate Speed"

Brown II's "all deliberate speed" formulation has been widely criticized. Consider the following arguments against the approach:

1. *If segregation is unconstitutional, the Court cannot legitimately tolerate continued segregation.* Given the fact that there were individual plaintiffs in the five consolidated cases before the Court, should the Court have simply ordered their admission to schools on a race-blind basis? Note that delay in

ordering a remedy would irreparably deprive the actual plaintiffs of the ability to attend a nonsegregated school.

2. Brown II *needlessly encouraged white resistance to desegregation by failing to demand an immediate remedy.* See, e.g., Black, The Unfinished Business of the Warren Court, 46 Wash. L. Rev. 3, 22 (1970). *Brown II* was followed by an extended period of "massive resistance" during which there was virtually no actual desegregation in the South. But the causal link between *Brown II* and the slow pace of desegregation is uncertain, and some have defended the decision on the ground that "any head-on challenge to the segregated South in 1955 would have produced civil strife sufficient to make Little Rock and Birmingham seem gatherings of good will." J. Wilkinson, From *Brown* to *Bakke* 68 (1979). What could the Court have done if an order for immediate desegregation had simply been defied? Note that in 1955 it was uncertain whether either the President or the Congress would support the Court if such an order were disobeyed.

Does *Brown II* prove that the Court "was a white court which would protect the interests of White America in the maintenance of stable institutions"? Steel, Nine Men in Black Who Think White, N.Y. Times Magazine, Oct. 13, 1968, at 112, col. 4. Or does the decision merely reflect the inherent limits of judicial power — limits that arguably influenced the formulation of the *Brown I* standard in the first place? See Gewirtz, Remedies and Resistance, 92 Yale L.J. 585 (1983).

3. Brown II *overstated the administrative difficulties of desegregation.* What precisely were the "varied local school problems" that might justify delay? Does the answer to that question depend in part on what *Brown I* required? If *Brown I* required no more than the repeal of laws prohibiting blacks from attending white schools, it is hard to see why this could not be accomplished instantly, or at least by the beginning of the next school year. Virtually every school system with more than one school, however, assigns individual pupils to particular schools. What administrative difficulties, if any, would reassigning students without taking race into account produce? If, however, *Brown I* required school boards to take affirmative steps to dismantle dual school systems and to produce actual integration, the process might be more complex. Did the Court act responsibly in authorizing a period of delay without specifying what was to be accomplished during that period?

4. *The Court acted unwisely in remitting the task of enforcement and elucidation of* Brown I *to the lower federal courts.* To the extent that difficulties were solely remedial and technical, it was perhaps appropriate to remand the cases to local federal judges familiar with local conditions. But could these courts be expected to devise appropriate remedies when the content of the right to be vindicated remained so vague? As the next Note indicates, *Brown II* was followed by an extended period during which the lower courts wrestled with the question of remedy in the face of intransigence and subterfuge. When, some fifteen years after *Brown II*, the Court finally returned to the question of rights, its views were crucially influenced by this remedial struggle.

4.   *The Meaning of* Brown

Note: *The Initial Response to* Brown

1. *Tokenism and massive resistance.* Suppose you were a southern governor in 1955 determined to minimize the impact of *Brown.* What policies would you

pursue? In retrospect, it seems at least possible that the immediate, good faith dismantling of the formal structure of segregation might have satisfied the courts while producing only minor disruption. Instead, *Brown* was greeted throughout the South with defiance and evasion. In the short term, this approach stymied judicial enforcement efforts. But in the longer term, the strategy had two unanticipated consequences. First, it helped to mobilize national political support for desegregation. Second, the long struggle to impose meaningful remedies in the face of "massive resistance" subtly influenced the way in which the fourteenth amendment was interpreted. See generally M. Klarman, From Jim Crow to Civil Rights: The Supreme Court and the Struggle for Racial Equality (2004).

Southern resistance took several different forms. In part, it was rhetorical. For example, most southern members of Congress signed the "Southern Manifesto" asserting the illegitimacy of *Brown* and the right of the states to ignore the decision. See 102 Cong. Rec. H3948, 4004 (daily ed. Mar. 12, 1956). Other southern politicians advanced their careers by vowing never to permit integration. In a number of communities, this verbal resistance was supplemented by intimidation and violence. And throughout the South, school districts devised a bewildering variety of legal strategies designed to slow or stop desegregation. A few communities, including one of the jurisdictions in a companion case to *Brown*, took the extreme measure of closing their public schools altogether to avoid desegregation. Others adopted complex pupil placement laws giving local officials discretion to place students in different schools on the basis of supposedly nonracial criteria. Still others adopted "freedom of choice" plans that assigned students to their old schools unless they applied for transfer, often subject to an intricate procedure. The common feature of all these plans was that they produced virtually no actual integration. For accounts of early efforts to circumvent *Brown*, see McKay, "With All Deliberate Speed," 31 N.Y.U. L. Rev. 991 (1956); Powe, The Road to *Swann:* Mobile County Crawls to the Bus, 51 Tex. L. Rev. 505 (1973). Some of the rhetoric from the period is collected in J. Wilkinson, From *Brown* to *Bakke* 69–74 (1979).

2. *The early judicial response.* The judicial response to these stratagems varied. Some courts upheld pupil placement, freedom of choice, and grade-per-year plans while others struck them down. In the face of massive community opposition, a few district court judges insisted on far-reaching and effective desegregation plans. See generally J. Peltason, Fifty-Eight Lonely Men (1971). But the more common judicial attitude toward *Brown* ranged from caution to outright hostility. In one widely quoted opinion written shortly after *Brown*, a district court held that *Brown* did not require "the states [to] mix persons of different races in the schools. [What] it has decided [is] that a state may not deny any person on account of race the right to attend any school that it maintains. [The] Constitution, in other words, does not require integration. [It] merely forbids the use of governmental power to enforce segregation." Briggs v. Elliott, 132 F. Supp. 776, 777 (E.D.S.C. 1955). Other judges read *Brown* even more narrowly. For example, one judge announced at the conclusion of a suit to desegregate the Dallas schools that "the white man has a right to maintain his racial integrity and it can't be done so easily in integrated schools. [We] will not name any date or issue any order." J. Peltason, supra, at 118–119. Overall, the pace of desegregation was painfully slow. By 1964, ten years after *Brown I*, only 2.3 percent of the black children in the South were attending desegregated schools. See Dunn, Title VI, the Guidelines, and School Desegregation in the South, 53 Va. L. Rev. 42, 44 n.9 (1967).

Despite the lack of uniformity and absence of progress, the Supreme Court remained almost entirely silent during this early period. It intervened only once — and then only in the face of outright defiance. Cooper v. Aaron, 358 U.S. 1 (1958), grew out of efforts to desegregate the Little Rock public school system. Pursuant to a plan developed by the Little Rock School Board, nine black children were scheduled to enroll in all-white Central High School at the start of the 1957 term. These plans were stymied by Arkansas Governor Orval Faubus, who ordered the Arkansas National Guard to block the entry of the children. The students were admitted only after President Eisenhower dispatched troops to enforce federal law. Under the protection of these troops and the federalized National Guard, the black students remained in Central High School through February 1958. The school board then sought permission from the federal district court to terminate the desegregation program because of the extreme public hostility. The district court granted the board's request, but the court of appeals reversed. In an extraordinary opinion, signed by all nine justices, the Supreme Court affirmed the court of appeals and ordered desegregation to proceed. The Court held that "the constitutional rights of respondents are not to be sacrificed or yielded to the violence and disorder which have followed upon the actions of the Governor and Legislature. [Law] and order are not here to be preserved by depriving the Negro children of their constitutional rights." In response to the Governor's assertion that he was not bound by Brown, the Court declared that "the federal judiciary is supreme in the exposition of the law of the Constitution," and that "the interpretation of the Fourteenth Amendment enunciated by this Court in the Brown case is the supreme law of the land."

3. *The end of deliberate speed.* Cooper v. Aaron was a powerful statement of judicial supremacy and an attack on outright defiance of Brown. It did little, however, to clarify the confusion concerning what Brown required. It was not until the early 1960s that the Court began to intervene more effectively and systematically to oversee the desegregation process. See Watson v. Memphis, 373 U.S. 526 (1963) (holding the "all deliberate speed" formulation inapplicable to segregated municipal recreation facilities and ordering immediate desegregation); Goss v. Board of Education, 373 U.S. 683 (1963) (invalidating "one-way transfer" plans permitting students to transfer from schools where they were in the racial minority to schools where they were in the majority); Griffin v. County School Board, 377 U.S. 218 (1964) (holding unconstitutional the closing of county schools to avoid desegregation).

The Court's renewed interest in the pace of school desegregation coincided with the reemergence for the first time since Reconstruction of an effective national political coalition supporting black equality. The changed political atmosphere resulted in part from extralegal events — in particular, "direct action" campaigns against southern segregation led by Martin Luther King and other civil rights activists. These campaigns, and the sometimes violent and brutal response that they engendered, helped to mobilize northern public opinion against segregation. See M. Klarman, supra, at 385–442.

An important turning point was passage of the Civil Rights Act of 1964, 42 U.S.C. §§2000a et seq. Although the most widely debated sections of the act prohibited racial discrimination in places of public accommodation, the act also had important provisions dealing with school desegregation. Title IV authorized the Attorney General to institute desegregation suits in the name of the United States, thereby ending the need to rely on individual lawsuits by private plaintiffs. More significantly, title VI established a parallel desegregation mechanism that avoided the necessity of lawsuits altogether. Racial discrimination was prohibited in any program receiving federal financial assistance — as most school systems throughout the nation did — and federal agencies were authorized to issue regulations enforcing this prohibition and to terminate funding upon non-compliance. Pursuant to this authority, the Department of Health, Education, and Welfare promulgated desegregation guidelines in 1966 that were considerably stiffer than the existing case law.

The guidelines were important not only because the threatened fund cutoff provided an impetus for desegregation but also because they allowed courts to escape from the morass of case-by-case litigation over individual desegregation plans. In a series of landmark decisions, the Fifth Circuit Court of Appeals used the guidelines to formulate model decrees, applicable throughout the circuit, which regulated every detail of the desegregation process. The percentage of southern black children attending desegregated schools jumped dramatically. For a discussion of the effect of the guidelines, see Note, The Courts, HEW, and Southern School Desegregation, 77 Yale L.J. 321 (1967).

What does this history suggest about the relative importance of legal and political forces in effecting social change? Consider Klarman, The Puzzling Resistance to Political Process Theory, 77 Va. L. Rev. 747, 813 (1991):

> [To] the extent that post-*Brown* Supreme Court decisions deserve even partial credit for the demise of southern school segregation, it is crucial to note that those decisions *post-dated* the emergence of a national political coalition committed to eliminating racial segregation and discrimination. [A] great deal of the school desegregation that ultimately flowed from *Brown* appears to have been more directly attributable to the intervention of a racially-enlightened national political process than to the Supreme Court.

Compare J. Greenberg, Crusaders in the Courts: How a Dedicated Band of Lawyers Fought for the Civil Rights Revolution 12 (1994) (arguing that *Brown* triggered the civil rights movement, which in turn produced civil rights legislation).

Four years after passage of the 1964 Civil Rights Act, the Court began dismantling the last barriers to desegregation in the rural South by questioning the "freedom of choice" plans widely used throughout the region. In Green v. County School Board, 391 U.S. 430 (1968), the Court invalidated a "freedom of choice" plan that the district had adopted to avoid loss of federal funds. The district had only two schools, one of which had been all-black and the other all-white prior to *Brown*. Since there was little residential segregation, a plan simply dividing the county in two would have created integrated schools. Instead, each pupil was required to choose between the two schools on entering first and eighth grades. Children in other grades were permitted to choose but were assigned to the school last attended if they made no choice. After the plan had been in effect for three years, 85 percent of the black children and none of the white children were attending the previously all-black school.

A unanimous Court held that this "freedom of choice" plan could not "be accepted as a sufficient step to 'effectuate a transition' to a unitary school system." Justice Brennan's opinion emphasized the Court's impatience at the pace of desegregation: "In determining whether [the board satisfied *Brown*] by adopting its 'freedom-of-choice' plan, it is relevant that this first step did not come until some 11 years after *Brown I* was decided and 10 years after *Brown II* directed the making of a 'prompt and reasonable start.' [The] burden on a school board today is to come forward with a plan that promises realistically to work, and promises realistically to work *now*."

The school board had an "affirmative duty to take whatever steps might be necessary to convert to a unitary system in which racial discrimination would be eliminated root and branch." The Court rejected the argument that adopting "freedom of choice" itself satisfied the board's constitutional obligation. Rather, "freedom of choice" had to be judged by its effectiveness as a means to achieve a unitary school system. The ultimate test was whether "the plan [promises] realistically to convert promptly to a system without a 'white' school and a 'Negro' school, but just schools."

Like most of the Court's pronouncements on school desegregation since *Brown II, Green* focused on the adequacy of remedy. Did the Court explain what *substantive* deprivation the board had failed to remedy? What made the *Green* school system nonunitary? As a practical matter, a network of formal and informal sanctions made black freedom wholly illusory under many "freedom of choice" plans. See, e.g., C. Curry, Silver Rights (1995) (describing how only one black family in Drew, Mississippi, was willing to send its children to the previously all-white schools and the difficulties the children faced). But *Green* did not rely on the illusory nature of the choice in invalidating the plan. Rather, it seems to have rested on some combination of prior, formal segregation and current results. The *Green* Court hinted that on the facts of the case, a plan for neighborhood schools would have made the system "unitary." In *Green*, and in much of the rural South, neighborhood schools would have produced substantial integration. But would a neighborhood school system be "unitary" in urban areas, where residential segregation patterns would be mirrored in school populations?

4. *Busing and the problem of race-conscious remedies.* The Court provided some answers to these questions in Swann v. Charlotte-Mecklenburg Board of Education, 402 U.S. 1 (1971). The case arose in a school district that had been segregated by law prior to 1954. Although geographic zoning and free transfers were introduced in 1965, in 1968 over half of the black students were still attending schools that were at least 99 percent black. In order to deal with this problem, the district court adopted a new plan that took race into account in drawing school zones and bused students between inner-city and suburban schools. In a unanimous opinion by Chief Justice Burger, the Supreme Court affirmed this order. Emphasizing the scope and flexibility of equitable remedies, the Court held that mathematical ratios and race-conscious assignments could be a useful starting point in fashioning relief. It also endorsed the busing of students outside their neighborhoods as "one tool of school desegregation." On the other hand, the Court emphasized that "[the] constitutional command to desegregate schools does not mean that every school in every community must always reflect the racial composition of the school system as a whole." And it warned that

> [absent] a constitutional violation there would be no basis for judicially ordering assignment of students on a racial basis. . . .
>
> At some point, these school authorities and others like them should have achieved full compliance with the Court's decision in *Brown I*. The systems will then be "unitary" in the sense required by our decisions. . . .
>
> Neither school authorities nor district courts are constitutionally required to make year-by-year adjustments of the racial composition of student bodies once the affirmative duty to desegregate has been [accomplished].

Swann thus articulated three principles that were to guide later school desegregation cases: first, that the constitutional violation stemmed from purposeful state manipulation of schools' racial composition; second, that the scope of judicial power was limited by the scope of the constitutional violation; and third, that once a school district achieved "unitary" status, judicial intervention should cease.

Note: The De Jure/De Facto Distinction and Limits on Courts' Remedial Powers

Swann was the last major desegregation decision that was entirely "southern" in its orientation. It thus ended an era begun with *Brown II*. In one sense, the Court's efforts to desegregate the South were stunningly successful. The Court's studied ambiguity concerning the scope of *Brown I* provided it with the flexibility to respond to each of the subterfuges advanced to defeat desegregation. Moreover, the "all deliberate speed" formulation allowed the Court to avoid defeat when significant progress was not politically feasible and then to push ahead when a coalition for change finally emerged. The results of this strategy speak for themselves: By 1971, 44 percent of the black students in the South attended majority white schools, compared to only 28 percent in the North and West. See 18 Cong. Rec. S564 (daily ed. Jan. 20, 1972) (remarks of Sen. Stennis). Much of this success was a product of demography: In rural areas, desegregation was easier to accomplish because, although residential segregation existed, the pattern did not involve large population concentrations; thus, any non-race-conscious geographic assignment of pupils was likely to produce desegregated schools. Some of it was an accident of history: The school system in *Swann*, for example, had consolidated inner-city urban and suburban school districts before *Brown* and thus it was relatively difficult for white families to leave the school system as it desegregated.

But although schools in the North were rarely segregated by statute — at least by the time *Brown* was decided — substantial numbers of black and Latino schoolchildren nonetheless attended monoracial schools. Starting in the 1970s, the Court confronted the question whether this situation violated the equal protection clause and, if it did, what remedial options were available.

1. Keyes *and the nature of the violation.* In Keyes v. School District No. 1, 413 U.S. 189 (1973), the Court considered the lawfulness of school segregation in Denver, Colorado, a northern city that had never mandated segregated education by statute. The district court found that the school board had deliberately segregated schools in the Park Hill section of the city through use of gerrymandered attendance zones and similar devices. Although the district court ordered desegregation of the Park Hill schools, it held that the finding of purposeful segregation in this area did not require the board to remedy racial imbalances in other areas of the city. The court of appeals affirmed this portion of the district court's order, but the Supreme Court, in an opinion by Justice Brennan, reversed and held that systemwide relief might be appropriate.

The Court assumed that plaintiffs bore the burden of establishing that segregated schools had been brought about or maintained by intentional state action. However, once such a showing had been made with regard to a substantial portion of the system, plaintiffs were not required to show deliberate segregation as to each school within the school system.

"[Common] sense dictates the conclusion that racially inspired school board actions have an impact beyond the particular schools that are subject to those actions." Although there might be "rare" cases where the effect of discriminatory conduct was isolated, in the more usual case proof of unlawful segregation in a substantial portion of a district was sufficient to support a finding of the existence of a dual school system, with a corresponding affirmative duty to dismantle segregated schools.

Justice Powell, the only white southerner then on the Court — and the former chairman of the Richmond, Virginia, school board from 1952 to 1961 — concurred in part and dissented in part:

> The situation in Denver is generally comparable to that in other large cities across the country in which there is a substantial minority population and where desegregation has not been ordered by the federal courts. There is segregation in the schools of many of these cities fully as pervasive as that in southern cities prior to the desegregation decrees of the past decade and a half. The focus of the school desegregation problem has now shifted from the South to the country as a whole. Unwilling and footdragging as the process was in most places, substantial progress toward achieving integration has been made in Southern States. No comparable progress has been made in many nonsouthern cities with large minority populations primarily because of the de facto/de jure distinction nurtured by the courts and accepted complacently by many of the same voices which denounced the evils of segregated schools in the South. But if our national concern is for those who attend such schools, rather than for perpetuating a legalism rooted in history rather than present reality, we must recognize that the evil of operating separate schools is no less in Denver than in Atlanta. . . .
>
> In my view we should abandon a distinction which long since has outlived its time, and formulate constitutional principles of national rather than merely regional application. . . .
>
> Whereas *Brown I* rightly decreed the elimination of state-imposed segregation in that particular section of the country where it did exist, *Swann* imposed obligations on southern school districts to eliminate conditions which are not regionally unique but are similar both in origin and effect to conditions in the rest of the country. [I] would hold, quite simply, that where segregated public schools exist within a school district to a substantial degree, there is a prima facie case that the duly constituted public authorities [are] sufficiently responsible to warrant imposing upon them a nationally applicable burden to demonstrate they nevertheless are operating a genuinely integrated school system. [This] means that school authorities, consistent with the generally accepted educational goal of attaining quality education for all pupils, must make and implement their customary decisions with a view toward enhancing integrated school opportunities. . . .
>
> Public schools are creatures of the State, and whether the segregation is state-created or state-assisted or merely state-perpetuated should be irrelevant to constitutional principle. The school board exercises pervasive and continuing responsibility over the long-range planning as well as the daily operations of the public school system. [School] board decisions obviously are not the sole cause of segregated school conditions. But if, after such detailed and complete public supervision, substantial school segregation still persists, the presumption is strong that the school board, by its acts or omissions, is in some part responsible. . . .

Although Justice Powell would thus have expanded the predicates for liability, he was more restrictive than the majority with respect to the courts' remedial powers. "Where desegregative steps are possible within the framework of a system of 'neighborhood education,' school authorities must pursue them," but he disapproved of "extensive student transportation solely to achieve integration" because it "infringes on what may fairly be regarded as other important community aspirations and personal rights."

Justice Rehnquist dissented on the ground that courts should not assume that a finding of manipulation with respect to a few attendance zones transformed all segregation within a school system into a constitutional violation justifying judicial intervention.

2. *Political and demographic factors.* The late 1960s and early 1970s were a time of tremendous political unrest. As the civil rights movement turned its attention to racial discrimination in the North and desegregation litigation occurred nationwide, the national consensus in support of desegregation began to wane. In 1968, for example, Richard Nixon, while seeking the presidential nomination, told southern Republican leaders that he thought "all deliberate speed" required reinterpretation, and that he opposed compulsory busing of students. See T. White, The Making of the President: 1968, at 137–138 (1969). When President Nixon assumed office, the Justice Department for the first time since 1954 intervened on behalf of a southern school board to seek additional time for desegregation. After *Swann,* Congress enacted legislation purporting to limit the use of busing as a remedy for desegregation.

This upsurge in political opposition to desegregation coincided with renewed doubts about the ability of courts to bring about integrated schools. Effective desegregation requires as a starting point the presence of both white and minority students within the pool of students being assigned to schools. While in 1954 many urban school districts, in both the South and the North, were majority-white, by the time real attempts at desegregation began in the 1970s, many of these districts were overwhelmingly black. Thus, it might be impossible to create integrated schools by simply reassigning students within a single district. Moreover, a phenomenon referred to as the "tipping point" made it even more difficult to achieve stable integration: as the proportion of black students within a particular school increased, white students might abandon the school with increasing velocity.

The extent to which court-ordered desegregation or the anticipation of court-ordered desegregation in fact caused whites to abandon urban public schools has been hotly debated in the social science literature. Compare, e.g., J. Coleman, S. Kelly, and J. Moore, Trends in School Segregation 1968–73 (1975), with Pettigrew and Green, School Desegregation in Large Cities: A Critique of the Coleman "White Flight" Thesis, 46 Harv. Educ. Rev. 1 (1976). See also G. Orfield, The Growth of Segregation in American Schools: Changing Patterns of Separation and Poverty since 1968, at 6 (1994) (concluding that "[the] great increase in the proportion of non-white students has not been a consequence of 'white flight' [but] the product of huge changes in birth rates and immigration patterns," and that "there has been no significant redistribution between the sectors of American education"). It is beyond dispute, however, that for whatever reason, the percentage of whites in many urban public schools declined.

3. *The Court's response.* How should the Court have responded to these new challenges to desegregation? In the 1960s, the Court had bravely announced that political opposition and "white flight" were no excuse for avoiding constitutional requirements. For example, in Monroe v. Board of Commissioners, 391 U.S. 450 (1968), a companion case to *Green,* the school board defended its "free transfer" plan on the ground that it was necessary to prevent whites from leaving the system altogether. A unanimous Court rejected the argument, citing *Brown II* for the

proposition that "[the] vitality of these constitutional principles cannot be allowed to yield simply because of disagreement with them." See also United States v. Scotland Neck City Board of Education, 407 U.S. 484, 490–491 (1972).

Some critics argued that this approach was simply unrealistic. Consider L. Graglia, Disaster by Decree 82 (1976): "Insistence on principle and legality in the face of threatened lawlessness can be justified even where great immediate costs are involved, but to ignore the existence of perfectly legal means of avoiding a requirement is to bury one's head in the sand." Compare Gewirtz, Remedies and Resistance, 92 Yale L.J. 585, 661 (1983): "[Realism] can be a dangerous aspiration for people, such as judges or law professors, who are often accused of not being realistic enough. Newly initiated into the jurisprudence of limitation, judges may become too realistic, taking reality to be more resistant than it is."

Whether justified or not, the Court (newly reconstituted with ten appointments by Republican Presidents, and none by Democratic Presidents, between 1969 and 1992) began to restrict the scope of constitutionally mandated desegregation.

a. *Interdistrict relief.* In Milliken v. Bradley, 418 U.S. 717 (1974) (*Milliken I*), the Court held that federal courts lack the power to impose interdistrict remedies for school segregation absent an interdistrict violation or interdistrict effects. After a lengthy trial, the district court found that the by-then overwhelmingly black Detroit school system had been deliberately segregated by school board decisions, and that any Detroit-only remedy "would make the Detroit school system more identifiably black [thereby] increasing the flight of whites from the city and the system." Consequently, the court ordered a desegregation plan encompassing fifty-three suburban school districts surrounding Detroit. The court of appeals affirmed after noting that "any less comprehensive [solution would] result in an all black school system immediately surrounded by practically all white suburban school systems, with an overwhelmingly white majority population in the local metropolitan area."

The Court, in an opinion by Chief Justice Burger, reversed. The Court rejected the "notion that school district lines may be casually ignored or treated as a mere administrative convenience. [No] single tradition in public education is more deeply rooted than local control over the operation of schools." To be sure, in cases where boundaries between school districts were deliberately drawn to create segregated school systems, a federal court could order a remedy that included reassigning pupils across district boundaries or redrawing school district boundaries. But the fact that a single school district had engaged in purposeful racial segregation did not authorize the federal courts to reach into adjacent districts.

The Court's conclusions in *Milliken I* were unaffected by the fact that the state of Michigan had exercised substantial control over the activity of local school districts, and that state agencies had participated in the deliberate segregation of the Detroit schools. Despite this state activity, "[disparate] treatment of white and Negro students occurred within the Detroit school system, and not elsewhere, and on this record the remedy must be limited to that system."

In a dissenting opinion that was joined by Justices Douglas, Brennan, and White, Justice Marshall complained that the Court had rendered the district judge

powerless to require the State to remedy its constitutional violation in any meaningful fashion. Ironically purporting to base its result on the principle that the scope of the remedy in a desegregation case should be determined by the nature and extent of the constitutional violation, the Court's answer is to provide no remedy at all for the violation proved in this case, thereby guaranteeing that Negro children in Detroit will receive the same separate and inherently unequal education in the future as they have been unconstitutionally afforded in the past.

b. *Intradistrict remediation.* On remand in *Milliken I*, the district court confronted the task of attempting to desegregate a school system that was approximately 70 percent black. The court rejected a plan that would have created a racial composition within each school that reflected the overall racial balance within the Detroit system — a plan that, inter alia, would have required busing large numbers of minority students from one majority-black school to another. Instead, the court ordered a plan providing each black student with at least some number of years in a racially integrated school and that also required extensive educational reform, including remedial education, counseling, and career guidance. In Milliken v. Bradley, 433 U.S. 267 (1977) (*Milliken II*), the Supreme Court affirmed. The Court rejected the notion that desegregation remedies were limited to pupil assignment and held that a district judge could order the expenditure of state funds for remedial education as part of an effort to place victims of unconstitutional conduct in the position they would have enjoyed but for the violation. Taken together, do *Milliken I* and *II* represent a turning away from *Brown* and a return to the "separate but equal" philosophy? Has the Court resolved the difficulties with that philosophy that caused its abandonment in the first place? What does it mean to say that but for unconstitutional school segregation, the plaintiffs would have attended schools with greater resources? In short, what is the connection between the remedy offered and the violation found?

The Court confronted this question repeatedly in the long-running Kansas City, Missouri, school desegregation case. After finding that the Kansas City public schools were unconstitutionally segregated, a district judge ordered a sweeping remedy designed to create "magnet schools" that would attract white children into the district as well as enhance the educational opportunities of black students already in the system. Ultimately, in Missouri v. Jenkins, 515 U.S. 70 (1995), the Court substantially restricted the power of district courts to order *Milliken II*–type remedies. At issue was a district court order mandating salary increases for instructional and non-instructional staff within the school district. The state argued that this order exceeded the district court's remedial authority because it was designed to serve the interdistrict goal of attracting white students from surrounding school districts. In a five-to-four decision, the Court, in an opinion by Chief Justice Rehnquist, agreed. Moreover, the Court expressed strong disagreement with the district court's position that a variety of educational enhancements were appropriate because achievement scores within the Kansas City district continued to lag behind those of adjacent suburban districts. The Court rejected the idea that those achievement differentials could be causally connected to the constitutional violation the district had committed in engaging in de jure segregation many years earlier.

c. *Resegregation and "unitary" status.* In a series of cases decided since the mid-1970s, the Court disapproved efforts by the lower courts to prevent resegregation and suggested guidelines for districts attempting to achieve unitary status. See Pasadena Board of Education v. Spangler, 427 U.S. 424 (1976) (disapproving lower court order requiring annual readjustment of school boundaries); Board of

Education of Oklahoma City Public Schools v. Dowell, 498 U.S. 237 (1991) (holding that a district would achieve unitary status upon a showing that it was "[operating] in compliance with the commands of the Equal Protection Clause [and] that it was unlikely that [it] would return to its former ways"); Freeman v. Pitts, 503 U.S. 467 (1992) (holding that "federal courts have the authority to relinquish supervision and control of school districts in incremental stages, before full compliance has been achieved in every area of school operations"). In the Charlotte-Mecklenburg schools that were the focus of the *Swann* litigation, this resulted in the lower federal courts ultimately holding not only that the school system had reached unitary status, but that the achievement of unitary status precluded even *voluntary* attempts by the school board to continue using race-conscious assignment practices to preserve racial integration. See Mickelson, The Academic Consequences of Desegregation and Segregation: Evidence from the Charlotte-Mecklenburg Schools, 81 N.C. L. Rev. 1513, 1521–1525 (2003).

Just as a decade elapsed between the Supreme Court's decision in *Brown* and its next significant intervention into public schools' pupil assignment policies, another decade elapsed between *Jenkins* and the court's next foray into school desegregation. This time, however, the Court addressed not the question of whether *courts* could compel school districts to use race-conscious student assignment to cure a constitutional violation, but whether *local school boards* could voluntarily use race-conscious student assignment policies to produce racially integrated schools in the absence of a constitutional violation. The Court's response in Parents Involved in Community Schools v. Seattle School District No. 1, 551 U.S. 701 (2007), rested not only on the line of cases decided following *Brown* but also on parallel developments in equal protection jurisprudence that occurred outside the context of public education. Accordingly, that opinion appears at pages 616-632, infra.

4. *The efficacy of judicial intervention.* What does the Court's long struggle to define and implement the principle of racial equality reveal about the efficacy of judicial review? Has the Court been able to achieve the objectives it established in *Brown*?

These questions raise difficult issues about the extent to which the Court can control social, historical, and political forces and the extent to which it is controlled by them. Many scholars have concluded that *Brown* was instrumental in sparking the civil rights movement. See, e.g., Gill, The Shaping of Race Relations by the Federal Judiciary in Court Decisions, 11 Negro Educ. Rev. 15, 15–16 (1960) ("It is clear that official action to improve the condition of the Negro minority probably would never have been taken in many instances had it not been for the Federal Courts."). See generally sources collected in Klarman, Civil Rights Law: Who Made It and How Much Did It Matter?, 83 Geo. L.J. 433, 452 n.91 (1994).

Much recent literature has been more skeptical, however. For example, in The Hollow Hope: Can Courts Bring about Social Change? 157 (1991), Gerald Rosenberg concludes that there is "little evidence that the judicial system [produced] much of the massive change in civil rights that swept the United States in the 1960s. [While] we can never know what would have happened if the Court had not acted as it did [the] existence and strength of pro–civil rights forces at least suggest that change would have occurred [without judicial intervention], albeit at a pace unknown." M. Klarman, From Jim Crow to Civil Rights: The Supreme Court and the Struggle for Racial Equality (2004) (elaborating on the relationship between *Brown,* southern resistance, and national support for civil rights).

Is there a plausible argument that *Brown* actually *weakened* the civil rights movement? Rosenberg suggests that civil rights litigation "siphon[ed] off crucial resources and talent [thereby] weakening political efforts":

> A further danger of litigation as a strategy for significant social reform is that symbolic victories may be mistaken for substantive ones, covering a reality that is distasteful. Rather than working to change that reality, reformers relying on a litigation strategy for reform may be misled (or content?) to celebrate the illusion of change.

Rosenberg, supra, at 340. See also Seidman, *Brown* and *Miranda,* 80 Cal. L. Rev. 673, 717 (1992):

> It came to be seen that the *Brown* Court offered the country a kind of deal, and, from the perspective of defenders of the status quo, not a bad one at that. Prior to *Brown* [contradictions] in the ideology of the separate-but-equal doctrine were permanently destabilizing and threatened any equilibrium.
>
> By purporting to resolve those contradictions, *Brown* also served to end their destabilizing potential. The Court resolved the contradictions by definitional fiat: separate facilities were now simply proclaimed to be inherently unequal. But the flip side of this aphorism was that once white society was willing to make facilities legally nonseparate, the demand for equality had been satisfied and blacks no longer had just cause for complaint. The mere existence of *Brown* thus served [to] legitimate current arrangements. True, many blacks remained poor and disempowered. But their status was now no longer a result of the denial of equality. Instead, it marked a personal failure to take advantage of one's definitionally equal status.

There is similar controversy about how much change was actually achieved, whatever its cause. The Court has been overwhelmingly successful in removing legally mandated segregation. The results in terms of actual integration are more mixed, however. Progress was substantial in the South during the 1960s and 1970s, but in 1988 the trend reversed itself, and since then segregation has risen substantially. While only 23 percent of black students in the South attended hypersegregated schools in 1980 (that is, schools that were more than 90 percent minority), by 2014, nearly 36 percent of black students were in such schools. See Frankenberg, Hawley, Ee, and Orfield, Southern Schools: More Than a Half Century After the Civil Rights Revolution 8 (May 2017).

Finally, even in schools that are formally integrated, the interracial contact envisioned by *Brown* has frequently not materialized. Thus, a significant percentage of blacks attending integrated schools are assigned to segregated, or substantially segregated, classrooms. See Fulfilling the Letter and Spirit of the Law: Desegregation of the Nation's Public Schools 233–234 (U.S. Commission on Civil Rights 1976). Indeed, "tracking" schemes and assignment of black children to special education programs in disproportionate numbers may have aggravated the sense of inferiority *Brown* was designed to combat. See G. Orfield, How to Make Desegregation Work: The Adaptation of Schools to Their Newly Integrated Bodies 327–328 (1976); see also J. Oakes, Keeping Track: How Schools Structure Inequality (2d ed. 2005).

If one asks whether integration, where it has occurred, has produced equal educational opportunity, the evidence is even more mixed. While there is no proof that integration has reduced white achievement levels, neither is there conclusive proof that it has aided blacks in any demonstrable fashion. See, e.g., St. John, The Effects of Desegregation on Children, in Yarmolinsky, Liebman, and Schelling, Race and Schooling in the City 85–102 (1981); Armor, The Evidence on Busing, Pub. Interest 90 (Summer 1972). But see Mickelson, The Academic Consequences of Desegregation and Segregation: Evidence from the Charlotte-Mecklenburg Schools, 81 N.C. L. Rev. 1513, 1546 (2003) (concluding on the bases of regression analyses conducted within the Charlotte-Mecklenburg school system that the more time both black and white students spend in desegregated elementary schools, the higher their standardized test scores in middle and high school, and the higher their track placements in secondary school); Schofield and Hausmann, The Conundrum of School Desegregation: Positive Student Outcomes and Waning Support, 66 U. Pitt. L. Rev. 83 (2004) (summarizing twenty years of social science research that suggests early integration is beneficial to black and white students, particularly by long-range social and academic measures and criticizing the reasons for abandoning it).

What if one asks, more broadly still, whether the Court has succeeded in implementing the great aims of the Reconstruction amendments — healing the wounds of slavery and integrating blacks into the mainstream of U.S. life?

Consider the following argument: *Brown* was a great success. Before *Brown*, it was constitutionally legitimate in our society for government to legislate the separation of the races. *Brown* put an end to the most degrading and most humiliating form of discrimination — state-sponsored, legally enforced racial separation. Moreover, *Brown* opened the door to the civil rights movement. In so doing, the Court took a critical first step toward forming the political coalition that produced the civil rights legislation of the 1960s. Whether or not *Brown* succeeded in transforming the education system, it triggered the desegregation of public facilities generally.

Compare with this optimistic view the following summary, which Derrick Bell puts into the mouth of his fictional heroine Geneva Crenshaw:

> [Because] the Supreme Court is unable or unwilling to recognize and remedy the real losses resulting from long-held, race-based, subordinated status, the relief the Court has been willing to grant, while welcome, proves of less value than expected and exacts the exorbitant price of dividing the black community along economic lines. . . .
>
> [There] seems little doubt that abandonment of overtly discriminatory policies has lowered racial barriers for some talented and skilled blacks seeking access to opportunity and advancement. Even their upward movement is, however, pointed to by much of the society as the final proof that racism is dead — a too hasty pronouncement which dilutes the achievement of those who have moved ahead and denies even society's sympathy to those less fortunate blacks whose opportunities and life fortunes are less promising today than they were twenty-five years ago.

D. Bell, And We Are Not Saved 48–49 (1987). See also D. Bell, Silent Covenants: Brown v. Board of Education and the Unfulfilled Hopes for Racial Reform (2004) (suggesting that blacks in America would be better off if the Supreme Court had retained, but had vigorously enforced, requirements of separate but equal).

Which of these views is most consistent with statistics concerning the current status of blacks in U.S. society? Blacks have made great strides in educational achievement since *Brown*. See H. Levin, Education and Earnings of Blacks and the *"Brown"* Decision 12 (1981). As recently as 1970, only 31 percent of African-American adults had completed four years of high school, as compared to 54 percent of white adults. By 2015, 87 percent of blacks and 93.3 percent of non-Hispanic whites had completed high school. See U.S. Bureau of the Census Educational Attainment in the United States: 2015, table 1.

Still, educational gains have not been uniformly translated into economic progress. In the second quarter of 2017, the total U.S. unemployment rate was 4.2 percent, while the black unemployment rate was 7.3 percent. U.S. Dep't of Labor, Bureau of Labor Statistics, Labor Force Statistics from the Current Population Survey (2017). Black median household income remains less than sixty percent of white household income. See U.S. Bureau of the Census, Income and Poverty in the United States: 2015, table 1. And the poverty rate for blacks is still more than double the rate for non-Hispanic whites. Id., table 3.

Do these statistics provide appropriate criteria by which to judge the Court's work? If not, what criteria would you suggest? In reviewing the Court's performance from before the Civil War through the modern desegregation controversies, think about the extent to which the Court has been able to function as an effective alternative power center for dealing with the race question. Has the Court's effectiveness been hampered (augmented?) by the necessity of formulating public policy through the litigation process? By the obligation to write opinions tying its conclusions to the constitutional text?

B. EQUAL PROTECTION METHODOLOGY: RATIONAL BASIS REVIEW

Despite the Supreme Court's prediction in The Slaughter-House Cases, 83 U.S. (16 Wall.) 36 (1873), that it "[doubted] very much whether any action of a State not directed by way of discrimination against the negroes as a class, or on account of their race, will ever be held to come within the purview of [the equal protection clause,]" see pages 476-477, supra, the equal protection clause has become a major doctrinal tool for analyzing controversies unrelated to race. (Indeed, Justice Oliver Wendell Holmes once referred to it as the "last resort of constitutional arguments." Buck v. Bell, 274 U.S. 200, 208 (1927).)

This section and the following sections examine the general methodology courts use to resolve equal protection disputes. Broadly speaking, equal protection claims involve a challenge to laws that allocate benefits or impose burdens on a defined class of individuals. (While it is possible to have a "class of one," see Village of Willowbrook v. Olech, 528 U.S. 562 (2000), discussed at page 529, infra, laws generally define classes more broadly.) The plaintiff in an equal protection case claims that the government has drawn the line between the favored and disfavored groups in an impermissible place. But the fact of treating individuals differently cannot invariably give rise to an equal protection violation: Such an approach would make government impossible, since nearly all government actions classify individuals. For example, a law that sets the driving age at sixteen treats fifteen-year-olds and seventeen-year olds differently, classifying on the basis of age, while a decision to set the passing score for the bar examination at 75 treats applicants who scored 74 differently from those who scored 76, classifying on the basis of test performance. Thus, the real question in equal protection cases involves deciding whether, under particular circumstances, a challenged classification is permissible. In addressing that issue, the Court's approach has focused on three basic questions: First, how has the government defined the group being benefited or burdened (the question of "means")? Second, what is the goal the government is pursuing (the question of "ends")? Third, is there a sufficient connection between the means the government is using and the ends it is pursuing (the question of "fit" or "nexus")?

The modern Supreme Court has largely analyzed these questions within a framework of "tiers." Normally, a reviewing court asks whether the line the government has drawn is related in a discernible way to the achievement of a permissible government purpose. This form of scrutiny, called rationality review, is generally quite deferential. But when the line the government has drawn is constitutionally troublesome — for reasons we shall examine later in this chapter — the level of judicial review is ratcheted up: The government may use constitutionally suspect classifications only when their use is more tightly tied to achieving a really significant government objective. To some extent, the tier of scrutiny a court applies can be outcome determinative: Policies that satisfy the default standard of rationality review might run afoul of the more demanding standards applied in cases involving suspect classifications. Thus, in reading the following materials, you should consider two major questions: How does the Court decide which form of scrutiny to apply and, having made that decision, how does the Court apply the form of scrutiny it has chosen?

New York City Transit Authority v. Beazer
440 U.S. 568 (1979)

MR. JUSTICE STEVENS delivered the opinion of the Court.

The New York City Transit Authority refuses to employ persons who use methadone. The District Court found that this policy violates the Equal Protection Clause of the Fourteenth Amendment. [The] Court of Appeals affirmed. [We] now reverse.

[A New York City Transit Authority (TA) rule prohibited employment of persons who use narcotic drugs. TA applied the rule to persons receiving methadone — a synthetic narcotic that, when taken orally, blocks the effect of heroin. The drug is widely used in the treatment of heroin addiction.]

The trial record contains extensive evidence concerning the success of methadone maintenance programs, the employability of persons taking methadone, and the ability of prospective employers to detect drug abuse or other undesirable characteristics of methadone users. In general, the District Court concluded that there are substantial numbers of methadone users who are just as employable as other members of the general population and that normal personnel-screening procedures — at least if augmented by some method of obtaining information from the staffs of methadone programs — would enable TA to identify the unqualified applicants on an individual basis. On the other hand, the District Court recognized that at least one-third of the persons receiving methadone treatment — and probably a good many more — would unquestionably be classified as unemployable.

[The District Court concluded that because] it is clear that substantial numbers of methadone users are capable of performing many of the jobs at TA, [the] Constitution will not tolerate a blanket exclusion of all users from all jobs.

The District Court enjoined TA from denying employment to any person solely because of participation in a methadone maintenance program. Recognizing, however, the special responsibility for public safety borne by certain TA employees and the correlation between longevity in a methadone maintenance program and performance capability, the injunction authorized TA to exclude methadone users from specific categories of safety-sensitive positions and also to condition eligibility on satisfactory performance in a methadone program for at least a year. In other words, the court held that TA could lawfully adopt general rules excluding all methadone users from some jobs and a large number of methadone users from all jobs. . . .

At its simplest, the District Court's conclusion was that TA's rule is broader than necessary to exclude those methadone users who are not actually qualified to work for TA. We may assume not only that this conclusion is correct but also that it is probably unwise for a large employer like TA to rely on a general rule instead of individualized consideration of every job applicant. But these assumptions concern matters of personnel policy that do not implicate the principle safeguarded by the Equal Protection Clause. As the District Court recognized, the special classification created by TA's rule serves the general objectives of safety and efficiency.[9]

[Because] the exclusionary line challenged by respondents . . . does not circumscribe a class of persons characterized by some unpopular trait or affiliation, it does not create or reflect any special likelihood of bias on the part of the ruling majority. Under these circumstances, it is of no constitutional significance that the degree of rationality is not as great with respect to certain ill-defined subparts of the classification as it is with respect to the classification as a whole.

No matter how unwise it may be for TA to refuse employment to individual car cleaners, track repairmen, or bus drivers simply because they are receiving methadone treatment, the Constitution does not authorize a federal court to interfere in that policy decision.

[Justice Powell's opinion, concurring in part and dissenting in part, and Justice Brennan's dissenting statement are omitted.]

MR. JUSTICE WHITE, with whom MR. JUSTICE MARSHALL joins, dissenting. . . .

The question before us is the rationality of placing successfully maintained or recently cured persons in the same category as those just attempting to escape heroin addiction or who have failed to escape it, rather than in with the general population. The asserted justification for the challenged classification is the objective of a capable and reliable work force, and thus the characteristic in question is employability. . . . Employability, as the District Court used it in reference to successfully maintained methadone users, means only that the employer is no more likely to find a member of that group to be an unsatisfactory employee than he would an employee chosen from the general population.

---

9. "[L]egislative classifications are valid unless they bear no rational relationship to the State's objectives. Massachusetts Bd. of Retirement v. Murgia, [427 U.S. 307, 314]. State legislation 'does not violate the Equal Protection Clause merely because the classifications [it makes] are imperfect.' Dandridge v. Williams, 397 U.S. 471, 485." Washington v. Yakima Indian Nation, 439 U.S. 463, 501–502. . . .

[TA] had every opportunity, but presented nothing to negative the employ-ability of successfully maintained methadone users. . . .

The District Court found that the fact of successful participation for one year could be discovered through petitioners' normal screening process without additional effort and, I repeat, that those who meet that criterion are no more likely than the average applicant to turn out to be poor employees. Accordingly, the rule's classification of successfully maintained persons as dispositively different from the general population is left without any justification and, with its irrationality and invidiousness thus uncovered, must fall before the Equal Protection Clause.[15]

Finally, even were the District Court wrong, and even were successfully maintained persons marginally less employable than the average applicant, the blanket exclusion of only these people, when but a few are actually unemployable and when many other groups have varying numbers of unemployable members, is arbitrary and unconstitutional. Many persons now suffer from or may again suffer from some handicap related to employability. But petitioners have singled out respondents — unlike ex-offenders, former alcoholics and mental patients, diabetics, epileptics, and those currently using tranquilizers, for example — for sacrifice to this at best ethereal and likely nonexistent risk of increased unemployability. Such an arbitrary assignment of burdens among classes that are similarly situated with respect to the proffered objectives is the type of invidious choice forbidden by the Equal Protection Clause.

Note: Equal Treatment and Relevant Differences

1. *The nature of equality.* What does it mean to treat two people, or two groups of people, "equally" for purposes of the equal protection clause? Consider, for example, whether each of the following hypothetical employment rules for the New York City Transit Authority provides for equal treatment:

a. No position shall be filled by a woman.
b. No position shall be filled by a person weighing less than 175 pounds.

---

15. [Heroin] addiction is a special problem of the poor, and the addict population is composed largely of racial minorities that the Court has previously recognized as politically powerless and historical subjects of majoritarian neglect. Persons on methadone maintenance have few interests in common with members of the majority, and thus are unlikely to have their interests protected, or even considered, in governmental decision-making. Indeed, petitioners stipulated that "[o]ne of the reasons for the . . . drug policy is the fact that [petitioners] fee[l] an adverse public reaction would result if it were generally known that [petitioners] employed persons with a prior history of drug abuse, including persons participating in methadone maintenance programs." It is hard for me to reconcile that stipulation of animus against former addicts with our past holdings that "a bare . . . desire to harm a politically unpopular group cannot constitute a legitimate governmental interest." United States Dept. of Agriculture v. Moreno, 413 U.S. 528, 534 (1973). On the other hand, the afflictions to which petitioners are more sympathetic, such as alcoholism and mental illness, are shared by both white and black, rich and poor.

Some weight should also be given to the history of the rule. Petitioners admit that it was not the result of a reasoned policy decision and stipulated that they had never studied the ability of those on methadone maintenance to perform petitioners' jobs. Petitioners are not directly accountable to the public, are not the type of official body that normally makes legislative judgments of fact such as those relied upon by the majority today, and are by nature more concerned with business efficiency than with other public policies for which they have no direct responsibility. . . .

    c. No position shall be filled by a person without a high school diploma.
    d. All positions shall be filled by lot.
    e. All persons applying for any position shall be hired.

In a trivial sense, each of these rules provides for equal treatment. Under each of them, every applicant is equally subject to the same criteria. Thus, under rule *c*, all applicants are equally subject to the requirement of a high school diploma, and under rule *a*, all applicants are equally subject to the requirement that they be male. Indeed, *all* rules, if they are applied as written, provide for equality in this sense. Thus, under rule *b*, it would violate equality of treatment for the Transit Authority to hire one individual who weighs 150 pounds, while refusing to hire another individual on the grounds that she weighs less than 175 pounds.

In a similarly trivial sense, each of the hypothetical employment rules denies equal treatment. Under each of them, some people are denied a benefit that is granted to others. Inequality in this sense is also inescapable. Even rule *e*, which requires hiring all people who apply for the position, discriminates against the class of people who did not apply for the position.

These examples illustrate another difficulty with the concept of equality: Providing similar treatment to two groups will not result in equal treatment if the groups are not similarly situated. Rule *b*, for example, provides similar treatment to all applicants: They cannot weigh less than 175 pounds. But in one obvious sense, the rule does not provide equal treatment because applicants are not similarly situated with respect to the rule. Similarly, rule *d* gives everyone an equal chance to win a job in a lottery. But even if the lottery is fairly conducted, the decision to use a lottery might generate complaints if the winner is less qualified for the job or less in need of it or less "deserving" of it than the loser.

This last point raises an important question about the perspective from which equality is to be measured. Equality might be measured with respect to formal treatment: As long as each individual is subjected to the same selection regime, the requirement of equality is satisfied. Or equality might be measured with respect to outcomes: As long as each individual obtains the same level of benefits, equality has been achieved. Suppose that all subway mechanics need protective helmets. Suppose, further, that some workers can use stock helmets that cost $100, but that other workers, either because of the size of their heads or because they wish to wear religious head coverings under their helmets, must obtain custom-made helmets that cost $200. Does equality require, prohibit, or permit the Transit Authority to provide each worker with the same helmet allowance?

2. *The normative appeal of equality.* Even if we could give substantive content to the equality requirement, it is not clear why it has any normative appeal. Although the demands of the equal protection clause can be satisfied by extending the contested benefit to a broader group, the government need not respond in this fashion. It may also fully satisfy the demand of equality by denying *both* groups the contested benefit. Suppose both A and B deserve a benefit, but B does not receive it. If A is also denied the benefit, does this make the outcome more or less just? How is A made better off by B's misfortune? Consider in this regard the problem posed by Heckler v. Mathews, 465 U.S. 728 (1984). Congress amended the Social Security Act to extend certain benefits to women but not to men. Concerned that the courts might invalidate the law on equal protection grounds, Congress also included a provision stating that, if the law were invalidated, neither men nor women would get the benefit. The Court upheld the right of a man to challenge the provision. Should it have? Consider also Sessions v.

Morales-Santana, 137 S. Ct. 1678 (2017). Federal law regarding transmission of citizenship to children born abroad treats children born to unmarried U.S. citizen mothers more favorably than children born to unmarried U.S. citizen fathers. The Court held that this differential treatment violated the equal protection clause. However, the Court went on to hold that it was "not equipped to grant the relief Morales-Santana seeks, *i.e.*, extending to his father (and, derivatively, to him) the benefit" of the more easily-met requirement "reserve[d] for unwed mothers." The Court left it to Congress to "address the issue and settle on a uniform prescription that neither favors nor disadvantages any person on the basis of gender." In the interim, the Court announced that the less favorable rule should also apply "prospectively, to children born to unwed U.S.-citizen mothers."

In thinking about the kinds of equal protection claims that get litigated and the kinds of remedies plaintiffs seek, consider Karlan, Race, Rights, and Remedies in Criminal Adjudication, 96 Mich. L. Rev. 2001, 2027 (1998):

> With few exceptions, the plaintiffs in the typical equal protection case seek to acquire, rather than to avoid, something: the vote, a job, admission to particular schools. The government distributes benefits and plaintiffs seek to receive the same benefits that [other] individuals . . . receive.
>
> The general assumption in contemporary equal protection law, which seems to play out most of the time, is that faced with a finding of unconstitutionality, the state will remedy the inequality by providing the benefit to the previously excluded group (that is, by "levelling up") rather than by depriving the previously included group ("levelling down"). The few examples in ordinary equal protection of levelling down . . . stand out precisely because of their rarity.

How much of the work being done in equality claims rests on the assumption that the benefit will be extended, rather than contracted, either because it is functionally impossible to deny the benefit to everyone — faced with the choice, it seems unlikely that New York would cease running a subway system rather than develop a different way of selecting Transit Authority employees — or because individuals already receiving the benefit will exert political pressure to retain their benefits even if the pool of beneficiaries must be expanded? Is leveling down incompatible with the norms of equality, even if it results in uniform treatment? See Brake, When Equality Leaves Everyone Worse Off: The Problem of Leveling Down in Equality Law, 46 Wm. & Mary L. Rev. 513 (2004).

3. *The "relevant difference" requirement.* One might say that the principle of equal treatment requires that individuals be treated similarly to the extent that they are the same and treated differently to the extent that they are different. But individuals are both the same and different in an infinite variety of respects. For example, although competing applicants under rule *a* are different in that some are men and some are women, they are the same in the sense that all are persons wishing to work for the Transit Authority.

Thus, the equality principle must be modified to provide that differences in treatment can be justified only by *relevant* differences between individuals. A difference is relevant if, but only if, it bears an empirical relationship to the purpose of the rule. This is presumably what the Court means in *Beazer* when it says that "legislative classifications are valid unless they bear no rational relationship to the State's objectives." Even though the Transit Authority's no-methadone rule treated methadone users and nonusers differently, the Court thought that the rule did not violate the equality principle because there was a difference between the two classes relevant to the state's objective of a safe and efficient transit system.

4. *Relevant differences and efficiency.* Is there a sound reason why we should insist that legislative classifications be based on relevant distinctions in this sense? This rule seems to turn the equality requirement into no more than a mandate for efficiency. Note, for example, that the requirement of a relevant distinction provides no guidance as to how the social costs of achieving the state's objective are to be distributed when different distributions are equally efficacious in achieving the state's goal. Nor does it provide any protection against the concentration of extreme costs on a small group when a "fairer" distribution of the costs over a larger group might be slightly less "efficient."

A more fundamental problem with this version of the "relevant difference" requirement is that it becomes meaningless unless some restriction is placed on the kinds of purposes the legislature may pursue. For example, imagine a Transit Authority whose director has decided that the public welfare would be best enhanced by promoting traditional family structures and that providing high-paying jobs to men while deterring women from entering the workforce will serve this goal. In this scenario, sex *is* a relevant difference among job candidates and rule *a* furthers the government's purpose.

Note: *Limitations on Permissible Government Purposes*

What makes a legislative purpose invalid under the equal protection clause? There are some purposes that are forbidden by other constitutional provisions; presumably a classification designed to accomplish one of those independently forbidden goals would be unconstitutional as well. For example, the first amendment protects the free exercise of religion. Thus, if a state denied a generally available government benefit — for example, drivers' licenses — to a class of people because of those individuals' religious beliefs, that law would be unconstitutional. But in such a case, reference to the equal protection clause would seem superfluous: A reviewing court could simply rely on the substantive constitutional provision to invalidate the law. Does the equal protection clause of its own force prohibit the government from pursuing certain ends? If so, what ends does it prohibit? Consider the following possibilities:

1. *Expressions of animus or disapproval.* To what extent is the government permitted to deny a benefit or impose a burden on a class of people because it disapproves of their conduct or beliefs or status? Many laws express moral judgments. For example, a state agency policy that provides health insurance to the spouses, but not to the unmarried partners, companions, or friends of state employees may in part rest on a judgment that marriage is a special relationship particularly deserving of state support. Similarly, a law criminalizing the mistreatment of animals — and thus treating individuals who treat animals in specified ways differently from other persons — may rest on the judgment that society thinks cruelty to animals is immoral.

But a principle that moral disapproval is always a permissible government purpose would swallow up the equal protection clause, since withholding a benefit or imposing a burden on a defined class can *always* be said to serve either the governmental purpose of expressing disapproval or the purpose of creating an incentive for individuals to forswear conduct of which the government disapproves. For example, a law that denies government-subsidized student loans to individuals who use illegal drugs both expresses disapproval of such drug use and may deter people who want such loans from using drugs.

What separates permissible from impermissible expressions of disapproval? Consider the following cases in which the Supreme Court has found violations of the equal protection clause. What accounts for the Court's holding that the government's purpose was impermissible?

U.S. DEPARTMENT OF AGRICULTURE v. MORENO, 413 U.S. 528 (1973). Section 3(e) of the Food Stamp Act of 1964 (as amended in 1971) excluded from participation in the food stamp program any low-income household containing an individual who was unrelated to any other member of the household. Individuals who satisfied the income eligibility requirements for the program brought suit to challenge this provision. For example, one plaintiff had a daughter with an acute hearing deficiency who required special instruction in a school for the deaf. Because the school was located in an area in which she could not otherwise afford to live, she agreed to share an apartment near the school with another woman on public assistance. Since she was not related to the woman, she was threatened with termination of food stamp assistance. The plaintiffs claimed that the "unrelated persons" provision created an irrational classification in violation of the equal protection component of the due process clause of the fifth amendment. Justice Brennan delivered the Court's opinion:

"Under traditional equal protection analysis, a legislative classification must be sustained if the classification itself is rationally related to a legitimate governmental interest. [The act stated that it was the policy of Congress to 'raise levels of nutrition among low-income households' and increase utilization of food so as to 'strengthen our agricultural economy.'] The challenged statutory classification [is] clearly irrelevant to [these purposes]. . . .

"Thus, if it is to be sustained, the challenged classification must rationally further some legitimate governmental interest other than those specifically stated in [the act]. Regrettably, there is little legislative history to illuminate the purposes of the [act]. The legislative history that does exist, however, indicates that that amendment was intended to prevent so-called 'hippies' and 'hippie communes' from participating in the food stamp program. The challenged classification clearly cannot be sustained by reference to this congressional purpose. For if the constitutional conception of 'equal protection of the laws' means anything, it must at the very least mean that a bare congressional desire to harm a politically unpopular group cannot constitute a *legitimate* governmental interest."

Justice Douglas wrote a separate concurring opinion.

Justice Rehnquist, with whom Chief Justice Burger joined, dissented: "I do not think it is unreasonable for Congress to conclude that the basic unit which it was willing to support with federal funding [is] some variation on the family as we know it — a household consisting of related individuals. This unit provides a guarantee which is not provided by households containing unrelated individuals that the household exists for some purpose other than to collect federal food stamps."

CITY OF CLEBURNE v. CLEBURNE LIVING CENTER, 473 U.S. 432 (1985). The City of Cleburne, Texas, had a municipal zoning ordinance that permitted a wide variety of structures to be built on a particular site, including "[hospitals], sanitariums, nursing homes or homes for convalescents or aged."

However, the ordinance specifically excluded "homes for [the] insane or feeble-minded or alcoholics or drug addicts." Pursuant to that ordinance, the city denied a special use permit for the operation of a group home for persons who were mentally retarded.

The Supreme Court held that the ordinance violated the equal protection clause. Justice White delivered the Court's opinion:

"To withstand equal protection review, legislation that distinguishes between the mentally retarded and others must be rationally related to a legitimate governmental purpose. . . .

"[The] mentally retarded as a group are indeed different from others not sharing their misfortune, and in this respect they may be different from those who would occupy other facilities that would be [permitted]. But this difference is largely irrelevant unless the [home] and those who would occupy it would threaten legitimate interests of the city in a way that other permitted uses such as boarding houses and hospitals would not. . . .

"[The city council] was concerned with the negative attitude of the majority of property owners located within 200 feet of the [facility], as well as with the fears of elderly residents of the neighborhood. But mere negative attitudes, or fear, unsubstantiated by factors which are properly cognizable in a zoning proceeding, are not permissible bases for treating a home for the mentally retarded differently from apartment houses, multiple dwellings, and the like. It is plain that the electorate as a whole [could] not order city action violative of the Equal Protection Clause, and the City may not avoid the strictures of that Clause by deferring to the wishes or objections of some fraction of the body politic. . . .

"[The] Council had two objections to the location of the facility. It was concerned that the facility was across the street from a junior high school, and it feared that the students might harass the occupants of the [home]. But the school itself is attended by about 30 mentally retarded students, and denying a permit based on such vague, undifferentiated fears is again permitting some portion of the community to validate what would otherwise be an equal protection violation. The other objection to the home's location was that it was located on 'a five hundred year flood plain.' This concern with the possibility of a flood, however, can hardly be based on a distinction between the [home] and, for example, nursing homes, homes for convalescents or the aged, or sanitariums or hospitals, any of which could be located on the [site] without obtaining a special use permit. . . .

"The short of it is that requiring the permit in this case appears to us to rest on an irrational prejudice against the mentally retarded, including those who would occupy the [facility] and who would live under the closely supervised and highly regulated conditions expressly provided for by state and federal law. . . ."

Justice Stevens concurred:

"[Our] cases reflect a continuum of judgmental responses to differing classifications which have been explained in opinions by terms ranging from 'strict scrutiny' at one extreme to 'rational basis' at the other. I have never been persuaded that these so called 'standards' adequately explain the decisional process. [In] my own approach to these cases, I have always asked myself whether I could find a 'rational basis' for the classification at issue. The term 'rational,' of course, includes a requirement that an impartial lawmaker could logically believe that the classification would serve a legitimate public purpose that transcends the harm to the members of the disadvantaged class. Thus, the word 'rational' — for me at least — includes elements of legitimacy and neutrality that must always characterize the performance of the sovereign's duty to govern impartially. . . .

"[The] Court of Appeals correctly observed that through ignorance and prejudice the mentally retarded 'have been subjected to a history of unfair and often grotesque mistreatment.' The discrimination against the mentally retarded that is at issue in this case is the city's decision to require an annual special use permit before property in an apartment house district may be used as a group home for persons who are mildly retarded. The record convinces me that this permit was required because of the irrational fears of neighboring property owners, rather than for the protection of the mentally retarded persons who would reside in [the] home."

Justice Marshall concurred in the judgment. He pointed out that the Court's rejection of "legitimate concerns for fire hazards or the serenity of the neighborhood" was atypical of the conventional form of rationality review.

ROMER v. EVANS, 517 U.S. 620 (1996). By statewide initiative, Colorado enacted a constitutional amendment prohibiting local governments from enacting antidiscrimination measures protecting "homosexual, lesbian, or bisexual orientation, conduct, practices or relationships." In a six-to-three decision, the Court, per Justice Kennedy, invalidated the amendment:

"Amendment 2 fails, indeed defies, [conventional rational basis] inquiry. First, the amendment has the peculiar property of imposing a broad and undifferentiated disability on a single named group, an exceptional and [invalid] form of legislation. Second, its sheer breadth is so discontinuous with the reasons offered for it that the amendment seems inexplicable by anything but animus toward the class that it affects; it lacks a rational relationship to legitimate state interests. . . .

"[Laws] of the kind now before us raise the inevitable inference that the disadvantage imposed is born of animosity toward the class of persons affected. 'If the constitutional conception of "equal protection of the laws" means anything, it must at the very least mean that a bare . . . desire to harm a politically unpopular group cannot constitute a legitimate governmental interest.' [*Moreno.*] Even laws enacted for broad and ambitious purposes often can be explained by reference to legitimate public policies which justify the incidental disadvantages they impose on certain persons. Amendment 2, however, in making a general announcement that gays and lesbians shall not have any particular protections from the law, inflicts on them immediate, continuing, and real injuries that outrun and belie any legitimate justifications that may be claimed for it."

Compare Justice Scalia's dissenting opinion, joined by Chief Justice Rehnquist and Justice Thomas:

"The Court's opinion contains grim, disapproving hints that Coloradans have been guilty of 'animus' or 'animosity' toward homosexuality, as though that has been established as Unamerican. Of course it is our moral heritage that one should not hate any human being or class of human beings. But I had thought that one could consider certain conduct reprehensible — murder, for example, or polygamy, or cruelty to animals — and could exhibit even 'animus' toward such conduct. Surely that is the only sort of 'animus' at issue here: moral disapproval of homosexual conduct, the same sort of moral disapproval that produced the centuries-old criminal laws [prohibiting sodomy] that we held constitutional in [Bowers v. Hardwick, 478 U.S. 186 (1986)]."

Several Justices revisited this issue in Lawrence v. Texas, 539 U.S. 558 (2003), which overruled Bowers v. Hardwick. (*Lawrence* is treated in more depth at pages 678-679 and 693-694, infra, and in Chapter 6.) The Court struck down a Texas criminal statute that prohibited homosexual, but not heterosexual sodomy, on due process grounds. Justice O'Connor concurred in the result on the ground that the distinction between heterosexual and homosexual sodomy violated equal protection because it reflected nothing beyond "a bare desire to harm the group, . . . an interest that is insufficient to satisfy rational basis review under the Equal Protection Clause. . . ."

Do you agree that the "desire to harm a politically unpopular group cannot constitute a *legitimate* governmental interest"? Does it matter *why* the group is politically unpopular? Is it really unconstitutional for the legislature to determine that one way of life is preferable to another and therefore more worthy of support? Would it be unconstitutional, for example, for the legislature to subsidize small family farms, but not large-scale industry, on the theory that farm life is "wholesome"? Is it a violation of the equal protection clause for a state agency to provide health insurance to the spouses of its employees, but not to unmarried companions of its workers, on the theory that marriage is an important stabilizing institution?

Does *Cleburne* suggest that laws should be subject to special scrutiny when they disadvantage groups based on immutable traits, since the immutability eliminates the possibility that the legislature is attempting to change behavior? See section C, infra. For example, although the *Moreno* statute could be justified as an attempt to discourage certain lifestyles, the zoning ordinance in *Cleburne* could not sensibly be defended as a measure designed to deter mental retardation. On which side of this line does the measure invalidated by *Romer* fall? And who should make the determination whether homosexuality is a mutable or immutable trait — courts, legislatures, the individual plaintiff? And aren't some traits relevant to legitimate governmental objectives even if a person is powerless to change them? Would denying drivers' licenses to blind people run afoul of the equal protection clause?

2. *Naked self-dealing.* Should rationality review be understood as a guarantor of a political process that is public-regarding and not merely the product of self-serving activity? On this view, differential treatment is illegitimate when its purpose is simply to advance the interests of politically powerful individuals. Consider Sunstein, Public Values, Private Interests, and the Equal Protection Clause, 1982 Sup. Ct. Rev. 127, 134:

> When the government operates to benefit A and burden B, it can do so only if it is prepared to justify its decision by reference to a public value. [Legislation] may not be merely the adjustment of private interests, or the transfer of wealth or opportunity from one person to another; it must be in some sense public-serving. [Nor] is political strength a legitimate justification. [The] institution that made the discrimination must be attempting to remedy a perceived public evil, and must not be responding only to the interests or preferences of some of its constituents.

Can the distinction between public and private interests, on which this theory rests, be maintained? What is the public interest if not the aggregation of the private preferences of individual participants in the political process?

Does this "public interest" requirement adequately capture the equality principle? Does it provide adequate protection against the infliction of very severe deprivations on small groups when those deprivations serve the public interest?

Note: "Actual Purpose" Review

Even if some purposes are impermissible, there still remain a wide variety of permissible government purposes. In deciding whether a particular classification is sufficiently related to a legitimate government purpose, what inquiry does the court need to make with respect to the purpose being pursued? In McGowan v. Maryland, 366 U.S. 420 (1961), the Court said that "[the] constitutional safeguard is offended only if the classification rests on grounds wholly irrelevant to the achievement of the State's objective. State legislatures are presumed to have acted within their constitutional power despite the fact that, in practice, their laws result in some inequality. A statutory discrimination will not be set aside if any state of facts reasonably may be conceived to justify it." Similarly in U.S. Railroad Retirement Board v. Fritz, 449 U.S. 166 (1980), Justice Rehnquist's opinion for the Court stated that "[where], as here, there are plausible reasons for Congress' action, our inquiry is at an end. It is, of course, "constitutionally irrelevant whether this reasoning in fact underlay the legislative decision," [quoting Flemming v. Nestor, 363 U.S. 603, 612 (1960)] because this Court has never insisted that a legislative body articulate its reasons for enacting a statute.

Does it make sense to invalidate a law that advances a legitimate state purpose simply because the legislators were not thinking of that purpose when they enacted it? On the other hand, why should deference to the legislature require upholding a statute that advances a policy that the legislature had no interest in pursuing?

1. *Putting the best face on dubious statutes.* To what extent does rationality review become an exercise in courts ignoring the real purpose behind self-dealing statutes and inventing more normatively attractive legislative goals? Consider the following examples:

MINNESOTA v. CLOVER LEAF CREAMERY CO., 449 U.S. 456 (1981). Minnesota law banned the retail sale of milk in plastic nonreturnable, nonrefillable containers but permitted such sale in nonreturnable paperboard milk cartons. A state trial court held the law violative of the equal protection clause in part because the "actual basis" for the law was to promote the economic interests of local dairy and pulpwood industries. On appeal, the Minnesota Supreme Court concluded that the law was actually designed to serve environmental objectives. Nonetheless, it affirmed the trial court on the ground that the ban on plastic containers was not rationally related to these purposes. The Supreme Court reversed. Justice Brennan wrote the Court's opinion:

"The parties agree that the standard of review applicable to this case under the Equal Protection Clause is the familiar 'rational basis' test. Moreover, they agree that the purposes of the Act cited by the legislature — promoting resource conservation, easing solid waste disposal problems, and conserving energy — are legitimate state purposes.[7]

7. [In] equal protection analysis, this court will assume that the objectives articulated by the legislature are actual purposes of the statute, unless an examination of the circumstances forces us to conclude that they "could not have been a goal of the legislation." [Weinberger v. Wiesenfeld, 420 U.S. 636, 648 n.16 (1975).] Here, a review of the legislative history supports the Minnesota Supreme Court's conclusion that the principal purposes of the Act were [environmental]. The contrary evidence cited by respondents [is] easily understood, in context, as economic defense of an Act genuinely proposed for environmental reasons. We will not invalidate a state statute under the Equal Protection Clause merely because some legislators sought to obtain votes for the measure on the basis of its beneficial side effects on state industry.

"[Respondents] apparently have not challenged the *theoretical* connection between a ban on plastic nonreturnables and the purposes articulated by the legislature; instead, they have argued that there is no *empirical* connection between the two. They produced impressive supporting evidence at trial to prove that the probable consequences of the ban on plastic nonreturnable milk containers will be to deplete natural resources, exacerbate solid waste disposal problems, and waste energy, because consumers unable to purchase milk in plastic containers will turn to paperboard milk cartons, allegedly a more environmentally harmful product.

"But States are not required to convince the courts of the correctness of their legislative judgments. . . .

"Although parties challenging legislation under the Equal Protection Clause may introduce evidence supporting their claim that it is irrational, they cannot prevail so long as 'it is evident from all the considerations presented to [the legislature], and those of which we may take judicial notice, that the question is at least debatable.' [United States v. Carolene Products Co., 304 U.S. 144, 154 (1938).] Where there was evidence before the legislature reasonably supporting the classification, litigants may not procure invalidation of the legislation merely by tendering evidence in court that the legislature was mistaken."

Does this formulation treat as "constitutionally irrelevant" the reasons that "in fact underlay the legislative decision" as *Fritz* requires?

More recently, in Armour v. City of Indianapolis, 566 U.S. 673 (2012), the Supreme Court upheld Indianapolis's decision to forgive the assessments for sewer improvement projects levied on property owners who had chosen to pay their assessment in periodic installments while refusing to refund the payments made by property owners who had chosen to pay in a lump sum. The assessment had been roughly $10,000. While the lump-sum payors had paid the entire amount, some of their neighbors had paid less than $500 at the time the forgiveness was announced.

Writing for the Court, Justice Breyer found that the city's decision satisfied the rational basis test. "Where 'ordinary commercial transactions' are at issue, rational basis review requires deference to reasonable underlying legislative judgments." Justice Breyer concluded that Indianapolis's differential treatment of installment and lump-sum payors had a rational basis: reducing the administrative costs entailed in continuing to seek payment from the installment-plan payors.

The Chief Justice, joined by Justices Scalia and Alito, dissented. He thought that the city's justifications for the differential treatment — "the desire to avoid administrative hassle and the 'fiscal[] challeng[e]' of giving back money it wanted to keep" — could not "pass constitutional muster, even under rational basis review":

> We have never before held that administrative burdens justify grossly disparate tax treatment of those the State has provided should be treated alike. . . . The reason we have rejected this argument is obvious: The Equal Protection Clause does not provide that no State shall "deny to any person within its jurisdiction the equal protection of the laws, unless it's too much of a bother." . . .
> The Court is willing to concede that "administrative considerations could not justify . . . an unfair system" in which "a city arbitrarily allocate[s] taxes among a few citizens while forgiving many others on the ground that it is cheaper and easier to collect taxes from a few people than from many." Cold comfort, that. If the

quoted language does not accurately describe this case, I am not sure what it would reach. . . .

Our precedents do not ask for much from government in this area — only "rough equality in tax treatment." . . . But every generation or so a case comes along when this Court needs to say enough is enough, if the Equal Protection Clause is to retain any force in this context. . . . Indiana law promised neighboring homeowners that they would be treated equally when it came to paying for sewer hookups. The City then ended up charging some homeowners 30 *times* what it charged their neighbors for the same hookups. The equal protection violation is plain.

2. *The epistemological problem.* Does the difficulty in discovering the legislature's "actual purpose" counsel against utilizing an actual purpose standard of review? See Shepsle, Congress Is a "They," Not an "It": Legislative Intent as Oxymoron, 12 Intl. Rev. L. & Econ. 239 (1992). Consider Kassel v. Consolidated Freightways Corp., 450 U.S. 662 (1981) (Rehnquist, J., dissenting):

> [Actual purpose review] assumes that individual legislators are motivated by one discernible "actual" purpose, and ignores the fact that different legislators may vote for a single piece of legislation for widely different reasons. [How], for example, would a court adhering to [actual purpose review] approach a statute, the legislative history of which indicated that 10 votes were based on [permissible considerations], 10 votes were based on [impermissible considerations] and the statute passed by a vote of 40-20?

Justice Rehnquist also pointed out that under actual purpose review, "litigants who wish to succeed in invalidating a law [must] have a certain schizophrenia if they are to be successful in their advocacy: They must first convince this Court that the legislature had a particular purpose in mind in enacting the law, and then convince it that the law was not at all suited to the accomplishment of that purpose." Trimble v. Gordon, 430 U.S. 762, 783 (1977) (dissenting opinion).

Are these problems insurmountable? Need an advocate be "schizophrenic" in a case where the statute itself or its legislative history makes plain that the legislature intended to accomplish results that fail to validate the statute?

3. *Requirement of statement of purpose.* Do these epistemological difficulties suggest that the Court should require or encourage the legislature to state explicitly the purposes it wishes a statute to achieve? Lawyers for the state would then be limited to these purposes in defending the constitutionality of the statute. Consider, for example, Justice Powell's dissenting opinion in Schweiker v. Wilson, 450 U.S. 221 (1981):

> The deference to which legislative accommodation of conflicting interests is entitled rests in part upon the principle that the political process of our majoritarian democracy responds to the wishes of the people. Accordingly, an important touchstone for equal protection review of statutes is how readily a policy can be discerned which the legislature intended to serve. When a legitimate purpose for a statute appears in the legislative history or is implicit in the statutory scheme itself, a court has some assurance that the legislature made a conscious policy choice. Our democratic system requires that legislation intended to serve a discernible purpose receive the most respectful deference. . . .
>
> In my view, the Court should receive with some skepticism post hoc hypotheses about legislative purpose, unsupported by the legislative history. When no indication of legislative purpose appears other than the current position of [an executive officer,] the Court should require that the classification bear a "fair and substantial

relation" to the asserted purpose. . . . This marginally more demanding scrutiny indirectly would test the plausibility of the tendered purpose and preserve equal protection review as something more than "a mere tautological recognition of the fact that Congress did what it intended to do." [*Fritz* (Stevens, J., concurring in the judgment).]

Presumably the heightened scrutiny Justice Powell would impose in the absence of a clearly discernible legislative purpose would provide incentives for the legislature to state its purpose explicitly. Might not the result of this requirement be no more than boilerplate statements of worthwhile purposes that fail to state the legislature's true objectives? Doesn't Justice Powell's position turn actual purpose review on its head by according "the most respectful deference" in precisely those cases where the legislative purpose is clear, and where rigorous judicial review is therefore possible?

Compare Justice Powell's views in *Schweiker* with Justice Brennan's *Fritz* dissent. Justice Brennan argued that "[where] Congress has expressly stated the purpose of a piece of legislation, but where the challenged classification is either irrelevant to or counter to that purpose, we must view any post hoc justifications proffered by Government attorneys with skepticism." Doesn't this suggest that legislative classifications may be subject to *more* rigorous review when the legislature articulates its purpose? Wouldn't such enhanced review discourage the legislators from candidly stating why they enacted the statute?

In any event, is there a legitimate constitutional basis for the Court skewing review in an effort to force legislative articulation of purpose? When it comes to federal statutes, does such an effort reflect disrespect for a coordinate branch of government?

Note: The Means-Ends Nexus

To survive equal protection review, a classification must bear some connection to a permissible government end. But when is a classification sufficiently related to justify conferring benefits or imposing burdens on the basis of the difference it tracks? Suppose that every member of the disadvantaged class has a trait that every member of the advantaged class lacks, and that the trait is related in some way to achievement of the state's goal. In *Beazer*, for example, suppose that every methadone user was an unsafe worker, while every nonuser was a safe one. Would this showing be sufficient to satisfy the equality requirement? Arguably the difference between users and nonusers would still not justify the difference in treatment unless the benefit derived, for example, from a safer transit system outweighed the cost imposed on users denied employment.

As complex as this analysis is, it vastly oversimplifies the problems encountered in the real world. For in almost all cases, the classification will not be perfectly efficient but will be either "overinclusive" or "underinclusive" or both. A classification is "overinclusive" if it disadvantages a larger class than is needed to achieve the state's purpose. A classification is "underinclusive" if some people are not disadvantaged even though the failure to include them undermines achievements of the state's interest.

1. *Overinclusion.* Consider, first, the problem of overinclusion in *Beazer*. If every methadone user were a safe and efficient worker, the exclusion of the class would not advance the state's purpose at all and hence would be

unconstitutional. Both the majority and the dissent seem to agree, however, that at least *some* methadone users are unsuited for transit work. Is it sufficient to uphold the classification to show that it advances the state's purpose to some extent — if, for example, the transit system would be somewhat safer without methadone users than with them? Such a test would permit the state to impose severe deprivations in exchange for trivial benefits.

A rule requiring the state to demonstrate that every member of the disadvantaged class possesses the trait relevant to the state's objective is no more satisfactory. This test would make legislation virtually impossible, for almost all laws group people together based on generalizations that do not universally hold. It may be that somewhere there is a ten-year-old who would make a perfectly safe transit worker. Yet the Transit Authority is surely justified in imposing a minimum age requirement on the individuals it employs.

It seems clear therefore that the permissibility of a legislative generalization must turn on the cost of the generalization as compared to the cost of a more individualized judgment. Making this comparison involves a complex process. In *Beazer*, for example, a no-methadone rule eliminates some unsafe workers but at the cost of eliminating some safe ones as well. A more individualized judgment would reduce the number of safe workers whom the selection criteria mistakenly exclude, but arguably at a higher administrative cost. And a less exclusionary categorical rule would reduce the number of safe workers whom the selection criteria mistakenly exclude, but arguably by increasing the costs that ensue from employing a greater number of unsafe workers who go undetected. To strike the balance, one must first weigh the importance of safety against the importance of employment and then discount each side of the equation by the risk of error. Moreover, even if one concludes that the cost imposed on safe methadone users who are wrongly denied employment under the no-methadone rule outweighs the cost imposed by unsafe methadone users who are wrongly employed under a more individualized approach, it does not follow that the no-methadone rule is invalid. The administrative costs associated with a more individualized assessment might still justify use of a prophylactic rule. For example, if the Transit Authority must conduct lengthy interviews with each methadone user to assure his or her safety, it might reasonably conclude that the cost of such interviews outweighs the cost of denying employment to those users who would be safe workers.

2. *Underinclusion.* A similarly complex weighing process is required when it is alleged that a classification is underinclusive. Is the Transit Authority's rule unconstitutional because it excludes methadone users on the grounds of safety, but does not exclude recovering alcoholics, mental patients, people with diabetes or epilepsy, and others who arguably pose an equal or greater safety risk? The Court has sometimes said that the equal protection clause permits the legislature to deal with one problem at a time or to proceed step by step. See, e.g., Williamson v. Lee Optical Co., 348 U.S. 483, 489 (1955). One cannot, however, take these statements literally. If the legislature were completely free to select which part of a problem to attack, the equal protection clause would be meaningless. For example, such a rule would permit the state to deny drivers' licenses to all people with green eyes on the theory that such people cause traffic accidents (albeit not at a greater rate than the population as a whole), and that their exclusion therefore advances the state's goal of traffic safety by decreasing the number of drivers.

One might therefore conclude that the equal protection clause prohibits any law that denies a benefit to a group but grants the benefit to other groups whose inclusion imposes equal or greater costs. Such a rule once again oversimplifies the analysis, however. Suppose, for example, 25 percent of persons with epilepsy would make unsafe transit workers, while only 10 percent of methadone users pose an unacceptable risk. But suppose further that only a small number of persons with epilepsy apply for employment with the Transit Authority, while large numbers of methadone users seek transit jobs. May the Transit Authority disqualify methadone users, but not persons with epilepsy, on the theory that by doing so, it is dealing with a larger share of the total problem?

Closely associated with this problem is the difficulty of relative administrative costs. It may be, for example, that methadone users are easier to identify than persons with epilepsy, or that unsafe persons with epilepsy are easier to identify than unsafe methadone users. In either event, the state might be justified in excluding users of methadone, even though they cause less of the problem, because the cost of exclusion is less.

Moreover, the cost calculation must include the cost of not achieving ancillary goals that may qualify the purpose of achieving a safe transit system. Suppose, for example, persons with epilepsy impose greater safety costs than methadone users. The Transit Authority might nonetheless employ persons with epilepsy, but not methadone users, if it believes that drug addicts, but not victims of epilepsy, are responsible for their plight.

In thinking about how the mixture of concerns might affect equal protection analysis, consider Fitzgerald v. Racing Association of Central Iowa, 539 U.S. 103 (2003). Iowa law imposed a higher tax on revenues gained from slot machines at racetracks than from slot machines on excursion riverboats. The Iowa Supreme Court held that this differential violated the equal protection clause. It reasoned that the "differential tax completely defeats the [statute's] alleged purpose [of helping] racetracks recover from economic distress" and that there could therefore be "no rational reason for this differential tax." In an opinion written by Justice Breyer, the Supreme Court unanimously reversed:

> [The] Iowa law, like most laws, might predominately serve one general objective, say, helping racetracks, while containing subsidiary provisions that seek to achieve other desirable (perhaps even contrary) ends as well, thereby producing a law that balances objectives but still serves the general objective when seen as a whole. . . .
>
> [The statute's] grant to the racetracks of authority to operate slot machines should help the racetracks economically to some degree — even if its simultaneous imposition of a tax on slot machine adjusted revenue means that the law provides less help than respondents might like. . . .
>
> [The] difference [in taxation rates], harmful to the racetracks, is helpful to the riverboats, which [were] also facing financial peril.

Finally, the underinclusion analysis is affected by the manner in which the advantaged class is characterized. In Beazer, for example, it may seem quite sensible to disadvantage methadone users, but not persons with epilepsy, if methadone users pose more of a problem. Still, methadone users might ask why the state is worried about the social cost of their unsafe conduct when it does nothing to control the arguably greater social cost imposed by automobile drivers who do not wear seat belts or cigarette smokers who pollute the air around them or parents who abuse their children.

3. *The relationship between fit and the Court's view of a statute's underlying purpose.* To what does the rationality requirement apply? Must proponents of the law demonstrate that a rational person would believe that the classification advances the legislative purpose to some extent? That a rational person would so believe if the facts were as the legislature supposed them to be? Or must the proponents demonstrate that the various trade-offs outlined between the costs of narrower and broader classifications are "rational"?

Regardless of the verbal distinctions, in practice the application of any of the standards has usually led to validation of the legislative scheme, particularly in cases involving what the Court sees as straightforward economic regulation. Two examples illustrate the Court's approach.

RAILWAY EXPRESS AGENCY v. NEW YORK, 336 U.S. 106 (1949). A New York traffic regulation prohibited the operation of "advertising vehicles," but permitted placing "business notices upon business delivery vehicles, so long as such vehicles are engaged in the usual business or regular work of the owner and not used merely or mainly for advertising." Justice Douglas delivered the Court's opinion:

"[The] regulation draws the line between advertisements of products sold by the owner of the truck and general advertisements. It is argued that unequal treatment on the basis of such a distinction is not justified by the aim and purpose of the regulation. It is said, for example, that one of appellant's trucks carrying the advertisement of a commercial house would not cause any greater distraction of pedestrians and vehicle drivers than if the commercial house carried the same advertisement on its own truck. . . .

"That, however, is a superficial way of analyzing the problem. [The] local authorities may well have concluded that those who advertise their own wares on their trucks do not present the same traffic problem in view of the nature or extent of the advertising which they use. [And] the fact that New York City sees fit to eliminate from traffic this kind of distraction but does not touch what may be even greater ones in a different category, such as the vivid displays on Times Square, is immaterial. It is no requirement of equal protection that all evils of the same genus be eradicated or none at all."

Justice Jackson wrote a concurring opinion: "There are two clauses of the Fourteenth Amendment which this Court may invoke to invalidate ordinances by which municipal governments seek to solve their local problems [— the due process clause and the equal protection clause]. . . .

"The burden should rest heavily upon one who would persuade us to use the due process clause to strike down a substantive law or ordinance. [Invalidation] of a statute [on] due process grounds leaves ungoverned and ungovernable conduct which many people find objectionable.

"Invocation of the equal protection clause, on the other hand, does not disable any governmental body from dealing with the subject at hand. It merely means that the prohibition or regulation must have a broader impact. I regard it as a salutary doctrine that [governments] must exercise their powers so as not to discriminate between their inhabitants except upon some reasonable differentiation fairly related to the object of regulation. [There] is no more effective practical guaranty against arbitrary and unreasonable government than to require that the principles of law which officials would impose upon a minority must be imposed generally. Conversely, nothing opens the door to arbitrary action so effectively as to allow those officials to pick and choose only a few to whom they will apply legislation and thus to escape the political retribution that might be visited upon them if larger numbers were affected. . . .

"This case affords an illustration. Even casual observations from the sidewalks of New York will show that an ordinance which would forbid all advertising on vehicles would run into conflict with many interests, including some, if not all, of the great metropolitan newspapers, which use that advertising extensively. [But] any regulation applicable to all such advertising would require much clearer justification in local conditions to enable its enactment than does some regulation applicable to a few. . . .

"There is not even a pretense here that the traffic hazard created by the advertising which is forbidden is in any manner or degree more hazardous than that which is permitted. It is urged with considerable force that this local regulation does not comply with the equal protection clause because it applies unequally upon classes whose differentiation is in no way relevant to the objects of the regulation. . . .

"The question in my mind comes to this. Where individuals contribute to an evil or danger in the same way and to the same degree, may those who do so for hire be prohibited, while those who do so for their own commercial ends but not for hire be allowed to continue? I think the answer has to be that the hireling may be put in a class by himself and may be dealt with differently than those who act on their own. But this is not merely because such a discrimination will enable the lawmaker to diminish the evil. That might be done by many classifications, which I should think wholly unsustainable. It is rather because there is a real difference between doing in self-interest and doing for hire, so that it is one thing to tolerate action from those who act on their own and it is another thing to permit the same action to be promoted for a price."

WILLIAMSON v. LEE OPTICAL, 348 U.S. 483 (1955). An Oklahoma statute made it unlawful for any person not a licensed optometrist or ophthalmologist to fit lenses to a face or to duplicate or replace lenses into frames except on a written prescription of an ophthalmologist or optometrist. In practical effect the statute prevented opticians from fitting old glasses into new frames or supplying new or duplicate lenses without a prescription. However, the statute specifically exempted sellers of ready-to-wear glasses. The district court held that this discrimination against opticians violated the equal protection clause.

In a unanimous opinion written by Justice Douglas, the Supreme Court reversed:

"The problem of legislative classification is a perennial one, admitting of no doctrinaire definition. Evils in the same field may be of different dimensions and proportions, requiring different remedies. Or so the legislature may think. Or the reform may take one step at a time, addressing itself to the phase of the problem which seems most acute to the legislative mind. The legislature may select one phase of one field and apply a remedy there, neglecting the others. The prohibition of the Equal Protection Clause goes no further than the invidious discrimination. We cannot say that the point has been reached here. For all this record shows, the ready-to-wear branch of this business may not loom large in Oklahoma or may present problems of regulation distinct from the other branch."

Contrast the fit the Court found adequate in *Railway Express* and *Lee Optical* with its rejection of the fit between means and ends in *Cleburne*, pages 516-518 supra. In addition to rejecting the city's claim that it could treat group homes for persons who are mentally retarded differently from other zoning uses because of other residents' discomfort, the Court also faced the city's claim that denial of the zoning variance was permissible because the proposed home was located on "a five hundred year flood plain." Certainly, avoiding the problems connected with locating a group home in a potentially hazardous area is a legitimate government concern. Nonetheless, the Court held that "[this] concern with the possibility of a flood, however, can hardly be based on a distinction between the [home] and, for example, nursing homes, homes for convalescents or the aged, or sanitariums or hospitals, any of which could be located on the [site] without obtaining a special use permit." How can this holding be reconciled with *Lee Optical*? Is this really an evaluation of the means-ends nexus or is this simply a form of actual purpose review?

4. *Evaluating the means-ends nexus: the problem of fact.* Whether a particular means is "rationally related" to the legislature's ends frequently turns on the answers to antecedent questions of fact — for example, will the prohibition of plastic milk containers in fact make for a cleaner environment, or how much expertise is necessary to fit lenses into an eyeglass frame. How should these answers be ascertained? Has the Court gone too far in curtailing the right of litigants to prove that the facts are not as the legislature supposed them to be? A court faced with a factual dispute generally resolves it pursuant to detailed procedural rules designed to give both parties a fair opportunity to bring to the fact-finder's attention all relevant evidence. Although legislatures frequently hold hearings before enacting statutes, their procedures tend to be far less careful and structured. Indeed, there is no requirement that a legislator hear any of the evidence or know anything about the subject before voting on a bill. If the court, after a full trial, determines that the legislature is factually mistaken, why should the statute nonetheless be upheld?

5. *Evaluating the means-ends nexus: the problem of value.* If we assume agreement about the underlying facts, should the Court be more aggressive in evaluating legislative means? Or are there sound institutional reasons for deference to the legislative judgment? Does aggressive rationality review depend on a court's making value judgments unconnected to the Constitution? For example, how is a court to balance the environmental benefits associated with the prohibition of plastic milk containers against the burden imposed on consumers?

Even if there is no problem with the judicial value judgments arguably inherent in rationality review, might there not still be a risk that the sporadic nature of judicial review will cause the Court to overlook the overall political context that makes a legislative judgment rational? For example, one might believe that requiring prescriptions from optometrists before opticians can replace lenses imposes costs that cannot be justified in terms of the marginal improvement in public safety. But suppose consumer groups agreed not to oppose the law in exchange for passage of measures that regulated the price that optometrists could charge their customers. Can a state defend an otherwise irrational classification on the ground that it is the product of compromise? Consider Bowen v. Owens, 476 U.S. 1137 (1986), where the Court defended deferential review of classifications contained in the Social Security law as follows:

> Congress' adjustments of this complex system of entitlements necessarily create distinctions among categories of beneficiaries, a result that could be avoided only by making sweeping changes in the Act instead of incremental ones. A constitutional rule that would invalidate Congress' attempts to proceed cautiously in awarding increased benefits might deter Congress from making any increases at all.

Compare the views of Justice Marshall expressed in a dissenting opinion:

[I] suspect that the Court is right to characterize the distinction drawn by [the act in question] as the product of Congress' decision to "take one step at a time." However under [equal protection principles] even legislative classifications that result from compromise must bear at least a rational relationship to a legitimate state purpose. Had Congress accommodated the House's reform goals with the Senate's more conservative outlook in this area by passing a law giving benefits to only those [born] on odd-numbered days of the calendar, we would surely have to strike the provision down as irrational.

Is a court competent to make judgments concerning the kinds of trade-offs between groups that are permissible?

6. *Means-ends scrutiny and the prohibition on sheer arbitrariness.* Can individuals bring equal protection claims based not on their membership in a disadvantaged class, but on their being singled out for unfair treatment? Consider in this connection Village of Willowbrook v. Olech, 528 U.S. 562 (2000). The plaintiffs, a married couple, asked the village to connect their property to the municipal water supply, but the village refused to do so unless the Olechs gave the village a thirty-three-foot easement. The Olechs alleged that the village required only a fifteen-foot easement from other property owners, that the difference in treatment was "irrational and wholly arbitrary," and that it was motivated by ill will resulting from a previous unrelated lawsuit, which plaintiffs had successfully brought against the village.

In a per curiam opinion, the Court held that the plaintiffs had stated a valid equal protection claim. According to the Court, a plaintiff can bring an equal protection claim even if she belongs to a "class of one" when she "alleges that she has been intentionally treated differently from others similarly situated and that there is no rational basis for the difference in treatment." The majority held that these allegations were sufficient "quite apart from the Village's subjective motivation" and that it was therefore unnecessary to reach the plaintiffs' alternative theory of subjective ill will.

In a concurring opinion, Justice Breyer expressed sympathy for the view that this holding might "transform many ordinary violations of city or state law into violations of the Constitution. [Zoning] decisions, for example, will often, perhaps almost always treat one landowner differently from another, and one might claim that, when a city's zoning authority takes an action that fails to conform to a city zoning regulation, it lacks a 'rational basis' for its [action]." Justice Breyer nonetheless concurred in the result on the ground that plaintiffs had also alleged "vindictive action."

Why does the majority limit its holding to plaintiffs who allege that they are *intentionally* treated differently? What does "intentionally" mean in this context?

In Engquist v. Oregon Department of Agriculture, 553 U.S. 591 (2008), the Court refused to recognize "class of one" claims by public employees. The plaintiff there brought suit, claiming that she had been fired for "arbitrary, vindictive, and malicious reasons" in violation of the equal protection clause. Chief Justice Roberts delivered the opinion of the Court. The Court distinguished between the government's exercise of its regulatory power with respect to individual citizens and its activities as an employer managing its internal operations. It pointed to a number of areas in which the government as employer is given more leeway with respect to constitutional constraints, such as under the first and fourth amendments. Employment, the Court declared, was a form of state action that by its nature "involve[s] discretionary decisionmaking based on a vast array of subjective, individualized assessments. In such cases the rule that people should be 'treated alike, under like circumstances and conditions' is not violated when one person is treated differently from others, because treating like individuals differently is an accepted consequence of the discretion granted. In such situations, allowing a challenge based on the arbitrary singling out of a particular person would undermine the very discretion that such state officials are entrusted to exercise." Recognizing class-of-one claims alleging that a public employer had treated an employee differently from others for a bad reason unconnected to a particular constitutional provision (such as discrimination on the basis of race or religion or gender) would undermine the concept of at-will employment, and the Court found that the "Constitution does not require repudiating that familiar doctrine." By contrast, the Court explained, in *Olech* and similar cases, there was "a clear standard against which departures, even for a single plaintiff, could be readily assessed."

Justice Stevens, joined by Justices Souter and Ginsburg, dissented. He saw no reason to treat property owners differently from employees and drew a distinction between discretion and arbitrariness: "A discretionary decision represents a choice of one among two or more rational alternatives," and while mistaken discretionary decisions do not violate the equal protection clause, the clause "proscribes arbitrary decisions — decisions unsupported by any rational basis."

7. *The underenforcement thesis.* Even if problems inherent in judicial review preclude vigorous judicial enforcement of the rationality requirement, might not that requirement still retain significance for other actors in the system? Consider the following view: Pure interest-group deals, justified by nothing other than the political strength of the beneficiaries, are prohibited by the equal protection clause. This prohibition is not subject to principled judicial enforcement because inquiries into the legislative process would prove unmanageable and strain judicial competence and authority. But although this prohibition is "underenforced," it nonetheless remains binding on legislators and administrators who have an obligation to obey the Constitution. See generally Sager, Fair Measure: The Status of Underenforced Constitutional Norms, 91 Harv. L. Rev. 1212 (1978).

C.   EQUAL PROTECTION METHODOLOGY: HEIGHTENED SCRUTINY AND THE PROBLEM OF RACE

This section, and those that follow it, explore the circumstances under which the Court has subjected classifications to some form of review more rigorous than the "rational relationship" test. What triggers such heightened scrutiny? What showing can satisfy the more demanding standard?

The best-established case for heightened review is for classifications based on race. Although the application of "strict scrutiny" to racial classifications is now taken as one of the cornerstones of equal protection doctrine, it was not until ten years after Brown v. Board of Education that the Supreme Court "both articulated *and* applied a more rigorous review standard to racial classifications" in

McLaughlin v. Florida, 379 U.S. 184 (1964). See Klarman, An Interpretive History of Modern Equal Protection, 90 Mich. L. Rev. 213, 255 (1991).

Thus, this section begins by considering the decisions that led the Court to articulate the requirement of strict scrutiny for racial classifications. It then turns to how strict scrutiny has operated. When do government decisions that do not explicitly rely on race nonetheless constitute racial classifications? Do *all* uses of race require strict scrutiny? When can the government take race into account?

1. The Origins and Rationale for Heightened Scrutiny in Race-Specific Classifications That Disadvantage Racial Minorities

Strauder v. West Virginia

100 U.S. (10 Otto) 303 (1880)

MR. JUSTICE STRONG delivered the opinion of the Court.

[Strauder, a black man, was convicted of murder before an all-white jury. A West Virginia statute limited jury service to "white male persons who are twenty-one years of age and who are citizens of this State." Strauder claimed that his conviction by a jury chosen pursuant to this provision violated the fourteenth amendment.]

[The] controlling [question is] whether by the Constitution and laws of the United States, every citizen of the United States has a right to a trial of an indictment against him by a jury selected and impanelled without discrimination against his race or color. . . .

It is to be observed that the [question] is not whether a colored man, when an indictment has been preferred against him, has a right to a grand or a petit jury composed in whole or in part of persons of his own race or color, but it is whether, in the composition or selection of jurors by whom he is to be indicted or tried, all persons of his race or color may be excluded by law, solely because of their race or color, so that by no possibility can any colored man sit upon the jury. . . .

[The fourteenth amendment] is one of a series of constitutional provisions having a common purpose; namely, securing to a race recently emancipated, a race that through many generations had been held in slavery, all the civil rights that the superior race enjoy. [At] the time when they were incorporated into the Constitution, it required little knowledge of human nature to anticipate that those who had long been regarded as an inferior and subject race would, when suddenly raised to the rank of citizenship, be looked upon with jealousy and positive dislike, and that State laws might be enacted or enforced to perpetuate the distinctions that had before existed. [The] colored race, as a race, was abject and ignorant, and in that condition was unfitted to command the respect of those who had superior intelligence. Their training had left them mere children, and as such they needed the protection which a wise government extends to those who are unable to protect themselves. They especially needed protection against unfriendly action in the States where they were resident. It was in view of these considerations the Fourteenth Amendment was framed and adopted. It was designed to assure to the colored race the enjoyment of all the civil rights that under the law are enjoyed by white persons, and to give to that race the protection of the general government, in that enjoyment, whenever it should be denied by the States. It not only gave citizenship and the privileges of citizenship to persons of color, but it denied to any State the power to withhold from them the equal protection of the laws, and authorized Congress to enforce its provisions by appropriate legislation. . . .

[What] is this but declaring that the law in the States shall be the same for the black as for the white; that all persons, whether colored or white, shall stand equal before the laws of the States, and, in regard to the colored race, for whose protection the amendment was primarily designed, that no discrimination shall be made against them by law because of their color? The words of the amendment, it is true, are prohibitory, but they contain a necessary implication of a positive immunity, or right, most valuable to the colored race, — the right to exemption from unfriendly legislation against them distinctively as colored, — exemption from legal discriminations, implying inferiority in civil society, lessening the security of their enjoyment of the rights which others enjoy, and discriminations which are steps towards reducing them to the condition of a subject race.

That the West Virginia statute respecting juries [is] such a discrimination ought not to be doubted. [The] very fact that colored people are singled out and expressly denied by a statute all right to participate in the administration of the law, as jurors, because of their color, though they are citizens, and may be in other respects fully qualified, is practically a brand upon them, affixed by the law, an assertion of their inferiority, and a stimulant to that race prejudice which is an impediment to securing to individuals of the race that equal justice which the law aims to secure to all others. . . .

[It] is well known that prejudices often exist against particular classes in the community, which sway the judgment of jurors, and which, therefore, operate in some cases to deny to persons of those classes the full enjoyment of that protection which others enjoy. . . .

In view of these considerations, it is hard to see why the statute of West Virginia should not be regarded as discriminating against a colored man when he is put upon trial for an alleged criminal offence against the State. It is not easy to comprehend how it can be said that while every white man is entitled to a trial by a jury selected from persons of his own race or color, or, rather, selected without discrimination against his color, and a Negro is not, the latter is equally protected by the law with the former. . . .

We do not say that within the limits from which it is not excluded by the amendment a State may not prescribe the qualifications of its jurors, and in so doing make discriminations. It may confine the selection to males, to freeholders, to citizens, to persons within certain ages, or to persons having educational qualifications. We do not believe the Fourteenth Amendment was ever intended to prohibit this. Looking at its history, it is clear it had no such purpose. Its aim was against discrimination because of race or color. . . .

[Justice Field and Justice Clifford dissented.]

Korematsu v. United States
323 U.S. 214 (1944)

MR. JUSTICE BLACK delivered the opinion of the Court.

[On February 19, 1942, some two months after the United States declared war against Japan, President Roosevelt issued Executive Order No. 9066, which authorized military commanders to "prescribe military areas [from] which any or all persons may be excluded, and with respect to which, the right of any person to enter, remain in, or leave shall be subject to whatever restrictions [the Military] Commander may impose in his discretion." On March 21, 1942, Congress enacted legislation making it a crime to violate an order issued by a military commander pursuant to this authority. Three days later, the military commander of the western defense command ordered imposition of a curfew on all persons of Japanese ancestry living on the West Coast. The Supreme Court upheld the constitutionality of this order in Hirabayashi v. United States, 320 U.S. 81 (1943).

On May 3, 1942, the same military commander issued one of a series of exclusion orders, requiring persons of Japanese descent, whether or not they were U.S. citizens, to leave their homes on the West Coast. Persons so ordered were required to report to "Assembly Centers." While some detainees were released from these centers on condition that they remain outside the prohibited zone, others were shipped to "Relocation Centers," which they were prohibited from leaving without permission of the military commander.

Korematsu, a U.S. citizen of unchallenged loyalty, but of Japanese descent, was tried and convicted for remaining in his home contrary to the exclusion order.]

It should be noted, to begin with, that all legal restrictions which curtail the civil rights of a single racial group are immediately suspect. That is not to say that all such restrictions are unconstitutional. It is to say that courts must subject them to the most rigid scrutiny. Pressing public necessity may sometimes justify the existence of such restrictions; racial antagonism never can. . . .

In the light of the principles we announced in the *Hirabayashi* case, we are unable to conclude that it was beyond the war power of Congress and the Executive to exclude those of Japanese ancestry from the West Coast war area at the time they did. True, exclusion from the area in which one's home is located is a far greater deprivation than constant confinement to the home from 8 p.m. to 6 a.m. Nothing short of apprehension by the proper military authorities of the gravest imminent danger to the public safety can constitutionally justify either. But exclusion from a threatened area, no less than curfew, has a definite and close relationship to the prevention of espionage and sabotage. The military authorities, charged with the primary responsibility of defending our shores, concluded that curfew provided inadequate protection and ordered exclusion. . . .

Here, as in the *Hirabayashi* case,

> . . . we cannot reject as unfounded the judgment of the military authorities and of Congress that there were disloyal members of that population, whose number and strength could not be precisely and quickly ascertained. We cannot say that the war-making branches of the Government did not have ground for believing that in a critical hour such persons could not readily be isolated and separately dealt with, and constituted a menace to the national defense and safety, which demanded that prompt and adequate measures be taken to guard against it.

Like curfew, exclusion of those of Japanese origin was deemed necessary because of the presence of an unascertained number of disloyal members of the group, most of whom we have no doubt were loyal to this country. It was because we could not reject the finding of the military authorities that it was impossible to bring about an immediate segregation of the disloyal from the loyal that we sustained the validity of the curfew order as applying to the whole group.

In the instant case, temporary exclusion of the entire group was rested by the military on the same ground. The judgment that exclusion of the whole group was for the same reason a military imperative answers the contention that the exclusion was in the nature of group punishment based on antagonism to those of Japanese origin. That there were members of the group who retained loyalties to Japan has been confirmed by investigations made subsequent to the exclusion. Approximately five thousand American citizens of Japanese ancestry refused to swear unqualified allegiance to the United States and to renounce allegiance to the Japanese Emperor, and several thousand evacuees requested repatriation to Japan.

We uphold the exclusion order as of the time it was made and when the petitioner violated it. [In] doing so, we are not unmindful of the hardships imposed by it upon a large group of American citizens. But hardships are part of war, and war is an aggregation of hardships. All citizens alike, both in and out of uniform, feel the impact of war in greater or lesser measure. Citizenship has its responsibilities as well as its privileges, and in time of war the burden is always heavier. Compulsory exclusion of large groups of citizens from their homes, except under circumstances of direst emergency and peril, is inconsistent with our basic governmental institutions. But when under conditions of modern warfare our shores are threatened by hostile forces, the power to protect must be commensurate with the threatened danger. . . .

It is said that we are dealing here with the case of imprisonment of a citizen in a concentration camp solely because of his ancestry, without evidence or inquiry concerning his loyalty and good disposition towards the United States. Our task would be simple, our duty clear, were this a case involving the imprisonment of a loyal citizen in a concentration camp because of racial prejudice. Regardless of the true nature of the assembly and relocation centers — we deem it unjustifiable to call them concentration camps with all the ugly connotations that term implies — we are dealing specifically with nothing but an exclusion order. To cast this case into outlines of racial prejudice, without reference to the real military dangers which were presented, merely confuses the issue. Korematsu was not excluded from the Military Area because of hostility to him or his race. He *was* excluded because we are at war with the Japanese Empire, because the properly constituted military authorities feared an invasion of our West Coast and felt constrained to take proper security measures, because they decided that the military urgency of the situation demanded that all citizens of Japanese ancestry be segregated from the West Coast temporarily, and finally, because Congress, reposing its confidence in this time of war in our military leaders — as inevitably it must — determined that they should have the power to do just this. There was evidence of disloyalty on the part of some, the military authorities considered that the need for action was great, and time was short. We cannot — by availing ourselves of the calm perspective of hindsight — now say that at that time these actions were unjustified.

[A concurring opinion by Justice Frankfurter and a dissenting opinion by Justice Roberts have been omitted.]

MR. JUSTICE MURPHY, dissenting.

This exclusion of "all persons of Japanese ancestry, both alien and non-alien," from the Pacific Coast area on a plea of military necessity in the absence of martial law ought not to be approved. Such exclusion goes over "the very brink of constitutional power" and falls into the ugly abyss of racism.

In dealing with matters relating to the prosecution and progress of a war, we must accord great respect and consideration to the judgments of the military authorities who are on the scene and who have full knowledge of the military facts. . . .

At the same time, however, it is essential that there be definite limits to military discretion, especially where martial law has not been declared. Individuals must not be left impoverished of their constitutional rights on a plea of military necessity that has neither substance nor support. Thus, like other claims conflicting with the asserted constitutional rights of the individual, the military claim must subject itself to the judicial process of having its reasonableness determined and its conflicts with other interests reconciled. . . .

It must be conceded that the military and naval situation in the spring of 1942 was such as to generate a very real fear of invasion of the Pacific Coast, accompanied by fears of sabotage and espionage in that area. The military command was therefore justified in adopting all reasonable means necessary to combat these dangers. In adjudging the military action taken in light of the then apparent dangers, we must not erect too high or too meticulous standards; it is necessary only that the action have some reasonable relation to the removal of the dangers of invasion, sabotage and espionage. But the exclusion, either temporarily or permanently, of all persons with Japanese blood in their veins has no such reasonable relation. And that relation is lacking because the exclusion order necessarily must rely for its reasonableness upon the assumption that *all* persons of Japanese ancestry may have a dangerous tendency to commit sabotage and espionage and to aid our Japanese enemy in other ways. It is difficult to believe that reason, logic or experience could be marshalled in support of such an assumption. . . .

The main reasons relied upon by those responsible for the forced evacuation, therefore, do not prove a reasonable relation between the group characteristics of Japanese Americans and the dangers of invasion, sabotage and espionage. The reasons appear, instead, to be largely an accumulation of much of the misinformation, half-truths and insinuations that for years have been directed against Japanese Americans by people with racial and economic prejudices — the same people who have been among the foremost advocates of the evacuation. A military judgment based upon such racial and sociological considerations is not entitled to the great weight ordinarily given the judgments based upon strictly military considerations. Especially is this so when every charge relative to race, religion, culture, geographical location, and legal and economic status has been substantially discredited by independent studies made by experts in these matters. . . .

[No] one denies, of course, that there were some disloyal persons of Japanese descent on the Pacific Coast who did all in their power to aid their ancestral land. Similar disloyal activities have been engaged in by many persons of German, Italian and even more pioneer stock in our country. But to infer that examples of individual disloyalty prove group disloyalty and justify discriminatory action against the entire group is to deny that under our system of law individual guilt is the sole basis for deprivation of rights. . . .

MR. JUSTICE JACKSON, dissenting. . . .

It would be impracticable and dangerous idealism to expect or insist that each specific military command in an area of probable operations will conform to conventional tests of constitutionality. When an area is so beset that it must be put under military control at all, the paramount consideration is that its measures be successful, rather than legal. . . .

But if we cannot confine military expedients by the Constitution, neither would I distort the Constitution to approve all that the military may deem expedient. That is what the Court appears to be doing, whether consciously or not. . . .

The [limitations] under which courts always will labor in examining the necessity for a military order are illustrated by this case. How does the Court know that these orders have a reasonable basis in necessity? No evidence whatever on that subject has been taken by this or any other court. . . .

Much is said of the danger to liberty from the Army program for deporting and detaining these citizens of Japanese extraction. But a judicial construction of the due process clause that will sustain this order is a far more subtle blow to liberty than the promulgation of the order itself. A military order, however unconstitutional, is not apt to last longer than the military emergency. Even during that period a succeeding commander may revoke it all. But once a judicial opinion rationalizes such an order to show that it conforms to the Constitution, or rather rationalizes the Constitution to show that the Constitution sanctions such an order, the Court for all time has validated the principle of racial discrimination in criminal procedure and of transplanting American citizens. The principle then lies about like a loaded weapon ready for the hand of any authority that can bring forward a plausible claim of an urgent need. Every repetition imbeds that principle more deeply in our law and thinking and expands it to new purposes. . . .

I should hold that a civil court cannot be made to enforce an order which violates constitutional limitations even if it is a reasonable exercise of military authority. The courts can exercise only the judicial power, can apply only law, and must abide by the Constitution, or they cease to be civil courts and become instruments of military policy.

Of course the existence of a military power resting on force, so vagrant, so centralized, so necessarily heedless of the individual, is an inherent threat to liberty. But I would not lead people to rely on this Court for a review that seems to me wholly delusive. The military reasonableness of these orders can only be determined by military superiors. If the people ever let command of the war power fall into irresponsible and unscrupulous hands, the courts wield no power equal to its restraint. The chief restraint upon those who command the physical forces of the country, in the future as in the past, must be their responsibility to the political judgments of their contemporaries and to the moral judgments of history.

My duties as a justice as I see them do not require me to make a military judgment as to whether General DeWitt's evacuation and detention program was a reasonable military necessity. I do not suggest that the courts should have attempted to interfere with the Army in carrying out its task. But I do not think they may be asked to execute a military expedient that has no place in law under the Constitution. I would reverse the judgment and discharge the prisoner.

Loving v. Virginia

388 U.S. 1 (1967)

MR. CHIEF JUSTICE WARREN delivered the opinion of the Court.

This case presents a constitutional question never addressed by this Court: whether a statutory scheme adopted by the State of Virginia to prevent marriages between persons solely on the basis of racial classifications violates the Equal Protection and Due Process Clauses of the Fourteenth Amendment.

For reasons which seem to us to reflect the central meaning of those constitutional commands, we conclude that these statutes cannot stand consistently with the Fourteenth Amendment. . . .

[The Lovings challenged their conviction under a Virginia statute making it a felony for "any white person [to] intermarry with a colored person, or any colored person [to] intermarry with a white person." The Supreme Court of Appeals of Virginia upheld the statute's constitutionality. The state court relied on its own earlier decision holding that the statute served the legitimate state purposes of preserving the "racial integrity" of its citizens and preventing "corruption of blood," the creation of "a mongrel breed of citizens," and "the obliteration of racial pride."]

[The] State argues that the meaning of the Equal Protection Clause, as illuminated by the statements of the Framers, is only that state penal laws containing an interracial element as part of the definition of the offense must apply equally to whites and Negroes in the sense that members of each race are punished to the same degree. Thus, the State contends that, because its miscegenation statutes punish equally both the white and the Negro participants in an interracial marriage, these statutes, despite their reliance on racial classifications, do not constitute an invidious discrimination based upon race. . . .

Because we reject the notion that the mere "equal application" of a statute containing racial classifications is enough to remove the classifications from the Fourteenth Amendment's proscription of all invidious racial discriminations, we do not accept the State's contention that these statutes should be upheld if there is any possible basis for concluding that they serve a rational purpose. The mere fact of equal application does not mean that our analysis of these statutes should follow the approach we have taken in cases involving no racial discrimination. . . .

[The] Equal Protection Clause requires the consideration of whether the classifications drawn by any statute constitute an arbitrary and invidious discrimination. The clear and central purpose of the Fourteenth Amendment was to eliminate all official state sources of invidious racial discrimination in the States.

There can be no question but that Virginia's miscegenation statutes rest solely upon distinctions drawn according to race. The statutes proscribe generally accepted conduct if engaged in by members of different races. [At] the very least, the Equal Protection Clause demands that racial classifications, especially suspect in criminal statutes, be subjected to the "most rigid scrutiny," [*Korematsu*], and, if they are ever to be upheld, they must be shown to be necessary to the accomplishment of some permissible state objective, independent of the racial discrimination which it was the object of the Fourteenth Amendment to eliminate. . . .

There is patently no legitimate overriding purpose independent of invidious racial discrimination which justifies this classification. The fact that Virginia prohibits only interracial marriages involving white persons demonstrates that the racial classifications must stand on their own justification, as measures designed to maintain White Supremacy.[11] We have consistently denied the constitutionality of measures which restrict the rights of citizens on account of

11. Appellants point out that the State's concern in these statutes, as expressed in the words of the 1924 Act's title, "An Act to Preserve Racial Integrity," extends only to the integrity of the white race. While Virginia prohibits whites from marrying any nonwhite, [Negroes], Orientals, and any other racial class may intermarry without statutory interference. Appellants contend that this distinction renders Virginia's miscegenation statutes arbitrary and unreasonable even assuming the constitutional validity of an official purpose to preserve "racial integrity." We need not reach this contention because we find the racial classifications in these statutes repugnant to the Fourteenth Amendment, even assuming an even-handed state purpose to protect the "integrity" of all races.

race. There can be no doubt that restricting the freedom to marry solely because of racial classifications violates the central meaning of the Equal Protection Clause. . . .

These convictions must be reversed.

It is so ordered.

MR. JUSTICE STEWART, concurring.

I have previously expressed the belief that "it is simply not possible for a state law to be valid under our Constitution which makes the criminality of an act depend upon the race of the actor." McLaughlin v. Florida, 379 U.S. 184, 198 (concurring opinion). Because I adhere to that belief, I concur in the judgment of the Court.

Note: Doctrinal Evolution in the Scrutiny Applied to Racial Classifications

1. *The move from rationality review to strict scrutiny. Loving* is one of the very first cases in which the Supreme Court articulated a different standard of review for racial classifications. Indeed, only two years earlier, in Anderson v. Martin, 375 U.S. 399 (1964), the Court unanimously struck down a Louisiana law requiring that a candidate's race be indicated on the ballot on the grounds that that there was no way in which the provision was "reasonably designed to meet legitimate governmental interests in informing the electorate as to candidates" or any other permissible state purpose — the standard language of rationality review. This raises the question whether strict scrutiny in fact enabled the Court to strike down laws that would have passed rationality review.

Conversely, *Korematsu* is frequently said to mark the last occasion on which the Supreme Court has upheld a race-specific statute disadvantaging a racial minority. It has been widely and severely criticized. See, e.g., E. Muller, Free to Die for Their Country: The Story of the Japanese American Draft Resisters in World War II (2001); P. Irons, Justice at War (1983); R. Daniels, Concentration Camps: North America — Japanese in the United States and Canada during World War II (rev. ed. 1981); J. TenBroek, E. Barnhart, and F. Matson, Prejudice, War and the Constitution (1954). Note that in a companion case to *Korematsu*, the Court held on statutory grounds that the "relocation camps" for Japanese Americans were illegal. See Ex parte Endo, 323 U.S. 283 (1944). For a discussion, see Gudridge, Remembering *Endo*, 116 Harv. L. Rev. 1933 (2003).

In 1984, a federal district court overturned Korematsu's conviction on the ground that the government had "knowingly withheld information from the courts when they were considering the critical question of military necessity." See Korematsu v. United States, 584 F. Supp. 1406 (N.D. Cal. 1984). Four years later, Congress enacted legislation acknowledging "the fundamental injustice" of the evacuation and providing restitution to individuals forced to leave their homes. See Pub. L. No. 100-338, 102 Stat. 903 (1988).

2. *The pragmatic consequences of heightened scrutiny.* If heightened scrutiny makes it more likely that the Court will strike down the challenged action, does this create pressures not to enunciate a broad principle of strict scrutiny for all racial classifications? In this light, consider the somewhat complex move from *Korematsu* — which articulated a requirement of heightened scrutiny but upheld the challenged practice — through *Brown* — which articulated no categorical

requirement but struck down the challenged statutes — to *Loving* — which both articulated a requirement of heightened scrutiny, perhaps unnecessarily, and applied the standard to strike down the challenged law.

The issue resolved in *Loving* was first presented to the Court over a decade earlier in Naim v. Naim. In *Naim*, a white husband sued under Virginia law to annul his marriage on the grounds that, his wife being of Chinese ancestry, their marriage ran afoul of the commonwealth's prohibition of interracial marriage. The Virginia state courts affirmed the annulment of the marriage in an opinion which rejected an equal protection challenge to the statute on the ground that "preserv[ing] the racial integrity of its citizens" was a permissible state interest. Naim v. Naim, 197 Va. 80 (1955). Although the Supreme Court had mandatory appellate jurisdiction over the case, it first remanded the case to the Virginia courts, ostensibly on the ground that the record on appeal was not entirely clear regarding some details related to the marriage, see Naim v. Naim, 350 U.S. 891 (1955), and, after the Virginia Supreme Court refused to take the hint and reconsider the question, see Naim v. Naim, 197 Va. 734 (1956), simply dismissed the succeeding appeal on the ground that the Virginia court's decision "in response to our order . . . leaves the case devoid of a properly presented federal question." At the time and since, the Court's actions in *Naim* were understood as a simple decision to dodge the underlying question. See, e.g., W. Eskridge and P. Frickey, An Historical and Critical Introduction to The Legal Process, in H. Hart and A. Sacks, The Legal Process: Basic Problems in the Making and Application of Law at cix–cx (W. Eskridge and P. Frickey eds., 1994); Hutchinson, Unanimity and Desegregation: Decisionmaking in the Supreme Court, 1948–1958, 68 Geo. L.J. 1, 62–67 (1979); Shapiro, Jurisdiction and Discretion, 60 N.Y.U. L. Rev. 543, 578 (1985).

In thinking about the Court's behavior, consider the view advanced by Bickel, who implicitly praises the Court for not deciding the case:

> [A] judgment legitimating such statutes would have been unthinkable, given the principle of the School Segregation Cases. . . . But would it have been wise, at a time when the Court had just pronounced its new integration principle, when it was subject to scurrilous attack by men who predicted that integration of the schools would lead directly to "mongrelization of the race," would it have been wise, just then, in the first case of its sort, on an issue that the Negro community as a whole can hardly be said to be pressing hard at the moment, to declare that the states may not prohibit racial intermarriage?

A. Bickel, The Least Dangerous Branch: The Supreme Court at the Bar of Politics 174 (1962). Thus, Bickel defended the Court's decision as an appropriate exercise of what he called the "passive virtues."

In thinking about whether the Court's actions in *Naim* were "virtuous," consider Seidman, The Secret Life of the Political Question Doctrine, 37 J. Marshall L. Rev. 441, 462–463 (2004):

> To many contemporary observers, the result in *Naim* seemed completely lawless and impossible to justify on the basis of principle. . . .
>
> [If] the passive virtues are to serve their intended function, they can do so only by misleading the country. Bickel must have assumed that the Court could maintain its reputation for apolitical, principled adjudication while still acting politically because the country paid more attention to what the Court decided than to what it chose not to decide. But not doing is, after all, also a kind of doing; for the parties

involved in *Naim*, the Court's disingenuous avoidance of the merits had precisely the same impact as a decision upholding the statute. If the two results differed at all, the difference lay in how the alternative dispositions were (or would have been) perceived. A decision upholding the Virginia antimiscegenation statute would "legitimate" naked racism, whereas a "nondecision," somehow getting rid of the case on unprincipled grounds, would not. But this difference, if indeed it exists at all, crucially depends upon the public's failure to understand the actual consequences of what the Court has done or failed to do. The Court was, in effect, betting on *Brown* creating banner headlines, while *Naim* slipped unreported through the news sieve. . . .

Note: *Justifications for Strict Scrutiny of Racial Classifications*

What specifically makes racial classifications especially problematic? Consider the following possibilities.

1. *The original intent of the fourteenth amendment was to protect African Americans from discrimination on the basis of race.* Note that the words of the fourteenth amendment do not provide for special treatment of racial classifications. (In this sense, contrast the fourteenth amendment to the fifteenth, which specifically forbids discrimination on the basis of race with respect to voting.) But even if a concern with discrimination against newly freed African American slaves was clearly the central concern of the fourteenth amendment's framers, it is far from clear that the Reconstruction Congress meant to invalidate all government uses of race that disadvantaged African Americans. Consider R. Berger, Government by Judiciary 10, 15 (1977):

> The key to an understanding of the Fourteenth Amendment is that the North was shot through with Negrophobia, that the Republicans, except for a minority of extremists, were swayed by the racism that gripped their constituents rather than by abolitionist ideology. [While] most men were united in a desire to protect the freedmen from outrage and oppression in the South by prohibiting discrimination with respect to "fundamental rights," without which freedom was illusory, to go beyond this with a campaign for political and social equality was, as Senator James R. Doolittle of Wisconsin confessed, "frightening" to the Republicans who "represented States containing the despised and feared negroes."

Note also that the argument from the framers' intent fails to explain the special scrutiny accorded statutes directed against racial groups other than African Americans, such as the Japanese and Japanese Americans whose rights were at issue in *Korematsu*. (And if the framers' intent was to protect African Americans from discrimination, how does this bear on the constitutionality of affirmative action? We return to this issue on pages 562–598, infra.)

2. *Race is rarely, if ever, relevant to any legitimate governmental purpose.* This argument is subject to two objections. First, it may not be empirically correct. For example, suppose that law enforcement officials are trying to describe a suspect, or are trying to decide whether a particular individual should be stopped and questioned with respect to a reported crime. Is an individual's race irrelevant to those decisions? See Banks, Race-Based Suspect Selection and Color Blind Equal Protection Doctrine and Discourse, 48 UCLA L. Rev. 1075 (2001) (discussing the ubiquitous use of race-based suspect descriptions and contrasting it to the more generalized use of race in decisions whether to stop and investigate particular individuals); Banks, Racial Profiling and Antiterrorism Efforts, 89

Cornell L. Rev. 1201 (2004) (describing the controversy over racial profiling in light of the post-9/11 concern with preventing terrorism). Moreover, for a variety of reasons, race may be correlated with traits or characteristics that are relevant to government decisionmaking. Certain racial and ethnic groups are far more susceptible to particular health problems with which the government may be concerned: For example, sickle-cell anemia is more prevalent among African Americans, while Tay-Sachs disease is more likely to strike individuals of Eastern European Jewish ancestry. *Strauder* itself seems to acknowledge that race may be correlated with differences that we might care about. If race were really irrelevant to the way jurors voted, it is hard to see how Strauder would be harmed by standing trial before an all-white jury. In this respect, consider whether Strauder's injury stems from the formal exclusion of black jurors: Would he face the same problems if as a matter of chance he were tried by a jury that happened to be all white?

Second, even if it were true that race is rarely relevant to legitimate government objectives, why does this factor militate in favor of a different standard of review? Doesn't it simply mean that most race classifications would fail rational basis review? Note that cases like Brown v. Board of Education and its progeny striking down de jure segregation, see pages 476–497, supra, did not invoke strict scrutiny, but simply held that racial separation was an impermissible government purpose. Similarly, given cases like United States Department of Agriculture v. Moreno, Cleburne v. Cleburne Living Center, and Romer v. Evans, discussed in the previous section, why couldn't the Court simply strike down laws that discriminate against racial minorities on the ground that the desire to stigmatize or injure an unpopular group is never an acceptable government purpose? Isn't that the approach taken by the Court in *Strauder* and Justice Murphy in dissent in *Korematsu*?

3. *Racial classifications violate a fundamental moral norm.* Perhaps strict scrutiny is simply a shorthand expression of a conclusion, reached after long experience with racial classifications, that such classifications generally express impermissible animus. Consider Brest, Foreword: In Defense of the Antidiscrimination Principle, 90 Harv. L. Rev. 1, 5–6 (1976):

> The antidiscrimination principle rests on fundamental moral values that are widely shared in our society. [The] text and history of the [equal protection] clause are vague and ambiguous and cannot, in any event, infuse the antidiscrimination principle with moral force or justify its extension to novel circumstances and new beneficiaries. Therefore, the argument [against racial classifications] does not ultimately turn on authority, but on whether it comports with the reader's reflective understanding of the antidiscrimination principle.

If the antidiscrimination principle really rests on widely shared views, does this suggests that when racial classifications *are* used, there is a very good reason for doing so? Does this argument lead to the conclusion that courts properly invalidate race-specific statutes adopted in only a few states, but not laws more widely adopted? See generally M. Klarman, From Jim Crow to Civil Rights: The Supreme Court and the Struggle for Racial Equality (2004) (suggesting that the Supreme Court acted to dismantle racial discrimination only after a national norm had emerged leaving the Deep South as an outlier). On the other hand, if the principle is not widely shared, and if it is not required by the text or history of the Constitution, what justification is there for judicial enforcement of it?

4. *Defects in the political process make it especially likely that racial classifications will be based on "hostility" or inaccurate stereotypes.* In United States v. Carolene Products, 304 U.S. 144 (1938), the Court used rational basis review to uphold a federal statute prohibiting interstate shipment of filled milk, which the statute defined as a milk product to which "any fat or oil other than milk fat" had been added. Today the case is less significant for its holding than for its famous footnote 4, in which Justice Stone, writing for the Court, intimated that a more stringent standard of review might apply to statutes "directed at particular religious or national or racial minorities." Justice Stone argued that stricter review might be appropriate in such cases because "prejudice against discrete and insular minorities may be a special condition, which tends seriously to curtail the operation of those political processes ordinarily to be relied upon to protect minorities." It followed that "correspondingly more searching judicial inquiry" was appropriate.

The *Carolene Products* footnote has been called "the most celebrated footnote in constitutional law." Powell, *Carolene Products* Revisited, 82 Colum. L. Rev. 1087, 1087 (1982). See also Fiss, Foreword: The Forms of Justice, 93 Harv. L. Rev. 1, 6 (1979) (describing the *Carolene Products* footnote as "[the] great and modern charter for ordering the relations between judges and other agencies of government"). It has been the subject of extensive scholarly commentary. See, e.g., Ackerman, Beyond *Carolene Products*, 98 Harv. L. Rev. 713 (1985); Ball, Judicial Protection of Powerless Minorities, 59 Iowa L. Rev. 1059 (1974); Cover, The Origins of Judicial Activism in the Protection of Minorities, 91 Yale L.J. 1287 (1982). For an interesting exposition of the history of the footnote, see Lusky, Footnote 4 Redux: A *Carolene Products* Reminiscence, 82 Colum. L. Rev. 1093 (1982).

Does the *Carolene Products* footnote provide a principled basis for judicial intervention to protect minorities? Why does the "discreteness" and "insularity" of these minorities interfere with their ability to protect themselves in the political process? Consider Ackerman, supra, at 728:

> In fact, for all our *Carolene* talk about the powerlessness of insular groups, we are perfectly aware of the enormous power such voting blocs have in American politics. The story of the protective tariff is [the] classic illustration of insularity's power in American history. Over the past half-century, we have been treated to an enormous number of welfare-state variations on the theme of insularity by the farm bloc, the steel lobby, the auto lobby, and others too numerous to mention. In this standard scenario of pluralistic politics, it is precisely the diffuse character of the majority forced to pay the bill for tariffs, agricultural subsidies, and the like, that allows strategically located Congressmen to deliver the goods to their well-organized constituents. Given these familiar stories, it is really quite remarkable to hear lawyers profess concern that insular interests have too little influence in Congress.

Is the problem, then, really one of "prejudice" rather than discreteness or insularity? The concept of prejudice lies at the heart of the most comprehensive, careful, and influential modern elaboration of the theory behind footnote 4: J. Ely, Democracy and Distrust (1980). Ely begins with the premise that "the Constitution [cannot] coherently be interpreted as outlining some 'appropriate' distributional pattern against which actual allocations of hurts and benefits can be traced to see if they are constitutional. The constitutionality of most distributions thus cannot be determined simply by looking to see who ended up with what, but rather can be approached intelligibly only by attending to the process that brought about the distribution in question." Generally, the Constitution prescribes a process of representative democracy to allocate costs and benefits. This process includes "the sort of pluralist wheeling and dealing by which the various minorities that make up our society typically interact to protect their interests."

This process sometimes breaks down. Prejudice directed at certain minorities may so obstruct their ability to form coalitions that "a system of 'mutual defense pacts' will prove recurrently unavailing." Under these circumstances, Ely argues, legislatures will systematically fail to take appropriate account of the allocation and magnitude of costs and benefits and courts must intervene to respond to this process failure.

Does Ely's analysis adequately distinguish between groups that are unfairly treated in the political process and groups that are simply outvoted? Consider the views of Justice Powell in *Carolene Products* Revisited, supra, at 1090:

> [In] one sense, any group that loses a legislative battle can be regarded as both "discrete" and "insular." It is discrete because it supported or opposed legislation not supported or opposed by the majority. It is insular because it was unable to form coalitions with other groups that would have enabled it to achieve its desired ends through the political process. On this view the drug culture — or for that matter public utilities — could be considered discrete and insular.

Ely would limit judicial intervention to cases where a group suffers political losses because of generalizations about its members that are more inaccurate than the legislature realizes. Is judicial review of racial classifications justified because racial prejudice is likely to be unconscious? Consider Lawrence, The Id, the Ego, and Equal Protection: Reckoning with Unconscious Racism, 39 Stan. L. Rev. 317, 349 (1987):

> [Unconscious] prejudice presents [a problem] in that it is not subject to self-correction within the political process. When racism operates at a conscious level, opposing forces can attempt to prevail upon the rationality and moral sensibility of racism's proponents. [But] when the discriminator is not aware of his prejudice and is convinced that he already walks in the path of righteousness, neither reason nor moral persuasion is likely to succeed. The process defect is all the more intractable, and judicial scrutiny becomes imperative.

But why should we assume that courts are more sensitive than legislatures to unconscious racism and inaccurate generalizations?

5. *The central concern of the equal protection clause involves preventing the subordination of groups, rather than simply the mistreatment of individuals.* Many of the arguments already presented are premised on the assumption that the equal protection clause protects *individuals* from being unfairly pigeonholed and treated as members of disfavored groups: "At the heart of the Constitution's guarantee of equal protection lies the simple command that the Government must treat citizens as individuals, not as simply components of a racial, religious, sexual or national class." Miller v. Johnson, 515 U.S. 900, 911 (1995) (internal quotation marks omitted).

Might heightened review be defended on the alternative theory that the equal protection clause protects the rights of particular social groups as such? Consider Fiss's view that the equal protection clause expresses an "ethical view against caste, one that would make it undesirable for any social group to occupy a position of subordination for any extended period of time." Fiss, Groups and the Equal Protection Clause, 5 J. Phil. & Pub. Aff. 107, 151 (1976). Under this view, strict scrutiny for racial classifications reflects the history of African Americans. Is Fiss's view of the equal protection clause too narrow because "it is unjust for society to attach negative significance to a morally irrelevant factor even when doing so does not eventuate in a specially disadvantaged group, but only in harm to, and suffering on the part of, the particular individual affected"? Perry, The Principle of Equal Protection, 32 Hastings L. Rev. 1133, 1146 (1981). Or is Fiss's view too broad because it protects members of a subjugated group, even if an individual member enjoying these rights is not himself subjugated?

6. *A synthesis.* For a detailed and insightful "unified framework" for strict scrutiny, see Rubin, Reconnecting Doctrine and Purpose: A Comprehensive Approach to Strict Scrutiny after *Adarand* and *Shaw*, 149 U. Pa. L. Rev. 1, 20–23 (2000). Rubin provides a taxonomy of the risks and harms that may accompany the use of race as a classificatory principle:

> 1. The risk that race is being used "to harm an unpopular group [or] to indicate that the members of that group are unfit to partake of something given to others [and] to convey in this way the community's judgment about the inherent worth of people of different kinds."
> 2. The risk that the classification "reflects nothing more than racial politics, a desire to reward the members of [one's] own racial group."
> 3. The risk that a racial classification "[reflects] nothing more than erroneous stereotypes."
> 4. The risk that racial classifications, even if related to a legitimate purpose, may perpetuate a negative racial stereotype.
> 5. The risk that decision-making based on race may "[deny] a person treatment as an individual in a way that other sorting mechanisms do not."
> 6. The risk that "the very use of race to identify people [will] [have] some divisive effect on the races by reinforcing the belief in inherent racial differences, regardless of [correlation] with traditional stereotypes."
> 7. The risk that the use of race will "cause a dignitary harm to individuals [regardless] of whether anyone is disadvantaged on the basis of their racial identity."

Rubin goes on to argue in considerable detail that "strict scrutiny must be flexible enough to recognize that different uses of race pose different risks and impose different harms. To determine what risks and harms are present requires a careful examination of the factual circumstances and social contexts in which the use of race by government has taken place." Id. at 25–26. Consider the extent to which this flexibility undermines the advantages of having formally distinct levels of review in the first place.

Note: The Structure of Strict Scrutiny

Korematsu held that racial classifications should be subject to "rigid scrutiny." How should this be accomplished? Can the scrutiny be structured to avoid the problem of judicial value judgments encountered in connection with rational relationship review? Consider the following possibilities:

1. *Limitation of what constitutes a sufficient government purpose. Korematsu* held that a racial classification must be supported by a "pressing public

necessity." The contemporary formulation of this requirement is that the government's interest be "compelling." Presumably this language means that the interests must be unusually weighty: Not every otherwise legitimate government consideration will suffice. But how should a court rank the importance of various constitutionally permissible ends?

Moreover, even once a court answers that question, it may not be clear that the government is pursuing *only* the "compelling goal." For example, winning World War II would clearly qualify as a "pressing public necessity." But was that the sole reason the government chose to use a racial classification to intern Japanese and Japanese-American individuals? Suppose racial prejudice also played a role in the government's decision. Is the decision then illegitimate, even if the compelling government interest was in fact a, or even the primary, reason for the government's decision?

What if the government's goal is actually compelling, but it accommodates illegitimate preferences? In this light, consider Palmore v. Sidoti, 466 U.S. 429 (1984). The case arose from a custody battle between Palmore and Sidoti (who were both white) following their divorce. Originally the trial court awarded custody of the couple's three-year-old daughter to the mother. When the mother married an African American, however, the court determined that the best interests of the child required that the father be awarded custody. The trial court ruled that, "despite the strides that have been made in bettering relations between the races in this country, it is inevitable that [the child] will, if allowed to remain in her present situation, [suffer] from the social stigmatization that is sure to come."

A unanimous Supreme Court reversed. Chief Justice Burger's opinion for the Court acknowledged that the state had "a duty of the highest order to protect the interests of minor children," and that "[there] is a risk that a child living with a step-parent of a different race may be subject to a variety of pressures and stresses not present if the child were living with parents of the same racial or ethnic origin." But the Court nonetheless held that the "reality of private biases and the possible injury they might inflict" were not "permissible considerations. [Private] biases may be outside the reach of the law, but the law cannot, directly or indirectly, give them effect."

Would the result in *Sidoti* have been the same if detailed empirical study demonstrated that children in mixed-race homes suffered psychological damage? Would the same analysis apply if the state were making adoption decisions, rather than child custody determinations? See Bartholet, Where Do Black Children Belong? The Politics of Race Matching in Adoption, 139 U. Pa. L. Rev. 1163 (1991); see also Banks, The Color of Desire: Fulfilling Adoptive Parents' Racial Preferences through Discriminatory State Action, 107 Yale L.J. 875 (1998); Bartholet, Private Race Preferences in Family Formation, 107 Yale L.J. 2351 (1998).

2. *Means scrutiny.* It is possible to read the *Korematsu* test as focusing not only on ends but also on means. Thus, even if winning World War II was a "pressing public necessity," it is hard to see how that necessity justified a racial classification that contributed only marginally to achieving the end. In other cases, the Court has been more explicit in requiring a tight fit between means and ends when reviewing racial classifications. In McLaughlin v. Florida, 379 U.S. 184, 196 (1964), for example, the Court said that racial classifications "[bear] a heavy burden of justification [and] will be upheld only if [necessary] and not merely rationally related, to the accomplishment of a permissible state policy." See also In re Griffiths, 413 U.S. 717, 721–722 (1973).

Does means-oriented strict scrutiny escape the problem of judicial value judgments? If the scrutiny is so strict that the existence of *any* alternative means, regardless of cost, is sufficient to invalidate a racial classification, then presumably the Court would be freed from the necessity of balancing. But could any racial classification survive this test? If, alternatively, a balance must be struck between the cost of the classification and the cost of forgoing it, must not the Court somehow attach values to these factors so that they can be weighed against each other?

Note how fact dependent means-oriented scrutiny is. In *Korematsu,* for example, the necessity of a racial classification turned on questions such as how serious the threat of sabotage was, how many Japanese Americans were disloyal, and how hard it would have been to separate the loyal from the disloyal. Did the *Korematsu* Court "rigidly scrutinize" the military commander's judgment? Would it be tolerable for nine justices in Washington to substitute their judgment for that of the military on questions such as these? Does "rigid scrutiny" amount to anything more than a rubber stamp if the Court is unwilling to look behind the factual judgments made by other branches?

3. *The interaction of means and ends.* Since announcing the requirement of strict scrutiny for racial classifications, the Supreme Court has applied the standard in a case involving a challenge by a black plaintiff to an explicit racial classification only once. In Johnson v. California, 543 U.S. 499 (2005), the Court addressed an unwritten policy of the California Department of Corrections (CDC) that assigned inmates to cells on the basis of race for up to sixty days each time a prisoner entered a new correctional facility, based on its view that such segregation prevented violence caused by racial gangs.

The court of appeals held that the policy's constitutionality should be reviewed under the deferential standard articulated in Turner v. Safley, 482 U.S. 78 (1987), which asks whether a regulation that burdens a prisoner's fundamental rights is "reasonably related" to "legitimate penological interests." Using that standard, the Ninth Circuit Court of Appeals upheld California's policy.

Justice O'Connor's opinion for the Court rejected that argument, reaffirming that "*all* racial classifications [imposed by government] . . . must be analyzed by a reviewing court under strict scrutiny."

> The need for strict scrutiny is no less important here, where prison officials cite racial violence as the reason for their policy. As we have recognized in the past, racial classifications "threaten to stigmatize individuals by reason of their membership in a racial group and to incite racial hostility." Indeed, by insisting that inmates be housed only with other inmates of the same race, it is possible that prison officials will breed further hostility among prisoners and reinforce racial and ethnic divisions. By perpetuating the notion that race matters most, racial segregation of inmates "may exacerbate the very patterns of [violence that it is] said to counteract." See also Trulson & Marquart, The Caged Melting Pot: Toward an Understanding of the Consequences of Desegregation in Prisons, 36 Law & Soc. Rev. 743, 774 (2002) (in a study of prison desegregation, finding that "over [10 years] the rate of violence between inmates segregated by race in double cells surpassed the rate among those racially integrated"). . . .

Even assuming that prevention of prison violence was a compelling government interest, the Court was not convinced that racial segregation was a necessary means of achieving that goal:

> [Virtually] all other States and the Federal Government manage their prison systems without reliance on racial segregation. [Indeed,] the United States argues,

based on its experience with the [Federal Bureau of Prisons], that it is possible to address "concerns of prison security through individualized consideration without the use of racial segregation, unless warranted as a necessary and temporary response to a race riot or other serious threat of race-related violence." As to transferees, in particular, whom the CDC has already evaluated at least once, it is not clear why more individualized determinations are not possible. . . .

Justice Thomas, joined by Justice Scalia, dissented. He saw the case as lying at the intersection of "two conflicting lines of precedent": one requiring strict scrutiny of all racial classifications and the other holding that a "relaxed" standard of review should apply "to all circumstances in which the needs of prison administration implicate constitutional rights." He would have followed the latter line. He ended his dissent by noting that given the level of violence in California prisons, if the plaintiff ultimately won his challenge to racial cell assignment, he "may well have won a Pyrrhic victory." A year later, in his concurrence in the judgment in Beard v. Banks, 548 U.S. 521 (2006), a prisoners' rights case involving the first amendment, Justice Thomas noted:

> Just last Term, this Court invalidated California's policy of racially segregating prisoners in its reception centers, notwithstanding that State's warning that its policy was necessary to prevent prison violence. California subsequently experienced several instances of severe race-based prison violence, including a riot that resulted in 2 fatalities and more than 100 injuries, and significant fighting along racial lines between newly arrived inmates, the very inmates that were subject to the policy invalidated by the Court in *Johnson*.

4. *What counts as a "facial" racial classification?* Must a law classify *individuals* on the basis of their race to count as a racial classification? Or is the fact that race is the explicit subject matter of a law sufficient to trigger strict scrutiny? In this light, consider Hunter v. Erickson, 393 U.S. 385 (1969). In response to the city council's passage of a fair housing ordinance that prohibited racial discrimination in real estate transactions, the citizens of Akron, Ohio, passed a referendum amending the city charter. The amendment (referred to as §137) provided that ordinances regulating real estate transactions "on the basis of race, color, religion, national origin or ancestry" had to be approved by the voters before taking effect. Other ordinances regulating real estate transactions could go into effect without first receiving popular approval. The Supreme Court held that the charter amendment violated the equal protection clause:

> Here, . . . there was an explicitly racial classification treating racial housing matters differently from other racial and housing matters. . . .
> It is true that the section draws no distinctions among racial and religious groups. Negroes and whites, Jews and Catholics are all subject to the same requirements if there is housing discrimination against them which they wish to end. But §137 nevertheless disadvantages those who would benefit from laws barring racial, religious, or ancestral discriminations as against those who would bar other discriminations or who would otherwise regulate the real estate market in their favor. The automatic referendum system does not reach housing discrimination on sexual or political grounds, or against those with children or dogs, nor does it affect tenants seeking more heat or better maintenance from landlords, nor those seeking rent control, urban renewal, public housing, or new building codes.
> Moreover, although the law on its face treats Negro and white, Jew and gentile in an identical manner, the reality is that the law's impact falls on the minority. The

majority needs no protection against discrimination and if it did, a referendum might be bothersome but no more than that. . . . [Section] 137 places special burdens on racial minorities within the governmental process. . . .

The Court went on to hold that the Akron charter amendment served no compelling government purpose. Does *Hunter* mean that all laws that refer to race involve racial classifications? Consider whether strict scrutiny should apply to the federal government's policy of asking citizens to identify their race on census forms or the government's ensuing publication of data that contains racial classifications. Does *Hunter* mean that all laws prohibiting discrimination on the basis of race would also trigger strict scrutiny? For example, suppose Akron had adopted a law that forbade housing discrimination on the basis of race, but left landlords free to discriminate "on sexual or political grounds, or against those with children or dogs." Would the city be subjected to more searching scrutiny of this choice that it would face if it made the opposite choice?

Compare Schuette v. Coalition to Defend Affirmative Action, 134 S. Ct. 1623 (2014), where the Court upheld a provision of the Michigan constitution that prohibited state and local governmental entities from "discriminat[ing] against, or grant[ing] preferential treatment to, any individual or group on the basis of race, sex, color, ethnicity, or national origin." The amendment was adopted in the wake of the Court's decision upholding a race-conscious affirmative action plan at the University of Michigan Law School. The justices in the 6-2 majority did not coalesce behind a single opinion. But none of them applied strict scrutiny to the Michigan provision.

5. *The meaning of "race."* History and constitutional context show quite clearly that discrimination against African Americans is "racial" discrimination. In *Korematsu*, the Court similarly treated discrimination against persons of Japanese origin as "racial." In Hirabayashi v. United States, 320 U.S. 81 (1943), on which *Korematsu* relied, the Court described the suspect classification more broadly, stating that "[distinctions] between citizens solely because of their ancestry are by their very nature odious to a free people whose institutions are founded upon the doctrine of equality."

Two weeks before the Supreme Court decided *Brown*, it addressed the question in Hernandez v. Texas, 347 U.S. 475 (1954). Hernandez, who was Mexican American and had been indicted for murder, alleged that persons of Mexican descent were being systematically excluded from juries in the county where he was to be tried in violation of the equal protection clause.

> The State of Texas would have us hold that there are only two classes — white and Negro — within the contemplation of the Fourteenth Amendment. The decisions of this Court do not support that view. . . .
>   Throughout our history differences in race and color have defined easily identifiable groups which have at times required the aid of the courts in securing equal treatment under the laws. But community prejudices are not static, and from time to time other differences from the community norm may define other groups which need the same protection. Whether such a group exists within a community is a question of fact. When the existence of a distinct class is demonstrated, and it is further shown that the laws, as written or as applied, single out that class for different treatment not based on some reasonable classification, the guarantees of the Constitution have been violated. The Fourteenth Amendment is not directed solely against discrimination due to a "two-class theory" — that is, based upon differences between "white" and Negro. . . .

The petitioner's initial burden in substantiating his charge of group discrimination was to prove that persons of Mexican descent constitute a separate class in Jackson County, distinct from "whites." One method by which this may be demonstrated is by showing the attitude of the community. Here the testimony of responsible officials and citizens contained the admission that residents of the community distinguished between "white" and "Mexican." The participation of persons of Mexican descent in business and community groups was shown to be slight. Until very recent times, children of Mexican descent were required to attend a segregated school for the first four grades. . . . On the courthouse grounds at the time of the hearing, there were two men's toilets, one unmarked, and the other marked "Colored Men" and "Hombres Aqui" ("Men Here"). No substantial evidence was offered to rebut the logical inference to be drawn from these facts, and it must be concluded that petitioner succeeded in his proof.

Does *Hernandez* hold that discrimination against Mexican Americans is racial discrimination or that it is somehow equivalent to racial discrimination because the position of Mexican Americans in Texas resembles, in important ways, the position of African Americans? In thinking about what counts as a "race," consider the Court's resolution of this question as a statutory matter in St. Francis College v. Al-Khazraji, 481 U.S. 604 (1987). That case concerned a claim of discrimination in employment brought under 42 U.S.C. §1981, a Reconstruction-era statute (indeed, part of the Civil Rights Act that prompted Congress to propose the fourteenth amendment, see pages 475-476, supra) that gave to all persons in the United States the same right "as is enjoyed by white citizens" to make and enforce contracts. Recognizing that §1981 had long been interpreted "to forbid all 'racial' discrimination" in the making of contracts, the Court held that Al-Khazraji had alleged racial discrimination when he claimed he had been denied tenure because of his status as an Arab American: "[W]e have little trouble in concluding that Congress intended to protect from discrimination identifiable classes of persons who are subjected to intentional discrimination solely because of their ancestry or ethnic characteristics. Such discrimination is racial discrimination that Congress intended §1981 to forbid, whether or not it would be classified as racial in terms of modern scientific theory." In a footnote, the Court described the contemporary debate over the nature of race, observing that "some, but not all, scientists" have concluded that "racial classifications are for the most part sociopolitical, rather than biological, in nature." As we will see in subsequent sections of this chapter, debates over what characteristics sufficiently resemble race to justify triggering strict scrutiny has been a recurring question in modern equal protection law.

2. *Facially Nonracial Classifications That Disadvantage Racial Minorities: When Does Heightened Scrutiny Apply?*

Washington v. Davis

426 U.S. 229 (1976)

MR. JUSTICE WHITE delivered the opinion of the Court.

[Respondents, unsuccessful black applicants for positions on the police force, claimed that a test measuring verbal ability, vocabulary, and reading comprehension unconstitutionally discriminated against them. According to the district court, respondents' evidence supported the conclusion that a higher percentage of blacks than whites failed the test, and that the test had not been empirically shown to reliably measure measuring subsequent job performance.]

The central purpose of the Equal Protection Clause of the Fourteenth Amendment is the prevention of official conduct discriminating on the basis of race. [But] our cases have not embraced the proposition that a law or other official act, without regard to whether it reflects a racially discriminatory purpose, is unconstitutional *solely* because it has a racially disproportionate impact.

Almost 100 years ago, Strauder v. West Virginia established that the exclusion of Negroes from grand and petit juries in criminal proceedings violated the Equal Protection Clause, but the fact that a particular jury or a series of juries does not statistically reflect the racial composition of the community does not in itself make out an invidious discrimination forbidden by the Clause. . . .

The school desegregation cases have also adhered to the basic equal protection principle that the invidious quality of a law claimed to be racially discriminatory must ultimately be traced to a racially discriminatory purpose. That there are both predominantly black and predominantly white schools in a community is not alone violative of the Equal Protection Clause. The essential element of de jure segregation is "a current condition of segregation resulting from intentional state action." Keyes v. School Dist. No. 1.

[The] Court has also recently rejected allegations of racial discrimination based solely on the statistically disproportionate racial impact of various provisions of the Social Security Act because "[t]he acceptance of appellants' constitutional theory would render suspect each difference in treatment among the grant classes, however lacking in racial motivation and however otherwise rational the treatment might be." Jefferson v. Hackney, 406 U.S. 535, 548 (1972).

This is not to say that the necessary discriminatory racial purpose must be express or appear on the face of the statute, or that a law's disproportionate impact is irrelevant in cases involving Constitution-based claims of racial discrimination. A statute, otherwise neutral on its face, must not be applied so as invidiously to discriminate on the basis of race. . . .

Necessarily, an invidious discriminatory purpose may often be inferred from the totality of the relevant facts, including the fact, if it is true, that the law bears more heavily on one race than another. It is also not infrequently true that the discriminatory impact — in the jury cases for example, the total or seriously disproportionate exclusion of Negroes from jury venires — may for all practical purposes demonstrate unconstitutionality because in various circumstances the discrimination is very difficult to explain on nonracial grounds. Nevertheless, we have not held that a law, neutral on its face and serving ends otherwise within the power of government to pursue, is invalid under the Equal Protection Clause simply because it may affect a greater proportion of one race than of another. Disproportionate impact is not irrelevant, but it is not the sole touchstone of an invidious racial discrimination forbidden by the Constitution. Standing alone, it does not trigger the rule, that racial classifications are to be subjected to the strictest scrutiny and are justifiable only by the weightiest of considerations. . . .

[We] have difficulty understanding how a law establishing a racially neutral qualification for employment is nevertheless racially discriminatory and denies "any person . . . equal protection of the laws" simply because a greater proportion of Negroes fail to qualify than members of other racial or ethnic groups. Had respondents, along with all others who had failed [the test], whether white or black, brought an action claiming that [it] denied each of them equal protection of the laws as compared with those who had passed with high enough scores to qualify them as police recruits, it is most unlikely that their challenge would have been sustained. [The test], which is administered generally to prospective Government employees, concededly seeks to ascertain whether those who take it have acquired a particular level of verbal skill; and it is untenable that the Constitution prevents the Government from seeking modestly to upgrade the communicative abilities of its employees rather than to be satisfied with some lower level of competence, particularly where the job requires special ability to communicate orally and in writing. Respondents, as Negroes, could no more successfully claim that the test denied them equal protection than could white applicants who also failed. The conclusion would not be different in the face of proof that more Negroes than whites had been disqualified by [the test]. That other Negroes also failed to score well would, alone, not demonstrate that respondents individually were being denied equal protection of the laws by the application of an otherwise valid qualifying test being administered to prospective police recruits.

Nor on the facts of the case before us would the disproportionate impact of [the test] warrant the conclusion that it is a purposeful device to discriminate against Negroes and hence an infringement of the constitutional rights of respondents as well as other black applicants. As we have said, the test is neutral on its face and rationally may be said to serve a purpose the Government is constitutionally empowered to pursue. Even agreeing with the District Court that the differential racial effect of [the test] called for further inquiry, we think the District Court correctly held that the affirmative efforts of the Metropolitan Police Department to recruit black officers, the changing racial composition of the recruit classes and of the force in general, and the relationship of the test to the training program negated any inference that the Department discriminated on the basis of race or that "a police officer qualifies on the color of his skin rather than ability." . . .

A rule that a statute designed to serve neutral ends is nevertheless invalid, absent compelling justification, if in practice it benefits or burdens one race more than another would be far reaching and would raise serious questions about, and perhaps invalidate, a whole range of tax, welfare, public service, regulatory, and licensing statutes that may be more burdensome to the poor and to the average black than to the more affluent white. . . .

MR. JUSTICE STEVENS, concurring. . . .

Frequently the most probative evidence of intent will be objective evidence of what actually happened rather than evidence describing the subjective state of mind of the actor. For normally the actor is presumed to have intended the natural consequences of his deeds. This is particularly true in the case of governmental action which is frequently the product of compromise, of collective decisionmaking, and of mixed motivation. It is unrealistic, on the one hand, to require the victim of alleged discrimination to uncover the actual subjective intent of the decisionmaker or, conversely, to invalidate otherwise legitimate action simply because an improper motive affected the deliberation of a participant in the decisional process. A law conscripting clerics should not be invalidated because an atheist voted for it.

My point in making this observation is to suggest that the line between discriminatory purpose and discriminatory impact is not nearly as bright, and perhaps not quite as critical, as the reader of the Court's opinion might assume. I agree, of course, that a constitutional issue does not arise every time some disproportionate impact is shown. On the other hand, when the disproportion is dramatic, [it] really does not matter whether the standard is phrased in terms of purpose or effect. Therefore, although I accept the statement of the general rule in the Court's opinion, I am not yet prepared to indicate how that standard should be applied in the many cases which have formulated the governing standard in different language. . . .

[A dissenting opinion by Justice Brennan is omitted.]

Note: *Rational Basis Review of Non–Race-Specific Classifications*

1. *Some preliminary questions.* After Washington v. Davis, a court confronted with a classification that disadvantages a racial minority must first determine whether it constitutes a "racial classification." If it does — either because the classification explicitly draws racial lines or because it is motivated by a racial purpose — the court will use strict scrutiny and probably invalidate it. If the classification is non–race-specific, the court will use rational basis review despite the classification's disproportionate impact on the minority group and probably uphold it. Has the Supreme Court given an adequate account of why facially neutral classifications that harm racial minorities should not be strictly scrutinized in the absence of a discriminatory purpose? Is it because such classifications are less likely to stigmatize? Because they are less likely to perpetuate stereotypes? Because it would be impractical to invalidate all the "tax, welfare, public service, regulatory, and licensing statutes that may be more burdensome to [the] average black than to the [average] white"? Even if strict scrutiny and virtual per se invalidation are inappropriate for non–race-specific classifications, should the fact that a challenged classification disproportionately affects racial minorities trigger some form of more rigorous review?

2. *The problem of remedy.* Many of the arguments against an effects test assume that, so long as a disproportionate impact is unintended, it is merely a matter of chance. Is this assumption warranted? Does it matter whether, and to what extent, blacks and whites are differently situated with respect to the challenged law because of *prior* unequal treatment by government? Consider Perry, The Disproportionate Impact Theory of Racial Discrimination, 125 U. Pa. L. Rev. 540, 558 (1977):

> Laws having a disproportionate racial impact burden blacks *because* of their especially disadvantaged position in American society. A failure to require government to take account of that especially disadvantaged social position by selecting and fine-tuning laws to avoid the unnecessary or thoughtless aggravation of the situation would effectively ignore American society's responsibility for that social position. Furthermore, the failure would compound the responsibility.

Compare Alexander, What Makes Wrongful Discrimination Wrong? Biases, Preferences, Stereotypes, and Proxies, 141 U. Pa. L. Rev. 149, 213 (1992):

> If one lacks a preferred trait that one would have possessed were one not the victim of wrongful discrimination, may one demand in addition to compensation from

one's victimizers that others overlook the absence of the trait? Surely not. If I was a promising neurosurgeon before my hands were mangled by a drunk driver, I cannot ask others to ignore my lack of dexterity in their choice of neurosurgeons. [Preferences] for scarce traits do not become immoral merely because the scarcity is in part due to the immoralities of others, even when just reparations have not been fully paid.

In Oregon v. Mitchell, 400 U.S. 112 (1970), the Supreme Court unanimously upheld Congress's nationwide ban of literacy tests as a prerequisite to voting, holding that the challenged statute reflected an appropriate use of congressional enforcement power under the Reconstruction amendments. Although there was no opinion for the Court, several of the justices pointed to the fact that official racial discrimination in education both before and after *Brown* was in part responsible for the racially disparate impact of such tests. Justice Black's opinion made the point most clearly:

> The children who were denied an equivalent education by the "separate but equal" rule of Plessy v. Ferguson, 163 U.S. 537 (1896), overruled in Brown v. Board of Education, 347 U.S. 483 (1954), are now old enough to vote. There is substantial, if not overwhelming, evidence from which Congress could have concluded that it is a denial of equal protection to condition the political participation of children educated in a dual school system upon their educational achievement. Moreover, the history of this legislation suggests that concern with educational inequality was perhaps uppermost in the minds of the congressmen who sponsored the Act. The hearings are filled with references to educational inequality. Faced with this and other evidence that literacy tests reduce voter participation in a discriminatory manner not only in the South but throughout the Nation, Congress was supported by substantial evidence in concluding that a nationwide ban on literacy tests was appropriate to enforce the Civil War amendments.

3. *Disproportionate impact and the theory of passive government.* Even if the government is not responsible for the fact that blacks are differently situated with respect to a non–race-specific classification, why should that fact matter? Doesn't treating people the same when they are relevantly different deny equality just as effectively as treating them differently when they are relevantly the same? Compare, for example, the following two hypothetical admissions policies followed by a state university:

a. No blind applicants will be admitted.
b. All applicants, whether sighted or blind, must take a written examination without assistance, and those receiving the highest scores will be admitted.

The first treats blind and sighted applicants differently, although they are (arguably) relevantly the same. The second treats blind and sighted applicants the same, although they are (arguably) relevantly different. Does either satisfy the equality principle?

Recall the suggestion that race-specific classifications are strictly scrutinized in order to deal with problems of legislative purpose. When the classification is race-specific, the purpose question is not whether the legislature intended to treat blacks and whites differently. The classification itself establishes that purpose. Rather, the question is whether the legislature intended to treat them differently simply for the sake of harming a racial minority rather than for the sake of achieving some permissible goal. The strict scrutiny doctrine holds that only a showing of a close fit and an overriding government interest can overcome the inference that the classification was motivated by a desire to harm the minority. See section C1 supra. See also Personnel Administrator of Massachusetts v. Feeney, 442 U.S. 256, 272 (1979). But why shouldn't the same inference be drawn, and the same strict scrutiny required, when a non–race-specific classification disproportionately disadvantages a racial minority? Isn't treating blacks and whites the same despite the fact that they are differently situated just as effective a strategy for disadvantaging blacks as treating them differently despite the fact that they are similarly situated?

Note: *What Constitutes a Racially Motivated Classification?: Questions of Discriminatory Purpose*

1. *What constitutes a discriminatory purpose?* Washington v. Davis provides that a court should apply strict scrutiny to a facially nonracial government action only if the plaintiff can show that the action was taken for a "discriminatory purpose." In Personnel Administrator of Massachusetts v. Feeney, 442 U.S. 256 (1979), a gender discrimination case, the Court elaborated on what "purpose" means. Under Massachusetts law, all veterans who qualified for state civil service positions had to be considered for appointment ahead of any qualifying nonveterans. The preference operated overwhelmingly to the advantage of males. In an opinion by Justice Stewart, the Court upheld the preference against equal protection attack. It conceded that it would be "disingenuous" to say that the legislation's effect on women was unintended "in the sense that [it] was not volitional or in the sense that [it] was not foreseeable." But

"discriminatory purpose" [implies] more than intent as volition or intent as awareness of consequences. It implies that the decisionmaker [selected] or reaffirmed a particular course of action at least in part "because of," not merely "in spite of" its adverse effects upon an identifiable group. Yet nothing in the record demonstrates that this preference for veterans was originally devised or subsequently re-enacted because it would accomplish the collateral goal of keeping women in a stereotypic or predefined place in the Massachusetts Civil Service.

Should the *Feeney* Court have focused on whether the Massachusetts legislature would have enacted the same preference if most veterans had been women? For a discussion of some problems with this approach, see Seidman, Public Principle and Private Choice: The Uneasy Case for a Boundary Maintenance Theory of Constitutional Law, 96 Yale L.J. 1006, 1038–1039 (1987).

2. *Mixed motives.* Does it make sense even to talk about "a purpose" when it comes to the decisions of collective bodies, often reaffirmed over long periods of time? Perhaps the Court tried to finesse this problem with its decision in Village of Arlington Heights v. Metropolitan Housing Development Corp., 429 U.S. 252 (1977). There, the Court held that

Davis does not require a plaintiff to prove that the challenged action rested solely on racially discriminatory purposes. Rarely can it be said that a legislature or administrative body operating under a broad mandate made a decision motivated solely by a single concern, or even that a particular purpose was the "dominant" or "primary" one. In fact, it is because legislators and administrators are properly concerned with balancing numerous competing considerations that courts refrain from reviewing the merits of their decisions, absent a showing of arbitrariness or irrationality. But racial discrimination is not just another competing consideration. When there is a proof that a discriminatory purpose has been a motivating factor in the decision, this judicial deference is no longer justified.

The Court went on to explain that proof that a decision "was motivated in part by a racially discriminatory purpose would not necessarily [require] invalidation of the challenged decision." Instead, such proof would shift to the government

> the burden of establishing that the same decision would have resulted even had the impermissible purpose not been considered. If this were established, the complaining party in a case of this kind no longer fairly could attribute the injury complained of to improper consideration of a discriminatory purpose. In such circumstances, there would be no justification for judicial interference with the challenged decision.

More broadly, consider also Justice Stevens's observation in his dissent in Rogers v. Lodge, 458 U.S. 613 (1982). There, the Court struck down the use of at-large elections in a county in Georgia on the grounds that the system "was being maintained for the invidious purpose of diluting the voting strength of the black population."

> The costs and the doubts associated with litigating questions of motive, which are often significant in routine trials, will be especially so in cases involving the "motives" of legislative bodies. Often there will be no evidence that the governmental system was adopted for a discriminatory reason. . . . In such a case the question becomes whether the system was maintained for a discriminatory purpose. Whose intentions control? Obviously not the voters, although they may be most responsible for the attitudes and actions of local government. Assuming that it is the intentions of the "state actors" that is critical, how will their mental processes be discovered? Must a specific proposal for change be defeated? What if different motives are held by different legislators or, indeed, by a single official? Is a selfish desire to stay in office sufficient to justify a failure to change a governmental system?

3. *Discriminatory administration of facially neutral statutes.* At what level ought purpose be evaluated? Can a law enacted for neutral reasons nonetheless be found purposefully discriminatory in practice?

In Yick Wo v. Hopkins, 118 U.S. 351 (1886), petitioner was convicted of violating a local ordinance prohibiting operation of a laundry not located in a brick or stone building without the consent of the board of supervisors. He alleged that he and more than two hundred other Chinese nationals had petitioned the board of supervisors for consent, but that all of their petitions were denied, whereas all but one of the petitions filed by non-Chinese were granted. The Court unanimously reversed Yick Wo's conviction. It held that

[*all challenges by chinese were denied*]

> the facts shown establish an administration directed so exclusively against a particular class of persons as to warrant and require the conclusion, that, whatever may have been the intent of the ordinances as adopted, they are applied by the public authorities charged with their administration, and thus representing the

State itself, with a mind so unequal and oppressive as to amount to a practical denial by the State of [equal] protection of the laws.

Note that there might be two separate explanations for the problem identified in *Yick Wo*. First, a statute might be passed for neutral reasons but administered in a discriminatory fashion unintended by the statute's drafters. Second, a legislative body might enact statutes that accord low-level government agents tremendous discretion with the understanding that such discretion will be administered in a discriminatory manner precisely because proving the purpose behind individual implementations of a policy would be relatively difficult.

In this light, consider the well-developed line of authority reversing convictions where it is shown that facially neutral jury selection statutes are administered in a discriminatory fashion. See page 560, infra, for treatment of these cases. See, e.g., Castaneda v. Partida, 430 U.S. 482 (1977); Carter v. Jury Commission, 396 U.S. 320 (1970); Avery v. Georgia, 345 U.S. 559 (1953). Moreover, in the jury context, reversal is required even in the absence of a showing that any prejudice (in the sense of a different outcome) resulted from the discriminatory policy. See Vasquez v. Hillery, 474 U.S. 254 (1986); Rose v. Mitchell, 443 U.S. 545 (1979). In Batson v. Kentucky, 476 U.S. 79 (1986), discussed at pages 560-561, infra, the Court extended these cases to the use of peremptory challenges by prosecutors to remove individual jurors on the basis of race.

4. *Statutes enacted for discriminatory purposes.* Is discriminatory purpose review less troublesome when a statute contains a classification that is deliberately "gerrymandered" to produce a disproportionate impact on racial minorities? Consider the following two examples in which the Court found such a motive.

Gomillion v. Lightfoot, 364 U.S. 339 (1960), concerned an Alabama statute that altered the shape of the city of Tuskegee from a square to an "uncouth twenty-eight sided figure." The plaintiffs alleged that the new boundary lines removed from the city all but four or five of the city's 400 black voters, while not removing a single white voter. The Court held that, if these allegations were proved, the statute infringed on the right of blacks to vote in violation of the fifteenth amendment:

> If these allegations upon a trial remained uncontradicted or unqualified, the conclusion would be irresistible, tantamount for all practical purposes to a mathematical demonstration, that the legislation is solely concerned with segregating white and colored voters by fencing Negro citizens out of town so as to deprive them of their pre-existing municipal vote. It is difficult to appreciate what stands in the way of adjudging a statute having this inevitable effect invalid.

Similarly, in Hunter v. Underwood, 471 U.S. 222 (1985), the Court confronted a provision of the Alabama Constitution, adopted in 1901, that disenfranchised all persons convicted of misdemeanors of moral turpitude. A unanimous Court, in an opinion by Justice Rehnquist, invalidated the provision because it was largely motivated by the desire to disenfranchise blacks: The list of disenfranchising misdemeanors was picked because the provision's drafters thought blacks were particularly prone to the specified offenses. Why should the motivation of the 1901 legislature determine the validity of the provision in 1985? Note also that the laws challenged in *Gomillion* and *Underwood* were both enacted during periods in which legislators were quite candid about the racial motivations behind their actions. Consider whether "gerrymandering" today is likely to be more sophisticated and less able to detect.

5. *"De facto" racial classifications.* Should a statute be subject to strict scrutiny even if it does not use race per se as a classifying principle and is not intended simply to circumvent the presumption against racial classifications if the classification correlates especially closely with race?

Consider Hernandez v. New York, 500 U.S. 352 (1991). Hernandez claimed that the prosecutor at his criminal trial had used peremptory challenges to exclude Latinos from the jury. The prosecutor told the trial judge that the challenges were based on his fear that the challenged jurors, who were bilingual, would have difficulty following only the official interpreter for Spanish-speaking witnesses rather than their own understanding of the testimony. The trial court rejected the defendant's claim, and the Supreme Court affirmed. According to Justice Kennedy, in an opinion joined by Chief Justice Rehnquist and Justices White and Souter, this was a disparate impact case and therefore governed by Washington v. Davis:

> As explained by the prosecutor, the challenges rested neither on the intention to exclude Latino or bilingual jurors, nor on stereotypical assumptions about Latinos or bilinguals. The prosecutor's articulated basis for these challenges divided potential jurors into two classes: those whose conduct during the *voir dire* would persuade him they might have difficulty in accepting the translator's rendition of Spanish-language testimony and those potential jurors who gave no such reason for doubt. Each category would include both Latinos and non-Latinos. While the prosecutor's criterion might well result in the disproportionate removal of prospective Latino jurors, that disproportionate impact does not turn the prosecutor's actions into a *per se* violation of the Equal Protection Clause.

Justice O'Connor, joined by Justice Scalia, concurred in the judgment:

> [I] believe that the plurality opinion goes farther than it needs to in assessing the constitutionality of the prosecutor's asserted justification for his peremptory strikes. . . .
>
> In this case, the prosecutor's asserted justification for striking certain Hispanic jurors was his uncertainty about the jurors' ability to accept the official translation of trial testimony. If this truly was the purpose of the strikes, they were not strikes because of race, and therefore did not violate the Equal Protection Clause. [They] may have acted like strikes based on race, but they were *not* based on race. No matter how closely tied or significantly correlated to race the explanation for a peremptory strike may be, the strike does not implicate the Equal Protection Clause unless it is based on race.

Compare *Hernandez* with Rice v. Cayetano, 528 U.S. 495 (2000). The Hawaiian constitution establishes the Office of Hawaiian Affairs (OHA), which is vested with authority to administer revenue from land held in trust for the betterment of the conditions of the descendants of the indigenous people who inhabited the island in 1778, the date when England's Captain Cook made landfall in Hawaii. (The constitutionality of this arrangement was not before the Court, and the Court expressed no opinion on this subject.) The right to vote for the nine trustees composing the governing body of the OHA was limited to descendants of people inhabiting Hawaii in 1778. Rice challenged this limitation on the ground that it violated the fifteenth amendment prohibition against racial restrictions on the right to vote. In a seven-to-two decision, the Supreme Court, per Justice Kennedy, agreed:

> Ancestry can be a proxy for race. It is that proxy here. Even if the residents of Hawaii in 1778 had been of more diverse ethnic backgrounds and cultures, it is far from clear that a voting test favoring their descendants would not be a race-based qualification. But that is not this case. For centuries Hawaii was isolated from migration. The inhabitants shared common physical characteristics, and by 1778 they had a common culture. . . .
>
> Simply because a class defined by ancestry does not include all members of the race does not suffice to make the classification race neutral. Here, the State's argument is undermined by its express racial purpose and by its actual effects.

Justice Stevens, in an opinion joined by Justice Ginsburg, dissented:

> The OHA voter qualification speaks in terms of ancestry and current residence, not of race or color. . . .
>
> Ancestry surely can be a proxy for race, or a pretext for invidious racial discrimination. But it is simply neither proxy nor pretext here. . . .
>
> [The] OHA election provision excludes all full-blooded Polynesians currently residing in Hawaii who are not descended from a 1778 resident of Hawaii. Conversely, [the] OHA scheme excludes no descendant of a 1778 resident because he or she is also part European, Asian, or African as a matter of race. The classification here is thus both too inclusive and not inclusive enough to fall strictly along racial lines.

Are *Hernandez* and *Cayetano* consistent?

6. *Racially motivated classifications that are not strictly scrutinized.* Does it follow from *Yick Wo* and *Gomillion* that racially motivated classifications should always be subject to strict scrutiny? The Court has demonstrated some reluctance to strictly scrutinize such classifications in three situations:

a. Palmer *and the problem of racially motivated classifications with neutral effects.* Compare *Gomillion* with Palmer v. Thompson, 403 U.S. 217 (1971), in which a city council closed municipal swimming pools following court-ordered integration. In a five-to-four decision, the Court held that the closing did not violate the equal protection clause. After observing that "no case in this Court has held that a legislative act may violate equal protection solely because of the motivations of the men who voted for it," the Court advanced several reasons why investigation of purpose was improper:

> First, it is extremely difficult for a court to ascertain the motivation, or collection of different motivations, that lie behind a legislative enactment. [Furthermore], there is an element of futility in a judicial attempt to invalidate a law because of the bad motives of its supporters. If the law is struck down for this reason, rather than because of its facial content or effect, it would presumably be valid as soon as the legislature or relevant governing body repassed it for different reasons.

The Court distinguished *Gomillion* as a case resting on the "actual effect" of the enactment, "not upon the motivation which led the [State] to behave as [it] did."

Is this explanation of *Gomillion* consistent with Washington v. Davis? The *Washington* Court attempted to explain *Palmer* on the ground that the pool closing extended "identical treatment to both whites and Negroes." Taken together, *Palmer* and *Washington* suggest that a facially neutral statute is subject to enhanced review only when it has *both* a discriminatory purpose *and* a disproportionate impact. However, it is difficult to see how a holding that the closing of integrated pools does not produce a disproportionate racial impact is consistent with Brown v. Board of Education. See Brest, Palmer v. Thompson: An Approach to the Problem of Unconstitutional Legislative Motive, 1971 Sup. Ct. Rev. 95, 132. Is it conceivable that the Court would uphold a statute that by its terms required the closing of any municipal facility ordered desegregated? Compare Bush v. Orleans Parish School Board, 187 F. Supp. 42 (E.D. La. 1960), aff'd, 365 U.S. 569 (1961) (statute providing for closing of all integrated schools unconstitutional).

b. *"Discretionary" decisions.* Should there be a class of "discretionary" governmental decisions not subject to improper purpose review? Suppose, for example, that the President chooses a nominee for the Supreme Court or for a cabinet post partially on the basis of racial or ethnic considerations. Will, or should, the courts review that choice? Is the absence of such suits a practical consequence of standing rules: What disappointed aspirant is likely to bring suit? And what would the remedy be?

c. *The causation requirement.* Should an improperly motivated classification be subject to strict scrutiny if the state is able to show that the same classification would have been used even in the absence of the improper motive? Note that *Arlington Heights* suggests that perhaps the answer to this question is "no." The Court has never suggested that a statute that discriminates on its face against racial minorities can be saved from strict scrutiny by a showing that the same classification would have been used in the absence of racial animus. Indeed, on one view the reason why the Court requires a compelling government interest and a tight fit between means and ends is to ascertain whether the same law would have been adopted if the legislature were not "prejudiced." Does it follow that strict scrutiny is also the appropriate technique for investigating the causation question when facially neutral statutes are infected by a discriminatory purpose?

7. *The transsubstantive nature of the discriminatory purpose inquiry.* Stated abstractly, there appears to be a sharp distinction between a "purpose" and an "effects" test for the constitutionality of facially neutral statutes that disproportionately disadvantage racial minorities. In practice, however, the importance of the distinction turns on the willingness of courts to infer discriminatory purpose from either discriminatory effect or the absence of other plausible purposes. The more willing the courts are to infer purpose from effect or to insist on proof of important nondiscriminatory purposes, the less important the distinction is. The Court's willingness to infer purpose from effect has varied across substantive areas. In this respect, consider Ortiz, The Myth of Intent in Equal Protection, 41 Stan. L. Rev. 1105, 1107 (1989):

> Instead of regulating the inputs to decisionmaking, intent serves, I believe, as a way of judging substantive outcomes. In particular, it works . . . by allocating burdens of proof between the individual and the state. Of particular interest is the way the doctrine allocates these burdens differently in different contexts. . . . The nature of the case makes all the difference.
>
> In my view, intent allocates these burdens differently in different contexts in order to "balance" individual and societal interests consistently with the ideology of traditional liberalism. Where (as in housing and employment) this ideology either relegates decisionmaking to markets or allows the state much leeway in allocating

goods, intent makes judicial supervision of decisionmaking difficult. On the other hand, where liberal ideology insists on particular types of nonmarket allocation (as in voting, jury selection, and sometimes education), intent makes judicial intervention more likely. . . . [Thus, the] intent doctrine serves to reinforce and protect many of our reigning political and economic values. The doctrine's significance lies in the way it simultaneously achieves and hides this purpose.

Note: *Distinctive Problems in the Administration of Criminal Justice*

Applying the equal protection clause to claims of racial discrimination in the criminal justice system poses many of the general problems associated with equal protection law in particularly acute form, especially with respect to determining whether facially neutral practices in fact reflect a discriminatory purpose.

Even though *Strauder* squarely established the principle that laws excluding blacks from serving on juries violate the equal protection clause, they continued in the South to be largely excluded from juries for a variety of reasons until the last half of the twentieth century. Some of this exclusion was the product of intentionally discriminatory enforcement of facially neutral laws regarding who could serve on juries. Particularly in jurisdictions where individual jury commissioners decided whom to call for jury service, exclusion was rampant. See, e.g., Castaneda v. Partida, 430 U.S. 482 (1977); Carter v. Jury Commission, 396 U.S. 320 (1970); Avery v. Georgia, 345 U.S. 559 (1953). Some of the exclusion was due to the interaction of laws regarding jury service with other laws that were intentionally discriminatory. For example, in jurisdictions where jury summonses were based on individuals being on the voting rolls, racial discrimination in registration would also affect jury composition.

When jury selection procedures are challenged as racially discriminatory, the Court has been relatively receptive to arguments based on disproportionate effects, at least as a device for shifting the burden of proof to the state. Castaneda v. Partida, 430 U.S. 482 (1977), sets out the standard method of proof. A defendant who claims he is a member of a racial group that has wrongly been excluded must show the "degree" of underrepresentation "by comparing the proportion of the group in the total population to the proportion called to serve as [jurors], over a significant period of time." If he also shows that the jury selection procedure is "susceptible of abuse or is not racially neutral," this will create a "presumption of discrimination," and "the burden then shifts to the State to rebut that case." What explains the Court's greater willingness to infer purpose from effect in the jury context?

The remedy the Court applied in cases where racial discrimination was proved was reversal of a defendant's conviction, even in the absence of a showing that any prejudice resulted from the discriminatory policy. See Vasquez v. Hillery, 474 U.S. 254 (1986); Rose v. Mitchell, 443 U.S. 545 (1979).

In Batson v. Kentucky, 476 U.S. 79 (1986), the Court extended these cases to the use of peremptory challenges by prosecutors to remove individual jurors on the basis of race. In an opinion by Justice Powell, the Court held that

[although] a prosecutor ordinarily is entitled to exercise permitted peremptory challenges "for any reason at all, as long as that reason is related to his view concerning the outcome" of the case to be tried, the Equal Protection Clause forbids the prosecutor to challenge potential jurors solely on account of their race or on the assumption that black jurors as a group will be unable impartially to consider the State's case against a black defendant.

In a dissenting opinion, Chief Justice Burger, joined by Justice Rehnquist, argued that

> peremptory challenges are often lodged, of necessity, for reasons "normally thought irrelevant to legal proceedings or official actions, namely, the race, religion, nationality, occupation or affiliation of people summoned for jury duty." Moreover, in making peremptory challenges, both the prosecutor and defense attorney necessarily act on only limited information or hunch. The process can not be indicted on the sole basis that such decisions are made on the basis of "assumption" or "intuitive judgment." As a result, unadulterated equal protection analysis is simply inapplicable to peremptory challenges exercised in any particular case.

Justice Rehnquist, joined by Chief Justice Burger, also wrote a dissenting opinion:

> [There] is simply nothing "unequal" about the State using its peremptory challenges to strike blacks from the jury in cases involving black defendants so long as such challenges are also used to exclude whites in cases involving white defendants, Hispanics in cases involving Hispanic defendants, Asians in cases involving Asian defendants, and so on. This case-specific use of peremptory challenges by the State does not single out blacks, or members of any other race for that matter, for discriminatory treatment. Such use of peremptories is at best based upon seat-of-the-pants instincts, which are undoubtedly crudely stereotypical and may in many cases be hopelessly mistaken. But as long as they are applied across the board to jurors of all races and nationalities, I do not see [how] their use violates the Equal Protection Clause.

See also Powers v. Ohio, 499 U.S. 400 (1991) (holding that *Batson* applied when the defendant and the excluded juror do not "share the same race"); Edmonson v. Leesville Concrete Co., 500 U.S. 614 (1991) (holding that race-based peremptory challenges by private litigants in civil litigation violated the Constitution); Georgia v. McCollum, 505 U.S. 42 (1992) (holding that *Batson* applied to defense, as well as prosecutorial, challenges).

Consider Justice Thomas's attack on *Batson* in his opinion concurring in the judgment in *McCollum*:

> [I] am certain that black criminal defendants will rue the day that this court ventured down this road that inexorably will lead to the elimination of peremptory strikes.
>
> In *Strauder*, [we] invalidated a state law that prohibited blacks from serving on juries. In the course of the decision, we observed that the racial composition of a jury may affect the outcome of a criminal case. . . .
>
> We reasonably surmised, without direct evidence in any particular case, that all-white juries might judge black defendants unfairly.

The *Batson* principle has proved notoriously difficult to enforce in practice. With nearly twenty years of hindsight, consider the observations made by Justice Breyer in his concurring opinion in Miller-El v. Dretke, 545 U.S. 213 (2005), a case involving a *Batson* claim that spawned two trips to the Supreme Court:

> As the Court's opinion makes clear, Miller-El marshaled extensive evidence of racial bias. But despite the strength of his claim, Miller-El's challenge has resulted in 17 years of largely unsuccessful and protracted litigation — including 8 different

judicial proceedings and 8 different judicial opinions, and involving 23 judges, of whom 6 found the *Batson* standard violated and 16 the contrary. . . .

Given the inevitably clumsy fit between any objectively measurable standard and the subjective decisionmaking at issue, I am not surprised to find studies and anecdotal reports suggesting that, despite *Batson*, the discriminatory use of peremptory challenges remains a problem. See, e.g., Baldus, Woodworth, Zuckerman, Weiner, & Broffitt, The Use of Peremptory Challenges in Capital Murder Trials: A Legal and Empirical Analysis, 3 U. Pa. J. Const. L. 3, 52–53, 73, n.197 (2001) (in 317 capital trials in Philadelphia between 1981 and 1997, prosecutors struck 51% of black jurors and 26% of nonblack jurors; defense counsel struck 26% of black jurors and 54% of nonblack jurors; and race-based uses of prosecutorial peremptories declined by only 2% after *Batson*); Rose, The Peremptory Challenge Accused of Race or Gender Discrimination? Some Data from One County, 23 Law and Human Behavior 695, 698–699 (1999) (in one North Carolina county, 71% of excused black jurors were removed by the prosecution; 81% of excused white jurors were removed by the defense). . . .

[Peremptory] challenges seem increasingly anomalous in our judicial system. On the one hand, the Court has widened and deepened *Batson*'s basic constitutional rule. [On] the other hand, the use of race- and gender-based stereotypes in the jury-selection process seems better organized and more systematized than ever before. . . .

[These] examples reflect a professional effort to fulfill the lawyer's obligation to help his or her client. Nevertheless, the outcome in terms of jury selection is the same as it would be were the motive less benign. And as long as that is so, the law's antidiscrimination command and a peremptory jury-selection system that permits or encourages the use of stereotypes work at cross-purposes. . . .

I recognize that peremptory challenges have a long historical pedigree. They may help to reassure a party of the fairness of the jury. But long ago, Blackstone recognized the peremptory challenge as an "arbitrary and capricious species of [a] challenge." 4 W. Blackstone, Commentaries on the Laws of England 346 (1769). If used to express stereotypical judgments about race, gender, religion, or national origin, peremptory challenges betray the jury's democratic origins and undermine its representative function. The "scientific" use of peremptory challenges may also contribute to public cynicism about the fairness of the jury system and its role in American government. And, of course, the right to a jury free of discriminatory taint is constitutionally protected — the right to use peremptory challenges is not.

Should the inability of the courts to police the *Batson* principle lead them to ban the use of peremptory challenges altogether?

McCleskey v. Kemp
481 U.S. 279 (1987)

JUSTICE POWELL delivered the opinion of the Court.

[McCleskey, an African American, was convicted in a Georgia state court of murdering a white police officer and sentenced to death. On habeas corpus, he alleged that the Georgia capital sentencing scheme was administered in a racially discriminatory manner in violation of the equal protection clause.

[In support of this claim, he proffered a statistical study prepared by Professor David Baldus (the "Baldus study"), which examined more than two thousand murder cases occurring in Georgia in the 1970s. The raw numbers collected by Baldus indicated that the death penalty was assessed in 22 percent of the cases involving black defendants and white victims; 8 percent of the cases involving white defendants and white victims; 1 percent of the cases involving black defendants and black victims; and 3 percent of the cases involving white defendants and black victims.

[Baldus then subjected his data to statistical analysis that attempted to account for other variables that might have explained these differences on nonracial grounds. After taking into account a variety of nonracial variables, he concluded that defendants charged with killing whites were 4.3 times more likely to receive a death sentence than defendants charged with killing blacks. The study further indicated that black defendants who killed white victims had the greatest likelihood of receiving a death sentence.

[The district court found the Baldus study flawed in several respects, held that it "[failed] to contribute anything of value" to McCleskey's claim, and dismissed the petition. The court of appeals affirmed. Although it assumed arguendo that the study was valid, the court held that the statistics were "insufficient to demonstrate discriminatory intent."]

Our analysis begins with the basic principle that a defendant who alleges an equal protection violation has the burden of proving "the existence of purposeful discrimination."[7] Thus, to prevail under the Equal Protection Clause, McCleskey must prove that the decisionmakers in *his* case acted with discriminatory purpose. He offers no evidence specific to his own case that would support an inference that racial considerations played a part in his sentence. . . .

[T]he nature of the capital sentencing decision, and the relationship of the statistics to that decision, are fundamentally different from the corresponding elements in the venire-selection or Title VII cases. Most importantly, each particular decision to impose the death penalty is made by a petit jury selected from a properly constituted venire. Each jury is unique in its composition, and the Constitution requires that its decision rest on consideration of innumerable factors that vary according to the characteristics of the individual defendant and the facts of the particular capital offense. Thus, the application of an inference drawn from the general statistics to a specific decision in a trial and sentencing simply is not comparable to the application of an inference drawn from general statistics to a specific venire-selection or Title VII case. In those cases, the statistics relate to fewer entities, and fewer variables are relevant to the challenged decisions.

Another important difference [is] that, in the venire-selection and Title VII contexts, the decisionmaker has an opportunity to explain the statistical disparity. Here, the State has no practical opportunity to rebut the Baldus study. [The] policy considerations behind a prosecutor's traditionally "wide discretion" suggest the impropriety of our requiring prosecutors to defend their decisions to seek death penalties, "often years after they were made." Moreover, absent far stronger proof, it is unnecessary to seek such a rebuttal, because a legitimate and unchallenged explanation for the decision is apparent from the record: McCleskey

---

7. [As] did the Court of Appeals, we assume the study is valid statistically without reviewing the factual findings of the District Court. Our assumption that the Baldus study is statistically valid does not include the assumption that the study shows that racial considerations actually enter into any sentencing decisions in Georgia. Even a sophisticated multiple regression analysis such as the Baldus study can only demonstrate a *risk* that the factor of race entered into some capital sentencing decisions and a necessarily lesser risk that race entered into any particular sentencing decision. [Relocated footnote. — Eds.]

committed an act for which the United States Constitution and Georgia laws permit imposition of the death penalty.

Finally, McCleskey's statistical proffer must be viewed in the context of his challenge. McCleskey challenges decisions at the heart of the State's criminal justice system. [Because] discretion is essential to the criminal justice process, we would demand exceptionally clear proof before we would infer that the discretion has been abused. . . .

McCleskey also suggests that the Baldus study proves that the State as a whole has acted with a discriminatory purpose. He appears to argue that the State has violated the Equal Protection Clause by adopting the capital punishment statute and allowing it to remain in force despite its allegedly discriminatory application. But "'[d]iscriminatory purpose' . . . implies more than intent as volition or intent as awareness of consequences. It implies that the decisionmaker, in this case a state legislature, selected or reaffirmed a particular course of action at least in part 'because of,' not merely 'in spite of,' its adverse effects upon an identifiable group." [Personnel Administrator v. Feeney, 442 U.S. 256 (1979).] For this claim to prevail, McCleskey would have to prove that the Georgia Legislature enacted or maintained the death penalty statute *because of* an anticipated racially discriminatory effect. [There is] no evidence [that] the Georgia Legislature enacted the capital punishment statute to further a racially discriminatory purpose. . . .

[The] capital sentencing decision requires the individual jurors to focus their collective judgment on the unique characteristics of a particular criminal defendant. It is not surprising that such collective judgments often are difficult to explain. But the inherent lack of predictability of jury decisions does not justify their condemnation. On the contrary, it is the jury's function to make the difficult and uniquely human judgments that defy codification and that "buil[d] discretion, equity, and flexibility into a legal system." H. Kalven & H. Zeisel, The American Jury 498 (1966).

McCleskey's argument that the Constitution condemns the discretion allowed decisionmakers in the Georgia capital sentencing system is antithetical to the fundamental role of discretion in our criminal justice system. [Of] course, "the power to be lenient [also] is the power to discriminate," K. Davis, Discretionary Justice 170 (1973), but a capital-punishment system that did not allow for discretionary acts of leniency "would be totally alien to our notions of criminal justice." Gregg v. Georgia, 428 U.S. 153, 200, n.50 (1976).

[Where] the discretion that is fundamental to our criminal process is involved, we decline to assume that what is unexplained is invidious. In light of the safeguards designed to minimize racial bias in the process, the fundamental value of jury trial in our criminal justice system, and the benefits that discretion provides to criminal defendants, we hold that the Baldus study does not demonstrate a constitutionally significant risk of racial bias affecting the Georgia capital sentencing process. . . .

McCleskey's claim, taken to its logical conclusion, throws into serious question the principles that underlie our entire criminal justice system. [If] we accepted McCleskey's claim that racial bias has impermissibly tainted the capital sentencing decision, we could soon be faced with similar claims as to other types of penalty. Moreover, the claim that his sentence rests on the irrelevant factor of race easily could be extended to apply to claims based on unexplained discrepancies that correlate to membership in other minority groups, and even to gender. [The] Constitution does not require that a State eliminate any

demonstrable disparity that correlates with a potentially irrelevant factor in order to operate a criminal justice system that includes capital punishment. . . .
[Affirmed.]

JUSTICE BRENNAN, with whom JUSTICE MARSHALL, [JUSTICE BLACKMUN, and JUSTICE STEVENS] join, dissenting. . . .

At some point in this case, Warren McCleskey doubtless asked his lawyer whether a jury was likely to sentence him to die. A candid reply to this question would have been disturbing. [The] story could be told in a variety of ways, but McCleskey could not fail to grasp its essential narrative line: there was a significant chance that race would play a prominent role in determining if he lived or died. . . .

The Baldus study indicates that, after taking into account some 230 nonracial factors that might legitimately influence a sentencer, the jury *more likely than not* would have spared McCleskey's life had his victim been black. . . .

Evaluation of McCleskey's evidence cannot rest solely on the numbers themselves. We must also ask whether the conclusion suggested by those numbers is consonant with our understanding of history and human experience. Georgia's legacy of a race-conscious criminal justice system, as well as this Court's own recognition of the persistent danger that racial attitudes may affect criminal proceedings, indicate that McCleskey's claim is not a fanciful product of mere statistical artifice.

For many years, Georgia operated openly and formally precisely the type of dual system the evidence shows is still effectively in place. The criminal law expressly differentiated between crimes committed by and against blacks and whites, distinctions whose lineage traced back to the time of slavery. . . .

This historical review of Georgia criminal law is not intended as a bill of indictment calling the State to account for past transgressions. Citation of past practices does not justify the automatic condemnation of current ones. But it would be unrealistic to ignore the influence of history in assessing the plausible implications of McCleskey's evidence. "[A]mericans share a historical experience that has resulted in individuals within the culture ubiquitously attaching a significance to race that is irrational and often outside their awareness." Lawrence, The Id, The Ego, and Equal Protection: Reckoning with Unconscious Racism, 39 Stan. L. Rev. 317 (1987). . . .

The Court maintains that petitioner's claim "is antithetical to the fundamental role of discretion in our criminal justice system." . . .

Reliance on race in imposing capital punishment, however, is antithetical to the very rationale for granting sentencing discretion. Discretion is a means, not an end. . . .

Considering the race of a defendant or victim in deciding if the death penalty should be imposed is completely at odds with [the] concern that an individual be evaluated as a unique human being. Decisions influenced by race rest in part on a categorical assessment of the worth of human beings according to color, insensitive to whatever qualities the individuals in question may possess. . . .

The Court next states that its unwillingness to regard the petitioner's evidence as sufficient is based in part on the fear that recognition of McCleskey's claim would open the door to widespread challenges to all aspects of criminal sentencing. Taken on its face, such a statement seems to suggest a fear of too much justice. Yet surely the majority would acknowledge that if striking evidence indicated that other minority groups, or women, or even persons with blond hair, were disproportionately sentenced to death, such a state of affairs would be repugnant to deeply rooted conceptions of fairness. The prospect that there may be more widespread abuse than McCleskey documents may be dismaying, but it does not justify complete abdication of our judicial role. . . .

[A dissenting opinion by Justice Blackmun, joined by Justices Marshall and Stevens and, in part, by Justice Brennan, and a dissenting opinion by Justice Stevens, joined by Justice Blackmun, are omitted.]

Note: *Racial Disparities in Investigating, Charging, and Sentencing*

1. *The problem of selective insensitivity.* Does the Court's formulation of the intent requirement in *McCleskey* adequately heed the risk that legislatures will be selectively indifferent to the welfare of politically powerless groups? Consider the following argument: Of course, the equal protection clause prohibits governmental action deliberately undertaken to harm racial and other minorities. But few laws are passed because legislators have a sadistic desire to inflict disabilities on these groups. The more common problem arises when the legislature is pursuing a neutral aim but, in doing so, is selectively indifferent to the welfare of certain groups. Thus, the question the *McCleskey* Court should have asked is not whether Georgia's capital punishment scheme was designed to harm African Americans, but rather whether the legislature would have been as willing to inflict the death penalty if most of the persons executed had been white. Compare Brest, Foreword: In Defense of the Antidiscrimination Principle, 90 Harv. L. Rev. 1, 6–8 (1976).

2. *Questions of stereotypes and statistical validity.* The Court returned to the problem of defining discriminatory purpose in a criminal justice context in United States v. Armstrong, 517 U.S. 456 (1996). Armstrong, an African American, had been charged with conspiring to possess with intent to distribute "crack" cocaine. He sought discovery from the prosecution to gather evidence supporting his claim that the government was not prosecuting similarly situated suspects of other races. The court of appeals upheld an order granting this request. In an eight-to-one decision the Supreme Court, per Chief Justice Rehnquist, reversed, holding that the defendant had failed to make a threshold showing:

> To establish a discriminatory effect in a race case, the claimant must show that similarly situated individuals of a different race were not prosecuted. . . .
>
> [If] the claim of selective prosecution were well founded, it should not have been an insuperable task to prove that persons of other races were being treated differently than respondents. . . . [We] think the required threshold — a credible showing of different treatment of similarly situated persons — adequately balances the Government's interest in vigorous prosecution and the defendant's interest in avoiding selective prosecution. . . .
>
> The Court of Appeals reached its decision in part because it started "with the presumption that people of *all* races commit *all types of crimes* — not with the premise that any type of crime is the exclusive province of any particular racial or ethnic group." It cited no authority for this proposition, which seems contradicted by the most recent statistics of the United States Sentencing Commission. Those statistics show that: More than 90% of the persons sentenced in 1994 for crack cocaine trafficking were black; 93.4% of convicted LSD dealers were white;

and 91% of those convicted for pornography or prostitution were white. Presumptions at war with presumably reliable statistics have no proper place in the analysis of this issue.

Do statistics about racial differentials in sentencing and conviction refute claims of racial discrimination in prosecution? Even more fundamentally, do they undermine the court of appeals' presumption that levels of criminal *behavior* are similar? But even if these statistics are valid, how can the Court's position in *Armstrong* be reconciled with *Batson* and other cases holding that the constitutional prohibition against race discrimination prevents the state from relying on even accurate racial generalizations?

Note that Armstrong did not allege that the statutory penalties for possession and distribution of "crack" were influenced by the racial composition of the class charged with violating the statute. How should such a claim be evaluated?

For discussion of the question whether decisions to use race as part of the calculus in deciding when to make investigatory stops, see D. Cole, No Equal Justice: Race and Class in the American Criminal Justice System 24–38 (1999) (arguing that pretextual traffic stops are conducted in a pervasively discriminatory manner). Professor Cole notes that police stops yield essentially the same "hit rates" — searches that actually find evidence of criminal behavior — for both white and nonwhite motorists and argues that this suggests that levels of criminal behavior among whites and nonwhites are similar; thus the fact that nonwhite motorists are stopped at much higher rates is evidence of discrimination. In response, consider the observations in Banks, Beyond Profiling: Race, Policing, and the Drug War, 56 Stan. L. Rev. 571, 592–593 (2003), that the studies' findings "are also consistent with the possibility that the extensive investigation of racial minorities reflects their higher rates of criminal activity, along with officers' rational use of racial profiling." Finally, consider Harcourt, Rethinking Racial Profiling: A Critique of the Economics, Civil Liberties, and Constitutional Literature, and of Criminal Profiling More Generally, 71 U. Chi. L. Rev. 1275 (2004). Harcourt argues that data upon which current research rests is of little empirical use. Absent data regarding natural offending rates by racial group and the comparative elasticity of offending to policing, Harcourt suggests, it is difficult to articulate how racial profiling should be used in policing.

Regardless of the empirical debate, racial profiling — at least with respect to "ordinary" crime (as opposed to profiling related to interdiction of terrorists) — has been largely condemned by politicians and citizens across the spectrum. Banks, supra at 574–575, suggests this "attests to the cultural resonance of antidiscrimination claims inflected by tropes of irrationality and innocence. The campaign against racial profiling has converted varied bases of drug war opposition and concerns about police treatment of minorities into a morally compelling and politically potent constitutional claim of discrimination."

3. *Difficulties of proof connected to one-time decisionmakers.* To what extent are cases involving the criminal justice system made more difficult to prove by the fact that so many decisions are delegated to low-level officials (such as individual police officers deciding whom to stop and investigate from among a universe of potential targets or individual assistants in a prosecutor's office deciding against whom to exercise peremptory challenges in a series of cases)? Is this problem exacerbated in the *McCleskey* context by the fact that individual juries make only one decision and are not required (and indeed, in some states are affirmatively discouraged) from ever providing any reason for their decision? See Alschuler,

The Supreme Court and the Jury: Voir Dire, Peremptory Challenges, and the Review of Jury Verdicts, 56 U. Chi. L. Rev. 153, 218–229 (1989) (discussing the various rules and decisions that limit inquiry into a jury's deliberations). For some observations regarding the possible effects of *judges'* race and sex on sentencing decisions, see Schanzenbach, Racial and Sex Disparities in Prison Sentences: The Effect of District-Level Judicial Demographics, 34 J. Legal Stud. 57 (2005).

In Pena-Rodriguez v. Colorado, 137 S. Ct. 855 (2017), the Court addressed the potential problem from a different angle. It held that the long-standing and widespread evidentiary rule that generally prohibits jurors from undermining the verdict by testifying as to statements made during deliberations must give way in cases where the testimony describes a clear statement by a juror that the juror relied on racial stereotypes or animus to convict a criminal defendant. During the deliberations in Pena-Rodriguez's trial, one of the jurors stated "I think he did it because he's Mexican and Mexican men take whatever they want," and expressed his disbelief of the defendant's alibi witness because the witness was "an illegal." (In fact, the witness testified that he was a legal resident of the United States.) Justice Kennedy's opinion for the Court pointed to the "imperative to purge racial prejudice from the administration of justice."

> "[T]he central purpose of the Fourteenth Amendment was to eliminate racial discrimination emanating from official sources in the States." In the years before and after the ratification of the Fourteenth Amendment, it became clear that racial discrimination in the jury system posed a particular threat both to the promise of the Amendment and to the integrity of the jury trial. . . .
>
> Permitting racial prejudice in the jury system damages "both the fact and the perception" of the jury's role as "a vital check against the wrongful exercise of power by the State.". . .
>
> A constitutional rule that racial bias in the justice system must be addressed — including, in some instances, after the verdict has been entered — is necessary to prevent a systemic loss of confidence in jury verdicts, a confidence that is a central premise of the Sixth Amendment trial right.

Justice Thomas filed a brief dissent, finding it dispositive that "[our] common-law history does not establish that — in either 1791 (when the Sixth Amendment was ratified) or 1868 (when the Fourteenth Amendment was ratified) — a defendant had the right to impeach a verdict with juror testimony of juror misconduct." Justice Alito, joined by Chief Justice Roberts and Justice Thomas, wrote a longer dissent. He took the position that no-impeachment rules served important interests and that impartiality among jurors was protected sufficiently by other mechanisms, such as voir dire and the use of extrinsic evidence. He also disputed the majority's position that, as a matter of Sixth Amendment law, racial bias was different than other forms of bias, none of which justified relaxing the no-impeachment rule.

4. *Questions of remedy.* Suppose that the Court had decided *McCleskey* in favor of the defendant. What remedy would the Court order? Would a state's decision to execute more individuals who killed black victims cure the equal protection violation? Consider Karlan, Race, Rights, and Remedies in Criminal Adjudication, 96 Mich. L. Rev. 2001, 2027–2028 (1998):

> The general assumption in contemporary equal protection law, which seems to play out most of the time, is that faced with a finding of unconstitutionality, the state will remedy the inequality by providing the benefit to the previously excluded

group (that is, by "levelling up") rather than by depriving the previously included group ("levelling down"). . . .

Precisely because prosecution is the converse of most government goods, [defendants will seek] levelling down. . . .

The problem with . . . mandating levelling up as a remedy instead, is that then no one will seek to vindicate the right: it is hard to imagine the defendant who would bring a selective-prosecution claim if the only available remedy is that his trial goes forward but someone else of a different race goes to prison as well. Misery loves company, but not that much.

3.   Race-Specific Classifications Designed to Benefit Racial Minorities

The Supreme Court did not articulate and apply the requirement that racial classifications be subjected to strict scrutiny until the mid-1960s, in cases like McLaughlin v. Florida, 379 U.S. 184 (1964) (striking down a Florida statute that prohibited interracial cohabitation), and Loving v. Virginia, 388 U.S. 1 (1967), reprinted at pages 536-538, supra. By then, the Court had already declared a wide range of racial classifications unconstitutional. And with only one exception — the California Department of Corrections' use of a policy that temporarily assigned cellmates to inmates on the basis of race, see Johnson v. California, 543 U.S. 499 (2005), discussed at pages 546-547, supra — the Supreme Court has not decided an equal protection case since *Loving* in which the plaintiff was a member of a minority group who was challenging an explicit racial classification.

Instead, the modern equal protection cases involving explicit racial classifications have all involved challenges by nonminority plaintiffs to affirmative action programs. Over time, the Court came to hold that strict scrutiny should apply to these programs as well. This decision then raised a series of subsidiary questions. Which government purposes count as sufficiently "compelling" to justify using race? What constraints does the Constitution impose on the design and operation of affirmative action programs? More fundamentally, does strict scrutiny operate the same way across different areas of law? Should it?

Note: The Imposition of Strict Scrutiny

For roughly a generation, the Supreme Court struggled with the question whether to apply strict scrutiny to racial classifications designed to benefit minorities. Almost as soon as the Court completed the project of requiring strict scrutiny for all racial classifications by whatever level of government, however, the Court started subtly to transform the content of strict scrutiny.

1. Bakke. The Court's first sustained encounter with affirmative action came in Regents of the University of California v. Bakke, 438 U.S. 265 (1978), a case concerning the constitutionality of a program designed to increase minority enrollment at the University of California at Davis medical school. Under the program, sixteen of the school's one hundred seats were set aside each year for members of specified minority groups found by a special committee to have suffered from economic or educational deprivation.

The case produced a splintered decision. Four justices (Brennan, White, Marshall, and Blackmun) would have upheld the program. They would have used an "intermediate" level of scrutiny somewhere between the rational basis test used for "ordinary" legislation and the strict scrutiny used for race-specific statutes that disadvantage minorities. As Justice Brennan explained:

> [Because] of the significant risk that racial classifications established for ostensibly benign purposes can be misused, causing effects not unlike those created by invidious classifications, it is inappropriate to inquire only whether there is any conceivable basis that might sustain such a classification. Instead, to justify such a classification an important and articulated purpose for its use must be shown. In addition, any statute must be stricken that stigmatizes any group or that singles out those least well represented in the political process to bear the brunt of a benign program.

For this group of justices, the purpose of remedying the continuing effects of prior discrimination was valid and sufficiently important to satisfy this test. Since the use of race was reasonable in light of the program's objectives, and since there was no evidence that the program stigmatized any individual or group, these justices would have upheld it.

Four other justices (Burger, Stewart, Rehnquist, and Stevens) thought that the program violated title VI of the 1964 Civil Rights Act and therefore would not have reached its constitutionality. (Title VI prohibits racial discrimination in programs receiving federal financial assistance.)

The Court's judgment was controlled by Justice Powell, although in some respects he disagreed with all eight of his colleagues. Justice Powell took the position that all racial classifications — including those supposedly benefiting racial minorities — were suspect and should be subject to strict scrutiny. Although the state had a "legitimate and substantial" interest in remedying prior discrimination, that interest did not justify the Davis program because there had been no prior judicial, administrative, or legislative findings of such discrimination. Although the university's interest in a diverse student body did justify some use of racial criteria in admission decisions, it did not justify Davis's rigid, two-track system under which nonminority applicants were precluded from competing for certain seats. Hence, Justice Powell joined Justices Burger, Stewart, Rehnquist, and Stevens to hold that Bakke had been unconstitutionally denied admission under the existing Davis plan. However, he also joined Justices Brennan, Marshall, White, and Blackmun in refusing to enjoin all use of race in the future. Instead, he would have permitted an admissions program under which "race [was] deemed a 'plus' in a particular applicant's file," but did not

> insulate the individual from comparison with all other candidates for the available seats. [An] admissions program operated in this way is flexible enough to consider all pertinent elements of diversity in light of the particular qualifications of each applicant, and to place them on the same footing for consideration, although not necessarily according them the same weight.

Consider how Justice Powell's view — that achieving "diversity" is a permissible state interest justifying considerations of race — which, at the time of *Bakke*, no other Justice advanced, later became the dominant position.

2. *Fullilove.* Two years after *Bakke*, in Fullilove v. Klutznick, 448 U.S. 448 (1980), the Court considered a federal affirmative action program. The results were again inconclusive. At issue was a provision of the Public Works Employment Act of 1977, which provided federal financial assistance to state and local

governments to build public facilities. The act required that, absent an administrative waiver, 10 percent of the funds granted for the projects had to be used to procure services or supplies from "minority business enterprises" (MBEs) — defined as businesses owned or controlled by "citizens of the United States who are Negroes, Spanish-speaking, Orientals, Indians, Eskimos, and Aleuts." On this occasion, the Court upheld the program but, once again, no opinion attracted the votes of a majority of the justices.

In an opinion announcing the Court's judgment and joined by Justices White and Powell, Chief Justice Burger emphasized the narrowness of the holding. The plurality noted that "a program that employs racial or ethnic criteria, even in a remedial context, calls for close examination." Here, the program was constitutional, albeit reaching the outer limits of congressional authority. In reaching this conclusion, the plurality relied in part on the limited duration of the program, on Congress's unique authority under section 5 of the fourteenth amendment to devise remedial measures for racial discrimination, on the fact that no nonminority contractor was severely injured by the program, and on the fact that a waiver provision permitted deviation from the 10 percent requirement in cases where the increased costs of nonminority contractors could be shown not to be caused by prior discrimination.

In a concurring opinion, Justice Powell repeated his view that "[racial] classifications must be assessed under the most stringent level of review because immutable characteristics, which bear no relation to individual merit or need, are irrelevant to almost every governmental decision." In this case, however, he agreed with the plurality that the statute was "justified as a remedy that serves the compelling governmental interest in eradicating the continuing effects of past discrimination identified by Congress."

Justice Marshall, joined by Justices Brennan and Blackmun, also concurred. He argued that Congress had a sound basis for finding that minority firms were hampered by the continuing effects of past discrimination, and that the means chosen by Congress were substantially related to the achievement of this remedial purpose.

In a dissenting opinion joined by Justice Rehnquist, Justice Stewart asserted that "[under] our Constitution, the government may never act to the detriment of a person solely because of that person's race." Justice Stevens also dissented in an opinion that emphasized the absence of congressional deliberation.

3. Croson. In City of Richmond v. J. A. Croson Co., 488 U.S. 469 (1989), a majority of the Court held that state and local affirmative action programs should be subject to strict scrutiny. The Justices rejected a Richmond, Virginia, set-aside program modeled on the one upheld in *Fullilove.*

In an opinion joined in relevant part by Chief Justice Rehnquist, and Justices White and Kennedy, Justice O'Connor rejected the argument that *Fullilove* required deference to the city's conclusion that race-conscious affirmative action was required. Far from principles of federalism supporting the city's position, the constitutional structure in fact undercut the city's claim:

> What appellant ignores is that Congress, unlike any State or political subdivision, has a specific constitutional mandate to enforce the dictates of the Fourteenth Amendment. The power to "enforce" may at times also include the power to define situations which *Congress* determines threaten principles of equality and to adopt prophylactic rules to deal with those situations. . . .

Section 1 of the Fourteenth Amendment is an explicit *constraint* on state power, and the States must undertake any remedial efforts in accordance with that provision. To hold otherwise would be to cede control over the content of the Equal Protection Clause to the 50 state legislatures and their myriad political subdivisions. . . .

In his concurrence in the judgment, Justice Scalia elaborated on this point:

A sound distinction between federal and state (or local) action based on race rests not only upon the substance of the Civil War Amendments, but upon social reality and governmental theory. . . . The struggle for racial justice has historically been a struggle by the national society against oppression in the individual States. And the struggle retains that character in modern times. Not all of that struggle has involved discrimination against blacks, and not all of it has been in the Old South. What the record shows, in other words, is that racial discrimination against any group finds a more ready expression at the state and local than at the federal level. To the children of the Founding Fathers, this should come as no surprise. An acute awareness of the heightened danger of oppression from political factions in small, rather than large, political units dates to the very beginning of our national history. As James Madison observed in support of the proposed Constitution's enhancement of national powers:

> The smaller the society, the fewer probably will be the distinct parties and interests composing it; the fewer the distinct parties and interests, the more frequently will a majority be found of the same party; and the smaller the number of individuals composing a majority, and the smaller the compass within which they are placed, the more easily will they concert and execute their plan of oppression. Extend the sphere and you take in a greater variety of parties and interests; you make it less probable that a majority of the whole will have a common motive to invade the rights of other citizens; or if such a common motive exists, it will be more difficult for all who feel it to discover their own strength and to act in unison with each other.

The Federalist No. 10, 82-84 (C. Rossiter ed., 1961).

Both Justice O'Connor and Justice Scalia also emphasized that a majority of the Richmond City Council was black. Consider the relevance of this point to the question whether the plan was remedial or simply represented a contemporary version of spoils politics.

Turning to the question whether strict scrutiny should apply, Justice O'Connor's plurality opinion disputed the proposition that strict scrutiny was unnecessary in cases involving benign uses of race:

[The] Richmond Plan denies certain citizens the opportunity to compete for a fixed percentage of public contracts based solely upon their race. To whatever racial group these citizens belong, their "personal rights" to be treated with equal dignity and respect are implicated by a rigid rule erecting race as the sole criterion in an aspect of public decisionmaking.

Absent searching judicial inquiry into the justification for such race-based measures, there is simply no way of determining what classifications are "benign" or "remedial" and what classifications are in fact motivated by illegitimate notions of racial inferiority or simple racial politics. Indeed, the purpose of strict scrutiny is to "smoke out" illegitimate uses of race by assuring that the legislative body is pursuing a goal important enough to warrant use of a highly suspect tool.

Applying strict scrutiny to Richmond's program, Justice O'Connor concluded that the program failed both prongs of the strict scrutiny inquiry. First, although remedying the city's own prior unconstitutional discrimination might serve as a compelling state purpose, Justice O'Connor rejected the idea that remedying the effects of "past societal discrimination" could serve as a compelling state interest.

> To accept Richmond's claim that past societal discrimination alone can serve as the basis for rigid racial preferences would be to open the door to competing claims for "remedial relief" for every disadvantaged group. The dream of a Nation of equal citizens in a society where race is irrelevant to personal opportunity and achievement would be lost in a mosaic of shifting preferences based on inherently unmeasurable claims of past wrongs. [We] think such a result would be contrary to both the letter and spirit of a constitutional provision whose central command is equality.

Second, with respect to the question whether Richmond's plan was narrowly tailored, Justice O'Connor, now delivering an opinion for the Court, observed that

> there does not appear to have been any consideration of the use of race-neutral means to increase minority business participation in city contracting. Many of the barriers to minority participation in the construction industry relied upon by the city to justify a racial classification appear to be race neutral. If MBEs disproportionately lack capital or cannot meet bonding requirements, a race-neutral program of city financing for small firms would, a fortiori, lead to greater minority participation.

Justices Brennan, Marshall, and Blackmun dissented. Consistent with their views in *Bakke*, they would have applied a form of intermediate scrutiny. Justice Marshall's dissent, which all three joined, argued that Richmond had "two powerful interests" justifying its set-aside program: "The first is the city's interest in eradicating the effects of past racial discrimination. It is far too late in the day to doubt that remedying such discrimination is a compelling, let alone an important, interest. . . . [A] second compelling interest" consisted in "the prospective one of preventing the city's own spending decisions from reinforcing and perpetuating the exclusionary effects of past discrimination." The dissenters thought Richmond's own experience undercut the notion that race-neutral means could achieve substantial minority participation and that the choice of the 30 percent figure was appropriate given the city's overall population.

Adarand Constructors, Inc. v. Pena

515 U.S. 200 (1995)

JUSTICE O'CONNOR announced the judgment of the Court and delivered an opinion with respect to Parts I, II, III-A, III-B, III-D, and IV, which is for the Court except insofar as it might be inconsistent with the views expressed in Justice Scalia's concurrence, and an opinion with respect to Part III-C in which JUSTICE KENNEDY joins.

Petitioner Adarand Constructors, Inc., claims that the Federal Government's practice of giving general contractors on government projects a financial incentive to hire subcontractors controlled by "socially and economically disadvantaged individuals," and in particular, the Government's use of race-based presumptions in identifying such individuals, violates the equal protection component of the Fifth Amendment's Due Process Clause. The Court of Appeals rejected Adarand's claim. We conclude, however, that courts should analyze cases of this kind under a different standard of review than the one the Court of Appeals applied. We therefore vacate the Court of Appeals' judgment and remand the case for further proceedings.

I

In 1989, the Central Federal Lands Highway Division (CFLHD), which is part of the United States Department of Transportation (DOT), awarded the prime contract for a highway construction project in Colorado to Mountain Gravel & Construction Company. Mountain Gravel then solicited bids from subcontractors for the guardrail portion of the contract. Adarand, a Colorado-based highway construction company specializing in guardrail work, submitted the low bid. Gonzales Construction Company also submitted a bid.

The prime contract's terms provide that Mountain Gravel would receive additional compensation if it hired subcontractors certified as small businesses controlled by "socially and economically disadvantaged individuals." Gonzales is certified as such a business; Adarand is not. Mountain Gravel awarded the subcontract to Gonzales, despite Adarand's low bid, and Mountain Gravel's Chief Estimator has submitted an affidavit stating that Mountain Gravel would have accepted Adarand's bid, had it not been for the additional payment it received by hiring Gonzales instead. Federal law requires that a subcontracting clause similar to the one used here must appear in most federal agency contracts, and it also requires the clause to state that "the contractor shall presume that socially and economically disadvantaged individuals include Black Americans, Hispanic Americans, Native Americans, Asian Pacific Americans, and other minorities, or any other individual found to be disadvantaged by the [Small Business] Administration pursuant to section 8(a) of the Small Business Act." Adarand claims that the presumption set forth in that statute discriminates on the basis of race in violation of the Federal Government's Fifth Amendment obligation not to deny anyone equal protection of the laws. . . .

III

The Government urges that "the Subcontracting Compensation Clause program is . . . a program based on disadvantage, not on race," and thus that it is subject only to "the most relaxed judicial scrutiny." To the extent that the statutes and regulations involved in this case are race neutral, we agree. The Government concedes, however, that "the race-based rebuttable presumption used in some certification determinations under the Subcontracting Compensation Clause" is subject to some heightened level of scrutiny. The parties disagree as to what that level should be. . . .

Adarand's claim arises under the Fifth Amendment to the Constitution, which provides that "No person shall . . . be deprived of life, liberty, or property, without due process of law." Although this Court has always understood that Clause to provide some measure of protection against arbitrary treatment by the Federal Government, it is not as explicit a guarantee of equal treatment as the Fourteenth Amendment, which provides that "No State shall . . . deny to any person within its jurisdiction the equal protection of the laws." Our cases have accorded varying degrees of significance to the difference in the language of those two Clauses. . . .

B. . . .

[T]he Court's cases through *Croson* had established three general propositions with respect to governmental racial classifications. First, skepticism: "any preference based on racial or ethnic criteria must necessarily receive a most searching examination." Second, consistency: "the standard of review under the Equal Protection Clause is not dependent on the race of those burdened or benefited by a particular classification." And third, congruence: "equal protection analysis in the Fifth Amendment area is the same as that under the Fourteenth Amendment." Taken together, these three propositions lead to the conclusion that any person, of whatever race, has the right to demand that any governmental actor subject to the Constitution justify any racial classification subjecting that person to unequal treatment under the strictest judicial scrutiny. . . .

[Accordingly,] we hold today that all racial classifications, imposed by whatever federal, state, or local governmental actor, must be analyzed by a reviewing court under strict scrutiny. In other words, such classifications are constitutional only if they are narrowly tailored measures that further compelling governmental interests. . . .

[In dissent,] Justice Stevens chides us for our "supposed inability to differentiate between 'invidious' and 'benign' discrimination," because it is in his view sufficient that "people understand the difference between good intentions and bad." But, [the] point of strict scrutiny is to "differentiate between" permissible and impermissible governmental use of race. And Justice Stevens himself has already explained in his dissent in *Fullilove* why "good intentions" alone are not enough to sustain a supposedly "benign" racial classification: "Even though it is not the actual predicate for this legislation, a statute of this kind inevitably is perceived by many as resting on an assumption that those who are granted this special preference are less qualified in some respect that is identified purely by their race. Because that perception — especially when fostered by the Congress of the United States — can only exacerbate rather than reduce racial prejudice, it will delay the time when race will become a truly irrelevant, or at least insignificant, factor. Unless Congress clearly articulates the need and basis for a racial classification, and also tailors the classification to its justification, the Court should not uphold this kind of statute." *Fullilove* (dissenting opinion). . . .

Perhaps it is not the standard of strict scrutiny itself, but our use of the concepts of "consistency" and "congruence" in conjunction with it, that leads Justice Stevens to dissent. According to Justice Stevens, our view of consistency "equates remedial preferences with invidious discrimination," and ignores the difference between "an engine of oppression" and an effort "to foster equality in society," or, more colorfully, "between a 'No Trespassing' sign and a welcome mat." It does nothing of the kind. The principle of consistency simply means that whenever the government treats any person unequally because of his or her race, that person has suffered an injury that falls squarely within the language and spirit of the Constitution's guarantee of equal protection. It says nothing about the ultimate validity of any particular law; that determination is the job of the court applying strict scrutiny. The principle of consistency explains the circumstances in which the injury requiring strict scrutiny occurs. The application of strict scrutiny, in turn, determines whether a compelling governmental interest justifies the infliction of that injury. . . .

D

Finally, we wish to dispel the notion that strict scrutiny is "strict in theory, but fatal in fact." *Fullilove* (Marshall, J., concurring in judgment). The unhappy persistence of both the practice and the lingering effects of racial discrimination against minority groups in this country is an unfortunate reality, and government is not disqualified from acting in response to it. When race-based action is necessary to further a compelling interest, such action is within constitutional constraints if it satisfies the "narrow tailoring" test this Court has set out in previous cases. . . .

JUSTICE SCALIA, concurring in part and concurring in the judgment.
I join the opinion of the Court, . . . except insofar as it may be inconsistent with the following: In my view, government can never have a "compelling interest" in discriminating on the basis of race in order to "make up" for past racial discrimination in the opposite direction. Individuals who have been wronged by unlawful racial discrimination should be made whole; but under our Constitution there can be no such thing as either a creditor or a debtor race. That concept is alien to the Constitution's focus upon the individual, [and] its rejection of dispositions based on [race]. To pursue the concept of racial entitlement — even for the most admirable and benign of purposes — is to reinforce and preserve for future mischief the way of thinking that produced race slavery, race privilege and race hatred. In the eyes of government, we are just one race here. It is American. . . .

JUSTICE THOMAS, concurring in part and concurring in the judgment.
I agree with the majority's conclusion that strict scrutiny applies to all government classifications based on race. I write separately, however, to express my disagreement with the premise underlying Justice Stevens' and Justice Ginsburg's dissents: that there is a racial paternalism exception to the principle of equal protection. I believe that there is a "moral [and] constitutional equivalence," (Stevens, J., dissenting), between laws designed to subjugate a race and those that distribute benefits on the basis of race in order to foster some current notion of equality. Government cannot make us equal; it can only recognize, respect, and protect us as equal before the law.
That these programs may have been motivated, in part, by good intentions cannot provide refuge from the principle that under our Constitution, the government may not make distinctions on the basis of race. . . .
These programs not only raise grave constitutional questions, they also undermine the moral basis of the equal protection principle. Purchased at the price of immeasurable human suffering, the equal protection principle reflects our Nation's understanding that such classifications ultimately have a destructive impact on the individual and our society. Unquestionably, "invidious [racial] discrimination is an engine of oppression." It is also true that "remedial" racial preferences may reflect "a desire to foster equality in society." But there can be no doubt that racial paternalism and its unintended consequences can be as poisonous and pernicious as any other form of discrimination. So-called "benign" discrimination teaches many that because of chronic and apparently immutable

handicaps, minorities cannot compete with them without their patronizing indulgence. Inevitably, such programs engender attitudes of superiority or, alternatively, provoke resentment among those who believe that they have been wronged by the government's use of race. These programs stamp minorities with a badge of inferiority and may cause them to develop dependencies or to adopt an attitude that they are "entitled" to preferences. . . .

In my mind, government-sponsored racial discrimination based on benign prejudice is just as noxious as discrimination inspired by malicious prejudice. In each instance, it is racial discrimination, plain and simple.

JUSTICE STEVENS, with whom JUSTICE GINSBURG joins, dissenting. . . .

II

The Court's concept of "consistency" assumes that there is no significant difference between a decision by the majority to impose a special burden on the members of a minority race and a decision by the majority to provide a benefit to certain members of that minority notwithstanding its incidental burden on some members of the majority. In my opinion that assumption is untenable. There is no moral or constitutional equivalence between a policy that is designed to perpetuate a caste system and one that seeks to eradicate racial subordination. Invidious discrimination is an engine of oppression, subjugating a disfavored group to enhance or maintain the power of the majority. Remedial race-based preferences reflect the opposite impulse: a desire to foster equality in society. No sensible conception of the Government's constitutional obligation to "govern impartially," should ignore this distinction. . . .

The consistency that the Court espouses would disregard the difference between a "No Trespassing" sign and a welcome mat. It would treat a Dixiecrat Senator's decision to vote against Thurgood Marshall's confirmation in order to keep African Americans off the Supreme Court as on a par with President Johnson's evaluation of his nominee's race as a positive factor. It would equate a law that made black citizens ineligible for military service with a program aimed at recruiting black soldiers. . . .

The Court's explanation for treating dissimilar race-based decisions as though they were equally objectionable is a supposed inability to differentiate between "invidious" and "benign" discrimination. But the term "affirmative action" is common and well understood. Its presence in everyday parlance shows that people understand the difference between good intentions and bad. As with any legal concept, some cases may be difficult to classify, but our equal protection jurisprudence has identified a critical difference between state action that imposes burdens on a disfavored few and state action that benefits the few "in spite of its adverse effects on the many." *Feeney.* . . .

Moreover, the Court may find that its new "consistency" approach to race-based classifications is difficult to square with its insistence upon rigidly separate categories for discrimination against different classes of individuals. For example, as the law currently stands, the Court will apply "intermediate scrutiny" to cases of invidious gender discrimination and "strict scrutiny" to cases of invidious race discrimination, while applying the same standard for benign classifications as for invidious ones. [The Court's articulation of an "intermediate" standard of review in cases of gender discrimination is discussed at pages 645-653, infra.] If this remains the law, then today's lecture about "consistency" will produce the anomalous result that the Government can more easily enact affirmative-action programs to remedy discrimination against women than it can enact affirmative-action programs to remedy discrimination against African Americans — even though the primary purpose of the Equal Protection Clause was to end discrimination against the former slaves. When a court becomes preoccupied with abstract standards, it risks sacrificing common sense at the altar of formal consistency.

III

The Court's concept of "congruence" assumes that there is no significant difference between a decision by the Congress of the United States to adopt an affirmative-action program and such a decision by a State or a municipality. In my opinion that assumption is untenable. It ignores important practical and legal differences between federal and state or local decisionmakers. . . .

[Federal] affirmative-action programs represent the will of our entire Nation's elected representatives, whereas a state or local program may have an impact on nonresident entities who played no part in the decision to enact it. Thus, in the state or local context, individuals who were unable to vote for the local representatives who enacted a race-conscious program may nonetheless feel the effects of that program. This difference recalls the goals of the Commerce Clause, which permits Congress to legislate on certain matters of national importance while denying power to the States in this area for fear of undue impact upon out-of-state residents. . . .

[Dissenting opinions by Justice Souter, with whom Justice Ginsburg and Justice Breyer joined, and Justice Ginsberg, with whom Justice Breyer joined, are omitted.]

Note: The Constitutionality of "Benign" Racial Classifications

Adarand and *Croson* establish that "benign" racial classifications, like those that harm racial minorities, are subject to strict scrutiny. The decisions leave uncertain, however, the exact nature of this scrutiny, as well as the kinds of justifications that will count as "compelling" government interests.

1. *The level of scrutiny for classifications that benefit racial minorities.* Recall the justifications for strict scrutiny for race-based classifications that harm racial minorities, discussed at pages 540-544, supra. Which, if any, of these arguments apply to affirmative action measures?

a. *Text and original intent.* By its terms, the fourteenth amendment says nothing about heightened review for racial classifications. As noted previously, see pages 475-476, supra, the original impetus for passage of the amendment was a desire to expand the scope of congressional power to enact the nineteenth-century analogue of affirmative action measures. For a discussion, see Schnapper, Affirmative Action and the Legislative History of the Fourteenth Amendment, 71 Va. L. Rev. 753 (1985). Congress wished to lay a firm constitutional grounding for Reconstruction statutes that had the specific purpose of benefiting and protecting the newly freed slaves. There is also a sense in which the amendment was designed to *restrict* judicial power. Members of the Reconstruction Congress feared that the Supreme Court would invalidate the 1866 Civil Rights Act and adopted the fourteenth amendment so as to avoid that result. In light of this history, is there an originalist justification for strict scrutiny of affirmative action measures?

b. *Race consciousness.* Do affirmative action measures merit strict scrutiny because of "the basic principle that the Fifth and Fourteenth Amendments to the Constitution protect persons, not groups"? *Adarand*, supra. The Court's statement cannot be taken literally in light of its regular application of low-level scrutiny to statutes that use group characteristics to categorize people in nonracial contexts. Perhaps, though, there are special dangers associated with group generalizations based on race

c. *History.* Does the fact that whites as a group have not suffered from a history of discrimination justify a lower standard of review for statutes disadvantaging them? Consider Lempert, The Force of Irony: On the Morality of Affirmative Action and United Steelworkers v. Weber, 95 Ethics 86, 89 (1984):

[A] claim made by a white person as a member of the dominant majority draws its moral force largely from our collective horror at centuries of oppressing black people. It would be ironic indeed if evils visited on blacks had lent enough force to the moral claims of whites to prevent what appears to many at this point to be the most effective means of eliminating the legacy of those evils.

Might not the same history be characterized as demonstrating the evils of racial discrimination regardless of the race against which it is directed?

d. *Political process.* Does the fact that whites have "adequate" political power justify a lower level of scrutiny when laws disadvantage them? Consider Ely, The Constitutionality of Reverse Racial Discrimination, 41 U. Chi. L. Rev. 723, 735–736 (1974):

When the group that controls the decision making process classifies so as to advantage a minority and disadvantage itself, the reasons for being unusually suspicious, and, consequently, employing a stringent brand of review are lacking. A White majority is unlikely to disadvantage itself for reasons of racial prejudice; nor is it likely to be tempted either to underestimate the needs and deserts of Whites relative to those of others, or to overestimate the cost of devising an alternative classification that would extend to certain Whites the advantages generally extended to Blacks. . . .

[Whether] or not it is more blessed to give than to receive, it is surely less suspicious.

Is it a necessary implication of this view that a race-conscious program might be constitutional if adopted by a city council dominated by whites but unconstitutional if adopted by a city council like Richmond's with a black majority? If the arguments for affirmative action are ultimately persuasive, why should it matter who is persuaded by them?

Does Ely's argument unrealistically assume that affirmative action disadvantages a monolithic white majority capable of protecting itself politically? Consider Greenberg, Affirmative Action in Higher Education: Confronting the Condition and Theory, 43 B.C. L. Rev. 521, 537 (2002):

In Regents of the University of California v. Bakke, the Supreme Court had never been informed that U.C. Davis's Dean personally admitted about a half-dozen applicants each year, including children of rich and influential physicians who had been rejected or wait-listed by the office of admissions. Allan Bakke challenged U.C. Davis's affirmative action program on the ground that it denied him a place in the incoming class; the identical criticism could have been made of the Dean's special admissions program.

e. *"Innocent victims."* It is sometimes argued that "benign" discrimination should be strictly scrutinized because it disadvantages individuals on the basis of immutable characteristics when those individuals are not themselves responsible for the evil to be corrected. Is it persuasive to insist on a general rule that the government should not disadvantage "innocent" individuals even when doing so promotes the general welfare? Does a merit-based system for dispensing scarce resources satisfy this requirement? Consider Karst and Horowitz, Affirmative Action and Equal Protection, 60 Va. L. Rev. 955, 962 (1974):

> Whether "merit" be defined in terms of demonstrated achievement or of potential achievement, it includes a large and hard-to-isolate ingredient of native talents. These talents resemble race in that they are beyond the control of the individual whose "merit" is being evaluated. If racial classifications are "suspect" partly for this reason, then it may be appropriate to insist that public rewards for native talents be justified by a showing of compelling necessity.

Is the "innocent victims" argument merely an artifact of an unduly narrow conception of the purposes of affirmative action programs? If, for example, the purpose of affirmative action is not to remedy past discrimination (particularly past discrimination against the beneficiaries of the affirmative action program), but rather to create integrated institutions for the future, would white claims of "innocence" count for less?

f. *Identifying affirmative action.* Is strict scrutiny for affirmative action programs necessary because, without such scrutiny, "there is simply no way of determining what classifications are 'benign' or 'remedial'"? *Croson,* supra.

In this respect, consider Justice Kennedy's observation in Metro Broadcasting v. FCC, 497 U.S. 547 (1990). There, the Court upheld FCC policies that gave a preference to minority-owned companies in competitions for new broadcast licenses and permitted sales of existing licenses to minority-owned companies under circumstances where other sales would be precluded. In dissent, Justice Kennedy wrote:

> The Court also justifies its result on the ground that "Congress and the Commission have determined that there may be important differences between the broadcasting practices of minority owners and those of their nonminority counterparts." The Court is all too correct that the type of reasoning employed by the Commission and Congress is not novel. Policies of racial separation and preference are almost always justified as benign, even when it is clear to any sensible observer that they are not. The following statement, for example, would fit well among those offered to uphold the Commission's racial preference policy: "The policy is not based on any concept of superiority or inferiority, but merely on the fact that people differ, particularly in their group associations, loyalties, cultures, outlook, modes of life and standards of development." See South Africa and the Rule of Law 37 (1968) (official publication of the South African Government).

2. *Justifications for affirmative action.* Under the strict scrutiny that *Adarand* and *Croson* require, "benign" classifications will be upheld only if they are narrowly tailored to achieve a compelling government interest. What interests are compelling? Remedying past discrimination? Assuring some prospective allocation of benefits and burdens? Complying with federal statutes that themselves go beyond constitutional prohibitions on purposeful racial discrimination to forbid practices with a racially disparate impact? Achieving representation of various groups or diversity within a government-sponsored program? These issues are fleshed out in several cases discussed in the remainder of this section.

3. *Empirical questions.* To what extent does the dispute about affirmative action turn on disagreement about empirical questions? For example, opponents and proponents of affirmative action may disagree about whether affirmative action helps or hurts its intended beneficiaries, about whether it increases or decreases racial antagonism, and about whether a "color-blind" regime eliminates or perpetuates discrimination.

For an excellent summary of the social psychological literature bearing on these and other questions, see Krieger, Civil Rights Perestroika: Intergroup Relations after Affirmative Action, 86 Cal. L. Rev. 1251, 1264, 1267–1268, 1294, 1331 (1998). According to Krieger, there is reason for concern that at least certain types of affirmative action may harm intended beneficiaries. The evidence that affirmative action produces self-derogating effects is mixed and largely depends on how the program is described and implemented. The effects of such programs on nonbeneficiaries are more troublesome. For example:

> In one group of studies, experimenters asked subjects to evaluate the qualifications of people supposedly selected for employment or admission to programs of higher education. Researchers indirectly informed subjects in one condition that the selecting institution had an affirmative action program. In a second condition, researchers made no mention of affirmative action. Subjects in the "affirmative action" condition consistently rated the files of selected women and minorities as reflecting lower levels of competence, qualification, and accomplishment than did subjects evaluating identical files in the "non-affirmative action" condition. . . .
>
> Absent some explanatory theory, the presence of women or minorities [in positions] [indicating] high levels of ability and accomplishment would disconfirm a variety of inconsistent, negative racial or gender stereotypes. [Preferential] selection, however, provides a plausible situational attribution for the stereotype-inconsistent information. Once female or minority presence in "high places" is attributed to preferential selection rather than to merit-related factors, pre-existing negative stereotypes are insulated from the potentially disconfirming effect of the otherwise stereotype disconfirming data.

To some degree these negative effects can be mitigated by programs that take into account both "merit" and group membership, by emphasizing a pattern of discrimination against the group in describing the programs, and by avoiding numerical quotas.
Krieger concludes that

> [for] better or for worse, the application of insights from social cognition and social identity theory complicates rather than simplifies the affirmative action debate. On the one hand, there is reason to fear that preferential forms of affirmative action, at least in some contexts, may indeed exacerbate intergroup tensions and perpetuate rather than reduce subtle forms of intergroup bias. [On] the other hand, insights

derived from these fields suggest that we are not yet ready to abandon preferential forms of affirmative action for the simple reason that we have nothing adequate with which to replace them.

For a detailed and mostly positive empirical study of the effects of affirmative action in higher education, see W. Bowen and D. Bok, The Shape of the River (1998).

How, if at all, do you think that such studies should affect the constitutional issue? For criticism of Bowen and Bok's study, see, e.g., Sandalow, Minority Preferences Reconsidered, 97 Mich. L. Rev. 1874 (1999).

Grutter v. Bollinger

539 U.S. 306 (2003)

JUSTICE O'CONNOR delivered the opinion of the Court.

This case requires us to decide whether the use of race as a factor in student admissions by the University of Michigan Law School [is] unlawful.

I

[The Law School's admission policy required admissions officials to evaluate each applicant based upon the entire file, including a personal statement, letters of recommendation, and an essay. Admissions officers were directed to take into account undergraduate grades and LSAT scores, but the policy made clear that no score led to either automatic admission or rejection. Instead, officials also looked to "soft variables" such as the enthusiasm of recommenders or the areas and difficulty of undergraduate course selection. The policy also emphasized diversity of various sorts. In this connection, the policy reaffirmed the Law School's commitment to "racial and ethnic diversity with special reference to the inclusion of students from groups which have been historically discriminated against, like African-Americans, Hispanics and Native Americans, who without this commitment might not be represented in our student body in meaningful numbers."

[Grutter, a white resident of Michigan whose application to the Law School was rejected, brought suit claiming she had not been admitted because the Law School had relied on race in violation of the equal protection clause.]

II

A . . .

Since this Court's splintered decision in *Bakke*, Justice Powell's opinion announcing the judgment of the Court has served as the touchstone for constitutional analysis of race-conscious admissions policies. Public and private universities across the Nation have modeled their own admissions programs on Justice Powell's views on permissible race-conscious policies. . . .

[For] the reasons set out below, today we endorse Justice Powell's view that student body diversity is a compelling state interest that can justify the use of race in university admissions.

B

We have held that all racial classifications imposed by government "must be analyzed by a reviewing court under strict scrutiny."[*Adarand*]. . . .

Although all governmental uses of race are subject to strict scrutiny, not all are invalidated by it. [When] race-based action is necessary to further a compelling governmental interest, such action does not violate the constitutional guarantee of equal protection so long as the narrow-tailoring requirement is also satisfied. . . .

III

A

[W]e turn to the question whether the Law School's use of race is justified by a compelling state interest. [The] Law School asks us to recognize, in the context of higher education, a compelling state interest in student body diversity.

We first wish to dispel the notion that the Law School's argument has been foreclosed, either expressly or implicitly, by our affirmative-action cases decided since *Bakke*. [We] have never held that the only governmental use of race that can survive strict scrutiny is remedying past discrimination. . . .

The Law School's educational judgment that such diversity is essential to its educational mission is one to which we defer. The Law School's assessment that diversity will, in fact, yield educational benefits is substantiated by respondents and their *amici*. Our scrutiny of the interest asserted by the Law School is no less strict for taking into account complex educational judgments in an area that lies primarily within the expertise of the university. Our holding today is in keeping with our tradition of giving a degree of deference to a university's academic decisions, within constitutionally prescribed limits.

As part of its goal of "assembling a class that is both exceptionally academically qualified and broadly diverse," the Law School seeks to "enroll a 'critical mass' of minority students." The Law School's interest is not simply "to assure within its student body some specified percentage of a particular group merely because of its race or ethnic origin." [*Bakke* (opinion of Powell, J.)]. That would amount to outright racial balancing, which is patently unconstitutional. . . . Rather, the Law School's concept of critical mass is defined by reference to the educational benefits that diversity is designed to produce.

These benefits are substantial. As the District Court emphasized, the Law School's admissions policy promotes "cross-racial understanding," helps to break down racial stereotypes, and "enables [students] to better understand persons of different races." These benefits are "important and laudable," because "classroom discussion is livelier, more spirited, and simply more enlightening and interesting" when the students have "the greatest possible variety of backgrounds."

The Law School's claim of a compelling interest is further bolstered by its *amici*, who point to the educational benefits that flow from student body diversity. . . .

These benefits are not theoretical but real, as major American businesses have made clear that the skills needed in today's increasingly global marketplace can only be developed through exposure to widely diverse people, cultures, ideas, and viewpoints. Brief for 3M et al. as *Amici Curiae*; Brief for General Motors Corp. as

Amicus Curiae. What is more, high-ranking retired officers and civilian leaders of the United States military assert that, "[b]ased on [their] decades of experience," a "highly qualified, racially diverse officer corps . . . is essential to the military's ability to fulfill its principle mission to provide national security." The primary sources for the Nation's officer corps are the service academies and the Reserve Officers Training Corps (ROTC) the latter comprising students already admitted to participating colleges and universities. At present, "the military cannot achieve an officer corps that is *both* highly qualified *and* racially diverse unless the service academies and the ROTC used limited race-conscious recruiting and admissions policies." (emphasis in original). . . .

Moreover, universities, and in particular, law schools, represent the training ground for a large number of our Nation's leaders. Sweatt v. Painter, 339 U.S. 629, 634 (1950) (describing law school as a "proving ground for legal learning and practice"). Individuals with law degrees occupy roughly half the state governorships, more than half the seats in the United States Senate, and more than a third of the seats in the United States House of Representatives. The pattern is even more striking when it comes to highly selective law schools. A handful of these schools accounts for 25 of the 100 United States Senators, 74 United States Courts of Appeals judges, and nearly 200 of the more than 600 United States District Court judges.

In order to cultivate a set of leaders with legitimacy in the eyes of the citizenry, it is necessary that the path to leadership be visibly open to talented and qualified individuals of every race and ethnicity. All members of our heterogeneous society must have confidence in the openness and integrity of the educational institutions that provide this training. As we have recognized, law schools "cannot be effective in isolation from the individuals and institutions with which the law interacts." See Sweatt v. Painter. Access to legal education (and thus the legal profession) must be inclusive of talented and qualified individuals of every race and ethnicity, so that all members of our heterogeneous society may participate in the educational institutions that provide the training and education necessary to succeed in America. . . .

B

To be narrowly tailored, a race-conscious admissions program cannot use a quota system — it cannot "insulat[e] each category of applicants with certain desired qualifications from competition with all other applicants." *Bakke* (opinion of Powell, J.). Instead, a university may consider race or ethnicity only as a "'plus' in a particular applicant's file, without 'insulat[ing]' the individual from comparison with all other candidates for the available seats." . . .

The Law School's goal of attaining a critical mass of underrepresented minority students does not transform its program into a quota. As the Harvard plan described by Justice Powell recognized, there is of course "some relationship between numbers and achieving the benefits to be derived from a diverse student body, and between numbers and providing a reasonable environment for those students admitted." [*Bakke*]. "[Some] attention to numbers," without more, does not transform a flexible admissions system into a rigid quota. Nor, as Justice Kennedy posits, does the Law School's consultation of the "daily reports," which keep track of the racial and ethnic composition of the class (as well as of residency and gender), "suggest[] there was no further attempt at individual review save for race itself during the final stages of the admissions process. To the contrary, the Law School's admissions officers testified without contradiction that they never gave race any more or less weight based on the information contained in these reports. Moreover, as Justice Kennedy concedes, between 1993 and 2000, the number of African-American, Latino, and Native-American students in each class at the Law School varied from 13.5 to 20.1 percent, a range inconsistent with a quota. . . .

Here, the Law School engages in a highly individualized, holistic review of each applicant's file, giving serious consideration to all the ways an applicant might contribute to a diverse educational environment. The Law School affords this individualized consideration to applicants of all races. There is no policy, either *de jure* or *de facto*, of automatic acceptance or rejection based on any single "soft" variable. Unlike the program at issue in *Gratz v. Bollinger* [discussed at pages 595–598, infra], the Law School awards no mechanical, predetermined diversity "bonuses" based on race or ethnicity. . . .

We also find that, like the Harvard plan Justice Powell referenced in *Bakke*, the Law School's race-conscious admissions program adequately ensures that all factors that may contribute to student body diversity are meaningfully considered alongside race in admissions decisions. With respect to the use of race itself, all underrepresented minority students admitted by the Law School have been deemed qualified. By virtue of our Nation's struggle with racial inequality, such students are both likely to have experiences of particular importance to the Law School's mission, and less likely to be admitted in meaningful numbers on criteria that ignore those experiences.

The Law School does not, however, limit in any way the broad range of qualities and experiences that may be considered valuable contributions to student body diversity. To the contrary, the 1992 policy makes clear "[t]here are many possible bases for diversity admissions," and provides examples of admittees who have lived or traveled widely abroad, are fluent in several languages, have overcome personal adversity and family hardship, have exceptional records of extensive community service, and have had successful careers in other fields. . . .

What is more, the Law School actually gives substantial weight to diversity factors besides race. The Law School frequently accepts nonminority applicants with grades and test scores lower than underrepresented minority applicants (and other nonminority applicants) who are rejected.

Petitioner and the United States argue that the Law School's plan is not narrowly tailored because race-neutral means exist to obtain the educational benefits of student body diversity that the Law School seeks. We disagree. Narrow tailoring does not require exhaustion of every conceivable race-neutral alternative. Nor does it require a university to choose between maintaining a reputation for excellence or fulfilling a commitment to provide educational opportunities to members of all racial groups. Narrow tailoring does, however, require serious, good faith consideration of workable race-neutral alternatives that will achieve the diversity the university seeks.

We agree with the Court of Appeals that the Law School sufficiently considered workable race-neutral alternatives. The District Court took the Law School to task for failing to consider race-neutral alternatives such as "using a lottery system" or "decreasing the emphasis for all applicants on undergraduate GPA and LSAT scores." But these alternatives would require a dramatic sacrifice of diversity, the academic quality of all admitted students, or both.

The Law School's current admissions program considers race as one factor among many, in an effort to assemble a student body that is diverse in ways broader than race. Because a lottery would make that kind of nuanced judgment impossible, it would effectively sacrifice all other educational values, not to mention every other kind of diversity. So too with the suggestion that the Law School simply lower admissions standards for all students, a drastic remedy that would require the Law School to become a much different institution and sacrifice a vital component of its educational mission. The United States advocates "percentage plans," recently adopted by public undergraduate institutions in Texas, Florida, and California to guarantee admission to all students above a certain class-rank threshold in every high school in the State. The United States does not, however, explain how such plans could work for graduate and professional schools. Moreover, even assuming such plans are race-neutral, they may preclude the university from conducting the individualized assessments necessary to assemble a student body that is not just racially diverse, but diverse along all the qualities valued by the university. . . .

We are mindful, however, that "[a] core purpose of the Fourteenth Amendment was to do away with all governmentally imposed discrimination based on race." Palmore v. Sidoti. Accordingly, race-conscious admissions policies must be limited in time. . . .

In the context of higher education, the durational requirement can be met by sunset provisions in race-conscious admissions policies and periodic reviews to determine whether racial preferences are still necessary to achieve student body diversity. Universities in California, Florida, and Washington State, where racial preferences in admissions are prohibited by state law, are currently engaged in experimenting with a wide variety of alternative approaches. Universities in other States can and should draw on the most promising aspects of these race-neutral alternatives as they develop. . . .

We take the Law School at its word that it would "like nothing better than to find a race-neutral admissions formula" and will terminate its race-conscious admissions program as soon as practicable. It has been 25 years since Justice Powell first approved the use of race to further an interest in student body diversity in the context of public higher education. Since that time, the number of minority applicants with high grades and test scores has indeed increased. We expect that 25 years from now, the use of racial preferences will no longer be necessary to further the interest approved today. . . .

JUSTICE GINSBURG, with whom JUSTICE BREYER joins, concurring. . . .

It is well documented that conscious and unconscious race bias, even rank discrimination based on race, remain alive in our land, impeding realization of our highest values and ideals. As to public education, data for the years 2000–2001 show that 71.6% of African-American children and 76.3% of Hispanic children attended a school in which minorities made up a majority of the student body. And schools in predominantly minority communities lag far behind others measured by the educational resources available to them.

However strong the public's desire for improved education systems may be, it remains the current reality that many minority students encounter markedly inadequate and unequal educational opportunities. Despite these inequalities, some minority students are able to meet the high threshold requirements set for admission to the country's finest undergraduate and graduate educational institutions. As lower school education in minority communities improves, an increase in the number of such students may be anticipated. From today's vantage point, one may hope, but not firmly forecast, that over the next generation's span, progress toward nondiscrimination and genuinely equal opportunity will make it safe to sunset affirmative action.

CHIEF JUSTICE REHNQUIST, with whom JUSTICE SCALIA, JUSTICE KENNEDY, and JUSTICE THOMAS join, dissenting. . . .

I do not believe, however, that the University of Michigan Law School's [means] are narrowly tailored to the interest it asserts. The Law School claims it must take the steps it does to achieve a "critical mass" of underrepresented minority students. But its actual program bears no relation to this asserted goal. Stripped of its "critical mass" veil, the Law School's program is revealed as a naked effort to achieve racial balancing. . . .

From 1995 through 2000, the Law School admitted between 1,130 and 1,310 students. Of those, between 13 and 19 were Native American, between 91 and 108 were African-Americans, and between 47 and 56 were Hispanic. If the Law School is admitting between 91 and 108 African-Americans in order to achieve "critical mass," thereby preventing African-American students from feeling "isolated or like spokespersons for their race," one would think that a number of the same order of magnitude would be necessary to accomplish the same purpose for Hispanics and Native Americans. Similarly, even if all of the Native American applicants admitted in a given year matriculate, which the record demonstrates is not at all the case, how can this possibly constitute a "critical mass" of Native Americans in a class of over 350 students? . . .

Only when the "critical mass" label is discarded does a likely explanation for these numbers emerge. . . .

[The] correlation between the percentage of the Law School's pool of applicants who are members of the three minority groups and the percentage of the admitted applicants who are members of these same groups is far too precise to be dismissed as merely the result of the school paying "some attention to [the] numbers." . . .

JUSTICE KENNEDY, dissenting. . . .

The Court's refusal to apply meaningful strict scrutiny will lead to serious consequences. By deferring to the law schools' choice of minority admissions programs, the courts will lose the talents and resources of the faculties and administrators in devising new and fairer ways to ensure individual consideration. Constant and rigorous judicial review forces the law school faculties to undertake their responsibilities as state employees in this most sensitive of areas with utmost fidelity to the mandate of the Constitution. [By contrast, under Michigan's system, one witness] testified that faculty members were "breathtakingly cynical" in deciding who would qualify as a member of underrepresented minorities. An example he offered was faculty debate as to whether Cubans should be counted as Hispanics: One professor objected on the grounds that Cubans were Republicans. Many academics at other law schools who are "affirmative action's more forthright defenders readily concede that diversity is merely the current rationale of convenience for a policy that they prefer to justify on other grounds." Schuck, Affirmative Action: Past, Present, and Future, 20 Yale L. & Pol'y Rev. 1, 34 (2002) (citing Levinson, Diversity, 2 U. Pa. J. Const. L. 573, 577–578 (2000); Rubenfeld, Affirmative Action, 107 Yale L.J. 427, 471 (1997)). This is not to suggest the faculty at Michigan or other law schools do not pursue aspirations they consider laudable and consistent with our constitutional traditions. It is but further evidence of the necessity for scrutiny that is real, not feigned, where the corrosive category of race is a factor in decisionmaking. . . .

JUSTICE SCALIA, with whom JUSTICE THOMAS joins, concurring in part and dissenting in part. . . .

The "educational benefit" that the University of Michigan seeks to achieve by racial discrimination consists, according to the Court, of "cross-racial understanding," and "better prepar[ation of] students for an increasingly diverse workforce and society," all of which is necessary not only for work, but also for good "citizenship." This is not, of course, an "educational benefit" on which students will be graded on their Law School transcript (Works and Plays Well with Others: B+) or tested by the bar examiners (Q: Describe in 500 words or less your cross-racial understanding). For it is a lesson of life rather than law — essentially the same lesson taught to (or rather learned by, for it cannot be "taught" in the usual sense) people three feet shorter and twenty years younger than the full-grown adults at the University of Michigan Law School, in institutions ranging from Boy Scout troops to public-school kindergartens. If properly considered an "educational benefit" at all, it is surely not one that is either uniquely relevant to law school or uniquely "teachable" in a formal educational setting. And therefore: If it is appropriate for the University of Michigan Law School to use racial discrimination for the purpose of putting together a "critical mass" that will convey generic lessons in socialization and good citizenship, surely it is no less appropriate — indeed, *particularly* appropriate — for the civil service system of the State of Michigan to do so. There, also, those exposed to "critical masses" of certain races will presumably become better Americans, better Michiganders, better civil servants. And surely private employers cannot be criticized — indeed, should be praised — if they also "teach" good citizenship to their adult employees through a patriotic, all-American system of racial discrimination in hiring. The nonminority individuals who are deprived of a legal education, a civil service job, or any job at all by reason of their skin color will surely understand.

Unlike a clear constitutional holding that racial preferences in state educational institutions are impermissible, or even a clear anticonstitutional holding that racial preferences in state educational institutions are OK, today's *Grutter-Gratz* split double header seems perversely designed to prolong the controversy and the litigation. . . .

JUSTICE THOMAS, with whom JUSTICE SCALIA joins as to Parts I–VII, concurring in part and dissenting in part.

Frederick Douglass, speaking to a group of abolitionists almost 140 years ago, delivered a message lost on today's majority:

> [I]n regard to the colored people, there is always more that is benevolent, I perceive, than just, manifested towards us. What I ask for the negro is not benevolence, not pity, not sympathy, but simply *justice*. The American people have always been anxious to know what they shall do with us. . . . I have had but one answer from the beginning. Do nothing with us! Your doing with us has already played the mischief with us. Do nothing with us! If the apples will not remain on the tree of their own strength, if they are worm-eaten at the core, if they are early ripe and disposed to fall, let them fall! . . . And if the negro cannot stand on his own legs, let him fall also. All I ask is, give him a chance to stand on his own legs! Let him alone! . . . [Y]our interference is doing him positive injury.

What the Black Man Wants: An Address Delivered in Boston, Massachusetts, on 26 January 1865, reprinted in 4 The Frederick Douglass Papers 59, 68 (J. Blassingame & J. McKivigan eds. 1991) (emphasis in original).

Like Douglass, I believe blacks can achieve in every avenue of American life without the meddling of university administrators. . . .

No one would argue that a university could set up a lower general admission standard and then impose heightened requirements only on black applicants. Similarly, a university may not maintain a high admission standard and grant exemptions to favored races. The Law School, of its own choosing, and for its own purposes, maintains an exclusionary admissions system that it knows produces racially disproportionate results. Racial discrimination is not a permissible solution to the self-inflicted wounds of this elitist admissions policy. . . .

I

The majority agrees that the Law School's racial discrimination should be subjected to strict scrutiny. . . .

Where the Court has accepted only national security, [*Korematsu*] and rejected even the best interests of a child, [Palmore v. Sidoti] as a justification for racial discrimination, I conclude that only those measures the State must take to provide a bulwark against anarchy, or to prevent violence, will constitute a "pressing public necessity." . . .

III . . .

B

Under the proper standard, there is no pressing public necessity in maintaining a public law school at all and, it follows, certainly not an elite law school. Likewise, marginal improvements in legal education do not qualify as a compelling state interest.

1

While legal education at a public university may be good policy or otherwise laudable, it is obviously not a pressing public necessity when the correct legal standard is applied. Additionally, circumstantial evidence as to whether a state activity is of pressing public necessity can be obtained by asking whether all States feel compelled to engage in that activity. [In] this sense, the absence of a public, American Bar Association (ABA) accredited, law school in Alaska, Delaware, Massachusetts, New Hampshire, and Rhode Island, provides further evidence that Michigan's maintenance of the Law School does not constitute a compelling state interest.

2

[Still,] even assuming that a State may, under appropriate circumstances, demonstrate a cognizable interest in having an elite law school, Michigan has failed to do so here.

This Court has limited the scope of equal protection review to interests and activities that occur within that State's jurisdiction. . . .

The only cognizable state interests vindicated by operating a public law school are, therefore, the education of that State's citizens and the training of that State's lawyers. . . .

The Law School today, however, does precious little training of those attorneys who will serve the citizens of Michigan. [Less] than 16% of the Law School's graduating class elects to stay in Michigan after law school. . . .

It does not take a social scientist to conclude that it is precisely the Law School's status as an elite institution that causes it to be a way-station for the rest of the country's lawyers, rather than a training ground for those who will remain in Michigan. The Law School's decision to be an elite institution does little to advance the welfare of the people of Michigan or any cognizable interest of the State of Michigan. . . .

IV . . .

With the adoption of different admissions methods, such as accepting all students who meet minimum qualifications, the Law School could achieve its vision of the racially aesthetic student body without the use of racial discrimination. . . .

B

1

The Court's deference to the Law School's conclusion that its racial experimentation leads to educational benefits will, if adhered to, have serious collateral consequences. The Court relies heavily on social science evidence to justify its deference. The Court never acknowledges, however, the growing evidence that racial (and other sorts) of heterogeneity actually impairs learning among black students. [Justice Thomas cites studies showing that black students attending historically black colleges (HBCs) report higher academic achievement than those attending predominantly white colleges.] . . .

The majority grants deference to the Law School's "assessment that diversity will, in fact, yield educational benefits." It follows, therefore, that an HBC's assessment that racial homogeneity will yield educational benefits would similarly be given deference. An HBC's rejection of white applicants in order to maintain racial homogeneity seems permissible, therefore, under the majority's view of the Equal Protection Clause. . . . Contained within today's majority opinion is the seed of a new constitutional justification for a concept I thought long and rightly rejected — racial segregation. . . .

C

The sky has not fallen at Boalt Hall at the University of California, Berkeley. Prior to Proposition 209's adoption of Cal. Const. Art. 1, §31(a), which bars the State from "grant[ing] preferential treatment . . . on the basis of race . . . in the operation of . . . public education," Boalt Hall enrolled 20 blacks and 28 Hispanics in its first-year class for 1996. In 2002, without deploying express racial discrimination in admissions, Boalt's entering class enrolled 14 blacks and 36 Hispanics. Total underrepresented minority student enrollment at Boalt Hall now exceeds 1996 levels. Apparently the Law School cannot be counted on to be as resourceful. The Court is willfully blind to the very real experience in California and elsewhere, which raises the inference that institutions with "reputation[s] for excellence" rivaling the Law School's have satisfied their sense of mission without resorting to prohibited racial discrimination.

V

Putting aside the absence of any legal support for the majority's reflexive deference, there is much to be said for the view that the use of tests and other measures to "predict" academic performance is a poor substitute for a system that gives every applicant a chance to prove he can succeed in the study of law. The rallying cry that in the absence of racial discrimination in admissions there would be a true meritocracy ignores the fact that the entire process is poisoned by numerous exceptions to "merit." For example, in the national debate on racial discrimination in higher education admissions, much has been made of the fact that elite institutions utilize a so-called "legacy" preference to give the children of alumni an advantage in admissions. This, and other, exceptions to a "true" meritocracy give the lie to protestations that merit admissions are in fact the order of the day at the Nation's universities. The Equal Protection Clause does not, however, prohibit the use of unseemly legacy preferences or many other kinds of arbitrary admissions procedures. What the Equal Protection Clause does prohibit are classifications made on the basis of race. So while legacy preferences can stand under the Constitution, racial discrimination cannot. I will not twist the Constitution to invalidate legacy preferences or otherwise impose my vision of higher education admissions on the Nation. The majority should similarly stay its impulse to validate faddish racial discrimination the Constitution clearly forbids.

In any event, there is nothing ancient, honorable, or constitutionally protected about "selective" admissions. The University of Michigan should be well aware that alternative methods have historically been used for the admission of students, for it brought to this country the German certificate system in the late-19th century. . . . Under this system, a secondary school was certified by a university so that any graduate who completed the course offered by the school was offered admission to the university. The certification regime supplemented, and later virtually replaced (at least in the Midwest), the prior regime of rigorous subject-matter entrance examinations. The facially race-neutral "percent plans" now used in Texas, California, and Florida are in many ways the descendents of the certificate system.

Certification was replaced by selective admissions in the beginning of the 20th century, as universities sought to exercise more control over the composition of their student bodies. Since its inception, selective admissions has been the vehicle for racial, ethnic, and religious tinkering and experimentation by university administrators. The initial driving force for the relocation of the selective function from the high school to the universities was the same desire to select racial winners and losers that the Law School exhibits today. Columbia, Harvard, and others infamously determined that they had "too many" Jews, just as today the Law School argues it would have "too many" whites if it could not discriminate in its admissions process.

Columbia employed intelligence tests precisely because Jewish applicants, who were predominantly immigrants, scored worse on such tests. . . .

Similarly no modern law school can claim ignorance of the poor performance of blacks, relatively speaking, on the Law School Admissions Test (LSAT). Nevertheless, law schools continue to use the test and then attempt to "correct" for black underperformance by using racial discrimination in admissions so as to obtain their aesthetic student body. The Law School's continued adherence to measures it knows produce racially skewed results is not entitled to deference by this Court. The Law School itself admits that the test is imperfect, as it must, given that it regularly admits students who score at or below 150 (the national median) on the test. . . .

Having decided to use the LSAT, the Law School must accept the constitutional burdens that come with this decision. The Law School may freely continue to employ the LSAT and other allegedly merit-based standards in whatever fashion it likes. What the Equal Protection Clause forbids, but the Court today allows, is the use of these standards hand-in-hand with racial discrimination. An infinite variety of admissions methods are available to the Law School. Considering all of the radical thinking that has historically occurred at this country's universities, the Law School's intractable approach toward admissions is striking. . . .

VI . . .

I believe what lies beneath the Court's decision today are the benighted notions that one can tell when racial discrimination benefits (rather than hurts) minority groups, and that racial discrimination is necessary to remedy general societal ills. . . .

I must contest the notion that the Law School's discrimination benefits those admitted as a result of it. . . .

The Law School tantalizes unprepared students with the promise of a University of Michigan degree and all of the opportunities that it offers. These over-matched students take the bait, only to find that they cannot succeed in the cauldron of competition. And this mismatch crisis is not restricted to elite institutions. Indeed, to cover the tracks of the aestheticists, this cruel farce of racial discrimination must continue — in selection for the Michigan Law Review, see University of Michigan Law School Student Handbook 2002–2003, pp. 39–40 (noting the presence of a "diversity plan" for admission to the review), and in hiring at law firms and for judicial clerkships — until the "beneficiaries" are no longer tolerated. While these students may graduate with law degrees, there is no evidence that they have received a qualitatively better legal education (or become better lawyers) than if they had gone to a less "elite" law school for which they were better prepared. And the aestheticists will never address the real problems facing "underrepresented minorities," instead continuing their social experiments on other people's children. . . .

It is uncontested that each year, the Law School admits a handful of blacks who would be admitted in the absence of racial discrimination. Who can differentiate between those who belong and those who do not? The majority of blacks are admitted to the Law School because of discrimination, and because of this policy all are tarred as undeserving. . . . When blacks take positions in the highest places of government, industry, or academia, it is an open question today whether their skin color played a part in their advancement. The question itself is the stigma. . . .

VII . . .

For the immediate future, [the] majority has placed its *imprimatur* on a practice. that can only weaken the principle of equality embodied in the Declaration of Independence and the Equal Protection Clause. "Our Constitution is color-blind, and neither knows nor tolerates classes among citizens." Plessy v. Ferguson (Harlan, J., dissenting). It has been nearly 140 years since Frederick Douglass asked the intellectual ancestors of the Law School to "[d]o nothing with us!" and the Nation adopted the Fourteenth Amendment. Now we must wait another 25 years to see this principle of equality [vindicated].

Note: The Contemporary Application of Strict Scrutiny

1. *What counts as a compelling interest?* The Court's opinion in *Grutter* rests on the conclusion that diversity in higher education — particularly in law schools — constitutes a compelling state interest. At the same time, the Court seems to abandon a retrospective, remedial justification for affirmative action in favor of a prospective, diversity-based rationale. Jeffries describes this as a significant shift. He locates its origins in Justice Powell's opinion in *Bakke:*

> Powell saw little prospect that the compensatory rationale would place any meaningful limit on the duration of [racial] preferences. Powell thought of affirmative action as a transition, a short-term departure from the ideal of color-blindness justified only by pressing necessity. Allowing minority set-asides to continue until all effects of past societal discrimination had been eliminated might mean they would last forever.
>
> Powell therefore crafted an approach designed both to permit affirmative action and to constrain it. He wanted to allow racial preferences in higher education while preserving the grounds for objecting to them, to permit race-conscious admissions under current conditions without conceding their long-term future. In short, he wanted to say "yes" now, while implying "no" later. . . .
>
> Diversity was a softer and more fluid concept. It directed attention to participation rather than to compensation, to the importance of some, though not necessarily perfect, representation from all groups. Because diversity was a less ambitious goal, it could plausibly be the sooner achieved. Most important, diversity put the justification for racial preferences squarely on improving the educational experience of all students, rather than on helping a favored few. . . .

Jeffries, *Bakke* Revisited, 2003 Sup. Ct. Rev. 1, 6–7.

Does the diversity rationale extend beyond higher education to other government decisions, such as government employment? Consider Professor Guinier's view:

> The task of constituting each [entering] class [at a selective public institution] is a political act because it implicates the institution's sense of itself as a community, as well as the larger society's sense of itself as a democracy. Such acts allocate resources in a way that affects those who are admitted to the institution, those who are rejected, those who fail to apply, and those who simply use the institution's selection criteria as an interpretive guide. Thus, they affect all members of society, both directly, as described above, and indirectly, by helping determine future political, economic, and social leaders. Directly or indirectly, taxpayers support these institutions, which function as gateways to upward mobility

and help legitimize democratic ideals of participation, fairness, and equal opportunity.

Guinier, Admissions Rituals as Political Acts: Guardians at the Gates of Our Democratic Ideals, 117 Harv. L. Rev. 113, 135 (2003). Consider also Post:

> In contrast to Powell's opinion in *Bakke*, *Grutter* does not offer an account of the intrinsic value of the educational process. It instead conceives of education as instrumental for the achievement of extrinsic social goods like professionalism, citizenship, or leadership. It follows from this way of conceptualizing the problem that the Law School can have a compelling interest in using diversity to facilitate the attainment of these social goods only if there is an independently compelling interest in the actual attainment of these goods. *Grutter*'s justifications for diversity thus potentially reach far more widely than do Powell's. . . .

Post, Foreward: Fashioning the Legal Constitution: Culture, Courts, and Law, 117 Harv. L. Rev. 4, 60, 62–63 (2003). In thinking about the extent of the diversity and citizenship rationales, consider the Court's later decision in Parents Involved in Community Schools v. Seattle School District No. 1, 551 U.S. 701 (2007), which appears at pages 616-632, infra. There, the Court struck down two public school systems' policies of taking race into account in assigning students to particular schools. In his opinion for the Court, Chief Justice Roberts wrote that public school assignment policies "are not governed by *Grutter*" because *Grutter* "relied upon considerations unique to institutions of higher education, noting that in light of 'the expansive freedoms of speech and thought associated with the university environment, universities occupy a special niche in our constitutional tradition.'" By contrast, in dissent, Justice Breyer emphasized as part of his view that the school districts had a compelling interest in taking race into account that "there is a democratic element: an interest in producing an educational environment that reflects the 'pluralistic society' in which our children will live. It is an interest in helping our children learn to work and play together with children of different racial backgrounds. It is an interest in teaching children to engage in the kind of cooperation among Americans of all races that is necessary to make a land of three hundred million people one Nation."

For criticism of the diversity argument, see Lawrence, Two Views of the River: A Critique of the Liberal Defense of Affirmative Action, 101 Colum. L. Rev. 928 (2001), which argues that "supporters of affirmative action have used the diversity argument to defend affirmative action at elite universities and law schools without questioning the ways that traditional admissions criteria continue to perpetuate race and class privilege."

2. *Who decides what counts as a compelling interest?* Note that the Court explicitly defers to the law school's determination that diversity constitutes a compelling interest. Is such deference to the defendant's views appropriate in deciding what counts as a compelling interest? Could another state conclude that diversity is *not* a weighty interest? Note that several states have forbidden consideration of race by state institutions as a matter of state constitutional law. In Schuette v. Coalition to Defend Affirmative Action, 134 S. Ct. 1623 (2014), the Supreme Court upheld such a prohibition against constitutional attack. Why was the Court prepared to defer to educational administrators in *Grutter* when it was skeptical of city council members in *Croson*?

Is there something distinctive about the very process of higher education that led the Court to defer here when it held in *Adarand* that "skepticism" is a core principle of equal protection review?

3. *The role of race in the admissions process.* The Court's opinion places great weight on the fact that the law school was using a "holistic" admissions process. What does this mean? In what ways does this process differ from the contracting processes at issue in *Croson* and *Adarand*? Is it that the fact of "merit" or "desert" is more contested or more complicated in the context of higher education admissions than in government contracting? Consider:

> [The] affirmative action cases that produced [the Supreme Court's] embrace of strict scrutiny — *Croson* and *Adarand* — involved the highly formal and thus somewhat atypical practice of competitive bidding. In competitive bidding, anonymity is easy to achieve, and, assuming the bid meets the specifications, bids can be ranked against each other along one entirely quantifiable dimension, namely, price. . . .
>
> [In] higher education, elite institutions could rely entirely on a few raw or mechanically adjusted numbers. . . . At most elite institutions, however, it would be possible to produce entering classes with vastly different characteristics, each made up entirely of well-qualified students. The numbers themselves, even when adjusted, may offer a spurious precision with respect to particular applicants. A school . . . may decide that a variety of other factors beyond standardized test scores and grade point averages will enhance its various missions. In that regard, it might decide, even in the complete absence of racial considerations, to take into account factors such as geographic diversity, choice of specialization, distinctive extra-curricular experiences, nonquantifiable evidence that an applicant's future promise is not adequately signaled by her past performance, and the like. Moreover, along [somewhat more] vaguely venal lines . . . , a school may decide to grant preferences to children of alumni or other financial or political supporters. . . .
>
> The reasons for going beyond the numbers are both "pluralist" and "republican." Within the institution, using multidimensional admissions criteria may be important for programmatic purposes. . . . In the broader world, the institution's continued vitality may depend on there being broad political support for its mission.

Karlan, Easing the Spring: Strict Scrutiny and Affirmative Action After the Redistricting Cases, 43 Wm. & Mary L. Rev. 1569, 1578, 1596–1597 (2002).

4. *The efficacy of law school affirmative action.* In the wake of *Grutter*, Sander offered a different critique of race-conscious affirmative action in law schools, claiming that black students admitted to law school through racial preferences are disadvantaged in the long term. As a result of affirmative action, Sander argues, black students are subject to an "academic mismatch": They have significantly lower credentials (LSAT scores and undergraduate grades) than students admitted without regard to race. Mismatched students, Sander argues, are less likely to perform well in law school (where instruction will be pitched toward students with better academic preparation), less likely to graduate, and less likely to pass the bar:

> [The] absolute number of black law graduates passing the bar on their first attempt — an achievement important both for a lawyer's self-esteem and for success in the legal market — would be much larger under a race-blind regime than under the current system of preferences. . . . [The] elimination of racial preferences would put blacks into schools where they were perfectly competitive with all

other students — and that would lead to dramatically higher performance in law school and on the bar. Black students' grades, graduation rates, and bar passage rates would all converge toward white students' rates. The overall rate of blacks graduating from law school and passing the bar on their first attempt would rise from . . . 45% . . . to somewhere between 64% and 70%. Conversely, the black students excluded by a switch to a race-blind system have such weak academic credentials that they add only a comparative handful of attorneys to total national production.

Sander, A Systemic Analysis of Affirmative Action in American Law Schools, 57 Stan. L. Rev. 367, 474 (2004). Sander's empirical methods, as well as the conclusions he draws from his data sets, have been extensively criticized. One study found that students with the same LSAT score, undergraduate GPA, and gender performed similarly on the bar regardless of which law school they attended and concluded that "[while] it is true that similarly qualified black students get lower grades as a result of going to a higher-tier school, they perform equally well on the bar irrespective of law school tier." Ho, Why Affirmative Action Does Not Cause Black Students to Fail the Bar, 114 Yale L.J. 1997, 2004 (2005). Another study found a "reverse mismatch" effect: For both white and black students, attending a higher-tier school was positively correlated with ultimately becoming a lawyer. Ayres and Brooks, Does Affirmative Action Reduce the Number of Black Lawyers?, 57 Stan. L. Rev. 1807, 1824–1825 (2005); see also Alon and Tienda, Assessing the "Mismatch" Hypothesis: Differential in College Graduation Rates by Institutional Selectivity, 78 Soc. Educ. 295 (2005) (finding that the likelihood of minority students graduating from college increases as the selectivity of the institution attended rises). For other empirical critiques of Sander's work, see, e.g., Harris and Kidder, The Black Student Mismatch Myth in Legal Education: The Systemic Flaws in Richard Sander's Affirmative Action Study, J. Blacks Higher Educ. 103 (Winter 2005); Johnson and Onwuachi-Willig, Cry Me a River: The Limits of "A Systemic Analysis of Affirmative Action in American Law Schools," 7 Afr.-Am. L. & Poly. Rep. 1 (2005).

Consider two goals of affirmative action: promoting diversity and remedying past wrongs. To what extent is Sander's argument useful in addressing these goals? In this regard, consider Wilkins, A Systematic Response to Systemic Disadvantage: A Response to Sander, 57 Stan. L. Rev. 1915, 1938 (2005):

Sander treats the success of the black graduates from elite law schools as if this were solely a benefit to the individuals involved. This seriously underestimates the importance of developing a viable black elite. Blacks who have achieved positions of power and influence in the legal profession, most of whom, as we have seen, are graduates of elite law schools, have played a critical role in opening the doors of opportunity for other black lawyers. Black partners routinely serve on hiring committees, form organizations dedicated to improving the hiring and retention of minority lawyers, and devote countless hours to mentoring black associates and law students. As many blacks have left law firms for in-house counsel positions, these newly minted purchasing agents have sought to use their new positions of authority to distribute work to minority lawyers and to press firms to report their progress on diversity and improve upon it.

Additionally, Sander recommends that schools make their admissions policies "transparent," so students can consider the grades and scores of students in their demographic group and make informed decisions about their chances of success at a particular law school. Do you agree? Would making this information more available serve the goals of affirmative action? Compare Ayres and Brooks, supra, at 1851 (suggesting better disclosure might be beneficial), with Wilkins, supra, at 1955–1959 (suggesting greater disclosure might undermine the goals of affirmative action).

5. *What counts as narrow tailoring?* Does *Grutter* significantly ease the tailoring inquiry? Note the Court's rejection of the idea that race-neutral means are always more narrowly tailored than race-conscious programs. Does this depend on the idea that the state is pursuing many goals simultaneously? Justices Scalia and Thomas criticize the majority by noting that the law school could achieve racial diversity quite easily if it simply abandoned its reliance on selection criteria that have a differential impact.

GRATZ v. BOLLINGER, 539 U.S. 244 (2003). This companion case to *Grutter* perhaps clarified the tailoring inquiry. The case concerned admissions to the undergraduate college of liberal arts and sciences at the University of Michigan. The University ranked college applicants according to a 150-point scale. Students receiving over 100 points were generally admitted, while those receiving under 75 points were generally delayed or rejected. Applicants received points based upon factors like high school grade point average, standardized test scores, the academic quality of an applicant's high school, in-state residency, and alumni relationships. Up to 110 points could be assigned for academic performance, and up to 40 points could be assigned for the other, nonacademic factors. Michigan residents, for example, received 10 points, and children of alumni received 4. Counselors could assign an outstanding essay up to 3 points and could award up to 5 points for an applicant's personal achievement, leadership, or public service. An applicant automatically received a 20-point bonus if he or she possessed any one of the following "miscellaneous" factors: membership in an underrepresented minority group; attendance at a predominantly minority or disadvantaged high school; or recruitment for athletics.

This point system was supplemented by the review of some applications by an Admissions Review Committee (ARC). Under this system, some applications were "flagged" for review by the Committee if it was determined that the applicant was academically prepared to succeed at the University, had received a minimum index score, and possessed characteristics important to the University's composition of its freshman class, such as high class rank, unique life experiences, challenges, circumstances, interests or talents, socioeconomic disadvantage, or underrepresented race, ethnicity, or geography. The Committee reviewed "flagged" applications individually and determined whether to admit or deny each applicant.

Chief Justice Rehnquist delivered the opinion of the Court: "Justice Powell's opinion in *Bakke* emphasized the importance of considering each particular applicant as an individual, assessing all of the qualities that individual possesses, and in turn, evaluating that individual's ability to contribute to the unique setting of higher education. . . .

"The [challenged] policy does not provide such individualized consideration. The [policy] automatically distributes 20 points to every single applicant from an 'underrepresented minority' group, as defined by the University. The only consideration that accompanies this distribution of points is a factual review of an application to determine whether an individual is a member of one of these minority groups. Moreover, unlike Justice Powell's example, where the race of a 'particular black applicant' could be considered without being decisive, see *Bakke*, the [University's] automatic distribution of 20 points has the effect of making 'the factor of race . . . decisive' for virtually every minimally qualified underrepresented minority applicant.

"Respondents emphasize the fact that the [college] has created the possibility of an applicant's file being flagged for individualized consideration by the ARC. . . .

"But the fact that the 'review committee can look at the applications individually and ignore the points,' once an application is flagged, is of little comfort under our strict scrutiny analysis. The record does not reveal precisely how many applications are flagged for this individualized consideration, but it is undisputed that such consideration is the exception and not the [rule]. Additionally, this individualized review is only provided *after* admissions counselors automatically distribute the University's version of a 'plus' that makes race a decisive factor for virtually every minimally qualified underrepresented minority applicant.

"Respondents contend that '[t]he volume of applications and the presentation of applicant information make it impractical for [the College] to use the . . . admissions system' upheld by the Court today in *Grutter*. But the fact that the implementation of a program capable of providing individualized consideration might present administrative challenges does not render constitutional an otherwise problematic system."

Justice O'Connor wrote a concurring opinion: "Although the Office of Undergraduate Admissions does assign 20 points to some 'soft' variables other than race, the points available for other diversity contributions, such as leadership and service, personal achievement, and geographic diversity, are capped at much lower levels. Even the most outstanding national high school leader could never receive more than five points for his or her accomplishments — a mere quarter of the points automatically assigned to an underrepresented minority solely based on the fact of his or her race. Of course, as Justice Powell made clear in *Bakke*, a university need not 'necessarily accor[d]' all diversity factors 'the same weight,' and the 'weight attributed to a particular quality may vary from year to year depending on the "mix" both of the student body and the applicants for the incoming class.' But the selection index, by setting up automatic, predetermined point allocations for the soft variables, ensures that the diversity contributions of applicants cannot be individually assessed. This policy stands in sharp contrast to the law school's admissions plan, which enables admissions officers to make nuanced judgments with respect to the contributions each applicant is likely to make to the diversity of the incoming class."

Justices Thomas and Breyer also wrote concurring opinions.

Justice Souter, joined by Justice Ginsburg, dissented: "The record does not describe a system with a quota like the one struck down in *Bakke*, which 'insulate[d]' all nonminority candidates from competition from certain seats. [The]-*Bakke* plan 'focused *solely* on ethnic diversity' and effectively told nonminority applicants that '[n]o matter how strong their qualifications, quantitative and extracurricular, including their own potential for contribution to educational diversity, they are never afforded the chance to compete with applicants from the preferred [groups].'

"The plan here, in contrast, lets all applicants compete for all places and values an applicant's offerings for any place not solely on the grounds of [race]. A nonminority applicant who scores highly in [other] categories can readily garner a selection index exceeding that of a minority applicant who gets the 20-point bonus. . . .

"[In] contrast to the college's forthrightness in saying just what plus factor it gives for membership in an underrepresented minority, it is worth considering the character of one alternative thrown up as preferable, because supposedly not based on race. Drawing on admissions systems used at public universities in California, Florida, and Texas, the United States contends that Michigan could get student diversity [by] guaranteeing admission to a fixed percentage of the top students from each high school in Michigan.

"While there is nothing unconstitutional about such a practice, it nonetheless suffers from a serious disadvantage. It is the disadvantage of deliberate obfuscation. The 'percentage plans' are just as race-conscious as the point system (and fairly so), but they get their racially diverse results without saying directly what they are doing or why they are doing it. In contrast, Michigan states its purpose directly and, if this were a doubtful case for me, I would be tempted to give Michigan an extra point of its own for its frankness. Equal protection cannot become an exercise in which the winners are the ones who hide the ball."

Justice Ginsburg, joined by Justice Souter, also dissented: "The stain of generations of racial oppression is still visible in our society, and the determination to hasten its removal remains vital. One can reasonably anticipate, therefore, that colleges and universities will seek to maintain their minority enrollment — and the networks and opportunities thereby opened to minority graduates — whether or not they can do so in full candor through adoption of affirmative action plans of the kind here at issue. Without recourse to such plans, institutions of higher education may resort to camouflage. For example, schools may encourage applicants to write of their cultural traditions in the essays they submit, or to indicate whether English is their second language. Seeking to improve their chances for admission, applicants may highlight the minority group associations to which they belong, or the Hispanic surnames of their mothers or grandparents. In turn, teachers' recommendations may emphasize who a student is as much as what he or she has accomplished. If honesty is the best policy, surely Michigan's accurately described, fully disclosed College affirmative action program is preferable to achieving similar numbers through winks, nods, and disguises."

In an opinion joined by Justice Souter, Justice Stevens dissented on the ground that the plaintiffs lacked standing.

Note: Scrutiny of Means

1. *The significance of candor.* Is the only difference between the law school and the undergraduate plans the frankness with which they admit the salience of race? Is holistic, individualized review necessarily less troubling than more mechanical processes? Or, to the contrary, does "mechanical decision making" better "restrain[] the state in its race consciousness"? See Rodriguez, Against Individualized Consideration, 83 Ind. L.J. 1405, 1409 (2008).

Are there methods of achieving the goals of affirmative action without utilizing facially racial classifications? Consider S. Cashin, Place Not Race: A New Vision of Opportunity in America xix (2014):

> The rub for proponents of affirmative action is that as long as they hold on to race as the sine qua non of diversity, they stymie possibilities for transformative change. The civil rights community, for example, expends energy on a policy that primarily benefits the most advantaged children of color, while contributing to a divisive

politics that makes it difficult to create quality K-12 education for all children. [The] next generation of diversity strategies should encourage rather than discourage cross-racial alliances and social mobility. [Meaningful] diversity can be achieved if institutions rethink exclusionary practices, cultivate strivers from overlooked places, and give special consideration to highly qualified applicants of all races that have had to overcome structural disadvantages like segregation.

In this regard, consider the history of affirmative action at the University of Texas. After the Fifth Circuit held in Hopwood v. Texas, 78 F.3d 932 (5th Cir. 1996), that the University of Texas's consideration of race in its admissions process violated the equal protection clause because it did not further a compelling government interest, the Texas legislature adopted a measure known as the Top Ten Percent Law. That statute granted automatic admission to the University (as well as other public institutions) to all students from Texas high schools who are in the top 10 percent of their class. The plan was expressly designed, in part, to enable the admission of black and Latino students, and took advantage of the fact that pervasive segregation in K-12 education guaranteed there would be a significant pool of black and Latino students graduating at the top of their classes. Following the Supreme Court's decision in *Grutter*, the University adopted an additional admissions program in which race was one factor taken into account in admitting the portion of the entering class that was not admitted under the Top Ten Percent Law.

Was the Top Ten Percent plan, standing alone, constitutionally unproblematic?

The Court's subsequent decisions addressing the combined plan are discussed on pages 601-607, infra.

2. *Deference to means?* The Supreme Court deferred to institutions' decisions about whether racial diversity is a compelling interest. By contrast, when it comes to the means of pursuing that racial diversity, the Supreme Court has been less deferential. In Fisher v. University of Texas, 133 S. Ct. 2411 (2013) (*Fisher I*), the Court, in an opinion by Justice Kennedy, held that the court of appeals had not applied "the correct standard of strict scrutiny":

The University must prove that the means chosen by the University to attain diversity are narrowly tailored to that goal. On this point, the University receives no deference. *Grutter* made clear that it is for the courts, not for university administrators, to ensure that "[t]he means chosen to accomplish the [government's] asserted purpose must be specifically and narrowly framed to accomplish that purpose." True, a court can take account of a university's experience and expertise in adopting or rejecting certain admissions processes. But, as the Court said in *Grutter*, it remains at all times the University's obligation to demonstrate, and the Judiciary's obligation to determine, that admissions processes "ensure that each applicant is evaluated as an individual and not in a way that makes an applicant's race or ethnicity the defining feature of his or her application."

Narrow tailoring also requires that the reviewing court verify that it is "necessary" for a university to use race to achieve the educational benefits of diversity. *Bakke*. This involves a careful judicial inquiry into whether a university could achieve sufficient diversity without using racial classifications. Although "[n]arrow tailoring does not require exhaustion of every conceivable race-neutral alternative," strict scrutiny does require a court to examine with care, and not defer to, a university's "serious, good faith consideration of workable race-neutral alternatives." See *Grutter*. Consideration by the university is of course necessary, but it is not sufficient to satisfy strict scrutiny: The reviewing court must ultimately be satisfied that no workable race-neutral alternatives would produce the educational benefits of diversity. If "'a nonracial approach . . . could promote the substantial interest about as well and at tolerable administrative expense,'" Wygant v. Jackson Bd. of Ed., 476 U.S. 267, 280, n.6 (1986) (quoting Greenawalt, Judicial Scrutiny of "Benign" Racial Preference in Law School Admissions, 75 Colum. L. Rev. 559, 578-579 (1975)), then the university may not consider race. A plaintiff, of course, bears the burden of placing the validity of a university's adoption of an affirmative action plan in issue. But strict scrutiny imposes on the university the ultimate burden of demonstrating, before turning to racial classifications, that available, workable race-neutral alternatives do not suffice.

Justice Scalia wrote a short concurring opinion adhering to the view he expressed in *Grutter* that the Fourteenth Amendment "proscribes government discrimination on the basis of race, and state-provided education is no exception," but noting that because Fisher had not asked the Court to overrule *Grutter*, he joined the Court's opinion.

Justice Thomas wrote a lengthier concurrence, reiterating his position that "a State's use of race in higher education admissions decisions is categorically prohibited by the Equal Protection Clause."

Justice Ginsburg issued a short dissent, stating that she would have upheld the University's admissions policy.

FISHER v. UNIVERSITY OF TEXAS (*FISHER II*), 136 S. Ct. 2198 (2016). After a remand, in which the court of appeals again upheld Texas's combined use of its Ten Percent Plan and race-conscious review, the case returned to the Supreme Court, which upheld the admissions process.

Justice Kennedy wrote the opinion for the Court. He described race as "but a 'factor of a factor of a factor' in the holistic-review calculus." And he emphasized that consideration of race was not limited to underrepresented minorities, but "'within the full context of the entire application, may be beneficial to any UT Austin applicant — including whites and Asian–Americans.'"

Much of his opinion seemed to turn on the distinctive posture of the case before the Court:

"Petitioner's acceptance of the Top Ten Percent Plan complicates this Court's review. In particular, it has led to a record that is almost devoid of information about the students who secured admission to the University through the [Ten Percent] Plan. The Court thus cannot know how students admitted solely based on their class rank differ in their contribution to diversity from students admitted through holistic review.

"In an ordinary case, this evidentiary gap perhaps could be filled by a remand to the district court for further factfinding. When petitioner's application was rejected, however, the University's combined percentage-plan/holistic-review approach to admission had been in effect for just three years. While studies undertaken over the eight years since then may be of significant value in determining the constitutionality of the University's current admissions policy, that evidence has little bearing on whether petitioner received equal treatment when her application was rejected in 2008. If the Court were to remand, therefore, further factfinding would be limited to a narrow 3-year sample, review of which might yield little insight. . . .

"Under the circumstances of this case, then, a remand would do nothing more than prolong a suit that has already persisted for eight years and cost the parties on both sides significant resources. Petitioner long since has graduated from another college, and the University's policy — and the data on which it first was based — may have evolved or changed in material ways."

Although the opinion thus resolved only a narrow question, Justice Kennedy emphasized that the University had a "continuing obligation to satisfy the burden of strict scrutiny in light of changing circumstances. The University engages in periodic reassessment of the constitutionality, and efficacy, of its admissions program. Going forward, that assessment must be undertaken in light of the experience the school has accumulated and the data it has gathered since the adoption of its admissions plan."

The Court rejected Fisher's argument that consideration of race was unnecessary because the University had been achieving a "critical mass" of black and Hispanic students through the Top Ten Percent Plan plus its prior race-neutral holistic review:

"To start, the demographic data the University has submitted show consistent stagnation in terms of the percentage of minority students enrolling at the University from 1996 to 2002. . . .

"Although demographics alone are by no means dispositive, they do have some value as a gauge of the University's ability to enroll students who can offer underrepresented perspectives.

"In addition to this broad demographic data, the University put forward evidence that minority students admitted under the *Hopwood* regime experienced feelings of loneliness and isolation.

"This anecdotal evidence is, in turn, bolstered by further, more nuanced quantitative data. In 2002, 52 percent of undergraduate classes with at least five students had no African-American students enrolled in them, and 27 percent had only one African-American student. In other words, only 21 percent of undergraduate classes with five or more students in them had more than one African-American student enrolled. Twelve percent of these classes had no Hispanic students, as compared to 10 percent in 1996. Though a college must continually reassess its need for race-conscious review, here that assessment appears to have been done with care, and a reasonable determination was made that the University had not yet attained its goals."

Building off a point made in *Parents Involved in Community Schools v. Seattle School Dist. No. 1*, 551 U.S. 701 (2007) — that there was a tension between arguing that race-conscious action is necessary and a claim that it has only a small effect — Fisher had argued that considering race was unnecessary because it affected the admissions of very few students. Justice Kennedy rejected this argument as well: "The fact that race consciousness played a role in only a small portion of admissions decisions should be a hallmark of narrow tailoring, not evidence of unconstitutionality."

Finally, the Court rejected the argument that there were workable race-neutral means available to the University:

"A review of the record reveals, however, that, at the time of petitioner's application, none of her proposed alternatives was a workable means for the University to attain the benefits of diversity it sought. For example, petitioner suggests that the University could intensify its outreach efforts to African-American and Hispanic applicants. But the University submitted extensive evidence of the many ways in which it already had intensified its outreach efforts to those students. The University has created three new scholarship programs, opened new regional admissions centers, increased its recruitment budget by half-a-million dollars, and organized over 1,000 recruitment events. Perhaps more significantly, in the wake of *Hopwood*, the University spent seven years attempting to achieve its compelling interest using race-neutral holistic review. None of these efforts succeeded, and petitioner fails to offer any meaningful way in which the University could have improved upon them at the time of her application.

"Petitioner also suggests altering the weight given to academic and socioeconomic factors in the University's admissions calculus. This proposal ignores the fact that the University tried, and failed, to increase diversity through enhanced consideration of socioeconomic and other factors. And it further ignores this Court's precedent making clear that the Equal Protection Clause does not force universities to choose between a diverse student body and a reputation for academic excellence.

"Petitioner's final suggestion is to uncap the Top Ten Percent Plan, and admit more — if not all — the University's students through a percentage plan. As an initial matter, petitioner overlooks the fact that the Top Ten Percent Plan, though facially neutral, cannot be understood apart from its basic purpose, which is to boost minority enrollment. Percentage plans are "adopted with racially segregated neighborhoods and schools front and center stage." *Fisher I*, 570 U.S., at —— (GINSBURG, J., dissenting). 'It is race consciousness, not blindness to race, that drives such plans.' *Ibid.* Consequently, petitioner cannot assert simply that increasing the University's reliance on a percentage plan would make its admissions policy more race neutral.

"Even if, as a matter of raw numbers, minority enrollment would increase under such a regime, petitioner would be hard-pressed to find convincing support for the proposition that college admissions would be improved if they were a function of class rank alone. That approach would sacrifice all other aspects of diversity in pursuit of enrolling a higher number of minority students. A system that selected every student through class rank alone would exclude the star athlete or musician whose grades suffered because of daily practices and training. It would exclude a talented young biologist who struggled to maintain above-average grades in humanities classes. And it would exclude a student whose freshman-year grades were poor because of a family crisis but who got herself back on track in her last three years of school, only to find herself just outside of the top decile of her class.

"These are but examples of the general problem. Class rank is a single metric, and like any single metric, it will capture certain types of people and miss others. This does not imply that students admitted through holistic review are necessarily more capable or more desirable than those admitted through the Top Ten Percent Plan. It merely reflects the fact that privileging one characteristic above all others does not lead to a diverse student body. Indeed, to compel universities to admit students based on class rank alone is in deep tension with the goal of educational diversity as this Court's cases have defined it."

Justice Thomas wrote a brief dissent restating his view that *Grutter* should be overruled.

Justice Alito, joined by the Chief Justice and Justice Thomas, wrote a lengthier dissent. He criticized the University's efforts in defense of its plan as "shifting, unpersuasive, and, at times, less than candid."

"Over the past 20 years, UT has frequently modified its admissions policies, and it has generally employed race and ethnicity in the most aggressive manner permitted under controlling precedent. . . .

"Although UT claims that race is but a 'factor of a factor of a factor of a factor,' UT acknowledges that 'race is the only one of [its] holistic factors that appears on the cover of every application,' Tr. of Oral Arg. 54 (Oct. 10, 2012). Because an applicant's race is identified at the front of the admissions file, reviewers are aware of it throughout the evaluation."

Justice Alito's dissent critiqued the university's claims regarding critical mass as being about anything other than sheer numbers. He then turned to a discussion of diversity and discrimination:

"Moreover, if UT is truly seeking to expose its students to a diversity of ideas and perspectives, its policy is poorly tailored to serve that end. UT's own study . . . demonstrated that classroom diversity was more lacking for students classified as Asian-American than for those classified as Hispanic. But the UT plan discriminates *against* Asian-American students. . . .

"Hispanics are better represented than Asian-Americans in UT classrooms. In fact, [the majority and the court of appeals] act almost as if Asian-American students do not exist. Only the District Court acknowledged the impact of UT's policy on Asian-American students. But it brushed aside this impact, concluding — astoundingly — that UT can pick and choose which racial and ethnic groups it would like to favor. According to the District Court, 'nothing in *Grutter* requires a university to give equal preference to every minority group,' and UT is allowed 'to exercise its discretion in determining which minority groups should benefit from the consideration of race.'

"This reasoning, which the majority implicitly accepts by blessing UT's reliance on the classroom study, places the Court on the 'tortuous' path of 'decid[ing] which races to favor.' *Metro Broadcasting*, 497 U.S., at 632 (Kennedy, J., dissenting). And the Court's willingness to allow this 'discrimination against individuals of Asian descent in UT admissions is particularly troubling, in light of the long history of discrimination against Asian Americans, especially in education.' [See, e.g.,] Gong Lum v. Rice, 275 U.S. 78, 81–82 (1927) (holding that a 9-year-old Chinese-American girl could be denied entry to a 'white' school because she was 'a member of the Mongolian or yellow race'). In sum, '[w]hile the Court repeatedly refers to the preferences as favoring 'minorities,' . . . it must be emphasized that the discriminatory policies upheld today operate to exclude' Asian-American students, who 'have not made [UT's] list' of favored groups. *Metro Broadcasting* (Kennedy, J., dissenting).

"Perhaps the majority finds discrimination against Asian-American students benign, since Asian-Americans are '*overrepresented*' at UT. But '[h]istory should teach greater humility.' . . .

"In addition to demonstrating that UT discriminates against Asian-American students, the classroom study also exhibits UT's use of a few crude, overly simplistic racial and ethnic categories. . . .

"For example, students labeled 'Asian American,' seemingly include 'individuals of Chinese, Japanese, Korean, Vietnamese, Cambodian, Hmong, Indian and other backgrounds comprising roughly 60% of the world's population.' It would be ludicrous to suggest that all of these students have similar backgrounds and similar ideas and experiences to share. So why has UT lumped them together and concluded that it is appropriate to discriminate against Asian-American students because they are 'overrepresented' in the UT student body? UT has no good answer. And UT makes no effort to ensure that it has a critical mass of, say, 'Filipino Americans' or 'Cambodian Americans.' As long as there are a sufficient number of 'Asian Americans,' UT is apparently satisfied. . . .

"Finally, it seems clear that the lack of classroom diversity is attributable in good part to factors other than the representation of the favored groups in the UT student population. UT offers an enormous number of classes in a wide range of subjects, and it gives undergraduates a very large measure of freedom to choose their classes. UT also offers courses in subjects that are likely to have special appeal to members of the minority groups given preferential treatment under its challenged plan, and this of course diminishes the number of other courses in which these students can enroll. Having designed an undergraduate program that virtually ensures a lack of classroom diversity, UT is poorly positioned to argue that this very result provides a justification for racial and ethnic discrimination, which the Constitution rarely allows.

"UT's purported interest in intraracial diversity, or 'diversity within diversity,' also falls short. At bottom, this argument relies on the unsupported assumption that there is something deficient or at least radically different about the African-American and Hispanic students admitted through the Top Ten Percent Plan. . . .

"UT complained that the Top Ten Percent Law hinders its efforts to assemble a broadly diverse class because the minorities admitted under that law are drawn largely from certain areas of Texas where there are majority-minority schools. These students, UT argued, tend to come from poor, disadvantaged families, and the University would prefer a system that gives it substantial leeway to seek broad diversity *within* groups of underrepresented minorities. In particular, UT asserted a need for more African-American and Hispanic students from privileged backgrounds. See, *e.g.*, Brief for Respondents in No. 11–345, at 34 (explaining that UT needs race-conscious admissions in order to admit '[t]he African-American or Hispanic child of successful professionals in Dallas'); *ibid.* (claiming that privileged minorities 'have great potential for serving as a 'bridge' in promoting cross-racial understanding, as well as in breaking down racial stereotypes'); *ibid.* (intimating that the underprivileged minority students admitted under the Top Ten Percent Plan '*reinforc[e]*' 'stereotypical assumptions'); Tr. of Oral Arg. 43–45 (Oct. 10, 2012) ('[A]lthough the percentage plan certainly helps with minority admissions, by and large, the minorities who are admitted tend to come from segregated, racially-identifiable schools,' and 'we want minorities from different backgrounds'). Thus, the Top Ten Percent Law is faulted for admitting *the wrong kind of African-American and Hispanic students. . . .*

"Remarkably, UT now contends that petitioner has 'fabricat[ed]' the argument that it is seeking affluent minorities. That claim is impossible to square with UT's prior statements to this Court in the briefing and oral argument in *Fisher I*. Moreover, although UT reframes its argument, it continues to assert that it needs affirmative action to admit privileged minorities. For instance, UT's brief highlights its interest in admitting '[t]he black student with high grades from Andover.' Similarly, at oral argument, UT claimed that its 'interests in the educational benefits of diversity would not be met if all of [the] minority students were . . . coming from depressed socioeconomic backgrounds.'

"Ultimately, UT's intraracial diversity rationale relies on the baseless assumption that there is something wrong with African-American and Hispanic students admitted through the Top Ten Percent Plan, because they are 'from the lower-performing, racially identifiable schools.' . . . UT's assumptions appear to be based on the pernicious stereotype that the African-Americans and Hispanics admitted through the Top Ten Percent Plan only got in because they did not have to compete against very many whites and Asian-Americans. . . . .

"In addition to relying on stereotypes, UT's argument that it needs racial preferences to admit privileged minorities turns the concept of affirmative action on its head. When affirmative action programs were first adopted, it was for the purpose of helping the disadvantaged. Now we are told that a program that tends to admit poor and disadvantaged minority students is inadequate because it does not work to the advantage of those who are more fortunate. This is affirmative action gone wild.

"It is also far from clear that UT's assumptions about the socioeconomic status of minorities admitted through the Top Ten Percent Plan are even remotely accurate. Take, for example, parental education. In 2008, when petitioner applied to UT, approximately 79% of Texans aged 25 years or older had a high school diploma, 17% had a bachelor's degree, and 8% had a graduate or professional degree. In contrast, 96% of African-Americans admitted through the Top Ten Percent Plan had a parent with a high school diploma, 59% had a parent with a bachelor's degree, and 26% had a parent with a graduate or professional degree. Similarly, 83% of Hispanics admitted through the Top Ten Percent Plan had a parent with a high school diploma, 42% had a parent with a bachelor's degree, and 21% had a parent with a graduate or professional degree. As these statistics make plain, the minorities that UT characterizes as 'coming from depressed socioeconomic backgrounds,' generally come from households with education levels exceeding the norm in Texas.

"Or consider income levels. In 2008, the median annual household income in Texas was $49,453. The household income levels for Top Ten Percent African-American and Hispanic admittees were on par: Roughly half of such admittees came from households below the Texas median, and half came from households above the median. And a large portion of these admittees are from households with income levels far exceeding the Texas median. Specifically, 25% of African-Americans and 27% of Hispanics admitted through the Top Ten Percent Plan in 2008 were raised in households with incomes exceeding $80,000. In light of this evidence, UT's actual argument is not that it needs affirmative action to ensure that its minority admittees are representative of the State of Texas. Rather, UT is asserting that it needs affirmative action to ensure that its minority students disproportionally come from families that are wealthier and better educated than the average Texas family. . . .

"[I]is simply not true that Top Ten Percent minority admittees are academically inferior to holistic admittees. In fact, as UT's president explained in 2000, 'top 10 percent high school students make much higher grades in college than non–top 10 percent students,' and '[s]trong academic performance in high school is an even better predictor of success in college than standardized test scores.' Indeed, the statistics in the record reveal that, for each year between 2003 and 2007, African-American in-state freshmen who were admitted under the Top Ten Percent Law earned a higher mean grade point average than those admitted outside of the Top Ten Percent Law. The same is true for Hispanic students. These conclusions correspond to the results of nationwide studies showing that high school grades are a better predictor of success in college than SAT scores. . . .

"It is important to understand what is and what is not at stake in this case. *What is not at stake* is whether UT or any other university may adopt an admissions plan that results in a student body with a broad representation of students from all racial and ethnic groups. UT previously had a race-neutral plan that it claimed had 'effectively compensated for the loss of affirmative action,' and UT could have taken other steps that would have increased the diversity of its admitted students without taking race or ethnic background into account.

"*What is at stake* is whether university administrators may justify systematic racial discrimination simply by asserting that such discrimination is necessary to achieve 'the educational benefits of diversity,' without explaining — much less proving — why the discrimination is needed or how the discriminatory plan is well crafted to serve its objectives. Even though UT has never provided any coherent explanation for its asserted need to discriminate on the basis of race, and even though UT's position relies on a series of unsupported and noxious racial assumptions, the majority concludes that UT has met its heavy burden. This conclusion is remarkable — and remarkably wrong."

Justice Kagan again did not participate.

Does *Fisher II* mark a significant change in the Court's approach to race-conscious affirmative action?

Note: The Special Problem of Facially Neutral but Race-Specific Voting Districts

1. *The problem.* How should standard principles of equal protection law apply to the construction of electoral districts? Gomillion v. Lightfoot, page 556, supra, and succeeding cases establish that when districts are purposely constructed to reduce the voting power of minorities, the plans are unconstitutional. (Indeed, the Court has not even applied strict scrutiny in such cases.) The Voting Rights Act of 1965, 52 U.S.C. §10301 et seq., goes further than the Constitution, to prohibit the use of districting plans that result in the dilution of minority voting strength regardless of the government's motivation in adopting or maintaining such plans.

The question is more complex when a legislature draws district lines in a fashion designed accurately to *reflect*, rather than to reduce, overall minority voting strength. Suppose, for example, that 30 percent of a state's population is African American. If district lines are drawn according to some "traditional" districting criteria (e.g., compactness or contiguity) and without regard to the racial composition of the ensuing districts, the result may produce few, if any, districts in which African Americans are a majority of the electorate. If voting is racially polarized, the result may be that black voters are unable to elect the candidates they prefer in any district. Is it permissible for the state to counteract this effect by deliberately drawing district lines so as to ensure that some percentage of the districts have African-American majorities? On the one hand, state efforts to ensure that groups are represented in proportion to their numbers might be thought desirable and, perhaps, even constitutionally mandatory. Yet on the other hand, deliberately placing individuals within districts based on race might be thought to run afoul of the prohibition on even facially neutral race-specific classifications.

2. Shaw. In Shaw v. Reno, 509 U.S. 630 (1993), plaintiffs challenged the constitutionality of a state reapportionment plan that included one "majority-minority" district with what the Court characterized as a "dramatically irregular" shape. In a five-to-four decision, the Court, per Justice O'Connor, held that the plaintiffs had stated a cognizable claim. A redistricting plan is unconstitutional when "though race-neutral on its face, [it] rationally cannot be understood as anything other than an effort to separate voters into different districts on the basis

of race, and that the separation lacks sufficient justification." This might be the case, for example, when a state "concentrated a dispersed minority population in a single district by disregarding traditional districting principles such as compactness, contiguity, and respect for political subdivisions." As the Court explained:

> [We] believe that reapportionment is one area in which appearances do matter. A reapportionment plan that includes in one district individuals who belong to the same race, but who are otherwise widely separated by geographical and political boundaries, and who may have little in common with one another but the color of their skin, bears an uncomfortable resemblance to political apartheid. It reinforces the perception that members of the same racial group — regardless of their age, education, economic status, or the community in which they live — think alike, share the same political interests, and will prefer the same candidates at the polls. We have rejected such perceptions elsewhere as impermissible racial stereotypes. By perpetuating such notions, a racial gerrymander may exacerbate the very patterns of racial bloc voting the majority-minority districting is sometimes said to counteract.

3. *The problem of injury.* Who is harmed by race-specific districting? In *Brown*, the Court thought that racial segregation generated "a feeling of inferiority as to [the] status [of black children] in the community that may affect their hearts and minds in a way unlikely ever to be undone." In *Loving*, the Court found that the ban on interracial marriages was "designed to maintain White Supremacy." In affirmative action cases, the Court has held that plaintiffs denied the possibility of competing for a benefit or position on equal terms are harmed by that denial. See Northeastern Florida Chapter of Associated General Contractors v. Jacksonville, 508 U.S. 656 (1993). Is it plausible that race-specific districting equalizing statewide representation has any of these effects?

In United States v. Hays, 515 U.S. 737 (1995), the Court held that plaintiffs living within a district subject to a racial gerrymander have standing to contest the districting, but that plaintiffs outside the district lack standing unless they can show that they have personally been subject to a racial classification. Is this distinction coherent? Haven't the voters who were excluded from a particular district because of their race also suffered an injury? See Sinkfield v. Kelley, 531 U.S. 28 (2000) (holding that white voters lacked standing to challenge the majority white district in which they were placed in order to create an adjacent majority-black district). Consider also Justice Stevens's discussion of the standing issue in his dissenting opinion in Shaw v. Hunt, 517 U.S. 899 (1996):

> [The] supposedly insidious messages that [*Shaw*] contends will follow from extremely irregular race-based districting will presumably be received in equal measure by all State residents. For that reason, the claimed violation of a shared right to a color-blind districting process would not seem to implicate the Equal Protection Clause at all precisely because it rests neither on a challenge to the State's decision to distribute burdens and benefits unequally, nor on a claim that the State's formally equal treatment of its citizens in fact stamps persons of one race with a badge of inferiority in a context that results in no race-based unequal treatment.

Does the Court's conception of harm match its restrictive standing rule? Compare Ely, Standing to Challenge Pro-Minority Gerrymanders, 111 Harv. L. Rev. 576, 594 (1997) (arguing that white voters "have standing basically because they've been deprived of a meaningful shot at helping to elect a representative whose race is the same as theirs"), with Issacharoff and Karlan, Standing and Misunderstanding in Voting Rights Law, 111 Harv. L. Rev. 2276 (1998) (arguing that the Court's standing doctrine is completely incoherent because it fails to explain the dividing line between those voters who have standing and those who lack standing and that the plaintiffs in the race-specific districting cases deliberately declined to claim vote dilution or the inability to elect their preferred candidates).

4. *The implementation of the* Shaw *principle.* The *Shaw* Court decided only that plaintiffs had presented a cognizable claim. The opinion left many questions unanswered, including the evidentiary showing necessary to trigger strict scrutiny; what interests might justify taking race into account; what to do about "mixed motive" cases when bizarrely shaped districts result from the intersection of ordinary political considerations and racial criteria; and how the narrow tailoring requirement should apply.

In Miller v. Johnson, 515 U.S. 900 (1995), the Court elaborated upon the question of what a plaintiff would have to show to trigger strict scrutiny. Following the 1990 census, and under substantial pressure from the U.S. Department of Justice, Georgia redrew its congressional districts to create two additional majority-black districts. The Eleventh Congressional District stretched from Atlanta, in the center of the state to Savannah, on the Atlantic coast, linking by narrow, relatively underpopulated corridors a set of majority black neighborhoods.

Justice Kennedy delivered the Court's opinion:

> [Just] as the State may not, absent extraordinary justification, segregate citizens on the basis of race in its public parks, buses, golf courses, beaches, and schools, so did we recognize in *Shaw* that it may not separate its citizens into different voting districts on the basis of race. . . .
>
> Our observation in *Shaw* of the consequences of racial stereotyping was not meant to suggest that a district must be bizarre on its face before there is a constitutional violation. [Shape] is relevant not because bizarreness is a necessary element of the constitutional wrong or a threshold requirement of proof, but because it may be persuasive circumstantial evidence that race for its own sake, and not other districting principles, was the legislature's dominant and controlling rationale in drawing its district lines. The logical implication, as courts applying *Shaw* have recognized, is that parties may rely on evidence other than bizarreness to establish race-based districting. . . .
>
> The plaintiff's burden is to show, either through circumstantial evidence of a district's shape and demographics or more direct evidence going to legislative purpose, that race was the predominant factor motivating the legislature's decision to place a significant number of voters within or without a particular district. To make this showing, a plaintiff must prove that the legislature subordinated traditional race-neutral districting principles, including but not limited to compactness, contiguity, respect for political subdivisions or communities defined by actual shared interests, to racial considerations. . . .
>
> In our view, the District Court applied the correct analysis, and its finding that race was the predominant factor motivating the drawing of the Eleventh District was not clearly erroneous.

Note the way in which *Miller* shifted the nature of the inquiry into whether a facially neutral law constitutes a racial classification. See also Bush v. Vera, 517 U.S. 952 (1996) (plurality opinion) (explaining that "[strict] scrutiny does not apply merely because redistricting is performed with consciousness of race. Nor does it apply to all cases of intentional creation of majority-minority districts. [For] strict scrutiny to apply, the plaintiffs must prove that other, legitimate districting principles were 'subordinated' to race. By that, we mean that race must be 'the predominant factor motivating the legislature's [redistricting] decision.'") Contrast *Miller* and *Vera* with Village of Arlington Heights v. Metropolitan Housing Development Corp., 429 U.S. 252, 265–266 (1977):

> Rarely can it be said that a legislature . . . made a decision motivated solely by a single concern, or even that a particular purpose was the "dominant" or "primary" one. In fact, it is because legislators and administrators are properly concerned with balancing numerous competing considerations that courts refrain from reviewing the merits of their decisions, absent a showing of arbitrariness or irrationality. But racial discrimination is not just another competing consideration. When there is a proof that a discriminatory purpose has been *a* motivating factor in the decision, this judicial deference is no longer justified.

Under the *Arlington Heights* test, "[proof] that the decision by the Village was motivated in part by a racially discriminatory purpose . . . would . . . have shifted to the [defendant] the burden of establishing that the same decision would have resulted even had the impermissible purpose not been considered. If this were established, the complaining party in a case of this kind no longer fairly could attribute the injury complained of to improper consideration of a discriminatory purpose."

Why does the Court treat voting cases differently? Is it because race serves a different function in the political process, correlating with political preferences rather than describing individuals? Is it because redistricting is inherently a process of treating people as members of groups? Consider Justice Ginsburg's point in dissent:

> Along with attention to size, shape, and political subdivisions, the Court recognizes as an appropriate districting principle, "respect for . . . communities defined by actual shared interests." The Court finds no community here, however, because a report in the record showed "fractured political, social, and economic interests within the Eleventh District's black population."
>
> But ethnicity itself can tie people together, as volumes of social science literature have documented — even people with divergent economic interests. . . .
>
> [To] accommodate the reality of ethnic bonds, legislatures have long drawn voting districts along ethnic lines. Our Nation's cities are full of districts identified by their ethnic character — Chinese, Irish, Italian, Jewish, Polish, Russian, for example. The creation of ethnic districts reflecting felt identity is not ordinarily viewed as offensive or demeaning to those included in the delineation.
>
> [In] adopting districting plans, [States] do not treat people as individuals. Apportionment schemes, by their very nature, assemble people in groups. States do not assign voters to districts based on merit or achievement, standards States might use in hiring employees or engaging contractors. . . .
>
> [That] ethnicity defines some of these groups is a political reality. Until now, no constitutional infirmity has been seen in districting Irish or Italian voters together, for example, so long as the delineation does not abandon familiar apportionment practices. If Chinese-Americans and Russian-Americans may seek and secure group recognition in the delineation of voting districts, then African-Americans should not be dissimilarly treated. Otherwise, in the name of equal protection, we would shut out "the very minority group whose history in the United States gave birth to the Equal Protection Clause." . . .

In Bethune-Hill v. Virginia State Bd. of Elections, 137 S. Ct. 788 (2017), the Court examined Virginia state legislative districts drawn after the 2010 census. The general assembly drew 12 districts with black voting-age populations of at least 55 percent. A three-judge district court rejected the plaintiffs' challenge to the districts, holding that strict scrutiny was triggered only if plaintiffs could show an actual conflict between traditional redistricting criteria and race. The Supreme Court, in an opinion by Justice Kennedy, disagreed. The Court held that in order to show that race predominated, a plaintiff could use either "circumstantial evidence of a district's shape and demographics or more direct evidence going to legislative purpose." Thus, race can predominate even if a plan respects traditional districting principles.

Easley v. Cromartie, 532 U.S. 234 (2001), revisited the North Carolina redistricting that first appeared before the Court in *Shaw*. This case involved a challenge to a redrawn version of North Carolina's Twelfth Congressional District, the district challenged originally in *Shaw* and struck down as unjustifiably race conscious in Shaw v. Hunt, 517 U.S. 899 (1996). This time around, the Court held that the district court had erred in finding that race, rather than politics, drove the legislature's districting decision.

Justice Breyer's opinion for the Court sharpened the distinction between race "simply hav[ing] been '*a* motivation for the drawing of a majority minority district'" — which would be permissible — and race being the "predominant factor," the showing that would trigger strict scrutiny. Justice Breyer cautioned against concluding that race was the predominant factor in situations "where the State has articulated a legitimate political explanation for its districting decision, and the voting population is one in which race and political affiliation are highly correlated."

Justice Breyer's opinion performed a painstakingly thorough review of the record, going beyond the district court's findings to examine the entire testimony of the expert witness on whom the trial court had relied. It also discounted the direct evidence relied on by the district court. One of the leaders of the redistricting process, State Senator Roy Cooper, testified before the legislative committee considering the plan that "overall it provides for a fair, geographic, racial and partisan balance throughout the State of North Carolina. . . ." Justice Breyer

> agree[d] that one can read the statement about "racial . . . balance" as the District Court read it — to refer to the current congressional delegation's racial balance. But even as so read, the phrase shows that the legislature considered race, along with other partisan and geographic considerations; and as so read it says little or nothing about whether race played a predominant role comparatively speaking. . . .
>
> We can put the matter more generally as follows: In a case such as this one where majority-minority districts (or the approximate equivalent) are at issue and where racial identification correlates highly with political affiliation, the party attacking the legislatively drawn boundaries must show at the least that the legislature could have achieved its legitimate political objectives in alternative ways that are comparably consistent with traditional districting principles. That party must also show that those districting alternatives would have brought about significantly greater racial balance.

Justice Thomas, joined by Chief Justice Rehnquist and Justices Scalia and Kennedy, dissented, stating that "[i]n light of the direct evidence of racial motive and the inferences that may be drawn from the circumstantial evidence, I am satisfied that the District Court's finding was permissible, even if not compelled by the record." Given the standard of review for district court findings of fact, he would have affirmed.

Two redistricting cycles later, the Court revisited the North Carolina congressional districts yet again. Prior to the 2010 redistricting, House Districts 1 and 12 had both consistently elected candidates preferred by the majority of African American voters in each district although neither district had a majority black voting-age population. Nevertheless, when the state legislature drew the new districts, it significantly increased the percentage of black citizens in each of the districts, making the districts majority-black. A three-judge district court held both districts unconstitutional, finding that race was the state's predominant motive for drawing the new lines and rejecting the state's claim that the increase in black population was required by the Voting Rights Act. The Supreme Court affirmed in Cooper v. Harris, 137 S. Ct. 1455 (2017). Justice Kagan wrote the Court's opinion. The Court agreed that race was the predominant factor explaining the configuration of House District 1, and it rejected the state's argument that the Voting Rights Act required those lines, especially because minority voters had been electing their preferred candidates for nearly twenty years from non-majority-black districts. With respect to House District 12, the Court rejected the state's argument that the mapmakers had moved voters in and out of the district as part of a "strictly" political gerrymander, without regard to race. And it rejected the state's argument that when race and politics are competing explanations for how a district was drawn, a court cannot conclude that race predominated unless the plaintiffs can show a different map that meets the state's political goals without relying so much on race.

Justice Thomas provided the fifth vote for the majority. He wrote a concurrence explaining that he thought "North Carolina's concession that it created [House District 1] as a majority-black district is by itself sufficient to trigger strict scrutiny." He emphasized that his position reflected deference to the district court's factual findings.

Justice Alito, joined by Chief Justice Roberts and Justice Kennedy, dissented. They thought that political considerations, rather than racial ones, best explained how North Carolina had drawn the challenged districts.

5. *Compelling state interests. Once strict scrutiny is triggered, what sort of government interest is sufficiently weighty to justify race-specific districting?*

a. *Compliance with the Voting Rights Act.* Recall that the Voting Rights Act, unlike the Constitution, does more than merely prohibit districting that has the purpose of reducing minority representation. To some extent, it also requires jurisdictions to avoid districting that has the "result" of understating such representation. Of course, to the extent that jurisdictions attempt to avoid this result, they run the risk of violating the *Miller* and *Shaw* restrictions on race-specific districting. This dilemma might be avoided if the Court treated compliance with the act as a compelling state interest sufficient to justify race-specific districting.

In Bush v. Vera, supra, Justice O'Connor, writing for a plurality of the Court, assumed, without deciding, that compliance with the act was such an interest. The Court found, however, that the act did not require "a State to create, on predominantly racial lines, a district that is not 'reasonably compact.'" Since Texas had created such a district, the Court did not have to reach the question whether the need to obey the act would provide a compelling government interest. A majority of the Court reached a similar conclusion in Shaw v. Hunt, supra. However, in an unusual concurrence to her own plurality opinion in *Bush*, Justice O'Connor stated her view that compliance with the "results" test mandated by the act was a compelling interest. See also League of United Latin American Citizens v. Perry, 548 U.S. 399 (2006), in which six justices, in two separate opinions, agreed that compliance with the Voting Rights Act can constitute a compelling interest that justifies race-conscious line drawing.

b. *Remedying the effects of prior discrimination.* In Bush v. Vera, Justice O'Connor's plurality opinion addressed the argument that remedying the effects of racially polarized voting, produced by prior discrimination, was a compelling government interest. Drawing from the Court's affirmative action jurisprudence, she concluded that the state has a compelling interest in remedying prior discrimination only when there is "specific, identified discrimination" and when the state has a "strong basis in evidence" to conclude that the remedial action is necessary. The Court returned to this issue in Shaw v. Hunt. Writing for the majority, Chief Justice Rehnquist acknowledged that "[a] State's interest in remedying the effects of past or present racial discrimination may in the proper case justify a government's use of racial distinctions." However, on the facts of this case, "the District Court found that an interest in ameliorating past discrimination did not actually precipitate the use of race in the redistricting plan." Compare Justice Stevens's dissenting opinion:

> [Some] legislators felt that the sorry history of race relations in North Carolina [was] sufficient reason for making it easier for more black leaders to participate in the legislative [process]. Even if that history does not provide the kind of precise guidance that will justify certain specific affirmative action programs in particular industries, it surely provides an adequate basis for a decision to facilitate the election of representatives of the previously disadvantaged minority.

In light of the history of redistricting litigation, consider Karlan, Easing the Spring: Strict Scrutiny and Affirmative Action After the Redistricting Cases, 43 Wm. & Mary L. Rev. 1569, 1586, 1602–1603 (2002):

> [The] redistricting cases suggest there is definitely more than one kind of strict scrutiny. Faced with the prospect of applying a form of strict scrutiny that threatened to resegregate state legislatures and congressional delegations, the Supreme Court has been unwilling to apply strict scrutiny strictly. It has constricted the domain in which strict scrutiny comes into play, permitting race to be taken into account when it is one factor among many and its inclusion produces districts that do not deviate too obviously from the sorts of districts created for other groups. It has also broadened the interests that can justify race-conscious redistricting, by holding that compliance with the Voting Rights Act's results tests can serve as a compelling state interest. The understanding of political equality embodied in the Act goes beyond what the Constitution itself demands. It requires states to arrange their electoral institutions to minimize the lingering effects of prior unconstitutional discrimination not otherwise chargeable to them, as well as to mitigate the impact of racially polarized voting that involves otherwise constitutionally protected private choice. In short, the theory of strict scrutiny yielded to the need for an electoral system that is equally open to members of minority groups.

Note: The "Special" Case of Indigenous People

Are the many statutes providing special treatment for American Indians and other native peoples consistent with the strict scrutiny supposedly accorded race-specific statutes? In his dissenting opinion in Rice v. Cayetano, 528 U.S. 495 (2000), Justice Stevens summarized the current state of the law:

> Throughout our Nation's history, this Court has recognized both the plenary power of Congress over the affairs of native Americans and the fiduciary character of the special federal relationship with descendants of those once sovereign peoples. . . . As our cases have consistently recognized, Congress' plenary power over these peoples has been exercised time and again to implement a federal duty to provide native peoples with special "care and protection." [Today], the Federal Bureau of Indian Affairs [administers] countless modern programs responding to [pragmatic] concerns, including health, education, housing, and impoverishment. Federal regulation in this area is not limited to the strictly practical but has encompassed as well the protection of cultural values. . . .
>
> [This] Court has taken account of the "numerous occasions" on which "legislation that singles out Indians for particular and special treatment" has been upheld, and has concluded that as "long as the special treatment can be tied rationally to fulfillment of Congress' unique obligations towards the Indians, such legislative judgments will not be disturbed."

Can this body of law be reconciled with the Court's treatment of race-based affirmative action in other contexts? What is it about sovereignty — as distinct from individual liberty — that justifies placing unique obligations on Congress with respect to Native Americans but not with respect to African Americans?

In Rice v. Cayetano itself, the Court held that Hawaii could not limit voting for the trustees who administer the Office of Hawaiian Affairs, which manages huge plots of land held in trust for the descendants of the Polynesians who occupied the Hawaiian Islands before the 1778 arrival of Captain Cook, to only the descendants of those persons. Writing for the Court, Justice Kennedy rejected the analogy to statutes dealing specially with American Indians:

> The decisions of this Court, interpreting the effect of treaties and congressional enactments on the subject, have held that various tribes retained some elements of quasi-sovereign authority, even after cession of their lands to the United States. In reliance on that theory the Court has sustained a federal provision giving employment preferences to persons of tribal ancestry. [Morton v. Mancari, 417 U.S. 535 (1974).] . . .
>
> It does not follow from *Mancari*, however, that Congress may authorize a State to establish a voting scheme that limits the electorate for its public officials to a class of tribal Indians, to the exclusion of all non-Indian citizens.
>
> [If] a non-Indian lacks the right to vote in tribal elections, it is for the reason that such elections are the internal affair of a quasi-sovereign. The OHA elections, by contrast, are the affair of the State of Hawaii. . . .
>
> To extend *Mancari* to this context would be to permit a State, by racial classification, to fence out whole classes of its citizens from decisionmaking in critical state affairs.

Justice Stevens, joined by Justice Ginsburg, dissented:

> The descendants of the native Hawaiians share with the descendants of the Native Americans on the mainland or in the Aleutian islands not only a history of subjugation at the hands of colonial forces, but also a purposefully created and specialized "guardian-ward" relationship with the Government of the United States. It follows that legislation targeting the native Hawaiians must be evaluated

according to the same understanding of equal protection that this Court has long applied to the Indians on the continental United States: that "special treatment . . . be tied rationally to the fulfillment of Congress' unique obligation" toward the native peoples. . . .

[The] Federal Government [has] not been limited in its special dealings with the native peoples to laws affecting tribes or tribal Indians alone. In light of this precedent, it is a painful irony indeed to conclude that native Hawaiians are not entitled to special benefits designed to restore a measure of native self-governance because they currently lack any vestigial native government — a possibility of which history and the actions of this Nation have deprived them.

Consider the extent to which the last paragraph of Justice Stevens's opinion might apply to African Americans as well. See Blacksher, Majority Black Districts, *Kiryas Joel*, and Other Challenges to American Nationalism, 26 Cumb. L. Rev. 407 (1996) (arguing that African Americans, like Native Americans, should be entitled to exercise a form of political sovereignty). See also Katz, Race and the Right to Vote after Rice v. Cayetano, 99 Mich. L. Rev. 491, 503 (2000).

For an examination of the equal protection problems posed by defining membership in Indian tribes based upon racial criteria, see Gould, Mixing Bodies and Beliefs: The Predicament of Tribes, 101 Colum. L. Rev. 702 (2001).

Note: A Comparative Perspective

Should the Constitution be amended to explicitly define the allowable scope of affirmative action (if any)? Does the inclusion of a specific provision dealing with affirmative action mean that the general equality provision would otherwise bar this practice?

Like the United States, India is a multicultural democracy with a history of class and religious divisions. Before independence in 1948, the British frequently distributed benefits based on membership in ethnic or communal groups. The original India Constitution sharply restricted these practices. The drafters rejected proposals to reserve legislative seats, cabinet posts, and public positions for minorities and included a broad provision prohibiting the state from discriminating "against any citizen on grounds only of religion, race, caste, sex, place of birth, or any of them." However, another, nonjusticiable provision provides that "[the] State shall promote with special care the educational and economic interests of the weaker sections of the people, and, in particular, of the Scheduled Castes and the Scheduled Tribes, and shall protect them from social injustice and all forms of exploitation."

In 1951, the India Supreme Court invalidated a state program that allocated seats in medical and engineering colleges on the basis of caste and religion. See State of Madras v. Champakam Dorairajan, A.I.R. 1951 S.C. 226, 1951 S.C.J. 313. Within two months of the decision, it had been reversed by a series of constitutional amendments. Among the amendments adopted was one providing that nothing in the constitution "shall prevent the State from making any special provision for the advancement of any socially and educationally backward classes of citizens or for the Scheduled Castes and Scheduled Tribes."

There has been considerable controversy about how to reconcile this and other amendments apparently authorizing affirmative action with the broader guarantee of equality. Some cases have treated the two sets of provisions as in conflict with each other and have therefore read the authorization for affirmative action narrowly. See, e.g., State of Andhra Pradesh v. Sagar, A.I.R. 1968 S.C. 1379, 1382 (broad reading would effectively eviscerate guarantee of equality). However, in a path-breaking decision in 1975, the India Supreme Court held that in some contexts affirmative action was *required* by the equality requirement rather than being in tension with it. See State of Kerala v. N. M. Thomas, A.I.R. 1976 S.C. 490. This decision has granted the government greater discretion as to its choice of means in pursuing compensatory measures, and today there are widespread "reservations" of positions in employment and education based on caste and minority status. For an account, see M. Galanter, Competing Equalities 363–395 (1985).

These reservations have produced considerable resentment and even violence. For conflicting accounts of their success in reducing inequality, compare M. Galanter, Law and Society in Modern India 185–197 (1989) (a costly success), with T. Sowell, Preferential Policies 90–103 (1990) (a failure). Galanter argues that compensatory discrimination has produced substantial redistribution, contributed to the growth of a middle class, and diminished stereotypes concerning ignorance and incompetence among the lower castes. Sowell argues that reserved seats in universities are often unused because they require supplemental assistance to take advantage of them, that they have led to a lowering of standards, that the most prosperous members of the benefited groups receive a disproportionate share of the benefits, and that resentment against preferential policies has led to a violent backlash.

Consider more generally the extent to which the Indian experience has relevance to the United States in light of the arguably unique history of race relations in this country.

4. The Synthesis of Brown and Affirmative Action

Parents Involved in Community Schools v. Seattle School District No. 1

551 U.S. 701 (2007)

CHIEF JUSTICE ROBERTS announced the judgment of the Court, and delivered the opinion of the Court with respect to Parts I, II, III-A, and III-C, and an opinion with respect to Parts III-B and IV, in which JUSTICES SCALIA, THOMAS, and ALITO join.

The school districts in these cases [from Seattle, Washington, and Jefferson County, Kentucky] voluntarily adopted student assignment plans that rely upon race to determine which public schools certain children may attend. . . . Parents of students denied assignment to particular schools under these plans solely because of their race brought suit, contending that allocating children to different public schools on the basis of race violated the Fourteenth Amendment guarantee of equal protection. The Courts of Appeals below upheld the plans. We granted certiorari, and now reverse.

I . . .

A

Seattle School District No. 1 operates 10 regular public high schools. In 1998, it adopted the plan at issue in this case for assigning students to these schools. The plan allows incoming ninth graders to choose from among any of the district's high schools, ranking however many schools they wish in order of preference.

Some schools are more popular than others. If too many students list the same school as their first choice, the district employs a series of "tiebreakers" to determine who will fill the open slots at the oversubscribed school. The first tiebreaker selects for admission students who have a sibling currently enrolled in the chosen school. The next tiebreaker depends upon the racial composition of the particular school and the race of the individual student. In the district's public schools approximately 41 percent of enrolled students are white; the remaining 59 percent, comprising all other racial groups, are classified by Seattle for assignment purposes as nonwhite. If an oversubscribed school is not within 10 percentage points of the district's overall white/nonwhite racial balance, it is what the district calls "integration positive," and the district employs a tiebreaker that selects for assignment students whose race "will serve to bring the school into balance." . . .

Seattle has never operated segregated schools — legally separate schools for students of different races — nor has it ever been subject to court-ordered desegregation. It nonetheless employs the racial tiebreaker in an attempt to address the effects of racially identifiable housing patterns on school assignments. . . .

B

Jefferson County Public Schools operates the public school system in metropolitan Louisville, Kentucky. In 1973 a federal court found that Jefferson County had maintained a segregated school system, and in 1975 the District Court entered a desegregation decree. Jefferson County operated under this decree until 2000, when the District Court dissolved the decree after finding that the district had achieved unitary status by eliminating "to the greatest extent practicable" the vestiges of its prior policy of segregation.

In 2001, after the decree had been dissolved, Jefferson County adopted the voluntary student assignment plan at issue in this case. Approximately 34 percent of the district's 97,000 students are black; most of the remaining 66 percent are white. The plan requires all nonmagnet schools to maintain a minimum black enrollment of 15 percent, and a maximum black enrollment of 50 percent.

At the elementary school level, based on his or her address, each student is designated a "resides" school to which students within a specific geographic area are assigned; elementary resides schools are "grouped into clusters in order to facilitate integration." The district assigns students to nonmagnet schools in one of two ways: Parents of kindergartners, first-graders, and students new to the district may submit an application indicating a first and second choice among the schools within their cluster; students who do not submit such an application are assigned within the cluster by the district. . . . If a school has reached the "extremes of the racial guidelines," a student whose race would contribute to the school's racial imbalance will not be assigned there. . . .

III

A

It is well established that when the government distributes burdens or benefits on the basis of individual racial classifications, that action is reviewed under strict scrutiny. Johnson v. California, 543 U.S. 499, 505–506 (2005); Grutter v. Bollinger, 539 U.S. 306, 326 (2003). . . . In order to satisfy this searching standard of review, the school districts must demonstrate that the use of individual racial classifications in the assignment plans here under review is "narrowly tailored" to achieve a "compelling" government interest.

Without attempting in these cases to set forth all the interests a school district might assert, it suffices to note that our prior cases, in evaluating the use of racial classifications in the school context, have recognized two interests that qualify as compelling. The first is the compelling interest of remedying the effects of past intentional discrimination. See Freeman v. Pitts, 503 U.S. 467, 494 (1992). Yet the Seattle public schools have not shown that they were ever segregated by law, and were not subject to court-ordered desegregation decrees. The Jefferson County public schools were previously segregated by law and were subject to a desegregation decree entered in 1975. In 2000, the District Court that entered that decree dissolved it, finding that Jefferson County had "eliminated the vestiges associated with the former policy of segregation and its pernicious effects," and thus had achieved "unitary" status. Jefferson County accordingly does not rely upon an interest in remedying the effects of past intentional discrimination in defending its present use of race in assigning students.

Nor could it. We have emphasized that the harm being remedied by mandatory desegregation plans is the harm that is traceable to segregation, and that "the Constitution is not violated by racial imbalance in the schools, without more." Milliken v. Bradley, 433 U.S. 267, 280, n.14 (1977). Once Jefferson County achieved unitary status, it had remedied the constitutional wrong that allowed race-based assignments. Any continued use of race must be justified on some other basis.

The second government interest we have recognized as compelling for purposes of strict scrutiny is the interest in diversity in higher education upheld in Grutter. . . .

The entire gist of the analysis in Grutter was that the admissions program at issue there focused on each applicant as an individual, and not simply as a member of a particular racial group. The classification of applicants by race upheld in Grutter was only as part of a "highly individualized, holistic review." . . .

In upholding the admissions plan in Grutter, . . . this Court relied upon considerations unique to institutions of higher education, noting that in light of "the expansive freedoms of speech and thought associated with the university environment, universities occupy a special niche in our constitutional tradition." . . . The present cases are not governed by Grutter.

B

Perhaps recognizing that reliance on Grutter cannot sustain their plans, both school districts assert additional interests, distinct from the interest upheld in Grutter, to justify their race-based assignments. In briefing and argument before this Court, Seattle contends that its use of race helps to reduce racial concentration in schools and to ensure that racially concentrated housing patterns do not prevent nonwhite students from having access to the most desirable schools. Jefferson County has articulated a similar goal, phrasing its interest in terms of educating its students "in a racially integrated environment." Each school district argues that educational and broader socialization benefits flow from a racially diverse learning environment, and each contends that because the diversity they seek is racial diversity — not the broader diversity at issue in *Grutter* — it makes sense to promote that interest directly by relying on race alone.

The parties and their *amici* dispute whether racial diversity in schools in fact has a marked impact on test scores and other objective yardsticks or achieves intangible socialization benefits. The debate is not one we need to resolve, however, because it is clear that the racial classifications employed by the districts are not narrowly tailored to the goal of achieving the educational and social benefits asserted to flow from racial diversity. In design and operation, the plans are directed only to racial balance, pure and simple, an objective this Court has repeatedly condemned as illegitimate. . . .

Accepting racial balancing as a compelling state interest would justify the imposition of racial proportionality throughout American society, contrary to our repeated recognition that "at the heart of the Constitution's guarantee of equal protection lies the simple command that the Government must treat citizens as individuals, not as simply components of a racial, religious, sexual or national class." . . . .

c

The districts assert, as they must, that the way in which they have employed individual racial classifications is necessary to achieve their stated ends. The minimal effect these classifications have on student assignments, however, suggests that other means would be effective. Seattle's racial tiebreaker results, in the end, only in shifting a small number of students between schools. Approximately 307 student assignments were affected by the racial tiebreaker in 2000–2001. . . .

Similarly, Jefferson County's use of racial classifications has only a minimal effect on the assignment of students. Elementary school students are assigned to their first- or second-choice school 95 percent of the time. . . . Jefferson County estimates that the racial guidelines account for only 3 percent of assignments. . . .

While we do not suggest that *greater* use of race would be preferable, the minimal impact of the districts' racial classifications on school enrollment casts doubt on the necessity of using racial classifications. . . .

IV

Justice Breyer's dissent takes a different approach to these cases. . . .

Justice Breyer speaks of bringing "the races" together (putting aside the purely black-and-white nature of the plans), as the justification for excluding individuals on the basis of their race. Again, this approach to racial classifications is fundamentally at odds with our precedent, which makes clear that the Equal Protection Clause "protects *persons*, not *groups*." This fundamental principle goes back, in this context, to *Brown* itself. See Brown v. Board of Education, 349 U.S. 294, 300 (1955) (*Brown II*) ("At stake is the *personal* interest of the plaintiffs in admission to public schools . . . on a nondiscriminatory basis" (emphasis added)). For the dissent, in contrast, "'individualized scrutiny' is simply beside the point." . . .

Justice Breyer's dissent ends on an unjustified note of alarm. . . .

[It] suggests that other means for achieving greater racial diversity in schools are necessarily unconstitutional if the racial classifications at issue in these cases cannot survive strict scrutiny. These other means — e.g., where to construct new schools, how to allocate resources among schools, and which academic offerings to provide to attract students to certain schools — implicate different considerations than the explicit racial classifications at issue in these cases, and we express no opinion on their validity — not even in dicta. Rather, we employ the familiar and well-established analytic approach of strict scrutiny to evaluate the plans at issue today, an approach that in no way warrants the dissent's cataclysmic concerns. Under that approach, the school districts have not carried their burden of showing that the ends they seek justify the particular extreme means they have chosen — classifying individual students on the basis of their race and discriminating among them on that basis. . . .

If the need for the racial classifications embraced by the school districts is unclear, even on the districts' own terms, the costs are undeniable. "Distinctions between citizens solely because of their ancestry are by their very nature odious to a free people whose institutions are founded upon the doctrine of equality." . . .

All this is true enough in the contexts in which these statements [have repeatedly been] made [by this Court — in] government contracting, voting districts, allocation of broadcast licenses, and electing state officers — but when it comes to using race to assign children to schools, history will be heard. In Brown v. Board of Education, 347 U.S. 483 (1954) (*Brown I*), we held that segregation deprived black children of equal educational opportunities regardless of whether school facilities and other tangible factors were equal, because government classification and separation on grounds of race themselves denoted inferiority. It was not the inequality of the facilities but the fact of legally separating children on the basis of race on which the Court relied to find a constitutional violation in 1954. The next Term, we accordingly stated that "full compliance" with *Brown I* required school districts "to achieve a system of determining admission to the public schools *on a nonracial basis.*" *Brown II,* 349 U.S., at 300–301 (emphasis added).

The parties and their *amici* debate which side is more faithful to the heritage of *Brown,* but the position of the plaintiffs in *Brown* was spelled out in their brief and could not have been clearer: "The Fourteenth Amendment prevents states from according differential treatment to American children on the basis of their color or race." Brief for Appellants in Nos. 1, 2, and 4 and for Respondents in No. 10 on Reargument in *Brown I,* O. T. 1953, p. 15 (Summary of Argument). What do the racial classifications at issue here do, if not accord differential treatment on the basis of race? As counsel who appeared before this Court for the plaintiffs in *Brown* put it: "We have one fundamental contention which we will seek to develop in the course of this argument, and that contention is that no State has any authority under the equal-protection clause of the Fourteenth Amendment to use race as a factor in affording educational opportunities among its citizens." Tr. of Oral Arg. in *Brown I,* p. 7 (Robert L. Carter, Dec. 9, 1952). There is no ambiguity in that statement. And it was that position that prevailed in this Court. . . .

JUSTICE THOMAS, concurring.

I

A . . .

Racial imbalance is not segregation.[2] Although presently observed racial imbalance might result from past *de jure* segregation, racial imbalance can also result from any number of innocent private decisions, including voluntary housing choices.

Although there is arguably a danger of racial imbalance in schools in Seattle and Louisville, there is no danger of resegregation. No one contends that Seattle has established or that Louisville has reestablished a dual school system that separates students on the basis of race. . . .

[margin note: no danger of resegregation]

B . . .

2

This Court has carved out a narrow exception to [the] general rule [forbidding government use of race] for cases in which a school district has a "history of maintaining two sets of schools in a single school system deliberately operated to carry out a governmental policy to separate pupils in schools solely on the basis of race." In such cases, race-based remedial measures are sometimes required. . . . [6]

Neither of the programs before us today is compelled as a remedial measure, and no one makes such a claim. . . .

II

Lacking a cognizable interest in remediation, neither of these plans can survive strict scrutiny because neither plan serves a genuinely compelling state interest. . . .

B . . .

2

[The] dissent argues that the interest in integration has an educational element. The dissent asserts that racially balanced schools improve educational outcomes for black children. In support, the dissent unquestioningly cites certain social science research to support propositions that are hotly disputed among social

[margin note: dissent critique]

2. The dissent refers repeatedly and reverently to "integration." However, outside of the context of remediation for past *de jure* segregation, "integration" is simply racial balancing. Therefore, the school districts' attempts to further "integrate" are properly thought of as little more than attempts to achieve a particular racial balance.

6. As I have explained elsewhere, the remedies this Court authorized lower courts to compel in early desegregation cases like *Green* and *Swann* were exceptional. Sustained resistance to *Brown* prompted the Court to authorize extraordinary race-conscious remedial measures (like compelled racial mixing) to turn the Constitution's dictate to desegregate into reality. Even if these measures were appropriate as remedies in the face of widespread resistance to *Brown*'s mandate, they are not forever insulated from constitutional scrutiny. . . .

scientists. In reality, it is far from apparent that coerced racial mixing has any educational benefits, much less that integration is necessary to black achievement.

Scholars have differing opinions as to whether educational benefits arise from racial balancing. Some have concluded that black students receive genuine educational benefits. . . . Others have been more circumspect. . . . And some have concluded that there are no demonstrable educational benefits. . . .

Add to the inconclusive social science the fact of black achievement in "racially isolated" environments. See T. Sowell, Education: Assumptions Versus History 7–38 (1986). Before *Brown*, the most prominent example of an exemplary black school was Dunbar High School. Id., at 29 ("In the period 1918–1923, Dunbar graduates earned fifteen degrees from Ivy League colleges, and ten degrees from Amherst, Williams, and Wesleyan"). Dunbar is by no means an isolated example. See id., at 10–32 (discussing other successful black schools). . . . Even after *Brown*, some schools with predominantly black enrollments have achieved outstanding educational results. . . .

The Seattle school board itself must believe that racial mixing is not necessary to black achievement. Seattle operates a K-8 "African-American Academy," which has a "nonwhite" enrollment of 99%. That school was founded in 1990 as part of the school board's effort to "increase academic achievement." This racially imbalanced environment has reportedly produced test scores "higher across all grade levels in reading, writing and math." Contrary to what the dissent would have predicted, the children in Seattle's African American Academy have shown gains when placed in a "highly segregated" environment.

Given this tenuous relationship between forced racial mixing and improved educational results for black children, the dissent cannot plausibly maintain that an educational element supports the integration interest, let alone makes it compelling. . . .

Perhaps recognizing as much, the dissent argues that the social science evidence is "strong enough to permit a democratically elected school board reasonably to determine that this interest is a compelling one." This assertion is inexplicable. It is not up to the school boards — the very government entities whose race-based practices we must strictly scrutinize — to determine what interests qualify as compelling under the Fourteenth Amendment to the United States Constitution. Rather, this Court must assess independently the nature of the interest asserted and the evidence to support it in order to determine whether it qualifies as compelling under our precedents. . . . To adopt the dissent's deferential approach would be to abdicate our constitutional responsibilities. . . .

III

Most of the dissent's criticisms of today's result can be traced to its rejection of the color-blind Constitution. The dissent attempts to marginalize the notion of a color-blind Constitution by consigning it to me and Members of today's plurality. But I am quite comfortable in the company I keep. My view of the Constitution is Justice Harlan's view in *Plessy*: "Our Constitution is colorblind, and neither knows nor tolerates classes among citizens." Plessy v. Ferguson, 163 U.S. 537, 559 (1896) (dissenting opinion). And my view was the rallying cry for the lawyers who litigated *Brown*. . . .

The dissent appears to pin its interpretation of the Equal Protection Clause to current societal practice and expectations, deference to local officials, likely practical consequences, and reliance on previous statements from this and other courts. Such a view was ascendant in this Court's jurisprudence for several decades. It first appeared in *Plessy*, where the Court asked whether a state law providing for segregated railway cars was "a reasonable regulation." The Court deferred to local authorities in making its determination, noting that in inquiring into reasonableness "there must necessarily be a large discretion on the part of the legislature." . . .

The segregationists in *Brown* embraced the arguments the Court endorsed in *Plessy*. Though *Brown* decisively rejected those arguments, today's dissent replicates them to a distressing extent. Thus, the dissent argues that "each plan embodies the results of local experience and community consultation." Similarly, the segregationists made repeated appeals to societal practice and expectation. The dissent argues that "weight [must be given] to a local school board's knowledge, expertise, and concerns," and with equal vigor, the segregationists argued for deference to local authorities. The dissent argues that today's decision "threatens to substitute for present calm a disruptive round of race-related litigation," and claims that today's decision "risks serious harm to the law and for the Nation." The segregationists also relied upon the likely practical consequences of ending the state-imposed system of racial separation. . . .

The similarities between the dissent's arguments and the segregationists' arguments do not stop there. Like the dissent, the segregationists repeatedly cautioned the Court to consider practicalities and not to embrace too theoretical a view of the Fourteenth Amendment. And just as the dissent argues that the need for these programs will lessen over time, the segregationists claimed that reliance on segregation was lessening and might eventually end.

What was wrong in 1954 cannot be right today. . . .

Justice Kennedy, concurring in part and concurring in the judgment. . . .

II

Our Nation from the inception has sought to preserve and expand the promise of liberty and equality on which it was founded. Today we enjoy a society that is remarkable in its openness and opportunity. Yet our tradition is to go beyond present achievements, however significant, and to recognize and confront the flaws and injustices that remain. This is especially true when we seek assurance that opportunity is not denied on account of race. The enduring hope is that race should not matter; the reality is that too often it does.

This is by way of preface to my respectful submission that parts of the opinion by The Chief Justice imply an all-too-unyielding insistence that race cannot be a factor in instances when, in my view, it may be taken into account. The plurality opinion is too dismissive of the legitimate interest government has in ensuring all people have equal opportunity regardless of their race. The plurality's postulate that "the way to stop discrimination on the basis of race is to stop discriminating on the basis of race," is not sufficient to decide these cases. Fifty years of experience since Brown v. Board of Education, 347 U.S. 483 (1954), should teach us that the problem before us defies so easy a solution. School districts can seek to reach *Brown*'s objective of equal educational opportunity. The plurality opinion is at least open to the interpretation that the Constitution requires school districts to ignore the problem of *de facto* resegregation in schooling. I cannot endorse that conclusion. To the extent the plurality opinion suggests the Constitution mandates that state and local school authorities must accept the status quo of racial isolation in schools, it is, in my view, profoundly mistaken.

The statement by Justice Harlan that "our Constitution is color-blind" was most certainly justified in the context of his dissent in Plessy v. Ferguson, 163 U.S. 537, 559 (1896). The Court's decision in that case was a grievous error it took far too long to overrule. . . . [A]s an aspiration, Justice Harlan's axiom must command our assent. In the real world, it is regrettable to say, it cannot be a universal constitutional principle.

In the administration of public schools by the state and local authorities it is permissible to consider the racial makeup of schools and to adopt general policies to encourage a diverse student body, one aspect of which is its racial composition. . . .

School boards may pursue the goal of bringing together students of diverse backgrounds and races through other means, including strategic site selection of new schools; drawing attendance zones with general recognition of the demographics of neighborhoods; allocating resources for special programs; recruiting students and faculty in a targeted fashion; and tracking enrollments, performance, and other statistics by race. These mechanisms are race conscious but do not lead to different treatment based on a classification that tells each student he or she is to be defined by race, so it is unlikely any of them would demand strict scrutiny to be found permissible. Executive and legislative branches, which for generations now have considered these types of policies and procedures, should be permitted to employ them with candor and with confidence that a constitutional violation does not occur whenever a decisionmaker considers the impact a given approach might have on students of different races. Assigning to each student a personal designation according to a crude system of individual racial classifications is quite a different matter; and the legal analysis changes accordingly. . . .

In the cases before us it is noteworthy that the number of students whose assignment depends on express racial classifications is limited. I join Part III-C of the Court's opinion because I agree that in the context of these plans, the small number of assignments affected suggests that the schools could have achieved their stated ends through different means. These include the facially race-neutral means set forth above or, if necessary, a more nuanced, individual evaluation of school needs and student characteristics that might include race as a component. The latter approach would be informed by *Grutter*, though of course the criteria relevant to student placement would differ based on the age of the students, the needs of the parents, and the role of the schools.

III . . .

C . . .

[If] it is legitimate for school authorities to work to avoid racial isolation in their schools, must they do so only by indirection and general policies? Does the Constitution mandate this inefficient result? Why may the authorities not recognize the problem in candid fashion and solve it altogether through resort to direct assignments based on student racial classifications? So, the argument proceeds, if race is the problem, then perhaps race is the solution.

The argument ignores the dangers presented by individual classifications, dangers that are not as pressing when the same ends are achieved by more indirect means. When the government classifies an individual by race, it must first define what it means to be of a race. Who exactly is white and who is nonwhite? To be forced to live under a state-mandated racial label is inconsistent with the dignity of individuals in our society. And it is a label that an individual is powerless to change. . . . On the other hand race-conscious measures that do not rely on differential treatment based on individual classifications present these problems to a lesser degree. . . .

* * *

This Nation has a moral and ethical obligation to fulfill its historic commitment to creating an integrated society that ensures equal opportunity for all of its children. A compelling interest exists in avoiding racial isolation, an interest that a school district, in its discretion and expertise, may choose to pursue. Likewise, a district may consider it a compelling interest to achieve a diverse student population. Race may be one component of that diversity, but other demographic factors, plus special talents and needs, should also be considered. What the government is not permitted to do, absent a showing of necessity not made here, is to classify every student on the basis of race and to assign each of them to schools based on that classification. Crude measures of this sort threaten to reduce children to racial chits valued and traded according to one school's supply and another's demand. . . .

The decision today should not prevent school districts from continuing the important work of bringing together students of different racial, ethnic, and economic backgrounds. Due to a variety of factors — some influenced by government, some not — neighborhoods in our communities do not reflect the diversity of our Nation as a whole. Those entrusted with directing our public schools can bring to bear the creativity of experts, parents, administrators, and other concerned citizens to find a way to achieve the compelling interests they face without resorting to widespread governmental allocation of benefits and burdens on the basis of racial classifications.

With this explanation I concur in the judgment of the Court.

JUSTICE STEVENS, dissenting. . . .

There is a cruel irony in the Chief Justice's reliance on our decision in Brown v. Board of Education, 349 U.S. 294 (1955). The first sentence in the concluding paragraph of his opinion states: "Before *Brown*, schoolchildren were told where they could and could not go to school based on the color of their skin." This sentence reminds me of Anatole France's observation: "The majestic equality of the law, forbids rich and poor alike to sleep under bridges, to beg in the streets, and to steal their bread." The Chief Justice fails to note that it was only black schoolchildren who were so ordered; indeed, the history books do not tell stories of white children struggling to attend black schools. In this and other ways, The Chief Justice rewrites the history of one of this Court's most important decisions. . . .

If we look at cases decided during the interim between *Brown* and *Adarand*, we can see how a rigid adherence to tiers of scrutiny obscures *Brown*'s clear message. Perhaps the best example is provided by our approval of the decision of the Supreme Judicial Court of Massachusetts in 1967 upholding a state statute mandating racial integration in that State's school system. See School Comm. of Boston v. Board of Education, 352 Mass. 693, 227 N.E.2d 729. Rejecting arguments comparable to those that the plurality accepts today, that court noted: "It would be the height of irony if the racial imbalance act, enacted as it was with the laudable purpose of achieving equal educational opportunities, should, by prescribing school pupil allocations based on race, founder on unsuspected shoals in the Fourteenth Amendment."

Invoking our mandatory appellate jurisdiction, the Boston plaintiffs prosecuted an appeal in this Court. Our ruling on the merits simply stated that the appeal was "dismissed for want of a substantial federal question." School Comm. of Boston v. Board of Education, 389 U.S. 572 (1968) (per curiam). That decision not only expressed our appraisal of the merits of the appeal, but it constitutes a precedent that the Court overrules today. The subsequent statements by the unanimous Court in Swann v. Charlotte-Mecklenburg Bd. of Ed., 402 U.S. 1, 16 (1971) . . . and by the host of state court decisions cited by Justice Breyer, were fully consistent with that disposition. Unlike today's decision, they were also entirely loyal to *Brown*.

The Court has changed significantly since it decided *School Comm. of Boston* in 1968. It was then more faithful to *Brown* and more respectful of our precedent than it is today. It is my firm conviction that no Member of the Court that I joined in 1975 would have agreed with today's decision.

JUSTICE BREYER, with whom JUSTICE STEVENS, JUSTICE SOUTER, and JUSTICE GINSBURG join, dissenting. . . .

I

FACTS . . .

Between 1968 and 1980, the number of black children attending a school where minority children constituted more than half of the school fell from 77% to 63% in the Nation (from 81% to 57% in the South) but then reversed direction by the year 2000, rising from 63% to 72% in the Nation (from 57% to 69% in the South). Similarly, between 1968 and 1980, the number of black children attending schools that were more than 90% minority fell from 64% to 33% in the Nation (from 78% to 23% in the South), but that too reversed direction, rising by the year 2000 from 33% to 37% in the Nation (from 23% to 31% in the South). As of 2002, almost 2.4 million students, or over 5% of all public school enrollment, attended schools with a white population of less than 1%. . . . Today, more than one in six black children attend a school that is 99–100% minority. In light of the evident risk of a return to school systems that are in fact (though not in law) resegregated, many school districts have felt a need to maintain or to extend their integration efforts.

The upshot is that myriad school districts operating in myriad circumstances have devised myriad plans, often with race-conscious elements, all for the sake of eradicating earlier school segregation, bringing about integration, or preventing retrogression. Seattle and Louisville are two such districts, and the histories of their present plans set forth typical school integration stories. . . .

In both Seattle and Louisville, the local school districts began with schools that were highly segregated in fact. In both cities plaintiffs filed lawsuits claiming unconstitutional segregation. In Louisville, a federal district court found that school segregation reflected pre-*Brown* state laws separating the races. In Seattle, the plaintiffs alleged that school segregation unconstitutionally reflected not only generalized societal discrimination and residential housing patterns, but also *school board policies and actions* that had helped to create, maintain, and aggravate racial segregation. In Louisville, a federal court entered a remedial decree. In Seattle, the parties settled after the school district pledged to undertake a desegregation plan. In both cities, the school boards adopted plans designed to achieve integration by bringing about more racially diverse schools. In each city the school board modified its plan several times in light of, for example, hostility to busing, the threat of resegregation, and the desirability of introducing greater student choice. And in each city, the school boards' plans have evolved over time in ways that progressively *diminish* the plans' use of explicit race-conscious criteria. . . .

II

THE LEGAL STANDARD

A longstanding and unbroken line of legal authority tells us that the Equal Protection Clause permits local school boards to use race-conscious criteria to achieve positive race-related goals, even when the Constitution does not compel it. Because of its importance, I shall repeat what this Court said about the matter in *Swann.* Chief Justice Burger, on behalf of a unanimous Court in a case of exceptional importance, wrote:

> School authorities are traditionally charged with broad power to formulate and implement educational policy and might well conclude, for example, that in order to prepare students to live in a pluralistic society each school should have a prescribed ratio of Negro to white students reflecting the proportion for the district as a whole. To do this as an educational policy is within the broad discretionary powers of school authorities.

The statement was not a technical holding in the case. But the Court set forth in *Swann* a basic principle of constitutional law — a principle of law that has found "wide acceptance in the legal culture." . . .

Courts are not alone in accepting as constitutionally valid the legal principle that *Swann* enunciated — i.e., that the government may voluntarily adopt race-conscious measures to improve conditions of race even when it is not under a constitutional obligation to do so. That principle has been accepted by every branch of government and is rooted in the history of the Equal Protection Clause itself. . . .

That *Swann*'s legal statement should find such broad acceptance is not surprising. For *Swann* is predicated upon a well-established legal view of the Fourteenth Amendment. That view understands the basic objective of those who wrote the Equal Protection Clause as forbidding practices that lead to racial exclusion. . . .

There is reason to believe that those who drafted an Amendment with this basic purpose in mind would have understood the legal and practical difference between the use of race-conscious criteria in defiance of that purpose, namely to keep the races apart, and the use of race-conscious criteria to further that purpose, namely to bring the races together. . . .

[The plurality claims] that later cases — in particular *Johnson, Adarand*, and *Grutter* — supplanted *Swann*. . . .

First, . . . [the] Court did not say in *Adarand* or in *Johnson* or in *Grutter* that it was overturning *Swann* or its central constitutional principle.

[In *Adarand*,] the Court . . . sought to "*dispel the notion* that strict scrutiny" is as likely to condemn *inclusive* uses of "race-conscious" criteria as it is to invalidate *exclusionary* uses. . . .

The Court in *Grutter* elaborated:

". . . Context matters when reviewing race-based governmental action under the Equal Protection Clause." . . .

Here, the context is one in which school districts seek to advance or to maintain racial integration in primary and secondary schools. It is a context, as *Swann* makes clear, where history has required special administrative remedies. And it is a context in which the school boards' plans simply set race-conscious limits at the outer boundaries of a broad range.

This context is *not* a context that involves the use of race to decide who will receive goods or services that are normally distributed on the basis of merit and which are in short supply. It is not one in which race-conscious limits stigmatize or exclude; the limits at issue do not pit the races against each other or otherwise significantly exacerbate racial tensions. They do not impose burdens unfairly upon members of one race alone but instead seek benefits for members of all races alike. The context here is one of racial limits that seek, not to keep the races apart, but to bring them together. . . .

Nonetheless, in light of *Grutter* and other precedents, . . . I shall apply the version of strict scrutiny that those cases embody. I shall consequently ask whether the school boards in Seattle and Louisville adopted these plans to serve a "compelling governmental interest" and, if so, whether the plans are "narrowly tailored" to achieve that interest. If the plans survive this strict review, they would survive less exacting review *a fortiori*. . . .

III

APPLYING THE LEGAL STANDARD

A

Compelling Interest

The principal interest advanced in these cases to justify the use of race-based criteria goes by various names. Sometimes a court refers to it as an interest in achieving racial "diversity." Other times a court, like the plurality here, refers to it as an interest in racial "balancing." I have used more general terms to signify that interest, describing it, for example, as an interest in promoting or preserving greater racial "integration" of public schools. By this term, I mean the school districts' interest in eliminating school-by-school racial isolation and increasing the degree to which racial mixture characterizes each of the district's schools and each individual student's public school experience.

Regardless of its name, however, the interest at stake possesses three essential elements. First, there is a historical and remedial element: an interest in setting right the consequences of prior conditions of segregation. . . .

Second, there is an educational element: an interest in overcoming the adverse educational effects produced by and associated with highly segregated schools. Studies suggest that children taken from those schools and placed in integrated settings often show positive academic gains.

Other studies reach different conclusions. But the evidence supporting an educational interest in racially integrated schools is well established and strong enough to permit a democratically elected school board reasonably to determine that this interest is a compelling one. . . .

Third, there is a democratic element: an interest in producing an educational environment that reflects the "pluralistic society" in which our children will live. It is an interest in helping our children learn to work and play together with children of different racial backgrounds. It is an interest in teaching children to engage in the kind of cooperation among Americans of all races that is necessary to make a land of three hundred million people one Nation.

Again, data support this insight. . . .

For his part, Justice Thomas faults my citation of various studies supporting the view that school districts can find compelling educational and civic interests in integrating their public schools. He is entitled of course to his own opinion as to which studies he finds convincing. . . . If we are to insist upon unanimity in the social science literature before finding a compelling interest, we might never find one. I believe only that the Constitution allows democratically elected school boards to make up their own minds as to how best to include people of all races in one America.

B

Narrow Tailoring . . .

First, the race-conscious criteria at issue . . . constitute but one part of plans that depend primarily upon other, nonracial elements. To use race in this way is not to set a forbidden "quota."

In fact, the defining feature of both plans is greater emphasis upon student choice. In Seattle, for example, in more than 80% of all cases, that choice alone determines which high schools Seattle's ninth graders will attend. . . . *Choice*, therefore, is the "predominant factor" in these plans. *Race* is not. . . .

Second, broad-range limits on voluntary school choice plans are less burdensome, and hence more narrowly tailored, than other race-conscious restrictions this Court has previously approved. Indeed, the plans before us are *more narrowly tailored* than the race-conscious admission plans that this Court approved in *Grutter*. Here, race becomes a factor only in a fraction of students' non-merit-based assignments — not in large numbers of students' merit-based applications. Moreover, the effect of applying race-conscious criteria here affects potentially disadvantaged students *less severely*, not more severely, than the criteria at issue in *Grutter*. Disappointed students are not rejected from a State's flagship graduate program; they simply attend a different one of the district's many public schools, which in aspiration and in fact are substantially equal. . . .

Third, the manner in which the school boards developed these plans itself reflects "narrow tailoring." Each plan was devised to overcome a history of segregated public schools. Each plan embodies the results of local experience and community consultation. Each plan is the product of a process that has sought to enhance student choice, while diminishing the need for mandatory busing. And each plan's use of race-conscious elements is *diminished* compared to the use of race in preceding integration plans. . . .

Nor could the school districts have accomplished their desired aims (e.g., avoiding forced busing, countering white flight, maintaining racial diversity) by other means. . . . [As] to "strategic site selection," Seattle has built one new high school in the last 44 years (and that specialized school serves only 300 students). In fact, six of the Seattle high schools involved in this case were built by the 1920's; the other four were open by the early 1960's. As to "drawing" neighborhood "attendance zones" on a racial basis, Louisville tried it, and it worked only when forced busing was also part of the plan. As to "allocating resources for special programs," Seattle and Louisville have both experimented with this; indeed, these programs are often referred to as "magnet schools," but the limited desegregation effect of these efforts extends at most to those few schools to which additional resources are granted. In addition, there is no evidence from the experience of these school districts that it will make any meaningful impact. As to "recruiting faculty" on the basis of race, both cities have tried, but only as one part of a broader program. As to "tracking enrollments, performance and other statistics by race," tracking *reveals* the problem; it does not cure it. . . .

V

CONSEQUENCES

The Founders meant the Constitution as a practical document that would transmit its basic values to future generations through principles that remained workable over time. Hence it is important to consider the potential consequences of the plurality's approach, as measured against the Constitution's objectives. To do so provides further reason to believe that the plurality's approach is legally unsound.

For one thing, consider the effect of the plurality's views on the parties before us and on similar school districts throughout the Nation. . . .

The districts' past and current plans are not unique. They resemble other plans, promulgated by hundreds of local school boards, which have attempted a variety of desegregation methods that have evolved over time in light of experience. . . .

At a minimum, the plurality's views would threaten a surge of race-based litigation. Hundreds of state and federal statutes and regulations use racial classifications for educational or other purposes. In many such instances, the contentious force of legal challenges to these classifications, meritorious or not, would displace earlier calm.

The wide variety of different integration plans that school districts use throughout the Nation suggests that the problem of racial segregation in schools, including *de facto* segregation, is difficult to solve. The fact that many such plans have used explicitly racial criteria suggests that such criteria have an important, sometimes necessary, role to play. The fact that the controlling opinion would make a school district's use of such criteria often unlawful (and the plurality's "color-blind" view would make such use always unlawful) suggests that today's opinion will require setting aside the laws of several States and many local communities. . . .

The plurality, or at least those who follow Justice Thomas' "color-blind" approach, may feel confident that, to end invidious discrimination, one must end *all* governmental use of race-conscious criteria including those with inclusive objectives. By way of contrast, I do not claim to know how best to stop harmful discrimination; how best to create a society that includes all Americans; how best to overcome our serious problems of increasing *de facto* segregation, troubled inner city schooling, and poverty correlated with race. But, as a judge, I do know that the Constitution does not authorize judges to dictate solutions to these problems. Rather, the Constitution creates a democratic political system through which the people themselves must together find answers. And it is for them to debate how best to educate the Nation's children and how best to administer America's schools to achieve that aim. The Court should leave them to their work. And it is for them to decide, to quote the plurality's slogan, whether the best "way to stop discrimination on the basis of race is to stop discriminating on the basis of race."

* * *

Finally, what of the hope and promise of *Brown*? For much of this Nation's history, the races remained divided. It was not long ago that people of different races drank from separate fountains, rode on separate buses, and studied in separate schools. In this Court's finest hour, Brown v. Board of Education challenged this history and helped to change it. For *Brown* held out a promise. It was a promise embodied in three Amendments designed to make citizens of slaves. It was the promise of true racial equality — not as a matter of fine words on paper, but as a matter of everyday life in the Nation's cities and schools. It was about the nature of a democracy that must work for all Americans. It sought one law, one Nation, one people, not simply as a matter of legal principle but in terms of how we actually live.

Not everyone welcomed this Court's decision in *Brown*. Three years after that decision was handed down, the Governor of Arkansas ordered state militia to block the doors of a white schoolhouse so that black children could not enter. The President of the United States dispatched the 101st Airborne Division to Little Rock, Arkansas, and federal troops were needed to enforce a desegregation decree. See Cooper v. Aaron, 358 U.S. 1 (1958). Today, almost 50 years later, attitudes toward race in this Nation have changed dramatically. Many parents, white and black alike, want their children to attend schools with children of different races. Indeed, the very school districts that once spurned integration now strive for it. The long history of their efforts reveals the complexities and difficulties they have faced. And in light of those challenges, they have asked us not to take from their hands the instruments they have used to rid their schools of racial segregation, instruments that they believe are needed to overcome the problems of cities divided by race and poverty. The plurality would decline their modest request.

The plurality is wrong to do so. The last half-century has witnessed great strides toward racial equality, but we have not yet realized the promise of *Brown*. To invalidate the plans under review is to threaten the promise of *Brown*. The plurality's position, I fear, would break that promise. This is a decision that the Court and the Nation will come to regret.

I must dissent.

Note: Parents Involved *and the Synthesis of Equal Protection Law*

1. *How the Court reads* Brown. In *Parents Involved,* the justices almost seem more focused on the meaning of *Brown* than on the meaning of the fourteenth amendment. Consider Karlan, The Law of Small Numbers: Gonzales v. Carhart, *Parents Involved in Community Schools,* and Some Themes from the First Full Term of the Roberts Court, 86 N.C. L. Rev. 1369, 1393, 1396 (2008):

> The Court was quite conscious in *Parents Involved* that the Justices were involved in a struggle over the meaning of Brown v. Board of Education. Chief Justice Roberts's opinion for the Court sought to end the debate by quoting what the counsel for the *Brown* plaintiffs said at oral argument. . . . The Court saw "no ambiguity in [his] statement." . . .
>
>   The attorney who made that statement, Robert L. Carter, is now a distinguished federal district judge. Asked for his reaction to the Court's statement, [he responded] . . . "'All that race was used for at that point in time was to deny equal opportunity to black people,' Judge Carter said of the 1950s. 'It's to stand that argument on its head to use race the way they use [it] now.'"

Consider also Liu, "History Will Be Heard": An Appraisal of the *Seattle/Louisville* Decision, 2 Harv. L. & Poly. Rev. 53, 62 (2008):

> Tellingly, the forty-one-page plurality opinion in *Seattle/Louisville* contains only one quotation from *Brown*: a paltry sentence fragment: "The impact [of segregation] is greater when it has the sanction of the law" — that omits the crucial adjacent words locating the illegality of segregation in its detrimental effects on black children. This inattention leads the plurality to identify the violation in 1954 as "differential treatment on the basis of race," again implying equal burdens on blacks and whites. But *Brown* did not speak of the violation that way. The Court nowhere used the term "colorblind" or availed itself of the familiar quotation from Harlan's dissent in *Plessy*. Instead, *Brown*'s most memorable utterance was its recognition that segregation harms black children by "generat[ing] a feeling of inferiority as to their status in the community that may affect their hearts and minds in a way unlikely ever to be undone." . . .

What strategic role did the justices' citation of *Brown* play in their positions? See Karlan, What Can *Brown*® Do for You?: Neutral Principles and the Struggle over the Equal Protection Clause, 58 Duke L.J. 1049 (2009).

2. *Justice Kennedy's position.* Justice Kennedy's concurrence plays a pivotal role in the case. Is he accurately describing the factors that trigger strict scrutiny, or, as he did with his opinion for the Court in Miller v. Johnson, 515 U.S. 900, 911 (1995), discussed at pages 609-610, supra, is he subtly recasting and relaxing the standard? Is his description here consistent with the Court's cases holding that strict scrutiny is triggered for facially neutral classifications that are intended to serve as proxies for racial classifications?

In this regard, consider Gerken, Justice Kennedy and the Domains of Equal Protection, 121 Harv. L. Rev. 104, 108, 114–117 (2007):

> Most of us think we already know the story of race. We tell the same story no matter what the domain. But every domain — schools, the marketplace, democracy — has an overarching narrative. What if we tried to fit race within that narrative rather than vice versa? . . .
>
> The way Justice Kennedy frames his opinion provides some evidence that a domain-centered narrative is driving him. . . . Chief Justice Roberts, for instance, opens his analysis by invoking general equal protection principles and ends with the aphorism that "the way to stop discrimination on the basis of race is to stop discriminating on the basis of race." Justice Thomas begins his concurrence by characterizing the case as being about "state entities" rather than public schools, and he ends by invoking general language on race from *Dred Scott* and Justice Harlan's dissent in *Plessy*.
>
> Justice Kennedy, in sharp contrast, anchors his concurrence in the domain of education. He opens his opinion by trumpeting the role that public schools play in teaching civic morality and explicitly linking that role to integration. . . . This opening certainly resonates with parts of *Brown*'s legacy. But its core narrative is less about equal educational opportunity, the dominant note in any equal protection story, than about the role schools play in teaching civic morality. . . .
>
> Public schools are, of course, a place where the state regulates pervasively, and at least on Kennedy's account, their job is to teach students to be citizens. This combination — pervasive regulation and an identifiable mission — makes it particularly hard to insist upon a race-neutral approach. . . . [Even] a judge committed to the colorblind ideal might worry, as Kennedy seems to, that the value of colorblindness cannot be learned in a racially segregated school. The narrative of the educational domain, then, may be what focuses Justice Kennedy on the poor fit between his preference for a race-neutral state and his desire for a race-neutral society. Perhaps this is why the question for Kennedy seems to have changed in the domain of education. It is no longer whether the state can act race consciously, but how. . . . [Perhaps] Justice Kennedy sincerely believes what Scalia suggested only sarcastically in *Grutter*: that "cross-racial understanding" and "good citizenship" are lessons to be learned by "people three feet shorter and 20 years younger than the full-grown adults at the University of Michigan Law School, in . . . public-school kindergartens."

Consider also the views in Siegel, The Virtue of Judicial Statesmanship, 86 Tex. L. Rev. 959, 1009–1013 (2008):

> In important ways, Kennedy's effort in *Parents Involved* seems to exhibit the practice of judicial statesmanship. He appeared not merely to tolerate but actually to entertain the strongly held moral claims of each party to the conflict over exactly whom equal protection protects and in what ways. . . .
>
> Perhaps most significant of all, he apprehended both the potentially balkanizing and stigmatizing consequences of government inaction in the face of widespread residential segregation and the potentially balkanizing and stigmatizing consequences of race-conscious state action aimed at ameliorating the problem.
>
> Kennedy, in short, seemed to appreciate what total defeat would mean for both sides. . . .
>
> Those commentators, including myself, who disagree with his analysis and resolution of the cases — whether because they would have upheld the plans or because they would have gone further in banning any use of race — should not

be quick to dismiss the ways in which Kennedy handled the controversy in a statesmanlike way. . . .

Yet it bears mention that throughout his opinion, Kennedy too was not completely transparent. He did not explain why addressing the problem of de facto segregation "in a general way" — "by indirection and general policies" — is less troubling than doing so through "individual typing by race." He did not specify why a racial classification that determines some student assignments "tells each student he or she is to be defined by race" to a greater extent than, say, a race-conscious attendance zone. He did not identify why it mattered so much that the "racial classifications at issue here" were "personal" and "explicit" — why it made a difference that the cases involved "official labels proclaiming the race of all persons in a broad class of citizens." He did not clarify why "individual classifications" present "dangers that are not as pressing when the same ends are achieved by more indirect means". . . .

Those are not trivial omissions. It is not as if race-conscious attendance zones avoid classifying groups of citizens in part based on their race. Nor is it the case that race-conscious attendance zones necessarily avoid imposing material harms on individuals based on their race: carving a district one way as opposed to another determines who goes to which schools. The primary difference between the methods that Kennedy approved and those that he disapproved may lie in the likelihood that the individual who is treated by the government in part as a member of a racial group will actually register that he or she is being so treated. In other words, the constitutional problem for Kennedy (and Powell and O'Connor) may lie not in "being forced to live under a state-mandated racial label" but in the individual's perception that he or she is living in that way. . . .

It is striking that three major efforts at judicial statesmanship in the area of race and equal protection put pressure on the rule-of-law value of transparency. . . .

3. *The judicial role.* In discussing the question whether local school boards have compelling interest in increasing racial integration within schools, does the Court adequately differentiate between what the Constitution would authorize judges to order over a jurisdiction's objection and what a jurisdiction can voluntarily undertake? In this regard, consider the observations of Judge J. Harvie Wilkinson, himself the author of an influential book on the meaning of *Brown*:

[Justice Breyer's] dissent rests in part on a shrewd tactical maneuver. The Justice seeks to co-opt all the traditional conservative arguments against race-based decisionmaking and harness them to his own ends. . . .

It has long been an article of faith among conservatives that the Constitution permits the use of race only for strictly remedial ends. . . . Justice Breyer converts the term "remedial" to his own uses. . . .

[It] has long been critical to the conservative self-perception that opponents were "activist" and that conservatives were guardians of "restraint." It was, after all, the Warren Court that made activism "a dirty word". . . . Conservatives saw themselves as protectors of restraint, stability, and the federal system with all its appreciation of democratic values and of the rights of states and localities to pursue their own distinctive policies.

In *Parents Involved*, Justice Breyer seeks to turn the tables. In some respects, the opinion is one long paean to the tradition of local control over local school systems. . . .

The Justice has left no stone unturned. It is his view, he says, that will foster the deference to democracy, the appreciation for local experimentation, the diminished litigation, the judicial restraint, and, above all, the binding ties to one nation that conservatives have wanted all along. The opinion consciously seeks to use the terminology of the other side and flip it. In one sense the dissent is unrelenting; in another it seeks to make a conciliatory case. The maneuver must be admired for its shrewdness and its attempt to appeal to opponents in a case made largely through their values and on their terms.

Why then does this best case fail ultimately to persuade? It fails because it recognizes few, if any, limits to the explicit use of race and ethnicity in public decisions. It fails because it risks abandoning America to a race-based course. . . . - Without the prospect of strict judicial scrutiny of race-based classifications, it is anything but certain that racial proportionality would not become more prevalent as citizens and their representatives demand that public benefits be based on race, namely their own. At a minimum, supporters of racial allocation must offer analytical breaks on a practice that, once blessed, would start rolling downhill.

Wilkinson, The Seattle and Louisville School Cases: There Is No Other Way, 121 Harv. L. Rev. 158, 176, 177–179 (2007).

4. *Affirmative action, democracy, and the standard of review.* In Schuette v. Coalition to Defend Affirmative Action, 134 S. Ct. 1623 (2014), the Supreme Court upheld a Michigan constitutional amendment, enacted through a popular initiative, that, among other things, forbid "discriminat[ion] against, or grant[ing] preferential treatment to, any individual or group on the basis of race . . . in the operation of . . . public education." In upholding the initiative, Justice Kennedy's opinion announcing the judgment of the Court (joined by Chief Justice Roberts and Justice Alito) expressed the view that "[it] is demeaning to the democratic process to presume that the voters are not capable of deciding an issue of this sensitivity on decent and rational grounds" and that "[freedom] embraces the right, indeed the duty, to engage in a rational, civic discourse in order to deter-mine how best to form a consensus to shape the destiny of the Nation and its people." Is this position consistent with the Court's insistence on strictly scruti-nizing decisions by the political branches to adopt affirmative action programs? Is the Court's insistence on strict scrutiny for these programs, even when their purpose is benign, consistent with its use of rational basis review when a facially neutral statute harms racial minorities for benign purposes?

Siegel, Foreword: Equality Divided, 127 Harv. L. Rev. 1, 50 (2013), argues that equal protection doctrine expresses more concern with the "racial meaning and impact of state action" in the context of affirmative action than it does with respect to facially neutral laws that disadvantage minority communities. Siegel concludes that the Court has thereby turned its traditional *Carolene Products* approach inside out to create "a form of judicial review that cares more about protecting members of majority groups from actions of representative govern-ment that promote minority opportunities than it cares about protecting 'discrete and insular minorities' from actions of representative government that reflect 'prejudice.'" Does this criticism place too little weight on the fact that affirmative action programs make facial distinctions whereas programs like the one upheld in *Feeney* are facially neutral? If so, why is this difference so significant?

5. *A more radical challenge to existing doctrine?* In Ricci v. DeStefano, 557 U.S. 557 (2009), Justice Scalia raised the possibility that strict scrutiny for racial classifications puts into doubt the constitutionality of much of the edifice of modern antidiscrimination law. Recall that many federal antidiscrimination sta-tutes — for example, Title VII of the Civil Rights Act of 1964, which deals with employment discrimination, and section 2 of the Voting Rights Act of 1965 — prohibit practices that have a disparate impact regardless of the defendant's

intent. In *Ricci*, the Court faced a Title VII and equal protection clause–based challenge to a city's decision not to certify the results of a promotional test for firefighters in light of the test's disparate impact on black and Latino applicants. The Court disposed of the case on statutory grounds, not reaching the constitutional question. In his concurrence, however, Justice Scalia observed that the Court's decision

> merely postpones the evil day on which the Court will have to confront the question: Whether, or to what extent, are the disparate-impact provisions of Title VII of the Civil Rights Act of 1964 consistent with the Constitution's guarantee of equal protection? The question is not an easy one. See generally Primus, Equal Protection and Disparate Impact: Round Three, 117 Harv. L. Rev. 493 (2003).
>
> The difficulty is this: . . . Title VII not only permits but affirmatively *requires* ["remedial"] actions when a disparate-impact violation *would* otherwise result. But if the Federal Government is prohibited from discriminating on the basis of race, *Bolling v. Sharpe*, 347 U.S. 497, 500 (1954), then surely it is also prohibited from enacting laws mandating that third parties — *e.g.*, employers, whether private, State, or municipal — discriminate on the basis of race. . . .
>
> Intentional discrimination is still occurring, just one step up the chain. Government compulsion of such design would therefore seemingly violate equal protection principles. Nor would it matter that Title VII requires consideration of race on a wholesale, rather than retail, level. . . .
>
> [T]he war between disparate impact and equal protection will be waged sooner or later, and it behooves us to begin thinking about how — and on what terms — to make peace between them.

In this light, consider also Texas Department of Housing and Community Affairs v. Inclusive Communities Project, Inc., 135 S. Ct. 2507 (2015). In that case, the Court, in an opinion by Justice Kennedy, interpreted the Fair Housing Act of 1968 to prohibit not just actions that had a discriminatory intent, but also actions that had a disproportionately adverse effect on minorities and are otherwise unjustified by a legitimate rationale. The Court noted, however, that remedial orders issued under a disparate impact theory "must be consistent with the Constitution." To meet this requirement, courts "should concentrate on the elimination of the offending practice that 'arbitrar[ily] . . . operate[s] invidiously to discriminate on the basis of rac[e].' If additional measures are adopted, courts should strive to design them to eliminate racial disparities through race-neutral means. [Remedial] orders that impose racial targets or quotas might raise more difficult constitutional questions." Nonetheless, the Court observed, race "may be considered in certain circumstances and in a proper fashion. [When] setting their larger goals, local housing authorities may choose to foster diversity and combat racial isolation with race-neutral tools, and mere awareness of race in attempting to solve the problems facing inner cities does not doom that endeavor at the outset."

Justice Thomas, and Justice Alito, joined by Chief Justice Roberts and Justices Scalia and Thomas, wrote opinions dissenting on the statutory construction question.

6. *Abandoning special scrutiny?* The plurality, Justice Kennedy's concurrence, and Justice Breyer's dissent all offer different formulations of what strict scrutiny means. And the Court seems to apply strict scrutiny quite differently to racial classifications in different contexts. Consider whether these decisions constitute a

dilution or abandonment of strict scrutiny, in fact if not in name. Karlan, Easing the Spring: Strict Scrutiny and Affirmative Action After the Redistricting Cases, 43 Wm. & Mary L. Rev. 1569 (2002), argues that these cases suggest that "strict scrutiny may be strict in theory, but . . . rather pliable in practice." Id. at 1573. Similarly, Goldberg, Equality without Tiers, 77 S. Cal. L. Rev. 481 (2004), argues that the Court has really adopted a far more fluid scale than the conventional account of strict scrutiny and rationality review captures.

In Griffin, Judicial Supremacy and Equal Protection in a Democracy of Rights, 4 U. Pa. J. Const. L. 281 (2002), the author argues that the Court should formally abandon strict scrutiny for racial classifications. From a strategic point of view, Griffin contends, recent decisions make clear that minorities gain little from such scrutiny. As Griffin puts it, "If you are a member of a racial minority, the Supreme Court is not your friend." Id. at 282. Moreover, "the protection against unjust discrimination all Americans receive from civil rights statutes is plainly superior to the protection provided by the Equal Protection Clause." Id. Would minorities be better off today if the Court were simply to announce that racial classifications were no longer subject to strict scrutiny?

D. EQUAL PROTECTION METHODOLOGY: HEIGHTENED SCRUTINY AND THE PROBLEM OF GENDER

Does the Constitution impose a special burden of justification when government action discriminates on the basis of gender? Under what circumstances can laws treat men and women differently?

1. The Early Cases

Until the 1970s, the Court applied only minimal scrutiny to gender classifications and consistently rejected constitutional attacks on statutes disadvantaging women. In Bradwell v. Illinois, 83 U.S. (16 Wall.) 130 (1873), for example, decided the day after The Slaughter-House Cases, pages 476-477, supra, the Court upheld Illinois' refusal to license a woman to practice law. In an opinion by Justice Miller, the author of The Slaughter-House Cases, the Court held that the right to practice law was not a privilege or immunity of national citizenship and therefore was not protected by the fourteenth amendment.

Justice Bradley, who had dissented in The Slaughter-House Cases, added a much-quoted concurring opinion. In The Slaughter-House Cases, Justice Bradley had written that "a law which prohibits a large class of citizens from adopting a lawful [employment deprives] them of liberty as well as property without due process of law." Thus, one might have assumed that he would be sympathetic to Bradwell's claim. In *Bradwell*, however, he asserted that

> [the] natural and proper timidity and delicacy which belongs to the female sex evidently unfits it for many of the occupations of civil life. The constitution of the family organization, which is founded in the divine ordinance, as well as in the nature of things, indicates the domestic sphere as that which properly belongs to the domain and functions of womanhood. The harmony, not to say identity, of

interests and views which belong or should belong to the family institution, is repugnant to the idea of a woman adopting a distinct and independent career from that of her husband. . . .

It is true that many women are unmarried and not affected by any of the duties, complications, and incapacities arising out of the married state but these are exceptions to the general rule. The paramount destiny and mission of woman are to fulfill the noble and benign offices of wife and mother. This is the law of the Creator. And the rules of civil society must be adapted to the general constitution of things, and cannot be based upon exceptional cases.

See also In re Lockwood, 154 U.S. 116 (1894).

Two years after *Bradwell*, in Minor v. Happersett, 88 U.S. (21 Wall.) 162 (1875), the Court acknowledged that women were "persons" and "citizens" within the meaning of the fourteenth amendment, but held that the right to vote was not a privilege of U.S. citizenship and that women could therefore be denied the franchise. (Note that in addition to the equal protection clause, the fourteenth amendment also contained a reduction-of-representation clause in section 2 that penalized states that denied the right to vote "to any of the male inhabitants" of the state.) *Minor* was overturned by the nineteenth amendment, which provides in pertinent part that "[the] right of citizens to vote shall not be denied or abridged by the United States or by any State on account of sex." Still, as late as Breedlove v. Suttles, 302 U.S. 277 (1937), the Supreme Court upheld the imposition of a poll tax on men only: "In view of burdens necessarily borne by them for the preservations of the race, the State reasonably may exempt [women] from poll taxes." Still, women were exempt from paying the tax only if they did not register to vote. In effect, the statute lifted the tax burden by discouraging women from participating in the political process. For extensive discussions of suffrage and equality, see L. Kerber, No Constitutional Right to Be Ladies 81–124 (1998); A. Keyssar, The Right to Vote: The Contested History of Democracy in the United States 172–223 (2000); Winkler, A Revolution Too Soon: Woman Suffragists and the "Living Constitution," 76 N.Y.U. L. Rev. 1456 (2001).

The early cases were decided against the backdrop of The Slaughter-House Cases, which had given an extremely narrow reading to the fourteenth amendment's due process and equal protection clauses. They therefore paid little attention to claims that gender discrimination violated these provisions. But even when the Court began to invalidate other legislation on due process and equal protection grounds, it resisted application of these clauses to gender discrimination.

In Muller v. Oregon, 208 U.S. 412 (1908), for example, the Court upheld an Oregon statute prohibiting the employment of women in factories for more than ten hours per day. In doing so, it distinguished its earlier decision in Lochner v. New York, 198 U.S. 45 (1905), in which it had held that the liberty of contract implicit in the due process clause prohibited a similar restriction on the working hours of bakers. In *Muller*, the Court maintained that "the inherent difference between the two sexes" justified limitations on a woman's right to contract. But see Adkins v. Children's Hospital, 261 U.S. 525 (1923) (invalidating minimum wage legislation for women on substantive due process grounds). *Adkins* was overruled in West Coast Hotel Co. v. Parrish, 300 U.S. 379 (1937). (For discussion of these cases, see generally Chapter 6, section D, infra.)

The Court was similarly unsympathetic to equal protection claims. In Goesaert v. Cleary, 335 U.S. 464 (1948), for example, the Court, in an opinion by

Justice Frankfurter, upheld a Michigan statute prohibiting a woman from working as a bartender unless she was the wife or daughter of a bar's male owner. See also Quong Wing v. Kirkendall, 223 U.S. 59 (1912). And in 1961, the Court, in Hoyt v. Florida, 368 U.S. 57, upheld as "rational" a jury selection system excluding women who did not affirmatively indicate a desire to serve.

2.   *The Road to Intermediate Scrutiny*

In the early 1970s, the Court became more receptive to constitutional attacks on gender classifications. Consider the extent to which the Court's position reflected an emerging popular view. What does this suggest about the willingness or ability of the Court to take positions that go far beyond contemporary views? See generally Siegel, Constitutional Culture, Social Movement, and Constitutional Change: The Case of the De Facto ERA, 94 Cal. L. Rev. 1323 (2006).

REED v. REED, 404 U.S. 71 (1971). This was the first Supreme Court decision to invalidate a gender classification under the equal protection clause. Idaho's law governing the estates of persons who had died intestate (that is, without a will) established a hierarchy of classes of persons eligible for appointment as administrators (e.g., the surviving spouse, the children, or the parents of the decedent). But within any class, the law provided that "of several persons claiming and equally entitled to administer, males must be preferred to females." Reed's parents were separated and when Reed died intestate, his mother filed a petition seeking to administer her son's estate. Reed's father subsequently filed a request that he be named administrator instead, and the state court judge appointed the father in light of the Idaho statute.

In a terse opinion, a unanimous Court held that this preference violated the equal protection clause. Chief Justice Burger, writing for the Court, characterized the issue as "whether a difference in the sex of competing applicants [bears] a rational relationship to a state objective that is sought to be advanced by the operation of [the statute]." The state defended the preference on the ground that it eliminated an area of controversy when two or more persons, otherwise equally entitled, sought to administer an estate. Although the Court acknowledged that reducing the workload of probate courts by eliminating one class of contests was legitimate, the Court maintained that the means used to achieve that objective — that is, a gender classification — was "the very kind of arbitrary legislative choice forbidden by the Equal Protection Clause."

If the decision to afford preference to men violated the equal protection clause because it was arbitrary, what other choices within otherwise similarly situated classes of potential administrators would *not* be unacceptably arbitrary? Would flipping a coin be non-arbitrary? Picking the older of two applicants?

FRONTIERO v. RICHARDSON, 411 U.S. 677 (1973). Under federal law, a male member of the uniformed armed services could automatically claim his spouse as a dependent, thereby receiving a larger housing allowance and higher medical benefits. However, a female service member could claim comparable benefits only if she demonstrated that her spouse was in fact dependent on her for over half his support. Although divided as to the appropriate standard of review, eight members of the Court agreed that this distinction violated the equal protection component of the fifth amendment's due process clause.

Writing for four justices, Justice Brennan argued that classifications based on gender are inherently suspect and, like racial classifications, should be subject to close scrutiny. Justice Brennan found "at least implicit support for such an approach" in *Reed*, since there the Court had "implicitly rejected appellee's apparently rational explanation of the statutory scheme." Moreover, this departure from "'traditional' rational-basis analysis" was "clearly justified" in Justice Brennan's opinion:

"There can be no doubt that our Nation has had a long and unfortunate history of sex discrimination. Traditionally, such discrimination was rationalized by an attitude of 'romantic paternalism' which, in practical effect, put women, not on a pedestal, but in a cage. . . .

"As a result of notions such as these, our statute books gradually became laden with gross, stereotyped distinctions between the sexes and, indeed, throughout much of the 19th century the position of women in our society was, in many respects, comparable to that of blacks under the pre–Civil War slave codes. Neither slaves nor women could hold office, serve on juries, or bring suit in their own names, and married women traditionally were denied the legal capacity to hold or convey property or to serve as legal guardians of their own children. And although blacks were guaranteed the right to vote in 1870, women were denied even that right [until] adoption of the Nineteenth Amendment half a century later.

"It is true, of course, that the position of women in America has improved markedly in recent decades. Nevertheless, it can hardly be doubted that, in part because of the high visibility of the sex characteristic, women still face pervasive, although at times more subtle, discrimination in our educational institutions, in the job market and, perhaps most conspicuously in the political arena.

"Moreover, since sex, like race and national origin, is an immutable characteristic determined solely by the accident of birth, the imposition of special disabilities upon the members of a particular sex because of their sex would seem to violate 'the basic concept of our system that legal burdens should bear some relationship to individual responsibility.' And what differentiates sex from such nonsuspect statuses as intelligence or physical disability, and aligns it with the recognized suspect criteria, is that the sex characteristic frequently bears no relation to ability to perform or contribute to society."

Finally, relying on title VII of the 1964 Civil Rights Act, which prohibited employment discrimination based on gender, and congressional approval of the equal rights amendment to the Constitution, Justice Brennan argued that "Congress itself has concluded that classifications based upon sex are inherently invidious, and this conclusion of a coequal branch of Government is not without significance." (At the time Justice Brennan wrote, the equal rights amendment had been submitted to the states for ratification. In 1982, the time period for ratification expired. See pages 677-678, infra.)

Turning to the classification at issue, Justice Brennan concluded that it could not survive strict scrutiny. The government argued that differential treatment of men and women served the purpose of administrative convenience, since, as an empirical matter, wives were usually dependent on their husbands for at least half their support, whereas husbands were rarely similarly dependent upon their wives.

"The Government offers no concrete evidence [tending] to support its view that such differential treatment in fact saves the Government any money. [In] any case, [when] we enter the realm of 'strict judicial scrutiny,' there can be no doubt that 'administrative convenience' is not a shibboleth, the mere recitation of which dictates constitutionality. On the contrary, any statutory scheme which draws a sharp line between the sexes, *solely* for the purpose of achieving administrative convenience, necessarily commands 'dissimilar treatment for men and women who are [similarly] situated,' and, therefore, involves the 'very kind of arbitrary legislative choice forbidden by the [Constitution.]' [*Reed*]."

In a separate opinion joined by Chief Justice Burger and Justice Blackmun, Justice Powell concurred in the judgment but expressly disassociated himself from Justice Brennan's assertion that classifications based on sex are suspect. Justice Powell thought that in light of *Reed* it was unnecessary to reach that question in order to invalidate the statute. Moreover, he noted that the equal rights amendment, which had been passed by Congress and was then pending ratification by the states, would, if adopted, resolve the issue.

"If this Amendment is duly adopted, it will represent the will of the people accomplished in the manner prescribed by the Constitution. By acting prematurely and unnecessarily, [the] Court has assumed a decisional responsibility at the very time when state legislatures, functioning within the traditional democratic processes, are debating the proposed Amendment."

Justice Stewart also concurred in the judgment.

Justice Rehnquist dissented without opinion.

Note: From Reed to Craig v. Boren: Evolution and Doctrinal Confusion

Reed inaugurated a period of intense judicial interest in gender classifications, and the Court began to use a variety of techniques to invalidate laws embodying distinctions based on sex.

1. *Due process and conclusive presumptions.* A few months after *Reed*, in Stanley v. Illinois, 405 U.S. 645 (1972), a divided Court struck down an Illinois statute that automatically made children of unwed fathers wards of the state on the death of their mothers. In contrast, unwed mothers could be deprived of their children only on a showing that they were unfit parents. The Court held that this scheme deprived fathers of due process of law by erecting a "conclusive presumption" of unfitness. In Cleveland Board of Education v. LaFleur, 414 U.S. 632 (1974), the Court used a similar technique to invalidate regulations requiring a school teacher to take maternity leave well before the expected birth date of her child. The Court held that the due process clause did not permit a "conclusive presumption" that pregnant women were medically unfit to teach. (In Weinberger v. Salfi, 422 U.S. 749 (1975), the Court sharply restricted use of the "conclusive presumption" technique for attacking statutory classifications. For a more detailed discussion of the problem, see Chapter 6, section G2, infra.)

In his concurrence in the judgment, Justice Powell declared that "[it] seems to me that equal protection analysis is the appropriate frame of reference":

> A range of possible school board goals emerge from the cases. Several may be put to one side. The records before us abound with proof that a principal purpose behind the adoption of the regulations was to keep visibly pregnant teachers out of the sight of school-children. The boards do not advance this today as a legitimate objective, yet its initial primacy casts a shadow over these cases. Moreover, most of the after-the-fact rationalizations proposed by these boards are unsupported in the records.

The boards emphasize teacher absenteeism, classroom discipline, the safety of schoolchildren, and the safety of the expectant mother and her unborn child. No doubt these are legitimate concerns. But the boards have failed to demonstrate that these interests are in fact threatened by the continued employment of pregnant teachers. . . .

[The] classifications chosen by these boards, so far as we have been shown, are either counterproductive or irrationally overinclusive even with regard to [the] significant, nonillusory goal [of ensuring continuity of personnel within a classroom.] Accordingly, in my opinion these regulations are invalid under rational-basis standards of equal protection review.

Although Justice Powell noted that "[most] school teachers are women, a certain percentage of them are pregnant at any given time, and pregnancy is a normal biological function," he did not think it necessary to decide "whether sex-based classifications invoke strict judicial scrutiny, for example, Frontiero v. Richardson, 411 U.S. 677 (1973), or whether these regulations involve sex classifications at all. Whether the challenged aspects of the regulations constitute sex classifications . . . , they must at least rationally serve some legitimate articulated or obvious state interest." Note that the due process approach in *LaFleur* did not rest on any showing that the challenged practice was gender-based or that male teachers were treated differently with respect to potentially disabling physical conditions.

2. *The sixth amendment and juries.* In Taylor v. Louisiana, 419 U.S. 522 (1975), the Court distinguished Hoyt v. Florida, page 639, supra, and held that the exclusion of women from jury service deprived the defendant of his sixth amendment right to a fair and impartial jury. The Court explained that "*Hoyt* did not involve a defendant's Sixth Amendment right to a jury drawn from a fair cross section of the community. [The] right to a proper jury cannot be overcome on merely rational grounds."

To what extent does the Court's holding rest simultaneously on both the ways in which men and women are the same — for example, in their ability to serve competently on juries — and the ways in which they are different — for example, in their perspective on the questions jurors are asked to decide? Justice White's opinion for the Court observed that "women are sufficiently numerous and distinct from men . . . that if they are systematically eliminated from jury panels, the Sixth Amendment's fair-cross-section requirement cannot be satisfied." He relied on the Court's earlier opinion in Ballard v. United States, 329 U.S. 187 (1946), where the Court had held that a federal court's exclusion of female potential jurors in a state where women were eligible as a matter of state law to serve violated the sixth amendment:

The thought is that the factors which tend to influence the action of women are the same as those which influence the action of men — personality, background, economic status — and not sex. Yet it is not enough to say that women when sitting as jurors neither act nor tend to act as a class. Men likewise do not act as a class. But, if the shoe were on the other foot, who would claim that a jury was truly representative of the community if all men were intentionally and systematically excluded from the panel? The truth is that the two sexes are not fungible; a community made up exclusively of one is different from a community composed of both; the subtle interplay of influence one on the other is among the imponderables. To insulate the courtroom from either may not in a given case make an iota of difference. Yet a flavor, a distinct quality is lost if either sex is excluded. The exclusion of one may indeed make the jury less representative of the community than would be true if an economic or racial group were excluded.

3. *Equal protection.* In Weinberger v. Wiesenfeld, 420 U.S. 636 (1975), the Court used equal protection analysis to strike down a section of the Social Security Act entitling a widowed mother, but not a widowed father, to benefits based on the earnings of the deceased spouse. The Court characterized *Frontiero* as standing for the proposition that gender classifications based on "archaic and overbroad [generalizations]" were unconstitutional. The statutory distinction between widows and widowers ran afoul of this principle by assuming "that male workers' earnings are vital to the support of their families, while the earnings of female wage earners do not significantly contribute to their families' support."

Less than a month after *Wiesenfeld,* the Court renewed its attack on "old notions" regarding sex roles as a sufficient justification for gender classifications. A Utah statute required parents to support their male children until age twenty-one, but required support of female children only until age eighteen. In Stanton v. Stanton, 421 U.S. 7 (1975), the Court held that this distinction violated the equal protection clause. The state argued that it was generally the responsibility of men to provide a home, and that they therefore needed a good education before undertaking this task. Women, in contrast, "tend generally to mature physically, emotionally and mentally before boys" and "tend to marry earlier." The Court categorically rejected this justification.

> Notwithstanding the "old notions" to which the [state refers], we perceive nothing rational in the distinction drawn by [the statute]. [No] longer is the female destined solely for the home and the rearing of the family, and only the male for the marketplace and the world of ideas. Women's activities and responsibilities are increasing and expanding.

4. *Unsuccessful challenges to gender classifications.* Although the post-*Reed* period was marked by dramatic advances for opponents of gender classifications, not all of their attacks were successful.

In Kahn v. Shevin, 416 U.S. 351 (1974), for example, the Court sustained a Florida statute providing a property tax exemption for widows but not for widowers. The Court held that the distinction was justified by the greater financial difficulties confronting a lone woman: "Whether from overt discrimination or from the socialization process of a male-dominated culture, the job market is inhospitable to the woman seeking any but the lowest paid jobs."

Similarly, in Schlesinger v. Ballard, 419 U.S. 498 (1975), the Court sustained a federal statute granting women in the Navy a longer period in which to achieve mandatory promotion than men. The Court reasoned that this distinction, unlike those disapproved in *Frontiero* and *Reed,* was not based on "archaic and overbroad generalizations." Rather, it reflected the "demonstrable fact that male and female line officers in the Navy are not similarly situated with respect to opportunities for professional service." Since women were precluded from participating in combat and most sea duty, they would "not generally have compiled records of seagoing service comparable to those of male lieutenants."

Can *Kahn* be distinguished from Reed v. Reed or *Frontiero*? Is the Florida statute an example of gender-conscious affirmative action or does it simply perpetuate stereotypes about the economic division of labor within marriages? This issue is explored further at pages 674-675, infra.

5. *What constitutes a gender-based distinction?* In Geduldig v. Aiello, 417 U.S. 484 (1974), the Court rejected an attack on a California disability insurance program that excluded pregnancy-related disabilities from coverage. The Court held that California's insurance limitation was justified by the state's "legitimate interest in maintaining the self-supporting nature of its insurance program." In a footnote, the Court added that the case was "a far cry from cases like [*Reed*] and [*Frontiero*], involving discrimination based on gender as such. The California insurance program does not exclude anyone from benefit eligibility because of gender but merely removes one physical condition — pregnancy — from the list of compensable disabilities."

Geduldig is one of the few equal protection cases involving a claim of sex discrimination in which the members of the Court disagreed over whether the challenged practice even involved gender-based discrimination. In a footnote, Justice Stewart's opinion for the Court denied that it did:

> Absent a showing that distinctions involving pregnancy are mere pretexts designed to effect an invidious discrimination against the members of one sex or the other, lawmakers are constitutionally free to include or exclude pregnancy from the coverage of legislation such as this on any reasonable basis, just as with respect to any other physical condition.
>
> The lack of identity between the excluded disability and gender as such under this insurance program becomes clear upon the most cursory analysis. The program divides potential recipients into two groups — pregnant women and non-pregnant persons. While the first group is exclusively female, the second includes members of both sexes. The fiscal and actuarial benefits of the program thus accrue to members of both sexes.

In dissent, Justice Brennan noted that under the California plan, "compensation is denied for disabilities suffered in connection with a 'normal' pregnancy — disabilities suffered only by women."

> In my view, by singling out for less favorable treatment a gender-linked disability peculiar to women, the State has created a double standard for disability compensation: a limitation is imposed upon the disabilities for which women workers may recover, while men receive full compensation for all disabilities suffered, including those that affect only or primarily their sex, such as prostatectomies, circumcision, hemophilia, and gout. In effect, one set of rules is applied to females and another to males. Such dissimilar treatment of men and women, on the basis of physical characteristics inextricably linked to one sex, inevitably constitutes sex discrimination.

In Coleman v. Maryland Court of Appeals, 566 U.S. 30 (2012) — a case concerning the sick-leave provision of the Family and Medical Leave Act — Justice Ginsburg, joined by Justices Breyer, Sotomayor, and Kagan, called for *Geduldig* to be overruled:

> First, "[a]s an abstract statement," it is "simply false" that "a classification based on pregnancy is gender-neutral." Rather, discriminating on the basis of pregnancy "[b]y definition . . . discriminates on account of sex; for it is the capacity to become pregnant which primarily differentiates the female from the male." . . .
>
> Second, pregnancy provided a central justification for the historic discrimination against women. . . . Relatedly, discrimination against pregnant employees was often "based not on the pregnancy itself but on predictions concerning the future

behavior of the pregnant woman when her child was born or on views about what her behavior should be." . . .

In sum, childbearing is not only a biological function unique to women. It is also inextricably intertwined with employers' "stereotypical views about women's commitment to work and their value as employees." Because pregnancy discrimination is inevitably sex discrimination, and because discrimination against women is tightly interwoven with society's beliefs about pregnancy and motherhood, I would hold that *Aiello* was egregiously wrong to declare that discrimination on the basis of pregnancy is not discrimination on the basis of sex.

6. *The legacy of* Reed. These mixed results in the period immediately following *Reed* sent confused signals. On the one hand, it was indisputable that the Court had become far more receptive to claims of sex discrimination. It seemed clear as well that, whatever it said in its opinions, the Court was subjecting gender classifications to some form of heightened scrutiny. Yet, on the other hand, the justices went to extraordinary lengths to leave intact prior equal protection doctrine that had supported the old approach. Thus, in *Taylor, Stanley,* and *LaFleur,* the Court managed to overturn gender classifications without any substantial reliance on equal protection analysis. While the Court did resort to equal protection principles in *Reed, Stanton,* and *Wiesenfeld,* it purported to use only low-level, rational basis review to invalidate the challenged statutes. And when confronted with an express invitation to afford heightened scrutiny for gender classifications in *Frontiero,* five justices declined to accept. In the case that follows, the Court for the first time applied heightened review to a gender classification.

Craig v. Boren

429 U.S. 190 (1976)

MR. JUSTICE BRENNAN delivered the opinion of the Court.

The interaction of two sections of an Oklahoma statute prohibits the sale of "nonintoxicating" 3.2% beer to males under the age of 21 and to females under the age of 18. The question to be decided is whether such a gender-based differential constitutes a denial to males 18–20 years of age of the equal protection of the laws in violation of the Fourteenth Amendment. . . .

[Analysis] may appropriately begin with the reminder that *Reed* emphasized that statutory classifications that distinguish between males and females are "subject to scrutiny under the Equal Protection Clause." To withstand constitutional challenge, previous cases establish that classifications by gender must serve important governmental objectives and must be substantially related to achievement of those objectives. Thus, in *Reed,* the objectives of "reducing the workload on probate courts," and "avoiding intrafamily controversy," were deemed of insufficient importance to sustain use of an overt gender criterion in the appointment of administrators of intestate decedents' estates. Decisions following *Reed* similarly have rejected administrative ease and convenience as sufficiently important objectives to justify gender-based classifications.[6] . . .

6. [*Kahn*] and [*Ballard*], upholding the use of gender-based classifications, rested upon the court's perception of the laudatory purposes of those laws as remedying disadvantageous conditions suffered by women in economic and military life. Needless to say, in this case Oklahoma does not suggest that the age-sex differential was enacted to ensure the availability of 3.2% beer for women as compensation for previous deprivations.

We turn then to the question whether, under *Reed*, the difference between males and females with respect to the purchase of 3.2% beer warrants the differential in age drawn by the Oklahoma statute. We conclude that it does not. . . .

We accept for purposes of discussion the District Court's identification of the objective underlying [the statute] as the enhancement of traffic safety. Clearly, the protection of public health and safety represents an important function of state and local governments. However, appellees' statistics in our view cannot support the conclusion that the gender-based distinction closely serves to achieve that objective and therefore the distinction cannot under *Reed* withstand equal protection challenge. . . .

Even [if the statistical evidence offered by the appellees were] accepted as accurate, it nevertheless offers only a weak answer to the equal protection question presented here. The most focused and relevant of the statistical surveys, arrests of 18–20-year-olds for alcohol-related driving offenses, exemplifies the ultimate unpersuasiveness of this evidentiary record. Viewed in terms of the correlation between sex and the actual activity that Oklahoma seeks to regulate — driving while under the influence of alcohol — the statistics broadly establish that .18% of females and 2% of males in that age group are arrested for that offense. While such a disparity is not trivial in a statistical sense, it hardly can form the basis for employment of a gender line as a classifying device. Certainly if maleness is to serve as a proxy for drinking and driving, a correlation of 2% must be considered an unduly tenuous "fit." Indeed, prior cases have consistently rejected the use of sex as a decisionmaking factor even though the statutes in question certainly rested on far more predictive empirical relationships than this.[13] . . .

There is no reason to belabor this line of analysis. It is unrealistic to expect either members of the judiciary or state officials to be well versed in the rigors of experimental or statistical technique. But this merely illustrates that proving broad sociological propositions by statistics is a dubious business, and one that inevitably is in tension with the normative philosophy that underlies the Equal Protection Clause. Suffice to say that the showing offered by the appellees does not satisfy us that sex represents a legitimate, accurate proxy for the regulation of drinking and driving. In fact, when it is further recognized that Oklahoma's statute prohibits only the selling of 3.2% beer to young males and not their drinking the beverage once acquired (even after purchase by their 18–20-year-old female companions), the relationship between gender and traffic safety becomes far too tenuous to satisfy *Reed*'s requirement that the gender-based difference be substantially related to achievement of the statutory objective.

We hold, therefore, that under *Reed*, Oklahoma's 3.2% beer statute invidiously discriminates against males 18–20 years of age. . . .

---

13. For example, we can conjecture that in *Reed*, Idaho's apparent premise that women lacked experience in formal business matters (particularly compared to men) would have proved to be accurate in substantially more than 2% of all cases. And in both *Frontiero* and *Wiesenfeld*, we expressly found appellees' empirical defense of mandatory dependency tests for men but not women to be unsatisfactory, even though we recognized that husbands are still far less likely to be dependent on their wives than vice versa.

MR. JUSTICE POWELL, concurring.

I join the opinion of the Court as I am in general agreement with it. I do have reservations as to some of the discussion concerning the appropriate standard for equal protection analysis and the relevance of the statistical evidence.

Reed and subsequent cases involving gender-based classifications make clear that the Court subjects such classifications to a more critical examination than is normally applied when "fundamental" constitutional rights and "suspect classes" are not present.[*]

I view this as a relatively easy case. No one questions the legitimacy or importance of the asserted governmental objective: the promotion of highway safety. The decision of the case turns on whether the state legislature, by the classification it has chosen, has adopted a means that bears a "fair and substantial relation" to this objective.

It seems to me that the statistics offered by appellees and relied upon by the District Court do tend generally to support the view that young men drive more, possibly are inclined to drink more, and — for various reasons — are involved in more accidents than young women. Even so, I am not persuaded that these facts and the inferences fairly drawn from them justify this classification based on a three-year age differential between the sexes, and especially one that is so easily circumvented as to be virtually meaningless. Putting it differently, this gender-based classification does not bear a fair and substantial relation to the object of the legislation.

MR. JUSTICE STEVENS, concurring.

There is only one Equal Protection Clause. It requires every State to govern impartially. It does not direct the courts to apply one standard of review in some cases and a different standard in other cases. Whatever criticism may be leveled at a judicial opinion implying that there are at least three such standards applies with the same force to a double standard.

I am inclined to believe that what has become known as the two-tiered analysis of equal protection claims does not describe a completely logical method of deciding cases, but rather is a method the Court has employed to explain decisions that actually apply a single standard in a reasonably consistent fashion. I also suspect that a careful explanation of the reasons motivating particular decisions may contribute more to an identification of that standard than an attempt to articulate it in all-encompassing terms. It may therefore be appropriate for me to state the principal reasons which persuaded me to join the Court's opinion.

In this case, the classification is not as obnoxious as some the Court has condemned, nor as inoffensive as some the Court has accepted. It is objectionable because it is based on an accident of birth, because it is a mere remnant of the now almost universally rejected tradition of discriminating against males in this

---

[*] As is evident from our opinions, the Court has had difficulty in agreeing upon a standard of equal protection analysis that can be applied consistently to the wide variety of legislative classifications. There are valid reasons for dissatisfaction with the "two-tier" approach that has been prominent in the Court's decisions in the past decade. Although viewed by many as a result-oriented substitute for more critical analysis, that approach — with its narrowly limited "upper-tier" — now has substantial precedential support. As has been true of *Reed* and its progeny, our decision today will be viewed by some as a "middle-tier" approach. While I would not endorse that characterization and would not welcome a further subdividing of equal protection analysis, candor compels the recognition that the relatively deferential "rational basis" standard of review normally applied takes on a sharper focus when we address a gender-based classification. So much is clear from our recent cases. . . .

age bracket, and because, to the extent it reflects any physical difference between males and females, it is actually perverse.[4] The question then is whether the traffic safety justification put forward by the State is sufficient to make an otherwise offensive classification acceptable.

The classification is not totally irrational. For the evidence does indicate that there are more males than females in this age bracket who drive and also more who drink. Nevertheless, there are several reasons why I regard the justification as unacceptable. It is difficult to believe that the statute was actually intended to cope with the problem of traffic safety, since it has only a minimal effect on access to a not very intoxicating beverage and does not prohibit its consumption. Moreover, the empirical data submitted by the State accentuate the unfairness of treating all 18–20-year-old males as inferior to their female counterparts. The legislation imposes a restraint on 100% of the males in the class allegedly because about 2% of them have probably violated one or more laws relating to the consumption of alcoholic beverages. It is unlikely that this law will have a significant deterrent effect either on that 2% or on the law-abiding 98%. But even assuming some such slight benefit, it does not seem to me that an insult to all of the young men of the State can be justified by visiting the sins of the 2% on the 98%.

[Concurring opinions by Justices Stewart and Blackmun and a dissenting opinion by Chief Justice Burger are omitted.]

MR. JUSTICE REHNQUIST, dissenting.

The Court's disposition of this case is objectionable on two grounds. First is its conclusion that *men* challenging a gender-based statute which treats them less favorably than women may invoke a more stringent standard of judicial review than pertains to most other types of classifications. Second is the Court's enunciation of this standard, without citation to any source, as being that "classifications by gender must serve *important* governmental objectives and must be *substantially* related to achievement of those objectives." The only redeeming feature of the Court's opinion, to my mind, is that it apparently signals a retreat by those who joined the plurality opinion in [*Frontiero*] from their view that sex is a "suspect" classification for purposes of equal protection analysis. I think the Oklahoma statute challenged here need pass only the "rational basis" equal protection analysis. . . .

Most obviously unavailable to support any kind of special scrutiny in this case, is a history or pattern of past discrimination, such as was relied on by the plurality in *Frontiero* to support its invocation of strict scrutiny. There is no suggestion in the Court's opinion that males in this age group are in any way peculiarly disadvantaged, subject to systematic discriminatory treatment, or otherwise in need of special solicitude from the courts. . . .

The Court's conclusion that a law which treats males less favorably than females "must serve important governmental objectives and must be substantially related to achievement of those objectives" apparently comes out of thin air. The Equal Protection Clause contains no such language, and none of our previous cases adopt that standard. I would think we have had enough difficulty with the two standards of review which our cases have recognized — the norm of "rational basis," and the "compelling state interest" required where a "suspect classification" is involved — so as to counsel weightily against the insertion of still another

4. Because males are generally heavier than females, they have a greater capacity to consume alcohol without impairing their driving ability than do females.

"standard" between those two. How is this Court to divine what objectives are important? How is it to determine whether a particular law is "substantially" related to the achievement of such objective, rather than related in some other way to its achievement? Both of the phrases used are so diaphanous and elastic as to invite subjective judicial preferences or prejudices relating to particular types of legislation, masquerading as judgments whether such legislation is directed at "important" objectives or, whether the relationship to those objectives is "substantial" enough. . . .

The Court "accept[s] for purposes of discussion" the District Court's finding that the purpose of the provisions in question was traffic safety, and proceeds to examine the statistical evidence in the record in order to decide if "the gender-based distinction *closely* serves to achieve that objective." [One] need not immerse oneself in the fine points of statistical analysis, however, in order to see the weaknesses in the Court's attempted denigration of the evidence at hand.

One survey of arrest statistics assembled in 1973 indicated that males in the 18–20 age group were arrested for "driving under the influence" almost 18 times as often as their female counterparts, and for "drunkenness" in a ratio of almost 10 to 1. Accepting, as the Court does, appellants' comparison of the total figures with 1973 Oklahoma census data, this survey indicates a 2% arrest rate among males in the age group, as compared to a .18% rate among females. . . .

The Court's criticism of the statistics relied on by the District Court conveys the impression that a legislature in enacting a new law is to be subjected to the judicial equivalent of a doctoral examination in statistics. Legislatures are not held to any rules of evidence such as those which may govern courts or other administrative bodies, and are entitled to draw factual conclusions on the basis of the determination of probable cause which an arrest by a police officer normally represents. In this situation, they could reasonably infer that the incidence of drunk driving is a good deal higher than the incidence of arrest.

And while, [such] statistics may be distorted as a result of stereotyping, the legislature is not required to prove before a court that its statistics are perfect. In any event, if stereotypes are as pervasive as the Court suggests, they may in turn influence the conduct of the men and women in question, and cause the young men to conform to the wild and reckless image which is their stereotype. . . .

[The] Court notes that only 2% of males (as against .18% of females) in the age group were arrested for drunk driving, and that this very low figure establishes "an unduly tenuous 'fit'" between maleness and drunk driving in the 18–20-year-old group. On this point the Court misconceives the nature of the equal protection inquiry. . . .

[The] clearest demonstration of this is the fact that the precise argument made by the Court would be equally applicable to a flat bar on such purchases by *anyone*, male or female, in the 18–20 age group. . . . What the Court's argument is relevant to is not equal protection, but due process — whether there are enough persons in the category who drive while drunk to justify a bar against purchases by all members of the group. . . .

Note: *Heightened Scrutiny for Gender Classifications?*

1. *The relevance of heightened scrutiny.* Since *Craig*, the Court has not been altogether consistent in how it articulates the appropriate standard of review in gender discrimination cases. For example, in Michael M. v. Sonoma County

Superior Court, page 664, infra, Justice Rehnquist, writing for a plurality of the Court, propounded a seemingly less stringent test: "[This] Court has consistently upheld statutes where the gender classification is not invidious, but rather realistically reflects the fact that the sexes are not similarly situated in certain circumstances." On the other hand, in United States v. Virginia, pages 654-661, infra, Justice Ginsburg, writing for the Court, announced a seemingly more stringent test: "[The] reviewing court must determine whether the proffered justification is 'exceedingly persuasive.' The burden of justification is demanding and it rests entirely on the State." As you read the material that follows, consider the extent to which the standard of review makes a difference. Is the Court evaluating fact situations under a predetermined standard of review, or is it manipulating the standard of review so as to justify a predetermined result?

To what extent is the pressure for an "intermediate" tier of scrutiny simply a product of the solidifying in the previous decade of a two-tiered structure treating racial classification as subject to a different test than virtually all other classifications? That is, once there are two tiers of scrutiny and the outcome seems to depend primarily on the tier into which a classification is placed, does this create a strong pressure for creating additional tiers?

2. *Arguments for heightened scrutiny.* Assuming that racial classifications require heightened scrutiny, are there persuasive reasons to accord gender classifications similar treatment? Consider the following possibilities:

a. *Original understandings.* In The Slaughter-House Cases, Justice Miller began his consideration of the fourteenth amendment by observing that its "one pervading purpose" was "the freedom of the slave race, the security and firm establishment of that freedom, and the protection of the newly-made freeman and citizen from the oppressions of those who had formerly exercised unlimited dominion over him." Is there anything in the history of the fourteenth amendment that provides analogous support for heightened scrutiny of gender classifications? Consider the following observations made by Justice O'Connor:

> The Civil War and the emancipation of former slaves brought the suffrage question to the forefront. If newly freed blacks were to be guaranteed the same civil rights, including suffrage, as all other citizens, there was no reason that women should not also be swept up by the momentum and included in the resulting expansion of the right to vote. The reformers were in for quite a shock, however. The draft of the Fourteenth Amendment, introduced into Congress in 1866, sought to incorporate an unprecedented gender restriction into the Constitution. The draft declared that the right to vote should not be "denied to any of the male inhabitants" of a state.
>
> The reformers realized that if this proposal were adopted, yet another constitutional amendment would be required to give women the right to vote in federal elections. Elizabeth Cady Stanton recognized what a monumental task securing such an amendment would be. She believed that the women's suffrage movement would be set back a full century if the proposal were adopted. In fact, she was not far wrong: it took another sixty years. The Fourteenth Amendment, which includes the word "male" not once but three times, was ratified in July 1868. The Fifteenth Amendment, which followed less than two years later, also failed to provide the suffragists with any cause for optimism. It decreed that no citizen could be denied the right to vote because of "race, color or previous condition of servitude," but made no mention of gender. Taken together, the Fourteenth and Fifteenth Amendments caused women to wonder if they were indeed fully citizens of the United States.

O'Connor, The History of the Women's Suffrage Movement, 49 Vand. L. Rev. 657, 660–661 (1996). As a result of their concern with section 2's provision requiring the reduction of representation in the House of Representatives for states that "denied [the right to vote] to any of the male inhabitants of such State, being twenty-one years of age, and citizens of the United States," infuriated feminists, such as Susan B. Anthony and Elizabeth Cady Stanton, actually worked to defeat the fourteenth amendment. See E. Flexner, Century of Struggle 146–148 (1975); A. Keyssar, The Right to Vote: The Contested History of Democracy in the United States 172–223 (2000).

Even apart from the history surrounding section 2 of the fourteenth amendment, it is hard to make the case that the framers had any intention of bringing into question laws that discriminated on the basis of gender. As Justice Ginsburg wrote in an article published before her appointment to the Court:

> Boldly dynamic interpretation, departing radically from the original understanding, is required to tie to the fourteenth amendment's equal protection clause a command that government treat men and women as individuals equal in rights, responsibilities, and opportunities. . . .
> When the post–Civil War amendments were added to the Constitution, women were not accorded the vote. [Married] women in many states could not contract, hold property, litigate on their own behalf, or even control their own earnings. The fourteenth amendment left all that untouched.?

Ginsburg, Sexual Equality under the Fourteenth and Equal Rights Amendments, 1979 Wash. U. L.Q. 161, 161–163. In a similar vein, Justice Scalia, asked whether "we've gone off in error by applying the 14th Amendment" to sex discrimination, responded: "Yes, yes. Sorry, to tell you that. . . . But, you know, if indeed the current society has come to different views, that's fine. You do not need the Constitution to reflect the wishes of the current society. Certainly the Constitution does not require discrimination on the basis of sex. The only issue is whether it prohibits it. It doesn't. Nobody ever thought that that's what it meant. Nobody ever voted for that. If the current society wants to outlaw discrimination by sex, hey we have things called legislatures, and they enact things called laws. You don't need a constitution to keep things up-to-date. All you need is a legislature and a ballot box." The Originalist, Cal. Law., Jan. 2011, at 33.

b. *Arguments by analogy.* Even if the framers of the equal protection clause did not specifically intend to ban gender discrimination, might the clause be read to require a special burden of justification for classifications that are similar in relevant respects to racial classifications? Does gender discrimination satisfy this test? For example, should gender discrimination be treated like racial discrimination because it is based on "a trait that is immutable and highly visible" and therefore "lends itself to a system of thought dominated by stereotype, which automatically consigns an individual to a general category [often] implying the inferiority of the person so categorized"? Karst, Foreword: Equal Citizenship under the Fourteenth Amendment, 91 Harv. L. Rev. 1, 23 (1977). Because the pervasive nature of sexual stereotypes and the historical subjugation of women make gender "like" race for purposes of the equal protection clause? Because women, like blacks, are effectively excluded from the political process?

For a criticism of the Court's reliance on the race analogy, see Siegel, She the People: The Nineteenth Amendment, Sex Equality, Federalism, and the Family, 115 Harv. L. Rev. 949, 960 (2002). Siegel argues that seeing gender discrimination through the lens of race

> [obscures] the extent to which gender status regulation had its own constitutional and common law history and distinctive social forms. Doctrinal effacement of this history [has] two important consequences. By enjoining sex discrimination on the ground that it resembled race discrimination prohibited by the Fourteenth Amendment, the Court suggested that the new body of sex discrimination doctrine lacked independent grounding in our constitutional history. At the same time, the Court's effort to reason by analogy deflected attention from the ways that race and gender status regulation intersect and [differ].

Instead of focusing on the fourteenth amendment alone, Siegel advocates a "synthetic" approach that reads the fourteenth amendment against the backdrop of the struggle to attain women's suffrage, which culminated in the nineteenth amendment. (For a more general defense of an approach that attempts to integrate language from different parts of the constitutional text, see Amar, Intratextualism, 112 Harv. L. Rev. 748 (1999).)

Of course, on its face, the nineteenth amendment does no more than guarantee women the right to vote. But Siegel argues that its adoption constituted a rejection of two interrelated arguments: that men adequately represented women within the family, and that the family, as so understood, was immune from federal regulation. Rejection of these arguments, in turn, should be read back into the fourteenth amendment conception of equality.

Given that the language of the nineteenth amendment more nearly tracks the language of the fifteenth amendment, which has been given an extremely narrow reading (protecting against racial discrimination only with respect to formal participation in the political process and not even reaching questions of vote dilution), does reading the nineteenth amendment in tandem with the fourteenth amendment instead raise interpretive problems?

c. *"Archaic" gender distinctions.* Should gender distinctions be subject to heightened scrutiny when they are "archaic"? Consider J. Ely, Democracy and Distrust 167 (1980):

> [Most] laws classifying by sex weren't passed this morning or even the day before yesterday: in fact, it is rare to see a gender-based classification enacted since the New Deal. In general, women couldn't even vote until the Nineteenth Amendment was ratified in 1920, and most of these laws probably predate even that: they should be invalidated.

Compare *Michael M.*, in which the Court upheld California's statutory rape law making men, but not women, criminally liable for acts of sexual intercourse involving a female under age eighteen. In a footnote to his plurality opinion, Justice Rehnquist noted that the California legislature had recently rejected a proposal to make the statute sex-neutral.

> That is enough to answer petitioner's contention that the statute was the "accidental byproduct of a traditional way of thinking about females." Certainly this decision of

the California Legislature is as good a source as is this Court in deciding what is "current" and what is "outmoded" in the perception of women.

d. *The problem of overgeneralization.* Can heightened scrutiny of even modern statutes be defended on the ground that gender classifications pose a peculiar risk of unthinking overgeneralization?

Consider the suggestion in Mississippi University for Women v. Hogan, 458 U.S. 718 (1982), that a skeptical attitude toward gender classifications is designed to ensure that government action is "determined through reasoned analysis rather than through the mechanical application of traditional, often inaccurate assertions about the proper roles of men and women." Under this view, judicial inspection of the means/ends connection and the substantiality of the state's interest is intended to ensure that such "reasoned analysis" is in fact at work.

3. *Gender segregation.* As the preceding discussion suggests, gender classifications are like racial classifications in some respects but different in others. Does the intermediate scrutiny announced in *Craig* therefore represent a sensible compromise, recognizing that the analogy has force in some contexts but not in others? In what contexts is the analogy inappropriate?

Consider in this connection the problem of gender segregation. In some situations, gender segregation is relatively uncontroversial:

> [The] primary evil of [racial segregation] was that [it] designedly and effectively marked off all black persons as degraded, dirty, less than fully developed persons who were unfit for full membership in the political, social, and moral community. [It] is worth observing that the social realities of sexually segregated bathrooms appear to be different. [There] is no notion of the possibility of contamination from use; or [of] inferiority or superiority. What seems to be involved — at least in part — is the importance of inculcating and preserving a sense of secrecy concerning the genitalia of the opposite sex.

R. Wasserstrom, Philosophy and Social Issues 21 (1980).

Is the analogy between gender and racial segregation more persuasive in other settings? In Mississippi University for Women v. Hogan, supra, the Court struck down the exclusion of men from the University's school of nursing, stating that "excluding males from admission to the School of Nursing tends to perpetuate the stereotyped view of nursing as an exclusively woman's job." The Court was careful to note, however, that it was not ruling on the constitutionality of the exclusion of males from other schools in the Mississippi University for Women or on the permissibility of a general policy of "separate but equal" education for men and women.

After *Hogan,* could the Mississippi University for Women establish an all-female school of mechanical engineering? Could it create two schools of nursing, each one sex-segregated (so that its maintenance of an all-female school did not deny anyone the ability to study nursing at the University)? The Court threw some light on these questions in United States v. Virginia, a case considered in more detail in the following section. Are state-supported, sexually segregated athletic programs unconstitutional because they reinforce stereotypes concerning women's athletic ability? Would integrated programs be unconstitutional because they fail to take account of differences between men and women and might therefore deny women an equal chance to participate?

3.   Archaic and Overbroad Generalizations versus "Real" Differences

In the cases decided since *Craig*, the Court has attempted to assimilate the analysis of gender discrimination into its basic equal protection methodology. Thus, it has looked (albeit with heightened scrutiny) to see whether a law or policy treats men and women differently. If it does, it has asked whether the difference in treatment corresponds to a relevant difference between the genders.

As applied to gender discrimination, this methodology has been criticized on a number of grounds. Some critics have complained that the differences between men and women that the Court has relied on to justify different treatment are not "natural" or inevitable. Instead, they are "constructed" by the very legal regime that they are used to defend. Others have argued that the Court's insistence on "facial" or "formal" equality has harmed women by ignoring important differences between the genders. Treating men and women identically is said to hold women to an implicitly male standard. Still others have complained that the preoccupation with "sameness" and "difference" is diversionary and that the Court should instead focus on fundamental power imbalances between the genders. On this view, constitutional doctrine should be reformulated so as to end male domination.

As you read the following material, consider which, if any, of these criticisms is valid. Has the Court responded to the most serious obstacles to gender equality? Is such a response possible from within standard constitutional methodology?

United States v. Virginia
518 U.S. 515 (1996)

JUSTICE GINSBURG delivered the opinion of the Court.

Virginia's public institutions of higher learning include an incomparable military college, Virginia Military Institute (VMI). The United States maintains that the Constitution's equal protection guarantee precludes Virginia from reserving exclusively to men the unique educational opportunities VMI affords. We agree.

I

Founded in 1839, VMI is today the sole single-sex school among Virginia's 15 public institutions of higher learning. VMI's distinctive mission is to produce "citizen-soldiers," men prepared for leadership in civilian life and in military service. VMI pursues this mission through pervasive training of a kind not available anywhere else in Virginia. Assigning prime place to character development, VMI uses an "adversative method" modeled on English public schools and once characteristic of military instruction. . . .

VMI has notably succeeded in its mission to produce leaders; among its alumni are military generals, Members of Congress, and business executives. The school's alumni overwhelmingly perceive that their VMI training helped them to realize their personal goals. VMI's endowment reflects the loyalty of its graduates; VMI has the largest per-student endowment of all undergraduate institutions in the Nation. . . .

II

A

VMI produces its "citizen-soldiers" through "an adversative, or doubting, model of education" which features "physical rigor, mental stress, absolute equality of treatment, absence of privacy, minute regulation of behavior, and indoctrination in desirable values." . . .

VMI cadets live in spartan barracks where surveillance is constant and privacy nonexistent; they wear uniforms, eat together in the mess hall, and regularly participate in drills. Entering students are incessantly exposed to the rat line, "an extreme form of the adversative model," comparable in intensity to Marine Corps boot camp. Tormenting and punishing, the rat line bonds new cadets to their fellow sufferers and, when they have completed the 7-month experience, to their former tormentors. . . .

[In 1990, the United States sued Virginia and VMI, alleging that VMI's admission policy violated the equal protection clause. At the conclusion of a trial, the district court found that "some women, at least" would want to attend VMI and were capable of all the activities required of VMI cadets. The district court nonetheless ruled in favor of VMI. The court acknowledged that women were denied a unique education opportunity available only at VMI, but held that if women were admitted, "some aspects of the [school's] distinctive method would be altered." Specifically, allowance for personal privacy would have to be made, physical education requirements would have to be altered, and the adversative environment could not survive unmodified. The court found that these changes would impinge on the state interest in diversity in public education.

The court of appeals reversed, holding that "neither the goal of producing citizen soldiers nor VMI's implementing methodology is inherently unsuitable to women." It remanded the case to the district court for purposes of selecting a remedy.]

C

In response to the Fourth Circuit's ruling, Virginia proposed a parallel program for women: Virginia Women's Institute for Leadership (VWIL). The 4-year, state-sponsored undergraduate program would be located at Mary Baldwin College, a private liberal arts school for women, and would be open, initially, to about 25 to 30 students. Although VWIL would share VMI's mission — to produce "citizen-soldiers" — the VWIL program would differ, as does Mary Baldwin College, from VMI in academic offerings, methods of education, and financial resources.

The average combined SAT score of entrants at Mary Baldwin is about 100 points lower than the score for VMI freshmen. Mary Baldwin's faculty holds "significantly fewer Ph.D.'s than the faculty at VMI," and receives significantly lower salaries. While VMI offers degrees in liberal arts, the sciences, and engineering, Mary Baldwin, at the time of trial, offered only bachelor of arts degrees. A VWIL student seeking to earn an engineering degree could gain one, without public support, by attending Washington University in St. Louis, Missouri, for two years, paying the required private tuition.

Experts in educating women at the college level composed the Task Force charged with designing the VWIL program; Task Force members were drawn from Mary Baldwin's own faculty and staff. Training its attention on methods of instruction appropriate for "most women," the Task Force determined that a military model would be "wholly inappropriate" for VWIL. . . .

In lieu of VMI's adversative method, the VWIL Task Force favored "a cooperative method which reinforces self-esteem." In addition to the standard bachelor of arts program offered at Mary Baldwin, VWIL students would take courses in leadership, complete an off-campus leadership externship, participate in community service projects, and assist in arranging a speaker series.

Virginia represented that it will provide equal financial support for in-state VWIL students and VMI cadets, and the VMI Foundation agreed to supply a $5.4625 million endowment for the VWIL program. Mary Baldwin's own endowment is about $19 million; VMI's is $131 million. Mary Baldwin will add $35 million to its endowment based on future commitments; VMI will add $220 million. The VMI Alumni Association has developed a network of employers interested in hiring VMI graduates. The Association has agreed to open its network to VWIL graduates, but those graduates will not have the advantage afforded by a VMI degree. . . .

D

[The district court approved this remedial plan, and the court of appeals affirmed.] . . .

IV

[Parties] who seek to defend gender-based government action must demonstrate an "exceedingly persuasive justification" for that action. . . .

[The] burden of justification is demanding and it rests entirely on the State. The State must show "at least that the [challenged] classification serves 'important governmental objectives and that the discriminatory means employed' are 'substantially related to the achievement of those objectives.'" The justification must be genuine, not hypothesized or invented post hoc in response to litigation. And it must not rely on overbroad generalizations about the different talents, capacities, or preferences of males and females.

The heightened review standard our precedent establishes does not make sex a proscribed classification. Supposed "inherent differences" are no longer accepted as a ground for race or national origin classifications. See Loving v. Virginia. Physical differences between men and women, however, are enduring. . . .

"Inherent differences" between men and women, we have come to appreciate, remain cause for celebration, but not for denigration of the members of either sex or for artificial constraints on an individual's opportunity. Sex classifications may be used to compensate women "for particular economic disabilities [they have] suffered," to "promote equal employment opportunity," to advance full development of the talent and capacities of our Nation's people. But such classifications may not be used, as they once were, to create or perpetuate the legal, social, and economic inferiority of women.

Measuring the record in this case against the review standard just described, we conclude that Virginia has shown no "exceedingly persuasive justification" for excluding all women from the citizen-soldier training afforded by VMI. We therefore affirm the Fourth Circuit's initial judgment, which held that Virginia had violated the Fourteenth Amendment's Equal Protection Clause. Because the remedy proffered by Virginia — the Mary Baldwin VWIL program — does not cure the constitutional violation, i.e., it does not provide equal opportunity, we reverse the Fourth Circuit's final judgment in this case.

V

[Virginia] asserts two justifications in defense of VMI's exclusion of women. First, the Commonwealth contends, "single-sex education provides important educational benefits," and the option of single-sex education contributes to "diversity in educational approaches." Second, the Commonwealth argues, "the unique VMI method of character development and leadership training," the school's adversative approach, would have to be modified were VMI to admit women. We consider these two justifications in turn.

A

Single-sex education affords pedagogical benefits to at least some students, Virginia emphasizes, and that reality is uncontested in this litigation. Similarly, it is not disputed that diversity among public educational institutions can serve the public good. But Virginia has not shown that VMI was established, or has been maintained, with a view to diversifying, by its categorical exclusion of women, educational opportunities within the State. In cases of this genre, . . . a tenable justification must describe actual state purposes, not rationalizations for actions in fact differently grounded. . . .

B

Virginia next argues that VMI's adversative method of training provides educational benefits that cannot be made available, unmodified, to women. Alterations to accommodate women would necessarily be "radical," so "drastic," Virginia asserts, as to transform, indeed "destroy," VMI's program. . . .

[It] is uncontested that women's admission would require accommodations, primarily in arranging housing assignments and physical training programs for female cadets. It is also undisputed, however, that "the VMI methodology could be used to educate women." ["Some] women," the expert testimony established, "are capable of all of the individual activities required of VMI cadets." The parties, furthermore, agree that "some women can meet the physical standards [VMI] now imposes on men." . . .

It may be assumed, for purposes of this decision, that most women would not choose VMI's adversative method. As Fourth Circuit Judge Motz observed, however, in her dissent from the Court of Appeals' denial of rehearing en banc, it is also probable that "many men would not want to be educated in such an environment." (On that point, even our dissenting colleague might agree.) [The] question is whether the State can constitutionally deny to women who have the will and capacity, the training and attendant opportunities that VMI uniquely affords.

The notion that admission of women would downgrade VMI's stature, destroy the adversative system and, with it, even the school, is a judgment hardly proved, a prediction hardly different from other "self-fulfilling prophecies," once routinely used to deny rights or opportunities. When women first sought admission to the bar and access to legal education, concerns of the same order were expressed. For example, in 1876, the Court of Common Pleas of Hennepin County, Minnesota, explained why women were thought ineligible for the practice of law. Women train and educate the young, the court said, which "forbids that they shall bestow that time (early and late) and labor, so essential in attaining to the eminence to which the true lawyer should ever aspire. It cannot therefore be said that the opposition of courts to the admission of females to practice . . . is to any extent the outgrowth of . . . 'old fogyism[.]' . . . It arises rather from a comprehension of the magnitude of the responsibilities connected with the successful practice of law, and a desire to grade up the profession." A like fear, according to a 1925 report, accounted for Columbia Law School's resistance to women's admission, although

> the faculty . . . never maintained that women could not master legal learning. . . . No, its argument has been . . . more practical. If women were admitted to the Columbia Law School, [the faculty] said, then the choicer, more manly and red-blooded graduates of our great universities would go to the Harvard Law School! . . .

Women's successful entry into the federal military academies, and their participation in the Nation's military forces, indicate that Virginia's fears for the future of VMI may not be solidly grounded. The State's justification for excluding all women from "citizen-soldier" training for which some are qualified, in any event, cannot rank as "exceedingly persuasive," as we have explained and applied that standard. . . .

The State's misunderstanding . . . is apparent from VMI's mission: to produce "citizen-soldiers," individuals "imbued with love of learning, confident in the functions and attitudes of leadership, possessing a high sense of public service, advocates of the American democracy and free enterprise system, and ready . . . to defend their country in time of national peril."

Surely that goal is great enough to accommodate women, who today count as citizens in our American democracy equal in stature to men. Just as surely, the State's great goal is not substantially advanced by women's categorical exclusion, in total disregard of their individual merit, from the State's premier "citizen-soldier" corps. Virginia, in sum, "has fallen far short of establishing the 'exceedingly persuasive justification,'" that must be the solid base for any gender-defined classification.

VI . . .

A

[V]irginia chose not to eliminate, but to leave untouched, VMI's exclusionary policy. For women only, however, Virginia proposed a separate program, different in kind from VMI and unequal in tangible and intangible facilities. Having violated the Constitution's equal protection requirement, Virginia was obliged to show that its remedial proposal "directly addressed and related to" the violation, i.e., the equal protection denied to women ready, willing, and able to benefit from educational opportunities of the kind VMI offers. . . .

VWIL affords women no opportunity to experience the rigorous military training for which VMI is famed. Instead, the VWIL program "deemphasizes" military education, and uses a "cooperative method" of education "which reinforces self-esteem." . . .

Virginia maintains that these methodological differences are "justified pedagogically," based on "important differences between men and women in learning and developmental needs," "psychological and sociological differences" Virginia describes as "real" and "not stereotypes." . . .

As earlier stated, generalizations about "the way women are," estimates of what is appropriate for most women, no longer justify denying opportunity to women whose talent and capacity place them outside the average description. Notably, Virginia never asserted that VMI's method of education suits most men. It is also revealing that Virginia accounted for its failure to make the VWIL experience "the entirely militaristic experience of VMI" on the ground that VWIL "is planned for women who do not necessarily expect to pursue military careers." By that reasoning, VMI's "entirely militaristic" program would be inappropriate for men in general or as a group, for "only about 15% of VMI cadets enter career military service."[19] . . .

B

In myriad respects other than military training, VWIL does not qualify as VMI's equal. VWIL's student body, faculty, course offerings, and facilities hardly match VMI's. Nor can the VWIL graduate anticipate the benefits associated with VMI's 157-year history, the school's prestige, and its influential alumni network. . . .

Virginia, in sum, while maintaining VMI for men only, has failed to provide any "comparable single-gender women's institution." Instead, the Commonwealth has created a VWIL program fairly appraised as a "pale shadow" of VMI in terms of the range of curricular choices and faculty stature, funding, prestige, alumni support and influence.

Virginia's VWIL solution is reminiscent of the remedy Texas proposed 50 years ago, in response to a state trial court's 1946 ruling that, given the equal protection guarantee, African Americans could not be denied a legal education at a state facility. See Sweatt v. Painter. Reluctant to admit African Americans to its flagship University of Texas Law School, the State set up a separate school for Herman Sweatt and other black law students. . . .

More important than the tangible features, the [Sweatt] Court emphasized, are "those qualities which are incapable of objective measurement but which make for greatness" in a school, including "reputation of the faculty, experience of the administration, position and influence of the alumni, standing in the community, traditions and prestige." Facing the marked differences reported in the Sweatt opinion, the Court unanimously ruled that Texas had not shown "substantial equality in the [separate] educational opportunities" the State offered. Accordingly, the Court held, the Equal Protection Clause required Texas to admit African Americans to the University of Texas Law School. In line with Sweatt, we rule here that Virginia has not shown substantial equality in the separate educational opportunities the State supports at VWIL and VMI. . . .

19. Admitting women to VMI would undoubtedly require alterations necessary to afford members of each sex privacy from the other sex in living arrangements, and to adjust aspects of the physical training programs. [Experience] shows such adjustments are manageable. [Relocated footnote. — EDS.]

JUSTICE THOMAS took no part in the consideration or decision of this case.

CHIEF JUSTICE REHNQUIST, concurring in the judgment.

The Court holds first that Virginia violates the Equal Protection Clause by maintaining [VMI's] all-male admissions policy, and second that establishing the [VWIL] program does not remedy that violation. While I agree with these conclusions, I disagree with the Court's analysis and so I write separately.

I

Two decades ago in Craig v. Boren, we announced that "to withstand constitutional challenge, . . . classifications by gender must serve important governmental objectives and must be substantially related to achievement of those objectives." We have adhered to that standard of scrutiny ever since. While the majority adheres to this test today, it also says that the State must demonstrate an "exceedingly persuasive justification" to support a gender-based classification. It is unfortunate that the Court thereby introduces an element of uncertainty respecting the appropriate test.

While terms like "important governmental objective" and "substantially related" are hardly models of precision, they have more content and specificity than does the phrase "exceedingly persuasive justification." That phrase is best confined, as it was first used, as an observation on the difficulty of meeting the applicable test, not as a formulation of the test itself. . . .

II

An adequate remedy in my opinion might be a demonstration by Virginia that its interest in educating men in a single-sex environment is matched by its interest in educating women in a single-sex institution. To demonstrate such, the State does not need to create two institutions with the same number of faculty PhD's, similar SAT scores, or comparable athletic fields. Nor would it necessarily require that the women's institution offer the same curriculum as the men's; one could be strong in computer science, the other could be strong in liberal arts. It would be a sufficient remedy, I think, if the two institutions offered the same quality of education and were of the same overall calibre.

If a state decides to create single-sex programs, the state would, I expect, consider the public's interest and demand in designing curricula. And rightfully so. But the state should avoid assuming demand based on stereotypes; it must not assume a priori, without evidence, that there would be no interest in a women's school of civil engineering, or in a men's school of nursing.

In the end, the women's institution Virginia proposes, VWIL, fails as a remedy, because it is distinctly inferior to the existing men's institution and will continue to be for the foreseeable future. VWIL simply is not, in any sense, the institution that VMI is. . . . I therefore ultimately agree with the Court that Virginia has not provided an adequate remedy.

JUSTICE SCALIA, dissenting.

Today the Court shuts down an institution that has served the people of the Commonwealth of Virginia with pride and distinction for over a century and a half. . . .

Much of the Court's opinion is devoted to deprecating the closed-mindedness of our forebears with regard to women's education, and even with regard to the treatment of women in areas that have nothing to do with education. Closed-minded they were — as every age is, including our own, with regard to matters it cannot guess, because it simply does not consider them debatable. The virtue of a democratic system with a First Amendment is that it readily enables the people, over time, to be persuaded that what they took for granted is not so, and to change their laws accordingly. That system is destroyed if the smug assurances of each age are removed from the democratic process and written into the Constitution. So to counterbalance the Court's criticism of our ancestors, let me say a word in their praise: they left us free to change. The same cannot be said of this most illiberal Court, which has embarked on a course of inscribing one after another of the current preferences of the society (and in some cases only the counter-majoritarian preferences of the society's law-trained elite) into our Basic Law. Today it enshrines the notion that no substantial educational value is to be served by an all-men's military academy — so that the decision by the people of Virginia to maintain such an institution denies equal protection to women who cannot attend that institution but can attend others. Since it is entirely clear that the Constitution of the United States — the old one — takes no sides in this educational debate, I dissent. . . .

Note: "Real Differences" and Formal Equality

1. *Integration or "separate but equal"?* As the *Virginia* Court acknowledges, only a small number of women are likely to benefit from the education VMI provides. Is the cause of gender equality significantly advanced by giving an opportunity to these women? Would the "separate but equal" approach suggested by Chief Justice Rehnquist's opinion do more or less to benefit women?

Virginia raises difficult questions about the extent to which the cause of gender equality is advanced by insisting on formally equal treatment. On the one hand, *Virginia* vindicates the right of individual women to be judged by the same standard used to judge men. It does so by refusing to permit the state to generalize about men and women as a group. On the other, to the extent that these generalizations are accurate, the decision leaves women as a group vulnerable to standards created for men. Notice in this regard that *Virginia* does not cast constitutional doubt on the "adversative" model itself.

In contrast to the majority's approach, Chief Justice Rehnquist would use VMI's policy as a lever to extract from the state resources that might provide a better education to a larger group of women. In doing so, however, he would provide no remedy for individual women who might benefit from adversative training. Moreover, his approach arguably leaves intact gender stereotypes that reinforce existing gender roles. Which approach better promotes gender equality?

In Hasday, The Principle and Practice of Women's "Full Citizenship": A Case Study of Sex-Segregated Public Education, 101 Mich. L. Rev. 755, 757–758 (2002), the author points out that sex-segregated public education has "historically been entangled in both racial and class stratification" and suggests that "a decisionmaker regulating single-sex public schools [would] be well-advised to consider whether some or all of those schools have different consequences for different groups of women." The author also argues that historically "the differences [between] sex-segregated and coeducational public education [may be] relatively unimportant in terms of their substantive impact on women's status." If this remains true, "it is hard to see why a jurisprudence committed to women's 'full citizenship' would want to emphasize form by absolutely prohibiting sex-segregated public schooling, or how transferring all public school students to coeducational schools would advance women's 'full citizenship stature' and fight their 'inferiority.'"

Virginia involves an institution of higher education. Would a different analysis apply to single-sex K–12 schools? In this light, consider the observation made in Simson, Separate But Equal and Single-Sex Schools, 90 Cornell L. Rev. 443, 456 (2005), that single-sex schools at the middle- or high-school level

> can be explained in terms that do not so obviously incorporate harmful gender stereotypes — that is, as an attempt to respond to special problems widely experienced by adolescent girls and as providing an environment in which teaching methods can most easily be tailored to ways of learning that girls generally seem to find most congenial. These explanations, however, are not unambiguously affirming of girls' abilities and potential, and altogether it is difficult to deny that there is some risk that the creation of the girls school sends a message to both girls and boys that girls are in some sense inferior to boys — whether that means more needy, less adaptable, more fragile, or some other disempowering comparative generalization.

2. *The role of gender in law school and other facially neutral institutions.* Kornhauser found significant gender segregation within law school faculties, finding that nearly 80 percent of courses had "a disproportionate number of men or women teaching the subject as compared to the gender composition of all law school professors" and that this disparity had increased over time:

> Courses with a female disparity — such as Juvenile Law, Poverty Law, and Legal Writing and Research — generally fit within a typical gender schema of "feminine." These courses are less central to the core of law and law school, less prestigious, and often associated with traditionally female traits such as care and relationships. Similarly, men are over-concentrated in the most traditional, and hence most "masculine," courses such as Constitutional Law, Evidence, Corporations, and Government Contracts. Men are also over-concentrated in "hot" or prestigious courses such as Law and Economics and Constitutional Law.

Kornhauser, Rooms of Their Own: An Empirical Study of Occupational Segregation by Gender among Law Professors, 73 UMKC L. Rev. 293, 324 (2004). Does it matter whether women and men voluntarily choose different teaching packages? Kornhauser notes that the question of prestige is complex. Does this complicate determining in which direction causation runs — that is, whether fields become less prestigious because they attract disproportionate numbers of female teachers or whether women are assigned to fields because they are less prestigious?

Is law school itself "gendered"? Empirical research suggests women are less comfortable than men participating in certain aspects of law school, such as volunteering answers and approaching professors outside of class. For an overview of research on race and gender in law school, see L. Guinier et al., Becoming Gentlemen: Women, Law School, and Institutional Change (1997); Cassman and Pruitt, A Kinder, Gentler Law School? Race, Ethnicity, Gender, and Legal Education at King Hall, 38 U.C. Davis L. Rev. 1209 (2005).

3. *In a different "voice"?* Is it ever permissible for the government to recognize that men and women speak with a different "voice" on some questions? Is there a plausible argument that the government might be constitutionally compelled to recognize these differences?

For an unusually candid debate among the justices on this topic, see J.E.B. v. Alabama ex rel. T.B., 511 U.S. 127 (1994). The case concerned the constitutionality of the state's use of gender-based peremptory challenges in a trial to determine whether the defendant was the father of a child and the extent of his child support obligations. (For a discussion of the constitutionality of race-based peremptory challenges, see pages 560-562, supra.) The state used nine of its ten peremptory strikes to remove male jurors. The defendant used all but one of his strikes to remove female jurors. As a result, all the selected jurors were female.

In an opinion by Justice Blackmun, the Court held that gender-based peremptory challenges were unconstitutional:

> Far from proffering an exceptionally persuasive justification for its gender-based peremptory challenges, respondent maintains that its decision to strike virtually all the males from the jury in this case "may reasonably have been based upon the perception, supported by history, that men otherwise totally qualified to serve upon a jury might be more sympathetic and receptive to the arguments of a man alleged in a paternity action to be the father of an out-of-wedlock child, while women equally qualified to serve upon a jury might be more sympathetic and receptive to the arguments of the complaining witness who bore the child."
>
> We shall not accept as a defense to gender-based peremptory challenges "the very stereotype the law condemns."

In a footnote, Justice Blackmun added that, even if "a measure of truth can be found in some of the gender stereotypes used to justify gender-based peremptory challenges," that fact was irrelevant. "[A] shred of truth may be contained in some stereotypes, but [the equal protection clause] requires that state actors look beyond the surface before making judgments about people that are likely to stigmatize as well as to perpetuate historical patterns of discrimination."

Consider Justice O'Connor's concurring opinion:

> We know that like race, gender matters. A plethora of studies make clear that in rape cases, for example, female jurors are somewhat more likely to vote to convict than male jurors. Moreover, though there have been no similarly definitive studies regarding, for example, sexual harassment, child custody, or spousal or child abuse, one need not be a sexist to share the intuition that in certain cases a person's gender and resulting life experience will be relevant to his or her view of the case.
>
> Today's decision severely limits a litigant's ability to act on this intuition. [But] to say that gender makes no difference as a matter of law is not to say that gender makes no difference as a matter of fact. [Today's] decision is a statement that, in an effort to eliminate the potential discriminatory use of the peremptory, gender is now governed by the special rule of relevance formerly reserved for race. Though we gain much from this statement, we cannot ignore what we lose.

Justice Kennedy also wrote a concurring opinion.

Is gender discrimination in jury selection unconstitutional because the law recognizes that the genders speak with different "voices" and that both require representation, or because it insists that they speak with the same "voice" and that distinctions between them are therefore irrational?

4. *Accommodation for "real differences."* In some cases, the Court has been willing to uphold sex-based distinctions to account for the supposed "real differences" between men and women. In doing so, has the Court escaped the gender stereotypes it purports to be policing?

In Michael M. v. Sonoma County Superior Court, 450 U.S. 464 (1981), the Court upheld a statute defining statutory rape as "an act of sexual intercourse accomplished with a female not the wife of the perpetrator, where the female is under the age of 18 years." Petitioner, a seventeen-year-old male, was convicted under the statute for having intercourse with a sixteen-year-old female. In an opinion for a plurality of the Court, Justice Rehnquist found that the purpose of the statute was to prevent illegitimate pregnancies and that the state had a strong interest in preventing such pregnancies:

> Because virtually all of the significant harmful and inescapably identifiable consequences of teenage pregnancy fall on the young female, a legislature acts well within its authority when it elects to punish only the participant who, by nature, suffers few of the consequences of his conduct. [Moreover], the risk of pregnancy itself constitutes a substantial deterrence to young females. No similar natural sanctions deter males. A criminal sanction imposed solely on males thus serves to roughly "equalize" the deterrents on the sexes.

Is it relevant, even if true, that more women than men are deterred by the risk of pregnancy from engaging in sexual intercourse? Since the California statute prohibits consensual intercourse, it applies only in cases where the female partner is undeterred by the risk of pregnancy (else the intercourse would not be consensual). What difference does it make, then, that there is another class of women, to whom the statute has no application in any event, who are deterred by this risk?

Might the result in *Michael M.* be justified on the ground that many rape laws fail to deal adequately with acts of intercourse that do not involve overt force, yet are also not fully consensual? See, e.g., S. Estrich, Real Rape 29–41 (1987); Olsen, Statutory Rape: A Feminist Critique of Rights Analysis, 63 Tex. L. Rev. 387, 427–428 (1984). Does this problem amount to the kind of "exceedingly persuasive" justification that *Virginia* requires?

NGUYEN v. IMMIGRATION AND NATURALIZATION SERVICE, **533 U.S. 53 (2001).** Nguyen was born in Vietnam to unmarried parents. His father was a U.S. citizen and his mother was a citizen of Vietnam. Nguyen spent much of his early childhood being raised by nonrelatives; he came to the United States at the age of six, became a lawful permanent resident, and was raised by his father. At age twenty-two, after being convicted of a felony, the Immigration and Naturalization Service initiated deportation proceedings against him as an alien who had been convicted of crimes of moral turpitude. While the matter was pending, Nguyen's father obtained an order of parentage from state court based on a DNA test that conclusively demonstrated paternity and Nguyen sought to claim U.S. citizenship.

Under federal law, a child born abroad to unmarried parents automatically acquires U.S. citizenship if the child's mother is a U.S. citizen who at some previous point in her life had been physically present in the United States for a continuous period of one year. By contrast, a child born abroad to unmarried parents does not automatically become a U.S. citizen if only the child's father is a U.S. citizen. Rather, such a child can be naturalized if the blood relationship between the child and his or her citizen father is "established by clear and convincing evidence," the father agrees in writing to provide support for the child, and, before the child turns eighteen, the child or the father obtains formal recognition of the father's paternity. See 8 U.S.C. §1409(a). Because Nguyen's father had not obtained a formal paternity order before Nguyen turned eighteen, the Board of Immigration Appeals rejected Nguyen's claim to U.S. citizenship. Nguyen and his father appealed.

In a five-to-four decision, the Court, in an opinion written by Justice Kennedy, upheld the statute.

Justice Kennedy began his analysis by noting the requirements that gender-based classifications serve important governmental objectives and be substantially related to the achievement of those objectives. "The first governmental interest to be served [by the statute] is the importance of assuring that a biological parent-child relationship exists. In the case of the mother, the relation is verifiable from the birth itself. . . .

"In the case of the father, the uncontestable fact is that he need not be present at the birth. If he is present, furthermore, that circumstance is not incontrovertible proof of fatherhood. . . .

"Petitioners argue that the requirement of [the statute] that a father provide clear and convincing evidence of parentage is sufficient to achieve the end of establishing paternity, given the sophistication of modern DNA tests. [The statute] does not actually mandate a DNA test, however. The Constitution, moreover, does not require that Congress elect one particular mechanism from among many possible methods of establishing paternity, even if that mechanism arguably might be the most scientifically advanced method. With respect to DNA testing, the expense, reliability, and availability of such testing in various parts of the world may have been a particular concern of Congress. . . .

"[To] require Congress to speak without reference to the gender of the parent with regard to its objective of ensuring a blood tie between parent and child would be to insist on a hollow neutrality. . . .

"[Here,] the use of gender specific terms takes into account a biological difference between the parents. The differential treatment is inherent in a sensible statutory scheme, given the unique relationship of the mother to the event of birth.

"The second important governmental interest furthered in a substantial manner by [the statute] is the determination to ensure that the child and the citizen parent have some demonstrated opportunity or potential to develop not just a relationship that is recognized, as a formal matter, by the law, but one that consists of the real, everyday ties that provide a connection between child and citizen parent and, in turn, the United States. In the case of a citizen mother and a child born overseas, the opportunity for a meaningful relationship between citizen parent and child inheres in the very event of birth, an event so often critical to our constitutional and statutory understandings of citizenship. The mother knows that the child is in being and is hers and has an initial point of contact with him. There is at least an opportunity for mother and child to develop a real, meaningful relationship.

"The same opportunity does not result from the event of birth, as a matter of biological inevitability, in the case of the unwed father. Given the 9-month interval between conception and birth, it is not always certain that a father will know that a child was conceived, nor is it always clear that even the mother will be sure of the father's identity. This fact takes on particular significance in the case of a child born overseas and out of wedlock. One concern in this context has always been with young people, men for the most part, who are on duty with the Armed Forces in foreign countries.

"[The] passage of time has produced additional and even more substantial grounds to justify the statutory distinction. The ease of travel and the willingness of Americans to visit foreign countries have resulted in numbers of trips abroad that must be of real concern when we contemplate the prospect of accepting petitioners' argument, which would mandate, contrary to Congress' wishes, citizenship by male parentage subject to no condition save the father's previous length of residence in this country. . . .

"The importance of the governmental interest at issue here is too profound to be satisfied merely by conducting a DNA test. [Scientific] proof of biological paternity does nothing, by itself, to ensure contact between father and child during the child's minority. . . .

"[This] difference does not result from some stereotype, defined as a frame of mind resulting from irrational or uncritical analysis. There is nothing irrational or improper in the recognition that at the moment of birth — the critical event in the statutory scheme and in the whole tradition of citizenship law — the mother's knowledge of the child and the fact of parenthood have been established in a way not guaranteed in the case of the unwed father. This is not a stereotype. . . .

"[The] question remains whether the means Congress chose to further its objective — the imposition of certain additional requirements upon an unwed father — substantially relate to [the ends of the statute].

"[It] should be unsurprising that Congress decided to require that an opportunity for a parent-child relationship occur during the formative years of the child's minority. . . .

"[Petitioners] assert that, although a mother will know of her child's birth, 'knowledge that one is a parent, no matter how it is acquired, does not guarantee a relationship with one's child.' They thus maintain that imposition of the additional requirements of [the statute] only on the children of citizen fathers must reflect a stereotype that women are more likely than men to actually establish a relationship with their children.

"[Congress] would of course be entitled to advance the interest of ensuring an actual, meaningful relationship in every case before citizenship is conferred. Or Congress could excuse compliance with the formal requirements when an actual father-child relationship is proved. It did neither here, perhaps because of the subjectivity, intrusiveness, and difficulties of proof that might attend an inquiry into any particular bond or tie. Instead, Congress enacted an easily administered scheme to promote the different but still substantial interest of ensuring at least an opportunity for a parent-child relationship to develop. . . .

"To fail to acknowledge even our most basic biological differences — such as the fact that a mother must be present at birth but the father need not be — risks making the guarantee of equal protection superficial, and so disserving it. Mechanistic classification of all our differences as stereotypes would operate to obscure those misconceptions and prejudices that are real. The distinction embodied in the statutory scheme here at issue is not marked by misconception and prejudice, nor does it show disrespect for either class. The difference between men and women in relation to the birth process is a real one, and the principle of equal protection does not forbid Congress to address the problem at hand in a manner specific to each gender."

Justice O'Connor, joined by Justices Souter, Ginsburg, and Breyer, dissented:

"While the Court invokes heightened scrutiny, the manner in which it explains and applies this standard is a stranger to our precedents. . . .

"It is [difficult] to see how [the statute's] limitation of the time allowed for obtaining proof of paternity substantially furthers the assurance of a blood relationship. Modern DNA testing, in addition to providing accuracy unmatched by other methods of establishing a biological link, essentially negates the evidentiary significance of the passage of time. . . .

"Assuming as the majority does, that Congress was actually concerned about ensuring a 'demonstrated opportunity' for a relationship, it is questionable whether such an opportunity qualifies as an 'important' governmental interest apart from the existence of an actual relationship. [It] is difficult to see how [anyone] profits from a 'demonstrated opportunity' for a relationship in the absence of the fruition of an actual tie. . . .

"Moreover, available sex-neutral alternatives would at least replicate, and could easily exceed, whatever fit there is between [the statute's] discriminatory means and the majority's asserted end. [Congress] could simply substitute for [the statute] a requirement that the parent be present at birth or have knowledge of birth. Congress could at least allow proof of such presence or knowledge to be one way of demonstrating an opportunity for a relationship. [Indeed], the idea that a mother's presence at birth supplies adequate assurance of an opportunity to develop a relationship while a father's presence at birth does not would appear to rest only on an overbroad sex-based generalization. . . .

"The claim that [the statute] substantially relates to the achievement of the goal of a 'real practical relationship' thus finds support not in biological differences but instead in a stereotype. . . .

"The majority asserts that a 'stereotype' is 'defined as a frame of mind resulting from irrational or uncritical analysis.' This Court has long recognized, however, that an impermissible stereotype may enjoy empirical support and thus be in a sense 'rational.' . . .

"Nor do stereotypes consist only of those overbroad generalizations that the reviewing court considers to 'show disrespect' for a class. [Indeed], arbitrary distinction between the sexes may rely on no identifiable generalization at all but may simply be a denial of opportunity out of pure caprice. Such a distinction, of course, would nonetheless be a classic equal protection violation."

SESSIONS v. MORALES-SANTANA, 137 S. Ct. 1678 (2017). *Ngyuyen* upheld differential treatment of parental transmission of citizenship predicated on women's and men's being differently situated at the moment of a child's birth. The Court subsequently rejected differential treatment in the transmission of citizenship absent such a difference.

The main rule for transmitting citizenship to children born abroad to parents only one of whom is a U.S. citizen appears in 8 U.S.C. §1401(g). It requires that the U.S. citizen parent have been physically present in the United States for ten years prior to the child's birth. That rule applies both to married couples and to unmarried couples where the father is the U.S. citizen. A separate rule applies to children born to unmarried couples where the mother is the U.S. citizen. Under that rule, which appears in 8 U.S.C. §1409(c), an unwed mother can transmit her citizenship to a child born abroad if she has lived in the United States for just one year prior to the child's birth.

Luis Ramón Morales-Santana's father, a U.S. citizen, was just 20 days short of meeting the physical-presence requirement when Luis was born in the Dominican Republic. (His mother, to whom his father was not then married, was Dominican.) Luis moved to the United States when he was 13. When Luis was 38 years old, the government placed him in removal proceedings after he was convicted of a number of state law offenses. An immigration judge rejected his claim to citizenship and the Board of Immigration Appeals rejected his constitutional challenge to the statutory regime for transmitting citizenship. The court of appeals agreed with Morales-Santana, holding first that the differential treatment of unwed mothers and fathers violated the equal protection component of the due process clause and second that "[t]o cure the constitutional flaw," Morales-Santana should be given citizenship.

The Supreme Court, in an opinion by Justice Ginsburg, affirmed in part and reversed in part. The Court began its analysis by declaring that the statutes providing differential treatment based on whether the U.S. citizen parent is a father or a mother "date from an era when the lawbooks of our Nation were rife with overbroad generalizations about the way men and women are. Today, laws of this kind are subject to review under the heightened scrutiny that now attends 'all gender-based classifications.'"

The Court found that the government had failed to supply an "'exceedingly persuasive justification,' for [the] 'gender-based' and 'gender-biased' disparity."

"History reveals what lurks behind §1409. . . . [That provision] ended a century and a half of congressional silence on the citizenship of children born abroad to unwed parents. During this era, two once habitual, but now untenable, assumptions pervaded our Nation's citizenship laws and underpinned judicial and administrative rulings: In marriage, husband is dominant, wife subordinate; unwed mother is the natural and sole guardian of a nonmarital child. . . .

"This unwed-mother-as-natural-guardian notion renders §1409's gender-based residency rules understandable. Fearing that a foreign-born child could turn out 'more alien than American in character,' the administration believed that a citizen parent with lengthy ties to the United States would counteract the influence of the alien parent. Concern about the attachment of foreign-born children to the United States explains the treatment of unwed citizen fathers, who, according to the familiar stereotype, would care little about, and have scant contact with, their nonmarital children. For unwed citizen mothers, however, there was no need for a prolonged residency prophylactic: The alien father, who might transmit foreign ways, was presumptively out of the picture. . . .

"[T]he Court has held that no 'important [governmental] interest' is served by laws grounded, as §1409(a) and (c) are, in the obsolescing view that 'unwed fathers [are] invariably less qualified and entitled than mothers' to take responsibility for nonmarital children. Overbroad generalizations of that order, the Court has come to comprehend, have a constraining impact, descriptive though they may be of the way many people still order their lives. . . ."

The Court rejected the government's argument that *Nguyen* should control the outcome.

"Unlike the paternal-acknowledgment requirement at issue in *Nguyen* . . . , the physical-presence requirements now before us relate solely to the duration of the parent's prebirth residency in the United States, not to the parent's filial tie to the child. . . ."

Having found that the statutory scheme violated equal protection principles, however, the Court went on to hold that it was "not equipped to grant the relief Morales-Santana seeks, i.e., extending to his father (and, derivatively, to him) the benefit of the one-year physical-presence term §1409(c) reserves for unwed mothers."

The Court pointed out that there were "two remedial alternatives" available. The first was to "extend the coverage" of the more favorable statute — here, the shorter residency period for unwed mothers — to the children of unwed fathers as well. The second was to declare the special provision benefiting the children of unwed mothers a nullity. Scholars refer to the former strategy as "levelling up" and the latter as "levelling down." See Karlan, Race, Rights, and Remedies in Criminal Adjudication, 96 Mich. L. Rev. 2001, 2027-29 (1998); Brake, When Equality Leaves Everyone Worse Off: The Problem of Leveling Down in Equality Law, 46 Wm. & Mary L. Rev. 513 (2004).

In this case, the Court explained that "[t]he choice between these outcomes is governed by the legislature's intent, as revealed by the statute at hand." While ordinarily courts level up, "[h]ere, however, the discriminatory exception consists of favorable treatment for a discrete group (a shorter physical-presence requirement for unwed U.S.-citizen mothers giving birth abroad). . . . [S]triking the discriminatory exception — leads here to extending the general rule of longer physical-presence requirements to cover the previously favored group." Moreover, "if §1409(c)'s one-year dispensation were extended to unwed citizen fathers, would it not be irrational to retain the longer term when the U.S.-citizen parent is married? Disadvantageous treatment of marital children in comparison to non-marital children is scarcely a purpose one can sensibly attribute to Congress." The Court therefore left it to Congress to "address the issue and settle on a uniform prescription that neither favors nor disadvantages any person on the basis of gender. In the interim, . . . the five-year requirement should apply, prospectively, to children born to unwed U.S.-citizen mothers."

Justice Gorsuch did not participate in the decision. Justice Thomas, joined by Justice Alito, concurred in the judgment. He took the position that the Court's remedial holding resolved the case so it was "unnecessary" for the Court to reach the constitutional question.

Note: The Relevance of "Real Differences"

1. *What makes a difference real?* In light of the cases discussed in this section, consider what makes a difference between the genders "real" for constitutional purposes. Must it be linked to some purely physiological distinction between the sexes? Which, if any, of the statutes considered in these cases can be justified on this basis alone? Are demonstrated differences in behavior sufficient? It is at least conceivable that some such differences are a product of cultural expectations reinforced by the very statutes under attack, rather than any "natural" difference. To the extent that this is true, the statutes become self-validating. Recall, for example, Justice O'Connor's concern in Mississippi University for Women v. Hogan that Mississippi's policy "makes the assumption that nursing is a field for women a self-fulfilling prophecy." Is it this phenomenon that concerned Justice Brennan in *Craig* when he wrote that statistical demonstrations are "in tension with the normative philosophy that underlies the Equal Protection Clause"?

Consider the argument that differences between the genders not only are socially constructed but also serve to reinforce male domination. See C. MacKinnon, Feminism Unmodified: Discourses on Life and Law 3, 8–9 (1987):

> The idea of gender difference helps keep the reality of male dominance in place. . . .
>
> Difference is the velvet glove on the iron fist of domination. This is as true when differences are affirmed as when they are denied, when their substance is applauded or when it is disparaged, when women are punished or [when] they are protected in their name. A sex inequality is not a difference gone wrong, a lesson the law of sex discrimination has yet to learn. One of the most deceptive antifeminisms in society, scholarship, politics, and law is the persistent treatment of gender as if it truly is a question of difference, rather than treating the gender difference as a construct of the difference gender makes.

If many gender differences are socially constructed, is the right question, what, if any, gender differences would exist in a "state of nature" before cultural forces have taken hold? Recall Justice Bradley's assertion over a century ago that a woman's duty "to fulfill the noble and benign offices of wife and mother" was "the law of the Creator." Is the current Court's search for "real differences" a modern-day analogue to this sort of reasoning? How likely is it that the justices can escape their own culture in deciding which differences are culturally determined?

Consider Case, Of Richard Epstein and Other Radical Feminists, 18 Harv. J.L. & Pub. Poly. 369, 375 (1995):

> Law is precisely that which fights against nature. If something were all that natural, a law would not be needed to bring it about. This is clear in almost every area of legal scholarship other than those pertaining to sex and gender. [The] evidence for natural human aggression is far stronger than any of the evidence [in] favor of difference between the sexes. No one [would], however, suggest that just because human beings are naturally aggressive there should be no laws of murder and assault.

With regard to the "naturalness" of gender differences, consider the possibility that current constitutional doctrine does not deal adequately with "people for whom gender and anatomical birth sex in some way diverge." Flynn, Transforming the Debate: Why We Need to Include Transgender Rights in the Struggles for Sex and Sexual Orientation Equality, 101 Colum. L. Rev. 392, 394 (2001). Flynn argues that this problem leads to the

> failure to remedy much of the discrimination experienced by women and sexual minorities, specifically the discrimination based on gender nonconformity. This failure is premised on a prevalent juridical assumption that the law should target discrimination based on sex (i.e., whether a person is anatomically male or female), rather than gender (i.e., whether a person has qualities that society considers masculine or feminine). In both law and life, though, conceptions of sex and gender are so firmly cemented together that courts' frequent refusals to address gender-based inequalities mean that much discrimination against women and sexual minorities goes unremedied.

Id. at 394–395.

For a discussion of the relationship between gender discrimination and discrimination based on sexual orientation, see pages 690-692, infra.

2. *Difference theory.* A second critique takes the opposite tack. It argues that there are significant differences between men and women, and sees the problem as the law's insistence on formal equality in the face of these differences. There are two ways in which this denial of difference might be problematic. First, practices might treat male traits as the norm and expect women to conform to these male traits. Alternatively, because traditional equal protection analysis focuses solely on legislative means (i.e., on whether a difference between men and women is relevant to a given legislative end), it may ignore ways in which legislative ends, which are treated as outside of the analysis, may themselves be the product of male domination.

How would constitutional doctrine have to be constructed to respond to these observations by Becker, Obscuring the Struggle: Sex Discrimination, Social Security, and Stone, Seidman, Sunstein and Tushnet's Constitutional Law, 89 Colum. L. Rev. 264, 283 (1989):

> [The] social security system fails to afford women as reliable an old-age security system as that afforded men. [Women] who lead ordinary lives are less likely to be well protected by the social security system than men who live ordinary lives because the system prefers those who have successfully fulfilled men's traditional breadwinner role over those who fulfilled women's traditional roles. Social security discriminates against women because it is designed so that women are at a much greater risk of poverty than are men. It exerts pressure on homemakers to depend economically on men in old age, despite the riskiness of such dependence.

In thinking about these questions, consider Nevada Department of Human Resources v. Hibbs, 538 U.S. 721 (2003). At issue was whether section 5 of the fourteenth amendment provided Congress with the power to authorize private suits for damages against state governments under the Family and Medical Leave Act. (The general question of congressional power under section 5 is covered in Chapter 3, section B, supra.) The act authorized eligible employees to take up to twelve weeks of unpaid leave annually to care for a spouse, child, or parent with a serious medical condition.

In a six-to-three decision, the Court upheld the statute. Chief Justice Rehnquist delivered the opinion of the Court:

> According to evidence that was before Congress, [States] continue to rely on invalid gender stereotypes in the employment context, specifically in the administration of leave benefits. . . .
> Congress [heard] testimony that "[p]arental leave for fathers . . . is rare. Even . . . [w]here child-care leave policies do exist, men, both in the public and private sectors, receive notoriously discriminatory treatment in their requests for such leave." [Many] States offer women extended "maternity" leave that far exceeded the typical 4- to 8-week period of physical disability due to pregnancy and childbirth, but very few States grant men a parallel [benefit]. This and other differential leave policies were not attributable to any differential physical needs of men and women, but rather to the pervasive sex-role stereotype that caring for family members is women's work.

Given the social roles commonly played by men and women, are the state practices upon which the Court relies evidence of gender discrimination or are they, instead, efforts to respond to gender discrimination? According to Chief Justice Rehnquist,

[Mutually] reenforcing stereotypes [that women have domestic responsibilities and men do not] created a self-fulfilling cycle of discrimination that forced women to continue to assume the role of primary family caregiver, and fostered employers' stereotypical views about women's commitment to work and their value as employees. . . .

By creating an across-the-board routine employment benefit for all eligible employees, Congress sought to ensure that family-care leave would no longer be stigmatized as an inordinate drain on the workplace caused by female employees, that the employers could not evade leave obligations simply by hiring men.

In the Court's view, a simple requirement that states administer leave benefits in a gender neutral fashion would not solve this problem:

Such a law would allow States to provide for no family leave at all. Where "[t]wo thirds of the nonprofessional caregivers for older, chronically ill, or disabled persons are working women" and state practices continue to reinforce the stereotype of women as caregivers, such a policy would exclude far more women than men from the workplace.

Why is this fact relevant? Isn't this mode of analysis in tension with the Court's own conclusion that official recognition of different social roles performed by men and women serves to reinforce stereotypes about those roles? In light of the statistics cited by the Court, would it be constitutional for Congress to mandate caretaker leave for women but not for men?

3. *Real differences and substantive values.* If we cannot rely on actual differences in behavior between men and women, and if we also cannot rely on suppositions about differences that would exist in the absence of cultural forces, what test should we use to evaluate gender discrimination claims? Is there in the end any way to judge the appropriateness of gender classifications without a substantive vision of the role gender would play in a just society?

4. *Beyond real differences.* Do the difficulties associated with the identification of "real differences" suggest that we might be better off, after all, with a virtual per se rule prohibiting gender classifications? Consider Brown, Emerson, Falk, and Freedman, The Equal Rights Amendment: A Constitutional Basis for Equal Rights for Women, 80 Yale L.J. 871, 873–874 (1971):

Many of the efforts to create a separate legal status for women stem from a good faith attempt to advance the interests of women. Nevertheless, the preponderant effect has been to buttress the social and economic subordination of women. [Whatever] the motivation for different treatment, the result is to create a dual system of rights and responsibilities in which the rights of each group are governed by a different set of values. History and experience have taught us that in such a dual system one group is always dominant and the other subordinate. As long as woman's place is defined as separate, a male-dominated society will define her place as inferior.

Is the cause of equality advanced by insisting on gender-neutral laws that disproportionately affect women because they are differently situated with respect to the laws? Consider Law, Rethinking Sex and the Constitution, 132 U. Pa. L. Rev. 955, 1007 (1984):

[Pregnancy,] abortion, reproduction, and creation of another human being are special — very special. Women have these experiences. Men do not. An equality doctrine that ignores the unique quality of these experiences implicitly says that women can claim equality only insofar as they are like men. Such doctrine demands that women deny an important aspect of who they are.

Note: Gender Discrimination as a Two-Edged Sword

A surprisingly high proportion of the Supreme Court's sex discrimination cases were brought by male plaintiffs. This was true both during the era when the Court laid down the basic doctrine, see Baer, Women's Rights and the Limits of Constitutional Doctrine, 44 W. Pol. Q. 821, 823 (1991) (men brought more than two-thirds of the constitutional sex discrimination cases adjudicated between 1971 and 1984), and in more recent years, see, e.g., Sessions v. Morales-Santana, 137 S. Ct. 1678 (2017); Coleman v. Maryland Court of Appeals, 566 U.S. 30 (2012); Nevada Department of Human Resources v. Hibbs, 538 U.S. 721 (2003); Nguyen v. Immigration & Naturalization Service, 533 U.S. 53 (2001). Why?

The conventional account focuses on strategic choices by sex discrimination litigators, most notably Ruth Bader Ginsburg, who was head of the American Civil Liberties Union's Women's Rights Project. It suggests that Ginsburg chose these plaintiffs to appeal to the empathy of an overwhelmingly male judiciary. See, e.g., Cole, Strategies of Difference: Litigating for Women's Rights in a Man's World, 2 Law & Ineq. 33 (1984); Torrey, Thirty Years, 22 Women's Rts. L. Rep. 147, 149 (2001). More recently, a revisionist account asserts that

[conventional] wisdom suggests that the WRP's reliance on male plaintiffs was a strategic and ultimately conservative choice designed to elicit sympathy and fellow feeling from male Justices. But this is not what happened. The first time a male plaintiff appeared before the Court in a sex-based equal protection case — as half of a married couple — the suggestion that he might be a victim of sex discrimination was treated as a joke. In subsequent cases, when it became clear that the WRP was serious about establishing the right of men to be free from sex discrimination, the laughter turned to confusion and disbelief, and, in some cases, to anger and disgust. . . .

To understand why "the fact that many of the cases Ruth Bader Ginsburg brought to the Court had male plaintiffs . . . did not make the Court's job any easier," it is useful to consider who these plaintiffs were. One of them, the first male plaintiff Ginsburg represented, was a lifelong bachelor and primary caregiver to his elderly and ailing mother. Another was a stay-at-home father. Several were married to women who contributed substantially to their support. Most of them, in one way or another, rejected or failed to satisfy masculine gender norms circa 1975. If Ginsburg's aim had been to "capitalize[] on sex-based ingroup biases," selecting gender-bending men as plaintiffs would not have been a wise strategy.

Ginsburg was well aware of this. The groundbreaking sex discrimination casebook she published in 1974 opened with a note explaining that men and women both encounter discrimination when they deviate from "assigned roles," but that "the very assurance of [male] dominance marks out for even greater social disapproval men whose unconventional interests and abilities lead them to choose different lifestyles." . . .

If Ginsburg knew male sex discrimination plaintiffs would strike the Justices as odd, why did she choose to represent them? . . . Ginsburg pressed the claims of male plaintiffs in order to promote a new theory of equal protection founded on an anti-stereotyping principle. This anti-stereotyping theory dictated that the state could not act in ways that reflected or reinforced traditional conceptions of men's and women's roles. It was not simply anti-classificationist: It permitted the state to classify on the basis of sex in instances where doing so served to dissipate sex-role stereotypes. Nor was it strictly anti-subordinationist: Because discrimination against women had traditionally been viewed as a benefit to them, Ginsburg was concerned that an anti-subordination principle would provide courts with too little guidance about which forms of regulation warrant constitutional concern. The anti-stereotyping approach was designed to provide such guidance; its aim was to direct courts' attention to the particular institutions and social practices that perpetuate inequality in the context of sex. . . .

Unlike the more radical critics of "the sex-role structure," the WRP aimed not to eradicate sex roles but to stop the state from enforcing them. [The] WRP began to challenge laws that reflected a "'separate-spheres' mentality" and reinforced the "breadwinner-homemaker dichotomy." By the mid-1970s, the Court itself had begun to reason about sex discrimination from an anti-stereotyping perspective. It recognized — particularly in male plaintiff cases we tend to overlook today — that laws that steer men out of traditionally female roles effectively require women to assume those roles, and it interpreted the Equal Protection Clause as a bar to such "role-typing."

Franklin, The Anti-Stereotyping Principle in Constitutional Law, 85 N.Y.U. L. Rev. 83, 86–90 (2010).

In thinking about who is being benefited and who is being burdened, note that many of the Court's cases involved laws that affected married couples. Consider the contrast between two cases, decided less than a month apart. In Califano v. Goldfarb, 430 U.S. 199 (1977), the Court struck down a federal benefits program that provided a widow with survivors' benefits based on the earnings of her deceased husband, while a widower received benefits based on the earnings of his deceased wife only if he had been receiving "at least one-half of his support" from her. Justice Brennan's opinion announcing the judgment of the Court treated the case as one involving discrimination against female workers because it "deprive[d] women of protection for their families which men receive as a result of their employment." A woman like Mrs. Goldfarb "worked and paid social security taxes for 25 years at the same rate as her male colleagues, but because of [the statute] the insurance protection received by the males was broader than hers. Plainly then [the statute] disadvantages women contributors to the social security system as compared to similarly situated men." Justice Stevens concurred in the judgment and focused on the differential treatment not of workers, but of their survivors. "Congress had simply assumed that all widows should be regarded as 'dependents' in some general sense, even though they could not satisfy the statutory support test later imposed on men." He was "persuaded that this discrimination against a group of males is merely the accidental byproduct of a traditional way of thinking about females."

Justice Rehnquist, joined by Chief Justice Burger, Justice Stewart, and Justice Blackmun, dissented.

In Califano v. Webster, 430 U.S. 313 (1977), by contrast, the Court upheld a provision of the Social Security Act that allowed women to exclude more years in which they had low earnings from the formula for computing monthly old-age benefits than men were permitted to exclude. As a result some retired female workers received higher benefits than similarly situated male workers. The Court's per curiam opinion noted that prior decisions had held that "[reduction] of the disparity in economic condition between men and women caused by the long history of discrimination against women" could constitute a sufficiently "important governmental objective" to justify sex-based distinctions. In the Court's opinion, the provision of the Social Security Act served that function:

> The more favorable treatment of the female wage earner enacted here was not a result of "archaic and overbroad generalizations" about women or of "the role-typing society has long imposed" upon women, such as casual assumptions that women are "the weaker sex" or are more likely to be child rearers or dependents. . . .
>
> [Rather, the] challenged statute operated directly to compensate women for past economic discrimination. Retirement benefits under the Act are based on past earnings. But as we have recognized: "Whether from overt discrimination or from the socialization process of a male-dominated culture, the job market is inhospitable to the woman seeking any but the lowest paid jobs." Thus, allowing women, who as such have been unfairly hindered from earning as much as men, to eliminate additional low-earning years from the calculation of their retirement benefits works directly to remedy some part of the effect of past discrimination.

Chief Justice Burger, with whom Justices Stewart, Blackmun, and Rehnquist joined, concurred in the judgment, but found it "somewhat difficult to distinguish the Social Security provision upheld here from that struck down so recently in [*Goldfarb*]."

Note: The Problem of "Benign" Gender Classifications

1. *Conceptualizing the victim of discrimination.* In what sense did the statute invalidated in *Goldfarb* discriminate against women, as opposed to men? Compare *Goldfarb* with Wengler v. Druggists Mutual Insurance Co., 446 U.S. 142 (1980), in which the Court invalidated a portion of Missouri's workers' compensation statute under which a widower of a deceased worker was entitled to death benefits only if he was mentally or physically incapacitated from wage earning or proved actual dependence on his wife's earnings. In contrast, a widow was automatically entitled to death benefits without having to demonstrate dependence. The Court concluded that the challenged statute discriminated against both men and women. Women were harmed because "[the] benefits [that] the working woman can expect to be paid to her spouse in the case of her work-related death are less than those payable to the spouse of the deceased male wage earner." Men were also discriminated against because "the surviving male spouse must prove his incapacity or dependency [while the] widow of a deceased wage earner [is] presumed dependent and is guaranteed a weekly benefit for life or until remarriage." If, as the Court asserts, the Missouri statute discriminated against women simply because their spouses were deprived of a benefit, don't virtually all laws that discriminate against men also discriminate against women? If, as the Court asserts, the Missouri statute discriminates against both men and women, in what sense does it involve gender discrimination? What argument is there for heightened scrutiny of statutes that classify on the basis of gender if neither men nor women as a class are disadvantaged by them?

If stereotyping is the problem, then are men victims of discrimination as well? Consider Kanowitz, "Benign" Sex Discrimination: Its Troubles and Their Cure, 31 Hastings L.J. 1379, 1394 (1980):

> [A] casual glance at the treatment males have received at the hands of the law solely because they are males suggests that they have paid an awesome price for other

advantages they have presumably enjoyed over females in our society. Whether one talks of the male's unique obligation of compulsory military service, his primary duty for spousal and child support, his lack of the same kinds of protective labor legislation that have traditionally been enjoyed by women, or the statutory or judicial preference in child custody disputes that has long been accorded to mothers vis-à-vis fathers of minor children, sex discrimination against males in statutes and judicial decisions has been widespread and severe.

It is, of course, possible that both men and women have been harmed in different ways by gender stereotyping. But if both sexes are harmed to equivalent degrees, what is the basis for judicial intervention? Kanowitz argues:

> Centuries of sex-role allocations, based on "habit, rather than analysis," simply disabled Americans of either sex from restructuring the duties of military service, family support, and protections in the work place so as to permit men and women to share the burdens and benefits of social existence more equitably. Viewed in this light, the apparent power of men to change their sex-based roles in the past can be seen as being more theoretical than real. In this respect, men were as powerless as any other discrete, insular minority.

Can *both* men and women be discrete and insular minorities? Under this expansive version of the political process argument, is there any group that cannot claim judicial protection?

Is the real point of *Goldfarb* and *Wengler* that, even though the laws invalidated in those cases superficially benefited women, they "really" discriminated against them by reinforcing stereotypes of dependence and passivity that make women the losers in the long run?

2. *Affirmative action for women.* The Court seems to have taken the view that affirmative action measures disadvantaging men are subject to intermediate scrutiny, and that remedying disparities between men and women, at least if caused by prior discrimination, qualifies as an "important government objective" for purposes of that test. However, the Court's pronouncements on this matter occurred at a time when the appropriate standard for *racial* affirmative action was still confused. The Court now insists that in the racial context, affirmative action statutes are subject to the same strict scrutiny as statutes disadvantaging racial minorities. See section C3 supra. What impact does this change have on the gender cases? Given the history of the equal protection clause, it seems implausible that efforts to remedy racial discrimination must satisfy a stricter test than efforts to remedy gender discrimination. Perhaps, then, gender affirmative action measures should also be subject to strict scrutiny. But this result is also deeply problematic, since it would leave laws disadvantaging women subject to a lower level of review than laws benefiting them.

Note: *Sex Discrimination Law and Constitutional Evolution*

1. *A comparative perspective.* Most modern constitutions contain explicit bans on sex discrimination (along with explicit reference to other forbidden classifications, such as race, religion, sexual orientation, caste, or disability). See, e.g., Can. Const. pt. I (Canadian Charter of Rights and Freedoms), §15 (providing both that every individual "has the right to the equal protection and equal benefit of the law without discrimination and, in particular, without discrimination based

on . . . sex" and that this prohibition "does not preclude any law, program or activity that has as its object the amelioration of conditions of disadvantaged individuals or groups including those that are disadvantaged because of . . . sex"); India Const. pt. III, art. 15 (providing that "[the] State shall not discriminate against any citizen on grounds . . . of . . . sex"); S. Afr. Const. §9(3) (providing that "[the] state may not unfairly discriminate directly or indirectly against anyone on one or more grounds, including . . . gender, sex, pregnancy, marital status"). Is the specific enumeration of prohibited classifications and protected classes a superior technique for constitutional drafting? Note that the U.S. Constitution is more than two hundred years old, while the average national constitution lasts for only a generation.

2. *The equal rights amendment.* In 1972, Congress approved and submitted to the states for ratification the following constitutional amendment:

> Section 1. Equality of rights under the law shall not be denied or abridged by the United States or by any State on account of sex.
>   Section 2. The Congress shall have the power to enforce, by appropriate legislation, the provisions of this article.
>   Section 3. This amendment shall take effect two years after the date of ratification.

Although about half of the required three-fourths of the states ratified the ERA within a few months of its submission, progress then became stalled. In 1978, Congress extended the period for ratification until June 30, 1982, but the second deadline expired with only thirty-five of the necessary thirty-eight states having approved the amendment.

The ERA was the subject of passionate debate, both within Congress and during the ratification process. And yet, even as the amendment was being defeated, the Supreme Court was interpreting the equal protection clause to provide much of the protection that the ERA would have afforded. Consider the following perspectives on the relationship between social movements, constitutional amendments, and constitutional interpretation. Did the ERA "fail[] partly *because it was widely seen as unnecessary*" in light of this changed judicial interpretation of the fifth and fourteenth amendments? C. Sunstein, The Second Bill of Rights 126 (2004). Consider also Siegel, Constitutional Culture, Social Movement Conflict and Constitutional Change: The Case of the De Facto ERA, 94 Cal. L. Rev. 1323, 1324, 1336, 1338–1339, 1369 (2006):

> The ERA was not ratified, but the amendment's proposal and defeat played a crucial role in enabling and shaping the modern law of sex discrimination. . . .
>   [Proponents] and opponents of the Equal Rights Amendment wanted their Article V struggles to reverberate through Article I, II, and III pathways, and shape judicial interpretation of equal protection under the Fifth and Fourteenth Amendments. Advocates understood that even without completed acts of constitutional law making, the Article V process offered a vehicle for influencing the constitutional judgments of judges and elected officials — offering a point of system feedback like debates over the nomination and confirmation of judges. They passionately supported and opposed the ERA on this understanding, and Congress and the Supreme Court seem to have interpreted the Constitution responsively. . . .
>   [An] extended and highly structured national conversation about questions of equal citizenship and the family focused public debate on how the abstract

principles of the constitutional tradition applied to concrete practices, and provided material on which different members of the Court would draw as they argued over the meaning of the Constitution's equal protection guarantee in the ensuing decade. Interaction between movements and the Court helped forge the understanding that the Equal Protection Clause prohibited classifications "on the basis of sex," as well as understandings about the particular practices this prohibition constrained. Long running dispute about whether to amend the Constitution's text changed public understandings of the Constitution's text, and so imbued the Court with authority to enforce the Constitution in new and unprecedented ways.

3. *Constitutional versus ordinary lawmaking.* Proponents of the equal rights amendment hoped to constitutionalize a wide variety of issues relating to gender discrimination. And yet, many of the most sweeping protections against sex discrimination — from title VII's prohibition on sex discrimination in employment (including in public employment since 1972) to title IX's prohibition on sex discrimination by institutions that receive federal funding (which, among other things, has provided a major impetus for the expansion in funding for girls' and women's athletic programs) to the Family Medical Leave Act have been the product of ordinary legislation. To what extent was the Supreme Court's doctrinal innovation in the area of sex discrimination simply a reflection of changes in cultural understanding? Note also that many contemporary statutes reach the actions of private parties, whose conduct would not be controlled by the Constitution directly. See Chapter 9 infra. Is sex discrimination so intimately linked with private ordering that legislation under the commerce clause or the spending clause, rather than judicial interpretation of the equal protection clause, better protects women's interests?

E. EQUAL PROTECTION METHODOLOGY: THE PROBLEM OF SEXUAL ORIENTATION

Should laws and policies that discriminate on the basis of sexual orientation be strictly scrutinized? If so, how should the protected class be defined?

Note: The Nature of the Class at Issue

What defines the class of people who might raise equal protection challenges to laws that discriminate on the basis of sexual orientation? Is the relevant group individuals who engage in homosexual acts (however defined) or individuals who have a desire or propensity to engage in such acts? Consider the alternative possibilities.

1. *Acts.* In Lawrence v. Texas, 539 U.S. 558 (2003), the Supreme Court held that the due process clause of the fourteenth amendment prohibits states from criminalizing private, noncommercial consensual sexual intimacy between two adults of the same sex. It therefore struck down a Texas statute that had criminalized oral and anal sex only between individuals of the same sex. (*Lawrence* is discussed in greater detail in Chapter 6, section F3, infra.)

Although the Court in *Lawrence* declined to rely explicitly on the equal protection clause, the Court stated that

> [equality] of treatment and the due process right to demand respect for conduct protected by the substantive guarantee of liberty are linked in important respects. . . . When homosexual conduct is made criminal by the law of the State, that declaration in and of itself is an invitation to subject homosexual persons to discrimination both in the public and in the private spheres.

In this respect, consider Karlan, Loving *Lawrence,* 102 Mich. L. Rev. 1447, 1457 (2004):

> The situation of gay people provokes an "analogical crisis" because in some ways it involves regulation of particular acts in which gay people engage, and so seems most amenable to analysis under the liberty prong of the Due Process Clause, while in other ways it involves regulation of a group of people who are defined not so much by what they do in the privacy of their bedrooms, but by who they *are* in the public sphere. As the Court itself phrased the issue, "[w]hen homosexual *conduct* is made criminal . . . that declaration . . . is an invitation to subject homosexual *persons* to discrimination." It is hard to substitute other adjectives for "homosexual" and continue to have the sentence make sense. No one, for example, would modify both "conduct" and "persons" with words like "larcenous" or "perjurious" or even, although it might be less initially jarring, "violent." . . . [This] must be in part because homosexuality straddles the line between conduct and status in ways that make it hard to apply conventional constitutional doctrine. A state cannot make it a crime to "be gay" since the Eighth Amendment prohibits states from criminalizing a particular status in the absence of "any antisocial behavior." So a state that wants to express its disapproval of gay people must instead craft a law that makes it a crime to engage in behaviors connected in some way with being gay. But the fact that the law explicitly targets behavior and not persons does not mean that it is not also class legislation.

How does this consideration map onto the ways in which other suspect classes are defined? Note that express racial and gender-based classifications distinguish among individuals on the basis of status rather than on the basis of particular acts. Even in the case of facially neutral classifications that are intended to disadvantage racial minorities or women, the classification is a proxy for underlying status, rather than some particular act.

2. *Desires.* Suppose the suspect class is defined in terms of "orientation" or "desires" rather than in terms of acts. Is the state ever justified in discriminating against an individual because of a wholly mental event? Consider in this regard Equality Foundation of Greater Cincinnati v. Cincinnati, 54 F.3d 261 (6th Cir. 1995), vacated and remanded for reconsideration, 518 U.S. 1001 (1996), reaffirmed, 128 F.3d 289 (6th Cir. 1997):

> [No] law can successfully be drafted that is calculated to burden or penalize [an] unidentifiable group or class of individuals whose identity is defined by subjective and unapparent characteristics such as innate desires, drives, and thoughts. Those persons having a homosexual "orientation" simply do not, as such comprise an identifiable class. Many homosexuals successfully conceal their orientation. Because homosexuals generally are not identifiable "on sight," unless they elect to be so identifiable by conduct, [they] cannot constitute a suspect [class].

Why must a characteristic be identifiable "on sight" to trigger strict scrutiny? Must individuals visibly possess the protected characteristic to bring equal protection claims? What about the long-standing practice of "passing" or "covering"? See K. Yoshino, Covering: The Hidden Assault on Our Civil Rights (2007).

3. *Relationships.* Does it make sense to discuss sexual orientation as an individual trait, in the way that sex or age is? Consider the argument that sexual orientation is always defined in relational terms: It concerns an individual's attraction to other people. Consider whether this view means that discrimination on the basis of sexual orientation is discrimination on the basis of sex, in the way that discrimination against individuals in interracial relationships is discrimination on the basis of race.

Romer v. Evans
517 U.S. 620 (1996)

JUSTICE KENNEDY delivered the opinion of the Court.

One century ago, the first Justice Harlan admonished this Court that the Constitution "neither knows nor tolerates classes among citizens." Plessy v. Ferguson (dissenting opinion). Unheeded then, those words now are understood to state a commitment to the law's neutrality where the rights of persons are at stake. The Equal Protection Clause enforces this principle and today requires us to hold invalid a provision of Colorado's Constitution.

I

["Amendment 2" was added to the state constitution by a statewide referendum held in 1992. It was enacted after a number of Colorado municipalities had adopted ordinances prohibiting discrimination on the basis of sexual orientation in many transactions and activities such as housing, employment, education, public accommodations, and health and welfare services. It provided:

NO PROTECTED STATUS BASED ON HOMOSEXUAL, LESBIAN, OR BISEXUAL ORIENTATION Neither the State of Colorado, through any of its branches or departments, nor any of its agencies, political subdivisions, municipalities or school districts, shall enact, adopt or enforce any statute, regulation, ordinance or policy whereby homosexual, lesbian or bisexual orientation, conduct, practices or relationships shall constitute or otherwise be the basis of or entitle any person or class of persons to have or claim any minority status, quota preferences, protected status or claim of discrimination. This Section of the Constitution shall be in all respects self-executing.]

II

The State's principal argument in defense of Amendment 2 is that it puts gays and lesbians in the same position as all other persons. So, the State says, the measure does no more than deny homosexuals special rights. This reading of the amendment's language is implausible. . . .

Homosexuals, by state decree, are put in a solitary class with respect to transactions and relations in both the private and governmental spheres. The amendment withdraws from homosexuals, but no others, specific legal protection from the injuries caused by discrimination, and it forbids reinstatement of these laws and policies.

The change that Amendment 2 works in the legal status of gays and lesbians in the private sphere is far-reaching, both on its own terms and when considered in light of the structure and operation of modern anti-discrimination laws. That structure is well illustrated by contemporary statutes and ordinances prohibiting discrimination by providers of public accommodations. "At common law, innkeepers, smiths, and others who 'made profession of a public employment,' were prohibited from refusing, without good reason, to serve a customer." The duty was a general one and did not specify protection for particular groups. The common law rules, however, proved insufficient in many instances, and it was settled early that the Fourteenth Amendment did not give Congress a general power to prohibit discrimination in public accommodations. In consequence, most States have chosen to counter discrimination by enacting detailed statutory schemes. . . .

These statutes and ordinances . . . depart from the common law by enumerating the groups or persons within their ambit of protection. Enumeration is the essential device used to make the duty not to discriminate concrete and to provide guidance for those who must comply. In following this approach, Colorado's state and local governments have not limited anti-discrimination laws to groups that have so far been given the protection of heightened equal protection scrutiny under our cases. Rather, they set forth an extensive catalogue of traits which cannot be the basis for discrimination, including age, military status, marital status, pregnancy, parenthood, custody of a minor child, political affiliation, physical or mental disability of an individual or of his or her associates and, in recent times, sexual orientation.

Amendment 2 bars homosexuals from securing protection against the injuries that these public-accommodations laws address. That in itself is a severe consequence, but there is more. Amendment 2, in addition, nullifies specific legal protections for this targeted class in all transactions in housing, sale of real estate, insurance, health and welfare services, private education, and employment.

[handwritten margin note: A2 bars homosexuals from seeking redress]

Not confined to the private sphere, Amendment 2 also operates to repeal and forbid all laws or policies providing specific protection for gays or lesbians from discrimination by every level of Colorado government. The State Supreme Court cited two examples of protections in the governmental sphere that are now rescinded and may not be reintroduced. The first is Colorado Executive Order D0035 (1990), which forbids employment discrimination against "'all state employees, classified and exempt' on the basis of sexual orientation." Also repealed, and now forbidden, are "various provisions prohibiting discrimination based on sexual orientation at state colleges." . . .

Amendment 2's reach may not be limited to specific laws passed for the benefit of gays and lesbians. It is a fair, if not necessary, inference from the broad language of the amendment that it deprives gays and lesbians even of the protection of general laws and policies that prohibit arbitrary discrimination in governmental and private settings. At some point in the systematic administration of these laws, an official must determine whether homosexuality is an arbitrary and thus forbidden basis for decision. Yet a decision to that effect would itself amount to a policy prohibiting discrimination on the basis of homosexuality, and so would appear to be no more valid under Amendment 2 than the specific prohibitions against discrimination the state court held invalid.

If this consequence follows from Amendment 2, as its broad language suggests, it would compound the constitutional difficulties the law creates. . . . In any event, even if . . . homosexuals could find some safe harbor in laws of general application, we cannot accept the view that Amendment 2's prohibition on specific legal protections does no more than deprive homosexuals of special rights. To the contrary, the amendment imposes a special disability upon those persons alone. Homosexuals are forbidden the safeguards that others enjoy or may seek without constraint. They can obtain specific protection against discrimination only by enlisting the citizenry of Colorado to amend the state constitution or perhaps, on the State's view, by trying to pass helpful laws of general applicability. This is so no matter how local or discrete the harm, no matter how public and widespread the injury. We find nothing special in the protections Amendment 2 withholds. These are protections taken for granted by most people either because they already have them or do not need them; these are protections against exclusion from an almost limitless number of transactions and endeavors that constitute ordinary civic life in a free society.

III

The Fourteenth Amendment's promise that no person shall be denied the equal protection of the laws must co-exist with the practical necessity that most legislation classifies for one purpose or another, with resulting disadvantage to various groups or persons. We have attempted to reconcile the principle with the reality by stating that, if a law neither burdens a fundamental right nor targets a suspect class, we will uphold the legislative classification so long as it bears a rational relation to some legitimate end. Amendment 2 fails, indeed defies, even this conventional inquiry. First, the amendment has the peculiar property of imposing a broad and undifferentiated disability on a single named group, an exceptional and, as we shall explain, invalid form of legislation. Second, its sheer breadth is so discontinuous with the reasons offered for it that the amendment seems inexplicable by anything but animus toward the class that it affects; it lacks a rational relationship to legitimate state interests.

Taking the first point, even in the ordinary equal protection case calling for the most deferential of standards, we insist on knowing the relation between the classification adopted and the object to be attained. . . .

Amendment 2 confounds this normal process of judicial review. It is at once too narrow and too broad. It identifies persons by a single trait and then denies them protection across the board. The resulting disqualification of a class of persons from the right to seek specific protection from the law is unprecedented in our jurisprudence. The absence of precedent for Amendment 2 is itself instructive; "discriminations of an unusual character especially suggest careful consideration to determine whether they are obnoxious to the constitutional provision."

It is not within our constitutional tradition to enact laws of this sort. Central both to the idea of the rule of law and to our own Constitution's guarantee of equal protection is the principle that government and each of its parts remain open on impartial terms to all who seek its assistance. "'Equal protection of the laws is not achieved through indiscriminate imposition of inequalities.'" Respect for this principle explains why laws singling out a certain class of citizens for disfavored legal status or general hardships are rare. A law declaring that in general it shall be more difficult for one group of citizens than for all others to seek aid from the government is itself a denial of equal protection of the laws in the most literal sense. . . .

A second and related point is that laws of the kind now before us raise the inevitable inference that the disadvantage imposed is born of animosity toward the class of persons affected. "If the constitutional conception of 'equal protection of the laws' means anything, it must at the very least mean that a bare . . . desire to harm a politically unpopular group cannot constitute a legitimate governmental interest." [Department of Agriculture v. Moreno.] Even laws enacted for broad and ambitious purposes often can be explained by reference to legitimate public policies which justify the incidental disadvantages they impose on certain persons. Amendment 2, however, in making a general announcement that gays and lesbians shall not have any particular protections from the law, inflicts on them immediate, continuing, and real injuries that outrun and belie any legitimate justifications that may be claimed for it. We conclude that, in addition to the far-reaching deficiencies of Amendment 2 that we have noted, the principles it offends, in another sense, are conventional and venerable; a law must bear a rational relationship to a legitimate governmental purpose, and Amendment 2 does not.

The primary rationale the State offers for Amendment 2 is respect for other citizens' freedom of association, and in particular the liberties of landlords or employers who have personal or religious objections to homosexuality. Colorado also cites its interest in conserving resources to fight discrimination against other groups. The breadth of the Amendment is so far removed from these particular justifications that we find it impossible to credit them. We cannot say that Amendment 2 is directed to any identifiable legitimate purpose or discrete objective. It is a status-based enactment divorced from any factual context from which we could discern a relationship to legitimate state interests; it is a classification of persons undertaken for its own sake, something the Equal Protection Clause does not permit. "Class legislation . . . [is] obnoxious to the prohibitions of the Fourteenth Amendment. . . ." Civil Rights Cases.

We must conclude that Amendment 2 classifies homosexuals not to further a proper legislative end but to make them unequal to everyone else. This Colorado cannot do. A State cannot so deem a class of persons a stranger to its laws. Amendment 2 violates the Equal Protection Clause, and the judgment of the Supreme Court of Colorado is affirmed.

State interest

JUSTICE SCALIA, with whom [CHIEF JUSTICE REHNQUIST] and JUSTICE THOMAS join, dissenting.

The Court has mistaken a Kulturkampf for a fit of spite. The constitutional amendment before us here is not the manifestation of a "bare . . . desire to harm" homosexuals, but is rather a modest attempt by seemingly tolerant Coloradans to preserve traditional sexual mores against the efforts of a politically powerful minority to revise those mores through use of the laws. That objective, and the means chosen to achieve it, are not only unimpeachable under any constitutional doctrine hitherto pronounced (hence the opinion's heavy reliance upon principles of righteousness rather than judicial holdings); they have been specifically approved by the Congress of the United States and by this Court.

In holding that homosexuality cannot be singled out for disfavorable treatment, the Court . . . places the prestige of this institution behind the proposition that opposition to homosexuality is as reprehensible as racial or religious bias.

Whether it is or not is precisely the cultural debate that gave rise to the Colorado constitutional amendment (and to the preferential laws against which the amendment was directed). Since the Constitution of the United States says nothing about this subject, it is left to be resolved by normal democratic means, including the democratic adoption of provisions in state constitutions. This Court has no business imposing upon all Americans the resolution favored by the elite class from which the Members of this institution are selected, pronouncing that "animosity" toward homosexuality, is evil. I vigorously dissent.

I

Let me first discuss Part II of the Court's opinion, its longest section, which is devoted to rejecting the State's arguments that Amendment 2 "puts gays and lesbians in the same position as all other persons," and "does no more than deny homosexuals special rights." . . .

The amendment prohibits special treatment of homosexuals, and nothing more. It would not affect, for example, a requirement of state law that pensions be paid to all retiring state employees with a certain length of service; homosexual employees, as well as others, would be entitled to that benefit. But it would prevent the State or any municipality from making death-benefit payments to the "life partner" of a homosexual when it does not make such payments to the long-time roommate of a nonhomosexual employee. . . .

Despite all of its hand-wringing about the potential effect of Amendment 2 on general antidiscrimination laws, the Court's opinion ultimately does not dispute all this, but assumes it to be true. The only denial of equal treatment it contends homosexuals have suffered is this: They may not obtain preferential treatment without amending the state constitution. That is to say, the principle underlying the Court's opinion is that one who is accorded equal treatment under the laws, but cannot as readily as others obtain preferential treatment under the laws, has been denied equal protection of the laws. If merely stating this alleged "equal protection" violation does not suffice to refute it, our constitutional jurisprudence has achieved terminal silliness.

The central thesis of the Court's reasoning is that any group is denied equal protection when, to obtain advantage (or, presumably, to avoid disadvantage), it must have recourse to a more general and hence more difficult level of political decisionmaking than others. The world has never heard of such a principle, which is why the Court's opinion is so long on emotive utterance and so short on relevant legal citation. And it seems to me most unlikely that any multilevel democracy can function under such a principle. . . .

III

[No] principle set forth in the Constitution, nor even any imagined by this Court in the past 200 years, prohibits what Colorado has done here. But the case for Colorado is much stronger than that. What it has done is not only unprohibited, but eminently reasonable, with close, congressionally approved precedent in earlier constitutional practice.

First, as to its eminent reasonableness. The Court's opinion contains grim, disapproving hints that Coloradans have been guilty of "animus" or "animosity" toward homosexuality, as though that has been established as Unamerican. Of course it is our moral heritage that one should not hate any human being or class of human beings. But I had thought that one could consider certain conduct reprehensible — murder, for example, or polygamy, or cruelty to animals — and could exhibit even "animus" toward such conduct. Surely that is the only sort of "animus" at issue here: moral disapproval of homosexual conduct, the same sort of moral disapproval that produced the centuries-old criminal laws that we held constitutional in [Bowers v. Hardwick, 478 U.S. 186 (1986)]. . . . *

But though Coloradans are, as I say, entitled to be hostile toward homosexual conduct, the fact is that the degree of hostility reflected by Amendment 2 is the smallest conceivable. The Court's portrayal of Coloradans as a society fallen victim to pointless, hate-filled "gay-bashing" is so false as to be comical. Colorado not only is one of the 25 States that have repealed their antisodomy laws, but was among the first to do so. But the society that eliminates criminal punishment for homosexual acts does not necessarily abandon the view that homosexuality is morally wrong and socially harmful; often, abolition simply reflects the view that enforcement of such criminal laws involves unseemly intrusion into the intimate lives of citizens.

There is a problem, however, which arises when criminal sanction of homosexuality is eliminated but moral and social disapprobation of homosexuality is meant to be retained. The Court cannot be unaware of that problem; it is evident in many cities of the country, and occasionally bubbles to the surface of the news, in heated political disputes over such matters as the introduction into local schools of books teaching that homosexuality is an optional and fully acceptable "alternate life style." The problem (a problem, that is, for those who wish to retain social disapprobation of homosexuality) is that, because those who engage in homosexual conduct tend to reside in disproportionate numbers in certain communities, have high disposable income, and of course care about homosexual-rights issues much more ardently than the public at large, they possess political power much greater than their numbers, both locally and statewide. Quite understandably, they devote this political power to achieving not merely a grudging social toleration, but full social acceptance, of homosexuality.

By the time Coloradans were asked to vote on Amendment 2, their exposure to homosexuals' quest for social endorsement was not limited to newspaper accounts of happenings in places such as New York, Los Angeles, San Francisco, and Key West. Three Colorado cities — Aspen, Boulder, and Denver — had enacted ordinances that listed "sexual orientation" as an impermissible ground for discrimination, equating the moral disapproval of homosexual conduct with racial and religious bigotry. The phenomenon had even appeared statewide: the Governor of Colorado had signed an executive order pronouncing that "in the State of Colorado we recognize the diversity in our pluralistic society and strive to bring an end to discrimination in any form," and directing state agency-heads to "ensure non-discrimination" in hiring and promotion based on, among other things, "sexual orientation." I do not mean to be critical of these legislative successes; homosexuals are as entitled to use the legal system for reinforcement of their moral sentiments as are the rest of society. But they are subject to being countered by lawful, democratic countermeasures as well.

* [Those laws were subsequently struck down by the Supreme Court in Lawrence v. Texas, 539 U.S. 558 (2003). — EDS.]

That is where Amendment 2 came in. It sought to counter both the geographic concentration and the disproportionate political power of homosexuals by (1) resolving the controversy at the statewide level, and (2) making the election a single-issue contest for both sides. It put directly, to all the citizens of the State, the question: Should homosexuality be given special protection? They answered no. The Court today asserts that this most democratic of procedures is unconstitutional. Lacking any cases to establish that facially absurd proposition, it simply asserts that it must be unconstitutional, because it has never happened before. . . .

[The constitutions] of the States of Arizona, Idaho, New Mexico, Oklahoma, and Utah to this day contain provisions stating that polygamy is "forever prohibited." Polygamists, and those who have a polygamous "orientation," have been "singled out" by these provisions for much more severe treatment than merely denial of favored status; and that treatment can only be changed by achieving amendment of the state constitutions. The Court's disposition today suggests that these provisions are unconstitutional, and that polygamy must be permitted in these States on a state-legislated, or perhaps even local-option, basis — unless, of course, polygamists for some reason have fewer constitutional rights than homosexuals.

The United States Congress, by the way, required the inclusion of these anti-polygamy provisions in the constitutions of Arizona, New Mexico, Oklahoma, and Utah, as a condition of their admission to statehood. (For Arizona, New Mexico, and Utah, moreover, the Enabling Acts required that the antipolygamy provisions be "irrevocable without the consent of the United States and the people of said State" — so that not only were "each of [the] parts" of these States not "open on impartial terms" to polygamists, but even the States as a whole were not; polygamists would have to persuade the whole country to their way of thinking.) [Thus], this "singling out" of the sexual practices of a single group for statewide, democratic vote — so utterly alien to our constitutional system, the Court would have us believe — has not only happened, but has received the explicit approval of the United States Congress. . . .

IV

[The] Court today, announcing that Amendment 2 "defies . . . conventional [constitutional] inquiry," and "confounds [the] normal process of judicial review," employs a constitutional theory heretofore unknown to frustrate Colorado's reasonable effort to preserve traditional American moral values. The Court's stern disapproval of "animosity" towards homosexuality might be compared with what an earlier Court (including the revered Justices Harlan and Bradley) said in Murphy v. Ramsey, 114 U.S. 15 (1885), rejecting a constitutional challenge to a United States statute that denied the franchise in federal territories to those who engaged in polygamous cohabitation:

> Certainly no legislation can be supposed more wholesome and necessary in the founding of a free, self-governing commonwealth, fit to take rank as one of the coordinate States of the Union, than that which seeks to establish it on the basis of the idea of the family, as consisting in and springing from the union for life of one man and one woman in the holy estate of matrimony; the sure foundation of all that is stable and noble in our civilization; the best guaranty of that reverent morality which is the source of all beneficent progress in social and political improvement.

I would not myself indulge in such official praise for heterosexual monogamy, because I think it no business of the courts (as opposed to the political branches) to take sides in this culture war.

But the Court today has done so, not only by inventing a novel and extravagant constitutional doctrine to take the victory away from traditional forces, but even by verbally disparaging as bigotry adherence to traditional attitudes. To suggest, for example, that this constitutional amendment springs from nothing more than "a bare . . . desire to harm a politically unpopular group" is nothing short of insulting. (It is also nothing short of preposterous to call "politically unpopular" a group which enjoys enormous influence in American media and politics, and which, as the trial court here noted, though composing no more than 4% of the population had the support of 46% of the voters on Amendment 2.)

When the Court takes sides in the culture wars, it tends to be with the knights rather than the villeins — and more specifically with the Templars, reflecting the views and values of the lawyer class from which the Court's Members are drawn. How that class feels about homosexuality will be evident to anyone who wishes to interview job applicants at virtually any of the Nation's law schools. The interviewer may refuse to offer a job because the applicant is a Republican; because he is an adulterer; because he went to the wrong prep school or belongs to the wrong country club; because he eats snails; because he is a womanizer; because she wears real-animal fur; or even because he hates the Chicago Cubs. But if the interviewer should wish not to be an associate or partner of an applicant because he disapproves of the applicant's homosexuality, then he will have violated the pledge which the Association of American Law Schools requires all its member-schools to exact from job interviewers: "assurance of the employer's willingness" to hire homosexuals. This law-school view of what "prejudices" must be stamped out may be contrasted with the more plebeian attitudes that apparently still prevail in the United States Congress, which has been unresponsive to repeated attempts to extend to homosexuals the protections of federal civil rights laws, and which took the pains to exclude them specifically from the Americans with Disabilities Act of 1990.

Today's opinion has no foundation in American constitutional law, and barely pretends to. The people of Colorado have adopted an entirely reasonable provision which does not even disfavor homosexuals in any substantive sense, but merely denies them preferential treatment. Amendment 2 is designed to prevent piecemeal deterioration of the sexual morality favored by a majority of Coloradans, and is not only an appropriate means to that legitimate end, but a means that Americans have employed before. Striking it down is an act, not of judicial judgment, but of political will. I dissent.

Note: *The Meaning of* Romer

1. *Baselines again.* The Court claims that its decision guarantees for homosexuals only "equal" and not "special" protection. This is so, the Court asserts, because under modern conditions the baseline is a general right to be free from discrimination. Protections against discrimination are "taken for granted by most people either because they already have them or do not need them; these are protections against exclusion from an almost limitless number of transactions and endeavors that constitute ordinary civic life in a free society." Suppose Colorado

had never enacted Amendment 2 but had simply failed to enact measures protecting homosexuals from discrimination. Does it follow from the Court's analysis that a state acts "irrationally" and therefore violates the Constitution if it provides general protection against discrimination for a wide range of group but fails to provide such protection for gay men and lesbians?

In Perry v. Brown, 671 F.3d 1052 (9th Cir. 2012), the Ninth Circuit Court of Appeals held that a California constitutional amendment ("Proposition 8") restoring the restriction of marriage to opposite-sex couples (after a California Supreme Court decision struck down a prior restriction and 18,000 same-sex marriages had taken place) violated equal protection. It reasoned that "Like Amendment 2, Proposition 8 [had] the 'peculiar property,' of 'withdraw[ing] from homosexuals, but no others,' an existing legal right — here, access to the official designation of 'marriage' — that had been broadly available, notwithstanding the fact that the Constitution did not compel the state to confer it in the first place." Furthermore, "like Amendment 2, Proposition 8 constitutionalizes that disability, meaning that gays and lesbians may overcome it 'only by enlisting the citizenry of [the state] to amend the State Constitution' for a second time." The court recognized that there were some significant differences between Amendment 2 and Proposition 8.

> [But] Proposition 8 is no less problematic than Amendment 2 merely because its effect is narrower; to the contrary, the surgical precision with which it excises a right belonging to gay and lesbian couples makes it even more suspect. A law that has no practical effect except to strip one group of the right to use a state-authorized and socially meaningful designation is all the more "unprecedented" and "'unusual'" . . . and raises an even stronger "inference that the disadvantage imposed is born of animosity toward the class of persons affected."

The Supreme Court vacated the Ninth Circuit's decision in light of its conclusion that the proponents of Proposition 8 had lacked standing to appeal the district court's decision striking it down. Hollingsworth v. Perry, 133 S. Ct. 2652 (2013).

2. *Justice Scalia's dissent.* What is the meaning of the first sentence of Justice Scalia's opinion? "Kulturkampf" is the German word for "culture war." The term refers to the effort by the German government in the late nineteenth century, under the leadership of Count Bismarck, to reduce the influence of the Roman Catholic Church. Among other things, Bismarck insisted that the state train and license priests and imprisoned priests and bishops who disobeyed his orders. Consider the possibility that our Constitution outlaws state-supported "Kulturkampfs" and that Amendment 2 violated the Constitution precisely because it formed part of an official "culture war" against a particular subsection of the population. Note that the majority and dissenting opinions each accuse the other of departing from a position of state neutrality in this conflict. What does state neutrality mean in this context? Is neutrality a desirable or constitutionally required objective? For a discussion of the equal rights/special rights distinction, see Rubin, Equal Rights, Special Rights, and the Nature of Antidiscrimination Law, 97 Mich. L. Rev. 564 (1998).

3. *Beyond equal protection.* Perhaps because the Court's opinion does not follow the conventional outline for equal protection decisions, commentators have read the opinion in a variety of ways. On the decision's reach, compare Sunstein, Foreword: Leaving Things Undecided, 110 Harv. L. Rev. 4 (1996)

(defending a "minimalist" interpretation), with Seidman, *Romer's* Radicalism: The Unexpected Revival of Warren Court Activism, 1996 Sup. Ct. Rev. 67 (defending a "radical" interpretation). On its meaning, see, e.g., Jeffries and Levinson, The Non-Retrogression Principle in Constitutional Law, 86 Cal. L. Rev. 1211 (1998) (analyzing and criticizing *Romer* as embodying a nonretrogression principle); Amar, Attainder and Amendment 2: *Romer's* Rightness, 95 Mich. L. Rev. 203 (1996) (analyzing *Romer* under the bill of attainder clause); Farber and Sherry, The Pariah Principle, 13 Const. Comment. 257 (1996) (analyzing *Romer* under the principle that "forbids government from designating any societal group as untouchable, regardless of whether the group in question is generally entitled to some special degree of judicial protection"); Alexander, Sometimes Better Boring and Correct: Romer v. Evans as an Exercise of Ordinary Equal Protection Analysis, 68 U. Colo. L. Rev. 335 (1996) (analyzing *Romer* in terms of "ordinary" equal protection principles). See generally Symposium, Gay Rights and the Courts: The Amendment 2 Controversy, 68 U. Colo. L. Rev. 285 (1996).

Note: *The Standard of Review*

Part of the Court's explanation for its decision in *Romer* was the very breadth of Amendment 2. Thus, the Court never confronted the conventional question of what level of scrutiny to apply to laws that discriminate on the basis of sexual orientation with respect to a particular burden or benefit. Consider the various possibilities.

1. *Strict scrutiny*. No court has held that discrimination on the basis of sexual orientation triggers strict scrutiny as a matter of federal equal protection law. But the California Supreme Court held that discrimination on the basis of sexual orientation triggers strict scrutiny under the state analogue to the equal protection clause:

> [Sexual] orientation is a characteristic (1) that bears no relation to a person's ability to perform or contribute to society, and (2) that is associated with a stigma of inferiority and second-class citizenship, manifested by the group's history of legal and social disabilities. . . .
>
> [It is irrelevant] that there is a question as to whether this characteristic is or is not "immutable." Although we noted in [an earlier case holding that sex-based distinctions trigger strict scrutiny] that generally a person's gender is viewed as an immutable trait, immutability is not invariably required in order for a characteristic to be considered a suspect classification for equal protection purposes. California cases establish that a person's religion is a suspect classification for equal protection purposes, and one's religion, of course, is not immutable but is a matter over which an individual has control. ([And] alienage [is] treated as a suspect classification notwithstanding circumstance that alien can become a citizen.) Because a person's sexual orientation is so integral an aspect of one's identity, it is not appropriate to require a person to repudiate or change his or her sexual orientation in order to avoid discriminatory treatment.
>
> In his briefing before this court, the Attorney General . . . argues that a *fourth* requirement should be imposed before a characteristic is considered a constitutionally suspect basis for classification for equal protection purposes — namely, that "a 'suspect' classification is appropriately recognized only for minorities who are unable to use the political process to address their needs." The Attorney General's

brief asserts that "[since] the gay and lesbian community in California is obviously able to wield political power in defense of its interests, this Court should not hold that sexual orientation constitutes a suspect classification."

Although some California decisions in discussing suspect classifications have referred to a group's "political powerlessness," our cases have not identified a group's *current* political powerlessness as a necessary *prerequisite* for treatment as a suspect class. Indeed, if a group's *current* political powerlessness were a prerequisite to a characteristic's being considered a constitutionally suspect basis for differential treatment, it would be impossible to justify the numerous decisions that continue to treat sex, race, and religion as suspect classifications. Instead, our decisions make clear that the most important factors in deciding whether a characteristic should be considered a constitutionally suspect basis for classification are whether the class of persons who exhibit a certain characteristic historically has been subjected to invidious and prejudicial treatment, and whether society now recognizes that the characteristic in question generally bears no relationship to the individual's ability to perform or contribute to society. Thus, "courts must look closely at classifications based on that characteristic lest *outdated* social stereotypes result in invidious laws or practices." This rationale clearly applies to statutory classifications that mandate differential treatment on the basis of sexual orientation. . . .

In re Marriage Cases, 43 Cal. 4th 757, 183 P.3d 384 (2008). Note that California also applies strict, rather than intermediate, scrutiny to classifications based on gender.

2. *Intermediate scrutiny.* Is discrimination on the basis of sexual orientation simply sex discrimination? Consider the sodomy statute at issue in Lawrence v. Texas, 539 U.S. 558 (2003). (*Lawrence* is discussed in more detail at pages 678-679 and 693-694, infra, and in Chapter 6, section F3, infra.) The statute criminalized consensual oral or anal sex between two adults of the same sex (but not the same acts when performed by individuals of different sexes). Or consider statutes that restrict marriage to persons of opposite sexes. In either situation, it would be accurate to say that a man challenging the statute would have been treated differently had he been a woman (and a woman challenging the statute would have been treated differently if she had been a man). Is something important gained (or lost) by differentiating between sex discrimination claims and sexual orientation discrimination claims?

Consider Koppelman, Why Discrimination against Lesbians and Gay Men Is Sex Discrimination, 69 N.Y.U. L. Rev. 197, 235 (1994) (emphasis omitted):

> Most Americans learn no later than high school that one of the nastier sanctions that one will suffer if one deviates from the behavior traditionally deemed appropriate for one's sex is the imputation of homosexuality. . . .
>
> [The] central outrage of male sodomy is that a man is reduced to the status of a woman, which is understood to be degrading. Just as miscegenation was threatening because it called into question the distinctive and superior status of being white, homosexuality is threatening because it calls into question the distinctive and superior status of being male. Male homosexuals and lesbians, respectively, are understood to be guilty of one aspect of the dual crime of the miscegenating white woman: self-degradation and insubordination. As with miscegenation, a member of the superior caste who allows his body to be penetrated is thereby polluted and degraded, and he assumes the status of the subordinate caste: he becomes womanlike.

For a skeptical examination of the gender discrimination argument, see Stein, Evaluating the Sex Discrimination Argument for Lesbian and Gay Rights, 49 UCLA L. Rev. 471 (2001).

In <u>Windsor v. United</u> States, 699 F.3d 169 (2d Cir. 2012), the Second Circuit became the first federal court of appeals to apply intermediate scrutiny to claims of discrimination on the basis of sexual orientation, not as a subset of sex discrimination claims more generally but because discrimination on the basis of sexual orientation should trigger heightened scrutiny in its own right. The case before it concerned a challenge to the federal Defense of Marriage Act (DOMA). Section 3 of DOMA provides that

> [in] determining the meaning of any Act of Congress, or of any ruling, regulation, or interpretation of the various administrative bureaus and agencies of the United States, the word "marriage" means only a legal union between one man and one woman as husband and wife, and the word "spouse" refers only to a person of the opposite sex who is a husband or a wife.

Edith Windsor, a widow whose marriage was recognized by New York State, sued for a refund of estate taxes levied on the estate of her deceased spouse: had Windsor's spouse been a man, rather than a woman, her estate would have passed to Windsor untaxed. The Second Circuit held that all four of the factors the Supreme Court had used "to decide whether a new classification qualifies as a quasi-suspect class" militated in favor of imposing heightened scrutiny here. First, the Second Circuit pointed to the fact that lesbian and gay people had experienced a history of official discrimination. Second, the court, quoting City of Cleburne v. Cleburne Living Center, 473 U.S. 432 (1985), concluded that sexual orientation had no "relation to ability to perform or contribute to society." To the contrary, "[t]he aversion homosexuals experience has nothing to do with aptitude or performance." Third, the court of appeals concluded that "homosexuality is a sufficiently discernible characteristic to define a discrete minority class." The court found that it did not matter whether sexual orientation was "necessarily fixed" or might "change over time, range along a continuum, and overlap (for bisexuals)." It pointed out that "[c]lassifications based on alienage, illegitimacy, and national origin are all subject to heightened scrutiny, even though these characteristics do not declare themselves, and often may be disclosed or suppressed as a matter of preference." Indeed, "[a]lienage and illegitimacy are actually subject to change." Finally, the court concluded that "homosexuals are still significantly encumbered" in using the political process to protect themselves from discrimination: "The question is not whether homosexuals have achieved political successes over the years; they clearly have. The question is whether they have the strength to politically protect themselves from wrongful discrimination."

The Second Circuit saw "parallels between the status of women at the time of *Frontiero* and homosexuals today: their position 'has improved markedly in recent decades,' but they still 'face pervasive, although at times more subtle, discrimination . . . in the political arena.'"

Applying intermediate scrutiny, the Second Circuit struck down Section 3 of DOMA, finding that it was not substantially related to any important governmental purpose.

The third and fourth factors discussed by the Second Circuit in *Windsor* map onto *Carolene Products*' identification of "prejudice against discrete and insular minorities" as "a special condition, which tends seriously to curtail the operation of those political processes ordinarily to be relied upon to protect minorities, and which may call for a correspondingly more searching judicial inquiry." Do these concerns operate differently with respect to gay men and lesbians than with respect to other groups receiving heightened scrutiny? See Sunstein, Homosexuality and the Constitution, 70 Ind. L.J. 1, 8 (1994):

> Homosexuals may well be politically powerless in the constitutionally relevant sense. [Precisely] because they are often anonymous [and] diffuse [they] face large barriers to exerting adequate political influence. [The] ability to conceal can actually make things worse from the standpoint of exercising political power. This problem, severe in itself, is heightened by the fact that people who challenge discrimination on the basis of sexual orientation are often "accused" of being homosexuals [themselves]. The existence of widespread hostility against homosexuals can thus make it difficult for homosexuals and heterosexuals alike to speak out against this form of discrimination.

See also Ackerman, Beyond *Carolene Products*, 98 Harv. L. Rev. 713, 718 (1985) (arguing that precisely because gay people are neither "discrete" — because they are not always easily identifiable, and thus can avoid being forced into political solidarity with one another — nor "insular" they face higher political organization costs and thus have a particularly strong claim "upon *Carolene*'s concern with the fairness of the political process").

Compare Duncan, Who Wants to Stop the Church?: Homosexual Rights Legislation, Public Policy, and Religious Freedom, 69 Notre Dame L. Rev. 393, 409 (1994):

> Not only are homosexuals an affluent and a highly educated class, they are also politically powerful. Homosexuals are far more likely than average to vote, and one of the fastest-growing political action organizations in Washington is the Human Rights Campaign, a pro-gay group that raised $4.5 million in 1992. During the Democratic primaries in [1992], all five of the leading Democratic candidates for president "actively courted the gay vote." And, of course, President Clinton is a strong supporter of the gay political agenda.

The Supreme Court affirmed the Second Circuit's judgment in United States v. Windsor, 133 S. Ct. 2675 (2013). The opinions in the case are described in Chapter 6, section F. Justice Kennedy, writing for the Court's majority, stated that "[t]he liberty protected by the Fifth Amendment's Due Process Clause contains within it the prohibition against denying to any person the equal protection of the laws. While the Fifth Amendment itself withdraws from Government the power to degrade or demean in the way this law does, the equal protection guarantee of the Fourteenth Amendment makes that Fifth Amendment right all the more specific and all the better understood and preserved." The Court's opinion, however, did not discuss the appropriate standard of review.

3. *Rationality review with "bite."* Another federal court of appeals faced with a challenge to the Defense of Marriage Act declined to apply intermediate scrutiny. In Massachusetts v. U.S. Department of Health & Human Services, 682 F.3d 1 (1st Cir. 2012), it offered a different view:

> [T]o create such a new suspect classification for same-sex relationships would have far-reaching implications. . . . Nothing indicates that the Supreme Court is about to adopt this new suspect classification. . . .

However, that is not the end of the matter. Without relying on suspect classifications, Supreme Court equal protection decisions have both intensified scrutiny of purported justifications where minorities are subject to discrepant treatment and have limited the permissible justifications. . . .

In a set of equal protection decisions, the Supreme Court has now several times struck down state or local enactments without invoking any suspect classification. In each, the protesting group was historically disadvantaged or unpopular, and the statutory justification seemed thin, unsupported or impermissible. . . .

[U.S. Department of Agriculture v. Moreno, 413 U.S. 528 (1973), City of Cleburne v. Cleburne Living Center, 473 U.S. 432 (1985), and Romer v. Evans, 517 U.S. 620 (1996)] did not adopt some new category of suspect classification or employ rational basis review in its minimalist form; instead, the Court rested on the case-specific nature of the discrepant treatment, the burden imposed, and the infirmities of the justifications offered. . . .

All three of the cited cases . . . stressed the historic patterns of disadvantage suffered by the group adversely affected by the statute. As with the women, the poor and the mentally impaired, gays and lesbians have long been the subject of discrimination. . . .

Accordingly, we conclude that the extreme deference accorded to ordinary economic legislation in cases like *Lee Optical* would not be extended to DOMA by the Supreme Court; and without insisting on "compelling" or "important" justifications or "narrow tailoring," the Court would scrutinize with care the purported bases for the legislation. . . .

Does the First Circuit's approach give any guidance as to how that court would analyze other statutes or policies that discriminate on the basis of sexual orientation?

4. *Conventional rationality review.* In Lawrence v. Texas, 539 U.S. 558 (2003), the Supreme Court held that laws criminalizing private, consensual sex between two adults of the same sex violate the due process clause. (*Lawrence* is discussed in more detail in Chapter 6, section F3, infra.) *Lawrence* overruled Bowers v. Hardwick, 478 U.S. 186 (1986), in which the Court had upheld a Georgia law criminalizing all oral or anal sex as applied to homosexual activity. (While the *Romer* majority never mentioned *Hardwick*, Justice Scalia's dissent spent considerable time arguing that if states were entitled to criminalize gay sexual activity, a fortiori they could refuse to accord special protection to gay men and lesbians.) The *Lawrence* Court recognized that *Romer* "cast [the Bowers v. Hardwick] holding into . . . doubt," but declined to rely on *Romer* in striking down the Texas statute because "[were] we to hold the statute invalid under the Equal Protection Clause some might question whether a prohibition would be valid if drawn differently, say, to prohibit the conduct both between same-sex and different-sex participants."

Was the Court correct? Does its concern rest on the probability that a facially neutral statute would be enforced in a selective manner? If it does, is the real problem the difficulty of teasing out discriminatory purpose?

In a concurrence in the judgment in *Lawrence*, Justice O'Connor embraced an equal protection clause basis for striking down Texas's statute. Notably, she did not argue for strict scrutiny. Rather, she concluded that Texas's law failed even to serve a legitimate state interest:

We have consistently held, however, that some objectives, such as "a bare . . . desire to harm a politically unpopular group," are not legitimate state interests. [*Moreno; Cleburne; Romer.*] When a law exhibits such a desire to harm a politically unpopular group, we have applied a more searching form of rational basis review to strike down such laws under the Equal Protection Clause.

We have been most likely to apply rational basis review to hold a law unconstitutional under the Equal Protection Clause where, as here, the challenged legislation inhibits personal relationships. . . .

The statute at issue here makes sodomy a crime only if a person "engages in deviate sexual intercourse with another individual of the same sex." Sodomy between opposite-sex partners, however, is not a crime in Texas. . . .

The Texas statute makes homosexuals unequal in the eyes of the law by making particular conduct — and only that conduct — subject to criminal sanction. . . .

The effect of Texas's sodomy law is not just limited to the threat of prosecution or consequence of conviction. Texas's sodomy law brands all homosexuals as criminals, thereby making it more difficult for homosexuals to be treated in the same manner as everyone else. Indeed, Texas itself has previously acknowledged the collateral effects of the law, stipulating in a prior challenge to this action that the law "legally sanctions discrimination against [homosexuals] in a variety of ways unrelated to the criminal law," including in the areas of "employment, family issues, and housing." . . .

This case raises [the question] . . . whether, under the Equal Protection Clause, moral disapproval is a legitimate state interest to justify by itself a statute that bans homosexual sodomy, but not heterosexual sodomy. It is not. Moral disapproval of this group, like a bare desire to harm the group, is an interest that is insufficient to satisfy rational basis review under the Equal Protection Clause. . . .

Is the desire to express disapproval of homosexual activity or to condemn gay people as immoral always an impermissible government purpose? If it is, is there any law that treats homosexuals and heterosexuals differently that can withstand rationality review?

In this light, consider the history of "don't ask, don't tell." For years, gay men and lesbians were barred from military service. See generally R. Shilts, Conduct Unbecoming (1993). In 1993, responding to President Clinton's indication that he might lift the ban, Congress enacted 10 U.S.C. §654. Declaring that "unit cohesion" was critical to combat capability and that combat troops were required "involuntarily to accept living conditions and working conditions that are often spartan, primitive, and characterized by forced intimacy with little or no privacy," Congress required that, under most circumstances, members of the armed forces should be separated from service if they stated that they were homosexual or bisexual or engaged in homosexual acts. The policy was repeatedly, and unsuccessfully, challenged as a denial of equal protection. See Cook v. Gates, 528 F.3d 42 (1st Cir. 2008) (holding that "don't ask, don't tell" was subject only to rationality review, which it satisfied because of the government's interest in service members' morale and unit cohesion); cf. Witt v. Department of the Air Force, 527 F.3d 806 (9th Cir. 2008) (affirming the dismissal of a service member's equal protection claim, but allowing her to go forward on her procedural and substantive due process claims).

If the major argument about unit cohesion rests on the potential disruption caused by other service members' dislike of or discomfort around gay people, can unit cohesion provide a legitimate or compelling reason for exclusion? In this regard, consider Palmore v. Sidoti, 466 U.S. 429 (1984), discussed on page 545, supra. There, the Supreme Court held that a court deciding a child custody case could not take into account the potential prejudice that would be suffered by a white child if custody were granted to a parent who had subsequently entered into an interracial marriage. Although the state had "a duty of the highest order to protect the interests of minor children," and there was "a risk that a child living with a step-parent of a different race may be subject to a variety of pressures and stresses," the "reality of private biases and the possible injury they might inflict" were not "permissible considerations. [Private] biases may be outside the reach of the law, but the law cannot, directly or indirectly, give them effect." Are the government interests served by unit cohesion more compelling? Does the answer to this question necessarily require considering whether sexual orientation is a suspect classification? Note also in this regard the Court's general deference to the military, even in cases involving sex discrimination, when military operations are at issue.

More generally, does *Palmore* undercut decisionmaking on the basis of sexual orientation with respect to family law matters, such as adoption or child custody decisions?

Although equal protection challenges to don't ask, don't tell failed, the policy was repealed by Congress.

5. *Same-sex marriage.* Do laws that restrict marriage to opposite-sex couples violate the equal protection clause? Beginning in the 1990s, several state supreme courts addressed this question under state constitutional provisions dealing with equality. See, e.g., Varnum v. Brien, 763 N.W.2d 862 (Iowa 2009); In re Marriage Cases, 43 Cal. 4th 757, 183 P.3d 384 (2008); Kerrigan v. Commissioner of Public Health, 289 Conn. 135, 957 A.2d 407 (2008); Baehr v. Lewin, 74 Haw. 645, 852 P.2d 44 (1993); Conaway v. Deane, 401 Md. 219, 932 A.2d 571 (2007); Goodridge v. Department of Public Health, 440 Mass. 309, 798 N.E.2d 941 (2003); Lewis v. Harris, 188 N.J. 415, 908 A.2d 196 (2006); Hernandez v. Robles, 7 N.Y.3d 338, 855 N.E.2d 1 (2006); Baker v. State, 170 Vt. 194, 744 A.2d 864 (1999); Andersen v. King County, 158 Wis. 2d 1, 138 P.3d 963 (2006).

Courts addressing the issue have applied a variety of legal standards, ranging from strict scrutiny (the California case), to intermediate scrutiny (the Connecticut case), to rationality review (the New York, Vermont, and Washington cases). Even when state courts applied rationality review, they reached different conclusions regarding the rationality of the state's proffered reasons for restricting marriage to opposite-sex couples.

In Obergefell v. Hodges, 135 S. Ct. 2584 (2015), the Court relied on both the due process clause and the equal protection clause to hold that state laws excluding same-sex couples from the right to marry are unconstitutional. Once again, the Court's discussion of the equal protection clause did not specify the standard of review that it was using. (The case is covered more fully in Chapter 6, section F.).

To what extent do the judicial and political responses to questions of sexual orientation generally, and same-sex marriage specifically, suggest the limits of constitutional adjudication as a mechanism for settling hotly contested social issues? For representative discussions of the relationship between judicial decisions, popular opinion, and social change, see D. Cole, Engines of Liberty: The Power of Citizen Activists to Make Constitutional Law 17–93 (2016); M. Klarman, From the Closet to the Altar: Courts, Backlash, and the Struggle for Same-Sex Marriage (2012); Egan, Persily, and Wallsten, Gay Rights, in Public Opinion and Constitutional Controversy (N. Persily, J. Citrin, and P. Egan eds.,

2008); Schacter, Sexual Orientation, Social Change, and the Courts, 54 Drake L. Rev. 861 (2006).

F. EQUAL PROTECTION METHODOLOGY: OTHER CANDIDATES FOR HEIGHTENED SCRUTINY

What, if any, other classifications should be regarded as "suspect"? What criteria should the Court use in assessing the claims of other "groups for heightened scrutiny"? Is the analogy to race and gender useful? If so, which characteristics of blacks and women must other candidates for heightened scrutiny share? Might heightened scrutiny for some classifications be justified even though the problems of the group are entirely different from those facing racial minorities and women? If so, what sorts of problems should trigger judicial intervention?

1. Alienage

One way to think about heightened scrutiny for suspect classifications is that it is the appropriate judicial response to efforts by the majority to exclude certain groups from the political community. In the famous footnote 4 of United States v. Carolene Products Co., 304 U.S. 144 (1938), the Supreme Court intimated that "more searching judicial inquiry" in cases involving discrete and insular minorities might rest on the fact that prejudice "tends seriously to curtail the operation of those political processes ordinarily to be relied upon to protect minorities." Yet the Constitution itself seems to contemplate different access to the political system for citizens and noncitizens: The amendments that explicitly protect the right to vote against discrimination on the basis of race, sex, and age, for example, each provide that the right "of citizens of the United States" cannot be denied on a forbidden basis. And the United States does not invariably owe the same protections to persons outside the nation as it does to those within its jurisdiction. See, e.g., United States v. Verdugo-Urquidez, 494 U.S. 259 (1990) (fourth amendment protection against unreasonable searches and seizures does not apply to a search of property owned by a nonresident alien in Mexico).

The moral and legal legitimacy of this power to define boundaries for the political community is intensely controversial. At one time, many groups we now include within the community — most notably racial minorities — were excluded. And yet at some point lines must be drawn. For example, some who claim that the U.S. government owes a duty to citizens of Mexico base the claim on physical proximity and are prepared to acknowledge that it may not owe the same duty to citizens of Pakistan. See Lopez, Undocumented Mexican Migration: In Search of a Just Immigration Law and Policy, 28 UCLA L. Rev. 615, 698–700 (1981).

Can the need to draw some boundaries around the political community be reconciled with heightened scrutiny for classifications disadvantaging some groups outside those boundaries? Are there principled limits on the way in which the boundaries can be defined? The Supreme Court's treatment of statutes disadvantaging aliens raises these questions.

Sugarman v. Dougall

413 U.S. 634 (1973)

MR. JUSTICE BLACKMUN delivered the opinion of the Court. . . .

[Appellees challenged the constitutionality of a New York statute that excluded aliens from all government civil service positions filled by competitive examination. Such positions included the "full range of work tasks [all] the way from the menial to the policy making." However, the exclusion did not apply to higher offices in the state executive departments and to elected officers and offices filled by the Governor or by legislative appointment.]

As is so often the case, it is important at the outset to define the precise and narrow issue that is here presented. The Court is faced only with the question whether New York's flat statutory prohibition against the employment of aliens in the competitive classified civil service is constitutionally valid. The Court is not asked to decide whether a particular alien, any more than a particular citizen, may be refused employment or discharged on an individual basis for whatever legitimate reason the State might possess.

Neither is the Court reviewing a legislative scheme that bars some or all aliens from closely defined and limited classes of public employment. . . .

It is established, of course, that an alien is entitled to the shelter of the Equal Protection Clause. [Appellants] argue, however, that [the statute] does not violate the equal protection guarantee of the Fourteenth Amendment because [it] "establishes a generic classification reflecting the special requirements of public employment in the career civil service." The distinction drawn between the citizen and the alien, it is said, "rests on the fundamental concept of identity between a government and the members, or citizens, of the state." The civil servant "participates directly in the formulation and execution of government policy," and thus must be free of competing obligations to another power. The State's interest in having an employee of undivided loyalty is substantial, for obligations attendant upon foreign citizenship "might impair the exercise of his judgment or jeopardize public confidence in his objectivity." [It] is at once apparent, however, that appellants' asserted justification proves both too much and too little. [The] State's broad prohibition of the employment of aliens applies to many positions with respect to which the State's proffered justification has little, if any, relationship. At the same time, the prohibition has no application at all to positions that would seem naturally to fall within the State's asserted purpose. Our standard of review of statutes that treat aliens differently from citizens requires a greater degree of precision.

In Graham v. Richardson, 403 U.S. 365, 372 (1971), we observed that aliens as a class "are a prime example of a 'discrete and insular' minority (see United States v. Carolene Products Co., 304 U.S. 144, 152–153, n.4 (1938))," and that classifications based on alienage are "subject to close judicial scrutiny."

[Graham concerned a constitutional challenge to state statutes disqualifying aliens from receipt of various forms of welfare assistance. Justice Blackmun's opinion for the Court held that "classifications based on alienage, like those based on nationality or race, are inherently suspect." Applying strict scrutiny to the challenged statutes, the Court found that the "State's desire to preserve limited welfare benefits for its own citizens is inadequate to justify [making] noncitizens ineligible for public assistance."]

Applying this standard to New York's purpose in confining civil servants in the competitive class to those persons who have no ties of citizenship elsewhere, [the statute] does not withstand the necessary close scrutiny. We recognize a State's interest in establishing its own form of government, and in limiting participation in that government to those who are within "the basic conception of a political community." Dunn v. Blumstein, 405 U.S. 330, 344 (1972). We recognize, too, the State's broad power to define its political community. But in seeking to achieve this substantial purpose, with discrimination against aliens, the means the State employs must be precisely drawn in light of the acknowledged purpose.

[The statute] is neither narrowly confined nor precise in its application. Its imposed ineligibility may apply to the "sanitation man, class B," to the typist, and to the office worker, as well as to the person who directly participates in the formulation and execution of important state policy. . . .

[We do not hold] that a State may not, in an appropriately defined class of positions, require citizenship as a qualification for office. Just as "the Framers of the Constitution intended the States to keep for themselves, as provided in the Tenth Amendment, the power to regulate elections," "[e]ach State has the power to prescribe the qualifications of its officers and the manner in which they shall be chosen." Such power inheres in the State by virtue of its obligation, already noted, "to preserve the basic conception of a political community." And this power and responsibility of the State applies, not only to the qualifications of voters, but also to persons holding state elective or important nonelective executive, legislative, and judicial positions, for officers who participate directly in the formulation, execution, or review of broad public policy perform functions that go to the heart of representative government. . . .

This Court has never held that aliens have a constitutional right to vote or to hold high public office under the Equal Protection Clause. Indeed implicit in many of this Court's voting rights decisions is the notion that citizenship is a permissible criterion for limiting such rights. A restriction on the employment of noncitizens, narrowly confined, could have particular relevance to this important state responsibility, for alienage itself is a factor that reasonably could be employed in defining "political community." . . .

MR. JUSTICE REHNQUIST, dissenting.

The Court [holds] that an alien is not really different from a citizen, and that any legislative classification on the basis of alienage is "inherently suspect." The Fourteenth Amendment, the Equal Protection Clause of which the Court interprets as invalidating the state legislation here involved, contains no language concerning "inherently suspect classifications," or for that matter, merely "suspect classifications." The principal purpose of those who drafted and adopted the Amendment was to prohibit the States from invidiously discriminating by reason of race, Slaughter-House Cases, and, because of this plainly manifested intent, classifications based on race have rightly been held "suspect" under the Amendment. But there is no language used in the Amendment, or any historical evidence as to the intent of the Framers, which would suggest to the slightest degree that it was intended to render alienage a "suspect" classification, that it was designed in any way to protect "discrete and insular minorities" other than racial minorities, or that it would in any way justify the result reached by the Court in these two cases. . . .

[The record contains] no indication that the aliens suffered any disability that precluded them, either as a group or individually, from applying for and being granted the status of naturalized citizens. [The] "status" of these individuals was not, therefore, one with which they were forever encumbered; they could take steps to alter it when and if they chose. . . . [1]

The Court, by holding in these cases and in Graham v. Richardson that a citizen-alien classification is "suspect" in the eyes of our Constitution, fails to mention, let alone rationalize, the fact that the Constitution itself recognizes a basic difference between citizens and aliens. That distinction is constitutionally important in no less than 11 instances in a political document noted for its brevity. . . .

Our society, consisting of over 200 million individuals of multitudinous origins, customs, tongues, beliefs, and cultures is, to say the least, diverse. It would hardly take extraordinary ingenuity for a lawyer to find "insular and discrete" minorities at every turn in the road. Yet, unless the Court can precisely define and constitutionally justify both the terms and analysis it uses, these decisions today stand for the proposition that the Court can choose a "minority" it "feels" deserves "solicitude" and thereafter prohibit the States from classifying that "minority" differently from the "majority." I cannot find, and the Court does not cite, any constitutional authority for such a "ward of the Court" approach to equal protection. . . .

It is not irrational to assume that aliens as a class are not familiar with how we as individuals treat others and how we expect "government" to treat us. An alien who grew up in a country in which political mores do not reject bribery or self-dealing to the same extent that our culture does; in which an imperious bureaucracy historically adopted a complacent or contemptuous attitude toward those it was supposed to serve; in which fewer if any checks existed on administrative abuses; in which "low-level" civil servants serve at the will of their superiors — could rationally be thought not to be able to deal with the public and with citizen civil servants with the same rapport that one familiar with our political and social mores would, or to approach his duties with the attitude that such positions exist for service, not personal sinecures of either the civil servant or his or her superior.

Note: *Strict Scrutiny for Classifications Based on Alienage: Defining the Political Community*

Is there an adequate justification for subjecting alienage classifications to special scrutiny? Consider the following arguments.

1. *History of discrimination.* Is strict scrutiny for alienage classifications required because aliens, like blacks and women, have suffered a history of discrimination in the United States? Historically, different states at different times have denied aliens the right to vote, prohibited them from engaging in a wide range of occupations, discriminated against them in taxation, and restricted their ownership of property. Moreover, a general sense of xenophobia has affected

---

1. Although some of the members of the class had not been residents of the United States for five years at the time the complaint was filed, and therefore were ineligible to apply immediately for citizenship, there is no indication that these members, assuming that they are in the same "class" as the named appellees, would be prohibited from seeking citizenship status after they had resided in this country for the required period. In any event, this circumstance only underscores the fact that it is not unreasonable to assume that they have not learned about and adapted to our mores and institutions to the same extent as one who had lived here for five years would have through social contact.

American attitudes and policies at various times in our history. In the Alien Act of 1798 and during the "Red Scare" after World War I, for example, the federal government adopted especially severe measures to deal with suspected subversion by aliens. See generally W. Gibson, Aliens and the Law (1940); M. Konvitz, The Alien and the Asiatic in American Law (1946); J. Smith, Freedom's Fetters (1956). See also Takahashi v. Fish & Game Commission, 334 U.S. 410 (1948) (invalidating a California law restricting the right of aliens to fish); Oyama v. California, 332 U.S. 633 (1948) (invalidating a California law restricting the right of aliens to own land); Truax v. Raich, 239 U.S. 33 (1915) (invalidating an Arizona law prohibiting any business employing five or more persons from employing more than 20 percent aliens).

2. *Alienage as an immutable characteristic.* Is strict scrutiny for alienage classifications required because it is an immutable characteristic over which the disadvantaged individual can exercise no control? Note that many resident aliens may be eligible for U.S. citizenship but choose not to become citizens. In Nyquist v. Mauclet, 432 U.S. 1 (1977), the Supreme Court rejected New York's argument that it was entitled to deny financial aid to noncitizen students who had neither applied for citizenship nor had affirmed their intent to apply as soon as they became eligible.

If aliens are free to change their status at will, why aren't classifications disadvantaging this group justified as a means of encouraging naturalization? Compare Plyler v. Doe, 457 U.S. 202 (1982), where the Court invalidated a Texas policy of refusing to provide free public education to illegally present alien children. The Court rejected the assertion that illegal aliens are a suspect class. "Unlike most of the classifications that we have recognized as suspect, entry into this class, by virtue of entry into this country, is the product of voluntary action. Indeed, entry into the class is itself a crime." But, although "[persuasive] arguments support the view that a State may withhold its beneficence from those whose very presence within the United States is the product of their own unlawful conduct," these arguments

> do not apply with the same force to classifications imposing disabilities on the minor *children* of such illegal entrants. [The] "parents have the ability to conform their conduct to societal norms," and presumably the ability to remove themselves from the State's jurisdiction; but the children who are plaintiffs in these cases "can affect neither their parents' conduct nor their own status" [quoting Trimble v. Gordon, 430 U.S. 762 (1977)]. Even if the State found it expedient to control the conduct of adults by acting against their children, legislation directing the onus of a parent's misconduct against his children does not comport with fundamental conceptions of justice.

Because Texas's policy "[imposed] a lifetime hardship on a discrete class of children not accountable for their disabling status," the Court concluded that the discrimination "can hardly be considered rational unless it furthers some substantial goal of the State." Chief Justice Burger filed a dissenting opinion, in which Justices White, Rehnquist, and O'Connor joined.

Illegal aliens are subject to deportation and, if deported, these aliens would be denied an education in the Texas public schools. Does it make sense, then, to say that their rights are violated when they are denied such an education while illegally residing in Texas? Like several of the other cases discussed in this section, *Plyler* raises a question — addressed more fully in Chapter 6, section E, infra — whether equal protection decisions are sometimes inflected by the underlying interests at stake.

3. *Aliens as a "discrete" and "insular" minority.* Are aliens members of a "discrete and insular [minority]" hampered by the kind of prejudice "which tends seriously to curtail the operation of those political processes ordinarily to be relied upon to protect minorities"? United States v. Carolene Products, 304 U.S. 144, 152 n.4 (1938). Consider Lusky, Footnote Redux: A *Carolene Products* Reminiscence, 82 Colum. L. Rev. 1087, 1093 n.72 (1982):

> As a matter of language, "discrete" means separate or distinct and "insular" means isolated or detached. The words do not describe aliens as such; many of them, who are anglophones, pass unnoticed, and many if not most others fit into the social scene with little difficulty. Of course, there are sizeable ethnic groups, and they include citizens as well as aliens, who are held at arm's length — Chicanos, Orientals, and so on — but that is quite another matter.

But compare Rosberg, The Protection of Aliens from Discriminatory Treatment by the National Government, 1977 Sup. Ct. Rev. 275, 309–310:

> Given the exclusion of aliens from the political process, it is [reasonable] for the Court to demand a special showing from the state if it is to classify on the basis of alienage. The state has presumably weighed its interest in giving a preference to the members of its polity against the aliens' interest in enjoying the benefits at issue. But aliens have had no opportunity to participate in the process of measuring the relative weight of these two interests. Since the legislature has denied aliens any chance to assert their own interests in the political forum, it cannot expect the courts to maintain their usual deference to the legislature's balancing of the interests.

Does basing strict scrutiny on the political disabilities that the law itself imposes on aliens involve circular reasoning? In the second paragraph of the *Carolene Products* footnote, Justice Stone suggested that strict scrutiny might be appropriate for laws that "[restrict] those political processes which can ordinarily be expected to bring about repeal of undesirable legislation." If aliens are politically vulnerable because they lack the franchise, why isn't the appropriate solution to scrutinize strictly the laws denying them the right to vote? See generally Rosberg, Aliens and Equal Protection: Why Not the Right to Vote?, 75 Mich. L. Rev. 1092 (1977). Note that the Court in *Sugarman* affirms the states' right to restrict the franchise and policymaking positions to citizens. Is there a justification for these restrictions that would survive strict scrutiny?

4. *Alienage and the political community.* In In re Griffiths, 413 U.S. 717 (1973), a case decided on the same day as *Sugarman*, the Court held that a state could not constitutionally exclude aliens from membership in the bar. However, in a series of subsequent cases the Court has upheld a number of state restrictions on employment of aliens on the theory that the positions involve the formulation or execution of broad public policy and may therefore be limited to members of the political community. See Foley v. Connelie, 435 U.S. 291 (1978) (upholding prohibition on aliens serving on state police force); Ambach v. Norwick, 441 U.S. 68 (1979) (upholding citizenship requirement for public school teachers); Cabell v. Chavez-Salido, 454 U.S. 432 (1982) (upholding citizenship requirement for probation officers). In Bernal v. Fainter, 467 U.S. 216 (1984), however, a unanimous Court invalidated a citizenship requirement for notaries public.

Can the results in these cases be reconciled? In Cabell v. Chavez-Salido, the Court acknowledged that the alienage decisions "have not formed an unwavering line over the years. [But] to say that the decisions do not fall into a neat pattern is not to say that they fall into no pattern." According to the Court:

> The cases through *Graham* dealt for the most part with attempts by the States to retain certain economic benefits exclusively for citizens. Since *Graham*, the Court has confronted claims distinguishing between the economic and sovereign functions of government. This distinction has been supported by the argument that although citizenship is not a relevant ground for the distribution of economic benefits, it is a relevant ground for determining membership in the political community.

Is this distinction sound? Note that the Court has relied on a similar distinction under the dormant commerce clause where it has been willing to uphold state actions as a "market participant" that would be invalidated if the state were acting as a "market regulator." See Chapter 2, section D, supra.

How does one separate the "economic" and "sovereign" functions of government? In *Cabell*, the Court set out a two-pronged test:

> First, the specificity of the classification will be examined: a classification that is substantially overinclusive or underinclusive tends to undercut the governmental claim that the classification serves legitimate political ends. [Second], even if the classification is sufficiently tailored, it may be applied in the particular case only to "persons holding state elective or important nonelective executive, legislative, and judicial positions," those officers who "participate directly in the formulation, execution, or review of broad public policy" and hence "perform functions that go to the heart of representative government." [*Sugarman.*]

Is this test workable? How can one determine whether a classification is over- or underinclusive without first settling on the level of review under which the fit is to be measured?

What is the justification for separating the "economic" and "sovereign" functions of government? Doesn't this distinction turn the *Carolene Products* theory on its head? That theory suggests that strict scrutiny is appropriate precisely when political, rather than economic, rights are at stake.

If "representation-reinforcement" for politically disadvantaged minorities is not the basis for the Court's intervention in this area, what is? Consider the possibility that the decisions reflect a concern that classifications in this area are peculiarly likely to reflect hostility or prejudice and not to respond to a legitimate effort by the state to promote the public interest. Is that a plausible distinction? How does it differ from an approach based on representation-reinforcement?

Note: *Alienage and Federal Preemption*

Can the alienage cases be explained on the ground that the states have only a narrow role to play when dealing with problems of immigration and naturalization? On this view, many state alienage classifications are invalid not simply because they discriminate against aliens, or because the policies they advance are inherently illegitimate, but rather because those policies are best pursued in a unified way on the national level. See Note, The Equal Treatment of Aliens: Preemption or Equal Protection?, 31 Stan. L. Rev. 1069 (1979).

In *Graham* itself, which first announced that alienage classifications were suspect for equal protection purposes, the Court also relied on federalism grounds as an alternative basis for invalidating the state law. State restrictions on the eligibility of aliens for welfare benefits, in the Court's view, conflicted with "overriding national policies in an area constitutionally entrusted to the Federal Government." Since *Graham*, federalism and preemption concerns have become an increasingly important theme in alienage cases. See, e.g., Arizona v. United States, 567 U.S. 387 (2012) (holding that a number of state provisions restricting aliens' employment were preempted by federal law).

1. *The federal cases.* In Mathews v. Diaz, 426 U.S. 67 (1976), a unanimous Court upheld a federal statute limiting participation in a federal medical insurance program to citizens and aliens who had continuously resided in the United States for five years and had been admitted for permanent residence. Writing for the Court, Justice Stevens explained:

> In the exercise of its broad power over naturalization and immigration, Congress regularly makes rules that would be unacceptable if applied to citizens. [In] particular, the fact that Congress has provided some welfare benefits for citizens does not require it to provide like benefits for *all aliens*. Neither the overnight visitor, the unfriendly agent of a hostile foreign power, the resident diplomat, nor the illegal entrant, can advance even a colorable constitutional claim to a share in the bounty that a conscientious sovereign makes available to its own citizens and *some* of its guests. The decision to share that bounty with our guests may take into account the character of the relationship between the alien and this country: Congress may decide that as the alien's tie grows stronger, so does the strength of his claim to an equal share of that munificence.

The Court asserted that the federalism prong of *Graham* supported its holding here because "it is the business of the political branches of the Federal Government, rather than that of either the States or the Federal Judiciary, to regulate the conditions of entry and residence of aliens" for while "the Constitution inhibits every State's power to restrict travel across its own borders, Congress is explicitly empowered to exercise that type of control over travel across the borders of the United States."

After *Diaz*, do any limits remain on the federal government's power to impose special rules governing the conduct of aliens? Could Congress prohibit resident aliens from having abortions? From working as lawyers? Could it insist that an alien doctor admitted to this country to practice medicine continue to do so while she or he remains here? See Reno v. American-Arab Anti-Discrimination Committee, 525 U.S. 936 (1999) (holding that in general aliens cannot challenge their deportations on the ground that they are being selectively prosecuted).

Can federal power over aliens be justified on the ground that the federal government could exclude aliens altogether, and that it therefore may condition their admission on the waiver of certain rights?

Compare *Diaz* with Hampton v. Mow Sun Wong, 426 U.S. 88 (1976), decided on the same day. In *Hampton*, the Court invalidated a Civil Service Commission policy excluding aliens from most civil service jobs. The Court, in an opinion by Justice Stevens, acknowledged that "there may be overriding national interests which justify selective federal legislation that would be unacceptable for an individual State. [The] paramount federal power over immigration and naturalization [forecloses] a simple extension of the holding in *Sugarman*." Nonetheless, the Court held that imposition of a citizenship requirement by the Civil Service Commission violated due process:

> We may assume [that] if the Congress or the President had expressly imposed the citizenship requirement, it would be justified by the national interest in providing an incentive for aliens to become naturalized, or possibly even as providing the President with an expendable token for treaty negotiating purposes; but we are not willing to presume that the Chairman of the Civil Service Commission [was] deliberately fostering an interest so far removed from his normal responsibilities. [By] broadly denying this class substantial opportunities for employment, the Civil Service Commission rule deprives its members of an aspect of liberty. Since these residents were admitted as a result of decisions made by the Congress and the President, [due process] requires that the decision to impose that deprivation of an important liberty be made either at a comparable level of government or, if it is to be permitted to be made by the Civil Service Commission, that it be justified by reasons which are properly the concern of that agency.

Justice Rehnquist wrote a dissenting opinion that was joined by Chief Justice Burger and Justices White and Blackmun.

If Congress could exclude aliens from civil service jobs, why is there a constitutional obstacle to congressional delegation of this power to the Civil Service Commission? Does *Hampton* suggest a revitalization of the nondelegation doctrine? See Chapter 4, section D2, supra.

In the wake of the September 11 attacks, the President ordered the establishment of military tribunals with jurisdiction to try aliens, but not American citizens, for, inter alia, engaging in acts of "international terrorism." (The order is discussed at greater length in Chapter 4, section C1, supra.) In light of *Diaz*, is there a plausible argument that the order unconstitutionally discriminates against noncitizens? Consider Katyal and Tribe, Waging War, Deciding Guilt: Trying the Military Tribunals, 111 Yale L.J. 1259, 1300-1301 (2002):

> [Deferential] review of federal distinctions between citizens and aliens [has] its roots in the wide berth accorded the political branches "in the area of immigration and naturalization." When a categorical preference for American citizens cannot be justified in terms of immigration and naturalization policy or as an adjunct to our international bargaining posture, the basis for relaxing the scrutiny otherwise applicable to discrimination against aliens as a class [evaporates].
>
> Even more important, the decisions manifesting relaxed [scrutiny] of federal discrimination [have] involved nothing beyond the preferential availability to our own citizens of government employment or other socioeconomic benefits that do not touch the raw nerve of equal justice under [law]. Crucially, the Military Order curtails rights that, at least when made available to others similarly situated, have long been deemed too fundamental to be dispensed with on a merely rational basis.

For a more general criticism of the government's treatment of aliens in the wake of the World Trade Center attack, see Cole, Enemy Aliens, 54 Stan. L. Rev. 953 (2002).

2. *The state cases.* Can the state cases also be read as resting on a concern that the proper unit of government make a judgment about the status of aliens rather than on a concern about the merits of the judgment itself? On occasion, the

Court has expressly relied on preemption grounds to invalidate state citizenship requirements. In Toll v. Moreno, 458 U.S. 1 (1982), for example, the Court considered a state policy denying in-state status to nonimmigrant aliens for purposes of qualifying for tuition reductions at state universities. Without reaching the equal protection question, the Court held the state policy unconstitutional under the supremacy clause. In light of the "long recognized [preeminent] role of the Federal Government with respect to the regulation of aliens within our borders," the Court held that "'state regulation not congressionally sanctioned that discriminates against aliens lawfully admitted to the country is impermissible if it imposes additional burdens not contemplated by Congress'" (quoting De Canas v. Bica, 424 U.S. 351 (1976)). Similarly, in Arizona v. United States, 567 U.S. 387 (2012), the Court held that an Arizona statute making it a misdemeanor for an unauthorized alien to seek or engage in work in the state was preempted by Congress's decision, in federal immigration law, to criminalize only the actions of the employer who hires such workers.

In other cases, however, federalism concerns have played a more indirect role in the Court's reasoning. Instead of relying directly on the supremacy clause, the Court has referred to the federal government's "preeminent role" regarding aliens when it assesses the legitimacy of state concerns that might otherwise justify the classification under the equal protection clause.

In Nyquist v. Mauclet, supra, for example, the state sought to justify its citizenship requirement for higher education financial assistance on the ground that it encouraged naturalization and ensured a "degree of national affinity." But the Court rejected this goal as "not a permissible one for a State. Control over immigration and naturalization is entrusted exclusively to the Federal Government, and a State has no power to interfere." Similarly, in Plyler v. Doe, supra, the Court was unimpressed by the state's claim that its refusal to enroll illegal aliens in public schools supported the federal policy against illegal immigration:

> To be sure, like all persons who have entered the United States unlawfully, these children are subject to deportation. But there is no assurance that a child subject to deportation will ever be deported. An illegal entrant might be granted federal permission to continue to reside in this country, or even to become a citizen. In light of the discretionary federal power to grant relief from deportation, a State cannot realistically determine that any particular undocumented child will in fact be deported until after deportation proceedings have been completed. It would of course be most difficult for the State to justify a denial of education to a child enjoying an inchoate federal permission to remain.

To what extent do arguments about preemption and heightened scrutiny depend on the assumption that states or localities are distinctively hostile to the rights of aliens? In recent years, some states have continued to provide social services to aliens, including undocumented aliens, despite federal authorization to deny such services, and have proposed providing additional rights, such as drivers' licenses to undocumented aliens. See Schuck, Taking Immigration Federalism Seriously, 2007 U. Chi. Legal F. 57. At the same time, other jurisdictions have embarked on ordinances designed to physically exclude undocumented aliens. For discussions of these developments, see Huntingdon, The Constitutional Dimension of Immigration Federalism, 61 Vand. L. Rev. 787 (2008); Motomura, Immigration Outside the Law, 108 Colum. L. Rev. 2037 (2008); Olivas, Immigration-Related State and Local Ordinances: Preemption,

Prejudice, and the Proper Role for Enforcement, 2007 U. Chi. Legal F. 27; Rodriguez, The Significance of the Local in Immigration Regulation, 106 Mich. L. Rev. 567 (2008).

2.   Wealth Classifications

Are the poor entitled to special judicial protection under the equal protection clause? In the late 1950s and 1960s, the Court repeatedly suggested that classifications based on indigence were suspect. See, e.g., Griffin v. Illinois, 351 U.S. 12 (1956) ("In criminal trials a State can no more discriminate on account of poverty than on account of religion, race, or color"); Harper v. Virginia Board of Elections, 383 U.S. 663 (1966) ("Lines drawn on the basis of wealth or property, like those of race, are traditionally disfavored"). By the 1970s, however, the Court had rejected the idea that "financial need alone identifies a suspect class for purposes of equal protection analysis." Maher v. Roe, 432 U.S. 464 (1977). The history of how the Court reached this conclusion illustrates some important themes in considering when strict scrutiny should apply.

Note: Defining the Class

1. *Poverty as a relative category*. If "the poor" are a suspect class, how should the class be defined? The concept of "poverty," unlike gender and alienage, is inherently relative: Individuals are poor by comparison to other individuals. Does it make sense to define a class without reference to the ability to purchase particular goods and services? *Harper*, for example, involved payment of a $1.50 poll tax as a prerequisite to voting in state elections. Most individuals were able to pay that tax. The Court held that denying individuals the right to vote for failure to pay the poll tax violated the equal protection clause. In *Harper*, the class of individuals unable to pay consisted of persons for whom the payment of a wide range of fees would be difficult. By contrast, many state institutions of higher education (particularly professional schools) charge tuition and fees that may be well beyond the average individual's ability to pay. Does who falls within the class of "the poor" shift depending on the goods or services involved? Is this a coherent way of defining a class of individuals?

2. *Facial discrimination against the poor*. Laws that explicitly single out poor individuals for different treatment are relatively rare. Historically, a number of state statutes treated "paupers" — persons who received public assistance — differently. See, e.g., Steinfeld, Property and Suffrage in the Early American Republic, 41 Stan. L. Rev. 335 (1989) (discussing how many states denied voting rights to individuals receiving various forms of public assistance); Belt, Ballots for Bullets?: Disabled Veterans and the Right to Vote, 69 Stan. L. Rev. 435 (2017) (discussing the disenfranchisement after the Civil War of disabled veterans living in soldiers' homes). In Edwards v. California, 314 U.S. 160 (1941), the Court addressed a California statute that made it a misdemeanor to bring or to assist in bringing into the state "an indigent person who is not a resident of the state." Although the Court relied solely on the commerce clause to invalidate the statute, it suggested in passing that it would not accept stereotypical judgments about the poor as justifications for laws disadvantaging them: "[We] do not think that it will now be seriously contended that because a person is without employment and without funds he

constitutes a 'moral pestilence.' Poverty and immorality are not synonymous."
Justice Jackson's concurring opinion went further. He urged the Court to
"say now, and in no uncertain terms, that a man's mere property status, without
more, cannot be used by a state to test, qualify, or limit his rights as a citizen of
the United States. 'Indigence' in itself is neither a source of rights nor a basis
for denying them. The mere state of being without funds is a neutral fact —
constitutionally an irrelevance, like race, creed or color."

3. *"De facto" wealth classifications.* The primary context in which equal protection claims involving wealth have arisen does not involve explicit distinctions
between individuals who are affluent and individuals who are not. Rather, it
involves challenges to government-imposed fees (for example, a poll tax or tuition
charge at a state university) or claims that the government has wrongly failed to
subsidize some activity that can be engaged in only if one has the money to
purchase it in private markets (for example, the failure to subsidize abortions
when the government subsidizes other medical care under Medicaid). Doesn't
defining the class in these terms amount to saying that there is a constitutional
right to the good in question?

Is defining the class entitled to heightened scrutiny in these terms inconsistent
with Washington v. Davis, discussed on pages 549-552, supra? There, the Court
held that proof of a disparate impact, without proof of a discriminatory purpose, is
insufficient to trigger strict scrutiny of a facially neutral government decision.
Consider in this connection M.L.B. v. S.L.J., 519 U.S. 102 (1996), where the
state relied on Washington v. Davis to defend its requirement that litigants pay
record preparation fees before appealing from decisions terminating parental
rights. The state reasoned that this requirement, like the practice at issue in
Washington v. Davis, involved no facial classification but at most had only a
disproportionate impact on the affected class. In a six-to-three decision, the Court
rejected this argument:

> Sanctions of [this] genre [are] not merely disproportionate in impact. Rather, they
> are wholly contingent on one's ability to pay, and thus "visit different consequences
> on two categories of persons" [citing Williams v. Illinois]; they apply to all indigents
> and do not reach anyone outside that class.

As a facial matter, doesn't the requirement that litigants pay the record preparation fee disadvantage everyone who, for whatever reason, does not pay the fee?
If so, in what sense does the requirement apply only to indigents?

Compare M.L.B. to James v. Valtierra, 402 U.S. 137 (1971). An amendment to
the state's constitution provided that no low-rent housing project should be developed, constructed, or acquired in any manner by a state public body until the
project was approved by a majority of those voting at a community election. The
Court upheld the provision, rejecting the claim that the amendment constituted
a violation of the equal protection clause "because it hampers persons desiring
public housing from achieving their objective when no such roadblock faces
other groups seeking to influence other public decisions to their advantage."
The Court held that "of course a lawmaking procedure that 'disadvantages' a
particular group does not always deny equal protection. Under any such holding,
presumably a State would not be able to require referendums on any subject
unless referendums were required on all, because they would always
disadvantage some group." Consider the possibility that, given Washington v.
Davis, both *M.L.B.* and *James* are wrongly decided: Unlike the statute invalidated

in *M.L.B.*, the provision upheld in *James* really does facially discriminate against the indigent since they are the only group who benefit from low-income housing.

Note: *Wealth Discrimination and the Problem of Affirmative Rights*

1. *The evolution of heightened scrutiny in the context of particular rights.* As suggested earlier, the cases in which the Supreme Court addressed wealth discrimination generally arose within the context of challenges to the denial of access to specific government programs. In the 1950s and 1960s, the Court ruled for the claimants in several such challenges. See, e.g., Griffin v. Illinois, 351 U.S. 12 (1956) (holding that the equal protection clause requires states to provide trial transcripts or their equivalent to indigents appealing their criminal convictions); Douglas v. California, 372 U.S. 353 (1963) (holding that states must provide indigents with counsel on a first appeal of right to challenge a criminal conviction); Harper v. Virginia Board of Elections, 383 U.S. 663 (1966) (holding a state law conditioning the vote on payment of a $1.50 poll tax denied equal protection); Cipriano v. City of Houma, 395 U.S. 701 (1969) (holding invalid a state statute restricting the franchise to property owners in a state election to approve issuance of revenue bonds by a municipal utility). (These cases are discussed more fully in conjunction with the "implied fundamental rights" strand of equal protection, Chapter 6, section E, infra.)

During the same period, the Court also hinted that strict judicial scrutiny might be appropriate when the state failed to provide the poor with "necessities." See, e.g., Shapiro v. Thompson, 394 U.S. 618 (1969) (classification "[denies] welfare aid upon which may depend the ability of the families to obtain the very means to subsist — food, shelter, and other necessities of life"); Goldberg v. Kelly, 397 U.S. 254 (1970) ("Welfare, by meeting the basic demands of subsistence, can help bring within the reach of the poor the same opportunities that are available to others to participate meaningfully in the life of the community. [Public] assistance, then, is not mere charity, but a means to 'promote the general Welfare, and secure the Blessings of Liberty to ourselves and our Posterity'").

But although some of the Court's rhetoric was sweeping, its actual holdings were far narrower. Those wealth classifications that were invalidated were all associated with access to "fundamental" rights, such as the franchise and the ability to challenge criminal convictions. No holding during this period established that it was unconstitutional as a general matter for the state to deny services or benefits to those who could not pay for them. Moreover, even with regard to fundamental rights, the Court never suggested that absolute equality was required so long as the poor were not denied minimal benefits (e.g., although the poor were entitled to representation on a first appeal of right, the Court never suggested that they had a constitutional right to the best lawyer that money could buy, and it later held that they were not entitled to appointed counsel for discretionary appeals or, with few exceptions, post-conviction proceedings). Finally, despite some suggestive dicta, no holding during this period established that the state had an affirmative constitutional obligation to guarantee subsistence to those in need.

In the 1970s, the Court veered sharply away from its earlier suggestions that wealth classifications were suspect. Although none of the earlier holdings were overturned, the Court was, in general, unwilling to extend these holdings. See, e.g., Ross v. Moffitt, 417 U.S. 600 (1974) (refusing to extend the *Douglas* principle to require counsel in discretionary appeals beyond a first appeal of right); United States v. Kras, 409 U.S. 434 (1973) (holding that there is no general equal protection principle barring the imposition of filing fees in ordinary civil litigation, even when they prevent the indigent from securing access to the courts).

At about the same time, the Court ended speculation that it might read the equal protection clause to impose an affirmative obligation on government to provide the poor with necessities. In Dandridge v. Williams, 397 U.S. 471 (1970), for example, the Court turned aside an equal protection challenge to Maryland's practice of imposing an upper limit on the size of grants under its Aid to Families with Dependent Children Program regardless of the size of the family. Similarly, in Lindsey v. Normet, 405 U.S. 56 (1972), the Court rejected a constitutional challenge to Oregon's summary eviction procedures.

The Court's most detailed treatment of a wealth discrimination claim during this period came in San Antonio Independent School District v. Rodriguez, 411 U.S. 1 (1973). The decision grew out of a constitutional challenge to the manner in which Texas, and many other states, financed public education. Much of the revenue needed for public schools was raised locally by an ad valorem property tax on the property located within each district. The result of this system was that children located in districts with more valuable property benefited from higher expenditures than children in districts with less valuable property, even though both districts made the same tax effort. Appellees claimed that this method of financing education should be strictly scrutinized under the equal protection clause because, inter alia, it discriminated against the poor. (Appellees also argued that it impinged on their fundamental right to education. This aspect of the case is discussed in greater detail in Chapter 6, section E5, infra.)

In a five-to-four decision, the Court rejected this claim and, applying rationality review, upheld the system. In its discussion of the wealth discrimination claim, the Court, in an opinion by Justice Powell, said that in prior cases,

> [the] individuals, or groups of individuals, who constituted the class discriminated against [shared] two distinguishing characteristics; because of their impecunity they were completely unable to pay for some desired benefit, and as a consequence, they sustained an absolute deprivation of a meaningful opportunity to enjoy that benefit. [Even] a cursory examination, however, demonstrates that neither of the two distinguishing characteristics of wealth classifications can be found here. First, in support of their charge that the system discriminates against the "poor," appellees have made no effort to demonstrate that it operates to the peculiar disadvantage of any class fairly definable as indigent. [There] is no basis on the record in this case for assuming that the poorest people — defined by reference to any level of absolute impecunity — are concentrated in the poorest districts.
>
> Second, [lack] of personal resources has not occasioned an absolute deprivation of the desired benefit. [Apart] from the unsettled and disputed question whether the quality of education may be determined by the amount of money expended for it, a sufficient answer to appellees' argument is that, at least where wealth is involved, the Equal Protection Clause does not require absolute equality or precisely equal advantages.

2. *Wealth discrimination and the efficient allocation of scarce resources.* Even if charging a price for a government service discriminates in some sense against the poor, might that decision be justified by the state's desire to allocate scarce

resources in an efficient manner? Consider, for example, Michelman, Foreword: On Protecting the Poor through the Fourteenth Amendment, 83 Harv. L. Rev. 7, 27–28 (1969):

> Unlike a de facto racial classification which usually must seek its justifications in purposes completely distinct from its race-related impacts, a de facto pecuniary classification typically carries a highly persuasive justification inseparable from the very effect which excites antipathy — i.e., the hard choices it forces upon the financially straitened. [A] de facto pecuniary classification [is] usually nothing more or less than the making of a market (e.g., in trial transcripts) or the failure to relieve someone of the vicissitudes of market pricing (e.g., for appellate legal services). But the risk of exposure to markets and their "decisions" is not normally deemed objectionable, to say the least, in our society. Not only do we not inveigh generally against unequal distribution of income or full-cost pricing for most goods. We usually regard it as both the fairest and most efficient arrangement to require each consumer to pay the full market price of what he consumes, limiting his consumption to what his income permits.

Is this argument persuasive when the government charges for "public goods" where the consumption of the goods by some does not interfere with their consumption by others? Is it constitutional, for example, for the government to charge an admission fee to cover the cost of running a municipal swimming pool when the cost remains constant regardless of the number of users? Does it matter whether the goods are uniquely within the control of the government? Note that this rationale played an important role in the Court's decision in Boddie v. Connecticut, 401 U.S. 371 (1971), that individuals could not be precluded from obtaining divorces for inability to pay a filing fee given the government's monopoly over marital status.

Is the argument persuasive when the government charges for goods in circumstances where the demand declines relatively little, even when the price rises? For example, could a government hospital refuse to perform life-saving surgery on a person too poor to pay the cost? Note that in many situations, statutes provide individuals with some version of the right in question; deprivation of those statutory rights without due process is an independent constitutional violation separate from any equal protection claim.

Is it constitutional for the state to substitute government regulation for the constraint normally exercised by the market when providing benefits to poor people? Would it be constitutional, for example, to provide appellate counsel for the poor only in cases where a preliminary review of the record demonstrated that there were nonfrivolous issues to be raised on appeal? Consider Draper v. Washington, 372 U.S. 487 (1963):

> The State [argues] that in practical effect there is no difference at all between the rights it affords indigents and nonindigents, because a moneyed defendant, motivated by a "sense of thrift," will choose not to appeal in exactly the same circumstances that an indigent will be denied a transcript. We reject this contention as untenable. It defies common sense to think that a moneyed defendant faced with long-term imprisonment and advised by counsel that he has substantial grounds for appeal, as petitioners were here, will choose not to appeal merely to save the cost of a transcript.

But see Smith v. Robbins, 528 U.S. 259 (2000), upholding a procedure under which appointed appellate counsel who believes that there are no nonfrivolous issues to appeal files a brief summarizing the procedural and factual history of the case and attesting that he has reviewed the record, explained his evaluation of the case to his client, provided the client with a copy of the brief, and informed the client of his right to file a pro se supplemental brief. Counsel then requests that the court independently examine the record for arguable issues.

3. *The Constitution and affirmative rights.* Are the wealth cases explicable in terms of a more general principle of constitutional construction under which the Constitution is seen primarily as a limitation on governmental power and not as an affirmative guarantee against conditions for which government is not responsible? Consider, for example, Justice Harlan's dissenting opinions in *Griffin* and *Douglas*, the cases establishing the equal protection right of the poor to a trial transcript and counsel in order to pursue an appeal of right in a criminal case. In *Griffin*, Justice Harlan wrote that "[all] that Illinois has done is to fail to alleviate the consequences of differences in economic circumstances that exist wholly apart from any state action. [The] issue here is not the typical equal protection question of the reasonableness of a 'classification' on the basis of which the State has imposed legal disabilities, but rather the reasonableness of the State's failure to remove natural disabilities." In *Douglas*, he added that

> every financial exaction which the State imposes on a uniform basis is more easily satisfied by the well-to-do than by the indigent. Yet I take it that no one would dispute the constitutional power of the State to levy a uniform sales tax, to charge tuition at a state university, to fix rates for the purchase of water from a municipal corporation, to impose a standard fine for criminal violations, or to establish minimum bail for various categories of offenses. Laws such as these do not deny equal protection to the less fortunate for one essential reason: the Equal Protection Clause does not impose on the States "an affirmative duty to lift the handicaps flowing from differences in economic circumstances" [quoting from his *Griffin* dissent]. To so construe it would be to read into the Constitution a philosophy of leveling that would be foreign to many of our basic concepts of the proper relations between government and society.

Note the affinity between this argument and the Washington v. Davis principle. One way to state that principle is that the equal protection clause does not impose on the states an affirmative obligation to compensate for unequal outcomes produced by a facially neutral governmental policy. The argument is also closely related to the "state action" doctrine. Under that doctrine, the Constitution in general protects individuals from state invasions of their rights and does not confer a right to affirmative governmental intervention to remedy privately imposed deprivations. (The state action doctrine is discussed in greater detail in Chapter 9 infra.) Finally, the argument is related to the more general orientation toward the equal protection clause pursuant to which different treatment of individuals similarly situated is viewed as more problematical than similar treatment of individuals differently situated.

Is Justice Harlan's argument persuasive? In what sense are the disabilities under which the poor labor "natural"? Why is the state not responsible for them? Consider L. Tribe, American Constitutional Law 1335–1336 (2d ed. 1988):

> [The] demise of the *Lochner* era [during which the Supreme Court read the due process clause to protect liberty of contract and thereby invalidated much social legislation] reflected the view that [the] system of governmental decisions — some

statutory and some made by common-law judges — bore an active responsibility for the plight of those who could not earn a decent living. [It] should be stressed that this perspective does *not* entail a judicially cognizable remedy against government for every instance of substandard wages or unmet needs. [But] at least sometimes, the person who is forced to work too hard for too little, or can find no work at all, must be regarded as the victim of the system of contract and property rights rather than the author of his own plight.

Is it sensible to suppose that a court could ever ascertain the extent to which the condition of the poor is the product of government action? Even if it were possible to do so in principle, why should the answer to this question matter? Why is the equality principle satisfied by government inaction that leaves the disadvantaged at the mercy of private forces?

In connection with these issues, consider Harris v. McRae, 448 U.S. 297 (1980), wherein the Court upheld the constitutionality of the so-called Hyde Amendment prohibiting virtually all federal funding for abortions under the Medicaid program. The Court acknowledged that the Constitution protected a woman's freedom of choice regarding abortions:

> But . . . it simply does not follow that a woman's freedom of choice carries with it a constitutional entitlement to financial resources to avail herself of the full range of protected choices. [Although] government may not place obstacles in the path of a woman's exercise of her freedom of choice, it need not remove those not of its own creation. Indigency falls in the latter category. [Although] Congress has opted to subsidize medically necessary services generally, but not certain medically necessary abortions, the fact remains that the Hyde Amendment leaves an indigent woman with at least the same range of choice in deciding whether to obtain a medically necessary abortion as she would have had if Congress had chosen to subsidize no health care costs at all.

In a footnote, the Court rejected the argument that the Hyde Amendment unconstitutionally "penalized" a woman's choice to abort the fetus because funding was available for live births. It noted, however:

> A substantial constitutional question would arise if Congress had attempted to withhold all Medicaid benefits from an otherwise eligible candidate simply because that candidate had exercised her constitutionally protected freedom to terminate her pregnancy by abortion. [But] the Hyde Amendment [does] not provide for such a broad disqualification from receipt of public benefits. Rather, the Hyde Amendment [represents] simply a refusal to subsidize certain protected conduct. A refusal to fund protected activity, without more, cannot be equated with the imposition of a "penalty" on that activity.

Is the Court's distinction between penalization and refusal to subsidize convincing? If one begins with the premise that it is important for women to have the abortion option, is there a sensible theory under which it is possible to distinguish between interference with that option by state action and interference by private action that the state fails to prevent?.

4. *Alternative doctrinal routes for protecting poor individuals.* Although in recent times, the Court has been generally reluctant to treat the poor as a "suspect" class for equal protection purposes, it has sometimes reached the same result through other doctrinal routes. Recall, for example, United States

Department of Agriculture v. Moreno, section B supra, where the Court used rational basis review to invalidate a law disqualifying from the federal food stamp program unrelated individuals who lived together. Similarly, some cases have extended rights to the poor through due process analysis. See, e.g., M.L.B. v. S.L.J., 519 U.S. 102 (1996) (using both due process and equal protection analysis to hold that the state may not condition appeals from decrees terminating parental rights on the parent's ability to pay record preparation fees); Ake v. Oklahoma, 470 U.S. 68 (1985) (due process requires the state to pay for psychiatric assistance for indigent defendant where there is preliminary showing that sanity is likely to be significant factor at trial); Evitts v. Lucey, 469 U.S. 387 (1985) (holding that due process requires effective assistance of counsel on first appeal of right, and suggesting that *Griffin-Douglas* line of cases rests in part on due process principles); Little v. Streater, 452 U.S. 1 (1981) (due process requires state to pay for blood test of indigent defendant in paternity action); Boddie v. Connecticut, 401 U.S. 371 (1971) (holding unconstitutional on due process grounds the imposition of court fees preventing an indigent from securing a divorce).

For an effort to build a case for the constitutional protection of welfare rights from strands in existing doctrine, see Edelman, Essay: The Next Century of Our Constitution: Rethinking Our Duty to the Poor, 39 Hastings L.J. 1 (1987). For skepticism that this can be done unless there are profound changes in the political climate, see Liu, Rethinking Constitutional Welfare Rights, 61 Stan. L. Rev. 203 (2008).

3. *Other Disadvantaged Groups*

Are there other "discrete and insular minorities" entitled to special judicial protection from the political process?

CITY OF CLEBURNE v. CLEBURNE LIVING CENTER, 473 U.S. 432 (1985). A city zoning ordinance prevented construction in a residential neighborhood of a group home for the individuals who were mentally retarded. Although it affirmed the decision below insofar as it invalidated the ordinance as applied — because the Court held that the refusal to grant a variance reflected illegitimate motives, see pages 516-517, supra — the Supreme Court held that the lower court had erred in applying heightened scrutiny. The Court, in an opinion by Justice White, advanced several reasons for rejecting heightened scrutiny:

"First, it is undeniable [that] those who are mentally retarded have a reduced ability to cope with and function in the everyday world. [They] are thus different, immutably so, in relevant respects, and the states' interest in dealing with and providing for them is plainly a legitimate one. How this large and diversified group is to be treated under the law is a difficult and often technical matter, very much a task for legislators guided by qualified professionals and not by the perhaps ill-informed opinions of the judiciary.

"Second, the distinctive legislative response, both national and state, to the plight of those who are mentally retarded demonstrates not only that they have unique problems, but also that the lawmakers have been addressing their difficulties in a manner that belies a continuing antipathy or prejudice and a corresponding need for more intrusive oversight by the judiciary. Thus, the federal government has not only outlawed discrimination against the mentally retarded in federally funded programs, but it has also provided the retarded with the right to receive 'appropriate treatment services and habilitation' in a setting that is 'least restrictive of [their] personal liberty.' . . .

"Such legislation thus singling out the retarded for special treatment reflects the real and undeniable differences between the retarded and others. That a civilized and decent society expects and approves such legislation indicates that governmental consideration of those differences in the vast majority of situations is not only legitimate but desirable. [Even] assuming that many of these laws could be shown to be substantially related to an important governmental purpose, merely requiring the legislature to justify its efforts in these terms may lead it to refrain from acting at all. [Especially] given the wide variation in the abilities and needs of the retarded themselves, governmental bodies must have a certain amount of flexibility and freedom from judicial oversight in shaping and limiting their remedial efforts.

"Third, the legislative response, which could hardly have occurred and survived without public support, negates any claim that the mentally retarded are politically powerless in the sense that they have no ability to attract the attention of lawmakers. . . .

"Fourth, if the large and amorphous class of the mentally retarded were deemed quasi-suspect [it] would be difficult to find a principled way to distinguish a variety of other groups who have perhaps immutable disabilities setting them off from others, who cannot themselves mandate the desired legislative responses, and who can claim some degree of prejudice from at least part of the public at large. One need mention in this respect only the aging, the disabled, the mentally ill, and the infirm. We are reluctant to set out on that course, and we decline to do so.

"Doubtless, there have been and there will continue to be instances of discrimination against the retarded that are in fact [invidious]. But the appropriate method of reaching such instances is not to create a new quasi-suspect classification and subject all governmental action based on that classification to more searching evaluation."

Justice Marshall, joined by Justices Brennan and Blackmun, wrote an opinion concurring in the judgment in part and dissenting in part:

"[The] mentally retarded have been subject to a 'lengthy and tragic history' of segregation and discrimination that can only be called grotesque. [By] the latter part of the [nineteenth] century and during the first decades of the new one, [social] views of the retarded underwent a radical transformation. Fueled by the rising tide of Social Darwinism, the 'science' of eugenics, and the extreme xenophobia of those years, leading medical authorities and others began to portray the 'feebleminded' as a 'menace to society and civilization [responsible] in a large degree for many, if not all, our social problems.' A regime of state-mandated segregation and degradation soon emerged that in its virulence and bigotry rivaled, and indeed paralleled, the worst excesses of Jim Crow. . . .

"Prejudice, once let loose, is not easily cabined. As of 1979, most states still categorically disqualified 'idiots' from voting, without regard to individual capacity and with discretion to exclude left in the hands of low-level officials. Not until Congress enacted the Education of the Handicapped Act were 'the door[s] of public education' opened wide to handicapped children. But most important, lengthy and continuing isolation of the retarded has perpetuated the ignorance, irrational fears, and stereotyping that long have plagued them.

"In light of the importance of the interest at stake and the history of discrimination the retarded have suffered, the Equal Protection Clause requires us to do more than review the distinctions drawn by Cleburne's zoning ordinance as if they appeared in a taxing statute or in economic or commercial legislation. The searching scrutiny I would give to restrictions on the ability of the retarded to establish community group homes leads me to conclude that Cleburne's vague generalizations for classifying the 'feeble-minded' with drug addicts, alcoholics, and the insane, and excluding them where the elderly, the ill, the boarder, and the transient are allowed, are not substantial or important enough to overcome the suspicion that the ordinance rests on impermissible assumptions or outmoded and perhaps invidious stereotypes."

Justice Stevens, joined by Chief Justice Burger, also wrote a concurring opinion.

Note: Evaluating the Claims of Other Disadvantaged Groups

1. *Individuals with cognitive deficits as a suspect class.* Does the *Cleburne* Court adequately explain why classifications disadvantaging persons who are mentally retarded need only survive low-level review? Do the courts really face problems of institutional competence here that don't exist with respect to other equal protection claims? Why does legislative protection for this group argue against heightened review, given that racial minorities and women have received legislative protection in recent decades? Even if "the real and undeniable differences between the retarded and others" make strict scrutiny inappropriate, why didn't the Court opt for intermediate review?

Does the broader category of people with physical or mental disabilities constitute a suspect class? In Tennessee v. Lane, 541 U.S. 509 (2004), the Court rejected a constitutional attack on title II of the Americans with Disabilities Act of 1990 (which prohibits qualified persons with disabilities from being "excluded from participation or denied the benefits of the services, programs or activities of a public entity") as applied to physically disabled individuals who claimed that their disabilities prevented them from gaining access to state courthouses. Tennessee argued that the measure exceeded Congress's enforcement power under section 5 of the fourteenth amendment. In the course of rejecting this argument, Justice Stevens, writing for the Court, stated the following:

> Congress enacted Title II against a backdrop of pervasive unequal treatment in the administration of state services and programs, including systematic deprivations of fundamental rights. . . . Similarly, a number of States have prohibited and continue to prohibit persons with disabilities from engaging in activities such as marrying and serving as jurors. The historical experience that Title II reflects is also documented in this Court's cases, which have identified unconstitutional treatment of disabled persons by state agencies in a variety of settings, including unjustified commitment; the abuse and neglect of persons committed to state mental health hospitals; and irrational discrimination in zoning decisions. The decisions of other courts, too, document a pattern of unequal treatment in the administration of a wide range of public services, programs, and activities, including the penal system, public education, and voting.

In light of this history, should disability discrimination be subject to heightened scrutiny? In *Lane*, the Court was not required to answer this question because it found that the Americans with Disabilities Act, as applied, was a permissible congressional effort to enforce the access to courts guaranteed by due process of law. Note that the Americans with Disabilities Act in some circumstances requires "reasonable accommodation" of persons with disabilities. If disability constituted a suspect classification, would this requirement be constitutionally vulnerable under the Court's affirmative action jurisprudence? Conversely, if disability were a suspect class, would governments be constitutionally required to accommodate persons with disabilities?

Although the Supreme Court upheld Congress's ability to authorize private damages lawsuits against states to enforce title II of the Americans with Disabilities Act in cases where individuals are denied access to the courts — itself a fundamental right whose denial would be subject to strict scrutiny — the Court rejected Congress's attempt to authorize private damages lawsuits against states to enforce title I of the act, which forbids discrimination in employment. See Board of Trustees of the University of Alabama v. Garrett, 531 U.S. 356 (2001). Does this suggest that the right being denied, rather than the class whose rights are being denied, is the key to the Court's holding in *Lane*? In this respect, consider Karlan, *Loving Lawrence*, 102 Mich. L. Rev. 1447, 1460 (2004): "By contrast to the incremental possibilities of fundamental rights/due process-based strict scrutiny, suspect classification/equal protection-based strict scrutiny seems far more binary: either a group is entitled to heightened scrutiny across the board or it isn't."

Is the problem here that applying strict scrutiny across the board to discrimination against persons with disabilities will either result in courts invalidating a range of justifiable legislation or somehow water down the concept of strict scrutiny?

2. *Other potentially suspect classifications.* In light of *Cleburne*, are there any other groups that can plausibly claim suspect status? In a series of cases beginning in 1968, the Court has invalidated a number of statutes disadvantaging children born to unmarried parents. Although the Court has refused formally to elevate discrimination against this group to "suspect" status, it has at least on occasion subjected them to something more than conventional rational basis review. See, e.g., Levy v. Louisiana, 391 U.S. 68 (1968) (invalidating statute that excluded nonmarital children from coverage of wrongful death statute); Glona v. American Guarantee & Liability Insurance Co., 391 U.S. 73 (1968) (same); Weber v. Aetna Casualty & Surety Co., 406 U.S. 164 (1972) (exclusion from workers' compensation invalidated); Gomez v. Perez, 409 U.S. 535 (1973) (failure to provide support rights for nonmarital children violates equal protection). But see Mathews v. Lucas, 427 U.S. 495 (1976) (upholding section of Social Security Act depriving certain nonmarital children of survivors' benefits); Lalli v. Lalli, 439 U.S. 259 (1978) (upholding statute providing that nonmarital children could inherit intestate from father only if court declared paternity during lifetime of father). In general, the Court has rejected the argument that statutes disadvantaging nonmarital children can be justified as a means of deterring or punishing their parents for illicit sexual activity. It has been somewhat more sympathetic to the argument that special problems concerning proof of paternity when parents are not married may justify different treatment. See, e.g., Nguyen v. INS, 533 U.S. 53 (2001), discussed at pages 664-667, supra.

In Massachusetts Board of Retirement v. Murgia, 427 U.S. 307 (1976), the Court rejected the argument that the aged were entitled to special judicial solicitude:

While the treatment of the aged in this Nation has not been wholly free of discrimination, such persons, unlike, say, those who have been discriminated against on the basis of race or national origin, have not experienced a "history of purposeful unequal treatment" or been subjected to unique disabilities on the basis of stereotyped characteristics not truly indicative of their abilities. [Old] age does not define a "discrete and insular" group in need of "extraordinary protection from the majoritarian political process." Instead, it marks a stage that each of us will reach if we live out our normal span.

See also Vance v. Bradley, 440 U.S. 93 (1979) (using rational basis review to uphold federal law requiring Foreign Service personnel to retire at age 60). Compare Schweiker v. Wilson, 450 U.S. 221 (1981) (avoiding the question whether persons who are mentally ill form a discrete and insular minority). As with persons with disabilities, older individuals are often protected statutorily, through such provisions as the Age Discrimination in Employment Act. But in contrast to its decision upholding the Family Medical Leave Act's authorization of private damages suits against state employers in Nevada Department of Human Resources v. Hibbs, 538 U.S. 721 (2003), as an appropriate exercise of congressional enforcement power to ensure sex equality, or its decision in *Lane* to uphold damages lawsuits claiming denials of access to the courts, the Supreme Court held that Congress lacked the power to authorize private damages lawsuits against states for discrimination on the basis of age. Kimel v. Florida Board of Regents, 528 U.S. 62 (2000).

For a discussion of whether and to what extent suspect categories should be expanded, see Scales-Trent, Black Women and the Constitution: Finding Our Place, Asserting Our Rights, 24 Harv. C.R.-C.L. L. Rev. 9 (1989).

Consider whether statutes disadvantaging any of the following groups should be strictly scrutinized: ethnic minorities; children; families with children; families without children; future generations; "ugly" persons; obese persons; residents of the District of Columbia; incarcerated individuals.

Do the Court's decisions provide reasonably clear standards under which the claims of these groups can be evaluated? Some of the Court's decisions indicate that heightened scrutiny is applied when there is a likelihood of impermissible motivation. But what is the motivation made impermissible by the equal protection clause? Can one distinguish between hostility or prejudice and good faith moral beliefs or empirical judgments? Is the notion that legislation must be based on "reasoned analysis" and reflect something other than power subject to judicial enforcement?

Do you agree with Justice Rehnquist that "[it] would hardly take extraordinary ingenuity for a lawyer to find 'insular and discrete' minorities at every turn in the road"? Sugarman v. Dougall (dissenting opinion), supra.

Consider the accuracy of the following description of how the Court goes about deciding which groups to protect:

[The] present Court [is] reluctant to strike down particular discriminations so long as the minority group is totally marginalized and powerless. [Once] an historically excluded group shows political clout and cultural and economic resonance, however, the Court becomes sensitive to discriminations against the group and increasingly willing to nullify some such discriminations at the retail level, but remains unenthusiastic about insisting on radical, or wholesale, revisions. Such revisions would be risky for the Court, because people whose status or values depend on discriminating against the minority group will be riled by any big constitutional entitlement for the group. The Court's current strategy is to send up trial balloons and to see what happens.

Eskridge, Destabilizing Due Process and Evolutive Equal Protection, 47 UCLA L. Rev. 1183, 1216–1217 (2000).

Consider also the suggestion in Dorf, Equal Protection Incorporation, 88 Va. L. Rev. 951 (2002), that the Court can give the strict scrutiny doctrine principled content by "incorporating" other provisions of the Constitution into equal protection analysis. Under this approach, the first, fourteenth, and nineteenth amendments make discrimination based upon religion, race, color, previous condition of servitude, and sex presumptively unconstitutional. Moreover, the twenty-sixth amendment raises important questions about the constitutionality of age discrimination. For another discussion of how the equal protection and due process clauses inform one another, see Karlan, Equal Protection, Due Process, and the Stereoscopic Fourteenth Amendment, 33 McGeorge L. Rev. 473 (2002).

3. *The relevance of suspectness.* In *Cleburne*, the Court insisted that it was not subjecting the statute to heightened scrutiny. Nonetheless, it looked closely enough at the purported justifications for the law to invalidate it. In this respect, the decision is reminiscent of the early gender discrimination cases in which the Court struck down a number of statutes disadvantaging women, while insisting that it was engaged in low-level review. Only in retrospect did the Court acknowledge that these cases in fact involved heightened scrutiny. See section D2 supra.

On the other hand, the Court has upheld a number of gender-based statutes, racial affirmative action measures, and laws disadvantaging aliens despite the supposedly heightened review to which these laws were subjected. These cases raise questions concerning the significance of the Court's categorization of levels of review. Is the Court really following a two-step process pursuant to which it first decides how closely to scrutinize a classification and then applies that level of scrutiny? Is it possible (desirable) to insulate the two steps of this process from each other? Might the Court's decisions more accurately be described as a series of ad hoc, intuitive judgments concerning the appropriateness of various classifications? For suggestions that heightened scrutiny has in fact taken on this flexible cast, see, e.g., Goldberg, Equality without Tiers, 77 S. Cal. L. Rev. 481 (2004); Winkler, Fatal in Theory and Strict in Fact: An Empirical Analysis of Strict Scrutiny in the Federal Courts, 59 Vand. L. Rev. 793 (2006).

Is the effort to single out particular groups entitled to special judicial protection from majoritarian processes a useful way to think about constitutional law? Is there a better alternative?

VI

Implied Fundamental Rights

A. INTRODUCTION

This chapter examines whether and in what sense the Constitution in general and the fourteenth amendment in particular create "implied" rights.

An important caveat: Although conventionally drawn, the line between express and implied rights is hardly clear. The right to equal protection of the laws is an express right. But what about the right to be free from racial segregation? The right to free speech is express. But what about the right to spend large sums of money on political campaigns? In disputed cases, the general express right does not answer the question whether the particular right at issue is entitled to protection. For this reason, there is a sense in which most controversial Supreme Court decisions involve the implication of rights.

Despite the haziness of the distinction between implied and express rights, both courts and commentators have often insisted upon it. The debate over implied rights goes back to the very beginning of constitutional interpretation. Recall Calder v. Bull, 3 U.S. (3 Dall.) 386 (1798), Chapter 1, section D, supra. Commentators and the Court itself have frequently treated the recognition of implied rights as particularly problematic. For example, many commentators have condemned the Court's decision in Lochner v. New York, 198 U.S. 45 (1905), striking down a state statute that restricted the working hours of bakers, because the Court enforced an implied liberty of contract that was not expressly provided for in the constitutional text. See the discussion at page 754, infra. Others have criticized the Court for creating a right to abortion without clear textual foundation in Roe v. Wade, 410 U.S. 113 (1973). And the Court itself acknowledged in Bowers v. Hardwick, 478 U.S. 186 (1986), that it was "most vulnerable and comes nearest to illegitimacy when it deals with judge-made constitutional law having little or no cognizable roots in the language or design of the Constitution."

As you read the material below, consider the extent to which these criticisms depend upon a sharp distinction between implied and express rights and the extent to which the distinction can be maintained.

One way to maintain the distinction is to insist that constitutional interpretation must be tightly tethered to the "original understanding" of constitutional text. The Note that follows discusses the plausibility of this interpretive technique.

Note: Theories of Constitutional Interpretation — "Originalism" and Its Critics

1. *The terms of the debate*. Originalism embodies the view that interpretation of the Constitution requires discovery of the Constitution's meaning, which was fixed at the time the Constitution was adopted. However, this simple statement papers over considerable disagreement among originalists. Depending on the type of originalism one embraces, the gap between originalists and nonoriginalists may be smaller or larger. For overviews of the varieties of originalism, see Colby and Smith, Living Originalism, 59 Duke L.J. 239 (2009); Fleming, The Balkanization of Originalism, 67 Md. L. Rev. 10 (2007).

2. *The beginnings of the modern debate*. Judges and scholars have been arguing about originalism for as long as there has been a Constitution, but the modern debate began with President Reagan's nomination of Robert Bork to the Supreme Court in 1987. While a professor at Yale Law School, Bork had written an article arguing that the Supreme Court acted illegitimately when it invalidated laws based upon principles not specified in the Constitution. See Bork, Neutral Principles and Some First Amendment Problems, 47 Ind. L.J. 1 (1971). Many of Bork's critics read the article as providing the intellectual foundations for a broad-based rejection of the work of the Warren and Burger Courts. The article included a critique of Griswold v. Connecticut, 381 U.S. 471 (1965), which struck down a state law prohibiting married couples from using contraceptive devices. Although Bork defended Brown v. Board of Education, 347 U.S. 483 (1954) in his article, his critics pointed to a large body of evidence indicating that the framers of the fourteenth amendment did not intend to outlaw segregation. They also argued that originalism could not accommodate many other Supreme Court decisions, including those striking down various forms of gender discrimination. Bork's nomination was ultimately defeated, but not before triggering an unusual public debate about the appropriate sources for constitutional decision making.

3. *The changing face of originalism.*

a. *"Expected application" originalism*. Many originalists at the time of the Bork nomination defended the view that what mattered was the original intent of the framers. Moreover, that intent was defined at a very specific level, sometimes referred to as the "expected application" approach. On this view, a court was required to determine how the authors of a constitutional provision believed it would apply to the specific question before the court. For example, a court asked to determine whether a statute excluding women from juries violated the equal protection clause should determine whether the framers of the fourteenth amendment meant to prohibit such statutes. For representative defenses of expected application originalism, see R. Berger, Government by Judiciary (1977); Maltz, Some New Thoughts on an Old Problem — The Role of the Intent of the Framers in Constitutional Theory, 63 B.U. L. Rev. 353 (1981);

Kay, Adherence to the Original Intentions in Constitutional Adjudication: Three Objections and Responses, 82 Nw. U. L. Rev. 226 (1988).

This form of originalism came under intense attack. Scholars pointed out that it was often impossible and perhaps conceptually incoherent to determine the intent of the large number of people who wrote or voted for constitutional provisions. They argued that this form of originalism provided no answer in cases where the framers had no specific intent, perhaps because they could not imagine how the provision would interact with facts that did not exist at the time of the drafting. They pointed out that some constitutional language was written in broad terms, which seemed to invite modern judgments about application of the language. And, they argued, this form of originalism produced some clearly unacceptable results. For early criticisms along these lines, see Brest, The Misconceived Quest for the Original Understanding, 60 B.U. L. Rev. 204 (1980); Tushnet, Following the Rules Laid Down: A Critique of Interpretivism and Neutral Principles, 96 Harv. L. Rev. 781 (1983).

b. The "new originalism." Some scholars continue to adhere to the expected application approach, and judicial opinions sometimes refer to how the authors of a provision meant to apply it. In recent years, however, many originalists have modified their approach. Instead of focusing on the intent of the framers, they have focused on the "original public meaning" of the Constitution's text. See, e.g., Scalia, Common-Law Courts in a Civil-Law System: The Role of United States Federal Courts in Interpreting the Constitution and Laws, in A Matter of Interpretation: Federal Courts and the Law 3 (A. Gutmann ed., 1997); R. Barnett, Restoring the Lost Constitution: The Presumption of Liberty (2004). On this approach, the relevant question is not what the framers expected or wanted, but what average members of the public would have understood the text to mean.

Some new originalists ground this approach in a theory about how language works in general. See, e.g., Lawrence B. Solum, The Fixation Thesis: The Role of Historical Fact in Original Meaning, 91 Notre Dame L. Rev. 1, 21, 22, 25 (2015):

> [If] you were reading a book of recipes written in the eighteenth century and [you] learned that "kale" was the eighteenth-century word for what we now call "radishes," you would be very unlikely to insist that the recipe actually referred to the acephala group of barassica oleracea, the green- or purple-leafed vegetable, which is quite unlike what we call a "radish." Of course, you might be inspired to try the recipe with some leaves from a plant in the acephala group of barassica oleracea, but that would be an experimental deviation from the recipe and not a case of following the recipe.

Even if this is a correct account of how language works when following a recipe, does it follow that language works this way when the reader has other purposes? Would the reader of a novel who had the purpose of getting the most aesthetic and intellectual satisfaction from it feel herself bound to interpret it according to the original understanding? What is the purpose of constitutional interpretation, and how does that purpose intersect with the way the language should be read?

Some new originalists distinguish between "interpretation" and "construction." See, e.g., K. Whittington, Constitutional Construction (1999); Solum, The Interpretation-Construction Distinction, 27 Const. Comment. 95 (2010); Solum, District of Columbia v. Heller and Originalism, 103 Nw. U. L. Rev. 923 (2009). Interpretation involves determining the semantic meaning of the provision in question. It requires discovery of a fact that exists in the world — how people at the time a measure was adopted would have understood the words in question. What would a new originalist do if historical inquiry discloses significant disagreements about a provision's meaning among reasonably well-informed people at the time the provision was adopted? In such a case, does the provision have no semantic meaning? For some new originalists, cases like this are within the domain of construction. Construction is the process by which semantic meaning is translated into a legal rule. It inevitably implicates normative rather than factual questions. For example, the semantic meaning of the word "equal" in the equal protection clause tells us little or nothing about whether different levels of scrutiny are required for different sorts of statutes.

In many cases, where constitutional language is clear, construction is quite unimportant. Once the semantic meaning of the requirement that the President be at least 35 years of age is established, there is very little to construe. In other cases, though, constitutional language is indeterminate either because it is ambiguous — it might have more than one semantic meaning — or it is vague — the boundaries of the semantic meaning are uncertain. Constitutional provisions that express broad principles or aspirations — that, for example, protect "the freedom of speech," prohibit "cruel or unusual punishment," or guarantee "equal protection of the laws" — are especially subject to this problem. When the semantic meaning is indeterminate, interpretation must necessarily be supplemented by construction. Most new originalists believe that construction must be consistent with semantic meaning. (Consider, though, the problem of stare decisis, where judges arguably enforce results that are inconsistent with their best interpretation of the Constitution's semantic meaning.) But many new originalists believe that construction is not fully determined by the Constitution's semantic meaning and may actually contradict the framers' expected application.

c. *New versus old.* Expected application originalism served two important functions. It provided theoretical grounding for a broad-based attack on Warren and Burger Court precedent that had, among other things, greatly expanded the rights of criminal defendants, created an abortion right, and expanded the protection of free speech. Its proponents asserted that it also legitimated constitutional law by constraining the discretion of judges and grounding constitutional doctrine in something other than the value judgments of unelected judges. As explained above, however, this form of originalism faced serious problems related to the difficulty of discovering and defining original intent and seemingly unacceptable results it sometimes produced.

The new originalism is designed to meet these problems. Does it do so successfully? For criticisms of the new originalism, see Berman, Originalism Is Bunk, 84 N.Y.U. L. Rev. 1 (2009); Dorf, The Undead Constitution, 125 Harv. L. Rev. 2011 (2012). Even if it does, it arguably achieves this end only by giving up on the objectives achieved by the old originalism. On the one hand, the new originalism provides less certain grounding for criticisms of "liberal" results. For example, "liberal" new originalists have argued that there is a good originalist case for recognition of a constitutional abortion right. See J. Balkin, Living Originalism 214–219 (2011). True, this was not the expected application of the fourteenth amendment, but neither is it inconsistent with the amendment's semantic meaning, and it might be the best construction of the amendment. On the other hand, depending on the size of the domains of interpretation and construction, the new originalism may leave considerable room for judicial discretion based upon judicial value choices. Consider, for example, the constitutional status of same-sex marriage. Once one abandons an expected application approach, is it really possible to determine whether same-sex and straight marriage are "the same" for purposes of the equal protection clause without making a contestable moral judgment about gay marriage? For a negative answer, see Seidman, Gay Sex and Marriage, the Reciprocal Disadvantage Problem, and the Crisis in Liberal Constitutional Theory, 31 Harv. J.L. & Pub. Poly. 135 (2008).

4. *Alternatives to originalism.* What would it mean to utilize a nonoriginalist approach to constitutional law? Opponents of originalism take a variety of positions that are not fully compatible with each other. As you consider these possibilities think about (a) whether the approaches really reject new originalism, or whether, alternatively, they are reactions to expected application originalism; and (b) whether the approaches resolve the problems of judicial discretion and create an uncontroversial normative foundation for constitutional law that motivated the creation of originalist approaches in the first place.

a. *Natural law.* Grey, Do We Have an Unwritten Constitution?, 27 Stan. L. Rev. 703, 715–716 (1975):

> For the generation that framed the Constitution, the concept of a "higher law," protecting "natural rights," and taking precedence over ordinary positive law as a matter of political obligation, was widely shared and deeply felt. An essential element of American constitutionalism was the reduction to written form — and hence to positive law — of some of the principles of natural rights. But at the same time, it was generally recognized that written constitutions could not completely codify the higher law. Thus in the framing of the original American constitutions it was widely accepted that there remained unwritten but still binding principles of higher law. [And as] it came to be accepted that the judiciary had the power to enforce the commands of the written Constitution when these conflicted with ordinary law, it was also widely assumed that judges would enforce as constitutional restraints the unwritten natural rights as well.

For a comprehensive historical discussion of the framers' intent, concluding that the "founding generation . . . expected the judiciary to keep legislatures from transgressing the natural rights of mankind, whether or not those rights found their way into the written Constitution," see Sherry, The Founders' Unwritten Constitution, 54 U. Chi. L. Rev. 1127, 1177 (1987). See also Grey, Origins of the Unwritten Constitution: Fundamental Law in American Revolutionary Thought, 30 Stan. L. Rev. 843 (1978); Corwin, The "Higher Law" Background of American Constitutional Law, 42 Harv. L. Rev. 149, 365 (1928–1929).

If the natural law argument has force, should we be bound by the framers' conception of natural law, by modern views, or by the objective content — if any — of natural law?

b. *Moral arguments and the search for "integrity."* A. Bickel, The Least Dangerous Branch 24–26 (1962):

> [Government] should serve not only what we conceive from time to time to be our immediate material needs but also certain enduring values. [But] such values do not present themselves ready-made. They [must] be continually derived, enunciated, and seen in relevant application. [Courts] have certain capacities for dealing with matters of principle that legislatures and executives do not possess. Judges have, or should have, the leisure, the training, and the insulation to follow the ways

of the scholar in pursuing the ends of government. This is crucial in sorting out the enduring values of a society.

See also R. Dworkin, Freedom's Law (1997). Dworkin's theory of interpretation — to simplify a complex argument — asks judges to provide the "best constructive account" of existing legal materials by putting constitutional text, and constitutional precedents, in the best possible light. On this view, judges have two obligations: to "fit" the existing legal materials and to "justify" them by making them sensible and good rather than senseless and bad. Judges therefore have obligations to constitutional text and history, but they also have an obligation to make the system fair and just rather than the opposite. See generally R. Dworkin, Law's Empire (1985). Moral philosophy plays a role in this account, not on the ground that judges should do what philosophy tells them to do, but on the ground that when the legal materials leave gaps and uncertainties, judges should try to put them in the best light, and here philosophical arguments, of one kind or another, are inevitable. Is this view meaningfully different from new originalism? Consider the possibility that under Dworkin's approach, originalism must be rejected, first because it does not "fit" our tradition, and second because it does not "justify" it, for a system of constitutional law based on originalism would offer an absurdly truncated set of constitutional rights. How might an originalist respond to these claims?

c. *Tradition.* Sandalow, Constitutional Interpretation, 79 Mich. L. Rev. 1033, 1036, 1068–1069, 1071 (1971):

> [There is a] need to accommodate the Constitution to changing circumstances and values. [Constitutional] law thus emerges not as exegesis, but as a process by which each generation gives formal expression to the values it holds [fundamental]. Judges [who] wish to appeal to the Constitution must demonstrate that the principles upon which they propose to confer constitutional status express values that [are] rooted in history. [The] relevant past for purposes of constitutional law, thus, is to be found not only in the intentions of those who drafted and ratified the document but in the entirety of our history.

d. *Common law and "living constitutionalism."* Perhaps constitutional law is a common law process in which judgments emerge from the cumulative impact of particular cases rather than from text or history. On this view, the "meaning" of the constitution is not fixed at the time of the framing, but, rather, evolves as new circumstances put pressure on old meanings and as language changes to deal with those pressures. See Strauss, Common Law Constitutional Interpretation, 63 U. Chi. L. Rev. 877 (1996), for a detailed treatment. See also Strauss, Foreword: Does the Constitution Mean What It Says?, 129 Harv. L. Rev. 1 (2015):

> [There] are times when established principles are simply inconsistent with the text. Beyond that, constitutional "interpretation" usually has little to do, in practice, with the words of the text. There are times when the text is decisive, and it is never acceptable to announce that you are ignoring the text. But routinely the text, although not flatly inconsistent with the outcome of a case, has very little to do with the way the case is argued or decided. In most litigated cases, constitutional law resembles the common law much more closely than it resembles a text-based system.

e. *Representation-reinforcement.* J. Ely, Democracy and Distrust 7–8, 87–88 (1980):

> [Rule] in accord with the consent of a majority [is] the core of the American governmental system. [But] that cannot be the whole story, since a majority with untrammeled power [is] in a position to deal itself benefits at the expense of the [minority]. The tricky task [is to devise] a way [of] protecting minorities from majority tyranny that is not a flagrant contradiction of the principle of majority [rule]. [To accomplish this task,] the Constitution [is] overwhelmingly concerned [with] procedural fairness [and] with ensuring broad participation in the processes [of] government. [Thus,] a representation-reinforcing approach to judicial review, [which focuses on "clearing the channels of political change" and "facilitating the representation of minorities," is] supportive of [the] underlying premises of the American system of representative democracy. [Moreover,] such an approach [involves] tasks that courts, as experts on process and [as] political outsiders, can sensibly claim to be better qualified [to] perform than political officials.

Under this view, courts are obligated to enforce unambiguous provisions in the Constitution. When interpreting open textured provisions, however, judges should read them in light of the Constitution's general commitment to democratic representation, but not to recognize or create fundamental rights unrelated to representation. This position would support decisions protecting minorities and rights of access to the political process. It would not readily support decisions recognizing rights of privacy or economic liberty. C. Sunstein, The Partial Constitution (1993), argues that the constitutional commitment to "deliberative democracy" should be the source of interpretative principles; this approach has a clear connection to Ely's. Consider the possibility that Ely's approach accepts the new originalist view of interpretation and offers a particular argument about construction that is not required by but not ruled out by the new originalism.

f. *Unsettlement.* On this view, originalism is misguided precisely because it attempts to use the Constitution to settle political disputes. Open textured constitutional text should, instead, be read so as to foster disagreement and debate about its meaning. See L. Seidman, Our Unsettled Constitution 8 (2001):

> Any constitutional settlement is bound to produce losers who will continue to nurse deep-seated grievances. [But] a constitution that unsettles creates no permanent losers. By destabilizing whatever outcomes are produced by the political process, it provides citizens with a forum and a vocabulary that they can use to continue the argument. Even when they suffer serious losses in the political sphere, citizens will have reason to maintain their allegiance to the community — not because constitutional law settles disputes, but because it provides arguments grounded in society's foundational commitments, for why the political settlement they oppose is unjust.

If open textured clauses of the Constitution are ambiguous or vague and if they embody no more than general principles, might not an insistence on adhering to their original public meaning produce unsettlement?

5. *Rebuttals.* Do the sources outlined above meet the objections from history and democracy? Consider the following objections:

a. *Natural law.* Ely, supra, at 48–50:

> At the time the original Constitution was ratified, [a] number of people espoused the existence of a system of natural law principles. [But the] historical record [is] not

so uncomplicated as it is sometimes made to appear. [In any event, the] idea is a discredited one in our society, [and] for good reason. "[A]ll theories of natural law have a singular vagueness which is both an advantage and disadvantage in the application of the theories." The advantage [is] that you can invoke natural law to support anything you want. The disadvantage is that everybody understands that.

b. *Moral arguments.* Ely, supra, at 56–58:

[The view] that judges, in seeking constitutional value judgments, should [employ] "the method of reason familiar to the discourse of moral philosophy" [assumes] that moral philosophy is what constitutional law is properly about, that there exists a correct way of doing such philosophy, and that judges are better than others at identifying and engaging in it. [But] surely the claim here cannot be that lawyers and judges are the best imaginable people to tell good moral philosophy from bad. [Moreover, this view assumes] that something exists called "the method of moral philosophy" whose contours sensitive experts will agree on. [That] is not the way things are. [There] simply does not exist a method of moral philosophy.

Consider the following response: The existence of competing methods of moral philosophy no more disqualifies moral philosophy as a source of constitutional interpretation than the existence of competing methods of ascertaining the original understanding disqualifies originalism as a source of constitutional interpretation. The critical issue is not whether there are unitary or uncontroversial answers to moral questions, but whether it is possible to engage in rational discourse about such questions — whether moral philosophy is ultimately about anything more than a wholly subjective and inevitably relativist choice of competing value preferences. But might we be nervous about moral reasoning by judges even if we are not nervous about moral reasoning in general? See R. Posner, The Problematics of Moral and Legal Theory (1998); C. Sunstein, Legal Reasoning and Political Conflict (1997), both emphasizing the problems with judge-made assessments of political philosophy.

c. *Tradition.* Ely, supra, at 60, 62:

Tradition is an obvious place to seek fundamental values, but one whose problems are also obvious. [Tradition] can be invoked in support of almost any cause. [Moreover, tradition's] overtly backward-looking character highlights its undemocratic nature: it is hard to square with the theory of our government that yesterday's majority [should not] control today's. [And] "[i]f the Constitution protects only interests which comport with traditional values, the persons most likely to be penalized for their way of life will be those least likely to receive judicial protection," and that flips the point of the [Constitution] exactly upside down.

d. *Common law and "living constitutionalism."* If, as common law advocates argue, it is never permissible for judges to expressly disavow or disregard constitutional text, how is this approach different from the new originalism? If the common law approach requires judges to continually "update" constitutional doctrine in light of changing conditions, what constrains their discretion? Consider in this regard, these comments by Justice Scalia:

the Constitution is not a living organism; it is a legal document. It says something and doesn't say other [things]. [Proponents of the living constitution want matters to be decided] not by the people, but by the justices of the Supreme Court. [They] are not looking for legal flexibility, they are looking for rigidity, whether it's the right to abortion or the right to homosexual activity, they want that right to be embedded from coast to coast and to be unchangeable.

e. *Representation-reinforcement.* Brest, The Substance of Process, 42 Ohio St. L.J. 131, 140, 142 (1981):

[Most] instances of representation-reinforcing review demand value judgments not different in kind or scope from the fundamental values sort. [Indeed, the] representation-reinforcing enterprise is shot full of value choices, starting with the decision of just how representative our various systems of government ought to be and who ought to be included in the political community, and ending with (covert) choices about who is justifiably the object of prejudice and whether legislative goals are sufficiently important to warrant the burdens they impose on some members of society. [In his] attempt to establish a value-free mode of constitutional adjudication, [Ely] has come as close as anyone could to proving that it can't be done.

f. *Unsettlement.* Samaha, Dead Hand Arguments and Constitutional Interpretation, 108 Colum. L. Rev. 606, 668–669 (2008):

[Even] assuming positive unifying effects from the situation, no one should blinker the decision costs associated with interpretive openness combined with supremacy. This combination encourages arguments over the content of supreme constitutional law, which require resources to resolve, even when short-term distributive consequences are the only stakes. At least some of the arguments surrounding the written Constitution involve nothing more majestic.

More important, the actual interpretive advice from an unsettlement theory is challenging to operationalize. What should an individual interpreter do when faced with a constitutional argument? In the unsettlement model, rights claims are supposed to be indeterminate. Should there be an institutional mechanism for assuring a plurality of interpretive perspectives at any given point in time, or perhaps shifting methods from time to time? Such a mechanism seems to qualify as a constitutional settlement forbidden by the theory.

6. *Concluding thoughts.* In reading the materials that follow, consider the following possibilities:

a. There is an ambiguous relation between originalism and judicial restraint. At least some versions of originalism are perfectly comfortable with relatively frequent judicial invalidation of democratic decisions; they insist only that such invalidation must follow from the original understanding. When it does, originalist judges let the chips fall where they may. Originalists are concerned to limit judicial discretion but not necessarily to restrict the number of invalidations. Some originalists believe in an active judicial role in invalidating statutes; others do not.

b. Originalism risks internal contradiction because, like any theory, it must offer reasons why it should be adopted. Those reasons, themselves, cannot be derived from originalist sources without arguing in a circle. Moreover, those reasons will inevitably involve contestable claims about the nature of a well-functioning constitutional democracy. Those who defend an active judicial role in (for example) protecting minorities will have to resort to something other than history. So, too, with those who defend originalism. In these respects, some kind of choice about values is inescapable — originalists themselves must defend their choices in terms of political theory — even though people often try to escape it.

c. Methods of construction through tradition and representation-reinforcement, and more, might be compatible with the new originalism. If so, does it matter whether we think of originalism, either in its old or new form, as the primary method of interpretation or, instead, as one of a repertoire of interactive techniques that include tradition, representation-reinforcement, and more?

d. The Court has not selected any particular "theory" of interpretation; it has not settled on any particular "method." Instead, it often brackets theoretical issues when it decides cases. See C. Sunstein, One Case at a Time (1999); Sunstein, Incompletely Theorized Agreements, 108 Harv. L. Rev. 1733 (1995). Does this make judicial review, as it is currently practiced, "unprincipled"? Would it be better if the Court made a decision in favor of a single method of interpretation? Could it? See Vermeule, The Judiciary Is a They, Not an It: Interpretive Theory and the Fallacy of Division, 14 J. Contemp. L. Issues 549 (2005).

B.   THE PRIVILEGES OR IMMUNITIES CLAUSE

Section 1 of the fourteenth amendment provides that "[no] State shall make or enforce any law which shall abridge the privileges or immunities of citizens of the United States." The enactment of the fourteenth amendment is examined in Chapter 5, section A, supra. Of the considerable body of literature concerning the adoption of the Civil War amendments, useful works are A. Amar, The Bill of Rights (1999); R. Berger, Government by Judiciary (1977); C. Fairman, Reconstruction and Reunion, 1864–1888, pt. 1, ch. 20 (1971); H. Flack, The Adoption of the Fourteenth Amendment (1908); J. James, The Framing of the Fourteenth Amendment (1956); Fairman, Does the Fourteenth Amendment Incorporate the Bill of Rights? The Original Understanding, 2 Stan. L. Rev. 5 (1949); Frank and Munro, The Original Understanding of "Equal Protection of the Laws," 1972 Wash. U. L.Q. 421.

What are the "privileges or immunities of citizens of the United States"?

The Slaughter-House Cases
83 U.S. (16 Wall.) 36 (1873)

Mr. Justice Miller delivered the opinion of the Court.

[A statute passed by the Louisiana legislature granted to the Crescent City Live-Stock Landing and Slaughter-House Company the exclusive right to engage in the livestock landing and slaughterhouse business within an area including the City of New Orleans. The company was required to permit any person to slaughter animals in its slaughterhouse at charges fixed by law. Plaintiffs, several butchers whose businesses were restricted by the statute, sued to invalidate the monopoly. They claimed that the statute violated various provisions of the thirteenth and fourteenth amendments, including the privileges and immunities clause.]

The most cursory glance at [the thirteenth and fourteenth amendments] discloses a unity of purpose, when taken in connection with the history of the times, which cannot fail to have an important bearing on any question of doubt concerning their true meaning. [For] in the light of [events,] almost too recent to be called history, but which are familiar to us all; and on the most casual examination of the language of these amendments, no one can fail to be impressed with the one pervading purpose found in them all, lying at the foundation of each, and without which none of them would have been even suggested; we mean the freedom of the slave race, the security and firm establishment of that freedom, and the protection of the newly-made freeman and citizen from the oppressions of those who had formerly exercised unlimited dominion over him. . . .

We do not say that no one else but the negro can share in this protection. [But] what we do say, and what we wish to be understood is, that in any fair and just construction of any section or phrase of these amendments, it is necessary to look to the purpose which we have said was the pervading spirit of them all. . . .

The first section of the fourteenth article, to which our attention is more specially invited, opens with a definition of citizenship — not only citizenship of the United States, but citizenship of the States. . . .

"All persons born or naturalized in the United States, and subject to the jurisdiction thereof, are citizens of the United States and of the State wherein they reside."

The first observation we have to make on this clause is, that it [overturns] the *Dred Scott* decision by making all persons born within the United States and subject to its jurisdiction citizens of the United States. . . .

The next observation is more important in view of the arguments of counsel in the present case. It is, that the distinction between citizenship of the United States and citizenship of a State is clearly recognized and established. [There] is a citizenship of the United States, and a citizenship of a State, which are distinct from each other, and which depend upon different characteristics or circumstances in the individual.

We think this distinction and its explicit recognition in this amendment of great weight in this argument, because the next paragraph of this same section, which is the one mainly relied on by the [plaintiffs], speaks only of privileges and immunities of citizens of the United States, and does not speak of those of citizens of the several States. . . .

If, then, there is a difference between the privileges and immunities belonging to a citizen of the United States as such, and those belonging to the citizen of the State as such, the latter must rest for their security and protection where they have heretofore rested; for they are not embraced by this paragraph of the amendment.

The first occurrence of the words "privileges and immunities" in our [Constitution] is to be found in [article IV, section 2, which provides that] "The citizens of each State shall be entitled to all the privileges and immunities of citizens of the several States." [The] first and the leading case on [this clause] is that of Corfield v. Coryell, decided by Mr. Justice Washington in the Circuit Court for the District of Pennsylvania in 1823.

"The inquiry," he says,

is, what are the privileges and immunities of citizens of the several States? We feel no hesitation in confining these expressions to those privileges and immunities which are fundamental; which belong of right to the citizens of all free governments, and which have at all times been enjoyed by citizens of the several States which compose this Union, from the time of their becoming free, independent, and sovereign. What these fundamental principles are, it would be more tedious than difficult to enumerate. They may all, however, be comprehended under the following general heads: protection by the government, with the right to acquire and possess property of every kind, and to pursue and obtain happiness and safety, subject, nevertheless, to such restraints as the government may prescribe for the general good of the whole. . . .

[Article IV, section 2] did not create those rights, which it called privileges and immunities of citizens of the States. [Its] sole purpose was to declare to the several States, that whatever those rights, as you grant or establish them to your own citizens, or as you limit or qualify, or impose restrictions on their exercise, the same, neither more nor less, shall be the measure of the rights of citizens of other States within your jurisdiction.

[Thus,] up to the adoption of the recent amendments, no claim or pretence was set up that those rights depended on the Federal government for their existence or protection. [Was] it the purpose of the fourteenth amendment, by the simple declaration that no State should make or enforce any law which shall abridge the privileges and immunities of citizens of the United States, to transfer the security and protection of all the civil rights which we have mentioned, from the States to the Federal government? And where it is declared that Congress shall have the power to enforce that article, was it intended to bring within the power of Congress the entire domain of civil rights heretofore belonging exclusively to the States?

All this and more must follow, if the proposition of the [plaintiffs] be sound. For not only are these rights subject to the control of Congress whenever in its discretion any of them are supposed to be abridged by State legislation, but that body may also pass laws in advance, limiting and restricting the exercise of legislative power by the States, in their most ordinary and usual functions, as in its judgment it may think proper on all such subjects. And still further, such a construction [would] constitute this court a perpetual censor upon all legislation of the States, on the civil rights of their own citizens, with authority to nullify such as it did not approve as consistent with those rights, as they existed at the time of the adoption of this amendment. The argument we admit is not always the most conclusive which is drawn from the consequences urged against the adoption of a particular construction of an instrument. But when, as in the case before us, these consequences are so serious, so far-reaching and pervading, so great a departure from the structure and spirit of our institutions; when the effect is to fetter and degrade the State governments by subjecting them to the control of Congress, in the exercise of powers heretofore universally conceded to them of the most ordinary and fundamental character; when in fact it radically changes the whole theory of the relations of the State and Federal governments to each other and of both these governments to the people; the argument has a force that is irresistible, in the absence of language which expresses such a purpose too clearly to admit of doubt. . . .

[Lest] it should be said that no [privileges] and immunities [of federal citizenship] are to be found if those we have been considering are excluded, we venture to suggest some which owe their existence to the Federal government, its National character, its Constitution, or its laws.

One of these is well described in the case of Crandall v. Nevada. [73 U.S. (6 Wall.) 35 (1867).] It is said to be the right of the citizen of this great country, protected by implied guarantees of its Constitution, "to come to the seat of government to assert any claim he may have upon that government, to transact any business he may have with it, to seek its protection, to share its offices, to engage in administering its functions. He has the right of free access to its sea-ports, through which all operations of foreign commerce are conducted, to the sub-treasuries, land offices, and courts of justice in the several States."

Another privilege of a citizen of the United States is to demand the care and protection of the Federal government over his life, liberty, and property when on the high seas or within the jurisdiction of a foreign government. [The] right to peaceably assemble and petition for redress of grievances, the privilege of the writ of habeas corpus, are rights of the citizen guaranteed by the Federal Constitution. The right to use the navigable waters of the United States, however they may penetrate the territory of the several States, all rights secured to our citizens by treaties with foreign nations, are dependent upon citizenship of the United States, and not citizenship of a State. [To] these may be added the rights secured by the thirteenth and fifteenth articles of amendment, and by the other [clauses] of the fourteenth. . . .

[The Court also rejected claims that the statute violated the thirteenth amendment and the equal protection and due process clauses of the fourteenth amendment.]

The judgments of the Supreme Court of Louisiana in these cases are affirmed.

MR. JUSTICE FIELD, dissenting. . . .

The act of Louisiana presents the naked case [where] a right to pursue a lawful and necessary calling, previously enjoyed by every citizen, [is] taken away and vested exclusively [in] a single corporation. . . .

The question presented is, therefore, one of the gravest importance, not merely to the parties here, but to the whole country. It is nothing less than the question whether the recent amendments to the Federal Constitution protect the citizens of the United States against the deprivation of their common rights by State legislation. In my judgment the fourteenth amendment does afford such protection, and was so intended by the Congress which framed and the States which adopted it. . . .

If [the privileges and immunities clause] only refers, as held by the majority of the court in their opinion, to such privileges and immunities as were before its adoption specially designated in the Constitution or necessarily implied as belonging to citizens of the United States, it was a vain and idle enactment, which accomplished nothing, and most unnecessarily excited Congress and the people on its passage. With privileges and immunities thus designated or implied no State could ever have interfered by its laws, and no new constitutional provision was required to inhibit such interference. The supremacy of the Constitution and the laws of the United States always controlled any State legislation of that character. But if the amendment refers to the natural and inalienable rights which belong to all citizens, the inhibition has a profound significance and consequence.

What, then, are the privileges and immunities which are secured against abridgment by State legislation?

[Justice Washington's interpretation of the "privileges and immunities" protected by article IV, section 2] appears to me to be a sound construction of the clause in question. The privileges and immunities designated are those which of right belong to the citizens of all free governments. Clearly among these must be placed the right to pursue a lawful employment in a lawful manner, without other restraint than such as equally affects all persons. . . .

I am authorized by THE CHIEF JUSTICE, MR. JUSTICE SWAYNE, and MR. JUSTICE BRADLEY, to state that they concur with me in this dissenting opinion.

MR. JUSTICE BRADLEY, also dissenting. . . .

The right of a State to regulate the conduct of its citizens is undoubtedly a very broad and extensive one, and not to be lightly restricted. But there are certain fundamental rights which this right of regulation cannot infringe. It may prescribe the manner of their exercise, but it cannot subvert the rights themselves. [In] this free country, the people of which inherited certain traditionary rights and privileges from their ancestors, citizenship means something. . . .

The people of this country brought with them to its shores the rights of Englishmen; the rights which had been wrested from English sovereigns at various periods of the nation's history. [Blackstone] classifies these fundamental rights under three heads, as the absolute rights of individuals, to wit: the right of personal security, the right of personal liberty, and the right of private property. [These] are the fundamental rights which can only be [interfered with] by lawful regulations necessary or proper for the mutual good of all. . . . [And among the privileges and immunities of citizens,] none is more essential and fundamental than the right to follow such profession or employment as each one may choose, subject only to uniform regulations equally applicable to all. . . .

[Great] fears are expressed that this construction of the amendment will lead to enactments by Congress interfering with the internal affairs of the States, and [that] it will lead the Federal courts to draw to their cognizance the supervision of State tribunals on every subject of judicial inquiry, on the plea of ascertaining whether the privileges and immunities of citizens have not been abridged.

In my judgment no such practical inconveniences would arise. Very little, if any, legislation on the part of Congress would be required to carry the amendment into effect. [And as] the privileges and immunities protected are only those fundamental ones which belong to every citizen, they would soon become so far defined as to cause but a slight accumulation of business in the Federal courts. [In any event, the] argument from inconvenience ought not to have a very controlling influence in questions of this sort. The National will and National interest are of far greater importance. . . .

[A dissenting opinion by Justice Swayne is omitted.]

Note: The Demise of the Privileges or Immunities Clause

1. *The Slaughter-House Cases.* Consider the following criticisms of Justice Miller's interpretation of the privileges or immunities clause:

a. "Unique among constitutional provisions, the privileges and [sic] immunities clause of the Fourteenth Amendment enjoys the distinction of having been rendered a 'practical nullity' by a single decision of the Supreme Court within five years after its ratification." E. Corwin, The Constitution of the United States of America 965 (1953). See Currie, The Constitution in the Supreme Court: Limitations on State Power, 1865–1873, 51 U. Chi. L. Rev. 329, 348 (1983):

[As Justice Field observed in dissent, the difficulty] was with Miller's apparent conclusion that the sole office of the clause was to protect rights already given by some other federal law. Apart from the amendment's less than conclusive reference to dual citizenship, his sole justification was that a broader holding would "radically [change] the whole theory of the relations of the State and Federal governments to each other and of both these governments to the people" — which quite arguably was precisely what the authors of the amendment had in mind.

b. Graham, Our "Declaratory" Fourteenth Amendment, 7 Stan. L. Rev. 3, 23, 25 (1954):

A single change was made in Section One after it had been reported by the Joint Committee. This was the addition of the first sentence defining citizenship. [Significantly,] no one observed that while citizenship was made dual in this first sentence, only the privileges or immunities of "citizens of the United States" were specifically protected in the second sentence against abridgment by the states. The reason for this apparent oversight is that [opponents] of slavery had regarded all the important "natural" and constitutional rights as being privileges or immunities of citizens of the United States. This had been the cardinal premise of anti-slavery theory. [The] real purpose of adding this citizenship definition was to [overrule *Dred Scott*]. [To] reach the conclusion of Justice Miller and the majority, one must disregard not only all antislavery from 1834 on, but one must ignore virtually every word said in the debates of 1865–66.

For a defense of Justice Miller's opinion, see Palmer, The Parameters of Constitutional Reconstruction: *Slaughter-House, Cruikshank*, and the Fourteenth Amendment, 1984 U. Ill. L. Rev. 739.

c. Kaczorowski, The Politics of Judicial Interpretation: The Federal Courts, Department of Justice and Civil Rights, 1866–1876, at 154–155, 161 (1985):

Theoretical rationalizations of legal doctrine are also means to achieve political objectives. [*Slaughter-House*] may thus be explained in terms of its political goals. Miller was quite explicit about the majority's desire to resist the nationalizing impact of the Civil War by redefining American federalism as a states rights–centered dual federalism. [Although the Court may not have] shared the political objectives and values of Democratic Conservatives of the South, [it clearly was] more concerned about preserving the states' regulatory functions [than] in establishing national authority to protect the civil rights of black Americans. [Moreover, the] revitalization of states rights was crucial to the success of Northern states in their struggle to cope with the stresses of industrialization, [for] it endorsed the state police power necessary to control the growing concentrations of monopolistic power of rising business.

2. *The* Slaughter-House *dissents.* The dissenters maintained that the "right to pursue a lawful employment in a lawful manner" is a "fundamental" right that belongs "to the citizens of all free governments." But perhaps this formulation is "question begging, because [the] question how lawfulness is to be determined is unresolved." Kurland, The Privileges or Immunities Clause: "Its Hour Come Round at Last"?, 1972 Wash. U. L.Q. 405, 409. If the *Slaughter-House* dissenters had prevailed, what other rights would constitute "privileges or immunities of citizens"?

3. *Alternative interpretations.*

a. *Justice Black's approach.* "My study of the historical events that culminated in the Fourteenth Amendment [persuades] me that one of the chief objects that [the] Amendment's first section [was] intended to accomplish was to make the Bill of Rights applicable to the states." Adamson v. California, 332 U.S. 46, 71–72 (1947) (Black, J., dissenting). "[The] words 'No State shall make or enforce any law which shall abridge the privileges or immunities of citizens of the United States' seem to me an eminently reasonable way of expressing the idea that henceforth the Bill of Rights shall apply to the States. What more precious 'privilege' of American citizenship could there be than that privilege to claim the protection of our great Bill of Rights?" Duncan v. Louisiana, 391 U.S. 145, 166 (1968) (Black, J., concurring).

In support of this view, note that Representative Bingham, the framer of the provision, stated that "the privileges and immunities of citizens of the United States [are] chiefly defined in the first eight amendments to the Constitution." Cong. Globe, 42d Cong., 1st Sess., app. 85 (1871). See also Kaczorowski, Revolutionary Constitutionalism in the Era of the Civil War and Reconstruction, 61 N.Y.U. L. Rev. 863 (1986). But note that the privileges and immunities of the original Constitution referred to something altogether different from the original bill of rights; and note also that the due process clause is included in the fourteenth amendment, an inclusion that would create redundancy if the bill of rights was already comprehended within the privileges and immunities clause.

b. *Academic criticism of Justice Black's approach.* Consider Fairman, Does the Fourteenth Amendment Incorporate the Bill of Rights? The Original Understanding, 2 Stan. L. Rev. 5, 132, 137–139 (1949):

> [Apart from a few isolated references, the theory that the] privileges and immunities clause incorporated Amendments I to VIII found no recognition in the practice of Congress, or the action of state legislatures, constitutional conventions, or courts. [The] freedom that the states traditionally [had] exercised to develop their own systems for administering justice repels any thought that the [Bill of Rights] provisions on grand jury, criminal jury, and civil jury were fastened upon them in 1868. Congress would not have attempted such a thing, the country would not have stood for it, the legislatures would not have ratified. . . .
>
> If the founders of the Fourteenth Amendment did not intend the privileges and immunities clause to impose Amendments I to VIII, then what, it may be asked, did they mean? [If] one seeks some inclusive and exclusive definition, such that one could say, this is precisely what they had in mind — pretty clearly there never was any such clear conception. [The opponents of the measure magnified] the proposal to render it odious. [The advocates] offered illustrations of particular evils that would be repressed; [but] stayed away from any explanation of a fundamental principle. [Brooding] over the matter [has] slowly brought [me to] the conclusion that [the protection of those rights that are] "implicit in the concept of ordered liberty" [comes] as close as one can to catching the vague aspirations that were hung upon the privileges and immunities clause.

In support of this view, note that Senator Howard, who presented the amendment to the Senate on behalf of the Joint Committee on Reconstruction, explained that the clause protects all "fundamental rights lying at the basis of all society," and that the precise scope of the rights incorporated in the clause would be left "to be discussed and adjudicated when they should happen practically to arise." Cong.

Globe, 39th Cong., 1st Sess. 2765–2766 (1866). Consider also R. Berger, Government by Judiciary 18, 20 (1977):

> The "privileges or immunities" clause was the central provision of the Amendment's §1 and the key to its meaning is furnished by the immediately preceding Civil Rights Act of 1866, which, all are agreed, it was the purpose of the Amendment to embody and protect. The objectives of the [Civil Rights] Act were quite limited. [The act provided that "there shall be no discrimination in civil rights or immunities on account of race [but] the inhabitants of every race [shall] have the same right to make and enforce contracts, to sue, be parties, and give evidence; to inherit, purchase, lease, sell, hold and convey real and personal property, and to full and equal benefit of all laws and proceedings for the security of person and property, and shall be subject to like punishment [and] no other."] The three clauses of §1 [of the fourteenth amendment] were [thus] three facets of one and the same concern: to insure that there would be no discrimination against [blacks] in respect of "fundamental rights," which had a clearly understood and narrow compass [as exemplified by the Civil Rights Act].

In support of this view, note Representative Garfield's comment that the proposed amendment will "lift [the Civil Rights Act] above the reach of political strife, [where] no storm of passion can shake it." Cong. Globe, 39th Cong., 1st Sess. 2462 (1866).

c. *The rights of citizens.* Amar, The Bill of Rights and the Fourteenth Amendment, 101 Yale L.J. 1193 (1992), argues for "refined incorporation":

> [All] of the privileges and immunities of citizens recognized in the Bill of Rights became applicable against states by dint of the Fourteenth Amendment. But not all of the provisions of the original Bill of Rights were indeed rights of citizens. Some instead were at least in part rights of states, and as such, awkward to incorporate fully against states. [The] right question is whether the provision really guarantees a privilege or immunity of individual citizens rather than a right of states or the public at large.

Amar's basic conclusion is that when a privilege or immunity of individual citizens is at issue, incorporation is appropriate. See also A. Amar, The Bill of Rights (1998).

4. *Subsequent developments.* Although the Court has generally adhered to the *Slaughter-House* interpretation of the privileges or immunities clause, it has on rare occasions relied upon it, most recently in Saenz v. Roe, 526 U.S. 489 (1999), with regard to the right to travel, discussed in more detail in section E3 infra.

In McDonald v. City of Chicago, 561 U.S. 742 (2010), a majority of the Court relied upon the fourteenth amendment's due process clause to hold that the second amendment right to bear arms was applicable to the states. (This portion of the Court's opinion is discussed at pages 738-746, infra). Writing for a plurality of the Court on whether the result should be justified under the privileges or immunities clause, Justice Alito refused to revisit the *Slaughter-House Cases.*

> [In] petitioners' view, the Privileges or Immunities Clause protects all of the rights set out in the Bill of Rights, as well as some others but petitioners are unable to identify the Clause's full scope. Nor is there any consensus on that question among scholars who agree that the *Slaughter-House Cases'* interpretation is flawed. We see no need to reconsider that interpretation here.

Compare Justice Thomas's opinion concurring in part and concurring in the judgment:

> As a consequence of this Court's marginalization of the [Privileges or Immunities] Clause, litigants seeking federal protection of fundamental rights turned to [the due process clause]. . . .
>
> [The] notion that a constitutional provision that guarantees only "process" [could] define the substance of those rights strains credulity for even the most casual user of words. Moreover, this fiction is a particularly dangerous one. The one theme that links the Court's substantive due process precedents together is their lack of a guiding principle to distinguish "fundamental" rights that warrant protection from nonfundamental rights that do not. . . .
>
> [I] believe the original meaning of the Fourteenth Amendment offers a superior alternative, and that a return to that meaning would allow this Court to enforce the rights the Fourteenth Amendment is designed to protect with greater clarity and predictability than the substantive due process framework has so far managed.

Justice Thomas's review of the legislative history of the privileges or immunities clause led him to conclude that the clause "enforces at least those fundamental rights enumerated in the Constitution against the States, including the Second Amendment right to keep and bear arms."

For other instances where individual justices have relied on the clause, see Hague v. CIO, 307 U.S. 496 (1939) (opinion of Roberts, J.) (right to assemble and discuss national issues is a privilege of national citizenship); Edwards v. California, 314 U.S. 160 (1941) (Douglas, J., concurring) (right of interstate travel is a privilege of national citizenship); Duncan v. Louisiana, 391 U.S. 145 (1968) (Black, J., concurring) (right to jury trial is a privilege of national citizenship).

As you read the material about substantive due process below, consider whether it would have made any difference if the Court had considered the same issues under the privileges or immunities clause.

C.   THE DUE PROCESS CLAUSE AND THE INCORPORATION CONTROVERSY

In Barron v. Baltimore, 32 U.S. (7 Pet.) 243 (1833), decided before the adoption of the fourteenth amendment, the Court, per Chief Justice Marshall, held that the rights guaranteed in the first eight amendments do not apply to the states. Did adoption of the fourteenth amendment effectively overrule Barron?

In Slaughter-House, the Court held that the rights guaranteed in the first eight amendments are not "privileges or immunities of citizens of the United States" and thus are not applicable to the states via the privileges or immunities clause of the fourteenth amendment. The fourteenth amendment also provides, however, that "[no] State shall [deprive] any person of life, liberty, or property, without due process of law." To what extent, if any, does the fourteenth amendment due process clause "incorporate" the specific guarantees of the bill of rights?

Note: Due Process and Incorporation

1. *The fundamental fairness approach.* In a series of cases decided during the first half of the twentieth century, the Court held that the due process clause did not incorporate the specific protections contained in the bill of rights. See Twining v. New Jersey, 211 U.S. 788 (1908) (self-incrimination clause); Palko v. Connecticut, 302 U.S. 319 (1937) (double jeopardy clause); Adamson v. California, 332 U.S. 46 (1947) (self-incrimination clause). The Court nonetheless held that the due process clause protected some fundamental rights that on occasion overlapped with rights protected by the bill of rights. The Court used this technique to hold that persons enjoyed the rights to freedom of speech, press, assembly, religion, and counsel, against state infringement.

What was the test for determining whether a particular right fell within the fundamental category? The Court used a variety of verbal formulations. In *Twining*, it said that the test was whether the right was "[a] fundamental principle of liberty and justice which inheres in the very idea of free government and is the inalienable right of a citizen of such a government." In *Palko*, the Court asked whether the right was "of the very essence of a scheme of ordered liberty" and whether "[to] abolish [it violates] a 'principle of justice so rooted in the tradition and conscience of our people as to be ranked as fundamental.'" In a concurring opinion in *Adamson*, Justice Frankfurter wrote that the test was whether state action offended "those canons of decency and fairness which express the notions of justice of English-speaking peoples."

2. *Total incorporation.* Beginning with *Adamson*, Justice Black wrote a series of separate opinions setting out his view that the fourteenth amendment was intended to incorporate the entire bill of rights. Part of Black's objection to the majority's approach was that it gave the Court the "power under 'natural law' periodically to expand and contract constitutional standards to conform to [its] conception of what at a particular time constitutes 'civilized decency' and 'fundamental liberty and justice.'" In addition, Black wrote that

> [my] study of the historical events that culminated in the Fourteenth Amendment, and the expressions of those who sponsored and favored, as well as those who opposed its submission and passage, persuades me that one of the chief objects that the provisions of the Amendment's first section, separately, and as a whole, were intended to accomplish was to make the Bill of Rights applicable to the states. With full knowledge of the import of the *Barron* decision, the framers and backers of the Fourteenth Amendment proclaimed its purpose to be to overturn the constitutional rule that case had announced. . . .

3. *Selective incorporation.* Although Black's "total incorporation" position never won majority support on the Court, the Court gradually moved away from *Twining*. Instead of either the fundamental fairness or the total incorporation approach, the Court endorsed "selective incorporation." On the one hand, the Court made separate determinations about whether individual provisions in the bill of rights were incorporated. In this respect, selective incorporation is consistent with *Twining*. But on the other hand, once a right was incorporated, its scope was fully determined by the scope of the bill of rights protection. Put differently, the due process right did not merely overlap with the federal right. Instead, it was completely determined by it. In this sense, the Court's approach drew on Justice Black's total incorporation position.

Duncan v. Louisiana, 391 U.S. 145 (1968), upholding a state criminal defendant's due process right to a jury trial, provides an example of how selective incorporation worked. Writing for the Court, Justice White stated that

> [in] one sense recent cases applying provisions of the first eight Amendments to the States represent a new approach to the "incorporation" debate. Earlier the Court can be seen as having asked [if] a civilized system could be imagined that would not accord the particular protection. [Citing *Palko.*] The recent cases, on the other hand, have proceeded upon the valid assumption that state criminal processes are not imaginary and theoretical schemes but actual systems bearing virtually every characteristic of the common-law system that has been developing contemporaneously in England and in this country. The question thus is whether given this kind of system a particular procedure is fundamental — whether, that is, a procedure is necessary to an Anglo-American regime of ordered liberty.

The Court utilized this test to incorporate almost all the bill of rights protections against the states. (The principal protections that have not been incorporated are the seventh amendment right to a civil jury and the fifth amendment right to a grand jury indictment. Is there something about these rights that makes them especially inappropriate candidates for incorporation?) Moreover, once a right was incorporated, it provided the same protection against the states that the original bill of rights provision provided against the federal government.

4. *The modern status of incorporation.* In recent years, the incorporation debate seemed settled. Although some scholars expressed lingering doubts about the coherence of the Court's approach and about whether it comported with the original understanding of the fourteenth amendment, none of the justices expressed interest in revisiting the issue. Then the Court decided District of Columbia v. Heller, 554 U.S. 570 (2008), holding that the second amendment made unconstitutional a District of Columbia statute prohibiting possession of any firearm. (*Heller* is discussed in detail in Chapter 1, section D, supra.) *Heller* left open whether second amendment guarantees extended to the states, and when the Court turned to that issue, it revived long dormant questions about the appropriate approach to incorporation.

McDonald v. City of Chicago
561 U.S. 742 (2010)

JUSTICE ALITO announced the judgment of the Court and delivered the opinion of the Court with respect to Parts I, II-A, II-B, II-D, III-A, and III-B, in which [CHIEF JUSTICE ROBERTS], JUSTICE SCALIA, JUSTICE KENNEDY, and JUSTICE THOMAS join, and an opinion with respect to Parts II-C, IV, and V, in which the CHIEF JUSTICE, JUSTICE SCALIA, and JUSTICE KENNEDY join.

[Chicago had a law similar to the District of Columbia statute invalidated in *Heller.* The City defended the law on the ground that the second amendment was not incorporated against the states.] We have previously held that most of the provisions of the Bill of Rights apply with full force to both the Federal Government and the States. Applying the standard that is well established in our case law, we hold that the Second Amendment right is fully applicable to the States. . . .

II

C

[In a portion of the opinion joined only by Chief Justice Roberts and Justices Kennedy and Scalia, the Court declined to read the privileges or immunities clause as incorporating the second amendment. This portion of the opinion is discussed at page 735, supra.]

D

[The Court outlined its "selective incorporation" approach, emphasizing that only a handful of bill of rights protections remain unincorporated and that once a right was incorporated it applied fully to the states.]

III

With this framework in mind, we now turn directly to the question whether the Second Amendment right to keep and bear arms is incorporated in the concept of due process. In answering that question, as just explained, we must decide whether the right to keep and bear arms is fundamental to our scheme of ordered liberty, or as we have said in a related context, whether this right is "deeply rooted in this Nation's history and tradition," *Washington v. Glucksberg*, 521 U.S. 702, 721 (1997) (internal quotation marks omitted).

A

Our decision in *Heller* points unmistakably to the answer. Self-defense is a basic right, recognized by many legal systems from ancient times to the present day, and in *Heller*, we held that individual self-defense is "the central component" of the Second Amendment right. . . .

B

1

By the 1850's, the perceived threat that had prompted the inclusion of the Second Amendment in the Bill of Rights — the fear that the National Government would disarm the universal militia — had largely faded as a popular concern, but the right to keep and bear arms was highly valued for purposes of self-defense. . . .

After the Civil War, many of the over 180,000 African Americans who served in the Union Army returned to the States of the old Confederacy, where systematic efforts were made to disarm them and other blacks. The laws of some States formally prohibited African Americans from possessing firearms. Throughout the South, armed parties, often consisting of ex-Confederate soldiers serving in the state militias, forcibly took firearms from newly freed slaves. . . .

Union Army commanders took steps to secure the right of all citizens to keep and bear arms, but the 39th Congress concluded that legislative action was necessary. Its efforts to safeguard the right to keep and bear arms demonstrate that the right was still recognized to be fundamental.

The most explicit evidence of Congress' aim appears in §14 of the Freedmen's Bureau Act of 1866, which provided that "the right . . . to have full and equal benefit of all laws and proceedings concerning personal liberty, personal security, and the acquisition, enjoyment, and disposition of estate, real and personal, including the constitutional right to bear arms, shall be secured to and enjoyed by all the citizens . . . without respect to race or color, or previous condition of slavery." Section 14 thus explicitly guaranteed that "all the citizens," black and white, would have "the constitutional right to bear arms."

The Civil Rights Act of 1866, which was considered at the same time as the Freedmen's Bureau Act, similarly sought to protect the right of all citizens to keep and bear arms. . . .

Congress, however, ultimately deemed these legislative remedies insufficient. . . .

In debating the Fourteenth Amendment, the 39th Congress referred to the right to keep and bear arms as a fundamental right deserving of protection. . . .

Evidence from the period immediately following the ratification of the Fourteenth Amendment only confirms that the right to keep and bear arms was considered fundamental. . . .

The right to keep and bear arms was also widely protected by state constitutions at the time when the Fourteenth Amendment was ratified. . . .

2

Despite all this evidence, municipal respondents contend that Congress, in the years immediately following the Civil War, merely sought to outlaw "discriminatory measures taken against freedmen, which it addressed by adopting a non-discrimination principle" and that even an outright ban on the possession of firearms was regarded as acceptable, "so long as it was not done in a discriminatory manner." [This] argument is implausible. [While] §1 of the Fourteenth Amendment contains "an antidiscrimination rule," namely, the Equal Protection Clause, municipal respondents can hardly mean that §1 does no more than prohibit discrimination. If that were so, then the First Amendment, as applied to the States, would not prohibit nondiscriminatory abridgments of the rights to freedom of speech or freedom of religion; the Fourth Amendment, as applied to the States, would not prohibit all unreasonable searches and seizures but only discriminatory searches and seizures — and so on. . . .

IV

[This portion of Justice Alito's opinion is joined only by Chief Justice Roberts and Justices Kennedy and Scalia.]

[Municipal] respondents' main argument is nothing less than a plea to disregard 50 years of incorporation precedent and return (presumably for this case only) to a by-gone era. Municipal respondents submit that the Due Process Clause protects only those rights "recognized by all temperate and civilized governments, from a deep and universal sense of [their] justice.'" According to municipal respondents, if it is possible to imagine any civilized legal system that does not recognize a particular right, then the Due Process Clause does not make that right binding on the States. . . .

This line of argument is, of course, inconsistent with the long-established standard we apply in incorporation cases. And the present-day implications of municipal respondents' argument are stunning. For example, many of the rights that our Bill of Rights provides for persons accused of criminal offenses are virtually unique to this country. . . .

JUSTICE SCALIA, concurring.

I join the Court's opinion. Despite my misgivings about Substantive Due Process as an original matter, I have acquiesced in the Court's incorporation of certain guarantees in the Bill of Rights "because it is both long established and narrowly limited." This case does not require me to reconsider that view, since straightforward application of settled doctrine suffices to decide it. I write separately only to respond to some aspects of Justice Stevens' dissent. . . .

The subjective nature of Justice Stevens' standard is [apparent] from his claim that it is the courts' prerogative — indeed their duty — to update the Due Process Clause so that it encompasses new freedoms the Framers were too narrow-minded to imagine. Courts, he proclaims, must "do justice to [the Clause's] urgent call and its open texture" by exercising the "interpretive discretion the latter embodies." (Why the people are not up to the task of deciding what new rights to protect, even though it is they who are authorized to make changes, see U.S. Const., Art. V, is never explained.) [It] is only we judges, exercising our "own reasoned judgment," who can be entrusted with deciding the Due Process Clause's scope — which rights serve the Amendment's "central values" — which basically means picking the rights we want to protect and discarding those we do not. . . .

Justice Stevens moves on to the "most basic" constraint on subjectivity his theory offers: that he would "esche[w] attempts to provide any all-purpose, top-down, totalizing theory of 'liberty.'" The notion that the absence of a coherent theory of the Due Process Clause will somehow curtail judicial caprice is at war with reason. Indeterminacy means opportunity for courts to impose whatever rule they like; it is the problem, not the solution. [If] there are no right answers, there are no wrong answers either. . . .

Justice Stevens also argues that requiring courts to show "respect for the democratic process" should serve as a constraint. That is true, but Justice Stevens would have them show respect in an extraordinary manner. In his view, if a right "is already being given careful consideration in, and subjected to ongoing calibration by, the States, judicial enforcement may not be appropriate." In other words, a right, such as the right to keep and bear arms, that has long been recognized but on which the States are considering restrictions, apparently deserves less protection, while a privilege the political branches (instruments of the democratic process) have withheld entirely and continue to withhold, deserves more. That topsy-turvy approach conveniently accomplishes the objective of ensuring that the rights this Court held protected in *Casey* [upholding a right to secure an abortion], *Lawrence* [upholding the right to gay sexual intimacy], and other such cases fit the theory — but at the cost of insulting rather than respecting the democratic process.

The next constraint Justice Stevens suggests is harder to evaluate. He describes as "an important tool for guiding judicial discretion" "sensitivity to the interaction between the intrinsic aspects of liberty and the practical realities of contemporary society." I cannot say whether that sensitivity will really guide judges because I have no idea what it is. Is it some sixth sense instilled in judges when they ascend to the bench? Or does it mean judges are more constrained when they agonize about the cosmic conflict between liberty and its potentially harmful consequences? Attempting to give the concept more precision, Justice Stevens explains that "sensitivity is an aspect of a deeper principle: the need to approach our work with humility and caution." Both traits are undeniably admirable, though what relation they bear to sensitivity is a mystery. But it makes no difference, for the first case Justice Stevens cites in support, *Casey*, dispels any illusion that he has a meaningful form of judicial modesty in mind. . . .

III

Justice Stevens' response to this concurrence makes the usual rejoinder of "living Constitution" advocates to the criticism that it empowers judges to eliminate or expand what the people have prescribed: The traditional, historically focused method, he says, reposes discretion in judges as well. . . .

I will stipulate to that. But the question to be decided is not whether the historically focused method is a perfect means of restraining aristocratic judicial Constitution writing; but whether it is the best means available in an imperfect world. Or indeed, even more narrowly than that: whether it is demonstrably much better than what Justice Stevens proposes. I think it beyond all serious dispute that it is much less subjective, and intrudes much less upon the democratic process. It is less subjective because it depends upon a body of evidence susceptible of reasoned analysis rather than a variety of vague ethicopolitical First Principles whose combined conclusion can be found to point in any direction the judges favor. [Moreover], the methodological differences that divide historians, and the varying interpretive assumptions they bring to their work, are nothing compared to the differences among the American people (though perhaps not among graduates of prestigious law schools) with regard to the moral judgments Justice Stevens would have courts pronounce. And whether or not special expertise is needed to answer historical questions, judges most certainly have no "comparative . . . advantage" in resolving moral disputes. What is more, his approach would not eliminate, but multiply, the hard questions courts must confront, since he would not replace history with moral philosophy, but would have courts consider both. . . .

[Justice Thomas's opinion concurring in part and concurring in the judgment is discussed at page 736, supra.]

JUSTICE STEVENS, dissenting.
[The] question we should be answering in this case is whether the Constitution "guarantees individuals a fundamental right," enforceable against the States, "to possess a functional, personal firearm, including a handgun, within the home." That is a different — and more difficult — inquiry than asking if the Fourteenth Amendment "incorporates" the Second Amendment. The so-called incorporation question was squarely and, in my view, correctly resolved in the late 19th century. [*Heller*] sheds no light on the meaning of the Due Process Clause of the Fourteenth Amendment. Our decisions construing that Clause to render various procedural guarantees in the Bill of Rights enforceable against the States likewise tell us little about the meaning of the word "liberty" in the Clause or about the scope of its protection of nonprocedural rights.

This is a substantive due process case.

I . . .

The first, and most basic, principle established by our cases is that the rights protected by the Due Process Clause are not merely procedural in nature. At first glance, this proposition might seem surprising, given that the Clause refers to "process." But substance and procedure are often deeply entwined. Upon closer inspection, the text can be read to "impos[e] nothing less than an obligation to give substantive content to the words 'liberty' and 'due process of law,'" *Washington v. Glucksberg* (1997) (Souter, J., concurring in judgment), lest superficially fair procedures be permitted to "destroy the enjoyment" of life, liberty, and property, *Poe v. Ullman* (Harlan, J., dissenting), and the Clause's prepositional modifier be permitted to swallow its primary command. Procedural guarantees are hollow unless linked to substantive interests; and no amount of process can legitimize some deprivations. . . .

The second principle woven through our cases is that substantive due process is fundamentally a matter of personal liberty. For it is the liberty clause of the Fourteenth Amendment that grounds our most important holdings in this field. It is the liberty clause that enacts the Constitution's "promise" that a measure of dignity and self-rule will be afforded to all persons. . . .

It follows that the term "incorporation," like the term "unenumerated rights," is something of a misnomer. Whether an asserted substantive due process interest is explicitly named in one of the first eight Amendments to the Constitution or is not mentioned, the underlying inquiry is the same: We must ask whether the interest is "comprised within the term liberty." . . .

The third precept to emerge from our case law flows from the second: The rights protected against state infringement by the Fourteenth Amendment's Due Process Clause need not be identical in shape or scope to the rights protected against Federal Government infringement by the various provisions of the Bill of Rights. . . .

II

[When] confronted with a substantive due process claim, we must ask whether the allegedly unlawful practice violates values "implicit in the concept of ordered liberty." If the practice in question lacks any "oppressive and arbitrary" character, if judicial enforcement of the asserted right would not materially contribute to "a fair and enlightened system of justice," then the claim is unsuitable for substantive due process protection. [Liberty] claims that are inseparable from the customs that prevail in a certain region, the idiosyncratic expectations of a certain group, or the personal preferences of their champions, may be valid claims in some sense; but they are not of constitutional stature. . . .

[This] test undeniably requires judges to apply their own reasoned judgment, but that does not mean it involves an exercise in abstract philosophy. [Historical] and empirical data of various kinds ground the analysis. Textual commitments laid down elsewhere in the Constitution, judicial precedents, English common law, legislative and social facts, scientific and professional developments, practices of other civilized societies, and, above all else, the "'traditions and conscience of our people,'" *Palko* (quoting *Snyder v. Massachusetts*, 291 U.S. 97, 105 (1934)), are critical variables. . . .

A rigid historical test is inappropriate in this case, most basically, because our substantive due process doctrine has never evaluated substantive rights in purely, or even predominantly, historical terms. . . .

[For] if it were really the case that the Fourteenth Amendment's guarantee of liberty embraces only those rights "so rooted in our history, tradition, and practice as to require special protection," *Glucksberg*, then the guarantee would serve little function, save to ratify those rights that state actors have already been according the most extensive protection. That approach is unfaithful to the expansive principle Americans laid down when they ratified the Fourteenth Amendment and to the level of generality they chose when they crafted its language; it promises an objectivity it cannot deliver and masks the value judgments that pervade any analysis of what customs, defined in what manner, are sufficiently "'rooted'"; it countenances the most revolting injustices in the name of continuity, for we must never forget that not only slavery but also the subjugation of women and other rank forms of discrimination are part of our history; and it effaces this Court's distinctive role in saying what the law is, leaving the development and safekeeping of liberty to majoritarian political processes. It is judicial abdication in the guise of judicial modesty. . . .

III

At this point a difficult question arises. In considering such a majestic term as "liberty" and applying it to present circumstances, how are we to do justice to its urgent call and its open texture — and to the grant of interpretive discretion the latter embodies — without injecting excessive subjectivity or unduly restricting the States' "broad latitude in experimenting with possible solutions to problems of vital local concern," *Whalen v. Roe*, 429 U.S. 589, 597 (1977)? One part of the answer, already discussed, is that we must ground the analysis in historical experience and reasoned judgment, and never on "merely personal and private notions." . . .

The most basic [guidepost] is that we have eschewed attempts to provide any all-purpose, top-down, totalizing theory of "liberty." That project is bound to end in failure or worse. The Framers did not express a clear understanding of the term to guide us, and the now-repudiated *Lochner* line of cases attests to the dangers of judicial overconfidence in using substantive due process to advance a broad theory of the right or the good. In its most durable precedents, the Court "has not attempted to define with exactness the liberty . . . guaranteed" by the Fourteenth Amendment. *Meyer*; see also, e.g., *Bolling*. By its very nature, the meaning of liberty cannot be "reduced to any formula; its content cannot be determined by reference to any code." *Poe* (Harlan, J., dissenting).

Yet while "the 'liberty' specially protected by the Fourteenth Amendment" is "perhaps not capable of being fully clarified," *Glucksberg*, it is capable of being refined and delimited. We have insisted that only certain types of especially significant personal interests may qualify for especially heightened protection.[24] . . .

---

24. That one eschews a comprehensive theory of liberty does not, pace Justice Scalia, mean that one lacks "a coherent theory of the Due Process Clause." It means that one lacks the hubris to adopt a rigid, context-independent definition of a constitutional guarantee that was deliberately framed in open-ended terms.

Rather than seek a categorical understanding of the liberty clause, our precedents have thus elucidated a conceptual core. The clause safeguards, most basically, "the ability independently to define one's identity," *Roberts v. United States Jaycees*; "the individual's right to make certain unusually important decisions that will affect his own, or his family's, destiny," *Fitzgerald*, 523 F.2d, at 719, and the right to be respected as a human being. Self-determination, bodily integrity, freedom of conscience, intimate relationships, political equality, dignity and respect — these are the central values we have found implicit in the concept of ordered liberty.

Another key constraint on substantive due process analysis is respect for the democratic process. If a particular liberty interest is already being given careful consideration in, and subjected to ongoing calibration by, the States, judicial enforcement may not be appropriate. . . .

As this discussion reflects, to acknowledge that the task of construing the liberty clause requires judgment is not to say that it is a license for unbridled judicial lawmaking. To the contrary, only an honest reckoning with our discretion allows for honest argumentation and meaningful accountability.

IV . . .

The question in this case, then, is not whether the Second Amendment right to keep and bear arms (whatever that right's precise contours) applies to the States because the Amendment has been incorporated into the Fourteenth Amendment. It has not been. The question, rather, is whether the particular right asserted by petitioners applies to the States because of the Fourteenth Amendment itself, standing on its own bottom. . . .

Understood as a plea to keep their preferred type of firearm in the home, petitioners' argument has real force. The decision to keep a loaded handgun in the house is often motivated by the desire to protect life, liberty, and property. It is comparable, in some ways, to decisions about the education and upbringing of one's children. For it is the kind of decision that may have profound consequences for every member of the family, and for the world beyond. . . .

While the individual's interest in firearm possession is thus heightened in the home, the State's corresponding interest in regulation is somewhat weaker . . .

V

While I agree with the Court that our substantive due process cases offer a principled basis for holding that petitioners have a constitutional right to possess a usable firearm in the home, I am ultimately persuaded that a better reading of our case law supports the city of Chicago. I would not foreclose the possibility that a particular plaintiff — say, an elderly widow who lives in a dangerous neighborhood and does not have the strength to operate a long gun — may have a cognizable liberty interest in possessing a handgun. But I cannot accept petitioners' broader submission. A number of factors, taken together, lead me to this conclusion. . . .

[First], in evaluating an asserted right to be free from particular gun-control regulations, liberty is on both sides of the equation. Guns may be useful for self-defense, as well as for hunting and sport, but they also have a unique potential to facilitate death and destruction and thereby to destabilize ordered liberty. . . .

Second, the right to possess a firearm of one's choosing is different in kind from the liberty interests we have recognized under the Due Process Clause. [It] does not appear to be the case that the ability to own a handgun, or any particular type of firearm, is critical to leading a life of autonomy, dignity, or political equality. . . .

[The] experience of other advanced democracies, including those that share our British heritage, undercuts the notion that an expansive right to keep and bear arms is intrinsic to ordered liberty. Many of these countries place restrictions on the possession, use, and carriage of firearms far more onerous than the restrictions found in this Nation. . . .

VI . . .

[Although] Justice Scalia aspires to an "objective," "neutral" method of substantive due process analysis, his actual method is nothing of the sort. Under the "historically focused" approach he advocates, numerous threshold questions arise before one ever gets to the history. At what level of generality should one frame the liberty interest in question? What does it mean for a right to be "'deeply rooted in this Nation's history and tradition'"? By what standard will that proposition be tested? Which types of sources will count, and how will those sources be weighed and aggregated? There is no objective, neutral answer to these questions. There is not even a theory — at least, Justice Scalia provides none — of how to go about answering them. . . .

It is hardly a novel insight that history is not an objective science, and that its use can therefore "point in any direction the judges favor." . . .

Justice Scalia's method invites not only bad history, but also bad constitutional law. [It] makes little sense to give history dispositive weight in every case. And it makes especially little sense to answer questions like whether the right to bear arms is "fundamental" by focusing only on the past, given that both the practical significance and the public understandings of such a right often change as society changes. What if the evidence had shown that, whereas at one time firearm possession contributed substantially to personal liberty and safety, nowadays it contributes nothing, or even tends to undermine them? Would it still have been reasonable to constitutionalize the right?

The concern runs still deeper. Not only can historical views be less than completely clear or informative, but they can also be wrong. Some notions that many Americans deeply believed to be true, at one time, turned out not to be true. . . .

[A dissenting opinion by Justice Breyer, joined by Justices Ginsburg and Sotomayor, is omitted].

D.   SUBSTANTIVE DUE PROCESS: THE PROTECTION OF ECONOMIC INTERESTS AND THE QUESTION OF REDISTRIBUTION

The Constitution contains several provisions that expressly restrict the government's power to interfere with market ordering and the private economic interests of individuals. The fifth and fourteenth amendments, for example, provide that "[no] person shall [be] deprived of [property,] without due process of law." Article I, section 10 provides that "[no] State shall [pass] any [Law] impairing the Obligation of Contracts." And the fifth amendment provides that "private property" shall not "be taken for public use, without just compensation." Although these provisions reflect the importance of private property, they have usually been understood to protect private economic interests only against certain narrowly defined forms of government interference. See section H infra. Is there a more general constitutional limitation on the power of government to interfere with private economic decisions?

In its 1905 decision in Lochner v. New York, infra, the Court held that the due process clauses of the fifth and fourteenth amendments protect liberty of contract and private property against putatively unwarranted government interference. The *Lochner* period has played a major role in defining the appropriate place of the Court in American government. This section traces the rise — and fall — of this exceptionally important doctrine.

Note: *The Road to* Lochner

1. *Early intimations.* Although the doctrine of economic substantive due process did not come into full flower until the Court's 1905 decision in *Lochner*, several pre-*Lochner* decisions flirted with analogous doctrines. In Calder v. Bull, Chapter 1, section D, supra, more than a century before *Lochner*, Justice Chase's "natural law" theory clearly reflected a concern with property rights, and in Fletcher v. Peck, 10 U.S. (6 Cranch) 87 (1810), in which the Court held that a state legislature could not constitutionally rescind land grants to individuals who had purchased the land in good faith, Chief Justice Marshall explained that the result was justified both by the contract clause and "by general principles which are common to our free institutions." In Wynehamer v. People, 13 N.Y. 378 (1856), the New York Court of Appeals relied expressly on the state due process clause in invalidating a liquor prohibition statute that prohibited the use or possession even of liquor owned prior to the enactment of the statute. The New York court explained that, when "a law annihilates the value of property, [the] owner is deprived of it [within] the spirit of a constitutional provision intended expressly to shield private rights from the exercise of arbitrary power." A year after *Wynehamer*, in Dred Scott v. Sanford, 60 U.S. (19 How.) 393 (1857), the Court held that Congress could not prohibit slavery in the territories. The Court observed, without explanation, that an "act of Congress which deprives a citizen of the United States of his liberty or property, merely because he came himself or brought his property into a particular [Territory,] could hardly be dignified with the name of due process of law."

These intermittent intimations of economic substantive due process did not seriously challenge the prevailing view that the due process guarantee was essentially procedural in nature. See Den ex dem. Murray v. Hoboken Land & Improvement Co., 59 U.S. (18 How.) 272 (1856). Moreover, in The Slaughter-House Cases, the Court held not only that the Louisiana statute did not violate the privileges or immunities clause of the fourteenth amendment, but also that it did not violate the fourteenth amendment due process clause.

Slaughter-House did not end the matter, however.

Lochner's *antecedents.* Shifting judicial attitudes toward substantive due process were produced in part by economic and social developments. The rise of industrial organization in the late nineteenth century transformed American society. As ownership of productive property became increasingly concentrated, inequalities in private economic power grew sharper, and the number of persons without significant productive property and dependent on industrial employment increased. As the twentieth century approached, state legislatures began to address the conditions accompanying the concentration of private power in business.

Opponents of the new regulatory laws maintained that "fundamental" rights of property were not being respected by the popularly controlled state legislatures. See, e.g., C. Tiedeman, A Treatise on the Limitations of the Police Power in the United States (1886). They relied in part on an older constitutional tradition of opposition to "class legislation" — that is, laws that benefitted specific groups rather than the general public. On this view, there was a sharp distinction between the "police power" — the general authority of the government to legislate do so as to protect public health, safety, and morals — and special interest legislation that impermissibly invaded the private sphere. For example, the minimum wage was said to increase unemployment, thus harming some of the most vulnerable members of society, for the benefit of better situated workers.

In Munn v. Illinois, 94 U.S. 113 (1877), the Court held that an Illinois law fixing the maximum charges for grain-storage warehouses did not violate the due process clause of the fourteenth amendment. The Court noted, however, that "under some circumstances," such statutes may violate due process. The critical inquiry was whether the "private property is 'affected with a public interest,' [for when] one devotes his property to a use in which the public has an interest, he, in effect, grants to the public an interest in that use, and must submit to be controlled by the public for the common good." The Court held that the businesses regulated in *Munn* were clearly "affected with a public interest," for they had a "virtual monopoly" on the storage of grain bound from the Midwest to national and international markets. In such circumstances, the Court would not consider the "reasonableness" of government-imposed rates.

In later cases, warnings about the limits of government regulatory power became more pointed. In The Railroad Commission Cases, 116 U.S. 307 (1886), the Court sustained state regulation of railroad rates but emphasized that there were bounds to judicial deference: "[The] power to regulate is not a power to [destroy]. Under pretence of regulating fares and freights, the State cannot require a railroad corporation to carry persons or property without reward; neither can it do that which in law amounts to a taking of private property for public use without just compensation, or without due process of law."

Later that same year, in Santa Clara County v. Southern Pacific Railroad, 116 U.S. 394 (1886), the Court held that corporations were "persons" within the meaning of the due process clause of the fourteenth amendment, thus opening the door for direct challenges to regulations by corporations. See Graham, The "Conspiracy Theory" of the Fourteenth Amendment, 47 Yale L.J. 371 (1938). The following year, in Mugler v. Kansas, 123 U.S. 623 (1887), the Court upheld a state law prohibiting the sale of alcoholic beverages but again cautioned that not every regulatory measure "is to be accepted as a legitimate exertion of the police powers of the State." In The Minnesota Rate Case (Chicago, Milwaukee & St. Paul Railway v. Minnesota), 134 U.S. 418 (1890), the Court held unconstitutional a state statute authorizing a commission to set final and unreviewable railroad rates, thus marking the first time that the Court relied directly on the due process clause to invalidate a state economic regulation. The Court explained that "[the] question of reasonableness of a rate of charge for transportation by a railroad company [is] eminently a question for judicial investigation, requiring due process of law for its determination." By the end of the decade, the Court was actively in the business of reviewing the reasonableness of rates. See Smith v. Ames, 169 U.S. 466 (1898) (establishing the rule that rates must yield a fair return on a fair present value); Federal Power Commission v. Hope Natural Gas Co., 320 U.S. 591 (1944) (tracing the evolution and eventual repudiation of the rule of Smith v. Ames); Siegel, Understanding the *Lochner* Era: Lessons from the Controversy over Railroad and Utility Rate Regulation, 70 Va. L. Rev. 187 (1984).

In Allgeyer v. Louisiana, 165 U.S. 578 (1897), the Court took the final step toward *Lochner. Allgeyer* invalidated a state statute that prohibited any person from issuing insurance on property in the state with companies that had not been admitted to do business in the state. Although Justice Peckham, writing for a unanimous Court, focused primarily on state power over foreign corporations, he also offered a comprehensive articulation of the "liberty of contract":

> The liberty mentioned in [the due process clause] means not only the right of the citizen to be free from the mere physical restraint of his person, as by incarceration, but the term is deemed to embrace the right of the citizen to be free in the enjoyment of all his faculties; to be free to use them in all lawful ways; to live and work where he will; to earn his livelihood by any lawful calling; to pursue any livelihood or avocation, and for that purpose to enter into all contracts which may be proper, necessary and essential to his carrying out to a successful conclusion the purposes mentioned above. [In] the privilege of pursuing an ordinary calling or trade and of acquiring, holding and selling property must be embraced the right to make all proper contracts in relation thereto, and although it may be conceded that this right to contract [or] to do business within the jurisdiction of the State may be regulated and sometimes prohibited when the contracts or business conflict with the policy of the State as contained in its statutes, yet the power does not and cannot extend to prohibiting a citizen from making contracts of the nature involved in this case outside of the limits and jurisdiction of the State, and which are also to be performed outside of such jurisdiction.

Lochner v. New York

198 U.S. 45 (1905)

MR. JUSTICE PECKHAM [delivered] the opinion of the Court.

[The Court held unconstitutional a New York statute providing that no employee shall "work in a biscuit, bread or cake bakery or confectionary establishment more than sixty hours in any one week, or more than ten hours in any one day."]

The statute necessarily interferes with the right of contract between the employer and employes [sic], concerning the number of hours in which the latter may labor in the bakery of the employer. The general right to make a contract in relation to his business is part of the liberty of the individual protected by the Fourteenth Amendment of the Federal Constitution. [*Allgeyer.*] Under that provision no State can deprive any person of life, liberty or property without due process of law. The right to purchase or to sell labor is part of the liberty protected by this amendment, unless there are circumstances which exclude the right. There are, however, certain powers, existing in the sovereignty of each State in the Union, somewhat vaguely termed police powers, the exact description and limitation of which have not been attempted by the courts. Those powers [relate] to the safety, health, morals and general welfare of the public. Both property and liberty are held on such reasonable conditions as may be imposed by the governing power of the State in the exercise of those powers, and with such conditions the Fourteenth Amendment was not designed to interfere. [*Mugler.*]

This court has recognized the existence and upheld the exercise of the police powers of the States in many cases. [Among] the [cases] where the state law has been upheld by this court is that of Holden v. Hardy, 169 U.S. 366 [1898]. A provision in the act of the legislature of Utah was there under consideration, the act limiting the employment of workmen in all underground mines or workings, to eight hours per day, "except in cases of emergency, where life or property is in imminent danger." [The] act was held to be a valid exercise of the police powers of the State. [It] was held that the kind of employment [and] the character of the employes [were] such as to make it reasonable and proper for the State to interfere to prevent the employes from being constrained by the rules laid down by the proprietors in regard to labor. [There] is nothing in Holden v. Hardy which covers the case now before us. . . .

It must, of course, be conceded that there is a limit to the valid exercise of the police power by the State. There is no dispute concerning this general proposition. Otherwise the Fourteenth Amendment would have no efficacy and the legislatures of the States would have unbounded power. [In] every case that comes before this court, therefore, where legislation of this character is concerned and where the protection of the Federal Constitution is sought, the question necessarily arises: Is this a fair, reasonable and appropriate exercise of the police power of the State, or is it an unreasonable, unnecessary and arbitrary interference with the right of the individual to his personal liberty or to enter into those contracts in relation to labor which may seem to him appropriate or necessary for the support of himself and his family? Of course the liberty of contract relating to labor includes both parties to it. The one has as much right to purchase as the other to sell labor.

This is not a question of substituting the judgment of the court for that of the legislature. If the act be within the power of the State it is valid, although the judgment of the court might be totally opposed to the enactment of such a law. But the question would still remain: Is it within the police power of the State? and that question must be answered by the court.

The question whether this act is valid as a labor law, pure and simple, may be dismissed in a few words. There is no reasonable ground for interfering with the liberty of person or the right of free contract, by determining the hours of labor, in the occupation of a baker. There is no contention that bakers as a class are not equal in intelligence and capacity to men in other trades or manual occupations, or that they are not able to assert their rights and care for themselves without the protecting arm of the State, interfering with their independence of judgment and of action. They are in no sense wards of the State. Viewed in the light of a purely labor law, with no reference whatever to the question of health, we think that a law like the one before us involves neither the safety, the morals nor the welfare of the public, and that the interest of the public is not in the slightest degree affected by such an act. The law must be upheld, if at all, as a law pertaining to the health of the individual engaged in the occupation of a baker. It does not affect any other portion of the public than those who are engaged in that occupation. Clean and wholesome bread does not depend upon whether the baker works but ten hours per day or only sixty hours a week. . . .

We think the limit of the police power has been reached and passed in this case. There is, in our judgment, no reasonable foundation for holding this to be necessary or appropriate as a health law to safeguard the public health or the health of the individuals who are following the trade of a baker. If this statute be valid, [there] would seem to be no length to which legislation of this nature might not go. . . .

We think that there can be no fair doubt that the trade of a baker, in and of itself, is not an unhealthy one to that degree which would authorize the legislature to interfere with the right to labor, and with the right of free contract on the part of the individual, either as employer or employe. In looking through statistics regarding all trades and occupations, it may be true that the trade of a baker does not appear to be as healthy as some other trades, and is also vastly more healthy than still others. To the common understanding the trade of a baker has never been regarded as an unhealthy one. [It] might be safely affirmed that almost all occupations more or less affect the health. There must be more than the mere fact of the possible existence of some small amount of unhealthiness to warrant legislative interference with liberty. It is unfortunately true that labor, even in any department, may possibly carry with it the seeds of unhealthiness. But are we all, on that account, at the mercy of legislative majorities? . . .

It is also urged, pursuing the same line of argument, that it is to the interest of the State that its population should be strong and robust, and therefore any legislation which may be said to tend to make people healthy must be valid as health laws, enacted under the police power. If this be a valid argument and a justification for this kind of legislation, it follows that the protection of the Federal Constitution from undue interference with liberty of person and freedom of contract is visionary, wherever the law is sought to be justified as a valid exercise of the police power. Scarcely any law but might find shelter under such Assumptions. [Not] only the hours of employes, but the hours of employers could be regulated, and doctors, lawyers, scientists, all professional men, as well as athletes and artisans, could be forbidden to fatigue their brains and bodies by prolonged hours of exercise, lest the fighting strength of the State be impaired. We mention these extreme cases because the contention is extreme. We do not believe in the soundness of the views which uphold this law. [The] act is not, within any fair meaning of the term, a health law, but is an illegal interference with the rights of individuals, both employers and employes, to make contracts regarding labor upon such terms as they may think best, or which they may agree upon with the other parties to such contracts. Statutes of the nature of that under review, limiting the hours in which grown and intelligent men may labor to earn their living, are mere meddlesome interferences with the rights of the individual, and they are not saved from condemnation by the claim that they are passed in the exercise of the police power and upon the subject of the health of the individual whose rights are interfered with, unless there be some fair ground, reasonable in and of itself, to say that there is material danger to the public health or to the health of the employes, if the hours of labor are not curtailed. [All that the State] could properly do has been done by it with regard to the conduct of bakeries, as provided for in the other sections of the act, [which] provide for the inspection of the premises where the bakery is carried on, with regard to furnishing proper wash-rooms and water-closets, [with] regard to providing proper drainage, plumbing and painting [and] for other things of that nature. . . .

It was further urged [that] restricting the hours of labor in the case of bakers was valid because it tended to cleanliness on the part of the workers, as a man was more apt to be cleanly when not overworked, and if cleanly then his "output" was also more likely to be so. [In] our judgment it is not possible in fact to discover the connection between the number of hours a baker may work in the bakery and the healthful quality of the bread made by the workman. The connection, if any exists, is too shadowy and thin to build any argument for the interference of the legislature. [When] assertions such as we have adverted to become necessary in order to give, if possible, a plausible foundation for the contention that the law is a "health law," it gives rise to at least a suspicion that there was some other motive dominating the legislature than the purpose to subserve the public health or welfare.

This interference on the part of the legislatures of the several States with the ordinary trades and occupations of the people seems to be on the increase. . . . It is impossible for us to shut our eyes to the fact that many of the laws of this character, while passed under what is claimed to be the police power for the purpose of protecting the public health or welfare, are, in reality, passed from other motives. We are justified in saying so when, from the character of the law and the subject upon which it legislates, it is apparent that the public health or welfare bears but the most remote relation to the law. . . .

It is manifest to us that the [law here] has no such direct relation to and no such substantial effect upon the health of the employe, as to justify us in regarding the section as really a health law. It seems to us that the real object and purpose were simply to regulate the hours of labor between the master and his employes (all being men, sui juris), in a private business, not dangerous in any degree to morals or in any real and substantial degree, to the health of the employes. Under such circumstances the freedom of master and employe to contract with each other in relation to their employment [cannot] be prohibited or interfered with, without violating the Federal Constitution. . . .

Reversed.

MR. JUSTICE HARLAN, with whom MR. JUSTICE WHITE and MR. JUSTICE DAY concurred, dissenting. . . .

[The] statute must be taken as expressing the belief of the people of New York that, as a general rule, and in the case of the average man, labor in excess of sixty hours during a week in such establishments may endanger the health of those who thus labor. Whether or not this be wise legislation it is not the province of the court to inquire. Under our systems of government the courts are not concerned with the wisdom or policy of legislation. So that in determining the question of power to interfere with liberty of contract, the court may inquire whether the means devised by the State are germane to an end which may be lawfully accomplished and have a real or substantial relation to the protection of health, as involved in the daily work of the persons, male and female, engaged in bakery and confectionery establishments. But when this inquiry is entered upon I find it impossible, in view of common experience, to say that there is here no real or substantial relation between the means employed by the State and the end sought to be accomplished by its legislation. . . .

Professor Hirt in his treatise on the "Diseases of the Workers" has said:

The labor of the bakers is among the hardest and most laborious imaginable, because it has to be performed under conditions injurious to the health of those engaged in it. It is hard, very hard work, not only because it requires a great deal of physical exertion in an overheated workshop and during unreasonably long hours, but more so because of the erratic demands of the public, compelling the baker to perform the greater part of his work at night, thus depriving him of an opportunity to enjoy the necessary rest and sleep, a fact which is highly injurious to his health.

baking is dangerous

Another writer says:

The constant inhaling of flour dust causes inflammation of the lungs and of the bronchial tubes. The eyes also suffer through this dust. . . . The long hours of toil to which all bakers are subjected produce rheumatism, cramps and swollen legs. The intense heat in the workshops [is] another source of a number of diseases of various organs. [The] average age of a baker is below that of other workmen; they seldom live over their fiftieth year, most of them dying between the ages of forty and fifty. . . .

I do not stop to consider whether any particular view of this economic question presents the sounder theory. What the precise facts are it may be difficult to say. It is enough for the determination of this case, and it is enough for this court to know, that the question is one about which there is room for debate and for an honest difference of opinion. There are many reasons of a weighty, substantial character, based upon the experience of mankind, in support of the theory that, all things considered, more than ten hours' steady work each day, from week to week, in a bakery or confectionery establishment, may endanger the health, and shorten the lives of the workmen, thereby diminishing their physical and mental capacity to serve the State, and to provide for those dependent upon them.

If such reasons exist that ought to be the end of this case, for the State is not amenable to the judiciary, in respect of its legislative enactments, unless such enactments are plainly, palpably, beyond all question inconsistent with the Constitution of the United States. . . .   *— Judicial Restraint*

MR. JUSTICE HOLMES, dissenting. . . .

This case is decided upon an economic theory which a large part of the country does not entertain. If it were a question whether I agreed with that theory, I should desire to study it further and long before making up my mind. But I do not conceive that to be my duty, because I strongly believe that my agreement or disagreement has nothing to do with the right of a majority to embody their opinions in law. It is settled by various decisions of this court that state constitutions and state laws may regulate life in many ways which we as legislators might think as injudicious or if you like as tyrannical as this, and which equally with this interfere with the liberty to contract. Sunday laws and usury laws are ancient examples. A more modern one is the prohibition of lotteries. The liberty of the citizen to do as he likes so long as he does not interfere with the liberty of others to do the same, which has been a shibboleth for some well-known writers, is interfered with by school laws, by the Post Office, by every state or municipal institution which takes his money for purposes thought desirable, whether he likes it or not. The Fourteenth Amendment does not enact Mr. Herbert Spencer's Social Statics. The other day we sustained the Massachusetts vaccination law. Jacobson v. Massachusetts, 197 U.S. 11. United States and state statutes and decisions cutting down the liberty to contract by way of combination are familiar to this court. [The] decision sustaining an eight hour law for miners is still recent.

[Holden v. Hardy.] Some of these laws embody convictions or prejudices which judges are likely to share. Some may not. But a constitution is not intended to embody a particular economic theory, whether of paternalism and the organic relation of the citizen to the State or of laissez faire. It is made for people of fundamentally differing views, and the accident of our finding certain opinions natural and familiar or novel and even shocking ought not to conclude our judgment upon the question whether statutes embodying them conflict with the Constitution of the United States.

General propositions do not decide concrete cases. The decision will depend on a judgment or intuition more subtle than any articulate major premise. But I think that the proposition just stated, if it is accepted, will carry us far toward the end. Every opinion tends to become a law. I think that the word liberty in the Fourteenth Amendment is perverted when it is held to prevent the natural outcome of a dominant opinion, unless it can be said that a rational and fair man necessarily would admit that the statute proposed would infringe fundamental principles as they have been understood by the traditions of our people and our law. It does not need research to show that no such sweeping condemnation can be passed upon the statute before us. A reasonable man might think it a proper measure on the score of health. Men whom I certainly could not pronounce unreasonable would uphold it as a first instalment of a general regulation of the hours of work. . . .

Note: The (Alleged?) Vices of Lochner

Lochner "is one of the most condemned cases in United States history and has been used to symbolize judicial dereliction and abuse." B. Siegan, Economic Liberties and the Constitution 23 (1980). But people have differed in their explanation of why the decision should be condemned, and not everyone is sure that it should be condemned. Embedded in the debate about *Lochner* are some of the most important arguments on the largest questions of constitutional law and theory.

Consider the following objections and the responses to them:

1. *The "liberty of contract" protected in* Lochner *is not within the "liberty" protected by the due process clause.* Consider the view of Justice Thomas: "[It] is hard to see how the 'liberty' protected by the [Due Process] Clause could be interpreted to include anything broader than freedom from physical restraint. That was the consistent usage of the time when 'liberty' was paired with 'life' and 'property.' And that usage avoids rendering superfluous those protections for 'life' and 'property.'"

Notice, though, that the fourteenth amendment was written in large part to ensure the constitutionality of the Civil Rights Act of 1868, and that that Act protected a wide range of "liberties" including the right to make contracts.

2. *Even if the "liberty of contract" is a "liberty" protected by the due process clause, workers, under the circumstances that then existed, were not acting freely when they entered labor contracts.* On this theory, these contracts were the product of a preexisting and unfair distribution of economic entitlements that in effect "coerced" laborers to accept contracts that they would have preferred to decline. The New York statute, by overcoming collective action problems, actually increased rather than decreased workers' liberty of contract. Does this argument sweep too broadly because it has the potential to unravel virtually any

constitutional right? For example, might some decisions to adhere to a particular religious faith, to marry, or to secure an abortion also be said to be the product of "coercive" circumstances that the individual making the decision did not choose?

3. *Even if the "liberty of contract" is a "liberty" protected by the due process clause, that clause does not guarantee substantive rights.* The due process clause is, by its own terms, concerned exclusively with "process," and thus has no relevance to the statute at issue in *Lochner*. "Substantive due process," is "a contradiction in terms — sort of like 'green pastel redness.'" J. Ely, Democracy and Distrust 18 (1980). In response, consider the argument that procedural protections are meaningless without some substantive substrate that the procedures attach to. Consider also the argument that statutes like the one invalidated in *Lochner* are premised on a set of findings made by the legislature — findings, for example, about the health effects of long hours of work in a bakery — and that opponents of the statute have a procedural right to contest these findings before a court. For further discussion, see section G infra.

Alternatively, one might argue that the due process clause accords substantive protection to all "fundamental" rights, but that the "liberty of contract" is not "fundamental." Under this view, "the error of [*Lochner*] lay not in judicial intervention to protect 'liberty' but in a misguided understanding of what liberty actually required." L. Tribe, American Constitutional Law 564 (1978).

Is the "liberty of contract" a "fundamental" right? Consider Siegan, supra, at 83:

A free society cannot exist unless government is prohibited from confiscating private property. If government can seize something owned by a private citizen, it can exert enormous power over people. One would be reluctant to speak, write, pray, or petition in a manner displeasing to the authorities lest he lose what he has already earned and possesses. As [Alexander] Hamilton stated, a power over a man's subsistence amounts to a power over his will.

The historical commitment to the "liberty of contract" and to rights of property runs deep: "[In the view of the Framers,] a major function of government was protecting and preserving property rights. [The] Framers probably subscribed to Blackstone's definition that the right of property is 'absolute . . . [and] consists in the free use, enjoyment and disposal [by man] of all his acquisitions, without any control or diminution, save only by the laws of the land.'" Siegan, supra, at 30–31. See also R. Epstein, Takings (1985). Moreover, in Calder v. Bull, Justice Chase maintained that "natural law" prohibits "a law that destroys or impairs the lawful private contracts of citizens [or] that takes property from A. and gives it to B." In Corfield v. Coryell, 6 F. Cas. 546 (1823), a decision recognized by all of the justices participating in *Slaughter-House* as defining the "fundamental" rights of individuals, Justice Washington declared that the "fundamental" privileges and immunities of individuals include the "right [to] take, hold and dispose of property." The Civil Rights Act of 1866, which provided the impetus for the fourteenth amendment, expressly protected the right of blacks "to make and enforce contracts [and to] purchase, lease, sell, hold and convey real and personal property."

On the other hand, it was also widely recognized that rights of contract and property were subject to "reasonable" regulation under the police power. How should a court decide what kinds of regulations are "reasonable."

4. *The means/ends connection: Even if the "liberty of contract" is entitled to "substantive" protection under the due process clause, the statute at issue in* Lochner *was justified by the state's interest in protecting the health of bakery employees.* In his opinion for the Court, Justice Peckham declared that, for the statute to be "saved from condemnation," there must "be some fair ground, reasonable in and of itself, to say that there is material danger to the public health or to the health of the employes, if the hours of labor are not curtailed." Is this standard too stringent? Perhaps the Court should have sustained the law because, as Justice Harlan observed, "the question is one about which there is room for debate and for an honest difference of opinion." And even if one assumes that Justice Peckham stated the appropriate standard, why weren't the data offered by Justice Harlan sufficient to satisfy that standard?

The Court's careful examination of the means/ends connection might be criticized on two grounds. The first is that judges do not have the fact-finding competence to engage in such inquiries; the second is that judges are unelected and therefore lack the accountability that would support such a role.

With regard to the first argument, why is a court with subpoena power and the ability to secure testimony from experts less able to make accurate fact-finding than a legislature? With regard to the second, is it proper to think of the case as posing a conflict between legislatures and courts, or, rather, between individuals and government? Put differently, if the health risks of being a baker are in fact contested, why shouldn't potential bakers decide for themselves whether the risks are worth taking?

In Muller v. Oregon, 208 U.S. 412 (1908), the Court sustained against due process attack an Oregon statute forbidding the employment of women "in any mechanical establishment, or factory, or laundry" for more than ten hours in any one day because the extensive evidence marshaled by Louis D. Brandeis in his "factual" brief convinced the Court that there was ample justification for the "widespread belief that woman's physical structure, and the functions she performs in consequence thereof, justify special legislation restricting or qualifying the conditions under which she should be permitted to toil." On the "Brandeis brief," see P. Freund, On Understanding the Supreme Court 86–91 (1949); Bikle, Judicial Determination of Questions of Fact Affecting the Constitutional Validity of Legislative Action, 38 Harv. L. Rev. 6 (1924); Karst, Legislative Facts in Constitutional Litigation, 1960 Sup. Ct. Rev. 75. Is *Muller* explainable on the ground that the Court regarded women as a dependent class analogous to children or workers in mining camps? Should the Court have viewed bakers as similarly dependent? Recall the discussion of gender discrimination in Chapter 5, section D, supra.

5. *The problem of ends: Even if the "liberty of contract" is entitled to "substantive" protection under the due process clause, the statute at issue in* Lochner *was justified as a "labor law, pure and simple."* Why wasn't the New York statute justified as a means of compensating for the unequal bargaining position of bakery workers? Here, the Court seems to have ruled certain kinds of redistributive regulation off limits. Consider, though, whether regulation of this sort ends up making workers even worse off. The minimum wage, for example, might increase unemployment or lead to the displacement of marginal workers with more skilled workers. What is especially notable is that the Court dismissed the "labor law" justification, unlike the health justification, as an effort to further an illegitimate end. What made this purpose illegitimate? Consider the following observations.

a. Coppage v. Kansas, 236 U.S. 1, 17–18 (1915):

[It] is said [that] "employees, as a rule, are not financially able to be as independent in making contracts for the sale of their labor as are employers in making contracts of purchase thereof." No doubt, wherever the right of private property exists, there must and will be inequalities of fortune. [Thus, it is] impossible to uphold freedom of contract and the right of private property without at the same time recognizing as legitimate those inequalities of fortune that are the necessary result of the exercise of those rights. [And] since a State may not strike [those rights] down directly it is clear that it may not do so indirectly, as by declaring in effect that the public good requires the removal of those inequalities that are but the normal and inevitable result of their [exercise]. The police power is broad, [but] it cannot be given the wide scope that is here asserted for it, without in effect nullifying the constitutional guaranty.

b. Sunstein, Naked Preferences and the Constitution, 84 Colum. L. Rev. 1689, 1697, 1718 (1984):

In the *Lochner* era, the Court attempted to create a separate category of impermissible ends, using the libertarian framework of the common law as a theoretical basis. Under that framework, the government's police power was sharply limited, and modern social legislation [appeared] not as an effort to promote a public value, but instead as a raw exercise of political power by the beneficiaries of the legislation. But the theoretical basis of the *Lochner* era [is undermined once one recognizes] that the market status quo [is] itself the product of government choices. [Once it becomes] clear that harms produced by the marketplace [are themselves] the products of public choices, efforts to alleviate those harms [must] be regarded as permissible exercises of government power.

c. Siegan, supra, at 123–124:

[Judges] who had received their education [during] the Civil War era viewed labor [in light of the antislavery tradition]. Freedom of contract for both employer and employee was strongly espoused by the antislavery movement. It was accepted that the right of the individual to bestow his labor as he pleased was among the rights for which the Civil War had been fought. [Accordingly, the Court's] contention [that] government has no legitimate interest in [protecting labor] was far less controversial than contemporary generations might suppose. The Court believed that the labor market itself would operate to support the welfare of both workers and employers.

For evaluations of this "belief," compare Kennedy, Distributive and Paternalistic Motives in Contract and Tort Law, with Special Reference to Compulsory Terms and Unequal Bargaining Power, 41 Md. L. Rev. 563 (1982), with Epstein, A Common Law for Labor Relations: A Critique of the New Deal Labor Legislation, 92 Yale L.J. 1357 (1983).

6. Lochner *and the political process.* Consider the following arguments.

a. *Lochner* is defensible in terms of "representation-reinforcement." There are circumstances in which statutes owe their existence primarily to the organized power of special interest groups and are enacted even though the majority does not approve of them and even though the majority may be harmed by their operation. Indeed, the theory of "public choice" postulates certain conditions in which even a properly functioning democratic process will frequently thwart majority values. See Stigler, The Theory of Economic Regulation, 2 Bell J. Econ.

& Mgmt. Sci. 3 (1971). The theory of "public choice" is examined in more detail in the context of the dormant commerce clause. See Chapter 2, section D, supra.

In *Lochner* itself, the New York statute was at least arguably the product of a political process in which labor unions had an organizational advantage (1) over consumers, who would ultimately pay for the regulation through higher prices for bread, and (2) over nonunionized, frequently immigrant workers who were willing or even eager to accept long-hour jobs in unregulated transactions with employers. Moreover, large employers and those already engaged in collective bargaining with unions had little incentive to oppose the legislation, for it simply imposed on all bakers regulations that had already been extracted in collective bargaining from some. In such circumstances, the unions were able, through maximum hour laws, to capture the legislative process to the disadvantage of the majority and to the disadvantage of otherwise competitive immigrant labor as well. The Court acted appropriately to rectify this defect in the operation of the representative process. For description of the political circumstances surrounding the adoption of the New York legislation, see D. Bernstein, Rehabilitating *Lochner*: Defending Individual Rights against Progressive Reform (2011); Siegan, supra, at 116–118; Tarrow, Lochner v. New York: A Political Analysis, 5 Lab. Hist. 277 (1964).

b. *Lochner* was wrongly decided because, as Justice Holmes recognized, the political process is inevitably a process of unprincipled compromises among competing social groups. Indeed, most "public policies are better explained as the outcome of a pure power struggle — clothed in a rhetoric of public interest that is a mere figleaf — among narrow interest or pressure groups." Posner, The DeFunis Case and the Constitutionality of Preferential Treatment of Racial Minorities, 1974 Sup. Ct. Rev. 1, 27. The due process clause cannot logically prohibit legislatures from passing laws merely because powerful groups want and press for them. Such an approach would ultimately prove counterproductive, for, if the courts prevent powerful groups from having their way in the legislative process, the political pressures will be bottled up and eventually emerge in even more destructive forms elsewhere.

Consider the view that, ironically, even though Justice Holmes's opinion denies that social Darwinism is constitutionally required, his own position rests on his general acceptance of social Darwinism: Note Holmes's reference to "the natural outcome of a dominant opinion." In another context, he wrote, "What proximate test of excellence can be found except correspondence to the actual equilibrium of force in the community — that is, conformity to the wishes of the dominant power. Of course, such conformity may lead to destruction, and it is desirable that the dominant power be wise. But wise or not, the proximate test of a good government is that the dominant power has its way." Justice Oliver Wendell Holmes: His Book Notices and Uncollected Letters and Papers 250 (H. C. Shriver ed. 1936). See generally A. Alschuler, Law without Values: The Life, Work, and Legacy of Oliver Wendell Holmes, Jr. (2002); Rogat, Mr. Justice Holmes: Some Modern Views — The Judge as Spectator, 31 U. Chi. L. Rev. 213 (1964).

7. *Are the reports of* Lochner's *death premature?* Consider Colby & Smith, The Return of *Lochner*, 100 Corn. L. Rev. 527 (2015):

[The] orthodoxy in modern conservative legal thought is on the verge of changing. There are increasing signs that the movement is ready, once again, to embrace

Lochner — although perhaps not in name — by recommitting to some form of robust judicial protection for economic rights. . . .

[Although] there are likely many factors contributing to this change, it has been greatly facilitated by important modifications to the theory of [originalism]. . . .

[Originalism] has slowly changed from a theory of judging, concerned principally with judicial restraint [to] an interpretive methodology that seeks objective semantic textual meaning. [Unlike] its forerunner, this "new originalism" can readily accommodate claims that the Fourteenth Amendment (and perhaps other provisions of the Constitution as well) protects an unenumerated right to freedom of contract.

As you read the material that follows, consider the extent to which *Lochner*-like ideas lie behind aspects of free speech, due process, takings clause, and state action doctrine. Notice also how the Court's contemporary dormant commerce clause jurisprudence, discussed in Chapter II, section D arguably sometimes treat market allocations as constitutionally mandatory. Can these constitutional provisions be given meaning without reference to a presumptive baseline formed by market transactions?

8. *Summary.* Objections to the *Lochner* decision generally fall into two camps. Some are institutional and emphasize that the Court overstepped its bounds in relation to the legislature. These objections focus on the Court's careful scrutiny of the means/ends connection and on its willingness to declare certain legislative ends impermissible. The problem here is that the Court interfered in a realm of policymaking; it does not matter what the basis for the interference was.

Other objections are substantive, in the sense that they have less to do with the role of the Court and more to do with the particular ideas at work in *Lochner* about the appropriate role of government. Here the problem is that the Court attempted to vindicate, as a matter of constitutional law, a laissez-faire conception of the role of government that could not be sustained. Under this view, *Lochner* saw the market status quo — market wages and prices — as a part of the state of nature rather than as a product of a set of legal choices defined in terms of common law categories. *Lochner* thus relied on a bad "baseline" from which to see whether there was impermissible redistribution. It took the existing distribution of rights and entitlements as a neutral or natural standpoint from which to see whether government had been impermissibly partisan.

Note that these two types of objections have very different implications. The institutional view suggests that courts should take a deferential approach to legislation — particularly in the realm of social and economic affairs. The substantive view leaves open the possibility that judicial deference might not be required if the Court acts in the service of some end other than laissez-faire.

Note: *The* Lochner *Era, 1905–1934*

From the decision in *Lochner* in 1905 to the mid-1950s, the Court invalidated approximately two hundred economic regulations, usually under the due process clause of the fourteenth amendment. These decisions centered primarily, although not exclusively, on labor legislation, the regulation of prices, and restrictions on entry into business. Although the Court employed substantive due process on many occasions, it sustained at least as many regulations as it struck down. See D. Bernstein, *Lochner's Legacy's Legacy,* 82 Tex. L. Rev. 1 (2003), for the suggestion with "a few famous exceptions," the Court upheld redistributive measures. Moreover, as reflected in *Lochner*, the Court was often divided. Justices Holmes, Brandeis, Stone, and Cardozo and Chief Justice Hughes dissented regularly from the Court's invalidation of economic regulations. This Note describes some of the more significant decisions. For comprehensive surveys, see Bernstein, supra; F. Strong, Substantive Due Process of Law: A Dichotomy of Sense and Nonsense (1986); The Constitution of the United States 1602–1612, 1643–1709 (Government Printing Office 1973 ed.); B. Wright, The Growth of American Constitutional Law 153–168 (1942); Jacobson, Federalism and Property Rights, 15 N.Y.U. L.Q. Rev. 319 (1938).

1. *Maximum hour legislation.* Although the Court invalidated maximum hour legislation in *Lochner*, three years later, in Muller v. Oregon, 208 U.S. 412 (1908), the Court upheld a statute prohibiting the employment of women in laundries for more than ten hours per day. The Court distinguished *Lochner* on the ground that "woman's physical structure" placed her at a disadvantage in the "struggle for subsistence" and legislation to protect women was thus "necessary to secure a real equality of right." In Bunting v. Oregon, 243 U.S. 426 (1917), the Court, in a rather cryptic opinion, upheld a statute establishing a maximum ten-hour day for factory workers of both sexes. Although *Bunting* overruled the specific holding of *Lochner* sub silentio, the constitutional theory on which *Lochner* was based continued to be enforced.

2. *"Yellow-dog" contracts.* In Adair v. United States, 208 U.S. 161 (1908), and Coppage v. Kansas, 236 U.S. 1 (1915), the Court invalidated federal and state legislation forbidding employers to require employees to agree not to join a union. The Court observed in *Adair* that "it is not within the functions of government [to] compel any person in the course of his business [to] retain the personal services of another." In *Coppage*, the Court emphasized that efforts to compensate for "unequal" bargaining power were beyond the legitimate scope of the police power and maintained that, although the individual has a right "to join the union, he has no inherent right to do this and still remain in the employ of one who is unwilling to employ a union man, any more than the same individual has a right to join the union without the consent of that organization."

3. *Minimum wages.* Although *Muller* upheld a law establishing maximum working hours for women, the Court invalidated a law establishing minimum wages for women in Adkins v. Children's Hospital, 261 U.S. 525 (1923). In distinguishing *Muller*, the Court observed:

> But the ancient inequality of the sexes, otherwise than physical, [has] continued "with diminishing intensity." In view of the great [changes] which have taken place since [*Muller*], in the contractual, political and civil status of women, culminating in the Nineteenth Amendment, it is not unreasonable to say that these differences have now come almost, if not quite, to the vanishing point. [Thus], while the physical differences must be recognized in appropriate cases, and legislation fixing hours or conditions of work may properly take them into account, we cannot accept the doctrine that women of mature age, sui juris, require or may be subjected to restrictions upon their liberty of contract which could not lawfully be imposed in the case of men under similar circumstances.

4. *Price regulation.* In a line of cases after *Munn*, the Court initially adopted a broad definition of "affected with a public interest" and thus upheld a wide range of laws regulating prices. See, e.g., German Alliance Insurance Co. v. Lewis, 233 U.S. 389 (1914) (fire insurance); Block v. Hirsh, 256 U.S. 135 (1921) (rental

housing). Thereafter, the Court increasingly narrowed the *Munn* standard and invalidated laws regulating prices with regard to such matters as gasoline, Williams v. Standard Oil Co., 278 U.S. 235 (1929); employment agencies, Ribnik v. McBride, 277 U.S. 350 (1928); and theater tickets, Tyson & Brother v. Banton, 273 U.S. 418 (1927).

5. *Business entry.* On several occasions, the Court invalidated laws restricting entry into particular lines of business. In New State Ice Co. v. Liebmann, 285 U.S. 262 (1932), for example, the Court invalidated a law prohibiting any person to manufacture ice without first obtaining a certificate of convenience and necessity. The Court explained that, as in the context of price regulation, the critical issue was "whether the business is [charged] with a public use," for "a regulation which has the effect of denying [the] common right to engage in a lawful private business, such as that under review, cannot be upheld." See also Louis K. Liggett Co. v. Baldridge, 278 U.S. 105 (1928) (invalidating a law limiting entry into the pharmacy business to pharmacists).

6. *The demise of* Lochner. As these decisions indicate, the Court's decisions in the *Lochner* era were often inconsistent. The unifying theme seemed to be the Court's perception of the "real" reason for the regulation. If the Court believed the regulation was truly designed to protect the health, safety, or morals of the general public, it was apt to uphold the law. But if the Court perceived the law to be an effort to readjust the market in favor of one party to the contract, it was more likely to hold the regulation invalid.

By the mid-1930s, the Court was prepared to abandon *Lochner.* This was due to changes in the composition of the Court, internal tensions in the doctrine, an attack on market ordering as a product of law and as sometimes inefficient and unjust, increasing judicial and academic criticism — and, perhaps most important, the economic realities of the Depression and President Franklin Delano Roosevelt's New Deal, which seemed to undermine *Lochner*'s central premises.

NEBBIA v. NEW YORK, 291 U.S. 502 (1934). During 1932, the prices received by farmers for milk fell much below the cost of production, and the situation of the families of dairy producers in New York grew "desperate." A legislative committee, established to investigate the matter, concluded that milk "is an essential item of diet," and that the failure "of producers to receive a reasonable return for their labor and investment over an extended period threatens a relaxation of vigilance against contamination." The committee further found that the "production and distribution of milk is a paramount industry of the state" and that the "milk industry is affected by factors of [price] instability [which] call for special methods of control." The legislature thus established the Milk Control Board, which was authorized to fix minimum and maximum retail prices for milk. Nebbia, the owner of a grocery store in Rochester, was convicted of selling milk below the minimum price fixed by the board. The Court, in a five-to-four decision, upheld the law.

Justice Roberts delivered the opinion of the Court:

"The legislature adopted [the law] as a method of correcting the evils, which the report of the committee showed could not be expected to right themselves through the ordinary play of the forces of supply and demand, owing to the peculiar and uncontrollable factors affecting the industry. [Under] our form of government the use of property and the making of contracts are normally matters of private and not of public concern. The general rule is that both shall be free of governmental interference. But neither property rights nor contract rights are absolute; for government cannot exist if the citizen may at will use his property to the detriment of his fellows, or exercise his freedom of contract to work them harm. [Thus] has this court from the early days affirmed that the power to promote the general welfare is inherent in government. [These] correlative rights, that of the citizen to exercise exclusive dominion over property and freely to contract about his affairs, and that of the state to regulate the use of property and the conduct of business, are always in collision. [But] subject only to constitutional restraint the private right must yield to the public need.

"The Fifth Amendment, in the field of federal activity, and the Fourteenth, as respects state action, do not prohibit governmental regulation for the public welfare. They merely condition the exertion of the admitted power, by securing that the end shall be accomplished by methods consistent with due process. And the guaranty of due process, as has often been held, demands only that the law shall not be unreasonable, arbitrary or capricious, and that the means selected shall have a real and substantial relation to the object sought to be attained. [The] Constitution does not guarantee the unrestricted privilege to engage in a business or to conduct it as one pleases. . . .

"But we are told that because the law essays to control prices it denies due process. Notwithstanding the admitted power to correct existing economic ills by appropriate regulation of business, [the] appellant urges that direct fixation of prices [is] per se unreasonable and unconstitutional, save as applied to businesses affected with a public interest; [and that no] business is so affected [unless it is in the nature of a public utility or a monopoly]. But this is a misconception. [There] is no closed class or category of businesses affected with a public interest, and the function of courts in the application of the Fifth and Fourteenth Amendments is to determine in each case whether circumstances vindicate the challenged regulation as a reasonable exertion of governmental authority or condemn it as arbitrary or discriminatory. [The] phrase 'affected with a public interest' can, in the nature of things, mean no more than that an industry, for adequate reason, is subject to control for the public good. . . .

"So far as the requirement of due process is concerned, [a] state is free to adopt whatever economic policy may reasonably be deemed to promote public welfare, and to enforce that policy by legislation adapted to its purpose. The courts are without authority either to declare such policy, or, when it is declared by the legislature, to override it. [If] the legislative policy be to curb unrestrained and harmful competition [it] does not lie with the courts to determine that the rule is unwise. [Times] without number we have said that the legislature is primarily the judge of the necessity of such an enactment, that every possible presumption is in favor of its validity, and that though the court may hold views inconsistent with the wisdom of the law, it may not be annulled unless palpably in excess of legislative power. [Price] control, like any other form of regulation, is unconstitutional only if arbitrary, discriminatory, or demonstrably irrelevant to the policy the legislature is free to adopt, and hence an unnecessary and unwarranted interference with individual liberty."

Justice McReynolds, joined by Justices Van Devanter, Sutherland, and Butler, dissented.

WEST COAST HOTEL CO. v. PARRISH, 300 U.S. 379 (1937). In a five-to-four decision, the Court explicitly overruled Adkins v. Children's Hospital and upheld a state law establishing a minimum wage for women. Chief Justice Hughes delivered the opinion of the Court:

[Handwritten margin note: argument against a min. wage for women]

"[The] violation alleged by those attacking minimum wage regulation for women is deprivation of freedom of contract. What is this freedom of contract? The Constitution does not speak of freedom of contract. It speaks of liberty and prohibits the deprivation of liberty without due process of law. [Regulation] which is reasonable in relation to its subject and is adopted in the interests of the community is due process. . . .

"What can be closer to the public interest than the health of women and their protection from unscrupulous and overreaching employers? And if the protection of women is a legitimate end of the exercise of state power, how can it be said that the requirement of the payment of a minimum wage fairly fixed in order to meet the very necessities of existence is not an admissible means to that end? The legislature of the State was clearly entitled to consider the situation of women in employment, the fact that they are in the class receiving the least pay, that their bargaining power is relatively weak, and that they are the ready victims of those who would take advantage of their necessitous circumstances. . . .

"There is an additional and compelling consideration which recent economic experience has brought into a strong light. The exploitation of a class of workers who are in an unequal position with respect to bargaining power and are thus relatively defenseless against the denial of a living wage is not only detrimental to their health and well being but casts a direct burden for their support upon the community. What these workers lose in wages the taxpayers are called upon to pay. The bare cost of living must be met. We may take judicial notice of the unparalleled demands for relief which arose during the recent period of depression. [The] community is not bound to provide what is in effect a subsidy for unconscionable employers. The community may direct its law-making power to correct the abuse which springs from their selfish disregard of the public interest. [*Adkins*] should be, and it is, overruled."

Justice Sutherland, joined by Justices Van Devanter, McReynolds, and Butler, dissented.

Note: *The End of an Era*

For discussion of the political context of West Coast Hotel, and the possible significance of President Roosevelt's "Court-packing plan," see Chapter 2, section C, supra. The decision may also have been influenced by extraordinary economic circumstances. The country was in the midst of the Great Depression, which caused massive economic dislocation and suffering and, some thought, threatened the very continuance of democratic governance.

However, the Court's disavowal of *Lochner*-style substantive due process review continued long after the immediate political and economic crisis had abated. In United States v. Darby, 312 U.S. 100 (1941), for example, the Court unanimously rejected a substantive due process challenge to the provisions of the Fair Labor Standards Act establishing maximum hours and minimum wages for all covered employees.

Later that term, in Phelps Dodge Corp. v. National Labor Relations Board, 313 U.S. 177 (1941), the Court upheld a provision of the National Labor Relations Act declaring it an unfair labor practice for an employer to encourage or discourage union membership. On the same day, in Olsen v. Nebraska, 313 U.S. 236 (1941), the Court unanimously upheld a state statute fixing the maximum fee that an employment agency could collect from employees, thus overruling

Ribnik v. McBride, 277 U.S. 350 (1928). The Court observed that "the only constitutional prohibitions or restraints which respondents have suggested for invalidation of this legislation are those notions of public policy embodied in earlier decisions of this Court but which, as Mr. Justice Holmes long admonished, should not be read into the Constitution."

In Lincoln Federal Union v. Northwestern Iron & Metal Co., 335 U.S. 525 (1949), the Court upheld a state right-to-work law that prohibited closed shops. The Court explained that it had abandoned "the *Allgeyer-Lochner-Adair-Coppage* constitutional doctrine" and returned "to the earlier constitutional principle that states have power to legislate against what are found to be injurious practices in their internal commercial and business affairs, so long as their laws do not run afoul of some specific federal constitutional prohibition." And in Day-Brite Lighting, Inc. v. Missouri, 342 U.S. 421 (1952), the Court upheld a law authorizing employees to take four hours' leave with full pay on election day, noting that, "if our recent cases mean anything, they leave debatable issues as respects business, economic, and social affairs to legislative decision." Consider the following three decisions.

UNITED STATES v. CAROLENE PRODUCTS CO., 304 U.S. 144 (1938). After extensive hearings, two congressional committees made the following findings:

> There is an extensive commerce in milk compounds made of condensed milk from which the butter fat has been extracted and an equivalent amount of vegetable oil [has been] substituted. [By] reason of the extraction of the natural milk fat the compounded product [known as "filled milk"] can be manufactured and sold at a lower cost than pure milk. Butter fat [is] rich in vitamins [that] are wanting in vegetable oils. The use of filled milk as a dietary substitute for pure milk results [in] undernourishment. [Despite] compliance with the branding and labeling requirements of the Pure Food and Drugs Act, there is widespread use of filled milk as a substitute for pure milk. This is aided by their identical taste and appearance, by the similarity of the containers in which they are sold, by the practice of dealers in offering the inferior product to customers as being as good as or better than pure condensed milk sold at a higher price, by customers' ignorance of the respective food values of the two products, and in many sections of the country by their inability to read the labels.

Based on these findings, Congress enacted the Filled Milk Act of 1923, which declared that "filled milk" is an "adulterated article of food, injurious to the public health," and that "its sale constitutes a fraud upon the public." The act therefore prohibited any person to ship filled milk in interstate commerce. In *Carolene Products*, the Court upheld the act. Justice Stone delivered the opinion of the Court:

"We may assume for present purposes that no pronouncement of a legislature can forestall attack upon the constitutionality of [a prohibition] by applying opprobrious epithets to the prohibited act, and that a statute would deny due process which precluded the disproof in judicial proceedings of all facts which would show or tend to show that a statute depriving the suitor of life, liberty or property had a rational basis.

"But such we think is not the purpose [of] the statutory characterization of filled milk as injurious to health and as a fraud upon the public. There is no need to consider it here as more than a declaration of the legislative findings deemed to support and justify the action taken, [aiding] informed judicial review, as do the reports of legislative committees, by revealing the rationale of the legislation. Even in the absence of such aids the existence of facts supporting the legislative judgment is to be presumed, for regulatory legislation affecting ordinary commercial transactions is not to be pronounced unconstitutional unless in the light of the facts made known or generally assumed it is of such a character as to preclude the assumption that it rests upon some rational basis. . . .

"Where the existence of a rational basis for legislation [depends] upon facts beyond the sphere of judicial notice, such facts may properly be made the subject of judicial inquiry, [and] the constitutionality of a statute predicated upon the existence of a particular state of facts may be challenged by showing to the court that those facts have ceased to exist. [Similarly] we recognize that the constitutionality of a statute, valid on its face, may be assailed by proof of facts tending to show that the statute as applied to a particular article is without support in reason because the article, although within the prohibited class, is so different from others of the class as to be without the reason for the prohibition, [though] the effect of such proof depends on the relevant circumstances of each case, as for example the administrative difficulty of excluding the article from the regulated class. [But] by their very nature such inquiries, where the legislative judgment is drawn in question, must be restricted to the issue whether any state of facts either known or which could reasonably be assumed affords support for it. Here the [appellee] challenges the validity of the statute on its face and it is evident from all the considerations presented to Congress, and those of which we may take judicial notice, that the question is at least debatable whether commerce in filled milk should be left unregulated, or in some measure restricted, or wholly prohibited. As that decision was for Congress, neither the finding of a court arrived at by weighing the evidence, nor the verdict of a jury can be substituted for it. [The act is] constitutional."

Does *Carolene Products* accord too much deference to legislative judgment?

For a detailed study of the problem in *Carolene Products*, see Miller, The True Story of *Carolene Products*, 1988 Sup. Ct. Rev. 397, 398–399, claiming that the

> statute upheld in the case was an utterly unprincipled "example of special interest legislation." The purported "public interest" justifications so credulously reported by Justice Stone were patently bogus. . . . The consequence of the decision was to expropriate the property of a lawful and beneficial industry; to deprive working and poor people of a healthful, nutritious, and low-cost food; and to impair the health of the nation's children by encouraging the use as baby food of a sweetened condensed milk product that was 42 percent sugar.

Suppose it is clear that Professor Miller's account is accurate. Was the case wrongly decided?

WILLIAMSON v. LEE OPTICAL OF OKLAHOMA, 348 U.S. 483 (1955). An ophthalmologist is a licensed physician who specializes in the care of the eyes. An optometrist examines for refractive error, recognizes diseases of the eye, and fills prescriptions for eyeglasses. An optician is an artisan qualified to grind lenses, fill prescriptions, and fit frames. In *Lee Optical*, the Court considered the constitutionality of an Oklahoma statute that made it unlawful for an optician to fit or duplicate lenses without a prescription from an ophthalmologist or optometrist. The district court held that through "ordinary skills the optician could take a broken lens or a fragment thereof, measure its power, and reduce it to prescriptive terms," that the requirement of a prescription from an ophthalmologist or optometrist was thus not "reasonably and rationally related to the health and welfare of the people," and that the law therefore "violated the Due Process Clause by arbitrarily interfering with the optician's right to do business." The Supreme Court reversed. Justice Douglas delivered the opinion of the Court:

"The Oklahoma law may exact a needless, wasteful requirement in many cases. But it is for the legislature, not the courts, to balance the advantages and disadvantages of the new requirement. It appears that in many cases the optician can easily supply the new frames or new lenses without reference to the old written prescription. [But] in some cases the directions contained in the prescription are essential. [The] legislature might have concluded that the frequency of occasions when a prescription is necessary was sufficient to justify this regulation of the fitting of eyeglasses. [Or] the legislature may have concluded that eye examinations were so critical, not only for correction of vision but also for detection of latent ailments or diseases, that every change in frames and every duplication of a lens should be accompanied by a prescription from a medical expert. To be sure, the present law does not require a new examination of the eyes every time the frames are changed or the lenses duplicated. [But] the law need not be in every respect logically consistent with its aims to be constitutional. It is enough that there is an evil at hand for correction, and that it might be thought that the particular legislative measure was a rational way to correct it. [The] day is gone when this Court uses the Due Process Clause [to] strike down state laws, regulatory of business and industrial conditions, because they may be unwise, improvident, or out of harmony with a particular school of thought."

FERGUSON v. SKRUPA, 372 U.S. 726 (1963). A Kansas statute declared it unlawful for any person to engage in the business of debt adjusting except as incident to "the lawful practice of law." The statute defined "debt adjusting" as the making of a contract with a debtor whereby the debtor pays money periodically to the adjuster who then distributes it to the debtor's creditors in accordance with an agreed-on plan. Skrupa, a debt adjuster who was put out of business by the statute, filed this action. The district court held that the statute was an unreasonable regulation of a "lawful business" and thus violative of due process. The Supreme Court reversed. Justice Black delivered the opinion of the Court:

"Under the system of government created by our Constitution, it is up to legislatures, not courts, to decide on the wisdom and utility of legislation. There was a time when the Due Process Clause was used by this Court to strike down laws which were thought unreasonable, that is, unwise or incompatible with some particular economic or social philosophy. [That doctrine] has long since been discarded. [It] is now settled that States 'have power to legislate against what are found to be injurious practices in their internal commercial and business affairs, so long as their laws do not run afoul of some specific federal constitutional prohibition. . . . ' [The] Kansas legislature was free to decide for itself that legislation was needed to deal with the business of debt adjusting. Unquestionably, there are arguments showing that the business of debt adjusting has social utility, but such arguments are properly addressed to the legislature, not to us. [The] Kansas debt adjusting statute may be wise or unwise. But relief, if any be needed, lies not with us but with the body constituted to pass laws for the State of Kansas." Justice Harlan concurred in the judgment "on the ground that this state measure bears a rational relation to a constitutionally permissible objective. See [*Lee Optical*]."

Note: Pluralism, Naked Wealth Transfers, and the Courts

1. *Economic substantive due process today.* In *Carolene Products*, the Court indicated that it would uphold economic legislation if any state of facts either known or reasonably inferable could support the legislative judgment. In *Lee Optical*, however, the Court went even further and resorted to wholly hypothetical facts and reasons to sustain the legislation. And in *Ferguson*, the Court appeared to uphold the legislation without any inquiry into the rationality of the means/ends connection.

It has been argued that economic substantive due process review has become so deferential in the post-*Lochner* era in part because "a wide range of justifications count as exercises of the police power and are not treated as naked wealth transfers." Sunstein, Naked Preferences and the Constitution, 84 Colum. L. Rev. 1689, 1718 (1984). Thus, almost all legislation — even that which reflects the untrammeled play of private self-interested groups, with the thinnest veil of public-regarding justifications — is upheld. In the post-*Lochner* era, what, if anything, constitutes an "impermissible" end? Are governmental actions based only on raw power and unsupported by any public value "impermissible"? Would *Carolene Products*, *Lee Optical*, and *Ferguson* pass muster under such a standard?

In any event, after decisions like *Carolene Products*, *Lee Optical*, and *Ferguson*, "there could be little doubt as to the practical result: no claim of substantive economic rights would now be sustained by the Supreme Court. The judiciary had abdicated the field." McCloskey, Economic Due Process and the Supreme Court: An Exhumation and Reburial, 1962 Sup. Ct. Rev. 34, 38. Indeed, the Court has not invalidated an economic regulation on substantive due process grounds since 1937. For decisions rejecting substantive due process challenges to economic regulation, see, e.g., Texaco v. Short, 454 U.S. 516 (1982); PruneYard Shopping Center v. Robins, 447 U.S. 74 (1980); Duke Power Co. v. Carolina Environmental Study Group, Inc., 438 U.S. 59 (1978); Exxon Corp. v. Governor of Maryland, 437 U.S. 117 (1978). But cf. Stop the Beach Renourishment v. Florida Department of Environmental Protection, 560 U.S. 702 (2010), where Justice Kennedy, in an opinion joined by Justice Sotomayor, noted that "[if] a judicial decision, as opposed to an act of the executive or the legislature, eliminates an established property right, the judgment could be set aside as a deprivation of property without due process of law. The Due Process Clause, in both its substantive and procedural aspects, is a central limitation upon the exercise of judicial power." Writing for a plurality of the Court on this point, Justice Scalia replied that "we have held for many years (logically or not) that the 'liberties' protected by Substantive Due Process do not include economic liberties. Justice Kennedy's language propels us back to what is referred to (usually deprecatingly) as 'the *Lochner* era.'"

2. *Alternatives to abdication?* Perhaps the Court has gone too far in its withdrawal from the substantive review of economic legislation. Should it continue to ask whether there was a substantial relationship between the statute at issue and legitimate statutory ends? Consider B. Siegan, Economic Liberties and the Constitution 260, 262, 284, 302–303 (1980):

The low esteem in which economic due process is held suggests to many that judicial review of economic matters is undesirable and harmful and that the judiciary should accept without reservation almost all legislative and administrative solutions to social and economic problems. Society was worse off, the proponents of this approach contend, as a result of the interventions of the "laissez-faire" Court. [But] studies effectively disclose the error in [the] New Deal emphasis on government intervention to solve existing economic problems. The studies demonstrate that the very people who [most] require the regulators' assistance — those at the lower end of the economic spectrum — actually suffer greatly from regulation. [The studies] are proving the wisdom of the Old Court's guiding principle, that freedom of contract is the rule and restraint the exception. [The] conclusion is warranted that the Old Court's policy of review is [preferable] to the contemporary Supreme Court's abdication.

But see Elhauge, Does Interest Group Theory Justify More Intrusive Judicial Review?, 101 Yale L.J. 31 (1991). Elhauge offers a number of arguments in favor of a negative answer to the conclusion posed in his title. He argues:

What interest group theory does identify are the factors that make certain groups more willing than others to expend resources on petitioning for governmental action. However, identifying those factors cannot alone demonstrate which groups' petitioning efforts are normatively disproportionate. Such a normative conclusion is only possible if we have some baseline for determining what level of petitioning activity is normatively proportional to each group's interest. Interest group theory does not itself provide such a normative baseline. Rather, implicit normative baselines are adopted, usually without any discussion, when analysis draws normative implications from the degree of political influence predicted by interest group theory.

Elhauge also claims that "interest group theory does not establish . . . that the litigation process is, overall, less defective than the political process," and that "more intrusive judicial review would have several adverse effects on the transaction costs of legal change."

3. *The implications of abdication: the decline of* Lochner *and the doctrine of governmental action.* Consider the following view: The position suggested in *West Coast Hotel* and other decisions marking the decline of *Lochner* — that government's apparent failure to act may in some circumstances amount to governmental action — does not justify judicial abdication as a general rule. To the contrary, the understanding that the "private" sphere is itself a governmental creation suggests that a wide range of practices might be vulnerable to constitutional attack. Perhaps most dramatically, the existence of poverty itself may be understood as in part the product of governmental "action." In fact President Roosevelt himself came to propose a second bill of rights, including the right to a useful and remunerative job; the right to a decent home; the right to adequate medical care and the opportunity to achieve and enjoy good health; and the right to a good education. See C. Sunstein, The Second Bill of Rights (2004). Many modern constitutions, in fact, recognize rights of this sort, as does the Universal Declaration of Human Rights. See id.

Alternatively: Some redistributions are in fact unprincipled and in fact hurt only the vulnerable members of society — including those nominally designed to help the disadvantaged. The wholesale exclusion of debt adjusters from the marketplace might well be an example; so, too, with the burdens placed on opticians. Is it so clear that the courts should do nothing about this? In this connection, consider the following:

The demise of the laissez-faire jurisprudence of the *Lochner* era [came] at a most inopportune time for black Americans. Federal labor law and policy of the 1930s cartelized the labor market on behalf of racist labor unions, while black workers remained unprotected by civil rights legislation. *Lochner*-style judicial intervention to protect free labor markets could have saved hundreds of thousands [of] blacks from being permanently deprived of their livelihoods. [It] is possible to imagine that but for the interruption of the Great Depression and the New Deal, entirely different forms of civil rights protections would have arisen — a laissez-faire combination of equal protection of the law, liberty of contract, and freedom of association, instead of the more statist combination of interest group liberalism, the welfare state, and government enforcement of nondiscrimination norms against private parties.

Bernstein, Roots of the "Underclass": The Decline of Laissez-Faire Jurisprudence and the Rise of Racist Labor Legislation, 43 Am. U. L. Rev. 85, 86–87, 135 (1993).

4. *The implications of abdication: The decline of* Lochner *and the rise of the "double standard."* Why is there a "presumption of constitutionality" when the Court reviews economic legislation? Does this presumption govern all constitutional review? All substantive due process review? All substantive due process review except where the right at issue is expressly guaranteed in the bill of rights? All substantive due process review except where the right at issue is "fundamental"?

Consider Justice Stone's famous footnote 4 in *Carolene Products*:

There may be narrower scope for operation of the presumption of constitutionality when legislation appears on its face to be within a specific prohibition of the Constitution, such as those of the first ten amendments, which are deemed equally specific when held to be embraced within the Fourteenth. . . .

It is unnecessary to consider now whether legislation which restricts those political processes [such as voting, expression, and political association] which can ordinarily be expected to bring about repeal of undesirable legislation, is to be subjected to more exacting judicial scrutiny under the general prohibitions of the Fourteenth Amendment than are most other types of legislation. . . .

Nor need we enquire whether similar considerations enter into the review of statutes directed at particular religious, [or] national, [or] racial minorities[;] whether prejudice against discrete and insular minorities may be a special condition, which tends seriously to curtail the operation of those political processes ordinarily to be relied upon to protect minorities, and which may call for a correspondingly more searching judicial inquiry.

For an interesting account of the origins of footnote 4, see Lusky, Footnote Redux: A *Carolene Products* Reminiscence, 82 Colum. L. Rev. 1093 (1982).

E.   FUNDAMENTAL INTERESTS AND THE EQUAL PROTECTION CLAUSE

This section explores the intersection of equal protection and implied fundamental rights jurisprudence. Chapter 5, supra, examined two basic models of equal protection analysis. The first model focuses on classification based on race or other "suspect" criteria. As we saw, the Court tests such classifications by varying forms of "strict" scrutiny. The second model focuses on classifications in the economic and social realm that do not involve "suspect" criteria. As we also saw, the Court tests such classifications by a highly usually deferential form of "rational basis" review, similar to the standard that the Court currently employs in considering substantive due process challenges to economic regulation.

This section asks whether there is a third model of equal protection analysis. That is: Should the degree of scrutiny vary not only with the "suspectness" of the criterion on which the classification is based but also with the "importance" or "fundamentality" of the interest that is distributed or affected "unequally"? Should inequalities involving "fundamental" interests be analyzed differently from inequalities involving "nonfundamental" interests? The inquiry is relevant here because the "fundamentality" of the interest is sometimes implied without clear textual support. Consider in this regard whether or how fundamental interest equal protection review differs from substantive due process review.

Skinner v. Oklahoma
316 U.S. 535 (1942)

MR. JUSTICE DOUGLAS delivered the opinion of the Court.

This case touches a sensitive and important area of human rights. Oklahoma deprives certain individuals of a right which is basic to the perpetuation of a race — the right to have offspring. . . .

The statute involved is Oklahoma's Habitual Criminal Sterilization Act. That Act defines an "habitual criminal" as a person who [has been convicted three] or more times for crimes "amounting to felonies involving moral turpitude." [Machinery] is provided for the institution by the Attorney General of a proceeding against such a person in the Oklahoma courts for a judgment that such person shall be rendered sexually sterile. [If] the court or jury finds that the defendant is an "habitual criminal" and that he "may be rendered sexually sterile without detriment to his or her general health," then the court "shall render judgment to the effect that said defendant be rendered sexually sterile" by the operation of vasectomy in case of a male, and of salpingectomy in case of a female. Only one other provision of the Act is material here, and that provides that "offenses arising out of the violation of the prohibitory laws, revenue acts, embezzlement, or political offenses, shall not come or be considered within the terms of this Act."

Petitioner was convicted in 1926 of the crime of stealing chickens, [and in 1929 and 1934] he was convicted of robbery with firearms. [In] 1936 the Attorney General instituted proceedings against him. [A] judgment directing that the operation of vasectomy be performed on petitioner was affirmed by the Supreme Court of Oklahoma. . . .

[The Act fails] to meet the requirements of the equal protection clause of the Fourteenth Amendment.

We do not stop to point out all of the inequalities in this Act. A few examples will suffice. In Oklahoma, [a] clerk who appropriates over $20 from his employer's till and a stranger who steals the same amount are [both] guilty of felonies. If the latter repeats his act and is convicted three times, he may be sterilized. But the clerk is not subject to the pains and penalties of the Act no matter how large his embezzlements nor how frequent his convictions. A person who enters a chicken coop and steals chickens commits a felony and he may be sterilized if he is thrice convicted. If, however, he is a bailee of the property and fraudulently appropriates it, he is an embezzler. Hence, no matter how habitual his proclivities for embezzlement are and no matter how often his conviction, he may not be sterilized. Thus, the nature of the two crimes is intrinsically the same and they are punishable in the same manner. . . .

[If] we had here only a question as to a State's classification of crimes, such as embezzlement or larceny, no substantial federal question would be raised. [For] a State is not constrained in the exercise of its police power to ignore experience which marks a class of offenders or a family of offenses for special treatment. Nor is it prevented by the equal protection clause from confining "its restrictions to those classes of cases where the need is deemed to be clearest." . . .

But the instant legislation runs afoul of the equal protection clause, though we give Oklahoma that large deference which the rule of the foregoing cases requires. We are dealing here with legislation which involves one of the basic civil rights of man. Marriage and procreation are fundamental to the very existence and survival of the race. The power to sterilize, if exercised, may have subtle, far-reaching and devastating effects. In evil or reckless hands it can cause races or types which are inimical to the dominant group to wither and disappear. There is no redemption for the individual whom the law touches. Any experiment which the State conducts is to his irreparable injury. He is forever deprived of a basic liberty. We mention these matters not to reexamine the scope of the police power of the States. We advert to them merely in emphasis of our view that strict scrutiny of the classification which a State makes in a sterilization law is essential, lest unwittingly, or otherwise, invidious discriminations are made against groups or types of individuals in violation of the constitutional guaranty of just and equal laws. The guaranty of "equal protection of the laws is a pledge of the protection of equal laws." When the law lays an unequal hand on those who have committed intrinsically the same quality of offense and sterilizes one and not the other, it has made as invidious a discrimination as if it had selected a particular race or nationality for oppressive treatment. . . .

Reversed.

MR. CHIEF JUSTICE STONE, concurring.

I concur in the result, but I am not persuaded that we are aided in reaching it by recourse to the equal protection clause.

If Oklahoma may resort generally to the sterilization of criminals on the assumption that their propensities are transmissible to future generations by inheritance, I seriously doubt that the equal protection clause requires it to apply the measure to all criminals in the first instance, or to none.

Moreover, if we must presume that the legislature knows — what science has been unable to ascertain — that the criminal tendencies of any class of habitual offenders are transmissible regardless of the varying mental characteristics of its individuals, I should suppose that we must likewise presume that the legislature, in its wisdom, knows that the criminal tendencies of some classes of offenders are more likely to be transmitted than those of others. And so I think the real question we have to consider is not one of equal protection, but whether the wholesale condemnation of a class to such an invasion of personal liberty, without opportunity to any individual to show that his is not the type of case which would justify resort to it, satisfies the demands of due process.

There are limits to the extent to which the presumption of constitutionality can be pressed, especially where the liberty of the person is concerned (see United States v. Carolene Products Co., 304 U.S. 144, 152, n.4) and where the presumption is resorted to only to dispense with a procedure which the ordinary dictates of prudence would seem to demand for the protection of the individual from arbitrary action. Although petitioner here was given a hearing to ascertain whether sterilization would be detrimental to his health, he was given none to discover whether his criminal tendencies are of an inheritable type. . . .

[A] law which condemns, without hearing, all the individuals of a class to so harsh a measure as the present because some or even many merit condemnation, is lacking in the first principles of due process. [The] state is called on to sacrifice no permissible end when it is required to reach its objective by a reasonable and just procedure adequate to safeguard rights of the individual which concededly the Constitution protects.

[A concurring opinion of Justice Jackson is omitted.]

Note: The Fundamental "Right to Have Offspring"

1. *Equal protection or due process?* Note that the state could cure the equal protection problem by extending the sterilization penalty to a larger class of offenders. If sterilization invades a fundamental right, how is the situation made better by invading the rights of a larger group of people?

2. *"Fundamental" interests and the equal protection clause.* *Skinner* might be thought inconsistent with the Court's essentially contemporaneous renunciation of economic substantive due process. Can the right to have offspring, unlike the liberty of contract, be thought to be a true "fundamental" right? Or is fundamental interest analysis more appropriate in equal protection jurisprudence than in due process jurisprudence?

Consider the following arguments: (a) Inequality with respect to a trivial interest is not as significant as inequality with respect to an important interest. (b) Inequality with respect to a fundamental interest is inherently irrational unless there are very good reasons for the inequality. (c) Inequality with respect to a fundamental interest suggests a possible improper motivation, for it is unlikely that those who framed the classification would have deprived themselves of the fundamental interest in the absence of extraordinary necessity. (d) The 1866 Civil Rights Act, on which the fourteenth amendment was based, protected African Americans against inequality only with respect to certain specified interests, thus suggesting that the importance of the interest affected is central to the constitutionality of a classification.

3. *Is the "right to have offspring" a "fundamental" interest?* Is it more "fundamental" than the "liberty of contract"? Suppose that Oklahoma sentenced some, but not all felons to life imprisonment without conjugal visits. Would such a sentence violate the equal protection clause? Consider the following views:

a. "[The] Court in *Skinner* was moved to recognize the fundamental personal character of a right to reproductive autonomy in part because of fear about the invidious and potentially genocidal way in which governmental control over reproductive matters might be exercised if the choice of whether or when to beget a child were to be transferred from the individual to the state." L. Tribe, American Constitutional Law 923 (1978). Note in this regard that the statutory distinction in *Skinner* was itself at least arguably class-based. White-collar crimes, and others likely to be committed by those relatively better off, would not be punished with sterilization. Should this bear on the equal protection issue?

b. "[The] right of procreation [rests] most securely on the interest in status and dignity. [The] choice to be [a] parent is, among other things, a choice of social role and of self-concept. For the state to deny such a choice is for the organized society to deny the individual [the] presumptive right to be treated as a person, one of equal worth among citizens." Karst, Foreword: Equal Citizenship under the Fourteenth Amendment, 91 Harv. L. Rev. 1, 32 (1977). On this view, would a statute prohibiting in vitro fertilization be unconstitutional as applied to a woman who could not otherwise become pregnant?

c. *Skinner* was simply wrong. The case is an example of the proposition that hard cases make bad law. Lacking a secure constitutional foundation for invalidating an oppressive law, the Court just made it up.

4. *A right not to have offspring?* In *Skinner*, the Court held that the right to have offspring is "fundamental." Is there also a fundamental right not to have offspring? Suppose, for example, that a married couple uses in vitro fertilization and freezes some of the resulting preembryos. If the parties then divorce, is it constitutional for the state to permit the wife to implant these preembryos if the husband objects? For an argument that there is no right not to be a genetic parent when genetic parenthood is divorced from gestational and legal parenthood, see Cohen, The Constitution and the Rights Not to Procreate, 60 Stan. L. Rev. 1135 (2008). See section F infra.

1.   Voting

In footnote 4 of *Carolene Products*, Chief Justice Stone suggested that there "may be a narrower scope for operation of the presumption of constitutionality when [legislation] restricts those political processes which can ordinarily be expected to bring about repeal of undesirable legislation." He then offered "restrictions upon the right to vote" as a specific example. This section examines three aspects of the right to vote: denial of the right to vote, dilution of the right to vote, and denial of access to the ballot.

a.   Denial of the "Right to Vote"

The original Constitution left the states free determine the qualifications of voters for both national and state elections, requiring only that electors for the House of Representatives "shall have the Qualifications requisite for Electors of the most numerous Branch of the State Legislature." See U.S. Const, art. I, §2, cl. 1; art. II, §1, cl. 2. The fourteenth amendment, enacted in 1868, did not directly prohibit discrimination in voting. Section 2 of the amendment, however, provided for a reduction in representation in the House of Representatives in proportion to the number of "male inhabitants of [the] State, being twenty-one years of age, and citizens of the United States," who were not permitted to vote. The fifteenth amendment, adopted in 1870, provided that the right of citizens to vote "shall not be denied or abridged [on] account of race, color or previous condition of servitude." The nineteenth amendment, enacted in 1920, provided that the right of citizens to vote "shall not be denied or abridged [on] account of sex." The twenty-fourth amendment, adopted in 1964, provided that the right of any citizen to vote in any election for president, vice-president, or members of Congress "shall not be denied or abridged [by] reason of failure to pay any poll tax or other tax." And the twenty-sixth amendment, enacted in 1971, provided that the right of any citizen eighteen years or older to vote "shall not be denied or abridged [on] account of age."

Until the 1960s, the Court generally deferred to the states in determining the qualifications to vote except where a particular qualification was expressly prohibited by a specific amendment. In Breedlove v. Suttles, 302 U.S. 277 (1937), for example, the Court unanimously upheld a Georgia statute requiring the payment of a $1 poll tax as a precondition for voting. Similarly, in Lassiter v. Northampton County Board of Elections, 360 U.S. 45 (1959), the Court unanimously upheld a North Carolina statute providing that to be eligible to vote an individual must "be able to read and write any section of the [state constitution] in the English language." The Court said that "in our society where newspapers, periodicals, books, and other printed matter canvass and debate campaign issues, a State might conclude that only those who are literate should exercise the franchise."

In 1964, however, in Reynolds v. Sims, section E1b, infra, a decision involving dilution of the right to vote, the Court observed: "[The] right of suffrage is a fundamental matter in a free and democratic society. Especially since the right to exercise the franchise in a free and unimpaired manner is preservative of other basic civil and political rights, any alleged infringement of the right of citizens to vote must be carefully and meticulously scrutinized." *Reynolds* opened the door to a more active judicial scrutiny of voter qualifications.

Harper v. Virginia State Board of Elections
383 U.S. 663 (1966)

[The Court, overruling Breedlove v. Suttles, invalidated a Virginia law requiring the payment of a poll tax not to exceed $1.50 as a precondition for voting. The Court held that "a State violates the Equal Protection Clause [whenever] it makes the affluence of the voter or payment of any fee an electoral standard."]

MR. JUSTICE DOUGLAS delivered the opinion of the Court. . . .

[The] right to vote in state elections is nowhere expressly mentioned [in the Constitution]. It is argued that the right to vote in state elections is implicit, particularly by reason of the First Amendment. [We] do not stop to canvass the relation between voting and political expression. For it is enough to say that once the franchise is granted to the electorate, lines may not be drawn which are inconsistent with the Equal Protection Clause of the Fourteenth Amendment. . . .

[The] *Lassiter* case does not govern the result here, because, unlike a poll tax, the "ability to read and write . . . has some relation to standards designed to promote intelligent use of the ballot." [Voter] qualifications have no relation to wealth nor to paying or not paying this or any other tax. . . .

It is argued that a State may exact fees from citizens for many different kinds of licenses; that if it can demand from all an equal fee for a driver's license, it can demand from all an equal poll tax for voting. But we must remember that the interest of the State, when it comes to voting, is limited to the power to fix qualifications. Wealth, like race, creed, or color, is not germane to one's ability to participate intelligently in the electoral process. Lines drawn on the basis of wealth or property, like those of race [are] traditionally disfavored. See [Griffin v.

Illinois and Douglas v. California, section E2, infra]. To introduce wealth or payment of a fee as a measure of a voter's qualifications is to introduce a capricious or irrelevant factor. . . .

We agree, of course, with Mr. Justice Holmes that the Due Process Clause of the Fourteenth Amendment "does not enact Mr. Herbert Spencer's Social Statics." [*Lochner.*] Likewise, the Equal Protection Clause is not shackled to the political theory of a particular era. In determining what lines are unconstitutionally discriminatory, we have never been confined to historic notions of [equality]. Notions of what constitutes equal treatment for purposes of the Equal Protection Clause do change. [Comparing Plessy v. Ferguson with Brown v. Board of Education.]

[We] have long been mindful that where fundamental rights and liberties are asserted under the Equal Protection Clause, classifications which might invade or restrain them must be closely scrutinized and carefully confined. See, e.g., [*Skinner*].

Those principles apply here. For to repeat, wealth or fee paying has, in our view, no relation to voting qualifications; the right to vote is too precious, too fundamental to be so burdened or conditioned.

Reversed.

MR. JUSTICE BLACK, dissenting. . . .

[Under] a proper interpretation of the Equal Protection Clause States are to have the broadest kind of leeway in areas where they have a general constitutional competence to act. [State] poll tax legislation can "reasonably," "rationally" and without an "invidious" or evil purpose to injure anyone be found to rest on a number of state policies including (1) the State's desire to collect its revenue, and (2) its belief that voters who pay a poll tax will be interested in furthering the State's welfare when they vote. [And] history is on the side of "rationality" of the State's poll tax policy. Property qualifications existed in the Colonies and were continued by many States after the Constitution was adopted. . . .

Another reason for my dissent [is that the Court] seems to be using the old "natural-law-due-process formula" to justify striking down state laws as violations of the Equal Protection Clause. . . .

MR. JUSTICE HARLAN, whom MR. JUSTICE STEWART joins, dissenting. . . .

[The Court uses] captivating phrases, but they are wholly inadequate to satisfy the standard governing adjudication of the equal protection issue: Is there a rational basis for Virginia's poll tax as a voting qualification? I think the answer to that question is undoubtedly "yes."

Property qualifications and poll taxes have been a traditional part of our political structure. In the Colonies the franchise was generally a restricted one. [It] is certainly a rational argument that payment of some minimal poll tax promotes civic responsibility, weeding out those who do not care enough about public affairs to pay $1.50 or thereabouts a year for the exercise of the franchise. It is also arguable, indeed it was probably accepted as sound political theory by a large percentage of Americans through most of our history, that people with some property have a deeper stake in community affairs, and are consequently more responsible, more educated, more knowledgeable, more worthy of confidence, than those without means, and that the community and Nation would be better managed if the franchise were restricted to such citizens. . . .

Note: Is the Right to Vote "Fundamental"?

1. *The basis of* Harper: *wealth as a "suspect classification."* The Court relied in *Harper* on both the "suspect classification" and the "fundamental interest" aspects of equal protection analysis. To what extent, if any, can *Harper* be explained on the ground that "lines drawn on the basis of wealth [are] tradition-ally disfavored"? Consider that (a) the poll tax does not expressly classify on the basis of wealth; (b) like ordinary license fees, and indeed any system that requires an expenditure, it might be seen to have a differential effect on the poor; and (c) the Court invalidated the poll tax in its entirety, not only as applied to the poor.

2. *The basis of* Harper: *voting as a fundamental interest.* The *Harper* Court assumed that there is no constitutional right to vote in state elections. This view is endorsed by some, but not all commentators. See R. Berger, Government by Judiciary ch. 4 (1977). But cf. Oregon v. Mitchell, 400 U.S. 112, 229 (1970) (Brennan, J.); Van Alstyne, The Fourteenth Amendment, the "Right" to Vote, and the Understanding of the Thirty-Ninth Congress, 1965 Sup. Ct. Rev. 33. Given the Court's assumption, how does it justify its conclusion that the right to vote is "fundamental"?

Consider J. Ely, Democracy and Distrust 77, 101–103 (1980):

> Malfunction occurs when [the] ins are choking off the channels of political change to ensure that they will stay in and the outs will stay out. [Unblocking] stoppages in the democratic process is what judicial review ought preeminently to be about, and denial of the vote seems the quintessential stoppage. [We] cannot trust the ins to decide who stays out, and it is therefore incumbent on the courts to ensure not only that no one is denied the vote for no reason, but also that where there is a reason [it] had better be a very convincing one.

3. *Bush v. Gore.* In connection with the putative "fundamental" character of the right to vote, consider the Supreme Court decision that brought to a con-clusion the disputed presidential election of 2000. (The decision is explored more generally in Chapter 1, section F3, supra.) With the presidential candidates separated by no more than a few hundred votes and the deadline for the casting of electoral ballots fast approaching, the Florida Supreme Court ordered a state-wide, manual recount of all ballots on which the voting machines had failed to detect a vote for president. In Bush v. Gore, 531 U.S. 98 (2000), the Supreme Court, in a five-to-four decision, reversed. In a per curiam opinion, joined by five justices, the Court held that the failure of the Florida court to specify standards for determining which votes would count violated the equal protection clause:

> When the state legislature vests the right to vote for President in its people, the right to vote as the legislature has prescribed is fundamental; and one source of its fundamental nature lies in the equal weight accorded to each vote and the equal dignity owned to each voter. . . .
>
> The right to vote is protected in more than the initial allocation of the franchise. Equal protection applies as well to the manner of its exercise. Having once granted the right to vote on equal terms, the State may not, by later arbitrary and disparate treatment, value one person's vote over that of another. . . .
>
> The recount mechanisms implemented in response to the decisions of the Florida Supreme Court do not satisfy the minimum requirement for non-arbitrary treatment of voters necessary to secure the fundamental right. [The] problem inheres in the absence of specific standards to ensure [equal] application. The

formulation of uniform rules to determine intent based on [recurring] circumstances is practicable and, we conclude, necessary. . . .

Our consideration is limited to the present circumstances, for the problem of equal protection in election processes generally presents many complexities.

The question before the Court is not whether local entities, in the exercise of their expertise, may develop different systems for implementing elections. Instead, we are presented with a situation where a state court with the power to assure uniformity has ordered a statewide recount with minimal procedural safeguards. When a court orders a statewide remedy, there must be at least some assurance that the rudimentary requirements of equal treatment and fundamental fairness are satisfied.

The Court went on to hold that it was impossible to conduct a recount satisfying equal protection standards before the deadline specified in 3 U.S.C. §5, which made conclusive state resolutions of election controversies if the determination was made at least six days prior to the date for the casting of electoral votes. (By the time the Court rendered its decision, this deadline was only hours away.) The Court also determined that the Florida legislature intended to take advantage of this "safe harbor." Accordingly, the Court held that the recount could not proceed. Chief Justice Rehnquist, joined by Justices Scalia and Thomas, wrote a concurring opinion. Justices Souter and Breyer both wrote opinions in which they agreed with the majority that the absence of uniform standards for the recount created constitutional difficulties. However, both would have remanded the case to the Florida court so that it could formulate such standards. Justices Ginsburg and Stevens also wrote dissenting opinions.

Does the result in Bush v. Gore follow from *Harper*? Note that Florida had a decentralized voting system under which the ballots had been counted in different ways before the recount was ordered. The Court nowhere suggested that the initial balloting was unconstitutional. From a constitutional perspective, did the recount make things worse or better?

Kramer v. Union Free School District

395 U.S. 621 (1969)

Mr. Chief Justice Warren delivered the opinion of the Court.

[Section 2012] of the New York Education Law [provides] that in certain New York school districts residents [may] vote in the school district election only if they (1) own (or lease) taxable real property within the district, or (2) are parents (or have custody of) children enrolled in the local public schools. Appellant, a bachelor who neither owns nor leases taxable real property, [claims] that §2012 denied him equal protection of the laws. . . .

In determining whether or not [this] law violates the Equal Protection Clause, [we] must give the statute a close and exacting examination. [This] careful examination is necessary because statutes distributing the franchise constitute the foundation of our representative society.

[Statutes] granting the franchise to residents on a selective basis always pose the danger of denying some citizens any effective voice in the governmental affairs which substantially affect their lives. Therefore, if a challenged state statute grants the right to vote to some bona fide residents of requisite age and citizenship and denies the franchise to others, the Court must determine whether the exclusions are necessary to promote a compelling state interest.

[The] presumption of constitutionality and the approval given "rational" classifications in other types of enactments are based on an assumption that the institutions of state government are structured so as to represent fairly all the people. However, when the challenge to the statute is in effect a challenge of this basic assumption, the assumption can no longer serve as the basis for presuming constitutionality. And, the assumption is no less under attack because the legislature which decides who may participate at the various levels of political choice is fairly elected. Legislation which delegates decision making to bodies elected by only a portion of those eligible to vote for the legislature can cause unfair representation. . . .

[We] turn therefore to question whether the exclusion is necessary to promote a compelling state interest. [Appellees] argue that the State has a legitimate interest in limiting the franchise in school district elections [to] those "primarily interested in such elections" [and] that the State may reasonably and permissibly conclude that "property taxpayers" (including lessees of taxable property who share the tax burden through rent payments) and parents of the children enrolled in the district's schools are those "primarily interested" in school affairs. . . .

We need express no opinion as to whether the State in some circumstances might limit the exercise of the franchise to those "primarily interested" or "primarily affected." [For,] assuming, arguendo, that New York legitimately might limit the franchise in these school district elections to those "primarily interested in school affairs," close scrutiny of the §2012 classifications demonstrates that they do not accomplish this purpose with sufficient precision to justify denying appellant the franchise.

[The] requirements of §2012 are not sufficiently tailored to limiting the franchise to those "primarily interested" in school affairs to justify the denial of the franchise to appellant and members of his class. . . .

Mr. Justice Stewart, with whom Mr. Justice Black and Mr. Justice Harlan join, dissenting. . . .

Clearly a State may reasonably assume that its residents have a greater stake in the outcome of elections held within its boundaries than do other persons. Likewise, it is entirely rational for a state legislature to suppose that residents, being generally better informed regarding state affairs than are nonresidents, will be more likely than nonresidents to vote responsibly. And the same may be said of legislative assumptions regarding the electoral competence of adults and literate persons on the one hand, and of minors and illiterates on the other. It is clear, of course, that lines thus drawn cannot infallibly perform their intended legislative function. Just as "[i]lliterate people may be intelligent voters," nonresidents or minors might also in some instances be interested, informed, and intelligent participants in the electoral process.

[Nor] is there any other justification for imposing the Court's "exacting" equal protection test. This case does not involve racial classifications [and] this statute is not one that impinges upon a constitutionally protected right, [for] "the Constitution of the United States does not confer the right of suffrage upon any one." . . .

Note: Kramer *and Its Progeny*

In examining the Court's decisions in the line inaugurated by *Kramer*, consider what the Court means in this context by "strict scrutiny."

1. *The meaning of strict scrutiny.* In the wake of *Kramer*, the Court has drawn an uncertain line between permissible and impermissible voting qualifications. For example, it has invalidated most property ownership requirements, see In Cipriano v. City of Houma, 395 U.S. 701 (1969); Phoenix v. Kolodziejski, 399 U.S. 204 (1970), but upheld them for "limited purpose governmental units. See Salyer Land Co. v. Tulare Lake Basin Water Storage District, 410 U.S. 719 (1973) (upholding a California statute permitting only landowners to vote in water storage district elections and allocating votes in proportion to the assessed valuation of the land); Ball v. James, 451 U.S. 355 (1981) (upholding a "one acre–one vote" scheme for voting for directors of a large water reclamation district in Arizona). It invalidated a one-year residency requirement in Dunn v. Blumstein, 405 U.S. 330 (1972), but upheld a fifty-day requirement in Marston v. Lewis, 410 U.S. 679 (1973), and Burns v. Fortson, 410 U.S. 686 (1973). See also McDonald v. Board of Election Commissioners, 394 U.S. 802 (1969) (upholding an Illinois statute that granted absentee ballots to some classes of persons but not to "unsentenced inmates awaiting trial" in circumstances where nothing in the record indicated that inmates could not vote at polling places); O'Brien v. Skinner, 414 U.S. 524 (1974) (invalidating a statute prohibiting absentee ballots for some persons incarcerated while awaiting trial when other inmates were granted absentee ballots); Richardson v. Ramirez, 418 U.S. 24 (1974) (upholding a statute that denied the vote to convicted felons even if they had completed their sentences and paroles). Compare Rosario v. Rockefeller, 410 U.S. 752 (1973) upholding a statute requiring voters to register their party affiliation at least thirty days before a general election in order to be eligible to vote in the next party primary) with Kusper v. Pontikes, 414 U.S. 51 (1973) (invalidating a statute that prohibited any person "from voting in the primary election of a political party if he has voted in the primary of any other party within the preceding 23 months").

2. *Strict scrutiny for laws requiring proof of voter qualification?* In Crawford v. Marion County Election Board, 553 U.S. 181 (2008), the Court rejected a facial challenge to an Indiana statute that required citizens to present a government-issued photo identification before voting. The state offered free photo identification to qualified voters who could establish their residence and identity. An indigent voter, or one who had a religious objection to being photographed, could cast a provisional ballot that would be counted only if she executed an appropriate affidavit with a circuit county clerk within ten days following the election. Voters who had photo identification but were unable to present the identification on election day could also file provisional ballots that would be counted if they brought photo identification to the clerk's office within the ten-day period.

Writing for himself, Chief Justice Roberts, and Justice Kennedy, Justice Stevens stated that the strict scrutiny applied in *Harper* was inapplicable because this was not a case where the restriction was an invidious limitation unrelated to voter qualifications. Instead, he applied the "general rule" that required the court to "identify and evaluate the interests put forward by the State as justifications for the burden imposed by its rule, and then make the 'hard judgment' that our adversary system demands."

In support of the rule, Justice Stevens emphasized the need to prevent voter fraud. Although noting that "[the] record contains no evidence of any such [in-person] fraud actually occurring in Indiana at any time in its history," the Court observed that there had been "flagrant examples of such fraud in other parts of the country" and that "[there] is no question about the legitimacy or importance of the State's interest in counting only the votes of eligible voters."

In Justice Stevens's view, this interest counterbalanced the burden placed upon voters who lacked, or failed to produce, photo identification.

> [On] the basis of the record that has been made in this litigation, we cannot conclude that the statute imposes "excessively burdensome requirements" on any class of voters. A facial challenge must fail where the statute has a "'plainly legitimate sweep.'" When we consider only the statute's broad application to all Indiana voters we conclude that it "imposes only a limited burden on voters' rights."

Justice Scalia, joined by Justices Thomas and Alito, concurred in the judgment. Although agreeing with Justice Stevens's conclusion, Justice Scalia would have applied "deferential" scrutiny on the ground that strict scrutiny was appropriate only for laws that "severely restrict the right to vote."

Justice Souter filed a dissenting opinion in which Justice Ginsburg joined. Justice Breyer also filed a dissenting opinion.

b.   Dilution of the "Right to Vote"

Until 1962, the Court held that legislative districting controversies were nonjusticiable. In Colegrove v. Green, 328 U.S. 549 (1946), for example, the Court declined to consider a claim that an Illinois law unconstitutionally prescribed congressional districts that were not approximately equal in population. Justice Frankfurter, writing for a plurality, explained that "this controversy concerns matters that bring courts into immediate and active relations with party contests. [It] is hostile to a democratic system to involve the judiciary in the politics of the people. [Courts] ought not to enter this political thicket."

In Baker v. Carr, 369 U.S. 186 (1962), however, the Court changed course. In a case involving a claim that the apportionment of the Tennessee General Assembly violated the appellants' rights under the equal protection clause "by virtue of the debasement of their votes," the Court held "that a justiciable cause of action is stated upon which appellants would be entitled to appropriate relief." *Baker* is examined more fully in Chapter 1, section F3, supra.

Reynolds v. Sims
377 U.S. 533 (1964)

[In *Reynolds* and five companion cases, the Court held that in six states the system of apportionment of one or both houses of the legislature was unconstitutional. *Reynolds* involved Alabama; the other cases involved Colorado, Delaware, Maryland, New York, and Virginia. The Court observed: "Legislative apportionment in Alabama is signally illustrative and symptomatic of the seriousness of this problem in a number of States. [There has] been no reapportionment of seats in the Alabama Legislature for over 60 years. [This has resulted] in the perpetuated scheme becoming little more than an irrational anachronism [enabling] a minority stranglehold on the State Legislature."]

Mr. Chief Justice Warren delivered the opinion of the Court. . . .

A predominant consideration in determining whether a State's legislative apportionment scheme constitutes an invidious discrimination violative of rights asserted under the Equal Protection Clause is that the rights allegedly impaired are individual and personal in nature. [Since] the right of suffrage is a fundamental matter in a free and democratic society [and] is preservative of other basic civil and political rights, any alleged infringement of the right of citizens to vote must be carefully and meticulously scrutinized. . . .

Legislators represent people, not trees or acres. Legislators are elected by voters, not farms or cities or economic interests. As long as ours is a representative form of government, [the] right to elect legislators in a free and unimpaired fashion is a bedrock of our political system. It could hardly be gainsaid that a constitutional claim had been asserted by an allegation that certain otherwise qualified voters had been entirely prohibited from voting for members of their state legislature. And, if a State should provide that the votes of citizens in one part of the State should be given two times, or five times, or 10 times the weight of votes of citizens in another part of the State, it could hardly be contended that the right to vote of those residing in the disfavored areas had not been effectively diluted. [Of] course, the effect of state legislative districting schemes which give the same number of representatives to unequal numbers of constituents is identical. . . .

Logically, in a society ostensibly grounded on representative government, it would seem reasonable that a majority of the people of a State could elect a majority of that State's legislators. [Since] the achieving of fair and effective representation for all citizens is concededly the basic aim of legislative apportionment, we conclude that the Equal Protection Clause guarantees the opportunity for equal participation by all voters in the election of state legislators. Diluting the weight of votes because of place of residence impairs basic constitutional rights under the Fourteenth Amendment. [Our] constitutional system amply provides for the protection of minorities by means other than giving them majority control of state legislatures. . . .

We are told that the matter of apportioning representation in a state legislature is a complex and many-faceted one. We are advised that States can rationally consider factors other than population in apportioning legislative representation. We are admonished not to restrict the power of the States to impose differing views as to political philosophy on their citizens. We are cautioned about the dangers of entering into political thickets and mathematical quagmires. Our answer is this: a denial of constitutionally protected rights demands judicial protection; our oath and our office require no less of us. [To] the extent that a citizen's right to vote is debased, he is that much less a citizen. [The] weight of a citizen's vote cannot be made to depend on where he lives. Population is, of necessity, the starting point for consideration and the controlling criterion for judgment in legislative apportionment controversies. A citizen, a qualified voter, is no more nor no less so because he lives in the city or on the farm. This is the clear and strong command of our Constitution's Equal Protection Clause. . . .

We hold that, as a basic constitutional standard, the Equal Protection Clause requires that the seats in both houses of a bicameral state legislature must be apportioned on a population basis. Simply stated, an individual's right to vote for state legislators is unconstitutionally impaired when its weight is in a substantial fashion diluted when compared with votes of citizens living in other parts of the State. . . .

[We] find the federal analogy inapposite and irrelevant to state legislative districting schemes. . . .

The system of representation in the two Houses of the Federal Congress is one ingrained in our Constitution [and] is based on the consideration that in establishing our type of federalism a group of formerly independent States bound themselves together under one national government. [A] compromise between the larger and smaller States on this matter averted a deadlock in the Constitutional Convention which had threatened to abort the birth of our Nation. . . .

Political subdivisions of States — counties, cities, or whatever — never were and never have been considered as sovereign entities. . . .

By holding that as a federal constitutional requisite both houses of a state legislature must be apportioned on a population basis, we mean that the Equal Protection Clause requires that a State make an honest and good faith effort to construct districts, in both houses of its legislature, as nearly of equal population as is practicable. We realize that it is a practical impossibility to arrange legislative districts so that each one has an identical number of residents, or citizens, or voters. [So] long as the divergences from a strict population standard are based on legitimate considerations incident to the effectuation of a rational state policy, some deviations from the equal-population principle are constitutionally permissible [but] neither history alone, nor economic or other sorts of group interests, are permissible factors in attempting to justify disparities from population-based representation. Citizens, not history or economic interests, cast votes. Considerations of area alone provide an insufficient justification for deviations from the equal-population principle. Again, people, not land or trees or pastures, vote. . . .

A consideration that appears to be of more substance in justifying some deviations from population-based representation in state legislatures is that of insuring some voice to political subdivisions, as political subdivisions. [In] many States much of the legislature's activity involves the enactment of so-called local legislation, directed only to the concerns of particular political subdivisions. [But] if, even as a result of a clearly rational state policy of according some legislative representation to political subdivisions, population is submerged as the controlling consideration in the apportionment of seats in the particular legislative body, then the right of all of the State's citizens to cast an effective and adequately weighted vote would be unconstitutionally impaired. . . .

[Affirmed and remanded.]

MR. JUSTICE HARLAN, dissenting [in all six cases]. . . .

[The] history of the adoption of the Fourteenth Amendment provides conclusive evidence that neither those who proposed nor those who ratified the Amendment believed that the Equal Protection Clause limited the power of the States to apportion their legislatures as they saw fit. Moreover, the history demonstrates that the intention to leave this power undisturbed was deliberate and was widely believed to be essential to the adoption of the Amendment. [Justice Harlan's extensive historical analysis is omitted.]

It is difficult to imagine a more intolerable and inappropriate interference by the judiciary with the independent legislatures of the States. . . .

[The] Court says [only] that "legislators represent people, not trees or acres." [This] may be conceded. But it is surely equally obvious, and, in the context of elections, more meaningful to note that people are not ciphers and that legislators can represent their electors only by speaking for their interests — economic, social, political — many of which do reflect the place where the electors live. . . .

[An opinion by Justice Stewart, joined by Justice Clark, dissenting in the Colorado and New York cases, is omitted]

Note: Reynolds *and Its Progeny*

1. *"One person, one vote."* Note that Kramer was denied the right to vote, whereas no one in *Reynolds* was denied that right. In this sense, the slogan "one person, one vote" that is often used to characterize *Reynolds* does not accurately describe its holding. Does the right to an equally weighted vote follow from the equality principle or from the conclusion that the "right to vote" is "fundamental"?

2. *Reapportionment: a "success story"?* Within four years of *Reynolds*, congressional and state legislative district lines had been redrawn on a one person–one vote basis in almost every state. Does this make *Reynolds* a success story? For an argument that it does, see McKay, Reapportionment: Success Story of the Warren Court, 67 Mich. L. Rev. 223 (1968). For more skeptical views, see A. Bickel, The Supreme Court and the Idea of Progress (1970); Bork, supra, at 88–90. Note also that the one person–one vote standard does nothing to limit partisan gerrymandering, a practice that remains very widespread. (The problem of vote dilution through gerrymandering is considered below.)

3. *Popularly mandated malapportionment.* *Reynolds* was designed, in part, to protect majoritarianism and to prevent "minority control of state legislative bodies." But malapportionment has been held unconstitutional even if it is approved by a majority of the state's voters. In Lucas v. Forty-Fourth General Assembly, 377 U.S. 713 (1964), a companion case to *Reynolds*, the Colorado scheme, which apportioned only one of the two Houses on the basis of population, had been approved in 1962 by a statewide referendum in which the voters specifically rejected a plan to apportion both Houses on the basis of population. Nonetheless, the Court held the scheme invalid: "An individual's constitutionally protected right to cast an equally weighted vote cannot be denied even by a vote of a majority of a State's electorate, if the apportionment scheme [fails] to measure up to the requirements of the Equal Protection Clause. [A] citizen's constitutional rights can hardly be infringed simply because a majority of the people choose that it be."

4. *Supermajorities.* If *Reynolds* was designed in part to protect majoritarianism and to prevent minority control of government, may a state constitutionally require the assent of a "supermajority" to enact legislation or take other action? In Gordon v. Lance, 403 U.S. 1 (1971), the Court upheld a West Virginia law prohibiting political subdivisions from incurring bonded indebtedness without the approval of 60 percent of the voters in a referendum election. The Court explained:

> [Any] departure from strict majority rule gives disproportionate power to the minority. But there is nothing in the language of the Constitution, our history or our cases that requires that a majority always prevail on every issue. [The] Constitution itself provides that a simple majority vote is insufficient on some issues. [We] conclude that so long as such provisions do not discriminate against or authorize

discrimination against any identifiable class they do not violate the Equal Protection Clause.

The Court added in a footnote: "We intimate no view on the constitutionality of a provision requiring unanimity or giving a veto power to a very small group. Nor do we decide whether a State may [require] extraordinary majorities for the election of public officers." See also See Lockport v. Citizens for Community Action, 430 U.S. 259 (1977) (upholding a provision that prohibited a new county charter from being adopted unless it was approved by "majorities of the voters who live in the cities within the county, and of those who live outside the cities").

5. *Local government units.* The Court extended *Reynolds* to local governmental units in Avery v. Midland County, 390 U.S. 474 (1968) and Hadley v. Junior College District, 397 U.S. 50 (1970).

6. *Permissible deviations from "one person, one vote."* The courts have developed a number of statistical indices to measure malapportionment. The most prominent index is the "maximum percentage deviation." For example, if a state with a population of ten million is allotted ten congressmen, the ideal district will have a population of one million. If the largest district has a population of 1.1 million (10 percent above the ideal) and the smallest has 0.9 million (10 percent below the ideal), the maximum percentage deviation is 20 percent. What is the maximum percentage deviation that should satisfy *Reynolds*?

a. *Congressional districting.* In Wesberry v. Sanders, 376 U.S. 1 (1964), the Court held that the provision of article I, section 2 that United States representatives "be chosen 'by the People of the several States' means that as nearly as is practicable one man's vote in a congressional election is to be worth as much as another's." The Court thus invalidated a Georgia congressional districting scheme with a maximum percentage deviation of more than 140 percent. The Court has relied on *Wesberry* to invalidate congressional districting plans with much smaller deviations. See Kirkpatrick v. Preisler, 394 U.S. 526 (1969) (5.97 percent); Wells v. Rockefeller, 394 U.S. 542 (1969) (13.1 percent); White v. Weiser, 412 U.S. 783 (1973) (4.13 percent); Karcher v. Daggett, 462 U.S. 725 (1983) (0.7 percent).

In *Kirkpatrick*, the Court held that no variance from absolute equality could be justified as de minimis. In *Karcher*, the Court reaffirmed *Kirkpatrick*. It again explained that states must "come as nearly as practicable to population equality."

b. *State districting.* The Court has tolerated significant deviations from the mathematical ideal in its review of districting plans for state and local offices. For example, in Harris v. Arizona Indep. Redistricting Commn., 136 S. Ct. 1301 (2016), the Court upheld a state redistricting scheme with a maximum population deviation of under 10 percent. Writing for a unanimous Court, Justice Breyer stated that

> those attacking a state-approved plan must show that it is more probable than not that a deviation of less than 10% reflects the predominance of illegitimate reapportionment factors rather than the "legitimate considerations" to which we have referred in Reynolds and other cases. Given the inherent difficulty of measuring and comparing factors that may legitimately account for small deviations from strict mathematical equality, we believe that attacks on deviations under 10% will succeed only rarely, in unusual cases.

7. *The unit of measurement.* The cases discussed above address the extent to which jurisdictions may depart from the ideal of equality. But how should equality be measured? Should the relevant population consist of eligible voters, registered voters, or total population? Suppose, for example, a district has a large number of undocumented noncitizens or a large prison facility where inmates are not permitted to vote within its borders. Is it unconstitutional to consider these persons for purposes of apportionment? How often (and with what degree of accuracy) must the measurement be taken?

Both article I, §2, cl.2 and §2 of the fourteenth amendment provide that members of Congress shall be apportioned among the states "according to their respective numbers." However, the Constitution is silent about how members of Congress should be apportioned within states and about how state legislators should be apportioned.

In practice, all states now utilize a total population measure as determined by the decennial census, but surprisingly, for more than a half century after its decisions in *Reynolds* and *Wesberry*, the Court said virtually nothing about the legality of this practice. It finally addressed the question in Evenwel v. Abbott, 136 S. Ct. 1120 (2016). Districting for the state senate of Texas yielded a maximum total-population deviation of 8.04 percent, well within the Supreme Court's guidelines, but if equality was measured by the total number of eligible or registered voters, the maximum population deviation exceeded 40 percent. Appellants, residents of a district with a large number of voters, claimed that their votes were unconstitutionally diluted under the *Reynolds* one person–one vote standard. In an opinion written by Justice Ginsburg, the Court held that the Constitution did not *require* a voter-based standard, but that "we need not and do not resolve whether [States] *may* draw districts to equalize voter-eligible population" (emphasis added).

According to the Court, a state is permitted (and perhaps required) to assume that a representative serves residents of her district even if they are not permitted to vote. Is this assumption plausible? If it is correct, why can't a state assume that a representative serves residents of the entire state, including people who cannot vote in her district because they live somewhere else?

City of Mobile v. Bolden

446 U.S. 55 (1980)

[Since 1911, the city of Mobile, Alabama, has been governed by a City Commission consisting of three commissioners who jointly exercise all legislative, executive, and administrative power. The commissioners are elected not by the residents of three distinct districts but by the residents of the city at large. This electoral system "is followed by literally thousands of municipalities." Although Mobile has a substantial black population, no black has ever been elected to the commission. In *Bolden*, the Court rejected a claim that the retention of the at-large electoral system in such circumstances unconstitutionally diluted the voting strength of blacks.]

MR. JUSTICE STEWART announced the judgment of the Court and delivered an opinion, in which [CHIEF JUSTICE BURGER], MR. JUSTICE POWELL, and MR. JUSTICE REHNQUIST joined.

[At the outset, Justice Stewart observed that the "claim that at-large electoral schemes" violate the equal protection clause "is rooted in their winner-take-all aspects, their tendency to submerge minorities." Stewart noted that, despite this feature, multimember legislative districts "are not unconstitutional per se." Rather, he maintained, they are invalid only if their purpose is "invidiously to minimize or cancel out the voting potential of racial or ethnic minorities." "A plaintiff," in other words, "must prove that the disputed plan was 'conceived or operated' as [a] purposeful devic[e] to further [racial] discrimination." Justice Stewart explained that this "burden of proof is simply one aspect of the basic principle that only if there is purposeful discrimination can there be a violation of the Equal Protection Clause." Applying the intent standard, Justice Stewart concluded that "the evidence [falls] far short of showing that the appellants 'conceived or operated [a] purposeful devic[e] to further racial [discrimination].'"]

We turn finally to the arguments advanced in [Mr.] Justice Marshall's dissenting opinion. The theory [appears] to be that every "political group," or at least every such group that is in the minority, has a federal constitutional right to elect candidates in proportion to its numbers.[22] Moreover, a political group's "right" to have its candidates elected is said to be a "fundamental interest," the infringement of which may be established without proof that a State has acted with the purpose of impairing anybody's access to the political process. This dissenting opinion finds the "right" infringed in the present case because no Negro has been elected to the Mobile City Commission.

Whatever appeal the dissenting opinion's view may have as a matter of political theory, it is not the law. The Equal Protection Clause [does] not require proportional representation as an imperative of political organization. The entitlement that the dissenting opinion assumes to exist simply is not to be found in the Constitution of the United States.

It is of course true that a law that impinges upon a fundamental right [is] presumptively unconstitutional. [And it is true] that the Equal Protection Clause confers a substantive right to participate in elections on an equal basis with other qualified voters. See [Dunn v. Blumstein; Reynolds v. Sims]. But this right to equal participation in the electoral process does not protect any "political group," however defined, from electoral defeat.

The dissenting opinion erroneously discovers the asserted entitlement to group representation within the "one person, one vote" principle of Reynolds v. Sims, supra, and its progeny. [The] Court [there] recognized that a voter's right to "have an equally effective voice" in the election of representatives is impaired where representation is not apportioned substantially on a population basis. [There] can be, of course, no claim that the "one person, one vote" principle has been violated in this case, because the city of Mobile is a unitary electoral district and the Commission elections are conducted at large. It is therefore obvious that nobody's vote has been "diluted" in the sense in which that word was used in

---

22. The dissenting opinion seeks to disclaim this description of its theory by suggesting that a claim of vote dilution may require, in addition to proof of electoral defeat, some evidence of "historical and social factors" indicating that the group in question is without political influence. [Putting] to the side the evident fact that these gauzy sociological considerations have no constitutional basis, it remains far from certain that they could, in any principled manner, exclude the claims of any discrete political group that happens, for whatever reason, to elect fewer of its candidates than arithmetic indicates it might. Indeed, the putative limits are bound to prove illusory if the express purpose informing their application would be, as the dissent assumes, to redress the "inequitable distribution of political influence."

the *Reynolds* case. [It] is, of course, true that the right of a person to vote on an equal basis with other voters draws much of its significance from the political associations that its exercise reflects, but it is an altogether different matter to conclude that political groups themselves have an independent constitutional claim to representation.[26]

[Reversed and remanded.]

[Opinions by Justices Blackmun and Stevens concurring in the judgment and by Justices Brennan and White dissenting are omitted].

Mr. Justice Marshall, dissenting. . . .

[The] equal protection problem attacked by the "one person, one vote" principle is [one] of vote dilution: under *Reynolds*, each citizen must have an "equally effective voice" in the election of representatives. In the present cases, the alleged vote dilution, though caused by the combined effects of the electoral structure and social and historical factors rather than by unequal population distribution, is analytically the same concept: the unjustified abridgment of a fundamental right. . . .

The plurality's response is that my approach amounts to nothing less than a constitutional requirement of proportional representation for groups. [I] explicitly reject the notion that the Constitution contains any such requirement. The constitutional protection against vote dilution [does] not extend to those situations in which a group has merely failed to elect representatives in proportion to its share of the population. To prove unconstitutional vote dilution, the group is also required to carry the far more onerous burden of demonstrating that it has been effectively fenced out of the political process. Typical of the plurality's mischaracterization of my position is its assertion that I would provide protection against vote dilution for "every 'political group,' or at least every such group that is in the minority." The vote-dilution doctrine can logically apply only to groups whose electoral discreteness and insularity allow dominant political factions to ignore them.

The plaintiffs [proved] that no Negro had ever been elected to the Mobile City Commission, despite the fact that Negroes constitute about one-third of the electorate, and that the persistence of severe racial bloc voting made it highly unlikely that any Negro could be elected at large in the foreseeable future. [The] plaintiffs convinced the District Court that Mobile Negroes were unable to use alternative avenues of political influence. They showed that Mobile Negroes still suffered pervasive present effects of massive historical official and private

---

26. It is difficult to perceive how the implications of the dissenting opinion's theory of group representation could rationally be cabined. Indeed, certain preliminary practical questions immediately come to mind: Can only members of a minority of the voting population in a particular municipality be members of a "political group"? How large must a "group" be to be a "political group"? Can any "group" call itself a "political group"? If not, who is to say which "groups" are "political groups"? Can a qualified voter belong to more than one "political group"? Can there be more than one "political group" among white voters (e.g., Irish-American, Italian-American, Polish-American, Jews, Catholics, Protestants)? Can there be more than one "political group" among nonwhite voters? Do the answers to any of these questions depend upon the particular demographic composition of a given city? Upon the total size of its voting population? Upon the size of its governing body? Upon its form of government? Upon its history? Its geographic location? The fact that even these preliminary questions may be largely unanswerable suggests some of the conceptual and practical fallacies in the constitutional theory espoused by the dissenting opinion, putting to one side the total absence of support for that theory in the Constitution itself.

discrimination, and that the City Commission had been quite unresponsive to the needs of the minority community. [Negroes] are grossly underrepresented on city boards and committees. [The] city's distribution of public services is racially discriminatory. . . .

[Even if] it is assumed that proof of discriminatory intent is necessary to support the vote-dilution claims in these cases, the question becomes what evidence will satisfy this requirement. . . .

I would apply the common-law foreseeability presumption to the present cases. . . .

The plurality [fails] to recognize that the maintenance of multimember districts in the face of foreseeable discriminatory consequences strongly suggests that officials are blinded by "racially selective sympathy and indifference." Like outright racial hostility, selective racial indifference reflects a belief that the concerns of the minority are not worthy of the same degree of attention paid to problems perceived by whites. When an interest as fundamental as voting is diminished along racial lines, a requirement that discriminatory purpose must be proved should be satisfied by a showing that official action was produced by this type of pervasive bias. . . .

Note: Vote Dilution and the Interests of Groups

1. A *"fundamental interest" in "proportional" representation?* Do you agree with Justice Stewart that there is no constitutional right to proportional representation? How would you distinguish between "one person, one vote" and "one group, one representative"? Consider Note, The Constitutional Imperative of Proportional Representation, 94 Yale L.J. 163, 172–173, 175–176, 182 (1984):

> Two fundamental values underlie the Supreme Court's debate about constitutional rights in voting: majority rule and minority representation. The debate has taken the traditional system of winner-take-all single-member districts as a given. [But this] system contains a strong majoritarian bias. If the supporters of two parties were distributed uniformly throughout the area of the elections, the party winning the most votes would win every seat in the legislature. The votes for the minority candidate would in effect be wasted. [Under the Court's analysis, majority] rule is conceptualized [as] an individual right deserving the strongest protection, whereas minority representation is conceptualized [as] a group right that will not be vindicated without proof of invidious discrimination. But the opposition of individual and group rights is logically [untenable]: The rights labeled as group rights are also individual rights and vice versa. [The] real distinction [is] not between individual and group rights but between the right to an equally weighted vote and the right to an equally powerful or equally meaningful vote.

Is it clear that proportional representation is always in the interest of an electoral minority? Might not a minority be better off with numerous representatives at least partly beholden to it than with one or two representatives wholly within its control? Consider also the view that it is false and pernicious to refer to something called "the interest of African Americans" and "the interest of whites," as if these were unitary things rather than to emphasize overlapping interests among racial and other groups.

2. *The permissibility of "fair representation."* City of Mobile holds that a "fair representation" system is not constitutionally mandatory. Is it constitutionally

permissible? In Gaffney v. Cummings, 412 U.S. 735 (1973), the challengers of the districting plan maintained that, even if the plan satisfied the one person–one vote requirement of *Reynolds*, it was nonetheless "invidiously discriminatory" because it was admittedly drawn to "achieve a rough approximation of statewide political strengths of the Democratic and Republican Parties." The Court held that the "political fairness principle" was not unconstitutional:

> Politics and political considerations are inseparable from districting and apportionment. [It] may be suggested that those who redistrict and reapportion should work with census, not political, data and achieve population equality without regard for political impact. But this politically mindless approach may produce, whether intended or not, the most grossly gerrymandered results. [Districting schemes may be invalid] if racial or political groups [are] fenced out of the political process and their voting strength invidiously minimized, [but there is no] constitutional warrant to invalidate a state plan, otherwise within tolerable population limits, because it undertakes, not to minimize or eliminate the political strength of any group or party, but to recognize it and, through districting, provide a rough sort of proportional representation in the legislative halls of the State.

Suppose that you are a Republican living in a district deliberately created under a "political fairness" plan to elect a Democrat. Is it a sufficient answer to your complaint about this districting that some other district has been deliberately created so as to elect a Republican?

The Court has been much more skeptical of the "fairness" principle when it has been utilized to insure "fair representation" of racial groups. In Miller v. Johnson, 515 U.S. 900 (1995), the Court held that where "race was the predominant factor motivating the legislature's decision to place a significant number of voters within or without a particular district," and where the legislature "subordinated traditional race-neutral districting principles," a fourteenth amendment violation had been made out. Taken together, *Gaffney* and *Miller* stand for the proposition that legislatures are constitutionally permitted to assure equal representation for political parties, but not for minority racial groups. Is this distinction consistent with the purposes and history that underlie the equal protection clause?

3. *Political gerrymandering.* Suppose that a legislature deliberately gerrymanders district lines not to produce fair representation of political groups, but to understate the voting strength of such a group.

a. Vieth. In Vieth v. Jubelirer, 541 U.S. 267 (2004), a four-justice plurality of the Court, per Justice Scalia, would have held that partisan gerrymandering posed a political question that should not be answered by courts. (This portion of the Court's opinion is excerpted at Chapter 1, section F3, supra.) Justice Kennedy concurred in the judgment, but would not have "[foreclosed] all possibility of judicial relief if some limited and precise rationale were found to correct an established violation of the Constitution in some redistricting cases." Justices Stevens, Souter (joined by Justice Ginsburg), and Breyer filed separate dissents. Consider the views of Justice Breyer:

> [One] should begin by asking why [the] Constitution does not insist that the membership of legislatures better reflect different political views held by different groups of voters. [The] answer [lies] in the fact that a single-member-district system helps to ensure certain democratic objectives better than many "more representative" (i.e., proportional) electoral systems. [Single-member] districts [diminish] the need for

coalition governments. And that fact makes it easier for voters to identify which party is responsible for government decision-making (and which rascals to throw out) while simultaneously providing greater legislative stability. . . .

If single-member districts are the norm, however, then political considerations will likely play an important, and proper, role in the drawing of district boundaries. [Given] a fairly large state population with a fairly large congressional delegation, districts assigned so as to be perfectly random in respect to politics would translate a small shift in political sentiment, say a shift from 51% Republican to 49% Republican, into a seismic shift in the makeup of the legislative delegation, say from 100% Republican to 100% Democratic. [Any] such exaggeration of tiny electoral changes — virtually wiping out legislative representation of the minority party — would itself seem highly undemocratic.

Given the resulting need for single-member districts with nonrandom boundaries, it is not surprising that "traditional" districting principles have rarely, if ever, been politically neutral. . . .

At the same time, these considerations can help identify at least one circumstance where use of purely political boundary-drawing factors can amount to a serious, and remediable, abuse, namely the unjustified use of political factors to entrench a minority in power. By entrenchment I mean a situation in which a party that enjoys only minority support among the populace has nonetheless contrived to take, and hold, legislative power. By unjustified entrenchment, I mean that the minority's hold on power is purely the result of partisan manipulation and not other factors. . . .

Courts need not intervene often to prevent the kind of abuse I have described, because those harmed constitute a political majority, and a majority normally can work its political will. . . .

But we cannot always count on a severely gerrymandered legislature itself to find and implement a remedy. . . .

When it is necessary, a court should prove capable of finding an appropriate remedy. . . .

[Courts] can identify a number of strong indicia of abuse. The presence of actual entrenchment, while not always unjustified (being perhaps a chance occurrence) is such a sign, particularly when accompanied by the use of partisan boundary drawing criteria[, i.e.], a use that both departs from traditional criteria and cannot be explained other than by efforts to achieve partisan advantage. [The] scenarios fall along a continuum: The more permanently entrenched the minority's hold on power becomes, the less evidence courts will need that the minority engaged in gerrymandering to achieve the desired result.

Compare Justice Scalia's response:

The criterion Justice Breyer proposes is nothing more precise than "the unjustified use of political factors to entrench a minority in power." While he invokes in passing the Equal Protection Clause, it should be clear to any reader that what constitutes unjustified entrenchment depends on his own theory of "effective government." While one must agree with Justice Breyer's incredibly abstract starting point that our Constitution sought to create a "basically democratic" form of government, that is a long and impassable distance away from the conclusion that the Judiciary may assess whether a group (somehow defined) has achieved a level of political power (somehow defined) commensurate with that to which they would be entitled absent unjustified political machinations (whatever that means).

b. Perry. In League of United Latin American Citizens v. Perry, 548 U.S. 399 (2006), the Court confronted a controversial effort by Texas Republicans to redraw congressional district lines in 2003 after they had gained control of both houses of the state legislature the year earlier. The redistricting was a radical departure from the normal practice of changing district lines only after the decennial census.

After the 1990 census, Democrats, then in control of the state legislature and governorship, redrew district lines in a fashion that led to only thirteen Republican seats out of thirty despite Republicans carrying 59 percent of the state-wide vote. After the 2000 census, the legislature, then divided between a Republican Senate and a Democratic House, could not agree on a districting plan. As a result, a federal district court imposed a new plan that, to the extent possible, tracked the 1990 plan. The Court-imposed plan gave the Republicans an advantage in twenty of the thirty-two congressional seats, but in the actual election (held in 2002), Republicans were unable to fully capitalize on this advantage and won only fifteen of the thirty-two seats.

When the Republicans gained control of the State House of Representatives, the Republican Governor called a special session of the legislature in order to replace the Court-imposed plan. The result was a dramatic standoff, with the legislature temporarily unable to act because Democratic Senators left the state so as to deprive the Senate of a quorum. Eventually, a plan was enacted which, the district court found, had the "single-minded purpose of [gaining] partisan advantage." In elections held under the new plan in 2004, Republicans gained six congressional seats over their 2002 total.

In a portion of his opinion announcing the judgment in which he wrote only for himself, Justice Kennedy rejected the argument that mid-decennial redistricting, when solely motivated by partisan objectives, is unconstitutional:

> [A] successful claim attempting to identify unconstitutional acts of partisan gerrymandering must do what appellants' sole-motivation theory explicitly disavows: show a burden, as measured by a reliable standard, on the complainants' representational rights. . . .
>
> [The new plan] can be seen as making the party balance more congruent to statewide party power. To be sure, there is no constitutional requirement of proportional representation, and equating a party's statewide share of the vote with its portion of the congressional delegation is a rough measure at best. Nevertheless, a congressional plan that more closely reflects the distribution of state party power seems a less likely vehicle for partisan discrimination than one that entrenches an electoral minority. By this standard [the new plan] can be seen as fairer than the plan that survived in *Vieth* and the two previous Texas [plans].

Justice Stevens, in an opinion joined by Justice Breyer, dissented from the Court's judgment upholding the mid-decennial partisan districting.

Justice Souter, in an opinion joined by Justice Ginsburg, stated that he saw "nothing to be gained by working through these cases on the standard I would have applied in *Vieth* because here as in *Vieth* we have no majority for any single criterion of impermissible gerrymander. [I] therefore treat the broad issue of gerrymander much as the subject of an improvident grant of certiorari." He added that he did not "share Justice Kennedy's seemingly flat rejection of any test of gerrymander turning on the process followed in redistricting."

Writing for himself and Justice Alito, Chief Justice Roberts agreed with the determination that appellants have not provided "a reliable standard for identifying unconstitutional political gerrymanders." He added that "[the] question whether any such standard exists — that is, whether a challenge to a political gerrymander presents a justiciable case or controversy — has not been argued in these cases. I therefore take no position on that question, which has divided the Court."

Writing for himself and Justice Thomas, Justice Scalia reaffirmed his position in *Vieth* that partisan gerrymandering claims are nonjusticiable.

In light of *Vieth* and *Perry*, how should lower courts treat cases of partisan gerrymandering?

c. *Nonpartisan redistricting.* In Arizona State Legislature v. Arizona Independent Redistricting Commn., 135 S. Ct. 2652 (2015), the Court, in an opinion by Justice Ginsburg, upheld Arizona's decision to vest redistricting decisions in an independent redistricting commission. Petitioners argued that the commission violated article I, §4, cl. 1 of the Constitution which provides that "[the] Times, Places and Manner of holding Elections for Senators and Representatives, shall be prescribed in each state by the Legislature [thereof]." The Court rejected this argument, noting that "[the] history and purpose of the Clause weigh heavily against such a preclusion, as does the animating principle of our Constitution that the people themselves are the originating source of all powers of government." Chief Justice Roberts, joined by Justices Scalia, Thomas, and Alito; Justice Scalia, joined by Justice Thomas; and Justice Thomas, joined by Justice Scalia filed dissenting opinions.

c.   Denial of "Access to the Ballot"

WILLIAMS v. RHODES, 393 U.S. 23 (1968). Under Ohio law, political parties that had received 10 percent of the vote in the prior gubernatorial election automatically qualified for the next presidential election ballot. Other political parties, however, could earn a place on the ballot only if they had an elaborate party structure, held "a primary election conforming to detailed and rigorous standards," and filed a petition nine months before the election signed "by qualified electors totaling 15 percent of the number of ballots cast in the last preceding gubernatorial election." Noting that the law had "made it virtually impossible for a new political party [to] be placed on [the] ballot," the Court invalidated the Ohio scheme.

Justice Black delivered the opinion of the Court: "In determining whether or not a state law violates the Equal Protection Clause, we must consider the facts and circumstances behind the law, the interests which the State claims to be protecting, and the interests of those who are disadvantaged by the classification. [Here] the state laws [burden] two different, although overlapping, kinds of rights — the right of individuals to associate for the advancement of political beliefs, and the right of qualified voters [to] cast their votes effectively. [The challenged laws] give the two old, established parties a decided advantage [and] thus place substantially unequal burdens on both the right to vote and the right to associate. [In] determining whether the State has power to place such unequal burdens on minority groups where rights of this kind are at stake, [we] have consistently held that 'only a compelling interest [can] justify limiting [such] freedoms.' . . .

"The State asserts that [it] may validly promote a two-party system in order to encourage compromise and political stability. [But] the Ohio system does not merely favor a 'two-party system'; it favors two particular parties — the

Republicans and the Democrats — and in effect [gives] them a complete monopoly. [Ohio argues further] that its highly restrictive provisions are justified because without them a large number of parties might qualify for the ballot, and the voters would then be confronted with a choice so confusing that the popular will could be frustrated. But [experience] demonstrates that no more than a handful of parties attempts to qualify for ballot positions even when a very low number of signatures, such as 1% of the electorate, is required. [Thus,] at the present time this danger [is] no more than 'theoretically imaginable.' No such remote danger can justify the immediate and crippling impact on the basic constitutional rights involved in this case."

Justice Harlan concurred in the result on the ground "that Ohio's statutory scheme violates the basic right of political association assured by the First Amendment." Chief Justice Warren and Justices Stewart and White dissented.

Note: Williams *and Its Progeny*

1. *Access to the ballot.* If there is a fundamental interest in gaining access to the franchise, is there necessarily also a fundamental interest in gaining access to the ballot? Whose right is the Court protecting? The candidate's? The party member's? The potential voter's?

2. *Petition requirements.* In Jenness v. Forston, 403 U.S. 431 (1971), the Court distinguished *Williams* and unanimously upheld a Georgia law providing that any political organization whose candidate received 20 percent of the vote at the most recent gubernatorial or presidential election automatically qualified for the ballot, but that a nominee of any other political organization must file a petition five months before the election signed by at least 5 percent of those eligible to vote at the last election for the office he is seeking. The Court explained:

> Unlike Ohio, Georgia freely provides for write-in votes, [it] does not require every candidate to be the nominee of a political party, [it] does not fix an unreasonably early filing deadline, [and it] does not impose upon a small party or a new party [the] requirement of establishing elaborate primary election [machinery]. In a word, Georgia in no way freezes the status [quo].

See also American Party of Texas v. White, 415 U.S. 767 (1974) (conditioning minor party ballot access on holding a nominating convention and obtaining signatures totaling at least 1 percent of the persons voting in the last preceding gubernatorial election); Illinois State Board of Elections v. Socialist Workers Party, 440 U.S. 173 (1979) (invalidating a state statute that had the effect of requiring more signatures to qualify for access to the ballot in Chicago elections than in statewide elections); Munro v. Socialist Workers Party, 479 U.S. 189 (1986) (upholding statute that required minor party to receive at least 1 percent of the votes cast in a "blanket primary" at which registered voters could vote for any candidate, irrespective of the candidate's political party affiliation).

3. *Filing fees.* In Lubin v. Panish, 415 U.S. 709 (1974), the Court invalidated as applied to indigents a California law requiring payment of a filing fee of 2 percent of the annual salary for the office sought. The Court pointed out that "a wealthy candidate with not the remotest chance of election may secure a place on the ballot by writing a check [while] impecunious but serious candidates may be

prevented from running" and held that "a State may [not] require from an indigent candidate filing fees he cannot pay."

4. *Party loyalty requirements.* In Storer v. Brown, 415 U.S. 724 (1974), the Court upheld a California statute forbidding a ballot position to an independent candidate who "had a registered affiliation with [a] political party at any time within one year prior to the immediately preceding primary election." The Court explained:

> [The challenged provision] involves no discrimination against independents. [Just as] the independent candidate must be clear of political party affiliations for a year before the primary, the party candidate must not have been registered with another party for a year before he files his [declaration]. [The challenged provision] protects the direct primary process by refusing to recognize independent candidates who do not make early plans to leave a [party]. It works against independent candidacies prompted by short-range political goals, pique, or personal quarrel. [It thus] furthers the State's [compelling] interest in the stability of its political system.

In Tashjian v. Republican Party, 479 U.S. 208 (1986), the Court distinguished *Storer* and invalidated a Connecticut statute requiring the voters in any party primary to be registered members of that party. The Republican Party, which had adopted a party rule permitting independents to vote in its primary, challenged the provision. Writing for the Court, Justice Marshall distinguished *Storer* as follows:

> The statute in *Storer* was designed to protect the parties and the party system against the disorganizing effect of independent candidacies launched by unsuccessful putative party nominees. This protection [was] undertaken to prevent the disruption of the political parties from without, and not, as in this case, to prevent the parties from taking internal steps affecting their own process for the selection of candidates. . . .
>
>   The Party's determination of the boundaries of its own association, and of the structure which best allows it to pursue its political goals, is protected by the Constitution.

Justice Stevens, joined by Justice Scalia, dissented. Justice Scalia also wrote a separate dissenting opinion, joined by Chief Justice Rehnquist and Justice O'Connor.

5. *Disqualification of public officials.* In Clements v. Fashing, 457 U.S. 957 (1982), the Court upheld two provisions of the Texas Constitution. Section 19 provides that certain public officials shall not "be eligible to the Legislature" until the expiration of their current term of office. Section 65 provides that certain public officials who run for any other state or federal office must automatically resign their current position.

In a plurality opinion, Justice Rehnquist, joined by Chief Justice Burger and Justices Powell and O'Connor, reasoned:

> [We have never held that] candidacy [is] a "fundamental right." [Rather, our] ballot access cases [focus] on the degree to which the challenged restrictions operate as a mechanism to exclude certain classes of candidates from the electoral process. The inquiry is whether the challenged restriction unfairly or unnecessarily burdens the "availability of political opportunity." [The] Court has departed from traditional equal protection analysis [in] two [lines] of ballot access cases. One line [involves]

classifications based on wealth. [E.g., *Lubin.*] The second [involves] classification schemes that impose burdens on new or small political parties or independent candidates. [E.g., *Williams; White; Storer.*] The provisions [challenged] in this case do not [fall within either of these lines]. [It is thus] necessary to examine the provisions in question in terms of the extent of the burdens that they place on the candidacy of current holders of public office. [Section 19] merely prohibits officeholders from cutting short their current term of office in order to serve in the Legislature. [As applied to appellee, a Justice of the Peace, section 19 establishes] a maximum "waiting period" of two [years]. A "waiting period" is hardly a significant barrier to candidacy. [Citing *Storer.*] We conclude that this sort of insignificant interference with access to the ballot need only rest on a rational predicate in order to [survive]. Section 19 clearly rests on a rational predicate [for] Texas has a legitimate interest in discouraging its Justices of the Peace from vacating their current terms of office. [The] burdens that §65 imposes on candidacy are even less substantial than those imposed by §19 [and the] two provisions [serve] essentially the same state interests.

6. *A different approach?* In Anderson v. Celebrezze, 460 U.S. 780 (1983), the Court invalidated an Ohio law requiring independent candidates to file their nominating petitions in mid-March in order to qualify for the ballot in the November election. Interestingly, Justice Stevens's majority opinion relied on the first amendment rather than the equal protection clause:

[We] base our conclusions directly on the First [Amendment] and do not engage in a separate Equal Protection Clause analysis. We rely, however, on the analysis in a number or our prior election cases resting on the Equal Protection Clause. [These] cases, applying the "fundamental rights" strand of equal protection analysis, have identified the First [Amendment] rights implicated by restrictions on the eligibility of voters and [candidates]. Constitutional challenges to specific provisions of a State's election laws [cannot] be resolved by any "litmus-paper test" that will separate valid from invalid restrictions. Instead, a court [must] first consider the character and magnitude of the asserted injury to [First Amendment rights]. It then must identify and evaluate the precise interests put forward by the State as justifications for the burden imposed. [The] Court must not only determine the legitimacy and strength of each of those interests; it also must consider the extent to which those interests make it necessary to burden [First Amendment] rights. Only after weighing all these factors is the reviewing court in a position to decide whether the challenged provision is unconstitutional.

The Court concluded that Ohio's interests in "voter education, equal treatment for partisan and independent candidates, and political stability" were either illegitimate or too remotely related to the early filing deadline to justify such a substantial barrier to independent candidates.

2.   Access to the Judicial Process

If there is a fundamental interest in equal access to the franchise, is there also a fundamental interest in equal access to the judicial process?

GRIFFIN v. ILLINOIS, 351 U.S. 12 (1956). The Court held that a state must furnish an indigent criminal defendant with a free trial transcript if such a transcript is necessary for "adequate and effective appellate review" of his conviction. In a plurality opinion, Justice Black, joined by Chief Justice Warren and Justices Douglas and Clark, explained: "[Our] constitutional guaranties of due process and equal protection both call for procedures in criminal trials which allow no invidious discriminations between persons and different groups of persons. [Plainly] the ability to pay costs in advance bears no rational relationship to a defendant's guilt or innocence and could not be used as an excuse to deprive a defendant of a fair trial. [It] is true that a State is not required by the Federal Constitution to provide appellate courts or a right to appellate review at all. See, e.g., McKane v. Durston, 153 U.S. 684 [1894]. But that is not to say that a State that does grant appellate review can do so in a way that discriminates against some convicted defendants on account of their poverty. . . .

"[To] deny adequate appellate review to the poor means that many of them may lose their life, liberty or property because of unjust convictions which appellate courts would set aside. [Such] a denial is a misfit in a country dedicated to affording equal justice to all and special privileges to none in the administration of its criminal law. There can be no equal justice where the kind of trial a man gets depends on the amount of money he has. Destitute defendants must be afforded as adequate appellate review as defendants who have money enough to buy transcripts."

Justice Frankfurter concurred in the judgment. Justices Burton, Minton, Reed, and Harlan dissented.

DOUGLAS v. CALIFORNIA, 372 U.S. 353 (1963). In a six-to-three decision, the Court held unconstitutional a California rule requiring state appellate courts, on the request of an indigent criminal defendant for counsel on appeal, to make "an independent investigation of the record" and to "appoint counsel [only] if in their opinion it would be helpful to the defendant or the court." Justice Douglas delivered the opinion of the Court:

"[The denial] 'of counsel on appeal [to an indigent] would seem to be at least as invidious [a discrimination] as that condemned in [Griffin].' [Under the California rule,] the type of an appeal a person is afforded [hinges] upon whether or not he can pay for the assistance of counsel. . . .

"When an indigent is forced to run this gauntlet of a preliminary showing of merit, the right to appeal does not comport with fair procedure. [The] discrimination is not between 'possibly good and obviously bad cases,' but between cases where the rich man can require the court to listen to argument of counsel before deciding on the merits, but a poor man cannot. There is lacking that equality demanded by the Fourteenth Amendment where the rich man, who appeals as of right, enjoys the benefit of counsel's examination into the record, research of the law, and marshalling of arguments on his behalf, while the indigent, already burdened by a preliminary determination that his case is without merit, is forced to shift for himself. The indigent, where the record is unclear or the errors are hidden, has only the right to a meaningless ritual, while the rich man has a meaningful appeal."

Justice Harlan, joined by Justice Stewart, dissented.

Note: Fundamental Interests and the Criminal Justice System

1. *The basis of* Griffin *and* Douglas: *wealth as a "suspect" classification.* As in *Harper,* section E1a, supra, the Court in *Griffin* and *Douglas* relied on both the

"suspect" classification and the "fundamental" interest aspects of equal protection analysis. To what extent, if any, can *Griffin* and *Douglas* be explained on the ground that "a State can no more discriminate on account of poverty than on account of religion, race, or color"? Consider that the rules invalidated in *Griffin* and *Douglas* (a) do not expressly classify on the basis of wealth but instead involved a fee of the sort that is charged in the private market and often by the state as it provides services; (b) like ordinary license fees, have a differential effect on the poor; and (c) unlike the poll tax, were invalidated not in their entirety but only as applied to the poor.

2. *The basis of* Griffin *and* Douglas: *equal access to appeal as a fundamental interest.* Justice Black conceded in *Griffin* that there is no constitutional right "to appellate review." How, then, does he justify his implicit conclusion that the right "to appellate review" is fundamental? In *Harper*, the Court suggested that the right to vote is fundamental because it is "preservative of all rights." Perhaps the "right to sue and defend in the courts" is similarly fundamental because "it is the right conservative of all other rights, and lies at the foundation of orderly government." Chambers v. Baltimore & Ohio Railroad, 207 U.S. 142, 148 (1907).

3. *Equal protection or due process?* What is the real concern in *Griffin* and *Douglas* — the inequality or the lack of an effective opportunity to appeal? If the due process clause guarantees a right to appeal, *Griffin* and *Douglas* would pose a coherent due process issue. But everyone seems to agree that the due process clause does not require the states to create an appellate system, and that there is thus no due process right to appeal. That being so, can one sensibly argue that the restrictions at issue in *Griffin* and *Douglas* violate due process because they limit the opportunity to appeal? Consider the following argument: Even if the due process clause does not require a state to create an appellate system, it does require a state that decides voluntarily to create such a system to permit access to the system unless its restrictions are justified by important government interests.

If there is no due process right to appeal, can one nonetheless argue that the interest in equal access to appeal is "fundamental" for purposes of the equal protection clause?

4. *The limits of* Griffin *and* Douglas. In Ross v. Moffitt, 417 U.S. 600 (1974), the Court held that the Constitution does not require states to provide counsel for indigent defendants petitioning for discretionary state appellate review or for review in the U.S. Supreme Court. Justice Rehnquist delivered the opinion of the Court:

> The precise rationale for the *Griffin* and *Douglas* lines of cases has never been explicitly stated, some support being derived from the Equal Protection Clause [and] some from the Due Process [Clause]. Neither clause by itself provides an entirely satisfactory basis for the result reached, each depending on a different inquiry which emphasizes different factors. . . .
>
> We do not believe that the Due Process Clause requires North Carolina to provide [counsel in this situation]. [T]he State need not provide any appeal at all. [The] fact that an appeal *has* been provided does not automatically mean that a State then acts unfairly by refusing to provide counsel to indigent defendants at every stage of the way. [Unfairness] results only if indigents are singled out by the State and denied meaningful access to the appellate system because of their poverty. That question is more profitably considered under an equal protection analysis. . . .

The [equal protection clause] "does not require absolute equality or precisely equal advantages," nor does it require the State to "equalize economic conditions." It does require that the state appellate system be "free of unreasoned distinctions," and that indigents have an adequate opportunity to present their claims fairly within the adversary system. The State cannot adopt procedures which leave an indigent defendant "entirely cut off from any appeal at all," by virtue of his indigency, or extend to such indigent defendants merely a "meaningless ritual" while others in better economic circumstances have a "meaningful appeal." That question is not one of absolutes, but one of degrees. . . .

North Carolina has followed the mandate of Douglas v. California [and] authorized appointment of counsel for a convicted defendant appealing to the intermediate Court of Appeals, but has not gone beyond *Douglas* to provide for appointment of counsel for a defendant who seeks [review] in the Supreme Court of North Carolina or a writ of certiorari here. We do not believe that [a] defendant in respondent's circumstances is denied meaningful access to the [state] Supreme Court [or to this Court] simply because the State does not appoint counsel to aid him in seeking [review]. At that stage he will have, at the very least, a transcript or other record of trial proceedings, a brief on his behalf in the Court of Appeals setting forth his claims of error, and in many cases an opinion by the Court of Appeals disposing of his case. These materials [would] appear to provide [an] adequate basis for [the] decision to grant or deny review.

Justice Douglas, joined by Justices Brennan and Marshall, dissented. See also United States v. MacCollom, 426 U.S. 317 (1976) (criminal defendant has no right to a free transcript to challenge federal conviction on collateral review); Fuller v. Oregon, 417 U.S. 40 (1974) (state may recoup legal expenses paid on behalf of a convicted defendant to the extent that he later becomes able to pay). But see James v. Strange, 407 U.S. 128 (1972) (invalidating a statute providing for the recoupment of all state expenditures for indigent defendants because the statute deprived such defendants of all the exemptions and restrictions ordinarily afforded civil judgment debtors and thus failed to accord "even treatment of indigent criminal defendants with other classes of debtors"); Rinaldi v. Yeager, 384 U.S. 305 (1966) (invalidating on similar grounds a statute requiring unsuccessful appellants confined to prison, but not those receiving suspended sentences, placed on probation, or penalized only by a fine, to repay the state for the cost of transcripts).

5. *Imprisonment for failure to pay a fine.* In Williams v. Illinois, 399 U.S. 235 (1970), appellant, who had been convicted of petty theft, received the maximum authorized sentence of one year in prison and a $500 fine. A state statute provided that defendants in default of payment of a fine must remain in jail to "work off" their obligations at a rate of $5 per day. "Applying the teaching [of] *Griffin*" the Court held the statute unconstitutional as applied to an indigent defendant insofar as it authorized imprisonment beyond the maximum statutory term. The Court reasoned that "when the aggregate imprisonment exceeds the maximum period fixed by the statute and results directly from an involuntary nonpayment of a fine or court costs we are confronted with an impermissible discrimination that rests on ability to pay." The Court concluded that no substantial state interest justified the discriminatory impact, for the state had "numerous alternatives," including the use of installment plans, for recouping the monetary penalties from indigents.

See also Tate v. Short, 401 U.S. 395 (1971), in which the Court held that a state could not constitutionally imprison an indigent defendant for failure to pay traffic fines not otherwise punishable by imprisonment, but added that *Williams* did not necessarily preclude imprisonment "as an enforcement method when alternative means are unsuccessful despite the defendant's reasonable efforts to satisfy the fines by those means"; Bearden v. Georgia, 461 U.S. 660 (1983), in which the Court, relying on *Williams* and *Tate*, held that probation may be revoked for nonpayment of a fine only if the probationer made no bona fide effort to pay or there are no "adequate alternative forms of punishment."

BODDIE v. CONNECTICUT, 401 U.S. 371 (1971). The Court held unconstitutional as applied to indigents a state requirement that individuals pay court fees and costs of about $60 in order to sue for divorce. Justice Harlan delivered the opinion of the Court: "American society [bottoms] its systematic definition of individual rights and duties [on] the common-law model. It is to courts [that] we ultimately look for the implementation of a regularized, orderly process of dispute settlement. [It] is upon this premise that this Court has [put] flesh upon the due process principle. [Past] litigation has, however, typically involved rights of defendants — not, as here, persons seeking access to the judicial process in the first instance. This is because our society has been so structured that resort to the courts is not usually the only available, legitimate means of resolving private disputes. Indeed, private structuring of individual relationships [is] largely encouraged in American life, [and] this Court has [thus] seldom been asked to view access to the courts as an element of due process. . . .

"As this Court [has] recognized, marriage involves interests of basic importance in our society. See, e.g., Loving v. Virginia [Chapter 5, section C1, supra]; Skinner v. Oklahoma [section E supra]; Meyer v. Nebraska [section F infra]. It is not surprising, then, that the States have seen fit to oversee many aspects of that institution. Without a prior judicial imprimatur, individuals may freely enter into and rescind commercial contracts, for example, but we are unaware of any jurisdiction where private citizens may covenant for or dissolve marriages without state approval. [The] State's refusal to admit these appellants to its courts, the sole means in Connecticut for obtaining a divorce, must be regarded as the equivalent of denying them an opportunity to be heard upon their claimed right to a dissolution of their marriages, and, in the absence of a sufficient countervailing [justification,] a denial of due process."

The Court emphasized that "[w]e do not decide that access for all individuals to the courts is a right that is, in all circumstances, guaranteed by the Due Process Clause," but only that, "given the basic position of the marriage relationship in this society's hierarchy of values and the concomitant state monopolization of the means for legally dissolving this relationship, due process does prohibit a State from denying, solely because of inability to pay, access to its courts to individuals who seek judicial dissolution of their marriages."

Justice Douglas and Justice Brennan concurred.

Justice Black dissented: "[*Griffin* is distinguishable.] Civil lawsuits [are] not like government prosecutions for crime. [In] such cases the government is not usually involved as a party, and there is no deprivation of life, liberty, or property as punishment for crime. [There] is consequently no necessity [why] government should in civil trials be hampered [by the strict] due process rules the

Constitution has provided to protect people charged with crime. [The] Court's opinion appears to rest solely on a philosophy that any law violates due process if it is unreasonable, arbitrary, indecent, deviates from the fundamental, is shocking to the conscience, or fails to meet other tests [equally] lacking in any possible constitutional precision. [The] Due Process and Equal Protection Clauses [do not justify] judges in trying [to] hold laws constitutional or not on the basis of a judge's sense of fairness."

Note: Access to the Judicial Process in Civil Cases

1. Boddie *extended.*
   a. *Little v. Streater, 452 U.S. 1 (1981).* A state law required the party moving for blood grouping tests in a paternity action to pay for the tests, as applied to an indigent party. In a unanimous opinion written by Chief Justice Burger, the Court held that the payment requirement violated the due process clause.
   b. *M.L.B. v. S.L.J., 519 U.S. 102 (1996).* A state law conditioned appeals from trial court decrees terminating parental rights on the affected party's payment of fees for preparation of the record. In an opinion written by Justice Ginsburg, the Court held that the law violated both the due process and the equal protection clauses. Justice Kennedy wrote an opinion concurring in the judgment. Chief Justice Rehnquist and Justice Thomas, joined by Justice Scalia and, in part, by Chief Justice Rehnquist, wrote dissenting opinions.
   c. *Turner v. Rogers, 564 U.S. 431 (2011).* The state failed to provide counsel to an indigent person faced with incarceration for civil contempt for failure to pay child support. In a five-to-four decision, the Court, in an opinion by Justice Breyer, held that the due process clause did not automatically require the provision of counsel, but that Turner's incarceration violated due process because the state had failed to provide him with alternative safeguards. Justice Thomas, joined by Justice Scalia and Chief Justice Roberts and Justice Alito in part, dissented.
2. Boddie *distinguished.*
   a. *United States v. Kras, 409 U.S. 434 (1973).* The Bankruptcy Act requires individuals seeking voluntary discharge to pay costs and fees of about $50. In a five-to-four decision, the Court, in an opinion written by Justice Blackmun, upheld the provision. The Court emphasized that bankruptcy, unlike divorce, was not an interest of fundamental importance under the Constitution and that the government's control over the dissolution of debt was not exclusive in the same way that its control over divorce was. Justice Stewart, joined by Justices Douglas, Brennan, and Marshall, and Justice Marshall wrote dissenting opinions.
   b. *Ortwein v. Schwab, 410 U.S. 656 (1973).* By a five-to-four vote, the Court, in a per curiam opinion, upheld a $25 appellate court filing fee as applied to indigents who sought to appeal administrative decisions reducing their welfare benefits. The Court again emphasized that the interest in increased welfare payments had less constitutional significance than the interest in divorce. Justices Douglas, Stewart, Brennan, and Marshall dissented. On welfare as a "fundamental" interest, see section E4 infra.
3. *Due process or equal protection?* Note Justice Harlan's reliance on due process rather than equal protection. Does Justice Harlan's analysis invalidate every limitation on the filing of divorce actions or only those that exclude the poor?

3. Travel

Shapiro v. Thompson
394 U.S. 618 (1969)

Mr. Justice Brennan delivered the opinion of the Court.

[Each of these three appeals is] from a decision [holding] unconstitutional a State or District of Columbia statutory provision which denies welfare assistance to residents [who] have not resided within their jurisdictions for at least one year immediately preceding their applications for such assistance. We affirm. . . .

There is no dispute that the effect of the waiting-period requirement [is] to create two classes of needy resident families indistinguishable from each other except that one is composed of residents who have resided a year or more, and the second of residents who have resided less than a year, in the jurisdiction. [The] second class is denied welfare aid upon which may depend the ability of the families to obtain the very means to subsist — food, shelter, and other necessities of life. [This scheme] constitutes an invidious discrimination [denying] equal protection of the laws. [The] interests which appellants assert are promoted by the classification either may not constitutionally be promoted by government or are not compelling governmental interests.

Primarily, appellants justify the waiting-period requirement as a protective device to preserve the fiscal integrity of state public assistance programs. It is asserted that people who require welfare assistance during their first year of residence in a State are likely to become continuing burdens on state welfare programs. Therefore, the argument runs, if such people can be deterred from entering the jurisdiction by denying them welfare benefits during the first year, state programs to assist long-time residents will not be impaired by a substantial influx of indigent newcomers. . . .

We do not doubt that the one-year waiting-period device is well suited to discourage the influx of poor families in need of assistance. An indigent who desires to migrate, resettle, find a new job, and start a new life will doubtless hesitate if he knows that he must risk making the move without the possibility of falling back on state welfare assistance during his first year of residence, when his need may be most acute. But the purpose of inhibiting migration by needy persons into the State is constitutionally impermissible.

This Court long ago recognized that the nature of our Federal Union and our constitutional concepts of personal liberty unite to require that all citizens be free to travel throughout the length and breadth of our land uninhibited by statutes, rules, or regulations which unreasonably burden or restrict this movement. . . .

We have no occasion to ascribe the source of this right to travel interstate to a particular constitutional provision. It suffices that, as Mr. Justice Stewart said for the Court in United States v. Guest, 383 U.S. 745, 757–758 (1966): "The constitutional right to travel from one State to another . . . occupies a position fundamental to the concept of our Federal Union. It is a right that has been firmly established and repeatedly recognized. . . ."

Thus, the purpose of deterring the in-migration of indigents cannot serve as justification for the classification created by the one-year waiting period, since that purpose is constitutionally impermissible. If a law has "no other purpose . . . than to chill the assertion of constitutional rights by penalizing those who choose to exercise them, then it [is] patently unconstitutional."

Alternatively, appellants argue that even if it is impermissible for a State to attempt to deter the entry of all indigents, the challenged classification may be justified as a permissible state attempt to discourage those indigents who would enter the State solely to obtain larger benefits. [But] a State may no more try to fence out those indigents who seek higher welfare benefits than it may try to fence out indigents generally. [We] do not perceive why a mother who is seeking to make a new life for herself and her children should be regarded as less deserving because she considers, among other factors, the level of a State's public assistance. Surely such a mother is no less deserving than a mother who moves into a particular State in order to take advantage of its better educational facilities.

Appellants argue further that the challenged classification may be sustained as an attempt to distinguish between new and old residents on the basis of the contribution they have made to the community through the payment of taxes. [But this] would logically permit the State to bar new residents from schools, parks, and libraries or deprive them of police and fire protection. Indeed it would permit the State to apportion all benefits and services according to the past tax contributions of its citizens. The Equal Protection Clause prohibits such an apportionment of state services.[10]

We recognize that a State [may] legitimately attempt to limit its expenditures, whether for public assistance, public education, or any other program. But a State may not accomplish such a purpose by invidious distinctions between classes of its citizens. It could not, for example, reduce expenditures for education by barring indigent children from its schools. Similarly, [appellants] must do more than show that denying welfare benefits to new residents saves money. The saving of welfare costs cannot justify an otherwise invidious classification. . . .

Appellants next advance as justification certain administrative and related governmental objectives allegedly served by the waiting-period requirement. They argue that the requirement (1) facilitates the planning of the welfare budget; (2) provides an objective test of residency; (3) minimizes the opportunity for recipients fraudulently to receive payments from more than one jurisdiction; and (4) encourages early entry of new residents into the labor force.

At the outset, we reject appellants' argument that a mere showing of a rational relationship between the waiting period and these four admittedly permissible state objectives will suffice to justify the classification, [for] in moving from State to State or to the District of Columbia appellees were exercising a constitutional right, and any classification which serves to penalize the exercise of that right, unless shown to be necessary to promote a compelling governmental interest, is unconstitutional. Cf. [Skinner].

[The Court rejects arguments that the waiting period is necessary to facilitate budget predictability, provides an objective test for residency minimizes fraud, or encourages work.]

We conclude therefore that appellants [have] no need to use the one-year requirement for the governmental purposes suggested. Thus, even under traditional equal protection tests a classification of welfare applicants according to whether they have lived in the State for one year would seem irrational and unconstitutional. But, of course, the traditional criteria do not apply in these cases. Since the classification here touches on the fundamental right of interstate

10. We are not dealing here with state insurance programs which may legitimately tie the amount of benefits to the individual's contributions.

movement, its constitutionality must be judged by the stricter standard of whether it promotes a compelling state interest. Under this standard, the waiting-period requirement clearly violates the Equal Protection Clause.[21]

[The Court also rejected the states' argument that Congress had expressly authorized the one-year waiting period and added that, "even if . . . Congress did approve the imposition of a . . . waiting period," such an approval "would be unconstitutional," for "Congress may not authorize the States to violate the Equal Protection Clause."]

MR. JUSTICE STEWART, concurring.

The Court today does *not* "pick out particular human activities, characterize them as 'fundamental,' and give them added protection. . . ." To the contrary, the Court simply recognizes, as it must, an established constitutional right, and gives to that right no less protection than the Constitution itself demands. [As] Mr. Justice Harlan wrote for the Court more than a decade ago, "[T]o justify the deterrent effect . . . on the free exercise . . . of their constitutionally protected right . . . a ' . . . subordinating interest of the State must be compelling.'" [NAACP v. Alabama, 357 U.S. 449 (1958).] . . .

[A dissenting opinion by Chief Justice Warren, joined by Justice Black, is omitted.]

MR. JUSTICE HARLAN, dissenting.

In upholding the equal protection argument, the Court has applied an equal protection doctrine of relatively recent vintage: the rule that statutory classifications which [affect] "fundamental rights" will be held to deny equal protection unless justified by a "compelling" governmental interest.

[I] think this [doctrine] particularly unfortunate [because] it creates an exception which threatens to swallow the standard equal protection rule. Virtually every state statute affects important rights. [The] doctrine is also unnecessary. When the right affected is one assured by the Federal Constitution, any infringement can be dealt with under the Due Process Clause. But when a statute affects only matters not mentioned in the Federal Constitution and is not arbitrary or irrational, I must reiterate that I know of nothing which entitles this Court to pick out particular human activities, characterize them as "fundamental," and give them added protection under an unusually stringent equal protection test. . . .

[If] the issue is regarded purely as one of equal protection, [this] classification should be judged by ordinary equal protection standards. [And in] light of [the] undeniable relation of residence requirements to valid legislative aims, [I] can find no objection to these residence requirements under the Equal Protection Clause. . . .

The next issue [is] whether a one-year welfare residence requirement amounts to an undue burden upon the right of interstate travel [which I conclude] is a "fundamental" right [which] should be regarded as having its source in the Due Process Clause of the Fifth Amendment. . . .

---

21. We imply no view of the validity of waiting-period or residence requirements determining eligibility to vote, eligibility for tuition-free education, to obtain a license to practice a profession, to hunt or fish, and so forth. Such requirements may promote compelling state interests on the one hand, or, on the other, may not be penalties upon the exercise of the constitutional right of interstate travel.

[The decisive question is] whether the governmental interests served by residence requirements outweigh the burden imposed upon the right to travel. [Taking] all of [the] competing considerations into account, I believe that the balance definitely favors constitutionality. In reaching that conclusion, I do not minimize the importance of the right to travel interstate. However, the impact of residence conditions upon that right is indirect and apparently quite insubstantial. On the other hand, the governmental purposes served by the requirements are legitimate and real, and the residence requirements are clearly suited to their accomplishment. To abolish residence requirements might well discourage highly worthwhile experimentation in the welfare field. The statutes come to us clothed with the authority of Congress and attended by a correspondingly heavy presumption of constitutionality. Moreover, although [it is argued] that the same objectives could have been achieved by less restrictive means, this is an area in which the judiciary should be especially slow to fetter [legislative] judgment. . . .

Residence requirements have advantages, such as administrative simplicity and relative certainty, which are not shared by the alternative solutions. . . .

In these circumstances, I cannot find that the burden imposed by residence requirements upon ability to travel outweighs the governmental interests in their continued employment. . . .

SAENZ v. ROE, 526 U.S. 489 (1999). The Court reaffirmed Shapiro v. Thompson, though on new grounds, and invalidated a California law imposing durational residence requirements by limiting welfare benefits during the recipient's first year of residence. More particularly, California amended its welfare program by limiting new residents to the benefits they would have received in the state of their prior residence — a change approved by the Secretary of Health and Human Services and subsequently by Congress. The Court held that the change violated the privileges or immunities clause of the fourteenth amendment.

The Court began by distinguishing three components of the right to travel: (1) the right to enter and leave another state, an inference from the federal structure without explicit textual support; (2) the right to be treated as "a welcome visitor rather than an unfriendly alien when temporarily present" in a second state, a right rooted in article IV, section 2; and (3) "for those travellers who elect to become permanent residents," the right to be treated like other citizens of that state. It was the third component of the right that was at issue in *Saenz*, and the Court squarely rooted that right on the fourteenth amendment ban on "any law which shall abridge the privileges or immunities of citizens of the United States." The discrimination at issue here, against those "who have completed their interstate travel," was clearly a "penalty" on the exercise of the right to travel.

Adhering to *Shapiro*, the Court said that it was illegitimate to defend the classifications "by a purpose to deter welfare applicants from migrating to California"; this was an impermissible purpose. Nor was the prospect of saving $10.9 million annually sufficient. The question is "whether the state may accomplish that end by the discriminatory means it has chosen." The citizenship clause of the fourteenth amendment "does not tolerate a hierarchy of 45 subclasses of similarly situated citizens based on the location of their prior residence." Nor was federal approval sufficient to save the law, since "Congress may not authorize the States to violate the Fourteenth Amendment," and since "the protection afforded to the citizen by the Citizenship Clause of that Amendment is a limitation on the powers of the National Government as well as the States."

Chief Justice Rehnquist, joined by Justice Thomas, dissented. He argued that the right to travel was not implicated, for anyone who has finished his journey is "no longer 'travelling.'" He also objected to what he saw as a new reading of the privileges or immunities clause, contending that the California provision was a reasonable and "bona fide residence requirement," akin to durational residence requirements for college eligibility and for divorce. Thus, this was a legitimate effort to ensure that services provided for state residents are enjoyed only by state residents. Justice Thomas, joined by Justice Rehnquist, urged the Court to investigate the original meaning of the privileges or immunities clause, which, he said, was quite limited. Thus the "privileges or immunities of citizens" were understood as "fundamental rights, rather than every public benefit established by positive law."

Note: The Right to Travel as a "Fundamental Interest"

1. *The right to travel.* As noted in *Shapiro*, the Court has long recognized a constitutional right to travel, even though the precise source of the right had been somewhat obscure before *Saenz*. In Crandall v. Nevada, 73 U.S. (6 Wall.) 35 (1867), for example, the Court invalidated a state law imposing a capitation tax of one dollar on "every person leaving the State by any [vehicle engaged] in the business of transporting passengers for hire." The Court explained that "[for] all the great purposes for which the Federal Government was formed we are one people, with one common country [and] as members of the same community must have the right to pass and repass through every part of it without interruption." Similarly, in Edwards v. California, 314 U.S. 160 (1941), the Court, relying on the commerce clause, invalidated a state statute prohibiting any person from "bringing into the State any indigent person who is not a resident of the State." Four justices concurred on the ground that the statute violated the privileges or immunities clause of the fourteenth amendment. Recall The Slaughter-House Cases, section B supra, and the Court's emphasis on the privileges or immunities clause in *Saenz*.

2. *The right to travel versus equal protection.* Given the Court's view that there is an independent constitutional right to travel, why did the *Shapiro* Court rely on the equal protection clause? Is the alternative approach of the *Saenz* Court more straightforward? Consider the possibility that the "fundamental interests" strand of equal protection jurisprudence provides the Court a lever with which to encourage the affirmative provision of "positive rights" like welfare. In contrast, substantive provisions of the Constitution have traditionally been limited to the protection of "negative rights" and the elimination of burdens rather than the mandating of benefits.

Do the durational residence requirements at issue in *Shapiro* violate the substantive right to travel? Abolition of a welfare program would not have violated the Constitution; perhaps this point makes reliance on the equal protection clause necessary for the *Shapiro* outcome. But if the abolition of a welfare program would be constitutional, and if the program at issue in *Shapiro* interfered with the right to travel less than that (admittedly permissible) outcome, consider whether reliance on the right to travel might not be misleading and the *Shapiro* outcome therefore incorrect. Does the rationale in *Saenz*, emphasizing equal treatment of new permanent residents, clear up the confusion?

Consider the possibility that the result in *Shapiro* actually discourages states from providing adequate levels of welfare. Without the ability to impose durational residency requirements, states confront a "race to the bottom." States are deterred from raising welfare levels because if any single state does so, it will be faced with an in-migration of individuals from surrounding states demanding the benefits. Should the federal government be constitutionally permitted to provide a solution to coordination problems of this sort? See the discussion of Steward Machine Co. v. Davis, 301 U.S. 548 (1937), and the Social Security Act in Chapter 3, section A, supra.

3. *The right to travel and the "necessities of life."* Note the Court's reference in *Shapiro* to the "necessities of life." To what extent does *Shapiro* turn on this aspect of the case? Do laws that unequally distribute the "necessities of life" infringe a "fundamental" interest? This issue is examined in section E4 infra.

Note: *"Penalizing" the Right to Travel*

1. *Impermissible purposes.* The Court in *Shapiro* distinguished between two types of state purposes — those that are "constitutionally impermissible" and those that are permissible but insufficient to satisfy the "compelling" interest standard. Is it "constitutionally impermissible" for a state (a) to attempt to deter "the in-migration of indigents"; (b) to "attempt to discourage those indigents who would enter the State solely to obtain larger benefits"; and (c) to "attempt to distinguish between new and old residents on the basis of the contribution they have made to the community through the payment of taxes"?

In Zobel v. Williams, 457 U.S. 55 (1982), the Court held that an Alaska statute distributing the income derived from its natural resources to adult citizens in varying amounts depending on length of residence in the state violated the equal protection clause. Citing *Shapiro*, the Court dismissed the state's objective of rewarding "citizens for past contributions" as "not a legitimate state purpose."

Consider Justice O'Connor's observations in a concurring opinion:

> [The] Court misdirects its criticism when it labels Alaska's objective illegitimate. A desire to compensate citizens for their prior contributions is neither inherently invidious nor irrational. [The] difficulty is that plans enacted to further this objective necessarily treat new residents of a State less favorably than the longer-term residents who have past contributions to "reward." This inequality [conflicts] with the constitutional purpose of maintaining a Union rather than a mere "league of States." [The] Court's task, therefore, should be (1) to articulate this constitutional principle, explaining its textual sources, and (2) to test the strength of Alaska's objective against the constitutional imperative. [The] Privileges and Immunities Clause of Article IV [addresses] just this type of discrimination. [In this case, the statute is invalid, not because the objective is illegitimate, but because] Alaska has not shown that its new residents are the "peculiar source" of any evil [or that there is] a "substantial relationship" between the evil and the discrimination practiced against the noncitizens.

Consider also the views expressed by Justice Brennan in a separate concurring opinion, joined by Justices Marshall, Blackmun, and Powell:

> [The] illegitimacy of [the] state purpose [reflects] not the structure of the Federal Union but the idea of constitutionally protected equality. [Even if] the Alaska plan

[did not] apply to migrants from sister States [the discrimination would] be constitutionally suspect. [Length] of residence has only the most tenuous relation to the actual service of individuals to the State. Thus, the past contribution rationale proves much too little to provide a rational predicate for discrimination on the basis of length of residence. But it also proves far too much, for "it would permit the State to apportion all benefits and services according to the [past] contributions of its citizens." [*Shapiro*.] In my view, it is difficult to escape from the recognition that underlying any scheme of classification on the basis of duration of residence, we shall almost invariably find the unstated premise that "some citizens are more equal than others." We rejected that premise [when] we adopted the Equal Protection Clause.

In Hooper v. Bernalillo County Assessor, 472 U.S. 612 (1985), the Court held that a New Mexico statute granting a special tax exemption to Vietnam veterans who were New Mexico residents before May 8, 1976, violated the equal protection clause. The Court distinguished *Shapiro*, Dunn v. Blumstein, Memorial Hospital v. Maricopa County, and Sosna v. Iowa, discussed infra, on the ground that they involved waiting periods, whereas the New Mexico statute, like the Alaska law invalidated in *Zobel*, "creates 'fixed, permanent distinctions between . . . classes of concededly bona fide residents' based on when they arrived in the State." The Court held that, "stripped of its asserted justifications, the New Mexico statute suffers from the same constitutional flaw as the Alaska statute in *Zobel*." See also Attorney General of New York v. Soto-Lopez, 476 U.S. 898 (1986) (invalidating on "right to travel" grounds a New York statute granting an employment preference to resident veterans who resided in New York at the time that they entered military service).

2. *Penalties and objectives.* In what circumstances may a state burden the right to travel in order to further a constitutionally *permissible* objective? In *Shapiro*, the Court invoked strict scrutiny because the durational residence requirements "penalized" the right to travel. Do you accept the "penalty" characterization? Consider the following arguments:

a. In the usual "penalty" case, the existence of a condition on eligibility for a state's program makes a person worse off with respect to the constitutional right in question than if there were no program at all. For example, if a state grants welfare benefits only to persons who agree not to vote, the right to vote is pressured in a way it would not be if there were no welfare program at all. The situation is different in *Shapiro*. If state X has a durational residence requirement for the receipt of welfare benefits, a person contemplating a move to state X is no worse off with respect to the right to travel than if state X had no welfare system at all.

b. In the usual "penalty" case, a state withholds an otherwise available benefit from an individual unless she forgoes a constitutional right. For example, if a state grants welfare benefits only to persons who agree not to vote, an individual who exercises her constitutional right to vote will lose a benefit she would otherwise receive. The benefit program thus "penalizes" the exercise of her right. The situation is different in *Shapiro*. If state X has a durational residence requirement for the receipt of welfare benefits, a person contemplating a move to state X will not receive benefits from state X even if she decides not to travel. If she exercises her right to travel, she does not lose a benefit she would otherwise have received from state X. Thus, insofar as state X is concerned, the individual is no worse off if she moves than if she stays put. State X's residence requirement therefore does not "penalize" her right to travel.

3. *Other penalties on the right to travel.* Are all durational residency requirements unconstitutional "penalties" on the right to travel? Note footnote 21 in
Shapiro, and consider the following cases:

a. *Voting.* In Dunn v. Blumstein, 405 U.S. 330 (1972), the Court, in a six-to-
one decision, held that Tennessee's one-year residence requirement for voting
violated the equal protection clause. The Court employed strict equal protection
scrutiny both because the requirement interfered with the "fundamental" right to
vote, see section E1 supra, and because it "penalized" the "fundamental" right to
travel. On the latter issue, the Court explained:

> Tennessee seeks to avoid the clear command of *Shapiro* by arguing that durational
> residence requirements for voting neither seek to nor actually do deter [travel]. This
> view represents a fundamental misunderstanding of the law. It is irrelevant whether
> disenfranchisement or denial of welfare is the more potent deterrent to travel.
> *Shapiro* did not rest upon a finding that denial of welfare actually deterred travel.
> [In] *Shapiro* we explicitly stated that the compelling-state-interest test would be
> triggered by "any classification which serves to *penalize* the exercise of that
> right. . . ." [Durational] residence laws impermissibly condition and penalize the
> right to travel by imposing their prohibitions on only those persons who have
> recently exercised that right. In the present case, such laws force a person [to]
> choose between travel and the basic right to vote. [Absent] a compelling state
> interest, a State may not burden the right to travel in this way.

b. *Nonemergency medical care.* In Memorial Hospital v. Maricopa County, 415
U.S. 250 (1974), the Court held that an Arizona statute requiring a year's residence in a county as a condition to receiving nonemergency medical care at
county expense violated the equal protection clause. The Court explained:

> Although any durational residence requirement imposes a potential cost on migra-
> tion, [*Shapiro*] cautioned that some "waiting-period[s] . . . may not be penalties."
> [In *Dunn*], the Court found that the denial of the franchise, "a fundamental polit-
> ical right," [was] a penalty requiring application of the compelling-state-interest
> test. In *Shapiro*, the Court found denial of the basic "necessities of life" to be a
> penalty. [Whatever] the ultimate parameters of the *Shapiro* penalty analysis, it is at
> least clear that medical care is as much "a basic necessity of life" to an indigent as
> welfare assistance. [It] would be odd, indeed, to find that [Arizona] was required to
> afford [appellant] welfare assistance to keep him from the discomfort of inadequate
> housing or the pangs of hunger but could deny him the medical care necessary to
> relieve him from the wheezing and gasping for breath that attend his illness. [Thus,
> the challenged requirement] penalizes indigents for exercising their right to
> migrate [and], "unless shown to be necessary to promote a compelling governmen-
> tal interest, is unconstitutional."

The Court held that the state's justifications for the requirement were not
"compelling."

c. *Divorce.* In Sosna v. Iowa, 419 U.S. 393 (1975), the Court upheld a one-year
residence requirement for bringing a divorce action against a nonresident. The
Court, in an opinion by Justice Rehnquist, explained:

> Appellant was not irretrievably foreclosed from obtaining some part of what she
> sought, as was the case with the welfare recipients in *Shapiro*, the voters in *Dunn*, or
> the indigent patient in *Maricopa County*. [Iowa's] requirement delayed her access
> to the courts, but, by fulfilling it, she could ultimately have obtained the same

opportunity for adjudication which she asserts ought to have been hers at an earlier point in time. [Moreover, unlike the residency requirements invalidated in *Shapiro, Dunn*, and *Maricopa County*,] Iowa's residency requirement may reasonably be justified on grounds other than purely budgetary considerations or administrative convenience. [A] decree of divorce [may affect the parties' marital status, their property rights, and their children]. With consequences of such moment riding on a divorce decree [Iowa] may insist that one seeking to initiate such a proceeding have the modicum of attachment to the State required here. Such a requirement additionally furthers the State's parallel interests both in avoiding officious intermeddling in matters in which another State has a paramount interest, and in minimizing the susceptibility of its own divorce decrees to collateral attack. [Iowa] may quite reasonably decide that it does not wish to become a divorce mill.

d. *Variations*. In the light of *Shapiro, Dunn, Maricopa County*, and *Sosna*, consider the following: (1) a one-year residency requirement for admittance to the bar, consider Supreme Court of New Hampshire v. Piper, 470 U.S. 274 (1985) (holding that a bona fide residency requirement for admission to the bar violates the privileges and immunities clause of article IV, section 2); (2) a one-year residency requirement for reduced tuition at a state university, consider Vlandis v. Kline, 412 U.S. 441 (1973) (invalidating such a requirement under the due process clause as an unconstitutional "irrebuttable presumption"); (3) a state statute making it a misdemeanor for a parent to abandon a dependent child and a felony for the parent to leave the state after the abandonment, consider Jones v. Helms, 452 U.S. 412 (1981) (upholding such a statute).

4. *Bona fide residency requirements*. *Shapiro* dealt with the right to travel in the sense of changing one's residence from one state to another. After *Shapiro*, could a state constitutionally deny welfare benefits to nonresidents who are in the state temporarily? Is such a law permissible because it does not implicate the right to travel?

Shapiro dealt with a classification between two groups of residents. After *Shapiro*, could a state constitutionally deny welfare benefits to former residents who had moved to another state? Consider McCarthy v. Philadelphia Civil Service Commission, 424 U.S. 645 (1976), in which the Court upheld the dismissal of an employee of the fire department who was terminated because he moved to New Jersey in violation of a requirement that city employees be residents of Philadelphia. In a summary per curiam disposition, the Court explained that *Shapiro* dealt only with durational residence requirements and "did not question 'the validity [of] bona fide residence requirements.'" Consider also Martinez v. Bynum, 461 U.S. 321 (1983), in which the Court upheld a bona fide residence requirement for attending a state's public schools. The Court explained: "A bona fide residence requirement [furthers] the substantial state interest in assuring that services provided for its residents are enjoyed only by residents. Such a requirement with respect to attendance in public free schools does not violate the Equal Protection Clause. [It] does not burden or penalize the constitutional right of interstate travel, for any person is free to move to a State and to establish residence there."

Is the issue in *McCarthy* and *Martinez* more sensibly analyzed under the privileges and immunities clause of article IV, section 2? See Supreme Court of New Hampshire v. Piper, supra (bona fide residence requirement for admission to the bar violates article IV, section 2); Supreme Court of Virginia v. Friedman, 487 U.S. 59 (1988) (same); United Building & Construction Trades

Council v. Mayor of Camden, 465 U.S. 208 (1984) (ordinance requiring at least 40 percent of employees of contractors working on city projects to be city residents may violate article IV, section 2); Hicklin v. Orbeck, 437 U.S. 518 (1978) (Alaska statute requiring private employers to grant hiring preferences to Alaska residents violates article IV, section 2); Baldwin v. Fish & Game Commission, 436 U.S. 371 (1978) (upholding against article IV, section 2 and equal protection attack a requirement that nonresidents pay higher fees than residents for hunting licenses).

4.   Welfare

In *Harper*, *Griffin*, and *Douglas*, the Court emphasized the impact of certain forms of inequality on the poor. In *Shapiro*, the Court observed that durational residence requirements for welfare affect "the ability [of] families to obtain the very means to subsist — food, shelter, and other necessities of life." After *Shapiro*, a number of courts and commentators maintained that welfare constituted a "fundamental" interest for purposes of equal protection review. In fact, this was a distinctive, but evidently short, period in the history of American constitutional thought.

Some people suggested that welfare, like voting and access to the judicial process, is a "fundamental" interest because it is "preservative of all rights." See, e.g, Michelman, Welfare Rights in a Constitutional Democracy, 1979 Wash. U. L.Q. 659 Michelman, Foreword: On Protecting the Poor through the Fourteenth Amendment, 83 Harv. L. Rev. 7, 9, 14–19 (1969). Many nations, including South Africa, have constitutionalized welfare rights in one or another form. Section 26 of the Constitution of South Africa states, "Everyone has the right to have access to adequate housing." It adds, "The state must take reasonable legislative and other measures, within its available resources, to achieve the progressive realization of this right." What does this mean? The South Africa Constitutional Court has said that denials of the right to housing are justiciable, but that the state is under no obligation to ensure that everyone has a decent home. For discussion, see C. Sunstein, The Second Bill of Rights (2004).

DANDRIDGE v. WILLIAMS, 397 U.S. 471 (1970). The Court upheld a provision of Maryland's Aid to Families with Dependent Children (AFDC) program that granted most eligible families their computed "standard of need," but imposed a maximum monthly grant of $250 per family regardless of family size or computed need. Justice Stewart delivered the opinion of the Court: "[Here] we deal with state regulation in the social and economic field, not affecting freedoms guaranteed by the Bill of Rights, and claimed to violate the Fourteenth Amendment only because the regulation results in some disparity in grants of welfare payments to the largest AFDC families. For this Court to approve the invalidation of state economic or social regulation [here] would be far too reminiscent of an era when the Court thought the Fourteenth Amendment gave it power to strike down state laws 'because they may be unwise, improvident, or out of harmony with a particular school of thought' [*Lee Optical*].

"In the area of economics and social welfare, a State does not violate the Equal Protection Clause merely because the classifications made by its laws are imperfect. If the classification has some 'reasonable basis,' it does not offend the [Constitution]. To be sure, the cases [enunciating] this [standard] have in the main involved state regulation of business or industry. The administration of public welfare assistance, by contrast, involves the most basic economic needs of impoverished human beings. We recognize the dramatically real factual difference between the [business] cases and this one, but we can find no basis for applying a different constitutional standard. . . .

"[The] maximum grant regulation is constitutionally valid. [By] keying the maximum family AFDC grants to the minimum wage a steadily employed head of a household receives, [the regulation encourages employment and avoids discrimination between welfare families and the families of the working poor]. [Although the regulation may be both over- and underinclusive,] the Equal Protection Clause does not require that a State must choose between attacking every aspect of a problem or not attacking the problem at all. [It] is enough that the State's action be rationally based and free from invidious discrimination. The regulation before us meets that test."

Justice Marshall, joined by Justice Brennan, dissented: "The cases [that used] a 'mere rationality' test [involved] the regulation of business interests. [But this] case, involving the literally vital interests of a powerless minority — poor families without breadwinners — is far removed from the area of business regulation. [On the other hand, in] my view, equal protection analysis of this case is not appreciably advanced by the a priori definition of a 'right,' fundamental or otherwise. Rather, concentration must be placed upon the character of the classification in question, the relative importance to individuals in the class discriminated against of the governmental benefits that they do not receive, and the asserted state interests in support of the classification. . . .

"It is the individual interests here at stake [that] most clearly distinguish this case from the 'business regulation' equal protection cases. AFDC support to needy dependent children provides the stuff that sustains those children's lives: food, clothing, shelter. And this Court has already recognized [that] when a benefit [is] necessary to sustain life, stricter constitutional standards, both procedural and substantive, are applied to the deprivation of that benefit. [Citing, e.g., Shapiro v. Thompson, section E3, supra; Goldberg v. Kelly, section G1, infra.] . . .

"Appellees are not a gas company or an optical dispenser, they are needy dependent children and families who are discriminated against by the State. The basis of that discrimination [is] too arbitrary, [the] impact on those discriminated against [too] great, and the supposed interests served [too] attenuated to meet the requirements of the Constitution."

Note: Dandridge and the Judicial Role in the Welfare Context

1. Dandridge and positive rights. Should the Court have subjected the regulation at issue in Dandridge to strict scrutiny because it imposed a penalty on the "fundamental" interest in procreation? Would it be constitutional for a state to impose a $250 fine on any poor family that had more than a certain number of children? Is a cap on welfare benefits for families over a certain size functionally different from such a fine? There is a sense in which a welfare claimant is not asking the government to leave him alone but is asking it to give him something. The Constitution is ordinarily thought of as creating limitations on government rather than as establishing affirmative rights. In this sense,

constitutional doctrine has a powerful libertarian dimension. Recall the discussion of *Lochner* in section D supra. Does this fact distinguish welfare from other interests that have been declared "fundamental"? Note that the eminent domain and contracts clauses also have a positive dimension, since private property rights depend on the state's willingness to have and to enforce trespass laws, and since courts have to be available to vindicate contractual rights.

Note also that spending decisions have a "polycentric" character. If the Court expands the class of beneficiaries, the state may simply reduce the benefits for all recipients. Thus, the effect of declaring welfare to be a fundamental interest may be not to benefit the poor as a class but to benefit some poor persons at the expense of others. On the relevance of this point, see S. Holmes and C. Sunstein, The Cost of Rights (1999).

2. *The reach of* Dandridge: *welfare.* Since *Dandridge*, the Court has generally adhered to the view that rational basis review is the appropriate standard for the evaluation of welfare classifications. See, e.g., Califano v. Boles, 443 U.S. 282 (1979) (upholding a provision of the Social Security Act restricting "mothers' insurance benefits" to widows and divorced wives of wage earners); Jefferson v. Hackney, 406 U.S. 535 (1972) (upholding a provision of a state welfare program authorizing payment of a lower percentage of need to recipients of AFDC than to recipients of other forms of categorical welfare assistance); Richardson v. Belcher, 404 U.S. 78 (1971) (upholding a provision of the Social Security Act reducing disability benefits for amounts received from workers' compensation but not for amounts received from private insurance).

3. *The reach of* Dandridge: *housing and health.* In Lindsey v. Normet, 405 U.S. 56 (1972), the Court upheld a state's summary "forcible entry and wrongful detainer" procedures for the eviction of tenants after alleged nonpayment of rent. The Court rejected a claim that "the 'need for decent shelter' and the 'right to retain peaceful possession of one's home' are fundamental interests which are particularly important to the poor and which may be trenched upon only after the State demonstrates some superior interest." Applying rational basis review, the Court found no constitutional defect in the fact that eviction actions are more summary than "other litigation," for the "unique factual and legal characteristics of the landlord-tenant relationship [justify] special statutory treatment." Justices Douglas and Brennan dissented.

The Court rejected a claim to governmental protection in Collins v. Texas, 484 U.S. 924 (1992). Larry Collins, a municipal employee, died of asphyxia after entering a manhole to unstop a sewer line. His widow brought suit, claiming that her husband had a constitutional right to be free from unreasonable risks of harm or at least to be protected from deliberate official indifference to employee safety. The Court concluded that the Constitution had not been violated, at least in the absence of an allegation of deliberate harm or of willful violation of rights: "Neither the text nor the history of the Due Process Clause supports petitioner's claim that the governmental employer's duty to provide its employees with a safe working environment is a substantive component of the Due Process Clause." Relying on the *DeShaney* case (see Chapter 9, section B1, infra) and the action/inaction distinction, the Court found "unprecedented" the suggestion that there is "a federal constitutional obligation to provide [employees] with certain minimal levels of safety and security." Nor was a duty of training or warning implied by the Constitution. "Decisions concerning the allocation of resources to individual programs, such as sewer maintenance, and to particular aspects of those programs, such as the training and compensation of employees, involve a host of policy choices that must be made by locally elected representatives."

The *Collins* Court acknowledged that there might be a constitutional claim if the state had coerced a citizen by placing him in hazardous conditions — for example, if a citizen confined in a facility for mental illness is not provided with "minimal custodial standards." What is the difference between such a case and *Collins* itself?

4. *The limits of* Dandridge: Moreno. In U.S. Department of Agriculture v. Moreno, 413 U.S. 528 (1973), the Court, in a seven-to-two decision, invalidated a provision of the Food Stamp Act excluding from participation in the program any household containing an individual who is unrelated to any other household member. The government argued that the challenged classification was rationally related to the legitimate government interest in minimizing fraud because "Congress might rationally have thought [that] households with one or more unrelated members are more likely than 'fully related' households to contain individuals who abuse the program by fraudulently failing to report sources of income." In rejecting this argument, the Court maintained that "the challenged classification [does] not operate so as rationally to further the prevention of fraud," for, "even if we were to accept as rational the Government's [assumptions] concerning the differences between 'related' and 'unrelated' households, we still could not agree" that the challenged provision "constitutes a rational effort to deal with" this concern, for "in practical operation," it "excludes from participation in [the] program, *not* those persons who are 'likely to abuse the program' but, rather, *only* those persons who are so desperately in need of aid that they cannot even afford to alter their living arrangements so as to retain their eligibility."

Does *Moreno* suggest that, despite *Dandridge*, the Court may apply a more stringent standard where a law involves not a mere *relative* deprivation of welfare benefits, as in *Dandridge*, but an *absolute* deprivation, as in *Moreno*?

5.   *Education*

San Antonio Independent School District v. Rodriguez

411 U.S. 1 (1973)

[Public school education has long been financed largely by means of property taxes imposed by local school districts. This suit challenged the constitutionality of Texas's use of this financing system on the ground that it produced substantial interdistrict disparities in per-pupil expenditures. For example, the Edgewood Independent School District, the least affluent of the seven school districts in metropolitan San Antonio, had an assessed property value of $5,960 per student. By imposing a property tax of $1.05 per $100 of assessed property value — the highest rate in the metropolitan area — the district raised $26 per student in local funds. In contrast, the Alamo Heights Independent School District, the most affluent in the area, had an assessed property value per student of more than $49,000 and with a tax rate of only $.85 per $100 was able to raise $333 per student. Although contributions from a state-funded "foundation program" tended to reduce interdistrict disparities, the inclusion of such funds still left a substantial difference — $248 per pupil in Edgewood as compared to $558 in

Alamo Heights. A federal district court, applying strict scrutiny, held that the
Texas scheme violated the equal protection clause. The Supreme Court
reversed.]

    Mr. Justice Powell delivered the opinion of the Court. . . .

I

[We] must decide, first, whether the Texas system of financing public education
operates to the disadvantage of some suspect class or impinges upon a
fundamental right explicitly or implicitly protected by the Constitution, thereby
requiring strict judicial scrutiny. If so, the judgment of the District Court should
be affirmed. If not, the Texas scheme must still be examined to determine
whether it rationally furthers some legitimate, articulated state purpose and therefore does not constitute an invidious discrimination in violation of the Equal
Protection Clause of the Fourteenth Amendment.

II

[We] find neither the suspect-classification nor the fundamental-interest analysis
persuasive.

A

[The Court rejected the claim that strict scrutiny was appropriate because the
Texas system discriminated against the "poor." The issue of wealth discrimination in *Rodriguez* is addressed more fully in Chapter 5 supra.]

B

In Brown v. Board of Education, a unanimous Court recognized that "education
is perhaps the most important function of state and local governments." . . .
    Nothing this Court holds today in any way detracts from our historic dedica-
tion to public education. [But] the importance of a service performed by the State
does not determine whether it must be regarded as fundamental for purposes of
examination under the Equal Protection Clause.
    [It] is not the province of this Court to create substantive constitutional rights
in the name of guaranteeing equal protection of the laws. Thus, the key to
discovering whether education is "fundamental" is not to be found in comparisons of the relative societal significance of education as opposed to subsistence or
housing. Nor is it to be found by weighing whether education is as important as
the right to travel. Rather, the answer lies in assessing whether there is a right to
education explicitly or implicitly guaranteed by the Constitution.[76]

---

76. [*Skinner*, for example,] applied the standard of close scrutiny to a state law permitting forced
sterilization of "habitual criminals." Implicit in the Count's opinion is the recognition that the
right of procreation is among the rights of personal privacy protected under the Constitution. See
Roe v. Wade, 410 U.S. 113, 152 (1973). [Relocated footnote. — Eds.]

Education, of course, is not among the rights afforded explicit protection under our Federal Constitution. Nor do we find any basis for saying it is implicitly so protected. [It] is appellees' contention, however, that education is distinguishable from other services and benefits provided by the State because it bears a peculiarly close relationship to other rights and liberties accorded protection under the Constitution. Specifically, they insist that education is itself a fundamental personal right because it is essential to the effective exercise of First Amendment freedoms and to intelligent utilization of the right to vote. In asserting a nexus between speech and education, appellees urge that the right to speak is meaningless unless the speaker is capable of articulating his thoughts intelligently and persuasively. . . .

A similar line of reasoning is pursued with respect to the right to vote.[78] Exercise of the franchise, it is contended, cannot be divorced from the educational foundation of the voter. . . .

We need not dispute any of these propositions. The Court has long afforded zealous protection against unjustifiable governmental interference with the individual's rights to speak and to vote. Yet we have never presumed to possess either the ability or the authority to guarantee to the citizenry the most *effective* speech or the most *informed* electoral choice. That these may be desirable goals [is] not to be doubted. [But] they are not values to be implemented by judicial intrusion into otherwise legitimate state activities.

[Whatever] merit appellees' argument might have if a State's financing system occasioned an absolute denial of educational opportunities to any of its children, that argument provides no basis for finding an interference with fundamental rights where only relative differences in spending levels are involved and where — as is true in the present case — no charge fairly could be made that the system fails to provide each child with an opportunity to acquire the basic minimal skills necessary for the enjoyment of the rights of speech and of full participation in the political process.

Furthermore, the logical limitations on appellees' nexus theory are difficult to perceive. How, for instance, is education to be distinguished from the significant personal interests in the basics of decent food and shelter? Empirical examination might well buttress an assumption that the ill-fed, ill-clothed, and ill-housed are among the most ineffective participants in the political process, and that they derive the least enjoyment from the benefits of the First Amendment. If so, appellees' thesis would cast serious doubt on the authority of Dandridge v. Williams and Lindsey v. Normet [405 U.S. 56 (1972)]. . . .

C

[We] have here nothing less than a direct attack on the way in which Texas has chosen to raise and disburse state and local tax revenues. [Appellees] would have the Court intrude in an area in which it has traditionally deferred to state legislatures. [No] scheme of taxation, whether the tax is imposed on property, income, or purchases of goods and services, has yet been devised which is free of all

---

78. Since the right to vote, per se, is not a constitutionally protected right, we assume that appellees' references to that right are simply shorthand references to the protected right, implicit in our constitutional system, to participate in state elections on an equal basis with other qualified voters whenever the State has adopted an elective process for determining who will represent any segment of the State's population.

discriminatory impact. In such a complex arena in which no perfect alternatives exist, the Court does well not to impose too rigorous a standard of scrutiny lest all local fiscal schemes become subjects of criticism under the Equal Protection Clause.

[Moreover], this case also involves the most persistent and difficult questions of educational policy, another area in which this Court's lack of specialized knowledge and experience counsels against premature interference with the informed judgments made at the state and local levels. Education, perhaps even more than welfare assistance, presents a myriad of "intractable economic, social, and even philosophical problems." . . .

III

[While] assuring a basic education for every child in the State, [the Texas system of school financing] permits and encourages a large measure of participation in and control of each district's schools at the local level. In an era that has witnessed a consistent trend toward centralization of the functions of government, local sharing of responsibility for public education has survived. [In] part, local control means [the] freedom to devote more money to the education of one's children. Equally important, however, is the opportunity it offers for participation in the decisionmaking process that determines how those local tax dollars will be spent. Each locality is free to tailor local programs to local needs. Pluralism also affords some opportunity for experimentation, innovation, and a healthy competition for educational [excellence]. Appellees suggest that local control could be preserved and promoted under other financing systems that resulted in more equality in educational expenditures. While it is no doubt true that reliance on local property taxation for school revenues provides less freedom of choice with respect to expenditures for some districts than for others, the existence of "some inequality" in the manner in which the State's rationale is achieved is not alone a sufficient basis for striking down the entire system.

[Nor] must the financing system fail because, as appellees suggest, other methods of satisfying the State's interest, which occasion "less drastic" disparities in expenditures, might be conceived. Only where state action impinges on the exercise of fundamental constitutional rights or liberties must it be found to have chosen the least restrictive alternative. [It] is also well to remember that even those districts that have reduced ability to make free decisions with respect to how much they spend on education still retain under the present system a large measure of authority as to how available funds will be allocated. They further enjoy the power to make numerous other decisions with respect to the operation of the schools. The people of Texas may be justified in believing that other systems of school financing, which place more of the financial responsibility in the hands of the State, will result in a comparable lessening of desired local autonomy. . . .

[The] constitutional standard under the Equal Protection Clause is whether the challenged state action rationally furthers a legitimate state purpose or interest. We hold that the Texas plan abundantly satisfies this standard. . . .

Reversed.

[The concurring opinion of Justice Stewart and the dissenting opinion of Justice Brennan are omitted.]

MR. JUSTICE WHITE, with whom MR. JUSTICE DOUGLAS and MR. JUSTICE BRENNAN join, dissenting.

[This] case would be quite different if it were true that the Texas system, while insuring minimum educational expenditures in every district through state funding, extended a meaningful option to all local districts to increase their per-pupil [expenditures. But for] districts with a low per-pupil real estate tax base [the] Texas system utterly fails to extend a realistic choice to parents because the property tax, which is the only revenue-raising mechanism extended to school districts, is practically and legally unavailable. . . .

In order to equal the highest yield in any other Bexar County district, [Edgewood] would be required to tax at the prohibitive rate of $5.76 per $100. But state law places a $1.50 per $100 ceiling on the maintenance tax rate. [Edgewood] is thus precluded in law, as well as in fact, from achieving a yield even close to that of some other districts. [Requiring] the State to establish only that unequal treatment is in furtherance of a permissible goal, without also requiring the State to show that the means chosen to effectuate that goal are rationally related to its achievement, makes equal protection analysis no more than an empty gesture. . . .

MR. JUSTICE MARSHALL, with whom MR. JUSTICE DOUGLAS concurs, dissenting.

[The] Court apparently seeks to establish today that equal protection cases fall into one of two neat categories which dictate the appropriate standard of review — strict scrutiny or mere rationality. But this Court's decisions in the field of equal protection defy such easy categorization. A principled reading of what this Court has done reveals that it has applied a spectrum of standards in reviewing discrimination allegedly violative of the Equal Protection Clause. This spectrum clearly comprehends variations in the degree of care with which the Court will scrutinize particular classifications, depending, I believe, on the constitutional and societal importance of the interest adversely affected and the recognized invidiousness of the basis upon which the particular classification is drawn. . . .

[I] would like to know where the Constitution guarantees the right to procreate [Skinner v. Oklahoma], or the right to vote in state elections [Reynolds v. Sims],[60] or the right to an appeal from a criminal conviction [Griffin].[61] These are instances in which, due to the importance of the interests at stake, the Court has displayed a strong concern with the existence of discriminatory state treatment. But the Court has never said or indicated that these are interests which independently enjoy full-blown constitutional protection. . . .

60. It is interesting that in its effort to reconcile the state voting rights cases with its theory of fundamentality the majority can muster nothing more than the contention that "[t]he constitutional underpinnings of the *right to equal treatment in the voting process* can no longer be doubted. . . ." If, by this, the Court intends to recognize a substantive constitutional "right to equal treatment in the voting process" independent of the Equal Protection Clause, the source of such a right is certainly a mystery to me.

61. It is true that *Griffin* [also] involved discrimination against indigents, that is, wealth discrimination. But, as the majority points out, the Court has never deemed wealth discrimination alone to be sufficient to require strict judicial scrutiny; rather, such review of wealth classifications has been applied only where the discrimination affects an important individual interest, see, e.g., [*Harper*]. Thus, I believe *Griffin* [can] only be understood as premised on a recognition of the fundamental importance of the criminal appellate process.

The majority is, of course, correct when it suggests that the process of determining which interests are fundamental is a difficult one. But I do not think the problem is insurmountable. [The] determination of which interests are fundamental should be firmly rooted in the text of the Constitution. The task in every case should be to determine the extent to which constitutionally guaranteed rights are dependent on interests not mentioned in the Constitution. As the nexus between the specific constitutional guarantee and the nonconstitutional interest draws closer, the nonconstitutional interest becomes more fundamental and the degree of judicial scrutiny applied when the interest is infringed on a discriminatory basis must be adjusted accordingly. Thus, it cannot be denied that interests such as procreation, the exercise of the state franchise, and access to criminal appellate processes are not fully guaranteed to the citizen by our Constitution. But these interests have nonetheless been afforded special judicial consideration in the face of discrimination because they are, to some extent, interrelated with constitutional guarantees. Procreation is now understood to be important because of its interaction with the established constitutional right of privacy. The exercise of the state franchise is closely tied to basic civil and political rights inherent in the First Amendment. And access to criminal appellate processes enhances the integrity of the range of rights implicit in the [guarantee] of due process of law. Only if we closely protect the related interests from state discrimination do we ultimately ensure the integrity of the constitutional guarantee itself. This is the real lesson that must be taken from our previous decisions involving interests deemed to be fundamental. . . .

[It] is true that this Court has never deemed the provision of free public education to be required by the Constitution. [Nevertheless] the fundamental importance of education is amply indicated by the prior decisions of this Court, by the unique status accorded public education by our society, and by the close relationship between education and some of our most basic constitutional values. . . .

Education directly affects the ability of a child to exercise his First Amendment rights, both as a source and as a receiver of information and ideas. [Of] particular importance is the relationship between education and the political process [and] the demonstrated effect of education on the exercise of the franchise by the electorate. [It] is this very sort of intimate relationship between a particular personal interest and specific constitutional guarantees that has heretofore caused the Court to attach special significance, for purposes of equal protection analysis, to individual interests such as procreation and the exercise of the state franchise.[74] [These factors] compel us to recognize the fundamentality of

74. I believe that the close nexus between education and our established constitutional values with respect to freedom of speech and participation in the political process makes this a different case from our prior decisions concerning discrimination affecting public welfare, see, e.g., [Dandridge] or housing, see, e.g., [Lindsey v. Normet]. There can be no question that, as the majority suggests, constitutional rights may be less meaningful for someone without enough to eat or without decent housing. But the crucial difference lies in the closeness of the relationship. Whatever the severity of the impact of insufficient food or inadequate housing on a person's life, they have never been considered to bear the same direct and immediate relationship to constitutional concerns for free speech and for our political processes as education has long been recognized to bear. Perhaps, the best evidence of this fact is the unique status which has been accorded public education as the single public service nearly unanimously guaranteed in the constitutions of our States. Education, in terms of constitutional values, is much more analogous, in my judgment, to the right to vote in state elections than to public welfare or public housing. Indeed, it is not without significance that we have long recognized education as an essential step in providing the disadvantaged with the tools necessary to achieve economic self-sufficiency.

education and to scrutinize with appropriate care the bases for state discrimination affecting equality of educational opportunity in Texas' school districts — a conclusion which is only strengthened when we consider the character of the classification in this case. . . .

[The] only justification offered [to] sustain the discrimination in educational opportunity caused by the Texas financing scheme is local educational control. [But] on this record, it is apparent that the State's purported concern with local control is offered primarily as an excuse rather than as a justification for inter-district inequality.

In Texas, statewide laws regulate [the] most minute details of local public education. [But] even if we accept Texas' general dedication to local control in educational matters, it is difficult to find any evidence of such dedication with respect to fiscal matters. [If] Texas had a system truly dedicated to local fiscal control, one would expect the quality of the educational opportunity provided in each district to vary with the decision of the voters in that district as to the level of sacrifice they wish to make for public education. In fact, the Texas scheme produces precisely the opposite result. Local school districts cannot choose to have the best education in the State by imposing the highest tax rate. Instead, the quality of the educational opportunity offered by any particular district is largely determined by the amount of taxable property located in the district — a factor over which local voters can exercise no control. . . .

In my judgment, any substantial degree of scrutiny of the operation of the Texas financing scheme reveals that the State has selected means wholly inappropriate to secure its purported interest in assuring its school districts local fiscal control. [Appellees] have pointed out a variety of alternative financing schemes which may serve the State's purported interest in local control as well as, if not better than, the present scheme without the current impairment of the educational opportunity of vast numbers of Texas schoolchildren.

I see no need, however, to explore the practical or constitutional merits of those suggested alternatives at this time for, whatever their positive or negative features, experience with the present financing scheme impugns any suggestion that it constitutes a serious effort to provide local fiscal control. . . .

Note: The Rodriguez Formulation

1. *Education as a fundamental interest.* To what extent does the Court's reiteration that the Texas system did not involve an "absolute deprivation" of education impeach its conclusion that education is not a "fundamental interest"? If the state is under no obligation to provide police services to protect life (as *DeShaney*, Chapter 9 infra, seems to suggest), how can it be under an obligation to provide some level of educational services?

If education *were* a "fundamental" interest, note that there would be serious problems in judicial assessment of what kind of education, and how much education, a person is entitled to receive. Would public schools be required to adopt standardized curricula? Would state universities be required to pay the tuition costs of indigents?

2. *Territorial discrimination.* The school financing scheme upheld in *Rodriguez* treats individuals differently depending on where they live in the state. How should the Court analyze such inequalities? Can a state constitutionally provide more money for the education of students who live in the northern part of the

state? For discussion, see Neuman, Territorial Discrimination, Equal Protection, and Self-Determination, 135 U. Pa. L. Rev. 261 (1987).

Compare *Rodriguez* to Papasan v. Allain, 478 U.S. 265 (1986). While Mississippi was still a territory, Congress reserved certain plots of land within each township for support of public schools. However, Congress failed to reserve such lands in northern Mississippi, which was then held by the Chickasaw Indian Nation. In 1836, Congress sought to remedy this oversight by vesting certain lands in the state for the use of schools within the Chickasaw Cession, but the state (with the permission of Congress) sold these lands and invested the proceeds in railroads that were destroyed during the Civil War. The result is that today school districts in most of the state receive an average income of $75.34 per pupil from reserved lands located within their borders, while Chickasaw Cession schools receive annual appropriations, designed to compensate for the lost lands, of only $.63 per pupil.

Petitioners filed an action claiming, inter alia, that the disparity in funding violated the equal protection clause. The court of appeals held that in light of *Rodriguez*, the trial court correctly granted respondent's motion to dismiss, but the Supreme Court, in an opinion by Justice White, reversed. Because petitioners had not alleged any facts supporting the contention that they were denied a minimally adequate education, the Court found it unnecessary to determine whether such a denial would infringe on a fundamental right and trigger strict scrutiny. Nonetheless, the Court ruled that the lower court had erred in holding that *Rodriguez* compelled dismissal of the suit:

> As we read their complaint, the petitioners do not challenge the overall organization of the Mississippi public school financing program. Instead, their challenge is restricted to one aspect of that program. . . .
> This case is [very] different from *Rodriguez*, where the differential financing available to school districts was traceable to school district funds available from local real estate taxation, not to a state decision to divide state resources unequally among school districts. The rationality of the disparity in *Rodriguez*, therefore, which rested on the fact that funding disparities based on differing local wealth were a necessary adjunct of allowing meaningful local control over school funding, does not settle the constitutionality of disparities alleged in this case.

The Court remanded the case so that the lower court could consider in the first instance whether, given state title to the lands, the equal protection clause permitted the state to distribute income from them unequally among school districts.

Justice Powell, joined by Chief Justice Burger and Justice Rehnquist, dissented. He pointed out that income from the lands accounted for only 1.5 percent of overall funding for the schools and argued that such de minimis variations in funding were insufficient to establish an equal protection clause violation.

Plyler v. Doe

457 U.S. 202 (1982)

JUSTICE BRENNAN delivered the opinion of the Court. . . .

[The Court held unconstitutional a Texas statute that authorized local school districts to deny free public education to children who had not been "legally admitted" into the United States. Pursuant to this statute, the Tyler Independent School District required "undocumented" children to pay a "tuition fee" in order to enroll.]

[In] applying the Equal Protection Clause to most forms of state action, we [seek] only the assurance that the classification at issue bears some fair relationship to a legitimate public purpose.

But we would not be faithful to our obligations under the Fourteenth Amendment if we applied so deferential a standard to every classification. [With] respect to [some] classifications, it is appropriate to enforce the mandate of equal protection by requiring the State to demonstrate that its classification has been precisely tailored to serve a compelling governmental interest. In addition, we have recognized that certain forms of legislative classification, while not facially invidious, nonetheless give rise to recurring constitutional difficulties; in these limited circumstances we have sought the assurance that the classification reflects a reasoned judgment consistent with the ideal of equal protection by inquiring whether it may fairly be viewed as furthering a substantial interest of the State. We turn to a consideration of the standard appropriate for the evaluation of [the challenged law].

Sheer incapability or lax enforcement of the laws barring entry into this country, [has] resulted in the creation of a substantial "shadow population" of illegal migrants — numbering in the millions — within our borders. This situation raises the specter of a permanent caste of undocumented resident aliens, encouraged by some to remain here as a source of cheap labor, but nevertheless denied the benefits that our society makes available to citizens and lawful residents. [The Court rejected the claim that "illegal aliens" are a suspect class on the ground that illegal status is at least partly voluntary and that that status is not irrelevant to legitimate government purposes.]

The children who are plaintiffs in these cases are special members of this underclass. [Adults] who elect to enter our territory by stealth and in violation of our law should be prepared to bear the consequences, including, but not limited to, deportation. But the children [of] illegal entrants are not comparably situated. [They] "can affect neither their parents' conduct nor their own status." [Trimble v. Gordon, 430 U.S. 762 (1977).]

[Of] course, undocumented status is not irrelevant to any proper legislative goal. Nor is undocumented status an absolutely immutable characteristic since it is the product of conscious, indeed unlawful, action. But [the challenged law] is directed against children, and imposes its discriminatory burden on the basis of a legal characteristic over which children can have little control. It is thus difficult to conceive of a rational justification for penalizing these children for their presence within the United States. Yet that appears to be precisely the effect of [the law].

Public education is not a "right" granted to individuals by the Constitution. [*Rodriguez.*] But neither is it merely some governmental "benefit" indistinguishable from other forms of social welfare legislation. Both the importance of education in maintaining our basic institutions, and the lasting impact of its deprivation on the life of the child, mark the distinction. ["Some] degree of education is necessary to prepare citizens to participate effectively and intelligently in our open political system if we are to preserve freedom and independence." [In] addition, education provides the basic tools by which individuals might lead economically productive lives to the benefit of us all. In sum, education has a fundamental role in maintaining the fabric of our society. We cannot ignore the significant social costs borne by our Nation when select groups are denied the means to absorb the values and skills upon which our social order rests.

In addition to the pivotal role of education in sustaining our political and cultural heritage, denial of education to some isolated group of children poses an affront to one of the goals of the Equal Protection Clause: the abolition of governmental barriers presenting unreasonable obstacles to advancement on the basis of individual merit. [Illiteracy] is an enduring disability. The inability to read and write will handicap the individual deprived of a basic education each and every day of his life. The inestimable toll of that deprivation on the social, economic, intellectual, and psychological well-being of the individual, and the obstacle it poses to individual achievement, make it most difficult to reconcile [a] status-based denial of basic education with the framework of equality embodied in the Equal Protection Clause.

These well-settled principles allow us to determine the proper level of deference to be afforded [the Texas statute]. Undocumented aliens [are not] a suspect class [and] education [is not] a fundamental [right]. But more is involved in [this case] than the abstract question whether [the Texas statute] discriminates against a suspect class, or whether education is a fundamental right. [The statute] imposes a lifetime hardship on a discrete class of children not accountable for their disabling status. [In] determining the rationality of [the challenged statute], we may appropriately take into account its costs to the Nation and to the innocent children who are its victims. In light of these countervailing costs, the discrimination contained in [the statute] can hardly be considered rational unless it furthers some substantial goal of the State.

It is the State's principal argument [that] the undocumented status of these children vel non establishes a sufficient rational basis for denying them benefits that a State might choose to afford other residents. The State notes that while other aliens are admitted "on an equality of legal privileges with all citizens under non-discriminatory laws," the asserted right of these children to an education can claim no implicit congressional imprimatur. Indeed, in the State's view, Congress' apparent disapproval of the presence of these children within the United States [provides] authority for its decision to impose upon them special disabilities. Faced with an equal protection challenge respecting the treatment of aliens, we agree that the courts must be attentive to congressional policy; [but] we are unable to find in the congressional immigration scheme any statement of policy that might weigh significantly in arriving at an equal protection balance concerning the State's authority to deprive these children of an education.

Congress has developed a complex scheme governing admission to our Nation and status within our borders. The obvious need for delicate policy judgments has counseled the Judicial Branch to avoid intrusion into this field. But this traditional caution does not persuade us that unusual deference must be shown the [challenged classification]. The States enjoy no power with respect to the classification of aliens. This power is "committed to the political branches of the Federal Government." [And although] the States do have some authority to act with respect to illegal aliens, at least where such action mirrors federal objectives and furthers a legitimate state [goal], there is no indication that the disability imposed by [the challenged law] corresponds to any identifiable congressional policy. . . .

To be sure, like all persons who have entered the United States unlawfully, these children are subject to deportation. But there is no assurance that a child subject to deportation will ever be deported. [We] are reluctant to impute to Congress the intention to withhold from these children, for so long as they are present in this country through no fault of their own, access to a basic education. In other contexts, undocumented status, coupled with some articulable federal policy, might enhance state authority with respect to the treatment of undocumented aliens. But in the area of special constitutional sensitivity presented by these cases, and in the absence of any contrary indication fairly discernible in the present legislative record, we perceive no national policy that supports the State in denying these children an elementary education. . . .

[The State argues further] that the classification at issue furthers an interest in the "preservation of the state's limited resources for the education of its lawful residents." [But the] State must do more than justify its classification with a concise expression of an intention to discriminate. [We] discern three colorable state interests that might support [the classification].

[The Court considers and rejects the state's arguments that the classification protects the state from an influx of illegal immigrants, that undocumented children pose a special burden on the educational system, and that these children are less likely to remain within the state.]

If the State is to deny a discrete group of innocent children the free public education that it offers to other children residing within its borders, that denial must be justified by a showing that it furthers some substantial state interest. No such showing was made here. . . .

Affirmed.

JUSTICE MARSHALL, concurring.

While I join the Court opinion, I do so without in any way retreating from my opinion in [*Rodriguez*].

JUSTICE BLACKMUN, concurring.

[This] conclusion is fully consistent with *Rodriguez*, [for the] Court there reserved judgment on the constitutionality of a state system that "occasioned an absolute denial of educational opportunities to any of its children." . . .

JUSTICE POWELL, concurring.

I join the opinion of the Court, and write separately to emphasize the unique character of the [case] before us. . . .

Although the analogy is not perfect, our holding today does find support in decisions of this Court with respect to the status of illegitimates. [In this case], Texas effectively denies to the school-age children of illegal aliens the opportunity to attend the free public schools that the State makes available to all residents. They are excluded only because of a status resulting from the violation by parents or guardians of our immigration laws and the fact that they remain in our country unlawfully. The appellee children are innocent in this respect.

[A] legislative classification that threatens the creation of an underclass of future citizens and residents cannot be reconciled with one of the fundamental purposes of the Fourteenth Amendment. In these unique circumstances, the Court properly may require that the State's interests be substantial and that the means bear a "fair and substantial relation" to these interests.[3] . . .

---

3. The Chief Justice argues [that] this heightened standard of review is inconsistent with [*Rodriguez*]. But in *Rodriguez* no group of children was singled out by the State and then penalized because of their parents' status. Rather, funding for education varied across the State because of the tradition of local control. Nor, in that case, was any group of children totally deprived of all education as in these cases.

CHIEF JUSTICE BURGER, with whom JUSTICE WHITE, JUSTICE REHNQUIST, and JUSTICE O'CONNOR join, dissenting.

[The] Court expressly — and correctly — rejects any suggestion that illegal aliens are a suspect class, or that education is a fundamental right. Yet by patching together bits and pieces of what might be termed quasi-suspect-class and quasi-fundamental-rights analysis, the Court spins out a theory custom-tailored to the facts of [this case]. If ever a court was guilty of an unabashedly result-oriented approach, this case is a prime example. . . .

Note: Plyler *and the Equal Protection Clause*

1. *The rationale and limits* of Plyler. What is the rationale *of Plyler?* Consider the view that the Court cobbled together a set of disparate doctrines in a way that creates decision akin to a "restricted railroad ticket, good for this day and train only." Smith v. Allwright, 321 U.S. 649, 669 (1944) (separate opinion of Roberts, J.). In Martinez v. Bynum, 461 U.S. 321 (1983), the Court upheld a Texas statute that authorized local school districts to deny tuition-free admission to public schools to minors who live apart from their parents or guardians and whose presence in the district is "for the primary purpose of attending the public free schools." Justice Powell wrote the opinion of the Court:

> [The challenged bona fide residence] requirement implicates no "suspect" classi-fication; [it] does not burden or penalize the constitutional right of interstate travel, for any person is free to move to [the] State and to establish residence there; [and] the "service" [denied] to nonresidents is not a fundamental right protected by the Constitution. [Citing *Plyler.*] [Moreover, as a bona fide residence requirement, the challenged statute furthers] the substantial state interest in assuring that [educa-tional] services provided for its residents are enjoyed only by residents. [The requirement thus] satisfies constitutional standards.

Justice Marshall dissented. Is *Martinez* consistent with *Plyler?*

2. *More limits of* Plyler: Kadrmas. In Kadrmas v. Dickinson Public Schools, 487 U.S. 450 (1988), the Court, in a five-to-four decision, upheld a program whereby North Dakota permitted local school boards to assess a user fee for transporting students to and from public schools. Relying primarily on *Plyler,* appellants contended that the user fee, which could not exceed the estimated cost to the school district of providing the service, unconstitutionally deprived those who could not "afford to pay it of 'minimum access to education.'" The Court explained that it had not extended *Plyler* beyond its "unique circumstances." Moreover, *Plyler* did not govern this case, for the children in this case "had not been penalized by the government for illegal conduct by [their] parents," and the Court saw no "reason to suppose that this user fee will 'promot[e] the creation and perpetuation of a sub-class of illiterates.'" The Court emphasized that, because the Constitution does not require the state to provide bus service at all, it surely does not require the state to provide free bus service to anyone.

3. *"Fundamental" interests and the equal protection clause: concluding thoughts.* What is the justification for special scrutiny of classifications affecting fundamental interests under the equal protection clause? Consider these ideas, which seem to run through the cases. (a) Sometimes the Constitution recognizes that the state need not provide certain things, but it constrains the distribution of

those things once the state has provided them. (b) Sometimes the government's justification for an inequality must become more persuasive as the interest being treated unequally becomes more important. (c) Sometimes there are constitutional constraints on the use of *wealth*, even the de facto use of wealth, in allocating interests that go to one's status as a citizen in a democratic nation. (d) Although the Constitution is mostly concerned with the protection of negative rights, sometimes positive rights also deserve protection.

But consider this evaluation:

> The relationship of [the] "fundamental personal right" analysis to the constitutional guarantee of equal protection of the law is approximately the same as that of "freedom of contract" to the constitutional guarantee that no person shall be deprived of life, liberty, or property without due process of law. It is an invitation for judicial exegesis over and above the commands of the Constitution, in which values that cannot possibly have their source in that instrument are invoked to either validate or condemn the countless laws enacted by the various States.

Weber v. Aetna Casualty & Surety Co., 406 U.S. 164, 182 (1972) (Rehnquist, J., dissenting).

F.   MODERN SUBSTANTIVE DUE PROCESS: PRIVACY, PERSONHOOD, AND FAMILY

Although the Court employed substantive due process in the *Lochner* era primarily in the realm of economic regulation and the liberty of contract, not all of its decisions were so limited. In Meyer v. Nebraska, 262 U.S. 390 (1923), for example, the Court invalidated a state law prohibiting the teaching of any modern language other than English in any public or private grammar school. The Court explained:

> [The "liberty" guaranteed by the due process clause of the fourteenth amendment] denotes not merely freedom from bodily restraint but also the right of the individual to contract, to engage in any of the common occupations of life, to acquire useful knowledge, to marry, establish a home and bring up children, to worship God according to the dictates of his own conscience, and generally to enjoy those privileges long recognized at common law as essential to the orderly pursuit of happiness by free men. [This] liberty may not be interfered with [by] legislative action which is arbitrary or without reasonable relation to some purpose within the competency of the state to effect. [That] the State may do much [to] improve the quality of its citizens [is] clear; but the individual has certain fundamental rights which must be respected. [Here, no] emergency has arisen which renders knowledge of a child of some language other than English so clearly harmful as to justify [its] infringement of the right long freely enjoyed.

[handwritten margin note: no harm to just knowing english]

Justice Holmes, joined by Justice Sutherland, dissented. Similarly, in Pierce v. Society of Sisters, 268 U.S. 510 (1925), the Court invalidated a state statute requiring students to attend public rather than private schools. The Court held that the statute "unreasonably [interfered] with the liberty of parents and guardians to direct the upbringing and education of children under their control."

1. *The Right of Privacy*

Griswold v. Connecticut

381 U.S. 479 (1965)

MR. JUSTICE DOUGLAS delivered the opinion of the Court.

Appellant Griswold is Executive Director of the Planned Parenthood League of Connecticut. Appellant Buxton is a licensed physician and a professor at the Yale Medical School who served as Medical Director for the League. . . .

They gave information, instruction, and medical advice to *married* persons as to the means of preventing conception. [Fees] were usually charged, although some couples were serviced free.

[A Connecticut statute prohibits any person from using "any drug, medicinal article or instrument for the purpose of preventing conception."]

The appellants were found guilty as accessories and fined $100 each, against the claim that the accessory statute as so applied violated the Fourteenth Amendment. . . .

We think that appellants have standing to raise the constitutional rights of the married people with whom they had a professional relationship. [Certainly] the accessory should have standing to assert that the offense which he is charged with assisting is not, or cannot constitutionally be, a crime. . . .

Coming to the merits, we are met with a wide range of questions that implicate the Due Process Clause of the Fourteenth Amendment. Overtones of some arguments suggest that [*Lochner*] should be our guide. But we decline that invitation as we did in [*West Coast Hotel* and *Lee Optical*, section D supra]. We do not sit as a super-legislature to determine the wisdom, need, and propriety of laws that touch economic problems, business affairs, or social conditions. This law, however, operates directly on an intimate relation of husband and wife and their physician's role in one aspect of that relation.

The association of people is not mentioned in the Constitution nor in the Bill of Rights. The right to educate a child in a school of the parents' choice — whether public or private or parochial — is also not mentioned. Nor is the right to study any particular subject or any foreign language. Yet the First Amendment has been construed to include certain of those rights. [As Pierce v. Society of Sisters, Meyer v. Nebraska, and other decisions suggest, the] right of freedom of speech and press includes not only the right to utter or to print, but the right to distribute, the right to receive, the right to read and freedom of inquiry, freedom of thought, and freedom to teach — indeed the freedom of the entire university community. Without those peripheral rights the specific rights would be less secure. And so we reaffirm the principle of the *Pierce* and the *Meyer* cases.

In NAACP v. Alabama, [Chapter 7, section E1, infra], we protected the "freedom to associate and privacy in one's associations," noting that freedom of association was a peripheral First Amendment right. Disclosure of membership lists of a constitutionally valid association, we held, was invalid. [In] other words, the First Amendment has a penumbra where privacy is protected from governmental intrusion. In like context, we have protected forms of "association" that are not political in the customary sense but pertain to the social, legal, and economic benefit of the members. NAACP v. Button, [Chapter 7, section E5, infra]. [While association] is not expressly included in the First Amendment its existence is necessary in making the express guarantees fully meaningful.

The foregoing cases suggest that specific guarantees in the Bill of Rights have penumbras, formed by emanations from those guarantees that help give them life and substance. See Poe v. Ullman, 367 U.S. 497, 516–522 [Douglas, J., dissenting]. Various guarantees create zones of privacy. The right of association contained in the penumbra of the First Amendment is one, as we have seen. The Third Amendment in its prohibition against the quartering of soldiers "in any house" in time of peace without the consent of the owner is another facet of that privacy. The Fourth Amendment explicitly affirms the "right of the people to be secure in their persons, houses, papers, and effects, against unreasonable searches and seizures." The Fifth Amendment in its Self-Incrimination Clause enables the citizen to create a zone of privacy which government may not force him to surrender to his detriment. The Ninth Amendment provides: "The enumeration in the Constitution, of certain rights, shall not be construed to deny or disparage others retained by the people." . . .

We have had many controversies over these penumbral rights of "privacy and repose." [Skinner v. Oklahoma and other] cases bear witness that the right of privacy which presses for recognition here is a legitimate one.

The present case, then, concerns a relationship lying within the zone of privacy created by several fundamental constitutional guarantees. And it concerns a law which, in forbidding the use of contraceptives rather than regulating their manufacture or sale, seeks to achieve its goals by means having a maximum destructive impact upon that relationship. Such a law cannot stand in light of the familiar principle, so often applied by this Court, that a "governmental purpose to control or prevent activities constitutionally subject to state regulation may not be achieved by means which sweep unnecessarily broadly and thereby invade the area of protected freedoms." [NAACP v. Alabama.] Would we allow the police to search the sacred precincts of marital bedrooms for telltale signs of the use of contraceptives? The very idea is repulsive to the notions of privacy surrounding the marriage relationship.

We deal with a right of privacy older than the Bill of Rights. [Marriage] is a coming together for better or for worse, hopefully enduring, and intimate to the degree of being sacred. It is an association that promotes a way of life, not causes; a harmony in living, not political faiths; a bilateral loyalty, not commercial or social projects. Yet it is an association for as noble a purpose as any involved in our prior decisions.

Reversed.

Mr. Justice Goldberg, whom The Chief Justice and Mr. Justice Brennan join, concurring.

[My] conclusion that the concept of liberty [embraces] the right of marital privacy though that right is not mentioned explicitly in the Constitution is supported both by numerous decisions of this Court, referred to in the Court's opinion, and by the language and history of the Ninth Amendment [which] reveal that the Framers of the Constitution believed that there are additional fundamental rights, protected from governmental infringement. . . .

The Ninth Amendment [was] proffered to quiet expressed fears that a bill of specifically enumerated rights could not be sufficiently broad to cover all essential rights and that the specific mention of certain rights would be interpreted as a denial that others were protected. . . .

While this Court has had little occasion to interpret the Ninth Amendment, "[i]t cannot be presumed that any clause in the constitution is intended to be without effect." [To] hold that a right so basic and fundamental and so deep-rooted in our society as the right of privacy in marriage may be infringed because that right is not guaranteed in so many words by the first eight amendments to the Constitution is to ignore the Ninth Amendment and to give it no effect whatsoever. . . .

I do not mean to imply that the Ninth Amendment is applied against the States by the Fourteenth. [Rather,] the Ninth Amendment [simply] lends strong support to the view that the "liberty" protected by the Fifth and Fourteenth Amendments from infringement by the Federal Government or the States is not restricted to rights specifically mentioned in the first eight amendments. . . .

In determining which rights are fundamental, judges are not left at large to decide cases in light of their personal and private notions. Rather, they must look to the "traditions and [collective] conscience of our people" to determine whether a principle is "so rooted [there] . . . as to be ranked as fundamental." The inquiry is whether a right involved "is of such a character that it cannot be denied without violating those 'fundamental principles of liberty and justice which lie at the base of all our civil and political institutions.' . . ."

The entire fabric of the Constitution and the purposes that clearly underlie its specific guarantees demonstrate that the rights to marital privacy and to marry and raise a family are of similar order and magnitude as the fundamental rights specifically protected.

Although the Constitution does not speak in so many words of the right of privacy in marriage, I cannot believe that it offers these fundamental rights no protection. The fact that no particular provision of the Constitution explicitly forbids the State from disrupting the traditional relation of the family — a relation as old and as fundamental as our entire civilization — surely does not show that the Government was meant to have the power to do so. . . .

The logic of the dissents would sanction federal or state legislation that seems to me even more plainly unconstitutional than the statute before us. Surely the Government, absent a showing of a compelling subordinating state interest, could not decree that all husbands and wives must be sterilized after two children have been born to them. Yet by their reasoning such an invasion of marital privacy would not be subject to constitutional challenge because, while it might be "silly," no provision of the Constitution specifically prevents the Government from curtailing the marital right to bear children and raise a family. . . .

[The] State, at most, argues that there is some rational relation between this statute and what is admittedly a legitimate subject of state concern — the dis-couraging of extra-marital relations. It says that preventing the use of birth-control devices by married persons helps prevent the indulgence by some in such extra-marital relations. The rationality of this justification is dubious, particularly in light of the admitted widespread availability to all persons [in] Connecticut, unmarried as well as married, of birth-control devices for the prevention of disease, as distinguished from the prevention of conception. But, in any event, it is clear that the state interest in safeguarding marital fidelity can be served by a more discriminately tailored statute, which does not, like the present one, sweep unnecessarily broadly, reaching far beyond the evil sought to be dealt with and intruding upon the privacy of all married couples. [Connecticut] does have statutes, the constitutionality of which is beyond doubt, which prohibit adultery and fornication. . . .

MR. JUSTICE HARLAN, concurring in the judgment.

[I] fully agree with the judgment of reversal, but [cannot] join the Court's opinion [because it evinces the view that] the Due Process Clause of the Fourteenth Amendment does not touch this Connecticut statute unless the enactment is found to violate some right assured by the letter or penumbra of the Bill of Rights. . . .

In my view, the proper constitutional inquiry in this case is whether this Connecticut statute infringes the Due Process Clause of the Fourteenth Amendment because the enactment violates basic values "implicit in the concept of ordered liberty," [Palko v. Connecticut, section C, supra]. For reasons stated at length in my dissenting opinion in Poe v. Ullman, [367 U.S. 497 (1961)], I believe that it does. While the relevant inquiry may be aided by resort to one or more of the provisions of the Bill of Rights, it is not dependent on them or any of their radiations. The Due Process Clause of the Fourteenth Amendment stands, in my opinion, on its own bottom. . . .

While I could not more heartily agree that judicial "self restraint" is an indispensable ingredient of sound constitutional adjudication, I do submit that the formula suggested [by the dissenters] for achieving it is more hollow than real. "Specific" provisions of the Constitution, no less than "due process," lend themselves as readily to "personal" interpretations by judges whose constitutional outlook is simply to keep the Constitution in supposed "tune with the times." . . .

Judicial self-restraint will not, I suggest, be brought about in the "due process" area by the historically unfounded incorporation formula long advanced by my Brother Black. It will be achieved in this area, as in other constitutional areas, only by continual insistence upon respect for the teachings of history, solid recognition of the basic values that underlie our society, and wise appreciation of the great roles that the doctrines of federalism and separation of powers have played in establishing and preserving American freedoms. . . .

[Justice Harlan dissented in Poe v. Ullman, in which the Court dismissed on justiciability grounds a challenge to the Connecticut statute invalidated in *Griswold*. Harlan argued:]

[I] believe that a statute making it a criminal offense for married couples to use contraceptives is an intolerable and unjustifiable invasion of privacy in the conduct of the most intimate concerns of an individual's personal life. [Since this contention draws its] basis from no explicit language of the Constitution, [I] feel it desirable [to] state the framework of Constitutional principles in which I think the issue must be judged.

[Because] it is the Constitution alone which warrants judicial interference in sovereign operations of the State, the basis of judgment as to the Constitutionality of state action must be a rational one, approaching the text [not] in a literalistic way, as if we had a tax statute before us, but as the basic charter of our society, setting out in spare but meaningful terms the principles of government. . . .

Due process has not been reduced to any formula; its content cannot be determined by reference to any code. The best that can be said is that through the course of this Court's decisions it has represented the balance which our Nation, built upon postulates of respect for the liberty of the individual, has struck between that liberty and the demands of organized society. If the supplying of content to this Constitutional concept has of necessity been a rational process, it certainly has not been one where judges have felt free to roam where unguided speculation might take them. The balance of which I speak is the balance struck by this country, having regard to what history teaches are the traditions from which it developed as well as the traditions from which it broke. That tradition is a living thing. . . .

[The] liberty guaranteed by the Due Process Clause [is] not a series of isolated points [represented by the Bill of Rights]. It is a rational continuum which, broadly speaking, includes a freedom from all substantial arbitrary impositions and purposeless restraints, [citing, e.g., Allgeyer v. Louisiana; Skinner v. Oklahoma], and which also recognizes, what a reasonable and sensitive judgment must, that certain interests require particularly careful scrutiny of the state needs asserted to justify their abridgment. . . .

The State [asserts] that it is acting to protect the moral welfare of its citizenry. [Society] has traditionally concerned itself with the moral soundness of its people. [Certainly,] Connecticut's judgment [here] is no more demonstrably correct or incorrect than are the varieties of judgment, expressed in law, on marriage and divorce, on adult consensual homosexuality, abortion, and sterilization, or euthanasia and suicide. If we had a case before us which required us to decide simply, and in abstraction, whether the moral judgment implicit in the [present statute] was a sound one, the very controversial nature of these questions would, I think, require us to hesitate long before concluding that the Constitution precluded Connecticut from choosing as it has. . . .

But, as might be expected, we are not presented simply with this moral judgment to be passed on as an abstract proposition. The secular state [must] operate in the realm of behavior, [and] where it does so operate, not only the underlying, moral purpose of its operations, but also the *choice of means* becomes relevant to any Constitutional judgment on what is done. . . .

Precisely what is involved here is this: the State is asserting the right to enforce its moral judgment by intruding upon the most intimate details of the marital relation with the full power of the criminal law. Potentially, this could allow the deployment of all the incidental machinery of the criminal law, arrests, searches and seizures; inevitably, it must mean at the very least the lodging of criminal charges, a public trial, and testimony as the corpus delicti. [The] statute allows the State to enquire into, prove and punish married people for the private use of their marital intimacy.

[This] enactment involves what, by common understanding throughout the English-speaking world, must be granted to be a most fundamental aspect of "liberty," the privacy of the home in its most basic sense, and it is this which requires that the statute be subjected to "strict scrutiny." [Skinner v. Oklahoma.]

That aspect of liberty which embraces the concept of the privacy of the home receives explicit Constitutional protection at two places only. These are the Third [and Fourth Amendments]. . . .

It is clear, of course, that this Connecticut statute does not invade the privacy of the home in the usual sense, since the invasion involved here may [be] accomplished without any physical intrusion [into] the home. [But it] would surely be an extreme instance of sacrificing substance to form were it to be held that the Constitutional principle of privacy against arbitrary official intrusion comprehends only physical invasions by the police. [If] the physical curtilage of the home is protected, it is surely as a result of solicitude to protect the privacies of the life within. Certainly the safeguarding of the home does not follow merely from the sanctity of property rights. The home derives its pre-eminence as the seat of family life. [Of the] whole "private realm of family life" it is difficult to imagine what is more private or more intimate than a husband and wife's marital relations. . . .

Of course, [there] are countervailing considerations. "[T]he family . . . is not beyond regulation," and it would be an absurdity to suggest either that offenses may not be committed in the bosom of the family or that the home can be made a sanctuary for crime. The right of privacy [is] not an absolute. Thus, I would not suggest that adultery, homosexuality, fornication and incest are immune from criminal enquiry, however privately practiced. [But] not to discriminate between what is involved in this case and either the traditional offenses against good morals or crimes which, though they may be committed anywhere, happen to have been committed or concealed in the home, would entirely misconceive the argument that is being made.

[The] intimacy of husband and wife is necessarily an essential and accepted feature of the institution of marriage, an institution which the State not only must allow, but which always and in every age it has fostered and protected. It is one thing when the State exerts its power either to forbid extra-marital sexuality altogether, or to say who may marry, but it is quite another when, having acknowledged a marriage and the intimacies inherent in it, it undertakes to regulate by means of the criminal law the details of that intimacy. . . .

But conclusive, in my view, is the utter novelty of this enactment. Although the Federal Government and many States have at one time or other had on their books statutes forbidding or regulating the distribution of contraceptives, none, so far as I can find, has made the *use* of contraceptives a crime. . . .

MR. JUSTICE WHITE, concurring in the judgment.

[The] State claims [that] its anti-use statute [serves its] policy against all forms of promiscuous or illicit sexual relationships, be they premarital or extramarital, concededly a permissible and legitimate legislative goal. [But I] fail to see how the ban on the use of contraceptives by married couples in any way reinforces the State's ban on illicit sexual relationships. [Perhaps] the theory is that the flat ban on use prevents married people from possessing contraceptives and without the ready availability of such devices for use in the marital relationship, there will be no or less temptation to use them in extramarital ones. This reasoning rests on the premise that married people will comply with the ban in regard to their marital relationship, notwithstanding total nonenforcement in this context and apparent nonenforcibility, but will not comply with criminal statutes prohibiting extra-marital affairs and the anti-use statute in respect to illicit sexual relationships, a premise whose validity has not been demonstrated and whose intrinsic validity is not very evident. [I] find nothing in this record justifying the sweeping scope of this statute. . . .

MR. JUSTICE BLACK, with whom MR. JUSTICE STEWART joins, dissenting. . . .

The Court talks about a constitutional "right of privacy" as though there is some constitutional [provision] forbidding any law ever to be passed which might abridge the "privacy" of individuals. But there is not. There are, of course, guarantees in certain specific constitutional provisions which are designed in part to protect privacy at certain times and places with respect to certain activities. Such, for example, is the Fourth Amendment's guarantee against "unreasonable searches and seizures." But I think it belittles that Amendment to talk about it as though it protects nothing but "privacy." [The] average man would very likely not have his feelings soothed any more by having his property seized openly than by having it seized privately and by stealth. [I] get nowhere in this case by talk about a constitutional "right of privacy" as an emanation from one or more constitutional provisions.¹ I like my privacy as well as the next one, but I am nevertheless compelled to admit that government has a right to invade it unless prohibited by some specific constitutional provision. . . .

[Of] the cases on which my Brothers White and Goldberg rely so heavily, undoubtedly the reasoning of two of them supports their result here — as would that of a number of others which they do not bother to name, e.g., [*Lochner*]. The two they do cite and quote from, [*Meyer* and *Pierce*], elaborated the same natural law due process philosophy found in [*Lochner*]. [That was a] philosophy which many later opinions repudiated, and which I cannot accept. . . .

My Brother Goldberg has adopted the recent discovery that the Ninth Amendment as well as the Due Process Clause can be used by this Court as authority to strike down all state legislation which this Court thinks violates "fundamental principles of liberty and justice," or is contrary to the "traditions and [collective] conscience of our people." He also states [that] in making decisions on this basis judges will not consider "their personal and private notions." One may ask how they can avoid considering them. Our Court certainly has no machinery with which to take a Gallup Poll. And the scientific miracles of this age have not yet produced a gadget which the Court can use to determine what traditions are rooted in the "[collective] conscience of our people." Moreover, one would certainly have to look far beyond the language of the Ninth Amendment to find that the Framers vested in this Court any such awesome veto powers over lawmaking, either by the States or by the Congress. [That] Amendment was passed [to] assure the people that the Constitution in all its provisions was intended to limit the Federal Government to the powers granted expressly or by necessary implication. [This] fact is perhaps responsible for the peculiar phenomenon that for a period of a century and a half no serious suggestion was ever made that the Ninth Amendment [could] be used as a weapon of federal power to prevent state legislatures from passing laws they consider appropriate to govern local affairs. . . .

I realize that many good and able men have eloquently spoken and written [about] the duty of this Court to keep the Constitution in tune with the times. [For] myself, I must with all deference reject that philosophy. The Constitution makers knew the need for change and provided for it. [The] Due Process Clause with an "arbitrary and capricious" or "shocking to the conscience" formula was liberally used by this Court to strike down economic legislation in the early decades of this century, threatening, many people thought, the tranquility and stability of the Nation. That formula, based on subjective considerations of "natural justice," is no less dangerous when used to enforce this Court's views about personal rights than those about economic rights. . . .

---

1. The phrase "right to privacy" appears first to have gained currency from an article written by Messrs. Warren and (later Mr. Justice) Brandeis in 1890 which urged that States should give some form of tort relief to persons whose private affairs were exploited by others. The Right to Privacy, 4 Harv. L. Rev. 193. [Today] this Court, which I did not understand to have power to sit as a court of common law, now appears to be exalting a phrase which Warren and Brandeis used in discussing grounds for tort relief, to the level of a constitutional rule which prevents state legislatures from passing any law deemed by this Court to interfere with "privacy."

MR. JUSTICE STEWART, whom MR. JUSTICE BLACK joins, dissenting. . . .

I think this is an uncommonly silly law. [But] we are not asked in this case to say whether we think this law is unwise, or even asinine. We are asked to hold that it violates the United States Constitution. And that I cannot do.

In the course of its opinion the Court refers to no less than six Amendments to the Constitution: the First, the Third, the Fourth, the Fifth, the Ninth, and the Fourteenth. But the Court does not say which of these Amendments, if any, it thinks is infringed by this Connecticut law.

[What] provision of the Constitution, then, does make this state law invalid? The Court says it is the right of privacy "created by several fundamental constitutional guarantees." With all deference, I can find no such general right of privacy in the Bill of Rights, in any other part of the Constitution, or in any case ever before decided by this Court. . . .

Note: Griswold *and the Right of Privacy*

1. Griswold. There is no explicit general right to privacy in the Constitution's text. What, then, grounds the Court's decision? Is the point that specific constitutional rights imply the existence of other rights necessary to make the specific rights meaningful? Or is it that open-textured provisions invite the Court to invent altogether new rights?

2. *The ninth amendment.* One such open textured provision is the ninth amendment, which provides that "[the] enumeration in the Constitution, of certain rights, shall not be construed to deny or disparage others retained by the people." Consider the following views:

a. J. Ely, Democracy and Distrust 34–38 (1980):

The received account of the Ninth Amendment, [offered by Justice Black in *Griswold*, goes] like this. There was fear that the inclusion of a bill of rights [would] be taken to imply that federal power was [not] limited to the authorities enumerated in Article I, Section 8, [but] extended all the way up to the edge of the rights stated in the first eight amendments. [The] Ninth Amendment, the received version goes, was attached to the Bill of Rights [to] negate that inference. [But the] Tenth Amendment, submitted and ratified at the same time, completely fulfills [that] function. [Moreover, the legislative history of the Ninth Amendment is consistent with Justice Goldberg's view, and] the conclusion that the Ninth Amendment was intended to signal the existence of federal constitutional rights beyond those specifically enumerated in the Constitution is the only conclusion its language seems comfortably able to support.

b. Berger, The Ninth Amendment, 66 Cornell L. Rev. 1, 23, 20, 14 (1980):

[The ninth and tenth amendments] are complementary: the ninth deals with *rights* "retained by the people," the tenth with *powers* "reserved" to the states or the people. [Madison] made clear that the retained rights [constitute] an area in which the "Government ought not to act." This means, in my judgment, that the courts have not been empowered to enforce the retained rights. [Rather, in] "retaining" the unenumerated rights, the people reserved to themselves power to add to or subtract from the rights enumerated in the Constitution by the process of amendment. [If] this be deemed supererogatory, be it remembered that according to Madison the ninth amendment itself was "inserted merely for greater caution."

c. Caplan, The History and Meaning of the Ninth Amendment, 69 Va. L. Rev. 223, 264–265, 227–228 (1983):

[The] ninth amendment was drafted in order to allay concern that the Constitution might abolish rights traditionally guaranteed by state law. [These] "other" rights were understood to refer to the common law, along with the state constitutions and statutes engrafted onto it. [But the] ninth amendment [did] not transform these unenumerated rights into constitutional [rights]. Instead, it simply provides that the individual rights contained in state law are to continue in force under the Constitution until modified or eliminated by state enactment, by federal preemption, or by a judicial determination of unconstitutionality.

d. Barnett, The Ninth Amendment: It Means What It Says, 85 Tex. L. Rev. 1, 1 (2006):

[The] evidence establishes that the Ninth Amendment actually meant at the time of its enactment what it appears now to say: the unenumerated (natural) rights that people possessed prior to the formation of government, and which they retain afterwards, should be treated in the same manner as those (natural) rights that were enumerated in the Bill of Rights. In short, the Amendment is what it appears to be: a meaningful check on federal power and a significant guarantee of individual liberty.

Note that the ninth amendment does not by its own terms create any rights. Instead, it mandates only a rule of construction. It provides that the "enumeration . . . of certain rights shall not be construed to deny or disparage others retained by the people." Consider the possibility that the framers of the amendment meant to leave open the contested question whether there were any such rights, or at least whether there were any such rights that were judicially enforceable. For an argument along these lines, see Seidman, Our Unsettled Ninth Amendment: An Essay on Unenumerated Rights and the Impossibility of Textualism, 98 Cal. L. Rev. 2129 (2010).

Since *Griswold*, various justices have alluded to the ninth amendment but without offering a comprehensive theory of precisely what unenumerated rights it protects. See, e.g., Richmond Newspapers v. Virginia, 448 U.S. 555, 579 n.15 (1980) (opinion of Burger, C.J.) (concerning the right of the people to attend criminal trials). For a broad range of views on the ninth amendment, see the Symposium on Interpreting the Ninth Amendment, 64 Chi.-Kent L. Rev. 37 (1988).

3. *Outdated norms.* Was the real problem in *Griswold* one of desuetude? Consider the view that the law at issue could not be enforced directly against married couples because the Connecticut citizenry would be aghast at any such enforcement action. In this sense, the law was out of step with democratic convictions. Perhaps a law should not be usable at all if the public would not permit it to be enforced in the way that it reads. This view, perhaps involving a genuinely procedural due process claim, would read the so-called privacy cases as involving a judicial insistence that, if laws cannot be enforced directly — through the criminal law prohibiting certain activities — they cannot be enforced through indirect, sporadic, discriminatory routes that escape the same degree of public accountability. See C. Sunstein, One Case at a Time (1999), for a defense of this approach.

4. *The right of "privacy."* What is the nature of the right of "privacy" protected in *Griswold*? Is *Griswold* about the privacy of the home? The privacy of information concerning intimate matters? The integrity of the marriage relationship? Sexual freedom? Autonomy over decisions relating to childbearing? Autonomy generally?

5. *The reach of* Griswold: *the unmarried.* In Eisenstadt v. Baird, 405 U.S. 438 (1972), the Court, in a six-to-one decision, held that a Massachusetts statute prohibiting the distribution of any drug or device to unmarried persons for the prevention of conception violated the equal protection clause because it provided dissimilar treatment for married and unmarried persons.

Purporting to apply traditional rational basis review, the Court, in an opinion by Justice Brennan, held that none of the interests asserted in defense of the statute was sufficient to justify the challenged classification. First, the Court concluded that the deterrence of premarital sex could not reasonably be regarded as the purpose of the law. This was so because (a) the statute did not prohibit the distribution of contraceptives to prevent the "spread of disease," and thus was "so riddled with exceptions" that its effect "has at best a marginal relation to the proffered objective"; and (b) in any event, it "would be plainly unreasonable to assume that Massachusetts has prescribed pregnancy and the birth of an unwanted child as punishment for fornication, which is a misdemeanor under Massachusetts [law]."

Second, the Court rejected the contention that the classification was designed to "serve the health needs of the community by regulating the distribution of potentially harmful articles." This was so because (a) "not all contraceptives are potentially dangerous," and (b) this rationale does not serve to distinguish between married and unmarried persons.

Finally, the Court rejected the argument that the statute could be sustained on moral grounds "as a prohibition on contraception." The Court explained:

> [Whatever] the rights of the individual to access to contraceptives may be, the rights must be the same for the unmarried and the married alike. If under *Griswold* the distribution of contraceptives to married persons cannot be prohibited, a ban on distribution to unmarried persons would be equally impermissible. It is true that in *Griswold* the right of privacy in question inhered in the marital relationship. Yet the marital couple is not an independent entity with a mind and heart of its own, but an association of two individuals each with a separate intellectual and emotional makeup. If the right of privacy means anything, it is the right of the *individual,* married or single, to be free from unwarranted governmental intrusion into matters so fundamentally affecting a person as the decision whether to bear or beget a child. [On] the other hand, if *Griswold* is no bar to a prohibition on the distribution of contraceptives, the State could not, consistently with the Equal Protection Clause, outlaw distribution to unmarried but not to married persons. In each case the evil, as perceived by the State, would be identical, and the underinclusion would be invidious.

6. *The reach of* Griswold: *access to contraceptives.* In Carey v. Population Services International, 431 U.S. 678 (1977), the Court, in a seven-to-two decision, invalidated a New York law prohibiting any person other than a licensed pharmacist from distributing contraceptives. The Court, in an opinion by Justice Brennan, explained:

Griswold may no longer be read as holding only that a State may not prohibit a married couple's use of contraceptives. Read in light of its progeny, the teaching of *Griswold* is that the Constitution protects individual decisions in matters of childbearing from unjustified intrusion by the State. Restrictions on the distribution of contraceptives clearly burden the freedom to make such decisions. [Limiting] the distribution of nonprescription contraceptives to licensed pharmacists clearly imposes a significant burden on the right of individuals to use contraceptives if they choose to do so. [Accordingly, the challenged law] "may be justified only by a 'compelling state interest' [and] must be narrowly drawn to express only the legitimate state interests at stake." [None of the interests asserted in defense of this statute is] compelling.

2.   *Abortion*

Roe v. Wade

410 U.S. 113 (1973)

MR. JUSTICE BLACKMUN delivered the opinion of the Court.

This [appeal presents] constitutional challenges to state criminal abortion legislation. The Texas statutes under attack here [make procuring an abortion a crime except "by medical advice for the purpose of saving the life of the mother." These statutes] are typical of those that have been in effect in many States for approximately a century. . . .

We forthwith acknowledge our awareness of the sensitive and emotional nature of the abortion controversy, of the vigorous opposing views, even among physicians, and of the deep and seemingly absolute convictions that the subject inspires. . . .

Our task, of course, is to resolve the issue by constitutional measurement, free of emotion and of predilection. We seek earnestly to do this, and, because we do, we have inquired into, and in this opinion place some emphasis upon, medical and medical-legal history and what that history reveals about man's attitudes toward the abortion procedure over the centuries. . . .

[The] restrictive criminal abortion laws in effect in a majority of States today are of relatively recent vintage. [They] derive from statutory changes effected, for the most part, in the latter half of the 19th century. . . .

[In this portion of its opinion, the Court examines the history of abortion regulation.]

Three reasons have been advanced to explain historically the enactment of criminal abortion laws in the 19th century and to justify their continued existence.

It has been argued occasionally that these laws were [designed] to discourage illicit sexual conduct. Texas, however, does not advance this justification in the present case. . . .

A second reason is concerned with abortion as a medical procedure. When most criminal abortion laws were first enacted, the procedure was [hazardous]. [Thus,] it has been argued that a State's real concern in enacting a criminal abortion law was to protect the pregnant woman. [Modern] medical techniques have altered this situation. [Mortality] rates for women undergoing early abortions [appear] to be as low as or lower than the rates for normal childbirth. [Of] course, important state interests in the areas of health and medical standards do remain. The State has a legitimate interest in seeing to it that abortion, like any other medical procedure, is performed under circumstances that insure maximum safety for the patient [and] the State retains a definite interest in protecting the woman's own health and safety when an abortion is proposed at a late stage of pregnancy.

The third reason is the State's interest [in] protecting prenatal life. Some of the argument for this justification rests on the theory that a new human life is present from the moment of conception. [But in] assessing the State's interest, recognition may [also] be given to the less rigid claim that [at] least potential life is involved. . . .

The Constitution does not explicitly mention any right of privacy. [But] the Court has recognized that a right of personal privacy, or a guarantee of certain areas or zones of privacy, does exist under the Constitution. In varying contexts, the Court or individual Justices have, indeed, found at least the roots of that right in the First Amendment, Stanley v. Georgia, [Chapter 7, section D4, infra]; in the Fourth and Fifth Amendments; in the penumbras of the Bill of Rights, [*Griswold*]; in the Ninth Amendment, id., (Goldberg, J., concurring); or in the concept of liberty guaranteed by the first section of the Fourteenth Amendment, see Meyer v. Nebraska. These decisions make it clear that only personal rights that can be deemed "fundamental" or "implicit in the concept of ordered liberty," are included in this guarantee of personal privacy. They also make it clear that the right has some extension to activities relating to marriage, Loving v. Virginia, [Chapter 5, section C3, supra]; procreation, [*Skinner*]; contraception, [*Eisenstadt*]; family relationships, Prince v. Massachusetts, 321 U.S. 158 (1944); and child rearing and education, [*Pierce; Meyer*].

This right of privacy, whether it be founded in the Fourteenth Amendment's concept of personal liberty [as] we feel it is, or [in] the Ninth [Amendment], is broad enough to encompass a woman's decision whether or not to terminate her pregnancy. The detriment that the State would impose upon the pregnant woman by denying this choice altogether is apparent. Specific and direct harm medically diagnosable even in early pregnancy may be involved. Maternity, or additional offspring, may force upon the woman a distressful life and future. Psychological harm may be imminent. Mental and physical health may be taxed by child care. There is also the distress, for all concerned, associated with the unwanted child, and there is the problem of bringing a child into a family already unable, psychologically and otherwise, to care for it. In other cases, [the] additional difficulties and continuing stigma of unwed motherhood may be involved. All these are factors the woman and her responsible physician necessarily will consider in consultation.

On the basis of elements such as these, appellant [argues] that the woman's right is absolute and that she is entitled to terminate her pregnancy at whatever time, in whatever way, and for whatever reason she alone chooses. With this we do not agree. [The] Court's decisions recognizing a right of privacy also acknowledge that some state regulation in areas protected by that right is appropriate. . . .

Where certain "fundamental rights" are involved, the Court has held that regulation limiting these rights may be justified only by a "compelling state interest," and that legislative enactments must be narrowly drawn to express only the legitimate state interests at stake. . . .

The appellee [argues] that the fetus is a "person" within the language and meaning of the Fourteenth Amendment. [If] this suggestion of personhood is established, the appellant's case, of course, collapses, for the fetus' right to life would then be guaranteed specifically by the Amendment. . . .

The Constitution does not define "person" in so many words. Section 1 of the Fourteenth Amendment contains three references to "person." ["Person"] is used in other places in the Constitution. [The Court surveys other uses of the word in the Constitution]. But in nearly all these instances, the use of the word is such that it has application only postnatally. None indicates, with any assurance, that it has any possible pre-natal application.

All this, together with our observation that throughout the major portion of the 19th century prevailing legal abortion practices were far freer than they are today, persuades us that the word "person," as used in the Fourteenth Amendment, does not include the unborn.

[Thus,] we pass on to other considerations. The pregnant woman cannot be isolated in her privacy. She carries an embryo and, later, a fetus. [The] situation therefore is inherently different from marital intimacy, or bedroom possession of obscene material, or marriage, or procreation, or education, with which *Eisenstadt* and *Griswold, Stanley, Loving, Skinner,* and *Pierce* and *Meyer* were respectively concerned. [It] is reasonable and appropriate for a State to decide that at some point in time another interest, that of health of the mother or that of potential human life, becomes significantly involved. . . .

Texas urges that, apart from the Fourteenth Amendment, life begins at conception and is present throughout pregnancy, and that, therefore, the State has a compelling interest in protecting that life from and after conception. We need not resolve the difficult question of when life begins. When those trained [in] medicine, philosophy, and theology are unable to arrive at any consensus, the judiciary, at this point in the development of man's knowledge, is not in a position to speculate as to the answer.

It should be sufficient to note briefly the wide divergence of thinking on [this] question. There has always been strong support for the view that life does not begin until live birth. This was the belief of the Stoics. It appears to be the predominant, though not the unanimous, attitude of the Jewish faith. It may be taken to represent also the position of a large segment of the Protestant community. [The] common law found greater significance in quickening. Physicians and their scientific colleagues have [tended] to focus either upon conception, upon live birth, or upon the interim point at which the fetus becomes "viable," that is, potentially able to live outside the mother's womb, albeit with artificial aid. Viability is usually placed at about seven months (28 weeks) but may occur earlier, even at 24 weeks. [The Catholic church recognizes] the existence of life from the moment of conception. . . .

In areas other than criminal abortion [such as torts and inheritance], the law has been reluctant to endorse any theory that life, as we recognize it, begins before live birth or to accord legal rights to the unborn except in narrowly defined situations and except when the rights are contingent upon live birth. . . .

In view of all this, we do not agree that, by adopting one theory of life, Texas may override the rights of the pregnant woman that are at stake. We repeat, however, that the State does have an important and legitimate interest in preserving and protecting the health of the pregnant woman [and] that it has still *another* important and legitimate interest in protecting the potentiality of human life. These interests are separate and distinct. Each grows in substantiality as the woman approaches term and, at a point during pregnancy, each becomes "compelling."

With respect to [the] interest in the health of the mother, the "compelling" point, in the light of present medical knowledge, is at approximately the end of the first trimester. This is so because of the now-established medical fact [that] until the end of the first trimester mortality in abortion may be less than mortality in normal childbirth. It follows that, from and after this point, a State may regulate the abortion procedure to the extent that the regulation reasonably relates to the preservation and protection of maternal health. Examples of permissible state regulation in this area are requirements as to the qualifications of the person who is to perform the abortion; [as] to the facility in which the procedure is to be performed; [and] the like.

This means, on the other hand, that, for the period of pregnancy prior to this "compelling" point, the attending physician, in consultation with his patient, is free to determine, without regulation by the State, that, in his medical judgment, the patient's pregnancy should be terminated. If that decision is reached, the judgment may be effectuated by an abortion free of interference by the State.

With respect to [the] interest in potential life, the "compelling" point is at viability. This is so because the fetus then presumably has the capability of meaningful life outside the mother's womb. State regulation protective of fetal life after viability thus has both logical and biological justifications. If the State is interested in protecting fetal life during that period, it may go so far as to proscribe abortion during that period, except when it is necessary to preserve the life or health of the mother.

Measured against these standards, [the Texas statute] sweeps too broadly [and] therefore, cannot survive the constitutional attack made upon it here. . . .

This holding, we feel, is consistent with the relative weights of the respective interests involved, with the lessons and examples of medical and legal history, with the lenity of the common law, and with the demands of the profound problems of the present day. . . .

MR. JUSTICE STEWART, concurring.
[The] Constitution nowhere mentions a specific right of personal choice in matters of marriage and family life, but the "liberty" protected by the Due Process Clause of the Fourteenth Amendment covers more than those freedoms explicitly named in the Bill of Rights. [In *Eisenstadt*], we recognized "the right of the *individual*, married or single, to be free from unwarranted governmental intrusion into matters so fundamentally affecting a person as the decision whether to bear or beget a child." That right necessarily includes the right of a woman to decide whether or not to terminate her pregnancy. . . .

It is evident that the Texas abortion statute infringes that right directly. [The] question then becomes whether the state interests advanced to justify this abridgment can survive the "particularly careful scrutiny" that the Fourteenth Amendment here requires.

The asserted state interests are protection of the health and safety of the pregnant woman, and protection of the potential future human life within her. These are legitimate objectives, [but as] the Court today has thoroughly demonstrated, [these] state interests cannot constitutionally support the broad abridgment of personal liberty worked by the existing Texas law. . . .

MR. JUSTICE DOUGLAS, concurring.
[The] Ninth Amendment [does] not create federally enforceable rights. [But] a catalogue of [the rights "retained by the people"] includes customary, traditional,

and time-honored rights, amenities, privileges, and immunities that come within the sweep of "the Blessings of Liberty" mentioned in the preamble to the Constitution. Many of them, in my view, come within the meaning of the term "liberty" as used in the Fourteenth Amendment.

First is the autonomous control over the development and expression of one's intellect, interests, tastes, and personality. . . .

Second is freedom of choice in the basic decisions of one's life respecting marriage, divorce, procreation, contraception, and the education and upbringing of children. . . .

Third is the freedom to care for one's health and person, freedom from bodily restraint or compulsion, freedom to walk, stroll, or loaf. . . .

[While] childbirth endangers the lives of some women, voluntary abortion at any time and place regardless of medical standards would impinge on a rightful concern of society. The woman's health is part of that concern; as is the life of the fetus after quickening. These concerns justify the State in treating the procedure as a medical one. . . .

[A concurring opinion of Chief Justice Burger, noting that "the Court today rejects any claim that the Constitution requires abortion on demand," is omitted.]

MR. JUSTICE WHITE, with whom MR. JUSTICE REHNQUIST joins, dissenting.

[I] find nothing in the language or history of the Constitution to support the Court's judgment. The Court simply fashions and announces a new constitutional right for pregnant mothers and, with scarcely any reason or authority for its action, invests that right with sufficient substance to override most existing state abortion statutes. The upshot is that the people and the legislatures of the 50 States are constitutionally disentitled to weigh the relative importance of the continued existence and development of the fetus, on the one hand, against a spectrum of possible impacts on the mother, on the other hand. As an exercise of raw judicial power, the Court perhaps has authority to do what it does today; but in my view its judgment is an improvident and extravagant exercise of the power of judicial review that the Constitution extends to this Court. . . .

MR. JUSTICE REHNQUIST, dissenting. . . .

I have difficulty in concluding [that] the right of "privacy" is involved in this case. Texas [bars] the performance of a medical abortion by a licensed physician on a plaintiff such as Roe. A transaction resulting in an operation such as this is not "private" in the ordinary usage of that word. Nor is the "privacy" that the Court finds here even a distant relative of the freedom from searches and seizures protected by the Fourth Amendment, . . .

If the Court means by the term "privacy" no more than that the claim of a person to be free from unwanted state regulation of consensual transactions may be a form of "liberty" protected by the Fourteenth Amendment, there is no doubt that similar claims have been upheld in our earlier decisions on the basis of that liberty. [The] test traditionally applied in the area of social and economic legislation is whether or not a law such as that challenged has a rational relation to a valid state objective. The Due Process Clause of the Fourteenth Amendment undoubtedly does place a limit, albeit a broad one, on legislative power to enact laws such as this. If the Texas statute were to prohibit an abortion even where the mother's life is in jeopardy, I have little doubt that such a statute would lack a rational relation to a valid state objective. But the Court's sweeping invalidation of any restrictions on abortion during the first trimester is impossible to justify under that standard, and the conscious weighing of competing factors that the Court's opinion apparently substitutes for the established test is far more appropriate to a legislative judgment than to a judicial one . . . .

The fact that a majority of the States reflecting, after all, the majority sentiment in those States, have had restrictions on abortions for at least a century is a strong indication, it seems to me, that the asserted right to an abortion is not "so rooted in the traditions and conscience of our people as to be ranked as fundamental." Even today, when society's views on abortion are changing, the very existence of the debate is evidence that the "right" to an abortion is not so universally accepted as the appellant would have us believe.

To reach its result, the Court necessarily has had to find within the scope of the Fourteenth Amendment a right that was apparently completely unknown to the drafters of the Amendment. [By] the time of the adoption of the Fourteenth Amendment in 1868, there were at least 36 laws enacted by state or territorial legislatures limiting abortion. [The] only conclusion possible from this history is that the drafters did not intend to have the Fourteenth Amendment withdraw from the States the power to legislate with respect to this matter. . . .

Note: The Abortion Decision

1. Griswold *to* Eisenstadt *to* Roe. A central issue in *Roe* was whether there was a constitutional basis for the woman's right of "privacy." The Court relied heavily on precedent to establish this right, but critics argue that the precedents did not establish a general right of privacy, let alone a right broad enough to reach abortion. Consider, for example, Ely, The Wages of Crying Wolf: A Comment on Roe v. Wade, 82 Yale L.J. 920, 930 (1973):

> [The] Court in *Griswold* stressed that it was invalidating only that portion of the Connecticut law that proscribed the use, as opposed to the manufacture, sale, or other distribution of contraceptives. That distinction [makes] sense [only] if the case is rationalized on the ground that [enforcement of the challenged provision] *would have been virtually impossible without* the most outrageous sort of governmental prying into the privacy of the home. [No] such rationalization is [possible in *Roe*], for whatever else may be involved, it is not a case about governmental snooping.

Defenders of *Roe*, on the other hand, argue that, taken together, the *Meyer/Pierce/Griswold/Eisenstadt* line of cases delineates a sphere of interests — which the Court now groups and denominates "privacy" — implicit in the "liberty" protected by the fourteenth amendment:

> At the core of this sphere is the right of the individual to make for himself [the] fundamental decisions that shape family life: whom to marry; whether and when to have children; and with what values to rear those children. [Plainly] the right [to an abortion] falls within [this] class of [interests]. The question of constitutionality [in *Roe*] is a more difficult one than that involved in *Griswold* and *Eisenstadt* only because the asserted state interest is more important, not because of any difference in the individual interests involved.

Heymann and Barzelay, The Forest and the Trees: Roe v. Wade and Its Critics, 53 B.U. L. Rev. 765, 772, 775 (1973).

2. *In defense of* Roe: *the question of a prima facie right to reproductive autonomy.* Consider the following two arguments:

a. Suppose that the state embarked upon a program of artificially inseminating unwilling women and forcing them to carry the resulting pregnancy to term. Is it conceivable that such a program would be constitutional? (Is it a sufficient answer to this hypothetical question that the circumstances it describes are very unlikely to arise?) Unlike any of the other privacy cases, *Roe* involved the interest to control over one's own body, or bodily integrity. This interest is far more tightly connected to the original or core concerns of the due process clause — and the common law itself — than the "privacy" right at issue in *Griswold*. Whether or not the government's justification is sufficient, surely the interest at issue is one that can be invaded only with special justification — unless the government can compel sterilization or involuntary medical treatment of multiple kinds.

Does the abortion right imply a right not to be a genetic, as opposed to a gestational parent? Suppose, for example, that a married couple uses in vitro fertilization and freezes some of the resulting preembryos. If the parties then divorce, is it unconstitutional for the state to prohibit one spouse from destroying these preembryos? For an argument that there is no right not to be a genetic parent when genetic parenthood is divorced from gestational and legal parenthood, see Cohen, The Constitution and the Rights Not to Procreate, 60 Stan. L. Rev. 1135 (2008).

b. The problem of abortion raises questions not of privacy, or not mostly of privacy, but instead, or in addition, of sex discrimination. The first point here is that only women become pregnant, and only women need abortions. Because laws prohibiting abortion are targeted at a class consisting exclusively of women, they should be understood as embodying a form of discrimination. On this view, the Court's decisions in *Griswold, Eisenstadt,* and *Roe,* and its decisions granting heightened scrutiny to gender classifications under the equal protection clause (see Chapter 5, section D, supra), "present various faces of a single issue: the roles women are to play in our society." It "is simply inconceivable that the majority Justices in *Roe* were indifferent to this question." Karst, Book Review, 89 Harv. L. Rev. 1028, 1036–1037 (1976).

Consider L. Tribe, Constitutional Choices 243 (1985):

> [Although] current law nowhere forces men to sacrifice their bodies and restructure their lives even in those tragic situations (of needed organ transplants, for example) where nothing less will permit their children to survive, those who would outlaw abortion [would] rely [on] physiological circumstances — the supposed dictates of the natural — to conscript women [as] involuntary incubators and thus to usurp a control over sexual activity and its consequences that men [take] for granted. To one who regards this outcome as unjust, a right to end pregnancy might be seen more plausibly as a matter of resisting sexual [domination] than as a matter of shielding from public control "private" transactions.

On this view, the problem with laws forbidding abortion is that they turn a biological difference with no necessary social consequences — women's capacity to bear children — into a social disadvantage. Such laws do not simply let nature run its course; instead, they compel women to be involuntary incubators. See also

Regan, Rewriting Roe v. Wade, 77 Mich. L. Rev. 1569 (1979). This view has the advantage of making it unnecessary, or arguably unnecessary, to decide on the moral status of the fetus. A selective cooptation of human bodies for the protection of third parties would be unconstitutional, even if those third parties are human beings. To this it might be added that laws forbidding abortion exist only because of traditional (and constitutionally barred) notions about the naturalness of women's roles as first and foremost childbearers. (In fact, restrictions on abortion rights have often been sought by people also enthusiastic about women's traditional role.) If men could get pregnant, it might be urged, abortion restrictions would not exist.

Is it true that the law forces only women "to sacrifice their bodies and restructure their lives"? Consider the military draft during time of war, which existed for much of the nation's history, and which applied only to men. Do laws that discriminate against persons who are pregnant in fact discriminate against women? See Geduldig v. Aiello, Chapter 5, section D, supra. Perhaps they do; but the point is not obvious. Even if they do, it does not necessarily follow that abortion restrictions are a form of sex discrimination.

For discussion of the abortion problem as one of sex discrimination, see Ginsburg, Some Thoughts on Autonomy and Equality in Relation to Roe v. Wade, 63 N.C. L. Rev. 375 (1985); Law, Rethinking Sex and the Constitution, 132 U. Pa. L. Rev. 955 (1984). For the view that the conception of the abortion right as one of "privacy" is fundamentally wrong, see MacKinnon, Roe v. Wade: A Study in Male Ideology in Abortion — Moral and Legal Perspectives 45, 49, 51 (J. Garfield ed., 1985):

> In feminist terms, [Roe] translates the ideology of the private sphere into the individual woman's legal right to privacy as a means of subordinating women's collective needs to the imperatives of male supremacy. [Under] conditions of gender inequality, [Roe] does not free women, it frees male sexual aggression. The availability of abortion [removes] the one remaining legitimized reason that women have had for refusing sex besides the headache.

On this account, the problem with the privacy notion is that it suggests that the realm of family, sex, and reproduction is essentially voluntary and free from power and politics. Notions of privacy in these arenas tend to confirm, rather than to undermine, the power of men over women.

3. *"Compelling state interest."* Even if (a) laws forbidding abortion are a form of sex discrimination or (b) there is a constitutional "right of privacy" and that right is "broad enough to encompass a woman's decision whether or not to terminate her pregnancy," the question remains whether the prohibition of abortion serves a "compelling state interest." In answering that question, can the Court avoid a decision about when life begins? If protection of potential life is a compelling state interest, doesn't it follow that potential of actual life is such an interest? Perhaps the inability of those trained in "medicine, philosophy, and theology [to] arrive at [a] consensus" means that the Court should simply have deferred to the legislative judgment. Consider, though, the alternative possibility that in the face of this disagreement, the Court should defer to the judgment of individual women. Note that, on this view of the case, the conflict it poses is not between legislative and judicial authority (after all, Roe nowhere suggests that courts should have the power to force women to have abortions) but between collective and individual choice.

4. *The fetus as "person" or as otherwise providing a sufficient end for government restrictions: a "dispositive" issue?* It is often assumed that, if the fetus is a "person," or if the interest in protecting it is "compelling," *Roe* is necessarily wrong. But consider the following views.

a. L. Tribe, American Constitutional Law 931 (1978):

[Prior to *Roe*, antiabortion laws] were not consistently enforced [either] against the affluent, who could evade them by obtaining lawful abortions outside their own restrictive jurisdictions, or against the poor, untold numbers of whom would unavoidably "subject themselves to the notorious backstreet abortion . . . fraught with the myriad possibilities of mutilation, infection, sterility and death." Thus, [in] view of the realities too commonplace to be ignored, the Court might understandably have viewed restrictive abortion laws less as meaningful protections for unborn life than as relatively pointless and economically skewed expressions of outdated worry about the health of the women involved coupled with disapproval of their moral choices.

Consider in this regard these (contestable but frequently agreed-upon) facts: (1) When abortion was unlawful, several thousand women died per year as a result of illegal abortions; (2) several more thousands of women faced serious health impairment, including emergency hospital admissions, as a result of illegal abortions; (3) the abortion rate before *Roe* was somewhere between 20 percent and 25 percent, whereas after *Roe* it is somewhere around 27 percent; (4) it is hard to demonstrate that there was a large increase in abortions as a result of *Roe*. Are any or all of these facts relevant? Consider the view that these contestable claims should play absolutely no role in constitutional law.

b. Thomson, A Defense of Abortion, 1 Phil. & Pub. Aff. 47, 48–49, 55–59 (1971):

I propose [that] we grant [for the sake of argument] that the fetus is a person from the moment of conception. . . .
[Now] let me ask you to imagine this. You wake up in the morning and find yourself back to back in bed with an unconscious violinist. [He] has been found to have a fatal kidney ailment, and the Society of Music Lovers has canvassed all the available medical records and found that you alone have the right blood type to help. They have therefore kidnapped you [and] plugged [the violinist's circulatory system] into yours. [To] unplug you would be to kill him. But never mind, it's only for nine months. By then he will have recovered [and] can safely be unplugged. [Is] it morally incumbent on you to accede to this situation? . . .
[The] right to life consists not in the right not to be killed, but rather in the right not to be killed unjustly. [This enables] us to square the fact that the violinist has a right to life with the fact that you do not act unjustly toward him in unplugging yourself, thereby killing him. For if you do not kill him unjustly, you do not violate his right to life. [But] if this emendation is accepted, the gap in the argument against abortion stares us plainly in the face: it is by no means enough to show that the fetus is a person, and to remind us that all persons have a right to life — we need to be shown also that killing the fetus violates its right to life, i.e., that abortion is unjust killing. And is it?

5. *Viability.* The Court held that, with "respect to [the] interest in potential life, the 'compelling' point is at viability [because] the fetus then presumably has the capability of meaningful life outside the mother's womb." Does this conclusion "mistake a definition for a syllogism"? Ely, supra, at 924. Consider Tribe,

Foreword: Toward a Model of Roles in the Due Process of Life and Law, 87 Harv. L. Rev. 1 (1973) at 27–28: "Once the fetus can be severed from the woman by a process which enables it to survive, leaving the abortion decision to private choice would confer not only a right to remove an unwanted fetus from one's body, but also an entirely separate right to ensure its death. [Viability] thus marks a point after which [the] state could properly conclude that permitting abortion would be tantamount to permitting murder."

The viability principle poses several potential problems.

a. *Shifting viability.* Viability is not biologically fixed. It will arrive earlier in gestation as better techniques are developed for sustaining existence outside the womb. Is this a problem? One might see this as a built-in social safety valve. If society really cares about fetal life, it can do something about it by advancing technology. See Tribe, Structural Due Process, 10 Harv. C.R.-C.L. L. Rev. 269 (1975).

Is the right of privacy recognized in *Roe* about the right not to continue an unwanted pregnancy, or is it about the right not to have unwanted children? If *Roe* is about the right not to be a mother, shifting viability should not matter. But the viability line itself suggests that *Roe* is about the right not to be pregnant, not the right not to be a mother.

b. *Uncertain viability.* The point of viability varies from fetus to fetus, and it is extremely difficult to determine the precise point of viability for any particular fetus. How, then, should viability be defined? At the point at which the average fetus is viable? At the earliest point at which a fetus has been found viable?

6. *The attack on* Roe. Recent scholarship has thrown doubt on the claim that Roe was strongly countermajoritarian and that the decision itself produced an immediate, large-scale backlash. See generally Greenhouse & Siegel, Before (and After) Roe v. Wade: New Questions About Backlash, 120 Yale L.J. 2028 (2011). Polls showed that a sizable majority of Americans favored legalization of abortion at the time that Roe was decided and that the percentage continued to grow in the immediate wake of the decision. Id. at 2081 n.83.

But whatever the cause, there can be no doubt that *Roe* became intensely controversial. In 1980, Ronald Reagan made *Roe* a major campaign issue, and his administration sought to persuade the Court to overrule its decision. The post-*Roe* cases that follow should be considered in the context of sustained political campaigns designed on the one hand to end, and on the other hand to preserve, the abortion right.

Note: *Abortion Regulation between* Roe *and* Casey

1. *Abortion Funding.* In Maher v. Roe, 432 U.S. 464 (1977) the Court, by a vote of six to three, upheld a state regulation granting Medicaid benefits for childbirth but denying such benefits for nontherapeutic abortions (i.e., abortions that are not "medically necessary"). Writing for the Court, Justice Powell emphasized that *Roe* implied "no limitation on the authority of a State to make a value judgment favoring childbirth over abortion, and to implement that judgment by the allocation of public funds" and that although the state had made childbirth "a more attractive alternative," it had "imposed no restriction on access to abortions that was not already there." See also Harris v. McRae, 448 U.S. 297 (1980) (extending *Maher* to uphold the "Hyde Amendment," which prohibited the use of federal Medicaid funds "to perform abortions except where the life of the mother would be endangered if the fetus were carried to term; or except for

such medical procedures necessary for the victims of rape or incest"). Cf. Rust v. Sullivan, 500 U.S. 173 (1991) (upholding the refusal of the government to fund speech that involved abortion in a context where it was subsidizing pregnancy counseling).

2. *The early cases.* With the exception of cases involving abortion funding, the Court generally resisted state regulation of abortion rights in the years immediately after *Roe.* Consider the extent to which these cases were influenced by the perception that the states were attempting to undermine the right rather than to regulate it in good faith. Compare the Court's reaction to the "massive resistance" that followed its decision in Brown v. Board of Education, discussed in Chapter 5, section A, supra.

For examples, see City of Akron v. Akron Center for Reproductive Health, Inc., 462 U.S. 416 (1983) (invalidating inter alia a requirement that second trimester abortions be performed in a hospital, that the physician inform the woman of the physical and emotional complications that may result from an abortion, and a twenty-four hour waiting period following the woman's signing of a consent form); Planned Parenthood of Central Missouri v. Danforth, 428 U.S. 52 (1976) (invalidating a statute requiring spousal consent to an abortion unless it was necessary to protect the life of the mother); Thornberg v. American College of Obstetricians & Gynecologists, 476 U.S. 747 (1986) (invalidating a statute requiring the use of the abortion technique most protective of the life of the fetus in postviability abortions); Colautti v. Franklin, 439 U.S. 379 (invalidating on vagueness grounds a statutory requirement that a physician determine whether a fetus is viable, and if it is determined that fetus "may be viable" to exercise the same care in preserving the life and health of the fetus as would be required "if the fetus were intended to be born alive"). But see Planned Parenthood Association of Kansas City v. Danforth, 462 U.S. 476 (1983) (upholding recordkeeping requirements for abortions); Planned Parenthood Association v. Ashcroft, 462 U.S. 476 (1983) (upholding requirement that tissue sample of aborted fetus be submitted to a certified pathologist); H. L. v. Matheson, 450 U.S. 398 (1981) (upholding a requirement that a physician notify a parent or guardian of a minor woman seeking an abortion in circumstances where the woman was living with and dependent on her parents, not emancipated, and made no claim or showing as to her maturity); Bellotti v. Baird, 443 U.S. 622 (1979) (indicating that a parental consent requirement would be permissible if it provided for a judicial bypass).

3. *Shifting attitudes on the Court.* The vote in *Roe* was seven to two, but as the composition of the Court gradually changed, it became less clear that a majority of the justices still favored an abortion right. When several provisions of a Missouri statute regulating abortion came before the Court in 1989, many commentators predicted that the Court would overrule *Roe.* In fact, a plurality of the Court in Webster v. Reproductive Health Services, 492 U.S. 490 (1989), upheld the Missouri statute and endorsed a significant reformulation of *Roe*'s trimester approach. However, the plurality was unable to attract the votes of a majority to overrule the decision.

The plurality found, first, that a statement in the statute's preamble that "the life of each human being begins at conception" was not in conflict with the statement in *Roe* that "a State may not adopt one theory of when life begins to justify its regulation of abortions." The preamble simply "express[ed] . . . [a] value judgment" in the abstract.

Relying on Harris v. McRae and related cases, the Court also upheld a bar on state employees performing abortions and a ban on the use of public facilities for performing abortions — even when the patient paid for the abortion herself.

The final provision at issue in *Webster*, as interpreted by the Court, required a physician, prior to performing an abortion "on a woman he has reason to believe is carrying an unborn child of twenty or more weeks gestational age," to perform tests that, in the physician's reasonable professional judgment, would be useful in determining the viability of the fetus. The plurality, in an opinion by Chief Justice Rehnquist, said that this statute, which regulated the performance of abortions in the second trimester in the interest not of maternal health, but of protecting potential human life, conflicted with the trimester system articulated in *Roe* and applied in *Colautti.* "It undoubtedly does superimpose state regulation on the medical determination of whether a particular fetus is viable." In addition, the plurality said that, "to the extent that the viability tests increase the cost of what are in fact second-trimester abortions" — in cases where the tests show that the fetus was not viable — "their validity may also be questioned under *Akron.*"

With respect to this issue, the plurality acknowledged that "[stare] decisis is a cornerstone of our legal system, but it has less power in constitutional cases, where, save for constitutional amendments, this Court is the only body able to make needed changes." In a key passage, the plurality argued that *Roe's* trimester system should be abandoned. "The rigid *Roe* framework is hardly consistent with the notion of a Constitution cast in general terms, as ours is, and usually speaking in general principles, as ours does."

However, the crucial fifth vote in the case was provided by Justice O'Connor, who wrote, "Unlike the plurality, I do not understand these viability testing requirements to conflict with any of the Court's past decisions concerning state regulation of abortion. Therefore, there is no necessity to accept the State's invitation to reexamine the constitutional validity of Roe v. Wade."

In an opinion concurring in part and concurring in the judgment, Justice Scalia urged the explicit overruling of *Roe:*

> The outcome of today's case will doubtless be heralded as a triumph of judicial statesmanship. It is not that, unless it is statesmanlike needlessly to prolong this Court's self-awarded sovereignty over a field where it has little proper business since the answers to most of the cruel questions posed are political and not juridical — a sovereignty which therefore quite properly, but to the great damage of the Court, makes it the object of the sort of organized public pressure that political institutions in a democracy ought to receive.

In an unusually personal opinion, concurring in part and dissenting in part, Justice Blackmun, the author of *Roe*, joined by Justices Brennan and Marshall, wrote:

> Today, Roe v. Wade, and the fundamental constitutional right of women to decide whether to terminate a pregnancy, survive but are not secure. Although the Court extricates itself from this case without making a single, even incremental, change in the law of abortion, the plurality and Justice Scalia would overrule *Roe* (the first silently, the other explicitly) and would return to the States virtually unfettered authority to control the quintessentially intimate, personal, and life-directing decision whether to carry a fetus to term. Although today, no less than yesterday, the Constitution and the decisions of this Court prohibit a State from enacting laws

that inhibit women from the meaningful exercise of that right, a plurality of this Court implicitly invites every state legislature to enact more and more restrictive abortion regulations in order to provoke more and more test cases, in the hope that sometime down the line the Court will return the law of procreative freedom to the severe limitations that generally prevailed in this country before January 22, 1973. Never in my memory has a plurality announced a judgment of this Court that so foments disregard for the law and for our standing decisions. . . .

I fear for the future. I fear for the liberty and equality of the millions of women who have lived and come of age in the 16 years since Roe was decided. I fear for the integrity of, and public esteem for, this Court. . . .

For today, at least, the law of abortion stands undisturbed. For today, the women of this Nation still retain the liberty to control their destinies. But the signs are evident and very ominous, and a chill wind blows.

Justice Stevens also filed an opinion concurring in part and concurring in the judgment.

Shortly after the decisions in *Webster*, President George H. W. Bush, a public opponent of *Roe*, appointed two new justices to the Court. The Court thereupon returned to the abortion issue in the case excerpted below. Consider the extent to which the decisions summarized in this Note survive the Court's new formulation of the abortion right.

Planned Parenthood of Southeastern Pennsylvania v. Casey

505 U.S. 833 (1992)

JUSTICE O'CONNOR, JUSTICE KENNEDY, and JUSTICE SOUTER announced the judgment of the Court and delivered the opinion of the Court with respect to Parts I, II, III, V-A, V-C, and VI, an opinion with respect to Part V-E, in which JUSTICE STEVENS joins, and an opinion with respect to Parts IV, V-B, and V-D.

I

Liberty finds no refuge in a jurisprudence of doubt. Yet 19 years after our holding that the Constitution protects a woman's right to terminate her pregnancy in its early stages, that definition of liberty is still questioned. Joining the respondents as amicus curiae, the United States, as it has done in five other cases in the last decade, again asks us to overrule *Roe*.

At issue in these cases are five provisions of the Pennsylvania Abortion Control Act of 1982 as amended in 1988 and 1989. [The] Act requires that a woman seeking an abortion give her informed consent prior to the abortion procedure, and specifies that she be provided with certain information at least 24 hours before the abortion is performed. For a minor to obtain an abortion, the Act requires the informed consent of one of her parents, but provides for a judicial bypass option if the minor does not wish to or cannot obtain a parent's consent. Another provision of the Act requires that, unless certain exceptions apply, a married woman seeking an abortion must sign a statement indicating that she has notified her husband of her intended abortion. The Act exempts compliance with these three requirements in the event of a "medical emergency." [In] addition to the above provisions regulating the performance of abortions, the Act imposes certain reporting requirements on facilities that provide abortion services.

[After] considering the fundamental constitutional questions resolved by *Roe*, principles of institutional integrity, and the rule of stare decisis, we are led to conclude this: the essential holding of Roe v. Wade should be retained and once again reaffirmed.

It must be stated at the outset and with clarity that *Roe*'s essential holding, the holding we reaffirm, has three parts. First is a recognition of the right of the woman to choose to have an abortion before viability and to obtain it without undue interference from the State. Before viability, the State's interests are not strong enough to support a prohibition of abortion or the imposition of a substantial obstacle to the woman's effective right to elect the procedure. Second is a confirmation of the State's power to restrict abortions after fetal viability, if the law contains exceptions for pregnancies which endanger a woman's life or health. And third is the principle that the State has legitimate interests from the outset of the pregnancy in protecting the health of the woman and the life of the fetus that may become a child.

II

Constitutional protection of the woman's decision to terminate her pregnancy derives from the Due Process Clause of the Fourteenth Amendment. [Although] a literal reading of the Clause might suggest that it governs only the procedures by which a State may deprive persons of liberty, for at least 105 years, [the] Clause has been understood to contain a substantive component as well.

[It] is also tempting [to] suppose that the Due Process Clause protects only those practices, defined at the most specific level, that were protected against government interference by other rules of law when the Fourteenth Amendment was ratified. See Michael H. v. Gerald D., 491 U.S. 110, 127–128, n.6 (1989) (opinion of Scalia, J.). But such a view would be inconsistent with our law. It is a promise of the Constitution that there is a realm of personal liberty which the government may not enter. We have vindicated this principle before. Marriage is mentioned nowhere in the Bill of Rights and interracial marriage was illegal in most States in the 19th century, but the Court was no doubt correct in finding it to be an aspect of liberty protected against state interference by the substantive component of the Due Process Clause in Loving v. Virginia. [Neither] the Bill of Rights nor the specific practices of States at the time of the adoption of the Fourteenth Amendment marks the outer limits of the substantive sphere of liberty which the Fourteenth Amendment protects. See U.S. Const., Amend. 9.

[Abortion] is a unique act. It is an act fraught with consequences for others: for the woman who must live with the implications of her decision; for the persons who perform and assist in the procedure; for the spouse, family, and society which must confront the knowledge that these procedures exist, procedures some deem nothing short of an act of violence against innocent human life; and, depending on one's beliefs, for the life or potential life that is aborted. [The] mother who carries a child to full term is subject to anxieties, to physical constraints, to pain that only she must bear. That these sacrifices have from the beginning of the human race been endured by woman with a pride that ennobles her in the eyes of others and gives to the infant a bond of love cannot alone be grounds for the State to insist she make the sacrifice. Her suffering is too intimate and personal for the State to insist, without more, upon its own vision of the woman's role, however dominant that vision has been in the course of our history and our culture. The destiny of the woman must be shaped to a large extent on her own conception of her spiritual imperatives and her place in society.

It should be recognized, moreover, that in some critical respects the abortion decision is of the same character as the decision to use contraception, to which Griswold v. Connecticut, Eisenstadt v. Baird, and Carey v. Population Services International afford constitutional protection. We have no doubt as to the correctness of those decisions. They support the reasoning in *Roe* relating to the woman's liberty because they involve personal decisions concerning not only the meaning of procreation but also human responsibility and respect for it. . . .

III

A. . . .

[When] this Court reexamines a prior holding, its judgment is customarily informed by a series of prudential and pragmatic considerations designed to test the consistency of overruling a prior decision with the ideal of the rule of law, and to gauge the respective costs of reaffirming and overruling a prior case. [In] this case we may inquire whether *Roe's* central rule has been found unworkable; whether the rule's limitation on state power could be removed without serious inequity to those who have relied upon it or significant damage to the stability of the society governed by the rule in question; whether the law's growth in the intervening years has left *Roe's* central rule a doctrinal anachronism discounted by society; and whether *Roe's* premises of fact have so far changed in the ensuing two decades as to render its central holding somehow irrelevant or unjustifiable in dealing with the issue it addressed.

1

Although *Roe* has engendered opposition, it has in no sense proven "unworkable," representing as it does a simple limitation beyond which a state law is unenforceable. While *Roe* has, of course, required judicial assessment of state laws affecting the exercise of the choice guaranteed against government infringement, and although the need for such review will remain as a consequence of today's decision, the required determinations fall within judicial competence.

2

The inquiry into reliance counts the cost of a rule's repudiation as it would fall on those who have relied reasonably on the rule's continued application. . . .

While neither respondents nor their amici in so many words deny that the abortion right invites some reliance prior to its actual exercise, one can readily imagine an argument stressing the dissimilarity of this case to one involving property or contract. Abortion is customarily chosen as an unplanned response to the consequence of unplanned activity or to the failure of conventional birth control, and except on the assumption that no intercourse would have occurred but for *Roe's* holding, such behavior may appear to justify no reliance claim. [To] eliminate the issue of reliance that easily, however, one would need to limit cognizable reliance to specific instances of sexual activity. But to do this would be simply to refuse to face the fact that for two decades of economic and social developments, people have organized intimate relationships and made choices that define their views of themselves and their places in society, in reliance on the availability of abortion in the event that contraception should fail. The ability of women to participate equally in the economic and social life of the Nation has been facilitated by their ability to control their reproductive lives. See, e.g., R. Petchesky, Abortion and Woman's Choice 109, 133, n.7 (rev. ed. 1990). The Constitution serves human values, and while the effect of reliance on *Roe* cannot be exactly measured, neither can the certain cost of overruling *Roe* for people who have ordered their thinking and living around that case be dismissed.

3

No evolution of legal principle has left *Roe*'s doctrinal footings weaker than they were in 1973. No development of constitutional law since the case was decided has implicitly or explicitly left *Roe* behind as a mere survivor of obsolete constitutional thinking.

It will be recognized, of course, that *Roe* stands at an intersection of two lines of decisions, but in whichever doctrinal category one reads the case, the result for present purposes will be the same. The *Roe* Court itself placed its holding in the succession of cases most prominently exemplified by Griswold v. Connecticut, 381 U.S. 479 (1965), see *Roe*, 410 U.S., at 152–153. [*Roe*,] however, may be seen not only as an exemplar of *Griswold* liberty but as a rule (whether or not mistaken) of personal autonomy and bodily integrity, with doctrinal affinity to cases recognizing limits on governmental power to mandate medical treatment or to bar its rejection. If so, our cases since *Roe* accord with *Roe*'s view that a State's interest in the protection of life falls short of justifying any plenary override of individual liberty claims. Cruzan v. Director, Missouri Dept. of Health [section F4 infra]. Finally, one could classify *Roe* as sui generis. If the case is so viewed, then there clearly has been no erosion of its central determination.

[The] soundness of this prong of the *Roe* analysis is apparent from a consideration of the alternative. If indeed the woman's interest in deciding whether to bear and beget a child had not been recognized as in *Roe*, the State might as readily restrict a woman's right to choose to carry a pregnancy to term as to terminate it, to further asserted state interests in population control, or eugenics, for example. Yet *Roe* has been sensibly relied upon to counter any such suggestions.

4

[Time] has overtaken some of *Roe*'s factual assumptions: advances in maternal health care allow for abortions safe to the mother later in pregnancy than was true in 1973. But these facts go only to the scheme of time limits on the realization of competing interests, and the divergences from the factual premises of 1973 have no bearing on the validity of *Roe*'s central holding, that viability marks the earliest point at which the State's interest in fetal life is constitutionally adequate to justify a legislative ban on nontherapeutic abortions. . . .

B

In a less significant case, stare decisis analysis could, and would, stop at the point we have reached. But the sustained and widespread debate *Roe* has provoked calls for some comparison between that case and others of comparable dimension that have responded to national controversies and taken on the impress of the controversies addressed. Only two such decisional lines from the past century present themselves for examination, and in each instance the result reached by the Court accorded with the principles we apply today.

The first example is that line of cases identified with Lochner v. New York. [West] Coast Hotel Co. v. Parrish signaled the demise *of Lochner* by overruling *Adkins*. In the meantime, the Depression had come and, with it, the lesson that seemed unmistakable to most people by 1937, that the interpretation of contractual freedom protected in *Adkins* rested on fundamentally false factual assumptions about the capacity of a relatively unregulated market to satisfy minimal levels of human welfare. As Justice Jackson wrote of the constitutional crisis of 1937 shortly before he came on the bench, "The older world of laissez faire was recognized everywhere outside the Court to be dead." R. Jackson, The Struggle for Judicial Supremacy 85 (1941). The facts upon which the earlier case had premised a constitutional resolution of social controversy had proved to be untrue, and history's demonstration of their untruth not only justified but required the new choice of constitutional principle that *West Coast Hotel* announced. Of course, it was true that the Court lost something by its misperception, or its lack of prescience, and the Court-packing crisis only magnified the loss; but the clear demonstration that the facts of economic life were different from those previously assumed warranted the repudiation of the old law.

The second comparison that 20th century history invites is with the cases employing the separate-but-equal rule for applying the Fourteenth Amendment's equal protection guarantee. They began with Plessy v. Ferguson. [The] *Plessy* Court considered "the underlying fallacy of the plaintiff's argument to consist in the assumption that the enforced separation of the two races stamps the colored race with a badge of inferiority. If this be so, it is not by reason of anything found in the act, but solely because the colored race chooses to put that construction upon it." [But] this understanding of the facts and the rule it was stated to justify were repudiated in *Brown*. As one commentator observed, the question before the Court in *Brown* was "whether discrimination inheres in that segregation which is imposed by law in the twentieth century in certain specific states in the American Union. And that question has meaning and can find an answer only on the ground of history and of common knowledge about the facts of life in the times and places aforesaid." Black, The Lawfulness of the Segregation Decisions, 69 Yale L.J. 421, 427 (1960).

The Court in *Brown* addressed these facts of life by observing that whatever may have been the understanding in *Plessy*'s time of the power of segregation to stigmatize those who were segregated with a "badge of inferiority," it was clear by 1954 that legally sanctioned segregation had just such an effect, to the point that racially separate public educational facilities were deemed inherently unequal. Society's understanding of the facts upon which a constitutional ruling was sought in 1954 was thus fundamentally different from the basis claimed for the decision in 1896. While we think *Plessy* was wrong the day it was decided, see *Plessy* (Harlan, J., dissenting), we must also recognize that the *Plessy* Court's explanation for its decision was so clearly at odds with the facts apparent to the Court in 1954 that the decision to reexamine *Plessy* was on this ground alone not only justified but required.

West Coast Hotel and *Brown* each rested on facts, or an understanding of facts, changed from those which furnished the claimed justifications for the earlier constitutional resolutions. Each case was comprehensible as the Court's response to facts that the country could understand, or had come to understand already, but which the Court of an earlier day, as its own declarations disclosed, had not been able to perceive. As the decisions were thus comprehensible they were also defensible, not merely as the victories of one doctrinal school over another by dint of numbers (victories though they were), but as applications of constitutional principle to facts as they had not been seen by the Court before. In constitutional adjudication as elsewhere in life, changed circumstances may impose new obligations, and the thoughtful part of the Nation could accept each decision to overrule a prior case as a response to the Court's constitutional duty.

Because the case before us presents no such occasion it could be seen as no such response. Because neither the factual underpinnings of *Roe*'s central holding nor our understanding of it has changed (and because no other indication of weakened precedent has been shown) the Court could not pretend to be reexamining the prior law with any justification beyond a present doctrinal disposition to come out differently from the Court of 1973. To overrule prior law for no other reason than that would run counter to the view repeated in our cases, that a decision to overrule should rest on some special reason over and above the belief that a prior case was wrongly decided. . . .

C

The examination of the conditions justifying the repudiation of *Adkins* by *West Coast Hotel* and *Plessy* by *Brown* is enough to suggest the terrible price that would have been paid if the Court had not overruled as it did. In the present case, however, as our analysis to this point makes clear, the terrible price would be paid for overruling. Our analysis would not be complete, however, without explaining why overruling *Roe*'s central holding would not only reach an unjustifiable result under principles of stare decisis, but would seriously weaken the Court's capacity to exercise the judicial power and to function as the Supreme Court of a Nation dedicated to the rule of law. . . .

[The] Court cannot buy support for its decisions by spending money and, except to a minor degree, it cannot independently coerce obedience to its decrees. The Court's power lies, rather, in its legitimacy, a product of substance and perception that shows itself in the people's acceptance of the Judiciary as fit to determine what the Nation's law means and to declare what it demands. . . .

[The] need for principled action to be perceived as such is implicated to some degree whenever this, or any other appellate court, overrules a prior case. [In] two circumstances, however, the Court would almost certainly fail to receive the benefit of the doubt in overruling prior cases. There is, first, a point beyond which frequent overruling would overtax the country's belief in the Court's good faith. [That] first circumstance can be described as hypothetical; the second is to the point here and now. Where, in the performance of its judicial duties, the Court decides a case in such a way as to resolve the sort of intensely divisive controversy reflected in *Roe* and those rare, comparable cases, its decision has a dimension that the resolution of the normal case does not carry. It is the dimension present whenever the Court's interpretation of the Constitution calls the contending sides of a national controversy to end their national division by accepting a common mandate rooted in the Constitution. [To] overrule under fire in the absence of the most compelling reason to reexamine a watershed decision would subvert the Court's legitimacy beyond any serious question. [A] decision to overrule *Roe*'s essential holding under the existing circumstances would address error, if error there was, at the cost of both profound and unnecessary damage to the Court's legitimacy, and to the Nation's commitment to the rule of law. It is therefore imperative to adhere to the essence of *Roe*'s original decision, and we do so today.

IV

[The] woman's liberty is not so unlimited, however, that from the outset the State cannot show its concern for the life of the unborn, and at a later point in fetal development the State's interest in life has sufficient force so that the right of the woman to terminate the pregnancy can be restricted.

[We] conclude the line should be drawn at viability, so that before that time the woman has a right to choose to terminate her pregnancy. We adhere to this principle for two reasons. First, as we have said, is the doctrine of stare decisis. [The] second reason is that the concept of viability, as we noted in *Roe*, is the time at which there is a realistic possibility of maintaining and nourishing a life outside the womb, so that the independent existence of the second life can in reason and all fairness be the object of state protection that now overrides the rights of the woman.

On the other side of the equation is the interest of the State in the protection of potential life. [It] must be remembered that Roe v. Wade speaks with clarity in establishing not only the woman's liberty but also the State's "important and legitimate interest in potential life." That portion of the decision in *Roe* has been given too little acknowledgement and implementation by the Court in its subsequent cases. [We] reject the trimester framework, which we do not consider to be part of the essential holding of *Roe*. [The] trimester framework suffers from these basic flaws: in its formulation it misconceives the nature of the pregnant woman's interest; and in practice it undervalues the State's interest in potential life, as recognized in *Roe*. . . .

[These] considerations of the nature of the abortion right illustrate that it is an overstatement to describe it as a right to decide whether to have an abortion "without interference from the State." [Not] all governmental intrusion is of necessity unwarranted; and that brings us to the other basic flaw in the trimester framework: even in *Roe*'s terms, in practice it undervalues the State's interest in the potential life within the woman. . . .

[Not] all burdens on the right to decide whether to terminate a pregnancy will be undue. In our view, the undue burden standard is the appropriate means of reconciling the State's interest with the woman's constitutionally protected liberty. . . .

A finding of an undue burden is a shorthand for the conclusion that a state regulation has the purpose or effect of placing a substantial obstacle in the path of a woman seeking an abortion of a nonviable fetus. A statute with this purpose is invalid because the means chosen by the State to further the interest in potential life must be calculated to inform the woman's free choice, not hinder it. And a statute which, while furthering the interest in potential life or some other valid state interest, has the effect of placing a substantial obstacle in the path of a woman's choice cannot be considered a permissible means of serving its legitimate ends. [Understood] another way, we answer the question, left open in previous opinions discussing the undue burden formulation, whether a law designed to further the State's interest in fetal life which imposes an undue burden on the woman's decision before fetal viability could be constitutional. The answer is no.

laws by fetal viability are unconstitutional

Some guiding principles should emerge. What is at stake is the woman's right to make the ultimate decision, not a right to be insulated from all others in doing so. Regulations which do no more than create a structural mechanism by which the State, or the parent or guardian of a minor, may express profound respect for the life of the unborn are permitted, if they are not a substantial obstacle to the woman's exercise of the right to choose. Unless it has that effect on her right of choice, a state measure designed to persuade her to choose childbirth over abortion will be upheld if reasonably related to that goal. Regulations designed to foster the health of a woman seeking an abortion are valid if they do not constitute an undue burden.

[We] give this summary:

(a) To protect the central right recognized by Roe v. Wade while at the same time accommodating the State's profound interest in potential life, we will employ the undue burden analysis as explained in this opinion. An undue burden exists, and therefore a provision of law is invalid, if its purpose or effect is to place a substantial obstacle in the path of a woman seeking an abortion before the fetus attains viability.

(b) We reject the rigid trimester framework of Roe v. Wade. To promote the State's profound interest in potential life, throughout pregnancy the State may take measures to ensure that the woman's choice is informed, and measures designed to advance this interest will not be invalidated as long as their purpose is to persuade the woman to choose childbirth over abortion. These measures must not be an undue burden on the right.

laws making abortions safe = good

(c) As with any medical procedure, the State may enact regulations to further the health or safety of a woman seeking an abortion. Unnecessary health regulations that have the purpose or effect of presenting a substantial obstacle to a woman seeking an abortion impose an undue burden on the right.

an obstacle? = bad

(d) Our adoption of the undue burden analysis does not disturb the central holding of Roe v. Wade, and we reaffirm that holding. Regardless of whether exceptions are made for particular circumstances, a State may not prohibit any woman from making the ultimate decision to terminate her pregnancy before viability.

(e) We also reaffirm Roe's holding that "subsequent to viability, the State in promoting its interest in the potentiality of human life may, if it chooses, regulate, and even proscribe, abortion except where it is necessary, in appropriate medical judgment, for the preservation of the life or health of the mother."

V

A

Because it is central to the operation of various other requirements, we begin with the statute's definition of medical emergency. Under the statute, a medical emergency is

> that condition which, on the basis of the physician's good faith clinical judgment so complicates the medical condition of a pregnant woman as to necessitate the immediate abortion of her pregnancy to avert her death or for which a delay will

Medical emergency

create serious risk of substantial and irreversible impairment of a major bodily function.

[The] District Court found that there were three serious conditions which would not be covered by the statute: preeclampsia, inevitable abortion, and premature ruptured membrane. Yet, as the Court of Appeals observed, it is undisputed that under some circumstances each of these conditions could lead to an illness with substantial and irreversible consequences. While the definition could be interpreted in an unconstitutional manner, the Court of Appeals construed the phrase "serious risk" to include those circumstances. [We] conclude that, as construed by the Court of Appeals, the medical emergency definition imposes no undue burden on a woman's abortion right.

This part doesn't work on abortions

B

[Except] in a medical emergency, the statute requires that at least 24 hours before performing an abortion a physician inform the woman of the nature of the procedure, the health risks of the abortion and of childbirth, and the "probable gestational age of the unborn child." The physician or a qualified nonphysician must inform the woman of the availability of printed materials published by the State describing the fetus and providing information about medical assistance for childbirth, information about child support from the father, and a list of agencies which provide adoption and other services as alternatives to abortion. An abortion may not be performed unless the woman certifies in writing that she has been informed of the availability of these printed materials and has been provided them if she chooses to view them. . . .

To the extent [*City of Akron*] and *Thornburgh* find a constitutional violation when the government requires, as it does here, the giving of truthful, nonmisleading information about the nature of the procedure, the attendant health risks and those of childbirth, and the "probable gestational age" of the fetus, those cases go too far, are inconsistent with *Roe*'s acknowledgment of an important interest in potential life, and are overruled. [In] attempting to ensure that a woman apprehend the full consequences of her decision, the State furthers the legitimate purpose of reducing the risk that a woman may elect an abortion, only to discover later, with devastating psychological consequences, that her decision was not fully informed. If the information the State requires to be made available to the woman is truthful and not misleading, the requirement may be permissible.

We also see no reason why the State may not require doctors to inform a woman seeking an abortion of the availability of materials relating to the consequences to the fetus, even when those consequences have no direct relation to her health. . . .

All that is left of petitioners' argument is an asserted First Amendment right of a physician not to provide information about the risks of abortion, and childbirth, in a manner mandated by the State. To be sure, the physician's First Amendment rights not to speak are implicated, but only as part of the practice of medicine, subject to reasonable licensing and regulation by the State. We see no constitutional infirmity in the requirement that the physician provide the information mandated by the State here. . . .

[In] [*City of Akron*] we said: "Nor are we convinced that the State's legitimate concern that the woman's decision be informed is reasonably served by requiring a 24-hour delay as a matter of course." We consider that conclusion to be wrong.

The idea that important decisions will be more informed and deliberate if they follow some period of reflection does not strike us as unreasonable, particularly where the statute directs that important information become part of the background of the decision. . . .

Whether the mandatory 24-hour waiting period is nonetheless invalid because in practice it is a substantial obstacle to a woman's choice to terminate her pregnancy is a closer question. The findings of fact by the District Court indicate that because of the distances many women must travel to reach an abortion provider, the practical effect will often be a delay of much more than a day because the waiting period requires that a woman seeking an abortion make at least two visits to the doctor. The District Court also found that in many instances this will increase the exposure of women seeking abortions to "the harassment and hostility of anti-abortion protestors demonstrating outside a clinic." As a result, the District Court found that for those women who have the fewest financial resources, those who must travel long distances, and those who have difficulty explaining their whereabouts to husbands, employers, or others, the 24-hour waiting period will be "particularly burdensome."

These findings are troubling in some respects, but they do not demonstrate that the waiting period constitutes an undue burden. We do not doubt that, as the District Court held, the waiting period has the effect of "increasing the cost and risk of delay of abortions," but the District Court did not conclude that the increased costs and potential delays amount to substantial obstacles. Rather, applying the trimester framework's strict prohibition of all regulation designed to promote the State's interest in potential life before viability, the District Court concluded that the waiting period does not further the state "interest in maternal health" and "infringes the physician's discretion to exercise sound medical judgment," Yet as we have stated, under the undue burden standard a State is permitted to enact persuasive measures which favor childbirth over abortion, even if those measures do not further a health interest. And while the waiting period does limit a physician's discretion, that is not, standing alone, a reason to invalidate it.

We also disagree with the District Court's conclusion that the "particularly burdensome" effects of the waiting period on some women require its invalidation. . . .

We are left with the argument that the various aspects of the informed consent requirement are unconstitutional because they place barriers in the way of abortion on demand. Even the broadest reading of *Roe*, however, has not suggested that there is a constitutional right to abortion on demand. Rather, the right protected by *Roe* is a right to decide to terminate a pregnancy free of undue interference by the State. Because the informed consent requirement facilitates the wise exercise of that right it cannot be classified as an interference with the right *Roe* protects. The informed consent requirement is not an undue burden on that right.

c

Section 3209 of Pennsylvania's abortion law provides, except in cases of medical emergency, that no physician shall perform an abortion on a married woman without receiving a signed statement from the woman that she has notified her spouse that she is about to undergo an abortion. The woman has the option of providing an alternative signed statement certifying that her husband is not the man who impregnated her; that her husband could not be located; that the pregnancy is the result of spousal sexual assault which she has reported; or that the woman believes that notifying her husband will cause him or someone else to inflict bodily injury upon her. A physician who performs an abortion on a married woman without receiving the appropriate signed statement will have his or her license revoked, and is liable to the husband for damages.

The District Court heard the testimony of numerous expert witnesses, and made detailed findings of fact regarding the effect of this statute.

> [279.] The "bodily injury" exception could not be invoked by a married woman whose husband, if notified, would, in her reasonable belief, threaten to (a) publicize her intent to have an abortion to family, friends or acquaintances; (b) retaliate against her in future child custody or divorce proceedings; (c) inflict psychological intimidation or emotional harm upon her, her children or other persons; (d) inflict bodily harm on other persons such as children, family members or other loved ones; or (e) use his control over finances to deprive of necessary monies for herself or her children. . . .
>
> 281. Studies reveal that family violence occurs in two million families in the United States. This figure, however, is a conservative one that substantially understates (because battering is usually not reported until it reaches life-threatening proportions) the actual number of families affected by domestic violence. In fact, researchers estimate that one of every two women will be battered at some time in their life. . . .
>
> 282. A wife may not elect to notify her husband of her intention to have an abortion for a variety of reasons, including the husband's illness, concern about her own health, the imminent failure of the marriage, or the husband's absolute opposition to the abortion. . . .
>
> [286.] Married women, victims of battering, have been killed in Pennsylvania and throughout the United States. . . .
>
> [289.] Mere notification of pregnancy is frequently a flashpoint for battering and violence within the family. The number of battering incidents is high during the pregnancy and often the worst abuse can be associated with pregnancy. . . .
>
> The battering husband may deny parentage and use the pregnancy as an excuse for abuse. . . .
>
> 290. Secrecy typically shrouds abusive families. Family members are instructed not to tell anyone, especially police or doctors, about the abuse and violence. Battering husbands often threaten their wives or her children with further abuse if she tells an outsider of the violence and tells her that nobody will believe her. A battered woman, therefore, is highly unlikely to disclose the violence against her for fear of retaliation by the abuser. . . .
>
> [298.] Because of the nature of the battering relationship, battered women are unlikely to avail themselves of the exceptions to section 3209 of the Act, regardless of whether the section applies to them.

These findings are supported by studies of domestic violence. [There] are millions of women in this country who are the victims of regular physical and psychological abuse at the hands of their husbands. Should these women become pregnant, they may have very good reasons for not wishing to inform their husbands of their decision to obtain an abortion. . . .

[Respondents] attempt to avoid the conclusion that §3209 is invalid by pointing out that [the] effects of §3209 are felt by only one percent of the women who obtain abortions. [We] disagree with respondents' basic method of analysis.

The analysis does not end with one percent of women upon whom the statute operates; it begins there. Legislation is measured for consistency with the

Constitution by its impact on those whose conduct it affects. [The] unfortunate yet persisting conditions we document above will mean that in a large fraction of the cases in which §3209 is relevant, it will operate as a substantial obstacle to a woman's choice to undergo an abortion. It is an undue burden, and therefore invalid.

This conclusion is in no way inconsistent with our decisions upholding parental notification or consent requirements. Those enactments, and our judgment that they are constitutional, are based on the quite reasonable assumption that minors will benefit from consultation with their parents and that children will often not realize that their parents have their best interests at heart. We cannot adopt a parallel assumption about adult women. . . .

It is an inescapable biological fact that state regulation with respect to the child a woman is carrying will have a far greater impact on the mother's liberty than on the father's. The effect of state regulation on a woman's protected liberty is doubly deserving of scrutiny in such a case, as the State has touched not only upon the private sphere of the family but upon the very bodily integrity of the pregnant woman. The Court has held that "when the wife and the husband disagree on this decision, the view of only one of the two marriage partners can prevail. Inasmuch as it is the woman who physically bears the child and who is the more directly and immediately affected by the pregnancy, as between the two, the balance weighs in her favor." *Danforth.* [The] Constitution protects individuals, men and women alike, from unjustified state interference, even when that interference is enacted into law for the benefit of their spouses.

[The] husband's interest in the life of the child his wife is carrying does not permit the State to empower him with this troubling degree of authority over his wife. The contrary view leads to consequences reminiscent of the common law. A husband has no enforceable right to require a wife to advise him before she exercises her personal choices. [A] State may not give to a man the kind of dominion over his wife that parents exercise over their children.

Section 3209 embodies a view of marriage consonant with the common-law status of married women but repugnant to our present understanding of marriage and of the nature of the rights secured by the Constitution. Women do not lose their constitutionally protected liberty when they marry. . . .

D

We next consider the parental consent provision. Except in a medical emergency, an unemancipated young woman under 18 may not obtain an abortion unless she and one of her parents (or guardian) provides informed consent as defined above. If neither a parent nor a guardian provides consent, a court may authorize the performance of an abortion upon a determination that the young woman is mature and capable of giving informed consent and has in fact given her informed consent, or that an abortion would be in her best interests. . . .

The only argument made by petitioners respecting this provision and to which our prior decisions do not speak is the contention that the parental consent requirement is invalid because it requires informed parental consent. For the most part, petitioners' argument is a reprise of their argument with respect to the informed consent requirement in general, and we reject it for the reasons given above. . . .

E . . .

Under the recordkeeping and reporting requirements of the statute, every facility which performs abortions is required to file a report stating its name and address as well as the name and address of any related entity, such as a controlling or subsidiary organization. In the case of state-funded institutions, the information becomes public. . . .

In *Danforth*, we held that recordkeeping and reporting provisions "that are reasonably directed to the preservation of maternal health and that properly respect a patient's confidentiality and privacy are permissible." We think that under this standard, all the provisions at issue here except that relating to spousal notice are constitutional. Although they do not relate to the State's interest in informing the woman's choice, they do relate to health. The collection of information with respect to actual patients is a vital element of medical research, and so it cannot be said that the requirements serve no purpose other than to make abortions more difficult. Nor do we find that the requirements impose a substantial obstacle to a woman's choice. At most they might increase the cost of some abortions by a slight amount. While at some point increased cost could become a substantial obstacle, there is no such showing on the record before us. . . .

VI

Our Constitution is a covenant running from the first generation of Americans to us and then to future generations. It is a coherent succession. Each generation must learn anew that the Constitution's written terms embody ideas and aspirations that must survive more ages than one. We accept our responsibility not to retreat from interpreting the full meaning of the covenant in light of all of our precedents. We invoke it once again to define the freedom guaranteed by the Constitution's own promise, the promise of liberty.

JUSTICE BLACKMUN, concurring in part, concurring in the judgment in part, and dissenting in part. . . .

State restrictions on abortion violate a woman's right of privacy in two ways. First, compelled continuation of a pregnancy infringes upon a woman's right to bodily integrity by imposing substantial physical intrusions and significant risks of physical harm. During pregnancy, women experience dramatic physical changes and a wide range of health consequences. Labor and delivery pose additional health risks and physical demands. In short, restrictive abortion laws force women to endure physical invasions far more substantial than those this Court has held to violate the constitutional principle of bodily integrity in other contexts. See, e.g., Winston v. Lee, 470 U.S. 753 (1985) (invalidating surgical removal of bullet from murder suspect); Rochin v. California, 342 U.S. 165 (1952) (invalidating stomach-pumping).

Further, when the State restricts a woman's right to terminate her pregnancy, it deprives a woman of the right to make her own decision about reproduction and family planning — critical life choices that this Court long has deemed central to the right to privacy. . . .

A State's restrictions on a woman's right to terminate her pregnancy also implicate constitutional guarantees of gender equality. State restrictions on abortion compel women to continue pregnancies they otherwise might terminate. By restricting the right to terminate pregnancies, the State conscripts women's bodies into its service, forcing women to continue their pregnancies, suffer the pains of childbirth, and in most instances, provide years of maternal care. The State does not compensate women for their services; instead, it assumes that they owe this duty as a matter of course. This assumption — that women can simply be forced to accept the "natural" status and incidents of motherhood — appears to rest upon a conception of women's role that has triggered the protection of the Equal Protection Clause. The joint opinion recognizes that these assumptions about women's place in society "are no longer consistent with our understanding of the family, the individual, or the Constitution." . . .

The 24-hour waiting period following the provision of the foregoing information is [clearly] unconstitutional. [The] Pennsylvania statute requires every facility performing abortions to report its activities to the Commonwealth. [The] Commonwealth attempts to justify its required reports on the ground that the public has a right to know how its tax dollars are spent. A regulation designed to inform the public about public expenditures does not further the Commonwealth's interest in protecting maternal health. Accordingly, such a regulation cannot justify a legally significant burden on a woman's right to obtain an abortion. . . .

JUSTICE STEVENS, concurring in part and dissenting in part. . . .

My disagreement with the joint opinion begins with its understanding of the trimester framework established in *Roe*. [It] is not a "contradiction" to recognize that the State may have a legitimate interest in potential human life and, at the same time, to conclude that that interest does not justify the regulation of abortion before viability (although other interests, such as maternal health, may). The fact that the State's interest is legitimate does not tell us when, if ever, that interest outweighs the pregnant woman's interest in personal liberty. It is appropriate, therefore, to consider more carefully the nature of the interests at stake.

[It] is clear that, in order to be legitimate, the State's interest must be secular; consistent with the First Amendment the State may not promote a theological or sectarian interest. . . .

Identifying the State's interests — which the States rarely articulate with any precision — makes clear that the interest in protecting potential life is not grounded in the Constitution. It is, instead, an indirect interest supported by both humanitarian and pragmatic concerns. Many of our citizens believe that any abortion reflects an unacceptable disrespect for potential human life and that the performance of more than a million abortions each year is intolerable; many find third-trimester abortions performed when the fetus is approaching personhood particularly offensive. The State has a legitimate interest in minimizing such offense. The State may also have a broader interest in expanding the population, believing society would benefit from the services of additional productive citizens — or that the potential human lives might include the occasional Mozart or Curie.

[Under] these principles, §§3205(a)(2)(i)-(iii) of the Pennsylvania statute are unconstitutional. Those sections require a physician or counselor to provide the woman with a range of materials clearly designed to persuade her to choose not to undergo the abortion. While the State is free, pursuant to §3208 of the Pennsylvania law, to produce and disseminate such material, the State may not inject such information into the woman's deliberations just as she is weighing such an important choice.

Under this same analysis, §§3205(a)(1)(i) and (iii) of the Pennsylvania statute are constitutional. Those sections, which require the physician to inform a woman of the nature and risks of the abortion procedure and the medical risks of carrying to term, are neutral requirements comparable to those imposed in other medical procedures. Those sections indicate no effort by the State to influence the woman's choice in any way. If anything, such requirements enhance, rather than skew, the woman's decisionmaking.

The 24-hour waiting period required by §§3205(a)(1)-(2) of the Pennsylvania statute raises even more serious concerns. . . .

A burden may be "undue" either because the burden is too severe or because it lacks a legitimate, rational justification.

The 24-hour delay requirement fails both parts of this test. . . .

The counseling provisions are similarly infirm. Whenever government commands private citizens to speak or to listen, careful review of the justification for that command is particularly appropriate. In this case, the Pennsylvania statute directs that counselors provide women seeking abortions with information concerning alternatives to abortion, the availability of medical assistance benefits, and the possibility of child-support payments. The statute requires that this information be given to all women seeking abortions, including those for whom such information is clearly useless, such as those who are married, those who have undergone the procedure in the past and are fully aware of the options, and those who are fully convinced that abortion is their only reasonable option. Moreover, the statute requires physicians to inform all of their patients of "the probable gestational age of the unborn child." This information is of little decisional value in most cases, because 90% of all abortions are performed during the first trimester when fetal age has less relevance than when the fetus nears viability. . . .

CHIEF JUSTICE REHNQUIST, with whom JUSTICE WHITE, JUSTICE SCALIA, and JUSTICE THOMAS join, concurring in the judgment in part and dissenting in part.

The joint opinion, following its newly-minted variation on stare decisis, retains the outer shell of Roe v. Wade, but beats a wholesale retreat from the substance of that case. We believe that *Roe* was wrongly decided, and that it can and should be overruled consistently with our traditional approach to stare decisis in constitutional cases. We would adopt the approach of the plurality in Webster v. Reproductive Health Services, and uphold the challenged provisions of the Pennsylvania statute in their entirety.

I

[Unlike] marriage, procreation and contraception, abortion "involves the purposeful termination of potential life." Harris v. McRae, 448 U.S. 297, 325 (1980). [One] cannot ignore the fact that a woman is not isolated in her pregnancy, and that the decision to abort necessarily involves the destruction of a fetus.

Nor do the historical traditions of the American people support the view that the right to terminate one's pregnancy is "fundamental." The common law which we inherited from England made abortion after "quickening" an offense. At the time of the adoption of the Fourteenth Amendment, statutory prohibitions or restrictions on abortion were commonplace. . . .

[We] think, therefore, both in view of this history and of our decided cases dealing with substantive liberty under the Due Process Clause, that the Court was mistaken in *Roe* when it classified a woman's decision to terminate her pregnancy as a "fundamental right" that could be abridged only in a manner which withstood "strict scrutiny."

II

[The] joint opinion [cannot] bring itself to say that *Roe* was correct as an original matter, but the authors are of the view that "the immediate question is not the soundness of *Roe*'s resolution of the issue, but the precedential force that must be accorded to its holding." Instead of claiming that *Roe* was correct as a matter of original constitutional interpretation, the opinion therefore contains an elaborate discussion of stare decisis. This discussion of the principle of stare decisis appears to be almost entirely dicta, because the joint opinion does not apply that principle in dealing with *Roe*. *Roe* decided that a woman had a fundamental right to an abortion. The joint opinion rejects that view. *Roe* decided that abortion regulations were to be subjected to "strict scrutiny" and could be justified only in the light of "compelling state interests." The joint opinion rejects that view. *Roe* analyzed abortion regulation under a rigid trimester framework, a framework which has guided this Court's decisionmaking for 19 years. The joint opinion rejects that framework.

[In] our view, authentic principles of stare decisis do not require that any portion of the reasoning in *Roe* be kept intact. [Erroneous] decisions in such constitutional cases are uniquely durable, because correction through legislative action, save for constitutional amendment, is impossible. . . .

The joint opinion discusses several stare decisis factors which, it asserts, point toward retaining a portion of *Roe*. Two of these factors are that the main "factual underpinning" of *Roe* has remained the same, and that its doctrinal foundation is no weaker now than it was in 1973. Of course, what might be called the basic facts which gave rise to *Roe* have remained the same — women become pregnant, there is a point somewhere, depending on medical technology, where a fetus becomes viable, and women give birth to children. But this is only to say that the same facts which gave rise to *Roe* will continue to give rise to similar cases. It is not a reason, in and of itself, why those cases must be decided in the same incorrect manner as was the first case to deal with the question. . . .

The joint opinion also points to the reliance interests involved in this context in its effort to explain why precedent must be followed for precedent's sake. Certainly it is true that where reliance is truly at issue, as in the case of judicial decisions that have formed the basis for private decisions, "considerations in favor of stare decisis are at their acme." But, as the joint opinion apparently agrees, any traditional notion of reliance is not applicable here.

[Apparently] realizing that conventional stare decisis principles do not support its position, the joint opinion advances a belief that retaining a portion of *Roe* is necessary to protect the "legitimacy" of this Court. Because the Court must take care to render decisions "grounded truly in principle," and not simply as political and social compromises, the joint opinion properly declares it to be this Court's duty to ignore the public criticism and protest that may arise as a result of a decision.

[But] the joint opinion goes on to state that when the Court "resolves the sort of intensely divisive controversy reflected in *Roe* and those rare, comparable cases," its decision is exempt from reconsideration under established principles of stare decisis in constitutional cases. [The] first difficulty with this principle lies in its assumption that cases which are "intensely divisive" can be readily distinguished from those that are not. The question of whether a particular issue is "intensely divisive" enough to qualify for special protection is entirely subjective and dependent on the individual assumptions of the members of this Court.

[The] joint opinion picks out and discusses two prior Court rulings that it believes are of the "intensely divisive" variety, and concludes that they are of comparable dimension to *Roe*. It appears to us very odd indeed that the joint opinion chooses as benchmarks two cases in which the Court chose not to adhere to erroneous constitutional precedent, but instead enhanced its stature by acknowledging and correcting its error, apparently in violation of the joint opinion's "legitimacy" principle. . . .

The joint opinion agrees that the Court's stature would have been seriously damaged if in *Brown* and *West Coast Hotel* it had dug in its heels and refused to apply normal principles of stare decisis to the earlier decisions. But the opinion contends that the Court was entitled to overrule *Plessy* and *Lochner* in those cases, despite the existence of opposition to the original decisions, only because both the Nation and the Court had learned new lessons in the interim. This is at best a feebly supported, post hoc rationalization for those decisions.

For example, the opinion asserts that the Court could justifiably overrule its decision in *Lochner* only because the Depression had convinced "most people" that constitutional protection of contractual freedom contributed to an economy that failed to protect the welfare of all. Surely the joint opinion does not mean to suggest that people saw this Court's failure to uphold minimum wage statutes as the cause of the Great Depression! In any event, the *Lochner* Court did not base its rule upon the policy judgment that an unregulated market was fundamental to a stable economy; it simply believed, erroneously, that "liberty" under the Due Process Clause protected the "right to make a contract." Lochner v. New York, 198 U.S., at 53. Nor is it the case that the people of this Nation only discovered the dangers of extreme laissez-faire economics because of the Depression. . . .

When the Court finally recognized its error in *West Coast Hotel*, it did not engage in the post hoc rationalization that the joint opinion attributes to it today; it did not state that *Lochner* had been based on an economic view that had fallen into disfavor, and that it therefore should be overruled. Chief Justice Hughes in his opinion for the Court simply recognized what Justice Holmes had previously recognized in his *Lochner* dissent, that "the Constitution does not speak of freedom of contract."

[The] Court in *Brown* simply recognized, as Justice Harlan had recognized beforehand, that the Fourteenth Amendment does not permit racial segregation. The rule of *Brown* is not tied to popular opinion about the evils of segregation; it is a judgment that the Equal Protection Clause does not permit racial segregation, no matter whether the public might come to believe that it is beneficial. . . .

JUSTICE SCALIA, with whom [CHIEF JUSTICE REHNQUIST], JUSTICE WHITE, and JUSTICE THOMAS join, concurring in the judgment in part and dissenting in part. . . .

[The] issue in these cases [is] not whether the power of a woman to abort her unborn child is a "liberty" in the absolute sense; or even whether it is a liberty of great importance to many women. Of course it is both. The issue is whether it is a liberty protected by the Constitution of the United States. I am sure it is not. I reach that conclusion [for] the same reason I reach the conclusion that bigamy is not constitutionally protected — because of two simple facts: (1) the Constitution says absolutely nothing about it, and (2) the longstanding traditions of American society have permitted it to be legally proscribed.

[Applying] the rational basis test, I would uphold the Pennsylvania statute in its entirety. I must, however, respond to a few of the more outrageous arguments in today's opinion, which it is beyond human nature to leave unanswered.

[The] Court's description of the place of *Roe* in the social history of the United States is unrecognizable. Not only did *Roe* not, as the Court suggests, resolve the deeply divisive issue of abortion; it did more than anything else to nourish it, by elevating it to the national level where it is infinitely more difficult to resolve. National politics were not plagued by abortion protests, national abortion lobbying, or abortion marches on Congress, before Roe v. Wade was decided. Profound disagreement existed among our citizens over the issue — as it does over other issues, such as the death penalty — but that disagreement was being worked out at the state level. As with many other issues, the division of sentiment within each State was not as closely balanced as it was among the population of the Nation as a whole, meaning not only that more people would be satisfied with the results of state-by-state resolution, but also that those results would be more stable. Pre-*Roe*, moreover, political compromise was possible.

Roe's mandate for abortion-on-demand destroyed the compromises of the past, rendered compromise impossible for the future, and required the entire issue to be resolved uniformly, at the national level. At the same time, *Roe* created a vast new class of abortion consumers and abortion proponents by eliminating the moral opprobrium that had attached to the act. ("If the Constitution guarantees abortion, how can it be bad?" — not an accurate line of thought, but a natural one.) Many favor all of those developments, and it is not for me to say that they are wrong. But to portray *Roe* as the statesmanlike "settlement" of a divisive issue, a jurisprudential Peace of Westphalia that is worth preserving, is nothing less than Orwellian. *Roe* fanned into life an issue that has inflamed our national politics in general, and has obscured with its smoke the selection of Justices to this Court in particular, ever since.

[What] makes all this relevant to the bothersome application of "political pressure" against the Court are the twin facts that the American people love democracy and the American people are not fools. As long as this Court thought (and the people thought) that we Justices were doing essentially lawyers' work up here — reading text and discerning our society's traditional understanding of that text — the public pretty much left us alone. Texts and traditions are facts to study, not convictions to demonstrate about.

[There] is a poignant aspect to the Court's opinion. Its length, and what might be called its epic tone, suggest that its authors believe they are bringing to an end a troublesome era in the history of our Nation and of our Court. "It is the dimension" of authority, they say, to "call the contending sides of national controversy to end their national division by accepting a common mandate rooted in the Constitution."

There comes vividly to mind a portrait by Emanuel Leutze that hangs in the Harvard Law School: Roger Brooke Taney, painted in 1859, the 82d year of his

life, the 24th of his Chief Justiceship, the second after his opinion in *Dred Scott*.
He is all in black, sitting in a shadowed red armchair, left hand resting upon a pad
of paper in his lap, right hand hanging limply, almost lifelessly, beside the inner
arm of the chair. He sits facing the viewer, and staring straight out. There seems to
be on his face, and in his deep-set eyes, an expression of profound sadness and
disillusionment. Perhaps he always looked that way, even when dwelling upon
the happiest of thoughts. But those of us who know how the lustre of his great
Chief Justiceship came to be eclipsed by *Dred Scott* cannot help believing that he
had that case — its already apparent consequences for the Court, and its soon-to-
be-played-out consequences for the Nation — burning on his mind. I expect that
two years earlier he, too, had thought himself "calling the contending sides of
national controversy to end their national division by accepting a common
mandate rooted in the Constitution."

It is no more realistic for us in this case, than it was for him in that, to think that
an issue of the sort they both involved — an issue involving life and death, freedom and subjugation — can be "speedily and finally settled" by the Supreme
Court, as President James Buchanan in his inaugural address said the issue of
slavery in the territories would be. Quite to the contrary, by foreclosing all democratic outlet for the deep passions this issue arouses, by banishing the issue from
the political forum that gives all participants, even the losers, the satisfaction of a
fair hearing and an honest fight, by continuing the imposition of a rigid national
rule instead of allowing for regional differences, the Court merely prolongs and
intensifies the anguish.

We should get out of this area, where we have no right to be, and where we do
neither ourselves nor the country any good by remaining.

Note: Casey *and the Role of the Court*

1. *Politics and judicial independence. Casey* raises a number of important
issues about stare decisis, liberty, equality, and the role of the Court in general.
Note first that five of the justices on the *Casey* Court were appointed by Presidents Reagan and Bush, both sharp critics of *Roe*. Does the decision contain
lessons about the power of the President to remake the Court? Does it suggest that
law does indeed operate in a way that is independent of politics?

2. Roe *and the democratic process.* Is it appropriate for the Court to "[call] the
contending sides of a national controversy to end their national division by
accepting a common mandate rooted in the Constitution"? Is such a call likely
to succeed? Might social fragmentation have been produced, not alleviated, by
Roe and *Casey*? If so, is the price worth paying?

Gonzales v. Carhart

550 U.S. 124 (2007)

JUSTICE KENNEDY delivered the opinion of the Court.

These cases require us to consider the validity of the Partial-Birth Abortion Ban
Act of 2003 (Act), a federal statute regulating abortion procedures. In recitations
preceding its operative provisions, the Act refers to the Court's opinion in

Stenberg v. Carhart [530 U.S. 914 (2000)] which also addressed the subject of abortion procedures used in the later stages of pregnancy.

[In *Stenberg*, the Court, in a five-to-four decision written by Justice Breyer, invalidated a Nebraska statute banning "partial birth abortion," which it defined as "an abortion procedure in which the person performing the abortion partially delivers vaginally a living unborn child before killing the unborn child and completing the delivery." The Court invalidated the statute on two separate grounds: that it contained no exception for the preservation of the health of the mother, as required by *Casey*; and that it imposed an undue burden on the abortion right. The second holding was premised on a finding that the statutory language covered not only the unusual "intact dilation and extraction" procedure, but also "standard dilation and extraction," which is the most commonly used procedure for abortions performed during the second trimester of pregnancy.]

Compared to the state statute at issue in *Stenberg*, the Act is more specific concerning the instances to which it applies and, in this respect, more precise in its coverage. We conclude the Act should be sustained against the objections lodged by the broad, facial attack brought against it. . . .

I

A

The Act proscribes a particular manner of ending fetal life, so it is necessary here, as it was in *Stenberg*, to discuss abortion procedures in some detail.

Three United States District Courts heard extensive evidence describing the procedures. . . .

[Between] 85 and 90 percent of the approximately 1.3 million abortions performed each year in the United States take place in the first three months of pregnancy, which is to say in the first trimester. The most common first trimester abortion method is vacuum aspiration (otherwise known as suction curettage) in which the physician vacuums out the embryonic tissue. Early in this trimester an alternative is to use medication, such as mifepristone (commonly known as RU-486), to terminate the pregnancy. The Act does not regulate these procedures.

Of the remaining abortions that take place each year, most occur in the second trimester. The surgical procedure referred to as "dilation and evacuation" or "D & E" is the usual abortion method in this trimester. Although individual techniques for performing D & E differ, the general steps are the same.

A doctor must first dilate the cervix at least to the extent needed to insert surgical instruments into the uterus and to maneuver them to evacuate the fetus. . . .

After sufficient dilation the surgical operation can commence. The woman is placed under general anesthesia or conscious sedation. The doctor, often guided by ultrasound, inserts grasping forceps through the woman's cervix and into the uterus to grab the fetus. The doctor grips a fetal part with the forceps and pulls it back through the cervix and vagina, continuing to pull even after meeting resistance from the cervix. The friction causes the fetus to tear apart. For example, a leg might be ripped off the fetus as it is pulled through the cervix and out of the woman. The process of evacuating the fetus piece by piece continues until it has been completely removed. A doctor may make 10 to 15 passes with the forceps to evacuate the fetus in its entirety, though sometimes removal is completed with fewer passes. Once the fetus has been evacuated, the placenta and any remaining fetal material are suctioned or scraped out of the uterus. The doctor examines the different parts to ensure the entire fetal body has been removed. . . .

The abortion procedure that was the impetus for the numerous bans on "partial-birth abortion," including the Act, is a variation of this standard D & E. [For] discussion purposes this D & E variation will be referred to as intact D & E. The main difference between the two procedures is that in intact D & E, a doctor extracts the fetus intact or largely intact with only a few passes. There are no comprehensive statistics indicating what percentage of all D & Es are performed in this manner. . . .

In an intact D & E procedure, the doctor extracts the fetus in a way conducive to pulling out its entire body, instead of ripping it apart. One doctor, for example, testified:

"If I know I have good dilation and I reach in and the fetus starts to come out and I think I can accomplish it, the abortion with an intact delivery, then I use my forceps a little bit differently. I don't close them quite so much, and I just gently draw the tissue out attempting to have an intact delivery, if possible."

Rotating the fetus as it is being pulled decreases the odds of dismemberment. A doctor also "may use forceps to grasp a fetal part, pull it down, and re-grasp the fetus at a higher level — 'sometimes using both his hand and a forceps' — to exert traction to retrieve the fetus intact until the head is lodged in the [cervix]."

Intact D & E gained public notoriety when, in 1992, Dr. Martin Haskell gave a presentation describing his method of performing the operation. In the usual intact D & E the fetus' head lodges in the cervix, and dilation is insufficient to allow it to pass. Haskell explained the next step as follows:

"'At this point, the right-handed surgeon slides the fingers of the left [hand] along the back of the fetus and hooks the shoulders of the fetus with the index and ring fingers (palm down).

"'While maintaining this tension, lifting the cervix and applying traction to the shoulders with the fingers of the left hand, the surgeon takes a pair of blunt curved Metzenbaum scissors in the right hand. He carefully advances the tip, curved down, along the spine and under his middle finger until he feels it contact the base of the skull under the tip of his middle finger.

"'[T]he surgeon then forces the scissors into the base of the skull or into the foramen magnum. Having safely entered the skull, he spreads the scissors to enlarge the opening.

"'The surgeon removes the scissors and introduces a suction catheter into this hole and evacuates the skull contents. With the catheter still in place, he applies traction to the fetus, removing it completely from the patient.'"

This is an abortion doctor's clinical description. Here is another description from a nurse who witnessed the same method performed on a 261/2-week fetus and testified before the Senate Judiciary Committee:

"'Dr. Haskell went in with forceps and grabbed the baby's legs and pulled them down into the birth canal. Then he delivered the baby's body and the arms — everything but the head. The doctor kept the head right inside the uterus. . . .

"'The baby's little fingers were clasping and unclasping, and his little feet were kicking. Then the doctor stuck the scissors in the back of his head, and the baby's arms jerked out, like a startle reaction, like a flinch, like a baby does when he thinks he is going to fall.

"'The doctor opened up the scissors, stuck a high-powered suction tube into the opening, and sucked the baby's brains out. Now the baby went completely limp. . . .

"'He cut the umbilical cord and delivered the placenta. He threw the baby in a pan, along with the placenta and the instruments he had just used.'"

Dr. Haskell's approach is not the only method of killing the fetus once its head lodges in the cervix, and "the process has evolved" since his presentation.

Another doctor, for example, squeezes the skull after it has been pierced "so that enough brain tissue exudes to allow the head to pass through." Still other physicians reach into the cervix with their forceps and crush the fetus' skull.

Others continue to pull the fetus out of the woman until it disarticulates at the neck, in effect decapitating it. These doctors then grasp the head with forceps, crush it, and remove it.

Some doctors performing an intact D & E attempt to remove the fetus without collapsing the skull. Yet one doctor would not allow delivery of a live fetus younger than 24 weeks because "the objective of [his] procedure is to perform an abortion," not a birth. The doctor thus answered in the affirmative when asked whether he would "hold the fetus' head on the internal side of the [cervix] in order to collapse the skull" and kill the fetus before it is born.

Another doctor testified he crushes a fetus' skull not only to reduce its size but also to ensure the fetus is dead before it is removed. For the staff to have to deal with a fetus that has "some viability to it, some movement of limbs," according to this doctor, "[is] always a difficult situation." . . .

B

In 2003, after this Court's decision in *Stenberg*, Congress passed the Act at issue here. . . .

The Act responded to *Stenberg* in two ways. First, Congress made factual findings. Congress determined that this Court in *Stenberg* "was required to accept the very questionable findings issued by the district court judge," but that Congress was "not bound to accept the same factual findings." Congress found, among other things, that "[a] moral, medical, and ethical consensus exists that the practice of performing a partial-birth abortion . . . is a gruesome and inhumane procedure that is never medically necessary and should be prohibited."

Second, and more relevant here, the Act's language differs from that of the Nebraska statute struck down in *Stenberg*. . . .

[The act criminalizes the performance of a "partial-birth abortion" except when such an abortion is necessary to save the life of the mother. It defines partial birth abortion as

> an abortion in which the person performing the abortion—
>   (A) deliberately and intentionally vaginally delivers a living fetus until, in the case of a head-first presentation, the entire fetal head is outside the body of the mother, or, in the case of breech presentation, any part of the fetal trunk past the navel is outside the body of the mother, for the purpose of performing an overt act that the person knows will kill the partially delivered living fetus; and
>   (B) performs the overt act, other than completion of delivery, that kills the partially delivered living fetus.

The act provides that a defendant accused of this offense may seek a hearing before a State medical board on whether the abortion was necessary to save the life of the mother and that the board's findings on that issue are admissible at the trial of the defendant. It further provides that a woman on whom a partial-birth abortion is performed may not be prosecuted under the act.]

II

The principles set forth in the joint opinion in Planned Parenthood of Southeastern Pa. v. Casey did not find support from all those who join the instant opinion. Whatever one's views concerning the *Casey* joint opinion, it is evident a premise central to its conclusion — that the government has a legitimate and substantial interest in preserving and promoting fetal life — would be repudiated were the Court now to affirm the judgments of the Courts of Appeals [which had invalidated the act]. . . .

We assume the following principles for the purposes of this opinion. Before viability, a State "may not prohibit any woman from making the ultimate decision to terminate her pregnancy." [*Casey*, plurality opinion.] It also may not impose upon this right an undue burden, which exists if a regulation's "purpose or effect is to place a substantial obstacle in the path of a woman seeking an abortion before the fetus attains viability." On the other hand, "[r]egulations which do no more than create a structural mechanism by which the State, or the parent or guardian of a minor, may express profound respect for the life of the unborn are permitted, if they are not a substantial obstacle to the woman's exercise of the right to choose." *Casey*, in short, struck a balance. The balance was central to its holding. We now apply its standard to the cases at bar.

III . . .

We conclude that the Act is not void for vagueness, does not impose an undue burden from any overbreadth, and is not invalid on its face.

A

The Act punishes "knowingly perform[ing]" a "partial-birth abortion." . . .

First, the person performing the abortion must "vaginally delive[r] a living fetus." The Act does not restrict an abortion procedure involving the delivery of an expired fetus. The Act, furthermore, is inapplicable to abortions that do not involve vaginal delivery (for instance, hysterotomy or hysterectomy). The Act does apply both previability and postviability because, by common understanding and scientific terminology, a fetus is a living organism while within the womb, whether or not it is viable outside the womb. . . .

Second, the Act's definition of partial-birth abortion requires the fetus to be delivered "until, in the case of a head-first presentation, the entire fetal head is outside the body of the mother, or, in the case of breech presentation, any part of the fetal trunk past the navel is outside the body of the mother." The Attorney General concedes, and we agree, that if an abortion procedure does not involve the delivery of a living fetus to one of these "anatomical 'landmarks'" — where, depending on the presentation, either the fetal head or the fetal trunk past the navel is outside the body of the mother — the prohibitions of the Act do not apply.

Third, to fall within the Act, a doctor must perform an "overt act, other than completion of delivery, that kills the partially delivered living fetus." For purposes of criminal liability, the overt act causing the fetus' death must be separate from delivery, and the overt act must occur after the delivery to an anatomical landmark. This is because the Act proscribes killing "the partially delivered" fetus, which, when read in context, refers to a fetus that has been delivered to an anatomical landmark.

Fourth, the Act contains scienter requirements concerning all the actions involved in the prohibited abortion. To begin with, the physician must have "deliberately and intentionally" delivered the fetus to one of the Act's anatomical landmarks. If a living fetus is delivered past the critical point by accident or inadvertence, the Act is inapplicable. In addition, the fetus must have been delivered "for the purpose of performing an overt act that the [doctor] knows will kill [it]." If either intent is absent, no crime has occurred. This follows from the general principle that where scienter is required no crime is committed absent the requisite state of mind.

B . . .

[U]nlike the statutory language in *Stenberg* that prohibited the delivery of a "'substantial portion'" of the fetus — where a doctor might question how much of the fetus is a substantial portion — the Act defines the line between potentially criminal conduct on the one hand and lawful abortion on the other.

Doctors performing D & E will know that if they do not deliver a living fetus to an anatomical landmark they will not face criminal liability. . . .

C

We next determine whether the Act imposes an undue burden, as a facial matter, because its restrictions on second-trimester abortions are too broad. A review of the statutory text discloses the limits of its reach. The Act prohibits intact D & E; and, notwithstanding respondents' arguments, it does not prohibit the D & E procedure in which the fetus is removed in parts.

1

The Act prohibits a doctor from intentionally performing an intact D & E. The dual prohibitions of the Act, both of which are necessary for criminal liability, correspond with the steps generally undertaken during this type of procedure. First, a doctor delivers the fetus until its head lodges in the cervix, which is usually past the anatomical landmark for a breech presentation. Second, the doctor proceeds to pierce the fetal skull with scissors or crush it with forceps. This step satisfies the overt-act requirement because it kills the fetus and is distinct from delivery. The Act's intent requirements, however, limit its reach to those physicians who carry out the intact D & E after intending to undertake both steps at the outset.

The Act excludes most D & Es in which the fetus is removed in pieces, not intact. If the doctor intends to remove the fetus in parts from the outset, the doctor will not have the requisite intent to incur criminal liability. . . .

The identification of specific anatomical landmarks to which the fetus must be partially delivered also differentiates the Act from the statute at issue in *Stenberg*. The Court in *Stenberg* interpreted "'substantial portion'" of the fetus to include an arm or a leg. The Act's anatomical landmarks, by contrast, clarify that the removal of a small portion of the fetus is not prohibited. . . .

By adding an overt-act requirement Congress sought further to meet the Court's objections to the state statute considered in *Stenberg*. . . .

The canon of constitutional avoidance, finally, extinguishes any lingering doubt as to whether the Act covers the prototypical D & E procedure. . . .

IV

Under the principles accepted as controlling here, the Act, as we have interpreted it, would be unconstitutional "if its purpose or effect is to place a substantial obstacle in the path of a woman seeking an abortion before the fetus attains viability." *Casey*, 505 U.S., at 878 (plurality opinion). The abortions affected by the Act's regulations take place both previability and postviability; so the quoted language and the undue burden analysis it relies upon are applicable. The question is whether the Act, measured by its text in this facial attack, imposes a substantial obstacle to late-term, but previability, abortions. The Act does not on its face impose a substantial obstacle, and we reject this further facial challenge to its validity.

A

The Act's purposes are set forth in recitals preceding its operative provisions. A description of the prohibited abortion procedure demonstrates the rationale for the congressional enactment. The Act proscribes a method of abortion in which a fetus is killed just inches before completion of the birth process. . . .

The Act expresses respect for the dignity of human life.

Congress was concerned, furthermore, with the effects on the medical community and on its reputation caused by the practice of partial-birth abortion. . . .

Casey reaffirmed these governmental objectives. The government may use its voice and its regulatory authority to show its profound respect for the life within the woman. . . .

Where it has a rational basis to act, and it does not impose an undue burden, the State may use its regulatory power to bar certain procedures and substitute others, all in furtherance of its legitimate interests in regulating the medical profession in order to promote respect for life, including life of the unborn.

The Act's ban on abortions that involve partial delivery of a living fetus furthers the Government's objectives. No one would dispute that, for many, D & E is a procedure itself laden with the power to devalue human life. . . .

Respect for human life finds an ultimate expression in the bond of love the mother has for her child. The Act recognizes this reality as well. Whether to have an abortion requires a difficult and painful moral decision. While we find no reliable data to measure the phenomenon, it seems unexceptionable to conclude some women come to regret their choice to abort the infant life they once created and sustained. See Brief for Sandra Cano et al. as Amici Curiae in No. 05-380, pp. 22–24. Severe depression and loss of esteem can follow. See ibid.

In a decision so fraught with emotional consequence some doctors may prefer not to disclose precise details of the means that will be used, confining themselves to the required statement of risks the procedure entails. From one standpoint this ought not to be surprising. Any number of patients facing imminent surgical procedures would prefer not to hear all details, lest the usual anxiety preceding invasive medical procedures become the more intense. This is likely the case with the abortion procedures here in issue.

It is, however, precisely this lack of information concerning the way in which the fetus will be killed that is of legitimate concern to the State. The State has an interest in ensuring so grave a choice is well informed. It is self-evident that a mother who comes to regret her choice to abort must struggle with grief more anguished and sorrow more profound when she learns, only after the event, what she once did not know: that she allowed a doctor to pierce the skull and vacuum the fast-developing brain of her unborn child, a child assuming the human form.

It is a reasonable inference that a necessary effect of the regulation and the knowledge it conveys will be to encourage some women to carry the infant to full term, thus reducing the absolute number of late-term abortions. The medical profession, furthermore, may find different and less shocking methods to abort the fetus in the second trimester, thereby accommodating legislative demand. The State's interest in respect for life is advanced by the dialogue that better informs the political and legal systems, the medical profession, expectant mothers, and society as a whole of the consequences that follow from a decision to elect a late-term abortion.

It is objected that the standard D & E is in some respects as brutal, if not more, than the intact D & E, so that the legislation accomplishes little. What we have already said, however, shows ample justification for the regulation. Partial-birth abortion, as defined by the Act, differs from a standard D & E because the former occurs when the fetus is partially outside the mother to the point of one of the Act's anatomical landmarks. It was reasonable for Congress to think that partial-birth abortion, more than standard D & E, "undermines the public's perception of the appropriate role of a physician during the delivery process, and perverts a process during which life is brought into the world." There would be a flaw in this Court's logic, and an irony in its jurisprudence, were we first to conclude a ban on both D & E and intact D & E was overbroad and then to say it is irrational to ban only intact D & E because that does not proscribe both procedures. . . .

B

The Act's furtherance of legitimate government interests bears upon, but does not resolve, the next question: whether the Act has the effect of imposing an unconstitutional burden on the abortion right because it does not allow use of the barred procedure where "necessary, in appropriate medical judgment, for [the] preservation of the . . . health of the mother." The prohibition in the Act would be unconstitutional, under precedents we here assume to be controlling, if it "subject[ed] [women] to significant health risks." In Ayotte [v. Planned Parenthood of Northern New England, 546 U.S. 320 (2006),] the parties agreed a health exception to the challenged parental-involvement statute was necessary "to avert serious and often irreversible damage to [a pregnant minor's] health." Here, by contrast, whether the Act creates significant health risks for women has been a contested factual question. The evidence presented in the trial courts and before Congress demonstrates both sides have medical support for their position.

Respondents presented evidence that intact D & E may be the safest method of abortion, for reasons similar to those adduced in *Stenberg*. Abortion doctors testified, for example, that intact D & E decreases the risk of cervical laceration or uterine perforation because it requires fewer passes into the uterus with surgical instruments and does not require the removal of bony fragments of the dismembered fetus, fragments that may be sharp. Respondents also presented evidence that intact D & E was safer both because it reduces the risks that fetal parts will remain in the uterus and because it takes less time to complete. Respondents, in addition, proffered evidence that intact D & E was safer for women with certain medical conditions or women with fetuses that had certain anomalies.

These contentions were contradicted by other doctors who testified in the District Courts and before Congress. They concluded that the alleged health advantages were based on speculation without scientific studies to support them. They considered D & E always to be a safe alternative.

There is documented medical disagreement whether the Act's prohibition would ever impose significant health risks on women. . . .

The question becomes whether the Act can stand when this medical uncertainty persists. The Court's precedents instruct that the Act can survive this facial attack. The Court has given state and federal legislatures wide discretion to pass legislation in areas where there is medical and scientific uncertainty.

This traditional rule is consistent with *Casey*, which confirms the State's interest in promoting respect for human life at all stages in the pregnancy. Physicians are not entitled to ignore regulations that direct them to use reasonable alternative procedures. The law need not give abortion doctors unfettered choice in the course of their medical practice, nor should it elevate their status above other physicians in the medical community. . . .

Medical uncertainty does not foreclose the exercise of legislative power in the abortion context any more than it does in other contexts. The medical uncertainty over whether the Act's prohibition creates significant health risks provides a sufficient basis to conclude in this facial attack that the Act does not impose an undue burden. . . .

In reaching the conclusion that the Act does not require a health exception, we reject certain arguments made by the parties on both sides of these cases. On the one hand, the Attorney General urges us to uphold the Act on the basis of the congressional findings alone. Although we review congressional fact-finding under a deferential standard, we do not in the circumstances here place dispositive weight on Congress' findings. The Court retains an independent constitutional duty to review factual findings where constitutional rights are at stake. . . .

As respondents have noted, and the District Courts recognized, some recitations in the Act are factually incorrect. Whether or not accurate at the time, some of the important findings have been superseded. Two examples suffice. Congress determined no medical schools provide instruction on the prohibited procedure. Congressional Findings. The testimony in the District Courts, however, demonstrated intact D & E is taught at medical schools. Congress also found there existed a medical consensus that the prohibited procedure is never medically necessary. The evidence presented in the District Courts contradicts that conclusion. Uncritical deference to Congress' factual findings in these cases is inappropriate.

On the other hand, relying on the Court's opinion in *Stenberg*, respondents contend that an abortion regulation must contain a health exception "if 'substantial medical authority supports the proposition that banning a particular procedure could endanger women's health.'" As illustrated by respondents' arguments and the decisions of the Courts of Appeals, *Stenberg* has been interpreted to leave no margin of error for legislatures to act in the face of medical uncertainty.

A zero tolerance policy would strike down legitimate abortion regulations, like the present one, if some part of the medical community were disinclined to follow the proscription. This is too exacting a standard to impose on the legislative power, exercised in this instance under the Commerce Clause, to regulate the medical profession. Considerations of marginal safety, including the balance of risks, are within the legislative competence when the regulation is rational and in pursuit of legitimate ends. . . .

V

The considerations we have discussed support our further determination that these facial attacks should not have been entertained in the first instance. In these circumstances the proper means to consider exceptions is by as-applied challenge. . . .

This is the proper manner to protect the health of the woman if it can be shown that in discrete and well-defined instances a particular condition has occurred or is likely to occur in which the procedure prohibited by the Act must be used. In an as-applied challenge the nature of the medical risk can be better quantified and balanced than in a facial attack. . . .

Respondents have not demonstrated that the Act, as a facial matter, is void for vagueness, or that it imposes an undue burden on a woman's right to abortion based on its overbreadth or lack of a health exception. For these reasons the judgments of the Courts of Appeals for the Eighth and Ninth Circuits are reversed.

It is so ordered.

[A concurring opinion by Justice Thomas, joined by Justice Scalia, is omitted.]

JUSTICE GINSBURG, with whom JUSTICE STEVENS, JUSTICE SOUTER, and JUSTICE BREYER join, dissenting. . . .

Today's decision is alarming. It refuses to take *Casey* and *Stenberg* seriously. It tolerates, indeed applauds, federal intervention to ban nationwide a procedure found necessary and proper in certain cases by the American College of Obstetricians and Gynecologists (ACOG). It blurs the line, firmly drawn in *Casey*, between previability and postviability abortions. And, for the first time since *Roe*, the Court blesses a prohibition with no exception safeguarding a woman's health.

I dissent from the Court's disposition. Retreating from prior rulings that abortion restrictions cannot be imposed absent an exception safeguarding a woman's health, the Court upholds an Act that surely would not survive under the close scrutiny that previously attended state-decreed limitations on a woman's reproductive choices.

I

A

In keeping with this comprehension of the right to reproductive choice, the Court has consistently required that laws regulating abortion, at any stage of pregnancy and in all cases, safeguard a woman's health. . . .

In *Stenberg*, we expressly held that a statute banning intact D & E was unconstitutional in part because it lacked a health exception. We noted that there existed a "division of medical opinion" about the relative safety of intact D & E, but we made clear that as long as "substantial medical authority supports the proposition that banning a particular abortion procedure could endanger women's health," a health exception is required. . . .

B

[The] congressional findings on which the Partial-Birth Abortion Ban Act rests do not withstand inspection, as the lower courts have determined and this Court is obliged to concede. . . .

Congress claimed there was a medical consensus that the banned procedure is never necessary. But the evidence "very clearly demonstrate[d] the opposite." . . .

C

In contrast to Congress, the District Courts made findings after full trials at which all parties had the opportunity to present their best evidence. . . .

During the District Court trials, "numerous" "extraordinarily accomplished" and "very experienced" medical experts explained that, in certain circumstances and for certain women, intact D & E is safer than alternative procedures and necessary to protect women's health. . . .

According to the expert testimony plaintiffs introduced, the safety advantages of intact D & E are marked for women with certain medical conditions, for example, uterine scarring, bleeding disorders, heart disease, or compromised immune systems. Further, plaintiffs' experts testified that intact D & E is significantly safer for women with certain pregnancy-related conditions, such as placenta previa and accreta, and for women carrying fetuses with certain abnormalities, such as severe hydrocephalus. . . .

Based on thoroughgoing review of the trial evidence and the congressional record, each of the District Courts to consider the issue rejected Congress' findings as unreasonable and not supported by the evidence. . . .

The Court acknowledges some of this evidence, but insists that, because some witnesses disagreed with the ACOG and other experts' assessment of risk, the Act can stand. In this insistence, the Court brushes under the rug the District Courts' well-supported findings that the physicians who testified that intact D & E is never necessary to preserve the health of a woman had slim authority for their opinions. They had no training for, or personal experience with, the intact D & E procedure, and many performed abortions only on rare occasions. . . .

II

A

The Court offers flimsy and transparent justifications for upholding a nationwide ban on intact D & E sans any exception to safeguard a women's health. Today's ruling, the Court declares, advances "a premise central to [*Casey*'s] conclusion" — i.e., the Government's "legitimate and substantial interest in preserving and promoting fetal life." But the Act scarcely furthers that interest: The law saves not a single fetus from destruction, for it targets only a method of performing abortion. . . .

As another reason for upholding the ban, the Court emphasizes that the Act does not proscribe the nonintact D & E procedure. But why not, one might ask. Nonintact D & E could equally be characterized as "brutal," involving as it does "tear[ing] [a fetus] apart" and "ripp[ing] off" its limbs. . . .

Delivery of an intact, albeit nonviable, fetus warrants special condemnation, the Court maintains, because a fetus that is not dismembered resembles an infant. But so, too, does a fetus delivered intact after it is terminated by injection a day or two before the surgical evacuation, or a fetus delivered through medical induction or cesarean. . . .

Ultimately, the Court admits that "moral concerns" are at work, concerns that could yield prohibitions on any abortion. . . .

By allowing such concerns to carry the day and case, overriding fundamental rights, the Court dishonors our precedent. See, e.g., *Casey*, 505 U.S., at 850 ("Some of us as individuals find abortion offensive to our most basic principles of morality, but that cannot control our decision. Our obligation is to define the liberty of all, not to mandate our own moral code."); Lawrence v. Texas, 539 U.S. 558, 571 (2003) (Though "[f]or many persons [objections to homosexual conduct] are not trivial concerns but profound and deep convictions accepted as ethical and moral principles," the power of the State may not be used "to enforce these views on the whole society through operation of the criminal law.").

Revealing in this regard, the Court invokes an antiabortion shibboleth for which it concededly has no reliable evidence: Women who have abortions come to regret their choices, and consequently suffer from "[s]evere depression and loss of esteem." Because of women's fragile emotional state and because of the "bond of love the mother has for her child," the Court worries, doctors may withhold information about the nature of the intact D & E procedure. The solution the Court approves, then, is not to require doctors to inform women, accurately and adequately, of the different procedures and their attendant risks. Instead, the Court deprives women of the right to make an autonomous choice, even at the expense of their safety.

This way of thinking reflects ancient notions about women's place in the family and under the Constitution — ideas that have long since been discredited.

Though today's majority may regard women's feelings on the matter as "self-evident," this Court has repeatedly confirmed that "[t]he destiny of the woman must be shaped . . . on her own conception of her spiritual imperatives and her place in society."

B

In cases on a "woman's liberty to determine whether to [continue] her pregnancy," this Court has identified viability as a critical consideration. "[T]here is no line [more workable] than viability," the Court explained in *Casey*, for viability is "the time at which there is a realistic possibility of maintaining and nourishing a life outside the womb, so that the independent existence of the second life can in reason and all fairness be the object of state protection that now overrides the rights of the woman. . . . In some broad sense it might be said that a woman who fails to act before viability has consented to the State's intervention on behalf of the developing child."

Today, the Court blurs that line, maintaining that "[t]he Act [legitimately] appl[ies] both previability and postviability because . . . a fetus is a living organism while within the womb, whether or not it is viable outside the womb." Instead of drawing the line at viability, the Court refers to Congress' purpose to differentiate "abortion and infanticide" based not on whether a fetus can survive outside the womb, but on where a fetus is anatomically located when a particular medical procedure is performed. . . .

III

A

The Court further confuses our jurisprudence when it declares that "facial attacks" are not permissible in "these circumstances," i.e., where medical uncertainty exists. ("In an as-applied challenge the nature of the medical risk can be better quantified and balanced than in a facial attack."). This holding is perplexing given that, in materially identical circumstances we held that a statute lacking a health exception was unconstitutional on its face. . . .

IV

Though today's opinion does not go so far as to discard *Roe* or *Casey*, the Court, differently composed than it was when we last considered a restrictive abortion regulation, is hardly faithful to our earlier invocations of "the rule of law" and the "principles of stare decisis." [Between *Stenberg* and *Gonzales*, Chief Justice Rehnquist was replaced by Chief Justice Roberts, and Justice O'Connor was replaced by Justice Alito.] . . .

In sum, the notion that the Partial-Birth Abortion Ban Act furthers any legitimate governmental interest is, quite simply, irrational. The Court's defense of the statute provides no saving explanation. In candor, the Act, and the Court's defense of it, cannot be understood as anything other than an effort to chip away at a right declared again and again by this Court — and with increasing comprehension of its centrality to women's lives. . . .

Whole Woman's Health v. Hellerstedt

136 S. Ct. 2292 (2016)

JUSTICE BREYER delivered the opinion of the Court.

[Texas House Bill 2 requires physicians performing abortions to "have active admitting privileges at a hospital that . . . is located not further than 30 miles from the location at which the abortion is performed" and to meet "the minimum standards . . . for ambulatory surgical centers." (ASC). These standards include detailed specifications concerning the nursing staff, building dimensions, and other building requirements. For example, the standards included a requirement for "a full surgical suite" with detailed specifications about the operating room and the recovery room, requirements for specific corridor widths and requirements for advanced heating, ventilation, and air conditioning systems.

[Petitioners, a group of abortion providers, filed suit in federal district court, claiming that House Bill 2 imposed an undue burden on the abortion right. After a four-day trial, the district court ruled in their favor and enjoined enforcement of the bill. Among other findings of fact, the district court determined that:

- the number of licensed abortion facilities in Texas dropped almost by half leading up to and in the wake of enforcement of the admitting-privileges requirement;
- if the surgical-center provision were allowed to take effect, the number of abortion facilities would be reduced to seven or eight for the entire state;
- all of these facilities would be in Houston, Austin, San Antonio, and the Dallas/Fort Worth area;
- these providers could not meet the demand of the entire state;
- if the requirements were allowed to go into effect, 2 million women of reproductive age would live more than 50 miles from an abortion provider, 1.3 million would live more than 100 miles from a provider, 900,000 would live more than 150 miles from a provider, and 750,000 would live more than 200 miles from a provider;
- abortion is much safer than many common medical procedures, such as colonoscopies, vasectomies, and plastic surgery, that are not covered by the regulations;
- risks are not appreciably lowered for patients undergoing abortions at ambulatory surgical centers.

[The court of appeals reversed the District Court and, with minor exceptions, found that the provisions were constitutional. It found that both the admitting privileges requirement and the surgical-center requirement were rationally related to the state interest in protecting the health and welfare of women seeking abortions and that the district court had erred by substituting its own judgment about these health effects for that of the legislature. Moreover, the court of appeals held, appellants had failed to show that the provisions imposed an undue burden on "a large fraction of women."

[The Supreme Court reversed the Court of Appeals and held that the Texas statute was facially unconstitutional.

[In an omitted section of the Court's opinion, it rejected appellee's argument that its claims were barred by res judicata. It then turned to the merits.]

III

Undue Burden — Legal Standard

The Court of Appeals' articulation of the relevant standard is incorrect. The first part of the Court of Appeals' test may be read to imply that a district court should not consider the existence or nonexistence of medical benefits when considering whether a regulation of abortion constitutes an undue burden. The rule announced in *Casey*, however, requires that courts consider the burdens a law imposes on abortion access together with the benefits those laws confer. And the second part of the test is wrong to equate the judicial review applicable to the regulation of a constitutionally protected personal liberty with the less strict review applicable where, for example, economic legislation is at issue. . . .

The statement that legislatures, and not courts, must resolve questions of medical uncertainty is also inconsistent with this Court's case law. Instead, the Court, when determining the constitutionality of laws regulating abortion procedures, has placed considerable weight upon evidence and argument presented in judicial proceedings. . . .

Unlike in *Gonzales*, the relevant statute here does not set forth any legislative findings. Rather, one is left to infer that the legislature sought to further a constitutionally acceptable objective (namely, protecting women's health). For a district court to give significant weight to evidence in the judicial record in these circumstances is consistent with this Court's case law. . . .

IV

Undue Burden — Admitting-Privileges Requirement . . .

The evidence upon which the [district] court based this conclusion included, among other things:

- A collection of at least five peer-reviewed studies on abortion complications in the first trimester, showing that the highest rate of major complications — including those complications requiring hospital admission — was less than one-quarter of 1%. . . .
- Expert testimony to the effect that complications rarely require hospital admission, much less immediate transfer to a hospital from an outpatient clinic. . . .

We add that, when directly asked at oral argument whether Texas knew of a single instance in which the new requirement would have helped even one woman obtain better treatment, Texas admitted that there was no evidence in the record of such a case. . . .

At the same time, the record evidence indicates that the admitting-privileges requirement places a "substantial obstacle in the path of a woman's choice." . . .

In our view, the record contains sufficient evidence that the admitting-privileges requirement led to the closure of half of Texas' clinics, or thereabouts. . . .

Those closures meant fewer doctors, longer waiting times, and increased crowding. Record evidence also supports the finding that after the admitting-privileges provision went into effect, the "number of women of reproductive age living in a county . . . more than 150 miles from a provider increased from approximately 86,000 to 400,000." . . .

[The] dissent suggests that one benefit of H. B. 2's requirements would be that they might "force un-safe facilities to shut down." To support that assertion, the dissent points to the Kermit Gosnell scandal. Gosnell, a physician in Pennsylvania, was convicted of first-degree murder and manslaughter. He "staffed his facility with unlicensed and indifferent workers, and then let them practice medicine unsupervised" and had "[d]irty facilities; unsanitary instruments; an absence of functioning monitoring and resuscitation equipment; the use of cheap, but dangerous, drugs; illegal procedures; and inadequate emergency access for when things inevitably went wrong." Gosnell's behavior was terribly wrong. But there is no reason to believe that an extra layer of regulation would have affected that behavior. Determined wrongdoers, already ignoring existing statutes and safety measures, are unlikely to be convinced to adopt safe practices by a new overlay of regulations. Regardless, Gosnell's deplorable crimes could escape detection only because his facility went uninspected for more than 15 years. Pre-existing Texas law already contained numerous detailed regulations covering abortion facilities, including a requirement that facilities be inspected at least annually. The record contains nothing to suggest that H. B. 2 would be more effective than pre-existing Texas law at deterring wrongdoers like Gosnell from criminal behavior.

V

UNDUE BURDEN — SURGICAL-CENTER REQUIREMENT . . .

There is considerable evidence in the record supporting the District Court's findings indicating that the statutory provision requiring all abortion facilities to meet all surgical-center standards does not benefit patients and is not necessary. The District Court found that "risks are not appreciably lowered for patients who undergo abortions at ambulatory surgical centers as compared to nonsurgical-center facilities." The court added that women "will not obtain better care or experience more frequent positive outcomes at an ambulatory surgical center as compared to a previously licensed facility." And these findings are well supported.

The record makes clear that the surgical-center requirement provides no benefit when complications arise in the context of an abortion produced through medication. That is because, in such a case, complications would almost always arise only after the patient has left the facility. The record also contains evidence indicating that abortions taking place in an abortion facility are safe — indeed, safer than numerous procedures that take place outside hospitals and to which Texas does not apply its surgical-center requirements. [Nationwide], childbirth is 14 times more likely than abortion to result in death, but Texas law allows a midwife to oversee childbirth in the patient's own home. [Medical] treatment after an incomplete miscarriage often involves a procedure identical to that involved in a nonmedical abortion, but it often takes place outside a hospital or surgical center. And Texas partly or wholly grandfathers (or waives in whole or in part the surgical-center requirement for) about two-thirds of the facilities to which the surgical-center standards apply. But it neither grandfathers nor provides waivers for any of the facilities that perform abortions. . . .

[In] the face of no threat to women's health, Texas seeks to force women to travel long distances to get abortions in crammed-to-capacity superfacilities. [Another] commonsense inference that the District Court made is that these effects would be harmful to, not supportive of, women's health. . . .

Finally, the District Court found that the costs that a currently licensed abortion facility would have to incur to meet the surgical-center requirements were considerable, ranging from $1 million per facility (for facilities with adequate space) to $3 million per facility (where additional land must be purchased). This evidence supports the conclusion that more surgical centers will not soon fill the gap when licensed facilities are forced to close. . . .

VI . . .

[Texas] claims that the provisions at issue here do not impose a substantial obstacle because the women affected by those laws are not a "large fraction" of Texan women "of reproductive age," which Texas reads *Casey* to have required. But *Casey* used the language "large fraction" to refer to "a large fraction of cases in which [the provision at issue] is relevant," a class narrower than "all women," "pregnant women," or even "the class of women seeking abortions identified by the State." Here, as in *Casey*, the relevant denominator is "those [women] for whom [the provision] is an actual rather than an irrelevant restriction." . . .

JUSTICE GINSBURG, concurring. . . .

When a State severely limits access to safe and legal procedures, women in desperate circumstances may resort to unlicensed rogue practitioners, faute de mieux, at great risk to their health and safety. Targeted Regulation of Abortion Providers laws like H. B. 2 that "do little or nothing for health, but rather strew impediments to abortion," cannot survive judicial inspection.

JUSTICE THOMAS, dissenting. . . .

I

[In this section of his opinion, Justice Thomas criticizes the Court for granting third-party standing to abortion providers whose own constitutional rights are not invaded by the statute.]

II . . .

I remain fundamentally opposed to the Court's abortion jurisprudence. Even taking *Casey* as the baseline, however, the majority radically rewrites the undue-burden test in three ways. First, today's decision requires courts to "consider the burdens a law imposes on abortion access together with the benefits those laws confer." Second, today's opinion tells the courts that, when the law's justifications are medically uncertain, they need not defer to the legislature, and must instead assess medical justifications for abortion restrictions by scrutinizing the record themselves. Finally, even if a law imposes no "substantial obstacle" to women's access to abortions, the law now must have more than a "reasonabl[e] relat[ion] to . . . a legitimate state interest." (Internal quotation marks omitted.) These precepts are nowhere to be found in *Casey* or its successors, and transform the undue-burden test to something much more akin to strict scrutiny. . . .

III

The majority's furtive reconfiguration of the standard of scrutiny applicable to abortion restrictions also points to a deeper problem. The undue-burden standard is just one variant of the Court's tiers-of-scrutiny approach to constitutional adjudication. And the label the Court affixes to its level of scrutiny in assessing whether the government can restrict a given right — be it "rational basis," intermediate, strict, or something else — is increasingly a meaningless formalism. As the Court applies whatever standard it likes to any given case, nothing but empty words separates our constitutional decisions from judicial fiat. . . .

[If] our recent cases illustrate anything, it is how easily the Court tinkers with levels of scrutiny to achieve its desired result. This Term, it is easier for a State to survive strict scrutiny despite discriminating on the basis of race in college admissions than it is for the same State to regulate how abortion doctors and clinics operate under the putatively less stringent undue-burden test. [Justice Thomas cites Fisher v. University of Tex. at Austin, discussed in Chapter 5, section C.] Yet the same State gets no deference under the undue-burden test, despite producing evidence that abortion safety, one rationale for Texas' law, is medically debated.

These more recent decisions reflect the Court's tendency to relax purportedly higher standards of review for less-preferred rights. . . .

The Court should abandon the pretense that anything other than policy preferences underlies its balancing of constitutional rights and interests in any given case.

IV

It is tempting to identify the Court's invention of a constitutional right to abortion in *Roe v. Wade* as the tipping point that transformed third-party standing doctrine and the tiers of scrutiny into an unworkable morass of special exceptions and arbitrary applications. But those roots run deeper, to the very notion that some constitutional rights demand preferential treatment. During the *Lochner* era, the Court considered the right to contract and other economic liberties to be fundamental requirements of due process of law. The Court in 1937 repudiated *Lochner*'s foundations. But the Court then created a new taxonomy of preferred rights.

In 1938, seven Justices heard a constitutional challenge to a federal ban on shipping adulterated milk in interstate commerce. Without economic substantive due process, the ban clearly invaded no constitutional right. See United States v. Carolene Products Co., 304 U.S. 144, 152-153 (1938). Within Justice Stone's opinion for the Court, however, was a footnote that just three other Justices joined — the famous Carolene Products Footnote 4. . . .

Though the footnote was pure dicta, the Court seized upon it to justify its special treatment of certain personal liberties like the First Amendment and the right against discrimination on the basis of race — but also rights not enumerated in the Constitution. As the Court identified which rights deserved special protection, it developed the tiers of scrutiny as part of its equal protection (and, later, due process) jurisprudence as a way to demand extra justifications for encroachments on these rights. And, having created a new category of fundamental rights, the Court loosened the reins to recognize even putative rights like abortion, which hardly implicate "discrete and insular minorities." . . .

Eighty years on, the Court has come full circle. The Court has simultaneously transformed judicially created rights like the right to abortion into preferred constitutional rights, while disfavoring many of the rights actually enumerated in the Constitution. But our Constitution renounces the notion that some constitutional rights are more equal than others. A plaintiff either possesses the constitutional right he is asserting, or not — and if not, the judiciary has no business creating ad hoc exceptions so that others can assert rights that seem especially important to vindicate. A law either infringes a constitutional right, or not; there is no room for the judiciary to invent tolerable degrees of encroachment. Unless the Court abides by one set of rules to adjudicate constitutional rights, it will continue reducing constitutional law to policy-driven value judgments until the last shreds of its legitimacy disappear.

* * *

Today's decision will prompt some to claim victory, just as it will stiffen opponents' will to object. But the entire Nation has lost something essential. The majority's embrace of a jurisprudence of rights-specific exceptions and balancing tests is "a regrettable concession of defeat — an acknowledgement that we have passed the point where 'law,' properly speaking, has any further application." Scalia, The Rule of Law as a Law of Rules, 56 U. Chi. L. Rev. 1175, 1189 (1989). I respectfully dissent.

JUSTICE ALITO, with whom [CHIEF JUSTICE ROBERTS] and JUSTICE THOMAS join, dissenting.

I

[In this section, and in section II of his opinion, Justice Alito argues that res judicata bars petitioners' claim.]

III . . .

Under our cases, petitioners must show that the admitting privileges and ASC requirements impose an "undue burden" on women seeking abortions. And in order to obtain the sweeping relief they seek — facial invalidation of those provisions — they must show, at a minimum, that these provisions have an unconstituional impact on at least a "large fraction" of Texas women of reproductive age. Such a situation could result if the clinics able to comply with the new requirements either lacked the requisite overall capacity or were located too far away to serve a "large fraction" of the women in question.

Petitioners did not make that showing. Instead of offering direct evidence, they relied on two crude inferences. First, they pointed to the number of abortion clinics that closed after the enactment of H. B. 2, and asked that it be inferred that all these closures resulted from the two challenged provisions. They made little effort to show why particular clinics closed. Second, they pointed to the number of abortions performed annually at ASCs before H. B. 2 took effect and, because this figure is well below the total number of abortions performed each year in the State, they asked that it be inferred that ASC-compliant clinics could not meet the demands of women in the State. See App. 237-238. Petitioners failed to provide any evidence of the actual capacity of the facilities that would be available to perform abortions in compliance with the new law. . . .

A

I do not dispute the fact that H. B. 2 caused the closure of some clinics. Indeed, it seems clear that H. B. 2 was intended to force unsafe facilities to shut down. The law was one of many enacted by States in the wake of the Kermit Gosnell scandal, in which a physician who ran an abortion clinic in Philadelphia was convicted for the first-degree murder of three infants who were born alive and for the manslaughter of a patient. Gosnell had not been actively supervised by state or local authorities or by his peers, and the Philadelphia grand jury that investigated the case recommended that the Commonwealth adopt a law requiring abortion clinics to comply with the same regulations as ASCs. If Pennsylvania had had such a requirement in force, the Gosnell facility may have been shut down before his crimes. And if there were any similarly un-safe facilities in Texas, H. B. 2 was clearly intended to put them out of business.

While there can be no doubt that H. B. 2 caused some clinics to cease operation, the absence of proof regarding the reasons for particular closures is a [problem]. [Justice Alito outlines other reasons why some clinics might have closed.]

we don't know why the closures occurred

B

Even if the District Court had properly filtered out immaterial closures, its analysis would have been incomplete for a second reason. Petitioners offered scant evidence on the capacity of the clinics that are able to comply with the admitting privileges and ASC requirements, or on those clinics' geographic distribution. Reviewing the evidence in the record, it is far from clear that there has been a material impact on access to abortion. . . .

Faced with increased demand, ASCs could potentially increase the number of abortions performed without prohibitively expensive changes. . . .

So much for capacity. The other potential obstacle to abortion access is the distribution of facilities throughout the State. This might occur if the two challenged H. B. 2 requirements, by causing the closure of clinics in some rural areas, led to a situation in which a "large fraction" of women of reproductive age live too far away from any open clinic. Based on the Court's holding in [Casey] it appears that the need to travel up to 150 miles is not an undue burden, and the evidence in this case shows that if the only clinics in the State were those that would have remained open if the judgment of the Fifth Circuit had not been enjoined, roughly 95% of the women of reproductive age in the State would live within 150 miles of an open facility (or lived outside that range before H. B. 2). Because the record does not show why particular facilities closed, the real figure may be even higher than 95%.

We should decline to hold that these statistics justify the facial invalidation of the H. B. 2 requirements. The possibility that the admitting privileges requirement might have caused a closure in Lubbock is no reason to issue a facial injunction exempting Houston clinics from that requirement. I do not dismiss the situation of those women who would no longer live within 150 miles of a clinic as a result of H. B. 2. But under current doctrine such localized problems can be addressed by narrow as-applied challenges. . . .

Note: The Future of Abortion Rights

1. Gonzales *and the government's interest.* Does the Court identify a legitimate government interest advanced by the Partial Birth Abortion Act? How does the Act "[express] respect for the dignity of human life" when it regulates only the method by which abortions are performed, not whether they are performed? Is it legitimate for the government to ban an abortion procedure because of speculation that "some women come to regret their choice to abort the infant life they once created and sustained"?

2. Gonzales *and undue burden.* In her dissenting opinion, Justice Ginsburg claims that "[the] law saves not a single fetus from destruction." If she is correct, how can it be that the statute unduly burdens the abortion right? Notice that the Court leaves open the possibility that individual women can challenge the statute as applied to them on the ground that a standard D & E would risk their health. Is this holding meaningfully different from reading a health exception into the statute? If the statute had had such an exception, would there be any question as to its constitutionality?

3. Hellerstedt *and the government's interest.* Under *Casey* an abortion statute is unconstitutional if it has the "purpose or effect" of placing a "substantial obstacle in the path of a woman seeking an abortion." In *Hellerstedt*, the Court assumes that the statute's purpose was constitutional but invalidates the statute because of its effect. The focus on effect, in turn, leads to a detailed analysis of the reasons why abortion clinics closed and the medical necessity for various regulatory procedures. Might this analysis have been avoided if the Court were more skeptical of the legislature's purpose? If one took seriously the claim that the legislature was in fact concerned about women's health, would the Court's careful scrutiny of the factual bases for the legislative decision be appropriate?

4. Hellerstedt *and Undue Burden.* The Court seems to acknowledge that an abortion regulation poses an undue burden only if it affects a "large fraction" of women seeking abortions. Is this test consistent with the status of abortion as an individual right? Perhaps it is, because the Court also claims that the denominator of the fraction is "those [women] for whom [the provision] is an actual rather than an irrelevant restriction." Doesn't this make the denominator the same as the numerator? If a single woman is unable to get an abortion because of a general regulatory scheme, does the scheme pose an undue burden?

5. *The law and politics of abortion.* Who are the long-term winners and losers in *Gonzales* and *Hellerstedt*? Consider the following possibilities:

a. Despite outward appearances, *Gonzales* aids the defenders of *Roe.* The decision itself has very little impact on the availability of abortions. It does, however, change the political dynamics of the abortion debate. On the one hand, it eliminates the most emotionally charged and problematic form of abortion, the existence of which was used effectively to mobilize "pro-life" forces. On the other hand, the decision produces anxiety among "pro-choice" forces that the basic abortion right is at risk, thereby promoting political mobilization on their side.

b. Despite outward appearances, *Hellerstedt* aids opponents of *Roe*. Instead of recognizing that most abortion regulation is impermissibly motivated by a desire to restrict the right, the Court has gotten itself bogged down in a fact-intensive analysis of the minutiae of abortion regulation. This approach leaves it unable to effectively control persistent local efforts to make abortion practically unattainable.

c. Both *Gonzales* and *Hellerstedt* are all about symbolism and will have very little real impact of any kind. The long-term future of the abortion right will be determined by cultural, political, economic, and technological developments rather than by constitutional doctrine.

3.   Same-Sex Intimacy

In Bowers v. Hardwick, 478 U.S. 186 (1986), the Supreme Court, in a five-to-four decision written by Justice White, refused to invalidate a statute prohibiting sodomy, defined as "any sexual act involving the sex organs of one person and the mouth or anus of another" as applied to two adult males who had sex in a private bedroom. The Court argued that "no connection between family, marriage, or procreation on the one hand and homosexual activity on the other has been demonstrated" and that "to claim that a right to engage in such conduct is 'deeply rooted in this Nation's history and tradition' or 'implicit on the concept of ordered liberty' is, at best, facetious." In response to the argument that objections to the immorality of homosexual conduct do not provide a rational basis for the law, the Court noted that "[the] law [is] constantly based on notions of morality, and if all laws representing essentially moral choices are to be invalidated under the Due Process Clause, the courts will be very busy indeed."

In a concurring opinion, Chief Justice Burger wrote that "to hold that the act of homosexual sodomy is somehow protected as a fundamental right would be to cast aside millennia of moral teaching."

Less than two decades later, the Court came to a very different conclusion.

Lawrence v. Texas
539 U.S. 558 (2003)

JUSTICE KENNEDY delivered the opinion of the Court.

Liberty protects the person from unwarranted government intrusions into a dwelling or other private places. In our tradition the State is not omnipresent in the home. And there are other spheres of our lives and existence, outside the home, where the State should not be a dominant presence. Freedom extends beyond spatial bounds. Liberty presumes an autonomy of self that includes freedom of thought, belief, expression, and certain intimate conduct. The instant case involves liberty of the person both in its spatial and more transcendent dimensions.

I

The question before the Court is the validity of a Texas statute making it a crime for two persons of the same sex to engage in certain intimate sexual conduct.

In Houston, Texas, officers of the Harris County Police Department were dispatched to a private residence in response to a reported weapons disturbance. They entered an apartment where one of the petitioners, John Geddes Lawrence, resided. The right of the police to enter does not seem to have been questioned. The officers observed Lawrence and another man, Tyron Garner, engaging in a sexual act. The two petitioners were arrested, held in custody overnight, and charged and convicted before a Justice of the Peace.

[Lawrence was charged under a statute that provides:] "A person commits an offense if he engages in deviate sexual intercourse with another individual of the same sex." The statute defines "[d]eviate sexual intercourse" as follows:

"(A) any contact between any part of the genitals of one person and the mouth or anus of another person; or

"(B) the penetration of the genitals or the anus of another person with an object." §21.01(1). . . .

[margin note: Violating statute]

II

We conclude the case should be resolved by determining whether the petitioners were free as adults to engage in the private conduct in the exercise of their liberty under the Due Process Clause of the Fourteenth Amendment to the Constitution. For this inquiry we deem it necessary to reconsider the Court's holding in *Bowers*. . . .

The Court began its substantive discussion in *Bowers* as follows: "The issue presented is whether the Federal Constitution confers a fundamental right upon homosexuals to engage in sodomy and hence invalidates the laws of the many States that still make such conduct illegal and have done so for a very long time." That statement, we now conclude, discloses the Court's own failure to appreciate the extent of the liberty at stake. To say that the issue in *Bowers* was simply the right to engage in certain sexual conduct demeans the claim the individual put forward, just as it would demean a married couple were it to be said marriage is simply about the right to have sexual intercourse. The laws involved in *Bowers* and here purport to do no more than prohibit a particular sexual act. Their penalties and purposes have more far-reaching consequences, touching upon the most private human conduct, sexual behavior, and in the most private of places, the home. They seek to control a personal relationship that, whether or not entitled to formal recognition in the law, is within the liberty of persons to choose without being punished as criminals. The liberty protected by the Constitution allows homosexual persons the right to choose to enter upon relationships in the confines of their homes and their own private lives and still retain their dignity as free persons. . . .

This, as a general rule, should counsel against attempts by the State, or a court, to define the meaning of the relationship or to set its boundaries absent injury to a person or abuse of an institution the law protects. It suffices for us to acknowledge that adults may choose to enter upon this relationship in the confines of their homes and their own private lives and still retain their dignity as free persons. When sexuality finds overt expression in intimate conduct with another person,

[margin note: the Bowers case was not just about sexual acts, but individual liberty/privacy]

the conduct can be but one element in a personal bond that is more enduring. The liberty protected by the Constitution allows homosexual persons the right to make this choice.

Having misapprehended the claim of liberty there presented to it, and thus stating the claim to be whether there is a fundamental right to engage in consensual sodomy, the *Bowers* Court said: "Proscriptions against that conduct have ancient roots." In academic writings, and in many of the scholarly amicus briefs filed to assist the Court in this case, there are fundamental criticisms of [this statement]. We need not enter this debate in the attempt to reach a definitive historical judgment, but the following considerations counsel against adopting the definitive conclusions upon which *Bowers* placed such reliance.

At the outset it should be noted that there is no longstanding history in this country of laws directed at homosexual conduct as a distinct matter. . . .

The absence of legal prohibitions focusing on homosexual conduct may be explained in part by noting that according to some scholars the concept of the homosexual as a distinct category of person did not emerge until the late 19th century. Thus early American sodomy laws were not directed at homosexuals as such but instead sought to prohibit nonprocreative sexual activity more generally. This does not suggest approval of homosexual conduct. It does tend to show that this particular form of conduct was not thought of as a separate category from like conduct between heterosexual persons.

Laws prohibiting sodomy do not seem to have been enforced against consenting adults acting in private . . .

In all events [the infrequency of prosecution] makes it difficult to say that society approved of a rigorous and systematic punishment of the consensual acts committed in private and by adults. The longstanding criminal prohibition of homosexual sodomy upon which the *Bowers* decision placed such reliance is as consistent with a general condemnation of nonprocreative sex as it is with an established tradition of prosecuting acts because of their homosexual character.

[Far] from possessing "ancient roots," American laws targeting same-sex couples did not develop until the last third of the 20th century. The reported decisions concerning the prosecution of consensual, homosexual sodomy between adults for the years 1880–1995 are not always clear in the details, but a significant number involved conduct in a public place.

It was not until the 1970's that any State singled out same-sex relations for criminal prosecution, and only nine States have done so. Post-*Bowers* even some of these States did not adhere to the policy of suppressing homosexual conduct. Over the course of the last decades, States with same-sex prohibitions have moved toward abolishing them.

In summary, the historical grounds relied upon in *Bowers* are more complex than the majority opinion and the concurring opinion by Chief Justice Burger indicate. Their historical premises are not without doubt and, at the very least, are overstated.

It must be acknowledged, of course, that the Court in *Bowers* was making the broader point that for centuries there have been powerful voices to condemn homosexual conduct as immoral. The condemnation has been shaped by religious beliefs, conceptions of right and acceptable behavior, and respect for the traditional family. For many persons these are not trivial concerns but profound and deep convictions accepted as ethical and moral principles to which they aspire and which thus determine the course of their lives. These considerations do not answer the question before us, however. The issue is whether the majority may use the power of the State to enforce these views on the whole society through operation of the criminal law. . . .

[We] think that our laws and traditions in the past half century are of most relevance here. These references show an emerging awareness that liberty gives substantial protection to adult persons in deciding how to conduct their private lives in matters pertaining to sex. . . .

This emerging recognition should have been apparent when *Bowers* was decided. In 1955 the American Law Institute promulgated the Model Penal Code and made clear that it did not recommend or provide for "criminal penalties for consensual sexual relations conducted in private." [In] 1961 Illinois changed its laws to conform to the Model Penal Code. Other States soon followed. . . .

The sweeping references by Chief Justice Burger to the history of Western civilization and to Judeo-Christian moral and ethical standards did not take account of other authorities pointing in an opposite direction. A committee advising the British Parliament recommended in 1957 repeal of laws punishing homosexual conduct. The Wolfenden Report: Report of the Committee on Homosexual Offenses and Prostitution (1963). Parliament enacted the substance of those recommendations 10 years later. Sexual Offences Act 1967, §1.

Of even more importance, almost five years before *Bowers* was decided the European Court of Human Rights considered a case with parallels to *Bowers* and to today's case. [The] court held that the laws proscribing the conduct were invalid under the European Convention on Human Rights. Dudgeon v. United Kingdom, 45 Eur. Ct. H. R. (1981) 152. Authoritative in all countries that are members of the Council of Europe (21 nations then, 45 nations now), the decision is at odds with the premise in *Bowers* that the claim put forward was insubstantial in our Western civilization.

In our own constitutional system the deficiencies in *Bowers* became even more apparent in the years following its announcement. The 25 States with laws prohibiting the relevant conduct referenced in the *Bowers* decision are reduced now to 13, of which 4 enforce their laws only against homosexual conduct. In those States where sodomy is still proscribed, whether for same-sex or heterosexual conduct, there is a pattern of nonenforcement with respect to consenting adults acting in private. The State of Texas admitted in 1994 that as of that date it had not prosecuted anyone under those circumstances.

Two principal cases decided after *Bowers* cast its holding into even more doubt. In [*Casey*], the Court reaffirmed the substantive force of the liberty protected by the Due Process Clause. The *Casey* decision again confirmed that our laws and tradition afford constitutional protection to personal decisions relating to marriage, procreation, contraception, family relationships, child rearing, and education. . . .

In explaining the respect the Constitution demands for the autonomy of the person in making these choices, we stated as follows:

"These matters, involving the most intimate and personal choices a person may make in a lifetime, choices central to personal dignity and autonomy, are central to the liberty protected by the Fourteenth Amendment. At the heart of liberty is the right to define one's own concept of existence, of meaning, of the universe, and of the mystery of human life. Beliefs about these matters could not define the attributes of personhood were they formed under compulsion of the State."

Persons in a homosexual relationship may seek autonomy for these purposes, just as heterosexual persons do. The decision in *Bowers* would deny them this right.

The second post-*Bowers* case of principal relevance is [Romer v. Evans, discussed in Chapter 5, section B]. There the Court struck down class-based legislation directed at homosexuals as a violation of the Equal Protection Clause. . . .

As an alternative argument in this case, counsel for the petitioners and some amici contend that *Romer* provides the basis for declaring the Texas statute invalid under the Equal Protection Clause. That is a tenable argument, but we conclude the instant case requires us to address whether *Bowers* itself has continuing validity. Were we to hold the statute invalid under the Equal Protection Clause some might question whether a prohibition would be valid if drawn differently, say, to prohibit the conduct both between same-sex and different-sex participants.

Equality of treatment and the due process right to demand respect for conduct protected by the substantive guarantee of liberty are linked in important respects, and a decision on the latter point advances both interests. If protected conduct is made criminal and the law which does so remains unexamined for its substantive validity, its stigma might remain even if it were not enforceable as drawn for equal protection reasons. When homosexual conduct is made criminal by the law of the State, that declaration in and of itself is an invitation to subject homosexual persons to discrimination both in the public and in the private spheres. The central holding of *Bowers* has been brought in question by this case, and it should be addressed. Its continuance as precedent demeans the lives of homosexual persons.

The stigma this criminal statute imposes, moreover, is not trivial. The offense, to be sure, is but a class C misdemeanor, a minor offense in the Texas legal system. Still, it remains a criminal offense with all that imports for the dignity of the persons charged. The petitioners will bear on their record the history of their criminal convictions. . . .

We are advised that if Texas convicted an adult for private, consensual homosexual conduct under the statute here in question the convicted person would come within the registration laws of at least four States were he or she to be subject to their jurisdiction. This underscores the consequential nature of the punishment and the state-sponsored condemnation attendant to the criminal prohibition. Furthermore, the Texas criminal conviction carries with it the other collateral consequences always following a conviction, such as notations on job application forms, to mention but one example.

The foundations of *Bowers* have sustained serious erosion from our recent decisions in *Casey* and *Romer*. When our precedent has been thus weakened, criticism from other sources is of greater significance. In the United States criticism of *Bowers* has been substantial and continuing, disapproving of its reasoning in all respects, not just as to its historical assumptions. The courts of five different States have declined to follow it in interpreting provisions in their own state constitutions parallel to the Due Process Clause of the Fourteenth Amendment.

To the extent *Bowers* relied on values we share with a wider civilization, it should be noted that the reasoning and holding in *Bowers* have been rejected elsewhere. The European Court of Human Rights has followed not *Bowers* but its own decision in Dudgeon v. United Kingdom. Other nations, too, have taken action consistent with an affirmation of the protected right of homosexual adults to engage in intimate, consensual conduct. The right the petitioners seek in this case has been accepted as an integral part of human freedom in many other countries. There has been no showing that in this country the governmental interest in circumscribing personal choice is somehow more legitimate or urgent.

The doctrine of stare decisis is essential to the respect accorded to the judgments of the Court and to the stability of the law. It is not, however, an inexorable command. In *Casey* we noted that when a Court is asked to overrule a precedent recognizing a constitutional liberty interest, individual or societal reliance on the existence of that liberty cautions with particular strength against reversing course. The holding in *Bowers*, however, has not induced detrimental reliance comparable to some instances where recognized individual rights are involved. Indeed, there has been no individual or societal reliance on *Bowers* of the sort that could counsel against overturning its holding once there are compelling reasons to do so. *Bowers* itself causes uncertainty, for the precedents before and after its issuance contradict its central holding.

[In] his dissenting opinion in *Bowers* Justice Stevens came to these conclusions:

> Our prior cases make two propositions abundantly clear. First, the fact that the governing majority in a State has traditionally viewed a particular practice as immoral is not a sufficient reason for upholding a law prohibiting the practice; neither history *nor tradition could save a law prohibiting miscegenation from constitutional attack.* Second, individual decisions by married persons, concerning the intimacies of their physical relationship, even when not intended to produce offspring, are a form of "liberty" protected by the Due Process Clause of the Fourteenth Amendment. Moreover, this protection extends to intimate choices by unmarried as well as married persons.

Justice Stevens' analysis, in our view, should have been controlling in *Bowers* and it should control here.

Bowers was not correct when it was decided, and it is not correct today. It ought not to remain binding precedent. *Bowers v. Hardwick* should be and now is overruled.

The present case does not involve minors. It does not involve persons who might be injured or coerced or who are situated in relationships where consent might not easily be refused. It does not involve public conduct or prostitution. It does not involve whether the government must give formal recognition to any relationship that homosexual persons seek to enter. The case does involve two adults who, with full and mutual consent from each other, engaged in sexual practices common to a homosexual lifestyle. The petitioners are entitled to respect for their private lives. The State cannot demean their existence or control their destiny by making their private sexual conduct a crime. Their right to liberty under the Due Process Clause gives them the full right to engage in their conduct without intervention of the government. The Texas statute furthers no legitimate state interest which can justify its intrusion into the personal and private life of the individual.

Had those who drew and ratified the Due Process Clauses of the Fifth Amendment or the Fourteenth Amendment known the components of liberty in its manifold possibilities, they might have been more specific. They did not presume to have this insight. They knew times can blind us to certain truths and later generations can see that laws once thought necessary and proper in fact serve only to oppress. As the Constitution endures, persons in every generation can invoke its principles in their own search for greater freedom. . . .

JUSTICE O'CONNOR, concurring in the judgment.

[I] joined *Bowers,* and do not join the Court in overruling it. Nevertheless, I agree with the Court that Texas' statute banning same-sex sodomy is unconstitutional. Rather than relying on the substantive component of the Fourteenth Amendment's Due Process Clause, as the Court does, I base my conclusion on the Fourteenth Amendment's Equal Protection Clause.

This case raises a different issue than *Bowers:* whether, under the Equal Protection Clause, moral disapproval is a legitimate state interest to justify by itself a statute that bans homosexual sodomy, but not heterosexual sodomy. It is not. Moral disapproval of this group, like a bare desire to harm the group, is an interest that is insufficient to satisfy rational basis review under the Equal Protection Clause. Indeed, we have never held that moral disapproval, without any other asserted state interest, is a sufficient rationale under the Equal Protection Clause to justify a law that discriminates among groups of persons. . . .

Texas' invocation of moral disapproval as a legitimate state interest proves nothing more than Texas' desire to criminalize homosexual sodomy. But the Equal Protection Clause prevents a State from creating "a classification of persons undertaken for its own sake." And because Texas so rarely enforces its sodomy law as applied to private, consensual acts, the law serves more as a statement of dislike and disapproval against homosexuals than as a tool to stop criminal behavior. . . .

A State can of course assign certain consequences to a violation of its criminal law. But the State cannot single out one identifiable class of citizens for punishment that does not apply to everyone else, with moral disapproval as the only asserted state interest for the law. The Texas sodomy statute subjects homosexuals to "a lifelong penalty and stigma." . . .

DISSENT:

JUSTICE SCALIA, with whom [CHIEF JUSTICE ROBERTS] and JUSTICE THOMAS join, dissenting. . . .

I.

I begin with the Court's surprising readiness to reconsider a decision rendered a mere 17 years ago in Bowers v. Hardwick. I do not myself believe in rigid adherence to stare decisis in constitutional cases; but I do believe that we should be consistent rather than manipulative in invoking the doctrine. Today's opinions in support of reversal do not bother to distinguish — or indeed, even bother to mention — the paean to stare decisis coauthored by three Members of today's majority in Planned Parenthood v. Casey. . . .

Today's approach to stare decisis invites us to overrule an erroneously decided precedent (including an "intensely divisive" decision) if: (1) its foundations have been "eroded" by subsequent decisions; (2) it has been subject to "substantial and continuing" criticism; and (3) it has not induced "individual or societal reliance" that counsels against overturning. The problem is that *Roe* itself — which today's majority surely has no disposition to overrule — satisfies these conditions to at least the same degree as *Bowers.* . . .

Scalia says Bowers
similar to Roe

I do not quarrel with the Court's claim that [*Romer*] "eroded" the "foundations" of *Bowers'* rational-basis holding. But *Roe* and *Casey* have been equally "eroded" by [Washington v. Glucksberg, 521 U.S. 707 (1997), discussed later in this chapter] which held that only fundamental rights which are "'deeply rooted in this Nation's history and tradition'" qualify for anything other than rational basis scrutiny under the doctrine of "substantive due process." *Roe* and *Casey*, of course, subjected the restriction of abortion to heightened scrutiny without even attempting to establish that the freedom to abort was rooted in this Nation's tradition.

Bowers, the Court says, has been subject to "substantial and continuing [criticism], disapproving of its reasoning in all respects, not just as to its historical assumptions." [Of] course, *Roe* too (and by extension *Casey*) had been (and still is) subject to unrelenting criticism. . . .

That leaves, to distinguish the rock-solid, unamendable disposition of *Roe* from the readily overrulable *Bowers*, only the third factor. "[T]here has been," the Court says, "no individual or societal reliance on *Bowers* of the sort that could counsel against overturning its holding. . . ." It seems to me that the "societal reliance" on the principles confirmed in *Bowers* and discarded today has been overwhelming. Countless judicial decisions and legislative enactments have relied on the ancient proposition that a governing majority's belief that certain sexual behavior is "immoral and unacceptable" constitutes a rational basis for regulation. . . . State laws against bigamy, same-sex marriage, adult incest, prostitution, masturbation, adultery, fornication, bestiality, and obscenity are likewise sustainable only in light of *Bowers'* validation of laws based on moral choices. Every single one of these laws is called into question by today's decision; the Court makes no effort to cabin the scope of its decision to exclude them from its holding. The impossibility of distinguishing homosexuality from other traditional "morals" offenses is precisely why *Bowers* rejected the rational-basis challenge. . . .

What a massive disruption of the current social order, therefore, the overruling of *Bowers* entails. Not so the overruling of *Roe*, which would simply have restored the regime that existed for centuries before 1973, in which the permissibility of and restrictions upon abortion were determined legislatively State-by-State.

To tell the truth, it does not surprise me, and should surprise no one, that the Court has chosen today to revise the standards of stare decisis set forth in *Casey*. It has thereby exposed *Casey*'s extraordinary deference to precedent for the result-oriented expedient that it is. . . .

II . . .

Our opinions applying the doctrine known as "substantive due process" hold that the Due Process Clause prohibits States from infringing fundamental liberty interests, unless the infringement is narrowly tailored to serve a compelling state interest. We have held repeatedly, in cases the Court today does not overrule, that only fundamental rights qualify for this so-called "heightened scrutiny" protection — that is, rights which are "'deeply rooted in this Nation's history and tradition.'" . . . All other liberty interests may be abridged or abrogated pursuant to a validly enacted state law if that law is rationally related to a legitimate state interest.

Bowers held, first, that criminal prohibitions of homosexual sodomy are not subject to heightened scrutiny because they do not implicate a "fundamental right" under the Due Process Clause. . . . Noting that "[p]roscriptions against that conduct have ancient roots," that "[s]odomy was a criminal offense at common law and was forbidden by the laws of the original 13 States when they ratified the Bill of Rights," ibid., and that many States had retained their bans on sodomy, *Bowers* concluded that a right to engage in homosexual sodomy was not "'deeply rooted in this Nation's history and tradition.'" . . .

The Court today does not overrule this holding. Not once does it describe homosexual sodomy as a "fundamental right" or a "fundamental liberty interest," nor does it subject the Texas statute to strict scrutiny. Instead, having failed to establish that the right to homosexual sodomy is "'deeply rooted in this Nation's history and tradition,'" the Court concludes that the application of Texas's statute to petitioners' conduct fails the rational-basis test, and overrules *Bowers*' holding to the contrary. . . .

IV.

[The Texas sodomy statute] undoubtedly imposes constraints on liberty. So do laws prohibiting prostitution, recreational use of heroin, and, for that matter, working more than 60 hours per week in a bakery. But there is no right to "liberty" under the Due Process Clause, though today's opinion repeatedly makes that claim. The Fourteenth Amendment expressly allows States to deprive their citizens of "liberty," so long as "due process of law" is provided. . . .

It is (as *Bowers* recognized) entirely irrelevant whether the laws in our long national tradition criminalizing homosexual sodomy were "directed at homosexual conduct as a distinct matter." Whether homosexual sodomy was prohibited by a law targeted at same-sex sexual relations or by a more general law prohibiting both homosexual and heterosexual sodomy, the only relevant point is that it was criminalized — which suffices to establish that homosexual sodomy is not a right "deeply rooted in our Nation's history and tradition." The Court today agrees that homosexual sodomy was criminalized and thus does not dispute the facts on which *Bowers* actually relied. . . .

Bowers' conclusion that homosexual sodomy is not a fundamental right "deeply rooted in this Nation's history and tradition" is utterly unassailable.

Realizing that fact, the Court instead says: "[W]e think that our laws and traditions in the past half century are of most relevance here. These references show an emerging awareness that liberty gives substantial protection to adult persons in deciding how to conduct their private lives in matters pertaining to sex." Apart from the fact that such an "emerging awareness" does not establish a "fundamental right," the statement is factually false. States continue to prosecute all sorts of crimes by adults "in matters pertaining to sex": prostitution, adult incest, adultery, obscenity, and child pornography. Sodomy laws, too, have been enforced "in the past half century," in which there have been 134 reported cases involving prosecutions for consensual, adult, homosexual sodomy. . . .

I turn now to the ground on which the Court squarely rests its holding: the contention that there is no rational basis for the law here under attack. This proposition is so out of accord with our jurisprudence — indeed, with the jurisprudence of any society we know — that it requires little discussion.

*Gratefully
of the
the floodgates*

The Texas statute undeniably seeks to further the belief of its citizens that certain forms of sexual behavior are "immoral and unacceptable" — the same interest furthered by criminal laws against fornication, bigamy, adultery, adult incest, bestiality, and obscenity. *Bowers* held that this was a legitimate state interest. The Court today reaches the opposite conclusion. [This] effectively decrees the end of all morals legislation. If, as the Court asserts, the promotion of majoritarian sexual morality is not even a legitimate state interest, none of the above-mentioned laws can survive rational-basis review. . . .

Today's opinion is the product of a Court, which is the product of a law-profession culture, that has largely signed on to the so-called homosexual agenda, by which I mean the agenda promoted by some homosexual activists directed at eliminating the moral opprobrium that has traditionally attached to homosexual conduct. . . .

One of the most revealing statements in today's opinion is the Court's grim warning that the criminalization of homosexual conduct is "an invitation to subject homosexual persons to discrimination both in the public and in the private spheres." It is clear from this that the Court has taken sides in the culture war, departing from its role of assuring, as neutral observer, that the democratic rules of engagement are observed. Many Americans do not want persons who openly engage in homosexual conduct as partners in their business, as scout-masters for their children, as teachers in their children's schools, or as boarders in their home. They view this as protecting themselves and their families from a lifestyle that they believe to be immoral and destructive. The Court views it as "discrimination" which it is the function of our judgments to deter. So imbued is the Court with the law profession's anti-anti-homosexual culture, that it is seemingly unaware that the attitudes of that culture are not obviously "mainstream"; that in most States what the Court calls "discrimination" against those who engage in homosexual acts is perfectly legal; that proposals to ban such "discrimination" under Title VII have repeatedly been rejected by Congress; that in some cases such "discrimination" is mandated by federal statute, see 10 U.S.C. §654(b)(1) (mandating discharge from the armed forces of any service member who engages in or intends to engage in homosexual acts); and that in some cases such "discrimination" is a constitutional right, see Boy Scouts of America v. Dale, 530 U.S. 640 (2000).

Let me be clear that I have nothing against homosexuals, or any other group, promoting their agenda through normal democratic means. Social perceptions of sexual and other morality change over time, and every group has the right to persuade its fellow citizens that its view of such matters is the best. That homosexuals have achieved some success in that enterprise is attested to by the fact that Texas is one of the few remaining States that criminalize private, consensual homosexual acts. But persuading one's fellow citizens is one thing, and imposing one's views in absence of democratic majority will is something else. I would no more require a State to criminalize homosexual acts — or, for that matter, display any moral disapprobation of them — than I would forbid it to do so. What Texas has chosen to do is well within the range of traditional democratic action, and its hand should not be stayed through the invention of a brand-new "constitutional right" by a Court that is impatient of democratic change. . . .

One of the benefits of leaving regulation of this matter to the people rather than to the courts is that the people, unlike judges, need not carry things to their logical conclusion. The people may feel that their disapprobation of homosexual conduct is strong enough to disallow homosexual marriage, but not strong enough to criminalize private homosexual acts — and may legislate accordingly. The Court today pretends that it possesses a similar freedom of action, so that we need not fear judicial imposition of homosexual marriage, as has recently occurred in Canada (in a decision that the Canadian Government has chosen not to appeal). At the end of its opinion — after having laid waste the foundations of our rational-basis jurisprudence — the Court says that the present case "does not involve whether the government must give formal recognition to any relationship that homosexual persons seek to enter." Do not believe it. More illuminating than this bald, unreasoned disclaimer is the progression of thought displayed by an earlier passage in the Court's opinion, which notes the constitutional protections afforded to "personal decisions relating to marriage, procreation, contraception, family relationships, child rearing, and education," and then declares that "[p]ersons in a homosexual relationship may seek autonomy for these purposes, just as heterosexual persons do." Today's opinion dismantles the structure of constitutional law that has permitted a distinction to be made between heterosexual and homosexual unions, insofar as formal recognition in marriage is concerned. If moral disapprobation of homosexual conduct is "no legitimate state interest" for purposes of proscribing that conduct and if, as the Court coos (casting aside all pretense of neutrality), "[w]hen sexuality finds overt expression in intimate conduct with another person, the conduct can be but one element in a personal bond that is more enduring"; what justification could there possibly be for denying the benefits of marriage to homosexual couples exercising "[t]he liberty protected by the Constitution." Surely not the encouragement of procreation, since the sterile and the elderly are allowed to marry. This case "does not involve" the issue of homosexual marriage only if one entertains the belief that principle and logic have nothing to do with the decisions of this Court. . . .

JUSTICE THOMAS, dissenting.

I join Justice Scalia's dissenting opinion. I write separately to note that the law before the Court today "is . . . uncommonly silly." Griswold v. Connecticut, 381 U.S. 479, 527 (1965) (Stewart, J., dissenting). If I were a member of the Texas Legislature, I would vote to repeal it. Punishing someone for expressing his sexual preference through noncommercial consensual conduct with another adult does not appear to be a worthy way to expend valuable law enforcement resources.

Notwithstanding this, I recognize that as a member of this Court I am not empowered to help petitioners and others similarly situated. My duty, rather, is to "decide cases 'agreeably to the Constitution and laws of the United States.'" And, just like Justice Stewart, I "can find [neither in the bill of rights nor in any other part of the Constitution a] general right of privacy," or as the Court terms it today, the "liberty of the person both in its spatial and more transcendent dimensions."

Note: The Legal and Political Landscape on the Eve of Obergefell

1. *Sex and Marriage.* The *Lawrence* Court noted that the case did "not involve whether the government must give formal recognition to any relationship that homosexual persons seek to enter." Does it make sense to hold that there is a constitutional right to casual sex, but not to sex within a committed, marital relationship?

At the time that *Lawrence* was decided, cases involving heterosexual relationships had already established that there was a fundamental right to marriage. For example, in Loving v. Virginia, 388 U.S. 1 (1967), the Court, in a nine-to-zero decision written by Justice Warren, invalidated a state prohibition on interracial marriage in part because "[the] freedom to marry has long been recognized as one of the vital personal rights essential to the orderly pursuit of happiness by free men." See also Zablocki v. Redhail, 434 U.S. 374 (1978) (invalidating a Wisconsin statute providing any resident "having minor issue not in his custody and which he is under an obligation to support by court order" may not marry without a prior judicial determination that the support obligation has been met, and that the children "are not then and are not likely thereafter to become public charges"); Turner v. Safley, 482 U.S. 78 (1987) (invalidating a prison regulation that permitted inmates to marry only when the superintendent found compelling reasons to grant permission). But see Califano v. Jobst, 434 U.S. 47 (1977) (upholding a statute providing that social security benefits received by a disabled dependent child of a covered wage earner terminate when the child marries an individual who is not independently entitled to benefits under the act, even though the individual is also disabled).

2. *Changes in public attitudes.* Consider the implications, if any, of the following public opinion data as reported by Gallup at http://www.gallup.com/poll/1651/gay-lesbian-rights.aspx:

> "Do you think gay and lesbian relations between consenting adults should be legal?"
> July 1986 (around the time that *Bowers* was decided): Yes 35%, No 57%, No Opinion 11%.
> July 2003 (around the time that *Lawrence* was decided): Yes 48%, No 46%, No Opinion 6%.
> July 2015 (around the time that *Obergefell,* discussed infra, upheld the constitutional right to same-sex marriage): Yes 68%, No 28%, No opinion 4%.
> May 2017: Yes 72%, No 23%, No opinion 5%.

> "Do you think that marriages between same-sex couples should or should not be recognized by law as valid with the same rights as traditional marriages?"
> January 2000: Valid 34%, Not Valid 62%, No Opinion 4%.
> July 2015: Valid 58%, Not Valid 40%, No Opinion 2%.
> May 2017: Valid 64%, Not Valid 34%, No Opinion 2%.

Which of the following conclusions do you find persuasive?

a. The polling data demonstrates that the Supreme Court's decisions in this area are broadly in line with public opinion and are, therefore, unproblematic.

b. The polling data demonstrates that the gay community is not a powerless minority and that, therefore, Supreme Court intervention was unnecessary and unjustified.

c. The polling data demonstrates that the Supreme Court has some power to shape public opinion.

d. Polls should have nothing to do with constitutional law.

3. *Legal Developments.* Consider the implications of the following legal developments that occurred between *Lawrence* and *Obergefell*:

a. *Developments on the state level.* In the wake of *Lawrence,* judicial decisions in a number of states, including Massachusetts, California, and Iowa, established a state constitutional right to same-sex marriage. In New York, Maryland, and the District of Columbia local legislatures enacted measures providing for same-sex marriages. On the other hand, a large number of states adopted state constitutional amendments prohibiting same-sex marriages, often by referenda, and sometimes overturning state court decisions establishing them.

b. *A federal constitutional amendment.* Congress considered a series of federal constitutional amendments which would have provided that marriage consisted only of the union of a man and a woman. In a test vote held on June 6, 2006, a version of the amendment failed to achieve the necessary two-thirds majority in the Senate, with forty-nine Senators voting in favor of the amendment and forty-eight against.

c. *The end of "Don't Ask, Don't Tell."* In December of 2010, President Obama signed into law the "Don't Ask, Don't Tell Repeal Act," Pub. L. 111-321, which set in motion the repeal of the military's "don't ask, don't tell" policy regarding gay and lesbian servicemen and permitted these individuals to serve openly in the armed forces.

d. Windsor. In 2013, the Supreme Court decided United States v. Windsor, 133 S. Ct. 2675, invalidating the "Defense of Marriage Act," 1 U.S.C. §7 (DOMA). The Act provided that, for purposes of federal law, the word "marriage" meant "only a legal union between one man and one woman as husband and wife." In a six-to-three decision, written by Justice Kennedy, the Court stated:

> [A] State's decision to give [same-sex couples] the right to marry conferred upon them a dignity and status of immense import. When the State used its historic and essential authority to define the marital relation in this way, its role and its power in making the decision enhanced the recognition, dignity, and protection of the class in their own community. DOMA, because of its reach and extent, departs from this history and tradition of reliance on state law to define marriage. . . .
>
> DOMA seeks to injure the very class [the state] seeks to protect. By doing so it violates basic due process and equal protection principles applicable to the Federal Government.

At the conclusion of its opinion, the Court noted that "By seeking to displace this protection and treating those persons as living in marriages less respected than others, the federal statute is in violation of the Fifth Amendment. This opinion and its holding are confined to those lawful marriages."

In a dissenting opinion, Justice Roberts stated that while he "[disagreed] with the result to which the majority's analysis leads it in this case, I think it more important to point out that its analysis leads no further. The Court does not have before it, and the logic of its opinion does not decide, the distinct question whether the States, in the exercise of their 'historic and essential authority to define the marital relation,' may continue to utilize the traditional definition of marriage." Consider Justice Scalia's views in a separate dissenting opinion joined in this respect by Justice Thomas:

> The penultimate sentence of the majority's opinion is a naked declaration that "[t]his opinion and its holding are confined" to those couples "joined in same-sex marriages made lawful by the State." I have heard such "bald, unreasoned disclaimer[s]" before. [*Lawrence.*] [It] takes real cheek for today's majority to assure us, as it is going out the door, that a constitutional requirement to give formal recognition to same-sex marriage is not at issue here — when what has preceded that assurance is a lecture on how superior the majority's moral judgment in favor of same-sex marriage is to the Congress's hateful moral judgment against it. I promise you this:

The only thing that will "confine" the Court's holding is its sense of what it can get away with.

I do not mean to suggest disagreement with The Chief Justice's view, that lower federal courts and state courts can distinguish today's case when the issue before them is state denial of marital status to same-sex couples — or even that this Court could theoretically do so. Lord, an opinion with such scatter-shot rationales as this one (federalism noises among them) can be distinguished in many ways. And deserves to be. State and lower federal courts should take the Court at its word and distinguish away.

In my opinion, however, the view that this Court will take of state prohibition of same-sex marriage is indicated beyond mistaking by today's opinion. . . .

As far as this Court is concerned, no one should be fooled; it is just a matter of listening and waiting for the other shoe.

e. *The lower courts respond.* Many lower courts apparently thought that Justice Scalia was the better prognosticator. Beginning in 2013, many courts invalidated state bans on same-sex marriages. See, e.g., Baskin v. Bogan, 766 F.3d 648 (7th Cir. 2014); Latta v. Otter, 771 F.3d 456 (9th Cir. 2014); Bishop v. Barton, 760 F.3d 1070 (10th Cir. 2014).

Were any of these developments relevant to the Court's ultimate decision concerning same-sex marriage?

Obergefell v. Hodges
135 S. Ct. 2584 (2015)

JUSTICE KENNEDY delivered the opinion of the Court.

The Constitution promises liberty to all within its reach, a liberty that includes certain specific rights that allow persons, within a lawful realm, to define and express their identity. The petitioners in these cases seek to find that liberty by marrying someone of the same sex and having their marriages deemed lawful on the same terms and conditions as marriages between persons of the opposite sex. . . .

II

Before addressing the principles and precedents that govern these cases, it is appropriate to note the history of the subject now before the Court.

A

From their beginning to their most recent page, the annals of human history reveal the transcendent importance of marriage. The lifelong union of a man and a woman always has promised nobility and dignity to all persons, without regard to their station in life. Marriage is sacred to those who live by their religions and offers unique fulfillment to those who find meaning in the secular realm. Its dynamic allows two people to find a life that could not be found alone, for a marriage becomes greater than just the two persons. Rising from the most basic human needs, marriage is essential to our most profound hopes and aspirations.

The centrality of marriage to the human condition makes it unsurprising that the institution has existed for millennia and across civilizations. . . .

That history is the beginning of these cases. The respondents say it should be the end as well. To them, it would demean a timeless institution if the concept and lawful status of marriage were extended to two persons of the same sex. Marriage, in their view, is by its nature a gender-differentiated union of man and woman. This view long has been held — and continues to be held — in good faith by reasonable and sincere people here and throughout the world. *[respondents' argument]*

The petitioners acknowledge this history but contend that these cases cannot end there. Were their intent to demean the revered idea and reality of marriage, the petitioners' claims would be of a different order. But that is neither their purpose nor their submission. To the contrary, it is the enduring importance of marriage that underlies the petitioners' contentions. This, they say, is their whole point. Far from seeking to devalue marriage, the petitioners seek it for themselves because of their respect — and need — for its privileges and responsibilities. And their immutable nature dictates that same-sex marriage is their only real path to this profound commitment.

Recounting the circumstances of three of these cases illustrates the urgency of the petitioners' cause from their perspective. Petitioner James Obergefell, [met] John Arthur over two decades ago. They fell in love and started a life together, establishing a lasting, committed relation. In 2011, however, Arthur was diagnosed with amyotrophic lateral sclerosi, or ALS. This debilitating disease is progressive, with no known cure. Two years ago, Obergefell and Arthur decided to commit to one another, resolving to marry before Arthur died. To fulfill their mutual promise, they traveled from Ohio to Maryland, where same-sex marriage was legal. It was difficult for Arthur to move, and so the couple were wed inside a medical transport plane as it remained on the tarmac in Baltimore. Three months later, Arthur died. Ohio law does not permit Obergefell to be listed as the surviving spouse on Arthur's death certificate. By statute, they must remain strangers even in death, a state-imposed separation Obergefell deems "hurtful for the rest of time." He brought suit to be shown as the surviving spouse on Arthur's death certificate. . . .

[The Court recounts the facts of two of the other cases before it.]

The cases now before the Court involve other petitioners as well, each with their own experiences. Their stories reveal that they seek not to denigrate marriage but rather to live their lives, or honor their spouses' memory, joined by its bond.

B

The ancient origins of marriage confirm its centrality, but it has not stood in isolation from developments in law and society. The history of marriage is one of both continuity and change. That institution — even as confined to opposite-sex relations — has evolved over time.

For example, marriage was once viewed as an arrangement by the couple's parents based on political, religious, and financial concerns; but by the time of the Nation's founding it was understood to be a voluntary contract between a man and a woman. As the role and status of women changed, the institution further evolved. Under the centuries-old doctrine of coverture, a married man and woman were treated by the State as a single, male-dominated legal entity. See 1 W. Blackstone, Commentaries on the Laws of England 430 (1765). As women gained legal, political, and property rights, and as society began to understand that women have their own equal dignity, the law of coverture was abandoned. These and other developments in the institution of marriage over the past centuries were not mere superficial changes. Rather, they worked deep transformations in its structure, affecting aspects of marriage long viewed by many as essential.

These new insights have strengthened, not weakened, the institution of marriage. Indeed, changed understandings of marriage are characteristic of a Nation where new dimensions of freedom become apparent to new generations, often through perspectives that begin in pleas or protests and then are considered in the political sphere and the judicial process.

This dynamic can be seen in the Nation's experiences with the rights of gays and lesbians. Until the mid–20th century, same-sex intimacy long had been condemned as immoral by the state itself in most Western nations, a belief often embodied in the criminal law. For this reason, among others, many persons did not deem homosexuals to have dignity in their own distinct identity. A truthful declaration by same-sex couples of what was in their hearts had to remain unspoken. Even when a greater awareness of the humanity and integrity of homosexual persons came in the period after World War II, the argument that gays and lesbians had a just claim to dignity was in conflict with both law and widespread social conventions. Same-sex intimacy remained a crime in many States. Gays and lesbians were prohibited from most government employment, barred from military service, excluded under immigration laws, targeted by police, and burdened in their rights to associate. . . .

[The Court recounts the history of judicial involvement with issues of homosexuality and same-sex marriage and notes that most federal courts of appeals and many state courts had upheld a right to same-sex marriage.]

After years of litigation, legislation, referenda, and the discussions that attended these public acts, the States are now divided on the issue of same-sex marriage.

III

Under the Due Process Clause of the Fourteenth Amendment, no State shall "deprive any person of life, liberty, or property, without due process of law." The fundamental liberties protected by this Clause include most of the rights enumerated in the Bill of Rights. In addition these liberties extend to certain personal choices central to individual dignity and autonomy, including intimate choices that define personal identity and beliefs.

The identification and protection of fundamental rights is an enduring part of the judicial duty to interpret the Constitution. That responsibility, however, "has not been reduced to any formula." Rather, it requires courts to exercise reasoned judgment in identifying interests of the person so fundamental that the State must accord them its respect. That process is guided by many of the same considerations relevant to analysis of other constitutional provisions that set forth broad principles rather than specific requirements. History and tradition guide and discipline this inquiry but do not set its outer boundaries. That method respects our history and learns from it without allowing the past alone to rule the present.

The nature of injustice is that we may not always see it in our own times. The generations that wrote and ratified the Bill of Rights and the Fourteenth Amendment did not presume to know the extent of freedom in all of its dimensions, and so they entrusted to future generations a charter protecting the right of all persons to enjoy liberty as we learn its meaning. When new insight reveals discord between the Constitution's central protections and a received legal stricture, a claim to liberty must be addressed.

Applying these established tenets, the Court has long held the right to marry is protected by the Constitution. . . .

It cannot be denied that this Court's cases describing the right to marry presumed a relationship involving opposite-sex partners. The Court, like many institutions, has made assumptions defined by the world and time of which it is a part. This was evident in Baker v. Nelson, a one-line summary decision issued in 1972, holding the exclusion of same-sex couples from marriage did not present a substantial federal question.

[margin handwriting: → reinforce that marriage as a concept is a right]

Still, there are other, more instructive precedents. This Court's cases have expressed constitutional principles of broader reach. In defining the right to marry these cases have identified essential attributes of that right based in history, tradition, and other constitutional liberties inherent in this intimate bond. And in assessing whether the force and rationale of its cases apply to same-sex couples, the Court must respect the basic reasons why the right to marry has been long protected.

This analysis compels the conclusion that same-sex couples may exercise the right to marry. The four principles and traditions to be discussed demonstrate that the reasons marriage is fundamental under the Constitution apply with equal force to same-sex couples.

A first premise of the Court's relevant precedents is that the right to personal choice regarding marriage is inherent in the concept of individual autonomy. . . .   *[margin: 1]*

Choices about marriage shape an individual's destiny. . . .

The nature of marriage is that, through its enduring bond, two persons together can find other freedoms, such as expression, intimacy, and spirituality. This is true for all persons, whatever their sexual orientation. There is dignity in the bond between two men or two women who seek to marry and in their autonomy to make such profound choices.

A second principle in this Court's jurisprudence is that the right to marry is fundamental because it supports a two-person union unlike any other in its importance to the committed individuals. . . .   *[margin: 2]*

The right to marry thus dignifies couples who "wish to define themselves by their commitment to each other." [*Windsor.*] Marriage responds to the universal fear that a lonely person might call out only to find no one there. It offers the hope of companionship and understanding and assurance that while both still live there will be someone to care for the other. . . .

A third basis for protecting the right to marry is that it safeguards children and families and thus draws meaning from related rights of childrearing, procreation, and education. [By] giving recognition and legal structure to their parents' relationship, marriage allows children "to understand the integrity and closeness of their own family and its concord with other families in their community and in their daily lives." [*Windsor.*] Marriage also affords the permanency and stability important to children's best interests.   *[margin: 3]*

As all parties agree, many same-sex couples provide loving and nurturing homes to their children, whether biological or adopted. And hundreds of thousands of children are presently being raised by such couples. . . .

Excluding same-sex couples from marriage thus conflicts with a central premise of the right to marry. Without the recognition, stability, and predictability marriage offers, their children suffer the stigma of knowing their families are somehow lesser. They also suffer the significant material costs of being raised by unmarried parents, relegated through no fault of their own to a more difficult and uncertain family life. The marriage laws at issue here thus harm and humiliate the children of same-sex couples.

That is not to say the right to marry is less meaningful for those who do not or cannot have children. An ability, desire, or promise to procreate is not and has not been a prerequisite for a valid marriage in any State. In light of precedent protecting the right of a married couple not to procreate, it cannot be said the Court or the States have conditioned the right to marry on the capacity or commitment to procreate. The constitutional marriage right has many aspects, of which childbearing is only one.

Fourth and finally, this Court's cases and the Nation's traditions make clear that marriage is a keystone of our social order. . . .

For that reason, just as a couple vows to support each other, so does society pledge to support the couple, offering symbolic recognition and material benefits to protect and nourish the union. Indeed, while the States are in general free to vary the benefits they confer on all married couples, they have throughout our history made marriage the basis for an expanding list of governmental rights, benefits, and responsibilities. These aspects of marital status include: taxation; inheritance and property rights; rules of intestate succession; spousal privilege in the law of evidence; hospital access; medical decisionmaking authority; adoption rights; the rights and benefits of survivors; birth and death certificates; professional ethics rules; campaign finance restrictions; workers' compensation benefits; health insurance; and child custody, support, and visitation rules. Valid marriage under state law is also a significant status for over a thousand provisions of federal law. The States have contributed to the fundamental character of the marriage right by placing that institution at the center of so many facets of the legal and social order.

There is no difference between same- and opposite-sex couples with respect to this principle. Yet by virtue of their exclusion from that institution, same-sex couples are denied the constellation of benefits that the States have linked to marriage. This harm results in more than just material burdens. Same-sex couples are consigned to an instability many opposite-sex couples would deem intolerable in their own lives. As the State itself makes marriage all the more precious by the significance it attaches to it, exclusion from that status has the effect of teaching that gays and lesbians are unequal in important respects. It demeans gays and lesbians for the State to lock them out of a central institution of the Nation's society. Same-sex couples, too, may aspire to the transcendent purposes of marriage and seek fulfillment in its highest meaning. . . .

Objecting that this does not reflect an appropriate framing of the issue, the respondents refer to Washington v. Glucksberg, 521 U.S. 701, 721 (1997), which called for a "'careful description'" of fundamental rights. They assert the petitioners do not seek to exercise the right to marry but rather a new and nonexistent "right to same-sex marriage." [Washington v. Glucksberg, upholding a statute that prohibited the causing or aiding of a suicide, and discussed infra] did insist that liberty under the Due Process Clause must be defined in a most circumscribed manner, with central reference to specific historical practices. Yet while that approach may have been appropriate for the asserted right there involved (physician-assisted suicide), it is inconsistent with the approach this Court has used in discussing other fundamental rights, including marriage and intimacy. Loving v. Virginia did not ask about a "right to interracial marriage"; *Turner* did not ask about a "right of inmates to marry"; and *Zablocki* did not ask about a "right of fathers with unpaid child support duties to marry." Rather, each case inquired about the right to marry in its comprehensive sense, asking if there was a sufficient justification for excluding the relevant class from the right.

That principle applies here. If rights were defined by who exercised them in the past, then received practices could serve as their own continued justification and new groups could not invoke rights once denied. This Court has rejected that approach, both with respect to the right to marry and the rights of gays and lesbians.

The right to marry is fundamental as a matter of history and tradition, but rights come not from ancient sources alone. They rise, too, from a better informed understanding of how constitutional imperatives define a liberty that remains urgent in our own era. Many who deem same-sex marriage to be wrong reach that conclusion based on decent and honorable religious or philosophical premises, and neither they nor their beliefs are disparaged here. But when that sincere, personal opposition becomes enacted law and public policy, the necessary consequence is to put the imprimatur of the State itself on an exclusion that soon demeans or stigmatizes those whose own liberty is then denied. Under the Constitution, same-sex couples seek in marriage the same legal treatment as opposite-sex couples, and it would disparage their choices and diminish their personhood to deny them this right.

The right of same-sex couples to marry that is part of the liberty promised by the Fourteenth Amendment is derived, too, from that Amendment's guarantee of the equal protection of the laws. The Due Process Clause and the Equal Protection Clause are connected in a profound way, though they set forth independent principles. Rights implicit in liberty and rights secured by equal protection may rest on different precepts and are not always co-extensive, yet in some instances each may be instructive as to the meaning and reach of the other. In any particular case one Clause may be thought to capture the essence of the right in a more accurate and comprehensive way, even as the two Clauses may converge in the identification and definition of the right. . . .

This dynamic also applies to same-sex marriage. It is now clear that the challenged laws burden the liberty of same-sex couples, and it must be further acknowledged that they abridge central precepts of equality. Here the marriage laws enforced by the respondents are in essence unequal: same-sex couples are denied all the benefits afforded to opposite-sex couples and are barred from exercising a fundamental right. Especially against a long history of disapproval of their relationships, this denial to same-sex couples of the right to marry works a grave and continuing harm. The imposition of this disability on gays and lesbians serves to disrespect and subordinate them. And the Equal Protection Clause, like the Due Process Clause, prohibits this unjustified infringement of the fundamental right to marry.

[The] Court now holds that same-sex couples may exercise the fundamental right to marry. No longer may this liberty be denied to them. Baker v. Nelson must be and now is overruled, and the State laws challenged by Petitioners in these cases are now held invalid to the extent they exclude same-sex couples from civil marriage on the same terms and conditions as opposite-sex couples.

There may be an initial inclination in these cases to proceed with caution — to await further legislation, litigation, and debate. The respondents warn there has been insufficient democratic discourse before deciding an issue so basic as the definition of marriage . . .

Yet there has been far more deliberation than this argument acknowledges. There have been referenda, legislative debates, and grassroots campaigns, as well as countless studies, papers, books, and other popular and scholarly writings. There has been extensive litigation in state and federal courts. Judicial opinions addressing the issue have been informed by the contentions of parties and counsel, which, in turn, reflect the more general, societal discussion of same-sex marriage and its meaning that has occurred over the past decades. As more than 100 amici make clear in their filings, many of the central institutions in American life — state and local governments, the military, large and small businesses, labor unions, religious organizations, law enforcement, civic groups, professional organizations, and universities — have devoted substantial attention to the question. This has led to an enhanced understanding of the issue — an understanding reflected in the arguments now presented for resolution as a matter of constitutional law.

Of course, the Constitution contemplates that democracy is the appropriate process for change, so long as that process does not abridge fundamental rights. [But] when the rights of persons are violated, "the Constitution requires redress by the courts," notwithstanding the more general value of democratic decision-making. This holds true even when protecting individual rights affects issues of the utmost importance and sensitivity. . . .

This is not the first time the Court has been asked to adopt a cautious approach to recognizing and protecting fundamental rights. In *Bowers*, a bare majority upheld a law criminalizing same-sex intimacy. That approach might have been viewed as a cautious endorsement of the democratic process, which had only just begun to consider the rights of gays and lesbians. Yet, in effect, *Bowers* upheld state action that denied gays and lesbians a fundamental right and caused them pain and humiliation. As evidenced by the dissents in that case, the facts and principles necessary to a correct holding were known to the *Bowers* Court. That is why *Lawrence* held *Bowers* was "not correct when it was decided." Although *Bowers* was eventually repudiated in *Lawrence*, men and women were harmed in the interim, and the substantial effects of these injuries no doubt lingered long after *Bowers* was overruled. Dignitary wounds cannot always be healed with the stroke of a pen.

A ruling against same-sex couples would have the same effect — and, like *Bowers*, would be unjustified under the Fourteenth Amendment. The petitioners' stories make clear the urgency of the issue they present to the Court. [Properly] presented with the petitioners' cases, the Court has a duty to address these claims and answer these questions. . . .

Were the Court to uphold the challenged laws as constitutional, it would teach the Nation that these laws are in accord with our society's most basic compact. Were the Court to stay its hand to allow slower, case-by-case determination of the required availability of specific public benefits to same-sex couples, it still would deny gays and lesbians many rights and responsibilities intertwined with marriage.

The respondents also argue allowing same-sex couples to wed will harm marriage as an institution by leading to fewer opposite-sex marriages. This may occur, the respondents contend, because licensing same-sex marriage severs the connection between natural procreation and marriage. That argument, however, rests on a counterintuitive view of opposite-sex couple's decisionmaking processes regarding marriage and parenthood. Decisions about whether to marry and raise children are based on many personal, romantic, and practical considerations; and it is unrealistic to conclude that an opposite-sex couple would choose not to marry simply because same-sex couples may do so. The respondents have not shown a foundation for the conclusion that allowing same-sex marriage will cause the harmful outcomes they describe. Indeed, with respect to this asserted basis for excluding same-sex couples from the right to marry, it is appropriate to observe these cases involve only the rights of two consenting adults whose marriages would pose no risk of harm to themselves or third parties.

Finally, it must be emphasized that religions, and those who adhere to religious doctrines, may continue to advocate with utmost, sincere conviction that, by divine precepts, same-sex marriage should not be condoned. The First Amendment ensures that religious organizations and persons are given proper protection as they seek to teach the principles that are so fulfilling and so central to their lives and faiths, and to their own deep aspirations to continue the family structure they have long revered. The same is true of those who oppose same-sex marriage for other reasons. In turn, those who believe allowing same-sex marriage is proper or indeed essential, whether as a matter of religious conviction or secular belief, may engage those who disagree with their view in an open and searching debate. The Constitution, however, does not permit the State to bar same-sex couples from marriage on the same terms as accorded to couples of the opposite sex. . . .

* * *

No union is more profound than marriage, for it embodies the highest ideals of love, fidelity, devotion, sacrifice, and family. In forming a marital union, two people become something greater than once they were. As some of the petitioners in these cases demonstrate, marriage embodies a love that may endure even past death. It would misunderstand these men and women to say they disrespect the idea of marriage. Their plea is that they do respect it, respect it so deeply that they seek to find its fulfillment for themselves. Their hope is not to be condemned to live in loneliness, excluded from one of civilization's oldest institutions. They ask for equal dignity in the eyes of the law. The Constitution grants them that right. . . .

CHIEF JUSTICE ROBERTS, with whom JUSTICE SCALIA and JUSTICE THOMAS join, dissenting.

Petitioners make strong arguments rooted in social policy and considerations of fairness. They contend that same-sex couples should be allowed to affirm their love and commitment through marriage, just like opposite-sex couples. That position has undeniable appeal; over the past six years, voters and legislators in eleven States and the District of Columbia have revised their laws to allow marriage between two people of the same sex.

But this Court is not a legislature. Whether same-sex marriage is a good idea should be of no concern to us. Under the Constitution, judges have power to say what the law is, not what it should be. . . .

Although the policy arguments for extending marriage to same-sex couples may be compelling, the legal arguments for requiring such an extension are not. The fundamental right to marry does not include a right to make a State change its definition of marriage. And a State's decision to maintain the meaning of marriage that has persisted in every culture throughout human history can hardly be called irrational. In short, our Constitution does not enact any one theory of marriage. The people of a State are free to expand marriage to include same-sex couples, or to retain the historic definition.

Today, however, the Court takes the extraordinary step of ordering every State to license and recognize same-sex marriage. Many people will rejoice at this decision, and I begrudge none their celebration. But for those who believe in a government of laws, not of men, the majority's approach is deeply disheartening. Supporters of same-sex marriage have achieved considerable success persuading their fellow citizens — through the democratic process — to adopt their view. That ends today. Five lawyers have closed the debate and enacted their own vision of marriage as a matter of constitutional law. Stealing this issue from the people will for many cast a cloud over same-sex marriage, making a dramatic social change that much more difficult to accept.

The majority's decision is an act of will, not legal judgment. The right it announces has no basis in the Constitution or this Court's precedent. The majority expressly disclaims judicial "caution" and omits even a pretense of humility, openly relying on its desire to remake society according to its own "new insight" into the "nature of injustice." As a result, the Court invalidates the marriage laws of more than half the States and orders the transformation of a social institution that has formed the basis of human society for millennia, for the Kalahari Bushmen and the Han Chinese, the Carthaginians and the Aztecs. Just who do we think we are? . . .

Understand well what this dissent is about: It is not about whether, in my judgment, the institution of marriage should be changed to include same-sex couples. It is instead about whether, in our democratic republic, that decision should rest with the people acting through their elected representatives, or with five lawyers who happen to hold commissions authorizing them to resolve legal disputes according to law. The Constitution leaves no doubt about the answer.

I . . .

A . . .

The premises supporting [the] concept of marriage [as supporting procreation] are so fundamental that they rarely require articulation. The human race must procreate to survive. Procreation occurs through sexual relations between a man and a woman. When sexual relations result in the conception of a child, that child's prospects are generally better if the mother and father stay together rather than going their separate ways. Therefore, for the good of children and society, sexual relations that can lead to procreation should occur only between a man and a woman committed to a lasting bond.

Society has recognized that bond as marriage. And by bestowing a respected status and material benefits on married couples, society encourages men and women to conduct sexual relations within marriage rather than without. . . .

This singular understanding of marriage has prevailed in the United States throughout our history. . . .

The Constitution itself says nothing about marriage, and the Framers thereby entrusted the States with "[t]he whole subject of the domestic relations of husband and wife." *Windsor.* There is no dispute that every State at the founding — and every State throughout our history until a dozen years ago — defined marriage in the traditional, biologically rooted way. . . .

As the majority notes, some aspects of marriage have changed over time. . . .

[The changes] did not, however, work any transformation in the core structure of marriage as the union between a man and a woman. If you had asked a person on the street how marriage was defined, no one would ever have said, "Marriage is the union of a man and a woman, where the woman is subject to coverture." The majority may be right that the "history of marriage is one of both continuity and change," but the core meaning of marriage has endured. . . .

II

Petitioners first contend that the marriage laws of their States violate the Due Process Clause. . . .

The majority purports to identify four "principles and traditions" in this Court's due process precedents that support a fundamental right for same-sex couples to marry. In reality, however, the majority's approach has no basis in principle or tradition, except for the unprincipled tradition of judicial policy-making that characterized discredited decisions such as Lochner v. New York. Stripped of its shiny rhetorical gloss, the majority's argument is that the Due Process Clause gives same-sex couples a fundamental right to marry because it will be good for them and for society. If I were a legislator, I would certainly consider that view as a matter of social policy. But as a judge, I find the majority's position indefensible as a matter of constitutional law. . . .

A

Allowing unelected federal judges to select which unenumerated rights rank as "fundamental" — and to strike down state laws on the basis of that determination — raises obvious concerns about the judicial role. Our precedents have accordingly insisted that judges "exercise the utmost care" in identifying implied fundamental rights, "lest the liberty protected by the Due Process Clause be subtly transformed into the policy preferences of the Members of this Court." . . .

The need for restraint in administering the strong medicine of substantive due process is a lesson this Court has learned the hard way. The Court first applied substantive due process to strike down a statute in Dred Scott v. Sandford. There the Court invalidated the Missouri Compromise on the ground that legislation restricting the institution of slavery violated the implied rights of slaveholders. . . .

Dred Scott's holding was overruled on the battlefields of the Civil War and by constitutional amendment after Appomattox, but its approach to the Due Process Clause reappeared. In a series of early 20th-century cases, most prominently Lochner v. New York, this Court invalidated state statutes that presented "meddlesome interferences with the rights of the individual," and "undue interference with liberty of person and freedom of contract." . . .

Eventually, the Court recognized its error and vowed not to repeat it. . . .

Rejecting Lochner does not require disavowing the doctrine of implied fundamental rights, and this Court has not done so. But to avoid repeating Lochner's error of converting personal preferences into constitutional mandates, our modern substantive due process cases have stressed the need for "judicial self-restraint." Our precedents have required that implied fundamental rights be "objectively, deeply rooted in this Nation's history and tradition," and "implicit in the concept of ordered liberty, such that neither liberty nor justice would exist if they were sacrificed." Glucksberg.

B

The majority acknowledges none of this doctrinal background, and it is easy to see why: Its aggressive application of substantive due process breaks sharply with decades of precedent and returns the Court to the unprincipled approach of *Lochner*.

1

The majority's driving themes are that marriage is desirable and petitioners desire it. [The] "right to marry" cases stand for the important but limited proposition that particular restrictions on access to marriage as traditionally defined violate due process. These precedents say nothing at all about a right to make a State change its definition of marriage, which is the right petitioners actually seek here. Neither petitioners nor the majority cites a single case or other legal source providing any basis for such a constitutional right. None exists, and that is enough to foreclose their claim.

2

Neither *Lawrence* nor any other precedent in the privacy line of cases supports the right that petitioners assert here. Unlike criminal laws banning contraceptives and sodomy, the marriage laws at issue here involve no government intrusion. They create no crime and impose no punishment. Same-sex couples remain free to live together, to engage in intimate conduct, and to raise their families as they see fit. No one is "condemned to live in loneliness" by the laws challenged in these cases — no one. At the same time, the laws in no way interfere with the "right to be let alone." . . .

[The] privacy cases provide no support for the majority's position, because petitioners do not seek privacy. Quite the opposite, they seek public recognition of their relationships, along with corresponding government benefits. Our cases have consistently refused to allow litigants to convert the shield provided by constitutional liberties into a sword to demand positive entitlements from the State. . . .

3

To be fair, the majority does not suggest that its individual autonomy right is entirely unconstrained. The constraints it sets are precisely those that accord with its own "reasoned judgment," informed by its "new insight" into the "nature of injustice," which was invisible to all who came before but has become clear "as we learn [the] meaning" of liberty. . . .

One immediate question invited by the majority's position is whether States may retain the definition of marriage as a union of two people. Although the majority randomly inserts the adjective "two" in various places, it offers no reason at all why the two-person element of the core definition of marriage may be preserved while the man-woman element may not. Indeed, from the standpoint of history and tradition, a leap from opposite-sex marriage to same-sex marriage is much greater than one from a two-person union to plural unions, which have deep roots in some cultures around the world. If the majority is willing to take the big leap, it is hard to see how it can say no to the shorter one. . . .

I do not mean to equate marriage between same-sex couples with plural marriages in all respects. There may well be relevant differences that compel different legal analysis. But if there are, petitioners have not pointed to any. . . . .

4

Near the end of its opinion, the majority offers perhaps the clearest insight into its decision. Expanding marriage to include same-sex couples, the majority insists, would "pose no risk of harm to themselves or third parties." This argument again echoes *Lochner*, which relied on its assessment that "we think that a law like the one before us involves neither the safety, the morals nor the welfare of the public, and that the interest of the public is not in the slightest degree affected by such an act."

Then and now, this assertion of the "harm principle" sounds more in philosophy than law. The elevation of the fullest individual self-realization over the constraints that society has expressed in law may or may not be attractive moral philosophy. But a Justice's commission does not confer any special moral, philosophical, or social insight sufficient to justify imposing those perceptions on fellow citizens under the pretense of "due process." . . .

III

In addition to their due process argument, petitioners contend that the Equal Protection Clause requires their States to license and recognize same-sex marriages. The majority does not seriously engage with this claim. Its discussion is, quite frankly, difficult to follow. The central point seems to be that there is a "synergy between" the Equal Protection Clause and the Due Process Clause, and that some precedents relying on one Clause have also relied on the other. . . .

[The majority] fails to provide even a single sentence explaining how the Equal Protection Clause supplies independent weight for its position, nor does it attempt to justify its gratuitous violation of the canon against unnecessarily resolving constitutional questions. In any event, the marriage laws at issue here do not violate the Equal Protection Clause, because distinguishing between opposite-sex and same-sex couples is rationally related to the States' "legitimate state interest" in "preserving the traditional institution of marriage."

It is important to note with precision which laws petitioners have challenged. Although they discuss some of the ancillary legal benefits that accompany marriage, such as hospital visitation rights and recognition of spousal status on official documents, petitioners' lawsuits target the laws defining marriage generally rather than those allocating benefits specifically. The equal protection analysis might be different, in my view, if we were confronted with a more focused challenge to the denial of certain tangible benefits. Of course, those more selective claims will not arise now that the Court has taken the drastic step of requiring every State to license and recognize marriages between same-sex couples.

IV

The legitimacy of this Court ultimately rests "upon the respect accorded to its judgments." That respect flows from the perception — and reality — that we exercise humility and restraint in deciding cases according to the Constitution and law. The role of the Court envisioned by the majority today, however, is anything but humble or restrained. Over and over, the majority exalts the role of the judiciary in delivering social change. . . .

Those who founded our country would not recognize the majority's conception of the judicial role. They after all risked their lives and fortunes for the precious right to govern themselves. They would never have imagined yielding that right on a question of social policy to unaccountable and unelected judges. And they certainly would not have been satisfied by a system empowering judges to override policy judgments so long as they do so after "a quite extensive discussion." In our democracy, debate about the content of the law is not an exhaustion requirement to be checked off before courts can impose their will. . . .

When decisions are reached through democratic means, some people will inevitably be disappointed with the results. But those whose views do not prevail at least know that they have had their say, and accordingly are — in the tradition of our political culture — reconciled to the result of a fair and honest debate. In addition, they can gear up to raise the issue later, hoping to persuade enough on the winning side to think again.

But today the Court puts a stop to all that. By deciding this question under the Constitution, the Court removes it from the realm of democratic decision. There will be consequences to shutting down the political process on an issue of such profound public significance. Closing debate tends to close minds. People denied a voice are less likely to accept the ruling of a court on an issue that does not seem to be the sort of thing courts usually decide. As a thoughtful commentator observed about another issue, "The political process was moving . . . , not swiftly enough for advocates of quick, complete change, but majoritarian institutions were listening and acting. Heavy-handed judicial intervention was difficult to justify and appears to have provoked, not resolved, conflict." Ginsburg, Some Thoughts on Autonomy and Equality in Relation to Roe v. Wade, 63 N.C. L. Rev. 375, 385–386 (1985) (footnote omitted). Indeed, however heartened the proponents of same-sex marriage might be on this day, it is worth acknowledging what they have lost, and lost forever: the opportunity to win the true acceptance that comes from persuading their fellow citizens of the justice of their cause. And they lose this just when the winds of change were freshening at their backs. . . .

Respect for sincere religious conviction has led voters and legislators in every State that has adopted same-sex marriage democratically to include accommodations for religious practice. The majority's decision imposing same-sex marriage cannot, of course, create any such accommodations. The majority graciously suggests that religious believers may continue to "advocate" and "teach" their views of marriage. The First Amendment guarantees, however, the freedom to "exercise" religion. Ominously, that is not a word the majority uses.

Hard questions arise when people of faith exercise religion in ways that may be seen to conflict with the new right to same-sex marriage — when, for example, a religious college provides married student housing only to opposite-sex married couples, or a religious adoption agency declines to place children with same-sex married couples. Indeed, the Solicitor General candidly acknowledged that the tax exemptions of some religious institutions would be in question if they opposed same-sex marriage. There is little doubt that these and similar questions will soon be before this Court. Unfortunately, people of faith can take no comfort in the treatment they receive from the majority today.

Perhaps the most discouraging aspect of today's decision is the extent to which the majority feels compelled to sully those on the other side of the debate. The majority offers a cursory assurance that it does not intend to disparage people who, as a matter of conscience, cannot accept same-sex marriage. That disclaimer is hard to square with the very next sentence, in which the majority explains that "the necessary consequence" of laws codifying the traditional definition of marriage is to "demea[n] or stigmatiz[e]" same-sex couples. . . .

* * *

If you are among the many Americans — of whatever sexual orientation — who favor expanding same-sex marriage, by all means celebrate today's decision. Celebrate the achievement of a desired goal. Celebrate the opportunity for a new expression of commitment to a partner. Celebrate the availability of new benefits. But do not celebrate the Constitution. It had nothing to do with it.

I respectfully dissent.

JUSTICE SCALIA, with whom JUSTICE THOMAS joins, dissenting. . . .

[It] is not of special importance to me what the law says about marriage. It is of overwhelming importance, however, who it is that rules me. Today's decree says that my Ruler, and the Ruler of 320 million Americans coast-to-coast, is a majority of the nine lawyers on the Supreme Court. The opinion in these cases is the furthest extension in fact — and the furthest extension one can even imagine — of the Court's claimed power to create "liberties" that the Constitution and its Amendments neglect to mention. This practice of constitutional revision by an unelected committee of nine, always accompanied (as it is today) by extravagant praise of liberty, robs the People of the most important liberty they asserted in the Declaration of Independence and won in the Revolution of 1776: the freedom to govern themselves.

I

Until the courts put a stop to it, public debate over same-sex marriage displayed American democracy at its best. Individuals on both sides of the issue passionately, but respectfully, attempted to persuade their fellow citizens to accept their views. . . .

The Constitution places some constraints on self-rule — constraints adopted by the People themselves when they ratified the Constitution and its Amendments. [These] cases ask us to decide whether the Fourteenth Amendment contains a limitation that requires the States to license and recognize marriages between two people of the same sex. Does it remove that issue from the political process?

Of course not. . . .

[When] the Fourteenth Amendment was ratified in 1868, every State limited marriage to one man and one woman, and no one doubted the constitutionality of doing so. That resolves these cases. . . .

But the Court ends this debate, in an opinion lacking even a thin veneer of law. Buried beneath the mummeries and straining-to-be-memorable passages of the opinion is a candid and startling assertion: No matter what it was the People ratified, the Fourteenth Amendment protects those rights that the Judiciary, in its "reasoned judgment," thinks the Fourteenth Amendment ought to protect. . . .

Judges are selected precisely for their skill as lawyers; whether they reflect the policy views of a particular constituency is not (or should not be) relevant. Not surprisingly then, the Federal Judiciary is hardly a cross-section of America. Take, for example, this Court, which consists of only nine men and women, all of them successful lawyers who studied at Harvard or Yale Law School. Four of the nine are natives of New York City. Eight of them grew up in east- and west-coast States. Only one hails from the vast expanse in-between. Not a single Southwesterner or even, to tell the truth, a genuine Westerner (California does not count). Not a single evangelical Christian (a group that comprises about one quarter of Americans), or even a Protestant of any denomination. The strikingly unrepresentative character of the body voting on today's social upheaval would be irrelevant if they were functioning as judges, answering the legal question whether the American people had ever ratified a constitutional provision that was understood to proscribe the traditional definition of marriage. But of course the Justices in today's majority are not voting on that basis; they say they are not. And to allow the policy question of same-sex marriage to be considered and resolved by a select, patrician, highly unrepresentative panel of nine is to violate a principle even more fundamental than no taxation without representation: no social transformation without representation.

II

But what really astounds is the hubris reflected in today's judicial Putsch. The five Justices who compose today's majority are entirely comfortable concluding that every State violated the Constitution for all of the 135 years between the Fourteenth Amendment's ratification and Massachusetts' permitting of same-sex marriages in 2003. They have discovered in the Fourteenth Amendment a "fundamental right" overlooked by every person alive at the time of ratification, and almost everyone else in the time since. They see what lesser legal minds — minds like Thomas Cooley, John Marshall Harlan, Oliver Wendell Holmes, Jr., Learned Hand, Louis Brandeis, William Howard Taft, Benjamin Cardozo, Hugo Black, Felix Frankfurter, Robert Jackson, and Henry Friendly — could not. They are certain that the People ratified the Fourteenth Amendment to bestow on them the power to remove questions from the democratic process when that is called for by their "reasoned judgment." These Justices know that limiting marriage to one man and one woman is contrary to reason; they know that an institution as old as government itself, and accepted by every nation in history until 15 years ago, cannot possibly be supported by anything other than ignorance or bigotry. And they are willing to say that any citizen who does not agree with that, who adheres to what was, until 15 years ago, the unanimous judgment of all generations and all societies, stands against the Constitution. . . .

* * *

Hubris is sometimes defined as o'erweening pride; and pride, we know, goeth before a fall. The Judiciary is the "least dangerous" of the federal branches because it has "neither Force nor Will, but merely judgment; and must ultimately depend upon the aid of the executive arm" and the States, "even for the efficacy of its judgments." With each decision of ours that takes from the People a question properly left to them — with each decision that is unabashedly based not on law, but on the "reasoned judgment" of a bare majority of this Court — we move one step closer to being reminded of our impotence.

JUSTICE THOMAS, with whom JUSTICE SCALIA joins, dissenting. . . .

II

Even if the doctrine of substantive due process were somehow defensible — it is not — petitioners still would not have a claim. To invoke the protection of the Due Process Clause at all — whether under a theory of "substantive" or "procedural" due process — a party must first identify a deprivation of "life, liberty, or property." The majority claims these state laws deprive petitioners of "liberty," but the concept of "liberty" it conjures up bears no resemblance to any plausible meaning of that word as it is used in the Due Process Clauses. . . .

Even assuming that the "liberty" in those Clauses encompasses something more than freedom from physical restraint, it would not include the types of rights claimed by the majority. In the American legal tradition, liberty has long been understood as individual freedom from governmental action, not as a right to a particular governmental entitlement. . . .

III . . .

B

Aside from undermining the political processes that protect our liberty, the majority's decision threatens the religious liberty our Nation has long sought to protect. . . .

In our society, marriage is not simply a governmental institution; it is a religious institution as well. Today's decision might change the former, but it cannot change the latter. It appears all but inevitable that the two will come into conflict, particularly as individuals and churches are confronted with demands to participate in and endorse civil marriages between same-sex couples. . . .

JUSTICE ALITO, with whom JUSTICE SCALIA and JUSTICE THOMAS join, dissenting. . . .

II

Attempting to circumvent the problem presented by the newness of the right found in these cases, the majority claims that the issue is the right to equal treatment. Noting that marriage is a fundamental right, the majority argues that a State has no valid reason for denying that right to same-sex couples. This reasoning is dependent upon a particular understanding of the purpose of civil marriage. Although the Court expresses the point in loftier terms, its argument is that the fundamental purpose of marriage is to promote the well-being of those who choose to marry. Marriage provides emotional fulfillment and the promise of support in times of need. And by benefiting persons who choose to wed, marriage indirectly benefits society because persons who live in stable, fulfilling, and supportive relationships make better citizens. It is for these reasons, the argument goes, that States encourage and formalize marriage, confer special benefits on married persons, and also impose some special obligations. This understanding of the States' reasons for recognizing marriage enables the majority to argue that same-sex marriage serves the States' objectives in the same way as opposite-sex marriage.

This understanding of marriage, which focuses almost entirely on the happiness of persons who choose to marry, is shared by many people today, but it is not the traditional one. For millennia, marriage was inextricably linked to the one thing that only an opposite-sex couple can do: procreate. . . .

If this traditional understanding of the purpose of marriage does not ring true to all ears today, that is probably because the tie between marriage and procreation has frayed. Today, for instance, more than 40% of all children in this country are born to unmarried women. This development undoubtedly is both a cause and a result of changes in our society's understanding of marriage.

While, for many, the attributes of marriage in 21st-century America have changed, those States that do not want to recognize same-sex marriage have not yet given up on the traditional understanding. They worry that by officially abandoning the older understanding, they may contribute to marriage's further decay. It is far beyond the outer reaches of this Court's authority to say that a State may not adhere to the understanding of marriage that has long prevailed, not just in this country and others with similar cultural roots, but also in a great variety of countries and cultures all around the globe. . . .

III . . .

[Today's decision] will be used to vilify Americans who are unwilling to assent to the new orthodoxy. In the course of its opinion, the majority compares traditional marriage laws to laws that denied equal treatment for African-Americans and women. The implications of this analogy will be exploited by those who are determined to stamp out every vestige of dissent.

Perhaps recognizing how its reasoning may be used, the majority attempts, toward the end of its opinion, to reassure those who oppose same-sex marriage that their rights of conscience will be protected. We will soon see whether this proves to be true. I assume that those who cling to old beliefs will be able to whisper their thoughts in the recesses of their homes, but if they repeat those views in public, they will risk being labeled as bigots and treated as such by governments, employers, and schools.

The system of federalism established by our Constitution provides a way for people with different beliefs to live together in a single nation. If the issue of same-sex marriage had been left to the people of the States, it is likely that some States would recognize same-sex marriage and others would not. It is also possible that some States would tie recognition to protection for conscience rights. The majority today makes that impossible. By imposing its own views on the entire country, the majority facilitates the marginalization of the many Americans who have traditional ideas. Recalling the harsh treatment of gays and lesbians in the past, some may think that turnabout is fair play. But if that sentiment prevails, the Nation will experience bitter and lasting wounds.

Today's decision will also have a fundamental effect on this Court and its ability to uphold the rule of law. If a bare majority of Justices can invent a new right and impose that right on the rest of the country, the only real limit on what future majorities will be able to do is their own sense of what those with political power and cultural influence are willing to tolerate. Even enthusiastic supporters of same-sex marriage should worry about the scope of the power that today's majority claims.

Today's decision shows that decades of attempts to restrain this Court's abuse of its authority have failed. A lesson that some will take from today's decision is that preaching about the proper method of interpreting the Constitution or the virtues of judicial self-restraint and humility cannot compete with the temptation to achieve what is viewed as a noble end by any practicable means. I do not doubt that my colleagues in the majority sincerely see in the Constitution a vision of liberty that happens to coincide with their own. But this sincerity is cause for concern, not comfort. What it evidences is the deep and perhaps irremediable corruption of our legal culture's conception of constitutional interpretation.

Most Americans — understandably — will cheer or lament today's decision because of their views on the issue of same-sex marriage. But all Americans, whatever their thinking on that issue, should worry about what the majority's claim of power portends.

Note: A Right to Same-Sex Marriage

1. Pavan. In Pavan v. Smith, 137 S. Ct. 2075 (2017), the Court in a per curiam opinion summarily reversed a state court decision upholding a statute that prohibited a same-sex couple from listing the nonbiological parent on a child's birth certificate in circumstances where the parent would have been listed if the spouse had been of the opposite sex. Justice Gorsuch, joined by Justices Thomas and Alito, filed a dissenting opinion.

2. *The argument from democracy.* Chief Justice Roberts accuses the majority of "stealing this issue from the people." Is this criticism fair? Note the polling data summarized above indicating that large majorities of Americans believe that same-sex marriage should be permitted. Note as well that constitutional provisions outlawing same-sex marriage in many states prevented majorities from legalizing same-sex marriages. Is it a sufficient answer to the latter point that these amendments were put in place by majorities or supermajorities?

3. *The argument from moral disagreement.* Justice Alito claims that by accepting the plaintiffs' equal protection argument, the Court is necessarily endorsing one view of marriage and rejecting another. This is so because if the purpose of marriage is procreation, same-sex and opposite-sex couples are not relevantly similar. But doesn't Justice Alito's rejection of the argument also entail the endorsement of a particular view of marriage? If the purpose of marriage is "self-fulfillment," then how are same-sex and opposite-sex marriages relevantly different?

Justice Alito also argues that if the Court had left the issue to the political process "some States would tie recognition [of same-sex marriage] to protection for conscience rights" and that "the majority today makes that impossible." Does anything in the Court's opinion require states to enact measures forcing private individuals to recognize same-sex marriages or prevent states from establishing "conscience rights" as an exception to antidiscrimination statutes?

4. *Plural marriages.* Does the Court have an answer to Chief Justice Roberts's contention that its argument entails constitutional protection for plural marriages? Note that the Court's opinion is focused on the individual right to marry. If it focused instead on the status of gay men and lesbians as a relevant social group, could the problem of plural marriages be distinguished?

5. *Dignity for the unmarried.* According to the Court, a failure to recognize same-sex marriage causes gay men and lesbians "pain and humiliation" and denies them "equal dignity in the eyes of the law." Does the Court's own glorification of marriage as "a keystone of our social order" denigrate the gay men and lesbians as well as straight people who reject or are unable to take advantage of the institution of marriage? For criticisms of same-sex marriage from within the gay community, see M. Warner, The Trouble with Normal: Sex, Politics, and the Ethics of Queer Life 81–141 (1999); Polikoff, We Will Get What We Ask For: Why Legalizing Gay and Lesbian Marriage Will Not "Dismantle the Legal Structure of Gender in Every Marriage," 79 Va. L. Rev. 1535 (1993).

4.   Other Family and Privacy Interests

The modern substantive due process decisions examined above — *Griswold*, *Eisenstadt*, *Roe*, and *Obergefell*, for example — have all involved the freedom to decide whether to marry or have a child. But modern substantive due process is not so limited.

   MOORE v. CITY OF EAST CLEVELAND, 431 U.S. 494 (1977). In *Moore*, the Court invalidated a city ordinance limiting occupancy of any dwelling unit to members of the same "family," where the ordinance narrowly defined "family" as including only "a few categories of related individuals." Appellant lived with her son, Dale, and her two grandsons, Dale, Jr., and John. Under the ordinance, John could not live in the home because he was not "sufficiently related" to his uncle, Dale, and his cousin, Dale, Jr., to constitute a "family" within the meaning of the ordinance. In a plurality opinion, Justice Powell, joined by Justices Brennan, Marshall, and Blackmun, concluded that the ordinance violated the due process clause of the fourteenth amendment:
   "The city argues that our decision in Village of Belle Terre v. Boraas, 416 U.S. 1 (1974), requires us to sustain the ordinance attacked here. Belle Terre, like East Cleveland, imposed limits on the types of groups that could occupy a single dwelling unit. [We] sustained the Belle Terre ordinance on the ground that it bore a rational relationship to permissible state objectives. But one overriding factor sets this case apart from *Belle Terre*. The ordinance there affected only *unrelated* individuals. It expressly allowed all who were related by 'blood, adoption, or marriage' to live [together]. East Cleveland, in contrast, has chosen to regulate the occupancy of its housing by slicing deeply into the family itself. [The ordinance] selects certain categories of relatives who may live together and declares that others may not. In particular, it makes a crime of a grandmother's choice to live with her grandson in circumstances like those presented here. . . .
   "Our decisions establish that the Constitution protects the sanctity of the family precisely because the institution of the family is deeply rooted in this Nation's history and tradition. It is through the family that we inculcate and pass down many of our most cherished values, moral and cultural. [And ours] is by no means a tradition limited to respect for [the] nuclear family. The tradition of uncles, aunts, cousins, and especially grandparents sharing a household along with parents has roots equally venerable and equally deserving of constitutional recognition. [Out] of choice, necessity, or a sense of family responsibility, it has been common for close relatives to draw [together]. Especially in times of adversity [the] broader family has tended to come together for mutual

[sustenance]. [The] choice of relatives in this degree of kinship to live together may not lightly be denied by the State. [The] Constitution prevents East Cleveland from standardizing its children — and its adults — by forcing all to live in certain narrowly defined family patterns."

Justice Stevens concurred in the result on the ground that the challenged ordinance "constitutes a taking of property without due process and without just compensation."

Justice Stewart, joined by Justice Rehnquist, Justice White, and Chief Justice Burger each filed dissenting opinions.

Note: Nontraditional Association

1. *Distinguishing* Belle Terre *and* Moore. Consider whether *Belle Terre* is distinguishable from *Moore* because the ordinance upheld in *Belle Terre* "allowed all who were related by 'blood, adoption, or marriage' to live [together]." If this distinction holds, it must be because the Court embraces a traditional definition of "family." Is its position consistent with its insistence on a nontraditional definition of "marriage" in *Obergefell*? After *Belle Terre* and *Moore*, could a city constitutionally prohibit "significant others" from living together?

2. *The Level of Generality*. Whether a relationship is "traditional" depends in part on the level of generality at which tradition is defined. If the tradition is defined very narrowly, the legislation at issue will almost always simply illustrate the tradition, thereby depriving the appeal to tradition of any power to check legislative action. But if the tradition is defined very broadly, judges will be able to appeal to it to invalidate whatever legislation they choose to characterize as inconsistent with tradition.

3. Michael H. The problem was the subject of an important exchange between Justices Scalia and Brennan in Michael H. v. Gerald D., 491 U.S. 110 (1989). A California statute provided that a child born to a married woman living with her husband is conclusively presumed to be a child of the marriage; this presumption has consequences for the visitation rights of the genetic father of such a child. A majority of the Court held that this statute did not violate the Constitution.

A plurality opinion by Justice Scalia said that, for the genetic father to have a liberty interest in establishing his paternity, that interest had to be both "fundamental" and "an interest traditionally protected by our society." To the plurality, the relevant tradition involved "the historic respect — indeed, sanctity would not be too strong a term — traditionally accorded to the relationships that develop within the unitary family." Because Michael H. was not part of such a unitary family, he had no interest of the necessary sort.

In a long footnote, Justice Scalia defended his reliance on "historical traditions specifically relating to the rights of an adulterous natural father, rather than [as Justice Brennan urged] inquiring more generally 'whether parenthood is an interest that historically has received our attention and protection.'" He asked,

> Why should the relevant category not be even more general — perhaps "family relationships"; or "personal relationships"; or even "emotional attachments in general"? Though [Justice Brennan] has no basis for the level of generality [he] would select, we do: We refer to the most specific level at which a relevant tradition protecting, or denying protection to, the asserted right can be identified. If [there] were no societal tradition, either way, regarding the rights of the natural father or a

child adulterously conceived, we would have to consult and if possible reason from, the traditions regarding natural fathers in general. But there is such a more specific tradition, and it unqualifiedly denies protection to such a parent. Because [general] traditions provide such imprecise guidance, they permit judges to dictate rather than discern the society's views. [Although] assuredly having the virtue (if it be that) of leaving judges free to decide as they think best when the unanticipated occurs, a rule of law that binds neither by text nor by any particular, identifiable tradition, is no rule of law at all.

Although Justices O'Connor and Kennedy joined most of the plurality opinion, they specifically declined to join this footnote. Justice Brennan responded:

If we had looked to tradition with such specificity in past cases, many a decision would have reached a different result. [*Eisenstadt*; *Griswold*; Stanley v. Illinois, infra.] [The] plurality's interpretative method [ignores] the good reasons for limiting the role of "tradition" in interpreting the Constitution's deliberately capacious language. [By] suggesting that our sole function is to "discern the society's views," the plurality acts as if the only purpose of the Due Process Clause is to confirm the importance of interests already protected by a majority of the States. [In] construing the Fourteenth Amendment to offer shelter only to those interests specifically protected by historical practice, [the] plurality ignores the kind of society in which our Constitution exists. We are not an assimilative, homogeneous society, but a facilitative, pluralistic one, in which we must be willing to abide someone else's unfamiliar or even repellant practice because the same tolerant impulse protects our own idiosyncracies. Even if we can agree [that] "family" and "parenthood" are part of the good life, it is absurd to assume that we can agree on the content of those terms and destructive to pretend that we do. In a community such as ours, "liberty" must include the freedom not to conform. The plurality today squashes this freedom by requiring specific approval from history before protecting anything in the name of liberty.

To Justice Brennan, the case merely involved the protection of "the interest of a parent and child in their relationship with each other."

Justice Stevens, who contributed the fifth vote to support the constitutionality of the California statute, agreed that Michael H. had a liberty interest but argued that the California statutes recognized that interest to the extent required by the due process clause.

Does *Obergefell* settle the dispute between Justices Scalia and Brennan?

4. Troxel. Compare *Michael H.* to Troxel v. Granville, 530 U.S. 57 (2000). *Troxel* involved a Washington statute that allowed any person to petition a court for visitation rights "at any time" and authorized the court to grant visitation rights whenever "visitation may serve the best interest of the child." The Troxels had petitioned a court for the right to visit their grandchildren; the mother, a single parent, sought a limitation on visitation rights, which the court overrode, ordering significantly more visitation than the mother wanted. The Supreme Court held that the statute was unconstitutional as applied. The Court reaffirmed *Meyer* and *Pierce*, suggesting that the due process clause has a substantive component encompassing "the fundamental right of parents to make decisions concerning the care, custody, and control of their children." The law at issue here infringed on this right, partly because it "is breathtakingly broad." There is "no requirement that a court accord a parent's decision that visitation would not be in the child's best interest a presumption of validity or any weight whatever." The decision to

reject the mother's judgment here "was based on precisely the type of mere disagreement we have just described and nothing more." There was no finding that the parent was unfit, and thus the court's framework "directly contravened the traditional presumption that a fit parent will act in the best interest of his or her child." The Constitution required "at least some special weight to the parent's own determination." Nor did the mother ever seek "to cut off visitation entirely." Justice Thomas concurred on the ground that neither party had argued "that our substantive due process cases were wrongly decided and that the original understanding of the Due Process Clause precludes judicial enforcement of unenumerated rights under that constitutional provision."

Justice Stevens dissented on the ground that the statute was constitutional on its face. He emphasized that "there may be circumstances in which a child has a stronger interest at stake than mere protection from serious harm caused by the termination of visitation by a 'person' other than a parent." Justice Scalia dissented on the ground that the Constitution does not protect the "unenumerated right" at issue in the case. Justice Kennedy also dissented, objecting to the Court's "concept that the conventional nuclear family ought to establish the visitation standard for every domestic relations case."

5. Reno *and* Stanley. In Reno v. Flores, 507 U.S. 292 (1993), the Court upheld against substantive due process challenge an Immigration and Naturalization Service (INS) regulation authorizing the arrest and holding of alien juveniles unaccompanied by parents or other related adults. The juveniles claimed a right to be released to "responsible adults," even if they were not family members. The Court doubted that "a child has a constitutional right not to be placed in a decent and humane custodial institution if there is available a responsible person unwilling to become the child's legal guardian but willing to undertake temporary legal custody." Because no fundamental right was involved — merely "the lesser" interest in being released into the custody of strangers — the Court required only a reasonable fit between the government purposes and the restriction in question. The Court said that the purpose of protecting juveniles was adequately advanced by the regulation in question, especially in light of the INS's lack of child-placement expertise and the fact that aliens were involved.

Justice O'Connor, joined by Justice Souter, wrote a lengthy concurring opinion, stressing that children have a "core liberty interest in remaining free from institutional confinement," that this freedom "is no narrower than an adult's," but that in this case "normal forms of custody," such as parents, close relatives, or legal guardians, have been unavailable, and therefore the INS program survives constitutional scrutiny. Justice Stevens, joined by Justice Blackmun, dissented on the ground that the "interest in minimizing administrative costs is a patently inadequate justification for the detention of harmless children."

In Stanley v. Illinois, 405 U.S. 645 (1972), the Court described the facts in this way: "Joan Stanley lived with Peter Stanley intermittently for 18 years, during which time they had three children. [Then Joan Stanley died.] Under Illinois law, the children of unwed fathers [automatically] become wards of the State upon the death of the mother. [Stanley maintained] that he had never been shown to be an unfit parent and that since married fathers [could] not be deprived of their children without such a showing, he had been deprived of the equal protection of the laws." The Court agreed. Justice White wrote:

[The] interest of a parent in the companionship, care, custody, and management of his or her children "come[s] to this Court with a momentum for respect lacking when appeal is made to liberties which derive merely from shifting economic arrangements." The Court has frequently emphasized the importance of the family. [Nor] has the law refused to recognize those family relationships unlegitimized by a marriage ceremony. ["To] say that the test of equal protection should be the 'legal' rather than the biological relationship is to avoid the issue. For the Equal Protection Clause necessarily limits the authority of a State to draw such 'legal' lines as it chooses." . . .

It may be [that] most unmarried fathers are unsuitable and neglectful parents. [But] all unmarried fathers are not in this category. [Given] the opportunity to make his case, Stanley may have been seen to be deserving of custody of his offspring. [Procedure] by presumption is always cheaper and easier than individualized determination. But when, as here, the procedure [needlessly] risks running roughshod over the important interests of both parent and child [it] cannot stand.

Justices Powell and Rehnquist did not participate.

5.   *The Right to Die*

CRUZAN V. DIRECTOR, MISSOURI DEPARTMENT OF HEALTH, 497 U.S. 261 (1991). Nancy Cruzan suffered a severe brain injury in a traffic accident and remained in a "persistent vegetative state" — a condition in which a person has motor reflexes but no significant cognitive functions. Doctors concluded that she had virtually no chance of regaining her mental faculties. Her parents asked state hospital officials to discontinue artificial nutrition and hydration procedures, an action that would cause death, but the officials refused without a court order. The Missouri Supreme Court held that because there was no clear and convincing evidence of Nancy's desire to have life-sustaining treatment withdrawn under such circumstances, such an order would violate state law. The Supreme Court granted certiorari to decide whether the Constitution required the hospital to withdraw life-sustaining treatment under these circumstances

Chief Justice Rehnquist delivered the opinion of the Court: "[The] principle that a competent person has a constitutionally protected liberty interest in refusing unwanted medical treatment may be inferred from our prior decisions.

"Although we think the logic of [these] cases would embrace such a liberty interest, the dramatic consequences involved in refusal of such treatment would inform the inquiry as to whether the deprivation of that interest is constitutionally permissible. But for purposes of this case, we assume that the United States Constitution would grant a competent person a constitutionally protected right to refuse lifesaving hydration and nutrition.

"Petitioners go on to assert that an incompetent person should possess the same right in this respect as is possessed by a competent person. [The] difficulty with petitioners' claim is that in a sense it begs the question: an incompetent person is not able to make an informed and voluntary choice to exercise a hypothetical right to refuse treatment or any other right. [Here], Missouri has in effect recognized that under certain circumstances a surrogate may act for the patient in electing to have hydration and nutrition withdrawn in such a way as to cause death, but it has established a procedural safeguard to assure that the action of the surrogate conforms as best it may to the wishes expressed by the patient while competent. Missouri requires that evidence of the incompetent's wishes as to withdrawal of treatment be proved by clear and convincing evidence. The question, then, is whether the United States Constitution forbids the establishment of this procedural requirement by the State. We hold that it does not.

"[Missouri] relies on its interest in the protection and preservation of human life, and there can be no gainsaying this interest. [The] majority of States in this country have laws imposing criminal penalties on one who assists another to commit suicide. We do not think a State is required to remain neutral in the face of an informed and voluntary decision by a physically-able adult to starve to death.

"But in the context presented here, a State has more particular interests at stake. The choice between life and death is a deeply personal decision of obvious and overwhelming finality. We believe Missouri may legitimately seek to safeguard the personal element of this choice through the imposition of heightened evidentiary requirements. . . .

"No doubt is engendered by anything in this record but that Nancy Cruzan's mother and father are loving and caring parents. If the State is required by the United States Constitution to repose a right of "substituted judgment" with anyone, the Cruzans would surely qualify. But we do not think the Due Process Clause requires the State to repose judgment on these matters with anyone but the patient herself."

Justice O'Connor wrote a concurring opinion: "[As] the Court notes the liberty interest in refusing medical treatment flows from decisions involving the State's invasions into the body. Because our notions of liberty are inextricably entwined with our idea of physical freedom and self-determination, the Court has often deemed state incursions into the body repugnant to the interests protected by the Due Process Clause. . . .

"[The] State's imposition of medical treatment on an unwilling competent adult necessarily involves some form of restraint and intrusion. [Artificial] feeding cannot readily be distinguished from other forms of medical treatment. . . .

"[I] also write separately to emphasize that the Court does not today decide the issue whether a State must also give effect to the decisions of a surrogate decision-maker. In my view, such a duty may well be constitutionally required to protect the patient's liberty interest in refusing medical treatment."

Justice Scalia also wrote a concurring opinion. Justice Brennan, joined by Justices Marshall and Blackmun, and Justice Stevens wrote dissenting opinions.

Washington v. Glucksberg

521 U.S. 707 (1997)

CHIEF JUSTICE REHNQUIST delivered the opinion of the Court.

The question presented in this case is whether Washington's prohibition against "caus[ing]" or "aid[ing]" a suicide offends the Fourteenth Amendment to the United States Constitution. We hold that it does not. . . .

I

We begin, as we do in all due-process cases, by examining our Nation's history, legal traditions, and practices. In almost every State — indeed, in almost every western democracy — it is a crime to assist a suicide. The States' assisted-suicide

bans are not innovations. Rather, they are longstanding expressions of the States'
commitment to the protection and preservation of all human life. [Indeed],
opposition to and condemnation of suicide — and, therefore, of assisting
suicide — are consistent and enduring themes of our philosophical, legal, and
cultural heritages. . . .

    More specifically, for over 700 years, the Anglo-American common-law tradi-
tion has punished or otherwise disapproved of both suicide and assisting
suicide. . . .

    Though deeply rooted, the States' assisted-suicide bans have in recent years
been reexamined and, generally, reaffirmed. Because of advances in medicine
and technology, Americans today are increasingly likely to die in institutions,
from chronic illnesses. Public concern and democratic action are therefore
sharply focused on how best to protect dignity and independence at the end
of life, with the result that there have been many significant changes in state
laws and in the attitudes these laws reflect. Many States, for example, now permit
"living wills," surrogate health-care decisionmaking, and the withdrawal or
refusal of life-sustaining medical treatment. [At] the same time, however, voters
and legislators continue for the most part to reaffirm their States' prohibitions on
assisting suicide. . . .

    Thus, the States are currently engaged in serious, thoughtful examinations of
physician-assisted suicide and other similar issues. . . .

II

[Our] established method of substantive-due-process analysis has two primary
features: First, we have regularly observed that the Due Process Clause specially
protects those fundamental rights and liberties which are, objectively, "deeply
rooted in this Nation's history and tradition," and "implicit in the concept of
ordered liberty," such that "neither liberty nor justice would exist if they were
sacrificed," Palko v. Connecticut, 302 U.S. 319, 325, 326 (1937). Second, we
have required in substantive-due-process cases a "careful description" of the
asserted fundamental liberty interest. Our Nation's history, legal traditions,
and practices thus provide the crucial "guideposts for responsible decisionmaking," that direct and restrain our exposition of the Due Process Clause. . . .

    [This] Court's substantive-due-process jurisprudence, has been a process
whereby the outlines of the "liberty" specially protected by the Fourteenth
Amendment — never fully clarified, to be sure, and perhaps not capable of
being fully clarified — have at least been carefully refined by concrete examples
involving fundamental rights found to be deeply rooted in our legal tradition.
This approach tends to rein in the subjective elements that are necessarily present
in due-process judicial review. In addition, by establishing a threshold requirement — that a challenged state action implicate a fundamental right — before
requiring more than a reasonable relation to a legitimate state interest to justify
the action, it avoids the need for complex balancing of competing interests in
every case.

    [We] now inquire whether this asserted right has any place in our Nation's
traditions. Here, as discussed above, we are confronted with a consistent and
almost universal tradition that has long rejected the asserted right, and continues
explicitly to reject it today, even for terminally ill, mentally competent adults. To
hold for respondents, we would have to reverse centuries of legal doctrine and

practice, and strike down the considered policy choice of almost every State. [Respondents] contend, however, that the liberty interest they assert is consistent with this Court's substantive-due-process line of cases, if not with this Nation's history and practice. Pointing to *Casey* and *Cruzan*, respondents read our jurisprudence in this area as reflecting a general tradition of "self-sovereignty," and as teaching that the "liberty" protected by the Due Process Clause includes "basic and intimate exercises of personal autonomy." According to respondents, our liberty jurisprudence, and the broad, individualistic principles it reflects, protects the "liberty of competent, terminally ill adults to make end-of-life decisions free of undue government interference." . . .

P's assert personal autonomy

[The] right assumed in *Cruzan* [was] not simply deduced from abstract concepts of personal autonomy. Given the common-law rule that forced medication was a battery, and the long legal tradition protecting the decision to refuse unwanted medical treatment, our assumption was entirely consistent with this Nation's history and constitutional traditions. The decision to commit suicide with the assistance of another may be just as personal and profound as the decision to refuse unwanted medical treatment, but it has never enjoyed similar legal protection. Indeed, the two acts are widely and reasonably regarded as quite distinct.

[Respondents] also rely on *Casey*. [The] opinion moved from the recognition that liberty necessarily includes freedom of conscience and belief about ultimate considerations to the observation that "though the abortion decision may originate within the zone of conscience and belief, it is more than a philosophic exercise." That many of the rights and liberties protected by the Due Process Clause sound in personal autonomy does not warrant the sweeping conclusion that any and all important, intimate, and personal decisions are so protected.

[The] history of the law's treatment of assisted suicide in this country has been and continues to be one of the rejection of nearly all efforts to permit it. That being the case, our decisions lead us to conclude that the asserted "right" to assistance in committing suicide is not a fundamental liberty interest protected by the Due Process Clause. The Constitution also requires, however, that Washington's assisted-suicide ban be rationally related to legitimate government interests. This requirement is unquestionably met here.

[The Court holds that Washington has a legitimate interest in the preservation of human life, in dealing with suicide as a public health problem, in protecting the ethics and integrity of the medical profession, in protecting vulnerable groups against subtle coercion, and in preventing a slide toward voluntary or involuntary euthanasia.]

JUSTICE O'CONNOR, concurring.

[I] join the Court's opinions because I agree that there is no generalized right to "commit suicide." But respondents urge us to address the narrower question whether a mentally competent person who is experiencing great suffering has a constitutionally cognizable interest in controlling the circumstances of his or her imminent death. I see no need to reach that question in the context of the facial challenges to the New York and Washington laws at issue here. [There] is no dispute that dying patients in Washington and New York can obtain palliative care, even when doing so would hasten their deaths. The difficulty in defining terminal illness and the risk that a dying patient's request for assistance in ending his or her life might not be truly voluntary justifies the prohibitions on assisted suicide we uphold here.

Narrower question

JUSTICE STEVENS, concurring in the judgments.

[Today], the Court decides that Washington's statute prohibiting assisted suicide is not invalid "on its face," that is to say, in all or most cases in which it might be applied. That holding, however, does not foreclose the possibility that some applications of the statute might well be invalid. . . .

[Although] as a general matter the State's interest in the contributions each person may make to society outweighs the person's interest in ending her life, this interest does not have the same force for a terminally ill patient faced not with the choice of whether to live, only of how to die. Allowing the individual, rather than the State, to make judgments "about the 'quality' of life that a particular individual may enjoy" does not mean that the lives of terminally-ill, disabled people have less value than the lives of those who are healthy. Rather, it gives proper recognition to the individual's interest in choosing a final chapter that accords with her life story, rather than one that demeans her values and poisons memories of her.

[Similarly,] the State's legitimate interests in preventing suicide, protecting the vulnerable from coercion and abuse, and preventing euthanasia are less significant in this context. I agree that the State has a compelling interest in preventing persons from committing suicide because of depression, or coercion by third parties. But the State's legitimate interest in preventing abuse does not apply to an individual who is not victimized by abuse, who is not suffering from depression, and who makes a rational and voluntary decision to seek assistance in dying. . . .

JUSTICE SOUTER, concurring in the judgments. . . .

[Justice Souter discusses the state's interest in "protecting terminally ill patients from involuntary suicide and euthanasia, both voluntary and nonvoluntary." He worries that the line between the patient's exercise of "responsible capacity" and her surrender to outside pressure might be difficult to enforce and that physicians might not fully respect the distinction.]

Respondents propose an answer to all this, the answer of state regulation with teeth. Legislation proposed in several States, for example, would authorize physician-assisted suicide but require two qualified physicians to confirm the patient's diagnosis, prognosis, and competence; and would mandate that the patient make repeated requests witnessed by at least two others over a specified time span; and would impose reporting requirements and criminal penalties for various acts of coercion.

But at least at this moment there are reasons for caution in predicting the effectiveness of the teeth proposed. Respondents' proposals, as it turns out, sound much like the guidelines now in place in the Netherlands, the only place where experience with physician-assisted suicide and euthanasia has yielded empirical evidence about how such regulations might affect actual practice. [There] is [a] substantial dispute today about what the Dutch experience shows. . . .

[The] experimentation that should be out of the question in constitutional adjudication displacing legislative judgments is entirely proper, as well as highly desirable, when the legislative power addresses an emerging issue like assisted suicide. The Court should accordingly stay its hand to allow reasonable legislative consideration. While I do not decide for all time that respondents' claim should not be recognized, I acknowledge the legislative institutional competence as the better one to deal with that claim at this time.

JUSTICE GINSBURG, concurring in the judgments.

I concur in the Court's judgments in these cases substantially for the reasons stated by Justice O'Connor in her concurring opinion.

JUSTICE BREYER, concurring in the judgments.

[I] would not reject the respondents' claim without considering a different formulation, for which our legal tradition may provide greater support. That formulation would use words roughly like a "right to die with dignity." But irrespective of the exact words used, at its core would lie personal control over the manner of death, professional medical assistance, and the avoidance of unnecessary and severe physical suffering — combined.

[I] do not believe, however, that this Court need or now should decide whether or a not such a right is "fundamental." That is because, in my view, the avoidance of severe physical pain (connected with death) would have to comprise an essential part of any successful claim and because, as Justice O'Connor points out, the laws before us do not force a dying person to undergo that kind of pain.

[Were] the legal circumstances different — for example, were state law to prevent the provision of palliative care, including the administration of drugs as needed to avoid pain at the end of life — then the law's impact upon serious and otherwise unavoidable physical pain (accompanying death) would be more directly at issue. And as Justice O'Connor suggests, the Court might have to revisit its conclusions in these cases.

Note: The Right to Die

1. *The distinction between active and passive.* In Vacco v. Quill, 521 U.S. 798 (1997), a companion case to *Glucksberg*, the Court rejected an equal protection challenge to the distinction made by New York law between doctor-assisted suicide (prohibited) and the patient's refusal of life-saving treatment (permitted). Is the distinction sensible?

2. *What is the precise holding of* Cruzan? The Court's opinion states that "[The] principle that a competent person has a constitutionally protected liberty interest in refusing unwanted medical treatment may be inferred from our prior decisions" and that "[the] choice between life and death is a deeply personal decision." But the opinion also states that "there can be no gainsaying" the state's interest "in the protection and preservation of human life" and that "[a] State is required [not] to remain neutral in the face of an informed and voluntary decision by a physically-able adult to starve to death." Which way is it? Note also Justice O'Connor's concurring opinion and the fact that her vote was necessary to achieve a majority. If Cruzan had been competent, or if she had clearly indicated her preference for the termination of treatment before she became incompetent, would she have a constitutional right to terminate treatment? On the facts of *Cruzan* is there a plausible case that it would be *unconstitutional* to terminate treatment?

3. *What is the precise holding of* Glucksberg? Suppose that you were a lawyer representing a terminally ill patient in uncontrolled pain. After *Glucksberg*, what argument could you make for a right to palliative care that hastened death? What argument could you make for a right to suicide that was not doctor-assisted?

4. Glucksberg *and* Obergefell. Recall the Court's treatment of *Glucksberg* in *Obergefell*: "[*Glucksberg*] did insist that liberty under the Due Process Clause

must be defined in a most circumscribed manner, with central reference to specific historical practices. Yet while that approach may have been appropriate for the asserted right there involved (physician-assisted suicide), it is inconsistent with the approach this Court has used in discussing other fundamental rights, including marriage and intimacy." Is there a good reason why "specific historical practices" should play a different role with respect to different liberties? If not, does *Obergefell* implicitly overrule *Glucksberg*?

G.   PROCEDURAL DUE PROCESS

The text of the due process clause — "nor shall any State deprive any person of life, liberty, or property, without due process of law" — suggests that the clause is concerned above all with procedure. This section explores the question when the clause requires procedural safeguards to accompany substantive choices. That question is an important aspect of the problem of identifying "implied" fundamental rights. As the preceding materials suggest, the terms "liberty" and "property" are not self-defining. In exploring the materials that follow, consider how and why the procedural and substantive contexts might differ.

1.   Liberty and Property Interests

Before Goldberg v. Kelly, 397 U.S. 254 (1970), the Court defined liberty and property interests by reference to the common law. If government took someone's property, or invaded his bodily integrity, the due process clause would require some kind of hearing. But the clause was inapplicable if government denied an individual some public benefit — employment, welfare, or some other advantageous opportunity. See, e.g., Bailey v. Richardson, 182 F.2d 46 (D.C. Cir. 1950), aff'd by an equally divided Court, 341 U.S. 918 (1951) (no hearing required for dismissal from government employment). This conclusion was a form of the traditional right/privilege distinction. "[Advantageous] relations with the government were mere 'privileges' or 'gratuities,' not legally protected rights. [But] with the expansion of the governmental role, it became less and less tolerable that the government should wield the degree of potentially arbitrary power over the lives of individuals implied by this doctrine." Stewart, The Reformation of American Administrative Law, 88 Harv. L. Rev. 1667, 1717–1718 (1975).

Reich, The New Property, 73 Yale L.J. 733 (1963), was an important critique of the original framework. According to Reich, that framework was anachronistic in a period in which individual security frequently depended on advantageous relationships with the government — insurance, Social Security benefits, employment, licenses, welfare, and so forth. In Reich's view, it was necessary to create a "new property" that would attach the traditional procedural safeguards to these benefits in order to furnish in the modern era the same kind of security promoted by "old property" under a common law regime. The idea was that without such safeguards, those dependent on governmental benefits would be subject to the arbitrary will of public officials.

The Supreme Court accepted Reich's approach in Goldberg v. Kelly, supra. The Court held that a welfare recipient's interest in continued receipt of welfare benefits was a "statutory entitlement" that amounted to "property" within the meaning of the due process clause. The Court referred to the "brutal need" of welfare recipients and held that a fairly elaborate hearing was required before benefits could be terminated. But what interests amount to "liberty" or "property" once it is concluded that at least some statutory benefits amount to rights?

BOARD OF REGENTS OF STATE COLLEGES v. ROTH, 408 U.S. 564 (1972). Roth was hired for a one-year term as assistant professor at Wisconsin State University. Under state law, he did not have tenure. The president of the university informed Roth that he would not be rehired; no explanation was given for the decision, and there was no opportunity to challenge it. Roth alleged that the failure to hold a hearing violated the due process clause. In an opinion by Justice Stewart, the Court rejected Roth's claim:

"The requirements of procedural due process apply only to the deprivation of interests encompassed by the Fourteenth Amendment's protection of liberty and property. [The] range of interests protected by procedural due process is not infinite.

"The District Court decided that procedural due process guarantees apply in this case by assessing and balancing the weights of the particular interests involved. [Undeniably,] the respondent's re-employment prospects were of major concern to him — concern that we surely cannot say was insignificant. And a weighing process has long been a part of any determination of the *form* of hearing required in particular situations by procedural due process. But, to determine whether due process requirements apply in the first place, we must look not to the weight, but to the *nature* of the interest at stake.

"'Liberty' and 'property' are broad and majestic terms. They are among the '[g]reat [constitutional] concepts . . . purposely left to gather meaning from experience. . . . [T]hey relate to the whole domain of social and economic fact, and the statesmen who founded this Nation knew too well that only a stagnant society remains unchanged.' For that reason, the Court has fully and finally rejected the wooden distinction between 'rights' and 'privileges' that once seemed to govern the applicability of procedural due process rights. The Court has also made clear that the property interests protected by procedural due process extend well beyond actual ownership of real estate, chattels, or money. . . .

"While this Court has not attempted to define with exactness the liberty [guaranteed] [by the fourteenth amendment], the term [denotes] not merely freedom from bodily restraint but also the right of the individual to contract, to engage in any of the common occupations of life, to acquire useful knowledge, to marry, establish a home and bring up children, to worship God according to the dictates of his own conscience, and generally to enjoy those privileges long recognized . . . as essential to the orderly pursuit of happiness by free men. In a Constitution for a free people, there can be no doubt that the meaning of 'liberty' must be broad indeed.

"The Fourteenth Amendment's procedural protection of property is a safeguard of the security of interests that a person has already acquired in specific benefits. These interests — property interests — may take many forms.

"Thus, the Court has held that a person receiving welfare benefits under statutory and administrative standards defining eligibility for them has an interest in continued receipt of those benefits that is safeguarded by procedural due process. [*Goldberg.*] [To] have a property interest in a benefit, a person clearly must have more than an abstract need or desire for it. He must have more than a unilateral expectation of it. He must, instead, have a legitimate claim of entitlement to it. It is a purpose of the ancient institution of property to protect those claims upon which people rely in their daily lives, reliance that must not be arbitrarily undermined. It is a purpose of the constitutional right to a hearing to provide an opportunity for a person to vindicate those claims.

"Property interests, of course, are not created by the Constitution. Rather, they are created and their dimensions are defined by existing rules or understandings that stem from an independent source such as state law — rules or understandings that secure certain benefits and that support claims of entitlement to those benefits.

"Just as [in *Goldberg*] the welfare recipient's 'property' interest in welfare payments was created and defined by statutory terms, so the respondent's 'property' interest in employment at Wisconsin State University-Oshkosh was created and defined by the terms of his appointment. [The] important fact in this case is that they specifically provided that the respondent's employment was to terminate on June 30. They did not provide for contract renewal absent 'sufficient cause.' Indeed, they made no provision for renewal whatsoever.

"Thus, the terms of the respondent's appointment secured absolutely no interest in re-employment for the next year. They supported absolutely no possible claim of entitlement to re-employment. Nor, significantly, was there any state statute or University rule or policy that secured his interest in re-employment or that created any legitimate claim to it. In these circumstances, the respondent surely had an abstract concern in being rehired, but he did not have a property interest sufficient to require the University authorities to give him a hearing when they declined to renew his contract of employment."

Justice Marshall dissented: "In my view, every citizen who applies for a government job is entitled to it unless the government can establish some reason for denying the employment. This is the 'property' right that I believe is protected by the Fourteenth Amendment and that cannot be denied 'without due process of law.' And it is also liberty — liberty to work — which is the 'very essence of the personal freedom and opportunity' secured by the Fourteenth Amendment. . . ."

PERRY v. SINDERMANN, 408 U.S. 593 (1972). This was a companion case to *Roth*. Sindermann was a professor at Odessa Junior College whose contract, like Roth's, was not renewed. Sindermann claimed that Odessa had a de facto tenure program. The college had stated in a faculty guide that, despite the absence of an actual tenure system, it "wishes each faculty member to feel that he has permanent tenure so long as his teaching services are satisfactory and as long as he displays a cooperative attitude." According to Sindermann, there was a mutual expectation that he would be renewed each year. Justice Stewart wrote the opinion of the Court:

"The respondent's lack of formal contractual or tenure security in continued employment at Odessa Junior College [may] not be entirely dispositive.

"[The] respondent's allegations [raise] a genuine issue as to his interest in continued employment at Odessa Junior College. He alleged that this interest, though not secured by a formal contractual tenure provision, was secured by a no less binding understanding fostered by the college administration. . . .

"[A] written contract with an explicit tenure provision clearly is evidence of a formal understanding that supports a teacher's claim of entitlement to continued employment unless sufficient 'cause' is shown. Yet absence of such an explicit contractual provision may not always foreclose the possibility that a teacher has a 'property' interest in re-employment. . . .

"A teacher, like the respondent, who has held his position for a number of years, might be able to show from the circumstances of this service — and from other relevant facts — that he has a legitimate claim of entitlement to job tenure."

Cleveland Board of Education v. Loudermill
470 U.S. 532 (1985)

JUSTICE WHITE delivered the opinion of the Court.

In these cases we consider what pretermination process must be accorded a public employee who can be discharged only for cause.

In 1979 the Cleveland Board of Education [hired] respondent James Louder-mill as a security guard. On his job application, Loudermill stated that he had never been convicted of a felony. Eleven months later, as part of a routine examination of his employment records, the Board discovered that in fact Lou-dermill had been convicted of grand larceny in 1968. By letter dated November 3, 1980, the Board's Business Manager informed Loudermill that he had been dismissed because of his dishonesty in filling out the employment application. Loudermill was not afforded an opportunity to respond to the charge of dishonesty or to challenge his dismissal. On November 13, the Board adopted a resolution officially approving the discharge.

Under Ohio law, Loudermill was a "classified civil servant." [Such] employees can be terminated only for cause, and may obtain administrative review if discharged. [Plaintiff's] federal constitutional claim depends on his having had a property right in continued employment. [If he did,] the State could not deprive [him] of this property without due process.

Property interests are not created by the Constitution, "they are created and their dimensions are defined by existing rules or understandings that stem from an independent source such as state law. . . ." [Roth.] [The] Ohio statute plainly creates such an interest. Respondents were "classified civil service employees," Ohio Rev. Code Ann. §124.11 (1984), entitled to retain their positions "during good behavior and efficient service," who could not be dismissed "except . . . - for . . . misfeasance, malfeasance, or nonfeasance in office." The statute plainly supports the conclusion, reached by both lower courts, that respondents possessed property rights in continued employment. [The lower court thus required a hearing.]

The [Board] argues, however, that the property right is defined by, and conditioned on, the legislature's choice of procedures for its deprivation. [The] Board stresses that in addition to specifying the grounds for termination, the statute sets out procedures by which termination may take place. The procedures were adhered to in these cases. According to petitioner, "[t]o require additional procedures would in effect expand the scope of the property interest itself." This argument, which was accepted by the District Court, has its genesis in the plurality opinion in Arnett v. Kennedy, 416 U.S. 134 (1974). Arnett involved a challenge by a former federal employee to the procedures by which he was dismissed. The plurality reasoned that where the legislation conferring the substantive right also sets out the procedural mechanism for enforcing that right, the two cannot be separated:

The employee's statutorily defined right is not a guarantee against removal without cause in the abstract, but such a guarantee as enforced by the procedures which Congress has designated for the determination of cause.

... [W]here the grant of a substantive right is inextricably intertwined with the limitations on the procedures which are to be employed in determining that right, a litigant in the position of appellee must take the bitter with the sweet.

This view garnered three votes in *Arnett,* but was specifically rejected by the other six Justices. [It] is [now] settled that the "bitter with the sweet" approach misconceives the constitutional guarantee. [The] point is straightforward: the Due Process Clause provides that certain substantive rights — life, liberty, and property — cannot be deprived except pursuant to constitutionally adequate procedures. The categories of substance and procedure are distinct. Were the rule otherwise, the Clause would be reduced to a mere tautology. "Property" cannot be defined by the procedures provided for its deprivation any more than can life or liberty. The right to due process "is conferred, not by legislative grace, but by constitutional guarantee. While the legislature may elect not to confer a property interest in [public] employment, it may not constitutionally authorize the deprivation of such an interest, once conferred, without appropriate procedural safeguards."

[Affirmed.]

[Justice Powell concurred in part and concurred in the result in part.]

JUSTICE REHNQUIST, dissenting.

In [*Arnett*] six Members of this Court agreed that a public employee could be dismissed for misconduct without a full hearing prior to termination. A plurality of Justices agreed that the employee was entitled to exactly what Congress gave him, and no more. The Chief Justice, Justice Stewart, and I said:

Here appellee did have a statutory expectancy that he not be removed other than for "such cause as will promote the efficiency of [the] service." But the very section of the statute which granted him that right, a right which had previously existed, only by virtue of administrative regulation, expressly provided also for the procedure by which "cause" was to be determined, and expressly omitted the procedural guarantees which appellee insists are mandated by the Constitution. Only by bifurcating the very sentence of the Act of Congress which conferred upon appellee the right not to be removed save for cause could it be said that he had an expectancy of that substantive right without the procedural limitations which Congress attached to it. . . .

In this case, the relevant Ohio statute provides in its first paragraph that "[t]he tenure of every officer or employee in the classified service [shall] be during good behavior and efficient service." The very next paragraph of this section [provides] that in the event of suspension of more than three days or removal the appointing authority shall furnish the employee with the stated reasons for his removal. The next paragraph provides that within ten days following the receipt of such a statement, the employee may appeal in writing to the State Personnel Board of Review or the Commission, such appeal shall be heard within 30 days from the time of its filing, and the Board may affirm, disaffirm, or modify the judgment of the appointing authority.

[Here,] as in *Arnett,* "[t]he employee's statutorily defined right is not a guarantee against removal without cause in the abstract, but such a guarantee as enforced by the procedures which [the Ohio legislature] has designated for the determination of cause." (Opinion of Rehnquist, J.)

Note: Defining "Liberty" and "Property"

1. *The purposes of hearings.* What goals are promoted by requiring a hearing before government deprives someone of a liberty or property interest?

a. *Obtaining more accurate factual determinations.* Suppose a welfare agency seeks to take away welfare benefits because the recipient's relatively high earnings disqualify her under the governing statute, but she disputes the government's claim that her earnings do in fact disqualify her. A hearing before an impartial arbiter might produce a more accurate resolution of the disputed factual issue than a unilateral decision by the administrator. (Note that the issue here is a dispute over the facts; hearings are generally not required on questions of law. Why?)

b. *Recognizing and promoting the dignity of those whose interests are at stake by allowing them to participate in the decision.* Consider Michelman, Formal and Associational Aims in Procedural Due Process, in NOMOS: Due Process 126, 127–128 (J. R. Pennock and J. Chapman eds., 1977):

> [Participatory] opportunity may [be] psychologically important to the individual: to have played a part in, to have made one's apt contribution to, decisions which are about oneself may be counted important even though the decision, as it turns out, is the most unfavorable one imaginable and one's efforts have not proved influential.

Hearings have costs as well. If government must spend money on procedural safeguards, it will have fewer resources at its command, and the result may be that welfare benefits or salaries are correspondingly diminished. Hearing requirements may therefore not prove beneficial for the class of intended beneficiaries as a whole. Fewer employees may be hired, fewer people may be allowed on the welfare rolls, and benefit levels and salaries may be decreased. Consider also the extent to which, for the very reasons that Michelman outlines above, hearings may lead to acceptance of outcomes that, in justice, should be rejected. What is the relevance of these possibilities?

2. *Statutory entitlements.* Under *Roth,* interests are defined by reference to positive law. The test for deciding whether a "property" interest has been created is to examine positive law to see whether the government's discretion has been confined by existing "rules or understandings." In *Perry,* the tenure system, if there was one, meant that professors could be discharged only "for cause." In *Roth,* there was no such "for cause" limitation of the discretion of the administrator as to renewal.

If the Court had ordered a hearing in *Roth,* what issue would be the subject of the hearing? Suppose Roth claimed that he had been discharged because of his exercise of first amendment rights or for some other reason that was unconstitutional? In a portion of the opinion not produced above, the *Roth* Court noted that "the respondent has alleged that the nonrenewal of his contract was based on his exercise of his right to freedom of speech. But this allegation is not now before us." If Roth lacked a property interest in his job, why would this case be different? Is the point that Roth's liberty interest created by the first amendment might be at stake?

In *Loudermill*, in contrast to *Roth*, the statute itself made concrete issues relevant to the decision. But if the due process clause does not require the government to create a "for cause" system at all, why does it bar the government from taking the intermediate step of providing a "for cause" system without procedural safeguards?

Note: *Statutory Entitlements, Property, and Natural Liberty*

1. Liberty interests apart from positive law. The Supreme Court has generally been reluctant to define "property" or "liberty" interests by reference to the importance of the interest at issue; even a "grievous loss" may not be enough. In some cases, however, the Court has concluded that a "liberty" interest is at issue even though there is no positive protection of the sort required in *Roth*. See, e.g., Ingraham v. Wright, 430 U.S. 651 (1977) (child's interest in bodily integrity, at stake because of practice of paddling children, is a liberty interest); Vitek v. Jones, 445 U.S. 480 (1980) (inmates' interest in preventing transfer from prison to mental institution is a liberty interest); Owen v. City of Independence, 445 U.S. 662 (1980) (the right to reputation when combined with dismissal from at-will employment is a liberty interest).

2. Doubts about natural liberty. In more recent years, some justices have expressed doubt about the recognition of nonstatutory liberty interests. Consider, for example, Kerry v. Din, 135 S. Ct. 2128 (2015). Petitioner, a United States citizen, challenged the refusal of the United States to grant an immigrant visa to her husband, a resident of Afghanistan. Under the applicable statute, a citizen may seek to have a noncitizen classified as an immediate relative. If the noncitizen is so classified, he may apply for a visa, but the visa cannot be granted if the statute makes him ineligible. The government classified petitioner's husband as an immediate relative, but then found him ineligible under a section of the statute that prohibited the granting of visas to individuals who had engaged in "terrorist activities." Petitioner then filed suit, claiming that she had been deprived of liberty without due process of law. She claimed a liberty interest in living with her husband in the United States and asserted that due process was denied with respect to that interest because the government failed to provide her with a further explanation of the denial. The Court of Appeals ruled in her favor, but the Supreme Court, in a five-to-four decision, reversed.

No single opinion gained majority support. Announcing the judgment of the Court, but writing only for himself, Chief Justice Roberts, and Justice Alito, Justice Scalia found that petitioner had failed to identify a constitutionally protected liberty interest. He began his analysis by noting that the due process clause "had its origin in Magna Carta," and that Edward Coke, writing at the close of the eighteenth century, had interpreted Magna Carta liberty protections to include guarantees like the right not to be subject to imprisonment, exile, or torture except under the law of the land. "[Petitioner] of course, could not conceivably claim that the denial of [her husband's] visa application deprived her — or for that matter even [her husband] — of life or property; and under the above described historical understanding, a claim that it deprived her of liberty is equally absurd."

Justice Scalia acknowledged that "the Court has seen fit on several occasions to expand the meaning of 'liberty' under the Due Process Clause to include certain implied 'fundamental rights.' (The reasoning presumably goes like this: If you have a right to do something, you are free to do it, and deprivation of freedom is a deprivation of 'liberty' — never mind the original meaning of that word in the Due Process Clause.)" These rights, Justice Scalia explained, were protected by substantive due process and could not be denied at all even if procedural protections were provided. But even if one were to accept "the textually unsupportable doctrine of implied fundamental rights," petitioner's argument would fail.

> [Before] conferring constitutional status upon previously unrecognized "liberty," we have required "a careful description of the asserted fundamental liberty interest," as well as a demonstration that the interest is "objectively, deeply rooted in this Nation's history and tradition, and implicit in the concept of ordered liberty." [Citing Washington v. Glucksberg, supra.]
>
> Petitioner relied upon her liberty interest in marriage or in being free from arbitrary restrictions on the right to live with a spouse.
>
> To be sure, this Court has at times indulged a propensity for grandiloquence when reviewing the sweep of implied rights, describing them so broadly that they would include not only the interests [petitioner] asserts but many others as well. [Citing Meyer v. Nebraska, supra.] But this Court is not bound by dicta, especially dicta that have been repudiated by the holdings of our subsequent cases. And the actual holdings of the cases [petitioner] relies upon hardly establish the capacious right she now asserts. . . .
>
> Nothing in the cases [petitioner] cites establishes a free-floating and categorical liberty interest in marriage (or any other formulation [petitioner] offers) sufficient to trigger constitutional protection whenever a regulation in any way touches an aspect of the marital relationship. Even if our cases could be construed so broadly, the relevant question is not whether the asserted interest "is consistent with this Court's substantive-due-process line of cases," but whether it is supported by "this Nation's history and practice."

Justice Scalia also rejected the assertion that there were procedural due process rights that attached to non-fundamental liberty interests. He characterized this notion as a "dangerous doctrine" that "vastly expands the scope of our implied-rights jurisprudence by setting it free from the requirement that the liberty interest be 'objectively, deeply rooted in this Nation's history and tradition, and implicit in the concept of ordered liberty.'"

Because Justice Scalia found no liberty interest, he thought that it was unnecessary to decide whether the process afforded petitioner would have been adequate if there had been a liberty interest.

Justice Kennedy, in an opinion joined by Justice Alito, concurred in the judgment. He would have found that even if petitioner had identified a protected liberty interest, the process afforded her was sufficient to satisfy the due process clause. (This aspect of the case is discussed at pages 945, infra.)

Justice Breyer, joined by Justices Ginsburg, Sotomayor, and Kagan, wrote a dissenting opinion:

> Our cases make clear that the Due Process Clause entitles [petitioner] to [procedural] rights as long as (1) she seeks protection for a liberty interest sufficiently important for procedural protection to flow "implicit[ly]" from the design, object, and nature of the Due Process Clause, or (2) nonconstitutional law (a statute, for example) creates "an expectation" that a person will not be deprived of that kind of liberty without fair procedures.
>
> The liberty for which [petitioner] seeks protection easily satisfies both standards. As this Court has long recognized, the institution of marriage, which encompasses

the right of spouses to live together and to raise a family, is central to human life, requires and enjoys community support, and plays a central role in most individuals' "orderly pursuit of happiness." . . .

At the same time, the law, including visa law, surrounds marriage with a host of legal protections to the point that it creates a strong expectation that government will not deprive married individuals of their freedom to live together without strong reasons and (in individual cases) without fair procedure.

Notice that only four justices supported the plurality opinion. On Justice Scalia's view, would the government be required to provide a hearing before it issued an order prohibiting a husband and wife from having contact with each other?

3. *Pre-*Din *cases.* In light of *Din,* consider the status of these older cases:

a. *Reputation.* Paul v. Davis, 424 U.S. 693 (1976), involved a person arrested on a charge of shoplifting; Davis's name was placed on a flyer sent to eight hundred merchants in Louisville, designating him as an active shoplifter. The charges were dismissed, and Davis brought suit, claiming that the action had deprived him of his constitutional interest in reputation. The Court concluded that reputation, standing alone, was not a constitutionally protected liberty interest. The Court acknowledged that in conjunction with some other injury — such as a failure to rehire or a deprivation of a right to purchase liquor, see Wisconsin v. Constantineau, 400 U.S. 433 (1971) (injury to reputation by "posting" is a liberty interest when accompanied by ban on purchase of liquor) — an injury to reputation would trigger the due process clause. The Court expressed concern that a contrary holding would allow the Constitution to swallow up state tort law, making it enforceable in the federal courts. Is it odd that under Paul v. Davis, zero (discharge of a probationary employee) plus zero (injury to reputation) equals one? For a sharply critical view of the decision, see Monaghan, Of "Liberty" and "Property," 62 Cornell L. Rev. 405 (1977).

b. *School suspension.* Compare *Paul* with Goss v. Lopez, 419 U.S. 565 (1975), where the Court found a liberty interest, as well as a property interest, in freedom from arbitrary suspension from a public school. "School authorities here suspended appellees from school for periods of up to 10 days based on charges of misconduct. If sustained and recorded, those charges could seriously damage the students' standing with their fellow students and their teachers as well as interfere with later opportunities for higher education and employment."

c. *Prisoners' rights.* Meachum v. Fano, 427 U.S. 215 (1976), found no constitutionally protected interest in a transfer of prisoners from a medium-security prison to a maximum-security prison on the basis of the prisoners' alleged responsibility for committing arson. The Court said:

We reject at the outset the suggestion that any grievous loss visited upon a person by the State is sufficient to invoke the procedural protections of the Due Process Clause. [The] determining factor is the nature of the interest involved rather than its weight. [Given] a valid conviction, the criminal defendant has been constitutionally deprived of his liberty, to the extent that the State may confine him and subject him to the rules of its prison system so long as the conditions of confinement do not otherwise violate the Constitution. [Confinement] in any of the State's institutions is within the normal limits or range of custody which the conviction has authorized the State to impose. That life in one prison is much more disagreeable than in another does not in itself signify that a Fourteenth Amendment liberty interest is implicated.

Justice Stevens, joined by Justices Brennan and Marshall, dissented on the ground that the Court's conception of liberty was

> fundamentally incorrect. [If] a man were a creature of the state, the analysis would be correct. But neither the Bill of Rights nor the laws of sovereign states create the liberty which the Due Process Clause protects. [I] had thought it self-evident that all men were endowed by their Creator with liberty, as one of the cardinal unalienable rights. It is that basic freedom which the Due Process Clause protects, rather than the particular rights or privileges conferred by specific laws or regulations.

Compare Vitek v. Jones, 445 U.S. 480 (1980), which involved a transfer of a prisoner to a state mental hospital for treatment. The Court held that the due process clause was triggered, distinguishing *Meachum* in two ways. First, the state statute at issue allowed transfer only upon a finding by a designated physician or psychologist that the prisoner "suffers from a mental disease or defect" and "cannot be given treatment in that facility." The prisoner therefore had a liberty interest under Arnett v. Kennedy. Second, the Court held that the prisoner "retained a residuum of liberty that would be infringed by a transfer to a mental hospital." The Court pointed to the stigmatic consequences of involuntary commitment to a mental hospital, the possibility of compelled treatment in the form of mandatory behavior modification programs, and the increased limitations on freedom of action. Assume there was no statutory entitlement in *Vitek*. If there is a constitutionally protected liberty interest, does it follow that there is a substantive constitutional right not to be transferred to a mental institution without just cause?

Greenholtz v. Inmates, 442 U.S. 1 (1979), held that without a statutory entitlement, there is no constitutionally protected interest in receiving parole. The Court acknowledged that a revocation of parole would trigger the due process clause but found a distinction between rescinding a benefit already conferred and refusing to grant a benefit in the first instance. In Board of Pardons v. Allen, 482 U.S. 369 (1987), the Court held that Montana's parole statute established a sufficient expectancy of release to create a liberty interest. Although acknowledging the subjective nature of the parole board's decision and the broad discretion vested in it, the Court held that the mandatory language of the parole statute created an expectancy of release. Justice O'Connor, joined by Chief Justice Rehnquist and Justice Scalia, dissented.

In Sandin v. Conner, 515 U.S. 472 (1995), the Court held that there was no due process violation when a prisoner was not permitted to present witnesses during a disciplinary hearing in which he was sentenced to disciplinary segregation for misconduct. The Court emphasized that judges should avoid involvement in "the ordinary incidents of prison life." It concluded that even if discipline was punitive, and even if state law appeared to create a statutory entitlement not to be disciplined except for "high misconduct," the due process clause would not be triggered unless it presented "a dramatic departure from the basic conditions" of the sentence. In the Court's view, the shift to segregated confinement was not such a dramatic departure, since disciplinary segregation involved conditions similar to those faced by inmates in administrative segregation and protective custody.

Finally, in Wilkinson v. Austin, 544 U.S. 209 (2005), the Court distinguished *Meachum* and *Sandin* and held that a prison inmate had a constitutionally protected liberty interest in avoiding transfer to a "Supermax" facility. Prisoners confined to this facility are held in cells measuring seven by fourteen feet for twenty-three hours per day for an indefinite period limited only by the length of the inmate's sentence. A light remains on in the cell at all times, although it is sometimes dimmed. The cells have solid metal doors with metal strips along the sides and bottoms designed to prevent any conversation or communication with other inmates. All meals are taken within the cells rather than in a common eating area.

Speaking for a unanimous court, Justice Kennedy noted that although the Constitution itself does not create a liberty interest in avoiding transfer to more adverse conditions of confinement, such an interest may arise from state policies and regulations. According to the Court, "the touchstone of the inquiry into the existence of [such] a protected, state-created liberty interest [is] not the language of regulations regarding those conditions but the nature of the conditions themselves 'in relation to ordinary incidents of prison life'" [quoting from *Sandin*]. The Court noted the difficulty under this test in "locating the appropriate baseline" against which to measure atypical hardships, but held that it "need not resolve the issue here, [for] we are satisfied that assignment to the [Supermax] imposes an atypical and significant hardship under any plausible baseline."

d. *DNA testing*. In District Attorney's Office for the Third Judicial District v. Osborne, 557 U.S. 52 (2009), the Court, in a five-to-four decision written by Chief Justice Roberts, held that there was no liberty interest in access to DNA evidence. Osborne had been convicted sixteen years earlier of kidnapping, assault, and sexual assault. He claimed that DNA evidence, in the possession of the state, would exonerate him. In the course of rejecting his claim, the Court acknowledged that Osborne had a liberty interest in demonstrating his innocence with new evidence under state law. It did not follow, however, that "the Due Process Clause requires that certain familiar preconviction trial rights be extended to protect Osborne's postconviction liberty interest. [A] criminal defendant proved guilty after a fair trial does not have the same liberty interests as a free man."

According to the Court, the standard was "whether consideration of Osborne's claim within the framework of the State's procedures for postconviction relief 'offends some principle of justice so rooted in the traditions and conscience of our people as to be ranked as fundamental,' or 'transgresses any recognized principle of fundamental fairness in operation.'" The Court found Alaska's procedures adequate under this standard.

4. *Property*. In contrast to the liberty cases, the Court has generally found a property interest only in circumstances where there is a state-created right.

a. *Police enforcement of a restraining order*. In Town of Castle Rock, Colorado v. Gonzales, 545 U.S. 748 (2005), the Court, in an opinion by Justice Scalia, held that an individual who had obtained a state-law restraining order did not have a constitutionally protected property interest in having the police enforce the order. The order in question, issued by a Colorado court, directed Gonzales's husband to stay away from her and her children and ordered the police to "use every reasonable means to enforce [the] order." The order was issued in conformance with a Colorado statute that required peace officers to "use every reasonable means to enforce a restraining order." When the husband violated the order by taking Gonzales's three daughters from their home, Gonzales repeatedly asked the police to respond, but they failed to do so. Ultimately, the husband killed the children.

The Court stated that Gonzales failed to identify a property interest in enforcement of the order because "Colorado law [did not] truly [make] enforcement of restraining orders *mandatory*. A well established tradition of police discretion has long coexisted with apparently mandatory arrest statutes." Moreover, even if the statute were mandatory,

> it is by no means clear that an individual entitlement to enforcement of a restraining order could constitute a "property" interest for purposes of the Due Process Clause. Such a right would not, of course, resemble any traditional conception of property. Although that alone does not disqualify it from due process protection, [the] right to have a restraining order enforced does not "have some ascertainable monetary value." [Perhaps] most radically, the alleged property interest here arises *incidentally*, not out of some new species of government benefit or service, but out of a function that government actors have always [performed].

b. *Failure to convene a hearing.* Compare the failure of the police to enforce the law in *Castle Rock* with the failure of an administrative agency to do so in Logan v. Zimmerman Brush Co., 455 U.S. 422 (1982). The case involved a state statute prohibiting discrimination on the basis of handicap and providing that within 120 days of the filing of a charge of unlawful discrimination, the state fair employment practices commission "shall convene a factfinding conference." In the *Logan* case, the commission failed through negligence to hold the hearing within the requisite time, and the plaintiff's claim was extinguished by state law. The Court held that the state-created right to redress of unlawful discrimination amounted to a property interest, and that under state law, that right was to be "assessed under what is, in essence, a 'for cause' standard, based upon the substantiality of the evidence." The plaintiff was therefore entitled to a hearing. Is *Logan* distinguishable from *Castle Rock*? For a fuller discussion of government inaction that allegedly violates constitutional interests, see Chapter 9 infra.

c. *Return of fees, court costs, and restitution.* In Nelson v. Colorado, 137 S. Ct. 1249 (2017), the Court, in a seven-to-one decision written by Justice Ginsburg, invalidated a Colorado statute that limited the ability of convicted criminal defendants to secure the return of fees, court costs, and restitution after their convictions were reversed on appeal and in circumstances where there would be no retrial. Under the state's Exoneration Act, these defendants could secure a refund only by filing a separate civil action and then only if they demonstrated by clear and convincing evidence that they were innocent.

Consider Justice Thomas's dissenting opinion:

> The Court assumes, without reference to either state or federal law, that defendants whose convictions have been reversed have a substantive right to any money exacted on the basis of [their] convictions. By doing so, the Court assumes away the real [issue]. . . .
>
> "Because the Constitution protects rather than creates property interests, the existence of a property interest is determined by reference to 'existing rules or understandings that stem from an independent source such as state law.'" Phillips v. Washington Legal Foundation, 524 U.S. 156, 164 (1998) (quoting [Board of Regents of State Colleges v. Roth]). [To] succeed on their procedural due process claim, petitioners must first point to a recognized property interest in that money, under state or federal law, within the meaning of the Fourteenth Amendment.

Justice Thomas concluded that petitioners had not demonstrated that they had such an interest and that, therefore, their claim should fail.

2. *What Process Is Due*

Mathews v. Eldridge
424 U.S. 319 (1976)

[Eldridge had received disability benefits since 1968. After considering Eldridge's response to a questionnaire about his condition, reports from Eldridge's physician and a psychiatric consultant, and Eldridge's files, the relevant state agency made a tentative determination that Eldridge's disability had ceased. Eldridge was so informed, given a statement of reasons, and offered an opportunity to submit a written response. He did so, disputing the agency's decision, but benefits were nonetheless terminated. Eldridge claimed that this procedure violated the due process clause. The Court below agreed.]

MR. JUSTICE POWELL delivered the opinion of the Court. . . .
This Court consistently has held that some form of hearing is required before an individual is finally deprived of a property interest. [Eldridge] agrees that the review procedures available to a claimant before the initial determination of ineligibility becomes final would be adequate if disability benefits were not terminated until after the evidentiary hearing stage of the administrative process. The dispute centers upon what process is due prior to the initial termination of benefits, pending review.
In recent years this Court increasingly has had occasion to consider the extent to which due process requires an evidentiary hearing prior to the deprivation of some type of property interest even if such a hearing is provided thereafter. In only one case, [*Goldberg*], has the Court held that a hearing closely approximating a judicial trial is necessary. In other cases requiring some type of pretermination hearing as a matter of constitutional right the Court has spoken sparingly about the requisite procedures. . . .
[Our] decisions underscore the truism that "'[d]ue process,' unlike some legal rules, is not a technical conception with a fixed content unrelated to time, place and circumstances." "[D]ue process is flexible and calls for such procedural protections as the particular situation demands." [Accordingly,] resolution of the issue whether the administrative procedures provided here are constitutionally sufficient requires analysis of the governmental and private interests that are affected. [*Arnett*.] More precisely, our prior decisions indicate that identification of the specific dictates of due process generally requires consideration of three distinct factors: First, the private interest that will be affected by the official action; second, the risk of an erroneous deprivation of such interest through the procedures used, and the probable value, if any, of additional or substitute procedural safeguards; and finally, the Government's interest, including the function involved and the fiscal and administrative burdens that the additional or substitute procedural requirement would entail.
[The Court described the relevant procedures. It noted that the worker bears a continuing burden of showing that he suffers from a medically determinable physical or mental impairment; that a state agency conducts continuing

eligibility investigations, in which there is communication with the disabled worker; that when an agency's tentative assessment differs from the worker's, the worker is informed that benefits may be terminated and is offered an opportunity to respond in writing and to furnish new evidence; that there is review by a federal official of any state decision to terminate; that after termination, there is a right to an evidentiary hearing, in which the claimant may be represented by counsel; and that the worker may recover retroactive payments if the termination is later found erroneous.]

[Despite] the elaborate character of the administrative procedures provided by the Secretary, the courts below held them to be constitutionally inadequate, concluding that due process requires an evidentiary hearing prior to termination. In light of the private and governmental interests at stake here and the nature of the existing procedures, we think this was error.

Since a recipient whose benefits are terminated is awarded full retroactive relief if he ultimately prevails, his sole interest is in the uninterrupted receipt of this source of income pending final administrative decision on his claim.

[Only] in *Goldberg* has the Court held that due process requires an evidentiary hearing prior to a temporary deprivation. It was emphasized there that welfare assistance is given to persons on the very margin of [subsistence. Eligibility] for disability benefits, in contrast, is not based upon financial need. . . .

As *Goldberg* illustrates, the degree of potential deprivation that may be created by a particular decision is a factor to be considered in assessing the validity of any administrative decisionmaking process. The potential deprivation here is generally likely to be less than in *Goldberg*, although the degree of difference can be overstated. As the District Court emphasized, to remain eligible for benefits a recipient must be "unable to engage in substantial gainful activity." Thus, in contrast to the discharged federal employee in *Arnett*, there is little possibility that the terminated recipient will be able to find even temporary employment to ameliorate the interim loss. [Further,] "the possible length of wrongful deprivation of . . . benefits [also] is an important factor in assessing the impact of official action on the private interests." The Secretary concedes that the delay between a request for a hearing before an administrative law judge and a decision on the claim is currently between 10 and 11 months. Since a terminated recipient must first obtain a reconsideration decision as a prerequisite to invoking his right to an evidentiary hearing, the delay between the actual cutoff of benefits and final decision after a hearing exceeds one year.

In view of the torpidity of this administrative review process, and the typically modest resources of the family unit of the physically disabled worker,[26] the hardship imposed upon the erroneously terminated disability recipient may be significant. Still, the disabled worker's need is likely to be less than that of a welfare recipient. In addition to the possibility of access to private resources, other forms of government assistance will become available where the termination of disability benefits places a worker or his family below the subsistence level.

---

26. Amici cite statistics compiled by the Secretary which indicate that in 1965 the mean income of the family unit of a disabled worker was $3,803, while the medial income for the unit was $2,836. The mean liquid assets — i.e., cash, stocks, bonds — of these family units was $4,862; the median was $940. These statistics do not take into account the family unit's nonliquid assets — i.e., automobile, real estate, and the like.

In view of these potential sources of temporary income, there is less reason here than in *Goldberg* to depart from the ordinary principle, [that] something less than an evidentiary hearing is sufficient prior to adverse administrative action.

An additional factor to be considered here is the fairness and reliability of the existing pretermination procedures, and the probable value, if any, of additional procedural safeguards. Central to the evaluation of any administrative process is the nature of the relevant inquiry. In order to remain eligible for benefits the disabled worker must demonstrate by means of "medically acceptable clinical and laboratory diagnostic techniques," that he is unable "to engage in any substantial gainful activity by reason of any *medically determinable* physical or mental impairment. . . ."

In short, a medical assessment of the worker's physical or mental condition is required. This is a more sharply focused and easily documented decision than the typical determination of welfare entitlement. . . .

[A] further safeguard against mistake is the policy of allowing the disability recipient's representative full access to all information relied upon by the state agency. In addition, prior to the cutoff of benefits the agency informs the recipient of its tentative assessment, the reasons therefor, and provides a summary of the evidence that it considers most relevant. Opportunity is then afforded the recipient to submit additional evidence or arguments, enabling him to challenge directly the accuracy of information in his file as well as the correctness of the agency's tentative conclusions.

Despite these carefully structured procedures, amici point to the significant reversal rate for appealed cases as clear evidence that the current process is inadequate. Depending upon the base selected and the line of analysis followed, the relevant reversal rates urged by the contending parties vary from a high of 58.6% for appealed reconsideration decisions to an overall reversal rate of only 3.3%. Bare statistics rarely provide a satisfactory measure of the fairness of a decisionmaking process. Their adequacy is especially suspect here since the administrative review system is operated on an open-file basis. A recipient may always submit new evidence, and such submissions may result in additional medical examinations. . . .

In striking the appropriate due process balance the final factor to be assessed is the public interest. This includes the administrative burden and other societal costs that would be associated with requiring, as a matter of constitutional right, an evidentiary hearing upon demand in all cases prior to the termination of disability benefits. The most visible burden would be the incremental cost resulting from the increased number of hearings and the expense of providing benefits to ineligible recipients pending decision. [The] parties submit widely varying estimates of the probable additional financial cost. We only need say that experience with the constitutionalizing of government procedures suggests that the ultimate additional cost in terms of money and administrative burden would not be insubstantial.

Financial cost alone is not a controlling weight in determining whether due process requires a particular procedural safeguard prior to some administrative decision. But the Government's interest, and hence that of the public, in conserving scarce fiscal and administrative resources is a factor that must be weighed. At some point the benefit of an additional safeguard to the individual affected by the administrative action and to society in terms of increased assurance that the action is just, may be outweighed by the cost. Significantly, the cost of protecting those whom the preliminary administrative process has identified as likely to be found undeserving may in the end come out of the pockets of the deserving since resources available for any particular program of social welfare are not unlimited. . . .

[In] assessing what process is due in this case, substantial weight must be given to the good-faith judgments of the individuals charged by Congress with the administration of social welfare programs that the procedures they have provided assure fair consideration of the entitlement claims of individuals. . . .

We conclude that an evidentiary hearing is not required prior to the termination of disability benefits and that the present administrative procedures fully comport with due process.

The judgment of the Court of Appeals is reversed.

Mr. Justice Stevens took no part in the consideration or decision of this case.

Mr. Justice Brennan, with whom Mr. Justice Marshall concurs, dissenting.

[The] Court's consideration that a discontinuance of disability benefits may cause the recipient to suffer only a limited deprivation is no argument. It is speculative. Moreover, the very legislative determination to provide disability benefits, without any prerequisite determination of need in fact, presumes a need by the recipient which is not this Court's function to denigrate. Indeed, in the present case, [because] disability benefits were terminated there was a foreclosure upon the Eldridge home and the family's furniture was repossessed, forcing Eldridge, his wife, and their children to sleep in one bed. Finally, it is also no argument that a worker, who has been placed in the untenable position of having been denied disability benefits, may still seek other forms of public assistance.

Note: Balancing Tests and the Due Process Clause

1. *The* Mathews *test in general.* In *Mathews,* the Court adopted a three-part "test," sometimes called one of balancing or "cost-benefit" analysis, that has played an important role in constitutional law. In almost all cases raising questions of procedural regularity, the Court refers to the *Mathews* test. On what grounds might the test be criticized?

a. *Ignoring nonutilitarian variables.* Perhaps the *Mathews* approach ignores participatory and dignitary concerns. Consider Mashaw, The Supreme Court's Due Process Calculus for Administrative Adjudication in Mathews v. Eldridge: Three Factors in Search of a Theory of Value, 44 U. Chi. L. Rev. 28, 49–51 (1976):

The Supreme Court's analysis in *Eldridge* is not informed by systematic attention to any theory of the values underlying due process review. The approach is implicitly utilitarian but incomplete, and the Court overlooks alternative theories that might have yielded fruitful inquiry. [The] increasingly secular, scientific, and collectivist character of the modern American state reinforces our propensity to define fairness in the formal, and apparently neutral language of social utility. [Yet] the popular moral presupposition of individual dignity, and its political counterpart, self-determination, persist. State coercion must be legitimized, not only by acceptable substantive policies, but also by political processes that respond to a democratic morality's demand for participation in decisions affecting individual and group interests. [A] dignitary theory of due process might have contributed significantly to the *Eldridge* analysis. [A] disability decision is a judgment of considerable social significance, and one that the claimant should rightly perceive as having a substantive moral content.

See also J. Mashaw, Due Process in the Administrative State (1985).

b. *Vagueness.* Perhaps the three-part analysis is not useful, or perhaps it fails to constrain judicial discretion in a helpful way. Note that in economics, cost-benefit analysis is usually based on the criterion of private willingness to pay. The benefit is measured by how much people would be willing to pay for the good in question; the cost is measured similarly. But how does one assess the benefits and costs in a case like *Mathews*? Might the various factors be thought incommensurable, in the sense that there is no metric along which they could be aligned? See Sunstein, Incommensurability and Valuation in Law, 92 Mich. L. Rev. 779 (1994).

c. *Susceptibility to misapplication.* Perhaps a utilitarian assessment of the three factors requires courts to duplicate legislative processes. That assessment, calling for ad hoc judgments of policy, may not be readily within judicial competence. What in the text of the due process clause or in acceptable conceptions of the judicial role authorizes such an approach?

This critique might be buttressed by reference to *Mathews* itself. Mashaw, The Supreme Court's Due Process Calculus for Administrative Adjudication, supra, argues that the Court misconceived the character of the disability determination. According to Mashaw, that determination is based much less on purely medical factors and much more on subjective impressions raising issues of credibility than the Court suggested. In these circumstances, oral rather than written testimony becomes more valuable. Note also the Court's confessed inability to evaluate the costs of additional safeguards, captured in its statement that it could not say that they would be "insubstantial."

Is there an alternative to the *Mathews* approach that would avoid these various critiques and at the same time provide a sensible approach for making decisions about the extent of procedural safeguards? Would bright-line rules — requiring, for example, trial-type hearings absent a special governmental showing or deference to the legislative determination absent special individual circumstances — be preferable? Consider also that (1) it is possible that detailed procedures may be requested only by the most educated and aggressive claimants, (2) the costs of such procedures may be taken out of the claimants' benefits elsewhere, and (3) formal procedures may increase the adversarial quality of relations that should be conducted in a more informal way.

See in this connection Walters v. National Association of Radiation Survivors, 473 U.S. 305 (1985), where the Court cited *Mathews* in upholding a statute providing that $10 is the maximum fee that may be paid to an attorney who represents a veteran seeking Veterans Administration benefits for service-related injuries. In a concurring opinion, Justice O'Connor, joined by Justice Blackmun, suggested that under the due process clause, courts should look at the individual claim to evaluate whether the statutory maximum is unconstitutional in particular applications. Justice Stevens, joined by Justices Brennan and Marshall, dissented, arguing in favor of a bright-line rule in favor of counsel.

Justice Stevens renewed his call for a bright-line rule in a dissenting opinion in Brock v. Roadway Express, Inc., 481 U.S. 252 (1987):

The Court's willingness to sacrifice due process to the Government's obscure suggestion of necessity reveals the serious flaws in its due process analysis. It is wrong to approach the due process analysis in each case by asking anew what procedures seem worthwhile and not too costly. Unless a case falls within a recognized exception, we should adhere to the strongest presumption that the Government may not take away life, liberty, or property before making a meaningful hearing available.

Compare Turner v. Rogers, 564 U.S. 431 (2011), where the Court, in an opinion by Justice Breyer, held that the due process clause did not automatically require the state to provide counsel to an indigent person confronting civil contempt for failure to pay child support, even if the individual faces incarceration. The Court nonetheless held that Turner's incarceration violated the due process clause because the state had failed to provide him with "alternative safeguards."

Using the *Mathews* balancing test, the Court conceded that the importance of the private interest at stake — loss of personal liberty through imprisonment — "argues strongly for the right to counsel." The Court nonetheless thought that three other considerations made counsel unnecessary. First, the critical issue in cases of nonsupport is ability to pay, but this issue would have to be resolved without counsel in any event to determine whether the defendant was indigent and therefore eligible for state-provided counsel. Second, the private individual opposing the nonpaying parent is often without counsel. Finally, alternative safeguards could reduce the risk of error without providing counsel. These safeguards included notice to the defendant that ability to pay was a critical issue, the use of a form to elicit relevant financial information, opportunity for the defendant to respond to statements and questions about his financial status at the hearing, and an express finding by the court that the defendant had the ability to pay. Because Turner had not been afforded these alternative safeguards, the Court held that his incarceration violated the due process clause.

In a dissenting opinion joined by Justice Scalia and joined in part by Chief Justice Roberts and Justice Alito, Justice Thomas agreed that the due process clause did not guarantee a right to counsel. However, because the issue was not raised by the parties, the dissenters would not have decided whether alternative procedural safeguards were required.

Compare Turner to Kerry v. Din, 135 S. Ct. 2128 (2015). Petitioner was a resident United States citizen. Her husband, a noncitizen, was denied a visa to enter the United States on the ground that he had engaged in "terrorist activities." The government refused to provide any additional information to support the denial. The Supreme Court rejected Petitioner's claim that this refusal denied her right to procedural due process, but no opinion gained majority support. Justice Scalia, in an opinion announcing the judgment of the Court and joined by Chief Justice Roberts and Justice Thomas, asserted that petitioner had failed to allege that a constitutionally protected liberty interest had been infringed. (This portion of the opinion is discussed at page 935, supra.) Justice Kennedy, in an opinion joined by Justice Alito, assumed arguendo that a liberty interest was implicated, but asserted that petitioner had received all the process that was due. He based this conclusion on "due consideration of the congressional power to make rules for the exclusion of aliens, and the ensuing power to delegate authority to the Attorney General to exercise substantial discretion in that field."

Absent an affirmative showing of bad faith on the part of the consular officer who denied [petitioner's husband] a visa — which [petitioner] has not plausibly alleged with sufficient particularity — [we should not] "look behind" the government's exclusion of [petitioner's husband] for additional factual details beyond what its express reliance on [the statute excluding those engaged in terrorist activity] encompasses. . . .

The government, furthermore, was not required [to] point to a more specific provision within [the statute even though] the statutory provision the consular officer cited covers a broad range of conduct. . . .

Congress evaluated the benefits and burdens of notice in this sensitive area and assigned discretion to the Executive to decide when more detailed disclosure is appropriate. This considered judgment gives additional support to the independent conclusion that the notice given was constitutionally adequate, particularly in light of the national security concerns that the terrorism bar addresses.

Justice Breyer, in an opinion joined by Justices Ginsburg, Sotomayor, and Kagan, dissented. He concluded that, at a minimum, the petitioner was entitled to "a statement of reasons, some kind of explanation, as to why the State Department denied her husband a visa."

[A] statement of reasons, even one provided after a visa denial, serves much the same function as a "notice" of a proposed action. It allows [petitioner], who suffered a "serious loss," a fair "opportunity to meet" "the case" that has produced separation from her husband. . . .

I recognize that our due process cases often determine the constitutional insistence upon a particular procedure by balancing, with respect to that procedure, the "private interest" at stake, "the risk of an erroneous deprivation" absent the sought-after protection, and the Government's interest in not providing additional procedure. Here "balancing" would not change the result. The "private interest" is important, the risk of an "erroneous deprivation" is significant, and the Government's interest in not providing a reason is normally small, at least administratively speaking.

2. *The problem of timing.* Must hearings be held before or after adverse action is taken? The traditional rule has been that a postdeprivation remedy is insufficient. In general, government must afford procedural safeguards before it harms someone. But in North American Cold Storage Co. v. Chicago, 211 U.S. 306 (1908), the Court held that a prior hearing was not required before state officers destroyed stored food deemed by health officials to be unfit for human consumption. The Court noted that the existence of the food posed a threat to public health, and that a subsequent tort action would provide sufficient protection to the owner. Would the *Mathews* approach support this outcome?

How far should the *North American Cold Storage* reasoning be taken? Consider whether it should apply to cases of termination of welfare benefits or of employment. In Arnett v. Kennedy, 416 U.S. 134 (1974), a majority of the Court held that a trial-type hearing was not required before termination of a federal employee accused of bribery. Justice Powell, undertaking a balancing approach, contended that the government "must have wide discretion and control over the management of its personnel and internal affairs. This includes the prerogative to remove employees whose conduct hinders efficient operation and to do so with dispatch. [The employee's] actual injury would consist of a temporary interruption of his income during the interim. [The] possible deprivation is considerably less severe than that involved in *Goldberg*." Note, however, that in *Arnett*, there was some predeprivation procedure as well.

In *Loudermill*, supra, the Court held that the Constitution did not permit discharge of state employees without any prior procedural safeguards. The

Court said: "In *Arnett* six Justices found constitutional minima satisfied where the employee had access to the material upon which the charge was based and could respond orally or in writing and present rebuttal affidavits. [The] need for some form of pretermination hearing [is] evident from a balancing of the competing interests at stake." The Court emphasized that the "private interest in retaining employment" was significant; that "some opportunity for the employee to present his side of the case is recurringly of obvious value in reaching an accurate decision," especially in light of the fact the discharge may involve a factual dispute; and that "affording the employee an opportunity to respond would impose neither a significant administrative burden nor intolerable delays."

The Court added that, even when the dispute was not factual, a hearing might allow an examination of the appropriateness or necessity of discharge, and that a hearing could serve governmental interests in retaining qualified employees. The Court said, however, that an employee's pretermination hearing need not be elaborate and could consist of "oral or written notice of the charges against him, an explanation of the employer's evidence, and an opportunity to present his side of the story."

In Brock v. Roadway Express, Inc., supra, the Court considered the converse of the problem posed by *Arnett* and *Loudermill* — that is, the kind of process that is due before an employer can be forced to reinstate a discharged worker. A federal statute protects employees in the transportation industry from discharge in retaliation for refusing to operate a motor vehicle that does not comply with state and federal safety regulations. The statute provides that, if the Secretary of Labor finds reasonable cause to believe that an employee has been discharged in violation of the act, he can issue an order reinstating the employee. An employer is entitled to a full evidentiary hearing only after the reinstatement.

In an opinion written by Justice Marshall, a plurality of the Court held that the Constitution did not require an evidentiary hearing and an opportunity to cross-examine witnesses before the government ordered temporary reinstatement. Although acknowledging the employer's substantial interest in controlling the makeup of its workforce, the plurality emphasized the government's countervailing interest in promoting highway safety and the employee's interest in retaining his job.

The plurality went on to hold, however, that the procedures would satisfy this reliability standard only if the employer received notice of the employee's allegations, notice of the substance of the relevant supporting evidence, an opportunity to submit a written response, and an opportunity to meet with the investigator and present statements from rebuttal witnesses.

In separate opinions, Justices Brennan and Stevens each argued that the due process clause required a full evidentiary hearing prior to a reinstatement order. Justice White, in an opinion joined by Chief Justice Rehnquist and Justice Scalia, argued that due process did not require that the employer be provided with information on which the reinstatement order is based, including names of witnesses, prior to reinstatement.

3. *How formal?* Goldberg v. Kelly required a trial-type hearing before termination of welfare benefits, including a number of features: a right to present oral evidence, a right to confront and cross-examine witnesses, a right to counsel, a statement by the arbiter of reasons and of the evidence relied on, and a right to an impartial decisionmaker. In recent cases, however, the Court has shown some reluctance to formalize the administrative process with such requirements.

At the opposite pole from *Goldberg,* for example, is Goss v. Lopez, 419 U.S. 565 (1975), in which the Court found that due process required only a conversation before temporary suspension of students. This included oral or written notice of the charges against them, an explanation of the evidence the authorities have, and a chance to provide the students' side of the story. The Court said:

> Even truncated trial-type procedures might well overwhelm administrative facilities in many places and, in diverting resources, cost more than it would save in educational effectiveness. Moreover, further formalizing the suspension process and escalating its formality and adversary nature may not only make it too costly as a regular disciplinary tool but also destroy its effectiveness as part of the teaching process. On the other hand, requiring effective notice and informal hearing permitting the student to give his version of the events will provide a meaningful hedge against erroneous action.

See also Board of Curators of University of Missouri v. Horowitz, 435 U.S. 78 (1978), declining to require elaborate procedures for discharge of a woman from medical school in part because of reluctance to "formalize the academic dismissal process." And note the various conclusions on the issue of formality in *Mathews, Arnett,* and *Loudermill.*

In Greenholtz v. Inmates, 442 U.S. 1 (1979), the Court held that in parole decisions, based on a subjective assessment of the whole person, an oral hearing was not required. A review of the prisoner's files, the Court said, was sufficient to satisfy due process. Compare Wilkinson v. Austin, 544 U.S. 209 (2005), where the Court upheld procedures under which, prior to transfer to a Supermax facility, inmates were provided with a written notice of reasons and a hearing at which they could offer explanations or objections but could not call witnesses.

For a discussion of the type of hearing that must be afforded an individual accused of being an enemy combatant, see Chapter 4, supra.

4. *State remedies as due process.* The Court has held that state tort remedies may sometimes provide all the process that is constitutionally "due." Ingraham v. Wright, 430 U.S. 651 (1977), involved a claim that the due process clause required some sort of procedural safeguard before teachers "paddled" students for asserted misconduct. The Court held that the interest in avoiding "paddling" was a constitutionally protected liberty but concluded that an after-the-fact state tort remedy provided sufficient procedural safeguards. "Because paddlings are usually inflicted in response to conduct directly observed by teachers in their presence, the risk that a child will be paddled without cause is typically insignificant. [In] those cases where severe punishment is contemplated, the available civil and criminal sanctions for abuse — considered in light of the openness of the school environment — afford significant protection against unjustified corporal punishment." Justice White, in a dissent joined by Justices Brennan, Marshall, and Stevens, complained that state law was inadequate in cases of a good faith mistake in school discipline, and that the "infliction of physical pain is final and irreparable."

Compare Memphis Light, Gas, & Water Division v. Craft, 436 U.S. 1 (1978), requiring a hearing in advance of termination of electricity service for nonpayment of a disputed bill. "The factors that have justified exceptions to the requirements of some prior process are not present here. Although utility service may be restored ultimately, the cessation of essential services for any appreciable time works a uniquely final deprivation. [Moreover], the probability of error in utility cut-off decisions is not so insubstantial as to warrant dispensing with all process prior to termination."

Ingraham was extended in Parratt v. Taylor, 451 U.S. 527 (1981), which involved a negligent loss of a prisoner's hobby kit. The Court held that state tort law provided a constitutionally adequate remedy. The Court noted that the case involved a "tortious loss of [property] as a result of a random and unauthorized act by a state employee [not] as a result of some established state procedure." A state tort remedy was therefore sufficient "process." See also Hudson v. Palmer, 468 U.S. 517 (1984), extending *Parratt* to intentional deprivations of property in the context of destruction of a prisoner's property during the search of his cell. Should it matter that property, rather than liberty, was at stake? That a prior hearing would seem impracticable?

In Logan v. Zimmerman Brush Co., section G1, supra, it was argued that *Parratt* was controlling, and that the state tort remedy provided sufficient procedural protection for the state's failure to hold a hearing on the plaintiff's claim of discrimination. The Court rejected that argument, reasserting the general principle requiring predeprivation hearings. Unlike in *Parratt*, moreover, "it is the state system itself that destroys a complainant's property interests, by operation of law, whenever the Commission fails to convene a timely conference."

In Daniels v. Williams, 474 U.S. 327 (1986), the Court overruled *Parratt* insofar as that case had suggested that a negligently inflicted loss could amount to a deprivation of due process in the absence of a state tort remedy. Although all nine justices joined the result in *Daniels*, a second case, also involving negligence by a state official and decided on the same day, evoked more controversy. In Davidson v. Cannon, 474 U.S. 344 (1986), the Court rejected the due process claim of a state prisoner who alleged that he was seriously injured when prison officials negligently failed to protect him from another inmate. Chief Justice Rehnquist wrote the Court's opinion: "[Where] a government official is merely negligent in causing the injury, no procedure for compensation is constitutionally required. [The] guarantee of due process has never been understood to mean that the State must guarantee due care on the part of its officials."

Justice Stevens wrote an opinion concurring in the results in both *Daniels* and *Davidson*, but solely on the ground that in neither case were state remedies for the deprivations constitutionally inadequate. In an extended opinion, Justice Blackmun, joined by Justice Marshall, dissented. Justice Brennan dissented separately.

In Nelson v. Colorado, 137 S. Ct. 1249 (2017), the Court, in a seven-to-one decision written by Justice Ginsburg, invalidated a Colorado statute that limited the ability of convicted criminal defendants to secure the return of fees, court costs, and restitution after their convictions were reversed on appeal and in circumstances where there would be no retrial. Under the state's Exoneration Act, these defendants could secure a refund only by filing a separate civil action and then only if they demonstrated by clear and convincing evidence that they were innocent. Applying the Mathews v. Eldridge test, the Court found that these limitations violated procedural due process. The Court reasoned that because their convictions had been reversed, the defendants must be presumed innocent and therefore should not have to establish their innocence. Moreover, even apart from this requirement, the Exoneration Act provided an inadequate remedy because "when amounts a defendant seeks to recoup are not large [the] cost of mounting a claim [and] retaining a lawyer to pursue it would be prohibitive." Accordingly, "a State may not impose anything more than minimal procedures on the refund of exactions dependent upon a conviction subsequently invalidated."

Does the Court's holding imply that an exonerated defendant is constitutionally entitled to compensation for the period during which the defendant was imprisoned? The Court stated that "the comparison is inapt" because petitioners "seek restoration of funds they paid to the State, not compensation for temporary deprivation of those funds. [Just] as the restoration of liberty on reversal of a conviction is not compensation, neither is the return of money taken by the State on account of the conviction."

Justice Alito wrote an opinion concurring in the judgment. Justice Thomas's dissenting opinion is discussed, supra.

5. *Bias.* Does the due process clause guarantee an unbiased decisionmaker? What does "bias" mean in this context?

Consider Caperton v. A. T. Massey Coal Co., 556 U.S. 868 (2009). A West Virginia jury found that defendant Massey was guilty of fraudulent misrepresentation, concealment, and tortious interference with existing contractual relations and awarded plaintiff Caperton $50 million in damages. Knowing that the Supreme Court of Appeals of West Virginia would consider an appeal in the case, Blankenship, Massey's chairman and chief executive officer, spent more than $3 million directly and indirectly supporting the election of Benjamin to a seat on the court. This was more than the total amount spent by all other Benjamin supporters, three times the amount spent by Benjamin's own committee, and, apparently, $1 million more than the total amount spent by the campaign committees of both candidates combined. Benjamin won the election. Despite repeated requests that he recuse himself, Benjamin sat on the appeal in the *Massey* case and cast the deciding vote in a three-to-two decision to reverse the result below.

In a five-to-four decision, the Court, in an opinion by Justice Kennedy, held that the due process clause required Benjamin's recusal. The Court noted that "[n]ot every campaign contribution by a litigant or attorney creates a probability of bias that requires a judge's recusal, but this is an exceptional case."

> [There] is a serious risk of actual bias — based on objective and reasonable perceptions — when a person with a personal stake in a particular case had a significant and disproportionate influence in placing the judge on the case by raising funds or directing the judge's election campaign when the case was pending or imminent. The inquiry centers on the contribution's relative size in comparison to the total amount of money contributed to the campaign, the total amount spent in the election, and the apparent effect such contribution had on the outcome of the election. . . .
>
> Just as no man is allowed to be a judge in his own cause, similar fears of bias can arise when — without the consent of the other parties — a man chooses the judge in his own cause. And applying this principle to the judicial election process, there was here a serious, objective risk of actual bias that required Justice Benjamin's recusal.

Chief Justice Roberts, joined by Justices Scalia, Thomas, and Alito, dissented:

> I, of course, share the majority's sincere concerns about the need to maintain a fair, independent, and impartial judiciary — and one that appears to be such. But I fear that the Court's decision will undermine rather than promote these values. . . .

Unlike the established grounds for disqualification, a "probability of bias" cannot be defined in any limited way. The Court's new "rule" provides no guidance to judges and litigants about when recusal will be constitutionally required. This will inevitably lead to an increase in allegations that judges are biased, however groundless those charges may be. The end result will do far more to erode public confidence in judicial impartiality than an isolated failure to recuse in a particular case.

Justice Scalia also wrote a dissenting opinion.

Compare Rippo v. Baker, 580 U.S. ___ (2017). Petitioner was charged with first-degree murder and unsuccessfully moved to recuse the trial judge on the ground that the District Attorney's Office was participating in a federal bribery probe of the trial judge. The Nevada Supreme Court held that petitioner was not entitled to discovery or an evidentiary hearing on his claim because his allegations "[did] not support the assertion that the trial judge was actually biased in this case." In a per curiam opinion, a unanimous Supreme Court vacated the state court's judgement because the state court had applied the wrong legal standard. "The Nevada Supreme Court did not ask the question our precedents require: whether, considering all the circumstances alleged, the risk of bias was too high to be constitutionally tolerable." Does this standard ask the right question, or does it merely beg the question?

Note: Procedural Due Process and "Legislative" Determinations

Congress and state legislatures may pass laws without affording procedural safeguards beyond those specifically required by the Constitution. The due process clause does not mean that, before passing laws, Congress must hear those who will be affected. Congress may, for example, reduce the welfare benefits of a class of people without offering anything in the way of procedure. Why? Does the same reasoning apply when administrative agencies make rules governing private conduct?

Some answers were spelled out in Bi-Metallic Investment Co. v. State Board of Equalization, 239 U.S. 441 (1915). *Bi-Metallic* involved an attempt to prevent the Denver Board of Equalization and the Colorado Tax Commission from increasing the valuation of all taxable property in Denver without affording a hearing. The Court held that no hearing was required:

> Where a rule of conduct applies to more than a few people it is impracticable that every one should have a direct voice in its adoption. The Constitution does not require all public acts to be done in town meeting or an assembly of the whole. General statutes within the state power are passed that affect the person or property of individuals, sometimes to the point of ruin, without giving them a chance to be heard. Their rights are protected in the only way that they can be in a complex society, by their power, immediate or remote, over those who make the rule.

This reasoning contains two points: Processes of representation are a sufficient guarantee of legitimacy, thus serving the same ends as a hearing; and it would be impracticable to require a hearing for determinations that affect large numbers of people. Kenneth Culp Davis has added that trial-type processes are best suited for "adjudicative" facts — facts "about the parties and their activities, business, and properties. Adjudicative facts usually answer the questions of who said what, where, when, how, why, with what motive or intent." K. Davis, Administrative Law Treatise §7.02 (1958). "Legislative" facts, by contrast, raise questions of policy that are better suited to a legislative forum.

How might one challenge these claims? Are representative processes a reliable safeguard when administrative agencies are making rules?

H.   THE CONTRACTS AND TAKINGS CLAUSES

This section explores the contracts clause and the eminent domain clause. The two clauses do not create "implied fundamental rights" in the sense that we have been discussing thus far, but they have a close association with decisions under the due process clause, and they therefore deserve treatment here.

The two clauses have been united by a single, quite general idea: Government ought not to be permitted to redistribute resources by "taking" resources from one person for the benefit of another. The contracts clause bars state government from disrupting voluntary agreements simply because government wants to help one or another side. The eminent domain clause bars the federal government (and, after incorporation, the states as well) from taking property from one person and giving it to someone else. Both clauses require the public as a whole, rather than distinct groups, to pay out funds to benefit people perceived to be in need of protection. Both clauses are in this sense allied by a fear of the power of "factions" — powerful private interests — over government and an associated belief that at least certain forms of redistribution should be banned.

Redistribution, particularly to the disadvantaged, has become an important part of the activity of the national and state governments in the aftermath of the New Deal. There has therefore been considerable pressure to limit the force of the contracts and the takings clauses. And when redistribution, to the disadvantaged or to anyone else, is perceived as inefficient or unjust, it should be unsurprising to see efforts to reinvigorate both clauses.

1.   The Contracts Clause

The contracts clause provides, "No State shall [pass] any [Law] impairing the Obligation of Contracts." U.S. Const. art. I, §10, cl. 1.

Note: Early Interpretive Problems

The contracts clause is one of the few "rights-protecting" provisions in the original Constitution. It is also one of the few such provisions that was directly applicable to the states before the adoption of the fourteenth amendment. Moreover, for a long period the contracts clause was among the most important provisions in the Constitution, at least if the structural provisions are excluded. Indeed, in the nineteenth century the clause "was the constitutional justification for more cases involving the validity of state law than all of the other clauses of the Constitution together." B. Wright, The Contract Clause of the Constitution 1 (1938). Some also highly valued the clause for its protection of a form of liberty. Sir

Henry Maine claimed that the clause "is the bulwark of American individualism against democratic impatience and socialistic fantasy." H. Maine, Popular Government 247–248 (1885). Why did the framers of the Constitution single out contractual freedom as one of the only rights entitled to protection against abridgment by state governments?

A partial answer lies in the history of the clause. Between the Revolution and the drafting of the Constitution, many states had enacted "debtor relief" laws — provisions that, among other things, postponed the time for payment of private debts, allowed for issuance and required acceptance of paper money, and allowed for payments in installments or at some percentage of the appraised value of commodities. Creditors, well-to-do or otherwise, regarded these measures as an indefensible intrusion on private ordering. Many debtors found such measures to be an indispensable protection against surprise or unfair dealing. Many observers, including some of the framers, saw such measures as general, long-term obstacles to trade and commercial development — obstacles that would ultimately harm everyone, including possible debtors themselves, by discouraging contractual arrangements.

Recall here that the contracts clause was applicable only to the states, and not to the federal government — unlike the eminent domain clause, which was at its inception applicable only to the federal government. Is this an accident of history, or might it reflect a broader set of structural concerns? See McConnell, Contract Rights and Property Rights: A Case Study in the Relationship between Individual Liberties and the Constitutional Structure, 76 Cal. L. Rev. 267 (1988).

The contracts clause was designed above all to prevent states from enacting debtor relief and similar laws. See Sturges v. Crowninshield, 17 U.S. (4 Wheat.) 122 (1819) (invalidating a New York law discharging debtors of their obligations upon surrender of their property); Green v. Biddle, 21 U.S. (8 Wheat.) 1 (1823) (invalidating a Kentucky law designed to make it harder for landowners to eject good-faith squatters). The first controversies over the clause involved three principal issues.

1. *Prospective or retrospective only?* What if a state does not reallocate rights under an existing contract but merely prohibits people from entering into certain sorts of contracts? In Ogden v. Saunders, 25 U.S. (12 Wheat.) 213 (1827), the Court was confronted with the critical question whether the prohibition of contractual impairments applies only to contracts made before the passage of the allegedly "impairing" law. The case involved a state bankruptcy law passed before the parties had entered into the relevant contract. According to the Court, the law in effect at the time a contract is formed is "the law of the contract," or a part of the contract, and therefore not an impairment at all within the meaning of the clause.

Chief Justice Marshall was in the minority — for the only time, in constitutional cases, during his thirty-four-year tenure as Chief Justice. He emphasized two points. First, in his view the text of the clause did not allow for a distinction between prospective and retrospective impairments. Second, Chief Justice Marshall stressed that the right to contractual freedom was a product of natural law. He said that the Court had forgotten that point by allowing positive law to dictate in advance the conditions under which contracts could go forward.

2. *Interference with contracts under the police power.* What if a state declares unenforceable existing contractual obligations through the exercise of its police power — as, for example, by prohibiting agreements calling for the sale of heroin, or for murder, or for a certain level of pollution? To what extent does the state's reserved authority operate as an implicit qualification of the contracts clause?

In early cases, the Court ruled that the clause does not prohibit even retroactive contractual impairments if the state is operating pursuant to the police power. In Manigault v. Springs, 199 U.S. 473 (1905), neighboring landowners quarreled over a dam that one of them had built. After negotiations, the landowners agreed that the obstruction might continue for four more months, after which it would be removed, so that there would be a clear passage through the creek. The dam was accordingly removed. Several years later a statute was enacted that authorized one of the landowners to build a dam on the same creek. The statute, of course, destroyed the contractual obligation not to build a dam on the creek.

The Court upheld the statute, stating that the police power "is an exercise of the sovereign right of the government to protect the lives, health, morals, comfort, and general welfare of the people, and is paramount to any rights under contracts between individuals." Thus, "parties by entering into contracts may not estop the legislature from enacting laws intended for the public good." See also Stone v. Mississippi, 101 U.S. 814 (1880), where the Court said that no "legislature can bargain away the public health or the public morals." (Should the state be required to give compensation in cases like *Manigault* and *Stone*? This question is explored in section H2 infra.)

In a sense, the police power exception is a direct outgrowth of the position that the contract clause does not prohibit prospective regulation. The police power itself is in place at the time that the contract is entered. Notice, though, that a police power "exception" might swallow the contract clause. If any effort that might be described as an attempt to protect the "general welfare" can justify a retroactive interference with rights acquired by contract, the clause furnishes little or no barrier to contractual impairments. Even debtor-relief legislation would be upheld, so long as the police power were understood to be sufficiently broad. For many years after *Manigault*, however, this risk did not materialize. The reason is that the police power comprehended a relatively narrow category of permissible government ends and certainly did not include the various forms of redistributive regulation characteristic of modern government.

3. *Regulation versus impairment.* In a number of early cases, the Court struggled with the issue of whether particular measures were "regulations" interfering with remedies or genuine impairments of contractual obligations. In this view, delays in time for performance might not interfere with "substantial rights"; they merely affected the remedy. But the distinction between rights and remedies might well be thought artificial. The line here was an "obscure" one, Worthen Co. v. Kavanaugh, 295 U.S. 56 (1935), but it did allow for some flexibility on the part of the legislature. See, e.g., Honeyman v. Jacobs, 306 U.S. 539 (1939) (upholding statute designed to prevent creditor from getting more by remedy than he would have obtained had contract been performed); Richmond Mortgage & Loan Corp. v. Wachovia Bank & Trust Co., 300 U.S. 124 (1937) (same); Curtis v. Whitney, 13 Wall. 68 (1872) (upholding statute providing that a deed may not issue unless a written notice had been served on any previous owner or occupant at least three months before; statute interfered with rights received by plaintiff who had received certificate entitling her to deed before statute had been passed); Bronson v. Kinzie, 1 How. 311 (1843) (noting that state may shorten the statute of limitations period or provide what articles may be liable to execution on judgment). See generally Hale, The Supreme Court and the Contract Clause, 57 Harv. L. Rev. 512, 621, 852 (1944); B. Wright, supra.

The following case is the starting point for modern contracts clause law.

Home Building & Loan Association v. Blaisdell
290 U.S. 398 (1934)

[In the midst of the Great Depression, Minnesota passed a mortgage moratorium law to provide relief for homeowners threatened with foreclosure. The law, passed in 1933, declared an emergency and said that during the emergency period, courts could postpone mortgage sales and periods of redemption. Its provisions were to apply "only during the continuance of the emergency and in no event beyond May 1, 1935." Pursuant to the statute, Blaisdell's period of redemption was extended to May 1, 1935, subject in general to the payment by Blaisdell of $40 a month through the extended period. There was no dispute that the extension modified the lenders' contractual rights of foreclosure. The lower court upheld the statute.]

MR. CHIEF JUSTICE HUGHES delivered the opinion of the Court.

In determining whether the provision for this temporary and conditional relief exceeds the power of the State by reason of the clause in the Federal Constitution prohibiting impairment of the obligations of contracts, we must consider the relation of emergency to constitutional power, the historical setting of the contract clause, the development of the jurisprudence of this Court in the construction of that clause, and the principles of construction which we may consider to be established.

Emergency does not create power. Emergency does not increase granted power or remove or diminish the restrictions imposed upon power granted or reserved. The Constitution was adopted in a period of grave emergency. Its grants of power to the Federal Government and its limitations of the power of the States were determined in the light of emergency and they are not altered by emergency. . . .

[In] the construction of the contract clause, the debates in the Constitutional Convention are of little aid. But the reasons which led to the adoption of that clause [are] not left in doubt. [The] widespread distress following the revolutionary period, and the plight of debtors, had called forth in the States an ignoble array of legislative schemes for the defeat of creditors and the invasion of contractual obligations. Legislative interferences had been so numerous and extreme that the confidence essential to prosperous trade had been undermined and the utter destruction of credit was threatened. . . .

[The] constitutional provision [is] qualified by the measure of control which the State [retains] to safeguard the vital interests of its people. [Not] only are existing laws read into contracts in order to fix obligations as between the parties, but the reservation of essential attributes of sovereign power is also read into contracts as a postulate of the legal order. The policy of protecting contracts against impairment presupposes the maintenance of a government by virtue of which contractual relations are worth while, — a government which retains adequate authority to secure the peace and good order of society. This principle of harmonizing the constitutional prohibition with the necessary residuum of state power has had progressive recognition in the decisions of this Court. . . .

The legislature cannot "bargain away the public health or the public morals." [The] question is not whether the legislative action affects contracts incidentally, or directly or indirectly, but whether the legislation is addressed to a legitimate end and the measures taken are reasonable and appropriate to that end. [It is argued] that the state power may be addressed directly to the prevention of the enforcement of contracts only when these are of a sort which the legislature in its discretion may denounce as being in themselves hostile to public morals, or public health, safety or welfare, or where the prohibition is merely of injurious practices; that interference with the enforcement of other and valid contracts according to appropriate legal procedure, although the interference is temporary and for a public purpose, is not permissible. . . .

Undoubtedly, whatever is reserved of state power must be consistent with the fair intent of the constitutional limitation of that power. The reserved power cannot be construed so as to destroy the limitation, nor is the limitation to be construed to destroy the reserved power in its essential aspects. They must be construed in harmony with each other. This principle precludes a construction which would permit the State to adopt as its policy the repudiation of debts or the destruction of contracts or the denial of means to enforce them. But it does not follow that conditions may not arise in which a temporary restraint of enforcement may be [constitutional]. . . .

[There] has been a growing appreciation of public needs and of the necessity of finding ground for a rational compromise between individual rights and public welfare. The settlement and consequent contraction of the public domain, the pressure of a constantly increasing density of population, the interrelation of the activities of our people and the complexity of our economic interests, have inevitably led to an increased use of the organization of society in order to protect the very bases of individual opportunity. Where, in earlier days, it was thought that only the concerns of individuals or of classes were involved, and that those of the State itself were touched only remotely, it has later been found that the fundamental interests of the State are directly affected; and that the question is no longer merely that of one party to a contract as against another, but of the use of reasonable means to safeguard the economic structure upon which the good of all depends.

It is no answer to say that this public need was not apprehended a century ago, or to insist that what the provision of the Constitution meant to the vision of that day it must mean to the vision of our time. If by the statement that what the Constitution meant at the time of its adoption it means today, it is intended to say that the great clauses of the Constitution must be confined to the interpretation which the framers, with the conditions and outlook of their time, would have placed upon them, the statement carries its own refutation. It was to guard against such a narrow conception that Chief Justice Marshall uttered the memorable warning — "We must never forget that it is *a constitution* we are expounding" [McCulloch v. Maryland] — "a constitution intended to endure for ages to come, and consequently, to be adapted to the various *crises* of human affairs." When we are dealing with the words of the Constitution, "we must realize that they have called into life a being the development of which could not have been foreseen completely by the most gifted of its begetters. . . . The case before us must be considered in the light of our whole experience and not merely in that of what was said a hundred years ago."

Nor is it helpful to attempt to draw a fine distinction between the intended meaning of the words of the Constitution and their intended application. When we consider the contract clause and the decisions which have expounded it in harmony with the essential reserved power of the States to protect the security of their peoples, we find no warrant for the conclusion that the clause has been warped by these decisions from its proper significance or that the founders of our Government would have interpreted the clause differently had they had occasion to assume that responsibility in the conditions of the later day. The vast body of law which has been developed was unknown to the fathers, but it is believed to have preserved the essential content and the spirit of the Constitution. With a growing recognition of public needs and the relation of individual right to public security, the court has sought to prevent the perversion of the clause through its use as an instrument to throttle the capacity of the States to protect their fundamental interests. This development is a growth from the seeds which the fathers planted. [The] principle of this development is, as we have seen, that the reservation of the reasonable exercise of the protective power of the State is read into all contracts. . . .

Applying the criteria established by our decisions we conclude:

1. An emergency existed in Minnesota which furnished a proper occasion for the exercise of the reserved power of the State to protect the vital interests of the community. [The] finding of the legislature and state court has support in the facts of which we take judicial notice. . . .

2. The legislation was addressed to a legitimate end, that is, the legislation was not for the mere advantage of particular individuals but for the protection of a basic interest of society.

3. In view of the nature of the contracts in question — mortgages of unquestionable validity — the relief afforded and justified by the emergency, in order not to contravene the constitutional provision, could only be of a character appropriate to that emergency and could be granted only upon reasonable conditions.

4. The conditions upon which the period of redemption is extended do not appear to be unreasonable. . . .

5. The legislation is temporary in operation. It is limited to the exigency which called it forth.

We are of the opinion that the Minnesota statute as here applied does not violate the contract clause of the Federal Constitution. Whether the legislation is wise or unwise as a matter of policy is a question with which we are not concerned. . . .

The judgment of the Supreme Court of Minnesota is affirmed.

MR. JUSTICE SUTHERLAND, dissenting.

[A] provision of the Constitution, it is hardly necessary to say, does not admit of two distinctly opposite interpretations. It does not mean one thing at one time and an entirely different thing at another time. If the contract impairment clause, when framed and adopted, meant that the terms of a contract for the payment of money could not be altered [by] a state statute enacted for the relief of hardly pressed debtors to the end and with the effect of postponing payment or enforcement during and because of an economic or financial emergency, it is but to state the obvious to say that it means the same now. . . .

Following the Revolution, and prior to the adoption of the Constitution, the American people found themselves in a greatly impoverished condition. Their commerce had been well-nigh annihilated. They were not only without luxuries, but in great degree were destitute of the ordinary comforts and necessities of life. In these circumstances they incurred indebtedness in the purchase of imported goods and otherwise, far beyond their capacity to pay. [The] circulation of depreciated currency became common. [This] state of things alarmed all thoughtful men, and led them to seek some effective remedy. . . .

The defense of the Minnesota law is made upon grounds which were discountenanced by the makers of the Constitution. [That] defense should not now succeed, because it constitutes an effort to overthrow the constitutional provision by an appeal to facts and circumstances identical with those which brought it into existence. With due regard for the processes of logical thinking, it legitimately cannot be urged that conditions which produced the rule may now be invoked to destroy it. . . .

It is quite true also that [general] statutes to put an end to lotteries, the sale or manufacture of intoxicating liquors, the maintenance of nuisances, to protect the public safety, etc., although they have the indirect effect of absolutely destroying private contracts previously made in contemplation of a continuance of the state of affairs then in existence but subsequently prohibited, have been uniformly upheld as not violating the contract impairment clause. The distinction between legislation of that character and the Minnesota statute, however, is readily observable. . . .

[The Minnesota] statute denies appellant for a period of two years the ownership and possession of the property — an asset which [is] of substantial character, and which possibly may turn out to be of great value. The statute, therefore, is not merely a modification of the remedy; it effects a material and injurious change in the obligation. . . .

If the provisions of the Constitution be not upheld when they pinch as well as when they comfort, they may as well be abandoned. Being unable to reach any other conclusion than that the Minnesota statute infringes the constitutional restriction under review, I have no choice but to say so.

[Justices Van Devanter, McReynolds, and Butler joined in this dissent.]

Note: Market Ordering and Constitutional Interpretation

1. *The changing scope of the police power.* The Court had long held that the contracts clause did not forbid states from impairing the obligations of contract if the impairment resulted from an exercise of the "police power," the state's traditional authority to protect its citizens from public harms. Why, then, was *Blaisdell* such an important case? The real shift came in the novel understanding of what the police power allowed, an understanding that resulted in a dramatic expansion of the permissible ends of government that would support a contractual impairment. That shift was part of the New Deal reformulation of the constitutional structure; it contemplated a large role for government in readjusting the benefits and burdens of social life. Was the Court correct to broaden the police power? Didn't the Minnesota statute implicate precisely the evil at which the clause was originally aimed?

Compare the Court's narrow interpretation of the contracts clause to its broad interpretation of free speech protection in the first amendment. See generally Chapter 7 infra. Is the Court justified in using the contracts clause to invalidate far less than its drafters intended, while using the first amendment to invalidate far more? Note in particular that the state's "police power" may be used only in very narrow circumstances to justify infringements on freedom of expression.

2. Blaisdell *and constitutional interpretation.* The Court suggests that the framers' own expected application of the contracts clause is not controlling. Indeed,

it says that the notion that "what the Constitution meant at the time of its adoption it means today [carries] its own refutation." This is one of the most candid statements by the Court that a constitutional decision is not based on the framers' original expected application. Is the statement consistent with the "new originalism?" See section A, supra. Is this merely another way of saying that "it is a Constitution we are expounding," or might it go far beyond what Chief Justice Marshall had in mind?

3. *The contracts clause after* Blaisdell. After *Blaisdell,* what does the contracts clause prohibit? The answer appears to be very little. Consider, for example, El Paso v. Simmons, 379 U.S. 497 (1965). The case grew out of a 1910 sale by the state of Texas, by contract, of public land. State law provided for the termination of the contract and forfeiture of the land for nonpayment of interest, and in such a case, the purchaser could reinstate his claim on request and with payment of delinquent interest. In 1941, the state amended the law, limiting reinstatement rights to claims asserted five years from the date of forfeiture. The 1941 law operated to impair rights acquired under the 1910 contract.

The Court upheld the law, referring to its purpose "to restore confidence in the stability and integrity of land titles" and to end "the imbroglio over land titles in Texas." Justice Black, in dissent, compared the Court's decision to "balancing away the First Amendment's unequivocally guaranteed rights." See also East New York Bank v. Hahn, 326 U.S. 230 (1945) (upholding an extension of mortgage moratorium legislation); Veix v. Sixth Ward, 310 U.S. 32 (1940) (upholding right of states to restrict right of certificate holders to withdraw or recover amounts of certificates).

UNITED STATES TRUST CO. v. NEW JERSEY, 431 U.S. 1 (1977). A New Jersey statute, in conjunction with a parallel New York provision, repealed a statutory covenant, made by the two states in 1962, that limited the ability of the Port Authority of New Jersey and New York to subsidize rail passenger transportation from revenues and reserves. The covenant had been adopted in order to provide special security for the bondholders against competition from rail transportation. But New Jersey and New York later concluded that subsidization was necessary to improve conservation and to advance rail transit. The Court, in an opinion by Justice Blackmun, invalidated the repeal of the covenant:

"The trial court concluded that repeal of the 1962 covenant was a valid exercise of New Jersey's police power because repeal served important public interests in mass transportation, energy conservation, and environmental protection. [Yet] the Contract Clause limits otherwise legitimate exercises of state legislative authority, and the existence of an important public interest is not always sufficient to overcome that limitation. . . .

"[In] applying this standard, [complete] deference to a legislative assessment of reasonableness and necessity is not appropriate [when] the State's self-interest is at stake. A governmental entity can always find a use for extra money, especially when taxes do not have to be raised. If a State could reduce its financial obligations whenever it wanted to spend the money for what it regarded as an important public purpose, the Contract Clause would provide no protection at all. . . .

"Mass transportation, energy conservation, and environmental protection are goals that are important and of legitimate public concern. Appellees contend that these goals are so important that any harm to bondholders from repeal of the 1962 covenant is greatly outweighed by the public benefit. We do not accept this invitation to engage in a utilitarian comparison of public benefit and private loss. Contrary to Mr. Justice Black's fear, expressed in sole dissent in [*El Paso*], the Court has not 'balanced away' the limitation on state action imposed by the Contract Clause. Thus a State cannot refuse to meet its legitimate financial obligations simply because it would prefer to spend the money to promote the public good rather than the private welfare of its creditors. We can only sustain the repeal of the 1962 covenant if that impairment was both reasonable and necessary to serve the admittedly important purposes claimed by the State.

"The more specific justification offered for the repeal of the 1962 covenant was the States' plan for encouraging users of private automobiles to shift to public transportation. The States intended to discourage private automobile use by raising bridge and tunnel tolls and to use the extra revenue from those tolls to subsidize improved commuter railroad service. Appellees contend that repeal of the 1962 covenant was necessary to implement this plan because the new mass transit facilities could not possibly be self-supporting and the covenant's 'permitted deficits' level had already been exceeded. We reject this justification because the repeal was neither necessary to achievement of the plan nor reasonable in light of the circumstances.

"The determination of necessity can be considered on two levels. First, it cannot be said that total repeal of the covenant was essential; a less drastic modification would have permitted the contemplated plan without entirely removing the covenant's limitations on the use of Port Authority revenues and reserves to subsidize commuter railroads. Second, without modifying the covenant at all, the States could have adopted alternative means of achieving their twin goals of discouraging automobile use and improving mass transit. . . .

"During the 12-year period between adoption of the covenant and its repeal, public perception of the importance of mass transit undoubtedly grew because of increased general concern with environmental protection and energy conservation. But these concerns were not unknown in 1962, and the subsequent changes were of degree and not of kind. We cannot say that these changes caused the covenant to have a substantially different impact in 1974 than when it was adopted in 1962. And we cannot conclude that the repeal was reasonable in the light of changed circumstances."

Justice Brennan, joined by Justices White and Marshall, dissented:

"One of the fundamental premises of our popular democracy is that each generation of representatives can and will remain responsive to the needs and desires of those whom they represent. Crucial to this end is the assurance that new legislators will not automatically be bound by the policies and undertakings of earlier days. In accordance with this philosophy, the Framers of our Constitution conceived of the Contract Clause primarily as protection for economic transactions entered into by purely private parties, rather than obligations involving the State itself. The Framers fully recognized that nothing would so jeopardize the legitimacy of a system of government that relies upon the ebbs and flows of politics to 'clean out the rascals' than the possibility that those same rascals might perpetuate their policies simply by locking them into binding contracts. [But Contract] Clause challenges [are] to be resolved by according unusual deference to the lawmaking authority of state and local governments. . . .

"I would not want to be read as suggesting that the States should blithely proceed down the path of repudiating their obligations, financial or otherwise. Their credibility in the credit market obviously is highly dependent on exercising their vast lawmaking powers with self-restraint and [discipline]. [But the] role to be played by the Constitution is at most a limited one. [For] this Court should have learned long ago that the Constitution — be it through the Contract or Due Process Clause — can actively intrude into such economic and policy matters only if my Brethren are prepared to bear enormous institutional and social costs. Because I consider the potential dangers of such judicial interference to be intolerable, I dissent."

ALLIED STRUCTURAL STEEL CO. v. SPANNAUS, 438 U.S. 234 (1978). Allied Structural Steel Co. maintained an office in Illinois with thirty employees. The company operated a general pension plan under which it retained unrestricted rights (1) to amend the plan in whole or in part and (2) to terminate the plan and to distribute the assets at any time and for any reason. Employees were thus entitled to benefits if they worked until reaching age sixty-five and if the company remained in business and elected to continue the plan. The Minnesota legislature enacted a Private Pension Benefits Protection Act, under which employers would be subject to a "pension funding charge" if they terminated the plan or closed a Minnesota office. The charge was assessed if pension funds did not cover full pensions for at least ten years. Under the act, employers must satisfy the deficiency by purchasing deferred annuities, payable to employees at their normal retirement age. Periods of employment prior to the effective date of the act were to be included in the ten-year employment criterion. Allied Structural Steel attempted to terminate its operation in Minnesota; the state informed the company that it owed a pension funding charge of $185,000; and the company brought suit, claiming that the act unconstitutionally impaired its contractual obligations.

The Court, in an opinion by Justice Stewart, responded:

"There can be no question of the impact of the Minnesota Private Pension Benefits Protection Act upon the company's contractual relationships with its employees. [The] Contract Clause remains part of the Constitution. It is not a dead letter. . . .

"[If] the Contract Clause is to retain any meaning at all, [it] must be understood to impose *some* limits upon the power of a State to abridge existing contractual relationships, even in the exercise of its otherwise legitimate police power. . . .

"In applying these principles to the present case, the first inquiry must be whether the state law has, in fact, operated as a substantial impairment of a contractual relationship. [Minimal] alteration of contractual obligations may end the inquiry at its first stage. Severe impairment, on the other hand, will push the inquiry to a careful examination of the nature and purpose of the state legislation. . . .

"Here, the company's contracts of employment with its employees included as a fringe benefit or additional form of compensation, the pension plan. The company's maximum obligation was to set aside each year an amount based on the plan's requirements for vesting. [The] company [had] no reason to anticipate that its employees' pension rights could become vested except in accordance with the terms of the plan. It relied heavily, and reasonably, on this legitimate contractual expectation in calculating its annual contributions to the pension fund.

"The effect of Minnesota's Private Pension Benefits Protection Act on this contractual obligation was severe. The company was required in 1974 to have made its contributions throughout the pre-1974 life of its plan as if employees' pension rights had vested after 10 years, instead of vesting in accord with the terms of the plan. Thus a basic term of the pension contract — one on which the company had relied for 10 years — was substantially modified. [The] Act thus forced a current recalculation of the past 10 years' contributions based on the new, unanticipated 10-year vesting requirement.

"[Moreover,] the retroactive state-imposed vesting requirement was applied only to those employers who terminated their pension plans or who, like the company, closed their Minnesota offices. The company was thus forced to make all the retroactive changes in its contractual obligations at one time. By simply proceeding to close its office in Minnesota, a move that had been planned before the passage of the Act, the company was assessed an immediate pension funding charge of approximately $185,000.

"[Yet] there is no showing in the record before us that this severe disruption of contractual expectations was necessary to meet an important general social problem. . . .

"[The statute] clearly has an extremely narrow focus. It applies only to private employers who have at least 100 employees, at least one of whom works in Minnesota, and who have established voluntary private pension plans, qualified under §401 of the Internal Revenue Code. And it applies only when such an employer closes his Minnesota office or terminates his pension plan. Thus, this law can hardly be characterized, like the law at issue in the *Blaisdell* case, as one enacted to protect a broad societal interest rather than a narrow class. [This] legislation, imposing a sudden, totally unanticipated, and substantial retroactive obligation upon the company to its employees, was not enacted to deal with a situation remotely approaching the broad and desperate emergency economic conditions of the early 1930's — conditions of which the Court in *Blaisdell* took judicial notice.

"[If] the Contract Clause means anything at all, it means that Minnesota could not constitutionally do what it tried to do to the company in this case."

Justice Brennan, joined by Justices White and Marshall, dissented:

"The Act does not relieve either the employer or his employees of any existing contract obligation. Rather, the Act simply creates an additional, supplemental duty of the employer, no different in kind from myriad duties created by a wide variety of legislative measures which defeat settled expectations but which have nonetheless been sustained by this Court. For this reason, the Minnesota Act, in my view, does not implicate the Contract Clause in any way. . . .

"[Under] the Court's opinion, any law that may be characterized as 'super-imposing' new obligations on those provided for by contract is to be regarded as creating 'sudden, substantial, and unanticipated burdens' and then to be sub-jected to the most exacting scrutiny. The validity of such a law will turn upon whether judges see it as a law that deals with a generalized social problem, whether it is temporary (as few will be) or permanent, whether it operates in an area previously subject to regulation, and, finally, whether its duties apply to a broad class of persons. [The] necessary consequence of the extreme malleability of these rather vague criteria is to vest judges with broad subjective discretion to protect property interests that happen to appeal to them.

"To permit this level of scrutiny of laws that interfere with contract-based expectations is an anomaly. There is nothing sacrosanct about expectations rooted in contract that justify according them a constitutional immunity denied other property rights."

Note: United States Trust, Spannaus, *and the Nonrevival of the Contracts Clause*

1. *"Heightened scrutiny" for a state's abrogation of its own contracts.* Two features of *United States Trust* are noteworthy: first, the willingness to adopt "heightened scrutiny" for a state's abrogation of its own contracts; second, the willingness to invalidate a state law under the contracts clause. The first element is in one sense familiar in constitutional law. The Court frequently adopts "heightened scrutiny" — in the form of a careful examination of means/ends connections and a search for less restrictive alternatives — when there is special reason for suspicion that an impermissible motivation is at work.

But which way does the state's involvement cut? Might not heightened scrutiny be appropriate when a state decides to bargain away its sovereign powers in a contract with a private party? One the other hand, one might think that the fact that a state abrogates a contract to which it is a party gives reason to believe that a state's self-interest, rather than some public good, is at stake. Is there a difference between a state's interest and some public good? If so, what is the impermissible end that the Court thought might be at work when a state abrogates its own contract? Note also the possibility that the Court was concerned with effects as well as purpose — the special obligation of government not to break its own promises.

2. *The police power and means/ends connections under the contracts clause.* In *United States Trust*, why did the Court conclude that the means/ends connection was too weak? Was *Spannaus* a stronger or weaker case in this regard?

3. *Subsequent developments. United States Trust* and *Spannaus* suggested that the Court might revive the contracts clause as a substantive constraint on legislation. But shortly thereafter the Court returned to its previous, more deferential approach. Consider in this regard Energy Reserves Group v. Kansas Power & Light, 459 U.S. 400 (1983). The contract at issue contained a price escalator clause that provided that, if a governmental authority fixes a price for natural gas that is higher than the price specified in the contract, the contract price would be increased to that level. A Kansas statute provided that the increase produced by a federal statute could not be taken into account in determining the contract price. The Energy Reserves Group attacked the statute on the ground that it impaired the contractual obligation by allowing for an increase in the price. In an opinion by Justice Blackmun, the Court responded:

> The threshold inquiry is "whether the state law has, in fact, operated as a substantial impairment of contractual relationship." The severity of the impairment is said to increase the level of scrutiny to which the legislation will be subjected. [In] determining the extent of the impairment, we are to consider whether the industry the complaining party has entered has been regulated in the past.
>
> If the state regulation constitutes a substantial impairment, the State, in justification, must have a significant and legitimate public purpose behind the regulation, such as the remedying of a broad and general social or economic problem. Furthermore, since *Blaisdell*, the Court has indicated that the public purpose need not be addressed to an emergency or temporary situation. One legitimate state interest is the elimination of unforeseen windfall profits. The requirement of a legitimate public purpose guarantees that the State is exercising its police power, rather than providing a benefit to special interests.
>
> Once a legitimate public purpose has been identified, the next inquiry is whether the adjustment of the rights and responsibilities of contracting parties is based upon

reasonable conditions and is of a character appropriate to the public purpose jus-tifying the legislation's adoption. Unless the state is itself a contracting party, "as is customary in reviewing economic and social regulation," [courts] properly defer to legislative judgment as to the necessity and reasonableness of a particular measure.

The Court upheld the statute. First, it suggested that there was no substantial impairment: "Significant here is the fact that the parties are operating in a heavily regulated industry." Thus, "ERG knew its contractual rights were subject to alteration by state price regulation. Price regulation existed and was foreseeable as the type of law that would alter contract obligations."

The Court also concluded that any contractual impairment "rests on, and is prompted by, significant and legitimate state interests." The Court referred to two such interests. The first was the protection of consumers from the escalation of prices caused by deregulation. "The State could reasonably find that higher gas prices have caused and will cause hardship among those who use gas heat but must exist on limited fixed incomes." The second interest was "correcting the imbalance between the interstate and intrastate markets by permitting intrastate prices to rise only to the [interstate] level." Justice Powell, joined by Chief Justice Burger and Justice Rehnquist, concurred, agreeing that there had been no substantial impairment but refusing to reach the question whether any impair-ment had in the circumstances been justified.

Consider also Exxon Corp. v. Eagerton, 462 U.S. 176 (1983), which involved a state statute prohibiting producers of oil and gas from passing on to consumers the costs of any increase in a state's severance tax. The Court replied that the con-tracts clause did not prohibit "a generally applicable rule of conduct designed to advance 'broad social interest,' protecting consumers from excessive prices." Do *Energy Reserves* and *Exxon* implicitly overrule *Spannaus*?

The Court adopted a similarly deferential stance in the face of a contract clause claim in Keystone Bituminous Coal Association v. DeBenedictis, 480 U.S. 470 (1987). A Pennsylvania statute had the effect of voiding damage waivers that coal companies had obtained from surface owners for damage to surface property caused by mining. The Court, in an opinion by Justice Stevens, upheld the statute. In the Court's view, the state had a strong public interest in preventing the environmental harm caused by the mining. Moreover, in cases where the state itself is not a contracting party, courts should defer to the legislative judg-ment as to the necessity and reasonableness of the contractual abrogation.

In General Motors Corp. v. Romein, 503 U.S. 181 (1992), the Court upheld a substantial change in a workers' compensation program. In 1980, Michigan had raised the level of maximum benefits; in 1981, it allowed employers to decrease the level of the relevant benefits to disabled employees who could receive com-pensation from other employer-funded sources. The Michigan Supreme Court ruled that under the 1981 law employers could reduce benefits to all workers, including those injured before the statute's effective date. In 1987, the legislature repudiated this ruling and said that employers must make refunds to the previ-ously disabled workers. According to the United States Supreme Court, there was no problem under the contracts clause because the allegedly impaired contracts contained "no contractual agreement regarding the specific workers' compensa-tion terms allegedly at issue." The Court rejected the claim that their statutory right to rely on past payment periods as "closed" was incorporated by law into employment contracts. "[W]e have not held that all state regulations are implied terms of every contract entered into while they are effective."

The Court added:

> The 1987 statute did not change the legal enforceability of the employment con-
> tracts here. Moreover, petitioners' suggestion that we should read every workplace
> regulation into the private arrangements of employers and employees would
> expand the definition of contract so far that the constitutional provision would
> lose its anchoring purpose, i.e., "[enabling] individuals to order their personal
> and business affairs according to their particular needs and interests." Instead,
> the Clause would protect against all changes in legislation.

4. *Concluding thoughts.* Consider the following evaluation: Modern review
under the contract clause is substantially identical to modern rationality review
under the due process and equal protection clauses. In all three contexts, the
Court engages in the same inquiry, identifying the legitimate state interests and
requiring a rough relation between the legitimate state interests and the measure
under review. But the class of legitimate state interests is extremely broad; the
Court has permitted any justification other than raw political power (the "special
interest" problem referred to in the *Energy Reserves* case). This idea seems to
follow from an understanding, prominent in the post–New Deal period, that
existing distributions are never prepolitical and often unjust, and therefore a
matter for democratic control. Moreover, the fit between the legitimate interest
and the measure under review need not be close.

Is it troublesome that the Court has adopted the same test in all three areas,
even though the contracts clause looks like an explicit limitation on contractual
impairment?

2.   *The Eminent Domain Clause*

The eminent domain clause provides, "[N]or shall private property be taken for
public use, without just compensation." The clause has two requirements: (1) All
takings must be for public use, and (2) even takings that are for public use must be
accompanied by compensation. Consider here, as with the contracts clause,
whether and how interpretation of the eminent domain clause differs from interpretation of the first amendment on the one hand, and treatment of "implied"
fundamental rights on the other. Consider also how the clause interacts with
competing notions about the role of government in redistributing wealth.

What is the evil at which the eminent domain clause is aimed? The history of
the clause is quite sparse, but the answer involves at least some sorts of redistribution of resources. The clause reflects a judgment that, if government is seeking
to produce some public benefit (the public use requirement), it is appropriate
that the payment come from the public at large — taxpayers — rather than from
identifiable individuals. The compensation requirement operates as insurance to
that effect. Note, in addition, that compensation tends to reduce the likelihood
that a transfer has occurred merely to benefit A at the expense of B. Public
willingness to pay for the transfer suggests that some general public good is at
work. We begin with the logically prior public use requirement.

In Hawaii Housing Authority v. Midkiff, 467 U.S. 229 (1984), a unanimous
Court, in an opinion by Justice O'Connor upheld a Hawaii statute that authorized Hawaii Housing Authority (HHA) to condemn the property on behalf of
tenants when it found that acquisition by the state effectuated the public purposes

of the Act. The Court held that the land condemnation was for a "public use." It quoted from its earlier decision, Berman v. Parker, 348 U.S. 26 (1954), where it had upheld a District of Columbia urban renewal plan:

> We deal [with] what traditionally has been known as the police power. An attempt to define its reach or trace its outer limits is fruitless, for each case must turn on its own facts. The definition is essentially the product of legislative determinations addressed to the purposes of government, purposes neither abstractly nor historically capable of complete definition. Subject to specific constitutional limitations, when the legislature has spoken, the public interest has been declared in terms well-nigh conclusive. In such cases the legislature, not the judiciary, is the main guardian of the public needs to be served by social legislation.

The *Midkiff* Court characterized its role as "extremely narrow."

> To be sure, the Court's cases have repeatedly stated that "one person's property may not be taken for the benefit of another private person without a justifying public purpose, even though compensation be paid." [But] where the exercise of the eminent domain power is rationally related to a conceivable public purpose, the Court has never held a compensated taking to be proscribed by the [clause].

In this case, the Court found that the statute was rationally related to the legitimate public purpose of reducing "the perceived social and economic evils of a land [oligopoly]" in Hawaii and that the condemnation was therefore constitutionally permissible.

KELO V. CITY OF NEW LONDON, 545 U.S. 469 (2005). Decades of decline in New London, Connecticut, caused state and city officials to target the city for economic revitalization. In 1998, Pfizer Inc. announced that it would build a $300 million research facility in the city. In an effort to capitalize on the new Pfizer facility, the city council approved a redevelopment plan requiring the acquisition of a ninety-acre area adjoining the facility. The plan called for the creation of a waterfront conference hotel, a marina, restaurants, retail stores, and offices. Petitioners, including Wilhelmina Dery, who had been born in her house in 1918 and lived there all her life, challenged the condemnation of their property pursuant to the plan on the ground that it violated the public use requirement.

Justice Stevens delivered the opinion of the Court:

"[Petitioners] urge us to adopt a new bright-line rule that economic development does not qualify as a public use. Putting aside the unpersuasive suggestion that the City's plan will provide only purely economic benefits, neither precedent nor logic supports petitioners' proposal. Promoting economic development is a traditional and long-accepted function of government. There is, moreover, no principled way of distinguishing economic development from the other public purposes that we have recognized. . . .

"It is further argued that without a bright-line rule nothing would stop a city from transferring citizen A's property to citizen B for the sole reason that citizen B will put the property to a more productive use and thus pay more taxes. Such a one-to-one transfer of property, executed outside the confines of an integrated development plan, is not presented in this case. While such an unusual exercise of government power would certainly raise a suspicion that a private purpose was afoot, the hypothetical cases posited by petitioners can be confronted if and when they arise. They do not warrant the crafting of an artificial restriction on the concept of public use.

"Alternatively, petitioners maintain that for takings of this kind we should require a 'reasonable certainty' that the expected public benefits will actually accrue. Such a rule, however, would represent an even greater departure from our precedent. 'When the legislature's purpose is legitimate and its means are not irrational, our cases make clear that empirical debates over the wisdom of takings — no less than debates over the wisdom of other kinds of socioeconomic legislation — are not to be carried out in the federal courts.' [*Midkiff*.]"

Justice Kennedy filed a concurring opinion. While agreeing with the majority that a rational basis approach was the appropriate level of review in public use cases, he emphasized that deferential review "does not [alter] the fact that transfers intended to confer benefits on particular, favored private entities, and with only incidental or pretextual public benefits, are forbidden by the Public Use Clause." According to Justice Kennedy, "[a] court applying rational-basis review under the Public Use Clause should strike down a taking that, by a clear showing, is intended to favor a particular private party, with only incidental or pretextual public benefits, just as a court applying rational-basis review under the Equal Protection Clause must strike down a government classification that is clearly intended to injure a particular class of private parties, with only incidental or pretextual public justifications." In addition, Justice Kennedy observed that

> a more stringent standard of review [might] be appropriate for a more narrowly drawn category of takings. There may be private transfers in which the risk of undetected impermissible favoritism of private parties is so acute that a presumption (rebuttable or otherwise) of invalidity is warranted under the Public Use Clause. This demanding level of scrutiny, however, is not required simply because the purpose of the taking is economic development.

Justice O'Connor dissented in an opinion joined by Chief Justice Rehnquist and Justices Scalia and Thomas:

"Today, the Court abandons [a] long-held, basic limitation on government power. Under the banner of economic development, all private property is now vulnerable to being taken and transferred to another private owner, so long as it might be upgraded — i.e., given to an owner who will use it in a way that the legislature deems more beneficial to the public — in the process. To reason, as the Court does, that the incidental public benefits resulting from the subsequent ordinary use of private property render economic development takings 'for public use' is to wash out any distinction between private and public use of property — and thereby effectively to delete the words 'for public use' from the Takings Clause of the Fifth Amendment."

Justice O'Connor distinguished *Midkiff* and Berman v. Parker on the ground that these cases had involved condemnation of property that was imposing an "affirmative harm on society — in *Berman* through blight resulting from extreme poverty and in *Midkiff* through oligopoly resulting from extreme wealth."

Justice Thomas filed a separate dissent in which he argued that the public use clause, as originally understood, allowed to government to take property only if after the condemnation the government owned the property or the public had a legal right to use the property. Consider also the following observations at the end of Justice Thomas's opinion:

"Allowing the government to take property solely for public purposes is bad enough, but extending the concept of public purpose to encompass any economically beneficial goal guarantees that these losses will fall disproportionately on poor communities. Those communities are not only systematically less likely to put their lands to the highest and best social use, but are also the least politically powerful. If ever there were justification for intrusive judicial review of constitutional provisions that protect 'discrete and insular minorities,' surely that principle would apply with great force to the powerless groups and individuals the Public Use Clause protects. . . .

"[The] legacy of this Court's 'public purpose' test [is] an unhappy one. In the 1950's, no doubt emboldened in part by the expansive understanding of 'public use' this Court adopted in *Berman*, cities 'rushed to draw plans' for downtown development. 'Of all the families displaced by urban renewal from 1949 through 1963, 63 percent of those whose race was known were nonwhite, and of these families, 56 percent of nonwhites and 38 percent of whites had incomes low enough to qualify for public housing, which, however, was seldom available to them.' Public works projects in the 1950's and 1960's destroyed predominantly minority communities in St. Paul, Minnesota, and Baltimore, Maryland. In 1981, urban planners in Detroit, Michigan, uprooted the largely 'lower-income and elderly' Poletown neighborhood for the benefit of the General Motors Corporation. Urban renewal projects have long been associated with the displacement of blacks; '[i]n cities across the country, urban renewal came to be known as "Negro removal."' Over 97 percent of the individuals forcibly removed from their homes by the 'slum-clearance' project upheld by this Court in *Berman* were black. Regrettably, the predictable consequence of the Court's decision will be to exacerbate these effects."

Note: The Public Use Requirement and the Takings Clause

1. *Public use after* Midkiff *and* Kelo. The public use requirement is designed to ensure against what might be called "naked" wealth transfers — takings from A in order to benefit B, supported by no "public" end, and only by a preference for B, or by B's political power. Compare Justice Chase's position in Calder v. Bull, Chapter 1 supra, also complaining about a taking from A to benefit B. Note that the requirement assumes that there are "public" ends that differ from the mere exercise of political power. Is the assumption warranted?

Assuming that it is, does the Court's deferential standard of review adequately protect against the evil it identifies?

2. *Poletown.* Consider Poletown Neighborhood Council v. City of Detroit, 410 Mich. 616, 304 N.W.2d 455 (1981), referred to in Justice Thomas's *Kelo* dissent, in which the city of Detroit condemned a neighborhood in order to permit General Motors to build a plant on the land. Was the taking for public use? Suppose the plant would employ a large number of people now on welfare or without jobs. If a General Motors plant was condemned and transferred for use by the community, would there also be a public use? Is it troublesome if the answer to both questions is yes? See also Rubenfeld, Usings, 102 Yale L.J. 1077 (1993), which argues that the takings clause is directed only against governmental "usings" of private property, that is, against situations in which government officials actually use the property that has been taken.

3. *Public use, compensation, and "takings."* Notice that even if a taking is for a public use, the owner is still entitled to "just compensation." But the compensation right applies only if "property" is "taken." What should count as a government "taking?" Consider the following:

Pennsylvania Coal Co. v. Mahon
260 U.S. 393 (1922)

MR. JUSTICE HOLMES delivered the opinion of the Court.

This is a bill in equity brought by the [plaintiffs] to prevent the Pennsylvania Coal Company from mining under their property in such way as to remove the supports and cause a subsidence of the surface and of their house. The bill sets out a deed executed by the Coal Company in 1878, under which the plaintiffs claim. The deed conveys the surface, but in express terms reserves the right to remove all the coal under the same, and the grantee takes the premises with the risk, and waives all claim for damages that may arise from mining out the coal. But the plaintiffs say that whatever may have been the Coal Company's rights, they were taken away by an Act of Pennsylvania, [commonly] known there as the Kohler Act. . . .

The statute forbids the mining of anthracite coal in such way as to cause the subsidence of, among other things, any structure used as a human habitation, with certain exceptions, including among them land where the surface is owned by the owner of the underlying coal and is distant more than one hundred and fifty feet from any improved property belonging to any other person. As applied to this case the statute is admitted to destroy previously existing rights of property and contract. The question is whether the police power can be stretched so far.

Government hardly could go on if to some extent values incident to property could not be diminished without paying for every such change in the general law. As long recognized, some values are enjoyed under an implied limitation and must yield to the police power. But obviously the implied limitation must have its limits, or the contract and due process clauses are gone. One fact for consideration in determining such limits is the extent of the diminution. When it reaches a certain magnitude, in most if not in all cases there must be an exercise of eminent domain and compensation to sustain the act. So the question depends upon the particular facts. The greatest weight is given to the judgment of the legislature, but it always is open to interested parties to contend that the legislature has gone beyond its constitutional power. . . .

[It] is our opinion that the act cannot be sustained as an exercise of the police power, so far as it affects the mining of coal under streets or cities in places where the right to mine such coal has been reserved. [What] makes the right to mine coal valuable is that it can be exercised with profit. To make it commercially impracticable to mine certain coal has very nearly the same effect for constitutional purposes as appropriating or destroying it. This we think that we are warranted in assuming that the statute does. . . .

The rights of the public in a street purchased or laid out by eminent domain are those that it has paid for. If in any case its representatives have been so short sighted as to acquire only surface rights without the right of support, we see no more authority for supplying the latter without compensation than there was for taking the right of way in the first place and refusing to pay for it because the public wanted it very much. The protection of private property in the Fifth Amendment presupposes that it is wanted for public use, but provides that it shall not be taken for such use without compensation. [When] this seemingly absolute protection is found to be qualified by the police power, the natural tendency of human nature is to extend the qualification more and more until at last private property disappears. But that cannot be accomplished in this way under the Constitution of the United States.

The general rule at least is, that while property may be regulated to a certain extent, if regulation goes too far it will be recognized as a taking. [In] general it is not plain that a man's misfortunes or necessities will justify his shifting the damages to his neighbor's shoulders. We are in danger of forgetting that a strong public desire to improve the public condition is not enough to warrant achieving the desire by a shorter cut than the constitutional way of paying for the change. As we already have said, this is a question of degree — and therefore cannot be disposed of by general propositions.

[We] assume, of course, that the statute was passed upon the conviction that an exigency existed that would warrant it, and we assume that an exigency exists that would warrant the exercise of eminent domain. But the question at bottom is upon whom the loss of the changes desired should fall. So far as private persons or communities have seen fit to take the risk of acquiring only surface rights, we cannot see that the fact that their risk has become a danger warrants the giving to them greater rights than they bought. . . .

Decree reversed.

MR. JUSTICE BRANDEIS, dissenting. . . .

[Coal] in place is land; and the right of the owner to use his land is not absolute. He may not so use it as to create a public nuisance; and uses, once harmless, may, owing to changed conditions, seriously threaten the public welfare. Whenever they do, the legislature has power to prohibit such uses without paying compensation; and the power to prohibit extends alike to the manner, the character and the purpose of the use. Are we justified in declaring that the Legislature of Pennsylvania has, in restricting the right to mine anthracite, exercised this power so arbitrarily as to violate the Fourteenth Amendment?

Every restriction upon the use of property imposed in the exercise of the police power deprives the owner of some right theretofore enjoyed, and is, in that sense, an abridgment by the State of rights in property without making compensation. But restriction imposed to protect the public health, safety or morals from dangers threatened is not a taking. The restriction here in question is merely the prohibition of a noxious use. The property so restricted remains in the possession of its owner. The state does not appropriate it or make any use of it. The State merely prevents the owner from making a use which interferes with paramount rights of the public. Whenever the use prohibited ceases to be noxious, — as it may because of further change in local or social conditions, — the restriction will have to be removed and the owner will again be free to enjoy his property as heretofore.

The restriction upon the use of this property cannot, of course, be lawfully imposed, unless its purpose is to protect the public. But the purpose of a restriction does not cease to be public, because incidentally some private persons may thereby receive gratuitously valuable special benefits. [Restriction] upon use does not become inappropriate as a means, merely because it deprives the owner of the only use to which the property can then be profitably put. [Nor] is a restriction imposed through exercise of the police power inappropriate as a means, merely because the same end might be effected through exercise of the power of eminent domain, or otherwise at public expense. Every restriction upon the height of buildings might be secured through acquiring by eminent domain the right of each owner to build above the limiting height; but it is settled that the State need not resort to that power. . . .

[If] by mining anthracite coal the owner would necessarily unloose poisonous gasses, I suppose no one would doubt the power of the State to prevent the mining, without buying his coal fields. And why may not the State, likewise, without paying compensation, prohibit one from digging so deep or excavating so near the surface, as to expose the community to like dangers? . . .

It is said that one fact for consideration in determining whether the limits of the police power have been exceeded is the extent of the resulting diminution in value; and that here the restriction destroys existing rights of property and con-tract. But values are relative. [For] aught that appears the value of the coal kept in place by the restriction may be negligible as compared with the value of the whole property, or even as compared with that part of it which is represented by the coal remaining in place and which may be extracted despite the statute.

[A] prohibition of mining which causes subsidence of [structures] and facilities is obviously enacted for a public purpose. [Yet] it is said that these provisions of the act cannot be sustained as an exercise of the police power where the right to mine such coal has been reserved. The conclusion seems to rest upon the assumption that in order to justify such exercise of the police power there must be "an average reciprocity of advantage" as between the owner of the property restricted and the rest of the community; and that here such reciprocity is absent. Reciprocity of advantage is an important consideration, and may even be an essential, where the State's power is exercised for the purpose of conferring benefits upon the property of a neighborhood. [But] where the police power is exercised, not to confer benefits upon property owners, but to protect the public from detriment and danger, there is, in my opinion, no room for considering reciprocity of advantage.

Miller v. Schoene

276 U.S. 272 (1928)

MR. JUSTICE STONE delivered the opinion of the Court.

Acting under the Cedar Rust Act of Virginia, [the] state entomologist ordered the plaintiffs in error to cut down a large number of ornamental red cedar trees growing on their property, as a means of preventing the communication of a rust or plant disease with which they were infected to the apple orchards in the vicinity. The plaintiffs in error appealed from the order to the circuit court of Shenandoah county which, after a hearing and a consideration of evidence, affirmed the order and allowed to plaintiffs in error $100 to cover the expense of removal of the cedars. Neither the judgment of the court nor the statute as interpreted allows compensation for the value of the standing cedars or the decrease in the market value of the realty caused by their destruction whether considered as ornamental trees or otherwise. . . .

[Cedar] rust is an infectious plant disease in the form of a fungoid organism which is destructive of the fruit and foliage of the apple, but without effect on the value of the cedar. Its life cycle has two phases which are passed alternately as a growth on red cedar and on apple trees. It is communicated by spores from one to the other over a radius of at least two miles. It appears not to be communicable between trees of the same species but only from one species to the other, and other plants seem not to be appreciably affected by it. The only practicable method of controlling the disease and protecting apple trees from its ravages is the destruction of all red cedar trees, subject to the infection, located within two miles of apple orchards.

The red cedar, aside from its ornamental use, has occasional use and value as lumber. It is indigenous to Virginia, is not cultivated or dealt in commercially on any substantial scale, and its value throughout the state is shown to be small as compared with that of the apple orchards of the state. Apple growing is one of the principal agricultural pursuits in Virginia. The apple is used there and exported in large quantities. Many millions of dollars are invested in the orchards, which furnish employment for a large portion of the population, and have induced the development of attendant railroad and cold storage facilities.

On the evidence we may accept the conclusion of the Supreme Court of Appeals that the state was under the necessity of making a choice between the preservation of one class of property and that of the other wherever both existed in dangerous proximity. It would have been none the less a choice if, instead of enacting the present statute, the state, by doing nothing, had permitted serious injury to the apple orchards within its borders to go on unchecked. When forced to such a choice the state does not exceed its constitutional powers by deciding upon the destruction of one class of property in order to save another which, in the judgment of the legislature, is of greater value to the public. It will not do to say that the case is merely one of a conflict of two private interests and that the misfortune of apple growers may not be shifted to cedar owners by ordering the destruction of their property; for it is obvious that there may be, and that here there is, a preponderant public concern in the preservation of the one interest over the other. [Where] the public interest is involved preferment of that interest over the property interest of the individual, to the extent even of its destruction, is one of the distinguishing characteristics of every exercise of the police power which affects property. . . .

We need not weigh with nicety the question whether the infected cedars constitute a nuisance according to the common law; or whether they may be so declared by statute. For where, as here, the choice is unavoidable, we cannot say that its exercise, controlled by considerations of social policy which are not unreasonable, involves any denial of due process.

[Reversed.]

Penn Central Transportation Co. v. New York City
438 U.S. 104 (1978)

Mr. Justice Brennan delivered the opinion of the Court.

The question presented is whether a city may, as part of a comprehensive program to preserve historical landmarks and historic districts, place restrictions on the development of individual historic landmarks — in addition to those imposed by applicable zoning ordinances — without effecting a "taking" requiring the payment of "just compensation." Specifically, we must decide whether the application of New York City's Landmarks Preservation Law to the parcel of land occupied by Grand Central Terminal has "taken" its owners' property in violation of the Fifth and Fourteenth Amendments.

Over the past 50 years, all 50 States and over 500 municipalities have enacted laws to encourage or require the preservation of buildings and areas with historic or aesthetic importance. These nationwide legislative efforts have been precipitated by two concerns. The first is recognition that, in recent years, large numbers of historic structures, landmarks, and areas have been destroyed without adequate consideration of either the values represented therein or the possibility of preserving the destroyed properties for use in economically productive ways. The second is a widely shared belief that structures with special historic, cultural, or architectural significance enhance the quality of life for all. Not only do these buildings and their workmanship represent the lessons of the past and embody precious features of our heritage, they serve as examples of quality for today. . . .

New York City [adopted] its Landmarks Preservation Law in 1965. The city acted from the conviction that "the standing of [New York City] as a worldwide tourist center and world capital of business, culture and government" would be threatened if legislation were not enacted to protect historic landmarks and neighborhoods from precipitate decisions to destroy or fundamentally alter their character. . . .

The New York City law is typical of many urban landmark laws in that its primary method of achieving its goals is not by acquisitions of historical properties, but rather by involving public entities in land-use decisions affecting these properties and providing services, standards, controls, and incentives that will encourage preservation by private owners and users. While the law does place special restrictions on landmark properties as a necessary feature to the attainment of its larger objectives, the major theme of the law is to ensure the owners of any such properties both a "reasonable return" on their investments and maximum latitude to use their parcels for purposes not inconsistent with the preservation goals.

[The Court noted that the law was administered by the Landmarks Preservation Commission, which identified especially important properties as designated "landmarks" and "historic districts."]

[Final] designation as a landmark results in restrictions upon the property owner's options concerning use of the landmark site. First, the law imposes a duty upon the owner to keep the exterior features of the building "in good repair" to assure that the law's objectives not be defeated by the landmark's falling into a state of irremediable disrepair. [Second,] the Commission must approve in advance any proposal to alter the exterior architectural features of the landmark or to construct any exterior improvement on the landmark site, thus ensuring that decisions concerning construction on the landmark site are made with due consideration of both the public interest in the maintenance of the structure and the landowner's interest in use of the property. . . .

In the event an owner wishes to alter a landmark site, [procedures] are available through which administrative approval may be obtained. . . .

Although the designation of a landmark and landmark site restricts the owner's control over the parcel, designation also enhances the economic position of the landmark owner in one significant respect. Under New York City's zoning laws, owners of real property who have not developed their property to the full extent permitted by the applicable zoning laws are allowed to transfer development rights to contiguous parcels on the same city block. . . .

This case involves the application of New York City's Landmarks Preservation Law to Grand Central Terminal (Terminal). [The Court noted that the terminal is one of New York City's most famous buildings and that it had been designated as occupying a landmark site. Penn Central submitted two plans to the Commission for construction of an office building atop the terminal. One plan called for a fifty-five-story office building; another called for tearing down some of its facade and constructing a fifty-three-story office building. The Commission denied permission to go forward with the plans. With respect to the second plan, the Commission observed, "To protect a Landmark, one does not tear it down." With respect to the first plan, the Commission referred primarily to the adverse effect of the proposed tower on the dramatic view of the terminal from Park Avenue South. "To balance a 55-story office tower above a flamboyant Beaux-Arts facade seems nothing more than an aesthetic joke. Quite simply, the tower would overwhelm the Terminal by its sheer mass."]

The [issue is whether] the restrictions imposed by New York City's law upon appellants' exploitation of the Terminal site effect a "taking" of appellants' property for a public use within the meaning of the Fifth Amendment. While this Court has recognized that the "Fifth Amendment's guarantee . . . [is] designed to bar Government from forcing some people alone to bear public burdens which, in all fairness and justice, should be borne by the public as a whole," Armstrong v. United States, 364 U.S. 40, 49 (1960), this Court, quite simply, has been unable to develop any "set formula" for determining when "justice and fairness" require that economic injuries caused by public action be compensated by the government, rather than remain disproportionately concentrated on a few persons.

In engaging in [essentially] ad hoc, factual inquiries, the Court's decisions have identified several factors that have particular significance. The economic impact of the regulation on the claimant and, particularly, the extent to which the regulation has interfered with distinct investment-backed expectations are, of course, relevant considerations. [So,] too, is the character of the governmental action. A "taking" may more readily be found when the interference with property can be characterized as a physical invasion by government, see, e.g., United States v. Causby, 328 U.S. 256 (1946), than when interference arises from some public program adjusting the benefits and burdens of economic life to promote the common good.

"Government hardly could go on if to some extent values incident to property could not be diminished without paying for every such change in the general law," [Mahon], and this Court has accordingly recognized, in a wide variety of contexts, that government may execute laws or programs that adversely affect recognized economic values. Exercises of the taxing power are one obvious example. A second are the decisions in which this Court has dismissed "taking" challenges on the ground that, while the challenged government action caused economic harm, it did not interfere with interests that were sufficiently bound up with the reasonable expectations of the claimant to constitute "property" for Fifth Amendment purposes. . . .

More importantly for the present case, in instances in which a state tribunal reasonably concluded that "the health, safety, morals, or general welfare" would be promoted by prohibiting particular contemplated uses of land, this Court has upheld land-use regulations that destroyed or adversely affected recognized real property interests. [Zoning] laws are, of course, the classic example, see Euclid v. Ambler Realty Co., 272 U.S. 365 (1926) (prohibition of industrial use). . . .

Zoning laws generally do not affect existing uses of real property, but "taking" challenges have also been held to be without merit in a wide variety of situations when the challenged governmental actions prohibited a beneficial use to which individual parcels had previously been devoted and thus caused substantial individualized harm. . . .

[We] emphasize what is not in dispute. Because this Court has recognized, in a number of settings, that States and cities may enact land-use restrictions or controls to enhance the quality of life by preserving the character and desirable aesthetic features of a city, [appellants] do not contest that [the] restrictions imposed on its parcel are appropriate means of securing the purposes of the New York City law. [Appellants also] accept for present purposes both that the parcel of land occupied by Grand Central Terminal must, in its present state, be regarded as capable of earning a reasonable return, and that the transferable development rights [TDRs] afforded appellants by virtue of the Terminal's designation as a landmark are valuable, even if not as valuable as the rights to construct above the Terminal. . . .

[Appellants] first observe that the airspace above the Terminal is a valuable property interest. [They] urge that the Landmarks Law has deprived them of any gainful use of their "air rights" above the Terminal and that, irrespective of the value of the remainder of their parcel, the city has "taken" their right to this superjacent airspace, thus entitling them to "just compensation" measured by the fair market value of these air rights.

[The] submission that appellants may establish a "taking" simply by showing that they have been denied the ability to exploit a property interest that they heretofore had believed was available for development is quite simply untenable. [Our] jurisprudence does not divide a single parcel into discrete segments and attempt to determine whether rights in a particular segment have been entirely abrogated. In deciding whether a particular governmental action has effected a taking, this Court focuses rather both on the character of the action and on the nature and extent of the interference with rights in the parcel as a whole — here, the city tax block designated as the "landmark site."

Secondly, appellants [argue] that [the law] effects a "taking" because its operation has significantly diminished the value of the Terminal site. [Appellants] argue that New York City's regulation of individual landmarks is fundamentally different from zoning or from historic-district legislation because the controls imposed by New York City's law apply only to individuals who own selected properties.

Stated baldly, appellants' position appears to be that the only means of ensuring that selected owners are not singled out to endure financial hardship for no reason is to hold that any restriction imposed on individual landmarks pursuant to the New York City scheme is a "taking" requiring the payment of "just compensation." [Contrary] to appellants' suggestions, landmark laws are not like discriminatory [zoning:] that is, a land-use decision which arbitrarily singles out a particular parcel for different, less favorable treatment than the neighboring ones. [In] contrast to discriminatory zoning, [the] New York City law embodies a comprehensive plan to preserve structures of historic or aesthetic interest wherever they might be found in the city, and [over] 400 landmarks and 31 historic districts have been designated pursuant to this plan.

Equally without merit is the related argument that the decision to designate a structure as a landmark "is inevitably arbitrary or at least subjective, because it is basically a matter of taste," [thus] unavoidably singling out individual landowners for disparate and unfair treatment. [A] landmark owner has a right to judicial review of any Commission decision, and, [there] is no basis whatsoever for a conclusion that courts will have any greater difficulty identifying arbitrary or discriminatory action in the context of landmark regulation than in the context of classic zoning or indeed in any other context.

Next, appellants observe that New York City's law differs from zoning laws and historic-district ordinances in that the Landmarks Law does not impose identical or similar restrictions on all structures located in particular physical communities. It follows, they argue, that New York City's law is inherently incapable of producing the fair and equitable distribution of benefits and burdens of governmental action [which] they maintain is a constitutional requirement if "just compensation" is not to be afforded. It is, of course, true that the Landmarks Law has a more severe impact on some landowners than on others, but that in itself does not mean that the law effects a "taking." Legislation designed to promote the general welfare commonly burdens some more than others.

In any event, appellants' repeated suggestions that they are solely burdened and unbenefited is factually inaccurate. This contention overlooks the fact that the New York City law applies to vast numbers of structures in the city in addition to the Terminal — all the structures contained in the 31 historic districts and over 400 individual landmarks, many of which are close to the Terminal. . . .

Appellants' final broad-based attack would have us treat the law as an instance, like that in United States v. Causby, in which government, acting in an enterprise capacity, has appropriated part of their property for some strictly governmental purpose. [But the] Landmarks Law neither exploits appellants' parcel for city purposes nor facilitates nor arises from any entrepreneurial operations of the city.

[The] Landmarks Law's effect is simply to prohibit appellants or anyone else from occupying portions of the airspace above the Terminal, while permitting appellants to use the remainder of the parcel in a gainful fashion. . . .

[We] now must consider whether the interference with appellants' property is of such a magnitude that "there must be an exercise of eminent domain and compensation to sustain [it]." [Mahon.] [That] inquiry may be narrowed to the question of the severity of the impact of the law on appellants' parcel, and its resolution in turn requires a careful assessment of the impact of the regulation on the Terminal site. [The] New York City law does not interfere in any way with the present uses of the Terminal. Its designation as a landmark [contemplates] that appellants may continue to use the property precisely as it has been used for the past 65 years; as a railroad terminal containing office space and concessions. So the law does not interfere with what must be regarded as Penn Central's primary expectation concerning the use of the parcel [or its ability] to obtain a "reasonable return" on its investment.

Appellants, moreover, exaggerate the effect of the law on their ability to make use of the air rights above the Terminal. [First, nothing] the Commission has said or done suggests an intention to prohibit any construction above the Terminal.

[Second,] it is not literally accurate to say that they have been denied all use of even [preexisting] air rights. [The] New York courts here supportably found that [the transferable development] rights afforded are valuable. While these rights may well not have constituted "just compensation" if a "taking" had occurred, the rights nevertheless undoubtedly mitigate whatever financial burdens the law has imposed on appellants and, for that reason, are to be taken into account in considering the impact of regulation.

On this record, we conclude that the application of New York City's Landmarks Law has not effected a "taking" of appellants' property. The restrictions imposed are substantially related to the promotion of the general welfare and not only permit reasonable beneficial use of the landmark site but also afford appellants opportunities further to enhance not only the Terminal site proper but also other properties.

Affirmed.

MR. JUSTICE REHNQUIST, with whom [CHIEF JUSTICE BURGER] and MR. JUSTICE STEVENS join, dissenting.

Only in the most superficial sense of the word can this case be said to involve "zoning." Typical zoning restrictions may, it is true, so limit the prospective uses of a piece of property as to diminish the value of that property in the abstract because it may not be used for the forbidden purposes. But any such abstract decrease in value will more than likely be at least partially offset by an increase in value which flows from similar restrictions as to use on neighboring properties. All property owners in a designated area are placed under the same restrictions, not only for the benefit of the municipality as a whole but also for the common benefit of one another. In the words of Mr. Justice Holmes, speaking for the Court in [Mahon,] there is "an average reciprocity of advantage."

Where a relatively few individual buildings, all separated from one another, are singled out and treated differently from surrounding buildings, no such reciprocity exists. [And] the cost associated with landmark legislation is likely to be of a completely different order of magnitude than that which results from the imposition of normal zoning restrictions. [Under] the historic-landmark preservation scheme adopted by New York, the property owner is under an affirmative duty to *preserve* his property *as a landmark* at his own expense. . . .

[Before] the city of New York declared Grand Central Terminal to be a landmark, Penn Central could have used its "air rights" over the Terminal to build a multistory office building, at an apparent value of several million dollars per year. Today, the Terminal cannot be modified in any form, including the erection of additional stories, without the permission of the Landmark Preservation Commission, a permission which appellants, despite good-faith attempts, have so far been unable to obtain. . . .

The nuisance exception to the taking guarantee is not coterminous with the police power itself. The question is whether the forbidden use is dangerous to the safety, health, or welfare of others. . . .

Appellees are not prohibiting a nuisance. The record is clear that the proposed addition to the Grand Central Terminal would be in full compliance with zoning, height limitations, and other health and safety requirements. Instead, appellees are seeking to preserve what they believe to be an outstanding example of beaux arts architecture. [The] city of New York, because of its unadorned admiration for the design, has decided that the owners of the building must preserve it unchanged for the benefit of sightseeing New Yorkers and tourists.

[Even] where the government prohibits a noninjurious use, the Court has ruled that a taking does not take place if the prohibition applies over a broad cross section of land and thereby "secure[s] an average reciprocity of advantage." [Mahon.] [While] zoning at times reduces *individual* property values, the burden is shared relatively evenly and it is reasonable to conclude that on the whole an individual who is harmed by one aspect of the zoning will be benefited by another.

Here, however, a multimillion dollar loss has been imposed on appellants; it is uniquely felt and is not offset by any benefits flowing from the preservation of some 400 other "landmarks" in New York City. Appellees have imposed a substantial cost on less than one one-tenth of one percent of the buildings in New York City for the general benefit of all its people. It is exactly this imposition of general costs on a few individuals at which the "taking" protection is directed. . . .

[A] taking does not become a noncompensable exercise of police power simply because the government in its grace allows the owner to make some "reasonable" use of his property. [Appellees] contend that, even if they have "taken" appellants' property, TDK's constitute "just compensation." [Because] the record on appeal is relatively slim, I would remand to the Court of Appeals for a determination of whether TDK's constitute a "full and perfect equivalent for the property taken."

KEYSTONE BITUMINOUS COAL ASSOCIATION v. DEBENEDICTIS, 480 U.S. 470 (1987). In this case, the Court upheld a modern-day analogue of the Kohler Act, invalidated in Pennsylvania Coal Co. v. Mahon, supra. A Pennsylvania statute enacted in 1966 prohibited mining that caused subsidence damage to public buildings, dwellings used for human habitation, and cemeteries. The administrative agency charged with enforcing the statute generally required 50 percent of the coal beneath such structures to be kept in place as a means of providing surface support. Moreover, the agency was authorized to revoke mining permits if removal of coal caused damage to such structures and the operator had not repaired or paid for the damage.

Justice Stevens delivered the Court's opinion: "Petitioners assert that disposition of their takings claim calls for no more than a straightforward application of the Court's decision in [Pennsylvania Coal]. Although there are some obvious similarities between the cases, we agree with the [court below] that the similarities are far less significant than the [differences]. . . .

"The two factors that the [Pennsylvania Coal] Court considered relevant have become integral parts of our takings analysis. We have held that land use regulation can effect a taking if it 'does not substantially advance legitimate state interests, . . . or denies an owner economically viable use of his land.' Agins v. Tiburon, 447 U.S. 255, 260 (1980).

"Application of these tests to petitioners' challenge demonstrates that they have not satisfied their burden of showing that the Subsidence Act constitutes a taking. First, unlike the Kohler Act, the character of the governmental action involved here leans heavily against finding a taking; the [state] has acted to arrest what it perceives to be a significant threat to the common welfare. Second, there is no record in this case to support a finding, similar to the one the Court made in Pennsylvania Coal, that the Subsidence Act makes it impossible for petitioners to profitably engage in their business, or that there has been undue interference with their investment-backed expectations. . . .

"Unlike the Kohler Act, [the] Subsidence Act does not merely involve a balancing of the private economic interests of coal companies against the private interests of the surface owners. The Pennsylvania Legislature specifically found that important public interests are served by enforcing a policy that is designed to minimize subsidence in certain areas. . . .

"The second factor that distinguishes this case from Pennsylvania Coal is the finding in that case that the Kohler Act made mining of 'certain coal' commercially impracticable. In this case, by contrast, petitioners have not shown any deprivation significant enough to satisfy the heavy burden placed upon one alleging a regulatory taking. . . .

"The parties have stipulated that enforcement of the [50%] rule will require petitioners to leave approximately 27 million tons of coal in place. Because they own that coal but cannot mine it, they contend that Pennsylvania has appropriated it for the public purposes described in the Subsidence Act.

"[But the] 27 million tons of coal do not constitute a separate segment of property for takings law purposes. . . .

"We do not consider Justice Holmes' statement that the Kohler Act made mining of 'certain coal' commercially impracticable as requiring us to focus on the individual pillars of coal that must be left in place. . . .

"When the coal that must remain beneath the ground is viewed in the context of any reasonable unit of petitioners' coal mining operations and financial-backed expectations, it is plain that the petitioners have not come close to satisfying their burden of proving that they have been denied the economically viable use of that property."

Chief Justice Rehnquist, in an opinion joined by Justices Powell, O'Connor, and Scalia, dissented.

Note: "Takings" and the Police Power

1. *In general.* To what does one look to decide whether there has been a "taking" of private property? Almost all government action — to take familiar examples: zoning, minimum wage and maximum hour legislation, the relocation of a highway, or other land use regulation — diminishes the value of some people's property and increases the value of the property of other people. Redistribution in this sense is almost always the result, and often the purpose, of government action. If compensation was required in all such cases, there would, of course, be far less redistribution. The need to calculate and hand out compensation (costs independent of compensation "itself") would often prevent its occurrence. There is an additional problem: Many people are "winners" from regulation, and they are not taxed accordingly; if government must compensate, but does not tax, its own incentives may be skewed against beneficial activities. Where one sets the line between taking and regulation will to a large degree determine how much redistribution (some of it perhaps efficient and just, some of it perhaps neither) will be permitted through the regulatory process.

2. *Distinguishing takings from regulation.* How does one tell whether there has been regulation or a taking? Some candidates for a test include the following.

a. *The extent of the intrusion.* Under this view, compensation will be required if, in Justice Holmes's words, regulation "goes too far." The compensation requirement is triggered by a significant invasion. But this approach raises the issue why the extent of the intrusion is relevant to the question whether compensation need be paid at all rather than to the question of the extent of compensation.

b. *The nature of the intrusion.* Under this approach, a court could take the notion of "taking" literally by examining whether property has "actually" been taken. Has there been, for example, a physical invasion? In fact, the Court has come close to holding that a physical invasion is a sufficient condition to find a taking. But compensation may not be required if the diminution in value produced by a regulatory measure does not actually "touch" the property in question — for example, occupational safety and health regulation, relocation of a highway, minimum wage legislation, or a zoning ordinance. Also relevant may be whether government has actually appropriated the property for its own or another's use rather than simply destroyed it.

Under this view, physical invasions present a stronger case for requiring compensation than government action that diminishes value without such an invasion. The theme of physical invasion is a prominent one in the law of eminent domain. But it is not easy to explain why government action that actually "invades" in a physical sense should be treated differently from government action that in some other way diminishes value. One response is that, where there has been a physical invasion, it is easy to identify those adversely affected, and one need not worry that the costs of identifying those people entitled to compensation will prevent necessary measures from going forward. Consider the zoning example, where the number of properties adversely affected may be extremely large and the costs of identifying them, calculating their losses, and compensating them may deter socially desirable measures. Cf. R. Posner, Economic Analysis of Law 40–48 (2d ed. 1977). Note, too, that there is no "givings" clause in the Constitution, allowing government to receive resources for the benefits that it grants to property owners.

c. *Balancing.* One might approach the takings versus regulation issue by asking: How important is the state's interest? How does it compare with the private interest? But consider, with respect to this approach, the view that "use of the balancing test for such a purpose seems to be a mistake, at best reflecting a careless confusion of two quite distinct questions. These are, first, whether a given measure would be in order assuming it was accompanied by compensation payments; and, second, whether the same measure, conceding that it would be proper under conditions of full compensation, ought to be enforced without payment of any compensation. The balancing test may have something to do with the first question, but cannot have anything to do with the second." Michelman, Property, Utility, and Fairness: Comments on the Ethical Foundations of "Just Compensation" Law, 80 Harv. L. Rev. 1165, 1193–1194 (1967). But note also a possible defense of a balancing approach as a means of testing whether the measure in question is "so obviously efficient as to quiet the potential outrage of persons 'unavoidably' sacrificed in its interest." Id. at 1235.

d. *The legitimacy of the state's interest: restraining harmful conduct, "mere" redistribution, and public benefit.* One might decide the takings question by asking, as the *Keystone* Court did, whether the state is attempting "merely" to redistribute property from one person to another or attempting instead to promote a more general good. In Lingle v. Chevron U.S.A., Inc., 544 U.S. 528 (2005), the Court repudiated the *Keystone* Court's statement that regulation can amount to a taking if it "does not substantially advance legitimate state interests." The court of appeals had struck down a Hawaii statute limiting the rent that oil companies could charge to dealers who leased service stations from the companies. The court of appeals reasoned that this measure did not "substantially advance" the state's interest in preventing concentration of the retail gasoline market and high prices for consumers, and that the statute therefore amounted to an uncompensated taking. The Supreme Court, in a unanimous decision written by Justice O'Connor, reversed. The Court held that, as an analytic matter, the "substantially advances" standard "prescribes an inquiry in the nature of a due process, not a takings, test, and that it has no proper place in our takings jurisprudence." The Court left open the possibility that a regulation that failed the "substantially advances" test might violate due process. It warned, however:

> The [formula] can be read to demand heightened means-ends review of virtually any regulation of private property. If so interpreted, it would require courts to scrutinize the efficacy of a vast array of state and federal regulations — a task for which courts are not well suited. Moreover, it would empower — and might often require — courts to substitute their predictive judgments for those of elected legislatures and expert agencies. . . .
>   We have long eschewed such heightened scrutiny when addressing substantive due process challenges to government regulation.

3. *Action and inaction.* In *Miller*, the Court stated that, if government had failed to act, "it would have been none the less a choice. [When] forced to such a choice the state does not exceed its constitutional powers by deciding upon the destruction of one class of property in order to save another." The implication is that government inaction is itself a form of regulation.

What consequences does this insight have for the eminent domain clause and the underlying principle of private property? Consider Sunstein, Naked Preferences and the Constitution, 84 Colum. L. Rev. 1689, 1776 (1984):

> The new conception of the market status quo as neither natural nor inviolate led the way toward a dramatically expanded understanding of the police power. [Indeed], the seeds of a destruction of the eminent domain clause may lie within the *Miller* Court's statement. If government inaction can be understood as government action — if a decision not to act is understood as an intrusion in the same way as "affirmative" regulation — then the traditional notion of private property [loses] much of its coherence.

Compare Arkansas Game & Fish Commission v. United States, 133 S. Ct. 511 (2012). The Commission owned a wildlife management area along the banks of the Black River and regularly harvested timber in the reserve as part of its forest management efforts. One hundred fifteen miles upstream from the management area is the Clearwater Dam (the Dam), constructed by the United States Corps of Engineers in 1948. Shortly after constructing the Dam, the Corps adopted a Water Control Manual, which determined the rates at which water would be released from the Dam. In 1993, the Corps approved a planned deviation from the release rate in response to requests from farmers to provide for a longer harvest period. To reduce accumulation of water in the lake behind the Dam, the Corps extended the period in which a high amount of water would be released, resulting in flooding in the management area above historical norms. The flooding resulted in the destruction of timber in the management area and necessitated costly reclamation measures. Had the Corps released the water at a lower rate, the farmers would have had a shorter harvest season, but the timber would not have been damaged. The Court, in a unanimous decision written by Justice Ginsburg, held that government-induced flooding can amount to a taking even if it is temporary in duration.

If the Corps had not released the water, the farmers would have had a shorter harvest season. Why wouldn't this have been a taking? Suppose that the management area would have been flooded if the Dam had not been built in the first place. Would release of the extra water still be a taking? Would the result be different if the Corps built the Dam but then tore it down? If the initial Water Control Manual had provided for release of water at the higher rate?

For an argument that the takings clause might make the government liable for regulatory inaction and that therefore "property owners could be constitutionally entitled either to governmental intervention on their behalf or to compensation if the government fails to act," see Serkin, Passive Takings: The State's Affirmative Duty to Protect Property, 113 Mich. L. Rev. 345 (2014). For a more general discussion of constitutional problems posed by government nonfeasance, see Chapter 9.

4. *Assorted cases.* Probably the best way to get a sense of eminent domain doctrine is to compare the holdings in different factual settings.

a. *Andrus v. Allard, 444 U.S. 51 (1979).* The Eagle Protection Act banned the sale of bald or golden eagle parts taken before the effective date of the statute. The act did not ban the possession or transportation of such parts. The Court upheld the statute, saying that government regulation often

> curtails some potential for the use or economic exploitation of private property. To require compensation in all such circumstances would effectively compel the government to regulate by purchase. [The] regulations challenged here do not compel the surrender of the artifacts, and there is no physical invasion or restraint upon them. Rather, a significant restriction has been imposed on one means of disposing of the artifacts. But the denial of one traditional property right does not always amount to a taking. At least where an owner possesses a full "bundle" of property rights, the destruction of one "strand" of the bundle is not a taking, because the aggregation must be viewed in its entirety. [It] is, to be sure, undeniable that the regulations here prevent the most profitable use of appellees' property. Again, however, that is not dispositive. When we review regulation, a reduction in the value of the property is not necessarily equated with a taking.

b. *Compare* Andrus *to Hodel v. Irving, 481 U.S. 704 (1987).* In the nineteenth century, Congress enacted a law that divided the communal property on the reservation of the Sioux Nation into individual allotments. The allotted lands were held in trust for the Indians by the United States, and after 1910 the allottees were permitted to dispose of their interests by will in accordance with regulations promulgated by the Secretary of the Interior. As successive generations came to hold the allotted lands, ownership became fractionated into extremely small, undivided interests, with the result that it became impractical to make productive use of the lands. To deal with this problem, Congress enacted the Indian Land Consolidation Act in 1983, which provided that undivided, fractional interests in trust land could not be devised, but instead would escheat to the tribe if the interest represented 2 percent or less of the total acreage of the tract and had earned its owner less than $100 in the previous year.

The Court, in an opinion by Justice O'Connor, held this escheat provision unconstitutional. "[The] regulation here amounts to virtually the abrogation of the right to pass on a certain type of property [to] one's heirs. In one form or another, the right to pass on property — to one's family in particular — has been part of the Anglo-American legal system since feudal times." The Court noted, however, that it would "surely" be permissible for the government to prevent owners from further subdividing the land among future heirs on pain of escheat and to abolish descent of such interest by rules of intestacy.

Justice Scalia, in a concurring opinion joined by Chief Justice Rehnquist and Justice Powell, noted that "the present statute, insofar as concerns the balance between rights taken and rights left untouched[, is] indistinguishable from the statute that was at issue in [*Allard*]" and that "in finding a taking today our decision effectively limits *Allard* to its facts." In another concurring opinion, Justice Brennan, joined by Justices Marshall and Blackmun, found "nothing in today's opinion that would limit [*Allard*]. Indeed, [I] am of the view that the unique negotiations giving rise to the property rights and expectations at issue here make this case the unusual one."

c. *Euclid v. Ambler Realty Co.*, 272 U.S. 365 (1926). *Euclid* involved a zoning ordinance. The tract at issue had been vacant and was held for purpose of sale and development for industrial uses; for such uses, it had a market value of about $10,000 per acre. The zoning ordinance would limit it to residential purposes, thus reducing its market value to $2,500 per acre.

The Court upheld the ordinance. It acknowledged that

the exclusion is in general terms of all industrial establishments, and it may thereby happen that not only offensive or dangerous industries will be excluded, but those which are neither offensive nor dangerous will share the same fate. But this is no more than happens in respect of many practice-forbidding laws which this Court has upheld although drawn in general terms so as to include individual cases that may turn out to be innocuous in themselves.

The Court went on to point to the various benefits of the zoning ordinance:

the segregation of residential, business, and industrial buildings will make it easier to provide fire apparatus suitable for the character and intensity of the development in each section; that it will increase the safety and security of home life; greatly tend to prevent street accidents, especially to children, by reducing the traffic and resulting confusion in residential sections; decrease noise and other conditions which produce or intensify nervous disorders; preserve a more favorable environment in which to rear children, etc.

In the Court's view, these factors were "sufficiently cogent to preclude us from saying, as it must be said before the ordinance can be declared unconstitutional, that such provisions are clearly arbitrary and unreasonable, having no substantial relation to the public health, safety, morals, or general welfare."

d. *Compare Kaiser Aetna v. United States, 444 U.S. 164 (1979), to United States v. Riverside Bayview Homes, 474 U.S. 121 (1985), and PruneYard Shopping Center v. Robins, 447 U.S. 74 (1980).* In *Kaiser Aetna*, the Army Corps of Engineers attempted to grant public access to Kuapa Pond, a lagoon in Hawaii that was contiguous to a navigable bay. Kaiser Aetna had obtained rights to use the lagoon and had dredged and filled parts of it, erected retaining walls, and built bridges. It also created accommodations for pleasure boats. Eventually there were about 1,500 marina waterfront lot lessees. Kaiser Aetna controlled access to and use of the marina and generally did not permit commercial use. The Army Corps of Engineers contended that Kaiser Aetna was required to allow public access to the lagoon, and that no compensation need be paid, since there was a federal navigational servitude on the property.

The Court concluded that "the Government's attempt to create a public right to access [goes] so far beyond ordinary regulation or improvement for navigation as to amount to a taking." The Court emphasized that (1) before Kaiser Aetna's improvements, the pond could not be used for navigation in interstate commerce; (2) the body of water was private property under Hawaiian law; (3) the intrusion at issue was on the right to exclude, "universally held to be a fundamental element of the property right"; and (4) there was an actual physical invasion.

In *Riverside Bayview Homes*, the Army Corps of Engineers issued regulations requiring landowners to secure permits before discharging fill material into wetlands adjacent to navigable bodies of water and their tributaries. The corps then brought this action against a landowner to enjoin respondents from placing fill material in adjacent wetlands. The district court granted the injunction, but the court of appeals reversed, holding that a narrow construction of the regulations was necessary in order to avoid a taking of private property without just compensation. The Court, in an opinion by Justice White, reversed the court of appeals. Although acknowledging that governmental land-use regulation may "under extreme circumstances" constitute a taking, the Court held that the mere assertion of regulatory jurisdiction does not amount to a taking: "A requirement that a person obtain a permit before engaging in a certain use of his or her property does not itself 'take' the property in any sense: after all, the very existence of a permit system implies that permission may be granted, leaving the landowner free to use the property as desired. Moreover, even if the permit is denied, there may be other viable uses available to the owner. Only when a permit is denied and the effect of the denial is to prevent 'economically viable' use of the land in question can it be said that a taking has occurred."

In *PruneYard*, the California Supreme Court had held that the state constitutional right of free speech compelled shopping center owners to allow protesters to exercise rights of free speech on shopping center property. The owners contended that there was a "taking" of their property. The Court said:

> Here the requirement that appellants permit appellees to exercise state-protected rights of free expression and petition on shopping center property clearly does not amount to an unconstitutional infringement of appellant's property rights under the Takings Clause. There is nothing to suggest that preventing appellants from prohibiting this sort of activity will unreasonably impair the value or use of their property as a shopping center. [The] decision of the California Supreme Court makes it clear that the PruneYard may restrict expressive activity by adopting time, place, and manner regulations. [Appellees] were orderly, and they limited their activity to the common areas of the shopping center.

What is the relevance of the last two sentences in this passage?

e. *Loretto v. Teleprompter Manhattan CATV Corp*, 458 U.S. 419 (1982). In *Loretto*, the issue was the constitutionality of a New York law providing that a landlord must permit a cable television company to install cable facilities on her property. The cable installation in the relevant case occupied portions of the plaintiff's roof and the side of her building. The Court concluded that the "permanent physical occupation authorized by government is a taking without regard to the public interests that it may serve." The Court added: "An owner suffers a special kind of injury when a stranger directly invades and occupies the owner's property. [The] traditional rule also avoids otherwise difficult line-drawing problems. [Whether] a permanent physical occupation has occurred presents relatively few problems of proof."

Is *Loretto* distinguishable from *PruneYard*?

The Court distinguished *Loretto* in FCC v. Florida Power Corp., 480 U.S. 245 (1987), and upheld a federal statute authorizing the Federal Communications Commission to regulate the rates utility companies charge cable operators for the use of utility poles. In a unanimous opinion written by Justice Marshall, the Court held that *Loretto* was inapplicable to these facts:

> [While] the statute we considered in *Loretto* specifically required landlords to permit permanent occupation of their property by cable companies, nothing in [this act gives] cable companies any right to occupy space on utility poles, or prohibits utility companies from refusing to enter into attachment agreements with cable operators. The Act authorizes the FCC [to] review the rents charged by public utility landlords who have voluntarily entered into leases with cable company tenants renting space on utility poles.

Compare Connolly v. Pension Benefit Guaranty Corp., 475 U.S. 211 (1986), upholding a statute requiring an employer withdrawing from a multiemployer pension plan to pay its proportionate share of the plan's unfunded vested benefits.

The Court relied on *Loretto* in Horne v. Dept. of Agriculture, 135 S. Ct. 1039 (2015), to invalidate a marketing order issued by the Department of Agriculture that required raisin growers to physically set aside a certain percentage of their crops for the government to dispose of in a way best suited to maintaining an orderly market. The order, issued under the Agricultural Marketing Agreement Act of 1937, gave the Raisin Administrative Committee, a government entity composed largely of growers appointed by the Secretary of Agriculture, the authority to determine the allocation. The Committee then disposed of the raisins, with raisin growers retaining an interest in any net proceeds from sales after deductions for export subsidies and the Committee's administrative expenses.

Petitioners refused to set aside raisins for the government, whereupon the government assessed a fine against them. Petitioners claimed that the assessment constituted a per se taking under *Loretto*. In an eight-to-one decision, the Court, per Chief Justice Roberts, agreed. The Court began its analysis by holding that the per se rule applied to the taking of personal, as well as real property. Although the Court had previously noted that regulation of personal property might make the property economically useless without constituting a taking, the same rule did not apply to the sort of direct appropriation that occurred in this case. Here, the actual raisins were transferred from the growers to the government and the growers lost "the entire 'bundle' of property rights in the appropriated raisins."

> The Government thinks it "strange" and the dissent "baffling" that the Hornes object to the reserve requirement, when they nonetheless concede that "the government may prohibit sale of raisins without effecting a per se taking." But that distinction flows naturally from the settled difference in our takings jurisprudence between appropriation and regulation. A physical taking of raisins and a regulatory limit on production may have the same economic impact on a grower. The Constitution, however, is concerned with means as well as ends.

This conclusion was not affected by the fact that the Government reserved to the growers a contingent interest in a portion of the value of the property. "[Once] there is a taking, as in the case of a physical appropriation, any payment from the

Government in connection with that action goes, at most, to the question of just compensation."

The Court also concluded that the requirement that growers relinquish some of the raisins could not be justified as a condition on permission to sell the remaining raisins in interstate commerce. (This portion of the opinion is discussed at page 990.)

Finally, the Court rejected the government's contention that the amount of compensation due should be reduced by the increased value of the raisins petitioner was able to sell due to the price support and other benefits from the regulatory program. (This portion of the opinion is discussed at page 993, supra.)

f. *United States v. Causby*, 328 U.S. 256 (1946). *Causby* raised the question whether frequent flights immediately above a landowner's property constituted a taking. The Court concluded that it did: "If, by reason of the frequency and altitude of the flights, respondents could not use this land for any purpose, their loss would be complete. It would be as complete as if the United States had entered upon the surface of the land and taken exclusive possession of it." See also Griggs v. Allegheny County, 369 U.S. 84 (1962).

g. *Is the takings clause violated when the government conditions the grant of a discretionary benefit on the recipient's willingness to give up property rights that could not be taken from him without compensation?*

In Bowen v. Gilliard, 483 U.S. 587 (1987), the Court considered a takings clause attack on an amendment to the Aid to Families with Dependent Children (AFDC) program that required recipient families to assign to the government child support payments received from a noncustodial parent for a child living in the covered household. The effect of the assignment was to reduce the level of support payments received by the household. Appellees argued that this reduction constituted a taking from the child because the child support payments could be legally used only for the individual child, while the compensating AFDC payments were available for the entire family. The Court, in an opinion by Justice Stevens, rejected the argument:

> Congress is not, by virtue of having instituted a social welfare program, bound to continue it at all, much less at the same benefit level. Thus, notwithstanding the technical legal arguments that have been advanced, it is imperative to recognize that the amendments at issue merely incorporate a definitional element into an entitlement program. It would be quite strange indeed if, by virtue of an offer to provide benefits to needy families through the entirely voluntary AFDC program, Congress or the States were deemed to have taken some of those very family members' property.

Compare *Bowen* to the following case.

NOLLAN v. CALIFORNIA COASTAL COMMISSION, 483 U.S. 825 (1987). The California Coastal Commission conditioned the grant of a permit to rebuild appellants' house on their transfer to the public of an easement across their beachfront property. The Court, in an opinion by Justice Scalia, held that the attempt to impose this condition was a taking:

"Had California simply required the [appellants] to make an easement across their beachfront available to the public on a permanent [basis] we have no doubt there would have been a taking. [We] think a 'permanent physical occupation' has occurred, for purposes of [*Loretto*], where individuals are given a permanent and continuous right to pass to and fro, so that the real property may continuously be traversed, even though no particular individual is permitted to station himself permanently upon the premises. . . .[2]

"Given, then, that requiring uncompensated conveyance of the easement outright would violate the Fourteenth Amendment, the question becomes whether requiring it to be conveyed as a condition for issuing a land use permit alters the outcome. . . .

"[If] the Commission attached to the permit some condition that would have protected the public's ability to see the beach notwithstanding construction of the new house — for example, a height limitation, a width restriction, or a ban on fences — so long as the Commission could have exercised its police power (as we [assume] it could) to forbid construction of the house altogether, imposition of the condition would also be constitutional. Moreover, [the] condition would be constitutional even if it consisted of the requirement that the [appellants] provide a viewing spot on their property for passersby with whose sighting of the ocean their new house would interfere. Although such a requirement [would] have to be considered a taking if it were not attached to a development permit, the Commission's assumed power to forbid construction of the house in order to protect the public's view of the beach must surely include the power to condition construction upon some concession by the owner, even a concession of property rights, that serves the same end. . . .

"The evident constitutional propriety disappears, however, if the condition substituted for the prohibition utterly fails to further the end advanced as the justification for the prohibition. When that essential nexus is eliminated, the situation becomes the same as if California law forbade shouting fire in a crowded theater, but granted dispensations to those willing to contribute $100 to the state treasury. [In] short, unless the permit condition serves the same governmental purpose as the development ban, the building restriction is not a valid regulation of land use but 'an out-and-out plan of extortion.' . . .

"Justice Brennan argues that imposition of the access requirement is not irrational. In his version of the Commission's argument, the reason for the requirement is that in its absence, a person looking toward the beach from the road will see a street of residential structures including the Nollans' new home and conclude that there is no public beach nearby. If, however, that person sees people passing and repassing along the dry sand behind the Nollans' home, he will realize that there is a public beach somewhere in the vicinity. The Commission's action, however, was based on the opposite factual finding that the wall of houses completely blocked the view of the beach and that a person looking from the road would not be able to see it at all.

2. "Justice Brennan [suggests] that the Commission's public announcement of its intention to condition the rebuilding of houses on the transfer of easements of access caused the Nollans to have 'no reasonable claim to any expectation of being able to exclude members of the public' from walking across their beach. . . . But the right to build on one's own property — even though its exercise can be subjected to legitimate permitting requirements — cannot remotely be described as a 'government benefit.' [Nor] are the Nollans' rights altered because they acquired the land well after the Commission had begun to implement its policy. So long as the Commission could not have deprived the prior owners of the easement without compensating them, the prior owners must be understood to have transferred their full property rights in conveying the lot." [Relocated footnote. — Eds.]

"Even if the Commission had made the finding that Justice Brennan proposes, however, it is not certain that it would suffice. [We] view the Fifth Amendment's property clause to be more than a pleading requirement, and compliance with it to be more than an exercise of cleverness and imagination. [Our] cases describe the condition for abridgement of property rights through the police power as '*substantially* advancing' a legitimate State interest. We are inclined to be particularly careful about the adjective where the actual conveyance of property is made a condition to the lifting of a land use restriction, since in that context there is heightened risk that the purpose is avoidance of the compensation requirement, rather than the stated police power objective."

Justice Brennan, joined by Justice Marshall, wrote a dissenting opinion:

"[The] Court imposes a standard of precision for the exercise of a State's police power that has been discredited for the better part of this century. . . .

"It is [by] now commonplace that this Court's review of the rationality of a State's exercise of its police power demands only that the State '*could rationally have decided*' that the measure adopted might achieve the State's objective. [Minnesota v. Clover Leaf Creamery Co.]

"The Court finds fault with [the Commission's conduct] because it regards the condition as insufficiently tailored to address the precise type of reduction in access produced by the new development. The Nollans' development blocks visual access, the Court tells us, while the Commission seeks to preserve lateral access along the coastline. Such a narrow conception of rationality, however, has long since been discredited as a judicial arrogation of legislative authority. . . .

"Even if we accept the Court's unusual demand for a precise match between the condition imposed and the specific type of burden on access created by the appellants, the State's action easily satisfies this requirement. First, the lateral access condition serves to dissipate the impression that the beach that lies behind the wall of homes along the shore is for private use only. It requires no exceptional imaginative powers to find plausible the Commission's point that the average person passing along the road in front of a phalanx of imposing permanent residences [is] likely to conclude that this particular portion of the shore is not open to the public. If, however, that person can see that numerous people are passing and repassing along the dry sand, this conveys the message that the beach is in fact open for use by the public. . . .

"The second flaw in the Court's analysis [is] more fundamental. The Court assumes that the only burden with which the Coastal Commission was concerned was blockage of visual access to the beach. This is incorrect. The Commission specifically stated in its report [that] '[t]he Commission finds that the applicants' proposed development would present an increase in view blockage, *an increase in private use of the shorefront,* and that this impact would burden the public's ability to traverse to and along the shorefront.'

"[Moreover,] appellants were clearly on notice when requesting a new development permit that a condition of approval would be a provision ensuring [the easement]. [In] this respect, this case is quite similar to Ruckelshaus v. Monsanto Co., 467 U.S. 986 (1984). In *Monsanto,* the respondent had submitted trade data to the Environmental Protection Agency for the purpose of obtaining registration of certain pesticides. [The] Court conceded that the data in question constituted property under state law. It also found, however, that certain of the data had been submitted to the agency after Congress had made clear that only limited confidentiality would be given data submitted for registration purposes. [The] Court rejected respondent's argument that the requirement that it relinquish some confidentiality imposed an unconstitutional condition upon receipt of a Government benefit."[10]

Justices Blackmun and Stevens also filed dissenting opinions.

Note: Nollan, *Unconstitutional Conditions, and Other Problems*

1. *Unconstitutional conditions.* Nollan might well be seen as an unconstitutional conditions case. On this view, *Nollan* raises the question whether government might condition the receipt of a benefit — here, permission to build — on the grant of an easement. *Nollan* treats this condition as impermissible partly on the theory that the right to build on one's own property is not a government "benefit," like welfare. But what is the difference between the two kinds of interests? Is one more "natural" than the other?

The Court also emphasized that the condition imposed by the state had no relation to the state's legitimate interest in preserving the view. The Court implied that a concession of property rights that involved a viewing spot rather than an easement might have been upheld. Here, however, the easement had no connection to the aesthetic goals at stake. As the Court had it, the problem was thus one of "extortion." See Epstein, Foreword: Unconstitutional Conditions, State Power, and the Limits of Consent, 102 Harv. L. Rev. 4, 62–63 (1988): "The doctrine of unconstitutional conditions limits the abuse of government discretion by severing the denial of the construction permit from the taking of the lateral easement. [The] 'relatedness' requirement [has] powerful functional roots, for it [reduces] the state's ability to extract concessions from individual owners by coordinating separate types of government initiatives."

But see Sullivan, Unconstitutional Conditions, 102 Harv. L. Rev. 1413, 1474 (1989): "Germaneness to the purpose of a benefit depends crucially on how broadly or how narrowly that purpose is defined. [The] condition invalidated in *Nollan* may be interpreted either as nongermane to the provision of visual access to the sea [or] as germane to a more general state interest in facilitating public use and enjoyment of the beach." How might a court resolve this problem?

For general discussion of this and related issues, see Symposium, The Jurisprudence of Takings, 88 Colum. L. Rev. 1581 (1988).

Compare Koontz v. St. Johns River Water Management District, 133 S. Ct. 2586 (2013). Petitioner owned a parcel of land that required state permits in order to develop. Petitioner suggested certain limitations on the development to mitigate the environmental damage, but the state Water Management District

---

10. "The Court suggests that [*Monsanto*] is distinguishable, because government regulation of property in that case was a condition on receipt of a 'government benefit,' while here regulation takes the form of a restriction on 'the right to build on one's own property.' This proffered distinction is not persuasive. Both Monsanto and the Nollans hold property whose use is subject to regulation; Monsanto may not sell its property without obtaining government approval and the Nollans may not build a new development on their property without government approval. Obtaining such approval is as much a 'government benefit' for the Nollans as it is for Monsanto. If the Court is somehow suggesting that 'the right to build on one's own property' has some privileged natural rights status, the argument is a curious one. By any traditional labor theory of value justification for property rights, for instance, see, e.g., J. Locke, The Second Treatise of Civil Government, Monsanto would have a superior claim, for the chemical formulae which constitute its property only came into being by virtue of Monsanto's efforts." [Relocated footnote. — EDS.]

found these insufficient. Instead, the District proposed that petitioner either take further measures to mitigate the damage on his own property or that he hire contractors to make improvements on other property owned by the District. Petitioner refused to take these measures, and the District denied petitioner's application. Relying upon *Nollan*, Petitioner then filed suit in state court, but the Florida Supreme Court held that *Nollan* was distinguishable because there the state had approved an application on the condition that the land owner acceded to the state's demands, whereas here, the state had denied the application because he refused to make the concessions.

The United States Supreme Court, in a five-to-four decision, rejected this distinction and reversed the judgment below. Writing for the Court, Justice Alito stated that the principles undergirding *Nollan* "do not change depending on whether the government approves a permit on the condition that the applicant turn over property or denies a permit because the applicant refuses to do so. We have often concluded that denials of governmental benefits were impermissible under the unconstitutional conditions doctrine."

Neither party disputed the proposition that the District could have simply refused to grant the permit. How was petitioner made worse off by the District's suggestion of actions petitioner could take that would lead it to grant the permit? Consider in this regard Justice Alito's observation that "land-use permit applicants are especially vulnerable to the type of coercion that the unconstitutional conditions doctrine prohibits because the government often has broad discretion to deny a permit that is worth far more than property it would like to take." Compare the following observations in Justice Kagan's dissenting opinion:

> Consider the matter from the standpoint of the District's lawyer. The District, she learns, has found that [petitioner's] permit applications do not satisfy legal requirements. It can deny the permits on that basis; or it can suggest ways for [petitioner] to bring his application into compliance. If every suggestion could become the subject of a lawsuit under *Nollan*, [the] lawyer can give but one recommendation: Deny the permits without giving [petitioner] any advice — even if he asks for guidance. [Nothing] in the Takings Clause requires that folly.

In Horne v. Department of Agriculture, 135 S. Ct. 1039 (2015), the Court rejected the argument that the government's taking of raisins from private producers as part of a program designed to regulate the raisin market could be justified as a condition on permission granted to the raisin owners to sell their product in interstate markets. The government relied on *Monsanto* (discussed at page 989), where the Court held that the Environmental Protection Agency could require companies manufacturing pesticides to disclose health and safety information as a condition to receiving a permit to sell their products. The *Monsanto* Court held that the even though the manufacturers had a property interest in these trade secrets, the disclosure was not a taking because the manufacturers received a "valuable Government benefit" in exchange — namely, permission to sell the chemicals. The *Horne* Court rejected this analogy:

> Selling produce in interstate commerce, although certainly subject to reasonable government regulation, is [not] a special governmental benefit that the Government may hold hostage, to be ransomed by the waiver of constitutional protection. Raisins are not dangerous pesticides; they are a healthy snack.

Justice Sotomayor wrote an opinion dissenting on this and other points. (*Horne* is discussed in greater detail at page 985.)

2. *Proportionality.* Compare *Nollan* to Dolan v. City of Tigard, 512 U.S. 374 (1994). Dolan sought permission from the City to expand her store and pave her parking lot. The City conditioned its permission on her willingness to dedicate a portion of her land to a public greenway along a creek, so as to minimize flooding, and a bicycle path designed to relieve vehicular congestion. In an opinion for written by Chief Justice Rehnquist, the Court held that the imposition of the condition was unconstitutional. Here, unlike in *Nollan*, the Court found that there was a nexus between the conditions imposed and the development sought by the landowner. Dolan's proposed parking lot would increase the amount of storm water runoff from the creek, and the bicycle path might reduce congestion caused by the expanded store. The Court nonetheless thought that the condition was improper because the extent of the deprivation was disproportionate to the harm caused by the development. "We think a term such as 'rough proportionality' best encapsulates what we hold to be the requirement of the Fifth Amendment. No precise mathematical calculation is required, but the city must make some sort of individualized determination that the required dedication is related both in nature and extent to the impact of the proposed development."

Justice Stevens wrote a dissenting opinion in which Justices Blackmun and Ginsburg joined. Justice Souter also dissented.

Suppose instead of demanding a property interest to which it was otherwise not entitled, the state simply demands cash in return for a permit application. As noted above, in Koontz v. St. Johns River Water Management District, supra, the District offered to allow petitioner to proceed with development if petitioner paid for improvements on a different parcel owned by the District. The Florida Supreme Court held that this situation was not governed by *Nollan* and *Dolan* because the requirement of a monetary payment did not constitute a "taking."

In his opinion for a five-to-four majority, Justice Alito rejected this reasoning: "[If] we accepted this argument it would be very easy for land-use permitting officials to evade the limitations of *Nollan* and *Dolan*. Because the government need only provide a permit applicant with one alternative that satisfies the nexus and rough proportionality standards, a permitting authority wishing to exact an easement could simply give the owner a choice of either surrendering an easement or making a payment equal to the easement's value."

The Court recognized that the takings clause does not apply to government-imposed financial obligations that do not operate upon or alter an identified property interest. Here, however, it found that the demand for money did operate upon such an interest "by directing the owner of a particular piece of property to make a monetary payment." The monetary obligation therefore "burdened petitioner's ownership of a specific parcel of land."

The Court acknowledged that neither a requirement that petitioner pay money to the state when not associated with a permit application nor the outright denial of a permit application would constitute a taking. How, then, can putting petitioner to a choice between these two options be a taking? Compare Rumsfeld v. FAIR, 547 U.S. 47 (2006). A federal statute provided that if a university denied access to military recruiters it would lose access to federal funds. The Court, in a unanimous opinion written by Chief Justice Roberts, upheld the amendment on the ground that universities did not have a constitutional right either to the federal funds or to exclude the military. Are *Rumsfeld* and *Koontz* consistent?

3. *Rent control.* In *Pennell v. City of San Jose,* 485 U.S. 1 (1988), the Supreme Court upheld an unusual rent control ordinance. The ordinance contained a mechanism for automatically increasing annual rents by as much as 8 percent. If a tenant objects to an increase greater than 8 percent, a hearing is provided, in which a mediation hearing officer decides whether the proposed increase is "reasonable under the circumstances." The decision about reasonableness is to include consideration of

the economic and financial hardship imposed on the present tenant or tenants of the unit or units to which such increases apply. If, on balance, the Hearing Officer determinates that the proposed increase constitutes an unreasonably severe financial or economic hardship on a particular tenant, he may order that the excess of the increase [be] disallowed. Any tenant whose household income and monthly housing expense meets [certain income requirements] shall be deemed to be suffering under financial and economic hardship which must be weighed.

The Court responded:

We think it would be premature to consider [the contention that the ordinance amounted to an unconstitutional taking] on the present record. As things stand, there simply is no evidence that the "tenant hardship clause" has in fact ever been relied upon by a Hearing Officer to reduce a rent below the figure it would have been set at on the basis of the other factors set forth in the Ordinance. In addition, there is nothing in the Ordinance requiring that a Hearing Officer in fact reduce a proposed rent increase on grounds of tenant hardship. . . . Given the "essentially ad hoc, factual inquir[y]" involved in the takings analysis, *Kaiser Aetna v. United States,* we have found it particularly important in takings cases to adhere to our admonition that "the constitutionality of statutes ought not be decided except in an actual factual setting that makes such a decision necessary." . . .

Petitioners argue, however, that it is "arbitrary, discriminatory, or demonstrably irrelevant," for appellees to attempt to accomplish the additional goal of reducing the burden of housing costs on low-income tenants by requiring that "hardship to a tenant" be considered in determining the amount of excess rent increase that is "reasonable under the circumstances." As appellants put it, "The objective of alleviating individual tenant hardship is . . . not a 'policy the legislature is free to adopt' in a rent control ordinance."

[But] the Ordinance establishes a scheme in which a Hearing Officer considers a number of factors in determining the reasonableness of a proposed rent increase which exceeds eight percent *and* which exceeds the amount deemed reasonable. . . . The first six factors [focus] on the individual landlord — the Hearing Officer examines the history of the premises, the landlord's costs, and the market for comparable housing. Section 5703.28(c)(5) also allows the landlord to bring forth any other financial evidence — including presumably evidence regarding his own financial status — to be taken into account by the Hearing Officer. It is in only this context that the Ordinance allows tenant hardship to be considered and . . . "balance[d]" with the other factors within this scheme. [The Ordinance] represents a rational attempt to accommodate the conflicting interests of protecting tenants from burdensome rent increases while at the same time ensuring that landlords are guaranteed a fair return on their investment. . . .

We accordingly find that the Ordinance, which so carefully considers both the individual circumstances of the landlord and the tenant before determining whether to allow an *additional* increase in rent over and above certain amounts that are deemed reasonable, does not on its face violate the Fourteenth Amendment's Due Process Clause. . . .

Compare Yee v. Escondido, 503 U.S. 519 (1992). At issue was a local rent control ordinance, applied to mobile home owners and in particular to owners of mobile home "parks." The ordinance set rents at a 1986 level, prohibited unapproved rent increases, and specified the factors that must be considered for any increases. Mobile home park owners contended that under this system they could no longer set rents or decide who their tenants would be, and that as a result the mobile home owner became an effective perpetual tenant of the park, indefinitely enabled to occupy the home's "pad." Thus, an interest in land — the right to occupy it at submarket rent — has been transferred from the park owner to the mobile home owner. According to the park owners, there was in this sense a physical invasion of their property.

The Court disagreed. It said that "government effects a physical taking only where it requires the landowner to submit to the physical occupation of the land." Here, however, "[p]etitioners voluntarily rented their land to mobile home owners. . . . [Neither] the City nor the State compels petitioners, once they have rented their property to tenants, to continue doing so." In the Court's view, "[No] government has required any physical invasions of petitioners' property. Petitioners' tenants were invited by petitioners, not forced upon them by the government." Thus, the laws at issue "merely regulate petitioners' use of their land by regulating the relationship between landlord and tenant."

The fact that there was a transfer of wealth from park owners to incumbent mobile home owners was not decisive, since many forms of land use regulation "can also be said to transfer wealth from the one who is regulated to another." But the Court noted that a "different case would be presented" if the statute compelled "a landowner over objection to rent his property or to refrain in perpetuity from terminating a tenancy."

4. *Remedies for takings.* When government regulation is sufficiently intrusive to constitute a taking, what remedy does the Constitution require? In First English Evangelical Lutheran Church of Glendale v. County of Los Angeles, 482 U.S. 304 (1987), the Court, in an opinion by Justice Rehnquist, held that the mere invalidation of the ordinance restricting use of the property in question was constitutionally insufficient. Although the state was free to end the taking by not enforcing the ordinance, it was also required to pay damages for the temporary taking effected during the period before the ordinance was invalidated. Justice Stevens, joined by Justices Blackmun and O'Connor, filed a dissenting opinion.

Compare Arkansas Game & Fish Commission v. United States, 133 S. Ct. 511 (2012), where the Court, in a unanimous decision by Justice Ginsburg, held that government action producing temporary flooding of property can constitute a compensable taking. Although the Court held that there was "no automatic exemption from Takings Clause inspection," it also noted that whether there was in fact a taking depended on factors like the length of time that the area was flooded, the degree to which the invasion was intended or foreseeable, the character of the land, and the owner's reasonable investment-backed expectations regarding the land's use.

In Horne v. Department of Agriculture, supra, the Court held that the government could not reduce the compensation due to growers whose product the government had taken by the value of the regulatory program to the growers.

[The] Government cites no support for [its] notion that general regulatory activity [can] constitute just compensation for a specific physical taking. Instead, our cases have set forth a clear and administrable rule for just compensation: "The Court has repeatedly held that just compensation normally is to be measured by 'the market value of the property at the time of the taking.'"

The Court distinguished cases "where the condemning authority may deduct special benefits — such as new access to a waterway or highway, or filling in of swampland — for the amount of compensation it seeks to pay a landowner suffering a partial taking. [Cases] of that sort can raise complicated questions involving the exercise of the eminent domain power, but they do not create a generally applicable exception to the usual compensation rule, based on asserted regulatory benefits of the sort at issue here."

In an opinion concurring in part and dissenting in part, Justice Breyer, joined by Justices Ginsburg and Kagan, disagreed:

> When the Government takes [a] percentage of the annual crop, the raisin owners retain the remaining [raisins]. The reserve requirement is intended [to] enhance the price that [the remaining] raisins will fetch on the open market. And any such enhancement matters. The Court's precedents indicate that, when calculating [just compensation] a court should deduct from the value of the taken [raisins] any enhancement caused by the taking to the value of the remaining [raisins].

Lucas v. South Carolina Coastal Council
505 U.S. 1003 (1992)

JUSTICE SCALIA delivered the opinion of the Court.

In 1986, petitioner David H. Lucas paid $975,000 for two residential lots on the Isle of Palms in Charleston County, South Carolina, on which he intended to build single-family homes. In 1988, however, the South Carolina Legislature enacted the Beachfront Management Act, which had the direct effect of barring petitioner from erecting any permanent habitable structures on his two parcels. A state trial court found that this prohibition rendered Lucas's parcels "valueless." This case requires us to decide whether the Act's dramatic effect on the economic value of Lucas's lots accomplished a taking of private property under the Fifth and Fourteenth Amendments requiring the payment of "just compensation."

I

A

South Carolina's expressed interest in intensively managing development activities in the so-called "coastal zone" dates from 1977 when, in the aftermath of Congress's passage of the federal Coastal Zone Management Act of 1972, the legislature enacted a Coastal Zone Management Act of its own. . . .

In the late 1970's, Lucas and others began extensive residential development of the Isle of Palms, a barrier island situated eastward of the City of Charleston. Toward the close of the development cycle for one residential subdivision known as "Beachwood East," Lucas in 1986 purchased the two lots at issue in this litigation for his own account. [At] the time Lucas acquired these parcels, he was not legally obliged to obtain a permit from the Council in advance of any development activity. His intention with respect to the lots was to do what the owners of the immediately adjacent parcels had already done: erect single-family residences. He commissioned architectural drawings for this purpose.

The Beachfront Management Act brought Lucas's plans to an abrupt end. Under that 1988 legislation, the Council was directed to establish a "baseline" connecting the landward-most "points of erosion . . . during the past forty years" in the region of the Isle of Palms that includes Lucas's lots. In action not challenged here, the Council fixed this baseline landward of Lucas's parcels. That was significant, for under the Act construction of occupiable improvements was flatly prohibited seaward of a line drawn 20 feet landward of, and parallel to, the baseline. The Act provided no exceptions.

Lucas promptly filed suit in the South Carolina Court of Common Pleas, contending that the Beachfront Management Act's construction bar effected a taking of his property without just compensation. Lucas did not take issue with the validity of the Act as a lawful exercise of South Carolina's police power, but contended that the Act's complete extinguishment of his property's value entitled him to compensation regardless of whether the legislature had acted in furtherance of legitimate police power objectives. Following a bench trial, the court agreed. Among its factual determinations was the finding that "at the time Lucas purchased the two lots, both were zoned for single-family residential construction and . . . there were no restrictions imposed upon such use of the property by either the State of South Carolina, the County of Charleston, or the Town of the Isle of Palms." The trial court further found that the Beachfront Management Act decreed a permanent ban on construction insofar as Lucas's lots were concerned, and that this prohibition "deprived Lucas of any reasonable economic use of the lots, . . . eliminated the unrestricted right of use, and rendered them valueless." The court thus concluded that Lucas's properties had been "taken" by operation of the Act, and it ordered respondent to pay "just compensation" in the amount of $1,232,387.50. . . .

Prior to Justice Holmes' exposition in Pennsylvania Coal Co. v. Mahon, 260 U.S. 393 (1922), it was generally thought that the Takings Clause reached only a "direct appropriation" of property, Legal Tender Cases, 12 Wall. 457, 551 (1871), or the functional equivalent of a "practical ouster of [the owner's] possession." Transportation Co. v. Chicago, 99 U.S. 635, 642 (1879). Justice Holmes recognized in *Mahon*, however, that if the protection against physical appropriations of private property was to be meaningfully enforced, the government's power to redefine the range of interests included in the ownership of property was necessarily constrained by constitutional limits. . . .

Nevertheless, our decision in *Mahon* offered little insight into when, and under what circumstances, a given regulation would be seen as going "too far" for purposes of the Fifth Amendment. In 70-odd years of succeeding "regulatory takings" jurisprudence, we have generally eschewed any "set formula" for determining how far is too far, preferring to "engage in . . . essentially ad hoc, factual inquiries," Penn Central Transportation Co. v. New York City, 438 U.S. 104, 124 (1978) (quoting Goldblatt v. Hempstead, 369 U.S. 590, 594 (1962)). See Epstein, Takings: Descent and Resurrection, 1987 Sup. Ct. Rev. 1, 4. We have, however, described at least two discrete categories of regulatory action as compensable without case-specific inquiry into the public interest advanced in support of the restraint. The first encompasses regulations that compel the property owner to suffer a physical "invasion" of his property. In general (at least with regard to permanent invasions), no matter how minute the intrusion, and no matter how weighty the public purpose behind it, we have required compensation. . . .

The second situation in which we have found categorical treatment appropriate is where regulation denies all economically beneficial or productive use of land. . . .[7]

We have never set forth the justification for this rule. Perhaps it is simply, as Justice Brennan suggested, that total deprivation of beneficial use is, from the landowner's point of view, the equivalent of a physical appropriation. Surely, at least, in the extraordinary circumstance when no productive or economically beneficial use of land is permitted, it is less realistic to indulge our usual assumption that the legislature is simply "adjusting the benefits and burdens of economic life," *Penn Central Transportation Co.*, in a manner that secures an "average reciprocity of advantage" to everyone concerned. *Mahon.* And the functional basis for permitting the government, by regulation, to affect property values without compensation — that "Government hardly could go on if to some extent values incident to property could not be diminished without paying for every such change in the general law" — does not apply to the relatively rare situations where the government has deprived a landowner of all economically beneficial uses.

On the other side of the balance, affirmatively supporting a compensation requirement, is the fact that regulations that leave the owner of land without economically beneficial or productive options for its use — typically, as here, by requiring land to be left substantially in its natural state — carry with them a heightened risk that private property is being pressed into some form of public service under the guise of mitigating serious public harm. . . .

We think, in short, that there are good reasons for our frequently expressed belief that when the owner of real property has been called upon to sacrifice all economically beneficial uses in the name of the common good, that is, to leave his property economically idle, he has suffered a taking.[8]

---

7. Regrettably, the rhetorical force of our "deprivation of all economically feasible use" rule is greater than its precision, since the rule does not make clear the "property interest" against which the loss of value is to be measured. When, for example, a regulation requires a developer to leave 90% of a rural tract in its natural state, it is unclear whether we would analyze the situation as one in which the owner has been deprived of all economically beneficial use of the burdened portion if the tract, or as one in which the owner has suffered a mere diminution in value of the tract as a whole. [Unsurprisingly,] this uncertainty regarding the composition of the denominator in our "deprivation" fraction has produced inconsistent pronouncements by the Court. The answer to this difficult question may lie in how the owner's reasonably expectations have been shaped by the State's law of property — i.e., whether and to what degree the State's law has accorded legal recognition and protection to the particular interest in land with respect to which the takings claimant alleges a diminution in (or elimination of) value. In any event, we avoid this difficulty in the present case, since the "interest in land" that Lucas has pleaded (a fee simple interest) is an estate with a rich tradition of protection at common law, and since the South Carolina Court of Common Pleas found that the Beachfront Management Act left each of Lucas's beachfront lots without economic value. [Relocated footnote. — EDS.]

8. Justice Stevens criticizes the "deprivation of all economically beneficial use" rule as "wholly arbitrary," in that "[the] landowner whose property is diminished in value 95% recovers nothing," while the landowner who suffers a complete elimination of value "recovers the land's full value." This analysis errs in its assumption that the landowner whose deprivation is one step short of complete is not entitled to compensation. Such an owner might not be able to claim the benefit of our categorical formulation, but, as we have acknowledged time and again, "the economic impact of the regulation on the claimant and . . . the extent to which the regulation has interfered with distinct investment-backed expectations" are keenly relevant to takings analysis generally. Penn Central Transportation Co. v. New York City, 438 U.S. 104, 124 (1978). . . .

The trial court found Lucas's two beachfront lots to have been rendered valueless by respondent's enforcement of the coastal-zone construction ban. . . .

It is correct that many of our prior opinions have suggested that "harmful or noxious uses" of property may be proscribed by government regulation without the requirement of compensation. For a number of reasons, however, we think the South Carolina Supreme Court was too quick to conclude that that principle decides the present case. . . .

When it is understood that "prevention of harmful use" was merely our early formulation of the police power justification necessary to sustain (without compensation) any regulatory diminution in value; and that the distinction between regulation that "prevents harmful use" and that which "confers benefits" is difficult, if not impossible, to discern on an objective, value-free basis; it becomes self-evident that noxious-use logic cannot serve as a touchstone to distinguish regulatory "takings" — which require compensation — from regulatory deprivations that do not require compensation. A fortiori the legislature's recitation of a noxious-use justification cannot be the basis for departing from our categorical rule that total regulatory takings must be compensated. If it were, departure would virtually always be allowed. The South Carolina Supreme Court's approach would essentially nullify *Mahon*'s affirmation of limits to the noncompensable exercise of the police power. . . .

Where the State seeks to sustain regulation that deprives land of all economically beneficial use, we think it may resist compensation only if the logically antecedent inquiry into the nature of the owner's estate shows that the proscribed use interests were not part of his title to begin with. This accords, we think, with our "takings" jurisprudence, which has traditionally been guided by the understandings of our citizens regarding the content of, and the State's power over, the "bundle of rights" that they acquire when they obtain title to property. [We] think the notion pressed by the Council that title is somehow held subject to the "implied limitation" that the State may subsequently eliminate all economically valuable use is inconsistent with the historical compact recorded in the Takings Clause that has become part of our constitutional culture.

Where "permanent physical occupation" of land is concerned, we have refused to allow the government to decree it anew (without compensation), no matter how weighty the asserted "public interests" involved, though we assuredly would permit the government to assert a permanent easement that was a preexisting limitation upon the landowner's title. We believe similar treatment must be accorded confiscatory regulations, i.e., regulations that prohibit all economically beneficial use of land: Any limitation so severe cannot be newly legislated or decreed (without compensation), but must inhere in the title itself, in the restrictions that background principles of the State's law of property and nuisance already place upon land ownership. A law or decree with such an effect must, in other words, do no more than duplicate the result that could have been achieved in the courts — by adjacent landowners (or other uniquely affected persons) under the State's law of private nuisance, or by the State under its complementary power to abate nuisances that affect the public generally, or otherwise.

On this analysis, the owner of a lake bed, for example, would not be entitled to compensation when he is denied the requisite permit to engage in a landfilling operation that would have the effect of flooding others' land. Nor the corporate owner of a nuclear generating plant, when it is directed to remove all improvements from its land upon discovery that the plant sits astride an earthquake fault.

Such regulatory action may well have the effect of eliminating the land's only economically productive use, but it does not proscribe a productive use that was previously permissible under relevant property and nuisance principles. The use of these properties for what are now expressly prohibited purposes was always unlawful, and (subject to other constitutional limitations) it was open to the State at any point to make the implication of those background principles of nuisance and property law explicit. . . .

The "total taking" inquiry we require today will ordinarily entail (as the application of state nuisance law ordinarily entails) analysis of, among other things, the degree of harm to public lands and resources, or adjacent private property, posed by the claimant's proposed activities, the social value of the claimant's activities and their suitability to the locality in question, and the relative ease with which the alleged harm can be avoided through measures taken by the claimant and the government (or adjacent private landowners) alike. The fact that a particular use has long been engaged in by similarly situated owners ordinarily imports a lack of any common-law prohibition (though changed circumstances or new knowledge may make what was previously permissible no longer so). So also does the fact that other landowners, similarly situated, are permitted to continue the use denied to the claimant.

It seems unlikely that common-law principles would have prevented the erection of any habitable or productive improvements on petitioner's land; they rarely support prohibition of the "essential use" of land, Curtin v. Benson, 222 U.S. 78, 86 (1911). The question, however, is one of state law to be dealt with on remand. We emphasize that to win its case South Carolina must do more than proffer the legislature's declaration that the uses Lucas desires are inconsistent with the public interest, or the conclusory assertion that they violate a common-law maxim such as sic utere tuo ut alienum non laedas. As we have said, a "State, by ipse dixit, may not transform private property into public property without compensation. . . ." Webb's Fabulous Pharmacies, Inc. v. Beckwith, 449 U.S. 155, 164 (1980). Instead, as it would be required to do if it sought to restrain Lucas in a common-law action for public nuisance, South Carolina must identify background principles of nuisance and property law that prohibit the uses he now intends in the circumstances in which the property is presently found. Only on this showing can the State fairly claim that, in proscribing all such beneficial uses, the Beachfront Management Act is taking nothing. . . .

The judgment is reversed and the cause remanded for proceedings not inconsistent with this opinion.

So ordered.

[Justice Souter would dismiss the writ of certiorari in this case as having been granted improvidently.]

JUSTICE KENNEDY, concurring in the judgment. . . .

In my view, reasonable expectations must be understood in light of the whole of our legal tradition. The common law of nuisance is too narrow a confine for the exercise of regulatory power in a complex and interdependent society. The State should not be prevented from enacting new regulatory initiatives in response to changing conditions, and courts must consider all reasonable expectations whatever their source. The Takings Clause does not require a static body of state property law; it protects private expectations to ensure private investment. I agree with the Court that nuisance prevention accords with the most common expectations of property owners who face regulation, but I do not believe this can be the sole source of state authority to impose severe restrictions. Coastal property may present such unique concerns for a fragile land system that the State can go further in regulating its development and use than the common law of nuisance might otherwise permit.

The Supreme Court of South Carolina erred, in my view, by reciting the general purposes for which the state regulations were enacted without a determination that they were in accord with the owner's reasonable expectations and therefore sufficient to support a severe restriction on specific parcels of property. The promotion of tourism, for instance, ought not to suffice to deprive specific property of all value without a corresponding duty to compensate. Furthermore, the means as well as the ends of regulation must accord with the owner's reasonable expectations. Here, the State did not act until after the property had been zoned for individual lot development and most other parcels had been improved, throwing the whole burden of the regulation on the remaining lots. This too must be measured in the balance.

With these observations, I concur in the judgment of the Court.

JUSTICE BLACKMUN, dissenting. . . .

I first question the Court's rationale in creating a category that obviates a "case-specific inquiry into the public interest advanced," if all economic value has been lost. If one fact about the Court's taking jurisprudence can be stated without contradiction, it is that "the particular circumstances of each case" determine whether a specific restriction will be rendered invalid by the government's failure to pay compensation. . . .

This Court repeatedly has recognized the ability of government, in certain circumstances, to regulate property without compensation no matter how adverse the financial effect on the owner may be. . . .

These cases rest on the principle that the State has full power to prohibit an owner's use of property if it is harmful to the public. "Since no individual has a right to use his property so as to create a nuisance or otherwise harm others, the State has not 'taken' anything when it asserts its power to enjoin the nuisance-like activity." *Keystone Bituminous Coal.* . . .

Ultimately even the Court cannot embrace the full implications of its per se rule: it eventually agrees that there cannot be a categorical rule for a taking based on economic value that wholly disregards the public need asserted. Instead, the Court decides that it will permit a State to regulate all economic value only if the State prohibits uses that would not be permitted under "background principles of nuisance and property law."

Until today, the Court explicitly had rejected the contention that the government's power to act without paying compensation turns on whether the prohibited activity is a common-law nuisance. . . .

[Common law] public and private nuisance law is simply a determination whether a particular use causes harm. There is nothing magical in the reasoning of judges long dead. They determined a harm in the same way as state judges and legislatures do today. If judges in the 18th and 19th centuries can distinguish a harm from a benefit, why not judges in the 20th century, and if judges can, why not legislators? There simply is no reason to believe that new interpretations of the hoary common law nuisance doctrine will be particularly "objective" or "value-free." . . .

The Court makes sweeping and, in my view, misguided and unsupported changes in our taking doctrine. While it limits these changes to the most narrow subset of government regulation — those that eliminate all economic value from land — these changes go far beyond what is necessary to secure petitioner Lucas' private benefit. One hopes they do not go beyond the narrow confines the Court assigns them to today.

I dissent.

JUSTICE STEVENS, dissenting. . . .

In addition to lacking support in past decisions, the Court's new rule is wholly arbitrary. A landowner whose property is diminished in value 95% recovers nothing, while an owner whose property is diminished 100% recovers the land's full value. . . .

Moreover, because of the elastic nature of property rights, the Court's new rule will also prove unsound in practice. In response to the rule, courts may define "property" broadly and only rarely find regulations to effect total takings. . . .

The Court's holding today effectively freezes the State's common law, denying the legislature much of its traditional power to revise the law governing the rights and uses of property. Until today, I had thought that we had long abandoned this approach to constitutional law. More than a century ago we recognized that "the great office of statutes is to remedy defects in the common law as they are developed, and to adapt it to the changes of time and circumstances." Munn v. Illinois, 94 U.S. 113, 134 (1877). As Justice Marshall observed about a position similar to that adopted by the Court today: "If accepted, that claim would represent a return to the era of Lochner v. New York, 198 U.S. 45 (1905), when common-law rights were also found immune from revision by State or Federal Government. Such an approach would freeze the common law as it has been constructed by the courts, perhaps at its 19th-century state of development. It would allow no room for change in response to changes in circumstance. The Due Process Clause does not require such a result." PruneYard Shopping Center v. Robins, 447 U.S. 74, 93 (1980) (concurring opinion).

Arresting the development of the common law is not only a departure from our prior decisions; it is also profoundly unwise. The human condition is one of constant learning and evolution — both moral and practical. Legislatures implement that new learning; in doing so they must often revise the definition of property and the rights of property owners. Thus, when the Nation came to understand that slavery was morally wrong and mandated the emancipation of all slaves, it, in effect, redefined "property." On a lesser scale, our ongoing self-education produces similar changes in the rights of property owners: New appreciation of the significance of endangered species, the importance of wetlands, and the vulnerability of coastal lands, shapes our evolving understandings of property rights.

Of course, some legislative redefinitions of property will effect a taking and must be compensated — but it certainly cannot be the case that every movement away from common law does so. There is no reason, and less sense, in such an absolute rule. We live in a world in which changes in the economy and the environment occur with increasing frequency and importance. If it was wise a century ago to allow Government "the largest legislative discretion" to deal with "the special exigencies of the moment," it is imperative to do so today. The rule that should govern a decision in a case of this kind should focus on the future, not the past. . . .

The Court's categorical approach rule will, I fear, greatly hamper the efforts of local officials and planners who must deal with increasingly complex problems in land-use and environmental regulation. . . .

[Even] assuming that petitioner's property was rendered valueless, the risk inherent in investments of the sort made by petitioner, the generality of the Act, and the compelling purpose motivating the South Carolina Legislature persuade me that the Act did not effect a taking of petitioner's property.

Accordingly, I respectfully dissent.

Note: Lucas, *the Environment, and Regulatory Takings*

1. Lucas's *importance. Lucas* appears to be one of the most important recent cases in the law of takings. But how could anyone object to the idea that compensation is due when government has rendered property completely "valueless"?

2. *The denominator problem.* Suppose Lucas had owned an additional, contiguous parcel of land that was not controlled by the regulation, so that the regulation did not render his property (consisting of both parcels) completely valueless. What result? What result if the second parcel was not contiguous?

Compare Murr v. Wisconsin, 137 S. Ct. 1933 (2017). Petitioners' family purchased adjoining Lots E and F along the St. Croix River in 1960 and 1961 and built a small, recreational cabin on Lot F. The lots were conveyed to petitioners in 1994 and 1995 and are now under common ownership. Petitioners wished to sell Lot E, but Wisconsin rules, designed to "guarantee the protection of the wild, scenic and recreational qualities of the river" prohibited the sale or development of adjacent lots under common ownership as separate lots. Petitioners claimed that this provision constituted a taking because it deprived them of all or practically all use of Lot E. In a five-to-three decision, written by Justice Kennedy, the Court rejected this claim.

The Court framed the case as posing a question about "the proper unit of property against which to assess the effect of the challenged governmental regulation." In answering that question, the Court rejected two approaches which it characterized as "unduly narrow."

First, the Court has declined to limit the parcel in an artificial manner to the portion of property targeted by the challenged regulation. That is because "defining the property interest taken in terms of the very regulation being challenged is circular." [Tahoe-Sierra Preservation Council, Inc. v. Tahoe Regional Planning Agency, 535 U.S. 322, 331 (2002).] . . .

The second concept about which the Court has expressed caution is the view that property rights under the Takings Clause should be coextensive with those under state law. States do not have the unfettered authority to "shape and define property rights and reasonable investment-backed expectations" leaving landowners without recourse against unreasonable regulations.

It followed that "no single consideration can supply the exclusive test for determining the denominator." Instead, the Court pointed to a number of factors including "the treatment of the land under state and local law; the physical characteristics of the land; and the prospective value of the regulated land."

The endeavor should determine whether reasonable expectations about property ownership would lead a landowner to anticipate that his holdings would be treated as one parcel, or, instead, as separate tracts. The inquiry is objective, and the reasonable expectations at issue derive from background customs and the whole of our legal tradition.

With regard to the first factor, "courts should give substantial weight to the treatment of the land [under] state and local law," and "[a] reasonable restriction that predates a landowner's acquisition, [can] be one of the objective factors that most landowners would reasonably consider in forming fair expectations about their property." On the other hand, "a use restriction which is triggered only after, or because of, a change in ownership should also guide a court's assessment of reasonable private expectations."

With regard to the second factor, "it may be relevant that the property is located in an area that is subject to, or likely to become subject to, environmental or other regulation."

Finally, with regard to the prospective value of the land, "[though] a use restriction may decrease the market value of the property, the effect may be tempered if the regulated land adds value to the remaining property, such as by increasing privacy, expanding recreational space, or preserving surrounding natural beauty."

Applying this test to the facts before it, the Court held that petitioners' property should be treated as a single parcel. Under state law, the lots were treated as a single unit, and the lots were subject to this provision because of petitioners "voluntary conduct in bringing the lots under common ownership after the regulations were enacted." The lots were contiguous, and because the Lower St. Croix River was regulated before they purchased the property, petitioners "could have anticipated public regulation that might affect their enjoyment of their property." Finally, although petitioners were "prohibited from selling Lots E and F separately or from building separate residential structures on each, [this] restriction [was] mitigated by the benefits of using the property as an integrated whole, allowing increased privacy and recreational space, plus the optimal location of any improvements."

When the two lots were considered as a single unit, the use regulation was insufficient to constitute a regulatory taking because the property had not lost all its economic value and the economic effect of the regulation was not severe.

Chief Justice Roberts, joined by Justices Thomas and Alito, dissented:

> [The Court's] bottom-line conclusion does not trouble me; the majority presents a fair case that the Murrs can still make good use of both lots and that the ordinance is a commonplace tool to preserve scenic areas. . . .
>
> Where the majority goes astray, however, is in concluding that the definition of the "private property" at issue [turns] on an elaborate test looking not only to state and local law. [Our] decisions have, time and again, declared that the Takings Clause protects property rights as state law creates and defines them. . . .
>
> I would therefore vacate the judgment below and remand for the court to identify the relevant property using ordinary principles of Wisconsin property law.

Justice Thomas filed a separate dissent, urging the Court "to take a fresh look at our regulatory takings jurisprudence, to see whether it can be grounded in the original public meaning of the Takings Clause of the Fifth Amendment or the Privileges or Immunities Clause of the Fourteenth Amendment."

3. *Takings and the common law.* Does the *Lucas* test depend on the common law background or instead on the legal background in general? Suppose the state had said by statute, *before* Lucas purchased the property, that certain lands must

not be developed in order to promote tourism and protect flora and fauna. Would the result be different? If it would be different, has the takings clause allowed the government to do basically whatever it wants through the simple redefinition of property rights?

4. *Sources of property rights.* There is a large question in the background: Where do property rights come from? Sometimes it is said that property rights come from "the state," which defines them; people who say this say that government can define property rights however it wishes. Such people might acknowledge that the takings clause requires compensation, but only if the state has changed the law after the time of purchase. Other people think that there are limits on how the state can define property rights, and that states cannot, for example, limit ownership in ways that go very far beyond the law of nuisance. How would this debate be resolved? Compare the debate over the source of property rights with respect to procedural due process discussed in section G, supra. Is there an explanation for the Court's different treatment of the issue in these two contexts?

5. *Temporary takings?* Is the government permitted to impose a moratorium on economic development? What if the moratorium deprives the property owner of all valuable use of the property? In Tahoe-Sierra Preservation Council, Inc. v. Tahoe Regional Planning Agency, 535 U.S. 302 (2002), the Court held that a moratorium, imposed during a period for studying the impact of development on Lake Tahoe, would not be treated as a categorical taking, subject to a per se requirement of compensation. The Court stressed that the case did not involve a physical taking, and it concluded that the rules for physical takings should not be used for "regulatory takings." Hence the *Penn Central* test, involving balancing, would be appropriate. The Court emphasized that *Lucas* involved a permanent taking, not a taking for a mere thirty-two months. The Court refused to accept the view "that we can effectively sever a 32-month segment from the remainder of each landowner's fee simple estate and then ask whether that segment has been taken in its entirety" by the moratorium. Hence the Court concluded that it was appropriate to rely on "the familiar *Penn Central* approach when deciding cases like this, rather than by attempting to craft a new categorical rule." Chief Justice Rehnquist dissented, in an opinion joined by Justices Scalia and Thomas.

6. *Judicial takings.* Can a judicial shift in common law property rules constitute an unconstitutional taking? The Court sharply divided on this question in Stop the Beach Renourishment v. Florida Department of Environmental Protection, 560 U.S. 702 (2010). At issue was a Florida program to repair beach erosion by depositing sand on eroded beaches. The program had the effect of turning previously submerged land into beachfront. The Florida Supreme Court held that under Florida common law property principles, this land belonged to the government rather than the private property owners whose land had previously extended to the shore line. A unanimous Court, in an opinion written by Justice Scalia, held that the Florida court's holding did not constitute a change in the common law and, therefore, was not an uncompensated taking. Writing for only four of the eight Justices participating, Justice Scalia, joined by Chief Justice Roberts and Justices Thomas and Alito, went on to state that

[the] Takings Clause [is] not addressed to the action of a specific branch or branches. It is concerned simply with the act, and not with the governmental actor. [It] would be absurd to allow a State to do by judicial decree what the Takings Clause forbids it to do by legislative fiat. . . .

If a legislature or a court declares that what was once an established right of private property no longer exists, it has taken that property, no less than if the State had physically appropriated it or destroyed its value by regulation.

Justice Scalia conceded that the framers did not envision that the takings clause would apply to judicial action:

They doubtless did not, since the Constitution was adopted in an era when courts had no power to "change" the common law. [Where] the text they adopted is clear, however, [what] counts is not what they envisioned but what they wrote.

Writing for himself and Justice Sotomayor, Justice Kennedy argued that the case did not require the Court to determine when or whether a judicial decision determining the rights of property owners violated the takings clause and pointed to "certain difficulties that should be considered before accepting [such a] theory." Justice Kennedy suggested that the due process clause might better serve the function of protecting settled property expectations in this situation.

Justice Breyer, joined by Justice Ginsburg, agreed that "[there] is no need now to decide more than [that] the Florida Supreme Court's decision in this case did not amount to a 'judicial taking.'" He argued that Justice Scalia's approach "would invite a host of federal takings claims without the mature consideration of potential procedural or substantive legal principles that might limit federal interference in matters that are primarily the subject of state law" and that the Court therefore should not resolve the issue in this case.

Justice Stevens did not participate.

Under Justice Scalia's approach, suppose that a state court overrules a prior decision, holding that the prior decision had misinterpreted the common law and that the new decision returned to common law principles. If the new decision diminishes property rights protected by the prior decision, is it a taking?

Palazzolo v. Rhode Island

533 U.S. 606 (2001)

JUSTICE KENNEDY delivered the opinion of the Court.

Petitioner Anthony Palazzolo owns a waterfront parcel of land in the town of Westerly, Rhode Island. Almost all of the property is designated as coastal wetlands under Rhode Island law. After petitioner's development proposals were rejected by respondent Rhode Island Coastal Resources Management Council (Council), he sued in state court, asserting the Council's application of its wetlands regulations took the property without compensation in violation of the Takings Clause of the Fifth Amendment, binding upon the State through the Due Process Clause of the Fourteenth Amendment. . . .

I. . . .

In 1959 petitioner, a lifelong Westerly resident, decided to invest in three undeveloped, adjoining parcels along this eastern stretch of Atlantic Avenue. [To] purchase and hold the property, petitioner and associates formed Shore Gardens,

Inc. (SGI). After SGI purchased the property petitioner bought out his associates and became the sole shareholder.

[During the first decade of SGI's ownership, several applications to develop the property were denied.]

No further attempts to develop the property were made for over a decade. Two intervening events, however, become important to the issues presented. First, in 1971, Rhode Island enacted legislation creating the Council, an agency charged with the duty of protecting the State's coastal properties. Regulations promulgated by the Council designated salt marshes like those on SGI's property as protected "coastal wetlands," on which development is limited to a great extent. Second, in 1978 SGI's corporate charter was revoked for failure to pay corporate income taxes; and title to the property passed, by operation of state law, to petitioner as the corporation's sole shareholder.

In 1983 petitioner, now the owner, renewed the efforts to develop the property. [Petitioner's applications to fill the marsh area and to establish a beach club were denied by the Council. He then filed this action, claiming that his property had been taken without just compensation.]

[We] hold [that] the owner is not deprived of all economic use of his property because the value of upland portions is substantial. We remand for further consideration of the claim under the principles set forth in *Penn Central*.

II

[Respondent argues that petitioner's claim should be denied because at the time the wetlands regulations were promulgated, the parcel was owned not by petitioner but by a corporation of which he was the sole shareholder.]

The theory underlying the argument that postenactment purchasers cannot challenge a regulation under the Takings Clause seems to run on these lines: Property rights are created by the State. So, the argument goes, by prospective legislation the State can shape and define property rights and reasonable investment-backed expectations, and subsequent owners cannot claim any injury from lost value. After all, they purchased or took title with notice of the limitation.

The State may not put so potent a Hobbesian stick into the Lockean bundle. [Were] we to accept the State's rule, the postenactment transfer of title would absolve the State of its obligation to defend any action restricting land use, no matter how extreme or unreasonable. A State would be allowed, in effect, to put an expiration date on the Takings Clause. This ought not to be the rule. Future generations, too, have a right to challenge unreasonable limitations on the use and value of land.

Nor does the justification of notice take into account the effect on owners at the time of enactment, who are prejudiced as well. Should an owner attempt to challenge a new regulation, but not survive the process of ripening his or her claim (which, as this case demonstrates, will often take years), under the proposed rule the right to compensation may not be asserted by an heir or successor, and so may not be asserted at all. The State's rule would work a critical alteration to the nature of property, as the newly regulated landowner is stripped of the ability to transfer the interest which was possessed prior to the regulation. The State may not by this means secure a windfall for itself. The proposed rule is, furthermore, capricious in effect. The young owner contrasted with the older owner, the owner with the resources to hold contrasted with the owner with the need to sell, would be in different positions. The Takings Clause is not so quixotic. A blanket rule that purchasers with notice have no compensation right when a claim becomes ripe is too blunt an instrument to accord with the duty to compensate for what is taken.

Direct condemnation, by invocation of the State's power of eminent domain, presents different considerations than cases alleging a taking based on a burdensome regulation. In a direct condemnation action, or when a State has physically invaded the property without filing suit, the fact and extent of the taking are known. In such an instance, it is a general rule of the law of eminent domain that any award goes to the owner at the time of the taking, and that the right to compensation is not passed to a subsequent purchaser. . . .

We have no occasion to consider the precise circumstances when a legislative enactment can be deemed a background principle of state law or whether those circumstances are present here. It suffices to say that a regulation that otherwise would be unconstitutional absent compensation is not transformed into a background principle of the State's law by mere virtue of the passage of title. . . .

III

[Petitioner] accepts the Council's contention and the state trial court's finding that his parcel retains $200,000 in development value under the State's wetlands regulations. He asserts, nonetheless, that he has suffered a total taking and contends the Council cannot sidestep the holding in *Lucas* "by the simple expedient of leaving a landowner a few crumbs of value."

Assuming a taking is otherwise established, a State may not evade the duty to compensate on the premise that the landowner is left with a token interest. This is not the situation of the landowner in this case, however. A regulation permitting a landowner to build a substantial residence on an 18-acre parcel does not leave the property "economically idle." *Lucas*. . . .

JUSTICE O'CONNOR, concurring.

I join the opinion of the Court but with my understanding of how the issues discussed in Part II of the opinion must be considered on remand.

Part II of the Court's opinion addresses the circumstance, present in this case, where a takings claimant has acquired title to the regulated property after the enactment of the regulation at issue. As the Court holds, the Rhode Island Supreme Court erred in effectively adopting the sweeping rule that the preacquisition enactment of the use restriction ipso facto defeats any takings claim based on that use restriction. Accordingly, the Court holds that petitioner's claim under Penn Central Transp. Co. v. New York City "is not barred by the mere fact that title was acquired after the effective date of the state-imposed restriction."

The more difficult question is what role the temporal relationship between regulatory enactment and title acquisition plays in a proper *Penn Central* analysis. Today's holding does not mean that the timing of the regulation's enactment relative to the acquisition of title is immaterial to the *Penn Central* analysis. Indeed, it would be just as much error to expunge this consideration from the takings inquiry as it would be to accord it exclusive significance. Our polestar instead remains the principles set forth in *Penn Central* itself and our other cases that govern partial regulatory takings. Under these cases, interference with investment-backed expectations is one of a number of factors that a court must examine. Further, the regulatory regime in place at the time the claimant acquires the property at issue helps to shape the reasonableness of those expectations.

If investment-backed expectations are given exclusive significance in the *Penn Central* analysis and existing regulations dictate the reasonableness of those expectations in every instance, then the State wields far too much power to redefine property rights upon passage of title. On the other hand, if existing regulations do nothing to inform the analysis, then some property owners may reap windfalls and an important indicium of fairness is lost. As I understand it, our decision today does not remove the regulatory backdrop against which an owner takes title to property from the purview of the *Penn Central* inquiry. It simply restores balance to that inquiry. Courts properly consider the effect of existing regulations under the rubric of investment-backed expectations in determining whether a compensable taking has occurred. As before, the salience of these facts cannot be reduced to any "set formula." *Penn Central* (internal quotation marks omitted). The temptation to adopt what amount to per se rules in either direction must be resisted. The Takings Clause requires careful examination and weighing of all the relevant circumstances in this context. The court below therefore must consider on remand the array of relevant factors under *Penn Central* before deciding whether any compensation is due.

JUSTICE SCALIA, concurring.

I write separately to make clear that my understanding of how the issues discussed in Part II of the Court's opinion must be considered on remand is not Justice O'Connor's.

The principle that underlies her separate concurrence is that it may in some (unspecified) circumstances be "[un]fai[r]," and produce unacceptable "windfalls," to allow a subsequent purchaser to nullify an unconstitutional partial taking (though, inexplicably, not an unconstitutional total taking) by the government. The polar horrible, presumably, is the situation in which a sharp real estate developer, realizing (or indeed, simply gambling on) the unconstitutional excessiveness of a development restriction that a naive landowner assumes to be valid, purchases property at what it would be worth subject to the restriction, and then develops it to its full value (or resells it at its full value) after getting the unconstitutional restriction invalidated.

This can, I suppose, be called a windfall — though it is not much different from the windfalls that occur every day at stock exchanges or antique auctions, where the knowledgeable (or the venturesome) profit at the expense of the ignorant (or the risk averse). There is something to be said (though in my view not much) for pursuing abstract "fairness" by requiring part or all of that windfall to be returned to the naive original owner, who presumably is the "rightful" owner of it. But there is nothing to be said for giving it instead to the government — which not only did not lose something it owned, but is both the cause of the miscarriage of "fairness" and the only one of the three parties involved in the miscarriage (government, naive original owner, and sharp real estate developer) which acted unlawfully — indeed unconstitutionally. Justice O'Connor would eliminate the windfall by giving the malefactor the benefit of its malefaction. It is rather like eliminating the windfall that accrued to a purchaser who bought property at a bargain rate from a thief clothed with the indicia of title, by making him turn over the "unjust" profit to the thief.

In my view, the fact that a restriction existed at the time the purchaser took title (other than a restriction forming part of the "background principles of the State's law of property and nuisance," Lucas v. South Carolina Coastal Council), should have no bearing upon the determination of whether the restriction is so substantial as to constitute a taking. The "investment-backed expectations" that the law will take into account do not include the assumed validity of a restriction that in fact deprives property of so much of its value as to be unconstitutional. Which is to say that a *Penn Central* taking, see Penn Central Transp. Co. v. New York City, no less than a total taking, is not absolved by the transfer of title.

[Justices Ginsburg and Breyer wrote separate opinions, dissenting on ripeness grounds.]

JUSTICE STEVENS, concurring in part and dissenting in part.

[I] have no doubt that [a property owner] has standing to challenge the restriction's validity whether she acquired title to the property before or after the regulation was adopted. For, as the Court correctly observes, even future generations "have a right to challenge unreasonable limitations on the use and value of land."

It by no means follows, however, that, as the Court assumes, a succeeding owner may obtain compensation for a taking of property from her predecessor in interest. A taking is a discrete event, a governmental acquisition of private property for which the state is required to provide just compensation. Like other transfers of property, it occurs at a particular time, that time being the moment when the relevant property interest is alienated from its owner. . . .

[To] the extent that the adoption of the regulations constitute the challenged taking, petitioner is simply the wrong party to be bringing this action. If the regulations imposed a compensable injury on anyone, it was on the owner of the property at the moment the regulations were adopted. Given the trial court's finding that petitioner did not own the property at that time, in my judgment it is pellucidly clear that he has no standing to claim that the promulgation of the regulations constituted a taking of any part of the property that he subsequently acquired. . . .

Note: Palazzolo — *Final Thoughts*

Question: What, exactly, is the "Lockean" bundle involved in this case? How can we know what the property right is at the time of acquisition without knowing what the state's law says at that time?

VII

Freedom of Expression

A. INTRODUCTION

The first amendment provides that "Congress shall make no law [abridging] the freedom of speech, or of the press; or the right of the people peaceably to assemble, and to petition the Government for a redress of grievances." Consider Justice Black's position: "The phrase 'Congress shall make no law' is composed of plain words, easily understood. [The] language [is] absolute. [Of] course the decision to provide a constitutional safeguard for [free speech] involves a balancing of conflicting interests. [But] the Framers themselves did this balancing when they wrote the [Constitution]. Courts have neither the right nor the power [to] make a different [evaluation]." Black, The Bill of Rights, 35 N.Y.U. L. Rev. 865, 874, 879 (1960).

The Court has never accepted Black's view. Rather, it has consistently held that "abridging" and "the freedom of speech" require interpretation, and that restraints on free expression may be "permitted for appropriate reasons." Elrod v. Burns, 427 U.S. 347, 360 (1976). This section examines two sources that might aid interpretation: the history and philosophy underlying the first amendment.

Note: The History of Free Expression

1. *The English background.* The notion that government "shall make no law [abridging] the freedom of speech, or of the press" received only gradual acceptance in Anglo-American law. Indeed, throughout much of English history the crown and Parliament attempted vigorously to suppress opinions deemed pernicious. Three forms of restraint were most commonly employed: the licensing of the press; the doctrine of constructive treason; and the law of seditious libel.

a. *Licensing.* The invention of printing greatly magnified the danger posed by "undesirable" opinions, and shortly after the first book was printed in England in 1476, the crown claimed an authority to control printing presses as a right of prerogative. The manuscript of any work intended for publication had to be submitted to crown officials empowered to censor objectionable passages and to approve or deny a license for the printing of the work. Anything published without an imprimatur was criminal. This system of "prior restraint" remained in effect until 1694, when the authorizing legislation expired and was not renewed. The decision not to renew licensing resulted not from any commitment to free expression but rather from considerations of expediency, for licensing had proved ineffective, difficult to enforce, and conducive to bribery. See generally L. Levy, Emergence of a Free Press ch. 1 (1985); F. Siebert, Freedom of the Press in England, 1476–1776 chs. 2–3, 6–12 (1952).

b. *Constructive treason.* The law of treason in England derived from the statute 25 Edward III (1352), which defined the crime as (1) compassing or imagining the king's death, (2) levying war against the king, or (3) adhering to his enemies. During the latter part of the seventeenth century, the English judges ruled that mere written or printed matter, as well as overt acts, could constitute treason. John Twyn was the first printer to suffer under this extension of the law of treason. Government officers searched Twyn's home and seized the proofs of a book suggesting that the king was accountable to the people, and that the people were entitled to self-governance. Twyn was convicted of constructive treason, hanged, drawn, and quartered.

Although constructive treason was invoked in only a few cases, the doctrine posed a serious threat to freedom of expression, for the few instances in which conviction and execution occurred served to remind potential publishers of the fate that awaited those who violated the law. The doctrine was abandoned after 1720 because juries were often reluctant to convict, the death penalty was in many cases considered too drastic, and the procedure was too detailed. See generally Siebert, supra, at 265–269.

c. *Seditious libel.* The doctrine of seditious libel first entered Anglo-American jurisprudence in a 1275 statute outlawing "any false news or tales whereby discord or occasion of discord or slander may grow between the king and his people." Violations were punished by the king's council sitting in the "starred chamber." The point of departure for the modern law of seditious libel was Sir Edward Coke's report of a Star Chamber case of 1606, which stated three central propositions: (1) A libel against a private person may be punished criminally because it may provoke revenge and thus cause a breach of the peace. (2) A libel against a government official is an even greater offense, "for it concerns not only the breach of the peace, but also the scandal of government." (3) Although the essence of the crime as fixed by the statute of 1275 was the falsity of the libel, even a true libel may be criminally punished.

The theory underlying seditious libel was explained by Chief Justice Holt in 1704: "If people should not be called to account for possessing the people with an ill opinion of the government, no government can subsist. For it is very necessary for all governments that the people should have a good opinion of it." Rex v. Tutchin, 14 Howell's State Trials 1095, 1128 (1704). Thus, a true libel is especially dangerous, for unlike a false libel, the dangers of truthful criticism cannot be defused by disproof. It was thus an oft-quoted maxim after 1606 that "the greater the truth the greater the libel."

In practice, then, seventeenth-century judges punished as seditious libel any "written censure upon any public man whatever for any conduct whatever, or upon any law or institution whatever." 2 J. Stephen, A History of the Criminal Law of England 350 (1883). As one commentator has observed, "no single method of restricting the press was as effective as the law of seditious libel as it was developed and applied by the common-law courts in the latter part of the seventeenth century." Siebert, supra, at 269. For general discussion, see

Hamburger, The Development of the Law of Seditious Libel and the Control of the Press, 37 Stan. L. Rev. 661 (1985).

In 1769, Blackstone summarized the law as follows:

> The liberty of the press [consists] in laying no *previous* restraints upon publications, and not in freedom from censure for criminal matter when published. [To] subject the press to the restrictive power of a licenser [is] to subject all freedom of sentiment to the prejudices of one man, and make him the arbitrary and infallible judge of all controverted points in learning, religion, and government. But to punish (as the law does at present) any dangerous or offensive writings, which, when published, shall on a fair and impartial trial be adjudged of a pernicious tendency, is necessary for the preservation of peace and good order, of government and religion, the only solid foundations of civil liberty.

4 W. Blackstone, Commentaries on the Laws of England *151–152.

2. *The colonial background.* The image of colonial America as a society in which freedom of expression was cherished seems largely inaccurate. Although colonial America was the scene of extraordinary diversity of opinion on religion, politics, social structure, and other subjects, each community "tended to be a tight little island clutching its own respective orthodoxy and [eager] to banish or extralegally punish unwelcome dissidents." Levy, supra, at 16.

Formal legal restraints on expression, however, were relatively rare. Licensing expired in 1725, and although there were hundreds of trials for seditious libel in England during the seventeenth and eighteenth centuries, there were not more than half a dozen such cases in colonial America. The most famous of these trials involved the prosecution of John Peter Zenger in New York in 1735. Zenger, publisher of the New York Weekly Journal, was charged with seditious libel by the Governor General of New York, whom he had criticized. Zenger argued unsuccessfully to the judge that the truth of the libel should be an absolute defense. The jury, responding to the popularity of Zenger's cause, disregarded the judge's instructions and returned a verdict of not guilty.

Although common law prosecutions for seditious libel were rare, the popularly elected colonial assemblies, imitating Parliament, assumed and vigorously exercised the power to punish "seditious" expression. Any criticism of an assembly or its members was likely to be regarded as a seditious scandal against the government punishable as a "breach of privilege." Levy, supra, at 14. To cite just one example, James Franklin, the older brother of Ben, ran a brief notice in his New England Courant that the government was preparing a ship to pursue coastal pirates "sometime this month, wind and weather permitting." The insinuation that the government was not dealing effectively with the pirates angered Massachusetts's popularly elected assembly. Franklin was arrested, and after a pro forma hearing, the assembly resolved that he had committed "a High affront to this Government." Franklin was imprisoned for the remainder of the session. For a lively account of the founding generation's understanding of freedom of speech and of the press, see S. Solomon, Revolutionary Dissent (2016).

3. *The first amendment.* Scholars have long puzzled over the actual intentions of the framers of the first amendment. The primary dispute is over whether the framers intended to adopt the Blackstonian view — that freedom of speech consists entirely in the freedom from prior restraints — or whether they intended some broader meaning. Consider the following views.

a. Z. Chafee, Free Speech in the United States 18–20 (1941):

If we [consider] what mischief in the existing law the [framers] wished to [remedy], we can be sure that it was not [licensing]. This had expired in England in 1695, and in the colonies by 1725. [There] was no need to go to all the trouble of pushing through a constitutional amendment just to settle an issue that had been dead for decades. What the framers did have plenty of reason to fear was an entirely different danger to political writers and speakers. For years the government here and in England had substituted for [licensing] rigorous and repeated prosecutions for seditious libel [and] for years these prosecutions were opposed by liberal opinion and popular agitation. [Two] different views of the relation of rulers and people were in conflict. According to one view, the rulers were the superiors of the people, and therefore must not be subjected to any censure that would tend to diminish their authority. [According] to the other view, the rulers were agents and servants of the people, who might therefore find fault with their servants and discuss questions of their punishment or dismissal, and of governmental policy. [In] the United States the people and not the government possess the absolute sovereignty, and [government is thus not free to punish seditious libel. Indeed, one] "of the objects of the Revolution was to get rid of the English common law on liberty of speech and of the press."

b. Levy, supra, at xii–xv:

[The proposition has been conventionally accepted] that it was the intent of the American Revolution or the Framers of the First Amendment to abolish the common law of seditious libel. [The] evidence suggests that the proposition is suppositious and unprovable. [We] may even have to confront the possibility that the intentions of the Framers were not the most [libertarian]. But this should be expected because the Framers were nurtured on the crabbed historicism of Coke and the narrow conservatism of Blackstone, as well as Zenger's case. The ways of thought of a lifetime are not easily broken. The Declaration of Independence severed the political connection with England but the American states continued the English common-law system except as explicitly rejected by statute. If the Revolution produced any radical libertarians on the meaning of freedom of speech and press, they were not present at the Constitutional Convention or the First Congress, which drafted the Bill of Rights. Scholars and judges have betrayed a penchant for what John P. Roche called "retrospective symmetry," by giving to present convictions a patriotic lineage and tradition — in this case, the fatherhood of the "Framers."

For critical analyses of this view, see D. Rabban, Free Speech in Its Forgotten Years (1997); Rabban, An Ahistorical Historian: Leonard Levy on Freedom of Expression in Early American History, 37 Stan. L. Rev. 795 (1985); Mayton, From a Legacy of Suppression to the "Metaphor of the Fourth Estate," 39 Stan. L. Rev. 139 (1986).

The framers themselves were unsure what a constitutional guarantee of "freedom of the speech or of the press" would mean. Benjamin Franklin observed, for example, that "Few of us, I believe, have distinct ideas of its nature and extent," and Alexander Hamilton asked "Who can give it any definition which would not leave the utmost latitude for evasion?" See Meyerson, The Neglected History of the Prior Restraint Doctrine, 34 Ind. L. Rev. 295, 320 (2001).

4. *The relevance of history.* To what extent, if any, is the preceding history relevant to interpretation of the first amendment? Is the English common law important because it was what the framers rejected or because it was what they accepted? Is it plausible that states that themselves punished seditious libel

intended to prohibit Congress from punishing it? And given the enormous changes in the media and politics since the adoption of the first amendment, to what extent, if any, should the intent of the framers control the contemporary resolution of first amendment issues?

5. *The Sedition Act of 1798.* The first serious challenge to freedom of expression in the United States came with the Sedition Act of 1798. Act of July 14, 1798, 1 Stat. 596. The United States was on the verge of war with France, and many of the ideas generated by the French Revolution aroused fear and hostility in segments of the U.S. population. A bitter political and philosophical debate raged between the Federalists, then in power, and the Republicans.

Against this backdrop, the Federalists enacted the Sedition Act of 1798. The act prohibited the publication of

> false, scandalous, and malicious [writings] against the government of the United States, or either house of the Congress of the United States, or the President of the United States, with intent to defame [them]; or to bring them [into] contempt or disrepute; or to excite against them [the] hatred of the good people of the United States. . . .

The act provided further that truth would be a defense and that malicious intent was an element of the crime. Thus, as the Federalists emphasized, the act eliminated those aspects of the English common law that had been the focus of attack during the eighteenth century. See Levy, supra, at xi.

The Sedition Act was vigorously enforced, but only against members or supporters of the Republican Party. Prosecutions were brought against the four leading Republican newspapers. The cases, often tried before openly hostile Federalist judges, resulted in ten convictions and no acquittals. Moreover, in the hands of these judges, the procedural reforms of the act proved largely illusory.

Consider, for example, the plight of Matthew Lyon, a Republican congressman from Vermont. During his reelection campaign, Lyon published an article in which he attacked the Adams administration, asserting that under President Adams "every consideration of the public welfare [was] swallowed up in a continual grasp for power, in an unbounded thirst for ridiculous pomp, foolish adulation, and selfish avarice." At Lyon's trial, the judge instructed the jury to find malicious intent unless the statement "could have been uttered with any other intent than that of making odious or contemptible the President and the government, and bringing them both into disrepute." Although Lyon was technically free to prove the "truth" of his statement in his defense, this was hardly possible, given the nature of the statement. Lyon was convicted and sentenced to a fine of $1,000 and four months in prison. The Federalist press rejoiced, but Lyon became an instant martyr and was reelected while in jail. See Trial of Matthew Lyon, in F. Wharton, State Trials 333 (1849).

The Supreme Court did not rule on the constitutionality of the Sedition Act, but it was upheld without dissent by the lower federal courts and by three Supreme Court justices sitting on circuit. The act expired of its own force on March 3, 1801. President Jefferson thereafter pardoned all those who had been convicted under the act, and Congress eventually repaid most of the fines. It is generally agreed that the act was a factor in the defeat of the Federalists in the election of 1800. Significant cases under the Sedition Act are printed in Wharton, supra. The story of the enforcement of the act is told in G. Stone,

Perilous Times: Free Speech in Wartime 15–78 (2004). What is the significance of the fact that the Sedition Act was approved by many of the same people who had earlier approved the first amendment?

6. *From the Sedition Act of 1798 to the Espionage Act of 1917.* The Supreme Court did not directly consider the first amendment's guarantee of free expression until Congress enacted the Espionage Act of 1917 at the outset of World War I. See section B1 infra. This is not to say, however, that controversies over free speech did not arise in the years between the Sedition Act of 1798 and the Espionage Act of 1917. See G. Stone, supra, 79–134 (free speech during the Civil War); M. Curtis, Free Speech: The People's Darling Privilege (2000) (abolitionist speech and free speech during the Civil War); D. Rabban, Free Speech in Its Forgotten Years (1997) (free speech between 1870 and 1920).

Note: The Philosophy of Free Expression

"Intuition at first may suggest that an individual ought to have more freedom to speak than he has liberty in other areas. There would seem to be some truth in the adage, 'sticks and stones can break my bones, but words will never hurt me.' Yet speech often hurts. It can offend, injure reputation, fan prejudice or passion, and ignite the world. Moreover, a great deal of other conduct that the state regulates has less harmful potential." Wellington, On Freedom of Expression, 88 Yale L.J. 1105, 1106–1107 (1979). Why, then, should expression have greater immunity from government regulation than most other forms of human conduct? Why should society prohibit the making of any law "abridging the freedom of speech"?

1. *Search for truth: the "marketplace of ideas."* The search for truth rationale for the protection of free expression rests on the premise that "when men have realized that time has upset many fighting faiths, they may come to believe even more than they believe the very foundations of their own conduct that the ultimate good desired is better reached by free trade in ideas — that the best test of truth is the power of the thought to get itself accepted in the competition of the market, and that truth is the only ground upon which their wishes safely can be carried out." Abrams v. United States, 250 U.S. 616, 630 (1919) (Holmes, J., dissenting).

The search for truth rationale was first fully enunciated by John Stuart Mill in On Liberty (1859):

> [The] peculiar evil of silencing the expression of an opinion is, that it is robbing the human race; posterity as well as the existing generation; those who dissent from the opinion, still more than those who hold it. . . . First: the opinion which it is attempted to suppress [may] be true. Those who desire to suppress it [are] not infallible. They have no authority to decide the question for all mankind, and exclude every other person from the means of judging. [Of course, it is not the case] that truth always triumphs over persecution. [But the] real advantage which truth has [is] that when an opinion is true, it may be extinguished once, twice, or many times, but in the course of ages there will generally be found persons to rediscover it, until [eventually] it has made such head as to withstand all subsequent attempts to suppress it. . . .
>
> [Second: the received opinion may be true. But however true an opinion] may be, if it is not fully, frequently, and fearlessly discussed, it will be held as a dead dogma, not a living truth. [He] who knows only his own side of the case, knows little of that. [Even if] the received opinion [is] true, a conflict with the opposite error is essential to a clear apprehension and deep feeling of its truth. . . .

[Finally:] the conflicting doctrines, instead of being one true and the other false, [may] share the truth between them; and the nonconforming opinion [may be] needed to supply the remainder of the truth, of which the received doctrine embodies only a part. [Every] opinion which embodies somewhat of the portion of truth which the common opinion omits, ought to be considered precious.

Consider the following observations.

a. Baker, Scope of the First Amendment Freedom of Speech, 25 UCLA L. Rev. 964, 974–978 (1978):

[The] hope that the marketplace leads to truth, or even to the best or most desirable decision, [is] implausible. [First, experience as well as discussion contributes to understanding. Thus,] restrictions on experience-generating conduct are as likely as restrictions on [debate] to stunt the progressive development of understanding, [but the marketplace theory gives no] constitutional protection [to] experience-producing conduct. [Second, the marketplace theory assumes] that people [use] their rational capacities to eliminate distortion caused by the form and frequency of message presentation. [This] assumption cannot be accepted. Emotional or "irrational" appeals have great [impact]. [Finally, in practice,] the marketplace of ideas appears improperly biased in favor of presently dominant groups.

b. Greenawalt, Free Speech Justifications, 89 Colum. L. Rev. 119, 135–136 (1989):

The critical question is not how well truth will advance absolutely in conditions of freedom, but how well it will advance in conditions of freedom as compared with some alternative set of conditions. Suppose one were highly pessimistic about the capacity of people to ascertain important kinds of truths, but believed that governments that suppress ideas almost always manage to promote [falsehoods]. One might then support freedom of speech as less damaging to truth than an alternative social practice. One's overall judgment on this subject must depend on a delicate judgment about people's responses to claimed truth, about the effects of inequality of private power over what is communicated, and about the soundness of government determinations about valid ideas.

c. Wellington, supra, at 1130–1132:

In the long run, true ideas do tend to drive out false ones. The problem is that the short run may be very long, that one short run follows hard upon another, and that we may become overwhelmed by the inexhaustible supply of freshly minted, often very seductive, false ideas. [Moreover,] most of us do believe that the book is closed on some issues. Genocide is an example. [Truth] may win, and in the long run it may almost always win, but millions of Jews were deliberately and systematically murdered in a very short period of time. [Before] those murders occurred, many individuals must have come "to have false beliefs."

2. *Self-governance.* The self-governance rationale is most closely identified with the work of Alexander Meiklejohn:

[The] Constitution [ordains] that all authority [to] determine common action, belongs to "We, the People." [Under this system, free men are governed] by themselves. [What,] then, does the First Amendment forbid? [The] town meeting suggests an answer. That meeting is called to discuss [and] to decide matters of public policy. [The] voters, therefore, must be made as wise as possible. [And] this, in turn, requires that so far as time allows, all facts and interests relevant to the problem shall be fully and fairly presented. . . .

The First Amendment, then, is not the guardian of unregulated talkativeness. It does not require that, on every occasion, every citizen shall take part in public debate. [Rather,] the vital point [is] that no suggestion of policy shall be denied a hearing because it is on one side of the issue rather than another. [Citizens] may not be barred [from speaking] because their views are thought to be false or dangerous. [The] reason for this equality of status in the field of ideas lies deep in the very foundation of the self-governing process. When men govern themselves, it is they — and no one else — who must pass judgment upon unwisdom and unfairness and danger. [Just] so far as, at any point, the citizens who are to decide an issue are denied acquaintance with information or opinion [which] is relevant to that issue, just so far the result must be ill-considered. [It] is that mutilation of the thinking process of the community against which the First Amendment [is] directed. The principle of the freedom of speech [is] not a Law of Nature or of Reason in the abstract. It is a deduction from the basic American agreement that public issues shall be decided by universal suffrage.

A. Meiklejohn, Free Speech and Its Relation to Self-Government 15–16, 24–27, 39 (1948).

Consider the following observations.

a. Chafee, Book Review, 62 Harv. L. Rev. 891, 899–900 (1949):

The most serious weakness in Mr. Meiklejohn's argument is that it rests on his supposed boundary between public speech and private speech. That line is extremely blurred. [The] truth is that there are public aspects to practically every subject. [Moreover, if Mr. Meiklejohn's public speech excludes scholarship,] art and literature, it is shocking to deprive these vital matters of the protection of [the] First Amendment. [Valuable] as self-government is, it is in itself only a small part of our lives. That a philosopher should subordinate all other activities to it is indeed surprising.

b. Meiklejohn's response:

The First Amendment [protects] the freedom of those activities of thought and communication by which we "govern." [But] voting is merely the external expression of a wide and diverse number of activities by means of which citizens attempt to meet the responsibilities of making judgments, which that freedom to govern lays upon them. [Self-government] can exist only insofar as the voters acquire the intelligence, integrity, sensitivity, and generous devotion to the general welfare that, in theory, casting a ballot is assumed to express. [Thus,] there are many forms of thought and expression within the range of human communications from which the voter derives the [necessary] knowledge, intelligence, [and] sensitivity to human values. [These], too, must suffer no abridgment of their freedom. [These include:] 1. Education, in all its phases. [2.] The achievements of philosophy and the sciences. [3.] Literature and the arts. [4.] Public discussions of public issues.

Meiklejohn, The First Amendment Is an Absolute, 1961 Sup. Ct. Rev. 245, 255–257.

c. Bork, Neutral Principles and Some First Amendment Problems, 47 Ind. L.J. 1, 26–28 (1971):

Professor Alexander Meiklejohn seems correct when he says: "The First Amendment [protects] the freedom of those activities of thought and communication by which we 'govern.'" [But Meiklejohn goes] further and would extend the protection of the first amendment beyond speech that is explicitly political. [I disagree.] [There is, of course,] an analogy between criticism of official behavior and the publication of a novel like Ulysses, for the latter may form attitudes that ultimately affect politics. But it is an analogy, not an identity. Other human activities and experiences also form personality, teach and create attitudes just as much as does the novel, but no one would on that account [suggest] that the first amendment strikes down regulations of economic activity, control of entry into trade, laws about sexual behavior, marriage and the like. Yet these activities, in their capacity to create attitudes that ultimately impinge upon the political process, are more like literature and science than literature and science are like political speech. If the dialectical progression is not to become an analogical stampede, the protection of the first amendment must be cut off when it reaches the outer limits of political speech. [The] notion that all valuable types of speech must be protected by the first amendment confuses the constitutionality of laws with their wisdom. Freedom of nonpolitical speech rests, as does freedom for other valuable forms of behavior, upon the enlightenment of society and its elected representatives.

d. Sunstein, Free Speech Now, 59 U. Chi. L. Rev. 255, 301, 304–306 (1992):

[The] First Amendment is principally about political deliberation. [We should] treat speech as political when it is both intended and received as a contribution to public deliberation about some issue. [An] approach that affords special protection to political speech, thus defined, is justified on numerous grounds. [It] receives firm support from history — not only from the Framers' theory of free expression, but also from the development of that principle through the history of American law. [In] addition, an insistence that government's burden is greatest when political speech is at issue responds well to the fact that here government is most likely to be biased. [Finally], this approach protects speech when regulation is most likely to be harmful. Restrictions on political speech have the distinctive feature of impairing the ordinary channels for political [change]. If there are controls on commercial advertising [or artistic and scientific expression], it always remains possible to argue that such controls should be lifted. [But] if the government forecloses political argument, the democratic corrective is unavailable. [Taken] in concert, these considerations suggest that government should be under a special burden of justification when it seeks to control speech intended and received as a contribution to public deliberation.

For additional perspectives on democracy and the First Amendment, see Post, Participatory Democracy and Free Speech, 97 Va. L. Rev. 477, 482-483, 486 (2011); Volokh, The Trouble with "Public Discourse" as a Limitation on Free Speech Rights, 97 Va. L. Rev. 567 (2011); M. Redish, The Adversary First Amendment 1–5 (2013).

3. *Self-fulfillment.* Consider the following views:

a. Richards, Free Speech and Obscenity Law: Toward a Moral Theory of the First Amendment, 123 U. Pa. L. Rev. 45, 62 (1974):

[People] are not to be constrained to communicate or not to communicate, to believe or not to believe, to associate or not to associate. The value placed on this cluster of ideas derives from the notion of self-respect that comes from a mature person's full and untrammelled exercise of capacities central to human rationality. Thus, the significance of free expression rests on the central human capacity to create and express symbolic systems, such as speech, writing, pictures, and [music]. Freedom of expression permits and encourages the exercise of these [capacities]. In so doing, it nurtures and sustains the self-respect of the mature person. [The] value of free expression, in this view, rests on its deep relation to self-respect arising from autonomous self-determination without which the life of the spirit is meager and slavish.

b. Bork, supra, at 25:

[The self-fulfillment/autonomy rationale does] not distinguish speech from any other human activity. An individual may develop his faculties or derive pleasure from trading on the stock market, [working] as a barmaid, engaging in sexual activity, [or] in any of thousands of other endeavors. Speech [can] be preferred to other activities [on the basis of this rationale] only by ranking forms of personal gratification. [One] cannot, on neutral grounds, choose to protect speech [on this basis] more than [one] protects any other claimed freedom.

4. *Other rationales.* Although courts and commentators have focused primarily on the search for truth, self-governance, and self-fulfillment/autonomy rationales for the protection of free expression, three further rationales merit note.

a. *The checking value.* Consider Blasi, The Checking Value in First Amendment Theory, 1977 Am. B. Found. Res. J. 521, 527–542:

[Another rationale for the protection of free expression] is the value that free speech [can] serve in checking the abuse of power by public officials. [The] central premise of the checking value is that the abuse of official power is an especially serious evil [because of government's unique] capacity to employ legitimized violence. [The] government's monopoly of legitimized violence means [that the] check on government must come from the power of public opinion. [Thus,] the checking value grows out of democratic theory, but it is the democratic theory of John Locke [and] not that of Alexander Meiklejohn. Under [this] view of democracy, the role of the ordinary citizen is not so much to contribute on a continuing basis to the formation of public policy as to retain a veto power to be employed when the decisions of officials pass certain bounds.

b. *Free speech and the development of character.* Consider Blasi, Free Speech and Good Character: From Milton to Brandeis to the Present, in L. Bollinger and G. Stone, Eternal Vigilance: Free Speech in the Modern Era 61, 62, 84–85 (2002):

[A] culture that prizes and protects expressive liberty nurtures in its members certain character traits such as inquisitiveness, distrust of authority, willingness to take initiative, and the courage to confront evil. Such character traits are valuable [for] their instrumental contribution to the collective well-being, social as well as political. [The] most important [consequence] of protecting free speech is the intellectual and moral pluralism, and thus disorder in a sense, thereby engendered. In matters of belief, conventional structures of authority are weakened, rebellion is facilitated, closure is impaired. Persons who live in a free-speech regime are forced to cope with persistent, and frequently intractable, differences of understanding. For most of us that is a painful challenge. . . . Being made to take account of such differences shapes our character.

(c) *Free speech and cultural democracy.* Consider Balkin, Cultural Democracy and the First Amendment, 110 Nw. U. L. Rev. 1053 (2016):

Freedom of speech does more than protect democracy; it also promotes a *democratic culture*. [Although] the right to participate in culture [helps] to legitimate political self-governance, it transcends that purpose. Cultural democracy, and therefore cultural freedom, is a necessary component of a free society, even in countries that are not fully democratic or democratic at all. Moreover, a cultural theory of free speech offers a much more convincing explanation of why a great deal of expression that seems to have little to do with political self-government enjoys full First Amendment protection.

[By] the end of the twentieth century, the political economy of communication had changed radically. In the age of the Internet, many of the assumptions that grounded Meiklejohn's model have fallen away. Vastly more people can communicate to others: not merely to small groups, but to the general public; and not merely within the United States, but around the globe. [A] theory of free expression for the digital age [has] to make sense of — and value — the explosion of popular appropriation, combination, and creativity in popular discussion, art, and culture. Culture, which had often taken a backseat to politics in twentieth-century discussions of the foundations of the First Amendment, came to the forefront in the early twenty-first century. [By] protecting the right to participate in culture, freedom of speech also promotes the growth and spread of mores, opinions, values, art, and knowledge.

5. *Philosophy and the first amendment.* To what extent, if any, are these rationales for the protection of free expression relevant to interpretation of the first amendment? Consider Bloustein, The Origin, Validity, and Interrelationships of the Political Values Served by Freedom of Expression, 33 Rutgers L. Rev. 372, 381 (1981): "[There] is no evidence [that these rationales were] discussed or debated during the period of the drafting and adoption of the [first] amendment [and we may thus conclude] that whatever validity and authority they may have do *not* derive directly from the intentions of the drafters." Whence, then, do the validity and authority of these rationales derive?

To what extent do these rationales, if relevant to interpretation of the first amendment, provide a coherent and workable basis for the decision of actual cases? Note that in some instances it may be necessary to choose among the competing rationales. For example, the self-fulfillment/autonomy rationale does not support a distinction between political and nonpolitical expression, whereas the self-governance theory seems to compel that distinction. Despite such potential conflicts, most commentators agree that any "adequate conception of freedom of speech must [draw] upon several strands of theory in order to protect a rich variety of expressional modes." L. Tribe, American Constitutional Law 789 (2d ed. 1988). As one commentator has observed, in the "democratic state," which "is founded on a tradition of free inquiry," the "attainment of knowledge," the "consensual participation in government," and the "dignity of self-expression" are "so interdependent that they really represent three aspects [of] a single value; their relationships define a kind of culture, embracing the individual, the state, and the system of knowledge, art and other such values that we call liberal." Bloustein, supra, at 395.

In light of all this, how would you address the question whether Jackson Pollock's paintings, Arnold Schoenberg's music, and Lewis Carroll's poem *Jabberwocky* are within the "freedom of speech" protected by the First Amendment? The Supreme Court has declared that all of these forms of expression are "unquestionably shielded" by the First Amendment. Does it make sense to conclude that "nonrepresentational art, instrumental music, and nonsense" are protected by the freedom of speech, "even though none involves what we typically think of as speech — the use of words to convey meaning"? M. Tushnet, A. Chen, and J. Blocher, Free Speech Beyond Words 1 (2017). See Hurley v. Irish-American. Gay, Lesbian and Bisexual Group of Boston, Inc., 515 U.S. 557, 568-69 (1969) infra section VII-E-5.

Note: Organization

The remaining sections in this chapter explore the Supreme Court's interpretation of the first amendment's guarantee of free speech, press, assembly, and petition. These sections are structured in accord with two distinctions that have played a central role in the Court's analysis. First, there is the distinction between content-based and content-neutral restrictions. Content-based restrictions restrict communication because of the message conveyed. Laws prohibiting the publication of "confidential" information, forbidding the hiring of teachers who advocate the violent overthrow of government, or banning the display of the swastika in certain neighborhoods illustrate this type of restriction. Content-neutral restrictions, on the other hand, restrict communication without regard to the message conveyed. Laws prohibiting noisy speeches near a hospital, banning the erection of billboards in residential communities, or requiring the disclosure of the names of all leafleteers are examples. The Court has generally employed different standards to test the constitutionality of these two types of restrictions.

Second, there is the distinction within the realm of content-based restrictions between "high"- and "low"-value expression. The Court has long adhered to the view that there are certain categories of expression that do not appreciably further the values underlying the first amendment. Examples are obscenity, commercial advertising, and false statements of fact. The Court has traditionally held that such categories of expression are either unprotected or only marginally protected by the first amendment.

In line with these distinctions, sections B and C focus primarily on government efforts to suppress "high" value speech; section D explores "low"-value expression; section E examines content-neutral restrictions and the issue of content-neutrality; and section F explores the "freedom of the press." The point of this structure is not to insulate these distinctions from challenge. It is rather to illuminate the Court's jurisprudence while at the same time facilitating critical scrutiny of the Court's analysis.

B.   CONTENT-BASED RESTRICTIONS: DANGEROUS IDEAS AND INFORMATION

In what circumstances, if any, may government, consonant with the first amendment, restrict speech because the expression of particular ideas or items of information might cause some harm to government, to private individuals, or to society in general? In addressing this question, this section examines four separate, but related, problems: speech that may induce hearers or listeners to engage in unlawful conduct; speech that "threatens" harm to others; speech that provokes a hostile audience response; and speech that discloses confidential information. In its effort to deal with these problems, the Court has struggled to identify the relevant considerations. The task is not easy. How serious must the harm be before speech may be suppressed? How likely must the harm be?

How imminent must it be? Should it matter whether the speaker intended to cause the harm? Can these and other considerations be integrated into a single, coherent standard?

1.   Speech That "Causes" Unlawful Conduct

The question whether government may constitutionally restrict expression because it might persuade, incite, or otherwise "cause" readers or listeners to engage in unlawful conduct has long absorbed the Court's attention. This was the first issue of first amendment interpretation to capture the Court's sustained interest, and the debate within the Court over this question has produced some of the most powerful and most eloquent opinions in the Court's history. That the question has played so central a role in the evolution of first amendment theory is not surprising, for it focuses on government efforts to restrict advocacy in many respects similar to the traditional concept of seditious libel and thus implicates values at the very core of the first amendment.

The Supreme Court first confronted this issue in a series of cases concerning agitation against the war and the draft during World War I. Such agitation was not uncommon:

> [When] the U.S. first entered the war, [many] influential groups of people were apathetic if not actually hostile to fighting. [Organizations] which identified themselves as against the war, [such as the Socialist Party of America], made strong gains during 1917 [and] over three hundred thirty thousand draft evaders or delinquents were reported during the war. [Antiwar] sentiment did not pose a threat of revolution or violence, but it did pose a threat of spreading disaffection which could paralyze the war effort. [Attorney] General Thomas Gregory, referring to war opponents in November, 1917, stated, "May God have mercy on them, for they need expect none from an outraged people and an avenging government."

R. Goldstein, Political Repression in Modern America 105–108 (1978).

Two months after our entry into the First World War, Congress enacted the Espionage Act of 1917. Although the act was directed primarily toward such matters as espionage and the protection of military secrets, the third section of title I of the act made it a crime when the nation is at war for any person (1) willfully to "make or convey false reports or false statements with intent to interfere" with the military success of the United States or "to promote the success of its enemies"; (2) willfully to "cause or attempt to cause insubordination, disloyalty, mutiny, or refusal of duty, in the military or naval forces of the United States"; or (3) willfully to "obstruct the recruiting or enlistment service of the United States." Violations were punishable by fines of up to $10,000, prison sentences of up to twenty years, or both. Act of June 15, 1917, ch. 30, tit. I, §3, 40 Stat. 219.

Eleven months later, Congress enacted the Sedition Act of 1918. The 1918 act, which was repealed in 1921, made it criminal, among other things, for any person to say anything with intent to obstruct the sale of war bonds; to utter, print, write, or publish any disloyal, profane, scurrilous, or abusive language intended to cause contempt or scorn for the form of government of the United States, the Constitution, or the flag; to urge the curtailment of production of war materials with the intent of hindering the war effort; or to utter any words supporting the cause of any country at war with the United States or opposing the cause of the United States. Act of May 16, 1918, ch. 75, §1, 40 Stat. 553.

During the war years, federal authorities initiated approximately two thousand prosecutions under these acts. Most of these prosecutions were brought under the 1917 statute. The opinions that follow represent three distinct analyses of the issue.

SHAFFER v. UNITED STATES, 255 F. 886 (9th Cir. 1919). Shaffer was convicted of violating the Espionage Act of 1917. The indictment alleged that Shaffer had mailed a book, The Finished Mystery, which contained several "treasonable, disloyal, and seditious utterances," specifying the following passages in particular:

> Standing opposite to these Satan has placed [a] certain delusion which is best described by the word patriotism, but which in reality is murder, the spirit of the very devil. [If] you say it is a war of defense against wanton and intolerable aggression, I must reply that [it] has yet to be proved that Germany has any intention or desire of attacking us. [The] war itself is wrong. Its prosecution will be a crime. There is not a question raised, an issue involved, a cause at stake, which is worth the life of one blue-jacket on the sea or one khaki-coat in the trenches.

The Court of Appeals affirmed the conviction: "It is true that disapproval of war and the advocacy of peace are not crimes under the Espionage Act; but the question here [is] whether the natural and probable tendency and effect of [the publication] are such as are calculated to produce the result condemned by the statute. [It cannot] be said, as a matter of law, that the reasonable and natural effect of [the] publication was not to obstruct [the] recruiting or enlistment service, and thus to injure the service of the United States. Printed matter may tend to obstruct [the] service, even if it contains no mention of recruiting or enlistment, and no reference to the military service of the United States. [The] service may be obstructed by attacking the justice of the cause for which the war is waged, and by undermining the spirit of loyalty which inspires men to enlist or to register for conscription in the service of their country. [To] teach that patriotism is murder and the spirit of the devil, and that the war against Germany was wrong and its prosecution a crime, is to weaken patriotism and the purpose to enlist or to render military service in the war. . . .

"It is argued that the evidence fails to show that [Shaffer] committed the act willfully and intentionally. But there is enough in the evidence to show the hostile attitude of his mind against the prosecution of the war by the United States, and that the books were intentionally concealed on his premises. He must be presumed to have intended the natural and probable consequences of what he knowingly did."

Masses Publishing Co. v. Patten
244 F. 535 (S.D.N.Y. 1917)

[In July 1917, the postmaster of New York, acting on the direction of the Postmaster General, advised the plaintiff, a publishing company engaged in the production of a monthly revolutionary journal called The Masses, that the August issue of the journal would be denied access to the mails under the

Espionage Act of 1917. The Masses regularly featured a remarkable collection of writers, poets, playwrights, and philosophers, including Max Eastman, John Reed, Vachel Lindsay, Emma Goldman, Carl Sandburg, Bertrand Russell, Louis Untermeyer, and Sherwood Anderson. Iconoclastic, impertinent, and confrontational, it was filled with sparkling social satire, intellectual commentary, and political criticism. Plaintiff applied for a preliminary injunction to forbid the postmaster to refuse to accept the August issue for mailing. While objecting generally that the whole purport of the issue was in violation of the law, on the ground that it tended to produce a violation of the law, to encourage the enemies of the United States, and to hamper the government in the conduct of the war, the postmaster specified four cartoons and four pieces of text as especially falling within the act.]

LEARNED HAND, DISTRICT JUDGE [after stating the facts as above]. . . .
It must be remembered at the outset, and the distinction is of critical consequence throughout, that no question arises touching the war powers of Congress. It may be that Congress may forbid the mails to any matter which tends to discourage the successful prosecution of the war. It may be that the fundamental personal rights of the individual must stand in abeyance, even including the right of the freedom of the press, though that is not here in question. . . .
[The postmaster's] position is that to arouse discontent and disaffection among the people with the prosecution of the war and with the draft tends to promote a mutinous and insubordinate temper among the troops. This [is] true; men who become satisfied that they are engaged in an enterprise dictated by the unconscionable selfishness of the rich, and effectuated by a tyrannous disregard for the will of those who must suffer and die, will be more prone to insubordination than those who have faith in the cause and acquiesce in the means. Yet to interpret the word "cause" so broadly would [involve] necessarily as a consequence the suppression of all hostile criticism, and of all opinion except what encouraged and supported the existing policies, or which fell within the range of temperate argument. It would contradict the normal assumption of democratic government that the suppression of hostile criticism does not turn upon the justice of its substance or the decency and propriety of its temper. Assuming that the power to repress such opinion may rest in Congress in the throes of a struggle for the very existence of the state, its exercise is so contrary to the use and wont of our people that only the clearest expression of such a power justifies the conclusion that it was intended.
The [postmaster's] position, therefore, in so far as it involves the suppression of the free utterance of abuse and criticism of the existing law, or of the policies of the war, is not, in my judgment, supported by the language of the statute. Yet there has always been a recognized limit to such expressions. [One] may not counsel or advise others to violate the law as it stands. Words are not only the keys of persuasion, but the triggers of action, and those which have no purport but to counsel the violation of law cannot by any latitude of interpretation be a part of that public opinion which is the final source of government in a democratic state. [To] counsel or advise a man to an act is to urge upon him either that it is his interest or his duty to do it. While, of course, this may be accomplished as well by indirection as expressly, since words carry the meaning that they impart, the definition is exhaustive, I think, and I shall use it. Political agitation, by the passions it arouses or the convictions it engenders, may in fact stimulate men to the violation of law. Detestation of existing policies is easily transformed into

forcible resistance of the authority which puts them in execution, and it would be folly to disregard the causal relation between the two. Yet to assimilate agitation, legitimate as such, with direct incitement to violent resistance, is to disregard the tolerance of all methods of political agitation which in normal times is a safeguard of free government. The distinction is not a scholastic subterfuge, but a hard-bought acquisition in the fight for freedom, and the purpose to disregard it must be evident when the power exists. If one stops short of urging upon others that it is their duty or their interest to resist the law, it seems to me one should not be held to have attempted to cause its violation. If that be not the test, I can see no escape from the conclusion that under this section every political agitation which can be shown to be apt to create a seditious temper is illegal. I am confident that by such language Congress had no such revolutionary purpose in view.

It seems to me, however, quite plain that none of the language and none of the cartoons in this paper can be thought directly to counsel or advise insubordination or mutiny, without a violation of their meaning quite beyond any tolerable understanding. I come, therefore, to the third phrase of the section, which forbids any one from willfully obstructing the recruiting or enlistment service of the United States. I am not prepared to assent to the plaintiff's position that this only refers to acts other than words, nor that the act thus defined must be shown to have been successful. One may obstruct without preventing, and the mere obstruction is an injury to the service; for it throws impediments in its way. Here again, however, since the question is of the expression of opinion, I construe the sentence, so far as it restrains public utterance, as [limited] to the direct advocacy of resistance to the recruiting and enlistment service. If so, the inquiry is narrowed to the question whether any of the challenged matter may be said to advocate resistance to the draft, taking the meaning of the words with the utmost latitude which they can bear.

As to the cartoons it seems to me quite clear that they do not fall within such a test. Certainly the nearest is that entitled "Conscription," and the most that can be said of that is that it may breed such animosity to the draft as will promote resistance and strengthen the determination of those disposed to be recalcitrant. There is no intimation that, however hateful the draft may be, one is in duty bound to resist it, certainly none that such resistance is to one's interest. I cannot, therefore, [assent] to the assertion that any of the cartoons violate the act.

The text offers more embarrassment. The poem to Emma Goldman and Alexander Berkman, at most, goes no further than to say that they are martyrs in the cause of love among nations. Such a sentiment holds them up to admiration, and hence their conduct to possible emulation. The paragraph in which the editor offers to receive funds for their appeal also expresses admiration for them, but goes no further. The paragraphs upon conscientious objectors are of the same kind. They go no further than to express high admiration for those who have held and are holding out for their convictions even to the extent of resisting the law. [That] such comments have a tendency to arouse emulation in others is clear enough, but that they counsel others to follow these examples is not so plain. Literally at least they do not, and while, as I have said, the words are to be taken, not literally, but according to their full import, the literal meaning is the starting point for interpretation. One may admire and approve the course of a hero without feeling any duty to follow him. There is not the least implied intimation in these words that others are under a duty to follow. The most that can be said is that, if others do follow, they will get the same admiration and the same approval.

Now, there is surely an appreciable distance between esteem and emulation; and unless there is here some advocacy of such emulation, I cannot see how the passages can be said to fall within the law. [The] question before me is quite the same as what would arise upon a motion to dismiss an indictment at the close of the proof: Could any reasonable man say, not that the indirect result of the language might be to arouse a seditious disposition, for that would not be enough, but that the language directly advocated resistance to the draft? I cannot think that upon such language any verdict would stand. . . .

It follows that the plaintiff is entitled to the usual preliminary injunction.

Schenck v. United States

249 U.S. 47 (1919)

MR. JUSTICE HOLMES delivered the opinion of the court. . . .

[The defendants were convicted of conspiracy to violate section 3 of the Espionage Act of 1917 by circulating "to men who had been called and accepted for military service" a document "alleged to be calculated" to obstruct the recruiting and enlistment service.]

The document in question, upon its first printed side, recited the 1st section of the Thirteenth Amendment, said that the idea embodied in it was violated by the Conscription Act, and that a conscript is little better than a convict. In impassioned language it intimated that conscription was despotism in its worst form and a monstrous wrong against humanity, in the interest of Wall Street's chosen few. It said: "Do not submit to intimidation"; but in form at least confined itself to peaceful measures, such as a petition for the repeal of the act. The other and later printed side of the sheet was headed, "Assert Your Rights." It stated reasons for alleging that anyone violated the Constitution when he refused to recognize "your right to assert your opposition to the draft," and went on: "If you do not assert and support your rights, you are helping to deny or disparage rights which it is the solemn duty of all citizens and residents of the United States to retain." It described the arguments on the other side as coming from cunning politicians and a mercenary capitalist press, and even silent consent to the Conscription Law as helping to support an infamous conspiracy. It denied the power to send our citizens away to foreign shores to shoot up the people of other lands, and added that words could not express the condemnation such cold-blooded ruthlessness deserves, etc., etc., winding up, "You must do your share to maintain, support, and uphold the rights of the people of this country." Of course the document would not have been sent unless it had been intended to have some effect, and we do not see what effect it could be expected to have upon persons subject to the draft except to influence them to obstruct the carrying of it out. The defendants do not deny that the jury might find against them on this point.

But it is said, suppose that that was the tendency of this circular, it is protected by the First Amendment to the Constitution. Two of the strongest expressions are said to be quoted respectively from well-known public men. It well may be that the prohibition of laws abridging the freedom of speech is not confined to previous restraints, although to prevent them may have been the main purpose, as intimated in Patterson v. Colorado, 205 U.S. 454, 462. We admit that in many places and in ordinary times the defendants, in saying all that was said in the circular, would have been within their constitutional rights. But the character of every act depends upon the circumstances in which it is done. The most stringent protection of free speech would not protect a man in falsely shouting fire in a theater, and causing a panic. It does not even protect a man from an injunction against uttering words that may have all the effect of force. The question in every case is whether the words used are used in such circumstances and are of such a nature as to create a clear and present danger that they will bring about the substantive evils that Congress has a right to prevent. It is a question of proximity and degree. When a nation is at war many things that might be said in time of peace are such a hindrance to its effort that their utterance will not be endured so long as men fight, and that no Court could regard them as protected by any constitutional right. It seems to be admitted that if an actual obstruction of the recruiting service were proved, liability for words that produced that effect might be enforced. The Statute of 1917, in §4, punishes conspiracies to obstruct as well as actual obstruction. If the act, (speaking, or circulating a paper,) its tendency and the intent with which it is done, are the same, we perceive no ground for saying that success alone warrants making the act a crime. Goldman v. United States, 245 U.S. 474, 477. Indeed, that case might be said to dispose of the present contention if the precedent covers all media concludendi. But as the right to free speech was not referred to specially we have thought fit to add a few words. . . .

Judgments affirmed.

Note: Shaffer, Masses, *and* Schenck

1. *The facts of* Masses. The following is one of the poems in the August 17 issues of The Masses magazine that led to the postmaster's action (Goldman and Berkman were in prison for obstructing the draft):

"A TRIBUTE"
JOSEPHINE BELL

. . .
Emma Goldman and Alexander Berkman
Are in prison tonight,
But they have made themselves elemental forces,
Like the water that climbs down the rocks:
Like the wind in the leaves:
Like the gentle night that holds us:
They are working on our destinies:
They are forging the love of the nations: . . .
Tonight they lie in prison.

2. *Bad tendency.* Shaffer reflects the then-prevailing view of the lower federal courts — that speech could constitutionally be punished as an attempt to cause some forbidden or otherwise undesirable conduct if the natural and reasonable tendency of the expression might be to bring about the conduct, and if the speaker intended such a result. Under this view, intent could be inferred from the tendency of the speech itself, on the theory that one intends the natural and foreseeable consequences of one's acts. Through the twin doctrines of bad tendency and constructive intent, decisions like *Shaffer* routinely converted criticism of the war and the draft into criminal attempts to cause insubordination or obstruct recruiting. The relatively modest provisions of the 1917 act were thus converted into essentially open-ended restrictions on seditious expression. For

detailed accounts of this era, see G. Stone, Perilous Times: Free Speech in Wartime 135–234 (2004); Z. Chafee, Free Speech in the United States 36–108 (1941); Rabban, The Emergence of Modern First Amendment Theory, 50 U. Chi. L. Rev. 1205 (1983).

3. *Express incitement.* Although Judge Hand technically limited himself in *Masses* to a mere interpretation of the Espionage Act, the opinion has clear constitutional overtones, and, as Hand himself made clear in private correspondence, *Masses* was "a distinctive, carefully considered alternative to the prevalent analyses of free speech issues." Gunther, Learned Hand and the Origins of Modern First Amendment Doctrine: Some Fragments of History, 27 Stan. L. Rev. 719, 720 (1975). In effect, Hand attempted in *Masses* to articulate a categorical, per se rule that would be "hard, conventional, difficult to evade." Id. at 749. Unlike the *Shaffer* and *Schenck* analyses, Judge Hand focused on the content of the speech rather than on the intent of the speaker or the consequences of the communication. Under Judge Hand's formula, the dispositive factor was whether the speaker employed express words of incitement. As Judge Hand intimated in his opinion and made explicit in correspondence, if the effect of such speech "upon the hearers is only to counsel them to violate the law, it is unconditionally illegal." Id. at 765. But if the speaker refrains from such incitement, the speech may not be restrained. Consider the following propositions.

a. *Hand's analysis of express incitement is underprotective of free speech.* Judge Hand's analysis accords little, if any, constitutional protection to express advocacy of criminal conduct. Is this defensible on the ground, urged by Judge Hand, that "words [which] have no purport but to counsel the violation of law cannot by any latitude of interpretation be a part of that public opinion which is the final source of government in a democratic state"? Consider Bork, Neutral Principles and Some First Amendment Problems, 47 Ind. L. Rev. 1, 31 (1971):

> Advocacy of law violation is a call to set aside the results that political speech has produced. The process of the "discovery and spread of political truth" is damaged or destroyed if the outcome is defeated by a minority that makes law enforcement, and hence the putting of political truth into practice, impossible or less effective. There should, therefore, be no constitutional protection for any speech advocating the violation of the law.

See also Stromberg v. California, 283 U.S. 359 (1931) ("The maintenance of the opportunity for free political discussion to the end that government may be responsible to the will of the people and that changes may be obtained *by lawful means* is a fundamental principle of our constitutional system.").

Even if express incitement is constitutionally "valueless," might there nonetheless be practical or institutional reasons to protect it? Consider T. Emerson, The System of Freedom of Expression 51–53 (1970):

> Groups which [would] abolish democratic institutions [do] not operate in a political vacuum. They advance other ideas that may be valid [and] groups [expressing] the prohibited views usually represent real grievances, which should be heard. [Moreover, suppression] of any group in a society destroys the atmosphere of freedom essential to the life and progress of a healthy community.

Should the rhetorical or hyperbolic use of express incitement ("Kill the umpire!") be constitutionally protected?

b. *The Hand formula is overprotective of the "clever" inciter.* Judge Hand's theory distinguishes between the speaker who uses express words of incitement and the speaker who specifically intends to incite but is clever enough to avoid the use of such language. Is this sensible? Consider the following arguments: (1) The express inciter is more dangerous because he is more likely to be effective. (2) Case-by-case inquiries into actual subjective intent are too slippery to provide adequate protection to innocent speakers. As Zechariah Chafee observed, "It is only in times of popular panic and indignation that freedom of speech becomes important as an institution, and it is precisely in those times that the protection of the jury proves [illusory]. 'Men believed during [the period of the Espionage Act prosecutions] that the only verdict in a war case, which could show loyalty, was a verdict of guilty.'" Chafee, supra, at 70. Thus, to avoid the dangers of "erroneous" fact-finding, and protect the rights of innocent dissenters, it is necessary to focus on more objective considerations than intent. (3) What really matters under the first amendment is not the intent of the speaker but the value of the expression. Since the clever inciter has not used "words [which] have no purport but to counsel the violation of law," the value of his speech is indistinguishable from that of the speaker who utters the same words with a more honorable intent.

c. *The Hand formula is overprotective of the dangerous speaker.* Suppose during a famine that a speaker angrily asserts "to an excited mob assembled before the house of a corn-dealer" that "corn-dealers are starvers of the poor," thus inflaming the mob to burn down the corn-dealer's house. J. S. Mill, On Liberty ch. 3 (1859). Is it sensible to accord absolute protection to such a speaker, without regard to the potential dangers of his speech, merely because he does not use express language of incitement? Consider the following arguments: (1) It is the actor, and not the speaker, who ultimately brings about the harm. Government should thus direct its punishment and deterrence toward actors, not speakers. (2) A central premise of the first amendment is that government may not restrict expression because it does not trust citizens to make wise decisions if they are exposed to the expression. Such "paternalism" is fundamentally at odds with the very notion of free expression. (3) As Judge Hand argued, "If that be not the test, I can see no escape from the conclusion that [every] political agitation which can be shown to be apt to create a seditious temper is illegal."

4. *The fate of* Masses. Judge Hand's opinion was reversed on appeal. Masses Publishing Co. v. Patten, 246 F. 24 (2d Cir. 1917). The court of appeals flatly rejected Judge Hand's construction of the act: "If the natural and reasonable effect of what is said is to encourage resistance to a law, and the words are used in an endeavor to persuade to resistance, it is immaterial that the duty to resist is not mentioned, or the interest of the persons addressed in resistance is not suggested." Other reactions to Judge Hand's formulation were equally unsupportive, and after 1921 Judge Hand himself abandoned his advocacy of the *Masses* approach. Parts of the formula, however, have reappeared in contemporary tests of subversive advocacy. See *Yates* and *Brandenburg*, infra, this section. The Masses itself was soon driven out of business, and its editors were prosecuted under the Espionage Act of 1917.

5. *Clear and present danger.* Whence does Justice Holmes derive the clear and present danger standard? Is Justice Holmes's famous reference to the false shout of fire helpful? Such speech, Justice Holmes implies, may be restricted because it creates a clear and present danger of panic. But suppose the shout is *true*. Would that change the analysis?

Was there a clear and present danger in *Schenck*? Of what? That the war effort would be jeopardized? That the recruiting and enlistment service would grind to a halt? That a single person might be influenced to refuse induction or not enlist? How should we deal with the possibility that there may be many Schencks?

Was Holmes's clear and present danger standard designed to supplant the prevailing bad tendency/constructive intent test? Note that the jury instructions in *Schenck* could not have embodied the clear and present danger standard, which did not yet exist. Why, then, didn't the Court remand for a new trial?

Consider the Court's decisions in *Frohwerk* and *Debs*, handed down on the same day in the spring of 1919, exactly one week after *Schenck*. Consider also the Court's decision, and Justice Holmes's dissent, in *Abrams*, handed down the following fall.

FROHWERK v. UNITED STATES, 249 U.S. 204 (1919). As a result of his participation in the preparation and publication of a series of articles in the Missouri Staats Zeitung, a German language newspaper, Frohwerk was convicted under the Espionage Act of 1917 of conspiring to cause disloyalty, mutiny, and refusal of duty in the military and naval forces of the United States. Frohwerk was sentenced to a fine and to ten years' imprisonment. The Court, speaking through Justice Holmes, unanimously rejected Frohwerk's contention that his conviction violated the first amendment. Illustrative of the articles was one that declared "it a monumental and inexcusable mistake to send our soldiers to France" and described our participation in the war as "outright murder."

Justice Holmes began his analysis by observing that the first amendment "cannot have been, and obviously was not, intended to give immunity for every possible use of language. Neither Hamilton nor Madison, nor any other competent person then or later ever supposed that to make criminal the counseling of murder within the jurisdiction of Congress would be an unconstitutional interference with free speech." Justice Holmes then turned to the crux of the issue: "It may be that all this may be said or written even in time of war in circumstances that would not make it a crime. [But] we must take the case on the record as it is, and on the record it is impossible to say that it might not have been found that the circulation of the paper was in quarters where a little breath would be enough to kindle a flame [and that that] fact was known and relied upon by those who sent the paper out." Justice Holmes therefore concluded that "we find ourselves unable to say that the articles could not furnish a basis for a conviction."

DEBS v. UNITED STATES, 249 U.S. 211 (1919). As a result of a speech delivered to a public assembly in Canton, Ohio, in July of 1918, Eugene V. Debs, national leader of the Socialist Party, was convicted under the Espionage Act of 1917 of attempting to obstruct the recruiting and enlistment service of the United States. Debs was sentenced to a prison term of ten years. The Supreme Court, speaking once again through Justice Holmes, unanimously rejected Debs's claim that the conviction violated the first amendment. Justice Holmes noted at the outset that "[the] main theme of the speech was socialism, its growth, and a prophecy of its ultimate success. With that we have nothing to do, but [if] one purpose of the speech, whether incidental or not does not matter, was to oppose [the] war, and if, in all the circumstances, that would be its probable effect, it would not be protected."

Turning to the speech itself, Justice Holmes observed that Debs had specifically praised several persons who previously had been convicted of aiding or encouraging others to refuse induction, and that toward the end of his address Debs had told his audience that "you need to know that you are fit for something better than slavery and cannon fodder." In such circumstances, Justice Holmes concluded that Debs's first amendment claim had in practical effect been "disposed of in [*Schenck*]." Justice Holmes emphasized that the jury in *Debs* had been "most carefully instructed that they could not find the defendant guilty for advocacy of any of his opinions unless the words used had as their natural tendency and reasonably probable effect to obstruct the recruiting service [and] unless the defendant had the specific intent to do so in his mind." As in *Frohwerk*, Justice Holmes made no reference in *Debs* to "clear and present danger."

In 1920, while in prison, Debs was the Socialist candidate for President. He again received almost a million votes. President Harding released him from prison in 1921.

Other representative prosecutions under the Espionage Act include the following:

(a) Rose Pastor Stokes was convicted for saying, "I am for the people and the government is for the profiteers," during an antiwar talk to the Women's Dining Club of Kansas City. Although there were no soldiers — indeed, no men — in her intended audience, the government successfully argued that she had violated the act because "our armies . . . can operate and succeed only so far as they are supported and maintained by the folks at home," and Stokes's statement had the tendency to "chill enthusiasm, extinguish confidence, and retard cooperation" of mothers, sisters, and sweethearts. She was sentenced to ten years in prison.

(b) The Reverend Clarence H. Waldron was convicted for distributing a pamphlet stating that "if Christians [are] forbidden to fight to preserve the Person of their Lord and Master, they may not fight to preserve themselves, or any city they should happen to dwell in." The government charged that in distributing this pamphlet Waldron had obstructed the recruiting service. He was sentenced to fifteen years in prison.

(c) Robert Goldstein was convicted for producing and exhibiting a motion picture about the American Revolution. The Spirit of '76 depicted Paul Revere's ride, the signing of the Declaration of Independence, and Washington at Valley Forge. But it also included a scene accurately portraying the Wyoming Valley Massacre, in which British soldiers bayoneted women and children. The government charged that this could promote insubordination because it negatively portrayed America's ally in the war against Germany. Goldstein was sentenced to ten years in prison. See G. Stone, Perilous Times: Free Speech in Wartime 170–173 (2004).

Abrams v. United States

250 U.S. 616 (1919)

[Although Czarist Russia, like the United States, had declared war on Germany, the Bolsheviks, on seizing power, signed a peace treaty with Germany. In the summer of 1918, the United States sent a contingent of marines to Vladivostok and Murmansk. The defendants in *Abrams*, a group of Russian immigrants who were self-proclaimed socialists and anarchists, perceived the expedition as an attempt to "crush the Russian Revolution." In protest, they distributed several thousand copies of each of two leaflets, one of which was written in English, the other in Yiddish. The leaflets, which were thrown from a window and circulated secretly, called for a general strike. The defendants were arrested by the military police, and after a controversial trial, they were convicted of conspiring to violate various provisions of the 1918 amendments to the Espionage Act of 1917. The overall flavor of the trial is captured in the trial judge's remarks just prior to sentencing:

> These defendants took the stand. They talked about capitalists and producers, and I tried to figure out what a capitalist and what a producer is as contemplated by them. After listening carefully to all they had to say, I came to the conclusion that a capitalist is a man with a decent set of clothes, a minimum of $1.25 in his pocket, and a good character. And when I tried to find out what the prisoners had produced, I was unable to find out anything at all. So far as I can learn, not one of them ever produced so much as a single potato. The only thing they know how to raise is hell, and to direct it against the government of the United States. [But] we are not going to help carry out the plans mapped out by the Imperial German Government, and which are being carried out by Lenin and Trotsky. I have heard of the reported fate of the poor little daughters of the Czar, but I won't talk about that now. I might get mad. I will now sentence the prisoners.

The defendants were sentenced to prison terms ranging from three to twenty years. The Supreme Court affirmed the convictions on two counts: one charging a violation of the provision prohibiting conspiracy "to incite, provoke or encourage resistance to the United States" (count 3); the other charging a violation of the provision prohibiting conspiracy to urge curtailment of the production of war materials "with intent [to] cripple or hinder the United States in the prosecution of the war" (count 4). Speaking for the Court, Justice Clarke summarily rejected the defendants' first amendment argument, noting simply that "[this] contention is sufficiently discussed and is definitely negatived in [*Schenck*] and [*Frohwerk*]."]

MR. JUSTICE HOLMES dissenting. . . .
The first of these leaflets says that the President's cowardly silence about the intervention in Russia reveals the hypocrisy of the plutocratic gang in Washington. It intimates that "German militarism combined with allied capitalism to crush the Russian revolution." [It] says that there is only one enemy of the workers of the world and that is capitalism; that it is a crime for workers of America, &c., to fight the workers' republic of Russia, and ends "Awake! Awake, you Workers of the World! Revolutionists." A note adds "It is absurd to call us pro-German. We hate and despise German militarism more than do you hypocritical tyrants. We have more reasons for denouncing German militarism than has the coward of the White House."
The other leaflet, headed "Workers — Wake Up," with abusive language says that [the] hypocrites shall not fool the Russian emigrants and friends of Russia in America. It tells the Russian emigrants that they now must spit in the face of the false military propaganda by which their sympathy and help to the prosecution of the war have been called forth and says that with the money they have lent or are going to lend "they will make bullets not only for the Germans but also for the Workers Soviets of Russia," and further, "Workers in the ammunition factories, you are producing bullets, bayonets, cannon, to murder not only the Germans, but also your dearest, best, who are in Russia and are fighting for freedom." It then appeals to the same Russian emigrants at some length not to consent to the "inquisitionary expedition to Russia," and says that the destruction of the Russian revolution is "the politics of the march to Russia." The leaflet winds up by saying

"Workers, our reply to this barbarous intervention has to be a general strike!," and after a few words on the spirit of revolution, exhortations not to be afraid, and some usual tall talk ends "Woe unto those who will be in the way of progress. Let solidarity live! The Rebels."

[After describing the leaflets, Justice Holmes argued that the conviction under the fourth count was invalid because the defendants did not have the intent, required by the act, "to cripple or hinder the United States in the prosecution of the war." The defendants' specific intent, Justice Holmes maintained, was to help Russia, with whom we were not at war. Although conceding that "the word *intent* as vaguely used in ordinary legal discussion means no more than knowledge at the time of the act that the consequences said to be intended will ensue," Justice Holmes insisted that "this statute must be taken to use its words in a strict and accurate sense." Otherwise, Justice Holmes reasoned, the act would "be absurd," for it would make it criminal for one who thought "we were wasting money on aeroplanes" successfully to advocate curtailment if such curtailment later turned out "to hinder the United States in the prosecution of the war." Justice Holmes then passed to what he referred to as "a more important aspect of the case" — the first amendment.]

I never have seen any reason to doubt that the questions of law that alone were before this Court in the cases of *Schenck, Frohwerk* and *Debs* were rightly decided. I do not doubt for a moment that by the same reasoning that would justify punishing persuasion to murder, the United States constitutionally may punish speech that produces or is intended to produce a clear and imminent danger that it will bring about forthwith certain substantive evils that the United States constitutionally may seek to prevent. The power undoubtedly is greater in time of war than in time of peace because war opens dangers that do not exist at other times.

But as against dangers peculiar to war, as against others, the principle of the right to free speech is always the same. It is only the present danger of immediate evil or an intent to bring it about that warrants Congress in setting a limit to the expression of opinion where private rights are not concerned. Congress certainly cannot forbid all effort to change the mind of the country. Now nobody can suppose that the surreptitious publishing of a silly leaflet by an unknown man, without more, would present any immediate danger that its opinions would hinder the success of the government arms or have any appreciable tendency to do so. Publishing those opinions for the very purpose of obstructing, however, might indicate a greater danger and at any rate would have the quality of an attempt. So I assume that the second leaflet if published for the purposes alleged in the fourth count might be punishable. But [I] do not see how anyone can find the intent required by the statute in any of the defendants' words. The second leaflet is the only one that affords even a foundation for the charge, and there, without invoking the hatred of German militarism expressed in the former one, it is evident from the beginning to the end that the only object of the paper is to help Russia and stop American intervention there against the popular government — not to impede the United States in the war that it was carrying on. To say that two phrases taken literally might import a suggestion of conduct that would have interference with the war as an indirect and probably undesired effect seems to me by no means enough to show an attempt to produce that effect.

In this case sentences of twenty years imprisonment have been imposed for the publishing of two leaflets that I believe the defendants had as much right to publish as the Government has to publish the Constitution of the United States now vainly invoked by them. Even if I am technically wrong and enough can be squeezed from these poor and puny anonymities to turn the color of legal litmus paper; I will add, even if what I think the necessary intent were shown; the most nominal punishment seems to me all that possibly could be inflicted, unless the defendants are to be made to suffer not for what the indictment alleges but for the creed that they avow — a creed that I believe to be the creed of ignorance and immaturity when honestly held, as I see no reason to doubt that it was held here, but which, although made the subject of examination at the trial, no one has a right even to consider in dealing with the charges before the Court.

Persecution for the expression of opinions seems to me perfectly logical. If you have no doubt of your premises or your power and want a certain result with all your heart you naturally express your wishes in law and sweep away all opposition. To allow opposition by speech seems to indicate that you think the speech impotent, as when a man says that he has squared the circle, or that you do not care whole-heartedly for the result, or that you doubt either your power or your premises. But when men have realized that time has upset many fighting faiths, they may come to believe even more than they believe the very foundations of their own conduct that the ultimate good desired is better reached by free trade in ideas — that the best test of truth is the power of the thought to get itself accepted in the competition of the market, and that truth is the only ground upon which their wishes safely can be carried out. That at any rate is the theory of our Constitution. It is an experiment, as all life is an experiment. Every year if not every day we have to wager our salvation upon some prophecy based upon imperfect knowledge. While that experiment is part of our system I think that we should be eternally vigilant against attempts to check the expression of opinions that we loathe and believe to be fraught with death, unless they so imminently threaten immediate interference with the lawful and pressing purposes of the law that an immediate check is required to save the country. I wholly disagree with the argument of the Government that the First Amendment left the common law as to seditious libel in force. History seems to me against the notion. I had conceived that the United States through many years had shown its repentance for the Sedition Act of 1798, by repaying fines that it imposed. Only the emergency that makes it immediately dangerous to leave the correction of evil counsels to time warrants making any exception to the sweeping command, "Congress shall make no law . . . abridging the freedom of speech." Of course I am speaking only of expressions of opinion and exhortations, which were all that were uttered here, but I regret that I cannot put into more impressive words my belief that in their conviction upon this indictment the defendants were deprived of their rights under the Constitution of the United States.

MR. JUSTICE BRANDEIS concurs with the foregoing opinion.

Note: Abrams *and the Emergence of the Holmes/Brandeis Tradition*

1. *Historical context.* For a lively telling of the full story of the *Abrams* case, see R. Polenberg, Fighting Faiths (1987). The defendants in *Abrams* were a fascinating group. One of Abrams's co-defendants, Mollie Steimer, arrived at Ellis Island in 1913 with her parents and her five brothers and sisters, part of the flood of immigrants fleeing poverty and anti-Semitism in csarist Russia. Two days after her arrival, the fifteen-year-old Steimer went to work in a grimy garment factory

amid the crowded tenements of New York's Lower East Side. Faced with continuing hardship and bleak prospects for the future, she began to explore radical literature and soon became a committed anarchist.

At the time of her trial, she was only twenty years old. At four feet nine inches and less than ninety pounds she was tiny, but she was tough as nails. After her conviction, she was sentenced to fifteen years in prison. In 1922, she was ordered deported to the Soviet Union. When she was informed of this action, she refused to leave the federal penitentiary, because there was a threatened railroad strike and she would not ride on a train run by strikebreakers. After the strike was resolved, she was shipped back to Russia.

Once there, she immediately began protesting the injustices of Soviet society. In 1923, the Soviets deported Steimer to Germany. Few other people have the distinction of having been deported by both the United States and the Soviet Union. In 1933, when Hitler came to power, Steimer fled to Paris. Her Jewish and anarchist identities caught up with her, however, and after the Nazis occupied France she escaped to Mexico. Steimer died in Cuernavaca in 1980 at the age of eighty-two. See G. Stone, Perilous Times: Free Speech in Wartime 138–140, 232–233 (2004).

2. *The Holmes transformation.* Most commentators have concluded that Justice Holmes moved from a narrow construction of the first amendment in *Schenck, Frohwerk,* and *Debs* to a more civil libertarian position in his dissent in *Abrams.* Holmes apparently was influenced during the summer of 1919 by a lively set of exchanges about free speech with Learned Hand, Zechariah Chafee, and Harold Laski. In 1922, Holmes confessed in a letter to Chafee that before the summer of 1919, when it came to issues of free speech and tolerance, "I was simply ignorant." See G. Stone, Perilous Times: Free Speech in Wartime 198–211 (2004); Rabban, The Emergence of Modern First Amendment Doctrine, 50 U. Chi. L. Rev. 1207, 1208–1209, 1311–1317 (1983). For a full account of Holmes's transformation, see T. Healy, The Great Dissent: How Oliver Wendell Holmes Changed His Mind — and Changed the History of Free Speech in America 201, 343 (2013).

3. *The administrability of clear and present danger.* Is Justice Holmes's formulation of clear and present danger in *Abrams* administratively workable? Judge Hand was largely unimpressed with Justice Holmes's effort. As he wrote to Chafee,

> I am not wholly in love with Holmesey's test, [for once] you admit that the matter is one of degree, [you] give to Tomdickandharry, D.J., so much latitude that the jig is at once up. Besides [the] Nine Elder Statesmen have not shown themselves wholly immune from the "herd instinct" and what seems "immediate and direct" to-day may seem very remote next year even though the circumstances surrounding the utterance be unchanged. I own I should prefer a qualitative formula, hard, conventional, difficult to evade.

In short, Judge Hand preferred "a test based upon the nature of the utterance itself." Gunther, Learned Hand and the Origins of Modern First Amendment Doctrine: Some Fragments of History, 27 Stan. L. Rev. 719, 749 (1975).

4. *Was there a clear and present danger in* Abrams? Consider Wigmore's criticism:

> [The *Abrams* dissent] is dallying with the facts and the law. [If] these [individuals] could, without the law's restraint, urge munition workers to a general strike and

armed violence, then others could lawfully do so; and a thousand disaffected undesirables, aliens and natives alike, were ready and waiting to do so. [If] such urgings were lawful, every munitions factory in the country could be stopped by them. The relevant amount of harm that one criminal act can effect is no measure of its criminality, and no measure of the danger of its criminality.

Wigmore, Abrams v. United States: Freedom of Speech and Freedom of Thuggery in War-Time and Peace-Time, 14 Ill. L. Rev. 539, 549–550 (1920).

5. *The rationale of clear and present danger.* Consider the following rationales for the clear and present danger standard: (a) The test balances competing speech and societal interests — speech is important, so government can restrict it only when there is an "emergency"; an "emergency" exists only if the danger is "clear" and "present." (b) The test marks off a broad area of protected expression to avoid Judge Hand's concern in *Masses* that government not be permitted to render unlawful "every political agitation which can be shown to be apt to create a seditious temper." (c) The test is designed to reduce the risk that government, in the guise of preventing "danger," will in fact suppress expression because it disapproves of the substantive message.

6. *"Sentences of twenty years imprisonment."* Holmes is clearly appalled that the defendants in *Abrams* were sentenced to terms "of twenty years imprisonment." He implies that the only plausible explanation for such severe punishment is that the defendants were being "made to suffer" not for any actual harm they might have caused to the nation (which he regards as trivial), but because of the government's hostility to their ideas (which he regards as impermissible). Suppose, then, that the defendants had been sentenced to a fine of $100 instead of to twenty years in prison. Should that have changed Holmes's analysis or the result? Should the nature or severity of the penalty be relevant to the constitutionality of a restriction of speech? See Coenen, Of Speech and Sanctions: Toward a Penalty-Sensitive Approach to the First Amendment, 112 Colum. L. Rev. 991 (2012).

7. *Other Espionage Act decisions.* In several post-*Abrams* decisions, the Court, over the dissents of Justices Holmes and Brandeis, upheld further convictions under the Espionage Act. See Pierce v. United States, 252 U.S. 239 (1920); Schaefer v. United States, 251 U.S. 466 (1920). See also Gilbert v. Minnesota, 254 U.S. 325 (1920).

Consider L. Weinrib, The Taming of Free Speech 123-24 (2016):

The Holmes and Brandeis dissents in [*Abrams*] and the remaining wartime speech cases galvanized liberal support for free speech. [But there] were details to be worked out. [Many] of the strongest advocates for expressive freedom continued to harbor deep reservations about advancing their agenda in the courts. [Felix Frankfurter, for example,] worried about expanding judicial oversight of the political branches [and University of Chicago law professor Ernst Freund [criticized] the Supreme Court's Espionage Act decisions for swapping an "arbitrary executive" with "arbitrary judicial power." [As] a correspondent complained to [Harvard law professor Zechariah] Chafee in 1921, "It seems the hardest thing in the world to straighten out the honest conservative mind on this question of free speech."

8. *The "Red Scare."* After World War I and the Russian Revolution, the United States entered a period of intense antiradicalism. In the years 1919 and 1920, an

era known as the "Red Scare," two-thirds of the states enacted laws prohibiting the advocacy of criminal syndicalism and criminal anarchy. In addition, two-thirds of the states adopted "red flag" laws, which made it a crime to display a red flag with a seditious intent. On the Red Scare, see G. Stone, supra, at 220–226; Z. Chafee, Free Speech in the United States 141–168 (1941). It was not long before the Court had to rule on the constitutionality of such legislation.

9. *Free Speech and Labor Agitation.* A central feature in the early battles over free speech in the United States involved disputes over labor agitation. In the early decades of the twentieth century, labor sympathizers turned bitterly against the courts for their refusal to recognize the free speech rights of labor. For an insightful telling of this story, see L. Weinrib, The Taming of Free Speech (2016).

Gitlow v. New York

268 U.S. 652 (1925)

MR. JUSTICE SANFORD delivered the opinion of the Court.

Benjamin Gitlow was indicted in the Supreme Court of New York, with three others, for the statutory crime of criminal anarchy. [He] was separately tried, convicted, and sentenced to imprisonment. . . .

The contention here is that the statute, by its terms and as applied in this case, is repugnant to the due process clause of the Fourteenth Amendment. Its material provisions are: . . .

§161. *Advocacy of criminal anarchy.* Any person [who] advocates, advises, or teaches the duty, necessity or propriety of overthrowing [organized] government by force or violence, or by assassination of [any] of the executive officials of government, or by any unlawful means; [is] guilty of a felony. . . .

[The] defendant is a member of the Left Wing Section of the Socialist Party, a dissenting branch or faction of that party formed in opposition to its dominant policy of "moderate Socialism." [The] Left Wing Section was organized nationally at a conference in New York City in June, 1919, attended by ninety delegates from twenty different States. The conference elected a National Council, of which the defendant was a member, and left to it the adoption of a "manifesto." This was published in The Revolutionary Age, the official organ of the Left Wing. The defendant [arranged] for the printing [and publication of the first issue of the paper, which contained the Left Wing Manifesto].

[The indictment charged that, as a result of his involvement in the publication of the manifesto, he "had advocated, advised and taught the duty, necessity and propriety of overthrowing and overturning organized government by force, violence and unlawful means." The Court conceded that there "was no evidence of any effect resulting from the publication and circulation of the Manifesto."]

The statute does not penalize the utterance or publication of abstract "doctrine" or academic discussion having no quality of incitement to any concrete action. It is not aimed against mere historical or philosophical essays. It does not restrain the advocacy of changes in the form of government by constitutional and lawful means. What it prohibits is language advocating, advising or teaching the overthrow of organized government by unlawful means. These words imply urging to action. . . .

The Manifesto, plainly, is neither the statement of abstract doctrine nor, as suggested by counsel, mere prediction that industrial disturbances and revolutionary mass strikes will result spontaneously in an inevitable process of evolution in the economic system. It advocates and urges in fervent language mass action which shall progressively foment industrial disturbances and through political mass strikes and revolutionary mass action overthrow and destroy organized parliamentary government. It concludes with a call to action in these words: "The proletariat revolution and the Communist reconstruction of society — *the struggle for these* — is now indispensable. . . . The Communist International calls the proletariat of the world to the final struggle!" This [is] the language of direct incitement. [That] the jury were warranted in finding that the Manifesto advocated not merely the abstract doctrine of overthrowing organized government by force, violence and unlawful means, but action to that end, is clear.

For present purposes we may and do assume that freedom of speech and of the press — which are protected by the First Amendment from abridgment by Congress — are among the fundamental personal rights and "liberties" protected by the due process clause of the Fourteenth Amendment from impairment by the States. . . .

It is a fundamental principle, long established, that the freedom of speech and of the press which is secured by the Constitution, does not confer an absolute right to speak or publish, without responsibility, whatever one may choose, or an unrestricted and unbridled license that gives immunity for every possible use of language and prevents the punishment of those who abuse this freedom. [A] State may punish utterances endangering the foundations of organized government and threatening its overthrow by unlawful means. These imperil its own existence as a constitutional State. Freedom of speech and press [does] not deprive a State of the primary and essential right of self preservation. . . .

By enacting the present statute the State has determined, through its legislative body, that utterances advocating the overthrow of organized government by force, violence and unlawful means, are so inimical to the general welfare and involve such danger of substantive evil that they may be penalized in the exercise of its police power. That determination must be given great weight. Every presumption is to be indulged in favor of the validity of the statute. Mugler v. Kansas, 123 U.S. 623, 661. [That] utterances inciting to the overthrow of organized government by unlawful means, present a sufficient danger of substantive evil to bring their punishment within the range of legislative discretion, is clear. Such utterances, by their very nature, involve danger to the public peace and to the security of the State. They threaten breaches of the peace and ultimate revolution. And the immediate danger is none the less real and substantial, because the effect of a given utterance cannot be accurately foreseen. The State cannot reasonably be required to measure the danger from every such utterance in the nice balance of a jeweler's scale. A single revolutionary spark may kindle a fire that, smouldering for a time, may burst into a sweeping and destructive conflagration. It cannot be said that the State is acting arbitrarily or unreasonably when in the exercise of its judgment as to the measures necessary to protect the public peace and safety, it seeks to extinguish the spark without waiting until it has enkindled the flame or blazed into the conflagration. It cannot reasonably be required to defer the adoption of measures for its own peace and safety until the revolutionary utterances lead to actual disturbances of the public peace or imminent and immediate danger of its own destruction; but it may, in the exercise of its judgment, suppress the threatened danger in its incipiency. . . .

We cannot hold that the present statute is an arbitrary or unreasonable exercise of the police power of the State unwarrantably infringing the freedom of speech or press; and we must and do sustain its constitutionality.

This being so it may be applied to every utterance — not too trivial to be beneath the notice of the law — which is of such a character and used with such intent and purpose as to bring it within the prohibition of the statute. [In] other words, when the legislative body has determined generally, in the constitutional exercise of its discretion, that utterances of a certain kind involve such danger of substantive evil that they may be punished, the question whether any specific utterance coming within the prohibited class is likely, in and of itself, to bring about the substantive evil, is not open to consideration. It is sufficient that the statute itself be constitutional and that the use of the language comes within its prohibition. . . .

Affirmed.

MR. JUSTICE HOLMES dissenting.

Mr. Justice Brandeis and I are of opinion that this judgment should be reversed. The general principle of free speech, it seems to me, must be taken to be included in the Fourteenth Amendment, in view of the scope that has been given to the word "liberty" as there used, although perhaps it may be accepted with a somewhat larger latitude of interpretation than is allowed to Congress by the sweeping language that governs, or ought to govern, the laws of the United States. If I am right, then I think that the criterion sanctioned by the full court in [*Schenck*] applies: "The question in every case is whether the words used are used in such circumstances and are of such a nature as to create a clear and present danger that they will bring about the substantive evils that [the state] has a right to prevent." It is true that in my opinion this criterion was departed from in [*Abrams*], but the convictions that I expressed in that case are too deep for it to be possible for me as yet to believe that it [has] settled the law. If what I think the correct test is applied, it is manifest that there was no present danger of an attempt to overthrow the government by force on the part of the admittedly small minority who shared the defendant's views. It is said that this Manifesto was more than a theory, that it was an incitement. Every idea is an incitement. It offers itself for belief, and, if believed, it is acted on unless some other belief outweighs it, or some failure of energy stifles the movement at its birth. The only difference between the expression of an opinion and an incitement in the narrower sense is the speaker's enthusiasm for the result. Eloquence may set fire to reason. But whatever may be thought of the redundant discourse before us, it had no chance of starting a present conflagration. If, in the long run, the beliefs expressed in proletarian dictatorship are destined to be accepted by the dominant forces of the community, the only meaning of free speech is that they should be given their chance and have their way.

If the publication of this document had been laid as an attempt to induce an uprising against government at once, and not at some indefinite time in the future, it would have presented a different question. The object would have been one with which the law might deal, subject to the doubt whether there was any danger that the publication could produce any result; or, in other words, whether it was not futile and too remote from possible consequences. But the indictment alleges the publication and nothing more.

Note: "Abstract Doctrine" versus "Urging to Action"

1. *Incitement.* Justice Sanford emphasized repeatedly in *Gitlow* that the New York statute was not directed against "abstract doctrine," "academic discussion," "historical or philosophical essays," or "advocacy of changes in the form of government by constitutional and lawful means." Rather, it restricted only "urging to action," "incitement to [concrete] action," and "the language of direct incitement." Justice Sanford thus seemed to be suggesting an analysis reminiscent of that of Judge Hand in *Masses*, arguing implicitly that whatever protection might be appropriate for "abstract doctrine" or for general political discussion, express "incitement" of unlawful conduct is an entirely different matter. Is Justice Holmes's reply to this argument that "every idea is an incitement" a satisfactory response?

2. *The marketplace of ideas.* In *Abrams*, Justice Holmes maintained that as an "experiment" our Constitution embraced the "theory" that "the best test of truth is the power of the thought to get itself accepted in the competition of the market." The market, however, is not perfect and in *Gitlow* Justice Holmes conceded that, "if, in the long run, the beliefs expressed in proletarian dictatorship are destined to be accepted by the dominant forces of the community, the only meaning of free speech is that they should be given their chance and have their way." What about ideas that, if accepted, would refuse to permit other ideas to compete in the "market"? Are some evils so grave that we cannot afford to "experiment"?

Consider Stone, Reflections on the First Amendment: The Evolution of the American Jurisprudence of Free Expression, 131 Proc. of the J. Am. Phil. Socy. 251, 253 (1987):

> [The central principle of first amendment jurisprudence is that] the Government may *never* restrict the expression of particular ideas because it fears that citizens may adopt those ideas in the political process. As Alexander Meiklejohn explained, this principle is rooted "in the very foundations of the self-governing process," for when individuals "govern themselves it is they — and no one else — who must pass judgment upon unwisdom, unfairness and danger." Under this view, "no suggestion of policy" may be denied a hearing "because someone in control thinks it unwise."
>
> Now, there is an anomaly in this principle, [for] if the essential goal is to preserve self-governance, why can't citizens, acting in their capacity as self-governors, decide that certain policies are simply out-of-bounds and thus prohibit further debate on such issues? Under this view, it is not the Government, as some independent entity, that is closing off debate, but citizens themselves, and they are doing so through the very self-governing process that the First Amendment is designed to promote.
>
> The answer, I think, is that the First Amendment [places] out of bounds any law that attempts to freeze public debate at a particular moment in time. Under this view, a majority at any moment has the power to decide an issue of policy for itself, but it has no power irrevocably to decide that issue for future citizens by preventing them from continuing to debate the issue. This is [what] Justice Holmes described as the great First Amendment "experiment."

Is there a difference under the marketplace theory between advocacy of change through political processes and advocacy of change through criminal conduct? Must those who seek to implement their ideas by the use of force or violence "be given their chance" to "have their way"?

Whitney v. California

274 U.S. 357 (1927)

MR. JUSTICE SANFORD delivered the opinion of the Court.

[In 1919, Anita Whitney attended the national convention of the Socialist Party in Chicago as a delegate of the local Oakland branch of the party. At this convention, the party split between the "radicals" and the old-line Socialists. The radicals, supported by the Oakland branch delegates, formed the Communist Labor Party and promulgated a platform similar in style and substance to the Left Wing Manifesto at issue in *Gitlow*. Shortly thereafter, Whitney attended a convention held in Oakland for the purpose of organizing a California branch of the Communist Labor Party. At this convention, she sponsored a moderate resolution calling for the achievement of the party's goals through the political process. This resolution was defeated, however, and the convention adopted the more militant national platform. Whitney remained at the convention until it adjourned and remained a member of the party. As a result of her activities at the Oakland convention, she was charged with violating the California Criminal Syndicalism Act, which prohibited any person to knowingly become a member of any organization that advocates "the commission of crime, sabotage, or unlawful acts of force and violence or unlawful methods of terrorism as a means of accomplishing a change in industrial ownership or control, or effecting any political change." For an excellent account of Ms. Whitney's life and of the trial and appellate proceedings in the case, see Blasi, The First Amendment and the Ideal of Civic Courage: The Brandeis Opinion in Whitney v. California, 29 Wm. & Mary L. Rev. 653 (1988).]

The first count of the information, on which the conviction was had, charged that [at the Oakland convention] the defendant, in violation of the Criminal Syndicalism Act, "did then and there [knowingly] became a member of [a group] organized [to advocate] criminal syndicalism." . . .

[At her trial, Whitney] testified that it was not her intention that the Communist Labor Party of California should be an instrument of terrorism or violence. [But by] enacting the provisions of the Syndicalism Act the State has declared, [for an individual] to knowingly be or become a member of [an organization that advocates criminal syndicalism] involves such danger to the public peace and the security of the State [that] these acts should be penalized in the exercise of its police power. That determination must be given great weight. . . .

The essence of the offense denounced by the Act [partakes] of the nature of a criminal conspiracy. [That] such united and joint action involves even greater danger to the public peace and security than the isolated utterances and acts of individuals, is clear. We cannot hold that, as here applied, the Act is an unreasonable or arbitrary exercise of the police power of the State. . . .

Affirmed.

MR. JUSTICE BRANDEIS, concurring. . . .

[Although] the rights of free speech and assembly are fundamental, they are not in their nature absolute. Their exercise is subject to restriction, if the particular restriction proposed is required in order to protect the state from destruction or from serious injury, political, economic or moral. That the necessity which is essential to a valid restriction does not exist unless speech would produce, or is intended to produce, a clear and imminent danger of some substantive evil which the state constitutionally may seek to prevent has been settled. See [*Schenck*].

It is said to be the function of the legislature to determine whether at a particular time and under the particular circumstances the formation of, or assembly with, a society organized to advocate criminal syndicalism constitutes a clear and present danger of substantive evil; and that by enacting the law here in question the legislature of California determined that question in the affirmative. [The] legislature must obviously decide, in the first instance, whether a danger exists which calls for a particular protective measure. But where a statute is valid only in case certain conditions exist, the enactment of the statute cannot alone establish the facts which are essential to its validity. . . .

This court has not yet fixed the standard by which to determine when a danger shall be deemed clear; how remote the danger may be and yet be deemed present; and what degree of evil shall be deemed sufficiently substantial to justify resort to abridgment of free speech and assembly as the means of protection. To reach sound conclusions on these matters, we must bear in mind why a state is, ordinarily, denied the power to prohibit dissemination of social, economic and political doctrine which a vast majority of its citizens believes to be false and fraught with evil consequence.

Those who won our independence believed that the final end of the state was to make men free to develop their faculties; and that in its government the deliberative forces should prevail over the arbitrary. They valued liberty both as an end and as a means. They believed liberty to be the secret of happiness and courage to be the secret of liberty. They believed that freedom to think as you will and to speak as you think are means indispensable to the discovery and spread of political truth; that without free speech and assembly discussion would be futile; that with them, discussion affords ordinarily adequate protection against the dissemination of noxious doctrine; that the greatest menace to freedom is an inert people; that public discussion is a political duty; and that this should be a fundamental principle of the American government. They recognized the risks to which all human institutions are subject. But they knew that order cannot be secured merely through fear of punishment for its infraction; that it is hazardous to discourage thought, hope and imagination; that fear breeds repression; that repression breeds hate; that hate menaces stable government; that the path of safety lies in the opportunity to discuss freely supposed grievances and proposed remedies; and that the fitting remedy for evil counsels is good ones. Believing in the power of reason as applied through public discussion, they eschewed silence coerced by law — the argument of force in its worst form. Recognizing the occasional tyrannies of governing majorities, they amended the Constitution so that free speech and assembly should be guaranteed.

Fear of serious injury cannot alone justify suppression of free speech and assembly. Men feared witches and burned women. It is the function of speech to free men from the bondage of irrational fears. To justify suppression of free speech there must be reasonable ground to fear that serious evil will result if free speech is practiced. There must be reasonable ground to believe that the danger apprehended is imminent. There must be reasonable ground to believe that the evil to be prevented is a serious one. Every denunciation of existing law tends in some measure to increase the probability that there will be violation of it. Condonation of a breach enhances the probability. Expressions of approval add to the probability. Propagation of the criminal state of mind by teaching syndicalism increases it. Advocacy of lawbreaking heightens it still further. But even advocacy of violation, however reprehensible morally, is not a justification for denying free speech where the advocacy falls short of incitement and there is nothing to indicate that the advocacy would be immediately acted on. The wide difference between advocacy and incitement, between preparation and attempt, between assembling and conspiracy, must be borne in mind. In order to support a finding of clear and present danger it must be shown either that immediate serious violence was to be expected or was advocated, or that the past conduct furnished reason to believe that such advocacy was then contemplated.

Those who won our independence by revolution were not cowards. They did not fear political change. They did not exalt order at the cost of liberty. To courageous, self-reliant men, with confidence in the power of free and fearless reasoning applied through the processes of popular government, no danger flowing from speech can be deemed clear and present, unless the incidence of the evil apprehended is so imminent that it may befall before there is opportunity for full discussion. If there be time to expose through discussion the falsehood and fallacies, to avert the evil by the processes of education, the remedy to be applied is more speech, not enforced silence. Only an emergency can justify repression. Such must be the rule if authority is to be reconciled with freedom. Such, in my opinion, is the command of the Constitution. It is, therefore, always open to Americans to challenge a law abridging free speech and assembly by showing that there was no emergency justifying it.

Moreover, even imminent danger cannot justify resort to prohibition of these functions essential to effective democracy, unless the evil apprehended is relatively serious. Prohibition of free speech and assembly is a measure so stringent that it would be inappropriate as the means for averting a relatively trivial harm to society. A police measure may be unconstitutional merely because the remedy, although effective as means of protection, is unduly harsh or oppressive. Thus, a state might, in the exercise of its police power, make any trespass upon the land of another a crime, regardless of the results or of the intent or purpose of the trespasser. It might, also, punish an attempt, a conspiracy, or an incitement to commit the trespass. But it is hardly conceivable that this court would hold constitutional a statute which punished as a felony the mere voluntary assembly with a society formed to teach that pedestrians had the moral right to cross unenclosed, unposted, waste lands and to advocate their doing so, even if there was imminent danger that advocacy would lead to a trespass. The fact that speech is likely to result in some violence or in destruction of property is not enough to justify its suppression. There must be the probability of serious injury to the state. Among freemen, the deterrents ordinarily to be applied to prevent crime are education and punishment for violations of the law, not abridgment of the rights of free speech and assembly.

The California Syndicalism Act recites, in §4:

> [This] act concerns and is necessary to the immediate preservation of the public peace and safety, for the reason that at the present time large numbers of persons are going from place to place in this state advocating, teaching and practicing criminal syndicalism. . . .

This legislative declaration satisfies the requirement of the Constitution of the state concerning emergency legislation. [But] it does not preclude inquiry into the question whether, at the time and under the circumstances, the conditions existed which are essential to validity under the Federal Constitution. As a statute, even if not void on its face, may be challenged because invalid as applied, [the] result of such an inquiry may depend upon the specific facts of the particular case. Whenever the fundamental rights of free speech and assembly are alleged to have been invaded, it must remain open to a defendant to present the issue whether there actually did exist at the time a clear danger; whether the danger, if any, was imminent; and whether the evil apprehended was one so substantial as to justify the stringent restriction interposed by the legislature. The legislative declaration, like the fact that the statute was passed and was sustained by the highest court of the state, creates merely a rebuttable presumption that these conditions have been satisfied. [For technical reasons, Justice Brandeis ultimately voted to uphold the conviction.]

MR. JUSTICE HOLMES joins in this opinion.

Note: The Brandeis Concurrence and the Road to Dennis

1. *Clear and present danger.* Justice Brandeis attempted in *Whitney* to explicate the underlying rationale of the clear and present danger standard. Was his reliance on the intent of the framers historically sound? Note that Justice Brandeis's conception of the function of free speech differs markedly from that of Justice Holmes. Whereas Justice Holmes speaks of "free trade in ideas," Justice Brandeis emphasizes the "development of the faculties" and the "deliberative" process, and suggests that "public discussion is a political duty" and that "the greatest menace to freedom is an inert people." See Blasi, The First Amendment and the Ideal of Civic Courage: The Brandeis Opinion in Whitney v. California, 29 Wm. & Mary L. Rev. 653 (1988). For a historical analysis of the Brandeis concurrence, see Collins and Skover, Curious Concurrence: Justice Brandeis's Vote in Whitney v. California, 2005 Sup. Ct. Rev. 333.

2. *The persuasion principle.* Justice Brandeis emphasized that, if the danger is not imminent, "the remedy to be applied is more speech, not enforced silence." Is the opportunity for counterspeech an adequate explanation of the imminence requirement? Consider Strauss, Persuasion, Autonomy, and Freedom of Expression, 91 Colum. L. Rev. 334–336, 346–347, 353–356 (1991):

> The government may not suppress speech on the ground that it is too persuasive. Except, perhaps, in extraordinary circumstances, the government may not restrict speech because it fears, however justifiably, that the speech will persuade those who hear it to do something of which the government disapproves. [This] principle [unifies] much of first amendment law.
>
> [T]he persuasion principle can[not] be justified on consequentialist grounds. [Justice Brandeis's] opinion in *Whitney* [argues that "good counsels"] are a "remedy" for "evil counsels." [The] suggestion is that "more" speech can accomplish practically everything that suppression could accomplish. [If] this were true, the persuasion principle would be easy to justify. [But] there will be many occasions on which this optimistic view is an illusion. The problem with the "more speech" approach is that it is not unusual for people to be persuaded to do bad things, and it will not always be possible to talk them out of it. . . .
>
> Brandeis's opinion in *Whitney*, in addition to suggesting a consequentialist argument, uses terms that we would today say reflect a conception of human autonomy: "the final end of the State" is to make people "free to develop their faculties," and liberty is valuable "both as an end and as a means." [The] persuasion principle can

be defended on autonomy grounds in the following way: Violations of the persuasion principle are similar in kind [to] lies that are told for the purpose of influencing behavior. Violating the persuasion principle is wrong for some of the same reasons that lies of this kind are wrong: both involve a denial of autonomy in the sense that they interfere with a person's control over her own reasoning processes. [When] the government violates the persuasion principle, it has determined that people [will] pursue [the government's] objectives, instead of their own.

For the proposition that in some circumstances more speech does not help to correct falsehoods, but only adds to polarization, see Glaeser and Sunstein, Does More Speech Correct Falsehoods?, 43 J. Legal Stud. 65 (2014).

3. *The limits of judicial dissent.* Consider H. Kalven, A Worthy Tradition: Freedom of Speech in America 158 (1988):

> Although *Whitney* marks the sixth consecutive decision in which the majority has either ignored the clear and present danger test or found it inapplicable, Justice Brandeis [continues to assert that it "has been settled" that clear and present danger is the test for restrictions of speech]. The stamina and tactics of these classic dissents are remarkable. In professional lawyering terms, the performance of Justices Holmes and Brandeis is outrageous. They keep insisting that they are adhering to the Court's true rule adopted in *Schenck* [even though they] have been told [repeatedly] by the majority that clear and present danger is not now and never was the general [test]. Yet we are all deeply in their debt for their outrageous behavior. They have kept alive a counter-tension in the tradition, and their towering prestige has invested the slogan with almost mesmerizing force. Like twin Moses come down from Mount Sinai bearing the true Commandment, they see little need to argue that the formula is rightly derived from the First Amendment, merely that it is.

4. *Association.* In the pre-*Whitney* cases, the various defendants were prosecuted for engaging personally in prohibited expression. The California Criminal Syndicalism Act, however, declared it unlawful for any person knowingly to be a *member* of any organization that engages in unlawful advocacy. *Whitney* thus posed, but did not necessarily answer, three new questions: First, is the act of associating with others for expression-related purposes in itself protected by the first amendment? Second, assuming association is a protected first amendment activity, in what circumstances, if any, can the state constitutionally punish membership in an organization that engages in unlawful advocacy? The Court in *Whitney* held "knowing" membership unprotected. Is that the appropriate line? Third, how does the Holmes-Brandeis conception of clear and present danger apply to association? Recall the argument of Wigmore that the legislature should be permitted to consider the cumulative danger posed by many individually harmless speakers in deciding whether there is sufficient danger to warrant the suppression of speech. On the "right to associate" as a distinct first amendment right, see Bhagwat, Associational Speech, 120 Yale L.J. 978 (2011).

5. A *new direction?* In the decade following *Whitney*, the Court handed down three decisions concerning subversive advocacy and the right of association. Although the Court did not expressly reconsider its earlier decisions in these cases, in each case the Court found a technical way to invalidate the conviction. Thus, after an era of nine consecutive affirmances of convictions for subversive advocacy, the Court in the next decade offered three consecutive reversals. See Fiske v. Kansas, 274 U.S. 380 (1927); De Jonge v. Oregon, 299 U.S. 353 (1937); Herndon v. Lowry, 301 U.S. 242 (1937).

6. *Clear and present danger from* Whitney *to* Dennis. In the quarter-century between *Whitney* and *Dennis*, the Court embraced clear and present danger as the appropriate test for a wide range of first amendment issues. See, e.g., Schneider v. State, section E1, infra (leafleting); Cantwell v. Connecticut, section B2 infra (hostile audience); Bridges v. California, section D3 infra (contempt by publication); Terminiello v. Chicago, section B2 infra (breach of peace). See also Strong, Fifty Years of "Clear and Present Danger": From *Schenck* to *Brandenburg* — and Beyond, 1969 Sup. Ct. Rev. 41.

Although there were no major Supreme Court decisions concerning subversive advocacy during World War II, there were several prosecutions of individuals under both the Espionage Act of 1917 and the Smith Act of 1940. Most often, these were prosecutions of individuals who were leaders of fascist organizations in the United States. See R. Steele, Free Speech in the Good War (1999); M. St. George and L. Dennis, The Great Sedition Trial of 1944 (1946); G. Stone, Perilous Times: Free Speech in Wartime 252–283 (2004).

7. *The war on communism.* With its 1951 decision in *Dennis*, the Court continued its quest for a satisfactory solution to the problem of subversive advocacy. During the post–World War II "cold war" era, fears over national security once again generated wide-ranging federal and state restrictions on "radical" speech. These restrictions included extensive loyalty programs, emergency detention plans, attempts to "outlaw" the Communist Party, requirements that all so-called communist-front and communist-action organizations register with the government, and extensive legislative investigations of suspected "subversives." *Dennis*, which involved the prosecution under the Smith Act of the national leaders of the Communist Party of the United States, represents but one facet of this era.

Dennis v. United States

341 U.S. 494 (1951)

MR. CHIEF JUSTICE VINSON announced the judgment of the Court and an opinion in which MR. JUSTICE REED, MR. JUSTICE BURTON and MR. JUSTICE MINTON join.

Petitioners were indicted for violation of the conspiracy provisions of the Smith Act during the period of April 1945 to July 1948. [A] verdict of guilty as to all the petitioners was returned by the jury. [The] Court of Appeals affirmed. . . .

Sections 2 and 3 of the Smith Act provide as follows:

> Sec. 2. It shall be unlawful for any person to knowingly or willfully advocate, abet, advise, or teach the duty, necessity, desirability, or propriety of overthrowing or destroying any government in the United States by force or violence, or by the assassination of any officer of such government. . . .
>
> Sec. 3. It shall be unlawful for any person to attempt to commit, or to conspire to commit, any of the acts prohibited by the provisions of . . . this title.

The indictment charged the petitioners with willfully and knowingly conspiring (1) to organize as the Communist Party of the United States of America a society, group and assembly of persons who teach and advocate the overthrow and destruction of the Government of the United States by force and violence, and (2) knowingly and willfully conspiring to advocate and teach the duty and necessity of overthrowing and destroying the Government of the United States by force and violence. . . .

The trial of the case extended over nine months, six of which were devoted to the taking of evidence, resulting in a record of 16,000 pages. Our limited grant of the writ of certiorari has removed from our consideration any question as to the sufficiency of the [evidence]. Whether on this record petitioners did in fact advocate the overthrow of the Government by force and violence is not before us, and we must base any discussion of this point upon the conclusion [of] the Court of Appeals, which [held] that the record in this case amply supports the necessary finding of the jury that petitioners, the leaders of the Communist Party in this country, [intended] to initiate a violent revolution whenever the propitious occasion appeared. . . .

[The petitioners attack] the statute on the grounds that by its terms it prohibits academic discussion of the merits of Marxism-Leninism, that it stifles ideas and is contrary to all concepts of a free speech and a free press. [But the] very language of the Smith Act [demonstrates that it] is directed at advocacy, not discussion. Thus, the trial judge properly charged the jury that they could not convict if they found that petitioners did "no more than pursue peaceful studies and discussions or teaching and advocacy in the realm of ideas." . . .

[In *Gitlow* and *Whitney*, the] legislature had found that a certain kind of speech was, itself, harmful and unlawful. [In such circumstances, the Court held that the test was] whether the statute was "reasonable." [Although] no case subsequent to *Whitney* and *Gitlow* has expressly overruled the majority opinions in those cases, there is little doubt that subsequent opinions have inclined toward the Holmes-Brandeis rationale. . . .

In this case we are [thus] squarely presented with the application of the "clear and present danger" test, and must decide what that phrase imports. We first note that [overthrow] of the Government by force and violence is certainly a substantial enough interest for the Government to limit speech. [If], then, this interest may be protected, the literal problem which is presented is what has been meant by the use of the phrase "clear and present danger." . . .

Obviously, the words cannot mean that before the Government may act, it must wait until the putsch is about to be executed, the plans have been laid and the signal is awaited. If Government is aware that a group aiming at its overthrow is attempting to indoctrinate its members and to commit them to a course whereby they will strike when the leaders feel the circumstances permit, action by the Government is required. The argument that there is no need for Government to concern itself, for Government is strong, it possesses ample powers to put down a rebellion, it may defeat the revolution with ease needs no answer. For that is not the question. Certainly an attempt to overthrow the Government by force, even though doomed from the outset because of inadequate numbers or power of the revolutionists, is a sufficient evil for Congress to prevent. The damage which such attempts create both physically and politically to a nation makes it impossible to measure the validity in terms of the probability of success, or the immediacy of a successful attempt. . . .

Chief Judge Learned Hand, writing for the majority below, interpreted the phrase as follows: "In each case [courts] must ask whether the gravity of the 'evil,' discounted by its improbability, justifies such invasion of free speech as is necessary to avoid the danger." [We] adopt this statement of the rule. As articulated by Chief Judge Hand, it is as succinct and inclusive as any other we might devise at this time. It takes into consideration those factors which we deem relevant, and relates their significances. More we cannot expect from words.

Likewise, we are in accord with the court below, which affirmed the trial court's finding that the requisite danger existed. The mere fact that from the period 1945 to 1948 petitioners' activities did not result in an attempt to overthrow the Government by force and violence is of course no answer to the fact that there was a group that was ready to make the attempt. The formation by petitioners of such a highly organized conspiracy, with rigidly disciplined members subject to call when the leaders, these petitioners, felt that the time had come for action, coupled with the inflammable nature of world conditions, similar uprisings in other countries, and the touch-and-go nature of our relations with countries with whom petitioners were in the very least ideologically attuned, convince us that their convictions were justified on this score. And this analysis disposes of the contention that a conspiracy to advocate, as distinguished from the advocacy itself, cannot be constitutionally restrained, because it comprises only the preparation. It is the existence of the conspiracy which creates the danger. . . .

[Affirmed.]

MR. JUSTICE CLARK took no part in the consideration or decision of this case.

MR. JUSTICE FRANKFURTER, concurring. . . .

Primary responsibility for adjusting the interests which compete in the situation before us of necessity belongs to the Congress. [We] are to set aside the judgment of those whose duty it is to legislate only if there is no reasonable basis for it. [After canvassing the entire corpus of the Court's first amendment jurisprudence, Justice Frankfurter set forth the following conclusions.]

First. Free-speech cases are not an exception to the principle that we are not legislators, that direct policy-making is not our province. [Second.] A survey of the relevant decisions indicates that the results which we have reached are on the whole those that would ensue from careful weighing of conflicting interests. [Third.] Not every type of speech occupies the same position on the scale of values. [On] any scale of values, [speech advocating the overthrow of the government by force and violence] ranks low. Throughout our decisions there has recurred a distinction between the statement of an idea which may prompt its hearers to take unlawful action, and advocacy that such action be taken. . . .

These general considerations underlie decision of the case before us. On the one hand is the interest in security. [In] determining whether application of the statute to the defendants is within the constitutional powers of Congress, we [must consider] whatever is relevant to a legislative judgment. [We] may take account of evidence brought forward at this trial and elsewhere, much of which has long been common knowledge, [that] would amply justify a legislature in concluding that recruitment of additional members of the Party would create a substantial danger to national security.

On the other hand is the interest in free speech. The right to exert all governmental powers in aid of maintaining our institutions and resisting their physical overthrow does not include intolerance of opinions and speech that cannot do harm although opposed and perhaps alien to dominant, traditional opinion. [Moreover, a] public interest is not wanting in granting freedom to speak their minds even to those who advocate the overthrow of the Government by force. For, as the evidence in this case abundantly illustrates, coupled with such advocacy is criticism of defects in our society. [We must also recognize that suppressing] advocates of overthrow inevitably will also silence critics who do not advocate overthrow but fear that their criticism may be so construed. [It] is self-delusion to think that we can punish [the defendants] for their advocacy without adding to the risks run by loyal citizens who honestly believe in some of the reforms these defendants advance. It is a sobering fact that in sustaining the convictions before us we can hardly escape restriction on the interchange of ideas. . . .

It is not for us to decide how we would adjust the clash of interests which this case presents were the primary responsibility for reconciling it ours. Congress has determined that the danger created by advocacy of overthrow justifies the ensuing restriction on freedom of speech. [To] make validity of legislation depend on judicial reading of events still in the womb of time [is] to charge the judiciary with duties beyond its equipment. . . .

Mr. Justice Jackson, concurring. . . .

I would save [the clear and present danger standard], unmodified, for application as a "rule of reason" in the kind of case for which it was devised. When the issue is criminality of a hot-headed speech on a street corner, or circulation of a few incendiary pamphlets, or parading by some zealots behind a red flag, [it] is not beyond the capacity of the judicial process to gather, comprehend, and weigh the necessary materials for decision whether it is a clear and present danger of substantive evil or a harmless letting off of steam. [But] unless we are to hold our government captive in a judge-made verbal trap, we must approach the problem of a well-organized, nation-wide conspiracy [as] realistically as our predecessors faced the trivialities that were being prosecuted until they were checked with a rule of reason. . . .

The highest degree of constitutional protection is due to the [individual]. But even an individual cannot claim that the Constitution protects him in advocating or teaching overthrow of government by force or violence. [I] think direct incitement by speech or writing can be made a crime, and I think there can be a conviction without also proving that the odds favored its success by 99 to 1, or some other extremely high ratio. . . .

Mr. Justice Black, dissenting. . . .

[The] other opinions in this case show that the only way to affirm these convictions is to repudiate directly or indirectly the established "clear and present danger" rule. This the Court does in a way which greatly restricts the protections afforded by the First Amendment. The opinions for affirmance indicate that the chief reason for jettisoning the rule is the expressed fear that advocacy of Communist doctrine endangers the safety of the Republic. Undoubtedly, a governmental policy of unfettered communication of ideas does entail dangers. To the Founders of this Nation, however, the benefits derived from free expression were worth the risk. . . .

Public opinion being what it now is, few will protest the conviction of these Communist petitioners. There is hope, however, that in calmer times, when present pressures, passions and fears subside, this or some later Court will restore the First Amendment liberties to the high preferred place where they belong in a free society.

Mr. Justice Douglas, dissenting.

If this were a case where those who claimed protection under the First Amendment were teaching the techniques of sabotage, the assassination of the President, the filching of documents from public files, the planting of bombs, the art of street warfare, and the like, I would have no doubts. The freedom to speak is not absolute; the teaching of methods of terror and other seditious conduct should be beyond the pale. [This] case was argued as if those were the facts. [But] the fact is that no such evidence was introduced at the trial. . . .

So far as the present record is concerned, what petitioners did was to organize people to teach and themselves teach the Marxist-Leninist doctrine contained chiefly in four books: Stalin, Foundations of Leninism (1924); Marx and Engels, Manifesto of the Communist Party (1848); Lenin, The State and Revolution (1917); History of the Communist Party of the Soviet Union (B.) (1939). . . .

The opinion of the Court does not outlaw these texts nor condemn them to the fire, as the Communists do literature offensive to their creed. But if the books themselves are not outlawed, if they can lawfully remain on library shelves, by what reasoning does their [use] become a crime? [The] Act, as construed, requires the element of intent — that those who teach the creed believe in it. The crime then depends not on what is taught but on who the teacher is. That is to make freedom of speech turn not on *what is said*, but on the *intent* with which it is said. Once we start down that road we enter territory dangerous to the liberties of every citizen. . . .

There comes a time when even speech loses its constitutional immunity. Speech innocuous one year may at another time fan such destructive flames that it must be halted in the interests of the safety of the Republic. That is the meaning of the clear and present danger test. When conditions are so critical that there will be no time to avoid the evil that the speech threatens, it is time to call a halt. . . .

[If] we are to take judicial notice of the threat of Communists within the nation, it should not be difficult to conclude that *as a political party* they are of little consequence. [Communism] in the world scene is no bogeyman; but Communism as a political faction or party in this country plainly is. Communism has been so thoroughly exposed in this country that it has been crippled as a political force. Free speech has destroyed it as an effective political party. . . .

How it can be said that there is a clear and present danger that this advocacy will succeed is, therefore, a mystery. [In] America, [the Communists] are miserable merchants of unwanted ideas; their wares remain unsold. The fact that their ideas are abhorrent does not make them powerful. [Thus], if we are to proceed on the basis of judicial notice, it is impossible for me to say that the Communists in this country are so potent or so strategically deployed that they must be suppressed for their speech. . . .

Note: Dennis *and the Communist "Conspiracy"*

1. *Clear and present danger: the Holmes/Brandeis formulation.* Could the Holmes/Brandeis formulation of clear and present danger sensibly be applied in *Dennis*? What "substantive evil" must be clear and present? Actual overthrow? Attempted overthrow? Conspiracy to overthrow? Conspiracy to advocate overthrow?

2. *Clear and present danger: the* Dennis *formulation.* Note that Judge Learned Hand, the author of *Masses*, also wrote the opinion for the court of appeals in *Dennis*. By the time of *Dennis*, Judge Hand had come to accept that *Masses* had found "little professional support." As he put it, he had "bid a long farewell to my

little toy ship which set out quite bravely on the shortest voyage ever made." As a lower court judge "who took seriously his obligation to follow Supreme Court precedents," Judge Hand did his best to make sense of "an array of rulings on 'clear and present danger' — a standard he disliked from the outset." Although upholding the convictions under his reformulated version of the standard, Judge Hand "insisted repeatedly" that the prosecution was "a mistake." As he wrote a friend shortly after the decision, we "should never have prosecuted those birds. . . . So far as all this will do anything, it will encourage the faithful and maybe help the [Party's] Committee on Propaganda." G. Gunther, Learned Hand: The Man and the Judge 600–603 (1994). Was Hand's opinion in *Dennis* a betrayal of the position he had staked out in *Masses*? Note that the Smith Act prohibited only the express advocacy of unlawful conduct. Consider G. Stone, Perilous Times: Free Speech in Wartime 402 (2004):

> In June 1951, [Hand] wrote Frankfurter, "[S]o far as the constitution goes, I cannot see why it should protect any speech which contains 'aid[ing], abetting, counsel[ing]' etc., to *violate* any law." Six months later he wrote [that] "every society which promulgates a law means that it shall be obeyed until it is changed, and any society which lays down means by which its laws can be changed makes those means exclusive. . . . If [this be] so, how in God's name can an incitement to do what will be unlawful if done, be itself lawful?" In this sense, then, not only was Learned Hand faithfully following Supreme Court precedents rather than his own inclinations in *Dennis*, but his own inclinations would have led him to the very same outcome, though for quite different reasons.

Is the *Dennis* version of clear and present danger "simply the remote bad tendency test dressed up in modern style"? M. Shapiro, Freedom of Speech: The Supreme Court and Judicial Review 65 (1966). In his concurring opinion in *Whitney*, Justice Brandeis first introduced the "seriousness" element as a means of intensifying the clear and present danger standard. The *Dennis* formulation, however, uses "gravity" to dilute the standard. Is this dilution unreasonable? If government may restrict speech that creates an immediate 70 percent chance of a relatively modest evil (such as persuading a few persons to refuse induction), shouldn't it also be permitted to restrict speech that creates a less immediate 30 percent chance of a very serious evil (such as attempted overthrow of government)? See Posner, The Speech Market and the Legacy of *Schenck*, in L. Bollinger and G. Stone, Eternal Vigilance: Free Speech in the Modern Era 121, 125–126 (2002).

3. *Deference.* In *Gitlow* and *Whitney* the Court held that when a legislature expressly prohibits a certain category of expression, the judiciary must defer to the legislative judgment so long as it is reasonable. Is this the "correct" approach to judicial review? The Court's present position on the deference issue is set out in Landmark Communications, Inc. v. Virginia, 435 U.S. 829 (1978):

> Deference to a legislative finding cannot limit judicial inquiry when First Amendment rights are at stake. "[A legislative declaration] does not preclude enquiry into the question whether, at the time and under the circumstances, the conditions existed which are essential to validity under the Federal Constitution." [A] legislature appropriately inquiries into and may declare the reasons impelling legislative action but the judicial function commands analysis of whether the specific conduct charged falls within the reach of the statute and if so whether the legislation is consonant with the Constitution. Were it otherwise, the scope of freedom of speech

and of the press would be subject to legislative definition and the function of the First Amendment as a check on legislative power would be nullified.

4. *The Smith Act in context — other anticommunist activity.* As noted earlier, in the post–World War II "cold war" era the federal government launched an intensive campaign against the Communist Party and its adherents that reached far beyond the Smith Act. Consider the following:

a. Because of a fear that communist officers of labor organizations might misuse their influence by calling strikes as a means of disrupting commerce and industry, section 9(h) of the Labor-Management Relations Act of 1947 prohibited the enforcement of employee representation rights of any labor union whose officers failed to execute affidavits that they were not members of the Communist Party. See American Communications Association v. Douds, 339 U.S. 382 (1950) (upholding section 9(h)).

b. The Internal Security Act of 1950 created a complex regulatory scheme requiring all "Communist-action organizations" to register with the Attorney General and to disclose a wide range of information, including membership lists. The act also established the Subversive Activities Control Board to administer the scheme and provided that, once a board order to register became final, various sanctions would automatically be imposed on the organization and its members. See Communist Party v. Subversive Activities Control Board, 367 U.S. 1 (1961) (upholding the registration requirement).

c. Both the state and federal governments created extensive loyalty programs for government employees, and at both the state and federal levels legislative committees were used extensively to investigate communist "infiltration." See Barenblatt v. United States, 360 U.S. 109 (1959) (upholding a contempt citation of a witness before a congressional investigating committee who refused to answer questions about his past and present membership in the Communist Party); Gibson v. Florida Legislative Investigating Committee, 372 U.S. 539 (1963) (invalidating a contempt citation of a witness before a state legislative investigating committee who refused to answer questions about whether certain identified members of the Communist Party were members of the NAACP).

d. There were also efforts during this era to prevent the importation of communist doctrine from abroad. See Lamont v. Postmaster General, 381 U.S. 301 (1965) (invalidating restrictions on the mailing of foreign "communist political propaganda"); Kleindienst v. Mandel, 408 U.S. 753 (1972) (upholding a law declaring foreign communists ineligible to visit the United States).

e. During this period, the FBI launched a wide-ranging campaign of anticommunist activities, including a program designed extra-legally to "expose, disrupt, and otherwise neutralize" the domestic communist movement. Consider the 1976 findings of a Senate committee:

The Government has often undertaken the secret surveillance of citizens on the basis of their political beliefs, even when those beliefs posed no threat of violence or illegal acts. [The] Government, operating primarily through secret informants, [has] swept in vast amounts of information about the personal lives, views, and associations of American citizens. Investigations of groups deemed potentially dangerous — and even of groups suspected of associating with potentially dangerous organizations — have continued for decades, despite the fact that those groups did not engage in unlawful activity. [FBI] headquarters alone has developed over 500,000 domestic intelligence files. [The] targets of intelligence activity have included political adherents of the right and the left, ranging from activists to casual supporters.

Senate Select Committee to Study Governmental Operations with Respect to Intelligence Activities, Final Report, Intelligence Activities and the Rights of Americans, Book II, S. Doc. No. 13133–4, 94th Cong., 2d Sess. 5–9 (1976). See also F. Donner, The Age of Surveillance (1980); A. Theoharis, Spying on Americans (1978).

5. *Understanding* Dennis. Consider Wiecek, The Legal Foundations of Domestic Anticommunism: The Background of Dennis v. United States, 2001 Sup. Ct. Rev. 375, 377–379, 417, 428–429:

> The [anticommunist] crusade after World War II [demonized] Communists, endowing them with extraordinary powers and malignity, making them both covert and ubiquitous. [Communists] became The Other. Popular culture, in movies like *On the Waterfront* [and] *Invasion of the Body Snatchers* effectively delivered this image to a mass audience. [The] manufactured image of the domestic Communist, cultivated and propagated by J. Edgar Hoover, the Catholic Church, the American Legion, and political opportunists, made of Communists something less than full humans, full [citizens]. [To] resist the ideological and emotional pressures of the Cold War era would have required superhuman wisdom and equanimity. Whatever else might be said of the Justices of the *Dennis* Court, the majority of them did not have those qualities.

Consider also Wells, Fear and Loathing in Constitutional Decision-Making, 2005 Wis. L. Rev. 115, 117–119:

> The [argument] that courts ought to protect civil liberties in times of crisis is an attractive one. [But courts] remain subject to the same passions, fears, and prejudices that sweep the rest of the nation. [Nowhere] is this more evident than in [*Dennis*]. [The evidence against the defendants] was weak, as there was no proof that they agreed to overthrow or advocate overthrow of the government. . . . Conventional wisdom roundly condemns *Dennis*, attributing the result to a Cold War hysteria that gripped the country and infected the judges' reasoning. [Conventional] wisdom, however, provides few answers regarding how to guard against *Dennis*'s failings in the future. We cannot simply assume that judges armed with an understanding of past errors will act courageously. [What] we need, then, is a doctrine that can counteract the effects of fear and prejudice that lead to such action. . . .

Note: The Road to Brandenburg

1. *Revising the* Dennis *approach: advocacy of doctrine versus advocacy of action.* Following *Dennis*, federal authorities initiated Smith Act prosecutions against more than 120 individuals constituting the secondary leadership of the Communist Party. By 1957, the government had secured convictions in almost all of these prosecutions. In Yates v. United States, 354 U.S. 298 (1957), however, the Court, in a six-to-one decision, adopted a narrow interpretation of the Smith Act to avoid constitutional doubts and overturned the convictions of several members of the Communist Party for conspiracy to violate the act. Justice Harlan delivered the opinion:

> [We are] faced with the question whether the Smith Act prohibits advocacy [of] forcible overthrow as an abstract principle, divorced from any effort to instigate

action to that end, so long as such advocacy [is] engaged in with evil intent. We hold that it does not.

The distinction between advocacy of abstract doctrine and advocacy directed at promoting unlawful action is one that has been consistently recognized in the opinions of this Court, [and] was heavily underscored in [*Gitlow*]. [We] need not, however, decide the issue before us in terms of constitutional compulsion, for our first duty is to construe this statute. In doing so we should not assume that Congress chose to disregard a constitutional danger zone so clearly marked. . . .

[We reject the proposition] that mere doctrinal justification of forcible overthrow, if engaged in with the intent to accomplish overthrow, is punishable [under] the Smith Act. That sort of advocacy, even though uttered with the hope that it may ultimately lead to violent revolution, is too remote from concrete action to be regarded as the kind of indoctrination preparatory to action which was condemned in *Dennis*. [The] essential distinction is that those to whom the advocacy is addressed must be urged to *do* something, now or in the future, rather than merely to *believe* in something.

Harlan's opinion in *Yates* was greeted with puzzlement. Nonetheless, "the Justice Department, faced with *Yates's* insistence upon proof of advocacy to '*do* something, now or in the future, rather than merely to *believe* in something,' soon admitted that 'we cannot satisfy the evidentiary requirements laid down by the Supreme Court' and dismissed" all remaining Smith Act conspiracy cases then pending. R. Lichtman, The Supreme Court and McCarthy Era Repression: One Hundred Decisions 95–96 (2012).

What is the basis of Justice Harlan's distinction between advocacy of action and advocacy of belief? Is it premised on the relative dangerousness of the expression? On the relative "value" of the speech? Consider Gunther, Learned Hand and the Origins of Modern First Amendment Doctrine: Some Fragments of History, 27 Stan. L. Rev. 719, 753 (1975):

Harlan found a way to curtail prosecutions under the Smith Act even though the constitutionality of the Act had been sustained in *Dennis*. He did it by [reading] the statute in terms of constitutional presuppositions; and he strove to find standards "manageable" by judges and capable of curbing jury discretion. He insisted on strict statutory standards of proof emphasizing the actual speech of the [defendants]. Harlan claimed to be interpreting *Dennis*. In fact, [*Yates*] represented doctrinal evolution in a new direction.

2. *Understanding* Yates. A dominant theme of Justice Harlan's opinion in *Yates* was that the Court had historically recognized an "essential distinction" between express advocacy of unlawful action on the one hand, and advocacy of "abstract doctrine" or general discussion of policies and ideas on the other. If the Court tests restrictions on express advocacy of unlawful action with the *Dennis* version of clear and present danger, what standard should it use to test restrictions on general discussion of policies and ideas? In reflecting on *Yates*, consider the Court's post-*Yates* decisions in *Kingsley Pictures* and *Bond*.

3. *Advocacy of immorality.* In Kingsley International Pictures Corp. v. Regents of New York, 360 U.S. 684 (1959), the Court held unconstitutional a New York statute prohibiting the issuance of a license to exhibit non-obscene motion pictures that "portray 'acts of sexual immorality [as] desirable, acceptable, or proper patterns of behavior.'" The state applied the statute to deny a license to the film Lady Chatterley's Lover because its "theme" was that adultery was "proper behavior."

The Court observed that the state was attempting "to prevent the exhibition of a motion picture because that picture advocates an idea — that adultery under certain circumstances may be proper behavior. Yet the First Amendment's basic guarantee is of freedom to advocate ideas. The state, quite simply, has thus struck at the heart of constitutionally protected liberty." In response to the state's argument that its "action was justified because the motion picture attractively portrays a relationship which is contrary to [the] legal code of its citizenry," the Court maintained that the state "misconceives what it is that the Constitution protects." The first amendment, the Court declared, "protects advocacy of the opinion that adultery may sometimes be proper, no less than advocacy of socialism or the single tax." Indeed, quoting Justice Brandeis's opinion in *Whitney*, the Court explained that "advocacy of conduct proscribed by law is [not] 'a justification for denying free speech where the advocacy falls short of incitement and there is nothing to indicate that the advocacy would be immediately acted on.'"

4. *Support for war resisters.* In Bond v. Floyd, 385 U.S. 116 (1966), the Court held that the Georgia House of Representatives could not constitutionally refuse to seat Julian Bond, a duly elected representative, because of his statements, and statements to which he subscribed, criticizing the policy of the federal government in Vietnam and the operation of the selective service system. Four days before Bond was scheduled to be sworn in, the Student Nonviolent Coordinating Committee (SNCC), a civil rights organization of which Bond was the communications director, issued a statement declaring its "opposition to United States' involvement in Viet Nam." The statement concluded by announcing: "We are in sympathy with, and support, the men in this country who are unwilling to respond to a military draft."

In a unanimous opinion, the Court observed that "Bond could not have been constitutionally convicted under [the federal statute] which punishes any person who 'counsels, aids, or abets another to refuse or evade registration.'" The Court explained that, although the SNCC statement expressed sympathy with, and support for, those who refused to respond to a military draft, that statement "alone cannot be interpreted as a call to unlawful refusal to be drafted." The Court thus concluded that "Bond could not have been convicted for these statements consistently with the First Amendment. [Citing *Yates.*]"

5. *Freedom of association.* In Scales v. United States, 367 U.S. 203 (1961), the Court revisited the constitutional status of membership in "subversive" organizations. In *Whitney*, the Court had concluded that mere "knowing" membership was sufficient to remove constitutional protection. In *Scales*, however, following up on *Yates*, the Court maintained that a "blanket prohibition" of knowing membership in organizations "having both legal and illegal aims" might pose "a real danger that legitimate political expression or association would be impaired." To avoid this danger, the Court interpreted the Smith Act as making membership unlawful only if the individual was an "active" member and not merely a "nominal, passive, inactive or purely technical" member, with knowledge of the organization's illegal advocacy, and with the "specific intent" to further the organization's illegal ends. Thus, a member could be punished under the act only if he was an "active" member who specifically intended "to bring about the overthrow of government as speedily as circumstances would permit."

Brandenburg v. Ohio
395 U.S. 444 (1969)

PER CURIAM.

The appellant, a leader of a Ku Klux Klan group, was convicted under the Ohio Criminal Syndicalism statute of "advocat[ing] . . . the duty, necessity, or propriety of crime, sabotage, violence, or unlawful methods of terrorism as a means of accomplishing industrial or political reform" and of "voluntarily assembl[ing] with any society, group or assemblage of persons formed to teach or advocate the doctrines of criminal syndicalism." He was fined $1,000 and sentenced to one to 10 years' imprisonment. . . .

The record shows that a man, identified at trial as the appellant, telephoned an announcer-reporter on the staff of a Cincinnati television station and invited him to come to a Ku Klux Klan "rally" to be held at a farm in Hamilton County. With the cooperation of the organizers, the reporter and a cameraman attended the meeting and filmed the events. Portions of the films were later broadcast on the local station and on a national network.

The prosecution's case rested on the films and on testimony identifying the appellant as the person who communicated with the reporter and who spoke at the rally. The State also introduced into evidence several articles appearing in the film, including a pistol, a rifle, a shotgun, ammunition, a Bible, and a red hood worn by the speaker in the films.

One film showed 12 hooded figures, some of whom carried firearms. They were gathered around a large wooden cross, which they burned. No one was present other than the participants and the newsman who made the film. Most of the words uttered during the scene were incomprehensible when the film was projected, but scattered phrases could be understood that were derogatory of Negroes and, in one instance, of Jews. Another scene on the same film showed the appellant, in Klan regalia, making a speech. The speech, in full, was as follows:

> This is an organizers' meeting. We have had quite a few members here today which are — we have hundreds, hundreds of members throughout the State of Ohio. I can quote from a newspaper clipping from the Columbus Ohio Dispatch, five weeks ago Sunday morning. The Klan has more members in the State of Ohio than does any other organization. We're not a revengent organization, but if our President, our Congress, our Supreme Court, continues to suppress the white, Caucasian race, it's possible that there might have to be some revengence taken. We are marching on Congress July the Fourth, four hundred thousand strong. From there we are dividing into two groups, one group to march on St. Augustine, Florida, the other group to march into Mississippi. Thank you.

The second film showed six hooded figures one of whom, later identified as the appellant, repeated a speech very similar to that recorded on the first film. The reference to the possibility of "revengence" was omitted, and one sentence was added: "Personally, I believe the nigger should be returned to Africa, the Jew returned to Israel." Though some of the figures in the films carried weapons, the speaker did not.

The Ohio Criminal Syndicalism Statute was enacted in 1919. From 1917 to 1920, identical or quite similar laws were adopted by 20 States and two territories. . . . In 1927, this Court sustained the constitutionality of California's

Criminal Syndicalism Act, [the] text of which is quite similar to that of the laws of Ohio. [*Whitney.*] The Court upheld the statute on the ground that, without more, "advocating violent means to effect political and economic change involves such danger to the security of the State that the State may outlaw it." [But] *Whitney* has been thoroughly discredited by later decisions. See [*Dennis*]. These later decisions have fashioned the principle that the constitutional guarantees of free speech and free press do not permit a State to forbid or proscribe advocacy of the use of force or of law violation except where such advocacy is directed to inciting or producing imminent lawless action and is likely to incite or produce such action.[1] As we [have said], "the mere abstract teaching [of] the moral propriety or even moral necessity for a resort to force and violence, is not the same as preparing a group for violent action and steeling it to such action." See also [*Bond*]. A statute which fails to draw this distinction impermissibly intrudes upon the freedoms guaranteed by the First and Fourteenth Amendments. It sweeps within its condemnation speech which our Constitution has immunized from governmental control. Cf. [*Yates*]. . . .

Measured by this test, Ohio's Criminal Syndicalism Act cannot be sustained. [Neither] the indictment nor the trial judge's instructions to the jury in any way refined the statute's bald definition of the crime in terms of mere advocacy not distinguished from incitement to imminent lawless action.

Accordingly, we are here confronted with a statute which, by its own words and as applied, purports to punish mere advocacy and to forbid, on pain of criminal punishment, assembly with others merely to advocate the described type of action. Such a statute falls within the condemnation of the First and Fourteenth Amendments. The contrary teaching of [*Whitney*] cannot be supported, and that decision is therefore overruled.

Reversed.

Mr. Justice Black, concurring.

I agree with the views expressed by Mr. Justice Douglas in his concurring opinion in this case that the "clear and present danger" doctrine should have no place in the interpretation of the First Amendment. I join the Court's opinion, which, as I understand it, simply cites [*Dennis*] but does not indicate any agreement on the Court's part with the "clear and present danger" doctrine on which *Dennis* purported to rely.

Mr. Justice Douglas, concurring. . . .

I see no place in the regime of the First Amendment for any "clear and present danger" test, whether strict and tight as some would make it, or free-wheeling as the Court in *Dennis* rephrased it. When one reads the opinions closely and sees when and how the "clear and present danger" test has been applied, great misgivings are aroused. First, the threats were often loud but always puny and made serious only by judges so wedded to the status quo that critical analysis made them nervous. Second, the test was so twisted and perverted in *Dennis* as to make

---

1. It was on the theory that the Smith Act [embodied] such a principle and that it had been applied only in conformity with it that this Court sustained the Act's constitutionality. [*Dennis.*] That this was the basis for *Dennis* was emphasized in [*Yates*], in which the Court overturned convictions for advocacy of the forcible overthrow of the Government under the Smith Act, because the trial judge's instructions had allowed convictions for mere advocacy, unrelated to its tendency to produce forcible action.

the trial of those teachers of Marxism an all-out political trial which was part and parcel of the cold war that has eroded substantial parts of the First Amendment. . . .

The line between what is permissible and not subject to control and what may be made impermissible and subject to regulation is the line between ideas and overt acts. The example usually given by those who would punish speech is the case of one who falsely shouts fire in a crowded theatre. This is, however, a classic case where speech is brigaded with action. [They] are indeed inseparable and a prosecution can be launched for the overt acts actually caused. Apart from rare instances of that kind, speech is, I think, immune from prosecution. . . .

Note: The Brandenburg Formulation

1. *The meaning of* Brandenburg. Although the Court maintained that the pre-*Brandenburg* "decisions [fashioned] the principle" adopted in *Brandenburg, Brandenburg* seems to have gone far beyond settled law. Indeed, it has been said that the *Brandenburg* formulation would "have demanded the contrary result in [both] the early Espionage Act cases and the later Communist cases," J. Ely, Democracy and Distrust 115 (1980), and that *Brandenburg* combined "the most [speech] protective ingredients of the *Masses* emphasis with the most useful elements of the clear and present danger heritage" to produce "the most speech-protective standard yet evolved by the Supreme Court." Gunther, Learned Hand and the Origins of Modern First Amendment Doctrine: Some Fragments of History, 27 Stan. L. Rev. 719, 754, 755 (1975). More specifically, *Brandenburg* has been interpreted as requiring "three things: (1) express advocacy of law violation; (2) the advocacy must call for *immediate* law violation; and (3) the immediate law violation must be *likely* to occur." Schwartz, Holmes versus Hand: Clear and Present Danger or Advocacy of Unlawful Action?, 1994 Sup. Ct. Rev. 209, 240-241.

Thus interpreted, and particularly when viewed in the light of *Yates* and *Bond, Brandenburg* appears by implication to accord absolute protection to the speaker so long as he does not use express words of incitement. If this is so, does *Brandenburg* suggest that, as a general first amendment principle, expression should be absolutely protected against direct criminal prohibition, regardless of dangerousness and intent, so long as it is not of "low" first amendment value?

2. *The lessons of history.* Consider Stone, Free Speech in the Twenty-First Century: Ten Lessons from the Twentieth Century, 36 Pepp. L. Rev. 273 (2008):

> As a result of its experience in the *Schenck-Brandenburg* line of decisions, the Court learned three very practical lessons about the workings of "the system of free expression" — lessons that have come to play a critical role in shaping contemporary First Amendment jurisprudence.
>
> First, the Court learned about the *chilling effect.* That is, the Court learned that people are easily deterred from exercising their freedom of speech. This is so because individual speakers usually gain very little personally from signing a petition, marching in a demonstration, handing out leaflets, or posting on a blog. [Thus,] if they know they might go to jail for speaking, they will often forego their right to speak. This makes perfect sense for each individual. But if many individuals make this same decision, the net effect may be to mutilate the thought process of the community. The Court's gradual recognition of this "chilling effect,"

and of the consequent power of government to use intimidation to silence its critics, was a critical insight in shaping twentieth-century free speech doctrine.

Second, the Court learned about the *pretext effect*. That is, the Court learned that government officials will often defend their restrictions of speech on grounds quite different from their real motivations for the suppression, which will often be [to] silence their critics, [insulate] themselves from criticism, and preserve their own authority. . . .

Third, the Court learned about the *crisis effect*. That is, the Court learned that in times of crisis, real or imagined, citizens and public officials tend to panic [and] to rush headlong to suppress speech that they demonize as dangerous, subversive, disloyal, or treasonable. Painful experience with this "crisis effect," especially dur-ing World War I and the Cold War, led the Court to embrace what Professor Vincent Blasi has termed a "pathological perspective" in crafting First Amendment doctrine. That is, the Court attempts to structure First Amendment doctrine to anticipate and to guard against the worst of times.

On the pathological perspective, see Blasi, The Pathological Perspective and the First Amendment, 85 Colum. L. Rev. 449, 449–500 (1985). On cost-benefit analysis and the problem of analyzing low-probability, high-magnitude harms (such as violent revolution), see Masur, Probability Thresholds, 92 Iowa L. Rev. 1293, 1296–1298 (2007).

3. *Subsequent decisions.* The Court has adhered to *Brandenburg.* In Hess v. Indiana, 414 U.S. 105 (1973), for example, the Court reversed the conviction for disorderly conduct of an individual who shouted, "We'll take the fucking street later [or again]," during an antiwar demonstration. The Court explained that at worst the statement "amounted to nothing more than advocacy of illegal action at some indefinite future time." Since there was no evidence that the "words were intended to produce, and likely to produce, *imminent* disorder," they could not constitutionally be punished "on the ground that they had a 'tendency to lead to violence.'"

NAACP v. Claiborne Hardware Co., 458 U.S. 886 (1982), involved an NAACP-sponsored boycott of racially discriminatory merchants in Claiborne County, Mississippi. During the course of the boycott, an NAACP official stated in a public speech to several hundred people that "[if] we catch any of you going in any of them racist stores, we're gonna break your damn neck." The Court held that this speech was protected by the First Amendment because the "mere *advocacy* of the use of force or violence does not remove speech from the protection of the First Amendment." The Court emphasized that "in this case, the acts of violence" that later occurred did not take place until "weeks or months after the speech." The Court concluded that "when such appeals do not incite [imme-diate] lawless action, they must be regarded as protected speech," for "to rule otherwise would ignore the 'profound national commitment' that 'debate on public issues should be uninhibited, robust, and wide-open.'"

4. *Additional variations.* Consider the following:

a. In Herceg v. Hustler Magazine, Inc., 814 F.2d 1017 (5th Cir. 1987), a fourteen-year-old boy was found hanging in his closet with a copy of Hustler on the floor beneath his feet, opened to an article entitled "Orgasms of Death," which detailed the procedures for autoerotic asphyxiation. The court invalidated a civil jury verdict against Hustler because *Brandenburg* was not satisfied.

b. In Olivia N. v. National Broadcasting Co., 178 Cal. Rptr. 888 (Ct. App. 1981), the court held that, even though the television movie Born Innocent, which described a rape using a "plumber's helper," had caused just such a rape of a nine-year-old girl by a group of teenage boys who had just seen Born Innocent shortly before, the rule in *Brandenburg* immunized NBC because no intent to injure could be shown.

c. In Rice v. The Paladin Enterprises, 128 F.3d 233 (4th Cir. 1997), a publisher distributed a book, entitled Hit Man, that extolled the lifestyle of contract murderers and offered detailed instructions on how to commit a contract murder. Following these instructions precisely, X killed Y in a contract murder, and Y's survivors thereafter sued the publisher for damages. The court held that *Brandenburg* does not control this situation and that the publisher could be held liable because the publisher "had intended . . . that the publication would be used by criminals to execute the crime of murder for hire."

d. *Encouraging a suicide.* Michelle Carter, a seventeen-year-old girl, sent a barrage of text messages to her boyfriend, eighteen-year-old Conrad Roy, urging him to commit suicide. She wrote him, for example: "If this is the only way you think you're gonna be happy, heaven will welcome you with open arms. You just need to do it." And he did. Can Carter constitutionally be convicted of involuntary manslaughter? See Michelle Carter Is Guilty of Manslaughter in Texting Suicide Case, New York Times (June 16, 2017).

e. *Crime-facilitating speech.* Note that these cases all involved "crime-facilitating speech." In what circumstances may the government prohibit such speech? See Volokh, Crime-Facilitating Speech, 57 Stan. L. Rev. 1095, 1105–1106 (2005).

5. *From* Schenck *to* Brandenburg, *and beyond.* Consider Bollinger, Epilogue, in L. Bollinger and G. Stone, Eternal Vigilance: Free Speech in the Modern Era 1, 312–313 (2002):

The question for the future [is] whether the scope of First Amendment rights articulated in the *Brandenburg* era reflects the distilled wisdom of historical experience, which makes it more likely to survive in future periods of social upheaval, or whether the *Brandenburg* era will turn out to be just one era among many, in which the freedom of speech varies widely and more or less according to the sense of security and tolerance prevailing in the nation at the time. The fact that the last thirty years since *Brandenburg* have been remarkably peaceful and prosperous means that the understandings we now have about the meaning of free speech have not really been tested. By the standards we now apply (that is, through the eyes of *Brandenburg*), just about every time the country has felt seriously threatened the First Amendment has retreated.

6. *Terrorism online.*
a. Consider C. Sunstein, #republic 236–251 (2017):

Terrorists and hate groups have long been communicating online, sometimes about conspiracies [and] formulas for making bombs. Members of such groups tend to communicate largely or mostly with one another, feeding various predilections. [According] to the FBI "[social] media is a critical tool for terror groups to exploit. [The] foreign terrorist now has direct access into the United States like never before." [Terrorists'] uses of the Internet and social media for recruitment, inspiration, and radicalization have put increasing pressure on [governments] to disrupt their online activities. [Other] democratic countries have enacted legislation to control access to online content that promotes terrorism. Under French law, for example, the government can block Internet sites that incite terrorist attacks or publicly glorify them. . . .

There is no question that terrorist uses of social media will continue to adapt and evolve, and that it will endanger human lives. [Frequently] what is involved is meeting dangerous speech with counterspeech, correcting the record or putting people on new paths. When the government uses counterspeech, it creates no constitutional issue. But the intensifying international focus on terrorism, and al-Qaeda and ISIL in particular, poses a fresh challenge to the greatest American contribution to the theory and practice of free speech: the clear and present danger test. [It] is at least worth asking whether that test may be ripe for reconsideration. . . .

One of the greatest and most influential judges in US history, with the unlikely name of Learned Hand, rejected the clear and present danger test [because] he believed that the free speech principle simply did not protect explicit or direct incitement to violence, even if no harm was imminent. [For] decades, the Supreme Court has shown zero interest in Hand's formula. [Brandeis] offered the best reason: "Only an emergency can justify repression." It is an appealing thought, and it is usually right. But is it convincing as applied to the recruitment and propaganda efforts of terrorist organizations? [In] free societies, it is almost always wrong to punish speech. But at the very least, the argument for the clear and present danger test is not quite as clear as it once was — and it might not be so well suited to the present.

b. Consider T. Ash, Free Speech: Ten Principles for a Connected World 133–34 (2016):

The American scholar Cass Sunstein was among the first to suggest that in practice the internet can contribute to what he calls group polarization. Far from being confronted with a diversity of viewpoints, as in an ideal liberal public sphere, people seek out and commune online with a like-minded minority. Jihadists read only jihadi websites, which link to each other; far-right extremists listen only to far-right extremists, atheists to atheists, flat-earthers to flat-earthers. [Unlike] in the physical world, the internet makes it easy for the conspiracy theorist to find the 957 other people across the planet who share his or her particular poisoned fantasy.

[This problem] clearly affects the analysis of speech and violence. Thus, for example, the Norwegian mass murderer Anders Behring Breivik was reinforced in his paranoid views by obsessive reading of anti-Islamic [websites], from which he quoted in his online "crusader" manifesto. Does that mean that such sites should be blocked and their content censored? Surely not. The yardstick for what speech is allowed [cannot] be its potential impact on a single unbalanced mind anywhere in the world.

7. *Material support.* A federal statute declares it unlawful for any person knowingly to provide "material support" to a designated foreign terrorist organization. "Material support'" includes, among other things, "training, expert advice or assistance." Plaintiffs wanted to train two designated foreign terrorist organizations, which engaged in political and humanitarian as well as violent terrorist activities, how to use international law to resolve disputes peacefully and to engage in political advocacy on behalf of these organizations and their causes. Plaintiffs asserted that the statute violates the first amendment because it does not require the government to prove that, in assisting these organizations, they specifically intended to further the organizations' unlawful activities. Plaintiffs relied on *Scales*, in which the Court held that an individual could not constitutionally be punished for being a "knowing" member of the Communist Party, which had "both legal and illegal aims," unless the government proved that he specifically intended to promote the Party's illegal aims (that is, in the context of *Scales*, "to

bring about the overthrow of government as speedily as circumstances would permit").

In *Holder v. Humanitarian Law Project*, 561 U.S. 1 (2010), the Court, in a six-to-three decision, upheld the material support provision. Writing for the Court, Chief Justice Roberts distinguished *Scales* on the ground that it dealt with mere membership, rather than with the provision of "material support." Roberts observed that "[e]veryone agrees that the Government's interest in combating terrorism is an urgent objective of the highest order." The plaintiffs maintained, however, that their speech was intended to "advance only the legitimate activities of the designated terrorist organizations, not their terrorism." Roberts responded that Congress had made specific findings that "any form of material support furnished 'to' a foreign terrorist organization" will have "harmful effects," regardless of the intent of the speaker. For example, such "support frees up other resources within the organization that may be put to violent ends" and "helps lend legitimacy to foreign terrorist groups — legitimacy that makes it easier for those groups to persist, to recruit members, and to raise funds — all of which facilitate more terrorist attacks."

Roberts insisted that the conclusions of Congress and the Executive about the dangers of such support were "entitled to deference" because the statute "implicates sensitive and weighty interests of national security and foreign affairs." Although "we do not defer to the Government's reading of the First Amendment, even when such interests are at stake," it is also the case that in these circumstances "conclusions must often be based on informed judgment rather than concrete evidence, and that reality affects what we may reasonably insist on from the Government" in terms of proof of danger. "Given the sensitive interests in national security and foreign affairs at stake, the political branches have adequately substantiated their determination that, to serve the Government's interest in preventing terrorism, it was necessary to prohibit providing material support in the form of training [and] expert advice [to] foreign terrorist groups, even if the supporters meant to promote only the groups' nonviolent ends."

Finally, Roberts made clear that "we in no way suggest that a regulation of independent speech would pass constitutional muster, even if the Government were to show that such speech benefits foreign terrorist organizations," and we "do not suggest that Congress could extend the same prohibition on material support [to] domestic organizations."

Justice Breyer, joined by Justices Ginsburg and Sotomayor, dissented: "'Coordination' with a group that engages in unlawful activity [does] not deprive the plaintiffs of the First Amendment's [protection]. [The] First Amendment protects advocacy of even *unlawful* action so long as that advocacy is not 'directed to inciting or producing *imminent lawless action* and . . . *likely to incite or produce* such action.' [Quoting *Brandenburg*.] Here the plaintiffs seek to advocate peaceful, *lawful* action to secure *political* ends; and they seek to teach others how to do the same. . . .

"[W]here, as here, a statute applies criminal penalties [for such speech], I should think we would scrutinize the statute and justifications 'strictly' — to determine whether the prohibition is justified by a 'compelling' need that cannot be 'less restrictively' accommodated. [I] doubt that the statute [can] survive any reasonably applicable First Amendment standard. [I] would read the statute as criminalizing First-Amendment protected pure speech [only] when the defendant knows or intends that those activities will assist the organization's unlawful terrorist actions. Under this reading, the Government would have to show, at a minimum, that such defendants provided support that they knew was significantly likely to help the organization pursue its unlawful terrorist aims."

Under the Court's approach, could a lawyer be convicted for filing a brief on behalf of an alleged terrorist asserting that his constitutional rights had been violated? See Tarkington, A First Amendment Theory for Protecting Attorney Speech, 45 U.C. Davis L. Rev. 27 (2011); Cole, The First Amendment's Borders: The Place of Holder v. Humanitarian Law Project in First Amendment Doctrine, 6 Harv. L. & Pol. Rev. 147, 149 (2012).

Note: *Abridgment of Speech Other Than by Direct Criminal Prohibition*

1. *Disclosure*. Up to now, we have focused on direct criminal prohibitions of speech or association. But there are other forms of regulation that may "abridge" the freedom of expression. In some circumstances, for example, government may "chill" the exercise of free expression merely by disclosing it. This is especially likely where the individual's speech or association is unpopular. Should such an "indirect" abridgment of speech trigger the same standards of constitutional review as direct criminal prohibition? Consider the following decisions:

a. In Barenblatt v. United States, 360 U.S. 109 (1959), an instructor at Vassar College was subpoenaed to appear as a witness before a subcommittee of the House Committee on Un-American Activities during an inquiry into alleged communist infiltration into the field of education. He was held in contempt of Congress for refusing to answer questions about his past and present membership in the Communist Party. The Court, in a five-to-four decision, held that this did not violate the first amendment.

b. In Gibson v. Florida Legislative Investigating Committee, 372 U.S. 539 (1963), the Florida legislature created a committee to investigate the infiltration of communists into various organizations. Gibson, who was president of the Miami branch of the NAACP, was adjudged in contempt for refusing to disclose whether fourteen individuals previously identified as communists were members of the NAACP. The Court, in an opinion by Justice Goldberg, distinguished *Barenblatt* and held that Gibson's conviction violated the first amendment:

> In *Barenblatt*, [it] was a refusal to answer [questions] concerning [membership] in the Communist Party which supported [the] conviction. [Here, however,] the entire thrust of the demands on the petitioner was that he disclose whether [certain] persons were members of the NAACP, itself a concededly legitimate and nonsubversive organization. [Such organizations do not] automatically forfeit their rights to privacy of association simply because the general subject matter of the legislative inquiry is Communist subversion or infiltration. [The] record in this case is insufficient to show a substantial connection between the Miami branch of the NAACP and Communist activities which [is] an essential prerequisite to demonstrating the immediate, substantial, and subordinating state interest necessary to sustain [the committee's] right of inquiry into the membership lists of the association.

After *Brandenburg* and *Scales*, what showing must the government make before "infiltrating" an allegedly organization with informers? Can the government investigate an organization because its advocacy raises concerns about possible future violence even if its speech does not meet the requirements of

Brandenburg? See Rosenthal, First Amendment Investigations and the Inescapable Pragmatism of the Common Law of Free Speech, 86 Ind. L.J. 1 (2011).

2. *Public employees.* Does firing a public employee for her speech pose the same constitutional issue as criminally punishing a citizen for her speech? Suppose the government refuses to hire an applicant for a position with the police department because she was once a member of an organization that advocates terrorism as a means of political change. Do *Brandenburg* and *Scales* govern these situations? Consider the following views:

a. McAuliffe v. Mayor of New Bedford, 155 Mass. 216, 29 N.E. 517 (1892) (in which Justice Holmes, speaking for the Supreme Judicial Court of Massachusetts, upheld a rule prohibiting police officers to "solicit money [for] any political purpose whatever"):

> The petitioner may have a constitutional right to talk politics, but he has no constitutional right to be a policeman. There are few employments for hire in which the servant does not agree to suspend his constitutional rights of free speech, as well as of idleness, by the implied terms of his contract. The servant cannot complain, as he takes the employment on the terms which are offered him.

b. Frost & Frost Trucking Co. v. Railroad Commission, 271 U.S. 583, 593–594 (1926):

> It would be a palpable incongruity to strike down an act of state legislation which [strips] the citizen of rights guaranteed by the federal Constitution, but to uphold an act by which the same result is accomplished under the guise of a surrender of a right in exchange for a valuable privilege which the State threatens otherwise to withhold. [It] is inconceivable that guarantees embedded in the Constitution [may] thus be manipulated out of existence.

The Court has generally followed *Frost* rather than *McAuliffe.* In Perry v. Sindermann, 408 U.S. 593, 597 (1972), for example, the Court announced that, "even though a person has no 'right' to a valuable government benefit and even though the government may deny him the benefit for any number of reasons, [it may not do so] on a basis that infringes his constitutionally protected interests — especially, his interest in freedom of speech."

Does the rejection of *McAuliffe* suggest that the first amendment rights of government employees are coextensive with those of private individuals? Consider Pickering v. Board of Education, 391 U.S. 563, 568 (1968):

> [The] State has interests as an employer in regulating the speech of its employees that differ significantly from those it possesses in [regulating] the speech of the citizenry in general. The problem in any case is to arrive at a balance between the interests of the [employee], as a citizen, in commenting upon matters of public concern, and the interests of the State, as an employer, in promoting the efficiency of the public services it performs through its employees.

3. *Subversive advocacy and the rights of public employees.* At the height of the post–World War II communist scare, more than one-sixth of the total civilian labor force was subject to some sort of loyalty qualification, and the federal government and most of the states excluded from many areas of public employment individuals who had been members of a "subversive" organization. What interests are served by the government's refusal to employ such individuals?

Consider Israel, Elfbrandt v. Russell: The Demise of the Oath?, 1966 Sup. Ct. Rev. 193, 219:

> [At] least three different state interests are commonly advanced to justify disqualification of individuals from public employment on the basis of membership in organizations advocating the violent overthrow of government: (1) The elimination of persons who present a potential for sabotage, espionage, or other activities directly injurious to national security. (2) The elimination of persons who are likely to be either incompetent or untrustworthy in the performance of their duties. (3) The elimination of persons who, aside from any question of danger or fitness, simply are not considered deserving of a government position because they oppose the basic principles on which the government is founded.

In what circumstances are these interests sufficient to justify a restriction on the subversive advocacy or associations of public employees?

4. *A first answer.* In Adler v. Board of Education, 342 U.S. 485 (1952), the Court upheld a New York law providing that no person who becomes a member of any organization that advocates the violent overthrow of government, with knowledge of the organization's proscribed advocacy, "shall be appointed to any [position] in a public school":

> A teacher works in a sensitive area in a schoolroom. There he shapes the attitude of young minds towards the society in which they live. [That] the school authorities have the right and the duty to screen [teachers] as to their fitness to maintain the integrity of the schools [cannot] be doubted. One's associates, past and present, as well as one's conduct, may properly be considered in determining [fitness]. If, under [the] New York law, a person is found to be unfit and is disqualified from employment in the public school system because of membership in a [subversive] organization, he is not thereby denied the right of free speech and assembly. His freedom of choice between membership in the organization and employment in the school system might be limited, but [such] limitation is not one the State may not make in the exercise of its police power to protect the schools from pollution and thereby to defend its own existence.

5. *A second answer.* In Elfbrandt v. Russell, 384 U.S. 11 (1966), the Court invalidated an Arizona statute requiring all state employees to take an oath that they are not "knowingly" a member of the Communist Party or of "any other organization" having for "one of its purposes" the overthrow of the government of Arizona:

> We recognized in *Scales* that [a] "blanket prohibition of association with a group having both legal and illegal aims" would pose "a real danger that legitimate political expression or association would be impaired." [Those] who join an organization but do not share its unlawful purposes and who do not participate in its unlawful activities surely pose no threat, either as citizens or as public employees. [A] law which applies to membership without the "specific intent" to further the illegal aims of the organization infringes unnecessarily on protected freedoms. It rests on the doctrine of "guilt by association" which has no place here. [Such] a law cannot stand.

Is *Elfbrandt*'s extension of *Scales* to the public employment context warranted? Does *Elfbrandt* suggest that the government may not refuse to employ an individual because of her advocacy or associations unless such advocacy or associations could constitutionally be declared unlawful?

6. *The reach of* Elfbrandt: Robel. In United States v. Robel, 389 U.S. 258 (1967), appellee, a member of the Communist Party who had worked at a shipyard for ten years "without incident," was charged with violating section 5(a)(1)(D) of the Subversive Activities Control Act of 1950, which prohibited any "knowing" member of a communist-action organization "to engage in any employment in any defense facility." The Court held that section 5(a)(1)(D) was an "unconstitutional abridgment of the right of association protected by the First Amendment":

> The Government [emphasizes] that the purpose of §5(a)(1)(D) is to reduce the threat of sabotage and espionage in the Nation's defense plants. The Government's interest in such a prophylactic measure is not insubstantial. But [the] means chosen to implement that governmental purpose in this instance cut deeply into the right of association. Section 5(a)(1)(D) [casts] its net across a broad range of associational activities, indiscriminately trapping membership which can be constitutionally punished [see *Scales*] and membership which cannot be so proscribed. [See *Elfbrandt.*] It is made irrelevant to the statute's operation that an individual may be a passive or inactive [member], that he may be unaware of the organization's unlawful aims, or that he may disagree with those unlawful aims. It is also made irrelevant that [the individual] may occupy a nonsensitive position in a defense facility. Thus, §5(a)(1)(D) contains the fatal defect of overbreadth because it seeks to bar employment both for association which may be proscribed and for association which may not be proscribed. [This] the Constitution will not tolerate.

After *Robel*, in what circumstances, if any, may the government refuse to employ an individual in a defense facility because of that individual's membership in a "terrorist" organization, where the individual's membership does not meet the requirements of *Scales*?

7. Brandenburg *and public employees.* Suppose a public school teacher publicly advocates the use of cocaine. Can she be fired even though such advocacy would not meet the requirements of *Brandenburg*? Does it matter whether the expression occurs on school premises? During class? Can a public school require a public school teacher to answer whether she has ever been a member of an organization that supports terrorism? For a comparative perspective, see Attis v. Board of School Trustees, 35 C.R.R.2d 1 (1996) (Canadian court upholding a rule prohibiting a public school teacher from making anti-Semitic statements and distributing anti-Semitic materials even during off-duty hours).

8. *The first amendment rights of students.* May a public university deny official recognition to a student group because it advocates the use of violence to effect change? Consider Healy v. James, 408 U.S. 169 (1972):

> [In] 1969–70, [a] climate of unrest prevailed on many college campuses in this country. There had been widespread civil disobedience on some college campuses, accompanied by the seizure of buildings, vandalism, and arson. Some colleges had been shut down altogether, while at others files were looted and manuscripts destroyed. SDS chapters on some of those campuses had been a catalytic force during this period. . . .
> [The College argues that its denial of recognition to SDS was justified because SDS adheres to] a philosophy of violence and disruption. [But as] repugnant as these views may [be], the mere expression of them would not justify the denial of First Amendment rights. Whether petitioners did in fact advocate a philosophy of "destruction" thus becomes immaterial. The College, acting here as the instrumentality of the State, may not restrict speech or association simply because it finds

the views expressed by any group to be abhorrent. [The] critical line [is] the line between mere advocacy and advocacy "directed to inciting or producing imminent lawless action and . . . likely to incite or produce such action." [*Brandenburg.*]

See also Papish v. Board of Curators of the University of Missouri, 410 U.S. 667 (1973) (a state university may not expel a student for distributing on campus a newspaper containing a political cartoon depicting policemen raping the Statue of Liberty); Tinker v. Des Moines School District, 393 U.S. 503 (1969) (a public school may not discipline students for wearing black armbands to school to publicize their objections to the war in Vietnam in the absence of a showing that the "forbidden conduct would 'materially and substantially interfere with the requirements of appropriate discipline in the operation of the school'").

On the other hand, in Morse v. Frederick, 551 U.S. 393 (2007) the Court upheld the suspension of a high school student for displaying at a school-sponsored event a fourteen-foot long banner bearing the phrase "BONG Hits 4 JESUS," on the theory that *Tinker* does not apply when a student's speech does not contribute to political debate and "can reasonably be regarded as encouraging illegal drug use."

9. *The first amendment rights of soldiers.* Does a soldier have a constitutional right to attempt to persuade other soldiers not to obey orders? Should *Brandenburg* govern? Consider Parker v. Levy, 417 U.S. 733 (1974), in which a captain in the army told enlisted personnel that "[the] United States is wrong in being involved in the Viet Nam War. I would refuse to go to Viet Nam if ordered to do so. I don't see why any colored soldier would go to Viet Nam; they should refuse to go [and] if sent should refuse to fight because they are discriminated against [in] the United States, and they are sacrificed and discriminated against in Viet Nam by being given all the hazardous duty." As a consequence of such statements, appellee was court-martialed for "conduct unbecoming an officer and gentleman." The Court, in a five-to-three decision, upheld the conviction:

> [The] military is, by necessity, a specialized society separate from civilian society. [It has] developed laws and traditions of its [own]. "An army is not a deliberative body. [No] question can be left open as to the right to command in the officer, or the duty of obedience in the soldier." [While] members of the military are not excluded from the protection granted by the First Amendment, the different character of the military community and of the military mission requires a different application of those protections. The fundamental necessity for obedience [may] render permissible within the military that which would be constitutionally impermissible outside it. [Appellee's] conduct, that of a commissioned officer publicly urging enlisted personnel to refuse to obey orders which might send them into combat, was unprotected under the most expansive notions of the First Amendment.

10. *The first amendment rights of government licensees.* To what extent can the government constitutionally regulate the speech of doctors, lawyers, psychologists, and other licensed professionals? In what circumstances, for example, can the government discipline a doctor for recommending sexual-orientation conversion therapy to gay patients? In what circumstances can the government compel a doctor to counsel her patients against abortion? For discussion of these

issues, see Haupt, Professional Speech, 125 Yale L.J. 1238 (2016); Zick, Professional Rights Speech, 47 Ariz. St. L.J. 1289 (2015).

2.   Speech That Provokes a Hostile Audience Reaction

This section examines the circumstances, if any, in which government may restrict speech because the ideas expressed might provoke a hostile audience response. To what extent does the first amendment protect the speaker whose expression provokes a "breach of the peace"? Must society tolerate speech that leads to fistfights, riots, or even mob violence? Is there a danger that, in attempting to maintain order, we may invite a "heckler's veto"?

TERMINIELLO v. CHICAGO, 337 U.S. 1 (1949). Terminiello was convicted of disorderly conduct based on a speech he delivered under the following circumstances: "The auditorium was filled to capacity with over eight hundred persons present. [Outside] a crowd of about one thousand persons gathered to protest against the meeting. A cordon of policemen was assigned to maintain order; but they were not able to prevent several disturbances. The crowd outside was angry and turbulent." Members of the crowd threw stink bombs and broke windows. Terminiello goaded his opponents, referring to them as "slimy scum," "snakes," and "bedbugs." In his condemnation of various political and racial groups, Terminiello "followed, with fidelity that [was] more than coincidental, the pattern of European fascist leaders." The Court found it unnecessary to decide the case on its facts. At Terminiello's trial, the jury was instructed that it could convict if it found that his speech included expression that "stirs the public to anger, invites dispute, brings about a condition of unrest, or creates a disturbance." The Court held that this instruction violated the first amendment:

> A function of free speech under our system of government is to invite dispute. It may indeed best serve its high purpose when it induces a condition of unrest, creates dissatisfaction with conditions as they are, or even stirs people to anger. [That] is why freedom of speech, though not absolute, [is] nevertheless protected against censorship or punishment, unless shown likely to produce a clear and present danger of a serious substantive evil that rises far above public inconvenience, annoyance, or unrest.

Terminiello stands for the proposition that speech may not be restricted because the ideas expressed offend the audience. Is that defensible? Because there is no clear and present danger? Because the harm is too insubstantial? Because the justification for suppression is fundamentally at odds with basic first amendment principles? Are no ideas sufficiently offensive to justify suppression on this basis?

Cantwell v. Connecticut

310 U.S. 296 (1940)

Mr. Justice Roberts delivered the opinion of the Court.

[In an effort to proselytize and solicit contributions, Jesse Cantwell, a Jehovah's Witness, played a phonograph record that sharply attacked the Roman Catholic religion to persons he encountered on the street. As a result of these activities, Cantwell was charged with inciting a breach of the peace.]

... When clear and present danger of riot, disorder, interference with traffic upon the public streets, or other immediate threat to public safety, peace, or order, appears, the power of the State to prevent or punish is obvious. Equally obvious is it that a State may not unduly suppress free communication of views, religious or other, under the guise of conserving desirable conditions. ...

Having these considerations in mind, we note that Jesse Cantwell, on April 26, 1938, was upon a public street, where he had a right to be, and where he had a right peacefully to impart his views to others. There is no showing that his deportment was noisy, truculent, overbearing or offensive. He requested of two pedestrians permission to play to them a phonograph record. The permission was granted. It is not claimed that he intended to insult or affront the hearers by playing the record. It is plain that he wished only to interest them in his propaganda. The sound of the phonograph is not shown to have disturbed residents of the street, to have drawn a crowd, or to have impeded traffic. Thus far he had invaded no right or interest of the public or of the men accosted.

The record [embodies] a general attack on all organized religious systems as instruments of Satan and injurious to man; it then singles out the Roman Catholic Church for strictures couched in terms which naturally would offend not only persons of that persuasion, but all others who respect the honestly held religious faith of their fellows. The hearers were in fact highly offended. One of them said he felt like hitting Cantwell and the other that he was tempted to throw Cantwell off the street. The one who testified he felt like hitting Cantwell said, in answer to the question "Did you do anything else or have any other reaction?" "No, sir, because he said he would take the victrola and he went." ...

Cantwell's conduct, in the view of the court below, considered apart from the effect of his communication upon his hearers, did not amount to a breach of the peace. One may, however, be guilty of the offense if he commit acts or make statements likely to provoke violence and disturbance of good order, even though no such eventuality be intended. Decisions to this effect are many, but examination discloses that, in practically all, the provocative language which was held to amount to a breach of the peace consisted of profane, indecent, or abusive remarks directed to the person of the hearer.

We find in the instant case no assault or threatening of bodily harm, no truculent bearing, no intentional discourtesy, no personal abuse. On the contrary, we find only an effort to persuade a willing listener to buy a book or to contribute money in the interest of what Cantwell, however misguided others may think him, conceived to be true religion.

In the realm of religious faith, and in that of political belief, sharp differences arise. In both fields the tenets of one man may seem the rankest error to his neighbor. To persuade others to his own point of view, the pleader, as we know, at times, resorts to exaggeration, to vilification of men who have been, or are, prominent in church or state, and even to false statement. But the people of this nation have ordained in the light of history, that, in spite of the probability of excesses and abuses, these liberties are, in the long view, essential to enlightened opinion and right conduct on the part of the citizens of a democracy. ...

Although the contents of the record not unnaturally aroused animosity, we think that, in the absence of a statute narrowly drawn to define and punish specific conduct as constituting a clear and present danger to a substantial interest of the State, the petitioner's communication, considered in the light of the constitutional guarantees, raised no such clear and present menace to public peace and order as to render him liable to conviction of the common law offense in question. . . .

Reversed.

Feiner v. New York

340 U.S. 315 (1951)

Mr. Chief Justice Vinson delivered the opinion of the Court.

Petitioner was convicted of the offense of disorderly conduct. . . .

On the evening of March 8, 1949, petitioner [was] addressing [a street-corner] meeting [in] the City of Syracuse. [The] police received a telephone complaint concerning the meeting, and two officers were detailed to investigate. [They] found a crowd of about seventy-five or eighty people, both Negro and white, filling the sidewalk and spreading out into the street. Petitioner, standing on a large wooden box on the sidewalk, was addressing the crowd through a loud-speaker system attached to an automobile. Although the purpose of his speech was to urge his listeners to attend a meeting to be held that night in the Syracuse Hotel, in its course he was making derogatory remarks concerning President Truman, the American Legion, the Mayor of Syracuse, and other local political officials. [Feiner referred to Truman as a "bum," to the mayor as a "champagne-sipping bum" who "does not speak for the Negro people," and to the American Legion as "a Nazi Gestapo."]

The police officers made no effort to interfere with petitioner's speech, but were first concerned with the effect of the crowd on both pedestrian and vehicular traffic. [The] crowd was restless and there was some pushing, shoving and milling around. . . .

At this time, petitioner was speaking in a "loud, high-pitched voice." He gave the impression that he was endeavoring to arouse the Negro people against the whites, urging that they rise up in arms and fight for equal rights. The statements before such a mixed audience "stirred up a little excitement." Some of the onlookers made remarks to the police about their inability to handle the crowd and at least one threatened violence if the police did not act. There were others who appeared to be favoring petitioner's arguments. Because of the feeling that existed in the crowd both for and against the speaker, the officers finally "stepped in to prevent it from resulting in a fight." One of the officers approached the petitioner, not for the purpose of arresting him, but to get him to break up the crowd. He asked petitioner to get down off the box, but the latter refused to accede to his request and continued talking. The officer waited for a minute and then demanded that he cease talking. Although the officer had thus twice requested petitioner to stop over the course of several minutes, petitioner not only ignored him but continued talking. During all this time, the crowd was pressing closer around petitioner and the officer. Finally, the officer told petitioner he was under arrest and ordered him to get down from the box, reaching up to grab him. Petitioner stepped down, announcing over the microphone that "the law has arrived, and I suppose they will take over now." In all, the officer had asked petitioner to get down off the box three times over a space of four or five minutes. Petitioner had been speaking for over a half hour.

On these facts, petitioner was specifically charged with violation of §722 of the Penal Law of New York, the pertinent part of which is set out in the margin.[1] . . .

We are not faced here with blind condonation by a state court of arbitrary police action. [The] courts below recognized petitioner's right to hold a street meeting at this locality, to make use of loud-speaking equipment in giving his speech, and to make derogatory remarks concerning public officials and the American Legion. They found that the officers in making the arrest were motivated solely by a proper concern for the preservation of order and protection of the general welfare, and that there was no evidence which could lend color to a claim that the acts of the police were a cover for suppression of petitioner's views and opinions. Petitioner was thus neither arrested nor convicted for the making or the content of his speech. Rather, it was the reaction which it actually engendered.

The language of [*Cantwell*] is appropriate here. ". . . When clear and present danger of riot, disorder, interference with traffic upon the public streets, or other immediate threat to public safety, peace, or order, appears, the power of the State to prevent or punish is obvious." . . .

We are well aware that the ordinary murmurings and objections of a hostile audience cannot be allowed to silence a speaker, and also mindful of the possible danger of giving overzealous police officials complete discretion to break up otherwise lawful public meetings. [But] we are not faced here with such a situation. It is one thing to say that the police cannot be used as an instrument for the suppression of unpopular views, and another to say that, when as here the speaker passes the bounds of argument or persuasion and undertakes incitement to riot, they are powerless to prevent a breach of the peace. . . .

Affirmed.

[A concurring opinion of Justice Frankfurter and a dissenting opinion of Justice Douglas, in which Justice Minton concurred, are omitted.]

MR. JUSTICE BLACK, dissenting.

The record before us convinces me that petitioner, a young college student, has been sentenced to the penitentiary for the unpopular views he expressed on matters of public interest while lawfully making a street-corner speech. . . .

The Court's opinion apparently rests on this reasoning: The policeman, under the circumstances detailed, could reasonably conclude that serious fighting or even riot was imminent; therefore he could stop petitioner's speech to prevent a breach of peace; accordingly, it was "disorderly conduct" for petitioner to continue speaking in disobedience of the officer's request. As to the existence of a dangerous situation on the street corner, it seems far-fetched to suggest that the "facts" show any imminent threat of riot or uncontrollable disorder. It is neither unusual nor unexpected that some people at public street meetings mutter, mill about, push, shove, or disagree, even violently, with the speaker. Indeed, it is rare where controversial topics are discussed that an outdoor crowd does not do some or all of these things. Nor does one isolated threat to assault the

---

1. "Section 722. Any person who with intent to provoke a breach of the peace, or whereby a breach of the peace may be occasioned, commits any of the following acts shall be deemed to have committed the offense of disorderly conduct:

"1.   Uses offensive, disorderly, threatening, abusive or insulting language, conduct or behavior;
"2.   Acts in such a manner as to annoy, disturb, interfere with, obstruct, or be offensive to others;
"3.   Congregates with others on a public street and refuses to move on when ordered by the police. . . .

speaker forebode disorder. Especially should the danger be discounted where, as here, the person threatening was a man whose wife and two small children accompanied him and who, so far as the record shows, was never close enough to petitioner to carry out the threat.

Moreover, assuming that the "facts" did indicate a critical situation, I reject the implication of the Court's opinion that the police had no obligation to protect petitioner's constitutional right to talk. The police of course have power to prevent breaches of the peace. But if, in the name of preserving order, they ever can interfere with a lawful public speaker, they first must make all reasonable efforts to protect him. Here the policeman did not even pretend to try to protect petitioner. According to the officers' testimony, the crowd was restless but there is no showing of any attempt to quiet it; pedestrians were forced to walk into the street, but there was no effort to clear a path on the sidewalk; one person threatened to assault petitioner but the officers did nothing to discourage this when even a word might have sufficed. Their duty was to protect petitioner's right to talk, even to the extent of arresting the man who threatened to interfere. Instead, they shirked that duty and acted only to suppress the right to speak.

Finally, I cannot agree with the Court's statement that petitioner's disregard of the policeman's unexplained request amounted to such "deliberate defiance" as would justify an arrest or conviction for disorderly conduct. On the contrary, I think that the policeman's action was a "deliberate defiance" of ordinary official duty as well as of the constitutional right of free speech. For at least where time allows, courtesy and explanation of commands are basic elements of good official conduct in a democratic society. Here petitioner was "asked" then "told" then "commanded" to stop speaking, but a man making a lawful address is certainly not required to be silent merely because an officer directs it. Petitioner was entitled to know why he should cease doing a lawful act. Not once was he told. I understand that people in authoritarian countries must obey arbitrary orders. I had hoped that there was no such duty in the United States. . . .

Note: The Search for Mechanisms of Control

1. *Incitement to riot.* Is *Feiner* consistent with *Cantwell*? Because Feiner triggered a clear and present danger? Because he passed "the bounds of argument or persuasion" and undertook "incitement to riot"? In what sense did Feiner "incite to riot"? Does "incitement" mean the same thing here as in the subversive advocacy context?

2. *Police orders.* Note that Feiner, unlike Cantwell, disobeyed a specific police order to stop speaking. What is the appropriate role of the police? Does the first amendment require the police to arrest the hostile members of the audience rather than to stop the speaker? Suppose the officers on the scene need support. Must they call in additional officers rather than stop the speaker? May an individual who is prosecuted for refusing to obey a police order to stop speaking assert the unconstitutionality of the order in his defense?

3. *Licensing.* Kunz v. New York, 340 U.S. 290 (1951), decided on the same day as *Feiner*, concerned the constitutionality of a city ordinance declaring it unlawful to hold public worship meetings on the streets without first obtaining a permit from the police commissioner. Kunz, an ordained Baptist minister, was issued a permit in 1946, but the permit was revoked after a hearing at which it was determined that Kunz had ridiculed and denounced other religious beliefs in such a way as to cause disorder. Thereafter, the city denied Kunz's permit applications,

and in 1948 he was convicted for holding a meeting without a permit in violation of the ordinance. The Court did not decide whether a permit could constitutionally be denied on the ground that the speaker had previously caused disorder, holding instead that the permit scheme was invalid on its face because it failed to provide clear standards to guide the discretion of the official charged with administering the scheme. On standardless licensing, see section C2 infra.

4. *Permit fees and the hostile audience.* In Forsyth County, Georgia v. The Nationalist Movement, 505 U.S. 123 (1992), the Court invalidated a municipal ordinance that authorized permit fees for parades, demonstrations, marches, and similar activities, up to a maximum of $1,000, based in part on the anticipated expense necessary to maintain the public order. The Court, in an opinion by Justice Blackmun, explained:

> The county envisions that the administrator [will] assess a fee to cover "the cost of necessary and reasonable protection of persons participating or observing [said] activity." [To perform this function, the administrator] "must necessarily examine the content of the message that is conveyed," [estimate] the response of others to that content, and judge the number of police necessary to meet that response. The fee assessed will depend on the administrator's measure of the amount of hostility likely to be created by the speech based on its content. Those wishing to express views unpopular with bottle throwers, for example, may have to pay more for their permit. [Speech] cannot be financially burdened, any more than it can be punished or banned, simply because it might offend a hostile mob. ["Regulations] which permit the Government to discriminate on the basis of the content of the message cannot be tolerated under the First Amendment." [The county] contends that the $1,000 cap on the fee [saves] its constitutionality. [But neither] the $1,000 cap [nor] even some lower nominal cap [could] save the ordinance because in this context the level of the fee is irrelevant. A tax based on the content of speech does not become more constitutional because it is a small tax.

5. A *"far cry"* from Feiner. In Edwards v. South Carolina, 372 U.S. 229 (1963), petitioners, 187 black high school and college students, walked to the South Carolina State House grounds, an area open to the general public, to protest discrimination. About thirty law enforcement officers, who had advance knowledge of the demonstration, were present. Petitioners walked in an orderly manner through the grounds carrying placards bearing such messages as "I am proud to be a Negro" and "Down with segregation." A crowd of about two hundred to three hundred onlookers gathered; although some were identified as "possible trouble makers," there were no threatening remarks, hostile gestures, or offensive comments. There was no significant interference with either vehicular or pedestrian traffic. After thirty to forty-five minutes, police authorities informed petitioners that they would be arrested if they did not disperse within fifteen minutes. One of the demonstrators then delivered a "religious harangue," inspiring petitioners to sing several patriotic songs while loudly clapping their hands and stamping their feet. After fifteen minutes, petitioners were arrested. They were convicted of the common law crime of breach of the peace.

The Court, in an opinion by Justice Stewart, held that the convictions "infringed the petitioners' constitutionally protected rights of free speech, free assembly, and freedom to petition for redress of their grievances." *Edwards*, the Court explained, "was a far cry" from *Feiner*. Here, "there was no violence or threat of violence on [the part of the petitioners], or on the part of any member of the crowd watching them." Moreover, "police protection at the scene was at all times sufficient to meet any foreseeable possibility of disorder." In the Court's view, then, petitioners had been convicted because "the opinions which they were peaceably expressing were sufficiently opposed to the views of the majority of the community to attract a crowd and necessitate police protection." The Constitution, however, "does not permit a State to make criminal the peaceful expression of unpopular views." The Court thus concluded that, "as in [*Terminiello*], the Courts of South Carolina have defined a criminal offense so as to permit conviction of the petitioners if their speech 'stirred people to anger, invited public dispute, or brought about a condition of unrest. A conviction resting on any of those grounds may not stand.'"

6. A *"far cry"* from Feiner II. In Cox v. Louisiana, 379 U.S. 536 (1965), Cox, an ordained minister, led a demonstration of approximately two thousand black students to protest the arrest the previous day of twenty-three black students who had picketed stores that maintained segregated lunch counters. The demonstration was to take place at the local courthouse, which contained the parish jail in which the twenty-three students were confined. The demonstrators walked to the courthouse in an orderly manner, two or three abreast. As they neared the courthouse, the police chief stopped the procession and inquired as to their purpose. Cox stated that they would sing the national anthem and a freedom song and recite the Lord's Prayer and the pledge of allegiance, and that he would deliver a short speech. The police chief instructed Cox to confine the demonstration to the west side of the street, across the street from the courthouse. The demonstrators lined up on the west sidewalk about five deep, spread along almost the entire length of the block. A group of about one hundred to three hundred whites, mostly courthouse personnel, gathered across the street on the steps of the courthouse. Seventy-five to eighty policemen, several members of the fire department, and a fire truck were stationed in the street between the two groups.

The demonstration proceeded according to plan until Cox, in the course of his speech, said: "It's lunch time. Let's go eat. There are twelve stores we are protesting. [These stores won't accept your money at one of their counters.] This is an act of racial discrimination. These stores are open to the public. You are members of the public." These remarks caused some "muttering" and "grumbling" among the white onlookers. The sheriff, deeming Cox's appeal to the students to sit in at the lunch counters to be "inflammatory," ordered the demonstrators to disperse. When Cox and the students ignored the sheriff, the police fired tear gas, causing the demonstrators to flee. The following day, Cox was arrested. He was thereafter convicted of breach of the peace.

In a unanimous decision, the Court overturned Cox's conviction. Justice Goldberg, speaking for the Court, found "no conduct which the State had a right to prohibit as a breach of the peace." The Court rejected the state's contention that the conviction could be sustained because "violence was about to erupt." The demonstrators themselves "were not violent and threatened no violence." Indeed, there was "no indication that the mood of the students was ever hostile, aggressive, or unfriendly." The fear of violence was thus "based upon the reaction of the group of white citizens looking on from across the street." Although there were some "mutterings," there was no evidence "that any member of the white group threatened violence." In any event, the police and other personnel present "could have handled the crowd." The Court thus concluded that the facts of *Cox* "are strikingly similar" to *Edwards* and, like *Edwards*, "a far cry" from *Feiner*.

7. A *"far cry"* from Feiner III. In Gregory v. City of Chicago, 394 U.S. 111 (1969), Gregory led a march of about eighty-five protesters to the home of Chicago Mayor Richard Daley to protest segregation in the city's public schools. The

protesters, accompanied by about one hundred police, arrived at the mayor's home at 8:00 P.M. and began marching continuously around the block. For the first thirty minutes, they sang civil rights songs and chanted slogans criticizing the mayor and referring to him as a "snake." After 8:30, the protesters marched quietly but continued to carry sharply critical placards. In the next hour, the crowd of white onlookers grew rapidly to more than one thousand, and, as the evening wore on, they became increasingly unruly. In several instances, spectators attempted physically to block the march. There were threatening shouts such as "Get out of here niggers — go back where you belong or we will get you out of here," and rocks and eggs were thrown at the marchers. At about 9:30, the police officer in charge informed Gregory that "the situation was dangerous and becoming riotous" and asked Gregory to lead the marchers out of the area. When Gregory refused, he and the other protesters were arrested. They were thereafter convicted under Chicago's disorderly conduct ordinance, which declared it unlawful for any person to make "any improper noise, riot, disturbance, breach of the peace, or diversion tending to a breach of the peace."

The Court, in an opinion by Chief Justice Warren, unanimously overturned the convictions. The Court announced that "this is a simple case." Noting that "there is no evidence in this record that petitioners' conduct was disorderly," the Court concluded that "convictions so totally devoid of evidentiary support violate due process."

8. *Evaluation.* Why were these cases "a far cry" from *Feiner?* Consider the following possibilities: (a) The demonstrators in these cases did not pass "the bounds of argument or persuasion and undertake incitement to riot"; (b) there was less likelihood in these cases of an imminent violent response; (c) the police were better able to handle the situations in *Edwards, Cox,* and *Gregory.* Were these cases really "a far cry" from *Feiner,* or do they limit its precedential force? Do the results in *Edwards, Cox,* and *Gregory* suggest that the Court has implicitly embraced a set of principles for dealing with the hostile audience problem analogous to those articulated at approximately the same time for dealing with the problem of subversive advocacy? Should the state *ever* be allowed to stop or punish a speaker because of a hostile audience response? Consider the argument that even allowing for that possibility will only invite threats of violence and discriminatory law enforcement against unpopular speakers. Might it be best simply to say: "Never"?

9. *The Heckler's Veto on Campus.* Consider the situation of a public university. Suppose a student group invites a highly controversial speaker to campus. If other students and community members threaten violence if the individual is permitted to speak, should the university disinvite the speaker and cancel the event? Would such action be consistent with the first amendment? Should it matter whether the speaker is controversial because she denounces affirmative action as a form of "black privilege," reviles evangelical Christians for their "ignorant and immoral" positions on abortion and homosexuality, denounces Muslims as "terrorists," or advocates violence against the police? Suppose the university allows the speaker to come to campus and protesters, including both students and community members, enter the hall and keep chanting "Get Her Out! Get Her Out!" in an effort to prevent her from speaking. What should the university do? What is the role of the first amendment in this situation? See Papandrea, The Free Speech Rights of University Students, 101 Minn. L. Rev. 1801 (2017); Tsesis, Campus Speech and Harassment, 101 Minn. L. Rev. 1863 (2017).

In April 2017, Richard B. Spencer, a white nationalist and one of the leaders of America's so-called alt-right movement, announced that he would be giving a speech on the campus of Auburn University in Alabama. Auburn, a public university, has a policy of permitting anyone who wants to rent meeting space to do so. Spencer is a controversial and divisive figure who has been decried as racist, anti-Semitic, un-American, and hateful. Knowing that his presence would upset many members of the university community, Auburn issued a statement: "We strongly deplore his views, which run counter to those of this institution. While his event isn't affiliated with the university, Auburn supports the constitutional right to free speech. We encourage the campus community to respond to speech they find objectionable with their own views in civil discourse and to do so with respect and inclusion."

Several days later, though, Auburn changed its tune. The university announced that it had decided to cancel the event because of "credible evidence that it will jeopardize the safety of students, faculty, staff and visitors." Was that justification for canceling the speech constitutionally permissible?

10. Is there such a thing as "low"-value speech in this context? The difficulties of defining "incitement" in cases like *Cantwell*, *Feiner*, *Edwards*, and *Cox* have already been noted. Consider also *Chaplinsky* and the "fighting words" doctrine.

Chaplinsky v. New Hampshire

315 U.S. 568 (1942)

Mr. Justice Murphy delivered the opinion of the Court.

Appellant, a member of the sect known as Jehovah's Witnesses, was convicted in the municipal court of Rochester, New Hampshire, for violation of Chapter 378, §2, of the Public Laws of New Hampshire:

> No person shall address any offensive, derisive or annoying word to any other person who is lawfully in any street or other public place, nor call him by an offensive or derisive name, nor make any noise or exclamation in his presence and hearing with intent to deride, offend or annoy him, or to prevent him from pursuing his lawful business or occupation.

The complaint charged that appellant,

> with force and arms, in a certain public place in said city of Rochester, to wit, on the public sidewalk on the easterly side of Wakefield Street, near unto the entrance of the City Hall, did unlawfully repeat, the words following, addressed to the complainant, that is to say, "You are a God damned racketeer" and "a damned Fascist and the whole government of Rochester are Fascists or agents of Fascists," the same being offensive, derisive and annoying words and names. . . .

There is no substantial dispute over the facts. Chaplinsky was distributing the literature of his sect on the streets of Rochester on a busy Saturday afternoon. Members of the local citizenry complained to the City Marshal, Bowering, that Chaplinsky was denouncing all religion as a "racket." Bowering told them that Chaplinsky was lawfully engaged, and then warned Chaplinsky that the crowd was getting restless. Some time later, a disturbance occurred and the traffic officer on duty at the busy intersection started with Chaplinsky for the police station, but did not inform him that he was under arrest or that he was going to be arrested. On the way, they encountered Marshal Bowering, who had been advised that a riot was under way and was therefore hurrying to the scene. Bowering repeated his earlier warning to Chaplinsky, who then addressed to Bowering the words set forth in the complaint.

Chaplinsky's version of the affair was slightly different. He testified that, when he met Bowering, he asked him to arrest the ones responsible for the disturbance. In reply, Bowering cursed him and told him to come along. Appellant admitted that he said the words charged in the complaint, with the exception of the name of the Deity.

Over appellant's objection the trial court excluded, as immaterial, testimony relating to appellant's mission "to preach the true facts of the Bible," his treatment at the hands of the crowd, and the alleged neglect of duty on the part of the police. This action was approved by the court below, which held that neither provocation nor the truth of the utterance would constitute a defense to the charge. . . .

Allowing the broadest scope to the language and purpose of the Fourteenth Amendment, it is well understood that the right of free speech is not absolute at all times and under all circumstances. There are certain well-defined and narrowly limited classes of speech, the prevention and punishment of which have never been thought to raise any Constitutional problem. These include the lewd and obscene, the profane, the libelous, and the insulting or "fighting" words — those which by their very utterance inflict injury or tend to incite an immediate breach of the peace. It has been well observed that such utterances are no essential part of any exposition of ideas, and are of such slight social value as a step to truth that any benefit that may be derived from them is clearly outweighed by the social interest in order and morality. "Resort to epithets or personal abuse is not in any proper sense communication of information or opinion safeguarded by the Constitution, and its punishment as a criminal act would raise no question under that instrument." [*Cantwell.*] . . .

On the authority of its earlier decisions, the state court declared that the statute's purpose was to preserve the public peace, no words being "forbidden except such as have a direct tendency to cause acts of violence by the persons to whom, individually, the remark is addressed." It was further said:

> The word "offensive" is not to be defined in terms of what a particular addressee thinks. . . . The test is what men of common intelligence would understand would be words likely to cause an average addressee to fight. . . . The English language has a number of words and expressions which by general consent are "fighting words" when said without a disarming smile. . . . Such words, as ordinary men know, are likely to cause a fight. So are threatening, profane or obscene revilings. Derisive and annoying words can be taken as coming within the purview of the statute as heretofore interpreted only when they have this characteristic of plainly tending to excite the addressee to a breach of the peace. . . . The statute, as construed, does no more than prohibit the face-to-face words plainly likely to cause a breach of the peace by the addressee, words whose speaking constitutes a breach of the peace by the speaker — including "classical fighting words," words in current use less "classical" but equally likely to cause violence, and other disorderly words, including profanity, obscenity and threats.

We are unable to say that the limited scope of the statute as thus construed contravenes the Constitutional right of free expression. It is a statute narrowly drawn and limited to define and punish specific conduct lying within the domain of state power, the use in a public place of words likely to cause a breach of the peace. . . .

Nor can we say that the application of the statute to the facts disclosed by the record substantially or unreasonably impinges upon the privilege of free speech. Argument is unnecessary to demonstrate that the appellations "damned racketeer" and "damned Fascist" are epithets likely to provoke the average person to retaliation, and thereby cause a breach of the peace.

The refusal of the state court to admit evidence of provocation and evidence bearing on the truth or falsity of the utterances, is open to no Constitutional objection. Whether the facts sought to be proved by such evidence constitute a defense to the charge, or may be shown in mitigation, are questions for the state court to determine. Our function is fulfilled by a determination that the challenged statute, on its face and as applied, does not contravene the Fourteenth Amendment.

Affirmed.

Note: Fighting Words

1. *The actual facts of* Chaplinsky. Consider Blasi and Shiffrin, The Real Story of West Virginia Board of Education v. Barnette, in Dorf, ed., Constitutional Law Stories 433 (2004):

> In April of 1940, Walter Chaplinsky, a vociferous Jehovah's Witness preaching in Rochester, New Hampshire, was surrounded by a group of men who scornfully invited him to salute the flag. While one veteran attempted to pummel Chaplinsky, the town marshal looked on, warned the Witness that things were turning ugly, but refused to arrest the assailant. After the marshal left, the assailant returned with a flag and attempted to impale Chaplinsky on the flagpole, eventually pinning him onto a car while other members of the crowd began to beat him. A police officer then arrived, not to detain or disperse members of the mob but to escort Chaplinsky to the police station. En route, the officer and others who joined the escort directed epithets at the hapless Witness. When Chaplinsky responded in kind, calling the marshal who had reappeared "a damn fascist and a racketeer," he was arrested for, and later convicted of, using offensive language in public.

2. *The two-level theory.* Building on dictum in *Cantwell,* the Court in *Chaplinsky* first fully enunciated what Professor Harry Kalven later termed the "two-level" theory of speech, under which speech is either "protected" or "unprotected" by the first amendment according to the Court's assessment of its relative "value." Kalven, The Metaphysics of the Law of Obscenity, 1960 Sup. Ct. Rev. 1, 10. The analytical underpinnings and historical evolution of this theory, and the other varieties of "unprotected" speech mentioned in *Chaplinsky,* such as the "obscene" and the "libelous," are examined more fully in section D infra.

3. *Fighting words as "low"-value speech.* Why was Chaplinsky's expression unprotected by the first amendment? Because it consisted of "epithets or personal abuse"? What distinguishes an "epithet" from bona fide criticism? The following arguments might be advanced for the proposition that fighting words are of only "low" first amendment value:

a. Fighting words are unprotected because, as "epithets or personal abuse," they are intended to inflict harm rather than to communicate ideas, and thus are not really "speech" at all. They are "verbal assaults," more akin to a "punch in the mouth" than to constitutionally protected expression of opinion. See Greenawalt, Insults and Epithets: Are They Protected Speech?, 42 Rutgers L. Rev. 287, 291–298 (1990). If Chaplinsky had actually punched Bowering, could he successfully claim that this was a constitutionally protected expression of his evaluation of Bowering's performance of his duties?

b. Fighting words are unprotected because they are "likely to provoke the average person to retaliation, and thereby cause a breach of the peace." On this view, the doctrine is merely an application of the Holmes/Brandeis version of clear and present danger. But is name-calling really likely to cause the *average* addressee to fight? Is the focus on the *average*, rather than the *actual*, addressee consistent with the Holmes/Brandeis formulation? How should we deal with the possibility that men may be more prone than women to respond with violence?

c. Fighting words are unprotected because they are "no essential part of any exposition of ideas." Does the Court undervalue the use of personal insults to dramatize one's point? Is the emotive impact worth protecting? Even if fighting words are not "essential" to the exposition of ideas, is this in itself a basis for holding them unprotected? Is it, in conjunction with other factors, a relevant consideration?

4. *Fighting words?* Consider whether the following constitute "fighting words": (1) Cantwell's phonograph record, which charged that Roman Catholicism "has by means of fraud and deception brought untold sorrow and suffering upon the people" and "operates the greatest racket ever employed amongst men and robs the people of their money," when played, as it was, to Roman Catholics. (2) Terminiello's speech, in which he called his opponents, who were outside the hall, "slimy scum," "snakes," and "bedbugs." (3) Kunz's public prayer meetings, in which he labeled Catholicism "a religion of the devil," declared that the Pope is "the anti-Christ," and described Jews as "Christ-killers" and "garbage that [should] have been burnt in the incinerators [of Nazi Germany]." (4) Gregory's repeated references to Mayor Daley as a "snake." Consider also the Court's post-*Chaplinsky* decisions:

a. In Street v. New York, 394 U.S. 576 (1969), Street, on learning that James Meredith, a civil rights leader, had been shot, burned an American flag in public. A small crowd gathered, and Street said, "We don't need no damn flag. [If] they let that happen to Meredith we don't need an American flag." The state argued, among other things, that Street could constitutionally be convicted for this speech because of "the possible tendency of [his] words to provoke violent retaliation." The Court disagreed: "Though it is conceivable that some listeners might have been moved to retaliate upon hearing [Street's] disrespectful words, we cannot say that [his] remarks were so inherently inflammatory as to come within that small class of 'fighting words' which are 'likely to provoke the average person to retaliation, and thereby cause a breach of the peace.' [Citing *Chaplinsky*.]"

b. In Cohen v. California, 403 U.S. 15 (1971), Cohen wore a jacket bearing the words "Fuck the Draft" in a corridor of a courthouse. As a consequence, he was convicted under a California statute prohibiting any person "maliciously and willfully [to disturb] the peace or quiet of any neighborhood or person [by] offensive conduct." The state courts interpreted the phrase "offensive conduct" as "behavior which has a tendency to provoke *others* to acts of violence." In overturning the conviction, the Court rejected the state's argument that Cohen's speech constituted fighting words: "While the four-letter word displayed by Cohen in relation to the draft is not uncommonly employed in a personally provocative fashion, in this instance it was clearly not 'directed to the person of the hearer.' [Citing *Cantwell*.] No individual actually or likely to be present could reasonably have regarded the words on appellant's jacket as a direct personal insult."

c. In Gooding v. Wilson, 405 U.S. 518 (1972), Gooding said to a police officer attempting to restore access to an army induction center during an antiwar demonstration, "White son of a bitch, I'll kill you" and "You son of a bitch, I'll choke you to death." He was thereafter convicted under a Georgia statute prohibiting any person to "use to or of another, and in his [presence] opprobrious words or abusive language, tending to cause a breach of the peace." The Court found it unnecessary to decide whether Gooding's speech could constitutionally be punished under a properly drawn statute, holding instead that the Georgia law was overbroad and hence unconstitutional on its face because the state courts had repeatedly interpreted it as reaching clearly protected expression. As examples of this overbreadth, the Court noted that the state courts had failed to construe the statute as "limited in application, as in *Chaplinsky*, to words that 'have a direct tendency to cause acts of violence by the person to whom, individually, the remark is addressed.'" On the overbreadth doctrine, see section C1 infra.

d. Rosenfeld v. New Jersey, 408 U.S. 901 (1972); Lewis v. New Orleans, 408 U.S. 913 (1972); and Brown v. Oklahoma, 408 U.S. 914 (1972), were decided as companion cases. In *Rosenfeld*, the appellant, in the course of a public school board meeting attended by approximately 150 people, about forty of whom were children, used the noun "mother-fucker" on four occasions to describe the teachers, the school board, the town, and the country. In *Lewis*, while the police were engaged in arresting appellant's son, she called them "god-damn-mother-fucker police." In *Brown*, appellant, a member of the Black Panthers, spoke by invitation to a large audience at the University of Tulsa's chapel. During the question-and-answer period, he referred to some police officers as "mother-fucking fascist pig cops" and to one officer in particular as a "black mother-fucking pig." Each appellant was convicted under a state law prohibiting, in varying forms, the use of profanity in public. In each case, the Court summarily vacated the judgment and reversed for reconsideration in light of *Gooding*.

e. In Texas v. Johnson, 491 U.S. 397 (1989), the Court invalidated a Texas statute that prohibited any person to "desecrate" the American flag "in a way that the actor knows will seriously offend [others] likely to observe or discover his action," as applied to an individual who publicly burned the flag in symbolic protest of national policy. The Court held that this "expressive conduct" did not fall within the fighting words doctrine because "no reasonable onlooker would have regarded [the defendant's] generalized expression of dissatisfaction with the policies of the Federal Government as a direct personal insult or an invitation to exchange fisticuffs."

5. *Fighting words reconsidered.* It has been suggested that the post-*Chaplinsky* decisions establish that the doctrine applies only to the use of insulting and provocative epithets that describe a particular individual and are addressed specifically to that individual in a face-to-face encounter. See Gard, Fighting Words as Free Speech, 58 Wash. U. L.Q. 531 (1980). Are these limitations defensible? Should the doctrine apply when an insult descriptive of a group is directed to an individual member of that group? Are insults descriptive of a group less likely to provoke a violent response? Are they, because of their generality, more likely to be of "high" first amendment value?

The Court has not upheld a conviction on the basis of the fighting words doctrine since *Chaplinsky*. It has been argued that the Court's post-*Chaplinsky* decisions have so narrowed the doctrine as to render it meaningless, and that the doctrine is "nothing more than a quaint remnant of an earlier morality that has no place in a democratic society dedicated to the principle of free expression." Gard, supra, at 536. Do you agree?

6. *The problem of underinclusion.* Suppose a law restricts only a subset of fighting words, such as (a) fighting words directed against blacks, (b) fighting words concerning religion, or (c) fighting words uttered in bars. Are such restrictions necessarily constitutional because the category of fighting words is itself "unprotected" by the first amendment? Are such restrictions subject to scrutiny,

even though the category is "unprotected," because of the inequalities created by the decision to restrict less than the entire category? This issue is addressed in R.A.V. v. City of St. Paul, section D8, infra.

Note: The Skokie Controversy

In 1977, the Village of Skokie, a northern Chicago suburb, had a population of about seventy thousand persons, forty thousand of whom were Jewish. Approximately five thousand of the Jewish residents were survivors of Nazi concentration camps during World War II. In March 1977, Frank Collin, leader of the National Socialist Party of America, informed village officials that the party intended to hold a peaceable public assembly in Skokie on May 1 to protest the village's requirement that a $350,000 insurance bond be posted before the village's parks could be used for purposes of assembly. Collin explained that the demonstration would last twenty to thirty minutes and would consist of thirty to fifty demonstrators marching in single file in front of the village hall. The marchers would wear uniforms reminiscent of those worn by members of the Nazi Party in Germany under Hitler, and they would wear swastika emblems or armbands. The marchers would carry a party banner containing a swastika emblem and signs bearing such messages as "White Free Speech" and "Free Speech for the White Man."

Village officials filed suit, seeking to enjoin the marchers from wearing their uniforms, displaying the swastika, or distributing or displaying any materials "which incite or promote hatred against persons of Jewish faith or ancestry." The complaint alleged that the march, as planned, was a "deliberate and willful attempt to exacerbate the sensitivities of the Jewish population in Skokie and to incite racial and religious hatred" and that the display of the swastika in Skokie "constitutes a symbolic assault against large numbers of the residents of the plaintiff village and an incitation to violence and retaliation."

At a hearing before the trial court, the village presented evidence that some fifteen to eighteen Jewish organizations, along with various other anti-Nazi organizations, planned to hold a counterdemonstration to protest the march. Between twelve thousand and fifteen thousand persons were expected to participate in the counterdemonstration. The village also presented evidence that there had already been many threats of violence, and that, if the party was permitted to demonstrate, "an uncontrollably violent situation would develop" and "bloodshed would occur." Finally, the village presented the testimony of a survivor of a Nazi concentration camp to the effect that for him and other survivors, "the swastika is a symbol that his closest family was killed by the Nazis, and that the lives of him and his children are not presently safe." The village maintained that the display of the swastika in such circumstances amounted to the intentional infliction of emotional harm. The witness testified further that, although he did not "intend to use violence against" the marchers, he did "not know if he [could] control himself." On April 29, the trial judge granted the injunction. The National Socialist Party appealed.

After the issuance of the injunction, the Illinois appellate courts refused to stay the injunction pending appeal, and the Illinois Supreme Court denied a petition for direct, expedited appeal. The party then sought a stay in the Supreme Court of the United States, which treated the petition as a petition for certiorari, granted the writ, and summarily reversed the state court's denial of the stay. In a five-to-four decision, the Court characterized the denial of the stay as a "final judgment for purposes of our jurisdiction" because it

> finally determined the merits of petitioners' claim that the outstanding injunction will deprive them of rights protected by the First Amendment during the period of appellate review which, in the normal course, may take a year or more to complete. If a State seeks to impose a restraint of this kind, it must provide strict procedural safeguards, [including] immediate appellate review. [Absent] such review, the State [must] allow a stay.

On remand, the Illinois appellate court in July modified the injunction, so as to enjoin the party only from displaying the swastika. Skokie v. Nationalist Socialist Party of America, 366 N.E.2d 347 (1977). The following January the Illinois Supreme Court held the entire injunction invalid. Skokie v. National Socialist Party of America, 373 N.E.2d 21 (1978).

During the course of the injunction litigation, Skokie enacted a series of ordinances designed to block the march. These ordinances (1) required applicants for parade permits to procure $300,000 in public liability insurance and $50,000 in property damage insurance; (2) prohibited the "dissemination of any material [including signs and clothing of symbolic significance] which promotes and incites hatred against persons by reason of their race, national origin, or religion, and is intended to do so"; and (3) prohibited anyone to demonstrate "on behalf of any political party while wearing a military-style uniform." All three ordinances were held to violate the first amendment. Collin v. Smith, 578 F.2d 1197 (7th Cir.), aff'g 477 F. Supp. 676 (N.D. Ill. 1978). With the march scheduled for June 25, 1978, the village requested the Supreme Court to stay the ruling of the court of appeals. The Court denied the stay, Justices Blackmun and Rehnquist dissenting. Smith v. Collin, 436 U.S. 953 (1978).

On June 22, Collin cancelled the march. He explained that he had used the threat of a march in Skokie as a means to win the right to demonstrate in Chicago, a right he had won while the Skokie litigation was proceeding. On July 9, 1978, the party held an hour-long rally in Chicago at which four hundred riot-helmeted policemen protected the twenty-five Nazi demonstrators. There were seventy-two arrests and some rock and bottle throwing, but no serious violence.

Consider Douglas-Scott, The Hatefulness of Protected Speech: A Comparison of the American and European Approaches, 7 Wm. & Mary Bill Rts. J. 305, 309, 317, 343–345 (1999):

> [Controls] on free speech long have been permitted in many European countries to curb incitement to race hatred. [For] example, in the United Kingdom, Part III of the Public Order Act of 1986 prohibits behavior intended to or likely to have the result of stirring up racial hatred. [The European approach to free speech emphasizes] particular values — dignity, protection of personal identity, and equality. [This] approach recognizes a different sort of harm caused by the abuse of freedom than the danger of imminent lawless action required under American law. The *Brandenburg* requirement that violence be imminent before hateful speech may be proscribed is objectionable. . . .
>
>   European case law looks not only to the harm caused by such expression, but also proceeds from a particular conception of individual personality and psychology. [European] case law rejects a conception of individuals as beings who merely should be left to their own devices to make up their own minds about the value of expression in the public domain, to be free to ignore it, or to counter it with more speech. Such an approach isolates human beings by forcing them to take the

consequences of painful conduct and ignores the particular susceptibility of certain groups to injury, especially when the offense of the speech seems to be targeted at such groups because of their identity. [Surely] it is not enough for societies that claim to be committed to the ideals of social and political equality and respect for individual dignity to remain neutral and passive when threats to these values exist. Sometimes the state must act to show its solidarity with vulnerable minority groups and its commitment to equality.

On the hate speech issue, see section D8, infra. Suppose a student group at a public university invites Frank Collin to speak. Can the university constitutionally veto the invitation? Suppose students and other protesters threaten to disrupt the event? Can a police officer be fired for marching in a Nazi Party demonstration?

SNYDER v. PHELPS, 562 U.S. 443 (2011). Suppose the Nazis had just marched in Skokie. Could individual residents who were shocked and outraged by their conduct have sued them for damages for the intentional infliction of emotional distress? Consider *Snyder*.

For at least 20 years, the congregation of the Westboro Baptist Church in Topeka, Kansas, picketed hundreds of military funerals to communicate its belief that God hates the United States for its tolerance of homosexuality, particularly in America's military. As part of this campaign, Fred Phelps, who founded the church, and six Westboro Baptist parishioners traveled to Maryland to picket the funeral of Marine Lance Corporal Matthew Snyder, who was killed in Iraq in the line of duty. The picketing took place on public land approximately one thousand feet from the church where the funeral was held. The picketers peacefully displayed their signs — stating, for example, "Thank God for Dead Soldiers," "Fags Doom Nations," "America is Doomed," and "You're Going to Hell" — for about thirty minutes before the funeral began.

Matthew Snyder's father (Snyder) saw the tops of the picketers' signs when driving to the funeral, but he did not learn what was written on them until he was watching a news broadcast later that night. Snyder filed a civil action against Phelps and Westboro asserting a state tort claim for intentional infliction of emotional distress. A jury held Westboro liable for millions of dollars in compensatory and punitive damages. The trial judge reduced the punitive damages award, but left the verdict otherwise intact. The court of appeals reversed, concluding that Westboro's statements were entitled to first amendment protection. The Supreme Court affirmed.

Chief Justice Roberts delivered the opinion of the Court: "Whether the First Amendment prohibits holding Westboro liable for its speech in this case turns largely on whether that speech is of public or private concern, as determined by all the circumstances of the case. [The] First Amendment reflects 'a profound national commitment to the principle that debate on public issues should be uninhibited, robust, and wide-open.' That is because 'speech concerning public affairs is more than self-expression; it is the essence of self-government.' [Accordingly], 'speech on public issues occupies the highest rung of the hierarchy of First Amendment values, and is entitled to special protection.' . . .

"Speech deals with matters of public concern when it can 'be fairly considered as relating to any matter of political, social, or other concern to the community' or when it 'is a subject of legitimate news interest; that is, a subject of general interest and of value and concern to the public.' [Deciding] whether speech is of public or private concern requires us to examine the 'content, form, and context' of that speech, as revealed by the whole record.' [The] 'content' of Westboro's signs plainly relates to broad issues of interest to society at large, rather than matters of 'purely private concern.' [While] these messages may fall short of refined social or political commentary, the issues they highlight — the political and moral conduct of the United States and its citizens, the fate of our Nation, [and] homosexuality in the military [are] matters of public import. The signs certainly convey Westboro's position on those issues, in a manner designed [to] reach as broad a public audience as possible. . . .

"Snyder goes on to argue that Westboro's speech should be afforded less than full First Amendment protection [because] the church members exploited the funeral 'as a platform to bring their message to a broader audience.' There is no doubt that Westboro chose to stage its picketing at the Naval Academy, the Maryland State House, and Matthew Snyder's funeral to increase publicity for its views and because of the relation between those sites and its views — in the case of the military funeral, because Westboro believes that God is killing American soldiers as punishment for the Nation's sinful policies. [Westboro's] choice of where and when to conduct its picketing is not beyond the Government's regulatory reach — it is 'subject to reasonable time, place, or manner restrictions.' [But the] record confirms that any distress occasioned by Westboro's picketing turned on the content and viewpoint of the message conveyed, rather than any interference with the funeral itself. A group of parishioners standing at the very spot where Westboro stood, holding signs that said 'God Bless America' and 'God Loves You,' would not have been subjected to liability. It was what Westboro said that exposed it to tort damages. [Given] that Westboro's speech was at a public place on a matter of public concern, [it] cannot be restricted simply because it is upsetting or arouses contempt. 'If there is a bedrock principle underlying the First Amendment, it is that the government may not prohibit the expression of an idea simply because society finds the idea itself offensive or disagreeable.'

"The jury here was instructed that it could hold Westboro liable for intentional infliction of emotional distress based on a finding that Westboro's picketing was 'outrageous.' 'Outrageousness,' however, is a highly malleable standard with 'an inherent subjectiveness about it which would allow a jury to impose liability on the basis of the jurors' tastes or views, or perhaps on the basis of their dislike of a particular expression.' In a case such as this, a jury is 'unlikely to be neutral with respect to the content of [the] speech,' posing 'a real danger of becoming an instrument for the suppression of . . . vehement, caustic, and sometimes unpleasan[t]' expression. Such a risk is unacceptable; 'in public debate [we] must tolerate insulting, and even outrageous, speech in order to provide adequate "breathing space" to the freedoms protected by the First Amendment.' [For] all these reasons, the jury verdict imposing tort liability on Westboro for intentional infliction of emotional distress must be set aside."

Justice Alito dissented: "Our profound national commitment to free and open debate is not a license for the vicious verbal assault that occurred in this case. [Phelps and Westboro] have strong opinions on certain moral, religious, and political issues, and the First Amendment ensures that they have almost limitless opportunities to express their views. They may write and distribute books, articles, and other texts; they may create and disseminate video and audio recordings; they may circulate petitions; they may speak to individuals and groups in public forums and in any private venue that wishes to accommodate them; they may picket peacefully in countless locations; they may appear on television and speak on the radio; they may post messages on the Internet and send out e-mails. And they may express their views in terms that are 'uninhibited,' 'vehement,' and 'caustic.' It does not follow, however, that they may intentionally inflict severe emotional injury on private persons at a time of intense emotional sensitivity by launching vicious verbal attacks that make no contribution to public debate. [I] think it is clear that the First Amendment does not entirely preclude liability for the intentional infliction of emotional distress by means of speech."

In the years since *Snyder*, many states enacted "buffer-zone" laws that prohibit any picketing within a certain distance of a funeral within a certain time before and after the funeral. Are such laws constitutional? See Heyman, To Drink the Cup of Fury: Funeral Picketing, Public Discourse, and the First Amendment, 45 Conn. L. Rev. 101 (2012).

3.   *Classified Information*

New York Times Co. v. United States; United States v. Washington Post Co.

403 U.S. 713 (1971)

[On June 12–14, 1971, the New York Times and, on June 18, the Washington Post published excerpts from a top secret Defense Department study of the Vietnam War. The study, which was commissioned by Robert McNamara in 1967, filled forty-seven volumes and reviewed in great detail the formulation of U.S. policy toward Indochina, including military operations and secret diplomatic negotiations. The newspapers obtained the study, known popularly as the Pentagon Papers, from Daniel Ellsberg, a former Pentagon official. The government filed suit in federal district courts in New York and Washington, D.C., seeking to enjoin further publication of the materials, claiming that such publication would interfere with national security and would lead to the death of soldiers, the undermining of our alliances, the inability of our diplomats to negotiate, and the prolongation of the war. Between June 15 and June 23, the cases worked their way through the federal courts, and on June 26 the Supreme Court heard argument. On June 30 the Court issued its decision. Restraining orders remained in effect throughout the Court's deliberations.]

PER CURIAM.

We granted certiorari in these cases in which the United States seeks to enjoin the New York Times and the Washington Post from publishing the contents of a classified study entitled "History of U.S. Decision-Making Process on Viet Nam Policy."

"Any system of prior restraints of expression comes to this Court bearing a heavy presumption against its constitutional validity." [The] Government "thus carries a heavy burden of showing justification for the imposition of such a restraint." [The] District Court for the Southern District of New York in the New York Times case and the District Court for the District of Columbia and the Court of Appeals for the District of Columbia Circuit in the

Washington Post case held that the Government had not met that burden. We agree.

The judgment of the Court of Appeals for the District of Columbia Circuit is therefore affirmed. The order of the Court of Appeals for the Second Circuit is reversed and the case is remanded with directions to enter a judgment affirming the judgment of the District Court for the Southern District of New York. The stays entered June 25, 1971, by the Court are vacated. The judgments shall issue forthwith.

So ordered.

MR. JUSTICE BLACK, with whom MR. JUSTICE DOUGLAS joins, concurring. . . .

[Every] moment's continuance of the injunctions against these newspapers amounts to a flagrant, indefensible, and continuing violation of the First Amendment. [For] the first time in the 182 years since the founding of the Republic, the federal courts are asked to hold that the First Amendment does not mean what it says, but rather means that the Government can halt the publication of current news of vital importance to the people of this country. . . .

In the First Amendment the Founding Fathers gave the free press the protection it must have to fulfill its essential role in our democracy. The press was to serve the governed, not the governors. The Government's power to censor the press was abolished so that the press would remain forever free to censure the Government. The press was protected so that it could bare the secrets of government and inform the people. Only a free and unrestrained press can effectively expose deception in government. . . .

[We] are asked to hold that despite the First Amendment's emphatic command, the Executive Branch, the Congress, and the Judiciary can make laws enjoining publication of current news and abridging freedom of the press in the name of "national security." . . .

The word "security" is a broad, vague generality whose contours should not be invoked to abrogate the fundamental law embodied in the First Amendment. The guarding of military and diplomatic secrets at the expense of informed representative government provides no real security for our Republic.

MR. JUSTICE DOUGLAS, with whom MR. JUSTICE BLACK joins, concurring. . . .

These disclosures may have a serious impact. But that is no basis for sanctioning a previous restraint on the press. [The] dominant purpose of the First Amendment was to prohibit the widespread practice of governmental suppression of embarrassing information. It is common knowledge that the First Amendment was adopted against the widespread use of the common law of seditious libel to punish the dissemination of material that is embarrassing to the powers-that-be. [A] debate of large proportions goes on in the Nation over our posture in Vietnam. That debate antedated the disclosure of the contents of the present documents. The latter are highly relevant to the debate in progress.

Secrecy in government is fundamentally anti-democratic, perpetuating bureaucratic errors. Open debate and discussion of public issues are vital to our national health. On public questions there should be "uninhibited, robust, and wide-open" debate. . . .

The stays in these cases that have been in effect for more than a week constitute a flouting of the principles of the First Amendment. . . .

MR. JUSTICE BRENNAN, concurring.

The error that has pervaded these cases from the outset was the granting of any injunctive relief whatsoever, interim or otherwise. The entire thrust of the Government's claim throughout these cases has been that publication of the material sought to be enjoined "could," or "might," or "may" prejudice the national interest in various ways. But the First Amendment tolerates absolutely no prior judicial restraints of the press predicated upon surmise or conjecture that untoward consequences may result.[*] Our cases, it is true, have indicated that there is a single, extremely narrow class of cases in which the First Amendment's ban on prior judicial restraint may be overridden. Our cases have thus far indicated that such cases may arise only when the Nation "is at war," [*Schenck*], during which times "[n]o one would question but that a government might prevent actual obstruction to its recruiting service or the publication of the sailing dates of transports or the number and location of troops." Near v. Minnesota, [section C2 infra]. Even if the present world situation were assumed to be tantamount to a time of war, or if the power of presently available armaments would justify even in peacetime the suppression of information that would set in motion a nuclear holocaust, in neither of these actions has the Government presented or even alleged that publication of items from or based upon the material at issue would cause the happening of an event of that nature. "[T]he chief purpose of [the First Amendment's] guaranty [is] to prevent previous restraints upon publication." [*Near.*] Thus, only governmental allegation and proof that publication must inevitably, directly, and immediately cause the occurrence of an event kindred to imperiling the safety of a transport already at sea can support even the issuance of an interim restraining order. [Every] restraint issued in this case, whatever its form, has violated the First Amendment — and not less so because that restraint was justified as necessary to afford the courts an opportunity to examine the claim more thoroughly. Unless and until the Government has clearly made out its case, the First Amendment commands that no injunction may issue.

MR. JUSTICE STEWART, with whom MR. JUSTICE WHITE joins, concurring.

In the governmental structure created by our Constitution, the Executive is endowed with enormous power in the two related areas of national defense and international relations. This power, largely unchecked by the Legislative and Judicial branches, has been pressed to the very hilt since the advent of the nuclear missile age. . . .

In the absence of the governmental checks and balances present in other areas of our national life, the only effective restraint upon executive policy and power in the areas of national defense and international affairs may lie in an enlightened citizenry — in an informed and critical public opinion which alone can here protect the values of democratic government. . . .

Yet it is elementary that the successful conduct of international diplomacy and the maintenance of an effective national defense require both confidentiality and

---

[*] Freedman v. Maryland, 380 U.S. 51 (1965), and similar cases regarding temporary restraints of allegedly obscene materials are not in point. For those cases rest upon the proposition that "obscenity is not protected by the freedoms of speech and press." [Here] there is no question but that the material sought to be suppressed is within the protection of the First Amendment; the only question is whether, notwithstanding that fact, its publication may be enjoined for a time because of the presence of an overwhelming national interest.

secrecy. Other nations can hardly deal with this Nation in an atmosphere of mutual trust unless they can be assured that their confidences will be kept. And within our own executive departments, the development of considered and intelligent international policies would be impossible if those charged with their formulation could not communicate with each other freely, frankly, and in confidence. In the area of basic national defense the frequent need for absolute secrecy is, of course, self-evident.

I think there can be but one answer to this dilemma, if dilemma it be. The responsibility must be where the power is. If the Constitution gives the Executive a large degree of unshared power in the conduct of foreign affairs and the maintenance of our national defense, then under the Constitution the Executive must have the largely unshared duty to determine and preserve the degree of internal security necessary to exercise that power successfully. [It] is clear to me that it is the constitutional duty of the Executive — as a matter of sovereign prerogative and not as a matter of law as the courts know law — through the promulgation and enforcement of executive regulations, to protect the confidentiality necessary to carry out its responsibilities in the fields of international relations and national defense.

This is not to say that Congress and the courts have no role to play. Undoubtedly Congress has the power to enact specific and appropriate criminal laws to protect government property and preserve government secrets. . . .

But in the cases before us we are asked neither to construe specific regulations nor to apply specific laws. We are asked, instead, to perform a function that the Constitution gave to the Executive, not the Judiciary. We are asked, quite simply, to prevent the publication by two newspapers of material that the Executive Branch insists should not, in the national interest, be published. I am convinced that the Executive is correct with respect to some of the documents involved. But I cannot say that disclosure of any of them will surely result in direct, immediate, and irreparable damage to our Nation or its people. That being so, there can under the First Amendment be but one judicial resolution of the issues before us. I join the judgments of the Court.

MR. JUSTICE WHITE, with whom MR. JUSTICE STEWART joins, concurring.

I concur in today's judgments, but only because of the concededly extraordinary protection against prior restraints enjoyed by the press under our constitutional system. I do not say that in no circumstances would the First Amendment permit an injunction against publishing information about government plans or operations. Nor, after examining the materials the Government characterizes as the most sensitive and destructive, can I deny that revelation of these documents will do substantial damage to public interests. Indeed, I am confident that their disclosure will have that result. But I nevertheless agree that the United States has not satisfied the very heavy burden that it must meet to warrant an injunction against publication in these cases, at least in the absence of express and appropriately limited congressional authorization for prior restraints in circumstances such as these. . . .

[Prior] restraints require an unusually heavy justification under the First Amendment; but failure by the Government to justify prior restraints does not measure its constitutional entitlement to a conviction for criminal publication. That the Government mistakenly chose to proceed by injunction does not mean that it could not successfully proceed in another way. . . .

The Criminal Code contains numerous provisions potentially relevant to these cases. [Section] 793(e)[8] makes it a criminal act for any unauthorized possessor of a document "relating to the national defense" either (1) willfully to communicate or cause to be communicated that document to any person not entitled to receive it or (2) willfully to retain the document and fail to deliver it to an officer of the United States entitled to receive it. . . .

It is thus clear that Congress has addressed itself to the problems of protecting the security of the country and the national defense from unauthorized disclosure of potentially damaging information. [It] has not, however, authorized the injunctive remedy against threatened publication. It has apparently been satisfied to rely on criminal sanctions and their deterrent effect on the responsible as well as the irresponsible press. I am not, of course, saying that either of these newspapers has yet committed a crime or that either would commit a crime if it published all the material now in its possession. That matter must await resolution in the context of a criminal proceeding if one is instituted by the United States. . . .

MR. JUSTICE MARSHALL, concurring.

I believe the ultimate issue in these cases [is] whether this Court or the Congress has the power to make law. . . .

The problem here is whether in these particular cases the Executive Branch has authority to invoke the equity jurisdiction of the courts to protect what it believes to be the national interest. [In] some situations it may be that under whatever inherent powers the Government may have, as well as the implicit authority derived from the President's mandate to conduct foreign affairs and to act as Commander in Chief, there is a basis for the invocation of the equity jurisdiction of this Court as an aid to prevent the publication of material damaging to "national security," however that term may be defined.

It would, however, be utterly inconsistent with the concept of separation of powers for this Court to use its power of contempt to prevent behavior that Congress has specifically declined to prohibit. [The] Constitution provides that Congress shall make laws, the President execute laws, and courts interpret laws. [It] did not provide for government by injunction in which the courts and the Executive Branch can "make law" without regard to the action of Congress. [It] is clear that Congress has specifically rejected passing legislation that would have clearly given the President the power he seeks here and made the current activity of the newspapers unlawful. When Congress specifically declines to make conduct unlawful it is not for this Court to redecide those issues — to overrule Congress. . . .

---

8. Section 793(e) of 18 U.S.C. provides that:

(e) Whoever having unauthorized possession of, access to, or control over any document, writing, code book, signal book, sketch, photograph, photographic negative, blueprint, plan, map, model, instrument, appliance, or note relating to the national defense, or information relating to the national defense which information the possessor has reason to believe could be used to the injury of the United States or to the advantage of any foreign nation, willfully communicates, delivers, transmits or causes to be communicated, delivered, or transmitted, or attempts to communicate, deliver, transmit or cause to be communicated, delivered, or transmitted the same to any person not entitled to receive it, or willfully retains the same and fails to deliver it to the officer or employee of the United States entitled to receive it; is guilty of an offense punishable by 10 years in prison, a $10,000 fine, or both.

MR. CHIEF JUSTICE BURGER, dissenting.

[In] these cases, the imperative of a free and unfettered press comes into collision with another imperative, the effective functioning of a complex modern government and specifically the effective exercise of certain constitutional powers of the Executive. Only those who view the First Amendment as an absolute in all circumstances — a view I respect, but reject — can find such cases as these to be simple or easy.

These cases are not simple for another and more immediate reason. We do not know the facts of the cases. No District Judge knew all the facts. No Court of Appeals judge knew all the facts. No member of this Court knows all the facts. . . .

I suggest we are in this posture because these cases have been conducted in unseemly haste. [It] seems reasonably clear now that the haste precluded reasonable and deliberate judicial treatment of these cases and was not warranted. The precipitate action of this Court aborting trials not yet completed is not the kind of judicial conduct that ought to attend the disposition of a great issue. . . .

It is not disputed that the Times has had unauthorized possession of the documents for three to four months, during which it has had its expert analysts studying them, presumably digesting them and preparing the material for publication. During all of this time, the Times, presumably in its capacity as trustee of the public's "right to know," has held up publication for purposes it considered proper and thus public knowledge was delayed. No doubt this was for a good reason; the analysis of 7,000 pages of complex material drawn from a vastly greater volume of material would inevitably take time and the writing of good news stories takes time. But why should the United States Government, from whom this information was illegally acquired by someone, along with all the counsel, trial judges, and appellate judges be placed under needless pressure? After these months of deferral, the alleged "right to know" has somehow and suddenly become a right that must be vindicated instanter. . . .

I would affirm the Court of Appeals for the Second Circuit and allow the District Court to complete the trial aborted by our grant of certiorari, meanwhile preserving the status quo in the Post case. I would direct that the District Court on remand give priority to the Times case to the exclusion of all other business of that court but I would not set arbitrary deadlines. . . .

We all crave speedier judicial processes but when judges are pressured as in these cases the result is a parody of the judicial function.

MR. JUSTICE HARLAN, with whom THE CHIEF JUSTICE and MR. JUSTICE BLACKMUN join, dissenting. . . .

With all respect, I consider that the Court has been almost irresponsibly feverish in dealing with these cases.

Both the Court of Appeals for the Second Circuit and the Court of Appeals for the District of Columbia Circuit rendered judgment on June 23. The New York Times' petition for certiorari, its motion for accelerated consideration thereof, and its application for interim relief were filed in this Court on June 24 at about 11 A.M. The application of the United States for interim relief in the Post case was also filed here on June 24 at about 7:15 P.M. This Court's order setting a hearing before us on June 26 at 11 A.M., a course which I joined only to avoid the possibility of even more peremptory action by the Court, was issued less than 24 hours before. The record in the Post case was filed with the Clerk shortly before 1 P.M. on June 25; the record in the Times case did not arrive until 7 or

8 o'clock that same night. The briefs of the parties were received less than two hours before argument on June 26.

This frenzied train of events took place in the name of the presumption against prior restraints created by the First Amendment. Due regard for the extraordinarily important and difficult questions involved in these litigations should have led the Court to shun such a precipitate timetable. . . .

Forced as I am to reach the merits of these cases, I dissent from the opinion and judgments of the Court. [It] is plain to me that the scope of the judicial function in passing upon the activities of the Executive Branch of the Government in the field of foreign affairs is very narrowly restricted. This view is, I think, dictated by the concept of separation of powers upon which our constitutional system rests. . . .

The power to evaluate the "pernicious influence" of premature disclosure is not, however, lodged in the Executive alone. I agree that, in performance of its duty to protect the values of the First Amendment against political pressures, the judiciary must review the initial Executive determination to the point of satisfying itself that the subject matter of the dispute does lie within the proper compass of the President's foreign relations power. Constitutional considerations forbid "a complete abandonment of judicial control." [Moreover], the judiciary may properly insist that the determination that disclosure of the subject matter would irreparably impair the national security be made by the head of the Executive Department concerned — here the Secretary of State or the Secretary of Defense — after actual personal consideration by that officer. . . .

But in my judgment the judiciary may not properly go beyond these two inquiries and redetermine for itself the probable impact of disclosure on the national security. [Even] if there is some room for the judiciary to override the executive determination, it is plain that the scope of review must be exceedingly narrow. I can see no indication in the opinions of either the District Court or the Court of Appeals in the Post litigation that the conclusions of the Executive were given even the deference owing to an administrative agency, much less that owing to a co-equal branch of the Government operating within the field of its constitutional prerogative. . . .

Pending further hearings in each case conducted under the appropriate ground rules, I would continue the restraints on publication. I cannot believe that the doctrine prohibiting prior restraints reaches to the point of preventing courts from maintaining the status quo long enough to act responsibly in matters of such national importance as those involved here.

MR. JUSTICE BLACKMUN, dissenting.

The First Amendment, after all, is only one part of an entire Constitution. Article II of the great document vests in the Executive Branch primary power over the conduct of foreign affairs and places in that branch the responsibility for the Nation's safety. Each provision of the Constitution is important, and I cannot subscribe to a doctrine of unlimited absolutism for the First Amendment at the cost of downgrading other provisions. First Amendment absolutism has never commanded a majority of this Court. [What] is needed here is a weighing, upon properly developed standards, of the broad right of the press to print and of the very narrow right of the Government to prevent. Such standards are not yet developed. The parties here are in disagreement as to what those standards should be. But even the newspapers concede that there are situations where restraint is in order and is constitutional. . . .

I therefore would remand these cases to be developed expeditiously, of course, but on a schedule permitting the orderly presentation of evidence from both sides. . . .

Note: The Pentagon Papers Controversy

1. *Prior restraint.* The Court emphasized repeatedly that the injunction in *New York Times* was a "prior restraint," and that a prior restraint bears a special "presumption against its constitutional validity." Why is an injunction more threatening to the values underlying the first amendment than a criminal prosecution for publication of the same material? For analysis of the doctrine of prior restraint, see section C2 infra.

2. *The Pentagon Papers: too much haste?* Publication of the Pentagon Papers offered the public valuable insights into the processes of government decision-making involving the Vietnam War. Moreover, by disclosing that the Eisenhower administration's attempt to undermine the new communist regime in North Vietnam directly involved the United States in the breakdown of the 1954 Geneva settlement, that the Johnson administration took steps toward waging an overt war against North Vietnam a full year before it disclosed the depth of its involvement to the American public, and that the infiltration of men and arms from North Vietnam into South Vietnam was more important as a means of publicly justifying our involvement than for its military effects, publication of the Papers sharpened the public's understanding of the war and altered public attitudes toward a central issue of American policy.

At the same time, however, one must ask whether, as the dissenters charged, the Court acted with "unseemly haste" in permitting publication of the documents. In light of the extraordinary seriousness of the government's contentions and the almost overwhelming length of the study, should the Court have permitted the injunctions to remain in effect pending a more thorough judicial determination of the risks? Was the Court, in other words, playing fast and loose with the national security? Consider in this regard Justice Brennan's argument that the very notion of an injunction against expression pending final resolution of the controversy is inherently incompatible with the first amendment.

3. *The Pentagon Papers: injunctions and the national security.* Note that the per curiam opinion did not define the precise circumstances in which a court may enjoin the publication of information relating to the national security. Does the standard enunciated by Justice Stewart, that there must be proof that the disclosure will "surely result in direct, immediate, and irreparable damage to our Nation or its people," come closest to representing the view of the Court? Why was that standard not satisfied in the *Pentagon Papers* case?

4. *The Pentagon Papers: criminal prosecution?* Suppose the New York Times and the Washington Post had been criminally prosecuted for their publication of the Pentagon Papers. What standard should govern? Is section 793(e) of the Federal Code, reproduced in footnote 8 of Justice White's opinion, constitutional? Should disclosure of historical information be absolutely protected? For such an argument, see Volokh, Freedom of Speech, Permissible Tailoring and Transcending Strict Scrutiny, 144 U. Pa. L. Rev. 2417, 2425–2431 (1996).

Suppose the government claimed in this hypothetical criminal prosecution that the newspapers' disclosure of some of the historical information weakened our alliances, increased the difficulty of negotiating with other nations, prolonged the war, and delayed the release of American prisoners of war. Could the newspapers constitutionally be convicted? Are these sorts of issues, as Justice Harlan suggested, beyond the competence of courts? Consider the following arguments: (a) The executive may consciously or unconsciously err on the side of suppression in order to prevent the revelation of potentially embarrassing information. (b) Newspapers, eager to boost sales, may undervalue the interest in national security.

In considering the Pentagon Papers controversy, recall the problem of the *true* cry of "fire." Even though the true cry may create a clear and present danger that some persons will be injured in the dash for the exit, the benefits of the speech may outweigh the harm. Do the decisions examined in this section, taken together, "leave little doubt that, except in cases involving imminent national military catastrophe, the Court will not permit previous restraints upon, or subsequent punishment for, publication in a mass medium of accurate information that the publisher has lawfully acquired"? Cox, Foreword: Freedom of Expression in the Burger Court, 94 Harv. L. Rev. 1, 17 (1980).

5. *Disclosure of the NSA surveillance program.* In January 2006, the New York Times publicly disclosed that President George W. Bush had secretly authorized the National Security Agency to intercept international telephone calls and emails between individuals inside the United States and individuals outside the United States whenever the NSA had "a reasonable basis to conclude that one party to the communication is a member of al Qaeda, affiliated with al Qaeda, or a member of an organization affiliated with al Qaeda, or working in support of al Qaeda." Critics of the program charged that it violated the Foreign Intelligence Surveillance Act of 1978, which prohibits such surveillance in the absence of probable cause and a warrant. Defenders of the program argued that FISA violates the inherent authority of the "President as commander in chief of the Army and Navy."

Attorney General Alberto Gonzales raised the possibility that the United States might prosecute the New York Times for violating the Espionage Act of 1917. Gonzales maintained that the disclosure of the program seriously undermined the national security by alerting terrorists to its existence. Suppose the United States had indicted the New York Times under section 793(e). What standard would apply in deciding whether the publication was protected by the first amendment? Note that the United States has never criminally prosecuted the press for publishing secret government information.

Suppose that in 2005 the NSA secretly broke the al Qaeda code, enabling the United States to thwart several terrorist attacks. Suppose further that in 2008 a newspaper published this information, with the result that the terrorists changed their cipher. In such circumstances, could the newspaper be punished for publishing this information?

Consider Stone, Government Secrecy v. Freedom of the Press, 1 Harv. L. & Pol. Rev. 185, 203-204 (2007):

> [The] reason for protecting the publication of the Pentagon Papers was not only that the disclosure would not "surely result in direct, immediate, and irreparable damage" to the nation, but also that the Pentagon Papers made a meaningful contribution to informed public discourse. Suppose a newspaper accurately reports that American troops in Iraq recently murdered twenty insurgents in cold blood. As a result of this publication, insurgents quite predictably kidnap and murder twenty

Americans. Could the newspaper constitutionally be punished for disclosing the initial massacre? I would argue that it could not. Even if there were a clear and present danger that the retaliation would follow, the information is simply too important to the American people to punish its publication.

What this suggests is that to justify the criminal punishment of the press for publishing classified information, the government must prove that the publisher knew that (a) it was publishing classified information, (b) the publication of which would result in likely, imminent, and serious harm to the national security, *and* (c) the publication of which would not meaningfully contribute to public debate.

6. *Restricting speech because it was obtained illegally.* Suppose a reporter gains access to confidential government information through an unlawful wiretap of a senator. Can the reporter be criminally punished for the wiretap? Can her newspaper be prohibited from publishing the information? Suppose the newspaper learns of the information as the result of a third party's unlawful act, such as theft of a document or an unlawful wiretap. Can the newspaper be enjoined, criminally punished, or held civilly liable for invasion of privacy for publishing the information? See Bartnicki v. Vopper, 532 U.S. 514 (2001), in which the Court held that federal and state anti-wiretap statutes cannot constitutionally be applied to a radio station that broadcasts the tape of an unlawfully intercepted telephone call, where the subject of the call was a matter of public concern and the broadcaster did not participate directly in the unlawful wiretap, even though the broadcaster knew that the material had been obtained unlawfully. Does this make any sense?

7. *Public employees.* The Court suggested in both *Nebraska Press* and *Pentagon Papers* that the state may keep information from the press by prohibiting government employees from disclosing that information. Suppose the government had prosecuted Daniel Ellsberg for releasing the Pentagon Papers. Should the government have greater authority to prohibit its employees from disclosing confidential information to the press than to prohibit the press from publishing such information once it comes into its hands? If an ultimate concern of the first amendment is the "public's right to know," isn't that right undermined just as much by restrictions on the press's ability to obtain information as by restrictions on its ability to publish?

Consider Snepp v. United States, 444 U.S. 507 (1980), in which Snepp, a former CIA agent, published a book about certain CIA activities in South Vietnam in violation of an express condition of his employment contract with the CIA in which he promised not to publish "any information or material relating to the Agency, its activities or intelligence activities generally, either during or after the term of [his] employment, [without] specific prior approval by the Agency." The Court, in a six-to-three decision, held that Snepp "breached a fiduciary obligation and that the proceeds of his breach are impressed with a constructive trust." The Court explained that the "Government has a compelling interest in protecting both the secrecy of information important to our national security and the appearance of confidentiality so essential to the effective operation of our foreign intelligence service." The Court concluded that the "agreement that Snepp signed is a reasonable means for protecting this vital interest."

Consider the following views:

a. The public employee gains access to confidential government information only by virtue of her employment. Thus, for government to prohibit her disclosure of such information does not limit any first amendment right the employee would have but for such employment.

b. Easterbrook, Insider Trading, Secret Agents, Evidentiary Privileges, and the Production of Information, 1981 Sup. Ct. Rev. 309, 345–347:

> Snepp [struck] a bargain. He learned of the CIA's activities by agreeing to limit his speech about them. [So] long as he enters into the agreement without fraud or coercion, he has made a judgment that he is better off with the agreement (and its restraints) than without; he can hardly complain that his rights have been reduced. [Constitutional] rights are waived every day.

c. Sunstein, Government Control of Information, 74 Cal. L. Rev. 889, 915 (1986):

> [The] first amendment is largely a structural provision. [Its] purpose is not only to protect private autonomy, but also to preserve a certain form of government. Citizens may often find it in their interest to give up rights of free speech in exchange for benefits from government. For many, these rights are not extremely valuable as individual possessions. But if government is permitted to obtain enforceable waivers, the aggregate effect may be considerable, and the deliberative processes of the public will be skewed. [Waivers] of first amendment rights thus affect people other than government employees, and effects on third parties are a classic reason to proscribe waivers. The analogy [is] to government purchases of voting rights, which are impermissible even if voters willingly assent.

In deciding whether government may constitutionally prohibit an employee's disclosure of particular "confidential" information, should courts consider not only the potential danger but also the potential value of the disclosure? For example, may an employee disclose "classified" information if it reveals a substantial abuse of power?

8. *Snowden.* If Edward Snowden returns to the United States, could he be prosecuted and convicted, consistent with the first amendment, for disclosing to journalists and thus to the world massive amounts of classified information about previously secret NSA surveillance programs? Consider the following positions:

a. Snowden accepted a position of trust in his relation to the government. He did not have to accept his job, but he did. A clear condition of that job was his voluntary agreement not to disclose any *classified* information. That agreement is binding. Period.

b. An individual government employee should never have the authority, on his own say, to override the judgments of the elected representatives of the American people and to decide for the nation that classified information should be disclosed to friends and foes alike. The question is *who* gets to decide when classified information should be made public. It should not be any tom-dick-and-harry government employee or private contractor with a security clearance who thinks he knows better than the President, the Congress, and the courts about how best to protect the nation's security.

c. Suppose the disclosure of the previously secret programs renders them ineffective in the future, thus seriously damaging the nation's ability to ferret out possible terrorist plots. Should Snowden nonetheless have a first amendment defense if, upon learning about the previously secret programs, the public opposes them as a matter of policy? If the programs are found to have been illegal? If some of the programs he disclosed were illegal and others were legal?

d. Does your view on any of these positions change if the prosecution is directed against the newspaper publishing Snowden's revelations rather than against Snowden himself?

e. Should Snowden's intent matter? Suppose he intended to aid the enemy? He intended to promote democratic review of secret decisions? He thought the disclosures wouldn't be harmful, but they were? For an analysis of the intent question, see Papandrea, National Security Information Disclosures and the Role of Intent, 56 Wm. & M. L. Rev. 1381 (2015).

For an historical analysis of government secrecy and an argument that "by seeking to keep secret so much for so long, the secrecy system cheapens and undermines our vital secrets," see F. Schwarz, Jr., Democracy in the Dark: The Seduction of Government Secrecy (2015). See also H. Kitrosser, Reclaiming Accountability: Transparency, Executive Power, and the U.S. Constitution (2015); Posen, The Leaky Leviathan: Why the Government Condemns and Condones Unlawful Disclosures of Information, 127 Harv. L. Rev. 512, 515 (2013).

9. "*Technical" information.* Suppose, in addition to general historical information, the Pentagon Papers had disclosed blueprints of secret military weapons, the identity of covert agents abroad, or secret codes? Is the disclosure of such information more readily subject to restriction? See Symposium, National Security and the First Amendment, 26 Wm. & Mary L. Rev. 715 (1985). Do you agree that "the law need not treat differently the crime of one man who sells a bomb to terrorists and that of another who publishes an instructional manual for terrorists on how to build their own bombs out of old Volkswagen parts"? Tribe, supra, at 837. For analysis of the constitutional status of technical data, see Sunstein, supra, at 905–912.

10. *Facts and the first amendment.* Note that in many cases the government is attempting to restrict the dissemination of facts rather than opinions. The seminal conception of the first amendment was about the "marketplace of ideas." How do facts fit into this marketplace? Should government efforts to restrict the dissemination of facts be treated the same way as government efforts to restrict the dissemination of ideas? In addition to the cases in this section, consider also the following: (a) an anti-abortion group publishes on its website the names and addresses of abortion providers; (b) a newspaper publishes the name of a rape victim; (c) a reporter discloses the names of covert American agents in Iran; (d) a terrorist posts on the internet instructions on how to make out of common household materials a bomb that is sufficiently powerful to destroy a large building; (e) a newspaper publishes classified information on how to make a nuclear bomb. See Bhagwat, Details: Specific Facts and the First Amendment, 86 S. Cal. L. Rev. 1 (2012); United States v. The Progressive, Inc., 467 F. Supp. 990 (W.D. Wis. 1979); Powe, The H-Bomb Injunction, 61 U. Colo. L. Rev. 55 (1990).

Consider Haig v. Agee, 453 U.S. 280 (1981), in which the Court upheld the revocation of Agee's passport because he engaged in activities abroad that caused "serious damage to the national security." Specifically, Agee, a former employee of the Central Intelligence Agency (CIA), engaged in a campaign "to expose CIA officers and agents and to take the measures necessary to drive them out of the countries where they are operating." Although Agee did not expressly incite "anyone to commit murder," there was evidence that his disclosures resulted in "episodes of violence against the persons and organizations identified."

The Court rejected Agee's claim that the passport revocation violated his rights under the first amendment: "Long ago, [this] Court recognized that 'No one would question but that a government might prevent actual obstruction to its recruiting service or the publication of the sailing dates of transports or the number and location of troops.' [*Near*, section C2, infra.] Agee's disclosures [have] the declared purpose of obstructing intelligence operations and the recruiting of personnel. They are clearly not protected by the Constitution."

Is *Agee* consistent with the *Pentagon Papers* decision? Are Agee's disclosures "not protected" because they consisted of "technical," rather than "historical," information? Because they were designed to effect change not through the political process but by directly obstructing the operations of government? Consider the constitutionality of the Intelligence Identities Protection Act, 50 U.S.C. §421 (1982), which prohibits any person "with reason to believe that such activities would impair or impede the foreign intelligence activities of the United States, [to disclose] any information that identifies an individual as a covert agent, [if the disclosure is part of a] pattern of activities intended to identify or expose covert action."

Note: *Dangerous Ideas and Information — Final Thoughts*

In what circumstances, if any, may government, consonant with the first amendment, restrict speech of "high" first amendment value because, if left unchecked, it might cause some harm to government, private individuals, or society in general? As the foregoing materials illustrate, the Court's efforts to define the perimeters of government power in this regard have focused primarily on the clear and present danger standard. Has that standard served well? In a different context, Justice Holmes, the author of the clear and present danger standard, warned of "the need of scrutinizing the reasons for the rules which we follow, and of not being contented with hollow forms of words merely because they have been used very [often]. We must think things not words, or at least we must constantly translate our words into the facts for which they stand, if we are to keep to the real and the true." O. Holmes, Collected Legal Papers 238 (1920). Has the Court been sensitive to this admonition, or has it "tended to seek [solutions] for problems of freedom of speech by invocation of magic phrases rather than hard rationalizations, if not by way of resolving the issues then by way of covering them up"? Kurland, The Irrelevance of the Constitution: The First Amendment's Freedom of Speech and Freedom of Press Clauses, 29 Drake L. Rev. 1, 5 (1979–1980).

Has the Court, in its results, been underprotective of free speech? Has it been overprotective? A canvass of what the Court has done may be more illuminating than an emphasis on what it has said. The Court has not upheld a direct prohibition of speech because it might induce readers or listeners to engage in criminal activity since *Dennis* (1951), and it has not upheld a direct prohibition of speech for this reason in the absence of express advocacy of crime since the Espionage Act cases following World War I. The Court has not upheld a restriction on speech because it might provoke a hostile audience response since *Feiner* (1951). With the exception of *Agee*, it has never upheld a restriction on the publication of truthful information because the government would prefer to keep it confidential. Has clear and present danger come to mean essentially absolute protection?

C. OVERBREADTH, VAGUENESS, AND PRIOR RESTRAINT

This section represents a brief interlude in our analysis of content-based restrictions. It focuses not on what speech government may restrict but rather on how government may restrict speech. The doctrines examined in this section may be explored either as a distinct unit or as they naturally arise in the course of the preceding and succeeding material.

In interpreting the first amendment, courts have often focused not only on what speech is "protected," but also on what means of restriction are constitutionally permissible. Indeed, "courts have [come] to realize that procedural guarantees play [a] large role in protecting freedom of speech; [for like] the substantive rules themselves, insensitive procedures can 'chill' the right of free expression. Accordingly, wherever first amendment claims are involved, sensitive procedural devices are necessary." Monaghan, First Amendment "Due Process," 83 Harv. L. Rev. 518, 518–519 (1970).

The overbreadth, vagueness, and prior restraint doctrines have played an especially important role in this aspect of first amendment jurisprudence. Under each of these doctrines, courts may invalidate restrictions on expression because the means of suppression are impermissible, even though the particular speech at issue might constitutionally be restricted by some other means.

1. Overbreadth and Vagueness

Gooding v. Wilson

405 U.S. 518 (1972)

[During an antiwar demonstration at an army induction center, police attempted to move appellee and his companions away from the door of the center. A scuffle ensued, and appellee said to several of the officers, "You son of a bitch, I'll choke you to death"; "White son of a bitch, I'll kill you"; and "You son of a bitch, if you ever put your hands on me again, I'll cut you all to pieces." Appellee was thereafter convicted of using opprobrious words and abusive language in violation of Georgia Code Ann. §26-6303, which provided: "Any person who shall, without provocation, use to or of another, and in his presence [opprobrious] words or abusive language, tending to cause a breach of the peace [shall] be guilty of a misdemeanor." The Supreme Court affirmed a decision of the U.S. Court of Appeals granting appellee's petition for federal habeas corpus relief.]

MR. JUSTICE BRENNAN delivered the opinion of the Court. . . .

Section 26-6303 punishes only spoken words. It can therefore withstand appellee's attack upon its facial constitutionality only if, as authoritatively construed by the Georgia courts, it is not susceptible of application to speech, although vulgar or offensive, that is protected by the First and Fourteenth Amendments. [Only] the Georgia courts can supply the requisite construction, since of course "we lack jurisdiction authoritatively to construe state legislation." [It] matters not that the words appellee used might have been constitutionally prohibited under a narrowly and precisely drawn statute. At least when statutes regulate or proscribe speech and when "no readily apparent construction suggests itself as a vehicle for rehabilitating the statutes in a single prosecution," [the] transcendent value to all society of constitutionally protected expression is deemed to justify allowing "attacks on overly broad statutes with no requirement that the person making the attack demonstrate that his own conduct could not be regulated by a statute drawn with the requisite narrow specificity." [This] is deemed necessary because persons whose expression is constitutionally protected may well refrain from exercising their rights for fear of criminal sanctions provided by a statute susceptible of application to protected expression. . . .

The constitutional guarantees of freedom of speech forbid the States to punish the use of words or language not within "narrowly limited classes of speech." [*Chaplinsky.*] [Statutes] must be carefully drawn or be authoritatively construed to punish only unprotected speech and not be susceptible of application to protected expression. "Because First Amendment freedoms need breathing space to survive, government may regulate in the area only with narrow specificity." . . .

Appellant does not challenge these principles but contends that the Georgia statute is narrowly drawn to apply only to a constitutionally unprotected class of words — "fighting" words — "those which by their very utterance inflict injury or tend to incite an immediate breach of the peace." [*Chaplinsky.*] In *Chaplinsky*, we sustained a conviction under [a statute] which provided: "No person shall address any offensive, derisive or annoying word to any other person who is lawfully in any street or other public place, nor call him by any offensive or derisive name. . . ." Chaplinsky was convicted for addressing to another on a public sidewalk the words, "You are a God damned racketeer," and "a damned Fascist and the whole government of Rochester are Fascists or agents of Fascists." Chaplinsky challenged the constitutionality of the statute as inhibiting freedom of expression because it was vague and indefinite. The Supreme Court of New Hampshire, however, "long before the words for which Chaplinsky was convicted," sharply limited the statutory language "offensive, derisive or annoying word" to "fighting" words. . . .

In view of that authoritative construction, this Court held: "We are unable to say that the limited scope of the statute as thus construed contravenes the Constitutional right of free expression. It is a statute narrowly drawn and limited to define and punish specific conduct lying within the domain of state power, the use in a public place of words likely to cause a breach of the peace." . . .

Appellant argues that the Georgia appellate courts have by construction limited the prescription of §26-6303 to "fighting" words, as the New Hampshire Supreme Court limited the New Hampshire statute. [We] have, however, made our own examination of the Georgia cases, both those cited and others discovered in research. That examination brings us to the conclusion, in agreement with the courts below, that the Georgia appellate decisions have not construed §26-6303 to be limited in application, as in *Chaplinsky*, to words that "have a direct tendency to cause acts of violence by the person to whom, individually, the remark is addressed." . . .

Moreover, [because Georgia has consistenly] applied §26-6303 to utterances where there was no likelihood that the person addressed would make an immediate violent response, it is clear that the standard allowing juries to determine guilt [does] not limit the application of §26-6303 to "fighting" words defined by *Chaplinsky*. . . .

Affirmed.

Mr. Justice Powell and Mr. Justice Rehnquist took no part in the consideration or decision of this case.

MR. CHIEF JUSTICE BURGER, dissenting.

I fully join in Mr. Justice Blackmun's dissent against the bizarre result reached by the Court. [The] Court apparently acknowledges that the conduct of the defendant in this case is not protected by the First Amendment, and does not contend that the Georgia statute is so ambiguous that he did not have fair notice that his conduct was prohibited. Nor does the Court deny that under normal principles of constitutional adjudication, appellee would not be permitted to attack his own conviction on the ground that the statute in question might in some hypothetical situation be unconstitutionally applied to the conduct of some party not before the Court. . . .

[Justice Blackmun also dissented.]

Note: Overbreadth

1. *The nature of overbreadth.* The traditional "as applied" mode of judicial review tests the constitutionality of legislation as it is applied to particular facts on a case-by-case basis. Suppose, for example, a state law prohibits any person to "advocate criminal conduct." Under "as applied" review, this law could constitutionally be applied to any expression that satisfies the requirements of *Brandenburg.* That the law fails "on its face" to comport with the strictures of *Brandenburg* is, under this approach, irrelevant.

The first amendment overbreadth doctrine, on the other hand, tests the constitutionality of legislation in terms of its *potential* applications. Under this approach, a state law prohibiting any person to "advocate unlawful conduct" is unconstitutional "on its face" because the law purports to forbid expression that the state may not constitutionally prohibit. That an individual defendant's own speech could constitutionally be restricted under a more narrowly drawn statute is irrelevant.

In effect, then, the overbreadth doctrine is an exception both to the traditional "as applied" mode of judicial review and to the general rule that an individual has no standing to litigate the rights of third persons. See United States v. Raines, 362 U.S. 17 (1960); Barrows v. Jackson, 346 U.S. 249 (1953); see also Note, Standing to Assert Constitutional Jus Tertii, 88 Harv. L. Rev. 423 (1974).

2. *Justifications and criticisms of overbreadth.* The overbreadth doctrine is "highly protective of first amendment interests, not only because it sometimes prescribes invalidation of an entire provision but also because of the alacrity with which it can accomplish that result." Note, The First Amendment Overbreadth Doctrine, 83 Harv. L. Rev. 844, 846 (1970). Are you persuaded by Justice Brennan's explanation in *Gooding* that this exception to ordinary standing rules is "necessary because persons whose expression is constitutionally protected may well refrain from exercising their rights for fear of criminal sanctions provided by a statute susceptible of application to protected expression"? Are you persuaded that "one of the evils of an overly broad statute is its potential for selective enforcement" and that the doctrine is thus justified because "it can minimize [this] danger by restricting the occasions for enforcement"? Karst, Equality as a Central Principle in the First Amendment, 43 U. Chi. L. Rev. 20, 38 (1975).

What are the costs of the overbreadth doctrine? Consider the following objections: (a) Because the doctrine permits an individual whose own rights have *not* been violated to "go free" or to otherwise benefit because the statute might conceivably interfere with the rights of others, it unjustifiably frustrates legitimate state interests. (b) The doctrine enables the Court to act "as if it had a roving commission" to find and to cure unconstitutionality and is thus inconsistent with a fundamental premise of judicial review — that judicial resolution of constitutional controversies is warranted only when unavoidable. A. Cox, The Warren Court 18 (1968). (c) The doctrine may promote judicial disingenuousness, for it invites the Court to escape possibly difficult decisions concerning the constitutionality of the statute "as applied" so long as it can hypothesize potentially unconstitutional applications not actually before the Court. (d) Because the Court may invalidate a statute for overbreadth without explaining precisely how the statute should have been drafted to pass constitutional muster, invocation of the doctrine "lacks intellectual coherence" and may leave legislatures with little or no guidance on how to avoid the Court's objections in the future. Id. at 53.

3. *The problem of narrowing construction.* As noted in *Gooding*, the statute at issue in *Chaplinsky* was clearly overbroad on its face but was saved by the state court's narrowing construction. When may a court narrowly construe a facially overbroad statute to save it from invalidation? In affirming the conviction of Gooding, could the Georgia Supreme Court have limited the statute to "fighting words" and thus avoided overbreadth invalidation? Was the legislative intent too clear in *Gooding* to permit a narrowing interpretation? Would a narrowing construction by the Georgia Supreme Court have come too late to affect Gooding?

Consider Osborne v. Ohio, 495 U.S. 103 (1990), in which the Court upheld a child pornography statute as construed by the state supreme court on appeal in the same case. Although the statute, as written, was unconstitutionally overbroad, the Court held that it was saved from invalidation by the state supreme court's narrowing construction, and that the statute, as construed, could "'be applied to conduct occurring prior to the construction, provided such application affords fair warning to the defendant.'" In *Osborne*, the Court concluded that the statute afforded "fair warning" because the defendant "would not [have been] surprised to learn that his possession of [the] photographs at issue [constituted] a crime."

Note that the Supreme Court of the United States had no authority to adopt a narrowing construction in *Gooding*. Is that sensible? Wouldn't a narrowing construction have involved a less drastic exercise of federal power than invalidation? Consider Virginia v. American Booksellers Association, Inc., 484 U.S. 383 (1988), in which the Court, rather than speculate on the reach of an ambiguous state statute, certified to the Virginia Supreme Court the question whether the challenged statute actually covered those acts of expression that gave rise to the overbreadth challenge. Is this a sensible approach?

Suppose that, while a criminal prosecution is on appeal, the state legislature amends the challenged statute to eliminate the unconstitutional overbreadth. May the defendant still take advantage of the fact that the statute was overbroad at the time he violated it? See Massachusetts v. Oakes, 491 U.S. 576 (1989) (defendant may still assert overbreadth).

4. *Broadrick: requiring "substantial" overbreadth.* Chief Justice Burger maintained in *Gooding* that the overbreadth doctrine should be invoked only when there is "a significant likelihood of deterring important First Amendment speech." In Broadrick v. Oklahoma, 413 U.S. 601 (1973), the Court, in a five-to-four decision, expressly adopted such a limitation. *Broadrick* involved a state law restricting the political activities of civil servants. The plaintiffs conceded that the state could constitutionally prohibit civil servants from doing what they had done — solicit funds for political candidates. They argued, however, that the law was unconstitutionally overbroad because it attempted also to prohibit civil

servants from engaging in such relatively innocuous and thus constitutionally protected activities as displaying political bumper stickers and buttons.

The Court, in an opinion by Justice White, observed that under the overbreadth doctrine, litigants "are permitted to challenge a statute not because their own rights of free expression are violated, but because of a judicial prediction or assumption that the statute's very existence may cause others not before the court to refrain from constitutionally protected speech or expression." Terming the doctrine "strong medicine," the Court argued that, although laws, "if too broadly worded, may deter protected speech to some unknown extent, there comes a point where that effect — at best a prediction — cannot, with confidence, justify invalidating a statute on its face and so prohibiting a State from enforcing the statute against conduct that is admittedly within its power to proscribe." Thus, the Court concluded, "we believe that the overbreadth of a statute must not only be real, but substantial as well, judged in relation to the statute's plainly legitimate sweep." Applying that standard to the statute in *Broadrick*, the Court concluded that, because the statute "regulates a substantial spectrum of conduct that [is] manifestly subject to state regulation," it "is not substantially overbroad [and] whatever overbreadth may exist should [thus] be cured through case-by-case analysis of the fact situations to which its sanctions, assertedly, may not be applied."

In dissent, Justice Brennan described *Broadrick* "as a wholly unjustified retreat from fundamental and previously well-established [principles]." The Court, Brennan noted, "makes no effort to define what it means by 'substantial overbreadth'" and "no effort to explain why the overbreadth of the Oklahoma Act, while real, is somehow not quite substantial."

5. *The impact of* Broadrick. In Los Angeles City Council v. Taxpayers for Vincent, 466 U.S. 789 (1984), the Court offered the following elaboration:

> The concept of "substantial overbreadth" is not readily reduced to an exact definition. It is clear, however, that the mere fact that one can conceive of some impermissible applications of a statute is not sufficient to render it susceptible to an overbreadth challenge. On the contrary, [there] must be a realistic danger that the statute itself will significantly compromise recognized First Amendment protections of parties not before the Court for it to be facially challenged on overbreadth grounds.

How should "substantiality" be measured: By the total number of unconstitutional applications? By the ratio of possible constitutional to possible unconstitutional applications? Should the state have to justify even an "insubstantial" overbreadth? See Redish, The Warren Court, the Burger Court and the First Amendment Overbreadth Doctrine, 78 Nw. U. L. Rev. 1031, 1067 (1983) (the "logical question [is] whether [a] more narrowly drawn [law] would inadequately achieve the state's goal").

The ultimate impact of *Broadrick* remains obscure. See New York v. Ferber, 458 U.S. 747 (1982), section D6, infra (upholding as not substantially overbroad a child pornography statute prohibiting any person to produce, exhibit, or sell any material depicting any "performance" by a child under the age of sixteen that includes "actual or simulated sexual intercourse, deviate sexual intercourse, sexual bestiality, masturbation, sado-masochistic abuse, or lewd exhibition of the genitals"); National Endowment for the Arts v. Finley, 524 U.S. 569 (1998), section E2d, infra (upholding as not substantially overbroad a federal statute directing the NEA, in establishing procedures to judge the artistic merit of grant applications, to "tak[e] into consideration general standards of decency and respect for the diverse beliefs and values of the American public").

Note: Vagueness

1. *The danger of vagueness.* Although not all overbroad laws are vague (e.g., "No person may expressly advocate criminal conduct"), and not all vague laws are overbroad (e.g., "No person may engage in any speech that the state may constitutionally restrict"), there is in most circumstances a close relation between the two doctrines. As a matter of due process, a law is void on its face if it is so vague that persons "of common intelligence must necessarily guess at its meaning and differ as to its application." Connally v. General Construction Co., 269 U.S. 385, 391 (1926). A law that fails to define clearly the conduct it proscribes "may trap the innocent by not providing fair warning" and may in practical effect impermissibly delegate "basic policy matters to policemen, judges and juries for resolution on an ad hoc and subjective basis, with the attendant dangers of arbitrary and discriminatory application." Grayned v. Rockford, 408 U.S. 104, 108–109 (1972).

These concerns are present whenever a law is vague, whether or not it touches on expression. The vagueness doctrine has special bite in the first amendment context, however, for "where First Amendment interests are affected, a precise statute 'evincing a legislative judgment that certain specific conduct [be] proscribed,' assures us that the legislature has focused on the First Amendment interests and determined that other governmental policies compel regulation." Moreover, "where a vague statute '[abuts] upon sensitive areas of basic First Amendment freedoms,' it 'operates to inhibit the exercise of [those] freedoms.'" Uncertain meanings inevitably lead citizens to "'steer far wider of the unlawful zone' [than] if the boundaries of the forbidden areas were clearly marked." Id. at 109 and n.5. In at least some instances, in other words, it may be difficult to determine whether a vague law proscribes — or purports to proscribe — constitutionally protected expression. In such circumstances, vague laws, like overbroad laws, may have a significant chilling effect and may invite selective enforcement. See Amsterdam, The Void-for-Vagueness Doctrine in the Supreme Court, 109 U. Pa. L. Rev. 67 (1960).

2. *How "vague" is "too vague"?* The degree of constitutionally tolerable vagueness "is not calculable with precision; in any particular area, the legislature confronts a dilemma: to draft with narrow particularity is to risk nullification by easy evasion of the legislative purpose; to draft with great generality is to risk ensnarement of the innocent in a net designed for others." L. Tribe, American Constitutional Law 1033 (2d ed. 1988). How vague must a law be for it to be held void on its face? Should it matter whether the vagueness is "avoidable"? Whether it is "substantial"? Consider the following:

a. A city ordinance provides that "no person, while on public or private grounds adjacent to any building in which a school [is] in session, shall willfully make [any] noise or diversion which disturbs or tends to disturb the peace or good order of such school." In Grayned v. City of Rockford, 408 U.S. 104 (1972), the Court rejected a vagueness challenge because "we think it is clear what the ordinance as a whole prohibits."

b. A Massachusetts statute provides that any person who "publicly mutilates, tramples upon, defaces or treats contemptuously the flag of the United States" shall be guilty of a misdemeanor. In Smith v. Goguen, 415 U.S. 566 (1974), the Court invalidated the statute because the statutory prohibition on treating the flag "contemptuously" failed "to draw reasonably clear lines between the kinds [of] treatment that are criminal and those that are not."

2. Prior Restraint

The doctrine of prior restraint has its roots in the sixteenth- and seventeenth-century English licensing systems under which all printing presses and printers were licensed by the state and no book or pamphlet could lawfully be published without the prior approval of a government censor. With the expiration of this system in England in 1695, the right of the press to be free from licensing gradually assumed the status of a common law right. Blackstone's definition of freedom of the press illustrates the importance of the doctrine of prior restraint in eighteenth-century thought: "The liberty of the press is indeed essential to the nature of a free state; but this consists in laying no *previous* restraints upon publications, and not in freedom from censure for criminal matter when published." 4 W. Blackstone, Commentaries *151–152.

Even after adoption of the first amendment, Justice Story and other early American commentators accepted the view that liberty of the press was limited to "the right to publish without any previous restraint or license." J. Story, Commentaries on the Constitution of the United States §1879 (1833); see also 2 J. Kent, Commentaries on American Law 23 (2d ed. 1832). Moreover, in its 1907 decision in Patterson v. Colorado, 205 U.S. 454, 462 (1907), the Court, speaking through Justice Holmes, announced that the Constitution prohibited "all such *previous restraints* upon publications as had been practiced by other governments," but not "the subsequent punishment of such as may be deemed contrary to the public welfare." And, although the Court, speaking again through Justice Holmes, recognized a dozen years later in *Schenck* that "the prohibition of laws abridging the freedom of speech is not confined to previous restraints," the doctrine of prior restraint has continued to play a central role in the jurisprudence of the first amendment. As indicated in the *Pentagon Papers* and *Nebraska Press* decisions, section B3 supra, the Court has steadfastly held that there is a special presumption under the first amendment against the use of prior restraints.

Like the vagueness and overbreadth concepts, the doctrine of prior restraint is concerned with the permissible means of restricting speech. A prior restraint may thus be invalid even if the particular expression at issue could constitutionally be restricted by some other means, such as subsequent criminal prosecution. Although the historical origins of the doctrine are clear, its analytical and functional underpinnings are often puzzling, at best. Apart from historical considerations, why are prior restraints special? After all, "whether the sanction be fine or imprisonment for criminal violation or fine or imprisonment for violation of [a prior restraint], the judicial sanction takes its bite after the [expression.]" Freund, The Supreme Court and Civil Liberties, 4 Vand. L. Rev. 533, 537–538 (1951).

Lovell v. Griffin

303 U.S. 444 (1938)

MR. CHIEF JUSTICE HUGHES delivered the opinion of the Court.

Appellant, Alma Lovell, was convicted in the Recorder's Court of the City of Griffin, Georgia, of the violation of a city ordinance and was sentenced to imprisonment for fifty days in default of the payment of a fine of fifty dollars. . . .

The ordinance in question is as follows:

> Section 1. That the practice of distributing, either by hand or otherwise, circulars, handbooks, advertising, or literature of any kind, whether said articles are being delivered free, or whether same are being sold, within the limits of the City of Griffin, without first obtaining written permission from the City Manager of the City of Griffin, such practice shall be deemed a nuisance, and punishable as an offense against the City of Griffin. . . .

The violation, which is not denied, consisted of the distribution without the required permission of a pamphlet and magazine in the nature of religious tracts, setting forth the gospel of the "Kingdom of Jehovah." Appellant did not apply for a permit. . . .

The ordinance in its broad sweep prohibits the distribution of "circulars, handbooks, advertising, or literature of any kind." [The] ordinance is not limited to "literature" that is obscene or offensive to public morals or that advocates unlawful conduct. [The] ordinance embraces "literature" in the widest sense. [Moreover, the] ordinance prohibits the distribution of literature of any kind at any time, at any place, and in any manner without a permit from the City Manager.

We think that the ordinance is invalid on its face. Whatever the motive which induced its adoption, its character is such that it strikes at the very foundation of the freedom of the press by subjecting it to license and censorship. The struggle for the freedom of the press was primarily directed against the power of the licensor. It was against that power that John Milton directed his assault by his "Appeal for the Liberty of Unlicensed Printing." And the liberty of the press became initially a right to publish *"without* a license what formerly could be published only *with* one." While this freedom from previous restraint upon publication cannot be regarded as exhausting the guaranty of liberty, the prevention of that restraint was a leading purpose in the adoption of the constitutional provision. . . .

Legislation of the type of the ordinance in question would restore the system of license and censorship in its baldest form. . . .

As the ordinance is void on its face, it was not necessary for appellant to seek a permit under it. She was entitled to contest its validity in answer to the charge against her. . . .

Reversed.

MR. JUSTICE CARDOZO took no part in the consideration and decision of this case.

Note: Licensing as Prior Restraint

1. *Standardless licensing.* What is the special vice of the licensing scheme in *Lovell?* Why not simply uphold the scheme on its face but permit any person

whose application for a license is unconstitutionally denied to challenge that denial in court? Is the Court's primary concern in *Lovell* the absence of standards to guide the city manager's discretion? See Kagan, Private Speech, Public Purpose: The Role of Governmental Motive in First Amendment Doctrine, 63 U. Chi. L. Rev. 415, 459–463 (1996) ("the rule against standardless licensing [serves the] function of flushing out bad motives by establishing a safeguard against administrative action based on the content of expression").

In City of Lakewood v. Plain Dealer Publishing Co., 486 U.S. 750 (1988), the Court applied the *Lovell* principle to invalidate an ordinance that gave a mayor standardless discretion to grant or deny permits to place newsracks on public property. The Court explained that the evils of standardless licensing "can be effectively alleviated only through a facial challenge":

> First, the mere existence of the licensor's unfettered discretion [intimidates] parties into censoring their own speech, even if the discretion and power are never actually abused. [Self-censorship] is immune to an "as applied" challenge, for it derives from the individual's own actions, not an abuse of government power. [Only] standards limiting the licensor's discretion will eliminate this danger by adding an element of certainty to fatal self-censorship. And only a facial challenge can effectively test the statute for these standards.
>
> Second, the absence of express standards makes it difficult to distinguish, "as applied," between a licensor's legitimate denial of a permit and its illegitimate abuse of censorial power. Standards provide the guideposts that check the licensor and allow courts quickly and easily to determine whether the licensor is discriminating against disfavored speech. Without these guideposts, post hoc rationalizations by the licensing official and the use of shifting or illegitimate criteria are far too easy, making it difficult for courts to determine in any particular case whether the licensor is permitting favorable, and suppressing unfavorable, expression.

Following *Lovell*, the Court has repeatedly held that a state "cannot vest restraining control over the right to speak [in] an administrative official where there are no appropriate standards to guide his action." Kunz v. New York, 340 U.S. 290, 295 (1951) (permit required for religious meetings); see also Shuttlesworth v. City of Birmingham, 394 U.S. 147 (1969) (permit required for parades); Staub v. City of Baxley, 355 U.S. 313 (1958) (permit required to solicit members for dues-paying organization); Saia v. New York, 334 U.S. 558 (1948) (permit required to operate sound amplifiers in public); Forsyth County, Georgia v. The Nationalist Movement, 505 U.S. 123 (1992) (even nominal permit fees for marches, demonstrations, and parades cannot be imposed in the absence of clear standards governing the setting of fees).

2. *Licensing with standards.* Suppose the authority of licensing officials to deny a permit is explicitly limited to only those circumstances in which the proposed expression could constitutionally be punished in a subsequent criminal prosecution. Would such a scheme, like that in *Lovell*, be unconstitutional on its face? Assume, for example, a state may constitutionally prohibit any person to participate in a parade that would physically interfere with another, ongoing parade. To prevent such conflicts from occurring, could the state constitutionally prohibit any person to participate in a parade without first obtaining a permit, where the licensing officials are authorized to deny a permit only on a finding that the proposed parade would physically interfere with another, previously authorized parade? Cf. Cox v. New Hampshire, 312 U.S. 569 (1941), section E2a, infra. Or assume a state may constitutionally make criminal the exhibition of "obscene"

motion pictures. May the state constitutionally create a licensing board to which all movies must be submitted prior to public exhibition, where the board is authorized to deny a license only on a finding that a movie is "obscene"? So long as the standards are clear, precise, and in conformity with the standards employed in subsequent criminal prosecutions, is there any reason to erect a special presumption against "prior" restraints?

3. *The objections to licensing.* Consider Emerson, The Doctrine of Prior Restraint, 20 Law & Contemp. Probs. 648, 656–660 (1955):

> [(1)] A system of prior restraint normally brings within the complex of govern-ment machinery a far greater amount of communication than a system of subsequent punishment. [The] pall of government control is, thus, likely to hang more pervasively over the area of communication.
>
> [(2)] Under a system of subsequent punishment, the communication has already been made before the government takes action. [Under] a system of prior restraint, the communication, if banned, never reaches the market place at all. Or the communication may be withheld until the issue of its release is finally settled, at which time it may have become obsolete.
>
> [(3)] A system of prior restraint is so constructed as to make it easier, and hence more likely, that in any particular case the government will rule adversely to free expression. [A] government official thinks longer and harder before deciding to undertake the serious task of subsequent punishment. [Under] a system of prior restraint, he can reach the result by a simple stroke of the pen.
>
> [(4)] Under a system of prior restraint, the issue of whether a communication is to be suppressed or not is determined by an administrative rather than a criminal procedure. This means that the procedural protections built around the criminal prosecution [are] not applicable to a prior restraint.
>
> [(5)] A system of prior restraint usually operates behind a screen of informality and partial concealment that seriously curtails opportunity for public appraisal and increases the chances of discrimination and other abuse.
>
> [(6)] [As] common experience [shows, the] attitudes, drives, emotions, and impulses [of licensers] all tend to carry them to excesses. [The] function of the censor is to censor. He has a professional interest in finding things to suppress. [These factors combine to produce] unintelligent, overzealous, and usually absurd administration.
>
> [(7)] A system of prior restraint is, in general, more readily and effectively enforced than a system of subsequent punishment. [A] penal proceeding to enforce a prior restraint normally involves only a limited and relatively simple issue — whether or not the communication was made without prior approval. The objec-tion to the content or manner of the communication need not be demonstrated. And furthermore, the violation of a censorship order strikes sharply at the status of the licenser, whose prestige thus becomes involved and whose power must be vindicated.

How weighty are these concerns? In light of these concerns, should licensing ever be permitted?

4. *The* Freedman *case: procedural safeguards.* In Freedman v. Maryland, 380 U.S. 51 (1965), appellant, in violation of a state motion picture censorship stat-ute, exhibited a film, conceded by the state not to be obscene or otherwise violative of the statutory standards, without first submitting it to the State Board of Censors for review. In a unanimous decision, the Court, speaking through Justice Brennan, held the statute invalid. At the outset, the Court empha-sized that the statute was unconstitutional not because it might "prevent even the first showing of a film whose exhibition may legitimately be the subject of an

obscenity prosecution," but rather because the administration of the censorship system "presents peculiar dangers to constitutionally protected speech." The Court explained that

> unlike a prosecution for obscenity, a censorship proceeding puts the initial burden on the exhibitor or distributor. Because the censor's business is to censor, there inheres the danger that he may well be less responsive than a court — part of an independent branch of government — to the constitutionally protected interests in free expression. And if it is made unduly onerous, by reason of delay or otherwise, to seek judicial review, the censor's determination may in practice be final.

The Court thus concluded that "a noncriminal process which requires the prior submission of a film to a censor avoids constitutional infirmity only if it takes place under procedural safeguards designed to obviate the dangers of a censorship system."

The Court then identified and explained several constitutionally required safeguards:

> First, the burden of proving that the film is unprotected expression must rest on the [censor]. Second, while the State may require advance submission of all films, in order to proceed effectively to bar all showings of unprotected films, the requirement cannot be administered in a manner which would lend an effect of finality to the censor's determination whether a film constitutes protected expression. [Because] only a judicial determination in an adversary proceeding ensures the necessary sensitivity to freedom of expression, only a procedure requiring a judicial determination suffices to impose a valid final restraint.
>
> [To] this end, the exhibitor must be assured, by statute or authoritative judicial construction, that the censor will, within a specified brief period, either issue a license or go to court to restrain showing the film. Any restraint imposed in advance of a final judicial determination on the merits must similarly be limited to preservation of the status quo for the shortest fixed period compatible with sound judicial resolution. Moreover, [the] procedure must also assure a prompt final judicial decision, to minimize the deterrent effect of an interim and possibly erroneous denial of a license. Without these safeguards, it may prove too burdensome to seek review of the censor's determination.

Because the Maryland scheme did not contain these procedural safeguards, the Court held it unconstitutional on its face. Justices Douglas and Black concurred on the ground that no "form of censorship — no matter how speedy or prolonged it may be — is permissible."

5. *The* Freedman *safeguards.* Should the *Freedman* safeguards be deemed a minimum requirement before *any* licensing scheme may pass constitutional muster? What about the parade permit scheme, noted earlier? See Blasi, Prior Restraints on Demonstrations, 68 Mich. L. Rev. 1481, 1536–1552 (1970); Monaghan, First Amendment "Due Process," 83 Harv. L. Rev. 518, 541–543 (1970). See Thomas v. Chicago Park District, 534 U.S. 316 (2002) (a content-neutral licensing scheme regulating the time, place and manner of use of a public forum need not employ the procedural safeguards required by *Freedman* because such a scheme "does not authorize a licensor to pass judgment on the content of speech").

To what extent do the *Freedman* safeguards mitigate the dangers of licensing? Does it follow from *Freedman* that a licensing scheme is always constitutional so long as (a) the licenser's authority to deny a permit is limited to only those circumstances in which the expression could constitutionally be subjected to subsequent criminal prosecution and (b) the *Freedman* safeguards are employed? *Freedman* involved the licensing of motion pictures. Can government constitutionally require that all *books* be submitted to a board of censors prior to publication in order to screen out those that are obscene or include libelous statements?

Near v. Minnesota
283 U.S. 697 (1931)

[A Minnesota statute provided for the abatement, as a public nuisance, of a "malicious, scandalous and defamatory newspaper, magazine or other periodical." The statute provided further that there "shall be available the defense that the truth was published with good motives and for justifiable ends." In November 1927, a county attorney sought to invoke this statute against The Saturday Press, which had run a series of articles charging "in substance that a Jewish gangster was in control of gambling, bootlegging and racketeering in Minneapolis, and that law enforcing officers and agencies were not energetically performing their duties." The Saturday Press was especially critical of the Chief of Police, who was charged "with gross neglect of duty, illicit relations with gangsters, and with participation in graft." Pursuant to the statute, a state trial court perpetually enjoined The Saturday Press and its owners from publishing or circulating "any publication whatsoever which is a malicious, scandalous or defamatory newspaper." The Supreme Court reversed.]

Mr. Chief Justice Hughes delivered the opinion of the Court. . . .

[The] object of the statute is not punishment, in the ordinary sense, but suppression of the offending newspaper or periodical. The reason for the enactment, as the state court has said, is that prosecutions to enforce penal statutes for libel do not result in "efficient repression or suppression of the evils of scandal." . . .

[The statute provides] that public authorities may bring [the] publisher of a newspaper or periodical before a judge upon a charge of conducting a business of publishing scandalous and defamatory matter [and] unless [the] publisher is able [to prove] that the charges are true and are published with good motives and for justifiable ends, his newspaper or periodical is suppressed and further publication is made punishable as a contempt. This is of the essence of censorship.

The question is whether a statute authorizing such proceedings [is] consistent with the conception of the liberty of the press as historically conceived and guaranteed. In determining the extent of the constitutional protection, it has been generally, if not universally, considered that it is the chief purpose of the guaranty to prevent previous restraints upon publication. [The] protection even as to previous restraint is not absolutely unlimited. But the limitation has been recognized only in exceptional cases. [No] one would question but that a government might prevent actual obstruction to its recruiting service or the publication of the sailing dates of transports or the number and location of troops. On similar grounds, the primary requirements of decency may be enforced against obscene publications. The security of the community life may be protected against incitements to acts of violence and the overthrow by force of orderly government. [These] limitations are not applicable here. . . .

The fact that for approximately one hundred and fifty years there has been almost an entire absence of attempts to impose previous restraints upon publications relating to the malfeasance of public officers is significant of the deep-seated conviction that such restraints would violate constitutional right. Public officers, whose character and conduct remain open to debate and free discussion in the press, find their remedies for false accusations in actions under libel laws providing for redress and punishment, and not in proceedings to restrain the publication of newspapers and periodicals. [The] fact that the liberty of the press may be abused by miscreant purveyors of scandal does not make any the less necessary the immunity of the press from previous restraint in dealing with official misconduct. Subsequent punishment for such abuses as may exist is the appropriate remedy, consistent with constitutional privilege. . . .

The statute in question cannot be justified by reason of the fact that the publisher is permitted to show, before injunction issues, that the matter published is true and is published with good motives and for justifiable ends. If such a statute, authorizing suppression and injunction on such a basis, is constitutionally valid, it would be equally permissible for the legislature to provide that at any time the publisher of any newspaper could be brought before a court, or even an administrative officer (as the constitutional protection may not be regarded as resting on mere procedural details) and required to produce proof of the truth of his publication, or of what he intended to publish, and of his motives, or stand enjoined. If this can be done, the legislature may provide machinery for determining in the complete exercise of its discretion what are justifiable ends and restrain publication accordingly. And it would be but a step to a complete system of censorship. The recognition of authority to impose previous restraint upon publication in order to protect the community against the circulation of charges of misconduct, and especially of official misconduct, necessarily would carry with it the admission of the authority of the censor against which the constitutional barrier was erected. . . .

For these reasons we hold the statute, so far as it authorized the proceedings in this action [to] be an infringement of the liberty of the press guaranteed by the Fourteenth Amendment. . . .

Judgment reversed.

Mr. Justice Butler, dissenting. . . .

The Minnesota statute does not operate as a *previous* restraint on publication within the proper meaning of that phrase. It does not authorize administrative control in advance such as was formerly exercised by the licensers and censors but prescribes a remedy to be enforced by a suit in equity. In this case there was previous publication made in the course of the business of regularly producing malicious, scandalous and defamatory periodicals. [There] is no question of the power of the State to denounce such transgressions. The restraint authorized is only in respect of continuing to do what has been duly adjudged to constitute a nuisance. [It] is fanciful to suggest similarity between the granting or enforcement of the decree authorized by this statute to prevent *further* publication of malicious, scandalous and defamatory articles and the *previous restraint* upon the press by licensers as referred to by Blackstone and described in the history of the times to which he alludes. . . .

It is well known, as found by the state supreme court, that existing libel laws are inadequate effectively to suppress evils resulting from the kind of business and publications that are shown in this case. The doctrine that measures such as the one before us are invalid because they operate as previous restraints [exposes] [every individual] to [the] false and malicious assaults of any insolvent publisher who [may] put into effect program[s] for oppression, blackmail or extortion.

The judgment should be affirmed.

Mr. Justice Van Devanter, Mr. Justice McReynolds, and Mr. Justice Sutherland concur in this opinion.

Note: Injunction as Prior Restraint

1. *Injunctions, criminal prosecutions, and licensing.* Assuming arguendo, as the Court apparently did in *Near*, that the speech prohibited by the injunction could constitutionally be punished in a subsequent criminal prosecution, why is the injunction invalid? Why isn't the injunction a *preferable* means of restraint? After all, unlike a criminal statute, an injunction is directed to a specific individual and is thus less likely to have a broad chilling effect. Moreover, unlike the licensing schemes in *Lovell* and *Freedman*, the injunctions in *Near*, the *Pentagon Papers* case, and *Nebraska Press* did not require prepublication submission to a censor for review. And, unlike licensing schemes, injunctions are issued and administered by judges rather than by censors whose "business is to censor." In what sense, then, is the injunction a prior restraint?

2. *Injunctions: Are they too effective?* It has been suggested that injunctions are especially threatening to free speech because they are more likely than criminal statutes to be obeyed. Does this make sense? If an injunction prohibits only speech that could constitutionally be punished in a subsequent criminal prosecution, is the greater effectiveness of the injunction a bad thing?

Suppose an injunction prohibits speech that could not constitutionally be punished in a subsequent criminal prosecution. Is the greater effectiveness of the injunction now a bad thing?

Are injunctions in fact more likely than criminal statutes to be obeyed? It has been argued that injunctions have a special "mystique," causing individuals to accord them an unusually high degree of respect, and that injunctions are more likely to be obeyed because they are more likely to be enforced. Injunctions, after all, are directed at specific individuals, thus increasing the probability that violations will be detected, and violations may be viewed as a direct affront to the issuing judge's authority, thus increasing the likelihood that violations will be punished. On the other hand, punishments imposed for violations of injunctions are typically less severe than those for violations of criminal statutes, thus reducing the potential costs of violation. For analyses of these issues, see O. Fiss, The Civil Rights Injunction 71–73 (1978); Barnett, The Puzzle of Prior Restraint, 29 Stan. L. Rev. 539, 551–552 (1977); Blasi, Toward a Theory of Prior Restraint: The Central Linkage, 66 Minn. L. Rev. 11, 24–49 (1981).

3. *The collateral bar rule.* It has been suggested that the critical feature of injunctions, making them far more likely to be obeyed than criminal statutes, and thus appropriately rendering them prior restraints, is the rule, applicable to injunctions generally, that an injunction "must be obeyed until it is set aside, and that persons subject to the [injunction] who disobey it may not defend against the ensuing charge of criminal contempt on the ground that the order was erroneous or even unconstitutional." Barnett, supra, at 552. In the ordinary criminal prosecution, the defendant may assert the unconstitutionality of the statute as

a defense. Thus, an individual whose planned expression is prohibited by a statute he believes to be invalid may elect to gamble and speak in defiance of the statute on the assumption that, if prosecuted, he will be able to persuade a court of the statute's unconstitutionality. An individual confronted with an injunction, however, has no such option, for under the "collateral bar" rule, "persons subject to an injunctive order issued by a court with jurisdiction are expected to obey that decree until it is modified or reversed, even if they have proper grounds to object to the order." GTE Sylvania v. Consumers Union, 445 U.S. 375, 386 (1980). This rule, which derives from the notion that "respect for judicial process is a small price to pay for the civilizing hand of law," has been held applicable even to injunctions directed against expression. In Walker v. City of Birmingham, 388 U.S. 307, 321 (1967), for example, a state trial court convicted eight black ministers of criminal contempt for leading mass street parades in violation of a temporary restraining order enjoining them from participating in such parades without first obtaining a permit as required by a city ordinance. The Court, invoking the collateral bar rule, upheld the contempt convictions without passing on the constitutionality of the injunction.

The collateral bar rule may have a significant impact on an individual's willingness to disobey even a patently unconstitutional order, for if the individual violates the injunction, he is subject to punishment even if the injunction is invalid. Consider Barnett, supra, at 553:

> [The rule places the individual] in a trilemma of chilling effects unique to a prior restraint situation. [He] can comply with the order and take no legal steps, thereby accepting the suppression. [He] can appeal the order directly, [but] must obey the interim restraint while [he] does so. [Or he] can [speak] in the face of [the] order, but only at the price of forfeiting [his] legal and constitutional objections to the order and thus, in all probability, embracing a contempt conviction.

With the collateral bar rule in force, the state in effect orders the enjoined individual to delay his speech unless and until a court lifts the injunction, whether or not the injunction itself is constitutionally permissible. The rule is thus strong medicine. In *Near*, for example, The Saturday Press was silenced for four years while courts debated the constitutionality of the injunction. In the *Skokie* controversy, section B2 supra, the injunction prohibited the Nazis from marching for more than eight months before it was set aside.

Does the existence of the collateral bar rule justify the observation that, whereas a "criminal statute chills," an injunction "freezes"? A. Bickel, The Morality of Consent 61 (1975). Does it justify the characterization of injunctions as prior restraints? See Jeffries, Rethinking Prior Restraint, 92 Yale L.J. 409 (1983). For a general analysis of the collateral bar rule, see Palmer, Collateral Bar and Contempt: Challenging a Court Order after Disobeying It, 88 Cornell L. Rev. 215 (2002).

4. *When is an injunction not a prior restraint?* Consider the following:

a. Suppose state law provides that the collateral bar rule is inapplicable to injunctions against expression. See cases cited in Rendleman, Free Press — Fair Trial: Review of Silence Orders, 52 N.C. L. Rev. 127, 153 n.181, 154 nn.182–185 (1973). Should injunctions in such a jurisdiction be treated as prior restraints?

b. In Pittsburgh Press Co. v. Pittsburgh Commission on Human Relations, 413 U.S. 376 (1973), the commission, after a hearing, found that the Pittsburgh Press had violated a city ordinance by displaying "help wanted" advertisements in its daily newspaper under headings designating job preference by sex. The commission therefore issued an order prohibiting the newspaper from carrying sex-designated ads in the future. In upholding the order, the Court explained that a criminal statute cast in such terms would be constitutionally permissible and then observed:

> [We have] never held that all injunctions are impermissible. [The] special vice of a prior restraint is that communication will be suppressed, either directly or by inducing excessive caution in the speaker, before an adequate determination that it is unprotected by the First Amendment. The present order does not endanger arguably protected speech. Because the order is based on a continuing course of repetitive conduct, this is not a case in which the Court is asked to speculate as to the effect of publication. Cf. [*Pentagon Papers* case]. Moreover, [because] no interim relief was granted, the order will not have gone into effect before our final determination that the actions of Pittsburgh Press were unprotected.

c. Should it matter whether an injunction is directed at the content of the restricted speech? Consider Madsen v. Women's Health Center, Inc., 512 U.S. 753 (1994), in which the Court held that an injunction prohibiting particular named individuals from demonstrating within thirty-six feet of an abortion clinic was not a "prior restraint" because the injunction was issued "not because of the content of petitioners' expression," but "because of their prior unlawful conduct" in earlier demonstrations. Consider also an injunction prohibiting the use of loudspeakers in demonstrations within one hundred feet of a hospital, school, or abortion clinic. In *Madsen*, the Court suggested that content-neutral injunctions are not "prior restraints," but that they nonetheless should be tested by more "rigorous" standards than other forms of content-neutral restrictions because injunctions "carry greater risks of censorship and discriminatory application than do general ordinances."

5. *Prior restraint revisited.* Consider Freund, The Supreme Court and Civil Liberties, 4 Vand. L. Rev. 533, 539 (1951): "In sum, it will hardly do to place 'prior restraint' in a special category for condemnation. What is needed is a pragmatic assessment of its operation in the particular circumstances. The generalization that prior restraint is particularly obnoxious in civil liberties cases must yield to more particularistic analysis."

D.   CONTENT-BASED RESTRICTIONS: "LOW" VALUE

As suggested in section B, the Court has articulated a two-level theory of free expression. Some speech, in other words, is said to possess only "low" first amendment value and is therefore accorded less than full constitutional protection. The two-level theory has its roots in the famous dictum of Chaplinsky v. New Hampshire, section B2 supra:

> There are certain well-defined and narrowly limited classes of speech, the prevention and punishment of which have never been thought to raise any Constitutional problem. These include the lewd and obscene, the profane, the libelous, and the insulting or "fighting" words — those which by their very utterance inflict injury or tend to incite an immediate breach of the peace. It has been well observed that such

utterances are no essential part of any exposition of ideas, and are of such slight social value as a step to truth that any benefit that may be derived from them is clearly outweighed by the social interest in order and morality.

This section examines the "low"-value theory in depth. In so doing, it poses several central first amendment questions: Is the very concept of low-value speech inherently incompatible with the guarantee of free expression? That is, does the determination that certain types of speech are of "slight social value as a step to truth" compel the Court to make "value judgments concerned with the content of expression, a role foreclosed to it by the basic theory of the First Amendment"? T. Emerson, The System of Freedom of Expression 326 (1970). Is the Court's exercise of this power tolerable so long as it confines itself to defining low-value speech in terms of discrete categories of expression rather than in terms of specific "good" or "bad" ideas? How is the Court to determine what speech is of low first amendment value? What follows from a determination that a certain category of expression is of low first amendment value? Is such expression wholly outside the protection of the first amendment, as suggested by *Chaplinsky*, or does such a determination trigger a form of "categorical balancing," according such speech some, but less than "full," first amendment protection?

It has been argued that the two-level theory is essential to "any well-functioning system of free expression" because without it one of two "unacceptable" results would follow — either (1) "the burden of justification imposed on government" when it regulates high-value speech, such as pure political expression, "would have to be lowered," or (2) "the properly stringent standards applied to efforts to regulate" high-value speech would have to be applied to low-value speech, with the result that government would not be able to regulate speech "that in all probability should be regulated." C. Sunstein, The Partial Constitution 233–234 (1993). Is there any answer to this argument?

Consider Lakier, The Invention of Low-Value Speech, 128 Harv. L. Rev. 2166 (2015):

> [The] doctrine of low-value speech allows the government to do what it is not supposed to be able to do: That is, it allows the government to remove ideas it dislikes from public [circulation]. By emphasizing the historical basis of the low-value categories, the Court has attempted to depict the distinction between high- and law-value speech as the product of something other than the perhaps idiosyncratic value judgments and preferences of its individual members. . . . There is little historical evidence, however, to back up the Court's claim that the categories of low-value speech we recognize [today] constituted, in the eighteenth and nineteenth centuries, well-defined and narrowly limited exceptions to the ordinary constitutional rule. . . .

This section examines several categories of arguably "low"-value expression — false statements of fact; nonnewsworthy disclosures of "private" facts; threats; commercial advertising; obscenity; child pornography; depictions of animal cruelty; violent expression; lewd, profane, and indecent speech; and hate speech and pornography.

1. False Statements of Fact

The Supreme Court has long maintained that "[under] the First Amendment there is no such thing as a false idea. However pernicious an opinion may seem, we depend for its correction not on the conscience of judges and juries but on the competition of other ideas." Gertz v. Robert Welch, Inc., infra this section. Government, in other words, may not restrict the expression of an idea or opinion because of *its* determination that the idea or opinion is "false." What, though, of false statements of *fact*? Recall Justice Holmes's example of the "false cry of fire."

The problem of false statements of fact arises most often in the context of defamation. At the time of adoption of the first amendment, civil and criminal actions for defamation were commonplace, and in *Chaplinsky* the Court expressly included libel within the class of utterances that "are no essential part of any exposition of ideas, and are of such slight social value as a step to truth that any benefit that may be derived from them is clearly outweighed by the social interest in order and morality." A decade later, in Beauharnais v. Illinois, section D8 infra, the Court announced that libelous utterances are not "within the area of constitutionally protected speech," and, accordingly, that "no one would contend that [they] may be punished only upon a showing" of clear and present danger.

New York Times v. Sullivan
376 U.S. 254 (1964)

MR. JUSTICE BRENNAN delivered the opinion of the Court.

We are required in this case to determine for the first time the extent to which the constitutional protections for speech and press limit a State's power to award damages in a libel action brought by a public official against critics of his official conduct.

Respondent L. B. Sullivan is one of the three elected Commissioners of the City of Montgomery, Alabama. [He] brought this civil libel action against the four individual petitioners, who are Negroes and Alabama clergymen, and against petitioner the New York Times. . . .

Respondent's complaint alleged that he had been libeled by statements in a full-page advertisement that was carried in the New York Times on March 29, 1960. Entitled "Heed Their Rising Voices," the advertisement [described the civil rights movement in the South and concluded with an appeal for funds].

Of the 10 paragraphs of text in the advertisement, the third and a portion of the sixth were the basis of respondent's claim of libel. They read as follows:

Third paragraph:

In Montgomery, Alabama, after students sang "My Country,' Tis of Thee" on the State Capital steps, their leaders were expelled from school, and truckloads of police armed with shotguns and tear-gas ringed the Alabama State College campus. When the entire student body protested to state authorities by refusing to re-register, their dining hall was padlocked in an attempt to starve them into submission.

Sixth paragraph:

Again and again the Southern violators have answered Dr. King's peaceful protests with intimidation and violence. They have bombed his home almost killing his wife and child. They have assaulted his person. They have arrested him seven times — for "speeding," "loitering" and similar "offenses." And now they have charged him with "perjury" — a *felony* under which they could imprison him for *ten years*. . . .

Although neither of these statements mentions respondent by name, he contended that the word "police" in the third paragraph referred to him as the Montgomery Commissioner who supervised the Police Department, so that he was being accused of "ringing" the campus with police. He further claimed that the paragraph would be read as imputing to the police, and hence to him, the padlocking of the dining hall in order to starve the students into submission. As to the sixth paragraph, he contended that since arrests are ordinarily made by the police, the statement "They have arrested [Dr. King] seven times" would be read as referring to him. . . .

It is uncontroverted that some of the statements contained in the two paragraphs were not accurate descriptions of events which occurred in Montgomery. Although Negro students staged a demonstration on the State Capitol steps, they sang the National Anthem and not "My Country,' Tis of Thee." Although nine students were expelled by the State Board of Education, this was not for leading the demonstration at the Capitol, but for demanding service at a lunch counter in the Montgomery County Courthouse on another day. Not the entire student body, but most of it, had protested the expulsion. [The] campus dining hall was not padlocked on any occasion. [Although] the police were deployed near the campus in large numbers on three occasions, they did not at any time "ring" the campus. [Dr.] King had not been arrested seven times, but only four. . . .

Respondent made no effort to prove that he suffered actual pecuniary loss as a result of the alleged libel.[3]

The trial judge submitted the case to the jury under instructions that the statements in the advertisement were "libelous per se" and were not privileged, so that petitioners might be held liable if the jury found that they had published the advertisement and that the statements were made "of and concerning" respondent. The jury was instructed that, because the statements were libelous per se, "the law . . . implies legal injury from the bare fact of publication itself," "falsity and malice are presumed," "general damages need not be alleged or proved but are presumed," and "punitive damages may be awarded by the jury even though the amount of actual damages is neither found nor shown." [The jury returned a judgment for respondent in the amount of $500,000.]

We reverse the judgment. We hold that the rule of law applied by the Alabama courts is constitutionally deficient for failure to provide the safeguards for freedom of speech and of the press that are required by the First and Fourteenth Amendments in a libel action brought by a public official against critics of his official conduct. We further hold that under the proper safeguards the evidence presented in this case is constitutionally insufficient to support the judgment for respondent.

I

We may dispose at the outset of [respondent's argument that the judgment of the state court is insulated from constitutional scrutiny because] "The Fourteenth Amendment is directed against State action and not private action." That

3. Approximately 394 copies of the edition of the Times containing the advertisement were circulated in Alabama. Of these, about 35 copies were distributed in Montgomery County. The total circulation of the Times for that day was approximately 650,000 copies. . . .

proposition has no application to this case. Although this is a civil lawsuit between private parties, the Alabama courts have applied a state rule of law which petitioners claim to impose invalid restrictions on their constitutional freedoms of speech and press. It matters not that that law has been applied in a civil action and that it is common law only. [The] test is not the form in which state power has been applied but, whatever the form, whether such power has in fact been exercised. . . .

II . . .

Respondent relies heavily, as did the Alabama courts, on statements of this Court to the effect that the Constitution does not protect libelous publications. Those statements do not foreclose our inquiry here. None of the cases sustained the use of libel laws to impose sanctions upon expression critical of the official conduct of public officials. [In] deciding the question now, we are compelled by neither precedent nor policy to give any more weight to the epithet "libel" than we have to other "mere labels" of state law. [Like] insurrection, contempt, advocacy of unlawful acts, breach of the peace, obscenity, solicitation of legal business, and the various other formulae for the repression of expression that have been challenged in this Court, libel can claim no talismanic immunity from constitutional limitations. It must be measured by standards that satisfy the First Amendment.

[We] consider this case against the background of a profound national commitment to the principle that debate on public issues should be uninhibited, robust, and wide-open, and that it may well include vehement, caustic, and sometimes unpleasantly sharp attacks on government and public officials. See [*Terminiello*]. The present advertisement, as an expression of grievance and protest on one of the major public issues of our time, would seem clearly to qualify for the constitutional protection. The question is whether it forfeits that protection by the falsity of some of its factual statements and by its alleged defamation of respondent.

Authoritative interpretations of the First Amendment guarantees have consistently refused to recognize an exception for any test of truth — whether administered by judges, juries, or administrative officials — and especially one that puts the burden of proving truth on the speaker. [Erroneous] statement is inevitable in free debate, [and] it must be protected if the freedoms of expression are to have the "breathing space" that they "need . . . to survive." . . .

Injury to official reputation affords no more warrant for repressing speech that would otherwise be free than does factual error. Where judicial officers are involved, this Court has held that concern for the dignity and reputation of the courts does not justify the punishment as criminal contempt of criticism of the judge or his decision. [*Bridges.*] If judges are to be treated as "men of fortitude, able to thrive in a hardy climate," [surely] the same must be true of other government officials, such as elected city commissioners. Criticism of their official conduct does not lose its constitutional protection merely because it is effective criticism and hence diminishes their official reputations.

If neither factual error nor defamatory content suffices to remove the constitutional shield from criticism of official conduct, the combination of the two elements is no less inadequate. This is the lesson to be drawn from the great controversy over the Sedition Act of 1798, which first crystallized a national awareness of the central meaning of the First Amendment. . . .

Although the Sedition Act was never tested in this Court, the attack upon its validity has carried the day in the court of history. Fines levied in its prosecution were repaid by Act of Congress on the ground that it was unconstitutional. [Jefferson], as President, pardoned those who had been convicted and sentenced under the Act and remitted their fines. [These] views reflect a broad consensus that the Act, because of the restraint it imposed upon criticism of government and public officials, was inconsistent with the First Amendment. . . .

What a State may not constitutionally bring about by means of a criminal statute is likewise beyond the reach of its civil law of libel. The fear of damage awards under a rule such as that invoked by the Alabama courts here may be markedly more inhibiting than the fear of prosecution under a criminal statute. [Alabama], for example, has a criminal libel law [which] allows as punishment upon conviction a fine not exceeding $500 and a prison sentence of six months. [The] judgment awarded in this case — without the need for any proof of actual pecuniary loss — was one thousand times greater than the maximum fine provided by the Alabama criminal statute, and one hundred times greater than that provided by the Sedition Act. [Whether] or not a newspaper can survive a succession of such judgments, the pall of fear and timidity imposed upon those who would give voice to public criticism is an atmosphere in which the First Amendment freedoms cannot survive. . . .

The state rule of law is not saved by its allowance of the defense of truth. [A] rule compelling the critic of official conduct to guarantee the truth of all his factual assertions — and to do so on pain of libel judgments virtually unlimited in amount — leads to a comparable "self-censorship." Allowance of the defense of truth, with the burden of proving it on the defendant, does not mean that only false speech will be deterred.[10] [Under] such a rule, would-be critics of official conduct may be deterred from voicing their criticism, even though it is believed to be true and even though it is in fact true, because of doubt whether it can be proved in court or fear of the expense of having to do so. They tend to make only statements which "steer far wider of the unlawful zone." [The] rule thus dampens the vigor and limits the variety of public debate. It is inconsistent with the First and Fourteenth Amendments.

The constitutional guarantees require, we think, a federal rule that prohibits a public official from recovering damages for a defamatory falsehood relating to his official conduct unless he proves that the statement was made with "actual malice" — that is, with knowledge that it was false or with reckless disregard of whether it was false or not. . . .

Such a privilege for criticism of official conduct is appropriately analogous to the protection accorded a public official when *he* is sued for libel by a private citizen. In Barr v. Matteo, 360 U.S. 564, 575, this Court held the utterance of a federal official to be absolutely privileged if made "within the outer perimeter" of his duties. The States accord the same immunity to statements of their highest officers. [The] reason for the official privilege is said to be that the threat of damage suits would otherwise "inhibit the fearless, vigorous, and effective administration of policies of government" and "dampen the ardor of all but the most resolute, or the most irresponsible, in the unflinching discharge of their duties."

10. Even a false statement may be deemed to make a valuable contribution to public debate, since it brings about "the clearer perception and livelier impression of truth, produced by its collision with error." Mill, On Liberty (Oxford: Blackwell, 1947), at 15; see also Milton, Areopagitica in Prose Works (Yale, 1959), Vol. II, at 561.

[Analogous] considerations support the privilege for the citizen-critic of government. It is as much his duty to criticize as it is the official's duty to administer. [As] Madison [said,] "the censorial power is in the people over the Government, and not in the Government over the people." . . .

III

We hold today that the Constitution delimits a State's power to award damages for libel in actions brought by public officials against critics of their official conduct. Since this is such an action,[23] the rule requiring proof of actual malice is applicable. . . .

Since respondent may seek a new trial, we deem that considerations of effective judicial administration require us to review the evidence in the present record to determine whether it could constitutionally support a judgment for respondent. [The] proof presented to show actual malice lacks the convincing clarity which the constitutional standard demands. [Although] there is evidence that the Times published the advertisement without checking its accuracy against the news stories in the Times' own files, [we] think the evidence against the Times supports at most a finding of negligence in failing to discover the misstatements, and is constitutionally insufficient to show the recklessness that is required for a finding of actual malice. . . .

We also think the evidence was constitutionally defective in another respect: it was incapable of supporting the jury's finding that the allegedly libelous statements were made "of and concerning" respondent. [The state courts embraced the proposition that criticism of government action could be treated as criticism of the officials responsible for that action for purposes of a libel suit.]

This proposition has disquieting implications for criticism of government conduct. [It would transmute] criticism of government, however impersonal it may seem on its face, into personal criticism, and hence potential libel, of the officials of whom the government is composed. [We] hold that such a proposition may not constitutionally be utilized to establish that an otherwise impersonal attack on governmental operations was a libel of an official responsible for those operations. . . .

Reversed and remanded.

MR. JUSTICE BLACK, with whom MR. JUSTICE DOUGLAS joins, concurring. . . .

"Malice," even as defined by the Court, is an elusive, abstract concept, hard to prove and hard to disprove. The requirement that malice be proved provides at best an evanescent protection for the right critically to discuss public affairs and certainly does not measure up to the sturdy safeguard embodied in the First Amendment. . . .

The half-million-dollar verdict [gives] dramatic proof [that] state libel laws threaten the very existence of an American press virile enough to publish unpopular views on public affairs and bold enough to criticize the conduct of public

---

23. We have no occasion here to determine how far down into the lower ranks of government employees the "public official" designation would extend for purposes of this rule, or otherwise to specify categories of persons who would or would not be included. Nor need we here determine the boundaries of the "official conduct" concept. It is enough for the present case that respondent's position as an elected city commissioner clearly made him a public official, and that the allegations in the advertisement concerned what was allegedly his official conduct as Commissioner in charge of the Police Department. . . .

officials. [There] is no reason to believe that there are not more such huge verdicts lurking just around the corner for the Times or any other newspaper or broadcaster which might dare to criticize public officials. In fact, briefs before us show that in Alabama there are now pending eleven libel suits by local and state officials against the Times seeking $5,600,000, and five such suits against the Columbia Broadcasting System seeking $1,700,000.

In my opinion the Federal Constitution has dealt with this deadly danger to the press in the only way possible without leaving the free press open to destruction — by granting the press an absolute immunity for criticism of the way public officials do their public duty. Compare Barr v. Matteo, 360 U.S. 564. Stopgap measures like those the Court adopts are in my judgment not enough. . . .

[In a separate concurring opinion, Justice Goldberg, joined by Justice Douglas, maintained that the first amendment affords "an absolute, unconditional privilege to criticize official conduct," but noted that "defamatory statements directed against the private conduct of a public official or private citizen" may be different, for "purely private defamation has little to do with the political ends of a self-governing society."]

Note: "The Central Meaning" of New York Times v. Sullivan

1. *The central meaning of the first amendment.* Professors Meiklejohn and Kalven maintained that the *New York Times* decision "is [an] occasion for dancing in the streets." Kalven, The *New York Times* Case: A Note on "The Central Meaning of the First Amendment," 1964 Sup. Ct. Rev. 191, 221 n.125. Consider id. at 208–209:

> The Court did not simply, in the face of an awkward history, definitively put to rest the status of the Sedition Act. More important, it found in the controversy over seditious libel the clue to "the central meaning of the First Amendment." The choice of language was unusually apt. The Amendment has a "central meaning" — a core of protection of speech without which democracy cannot function, without which, in Madison's phrase, "the censorial power" would be in the Government over the people and not "in the people over the Government." This is not the whole meaning of the Amendment. There are other freedoms protected by it. But at the center there is no doubt what speech is being protected and no doubt why it is being protected. The theory of the freedom of speech clause was put right side up for the first time. [The] central meaning of the Amendment is that seditious libel cannot be made the subject of government sanction.

2. *Low value?* Does *New York Times* reject the view of *Chaplinsky* and *Beauharnais* (section D8 infra) that false statements of fact are of "slight social value" and hence not "within the area of constitutionally protected speech"? Consider footnote 10. Is the Court's primary concern with the protection of false statements of fact or with the risk that libel laws might generate a self-censorship that invades the zone of "high" value speech?

3. *Categorical balancing.* Consider Nimmer, The Right to Speak from *Times* to *Time:* First Amendment Theory Applied to Libel and Misapplied to Privacy, 56 Cal. L. Rev. 935, 942–943 (1968):

> [*New York Times*] points the way to the employment of the balancing process on the [categorical level]. That is, the Court employs balancing [for] the purpose of

[determining when certain categories of speech can be restricted] within the meaning of the first amendment. [By] in effect holding that [false statements of fact can be restricted when they are] knowingly and recklessly false [the] Court implicitly [balanced] certain competing policy considerations.

Is such "categorical balancing" an appropriate way to formulate first amendment doctrine? Contrast the "definitional balancing" in *New York Times* with that in *Brandenburg*. How does each treat the issue of intent? For a critique of categorical balancing, see Aleinikoff, Constitutional Law in the Age of Balancing, 96 Yale L.J. 943, 979–981 (1987).

4. *Is* New York Times *overprotective of false speech?* Consider the following views:

a. Even if the first amendment protects false statements of fact in the sense that government may not criminally punish them, does it necessarily follow that newspapers should not have to pay for the costs of their speech? Why should the first amendment require the victims of false statements to bear the loss and in effect to *subsidize* newspapers?

b. *New York Times* rests on the assumption that traditional libel law chills true speech. But an "argument based on chilling effect necessarily rests [on] intractable empirical suppositions" that might not be correct. See Kendrick, Speech, Intent, and the Chilling Effect, 54 Wm. & Mary L. Rev. 1633 (2013).

c. *New York Times* rests on the assumption that the marketplace of ideas will function better with the Court's rule than without it. But the opposite assumption seems at least equally plausible. First, self-censorship is not intrinsically a bad thing. It all depends on what speech is discouraged. Although traditional libel law may "chill" more valuable speech than the *New York Times* rule, it also "chills" more false speech. It is by no means clear that the effect of *New York Times* will be to improve the overall quality of public debate. Second, *New York Times* may actually reduce "the quality of information [available to the public by eliminating jury judgments] as to the truth or falsity of some accusations." Nagel, How Useful Is Judicial Review in Free Speech Cases?, 69 Cornell L. Rev. 302, 323 (1984). Finally, *New York Times* may so expose public officials to journalistic abuse that it will drive capable persons away from government service, thus frustrating, rather than furthering, the political process.

d. Dun & Bradstreet v. Greenmoss Builders, 472 U.S. 749 (1985) (White, J., concurring):

> Instead of escalating the plaintiff's burden of proof to an almost impossible level, [the Court] could have achieved [its] goal by limiting the recoverable damages to a level that would not unduly threaten the press. Punitive [and presumed damages] might have been prohibited, or limited. Had that course been taken and the common-law standard of liability been retained, the defamed public official, upon proving falsity, could at least have had a judgment to that effect. His reputation would then be vindicated; and to the extent possible, the misinformation circulated would have been countered. He might also have recovered a modest amount, enough perhaps to pay his litigation expenses. [In] this way, both First Amendment and reputational interests would have been far better served.

5. *Is* New York Times *underprotective of false speech?* Consider Smolla, Let the Author Beware: The Rejuvenation of the American Law of Libel, 132 U. Pa. L. Rev. 1, 4–7, 12, 91–93 (1984):

> The data show a trend toward more generous jury awards, and a corresponding trend toward the media settling suits at a substantial cost. [One] study showed that

thirty out of forty-seven damage awards included punitive damages, and seven of those punitive damage awards were for $1 million or more. [The] prospect of such lucrative awards is likely to entice more potential defamation plaintiffs to bring [suit]. A failure to adjust defamation doctrine [can] be expected to have a severe impact on the media. [Many] media outlets [defend] libel actions under the peril of shutdown if they lose. [One] alternative to current law is to allow punitive damages only when the plaintiff, in addition to proving actual malice, proves common law ill-will malice. [Preferably,] punitive damages should be [abolished altogether].

6. *The limits of* New York Times. What does the Court mean by "reckless disregard"? Does *New York Times* implicitly prohibit criminal prosecutions for libel of public officials? Are all public employees "public officials" within the meaning of *New York Times*?

Consider the following decisions, which shed light on these and related issues: Milkovich v. Lorain Journal Co., 497 U.S. 1 (1990) (a statement "must be provable as false before there can be liability"); Harte-Hanks Communications v. Connaughton, 491 U.S. 657 (1989) (neither failure to comply with "professional standards" nor publication of falsehood in order to increase profits is in itself sufficient to establish "actual malice," but "purposeful avoidance of the truth" may be sufficient); Philadelphia Newspapers, Inc. v. Hepps, 475 U.S. 767 (1986) (the "plaintiff must bear the burden of proving that the statements at issue are false"); Monitor Patriot Co. v. Roy, 401 U.S. 265 (1971) ("a charge of criminal conduct, no matter how remote in time or place, can never be irrelevant to an official's or a candidate's fitness for office for purposes of application of" *New York Times*); St. Amant v. Thompson, 390 U.S. 727 (1968) (failure to investigate or otherwise seek corroboration prior to publication is not reckless disregard for the truth unless the publisher acts with a "high degree of awareness of [probable] falsity"); Garrison v. Louisiana, 379 U.S. 64 (1964) (first amendment does not absolutely prohibit criminal prosecution for libel even of public officials, but *New York Times* standard applies).

Perhaps the most important question remaining after *New York Times* was whether the privilege it recognized governed only libel of public officials or whether it extended to libel of other persons as well.

CURTIS PUBLISHING CO. v. BUTTS; ASSOCIATED PRESS v. WALKER, 388 U.S. 130 (1967). In these companion cases, the Court examined the question whether a libel action brought by an individual who is a "public figure," but not a "public official," must also be governed by the *New York Times* standard. Butts brought an action for libel, alleging that the defendant had published an article falsely accusing him of conspiring to "fix" a football game between the University of Georgia and the University of Alabama. At the time of the article, Butts was the athletic director of the University of Georgia, a state university, but was employed by the Georgia Athletic Association, a private corporation. Butts had served previously as head football coach at the university and had an established national reputation. In the companion case, Walker sued the Associated Press for libel, claiming that it had distributed a news dispatch falsely reporting that, when a riot erupted on the campus of the University of Mississippi because of federal efforts to enforce court-ordered desegregation, Walker had taken command of the crowd, encouraged it to use violence, and personally led a charge against the federal marshals. Walker, a private citizen at the time of the riot and publication, had pursued a distinguished military career and was a figure of national prominence. In each case, the jury found the defendant liable under state law, the trial judge approved a damage award of about $500,000, and the defendant maintained that *New York Times* should govern and that it thus could not be held liable without proof that it had published the story either knowing it to be false or with reckless disregard for the truth.

In a sharply divided set of opinions, the Court held the *New York Times* standard applicable to "public figures" as well as to "public officials," and, further, that both Butts and Walker constituted "public figures" for purposes of the rule. Chief Justice Warren, joined by Justices Brennan and White, observed that "increasingly in this country, the distinctions between governmental and private sectors are blurred," and that many individuals "who do not hold public office at the moment are nevertheless intimately involved in the resolution of important public questions or, by reason of their fame, shape events in areas of concern to society at large." Moreover, Chief Justice Warren argued, "as a class these 'public figures' have as ready access as 'public officials' to mass media of communication, both to influence policy and to counter criticism of their views and activities." Thus, Chief Justice Warren concluded, "differentiation between 'public figures' and 'public officials' and adoption of separate standards of proof for each have no basis in law, logic, or First Amendment policy." Justice Black, joined by Justice Douglas, maintained that "the First Amendment was intended to leave the press [absolutely] free from the harassment of libel judgments," but accepted the narrower rationale of Chief Justice Warren "'in order for the Court to be able at this time to agree on [a disposition of] this important case.'" Justice Harlan, joined by Justices Clark, Stewart, and Fortas, concurred in the result.

Is the extension of *New York Times* to "public figures" mandated by "the central meaning of the first amendment"?

GERTZ v. ROBERT WELCH, INC., 418 U.S. 323 (1974). In 1968, a Chicago policeman named Nuccio shot and killed a youth named Nelson. The state prosecuted Nuccio and obtained a conviction for murder. The Nelson family retained Gertz, a Chicago attorney, to represent them in civil litigation against Nuccio. In 1969, respondent, publisher of American Opinion, a monthly outlet for the views of the John Birch Society, ran an article in which it accused Gertz of being the architect of a "frame-up" of Nuccio and stated that Gertz had a criminal record and long-standing communist affiliations. Gertz filed this action for libel. After the jury returned a $50,000 verdict for Gertz, the trial court entered judgment for respondent, concluding that the *New York Times* standard applied to any discussion of a "public issue."

The Supreme Court, in an opinion by Justice Powell, reversed: "The principal issue in this case is whether a newspaper or broadcaster that publishes defamatory falsehoods about an individual who is neither a public official nor a public figure may claim a constitutional privilege against liability for the injury inflicted by those statements. [We] begin with the common ground. Under the First Amendment there is no such thing as a false idea. However pernicious an opinion may seem, we depend for its correction not on the conscience of judges and juries but on the competition of other ideas. But there is no constitutional value in false statements of fact. Neither the intentional lie nor the careless error materially advances society's interest in 'uninhibited, robust, and wide-open' debate on public issues. [New York Times Co. v. Sullivan.] They belong to that category of utterances which 'are no essential part of any exposition of ideas, and are of such slight social value as a step to truth that any benefit that may be derived from them is clearly outweighed by the social interest in order and morality.' [*Chaplinsky.*]

"Although the erroneous statement of fact is not worthy of constitutional protection, it is nevertheless inevitable in free debate. [And] punishment of error runs the risk of inducing a cautious and restrictive exercise of the constitutionally guaranteed freedoms of speech and press. Our decisions recognize that a rule of strict liability that compels a publisher or broadcaster to guarantee the accuracy of his factual assertions may lead to intolerable self-censorship. [The] First Amendment requires that we protect some falsehood in order to protect speech that matters.

"The need to avoid self-censorship by the news media is, however, not the only societal value at issue. If it were, this Court would have embraced long ago the view that publishers and broadcasters enjoy an unconditional and indefeasible immunity from liability for defamation. [The] legitimate state interest underlying the law of libel is the compensation of individuals for the harm inflicted on them by defamatory falsehood. We would not lightly require the State to abandon this purpose, for [the] individual's right to the protection of his own good name 'reflects [our] basic concept of the essential dignity and worth of every human being — a concept at the root of any decent system of ordered [liberty].' . . .

"The *New York Times* standard defines the level of constitutional protection appropriate to the context of defamation of a public person. [We] have no difficulty in distinguishing among defamation plaintiffs. The first remedy of any victim of defamation is self-help — using available opportunities to contradict the lie or correct the error and thereby to minimize its adverse impact on reputation. Public officials and public figures usually enjoy significantly greater access to the channels of effective communication and hence have a more realistic opportunity to counteract false statements than private individuals normally enjoy. Private individuals are therefore more vulnerable to injury, and the state interest in protecting them is correspondingly greater.

"[Moreover, an] individual who decides to seek governmental office must accept certain necessary consequences of that involvement in public affairs. He runs the risk of closer public scrutiny than might otherwise be the case. [Those] classed as public figures stand in a similar position. [For] the most part those who attain this status have assumed roles of especial prominence in the affairs of society. Some occupy positions of such persuasive power and influence that they are deemed public figures for all purposes. More commonly, those classed as public figures have thrust themselves to the forefront of particular public controversies in order to influence the resolution of the issues involved. In either event, they invite attention and comment.

"Even if the foregoing generalities do not obtain in every instance, the communications media are entitled to act on the assumption that public officials and public figures have voluntarily exposed themselves to increased risk of injury from defamatory falsehood concerning them. No such assumption is justified with respect to a private individual. He has not accepted public office or assumed an 'influential role in ordering society.' [He] has relinquished no part of his interest in the protection of his own good name, and consequently he has a more compelling call on the courts for redress of injury inflicted by defamatory falsehood. Thus, private individuals are not only more vulnerable to injury than public officials and public figures; they are also more deserving of recovery.

"For these reasons we conclude that the States should retain substantial latitude in their efforts to enforce a legal remedy for defamatory falsehood injurious to the reputation of a private individual. The extension of the *New York Times* test [to defamatory falsehoods relating to private persons if the statements concerned matters of general or public interest] would abridge this legitimate state interest to a degree that we find unacceptable. [We] hold that, so long as they do not impose liability without fault, the States may define for themselves the appropriate standard of liability for a publisher or broadcaster of defamatory falsehood injurious to a private individual. . . .

"[We] endorse this approach in recognition of the strong and legitimate state interest in compensating private individuals for injury to reputation. But this countervailing state interest extends no further than compensation for actual injury. [We] hold that the States may not permit recovery of presumed or punitive damages, at least when liability is not based on a showing of knowledge of falsity or reckless disregard for the truth."

Justice Douglas dissented: "The Court describes this case as a return to the struggle of 'defin[ing] the proper accommodation between the law of defamation and the freedoms of speech and press protected by the First Amendment.' [I] would suggest that the struggle is a quite hopeless one, for, in light of the command of the First Amendment, no 'accommodation' of its freedoms can be 'proper' except those made by the Framers themselves."

Justice Brennan dissented: "[We] strike the proper accommodation between avoidance of media self-censorship and protection of individual reputations only when we require States to apply the [*New York Times*] knowing-or-reckless-falsity standard in civil libel actions concerning media reports of the involvement of private individuals in events of public or general interest."

Justice White dissented: "To me, it is quite incredible to suggest that threats of libel suits from private citizens are causing the press to refrain from publishing the truth. I know of no hard facts to support that proposition, and the Court furnishes none. [In] any event, if the Court's principal concern is to protect the communications industry from large libel judgments, it would appear that its new requirements with respect to general and punitive damages would be ample protection. Why it also feels compelled to escalate the threshold standard of liability I cannot fathom, particularly when this will eliminate in many instances the plaintiff's possibility of securing a judicial determination that the damaging publication was indeed false, whether or not he is entitled to recover money damages. Under the Court's new rules, the plaintiff must prove not only the defamatory statement but also some degree of fault accompanying it. The publication may be wholly false and the wrong to him unjustified, but his case will nevertheless be dismissed for failure to prove negligence or other fault on the part of the publisher. I find it unacceptable to distribute the risk in this manner and force the wholly innocent victim to bear the injury; for, as between the two, the defamer is the only culpable party. It is he who circulated a falsehood that he was not required to publish."

Chief Justice Burger also filed a dissenting opinion.

Note: *Public and Private Figures, Public and Private Speech*

1. *Was Gertz a "public figure"?* Consider Justice Powell's analysis of this question:

[The public figure] designation may rest on either of two alternative bases. In some instances an individual may achieve such pervasive fame or notoriety that he becomes a public figure for all purposes and in all contexts. More commonly, an individual voluntarily injects himself or is drawn into a particular public controversy and thereby becomes a public figure for a limited range of issues. In either case such persons assume special prominence in the resolution of public questions.

Petitioner has long been active in community and professional affairs. He has served as an officer of local civic groups and of various professional organizations, and he has published several books and articles on legal subjects. Although petitioner was consequently well known in some circles, he had achieved no general fame or notoriety in the community. [Absent] clear evidence of general fame or notoriety in the community, and pervasive involvement in the affairs of society, an individual should not be deemed a public personality for all aspects of his life. It is preferable to reduce the public-figure question to a more meaningful context by looking to the nature and extent of an individual's participation in the particular controversy giving rise to the defamation.

In this context it is plain that petitioner was not a public figure. He played a minimal role at the coroner's inquest, and his participation related solely to his representation of a private client. He took no part in the criminal prosecution of Officer Nuccio. Moreover, he never discussed either the criminal or civil litigation with the press and was never quoted as having done so. He plainly did not thrust himself into the vortex of this public issue, nor did he engage the public's attention in an attempt to influence its outcome. We are persuaded that the trial court did not err in refusing to characterize petitioner as a public figure for the purpose of this litigation.

2. *Public figures.* Consider the following:

a. Plaintiff was divorced by Russell Firestone, the scion of one of America's wealthiest families. Time magazine erroneously reported that the divorce was granted on the ground of adultery. Plaintiff sued Time for libel. In Time, Inc. v. Firestone, 424 U.S. 448 (1976), the Court rejected Time's claim that Mrs. Firestone was a public figure: "[She] did not assume any role of especial prominence in the affairs of society, other than perhaps Palm Beach society, and she did not thrust herself to the forefront of any particular public controversy in order to influence the resolution of the issues involved in it."

b. In the late 1950s, in a widely publicized case, plaintiff was convicted of contempt for his refusal to appear before a grand jury investigating Soviet espionage. Sixteen years later, defendant published a book erroneously identifying plaintiff as a Soviet agent. Plaintiff sued for libel. In Wolston v. Reader's Digest Association, 443 U.S. 157 (1979), the Court rejected the publisher's claim that plaintiff was a "limited-purpose public figure." The Court emphasized that plaintiff had not "engaged the attention of the public in an attempt to influence the resolution of the issues involved" and explained that one who commits a crime does not become a public figure, even for the purpose "of comment on a limited range of issues relating to his conviction," for "[to] hold otherwise would create an 'open season' for all who sought to defame persons convicted of a crime."

c. Over the course of several years, various federal agencies spent almost half a million dollars funding plaintiff's research into aggressive monkey behavior. Senator Proxmire awarded the federal agencies his Golden Fleece of the Month Award, an award designed to publicize what Proxmire believed to be the most egregious examples of wasteful government spending. Claiming Proxmire's description of his research to be inaccurate, plaintiff sued for libel. In Hutchinson v. Proxmire, 443 U.S. 111 (1979), the Court rejected Proxmire's argument that plaintiff was a "limited-purpose public figure" for the "purpose of comment on his receipt of federal funds for research projects." The Court concluded that plaintiff "at no time assumed any role of public prominence in the broad question of concern about expenditures," and that "neither his applications for federal grants nor his publications in professional journals can be said to have invited that degree of public attention and comment on his receipt of federal grants essential to meet the public figure level."

3. *The need for vindication.* Justice White expressed concern in *Gertz* that the Court's decision would eliminate the private plaintiff's opportunity to vindicate himself by obtaining a judicial declaration of falsity. Is there any way to deal with this concern after *Gertz*? Consider Freund, Political Libel and Obscenity, 42 F.R.D. 491, 497 (1966): "Plaintiffs [should] be permitted to request a special verdict, so that if there is a verdict for the defendant based solely and simply on [the *New York Times* or *Gertz* privileges, the jury could nevertheless find] that the utterances were untrue." Consider also Justice Brennan's suggestion in *Gertz* that states could enact statutes "not requiring proof of fault, which provide for an action for retraction or for publication of a court's determination of falsity if the plaintiff is able to demonstrate that false statements have been published concerning his activities." Would such a statute violate the first amendment "right" of newspapers not to publish information against their will? See Miami Herald Publishing Co. v. Tornillo, 418 U.S. 241 (1974), section F4, infra.

4. *The limits of* Gertz. Does *Gertz*'s "fault" standard govern all libelous statements not involving public officials or public figures, whether or not such statements concern matters of "general or public interest"? Is the *Gertz* privilege available only to media defendants? Note Justice Powell's consistent references to the media. Can denial of the privilege to nonmedia defendants be justified on the ground that the "press" is entitled to special constitutional protection? See section F infra.

DUN & BRADSTREET v. GREENMOSS BUILDERS, 472 U.S. 749 (1985). Petitioner, a credit reporting agency, provides subscribers with financial information about businesses. Petitioner sent a report to five subscribers indicating that respondent, a construction contractor, had filed a voluntary petition for bankruptcy. This report was inaccurate. In respondent's defamation action against petitioner, the trial judge instructed the jury that it could award presumed and punitive damages without a showing of "actual malice." The jury returned a verdict in favor of respondent and awarded $50,000 in compensatory or presumed damages and $300,000 in punitive damages. The Supreme Court, in a five-to-four decision, affirmed the judgment.

Justice Powell's plurality opinion was joined by Justices Rehnquist and O'Connor: "We have never considered whether the *Gertz* balance obtains when the defamatory statements involve no issue of public concern. [The] state interest [here] is identical to the one weighed in *Gertz*. [The] First Amendment interest, on the other hand, is less important than the one weighed in *Gertz*. We have long recognized that not all speech is of equal First Amendment importance. It is speech on 'matters of public concern' that is 'at the heart of the First Amendment's protection.' In contrast, speech on matters of purely private concern is of less First Amendment concern. [When the state regulates such expression], 'There is no threat to the free and robust debate of public issues, [and] there is no potential interference with a meaningful dialogue of ideas concerning self-government.' [While] such speech is not totally unprotected by the First Amendment, its protections are less stringent. [In] light of the reduced constitutional value of speech involving no matters of public concern, we hold that the state interest adequately supports awards of presumed and punitive damages — even absent a showing of 'actual malice.'"

Chief Justice Burger and Justice White concurred in the judgment. Justice Brennan, joined by Justices Marshall, Blackmun, and Stevens, dissented on the ground that, under *Gertz*, respondent "should be required to show actual malice to receive presumed or punitive damages."

Note: Other False Statements of Fact

In *Gertz*, the Court again made explicit its conclusion that "there is no constitutional value in false statements of fact." Nonetheless, in its *New York Times/Gertz* line of authority, the Court granted substantial first amendment protection to false statements of fact in the libel context to avoid "self-censorship" and "to protect speech that matters." How should false statements of fact be dealt with in other contexts? Consider the following:

a. Suppose an individual falsely asserts that a particular law was enacted because a majority of the legislators had been "paid off." In what circumstances, if any, may government criminally punish an individual for factually false utterances that defame government itself?

b. Recall section 3 of the Espionage Act of 1917, section B1 supra: "Whoever, when the United States is at war, shall willfully make or convey false reports [with] intent to interfere with [the] success of the military [forces] of the United States [shall be guilty of a felony]." Is the act constitutional in light of the *New York Times/Gertz* line of authority? If not, how might it be redrafted to satisfy the first amendment? For discussion of the prosecution of an American Nazi under this provision during World War II, see G. Stone, Perilous Times: Free Speech in Wartime 258–275 (2004).

c. The problem of false statements of fact arises often in the context of political campaigns. Suppose, for example, a supporter of a candidate's opponent falsely accuses the candidate of some impropriety. So long as the candidate can meet the demands of *New York Times*, he can, of course, sue for libel. That may be small consolation, however, if he loses the election. To avoid that result, can the candidate obtain an injunction against further dissemination of the falsehood? Can a state electoral commission prohibit distribution of any campaign literature containing the falsehood? Suppose, instead of defaming an opponent, a candidate or his supporters falsely inflate the candidate's own qualifications. In what circumstances, and by what means, may such speech be restricted? See Pestrak v. Ohio Elections Commission, 926 F.2d 573 (6th Cir. 1991) (upholding state election commission's restriction on the dissemination of false statements in the context of political campaigns); Tomei v. Finley, 512 F. Supp. 695 (N.D. Ill. 1981) (granting a preliminary injunction against a candidate's use of a misleading campaign slogan); Stone, The Rules of Evidence and the Rules of Public Debate, 1993 U. Chi. Legal F. 127, 137–141 (arguing that such restrictions are invalid because of the "great danger" inherent in permitting "government to involve itself in the political process in this manner"); Marshall, False Campaign Speech and the First Amendment, 53 U. Pa. L. Rev. 285, 299 (2004) ("authorizing the government to decide what is true or false in campaign speech opens the door to partisan abuse"); Ashdown, Distorting Democracy: Campaign Lies in the 21st Century, 20 Wm. & Mary Bill Rts. J. 1085 (2012).

d. In a state law defamation action filed by attorney Johnnie Cochran, a California trial court found that defendant Tory had falsely claimed that Cochran owed him money, picketed Cochran's office with signs containing insults, and pursued him in public, chanting similar insults, in order to coerce Cochran into paying Tory money to get him to desist from such defamatory activity. Because Tory was judgment-proof, the California court enjoined him from continuing in this conduct. Is such a prior restraint permissible in these circumstances? See Tory v. Cochran, 544 U.S. 734 (2004) (invalidating the injunction in light of Cochran's death).

e. In light of changes in social media since the leading Supreme Court decisions on these issues, and the rise of so-called "fake news" that is said to undermine democratic discourse and deliberation, can the government intervene to make the publication of such "fake news" a crime?

UNITED STATES v. ALVAREZ, 567 U.S. — (2012). The federal Stolen Valor Act makes it a crime for any person to falsely state that he was "awarded any decoration or medal authorized by Congress for the Armed Forces of the United States." At a public meeting, Alvarez falsely stated to the persons present that he had received the Congressional Medal of Honor. This statement was made not to secure any particular benefit, but as "a pathetic attempt to gain respect that eluded him." He was prosecuted and convicted for violating the Act. The Supreme Court held the Act unconstitutional.

Justice Kennedy delivered a plurality opinion joined by Chief Justice Roberts and Justices Ginsburg and Sotomayor: "The Government [argues] that false statements 'have no First Amendment value in themselves,' and [are thus] beyond constitutional protection. [But the] Court has never endorsed the categorical rule [that] false statements receive no First Amendment protection." Although conceding that some false statement could be restricted, including defamatory statements, perjury, and fraudulent statements intended to extract something from another, Kennedy noted that the Stolen Valor Act applies broadly, without regard to whether anyone else is harmed by the falsehood. "Permitting the government to decree this speech to be a criminal offense [without regard to the circumstances] would endorse government authority to compile a list of subjects about which false statements are punishable. That governmental power has no clear limiting principle. Our constitutional tradition stands against the idea that we need Oceania's Ministry of Truth [citing George Orwell's *Nineteen-Eighty-Four*]. Were the Court to hold that the interest in truthful discourse alone is sufficient to sustain a ban on speech, [] would give government a broad censorial power unprecedented in [our] constitutional tradition."

Although agreeing that the "Government's interest in protecting the integrity of the Medal of Honor is beyond question," Kennedy concluded that in order to satisfy "exacting scrutiny" the restriction must "be 'actually necessary' to achieve" the Government's interests. Here, the "Government points to no evidence [that] the public's general perception of military awards is diluted by false claims such as those made by Alvarez." Moreover, the "Government has not shown, and cannot show, why counterspeech would not suffice to achieve its interest." Indeed, if the Government really wants to address this interest it can simply create an online database that "could list Congressional Medal of Honors winners." It would then "be easy to verify and expose false claims." In such circumstances, Kennedy held that the Act was unconstitutional.

Justice Breyer, joined by Justice Kagan, concurred. Breyer argued that "intermediate scrutiny" was appropriate in this situation, because "false factual statements are less likely than are true factual statements to make a valuable contribution to the marketplace of ideas [and] the government often has good reasons to prohibit such false speech." Although noting that the Court "has frequently [said] that false factual statements enjoy little First Amendment protection," Breyer observed that this does not mean "no protection at all." After all, he argued, false "factual statements can serve useful human objectives." In social contexts, for example, they can "prevent embarrassment, protect privacy, shield a person from prejudice, provide the sick with comfort, or preserve a child's innocence; in public contexts [they can] stop a panic or otherwise preserve calm in the face of danger."

Moreover, Breyer noted, there are dangers to free speech in allowing the government to punish even lies. As the Court recognized in New York Times v. Sullivan, "the threat of criminal prosecution for making a false statement can inhibit the speaker from making true statements, thereby 'chilling' a kind of speech that lies at the First Amendment's heart." In addition, he recognized, the inevitability of inaccurate statements in public discourse "provides a weapon to a government broadly empowered to prosecute falsity without more. And those who are unpopular may fear that the government will use that weapon selectively, say by prosecuting a pacifist who supports his cause by (falsely) claiming to have been a war hero, while ignoring members of other political groups who might make similar claims."

Like Justice Kennedy, though, Breyer conceded that the government can constitutionally restrict some types of factually false statements, such as fraud, defamation, perjury, false statements about terrorist threats, and impersonating a government official. But in such instances, he reasoned, "limitations of context, requirements of proof of injury, and the like, narrow the statute to a subset of lies where specific harm is more likely to occur," whereas the "statute before us lacks any such limiting features." Because the "government has provided no convincing explanation as to why a more finely tailored statute would not work," he concluded that "the statute as presently drafted works disproportionate constitutional harm. It consequently fails intermediate scrutiny, and so violates the First Amendment."

Justice Alito, joined by Justices Scalia and Thomas, dissented: "The [Act] was enacted to stem an epidemic of false claims about military decorations. [It] is a narrow statute that presents no threat to the freedom of speech. The statute reaches only knowingly false statements about hard facts directly within a speaker's personal knowledge. These lies have no value in and of themselves, and proscribing them does not chill any valuable speech. [Moreover,] the Act is strictly viewpoint neutral. [It] applies equally to all false statements, whether they tend to disparage or commend the Government, the military, or the system of military honors.

"[At the same time, these lies] inflict substantial harm. In many instances, the harm is tangible in nature: Individuals often falsely represent themselves as award recipients in order to obtain financial or other material rewards. [In] other cases the harm is less tangible, but nonetheless significant. The lies proscribed by the [Act] tend to debase the distinctive honor of military awards. [It] is well recognized in trademark law that the proliferation of cheap imitations of luxury goods blurs the '"signal" given out by the purchasers of the originals.' [Surely] it was reasonable for Congress to conclude that the goal of preserving the integrity of our country's top military honors is at least as worthy as that of protecting the prestige associated with fancy watches and designer handbags. . . .

"Time and again, this Court has recognized that as a general matter false factual statements possess no intrinsic First Amendment value. [There] are more than 100 federal criminal statutes that punish false statements made in connection with areas of federal agency concern. [Of course,] there are broad areas in which any attempt by the state to penalize purportedly false speech would present a grave and unacceptable danger of suppressing truthful speech. [But] the Stolen Valor Act presents no risk at all that valuable speech will be suppressed. The speech punished by the Act is not only verifiably false and entirely lacking in intrinsic value, but it also fails to serve any instrumental purpose that the First Amendment might protect. . . .

"The plurality [worries] that a decision sustaining the Stolen Valor Act might prompt Congress and the state legislatures to enact laws criminalizing lies about 'an endless list of subjects.' The plurality apparently fears that we will see laws making it a crime to lie about civilian awards such as college degrees. [This] concern is likely unfounded. With very good reason, military honors have traditionally been regarded as quite different from civilian awards. [In] any event, if the plurality's concern is not entirely fanciful, it falls outside the purview of the First Amendment. [If] there is a problem with, let us say, a law making it a criminal offense to falsely claim to have been a high school valedictorian, the problem is not the suppression of speech but the misuse of the criminal law, which should be reserved for conduct that inflicts or threatens truly serious societal harm. The objection to this hypothetical law would be the same as the objection to a law making it a crime to eat potato chips during the graduation ceremony. [The] safeguard against such laws is democracy, not the First Amendment. Not every foolish law is unconstitutional.

". . . The Stolen Valor Act is a narrow law enacted to address an important problem, and it presents no threat to freedom of expression."

Is there any good reason not to allow the government to punish "knowingly false statements about hard facts directly within a speaker's personal knowledge"? Because an individual knows to a virtual certainty whether or not he's won the Congressional Medal of Honor, does enforcement of the Stolen Valor Act pose *any* realistic risk of chilling valuable speech? Certainly, there would be a significant chilling effect if the government made it a crime to tell lies. After all, from a fact-finding standpoint, it is not usually not possible to determine with 100 percent certainty (a) whether a statement is objectively false, and (b) if it is, whether the speaker knew it to be false. But are those problems present in the context of the Stolen Valor Act? If there is zero risk of chilling valuable speech, is there any reason to protect lies of this sort?

Suppose a reporter lies about his identity in order to obtain information that reveals serious government corruption or suppose an investigator lies about his interest in purchasing a home in order to do a study of racial discrimination in housing. Do such lies have only low first amendment value? Can they constitutionally be forbidden? On the issue of high-value lies, see Chen & Marceau, High Value Lies, Ugly Truths, and the First Amendment, 68 Vand. L. Rev. 1435 (2015); Porat & Yadlin, A Welfarist Perspective on Lies, 91 Ind. L.J. 617

(2016); Han, Autobiographical Lies and the First Amendment's Protection of Self-Defining Speech, 87 N.Y.U. L. Rev. 70 (2012).

Assuming Justice Alito is correct that the government can constitutionally punish "knowingly false statements about hard facts directly within a speaker's personal knowledge" because such speech has no first amendment value and such restrictions chill no valuable speech, should it matter that the Stolen Valor Act punishes only some speech falling within the category, but not other speech falling within it? For example, is it constitutional for the government to punish "knowingly false statements about hard facts directly within a speaker's personal knowledge" if the statements relate to military medals but not if they relate to college degrees? Is there any first amendment problem in the government picking and choosing which of those statements to punish and which to leave alone? Is Justice Alito right that such choices pose no first amendment issue? See R.A.V. v. City of St. Paul, section D8 infra. For a helpful analysis, see Norton, Lies and the Constitution, 2012 Sup. Ct. Rev. 161.

Why is perjury different from what Alvarez did? Consider Tushnet, The Coverage/Protection Distinction in the Law of Freedom of Speech, 25 Wm. & Mary Bill Rts. J. 1073, 1100 (2017):

> Perhaps making perjury a crime could be defended as advancing the interest in preserving the integrity of judicial proceedings, or as penalizing insults to the legal system. *Alvarez* characterizes these as compelling interests, as it also characterizes the interest in preserving the integrity of the government's system of military honors. But, with respect to the Stolen Valor Act the Court saw no "direct causal link between the restriction imposed and the injury to be prevented." It is not clear to me how one could prove a causal link between an utterance and a harm as generalized as impairing the "integrity" of a system. Discussing the required causal connection, Justice Kennedy wrote, "The Government points to no evidence to support its claim that the public's general perception of military awards is diluted by false claims such as those made by Alvarez." Justice Kennedy did not discuss the existence or not of such evidence when he dealt with the way perjury "threatens the integrity of judgments that are the basis of the legal system[,]" and as far as I can tell none of the cases discussing the relation between perjury and the First Amendment offers such evidence.

HUSTLER MAGAZINE v. FALWELL, 485 U.S. 46 (1988). Hustler magazine published a "parody" of an advertisement concerning the nationally known minister Jerry Falwell. The relevant item contained the name and picture of Reverend Falwell and an "interview" in which Falwell says that his "first time" was during a drunken incestuous rendezvous with his mother in an outhouse. Small print at the bottom of the page noted "ad parody — not to be taken seriously." Falwell brought suit for libel and intentional infliction of emotional distress. The jury found against Falwell on the libel claim because the ad parody could not "reasonably be understood as describing actual facts" about Falwell. The jury found in favor of Falwell on the intentional infliction of emotional distress claim, however, and awarded $100,000 in compensatory damages and $50,000 in punitive damages. The court of appeals affirmed. The Supreme Court, in a unanimous decision, reversed.

Chief Justice Rehnquist wrote the opinion: "The sort of robust political debate encouraged by the First Amendment is bound to produce speech that is critical of [public officials and public figures]. Such criticism, inevitably, will not always be reasoned or moderate; public figures as well as public officials will be subject to 'vehement, caustic, and sometimes unpleasantly sharp attacks.' [*New York Times.*]

"Of course, this does not mean that *any* speech about a public figure is immune from sanction in the form of damages. [To the contrary, because] false statements of fact are particularly valueless, [we have consistently held since *New York Times*] that a public figure may hold a speaker liable for the damage to reputation caused by publication of a defamatory falsehood, but only if the statement was made 'with knowledge that it was false or with reckless disregard of whether it was false or not.' . . .

"Respondent argues [that] a different standard should apply in this case because here the State seeks to prevent not reputational damage, but the severe emotional distress suffered by the person who is the subject of an offensive publication. In respondent's view, [so] long as the utterance was intended to inflict emotional distress, was outrageous, and did in fact inflict serious emotional distress, it is of no constitutional import whether the statement was a fact or an opinion, or whether it was true or false. It is the intent to cause injury that is the gravamen of the tort, and the State's interest in preventing emotional harm simply outweighs whatever interest a speaker may have in speech of this type.

"Generally speaking the law does not regard the intent to inflict emotional distress as one which should receive much [solicitude]. But [while a] bad motive may be deemed controlling for purposes of tort liability in other areas of the law, we think the First Amendment prohibits such a result in the area of public debate about public figures. Were we to hold otherwise, there can be little doubt that political cartoonists and satirists would be subjected to damage awards without any showing that their work falsely defamed its subject. [The] appeal of the political cartoon or caricature is often based on exploration of unfortunate physical traits or politically embarrassing events — an exploration often calculated to injure the feelings of the subject of the portrayal. The art of the cartoonist is often not reasoned or evenhanded, but slashing and one-sided. . . .

"Respondent contends, however, that the caricature in question was so 'outrageous' as to distinguish it from more traditional political cartoons. [If] it were possible by laying down a principled standard to separate the one from the other, public discourse would probably suffer little or no harm. But we doubt that there is any such standard, and we are quite sure that the pejorative description 'outrageous' does not supply one. 'Outrageousness' in the area of political and social discourse has an inherent subjectiveness about it which would allow a jury to impose liability on the basis of the jurors' tastes or views, or perhaps on the basis of the dislike of a particular expression. An 'outrageousness' standard thus runs afoul of our longstanding refusal to allow damages to be awarded because the speech in question may have an adverse emotional impact on the audience. . . .

"We conclude that public figures and public officials may not recover for the tort of intentional infliction of emotional distress by reason of publications such as the one here at issue without showing in addition that the publication contains a false statement of fact which was made with 'actual malice,' i.e., with knowledge that the statement was false or with reckless disregard as to whether or not it was true. . . ."

Suppose X posts online a parody analogous to the one in *Hustler* about Y, a non-public figure whom he particularly dislikes. Can Y sue X for intentional infliction of emotional distress? Recall Snyder v. Phelps. Can Y sue X for invasion of privacy? Suppose X calls Y and, pretending to be a doctor, falsely tells him that his son has been killed in a car accident. Can Y sue X for intentional infliction of emotional distress in that situation after *Snyder* and *Hustler*?

Did the Court in *Hustler* give sufficient weight to Falwell's dignitary interests? Consider *Strauss Caricature*, 75 BVerfGE 369 (1987), in which the German Constitutional Court reviewed a civil action for damages brought by Bavarian Prime Minister Franz Josef Strauss against the magazine *Konkret*, which had published a series of disparaging cartoons portraying Strauss as a rutting pig. One cartoon, for example, depicted a pig, clearly drawn to be a caricature of Strauss, copulating with other pigs dressed in judicial robes. Noting that individual dignity is a "preferred constitutional value," the court held that the cartoons were not protected by Germany's constitutional guarantee of freedom of speech. The court explained that by depicting the Prime Minister as a pig engaged in bestial sexual conduct, the cartoons were clearly "intended to devalue the person concerned as a person, to deprive him of his dignity as a human being," and therefore went "too far" to merit constitutional protection. See Ronald Krotoszynski, The First Amendment in Cross-Cultural Perspective 112 (2006); Carmi, Dignity — The Enemy from Within: A Theoretical and Comparative Analysis of Human Dignity as a Free Speech Justification, 9 U. Pa. J. Const. L. 957 (2007).

2.   *"Nonnewsworthy" Disclosures of "Private" Information*

In the Pentagon Papers case, the Supreme Court took a strong position against government efforts to prohibit the publication of truthful information. In the years since, the Court has extended this position beyond the context of classified national security information. In Landmark Communications, Inc. v. Virginia, 435 U.S. 829 (1978), for example, the Court invalidated a state statute making it a crime for any person to divulge information regarding confidential matters pending before the state's Judicial Inquiry and Review Commission. Although the state argued that the disclosure of confidential information about pending investigations would create a clear and present danger to the effective operation of the commission by chilling the willingness of individuals to file complaints, the Court held that if the state wanted to protect this interest it had to do so by means other than restricting the press's publication of truthful information, for example, by adopting "careful internal procedures" to preserve confidentiality and by prohibiting participants in commission's proceedings from divulging confidential information.

Similarly, in Nebraska Press Association v. Stuart, 427 U.S. 539 (1976), the Court unanimously held unconstitutional a judge's order, issued in anticipation of a trial for a multiple murder that had attracted widespread news coverage, that restrained newspapers and broadcasters from disseminating accounts of confessions made by the accused or any other facts "strongly implicative" of the accused. The Court explained that even though the Constitution guarantees trial "by an impartial jury," and that a trial judge therefore "has a major responsibility" to protect the rights of a defendant against unduly prejudicial pretrial publicity, the judge must use alternative means to mitigate the danger, such as changing the trial venue, postponing the trial, questioning prospective jurors about their knowledge, sequestering jurors, and restricting what the lawyers, police, and witnesses may "say to anyone."

Are some types of information so private and so non-newsworthy, however, that government can constitutionally restrict their publication on the theory that, unlike the information in Pentagon Papers, *Landmark Communications* and *Nebraska Press*, they are of only "low" First Amendment value?

Cox Broadcasting Corp. v. Cohn

420 U.S. 469 (1975)

MR. JUSTICE WHITE delivered the opinion of the Court.

The issue before us in this case is whether, consistently with the First and Fourteenth Amendments, a State may extend a cause of action for damages for invasion of privacy caused by the publication of the name of a deceased rape victim which was publicly revealed in connection with the prosecution of the crime.

In August 1971, appellee's 17-year-old daughter was the victim of a rape and did not survive the incident. Six youths were soon indicted for murder and rape. Although there was substantial press coverage of the crime and of subsequent developments, the identity of the victim was not disclosed pending trial, perhaps because of Ga. Code Ann. §26-9901 (1972), which makes it a misdemeanor to publish or broadcast the name or identity of a rape victim. In April 1972, some eight months later, the six defendants appeared in court. . . .

In the course of the proceedings that day, appellant Wassell, a reporter covering the incident for his employer, learned the name of the victim from an examination of the indictments which were made available for his inspection in the courtroom. That the name of the victim appears in the indictments and that the indictments were public records available for inspection are not disputed. Later that day, Wassell broadcast over the facilities of station WSB-TV, a television station owned by appellant Cox Broadcasting Corp., a news report concerning the court proceedings. The report named the victim of the crime and was repeated the following day.

In May 1972, appellee brought an action for money damages against appellants, relying on §26-9901 and claiming that his right to privacy had been invaded by the television broadcasts giving the name of his deceased daughter. Appellants admitted the broadcasts but claimed that they were privileged under [the] First and Fourteenth Amendments. . . .

Georgia stoutly defends both §26-9901 and the State's common-law privacy action challenged here. Its claims are not without force, for powerful arguments can be made, and have been made, that however it may be ultimately defined, there *is* a zone of privacy surrounding every individual, a zone within which the State may protect him from intrusion by the press, with all its attendant publicity. Indeed, the central thesis of the root article by Warren and Brandeis, The Right to Privacy, 4 Harv. L. Rev. 193, 196 (1890), was that the press was overstepping its prerogatives by publishing essentially private information and that there should be a remedy for the alleged abuses.[16]

More compellingly, the century has experienced a strong tide running in favor of the so-called right of privacy. "[I]n one form or another, the right of privacy is by this time recognized and accepted in all but a very few jurisdictions." W. Prosser, Law of Torts 804 (4th ed.). . . .

These are impressive credentials for a right of privacy. [The] version of the privacy tort now before us — termed in Georgia "the tort of public disclosure," [is] that in which the plaintiff claims the right to be free from unwanted publicity about his private affairs, which, although wholly true, would be offensive to a person of ordinary sensibilities. [In] this sphere of collision between claims of privacy and those of the free press, the interests on both sides are plainly rooted in the traditions and significant concerns of our society. Rather than address the broader question whether truthful publications may ever be subjected to civil or criminal liability, [it] is appropriate to focus on the narrower interface between press and privacy that this case presents, namely, whether the State may impose sanctions on the accurate publication of the name of a rape victim obtained from public records — more specifically, from judicial records which are maintained in connection with a public prosecution and which themselves are open to public inspection. We are convinced that the State may not do so.

[In] a society in which each individual has but limited time and resources with which to observe at first hand the operations of his government, he relies necessarily upon the press to bring to him in convenient form the facts of those operations. [With] respect to judicial proceedings in particular, the function of the press serves to guarantee the fairness of trials and to bring to bear the beneficial effects of public scrutiny upon the administration of justice. [The] commission of crime, prosecutions resulting from it, and judicial proceedings arising from the prosecutions [are] without question events of legitimate concern to the public and consequently fall within the responsibility of the press to report the operations of government. . . .

[Moreover, the] interests in privacy fade when the information involved already appears on the public record. [The] publication of truthful information available on the public record contains none of the indicia of those limited categories of expression, such as "fighting" words, which "are no essential part of any exposition of ideas, and are of such slight social value as a step to truth that any benefit that may be derived from them is clearly outweighed by the social interest in order and morality." [*Chaplinsky.*]

By placing the information in the public domain on official court records, the State must be presumed to have concluded that the public interest was thereby

---

16. "Of the desirability — indeed of the necessity — of some such protection [of the right of privacy], there can, it is believed, be no doubt. The press is overstepping in every direction the obvious bounds of propriety and of decency. Gossip is no longer the resource of the idle and of the vicious, but has become a trade, which is pursued with industry as well as effrontery. To satisfy a prurient taste the details of sexual relations are spread broadcast in the columns of the daily papers. To occupy the indolent, column upon column is filled with idle gossip, which can only be procured by intrusion upon the domestic circle. The intensity and complexity of life, attendant upon advancing civilization, have rendered necessary some retreat from the world, and man, under the refining influence of culture, has become more sensitive to publicity, so that solitude and privacy have become more essential to the individual; but modern enterprise and invention have, through invasions upon his privacy, subjected him to mental pain and distress, far greater than could be inflicted by mere bodily injury. . . ."

being served. Public records by their very nature are of interest to those concerned with the administration of government, and a public benefit is performed by the reporting of the true contents of the records by the media. . . .

We are reluctant to embark on a course that would make public records generally available to the media but forbid their publication if offensive to the sensibilities of the supposed reasonable man. Such a rule would make it very difficult for the media to inform citizens about the public business and yet stay within the law. The rule would invite timidity and self-censorship and very likely lead to the suppression of many items that would otherwise be published and that should be made available to the public. At the very least, the First and Fourteenth Amendments will not allow exposing the press to liability for truthfully publishing information released to the public in official court records. If there are privacy interests to be protected in judicial proceedings, the States must respond by means which avoid public documentation or other exposure of private information. Their political institutions must weigh the interests in privacy with the interests of the public to know and of the press to publish. Once true information is disclosed in public court documents open to public inspection, the press cannot be sanctioned for publishing it. In this instance as in others reliance must rest upon the judgment of those who decide what to publish or broadcast. . . .

Reversed.

[Concurring opinions of Chief Justice Burger and Justices Powell and Douglas are omitted, as is Justice Rehnquist's dissenting opinion, which argues that there is a "want of jurisdiction."]

Note: *Invasion of Privacy and the First Amendment*

1. *The reach of* Cox Broadcasting. For similar decisions, see The Florida Star v. B.J.F., 491 U.S. 524 (1989) (newspaper cannot be held liable in damages for publishing a rape victim's name where the name was obtained from a publicly released police report); Oklahoma Publishing Co. v. District Court, 430 U.S. 308 (1977) (reporter cannot be prohibited from disclosing the name of a juvenile offender where the name was obtained at court proceedings that were open to the public); Smith v. Daily Mail Publishing Co., 443 U.S. 97 (1979) (newspaper cannot be punished for publishing the name and photograph of a juvenile offender where the newspaper had learned the suspect's name from several witnesses to the shooting and from police and prosecutors at the scene).

2. *Other sources of information.* Suppose a reporter learns the name of a rape victim from a witness rather than from a public document or proceeding. Consider also the following:

a. William Sidis was a famous child prodigy in 1910. His name and prowess were well known to newspaper readers of the period. At the age of eleven, he lectured to distinguished mathematicians on the subject of four-dimensional bodies, and at the age of sixteen, he graduated from Harvard College amid considerable public attention. Thereafter, Sidis sought to live as unobtrusively as possible, and his name disappeared from public view. In 1937, however, The New Yorker ran a biographical sketch of Sidis in its Where Are They Now? feature. The article described Sidis's early achievements, his general breakdown, and his attempts to conceal his identity through his chosen career as an insignificant clerk. The article further described in intimate detail Sidis's enthusiasm for collecting streetcar transfers, his interest in the lore of the Okamakammessett Indians, and his personal lifestyle and habits. Sidis sued for invasion of privacy. Sidis v. F-R Publishing Corp., 113 F.2d 806 (2d Cir. 1940).

b. Dorothy Barber suffered from a rare condition that caused her to lose weight, even though she ate often. In its Medicine section, Time magazine reported on Barber's condition, disclosing her name and publishing a photograph that showed "her face, head and arms, with bedclothes over her chest." The article was titled Starving Glutton. Barber sued for invasion of privacy. Barber v. Time, Inc., 348 Mo. 1199, 159 S.W.2d 291 (1942).

c. In 1956, Marvin Briscoe and another man hijacked a truck. After paying his debt to society, Briscoe abandoned his life of crime, led an exemplary life, and made many friends who were unaware of the incident in his earlier life. In 1967, Reader's Digest published an article on The Big Business of Hijacking, which reported: "Typical of many beginners, Marvin Briscoe and [another man] stole a 'valuable-looking' truck in Danville, Ky., and then fought a gun battle with the local police only to learn that they had hijacked four bowling-pin spotters." Briscoe sued for invasion of privacy. Briscoe v. Reader's Digest Association, 4 Cal. 3d 529, 93 Cal. Rptr. 866, 483 P.2d 34 (1971).

3. *Nonnewsworthiness and "low" value.* As Justice White suggested in *Cox Broadcasting,* in most states the truthful disclosure of "private" facts concerning an individual constitutes a tort if the disclosure would be "highly offensive" to a reasonable person and is not in itself newsworthy. Is the tort of public disclosure compatible with the first amendment? Should it matter that the harm caused by such speech cannot be corrected by counterspeech? That there is no significant "risk that government will [use the tort to] insulate itself from the critical views of its enemies"? L. Tribe, American Constitutional Law 889 (2d ed. 1988).

Is "nonnewsworthy" information of "low" first amendment value? Consider Bloustein, The First Amendment and Privacy: The Supreme Court Justice and the Philosopher, 28 Rutgers L. Rev. 41, 56–57 (1974): "[The] weight to be given 'the public interest in obtaining information' should depend on whether or not the information is relevant to the public's governing purposes. 'Public interest,' taken to mean curiosity, must be distinguished from 'public interest,' taken to mean value to the public of receiving information of governing importance. There is [no first amendment] right to satisfy public curiosity and publish lurid gossip about private lives."

On the other hand, consider Zimmerman, Requiem for a Heavyweight: A Farewell to Warren and Brandeis's Privacy Tort, 68 Cornell L. Rev. 291, 332–334 (1983):

> [Contemporary] society [uses] knowledge about the private lives of individual members [to] preserve and enforce social norms. [By] providing people with a way to learn about social groups to which they do not belong, gossip increases intimacy and a sense of community among disparate groups and individuals. [It] is a basic form of information exchange that teaches about other lifestyles and attitudes, and through which community values are changed or reinforced. [Perceived] in this way, gossip contributes directly to the first amendment "marketplace of ideas."

Even if "nonnewsworthy" information has only "low" first amendment value, might there nonetheless be sound reasons to reject such a standard? In *Gertz* the Court expressed "doubt" as to "the wisdom of committing [the task of deciding what information is relevant to self-government] to the conscience of judges." Is the "nonnewsworthiness" concept simply too vague to protect first amendment rights? Consider Kalven, Privacy in Tort Law — Were Warren and Brandeis Wrong?, 31 Law & Contemp. Probs. 326, 336 (1966): "What is at issue [is] whether the claim of privilege is not so overpowering as virtually to swallow the tort. [Surely] there is force to the simple contention that whatever is in the news media is by definition newsworthy, that the press must in the nature of things be the final arbiter of newsworthiness."

4. *The interest in "privacy."* Are the interests protected by the public disclosure tort of sufficient importance to justify a restriction of even "low"-value expression? How would you compare the gravity of the harm caused by speech that "invades privacy" with the gravity of the harm in the incitement, fighting words, and libel contexts? Consider Bloustein, supra, at 54: "In [public disclosure] cases the individual has been profaned by laying a private life open to public view. The intimacy and private space necessary to sustain individuality and human dignity has been impaired by turning a private life into a public spectacle. The innermost region of being [has] been bruised by exposure to the world." See also Gewirtz, Privacy and Speech, 2001 Sup. Ct. Rev. 139. On the other hand, consider Posner, The Right of Privacy, 12 Ga. L. Rev. 393, 419 (1978): "If what is revealed is something the individual has concealed for purposes of misrepresenting himself to others, the fact that disclosure is offensive to him and of limited interest to the public at large is no better reason for protecting his privacy than if a seller advanced such arguments for being allowed to continue to engage in false advertising of his goods."

5. *Privacy and the internet.* Consider the following views:

a. Stone, Privacy, the First Amendment, and the Internet, in Levmore & Nussbaum, eds., The Offensive Internet 174, 194 (2010):

> [L]egal enforcement of the concept of non-newsworthiness [is now] staggeringly problematic. Consider [a] student who posts accurately on a blog dealing with her school that a teacher [was] seen in a gay bar. Within the confines of the school community, it would be difficult to argue that this is nonnewsworthy information or that the student could be punished for revealing it to others. But with modern technology, this information will be available not only to those in the particular school community, at that time and place, but to all Internet users and forever. [In] the world of the Internet it is no longer possible to segregate audiences based on immediate relevance of information to the community. [This] may be liberating or it may be unnerving and unwelcome, but in no event is it a state of affairs that can meaningfully be addressed by the invasion of privacy tort. [As a practical matter, the disclosure tort is a relic] of an earlier and vastly simpler era. . . .
>
> The most realistic way to protect privacy today is at its source. By prohibiting highly intrusive methods of gaining information that people want to keep confidential it is still possible to enable individuals who truly care about their privacy to preserve it, if they act carefully and with discretion. But once information is out of the bottle, once we share it with others, once others know it, we can longer hope to put it back. If that era ever existed, it is now the past.

b. Solove, Speech, Privacy, and Reputation on the Internet, in Levmore & Nussbaum, eds., The Offensive Internet 15, 16, 18, 21, 28 (2010):

> Before the Internet, gossip would spread by word of mouth and remain within the boundaries of a social circle. [In] the village of yesteryear, people had to live under

the ever-present judgmental eye of their fellow villagers. [One] of the benefits of the modern world was that people could escape from the oppressiveness of the small village fishbowl. But no longer. We now live in a "global village," [but] with a pernicious twist. In the small village, people knew each other well, and disreputable information would be judged within the context of a person's entire life. Now, people are judged out of context based on information fragments found online. . . .

It is still possible to protect privacy, but doing so requires that we rethink outdated understandings of the concept. [The modern understanding of privacy should recognize] that a person should retain some control over personal information that becomes publicly available. [For example, suppose] a person discloses information on a Facebook page that is set up so that only the person's friends can view it. Suppose the person has fifty friends. Is the information still private? I believe [that] it is. [If] one of the person's friends were to disseminate the information beyond the group of friends, such a disclosure could be understood to be a breach of confidentiality.

6. *"Revenge porn."* Would a prohibition on "revenge porn" be constitutional? "Revenge porn" refers to the practice of posting nude or sexually suggestive photographs or videos online without the consent of the person depicted. Consider the following proposed statute:

> An actor commits criminal invasion of privacy if the actor harms another person by knowingly disclosing an image of another person whose intimate parts are exposed or who is engaged in a sexual act, when the actor knows that the other person did not consent to the disclosure and when the actor knows that the other person expected that the image would be kept private, under circumstances where the other person had a reasonable expectation that the image would be kept private. The fact that a person has consented to the possession of an image by another person does not imply consent to disclose that image more broadly.

D. Citron, Hate Crimes in Cyberspace (2014). The proposed statute contains exceptions for "lawful and common practices of law enforcement, criminal reporting, legal proceedings; or medical treatment," for the reporting of unlawful conduct, for voluntary exposures in public or commercial settings, and for disclosures that relate to the public interest.

Is the proposed statute constitutional? If so, how (if at all) is this disclosure different from unconsented disclosure of verbal descriptions of sexual acts or from disclosure of other forms of embarrassing information gained through an intimate relationship? Consider Waldman, A Breach of Trust: Fighting Nonconsensual Pornography, 102 Iowa L. Rev. 709 (2017): "The distribution of sexually graphic or intimate images of individuals without their consent [can] have devastating effects: Victims experience severe anxiety and depression and they are often placed in physical danger. They lose their jobs and have difficulty finding new ones. Many have to recede from online life, move far away, and even change their names to escape revenge porn's long shadow."

For the argument that laws against revenge porn violate the first amendment, see Goldberg, Free Speech Consequentialism, 116 Colum. L. Rev. 687, 743-749 (2016):

> [Advocates for the criminalization of revenge porn maintain that such speech is socially harmful and does not] "contribute any benefits to society." Yet this does not separate revenge porn from any number of categories of protected speech that may

cause others emotional distress and are considered by some to possess little value. . . . There is not a principled way to create, at the wholesale level, an unprotected category of speech around revenge porn. . . . However, partners can protect their own interests by explicitly asking their partners to agree not to [disclose such images.] The best way to regulate revenge porn is through private (noncriminal) law, as a breach of implied contract. . . .

7. *Unlawfully obtained information.* In *Cox Broadcasting*, the Court emphasized that the information had been obtained lawfully by the press from government documents. Suppose, however, the information is obtained unlawfully? In *Bartnicki v. Vopper*, 532 U.S. 514 (2001), a radio station aired a tape of a telephone conversation that the station received from an anonymous source. In the circumstances, the station knew that the tape had been made in violation of federal and state anti-wiretap statutes. The Court held that these statutes could not constitutionally be applied to the radio station because the topic of the call was a matter of public concern (collective-bargaining negotiations between a union representing teachers at a public high school and the local school board) and the broadcaster had not participated directly in the unlawful interception (even though the broadcaster knew that the material had been obtained unlawfully). Without deciding whether there might be some circumstances in which the privacy interest is "strong enough to justify the application" of the statute, such as when there is disclosure of "domestic gossip [of] purely private concern," the Court held that the enforcement of the statute in this case "implicates core purposes of the First Amendment because it imposes sanctions on the publication of truthful information of public concern." In this situation, "privacy concerns give way when balanced against the interest in publishing matters of public importance." Recall the *Pentagon Papers* case. Suppose in *Bartnicki* that the radio station itself had unlawfully intercepted the phone call. Should that lead to a different result?

3.   Threats

A "threat" is generally defined as "a statement of an intention to inflict pain, injury, damage, or other hostile action on someone if she does not do something the person making the statement wants her to do." In what circumstances, and for what reasons, can the state constitutionally punish individuals who make threats? Are threats of only "low" First Amendment value?

BRIDGES v. CALIFORNIA, 314 U.S. 252 (1941). *Bridges* arose out of litigation between two rival unions. While a motion for new trial was pending, Bridges, president of the union against whom the trial judge had ruled, published a copy of a telegram he had sent to the Secretary of Labor describing the judge's decision as "outrageous" and suggesting that, if the decision were enforced, his union would call a strike that would tie up the port of Los Angeles. As a result of this publication, Bridges was found guilty of contempt of court.

In an opinion by Justice Black, the Court held the contempt conviction unconstitutional: "The 'clear and present danger' language of the *Schenck* case has afforded practical guidance in a great variety of cases in which the scope of constitutional protections of freedom of expression was in issue. [What] finally emerges from the 'clear and present danger' cases is a working principle that the substantive evil must be extremely serious and the degree of imminence extremely high before utterances can be punished . . . .

"Let us assume that the telegram could be construed as an announcement of Bridges' intention to call a strike, something which [neither] the general law of California nor the court's decree prohibited. With an eye on the realities of the situation, we cannot assume that Judge Schmidt was unaware of the possibility of a strike as a consequence of his decision. If he was not intimidated by the facts themselves, we do not believe that the most explicit statement of them could have sidetracked the course of justice."

Justice Frankfurter, joined by Chief Justice Stone and Justices Roberts and Byrnes, dissented: "Of course freedom of speech and of the press [should] be employed in comment upon the work of [courts]. But [freedom] of expression can hardly carry implications that nullify the guarantees of impartial trials. [Comment] however forthright is one thing. Intimidation with respect to specific matters still in judicial suspense, quite another. [To be punishable, a publication] must refer to a matter under consideration and constitute in effect a threat to its impartial disposition. It must be calculated to create an atmospheric pressure incompatible with rational, impartial adjudication. But to interfere with justice it need not succeed. As with other offenses, the state should be able to proscribe attempts that fail because of the danger that attempts may succeed. . . .

"The publication of the telegram was regarded by the state supreme court as 'a threat that if an attempt was made to enforce the decision, the ports of the entire Pacific Coast would be tied up.' [This] occurred immediately after counsel had moved to set aside the judgment which was criticized, so unquestionably there was a threat to litigation obviously alive. It would be inadmissible dogmatism for us to say that in the context of the immediate case [this] could not have dominated the mind of the judge before whom the matter was pending."

Is clear and present danger the correct standard in a case like *Bridges*? Is Justice Frankfurter correct in asserting that Bridges "threatened" the judge? Should a threat be thought of only "low"-value speech "because it operates more like a physical action than [a] communication of ideas or emotions"? Gey, The Nuremberg Files and the First Amendment Value of Threats, 78 Tex. L. Rev. 541, 591–593 (2000). See K. Greenawalt, Speech, Crime and the Uses of Language 94 (1989) (the first amendment does not protect speech that "involves the creation of prospective harmful consequences in order to achieve one's objective").

Consider the following situations: (a) X threatens to kill Judge Y unless she acquits Z. (b) X threatens to disclose that Judge Y is having a lesbian relationship unless she acquits Z. (c) X threatens to oppose Judge Y's reelection unless she acquits Z. (d) X threatens to call a general strike unless Judge Y convicts Z. If a "threat" is subject to regulation because it affects behavior by coercion rather than by persuasion, does that rationale support any distinction among situations (a), (b), (c), and (d)?

WATTS v. UNITED STATES, 394 U.S. 705 (1969). Petitioner, during a public rally at the Washington Monument, stated to a small group of persons: "I have already received my draft classification as 1-A and I have got to go for my physical this Monday coming. I am not going. If they ever make me carry a rifle the first man I want to get in my sights is L.B.J." For this remark, petitioner was convicted of violating a federal statute prohibiting any person "knowingly and willfully [to make] any threat to take the life of or to inflict bodily harm upon the President of the United States." Although conceding that the statute was constitutional "on its face," the Court reversed the conviction on the ground that "the kind of political hyperbole indulged in by petitioner" did not constitute a "threat" within the meaning of the statute. Petitioner's "only offense," the Court concluded, "was 'a kind of very crude offensive method of stating a political opposition to the President.'" Do you agree that the statute is constitutional "on its face"? Is a threat to kill the President of "low" first amendment value?

PLANNED PARENTHOOD v. AMERICAN COALITION OF LIFE ACTIVISTS, 290 F.3d 1058 (9th Cir. 2002). Suppose defendant establishes a website (called the "Nuremberg Files") that states that its purpose is to "collect dossiers on abortionists in anticipation that one day we may be able to hold them on trial for crimes against humanity," lists the names and addresses of abortion providers, includes photographs of abortion providers in Wild-West-style "Wanted" posters, and crosses out the names of abortion providers who have been murdered. Can this expression be restricted on the ground that the website constitutes "incitement"? On the ground that it constitutes a "threat"? Should it matter that the website was established after an unrelated individual had murdered three abortion providers after distributing similar posters naming them as "Wanted" persons?

The Court of Appeals, in a six-to-five *en banc* decision, held that the operators of the Nuremberg Files website could be held liable in damages and enjoined because the site constituted an unprotected threat: "If ACLA had merely endorsed or encouraged the violent actions of others, its speech would be protected. [Citing *Brandenburg*.] However, while advocating violence is protected, threatening a person with violence is not. [Although the] posters contain no language that is [literally] a threat, whether a particular statement may properly be considered to be a threat is governed by an objective standard — whether a reasonable person would foresee that the statement would be interpreted by those to whom the maker communicates the statement as a serious expression of intent to harm or assault. [It] is not necessary that the defendant intend to, or be able to carry out his threat; the only intent requirement for a true threat is that the defendant intentionally or knowingly communicate the [threat] *with the intent to intimidate*. [It] is making a threat to intimidate that makes ACLA's conduct unlawful. . . .

"The true threats analysis [in this case] turns on the poster pattern. [The website does not contain] any language that is overtly threatening. [It] is use of the 'Wanted'-type format in the context of the poster pattern — poster followed by murder — that constitutes the threat. Because of the pattern, a 'Wanted'-type poster naming a specific doctor who provides abortions was perceived by physicians, who are providers of reproductive health services, as a serious threat of death or bodily harm. [The] posters are a true threat because, [like] burning crosses, they connote something they do not literally say, yet both the actor and the recipient get the message. To the doctor who performs abortions, these posters meant 'You'll be shot or killed.' [As] a direct result of having [a] poster out on them, physicians wore bullet-proof vests and took other extraordinary security measures to protect themselves and their families. ACLA had every reason to foresee that its expression [would] elicit this reaction. Physicians' fear did not simply happen; ACLA intended to intimidate them from doing what they do. This [is] conduct that [lacks] any protection under the First Amendment.

Violence is not a protected value. Nor is a true threat of violence with intent to intimidate."

The dissenting judges argued as follows: "[I]t is not illegal — and cannot be made so — merely to say things that would frighten or intimidate the listener. For example, when a doctor says, 'You have cancer and will die within six months,' it is not a threat, even though you almost certainly will be frightened. [By] contrast, 'If you don't stop performing abortions, I'll kill you' is a true threat and surely illegal. The difference between a true threat and protected expression is this: A true threat warns of violence or other harm that the speaker controls. . . .

"[As the majority argues,] because context matters, the statements [in this case] could reasonably be interpreted as an effort to intimidate plaintiffs into ceasing their abortion-related activities. If that were enough to strip the speech of First Amendment protection, there would be nothing left to decide. But the Supreme Court has told us that '[s]peech does not lose its protected character . . . simply because it may embarrass others *or coerce them into action.*' [*Claiborne Hardware.*] In other words, some forms of intimidation enjoy constitutional protection. The majority does not point to any statement by defendants that they intended to inflict bodily harm on plaintiffs, nor is there any evidence that defendants took any steps whatsoever to plan or carry out physical violence against anyone. Rather, the majority relies on the fact that 'the poster format itself had acquired currency as a death threat for abortion providers.' [But none of the doctors who were killed were killed by anyone connected with this Web page.]

"The majority tries to fill this gaping hole in the record by noting that defendants 'kn[ew] the fear generated among those in the reproductive health services community who were singled out for identification on a "Wanted"-type poster.' But a statement does not become a true threat because it instills fear in the listener; as noted above, many statements generate fear in the listener, yet are not true threats and therefore may not be punished or enjoined consistent with the First Amendment. In order for the statement to be a threat, it must send the message that the speakers themselves — or individuals acting in concert with them — will engage in physical violence. [Yet] the opinion points to no evidence that defendants [would] have been understood by a reasonable listener as saying that *they* will cause the harm.

"From the point of view of the victims, it makes little difference whether the violence against them will come from the makers of the posters or from unrelated third parties; bullets kill their victims regardless of who pulls the trigger. But it makes a difference for the purpose of the First Amendment. Speech — especially political speech, as this clearly was — may not be punished or enjoined unless it falls into one of the narrow categories of unprotected speech recognized by the Supreme Court: true threat, incitement, fighting words, etc. [The] posters can be viewed, at most, as a call to arms for *other* abortion protesters to harm plaintiffs. However, the Supreme Court made it clear that under *Brandenburg*, encouragement or even advocacy of violence is protected by the First Amendment [unless the harm is both likely and imminent]. . . .

"The Nuremberg Files website is clearly an expression of a political point of view. The posters and the website are designed both to rally political support for the views espoused by defendants, and to intimidate plaintiffs and others like them into desisting abortion related activities. This political agenda may not be to the liking of many people — political dissidents are often unpopular — but the speech, including the intimidating message, does not constitute a direct threat because there is no evidence [that] the speakers intend to resort to physical violence if their threat is not heeded. We have recognized that statements communicated directly to the target are much more likely to be true threats than those, as here, communicated as part of a public protest. [In] deciding whether the coercive speech is protected, it makes a big difference whether it is contained in a private communication — a face-to-face confrontation, a telephone call, a dead fish wrapped in newspaper — or is made during the course of public discourse. The reason for this distinction is obvious: Private speech is aimed only at its target. Public speech, by contrast, seeks to move public opinion and to encourage those of like mind. Coercive speech that is part of public discourse enjoys far greater protection than identical speech made in a purely private context. In this case, defendants said nothing remotely threatening, yet they find themselves crucified financially. Who knows what other neutral statements a jury might imbue with a menacing meaning based on the activities of unrelated parties. ..."

See Rothman, Freedom of Speech and True Threats, 25 Harv. J.L. & Pub. Poly. 283 (2001) (to prove a "true" threat, the prosecution should have to prove (a) that the speaker knowingly or recklessly made a statement that would frighten or intimidate the victim with the threat of harm; (b) that the speaker knowingly or recklessly suggested that the threat would be carried out by the speaker or his co-conspirators; and (c) that a reasonable person who heard the statement would conclude that it was meant to threaten the victim with harm).

In what circumstances, if any, might the display of a swastika or a burning cross constitute a "true threat"? Suppose a black family moves into an all-white community and the next day wakes up to discover a burning cross on the street in front of their home. Can the persons who erected the cross be punished for making a threat? In the incitement situation, the Court, following the leading of Judge Learned Hand in *Masses*, seems to require that for incitement of unlawful conduct to come within the low-value category of express incitement the incitement must be *express*. Is a burning cross an *express* threat? Does it make any sense to require express incitement but not express threats? On cross-burning as a threat, see Virginia v. Black, section D8, infra.

Can an individual be punished for threatening words if she does not intend for them to be perceived as a threat? In Elonis v. United States, 135 S. Ct. 2001 (2015), the petitioner posted on Facebook a series of threatening statements directed toward his wife and others. He maintained that he was an aspiring rap artists and that his speech was intended as mere hyperbole, analogizing it to the violence sometimes expressed in rap music. He was convicted under a federal statute making it a crime to transmit in interstate commerce "any threat . . . to injure the person of another." The trial court instructed the jury that it could convict if a reasonable person would regard the statements as threats and declined to instruct the jury that the petitioner had to intend to communicate a threat.

The Supreme Court, in an opinion by Chief Justice Roberts, reversed the conviction, but declined to reach the constitutional question. As a matter of statutory construction, the Court held that the government was required to prove more than mere negligence, but did not specify what mental state was required.

In a separate opinion, Justice Alito argued that recklessness, meaning disregard of a risk of which the speaker was aware, was sufficient to satisfy the demands of the first amendment. In Alito's view, "threats inflict great harm and have little if any social value," and "whether or not the person making a threat intends to cause harm, the damage is the same." Drawing an analogy to libel law, he concluded that "reckless disregard" for the harm caused should be sufficient to meet the demands of the first amendment in the threat context as well.

In another separate opinion, Justice Thomas, adopting an originalist approach that invoked state statutes and English precedent at the time of the framing, argued that the first amendment in this situation requires a showing of neither specific intent to threaten nor recklessness. Mere negligence, he concluded, is sufficient.

4.   Commercial Advertising

Although the *Chaplinsky* dictum made no reference to commercial advertising, only a month after *Chaplinsky* the Court added commercial advertising to its list of "unprotected" expression in Valentine v. Chrestensen, 316 U.S. 52 (1942). In *Chrestensen*, the Court upheld a prohibition on the distribution of any "handbill [or] other advertising matter [in] or upon any street." Although conceding that a similar prohibition on noncommercial expression would violate the first amendment, the Court announced, without explanation or analysis, that the amendment imposed "no such restraint on government as respects purely commercial advertising." See also Breard v. Alexandria, 341 U.S. 622 (1951) (upholding a prohibition on door-to-door solicitation of magazine subscriptions).

Despite *Chrestensen*, the precise contours and rationale of the commercial advertising doctrine remained obscure. The mere presence of a commercial motive, for example, was not deemed dispositive, as evidenced by the Court's continued protection of books, movies, newspapers, and other forms of expression produced and sold for profit. Moreover, in New York Times v. Sullivan, section D1 supra, the Court rejected an argument that the paid "political" advertisement there at issue was unprotected commercial expression:

> The publication here was not a "commercial" advertisement in the sense in which the word was used in *Chrestensen*. It communicated information, expressed opinion, recited grievances, [and] protested claimed abuses. [That] the Times was paid for publishing the advertisement is as immaterial in this connection as is the fact that newspapers and books are sold. [Any] other conclusion would discourage newspapers from carrying "editorial advertisements" of this type, and so might shut off an important outlet for the promulgation of information and ideas by persons who do not themselves have access to publishing facilities.

In the 1970s, the Court began to narrow the scope of the commercial speech doctrine. In Bigelow v. Virginia, 421 U.S. 809 (1975), for example, the Court reversed the conviction of an individual who, prior to the Court's decision in Roe v. Wade, 410 U.S. 113 (1973), and in violation of Virginia law, published in his newspaper an advertisement announcing the availability of legal abortions in New York. The Court distinguished *Chrestensen* on the ground that the advertisement in *Bigelow* "did more than simply propose a commercial transaction. It contained factual material of clear 'public interest.'" The Court emphasized that *Chrestensen*'s holding was "distinctly a limited one."

Virginia State Board of Pharmacy v. Virginia Citizens Consumer Council
425 U.S. 748 (1976)

[An organization of prescription drug consumers challenged as violative of the first and fourteenth amendments a Virginia statute providing that a pharmacist licensed in Virginia is guilty of unprofessional conduct if he "publishes, advertises, or promotes, directly or indirectly, in any manner whatsoever, any amount, price, fee, premium, discount, rebate or credit terms [for] any drugs which may be dispensed only by prescription." Although drug prices varied strikingly throughout the state and even within the same locality, the challenged law effectively prevented the dissemination of any prescription drug price information, since only licensed pharmacists were authorized to dispense such drugs. A three-judge district court held the law invalid. The Supreme Court affirmed.]

MR. JUSTICE BLACKMUN delivered the opinion of the Court. . . . *

IV

The appellants contend that the advertisement of prescription drug prices is outside the protection of the First Amendment because it is "commercial speech." There can be no question that in past decisions the Court has given some indication that commercial speech is unprotected. [Discussing *Chrestensen*, *Breard*, and *Bigelow*.] . . .

[The] question whether there is a First Amendment exception for "commercial speech" is squarely before us. Our pharmacist does not wish to editorialize on any subject, cultural, philosophical, or political. He does not wish to report any particularly newsworthy fact, or to make generalized observations even about commercial matters. The "idea" he wishes to communicate is simply this: "I will sell you the X prescription drug at the Y price." Our question, then, is whether this communication is wholly outside the protection of the First Amendment.

V

We begin with several propositions that already are settled or beyond serious dispute. It is clear, for example, that speech does not lose its First Amendment protection because money is spent to project it, as in a paid advertisement of one form or another. [Citing New York Times v. Sullivan.] Speech likewise is protected even though it is carried in a form that is "sold" for profit, [and] even though it may involve a solicitation to purchase or otherwise pay or contribute money. . . .

---

* [At the outset, Justice Blackmun rejected a claim that, even if first amendment protection attached to the flow of drug price information, it is a protection enjoyed only by advertisers and not by the appellees, who were mere recipients of such information. Justice Blackmun reasoned that, "where a speaker exists, [the] protection afforded is to the communication, to its source and to its recipients both." Thus, "if there is a right to advertise, there is a reciprocal [first amendment] right to receive the advertising." — Eds.]

If there is a kind of commercial speech that lacks all First Amendment protection, therefore, it must be distinguished by its content. Yet the speech whose content deprives it of protection cannot simply be speech on a commercial subject. No one would contend that our pharmacist may be prevented from being heard on the subject of whether, in general, pharmaceutical prices should be regulated, or their advertisement forbidden. Nor can it be dispositive that a commercial advertisement is noneditorial, and merely reports a fact. Purely factual matter of public interest may claim protection. . . .

Our question is whether speech which does "no more than propose a commercial transaction" is so removed from any "exposition of ideas," [*Chaplinsky*], and from "'truth, science, morality, and arts in general, in its diffusion of liberal sentiments on the administration of Government,'" that it lacks all protection. Our answer is that it is not.

Focusing first on the individual parties to the transaction that is proposed in the commercial advertisement, we may assume that the advertiser's interest is a purely economic one. That hardly disqualifies him from protection under the First Amendment. The interests of the contestants in a labor dispute are primarily economic, but it has long been settled that both the employee and the employer are protected by the First Amendment when they express themselves on the merits of the dispute in order to influence its outcome. [We] know of no requirement that, in order to avail themselves of First Amendment protection, the parties to a labor dispute need address themselves to the merits of unionism in general or to any subject beyond their immediate dispute. . . .

As to the particular consumer's interest in the free flow of commercial information, that interest may be as keen, if not keener by far, than his interest in the day's most urgent political debate. Appellees' case in this respect is a convincing one. Those whom the suppression of prescription drug price information hits the hardest are the poor, the sick, and particularly the aged. A disproportionate amount of their income tends to be spent on prescription drugs; yet they are the least able to learn, by shopping from pharmacist to pharmacist, where their scarce dollars are best spent. When drug prices vary as strikingly as they do, information as to who is charging what becomes more than a convenience. It could mean the alleviation of physical pain or the enjoyment of basic necessities.

Generalizing, society also may have a strong interest in the free flow of commercial information. Even an individual advertisement, though entirely "commercial," may be of general public interest. The facts of decided cases furnish illustrations: advertisements stating that referral services for legal abortions are available, [*Bigelow*]; that a manufacturer of artificial furs promotes his product as an alternative to the extinction by his competitors of fur-bearing mammals, and that a domestic producer advertises his product as an alternative to imports that tend to deprive American residents of their jobs. [Obviously,] not all commercial messages contain the same or even a very great public interest element. There are few to which such an element, however, could not be added. Our pharmacist, for example, could cast himself as a commentator on store-to-store disparities in drug prices, giving his own and those of a competitor as proof. We see little point in requiring him to do so, and little difference if he does not.

Moreover, there is another consideration that suggests that no line between publicly "interesting" or "important" commercial advertising and the opposite kind could ever be drawn. Advertising, however tasteless and excessive it sometimes may seem, is nonetheless dissemination of information as to who is producing and selling what product, for what reason, and at what price. So long as we preserve a predominantly free enterprise economy, the allocation of our resources in large measure will be made through numerous private economic decisions. It is a matter of public interest that those decisions, in the aggregate, be intelligent and well informed. To this end, the free flow of commercial information is indispensable. [And] if it is indispensable to the proper allocation of resources in a free enterprise system, it is also indispensable to the formation of intelligent opinions as to how that system ought to be regulated or altered. Therefore, even if the First Amendment were thought to be primarily an instrument to enlighten public decisionmaking in a democracy, we could not say that the free flow of information does not serve that goal.

Arrayed against these substantial individual and societal interests are a number of justifications for the advertising ban. These have to do principally with maintaining a high degree of professionalism on the part of licensed pharmacists. Indisputably, the State has a strong interest in maintaining that professionalism. . . .

Price advertising, it is argued, will place in jeopardy the pharmacist's expertise and, with it, the customer's health. It is claimed that the aggressive price competition that will result from unlimited advertising will make it impossible for the pharmacist to supply professional services in the compounding, handling, and dispensing of prescription drugs. Such services are time consuming and expensive; if competitors who economize by eliminating them are permitted to advertise their resulting lower prices, the more painstaking and conscientious pharmacist will be forced either to follow suit or to go out of business. It is also claimed that prices might not necessarily fall as a result of advertising. If one pharmacist advertises, others must, and the resulting expense will inflate the cost of drugs. [Finally] it is argued that damage will be done to the professional image of the pharmacist. This image, that of a skilled and specialized craftsman, attracts talent to the profession and reinforces the better habits of those who are in it. Price advertising, it is said, will reduce the pharmacist's status to that of a mere retailer.

The strength of these proffered justifications is greatly undermined by the fact that high professional standards, to a substantial extent, are guaranteed by the close regulation to which pharmacists in Virginia are subject. [At] the same time, we cannot discount the Board's justifications entirely. The Court regarded justifications of this type sufficient to sustain the advertising bans challenged on due process and equal protection grounds. [Citing, e.g., Williamson v. Lee Optical of Oklahoma, 348 U.S. 483 (1955).]

The challenge now made, however, is based on the First Amendment. This casts the Board's justifications in a different light, for on close inspection it is seen that the State's protectiveness of its citizens rests in large measure on the advantages of their being kept in ignorance. The advertising ban does not directly affect professional standards one way or the other. It affects them only through the reactions it is assumed people will have to the free flow of drug price information. . . .

It appears to be feared that if the pharmacist who wishes to provide low cost, and assertedly low quality, services is permitted to advertise, he will be taken up on his offer by too many unwitting customers. They will choose the low-cost, low-quality service and drive the "professional" pharmacist out of business. They will respond only to costly and excessive advertising, and end up paying the price. They will go from one pharmacist to another, following the discount, and destroy the pharmacist-customer relationship. They will lose respect for the profession because it advertises. All this is not in their best interests, and all this can be avoided if they are not permitted to know who is charging what.

There is, of course, an alternative to this highly paternalistic approach. That alternative is to assume that this information is not in itself harmful, that people will perceive their own best interests if only they are well enough informed, and that the best means to that end is to open the channels of communication rather than to close them. If they are truly open, nothing prevents the "professional" pharmacist from marketing his own assertedly superior product, and contrasting it with that of the low-cost, high-volume prescription drug retailer. But the choice among these alternative approaches is not ours to make or the Virginia General Assembly's. It is precisely this kind of choice, between the dangers of suppressing information, and the dangers of its misuse if it is freely available, that the First Amendment makes for us. . . .

VI

In concluding that commercial speech, like other varieties, is protected, we of course do not hold that it can never be regulated in any way. Some forms of commercial speech regulation are surely permissible. We mention a few only to make clear that they are not before us and therefore are not foreclosed by this case.

There is no claim, for example, that the prohibition on prescription drug price advertising is a mere time, place, and manner restriction. We have often approved restrictions of that kind provided that they are justified without reference to the content of the regulated speech, that they serve a significant governmental interest, and that in so doing they leave open ample alternative channels for communication of the information. [Whatever] may be the proper bounds of time, place, and manner restrictions on commercial speech, they are plainly exceeded by this Virginia statute, which singles out speech of a particular content and seeks to prevent its dissemination completely.

Nor is there any claim that prescription drug price advertisements are forbidden because they are false or misleading in any way. Untruthful speech, commercial or otherwise, has never been protected for its own sake. [*Gertz.*] Obviously, much commercial speech is not provably false, or even wholly false, but only deceptive or misleading. We foresee no obstacle to a State's dealing effectively with this problem.[24] The First Amendment, as we construe it today,

---

24. In concluding that commercial speech enjoys First Amendment protection, we have not held that it is wholly undifferentiable from other forms. There are commonsense differences between speech that does "no more than propose a commercial transaction," and other varieties. Even if the differences do not justify the conclusion that commercial speech is valueless, and thus subject to complete suppression by the State, they nonetheless suggest that a different degree of protection is necessary to insure that the flow of truthful and legitimate commercial information is unimpaired. The truth of commercial speech, for example, may be more easily verifiable by its disseminator than, let us say, news reporting or political commentary, in that ordinarily the advertiser seeks to disseminate information about a specific product or service that he himself provides and presumably knows more about than anyone else. Also, commercial speech may be more durable than other kinds. Since advertising is the sine qua non of commercial profits, there is little likelihood of its being chilled by proper regulation and forgone entirely.

Attributes such as these, the greater objectivity and hardiness of commercial speech, may make it less necessary to tolerate inaccurate statements for fear of silencing the speaker. [They] may also make it appropriate to require that a commercial message appear in such a form, or include such additional information, warnings, and disclaimers, as are necessary to prevent its being deceptive. [They] may also make inapplicable the prohibition against prior restraints. . . .

does not prohibit the State from insuring that the stream of commercial information flows cleanly as well as freely. . . .

Also, there is no claim that the transactions proposed in the forbidden advertisements are themselves illegal in any way. [Finally,] the special problems of the electronic broadcast media are likewise not in this case. . . .

What is at issue is whether a State may completely suppress the dissemination of concededly truthful information about entirely lawful activity, fearful of that information's effect upon its disseminators and its recipients. Reserving other questions,[25] we conclude that the answer to this one is in the negative.

The judgment of the District Court is affirmed.

[Justice Stevens did not participate. Chief Justice Burger concurred in an opinion emphasizing the reservations set out in footnote 25. Justice Stewart concurred in an opinion emphasizing that government still should be free to regulate false or misleading commercial advertising.]

MR. JUSTICE REHNQUIST, dissenting.

The logical consequences of the Court's decision in this case, a decision which elevates commercial intercourse between a seller hawking his wares and a buyer seeking to strike a bargain to the same plane as has been previously reserved for the free marketplace of ideas, are far reaching indeed. Under the Court's opinion the way will be open not only for dissemination of price information but for active promotion of prescription drugs, liquor, cigarettes, and other products the use of which it has previously been thought desirable to discourage. Now, however, such promotion is protected by the First Amendment so long as it is not misleading or does not promote an illegal product or enterprise. . . .

The Court speaks of the consumer's interest in the free flow of commercial information, particularly in the case of the poor, the sick, and the aged. It goes on to observe that "society also may have a strong interest in the free flow of commercial information." [One] need not disagree with either of these statements in order to feel that they should presumptively be the concern of the Virginia Legislature, which sits to balance these and other claims in the process of making laws such as the one here under attack. The Court speaks of the importance in a "predominantly free enterprise economy" of intelligent and well-informed decisions as to allocation of resources. While there is again much to be said for the Court's observation as a matter of desirable public policy, there is certainly nothing in the United States Constitution which requires the Virginia Legislature to hew to the teachings of Adam Smith in its legislative decisions regulating the pharmacy profession. E.g., Nebbia v. New York, 291 U.S. 502 (1934); Olsen v. Nebraska, 313 U.S. 236 (1941). . . .

The Court insists that the rule it lays down is consistent even with the view that the First Amendment is "primarily an instrument to enlighten public decision-making in a democracy." I had understood this view to relate to public decision-making as to political, social, and other public issues, rather than the decision of a particular individual as to whether to purchase one or another kind of shampoo.

---

25. We stress that we have considered in this case the regulation of commercial advertising by pharmacists. Although we express no opinion as to other professions, the distinctions, historical and functional, between professions may require consideration of quite different factors. Physicians and lawyers, for example, do not dispense standardized products; they render professional *services* of almost infinite variety and nature, with the consequent enhanced possibility for confusion and deception if they were to undertake certain kinds of advertising.

It is undoubtedly arguable that many people in the country regard the choice of shampoo as just as important as who may be elected to local, state, or national political office, but that does not automatically bring information about competing shampoos within the protection of the First Amendment. . . .

In the case of "our" hypothetical pharmacist, he may now presumably advertise not only the prices of prescription drugs, but may attempt to energetically promote their sale so long as he does so truthfully. Quite consistently with Virginia law requiring prescription drugs to be available only through a physician, "our" pharmacist might run any of the following representative advertisements in a local newspaper:

> Pain getting you down? Insist that your physician prescribe Demerol. You pay a little more than for aspirin, but you get a lot more relief.

> Can't shake the flu? Get a prescription for Tetracycline from your doctor today.

> Don't spend another sleepless night. Ask your doctor to prescribe Seconal without delay.

Unless the State can show that these advertisements are either actually untruthful or misleading, it presumably is not free to restrict in any way commercial efforts on the part of those who profit from the sale of prescription drugs to put them in the widest possible circulation. But such a line simply makes no allowance whatever for what appears to have been a considered legislative judgment in most States that while prescription drugs are a necessary and vital part of medical care and treatment, there are sufficient dangers attending their widespread use that they simply may not be promoted in the same manner as hair creams, deodorants, and toothpaste. The very real dangers that general advertising for such drugs might create in terms of encouraging, even though not sanctioning, illicit use of them by individuals for whom they have not been prescribed, or by generating patient pressure upon physicians to prescribe them, are simply not dealt with in the Court's opinion. . . .

Note: Virginia Pharmacy *and the "Free Flow of Commercial Information"*

1. *Is commercial speech of "low" first amendment value?* Consider the following:
a. Jackson and Jeffries, Commercial Speech: Economic Due Process and the First Amendment, 65 Va. L. Rev. 1, 17–18, 30–31 (1979):

> [The Court's conclusion in *Virginia Pharmacy* that commercial speech is relevant to self-government is] a non sequitur. It apparently rests on the assertion that because regulation of the free enterprise system is a matter of political choice, commercial advertising that plays a part in the functioning of the free enterprise system is *for that reason* politically significant speech. But in terms of relevance to political decisionmaking, advertising is neither more nor less significant than a host of other market activities that legislatures concededly may regulate. [The] decisive point is the absence of any principled distinction between commercial soliciting and other aspects of economic activity. [In *Virginia Pharmacy*,] economic due process is resurrected, clothed in the ill-fitting garb of the first amendment.

For a critique of this argument, see Shiffrin, The First Amendment and Economic Regulation: Away from a General Theory of the First Amendment, 78 Nw. U. L. Rev. 1212, 1225-1239 (1983).

b. Redish, The First Amendment in the Marketplace: Commercial Speech and the Values of Free Expression, 39 Geo. Wash. L. Rev. 429, 433, 441-444 (1971):

> If the individual is to achieve the maximum degree of material satisfaction permitted by his resources, he must be presented with as much information as possible concerning the relative merits of competing products. After receiving the competing information, the individual will then be in a position [to] rationally decide which combination of features best satisfies his personal needs. [Viewed in this light,] informational commercial speech furthers legitimate first amendment purposes. When the individual is presented with rational grounds for preferring one product or brand over another, he is encouraged to consider the competing information [and to] exercise his abilities to reason and think; this aids him towards the intangible goal of rational self-fulfillment.

Compare R. Collins and D. Skover, The Death of Discourse 77, 80, 105, 114 (1996):

> On the eve of the twenty-first century, America's marketplace of ideas has largely become a junkyard of commodity ideology. [Today's] mass advertising often has less to do with products than lifestyles, less to do with facts than image, and less to do with reason than romance. [In modern mass advertising, entire] categories of commercial communication are essentially bereft of any real informational content. [If] commercial communication is safe [in the free speech marketplace], it is not because it *actually* furthers the First Amendment's traditional values of rational decisionmaking and self-realization. [The] real reason for constitutional protection of modern mass advertising is less ennobling: It is speech in the service of selling.

c. Coase, Advertising and Free Speech, 6 J. Legal Stud. 1, 2, 14 (1977):

> It seems to be believed that [if the government intervened in the market for ideas, it] would be inefficient and wrongly motivated. [How] different is the government assumed to be when we come to economic regulation. In this area government is considered to be competent in action and pure in motivation. [Since] we are concerned with [the] same government, why is it that it is regarded as incompetent and untrustworthy in the one market and efficient and reliable in the other? [It] seems to me that the arguments [used] to support freedom in the market for ideas are equally applicable in the market for goods.

Compare Scanlon, Freedom of Expression and Categories of Expression, 40 U. Pitt. L. Rev. 519, 541 (1979): "[Commercial speech deserves less than full first amendment protection because] we regard the government as much less partisan in the competition between commercial firms than in the struggle between religious or political views." See also Stone, Ronald Coase's First Amendment, 54 J. Law & Econ. 367, 374 (2011); Brudney, The First Amendment and Commercial Speech, 53 B.C. L. Rev. 1153, 1179, 1168 (2013).

d. Blasi, The Pathological Perspective and the First Amendment, 85 Colum. L. Rev. 449, 486, 488 (1985):

> Commercial advertising was never a concern in any of the historical political struggles over freedom of expression. The first amendment claimants in disputes over commercial advertising often are sophisticated and driven by the profit motive. The speech in question is brief and intended to evoke a reflexive, even if somewhat delayed, response from listeners. There is a strong tradition of government regulation of [advertising]. [Perhaps] most important, [the] spectacle of voluminous litigation over [product] advertising, conducted in the name of the first amendment, [would] undercut [society's] belief that first amendment freedoms represent a noble commitment well worth preserving even in the face of serious anxieties, risks, and costs. [Thus, we should] exclude commercial advertising from the protection of the first amendment.

e. Justice Powell's opinion for the Court in Ohralik v. Ohio State Bar, 436 U.S. 447 (1978):

> In rejecting the notion [that expression concerning purely commercial transactions] "is wholly outside the protection of the First Amendment," [we] were careful [in *Virginia Pharmacy* not to discard] the "commonsense distinction between speech proposing a commercial transaction [and] other varieties of speech." [Indeed,] to require a parity of constitutional protection for commercial and non-commercial speech alike could invite dilution, simply by a leveling process, of the force of the Amendment's guarantee with respect to the latter kind of speech. Rather than subject the First Amendment to such a devitalization, we have instead afforded commercial speech a limited measure of protection, commensurate with its subordinate position in the scale of First Amendment values. . . .

2. *What is "commercial" speech?* In *Virginia Pharmacy*, the Court reaffirmed that the content of the speech, rather than the speaker's commercial or profit motivation, is determinative. What matters, in other words, is not whether the speaker is out to make money, but whether the expression does "no more than propose a commercial transaction." Is this definition satisfactory? Does a billboard displaying a cigarette package in a pastoral setting constitute "commercial" speech under this definition? What about corporate issue advertising that describes the corporation, its activities, or its policies without explicitly identifying any of the corporation's products or services? Consider Comment, First Amendment Protection for Commercial Advertising: The New Constitutional Doctrine, 44 U. Chi. L. Rev. 205, 236 (1976): "[Commercial speech should be defined as] (1) speech that refers to a specific brand name product or service, (2) made by a speaker with a financial interest in the sale of the advertised product or service, in the sale of a competing product or service, or in the distribution of the speech, (3) that does not advertise an activity itself protected by the first amendment."

Is a law regulating the manner in which companies can state their prices a regulation of commercial speech? See Expressions Hair Design v. Schneiderman, 582 U.S. — (2017).

In Bolger v. Youngs Drug Products Corp., 463 U.S. 60 (1983), the Court held that various "informational pamphlets" dealing with contraceptives constituted "commercial" speech. "One of [the] pamphlets, 'Condoms and Human Sexuality,' specifically [referred] to a number of Trojan-brand condoms manufactured by [Youngs] and [described] the advantages of each type. [Another], 'Plain Talk about Venereal Disease,' [discussed] condoms without any specific reference to those manufactured by [Youngs]." The Court explained:

> The mere fact that these pamphlets are conceded to be advertisements clearly does not compel the conclusion that they are commercial speech. [Citing New York Times v. Sullivan.] Similarly, the reference to a specific product does not by itself render the pamphlets commercial speech. Finally, the fact that Youngs has an economic motivation for mailing the pamphlets would clearly be insufficient by itself to turn the materials into commercial speech. [The] combination of *all* these characteristics, however, provides strong support for [the] conclusion that the informational pamphlets [are] commercial speech. [Moreover, the pamphlets] constitute commercial speech notwithstanding the fact that they contain discussions of important public issues such as venereal disease and family planning. [Advertising] which "links a product to a current public debate" is not thereby entitled to the constitutional protection afforded noncommercial speech. [Finally, that] a product is referred to generically [and not by brand name] does not [remove] it from the realm of commercial speech. [For] a company with sufficient control of the market for a product may be able to promote the product without reference to specific brand names. [Indeed, in] this case, Youngs describes itself as "the leader in the manufacture and sale" of contraceptives.

Note: *Truthful, Nondeceptive Commercial Advertising after Virginia Pharmacy*

In the years immediately after *Virginia Pharmacy*, the Court reaffirmed and expanded its protection of truthful, nondeceptive commercial speech:

1. *Lawyer advertising.* In Bates v. State Bar of Arizona, 433 U.S. 350 (1977), the Court invalidated a state court rule prohibiting attorney advertising, as applied to a newspaper advertisement stating "DO YOU NEED A LAWYER? Legal Services at Very Reasonable Fees" and listing fees for a variety of services, such as uncontested divorce, uncontested adoption, uncontested nonbusiness bankruptcy, and name change. The Court rejected the state's argument that attorney advertising of routine services would adversely affect professionalism and the quality of legal services, stir up unnecessary litigation, increase the overhead costs of lawyers, cause increased fees, and create difficulties in enforcing the line between protected and unprotected advertisements. Without specifying precisely what standard it was applying, the Court concluded that none "of the proffered justifications [rises] to the level of an acceptable reason for the suppression of all advertising by attorneys."

2. *"For sale" signs.* In Linmark Associates v. Township of Willingboro, 431 U.S. 85 (1977), the Court invalidated an ordinance prohibiting the display of "For Sale" or "Sold" signs on all but model homes. The ordinance was designed to prevent "panic selling" in a racially integrated residential community that had recently experienced "white flight" in response to a sharp increase in the nonwhite proportion of the population. The Court recognized that the goal of "promoting stable, racially integrated housing" is "vital," but nonetheless held that the township had failed to establish that the ordinance "was necessary to achieve this objective." In any event, "the constitutional defect in this ordinance [is] far more basic," for the township "has sought to restrict the free flow of these data because it fears that otherwise homeowners will make decisions inimical to what the [town council] views as the homeowners' self-interest and the corporate interest of the township: they will choose to leave the town. [If] dissemination of

this information can be restricted, then every locality in the country can suppress any facts that reflect poorly on the locality, so long as a plausible claim can be made that disclosure would cause the recipients of the information to act 'irrationally.' [*Virginia Pharmacy*] denies government such sweeping powers."

3. *Contraceptive advertising.* In Carey v. Population Services International, 431 U.S. 678 (1977), the Court invalidated a prohibition on the advertising of contraceptives because the state's concerns "that advertisements of contraceptive products would be offensive and embarrassing to those exposed to them, and that permitting them would legitimate sexual activity of young people" are "classically not justifications validating the suppression of expression protected by the First Amendment." See also Bolger v. Youngs Drug Products Corp., 463 U.S. 60 (1983) (invalidating a federal statute prohibiting the mailing of unsolicited advertisements for contraceptives because the interest in shielding "recipients of mail from materials that they are likely to find offensive" is not sufficiently substantial to justify the suppression of "protected speech").

CENTRAL HUDSON GAS v. PUBLIC SERVICE COMMISSION OF NEW YORK, 447 U.S. 557 (1980). The commission permitted electric utilities to engage in institutional and informational advertising, but, to further the conservation of energy, prohibited such utilities to engage in promotional advertising designed to stimulate the use of electricity. The Court, in an opinion by Justice Powell, held the order invalid. After observing that the "Constitution [accords] a lesser protection to commercial speech than to other constitutionally guaranteed expression," the Court maintained that in its prior decisions, it had implicitly "developed" a "four-part analysis" for commercial speech cases:

"[First], we must determine whether the expression is protected by the First Amendment. For commercial speech to come within that provision, it at least must concern lawful activity and not be misleading. [Second], we ask whether the asserted governmental interest is substantial. [Third, if] both inquiries yield positive answers, we must determine whether the regulation directly advances the governmental interest. [And fourth], if the governmental interest could be served as well by a more limited restriction on commercial speech, the excessive restrictions cannot survive."

Applying this analysis to the ban on promotional advertising, the Court noted that the "Commission does not claim that the expression at issue is either inaccurate or relates to unlawful activity." Moreover, "in view of our country's dependence on energy resources beyond our control, no one can doubt the importance of energy conservation. Plainly, therefore, the state interest asserted is substantial." Further, "the State's interest in energy conservation is directly advanced by the Commission order." Thus, "the critical inquiry" is whether the commission's complete suppression of speech ordinarily protected by the first amendment is "no more extensive than necessary to further the State's interest." The Court found the complete ban on promotional advertising to be too "extensive" because the commission "has not demonstrated that its interest in conservation cannot be protected adequately by more limited regulation of [the] format and content of Central Hudson's advertising. It might, for example, require that the advertisements include information about the relative efficiency and expense of the offered service." The Court thus concluded that, "in the absence of a showing that more limited speech regulation would be ineffective, we cannot approve the complete suppression of Central Hudson's advertising."

Justice Blackmun, joined by Justice Brennan, concurred, but argued that the Court's standard weakened the protection accorded commercial advertising in *Virginia Pharmacy*. Justice Rehnquist dissented. He argued that New York's order is essentially "an economic regulation to which virtually complete deference should be accorded by this Court," for "in terms of constitutional values," the ban on promotional advertising is "virtually indistinguishable" from a decision of the commission to raise the price of electricity in order to conserve energy.

Note: Truthful, Nondeceptive Commercial Advertising

1. *Retreat?* Confirming Justice Blackmun's concern that *Central Hudson* seemed to retreat from the Court's prior understanding of the first amendment's protection of truthful, nondeceptive commercial advertising, in a few post–*Central Hudson* decisions the Court did seem to take a relatively deferential approach to laws regulating commercial advertising.

In Posadas de Puerto Rico Associates v. Tourism Co. of Puerto Rico, 478 U.S. 328 (1986), for example, the Court, in a five-to-four decision, upheld a Puerto Rican statute that prohibited any advertising of legal casino gambling aimed at the residents of Puerto Rico. In an opinion by Justice Rehnquist, the Court explained that Puerto Rico apparently believed that "[excessive] casino gambling among local residents [would] produce serious harmful effects" similar to those that had "motivated the vast majority of the 50 States to prohibit casino gambling." The Court held this was a "substantial" government interest and declared that the law directly advanced that interest, within the meaning of *Central Hudson*.

In response to the argument that, having chosen to legalize casino gambling for residents of Puerto Rico, the first amendment prohibited the legislature from using restrictions on advertising to accomplish its goal of reducing demand for such gambling, the Court reasoned that because "the government could have enacted a wholesale prohibition of the underlying conduct" it was permissible for the government to take the "less intrusive step of allowing the conduct, but reducing the demand through restrictions on advertising." The Court observed that "the greater power to completely ban casino gambling necessarily includes the lesser power to ban advertising of casino gambling," and that it would "be a strange constitutional doctrine which would concede to the legislature the authority to totally ban a product or activity, but deny to the legislature the authority to forbid the stimulation of demand for the product or activity through advertising." After *Posadas*, could a state constitutionally ban all cigarette advertising?

See also Florida Bar v. Went for It, 515 U.S. 618 (1995) (upholding a rule of the Florida bar prohibiting any lawyer to send "a written communication to a prospective client for the purpose of obtaining professional employment if [the] communication concerns an action for personal injury [arising out of] an accident [involving] the person to whom the communication is addressed," because the challenged rule protects "in a direct and material way" the "privacy and tranquility of personal injury victims [against] intrusive, unsolicited contact by lawyers").

2. *Retreat from retreat.* The retreat from *Virginia Pharmacy* was short-lived, however. Consider the following decisions:

a. In Rubin v. Coors Brewing Co., 514 U.S. 476 (1995), the Court invalidated section 205(e)(2) of the Federal Alcohol Administration Act, which prohibited beer labels from displaying alcohol content. The government had argued that the labeling ban was necessary to prevent "strength wars" among brewers who, without regulation, would seek to compete in the marketplace based on the potency of their beer.

b. In Greater New Orleans Broadcasting Association, Inc. v. United States, 527 U.S. 173 (1999), the Court unanimously invalidated 18 U.S.C. §1304, which prohibited radio and television broadcasters from carrying advertisements about privately operated commercial casino gambling, as applied to broadcast stations located in states where such gambling is legal.

c. In 44 Liquormart, Inc. v. Rhode Island, 517 U.S. 484 (1996), the Court invalidated a Rhode Island statute prohibiting "advertising in any manner whatsoever" of the price of any alcoholic beverage, except for price tags or signs displayed within licensed premises and not visible from the street: "[When] a State [prohibits] the dissemination of truthful, nonmisleading commercial [messages], there is [little] reason to depart from the rigorous review that the First Amendment generally demands. [Bans] against truthful, nonmisleading commercial speech [usually] rest solely on the offensive assumption that the public will respond 'irrationally' to the truth. The First Amendment directs us to be especially skeptical of regulations that seek to keep people in the dark for what the government perceives to be their own good. . . .

"The State [cannot] satisfy the requirement that its restriction on speech be no more extensive than necessary. It is perfectly obvious that alternative forms of regulation that would not involve any restriction on speech would be more likely to achieve the State's goal of promoting temperance. [Higher] prices can be maintained [by] increased taxation. Per capita purchases could be limited as is the case with prescription drugs. Even educational campaigns focused on the problems [of] drinking might prove to be more effective. [Thus,] the price advertising ban cannot survive the more stringent constitutional review that *Central Hudson* [concluded] was appropriate for the complete suppression of truthful, nonmisleading commercial speech."

Justice Thomas filed a concurring opinion: "In cases such as this, in which the government's asserted interest is to keep legal users of a product or service ignorant in order to manipulate their choices in the marketplace, [the state's interest] is per se illegitimate and can no more justify regulation of 'commercial' speech than it can justify regulation of 'noncommercial' speech. [I] would [hold that] all attempts to dissuade legal choices by citizens by keeping them ignorant are impermissible."

d. In Lorillard Tobacco Co. v. Reilly, 533 U.S. 525 (2001), the Court invalidated Massachusetts regulations governing the advertising of cigarettes, smokeless tobacco products, and cigars. The regulations prohibited outdoor advertising of such products within one thousand feet of a public playground or elementary or secondary school: "The State's interest in preventing underage tobacco use is substantial, and even compelling, but it is no less true that the sale and use of tobacco products by adults is a legal activity. [Tobacco] retailers and manufacturers have an interest in conveying truthful information about their products to adults, and adults have a corresponding interest in receiving truthful information about tobacco products. [The state] has failed to show that [these regulations] are not more extensive than necessary to advance the State's substantial interest in preventing underage tobacco use."

In a concurring opinion, Justice Thomas argued that "there is no 'philosophical or historical basis for asserting that "commercial" speech is of "lower value" than "noncommercial" speech.'" Thus, the "asserted government interest in keeping people ignorant by suppressing expression 'is per se illegitimate and can no more justify regulation of "commercial" speech than it can justify regulation of "noncommercial" speech.'"

e. Thompson v. Western States Medical Center, 535 U.S. 357 (2002) concerned the regulation of drug compounding, a process by which a pharmacist combines ingredients to create a medication tailored to the needs of an individual patient. Compounding is typically used to prepare medications that are not commercially available. It is a traditional component of the practice of pharmacy. The federal Food, Drug and Cosmetic Act of 1938 prohibits any person to manufacture or sell any "new drug" without prior FDA approval. Until the early 1990s, the FDA left the regulation of drug compounding to the states. In the early 1990s, however, the FDA became increasingly concerned about the practice. In 1997 Congress enacted the Food and Drug Administration Modernization Act which, among other things, expressly exempted compounded drugs from the FDA's standard drug approval requirements if, but only if, the providers of those drugs did not advertise them.

The Court, in a five-to-four decision, held this restriction unconstitutional: "[The] Government [notes] that the FDCA's [general] drug approval requirements are critical to the public health [because the safety] of a new drug needs to be established by rigorous, scientifically valid clinical studies, [rather than by the] impressions of individual doctors, who cannot themselves compile sufficient [data]. [But] 'because obtaining FDA approval for a new drug is a costly process, requiring [such] approval of all drug products compounded by pharmacies for the particular needs of an individual patient would, as a practical matter, eliminate the practice of compounding, and thereby [eliminate] compounded drugs for those patients who have no alternative treatment.' [Thus], the Government needs to be able to draw a line between small-scale compounding and large-scale drug manufacturing. That line must distinguish compounded drugs produced on such a small scale that they could not [realistically] undergo [costly] safety and efficacy testing from drugs produced and sold on a large enough scale that they could undergo such testing and therefore must do so.

"[The] Government has failed to demonstrate that the speech restrictions are 'not more extensive than is necessary to serve [its] interest[s].' [Several] non-speech related means of drawing a line between compounding and large-scale manufacturing might be possible here. [For] example, the Government could ban the use of 'commercial scale manufacturing [for] compounding drug products.' [It could cap] the amount of any particular compounded drug [that] a pharmacist may make or sell in a given period of time. [The] Government has not offered any reason why these possibilities, alone or in combination, would be insufficient to prevent compounding from occurring on such a scale as to undermine the new drug approval process."

Justice Breyer, joined by Chief Justice Rehnquist and Justices Stevens and Ginsburg, dissented: "There is considerable evidence that consumer oriented advertising will create strong consumer-driven demand for a particular drug, [and] there is strong evidence that doctors will often respond affirmatively to a patient's request for a specific drug that the patient has seen advertised. [I] do not deny that the statute restricts the circulation of some truthful information. [Nonetheless], this Court has not previously held that commercial advertising restrictions automatically violate the First Amendment. Rather, the Court has applied a more flexible test. [It] has done so because it has concluded that, from a constitutional perspective, commercial speech does not warrant application of the Court's strictest speech-protective tests. [The] Court, in my view, gives insufficient weight [in this case] to the Government's regulatory rationale, and too readily assumes the existence of practical alternatives. It thereby applies the commercial speech doctrine too strictly."

f. Sorrell v. IMS Health Inc., 564 U.S. 552 (2011) involved the process of "detailing," by which pharmaceutical manufacturers market their drugs to doctors. This typically involves a salesman's (or detailer's) visit to a doctor's office to persuade the doctor to prescribe a particular brand-name drug. Knowledge of the doctor's prescription practices — called "prescriber-identifying information" — enables the detailer to determine which doctors are likely to be interested in particular drugs and how best to present the sales pitch. Pharmacies receive prescriber-identifying information whenever they fill prescriptions. Many pharmacies sell this information to data miners, who then analyze the information and sell it to pharmaceutical manufacturers, who then give it to their detailers to enable them to refine their marketing approach and increase sales. In 2007, Vermont enacted legislation prohibiting pharmacies from selling prescriber-identifying information for the purpose of marketing prescription drugs.

The Court, in a six-to-three decision, held that this law violated the First Amendment: "[The State] contends that [its law] advances important public policy goals by lowering the costs of medical services and promoting public health. If prescriber-identifying information were available for use by detailers, the State contends, then detailing would be effective in promoting brand-name drugs that are more expensive and less safe than generic alternatives. [While these] goals may be proper, [the law] does not advance them in a permissible way. [Those] who seek to censor [expression] often assert that disfavored speech has adverse effects. But the 'fear that people would make bad decisions if given truthful information' cannot justify content-based burdens on speech. [Citing *Thompson, Virginia Board of Pharmacy*, and *44 Liquormart*]."

Justice Breyer, joined by Justices Ginsburg and Kagan, dissented: "[O]ur cases make clear that the First Amendment offers considerably less protection to the maintenance of a free marketplace for goods and services [than for] a marketplace that provides access to 'social, political, esthetic, moral, and other ideas and experiences.' [To] apply a 'heightened' standard of review [in a case like this] would risk what then-Justice Rehnquist [once described] as a 'retur[n] to the bygone era of *Lochner*.' [By] inviting courts to scrutinize whether a State's legitimate regulatory interests can be achieved in less restrictive ways whenever they touch (even indirectly) upon commercial speech, today's majority risks repeated the mistakes of the past."

3. *The implications of* Rubin, Greater New Orleans, Liquormart, Lorillard, Thompson, *and* Sorrell. After these six decisions, can you envision any circumstances in which the Court would uphold the regulation of truthful, nondeceptive commercial advertising of a lawful product or service because the advertising might cause consumers to make undesirable decisions? Is the Court's concern with paternalism in these cases warranted? For a skeptical view, see Brudney, The First Amendment and Commercial Speech, 53 B.C. L. Rev. 1153, 1194-1197 (2013). What about advertising directed at children? Can the state constitutionally ban cigarette advertisements in school newspapers? In comic books?

4. *A Corporate Takeover of the First Amendment?* A recent analysis of Supreme Court and lower court decisions finds that in the wake of *Virginia Pharmacy* "corporations have begun to displace individuals" as the primary beneficiaries of

the first amendment. This analysis finds that until *Virginia Pharmacy* only expressive businesses, like media companies, were able to convince the Court to strike down laws regulating their expressive activity, but that since that decision the number of cases in which non-expressive businesses have successfully invoked the protection of the first amendment has increased dramatically, substantially displacing cases in which individuals are the primary beneficiary of the first amendment. See Coates, Corporate Speech and the First Amendment: History, Data, and Implications, 30 Const. Comment. 223 (2015); Kessler, The Early Years of First Amendment Lochnerism, 116 Colum. L. Rev. 1915 (2016).

Note: Other Regulations of Commercial Advertising

1. *Regulating the means of commercial advertising.* The cases considered above involved restrictions on the advertising of particular services or products. Suppose the government restricts *all* commercial advertising, as a class. How might that affect the analysis? Consider City of Cincinnati v. Discovery Network, 507 U.S. 410 (1993). In 1989, Cincinnati authorized respondent companies to place sixty-two freestanding newsracks on public property for the purpose of distributing free magazines that consisted primarily of advertisements for respondents' services. In 1990, motivated by its interest in the safety and attractive appearance of its streets and sidewalks, Cincinnati revoked respondents' permits on the ground that the magazines were "commercial handbills" whose distribution on public property could be prohibited. The Court, in an opinion by Justice Stevens, invalidated the restriction:

> [Respondents] do [not] question the substantiality of the city's interest in safety and esthetics. [The critical issue is whether the city has met its burden under *Central Hudson* and *Fox*] to establish a "reasonable fit" between its legitimate interests [and] its [ban] on newsracks dispensing "commercial handbills." . . .
>
> The city argues that there is a close fit [because] every decrease in the number of such dispensing devices necessarily effects an increase in safety and an improvement in the attractiveness of the cityscape. [This is] an insufficient justification for the discrimination against respondents' use of newsracks that are no more harmful than the [1,500 to 2,000 noncommercial newsracks that the city permits]. The major premise supporting the city's argument is the proposition that commercial speech has only a low value. Based on that premise, the city contends that the fact that assertedly more valuable publications are allowed to use newsracks does not undermine its judgment that its esthetic and safety interests are stronger than the interest in allowing commercial speakers to have similar access to the reading public.
>
> We cannot agree. [In] this case, the distinction [between commercial and non-commercial speech] bears no relationship whatsoever to the particular interests that the city has asserted. It is therefore an impermissible means of responding to the city's admittedly legitimate interests. [Respondents'] newsracks are no greater an eyesore than the newsracks permitted to remain on Cincinnati's sidewalks. [In] the absence of some basis for distinguishing between "newspapers" and "commercial handbills" that is relevant to an interest asserted by the city, we are unwilling to recognize Cincinnati's bare assertion that the "low value" of commercial speech is a sufficient justification for its selective and categorical ban on newsracks dispensing "commercial handbills."

Chief Justice Rehnquist, joined by Justices White and Thomas, dissented, arguing that one "would have thought that the city [could] have decided to place the burden of its regulatory scheme on less protected speech [without] running afoul of the First Amendment."

2. *Regulating commercial billboards.* In light of *Discovery Network*, how would you expect the Court to rule on the constitutionality of a city ordinance banning all commercial (but not political or public service) billboards? Consider Metromedia, Inc. v. San Diego, 453 U.S. 490 (1981), which involved the constitutionality of a San Diego ordinance prohibiting virtually all outdoor advertising display signs. The ordinance was designed to eliminate hazards to pedestrians and motorists and to improve the appearance of the city. Although the Court invalidated the ordinance as applied to *noncommercial* advertising, it sustained the ordinance as applied to *commercial* messages. The Court explained that the "critical" question concerned "the third of the *Central Hudson* criteria: Does the ordinance 'directly advance' governmental interests in traffic safety and in the appearance of the city?" Although noting that there was no direct evidence in the record "to show any connection between billboards and traffic safety," the Court was reluctant "to disagree with the accumulated, common-sense judgments of local lawmakers [that] billboards are real and substantial hazards to traffic safety. There is nothing here to suggest that these judgments are unreasonable." Similarly, although noting that "esthetic judgments are necessarily subjective," the Court concluded that the city's esthetic judgment was reasonable. Can *Metromedia* be squared with *Discovery Network*?

3. *Regulating commercial spam.* Commercial advertisers often send unsolicited, bulk emails to thousands of recipients. This has the potential to overwhelm individuals' electronic mailboxes and thus to discourage the use of email generally. Could Congress constitutionally prohibit any person to send unsolicited commercial advertisements via email? Could it constitutionally prohibit any person to send unsolicited commercial advertisements via regular mail?

4. *Regulating commercial advertisements of unlawful products or services.* The Court has repeatedly stated that commercial advertisements offering to enter into unlawful transactions are not protected by the first amendment. See, e.g., Hoffman Estates v. Flipside, 455 U.S. 489 (1982) ("government may regulate or ban entirely" commercial "speech proposing an illegal transaction"). Is this reconcilable with *Brandenburg*?

5. *Regulating the viewpoints expressed in commercial advertising.* Suppose a law forbids any commercial advertisement that demeans any person or group. Should the constitutionality of such a law be evaluated under the *Central Hudson* standard or under the more general First Amendment standard that demands strict scrutiny for any law that discriminates on the basis of viewpoint? The Court confronted this question in *Matal v. Tam*, 582 U.S. — (2017). "Slants" is a derogatory term for persons of Asian descent. Simon Tam, lead singer of the rock group "The Slants," whose members are Asian-Americans, chose the name in order to "reclaim" the term and drain it of its denigrating force. The federal Patent and Trademark Office denied Tam's application for federal trademark registration of the name because it violated a federal law prohibiting the registration of any trademarks that "disparage . . . or bring . . . into contemp[t] or disrepute" any "persons." The government argued that trademarks are commercial speech and that the law should therefore be tested under *Central Hudson*. Although the eight justices participating in the case were unanimous in invalidating the law, four justices held that strict scrutiny is the appropriate standard for all viewpoint discrimination even in the context of commercial advertising, and four justices held that there was no need to decide whether

trademarks constitute commercial advertising because the statute failed to pass muster even under *Central Hudson.*

6. *Regulating factually false commercial advertising.* In footnote 24 of *Virginia Pharmacy,* the Court offered several arguments as to why factually false commercial speech may constitutionally be regulated more extensively than other forms of factually false expression. Consider the following criticisms: (a) "Commercial speech is not necessarily more verifiable than other speech. There may well be uncertainty about some quality of a product, such as the health effect of eggs. [On] the other hand, political speech is often quite verifiable by the speakers. A political candidate knows the truth about his own past and present intentions, yet misrepresentations on these subjects are immune from state regulation." Farber, Commercial Speech and First Amendment Theory, 74 Nw. U. L. Rev. 372, 385–386 (1979). (b) "[It] is also incorrect to distinguish commercial from political expression on the ground that the former is somehow hardier because of the inherent profit motive. It could just as easily be said that we need not fear that commercial magazines and newspapers will cease publication for fear of government regulation, because they are in business for profit." Redish, The Value of Free Speech, 130 U. Pa. L. Rev. 591, 633 (1982).

7. *Regulating deceptive or misleading commercial advertising. Virginia Pharmacy* suggests that commercial advertising may be regulated or prohibited, even if it is not factually false, if it is deceptive or misleading. Is this defensible? The Court observed in *Gertz* that "there is no constitutional value in false statements of fact." Can the same be said of misleading or deceptive expression? Do you agree with the Court in *Central Hudson* that, since "the First Amendment's concern for commercial speech is based on the informational function of advertising, [there] can be no constitutional objection to the suppression of commercial messages that [are] more likely to deceive the public than to inform it"? When is an advertisement "misleading"? See Friedman v. Rogers, 440 U.S. 1 (1979) (upholding a state statute prohibiting the practice of optometry under "any trade name" as a permissible restriction of misleading advertising); Peel v. Attorney Registration & Disciplinary Commission of Illinois, 496 U.S. 91 (1990) (rejecting a state's claim that it is "inherently misleading" for lawyers to hold themselves out as "specialists" in particular fields); Ibanez v. Florida Department of Business and Professional Regulation, 512 U.S. 136 (1994) (rejecting a state's claim that it is "inherently misleading" for an attorney truthfully to advertise that she is also a certified public accountant).

8. *Compelled disclosure.* In Zauderer v. Office of Disciplinary Counsel, 471 U.S. 626 (1985), an attorney advertised in a certain type of case, "if there is no recovery, no legal fees are owed by our clients." The Court upheld a disciplinary rule requiring the attorney to disclose in the advertisement that clients would have to pay "costs" even if the lawsuits were unsuccessful. The Court explained that "because the extension of First Amendment protection to commercial speech is justified principally by the value to consumers of the information such speech provides," the state may constitutionally require advertisers to disclose specific information in their advertisements if that requirement is "reasonably related to the State's interest in preventing deception of consumers."

9. *Compelled commercial speech.* The Agricultural Marketing Agreement Act of 1937, which is designed to maintain orderly agricultural markets, authorizes collective action by groups of agricultural producers on such matters as uniform prices, product standards, and generic advertising. The cost of such collective action, which must be approved by two-thirds of the affected producers, is

covered by compulsory assessments on the producers. In Glickman v. Wileman Brothers & Elliott, Inc., 512 U.S. 1145 (1997), the Court held that marketing orders promulgated by the Secretary of Agriculture, which assessed respondent producers for the cost of generic advertising of California tree fruits, did not violate respondents' first amendment rights, even though respondents objected to the requirement that they pay for such advertising. The Court explained:

> [The] regulatory scheme at issue [is distinguishable] from laws that we have found to abridge [the] First Amendment [see Chapter 6, section C, supra] [because] they do not compel the producers to endorse or to finance any political or ideological views. [None] of the advertising in this record promotes any particular message other than encouraging consumers to buy California tree fruit. Neither the fact that respondents may prefer to foster that message independently in order to promote and distinguish their own products, nor the fact that they think more or less money should be spent fostering it, makes this case comparable to those in which an objection rested on political or ideological disagreement with the content of the message. The mere fact that the objectors believe their money is not being well spent "does not mean [that] they have a First Amendment complaint."

In such circumstances, the Court concluded that the wisdom of the overall program "is simply a question of economic policy for Congress and the Executive to resolve." Justice Souter, joined by Chief Justice Rehnquist and Justices Scalia and Thomas, dissented.

See also United States v. United Foods, 533 U.S. 405 (2001) (invalidating a federal statute requiring producers of fresh mushrooms to fund a common advertising program promoting mushroom sales on the ground that, unlike the situation in Glickman, where the compelled assessments were ancillary to a comprehensive regulatory scheme, the requirements in United Foods were not part of such a comprehensive scheme); Johanns v. Livestock Marketing Association, 544 U.S. 550 (2005) (upholding a federal statute imposing an assessment on all sales of cattle to fund, among other things, beef promotional campaigns, on the ground that, unlike the situation in United Foods, the promotional materials in this case are "government speech" rather than government-compelled private speech because the Secretary of Agriculture directly controls "every word" in the promotional materials). See Post, Compelled Subsidization of Speech: Johanns v. Livestock Marketing Association, 2005 Sup. Ct. Rev. 195. For more on the problem of government speech, see section E2d.

5. Obscenity

In the first reported obscenity case in the United States, a Pennsylvania court declared it an offense at common law to exhibit for profit a picture of a nude couple. Commonwealth v. Sharpless, 2 Serg. & Rawle 91 (1815). Despite *Sharpless*, there were few serious efforts to restrict "obscene" expression prior to the Civil War. In the late 1860s, however, Anthony Comstock, a grocer, initiated a campaign to suppress obscenity. Comstock's efforts resulted in the enactment of anti-obscenity legislation in virtually every state. In applying this legislation, most courts adopted the *Hicklin* definition of obscenity: The "test of obscenity" is "whether the tendency of the matter [is] to deprave and corrupt those whose minds are open to such immoral influences." Regina v. Hicklin, 3 L.R-Q.B. 360, 371 (1868). Under this test, which resulted in the suppression of such works as

Theodore Dreiser's An American Tragedy and D. H. Lawrence's Lady Chatterley's Lover, a work could be deemed obscene because of the potential effect of even isolated passages on the most susceptible readers or viewers. See Commonwealth v. Friede, 271 Mass. 318, 171 N.E. 472 (1930) (An American Tragedy); Commonwealth v. DeLacey, 271 Mass. 327, 171 N.E. 455 (1930) (Lady Chatterley's Lover).

In an influential decision reviewing the suppression of James Joyce's Ulysses in the early 1930s, a federal court rejected the *Hicklin* test and adopted instead a standard focusing on the effect on the average person of the dominant theme of the work as a whole. United States v. One Book Called "Ulysses," 5 F. Supp. 182 (S.D.N.Y. 1933), aff'd, 72 F.2d 705 (2d Cir. 1934). On the evolution of obscenity doctrine in this era, see G. Stone, Sex and the Constitution 145–148, 153–178 (2017).

Throughout this era, it was generally assumed that the first amendment posed no barrier to the suppression of obscenity. Indeed, the *Chaplinsky* dictum prominently featured the "obscene" in its catalogue of "unprotected" utterances. The Supreme Court first considered the obscenity issue in a 1948 case arising out of New York's attempt to suppress Memoirs of Hecate County, a highly regarded book written by Edmund Wilson, one of America's foremost literary critics. The Court divided equally on the issue, however, and thus affirmed the conviction without opinion. Doubleday & Co. v. New York, 335 U.S. 848 (1948).

Nine years later, in Roth v. United States, infra, the Court finally addressed the obscenity question. There have been two distinct periods in the Court's efforts to come to grips with obscenity. The first period, which lasted from the 1957 decision in *Roth* until 1973, was dominated by the Warren Court's frustrating and largely unsuccessful efforts to define "obscenity." The second period, which began with the Court's 1973 decisions in Miller v. California and Paris Adult Theatre I v. Slaton, infra, has been dominated by the Court's subsequent efforts to reformulate the doctrine. This section focuses on three questions: Is obscenity "low"-value speech? What is "obscenity"? What interests justify the suppression of obscenity?

ROTH v. UNITED STATES; ALBERTS v. CALIFORNIA, 354 U.S. 476 (1957). Roth was convicted of violating a federal statute prohibiting any person to mail any "obscene" publication. Alberts was convicted of violating a California statute prohibiting any person to write, print, or sell any "obscene" writing. The Supreme Court affirmed the convictions. Justice Brennan delivered the opinion of the Court:

"The dispositive question is whether obscenity is utterance within the area of protected speech and press. [All] ideas having even the slightest redeeming social importance — unorthodox ideas, controversial ideas, even ideas hateful to the prevailing climate of opinion — have the full protection of the guarantees, unless excludable because they encroach upon the limited area of more important interests. But implicit in the history of the First Amendment is the rejection of obscenity as utterly without redeeming social importance. [Thirteen] of the 14 States which by 1792 had ratified the Constitution [provided] for the prosecution of libel, and all of those States made either blasphemy or profanity, or both, statutory crimes. [In] light of this history, it is apparent [that] obscenity, [like] libel, [was] outside the protection intended for speech and press. [We therefore] hold that obscenity is not within the area of constitutionally protected speech or press. [Accordingly,] obscene material [may be suppressed] without proof [that it will] create a clear and present danger of antisocial conduct.

"However, sex and obscenity are not synonymous. Obscene material is material which deals with sex in a manner appealing to prurient interest. The portrayal of sex, e.g., in art, literature, and scientific works, is not itself sufficient reason to deny material the constitutional protection of freedom of speech and press. Sex, a great and mysterious motive in human life, has indisputably been a subject of absorbing interest to mankind through the ages; it is one of the vital problems of human interest and public concern. [It] is therefore vital that the standards for judging obscenity safeguard the protection of freedom of speech and press for material which does not treat sex in a manner appealing to prurient interest. [The proper test is] whether to the average person, applying contemporary community standards, the dominant theme of the material taken as a whole appeals to the prurient interest."

Chief Justice Warren concurred in the result: "It is not the book that is on trial; it is a person. [The] defendants [in] these cases [were] plainly engaged in the commercial exploitation of the morbid and shameful craving for materials with prurient effect. [State] and Federal Governments can constitutionally punish such conduct. That is all that [we] need to decide."

Justice Harlan concurred in the result in *Alberts*, but dissented in *Roth* on the ground that the states have broader authority to regulate obscene expression than the federal government, which may restrict only "hard-core pornography."

Justice Douglas, joined by Justice Black, dissented: "I do not think that the problem can be resolved by the Court's statement that 'obscenity is not expression protected by the First Amendment.' [There] is no special historical evidence that literature dealing with sex was intended to be treated in a special manner by those who drafted the First Amendment. [Moreover,] I reject [the] implication that problems of freedom of speech [are] to be resolved by weighing against the values of free expression, the judgment of the Court that a particular form of expression has 'no redeeming social importance.' The First Amendment [was] designed to preclude courts as well as legislatures from weighing the values of speech against silence. [I] have the same confidence in the ability of our people to reject noxious literature as I have in their capacity to sort out the true from the false in theology, economics, politics, or any other field."

Note: *Obscenity and Free Expression*

1. *Samuel Roth*. Samuel Roth was a character. Born in 1893 in the Carpathian Mountains in Eastern Europe, he emigrated to America as a child and grew up in the tenements on the Lower East Side of New York, in the same neighborhood as Mollie Steimer, one of the defendants in *Abrams*. As a young man he started a poetry magazine called *The Lyric*, in which he published not only his own work, but also poems by such then-unknown authors as Archibald MacLeish and D. H. Lawrence. He established a bookstore in Greenwich Village that became famous as the Poetry Bookshop.

During a trip to England, when he was in his early twenties, Roth was intrigued by a German sex manual that he picked up from one of the many pornography stalls in London. When he returned to New York, he translated, advertised, and distributed the pamphlet, but he soon got in trouble with the postal authorities. Several years later, in 1927, he began circulating advertisements for his impending publication of *The Perfumed Garden*, a pornographic fifteenth-century Arabian classic. The New York Society for the Suppression of Vice, which had been founded by Anthony Comstock, promptly had Roth arrested.

Over the next thirty years, Roth was repeatedly arrested for the publication of such works as D. H. Lawrence's *Lady Chatterley's Lover* and a growing list of pornographic titles, such as *Celestine: The Diary of a Chambermaid*, *Her Candle Burns Hot*, and *Beautiful Sinners of New York*. Through it all, and through a series of jail terms, Roth insisted that individuals had a right to read such material. In his early sixties, and after being sentenced to five years in prison for publishing several ever-more sexually explicit works like *Wild Passion* and *Wanton at Night*, he finally made it to the Supreme Court of the United States. See G. Stone, Sex and the Constitution 269–271 (2017).

2. *Entertainment, art, literature, and the first amendment*. Does the first amendment protect not only speech that expressly addresses "public" issues but also "speech" in the form of entertainment, art, and literature? Does the latter form of "speech" have a "subordinate position" in the scale of first amendment values? Consider Kalven, The Metaphysics of the Law of Obscenity, 1960 Sup. Ct. Rev. 1, 15–16:

> The classic defense of John Stuart Mill and the modern defense of Alexander Meiklejohn do not help much when the question is why the novel, the poem, the painting, the drama, or the piece of sculpture falls within the protection of the First Amendment. Nor do the famous opinions of Hand, Holmes, and Brandeis. The emphasis is all on truth winning out in a fair fight between competing ideas [and on the] argument that free speech is indispensable to the informed citizenry required to make self-government work. The people need free speech because they vote. [But not] all communications are relevant to the political process. The people do not need novels or dramas or paintings or poems because they will be called upon to vote. Art and belles-lettres do not deal in such ideas — at least not good art or belles-lettres. [Thus] there seems to be a hiatus in our basic free-speech theory.

Consider Meiklejohn's response:

> [There] are many forms of thought and expression within the range of human communications from which the voter derives the knowledge, intelligence, sensitivity to human values: the capacity for sane and objective judgment which, so far as possible, a ballot should express. [The] people do need novels and dramas and paintings and poems, "because they will be called upon to vote." The primary social fact which blocks and hinders the success of our experiment in self-government is that our citizens are not educated for self-government.

Meiklejohn, The First Amendment Is an Absolute, 1961 Sup. Ct. Rev. 245, 256, 263. Does the "self-fulfillment" defense of free expression fill Kalven's "hiatus" and offer a more persuasive rationale for the protection of art, literature, and entertainment?

The Court has generally assumed that non-obscene literature and entertainment are entitled to "full" first amendment protection. In Winters v. New York, 333 U.S. 507, 510 (1948), for example, the Court explained that "[the] line between the informing and the entertaining is too elusive for the protection of the basic right. Everyone is familiar with instances of propaganda through fiction. What is one man's amusement, teaches another's doctrine." See also Schad v. Borough of Mount Ephraim, 452 U.S. 61 (1981) (holding unconstitutional a prohibition on all live entertainment in the borough). For a more thorough explication of the values of aesthetic expression, see Bezanson, Art and the Constitution, 93 Iowa L. Rev. 1593 (2008); Nahmod, Artistic Expression and Aesthetic Theory: The Beautiful, The Sublime and The First Amendment, 1987 Wis. L. Rev. 221; Hamilton, Art Speech, 49 Vand. L. Rev. 73 (1996).

3. *Is obscenity of only "low" first amendment value?* Does obscenity further any of the values underlying the protection of free expression? Consider the following arguments:

a. As the Court demonstrated in *Roth*, the historical evidence shows that obscenity "was outside the protection intended for speech and press." But consider Kalven, supra, at 9: "[The] Court's use of history was so casual as to be [alarming]. Is it clear, for example, that blasphemy can constitutionally be made a crime today? And what would the Court say to an argument along the same lines appealing to the Sedition Act of 1798 as justification for the truly liberty-defeating crime of seditious libel?"

b. Stone, Sex, Violence, and the First Amendment, 74 U. Chi. L. Rev. 1857, 1861–1863 (2007):

> In *Roth*, the Court maintained that "implicit in the history of the First Amendment is the rejection of obscenity as utterly without redeeming social importance." [But] unlike libel, blasphemy, and profanity, obscenity was not unlawful under either English or American law in 1792.
>
> In England, the state first punished an obscene publication in 1727. In King v. Curll [2 Stra. 788], the court sustained the conviction of Edward Curll for publishing *Venus in the Cloister or the Nun in her Smock*, [a] sexually explicit depiction of supposedly rampant sex among monks and nuns in a convent. It dealt quite graphically with voyeurism, masturbation, fornication, dildos, and flagellation. In a two-to-one decision, the King's Bench held that Curll's publication was "punishable at common law, as an offense against the peace, in tending to weaken the bonds of civil society, virtue, and morality." In fact, the prosecution had less to do with the sexual nature of the material than with Curll's [publication] of several politically libelous works that had infuriated public officials.
>
> Thereafter, obscenity prosecutions remained essentially unknown in England throughout the 18th century, despite a profusion of sexually explicit writings. [In] the 1790s, when the United States was contemplating the First Amendment, England was awash with all sorts of sexually explicit material, [and the] first prosecution for obscenity in the United States did not occur until [almost] a quarter-century *after* the adoption of the First Amendment. . . .

For a fuller account of this history, see G. Stone, Sex and the Constitution 145–148, 153–178, 269–278 (2017).

c. Schauer, Speech and "Speech" — Obscenity and "Obscenity": An Exercise in the Interpretation of Constitutional Language, 67 Geo. L.J. 899, 906, 922, 923, 926 (1979):

> Certain uses of words, although speech in the ordinary sense, clearly are not speech in the constitutional sense. ["Speech" for first amendment purposes is defined by] the idea of cognitive content, of mental effect, of a communication designed to appeal to the intellectual process. This [includes] the artistic and the emotive as well as the propositional. [But] hardcore pornography is [by definition] designed to produce a purely physical effect. [It is] essentially a physical rather than a mental stimulus. [A] pornographic item is in a real sense a sexual surrogate. [Consider] rubber, plastic, or leather sex aids. It is hard to find any free speech aspects in their

sale or use. [The] mere fact that in pornography the stimulating experience is initiated by visual rather than tactile means is irrelevant. [Neither] means constitutes communication in the cognitive sense. [Thus,] hardcore pornography *is sex*, [not "speech"].

Is this what the Court meant in *Roth* when it defined obscenity as "material which deals with sex in a manner appealing to prurient interest"? For a critique of Schauer's view, see Gey, The Apologetics of Suppression: The Regulation of Pornography as Act and Idea, 86 Mich. L. Rev. 1564 (1988).

d. Laws directed against obscenity are not restrictions on ideas as such, for they limit the *means* of expression rather than the *ideas* expressed. As the Court said in *Chaplinsky*, obscene "utterances are no essential part of any exposition of ideas." Moreover, to the extent that obscenity is associated with a particular ideological message, such as "sexual freedom," it is an especially problematic *means* of expression, for it alters "one's tastes and preferences" not by direct persuasion or rational argument but by "a process that is, like subliminal advertising, both outside of one's rational control and quite independent of the relevant grounds for preference." Scanlon, Freedom of Expression and Categories of Expression, 40 U. Pitt. L. Rev. 519, 547 (1979). On the other hand, might it be said that the very concept of "obscenity" embodies a forbidden "viewpoint-based restriction" because "it is justified by moral objections to the ideas or messages that sexual speech is said to convey"? Heins, Viewpoint Discrimination, 24 Hast. Const. L.Q. 99, 103 (1996).

4. *The interests furthered by the suppression of obscenity.* Because the Court in *Roth* accepted the underlying premise of the *Chaplinsky* dictum — that obscene utterances are wholly "unprotected" by the first amendment — the Court found it unnecessary to inquire into the nature or substantiality of the state interests said to justify the suppression of obscene expression. The gradual breakdown of the rigid "two-level" theory (under which speech is either "protected" or "unprotected") and the increased use of "categorical" balancing in such areas as libel and commercial speech would seem to raise doubts about this approach. Do the decisions to "balance" conflicting state and speech interests in the libel and commercial speech contexts suggest a need for similar balancing in the obscenity context? If so, what state interests are sufficiently important to justify restrictions on obscene expression? Consider the following:

a. The state may suppress obscenity because it may cause antisocial conduct. Must the state "prove" causation? What must be the nature of the correlation — clear and present danger? Bad tendency? For analysis of the "correlation," see the Report of the Commission on Obscenity and Pornography 26–27 (1970) (finding "no evidence to date that exposure to explicit sexual materials plays a significant role in the causation of delinquent or criminal behavior").

Sixteen years after publication of the Commission on Obscenity and Pornography's report, a new government commission — the Attorney General's Commission on Pornography — determined that at least certain forms of obscenity could cause some types of antisocial conduct. For criticism of the report, see G. Hawkins and F. Zimring, Pornography in a Free Society (1988). For further discussion of the causation issue, see Schauer, Causation Theory and the Causes of Sexual Violence, 1987 Am. B. Found. Res. J. 737. On the two presidential commissions, see G. Stone, Sex and the Constitution 284–286, 297–298 (2017).

b. The state may suppress obscenity because it "corrupts character," impairs "mental health," and "has a deleterious effect on the individual from which the community should protect him." Henkin, Morals and the Constitution: The Sin of Obscenity, 63 Colum. L. Rev. 391, 394 (1963). But see Koppelman, Does Obscenity Cause Moral Harm?, 105 Colum. L. Rev. 1635 (2005) (analogizing regulation of the moral of harm supposedly caused by obscenity to the regulation of religious values).

c. The state may suppress obscenity to prevent the erosion of moral standards. Consider Lockhart and McClure, Literature, the Law of Obscenity, and the Constitution, 38 Minn. L. Rev. 295, 374–375 (1954):

> The view that literature may be proscribed because [it] may [change] accepted moral standards [flies] squarely in the face of the [guarantee of free] expression. Back of this fundamental freedom lies the basic conviction that our democratic society must be free to perfect its own standards of conduct and belief [through] the heat of unrepressed controversy and debate. The remedy against those who attack currently accepted standards is [defense] of those standards, not censorship.

d. The state may suppress obscenity because it erodes moral standards not by rational persuasion but by indirect degradation of values. Consider H. Clor, Obscenity and Public Morality 121, 170–171 (1969):

> [Obscene materials] do not make arguments which are to be met by intelligent defense. While they attack moral values, they do not [do so] in any sense relevant to [public debate]. [Rather,] they have an [effect] upon feeling, upon motivations — ultimately upon character and the basic attitudes which arise from character. [Constant] exposure to [obscene] materials which overemphasize sensuality and brutality, reduce love to sex, and blatantly expose to public view intimacies which have been thought [private] must eventually [erode] moral standards. [The] ethical convictions of man do not rest simply upon his explicit opinions. They rest also upon a delicate network of moral and aesthetic feelings, sensibilities, [and] tastes. [These] "finer feelings" [may be eroded] by a steady stream of [obscenity]. Men whose sensibilities are frequently assaulted by prurient and lurid impressions may become desensitized. [This] is what is meant by "an erosion of the moral fabric."

e. The state may suppress the dissemination of obscenity to minors because they are especially vulnerable to its "harmful" effects. But is there really anything to the notion that children need to be protected from exposure to sexual images? Consider Garfield, Protecting Children from Speech, 57 Fla. L. Rev. 565 (2005): "[The] concept of sheltering children from [sexual] speech is largely a modern conceit. The concept, after all, presupposes a 'childhood' — a prolonged period of innocence — that was rare in premodern times and continues to be rare in many parts of the world. Put bluntly, children in the Middle Ages, who slept in their parents' beds . . . did not need sheltering from sexually-explicit speech."

Note: Developments in the Law of "Obscenity" — 1957-1973

1. *The definition of obscenity: the breakdown of consensus.* In *Roth*, the Court embraced the view that material is "obscene" if, "to the average person, applying contemporary community standards, the dominant theme of the material taken as a whole appeals to prurient interest." But agreement on the definition of obscenity was short-lived. Only a decade after *Roth*, Justice Harlan aptly observed that "[the] subject of obscenity has produced a variety of views among the

members of the Court unmatched in any other course of constitutional adjudication." As evidence, Justice Harlan noted that in the thirteen obscenity cases decided in the decade after *Roth*, there were "a total of 55 separate opinions among the Justices." Interstate Circuit, Inc. v. Dallas, 390 U.S. 676, 704–705, 705 n.1 (1968) (Harlan, J., dissenting).

By 1968, the following views had emerged:

a. Justices Clark and White adhered to the initial *Roth* formulation. See Memoirs v. Massachusetts, 383 U.S. 413, 441 (1966) (Clark, J., dissenting); id. at 460–462 (White, J., dissenting).

b. Justices Black and Douglas adhered to their view, expressed in *Roth*, that government is wholly powerless to regulate sexually oriented expression on the ground of its obscenity. See Jacobellis v. Ohio, 378 U.S. 184, 196–197 (1964) (Black, J., joined by Douglas, J., concurring).

c. Justice Harlan adhered to the view he expressed in *Roth*. See Jacobellis v. Ohio, 378 U.S. at 204 (Harlan, J., dissenting).

d. Justice Stewart "reached the conclusion [that] under the First and Fourteenth Amendments criminal laws in this area are constitutionally limited to hard-core pornography." Justice Stewart continued: "I shall not today attempt further to define the kinds of material I understand to be embraced within that shorthand description; and perhaps I could never succeed in intelligibly doing so. But I know it when I see it, and the motion picture involved in this case is not that." Jacobellis v. Ohio, id. at 197 (Stewart, J., concurring).

e. Justice Brennan, Chief Justice Warren, and Justice Fortas adopted the view that, for material to be deemed obscene, "three elements must coalesce: it must be established that (a) the dominant theme of the material taken as a whole appeals to a prurient interest in sex; (b) the material is patently offensive because it affronts contemporary community standards relating to the description or representation of sexual matters; and (c) the material is utterly without redeeming social value." Memoirs v. Massachusetts, 383 U.S. at 418 (Brennan, J., joined by Warren, C.J., and Fortas, J.). Although this formulation represented the view of only three justices, it was the formulation most often followed by state and federal courts from 1966 until the Court's 1973 decision in *Miller*, infra. Note the addition of elements (b) and (c) to the initial *Roth* formulation.

2. *The definition of obscenity: pandering.* To complicate matters further, there was substantial disagreement within the Court over the extent to which factors extrinsic to the material should be considered in the obscenity determination. In Ginzburg v. United States, 383 U.S. 463 (1966), the Court held that "the question of obscenity may include consideration of the setting in which the publications were presented." Here, the publisher had "sought mailing privileges from the postmasters of Intercourse and Blue Ball, Pennsylvania" in order to sell the "publications on the basis of salacious appeal." The Court held that such "commercial exploitation of erotica solely for the sake of their prurient appeal [may] support the determination that the material is obscene even though in other contexts the material would escape such condemnation."

3. *The definition of obscenity: material that is "obscene for minors."* Ginsberg v. New York, 390 U.S. 629 (1968), another "variable obscenity" case, involved the problem of children. The Court had previously addressed the problem of obscenity and children in Butler v. Michigan, 352 U.S. 380 (1957). In *Butler*, the Court held invalid a law prohibiting the sale of "lewd" material that might have a deleterious influence on youth. Justice Frankfurter, speaking for a unanimous Court, explained that the state may not "reduce the adult population of Michigan

to reading only what is fit for children." In *Ginsberg*, the Court held that a state can constitutionally prohibit "the sale to minors under seventeen years of age of material defined to be obscene on the basis of its appeal to them whether or not it would be obscene to adults." In recognizing this principle, the Court observed that (1) "the power of the state to control the conduct of children reaches beyond the scope of its authority over adults"; (2) the claim of parents "to direct the rearing of their children is basic in the structure of our society," and "the legislature could properly conclude that parents [are] entitled to the support of laws designed to aid discharge of that responsibility"; and (3) the state "has an independent interest in the well-being of its youth" and in seeing to it "that they are 'safeguarded from abuses' which might prevent their 'growth into free and independent well-developed men and citizens.'"

Consider the following regulations: (1) No bookstore may display any book or magazine that is obscene for children, except in a separate "adults only" section. (2) No television station may broadcast any material that is obscene for children, except between the hours of 11:00 P.M. and 6:00 A.M. (3) No person may post on the internet any material that is obscene for children. (4) No person may display on any billboard any image that is obscene for children.

4. *The definition of obscenity*: Redrup. The inability of the Court to articulate a definition of obscenity that could command the allegiance of a majority, compounded by the potential relevance of factors extrinsic to the material itself, led to an era of chaos. In Redrup v. New York, 386 U.S. 767 (1967), the Court began the practice of per curiam reversals of convictions for the sale or exhibition of materials that at least five members of the Court, applying their separate tests, deemed not to be obscene. From 1967 to 1973, some thirty-one cases were disposed of in this fashion. The full opinion of the Court in Walker v. Ohio, 398 U.S. 434 (1970), is typical: "The judgment of the Supreme Court of Ohio is reversed. [*Redrup*.]" As Justice Brennan later commented: "[The *Redrup* approach] resolves cases as between the parties, but offers only the most obscure guidance to legislation, adjudication by other courts, and primary conduct. [It] comes as no surprise that judicial attempts to follow our lead conscientiously have often ended in hopeless confusion." Paris Adult Theatre I v. Slaton, 413 U.S. 49, 83 (1973) (Brennan, J., dissenting).

5. *The interests furthered by the suppression of obscenity*. Although debating the definitional issue endlessly, the justices in this era said almost nothing about the nature of the interests that assertedly justified the suppression of obscene expression. As noted earlier, this was due largely to *Roth*'s acceptance of the underlying premise of the *Chaplinsky* dictum — obscene utterances are wholly "unprotected" by the first amendment and their restriction thus does not necessitate an inquiry into the nature or substantiality of the state interests.

There was, however, one notable exception to the Court's silence on this issue. In Stanley v. Georgia, 394 U.S. 557 (1969), the Court, speaking through Justice Marshall, held that "the mere private possession of obscene matter cannot constitutionally be made a crime." In reaching this result, the Court announced that the "right to receive information and ideas, regardless of their social worth, [is] fundamental to our free society," and that "in the context of this case — a prosecution for mere possession of printed or filmed matter in the privacy of a person's own home — that right takes on an added dimension," for "also fundamental is the right to be free, except in very limited circumstances, from unwanted governmental intrusions into one's privacy." In light of these interests, "mere categorization of these films as 'obscene' is insufficient justification for such a drastic invasion of personal liberties," for "if the First Amendment means anything, it means that a State has no business telling a man, sitting alone in his own house, what books he may read or what films he may watch."

6. *The implications of* Stanley: Reidel. In United States v. Reidel, 402 U.S. 351 (1971), a federal district court, relying on *Stanley*, held a federal statute prohibiting the knowing use of the mails for the delivery of obscene matter unconstitutional as applied to the distribution of such matter to willing recipients who state that they are adults. The district court reasoned that, "if a person has the right to receive and possess this material, then someone must have the right to deliver it to him." The Supreme Court reversed. The Court explained that the "focus of [*Stanley*] [was] on freedom of mind and thought and on the privacy of one's home." "Reidel," however, "is in a wholly different position," for "he has no complaints about governmental violations of his private thoughts or fantasies, but stands squarely on a claimed First Amendment right to do business in obscenity and use the mails in the process. [*Stanley*] did not overrule *Roth* and we decline to do so now." To the same effect, see United States v. Thirty-Seven Photographs, 402 U.S. 363 (1971); United States v. 12 200 Ft. Reels, 413 U.S. 123 (1973); United States v. Orito, 413 U.S. 139 (1973). See also Osborne v. Ohio, 495 U.S. 103 (1990) (holding *Stanley* inapplicable to the possession of child pornography).

7. *Reformulation.* By 1973, then, the law of obscenity was in a state of considerable confusion. Two questions were especially troublesome: How should obscenity be defined? When may it be restricted? With Richard Nixon's appointment of four new justices shortly after assuming office, the newly-constituted Burger Court was eager to address these questions. Indeed, "Warren Burger loathed pornography. He despised 'smut peddlers' and was determined that 'something had to be done to suppress them.'" As the new Chief Justice, he "could hardly wait" to get his "hands on the obscenity issue. Burger considered it fortunate that the justices of the Warren Court had never managed to get five votes to agree on a definition, because that would have settled the law. Their failure to agree on a single approach left the door open for him to reshape a critically important area of the law on which the Court, in his view, had been 'stumbling' since 1957. He eagerly awaited the challenge." G. Stone, Sex and the Constitution 288 (2017). In its 1973 decisions in *Miller* and *Paris Adult Theatre*, the Burger Court took on that challenge.

Miller v. California

413 U.S. 15 (1973)

Mr. Chief Justice Burger delivered the opinion of the Court.

This is one of a group of "obscenity-pornography" cases being reviewed by the Court in a re-examination of [the standards] which must be used to identify obscene material that a State may regulate. . . .

[In this case, appellant] conducted a mass mailing campaign to advertise the sale of illustrated books, euphemistically called "adult" material. [Appellant's] conviction was specifically based on his conduct in causing five unsolicited advertising brochures to be sent through the mail. [The] brochures [consist primarily] of pictures and drawings very explicitly depicting men and women in groups of two or more engaging in a variety of sexual activities, with genitals often prominently displayed. [This] case [thus] involves the application of a

State's criminal obscenity statute to a situation in which sexually explicit materials have been thrust by aggressive sales action upon unwilling recipients. . . .

II

[Obscene] material is unprotected by the First Amendment. [*Roth.*] [However,] State statutes designed to regulate obscene materials must be carefully limited. [Thus,] we now confine the permissible scope of such regulation to works which depict or describe sexual conduct. That conduct must be specifically defined by the applicable state law, as written or authoritatively construed. . . .

The basic guidelines for the trier of fact must be: (a) whether "the average person, applying contemporary community standards" would find that the work, taken as a whole, appeals to the prurient interest; (b) whether the work depicts or describes, in a patently offensive way, sexual conduct specifically defined by the applicable state law; and (c) whether the work, taken as a whole, lacks serious literary, artistic, political, or scientific value. We do not adopt as a constitutional standard the "*utterly* without redeeming social value" test of [*Memoirs*]. . . .

We emphasize that it is not our function to propose regulatory schemes for the States. [It] is possible, however, to give a few plain examples of what a state statute could define for regulation under part (b) of the standard announced in this opinion, supra:

(a) Patently offensive representations or descriptions of ultimate sexual acts, normal or perverted, actual or simulated.
(b) Patently offensive representations or descriptions of masturbation, excretory functions, and lewd exhibition of the genitals.

Sex and nudity may not be exploited without limit by films or pictures exhibited or sold in places of public accommodation any more than live sex and nudity can be exhibited or sold without limit in such public places. At a minimum, prurient, patently offensive depiction or description of sexual conduct must have serious literary, artistic, political, or scientific value to merit First Amendment protection. [In] resolving the inevitably sensitive questions of fact and law, we must continue to rely on the jury system, accompanied by the safeguards that judges, rules of evidence, presumption of innocence, and other protective features provide, as we do with [other] offenses against society and its individual members.

Mr. Justice Brennan [now] maintains that no formulation of this Court, the Congress, or the States can adequately distinguish obscene material unprotected by the First Amendment from protected expression, [*Paris Adult Theatre*, infra]. (Brennan J., dissenting.) [But under] the holdings announced today, no one will be subject to prosecution for the sale or exposure of obscene materials unless these materials depict or describe patently offensive "hard core" sexual conduct specifically defined by the regulating state law, as written or construed. We are satisfied that these specific prerequisites will provide fair notice to a dealer in such materials that his public and commercial activities may bring prosecution. See [*Roth*]. . . .

Mr. Justice Brennan also emphasizes "institutional stress" in justification of his change of view. [It] is certainly true that the absence, since *Roth*, of a single majority view of this Court as to proper standards for testing obscenity has placed a strain on both state and federal courts. But today, for the first time since *Roth* was decided in 1957, a majority of this Court has agreed on concrete guidelines to isolate "hard core" pornography from expression protected by the First Amendment. Now we may abandon the casual practice of [*Redrup*] and attempt to provide positive guidance to federal and state courts alike.

This may not be an easy road, free from difficulty. But no amount of "fatigue" should lead us to adopt a convenient "institutional" rationale — an absolutist, "anything goes" view of the First Amendment — because it will lighten our burdens. . . .

III

Under a National Constitution, fundamental First Amendment limitations on the powers of the States do not vary from community to community, but this does not mean that there are, or should or can be, fixed, uniform national standards of precisely what appeals to the "prurient interest" or is "patently offensive." These are essentially questions of fact, and our Nation is simply too big and too diverse for this Court to reasonably expect that such standards could be articulated for all 50 States in a single formulation, even assuming the prerequisite consensus exists. [It] is neither realistic nor constitutionally sound to read the First Amendment as requiring that the people of Maine or Mississippi accept public depiction of conduct found tolerable in Las Vegas, or New York City.[13] [People] in different States vary in their tastes and attitudes, and this diversity is not to be strangled by the absolutism of imposed uniformity. We hold that the requirement that the jury evaluate the materials with reference to "contemporary standards of the State of California" [is] constitutionally adequate.

IV

The dissenting Justices sound the alarm of repression. But, in our view, to equate the free and robust exchange of ideas and political debate with commercial exploitation of obscene material demeans the grand conception of the First Amendment. [The] First Amendment protects works which, taken as a whole, have serious literary, artistic, political, or scientific value, regardless of whether the government or a majority of the people approve of the ideas these works represent. [But] the public portrayal of hard-core sexual conduct for its own sake, and for the ensuing commercial gain, is a different matter. [There] is no evidence, empirical or historical, that the stern 19th century American censorship of public distribution and display of material relating to sex [in] any way

---

13. In [*Jacobellis*] two Justices argued that application of "local" community standards would run the risk of preventing dissemination of materials in some places because sellers would be unwilling to risk criminal conviction by testing variations in standards from place to place. [The] use of "national" standards, however, necessarily implies that materials found tolerable in some places, but not under the "national" criteria, will nevertheless be unavailable where they are acceptable. Thus, in terms of danger to free expression, the potential for suppression seems at least as great in the application of a single nationwide standard as in allowing distribution in accordance with local tastes. . . .

limited or affected expression of serious literary, artistic, political, or scientific ideas. . . .

In sum, we (a) reaffirm the *Roth* holding that obscene material is not protected by the First Amendment; (b) hold that such material can be regulated by the States, subject to the specific safeguards enunciated above, without a showing that the material is "*utterly* without redeeming social value"; and (c) hold that obscenity is to be determined by applying "contemporary community standards." . . .

Vacated and remanded.

MR. JUSTICE DOUGLAS, dissenting. . . .

[The] idea that the First Amendment permits punishment for ideas that are "offensive" to the particular judge or jury sitting in judgment is astounding. No greater leveler of speech or literature has ever been designed. . . .

I do not think we, the judges, were ever given the constitutional power to make definitions of obscenity. If it is to be defined, let the people [decide] by a constitutional amendment what they want to ban as [obscene]. Whatever the choice, the courts will have some guidelines. Now we have none except our own predilections.

MR. JUSTICE BRENNAN, with whom MR. JUSTICE STEWART and MR. JUSTICE MARSHALL join, dissenting.

In my dissent in [*Paris Adult Theatre*, infra], I noted that I had no occasion to consider the extent of state power to regulate the distribution of sexually oriented material [to] unconsenting adults. [I] need not now decide [that question, for] it is clear that under my dissent in *Paris Adult Theatre* the statute under which the prosecution was brought is unconstitutionally overbroad, and therefore invalid on its face. . . .

Paris Adult Theatre I v. Slaton
413 U.S. 49 (1973)

MR. CHIEF JUSTICE BURGER delivered the opinion of the Court.

[Petitioners are two Atlanta, Georgia, movie theaters and their owners and managers, operating in the style of "adult" theaters. The theaters have a conventional, inoffensive entrance, without any pictures, but with signs indicating that the theaters exhibit "Atlanta's Finest Mature Feature Films." On the door is a sign saying "Adult Theater — You must be 21 and able to prove it. If viewing the nude body offends you, Please Do Not Enter." The local state district attorney filed civil complaints alleging that petitioners were exhibiting to the public for paid admission two allegedly obscene films, Magic Mirror and It All Comes Out in the End, which depict scenes of simulated fellatio, cunnilingus, and group sex intercourse. Respondent's complaints demanded that the two films be declared obscene, and that petitioners be enjoined from exhibiting the films. The trial judge found the films obscene, but dismissed the complaints on the ground that "the display of these films in a commercial theatre, when surrounded by requisite notice to the public of their nature and by reasonable protection against the exposure of these films to minors, is constitutionally permissible." The Georgia Supreme Court reversed and held that exhibition of the films should be enjoined. The U.S. Supreme Court vacated and remanded for reconsideration in light of *Miller*.]

We categorically disapprove the theory [that] obscene, pornographic films acquire constitutional immunity from state regulation simply because they are exhibited for consenting adults only. [Although] we have often pointedly recognized the high importance of the state interest in regulating the exposure of obscene materials to juveniles and unconsenting adults, [this] Court has never declared these to be the only legitimate state interests permitting regulation of obscene material. . . .

In particular, we hold that there are legitimate state interests at stake in stemming the tide of commercialized obscenity, even assuming it is feasible to enforce effective safeguards against exposure to juveniles and to passersby.[7] Rights and interests "other than those of the advocates are involved." [These] include the interest of the public in the quality of life and the total community environment, the tone of commerce in the great city centers, and, possibly, the public safety itself. The Hill-Link Minority Report of the Commission on Obscenity and Pornography indicates that there is at least an arguable correlation between obscene material and crime. Quite apart from sex crimes, however, there remains one problem of large proportions aptly described by Professor Bickel:

> It concerns the tone of the society, the mode, or to use terms that have perhaps greater currency, the style and quality of life, now and in the future. A man may be entitled to read an obscene book in his room, or expose himself indecently there. . . . We should protect his privacy. But if he demands a right to obtain the books and pictures he wants in the market, and to foregather in public places — discreet, if you will, but accessible to all — with others who share his tastes, *then to grant him his right is to affect the world about the rest of us, and to impinge on other privacies.* Even supposing that each of us can, if he wishes, effectively avert the eye and stop the ear (which, in truth, we cannot), what is commonly read and seen and heard and done intrudes upon us all, want it or not.

22 The Public Interest 25–26 (Winter 1971). (Emphasis added.) As Mr. Chief Justice Warren stated, there is a "right of the Nation and of the States to maintain a decent society . . ." [*Jacobellis*] (dissenting opinion). . . .

But, it is argued, there are no scientific data which conclusively demonstrate that exposure to obscene material adversely affects men and women or their society. It is urged on behalf of the petitioners that, absent such a demonstration, any kind of state regulation is "impermissible." We reject this argument. It is not for us to resolve empirical uncertainties underlying state legislation, save in the exceptional case where that legislation plainly impinges upon rights protected by the Constitution itself. [Although] there is no conclusive proof of a connection between antisocial behavior and obscene material, the legislature of Georgia could quite reasonably determine that such a connection does or might exist. In deciding *Roth*, this Court implicitly accepted that a legislature could legitimately act on such a conclusion to protect *"the social interest in order and morality."* . . .

---

7. It is conceivable that an "adult" theater can — if it really insists — prevent the exposure of its obscene wares to juveniles. An "adult" bookstore, dealing in obscene books, magazines, and pictures, cannot realistically make this claim. The legitimate interest in preventing exposure of juveniles to obscene material cannot be fully served by simply barring juveniles from the immediate physical premises of "adult" bookstores, when there is a flourishing "outside business" in these materials.

Finally, petitioners argue that conduct which directly involves "consenting adults" only has, for that sole reason, a special claim to constitutional protection. Our Constitution establishes a broad range of conditions on the exercise of power by the States, but for us to say that our Constitution incorporates the proposition that conduct involving consenting adults only is always beyond state regulation, is a step we are unable to take.[15] [The] issue in this context goes beyond whether someone, or even the majority, considers the conduct depicted as "wrong" or "sinful." The States have the power to make a morally neutral judgment that public exhibition of obscene material, or commerce in such material, has a tendency to injure the community as a whole, to endanger the public safety, or to jeopardize [the] States' "right [to] maintain a decent society." . . .

Vacated and remanded.

MR. JUSTICE BRENNAN, with whom MR. JUSTICE STEWART and MR. JUSTICE MARSHALL join, dissenting. [A dissenting opinion of Justice Douglas is omitted.]

[I] am convinced that the approach initiated 16 years ago in [*Roth*], and culminating in the Court's decision today, cannot bring stability to this area of the law without jeopardizing fundamental First Amendment [values]. The vagueness of the standards in the obscenity area produces a number of separate problems, [including a] lack of fair notice, [a] chill on protected expression, and [a severe] stress [on the] judicial machinery. [These concerns] persuade me that a significant change in direction is urgently required. I turn, therefore, to the alternatives that are now open.

[One] approach [would] be to draw a new line between protected and unprotected [speech] that resolves all doubt in favor of state [power]. We could hold, for example, that any depiction [of] human sexual organs [is] outside the protection of the First [Amendment]. That formula would [reduce the problems of vagueness]. But [it] would be appallingly [overbroad]. . . .

The alternative adopted by the Court [today] adopts a restatement of the *Roth-Memoirs* definition of obscenity. [The] Court today permits suppression if the government can prove that the materials lack "*serious* literary, artistic, political or scientific value." But [*Roth*] held that certain expression is obscene, and thus outside the protection of the First Amendment, precisely *because* it lacks even the slightest redeeming social value. [The] Court's approach [is thus] nothing less than a rejection of the fundamental First Amendment premises [of *Roth*] and an invitation to widespread suppression of sexually oriented speech. . . .

In any case, [the Court's approach] can have no ameliorative impact on [the] problems that grow out of the vagueness of our current standards. [Although] the Court's [test] does limit the definition of obscenity to depictions [of] explicit sexual acts, [even] a confirmed optimist could find little realistic comfort in the adoption of such a test. Indeed, the valiant attempt of one lower federal court to draw the constitutional line at depictions of explicit sexual conduct seems to belie any suggestion that this approach marks the road to clarity.[16] . . .

---

15. The state statute books are replete with constitutionally unchallenged laws against prostitution, suicide, voluntary self-mutilation, brutalizing "bare fist" prize fights, and duels, although these crimes may only directly involve "consenting adults." Statutes making bigamy a crime surely cut into an individual's freedom to associate, but few today seriously claim such statutes violate the First Amendment or any other constitutional provision. . . .

16. Huffman v. United States, 152 U.S. App. D.C. 238, 470 F.2d 386 (1971). The test apparently requires an effort to distinguish between "singles" and "duals," between "erect penises" and "semi-erect penises," and between "ongoing sexual activity" and "imminent sexual activity."

Finally, I have considered the view, urged so forcefully since 1957 by our Brothers Black and Douglas, that the First Amendment bars the suppression of any sexually oriented expression. That position would [strip] the States of power to an extent that cannot be justified by the commands of the Constitution, at least so long as there is available an alternative approach that strikes a better balance between the guarantee of free expression and the States' legitimate interests. . . .

[Given the] inevitable side effects of state efforts to suppress [obscenity], we must scrutinize with care the state interests that are asserted to justify the suppression. For in the absence of some very substantial interest in suppressing such speech, we can hardly condone the ill effects that seem to flow inevitably from the effort. . . .

[The] state interests in protecting children and in protecting unconsenting adults [stand] on a different footing from the other asserted state interests. [But] whatever the strength of [those] interests, [they] cannot be asserted [where, as] in this case, [the] films [were] exhibited only to persons over the age of 21 who viewed them willingly and with prior knowledge of the nature of their contents. [The] justification for the suppression must be found, therefore, in some independent interest in regulating the reading and viewing habits of consenting adults. . . .

In *Stanley* we pointed out that "[t]here appears to be little empirical basis for" the assertion that "exposure to obscene materials may lead to deviant sexual behavior or crimes of sexual violence."[26] [In] any event, we added that "if the State [is] concerned about [sexual] materials inducing antisocial conduct, [we] should adhere to the view that '[a]mong free men, the deterrents ordinarily to be applied to prevent crime are education and punishment for violations of the law. . . .'"

Moreover, in *Stanley* we rejected as "wholly inconsistent with the philosophy of the First Amendment" [the] notion that there is a legitimate state concern in the "control [of] the moral content of a person's thoughts." [That] is not to say, of course, that a State must remain utterly indifferent to — and take no action bearing on — the morality of the community. The traditional description of state police power does embrace the regulation of morals as well as the health, safety, and general welfare of the citizenry. [But] the State's interest in regulating morality by suppressing obscenity, while often asserted, remains essentially unfocused and ill defined. And, since the attempt to curtail unprotected speech necessarily spills over into the area of protected speech, the effort to serve this speculative interest through the suppression of obscene material must tread heavily on rights protected by the First Amendment. [I] would hold, therefore, that at least in the absence of distribution to juveniles or obtrusive exposure to unconsenting adults, the First and Fourteenth Amendments prohibit the State and Federal Governments from attempting [to] suppress sexually oriented materials on the basis of their allegedly "obscene" contents. . . .

---

26. Indeed, since *Stanley* was decided, [the] President's Commission on Obscenity and Pornography has concluded: "In sum, empirical research designed to clarify the question has found no evidence to date that exposure to explicit sexual materials plays a significant role in the causation of delinquent or criminal behavior among youth or adults. The Commission cannot conclude that exposure to erotic materials is a factor in the causation of sex crime or sex delinquency. . . ."

Note: The 1973 Reformulation and Its Aftermath

1. Miller *and* Roth. Does the *Miller* reformulation constitute a "rejection of the fundamental first amendment premises" of *Roth*? Does its elimination of the "utterly without redeeming social value" criterion fatally undermine the notion that obscenity is of only "low" first amendment value?

2. Miller *and vagueness.* Is the *Miller* reformulation likely significantly to reduce the problems generated by the prior vagueness of the definition of obscenity? Are there any limits on the sorts of "sexual conduct" that might constitutionally be deemed "patently offensive"? In Jenkins v. Georgia, 418 U.S. 153 (1974), the Court, in an opinion by Justice Rehnquist, overturned a state court determination that the highly acclaimed movie Carnal Knowledge was obscene. The Court explained that *Miller* "intended to fix substantive constitutional limitations, deriving from the First Amendment, on the type of material subject to [a determination of patent offensiveness]." As an example, the Court observed that "it would be wholly at odds with this aspect of *Miller* to uphold an obscenity conviction based upon a defendant's depiction of a woman with a bare midriff." As for Carnal Knowledge, the Court noted that "our own viewing of the film satisfies us that [it] could not be found under the *Miller* standards to depict sexual conduct in a patently offensive way." The Court explained that, "while the subject of the picture is, in a broader sense, sex, and there are scenes in which sexual conduct including 'ultimate sexual acts' is to be understood to be taking place, the camera does not focus on the bodies of the actors at such times. There is no exhibition of the actor's genitals, lewd or otherwise, during these scenes. There are occasional scenes of nudity, but nudity alone is not enough to make material legally obscene under the *Miller* standards." Thus, "the film could not, as a matter of constitutional law, be found to depict sexual conduct in a patently offensive way, [and] is therefore not outside the protection of the First and Fourteenth Amendments because it is obscene."

3. *Local versus national standards.* What interests are furthered by the Court's conclusion in *Miller* that "appeal to prurient interest" and "patent offensiveness" may be determined according to local rather than national standards? Consider the following objections to local standards:

a. Smith v. United States, 431 U.S. 291, 313–315 (1977) (Stevens, J., dissenting):

> The geographic boundaries of [a local] community are not easily defined. They are [thus] subject to elastic adjustment to suit the needs of the prosecutor. Moreover, although a substantial body of evidence and decisional law concerning the content of a national standard could have evolved through its consistent use, the derivation of the relevant community standard for each of our countless communities is necessarily dependent on the perceptions of the individuals who happen to compose the jury in a given case.

b. Hamling v. United States, 418 U.S. 87, 144–145 (1974) (Brennan, J., dissenting):

> Under [a local standards approach national] distributors [will] be forced to cope with the community standards of every hamlet into which their goods may wander. [Because] these variegated standards are impossible to discern, national distributors, fearful of risking the expense and difficulty of defending against prosecution in any of several remote communities, must inevitably [retreat] to debilitating

self-censorship. [As a result], the people of many communities will be "protected" far beyond government's constitutional power to deny them access to sexually oriented materials.

4. *Local standards: post-*Miller *decisions.* The Court has handed down several post-*Miller* rulings concerning local standards. See *Jenkins,* supra (in a state obscenity prosecution, jurors need not "apply the standards of a hypothetical statewide community," but may "rely on their understanding of community from which they come"); Hamling v. United States, 418 U.S. 87 (1974) (in a federal obscenity prosecution, jurors need not rely on national standards, but may rely on their "knowledge of the community or vicinage" from which they come); *Paris Adult Theatre,* supra (the first amendment does not "require 'expert' affirmative evidence that the materials [are] obscene when the materials themselves [are] actually placed in evidence"); Pope v. Illinois, 481 U.S. 497 (1987) (a trial court may not use community standards to decide whether a work lacks serious literary, artistic, political, or scientific value, for "the value of a work does not vary from community to community").

5. *Community standards on the internet.* In Ashcroft v. American Civil Liberties Union, 535 U.S. 564 (2002), the Court held that a federal statute (the Child Online Protection Act) regulating obscene material on the internet was not invalid on its face because it applies local community standards in determining whether particular material is obscene, even though an individual posting sexually explicit material on the internet has no control over the geographic areas in which the material is accessible. The majority left open the question, however, whether the statute might be unconstitutional as applied in specific circumstances. As Justice O'Connor observed, "given Internet speakers' inability to control the geographic location of their audience, expecting them to bear the burden of controlling the recipients of their speech [may] be entirely too much to ask, and would potentially suppress an inordinate amount of expression." Justice Stevens would have held the law invalid on its face.

6. *Intent.* What state of mind must the seller or distributor have in an obscenity prosecution? As the incitement and libel cases make clear, intent can play a central role in "definitional" balancing and can do much to reduce problems caused by the vagueness of the underlying concepts.

In Smith v. California, 361 U.S. 147 (1959), appellant was convicted of violating a city ordinance construed by the state courts as imposing strict liability on the proprietor of any bookstore who possessed in his store any book later judicially determined to be obscene — even if the proprietor had no personal knowledge of the contents of the book. The Court held the imposition of strict liability invalid. This feature of the ordinance, the Court noted, "tends to impose a severe limitation on the public's access to constitutionally protected matter. For if the bookseller is criminally liable without knowledge of the contents [he] will tend to restrict the books he sells to those he has inspected." Such a state of affairs would generate a "self-censorship [affecting] the whole public."

In Hamling v. United States, supra, however, the Court approved a jury instruction to the effect that, to satisfy its burden on intent, the prosecution need only prove that the defendants "had knowledge of the character of the materials." The Court explained that the prosecution did not need to prove that the defendants knew that the materials were obscene because to "require proof of a defendant's knowledge of the legal status of the materials would permit the defendant to avoid prosecution by simply claiming that he had not brushed up on the law." Is this reconcilable with the Court's analysis of intent in the libel context? Consider Lockhart, Escape from the Chill of Uncertainty: Explicit Sex and the First Amendment, 9 Ga. L. Rev. 533, 563 (1975): "My suggestion is that [the first amendment establishes] as a defense to a criminal obscenity prosecution that the defendant *reasonably believed* that the material involved was not obscene."

7. *The regulation of obscenity.* The procedural issues involved in the regulation of obscenity have proved especially difficult. See, e.g., Times Film Corp. v. Chicago, 365 U.S. 43 (1961) (licensing); Bantam Books v. Sullivan, 372 U.S. 58 (1963) (blacklisting); *Paris Adult Theatre,* supra (injunction); Heller v. New York, 413 U.S. 483 (1973) (search and seizure); Alexander v. United States, 509 U.S. 544 (1993) (forfeiture).

8. *Internet filters for public libraries.* Can a public library use filters on its internet terminals designed to preclude patrons from accessing obscene websites? Suppose the filter is imprecise and inevitably will block access to non-obscene as well as obscene websites? See United States v. American Library Association, 539 U.S. 194 (2003), section E2, infra.

9. *The end of obscenity?* Consider the following proposition: In the forty years since the Court's 1973 decisions, a combination of technological innovation and changing social mores have rendered the obscenity doctrine irrelevant. The advent of video rentals, DVDs, cable television, and the internet have completely overwhelmed the capacity of law enforcement to keep up with the flood of sexually oriented material. As more and more individuals have been exposed to more and more of that material, "contemporary community standards" about what is "patently offensive" have evolved (some might say deteriorated) to the point where today virtually nothing is obscene. Rather than focus their limited resources on ferreting out the few extreme images that a jury today might still find obscene, most prosecutors have moved on to more important matters and left obscenity in the dust. Thus, although there are still calls from moral crusaders for government to initiate obscenity prosecutions, such prosecutions now seem more symbolic than real — except, of course, for those few defendants who are unlikely enough to be targeted. Does this seem an accurate statement of reality? If so, is it a good or a bad thing? See G. Stone Sex and the Constitution 295–312, 340–347 (2017).

10. *Obscenity and substantive due process.* Even if obscenity is not protected by the First Amendment, is it protected from prohibition by the doctrine of substantive due process, as articulated in such decisions as Griswold v. Connecticut, Roe v. Wade, Planned Parenthood v. Casey, and Lawrence v. Texas, supra Chapter 6, section F? In *Lawrence,* the Court observed that "liberty gives substantial protection to adult persons in deciding how to conduct their private lives in matters pertaining to sex." Does "the right of autonomous decision-making" in private matters include "the protection of both intimate sexual conduct and the commercial transactions that enable and promote sexual intimacy"? Kinsley, Sexual Privacy in the Internet Age: How Substantive Due Process Protects Online Obscenity, 16 Vand. J. Ent. & Tech. L. 103 (2013). See Reliable Consultants, Inc. v. Earle, 517 F.3d 738 (5th Cir. 2008) (invalidating on substantive due process grounds a Texas law prohibiting any person to sell, advertise, give away or lend any device "designed or marketed for sexual stimulation").

6.   *Child Pornography, Animal Cruelty, and Violent Expression*

The Court's conclusion that obscenity can constitutionally be regulated inevitably invited analogies. To what extent does the obscenity doctrine open the door to other forms of speech restriction?

NEW YORK v. FERBER, 458 U.S. 747 (1982). Ferber, the proprietor of a Manhattan bookstore specializing in sexually oriented products, was prosecuted for selling two films to an undercover police officer. The films were devoted almost entirely to depicting young boys masturbating. A jury held that the films were not obscene, but convicted Ferber of violating a New York statute prohibiting any person knowingly to produce, promote, direct, exhibit, or sell any material depicting a "sexual performance" by a child under the age of sixteen. The statute defined "sexual performance" as any performance that includes "actual or simulated sexual intercourse, deviate sexual intercourse, sexual bestiality, masturbation, sado-masochistic abuse, or lewd exhibition of the genitals." The Court unanimously upheld the conviction. Justice White delivered the opinion:

"In [the *Chaplinsky* dictum], the Court laid the foundation for the excision of obscenity from the realm of constitutionally protected expression. [For the following reasons, we are persuaded that pornographic depiction of children, like obscenity, is unprotected by the first amendment.]

"First. It is evident beyond the need for elaboration that a state's interest in 'safeguarding the physical and psychological well-being of a minor' is 'compelling.' [The] use of children as subjects of pornographic materials is harmful to the physiological, emotional, and mental health of the child.

"Second. The distribution of photographs and films depicting sexual activity by juveniles is intrinsically related to the sexual abuse of children in at least two ways. First, the materials produced are a permanent record of the children's participation and the harm to the child is exacerbated by their circulation. Second, the distribution network for child pornography must be closed if the production of material which requires the sexual exploitation of children is to be effectively controlled. . . .

"Third. The advertising and selling of child pornography provides an economic motive for and is thus an integral part of the production of such materials, an activity illegal throughout the nation. [Were] the statutes outlawing the employment of children in these films and photographs fully effective, and the constitutionality of these laws have not been questioned, the First Amendment implications would be no greater than that presented by laws against distribution: enforceable production laws would leave no child pornography to be marketed.

"Fourth. The value of permitting live performances and photographic reproductions of children engaged in lewd sexual conduct is exceedingly modest, if not de minimis. We consider it unlikely that visual depictions of children performing sexual acts or lewdly exhibiting their genitals would often constitute an important and necessary part of a literary performance or scientific or educational work. [If] it were necessary for literary or artistic value, a person over the statutory age who perhaps looked younger could be utilized. Simulation outside of the prohibition of the statute could provide another alternative. Nor is there any question here of censoring a particular literary theme or portrayal of sexual activity. The First

Amendment interest is limited to that of rendering the portrayal somewhat more 'realistic' by utilizing or photographing children.

"Fifth. Recognizing and classifying child pornography as a category of material outside the protection of the First Amendment is not incompatible with our earlier decisions. [It] is not rare that a content-based classification of speech has been accepted because it may be appropriately generalized that within the confines of the given classification, the evil to be restricted so overwhelmingly outweighs the expressive interests, if any, at stake, that no process of case-by-case adjudication is required. . . .

"There are, of course, limits on the category of child pornography which, like obscenity, is unprotected by the First Amendment. As with all legislation in this sensitive area, the conduct to be prohibited must be adequately defined by the applicable state law, as written or authoritatively construed. [The] test for child pornography is separate from the obscenity standard enunciated in *Miller*, but may be compared to it for purpose of clarity. The *Miller* formulation is adjusted in the following respects: A trier of fact need not find that the material appeals to the prurient interest of the average person; it is not required that sexual conduct portrayed be done so in a patently offensive manner; and the material at issue need not be considered as a whole. . . .

"It remains to address the claim that the New York statute is unconstitutionally overbroad because it would forbid the distribution of material with serious literary, scientific, or educational value or material which does not threaten the harms sought to be combated by the State. [The New York Court of Appeals, which invalidated the statute,] was understandably concerned that some protected expression, ranging from medical textbooks to pictorials in National Geographic would fall prey to the statute. [Yet] we seriously doubt, and it has not been suggested, that these arguably impermissible applications of the statute amount to more than a tiny fraction of the materials within the statute's reach. [Under] these circumstances, [the statute] is 'not substantially overbroad and whatever overbreadth exists should be cured through case-by-case analysis of the fact situations to which its sanctions, assertedly, may not be applied.' [Broadrick v. Oklahoma, section C1, supra]. As applied to [Ferber] and to others who distribute similar material, the statute does not violate the First Amendment."

Should the Court have analyzed the New York statute not as a content-based restriction of "unprotected" speech but as a content-neutral restriction on the "means" of expression? Child abuse is unlawful. Consider the following propositions: (1) There is no first amendment right to violate an otherwise valid criminal law that is unrelated to the suppression of free expression merely because the violation would render one's speech more effective. Can one, for example, steal a camera in order to make a movie? Could the government have punished Daniel Ellsberg for "stealing" the Pentagon Papers? (2) There is no first amendment right to depict the commission of a criminal act where the criminal act was committed solely in order to produce the depiction. In other words, if X stabs Y in order to film a real stabbing, X can be punished for the assault. But can the film be banned? If so, is that true of the Pentagon Papers as well?

Consider Bartnicki v. Vopper, 532 U.S. 514 (2001), in which the Court held that federal and state antiwiretap statutes cannot constitutionally be applied to a radio station that broadcasts the tape of an unlawfully intercepted telephone call, where the subject of the call was a matter of public concern and the broadcaster did not participate directly in the unlawful wiretap, even though the broadcaster knew that the material had been obtained unlawfully. The Court expressly distinguished *Ferber* on the ground that *Ferber* involved speech "considered of minimal value." Suppose a documentary filmmaker secretly films the actual sexual abuse of a child in a foster home. Can the government make it unlawful for the filmmaker to show the documentary? Can it require the filmmaker to block out the face and identity of the child?

Suppose a film depicts *simulated* sex between an adult and a child but was made entirely with adult actors or by computer imaging. Can the exhibition of the film be prohibited after *Ferber* on the ground that it will encourage pederasty? What about an animated film?

ASHCROFT v. THE FREE SPEECH COALITION, 535 U.S. 234 (2002). The Court invalidated the Child Pornography Prevention Act of 1996 (CPPA), which extended the prohibition against child pornography to sexually explicit images that *appear* to depict minors, but were in fact produced without using real children — either by computer imaging or by using adults who look like children. Justice Kennedy delivered the opinion of the Court:

"By prohibiting child pornography that does not depict an actual child, the statute goes beyond *Ferber*, which distinguished child pornography from other sexually explicit speech because of the State's interest in protecting the children exploited by the production process. [Although the statute] captures a range of depictions [that] do not [harm] any children in the production process, [Congress] decided the materials threaten children in other, less direct, ways. Pedophiles might use the materials to encourage children to participate in sexual activity [or they] might 'whet their own sexual appetites' with the pornographic images, 'thereby increasing the creation and distribution of child pornography and the sexual abuse and exploitation of actual children.' Under these rationales, harm flows from the content of the images, not from the means of their production. In addition, Congress [was concerned that the existence of] computer-generated images [can] can make it harder to prosecute pornographers who [use] real minors. As imaging technology improves, Congress found, it becomes more difficult to prove that a particular picture was produced using actual children. To ensure that defendants possessing child pornography using real minors cannot evade prosecution, Congress extended the ban to virtual child pornography. . . .

"The sexual abuse of a child is a most serious crime and an act repugnant to the moral instincts of a decent people. [Congress] may pass valid laws to protect children from abuse, and it has. The prospect of crime, however, by itself does not justify laws suppressing protected speech. See *Kingsley Pictures.* ('Among free men, the deterrents ordinarily to be applied to prevent crime are education and punishment for violations of the law, not abridgment of the rights of free speech'). . . .

"As a general principle, the First Amendment bars the government from dictating what we see or read or speak or hear. The freedom of speech has its limits; it does not embrace certain categories of speech, including defamation, incitement, obscenity, and pornography produced with real children. While these categories may be prohibited without violating the First Amendment, none of them includes the speech prohibited by the CPPA. . . .

"[T]he CPPA [does not deal with] obscenity. Under *Miller*, the Government must prove that the work, taken as a whole, appeals to the prurient interest, is patently offensive in light of community standards, and lacks serious literary, artistic, political, or scientific value. The CPPA, however, [applies] without regard to the *Miller* requirements. . . .

"The Government seeks to address this deficiency by arguing that speech prohibited by the CPPA is virtually indistinguishable from child pornography, which may be banned without regard to whether it depicts works of value. See *Ferber*. Where the images are themselves the product of child sexual abuse, *Ferber* recognized that the State had an interest in stamping it out without regard to any judgment about its content. The production of the work, not its content, was the target of the statute. The fact that a work contained serious literary, artistic, or other value did not excuse the harm it caused to its child participants. [*Ferber*] upheld a prohibition on the distribution and sale of child pornography, as well as its production, because these acts were 'intrinsically related' to the sexual abuse of children in two ways. First, as a permanent record of a child's abuse, the continued circulation itself would harm the child who had participated. Like a defamatory statement, each new publication of the speech would cause new injury to the child's reputation and emotional well-being. Second, because the traffic in child pornography was an economic motive for its production, the State had an interest in closing the distribution network. [Under] either rationale, the speech had what the Court in effect held was a proximate link to the crime from which it came. . . .

"In contrast to the speech in *Ferber*, [the] CPPA prohibits speech that records no crime and creates no victims by its production. Virtual child pornography is not 'intrinsically related' to the sexual abuse of children, as were the materials in *Ferber*. While the Government asserts that the images can lead to actual instances of child abuse, the causal link is contingent and indirect. The harm does not necessarily follow from the speech, but depends upon some unquantified potential for subsequent criminal acts.

"The Government says these indirect harms are sufficient because, as *Ferber* acknowledged, child pornography rarely can be valuable speech. This argument, however, suffers from two flaws. First, *Ferber*'s judgment about child pornography was based upon how it was made, not on what it communicated. [Second,] *Ferber* did not hold that child pornography is by definition without value. On the contrary, the Court recognized some works in this category might have significant value, but relied on virtual images — the very images prohibited by the CPPA — as an alternative and permissible means of expression. *Ferber*, then, not only referred to the distinction between actual and virtual child pornography, it relied on it as a reason supporting its holding. *Ferber* provides no support for a statute that eliminates the distinction and makes the alternative mode criminal as well.

"The CPPA [is thus] inconsistent with *Miller* and finds no support in *Ferber*. The Government seeks to justify its prohibitions in other ways. It argues that the CPPA is necessary because pedophiles may use virtual child pornography to seduce children. There are many things innocent in themselves, however, such as cartoons, video games, and candy, that might be used for immoral purposes, yet we would not expect those to be prohibited because they can be misused. The Government, of course, may punish adults who provide unsuitable materials to children, see *Ginsberg*, and it may enforce criminal penalties for unlawful solicitation. The precedents establish, however, that speech within the rights of adults to hear may not be silenced completely in an attempt to shield children from it. [Here, the] evil in question depends upon the actor's unlawful conduct, conduct defined as criminal quite apart from any link to the speech in question. This establishes that the speech ban is not narrowly drawn. The objective is to prohibit illegal conduct, but this restriction goes well beyond that interest by restricting the speech available to law-abiding adults.

"The Government submits further that virtual child pornography whets the appetites of pedophiles and encourages them to engage in illegal conduct. This rationale cannot sustain the provision in question. The mere tendency of speech to encourage unlawful acts is not a sufficient reason for banning it. [The] Court's First Amendment cases draw vital distinctions between words and deeds, between ideas and conduct. The government may not prohibit speech because it increases the chance an unlawful act will be committed 'at some indefinite future time.' [The] Government has shown no more than a remote connection between speech that might encourage thoughts or impulses and any resulting child abuse. Without a significantly stronger, more direct connection, the Government may not prohibit speech on the ground that it may encourage pedophiles to engage in illegal conduct. . . .

"Finally, the Government says that the possibility of producing images by using computer imaging makes it very difficult for it to prosecute those who produce pornography by using real children. Experts, we are told, may have difficulty in saying whether the pictures were made by using real children or by using computer imaging. The necessary solution, the argument runs, is to prohibit both kinds of images. The argument, in essence, is that protected speech may be banned as a means to ban unprotected speech. This analysis turns the First Amendment upside down. The Government may not suppress lawful speech as the means to suppress unlawful speech. Protected speech does not become unprotected merely because it resembles the latter."

Justice Thomas filed a concurring opinion in which he observed that "if technological advances" eventually reach a point where they actually (as opposed to speculatively) "thwart prosecution of 'unlawful speech,' the Government may well have a compelling interest [in] regulating some narrow category of 'lawful speech' in order to enforce effectively laws against pornography made through the abuse of real children."

Justice O'Connor, joined in part by Chief Justice Rehnquist and Justice Scalia, dissented in part. Justice O'Connor concluded that the CPPA was unconstitutional insofar as it restricts material created by using youthful-looking adults, but that it was constitutional insofar as it restricts virtual-child pornography. With respect to the latter, Justice O'Connor argued that if the CPPA is narrowly construed to limit only computer-generated images that are "virtually indistinguishable" from real child pornography, it would satisfy "strict scrutiny" because it would then be narrowly tailored to serve the compelling governmental interest in eliminating real child pornography. She also noted that if any work falling within this category in fact has serious social, political, literary or scientific value, the possible "overbreadth" of the law in that regard could be considered in an "as applied" challenge. On the other hand, Justice O'Connor concurred with the Court in invalidating the law insofar as it restricts material created with youthful-looking adults because such material would not pose the same problem to the enforcement of the prohibition on actual child pornography as material created using computer images.

Note: Child Pornography

1. *Morphing.* Another provision of the CPPA, not at issue in this case, prohibits the use of computer morphing to alter the images of real children so they appear to be engaged in sexual activity. Is this different from the issues addressed in *Ashcroft?* The Court noted in passing that because such morphed images "implicate the interests of real children" they are closer to the issue considered in *Ferber.* Might this better be analyzed as a form of libel?

2. *An affirmative defense.* Suppose Congress re-enacted the CPPA verbatim, but recognized an affirmative defense to enable the defendant to prove that the image had been created without the abuse of a real child. Would that satisfy the first amendment?

3. *Child pornography in the home.* In Osborne v. Ohio, 495 U.S. 103 (1990), the Court held that Stanley v. Georgia does not extend to the private possession of child pornography. The Court, in an opinion by Justice White, explained: "[The] interests underlying child pornography prohibitions far exceed the interests justifying [the] law at issue in *Stanley.* [In] *Stanley,* Georgia primarily sought to proscribe the private possession of obscenity because it was concerned that obscenity will poison the mind of its viewers. [The] difference here is obvious: the State does not rely on a paternalistic interest in regulating [the defendant's] mind. Rather, [the law is designed] to protect the victims of child pornography; it hopes to destroy a national market for the exploitative use of children." Justices Brennan, Marshall, and Stevens dissented.

4. *Offers to sell child pornography.* In response to Ashcroft v. Free Speech Coalition, Congress in 2003 enacted the Prosecutorial Remedies and Other Tools to end the Exploitation of Children Today Act (the PROTECT Act), which made it a crime for any person "knowingly" to "advertise, promote, present, distribute, or solicit through the mails, or in interstate or foreign commerce [any] material or purported material in a manner that reflects the belief, or that is intended to cause another to believe, that the material or purported material is, or contains, [a] visual depiction of an actual minor engaging in sexually explicit conduct." The act defined "sexually explicit conduct" in a manner consistent with the New York law upheld in *Ferber.*

Congress enacted the act because it was concerned that "limiting the child-pornography prohibition to material that could be *proved* to feature actual children [would] enable many child pornographers to evade conviction." Congress found that the "emergence of new technology and the repeated retransmission of picture files over the Internet could make it nearly impossible to prove that a particular image was produced using real children — even though '[t]here is no substantial evidence that any of the child pornography images being trafficked today were made other than by the abuse of real children.'" The Court of Appeals held that the act was unconstitutionally overbroad, because it makes it a crime to distribute constitutionally protected material, that is, material that does *not* constitute child pornography within the meaning of *Free Speech Coalition.*

The Supreme Court, in an opinion by Justice Scalia, reversed: "Offers to engage in illegal transactions are categorically excluded from First Amendment protection. One would think that this principle resolves the present case, since the statute criminalizes only offers to provide or requests to obtain contraband — child [pornography] involving actual children. [The position of the Court of Appeals] would forbid the government from punishing *fraudulent offers to provide illegal products.* We see no logic in that position. [According] to the dissent, Congress has made an end-run around the First Amendment's protection of virtual child pornography by prohibiting proposals to transact in such images rather than prohibiting the images themselves. But an offer to provide or request to receive virtual child pornography is not prohibited by the statute. A crime is committed only when the speaker believes or intends the listener to believe that the subject of the proposed transaction depicts *real* children. [Simulated] child pornography will be as available as ever, so long as it is offered and sought *as such*, and not as real child pornography."

Justice Souter, joined by Justice Ginsburg, dissented: "What justification can there be for making independent crimes of proposals to engage in transactions that [actually distribute] constitutionally protected materials? [The Court argues] that a proposal to commit a crime enjoys no speech protection. [But why] should [this] general rule [cover] a case like the proposal to transfer what [turns] out to be [constitutionally protected speech?] If the Act can be enforced, it will function just as it was meant to do, by merging the whole subject of child pornography into the offense of proposing a transaction, dispensing with the real-child element in the underlying subject. [We] should hold that a transaction in what turns out to be [constitutionally protected speech] is better understood, not as an incomplete attempt to commit a crime, but as a completed series of intended acts that simply do not add up to a crime, owing to the privileged character of the material the parties were in fact about to deal in."

UNITED STATES v. STEVENS, 559 U.S. 460 (2010). 18 U.S.C. §48 establishes a criminal penalty of up to five years in prison for anyone who knowingly "creates, sells, or possesses a depiction of animal cruelty" for "commercial gain" in interstate or foreign commerce. A depiction of "animal cruelty" is defined as one "in which a living animal is intentionally maimed, mutilated, tortured, wounded, or killed," if that conduct violates federal or state law where "the creation, sale, or possession takes place." The law exempts from prohibition any depiction "that has serious religious, political, scientific, educational, journalistic, historical, or artistic value."

The legislative background of §48 focused primarily on the interstate market for "crush videos," which depict women crushing small animals like mice and hamsters to death with their bare feet or while wearing high heeled shoes, sometimes while talking to the animals in a kind of dominatrix patter. Apparently these depictions appeal to persons with a very specific sexual fetish. The acts depicted in crush videos are typically prohibited by the animal cruelty laws enacted by all 50 States and the District of Columbia, but because crush videos rarely disclose the participants' identities, prosecution of the underlying conduct is often impossible.

This case involved an application of §48 not to crush videos, but to depictions of dogfighting. Dogfighting is unlawful in all 50 States and the District of Columbia, and has been restricted by federal law since 1976. Robert Stevens ran a business, "Dogs of Velvet and Steel," and an associated Web site, through which he sold videos of pit bulls engaging in dogfights and attacking other animals. His videos included contemporary footage of dogfights in Japan (where such conduct is legal) as well as footage of American dogfights from the 1960's and 1970's. On the basis of these videos, Stevens was convicted of violating §48. The court of appeals declared §48 facially unconstitutional and vacated Stevens's conviction.

In an eight-to-one decision, the Supreme Court affirmed. Chief Justice Roberts delivered the opinion of the Court:

"The Government's primary submission is that §48 necessarily complies with the Constitution because the banned depictions of animal cruelty, as a class, are categorically unprotected by the First Amendment. We disagree. . . .

"From 1791 to the present, [the] First Amendment has 'permitted restrictions upon the content of speech in a few limited areas,' [including, for example, obscenity, defamation, threats, and incitement]. [Citing *Chaplinsky*.] The Government argues that 'depictions of animal cruelty' should be added to the list. It contends that depictions of 'illegal acts of animal cruelty' that are 'made, sold, or possessed for commercial gain' necessarily 'lack expressive value,' and may accordingly 'be regulated as *unprotected* speech.' [The] prohibition of animal cruelty [has] a long history in American law, [but] we are unaware of any similar tradition excluding *depictions* of animal cruelty from 'the freedom of speech' codified in the First Amendment. . . .

"The Government contends that 'historical evidence' about the reach of the First Amendment is not 'a necessary prerequisite for regulation today,' and that categories of speech may be exempted from the First Amendment's protection without any long-settled tradition of subjecting that speech to regulation. Instead, the Government points to Congress's 'legislative judgment that . . . depictions of animals being intentionally tortured and killed [are] of such minimal redeeming value as to render [them] unworthy of First Amendment protection,' and asks the Court to uphold the ban on the same basis. The Government thus proposes that a claim of categorical exclusion should be considered under a simple balancing test: 'Whether a given category of speech enjoys First Amendment protection depends upon a categorical balancing of the value of the speech against its societal costs.' [Quoting Brief for United States].

"As a free-floating test for First Amendment coverage, that sentence is startling and dangerous. The First Amendment's guarantee of free speech does not extend only to categories of speech that survive an ad hoc balancing of relative social costs and benefits. The First Amendment itself reflects a judgment by the American people that the benefits of its restrictions on the Government outweigh the costs. Our Constitution forecloses any attempt to revise that judgment simply on the basis that some speech is not worth it. . . .

"When we have identified categories of speech as fully outside the protection of the First Amendment, it has not been on the basis of a simple cost-benefit analysis. [Our decisions] cannot be taken as establishing a freewheeling authority to declare new categories of speech outside the scope of the First Amendment. Maybe there are some categories of speech that have been historically unprotected, but have not yet been specifically identified or discussed as such in our case law. But if so, there is no evidence that 'depictions of animal cruelty' is among them. We need not foreclose the future recognition of such additional categories to reject the Government's highly manipulable balancing test as a means of identifying them. . . .

"We read §48 to create a criminal prohibition of alarming breadth. [The] only thing standing between defendants who sell such depictions and five years in federal prison — other than the mercy of a prosecutor — is the statute's exceptions clause. Subsection (b) exempts from prohibition 'any depiction that has serious religious, political, scientific, educational, journalistic, historical, or artistic value.' The Government argues that this clause substantially narrows the statute's reach: News reports about animal cruelty have 'journalistic' value;

pictures of bullfights in Spain have 'historical' value; and instructional hunting videos have 'educational' value. [But much valuable speech under the First Amendment does not] fall within one of the enumerated categories. [Most] hunting videos, for example, are not obviously instructional in nature, [but] 'have primarily entertainment value.' [The] Government offers no principled explanation why these depictions of hunting or depictions of Spanish bullfights would be *inherently* valuable while those of Japanese dog-fights are not. . . .

"The Government explains that the language of §48(b) was largely drawn from our opinion in *Miller* v. *California*, which excepted from its definition of obscenity any material with 'serious literary, artistic, political, or scientific value.' According to the Government, this incorporation of the *Miller* standard into §48 is therefore surely enough to answer any First Amendment objection. In *Miller* we held that 'serious' value shields depictions of sex from regulation as obscenity. We did not, however, determine that serious value could be used as a general precondition to protecting *other* types of speech in the first place. *Most* of what we say to one another lacks 'religious, political, scientific, educational, journalistic, historical, or artistic value' (let alone serious value), but it is still sheltered from government regulation. [Thus,] the protection of the First Amendment presumptively extends to many forms of speech that do not qualify for the serious-value exception of §48(b), but nonetheless fall within the broad reach of §48(c)."

Why are depictions of animal cruelty different from depictions of child sexual abuse? Consider Chief Justice Roberts's explanation: "In *Ferber*, [we] classified child pornography as [unprotected speech]. We noted that the State [had] a compelling interest in protecting children from abuse, and that the value of using children in these works (as opposed to simulated conduct or adult actors) was *de minimis*. But our decision did not rest on this 'balance of the competing interests' alone. We made clear that *Ferber* presented a special case: The market for child pornography was 'intrinsically related' to the underlying abuse, and was 'an integral part of the production of such materials, an activity illegal throughout the Nation.' As we noted, '[i]t rarely has been suggested that the constitutional freedom for speech and press extends its immunity to speech or writing used as an integral part of conduct in violation of a valid criminal statute.' *Ferber* thus grounded its analysis in a previously recognized, long-established category of unprotected speech." Is this persuasive?

The Court held in *Ferber* and *Ashcroft* that the government can constitutionally prohibit the sale or exhibition of child pornography only because the government has a "compelling" interest in "safeguarding the physical and psychological well-being of a minor." The Court explained that the prohibition of child pornography serves this "compelling" interest in two ways: (1) by drying up the market for such materials and thereby eliminating the incentive to create them, and (2) by protecting the victims from the emotional and psychological harm caused by the continued circulation of the images. Does the government have a similarly "compelling" argument in the animal cruelty context?

Consider the following arguments: (1) As evidenced by the many circumstances (including hunting and slaughtering food animals) in which we permit cruelty to animals, we clearly do not take the interest in preventing animal cruelty as seriously as we take the interest in preventing child sexual abuse, which is never permitted. (2) Unlike people, animals have no consciousness of the continuing exhibition of the depiction of their abuse and therefore suffer no comparable emotional or psychological injury.

Justice Alito was the lone dissenter: "The Court strikes down in its entirety a valuable statute [that] was enacted not to suppress speech, but to prevent horrific acts of animal cruelty — in particular, the creation and commercial exploitation of 'crush videos,' a form of depraved entertainment that has no social value. The Court's approach [is] unwarranted. [The] most relevant of our prior decisions is *Ferber*. [In] *Ferber*, an important factor — I would say the most important factor — was that child pornography involves the commission of a crime that inflicts severe personal injury to the 'children who are made to engage in sexual conduct for commercial purposes.' [As] later noted in Ashcroft v. Free Speech Coalition, in *Ferber* '[t]he production of the work, not its content, was the target of the statute.' [*Ferber* also] emphasized [that] these underlying crimes could not be effectively combated without targeting the distribution of child pornography. [And, finally,] the *Ferber* Court noted that the value of child pornography 'is exceedingly modest, if not *de minimis*,' and that any such value was 'overwhelmingly outweigh[ed]' by 'the evil to be restricted.'

"All three of these characteristics are shared by §48, as applied to crush videos. [It] must be acknowledged that §48 differs from a child pornography law in an important respect: preventing the abuse of children is certainly much more important than preventing the torture of the animals used in crush videos. But while protecting children is unquestionably *more* important than protecting animals, the Government also has a compelling interest in preventing the torture depicted in crush videos. [The] animals used in crush videos are living creatures that experience excruciating pain. [Applying] the principles set forth in *Ferber*, I would hold that crush videos are not protected by the First Amendment."

BROWN v. ENTERTAINMENT MERCHANTS ASS'N, 564 U.S. 786 (2011). In *Brown*, the Court invalidated a California law imposing restrictions on violent video games. Justice Scalia delivered the opinion of the Court: "California Assembly Bill 1179 prohibits the sale or rental of 'violent video games' to [minors]. The Act covers games 'in which the range of options available to a player includes killing, maiming, dismembering, or sexually assaulting an image of a human being, if those acts are depicted' in a manner that 'a reasonable person, considering the game as a whole, would find appeals to a deviant or morbid interest of minors,' that is 'patently offensive to prevailing standards in the community as to what is suitable for minors,' and that 'causes the game, as a whole, to lack serious literary, artistic, political, or scientific value for minors.' . . .

"[V]ideo games qualify for First Amendment protection. The Free Speech Clause exists principally to protect discourse on public matters, but we have long recognized that it is difficult to distinguish politics from entertainment, and dangerous to try. [Like] the protected books, plays, and movies that preceded them, video games communicate ideas — and even social messages — through many familiar literary devices (such as characters, dialogue, plot, and music) and through features distinctive to the medium (such as the player's interaction with the virtual world). That suffices to confer First Amendment protection. [W]hatever the challenges of applying the Constitution to ever-advancing technology, 'the basic principles of freedom of speech and the press, like the First Amendment's command, do not vary' when a new and different medium for communication appears.

"The most basic of those principles is this: '[A]s a general matter, . . . government has no power to restrict expression because of its message, its ideas, its subject matter, or its content.' There are of course exceptions. '"From 1791 to the present," ... the First Amendment has "'permitted restrictions upon the content of speech in a few limited areas].'" These limited areas — such as obscenity [*Roth*, incitement [*Brandenburg*], and fighting words [*Chaplinsky*] — represent 'well-defined and narrowly limited classes of speech, the prevention and punishment of which have never been thought to raise any Constitutional problem.' Last Term, in *Stevens*, we held that new categories of unprotected speech may not be added to the list by a legislature that concludes certain speech is too harmful to be tolerated. [There] was no American tradition of forbidding the *depiction of* animal cruelty — though States have long had laws against *committing* it. [As] in *Stevens*, California has tried to make violent-speech regulation look like obscenity regulation, [but] the obscenity exception to the First Amendment does not cover whatever a legislature finds shocking, but only depictions of 'sexual conduct.'

"[B]ecause speech about violence is not obscene, it is of no consequence that California's statute mimics the New York statute regulating obscenity for minors that we upheld in *Ginsberg*. [The] California Act [does] not adjust the boundaries of an existing category of unprotected speech to ensure that a definition designed for adults is not uncritically applied to children. California does not argue that it is empowered to prohibit selling offensively violent works *to adults*. ... Instead, it wishes to create a wholly new category of content-based regulation that is permissible only for speech directed at children. That is unprecedented and mistaken. [No] doubt a State possesses legitimate power to protect children from harm, but that does not include a free-floating power to restrict the ideas to which children may be exposed. [California's] argument would fare better if there were a long standing tradition in this country of specially restricting children's access to depictions of violence, but there is none. Certainly the *books* we give children to read — or read to them when they are younger — contain no shortage of gore. [As] her just deserts for trying to poison Snow White, the wicked queen is made to dance in red hot slippers 'till she fell dead on the [floor].' Hansel and Gretel (children!) kill their captor by baking her in an oven. High-school reading lists are full of similar fare. Homer's Odysseus blinds Polyphemus the Cyclops by grinding out his eye with a heated stake. [And] Golding's Lord of the Flies recounts how a schoolboy called Piggy is savagely murdered *by other children* while marooned on an island. ...

"California claims that video games present special problems because they are 'interactive,' [but as] Judge Posner has observed, all literature is interactive. '[T]he better it is, the more interactive. ...' American Amusement Machine Assn. v. Kendrick, 244 F. 3d 572, 577 (CA7 2001). [Justice] Alito has done considerable independent research to identify, video games in which 'the violence is astounding.' 'Victims are dismembered, decapitated, disemboweled, set on fire, and chopped into little pieces. ... Blood gushes, splatters, and pools.' Justice Alito recounts all these disgusting video games in order to disgust us — but disgust is not a valid basis for restricting expression. ...

"Because the Act imposes a restriction on the content of protected speech, it is invalid unless California can demonstrate that it passes strict scrutiny — that is, unless it is justified by a compelling government interest and is narrowly drawn to serve that interest. [California] cannot meet that standard. At the outset, it acknowledges that it cannot show a direct causal link between violent video games and harm to minors. [Indeed,] the State's evidence is not compelling. California relies primarily [on a few] research psychologists whose studies purport to show a connection between exposure to violent video games and harmful effects on children. These studies have been rejected by every court to consider them, and with good reason: They do not prove that violent video games *cause* minors to *act* aggressively (which would at least be a beginning). Instead, '[n]early all of the research is based on correlation, not evidence of causation, and most of the studies suffer from [significant] flaws in methodology.' [Even] taking for granted [the conclusion] that violent video games produce some effect on children's feelings of aggression, those effects are both small and indistinguishable from effects produced by other media. [It appears that] the 'effect sizes' of children's exposure to violent video games are 'about the same' as that produced by their exposure to [cartoons] starring Bugs Bunny or the Road Runner, [or] video games like Sonic the Hedgehog that are rated 'E' (appropriate for all ages), or even when they 'vie[w] a picture of a gun.'

"Of course, California has (wisely) declined to restrict Saturday morning cartoons, the sale of games rated for young children, or the distribution of pictures of guns. The consequence is that its regulation is wildly underinclusive when judged against its asserted justification, which in our view is alone enough to defeat it. Underinclusiveness raises serious doubts about whether the government is in fact pursuing the interest it invokes, rather than disfavoring a particular speaker or viewpoint. Here, California has singled out the purveyors of video games for disfavored treatment — at least when compared to booksellers, cartoonists, and movie producers — and has given no persuasive reason why.

"The Act is also seriously underinclusive in another respect. The California Legislature is perfectly willing to leave this dangerous, mind-altering material in the hands of children so long as one parent (or even an aunt or uncle) says it's OK. [That] is not how one addresses a serious social problem.

"California claims that the Act is justified in aid of parental authority: By requiring that the purchase of violent video games can be made only by adults, the Act ensures that parents can decide what games are appropriate. [But] California cannot show that the Act's restrictions meet a substantial need of parents who wish to restrict their children's access to violent video games but cannot do so. The video-game industry has in place a voluntary rating system designed to inform consumers about the content of games. [Moreover,] the Act's purported aid to parental authority is vastly overinclusive. Not all of the children who are forbidden to purchase violent video games on their own have parents who *care* whether they purchase violent video games. While some of the legislation's effect may indeed be in support of what some parents of the restricted children actually want, its entire effect is only in support of what the State thinks parents *ought* to want. This is not the narrow tailoring to 'assisting parents' that restriction of First Amendment rights requires."

Justice Alito, joined by Chief Justice Roberts, concurred in the result because "the law's definition of 'violent video game' is impermissibly vague." Justice Alito argued that it was unnecessary to go beyond that conclusion to resolve the case, but he nonetheless suggested that he disagreed "with the approach taken in the Court's opinion." He reasoned that in "considering the application of unchanging constitutional principles to new and rapidly evolving technology, [we] should not jump to the conclusion that new technology is fundamentally the same as some older thing with which we are familiar. And we should not hastily dismiss the judgment of legislators, who may be in a better position than we are to assess the implications of new technology."

Justice Thomas dissented: "The Court's decision [does] not comport with the original public understanding of the First Amendment. [The] practices and beliefs of the founding generation establish that 'the freedom of speech,' as originally understood, does not include a right to speak to minors (or a right of minors to access speech) without going through the minors' parents or guardians. [Because] the Constitution is a written instrument, 'its meaning does not alter.' 'That which it meant when adopted, it means now.' [The] founding generation would not have considered it an abridgment of 'the freedom of speech' to support parental authority by restricting speech that bypasses minors' parents."

Justice Breyer also dissented: "In my view, California's statute provides 'fair notice' of what is prohibited,' and consequently is not impermissibly vague. [I] can find no vagueness-related differences between California's law and the New York law upheld in *Ginsberg*. . . .

"Like the majority, I believe that the California law must be 'narrowly tailored' to further a 'compelling interest,' without there being a 'less restrictive' alternative that would be 'at least as effective.' [But I would not apply this strict standard mechanically. Rather, in applying it, I would evaluate the degree to which the statute injures speech-related interests, the nature of the potentially-justifying 'compelling interests,' the degree to which the statute furthers that interest, the nature and effectiveness of possible alternatives, and, in light of this evaluation, whether, overall, 'the statute works speech-related harms . . . out of proportion to the benefits that the statute seeks to provide.' First Amendment standards applied in this way are difficult but not impossible to satisfy. [Citing his dissenting opinion in *Holder v. Humanitarian Law Project*.] . . .

"California's law imposes no more than a modest restriction on expression. [All] it prevents is a child or adolescent from buying, without a parent's assistance, a gruesomely violent video [game]. The interest that California advances in support of the statute is compelling. As the Court has previously described that interest, it consists of both (1) the 'basic' parental claim 'to authority in their own household to direct the rearing of their children,' which makes it proper to enact 'laws designed to aid discharge of [parental] responsibility, and (2) the State's 'independent interest in the well-being of its youth.' [Quoting *Ginsberg*.] Both interests are present here. . . .

"[Moreover,] there is considerable evidence that California's statute significantly furthers this compelling interest. [There] are many scientific studies that support California's views. [Some] of these studies [explain] that the closer a child's behavior comes, not to watching, but to *acting* out horrific violence, the greater the potential psychological harm. [Of course, experts] debate the conclusions of all these studies [and] critics have produced studies [that] reach different conclusions. [I], like most judges, lack the social science expertise to say definitively who is right. [But unlike] the majority, I would find sufficient grounds in these studies [for] this Court to defer to an elected legislature's conclusion that the video games in question are particularly likely to harm children. . . .

"I add that the majority's [conclusion] creates a serious anomaly in First Amendment law. [What] sense does it make to forbid selling to a 13-year-old boy a magazine with an image of a nude woman, while protecting a sale to that 13-year-old of an interactive video game in which he actively, but virtually, binds and gags the woman, then tortures and kills her?"

Are video games "speech" within the meaning of the first amendment? Are games such as bingo, blackjack, chess, and baseball "speech"? After *Brown*, how would you analyze the constitutionality of a state law prohibiting anyone to engage in mixed martial arts? Suppose the law prohibited only public "exhibitions" of mixed martial arts?

Does the Court's emphasis on history in the low-value analysis make sense? Consider Magarian, The Marrow of Tradition: The Roberts Court and Categorical First Amendment Speech Exclusions, 56 Wm. & M. L. Rev. 1339 (2015): "Most of the Court's [major] categorical decisions — *Chaplinsky, Brandenburg, Virginia Pharmacy, Ferber* — have said little or nothing about tradition, concentrating almost entirely on substantive justifications for excluding certain speech from First Amendment protection. [The] most transparent way for the Court to decide categorical exclusion cases would be for the Justices to talk openly about which values matter and why. By rejecting that substantive analysis in favor of a tradition-bound analysis, the Roberts Court hides the analytic ball." For a similar critique, see Lakier, The Invention of Low-Value Speech, 128 Harv. L. Rev. 2166 (2015).

7.   The Lewd, the Profane, and the Indecent

In what circumstances, if any, may government restrict the public use of profane or sexually oriented, but non-obscene, expression because of its offensive character? Recall that in *Chaplinsky* the Court's list of utterances "the prevention and punishment of which have never been thought to raise any Constitutional problem" expressly included not only "fighting words," the "libelous," and the "obscene," but also the "lewd" and the "profane." Moreover, in explaining why such utterances are "unprotected," the Court in *Chaplinsky* noted not only that they might "tend to incite an immediate breach of the peace," but also that they might "by their very utterance inflict injury."

Cohen v. California

403 U.S. 15 (1971)

MR. JUSTICE HARLAN delivered the opinion of the Court.

This case may seem at first blush too inconsequential to find its way into our books, but the issue it presents is of no small constitutional significance.

Appellant Paul Robert Cohen was convicted in the Los Angeles Municipal Court of violating that part of California Penal Code §415 which prohibits "maliciously and willfully disturb[ing] the peace or quiet of any neighborhood or person . . . by . . . offensive conduct. . . ." He was given 30 days' imprisonment. The facts upon which his conviction rests are detailed in the opinion of the [state court]:

> On April 26, 1968, the defendant was observed in the Los Angeles County Courthouse in the corridor outside [of] the municipal court wearing a jacket bearing the words "Fuck the Draft." There were women and children present in the corridor. The defendant was arrested. The defendant testified that he wore the jacket [as] a means of informing the public of the depth of his feelings against the Vietnam War and the draft.
>
> The defendant did not engage in, nor threaten to engage in, nor did anyone as the result of his conduct in fact commit or threaten to commit any act of violence.

The defendant did not make any loud or unusual noise, nor was there any evidence that he uttered any sound prior to his arrest. . . .

[We reverse.]

I

In order to lay hands on the precise issue which this case involves, it is useful first to canvass various matters which this record does *not* present.

The conviction quite clearly rests upon the asserted offensiveness of the *words* Cohen used, [for] the State certainly lacks power to punish Cohen for [the] message the inscription conveyed. [Moreover], this is not [an] obscenity case. Whatever else may be necessary to give rise to the States' broader power to prohibit obscene expression, such expression must be, in some significant way, erotic. [*Roth.*] It cannot plausibly be maintained that this vulgar allusion to the Selective Service System would conjure up such psychic stimulation in anyone likely to be confronted with Cohen's crudely defaced jacket.

This Court has [held] that the States are free to [ban] so-called "fighting words," those personally abusive epithets which, when addressed to the ordinary citizen, [are] inherently likely to provoke violent reaction. [*Chaplinsky.*] While the four-letter word displayed by Cohen in relation to the draft is not uncommonly employed in a personally provocative fashion, in this instance it was clearly not "directed to the person of the hearer." [No] individual actually or likely to be present could reasonably have regarded the words on appellant's jacket as a direct personal insult. Nor do we have here an instance of the exercise of the State's police power to prevent a speaker from intentionally provoking a given group to hostile reaction. Cf. [*Feiner*]. There [is] no showing that anyone who saw Cohen was in fact violently aroused or that appellant intended such a result.

Finally, in arguments before this Court much has been made of the claim that Cohen's distasteful mode of expression was thrust upon unwilling or unsuspecting viewers, and that the State might therefore legitimately act as it did in order to protect the sensitive from otherwise unavoidable exposure to appellant's crude form of protest. Of course, the mere presumed presence of unwitting listeners or viewers does not serve automatically to justify curtailing all speech capable of giving offense. [While] this Court has recognized that government may properly act in many situations to prohibit intrusion into the privacy of the home of unwelcome views and ideas which cannot be totally banned from the public dialogue, e.g., Rowan v. Post Office Dept., 397 U.S. 728 (1970), we have at the same time consistently stressed that "we are often 'captives' outside the sanctuary of the home and subject to objectionable speech." [The] ability of government, consonant with the Constitution, to shut off discourse solely to protect others from hearing it is, in other words, dependent upon a showing that substantial privacy interests are being invaded in an essentially intolerable manner. Any broader view of this authority would effectively empower a majority to silence dissidents simply as a matter of personal predilections.

In this regard, persons confronted with Cohen's jacket were in a quite different posture than, say, those subjected to the raucous emissions of sound trucks blaring outside their residences. Those in the Los Angeles courthouse could effectively avoid further bombardment of their sensibilities simply by averting their eyes. And, while it may be that one has a more substantial claim to a recognizable privacy interest when walking through a courthouse corridor than, for example, strolling through Central Park, surely it is nothing like the interest in being free from unwanted expression in the confines of one's own home. . . .

II

Against this background, the issue flushed by this case stands out in bold relief. It is whether California can excise, as "offensive conduct," one particular scurrilous epithet from the public discourse, either upon the theory [that] its use is inherently likely to cause violent reaction or upon a more general assertion that the States, acting as guardians of public morality, may properly remove this offensive word from the public vocabulary.

The [first rationale] is plainly untenable. At most it reflects an "undifferentiated fear or apprehension of disturbance [which] is not enough to overcome the right to freedom of expression." [We] have been shown no evidence that substantial numbers of citizens are standing ready to strike out physically at whoever may assault their sensibilities with execrations like that uttered by Cohen. There may be some persons about with such lawless and violent proclivities, but that is an insufficient base upon which to erect, consistently with constitutional values, a governmental power to force persons who wish to ventilate their dissident views into avoiding particular forms of expression. The argument amounts to little more than the self-defeating proposition that to avoid physical censorship of one who has not sought to provoke such a response by a hypothetical coterie of the violent and lawless, the States may more appropriately effectuate that censorship themselves. . . .

Admittedly, it is not so obvious that the First and Fourteenth Amendments must be taken to disable the States from punishing public utterance of this unseemly expletive in order to maintain what they regard as a suitable level of discourse within the body politic. We think, however, that examination and reflection will reveal the shortcomings of a contrary viewpoint.

At the outset, we cannot overemphasize that, in our judgment, most situations where the State has a justifiable interest in regulating speech will fall within one or more of the various established exceptions, discussed above but not applicable here, to the usual rule that governmental bodies may not prescribe the form or content of individual expression. Equally important to our conclusion is the constitutional backdrop against which our decision must be made. The constitutional right of free expression is powerful medicine in a society as diverse and populous as ours. It is designed and intended to remove governmental restraints from the arena of public discussion, putting the decision as to what views shall be voiced largely into the hands of each of us, in the hope that use of such freedom will ultimately produce a more capable citizenry and more perfect polity and in the belief that no other approach would comport with the premise of individual dignity and choice upon which our political system rests. See [*Whitney* (Brandeis, J., concurring)].

To many, the immediate consequence of this freedom may often appear to be only verbal tumult, discord, and even offensive utterance. These are, however, within established limits, in truth necessary side effects of the broader enduring values which the process of open debate permits us to achieve. That the air may at times seem filled with verbal cacophony is, in this sense not a sign of weakness but of strength. We cannot lose sight of the fact that, in what otherwise might seem a trifling and annoying instance of individual distasteful abuse of a privilege, these fundamental societal values are truly implicated. . . .

Against this perception of the constitutional policies involved, we discern certain more particularized considerations that peculiarly call for reversal of this conviction. First, the principle contended for by the State seems inherently boundless. How is one to distinguish this from any other offensive word? Surely the State has no right to cleanse public debate to the point where it is grammatically palatable to the most squeamish among us. Yet no readily ascertainable general principle exists for stopping short of that result were we to affirm the judgment below. For, while the particular four-letter word being litigated here is perhaps more distasteful than most others of its genre, it is nevertheless often true that one man's vulgarity is another's lyric. Indeed, we think it is largely because governmental officials cannot make principled distinctions in this area that the Constitution leaves matters of taste and style so largely to the individual.

Additionally, we cannot overlook the fact, because it is well illustrated by the episode involved here, that much linguistic expression serves a dual communicative function: it conveys not only ideas capable of relatively precise, detached explication, but otherwise inexpressible emotions as well. In fact, words are often chosen as much for their emotive as their cognitive force. We cannot sanction the view that the Constitution, while solicitous of the cognitive content of individual speech, has little or no regard for that emotive function which, practically speaking, may often be the more important element of the overall message sought to be communicated. . . .

Finally, and in the same vein, we cannot indulge the facile assumption that one can forbid particular words without also running a substantial risk of suppressing ideas in the process. Indeed, governments might soon seize upon the censorship of particular words as a convenient guise for banning the expression of unpopular views. We have been able, as noted above, to discern little social benefit that might result from running the risk of opening the door to such grave results.

It is, in sum, our judgment that, absent a more particularized and compelling reason for its actions, the State may not, consistently with the First and Fourteenth Amendments, make the simple public display here involved of this single four-letter expletive a criminal offense. . . .

Reversed.

Mr. Justice Blackmun, with whom The Chief Justice and Mr. Justice Black join.

I dissent. . . .

Cohen's absurd and immature antic, in my view, was mainly conduct and little speech. [Further,] the case appears to me to be well within the sphere of [Chaplinsky], where Mr. Justice Murphy, a known champion of First Amendment freedoms, wrote for a unanimous bench. As a consequence, this Court's agonizing over First Amendment values seems misplaced and unnecessary.

[Justice White dissented on other grounds.]

Note: Profanity, Cohen, and the Captive Audience

1. Profanity as "low"-value speech. Does Cohen repudiate Chaplinsky's assumption that profanity is of only "low" first amendment value? If obscenity

has "no redeeming social value," why isn't the same true of profanity? Consider the following proposition: Profanity has "high" first amendment value because (a) its use may be necessary to convey "otherwise inexpressible emotions," (b) its suppression creates "a substantial risk of suppressing ideas in the process," and (c) there exists "no readily ascertainable general principle" for distinguishing between prohibitable and nonprohibitable offensive language.

Consider W. Berns, The First Amendment and the Future of American Democracy 200 (1976):

> This country managed to live most of its years under rules, conventional and legal, that forbade the public use of profanity [and] it would be an abuse of language to say that its freedom was thereby restricted in any important respect. Now, suddenly, and for reasons that ought to persuade no one, we are told that it is a violation of the First Amendment for the law to enforce these rules; that however desirable it might be to see them preserved, there is no way for the law to do this except by threatening the freedom of all speech. [Do] we really live in a world so incapable of communication that it can be said that "one man's vulgarity is another's lyric"?

2. *Profanity and fighting words.* As evident in *Chaplinsky*, the problems of fighting words and profanity are closely related. In *Cohen*, however, the Court "made clear that [the phrase 'fighting words'] was no longer to be understood as a euphemism for controversial or dirty talk but was to require instead a quite unambiguous invitation to a brawl." J. Ely, Democracy and Distrust 114 (1980). The Court thus recognized in *Cohen* that the fighting words and profanity problems are analytically distinct — although fighting words typically involve the use of profanity, this is not essential; although fighting words usually involve insults directed personally to the addressee, the problem of profanity is not so limited; and although the fighting words doctrine is designed primarily to forestall an addressee's violent response, government efforts to suppress offensive language are designed primarily to raise the level of public discourse and to protect the sensibilities of an unconsenting audience. The fighting words doctrine is examined in section B3 supra.

3. *Profanity: manner or content?* Is a law restricting the use of profanity in public more akin to a law restricting the public expression of an "offensive" idea or to a law restricting the use of an "offensive" means of expression? Compare, for example, a law prohibiting the expression of "offensive ideas" in a public park, a law prohibiting the use of profanity in a public park, and a law prohibiting the use of loudspeakers in a public park. Is the prohibition on profanity more akin to the prohibition on loudspeakers because both are directed against "consequences unrelated" to the particular ideas expressed? Cox, Foreword: Freedom of Expression in the Burger Court, 94 Harv. L. Rev. 1, 40 (1980). Is it more akin to the prohibition on "offensive ideas" because the "harms of shock and offense [flow] entirely from the communicative content of [the] message"? Ely, supra, at 114.

Consider the following views:

a. Haiman, Speech v. Privacy: Is There a Right Not to Be Spoken To?, 67 Nw. U. L. Rev. 153, 189 (1972):

> The problem with the position [that prohibitions on the use of profanity are merely restrictions on the manner of expression] is that the form and content of communications are so inextricably tied that to control the former is, in fact, to modify the latter. [For] example, it can hardly be maintained that phrases like, "Repeal the

Draft," "Resist the Draft," or "The Draft Must Go" convey essentially the same message as "Fuck the Draft." Clearly something is lost in the translation.

b. Stone, Content Regulation and the First Amendment, 25 Wm. & Mary L. Rev. 189, 243–244 (1983):

> Governmental efforts to limit speech because it is offensively *noisy* [do] not implicate the same kind of censorial or heckler's veto concerns as governmental efforts to limit speech because the *ideas* are offensive. Analytically, offense at language is more like offense at noise than offense at ideas. [Moreover, although] restrictions on the use of profanity may affect some speakers more than others, [this] is also true of most content-neutral restrictions.

4. *The captive audience.* Does Justice Harlan undervalue the interests of the "audience" in *Cohen*? Consider A. Bickel, The Morality of Consent 72 (1975): "There is such a thing as verbal violence, a kind of cursing, assaultive speech that amounts to almost physical aggression. [The sort of speech at issue in *Cohen*] constitutes an assault." As noted in *Chaplinsky*, such profanities "by their very utterance inflict injury." Why, then, can't such expression be suppressed? Is the interest in protecting the sensibilities of unconsenting individuals against such "assaults" simply too insubstantial to justify restrictions on "offensive" expression? Note Justice Harlan's conclusion in *Cohen* that "[the] ability of government [to] shut off discourse solely to protect others from hearing it is [dependent] upon a showing that substantial privacy interests are being invaded in an essentially intolerable manner."

Consider the following:

a. Suppose Congress enacts a law authorizing any homeowner who no longer wishes to receive mail from a particular person or organization to instruct the Postmaster General to direct that person or organization to refrain from further mailings to the homeowner. Consider Rowan v. Post Office Department, 397 U.S. 728 (1970):

> In today's complex society we are inescapably captive audiences for many purposes, but a sufficient measure of individual autonomy must survive to permit every householder to exercise control over unwanted mail. To make the householder the exclusive and final judge of what will cross his threshold undoubtedly has the effect of impeding the flow of ideas, information, and arguments that, ideally, he should receive and consider. [But] nothing in the Constitution compels us to listen to or view any unwanted communication, whatever its merit. [The] ancient concept that "a man's home is his castle" into which "not even the king may enter" has lost none of its vitality, [and we] therefore categorically reject the argument that [an individual] has a right under the Constitution [to] send unwanted material into the home of another.

b. Suppose Congress enacts a law prohibiting any person to mail to another any materials containing profanity or photographs revealing bare human pubic areas without the recipient's prior written consent. In Bolger v. Youngs Drug Products Corp., 463 U.S. 60 (1983), the Court invalidated a federal statute prohibiting the mailing of unsolicited advertisements for contraceptives. The Court explained:

> We [have] recognized the important interest in allowing addressees to give notice to a mailer that they wish no further mailings [citing *Rowan*]. But we have never held

that the government itself can shut off the flow of mailings to protect those recipients who might potentially be offended. The First Amendment "does not permit the government to prohibit speech as intrusive unless the 'captive' audience cannot avoid objectionable speech." [The] "short, regular, journey from mail box to trash can [is] an acceptable burden, at least so far as the Constitution is concerned."

In light of *Rowan* and *Bolger*, could Congress constitutionally require all televisions to have a chip that enables the owner to block out unwanted channels or shows? Could it constitutionally require all televisions to have a chip that enables the owner to block out only unwanted channels or shows that are rated as especially violent or sexual? See Balkin, Media Filters, the V-Chip, and the Foundations of Broadcast Regulation, 45 Duke L.J. 1131 (1996).

c. Suppose a city operates a public bus system and each bus contains twenty interior advertising spaces available for lease by private persons. May the city, to protect the sensibilities of "captive" commuters, exclude such "highly offensive" messages as "Welfare Is Black Theft," "God Is Dead," and "Abortion Is Murder"? Is this a situation in which, as in *Cohen*, the audience "could effectively avoid further bombardment of their sensibilities simply by averting their eyes"? Suppose the city excludes ads that contain profanity? Nudity? Cf. Lehman v. City of Shaker Heights, 418 U.S. 298 (1974) (plurality opinion upholding city policy permitting the display of commercial but not generally more "controversial" political or public issue advertisements in the interior of city buses), section E2c infra. Note that in the bus situation, unlike the situation in *Cohen*, the city could protect the "captive" audience by adopting a content-neutral restriction excluding *all* speech. Is a content-neutral restriction preferable to a "narrower" restriction based on content? Consider Stone, supra, at 280: "If a 'true' captive audience exists, the state may protect the sensibilities of unwilling listeners by banning all speech, regardless of content. It should never, however, be permitted to use the captive audience as a lever for censorship." Should that conclusion, however justified as applied to offensive ideas, apply also to the use of profanity and to the display of "lewd" pictures?

ERZNOZNIK v. JACKSONVILLE, 422 U.S. 205 (1975). In *Erznoznik*, the Court invalidated a Jacksonville, Florida, ordinance that declared it a public nuisance for any drive-in movie theater to exhibit any motion picture "in which the human male or female bare buttocks, human female bare breasts, or human bare pubic areas are shown, if such motion picture [is] visible from any public street or place." Justice Powell delivered the opinion of the Court:

"[The city] concedes that its ordinance sweeps far beyond the permissible restraints on obscenity [and] thus applies to films that are protected by the First Amendment. [Nevertheless], it maintains that any movie containing nudity which is visible from a public place may be suppressed as a nuisance. . . .

"[The city's] primary argument is that it may protect its citizens against unwilling exposure to materials that may be offensive. Jacksonville's ordinance, however, does not protect citizens from all movies that might offend; rather it singles out films containing nudity, presumably because the lawmakers considered them especially offensive to passersby. [A] State or municipality may protect individual privacy by enacting reasonable time, place, and manner regulations applicable to all speech irrespective of content. [But] when government [undertakes] selectively to shield the public from some kinds of speech on the ground that they are more offensive than others, the First Amendment strictly limits its power. [Absent extraordinary circumstances], the burden normally falls upon the viewer to 'avoid further bombardment of [his] sensibilities simply by averting [his] eyes.' [*Cohen.*] [The] limited privacy interest of persons on the public streets cannot justify this censorship of otherwise protected speech on the basis of its content. . . .

"[The city] also attempts to support the ordinance as an exercise of the city's undoubted police power to protect children. [But] the ordinance is not directed [only] against sexually explicit [nudity]. Rather, it sweepingly forbids display of all films containing *any* uncovered buttocks or breasts, irrespective of context or pervasiveness. [Clearly] all nudity cannot be deemed obscene even as to minors. [Thus], if Jacksonville's ordinance is intended to regulate expression accessible to minors it is overbroad in its proscription. . . .

"[Finally, the city attempts] to justify the ordinance [on the ground] that nudity on a drive-in movie screen distracts passing motorists, thus slowing the flow of traffic and increasing the likelihood of accidents. [But] the legislative classification is strikingly underinclusive. There is no reason to think that a wide variety of other scenes in the customary screen diet, ranging from soap opera to violence, would be any less distracting to the passing motorist."

Justice Douglas filed a concurring opinion.

Chief Justice Burger, joined by Justice Rehnquist, dissented: "Whatever validity the notion that passersby may protect their sensibilities by averting their eyes may have when applied to words printed on an individual's jacket, see [*Cohen*], it distorts reality to apply that notion to the outsize screen of a drive-in movie theater. [It] is not unreasonable for lawmakers to believe that public nudity on a giant screen, visible at night to hundreds of [drivers], may have a tendency to divert attention from their task and cause accidents. [Moreover], those persons who legitimately desire to [view such films] are not foreclosed from doing so. [Such films may be] exhibited [in] indoor theaters [and in any] drive-in movie theater [whose] screen [is shielded] from public view. Thus, [the challenged] ordinance [is] not a restriction of any 'message.' [The] First Amendment interests involved in this case are trivial at best."

Justice White also dissented.

FCC v. PACIFICA FOUNDATION, 438 U.S. 726 (1978). At about 2 o'clock in the afternoon on October 30, 1973, a New York radio station, owned by Pacifica Foundation, broadcast George Carlin's monologue entitled "Filthy Words." In this twelve-minute monologue, Carlin discussed "the words you couldn't say on the public, ah, airwaves, um, the ones you definitely wouldn't say, ever." He proceeded to list those words ("shit, piss, fuck, cunt, cocksucker, motherfucker, and tits"), which he described as the "ones that will curve your spine [and] grow hair on your hands," and then repeated them in a variety of colloquialisms. The recording includes frequent laughter from the live audience. A few weeks later, a man who had heard the broadcast while driving with his young son wrote a letter complaining to the Commission.

Pacifica responded to the complaint by explaining that the monologue had been played during a program about contemporary society's attitude toward language and that, immediately before its broadcast, listeners had been advised that it included "sensitive language which might be regarded as offensive to some." Pacifica characterized Carlin as "a significant social satirist" who uses "words to satirize as harmless and essentially silly our attitudes towards those words." There were no other complaints about the broadcast.

The Commission issued a declaratory order granting the complaint. Characterizing Carlin's language as "patently offensive," though not obscene, the Commission explained that such "indecent" speech should be regulated by principles analogous to those found in the law of nuisance. Specifically, the Commission announced that broadcasters may not air language that describes sexual or excretory activities or organs in terms that are patently offensive as measured by contemporary community standards at times of the day when children are likely to be in the audience. Although the Commission did not impose formal sanctions, it stated that the complaint would be "associated with the station's license [file]." . . .

The Court upheld the Commission, although there was no majority opinion. In a plurality opinion, joined by Chief Justice Burger and Justice Rehnquist, Justice Stevens noted that a "requirement that indecent language be avoided will have its primary effect on the form, rather than the content, of serious communication. There are few, if any, thoughts that cannot be expressed by the use of less offensive language." Although affirming that "the government must remain neutral in the marketplace of ideas," Stevens maintained that the FCC's action had nothing to do with the substance of Carlin's political ideas or opinions. Rather, the Commission objected only to the "way" in which Carlin expressed those ideas. In such circumstances, "we must consider its context in order to determine whether the Commission's action was constitutionally permissible."

Applying that approach, Justice Stevens upheld the FCC's order: "The broadcast media have established a uniquely pervasive presence in the lives of all Americans. Patently offensive, indecent material presented over the airwaves confronts the citizen, not only in public, but also in the privacy of the home, where the individual's right to be left alone plainly outweighs the First Amendment rights of an intruder. [*Rowan.*] Because the broadcast audience is constantly tuning in and out, prior warnings cannot completely protect the listener or viewer from unexpected program content. [Moreover], broadcasting is uniquely accessible to children, even those too young to read. Although Cohen's written message might have been incomprehensible to a first grader, Pacifica's broadcast could have enlarged a child's vocabulary in an instant. Other forms of offensive expression may be withheld from the young without restricting the expression at its source. Bookstores and motion picture theaters, for example, may be prohibited from making indecent material available to children. [Citing *Ginsberg*, section D5, supra.] The ease with which children may obtain access to broadcast material, coupled with the concerns recognized in *Ginsberg*, amply justify special treatment of indecent broadcasting.

"It is appropriate [to] emphasize the narrowness of our holding. [As] Mr. Justice Sutherland wrote, a 'nuisance may be merely a right thing in the wrong place, — like a pig in the parlor instead of the barnyard.' [We] simply hold that when the Commission finds that a pig has entered the parlor, the exercise of its regulatory power does not depend on proof that the pig is obscene."

Justice Powell, joined by Justice Blackmun, filed a concurring opinion: "The Commission sought to 'channel' the monologue to hours when the fewest unsupervised children would be exposed to it. [This] consideration provides strong support for the Commission's holding. [The] Commission properly held that [the] language involved in this case is as potentially degrading and harmful to children as representations of many erotic acts. In most instances, the dissemination of this kind of speech to children may be limited without also limiting willing adults' access to it. [The] difficulty is that such a physical separation of the audience cannot be accomplished in the broadcast media. [In] my view, the Commission was entitled to give substantial weight to this difference [between the broadcast and other media] in reaching its decision in this case. . . .

"The Commission's holding does not prevent willing adults from purchasing Carlin's record, from attending his performances, or, indeed, from reading the transcript reprinted as an appendix to the Court's opinion. [It] does not prevent Pacifica Foundation from broadcasting the monologue during late evening hours when fewer children are likely to be in the audience, nor from broadcasting discussions of the contemporary use of language at any time during the day."

Justice Brennan, joined by Justice Marshall, dissented: "[An] individual's actions in switching on and listening to communications transmitted over the public airways and directed to the public at large do not implicate fundamental privacy interests, even when engaged in within the home. Instead, [these] actions are more properly viewed as a decision to take part, if only as a listener, in an ongoing public discourse. [Moreover], unlike other intrusive modes of communication, such as sound trucks, '[t]he radio can be turned off.' [The Court] fails to accord proper weight to the interests of listeners who wish to hear broadcasts the FCC deems offensive. It permits majoritarian tastes completely to preclude a protected message from entering the homes of a receptive, unoffended minority. No decision of this Court supports such a result. . . .

"[The] government unquestionably has a special interest in the well-being of children and consequently 'can adopt more stringent controls on communicative materials available to youths than on those available to adults.' [But] '[s]peech that is neither obscene as to youths nor subject to some other legitimate proscription cannot be suppressed solely to protect the young from ideas or images that a legislative body thinks unsuitable for them.' [*Erznoznik*.] [Thus, the Court's] result violates in spades the principle of Butler v. Michigan [that government may not] 'reduce the adult population [to] reading only what is fit for children.'"

Justice Stewart, joined by Justices Brennan, White, and Marshall, dissented on the ground that the FCC had statutory authority to regulate only "obscene" material.

Note: Fleeting Expletives

In 2004, the Federal Communications Commission amended the indecency rule that the Court had upheld twenty-five years earlier in *Pacifica* to provide for the first time that *any* use of indecent words could be actionable, even if the words were not used in a sexual manner and even if they were used spontaneously and only in passing. The 2004 order arose out of several incidents involving so-called "fleeting" expletives. In one incident, Cher exclaimed during an unscripted acceptance speech at the 2002 Billboard Music Awards, "I've had my critics for the last 40 years saying that I was on my way out every year. Right. So fuck 'em." In another incident, at the 2003 Golden Globe Awards, Bono, upon winning the award for Best Original Song, exclaimed, "This is really, really, fucking brilliant." For these and similar incidents involving fleeting expletives, the FCC levied fines on broadcasters totaling some $8 million. The Commission defended its new rule on the ground that the word "fuck" "is one of the most vulgar, graphic and explicit descriptions of sexual activity in the English language." It therefore argued that its action was necessary to "safeguard the well-being of the nation's children from the most objectionable, most offensive language."

In 2008, the United States Court of Appeals ruled that the FCC lacked statutory authority to punish broadcasters for mere fleeting expletives. In 2009, in FCC v. Fox Television Stations, 566 U.S. 502 (2009), the Supreme Court, in a five-to-four decision, reversed, holding that the FCC did, indeed, have statutory authority for its rule. But the Court remanded the case to the Court of Appeals to decide whether the FCC's new rule violated the first amendment.

On remand, the Court of Appeals held that the FCC's indecency policy did, indeed, violate the first amendment because the Commission, in applying its rule, had made ad hoc and inconsistent judgments about the circumstances in which the use of the word fuck was forbidden. In FCC v. Fox Television Stations, 132 S.Ct. 2307 (2012) (*Fox II*), the Supreme Court vacated the Court of Appeals' first amendment holding, but unanimously ruled that the FCC's standard violated the due process clause because the FCC had failed to give the broadcasters fair notice that fleeting expletives could be found indecent.

Perhaps the most interesting thing about the Court's opinions in these cases is that unlike the opinions in *Cohen* and *Pacifica*, in which the justices used the words fuck, cunt, shit, and cocksucker in their opinions, because they were the relevant facts in the cases, in their opinions in *Fox I* and *Fox II*, Justices Scalia and Kennedy insisted on using f***, s***, and f***ing. What do you think of the following argument:

> This is not what lawyers and judges do. Lawyers and judges must deal forthrightly with the real world. They deal with murder and greed and rape; they deal with torture and brutality and gruesome wounds. It is their responsibility as *professionals* to deal in a mature and straightforward manner with all sorts of unpleasantness. Especially in a First Amendment case, lawyers and judges have to be willing to say the words out loud, even if it makes them uncomfortable. To do otherwise is to deny the realities of the case before them. It is to put their own sensitivities above their obligations to their clients and to the law. It is, in short, unprofessional.

SABLE COMMUNICATIONS, INC. v. FCC, 492 U.S. 115 (1989). The Court unanimously held unconstitutional a federal statute prohibiting the interstate transmission of "indecent" commercial telephone messages ("dial-a-porn" services). In an opinion by Justice White, the Court distinguished the "emphatically narrow holding" of *Pacifica*. The Court explained that telephone communications are different, for they require the caller to take "affirmative steps" to receive the message: "Placing a telephone call is not the same as turning on a radio and being taken by surprise by an indecent message." Moreover, the government's interest in protecting children could be served by various technical means other than a total ban of the transmission of such messages; although some limited numbers of children might be able to defeat these devices, the prohibition "has the invalid effect of limiting the content of adult telephone conversations to that which is suitable for children to hear."

RENO v. AMERICAN CIVIL LIBERTIES UNION, 521 U.S. 844 (1997). In an opinion by Justice Stevens, the Court invalidated two sections of the Communications Decency Act of 1996 (CDA) that were designed to protect minors from "indecent" and "patently offensive" communications on the internet. Section 223(a) prohibited any person from making any communication over the internet "which is . . . indecent, knowing that the recipient of the communication is under eighteen years of age." Section 223(d) prohibited any person from knowingly sending over the internet any communication that will be available to a person under 18 years of age and "that, in context, depicts or describes, in terms patently offensive as measured by contemporary community standards, sexual or excretory activities or organs."

At the outset, the Court distinguished *Pacifica*: "[There] are significant differences between the order upheld in *Pacifica* and the CDA. First, the order in *Pacifica* [focused on when — rather than whether — it would be permissible to air such a program in that particular medium. The CDA's broad categorical prohibitions are not limited to particular [times]. Second, [the] Commission's order [in *Pacifica*] applied to a medium which as a matter of history had 'received the most limited First Amendment protection,' in large part because warnings could not adequately protect the listener from unexpected program content. The Internet, however, has no comparable history. Moreover, [the] risk of encountering indecent material [on the Internet] by accident is remote because a series of affirmative steps is required to access specific material."

The Court next noted "the many ambiguities" concerning the act's coverage, which "render it problematic" for purposes of the first amendment: "For instance, each of the two parts of the CDA uses a different linguistic form. The first uses the word 'indecent,' while the second speaks of material that 'in context, depicts or describes, in terms patently offensive as measured by contemporary community standards, sexual or excretory activities or organs.' Given the absence of a definition of either term, this difference in language will provoke uncertainty among speakers about how the two standards relate to each other and just what they mean."

The Court found this "lack of precision" fatal: "In order to deny minors access to potentially harmful speech, the CDA effectively suppresses a large amount of speech that adults have a constitutional right to receive and to address to one another. That burden on adult speech is unacceptable if less restrictive alternatives would be at least as effective in achieving the legitimate purpose that the statute was enacted to serve. In evaluating the free speech rights of adults, we have made it perfectly clear that '[s]exual expression which is indecent but not obscene is protected by the First Amendment.' [It] is true that we have repeatedly recognized the governmental interest in protecting children from harmful materials. [Citing *Ginsberg; Pacifica*.] But that interest does not justify an unnecessarily broad suppression of speech addressed to adults. As we have explained, the Government may not 'reduc[e] the adult population [to] only what is fit for children.'"

ASHCROFT v. AMERICAN CIVIL LIBERTIES UNION, 535 U.S. 564 (2004). In response to *Reno*, Congress enacted the Child Online Protection Act (COPA), which was designed to address the constitutional defects the Court had identified in the Communications Decency Act. COPA imposes criminal penalties of a $50,000 fine and six months in prison for the knowing posting, for "commercial purposes," of World Wide Web content that is "harmful to minors." The act defines material that is "harmful to minors" as: "any communication, picture, image, graphic image file, article, recording, writing, or other matter of any kind that is obscene or that (A) the average person, applying contemporary community standards, would find, taking the material as a whole and *with respect to minors*, is designed to appeal to, or is designed to pander to, the prurient interest; (B) depicts, describes, or represents, in a manner patently offensive *with respect to minors*, an actual or simulated sexual act or sexual contact, an actual or simulated normal or perverted sexual act, or a lewd exhibition of the genitals or post-pubescent female breast; and (C) taken as a whole, lacks serious literary, artistic, political, or scientific value for minors."

COPA defines "minor" as "any person under 17 years of age" and specifies that a person acts for "commercial purposes" only if he "makes a communication, or offers to make a communication, by means of the World Wide Web, that includes any material that is harmful to minors, . . . as a regular course of such person's trade or business, with the objective of earning a profit as a result of such activities." COPA recognizes an affirmative defense for those who attempt to prevent minors from gaining access to the prohibited materials "(A) by requiring use of a credit card, debit account, adult access code, or adult personal identification number; (B) by accepting a digital certificate that verifies age; or (C) by any other reasonable measures that are feasible under available technology."

In a five-to-four decision, the Court held that the federal district court did not "abuse its discretion" in entering a preliminary injunction against enforcement of COPA. In its opinion, written by Justice Kennedy, the Court explained that the district court had issued the preliminary injunction because it found that there "are plausible, less restrictive alternatives to COPA."

The Court continued: "The primary alternative considered by the District Court was blocking and filtering software. [Filters] are less restrictive than COPA. They impose selective restrictions on speech at the receiving end, not universal restrictions at the source. Under a filtering regime, adults without children may gain access to speech they have a right to see without having to identify themselves or provide their credit card information. Even adults with children may obtain access to the same speech on the same terms simply by turning off the filter on their home computers. . . .

"Filters also may well be more effective than COPA. First, a filter can prevent minors from seeing all pornography, not just pornography posted to the Web from America. The District Court noted [that] 40% of harmful-to-minors content comes from overseas. COPA does not prevent minors from having access to those foreign harmful materials. That alone makes it possible that filtering software might be more effective in serving Congress' goals. [It] is not an answer to say that COPA reaches some amount of materials that are harmful to minors; the question is whether it would reach more of them than less restrictive alternatives. In addition, the District Court found that verification systems may be subject to evasion and circumvention, for example by minors who have their own credit cards. [The] Commission on Child Online Protection, a blue-ribbon commission created by Congress, unambiguously found that filters are more effective than age-verification requirements. . . .

"Filtering software, of course, is not a perfect solution to the problem of children gaining access to harmful-to-minors materials. It may block some materials that are not harmful to minors and fail to catch some that are. Whatever the deficiencies of filters, however, the Government failed to introduce specific evidence proving that existing technologies are less effective than the restrictions in COPA. In the absence of a showing as to the relative effectiveness of COPA and the alternatives proposed by respondents, it was not an abuse of discretion for the District Court to grant the preliminary injunction . . . .

One argument to the contrary is worth mentioning — the argument that filtering software is not an available alternative because Congress may not require it to be used. That argument carries little weight, because Congress undoubtedly may act to encourage the use of filters. [The] need for parental cooperation does not automatically disqualify a proposed less restrictive alternative. [By] enacting programs to promote use of filtering software, Congress could give parents that ability without subjecting protected speech to severe penalties."

Justice Breyer, joined by Chief Justice Rehnquist and Justice O'Connor, dissented: "Like the Court, I would subject the Act to 'the most exacting scrutiny.' [But] my examination of (1) the burdens the Act imposes on protected expression, (2) the Act's ability to further a compelling interest, and (3) the proposed 'less restrictive alternatives' convinces me that the Court is wrong. . . .

"[The] Act, properly interpreted, imposes a burden on protected speech that is no more than modest. [The] Act does not censor the material it covers. Rather, it requires providers of the 'harmful to minors' material to restrict minors' access to it by verifying age. [I] recognize that the screening requirement imposes some burden on adults who seek access to the regulated material, as well as on its providers. The [burden] is, in part, monetary [and, in part, the fear of embarrassment caused by the identification requirement]. Both monetary costs and potential embarrassment can deter potential viewers and, in that sense, the statute's requirements may restrict access to a site. . . .

"I turn next to the question of 'compelling interest,' that of protecting minors from exposure to commercial pornography. No one denies that such an interest is 'compelling.' Rather, the question here is whether the Act, given its restrictions on adult access, significantly advances that interest. [Filtering] software, as presently available, does not solve the 'child protection' problem. It suffers from four serious inadequacies that prompted Congress to pass legislation instead of relying on its voluntary use. First, its filtering is faulty, allowing some pornographic material to pass through without hindrance. [Second], filtering software costs money. Not every family has the $40 or so necessary to install it. Third, filtering software depends upon parents willing to decide where their children will surf the Web and able to enforce that decision. [Fourth], software blocking lacks precision, with the result that those who wish to use it to screen out pornography find that it blocks a great deal of material that is valuable. [Thus], Congress could reasonably conclude that a system that relies entirely upon the use of such software is not an effective system. And a law that adds to that system an age-verification screen requirement significantly increases the system's efficacy. That is to say, at a modest additional cost to those adults who wish to obtain access to a screened program, that law will bring about better, more precise blocking, both inside and outside the home. . . ."

Justice Scalia also dissented.

Note: "Indecent" Expression

1. Reno: right result, wrong reason? Consider Volokh, Freedom of Speech, Shielding Children, and Transcending Balancing, 1997 Sup. Ct. Rev. 141, 148–149, 165–166:

The CDA is invalid, the Court said, because it is possible to protect speech in this context without *any* sacrifice of shielding of children. [But] the Court is wrong. None of the Court's proposed alternatives to the CDA [would] have been as effective [in protecting children] as the CDA's more or less total ban. [This] error is more than just a harmless misstatement, [for the] pregnant negative in the Court's reasoning is that, had there really been no equally effective alternatives, the CDA should have been upheld. [This view] is unsound. As Butler v. Michigan [section D5 supra] correctly holds, the government may not reduce adults to reading only what is fit for children. This is true even though letting adults access indecent material would necessarily sacrifice a great deal of shielding of children — even though a total ban would genuinely be the only means to effectively further the interest. [Thus, the correct approach would provide that if] the law imposes a substantial burden on generally protected speech, then it is per se impermissible, even if this means we must sacrifice a significant amount of shielding of children. [Under this approach, the] CDA would be unconstitutional because [banning such] communications substantially burdens speech to adults, [even if there are no less restrictive alternatives].

2. *Discrimination against "indecent" expression.* The Cable Act of 1984 required cable operators to reserve approximately 15 percent of their channels for commercial lease. The act expressly prohibited cable operators from exercising *any* editorial control over the content of programs broadcast on "leased access" channels. In Denver Area Educational Telecommunications Consortium, Inc. v. FCC, 518 U.S. 727 (1966), the Court considered the constitutionality of several provisions of the Cable Television Consumer Protection and Competition Act of 1992, which altered this scheme with respect to "indecent programming," defined as programming that depicts or describes "sexual activities or organs in a patently offensive manner."

Section 10(a) authorized cable operators to prohibit "indecent" programming on leased access channels. In defense of this provision, the FCC argued that a cable operator is analogous to a newspaper, which, as a private actor, can refuse to carry such material without violating the first amendment. Petitioners (a consortium of leased access channel programmers) offered a different view. Noting that section 10(a) is an exception to the general statutory prohibition against cable operators exercising editorial control over leased access programming, they argued that it was an unconstitutional content-based discrimination against "indecent" speech because it authorized cable operators to exercise editorial control over *only* this form of expression.

The Court upheld the provision. In a plurality opinion, Justice Breyer, joined by Justices Stevens, O'Connor, and Souter, argued that "the permissive nature of the provision, coupled with its viewpoint-neutral application, [suggests that section 10(a) is] a constitutionally permissible way to protect [children]." Justice Thomas, joined by Chief Justice Rehnquist and Justice Scalia, concurred in the result. Justice Kennedy, joined by Justice Ginsburg, dissented. Kennedy emphasized that in section 10(a) "Congress singles out one sort of speech for vulnerability to private censorship in a context where [it does not otherwise permit] content-based discrimination." Kennedy argued that, in such circumstances, "strict scrutiny applies," and however "compelling Congress' interest in shielding children from indecent programming," section 10(a) "cannot survive this exacting review" because of the availability of other means of regulating such expression, such as blocking mechanisms available to individual subscribers.

3. *Blocking versus unblocking.* Section 10(b) of the 1992 Cable Act required cable operators who choose to carry "indecent" programming to segregate such programming on a single channel, to block that channel from viewer access, and to unblock it only on a subscriber's written request. In *Denver Area*, the Court invalidated this provision. In an opinion by Justice Breyer, the Court explained that this provision "significantly differs" from section 10(a) because "it does not

simply permit, but rather requires cable operators to restrict [such] speech." The Court observed that this provision had a potentially significant chilling effect because of its "written notice" requirement, which might affect subscribers who may "fear for their reputations should the operator, advertently or inadvertently, disclose the list of those who wish to watch the 'patently offensive' channel." Although agreeing with the government that the "protection of children is a 'compelling interest,'" the Court concluded that this provision was nonetheless invalid because it was not the "'least restrictive alternative.'" An obvious alternative, for example, was to require those who did not want to receive such channels to bear the burden of requesting that they be blocked. Justice Thomas, joined by Chief Justice Rehnquist and Justice Scalia, dissented.

4. *Scrambling and blocking.* Section 505 of the Telecommunications Act of 1996 requires cable operators who provide channels "primarily dedicated to sexually-oriented programming" either to "fully scramble" those channels or to limit their transmission to between 10 P.M. and 6 A.M. Even before the enactment of section 505, cable operators used scrambling to ensure that only paying customers had access to such programming, but the technology of scrambling is imperfect and the scrambled programs occasionally "bleed" through to the viewer. The purpose of section 505 was to shield children from exposure to sexually-oriented "signal bleed." Because the technology to "fully" eliminate signal bleed is very expensive, most cable operators conformed to the requirements of section 505 by limiting transmission to only the eight authorized hours.

In United States v. Playboy Entertainment Group, Inc., 529 U.S. 803 (2000), the Court invalidated section 505. Justice Kennedy wrote the opinion of the Court:

> The only reasonable way for a substantial number of cable operators to comply with [section 505] is to time channel, which silences the protected speech for two-thirds of the day in every [home], regardless of the presence or [absence] of children or of the wishes of the viewers. According to the District Court, 30% to 50% of all adult programming is viewed by households prior to 10 P.M. [To] prohibit this much speech is a significant restriction of communication. [There is a] key difference between cable television and the broadcasting media, which is the point on which this case turns: Cable systems have the capacity to block unwanted channels on a household-by-household basis. [Simply] put, targeted blocking is less restrictive than banning, and the Government cannot ban speech if targeted blocking is a feasible and effective means of furthering its compelling interests. . . .
>
> [The] Government [argues] that society's independent interests will be unserved if parents fail to act [by failing to use the blocking alternative. But even] upon the assumption that the Government has an interest in substituting itself for informed and empowered parents, its interest is not sufficiently compelling to justify this widespread restriction on speech. The Government's argument stems from the idea that parents do not know their children are viewing the material on a scale or frequency to cause concern, or if so, that parents do not want to take affirmative steps to block it and their decisions are to be superceded. [The] Government has not [shown, however,] that [the voluntary blocking] alternative [would] be insufficient to secure its objective, or that any overriding harm justifies its intervention.

Justice Breyer, joined by Chief Justice Rehnquist and Justices O'Connor and Scalia, dissented.

5. *Indecent expression and subsidies for the arts.* In considering the constitutionality of government regulations of "indecent" expression, to what extent

should it matter whether the government directly restricts such expression (as in *Reno, Pacifica,* and *Sable*) or merely refuses to subsidize it in a government-sponsored grant program? See National Endowment for the Arts v. Finley, section E2d, infra, in which the Court upheld against both overbreadth and vagueness challenges a federal statute that directs the National Endowment for the Arts, in establishing procedures to judge the artistic merit of grant applications, to take "into consideration general standards of decency." The subsidy issue is closely related to the issue of "unconstitutional conditions." See Chapter 9, section E, infra. See G. Stone, Sex and the Constitution 334–340 (2017).

6. *Indecent expression and public employees.* In City of San Diego v. John Roe, 543 U.S. 77 (2004), the Court unanimously upheld the discharge of a police officer for selling on the adults-only section of eBay videotapes of himself stripping off a police uniform (not his official uniform) and then masturbating. His eBay user profile identified him as a person "employed in the field of law enforcement." The Court explained that "a governmental employer may impose certain restraints on the speech of its employees, restraints that would not be constitutional if applied to the general public." Indeed, *Pickering* balancing applies only when an employee speaks on "matters of public concern." When an employee speaks on matters unrelated to his employment and of no "public concern," the governmental employer may discipline or discharge him if "legitimate and substantial interests [are] compromised by his speech."

The Court held that the police officer's speech "does not qualify as a matter of public concern under any view of the public concern test." Because the officer "took deliberate steps to link his videos [to] his police work," and because his "debased parody of an officer performing indecent acts while in the course of his official duties brought the mission of the employer and the professionalism of its officers into serious disrepute," he could be discharged consistent with the first amendment. To what extent does this decision turn on the officer's sexual activity? Suppose he had performed in a skit mocking the police department's respect for the Constitution? Suppose he had performed in black-face in order to parody the department's treatment of African Americans?

7. *Indecent expression and students.* In Bethel School District No. 403 v. Fraser, 478 U.S. 675 (1986), the Court rejected a first amendment attack on a public high school's decision to discipline a student for speech containing sexual innuendo. Respondent delivered the speech, nominating a fellow student for student elective office, to a high school assembly of approximately six hundred students:

> I know a man who is firm — he's firm in his pants, he's firm in his shirt, his character is firm — but most [of] all, his belief in you, the students of Bethel, is firm. Jeff Kuhlman is a man who takes his point and pounds it in. If necessary, he'll take an issue and nail it to the wall. He doesn't attack things in spurts — he drives hard, pushing and pushing until finally — he succeeds. Jeff is a man who will go to the very end — even the climax, for each and every one of you.

There was evidence before the trial court that during the speech, some students hooted, yelled, and made gestures simulating the sexual activities alluded to in the speech, while others appeared bewildered and embarrassed. One teacher reported that she found it necessary to forgo a portion of her scheduled class on the following day to discuss the speech.

In an opinion by Chief Justice Burger, the Court emphasized the "sexual content" of the student's speech:

> [The] penalties imposed in this case were unrelated to any political viewpoint. The First Amendment does not prevent the school officials from determining that to permit a vulgar and lewd speech such as respondent's would undermine the school's basic educational mission. A high school assembly or classroom is no place for a sexually explicit monologue [and] it was perfectly appropriate for the school to disassociate itself to make the point to the pupils that vulgar speech [is] wholly inconsistent with the "fundamental values" of public school education.

Note: Zoning Theaters with Adult Movies and Bars with Nude Dancing

1. *Zoning adult movie theaters.* In the mid-1970s, Detroit adopted zoning ordinances providing that no adult theater may be located within one thousand feet of any two other "regulated uses" or within five hundred feet of a residential area. Other "regulated uses" included cabarets, bars, hotels, motels, pawnshops, pool halls, shoeshine parlors, and secondhand stores. The ordinance classified a theater as "adult" if it was used to present "material distinguished or characterized by an emphasis on matter depicting, describing or relating to 'Specified Sexual Activities' or 'Specified Anatomical Areas.'"

In Young v. American Mini-Theatres, 427 U.S. 50 (1976), the Court, in an opinion by Justice Stevens, upheld the constitutionality of the ordinances: "In the opinion of urban planners and real estate experts who supported the ordinances, the location of several regulated uses in the same neighborhood tends to attract an undesirable quantity and quality of transients, adversely affects property values, causes an increase in crime, [and] encourages residents and businesses to move elsewhere. [The] ordinances are not challenged on the ground that they impose a limit on the total number of adult theaters which may operate in the city of Detroit. There is no claim that distributors or exhibitors of adult films are denied access to the market or, conversely, that the viewing public is unable to satisfy its appetite for sexually explicit fare. Viewed as an entity, the market for this commodity is essentially unrestrained. [Thus,] apart from the fact that the ordinances treat adult theaters differently from other theaters and the fact that the classification is predicated on the content of material shown in the respective theaters, the regulation of the place where such films may be exhibited does not offend the First Amendment.

"[The Detroit ordinances draw a line] on the basis of content without violating the government's paramount obligation of neutrality in its regulation of protected communication. For the regulation of the places where sexually explicit films may be exhibited is unaffected by whatever social, political, or philosophical message a film may be intended to communicate; whether a motion picture ridicules or characterizes one point of view or another, the effect of the ordinances is exactly the same. [Moreover,] even though we recognize that the First Amendment will not tolerate the total suppression of erotic materials that have some arguably artistic value, it is manifest that society's interest in protecting this type of expression is of a wholly different, and lesser, magnitude than the interest in untrammeled political debate. . . . [Even] though the First Amendment protects communication in this area from total suppression, we hold that the State may legitimately use the content of these materials as the basis for placing them in a different classification from other motion pictures.

"The remaining question is whether the line drawn by these ordinances is justified by the city's interest in preserving the character of its neighborhoods. [The] record discloses a factual basis for the Common Council's conclusion that this kind of restriction will have the desired effect. It is not our function to appraise the wisdom of its decision to require adult theaters to be separated. . . . The city's interest in attempting to preserve the quality of urban life is one that must be accorded high respect [and it] must be allowed a reasonable opportunity to experiment with solutions to admittedly serious problems."

Justice Stewart, joined by Justices Brennan, Marshall and Blackmun, dissented: "This case does not involve a simple zoning ordinance, or a content-neutral time, place, and manner restriction, or a regulation of obscene expression or other speech that is entitled to less than the full protection of the First Amendment. The kind of expression at issue here is no doubt objectionable to some, but that fact does not diminish its protected status any more than did the particular content of the 'offensive' expression in [*Erznoznik* or *Cohen*]. What this case does involve is the constitutional permissibility of selective interference with protected speech whose content is thought to produce distasteful effects. It is elementary that a prime function of the First Amendment is to guard against just such interference. By refusing to invalidate Detroit's ordinance the Court rides roughshod over cardinal principles of First Amendment law, which require that time, place, and manner regulations that affect protected expression be content neutral . . . ."

Presumably, the Court would not uphold a law requiring cable operators to confine antiwar or Nazi programming to certain hours or restricting the location of movie theaters that show racist films or films that portray adultery or homosexuality in a positive light. What, then, explains *Young*? Is it that "indecent" (but non-obscene) speech is of only "low" first amendment value? Is it that regulations of such expression are "viewpoint-neutral"? Does *Young* make any sense? Recall *Denver Area*, supra.

2. *Making sense of* Young? Ten years later, in City of Renton v. Playtime Theatres, 475 U.S. 41 (1986), the Court considered the constitutionality of an ordinance prohibiting adult movie theaters from locating within one thousand feet of any residential zone, single- or multiple-family dwelling, church, park, or school. In an opinion by Justice Rehnquist, the Court upheld the ordinance. At the outset, the Court observed that "the resolution of this case is largely dictated by [*Young*]." After noting the distinction between "regulations enacted for the purpose of restraining speech on the basis of its content," which "presumptively violate the First Amendment," and "'content-neutral' time, place, and manner regulations," which "are acceptable so long as they are designed to serve a substantial governmental interest and do not unreasonably limit alternative avenues of communication," the Court concluded that, because "the Renton ordinance is aimed not at the *content* of the films, [but] at the *secondary effects* of such theaters on the surrounding community," it is "completely consistent with our definition of 'content-neutral' speech regulations as those that 'are *justified* without regard to the content of the regulated speech.'" This being so, the Court held that the Renton ordinance must be tested as a content-neutral restriction. Applying that standard, the Court echoed its finding in *Young* that "a city's 'interest in attempting to preserve the quality of urban life is one that must be accorded high respect.'"

Justice Brennan, joined by Justice Marshall, dissented. Brennan lamented the Court's "misguided" conclusion that the Renton ordinance was "content-neutral." In Justice Brennan's view, the "fact that adult movie theaters may cause harmful 'secondary' land use effects" does not mean that the regulation is content-neutral. To the contrary, because the ordinance explicitly "discriminates on its face against certain forms of speech based on content," it must be tested as a content-based restriction.

Was the *Renton* ordinance "content-neutral"? Does it make sense to treat a law that expressly "discriminates on its face against certain forms of speech based on content" more leniently than other content-based laws because it is "justified" in terms of the "secondary effects" of the speech? The issue of content-neutrality is taken up in section E infra.

3. *Making sense of* Renton? In 1977, the city of Los Angeles conducted a study that concluded that concentrations of adult entertainment establishments are associated with higher crimes rates. Accordingly, it enacted an ordinance prohibiting such establishments within one thousand feet of each other or within five hundred feet of a religious institution, school, or public park. In 1983, to close a "loophole" in the original ordinance, the city amended the ordinance to prohibit "more than one adult entertainment business in the same building." Alameda Books, which operated a combined adult book store and adult video arcade in a single location, challenged the amendment on the ground that there was no evidence that combining these two activities in a single location caused higher crime rates. The lower court granted summary judgment to Alameda Books. The Supreme Court reversed.

Justice O'Connor, joined by Chief Justice Rehnquist and Justices Scalia and Thomas, delivered the plurality opinion: "[In *Renton*,] we stated that the ordinance would be upheld so long as the city [showed] that [it] was designed to serve a substantial government interest and that reasonable alternative avenues of communication remained available. [It was] rational for the city to infer that reducing the concentration of adult operations in a neighborhood, whether within separate establishments or in one large establishment, will reduce crime rates. [We] conclude that the city [has sufficiently] complied with the evidentiary requirement in *Renton* [to withstand a motion for summary judgment]."

Justice Kennedy concurred in the judgment: "If a city can decrease the crime and blight associated with certain speech by the traditional exercise of its zoning power, and at the same time leave the quantity and accessibility of the speech substantially undiminished, there is no First Amendment objection. [But] the purpose and effect of [such] a zoning ordinance must be to reduce secondary effects and not to reduce speech. [In *Renton*,] the Court designated the restriction 'content neutral.' [This] was something of a fiction. [Whether] a statute is content-based or content neutral is something that can be determined on the face of it; if the statute describes speech by content then it is content based. [This ordinance is] content based and we should call [it] so. [Nevertheless], the central holding of *Renton* is sound: [Zoning] regulations do not automatically raise the specter of impermissible content discrimination, even if they are content based, [because the] zoning context provides a built-in legitimate rationale, which rebuts the usual presumption that content-based restrictions are unconstitutional. [But] the necessary rationale for applying intermediate [rather than strict] scrutiny is the promise that zoning ordinances like this one [will] reduce [the] secondary effects without substantially reducing speech."

Justice Souter, joined by Justices Stevens, Ginsburg, and Breyer, dissented: "Because content-based regulation applies to expression by very reason of what is said, it carries a high risk that expressive limits are imposed for the sake of suppressing a message that is disagreeable to listeners or readers, or the government. [The] risk lies in the fact that when a law applies selectively only to speech of particular content, the more precisely the content is identified, the greater is the opportunity for government censorship. [The] capacity of zoning regulations to address the [secondary effects] without eliminating the speech [is] the only possible excuse for [treating them] as akin to time, place and manner regulations. [In] this case, [the] government has not shown that bookstores containing viewing booths [increase] negative secondary effects, [and] we are thus left without substantial justification for viewing the [restriction as content neutral]."

Is it credible to call these regulations "content-neutral"? In Reed v. Town of Gilbert, 135 S. Ct. 2218 (2015), the Supreme Court invalidated an ordinance that treated different types of signs differently based on their content. Temporary political signs, for example, were treated differently in terms of their permissible size and the length of time they could be displayed than were temporary directional signs. The lower court upheld the ordinance as a content-neutral regulation because the town's justifications for regulating the signs differently were "unrelated to the content of the sign." The Supreme Court, in an opinion authored by Justice Thomas, rejected this argument, stating emphatically that a "law that is content-based on its face is subject to strict scrutiny regardless of the government's benign motive, content-neutral justification, or lack of 'animus toward the ideas contained' in the regulated speech." Does *Reed* effectively overrule this line of cases? If the laws in these cases cannot defensibly be characterized as "content-neutral," is there any other way to uphold them? See Lakier, Reed v. Town of Gilbert, Arizona, and the Rise of the Anticlassificatory First Amendment, 2016 Sup. Ct. Rev. 233, noting that *Reed* effectively overruled the Court's prior decisions that had suggested that "a law that made facial content distinctions" should be analyzed as content-neutral if "it could be justified by reference to a content-neutral purpose."

4. *Nude dancing.* In Schad v. Borough of Mt. Ephraim, 452 U.S. 61 (1981), appellants, who operated an adult bookstore, installed a coin-operated mechanism permitting a customer to watch a live dancer, usually nude, performing behind a glass panel. Appellants were convicted of violating a Mount Ephraim zoning ordinance prohibiting all live entertainment within the borough. The Court, in an opinion by Justice White, held the ordinance invalid. The Court noted that, as a form of entertainment, "nude dancing is not without its First Amendment protections." The Court explained that "this case is not controlled by *Young*," for unlike the situation in *Young*, there was "no evidence" in *Schad* "that the kind of entertainment appellants wish to provide is available in reasonably nearby areas." Chief Justice Burger, joined by Justice Rehnquist, dissented, observing that "to invoke the First Amendment to protect the activity involved in this case trivializes and demeans that great Amendment."

See also California v. LaRue, 409 U.S. 109 (1972) (upholding as "reasonable" under the twenty-first amendment an administrative regulation prohibiting nude dancing in bars and nightclubs that are licensed to sell liquor because of administrative findings that such explicitly sexual performances in establishments licensed to sell liquor tend to promote rape and prostitution and often result in the commission by customers of unlawful public acts of sexuality); New York State Liquor Authority v. Bellanca, 452 U.S. 714 (1981) (upholding a statute prohibiting nude dancing in establishments licensed by the state to sell liquor for on-premises consumption); Newport v. Iacobucci, 479 U.S. 92 (1986) (same); 44

Liquormart, Inc. v. Rhode Island, 517 U.S. 484 (1996) (disavowing *LaRue's* reliance on the twenty-first amendment and concluding that the twenty-first amendment does not qualify the first amendment's prohibition against laws abridging the freedom of speech).

In Barnes v. Glen Theatre, Inc., 501 U.S. 560 (1991), the Court upheld an Indiana statute prohibiting any person to appear "in a state of nudity" in any "public place," as applied to establishments that present nude dancing as entertainment. Although there was no opinion of the Court, a majority of the justices concluded that nude performance dancing "is expressive conduct within the outer perimeters of the First Amendment." A majority also concluded, however, that the requirement that such dancers wear pasties and a G-string does not violate the first amendment because the nudity statute was not directed at nude dancing as such and had only an "incidental effect" on constitutionally protected activity. See also City of Erie v. Pap's A.M., 529 U.S. 277 (2000) (upholding a city ordinance banning public nudity, as applied to nude performance dancing). For a fuller account of *Barnes* and *Pap's A.M.*, see section E3 infra.

8.   *Hate Speech and Pornography*

Beauharnais v. Illinois
343 U.S. 250 (1952)

[Beauharnais, president of the White Circle League, organized the distribution of a leaflet setting forth a petition calling on the mayor and city council of Chicago "to halt the further encroachment, harassment and invasion of white people, their property, neighborhoods and persons, by the Negro." The leaflet called for "[one] million self respecting white people in Chicago to unite" and added that, "[if] persuasion and the need to prevent the white race from becoming mongrelized by the negro will not unite us, then the aggressions, [rapes], robberies, knives, guns and marijuana of the negro surely will." Attached to the leaflet was an application for membership in the White Circle League. As a result of his participation in the distribution of this leaflet, Beauharnais was convicted under an Illinois statute declaring it unlawful for any person to [distribute] any publication that "portrays depravity, criminality, unchastity, or lack of virtue of a class of citizens, of any race, color, creed or religion, which [publication] exposes the citizens of any race, color, creed or religion to contempt, derision, or obloquy or which is productive of breach of the peace or riots." At Beauharnais's trial, the judge refused to instruct the jury that, in order to convict, they must find "that the article complained of was likely to produce a clear and present danger of a serious substantive evil that rises far above public inconvenience, annoyance or unrest." The trial judge also refused to consider Beauharnais's offer of proof on the issue of truth, for under Illinois law, the defense of truth is unavailable in a prosecution for criminal libel unless "the truth of all facts in the utterance [be] shown together with good motive for publication." The Supreme Court, in a five-to-four decision, affirmed the conviction.]

MR. JUSTICE FRANKFURTER delivered the opinion of the Court. . . .
Libel of an individual was a common-law crime, and thus criminal in the colonies. Indeed, at common law, truth or good motives was no defense. In the first decades after the adoption of the Constitution, this was changed by

judicial decision, statute or constitution in most States, but nowhere was there any suggestion that the crime of libel be abolished. [As we have observed, "libelous] utterances are no essential part of any exposition of ideas, and are of such slight social value as a step to truth that any benefit that may be derived from them is clearly outweighed by the social interest in order and morality. . . ." [*Chaplinsky.*]

No one will gainsay that it is libelous falsely to charge another with being a rapist, robber, carrier of knives and guns, and user of marijuana. The precise question before us, then, is whether the [Constitution] prevents a State from punishing such libels — as criminal libel has been defined, limited and constitutionally recognized time out of mind — directed at designated collectivities and flagrantly disseminated. [If] an utterance directed at an individual may be the object of criminal sanctions, we cannot deny to a State power to punish the same utterance directed at a defined group, unless we can say that this is a willful and purposeless restriction unrelated to the peace and well-being of the State.

Illinois did not have to look beyond her own borders or await the tragic experience of the last three decades to conclude that wilful purveyors of falsehood concerning racial and religious groups promote strife and tend powerfully to obstruct the manifold adjustments required for free, ordered life in a metropolitan, polyglot community. From the murder of the abolitionist Lovejoy in 1837 to the Cicero riots of 1951, Illinois has been the scene of exacerbated tension between races, often flaring into violence and destruction. In many of these outbreaks, utterances of the character here in question, so the Illinois legislature could conclude, played a significant part. . . .

In the face of this history and its frequent obligato of extreme racial and religious propaganda, we would deny experience to say that the Illinois legislature was without reason in seeking ways to curb false or malicious defamation of racial and religious groups, made in public places and by means calculated to have a powerful emotional impact on those to whom it was presented. [Moreover, it would be] quite outside the scope of our authority [for] us to deny that the Illinois legislature may warrantably believe that a man's job and his educational opportunities and the dignity accorded him may depend as much on the reputation of the racial and religious group to which he willy-nilly belongs, as on his own merits. This being so, we are precluded from saying that speech concededly punishable when immediately directed at individuals cannot be outlawed if directed at groups with whose position and esteem in society the affiliated individual may be inextricably involved.

As to the defense of truth, Illinois in common with many States requires a showing not only that the utterance state the facts, but also that the publication be made "with good motives and for justifiable ends." Both elements are necessary if the defense is to prevail . . . .

Libelous utterances not being within the area of constitutionally protected speech, it is unnecessary, either for us or for the State courts, to consider the issues behind the phrase "clear and present danger." Certainly no one would contend that obscene speech, for example, may be punished only upon a showing of such circumstances. Libel, as we have seen, is in the same class.

We find no warrant in the Constitution for denying to Illinois the power to pass the law here under attack. . . .

Affirmed.

MR. JUSTICE BLACK, with whom MR. JUSTICE DOUGLAS concurs, dissenting. . . .

The Court condones this expansive state censorship by painstakingly analogizing it to the law of criminal libel. As a result of this refined analysis, the Illinois statute emerges labeled a "group libel law." This label may make the Court's holding more palatable for those who sustain it, but the sugar-coating does not make the censorship less deadly. However tagged, the Illinois law is not that criminal libel which has been "defined, limited and constitutionally recognized time out of mind." For as "constitutionally recognized" that crime has provided for punishment of false, malicious, scurrilous charges against individuals, not against huge groups. This limited scope of the law of criminal libel is of no small importance. It has confined state punishment of speech and expression to the narrowest of areas involving nothing more than purely private feuds. Every expansion of the law of criminal libel so as to punish discussions of matters of public concern means a corresponding invasion of the area dedicated to free expression by the First Amendment. . . .

Moreover, the leaflet used here was [the] means adopted by an assembled group to enlist interest in their efforts to have legislation enacted. [Freedom] of petition, assembly, speech and press could be greatly abridged by a practice of meticulously scrutinizing every editorial, speech, sermon or other printed matter to extract two or three naughty words on which to hang charges of "group libel." The *Chaplinsky* case makes no such broad inroads on First Amendment freedoms. . . .

If there be minority groups who hail this holding as their victory, they might consider the possible relevancy of this ancient remark: "Another such victory and I am undone."

MR. JUSTICE DOUGLAS, dissenting. . . .

My view is that if in any case other public interests are to override the plain command of the First Amendment, the peril of speech must be clear and present, leaving no room for argument, raising no doubts as to the necessity of curbing speech in order to prevent disaster. . . .

[Dissenting opinions of Justices Reed and Jackson are omitted.]

Note: Group Defamation and "Hate Speech"

1. *The* Skokie *controversy.* Reconsider the *Skokie* controversy, section B2 supra, in light of *Beauharnais.* Does the display of a swastika constitute "group libel"?

2. *Group defamation as "libel."* Central to Justice Frankfurter's analysis was the conclusion that "group libel," as defined in the Illinois statute, is not "within the area of constitutionally protected speech" and thus need not be tested by the clear and present danger standard. In justifying this conclusion, Justice Frankfurter relied primarily on *Chaplinsky*'s characterization of "libelous" utterances as "unprotected" speech. In New York Times v. Sullivan, however, the Court held that "libel can claim no talismanic immunity from constitutional limitations." Moreover, the concept of "group libel," held in *Beauharnais* to be "unprotected" expression, was not limited to false statements of fact. Subsequent opinions, however, such as *New York Times* and *Hustler,* have unequivocally held that "libel" is of "low" first amendment value only insofar as it consists of false statements of fact. These decisions have generally been understood to pull the rug out from under *Beauharnais.* See, e.g., Collin v. Smith, 578 F.2d 1197 (7th Cir. 1978) (the "approach sanctioned [in] *Beauharnais* would [not] pass constitutional muster today").

3. *False statements of fact.* Suppose the Illinois statute prohibited only false statements of fact that portray "depravity, criminality, unchastity, or lack of virtue of a class of citizens, of any race, color, creed or religion." Are the interests threatened by such expression too diffuse to warrant restriction? Given the statements in the *Beauharnais* leaflet, what sort of showing would be necessary to establish "truth" or "falsity"? Consider Arkes, Civility and the Restriction of Speech: Rediscovering the Defamation of Groups, 1974 Sup. Ct. Rev. 281, 301: "One can think of few things worse than having a jury pronounce on the 'truth' of Beauharnais's charges, with all the solemnity and authority of the legal process. [These] are not the kinds of questions that we typically trust to the judgment of juries."

4. *Other bases for "low"-value status.* If the conclusion that group libel constitutes "low"-value speech can no longer be sustained solely by invocation of the term "libel," is there any other basis for attributing to such expression only "low" first amendment value? Consider the following arguments:

a. The group libel doctrine is a logical extension of the fighting words doctrine. The fighting words doctrine declares the malicious use of personal epithets to be of "low" first amendment value, see section B2 supra; the group libel doctrine accords equivalent treatment to the similarly malicious use of what amount to epithets directed against groups.

b. Group libel is of "low" first amendment value because it operates not by persuasion but by insidiously undermining social attitudes and beliefs, as evidenced by the experience of Nazi Germany. See Riesman, Democracy and Defamation: Control of Group Libel, 42 Colum. L. Rev. 727 (1942). For a description of contemporary anti-Nazi legislation in Germany, see Stein, History against Free Speech: The New German Law against the "Auschwitz" — and Other — Lies, 85 Mich. L. Rev. 277 (1986).

c. It cannot seriously be maintained that the first amendment was intended to protect speech that maliciously "portrays depravity, criminality, unchastity, or lack of virtue of a class of citizens, of any race, color, creed or religion." Just as express language of incitement to crime is incompatible with the fundamental assumptions of our democratic system, and is thus of "low" first amendment value, group libel is likewise of "low" value because it is incompatible with our fundamental commitment to human dignity and equality. Indeed, this issue poses a clash of constitutional rights and calls for the first amendment to be interpreted and applied in light of the fourteenth amendment's equally important guarantee of "equal protection of the laws."

d. Waldron, Dignity and Defamation: The Visibility of Hate, 123 Harv. L. Rev. 1597, 1599-1600, 1627 (2010):

[H]ate speech regulation can be understood as the protection of a certain sort of precious public good: a visible assurance offered by society to all of its members that they will not be subject to abuse, defamation, humiliation, discrimination, and violence on grounds of race, ethnicity, religion, gender, and in some cases sexual orientation. [The] most important aim of these laws [is] simply to diminish the presence of visible hatred in society by protecting the public commitment to their equal standing in society against public denigration. [In] a well-ordered society, [people] know that when they leave home in the morning they can reasonably count on not being discriminated against, humiliated, or terrorized. [When] a society is defaced with anti-Semitic signage, burning crosses, or defamatory racial leaflets, that sort of assurance evaporates. [In a society that tolerates hate speech], people no longer have the benefit of a general public assurance [of] human dignity.

[The] security that people look for is security against the soul-shriveling humiliation that accompanies the manifestation of injustice in society.

e. Matsuda, Public Response to Racist Speech: Considering the Victim's Story, 87 Mich. L. Rev. 2320, 2332, 2336–2337, 2357, 2359 (1989):

The claim that a legal response to racist speech is required stems from a recognition of the structural reality of racism in America. Racism, as used here, comprises the ideology of racial supremacy and the mechanisms for keeping selected victim groups in subordinated positions. [Victims of] hate propaganda have experienced [fear, nightmares], post-traumatic stress disorder, hypertension, psychosis, and suicide. [In] order to avoid receiving hate messages, victims [of such speech] have had to quit jobs, forego education, leave their homes, avoid certain public places, curtail their own exercise of free speech rights, and otherwise modify their behavior. . . .

Racist speech is best treated as a *sui generis* category, presenting an idea so historically untenable, so dangerous, and so tied to perpetuation of violence and degradation [that] it is properly treated as outside the realm of protected discourse. [The] identifying characteristics [of] racist hate [speech are]: 1. The message is of racial inferiority; 2. The message is directed against a historically oppressed group; and 3. The message is persecutorial, hateful, and degrading. . . .

How can one argue for censorship of racist hate messages without encouraging a revival of McCarthyism? There is an important difference that comes from human experience, our only source of collective knowledge. [The] doctrines of racial supremacy and racial hatred [are] uniformly rejected. [We] have fought wars and spilled blood to establish [this principle]. The universality of this principle, in a world bereft of agreement on many things, is a mark of collective human progress.

In light of Matsuda's argument that hate speech causes its victims to "curtail their own exercise of free speech rights," can it be said that the regulation of hate speech is justified because it maximizes free expression in the aggregate?

Consider also Powell, As Justice Requires/Permits: The Delimitation of Harmful Speech in a Democratic Society, 16 Law & Inequality 97, 103, 147–149 (1998):

[The] insights proffered by critical race and post-modern theorists [suggest] that the classic remedy for harmful speech — that is, more speech — will, in some instances, perpetuate disparities of power and destabilize our sense of self. The marketplace of ideas cannot self-regulate so long as objections to lack of participatory access are subsumed by claims that the liberty interest in expression is primary to the equality interest in participatory access. A self-regulating marketplace presupposes an equal starting line — an assumption that has never been a reality in American political life.

[A decision of the Canadian Supreme Court, Regina v. Keegstra, 2 W.W.R. 1 (1991), illustrates] an alternative way of using democratic principles to valorize liberty and equality. [In *Keegstra*, a Canadian high school teacher was convicted of "communicating statements [that] willfully promote hatred against any identifiable group" for communicating anti-Semitic statements to his students. The Canadian Supreme Court rejected Keegstra's claim that his conviction violated the Canadian Charter of Rights and Freedoms because his speech] was not expression that "serves individual and societal values in a free and democratic society." [This decision reflects] a commitment to both liberty and equality, and mediates between these values by recourse to a collective concern for the underlying values and principles of the society, including social justice. [Commenting] that it is destructive of free expression values themselves, as well as other democratic values, "to treat all expression as equally crucial to those principles at the core" of free expression, the Court suggested that democratic principles recommend viewing free expression as a function of three underlying goals. These goals are truth attainment, ensuring [the] development of self-identity, and most importantly, [the] guarantee that the opportunity for participation in the democratic process is open to all. The Court simultaneously supports these rationales with the observations that hate speech can impede the search for truth, impinge on the autonomy necessary to individual development, and subvert the democratic process. Cognizant that the regulation "muzzles the participation of a [few]," the Court remains certain that the loss of that voice is not substantial. [What] is most instructive about the decision is that the Court was willing to employ a democratic calculus.

See also A. Tsesis, Destructive Messages 180, 192 (2002) ("A general consensus among nations holds that hate propaganda [threatens] both outgroup participation in democracy and minority rights. Countries that have enacted laws penalizing the dissemination of hate speech include Austria, Belgium, Brazil, Canada, Cyprus, England, France, Germany, India, Israel, Italy, Netherlands, and Switzerland. [These] international examples demonstrate that the United States's pure speech jurisprudence is anomalous.").

f. Graber, Old Wine in New Bottles: The Constitutional Status of Unconstitutional Speech, 48 Vand. L. Rev. 349, 352, 364, 367–368, 371–372 (1995):

Scholars who would ban [hate speech] insist that government can regulate certain expressions of prejudice without violating First Amendment values [because] the First Amendment does not fully protect unconstitutional speech — speech that denies or threatens the realization of fundamental constitutional values. [But what proponents of hate speech regulation] fail to realize is that the leading opponents of free speech in every generation [have] insisted that the First Amendment does not fully protect the right to deny or criticize what their generation regards to be fundamental constitutional values.

[The leading] proponents of restrictions on speech during World War I, [for example, maintained] that persons had no constitutional right to attack what they believed to be the essential principles of republican government. [Similarly,] proponents of the freedom of contract [argued] that the First Amendment did not protect [attacks] on private property because such advocacy [was] unconstitutional speech, [and proponents of restricting the speech of communists asserted] that "[n]o democratic or constitutional principle is violated [when] a democracy acts to exclude those groups from entering the struggle for political power which, if victorious, will not permit that struggle to continue in accordance with the democratic way."

g. Post, Racist Speech, Democracy, and the First Amendment, 32 Wm. & Mary L. Rev. 267, 312–317 (1991):

[If] representations in the current literature are accepted as true, [the members of victim groups] confront in public discourse an undifferentiated complex of circumstances in which they are systematically demeaned, stigmatized, ignored; in which the very language of debate resists the articulation of their claims; in which they are harassed, abused, intimidated, and systematically [injured] both individually and collectively. The question [posed is] whether this unacceptable situation would be cured by restraints on speech. . . .

Bluntly expressed, the argument requires us to balance the integrity of public discourse [against] the importance of enhancing the experience [of] members of victim groups. [This] invitation to balance ought to be declined [because] the temptation to balance rests on what might be termed the fallacy of immaculate isolation. The effect on public discourse is acceptable only if it is de minimis, and it is arguably de minimis only when a specific claim is evaluated in isolation from other, similar claims. But no claim is in practice immaculately isolated in this manner. As the flag burning [issue] suggests, there is no shortage of powerful groups contending that uncivil speech [ought] to be "minimally" regulated for highly pressing symbolic reasons. [This] is already plain in the regulations that have pro-liferated on college campuses, which commonly proscribe not merely speech that degrades persons on the basis of their race, but also [on] the basis of their "color, national origin, religion, sex, sexual orientation, age, handicap, or veteran's status." The claim of de minimis impact loses credibility as the list of claimants to special protection grows longer.

h. R. Kennedy, Nigger 151, 154, 158–159 (2002):

[Proponents] of enhanced hate-speech regulation have typically failed to establish persuasively the asserted predicate for their campaign — that is, that verbal abuse [is] a "rising" [development] demanding countermeasures. Regulationists do cite racist incidents [but] too often the dramatic retelling of an anecdote is permitted to substitute for a more systematic, quantitative analysis. [An] examination of the substance of the regulationists' proposals turns up suggested reforms that are puzzlingly narrow, frighteningly broad, or disturbingly susceptible to discrimina-tory manipulation. . . .

The cumulative effect of [the Supreme Court's] speech-protective doctrines is a conspicuous toleration of speech [that] many people — in some instances the vast majority of people — find deeply, perhaps even viscerally, obnoxious, includ-ing flag burning, pornography, Nazis' taunting of Holocaust survivors, a jacket emblazoned with the phrase "Fuck the Draft," *The Satanic Verses, The Birth of a Nation, The Last Temptation of Christ.* And just as acute wariness [of] censorship has long furthered struggles for freedom of expression in all its many guises, so has resistance against censorship always been an important and positive feature of the great struggles against racist tyranny in the United States, from the fight against slavery to the fight against Jim Crow. For this reason, we may count ourselves fortunate that the anti-hate-speech campaign [has] fizzled and largely subsided. This [effort] was simply not worth the various costs that success would have exacted.

i. T. Ash, Free Speech: Ten Principles for a Connected World 90–94 (2016):

Today's veto statements come most often in the form of claimed offence to a group identity. [Do] we want to be the kind of human beings who are habitually at the ready to take offense, and our children to be educated and socialized that way? [Should] our role model be the thin-skinned identity activist who is constantly crying, "I am offended"? Or should it be the Mandela, Baldwin, or Gandhi who says, in effect, "although what I see written or depicted is grossly offensive, I hold it beneath my dignity to take offense. It is those who abuse me who are demeaning themselves." [However,] we should take positive steps of many different kinds, whether in education, journalism, local communities or our own personal conduct, not merely to equip us to live with offence but to develop a culture of open debate and robust civility. These are twin tasks. The better we succeed in the latter, the less we will have need of the former.

j. Goldberg, Free Speech Consequentialism, 116 Colum. L. Rev. 687 (2016):

[As many proponents of laws forbidding hate speech have observed, the] emotional burdens of speech may not be shared equally. This is a significant concern, especially when the burdens of speech fall on particularly vulnerable members of the population, or those who have been historically oppressed. [Proponents] of laws regulating hate speech [maintain] that [such laws make] society overall more tolerant and more welcoming to marginalized groups . . . .

   It is unclear whether members of minority groups fare better in societies where speech damaging to these groups is aired or in cultures that prohibit this type of speech and force it underground. There is reason to believe that suppressing the types of speech most damaging to women and minorities may not actually benefit members of these groups in the long term. Some feminists, generally associated with third-wave feminism, convincingly argue that the association of women with emotional trauma, and the law's efforts to specifically cater to women's emotional distress, has actually deprived women of autonomy and the ability to make their own choices. Further, instead of feeling victimized, many are empowered by collective efforts to speak out against expressions of bigotry. The U.S. approach of tolerating the intolerant may actually make society overall more tolerant and more welcoming to marginalized groups.

R.A.V. v. City of St. Paul

505 U.S. 377 (1992)

JUSTICE SCALIA delivered the opinion of the Court.

   [After allegedly burning a cross on a black family's lawn, petitioner, a teenager, was charged under the St. Paul, Minnesota, Bias-Motivated Crime Ordinance, which prohibits the display of a burning cross, a swastika, or other symbol that one knows or has reason to know "arouses anger, alarm or resentment in others" on the basis of race, color, creed, religion, or gender. The state supreme court rejected a claim that the ordinance was unconstitutionally overbroad, because the phrase "arouses anger, alarm or resentment in others" had been construed in earlier state cases to limit the ordinance's reach to fighting words within the meaning of *Chaplinsky*. It also rejected the claim that the ordinance was impermissibly content-based, because it was narrowly tailored to serve a compelling governmental interest. The U.S. Supreme Court reversed.]

I

[We] accept the Minnesota Supreme Court's authoritative statement that the ordinance reaches only those expressions that constitute "fighting words" within the meaning of *Chaplinsky*. [Assuming,] arguendo, that all of the expression reached by the ordinance is proscribable under the "fighting words" doctrine, we nonetheless conclude that the ordinance is facially unconstitutional in that it [prohibits] speech solely on the basis of the subjects the speech addresses.

   The First Amendment generally prevents government from proscribing speech [because] of disapproval of the ideas expressed. Content-based regulations are presumptively invalid. From 1791 to the present, however, our society [has] permitted restrictions upon the content of speech in a few limited areas, which are "of such slight social value as a step to truth that any benefit that may be derived from them is clearly outweighed by the social interest in order and morality." [*Chaplinsky.*] [We] have sometimes said that these categories of expression are "not within the area of constitutionally protected speech." [Such] statements must be taken in context, however. [What] they mean is that these areas of speech can, consistently with the First Amendment, be regulated because of their constitutionally proscribable content (obscenity, defamation, etc.) — not that they are categories of speech entirely invisible to the Constitution, so that they may be made the vehicles for content discrimination unrelated to their distinctively proscribable content. Thus, the government may proscribe libel; but it may not make the further content discrimination of proscribing only libel critical of the government, [and although a city may proscribe obscenity, it may not prohibit] only those legally obscene works that contain criticism of the city government. . . .

Even the prohibition against content discrimination [is] not absolute. It applies differently in the context of proscribable speech than in the area of fully protected speech. [When] the basis for the content discrimination consists entirely of the very reason the entire class of speech at issue is proscribable, no significant danger of idea or viewpoint discrimination exists. Such a reason, having been adjudged neutral enough to support exclusion of the entire class of speech from First Amendment protection, is also neutral enough to form the basis of distinction within the class. To illustrate: A State might choose to prohibit only that obscenity which is the most patently offensive in its prurience — i.e., that which involves the most lascivious displays of sexual activity. But it may not prohibit, for example, only that obscenity which includes offensive political messages. And the Federal Government can criminalize only those threats of violence that are directed against the President — since the reasons why threats of violence are outside the First Amendment (protecting individuals from the fear of violence, from the disruption that fear engenders, and from the possibility that the threatened violence will occur) have special force when applied to the person of the President. But the Federal Government may not criminalize only those threats against the President that mention his policy on aid to inner cities. And to take a final example, [a] State may choose to regulate price advertising in one industry but not in others, because the risk of fraud (one of the characteristics of commercial speech that justifies depriving it of full First Amendment protection), is in its view greater there. But a State may not prohibit only that commercial advertising that depicts men in a demeaning fashion. . . .

II

Applying these principles to the St. Paul ordinance, we conclude that, even as narrowly construed by the Minnesota Supreme Court, the ordinance is facially unconstitutional. Although the phrase in the ordinance, "arouses anger, alarm or resentment in others," has been limited by the Minnesota Supreme Court's construction to reach only those symbols or displays that amount to "fighting words," the remaining, unmodified terms make clear that the ordinance applies only to "fighting words" that insult, or provoke violence, "on the basis of race, color, creed, religion or gender." Displays containing abusive invective, no matter how vicious or severe, are permissible unless they are addressed to one of the specified disfavored topics. Those who wish to use "fighting words" in connection with other ideas — to express hostility, for example, on the basis of political affiliation, union membership, or homosexuality — are not covered. The First Amendment does not permit St. Paul to impose special prohibitions on those speakers who express views on disfavored subjects.

In its practical operation, moreover, the ordinance goes even beyond mere content discrimination, to actual viewpoint discrimination. Displays containing some words — odious racial epithets, for example — would be prohibited to proponents of all views. But "fighting words" that do not themselves invoke race, color, creed, religion, or gender — aspersions upon a person's mother, for example — would seemingly be usable ad libitum in the placards of those arguing in favor of racial, color, etc. tolerance and equality, but could not be used by that speaker's opponents. One could hold up a sign saying, for example, that all "anti-Catholic bigots" are misbegotten; but not that all "papists" are, for that would insult and provoke violence "on the basis of religion." St. Paul has no such authority to license one side of a debate to fight freestyle, while requiring the other to follow Marquis of Queensbury Rules.

What we have here [is] a prohibition of fighting words that contain (as the Minnesota Supreme Court repeatedly emphasized) messages of "bias-motivated" hatred and in particular, as applied to this case, messages "based on virulent notions of racial supremacy." One must wholeheartedly agree with the Minnesota Supreme Court that "it is the responsibility, even the obligation, of diverse communities to confront such notions in whatever form they appear," but the manner of that confrontation cannot consist of selective limitations upon speech. St. Paul's brief asserts that a general "fighting words" law would not meet the city's needs because only a content-specific measure can communicate to minority groups that the "group hatred" aspect of such speech "is not condoned by the majority." The point of the First Amendment is that majority preferences must be expressed in some fashion other than silencing speech on the basis of its content. . . .

The content-based discrimination reflected in the St. Paul ordinance [does] not fall within the exception for content discrimination based on the very reasons why the particular class of speech at issue (here, fighting words) is proscribable. [The] reason why fighting words are categorically excluded from the protection of the First Amendment is not that their content communicates any particular idea, but that their content embodies a particularly intolerable (and socially unnecessary) mode of expressing whatever idea the speaker wishes to convey. St. Paul has not singled out an especially offensive mode of expression — it has not, for example, selected for prohibition only those fighting words that communicate ideas in a threatening (as opposed to a merely obnoxious) manner. Rather, it has proscribed fighting words of whatever manner that communicate messages of racial, gender, or religious intolerance. Selectivity of this sort creates the possibility that the city is seeking to handicap the expression of particular ideas. . . .

Finally, St. Paul [argues] that, even if the ordinance regulates expression based on hostility towards its protected ideological content, this discrimination is nonetheless justified because it is narrowly tailored to serve compelling state interests. Specifically, [it asserts] that the ordinance helps to ensure the basic human rights of members of groups that have historically been subjected to discrimination, including the right of such group members to live in peace where they wish. We do not doubt that these interests are compelling, and that the ordinance can be said to promote them. But the "danger of censorship" presented by a facially content-based statute requires that that weapon be employed only where it is "necessary to serve the asserted [compelling] interest." The existence of adequate content-neutral alternatives thus "undercuts significantly" any defense of such a statute, casting considerable doubt on the government's protestations that "the asserted justification is in fact an accurate description of the purpose and effect of the law." The dispositive question in this case, therefore, is whether content discrimination is reasonably necessary to achieve St. Paul's compelling interests; it plainly is not. An ordinance not limited to the favored topics, for example, would have precisely the same beneficial effect. In fact the only interest distinctively served by the content limitation is that of displaying the city council's special hostility towards the particular biases thus singled out. That is precisely what the First Amendment forbids. . . .

Let there be no mistake about our belief that burning a cross in someone's front yard is reprehensible. But St. Paul has sufficient means at its disposal to prevent such behavior[1] without adding the First Amendment to the fire.

The judgment of the Minnesota Supreme Court is reversed. . . .

JUSTICE WHITE, with whom JUSTICE BLACKMUN and JUSTICE O'CONNOR join, and with whom JUSTICE STEVENS joins except as to Part I(A), concurring in the judgment. . . .

I

A

This Court's decisions have plainly stated that expression falling within certain limited categories so lacks the values the First Amendment was designed to protect that the Constitution affords no protection to that expression. [Nevertheless], the majority holds that the First Amendment protects those narrow categories of expression long held to be undeserving of First Amendment protection — at least to the extent that lawmakers may not regulate some fighting words more strictly than others because of their content. [It] is inconsistent to hold that the government may proscribe an entire category of speech because the content of that speech is evil; but that the government may not treat a subset of that category differently without violating the First Amendment; the content of the subset is by definition worthless and undeserving of constitutional protection. . . .

II

Although I disagree with the Court's analysis, I do agree with its conclusion: The St. Paul ordinance is unconstitutional. However, I would decide the case on overbreadth grounds. [In] construing the St. Paul ordinance, the Minnesota Supreme Court drew upon the definition of fighting words that appears in *Chaplinsky* — words "which by their very utterance inflict injury or tend to incite an immediate breach of the peace." [The court also stated, however,] "the ordinance censors only those displays that one knows or should know will create anger, alarm or resentment based on racial, ethnic, gender or religious bias."

---

1. The conduct might have violated Minnesota statutes [prohibiting "terrorist threats," arson, or criminal damage to property]. [Relocated footnote. — EDS.]

[Our] fighting words cases have made clear, however, that such generalized reactions are not sufficient to strip expression of its constitutional protection. The mere fact that expressive activity causes hurt feelings, offense, or resentment does not render the expression unprotected. [Citing, e.g., Cohen v. California; Terminiello v. Chicago.] [Thus, although] the ordinance reaches conduct that is unprotected, it also makes criminal expressive conduct that causes only hurt feelings, offense, or resentment, and is protected by the First Amendment. The ordinance is therefore fatally overbroad and invalid on its face. . . .

JUSTICE BLACKMUN, concurring in the judgment.
I regret what the Court has done in this case. [I] fear that the Court has been distracted from its proper mission by the temptation to decide the issue over "politically correct speech" and "cultural diversity," neither of which is presented here. [I] see no First Amendment values that are compromised by a law that prohibits hoodlums from driving minorities out of their homes by burning crosses on their lawns, but I see great harm in preventing the people of Saint Paul from specifically punishing the race-based fighting words that so prejudice their community.
I concur in the judgment, however, because I agree with Justice White that this particular ordinance reaches beyond fighting words to speech protected by the First Amendment.

JUSTICE STEVENS, concurring in the judgment. . . .
[The] St. Paul ordinance regulates [fighting words] not on the basis of [content], but rather on the basis of the harm the speech causes. [Contrary] to the Court's suggestion, the ordinance regulates [a] subcategory of expression that causes injuries based on "race, color, creed, religion or gender," not a subcategory that involves discussions [of] those characteristics. [Moreover], even if the St. Paul ordinance did regulate fighting words based on its subject matter, such a regulation would, in my opinion, be constitutional. [Subject matter restrictions] generally do not raise the same concerns of government censorship and the distortion of public discourse presented by viewpoint regulations. [Contrary] to the suggestion of the majority, the St. Paul ordinance does not regulate expression based on viewpoint. [The] St. Paul ordinance is evenhanded. In a battle between advocates of tolerance and advocates of intolerance, the ordinance does not prevent either side from hurling fighting words at the other on the basis of their conflicting ideas, but it does bar both sides from hurling such words on the basis of the target's "race, color, creed, religion or gender." To extend the Court's pugilistic metaphor, the St. Paul ordinance simply bans punches "below the belt" — by either party. It does not, therefore, favor one side of any debate. . . .

WISCONSIN v. MITCHELL, 508 U.S. 476 (1993). After viewing the motion picture Mississippi Burning, in which a white man beat a young black who was praying, Mitchell, who is black, urged a group of blacks to assault a young white boy who happened to be walking by. The group, including Mitchell, beat the white boy severely. Mitchell was convicted of aggravated battery, which ordinarily carries a maximum sentence of two years' imprisonment. But because the jury found that Mitchell had intentionally selected his victim because of the boy's race, the maximum sentence for his offense was increased to seven years under the state's hate-crime penalty enhancement statute, which enhances the maximum penalty for an offense whenever the defendant "intentionally selects the person against whom the crime . . . is committed . . . because of the race, religion, color, disability, sexual orientation, national origin or ancestry of that person." The Court overturned the holding of the Wisconsin Supreme Court that the statute violated the first amendment. Chief Justice Rehnquist delivered the opinion for a unanimous Court:

"[A] physical assault is not by any stretch of the imagination expressive conduct protected by the First Amendment. [But this does not end the matter, for] although the statute punishes criminal conduct, it enhances the maximum penalty for conduct motivated by a discriminatory point of view more severely than the same conduct engaged in for some other reason or for no reason at all. Because the only reason for the enhancement is the defendant's discriminatory motive for selecting his victim, Mitchell argues (and the Wisconsin Supreme Court held) that the statute violates the First Amendment by punishing offenders' bigoted beliefs. [But] motive plays the same role under the Wisconsin statute as it does under federal and state antidiscrimination [laws]. Title VII, for example, makes it unlawful for an employer to discriminate against an employee 'because of such individual's race, color, religion, sex, or national origin.' [In Hishon v. King & Spalding, 467 U.S. 69 (1984), we] rejected the argument that Title VII infringed employers' First Amendment rights. . . .

"Nothing in our decision last Term in R.A.V. compels a different result here, [for] whereas the ordinance struck down in R.A.V. was explicitly directed at expression (i.e., 'speech' or 'messages'), the statute in this case is aimed at conduct unprotected by the First Amendment. Moreover, the Wisconsin statute singles out for enhancement bias-inspired conduct because this conduct is thought to inflict greater individual and societal harm. For example, according to the [State], bias-motivated crimes are more likely to provoke retaliatory crimes, inflict distinct emotional harms on their victims, and incite community unrest. The State's desire to redress these perceived harms provides an adequate explanation for its penalty-enhancement provision over and above mere disagreement with offenders' beliefs or biases."

Note: R.A.V. and Mitchell

1. *Variations on* R.A.V.

a. Consider the following law: "No public official may sue for libel for any statement concerning the performance of her official duties." Is this distinguishable from R.A.V.? If so, is it because the "content discrimination is based on the very reason why the particular class of speech at issue is proscribable"? Is it because the state can adequately justify the exemption of defamatory statements concerning the performance of a public official's duties from the "content-neutral" alternative of restricting all defamatory statements governed by New York Times v. Sullivan?

b. After R.A.V., how would you assess the constitutionality of 18 U.S.C. §241, which prohibits any person to "injure, oppress, threaten, or intimidate" others in the enjoyment of their civil rights, as applied to a white who burns a cross in front of a black's home?

c. The civil rights laws prohibit an employer from firing an employee because of her race, even though the employer may fire her for many other reasons. Are the civil rights laws invalid after R.A.V. because they penalize the employer for his political convictions? That is, if the employer fires an employee because he does not like blacks he is penalized, but if he fires an employee because he does not like Democrats, he is not. Why is *R.A.V.* different? Because the employer is not engaged in "speech"?

d. In United States v. Alvarez, section D1 supra, Justices Alito, Scalia and Thomas voted to uphold the Stolen Valor Act. Can their position be squared with *R.A.V.*?

2. *Hate speech and viewpoint-discrimination.* The Court in *R.A.V.* makes clear that laws banning hate speech are unconstitutional because they constitute viewpoint discrimination. In that light, consider Matal v. Tam, 582 U.S. — (2017). "Slants" is a derogatory term for persons of Asian descent. Simon Tam, lead singer of the rock group "The Slants," whose members are Asian-Americans, chose the name in order to "reclaim" the term and drain it of its denigrating force. The federal Patent and Trademark Office denied Tam's application for federal trademark registration of the name because it violated a federal law prohibiting the registration of any trademarks that "disparage . . . or bring . . . into contemp[t] or disrepute" any "persons, living or dead."

In a plurality opinion joined by Chief Justice Roberts and Justices Breyer and Thomas, Justice Alito concluded that even though the statute did not forbid a *specific* viewpoint, but forbade *any* trademark that disparaged or brought into contempt or disrepute any person or group, it nonetheless constituted unconstitutional "viewpoint discrimination." Alito explained that although the statute "evenhandedly prohibits disparagement of all groups," and "applies equally to marks that damn Democrats and Republicans, capitalists and socialists, and those arrayed on both sides of every possible issue," it nonetheless constituted "viewpoint discrimination" because "giving offense is a viewpoint." In short, he concluded, it was well established that "the public expression of ideas may not be prohibited merely because the ideas are themselves offensive to some of their hearers." Indeed, "no matter how the point is phrased, its unmistakable thrust is this: The Government has no interest in preventing speech expressing ideas that offend." Thus, "[s]peech that demeans on the basis of race, ethnicity, gender, religion, age, disability, or any other similar ground is hateful, but the proudest boast of our free speech jurisprudence is that we protect the freedom to express 'the thought that we hate.'"

In a separate concurring opinion, Justice Kennedy, joined by Justices Ginsburg, Sotomayor, and Kagan, agreed. Kennedy explained that because the statute "reflects the Government's disapproval of a subset of messages it finds offensive," it embodies "the essence of viewpoint discrimination." Although the government argued that "the law is viewpoint neutral because it applies in equal measure to any trademark that demeans or offends," that argument "misses the point." "To prohibit all sides from criticizing their opponents makes a law more viewpoint based, not less so." "The danger of viewpoint discrimination," Kennedy added, "is that the government is attempting to remove certain ideas or perspectives from a broader debate. That danger is all the greater if the ideas or perspectives are ones a particular audience might think offensive."

3. Mitchell *and* R.A.V. On what principle is *Mitchell* consistent with *R.A.V.*? Is the difference that, unlike the defendant in *Mitchell*, the cross-burner was engaged in "speech"? But if cross-burning is "speech," why isn't the act of beating an individual "because of his race" speech as well? After all, the assault "communicates" the defendant's views both to the victim and to observers. Is the assault not "speech" within the meaning of the first amendment because the message is communicated by conduct rather than by words? But then what of

cross-burning? Is the difference that in *R.A.V.* the harm was caused by the communicative element of the conduct, whereas in *Mitchell* the harm was caused directly by the conduct itself? But would any of the harms identified by the Court in *Mitchell* to justify the enhanced punishment arise if the act did *not* communicate a message of racial hatred? On the problem of symbolic expression, see section E3 infra.

4. *Harassment in the workplace.* Title VII of the 1964 Civil Rights Act prohibits discrimination in conditions of employment by race, religion, national origin, and sex. Courts have held that various kinds of harassment at work can be so severe that an employee effectively suffers from "discrimination" within the meaning of title VII. Such harassment generally takes two forms. First, there is quid pro quo harassment. This typically arises when an employer conditions an individual's hiring, promotion, or continued employment on sexual involvement, as when a supervisor tells an employee that he will fire her unless she has sex with him. This sort of harassment is generally regarded as an explicit threat that, at least in this context, is not protected by the first amendment.

The second form of harassment is more complex. It may arise when an employer or coworker creates a situation in which the work environment becomes hostile or abusive. Consider the following situations: (a) A white supervisor repeatedly says that black workers are lazy. (b) A male employee repeatedly compliments a female employee on her appearance. (c) Christian employees post pictures of Jesus at their workstations, over the objections of Jewish employees. (d) Male employees post pictures of naked women at their workstations, over the objections of female employees. To what extent, and on what theories, can the government constitutionally prohibit such speech?

Consider the following arguments: (a) Workplace harassment is not speech. It is discrimination. (b) The workplace is for work, not speech. (c) Workplace harassment is private conversation, not public discourse. (d) Workers are a captive audience. (e) Workplace harassment is of "low" first amendment value. For further discussion of workplace harassment, see Estlund, Freedom of Expression in the Workplace and the Problem of Discriminatory Harassment, 75 Tex. L. Rev. 687 (1997); Fallon, Sexual Harassment, Content-Neutrality, and the First Amendment Dog That Didn't Bark, 1994 Sup. Ct. Rev. 1; Volokh, Freedom of Speech and Workplace Harassment, 39 UCLA L. Rev. 1791 (1992); Strauss, Sexist Speech in the Workplace, 25 Harv. C.R.-C.L. L. Rev. 1 (1990).

Virginia v. Black

538 U.S. 343 (2003)

Justice O'Connor announced the judgment of the Court and delivered the opinion of the Court with respect to Parts I, II, and III, and an opinion with respect to Parts IV and V, in which The Chief Justice, Justice Stevens, and Justice Breyer join.

In this case we consider whether the Commonwealth of Virginia's statute banning cross burning with "an intent to intimidate a person or group of persons" violates the First Amendment. Va. Code Ann. §18.2-423 (1996). We conclude that while a State, consistent with the First Amendment, may ban cross burning carried out with the intent to intimidate, the provision in the Virginia statute treating any cross burning as prima facie evidence of intent to intimidate renders the statute unconstitutional. . . .

I

Respondents Barry Black, Richard Elliott, and Jonathan O'Mara were convicted separately of violating Virginia's cross-burning statute, §18.2-423. That statute provides:

> It shall be unlawful for any person or persons, with the intent of intimidating any person or group of persons, to burn, or cause to be burned, a cross on the property of another, a highway or other public place. . . . Any such burning of a cross shall be prima facie evidence of an intent to intimidate a person or group of persons.

Law

On August 22, 1998, Barry Black led a Ku Klux Klan rally in Carroll County, Virginia. Twenty-five to thirty people attended this gathering, which occurred on private property with the permission of the owner, who was in attendance. The property was located on an open field. . . .

When the sheriff of Carroll County learned that a Klan rally was occurring in his county, he went to observe it from the side of the road. During the approximately one hour that the sheriff was present, about 40 to 50 cars passed the site, a "few" of which stopped to ask the sheriff what was happening on the property. [Rebecca] Sechrist, who was related to the owner of the property where the rally took place, "sat and watched to see what [was] going on" from the lawn of her in-laws' house. She looked on as the Klan prepared for the gathering and subsequently conducted the rally itself.

During the rally, Sechrist heard Klan members speak about "what they were" and "what they believed in." The speakers "talked real bad about the blacks and the Mexicans." One speaker told the assembled gathering that "he would love to take a .30/.30 and just random[ly] shoot the blacks." The speakers also talked about "President Clinton and Hillary Clinton," and about how their tax money "goes to . . . the black people." Sechrist testified that this language made her "very . . . scared."

At the conclusion of the rally, the crowd circled around a 25- to 30-foot cross. The cross was between 300 and 350 yards away from the road. According to the sheriff, the cross "then all of a sudden . . . went up in a flame." As the cross burned, the Klan played Amazing Grace over the loudspeakers. Sechrist stated that the cross burning made her feel "awful" and "terrible."

When the sheriff observed the cross burning, he informed his deputy that they needed to "find out who's responsible and explain to them that they cannot do this in the State of Virginia." The sheriff then went down the driveway, entered the rally, and asked "who was responsible for burning the cross." Black responded, "I guess I am because I'm the head of the rally." The sheriff then told Black, "[T]here's a law in the State of Virginia that you cannot burn a cross and I'll have to place you under arrest for this."

Black was charged with burning a cross with the intent of intimidating a person or group of persons, in violation of §18.2-423. At his trial, the jury was instructed that "intent to intimidate means the motivation to intentionally put a person or a group of persons in fear of bodily harm. Such fear must arise from the willful conduct of the accused rather than from some mere temperamental timidity of the victim." The trial court also instructed the jury that "the burning of a cross by itself is sufficient evidence from which you may infer the required intent." [The] jury found Black guilty, and fined him $2,500. The Court of Appeals of Virginia affirmed Black's conviction.

On May 2, 1998, respondents Richard Elliott and Jonathan O'Mara, as well as a third individual, attempted to burn a cross on the yard of James Jubilee. Jubilee, an African-American, was Elliott's next-door neighbor in Virginia Beach, Virginia. Four months prior to the incident, Jubilee and his family had moved from California to Virginia Beach. Before the cross burning, Jubilee spoke to Elliott's mother to inquire about shots being fired from behind the Elliott home. Elliott's mother explained to Jubilee that her son shot firearms as a hobby, and that he used the backyard as a firing range.

On the night of May 2, respondents drove a truck onto Jubilee's property, planted a cross, and set it on fire. Their apparent motive was to "get back" at Jubilee for complaining about the shooting in the backyard. Respondents were not affiliated with the Klan. The next morning, as Jubilee was pulling his car out of the driveway, he noticed the partially burned cross approximately 20 feet from his house. After seeing the cross, Jubilee was "very nervous" because he "didn't know what would be the next phase," and because "a cross burned in your yard . . . tells you that it's just the first round."

Elliott and O'Mara were charged with attempted cross burning and conspiracy to commit cross burning. O'Mara pleaded guilty to both counts, reserving the right to challenge the constitutionality of the cross-burning statute. The judge sentenced O'Mara to 90 days in jail and fined him $2,500. The judge also suspended 45 days of the sentence and $1,000 of the fine. At Elliott's trial, the judge [instructed] the jury that the Commonwealth must prove that "the defendant intended to commit cross burning," that "the defendant did a direct act toward the commission of the cross burning," and that "the defendant had the intent of intimidating any person or group of persons." The court did not instruct the jury on the meaning of the word "intimidate," nor on the prima facie evidence provision of §18.2-423. The jury found Elliott guilty of attempted cross burning and acquitted him of conspiracy to commit cross burning. It sentenced Elliott to 90 days in jail and a $2,500 fine. The Court of Appeals of Virginia affirmed the convictions of both Elliott and O'Mara. O'Mara v. Commonwealth, 33 Va. App. 525, 535 S.E. 2d 175 (2000).

Each respondent appealed to the Supreme Court of Virginia, arguing that §18.2-423 is facially unconstitutional. The Supreme Court of Virginia consolidated all three cases, and held that the statute is unconstitutional on its face. 262 Va. 764, 553 S.E. 2d 738 (2001). It held that the Virginia cross-burning statute "is analytically indistinguishable from the ordinance found unconstitutional in [R.A.V. v. St. Paul]. The Virginia statute, the court held, discriminates on the basis of content since it "selectively chooses only cross burning because of its distinctive message." The court also held that the prima facie evidence provision renders the statute overbroad because "[t]he enhanced probability of prosecution under the statute chills the expression of protected speech." . . .

II

. . . Burning a cross in the United States is inextricably intertwined with the history of the Ku Klux Klan. [Since at least 1905], cross burnings have been used to communicate both threats of violence and messages of shared ideology. [Often] the Klan used cross burnings as a tool of intimidation and a threat of impending violence. For example, [in] 1941, the Klan burned four crosses in front of a proposed housing project, declaring, "We are here to keep niggers out of your town. . . . When the law fails you, call on us." [These] threats had special force given the long history of Klan violence. [The] Klan continued to use cross burnings to intimidate after World War II. [These] incidents of cross burning, among others, helped prompt Virginia to enact its first version of the cross-burning statute in 1950. . . .

Throughout the history of the Klan, cross burnings have also remained potent symbols of shared group identity and ideology. The burning cross became a symbol of the Klan itself and a central feature of Klan gatherings. [The] Klan has often published its newsletters and magazines under the name The Fiery Cross. [At] Klan gatherings across the country, cross burning became the climax of the rally or the initiation. [Throughout] the Klan's history, the Klan continued to use the burning cross in their ritual ceremonies. [For] its own members, the cross was a sign of celebration and ceremony. . . .

To this day, regardless of whether the message is a political one or whether the message is also meant to intimidate, the burning of a cross is a "symbol of hate." And while cross burning sometimes carries no intimidating message, at other times the intimidating message is the *only* message conveyed. For example, when a cross burning is directed at a particular person not affiliated with the Klan, the burning cross often serves as a message of intimidation, designed to inspire in the victim a fear of bodily harm. Moreover, the history of violence associated with the Klan shows that the possibility of injury or death is not just hypothetical. The person who burns a cross directed at a particular person often is making a serious threat, meant to coerce the victim to comply with the Klan's wishes unless the victim is willing to risk the wrath of the Klan. Indeed, as the cases of respondents Elliott and O'Mara indicate, individuals without Klan affiliation who wish to threaten or menace another person sometimes use cross burning because of this association between a burning cross and violence.

In sum, while a burning cross does not inevitably convey a message of intimidation, often the cross burner intends that the recipients of the message fear for their lives. And when a cross burning is used to intimidate, few if any messages are more powerful.

III

A . . .

The protections afforded by the First Amendment [are] not absolute, and we have long recognized that the government may regulate certain categories of expression consistent with the Constitution. The First Amendment permits "restrictions upon the content of speech in a few limited areas, which are 'of such slight social value as a step to truth that any benefit that may be derived from them is clearly outweighed by the social interest in order and morality.'" [R.A.V., quoting *Chaplinsky*]. . . .

Thus, for example, a State may punish [a] "true threat." [*Watts.*] "True threats" encompass those statements where the speaker means to communicate a serious expression of an intent to commit an act of unlawful violence to a particular individual or group of individuals. The speaker need not actually intend to carry out the threat. Rather, a prohibition on true threats "protect[s] individuals from the fear of violence" and "from the disruption that fear engenders," in addition to protecting people "from the possibility that the threatened violence will occur." Intimidation in the constitutionally proscribable sense of the word is a type of true threat, where a speaker directs a threat to a person or group of persons with the intent of placing the victim in fear of bodily harm or death. Respondents do not contest that some cross burnings fit within this meaning of intimidating speech, and rightly so. As noted in Part II, *supra*, the history of cross burning in this country shows that cross burning is often intimidating, intended to create a pervasive fear in victims that they are a target of violence.

B

The Supreme Court of Virginia ruled that in light of *R.A.V.*, even if it is constitutional to ban cross burning in a content-neutral manner, the Virginia cross-burning statute is unconstitutional because it discriminates on the basis of content and viewpoint. It is true [that] the burning of a cross is symbolic expression. The reason why the Klan burns a cross at its rallies, or individuals place a burning cross on someone else's lawn, is that the burning cross represents the message that the speaker wishes to communicate. Individuals burn crosses as opposed to other means of communication because cross burning carries a message in an effective and dramatic manner.

The fact that cross burning is symbolic expression, however, does not resolve the constitutional question. [In] *R.A.V.*, we held that a local ordinance that banned certain symbolic conduct, including cross burning, when done with the knowledge that such conduct would "'arouse anger, alarm or resentment in others on the basis of race, color, creed, religion or gender'" was unconstitutional. We held that the ordinance did not pass constitutional muster because it discriminated on the basis of content by targeting only those individuals who "provoke violence" on a basis specified in the law. The ordinance did not cover "[t]hose who wish to use 'fighting words' in connection with other ideas — to express hostility, for example, on the basis of political affiliation, union membership, or homosexuality." This content-based discrimination was unconstitutional because it allowed the city "to impose special prohibitions on those speakers who express views on disfavored subjects."

We did not hold in *R.A.V.* that the First Amendment prohibits *all* forms of content-based discrimination within a proscribable area of speech. Rather, we specifically stated that some types of content discrimination did not violate the First Amendment: "When the basis for the content discrimination consists entirely of the very reason the entire class of speech at issue is proscribable, no significant danger of idea or viewpoint discrimination exists. Such a reason, having been adjudged neutral enough to support exclusion of the entire class of speech from First Amendment protection, is also neutral enough to form the basis of distinction within the class."

Indeed, we noted that it would be constitutional to ban only a particular type of threat: "[T]he Federal Government can criminalize only those threats of violence that are directed against the President . . . since the reasons why threats of violence are outside the First Amendment . . . have special force when applied to the person of the President." And a State may "choose to prohibit only that obscenity which is the most patently offensive *in its prurience — i.e.*, that which involves the most lascivious displays of sexual activity." Consequently, while the holding of *R.A.V.* does not permit a State to ban only obscenity based on "offensive *political* messages," or "only those threats against the President that mention his policy on aid to inner cities," the First Amendment permits content discrimination "based on the very reasons why the particular class of speech at issue . . . is proscribable."

Similarly, Virginia's statute does not run afoul of the First Amendment insofar as it bans cross burning with intent to intimidate. Unlike the statute at issue in *R.A.V.*, the Virginia statute does not single out for opprobrium only that speech directed toward "one of the specified disfavored topics." It does not matter whether an individual burns a cross with intent to intimidate because of the victim's race, gender, or religion, or because of the victim's "political affiliation, union membership, or homosexuality." . . .

The First Amendment permits Virginia to outlaw cross burnings done with the intent to intimidate because burning a cross is a particularly virulent form of intimidation. Instead of prohibiting all intimidating messages, Virginia may choose to regulate this subset of intimidating messages in light of cross burning's long and pernicious history as a signal of impending violence. Thus, just as a State may regulate only that obscenity which is the most obscene due to its prurient content, so too may a State choose to prohibit only those forms of intimidation that are most likely to inspire fear of bodily harm. A ban on cross burning carried out with the intent to intimidate is fully consistent with our holding in *R.A.V.* and is proscribable under the First Amendment.

IV

The Supreme Court of Virginia ruled in the alternative that Virginia's cross-burning statute was unconstitutionally overbroad due to its provision stating that "[a]ny such burning of a cross shall be prima facie evidence of an intent to intimidate a person or group of persons." [The] Supreme Court of Virginia has . . . stated that "the act of burning a cross alone, with no evidence of intent to intimidate, [will] suffice for arrest and prosecution and will insulate the Commonwealth from a motion to strike the evidence at the end of its case-in-chief." . . .

The prima facie evidence provision . . . renders the statute unconstitutional. [The] prima facie provision strips away the very reason why a State may ban cross burning with the intent to intimidate. The prima facie evidence provision permits a jury to convict in every cross-burning case in which defendants exercise their constitutional right not to put on a defense. And even where a defendant [presents] a defense, the prima facie evidence provision makes it more likely that the jury will find an intent to intimidate regardless of the particular facts of the case. The provision permits the Commonwealth to arrest, prosecute, and convict a person based solely on the fact of cross burning itself.

It is apparent that the provision as so interpreted "'would create an unacceptable risk of the suppression of ideas.'" The act of burning a cross may mean that a person is engaging in constitutionally proscribable intimidation. But that same act may mean only that the person is engaged in core political speech. The prima facie evidence provision in this statute blurs the line between these two meanings of a burning cross. As interpreted by the jury instruction, the provision chills constitutionally protected political speech because of the possibility that a State will prosecute — and potentially convict — somebody engaging only in lawful political speech at the core of what the First Amendment is designed to protect.

As the history of cross burning indicates, a burning cross is not always intended to intimidate. Rather, sometimes the cross burning is a statement of ideology, a symbol of group solidarity. It is a ritual used at Klan gatherings, and it is used to represent the Klan itself. Thus, "[b]urning a cross at a political rally would almost certainly be protected expression." . . .

The prima facie provision makes no effort to distinguish among these different types of cross burnings. It [may] be true that a cross burning, even at a political rally, arouses a sense of anger or hatred among the vast majority of citizens who see a burning cross. But this sense of anger or hatred is not sufficient to ban all cross burnings. [The] prima facie evidence provision in this case ignores all of the contextual factors that are necessary to decide whether a particular cross burning is intended to intimidate. The First Amendment does not permit such a shortcut. . . .

JUSTICE STEVENS, concurring.

Cross burning with "an intent to intimidate" unquestionably qualifies as the kind of threat that is unprotected by the First Amendment. For the reasons stated in the separate opinions that Justice White and I wrote in R.A.V., that simple proposition provides a sufficient basis for upholding the basic prohibition in the Virginia statute even though it does not cover other types of threatening expressive conduct. With this observation, I join Justice O'Connor's opinion.

JUSTICE THOMAS, dissenting.

In every culture, certain things acquire meaning well beyond what outsiders can comprehend. That goes for both the sacred, see Texas v. Johnson [section E3 infra] (describing the unique position of the American flag in our Nation's 200 years of history), and the profane. I believe that cross burning is the paradigmatic example of the latter.

Although I agree with the majority's conclusion that it is constitutionally permissible to "ban . . . cross burning carried out with intent to intimidate," I believe that the majority errs in imputing an expressive component to the activity in question. [In] our culture, cross burning has almost invariably meant lawlessness and understandably instills in its victims well-grounded fear of physical violence. [This] statute prohibits only conduct, not expression. And, just as one cannot burn down someone's house to make a political point and then seek refuge in the First Amendment, those who hate cannot terrorize and intimidate to make their point. In light of my conclusion that the statute here addresses only conduct, there is no need to analyze it under any of our First Amendment tests. [Because] I would uphold the validity of this statute, I respectfully dissent.*

JUSTICE SOUTER, with whom JUSTICE KENNEDY and JUSTICE GINSBURG join, concurring in the judgment in part and dissenting in part.

I agree with the majority that the Virginia statute makes a content-based distinction within the category of punishable intimidating or threatening expression, [but] I disagree that [the Virginia statute can be saved even in part] from unconstitutionality under the holding in R.A.V. . . .

The [prohibition] of cross burning with intent to intimidate selects a symbol with particular content from the field of all proscribable expression meant to intimidate. [The] issue is whether the statutory prohibition restricted to this symbol falls within one of the exceptions to R.A.V.'s general condemnation of

---

* Justice Scalia, joined by Justice Thomas, also filed a separate opinion, concurring in part and dissenting in part.

limited content-based proscription within a broader category of expression pro-scribable generally. [R.A.V.] defines the special virulence exception [this] way: prohibition by subcategory [is] constitutional if it is made "entirely" on the "basis" of "the very reason" that "the entire class of speech at issue is proscribable" at all. The Court explained that when the subcategory is confined to the most obviously proscribable instances, "no significant danger of idea or viewpoint discrimination exists." . . .

The first example of permissible distinction is for a prohibition of obscenity unusually offensive "in its prurience." [Distinguishing] obscene publications on this basis does not suggest discrimination on the basis of the message conveyed. The opposite is true, however, when a general prohibition of intimidation is rejected in favor of a distinct proscription of intimidation by cross burning. The cross may have been selected because of its special power to threaten, but it may also have been singled out because of disapproval of its message of white supremacy, either because a legislature thought white supremacy was a perni-cious doctrine or because it found that dramatic, public espousal of it was a civic embarrassment. Thus, there is no kinship between the cross-burning statute and the core prurience example.

Nor does this case present any analogy to the statute prohibiting threats against the President. [The] content discrimination in that statute [reflects] the special risks and costs associated with threatening the President. Again, however, threats against the President are not generally identified by reference to the content of any message that may accompany the threat, let alone any viewpoint, and there is no obvious correlation in fact between victim and message. [Differential] treatment of threats against the President, then, selects nothing but special risks, not special messages. A content-based proscription of cross burning, on the other hand, may be a subtle effort to ban not only the intensity of the intimidation cross burning causes when done to threaten, but also the particular message of white supremacy that is broadcast even by non-threatening cross burning. [I] thus read R.A.V.'s examples of the particular virulence exception as covering prohibitions that are not clearly associated with a particular viewpoint, and that are consequently different from the Virginia statute. . . .

Note: R.A.V. *and* Black

Consider the following views:

a. Schauer, Intentions, Conventions, and the First Amendment: The Case of Cross-Burning, 2003 Sup. Ct. Rev. 197, 206–208:

> [Because] Justice O'Connor saw the Virginia statute as singling [out] intimidation with special intimidating power, she concluded [that] the statute was [a] constitu-tionally permissible prohibition on unprotected intimidation. [But] a closer look at the dynamics of what causes cross-burning to be especially intimidating [makes] the Court's distinction between *Black* and *R.A.V.* difficult to accept. What makes cross-burning more intimidating than, say, flag-burning or leaf-burning, [is] a function of the racist [point] of view it embodies. [Virginia's] belief that burning a cross is especially intimidating is based solely on the viewpoint-based judgment that sym-bols with one point of view have effects that symbols with another point of view do not have.

b. Gey, A Few Questions About Cross Burning, Intimidation, and Free Speech, 80 Notre Dame L. Rev. 1287, 1373–1374 (2005):

> *Black* is just one example of a disturbing [proliferation] of alternative First Amendment constructs to regulate antisocial speech. These constructs appear uncoordinated by any central principle and seem limited only by the ingenuity of plaintiffs and prosecutors in fitting familiar examples of antisocial speech into the new regulatory patterns. [Some] overriding constitutional framework is needed to limit the expansion of the new categories and constrain the use of flexible terms such as "intimidation" and "terrorism." The *Brandenburg* [explicitness and immediate harm] paradigm was devised to serve precisely that function, if the courts would only use it.

c. In the incitement situation, the Court, following the lead of Judge Learned Hand in *Masses*, seems to require that for incitement of unlawful conduct to come within the low-value category of express incitement the incitement must be express. Is *Black*'s treatment of threats consistent with that requirement? Is a burning cross an *express* threat? Does it make any sense to require express incitement but not express threats? See Taylor, Free Expression and Expressiveness, 33 N.Y.U. Rev. L. & Soc. Ch. 375 (2009). Is a noose on someone's front lawn equivalent to a burning cross?

Note: *Pornography and the Victimization of Women*

1. *A model statute.* Consider the constitutionality of the following law:

> Pornography is the sexually explicit subordination of women, graphically depicted, whether in words or pictures, that also includes one or more of the following: (i) women are presented dehumanized as sexual objects, things or commodities; (ii) women are presented as sexual objects who enjoy pain, humiliation or rape; (iii) women are presented as sexual objects tied up or cut up or mutilated or physically hurt; (iv) women are presented in postures of sexual submission or sexual servility, including by inviting penetration; or (v) women are presented as whores by nature. No person may sell, exhibit, or distribute pornography.

2. *Evaluation.* Consider the following views:
a. MacKinnon, Not a Moral Issue, 2 Yale L. & Soc. Poly. Rev. 321, 322–324 (1984):

> Obscenity law is concerned with morality, specifically morals from the male point of view, meaning the standpoint of male dominance. The feminist critique of pornography is politics, specifically politics from the women's point of view, meaning the standpoint of the subordination of women to men. Morality here means good and evil; politics means power and powerlessness. Obscenity is a moral idea; pornography is a political practice. The two concepts represent entirely different things. Nudity, explicitness, excess of candor, [these] qualities bother obscenity law when sex is depicted or portrayed. [Sex] forced on real women so that it can be sold at a profit to be forced on other real women; women's bodies trussed and maimed and raped and made into things to be hurt and obtained and accessed and this presented as the nature of women; the coercion that is visible and the coercion that has become invisible — this and more bothers feminists about pornography. Obscenity as such probably does little harm; pornography causes

attitudes and behaviors of violence and discrimination which define the treatment and status of half of the population.

b. Clark, Liberalism and Pornography, in Pornography and Censorship 52–57 (D. Copp and S. Wendells eds. 1983):

[Pornography] has very little to do with sex, [but] it has everything to do with [the] use of sexuality as an instrument of active oppression. [Pornography is] a species of hate literature. [It depicts] women [as inviting] humiliating, degrading, and violently abusive [treatment]. [It feeds] traditional male phantasies [and glorifies] the traditional advantages men have enjoyed in relation to exploitation of female sexuality. [Pornography] is a method of socialization; [it] "teaches society to view women as less than human." [It is thus an] affront to [the dignity of women] as equal persons. [Moreover,] role modeling has a powerful effect on human behavior. [People] tend to act out and operationalize the behavior that they see typically acted out around them.

See also A. Dworkin, Pornography: Men Possessing Women (1981); Take Back the Night: Women on Pornography (L. Lederer ed. 1980).

c. MacKinnon, Pornography, Civil Rights, and Speech, 20 Harv. C.R.-C.L. L. Rev. 1, 52–54 (1985):

Recent experimental research on pornography shows that [pornographic material may cause] measurable harm to women through increasing men's attitudes and behaviors of discrimination in both violent and nonviolent forms. Exposure to [pornography] increases men's immediately subsequent willingness to aggress against women under laboratory conditions. It [significantly] increases attitudinal measures known to correlate with rape, [such as] hostility toward women, [condoning] rape, and predicting that one would rape [if] one knows one would not get caught.

d. West, The Feminist-Conservative Anti-Pornography Alliance and the 1986 Attorney General's Commission on Pornography Report, 1987 Am. B. Found. Res. J. 681, 686, 691–692:

A woman-centered conception of pornography [has] two dimensions: for many women (perhaps most), pornography is primarily victimizing, threatening and oppressive, [but] for others [it] is on occasion liberating and transformative. [Indeed, some pornography assaults] a source of oppression: the marital, familial, productive, and reproductive values that the conservative wrongly identifies as necessary to the creation of a virtuous life and a virtuous society. [According] to women who enjoy pornography, the validation of pleasure, desire, and sexuality found in some pornography is [a] healthy attack on a stifling and oppressive societal denial of female sexuality. [It can be] something to celebrate, rather than something to condemn.

e. In American Booksellers Association v. Hudnut, 771 F.2d 323 (7th Cir. 1985), the Court of Appeals for the Seventh Circuit held unconstitutional an Indianapolis antipornography ordinance similar to the model antipornography law set forth above. The court of appeals accepted the factual premises of the ordinance, conceding that "depictions of subordination tend to perpetuate subordination," and that the "subordinate status of women in turn leads to affront and lower pay at work, insult and injury at home, battery and rape on the streets."

The court of appeals observed, however, that "racial bigotry, anti-semitism, violence on television [and other forms of expression also] influence the culture and shape our socialization. [Yet] all is protected speech, however insidious. Any other answer leaves the government in control of all of the institutions of culture, the great censor and director of which thoughts are good for us." Moreover, the court of appeals rejected the argument that pornography, as defined in the ordinance, is "low"-value speech: "True, pornography and obscenity have sex in common. But Indianapolis left out of its definition any reference to literary, artistic, political, or scientific value. [Moreover, although the Supreme] Court sometimes balances the value of speech against the costs of its restriction, [it] does this by category of speech and not by the content of particular works." The Court emphasized that the Indianapolis ordinance expressly discriminated against a particular viewpoint: "Under the ordinance graphic sexually explicit speech is 'pornography' or not depending on the perspective the author adopts. Speech that 'subordinates' women [is] forbidden, [but speech] that portrays women in positions of equality is [lawful]. This is thought control. [Those] who espouse that approved view may use sexual images; those who do not, may not." The court of appeals concluded that, because the ordinance "created an approved point of view," it could not be defended as a restriction of only "low"-value speech. See also Stone, Anti-Pornography Legislation as Viewpoint Discrimination, 9 Harv. J.L. & Pub. Poly. 701 (1986). For the Supreme Court's summary affirmance of *Hudnut*, see 475 U.S. 1001 (1986). The Canadian Supreme Court has unanimously upheld legislation that is similar to the model antipornography ordinance. See Butler v. Regina, File No. 22191 (1992).

f. Consider Posner, The Speech Market and the Legacy of *Schenck*, in L. Bollinger and G. Stone, Eternal Vigilance: Free Speech in the Modern Era 121, 136–137 (2002):

> In the case of both pornography and hate speech, [one] has the sense that the desire to crack down on these forms of speech has little to do with demonstrable harms [but] with an ideological project — [that] of denying or occluding the existence of deep-seated differences between groups (in particular men and women, and blacks and whites). Hate speakers are vociferous deniers of equality, and pornography caters primarily to a specifically male interest in women as sexual playthings for men. . . . Insofar as campaigns for the regulation of hate speech and pornography have the purpose and effect of correcting ideological or political "error," giving them the backing of the law interferes arbitrarily with the market in ideas and opinions.

3. *Alternative approaches.* Consider the following:

a. Suppose a city enacted an ordinance that prohibited obscenity, which is concededly of "low" first amendment value, only insofar as it is also pornographic, within the meaning of the ordinance invalidated in *Hudnut*. Would such a law be constitutional? Recall *R.A.V.*

b. In light of *Ferber*, could the antipornography ordinance be justified on the ground that pornography harms women participants in the same way that child pornography harms children? Consider Note, Anti-Pornography Laws and First Amendment Values, 98 Harv. L. Rev. 460, 473 (1984): "Because the Court is probably not disposed to presume that adult models are incapable of refusing to participate in pornographic films or photographs, it is unlikely to reason that adult pornography [can] be banned irrespective of a work's social merit."

Note: "Low"-Value Speech — Final Thoughts

Has the doctrine of "low"-value speech injected the Court "into value judgments [foreclosed] to it by the basic theory of the First Amendment"? T. Emerson, The System of Free Expression 326 (1970). Reconsider the various categories of "low" or arguably "low"-value expression — express incitement, fighting words, threats, technical military information, false statements of fact, nonnewsworthy invasions of privacy, commercial speech, obscenity, offensive language, offensive sexually oriented expression, group defamation, hate speech, pornography. Has the Court developed a coherent theory of first amendment "value"? What considerations are relevant in deciding whether particular categories of expression constitute "low"-value speech?

Consider Sunstein, Pornography and the First Amendment, 1986 Duke L.J. 589, 603–604:

> [In] determining whether speech qualifies as low-value, the cases suggest that four factors are relevant. First, the speech must be far afield from the central concern of the first amendment, which, broadly speaking, is effective popular control of public affairs. [Second], a distinction is drawn between cognitive and noncognitive aspects of speech. [Third], the purpose of the speaker is relevant: if the speaker is seeking to communicate a message, he will be treated more favorably than if he is not. Fourth, the various classes of low-value speech reflect judgments that in certain areas, government is unlikely to be acting for constitutionally impermissible reasons or producing constitutionally troublesome harms.

For a slightly different formulation, consider Stone, Sex, Violence and the First Amendment, 74 U. Chi. L. Rev. 1857, 1863–1864 (2007):

> The Supreme Court has never offered a clearly-defined theory of low-value speech. The case law, however, suggests that several factors are relevant to the analysis. First, categories of low-value speech (for example, false statements of fact, threats, commercial advertising, fighting words, express incitement of unlawful conduct, and obscenity) do not primarily advance political discourse. Second, categories of low-value speech are not defined in terms of disfavored ideas or political viewpoints. Third, low-value speech usually has a strong noncognitive impact on its audience. Fourth, categories of low-value speech have long been regulated without undue harm to the overall system of free expression.

Does either of these four-factor analyses adequately explain (or at least describe) the Court's decisions? Are these the right factors to consider? What role should the history of regulation of different categories of speech play in the "low"-value analysis? See Lakier, The Invention of Low-Value Speech, 128 Harv. L. Rev. 2166 (2015).

How would you assess the overall impact of the "low"-value doctrine? Have any of the restrictions upheld under this doctrine seriously threatened the system of free expression?

Consider the following evaluations:

(1) The Court's use of the "low"-value theory "has been marked by vacillation and uncertainty." It is a highly "result-oriented" approach that is susceptible to an endless expansion of the list of "low"-value categories "whenever another kind of expression [gains] a renewed disfavor." To the extent that fighting words, commercial speech, obscenity, and libel are "subject to regulation, it should

be because they cause harm and not because they are presumed to be low in communicative value." Shaman, The Theory of Low-Value Speech, 48 S.M.U. L. Rev. 297, 339, 348 (1995).

(2) "The important line for resolving whether restrictions on the content of speech [should] receive highest scrutiny [should turn not on judgments about the 'value' of the speech, but on the distinction] between censorial and non-censorial theories of harm. [Censorial] restrictions are those that rest on the possibility that expression of a dangerous idea will cause social harm through the processing, influence, and spread of that idea or message. [Non-censorial] restrictions, on the other hand, [are directed at categories of speech such as libel, obscenity, child pornography, hate speech, animal cruelty videos, fighting words, violent video games, misogynistic pornography, and threats, that cause harm] by virtue of some kind of non-rational impact that the expression can be expected to have by its utterance, not dependent on any idea or message that it may also contain. [Once] a law is determined to fall on the non-censorial side of the [line], then it must still be justified and tested for scope and possible pretext, but without the heavy presumption of invalidity that comes with the suppression of ideas." Brown, The Harm Principle and Free Speech, 89 S. Cal. L. Rev. 953 (2016).

(3) The "low"-value doctrine has served a salutary function, for it has operated as a critical "safety valve," enabling the Court to deal sensibly with somewhat harmful, but relatively insignificant, speech without running the risk of diluting the protection accorded expression at the very heart of the guarantee.

(4) In the decades after *Chaplinsky*, defenders of free speech viewed the *Chaplinsky* dictum as an "unfortunate" invitation to the Court to make open-ended value judgments about which speech is and is not to be protected by the First Amendment. Indeed, Harry Kalven criticized it as a "broad dictum" that "haunted constitutional law." H. Kalven, A Worthy Tradition: Freedom of Speech in America 18 (1988). In light of the Roberts Court's decisions in *Stevens*, *Snyder*, *Brown*, and *Alvarez*, however, the *Chaplinsky* dictum seems to have taken on a somewhat different cast. Indeed, one might say that the Roberts Court "has generally declined to expressly invoke *Chaplinsky*'s low-value [doctrine] as a rationale for enlarging the realm of unprotected expression" and instead has "moved in the opposite direction." Collins, Exceptional Freedom: The Roberts Court, the First Amendment, and the New Absolutism, 76 Alb. L. Rev. 409, 424 (2013).

E. CONTENT-NEUTRAL RESTRICTIONS: LIMITATIONS ON THE MEANS OF COMMUNICATION AND THE PROBLEM OF CONTENT-NEUTRALITY

Content-neutral restrictions limit expression without regard to its content. They turn neither on their face nor as applied on the content or communicative impact of speech. Such restrictions encompass a broad spectrum of limitations on expressive activity, ranging from a prohibition on the use of loudspeakers, to a ban on billboards, to a limitation on campaign contributions, to a prohibition on the mutilation of draft cards. To what extent, and in what manner, do content-neutral restrictions implicate the concerns and values underlying the first amendment?

How do they differ in this regard from content-based restrictions? Should the doctrines devised to govern content-based restrictions also govern content-neutral restrictions? In exploring these and related questions, this section begins with a search for general principles and then examines four specific areas: the right to a public forum; symbolic speech; regulation of the electoral process; and litigation, association, and the right not to speak. Throughout, this section questions the meaning of "content-neutrality" and tests the occasionally elusive line between content-based and content-neutral restrictions.

1. General Principles

SCHNEIDER v. STATE, 308 U.S. 147 (1939). Appellants, who distributed leaflets on a public street announcing a protest meeting, were convicted of violating an ordinance prohibiting any person to distribute leaflets in "any street or way." The Court held the ordinance invalid. Justice Roberts delivered the opinion:

"Municipal authorities, as trustees for the public, have the duty to keep their communities' streets open and available for movement of people and property, the primary purpose to which the streets are dedicated. So long as legislation to this end does not abridge the constitutional liberty of one rightfully upon the street to impart information through speech or the distribution of literature, it may lawfully regulate the conduct of those using the streets. For example, a person could not exercise this liberty by taking his stand in the middle of a crowded street, contrary to traffic regulations, and maintain his position to the stoppage of all traffic; [nor] does the guarantee of freedom of speech or of the press deprive a municipality of power to enact regulations against throwing literature broadcast in the streets. Prohibition of such conduct would not abridge the constitutional liberty since such activity bears no necessary relationship to the freedom to speak, write, print or distribute information or opinion.

"This court has characterized the freedom of speech and freedom of press as fundamental personal rights and liberties. [Mere] legislative preferences or beliefs respecting matters of public convenience may well support regulation directed at other personal activities, but be insufficient to justify such as diminishes the exercise of rights so vital to the maintenance of democratic institutions. And so, as cases arise, the delicate and difficult task falls upon the courts to weigh the circumstances and to appraise the substantiality of the reasons advanced in support of the regulation of the free enjoyment of the rights.

"[The] legislation under attack [is designed to prevent littering]. Although the alleged offenders were not charged with themselves scattering paper in the streets, their convictions were sustained upon the theory that distribution by them [resulted] in such littering. We are of opinion that the purpose to keep the streets clean and of good appearance is insufficient to justify an ordinance which prohibits a person rightfully on a public street from handing literature to one willing to receive it. Any burden imposed upon the city authorities in cleaning and caring for the streets as an indirect consequence of such distribution results from the constitutional protection of the freedom of speech and press. This constitutional protection does not deprive a city of all power to prevent street littering. There are obvious methods of preventing littering. Amongst these is the punishment of those who actually throw papers on the streets. . . .

"It is suggested that the [ordinance is] valid because [its] operation is limited to streets and alleys and leaves persons free to distribute printed matter in other places. [But] the streets are natural and proper places for the dissemination of information and opinion; and one is not to have the exercise of his liberty of expression in appropriate places abridged on the plea that it may be exercised in some other place."

MARTIN v. CITY OF STRUTHERS, 319 U.S. 141 (1943). Appellant, a Jehovah's Witness, went to the homes of strangers, knocking on doors and ringing doorbells in order to distribute leaflets advertising a religious meeting. She was convicted of violating a municipal ordinance prohibiting any person "to ring the doorbell [or] otherwise summon the inmate [of] any residence [for] the purpose of [distributing] handbills." The Court held the ordinance invalid. Justice Black delivered the opinion of the Court:

"We are faced [with] the necessity of weighing the conflicting interests of the appellant in the civil rights she claims, as well as the right of the individual householder to determine whether he is willing to receive her message, against the interest of the community which by this ordinance offers to protect the interests of all its citizens, whether particular citizens want that protection or not. [In] considering legislation which thus limits the dissemination of knowledge, we [must] 'weigh the circumstances [and] appraise the substantiality of the reasons advanced in support of the regulation.' [Schneider.] ...

"While door to door distributors of literature may be either a nuisance or a blind for criminal activities, they may also be useful members of society engaged in the dissemination of ideas in accordance with the best tradition of free discussion. The widespread use of this method of communication by many groups espousing various causes attests its major importance. [Door] to door distribution of circulars is essential to the poorly financed causes of little people.

"Freedom to distribute information to every citizen whenever he desires to receive it is so clearly vital to the preservation of a free society that, putting aside reasonable police and health regulations of time and manner of distribution, it must be fully preserved. [Traditionally] the American law punishes persons who enter onto the property of another after having been warned by the owner to keep off. [Thus], the city may make it an offense for any person to ring the bell of a householder who has appropriately indicated that he is unwilling to be disturbed. This or any similar regulation leaves the decision as to whether distributors of literature may lawfully call at a home where it belongs — with the homeowner himself. [Because] the dangers of distribution can so easily be controlled by traditional legal methods, [the challenged ordinance] can serve no purpose but that forbidden by the Constitution, the naked restriction of the dissemination of ideas."

Justice Frankfurter filed a separate opinion: "[The] ordinance before us [penalizes only] the distribution of 'literature.' [It does not penalize door-to-door canvassing for other purposes, such as the sale of pots and pans.] The Court's opinion leaves one in doubt whether prohibition of [all door-to-door canvassing] would be deemed an infringement of free speech. It would be fantastic to suggest that a city has power [to] forbid house-to-house canvassing generally, but the Constitution prohibits the inclusion in such prohibition of door-to-door [distribution of] printed matter." Is Justice Frankfurter right that this would be a different case?

KOVACS v. COOPER, 336 U.S. 77 (1949). In *Kovacs*, the Court, in a five-to-four decision, upheld a city ordinance prohibiting any person to use any sound truck or other instrument that emits "loud and raucous noises" on any public street. Justice Reed wrote a plurality opinion: "City streets are recognized as a normal place for the exchange of [ideas]. But this does not mean the freedom is beyond all control. We think it is a permissible exercise of legislative discretion to bar sound [trucks], amplified to a loud and raucous volume, from the public ways of municipalities. [That] more people may be more easily and cheaply reached by sound trucks [is] not enough to call forth constitutional protection for what those charged with public welfare reasonably think is a nuisance when easy means of publicity are open."

Justice Frankfurter concurred in the result: "Surely there is not a constitutional right to force unwilling people to listen. [So] long as a legislature does not prescribe what ideas may be noisily expressed, [it] is not for us to supervise the limits it may impose in safeguarding the steadily narrowing opportunities for serenity and reflection."

Justice Black, joined by Justices Douglas and Rutledge, dissented: "The basic premise of the First Amendment is that all present instruments of communication, as well as others that inventive genius may bring into being, shall be free from governmental censorship or prohibition. Laws which hamper the free use of some instruments of communication [favor] competing channels. Thus, [laws] like [this] ordinance can give an overpowering influence to views of owners of legally favored instruments of communication. [There] are many people who have ideas that they wish to disseminate but who do not have enough money to own or control publishing plants, newspapers, radios, moving picture studios, or chains of show places. [Transmission] of ideas through public speaking is [thus] essential to the sound thinking of a fully informed citizenry. [And] it is an obvious fact that public speaking today without sound amplifiers is a wholly inadequate way to reach the people on a large scale. . . .

"I am aware that the 'blare' of this new method of carrying ideas is susceptible of abuse and may under certain circumstances constitute an intolerable nuisance. But ordinances can be drawn which adequately protect a community from unreasonable use of public speaking devices without absolutely denying to the community's citizens all information that may be disseminated or received through this new avenue for trade in ideas. [A] city ordinance that reasonably restricts the volume of sound, or the hours during which an amplifier may be used, does not, in my mind, infringe the constitutionally protected area of free speech. [But the challenged] ordinance [is] an absolute prohibition of all uses of an amplifier on any of the streets of [the city]."

METROMEDIA, INC. v. SAN DIEGO, 453 U.S. 490 (1981). A San Diego ordinance banned virtually all billboards. Justice Brennan, joined by Justice Blackmun, argued that the ordinance was unconstitutional: "[The] *practical* effect of the San Diego ordinance is to eliminate the billboard as an effective medium of communication. [Thus, it is necessary to assess] the 'substantiality of the governmental interests asserted' and 'whether those interests could be served by means that would be less intrusive on activity protected by the First Amendment.' [*Schneider; Struthers.*] Applying that test to the instant case, I would invalidate the San Diego ordinance. [First], although I have no quarrel with the substantiality of the city's interest in traffic safety, the city has failed to come forward with evidence demonstrating that billboards actually impair traffic safety in San Diego. [Second], the city has failed to show that its asserted interest in aesthetics is sufficiently substantial in the commercial and industrial areas of San Diego. . . .

"It is no doubt true that the appearance of certain areas of the city would be enhanced by the elimination of billboards, but 'it is not immediately [apparent]' that their elimination in all other areas as well would have more than a negligible impact on aesthetics. [A] billboard is not *necessarily* inconsistent with oil storage tanks, blighted areas, or strip development. Of course, it is not for a court to impose its own notion of beauty on San Diego. But before deferring to a city's judgment, a court must be convinced that the city is seriously and comprehensively addressing aesthetic concerns with respect to its environment. Here, San Diego has failed to demonstrate a comprehensive coordinated effort in its commercial and industrial areas to address other obvious contributors to an unattractive environment. In this sense the ordinance is underinclusive."

Justice Stevens disagreed: "[The] net effect of the city's ban on billboards will be a reduction in the total quantity of communication in San Diego. [But that does not in itself render the ordinance invalid.] Graffiti [is] an inexpensive means of communicating [to] large numbers of people; some creators of graffiti have no effective alternative means of publicly expressing themselves. Nevertheless, I believe a community has the right to decide that its interests [in] securing beautiful surroundings outweigh the countervailing interest in uninhibited expression by means of words and pictures in public places. . . .

"It seems to be accepted by all that a zoning regulation excluding billboards from residential neighborhoods is justified by the interest in maintaining pleasant surroundings and enhancing property values. The same interests are at work in commercial and industrial zones, [for the] character of the environment affects property values and the quality of life not only for the suburban resident but equally so for the individual who toils in a factory or invests his capital in industrial properties.

"Because the legitimacy of the interests [is] beyond dispute, [the] constitutionality of the prohibition of outdoor advertising involves two separate questions. First, is there any reason to believe that the regulation is biased in favor of one point of view? Second, is it fair to conclude that the market which remains open for the communication [of] ideas is ample and not threatened with gradually increasing restraints? In this case, there is not even a hint of bias or censorship in the city's actions. Nor is there any reason to believe that the overall communications market in San Diego is inadequate. [Thus,] nothing in this record suggests that the ordinance poses a threat to the interests protected by the First Amendment." Chief Justice Burger and Justice Rehnquist agreed with Justice Stevens because "there has been no suggestion that billboards [advance] any particular viewpoint or issue disproportionately." The remaining justices found it unnecessary to address this issue.

CITY OF LADUE v. GILLEO, 512 U.S. 43 (1994). In a unanimous opinion, the Court held that a city could not constitutionally prohibit homeowners from displaying signs on their property. The purpose of the ordinance was to minimize "visual clutter." At issue was respondent's desire to place on her front lawn a 24-by-36-inch sign printed with the words "Say No to War in the Persian Gulf, Call Congress Now." Justice Stevens delivered the opinion of the Court:

"Ladue has almost completely foreclosed a venerable means of communication that is both unique and important. [Although] prohibitions foreclosing entire media may be completely free of content or viewpoint discrimination, the danger they pose to freedom of speech is readily apparent — by eliminating a common means of speaking, such measures can suppress too much speech. . . .

"Ladue contends, however, that its ordinance is a mere regulation of the 'time, place, or manner' of speech because residents remain free to convey their desired messages by other means, such as hand-held signs, 'letters, handbills, flyers, telephone calls, newspaper advertisements, bumper stickers, speeches, and neighborhood or community meetings.' However, even regulations [of] time, place, or manner [must] 'leave open ample alternative channels for communication.' In this case, we are not persuaded that adequate substitutes exist for the important medium of speech that Ladue has closed off.

"Displaying a sign from one's own residence often carries a message quite distinct from placing the same sign someplace else, or conveying the same text or picture by other means. Precisely because of their location, such signs provide information about the identity of the 'speaker.' [Moreover, residential] signs are an unusually cheap and convenient form of communication. Especially for persons of modest means or limited mobility, a yard or window sign may have no practical substitute. . . .

"A special respect for individual liberty in the home has long been part of our culture and our law; that principle has special resonance when the government seeks to constrain a person's ability to speak there. Most Americans would be understandably dismayed, given that tradition, to learn that it was illegal to display from their window [a] sign expressing their political views. . . .

"Our decision [by] no means leaves the City powerless to address the ills that may be associated with residential signs. [We] are not confronted here with mere regulations short of a ban. [We] are confident that more temperate measures could in large part satisfy Ladue's stated regulatory needs without harm to the First Amendment rights of its citizens. As currently framed, however, the ordinance abridges those rights."

BARTNICKI v. VOPPER, 532 U.S. 514 (2001). During contentious collective-bargaining negotiations between a union representing teachers at a public high school and the local school board, an unidentified person intercepted and recorded a cell phone conversation between the union negotiator and the union president. Vopper, a radio commentator, played a tape of the intercepted conversation on his public affairs talk show in connection with news reports about the settlement. The Court held that Vopper could not be held liable for damages under federal or state wiretap laws for broadcasting the unlawfully recorded phone call.

Justice Stevens delivered the opinion of the Court. The Court accepted that the information on the tapes had been obtained unlawfully by an unknown party, that Vopper had played no part in the illegal interception, that he knew or should have known that the phone call had been intercepted unlawfully, and that "the subject matter of the conversation was a matter of public concern."

The Court explained that the relevant statutes, which prohibited the unauthorized disclosure of unlawfully intercepted communications, were "content-neutral" laws of general applicability. The Court then defined the issue as follows: "Where the punished publisher of information has obtained the information [in] a manner lawful in itself but from a source who has obtained it unlawfully, may the government punish the ensuing publication of that information?" The Court explained that, as a general proposition, "'if a newspaper unlawfully obtains truthful information about a matter of public significance then [government] officials may not constitutionally punish publication of the information, absent a need of the highest order,'" [quoting Smith v. Daily Mail Publishing Co.].

The Court identified "two interests served by the statutes — first, the interest in removing an incentive for parties to intercept private conversations, and second, the interest in minimizing the harm to persons whose conversations have been illegally intercepted." With respect to the first of these interests, the Court reasoned that "the normal method of deterring unlawful conduct is to impose an appropriate punishment on the person who engages in it. If the sanctions that presently attach to [these unlawful acts] do not provide sufficient deterrence, perhaps those sanctions should be made more severe. But it would be quite remarkable to hold that speech by a law-abiding possessor of information can be suppressed in order to deter conduct by a non-law abiding third party."

The Court conceded that the second interest "is considerably stronger" because "privacy of communications is an important interest" and "the fear of public disclosure of private conversations might well have a chilling effect on private speech." Without deciding whether there might be some circumstances in which the privacy interest is "strong enough to justify the application" of the statutes, such as when there is disclosure of a trade secret or "domestic gossip [of] purely private concern," the Court held that the enforcement of the statutes in this case "implicates core purposes of the First Amendment because it imposes sanctions on the publication of truthful information of public concern." In such circumstances, "privacy concerns give way when balanced against the interest in publishing matters of public importance." Justice Breyer, joined by Justice O'Connor, filed a concurring opinion.

Chief Justice Rehnquist, joined by Justices Scalia and Thomas, dissented: "[The] Court's decision diminishes, rather than enhances, the purposes of the First Amendment: chilling the speech of the millions of Americans who rely upon electronic technology to communicate each day. [These] laws are content-neutral; they only regulate information that was illegally obtained; they do not restrict republication of what is already in the public domain; they impose no special burdens upon the media; they have a scienter requirement to provide fair warning; and they promote the privacy and free speech of those using cellular telephones. [These] laws should [be] upheld if they further a substantial governmental interest unrelated to the suppression of free speech, and they do."

Note: The Search for Principles

1. *Balancing.* Is "balancing" underprotective of free speech? Should content-neutral restrictions be governed by the same standards as content-based restrictions? Consider Redish, The Content Distinction in First Amendment Analysis, 34 Stan. L. Rev. 113, 128 (1981):

> The most puzzling aspect of the distinction between content-based and content-neutral restrictions is that either restriction reduces the sum total of information or opinion disseminated. That governmental regulation impedes all forms of speech, rather than only selected viewpoints or subjects, does not alter the fact that the regulation impairs the free flow of expression. Whatever rationale one adopts for the constitutional protection of speech, the goals behind that rationale are undermined by *any* limitation on expression, content-based or not.

Consider the following responses: (a) Content-based restrictions generally are more dangerous than content-neutral restrictions because they are more likely significantly to distort the "marketplace of ideas." (b) Content-based restrictions are more dangerous than content-neutral restrictions because they are more likely to be enacted for the constitutionally impermissible purpose of suppressing "erroneous," "undesirable," or "unpopular" ideas. (c) Content-based restrictions are more dangerous than content-neutral restrictions because they are more likely to restrict speech because of its "communicative impact" (i.e., because of government's fear of how people will react to the content of the speaker's message).

For further commentary on the content-based/content-neutral distinction, see Ely, Flag Desecration: A Case Study in the Roles of Categorization and Balancing in First Amendment Analysis, 88 Harv. L. Rev. 1482 (1975); Stephan, The First Amendment and Content Discrimination, 68 Va. L. Rev. 203 (1982); Stone, Content-Neutral Restrictions, 54 U. Chi. L. Rev. 46 (1987); Williams, Content Discrimination and the First Amendment, 139 U. Pa. L. Rev. 615 (1991); Kagan, Private Speech, Public Purpose: The Role of Governmental Motive in First Amendment Doctrine, 63 U. Chi. L. Rev. 415, 446–463 (1996) (arguing that the concern with improper government motivation best explains the content-based/content-neutral distinction). For a critique of the Court's use of "intermediate scrutiny" across a broad range of First Amendment issues, see Bhagwat, The Test that Ate Everything: Intermediate Scrutiny in First Amendment Jurisprudence, 2007 U. Ill. L. Rev. 783.

2. *Striking the balance.* If content-neutral restrictions are tested by "balancing," what factors should be weighed in the balance? Consider the following propositions:

a. Although "the purpose to keep the streets clean and of good appearance is insufficient to justify" a prohibition on leafleting, the first amendment does not "deprive a municipality of power to enact regulations against throwing literature broadcast in the streets [since] such activity bears no necessary relationship to the freedom to speak, write, print or distribute information or opinion."

b. "[One] is not to have the exercise of his liberty of expression in appropriate places abridged on the plea that it may be exercised in some other place." Suppose a city permits soapbox orators to make public speeches in only four of its six municipal parks.

c. "That more people may be more easily and cheaply reached by sound trucks [is] not enough to call forth constitutional protection for what those charged with public welfare reasonably think is a nuisance when [alternative] means of publicity are open." Is this consistent with b? Should the existence of alternative means of communication affect the balance?

d. "The dangers of [door-to-door distribution of leaflets] can so easily be controlled by traditional legal methods [that] stringent prohibition can serve no purpose but [the] naked restriction of the dissemination of ideas." Should it matter that the state may be able to achieve part or all of its goals through alternative means that may have a less restrictive effect on expression?

e. "It would be fantastic to suggest that a city has power [to] forbid house-to-house canvassing generally, but that the Constitution prohibits the inclusion in such prohibition of door-to-door [distribution of] printed matter." Should it matter whether a law specifically restricts expression or restricts a broader range of activities in a manner that has only an incidental effect on expression?

f. "There has been no suggestion that billboards heretofore have advanced any particular viewpoint or issue disproportionately. . . . Thus, the ideas billboard advertisers have been presenting are not *relatively* disadvantaged vis-à-vis the messages of those who heretofore have chosen other methods of spreading their views." Should it matter whether a content-neutral restriction has "content-differential" effects?

Note: The Meaning of "Content-Neutrality"

In most cases, a law's content-neutrality is self-evident. There are several situations, however, in which the matter is more complex:

1. *Communicative impact.* A law may be content-neutral on its face but may turn in application on communicative impact — that is, "on how people will react to what the speaker is saying." J. Ely, Democracy and Distrust 111 (1980). Consider, for example, a law declaring it unlawful for any person to "disturb the peace" by making any public speech that "may cause a hostile audience response." Although such laws are "neutral" on their face, the Court has analyzed them as content-based because it is the content of the message that triggers the restriction. Recall, for example, *Terminiello, Cantwell,* and *Edwards,* section B2 supra. For analysis of this issue, see Stone, Content Regulation and the First Amendment, 25 Wm. & Mary L. Rev. 189, 207–217 (1983); Rubenfeld, The First Amendment's Purpose, 53 Stan. L. Rev. 767 (2001).

2. *Secondary effects.* A law may be content-based on its face but may be defended in terms that are unrelated to communicative impact. In *Renton,* section D7, supra, for example, the Court characterized a zoning ordinance that restricted the location of movie theaters that exhibit movies emphasizing "specified sexual activities" as "content-neutral" because it was defended not in terms of the communicative impact of the restricted expression but in terms of "the secondary effects of such theaters on the surrounding community." As noted in section D7, however, in its decisions since *Renton* the Court seems to have backed away from this approach. See Boos v. Barry, 485 U.S. 312 (1988); City of Cincinnati v. Discovery Network, 507 U.S. 410 (1993); City of Los Angeles v. Alameda Books, 535 U.S. 425 (2002); Reed v. Town of Gilbert, 135 S. Ct. 2218 (2015). Indeed, in *Reed* the Court made clear that a "law that is content-based on its face" must be treated as content-based "regardless of the government's . . . content-neutral justification" for the restriction. See Lakier, Reed v. Town of Gilbert, Arizona, and the Rise of the Anticlassificatory First Amendment, 2016 Sup. Ct. Rev. 233, noting that *Reed* effectively overruled the Court's prior decisions that had suggested that "a law that made facial content distinctions" should be analyzed as content-neutral if "it could be justifed by reference to a content-neutral purpose."

3. *Impermissible motive.* A law may be content-neutral on its face but may have been enacted with the purpose of suppressing a particular message. Consider, for example, a law prohibiting any person to destroy a draft card, enacted for the purpose of punishing those individuals who publicly burn their draft cards to protest national policy. For analysis of this issue, see section E3 infra.

Consider McDonald, Speech and Distrust: Rethinking the Content Approach to Protecting the Freedom of Expression, 81 Notre Dame L. Rev. 1347, 1387 (2006):

Consider [laws] currently being enacted by states that prohibit picketing and demonstrating within a certain distance of funerals shortly before and after a service. These laws are being passed in response to an alleged pastor and members of a church who are using funerals of American soldiers killed in Iraq as opportunities to get out their message that the war and soldiers' deaths constitute divine retribution for the country's tolerant attitude towards homosexuals Apparently, the church group assembles across the street from such funerals, engaging in expletive-laden chants and displaying signs containing messages such as "Thank God for Dead Soldiers," "Thank God for IEDs" (improvised explosive devices that frequently kill soldiers), and "God Hates Fags."

Should such laws be analyzed as content-based or content-neutral? In Reed v. Town of Gilbert, supra, the Court made clear that "facially content neutral" laws "will be considered content-based" if they "were adopted by the government 'because of disagreement with the message [the speech] conveys.'" How should a court go about determining whether any particular law was adopted for such a reason?

4. *Content-differential effects.* Some laws are content-neutral on their face but have content-differential effects. Recall, for example, Justice Black's observation in *Struthers* that "door to door distribution of circulars is essential to the poorly financed causes of little people." To what extent should this factor convert a content-neutral regulation into one that is treated as content-based? See Williams, Content Discrimination and the First Amendment, 139 U. Pa. L. Rev. 615 (1991) (disparate impact should trigger content-based analysis); Stone, Content-Neutral Restrictions, 54 U. Chi. L. Rev. 46, 81–86 (1987) (disparate impact should merely be a relevant factor in content-neutral analysis).

5. *Speaker-based restrictions.* Is an injunction prohibiting specifically named antiabortion protestors from demonstrating near an abortion clinic content-based or content-neutral? In Madsen v. Women's Health Center, Inc., 512 U.S. 753 (1994), the Court held that such an injunction, issued after the specifically named petitioners had previously violated a narrower order enjoining them from blocking access to the clinic, was content-neutral:

> We [reject] petitioners' contention that the [order is content-based because it] restricts only the speech of antiabortion protestors. [The] injunction, by its very nature, applies only to a particular group. [It] does so, however, because of the group's past actions in the context of a specific dispute. [The] fact that the injunction in the present case did not prohibit activities of those demonstrating in favor of abortion is justly attributable to the lack of any similar demonstrations by those in favor of abortion, and of any consequent request that their demonstrations be regulated by injunction. There is no suggestion [that] Florida law would not equally restrain similar conduct directed at a target having nothing to do with abortion; none of the restrictions [were] directed at the contents of petitioners' message. [The] state court imposed restrictions on petitioners incidental to their abortion message because they repeatedly violated the court's original order. That petitioners all share the same viewpoint regarding abortion does not in itself demonstrate that some invidious content or viewpoint-based purpose motivated the issuance of the order. It suggests only that those in the group whose conduct violated the court's order happen to share the same opinion regarding abortions being performed in the clinic.

Suppose the injunction had prohibited "any antiabortion protestor from demonstrating within thirty-six feet of an abortion clinic"? Would that be content-neutral? Speaker-based restrictions, which treat some speakers differently than others but define the distinction in terms other than content, do not fit neatly within the Court's content-based/content-neutral distinction. For example, suppose a city bans all door-to-door canvassing after 8:00 P.M., except for canvassing by veterans' groups. How should such a law be analyzed? For commentary on speaker-based restrictions, see Stone, Content Regulation, supra, at 244–251. See also Regan v. Taxation with Representation, Perry Educators' Assocation v. Perry Local Educators' Association, and Cornelius v. NAACP Legal Defense and Educational Fund, sections E2c and E2d, infra.

6. *Content or not?* In McCullen v. Coakley, 134 S. Ct. 2518 (2014), the Supreme Court considered the constitutionality of a Massachusetts statute that made it a crime for any person knowingly to stand on a "public way or sidewalk" within 35 feet of an entrance or driveway to any place, other than a hospital, where abortions are performed. The law was designed to eliminate clashes between abortion opponents and advocates of abortion rights that had occurred outside clinics where abortions were performed. The law was challenged by individuals "who approach and talk to women outside such facilities, attempting to dissuade them from having abortions." According to testimony presented at the trial, such individuals have, over time, "persuaded hundreds of women to forgo abortions." The Act exempted persons entering or leaving the facility, employees or agents of the facility, law enforcement and similar personnel, and persons using the sidewalk area solely for the purpose of reaching another destination. The Court, in an opinion by Chief Justice Roberts, invalidated the law as an unconstitutional content-neutral restriction of speech in a traditional public forum. This facet of the decision is examined in section 2a, infra.

The challengers also argued, however, that the law was an unconstitutional content-based restriction because it applied only at facilities that performed abortions and therefore had a disparate impact on those who oppose abortion. Chief Justice Roberts rejected this argument:

> To begin, the Act does not draw content based distinctions on its face. The Act would be content based if it required "enforcement authorities" to "examine the content of the message that is conveyed to determine whether" a violation has occurred. But it does not. Whether petitioners violate the Act "depends" not "on what they say," but simply on where they say it. Indeed, petitioners can violate the Act merely by standing in a buffer zone, without displaying a sign or uttering a word.
>
> It is true, of course, that by limiting the buffer zones to abortion clinics, the Act has the "inevitable effect" of restricting abortion-related speech more than speech on other subjects. But a facially-neutral law does not become content based simply because it may disproportionately affect speech on certain topics. [The] question in such a case is whether the law is "justified without reference to the content of the regulated speech." [The] Massachusetts Act is. Its stated purpose is to "increase public safety at reproductive health care facilities." [Obstructed] access and congested sidewalks are problems no matter what caused them. A group of individuals can obstruct clinic access and clog sidewalks just as much when they loiter as when they protest abortion or counsel patients. . . .
>
> [The challengers argue, however, that] by choosing to pursue these interests only at abortion clinics, [the] Massachusetts Legislature evinced a purpose to "single[ ] out for regulation speech about one particular topic: abortion." We cannot infer such a purpose from the Act's limited scope. [The] Massachusetts Legislature [enacted the statute] in response to a problem that was, in its experience, limited to abortion clinics. There was a record of crowding, obstruction, and even violence outside such clinics. There were apparently no similar recurring problems associated with other kinds of healthcare facilities [or other kinds of buildings or activities]. In light of

the limited nature of the problem, it was reasonable for the Massachusetts Legislature to enact a limited solution. [W]e thus conclude that the Act is neither content nor viewpoint based and therefore need not be analyzed under strict scrutiny.

Justice Scalia, joined by Justices Kennedy and Thomas, filed a concurring opinion in which he maintained that the challenged statute "is content based and fails strict scrutiny": "[It] blinks reality to say [that] a blanket prohibition on the use of streets and sidewalks where speech on only one politically controversial topic is likely to occur — and where that speech can most effectively be communicated — is not content based. Would the Court exempt from strict scrutiny a law banning access to the streets and sidewalks surrounding the site of the Republican National Convention? Or those used annually to commemorate the 1965 Selma-to-Montgomery civil rights marches? Or those outside the Internal Revenue Service? Surely not. . . ." Justice Alito also filed a concurring opinion arguing that the law was content-based and therefore unconstitutional. For a thoughtful analysis of *McCullen*, see Kendrick, Nonsense on Sidewalks: Content Discrimination in McCullen v. Coakley, 2014 Sup. Ct. Rev. 215.

2.   Speech on Public Property: The Public Forum

In what circumstances, if any, does the first amendment guarantee the individual the right to commandeer publicly owned property for the purpose of exercising the freedom of speech? The Court has been highly solicitous of the right of owners of *private* property to prevent others from using their property for speech purposes. In *Struthers*, for example, the Court left no doubt that the city could constitutionally "punish those who call at a home in defiance of the previously expressed will of the occupant." More generally, the Court has accepted the view that in most circumstances "an uninvited guest may [not] exercise general rights of free speech on property privately owned," for it "would be an unwarranted infringement of property rights to require them to yield to the exercise of First Amendment rights." Lloyd Corp. v. Tanner, 407 U.S. 551, 568, 567 (1972).

To what extent does the first amendment supersede the "property rights" of the state? Must the state "subsidize" speech by allowing individuals to use publicly owned property for speech purposes? For early commentary on the "public forum," see Kalven, The Concept of the Public Forum: Cox v. Louisiana, 1965 Sup. Ct. Rev. 1; Stone, Fora Americana: Speech in Public Places, 1974 Sup. Ct. Rev. 233.

Public forum theory has evolved along two separate, but related, lines — one governing streets and parks, the other governing all other publicly owned property. The first two parts of this section track this distinction. The remaining two parts of this section examine the problem of inequality of access to public property for speech purposes.

a.   The Public Forum: Streets and Parks

COMMONWEALTH v. DAVIS, 162 Mass. 510, 39 N.E. 113 (1895), aff'd sub nom. DAVIS v. MASSACHUSETTS, 167 U.S. 43 (1897). Davis, a preacher whose congregation apparently consisted of the crowds on the Boston Common, was convicted under a city ordinance that forbade, among other things, "any public address" on any publicly owned property "except in accordance with a permit from the mayor." The Supreme Judicial Court of Massachusetts, speaking through Justice Holmes, affirmed the conviction. Justice Holmes explained that the ordinance "is directed against free speech generally, [whereas] in fact it is directed toward the modes in which Boston Common may be used," and that, "as representative of the public," the legislature "may and does exercise control over the use which the public may make of such places," and for "the Legislature absolutely or conditionally to forbid public speaking in a highway or public park is no more an infringement of the rights of a member of the public than for the owner of a private house to forbid it in his house." Since the legislature "may end the right of the public to enter upon the public place by putting an end to the dedication to public uses," it necessarily "may take the lesser step of limiting the public use to certain purposes."

On appeal, the Supreme Court unanimously embraced Justice Holmes's position. Chief Justice White, speaking for the Court, maintained that the federal Constitution "does not have the effect of creating a particular and personal right in the citizen to use public property in defiance of the constitution and laws of the State." Indeed, the "right to absolutely exclude all right to use, necessarily includes the authority to determine under what circumstances such use may be availed of, as the greater power contains the lesser."*

Is this a satisfactory resolution of the public forum issue? Consider Stone, Fora Americana: Speech in Public Places, 1974 Sup. Ct. Rev. 233, 237: "[Under] the Holmes-White approach, the state possessed the power absolutely to prohibit the exercise of First Amendment rights [on] public property simply by asserting the prerogatives traditionally associated with the private ownership of land. [The] problem of the public forum had been 'solved' by resort to common law concepts of private property."

HAGUE v. CIO, 307 U.S. 496 (1939). Forty-two years later, the Court reopened the question. In *Hague*, the Court considered the constitutionality of a municipal ordinance forbidding all public meetings in the streets and other public places without a permit. The city maintained that the ordinance was clearly constitutional under *Davis*. The dispute in *Hague* was a bitter one. Frank Hague, the Mayor of Jersey City, was a fierce opponent of the labor movement. Hague cast labor organizers and their defenders as "Communist interlopers," and his "police force harassed, beat, and arrested agitators and shut down union picketing, meetings, and leafleting." For a full telling of the *Hague* case, see L. Weinrib, The Taming of Free Speech 226–269 (2016). Although the Court did not directly decide the question presented in *Hague*, Justice Roberts, in a plurality opinion, flatly rejected the city's contention in a dictum that has played a central role in the evolution of public forum theory:

---

* [At the time of *Davis*, the Court had not as yet held the first amendment applicable to the states, thus undermining the precedential force of *Davis* as a "free speech" decision. It appears that the primary constitutional issue before the Court concerned dictum in Yick Wo v. Hopkins, 118 U.S. 356 (1886), suggesting that the equal protection clause prohibited all forms of standardless licensing. This dictum was rejected more clearly in a series of subsequent decisions. See Lieberman v. Van de Carr, 199 U.S. 552 (1905); Gundling v. Chicago, 177 U.S. 183 (1900); Wilson v. Eureka, 173 U.S. 32 (1899). — Eds.]

Wherever the title of streets and parks may rest, they have immemorially been held in trust for the use of the public and, time out of mind, have been used for purposes of assembly, communicating thought between citizens, and discussing public questions. Such use of the streets and public places has, from ancient times, been a part of the privileges, immunities, rights, and liberties of citizens. The privilege of a citizen of the United States to use the streets and parks for communication of views on national questions may be regulated in the interest of all; it is not absolute, but relative, and must be exercised in subordination to the general comfort and convenience, and in consonance with peace and good order; but it must not, in the guise of regulation, be abridged or denied.

Consider Stone, supra, at 238:

Perhaps the most interesting aspect of the Roberts dictum is its implicit acceptance of the underlying premise of the Holmes-White position — that the public forum issue must be defined in terms of the common law property rights of the state. Rather than challenging that premise head-on, Roberts conveniently adapted it to his own advantage, predicating the public forum right upon established common law notions of adverse possession and public trust. [In effect, Roberts concluded that] the streets, parks, and similar public places are subject to what Professor Kalven has termed "a kind of First-Amendment easement." [Citing Kalven, The Concept of the Public Forum: Cox v. Louisiana, 1965 Sup. Ct. Rev. 1, 13.] Since such places have been used, "time out of mind," for purposes of speech and assembly, the Constitution now requires that their continued use for these purposes not "be abridged or denied."

Is this a sound rationale for the right to a public forum? Note that the Roberts rationale creates by implication two distinct classes of public property. Although streets, parks, and similar public places may constitute public fora, publicly owned property that cannot satisfy the "time out of mind" requirement remains subject to the *Davis* dictum, and access to such places for purposes of speech and assembly may thus be denied absolutely upon the state's naked assertion of title. Would it be preferable to base public forum theory on the notion that access to public property for speech purposes is essential to effective exercise of first amendment rights?

Consider C. Sunstein, republic.com 30–32 (2001):

[The] public forum doctrine promotes three important goals. First, it ensures that speakers can have access to a wide array of people. [It allows speakers] to press their concerns that might otherwise be ignored by their fellow citizens. [Second, the doctrine] allows speakers [to have access] to specific people and specific institutions with whom they have a complaint. [The] public forum doctrine ensures that you can make your views heard by legislators, for example, by protesting in front of the state legislature. [Third, the doctrine] increases the likelihood that people generally will be exposed to a wide variety of people and views. [It] tends to ensure a range of experiences that are widely shared [and] a set of exposures to diverse views. [These] exposures can help promote understanding.

SCHNEIDER v. STATE, 308 U.S. 147 (1939). In *Schneider*, section E1, supra, decided only eight months after *Hague*, the Court held that a city's interest in keeping "the streets clean and of good appearance" was "insufficient" to justify a municipal ordinance prohibiting the distribution of leaflets on public property. Although the Court did not explicitly address the status of *Davis*, the impact of

Hague and *Schneider* was made clear several years later in Jamison v. Texas, 318 U.S. 413 (1943), in which the Court, following *Schneider*, invalidated a city ordinance prohibiting the dissemination of leaflets. Relying on *Davis*, the city maintained that "it has the power absolutely to prohibit the use of the streets for the communication of ideas." The Court responded: "This same argument, made in reliance upon the same decision, has been directly rejected by this Court. [Citing Justice Roberts's concurring opinion in *Hague*.]"

Consider Kalven, supra, at 18–21:

> The result [in *Schneider*] had an impressive bite. Leaflet distribution in public places in a city is a method of communication that carries as an inextricable and expected consequence substantial littering of the streets, which the city has an obligation to keep clean. It is also a method of communication of some annoyance to a majority of people so addressed; that its impact on its audience is very high is doubtful. Yet the constitutional balance in *Schneider* was struck emphatically in favor of keeping the public forum open for this mode of communication. [At stake in *Schneider* was] the immemorial claim of the free man to use the streets as a forum. [The state], the Court was telling us, must recognize the special nature and value of that claim to be on the street. [The] operative theory of the Court, at least for the leaflet situation, is that [the] right to use the streets as a public forum [cannot] be prohibited and can be regulated only for weighty reasons.

How does the *Hague/Schneider* theory of the public forum relate to the analysis of content-neutral restrictions generally? Consider the following propositions:

1. Although the *Hague/Schneider* theory holds that the property rights of the state do not in themselves permit the state absolutely to exclude expression from public property that has been used "time out of mind" for speech purposes, it does not hold that government property rights are irrelevant. Thus, content-neutral restrictions governing streets and parks should be tested by more lenient standards of justification than content-neutral restrictions that do not implicate the property rights of the state.

2. The *Hague/Schneider* theory holds that government property rights are irrelevant when the property has been used "time out of mind" for speech purposes. Thus, content-neutral restrictions governing streets and parks should be tested by the same standards of justification that are used to test content-neutral restrictions that do not implicate the property rights of the state.

3. The *Hague/Schneider* theory holds that the streets and parks are "public fora" in which the state must be especially solicitous of free expression. Thus, content-neutral restrictions governing streets and parks should be tested by more stringent standards of justification than content-neutral restrictions that do not implicate "public forum" rights.

Note: Regulating the Public Forum

1. *Signs near a courthouse.* In United States v. Grace, 461 U.S. 171 (1983), the Court invalidated a federal statute prohibiting any person to display on the public sidewalks surrounding the Supreme Court building "any flag, banner, or device designed [to] bring into public notice any party, organization or movement." The Court explained that the "public sidewalks forming the perimeter of the Supreme Court grounds [are] public forums," and that "the government's ability" to restrict expression in such places "is very limited." Indeed, "the government may enforce

reasonable time, place, and manner restrictions" in public forums only if "the restrictions 'are content-neutral, are narrowly tailored to serve a significant government interest, and leave open ample alternative channels of communication,'" and it may absolutely prohibit "a particular type of expression" only if the prohibition is "narrowly drawn to accomplish a compelling governmental interest."

The Court held that this statute could not be justified as a means "to maintain proper order and decorum" near the Supreme Court, for a "total ban" was not necessary to achieve these ends. And the restriction could not be justified as a means to prevent the appearance "that the Supreme Court is subject to outside influence," for the restriction did not "sufficiently serve" that purpose "to sustain its validity."

2. *Noise near a school.* In Grayned v. Rockford, 408 U.S. 104 (1972), approximately two hundred demonstrators marched on a public sidewalk about one hundred feet from a public high school to protest the school's racial policies. Appellant, a participant in the demonstration, was convicted of violating a Rockford ordinance prohibiting any "person, while on public or private grounds adjacent to any building in which a school or any class thereof is in session, [to make] any noise or diversion which disturbs or tends to disturb the peace or good order of such school." The Court, in an eight-to-one decision, affirmed the conviction.

The Court explained that, although "the public sidewalk adjacent to school grounds may not be declared off limits for expressive activity, [such] activity may be prohibited if it 'materially disrupts classwork or involves substantial disorder or invasion of the rights of others.'" In this case, the Court held that the "antinoise" ordinance "is narrowly tailored to further Rockford's compelling interest in having an undisrupted school session conducive to the students' learning"; "punishes only conduct which disrupts or is about to disrupt normal school activities"; requires that the "decision [be] made [on] an individualized basis"; and "gives no license to punish anyone because of what he is saying." The Court concluded that "such a reasonable regulation is not inconsistent with the First and Fourteenth Amendments."

3. *Picketing near a home.* In Frisby v. Shultz, 487 U.S. 474 (1988), a group varying in size from eleven to forty people picketed in protest on six occasions within one month on the public street outside the residence of a doctor who performed abortions. The picketing was orderly and peaceful. Thereafter, the town enacted an ordinance that prohibited residential picketing that focuses on and takes place in front of a particular residence. The Court, in a six-to-three decision, upheld the ordinance.

Although emphasizing that "a public street does not lose its status as a traditional public forum because it runs through a residential neighborhood," the Court nonetheless concluded that the ordinance was constitutional because it left "open ample alternative channels of communication" and was "narrowly tailored to serve a significant government interest." The Court found the first requirement "readily" satisfied because the ordinance left protestors free to march, proselytize door-to-door, leaflet, and even picket in a manner that did not focus exclusively on a particular residence.

As to the second requirement, the Court observed that "privacy of the home is [of] the highest order in a free and civilized society." Moreover, the "type of picketers banned by [this ordinance] generally do not seek to disseminate a message to the general public, but to intrude upon the targeted resident, and to do so in an especially offensive way. [And] even if some such picketers have a

broader communicative purpose, their activity nonetheless inherently and offensively intrudes on residential privacy." Indeed, "even a solitary picket can invade
residential privacy, [for the] target of the focused picketing banned by [this]
ordinance is [a] 'captive,' [figuratively], and perhaps literally, trapped within
the home." The Court thus concluded that the ordinance was "narrowly tailored"
because "the 'evil' of targeted residential picketing, 'the very presence of an
unwelcome visitor at the home,' is 'created by the medium of expression itself.'"
Justices Brennan, Marshall, and Stevens dissented.

4. *Sleeping in a park.* In Clark v. Community for Creative Non-Violence, 468
U.S. 288 (1983), the National Park Service permitted CCNV to erect symbolic
tent cities, consisting of between twenty and forty tents, in Lafayette Park and on
the Mall in Washington, D.C., for the purpose of conducting a round-the-clock
demonstration designed to dramatize the plight of the homeless. Pursuant to a
National Park Service regulation prohibiting "camping" in these parks, however,
the Park Service prohibited CCNV demonstrators from sleeping overnight in the
tents. The Court assumed arguendo "that overnight sleeping in connection with
the demonstration is expressive conduct protected [by] the First Amendment,"
but upheld the regulation as a "reasonable time, place, and manner restriction."

The Court emphasized that the regulation is "content neutral," that it does not
prevent CCNV from demonstrating the "plight of the homeless [in] other ways,"
and that it "narrowly focuses on the Government's substantial interest in maintaining the parks [in] an attractive and intact condition." The Court rejected
CCNV's argument that, once the Park Service decided to permit "the symbolic
city of tents," the "incremental benefit to the parks was insufficient to justify the
ban on sleeping." Justice Marshall, joined by Justice Brennan, dissented.

5. *Noise in a park.* In Ward v. Rock against Racism, 491 U.S. 781 (1989), the
Court upheld a New York City regulation requiring the use of city-provided
sound systems and technicians for concerts in the Bandshell in Central Park.
The principal justification for the regulation was the city's desire to control noise
levels to avoid undue intrusion into other areas of the park and adjacent residential areas. The Court held that government clearly "'ha[s] a substantial interest in
protecting its citizens from unwelcome noise,'" and that the regulation clearly
leaves "open ample alternative channels of communication." Justice Marshall,
joined by Justices Brennan and Stevens, dissented.

6. *Demonstrating near an abortion clinic.* In Madsen v. Women's Health
Center, Inc., 512 U.S. 753 (1994), after petitioners repeatedly violated an injunction prohibiting them from blocking access to an abortion clinic and engaging in
other activities that harassed patients and doctors both at the clinic and at their
homes, a state court issued a new injunction prohibiting the petitioners from,
inter alia, demonstrating within thirty-six feet of the clinic; making excessive
noise near the clinic by "singing, chanting, whistling, shouting, yelling, use of
bullhorns, auto horns [or] sound amplification equipment"; exhibiting "images
observable" by patients within the clinic; approaching patients within three
hundred feet of the clinic who did not voluntarily indicate a desire to speak
with them; and demonstrating within three hundred feet of the residence of
any of the clinic's employees.

The Court upheld the thirty-six-foot buffer zone as a reasonable way to protect
"access to the clinic" and the restriction on excessive noise because noise "control
is particularly important around hospitals and medical facilities." On the other
hand, the Court invalidated the restriction on exhibiting "images observable" to
patients within the clinic because the proper remedy is for the clinic to "pull its

curtains." It also invalidated that portion of the injunction that prohibited petitioners from "approaching any person seeking services of the clinic 'unless such person indicates a desire to communicate' in an area within 300 feet of the clinic." The Court held that, "[absent] evidence that the protesters' speech is independently proscribable (i.e., 'fighting words' or threats), [this] provision cannot stand." Finally, the Court invalidated the provision enjoining petitioners from demonstrating within three hundred feet of the residences of clinic staff. The Court explained that "the 300-foot zone [is] much larger than the zone [upheld] in *Frisby*. [A] limitation of the time, duration of picketing, and number of pickets outside a smaller zone could have accomplished the desired result."

7. *Demonstrating near an abortion clinic II.* In Schenck v. Pro-Choice Network of Western New York, 519 U.S. 357 (1997), several abortion clinics in upstate New York were subjected to a series of large-scale blockades in which antiabortion protesters marched, stood, knelt, or lay in clinic parking lots and doorways, blocking cars from entering the lots and interfering with patients and clinic employees who attempted to enter the clinics. Smaller groups of protesters, called "sidewalk counselors," crowded, jostled, pushed, and yelled and spit at women entering the clinics. Police officers who attempted to control the protests often were harassed by the protesters both verbally and by mail. A federal district court issued an injunction against fifty individuals and three organizations (including Operation Rescue), which, among other things, (a) prohibited them from demonstrating within fifteen feet of clinic doorways, parking lots, and driveways ("fixed buffer zones"); and (b) prohibited them from demonstrating within fifteen feet of any person or vehicle seeking access to or leaving a clinic ("floating buffer zones").

In upholding the "fixed buffer zones," the Court explained that, in light of the prior conduct of the protesters, the district court "was entitled to conclude" that fixed buffer zones were necessary to prevent the protesters from doing "what they had done before: aggressively follow and crowd individuals right up to the clinic door and then refuse to move, or purposefully mill around parking lot entrances in an effort to impede or block the progress of cars." On the other hand, the Court invalidated the "floating buffer zones" because they would effectively prevent protesters "from communicating a message from a normal conversational distance or handing leaflets to people entering or leaving the clinics [on] the public sidewalks."

8. *Demonstrating near an abortion clinic III.* In Hill v. Colorado, 530 U.S. 703 (2000), the Court, in a six-to-three decision, upheld a Colorado statute that makes it unlawful for any person within one hundred feet of a health care facility to "knowingly approach" within eight feet of another person, without that person's consent, in order to pass "a leaflet or handbill to, [display] a sign to, or [engage] in oral protest, education, or counseling with, such other person." Citing *Frisby*, the Court explained that although the right to free speech "includes the right to attempt to persuade others to change their views, and may not be curtailed simply because the speaker's message may be offensive to his audience," the "protection afforded to offensive messages does not always embrace offensive speech that is so intrusive that the unwilling audience cannot avoid it." Indeed, "no one has a right to press even 'good' ideas on an unwilling recipient," and "none of our decisions has minimized the enduring importance of 'the right to be free' from persistent 'importunity, following and dogging' after an offer to communicate has been declined." The Court thus concluded that the statute "is a valid time, place, and manner regulation [because it] serves governmental interests that are

significant and legitimate and [is] 'narrowly tailored' to serve those interests and . . . leaves open ample alternative channels for communication."

9. *Demonstrating near an abortion clinic IV.* In McCullen v. Coakley, 134 S. Ct. 2518 (2014), the Supreme Court invalidated a Massachusetts statute that made it a crime for any person knowingly to stand on a "public way or sidewalk" within 35 feet of an entrance or driveway to any place, other than a hospital, where abortions are performed. The law was designed to eliminate clashes between abortion opponents and advocates of abortion rights that had occurred outside clinics where abortions were performed. The law was challenged by individuals "who approach and talk to women outside such facilities, attempting to dissuade them from having abortions." According to testimony presented at the trial, such individuals have, over time, "persuaded hundreds of women to forgo abortions."

The Court unanimously invalidated the ordinance. Chief Justice Roberts authored the opinion of the Court: "[We] have held that the government's ability to restrict speech in [traditional public fora] is 'very limited.' [Even if such laws are content neutral, they must be] narrowly tailored to serve a significant governmental interest. [The] buffer zones burden substantially more speech than necessary to achieve the Commonwealth's asserted interests. [The] Commonwealth's interests include ensuring public safety outside abortion clinics, preventing harassment and intimidation of patients and clinic staff, and combating deliberate obstruction of clinic entrances. [The Act] itself contains a separate provision [that] prohibits much of this conduct. That provision subjects to criminal punishment '[a]ny person who knowingly obstructs, detains, hinders, impedes or blocks another person's entry to or exit from a reproductive health care facility.' [If] Massachusetts determines that broader prohibitions along the same lines are necessary, it could enact legislation similar to the federal Freedom of Access to Clinic Entrances Act of 1994, which subjects to both criminal and civil penalties anyone who 'by force or threat of force or by physical obstruction, intentionally injures, intimidates or interferes with or attempts to injure, intimidate or interfere with any person because that person is or has been, or in order to intimidate such person or any other person or any class of persons from, obtaining or providing reproductive health services.' [If] the Commonwealth is particularly concerned about harassment, it could also consider an ordinance such as the one adopted in New York City that not only prohibits obstructing access to a clinic, but also makes it a crime 'to follow and harass another person within 15 feet of the premises of a reproductive health care facility.' [The] point is not that Massachusetts must enact all or even any of the proposed measures discussed above. The point is instead that the Commonwealth has available to it a variety of approaches that appear capable of serving its interests without excluding individuals from areas historically open for speech and debate." Justices Scalia, Kennedy Thomas, and Kennedy concurred in the result.

10. *Picketing near military funerals.* In recent years, members of the Westboro Baptist Church have protested at the funerals of American soldiers, carrying placards and shouting such phrases as "Thank God for Dead Soldiers," "God Is Your Enemy," and "Thank God for 9/11." The church's predominant message is one of virulent anti-homosexuality, and these protests are designed to convey the message that the United States is being punished for its toleration of such conduct.

To rein in such protests, most states have enacted laws designed to restrict demonstrations near military funerals. What do you think of the constitutionality of the federal Respect for America's Fallen Heroes Act, which was enacted in 2006? The act, which governs funerals at national cemeteries, prohibits any "demonstration" "during the period beginning 60 minutes before and ending 60 minutes" after a funeral at a national cemetery if the demonstration is "within 150 feet of a road pathway, or other route of ingress to or egress from such cemetery property" and the demonstrators willfully makes "any noise or diversion that disturbs or tends to disturb the peace or good order" of the funeral or is "within 300 feet of such cemetery" if the demonstration "impedes the access to or egress from such cemetery." The act defines "demonstration" to include "any picketing or similar conduct," "any oration, speech, use of sound amplification equipment" that is not part of the funeral, "the display of any placard, banner, flag, or similar device" that is not part of the funeral, and the "distribution of any handbill, pamphlet, or other written or printed matter" that is not part of the funeral. Is this law a reasonable regulation of public property? Is it content-neutral? See Wells, Privacy and Funeral Protests, 87 N.C. L. Rev. 151 (2008); McAllister, Funeral Picketing Laws and Free Speech, 55 U. Kan. L. Rev. 575 (2007).

11. *Free speech zones.* Consider Zick, Speech and Spatial Tactics, 84 Tex. L. Rev. 581, 584–589 (2006):

> Governments have learned to manipulate geography in a manner that now seriously threatens basic First Amendment principles. [The] state has moved from *regulating* place to actually . . . *creating* places [such as "buffer zones," "free speech zones," and "speech-free zones"] for the express purpose of controlling and disciplining protest and dissent. [By] design, these places mute and even suppress messages, depress participation in social and political protests, and send negative signals to those on the outside regarding those confined within. [Protests in such] places are docile; they are tightly scripted and ineffectual imitations of past social and political movements. [Passively] filing into cages, zones, and other tactical places is an utter capitulation to the status quo. [Such places are] being used to marginalize dissent, to capture and confine it. [Courts] should view [such manipulation of protests] with far greater skepticism than they currently do [and should] take far more seriously the notion that "one is not to have the exercise of his liberty of expression in appropriate places abridged on the plea that it may be exercised elsewhere." [Quoting Schneider v. State.]

12. *Unlawful assembly.* In what circumstances can the police constitutionally arrest individuals who are participating in an otherwise lawful assembly because of a concern that the event seems likely to get out of hand and result in damage to persons or property? In what circumstances can the police order individuals to disperse because of such concerns? Must there be a clear and present danger of violence or of serious damage to property? What if some demonstrators begin throwing rocks through windows? Can the police order the entire crowd to disband? See Inazu, Unlawful Assembly as Social Control, 64 UCLA L. Rev. 2 (2017).

13. *Unattended structures.* Does an individual have a constitutional right to erect an unattended display in a public park? Suppose, for example, an individual wants to construct a statue, or a cross, or a billboard in such a park? Can the state prohibit this completely? If prohibition is impermissible, what sorts of regulations would be appropriate? In Capitol Square Review and Advisory Board v. Pinette, 515 U.S. 753 (1995), the Court strongly suggested, but did not decide, that "a ban on all unattended displays" might be constitutional. As Justice Stevens explained

in a separate opinion, such a display "creates a far greater intrusion on government property and interferes with the Government's ability to differentiate its own message from those of private individuals."

Note: Devices for Regulating the Public Forum

1. *Licensing.* In Cox v. New Hampshire, 312 U.S. 569 (1941), a group of Jehovah's Witnesses were convicted of violating a state statute prohibiting any "parade or procession" upon a public street without first obtaining a permit. The Court, in a unanimous decision, affirmed the convictions. Chief Justice Hughes, speaking for the Court, explained that, "as regulation of the use of the streets for parades and processions is a traditional exercise of control by local government, the question in a particular case is whether that control is exerted so as not to deny or unwarrantedly abridge the right of assembly and the opportunities for the communication of [thought] immemorially associated with resort to public places."

The Court emphasized that the state court had "construed the statute" as authorizing "the licensing authority" to take into account only "considerations of time, place and manner so as to conserve the public convenience." Such a limited permit requirement had the "obvious advantage" of "giving the public authorities notice in advance so as to afford opportunity for proper policing" and, "in fixing time and place, '[to] prevent confusion by overlapping parades or processions, to secure convenient use of the streets by other travelers, and to minimize the risk of disorder.'" Moreover, the Court emphasized that the state court had stressed that "the licensing board was not vested with arbitrary power [and] that its discretion must be [exercised] 'free [from] unfair discrimination.'" The Court concluded that under this construction of the statute, it is "impossible to say that the limited authority conferred by the licensing provisions [contravened] any constitutional right."

For a critical view, see Baker, Unreasoned Reasonableness: Mandatory Parade Permits and Time, Place, and Manner Regulations, 78 Nw. U. L. Rev. 937 (1983). For analysis of licensing generally, see section C2 supra. See also Thomas v. Chicago Park District, 534 U.S. 316 (2002) (a content-neutral licensing scheme regulating the time, place and manner of use of a public forum need not employ the *Freedman* safeguards because such a scheme "does not authorize a licensor to pass judgment on the content of speech").

If a city can use a "time, place, and manner" based licensing scheme for individuals who want to parade on public streets, can it also use such a licensing scheme for speakers who want to go door-to-door to speak with homeowners and distribute literature? In Watchtower Bible & Tract Society v. Village of Stratton, 536 U.S. 150 (2002), the Court, in an eight-to-one decision, held such a scheme unconstitutional. Although acknowledging that the Village's interests in preventing fraud, preventing crime and protecting privacy are "important," the Court nonetheless held that the effect of the licensing scheme on the interests of speakers who want to maintain their anonymity, the administrative burden the scheme imposes on speakers, and the potential impact of the licensing requirement on "spontaneous speech" rendered the ordinance unconstitutional. The Court indicated that such a scheme limited to commercial activities and the solicitation of funds might not be invalid.

2. *Fees.* To what extent may the state charge for use of the public forum? In Murdock v. Pennsylvania, 319 U.S. 105 (1943), the Court held that the state

may not impose a "flat license tax [as] a condition to the pursuit of activities whose enjoyment is guaranteed by the First Amendment" where the tax "is not a nominal fee imposed as a regulatory measure to defray the expenses of policing the activities in question." In Cox v. New Hampshire, supra, the licensing statute provided that "every licensee shall pay in advance" a fee ranging from a nominal amount to $300 per day. The state court construed the statute as requiring "a reasonable fixing of the amount of the fee." That is, the amount of the fee must in each instance turn on the size of the "parade or procession," the size of the crowd, and the "public expense of policing" the event. The state court explained that the fee was "not a revenue tax, but one to meet the expense incident to the administration of the Act and to the maintenance of public order in the matter licensed." The Court held that in such circumstances "there is nothing contrary to the Constitution in the charge of a fee limited to the purpose stated." Moreover, the Court rejected "the suggestion that a flat fee should have been charged," explaining that it is difficult to frame "a fair schedule to meet all circumstances," and that there is "no constitutional ground for denying to local governments that flexibility of adjustment of fees which in the light of varying conditions would tend to conserve rather than impair the liberty sought."

During the Skokie controversy, section B2 supra, the village enacted an ordinance requiring applicants for parade or public demonstration permits to procure public liability insurance in the amount of $350,000 and property damage insurance in the amount of $50,000. Is this ordinance constitutional under the doctrine of Cox? Consider Forsyth County, Georgia v. The Nationalist Movement, 505 U.S. 123 (1992), in which the Court invalidated a municipal ordinance that authorized permit fees for parades, demonstrations, marches, and similar activities, up to a maximum of $1,000, based in part on the anticipated expense necessary to maintain the public order. The Court, in an opinion by Justice Blackmun, explained that under this scheme the fee "will depend on the administrator's measure of the amount of hostility likely to be created by the speech." As a result, those "wishing to express views unpopular with bottle throwers [may] have to pay more for their permit." The Court announced that speech "cannot be financially burdened, any more than it can be punished or banned, simply because it might offend a hostile mob," and that "regulations which permit the Government to discriminate on the basis of the content of the message cannot be tolerated under the First Amendment."

3. *Disclosure.* To what extent may the state, in order to prevent abuse, require speakers to disclose their identities? In Talley v. California, 362 U.S. 60 (1960), a distributor of handbills protesting employment discrimination was prosecuted for violating a Los Angeles ordinance prohibiting any person to distribute "any handbill [which] does not have printed on [the] face thereof, the name and address of [the] person who printed, wrote, compiled, or manufactured [it]." The Court held the ordinance invalid:

[It is] urged that this ordinance is aimed at providing a way to identify those responsible for fraud, false advertising and libel. [But] such an identification requirement would tend to restrict freedom to distribute information and thereby freedom of expression. [Anonymous] pamphlets, leaflets, brochures and even books have played an important role in the progress of mankind. Persecuted groups [throughout] history have been able to criticize oppressive practices [either] anonymously or not at all. [Identification] and fear of reprisal might deter perfectly peaceful discussions of public matters of importance. This broad Los Angeles ordinance is subject to the same infirmity.

See also McIntyre v. Ohio Elections Commission, 514 U.S. 334 (1995), in which the Court invalidated a state statute prohibiting the distribution of campaign literature that does not contain the name and address of the person issuing the literature: "Under our Constitution, anonymous pamphleteering is not a pernicious, fraudulent practice, but an honorable tradition of advocacy and of dissent. Anonymity is a shield from the tyranny of the majority. It thus exemplifies the purpose behind the Bill of Rights, and of the First Amendment in particular: to protect unpopular individuals from retaliation — and their ideas from suppression — at the hand of an intolerant society." See also Buckley v. American Constitutional Law Foundation, 525 U.S. 182 (1999) (invalidating a state law requiring petition circulators to wear a badge identifying them by name).

Are there any circumstances in which compelled disclosure is constitutional? See Buckley v. Valeo, section E4 infra (upholding compelled disclosure of campaign contributions). Are there any circumstances in which compelled disclosure is generally constitutional, but is unconstitutional as applied to particular speakers who can demonstrate a meaningful risk of "economic reprisal, loss of employment, threat of physical coercion [or] other manifestations of public hostility"? See NAACP v. Alabama, section E5 infra (invalidating an Alabama statute requiring disclosure of the names of members of registered organizations, as applied to the NAACP); Brown v. Socialists Workers '74 Campaign Committee, 459 U.S. 87 (1982) (invalidating the statute compelling disclosure of campaign contributions that had been upheld in *Buckley*, as applied to the Socialist Workers Party).

b. The Public Forum: Other Publicly Owned Property

If there is a first amendment right to use streets and parks for purposes of expression, to what extent, if any, is there an analogous right to use other publicly owned property, ranging from the grounds surrounding a jail, to a military base, to a state fair? Does the *Hague* dictum's definition of the right to a "public forum" in terms of the common law property rights of the state suggest that the right does not extend to property that has not been used "time out of mind" for speech purposes?

Adderley v. Florida
385 U.S. 39 (1966)

[About two hundred Florida A. & M. students marched to the county jail to protest the arrest the previous day of several of their schoolmates who had engaged in a civil rights demonstration. The protestors went directly to the jail entrance, where they were met by a deputy sheriff who explained that they were blocking the entrance to the jail and asked them to move back. The protestors moved back part of the way, where they stood or sat, singing, clapping, and dancing, on the jail driveway and on an adjacent grassy area on the jail premises. This jail entrance and driveway were normally used not by the public, but by the sheriff's department for transporting prisoners and by commercial concerns for servicing the jail. [The] county sheriff, who was legal custodian of the jail and jail grounds, [ordered the students] to leave and informed them that, if they did not leave within ten minutes, he would arrest them for trespassing. Some protestors left, but 107 others, including petitioners, remained and were arrested. They were convicted of violating a Florida statute declaring unlawful "every trespass upon the property of another, committed with a malicious and mischievous intent." The Court, in a five-to-four decision, affirmed the convictions.]

MR. JUSTICE BLACK delivered the opinion of the Court. . . .
[Petitioners maintain that conviction under the trespass statute] unconstitutionally deprives [them] of their rights to freedom of speech, press, assembly, or petition. We hold that it does not. The sheriff, as jail custodian, had power [to] direct that this large crowd of people get off the grounds. There is not a shred of evidence in this record that this power was exercised [because] the sheriff objected to what was being sung or said by the demonstrators or because he disagreed with the objectives of their protest. The record reveals that he objected only to their presence on that part of the jail grounds reserved for jail uses. There is no evidence at all that on any other occasion had similarly large groups of the public been permitted to gather on this portion of the jail grounds for any purpose. Nothing in the Constitution of the United States prevents Florida from even-handed enforcement of its general trespass statute against those refusing to obey the sheriff's order to remove themselves from what amounted to the curtilage of the jailhouse. The State, no less than a private owner of property, has power to preserve the property under its control for the use to which it is lawfully dedicated. For this reason there is no merit to the petitioners' argument that they had a constitutional right to stay on the property, over the jail custodian's objections, because this "area chosen for the peaceful civil rights demonstration was not only 'reasonable' but also particularly appropriate. . . ." Such an argument has as its major unarticulated premise the assumption that people who want to propagandize protests or views have a constitutional right to do so whenever and however and wherever they please. [We] reject [that concept]. The United States Constitution does not forbid a State to control the use of its own property for its own lawful nondiscriminatory purpose.
These judgments are affirmed.

MR. JUSTICE DOUGLAS, with whom THE CHIEF JUSTICE, MR. JUSTICE BRENNAN, and MR. JUSTICE FORTAS concur, dissenting. . . .
The jailhouse, like an executive mansion, a legislative chamber, a courthouse, or the statehouse itself [is] one of the seats of government, whether it be the Tower of London, the Bastille, or a small county jail. And when it houses political prisoners or those who many think are unjustly held, it is an obvious center for protest. The right to petition for the redress of grievances has an ancient history and is not limited to writing a letter or sending a telegram to a congressman; it is not confined to appearing before the local city council, or writing letters to the President or Governor or Mayor. [Conventional] methods of petitioning may be, and often have been, shut off to large groups of our citizens. [Those] who do not control television and radio, those who cannot afford to advertise in newspapers or circulate elaborate pamphlets may have only a more limited type of access to public officials. Their methods should not be condemned as tactics of obstruction and harassment as long as the assembly and petition are peaceable, as these were.

There is no question that petitioners had as their purpose a protest against the arrest of Florida A. & M. students for trying to integrate public theatres. [There] was no violence; no threat of violence; no attempted jail break; no storming of a prison; no plan or plot to do anything but protest. . . .

We do violence to the First Amendment when we permit this "petition for redress of grievances" to be turned into a trespass action. [To] say that a private owner could have done the same if the rally had taken place on private property is to speak of a different case, as an assembly and a petition for redress of grievances run to government, not to private proprietors.

The Court forgets that prior to this day our decisions have drastically limited the application of state statutes inhibiting the right to go peacefully on public property to exercise First Amendment rights. [Citing Justice Roberts's plurality opinion in *Hague*. There] may be some public places which are so clearly committed to other purposes that their use for the airing of grievances is anomalous. There may be some instances in which assemblies and petitions for redress of grievances are not consistent with other necessary purposes of public property. A noisy meeting may be out of keeping with the serenity of the statehouse or the quiet of the courthouse. No one, for example, would suggest that the Senate gallery is the proper place for a vociferous protest rally. And in other cases it may be necessary to adjust the right to petition for redress of grievances to the other interests inhering in the uses to which the public property is normally put. [See Cox v. New Hampshire.] But this is quite different from saying that all public places are off limits to people with grievances. . . .

Note: "No Less Than a Private Owner of Property"?

1. Davis *revisited?* Does *Adderley* turn on Justice Black's assertion that "the State, no less than a private owner of property, has power to preserve the property under its control for the use to which it is lawfully dedicated"? Does *Adderley* undervalue the interest of the speaker in selecting a "particularly appropriate" location for his speech?

2. *The* Grayned *dictum.* In Grayned v. Rockford, section E2a, supra, decided in 1972, the Court, although upholding the antinoise ordinance as a reasonable time, place, and manner regulation, offered the following analysis of the public forum issue:

> The nature of a place, "the pattern of its normal activities, dictate the kinds of regulations of time, place, and manner that are reasonable." [The] crucial question is whether the manner of expression is basically incompatible with the normal activity of a particular place at a particular time. Our cases make clear that in assessing the reasonableness of a regulation, we must weigh heavily the fact that communication is involved; the regulation must be narrowly tailored to further the State's legitimate interest.

What are the implications of *Grayned?* Does it reject the central premise of *Adderley?* Consider Stone, Fora Americana: Speech in Public Places, 1974 Sup. Ct. Rev. 233, 251–252:

> In [the *Grayned* dictum], the right to a public forum came of age. No longer does the right to effective freedom of expression turn on the common law property rights of the state, and no longer does it turn on whether the particular place at issue has

historically been dedicated to the exercise of First Amendment rights. The streets, parks, public libraries, and other publicly owned places are all brought under the same roof. In each case, the "crucial question is whether the manner of expression is basically incompatible with the normal activity of a particular place at a particular time."

As events turned out, this celebration proved premature. Consider the following post-*Grayned* decisions.

3. *A military base*. The Fort Dix Military Reservation is a U.S. Army post. Although the federal government exercises exclusive jurisdiction over the base, civilian vehicular traffic is permitted on paved roads within the reservation, and civilians are freely permitted to visit unrestricted areas of the base. In 1972, Benjamin Spock, the People's Party's candidate for President of the United States, requested permission to enter the base to hold a meeting to discuss election issues with service personnel and their dependents. The commanding officer of the base rejected the request, citing a Fort Dix regulation providing that "demonstrations, picketing, sit-ins, protest marches, political speeches and similar activities are prohibited and will not be conducted on the Fort Dix Military Reservation."

In Greer v. Spock, 424 U.S. 828 (1976), the Court, in a six-to-two decision, upheld the regulation. In an opinion by Justice Stewart, the Court rejected "the principle that whenever members of the public are permitted freely to visit a place owned or operated by the Government, then that place becomes a 'public forum' for purposes of the First Amendment." Quoting *Adderley*, the Court explained that "'[t]he State, no less than a private owner of property, has power to preserve the property under its control for the use to which it is lawfully dedicated.'" The Court added that it is "the business of a military installation like Fort Dix to train soldiers, not to provide a public forum," and that the challenged regulation reflects "a considered [policy], objectively and evenhandedly applied, of keeping official military activities [free] of entanglement with partisan political campaigns of any kind [in order to insulate] the military [from] both the reality and the appearance of acting as a handmaiden for partisan political causes or candidates."

Justice Brennan, joined by Justice Marshall, dissented. Justice Brennan maintained that the Court's emphasis on whether the base was a "public forum" was misplaced, for "the determination that a locale is a 'public forum' has never been erected as an absolute prerequisite to all forms of demonstrative First Amendment activity." What is needed, Justice Brennan explained, is a "flexible approach [for] determining when public expression should be protected." Justice Brennan reasoned that the speech in this case was "basically compatible with the activities otherwise occurring" at the base, and he rejected the contention that the interest in "military neutrality" could justify the restriction, for "it borders on casuistry to contend that by evenhandedly permitting public expression to occur in unrestricted portions of a military installation, the military will be viewed as sanctioning the causes there espoused."

4. *A state fair*. The Minnesota State Fair is conducted each year on a 125-acre site. The average daily attendance exceeds 100,000. Minnesota State Fair Rule 6.05 prohibits the sale or distribution of any merchandise, including printed or written material, except from a booth rented from the state. Booths are rented to all comers in a nondiscriminatory manner on a first-come, first-served basis. The rental charge is based on the size and location of the booth.

The International Society for Krishna Consciousness (ISKCON), an international religious society espousing the views of the Krishna religion, challenged Rule 6.05 on the ground that it would impair ISKCON's ability effectively to distribute its literature.

In Heffron v. International Society for Krishna Consciousness, 452 U.S. 640 (1981), the Court upheld the rule. In an opinion by Justice White, the Court rejected ISKCON's effort to analogize "the fairgrounds [to] city streets which have 'immemorially been [used] for purposes [of] assembly [and] discussing public questions'":

> A street is continually open, often uncongested, [and] a place where people may enjoy the open air or the company of friends [in] a relaxed environment. The Minnesota Fair [is] a temporary event attracting great numbers of visitors who come to the event for a short period to see [the] host of exhibits [at] the Fair. The flow of the crowd and the demands of safety are more pressing in the context of the Fair. As such, any comparisons to public streets are necessarily inexact." [Thus, given the] threat to the State's interest in crowd control if [all] organizations [could] move freely about the fairgrounds distributing and selling literature and soliciting funds at will, [the] State's interest in confining distribution, selling, and fund solicitation activities to fixed locations is sufficient to satisfy the requirement that a place or manner restriction must serve a substantial state interest.

Justice Brennan, joined by Justices Marshall and Stevens, concurred in part and dissented in part. Although conceding that "the State has a significant interest in maintaining crowd control on its fairgrounds," Justice Brennan concluded that the "booth rule is an overly intrusive means of achieving [that interest]." "A state fair," Justice Brennan maintained, "is truly a marketplace of ideas and a public forum for the communication of ideas and information." Thus, Rule 6.05 constitutes a "significant restriction on First Amendment rights," for "by prohibiting distribution of literature outside the booths, the fair officials sharply limit the number of fairgoers to whom the proselytizers [can] communicate their messages."

5. A *mailbox*. In U.S. Postal Service v. Council of Greenburgh Civic Associations, 453 U.S. 114 (1981), the Court upheld a federal statute prohibiting the deposit of unstamped "mailable matter" in a letter box approved by the U.S. Postal Service, as applied to appellee civic association, which routinely delivered its messages by placing unstamped notices in the letter boxes of private homes. In an opinion by Justice Rehnquist, the Court explained:

> There is neither historical nor constitutional support for the characterization of a letter box as a public forum. [At least since 1934, when the statute was promulgated,] access to [letter boxes] has been unlawful except under the terms and conditions specified by Congress and the Postal Service. As such, it is difficult to accept appellees' assertion that because it may be somewhat more efficient to place their messages in letter boxes there is a First Amendment right to do so. [Indeed,] it is difficult to conceive of any reason why this Court should treat a letter box differently for First Amendment [purposes] than it has in the past treated the military base in [*Greer* or] the jail [in *Adderley*]. . . . What we hold is the principle reiterated by cases such as [*Adderley*] and [*Greer*], that property owned or controlled by the government which is *not* a public forum may be subject to a prohibition of speech, leafleting, picketing, or other forms of communication without running afoul of the First Amendment. Admittedly, the government must act reasonably in imposing

such restrictions [and] the prohibition must be content-neutral. [But] this statute is both a reasonable and content-neutral regulation.

Justices Marshall and Stevens dissented.

6. *A public utility pole.* In Members of the City Council of Los Angeles v. Taxpayers for Vincent, 466 U.S. 789 (1984), the Court upheld a Los Angeles ordinance prohibiting the posting of signs on public property as applied to individuals who tied political campaign signs to public utility poles. Justice Stevens delivered the opinion:

> The ordinance [diminishes] the total quantity of [appellees'] communication in the City. [But] the state [may] curtail speech [in a content-neutral manner if the restriction] "furthers an important or substantial governmental interest [and if the] restriction on [free speech] is no greater than is essential to the furtherance of that interest." [It is undisputed that the] problem addressed by this ordinance — the visual assault [on] citizens [presented] by an accumulation of signs posted on public property — constitutes a significant substantive evil. [Moreover, the] restriction on appellees' expressive activity is [no] broader than necessary to protect the City's interest. [By] banning these signs, the City did no more than eliminate the exact source of the evil it sought to remedy. [Appellees] suggest that the public property covered by the ordinance is [a] "public forum," [but they] fail to demonstrate the existence of a traditional right of access respecting such items as utility poles for purposes [of] communication comparable to that recognized for public streets and parks. [The] mere fact that government property can be used as a vehicle for communication does not mean that the Constitution requires such uses to be permitted.

Justice Brennan, joined by Justices Marshall and Blackmun, dissented. Is *Vincent* consistent with *Schneider*? Consider Justice Stevens's answer in *Vincent*: "It is true that the esthetic interest in preventing [litter] cannot support a prophylactic prohibition against [leafleting. But the] rationale of *Schneider* is inapposite in the context of this case. [In *Schneider*,] an anti-littering statute could have addressed the substantive evil without prohibiting expressive activity. [Here], the substantive evil — visual blight — is not merely a possible by-product of the activity, but is created by the medium of expression itself. [Thus, the] ordinance curtails no more speech than is necessary to accomplish its purpose."

7. *A post office sidewalk.* In United States v. Kokinda, 497 U.S. 720 (1990), respondents, members of a political advocacy group, set up a table on a sidewalk near the entrance to a United States Post Office to distribute literature and solicit contributions. The sidewalk, which is located entirely on Postal Service property, is the sole means by which customers may travel from the parking lot to the post office building. Respondents were convicted of violating a federal regulation prohibiting any person from soliciting contributions "on postal premises." The Court upheld the regulation as applied.

Justice O'Connor, in a plurality opinion joined by Chief Justice Rehnquist and Justices White and Scalia, explained that the "postal sidewalk [does] not have the characteristics of public sidewalks traditionally open to expressive activity." Rather, "the postal sidewalk was constructed solely to provide for the passage of individuals engaged in postal business." Although conceding that individuals had generally "been permitted to leaflet, speak, and picket on postal premises," Justice O'Connor argued this did "not add up to the dedication of postal property to speech activities." Justice O'Connor therefore concluded that "the regulation

[must] be analyzed under the standards set forth for nonpublic fora: it must be reasonable and 'not an effort to suppress expression merely because public officials oppose the speaker's view.'" Applying that standard, Justice O'Connor noted that, "based on its long experience with solicitation," the Postal Service had concluded that "solicitation is inherently disruptive of the postal service's business" because it "impedes the normal flow of traffic" and "is more intrusive and intimidating than an encounter with a person giving out information." Justice O'Connor concluded that the challenged regulation therefore "passes constitutional muster under [the] usual test for reasonableness." Justice Kennedy concurred in the result. Justice Brennan, joined by Justices Marshall, Blackmun, and Stevens, dissented.

What about an airport terminal?

INTERNATIONAL SOCIETY FOR KRISHNA CONSCIOUSNESS v. LEE, 505 U.S. 672 (1992). The Port Authority of New York and New Jersey, which owns and operates three major airports in the New York City area, forbids within the airport terminals the repetitive solicitation of money and the repetitive sale or distribution of any merchandise, "including but not limited to jewelry, food stuffs, candles, flowers, . . . flyers, brochures, pamphlets, books or any other printed or written material." The regulation governs only the terminal buildings. It does not restrict such activities on the public sidewalks outside the buildings. In a bewildering array of opinions, the Court upheld the ban on solicitation but invalidated the ban on the sale or distribution of literature.

Solicitation. Chief Justice Rehnquist delivered the opinion of the Court upholding the ban on solicitation. The Court explained that airport terminals are not traditional public fora because, "given the lateness with which the modern air terminal has made its appearance, it hardly qualifies for the description of having 'immemorially . . . time out of mind' been held in the public trust and used for purposes of expressive activity." Moreover, such terminals have not "been intentionally opened by their operators to such activity." To the contrary, "the frequent and continuing litigation evidencing the operators' objections belies any such claim." Moreover, "airports are commercial establishments funded by use fees and designed to make a regulated profit." The Court thus concluded that, "because it cannot fairly be said that an airport terminal has as a principal purpose 'promoting the free exchange of ideas,'" it is not a public forum.

This being so, the prohibition of solicitation "need only satisfy a requirement of reasonableness," a standard the Court held was easily satisfied because of "the disruptive effect that solicitation may have on business." Specifically, the Court observed that solicitation impedes "the normal flow of traffic," and that such "delays may be particularly costly in this setting, as a flight missed by only a few minutes can result in hours worth of subsequent inconvenience." Moreover, "face to face solicitation presents risk of duress" and "fraud," and it may be especially difficult for airport authorities to enforce rules against such abuses because passengers "frequently are on tight schedules" and are "unlikely to stop and formally complain." Finally, the prohibition is reasonable because solicitation is permitted on the "sidewalk areas outside the terminals," where the "overwhelming" majority of airport users can be reached.

Justice Kennedy, joined by Justices Blackmun, Stevens, and Souter, offered a very different approach to the public forum issue and, contrary to the majority, concluded that airport terminals are public fora. Justice Kennedy complained that "our public forum doctrine ought [not] convert what was once an analysis protective of expression into one which grants the government authority to restrict speech by fiat." Justice Kennedy observed that the Court's analysis, which "holds that traditional public forums are limited to public property which have as their 'principal purpose . . . the free exchanges of ideas,'" as "evidenced by a longstanding historical practice of permitting speech," leaves "the government with almost unlimited authority to restrict speech on its property," for "the critical step in the Court's analysis" is "the government's own definition or decision, unconstrained by an independent duty to respect the speech its citizens can voice" on public property. Justice Kennedy argued that this view "is contrary to the underlying purposes of the public forum doctrine," for "at the heart of our jurisprudence lies the principle that in a free nation citizens must have the right to gather and speak with other persons in public places."

Justice Kennedy therefore argued that the purposes of the public forum doctrine "cannot be given effect unless we recognize that open, public spaces and thoroughfares which are suitable for discourse may be public forums, whatever their historical pedigree and without concern for a precise classification of the property." Indeed, "without this recognition our forum doctrine retains no relevance in times of fast-changing technology and increasing insularity," and the Court's failure to "recognize the possibility that new types of government property may be appropriate forums for speech will lead to a serious curtailment of our expressive activity." Justice Kennedy thus maintained that, "if the objective, physical characteristics of the property at issue and the actual public access and uses which have been permitted by the government indicate that expressive activity would be appropriate and compatible with those uses, the property is a public forum."

Turning to the issue of airport terminals, Justice Kennedy observed that "in these days an airport is one of the few government-owned spaces where people have extended contact with other members of the public." Although an "airport corridor [is] not a street," it bears important "physical similarities" to a street, the relevant areas "are open to the public without restriction," and the "recent history of airports [demonstrates] that when adequate time, place, and manner regulations are in place, expressive activity is quite compatible with the uses of major airports." Justice Kennedy thus found that the public areas of an airport terminal constitute a public forum.

Despite this disagreement with the Court, Justice Kennedy, writing only for himself, concurred that the ban on solicitation was constitutional as "a reasonable time, place, and manner restriction" because of the risks of fraud and duress. Justice Souter, joined by Justices Blackmun and Stevens, adopted Justice Kennedy's analysis of the general public forum issue but dissented on the constitutionality of the ban on solicitation. In Justice Souter's view, "the claim to be preventing coercion is weak" because, "while a solicitor can be insistent," a pedestrian on the street or airport concourse can simply "walk away." Moreover, Justice Souter found the claim to be preventing fraud unpersuasive because, once it is accepted that the terminal is a public forum, the absolute ban on solicitation does not meet "the requirement of narrow tailoring."

Sale or distribution of literature. In a plurality opinion, Justice Kennedy, joined by Justices Blackmun, Stevens, and Souter, concluded that the ban on the sale or distribution of literature violated the first amendment. After finding, for the reasons set forth above, that airport terminals are public fora, Justice Kennedy explained that the ban was invalid because "the right to distribute flyers and literature lies at the heart of the liberties guaranteed" by the first amendment, the challenged "regulation is not drawn in narrow terms [and] does not leave open ample alternative channels for communication," and the "Port Authority's concerns with the problem of congestion can be addressed through narrow restrictions on the time and place of expressive activity."

Justice O'Connor concurred in the result. Although agreeing with the dissent that airport terminals are not public fora, she nonetheless concluded that the ban on the sale or distribution of literature was invalid because it was an "unreasonable" restriction. Justice O'Connor explained that "leafleting does not necessarily entail the same kinds of problems presented by face-to-face solicitation." Indeed, "with the possible exception of avoiding litter, it is difficult to point to any problems intrinsic to the act of leafleting that would make it naturally incompatible with a large, multipurpose forum such as those at issue here."

Chief Justice Rehnquist, joined by Justices White, Scalia, and Thomas, dissented. Having found that airport terminals are not public fora, Chief Justice Rehnquist reasoned that "the distribution ban, no less than the solicitation ban, is reasonable." He argued that "the weary, harried or hurried traveler may have no less desire and need to avoid the delays generated by having literature foisted upon him than he does to avoid delays from a financial solicitation." Moreover, like solicitation, leafleting can cause congestion. Finally, leafleting is even worse than solicitation insofar as leafleting may produce litter, thereby "creating an eyesore, a safety hazard, and additional clean-up work for the airport staff."

Note: Modern Public Forum Doctrine

1. *Deference to regulators.* Consider Goldberger, Judicial Scrutiny in Public Forum Cases: Misplaced Trust in the Judgment of Public Officials, 32 Buff. L. Rev. 175, 206–207, 217–218 (1983):

> By employing [low] levels of scrutiny in [these cases], the Court [assumes] that regulatory decision making is [generally] trustworthy. [The] Court has failed to recognize [that] public officials [often] have strong incentives to overregulate. [These incentives come] from two sources. First, there is the tendency of forum regulators to be disproportionately sensitive to threats of [disruption]. Second, forum regulators tend to be particularly sensitive toward protecting public services [when] the communication is controversial or is of interest to only a small segment of the population. [To compensate for these incentives, the Court in these cases should have required state] officials to prove that the activities regulated were as disruptive [as] claimed.

See also Post, Between Governance and Management: The History and Theory of the Public Forum, 34 UCLA L. Rev. 1713, 1809–1824 (1987).

2. *Evaluation.* Consider the following assessment: The dispute over access to nonpublic forum public property turns on a conflict between two competing views. Under one view, the first amendment requires government to permit the widest possible opportunity for free expression. The greater the opportunity for free expression, the healthier the marketplace of ideas. Thus, any law that restricts free expression must be invalidated unless the government interest served by the restriction outweighs the effect on free expression. Under the competing view, the traditional means of expression — radio, television, newspapers, speeches, parades, picketing, leaflets, and the like — provide ample opportunity for free

expression. Although access to nonpublic forum public property might make some speech marginally more effective, a denial of access to such property poses no real threat to the marketplace of ideas. But to require such access would necessarily interfere with competing government interests and involve the courts in an endless series of highly subjective and unpredictable judgments. Thus, the costs of such inquiries far exceed the benefits. In recent years, the Court has embraced this second view.

Note: The Right to a "Private" Forum

To what extent, if any, does the first amendment guarantee the individual a right to commandeer some other person's private property for speech purposes? Do the property rights of private owners absolutely preclude such an interpretation of the first amendment? Does the state action requirement foreclose such an interpretation? On the state action doctrine, see Chapter 9.

1. *The company town.* In Marsh v. Alabama, 326 U.S. 501 (1946), the Court considered whether a state could constitutionally "impose criminal punishment on a person who undertakes to distribute religious literature on the premises of a company-owned town contrary to the wishes of the town's management." The town, a suburb of Mobile, Alabama, known as Chickasaw, was owned by the Gulf Shipbuilding Corporation. The town was freely used by the public, and there was "nothing to distinguish [it] from any other town [except] the fact that the title to the property [belonged] to a private corporation." Appellant, a Jehovah's Witness, attempted to distribute literature on one of the town's sidewalks. She was informed that, pursuant to a formal corporation policy, she could not distribute literature without a permit, and that no permit would be issued her. When asked to leave, she declined. She was eventually convicted of violating a state statute prohibiting any person to enter or remain on the premises of another after having been warned not to do so.

The Court overturned the conviction. Justice Black, speaking for the Court, observed:

> Had the title to Chickasaw belonged not to a private, but to a municipal corporation [it] would have been clear that appellant's conviction must be reversed. [The] State urges [that] the corporation's right to control the inhabitants of Chickasaw is coextensive with the right of a homeowner to regulate the conduct of his guests. We cannot accept that contention. Ownership does not always mean absolute dominion. The more an owner, for his advantage, opens up his property for use by the public in general, the more do his rights become circumscribed by the statutory and constitutional rights of those who use it. [In] our view the circumstance that the property rights to the premises where the deprivation of liberty, here involved, took place, were held by others than the public, is not sufficient to justify the State's permitting a corporation to govern a community of citizens so as to restrict their fundamental liberties and the enforcement of such restraint by the application of a state statute.

2. *Privately owned shopping centers.* Suppose a privately owned shopping center bans all leafleting in the shopping center. Does that violate the first amendment? Consider the following argument:

> [The] similarities between the business block in *Marsh* and the [modern day] shopping center [are] striking. [The] shopping center premises are open to the

public to the same extent as the commercial center of a normal town. [Because the] shopping center [is] clearly the functional equivalent of the business district of Chickasaw involved in *Marsh*, [the] State may not delegate the power, through the use of its trespass laws, wholly to exclude those members of the public wishing to exercise their First Amendment rights on the premises in a manner and for a purpose generally consonant with the use to which the property is actually put.

Food Employees Local 590 v. Logan Valley Plaza, 391 U.S. 308 (1968) (holding that the "peaceful [labor] picketing of a business enterprise located within a shopping center" cannot constitutionally be prohibited by the owner of the shopping center). In Hudgens v. NLRB, 424 U.S. 507 (1976), the Court overruled *Logan Valley*. For a critical evaluation, consider C. Sunstein, The Partial Constitution 208 (1993):

> The [Court] has said that the First Amendment is not implicated [in cases like *Hudgens* because] no government regulation of speech is involved. All that has happened is that private property owners have barred people from their land. [But] this is a poor way to understand the situation. [The] owners of the shopping center are able to exclude the protestors only because government has conferred on them a legal right to do so. The conferral of that right is an exercise of state power. It is this action that restricts the speech of the protestors. Surely it is a real question whether the grant of exclusionary power violates the First Amendment.

3. *Does the appropriation of private property for speech purposes violate the constitutional rights of owners?* Suppose the state, in an effort to promote free expression, grants the individual a right under state law to enter on private property for speech purposes. Might that in itself violate the property or speech rights of the property owner? In PruneYard Shopping Center v. Robins, 447 U.S. 74 (1980), a group of high school students who sought to solicit support for their opposition to a United Nations resolution against Zionism set up a card table in the PruneYard Shopping Center and asked passersby to sign petitions. Pursuant to a policy prohibiting any visitor to engage in any publicly expressive activity not directly related to the shopping center's commercial purposes, a security guard ordered the students to leave. The California Supreme Court held that the California Constitution protects "speech and petitioning, reasonably exercised, in shopping centers even when the centers are privately owned." The U.S. Supreme Court rejected PruneYard's contention that the California Supreme Court's decision violated the federal constitutional rights of the shopping center owner. The Court explained:

> [PruneYard contends] that a right to exclude others underlies the Fifth Amendment guarantee against the taking of property without just compensation. [But] "not every destruction or injury to property by governmental action has been held to be a 'taking' in the constitutional sense." [Here, there] is nothing to suggest that preventing [PruneYard] from prohibiting this sort of activity will unreasonably impair the value or use of [the] property as a shopping center. [PruneYard contends further] that a private property owner has a First Amendment right not to be forced by the State to use his property as a forum for the speech of others. [Although there are circumstances in which] a State may not constitutionally require an individual to participate in the dissemination of an ideological message by displaying it on his private property, [this is not such a case. First, PruneYard is] a business establishment that is open to the public to come and go as they please. The views expressed

by members of the public in passing out pamphlets or seeking signatures for a petition thus will not likely be identified with those of the owner. Second, no specific message is dictated by the State to be displayed. [There] consequently is no danger of governmental discrimination for or against a particular message. Finally, [PruneYard] can expressly disavow any connection with the message by simply posting signs in the area where the speakers or handbillers stand.

On the right "not to speak," see section E5 infra. On the problem of "takings," see Chapter 6.

c.   The Public Forum: Unequal Access and the Problem of Content-Neutrality

As we have seen, there are many situations in which government can constitutionally restrict expression on public property in a content-neutral manner. Suppose, however, government decides voluntarily to permit some, but not all, speech? For example, the Court held in *Lee* that government can constitutionally prohibit all solicitation in airport terminals. Suppose government decides to permit solicitation by antiabortion groups, or local political candidates, or groups interested in issues relating to air travel?

The issue is one of "underinclusion." That is, such a regulation restricts *less* speech than a broader and concededly constitutional content-neutral restriction. But in so doing, it adopts a potentially problematic inequality. To avoid this inequality, the regulation could be broadened to restrict *more* speech. Can it be that a law that restricts *more* speech is constitutional but a law that restricts *less* speech is unconstitutional? Recall *R.A.V.*, section D8 supra.

Consider Kagan, The Changing Faces of First Amendment Neutrality, 1992 Sup. Ct. Rev. 38–40:

> Such underinclusion [is] a particular kind of content-based restriction. . . . In [most] cases of content-based restrictions, the question [is] the permissibility of the burden placed on the speech affected. Consider, for example, [a] statute that [criminalizes] seditious advocacy. In deciding [on the constitutionality of such a statute], the Court usually will not ask whether the government has a sufficient reason to treat speech of one kind (seditious advocacy) differently from speech of another; rather, the Court will ask merely whether the government has a sufficient reason to restrict the speech actually affected. [In] such a case, the issue is not underinclusion, for the government could not cure the constitutional flaw by extending the restriction to [other speech]. By contrast, in a content-based underinclusion case, equality is all that is at issue.

Police Department of Chicago v. Mosley

408 U.S. 92 (1972)

MR. JUSTICE MARSHALL delivered the opinion of the Court.

At issue in this case is the constitutionality of [a] Chicago ordinance [providing that a] "person commits disorderly conduct when he knowingly [pickets] or demonstrates on a public way within 150 feet of [any] school building while the school is in [session], provided that this subsection does not prohibit the peaceful picketing of any school involved in a labor dispute. . . ."

[For] seven months prior to the enactment of [this ordinance], Earl Mosley, a federal postal employee, [frequently] picketed Jones Commercial High School in Chicago. During school hours and usually by himself, Mosley would walk the public sidewalk adjoining the school, carrying a sign that read: "Jones High School practices black discrimination. Jones High School has a black quota." His lonely crusade was always peaceful, orderly, and quiet, and was conceded to be so by the city of Chicago. [Mosley brought this action] seeking declaratory and injunctive relief. [We] hold that the ordinance is unconstitutional because it makes an impermissible distinction between labor picketing and other peaceful picketing.

Because Chicago treats some picketing differently from others, we analyze this ordinance in terms of the Equal Protection Clause of the Fourteenth Amendment. Of course, the equal protection claim in this case is closely intertwined with First Amendment interests; the Chicago ordinance affects picketing, which is expressive conduct; moreover, it does so by classifications formulated in terms of the subject of the picketing. As in all equal protection cases, however, the crucial question is whether there is an appropriate governmental interest suitably furthered by the differential treatment.

The central problem with Chicago's ordinance is that it describes permissible picketing in terms of its subject matter. Peaceful picketing on the subject of a school's labor-management dispute is permitted, but all other peaceful picketing is prohibited. The operative distinction is the message on a picket sign. But, above all else, the First Amendment means that government has no power to restrict expression because of its message, its ideas, its subject matter, or its content. [Citing Cohen v. California; New York Times v. Sullivan; Terminiello v. Chicago.] . . .

Necessarily, [then], government may not grant the use of a forum to people whose views it finds acceptable, but deny use to those wishing to express less favored or more controversial views. And it may not select which issues are worth discussing or debating in public facilities. There is an "equality of status in the field of ideas," and government must afford all points of view an equal opportunity to be heard. Once a forum is opened up to assembly or speaking by some groups, government may not prohibit others from assembling or speaking on the basis of what they intend to say. Selective exclusions from a public forum may not be based on content alone, and may not be justified by reference to content alone. . . .

This is not to say that all picketing must always be allowed. We have continually recognized that reasonable "time, place and manner" regulations of picketing may be necessary to further significant governmental interests. [Cox v. New Hampshire; Adderley v. Florida.] Conflicting demands on the same place may compel the State to make choices among potential users and uses. And the State may have a legitimate interest in prohibiting some picketing to protect public order. But these justifications for selective exclusions from a public forum must be carefully scrutinized [and such discriminations] among pickets must be tailored to serve a substantial governmental interest.

In this case, the ordinance itself describes impermissible picketing not in terms of time, place, and manner, but in terms of subject matter. The regulation "thus slip[s] from the neutrality of time, place, and circumstance into a concern about content." This is never permitted. In spite of this, Chicago urges that the ordinance is not improper content censorship, but rather a device for preventing disruption of the school. [Although] preventing school disruption is a city's legitimate concern, Chicago itself has determined that peaceful labor picketing during school hours is not an undue interference with school. Therefore, [Chicago] may not maintain that other picketing disrupts the school unless that picketing is clearly more disruptive than the picketing Chicago already permits. "Peaceful" nonlabor picketing, [however], is obviously no more disruptive than "peaceful" labor picketing. . . .

Similarly, we reject the city's argument that, although it permits peaceful labor picketing, it may prohibit all nonlabor picketing because, as a class, nonlabor picketing is more prone to produce violence than labor picketing. Predictions about imminent disruption from picketing involve judgments appropriately made on an individualized basis, not by means of broad classifications, especially those based on subject matter. [Some] labor picketing is peaceful, some disorderly; the same is true of picketing on other themes. [Given] what Chicago tolerates from labor picketing, the excesses of some nonlabor picketing may not be controlled by a broad ordinance prohibiting both peaceful and violent picketing. Such excesses "can be controlled by narrowly drawn statutes," [focusing] on the abuses and dealing even handedly with picketing regardless of subject matter. [Far] from being tailored to a substantial governmental interest, the discrimination among pickets is based on the content of their expression. Therefore, under the Equal Protection Clause, it may not stand.

Affirmed.

Mr. Justice Blackmun and Mr. Justice Rehnquist concur in the result.

Note: Mosley *and the "Equality" of Ideas*

1. *Equality and underinclusion.* Is the Chicago ordinance, absent the labor picketing exemption, a permissible content-neutral restriction? Recall Grayned v. Rockford, section E2a, supra. If the ordinance is constitutional absent the labor-picketing exemption, should the exemption render it invalid? Is it anomalous that under the Court's reasoning the ordinance would be more likely to be constitutional if it restricted *more* speech? Consider the following arguments:

a. The city's willingness to enact the labor exemption undermines the credibility of its asserted justifications for the restriction of nonlabor speech. Thus, even under the ordinary standards of content-neutral review, the restriction of nonlabor picketing may be invalid, even though a restriction of all picketing might be valid.

b. The standard of review should be higher when the city distinguishes between labor and nonlabor speech than when it acts in a content-neutral manner. That is, from a constitutional perspective, the inequality between labor and nonlabor picketing is more problematic than the broader, but more "equal," restriction of all picketing near a school. (On the other hand, consider the following argument: The standard of review should be especially *lenient* in a case like *Mosley* because the ordinance was designed not to restrict but to expand the opportunities for free expression.)

2. *Subject matter restrictions.* Note that in *Mosley* the content-based restriction was directed not against a particular viewpoint but against an entire subject of discussion — all nonlabor expression. Should the first amendment's hostility to content-based regulation extend not only to restrictions on particular viewpoints but also to restrictions on entire topics? Recall the debate on this issue in R.A.V. v.

City of St. Paul, section D8 supra. Consider Stone, Restrictions of Speech because of Its Content: The Peculiar Case of Subject-Matter Restrictions, 46 U. Chi. L. Rev. 81, 83, 108 (1978):

> [Although] "subject-matter" distinctions unquestionably regulate content, they [do] not fit neatly within the Court's general framework. [The] Court's rigorous approach to content-based restrictions stems in part from the realization that such restrictions generally have an especially potent viewpoint-differential impact upon the "marketplace of ideas." [Because] they are at least facially viewpoint-neutral, [however, subject-matter restrictions] do not have the same sort of skewing effect on "the thinking process of the community" as restrictions directed against speech taking a particular side in an ongoing debate. Moreover, because of their apparent viewpoint-neutrality, subject-matter restrictions seem much less likely than other forms of content-based restrictions to be the product of government hostility to the ideas suppressed. In general, one is more likely to be hostile to speech espousing a specific point of view than to speech about an entire subject. As a result, one [might] argue that subject-matter restrictions are in general less threatening than other sorts of content-based restrictions and, like content-neutral restrictions, need not be subjected to the most stringent standards of review.

3. *The reach of* Mosley: *residential picketing.* In Carey v. Brown, 447 U.S. 455 (1980), appellees participated in a peaceful demonstration in front of the home of the mayor of Chicago, protesting his alleged failure to support the busing of school children to achieve racial integration. As a result of this demonstration, appellees were convicted of violating an Illinois statute declaring it "unlawful to picket before or about the residence [of] any person, except when the residence" is "a place of employment involved in a labor dispute."

The Court held that the residential picketing statute was "constitutionally indistinguishable from the ordinance invalidated in *Mosley*":

> [The] Act accords preferential treatment to the expression of views on one particular subject; information about labor disputes may be freely disseminated, but discussion of all other issues is restricted. [When] government regulation discriminates among speech-related activities in a public forum, the Equal Protection Clause mandates that the legislation be finely tailored to serve substantial state interests, and the justifications offered for and distinctions it draws must be carefully scrutinized. [*Mosley.*] . . .

Justice Rehnquist, joined by Chief Justice Burger and Justice Blackmun, dissented.

4. *The reach of* Mosley: *universities and the problem of religious expression.* The University of Missouri at Kansas City, which officially recognizes more than one hundred student groups and routinely permits such groups to meet in university facilities, adopted a regulation prohibiting the use of university buildings for "purposes of religious worship or religious teaching." Several university students who were members of an organization of evangelical Christian students challenged the regulation.

In Widmar v. Vincent, 454 U.S. 263 (1981), the Court invalidated the regulation:

> [The] campus of a public university, at least for its students, possesses many of the characteristics of a public forum. [At] the same time, however, [a] university differs

in significant respects from public forums such as streets or parks. [A] university's mission is education, and [it may] impose reasonable regulations compatible with that mission upon the use of its campus and facilities. [Here, through] its policy of accommodating their meetings, the University has created a forum generally open for use by student groups. [The] Constitution forbids a State to enforce certain exclusions from a forum generally open to the public, even if it was not required to create the forum in the first place. [In] order to justify discriminatory exclusion from a public forum based on the religious content of a group's intended speech, the University [must] show that its regulation is necessary to serve a compelling state interest and that it is narrowly drawn to achieve that end. See [Carey v. Brown]. In this case the University claims a compelling interest in maintaining a strict separation of church and state. [We] agree that the interest of the University in complying with its constitutional obligations may be characterized as compelling. It does not follow, however, that an "equal access" policy would be incompatible with [the establishment clause]. It is possible — perhaps even foreseeable — that religious groups will benefit from access to University facilities. But [a] religious organization's enjoyment of merely "incidental" benefits does not violate the prohibition against the "primary advancement" of religion.

Justice Stevens concurred in the judgment. Justice White dissented.

See also Lamb's Chapel v. Center Moriches Union Free School District, 508 U.S. 384 (1993) (relying on *Widmar* to invalidate a school district rule permitting school property to be used after school for social, civic, and recreational uses, but prohibiting the use of such property for religious purposes); Rosenberger v. Rector and Visitors of the University of Virginia, 515 U.S. 819 (1995) (relying on *Lamb's Chapel* to invalidate a University of Virginia policy authorizing payment from the Student Activities Fund for the printing costs of a variety of student publications, but prohibiting payment for any student publication that "primarily promotes or manifests a particular belief in or about a deity or an ultimate reality").

5. *The reach of* Mosley: *the "careful scrutiny" standard.* Are there circumstances in which a content-based law, like the ones invalidated in *Mosley, Carey,* and *Widmar,* can withstand "careful scrutiny"? See Burson v. Freeman, 504 U.S. 191 (1992) (upholding a law prohibiting the solicitation of votes and the display or distribution of campaign materials within one hundred feet of the entrance to a polling place).

Lehman v. City of Shaker Heights

418 U.S. 298 (1974)

MR. JUSTICE BLACKMUN announced the judgment of the Court and an opinion, in which THE CHIEF JUSTICE, MR. JUSTICE WHITE, and MR. JUSTICE REHNQUIST join.

This case presents the question whether a city which operates a public rapid transit system and sells [commercial and public service] advertising space for car cards on its vehicles is required by the First and Fourteenth Amendments to accept paid political advertising on behalf of a candidate for public office.

[Petitioner, a candidate for the office of state representative,] sought to promote his candidacy by purchasing car card space on the Shaker Heights Rapid Transit System for the months of August, September, and October.

[He] was informed [that], although space was then available, [the] city did not permit political advertising. The system, however, accepted ads from cigarette companies, banks, savings and loan associations, liquor companies, retail and service establishments, churches, and civic and public-service oriented groups. . . .

When petitioner did not succeed in his effort to have his copy accepted, he sought declaratory and injunctive relief in the state courts of Ohio without success. . . . It is urged that the car cards here constitute a public forum protected by the First Amendment, and that there is a guarantee of nondiscriminatory access to such publicly owned and controlled areas of communication "regardless of the primary purpose for which the area is dedicated." [We] disagree.

[This situation is] different from the traditional settings where First Amendment values inalterably prevail. [Although] American constitutional jurisprudence, in the light of the First Amendment, has been jealous to preserve access to public places for purposes of free speech, the nature of the forum and the conflicting interests involved have remained important in determining the degree of protection afforded by the Amendment to the speech in question. . . .

Here, we have no open spaces, no meeting hall, park, street corner, or other public thoroughfare. Instead, the city is engaged in commerce. It must provide rapid, convenient, pleasant, and inexpensive service to the commuters of Shaker Heights. The car card space, although incidental to the provision of public transportation, is a part of the commercial venture. In much the same way that a newspaper or periodical, or even a radio or television station, need not accept every proffer of advertising from the general public, a city transit system has discretion to develop and make reasonable choices concerning the type of advertising that may be displayed in its vehicles. . . .

Because state action exists, however, the policies and practices governing access to the transit system's advertising space must not be arbitrary, capricious, or invidious. Here, the city has decided that "[p]urveyors of goods and services saleable in commerce may purchase advertising space on an equal basis, whether they be house builders or butchers." This decision is little different from deciding to impose a 10-, 25-, or 35-cent fare, or from changing schedules or the location of bus stops. [Revenue] earned from long-term commercial advertising could be jeopardized by a requirement that short-term candidacy or issue-oriented advertisements be displayed on car cards. Users would be subjected to the blare of political propaganda. There could be lurking doubts about favoritism, and sticky administrative problems might arise in parceling out limited space to eager politicians. In these circumstances, the managerial decision to limit car card space to innocuous and less controversial commercial and service oriented advertising does not rise to the dignity of a First Amendment violation. . . .

[The] city consciously has limited access to its transit system advertising space in order to minimize chances of abuse, the appearance of favoritism, and the risk of imposing upon a captive audience. These are reasonable legislative objectives advanced by the city in a proprietary capacity. [There] is no First or Fourteenth Amendment violation.

[Affirmed.]

MR. JUSTICE DOUGLAS, concurring in the judgment. . . .

[If] the streetcar or bus were a forum for communication akin to that of streets or public parks, considerable problems would be presented. [But] a streetcar or bus is plainly not a park or sidewalk or other meeting place for discussion.

[It] is only a way to get to work or back home. The fact that it is owned and operated by the city does not without more make it a forum.

[If] we are to turn a bus or streetcar into either a newspaper or a park, we take great liberties with people who because of necessity become commuters and at the same time captive viewers or listeners.

In asking us to force the system to accept his message as a vindication of his constitutional rights, the petitioner overlooks the constitutional rights of the commuters. While petitioner clearly has a right to express his views to those who wish to listen, he has no right to force his message upon an audience incapable of declining to receive it. In my view the right of the commuters to be free from forced intrusions on their privacy precludes the city from transforming its vehicles of public transportation into forums for the dissemination of ideas upon this captive audience. . . .

I do not view the content of the message as relevant either to petitioner's right to express it or to the commuters' right to be free from it. Commercial advertisements may be as offensive and intrusive to captive audiences as any political message. But the validity of the commercial advertising program is not before us since we are not faced with one complaining of an invasion of privacy through forced exposure to commercial ads. Since I do not believe that petitioner has any constitutional right to spread his message before this captive audience, I concur in the Court's judgment.

MR. JUSTICE BRENNAN, with whom MR. JUSTICE STEWART, MR. JUSTICE MARSHALL, and MR. JUSTICE POWELL join, dissenting. . . .

In the circumstances of this case, [we] need not decide whether public transit cars *must* be made available as forums for the exercise of First Amendment rights. By accepting commercial and public service advertising, the city effectively waived any argument that advertising in its transit cars is incompatible with the rapid transit system's primary function of providing transportation. A forum for communication was voluntarily established when the city installed the physical facilities for the advertisements [and] created the necessary administrative machinery for regulating access to that forum.

The plurality opinion, however, contends that as long as the city limits its advertising space to "innocuous and less controversial commercial and service oriented advertising," no First Amendment forum is created. I find no merit in that position. Certainly, noncommercial public service advertisements convey messages of public concern and are clearly protected by the First Amendment. And while it is possible that commercial advertising may be accorded *less* First Amendment protection than speech concerning political and social issues of public importance, [it] is "speech" nonetheless, often communicating information and ideas found by many persons to be controversial. [Once] such messages have been accepted and displayed, the existence of a forum for communication cannot be gainsaid. To hold otherwise, and thus sanction the city's preference for bland commercialism and noncontroversial public service messages over "uninhibited, robust, and wide-open" debate on public issues, would reverse the traditional priorities of the First Amendment.

Once a public forum for communication has been established, both free speech and equal protection principles prohibit discrimination based *solely* upon subject matter or content. See, e.g., [Mosley]. That the discrimination is among entire classes of ideas, rather than among points of view within a particular class, does not render it any less odious. Subject matter or content censorship in any form is forbidden. [Few] examples are required to illustrate the scope of the city's policy and practice.[10]

The city contends that its ban against political advertising is bottomed upon its solicitous regard for "captive riders" of the rapid transit system, who are "forced to endure the advertising thrust upon [them]." Whatever merit the city's argument might have in other contexts, it has a hollow ring in the present case, where the city has voluntarily opened its rapid transit system as a forum for communication. In that circumstance, the occasional appearance of provocative speech should be expected. . . .

The line between ideological and nonideological speech is impossible to draw with accuracy. By accepting commercial and public service advertisements, the city opened the door to "sometimes controversial or unsettling speech" and determined that such speech does not unduly interfere with the rapid transit system's primary purpose of transporting passengers. In the eyes of many passengers, certain commercial or public service messages[11] are as profoundly disturbing as some political advertisements might be to other passengers. There is certainly no evidence in the record of this case indicating that political advertisements, as a class, are so disturbing when displayed that they are more likely than commercial or public service advertisements to impair the rapid transit system's primary function of transportation. . . .

Moreover, even if it were possible to draw a manageable line between controversial and noncontroversial messages, the city's practice of censorship for the benefit of "captive audiences" still would not be justified. [The] advertisements accepted by the city [are] not broadcast over loudspeakers in the transit cars. The privacy of the passengers is not, therefore, dependent upon their ability "to sit and to try *not* to listen." [Rather], all advertisements accepted for display are in *written* form. [Should] passengers chance to glance at advertisements they find offensive, they can "effectively avoid further bombardment of their sensibilities simply by averting their eyes." [Cohen v. California.] Surely that minor inconvenience is a small price to pay for the continued preservation of so precious a liberty as free speech.

The city's remaining justification is equally unpersuasive. The city argues that acceptance of "political advertisements [would] suggest [that] the candidate so

---

10. In declaring unconstitutional an advertising policy remarkably similar to the city's policy in the present case, the California Supreme Court detailed "the paradoxical scope of the [transit] district's policy [banning political advertising]" in the following manner:

> A cigarette company is permitted to advertise the desirability of smoking its brand, but a cancer society is not entitled to caution by advertisement that cigarette smoking is injurious to health. A theater may advertise a motion picture that portrays sex and violence, but the Legion for Decency has no right to post a message calling for clean films. A lumber company may advertise its wood products, but a conservation group cannot implore citizens to write to the President or Governor about protecting our natural resources. An oil refinery may advertise its products, but a citizens' organization cannot demand enforcement of existing air pollution statutes. An insurance company may announce its available policies, but a senior citizens' club cannot plead for legislation to improve our social security program. Advertisements for travel, foods, clothing, toiletries, automobiles, legal drugs — all these are acceptable, but the American Legion would not have the right to place a paid advertisement reading, "Support Our Boys in Viet Nam. Send Holiday Packages."

Wirta v. Alameda-Contra Costa Transit District, 63 Cal. 2d 51, 57–58, 434 P.2d 982, 986–987 (1967).

11. For example, the record indicates that *church advertising* was accepted for display on the Shaker Heights Rapid Transit System.

advertised is being supported or promoted by the government of the City." Clearly, such ephemeral concerns do not provide the city with *carte blanche* authority to exclude an entire category of speech from a public forum. . . .

Moreover, neutral regulations, which do not distinguish among advertisements on the basis of subject matter, can be narrowly tailored to allay the city's fears. The impression of city endorsement can be dispelled by requiring disclaimers to appear prominently on the face of every advertisement. And while problems of accommodating all potential advertisers may be vexing at times, the appearance of favoritism can be avoided by the even-handed regulation of time, place, and manner for all advertising, irrespective of subject matter. . . .

Note: Lehman *and the Limits of* Mosley

1. *Analysis of* Lehman. In *Mosley*, the Court announced that laws granting unequal access to government property for speech purposes "must be carefully scrutinized" and "must be tailored to serve a substantial governmental interest." But in *Lehman*, Justice Blackmun, speaking for the plurality, upheld such a law because it was not "arbitrary, capricious, or invidious." Is Justice Blackmun's analysis in *Lehman* consistent with *Mosley*? Consider the following:

a. *In its operation of the transit system and its sale of advertising space, "the city is engaged in commerce."* Consider Wells and Hellerstein, The Governmental-Proprietary Distinction in Constitutional Law, 66 Va. L. Rev. 1073, 1116 (1980):

> As a regulator of the general public, the government must base its proscription of an activity on the premise that the proscription will act to enhance the general welfare. [As] a procurer or provider of goods and services, however, it may assert a different, more specific kind of interest — the interest of an employer who needs an efficient workforce, a landlord who would prefer not to deal with tenants who do not pay rent, or a purchaser who wishes to contract with a trustworthy seller. This quasi-business interest may adequately support regulation that a court might strike down if applied to the public at large and the state supported it with arguments that it promotes the general welfare. [That government acts in a proprietary capacity, however,] legitimately serves only to identify a state interest not present when the state regulates the general public. It should be but one element in the analysis and should not by itself determine the outcome.

See also International Society for Krishna Consciousness, Inc. v. Lee, supra (invoking the proprietary/governmental distinction in upholding a ban on solicitation in airport terminals); United States v. Kokinda, section E2b, supra (invoking the distinction in upholding a Postal Service regulation prohibiting any person from soliciting contributions on post office property).

b. *Streetcar passengers are a "captive audience."* Recall Cohen v. California, section D7, supra: "The ability of government, consonant with the Constitution, to shut off discourse solely to protect others from hearing it is [dependent] upon a showing that substantial privacy interests are being invaded in an essentially intolerable manner." Is that test satisfied in *Lehman*? If so, is the exclusion of all political speech an appropriate device for protecting the sensibilities of captive commuters? Suppose that, after polling its commuters, the city finds that, although the vast majority do not object to the ideas of Democratic and Republican candidates, they "deeply resent" the views expressed by Socialist candidates. Based on this finding, may the city permit Democratic and

Republican candidates to purchase car card space to espouse their "inoffensive" ideas, while excluding the "offensive" Socialist messages? For analysis of the "captive" audience, see section D7 supra.

c. *"No First Amendment forum is here to be found."* Do you agree with Justice Brennan that, even if the car card space did not inherently constitute a public forum, the city's acceptance of commercial and public service advertisements "created" such a forum? Recall *Widmar*. Consider Emerson, The Affirmative Side of the First Amendment, 15 Ga. L. Rev. 795, 813 (1981): "The dissenters fail to recognize the complications arising when the government is affirmatively promoting expression by providing facilities for a selected area of expression. They argue that, once the 'forum' has been opened, the government may not regulate on the basis of content. The issue before the Court, however, was what the scope of the forum was."

Would any of these "explanations" of *Lehman* justify a content-based restriction defined in terms of viewpoint rather than subject matter?

2. *The reach of* Lehman: *military bases.* In Greer v. Spock, section E2b, supra, the base commander of the Fort Dix Military Reservation, acting under the authority of a regulation prohibiting "demonstrations, picketing, sit-ins, protest marches, political speeches and similar activities" on the base, denied the request of a political candidate to make a speech on the base to discuss election issues with service personnel and their dependents. The candidate maintained that the regulation was invalid because the ban on civilian access to the base for expressive purposes was not content-neutral: "Civilian speakers have occasionally been invited to the base to address military personnel. The subjects of their talks have ranged from business management to drug abuse. Visiting clergymen have, by invitation, participated in religious services at the base chapel. Theatrical exhibitions and musical productions have also been presented on the base."

The Court upheld the regulation. Although the base was generally open to the public, the Court explained that "the business of a military installation [is] to train soldiers, not to provide a public forum." Moreover, the Court emphasized that there was "no claim that the military authorities discriminated in any way among candidates for public office based upon the candidates' supposed political views." In such circumstances, the ban on partisan political expression was not unconstitutional. Justices Brennan and Marshall dissented. Is *Greer* reconcilable with *Mosley* and *Widmar*?

PERRY EDUCATORS' ASSOCIATION v. PERRY LOCAL EDUCATORS' ASSOCIATION, 460 U.S. 37 (1983). The school district of Perry Township, Indiana, operates an interschool mail system to transmit messages among the teachers and between the teachers and the school administration. In addition, some private organizations, such as the YMCA and the Cub Scouts, have been permitted to use the system. After the Perry Educators' Association (PEA) was certified as the exclusive bargaining representative of the district's teachers, the school district and PEA entered into a collective bargaining agreement granting PEA, but no other union, access to the mail system. The Perry Local Educators' Association (PLEA), a rival union, brought this suit claiming that the district's access policy violated the Constitution.

The Court, in a five-to-four decision, upheld the challenged policy. Justice White delivered the opinion: "The existence of a right of access to public property [depends] on the character of the property at issue. [First, there are the] streets and [parks]. In these quintessential public forums, the government may not [enforce] a content-based exclusion [unless the exclusion] is necessary to serve a compelling state interest and [is] narrowly drawn to achieve that end. [*Mosley; Carey.*] [A] second category consists of public property which the state has [voluntarily] opened for use by the public as a place for expressive activity. [Although] a state is not required to indefinitely retain the open character of [such facilities], as long as it does so it is bound by the same standards as apply in a traditional public forum. [*Widmar.*] [A third category consists of public] property which is not by tradition or designation a forum for public communication. [The] state may reserve [such property] for its intended purposes, communicative or otherwise, so long as the regulation of speech is reasonable and not an effort to suppress expression merely because public officials oppose the speaker's view. . . .

"The school mail facilities [fall] within the third category. [The] interschool mail system is not a traditional public forum [and it] is not held open to the general public. [PLEA argues, however,] that the school mail facilities have become a 'limited public forum' from which it may not be excluded because of the periodic use of the system by private non-school connected groups, [such as] the YMCA, Cub Scouts, and other civic and church organizations. [The] use of the [mail system] by [such] groups [is] no doubt a relevant consideration. [Indeed, had the school district] opened its mail system for indiscriminate use by the general public, then PLEA could justifiably argue a public forum [had] been created. [But that] is not the case. [And the] type of selective access [involved here] does not transform government property into a public forum. [*Greer; Lehman.*] Moreover, even if [the grant of] access to the Cub Scouts, YMCAs, and parochial schools [had] created a 'limited' public forum, the constitutional right of access [would] extend only to other entities of similar character. While the school mail facilities thus might be a forum generally open for [other] organizations that engage in activities of interest [to] students, they would not [be] open to an organization such as PLEA, which is concerned with the terms and conditions of teacher employment. . . .

"[PLEA argues further that by allowing PEA and not PLEA to use the mail facilities,] the access policy [favors] a particular viewpoint, that of the PEA, on labor relations, and consequently must be strictly scrutinized regardless of whether a public forum is involved. There is, however, no indication that the school board intended to discourage one viewpoint and advance another. [It] is more accurate to characterize the access policy as based on the *status* of the respective unions rather than their views. Implicit in the concept of the nonpublic forum is the right to make distinctions in access on the basis of subject matter and speaker identity. These distinctions may be impermissible in a public forum but are inherent and inescapable in the process of limiting a nonpublic forum to activities compatible with the intended purpose of the property. The touchstone for evaluating these distinctions is whether they are reasonable in light of the purpose which the forum at issue serves. [Access to the] mail service [clearly] could be restricted to those with teaching and operational responsibility in the schools. [By] the same token — and upon the same principle — the system was properly opened to PEA, when it [was] designated the collective bargaining agent for all teachers in the Perry schools. PEA thereby assumed an official position in the operational structure of [the schools]. [The] differential access provided PEA and PLEA is reasonable because it is wholly consistent with the district's legitimate interest in 'preserv[ing] the property [for] the use to which it is lawfully dedicated.'"

Justice Brennan, joined by Justices Marshall, Powell, and Stevens, dissented: "In focusing on the public forum issue, the Court disregards the First Amendment's central proscription [against] viewpoint discrimination, in any forum, public or nonpublic. [As the] Court of Appeals [noted], 'the access policy [favors] a particular viewpoint on labor relations in the Perry schools: the teachers inevitably will receive from [PEA] self-laudatory descriptions of its activities [and] will be denied the critical perspective offered by [PLEA].' [Indeed], the only reason for [PEA] to seek an exclusive access policy is to deny its rivals access to an effective channel of communication. [In effect, the school district] has agreed to amplify the speech of [PEA], while repressing the speech of [PLEA] based on [PLEA's] point of view. [Such viewpoint discrimination] can be sustained 'only if the government can show that the regulation is a precisely drawn means of serving a compelling state interest.' [The state interests here] are not sufficient to sustain the [challenged] policy."

Note: Quintessential, Designated, and Nonpublic Forums

1. *Distinctions among charities*. The Combined Federal Campaign (CFC) is an annual charitable fund-raising drive conducted in the federal workplace during working hours largely through the voluntary efforts of federal employees. In Cornelius v. NAACP Legal Defense & Educational Fund, 473 U.S. 788 (1985), the Court, in a four-to-three decision, upheld an Executive Order limiting participation in the CFC to voluntary, tax-exempt, nonprofit charitable agencies that provide direct health and welfare services to individuals and expressly excluding legal defense and political advocacy organizations.

In an opinion by Justice O'Connor, the Court first held that the CFC is a nonpublic forum:

> Respondents argue [that] the Government created a limited public forum for use by all charitable organizations to solicit funds from federal employees. [We do not agree.] The Government's consistent policy has been to limit participation in the CFC to "appropriate" voluntary [agencies]. Such selective access, unsupported by evidence of a purposeful designation for public use, does not create a public forum.

Citing *Perry*, the Court explained that "control over access to a nonpublic forum can be based on subject matter and speaker identity so long as the distinctions drawn are reasonable in light of the purpose served by the forum and are viewpoint neutral." The Court held that the challenged limitation was reasonable because "the President could reasonably conclude" that (1) "a dollar directly spent on providing food or shelter to the needy is more beneficial than a dollar spent on litigation that might or might not result in aid to the needy"; (2) the participation of legal defense and political advocacy groups would generate controversy and thus "be detrimental to the Campaign and disruptive of the federal workplace"; and (3) the exclusion of legal defense and political advocacy groups would "avoid the reality and the appearance of government favoritism or entanglement with particular viewpoints." Justices Blackmun, Brennan, and Stevens dissented.

2. *Payroll deductions for union political activities*. Until 2003, public employees in Idaho could authorize both a payroll deduction for general union dues and a separate payroll deduction for union political activities. In 2003, the Idaho

legislature prohibited payroll deductions for political purposes. A group of Idaho public employee unions challenged the 2003 legislation on the ground that it violated the first amendment. In Ysursa v. Pocatello Education Association, 555 U.S. 353 (2009), the Court rejected this claim.

Chief Justice Roberts wrote the opinion of the Court: "Restrictions on speech based on its content are 'presumptively invalid' and subject to strict scrutiny. [But 'a] legislature's decision not to subsidize the exercise of a fundamental right does not infringe the right, and thus is not subject to strict scrutiny.' [The] State is not constitutionally obligated to provide payroll deductions at all. [While] publicly administered payroll deductions for political purposes can enhance the unions' exercise of First Amendment rights, Idaho is under no obligation to aid the unions in their political activities. And the State's decision not to do so is not an abridgment of the unions' speech. [Given] that the State has not infringed the unions' First Amendment rights, the State need only demonstrate a rational basis to justify the ban on political payroll deductions. [The] prohibition is [justified] by the State's interest in avoiding the reality or appearance of government favoritism or entanglement with partisan politics."

Justice Ginsburg filed a concurring opinion. Justices Stevens, Breyer, and Souter filed dissenting opinions. Would the outcome be different if the State prohibited payroll deductions to support the Democratic Party?

3. *Distinctions among political candidates.* The Arkansas Educational Television Commission is a state agency that owns and operates five noncommercial television stations in the Arkansas. In 1992, the AETC planned a series of debates between candidates for federal office. Given the time constraints of such debates, the AETC decided to limit participation "to the major party candidates or any other candidate who had strong popular support." Forbes, an independent candidate for Congress, had satisfied the Arkansas requirement that he obtain two thousand signatures to qualify him to appear on the ballot, but the AETC nonetheless refused to include him in the debates because he "had not generated appreciable voter support" and "was not regarded as a serious candidate by the press." It was undisputed that the AETC did not exclude Forbes because of any "disagreement with his views." Forbes claimed that his exclusion violated the first amendment.

In Arkansas Educational Television Commission v. Forbes, 523 U.S. 666 (1998) the Court, in an opinion by Justice Kennedy, rejected this claim. At the outset, the Court asked whether the debate was a designated public forum or a nonpublic forum:

> To create a [designated public forum], the government must intend to make the property 'generally available' to a class of speakers. [A] designated public forum is not created when the government allows selective access for individual speakers rather than general access for a class of speakers. [Citing *Perry*, *Cornelius*, and *Widmar*.] These cases illustrate the distinction between 'general access,' which indicates the property is a designated public forum, and 'selective access,' which indicates the property is a nonpublic forum. [By] recognizing the distinction, we encourage the government to open its property to some expressive activity in cases where, if faced with an all-or-nothing choice, it might not open the property at all.

Applying this analysis, the Court held that the "AETC debate was not a designated public forum":

> Here, the debate did not have an open-microphone format. [The] AETC did not make its debate generally available to candidates for [this congressional] seat.

Instead, just as the [government] in *Cornelius* reserved eligibility for participation in the CFC program to certain classes of voluntary agencies, AETC reserved eligibility for participation in the debate to candidates for [this congressional] seat (as opposed to some other seat). [Just] as the government in *Cornelius* made agency-by-agency determinations as to which of the eligible agencies would participate in the CFC, AETC made candidate-by-candidate determinations as to which of the eligible candidates would participate in the debate. "Such selective access, unsupported by evidence of a purposeful designation for public use, does not create a public forum." Thus the debate was a nonpublic forum.

Applying the standard for exclusions from a nonpublic forum, the Court concluded that the decision to exclude Forbes "because he had generated no appreciable public support" was constitutionally permissible because it was not "based on the speaker's viewpoint" and was "reasonable in light of the purpose of the property."

Justice Stevens, joined by Justices Souter and Ginsburg, dissented. Although agreeing with the general analysis of the Court, Justice Stevens objected that the broad "flexibility of AETC's purported standard" for excluding individual candidates gave it "nearly limitless discretion to exclude Forbes from the debate based on ad hoc justifications."

4. *Specialty license plates.* In Walker v. Texas Div., Sons of Confederate Veterans, Inc., 135 S. Ct. 2239 (2015), the Court, in a five-to-four decision written by Justice Breyer, held that Texas had not created a limited or nonpublic forum when it permitted private groups to submit proposals for specialty license plates. It upheld the refusal of the Texas Department of Motor Vehicles to approve a license plate featuring the Confederate battle flag on the ground that the plate constituted government, rather than private, speech. In the Court's view, the license plates were not a nonpublic forum because the state was "not simply managing government property, but instead is engaging in expressive conduct." It based this conclusion on the historical context, observers' reasonable interpretation of the messages conveyed by Texas specialty plates, and the "effective control that Texas exerted over the design selection process." Justice Alito, joined by Chief Justice Roberts and Justices Scalia and Kennedy, dissented.

5. *Distinctions among means of expression.* In United States v. Kokinda, supra, respondents, members of a political advocacy group, set up a table on a sidewalk near the entrance to a United States Post Office to distribute literature and solicit contributions. The sidewalk is located entirely on post office property and is the sole means by which customers travel from the parking lot to the post office building. Respondents were convicted of violating a regulation prohibiting any person from soliciting contributions on postal premises. The Court upheld the regulation as applied.

In a plurality opinion, Justice O'Connor, joined by Chief Justice Rehnquist and Justices White and Scalia, concluded that the sidewalk is not a "traditional" public forum because the "postal sidewalk at issue does not have the characteristics of public sidewalks traditionally open to expressive activity." Justice O'Connor then rejected the claim that the sidewalk, which was available for all conventional forms of expressive activity other than solicitation, was a "limited-purpose" public forum:

The Postal Service has not expressly dedicated its sidewalks to any expressive activity. [Although] individuals or groups have been permitted to leaflet, speak, and picket on postal premises, [the] practice of allowing some speech activities on postal property [does] not add up to the dedication of postal property to speech activities. ["The] government does not create a public forum by . . . *permitting* limited discourse, but only by intentionally opening a nontraditional forum for public discourse." [*Cornelius*]. [It] is anomalous [to suggest] that the Service's allowance of some avenues of speech would be relied upon as evidence that it is impermissibly suppressing other speech. If anything, the Service's generous accommodation of some types of speech testifies to its willingness to provide as broad a forum as possible, consistent with its postal mission. [Any other view] would create, in the name of the First Amendment, a disincentive for the Government to dedicate its property to any speech activities at all.

Justice Kennedy concurred in the result. Justice Brennan, joined by Justices Marshall, Blackmun, and Stevens, dissented. Would it be constitutional for the post office to permit only charities eligible to participate in the CFC to distribute literature on this sidewalk?

6. *Speaker-based restrictions.* Note that *Perry, Cornelius,* and *Forbes* involved "speaker-based" restrictions. Such restrictions, which treat some speakers differently than others, but define the distinction in terms other than content, do not fit neatly within the Court's content-based/content-neutral distinction. In these cases, the Court sharply distinguished speaker-based from viewpoint-based restrictions and, at least in the nonpublic forum context, tested speaker-based restrictions by a standard of reasonableness. But speaker-based restrictions often have clear viewpoint-differential effects. In *Perry,* for example, the challenged policy unquestionably favored some viewpoints over others, for recognized bargaining agents are likely to take consistent and predictable positions on particular issues. Indeed, in some instances, speaker-based restrictions may correlate almost perfectly with viewpoint. Consider, for example, laws granting special subsidies to veterans' organizations or denying tax deductions to individuals who contribute to the Communist Party. How should we deal with such restrictions? See Stone, Content Regulation and the First Amendment, 25 Wm. & Mary L. Rev. 189, 244–251 (1983).

7. *Evaluation.* Consider the Court's categorization of "quintessential," "limited," and "non" public forums. Do these categories make sense? Do you agree that the Court in *Perry* "indulged in a shell game, [throwing] out a circular definition of the public forum"? L. Tribe, Constitutional Choices 207 (1985). Consider the following views:

a. Subject matter classifications should be subjected to closer scrutiny in "quintessential" public forums than in "non" public forums for the same reasons that content-neutral restrictions are subjected to closer scrutiny in quintessential public forums.

b. Whether a particular public facility constitutes a "limited" public forum, rather than a "non" public forum, turns on the amount of speech government has allowed. If the government allows almost all speech, and excludes only a narrow category, as in *Widmar,* it has created a public forum. If it excludes almost all speech, and allows only a narrow category, as in *Lehman, Greer,* and *Perry,* it has not created a public forum.

c. "Classification of public places as various types of forums has only confused judicial opinions by diverting attention from the real first amendment [issues]. Like the fourth amendment, the first amendment 'protects people, not places.' Constitutional protection should depend not on labeling the speaker's physical location but on the first amendment values and governmental interests involved in the case." Farber and Nowak, The Misleading Nature of Public Forum Analysis: Content and Context in First Amendment Adjudication, 70 Va. L. Rev. 1219, 1234 (1984).

d. Contrary to the Court's doctrine, government should be permitted to impose viewpoint-based restrictions in non-public forums, such as "vanity license plates, ads on public transit vehicles, and public school classrooms used for after-school programs," at least insofar as it forbids "demeaning speech based on race and other characteristics that we protect in various ways through equality doctrine, either constitutional or statutory." This makes sense because when the government decides to permit speech in non-public forums, it is acting not as a censor but as a "participant" in "the speech market." In sum, "we should overcome" our concerns about viewpoint discrimination in such settings "because criminal and civil sanctions are not involved, and we want the state to provide space for a wide variety of private speech while permitting it to avoid fostering certain kinds of hateful messages." Greene, The Concept of the Speech Platform: Walker v. Texas Division, 68 Ala. L. Rev. 337 (2016).

Note: Religious Expression and the Meaning of "Viewpoint Neutrality"

1. *Viewpoint versus subject matter.* In Lamb's Chapel v. Moriches Union Free School District, supra, the Court considered the constitutionality of a school district rule that permitted after-school social, civic, and recreational uses of school property, but prohibited the use of such property for religious purposes. Applying this rule, the school district rejected Lamb's Chapel's request to show on school property religious-oriented films concerning family values and childrearing. The lower courts upheld the rule on the theory that the school property was "a limited public forum open only for designated purposes," and that access to such a forum "can be based on subject matter [so] long as the distinctions drawn are reasonable [and] viewpoint neutral." The Supreme Court accepted this analysis, but nonetheless invalidated the rule because it was not "viewpoint neutral."

In reaching this result, the Court rejected the lower courts' conclusion that the challenged rule was based on subject matter, rather than viewpoint, "because it [would] be applied in the same way to all uses of school property for religious purposes." Although conceding that "all religions and all uses for religious purposes are treated alike under the rule," the Court observed that this "does not answer the critical question" whether it constitutes discrimination "on the basis of viewpoint to permit the school property to be used for the presentation of all views about family issues [except] those dealing with the subject matter from a religious standpoint." The Court reasoned that the "film involved here [dealt] with a subject otherwise permissible under [the rule], and its exhibition was denied solely because the film dealt with the subject from a religious standpoint." The Court therefore concluded that the rule "violates the First Amendment" because it denied "access to a speaker solely to suppress the point of view he espouses on an otherwise included subject."

Consider Stone, The Equal Access Controversy: The Religion Clauses and the Meaning of "Neutrality," 81 Nw. U. L. Rev. 168, 169–170 (1986):

> The protection of political speech, like religious speech, lies at the very core of the first amendment. The Court often has recognized, however, that government may

grant special benefits to nonpolitical speech without extending those benefits to political speech, so long as it does not expressly favor any particular political viewpoint. [Citing *Lehman, Greer,* and *Cornelius.*] This is so because policies that disadvantage political speech as a class are less threatening to first amendment values than laws that expressly disadvantage specific points of view.

A similar principle [should govern] religious expression. As the Supreme Court has long recognized, the "clearest command" of the religion clauses is that "one religious denomination cannot be officially preferred over another." [Denominational] discrimination in the religious context is the analog of viewpoint discrimination in the political context. [The] corollary is also true, however. Governmental policies that grant special benefits to nonreligious expression as a class should be tested by the same — less demanding — standards that the Court uses to test the constitutionality of governmental policies that grant special benefits to nonpolitical expression as a class. In the religious, as in the political, realm the broader subject-matter classification is less threatening to core first amendment values.

2. Lamb's Chapel *revisited: further debate on the meaning of viewpoint neutrality.* In Rosenberger v. Rector and Visitors of University of Virginia, 515 U.S. 819 (1995), the Court, in a five-to-four decision, invalidated a University of Virginia policy authorizing payment from the Student Activities Fund for the printing costs of a variety of student publications, but prohibiting payment for any student publication that "primarily promotes or manifests a particular belief in or about a deity or an ultimate reality." The suit was brought by a student organization that was denied funding because it publishes a journal that "offers a Christian perspective on both personal and community issues," such as "racism, crisis pregnancy, [and] homosexuality."

The Court, in an opinion by Justice Kennedy, explained that, although the "necessities of confining a forum to the limited and legitimate purposes for which it was created may justify the State in reserving it for certain groups or for the discussion of certain topics," it may not "discriminate against speech on the basis of its viewpoint." The Court then observed that these "same principles apply" to the Student Activities Fund, which the Court described as a "forum," albeit "more in a metaphysical than in a spatial or geographic sense."

Acknowledging that the definition of viewpoint discrimination "is not a precise one," the Court nonetheless concluded that "here, as in *Lamb's Chapel,* viewpoint discrimination is the proper way to interpret the University's" policy. The Court explained that this was so because it was the religious "perspective" of the journal, rather than the "subjects discussed," such as racism, pregnancy or homosexuality, that resulted in the university's refusal to pay the journal's printing costs.

In dissent, Justice Souter, joined by Justices Stevens, Ginsburg, and Breyer, maintained that the "issue whether a distinction is based on viewpoint does not turn simply on whether a government regulation happens to be applied to a speaker who seeks to advance a particular viewpoint," but "on whether the burden on speech is explained by reference to viewpoint." Thus, citing *Lehman,* Justice Souter observed that "a municipality's decision to prohibit political advertising on bus placards" does not "amount to viewpoint discrimination when in the course of applying this policy it denies space to a person who wishes to speak in favor of a particular political candidate."

Justice Souter argued that it is the "element of taking sides in a public debate that identifies viewpoint discrimination and makes it the most pernicious of all distinctions based on content." Justice Souter reasoned that, given this understanding, there was "no viewpoint discrimination" in this case:

> If the [policy] were written [so] as to limit [only] Christian advocacy, [the] discrimination would be based on viewpoint. But that is not what the regulation authorizes; it applies to Muslim and Jewish and Buddhist advocacy as well as Christian. And since it limits funding to activities promoting or manifesting a particular belief not only "in" but "about" a deity or ultimate reality, it applies to agnostics and atheists as well as [to] deists and theists. [Thus, the policy does] not skew debate by funding one position but not its competitors. [It simply denies] funding for hortatory speech that "primarily promotes or manifests" any view on the merits of religion; [it denies] funding for the entire subject matter of religious apologetics.

Justice Souter therefore concluded that this case was distinguishable from *Lamb's Chapel*, where the "regulation did not purport to deny access to any speaker wishing to express a non-religious or expressly antireligious point of view." He concluded that, if the policy at issue in this case "amounts to viewpoint discrimination, the Court has all but eviscerated the line between viewpoint and content."

Recall the debate over a similar issue in R.A.V. v. City of St. Paul, section D8, supra. In light of the Court's reasoning in *Lamb's Chapel* and *Rosenberger*, does it follow that the regulation of "obscenity" is also impermissibly viewpoint-based "because it is justified by moral objections to the ideas or messages that sexual speech is said to convey"? Heins, Viewpoint Discrimination, 24 Hast. Const. L.Q. 99, 103 (1996).

3. *Religious speech as viewpoint discrimination: another look.* In Good News Club v. Milford Central School, 533 U.S. 98 (2001), the school district authorized district residents to use school buildings after school hours for "instruction in education, learning, or the arts" and for "social, civic, recreational, and entertainment uses pertaining to the community welfare," but not for "religious purposes." The school district denied a request by the Good News Club, a private Christian organization for children ages six to twelve, to use school property to "sing songs, hear Bible lessons, memorize scripture and pray" on the ground that this constituted "religious purposes."

The Court, in a six-to-three decision, held that this was unconstitutional viewpoint discrimination in a limited public forum. In his opinion for the Court, Justice Thomas explained that "the Club seeks to address a subject otherwise permitted under the rule, the teaching of morals and character, from a religious standpoint." He therefore concluded that this case was indistinguishable from *Lamb's Chapel* and *Rosenberger*.

In dissent, Justice Stevens argued that "speech for 'religious purposes' may reasonably be understood to encompass three different categories. First, there is religious speech that is simply speech about a particular topic from a religious point of view. [Second], there is religious speech that amounts to worship. [Third], there is [speech] that is aimed principally at proselytizing or inculcating a belief in a particular religious faith." In Justice Stevens's view, "the question is whether a school can [create] a limited public forum that admits the first type of religious speech without allowing the other two." He concluded that "just as a school may allow meetings to discuss current events from a political perspective without also allowing organized political recruitment, so too can a school allow discussion of topics such as moral development from a religious (or nonreligious) perspective without thereby opening its forum to religious proselytizing or worship."

In a separate dissenting opinion, Justice Souter, joined by Justice Ginsburg, argued that this case was distinguishable from *Lamb's Chapel* and *Rosenberger* because "Good News intends to use the public school premise not for the mere discussion of a subject from a particular, Christian point of view, but for an evangelical service of worship calling children to commit themselves in an act of Christian conversion." He maintained that the majority's position stands "for the remarkable proposition that any public school opened for civic meetings must be opened for use as a church, synagogue, or mosque."

In a concurring opinion, Justice Scalia responded to the dissenters: "The dissenters emphasize that the religious speech [of the Club is] 'aimed principally at proselytizing or inculcating belief in a particular religious faith. [But this] does not distinguish the Club's activities from those of [political, social, and cultural organizations that also] may seek to inculcate children with their beliefs [and try to] 'recruit others to join their respective groups.'"

CHRISTIAN LEGAL SOCIETY CHAPTER v. MARTINEZ, 561 U.S. 661 (2011). Hastings College of the Law, a public law school within the University of California system, extends official recognition to student groups through its "Registered Student Organization" (RSO) program. RSOs receive certain benefits, including the use of school funds, facilities, and channels of communication, as well as the use of Hastings' name and logo. In exchange for such recognition, RSOs must abide by certain conditions. All RSOs, for example, must comply with the school's Nondiscrimination Policy, which forbids discrimination on the basis of race, religion, gender, national origin, age, disability, ancestry, and sexual orientation. Hastings interprets this policy to mandate acceptance of *all* students.

In 2004, students at Hastings created the Christian Legal Society by affiliating with a national Christian association that charters student chapters at law schools throughout the country. These chapters must adopt bylaws that, *inter alia*, require members and officers to sign a "Statement of Faith" and to conduct their lives in accord with prescribed principles. CLS excludes from affiliation anyone who engages in "unrepentant homosexual conduct" or holds religious convictions different from those in the Statement of Faith. Hastings rejected CLS's application for RSO status on the ground that the group excluded students based on religion and sexual orientation. CLS filed this action asserting that Hastings' "accept all-comers" policy violates its First Amendment rights of expression and association.

The Court, in a five-to-four decision, rejected CLS's claim. Justice Ginsburg delivered the opinion of the Court: "[Hastings], through its RSO program, established a limited public forum. [See *Rosenberger*]. [The] Court has permitted restrictions on access to a limited public forum, like the RSO program here, [if they are] reasonable and viewpoint neutral. [We first] consider whether the Hastings' policy is reasonable. [With] appropriate regard for school administrators' judgment, we review the justifications Hastings offers in defense of its all-comers requirement. First, the open-access policy 'ensures that the leadership, educational, and social opportunities afforded by [RSOs] are available to all students. [Second], the all-comers requirement helps Hastings police the written terms of its Nondiscrimination Policy without inquiring into an RSO's motivation for membership restrictions. [Third], the Law School reasonably adheres to the view that an all-comers [policy] 'encourages tolerance, cooperation, and learning among students.' [Fourth], Hastings' policy [conveys] the Law School's decision 'to decline to subsidize with public monies and benefits [discriminatory conduct].' . . .

"The Law School's policy is all the more creditworthy in view of the substantial alternative channels that remain open for [CLS-student] communication to take place. [Student groups] commonly maintain a presence at universities without official school affiliation. Based on the record before us, CLS [hosted] a variety of activities the year after Hastings denied it recognition. [It bears emphasizing] that nonrecognition of a student organization is [not] equivalent to prohibiting its members from speaking. . . .

"CLS [assails] the reasonableness of the all-comers policy [by forecasting] that the policy will facilitate hostile takeovers; if organizations must open their arms to all, CLS contends, saboteurs will infiltrate groups to subvert their mission and message. This supposition strikes us as more hypothetical than real, [but if] students begin to exploit an all-comers policy by hijacking organizations to distort or destroy their missions, Hastings presumably would revisit and revise its policy. . . .

"We next consider whether Hastings' all-comers policy is viewpoint neutral. [It is] hard to imagine a more viewpoint-neutral policy than one requiring *all* student groups to accept *all* comers. [CLS] attacks the regulation by pointing to its effect: The policy is vulnerable to constitutional assault, CLS contends, because 'it systematically and predictably burdens most heavily those groups whose viewpoints are out of favor with the campus mainstream.' [This] argument stumbles from its first step because '[a] regulation that serves purposes unrelated to the content of expression is deemed neutral, even if it has an incidental effect on some speakers or messages but not others.' [Moreover,] Hastings' requirement that student groups accept all [comers] 'is justified without reference to the content [or viewpoint] of the regulated speech.' The Law School's policy aims at the *act* of rejecting would-be group members without reference to the reasons motivating that [behavior]. CLS' conduct — not its Christian perspective — is [what] stands between the group and RSO status. [Finding] Hastings' open-access condition on RSO status reasonable and viewpoint neutral, we reject CLS' free-speech and expressive-association claims."

Note that the Court decided the case on the basis of a stipulation by the parties that Hastings had interpreted and applied the Nondiscrimination Policy as an "accept all-comers" policy. Would it change the analysis if the Court had considered the constitutionality of the Nondiscrimination Policy itself — that is, as a policy denying RSO status to organizations discriminating on the basis of certain *particular* characteristics (that is, race, religion, gender, sexual orientation, etc.)?

Does it matter that this case involves a subsidy rather than a prohibition? Suppose, for example, the state made it unlawful for any group or organization to deny membership to any person. Would such a law be constitutional as applied to the Democratic Party, if it wants to exclude Republicans from voting in its upcoming primary? Would it be constitutional as applied to a synagogue that restricts membership only to Jews? Suppose that, instead of prohibiting such selective membership, the state merely denied tax-exempt status to any group or organization that isn't open to all comers?

Consider the Court's response to this question: "CLS, in seeking what is effectively a state subsidy, faces only indirect pressure to modify its membership policies; CLS may exclude any person for any reason if it forgoes the benefits of official recognition. [Our] decisions have distinguished between policies that require action and those that withhold benefits. [The] First Amendment shields CLS against state prohibition of the organization's expressive activity, [but] CLS enjoys no constitutional right to state subvention of its selectivity." Suppose Hastings denied RSO status only to student organizations that promote religion? On compelled association, see Section 5e2 infra.

Justice Alito, joined by Chief Justice Roberts and Justices Scalia and Thomas, dissented: "The proudest boast of our free speech jurisprudence is that we protect the freedom to express 'the thought that we hate.' Today's decision rests on a very different principle: no freedom for expression that offends prevailing standards of political correctness in our country's institutions of higher learning. [Hastings] currently has more than 60 registered groups and, in all its history, has denied registration to exactly one: the Christian Legal Society."

Justice Alito maintained that, for procedural reasons, the Nondiscrimination Policy rather than the accept-all-comers policy was properly at issue in the case, and he therefore proceeded to consider the constitutionality of that policy: "[Many RSOs at Hastings] are dedicated to expressing a message. For example, Silenced Right, a pro-life group, [teaches] that 'all human life [is] sacred and has inherent dignity,' while [the] American Constitution Society [seeks] 'to counter [a] narrow conservative vision' of American law.' [Under the Nondiscrimination Policy, such groups may exclude members who do not share the organization's views, without losing their RSO status, because discrimination of the basis of political, philosophical, cultural, or social viewpoints is not prohibited. The Nondiscrimination Policy] singled out one category of expressive associations for disfavored treatment: groups formed to express a religious message. Only religious groups were required to admit students who did not share their views. An environmentalist group was not required to admit students who rejected global warming. [But] CLS was required to admit avowed atheists. This was patent viewpoint discrimination. It is no wonder that the Court makes no attempt to defend the constitutionality of the Nondiscrimination Policy."

Although the Court found it unnecessary to consider the constitutionality of the Nondiscrimination Policy because of the parties' stipulation, Justice Stevens filed a separate concurring opinion responding to Justice Alito: "In the dissent's view, by refusing to grant CLS an exemption from the Nondiscrimination Policy, Hastings violated CLS's rights, for by proscribing unlawful discrimination on the basis of religion, the policy discriminated unlawfully on the basis of religion. [But] the Nondiscrimination Policy is content and viewpoint neutral. It does not reflect a judgment by school officials about any student group's speech. [Indeed], it does not regulate expression or belief at all. [What] the policy does reflect is a judgment that discrimination [on] the basis of certain factors, such as race and religion, is less tolerable than discrimination on the basis of other factors."

Justice Alito responded to this argument: "Justice Stevens [argues] that the Nondiscrimination Policy is viewpoint neutral because it 'does not regulate expression or belief at all' but instead regulates conduct. This Court has held, however, that the particular conduct at issue here constitutes a form of expression that is protected by the First Amendment. It is [well] established that the First Amendment shields the right of a group to engage in expressive association by limiting membership to persons whose admission does not significantly interfere with the group's ability to convey its views. [Citing *Boy Scouts v. Dale*, section E5 infra.] [Moreover, the Nondiscrimination Policy] also discriminates on the basis of viewpoint regarding sexual morality. CLS has a particular viewpoint on this subject, namely, that sexual conduct outside marriage [is] wrongful. Hastings would not allow CLS to express this viewpoint by limiting membership to persons willing to express a sincere agreement with CLS's views. By contrast, [a] Free Love Club could require members to affirm that they reject the traditional view of sexual morality to which CLS adheres. It is hard to see how this can be viewed as anything other than viewpoint discrimination."

Justice Alito then turned to the "accept-all-comers" version of the Hastings policy: "There can be no dispute that [the first amendment] would not permit a generally applicable law mandating that private religious groups admit members who do not share the group's beliefs. Religious groups like CLS obviously engage in expressive association, and no legitimate state interest could override the powerful effect that an accept-all-comers law would have on the ability of religious groups to express their views. The State of California surely could not demand that all Christian groups admit members who believe that Jesus was merely human. [Muslim] groups could not be forced to admit person who are viewed as slandering Islam. [But] the Court now holds that Hastings [may] impose these very same requirements on students who wish to [gain the benefits of RSO status]. The Court lists four justifications offered by Hastings in defense of the accept-all-comers policy, [but these justifications] are insufficient. [Moreover], statements in the majority opinion make it seem as if the denial of registration did not hurt CLS at all. [Beyond that, though, the] majority's emphasis on CLS's ability to endure [by] using private facilities and means of communication [is] quite amazing. This Court does not customarily brush aside a claim of unlawful discrimination with the observation that the effects of the discrimination were really not so bad. . . .

"The Court is also wrong in holding that the accept-all-comers policy is viewpoint neutral. The Court proclaims that it would be 'hard to imagine a more viewpoint-neutral policy,' but I would not be so quick to jump to this conclusion. Even if it is assumed that the policy is viewpoint neutral on its face, there is strong evidence in the record that the policy was announced as a pretext. The adoption of a facially neutral policy for the purpose of suppressing the expression of a particular viewpoint is viewpoint discrimination. Here, CLS has made a strong showing that Hastings's sudden adoption [of] its accept-all-comers policy was a pretext for the law school's unlawful denial of CLS's registration application under the Nondiscrimination Policy. . . .

"I do not think it is an exaggeration to say that today's decision is a serious setback for freedom of expression in this country. [I] can only hope this decision will turn out to be an aberration."

REED v. TOWN OF GILBERT, 135 S. Ct. 2218 (2015). The Court in *Mosley* held that even subject-matter restrictions in public forums must be subjected to heightened scrutiny because they distinguish among speakers on the basis of the content of their expression. In subsequent decisions, the Court made clear that a less demanding standard of review applies to subject-matter restrictions in nonpublic forums. What rule should apply to subject-matter restrictions that regulate speech on private property? The Court addressed the private property issue in *Reed v. Town of Gilbert*. The Town of Gilbert comprehensively regulated signs displayed on private property in ways that made distinctions between different types of signs. For example, "temporary directional signs" could be no larger than six square feet and could be in place for no longer than twelve hours before the event and one hour afterward, while "political signs" could be up to thirty-two square feet and could be displayed up to sixty days before a primary election and up to fifteen days following a general election. In total, the regulations imposed different rules for twenty-three categories of signs.

Applying this regulation, the Good News Community Church was cited for exceeding the permissible time limit for a sign displaying the time and location of an upcoming service. What standard of review should apply in such a case? Should this regulation be tested by the same standard of review as a law that distinguished between signs on the basis of viewpoint (distinguishing, for example, between the permissible size of anti-war and pro-war signs), or should it be tested by some less demanding standard?

The Court, in an opinion by Justice Thomas, held the challenged ordinance unconstitutional. Invoking *Mosley*, Thomas declared that because the Town's code was "content based on its face" it must be subjected to "strict scrutiny," explaining that although "this type of ordinance may seem like a perfectly rational way to regulate signs, . . . a clear and firm rule governing content neutrality is an essential means of protecting the freedom of speech." Thomas conceded that "government discrimination among viewpoints" may be the most "blatant and egregious form of content discrimination," but he insisted that "the First Amendment's hostility to content-based regulations extends not only to restrictions on particular viewpoints, but also to prohibition of public discussion of an entire topic." Thus, Thomas concluded, because the challenged ordinance "singles out specific subject matter for differential treatment, even if it does not target viewpoints within that subject matter," it must be tested by strict scrutiny, "which requires the Government to prove that the restriction furthers a compelling interest and is narrowly tailored to achieve that interest."

Does it make sense to treat all content-based restrictions in the same way that viewpoint-based restrictions are treated? What are the costs and benefits of such an approach? Although concurring in the result because the particular distinctions drawn by the ordinance could not pass "even the laugh test," Justice Kagan, joined by Justices Ginsburg and Breyer, emphatically disagreed with the Court's analysis. Indeed, she noted, given the Court's approach many perfectly sensible "sign ordinances [are] now in jeopardy." The courts, she noted, will now "have to determine that a town has a compelling interest in informing passersby where George Washington slept. And likewise, courts [will] have to find that a town has no way to prevent hidden-driveway mishaps than by specially treating hidden-driveway signs. [The] consequence — unless courts water down strict scrutiny to something unrecognizable — is that our communities will find themselves in an unenviable bind: They will have to either repeal the exemptions that allow for helpful signs on streets and sidewalks, or else lift their sign restrictions altogether and resign themselves to the resulting clutter."

In a separate concurring opinion, Justice Breyer also rejected the majority's reasoning. He maintained that although it makes sense to use strict scrutiny to evaluate the constitutionality of laws that discriminate on the basis of viewpoint or that restrict speech on the basis of content in "a traditional public form," it makes no sense to hold that content discrimination *always* triggers strict scrutiny. Such a rule, he observed, would require the Court to invalidate a broad range of perfectly sensible content-based regulations, including, for examples, regulations of "securities," of "energy conservation labeling-practices," of "prescription-drugs," of "doctor-patient confidentiality," of "signs at petting zoos," and so on. Breyer warned that the likely outcome of the Court's approach will be the "watering down" of "strict scrutiny" in order to reach sensible results in such cases, with the dangerous consequence of weakening "the First Amendment's protection in instances where 'strict scrutiny' should apply in full force."

For an especially thoughtful analysis of this puzzle, see Lakier, Reed v. Town of Gilbert, Arizona, and the Rise of the Anticlassificatory First Amendment, 2016 Sup. Ct. Rev. 233. See also Armijo, Reed v. Town of Gilbert, Relax, Everybody, 58 B.C. L. Rev. 65 (2017).

d.   Unequal Access and the Problem of Government Speech

To what extent, if any, should the principles and doctrines that govern access to public parks, airport terminals, and military bases also govern public auditoriums, school libraries, and government-funded programs to support the arts? To what extent may the government itself engage in speech? When the government speaks, must it do so in an even-handed manner?

Consider Matal v. Tam, 582 U.S. — (2017): "'[The] Free Speech Clause . . . does not regulate government speech.' ['The] First Amendment forbids the government to regulate speech in ways that favor some viewpoints or ideas at the expense of others,' [but] imposing a requiring of viewpoint neutrality on government speech would be paralyzing. [Here] is a simply example. During the Second World War, the Federal Government produced and distributed millions of posters to promote the war effort. [These] posters expressed a viewpoint, but the First Amendment did not demand that the Government balance the message on these posters by producing and distributing posters [opposing the war effort.]" What are limits of this doctrine?

SOUTHEASTERN PROMOTIONS v. CONRAD, 420 U.S. 546 (1975). Petitioner, a promoter of theatrical productions, applied to a municipal board charged with managing a city auditorium and a city-leased theater to present the musical Hair at the theater. Although no conflicting engagement was scheduled, the board, based on reports that the musical was sexually explicit, involved nudity, and might be "obscene," rejected the application because the production would not be "in the best interest of the community." The Court held that this action constituted an unconstitutional prior restraint. Justice Blackmun, speaking for the Court, explained:

"The elements of prior restraint [were] clearly present in the system by which [the] board regulated the use of its theaters. One seeking to use a theater was required to apply to the board. The board was empowered to determine whether the applicant should be granted permission — in effect, a license or permit — on the basis of its review of the content of the proposed production. [The board's] action was no less a prior restraint because the public facilities under [its] control happened to be municipal theaters. The Memorial Auditorium and the [city-leased theater] were public forums designed for and dedicated to expressive activities. [Thus, in] order to be held lawful, [the board's] action [must] have been accomplished with procedural safeguards that reduce the danger of suppressing constitutionally protected speech. [We] held in [Freedman v. Maryland, section C2 supra], that a system of prior restraint runs afoul of the First Amendment if it lacks certain safeguards. [Such] safeguards were lacking here."

Justice Douglas dissented in part and concurred in the result in part: "The critical flaw in this case lies, not in the absence of procedural safeguards, but rather in the very nature of the content screening in which respondents have engaged. [A] municipal theater is no less a forum for the expression of ideas than is a public park, or a sidewalk. [As] soon as municipal officials are permitted to pick and choose [between] those productions which are 'clean and healthful and culturally uplifting' in content and those which are not, the path is cleared for a regime of censorship under which full voice can be given only to those views which meet with the approval of the powers that be."

Justice White, joined by Chief Justice Burger, dissented: "[The District Court described] the play as involving not only nudity but repeated 'simulated acts of anal intercourse, frontal intercourse, heterosexual intercourse, homosexual intercourse, and group intercourse.' Given this description of 'Hair,' the First Amendment in my view does not compel municipal authorities to permit production of the play in municipal facilities. Whether or not a production as described by the District Court is obscene and may be forbidden to adult audiences, it is apparent to me that the [State] could constitutionally forbid exhibition of the musical to children, [Ginsberg v. New York, section D5, supra], and that [the city] may reserve its auditorium for productions suitable for exhibition to all citizens of the city, adults and children alike."

Justice Rehnquist also dissented: "[Until] this case the Court has not equated a public auditorium, which must of necessity schedule performances by a process of inclusion and exclusion, with public streets and parks. [Moreover, here] we deal with municipal [action], not prohibiting or penalizing the expression of views in dramatic form [in privately owned theaters], but rather managing its municipal auditorium. [If] it is the desire of the citizens of [the city], who presumably have paid for and own the facilities, that the attractions to be shown there should not be of the kind which would offend any substantial number of potential theatergoers, I do not think the policy can be described as arbitrary or unreasonable. [May] an opera house limit its production to operas, or must it also show rock musicals? May a municipal theater devote an entire season to Shakespeare, or is it required to book any potential producer on a first come, first served basis?"

What substantive standards should govern the use of municipal auditoriums? Consider Shiffrin, Government Speech, 27 UCLA L. Rev. 565, 584 (1980): "*Conrad* does not appreciate the complicated relationships between public forum doctrine and government interests in speech. *Conrad* supposes that the government could not choose between competing applicants on a content basis. Yet such a supposition denies any legitimate government speech interest." What is the city's "speech interest" in *Conrad*? May the city limit use of the auditorium to the presentation of Shakespeare? To "family" productions? To "competently performed" productions?

Suppose a city allocates $50,000 per year to "promote the arts." What factors may it consider in awarding its grants? Consider the following statute, which was proposed by Senator Jesse Helms in 1990:

None of the funds authorized to be appropriated pursuant to this Act may be used by [the National Endowment for the Arts] to promote, disseminate, or produce —

- obscene or indecent material, including but not limited to depictions of sadomasochism, homo-eroticism, the exploitation of children, or individuals engaged in sex acts; or

- material which denigrates the objects or beliefs of the adherents of a particular religion or non-religion; or
- material which denigrates, debases, or reviles a person, group, or class of citizens on the basis of race, creed, sex, handicap, age, or national origin.

Are government subsidies of expression less problematic than government restrictions? Is the ordinance in *Mosley* a subsidy or a restriction?

BOARD OF EDUCATION, ISLAND TREES UNION FREE SCHOOL DISTRICT v. PICO, 457 U.S. 853 (1982). In 1975, several members of the petitioner Board of Education attended a conference sponsored by a politically conservative organization at which they obtained lists of books described as "objectionable" and as "improper fare for school students." Thereafter, the board removed eleven of the listed books from the district's school libraries "so that Board members could read them." In a press release justifying this action, the board characterized the books as "anti-American, anti-Christian, anti-Semitic, and just plain filthy." Among the books removed were Slaughterhouse Five, by Kurt Vonnegut, Jr.; The Naked Ape, by Desmond Morris; Best Short Stories of Negro Writers, edited by Langston Hughes; Soul on Ice, by Eldridge Cleaver; and Go Ask Alice, of anonymous authorship. The board appointed a Book Review Committee, consisting of parents and teachers, to recommend whether the books should be retained. Although the committee recommended that most of the books should be retained, the board decided to remove nine of the books and to make one other available subject to parental approval. Respondents, students in the Island Trees school system, brought this action claiming that the board's decision violated the first amendment. The district court, finding that the board acted not on religious or political principles, but "on its belief that the [books] were irrelevant, vulgar, immoral, and in bad taste," granted summary judgment to the board. The court of appeals reversed and remanded for a trial on the merits. The Supreme Court affirmed. Justice Brennan delivered an opinion joined by Justices Marshall and Stevens and joined in part by Justice Blackmun:

"[Although petitioners] rightly possess significant discretion to determine the content of their school [libraries, that] discretion may not be exercised in a narrowly partisan or political manner. If a Democratic school board, motivated by party affiliation, ordered the removal of all books written by or in favor of Republicans, few would doubt that the order violated the [first amendment]. The same conclusion would surely apply if an all-white school board, motivated by racial animus, decided to remove all books authored by blacks or advocating racial equality and integration. Our Constitution does not permit the official suppression of *ideas*. Thus, whether petitioners' removal of the books from their school libraries [violated the first amendment] depends upon the motivation behind petitioners' actions. If petitioners *intended* by their removal decision to deny respondents access to ideas with which petitioners disagreed, and if this intent was the decisive factor in petitioners' decision, then petitioners have exercised their discretion in violation of the Constitution. On the other hand, [an] unconstitutional motivation would *not* be demonstrated if it were shown that petitioners had decided to remove the books at issue because those books were pervasively vulgar [or educationally unsuitable. Such motivations] would not carry the danger of an official suppression of ideas, and thus would not violate respondents' First Amendment rights." Justices White and Blackmun filed concurring opinions.

Justice Rehnquist, joined by Chief Justice Burger and Justice Powell, filed a dissenting opinion: "[When the government] acts as an educator, at least at the elementary and secondary school level, [it] is engaged in inculcating social values and knowledge in relatively impressionable young people. Obviously there are innumerable decisions to be made as to what courses should be taught, what books should be purchased, or what teachers should be employed. [In my view,] it is 'permissible and appropriate for local boards to make educational decisions based upon their personal, social, political and moral views.' [Actions] by the government as educator do not raise the same First Amendment concerns as actions by the government as sovereign." Chief Justice Burger and Justices Powell and O'Connor also filed dissenting opinions.

Do you agree with the plurality that a school board cannot constitutionally remove books "simply because they dislike the ideas" espoused? Consider Justice Powell's evaluation, set forth in his *Pico* dissent: "[Under the plurality's approach, books] may not be removed because they are indecent; extoll violence, intolerance and racism; or degrade the dignity of the individual. [I] would not require a school board to promote ideas and values repugnant to a democratic society."

Suppose a school or public library has computer terminals to connect users to the internet. To what extent, and in what circumstances, may the library use filters to prevent students or library patrons from accessing "inappropriate" material?

Consider United States v. American Library Association, 539 U.S. 194 (2003): Two federal programs provided funds to public libraries to help them expand access to the internet. The Children's Internet Protection Act (CIPA), however, forbade public libraries to receive federal funds under these programs unless they installed software to block obscenity and child pornography and to prevent minors from accessing material that is "harmful to minors." A group of libraries, library patrons, and Web site publishers brought suit challenging CIPA's filtering provisions. The lower federal court held CIPA unconstitutional, but the Supreme Court reversed.

Chief Justice Rehnquist, joined by Justices O'Connor, Scalia, and Thomas, authored a plurality opinion: "Congress has wide latitude to attach conditions to the receipt of federal assistance in order to further its policy objectives. But Congress may not 'induce' the recipient 'to engage in activities that would themselves be unconstitutional.' To determine whether libraries would violate the First Amendment by employing the filtering software that CIPA requires, we must [examine] the role of libraries in our society. Public libraries pursue the worthy missions of facilitating learning and cultural enrichment. [To] fulfill [these] missions, public libraries must have broad discretion to decide what material to provide to their patrons. Although they seek to provide a wide array of information, their goal has never been to provide 'universal coverage.' Instead, public libraries seek to provide materials 'that would be of the greatest direct benefit or interest to the community.' To this end, libraries collect only those materials deemed to have 'requisite and appropriate quality.' [Most] libraries already exclude pornography from their print collections because they deem it inappropriate for inclusion. We do not subject these decisions to heightened scrutiny; it would make little sense to treat libraries' judgments to block online pornography any differently, when these judgments are made for just the same reason. . . .

"Appellees urge us to affirm the District Court's judgment on [the] ground that CIPA imposes an unconstitutional condition on the receipt of federal assistance. Under this doctrine, 'the government may not deny a benefit to a person on a basis that infringes his constitutionally protected . . . freedom of speech even if he has no entitlement to that benefit.' Appellees argue that CIPA imposes an unconstitutional condition on libraries that receive [federal] subsidies by requiring them, as a condition on their receipt of federal funds, to surrender their First Amendment right to provide the public with access to constitutionally protected speech. . . .

"Within broad limits, 'when the Government appropriates public funds to establish a program it is entitled to define the limits of that program.' [Citing *Rust.*] The [internet subsidy] programs were intended to help public libraries fulfill their traditional role of obtaining material of requisite and appropriate quality for educational and informational purposes. Congress may certainly insist that these 'public funds be spent for the purposes for which they were authorized.' Especially because public libraries have traditionally excluded pornographic material from their other collections, Congress could reasonably impose a parallel limitation on its Internet assistance programs. As the use of filtering software helps to carry out these programs, it is a permissible condition under *Rust.* [CIPA does not prohibit public libraries from providing computers to adult patrons that enable them to access material that is obscene for minors, it] simply reflects Congress' decision not to subsidize their doing so. ['A] refusal to fund protected activity, without more, cannot be equated with the imposition of a "penalty" on that activity.'" [Quoting *Rust.*] Justices Kennedy and Breyer filed concurring opinions. Justices Stevens, Souter, and Ginsburg dissented.

REGAN v. TAXATION WITH REPRESENTATION OF WASHINGTON, 461 U.S. 540 (1983). In a unanimous decision, the Court upheld a federal statute providing that contributions to an otherwise tax-exempt organization, other than a tax-exempt veterans' organization, are not tax deductible if a substantial part of the organization's activities consists of attempts to influence legislation. Justice Rehnquist delivered the opinion of the Court:

"Congress is not required by the First Amendment to subsidize lobbying. [Respondent contends, however, that the challenged provision is unconstitutional because of its distinction between veterans' and other tax-exempt organizations. We do not agree.] The case would be different if Congress were to discriminate invidiously in its subsidies in such a way as to '"aim[] at the suppression of dangerous ideas."' [But] veterans' organizations [receive] tax-deductible contributions regardless of the content of [their speech]. We find no indication that the statute was intended to suppress any ideas or any demonstration that it has had that effect. . . .

"It [is] not irrational for Congress to decide that, even though it will not subsidize substantial lobbying by charities generally, it will subsidize lobbying by veterans' organizations. Veterans have [made a unique contribution to the nation]. Our country has a long standing policy of compensating veterans for [this contribution] by providing them with numerous advantages. This policy has 'always been deemed to be legitimate.'"

Justice Blackmun, joined by Justices Brennan and Marshall, filed a concurring opinion: "Because [the] discrimination between veterans' organizations and charitable organizations is not based on the content of their speech, [it] does not deny charitable organizations equal protection of the law. [As] the Court says, a statute designed to discourage the expression of particular views would present a very different question."

Consider the following: (a) "No organization, other than a veterans' organization, may demonstrate on a military base." (b) "Contributions to an otherwise tax-exempt organization are not deductible if the organization engages in substantial lobbying activities, unless those activities concern the subject of abortion." (c) "Contributions to an otherwise tax-exempt organization are not deductible if the organization advocates the violent overthrow of government."

In FCC v. League of Women Voters, 468 U.S. 364 (1984), the Court invalidated section 399 of the Public Broadcasting Act of 1967, which prohibited any noncommercial educational station that receives a grant from the Corporation for Public Broadcasting to "engage in editorializing." The Court distinguished *Taxation with Representation* on the ground that, under the statute at issue in *Taxation with Representation*, "a charitable organization could create [an] affiliate to conduct its non-lobbying activities using tax-deductible contributions, and, at the same time, establish [a] separate affiliate to pursue its lobbying efforts without such contributions," whereas in *League of Women Voters* "a noncommercial educational station that receives [even] 1% of its overall income from [the CPB] is barred absolutely from all editorializing." Thus, in *Taxation with Representation* the law prevented only the use of *government funds* for lobbying, whereas in *League of Women Voters* the law prohibited any station that accepted government funds from editorializing, whether or not the editorializing was paid for with government funds.

NATIONAL ENDOWMENT FOR THE ARTS v. FINLEY, 524 U.S. 569 (1998). Since its creation by Congress in 1965, the NEA has made more than 100,000 grants, totaling some three billion dollars, to promote "public knowledge, education, understanding and appreciation of the arts." In 1989, two provocative works that were supported by NEA grants — a series of homoerotic photographs by Robert Mapplethorpe and a photograph by Andres Serrano that depicted a crucifix immersed in urine ("Piss Christ") — prompted a public controversy that led to a congressional reevaluation of the NEA's funding priorities and procedures. Senator Jesse Helms (R-North Carolina), for example, declared that public funding for such "art" was "an insult to taxpayers," who "have a right not to be denigrated, offended, or mocked with their own tax dollars." In light of those controversies, in 1990 Congress enacted section 954(d)(1), which directs the NEA, in establishing procedures to judge the artistic merit of grant applications, to "tak[e] into consideration general standards of decency and respect for the diverse beliefs and values of the American public." In implementing this provision, the NEA concluded that it was not required to do anything more than ensure that its peer review panels were constituted in such a way as to represent geographic, ethnic, and aesthetic diversity. Invoking that provision, the NEA denied a grant to support the work of the performance artist Karen Finley, who "was well known in the late 1980s for her use of food, nudity, music, and discourse on stage to address such issues as incest, rape, domination, the sexualization of women, violence, and AIDS." See G. Stone, Sex and the Constitution 337–339 (2017).

The Court, in an opinion by Justice O'Connor, held that section 954(d)(1) is not unconstitutional "on its face": "Respondents argue that the provision is a paradigmatic example of viewpoint discrimination. [But the challenged provision merely] adds 'considerations' to the grant-making process; it does not preclude awards to projects that might be deemed 'indecent' or 'disrespectful,' [or] even specify that those factors be given any particular weight in reviewing an application. . . .

"[Moreover], the considerations that the provision introduces [do] not engender the kind of directed viewpoint discrimination that would prompt this Court to invalidate a statute on its face. [The considerations enumerated in section 954(d)(1) are] susceptible to multiple interpretations, [and particularly because the NEA considers grant applications through the decisions of many diverse review panels], the provision does not introduce considerations that, in practice, would effectively preclude or punish the expression of particular views."

Although acknowledging that the provision could conceivably be applied in ways that could violate the first amendment, the Court was "reluctant . . . to invalidate legislation 'on the basis of its hypothetical application to situations not before the Court,'" particularly where, as here, there are numerous "constitutional applications" for both the "decency" and "respect" criteria. For example, "educational programs are central to the NEA's mission," and "it is well-established that 'decency' is a permissible factor where 'educational suitability' motivates its consideration. [Citing *Pico.*]" And "permissible applications of the mandate to consider 'respect for the diverse beliefs and values of the American public' are also apparent, [for the] agency expressly takes diversity into account, giving special consideration to 'projects and productions . . . that reach, or reflect the culture of, a minority, inner city, rural, or tribal community.'"

The Court was unpersuaded that "the language of §954(d)(1) itself will give rise to the suppression of protected expression": "Any content-based considerations that may be taken into account in the grant-making process are a consequence of the nature of arts funding. The NEA has limited resources and it must deny the majority of the grant applications that it receives, including many that propose 'artistically excellent' projects. The agency may decide to fund particular projects for a wide variety of reasons, 'such as the technical proficiency of the artist, the creativity of the work, the anticipated public interest in or appreciation of the work, the work's contemporary relevance, its educational value, its suitability for or appeal to special audiences (such as children or the disabled), its service to a rural or isolated community, or even simply that the work could increase public knowledge of an art form.' [The] very 'assumption' of the NEA is [that] absolute neutrality is simply 'inconceivable.'"

The Court therefore distinguished its decision in *Rosenberger* on the ground that, in "the context of arts funding, in contrast to many other subsidies, the Government does not indiscriminately 'encourage a diversity of views from private speakers.' The NEA's mandate is to make aesthetic judgments, and the inherently content-based 'excellence' threshold for NEA support sets it apart from the subsidy issue in *Rosenberger* — which was available to all student organizations that were 'related to the educational purpose of the University' — and from comparably objective decisions on allocating public benefits, such as access to a school auditorium or a municipal theater [citing *Lamb's Chapel* and *Southeastern Promotions*]."

The Court emphasized that "we have no occasion here to address an as-applied challenge in a situation where the denial of a grant may be shown to be the product of invidious viewpoint discrimination. If the NEA were to leverage its power to award subsidies on the basis of subjective criteria into a penalty on disfavored viewpoints, then we would confront a different case. [Even] in the provision of subsidies, the Government may not 'ai[m] at the suppression of dangerous ideas,' and if a subsidy were 'manipulated' to have a 'coercive effect,' then relief could be appropriate. In addition, as the NEA itself concedes, a more pressing constitutional question would arise if government funding resulted in the imposition of a disproportionate burden calculated to drive 'certain ideas or viewpoints from the marketplace.'"

Justice Scalia, joined by Justice Thomas, concurred in the result: "[Under the challenged provision, to] the extent a particular applicant exhibits disrespect for the diverse beliefs and values of the American public or fails to comport with general standards of decency, the likelihood that he will receive a grant diminishes. [This] unquestionably constitutes viewpoint discrimination. That conclusion is not altered by the fact that the statute does not 'compel' the denial of funding, any more than a provision imposing a five-point handicap on all black applicants for civil service jobs is saved from being race discrimination by the fact that it does not compel the rejection of black applicants. . . .

"[The challenged provision does] not *abridge* the speech of those who disdain the beliefs and values of the American public, nor [does] it *abridge* indecent speech. Those who wish to create indecent and disrespectful art are as unconstrained now as they were before the enactment of this statute. [They] are merely deprived of the [satisfaction] of having the [public] taxed to pay for it. It is preposterous to equate the denial of taxpayer subsidy with measures 'aimed at the *suppression* of dangerous ideas.' 'The reason that denial of participation in a tax exemption or other subsidy scheme does not necessarily "infringe" a fundamental right is that — unlike direct restriction or prohibition — such a denial does not, as a general rule, have any significant coercive effect.' . . ."

Justice Souter dissented: "The decency and respect proviso mandates viewpoint-based decisions in the disbursement of government subsidies, and the Government has wholly failed to explain why the statute should be afforded an exemption from the fundamental rule of the First Amendment that viewpoint discrimination in the exercise of public authority over expressive activity is unconstitutional. ['If] there is a bedrock principle underlying the First Amendment, it is that the government may not prohibit the expression of an idea simply because society finds the idea itself offensive or disagreeable.' [Because] this principle applies not only to affirmative suppression of speech, but also to disqualification for government favors, Congress is generally not permitted to pivot discrimination against otherwise protected speech on the offensiveness or unacceptability of the views it expresses. [Citing *Rosenberger* and *Lamb's Chapel.*] One need do nothing more than read the text of [this] statute to conclude that Congress's purpose in imposing the decency and respect criteria was to prevent the funding of art that conveys an offensive message; the [provision] on its face is quintessentially viewpoint-based, [for] it penalizes [art] that disrespects the ideology, opinions, or convictions of a significant segment of the American [public, but not] art that reinforces those values. . . .

"[Another] basic strand in the Court's [analysis], and the heart of Justice Scalia's, in effect assumes that whether or not the statute mandates viewpoint discrimination, [government] art subsidies fall within a zone of activity free from

First Amendment restraints. [This argument] calls attention to the roles of government-as-speaker and government-as-buyer, in which the government is of course entitled to engage in viewpoint discrimination: if the Food and Drug Administration launches an advertising campaign on the subject of smoking, it may condemn the habit without also having to show a cowboy taking a puff on the opposite page; and if the Secretary of Defense wishes to buy a portrait to decorate the Pentagon, he is free to prefer George Washington over George the Third.

"[But the government] neither speaks through the expression subsidized by the NEA, nor buys anything itself with NEA grants. On the contrary, [in this context] the government acts as a patron, financially underwriting the production of art by private artists [for] independent consumption. [And] outside of the contexts of government-as-buyer and government-as-speaker, we have held time and again that Congress may not 'discriminate invidiously in its subsidies in such a way as to aim at the suppression of ideas.' [As we held in *Rosenberger*, when] the government acts as patron, subsidizing the expression of others, it may not prefer one lawfully stated view over another. [The Court attempts] to distinguish *Rosenberger* on the ground that the student activities funds in that case were generally available to most applicants, whereas NEA funds are disbursed selectively and competitively to a choice few. But the Court in *Rosenberger* [specifically] rejected just this distinction when it held [that] '[t]he government cannot justify viewpoint discrimination among private speakers on the economic fact of scarcity.' Scarce money demands choices, of course, but choices 'on some acceptable [viewpoint] neutral principle,' like artistic excellence; 'nothing in our decision[s] indicates that scarcity would give the State the right to exercise viewpoint discrimination that is otherwise impermissible.'"

RUST v. SULLIVAN, 500 U.S. 173 (1991). Title X of the Public Health Service Act, enacted in 1970, provides that none of the federal funds appropriated under the act for family planning services "shall be used in programs where abortion is a method of family planning." In 1988, respondent, the Secretary of Health and Human Services, issued new regulations attaching three conditions on the grant of federal funds for title X projects. First, a "[title] X project may not provide counseling concerning the use of abortion or provide referral for abortion as a method of family planning," even upon request. Second, a title X project may not engage in activities that "encourage, promote or advocate abortion as a method of family planning." Forbidden activities include lobbying for legislation and disseminating materials, providing speakers, and using legal action to increase the availability of abortion. Third, title X projects must be organized so that they are "physically and financially separate" from prohibited abortion activities.

Petitioners, title X grantees and doctors suing on behalf of themselves and their patients, challenged these regulations. The Court, in a five-to-four decision, upheld the regulations. Chief Justice Rehnquist delivered the opinion of the Court:

"Petitioners contend that the regulations violate the first amendment by impermissibly discriminating based on viewpoint because they prohibit 'all discussion about abortion as a lawful option — including counseling, referral, and the provision of neutral and accurate information about ending a pregnancy — while compelling the clinic or counselor to provide information that promotes continuing a pregnancy to term.' [In] Maher v. Roe, [432 U.S. 464 (1977)], we upheld a state welfare regulation under which Medicaid recipients received payments for services related to childbirth, but not for nontherapeutic abortions. The Court rejected the claim that this unequal subsidization worked a violation of the Constitution. We held that the government may 'make a value judgment favoring childbirth over abortion, and . . . implement that judgment by the allocation of public funds.' Here the Government is exercising the authority it possesses under *Maher* [to] subsidize family planning services [while] declining to 'promote or encourage abortion.' The Government can, without violating the Constitution, selectively fund a program to encourage certain activities it believes to be in the public interest, without at the same time funding an alternate program which seeks to deal with the problem in another way. In so doing, the Government has not discriminated on the basis of viewpoint; it has merely chosen to fund one activity to the exclusion of the other. '[A governmental] decision not to subsidize the exercise of a fundamental right does not infringe that right.' [Quoting *Taxation with Representation.*] The challenged regulations [are] designed to ensure that the limits of the federal program are observed. [This] is not a case of the Government 'suppressing a dangerous idea,' but of a prohibition on a project grantee or its employees from engaging in activities outside of its scope.

"To hold that the Government unconstitutionally discriminates on the basis of viewpoint when it chooses to fund a program dedicated to advance certain permissible goals, because the program in advancing those goals necessarily discourages alternate goals, would render numerous government programs constitutionally suspect. When Congress established a National Endowment for Democracy to encourage other countries to adopt democratic principles, it was not constitutionally required to fund a program to encourage competing lines of political philosophy such as Communism and Fascism. Petitioners' assertions ultimately boil down to the position that if the government chooses to subsidize one protected right, it must subsidize analogous counterpart rights. But the Court has soundly rejected that proposition. [Citing *Taxation with Representation; Maher.*] Within far broader limits than petitioners are willing to concede, when the government appropriates public funds to establish a program it is entitled to define the limits of that program. [We] have here not the case of a general law singling out a disfavored group on the basis of speech content, but a case of the Government refusing to fund activities, including speech, which are specifically excluded from the scope of the project funded.

"[Relying on *League of Women Voters*, petitioners] contend that the restrictions on the subsidization of abortion-related speech [are] impermissible because they condition the receipt of a benefit [on] the relinquishment of [the constitutional] right to engage in abortion advocacy and counseling. [Petitioners'] reliance on [this case] is unavailing, however, because here the Government is not denying a benefit to anyone, but is instead simply insisting that public funds be spent for the purposes for which they were authorized. The [regulations] do not force the Title X grantee to give up abortion-related speech; they merely require that the grantee keep such activities separate and distinct from Title X activities. [By] requiring that the Title X grantee engage in abortion-related activity separately from activity receiving federal funding, Congress has, consistent with our teaching in *League of Women Voters* and *Taxation with Representation*, not denied it the right to engage in abortion-related activities. Congress has merely refused to fund such activities out of the public fisc. . . .

"This is not to suggest that funding by the Government, even when coupled with the freedom of the fund recipients to speak outside the scope of the Government-funded project, is invariably sufficient to justify government control over the content of expression. For example, this Court has recognized that the existence of a Government 'subsidy,' in the form of Government-owned property, does not justify the restriction of speech in areas that have 'been traditionally open to the public for expressive activity' [or] have been 'expressly dedicated to speech activity.' [Citing *Kokinda*; *Hague*; *Perry*.] In [the] circumstances [of this case, however], the general rule that the Government may choose not to subsidize speech applies with full force."

Justice Blackmun, joined by Justices Marshall and Stevens, dissented: "Until today, the Court has never upheld viewpoint-based suppression of speech simply because that suppression was a condition upon the acceptance of public funds. [Nothing in *Taxation with Representation*] can be said to challenge this long-settled understanding. In [*Taxation with Representation*], the Court upheld a content-neutral provision [and emphasized that the] 'case would be different if Congress were to discriminate invidiously in its subsidies in such a way as to "[aim] at the suppression of dangerous ideas."' [The regulations at issue here are] clearly viewpoint-based. [Indeed, if] a client asks directly about abortion, a Title X physician or counselor is required to say, in essence, that the project does not consider abortion to be an appropriate method of family planning. [The] regulations pertaining to 'advocacy' are even more explicitly viewpoint-based. [The] majority's reliance on the fact that the regulations pertain solely to funding decisions simply begs the question. Clearly, there are some bases upon which government may not rest its decisions to fund or not to fund. For example, [the] majority surely would agree that government may not base its decision to support an activity upon considerations of race. [Our] cases make clear that ideological viewpoint is a similarly repugnant ground upon which to base funding decisions. . . .

"In the cases at bar, the speaker's interest in the communication is both clear and vital. In addressing the family planning needs of their clients, the physicians and counselors who staff Title X projects seek to provide them with the full range of information and options regarding their health and reproductive freedom. Indeed, the legitimate expectations of the patient and the ethical responsibilities of the medical profession demand no less. [Indeed], it is of no small significance that the speech the Secretary would suppress is truthful information regarding constitutionally protected conduct of vital importance to the listener. One can imagine no legitimate governmental interest that might be served by suppressing such information." Justice O'Connor dissented on statutory grounds.

Note: The Implications of Rust

1. *Abortions versus smoking.* Suppose government establishes a program to give grants to organizations that help people quit smoking. Does the first amendment require government also to give grants to organizations that encourage people to smoke? Consider the following argument: The cigarette regulation is constitutional, even though *Rust* was wrong. This is so because in the cigarette case the information relates only to the individual's decision whether to smoke, whereas in *Rust* the information relates to the individual's decision whether to

exercise a constitutional right (abortion). Along these lines, suppose the government instructs all public defenders not to advise their clients of their rights under the fourth amendment exclusionary rule. Is *Rust* distinguishable? After *Rust*, could the government constitutionally fund the Democratic, but not the Republican, Convention?

2. *Government speech.* At least part of the Court's argument in *Rust* turned on the notion that government does not unconstitutionally discriminate "on the basis of viewpoint when it chooses to fund a program dedicated to advance certain permissible goals." Consider Rosenberger v. Rector and Visitors of University of Virginia, 515 U.S. 819 (1995), in which the Court invalidated a University of Virginia policy authorizing payment from the Student Activities Fund for the printing costs of a variety of student publications but prohibiting payment for any student publication that "primarily promotes or manifests a particular belief in or about a deity or an ultimate reality." Citing *Rust*, the University argued that it "must have substantial discretion in determining how to allocate scarce resources to accomplish its educational mission," and that the challenged policy was reasonably designed to serve the permissible goal of preserving the separation of church and state. The Court rejected this argument:

> [We] have permitted the government to regulate the content of what is or is not expressed when it is the speaker or when it enlists private entities to convey its own message. [In *Rust*, for example,] the government did not create a program to encourage private speech but instead used private speakers to transmit specific information pertaining to its own program. We recognized that when the government appropriates public funds to promote a particular policy of its own it is entitled to say what it wishes [and] it may take [appropriate] steps to ensure that its message is neither garbled nor distorted by the grantee. It does not follow, however, [that] viewpoint-based restrictions are proper when the [government] does not itself speak or subsidize transmittal of a message it favors but instead expends funds to encourage a diversity of views from private speakers. [The] distinction between the University's own favored message and the private speech of students is evident in the case before us. [The] University declares that the student groups eligible for Student Activities Fund support are not the University's agents, are not subject to its control, and are not its responsibility. Having offered to pay [the printing costs] of private speakers who convey their own messages, the University may not silence the expression of selected viewpoints.

3. *What's wrong with* Rust? Consider Redish and Kessler, Government Subsidies and Free Expression, 80 Minn. L. Rev. 543, 576–577 (1996):

> The problem with the [Court's analysis in *Rust*] is that it allows the government to define its subsidization programs in a wholly unchecked, self-referential manner. [The] fallacy of [this approach] becomes clear if one visualizes the subsidization of private expression exclusively in favor of such ideas as a free-market economic philosophy, or the political theories of Mao Zedong or Rush Limbaugh. [Government] may appropriately choose neutrally to fund works on family planning, on the viability of free-market economic philosophy, or on the wisdom of Mao Zedong's or Rush Limbaugh's political thought. Each of these subsidies would foster First Amendment values by adding to the public's knowledge. [But] government may not foster public acceptance of its own viewpoints on these issues by manipulating private expression [in a viewpoint-based manner].

Consider also Norton, The Measure of Government Speech: Identifying Expression's Source, 88 B.U. L. Rev. 587, 589, 595-597, 629–630 (2008):

> [T]he Supreme Court has shielded the government's expression from Free Speech Clause scrutiny. [Government] speech merits this insulation because it is both inevitable and valuable. [One danger of government speech, though, is] that the government may manipulate the public's attitudes towards its views by deliberately obscuring its identity as a message's source. [In] *Rust*, [doctors and nurses] delivered the contested counseling [without] any requirement that its governmental origins be disclosed. Under these circumstances, patients might well misunderstand clinic employees to be offering their own independent counsel, rather than speaking as agents required to espouse the government's view. [*Rust*] thus illustrates the danger of treating expression that fails to satisfy the demands of functional transparency as government speech free from First Amendment scrutiny.

4. *Professional Speech.* Wholly apart from the question of government speech, to what extent can the government constitutionally regulate the speech of doctors, lawyers, and other professionals? In what circumstances can the state forbid doctors to give certain medical advice to their patients? Can it constitutionally forbid doctors to use certain psychological treatments to "cure" patients of homosexuality? Similar questions arise, of course, in the regulation of lawyers. See Haupt, Professional Speech, 125 Yale L.J. 1238 (2016).

LEGAL SERVICES CORPORATION v. VELAZQUEZ, 531 U.S. 533 (2001). In 1974, Congress established the Legal Services Corporation (LSC), whose mission is to distribute funds appropriated by Congress to eligible local grantee organizations "for the purpose of providing financial support for legal assistance in noncriminal proceedings . . . to persons financially unable to afford legal assistance." LSC grantees consist of hundreds of local organizations governed by local boards of directors. In many instances, the grantees are funded by a combination of LSC funds and other public or private sources. The grantee organizations hire and supervise lawyers to provide free legal assistance to indigent clients.

In a five-to-four decision, the Court distinguished *Rust* and held unconstitutional a congressionally imposed restriction prohibiting LSC-funded attorneys from challenging the legality or constitutionality of existing welfare laws. Justice Kennedy delivered the opinion of the Court: "The Court in *Rust* did not place explicit reliance on the rationale that the counseling activities of the doctors under Title X amounted to governmental speech; when interpreting the holding in later cases, however, we have explained *Rust* on this understanding. We have said that viewpoint-based funding decisions can be sustained in instances in which the government is itself the speaker, or instances, like *Rust*, in which the government 'used private speakers to transmit information pertaining to its own program.' As we said in *Rosenberger*, '[w]hen the government disburses public funds to private entities to convey a governmental message, it may take legitimate and appropriate steps to ensure that its message is neither garbled nor distorted by the grantee.' . . .

"[But] '[i]t does not follow . . . that viewpoint-based restrictions are proper when the [government] does not itself speak or subsidize transmittal of a message it favors but instead expends funds to encourage a diversity of views from private speakers.' *Rosenberger.* Although the LSC program differs from the program at issue in *Rosenberger* in that its purpose is not to 'encourage a diversity of views,' the salient point is that, like the program in *Rosenberger*, the LSC program was designed to facilitate private speech, not to promote a governmental message. Congress funded LSC grantees to provide attorneys to represent the interests of indigent clients. [In] this vital respect this suit is distinguishable from *Rust*.

"The private nature of the speech involved here, and the extent of LSC's regulation of private expression, are indicated further by the circumstance that the Government seeks to use an existing medium of expression and to control it, in a class of cases, in ways which distort its usual functioning. Where the government uses or attempts to regulate a particular medium, we have been informed by its accepted usage in determining whether a particular restriction on speech is necessary for the program's purposes and limitations. [Citing FCC v. League of Women Voters; Arkansas Educational Television Commission v. Forbes; and *Rosenberger*.]

"[Restricting] LSC attorneys in advising their clients and in presenting arguments and analyses to the courts distorts the legal system by altering the traditional role of the attorneys in much the same way broadcast systems or student publication networks were changed in the limited forum cases we have cited. Just as government in those cases could not elect to use a broadcasting network or a college publication structure in a regime which prohibits speech necessary to the proper functioning of those systems, it may not design a subsidy to effect this serious and fundamental restriction on advocacy of attorneys and the functioning of the judiciary. . . .

"Congress was not required to fund an LSC attorney to represent indigent clients; and when it did so, it was not required to fund the whole range of legal representations or relationships. The LSC and the United States, however, in effect ask us to permit Congress to define the scope of the litigation it funds to exclude certain vital theories and ideas. The attempted restriction is designed to insulate the Government's interpretation of the Constitution from judicial challenge. The Constitution does not permit the Government to confine litigants and their attorneys in this manner. We must be vigilant when Congress imposes rules and conditions which in effect insulate its own laws from legitimate judicial challenge."

Justice Scalia, joined by Chief Justice Rehnquist and Justices O'Connor and Justice Thomas, dissented: "The LSC Act is a federal subsidy program, not a federal regulatory program, and '[t]here is a basic difference between [the two].' Regulations directly restrict speech; subsidies do not. [In *Rust*, the Court upheld] a statutory scheme that is in all relevant respects indistinguishable from [the provision challenged in this case]. The LSC Act, like the scheme in *Rust*, does not [discriminate] on the basis of viewpoint, since it funds neither challenges to nor defenses of existing welfare law. The provision simply declines to subsidize a certain class of litigation, and under *Rust* that decision 'does not infringe the right' to bring such litigation. . . . There is no legitimate basis for declaring [this law] unconstitutional."

Is there a coherent distinction between *Rust* and *Velazquez*? If so, what is it? Note that Justice Kennedy was the only justice to vote differently in the two cases.

AGENCY FOR INTERNATIONAL DEVELOPMENT v. ALLIANCE FOR OPEN SOCIETY INTERNATIONAL, 133 S. Ct. 2321 (2013). The United States Leadership Against HIV/AIDS, Tuberculosis, and Malaria Act of 2003 (Leadership Act) authorized the appropriation of billions of dollars to fund efforts by nongovernmental organizations to combat HIV/AIDS worldwide. The

Act imposed a condition ("The Policy Requirement") on all recipients of funds under the Act: All recipients must explicitly oppose prostitution. This requirement was challenged by recipients of Leadership Act funds who wish to remain neutral on the issue of prostitution. The Court, in a six-to-two decision, held that this requirement violated the First Amendment rights of recipients.

Chief Justice Roberts delivered the opinion of the Court: "The Policy Requirement mandates that recipients of Leadership Act funds explicitly agree with the Government's policy to oppose prostitution. . . . It is, however, a basic First Amendment principle that 'freedom of speech prohibits the government from telling people what they must say.' [Citing West Virginia Bd. of Educ. v. Barnette; Wooley v. Maynard]. [Were The Policy Requirement] enacted as a direct regulation of speech, [it] would plainly violate the First Amendment. The question is whether the Government may nonetheless impose that requirement as a condition on the receipt of federal funds. . . .

"[As] a general matter, if a party objects to a condition on the receipt of federal funding, its recourse is to decline the funds. This remains true when the objection is that a condition may affect the recipient's exercise of its First Amendment rights. [At] the same time, however, we have held that the Government 'may not deny a benefit to a person on a basis that infringes his constitutionally protected . . . freedom of speech even if he has no entitlement to that benefit.' In some cases, a funding condition can result in an unconstitutional burden on First Amendment rights. . . .

"The dissent thinks that can only be true when the condition is not relevant to the objectives of the program [or] when the condition is actually coercive, in the sense of an offer that cannot be refused. Our precedents, however, are not so limited. In the present context, the relevant distinction that has emerged from our cases is between conditions that define the limits of the government spending program — those that specify the activities Congress wants to subsidize — and conditions that seek to leverage funding to regulate speech outside the contours of the program itself. The line is hardly clear, in part because the definition of a particular program can always be manipulated to subsume the challenged condition. We have held, however, that 'Congress cannot recast a condition on funding as a mere definition of its program in every case, lest the First Amendment be reduced to a simple semantic exercise.'" [Velazquez.]

As an example, Chief Justice Roberts invoked FCC v. League of Women Voters, in which "the Court struck down a condition on federal financial assistance to noncommercial broadcast television and radio stations that prohibited all editorializing, including with private funds. Even a station receiving only one percent of its overall budget from the Federal Government, the Court explained, was 'barred absolutely from all editorializing.' [The] law provided no way for a station to limit its use of federal funds to non-editorializing activities, while using private funds 'to make known its views on matters of public importance.' The prohibition thus went beyond ensuring that federal funds not be used to subsidize 'public broadcasting station editorials,' and instead leveraged the federal funding to regulate the stations' speech outside the scope of the program.

"Our decision in Rust elaborated on the approach [in] League of Women Voters. In Rust, [the] organizations received funds from a variety of sources other than the Federal Government for a variety of purposes. The Act, however, prohibited the Title X federal funds from being 'used in programs where abortion is a method of family planning.' To enforce this provision, HHS regulations barred Title X projects from advocating abortion as a method of family planning, and required grantees to ensure that their Title X projects were 'physically and financially separate' from their other projects that engaged in the prohibited activities. . . .

"We explained that Congress can, without offending the Constitution, selectively fund certain programs to address an issue of public concern, without funding alternative ways of addressing the same problem. In Title X, Congress had defined the federal program to encourage only particular family planning methods. The challenged regulations were simply 'designed to ensure that the limits of the federal program are observed,' and 'that public funds [are] spent for the purposes for which they were authorized.' [The] regulations governed only the scope of the grantee's Title X projects, leaving it 'unfettered in its other activities.' [Title X grantees could continue to engage in abortion advocacy as long as they conducted] 'those activities through programs that are separate and independent from the project that receives Title X funds.' Because the regulations did not 'prohibit[ ] the recipient from engaging in the protected conduct outside the scope of the federally funded program,' they did not run afoul of the First Amendment. Here, however, [the] Policy Requirement falls on the unconstitutional side of the line. [By] demanding that funding recipients adopt — as their own — the Government's view on an issue of public concern, the condition by its very nature affects 'protected conduct outside the scope of the federally funded program.' [By] requiring recipients to profess a specific belief, the Policy Requirement goes beyond defining the limits of the federally funded program to defining the recipient. [In] so doing, it violates the First Amendment and cannot be sustained."

Justice Scalia, joined by Justice Thomas, dissented: "The First Amendment does not mandate a viewpoint neutral government. Government must choose between rival ideas and adopt some as its own: competition over cartels, solar energy over coal, weapon development over disarmament, and so forth. Moreover, the government may enlist the assistance of those who believe in its ideas to carry them to fruition; and it need not enlist for that purpose those who oppose or do not support the ideas. That seems to me a matter of the most common common sense. . . .

"The argument is that this commonsense principle will enable the government to discriminate against, and injure, points of view to which it is opposed. Of course the Constitution does not prohibit government spending that discriminates against, and injures, points of view to which the government is opposed; every government program which takes a position on a controversial issue does that. Anti-smoking programs injure cigar aficionados, programs encouraging sexual abstinence injure free-love advocates, etc. The constitutional prohibition at issue here is not a prohibition against discriminating against or injuring opposing points of view, but the First Amendment's prohibition against the coercing of speech. I am frankly dubious that a condition for eligibility to participate in a minor federal program such as this one runs afoul of that prohibition even when the condition is irrelevant to the goals of the program. Not every disadvantage is a coercion.

"But that is not the issue before us here. Here the views that the Government demands an applicant forswear — or that the Government insists an applicant favor — are relevant to the program in question. The program is valid only if the Government is entitled to disfavor the opposing view (here, advocacy of or toleration of prostitution). And if the program can disfavor it, so can the selection of those who are to administer the program. There is no risk that this principle will enable the Government to discriminate arbitrarily against positions it disfavors. It would not, for example, permit the Government to exclude from bidding on defense contracts anyone who refuses to abjure prostitution. But here a central part of the Government's HIV/AIDS strategy is the suppression of prostitution, by which HIV is transmitted. It is entirely reasonable to admit to participation in the program only those who believe in that goal. . . ."

Note: The Reach of Government Speech: Summum, Walker, and Matal

1. *Monuments in a public park.* Presumably, there is no first amendment right to erect monuments in a public park. But what if the government erects some monuments but not others? Pioneer Park, a public park in Pleasant Grove City, contains fifteen permanent displays, eleven of which were donated to the city by private groups. These include an historic granary, a wishing well, a September 11 monument, and a Ten Commandments monument donated by the Fraternal Order of Eagles in 1971. Summum is a religious organization founded in 1975 and headquartered in Salt Lake City. In 2003, Summum's president requested permission to erect a stone monument in Pioneer Park. The monument would contain the Seven Aphorisms of Summum, which according to Summum doctrine were inscribed on the original tablet handed down by God to Moses on Mount Sinai. The city denied the request, explaining that it permitted monuments to be displayed in the park only if they "directly related to the history of Pleasant Grove" or they "were donated by groups with longstanding ties to the Pleasant Grove community." The Court of Appeals for the Tenth Circuit held that because public parks have traditionally been regarded as public forums, the city could not constitutionally reject the Seven Aphorisms monument absent a compelling justification for doing so.

In a unanimous decision in Pleasant Grove City, Utah v. Summum, 555 U.S. 460 (2009), the Supreme Court reversed. Justice Alito delivered the opinion of the Court: "The [fundamental] disagreement [centers] on the nature of [the city's] conduct when [it] permitted privately donated monuments to be erected in Pioneer Park. [Was the city] engaging in [its] own expressive conduct? Or [was it] providing a forum for private speech? [If the city was] engaging in [its] own expressive conduct, then the Free Speech Clause has no application. The Free Speech Clause restricts government regulation of private speech; it does not regulate government speech. [Citing *Rust.*] [Indeed,] it is not easy to imagine how government could function if it lacked this freedom. . . .

"[There] may be situations in which it is difficult to tell whether a government entity is speaking on its own behalf or is providing a forum for private speech, but this case does not present such a situation. Permanent monuments displayed on public property typically represent government speech. [When] a government entity arranges for the construction of a monument, it does so because it wishes to convey some thought or instill some feeling in those who see the structure. [Just] as government-commissioned and government-financed monuments speak for the government, so do privately financed and donated monuments that the government accepts and displays to the public on government land. [The] monuments that are accepted [are] meant to convey and have the effect of conveying a government message, and they thus constitute government speech. . . .

"[Summum] voices the legitimate concern that the government speech doctrine not be used as a subterfuge for favoring certain private speakers over others based on viewpoint. [Summum] and the Court of Appeals analogize the installation of permanent monuments in a public park to the delivery of speeches and the holding of marches and demonstrations, and they thus invoke the rule that a public park is a traditional public forum for these activities. But 'public forum principles . . . are out of place in the context of this case.' The forum doctrine has been applied in situations in which government-owned property or a government program was capable of accommodating a large number of public speakers without defeating the essential function of the land or the program. For example, a park can accommodate many speakers and, over time, many parades and demonstrations. [A] public university's student activity fund can provide money for many campus activities. [Citing *Rosenberger*.] A public university's buildings may offer meeting space for hundreds of student groups. [Citing *Widmar*.]

[By] contrast, public parks can accommodate only a limited number of permanent monuments. [It] is hard to imagine how a public park could be opened up for the installation of permanent monuments by every person or group wishing to engage in that form of expression. [Indeed,] if public parks were considered to be traditional public forums for the purpose of erecting privately donated monuments, most parks would have little choice but to refuse all such donations. And where the application of forum analysis would lead almost inexorably to closing of the forum, it is obvious that forum analysis is out of place. [Therefore,] forum analysis simply does not apply to the installation of permanent monuments on public property. [We therefore] hold that the City's decision to accept certain privately donated monuments while rejecting [Summum's] is best viewed as a form of government speech. As a result, the City's decision is not subject to the Free Speech Clause. . . ."

2. *Specialty license plates.* Suppose a state permits individuals to purchase vanity license plates. Can it constitutionally refuse to sell such plates if the message would be demeaning to any person on the basis of race, religion, gender, or sexual orientation? In Walker v. Texas Div., Sons of Confederate Veterans, Inc., 135 S. Ct. 2239 (2015), the Court upheld the refusal of the Texas Department of Motor Vehicles to approve a specialty license plate design submitted by the Sons of Confederate Veterans and featuring the Confederate battle flag. In a five-to-four decision, written by Justice Breyer, the Court relied heavily upon *Summum* to conclude that the plate was government speech and therefore did not have to be viewpoint neutral. In the Court's view, license plates, like monuments in public parks, "long have communicated messages from the States," are "'often closely identified in the public mind with the [State]'" and are subject to direct government control. The fact that private parties took part in the design and propagation of the message did not extinguish the governmental nature of the message.

Consider Justice Alito's dissent, joined by Chief Justice Roberts and Justices Scalia and Kennedy: "Here is a test. Suppose you sat by the side of a Texas highway and studied the license plates on the vehicles passing by. You would see, in addition to the standard Texas plates, an impressive array of specialty plates. (There are now more than 350 varieties.) . . . [Would] you really think that the sentiments reflected in these specialty plates are the views of the State of Texas and not those of the owners of the cars? If a car had a plate that says 'Rather Be Golfing' passed by at 8:30 A.M. on a Monday morning, would you think: 'This is the official policy of the State — better to golf than to work?'

Consider Papandrea, The Government Brand, 110 Nw. U. L. Rev. 1195 (2016):

[A major] problem with the government speech doctrine after *Summum* and *Walker* is that the government is not required to articulate any particular message. The Court first expressly rejected any such requirement in *Summum*, where Justice Alito waxed eloquently for the Court about how the meaning of public monuments is potentially different for each observer and changes over time. Although it may not be possible to declare definitively what message a permanent government monument is intended to express, the wide variety of the over 400 Texas specialty license plates indicates that the government has no message at all. . . .

Because Texas does not exercise any meaningful selectivity over the specialty license plates it chooses, the program appears to be some sort of forum like the one in *Rosenberger,* where the university did not "speak or subsidize . . . a message it favors but instead expends funds to encourage a diversity of views from private speakers." By rejecting the SCV plate, Texas appears to be doing nothing but blatantly and impermissibly "manipulating private expression" in a viewpoint-based manner. [The] ramifications of *Walker* are potentially staggering. Using this decision as a guide, the government will likely assert the government speech doctrine in a wide variety of contexts in order to justify content-based and even viewpoint-based censorship of private speech.

Along similar lines, see Strasser, Government Speech and the Circumvention of the First Amendment, 44 Hast. Const. L.Q. 37 (2016); Schauer, Not Just About License Plates: Walker v. Sons of Confederate Veterans, Government Speech, and Doctrinal Overlap in the First Amendment, 2015 Sup. Ct. Rev. 265.

3. *Trademarks.* "Slants" is a derogatory term for persons on Asian descent. Simon Tam, lead singer of the rock group "The Slants," whose members are Asian-Americans, chose the name to "reclaim" the term and drain it of its denigrating force. The federal Patent and Trademark Office denied Tam's application for federal trademark registration of the name because it violated a federal law prohibiting the registration of any trademarks that "disparage . . . or bring . . . into contemp[t] or disrepute" any "persons, living or dead." The government argued that federally-registered trademarks are government speech and that, as in *Summum* and *Walker,* the statute therefore did not violate the First Amendment. In a unanimous decision, the Supreme Court in *Matal v. Tam,* 582 U.S. — (2017) disagreed and held that the statutory provision violated the First Amendment.

In his opinion for the Court, Justice Alito explained that "while the government-speech doctrine is important — indeed, essential — it is a doctrine that is susceptible to dangerous misuse." This is so because if "private speech could be passed off as government speech by simply affixing a government seal of approval, government could silence or muffle the expression of disfavored viewpoints." Thus, Alito insisted, "we must exercise great caution before extending our government-speech precedents."

Alito maintained that because the federal government "does not dream up these marks, and it does not edit marks submitted for registration, [it] is far-fetched to suggest that the content of a registered mark is government speech." Indeed, if "the federal registration of a trademark makes the mark government speech, the Federal Government is babbling prodigiously and incoherently [and it] is unashamedly endorsing a vast array of commercial products and services." Moreover, it "is unlikely that more than a tiny fraction of the public has any idea what federal registration of a trademark means."

Alito insisted that "[n]one of our government speech cases even remotely supports the idea that registered trademarks are government speech." In *Summum*, for example, "we cited many factors. Governments have used monuments to speak to the public since ancient times; parks have traditionally been selective in accepting and displaying donated monuments; parks would be overrun if they were obliged to accept all monuments offered by private groups; [and] monuments that are accepted . . . are meant to convey and have the effect of conveying a government message." Trademarks, Alito reasoned, "share none of these characteristics."

Alito also distinguished *Walker*, which, he noted, "likely marks the outer bounds of the government speech doctrine." The Court in *Walker*, Alito explained, "cited three factors distilled from *Summum*. First, license plates have long been used by the States to convey state messages." Second, "license plates 'are often closely identified in the public mind' with the State. . . . Third, Texas 'maintain[ed] direct control over the messages conveyed on its specialty plates.'" Alito maintained that "none of these factors are present in this case." In sum, then, "the federal registration of trademarks is vastly different from [the] monuments in *Summum*, and even the specialty license plates in *Walker*." Moreover, "[h]olding that the registration of a trademark converts the mark into government speech would constitute a huge and dangerous extension of the government-speech doctrine." Thus, he concluded, "trademarks are private, not government speech."

Are you persuaded that *Matal* is distinguishable from *Summum* and *Walker*? Suppose the government allows individuals to display signs inside public buses. Is that case governed by *Walker* or *Matal*? Suppose the government excludes any sign that "disparages or brings into contempt or disrepute any person or group"? Is that case governed by *Walker* or *Matal*? Or is it instead a created public forum case? How does one know the difference? On the problem of competing modes of analysis, see Schauer, supra. The Court made clear in *Matal* that even if the case were analyzed in terms of public forum analysis, the statute embodied an unconstitutional viewpoint based restriction.

3.   *Symbolic Conduct*

This section explores the use of nonverbal conduct — such as burning a draft card or mutilating a flag — as a means of "symbolic" expression. In what circumstances, if any, does such nonverbal conduct constitute protected "speech" within the meaning of the first amendment? Consider Henkin, Foreword: On Drawing Lines, 82 Harv. L. Rev. 63, 79–80 (1968): "A constitutional distinction between speech and conduct is specious. Speech *is* conduct, and actions speak. There is nothing intrinsically sacred about wagging the tongue or wielding a pen; there is nothing intrinsically more sacred about words than other symbols. [The] meaningful constitutional distinction is not between speech and conduct, but between conduct that speaks, communicates, and other kinds of conduct." In fact, the Court has long recognized that at least some forms of conduct may constitute "speech" within the meaning of the first amendment. In West Virginia State Board of Education v. Barnette, 319 U.S. 624 (1943), for example, Justice Jackson explained that "symbolism is a primitive but effective way of communicating ideas. [It] is a short cut from mind to mind." See also R.A.V. v. City of St. Paul, section D8, supra (cross-burning); Tinker v. Des Moines Independent

Community School District, 393 U.S. 503 (1969) (black armbands); Brown v. Louisiana, 383 U.S. 131 (1966) (sit-in); Stromberg v. California, 283 U.S. 359 (1931) (red flag).

If it is assumed that some forms of nonverbal conduct may constitute "speech," the question remains, how are we to determine what nonverbal conduct merits first amendment protection? At one level, it seems clear that "[everything] that one does, every action that one takes or fails to take, 'speaks' to anyone who is interested in looking for a message." That is, "all behavior is *capable of being understood* as communication." F. Haiman, Speech and Law in a Free Society 31 (1981). Surely, however, not all behavior that is "capable of being understood as communication" constitutes "speech," for that would bring all conduct within the ambit of the first amendment.

Consider Nimmer, The Meaning of Symbolic Speech under the First Amendment, 21 UCLA L. Rev. 29, 36 (1973):

> A further element must be added to the mix before conduct may be considered to be speech. Whatever else may or may not be true of speech, as an irreducible minimum it must constitute a communication. That, in turn, implies both a communicator and a communicate — a speaker and an audience. [Without] an actual or potential audience there can be no first amendment speech right. Nor may the first amendment be invoked if there is an audience but no actual or potential "speaker." [Unless] there is a human communicator intending to convey a meaning by his conduct, it would be odd to think of it as conduct constituting a communication protected by the first amendment.

Does all nonverbal conduct that is intended to communicate constitute "speech"? Note that such a doctrine might create a serious "imposter problem." That is, it would invite fraudulent claims by "criminals" that their actual intent was to communicate. Should courts be in the business of inquiring into the sincerity of individuals who claim to have exercised first amendment rights? Is there any way to avoid such inquiries? The issue of inquiry into sincerity in the religion context is examined in Chapter 8, section C, infra. Note also that, depending on the circumstances, nonverbal conduct that is intended to communicate may range across the entire spectrum of human behavior. It may include assassination, refusal to pay taxes, public nudity, flag burning, and urination on the steps of the state capitol. Does all such conduct constitute constitutionally protected "speech," so long as the actor intended to communicate?

United States v. O'Brien
391 U.S. 367 (1968)

Mr. Chief Justice Warren delivered the opinion of the Court.

On the morning of March 31, 1966, David Paul O'Brien and three companions burned their Selective Service registration certificates on the steps of the South Boston Courthouse. A sizable crowd, including several agents of the Federal Bureau of Investigation, witnessed the event. Immediately after the burning, [O'Brien] stated to FBI agents that he had burned his registration certificate because of his beliefs, knowing that he was violating federal law.

For this act, O'Brien was indicted, tried, convicted, and sentenced in the United States District Court for the District of Massachusetts. He did not contest the fact that he had burned the certificate. He stated in argument to the jury that he burned the certificate publicly to influence others to adopt his antiwar beliefs, as he put it, "so that other people would reevaluate their positions with Selective Service, with the armed forces, and reevaluate their place in the culture of today, to hopefully consider my position."

The indictment upon which he was tried charged that he "willfully and knowingly did mutilate, destroy, and change by burning [his] registration Certificate [in] violation of [§462(b)(3) of the Universal Military Training and Service Act of 1948]." Section 462(b)(3) [was] amended by Congress in 1965 (adding the words italicized below) so that at the time O'Brien burned his certificate an offense was committed by any person, "who forges, alters, *knowingly destroys, knowingly mutilates,* or in any manner changes any such certificate...." (Italics supplied.) . . .

[The] Court of Appeals [held] the 1965 Amendment unconstitutional as a law abridging freedom of speech. At the time the Amendment was enacted, a regulation of the Selective Service System required registrants to keep their registration certificates in their "personal possession at all times." 32 C.F.R. §1617.1 (1962). [The] Court of Appeals [was] of the opinion that conduct punishable under the 1965 Amendment was already punishable under the non-possession regulation, and consequently that the Amendment served no valid purpose; further, that in light of the prior regulation, the Amendment must have been "directed at public as distinguished from private destruction." On this basis, the court concluded that the 1965 Amendment ran afoul of the First Amendment by singling out persons engaged in protests for special treatment. [We] hold that the 1965 Amendment is constitutional both as enacted and as applied. . . .

[The] 1965 Amendment plainly does not abridge free speech on its face, and we do not understand O'Brien to argue otherwise. Amended §12(b)(3) on its face deals with conduct having no connection with speech. It prohibits the knowing destruction of certificates issued by the Selective Service System, and there is nothing necessarily expressive about such conduct. The Amendment does not distinguish between public and private destruction, and it does not punish only destruction engaged in for the purpose of expressing views. Compare Stromberg v. California, 283 U.S. 359 (1931). A law prohibiting destruction of Selective Service certificates no more abridges free speech on its face than a motor vehicle law prohibiting the destruction of drivers' licenses, or a tax law prohibiting the destruction of books and records.

O'Brien nonetheless argues that the 1965 Amendment is unconstitutional in its application to him, and is unconstitutional as enacted because what he calls the "purpose" of Congress was "to suppress freedom of speech." We consider these arguments separately.

II

O'Brien first argues that the 1965 Amendment is unconstitutional as applied to him because his act of burning his registration certificate was protected "symbolic speech" within the First Amendment. His argument is that the freedom of expression which the First Amendment guarantees includes all modes of "communication of ideas by conduct," and that his conduct is within this definition because he did it in "demonstration against the war and against the draft."

We cannot accept the view that an apparently limitless variety of conduct can be labeled "speech" whenever the person engaging in the conduct intends thereby to express an idea. However, even on the assumption that the alleged communicative element in O'Brien's conduct is sufficient to bring into play the First Amendment, it does not necessarily follow that the destruction of a registration certificate is constitutionally protected activity. This Court has held that when "speech" and "nonspeech" elements are combined in the same course of conduct, a sufficiently important governmental interest in regulating the nonspeech element can justify incidental limitations on First Amendment freedoms. To characterize the quality of the governmental interest which must appear, the Court has employed a variety of descriptive terms: compelling; substantial; subordinating; paramount; cogent; strong. Whatever imprecision inheres in these terms, we think it clear that a government regulation is sufficiently justified if it is within the constitutional power of the Government; if it furthers an important or substantial governmental interest; if the governmental interest is unrelated to the suppression of free expression; and if the incidental restriction on alleged First Amendment freedoms is no greater than is essential to the furtherance of that interest. We find that the 1965 Amendment [meets] all of these requirements, and consequently that O'Brien can be constitutionally convicted for violating it.

The constitutional power of Congress to raise and support armies and to make all laws necessary and proper to that end is broad and sweeping. [Pursuant] to this power, Congress may establish a system of registration for individuals liable for training and service, and may require such individuals within reason to cooperate in the registration system. The issuance of certificates indicating the registration and eligibility classification of individuals is a legitimate and substantial administrative aid in the functioning of this system. And legislation to insure the continuing availability of issued certificates serves a legitimate and substantial purpose in the system's administration. . . .

1. The registration certificate serves as proof that the individual described thereon has registered for the draft. The classification certificate shows the eligibility classification of a named but undescribed individual. Voluntarily displaying the two certificates is an easy and painless way for a young man to dispel a question as to whether he might be delinquent in his Selective Service obligations. [Additionally] in a time of national crisis, reasonable availability to each registrant of the two small cards assures a rapid and uncomplicated means for determining his fitness for immediate induction, no matter how distant in our mobile society he may be from his local board.

2. The information supplied on the certificates facilitates communication between registrants and local boards, simplifying the system and benefiting all concerned. To begin with, each certificate bears the address of the registrant's local board, an item unlikely to be committed to memory. Further, each card bears the registrant's Selective Service number, and a registrant who has his number readily available so that he can communicate it to his local board when he supplies or requests information can make simpler the board's task in locating his file. . . .

3. Both certificates carry continual reminders that the registrant must notify his local board of any change of address, and other specified changes in his status. . . .

The many functions performed by Selective Service certificates establish beyond doubt that Congress has a legitimate and substantial interest in preventing their wanton and unrestrained destruction and assuring their continuing availability by punishing people who knowingly and wilfully destroy or mutilate them. And we are unpersuaded that the pre-existence of the non-possession regulations in any way negates this interest.

In the absence of a question as to multiple punishment, it has never been suggested that there is anything improper in Congress' providing alternative statutory avenues of prosecution to assure the effective protection of one and the same interest. [Here], the pre-existing avenue of prosecution was not even statutory. Regulations may be modified or revoked from time to time by administrative discretion. Certainly, the Congress may change or supplement a regulation.

Equally important, a comparison of the regulations with the 1965 Amendment indicates that they protect overlapping but not identical governmental interests, and that they reach somewhat different classes of wrongdoers. The gravamen of the offense defined by the statute is the deliberate rendering of certificates unavailable for the various purposes which they may serve. Whether registrants keep their certificates in their personal possession at all times, as required by the regulations, is of no particular concern under the 1965 Amendment, as long as they do not mutilate or destroy the certificates so as to render them unavailable. . . .

We think it apparent that the continuing availability to each registrant of his Selective Service certificates substantially furthers the smooth and proper functioning of the system that Congress has established to raise armies [and] that the 1965 Amendment specifically protects this substantial governmental interest. We perceive no alternative means that would more precisely and narrowly assure the continuing availability of issued Selective Service certificates than a law which prohibits their wilful mutilation or destruction.

[Moreover,] both the governmental interest and the operation of the 1965 Amendment are limited to the noncommunicative aspect of O'Brien's conduct. The governmental interest and the scope of the 1965 Amendment are limited to preventing harm to the smooth and efficient functioning of the Selective Service System. When O'Brien deliberately rendered unavailable his registration certificate, he wilfully frustrated this governmental interest. For this noncommunicative impact of his conduct, and for nothing else, he was convicted.

The case at bar is therefore unlike one where the alleged governmental interest in regulating conduct arises in some measure because the communication allegedly integral to the conduct is itself thought to be harmful. In Stromberg v. California, 283 U.S. 359 (1931), for example, this Court struck down a statutory phrase which punished people who expressed their "opposition to organized government" by displaying "any flag, badge, banner, or device." Since the statute there was aimed at suppressing communication it could not be sustained as a regulation of noncommunicative conduct. . . .

In conclusion, we find that because of the Government's substantial interest in assuring the continuing availability of issued Selective Service certificates, because amended §462(b) is an appropriately narrow means of protecting this interest and condemns only the independent noncommunicative impact of conduct within its reach, and because the noncommunicative impact of O'Brien's act of burning his registration certificate frustrated the Government's interest, a sufficient governmental interest has been shown to justify O'Brien's conviction.

III

O'Brien finally argues that the 1965 Amendment is unconstitutional as enacted because what he calls the "purpose" of Congress was "to suppress freedom of speech." We reject this argument because under settled principles the purpose of Congress, as O'Brien uses that term, is not a basis for declaring this legislation unconstitutional.

It is a familiar principle of constitutional law that this Court will not strike down an otherwise constitutional statute on the basis of an alleged illicit legislative motive. . . .

Inquiries into congressional motives or purposes are a hazardous matter. When the issue is simply the interpretation of legislation, the Court will look to statements by legislators for guidance as to the purpose of the legislature, because the benefit to sound decision-making in this circumstance is thought sufficient to risk the possibility of misreading Congress' purpose. It is entirely a different matter when we are asked to void a statute that is, under well-settled criteria, constitutional on its face, on the basis of what fewer than a handful of Congressmen said about it. What motivates one legislator to make a speech about a statute is not necessarily what motivates scores of others to enact it, and the stakes are sufficiently high for us to eschew guesswork. We decline to void [legislation] which could be reenacted in its exact form if the same or another legislator made a "wiser" speech about it. . . .

We think it not amiss, in passing, to comment upon O'Brien's legislative-purpose argument. There was little floor debate on this legislation in either House. Only Senator Thurmond commented on its substantive features in the Senate. [After] his brief statement, and without any additional substantive comments, the [bill] passed the Senate. [In] the House debate only two Congressmen addressed themselves to the Amendment — Congressmen Rivers and Bray. [The] bill was passed after their statements without any further debate by a vote of 393 to 1. It is principally on the basis of the statements by these three Congressmen that O'Brien makes his congressional-"purpose" argument. We note that if we were to examine legislative purpose in the instant case, we would be obliged to consider not only these statements but also the more authoritative reports of the Senate and House Armed Services Committees. [While] both reports make clear a concern with the "defiant" destruction of so-called "draft cards" and with "open" encouragement to others to destroy their cards, both reports also indicate that this concern stemmed from an apprehension that unrestrained destruction of cards would disrupt the smooth functioning of the Selective Service System.

IV

Since the 1965 Amendment to §12(b)(3) of the Universal Military Training and Service Act is constitutional as enacted and as applied, the Court of Appeals should have affirmed the judgment of conviction entered by the District Court. . . .

MR. JUSTICE MARSHALL took no part in the consideration or decision of these cases.

MR. JUSTICE HARLAN, concurring. . . .
I wish to make explicit my understanding that this [decision] does not foreclose consideration of First Amendment claims in those rare instances when an "incidental" restriction upon expression, imposed by a regulation which furthers an "important or substantial" governmental interest and satisfies the Court's other criteria, in practice has the effect of entirely preventing a "speaker" from reaching a significant audience with whom he could not otherwise lawfully communicate. This is not such a case, since O'Brien manifestly could have conveyed his message in many ways other than by burning his draft card.

MR. JUSTICE DOUGLAS, dissenting. . . .
[Justice Douglas maintained that the "underlying and basic [issue] in this case [is] whether conscription is permissible in the absence of a declaration of war." Justice Douglas therefore suggested that "this case should be put down for reargument" on that question. Justice Douglas briefly addressed the symbolic conduct issue in his concurring opinion the following term in Brandenburg v. Ohio, section B1 supra: "Action is often a method of expression and within the protection of the First Amendment. Suppose one tears up his own copy of the Constitution in eloquent protest to a decision of this Court. May he be indicted? Suppose one rips his own Bible to shreds to celebrate his departure from one 'faith' and his embrace of atheism. May he be indicted? [This] Court's affirmance of [O'Brien's conviction for burning the draft card] was not, with all respect, consistent with the First Amendment."]

Note: Draft Card Burning and the First Amendment

1. *Is draft card burning "speech"?* Did the Court decide that question? How would you decide it? Why was Chief Justice Warren reluctant in *O'Brien* to "accept the view that an apparently limitless variety of conduct can be labeled 'speech' whenever the person engaging in the conduct intends thereby to express an idea"? Consider the following propositions: (a) If nonverbal conduct that is intended "to express an idea" constitutes "speech," government may not restrict that conduct unless it poses a "clear and present danger" within the meaning of the Holmes/Brandeis formulation. (b) Even if nonverbal conduct that is intended to communicate constitutes "speech," the first amendment does not "afford the same kind of freedom to those who would communicate ideas by conduct [as it affords] to those who communicate by pure speech." Cox v. Louisiana, 379 U.S. 536, 555 (1965).

2. *Symbolic conduct and the content-based/content-neutral distinction.* Should a distinction be drawn between laws that restrict symbolic conduct because of its content and laws that restrict symbolic conduct for reasons unrelated to content? Compare, for example, a law prohibiting "any person to urinate in public" with a law prohibiting "any person to urinate on a public building as a symbolic act of opposition to government." Does the content-based/content-neutral distinction provide a useful framework for analyzing the constitutionality of such laws? Does *O'Brien* adopt such an analysis?

3. *Restrictions related "to the suppression of free expression":* Stromberg, Tinker, *and* Schacht. In Stromberg v. California, discussed in *O'Brien,* the Court invalidated a

statute prohibiting any person to display "a red flag [in] any public place [as] a [symbol] of opposition to organized government." The Court explained that the law might be construed to prohibit "peaceful and orderly opposition to government by legal means" and thus curtail "the opportunity for free political discussion."

In Tinker v. Des Moines Independent Community School District, 393 U.S. 503 (1969), decided a year after O'Brien, school officials, fearing possible disruption of school activities, suspended three public school students because they wore black armbands to school to protest the government's policy in Vietnam. In invalidating the suspensions, the Court observed that "the wearing of an armband for the purpose of expressing certain views is the type of symbolic act that is within [the] First Amendment" and is "closely akin to 'pure speech.'" The Court observed further that "the school authorities did not purport to prohibit the wearing of all symbols of political or controversial significance; [rather], a particular symbol — black armbands worn to exhibit opposition to this Nation's involvement in Vietnam — was singled out for prohibition." Consider Ely, Flag Desecration: A Case Study in the Roles of Categorization and Balancing in First Amendment Analysis, 88 Harv. L. Rev. 1482, 1498 & n.63 (1975): "[In] Tinker the state regulated [the armbands] because it feared the effect that the message those armbands conveyed would have on the other children. [Tinker] would have been quite a different case had it arisen [in] the context of a school regulation banning armbands in woodworking class along with all other sartorial embellishments liable to become safety hazards."

In Schacht v. United States, 398 U.S. 58 (1970), petitioner, who participated in a skit demonstrating opposition to American involvement in Vietnam, was convicted of violating 18 U.S.C. §702, which made criminal the unauthorized wearing of an American military uniform. The Court reversed the conviction. Citing O'Brien, the Court observed that section 702 "is, standing alone, a valid statute on its face." The Court noted, however, that another statute, 10 U.S.C. §772(f), authorized the wearing of an American military uniform in a theatrical production "if the portrayal does not tend to discredit [the armed forces]." Finding that petitioner's skit constituted a "theatrical production" within the meaning of section 772(f), the Court concluded: "[Petitioner's] conviction can be sustained only if he can be punished for speaking out against the role of our Army and our country in Vietnam. Clearly punishment for this reason would be an unconstitutional abridgement of freedom of speech. [Section 772(f)], which leaves Americans free to praise the war in Vietnam but can send persons like [petitioner] to prison for opposing it, cannot survive in a country which has the First Amendment."

4. *Restrictions "unrelated to the suppression of free expression."* O'Brien's analysis of restrictions that are "unrelated to the suppression of free expression" applies the general principles of content-neutral balancing to the specific context of symbolic conduct. Is O'Brien's application of those principles sufficiently speech-protective?

Consider Alfange, The Draft-Card Burning Case, 1968 Sup. Ct. Rev. 1, 23, 26:

[As] the Court's own inventory of possible draft-card uses indicates, [the certificates] serve functions of dispensable convenience rather than urgent necessity. The Court's use of "substantial," therefore, is more appropriate if the term is understood in its sense of "having substance" or "not imaginary," rather than the sense of "considerable" or "large." [Moreover, the Court should have weighed] the importance of the government's interest against the impact of the draft law amendment on freedom of speech.

Should the Court have "balanced" the competing interests in *O'Brien*? How would you assess the importance of the draft law amendment's impact on free speech? Consider the following arguments:

a. "In view of the fact that the amendment does not punish dissent per se, but merely forbids one very specific means of conveying the expression of dissent, it cannot seriously be contended that the amendment's effect upon speech is anything but minor." Id. at 27.

b. "Burning a draft card [is] the ordinary person's way of attracting the attention of the national news media. [To] [prohibit] such an effective form of propagating one's views [is] to greatly diminish the effectiveness of the individual's right [to] make his dissent known." Velvel, Freedom of Speech and the Draft Card Burning Cases, 16 U. Kan. L. Rev. 149, 153 (1968).

c. "[Symbolic] conduct deserves a high degree of constitutional protection. [The] kind of stimulus necessary to activate the political conscience of [the] populace sometimes can be created only by transcending rationality and appealing to more primitive, more basic instincts. [The] communication achieved by the wave of draft-card burnings at the height of the United States involvement in Vietnam represents a paradigm example of the 'speech' with which the First Amendment is concerned." Blasi, The Checking Value in First Amendment Theory, 1977 Am. B. Found. Res. J. 521, 640.

d. "[Much] of the effectiveness of O'Brien's communication [derived] precisely from the fact that it was illegal. Had there been no law prohibiting draft card [burning], he might have attracted no more attention than he would have by swallowing a goldfish." Ely, supra, at 1489–1490. See G. Stone, Perilous Times: Free Speech in Wartime 471–472 (2004): "By 1965, the act of publicly burning one's draft card had become a potent means of protest. This was more than a clever way to express one's opposition to the war. Burning a copy of the Constitution is also a clever way to express opposition, but burning a copy of the Constitution (as distinct from burning the original) was not a crime. Burning a draft card was. Thus, this act represented not only symbolic dissent but direct resistance. Those who publicly burned their draft cards [crossed] the line between protest and civil disobedience."

e. "As applied to expression, the [O'Brien] statute had [a] disparate impact on those who opposed government policy, for who would destroy a draft card as an expression of *support* for government policy? [Indeed], in practical effect, the statute had essentially the same content-differential effect as a law prohibiting any person [to destroy] a draft card 'as a symbolic expression of protest against government policy.'" Stone, Content Regulation and the First Amendment, 25 Wm. & Mary L. Rev. 189, 222–223 (1983).

Is the Court's analysis of symbolic expression in *O'Brien* consistent with its analysis of content-neutral restrictions generally? Consider Ely, supra, at 1488–1489: "What was unconsciously going on in *O'Brien* [was] a reservation [of] serious balancing [for] relatively familiar [means] of expression, such as pamphlets, pickets, public speeches and rallies, [and a relegation of] other, less orthodox modes of communication to the [highly deferential approach] that sustained the draft card burning law."

5. *"Incidental" restrictions on free speech.* Note that, unlike most content-neutral restrictions, such as laws prohibiting leafleting, the law at issue in *O'Brien* was not expressly directed at speech. Its effect on speech was merely "incidental." Should it matter whether a content-neutral law expressly restricts

speech or whether it restricts a broader range of activities but has only an incidental effect on speech? For analysis of incidental restrictions, see Kagan, Private Speech, Public Purpose: The Role of Governmental Motive in First Amendment Doctrine, 63 U. Chi. L. Rev. 415, 494–508 (1996) (the distinction between direct and incidental restrictions can be explained largely in terms of the concern with avoiding possible improper governmental motivation); Rubenfeld, The First Amendment's Purpose, 53 Stan. L. Rev. 767, 769 (2001) ("there is no such thing as a free speech immunity based on the claim that someone wants to break an otherwise constitutional law for expressive purposes"); Dorf, Incidental Burdens on Fundamental Rights, 109 Harv. L. Rev. 1175 (1996) ("sound reasons can be advanced for taking direct burdens more seriously than incidental burdens," but "*substantial* incidental burdens" raise "a bona fide constitutional problem"); Stone, Content-Neutral Restrictions, 54 U. Chi. L. Rev. 46, 114 (1987) (incidental restrictions may be unconstitutional if they have a highly disproportionate and significant impact on particular viewpoints).

For an example of a (relatively rare) decision in which the Court has invalidated an incidental restriction on expression, see NAACP v. Alabama, section E5, infra, in which the Court held at the height of the civil rights movement that an Alabama statute requiring all out-of-state corporations doing business in the state to disclose the names and addresses of all Alabama "members" was invalid as applied to the NAACP, because "on past occasions revelation of the identity of [the NAACP's] rank-and-file members has exposed these members to economic reprisal, loss of employment, threat of physical coercion, and other manifestations of public hostility." The Court concluded that, "under these circumstances, [compelled] disclosure of [the NAACP's] Alabama membership is likely to affect adversely the ability of [the NAACP] and its members to pursue their [constitutional rights]." For a more recent example, see Boy Scouts of America v. Dale, section E5, infra.

6. *When is an incidental restriction not "incidental"*? A paradigm example of an incidental restriction might be a law prohibiting any person to speed, as applied to an individual who speeds in order to express his opposition to speed limits. Note that two factors are present in this situation: (1) the law is not directed at speech, and (2) it is not the expressive element of the act that causes the harm the state seeks to prevent. Both factors must be present for the incidental effect doctrine to apply. Consider, for example, a prosecution for breach of the peace based on an inflammatory speech given by an individual on a street corner that causes a fight. The breach of the peace statute is not directed at speech, as such. It applies to all sorts of nonspeech conduct, such as making loud noises late at night in a residential neighborhood or parking one's car on a sidewalk. In that sense, the statute has only an incidental effect on speakers. But because the speaker has breached the peace because of the response of others to the message he has conveyed, the Court does not treat this as a mere incidental effect. Indeed, this is implicit in the World War I cases in which defendants were prosecuted for "obstructing the draft" and in the hostile audience cases in which they were prosecuted for breach of the peace. Put simply, where the relevant harm is caused by the message, the incidental effects doctrine is inapplicable.

Along these lines, consider Holder v. Humanitarian Law Project, 561 U.S. 1 (2010), which involved the constitutionality of a federal statute declaring it unlawful for any person knowingly to provide "material support" to a foreign terrorist organization, where the statute defined "material support" as including, among other things, property, money, lodging, safehouses, facilities, weapons, and expert advice. Plaintiffs, who wanted to advise foreign terrorist organizations how to further their ends through legal channels, challenged the constitutionality of the statute as applied to them. The government argued that the statute had only an incidental effect on speech and that *O'Brien* should govern. Although the Court upheld the statute on other grounds, it unanimously rejected the government's argument:

> *O'Brien* does not provide the applicable standard for reviewing a content-based regulation of speech, and [this statute] regulates speech on the basis of its content. [The government] argues that [the statute falls under *O'Brien*] because it *generally* functions as a regulation of conduct. That argument runs headlong into a number of our precedents, most prominently Cohen v. California, [which] involved a generally applicable regulation of conduct, barring breaches of the peace. But when Cohen was convicted for wearing a jacked bearing an epithet, we did not apply *O'Brien*. Instead, we recognized that the generally applicable law was directed at Cohen because of what his speech communicated — he violated the breach of the peace statute because of the offensive content of his particular message. We accordingly applied more rigorous scrutiny and reversed his conviction. This suit falls into the same category.

7. *The problem of legislative motivation.* Should the Court in *O'Brien* have invalidated the 1965 amendment because "the 'purpose' of Congress was 'to suppress freedom of speech'"? As the Court noted, only two Representatives and one Senator commented directly on the legislation. Congressman Bray's comments are representative: "The need of this legislation is clear. Beatniks and so-called 'campus cults' have been publicly burning their draft cards to demonstrate their contempt for the United States and our resistance to Communist takeovers. [If] these 'revolutionaries' are permitted to deface and destroy their draft cards, our entire Selective Service System is dealt a serious blow."

Consider Alfange, supra, at 15, 16: "[What] emerges with indisputable clarity from an examination of the legislative history of the amendment is that the intent of its framers was purely and simply to put a stop to this particular form of antiwar protest, which they deemed extraordinarily contemptible and vicious — even treasonous — at a time when American troops were engaged in combat. [The Court's contrary conclusion blinked] the facts."

The Court has often inquired into the motivation underlying executive and administrative decisions. See, e.g., Cornelius v. NAACP Legal Defense & Educational Fund, 473 U.S. 788 (1985) ("the existence of reasonable grounds for limiting access to a nonpublic forum [will] not save a regulation that is in reality a facade for viewpoint-based discrimination"); Mt. Healthy City School District Board of Education v. Doyle, 429 U.S. 274 (1977) (although untenured teacher can be dismissed for "no reason whatever," he cannot be fired for exercise of first amendment rights); Keyes v. School District No. 1, 413 U.S. 189 (1973) (Denver schools held unlawfully segregated because school board decisions concerning the location of schools were motivated by racial considerations); Yick Wo v. Hopkins, 118 U.S. 356 (1886) (licensing law invalidated because of discriminatory administration).

As indicated in *O'Brien*, however, the Court has been reluctant to inquire into the motivation underlying legislative actions. Three explanations have usually been offered for this reluctance: the difficulty of ascertaining the "actual" motivation of a collective body; the futility of invalidating a law that could be reenacted with a show of "wiser" motives; and the inappropriateness of impugning the integrity of a coordinate branch of government. Are these explanations sufficiently weighty to justify the conclusion that "the purpose of Congress [is] not a basis for declaring [legislation] unconstitutional"? See Brest, Palmer v. Thompson: An Approach to the Problem of Unconstitutional Legislative Motive, 1971 Sup. Ct. Rev. 95; Ely, Legislative and Administrative Motivation in Constitutional Law, 79 Yale L.J. 1205 (1970). For more on the problem of "motivation," see Chapter 5, section C2, supra.

Note: *Flag Desecration and Misuse*

1. *Flag burning.* In Street v. New York, 394 U.S. 576 (1969), appellant, after hearing a news report that civil rights leader James Meredith had been shot, took his American flag out of a drawer, carried it to a nearby street corner, and lit it with a match. As it burned on the pavement, appellant said to a group of onlookers, "We don't need no damn flag. [If] they let that happen to Meredith we don't need an American flag." Appellant was convicted of violating a New York statute declaring it a misdemeanor "publicly [to] mutilate, deface, defile, trample upon, or cast contempt upon either by words or acts [any flag of the United States]." The Court, in a five-to-four decision, overturned appellant's conviction. The Court found it unnecessary, however, to address appellant's assertion "that New York may not constitutionally punish one who publicly destroys or damages an American flag as a means of protest," holding instead that the statute "was unconstitutionally applied in appellant's case because it permitted him to be punished merely for *speaking* defiant or contemptuous *words about* the American flag."

Chief Justice Warren and Justices Black, White, and Fortas dissented. Chief Justice Warren chastised the Court for ducking "the basic question presented": "'whether the deliberate act of burning an American flag in public as a "protest" may be punished as a crime.'" On that question, Chief Justice Warren concluded that "the States and the Federal Government [have] the power to protect the flag from acts of desecration and disgrace." In a separate dissenting opinion, Justice Fortas elaborated:

> If a state statute provided that it is a misdemeanor to burn one's shirt [on] the public thoroughfare, it could hardly be asserted that the citizen's constitutional right is violated. [And if] the arsonist asserted that he was burning his shirt [as] a protest against the Government's fiscal policies, [it] is hardly possible that his claim to First Amendment shelter would prevail against the State's claim of a right to avert danger to the public and to avoid obstruction to traffic as a result of the fire. [If], as I submit, it is permissible to prohibit the burning of personal property on the public sidewalk, there is no basis for applying a different rule to flag burning. And the fact that the law is violated for purposes of protest does not immunize the violator. [Citing *O'Brien*.]

Suppose Street had been convicted of violating a law prohibiting any person to make any "open fire in public." Is the flag desecration statute distinguishable?

2. *Contemptuous treatment.* In Smith v. Goguen, 415 U.S. 566 (1974), appellee, who wore a small cloth replica of the United States flag sewn to the seat of his trousers, was convicted of violating a Massachusetts statute prohibiting any person to "publicly mutilate, trample upon, deface or treat contemptuously

the flag of the United States." The Court, in an opinion by Justice Powell, over-turned the conviction. The Court found it unnecessary to decide whether the statute was unconstitutionally overbroad, holding instead that it was "void for vagueness." The Court emphasized that appellee was charged not "with any act of physical desecration," but with "'publicly [treating] contemptuously the flag of the United States.'" Noting that "the flag has become 'an object of youth fashion and high camp,'" and that "casual treatment of the flag in many contexts has become a widespread contemporary phenomenon," the Court concluded that this aspect of the statute was "inherently vague" and hence violative of due process. Chief Justice Burger and Justices Blackmun and Rehnquist dissented.

3. *Flag misuse.* In Spence v. Washington, 418 U.S. 405 (1974), appellant, to protest the invasion of Cambodia and the killings at Kent State University, dis-played a United States flag, which he owned, out of the window of his apartment. Affixed to the flag was a large peace symbol made of removable tape. Appellant was convicted under Washington's "flag misuse" statute, which prohibited the exhibition of a United States flag to which is attached or superimposed "any word, figure, mark, design, drawing, or advertisement." The Court held, in a per curiam opinion, that, "as applied to appellant's activity," which the Court described as "a pointed expression of anguish by appellant about [the] affairs of his government," the Washington statute "impermissibly infringed free expression":

[The state maintains that it] has an interest in preserving the national flag as an unalloyed symbol of our country. [This] interest might be seen as an effort to prevent the appropriation of a revered national symbol by an individual, interest group, or enterprise where there was a risk that association of the symbol with a particular product or viewpoint might be taken erroneously as evidence of govern-mental endorsement. [Alternatively], the interest [may be understood as] based on the uniquely universal character of the national flag as a symbol. [If] it may be destroyed or permanently disfigured, it [could] lose its capability of mirroring the sentiments of all who view it.

[We] need not decide in this case whether the interest advanced by the [state] is valid. We assume, arguendo, that it is. [But even if] it is valid, [it] is directly related to expression in the context of activity like that undertaken by appellant. For that reason [the] four-step analysis of [O'Brien] is inapplicable. [We hold that the statute is] unconstitutional as applied to appellant's activity. There was no risk that appel-lant's acts would mislead viewers into assuming that the Government endorsed his viewpoint. [Moreover, appellant] did [not] permanently disfigure the flag or destroy it. [And] his message was direct, likely to be understood, and within the contours of the First Amendment. [The] conviction must be reversed.

Justice Rehnquist, joined by Chief Justice Burger and Justice White, dissented:

[The] Court's treatment [of the state's interest] lacks all substance. The suggestion that the State's interest somehow diminishes when the flag is decorated with *remov-able* tape trivializes something which is not trivial. The State [is] hardly seeking to protect the flag's resale value. [The] true nature of the State's interest in this case is [one] of preserving the flag as "an important symbol of nationhood and unity." [It] is the character, not the cloth, of the flag which the State seeks to protect. "[The] flag is a national property, and the Nation may regulate those who would make, imitate, sell, possess, or use it." . . .

[That] the State has a valid interest in preserving the character of the flag does not mean, of course, that it can employ all conceivable means to enforce it. It certainly could not require all citizens to own the flag or compel citizens to salute one. [It] presumably cannot punish criticism of the flag, or the principles for which it stands, any more than it could punish criticism of this country's policies or ideas. But the statute in this case demands no such allegiance. Its operation does not depend upon whether [the] use of the flag is respectful or contemptuous. [It] simply withdraws a unique national symbol from the roster of materials that may be used as a background for communications. [The] Constitution [does not prohibit] Washington from making that decision.

Is *Spence* consistent with *O'Brien*? Do you agree with the Court that the interests underlying flag misuse statutes are "directly related to expression," and that the *O'Brien* standard thus should not govern? Consider Ely, Flag Desecration: A Case Study in the Roles of Categorization and Balancing in First Amendment Analysis, 88 Harv. L. Rev. 1482, 1503–1504, 1506–1508 (1975):

[The flag misuse statute is] ideologically neutral on its face, and would proscribe the superimposition of "Buy Mother Fletcher's Ambulance Paint" [as] fully as it would the addition of a swastika. Such "improper use" provisions are [thus] more complicated constitutionally than the ideologically tilted "desecration" provisions. [In the flag misuse context], the state may assert an interest [similar] to that asserted in [defense of a content-neutral law prohibiting any person to interrupt a public speaker]. The state's interest in both of these cases might be characterized as an interest in preventing the [defendant] from interfering with the expression of others. [As with interruption of a public speaker, the] state does not care what message the defendant is conveying by altering the flag: all that matters is that he is interrupting the message conveyed by the flag. [There is, however, an answer to this argument, for] although improper use statutes do not single out certain messages for proscription, they *do* single out one set of messages, namely the set of messages conveyed by the American flag, for protection. That, of course, is not true of a law that generally prohibits the interruption of speakers. [In reality, then, an improper use statute] is, at best, analogous to a law prohibiting the interruption of patriotic speeches, and that is a law that is hardly "unrelated to the suppression of free expression."

4. *Flag desecration.* The Court directly confronted the issue of flag desecration in Texas v. Johnson, 491 U.S. 397 (1989). During the 1984 Republican National Convention, Johnson burned an American flag as part of a political demonstration protesting the policies of the Reagan administration. Johnson was arrested and convicted of violating a Texas flag desecration statute, which made it a crime for any person to "deface, damage or otherwise physically mistreat" the flag "in a way that the actor knows will seriously offend one or more persons likely to observe or discover his action." The Court, in a five-to-four decision, overturned the conviction.

In an opinion by Justice Brennan, the Court began by concluding that "Johnson's flag-burning was 'conduct' sufficiently imbued with elements of 'communication' to implicate the First Amendment." After rejecting the claim that the statute could be justified in terms of the state's interest in "preventing breaches of the peace," see section B2 supra, the Court turned to the heart of the issue:

The Government generally has a freer hand in restricting expressive conduct than it has in restricting the written or spoken word. It may not, however, proscribe particular conduct *because* it has expressive elements. [Thus], although we have recognized that where "'speech' and 'nonspeech' elements are combined in the same course of conduct, a sufficiently important governmental interest in regulating the nonspeech element can justify incidental limitations on First Amendment freedoms," [O'Brien], we have limited the applicability of O'Brien's relatively lenient standard to those cases in which "the governmental interest is unrelated to the suppression of free expression." . . .

The State [asserts] an interest in preserving the flag as a symbol of nationhood and national unity. [We are] persuaded that this interest is related to expression in the case of Johnson's burning of the flag. The State, apparently, is concerned that such conduct will lead people to believe either that the flag does not stand for nationhood and national unity, but instead reflects other, less positive concepts, or that the concepts reflected in the flag do not in fact exist, that is, we do not enjoy unity as a Nation. These concerns blossom only when a person's treatment of the flag communicates some message, and thus are related "to the suppression of free expression" within the meaning of O'Brien. . . .

It remains to consider whether the State's interest in preserving the flag as a symbol of nationhood and national unity justifies Johnson's conviction. [Johnson] was prosecuted because he knew that his politically charged expression would cause "serious offense." [The] Texas law is thus not aimed at protecting the physical integrity of the flag in all circumstances, but is designed instead to protect it only against impairments that would cause serious offense to others. [Whether] Johnson's treatment of the flag violated Texas law thus depended on the likely communicative impact of his expressive conduct. [Because] this restriction [is] content-based, [we must] subject the State's asserted interest [to] "the most exacting scrutiny." . . .

If there is a bedrock principle underlying the First Amendment, it is that the Government may not prohibit the expression of an idea simply because society finds the idea itself offensive or disagreeable. We have not recognized an exception to this principle even where our flag is involved. [Citing *Street; Spence;* and *Goguen.*] [Nothing] in our precedents suggests that a State may foster its own view of the flag by prohibiting expressive conduct related to it. [If] we were to hold that a State may forbid flag-burning wherever it is likely to endanger the flag's symbolic role, but allow it wherever burning a flag promotes that role — as where, for example, a person ceremoniously burns a dirty flag — we would be saying that when it comes to impairing the flag's physical integrity, the flag itself may be used as a symbol [only] in one direction. We would be permitting a State to "prescribe what shall be orthodox" by saying that one may burn the flag to convey one's attitude toward it and its referents only if one does not endanger the flag's representation of nationhood and national unity.

We never before have held that the Government may ensure that a symbol be used to express only one view of that symbol or its referents. [Citing *Schacht.*] To conclude that the Government may permit designated symbols to be used to communicate only a limited set of messages would be to enter territory having no discernible or defensible boundaries. Could the Government, on this theory, prohibit the burning of state flags? Of copies of the presidential seal? Of the Constitution? . . .

Chief Justice Rehnquist, joined by Justices White and O'Connor, dissented:

The flag is not simply another "idea" or "point of view" competing for recognition in the marketplace of ideas. [Flag burning is] no essential part of any expression of ideas, [citing *Chaplinsky*], and [Johnson's] act [conveyed] nothing that could not have been conveyed [in] a dozen different ways. [Far] from being a case of "one picture being worth a thousand words," flag burning is the equivalent of an inarticulate grunt or roar that [is] most likely to be indulged in not to express any particular idea, but to antagonize others. [The] Texas statute deprived Johnson of only one rather inarticulate symbolic form of protest — a form of protest that was profoundly offensive to many — and left him with a full panoply of other symbols and every conceivable form of verbal expression to express his deep disapproval of national policy. Thus, in no way can it be said that Texas is punishing him because his hearers — or any other group of people — were profoundly opposed to the message that he sought to convey. [It] was Johnson's use of this particular symbol, and not the idea that he sought to convey by [it], for which he was punished.

Justice Stevens also dissented.

5. *Flag desecration revisited.* Almost immediately after the decision in *Johnson*, Congress enacted the Flag Protection Act of 1989, which made it a crime for any person knowingly to mutilate, deface, physically defile, burn, maintain on the floor or ground, or trample upon any flag of the United States. The government maintained that this act was constitutional because, unlike the statute addressed in *Johnson*, the act was designed to protect "the physical integrity of the flag under all circumstances," did "not target expressive conduct on the basis of the content of its message," and proscribed "conduct (other than disposal) that damages or mistreats a flag, without regard to the actor's motive, his intended message, or the likely effects of his conduct on onlookers." In United States v. Eichman, 496 U.S. 310 (1990), the Court, in a five-to-four decision, invalidated this act.

Justice Brennan delivered the opinion:

Although the [act] contains no explicit content-based limitation on the scope of prohibited conduct, it is nevertheless clear that the Government's asserted *interest* is "related to the suppression of free expression" and concerned with the content of such expression. The Government's interest in protecting the "physical integrity" of a privately owned flag rests upon a perceived need to preserve the flag's status as a symbol of our Nation and certain national ideals. But the mere destruction or disfigurement of a particular physical manifestation of the symbol, without more, does not diminish or otherwise affect the symbol itself in any way. For example, the secret destruction of a flag in one's own basement would not threaten the flag's recognized meaning. Rather, the Government's desire to preserve the flag as a symbol for certain national ideals is implicated "only when a person's treatment of the flag communicates [a] message" to others that is inconsistent with those ideals.

Moreover, the precise language of the Act's prohibitions confirms Congress' interest in the communicative impact of flag destruction. The Act criminalizes the conduct of anyone who "knowingly mutilates, defaces, physically defiles, burns, maintains on the floor or ground, or tramples upon any flag." Each of the specified terms — with the possible exception of "burns" — unmistakably connotes disrespectful treatment. . . .

Although Congress cast the [act] in somewhat broader terms than the Texas statute at issue in *Johnson*, the Act still suffers from the same fundamental flaw: it suppresses expression out of concern for its likely communicative impact. Despite the Act's wider scope, its restriction on expression cannot be "'justified without reference to the content of the regulated speech.'" The Act therefore must be subjected to "the most exacting scrutiny," and for the reasons stated in *Johnson*, the Government's interest cannot justify its infringement on First Amendment rights.

Justice Stevens, joined by Chief Justice Rehnquist and Justices White and O'Connor, dissented.

Central to the Court's reasoning in *Eichman* is its assertion that the Flag Protection Act was "related to the suppression of free expression" because "the Government's desire to preserve the flag as a symbol for certain national ideals" is implicated "only when a person's treatment of the flag 'communicates [a] message' to others that is inconsistent with those ideals." Is that assertion persuasive? Suppose Congress enacts the following statute: "No person may knowingly impair the physical integrity of the American flag." Do *Johnson* and *Eichman* require the invalidation of this law? See Stone, Flag Burning and the Constitution, 75 Iowa L. Rev. 111 (1989). Could government constitutionally protect the flag as a matter of copyright law? See Kmiec, In the Aftermath of *Johnson* and *Eichman*, 1990 B.Y.U. L. Rev. 577.

BARNES v. GLEN THEATRE, INC., 501 U.S. 560 (1991). Respondents, two Indiana establishments that present nude dancing as entertainment, brought suit to enjoin enforcement of Indiana's public indecency statute, which prohibits any person to appear "in a state of nudity" in any "public place." The state courts interpreted the statute as requiring nude dancers in such establishments to wear pasties and a G-string. The Court, in a five-to-four decision, rejected the claim that this statute, as applied to respondents, violates the first amendment.

Chief Justice Rehnquist, joined by Justices O'Connor and Kennedy, delivered the plurality opinion: "[Nude] dancing of the kind sought to be performed here is expressive conduct within the outer perimeters of the First Amendment, though we view it as only marginally so. [Indiana], of course, has not banned nude dancing as such, but has proscribed public nudity across the board. [Applying] the four-part *O'Brien* test, we find that Indiana's public indecency statute is justified despite its incidental limitations on some expressive activity. The public indecency statute is clearly within the constitutional power of the State and furthers substantial governmental interests. [Such statutes, which] are of ancient origin, and presently exist in at least 47 States, [reflect] moral disapproval of people appearing in the nude among strangers in public places. [The] traditional police power of the States is defined as the authority to provide for the public health, safety, and morals, and we have upheld such a basis for legislation. [Citing *Roth*, section D5 supra; *Paris Adult Theatre*, section D5, supra.]

"This interest is unrelated to the suppression of free expression. [Respondents contend] that even though prohibiting nudity in public generally may not be related to suppressing expression, prohibiting the performance of nude dancing is related to expression because the state seeks to prevent its erotic message. [But] we do not think that when Indiana applies its statute to the nude dancing in these nightclubs it is proscribing nudity because of the erotic message conveyed by the dancers. Presumably numerous other erotic performances are presented at these establishments [without] any interference from the state, so long as the performers wear a scant amount of clothing. Likewise, the requirement that the dancers don pasties and a G-string does not deprive the dance of whatever erotic message it conveys; it simply makes the message slightly less graphic. The perceived evil that Indiana seeks to address is not erotic dancing, but public nudity. The appearance of people of all shapes and sizes in the nude at a beach, for example, would convey little if any erotic message, yet the state still seeks to prevent it. Public nudity is the evil the state seeks to prevent, whether or not it is combined with expressive activity. . . ."

Justice Scalia filed a separate concurring opinion: "[The] challenged regulation must be upheld [because], as a general law regulating conduct and not specifically directed at expression, it is not subject to First Amendment scrutiny at all. [Virtually] every law restricts conduct, and virtually any prohibited conduct can be performed for an expressive purpose — if only expressive of the fact that the actor disagrees with the prohibition. It cannot reasonably be demanded, therefore, that every restriction of expression incidentally produced by a general law regulating conduct pass normal First Amendment scrutiny, or even — as some of our cases have suggested, see, e.g., *O'Brien* — that it be justified by an 'important or substantial' government interest. . . .

"This is not to say that the first amendment affords no protection to expressive conduct. Where the government prohibits conduct precisely because of its communicative attributes, we hold the regulation unconstitutional. See, e.g., *Eichman; Johnson; Spence*. [In] each of the foregoing cases, we explicitly found that suppressing communication was the object of the regulation of conduct. Where that has not been the case, however — where suppression of communicative use of the conduct was merely the incidental effect of forbidding the conduct for other reasons — we have allowed the regulation to stand. [All] our holdings (though admittedly not some of our discussion) support the conclusion that 'the only First Amendment analysis applicable to laws that do not directly or indirectly impede speech is the threshold inquiry of whether the purpose of the law is to suppress communication. If not, that is the end of the [matter].' We have explicitly adopted such a regime in another First Amendment context: that of Free Exercise. [Citing Employment Division, Department of Human Resources v. Smith, Chapter 8, section C, infra.] I think we should avoid wherever possible [a] mode of analysis that requires judicial assessment of the 'importance' of government interests — and especially of government interests in various aspects of morality."

Justice Souter also filed a concurring opinion: "[I] agree with the plurality that the appropriate analysis to determine the actual protection required by the First Amendment is the four-part enquiry described in *O'Brien*. [I rest my concurrence, however,] not on the possible sufficiency of society's moral views [but] on the State's substantial interest in combating the secondary effects of adult establishments of the sort typified by respondents' establishments. [In] my view, the interest [in] preventing prostitution, sexual assault, and other criminal activity, although presumably not a justification for all applications of the statute, is sufficient under *O'Brien* to justify the State's enforcement of the statute against the type of adult entertainment at issue here. [Citing *Renton* and *Young*, section D7 supra.] [This] justification of the statute may not be ignored merely because it is unclear to what extent this purpose motivated the Indiana Legislature in enacting the statute. Our appropriate focus is not an empirical enquiry into the actual intent of the enacting legislature, but rather the existence [of a] governmental interest in the service of which the challenged application of the statute may be constitutional. [The] secondary effects rationale on which I rely would be open to question if the State were to seek to enforce the statute by barring expressive nudity in classes of productions that could not readily be analogized to the adult films at issue in *Renton*. It is difficult to see, for example, how the enforcement of Indiana's statute against nudity in a production of 'Hair' or 'Equus' somewhere other than in an 'adult' theater would further the State's interest in avoiding harmful secondary effects. . . ."

Justice White, joined by Justices Marshall, Blackmun, and Stevens, dissented: "The purpose of forbidding people from appearing nude in parks, beaches, hot dog stands, and like public places is to protect others from offense. But that could not possibly be the purpose of preventing nude dancing in theaters and barrooms since the viewers are exclusively consenting adults who pay money to see these dances. The purpose of the proscription in these contexts is to protect the viewers from what the State believes is the harmful message that nude dancing communicates. [This] being the case, it cannot be that the statutory prohibition is unrelated to expressive conduct. [It] is only because nude dancing performances may generate emotions and feelings of eroticism and sensuality among the spectators that the State seeks to regulate such expressive activity, apparently on the assumption that creating or emphasizing such thoughts and ideas in the minds of the spectators may lead to increased prostitution and the degradation of women. But generating thoughts, ideas, and emotions is the essence of communication. The nudity element of nude dancing performances cannot be neatly pigeonholed as mere 'conduct' independent of any expressive component of the dance. That fact dictates the level of First Amendment protection to be accorded the performances at issue here. [Content] based restrictions 'will be upheld only if narrowly drawn to accomplish a compelling governmental interest.' [Neither] the Court nor the State suggests that the statute could withstand scrutiny under that standard."

Consider Justice Scalia's response to Justice White's dissent: "The dissent confidently asserts that the purpose of restricting nudity in public places in general is to protect nonconsenting parties from offense; and argues that since only consenting, admission-paying patrons see respondents dance, that purpose cannot apply and the only remaining purpose must relate to the communicative elements of the performance. Perhaps the dissenters believe that 'offense to others' ought to be the only reason for restricting nudity in public places generally, but there is no basis for thinking that our society has ever shared that Thoreauvian 'you-may-do-what-you-like-so-long-as-it-does-not-injure-someone-else' beau ideal — much less for thinking that it was written into the Constitution. The purpose of Indiana's nudity law would be violated, I think, if 60,000 fully consenting adults crowded into the Hoosierdome to display their genitals to one another, even if there were not an offended innocent in the crowd. Our society prohibits, and all human societies have prohibited, certain activities not because they harm others but because they are considered in the traditional phrase, 'contra bonos mores,' i.e., immoral. [The] purpose of the Indiana statute [is] to enforce the traditional moral belief that people should not expose their private parts indiscriminately, regardless of whether those who see them are disedified. Since that is so, the dissent has no basis for positing that, where only thoroughly edified adults are present, the purpose must be repression of communication."

Consider the constitutionality, after *Barnes*, of the application of Indiana's public nudity statute to movies, art exhibits, and television productions depicting nudity. For the argument that "the outcome in *Barnes* would have been different" had Indiana attempted to apply its "statute to accepted media for the communication of ideas, as for example by attempting to prohibit nudity in movies or in the theater," see Post, Recuperating First Amendment Doctrine, 47 Stan. L. Rev. 1249, 1255–1259 (1995); Kagan, Regulation of Hate Speech and Pornography after *R.A.V.*, 60 U. Chi. L. Rev. 873, 887–888 (1993) (arguing that the application of pandering statutes to the producers of sexually-explicit but non-obscene movies is "questionable" because of the "potential for applying such statutes to large amounts of speech at the core of constitutional protection"); People v. Freeman, 758 P.2d 1128 (1988) (reversing the pandering conviction of a film producer who had paid actors to copulate on screen).

CITY OF ERIE v. PAP'S A.M., 529 U.S. 277 (2000). Erie, Pennsylvania, enacted an ordinance banning public nudity. The preamble stated that the "purpose" of the ordinance was to respond to "a recent increase in nude live entertainment within the City, which activity adversely impacts . . . the public health, safety and welfare by providing an atmosphere conducive to violence, sexual harassment, public intoxication, prostitution, the spread of sexually trans-mitted diseases and other deleterious effects." The ordinance was challenged by the owner of Kandyland, a nude dancing establishment. Does the existence of this preamble distinguish this case from *Barnes*? The Court, in a six-to-three decision, upheld the ordinance.

Justice O'Connor delivered a plurality opinion, joined by Chief Justice Rehn-quist and Justices Kennedy and Breyer: "The ordinance here, like the statute in *Barnes*, is on its face a general prohibition on public nudity. [It] bans all public nudity, regardless of whether that nudity is accompanied by expressive activity. [Moreover, the] State's interest in preventing harmful secondary effects is not related to the suppression of expression. In trying to control the secondary effects of nude dancing, the ordinance seeks to deter crime and the other deleterious effects caused by the presence of such an establishment in the neighborhood. [Citing *Renton.*]

"[Even] if Erie's public nudity ban has some minimal effect on the erotic message by muting that portion of the expression that occurs when the last stitch is dropped, [erotic dancers] are free to perform wearing pasties and G-strings. Any effect on the overall expression is *de minimis.* . . .

"[This] case is, in fact, similar to [*O'Brien*]. The justification for the govern-ment regulation in each case prevents harmful 'secondary' effects that are unre-lated to the suppression of expression. [While] the doctrinal theories behind 'incidental burdens' and 'secondary effects' are, of course, not identical, there is nothing objectionable about a city passing a general ordinance to ban public nudity (even though such a ban may place incidental burdens on some protected speech) and at the same time recognizing that one specific occurrence of public nudity — nude erotic dancing — is particularly problematic because it produces harmful secondary effects. . . .

"We conclude that Erie's asserted interest in combating the negative secondary effects associated with adult entertainment establishments [is] unrelated to the suppression of the erotic message conveyed by nude dancing. The ordinance [is] therefore valid if it satisfies the four-factor test from *O'Brien* for evaluating restric-tions on symbolic speech." Justice O'Connor then went on to find that the ordinance did, indeed, satisfy the *O'Brien* test.

Justice Scalia, joined by Justice Thomas, concurred in the judgment, reaffirm-ing his position in *Barnes* that because the public nudity ordinance is "a general law regulating conduct and not specifically directed at expression, it is not subject to First Amendment scrutiny at all." Justice Scalia argued further that the exist-ence of the preamble is irrelevant to the constitutionality of the ordinance because it neither "make[s] the law any less general in its reach nor demon-strate[s] that what the municipal authorities *really* find objectionable is expres-sion rather than public nakedness."

Justice Stevens, joined by Justice Ginsburg, dissented: "The censorial purpose of Erie's ordinance precludes reliance on [Barnes]. As its preamble forthrightly admits, the ordinance's 'purpose' is to 'limit' a protected form of speech. [Moreover,] Erie's ordinance differs from the statute in Barnes in another respect, [for in] an earlier proceeding in this case, [the city stipulated that it had] permitted a production of [the play] Equus to proceed without prosecution [even though it included public nudity]. [Thus, unlike the statute in Barnes, the Erie] ordinance is deliberately targeted at Kandyland's type of nude dancing (to the exclusion of plays like Equus)."

In her plurality opinion, Justice O'Connor offered the following response to Justice Stevens's argument about the purpose of the ordinance: "The argument that the ordinance is 'aimed' at suppressing expression through a ban on nude dancing — an argument [supported] by pointing to statements [that] the public nudity ban was not intended to apply to 'legitimate' theater productions — is really an argument that the city council [had] an illicit motive in enacting the ordinance. [But] this Court will not strike down an otherwise constitutional statute on the basis of an alleged illicit motive. [Citing O'Brien.]" Justice Souter also dissented.

Note: Other Forms of Symbolic Speech

1. *Political boycotts.* Suppose an antiabortion group boycotts all manufacturers who sell supplies to abortion clinics. Is such a concerted refusal to deal "speech"? May the group constitutionally be punished under a statute that prohibits "two or more persons, acting in concert, to refuse to deal with any merchant in an effort to induce such merchant to adopt a policy it would not otherwise choose to adopt"? See NAACP v. Claiborne Hardware Co., 458 U.S. 886 (1982), in which the Court invalidated a civil judgment against the NAACP for instituting a boycott of white merchants designed to induce business and civic leaders to adopt a number of reforms, including the desegregation of public facilities. The Court explained that "speech does not lose its protected character . . . simply because it may . . . coerce [others] into action." And while "States have broad powers to regulate economic activity, we do not find a comparable right to prohibit peaceful political activity such as that found in the boycott in this case."

2. *Banning military recruiters.* Suppose law schools exclude from their placement facilities any employer, including the military, who discriminates against gays and lesbians. Suppose also that the government makes it a crime for any institution of higher education to discriminate against the military in the use of its placement facilities. Is the exclusion of military recruiters "speech" within the meaning of the first amendment? Is the constitutionality of the statute governed by O'Brien?

In Rumsfeld v. FAIR, 547 U.S. 47 (2006), the Court, in an opinion by Chief Justice Roberts, declared that "we have extended First Amendment protection only to conduct that is *inherently* expressive." Unlike burning a draft card, the exclusion by law schools of military recruiters "is not inherently expressive," because such conduct has meaning only if the law schools accompany "their conduct with speech explaining it." Indeed, "an observer who sees military recruiters interviewing away from the law school has no way of knowing whether the law school is expressing its disapproval of the military, all the law school's interview rooms are full, or the military recruiters decided for reasons of their own that they would rather interview someplace else." The Court concluded that the fact that "explanatory speech is necessary" to give content to the act "is strong evidence that the conduct [is] not so inherently expressive that it warrants protection under *O'Brien*." In any event, the Court held that even if the law were regarded as incidentally burdening speech it would satisfy *O'Brien* because it serves the government's legitimate interest in facilitating military recruitment. For more on *FAIR*, see section E5 infra.

3. *Are signatures on a referendum petition "speech" within the meaning of the First Amendment?* In Doe v. Reed, 561 U.S. 186 (2010), the Court considered the constitutionality of a Washington state public records statute that authorizes the public disclosure of the names of individuals who sign referendum petitions. The plaintiffs argued that public disclosure would chill the willingness of individuals to sign such petitions. Although upholding the statute on its face, the Court rejected the argument that such signatures are not "speech" because "signing a petition is a legally operative legislative act and therefore 'does not involve any significant expressive element.'" The Court concluded that "[p]etition signing remains expressive even when it has legal effect in the electoral process."

4. *Are legislative votes "speech" within the meaning of the First Amendment?* In Nevada Comm'n on Ethics v. Carrigan, 564 U.S. 117 (2011), Carrigan, a state legislator, voted to approve a casino project that had used his long-time friend and campaign manager as a paid consultant. The commission held that, by so doing, Carrigan had violated a state ethics rule prohibiting public officials from voting on legislative matters with respect to which they have a conflict of interest. Carrigan claimed that this finding violated his rights under the First Amendment. The key issue was whether the casting of a vote by a state legislator is constitutionally protected speech. In a unanimous decision, the Court rejected Carrigan's claim.

Justice Scalia delivered the opinion of the Court: "Laws punishing libel and obscenity are not thought to violate 'the freedom of speech' [because] such laws existed in 1791 and have been in place ever since. The same is true of legislative recusal rules. [Such] rules have been commonplace for over 200 years. '[E]arly congressional enactments "provid[e] contemporaneous and weighty evidence of the Constitution's meaning,'" [and that] evidence is dispositive here. Within 15 years of the founding, both the House of Representatives and the Senate adopted recusal rules. [Moreover, today,] virtually every State has enacted some type of recusal law. . . .

"But how can it be that restrictions upon legislators' voting are not restrictions upon legislators' protected speech? The answer is that a legislator's vote is the commitment of his apportioned share of the legislature's power to the passage or defeat of a particular proposal. The legislative power thus committed is not personal to the legislator but belongs to the people; the legislator has no personal right to it. [In] this respect, voting by a legislator is different from voting by a citizen. . . .

"Carrigan and Justice Alito [cite] Doe v. Reed as establishing 'the expressive character of voting.' But *Reed* did no such thing. That case held only that a citizen's signing of a petition — "'core political speech'" — was not deprived of its protected status simply because, under state law, a petition that garnered a sufficient number of signatures would suspend the state law to which it pertained, pending a referendum. It is one thing to say that an inherently expressive act remains so despite its having governmental effect, but it is altogether another thing to say that a governmental act becomes expressive simply because the governmental actor wishes it to be so." Justices Alito and Kennedy filed concurring opinions.

Are you persuaded by the Court's distinction of Doe v. Reed? What do you think of the Court's "originalist" argument? Note that Justice Scalia was wrong about obscenity laws. In fact, there were no anti-obscenity laws in the United States until the nineteenth century. See Stone, Sex, Violence, and the First Amendment, 74 U. Chi. L. Rev. 1857, 1861–1863 (2007). What does this tell you about the dangers of "originalism" as a method of constitutional interpretation? Does Carrigan suggest that New York Times v. Sullivan was wrong and that a modern Sedition Act based on the Sedition Act of 1798 would be constitutional?

4. Other Means of Expression: Litigation, Association, and the Right Not to Speak

NAACP v. BUTTON, 371 U.S. 415 (1963). For more than a decade, the Virginia Conference of the NAACP had financed litigation aimed at ending racial segregation in the public schools of Virginia. In 1956, the Virginia legislature enacted chapter 33, which prohibited any organization to retain a lawyer in connection with litigation to which it was not a party and in which it had no pecuniary right or liability. The Supreme Court held that, as applied to the NAACP's activities, chapter 33 violated the first amendment. Justice Brennan delivered the opinion:

"In the context of NAACP objectives, litigation is not a technique of resolving private differences; it is a means for [achieving] equality of treatment [for] the members of the Negro [community]. It is [a] form of political expression. Groups which find themselves unable to achieve their objectives through the ballot frequently turn to the courts. [Under] Chapter 33, [a] person who advises another that his legal rights have been infringed and refers him to a particular attorney [for] assistance has committed a [crime]. There thus inheres in the statute the gravest danger of smothering all discussion looking to the eventual institution of litigation on behalf of the rights of members of an unpopular minority. [We] cannot close our eyes to the fact that the militant Negro civil rights movement has engendered the intense resentment and opposition of the politically dominant white community of Virginia. [In] such circumstances, a statute broadly curtailing group activity leading to litigation may easily become a weapon of oppression, however even-handed its terms appear. Its mere existence could well freeze out of existence all such activity on behalf of the civil rights of Negro citizens.

"It is apparent, therefore, that Chapter 33 as construed limits First Amendment freedoms. [However] valid may be Virginia's interest in regulating the traditionally illegal practices of barratry, maintenance and champerty, that interest does not justify the prohibition of the NAACP activities disclosed by this record. Malicious intent was the essence of the common-law offenses of fomenting or stirring up litigation. [The exercise] of First Amendment rights to enforce constitutional rights through litigation, as a matter of law, cannot be deemed malicious. . . ."

Justice White concurred in part and dissented in part.

Justice Harlan, joined by Justices Clark and Stewart, dissented: "Freedom of expression embraces more than the right of an individual to speak his mind. It includes also his right to advocate and his right to join with his fellows in an effort to make that advocacy effective. And just as it includes the right jointly to petition the legislature for redress of grievances, so it must include the right to join together for purposes of obtaining judicial redress. . . .

"But to declare that litigation is a form of conduct that may be associated with political expression does not resolve this case. [For this Court has repeatedly held that] 'general regulatory statutes, not intended to control the content of speech but incidentally limiting its unfettered exercise,' are permissible 'when they have been found justified by subordinating valid governmental interests.' . . .

"The important function of organizations like petitioner in vindicating constitutional rights is [not] substantially impaired by this statute. [This] enactment [does] not in any way suppress [advocacy] of litigation in general or in particular. [Moreover, it does not] prevent petitioner from recommending the services of attorneys who are not subject to its directions and control. [It] prevents only the solicitation of business for attorneys subject to petitioner's control, and as so limited, should be sustained."

Note: Litigation and the First Amendment

1. Button *in context.* Consider H. Kalven, The Negro and the First Amendment 66–69, 75–79 (1965):

> One of the most distinctive features of the Negro revolution [of the 1950s and 1960s was] its almost military assault on the Constitution via the strategy of systematic litigation. [Chapter 33 was designed] to slow down [NAACP litigation]. Unless the NAACP [could go] out and sign up the client, pay for the case, and deliver the client to one of its expert lawyers, it [would have been] unable to recruit the needed flow of litigation. Unless it [could] control the timing and line of attack in the litigation once it was begun, its grand strategy of war by lawsuit [would have been] frustrated. [The] case thus raised a profound question for our scheme of constitutional adjudication.

2. *Litigation as "speech."* Why does *Button* pose a first amendment issue? Because the law might be discriminatorily applied against persons espousing a particular view? Because association for the purpose of litigation is "speech"? Because litigation is "speech"? Because litigation is "speech" when it attempts to enforce constitutional rights?

3. *The reach of* Button: Primus. In In re Primus, 436 U.S. 412 (1978), an ACLU "cooperating lawyer" wrote a letter to a woman who had been sterilized, informing her of the ACLU's willingness to provide free legal representation to women in her position in a proposed lawsuit challenging the constitutionality of an alleged program of sterilizing pregnant mothers as a condition of their continued receipt of Medicaid benefits. The Disciplinary Board of the South Carolina Supreme Court reprimanded the ACLU lawyer for violating a disciplinary rule prohibiting any "lawyer who has given unsolicited advice to a layman that he should [take] legal action [to] accept employment resulting from that advice."

The Court held the reprimand unconstitutional. The Court emphasized that "for the ACLU, as for the NAACP, 'litigation is not a technique of resolving private differences'; it is 'a form of political expression' and 'political association.'" To justify a restriction on such "'core First Amendment rights,'" the state must demonstrate that the attorney's "activity in fact involved the type of misconduct at which South Carolina's [prohibition on solicitation] is said to be directed." Since the record did "not support [the state's] contention that undue influence, over-reaching, misrepresentation, or invasion of privacy [had] actually occurred," the reprimand violated the first amendment.

See also United Transportation Union v. State Bar of Michigan, 401 U.S. 576 (1971) (invalidating an injunction prohibiting the union from recommending attorneys to its members only if the attorneys agreed that their fees would not exceed 25 percent of the recovery); United Mine Workers v. Illinois Bar Association, 389 U.S. 217 (1967) (invalidating an injunction prohibiting the union from employing a salaried attorney to assist its members with workers' compensation claims); Brotherhood of Railroad Trainmen v. Virginia State Bar, 377 U.S. 1 (1964) (invalidating an injunction prohibiting a union from recommending lawyers to its members to represent them in railroad personal injury litigation).

4. *The reach of* Button: Ohralik. In Ohralik v. Ohio State Bar Association, 436 U.S. 447 (1978), decided on the same day as *Primus*, appellant, an attorney, after learning about an automobile accident, personally contacted two young women who had been injured in the accident and arranged to represent them in subsequent litigation. As a result of this "ambulance chasing," Ohralik was suspended by the Ohio State Bar for violation of a disciplinary rule prohibiting any "lawyer who has given unsolicited advice to a layman that he should obtain counsel" to accept "employment resulting from that advice."

The Court upheld the suspension. The Court explained that *Ohralik* was not governed by *Button* and *Primus*, for appellant's "approaches to the young women [did not involve] political expression or an exercise of associational freedom '[to] secure constitutionally guaranteed civil rights.'" Moreover, *Ohralik* was not governed by the union cases, for "[appellant cannot] compare his solicitation to the mutual assistance in asserting legal rights that was at issue [in those cases]." Indeed, a "lawyer's procurement of remunerative employment is a subject only marginally affected with First Amendment concerns. It falls within the State's proper sphere of economic and professional regulation." Appellant's conduct, the Court added, was analogous to commercial expression, which occupies only a "subordinate position in the scale of First Amendment values." In light of changes in the commercial speech doctrine, is *Ohralik* still good law?

NAACP v. ALABAMA, 357 U.S. 449 (1958). Alabama has a statute, similar to those of many other states, that requires out-of-state corporations to qualify before doing business in the state. For membership organizations, this requirement includes disclosure of the names and addresses of all Alabama members of the organization. In an opinion by Justice Harlan, the Court held at the height of the civil rights movement in the South that this otherwise valid requirement could not constitutionally be applied to the NAACP:

"It is hardly a novel perception that compelled disclosure of affiliation with groups engaged in advocacy may constitute [an effective] restraint on freedom of association. [There is a] vital relationship between freedom to associate and privacy in one's associations. [Inviolability] of privacy in group association may in many circumstances be indispensable to preservation of freedom of association, particularly where a group espouses dissident beliefs. . . .

"We think that the production order [must] be regarded as entailing the likelihood of a substantial restraint upon the exercise by petitioner's members of their right to freedom of association. Petitioner has made an uncontroverted showing that on past occasions revelation of the identity of its rank-and-file members has exposed these members to economic reprisal, loss of employment, threat of physical coercion, and other manifestations of public hostility. Under these circumstances, we think it apparent that compelled disclosure of petitioner's Alabama membership is likely to affect adversely the ability of petitioner and its members to pursue their collective effort to foster beliefs which they admittedly have the right to advocate, in that it may induce members to withdraw from the Association and dissuade others from joining it because of fear of exposure of their beliefs shown through their associations and of the consequences of this exposure. . . .

"We turn to the final question whether Alabama has demonstrated an interest in obtaining the disclosures it seeks from petitioner which is sufficient to justify the deterrent effect which we have concluded these disclosures may well have on the free exercise by petitioner's members of their constitutionally protected right of association. [Whatever] interest the State may have in obtaining names of ordinary members has not been shown to be sufficient to overcome petitioner's constitutional objections to the production order."

ROBERTS v. U.S. JAYCEES, 468 U.S. 609 (1984). The Jaycees is a nonprofit membership corporation whose objective is to provide young men with an "opportunity for personal development and achievement and an avenue for intelligent participation [in] the affairs of [the] community." Regular membership in the Jaycees is limited to men between the ages of eighteen and thirty-five. Associate membership is open to older men and to women. Associate members may not vote, hold office, or participate in certain leadership training programs. The Minnesota Department of Human Rights found that the Jaycees' membership policy violated the Minnesota Human Rights Act, which prohibits discrimination on the basis of sex. The Court held that the act does not violate the first amendment right of association. Justice Brennan delivered the opinion of the Court:

"[We have long] recognized a right to associate for the purpose of engaging in those activities protected by the First Amendment, [for an] individual's freedom to speak [and] to petition the Government for the redress of grievances could not be vigorously protected [unless] a correlative freedom to engage in group effort toward those ends were not also guaranteed. [There] can be no clearer example of an intrusion into the internal structure [of] an association than a regulation that forces the group to accept members it does not desire. . . .

"The right to associate for expressive purposes is not, however, absolute. Infringements on that right may be justified by regulations adopted to serve compelling state interests, unrelated to the suppression of ideas, that cannot be achieved through means significantly less restrictive of associational freedoms. [We] are persuaded that Minnesota's compelling interest in eradicating discrimination against its female citizens justifies the impact that application of the statute to the Jaycees may have on the male members' associational freedoms. . . .

"[The challenged act] does not aim at the suppression of speech [and it] does not distinguish between prohibited and permitted activity on the basis of viewpoint. [The] Act reflects the State's strong historical commitment to eliminating [discrimination]. That goal, which is unrelated to the suppression of expression, plainly serves compelling state interests of the highest order. . . .

"[Moreover], the Jaycees have failed to demonstrate that the Act imposes any serious burdens on the male members' freedom of expressive association. [To] be sure, [a] 'not insubstantial part' of the Jaycees' activities constitutes protected expression on political, economic, cultural, and social affairs. [There] is, however, no basis [for] concluding that admission of women as full voting members will impede the organization's ability to engage in these protected activities or to disseminate its preferred views. The Act requires no change in the Jaycees' creed of promoting the interests of young men, and it imposes no restrictions on the organization's ability to exclude individuals with ideologies [different] from those of its existing members. . . .

"It [is] arguable that, insofar as the Jaycees is organized to promote the views of young [men], admission of women as voting members will change the message communicated by the group's [speech]. [In] claiming that women might have a different attitude about such issues as the federal budget, school prayer, voting rights, and foreign relations, [the] Jaycees rely solely on unsupported generalizations about the relative interests and perspectives of men and women. Although such generalizations may or may not have a statistical basis in fact with respect to particular positions adopted by the Jaycees, we have repeatedly condemned legal decisionmaking that relies uncritically on such assumptions. [In] the absence of a showing far more substantial than that attempted by the Jaycees, we decline to indulge in the sexual stereotyping that underlies the [contention] that, by allowing women to vote, the [act] will change the content or impact of the organization's speech."

Justices O'Connor and Rehnquist concurred in the judgment. Chief Justice Burger and Justice Blackmun did not participate.

Note: Association and the First Amendment

1. *Incidental restrictions.* Note that analytically NAACP v. Alabama and *Roberts* are variants of *O'Brien.* That is, in all these cases a law that arguably was not directed at expression was challenged on the ground that it had an incidental effect on speech. In what circumstances does a law that has only an incidental effect on speech violate the first amendment?

2. *The reach of* Roberts: *social and business clubs.* In Board of Directors of Rotary International v. Rotary Club of Duarte, 481 U.S. 537 (1987), the Court unanimously upheld a California antidiscrimination statute that required the Rotary Club to admit women. The Court explained that, although "the right to engage in activities protected by the First Amendment implies 'a corresponding right to associate with others in pursuit of a wide variety of political, social, economic, educational, religious, and cultural ends,' [the] evidence [in this case] fails to demonstrate that admitting women to Rotary Clubs will affect in any significant way the existing members' ability to carry out their various purposes." See also New York State Club Association, Inc. v. City of New York, 487 U.S. 1 (1988) (upholding a New York City human rights law that banned discrimination on the basis of race, creed, or sex in any institution, club, or place of accommodation that has more than four hundred members, provides regular meal service, and regularly receives payment from nonmembers for the furtherance of trade or business).

3. *The reach of* Roberts: *political associations.* After *Roberts,* can a state prohibit the Nazi Party of America from excluding Jews? Is that case different because the Nazis, unlike the Jaycees, are engaged principally in political expression? Is it different because the admission of Jews would *symbolically* interfere with the essential message of the party? In *Roberts,* the Court rejected the argument that the act was invalid as applied to the Jaycees because the admission of women would

interfere with the symbolic message inherent in an all-male organization: "[Even] if enforcement of the Act causes some incidental abridgment of the Jaycees' protected speech, that effect is no greater than is necessary to accomplish the State's legitimate purposes. [Like] violence or other types of potentially expressive activities that produce special harms distinct from their communicative impact, [discrimination on the basis of gender is] entitled to no constitutional protection."

After *Roberts*, can a state permit Republicans to vote in a Democratic primary? See California Democratic Party v. Jones, 530 U.S. 567 (2000), in which the Court held that a state may not require political parties to allow individuals who are not members of the party to vote in the party's primary. The Court explained that such a law "forces political parties to associate with — to have their nominees and hence their positions, determined by — those who, at best, have refused to affiliate with the party, and, at worst, have expressly affiliated with a rival." The Court explained that "freedom of association would prove an empty guarantee if associations could not limit control over their decisions to those who share the interests and persuasions that underlie the association's being."

Compare Rosario v. Rockefeller, 410 U.S. 752 (1973) (upholding a New York statute requiring voters to register their party affiliation eleven months prior to the next party primary in order to inhibit "party raiding"); Storer v. Brown, 415 U.S. 724 (1974) (upholding a California statute forbidding ballot position to an independent candidate who "had a registered affiliation with [any] political parties at any time within one year prior to the immediately preceding primary election"); Tashjian v. Republican Party, 479 U.S. 208 (1987) (invalidating a state law prohibiting independents from voting in party primaries).

4. *The reach of* Roberts: *dance halls.* In City of Dallas v. Stanglin, 490 U.S. 19 (1989), the Court unanimously upheld a Dallas ordinance restricting admittance to certain dance halls to persons between the ages of fourteen and eighteen:

> [The opportunities to dance with adults, and for adults to dance with minors] do not involve the sort of expressive association that the First Amendment has been held to protect. The hundreds of teenagers who congregate each night at this particular dance hall are not members of any organized association; they are patrons of the same business establishment. Most are strangers to one another, and the dance hall admits all who are willing to pay the admission fee. [These patrons do not] "take positions on public questions," or perform any of the other [activities that constitute First Amendment expression]. The activity of these dance-hall patrons — coming together to engage in recreational dancing — is not protected by the First Amendment. Thus this activity [does not qualify] as a form of "expressive association" as [that term was used] in *Roberts*.

BOY SCOUTS OF AMERICA v. DALE, 530 U.S. 640 (2000). Dale's position as an adult scoutmaster in the Boy Scouts was revoked when the Boy Scouts learned that he is an "avowed homosexual" and a gay rights activist. New Jersey's public accommodations law, which prohibits discrimination on the basis of sexual orientation, was interpreted by the New Jersey courts to prohibit the Boy Scouts from revoking Dale's position. The Court, in a five-to-four decision, held that this application of the New Jersey public accommodations law violates the Boy Scouts' first amendment right of expressive association. Chief Justice Rehnquist delivered the opinion of the Court:

"The forced inclusion of an unwanted person in a group infringes the group's freedom of expressive association if the presence of that person affects in a significant way the groups ability to advocate public or private viewpoints. [But] the freedom of expressive association, like many freedoms, is not absolute. We have held that the freedom could be overridden 'by regulations adopted to serve compelling state interests, unrelated to the suppression of ideas, that cannot be achieved through means significantly less restrictive of associational freedoms.' [*Roberts.*]

"To determine whether a group is protected by the First Amendment's expressive associational right, we must determine whether the group engages in 'expressive association.' The First Amendment's protection of expressive association is not reserved for advocacy groups. But to come within its ambit, a group must engage in some form of expression, whether it be public or private. . . .

"The Boy Scouts is a private, nonprofit organization. According to its 'mission statement,' [the] general mission of the Boy Scouts is '[t]o instill values in young people.' The Boy Scouts seeks to instill these values by having its adult leaders spend time with the youth members, instructing and engaging them in activities like camping, archery, and fishing. During the time spent with the youth members, the scoutmasters and assistant scoutmasters inculcate them with the Boy Scouts' values — both expressly and by example. It seems indisputable that an association that seeks to transmit such a system of values engages in expressive activity. . . .

"Given that the Boy Scouts engages in expressive activity, we must determine whether the forced inclusion of Dale as an assistant scoutmaster would significantly affect the Boy Scouts' ability to advocate public or private viewpoints. This inquiry necessarily requires us first to explore, to a limited extent, the nature of the Boy Scouts' view of homosexuality. [Although the] Boy Scout Oath and Law do not expressly mention sexuality or sexual orientation, [the] Boy Scouts asserts that it 'teach[es] that homosexual conduct is not morally straight' [and] that it does 'not want to promote homosexual conduct as a legitimate form of behavior.' [We] accept the Boy Scouts' assertion. . . .

"We must then determine whether Dale's presence as an assistant scoutmaster would significantly burden the Boy Scouts' desire to not 'promote homosexual conduct as a legitimate form of behavior.' As we give deference to an association's assertions regarding the nature of its expression, we must also give deference to an association's view of what would impair its expression. [That] is not to say that an expressive association can erect a shield against antidiscrimination laws simply by asserting that mere acceptance of a member from a particular group would impair its message. But here Dale, by his own admission, is one of a group of gay Scouts who have 'become leaders in their community and are open and honest about their sexual orientation.' Dale was the co-president of a gay and lesbian organization at college and remains a gay rights activist. Dale's presence in the Boy Scouts would, at the very least, force the organization to send a message, both to the youth members and the world, that the Boy Scouts accepts homosexual conduct as a legitimate form of behavior.

"The New Jersey Supreme Court determined that the Boy Scouts' ability to disseminate its message was not significantly affected by the forced inclusion of Dale as an assistant scoutmaster because 'Boy Scout members do not associate for the purpose of disseminating the belief that homosexuality is immoral.' [We] disagree with the New Jersey Supreme Court's [reasoning]. First, associations do not have to associate for the 'purpose' of disseminating a certain message in order to be entitled to the protections of the First Amendment. An association must merely engage in expressive activity that could be impaired in order to be entitled to protection. Second, [the] First Amendment simply does not require that every member of a group agree on every issue in order for the group's policy to be 'expressive association.' The Boy Scouts takes an official position with respect to homosexual conduct, and that is sufficient for First Amendment purposes. . . .

"Having determined that the Boy Scouts is an expressive association and that the forced inclusion of Dale would significantly affect its expression, we inquire whether the application of New Jersey's public accommodations law to require that the Boy Scouts accept Dale as an assistant scoutmaster runs afoul of the Scouts' freedom of expressive association. We conclude that it does. . . .

"We recognized in cases such as *Roberts* [that] States have a compelling interest in eliminating discrimination against women in public accommodations. But in each of these cases we went on to conclude that the enforcement of these statutes would not materially interfere with the ideas that the organization sought to express. In *Roberts*, we said '[i]ndeed, the Jaycees has failed to demonstrate [any] serious burden on the male members' freedom of expressive association.' We thereupon concluded in each of these cases that the organizations' First Amendment rights were not violated by the application of the States' public accommodations laws.

"[We] have already concluded that a state requirement that the Boy Scouts retain Dale as an assistant scoutmaster would significantly burden the organization's right to oppose or disfavor homosexual conduct. The state interests embodied in New Jersey's public accommodations law do not justify such a severe intrusion on the Boy Scouts' rights to freedom of expressive association. That being the case, we hold that the First Amendment prohibits the State from imposing such a requirement through the application of its public accommodations law."

Justice Stevens, joined by Justices Souter, Ginsburg, and Breyer, dissented: "[Until] today, we have never once found a claimed right to associate in the selection of members to prevail in the face of a State's antidiscrimination law. To the contrary, we have squarely held that a State's antidiscrimination law does not violate a group's right to associate simply because the law conflicts with that group's exclusionary membership policy. [Citing *Roberts*.]

"Surely there are instances in which an organization that truly aims to foster a belief at odds with the purposes of a State's antidiscrimination laws will have a First Amendment right to association that precludes forced compliance with those laws. But that right is not a freedom to discriminate at will, nor is it a right to maintain an exclusionary membership policy simply out of fear of what the public reaction would be if the group's membership were opened up. It is an implicit right designed to protect the enumerated rights of the First Amendment, not a license to act on any discriminatory impulse. To prevail in asserting a right of expressive association as a defense to a charge of violating an antidiscrimination law, the organization must at least show it has adopted and advocated an unequivocal position inconsistent with a position advocated or epitomized by the person whom the organization seeks to exclude. . . .

"Dale's inclusion in the Boy Scouts [sends] no cognizable message to the Scouts or to the world. [If] there is any kind of message being sent, [it] is by the mere act of joining the Boy Scouts. [The] only apparent explanation for the majority's holding [is] that homosexuals are simply so different from the rest of society that their presence alone — unlike any other individual's — should be singled out for special First Amendment treatment. Under the majority's reasoning, an openly gay male is irreversibly affixed with the label 'homosexual.' [Reliance] on such a justification is tantamount to a constitutionally prescribed symbol of inferiority. . . .

"Furthermore, it is not likely that BSA would be understood to send any message, either to Scouts or to the world, simply by admitting someone as a member. Over the years, BSA has generously welcomed over 87 million young Americans into its ranks. In 1992 over one million adults were active BSA members. [The] notion that an organization of that size and enormous prestige implicitly endorses the views that each of those adults may express in a non-Scouting context is simply mind boggling. Indeed, in this case there is no evidence that the young Scouts in Dale's troop, or members of their families, were even aware of his sexual [orientation]. It is equally farfetched to assert that Dale's open declaration of his homosexuality, reported in a local newspaper, will effectively force BSA to send a message to anyone simply because it allows Dale to be an Assistant Scoutmaster."

Note: The Meaning of Dale

1. *Competing analogies.* Should *Dale* have been governed by *Roberts* or by *California Democratic Party*? Is the Boy Scouts more of an "expressive associa-tion" than the Jaycees? Is the compelled inclusion of a gay Boy Scout more intrusive upon the right of expressive association than the compelled inclusion of a woman Jaycee? Is *Dale* reconcilable with *O'Brien*? Because the government's interests in preventing the destruction of draft cards are more important that its interests in preventing discrimination against gays? Because it is more important for the Boy Scouts to discriminate against gays than it is for antiwar protesters to burn draft cards? Is the incidental effect of the law in *Dale* equivalent to the incidental effect of the law in NAACP v. Alabama?

2. *The rationale and reach of* Dale. Consider Rubenfeld, The First Amend-ment's Purpose, 53 Stan. L. Rev. 767, 768–769 (2001):

> [The] Boy Scouts claim was a simple one. The Scouts wanted [to] discriminate for expressive reasons. If they could not exclude homosexuals, they would not be able effectively — or as effectively — to express their sincerely held anti-homosexual views. [But] people constantly want to violate laws for expressive reasons. Every person and every organization that wants to discriminate probably has good expres-sive reasons for doing so. Discrimination is profoundly expressive. It is by far the most effective way most people have of expressing their view of the superiority of their own group and the inferiority of others.
>
>   Title VII has "significantly affected" the ability of countless employers to express their views about race or sex. Indeed, it has forced them to "send a message" of equality that many presumably oppose (or would oppose if permitted to do so), in the same way that New Jersey's law forced the Boy Scouts to do so. Should racist and sexist employers be able to come to court with First Amendment challenges to Title VII, demanding that judges accord them the same strict scrutiny that the Boy Scouts received?

3. *Prohibition v. subsidy.* Suppose *Dale* involved not a state law prohibiting discrimination, but a state law denying tax-exempt status to any organization that discriminates on the basis of sexual orientation or a public high school's policy that denies any student group the right to use school facilities if it discriminates on that basis. As applied to the Boy Scouts, would such restric-tions be constitutional? See *Christian Legal Society v. Martinez*, section E2c supra.

PRUNEYARD SHOPPING CENTER v. ROBINS, 447 U.S. 74 (1980). The PruneYard is a privately owned shopping center containing more than seventy-five shops and restaurants. It prohibits any visitors or tenants from engaging in any publicly expressive activity, including the circulation of petitions. Several high school students seeking support for their opposition to a United Nations resolution against Zionism set up a card table in PruneYard's central courtyard. They distributed leaflets and asked passersby to sign petitions. They were asked to leave and thereafter filed suit to enjoin PruneYard from denying them access to the premises for the purpose of circulating their petitions. The California Supreme Court held that the California Constitution protects "speech and petitioning, reasonably exercised, in shopping centers even when the centers are privately owned." Appellants, the owners of PruneYard, maintained that "a private property owner has a First Amendment right not to be forced by the State to use his property as a forum for the speech of others." The Court, in an opinion by Justice Rehnquist, rejected appellants' claim:

"[The] shopping center [is] a business establishment that is open to the public. [The] views expressed by members of the public in passing out pamphlets or seeking signatures for a petition thus will not likely be identified with those of the owner. [Moreover], no specific message is dictated by the State. [There] consequently is no danger of governmental discrimination for or against a particular message. Finally, [appellants] can expressly disavow any connection with the message by simply posting signs [disclaiming] any sponsorship of the message and [explaining] that the persons are communicating their own messages by virtue of state law. [Appellants here are not] compelled to affirm their belief in any governmentally prescribed position or view, and they are free to publicly dissociate themselves from the views of the speakers or handbillers." Justice Powell, joined by Justice White, concurred in the result.

Note: Compelled Affirmation, Expression, and Association: The Right Not to Speak

1. *The pledge of allegiance.* Are there any circumstances in which there is a right not to be compelled to support or express ideas with which one disagrees? This right first received articulation in West Virginia State Board of Education v. Barnette, 319 U.S. 624 (1943), in which the Court overruled its prior decision in Minersville School District v. Gobitis, 310 U.S. 586 (1940), and held unconstitutional a state law requiring all children in the public schools to salute and pledge allegiance to the flag of the United States. Justice Jackson, speaking for the Court, explained:

> [The] compulsory flag salute and pledge requires affirmation of a belief and an attitude of mind. [To] sustain the compulsory flag salute we are required to say that a Bill of Rights which guards the individual's right to speak his own mind, left it open to public authorities to compel him to utter what is not in his mind. [But if] there is any fixed star in our constitutional constellation, it is that no official, high or petty, can prescribe what shall be orthodox in politics, nationalism, religion, or other matters of opinion or force citizens to confess by word or act their faith therein. If there are any circumstances which permit an exception, they do not now occur to us.

Justice Frankfurter dissented. Is *PruneYard* reconcilable with *Barnette*? In *PruneYard*, the Court explained that "*Barnette* is inapposite because it involved the compelled recitation of a message containing an affirmation of belief," whereas in *PruneYard* "no specific message [was] dictated by the State."

2. *"Live free or die."* In Wooley v. Maynard, 430 U.S. 705 (1977), the Court, in an opinion by Chief Justice Burger, held that New Hampshire could not criminally punish individuals who covered up the state motto "Live Free or Die" on their passenger vehicle license plates because the motto was repugnant to their moral, political, and religious beliefs:

> [Here,] as in *Barnette,* we are faced with a state measure which forces an individual, as part of his daily life [to] be an instrument for fostering public adherence to an ideological point of view he finds unacceptable. [Thus, we must] determine whether the State's countervailing interest is sufficiently compelling to justify requiring appellees to display the state motto on their license plates. The two interests advanced by the State are that display of the motto (1) facilitates the identification of passenger [as distinct from other] vehicles, and (2) promotes appreciation of history, individualism, and state pride. [The first argument is insufficient] "in the light of less drastic means for achieving the same basic purpose." [The] State's second claimed interest is not ideologically neutral. [The State's interest in disseminating an ideology] cannot outweigh an individual's First Amendment right to avoid becoming the courier for such message.

The Court in *Wooley* distinguished *PruneYard* as follows: "[In *Wooley,*] the government itself prescribed the message, required it to be displayed openly on appellee's personal property that was used 'as part of his daily life,' and refused to permit him to take any measures to cover up the motto even though the Court found that the display of the motto served no important state interest." Justice Rehnquist, joined by Justice Blackmun, dissented.

Does it follow from *Wooley* that the government may not engage in viewpoint discrimination when it chooses between specialty license plates designed and submitted by motorists? The Court answered this question in the negative in Walker v. Texas Div., Sons of Confederate Veterans, Inc., 135 S. Ct. 2239 (2015), where, in a five-to-four decision written by Justice Breyer, it upheld the refusal of the Texas Department of Motor Vehicles to issue a license plate featuring the Confederate battle flag on the ground that the plate consisted of government, rather than private, speech:

> Our determination that Texas's specialty license plate designs are government speech does not mean that the designs do not also implicate the free speech rights of private persons. We have acknowledged that drivers who display a State's selected license plate designs convey the messages communicated through those designs. [*Wooley.*] And we have recognized that the First Amendment stringently limits a State's authority to compel a private party to express a view with which the private party disagrees. But here, compelled private speech is not at issue. And just as Texas cannot require [The Sons of Confederate Veterans] to convey "the State's ideological message," [*Wooley*], [The Sons of Confederate Veterans] cannot force Texas to include a Confederate battle flag on its specialty license plates.

3. *A St. Patrick's Day parade.* The City of Boston authorized the South Boston Allied War Veterans Council to organize the annual St. Patrick's Day Parade. The council refused a place in the parade to GLIB, an organization formed for the purpose of expressing its members' pride in their Irish heritage as openly gay, lesbian, and bisexual individuals. GLIB filed suit claiming that this refusal

violated a Massachusetts law prohibiting discrimination on account of sexual orientation in places of public accommodation. In Hurley v. Irish-American Gay, Lesbian and Bisexual Group of Boston, 515 U.S. 557 (1995), the Court, in a unanimous opinion by Justice Souter, held that application of the statute in this context violated the first amendment rights of the council.

The Court explained that, because "every participating unit affects the message conveyed by the private organizers," application of the statute in this context effectively required the council "to alter the expressive content" of its parade. The Court declared that "this use of the State's power violates the fundamental rule" that "a speaker has the autonomy to choose the content of his own message." Thus, if the council "objects," for example, to GLIB's implicit assertion that homosexuals and bisexuals are entitled to full and equal "social acceptance," it has a right "not to propound" this message.

The Court held that PruneYard was distinguishable because (1) the proprietors of the shopping center "were running 'a business establishment that [was] open to the public,'" (2) they "could 'expressly disavow any connection with the message by simply posting signs in the areas where the speakers or handbillers stand,'" and (3) the shopping center owners' own right to speak was not implicated because they "did not even allege that [they] objected to the content" of the speech. On the disclaimer issue, the Court observed that disclaimers would not be sufficient to protect the interests of the council because "such disclaimers would be quite curious in a moving parade."

4. *Military recruiting in law schools.* Most law schools do not permit employers who discriminate on the basis of race, religion, gender, national origin, or sexual orientation to use their placement facilities. In the 1980s, most law schools extended this policy to the U.S. military, because it discriminated on the basis of sexual orientation. In response, Congress enacted the Solomon Amendment, which provided that if any part of an institution of higher education denied military recruiters access equal to that provided other recruiters, the entire institution would lose access to federal funds. Because most universities are heavily dependent on federal support for research and financial aid, most law schools waived their nondiscrimination policy as applied to the military. The Forum for Academic and Institutional Rights (FAIR), an association of law schools and law faculties, filed suit to enjoin the application of the Solomon Amendment on the ground that it violated the first amendment.

In a unanimous decision, the Court rejected this argument in Rumsfeld v. FAIR, 547 U.S. 47 (2006). In his opinion for the Court, Chief Justice Roberts observed that the Solomon Amendment "gives universities a choice: Either allow military recruiters the same [access] afforded any other recruiter or forgo certain federal funds." Roberts distinguished *Hurley* on the ground that in that case "the complaining speaker's own message was affected by the speech it was forced to accommodate." Indeed, he explained, the "expressive nature of a parade was central" to the result in *Hurley*. In this case, however, "accommodating the military's message does not affect the law schools' speech, because the schools are not speaking when they host interviews and recruiting receptions. Unlike a parade organizer's choice of parade contingents, a law school's decision to allow recruiters on campus is not inherently expressive." Roberts concluded that, in this respect, the case was governed by *PruneYard*.

5. *Union dues.* May a state compel government employees to pay union dues? See Abood v. Detroit Board of Education, 431 U.S. 209 (1977) (upholding a state statute authorizing unions representing government employees to charge

members dues insofar as the dues are used to support collective bargaining and related activities, but invalidating the statute insofar as the union uses the dues "to contribute to political candidates and to express political views unrelated to its duties as exclusive bargaining representative"); Ellis v. Brotherhood of Railway, Airline & Steamship Clerks, 466 U.S. 85 (1984) (compelled contributions may constitutionally be used to pay for union conventions, social activities, and publications); Keller v. State Bar of California, 496 U.S. 1 (1990) (an integrated state bar association may not use compulsory dues to finance political and ideological activities with which particular members disagree when such expenditures are not "necessarily or reasonably incurred for the purpose of regulating the legal profession or improving the quality of legal services"); Lehnert v. Ferris Faculty Association, 500 U.S. 507 (1991) (a union may constitutionally charge dissenting employees only for those activities that are (1) "germane" to collective bargaining; (2) justified by the government's interests in labor peace and avoiding free riders; and (3) not significantly burdening of speech); Davenport v. Washington Education Association, 551 U.S. 177 (2007) (a state may constitutionally require public-sector unions to receive affirmative authorization from nonmembers before spending their agency fees for election-related purposes); Knox v. Service Employees International Union, 567 U.S. 310 (2012) (when a public-sector union imposes a special assessment or mid-year dues increase, the union cannot constitutionally require nonmembers to pay the increased amount unless they choose to opt in by affirmatively consenting).

In Harris v. Quinn, 134 S. Ct. 2618 (2014), the Court considered the constitutionality of an Illinois law that allowed Medicaid recipients who normally would need institutional care to hire a "personal assistant" (PA) to provide homecare services. Under the law, the Medicaid homecare recipients and the state both play a role in the employment relationship with the PAs. Pursuant to this program, the Service Employees International Union (SEIU) was designated the exclusive union representative for the PAs. SEIU entered into collective-bargaining agreements with the state that included an agency-fee provision, which requires PAs who do not wish to join the union to pay the union a fee for the cost of collective-bargaining expenses, but not for the cost of any political activities of the union unrelated to collective bargaining. A group of PAs who had not joined the union and did not want to pay *any* union fees brought this suit claiming that the law violated their First Amendment right not to be compelled to support the union. Pursuant to *Abood*, the lower courts rejected this challenge and upheld the law.

In a five-to-four decision, the Supreme Court reversed. In an opinion by Justice Alito, the Court cast serious doubt on *Abood*, insofar as it permitted the state to compel non-union members to pay union fees even for the costs of collective-bargaining activities that benefit them. Ultimately, though, the Court invalidated the law without overruling *Abood*, by distinguishing the specific factual situation in the context of PAs from the situations in other public union arrangements. Justice Kagan, joined by Justices Ginsburg, Breyer, and Sotomayor, dissented. Kagan insisted that *Abood* reflected sound First Amendment principles and that the situation in this case was not in any principled way distinguishable from the Court's prior decisions. For an analysis of the implications of Harris v. Quinn, see Estlund, Are Unions a Constitutional Anomaly?, 114 Mich. L. Rev. 169 (2015).

6. *Student activity fees.* Board of Regents of the University of Wisconsin System v. Southworth, 529 U.S. 217 (2000), concerned the constitutionality of

the University of Wisconsin's requirement that all full-time students pay an annual activities fee, part of which is allocated by the student government to support registered student organizations that engage in a broad range of expressive and other activities. Examples of the more than six hundred registered student organizations at the University of Wisconsin are the College Democrats, the College Republicans, the International Socialist Organization, and the Future Financial Gurus of America. Citing *Abood*, respondents challenged the constitutionality of this program on the ground that by compelling them financially to support political and ideological expression with which they disagree, the program violates their first amendment right "not to speak."

In a unanimous decision, the Court rejected this challenge. Justice Kennedy authored the opinion of the Court:

> In *Abood* [the] constitutional rule took the form of limiting the required subsidy to speech germane to the purposes of the [union]. The standard of germane speech as applied to student speech at a university is [unworkable]. The speech the University seeks to encourage in the program before us is distinguished not by discernable limits but by its vast, unexplored bounds. To insist upon asking what speech is germane would be contrary to the very goal the University seeks to pursue. It is not for the Court to say what is or is not germane to the ideas to be pursued in an institution of higher learning. . . .

7. *The right not to publish or broadcast.* In what circumstances, if any, may government constitutionally compel a broadcaster or publisher to broadcast or publish material? See Denver Area Education Telecommunications Consortium, Inc. v. FCC, 518 U.S. 727 (1996) (considering the constitutionality of several provisions of the Cable Television Consumer Protection and Competition Act of 1992 concerning the broadcasting of "indecent" programming on public access and leased access channels); Turner Broadcasting System Inc. v. FCC, 512 U.S. 622 (1994) (upholding "must carry" provisions for cable television); Columbia Broadcasting System v. FCC, 453 U.S. 367 (1981) (upholding an FCC rule requiring broadcasters "to allow reasonable access [by] a legally qualified candidate for Federal elective office on behalf of his candidacy"); Miami Herald Publishing Co. v. Tornillo, 418 U.S. 241 (1974) (invalidating a "right of reply" statute requiring any newspaper that "assails" the character of a political candidate to print the candidate's reply); Red Lion Broadcasting Co. v. FCC, 395 U.S. 367 (1969) (upholding the FCC's "fairness doctrine"). See section F infra.

5.   Regulation of Political Solicitation, Contribution, Expenditure, and Activity

It has been suggested that the "critical problem for contemporary First Amendment theory is the unequal access that wealth can buy." Carter, Technology, Democracy, and the Manipulation of Consent, 93 Yale L.J. 581 (1984). This section explores that "problem." To what extent is the solicitation, contribution, or expenditure of money "speech" within the meaning of the first amendment? To what extent may government regulate or restrict such activities in order to "enhance" the quality of public debate?

Buckley v. Valeo

424 U.S. 1 (1976)

PER CURIAM.

These appeals present constitutional challenges to the key provisions of the Federal Election Campaign Act of 1971 (Act), and related provisions of the Internal Revenue Code of 1954, all as amended in 1974. . . .

[The] statutes at issue [contain] the following provisions: (a) individual political contributions [and expenditures] "relative to a clearly identified candidate" are limited, [and] campaign spending by candidates for various federal offices [is] subject to prescribed limits; (b) contributions and expenditures above certain threshold levels must be reported and publicly disclosed; (c) a system for public funding of Presidential campaign activities is established; [and] (d) a Federal Election Commission is established to administer and enforce the legislation. . . .

[The Court upheld the constitutionality of the individual contribution limits, the disclosure and reporting provisions, and the public financing scheme. The Court invalidated the composition of the Federal Election Commission and the limitations on expenditures. The following excerpts relate to the contribution and expenditure limitations.]

I. CONTRIBUTION AND EXPENDITURE LIMITATION

The intricate statutory scheme adopted by Congress to regulate federal election campaigns includes restrictions on political contributions and expenditures that apply broadly to all phases of and all participants in the election process. The major contribution and expenditure limitations in the Act prohibit individuals from contributing more than $25,000 in a single year or more than $1,000 to any single candidate for an election campaign and from spending more than $1,000 a year "relative to a clearly identified candidate." Other provisions restrict a candidate's use of personal and family resources in his campaign and limit the overall amount that can be spent by a candidate in campaigning for federal office. . . .

A. GENERAL PRINCIPLES

The Act's contribution and expenditure limitations operate in an area of the most fundamental First Amendment activities. Discussion of public issues and debate on the qualifications of candidates are integral to the operation of the system of government established by our Constitution. . . .

In upholding the constitutional validity of the Act's contribution and expenditure provisions on the ground that those provisions should be viewed as regulating conduct, not speech, the Court of Appeals relied upon [O'Brien].

We cannot share the view that the present Act's contribution and expenditure limitations are comparable to the restrictions on conduct upheld in O'Brien. The expenditure of money simply cannot be equated with such conduct as destruction of a draft card. Some forms of communication made possible by the giving and spending of money involve speech alone, some involve conduct primarily, and some involve a combination of the two. Yet this Court has never suggested that the dependence of a communication on the expenditure of money operates itself to introduce a nonspeech element or to reduce the exacting scrutiny required by the First Amendment. . . .

Even if the categorization of the expenditure of money as conduct were accepted, the limitations challenged here would not meet the *O'Brien* test because the governmental interests advanced in support of the Act involve "suppressing communication." The interests served by the Act include restricting the voices of people and interest groups who have money to spend and reducing the overall scope of federal election campaigns. Although the Act does not focus on the ideas expressed by persons or groups subject to its regulations, it is aimed in part at equalizing the relative ability of all voters to affect electoral outcomes by placing a ceiling on expenditures for political expression by citizens and groups. Unlike *O'Brien*, where the Selective Service System's administrative interest in the preservation of draft cards was wholly unrelated to their use as a means of communication, it is beyond dispute that the interest in regulating the alleged "conduct" of giving or spending money "arises in some measure because the communication allegedly integral to the conduct is itself thought to be harmful." . . .

Nor can the Act's contribution and expenditure limitations be sustained, as some of the parties suggest, by reference to the constitutional principles reflected in such decisions as [Adderley v. Florida and Kovacs v. Cooper, supra]. Those cases stand for the proposition that the government may adopt reasonable time, place, and manner regulations, which do not discriminate among speakers or ideas, in order to further an important governmental interest unrelated to the restriction of communication. [In] contrast to *O'Brien*, where the method of expression was held to be subject to prohibition, [*Adderley*] and *Kovacs* involved place or manner restrictions on legitimate modes of expression — picketing, parading, demonstrating, and using a soundtruck. The critical difference between this case and those time, place, and manner cases is that the present Act's contribution and expenditure limitations impose direct quantity restrictions on political communication and association by persons, groups, candidates, and political parties in addition to any reasonable time, place, and manner regulations otherwise imposed.[17]

A restriction on the amount of money a person or group can spend on political communication during a campaign necessarily reduces the quantity of expression by restricting the number of issues discussed, the depth of their exploration, and the size of the audience reached.[18] This is because virtually every means of communicating ideas in today's mass society requires the expenditure of money. . . .

The expenditure limitations contained in the Act represent substantial rather than merely theoretical restraints on the quantity and diversity of political speech. The $1,000 ceiling on spending "relative to a clearly identified candidate," [for example,] would appear to exclude all citizens and groups except candidates,

17. The nongovernmental appellees argue that just as the decibels emitted by a sound truck can be regulated consistently with the First Amendment, [*Kovacs*,] the Act may restrict the volume of dollars in political campaigns without impermissibly restricting freedom of speech. [This] comparison underscores a fundamental misconception. The decibel restriction upheld in *Kovacs* limited the *manner* of operating a soundtruck, but not the *extent* of its proper use. By contrast, the Act's dollar ceilings restrict the extent of the reasonable use of virtually every means of communicating information. . . .

18. Being free to engage in unlimited political expression subject to a ceiling on expenditures is like being free to drive an automobile as far and as often as one desires on a single tank of gasoline.

political parties, and the institutional press from any significant use of the most effective modes of communication.[20] . . .

By contrast with a limitation upon expenditures for political expression, a limitation upon the amount that any one person or group may contribute to a candidate or political committee entails only a marginal restriction upon the contributor's ability to engage in free communication, [for] it permits the symbolic expression of support evidenced by a contribution but does not in any way infringe the contributor's freedom to discuss candidates and issues. While contributions may result in political expression if spent by a candidate or an association to present views to the voters, the transformation of contributions into political debate involves speech by someone other than the contributor.

Given the important role of contributions in financing political campaigns, contribution restrictions could have a severe impact on political dialogue if the limitations prevented candidates and political committees from amassing the resources necessary for effective advocacy. There is no indication, however, that the contribution limitations imposed by the Act would have any dramatic adverse effect on the funding of campaigns and political associations.[23] The overall effect of the Act's contribution ceilings is merely to require candidates and political committees to raise funds from a greater number of persons and to compel people who would otherwise contribute amounts greater than the statutory limits to expend such funds on direct political expression, rather than to reduce the total amount of money potentially available to promote political expression. . . .

In sum, although the Act's contribution and expenditure limitations both implicate fundamental First Amendment interests, its expenditure ceilings impose significantly more severe restrictions on protected freedoms of political expression and association than do its limitations on financial contributions.

B. CONTRIBUTION LIMITATIONS

Section 608(b) provides, with certain limited exceptions, that "no person shall make contributions to any candidate with respect to any election for Federal office which, in the aggregate, exceed $1,000." . . .

[The] primary First Amendment problem raised by the Act's contribution limitations is their restriction of one aspect of the contributor's freedom of political association. The Court's decisions involving associational freedoms establish that the right of association is a "basic constitutional freedom," [and that] governmental "action which may have the effect of curtailing the freedom to associate is subject to the closest scrutiny." Yet, it is clear that "Neither the right to associate nor the right to participate in political activities is absolute." [Even] a "'significant interference' with protected rights of political association" may be sustained if the State demonstrates a sufficiently important interest and employs

20. The record indicates that, as of January 1, 1975, one full-page advertisement in a daily edition of a certain metropolitan newspaper cost $6,971.04 — almost seven times the annual limit on expenditures "relative to" a particular candidate imposed on the vast majority of individual citizens and associations by [the act].

23. Statistical findings agreed to by the parties reveal that approximately 5.1% of the $73,483,613 raised by the 1,161 candidates for Congress in 1974 was obtained in amounts in excess of $1,000. . . .

means closely drawn to avoid unnecessary abridgment of associational freedoms. . . .

It is unnecessary to look beyond the Act's primary purpose — to limit the actuality and appearance of corruption resulting from large individual financial contributions — in order to find a constitutionally sufficient justification for the $1,000 contribution limitation. [The] increasing importance of the communications media and sophisticated mass-mailing and polling operations to effective campaigning make the raising of large sums of money an ever more essential ingredient of an effective candidacy. To the extent that large contributions are given to secure a political quid pro quo from current and potential office holders, the integrity of our system of representative democracy is undermined. . . .

Of almost equal concern [is] the appearance of corruption stemming from [the] opportunities for abuse inherent in a regime of large individual financial contributions. [Congress] could legitimately conclude that the avoidance of the appearance of improper influence [is] "critical [if] confidence in the system of representative Government is not to be [eroded]." . . .

Appellants contend that the contribution limitations must be invalidated because bribery laws and narrowly drawn disclosure requirements constitute a less restrictive means of dealing with "proven and suspected quid pro quo arrangements." But laws making criminal the giving and taking of bribes deal with only the most blatant and specific attempts of those with money to influence governmental action. And while disclosure requirements serve [many salutary purposes] Congress was surely entitled to conclude that disclosure was only a partial measure, and that contribution ceilings were a necessary legislative concomitant to deal with the reality or appearance of corruption. . . .

We find that, under the rigorous standard of review established by our prior decisions, the weighty interests served by restricting the size of financial contributions to political candidates are sufficient to justify the limited effect upon First Amendment freedoms caused by the $1,000 contribution ceiling.

[Appellants argue further, however,] that the contribution limitations work [an] invidious discrimination between incumbents and [challengers].[33] [But] there is [no] evidence [that] contribution limitations [discriminate] against major-party challengers to incumbents, [and although] the charge of discrimination against minor-party and independent candidates is more troubling, [the] record provides no basis for concluding that the Act invidiously disadvantages such candidates. [Indeed, in some circumstances] the restriction would appear to benefit minor-party and independent candidates relative to their major-party

---

33. In this discussion, we address only the argument that the contribution limitations alone impermissibly discriminate against nonincumbents. We do not address the more serious argument that these limitations, in combination with the limitation on expenditures [invidiously] discriminate against major-party challengers and minor-party candidates.

Since an incumbent is subject to these limitations to the same degree as his opponent, the Act, on its face, appears to be evenhanded. The appearance of fairness, however, may not reflect political reality. Although some incumbents are defeated in every congressional election, it is axiomatic that an incumbent usually begins the race with significant advantages. [In some circumstances] the overall effect of the contribution and expenditure limitations enacted by Congress could foreclose any fair opportunity of a successful challenge.

However, since we decide in Part I-C, infra, that the ceilings on [expenditures] are unconstitutional under the First Amendment, we need not express any opinion with regard to the alleged invidious discrimination resulting from the full sweep of the legislation as enacted.

opponents because major-party candidates receive far more money in large contributions. . . .

In view of these considerations, we conclude that the impact of the Act's $1,000 contribution limitation on major-party challengers and on minor-party candidates does not render the provision unconstitutional on its face.

[For similar reasons, the Court also upheld the $5,000 limit on contributions by "political committees," the limits on volunteers' incidental expenses, and the $25,000 limit on total political contributions by an individual during a single calendar year.]

C. EXPENDITURE LIMITATIONS

The Act's expenditure ceilings impose direct and substantial restraints [on] the quantity of campaign speech by individuals, groups, and candidates. The restrictions, while neutral as to the ideas expressed, limit political expression "at the core of our electoral process and of the First Amendment freedoms." . . .

The $1,000 Limitation on Expenditures "Relative to a Clearly Identified Candidate"

Section 608(e)(1) provides that "[n]o person may make any expenditure . . . relative to a clearly identified candidate during a calendar year [which] exceeds $1,000." [Appellants maintain] that the provision is unconstitutionally vague. [The] use of so indefinite a phrase as "relative to" a candidate fails to clearly mark the boundary between permissible and impermissible [speech]. "Such a distinction offers no security for free [discussion]." [To] preserve the provision against invalidation on vagueness grounds, §608(e)(1) must be construed to apply only to expenditures for communications that in express terms advocate the election or defeat of a clearly identified candidate for federal office.

We turn then to the basic First Amendment question — whether §608(e)(1), even as thus narrowly and explicitly construed, impermissibly burdens the constitutional right of free expression. . . .

The discussion in Part I-A supra, explains why the Act's expenditure limitations impose far greater restraints on the freedom of speech and association than do its contribution limitations. . . .

We find that the governmental interest in preventing corruption and the appearance of corruption is inadequate to justify §608(e)(1)'s ceiling on independent expenditures. [First], §608(e)(1) prevents only some large expenditures. So long as persons and groups eschew expenditures that in express terms advocate the election or defeat of a clearly identified candidate, they are free to spend as much as they want to promote the candidate and his views. The exacting interpretation of the statutory language necessary to avoid unconstitutional vagueness thus undermines the limitation's effectiveness. . . .

Second, [although the] parties defending §608(e)(1) contend that it is necessary to prevent would-be contributors from avoiding the contribution limitations [by] paying directly for media advertisements or for other portions of the candidate's campaign activities, [such] coordinated expenditures are treated as contributions rather than expenditures under the Act [and are thus limited by the] contribution ceilings. [Thus], §608(e)(1) limits [only] expenditures [made] totally independently of the candidate and his campaign. [But the] absence of [coordination with respect to such expenditures] undermines the value of the expenditure to the candidate [and] alleviates the danger that expenditures will be given as a quid pro quo for improper commitments. [Thus,] §608(e)(1) severely [restricts] independent advocacy despite its substantially diminished potential for abuse. . . .

It is argued [further, however, that the] governmental interest in equalizing the relative ability of individuals [to] influence the outcome of elections [justifies the] expenditure ceiling. But the concept that government may restrict the speech of some [in] order to enhance the relative voice of others is wholly foreign to the First Amendment, which was designed "to secure 'the widest possible dissemination of information from diverse and antagonistic sources.'" [The] First Amendment's protection against governmental abridgment of free expression cannot properly be made to depend on a person's financial ability to engage in public discussion. [Section] 608(e)(1)'s [expenditure] limitation is unconstitutional under the First Amendment.

Limitation on Expenditures by Candidates from Personal or Family Resources

The Act also [limits] expenditures by a candidate "from his personal funds, or the personal funds of his immediate family, in connection with his campaigns during any calendar year." . . .

The ceiling on personal expenditures by candidates on their own [behalf] imposes a substantial restraint on the ability of persons to engage in protected First Amendment expression. The candidate, no less than any other person, has a First Amendment right to engage in the discussion of public issues and [to] advocate his own election. . . .

The [interest] in equalizing the relative financial resources of candidates competing for elective office is clearly not sufficient to justify the provision's infringement of fundamental First Amendment rights. . . .

Limitations on Campaign Expenditures

Section 608(c) places limitations on overall campaign expenditures by candidates seeking nomination for election and election to federal office. [For example, the] Act imposes blanket $70,000 limitations on both primary campaigns and general election campaigns for the House of Representatives. . . .

No governmental interest that has been suggested is sufficient to justify the restriction on the quantity of political expression imposed by §608(c)'s campaign expenditure limitations. [The] interest in alleviating the corrupting influence of large contributions is served by the Act's contribution limitations and disclosure provisions, [and the] interest in equalizing the financial resources of candidates [is not a] convincing justification for restricting the scope of federal election campaigns. [The] campaign expenditure ceilings appear to be designed primarily to [reduce] the allegedly skyrocketing costs of political campaigns. [But the] First Amendment denies government the power to determine that spending to promote one's political views is wasteful, excessive, or unwise. In the free society ordained by our Constitution it is not the government, but the people — individually as citizens and candidates and collectively as associations and political committees — who must retain control over the quantity and range of debate on public issues in a political campaign.

For these reasons we hold that §608(c) is constitutionally invalid.

In sum, the provisions of the Act that impose a $1,000 [limitation on contributions] are constitutionally valid. These limitations [serve] the basic governmental interest in safeguarding the integrity of the electoral process without directly impinging upon the rights of individual citizens and candidates to engage in political debate and discussion. By contrast, the First Amendment requires the invalidation of the Act's independent expenditure [ceilings]. These provisions place substantial and direct restrictions on the ability of candidates, citizens, and associations to engage in protected political expression, restrictions that the First Amendment cannot tolerate. . . .

[Affirmed] in part and reversed in part.

Mr. Chief Justice Burger, concurring in part and dissenting in part. . . .

[The contribution limitations are unconstitutional. Contributions] and expenditures are two sides of the same First Amendment coin. [Limiting] contributions, as a practical matter, will limit expenditures and will put an effective ceiling on the amount of political activity [that] the Government will permit to take place. . . .

The Court's attempt to distinguish the communication inherent in political *contributions* from the speech aspects of political *expenditures* simply "will not wash." We do little but engage in word games unless we recognize that people — candidates and contributors — spend money on political activity because they wish to communicate ideas, and their constitutional interest in doing so is precisely the same whether they or someone else utters the words. [Moreover, the contribution] restrictions are hardly incidental in their effect upon particular campaigns. [Such restrictions] will foreclose some candidacies,[9] [and] alter the nature of some electoral contests drastically.[10]

At any rate, the contribution limits are a far more severe restriction on First Amendment activity than the sort of "chilling" legislation for which the Court has shown such extraordinary concern in the past. See, e.g., [Cohen v. California, section D7 supra]. If such restraints can be justified at all, they must be justified by the very strongest of state interests. . . .

Mr. Justice White, concurring in part and dissenting in part. . . .

I dissent [from] the Court's view that the expenditure limitations [violate] the First Amendment. . . .

The congressional judgment [was that expenditure limitations are necessary] to counter the corrosive effects of money in federal election campaigns. [The] Court strikes down [§608(e)], strangely enough claiming more [knowledge] as to what may improperly influence candidates than is possessed by the majority of Congress that passed this bill and the President who signed it. [I] would take the word of those who know — that limiting independent expenditures is essential to prevent transparent and widespread evasion of the contribution limits. . . .

The Court also rejects Congress' judgment manifested in §608(c) that the federal interest in limiting total campaign expenditures by individual candidates justifies the incidental effect on their opportunity for effective political speech. I disagree. . . .

---

9. Candidates who must raise large initial contributions in order to appeal for more funds to a broader audience will be handicapped. . . .

10. Under the Court's holding, candidates with personal fortunes will be free to contribute to their own campaigns as much as they like, since the Court chooses to view the Act's provisions in this regard as unconstitutional "expenditure" limitations rather than "contribution" limitations. . . .

[The] argument that money is speech and that limiting the flow of money to the speaker violates the First Amendment proves entirely too much. Compulsory bargaining [has] increased the labor costs of those who publish newspapers, [and] taxation directly removes from company coffers large amounts of money that might be spent on larger and better newspapers. [But] it has not been suggested [that] these laws, and many others, are invalid because they siphon [off] large sums that would otherwise be available for communicative activities.

[The] judgment of Congress was that reasonably effective campaigns could be conducted within the limits established by the Act. [There] is no sound basis for invalidating the expenditure limitations, so long as the purposes they serve are legitimate and sufficiently substantial, which in my view they are.

[Expenditure] ceilings reinforce the contribution limits and help eradicate the hazard of corruption. [Without] limits on total expenditures, campaign costs will [inevitably] escalate, [creating an incentive to accept unlawful contributions. Moreover,] the corrupt use of money by candidates is as much to be feared as the corrosive influence of large contributions. There are many illegal ways of spending money to influence elections. [The] expenditure limits could play a substantial role in preventing unethical practices. There just would not be enough of "that kind of money" to go around. . . .

It is also important to [restore] public confidence in federal elections. It is critical to obviate [the] impression that federal elections are purely and simply a function of money. [The] ceiling on candidate expenditures represents the considered judgment of Congress that elections are to be decided among candidates none of whom has overpowering advantage by reason of a huge campaign war chest. [This] seems an acceptable purpose and the means chosen a common-sense way to achieve it. . . .

I also disagree with the Court's judgment that §608(a), which limits the amount of money that a candidate or his family may spend on his campaign, violates the Constitution. [By] limiting the importance of personal wealth, §608(a) helps to assure that only individuals with a modicum of support from others will be viable candidates. [This] would tend to discourage any notion that the outcome of elections is primarily a function of money. Similarly, §608(a) tends to equalize access to the political arena, encouraging the less wealthy [to] run for political office. [Congress] was entitled to determine that personal wealth ought to play a less important role in political campaigns than it has in the past. Nothing in the First Amendment stands in the way of that determination. . . .

MR. JUSTICE MARSHALL, concurring in part and dissenting in part.

[The] Court invalidates §608(a), [which limits the amount a candidate may spend from personal or family funds], as violative of the candidate's First Amendment Rights. [I] disagree.

[The] perception that personal wealth wins elections may not only discourage potential candidates without significant personal wealth from entering the political arena, but also undermine public confidence in the integrity of the electoral process.[1]

The concern that candidacy for public office not become, or appear to become, the exclusive province of the wealthy assumes heightened significance when one considers the impact of §608(b), which the Court today upholds. That

---

1. "In the Nation's seven largest States in 1970, 11 of the 15 major senatorial candidates were millionaires. The four who were not millionaires lost their bid for election." . . .

provision prohibits contributions from individuals and groups to candidates in excess of $1,000, and contributions from political committees in excess of $5,000. While the limitations on contributions are neutral there can be no question that large contributions generally mean more to the candidate without a substantial personal fortune to spend on his campaign. Large contributions are the less wealthy candidate's only hope of countering the wealthy candidate's immediate access to substantial sums of money. [Section 608(a) thus provides] some symmetry to a regulatory scheme that otherwise enhances the natural advantage of the wealthy. . . .

MR. JUSTICE BLACKMUN, concurring in part and dissenting in part.

I am not persuaded that the Court makes [a] principled constitutional distinction between the contribution limitations [and] the expenditure limitations. [I] therefore do not join Part I-B of the Court's opinion or those portions of Part I-A that are consistent with Part I-B. As to those, I dissent. . . .

Note: Buckley *and the Problem of Abridging Speech to "Enhance" the Electoral Process*

1. *The problem of unequal resources.* In upholding the expenditure and contribution limitations in *Buckley*, the court of appeals explained:

> [The] statute taken as a whole affirmatively enhances First Amendment values. By reducing in good measure disparity due to wealth, the Act tends to equalize both the relative ability of all voters to affect electoral outcomes, and the opportunity of all interested citizens to become candidates for elective federal office. This broadens the choice of candidates and the opportunity to hear a variety of views.

519 F.2d 817, 841 (D.C. Cir. 1975). Do you agree that, if the purpose and "net effect of the legislation [are] to enhance freedom of speech, the exacting review reserved for abridgements of free speech is inapposite"? L. Tribe, American Constitutional Law 1135 (2d ed. 1988). Do you agree with the Court that "the concept that government may restrict the speech of some elements of our society in order to enhance the relative voice of others is wholly foreign to the First Amendment"?

Note that *Buckley* posed a conflict between two conceptions of a properly functioning system of free expression, and between two conceptions of the role of the state. Under one view, government should take the "private" status quo for granted and all persons, no matter their resources, are free to press their interests on the political process. If some people have more money than others, and if their greater resources permit more speech, that result is something for which government is not itself responsible and which cannot be "remedied" consistent with the first amendment. The role of government is to remain "neutral" as people in the private sphere compete in the political marketplace.

Under the competing view, a system of free expression is one in which there is fair deliberation on what the public good requires, and inequality of resources, which can seriously distort that deliberation, is understood to be at least in part the product of governmental choices. If government permits the process of political deliberation to become distorted by this inequality of resources, the result is inconsistent with first amendment aspirations. Under this view, government efforts to equalize resources are permitted (and perhaps even required) in order to promote a more fair public debate. See Balkin, Some Realism about Pluralism: Legal Realist Approaches to the First Amendment, 1990 Duke L.J. 375.

2. *Competing views.* Consider the following:

a. Wright, Politics and the Constitution: Is Money Speech?, 85 Yale L.J. 1001, 1005, 1015–1019 (1976):

> Nothing in the First Amendment prevents us, as a political community, from [choosing] to move closer to the kind of community process that lies at the heart of the First Amendment conception — a process wherein ideas and candidates prevail because of their inherent worth, not because [one] side puts on a more elaborate show of support. [The] picture of the political process that emerges from [*Buckley*] corresponds [to the] pluralist model. [To] the pluralist, the political process consists [of] the pulling and hauling of various competing interest groups. [Force] collides with counterforce, [and] the strongest force [determines] the outcome of [the] process. [This model] gives undeserved weight [to] highly organized and wealthy groups [and drains] politics of its moral and intellectual content.

b. Kagan, Private Speech, Public Purpose: The Role of Governmental Motive in First Amendment Doctrine, 63 U. Chi. L. Rev. 415, 467–475 (1996):

> In what has become one of the most castigated passages in modern First Amendment case law, the Court pronounced in *Buckley* that "the concept that government may restrict the speech of some elements of our society in order to enhance the relative voice of others is wholly foreign to the First Amendment. . . ." [The] *Buckley* principle emerges not from the view that redistribution of speech opportunities is itself an illegitimate end, but from the view that governmental actions justified as redistributive devices often (though not always) stem partly from hostility or sympathy toward ideas — or, even more commonly, from self-interest. [The] nature of [such] regulations, as compared with other content-neutral regulations, creates [a special problem]: that governmental officials (here, legislators) more often will take account of improper factors. [This] increased probability of taint arises [from] the very design of laws directed at equalizing the realm of public expression. Unlike most content-neutral regulations, these laws not only have, but are supposed to have, content-based effects. . . . In considering such a law, a legislator's own views of the ideas (or speakers) that the equalization effort means to suppress or promote may well intrude, consciously or not, on her decisionmaking process. [Thus,] there may be good reason to distrust the motives of politicians when they apply themselves to reconstructing the realm of expression.

c. Strauss, Corruption, Equality, and Campaign Finance, 94 Colum. L. Rev. 1369, 1383–1384 (1994):

> [The principle] "one person, one vote" is [the] decisive counterexample to the suggestion [in *Buckley*] that the aspiration [of equalizing "speech"] is foreign to the First Amendment. We do not think of "one person, one vote" as an example of reducing the speech of some to enhance the relative speech of others, but that is only because the principle seems so natural. When legislatures were malapportioned, rural voters had a more effective voice than urban voters. Reapportionment reduced their influence in order to enhance the relative influence of others. We might unreflectively say that the rural voters were deprived of voting power that was not rightfully theirs, while my ability to make a campaign contribution is rightfully

[mine]. But this formulation begs the question. We have to explain why superior spending power is rightfully mine but superior voting power is not. . . .

d. B. Neuborne, Madison's Music 67–68 (2015):

By treating independent campaign *expenditures* much more favorably than campaign *contributions* to a candidate, the Court undermined the ability of candidates (and political parties) to define their own political agendas, licensing "independent" ideological outriders to spend unlimited funds to dominate the electoral agenda, while candidates must struggle to raise tightly regulated contributions. [*Buckley*] left us with a judge-made campaign finance system that turns American democracy over to ideologues in the top 1 percent of the economic tree, a system that no legislator has ever supported and one that would astound the Founders. [Tell] the truth. If you tried, could you have come up with a worse way to structure and finance our democracy?

3. *A comparative perspective.* The Canada Elections Act of 2000 set limits for third party spending in elections. Specifically, the Act provides that a third-party (that is, a group or individual who is not a candidate) "shall not incur election advertising expenses of a total amount of more than $150,000 during an election period in relation to a general election" and "not more than $3,000 [to] promote or oppose the election of one or more candidates in a given electoral district." The act defines "election advertising expenses" as including any paid message that names candidates, shows their likeness, or takes a position on an issue "with which they are particularly associated." Stephen Harper, the head of a conservative political group, brought suit claiming that the act violated the Canadian Charter of Rights and Freedoms, which guarantees to every person the fundamental "freedom of thought, belief, opinion and expression." The Charter provides that fundamental freedoms may be subjected "only to such reasonable limits [as] can be demonstrably justified in a free and democratic society." In Harper v. Canada, 1 S.C.R. 827 (2004), excerpted in Hasen, Regulation of Campaign Finance, in V. Amar and M. Tushnet, Global Perspectives on Constitutional Law 198 (2009), the Supreme Court of Canada upheld these provisions of the act, therefore reaching a different result than the Supreme Court of the United States in *Buckley*.

Justice Bastarache delivered the opinion of the court: "Third party advertising is political expression. [As such, it] lies at the core of the expression guaranteed by the Charter and warrants a high degree of constitutional protection. [In] some circumstances, however, third party advertising will be less deserving of constitutional protection. Indeed, it is possible that third parties who have access to significant financial resources can manipulate political discourse to their advantage through political advertising. [Advertising] expense limits may restrict free expression to ensure that participants are able to meaningfully participate in the electoral process. For candidates, political parties and third parties, meaningful participation means the ability to inform voters of their position. For voters, meaningful participation means the ability to hear and weigh many points of view. The difficulties of striking this balance are evident. . . .

"The question, then, is what promotes an informed voter? For voters to be able to hear all points of view, the information disseminated by third parties, candidates, and political parties cannot be unlimited. In the absence of spending limits, it is possible for the affluent or a number of persons or groups pooling their resources and acting in concert to dominate the political discourse. [If] a few groups are able to flood the electoral discourse with their message, it is possible, indeed likely, that the voices of some will be drowned out. Where those having access to the most resources monopolize the election discourse, their opponents will be deprived of a reasonable opportunity to speak and be heard. This unequal dissemination of points of view undermines the voter's ability to be adequately informed of all views. In this way, equality in the political discourse is necessary for meaningful participation in the electoral process and ultimately enhances the right to vote."

Note: Subsidy and Disclosure

1. *Public financing of campaigns. Buckley* concluded that, absent extraordinary circumstances, government cannot constitutionally *restrict* speech in order to eliminate imbalance in the marketplace. What other means, if any, might government employ to achieve this objective? Consider Powe, Mass Speech and the Newer First Amendment, 1982 Sup. Ct. Rev. 243, 268–269, 282–283:

> [To] attempt to tone down a debate [in] the interests of enhancing the marketplace [is] wildly at odds with the normal First Amendment belief that more speech is better. [If the problem is that] the wealthy are too powerful, [we should provide] significant additional public funding [for] electoral campaigns, so that the advantages of wealth can [be] minimized.

2. *Subtitle H.* In *Buckley,* the Court considered the constitutionality of subtitle H of the Internal Revenue Code, which established a scheme of campaign "subsidies" to equalize the financial resources of political candidates. Under subtitle H, major political parties (those that had received more than 25 percent of the vote in the preceding presidential election) qualified for subsidies of up to $20 million for their candidates' presidential campaigns. Minor parties (those that had received between 5 and 25 percent of the vote in the preceding presidential election) qualified for subsidies proportional to their share of the vote in the preceding or current election, whichever was higher. All other political parties qualified for subsidies only if they received more than 5 percent of the vote in the current election. Subtitle H provided for public financing of primaries and party nominating conventions on similar terms. All subsidies were indexed to inflation. Major party candidates were eligible for public funding only if they agreed to forgo all private contributions and to limit their expenditures to the amount of the subsidy. Other candidates who accepted subsidies were permitted to supplement their public funding with private contributions as long as they agreed to limit their total expenditures to the amount of the major party subsidy.

The Court upheld the public financing provisions: "Subtitle H is a congressional effort, not to abridge, restrict, or censor speech, but rather to use public money to facilitate and enlarge public discussion and participation in the electoral process, goals vital to a self-governing people. Thus, Subtitle H furthers, not abridges, pertinent First Amendment values." Is this consistent with the Court's analysis in other parts of the opinion?

The Court held further that subtitle H's requirement that a candidate who accepts public financing agree to limit total campaign expenditures to the amount of the major party subsidy did not independently violate the first amendment: "Congress [may] condition acceptance of public funds on an agreement by the candidate to abide by specified expenditure limitations. Just as a candidate may voluntarily limit the size of the contributions he chooses to accept, he may decide to forgo private fundraising and accept public funding."

3. *Subsidizing individuals rather than parties.* Consider the following proposal: "The principle of equal-dollars-per-voter means that each eligible voter should receive the same amount of financial resources for the purpose of participating in electoral politics. [The] only money that voters would be permitted to [spend or contribute] would be the money they receive from the government." Foley, Equal-Dollars-Per-Voter: A Constitutional Principle of Campaign Finance, 94 Colum. L. Rev. 1204, 1206–1207 (1994). For a variant of this proposal, consider B. Ackerman and I. Ayres, Voting with Dollars 4–8, 156–157 (2002):

> [The] American citizen should [be] given a more equal say in [campaign] funding decisions. Just as he receives a ballot on election day, he should also receive a special credit card to finance his favorite candidate. [Suppose] that Congress seeded every voter's account with fifty [dollars, which each voter could then allocate among the candidates for federal office as he sees fit. Additional private contributions should be permitted, but contributors should] be barred from giving money directly to candidates. They [should] instead pass their checks through a blind trust [so candidates] won't be able to identify who provided the funds. [There] are lots of reasons for contributing to campaigns, and this [approach] undercuts only one of them — the desire to obtain a quid pro quo from a victorious candidate. [This two-pronged approach] promises an effective increase in both political equality *and* political expression.

See Karlan, Elections and Change Under "Voting with Dollars," 91 Cal. L. Rev. 706 (2003) (suggesting some contradictions between first amendment theory and the proposal's reliance on anonymous donation).

4. *Disclosure.* To what extent is disclosure of the identity of contributors an effective and constitutional means of preventing undue influence? The Federal Election Campaign Act of 1971 requires every political candidate and "political committee" to maintain records of the names and addresses of all persons who contribute more than $10 in a calendar year and to make such records available for inspection by the commission. Moreover, the act provides that such reports are to be available "for public inspection and copying." In *Buckley,* the Court upheld these provisions:

> The governmental interests sought to be vindicated by the disclosure requirements [fall] into three categories. First, disclosure provides the electorate with information "as to where political campaign money comes [from]" in order to aid the voters in evaluating those who seek federal office. [Second,] disclosure requirements deter actual corruption and avoid the appearance of corruption by exposing [contributions] to the light of publicity. [Third, such] requirements are an essential means of gathering the data necessary to detect violations of the contribution limitations. [Thus, the] disclosure requirements [directly] serve substantial governmental interests. . . .

In subsequent decisions, the Court has reaffirmed *Buckley's* conclusion that disclosure requirements in the context of campaign finance regulations are presumptively constitutional. See McConnell v. Federal Election Commission, 540 U.S. 93 (2003) (upholding disclosure requirements in the Bipartisan Campaign

Reform Act of 2002); Citizens United v. Federal Election Commission, 558 U.S. 310 (2010) (same).

At the same time, though, the Court has recognized constitutional limits on disclosure requirements. In Brown v. Socialist Workers '74 Campaign Committee, 459 U.S. 87 (1982), the Court held that the disclosure provisions of the Ohio campaign reporting law could not constitutionally be applied to the Socialist Workers Party, "a minor political party which historically has been the object of harassment by government officials and private parties."

The Court followed *Buckley* and *Brown* in Doe v. Reed, 561 U.S. 186 (2010), which involved the constitutionality of a Washington state public records statute, which authorizes the public disclosure of the names of individuals who sign referendum petitions. The plaintiffs argued that public disclosure would chill the willingness of individuals to sign such petitions. The Court held that the state's interest in "preserving the integrity of the electoral process by combating fraud, detecting invalid signatures, and fostering government transparency and accountability" is sufficient to justify the generally modest impact on those who sign such petitions. On the other hand, the Court made clear that if those who sign any *particular* petition can demonstrate "a reasonable probability that the compelled disclosure [of personal information] will subject them to threats, harassment, or reprisals from either Government officials or private parties," then disclosure might well violate the First Amendment.

Note: Campaign Finance Regulation in the Thirty Years After Buckley

1. *Contribution limits.* In Nixon v. Shrink Missouri Government PAC, 523 U.S. 666 (2000), the Court upheld a Missouri statute imposing limits ranging from $275 to $1,075 on contributions to candidates for state offices (different limits were applicable to different offices). In an opinion by Justice Souter, the Court rejected the argument that "*Buckley* set a minimum constitutional threshold for contribution limits, which in dollars adjusted for loss of purchasing power are now well above the lines drawn by Missouri." The key question, he explained, was whether "the limits were so low as to impede the ability of candidates to 'amas[s] the resources necessary for effective advocacy.'" The Court found no such showing in this case. Justices Kennedy, Scalia, and Thomas dissented.

In Randall v. Sorrell, 548 U.S. 230 (2006), the Court, in a six-to-three decision, invalidated Vermont's Act 64, which stringently limited the amount that individuals, organizations, and political parties could contribute to state and local political candidates. The act limited contributions to candidates for governor to $200 over a two-year period, with substantially lower limits for contributions to candidates for state senator and state representative. In a plurality opinion joined by Chief Justice Roberts and Justice Alito, Justice Breyer concluded that Act 64's limits were so "low as to generate suspicion" that they were "not closely drawn" to serve the state's legitimate interest in preventing the reality and appearance of corruption. Justice Souter, joined by Justices Stevens and Ginsburg, dissented.

2. *Political action committees.* The Court has handed down several decisions concerning political action committees (PACs) and related organizations. See, e.g., Federal Election Commission v. National Conservative Political Action Committee, 470 U.S. 480 (1985) (invalidating a statute prohibiting any independent political action committee to spend more than $1,000 to further

the election of a presidential candidate who receives public financing); California Medical Association v. Federal Election Commission, 453 U.S. 182 (1981) (upholding a statute prohibiting individuals and unincorporated associations from contributing more than $5,000 per year to any multicandidate political committee); Federal Election Commission v. National Right to Work Committee, 459 U.S. 197 (1982) (upholding a statute prohibiting nonstock corporations from soliciting contributions from persons other than their "members" for the purpose of generating funds to be spent in federal election campaigns); Citizens against Rent Control v. Berkeley, 454 U.S. 290 (1981) (invalidating an ordinance imposing a $250 limit on contributions to committees formed to support or oppose ballot measures submitted to a popular vote).

3. *Political parties.* After *Buckley*, can the government constitutionally limit the amount a political party can spend in support of its own candidates? Are such expenditures "contributions" or "expenditures" within the meaning of *Buckley*? See Colorado Republican Federal Campaign Committee v. Federal Election Commission, 518 U.S. 604 (1996), in which the Court held that the first amendment prohibits the application of a provision of the Federal Election Campaign Act that imposes dollar limits on political party "expenditures in connection with the general election campaign of a [congressional] candidate." In a plurality opinion, Justice Breyer, joined by Justices O'Connor and Souter, held that, under *Buckley*, the first amendment prohibits the application of this provision to expenditures that the political party makes "independently, without coordination with a candidate."

In Federal Election Commission v. Colorado Republican Federal Campaign Committee, 533 U.S. 431 (2001) (*Colorado II*), the Court rejected the claim that a political party's *coordinated* expenditures on behalf of its electoral candidates should be treated as expenditures rather than contributions. The Court explained that "a party's right to make unlimited expenditures coordinated with a candidate would induce individual and other nonparty contributors to give to the party in order to finance coordinated spending for a favored candidate beyond the contribution limits, [and thus bypass the very limits] that *Buckley* upheld." Chief Justice Rehnquist and Justices Scalia, Kennedy, and Thomas dissented.

4. *Corporate speech.* First National Bank of Boston v. Bellotti, 435 U.S. 765 (1978), involved a Massachusetts statute that prohibited any corporation to make contributions or expenditures "for the purpose [of] influencing or affecting the vote on any question submitted to the voters, other than one materially affecting any of the property, business or assets of the corporation." The statute specified further that "[n]o question submitted to the voters solely concerning the taxation of the income, property or transactions of individuals shall be deemed materially to affect the property, business or assets of the corporation." The state court, in upholding the statute, held that the first amendment rights of a corporation are limited to issues that materially affect its business, property, or assets.

The Court, in a five-to-four decision, reversed. In an opinion by Justice Powell, the Court explained that the state court had "posed the wrong question." The proper question "is not whether corporations 'have' First Amendment rights and, if so, whether they are coextensive with those of natural persons, [but] whether [the statute] abridges expression that the First Amendment was meant to protect." The statute is directed against speech that is "indispensable to decisionmaking in a democracy," and that lies "at the heart of the First Amendment's protection." Moreover, the Court could "find no support in the First [Amendment], or in the decisions of this Court, for the proposition that speech that otherwise would be within the protection of the First Amendment loses that protection simply because its source is a corporation that cannot prove, to the satisfaction of a court, a material effect on its business or property."

Justice White, joined by Justices Brennan and Marshall, dissented: "[The] special status of corporations has placed them in a position to control vast amounts of economic power which may, if not regulated, dominate not only the economy but also the very heart of our democracy, the electoral process. Although [*Buckley*] provides support for the position that the desire to equalize the financial resources available to candidates does not justify the limitation upon the expression of support which a restriction upon individual contributions entails, the interest of Massachusetts [is] quite different. It is not one of equalizing the resources of opposing candidates or opposing positions, but rather of preventing institutions which have been permitted to amass wealth as a result of special advantages extended by the State for certain economic purposes from using that wealth to acquire an unfair advantage in the political process. [The] State need not permit its own creation to consume it." Justice Rehnquist also dissented.

5. *Corporate speech II*. In Austin v. Michigan Chamber of Commerce, 494 U.S. 652 (1990), the Court, in a six-to-three decision, upheld section 54(1) of the Michigan Campaign Finance Act, which prohibited corporations from using corporate treasury funds for independent expenditures in support of or in opposition to any candidate for state office. In an opinion by Justice Marshall, the Court observed that "the unique legal and economic characteristics of corporations" — such as "limited liability, perpetual life, and favorable treatment of the accumulation and distribution of assets" — enable corporations "to use 'resources amassed in the economic marketplace' to obtain 'an unfair advantage in the political marketplace.'" Noting that section 54(1) was designed to deal with "the corrosive and distorting effects of immense aggregations of wealth that are accumulated with the help of the corporate form and that have little or no correlation to the public's support for the corporation's political ideas," the Court held that "the State has articulated a sufficiently compelling rationale to support its restriction on independent expenditures by corporations."

Justice Scalia dissented: "[Corporations] are, to be sure, given special advantages, [but] so are other associations and private individuals, [ranging] from tax breaks to contract awards to public employment to outright cash subsidies. It is rudimentary that the State cannot exact as the price of those special advantages the forfeiture of First Amendment rights. [Moreover], the fact that corporations 'amas[s] large treasuries' [is] not sufficient justification for the suppression of political speech, unless one thinks it would be lawful to prohibit men and women whose net worth is above a certain figure from endorsing political candidates."

6. *Advocacy corporations*. North Carolina Right to Life, a nonprofit advocacy corporation that counsels pregnant women how to deal with unwanted pregnancies without resorting to abortion, challenged the constitutionality of 2 U.S.C. §441, which prohibits corporations from making political contributions directly to candidates for federal office, but permits them to establish, administer, and solicit contributions to separately created PACs, which can themselves make such contributions. In Federal Election Commission v. Beaumont, 539 U.S. 146 (2003), the Court upheld §441, even as applied to nonprofit advocacy corporations. In an opinion by Justice Souter, the Court noted that nonprofit advocacy corporations, like for-profit corporations, benefit from state-created advantages and may thus be able to amass substantial political war chests.

Moreover, §441 helps to prevent individuals and organizations from circumventing the contribution limits upheld in *Buckley*. Because restrictions on political contributions are "merely 'marginal' speech restrictions," and "lie closer to the edges than to the core of political expression," they are constitutional if they are "closely drawn" to serve a "sufficiently important interest," a test the Court held was satisfied in this case. Justice Thomas, joined by Justice Scalia, dissented. See also McConnell v. Federal Election Commission, infra.

7. *The thirty years after* Buckley. As evident from the above decisions, in the thirty years after *Buckley* the Court, often in five-to-four decisions, took an increasingly moderate approach to campaign finance regulation. In part, this was due to concerns about the steadily growing influence of money in the political process. Perhaps the most revealing and most important decision in this era was McConnell v. Federal Election Commission, in which the Court, again by a five-to-four vote, upheld the constitutionality of the Bipartisan Campaign Reform Act of 2002 (BCRA), which was signed into law by President George W. Bush, and which amended the Federal Election Campaign Act of 1971 (FECA).

McCONNELL v. FEDERAL ELECTION COMM'N, 540 U.S. 93 (2003). The Bipartisan Campaign Reform Act of 2002 (BCRA) sought to address several important developments in the years since *Buckley*, including the increased importance of "soft money" and the disturbing findings of a Senate investigation into campaign practices related to the 1996 federal elections. Prior to BCRA, FECA's contribution limitations extended only to so-called "hard money" contributions made for the purpose of influencing an election for federal office. Political parties and candidates were able to contribute "soft money" — money unregulated under FECA — to support activities intended to influence state or local elections, to support get-out-the-vote (GOTV) drives and generic party advertising, and to pay for legislative advocacy advertisements, even if they mentioned a federal candidate's name, as long as the ads did not expressly advocate the candidate's election or defeat. In BCRA, Congress sought to close these soft-money "loopholes" on the premise that they facilitated widespread circumvention of FECA's requirements.

Justices Stevens and O'Connor, joined by Justices Souter, Ginsburg, and Breyer, delivered the opinion of the Court: "The solicitation, transfer, and use of soft money [has] enabled parties and candidates to circumvent FECA's limitations on the source and amount of contributions in connection with federal elections.

"In 1998 the Senate Committee on Governmental Affairs issued a six-volume report summarizing the results of an extensive investigation into the campaign practices in the 1996 federal elections. The report gave particular attention to the effect of soft money on the American political system, including elected officials' practice of granting special access in return for political contributions. [The report concluded] that both parties promised and provided special access to candidates and senior Government officials in exchange for large soft-money contributions. . . .

"The cornerstone of Title I [of the BCRA is] §323(a), which prohibits national party committees and their agents from soliciting, receiving, directing, or spending any soft money. [In] *Buckley*, [we] recognized that contribution limits, unlike limits on expenditures, 'entai[l] only a marginal restriction upon the contributor's ability to engage in free communication.' [The] less rigorous standard of review we have applied to contribution limits [shows] proper deference to Congress' ability to weigh competing constitutional interests in an area in which it enjoys particular expertise. [Like] the contribution limits we upheld in *Buckley*, §323's restrictions have only a marginal impact on the ability of contributors, candidates, officeholders, and parties to engage in effective political speech. Complex as its provisions may be, §323, in the main, does little more than regulate the ability of wealthy individuals, corporations, and unions to contribute large sums of money to influence federal elections, federal candidates, and federal officeholders. . . .

"[§323(a)] provides that 'national committee[s] of a political party . . . may not solicit, receive, or direct to another person a contribution, donation, or transfer of funds or any other thing of value, or spend any funds, that are not subject to the limitations, prohibitions, and reporting requirements of this Act.' [Before the enactment of this provision], national parties were able to use vast amounts of soft money in their efforts to elect federal candidates. Consequently, as long as they directed the money to the political parties, donors could contribute large amounts of soft money for use in activities designed to influence federal elections. New §323(a) is designed to put a stop to that practice.

"The Government defends §323(a)'s ban on national parties' involvement with soft money as necessary to prevent the actual and apparent corruption of federal candidates and officeholders. Our cases have made clear that the prevention of corruption or its appearance constitutes a sufficiently important interest to justify political contribution limits. [The] idea that large contributions to a national party can corrupt or, at the very least, create the appearance of corruption of federal candidates and officeholders is neither novel nor implausible. . . .

"The question for present purposes is whether large *soft-money* contributions to national party committees have a corrupting influence or give rise to the appearance of corruption. Both common sense and the ample record in these cases confirm Congress' belief that they do. [The] evidence in the record shows that candidates and donors alike [have] exploited the soft-money loophole, the former to increase their prospects of election and the latter to create debt on the part of officeholders, with the national parties serving as willing intermediaries. . . .

"The core of §323(b) is a straightforward contribution regulation: It prevents donors from contributing [soft-money] to state and local party committees to help finance 'Federal election activity.' The term 'Federal election activity' encompasses four distinct categories of electioneering: (1) voter registration activity during the 120 days preceding a regularly scheduled federal election; (2) voter identification, get-out-the-vote (GOTV), and generic campaign activity that is 'conducted in connection with an election in which a candidate for Federal office appears on the ballot'; (3) any 'public communication' that 'refers to a clearly identified candidate for Federal office' and 'promotes,' 'supports,' 'attacks,' or 'opposes' a candidate for that office; and (4) the services provided by a state committee employee who dedicates more than 25% of his or her time to 'activities in connection with a Federal election.' . . .

"[In] addressing the problem of soft-money contributions to state committees, Congress both drew a conclusion and made a prediction. Its conclusion, based on the evidence before it, was that the corrupting influence of soft money does not insinuate itself into the political process solely through national party committees. Rather, state committees function as an alternate avenue for precisely the same corrupting forces. [Congress] also made a prediction. Having been taught the hard lesson of circumvention by the entire history of campaign finance regulation, Congress knew that soft-money donors would react to §323(a) by scrambling to find another way to purchase influence. [We] 'must accord substantial deference to the predictive judgments of Congress.' [Preventing] corrupting activity from shifting wholesale to state committees and thereby eviscerating FECA clearly qualifies as an important governmental interest. [Because] voter registration, voter identification, GOTV, and generic campaign activity all confer substantial benefits on federal candidates, the funding of such activities creates a significant risk of actual and apparent corruption. Section 323(b) is a reasonable response to that risk."

Justice Scalia concurred in part and dissented in part: "We are governed by Congress, and this legislation prohibits the criticism of Members of Congress by those entities most capable of giving such criticism loud voice: national political parties. [To] be sure, the legislation is evenhanded: It similarly prohibits criticism of the candidates who oppose Members of Congress in their reelection bids. But as everyone knows, this is an area in which evenhandedness is not fairness. [If] incumbents and challengers are limited to the same quantity of electioneering, incumbents are favored. [Beyond] that, however, the present legislation *targets* for prohibition certain categories of campaign speech that are particularly harmful to incumbents. Is it accidental, do you think, that incumbents raise about three times as much 'hard money'—the sort of funding generally *not* restricted by this legislation—as do their challengers? Or that lobbyists [give] 92 percent of their money in 'hard' contributions? [Is] it mere happenstance [that] national-party funding, which is severely limited by the Act, is more likely to assist cash-strapped challengers than flush-with-hard-money incumbents[?]"

Justice Kennedy, joined in part by Chief Justice Rehnquist and Justices Scalia and Thomas, filed an opinion concurring in part and dissenting in part: "Today's decision [replaces] respected First Amendment principles with new, amorphous, and unsound rules, rules which dismantle basic protections for speech. [Our] precedents teach, above all, that Government cannot be trusted to moderate its own rules for suppression of speech. The dangers posed by speech regulations have led the Court to insist upon principled constitutional lines and a rigorous standard of review. The majority now abandons these distinctions and limitations. . . .

"In *Buckley*, the Court held that one, and only one, interest justified the significant burden on the right of association involved there: eliminating, or preventing, actual corruption or the appearance of corruption stemming from contributions to candidates. [The] Court [today] ignores these constitutional bounds and in effect interprets the anticorruption rationale to allow regulation not just of 'actual or apparent *quid pro quo* arrangements,' but of any conduct that wins goodwill from or influences a Member of Congress. [The] very aim of *Buckley*'s standard [was] to define undue influence by reference to the presence of *quid pro quo* involving the officeholder. The Court, in contrast, concludes that access, without more, proves influence is undue. [This] new definition of corruption sweeps away all protections for speech that lie in its path." Justice Thomas, joined in part by Justice Scalia, also concurred in part and dissented in part.

In another aspect of *McConnell*, the Court, in by the same five-to-four vote, upheld §203 of The Bipartisan Campaign Reform Act, which prohibited corporations and labor unions from funding "electioneering communications" from their general treasuries. The BCRA defined an "electioneering communication" as any "broadcast, cable, or satellite communication" that refers to a clearly identified candidate for federal office, is made within 60 days before a general election or 30 days before a primary election, and is targeted to the relevant electorate.

Justices Stevens and O'Connor delivered the opinion of the Court. At the outset, the Court noted that Congress's "power to prohibit corporations and unions from using funds in their treasuries to finance advertisements expressly advocating the election or defeat of [particular] candidates in federal elections has been firmly embedded in our law." The ability of such organizations to create PACs, the Court observed, has "provided corporations and unions with a constitutionally sufficient opportunity to engage in [such] advocacy." In the Court's view, all BCRA did was to extend this principle from advertisements that expressly advocate the election or defeat of named candidates ("Vote Against Smith") to advertisements that purport to address general issues but that expressly refer to named candidates, without literally calling for their election or defeat, in circumstances in which the underlying point of the advertisement is clear ("Tell Smith to stop raising your taxes.").

Justice Kennedy, joined in part by Chief Justice Rehnquist and Justices Scalia and Thomas, dissented: "The majority permits a new and serious intrusion on speech when it upholds §203, [which] prohibits corporations and labor unions from using money from their general treasury to fund electioneering communications. The majority compounds the error made in *Austin*, and silences political speech central to the civic discourse that sustains and informs our democratic processes. Unions and corporations, including nonprofit corporations, now face severe criminal penalties for broadcasting advocacy messages that 'refe[r] to a clearly identified candidate' in an election season."

Note: *Campaign Finance and the Roberts Court*

1. *A critical shift in the Court.* The appointment of Samuel Alito to replace Sandra Day O'Connor led to a sudden shift in the Court. Only four years after the decision in *McConnell*, after Justice Alito had replaced O'Connor, who had voted with the majority in *McConnell*, the Court in a five-to-four decision in Federal Election Commission v. Wisconsin Right to Life, 551 U.S.449 (2007), now held §203 of BCRA *unconstitutional* as applied to Wisconsin Right to Life's televised political advertisements that criticized Wisconsin's senators for participating in a filibuster to block the confirmation of several of President Bush's judicial nominees. Because the ads expressly mentioned Senator Russ Feingold by name and called upon viewers to contact Feingold to urge him to oppose the filibuster, they clearly violated §203.

In an opinion joined only by Justice Alito, Chief Justice Roberts argued that the Court in *McConnell* had upheld §203 only insofar as it regulated political advertising that "was the 'functional equivalent' of express campaign speech." The question in this case, Roberts declared, was whether the WRTL ads were "the 'functional equivalent' of speech expressly advocating the election or defeat of a candidate for federal office," which could constitutionally be regulated under *McConnell*, or whether they were "genuine" issue ads, which, he maintained, could not be regulated consistent with the First Amendment:

"In drawing that line, the First Amendment requires us to err of the side of protecting political speech rather than suppressing it. We conclude that the speech at issue in this as-applied challenge is not the 'functional equivalent' of express campaign speech. We further conclude that the interests held to justify restricting corporate campaign speech or its functional equivalent do not justify restricting issue advocacy, and accordingly we hold that BCRA §203 is unconstitutional as applied to the advertisements at issue."

Justice Scalia, joined by Justices Kennedy and Thomas, concurred in the result: "[It] was adventurous for *McConnell* to extend *Austin* beyond corporate speech constituting express advocacy. [I] would overrule that part of the Court's decision in *McConnell* upholding §203(a) of the BCRA."

Justice Souter, joined by Justices Stevens, Ginsburg, and Breyer, dissented: "[In] *McConnell*, we found [§203] to be 'easily understood and objective[e]' [and] we held that the [line] separating regulated election speech from general political discourse does not, on its face, violate the First Amendment. [We] found '[l]ittle difference . . . between an ad that urged viewers to "vote against Jane Doe" and one that condemned Jane Doe's record on a particular issue before exhorting viewers to "call Jane Doe and tell her what you think."' *McConnell*'s "holding that §203 is facially constitutional is overruled. [The] price of *McConnell*'s demise [seems] to me a high one. The Court (and I think the country) loses when important precedent is overruled without good reason, and there is no justification for departing from our usual rule of *stare decisis* here."

2. *The "Millionaire's Amendment."* The next year, the Court considered the constitutionality of §319(a) of BCRA, the so-called "Millionaire's Amendment," which provided that if a candidate for Congress spends $350,000 or more of his own money in order to secure his own election, the opposing candidate was then permitted to accept individual campaign contributions up to three-times larger than would otherwise be allowed. (The opposing candidate could not accept additional contributions under this provision that would in total exceed the "millionaire" candidate's personal expenditures.) In Davis v. Federal Election Commission, 554 U.S. 724 (2008), the Court, in a five-to-four decision, held the provision unconstitutional.

Justice Alito delivered the opinion of the Court: "In *Buckley*, we soundly rejected a cap on a candidate's expenditure of personal funds to finance campaign speech. [We] rejected the argument that [such] an expenditure cap could be justified on that ground that it served [the] 'interest in equalizing the relative financial resources of candidates competing for elective office.' [While §319(a)] does not impose a cap on a candidate's expenditure of personal funds, it imposes [a] penalty on any candidate who robustly exercises that First Amendment right. Section 319(a) requires a candidate to choose between the First Amendment right to engage in unfettered political speech and subjection to discriminatory fundraising limitations. [Under] §319(a), the vigorous exercise of the right to use personal funds to finance campaign speech produces fundraising advantages for opponents in the competitive context of electoral politics. [Because] §319(a) imposes a substantial burden on the exercise of the First Amendment right to use personal funds for campaign speech, [it] cannot stand unless it is 'justified by a compelling state interest.' No such justification is present here."

Justice Stevens, joined by Justices Souter, Ginsburg and Breyer, dissented: "The Millionaire's Amendment [is] the product of a congressional judgment that candidates who are willing and able to spend over $350,000 of their own money in seeking election to Congress enjoy an advantage over opponents who must rely on contributions to finance their campaigns. To reduce that advantage, and to combat the perception that congressional seats are for sale to the highest bidder, Congress has relaxed the amount of contributions that the opponents of self-funding candidates may accept from their supporters. [Because] the Millionaire's Amendment does not impose any burden [on] the self-funding candidate's freedom to speak [and] because it does no more than diminish the unequal strength of the self-funding candidate, it does not violate the [Constitution]."

3. *Arizona Free Enterprise*. The Arizona Citizens Clean Elections Act of 1998 created a voluntary public financing system to fund the primary and general election campaigns of candidates for state office. All eligible candidates may opt to receive public funding. Eligibility is contingent on the collection of a specified number of five-dollar contributions from Arizona voters and the acceptance of certain campaign restrictions and obligations. Publicly funded candidates must agree to limit their expenditure of personal funds to $500, participate in at least one public debate, adhere to an overall expenditure cap, and return all unspent public moneys to the State.

In exchange for accepting these conditions, participating candidates are granted public funds to conduct their campaigns. When certain conditions are met, publicly funded candidates are granted additional "equalizing" or matching funds. Equalizing funds are made available to a publicly funded candidate when the amount of money a *privately* financed candidate receives in contributions (including expenditures of his own funds), combined with the expenditures of independent groups made in support of the privately financed candidate or in opposition to the publicly financed candidate, exceed the initial allotment of funds to the publicly financed candidate. Once matching funds are triggered, each additional dollar that a privately financed candidate spends or is spent on his behalf results in one dollar in additional state funding to his publicly financed opponent. Matching funds top out at two times the initial authorized grant of public funding to the publicly financed candidate. Under Arizona law, a privately financed candidate may raise and spend unlimited funds.

In Arizona Free Enterprise Club's Freedom Club PAC v. Bennett, 564 U.S. 721 (2011), the Court, in another five-to-four decision, held that this scheme violates the First Amendment. Chief Justice Roberts wrote the opinion of the Court: "Although the speech of the candidates and independent expenditure groups that brought this suit is not directly capped by Arizona's matching funds provision, those parties contend that their political speech is substantially burdened by the state law in the same way that speech was burdened by the law we recently found invalid in *Davis*. [The] logic of *Davis* largely controls our approach to this case. Much like the burden placed on speech in *Davis*, the matching funds provision "imposes an unprecedented penalty on any candidate who robustly exercises [his] First Amendment right[s]."

Justice Kagan, joined by Justices Ginsburg, Breyer, and Sotomayor, dissented: "The First Amendment's core purpose is to foster a healthy, vibrant political system full of robust discussion and debate. [Campaign] finance reform over the last century has focused on one key question: how to prevent massive pools of private money from corrupting our political system. If an officeholder owes his election to wealthy contributors, he may act for their benefit alone, rather than on behalf of all the people. [To] prevent both corruption and the appearance of corruption — and so to protect our democratic system of governance — citizens have implemented reforms designed to curb the power of special interests. Among these measures, public financing of elections has emerged as a potentially potent mechanism to preserve elected officials' independence. By supplanting private cash in elections, public financing eliminates the source of political corruption. For this reason, [almost] one-third of the States have adopted some form of public financing, and so too has the Federal Government for presidential elections. . . .

"We declared the presidential public financing system constitutional in *Buckley*. [We] reiterated "that public financing as a means of eliminating the improper influence of large private contributions furthers a significant governmental interest." And finally, in rejecting a challenge based on the First Amendment, we held that the program did not 'restrict[] or censor speech, but rather . . . use[d] public money to facilitate and enlarge public discussion and participation in the electoral process.' [But] this model, which distributes a lump-sum grant at the beginning of an election cycle, has a significant weakness: It lacks a mechanism for setting the subsidy at a level that will give candidates sufficient incentive to participate, while also conserving public resources. [Candidates] will choose to sign up only if the subsidy provided enables them to run competitive races. If the grant is pegged too low, it puts the participating candidate at a disadvantage: Because he has agreed to spend no more than the amount of the subsidy, he will lack the means to respond if his privately funded opponent spends over that threshold. [But] if the subsidy is set too high, it may impose an unsustainable burden on the public fisc. [The] difficulty, then, is in finding the Goldilocks solution — not too large, not too small, but just right. . . .

". . . The hallmark of Arizona's program is its inventive approach to the challenge that bedevils all public financing schemes: fixing the amount of the subsidy. [Arizona's] matching funds arrangement responds to the shortcoming of the lump-sum model by adjusting the public subsidy in each race to reflect the expenditures of a privately financed candidate and the independent groups that support him. Arizona can therefore assure candidates that, if they accept public funds, they will have the resources to run a viable race against those who rely on private money. And at the same time, Arizona avoids wasting taxpayers' dollars. In this way, the Clean Elections Act creates an effective and sustainable public financing system. [The] majority contends that the matching funds provision 'substantially burdens protected political speech' and does not 'serv[e] a compelling state interest.' But the Court is wrong on both counts.

"Arizona's statute does not impose a 'restriction,' or 'substantia[l] burde[n],' on expression. The law has quite the opposite effect: It subsidizes and so produces *more* political speech. [Except] in a world gone topsy-turvy, additional campaign speech and electoral competition is not a First Amendment injury.

"At every turn, the majority tries to convey the impression that Arizona's matching fund statute is of a piece with laws prohibiting electoral speech. The majority [insists] that the statute 'restrict[s] the speech of some elements of our society' to enhance the speech of others. And it concludes by reminding us that the point of the First Amendment is to protect 'against unjustified government restrictions on speech.' There is just one problem. Arizona's matching funds provision does not restrict, but instead subsidizes, speech. The law 'impose[s] no ceiling on [speech] and do[es] not prevent anyone from speaking.' [What] the law does — all the law does — is fund more speech. And under the First Amendment, that makes all the difference. In case after case, we have distinguished between speech restrictions and speech subsidies. [No] one can claim that Arizona's law discriminates against particular [ideas.] Republicans and Democrats, conservatives and liberals may [participate.] Arizona disburses funds based not on a candidate's (or supporter's) ideas, but on the candidate's decision to sign up for public funding. So under our precedent, Arizona's subsidy statute should easily survive First Amendment scrutiny."

Citizens United v. Federal Elections Commission
558 U.S. 310 (2010)

JUSTICE KENNEDY delivered the opinion of the Court.

Federal law prohibits corporations and unions from using their general treasury funds to make independent expenditures for speech defined as an "electioneering communication" or for speech expressly advocating the election or defeat of a candidate. Limits on electioneering communications were upheld in [McConnell]. The holding of McConnell rested to a large extent on [Austin, which] had held that political speech may be banned based on the speaker's corporate identity.

In this case we are asked to reconsider Austin and, in effect, McConnell. [We] hold that stare decisis does not compel the continued acceptance of Austin. . . .

Citizens United is a nonprofit corporation. [In] January 2008 Citizens United released a film entitled Hillary: The Movie. [It] is a 90-minute documentary about then-Senator Hillary Clinton, who was a candidate in the Democratic Party's 2008 Presidential primary elections. . . .

Before the Bipartisan Campaign Reform Act of 2002 (BCRA), federal law prohibited—and still does prohibit—corporations and unions from using general treasury funds [to] make independent expenditures that expressly advocate the election or defeat of a candidate. 2 U.S.C. §441b. [BCRA §203 prohibited] any "electioneering communication" as well. [The Federal Elections Commission held that Hillary was an "electioneering communication" within the meaning of BCRA §203.] . . .

III

. . . The law before us is an outright ban [on speech], backed by criminal sanctions. Section 441b makes it a felony for all corporations [either] to expressly advocate the election or defeat of candidates or to broadcast electioneering communications within 30 days of a primary election and 60 days of a general election. [If] §441b applied to individuals, [it would clearly be unconstitutional under Buckley.] Laws that burden political speech are "subject to strict scrutiny," which requires the Government to prove that the restriction "furthers a compelling interest and is narrowly tailored to achieve that interest." [WRTL]. . . .

Premised on mistrust of governmental power, the First Amendment stands against attempts to disfavor certain subjects or viewpoints. Prohibited, too, are restrictions distinguishing among different speakers, allowing speech by some but not others. [Citing Bellotti.] As instruments to censor, these categories are interrelated: Speech restrictions based on the identity of the speaker are all too often simply a means to control content. [By] taking the right to speak from some and giving it to others, the Government deprives the disadvantaged person or class of the right to use speech to strive to establish worth, standing, and respect for the speaker's voice. The Government may not by these means deprive the public of the right and privilege to determine for itself what speech and speakers are worthy of consideration. The First Amendment protects speech and speaker, and the ideas that flow from each. [We] find no basis for the proposition that, in the context of political speech, the Government may impose restrictions on certain disfavored speakers. . . .

A

The Court has recognized that First Amendment protection extends to corporations. [Citing *Bellotti*; *Cox Broadcasting*; *New York Times v. United States*; *New York Times v. Sullivan*.] Under the rationale of these precedents, political speech does not lose First Amendment protection "simply because its source is a corporation." [*Bellotti*]. The Court [has] rejected the argument that political speech of corporations or other associations should be treated differently under the First Amendment simply because such associations are not "natural persons." [*Bellotti*.] . . .

   Austin "uph[eld] a direct restriction on the independent expenditure of funds for political speech for the first time in [this Court's] history." [To] bypass *Buckley* and *Bellotti*, the *Austin* Court identified a new governmental interest in limiting political speech: an antidistortion interest. *Austin* found a compelling governmental interest in preventing "the corrosive and distorting effects of immense aggregations of wealth that are accumulated with the help of the corporate form and that have little or no correlation to the public's support for the corporation's ideas."

B

This Court is thus confronted with conflicting lines of precedent: a pre-*Austin* line that forbids restrictions on political speech based on the speaker's corporate identity and a post-*Austin* line that permits them. [In] its defense of the corporate-speech restrictions in §441b, the Government notes the antidistortion rationale. . . . [This] rationale cannot support §441b. If the First Amendment has any force, it prohibits Congress from fining or jailing citizens, or associations of citizens, for simply engaging in political speech. If the antidistortion rationale were to be accepted, however, it would permit Government to ban political speech simply because the speaker is an association that has taken on the corporate form. [*Austin*] sought to defend the antidistortion rationale as a means to prevent corporations from obtaining "an unfair advantage in the political marketplace" by using "resources amassed in the economic marketplace." But *Buckley* rejected the premise that the Government has an interest "in equalizing the relative ability of individuals and groups to influence the outcome of elections."

   [T]he *Austin* majority undertook to distinguish wealthy individuals from corporations on the ground that "[s]tate law grants corporations special advantages — such as limited liability, perpetual life, and favorable treatment of the accumulation and distribution of assets." This does not suffice, however, to allow laws prohibiting speech. "It is rudimentary that the State cannot exact as the price of those special advantages the forfeiture of First Amendment rights.". . . .

   The censorship we now confront is vast in its reach. The Government has "muffle[d] the voices that best represent the most significant segments of the economy." The purpose and effect of this law is to prevent corporations [from] presenting both facts and opinions to the public. [The] speech that §441b forbids [is] public, and all can judge its content and purpose. References to massive corporate treasuries should not mask the real operation of this law. Rhetoric ought not obscure reality. [When] Government seeks to use its full power, including the criminal law, to command where a person may get his or her information or what distrusted source he or she may not hear, it uses censorship to control thought. This is unlawful. The First Amendment confirms the freedom to think for ourselves. . . .

What we have said also shows the invalidity of other arguments made by the Government. [The] Government falls back on the argument that corporate political speech can be banned in order to prevent corruption or its appearance. In *Buckley*, the Court found this interest "sufficiently important" to allow limits on contributions but did not extend that reasoning to expenditure limits. [Indeed], 26 States do not restrict independent expenditures by for-profit corporations. The Government does not claim that these expenditures have corrupted the political process in those States. [The] appearance of influence or access, furthermore, will not cause the electorate to lose faith in our democracy. [The] fact that a corporation, or any other speaker, is willing to spend money to try to persuade voters presupposes that the people have the ultimate influence over elected officials. . . .

When Congress finds that a problem exists, we must give that finding due deference; but Congress may not choose an unconstitutional remedy. If elected officials succumb to improper influences from independent expenditures; if they surrender their best judgment; and if they put expediency before principle, then surely there is cause for concern. [The] remedies enacted by law, however, must comply with the First Amendment; and, it is our law and our tradition that more speech, not less, is the governing rule. An outright ban on corporate political speech is not a permissible remedy. . . .

The Government contends further that corporate political expenditures can be limited because of its interest in protecting dissenting shareholders from being compelled to fund corporate political speech. This asserted interest, like *Austin's* antidistortion rationale, would allow the Government to ban the political speech even of media corporations. [In any event], the remedy is not to restrict speech but to consider and explore other regulatory mechanisms. . . .

C

. . . For the reasons above, it must be concluded that *Austin* was not well reasoned. [Due] consideration leads to this conclusion: *Austin* should be and now is overruled. We return to the principle established [in] *Bellotti* that the Government may not suppress political speech on the basis of the speaker's corporate identity. No sufficient governmental interest justifies limits on the political speech [of] corporations. [Given] our conclusion we are further required to overrule the part of *McConnell* that upheld BCRA §203's extension of §441b's restrictions on corporate independent expenditures.

CHIEF JUSTICE ROBERTS, with whom JUSTICE ALITO joins, concurring.
. . . The text and purpose of the First Amendment point in the same direction: Congress may not prohibit political speech, even if the speaker is a corporation or union. What makes this case difficult is the need to confront our prior decision in *Austin*. [Fidelity] to precedent — the policy of *stare decisis* — is vital to the proper exercise of the judicial function. "*Stare decisis* is the preferred course because it promotes the evenhanded, predictable, and consistent development of legal principles, fosters reliance on judicial decisions, and contributes to the actual and perceived integrity of the judicial process." For these reasons, we have long recognized that departures from precedent are inappropriate in the absence of a "special justification." [But] *stare decisis* is neither an "inexorable command," nor

"a mechanical formula of adherence to the latest decision," especially in constitutional cases. If it were, segregation would be legal, minimum wage laws would be unconstitutional, and the Government could wiretap ordinary criminal suspects without first obtaining warrants. . . . *Stare decisis* is instead a "principle of policy." When considering whether to reexamine a prior erroneous holding, we must balance the importance of having constitutional questions *decided* against the importance of having them *decided right*. . . .

[Several] considerations weigh against retaining our decision in *Austin*. First, [that] decision was an "aberration" insofar as it departed from the robust protections we had granted political speech in our earlier cases. *Austin* undermined the careful line that *Buckley* drew to distinguish limits on contributions to candidates from limits on independent expenditures on speech. [Second,] the validity of *Austin*'s rationale [has] proved to be the consistent subject of dispute among Members of this Court ever since. [Citing *WRTL* and *McConnell*]. In such circumstances, it is entirely appropriate for the Court [to] address the matter with a greater willingness to consider new approaches capable of restoring our doctrine to sounder footing. [Because] continued adherence to *Austin* threatens to subvert the "principled and intelligible" development of our First Amendment jurisprudence, I support the Court's determination to overrule that decision.

JUSTICE SCALIA, with whom JUSTICE ALITO joins, and with whom JUSTICE THOMAS joins in part, concurring.

I join the opinion of the Court. I write separately to address Justice Stevens' discussion of "*Original Understandings*." This section of the dissent purports to show that today's decision is not supported by the original understanding of the First Amendment. The dissent attempts this demonstration, however, in splendid isolation from the text of the First Amendment. It never shows why "the freedom of speech" that was the right of Englishmen did not include the freedom to speak in association with other individuals, including association in the corporate form. To be sure, in 1791 (as now) corporations could pursue only the objectives set forth in their charters; but the dissent provides no evidence that their speech in the pursuit of those objectives could be censored.

Instead of taking this straightforward approach to determining the Amendment's meaning, the dissent embarks on a detailed exploration of the Framers' views about the "role of corporations in society." The Framers didn't like corporations, the dissent concludes, and therefore it follows (as night the day) that corporations had no rights of free speech. Of course the Framers' personal affection or disaffection for corporations is relevant only insofar as it can be thought to be reflected in the understood meaning of the text they enacted — not, as the dissent suggests, as a freestanding substitute for that text. [Even] if we thought it proper to apply the dissent's approach of excluding from First Amendment coverage what the Founders disliked, and even if we agreed that the Founders disliked founding-era corporations; modern corporations might not qualify for exclusion. Most of the Founders' resentment towards corporations was directed at the state-granted monopoly privileges that individually chartered corporations enjoyed. Modern corporations do not have such privileges, and would probably have been favored by most of our enterprising Founders. . . .

But to return to, and summarize, my principal point, which is the conformity of today's opinion with the original meaning of the First Amendment. [Its] text offers no foothold for excluding any category of speaker, from single individuals to partnerships of individuals, to unincorporated associations of individuals, to incorporated associations of individuals — and the dissent offers no evidence about the original meaning of the text to support any such exclusion. . . .

JUSTICE STEVENS, with whom JUSTICE GINSBURG, JUSTICE BREYER, and JUSTICE SOTOMAYOR join, concurring in part and dissenting in part.
   . . . The basic premise underlying the Court's ruling is its iteration, and constant reiteration, of the proposition that the First Amendment bars regulatory distinctions based on a speaker's identity, including its "identity" as a corporation. While that glittering generality has rhetorical appeal, it is not a correct statement of the law. [In] the context of election to public office, the distinction between corporate and human speakers is significant. Although they make enormous contributions to our society, corporations are not actually members of it. They cannot vote or run for office. [The] financial resources, legal structure, and instrumental orientation of corporations raise legitimate concerns about their role in the electoral process. Our lawmakers have a compelling constitutional basis, if not also a democratic duty, to take measures designed to guard against the potentially deleterious effects of corporate spending in local and national races.
   The majority's approach to corporate electioneering marks a dramatic break from our past. Congress has placed special limitations on campaign spending by corporations ever since the passage of the Tillman Act in 1907. [The] Court today rejects a century of history when it treats the distinction between corporate and individual campaign spending as an invidious novelty born of *Austin*. Relying largely on individual dissenting opinions, the majority blazes through our precedents, overruling or disavowing a body of case law including *WRTL* [and] *McConnell*. . . .

II

. . . I am not an absolutist when it comes to *stare decisis*, [but] if this principle is to do any meaningful work in supporting the rule of law, it must at least demand a significant justification, beyond the preferences of five Justices, for overturning settled doctrine. [No] such justification exists in this case, and to the contrary there are powerful prudential reasons to keep faith with our precedents. The Court's central argument for why *stare decisis* ought to be trumped is that it does not like *Austin*. [I] am perfectly willing to concede that if one of our precedents were dead wrong in its reasoning or irreconcilable with the rest of our doctrine, there would be a compelling basis for revisiting it. But neither is true of *Austin*. [The] Court proclaims that "*Austin* is undermined by experience since its announcement." [But it] has no empirical evidence with which to substantiate [this claim.] Nor does the majority bother to specify in what sense *Austin* has been "undermined." . . .
   In the end, the Court's rejection of *Austin* and *McConnell* comes down to nothing more than its disagreement with their results. Virtually every one of its arguments was made and rejected in those cases, and the majority opinion is essentially an amalgamation of resuscitated dissents. The only relevant thing that has changed since *Austin* and *McConnell* is the composition of this Court. Today's ruling thus strikes at the vitals of *stare decisis*, "the means by which we ensure that the law will not merely change erratically, but will develop in a principled and intelligible fashion" that "permits society to presume that bedrock principles are founded in the law rather than in the proclivities of individuals."

III

The novelty of the Court's [approach] to *stare decisis* is matched by the novelty of its ruling on the merits. The ruling rests on several premises. First, the Court claims [that] the First Amendment precludes regulatory distinctions based on speaker identity, including the speaker's identity as a corporation. [Second], it claims that *Austin* and *McConnell* were radical outliers in our First Amendment tradition. . . . Each of these claims is wrong. . . .

IDENTITY-BASED DISTINCTIONS

[The majority asserts] that "the Government cannot restrict political speech based on the speaker's . . . identity." [But in] a variety of contexts, we have held that speech can be regulated differentially on account of the speaker's identity, when identity is understood in categorical or institutional terms. The Government routinely places special restrictions on the speech rights of students, prisoners, members of the Armed Forces, foreigners, and its own employees. [In] contrast to the blanket rule that the majority espouses, our cases recognize that the Government's interests may be more or less compelling with respect to different classes of speakers. . . . .

The election context is distinctive in many ways, and the Court, of course, is right that the First Amendment closely guards political speech. But in this context, too, the authority of legislatures to enact viewpoint-neutral regulations based on content and identity is well settled. We have, for example, allowed state-run broadcasters to exclude independent candidates from televised debates. [Citing *Forbes*. Recall also *Perry*]. The same logic applies to this case with additional force because it is the identity of corporations, rather than individuals, that the Legislature has taken into account. [Not] only has the distinctive potential of corporations to corrupt the electoral process long been recognized, but [campaign] finance distinctions based on corporate identity tend to be less worrisome [because] the "speakers" are not natural persons, much less members of our political [community]. . . .

In short, the Court dramatically overstates its critique of identity-based distinctions, without ever explaining why corporate identity demands the same treatment as individual identity. Only the most wooden approach to the First Amendment could justify the unprecedented line it seeks to draw.

OUR FIRST AMENDMENT TRADITION

[Another] fulcrum of the Court's opinion is the idea that *Austin* and *McConnell* are radical outliers [in] our First Amendment tradition. The Court has it exactly backwards. It is today's holding that is the radical departure from what had been settled First Amendment law. To see why, it is useful to take a long view.

1. Original Understandings

[T]here is not a scintilla of evidence to support the notion that anyone believed [the First Amendment] would preclude regulatory distinctions based on the corporate form. To the extent that the Framers' views are discernible and relevant to the disposition of this case, they would appear to cut strongly against the majority's position.

[T]he Framers [held] very different views [than the majority does today] about the nature of the First Amendment right and the role of corporations in society.

Those few corporations that existed at the founding were authorized by grant of a special legislative charter. [Corporations] were created, supervised, and conceptualized as quasi-public entities, "designed to serve a social function for the state." It was "assumed that [they] were legally privileged organizations that had to be closely scrutinized by the legislature because their purposes had to be made consistent with public welfare." [The] Framers thus took it as a given that corporations could be comprehensively regulated in the service of the public welfare. Unlike our colleagues, [the Framers] had little trouble distinguishing corporations from human beings, and when they constitutionalized the right to free speech in the First Amendment, it was the free speech of individual Americans that they had in mind. . . .

Justice Scalia criticizes the foregoing discussion for failing to adduce statements from the founding era showing that corporations were understood to be excluded from the First Amendment's free speech guarantee. Of course, Justice Scalia adduces no statements to suggest the contrary proposition. . . . Nothing in his account dislodges my basic point that members of the founding generation held a cautious view of corporate power and a narrow view of corporate rights (not that they "despised" corporations), and that they conceptualized speech in individualistic terms. If no prominent Framer bothered to articulate that corporate speech would have lesser status than individual speech, that may well be because the contrary proposition — if not also the very notion of "corporate speech" — was inconceivable. . . .

2. Legislative and Judicial Interpretation

A century of more recent history puts to rest any notion that today's ruling is faithful to our First Amendment tradition. At the federal level, the express distinction between corporate and individual political spending on elections stretches back to 1907, when Congress passed the Tillman Act, banning all corporate contributions to candidates. [By] the time Congress passed FECA in 1971, the bar on corporate contributions and expenditures had become such an accepted part of federal campaign finance regulation that [in *Buckley*] no one even bothered to argue that the bar as such was unconstitutional. [Thus], it was unremarkable, that [in FEC v. National Right to Work Committee, 459 U.S. 197 (1982)] then-Justice Rehnquist wrote for a unanimous Court that "[the] governmental interest in preventing both actual corruption and the appearance of corruption of elected representatives has long been recognized" [and that] "there is no reason why it may not . . . be accomplished by treating . . . corporations . . . differently from individuals." [Several] years later, in *Austin*, we [held that] corporations [could] be barred from using general treasury funds to make independent expenditures in support of, or in opposition to, candidates. In the 20 years since *Austin*, we have reaffirmed its holding and rationale a number of times, most importantly in *McConnell*, where we upheld the provision challenged here. . . .

3. Buckley and Bellotti

Against [the] extensive background of congressional regulation of corporate campaign spending, and our repeated affirmation of this regulation as constitutionally sound, the majority dismisses *Austin* as "a significant departure from ancient First Amendment principles." How does the majority attempt to justify this claim? Selected passages from two cases, *Buckley* and *Bellotti*, do all of the work. [The] case on which the majority places [its primary emphasis] is *Bellotti*, claiming it "could not have been clearer" that *Bellotti's* holding forbade distinctions between corporate and individual [expenditures]. The Court's reliance is odd. The only thing about *Bellotti* that could not be clearer is that it declined to adopt the majority's position. *Bellotti* ruled, in an explicit limitation on the scope of its holding, that "our consideration of a corporation's right to speak on issues of general public interest implies no comparable right in the quite different context of participation in a political campaign for election to public office." *Bellotti*, in other words, did not touch the question presented in *Austin* and *McConnell*, and the opinion squarely disavowed the proposition for which the majority cites it. . . .

IV

Having explained [why] *Austin* and *McConnell* [sit] perfectly well with "First Amendment principles," I come at last to the interests that are at stake. . . .

THE ANTICORRUPTION INTEREST

. . . On numerous occasions we have recognized Congress' legitimate interest in preventing the money that is spent on elections from exerting an "'undue influence on an officeholder's judgment'" and from creating "'the appearance of such influence,'" beyond the sphere of *quid pro quo* relationships. [Our] "undue influence" cases [have recognized that when] private interests are seen to exert outsized control over officeholders solely on account of the money spent on (or withheld from) their campaigns, the result can depart so thoroughly "from what is pure or correct" in the conduct of Government that it amounts to a "subversion . . . of the electoral process." [This] understanding of corruption has deep roots in the Nation's history. . . .

Rather than show any deference to a coordinate branch of Government, the majority [rejects] the anticorruption rationale without serious analysis. Today's opinion provides no clear rationale for being so dismissive of Congress, but the prior individual opinions on which it relies have offered one: the incentives of the legislators who passed BCRA. Section 203, our colleagues have suggested, may be little more than "an incumbency protection plan," a disreputable attempt at legislative self-dealing rather than an earnest effort to facilitate First Amendment values and safeguard the legitimacy of our political system. This possibility, the Court apparently believes, licenses it to run roughshod over Congress' handiwork.

In my view, we should instead start by acknowledging that "Congress surely has both wisdom and experience in these matters that is far superior to ours." [This] is not to say that deference would be appropriate if there were a solid basis for believing that a legislative action was motivated by the desire to protect incumbents or that it will degrade the competitiveness of the electoral process. [But] it is the height of recklessness to dismiss Congress' years of bipartisan deliberation and its reasoned judgment on this basis, without first confirming that the statute in question was intended to be, or will function as, a restraint on electoral competition. [In fact, we] have no record evidence from which to conclude that BCRA §203, or any of the dozens of state laws that the Court today calls into question, reflects or fosters such invidious discrimination. . . .

AUSTIN AND CORPORATE EXPENDITURES

Just as the majority gives short shrift to the general societal interests at stake in campaign finance regulation, it also overlooks the distinctive considerations raised by the regulation of *corporate* expenditures. The majority fails to appreciate that *Austin*'s antidistortion rationale is itself an anticorruption rationale, tied to the special concerns raised by corporations. Understood properly, "antidistortion" is simply a variant on the classic governmental interest in protecting against improper influences on officeholders that debilitate the democratic process. It is manifestly not just an "'equalizing'" ideal in disguise. . . .

1. Antidistortion

The fact that corporations are different from human beings might seem to need no elaboration, except that the majority opinion almost completely elides it. *Austin* set forth some of the basic differences. Unlike natural persons, corporations have "limited liability" for their owners and managers, "perpetual life," separation of ownership and control, "and favorable treatment of the accumulation and distribution of assets . . . that enhance their ability to attract capital and to deploy their resources in ways that maximize the return on their shareholders' investments." "'[T]he resources in the treasury of a business corporation [are] not an indication of popular support for the corporation's political ideas.'" "'They reflect instead the economically motivated decisions of investors and customers. The availability of these resources may make a corporation a formidable political presence, even though the power of the corporation may be no reflection of the power of its ideas.'" [Corporations] help structure and facilitate the activities of human beings, to be sure, and their "personhood" often serves as a useful legal fiction. But they are not themselves members of "We the People" by whom and for whom our Constitution was established. These basic points help explain why corporate electioneering is not only more likely to impair compelling governmental interests, but also why restrictions on that electioneering are less likely to encroach upon First Amendment freedoms. . . .

. . . Recognizing the weakness of a speaker-based critique of *Austin*, the Court places primary emphasis not on the corporation's right to electioneer, but rather on the listener's interest in hearing what every possible speaker may have to say. [There] are many flaws in this argument. [*Austin*] recognized that there are substantial reasons why a legislature might conclude that unregulated general treasury expenditures will give corporations "unfai[r] influence" in the electoral process and distort public debate in ways that undermine rather than advance the interests of listeners. [In] addition to [the] drowning out of noncorporate voices, [corporate] "domination" of electioneering can generate the impression that corporations dominate our democracy. [Citizens] may lose faith in their capacity, as citizens, to influence public policy. [The] predictable result is cynicism and disenchantment. [The] Court's facile depiction of corporate electioneering assumes away all of these complexities. . . .

2. Shareholder Protection

There is yet another way in which laws such as §203 can serve First Amendment values. Interwoven with *Austin*'s concern to protect the integrity of the electoral process is a concern to protect the rights of shareholders from a kind of coerced [speech]. When corporations use general treasury funds to praise or attack a particular candidate for office, it is the shareholders [who] are effectively footing the bill. Those shareholders who disagree with the corporation's electoral message may find their financial investments being used to undermine their political convictions. [*Austin's*] acceptance of restrictions on general treasury spending "simply allows people who have invested in the business corporation for purely economic reasons" — the vast majority of investors, one assumes — "to avoid being taken advantage of, without sacrificing their economic objectives."

The concern to protect dissenting shareholders and union members has a long history in campaign finance reform. [Indeed], we have unanimously recognized the governmental interest in "protect[ing] the individuals who have paid money into a corporation or union for purposes other than the support of candidates from having that money used to support political candidates to whom they may be opposed." [See section E infra.]

V

. . . Our colleagues have arrived at the conclusion that *Austin* must be overruled [only] after mischaracterizing both the reach and rationale of [the relevant] authorities, and after bypassing or ignoring rules of judicial restraint used to cabin the Court's lawmaking power. [While] American democracy is imperfect, few outside the majority of this Court would have thought its flaws included a dearth of corporate money in politics. . . .

Note: *Reflections on* Citizens United

Consider the following views:

a. Ansolabehere, Arizona Free Enterprise v. Bennett and the Problem of Campaign Finance, 2011 Sup. Ct. Rev. 39, 71–77:

> Since the 1970s, political scientists have documented severe inequities in the amount of money raised and spent by candidates. [If] the ultimate objective is to create a robust marketplace of ideas where the public can learn about the choices and reach a reasoned judgment, then the approach in *Buckley,* [*Bennett*, and *Citizens United*] has failed. Campaign finance law in the United States has not served the ultimate purpose of the First Amendment. Rather, it has generally produced elections with one-sided political competition — a lecture, not a debate. . . .
>
> The past forty years of full private financing of elections have exposed serious deficiencies — especially the inadequacy of resources, the threat of corruption and bias, and the public distrust that such an approach engenders. As the Court continues to push the United States away from more modest attempts at campaign finance regulation, then, it is increasingly pushing public policy toward the one alternative that many conservatives most abhor: full public financing of all federal elections. . . .

b. In Brown & Martin, Rhetoric and Reality: Testing the Harm of Campaign Spending, 90 NYU L. Rev. 1066 (2015), the authors note that the Court in *Citizens United* insisted that any perceptions members of the public might have that their elected representatives are ingratiated to large donors "would not undermine the electorate's faith in democracy." The authors argue that "a loss of faith by the electorate implicates a central constitutional value and is a sufficiently compelling interest to justify campaign finance regulation." More-over, they offer empirical evidence to demonstrate that "the Court should not have been so confident that the electorate's faith in democracy is unaffected either by the appearance of influence or access due to campaign spending or by independent expenditures." If it is true that large campaign expenditures undermine the faith of citizens in democracy, should that be a sufficiently compelling concern to justify otherwise unconstitutional campaign finance restrictions?

c. In Western Tradition Partnership, Inc. v. Attorney General of Montana, 271 P. 3d 1 (2010), the Montana Supreme Court distinguished *Citizens United* and upheld a Montana law providing that "a corporation may not make . . . an expen-diture in connection with a candidate or a political party." The Montana court explained that in *Citizens United* the Court "found that the Government did not claim that corporate expenditures had actually corrupted the political process and concluded that 'independent expenditures, including those made by cor-porations, do not give rise to corruption or the appearance of corruption.'" Thus, the Court in *Citizens United* "determined that the government had not provided a compelling interest to justify the speech restriction at issue." In *Western Tra-dition Partnership*, however, the Montana court found that the state had pre-sented sufficient evidence to satisfy the strict scrutiny standard of *Citizens United*.

Specifically, the Montana court observed that Montana had had a long and bitter history in which its political elections had been dominated by "mining and industrial enterprises controlled by foreign trusts or corporations." Indeed, it was precisely that history that had led the state to enact the challenged law in the first place. Moreover, the Montana court pointed to recent studies that showed that prior to *Citizens United* the "percentage of campaign contributions from individual voters drops sharply from 48% in states with restrictions on corporate spending to 23% in states without." Thus, the court concluded that the chal-lenged statute furthered "the compelling interest of the people of Montana in strong voter participation in the process."

In American Tradition Partnership, Inc. v. Bullock, 567 U.S. 516 (2012), the Supreme Court summarily reversed in a per curiam opinion, declaring that "Montana's arguments . . . either were already rejected in *Citizens United*, or fail to meaningfully distinguish that case." Justice Breyer, joined by Justices Ginsburg, Sotomayor, and Kagan, dissented: "[E]ven if I were to accept *Citizens United*, this Court's legal conclusion should not bar the Montana Supreme Court's finding, made on the record before it, that independent expenditures by corporations did in fact lead to corruption or the appearance of corruption in Montana," contrary to the Court's assertion in *Citizens United*. [Thus,] Monta-na's experience, like considerable experience elsewhere since the Court's decision in *Citizens United*, casts grave doubt on the Court's supposition that independent expenditures do not corrupt or appear to do so."

d. *SuperPacs.* What is the connection between *Citizens United* and the sudden emergence since 2010 of so-called SuperPacs, which now raise and spend unlim-ited amounts of money in the electoral process? Political organizations known as 527s (a reference to a provision of the Internal Revenue Code) raised money from contributions and then make independent expenditures (that is, expenditures that are not coordinated with any candidate) to support or oppose the election of federal candidates. Prior to *Citizens United*, 527s were governed by provisions of the Federal Election Campaign Act. Those provisions prohibited individuals from contributing more than $5,000 in any calendar year to any 527 and from contributing more than $69,900 in total to 527s over the course of two years. Thus, although 527s could spend as much as they wished to support or oppose the election of federal candidates, they could not receive large contributions. Until *Citizens United*, no one questioned the constitutionality of this scheme.

In SpeechNow.org v. Federal Election Commission, 599 F.3d 686 (D.C. Cir. 2010), however, the D.C. Circuit held that, in light of *Citizens United*, those limitations on 527s were unconstitutional. The court explained:

> [The] Supreme Court has recognized only one interest as sufficiently important to outweigh the First Amendment interests implicated by contributions for political speech: preventing corruption or the appearance of corruption. [In] *Citizens United*, [the] Court held that the government has *no* anti-corruption interest in limiting independent expenditures. [The] Court stated, "[W]e now conclude that independent expenditures, including those made by corporations, do not give rise to corruption or the appearance of corruption." [The Court justified this conclusion by rejecting the logic of *McConnell* and other prior decisions, and narrowly construing the concept of corruption as limited *only* to the interest in preventing the reality or appearance of *quid pro quo* corruption].
>
> In light of the Court's holding as a matter of law that independent expenditures do not corrupt or create the appearance of *quid pro quo* corruption, contributions to groups that make only independent expenditures also cannot corrupt or create the appearance of corruption. The Court has effectively held that there is no corrupting "quid" for which a candidate might in exchange offer a corrupt "quo."
>
> Given this analysis from *Citizens United*, we must conclude that the government has no anti-corruption interest in limiting contributions to an independent expenditure group such as SpeechNow. This simplifies the task of weighing the First Amendment interests implicated by contributions to SpeechNow against the government's interest in limiting such contributions. [After all], "something . . . outweighs nothing every time." . . .

For criticism of the conception of corruption that underlies the Court's decision in *Citizens United*, see Z. Teachout, Corruption in America (2014), which argues that the modern Supreme Court has ignored the way earlier generations conceived of corruption.

McCUTCHEON v. FEDERAL ELECTION COMMISSION, 572 U.S. — (2014). The federal Bipartisan Campaign Reform Act imposes two types of limits on campaign contributions. The first, called base limits, restricts how much money a donor may contribute to a particular candidate or committee. The second, called aggregate limits, restricts how much money a donor may contribute in total to all candidates or committees. In *Buckley*, the Court upheld the constitutionality of the base contribution limits. This case concerned the constitutionality of the aggregate contribution limits.

For the 2013–2014 election cycle, the aggregate limits permitted an individual to contribute a total of $48,600 to federal candidates and a total of $74,600 to other political committees. In the 2011–2012 election cycle, Shaun McCutcheon contributed a total of $33,088 to sixteen different federal candidates, in compliance with the then-applicable base limits. McCutcheon wanted to contribute $1,776 to each of twelve additional candidates, but was prevented from doing so by the aggregate limit on contributions to candidates. He also wanted to contribute to several additional political committees, including $25,000 to each of the three Republican national party committees, but again he was prevented from doing so by the aggregate limit on contributions to political committees. The Republican National Committee wanted to receive the contributions that McCutcheon and other potential contributors wanted to make to it — contributions otherwise permissible under the base limits for national party committees, but foreclosed by the aggregate limit on contributions to political committees.

In June 2012, McCutcheon and the RNC filed a complaint before a three-judge panel of the U.S. District Court for the District of Columbia, maintaining that the aggregate limits on contributions to candidates and to noncandidate political committees were unconstitutional under the First Amendment. The three-judge court dismissed the complaint, holding that the aggregate limits survived First Amendment scrutiny.

The Supreme Court, in a five-to-four decision, held the aggregate contribution limits unconstitutional. Chief Justice Roberts announced the judgment of the Court and delivered an opinion, in which Justices Scalia, Kennedy, and Alito joined:

"The right to participate in democracy through political contributions is protected by the First Amendment, but that right is not absolute. Our cases have held that Congress may regulate campaign contributions to protect against corruption or the appearance of corruption. [Citing *Buckley*.] At the same time, we have made clear that Congress may not regulate contributions simply to reduce the amount of money in politics, or to restrict the political participation of some in order to enhance the relative influence of others. [Citing *Bennett*]. . . .

"In a series of cases over the past 40 years, we have spelled out how to draw the constitutional line between the permissible goal of avoiding corruption in the political process and the impermissible desire simply to limit political speech. We have said that government regulation may not target the general gratitude a candidate may feel toward those who support him or his allies, or the political access such support may afford. [Any] regulation must instead target what we have called 'quid pro quo' corruption or its appearance. That Latin phrase captures the notion of a direct exchange of an official act for money. [Campaign] finance restrictions that pursue other objectives . . . impermissibly inject the Government 'into the debate over who should govern.' [Quoting *Bennett*.]

"The statute at issue in this case [restricts] how much money a donor may contribute in total to all candidates or committees. This case does not involve any challenge to the base limits, which we have previously upheld as serving the permissible objective of combatting corruption. [We conclude] that the aggregate limits do little, if anything, to address that concern, while seriously restricting participation in the democratic process. The aggregate limits are therefore invalid under the First Amendment. . . .

"To put it in the simplest terms, the aggregate limits prohibit an individual from fully contributing to the campaigns of [all the candidates he wants to support], even if all contributions fall within the base limits Congress views as adequate to protect against corruption. [It] is no answer to say that the individual can simply contribute less money to more people. To require one person to contribute at lower levels than others because he wants to support more candidates or causes is to impose a special burden on broader participation in the democratic process. . . .

"With the significant First Amendment costs for individual citizens in mind, we turn to the governmental interests asserted in this case. This Court has identified only one legitimate governmental interest for restricting campaign finances: preventing corruption or the appearance of corruption. We have consistently rejected attempts to suppress campaign speech based on other legislative objectives. No matter how desirable it may seem, it is not an acceptable governmental objective to 'level the playing field,' or to 'level electoral opportunities,' or to 'equaliz[e] the financial resources of candidates.' . . .

"Moreover, while preventing corruption or its appearance is a legitimate objective, Congress may target only a specific type of corruption — 'quid pro quo' corruption. [Spending] large sums of money in connection with elections, but not in connection with an effort to control the exercise of an officeholder's official duties, does not give rise to such quid pro quo corruption. Nor does the possibility that an individual who spends large sums may garner 'influence over or access to' elected officials or political parties. . . .

"'When the Government restricts speech, the Government bears the burden of proving the constitutionality of its actions.' Here, the Government seeks to carry that burden by arguing that the aggregate limits further the permissible objective of preventing quid pro quo corruption. The difficulty is that once the aggregate limits kick in, they ban all contributions of any amount. But Congress's selection of a $5,200 base limit indicates its belief that contributions of that amount or less do not create a cognizable risk of corruption. . . .

"For the past 40 years, our campaign finance jurisprudence has focused on the need to preserve authority for the Government to combat corruption, without at the same time compromising the political responsiveness at the heart of the democratic process, or allowing the Government to favor some participants in that process over others. [The] Government has a strong interest, no less critical to our democratic system, in combatting corruption and its appearance. We have, however, held that this interest must be limited to a specific kind of corruption — quid pro quo corruption — in order to ensure that the Government's efforts do not have the effect of restricting the First Amendment right of citizens to choose who shall govern them. [We] conclude that the aggregate limits on contributions do not further the only governmental interest this Court accepted as legitimate in *Buckley*. They instead intrude without justification on a citizen's ability to exercise 'the most fundamental First Amendment activities.'"

Justice Thomas concurred in the judgment: "I adhere to the view that this Court's decision in *Buckley* denigrates core First Amendment speech and should be overruled. [Contributions] to political campaigns, no less than direct expenditures, 'generate essential political speech' by fostering discussion of public issues and candidate qualifications. [This] case represents yet another missed opportunity to right the course of our campaign finance jurisprudence by restoring a standard that is faithful to the First Amendment."

Justice Breyer, joined by Justices Ginsburg, Sotomayor, and Kagan, dissented: "Taken together with *Citizens United*, today's decision eviscerates our Nation's campaign finance laws, leaving a remnant incapable of dealing with the grave problems of democratic legitimacy that those laws were intended to resolve. The plurality's [claim] that large aggregate contributions do not 'give rise' to 'corruption' is plausible only because the plurality defines 'corruption' too narrowly. [Its] definition of 'corruption' is inconsistent with the Court's prior case law (with the possible exception of *Citizens United*) [and] it misunderstands the constitutional importance of the interests at stake. [The] history of campaign finance reform shows [that] the anticorruption interest that drives Congress to regulate campaign contributions is a far broader, more important interest than the plurality acknowledges. It is an interest in maintaining the integrity of our public governmental institutions. And it is an interest rooted in the Constitution and in the First

Amendment itself. [Speech] does not exist in a vacuum. Rather, political communication seeks to secure government action. A politically oriented 'marketplace of ideas' seeks to form a public opinion that can and will influence elected representatives. This is not a new idea. [Citing Whitney v. California (Brandeis, J., concurring).] [Accordingly], the First Amendment advances not only the individual's right to engage in political speech, but also the public's interest in preserving a democratic order in which collective speech matters.

"What has this to do with corruption? It has everything to do with corruption. Corruption breaks the constitutionally necessary 'chain of communication' between the people and their representatives. [Where] enough money calls the tune, the general public will not be heard. Insofar as corruption cuts the link between political thought and political action, a free marketplace of political ideas loses its point. [The] 'appearance of corruption' can make matters worse. It can lead the public to believe that its efforts to communicate with its representatives or to help sway public opinion have little purpose. And a cynical public can lose interest in political participation altogether. The upshot is that the interests the Court has long described as preventing 'corruption' or the 'appearance of corruption' are more than ordinary factors to be weighed against the constitutional right to political speech. Rather, they are interests rooted in the First Amendment itself. They are rooted in the constitutional effort to create a democracy responsive to the people — a government where laws reflect the very thoughts, views, ideas, and sentiments, the expression of which the First Amendment protects. Given that end, we can and should understand campaign finance laws as resting upon a broader and more significant constitutional rationale than the plurality's limited definition of 'corruption' suggests. We should see these laws as seeking in significant part to strengthen, rather than weaken, the First Amendment. To say this is not to deny the potential for conflict between (1) the need to permit contributions that pay for the diffusion of ideas, and (2) the need to limit payments in order to help maintain the integrity of the electoral process. But that conflict takes place within, not outside, the First Amendment's boundaries. . . .

"Here, as in *Buckley*, in the absence of limits on aggregate political contributions, donors can and likely will find ways to channel millions of dollars to parties and to individual candidates, [producing] 'corruption' or 'appearance of corruption.' The methods for using today's opinion to evade the law's individual contribution limits are complex, but they are well known, or will become well known, to party fundraisers. [Justice Breyer then described three such methods in detail.] The plurality [substitutes its limited understanding] of how the political process works for the understanding of Congress, [and in so doing it] creates huge loopholes in the law [and] undermines, perhaps devastates, what remains of campaign finance reform."

———————————

Consider the following views:

a. Hellman, Defining Corruption and Constitutionalizing Democracy, 111 Mich. L. Rev. 1385 (2013):

The main front in the battle over the constitutionality of campaign finance laws has long focused on defining corruption. [But] corruption is a derivative concept, meaning it depends on a theory of the institution or official involved. [What] constitutes corruption in a democracy depends on a theory of democracy. To put the point in a more grounded fashion, what constitutes corruption of legislators depends on a view of the proper basis for decisionmaking by elected officials. [Our] campaign finance case law contains at least three distinct conceptions of legislative corruption. I call these "corruption as the deformation of judgment," "corruption as the distortion of influence," and "corruption as the sale of favors." . . .

On one view, a legislator ought to exercise his own independent judgment about each decision he faces. [The] legislator, according to this view, should consider only the merits-based reasons that bear on the decision at hand. [Corruption as the "deformation of judgment"] occurs when non-merits-based factors influence the legislator's judgment. . . .

Corruption as the distortion of influence sees the legislator as properly attentive to the desires and preferences of those he represents. In a well-functioning democracy, the legislator responds to these desires and preferences. [On this view,] corruption occurs when a legislator weighs the preferences of some too heavily, especially when the legislator considers the wishes of wealthy contributors more than others. . . .

A third view of proper legislative conduct [requires] only that the legislator not actually exchange votes or favors for money. [Corruption], on this view, is narrowly defined as quid pro quo corruption — that is, the sale of some public favor. . . .

[W]hen the Court defines corruption [in its campaign finance case law], it inescapably puts forward a conception of the proper role of a legislator in a democracy. That is a task that the Court should be cautious to take up. [Because there] are many reasonable ways to instantiate representative democracy, [we] should eschew judicial actions that adopt one view of representative democracy [over another]. Because judicial pronouncements about what constitutes corruption entail commitments to contested conceptions of democracy, there are strong reasons for courts to avoid defining corruption.

b. R. Post, Citizens Divided: Campaign Finance Reform and the Constitution 4, 60–65 (2014):

[F]irst Amendment rights presuppose that elections [have] the property of choosing candidates whom the people trust [to act in their interests]. If the people do not believe that elected officials listen to public opinion, participation in public discourse, no matter how free, cannot create the experience of self-government. [The] democratic structure and legitimacy of our government depend on [this understanding of] electoral integrity.

Yet the Court in its campaign finance opinions has not considered the state's interest in promoting the electoral integrity required by the First Amendment. The Court has instead been preoccupied by the attempt to balance First Amendment rights against the need to prevent [quid pro quo] corruption. . . .

If [we] reformulate our campaign finance jurisprudence upon the principle of electoral integrity, [we] may create a more enduring foundation for the contested area of campaign finance reform. [This] formulation of the issue [requires] us merely to affirm [that] Americans cannot maintain the blessings of self-government unless they believe that elections produce representatives who are responsive to public opinion. [Electoral] integrity is a compelling government interest because without it Americans have no reason to exercise the communicative rights guaranteed by the First Amendment.

[There] are good reasons to worry that electoral integrity is today under threat. Americans' trust and confidence in their representative institutions has fallen to record lows; we are [experiencing] what most regard as a crisis of representation. In such circumstances it is especially disappointing that the Court seems unwilling to recognize even the existence of the constitutional principle of electoral integrity. . . .

c. Lessig, What an Originalist Would Understand "Corruption" to Mean, 102 Cal. L. Rev. 1, 3–11 (2014):

The United States [effectively] has two distinct elections. One election is discrete — call it the "voting election." [All] "voters" are permitted to participate in that election. [The] other election is continuous — call it the "money election." It happens throughout the election cycle. Any citizen [is] permitted to participate in that money election. [To] be allowed to run in the voting election [one] has to do extremely well in the money election. [In] the 2012 election cycle, 84 percent of the House candidates and 67 percent of the Senate candidates with more money than their opponents won. [The] money election produces a subtle, perhaps camouflaged bending [of the process] to keep the funders of the money election happy. [Importantly,] the relevant number of funders is [small]. [In] the 2012 presidential election 0.000032 percent [of Americans] — or 99 Americans — provided 60 percent of the individual Super PAC money spent. . . .

[The] way we fund elections has created a dependency that conflicts with the dependency intended by the Constitution. That conflict is a corruption. [In] the Framers' language, [the concept of "corruption"] included a collective sense — the corruption of an institution, or a people, and not just a person. [Congress] was intended to be "dependent on the people alone." It has become dependent upon an additional dependence, "the funders" of campaigns. Because of who "the funders" are, this additional dependence is a conflicting dependence, and that conflict constitutes "corruption."

This sense of corruption [was] perfectly familiar to the Framers. [For] the Framers, Congress was [to] have an intended dependence. That dependence was to be, as James Madison wrote in The Federalist No. 52, "on the people." [For the Framers,] the anti-corruption challenge was [how to protect the institution] from improper dependence. [It] is this fact that makes the current Supreme Court's jurisprudence about "corruption" so weird. [Only] a non-originalist could embrace [the Court's] position.

d. L. Tribe and J. Matz, Uncertain Justice: The Roberts Court and the Constitution 100–101, 104–105, 108–109, 112–113 (2014):

Citizens United decisively rejected the anti-distortion justification for campaign finance laws. . . . To be sure, money can powerfully advantage a speaker in the marketplace of ideas [and] concentrated wealth, left unregulated, can create a risk that most headlines and TV ads will be controlled by a small group. . . . Still, it would be a mistake to leave judgments about the "proper" distribution of speech to politicians. Arming them with a roving license to level the playing field by silencing or adjusting the volume of disfavored speakers is an invitation to self-serving behavior and, ultimately, tyranny. The anti-distortion argument can too easily lead down this dangerous path, and [the Court] rightly discarded it. . . .

[Another argument made against the Court's approach in these cases focuses on a broad conception of "corruption."] "Corruption," in this view, occurs when politicians become dependent on a wealthy clique and government is no longer responsive to the public interest. [The justices in the majority in these cases] are unreservedly hostile to such arguments. They worry that noble-sounding rationales for campaign finance laws can too easily conceal efforts by incumbents to protect themselves and punish their enemies. [The Court has not adopted] a narrow definition of corruption because it is naïve or apathetic. It has done so because it doubts that the Court [can] create workable First Amendment law that adequately guards against abuse by politicians. Embracing a broader view of the anti-corruption interest risked creating an exception that swallowed the rule. . . .

In an age of political dysfunction, the extraordinary sums of money that candidates avidly pursue present hard questions about how to reconcile competing national values. [The Court's decisions in these cases will likely affect] policy outcomes by causing an across-the-board realignment of government priorities toward interests backed by big money. Every capable politician has an eye on the next election and a keen sense of who provided support last time, who didn't, who might be persuaded to shift their opinions, and how that might be achieved. [The Court's decisions are] therefore likely to trigger a self-reinforcing cycle. [As] the group of victorious candidates comes to consist mainly of politicians who can successfully navigate these structures and depend on them for reelection, the impetus for change among officeholders will fade. [Perhaps the best solution would be the enactment of new disclosure requirements.] In the post-*Citizens United* era, transparency would provide at least a measure of reassurance. . . .

See also Tribe, Dividing Citizens United: The Case and The Controversy, 30 Const. Comment. 463 (2015).

e. Given that the Court has dismissed the equality, corruption, and distortion justifications for campaign finance regulation, might the case for such regulation be strengthened by invoking an "alignment" rationale? That is, is it a problem for democracy if elected officials systematically do not represent the interests of the majority of their constituents? Consider the fact that "individuals who contribute at least $200 to federal candidates are overwhelmingly wealthy, highly educated, male, and white." In 2012, "these donors amounted to just 0.4% of the population, but supplied 64% of the funds received by candidates from individuals." Does it matter that individuals falling within this select group tend to hold views on critical issues of public policy that are very different from those of the majority of the American people, and that legislators tend to act in accord with the views of this tiny minority of very wealthy individuals, even when they conflict with the views of the vast majority of their constituents? Is such "non-alignment" between the views of American citizens and the votes of their elected representatives a sufficiently important concern in a democracy to justify campaign finance regulations of the sort that have thus far been invalidated by the Supreme Court? See Stephanopolous, Aligning Campaign Finance Law, 101 Va. L. Rev. 1425 (2015).

f. For an excellent overview of the evolution of the Supreme Court's jurisprudence in this line of cases, and for an analysis of the fundamental shift caused by the appointments of John Roberts and Samuel Alito to replace William Rehnquist and Sandra Day O'Connor, see Kang, The Brave New World of Party Campaign Finance Law, 101 Cornell L. Rev. 531 (2016).

g. In Six Amendments: How and Why We Should Change the Constitution (2014), former Justice John Paul Stevens proposed the following amendment to the Constitution: "Neither the First Amendment nor any other provision of this Constitution shall be construed to prohibit the Congress or any state from imposing reasonable limits on the amount of money that candidates for public office, or their supporters, may spend in election campaigns."

Note: *Additional Regulation of the Electoral Process*

1. *Prohibiting paid petitioners.* In Meyer v. Grant, 486 U.S. 414 (1988), the Court invalidated a Colorado statute prohibiting the use of paid circulators to

obtain signatures for petitions to qualify proposed state constitutional amendments for inclusion on the general election ballot:

> The refusal to permit appellees to pay petition circulators restricts political expression in two ways: First, it limits the number of voices who will convey appellees' message and the hours they can speak and, therefore, limits the size of the audience they can reach. Second, it makes it less likely that appellees will garner the number of signatures necessary to place the matter on the ballot, thus limiting their ability to make the matter the focus of statewide attention. [Colorado's] prohibition of paid petition circulators restricts access to the most effective, fundamental, and perhaps economical avenue of political discourse, direct one-on-one communication.

See also Buckley v. American Constitutional Law Foundation, 525 U.S. 182 (1999), in which the Court, relying upon *Meyer*, invalidated a state law providing that (a) only registered voters may circulate ballot-initiative petitions; (b) petition circulators must wear a badge identifying them by name; and (c) ballot-initiative proponents must file a report listing each petition circulator by name and stating the amount paid to each circulator.

2. *Regulating campaign promises.* In Brown v. Hartlage, 456 U.S. 46 (1982), petitioner, a candidate for local office in Kentucky, promised the voters that, if elected, he would reduce the salary of the office "to a more realistic level." Petitioner was elected, but a state court declared the election void on the ground that petitioner had violated Kentucky's Corrupt Practices Act. The Supreme Court reversed:

> The [Act] prohibits a political candidate from giving, or promising to give, anything of value to a voter in exchange for his vote or support. In many of its possible applications, this provision would appear to present little constitutional difficulty, for a State may surely prohibit a candidate from buying votes. [But here, petitioner's promise] was made openly, subject to the comment and criticism of his political opponent and to the scrutiny of the voters. [His] was a declaration of intention to exercise the fiscal powers of government office within what he believed [to] be the recognized framework of office. [Petitioner's] promise to reduce his salary cannot be considered as inviting the kind of corrupt arrangement the appearance of which a State may have a compelling interest in avoiding.

3. *Regulating the speech of judicial candidates.* Minnesota elects its judges. It prohibits candidates for judicial office from announcing their views of any disputed legal issues that might come before them as judges. In Republican Party of Minnesota v. White, 536 U.S. 735 (2002), the Court, in a five-to-four decision, held that this prohibition (known as the "announce clause") violated the first amendment.

Justice Scalia delivered the opinion of the Court. At the outset, Justice Scalia reasoned that because the "announce clause both prohibits speech on the basis of its content and burdens a category of speech that is 'at the very core of our First Amendment freedoms' — speech about the qualifications for public office," the State must "prove that the announce clause is (1) narrowly tailored, to serve (2) a compelling state interest." He then observed that the State asserts two interests: "preserving the impartiality of the state judiciary and preserving the appearance of the impartiality of the state judiciary." Defining the interest in "impartiality" as meaning that a judge should not have "a preconception in favor or against a particular legal view," Justice Scalia said that "it is virtually impossible to find a judge who does not have preconceptions about the law," and "pretending otherwise by attempting to preserve the 'appearance' of that type of impartiality can hardly be a compelling interest."

Justice Scalia also considered another version of impartiality: "open-mindedness." This "sort of impartiality seeks to guarantee each litigant, not an *equal* chance to win the legal points in the case, but at least *some* chance of doing so." Justice Scalia conceded that impartiality and the appearance of impartiality in this sense "may well be . . . desirable in the judiciary" and that the announce clause serves these interests "because it relieves a judge from pressure to rule a certain way in order to maintain consistency with statements the judge has previously made." Scalia nonetheless concluded, however, that "statements in election campaigns are such an infinitesimal portion of the public commitments to legal positions that judges (or judges to be) undertake, that this object of the prohibition is implausible." Scalia offered as examples of such other statements rulings in earlier cases, statements made in classes judges teach, statements made in books, articles, speeches, and so on.

Justice Ginsburg, joined by Justices Stevens, Souter, and Breyer, dissented:

> Legislative and executive officials act on behalf of the voters who placed them in office; "judge[s] represen[t] the Law." Unlike their counterparts in the political branches, judges are expected to refrain from catering to particular constituencies or committing themselves on controversial issues in advance of adversarial presentation. [I] would differentiate elections for political offices, in which the First Amendment holds full sway, from elections designed to select those whose office it is to administer justice without respect to persons. Minnesota's choice to elect its judges [does] not preclude [it] from installing an election process geared to the judicial office. [The] rationale underlying unconstrained speech in elections for political office — that representative government depends on the public's ability to choose agents who will act at its behest — does not carry over to campaigns for the bench.

The Supreme Court returned to the problem posed by judicial candidates in Williams-Yulee v. Florida Bar, 575 U.S. — (2015). On this occasion, though, the Court upheld a Florida rule that prohibited judicial candidates from "personally [soliciting] campaign funds." Justices Scalia, Thomas, Kennedy, and Alito dissented.

Note: *Regulating the Political Activities of Public Employees*

1. *Partisan political activity.* U.S. Civil Service Commission v. National Association of Letter Carriers, 413 U.S. 548 (1973), concerned the constitutionality of §9(a) of the Hatch Act, now codified in 5 U.S.C. §7324(a)(2), which prohibits federal employees from soliciting contributions for a partisan political purpose, taking an active part in a political campaign, soliciting votes for any candidate, or endorsing any candidate. The Court, in an opinion by Justice White, expressly reaffirmed United Public Workers v. Mitchell, 330 U.S. 75 (1947), and upheld the act:

> [Until] after the Civil War, the spoils system under which federal employees came and went depending upon party service and changing administrations, was the prevalent basis for governmental employment and advancement. [That] system

did not survive. [It is now] the judgment of Congress, the Executive, and the country [that] partisan political activities by federal employees must be limited if the Government is to operate effectively and fairly, elections are to play their proper part in representative government, and employees themselves are to be sufficiently free from improper influences. The restrictions [imposed] on federal employees are not aimed at particular parties, groups, or points of view, but apply equally to all partisan activities of the type described. . . .

[The] problem in any case is to arrive at a balance between the interests of the [employee] and the [interests] of the [government]. Although Congress is free to strike a different balance than it has, [we] think the balance it [has] struck is sustainable by the obviously important interests sought to be served by [the] Hatch Act.

It seems fundamental [that] employees [of] the Government [should] administer the law in accordance with the will of Congress, rather than in accordance with [the] will of a political party. [Moreover,] it is not only important that [Government] employees in fact avoid practicing political justice, but [also] that they appear to the public to be avoiding it, if confidence in the system of representative Government is not to be eroded. [Another] major concern [is] the conviction that the rapidly expanding Government work force should not be employed to build a powerful, invincible, and perhaps corrupt political machine. [A] related concern [is] to make sure that Government employees [are] free from pressure [to] vote in a certain way or perform political chores in order to curry favor with their superiors rather than to act out of their own beliefs.

Justices Douglas, joined by Justices Brennan and Marshall, dissented: "The Hatch Act [prohibits] federal employees from taking 'an active part in political management or in political campaigns.' [No] one could object if employees were barred from using office time to engage in outside activities whether political or otherwise. But it is of no concern of Government what an employee does in his spare time, [unless] what he does impairs efficiency or other facets of the merits of his job. Some [activities may] affect the employee's job performance. But his political creed, like his religion, is irrelevant. In the areas of speech, like religion, it is of no concern what the employee says in private to his wife or to the public in Constitution Hall."

In Broadrick v. Oklahoma, 413 U.S. 601 (1973), decided on the same day as *Letter Carriers*, the Court upheld Oklahoma's Merit System of Personnel Administration Act, which "serves roughly the same function as the analogous provisions of the other 49 States, and is patterned on §9(a) of the Hatch Act." Appellants, several state employees charged with violating the Oklahoma act, maintained that the act was unconstitutionally overbroad because it had been construed to prohibit public employees from wearing political buttons and displaying political bumper stickers. Finding that appellants' own activities could clearly be proscribed, and that the act was not "substantially" overbroad, the Court found it unnecessary to decide the overbreadth issue. See section C1 supra. Can Oklahoma constitutionally prohibit its public employees from wearing political buttons and displaying political bumper stickers? For an interesting variation, see United States v. National Treasury Employees Union, 513 U.S. 454 (1995) (invalidating a provision of the Ethics in Government Act that prohibited a broad class of government employees from accepting any compensation for making speeches or writing articles without regard to whether the subject of the speech or article or the person or group paying the honorarium had any connection with the employee's official duties).

2. *Criticizing government policy.* In Pickering v. Board of Education, 391 U.S. 563 (1968), a teacher was dismissed from his position by the Board of Education for sending a letter to a local newspaper in connection with a recently proposed tax increase that was critical of the way in which the Board and the district superintendent of schools had handled past proposals to raise new revenue for the schools. The teacher's dismissal resulted from a determination by the Board, after a full hearing, that the publication of the letter was "detrimental to the efficient operation and administration of the schools of the district." The Court, in an opinion by Justice Marshall, held that the teacher's right to freedom of speech had been violated:

> An examination of the statements in appellant's letter objected to by the Board reveals that [they] consist essentially of criticism of the Board's allocation of school funds between educational and athletic programs. [The] statements are in no way directed towards any person with whom appellant would normally be in contact in the course of his daily work as a teacher. Thus no question of maintaining either discipline by immediate superiors or harmony among coworkers is presented here. Appellant's employment relationships with the Board and, to a somewhat lesser extent, with the superintendent are not the kind of close working relationships for which it can persuasively be claimed that personal loyalty and confidence are necessary to their proper functioning. Accordingly, to the extent that the Board's position here can be taken to suggest that even comments on matters of public concern that are substantially correct [may] furnish grounds for dismissal if they are sufficiently critical in tone, we unequivocally reject it.

Suppose the teacher's speech had been personal in nature — for example, suppose the teacher had made statements critical of another teacher's driving, causing tension between them. Would *Pickering* govern? See Connick v. Meyers, 461 U.S. 138 (1983) ("when employee expression cannot fairly be considered as relating to any matter of political, social, or other concern to the community, [but concerns only matters of personal interest,] officials should enjoy wide latitude in managing their offices, without intrusive oversight by the judiciary in the name of the First Amendment"); Rankin v. McPherson, 483 U.S. 378 (1987) (*Pickering* rather than *Connick* governs in a situation in which a clerical employee in the office of a county constable was fired because, after hearing of an assassination attempt against the President, she remarked to a coworker, "If they go for him again, I hope they get him," because the remark constituted speech "on a matter of public concern.").

Suppose the teacher's statements in *Pickering* had been false? The Court noted in *Pickering* that "in a case such as this, absent proof of false statements knowingly or recklessly made by him, a teacher's exercise of his right to speak on issues of public importance may not furnish the basis for his dismissal from public employment."

On related issues, see Waters v. Churchill, 511 U.S. 661 (1994) (there is no violation of the first amendment when a government employer fires an employee for constitutionally protected speech if the employer reasonably believed that the speech was unprotected); Board of County Commissioners, Wabaunsee County, Kansas v. Umbehr, 518 U.S. 668 (1996) (independent contractors are governed by *Pickering*); O'Hare Truck Service, Inc. v. City of Northlake, 518 U.S. 712 (1996) (same); Gentile v. State Bar of Nevada, 501 U.S. 1030 (1991) (government licensees, such as attorneys participating in judicial proceedings, are governed by *Pickering*); Tennessee Secondary School Athletic Association v. Brentwood

Academy, 551 U.S. 291 (2007) (voluntary associations are governed by *Pickering*); Garcetti v. Ceballos, 461 U.S. 138 (2006) (public employee who speaks pursuant to a public duty is not protected by *Pickering*); Borough of Duryea, Pennsylvania v. Guarnieri, 564 U.S. 379 (2011) (litigation by public employees against the government is governed by public concern standard); Lane v. Franks, 134 S. Ct. 2369 (2014) (public employee who testifies under subpoena about a matter related to his public employment is protected by the First Amendment, despite *Garcetti*, where his testimony was not required by "his ordinary job responsibilities"). For a thoughtful analysis of the value of public employee speech, see Kitrosser, The Special Value of Public Employee Speech, 2015 Sup. Ct. Rev. 301.

3. *Patronage.* In December 1970, the Sheriff of Cook County, Illinois, a Republican, was replaced by Richard Elrod, a Democrat. At that time, respondents, all Republicans, were non–civil service employees of the Cook County Sheriff's Office. Respondent Burns was a process server; respondent Vargas was a bailiff and security guard. Following prior practice, Sheriff Elrod discharged respondents from their employment solely because they did not support and were not members of the Democratic Party. In Elrod v. Burns, 427 U.S. 347 (1976), the Court held this practice unconstitutional. In a plurality opinion, Justice Brennan explained:

> The [practice] of dismissing employees on a partisan basis [is] one form of the general practice of political patronage. Patronage practice is not new to American politics. It has existed at the federal level at least since the Presidency of Thomas Jefferson. [More] recent times have witnessed a strong decline in its use, [however, and] merit systems have increasingly displaced the practice. [The] cost of the practice of patronage is the restraint it places on freedoms of belief and association. In order to maintain their jobs, respondents were required to pledge their political allegiance to the Democratic Party, work for the election of other candidates of the Democratic Party, contribute a portion of their wages to the Party, or obtain the sponsorship of a member of the Party, usually at the price of one of the first three alternatives. [An] individual who is a member of the out-party maintains affiliation with his own party at the risk of losing his job. . . .
>
> One interest which has been offered in justification of patronage is the need to insure effective government and the efficiency of public employees. It is argued that employees of political persuasions not the same as that of the party in control of public office will not have the incentive to work effectively and may even be motivated to subvert the incumbent administration's efforts to govern effectively. We are not persuaded. [It] is doubtful that the mere difference of political persuasion motivates poor performance. [At] all events, less drastic means for insuring government effectiveness and employee efficiency are available to the State. Specifically, employees may always be discharged for good cause, such as insubordination or poor job performance, when those bases in fact exist. . . .
>
> A second interest advanced in support of patronage is the need for political loyalty of employees [to] the end that representative government not be undercut by tactics obstructing the implementation of policies of the new administration, policies presumably sanctioned by the electorate. The justification is not without force, but is nevertheless inadequate to validate patronage wholesale. Limiting patronage dismissals to policymaking positions is sufficient to achieve this governmental end. Nonpolicymaking individuals usually have only limited responsibility and are therefore not in a position to thwart the goals of the in-party. . . .

Justice Powell, joined by Chief Justice Burger and Justice Rehnquist, dissented.

See also Branti v. Finkel, 445 U.S. 507 (1980) (the position of assistant public defender is not a "policymaking" position within the meaning of *Elrod* and the first amendment therefore prohibits the discharge of two assistant public defenders solely because they were Republicans and were unable to provide the necessary Democratic sponsorship when a Democratic Public Defender took office); Rutan v. Republican Party of Illinois, 497 U.S. 62 (1990) (rejecting the argument that only those employment decisions that are the "substantial equivalent of a dismissal" violate a public employee's rights under the first amendment and holding that *Elrod* also governs decisions about hiring, "promotions, transfers and recalls after layoffs based on political affiliation or support"); O'Hare Truck Service, Inc. v. City of Northlake, 518 U.S. 712 (1996) (*Elrod* protects independent contractors as well as government employees.).

Note: Content-Neutral Restrictions — Final Thoughts

Consider the following evaluation: The Court has long recognized that by limiting the availability of particular means of communication, content-neutral restrictions can significantly impair the ability of individuals to communicate their views to others. This is a central first amendment concern. The Court generally tests content-neutral restrictions with an implicit balancing approach: The greater the interference with the opportunities for free expression, the greater the burden on government to justify the restriction. When the challenged restriction has a relatively severe effect, the Court invokes strict scrutiny. See, e.g., *Button*; *Buckley* (expenditure limitations); *Roberts*. When the challenged restriction has a significant, but not severe, effect, the Court employs intermediate scrutiny. See, e.g., *Schneider*; *Buckley* (contribution limitations); *Martin*. And when the restriction has a relatively modest effect, the Court applies deferential scrutiny. See, e.g., *O'Brien*; *Heffron*, section E2b, supra; *Clark*, section E2a. There are exceptions to this pattern, and the exceptions are often quite revealing, for they suggest the impact of additional factors, such as "public property" or "incidental effect," that may trump the central concern of content-neutral analysis. But the general pattern is clear: As the restrictive effect increases, the standard of review increases as well. Is this an accurate description of the Court's analysis? If so, does it reflect a satisfactory approach? See Stone, Content-Neutral Restrictions, 54 U. Chi. L. Rev. 46 (1987).

For critical analyses of the Court's content-based/content-neutral distinction, see Bhagwat, Purpose Scrutiny in Constitutional Analysis, 85 Cal. L. Rev. 297 (1997); McDonald, Speech and Distrust: Rethinking the Content Approach to Protecting the Freedom of Expression, 81 Notre Dame L. Rev. 1347 (2006); Huhn, Assessing the Constitutionality of Laws That Are Both Content-Based and Content-Neutral: The Emerging Constitutional Calculus, 79 Ind. L.J. 801 (2004).

F. FREEDOM OF THE PRESS

This section examines the first amendment's guarantee of "freedom [of] the press." The focus is on four questions. First, in what circumstances, if any, is the press, because of its constitutionally protected status, exempt from laws of otherwise general application? Second, to what extent, if any, does the first amendment guarantee a right to "gather" news? Third, in what circumstances, if any, may government treat the press differently from other institutions? Fourth, in what circumstances, if any, may government regulate the press in order to improve the "marketplace of ideas"?

1.   A "Preferred" Status for the Press?

The first amendment prohibits any law "abridging the freedom of speech, or of the press." Does the press clause confer any rights that would not be conferred by the speech clause alone? Consider the views of Justice Stewart and Chief Justice Burger:

a. Stewart, "Or of the Press," 26 Hastings L.J. 631, 633–634 (1975):

> The publishing business is the only organized private business that is given explicit constitutional protection. [If] the Free Press guarantee meant no more than freedom of expression, it would be a constitutional redundancy. [By] including both [the speech and press] guarantees in the First Amendment, the Founders quite clearly recognized the distinction between the two. [In] setting up the three branches of the Federal Government, the Founders deliberately created an internally competitive system. [The] primary purpose of the constitutional guarantee of a free press was [to] create a fourth institution outside the Government as an additional check on the three official branches. [The] relevant metaphor [is that] of the Fourth Estate. [The first amendment thus protects] the institutional autonomy of the press.

b. First National Bank of Boston v. Bellotti, 435 U.S. 765, 797–801 (1978) (Burger, C.J., concurring):

> [There are those] who view the Press Clause as somehow conferring special and extraordinary privileges or status on the "institutional press." [I] perceive two fundamental difficulties with [such a] reading of the Press Clause. First, although certainty on this point is not possible, the history of the Clause does not suggest that the authors contemplated a "special" or "institutional" privilege. [Most] pre-First Amendment commentators "who employed the term 'freedom of speech' [used] it synonymously with freedom of the press." [The] second fundamental difficulty with interpreting the Press Clause as conferring special status on a limited group is one of definition. [The] very task of including some entities within the "institutional press" while excluding others [is] reminiscent of the abhorred licensing system [that] the First Amendment was intended to ban. [In my view,] the First Amendment does not "belong" to any definable category of persons or entities: It belongs to all who exercise its freedoms.

Consider also Associated Press v. NLRB, 301 U.S. 103 (1937). The Associated Press is a cooperative organization whose members in 1937 included approximately 1,350 newspapers. It collects, compiles, and distributes news to its members. The NLRB found that the Associated Press discharged an employee in violation of section 7 of the National Labor Relations Act, which confers on employees the right to organize and to bargain collectively. The Court, in a five-to-four decision, held that application of section 7 to the Associated Press did not violate the first amendment:

> The business of the Associated Press is not immune from regulation because it is an agency of the press. The publisher of a newspaper has no special immunity from the application of general laws. He has no special privilege to invade the rights and liberties of others. He must answer for libel. He may be punished for contempt of court. He is subject to the anti-trust laws. Like others he must pay equitable and nondiscriminatory taxes on his business. The regulation here in question has no relation whatever to the impartial distribution of news.

See also Dun & Bradstreet v. Greenmoss Builders, section D1, supra (the media are not entitled to any greater protection against actions for libel than other speakers); Citizen Publishing Co. v. United States, 394 U.S. 131 (1969) (Sherman Antitrust Act); Oklahoma Press Publishing Co. v. Walling, 327 U.S. 186 (1946) (Fair Labor Standards Act); cf. Grosjean v. American Press Co., 297 U.S. 233 (1936) (taxation). Are these decisions consistent with Justice Stewart's contention that the "publishing business is the only organized private business that is given explicit constitutional protection"? Are there *some* circumstances in which the first amendment exempts the press from tax, labor, antitrust, or other laws of general application?

For a particularly thoughtful analysis of the Framers' understanding of the Press Clause, see West, The "Press," Then & Now, 77 Ohio St. L.J. 49 (2016), noting that "press freedom was of paramount importance at the time of the framing. James Madison referred to liberty of the press as one of the 'choicest privileges of the people' and proposed language to make press freedom 'inviolable.' So clear was the significance of securing freedom of the press that it surpassed even the push for speech rights."

2.   A Right to "Gather" News?

Branzburg v. Hayes

408 U.S. 665 (1972)

Opinion of the Court by MR. JUSTICE WHITE. . . .

[Branzburg, a newspaper reporter, published several articles describing unlawful drug activities in Frankfort, Kentucky. He refused, on first amendment grounds, to disclose to a state grand jury the identities of the persons whose activities he had described.]

The issue in these cases is whether requiring newsmen to appear and testify before state or federal grand juries abridges the freedom of speech and press guaranteed by the First Amendment. We hold that it does not.

Petitioners [press] First Amendment claims that may be simply put: that to gather news it is often necessary to agree either not to identify the source of information published or to publish only part of the facts revealed, or both; that if the reporter is nevertheless forced to reveal these confidences to a grand jury, the source so identified and other confidential sources of other reporters will be measurably deterred from furnishing publishable information, all to the detriment of the free flow of information protected by the First Amendment. Although the newsmen [do] not claim an absolute privilege against official interrogation in all circumstances, they assert that the reporter should not be forced either to appear or to testify before a grand jury or at trial until and unless sufficient grounds are shown for believing that the reporter possesses information relevant to a crime the grand jury is investigating, that the information the reporter has is unavailable from other sources, and that the need for the information is sufficiently compelling to override the claimed invasion of First Amendment interests occasioned by the disclosure. [The] heart of the claim is that the burden on news gathering resulting from compelling reporters to disclose confidential information outweighs any public interest in obtaining the information.

We do not question the significance of free speech, press, or assembly to the country's welfare. Nor is it suggested that news gathering does not qualify for First Amendment protection; without some protection for seeking out the news, freedom of the press could be eviscerated. But these cases involve no [restriction] on what the press may publish, and no express or implied command that the press publish what it prefers to withhold. [The] use of confidential sources by the press is not forbidden or restricted. [The] sole issue before us is the obligation of reporters to respond to grand jury subpoenas as other citizens do and to answer questions relevant to an investigation into the commission of crime. . . .

[The] First Amendment does not invalidate every incidental burdening of the press that may result from the enforcement of civil or criminal statutes of general applicability. [Citing Associated Press v. NLRB; Oklahoma Press Publishing Co. v. Walling.] . . .

It has generally been held that the First Amendment does not guarantee the press a constitutional right of special access to information not available to the public generally. [In Zemel v. Rusk, 381 U.S. 1 (1965)], for example, the Court sustained the Government's refusal to validate passports to Cuba even though that restriction "render[ed] less than wholly free the flow of information concerning that country." The ban on travel was held constitutional, for "[t]he right to speak and publish does not carry with it the unrestrained right to gather information."

Despite the fact that news gathering may be hampered, the press is regularly excluded from grand jury proceedings, our own conferences, the meetings of other official bodies gathered in executive session, and the meetings of private organizations. Newsmen have no constitutional right of access to the scenes of crime or disaster when the general public is excluded, and they may be prohibited from [attending] trials if such restrictions are necessary to assure a defendant a fair trial before an impartial tribunal. . . .

It is thus not surprising that the great weight of authority is that newsmen are not exempt from the normal duty of appearing before a grand jury and answering questions relevant to a criminal investigation. [The] prevailing constitutional view of the newsman's privilege is very much rooted in the ancient role of the grand jury. [Because] its task is to inquire into the existence of possible criminal conduct and to return only well-founded indictments, its investigative powers are necessarily broad. [On] the records now before us, we perceive no basis for holding that the public interest in law enforcement and in ensuring effective grand jury proceedings is insufficient to override the consequential, but uncertain, burden on news gathering that is said to result from insisting that reporters, like other citizens, respond to relevant questions put to them in the course of a valid grand jury investigation or criminal trial.

This conclusion [does not] threaten the vast bulk of confidential relationships between reporters and their sources. [Only] where news sources themselves are implicated in crime or possess information relevant to the grand jury's task need they or the reporter be concerned about grand jury subpoenas. Nothing before us indicates that a large number or percentage of *all* confidential news sources falls into either category and would in any way be deterred by our holding. . . .

[Moreover, although the] argument that the flow of news will be diminished by compelling reporters to aid the grand jury in a criminal investigation is not [irrational, we] remain unclear how often and to what extent informers are actually deterred from furnishing information when newsmen are forced to testify before a grand jury. [The] evidence fails to demonstrate that there would be a significant constriction of the flow of news to the public if this Court reaffirms the prior common-law and constitutional rule regarding the testimonial obligations of newsmen.[33]

[Furthermore, the] administration of a constitutional newsman's privilege would present practical and conceptual difficulties of a high order. Sooner or later, it would be necessary to define those categories of newsmen who qualified for the privilege, a questionable procedure in light of the traditional doctrine that liberty of the press is the right of the lonely pamphleteer [just] as much as of the large metropolitan publisher. [Almost] any author may [assert] that he is contributing to the flow of information to the public, that he relies on confidential sources of information, and that these sources will be silenced if he is forced to make disclosures before a grand jury.

In each instance where a reporter is subpoenaed to testify, the courts would also be embroiled in preliminary factual and legal determinations with respect to whether the proper predicate had been laid for the reporter's appearance: Is there probable cause to believe a crime has been committed? Is it likely that the reporter has useful information gained in confidence? Could the grand jury obtain the information elsewhere? Is the official interest sufficient to outweigh the claimed privilege? . . .

Finally, as we have earlier indicated, news gathering is not without its First Amendment protections, and grand jury investigations if instituted or conducted other than in good faith, would pose wholly different issues for resolution under the First Amendment. Official harassment of the press undertaken not for purposes of law enforcement but to disrupt a reporter's relationship with his news sources would have no justification. Grand juries are subject to judicial control and subpoenas to motions to quash. We do not expect courts will forget that grand juries must operate within the limits of the First Amendment. . . .

MR. JUSTICE POWELL, concurring.

I add this brief statement to emphasize what seems to me to be the limited nature of the Court's holding. The Court does not hold that newsmen, subpoenaed to testify before a grand jury, are without constitutional rights with respect to the gathering of news or in safeguarding their sources. . . .

As indicated in the concluding portion of the opinion, the Court states that no harassment of newsmen will be tolerated. If a newsman believes that the grand

---

33. In his Press Subpoenas: An Empirical and Legal Analysis, Study Report of the Reporters' Committee on Freedom of the Press 6–12, Prof. Vince Blasi [found] that slightly more than half of the 975 reporters questioned said that they relied on regular confidential sources for at least 10% of their stories. Of this group of reporters, only 8% were able to say with some certainty that their professional functioning had been adversely affected by the threat of subpoena; another 11% were not certain whether or not they had been adversely affected. [Relocated footnote. — EDS.]

jury investigation is not being conducted in good faith he is not without remedy. Indeed, if the newsman is called upon to give information bearing only a remote and tenuous relationship to the subject of the investigation, or if he has some other reason to believe that his testimony implicates confidential source relationships without a legitimate need of law enforcement, he will have access to the court on a motion to quash and an appropriate protective order may be entered. The asserted claim to privilege should be judged on its facts by the striking of a proper balance between freedom of the press and the obligation of all citizens to give relevant testimony with respect to criminal conduct. The balance of these vital constitutional and societal interests on a case-by-case basis accords with the tried and traditional way of adjudicating such questions.

In short, the courts will be available to newsmen under circumstances where legitimate First Amendment interests require protection.

MR. JUSTICE DOUGLAS, dissenting. . . .

Today's decision will impede the wide-open and robust dissemination of ideas and counter thought which a free press both fosters and protects and which is essential to the success of intelligent self-government. . . .

I see no way of making mandatory the disclosure of a reporter's confidential source of the information on which he bases his news story. . . .

MR. JUSTICE STEWART, with whom MR. JUSTICE BRENNAN and MR. JUSTICE MARSHALL join, dissenting.

The Court's crabbed view of the First Amendment reflects a disturbing insensitivity to the critical role of an independent press in our society. [While] Mr. Justice Powell's enigmatic concurring opinion gives some hope of a more flexible view in the future, the Court in these cases holds that a newsman has no First Amendment right to protect his sources when called before a grand jury. The Court thus invites state and federal authorities to undermine the historic independence of the press by attempting to annex the journalistic profession as an investigative arm of government. . . .

A corollary of the right to publish must be the right to gather news. [The] right to gather news implies, in turn, a right to a confidential relationship between a reporter and his source. [Informants] are necessary to the news-gathering process as we know it today. [And] the promise of confidentiality may be a necessary prerequisite to a productive relationship between a newsman and his informants. . . .

The impairment of the flow of news cannot, of course, be proved with scientific precision, as the Court seems to demand. [But] we have never before demanded that First Amendment rights rest on elaborate empirical studies demonstrating beyond any conceivable doubt that deterrent effects exist. . . .

Rather, on the basis of common sense and available information, we have asked, often implicitly, (1) whether there was a rational connection between the cause (the governmental action) and the effect (the deterrence or impairment of First Amendment activity), and (2) whether the effect would occur with some regularity, i.e., would not be de minimis. [Citing, e.g., NAACP v. Alabama; New York Times v. Sullivan.] Once this threshold inquiry has been satisfied, we have then examined the competing interests in determining whether there is an unconstitutional infringement of First Amendment freedoms. . . .

Surely [the] claim of deterrence here is as securely grounded in evidence and common sense as the claims in the cases cited above. [To] require any greater burden of proof is to shirk our duty to protect values securely embedded in the Constitution. . . .

Posed against the First Amendment's protection of the newsman's confidential relationships in these cases is society's interest in the use of the grand jury to administer justice fairly and effectively. [To] perform these functions the grand jury must have available to it every man's relevant evidence. [But] the longstanding rule making every person's evidence available to the grand jury is not absolute. The rule has been limited by the Fifth Amendment, the Fourth Amendment, and the evidentiary privileges of the common law. . . .

In striking the proper balance between the public interest in the efficient administration of justice and the First Amendment guarantee of the fullest flow of information, we must begin with the basic proposition [that] First Amendment rights require special safeguards. . . .

Accordingly, when a reporter is asked to appear before a grand jury and reveal confidences, I would hold that the government must (1) show that there is probable cause to believe that the newsman has information that is clearly relevant to a specific probable violation of law; (2) demonstrate that the information sought cannot be obtained by alternative means less destructive of First Amendment rights; and (3) demonstrate a compelling and overriding interest in the information. . . .

No doubt the courts would be required to make some delicate judgments in working out this accommodation. But that, after all, is the function of courts of law. Better such judgments, however difficult, than the simplistic and stultifying absolutism adopted by the Court in denying any force to the First Amendment in these cases. . . .

Note: A Right to Gather News?

1. *Newsgathering.* Does the first amendment guarantee the press a right to gather as well as to publish the news? Has the press a first amendment right to gather news through such practices as deception, burglary, wiretapping, and the bribing of sources? Suppose a reporter breaks into a government official's home to uncover evidence of corruption. Can the reporter be prosecuted? Note that this issue implicates the incidental effects doctrine. Recall *O'Brien.* If fraud, burglary, wiretapping, and bribery are generally unlawful, does the first amendment create a special exemption for the press? If the reporter can constitutionally be prosecuted for the break-in, the wiretap, or the bribery, does it follow that her newspaper can be punished for publishing the information? Recall *Pentagon Papers, Bartnicki,* and *Ferber.* See Stone, Government Secrecy v. Freedom of the Press, 1 Harv. L. & Pol. Rev. 185 (2007).

2. *Journalist's privilege.* In light of Justice Powell's concurring opinion, is it fair to say that the Court divided "by a vote of four and a half to four and a half"? Stewart, "Or of the Press," 26 Hastings L. Rev. 631, 635 (1975). Note that Justice Powell joined the majority opinion in *Branzburg.* Suppose he had filed his concurring opinion without joining Justice White's opinion. Would that have affected the meaning of the decision?

Forty-nine states and the District of Columbia have adopted some form of journalist-source privilege, but the federal government had no such privilege. Three questions are especially vexing in crafting such a privilege: (1) Should the privilege be absolute or qualified? That is, should the government be able to overcome the privilege with a sufficient showing of need? (2) Should the privilege protect the confidentiality of a source whose disclosure is *unlawful?* If the purpose of the privilege is to encourage a source to communicate, does it make any sense to extend the privilege to unlawful communications? Note that this query has particular relevance to unlawful leaks of classified information. (3) Who should be able to assert the privilege? Presumably, the privilege would cover disclosures to a reporter for the Washington Post or CNN, but what about disclosures to a professor who is writing a book, to bloggers, or to the editor of a high school newspaper? See Papandrea, Citizen Journalism and the Reporter's Privilege, 91 Minn. L. Rev. 515 (2007); Stone, Why We Need a Federal Reporter's Privilege, 34 Hofstra L. Rev. 39 (2005).

3. *Investigative journalism or criminal solicitation?* Suppose a reporter persuades a public employee unlawfully to leak classified information. Can the reporter constitutionally be convicted of the crime of criminal solicitation? Recall *O'Brien.* Suppose a journalist conducts an illegal wiretap in order to prove that a congressman took a bribe. Would her conduct be protected by the first amendment? If not, is criminal solicitation any different? See G. Stone, Top Secret: When Government Keeps Us in the Dark 29–38 (2007) (arguing that because prosecution of journalists for the crime of solicitation would interject "government into the very heart of the journalist-source relationship" and thus "have a serious chilling effect" on legitimate and important journalist-source exchanges, the government should not be able to punish journalists for encouraging public employees to disclose classified information unless the journalist (a) expressly incites the leak and (b) knows that publication of the information would likely cause imminent and grave harm to the national security). Can that position be reconciled with the wiretap example or with *Branzburg?*

4. *Newsroom searches.* In Zurcher v. Stanford Daily, 436 U.S. 547 (1978), the Daily, a student newspaper, published articles and photographs concerning a violent clash on campus between demonstrators and police. Thereafter, the police obtained a warrant for an immediate search of the newspaper's offices for negatives, films, and pictures that might enable them to identify some of the demonstrators. The Daily's photographic laboratories, filing cabinets, desks, and wastepaper baskets were searched, but the police found only those photographs that had already been published. The Daily brought this civil action on the theory that the decision of the police to conduct a search, rather than to proceed by subpoena duces tecum, violated the first amendment. The Daily maintained that, unlike subpoenas, "searches of newspaper offices for evidence of [crime] seriously threaten the ability of the press to gather, analyze, and disseminate news." In a five-to-three decision, the Court, in an opinion by Justice White, rejected this argument:

> Properly administered, the preconditions for a warrant — probable cause, specificity with respect to the place to be searched and the things to be seized, and overall reasonableness — should afford sufficient protection against the harms that are assertedly threatened by warrants for searching newspaper offices. [Nor] are we convinced, any more than we were in [*Branzburg*], that confidential sources will disappear. [Whatever] incremental effect there may be in this regard [does] not make a constitutional difference.

In the Privacy Protection Act of 1980, 42 U.S.C. §2000aa, Congress prohibited any government officer to search for work product or other documents of any "person reasonably believed to have a purpose to disseminate to the public a newspaper, book, broadcast, or other similar form of public communication," unless there is either probable cause to believe that the person is involved in the crime being investigated or there is otherwise reason to believe that giving notice by subpoena would result in the loss of the evidence.

5. *Breach of promise.* In Cohen v. Cowles Media Co., 501 U.S. 663 (1991), petitioner, who was associated with one party's campaign during the 1982 Minnesota gubernatorial race, gave court records disclosing derogatory information about another party's candidate to respondent newspapers after receiving a promise of confidentiality from the reporters. Despite this promise, the newspapers identified him in their stories, and petitioner was thereafter fired from his job. In a five-to-four decision, the Court held that the first amendment did not bar petitioner's state law action for damages for breach of promise. Justice White delivered the opinion of the Court:

> Generally applicable laws do not offend the First Amendment simply because their enforcement against the press has incidental effects on its ability to gather and report the news. [There] can be little doubt that the Minnesota doctrine of promissory estoppel is a law of general applicability. It does not target or single out the press. [The] First Amendment does not forbid its application to the press.

Justices Souter, Marshall, Blackmun, and O'Connor dissented:

6. *Does the press have a right to publish someone else's "property"?* Consider Zacchini v. Scripps-Howard Broadcasting Co., 433 U.S. 562 (1977), in which petitioner's fifteen-second "human cannonball" act, in which he is shot from a cannon into a net some two hundred feet away, was, without his consent, filmed in its entirety at a county fair and shown on a television news program later the same day. Petitioner filed a damage action alleging an "unlawful appropriation" of his "professional property." The Court held that the first amendment did not bar petitioner's action: "[The first amendment does not give the media a right to] broadcast a performer's entire act without his consent. The Constitution no more prevents a State from requiring respondent to compensate petitioner for broadcasting his act on television than it would privilege respondent to film and broadcast a copyrighted dramatic work without liability to the copyright owner."

7. *The first amendment and copyright.* Is copyright protection consistent with the first amendment? See Harper & Row, Publishers v. Nation Enterprises, 471 U.S. 539 (1985) (a magazine's unauthorized publication of verbatim quotes from President Ford's unpublished memoirs constituted an actionable copyright infringement); Eldred v. Ashcroft, 537 U.S. 186 (2003) (upholding the 1998 Copyright Extension Act, which extended the duration of existing copyrights by an additional twenty years).

Does an artist have a first amendment right to use a famous movie star's image in one of her paintings? Does the first amendment protect an individual who produces and sells t-shirts that mock well-known politicians or products? See R. Tushnet, Copy This Essay: How the Fair Use Doctrine Harms Free Speech and How Copying Serves It, 114 Yale L.J. 535 (2004); Rothman, Commercial Speech, Commercial Use, and the Intellectual Property Quagmire, 101 Va. L. Rev. 1929 (2015).

For an interesting twist on this problem, see Simon & Schuster, Inc. v. Members of the New York State Crime Victims Board, 502 U.S. 428 (1991) (invalidating New York's Son of Sam law, which required any entity contracting with a person convicted of a crime to publish any depiction of the crime to turn over any income under the contract to the Crime Victims Board, which was then required to deposit the payments in an escrow account for the benefit of any victims).

Note: A Press Right of Access to Information?

1. A *right of access?* To what extent, if any, does the press have a first amendment right of access to information from the government? For example, do members of the press ever have a constitutional right to be present during military operations, to interview prisoners, to demand information from government officials, or to attend criminal trials? If the right of the press to *publish* information about the activities of government is central to the first amendment, isn't the right of the press to *obtain* such information equally central? Consider BeVier, An Informed Public, An Informing Press: The Search for a Constitutional Principle, 68 Cal. L. Rev. 482, 498–499 (1980):

> The effect on the flow of information [of] government denials of access to information [is] similar to the [effect of such direct restrictions on publication as punishment and censorship. But] the failure of government to [grant] access cannot be credibly argued to be the constitutional equivalent of [such direct restrictions. Punishment and censorship] interfere quite directly with the freedom to publish. When the government denies access to information, however, it poses no threat to freedom, at least if that word is given its ordinary legal meaning. [Punishment and] censorship directly undermine the value of *free* speech, while the denial of access to information undermines [only] the value of *well-informed* speech.

If there is a first amendment right of press access to government information, what are its limits? Is government under a constitutional obligation to make public all information that might enhance "the ability of our people through free and open debate to consider and resolve their own destiny"? Is it "impossible to conceive of a court making case-by-case determinations of the 'necessity' of nondisclosure in any way that would bear even the faintest resemblance [to] 'reasoned elaboration'"? BeVier, supra, at 510.

2. *Access to prisons.* In Pell v. Procunier, 417 U.S. 817 (1974), the Court held that professional journalists had no first amendment right to conduct face-to-face interviews of prison inmates:

> The First and Fourteenth Amendments bar government from interfering in any way with a free press. The Constitution does not, however, require government to accord the press special access to information not shared by members of the public generally. It is one thing to say that a journalist is free to seek out sources of information not available to members of the general public, that he is entitled to some constitutional protection of the confidentiality of such sources, cf. [*Branzburg*], and that government cannot restrain the publication of news emanating from such sources. Cf. [*Pentagon Papers*, section B3 supra]. It is quite another thing to suggest that the Constitution imposes upon government the affirmative duty to make available to journalists sources of information not available to members of the public generally. That proposition finds no support in the words of the Constitution or in any decision of this Court.

Justices Douglas, Brennan, Marshall, and Powell dissented.

3. *Access to the military*. Consider Anderson, Freedom of the Press in Wartime, 77 U. Colo. L. Rev. 49, 66, 95–98 (2006): "So far as existing case law is concerned, there appears to be nothing to prevent the Pentagon from eliminating on-scene coverage of military operations, detention facilities, military hospitals, and other auxiliaries of war. [A] judicial response that leaves news about the conduct of war at the sufferance of the military is an abdication of constitutional responsibility."

4. *Are there potential dangers in recognizing a "preferred" status for the press?* Consider Van Alstyne, The First Amendment and the Free Press: A Comment on Some New Trends and Some Old Theories, 9 Hofstra L. Rev. 1, 19–23 (1980):

> [If] journalists may assert access to certain public facilities [in] "first amendment preference" to laypersons, [it] may follow symmetrically that the ensuing published story must meet a standard of professionalism commensurate with the privileged standing of the reporter. [The press operates] most effectively and most legitimately precisely because it forms no part of government. [The] security of the [press] from the encumbrance of public regulation [may] be at risk if one's accent is not on the freedom of the press but is, rather, on the public's right to know. [We] have already imposed upon radio and television substantial "public" obligations — in exchange for exclusive, cost-free licensing privileges. [There] is no reason to suppose that the matter will be different for newspapers should they, too, "succeed" in securing particular rights [that others] cannot claim under a single and indivisible amendment.

5. *Access to judicial proceedings*. In Gannett v. DePasquale, 443 U.S. 368 (1979), the defendants in a murder prosecution requested that the public and the press be excluded from a pretrial hearing on a motion to suppress allegedly involuntary confessions. The district attorney did not oppose the request, and the trial judge, finding that the adverse publicity might jeopardize the defendants' right to a fair trial, granted the closure motion. In upholding this order, the Court focused primarily on the claim that the order violated the sixth amendment's guarantee that "[in] all criminal prosecutions, the accused shall enjoy the right to a [public] trial." Although conceding that "there is a strong societal interest in public trials," the Court concluded that the sixth amendment guarantee "is personal to the accused," and that "members of the public" thus "have no constitutional right under the Sixth [Amendment] to attend criminal trials."

RICHMOND NEWSPAPERS v. VIRGINIA, 448 U.S. 555 (1980). In 1976, Stevenson was convicted of murder. The conviction was reversed, however, and two subsequent trials ended in mistrials. At the outset of his fourth trial, Stevenson moved that the proceeding be closed to the public. Neither the prosecutor nor anyone else present, including two of appellant's reporters, objected to the motion. The trial judge, acting pursuant to a Virginia statute authorizing the court, "in its discretion," to "exclude from the trial any persons whose presence would impair the conduct of a fair trial," ordered "that the Courtroom be kept clear of all parties except the witnesses when they testify." Later that day appellant moved to vacate the closure order. In defense of the order, Stevenson argued that he "didn't want information to leak out," be published by the media, perhaps inaccurately, and then be seen by the jurors. The trial judge, noting also that "having people in the Courtroom is distracting to the jury," denied the motion to vacate and ordered the trial to continue "with the press and public excluded."

The following day the trial judge excused the jury and found Stevenson "not guilty." As soon as the trial ended, tapes of the proceeding were made available to the public.

In a divided set of opinions, the Court held that the order closing the trial to the press and the public was unconstitutional. Chief Justice Burger, joined by Justices White and Stevens, authored a plurality opinion: "The narrow question presented in this case is whether the right of the public and press to attend criminal trials is guaranteed under the United States Constitution. [The] origins of [the] modern criminal trial in Anglo-American justice can be traced back beyond reliable historical records. [Throughout] its evolution, the trial has been open to all who cared to observe. [This] is no quirk of history; rather, it has long been recognized as an indispensable attribute of an Anglo-American trial. [Such openness gives] assurance that the proceedings [are] conducted fairly to all concerned, and it [discourages] perjury, the misconduct of participants, and decisions based on secret bias or partiality. [Moreover,] public trials [have] significant community therapeutic value. [When] a shocking crime occurs, a community reaction of outrage and public protest often follows. Thereafter the open processes of justice serve an important prophylactic purpose, providing an outlet for community concern, hostility, and emotion. . . .

"The Bill of Rights was enacted against the backdrop of the long history of trials being presumptively open. [In] guaranteeing freedoms such as those of speech and press, the First Amendment can be read as protecting the right of everyone to attend trials so as to give meaning to those explicit guarantees. [The] explicit, guaranteed rights to speak and to publish concerning what takes place at a trial would lose much meaning if access to observe the trial could, as it was here, be foreclosed arbitrarily. [We] hold that the right to attend criminal trials[17] is implicit in the guarantees of the First Amendment; without the freedom to attend such trials, which people have exercised for centuries, important aspects of freedom of speech and 'of the press could be eviscerated.'

"Having concluded there was a guaranteed right of the public under the First and Fourteenth Amendments to attend the trial of Stevenson's case, we return to the closure order challenged by appellants. [The] trial judge made no findings to support closure; no inquiry was made as to whether alternative solutions would have met the need to ensure fairness; there was no recognition of any right under the Constitution for the public or press to attend the trial. [Absent] an overriding interest articulated in findings, the trial of a criminal case must be open to the public."[18]

Justice Brennan, joined by Justice Marshall, filed a concurring opinion: "Customarily, First Amendment guarantees are interposed to protect communication

17. Whether the public has a right to attend trials of civil cases is a question not raised by this case, but we note that historically both civil and criminal trials have been presumptively open.

18. We have no occasion here to define the circumstances in which all or parts of a criminal trial may be closed to the public, but our holding today does not mean that the First Amendment rights of the public and representatives of the press are absolute. Just as a government may impose reasonable time, place, and manner restrictions upon the use of its streets in the interest of such objectives as the free flow of traffic, see, e.g., Cox v. New Hampshire, [section E2a supra], so may a trial judge, in the interest of the fair administration of justice, impose reasonable limitations on access to a trial. [Moreover], since courtrooms have limited capacity, there may be occasions when not every person who wishes to attend can be accommodated. In such situations, reasonable restrictions on general access are traditionally imposed, including preferential seating for media representatives. . . .

between speaker and listener. [But] the First Amendment embodies more than a commitment to free expression and communicative interchange for their own sakes; it has a *structural* role to play in securing and fostering our republican system of self-government. Implicit in this structural role is [the] assumption that valuable public debate [must] be informed. The structural model links the First Amendment to that process of communication necessary for a democracy to survive, and thus entails solicitude not only for communication itself, but also for the indispensable conditions of meaningful communication.

"However, because 'the stretch of this protection is theoretically endless,' it must be invoked with discrimination and temperance. [At] least two helpful principles may be sketched. First, the case for a right of access has special force when drawn from an enduring and vital tradition of public entree to particular proceedings or information. [Second], the value of access must be measured in specifics. Analysis is not advanced by rhetorical statements that all information bears upon public issues; what is crucial in individual cases is whether access to a particular government process is important in terms of that very process. [Our] ingrained tradition of public trials and the importance of public access to the broader purposes of the trial process tip the balance strongly toward the rule that trials be open. What countervailing interests might be sufficiently compelling to reverse this presumption of openness need not concern us now,[24] for the statute at stake here authorizes trial closures at the unfettered discretion of the judge and parties."

Justice Stewart concurred in the judgment. Justice Rehnquist dissented.

GLOBE NEWSPAPER CO. v. SUPERIOR COURT, 457 U.S. 596 (1982). To protect the minor victims of sex crimes from further trauma and embarrassment and to encourage such victims to come forward and testify in a truthful and credible manner, section 16A of chapter 278 of Massachusetts General Laws requires trial judges, at trials for specified sexual offenses involving a victim under age eighteen, to exclude the press and general public from the courtroom during the testimony of the victim. The Court, in a six-to-three decision, held section 16A unconstitutional. Justice Brennan delivered the opinion of the Court:

"*Richmond Newspapers* firmly established for the first time that the press and general public have a constitutional right of access to criminal trials. [Where], as in the present case, the State attempts to deny the right of access in order to inhibit the disclosure of sensitive information, it must be shown that the denial is necessitated by a compelling governmental interest, and is narrowly tailored to serve that interest. . . .

"We agree [that the Commonwealth's interest in] safeguarding the physical and psychological well-being of a minor [is] a compelling one. But as compelling as that interest is, it does not justify a *mandatory*-closure rule, for it is clear that the circumstances of the particular case may affect the significance of the interest. A trial court can determine on a case-by-case basis whether closure is necessary to protect the welfare of a minor victim. Among the factors to be weighed are the minor victim's age, psychological maturity and understanding, the nature of the crime, the desires of the victim, and the interests of parents and relatives.

---

24. For example, national security concerns about confidentiality may sometimes warrant closures during sensitive portions of trial proceedings, such as testimony about state secrets. Cf. United States v. Nixon, 418 U.S. 683, 714–716 (1974).

[Section] 16A cannot be viewed as a narrowly tailored means of accommodating the State's asserted interest. . . .

"Nor can §16A be justified on the basis of the Commonwealth's [interest in] the encouragement of minor victims of sex crimes to come forward and provide accurate testimony. The Commonwealth has offered no empirical support for the claim that the rule of automatic closure [will] lead to an increase in the number of minor sex victims coming forward and cooperating with state authorities. . . ." Chief Justice Burger, joined by Justice Rehnquist, dissented.

Note: Variations on the Press Right of Access

1. *Voir dire hearings.* In Press-Enterprise Co. v. Superior Court, 464 U.S. 501 (1984), the Court held that a state court order closing the voir dire examination of prospective jurors in a criminal trial violated the first amendment. The Court explained that the "presumption of openness may be overcome only by an overriding interest based on findings that closure is essential to preserve higher values and is narrowly tailored to serve that interest." Although conceding that the "jury selection process may, in some circumstances, give rise to a compelling [privacy] interest of a prospective juror when interrogation touches on deeply personal matters," the Court concluded that the trial court in this case had not adequately considered the alternatives to closure. See also Press-Enterprise Co. v. Superior Court, 478 U.S. 1 (1986) (holding that a newspaper has a first amendment right of access to the transcript of a preliminary hearing).

In what circumstances, if any, does the first amendment guarantee the media a right at attend civil trials? Deportation hearings? Congressional hearings? To what extent, if any, does the first amendment give the media a right to televise criminal trials? *Richmond Newspapers* was premised on a long-standing tradition of public access to criminal trials. To what extent is that an inadequate basis for the right of access? Should the First Amendment "be understood to embody an affirmative right of access to information held by the courts, which by virtue of their unique institutional position possess information that is essential for the public to effectively evaluate the workings of government and, therefore, to act as sovereigns over the government," without regard to historical precedent? Ardia, Court Transparency and the First Amendment, 38 Cardozo L. Rev. 835 (2017).

2. *Conditioned access to information.* Despite *Richmond Newspapers*, government is under no general constitutional obligation to disclose information to the press or public and indeed may ordinarily prohibit its employees from disclosing "confidential" information. To what extent, then, may government condition its voluntary disclosure of information on the press's agreement not to publish?

Consider Seattle Times Co. v. Rhinehart, 467 U.S. 20 (1984). In a defamation action against the Seattle Times, a state court ordered the plaintiff to disclose certain information in discovery. The state court entered a protective order prohibiting the newspaper from using the disclosed information, which included the names of contributors to a controversial religious group, for any purpose other than trial of the case. The Supreme Court unanimously rejected the newspaper's claim that the order violated the first amendment:

[The newspaper] gained the information [only] by virtue of the trial court's discovery processes. [It had] no First Amendment right of access to [the information]. [Moreover, the] protective order prevents [the dissemination only of] information obtained through [discovery. The newspaper is free to] disseminate the identical information [if it obtains it] through means independent of the court's processes. [Thus], continued court control over the discovered information does not raise the same spectre of government censorship that such control might suggest in other situations. [We] therefore hold that where [a] protective order is entered on a showing of good cause, [is] limited to the context of pretrial civil discovery, and does not restrict the dissemination of the information if gained from other sources, it does not offend the First Amendment.

3.   Differential Treatment of the Press

Consider the constitutionality of the following laws: (1) A sales tax of 4 percent on all sales of goods. This is challenged by a newspaper publisher who argues that, as applied to his sales, the tax constitutes an impermissible "tax on the press." (2) A sales tax of 4 percent on all sales of goods, except that sales of newspapers, books, and periodicals are taxed at the rate of 6 percent. (3) A sales tax of 4 percent on all sales of goods, except that sales of newspapers, books, and periodicals are taxed at the rate of 2 percent. (4) A sales tax of 4 percent on all sales of goods, except that sales of newspapers are taxed at the rate of 2 percent. This is challenged by a publisher of magazines. (5) A sales tax of 4 percent on all sales of goods, except that sales of newspapers, books, and periodicals are taxed at 2 percent if the publisher has an annual profit of less than $1 million. This is challenged by the only publisher in the state who has an annual profit of more than $1 million.

MINNEAPOLIS STAR & TRIBUNE CO. v. MINNESOTA COMMISSIONER OF REVENUE, 460 U.S. 575 (1983). Minnesota imposes a sales tax on retail sales. To avoid double taxation, sales of components to be used in the production of goods that will themselves be sold at retail are exempt from the sales tax. Minnesota also imposes a use tax on the use or consumption of goods that were purchased without payment of the sales tax. The use tax is designed to eliminate the incentive of residents to buy goods in states with lower sales taxes. Until 1971, periodic publications were exempt from both the sales and the use taxes. In 1971, however, Minnesota imposed a use tax on the cost of paper and ink products consumed in the production of periodic publications. As a result, ink and paper used in such publications became the only components of goods to be sold at retail subject to the use tax. In 1974, Minnesota amended the use tax to exempt the first $100,000 worth of ink and paper consumed by a publication in any calendar year. After enactment of the $100,000 exemption, eleven publishers, producing fourteen of the 388 newspapers in Minnesota, incurred a tax liability in 1974. Appellant was one of the eleven. Because of its size, it paid approximately $600,000, or about two-thirds of the total revenue raised by the tax. The Court held that this taxing scheme violated appellant's rights under the first amendment. Justice O'Connor delivered the opinion of the Court:

"Minnesota has [created] a special tax that applies only to certain publications protected by the First Amendment. [We] must determine whether the First Amendment permits such special taxation. [There] is substantial evidence that differential taxation of the press would have troubled the Framers of the First Amendment. [The] fears of the [framers] were well-founded. [When] a State singles out the press [for special taxation], the political constraints that prevent a legislature from passing crippling taxes of general applicability are weakened, and the threat of burdensome taxes becomes acute. That threat can operate as effectively as a censor to check critical comment by the press. [Differential] taxation of the press, then, places such a burden on the interests protected by the First Amendment and we cannot countenance such treatment unless the State asserts a counterbalancing interest of compelling importance that it cannot achieve without differential taxation. . . .

"Minnesota invites us to look beyond the form of the tax to its substance. The tax is, according to the State, merely a substitute for the sales tax, which, as a generally applicable tax, would be constitutional as applied to the press. [But] the State has offered no explanation of why it chose to use a substitute for the sales tax rather than the sales tax itself.

"[The State argues further] that this scheme actually *favors* the press over other businesses, because the same rate of tax is applied, but, for the press, the rate applies to the cost of components rather than to the sales price. [But we] would be hesitant to fashion a rule that automatically allowed the State to single out the press for a different method of taxation as long as the effective burden was no different from that on other taxpayers or the burden on the press was lighter than that on other businesses. One reason for this reluctance is that the very selection of the press for special treatment threatens the press not only with the current *differential* treatment, but with the possibility of subsequent differentially *more burdensome* treatment. Thus, even without actually imposing an extra burden on the press, the government might be able to achieve censorial effects, for '[t]he threat of sanctions may deter [the] exercise of [First Amendment] rights almost as potently as the actual application of sanctions.' [A] second reason to avoid the proposed rule is that courts as institutions are poorly equipped to evaluate with precision the relative burdens of various methods of taxation. [The] possibility of error inherent in the proposed rule poses too great a threat to concerns at the heart of the First Amendment, and we cannot tolerate that possibility.[13] Minnesota, therefore, has offered no adequate justification for the special treatment of newspapers. . . .

"Minnesota's ink and paper tax violates the First Amendment not only because it singles out the press, but also because it targets a small group of newspapers. The effect of the $100,000 exemption [is] that only a handful of publishers pay any tax at [all]. The State explains this exemption as part of a policy favoring an 'equitable' tax system, [but] there are no comparable exemptions for small enterprises outside the press. [We] think that recognizing a power in the State [to] tailor the tax so that it singles out only a few members of the press presents such a potential for abuse that [Minnesota's interest in an 'equitable' tax system cannot] justify the scheme. [The] tax violates the First Amendment."

Justice Rehnquist dissented. Justice White concurred in part and dissented in part.

---

13. If a State employed the same *method* of taxation but applied a lower *rate* to the press, so that there could be no doubt that the legislature was not singling out the press to bear a more burdensome tax, we would, of course, be in a position to evaluate the relative burdens. And, given the clarity of the relative burdens, as well as the rule that differential methods of taxation are not automatically permissible if less burdensome, a lower tax rate for the press would not raise the threat that the legislature might later impose an extra burden that would escape detection by the courts.

Note: Differential Treatment

1. *Preserving press neutrality.* Consider Bezanson, Political Agnosticism, Editorial Freedom, and Government Neutrality toward the Press, 72 Iowa L. Rev. 1359, 1371 (1987): "[A sound] reason for making constitutionally suspect any formal singling out of the press [is] to protect the political neutrality of the press [and to] prevent the government from undermining the [neutrality of the press] by forcing [it] to engage actively in the political process [to] protect its own self-interest." Does this mean that even a law expressly benefiting the press, such as an exemption from a state's sales tax, should be invalid? Consider footnote 13 in *Minneapolis Star.*

2. *Content-based differentiation.* The Court relied on *Minneapolis Star* in Arkansas Writers' Project, Inc. v. Ragland, 481 U.S. 221 (1987), to invalidate an Arkansas statute that imposed a state sales tax on general interest magazines but exempted religious, professional, trade, and sports journals. In an opinion by Justice Marshall, the Court invalidated the law because the discrimination was "content-based." Justice Scalia, joined by Chief Justice Rehnquist, dissented.

3. *Intermedia differentiation: Leathers.* In Leathers v. Medlock, 499 U.S. 439 (1991), the Court considered the constitutionality of the Arkansas Gross Receipts Act, which imposes a 4 percent tax. The act expressly exempts receipts from subscription and over-the-counter newspaper and magazine sales but imposes the tax on cable television. The Court, in an opinion by Justice O'Connor, rejected petitioners' argument that such "intermedia discrimination" violates the first amendment. The Court explained that such a tax is "suspect" only if it "threatens to suppress the expression of particular ideas or viewpoints," "singles out the press," "targets a small group of speakers," or "discriminates on the basis [of] content." Because the "Arkansas tax [presents] none of these types of discrimination," the Court concluded that Arkansas's "extension of its generally applicable sales tax to [cable television], while exempting the print media, does not violate the First Amendment." Justice Marshall, joined by Justice Brennan, dissented.

4. *Intermedia discrimination: Turner.* In Turner Broadcasting Inc. v. FCC, 512 U.S. 622 (1994), section F4, infra, the Court upheld "must carry" provisions for cable television that favored broadcast over cable programmers. The Court observed:

> Regulations that discriminate among media, or among different speakers within a single medium, often present serious First Amendment concerns. [Citing *Minneapolis Star* and *Arkansas Writers' Project*.] It would be error to conclude, however, that the First Amendment mandates strict scrutiny for any speech regulation that applied to one medium (or a subset thereof) but not others. [The] taxes invalidated in *Minneapolis Star* and *Arkansas Writers' Project* [targeted] a small number of speakers [and] were structured in a manner that raised suspicions that their objective [was] the suppression of certain ideas.
>
> But such heightened scrutiny is unwarranted [where, as here,] the differential treatment [is] not structured in a manner that carries the inherent risk of undermining First Amendment interests. The [must carry] regulations [apply] to almost all cable systems in the country, rather than just a select few. As a result, [they] do not pose the same dangers of suppression and manipulation that were posed by the more narrowly targeted regulations in *Minneapolis Star* and *Arkansas Writers' Project*.

5. *Intermedia discrimination: shield laws.* Suppose a journalist-shield law allows reporters for mainstream newspapers and television and radio stations to invoke the journalist-source privilege, but does not extend to bloggers. Does such intermedia discrimination violate the first amendment? Consider Stone, Why We Need a Federal Reporter's Privilege, 34 Hofstra L. Rev. 39, 48 (2005):

> [Although the issue of "who is a member of the press"] was a serious constraint on the Court in *Branzburg*, it poses a much more manageable issue in the context of legislation. Government often treats different speakers and publishers differently from one another. Which reporters are allowed to attend a White House briefing? Which are eligible to be embedded with the military? Broadcasting is regulated, but print journalism is not. Legislation treats the cable medium differently from both broadcasting and print journalism. These categories need not conform perfectly to the undefined phrase "the press" in the First Amendment. Differentiation among different elements of the media is constitutional, as long as it is not based on viewpoint or any other invidious consideration, and as long as the differential is reasonable.

4.   Regulating the Press to "Improve" the Marketplace of Ideas

In what circumstances, if any, is it appropriate for government to regulate the media in order to "improve" the system of free expression? Recall the discussion of this issue in the electoral context in section E4 supra.

MIAMI HERALD PUBLISHING CO. v. TORNILLO, 418 U.S. 241 (1974). In *Tornillo*, the Court considered the constitutionality of a Florida "'right of reply' statute which [provided] that if a candidate for [political office] is assailed regarding his personal character or official record by any newspaper, the candidate has the right to demand that the newspaper print, free of cost to the candidate, any reply the candidate may make to the newspaper's charges. The reply must appear in as conspicuous a place and in the same kind of type as the charges which prompted the reply, provided it does not take up more space than the charges." The Court, in a unanimous decision, held the statute invalid. Chief Justice Burger delivered the opinion of the Court:

"[Advocates] of an enforceable right of access to the press [urge] that at the time the First Amendment [was ratified] the press was broadly representative of the people it was serving. [Entry] into publishing was inexpensive [and a] true marketplace of ideas existed in which there was relatively easy access to the channels of communication. Access advocates submit that [the press of today is] very different. [Newspapers] have become big business and [the press] has become noncompetitive and enormously powerful and influential in its capacity to manipulate popular opinion. [The] result of these vast changes has been to place in a few hands the power to inform the American people and shape public opinion. [There] tends to be a homogeneity of editorial opinion, commentary, and interpretative analysis. [The] obvious solution [would] be to have additional newspapers. But [economic factors] have made entry into the marketplace of ideas served by the print media almost impossible. [The] First Amendment interest of the public in being informed is said to be in peril. . . .

"However much validity may be found in these arguments, [the] implementation of a remedy such as an enforceable right of access necessarily [brings] about a confrontation with the express provisions of the First Amendment. [The] argument that the Florida statute does not amount to a restriction of [the newspaper's] right to speak because 'the statute in question here has not prevented [the newspaper] from saying anything it wished' begs the core question. Compelling editors or publishers to publish that which "'reason' tells them should not be published" is what is at issue in this case. The Florida statute operates as a command in the same sense as a statute or regulation forbidding [the newspaper] to publish specified matter. [The] Florida statute exacts a penalty on the basis of the content of a newspaper. The first phase of the penalty [is] exacted in terms of the cost in printing [and] in taking up space that could be devoted to other material the newspaper may have preferred to print. [Faced with such a penalty,] editors might well conclude that the safe course is to avoid controversy. [Thus, the government-enforced] right of access inescapably 'dampens the vigor and limits the variety of public debate.' . . .

"[Moreover, even] if a newspaper would face no additional costs to comply with a compulsory access law and would not be forced to forgo publication of news or opinion by the inclusion of a reply, the Florida statute fails to clear the barriers of the First Amendment because of its intrusion into the function of editors. A newspaper is more than a passive receptacle or conduit for news, comment, and advertising. The choice of material to go into a newspaper [constitutes] the exercise of editorial control and judgment. It has yet to be demonstrated how governmental regulation of this crucial process can be exercised consistent with First Amendment guarantees of a free press as they have evolved to this time."

Consider the possibility that the law in *Tornillo* was a kind of "candidate protection act," and illegitimate because its purpose and effect were to insulate political figures from criticism. In a concurring opinion in *Tornillo*, Justice Brennan asserted that "the Court's opinion [implies] no view upon the constitutionality of 'retraction' statutes affording plaintiffs able to prove defamatory falsehoods a statutory action to require publication of a retraction." Do you agree? Suppose, instead of a "right-of-reply" law, Florida adopted a "right-of-access" law, requiring every newspaper to set aside one page each issue for letters to the editor, not to exceed five hundred words, to be selected for publication without regard to content. Would such a law be invalid under *Tornillo*? Recall *PruneYard*, section E4, supra.

RED LION BROADCASTING CO. V. FCC, 395 U.S. 367 (1960). In *Red Lion*, the Court upheld the constitutionality of the Federal Communication Commission's fairness doctrine and its component regulations governing personal attacks and political editorializing. The fairness doctrine, which originated "very early in the history of broadcasting," imposes "on radio and television broadcasters the requirement that discussion of public issues be presented on broadcast stations, and that each side of those issues must be given fair coverage." The personal attack rule requires that when, "during the presentation of views on a controversial issue of public importance, an attack is made upon the honesty, character, integrity or like personal qualities of an identified person or group," the attacked person or group must be given notice, a transcript, and a reasonable opportunity to respond. The political editorializing rule requires that when, in an editorial, a broadcaster endorses or opposes a political candidate, the broadcaster must notify the opposed candidate or the opponents of the endorsed candidate and give them a "reasonable opportunity" to reply.

Justice White delivered the opinion of the Court: "The broadcasters [allege] that the [challenged] rules abridge their freedom of speech and press. Their contention is that the First Amendment protects their desire to use their allotted frequencies continuously to broadcast whatever they choose, and to exclude whomever they choose from ever using that frequency. [Although] broadcasting is clearly a medium affected by a First Amendment interest, differences in the characteristics of new media justify differences in the First Amendment standards applied to them. [Where] there are substantially more individuals who want to broadcast than there are frequencies to allocate, it is idle to posit an unabridge-able First Amendment right to broadcast comparable to the right of every individual to speak, write, or publish. If 100 persons want broadcast licenses but there are only 10 frequencies to allocate, all of them may have the same "right" to a license; but if there is to be any effective communication by radio, only a few can be licensed and the rest must be barred from the airwaves. It would be strange if the First Amendment, aimed at protecting and furthering communications, prevented the Government from making radio communication possible by requiring licenses to broadcast and by limiting the number of licenses so as not to overcrowd the spectrum. . . .

"By the same token, as far as the First Amendment is concerned those who are licensed stand no better than those to whom licenses are refused. A license permits broadcasting, but the licensee has no constitutional right to be the one who holds the license or to monopolize a radio frequency to the exclusion of his fellow citizens. There is nothing in the First Amendment which prevents the Government from requiring a licensee to share his frequency with others and to conduct himself as a proxy or fiduciary with obligations to present those views and voices which are representative of his community and which would otherwise, by necessity, be barred from the airwaves. [The] people as a whole retain their interest in free speech by radio and their collective right to have the medium function consistently with the ends and purposes of the First Amendment. It is the right of the viewers and listeners, not the right of the broadcasters, which is paramount. [It] is the right of the public to receive suitable access to social, political, esthetic, moral, and other ideas and experiences which is crucial here. . . .

"[We cannot] say that it is inconsistent with the First Amendment goal of producing an informed public capable of conducting its own affairs to require a broadcaster to permit answers to personal attacks occurring in the course of discussing controversial issues, or to require that the political opponents of those endorsed by the station be given a chance to communicate with the public. Otherwise, station owners and a few networks would have unfettered power to make time available only to the highest bidders, to communicate only their own views on public issues, people and candidates, and to permit on the air only those with whom they agreed. There is no sanctuary in the First Amendment for unlimited private censorship operating in a medium not open to all. . . .

"It is strenuously argued, however, that if political editorials or personal attacks will trigger an obligation in broadcasters to afford the opportunity for expression to speakers who need not pay for time and whose views are unpalatable to the licensees, then broadcasters will be irresistibly forced to self-censorship and their coverage of controversial public issues will be eliminated or at least rendered wholly ineffective. Such a result would indeed be a serious matter, for should licensees actually eliminate their coverage of controversial issues, the purposes of the doctrine would be stifled. [At] this point, however, as the Federal Communications Commission has indicated, that possibility is at best speculative. [And] if experience with the administration of these doctrines indicates that they have the net effect of reducing rather than enhancing the volume and quality of coverage, there will be time enough to reconsider the constitutional implications. . . .

"It is argued that even if at one time the lack of available frequencies for all who wished to use them justified the Government's choice of those who would best serve the public interest by acting as proxy for those who would present differing views, or by giving the latter access directly to broadcast facilities, this condition no longer prevails so that continuing control is not justified. To this there are several answers. Scarcity is not entirely a thing of the past. Advances in technology, such as microwave transmission, have led to more efficient utilization of the frequency spectrum, but uses for that spectrum have also grown apace. [Nothing] in this record, or in our own researches, convinces us that the resource is no longer one for which there are more immediate and potential uses than can be accommodated. . . .

"[Moreover], the fact remains that existing broadcasters have often attained their present position because of their initial government selection in competition with others before new technological advances opened new opportunities for further uses. Long experience in broadcasting, confirmed habits of listeners and viewers, network affiliation, and other advantages in program procurement give existing broadcasters a substantial advantage over new entrants, even where new entry is technologically possible. These advantages are the fruit of a preferred position conferred by the Government. Some present possibility for new entry by competing stations is not enough, in itself, to render unconstitutional the Government's effort to assure that a broadcaster's programming ranges widely enough to serve the public interest.

"In view of the scarcity of broadcast frequencies, the Government's role in allocating those frequencies, and the legitimate claims of those unable without governmental assistance to gain access to those frequencies for expression of their views, we hold the [regulations] constitutional."[28]

Note: Regulating the Airwaves

1. *Licensing the airwaves.* In the Communications Act of 1934, the government, "to maintain the control of the United States over [the channels of] radio transmission; and to provide for the use of such channels, but not the ownership thereof, by persons for limited periods of time," established the FCC and granted

---

28. We need not deal with the argument that even if there is no longer a technological scarcity of frequencies limiting the number of broadcasters, there nevertheless is an economic scarcity in the sense that the Commission could or does limit entry to the broadcasting market on economic grounds and license no more stations than the market will support. Hence, it is said, the fairness doctrine or its equivalent is essential to satisfy the claims of those excluded and of the public generally. A related argument, which we also put aside, is that quite apart from scarcity of frequencies, technological or economic, Congress does not abridge freedom of speech or press by legislation directly or indirectly multiplying the voices and views presented to the public through time sharing, fairness doctrines, or other devices which limit or dissipate the power of those who sit astride the channels of communication with the general public. . . .

it broad power to license and regulate the broadcast spectrum "as public convenience, interest, or necessity requires." In National Broadcasting Co. v. United States, 319 U.S. 190 (1943), the Court held that such government licensing did not violate the first amendment because, "[unlike] other modes of expression, radio inherently is not available to all." Consider the following arguments:

a. Coase, The Federal Communications Commission, 2 J.L. & Econ. 1, 14–18 (1959):

[The Court] seems to believe that federal regulation is needed because radio frequencies are limited in number and people want to use more of them than are available. But it is a commonplace of economics that almost all resources used in the economic system (and not simply radio and television frequencies) are limited in amount and scarce, in that people would like to use more than exists. [It] is true that some mechanism has to be employed to decide who [should] be allowed to use the scarce resource. But the way this is usually done [is] to employ the price mechanism, and this allocates resources to users without the need for government regulation. [An] administrative agency which attempts to perform the function normally carried out by the pricing mechanism [cannot], by the nature of things, be [fully aware] of the preferences of consumers. [Allocation by means of the pricing mechanism is thus more likely than allocation by administrative action to serve the "public convenience, interest, or necessity."]

b. Van Alstyne, The Mobius Strip of the First Amendment: Perspectives on Red Lion, 29 S.C. L. Rev. 539, 562 (1978):

The [Coase] argument is appealing, but it is based on a fatal myopia in its failure to see how clearly freedom of speech [is] abridged by a government policy that adheres only to a private property system and a market-pricing mechanism in determining who shall be able to speak. [Allocation by means of the pricing mechanism would winnow] the field of otherwise eligible applicants strictly according to their ability to pay; it [would eliminate] from the licensing competition those who lack dollars to put in an effective bid.

c. In FCC v. Fox Television Stations, 556 U.S. 502 (2009), section D7 supra, Justice Thomas called Red Lion into question in a separate concurring opinion:

Red Lion [was] unconvincing when [it was] issued, and the passage of time has only increased doubt regarding [its] continued validity. [Red Lion] relied heavily on the scarcity of available broadcast frequencies. [Dramatic] technological advances have eviscerated the factual assumptions underlying [that decision]. Broadcast spectrum is significantly less scarce than it was 40 years ago. [And] the trend should continue. [Moreover], traditional broadcast television and radio are no longer the 'uniquely pervasive' media forms they once were. For most consumers, traditional broadcast media programming is now bundled with cable or satellite services. Broadcast and other video programming is also widely available over the Internet. [The] extant facts that drove this Court to subject broadcasters to unique disfavor under the First Amendment simply do not exist today.

2. *Regulating the airwaves.* Assuming licensing of the airwaves is not itself unconstitutional, what factors may the FCC consider in its allocation of licenses?

a. May the FCC compel an applicant for a broadcast license to ascertain the problems, needs, and interests of his community and to provide programming to meet those needs? See Ascertainment of Community Problems by Broadcast

Applicants Primer, 57 F.C.C.2d 418 (1976). May the FCC, for example, deny a license to an applicant for a radio station in a community with a significant minority population unless the applicant agrees to devote a significant portion of her programming to information and entertainment designed specifically for the minority community?

b. May the FCC prohibit broadcasters from airing programs that contain profanity? May it prohibit programs that incite to crime? That are sexually explicit? That depict a racial or religious group in a degrading manner? Recall FCC v. Pacifica Foundation, section D7, supra.

c. Consider the following proposal made by Reed Hundt, then-chair of the FCC, in Hundt, The Public's Airwaves: What Does the Public Interest Require of Television Broadcasters?, 45 Duke L.J. 1089, 1099–1100, 1105–1106 (1996):

> In the aggregate, political candidates at all levels spent [$500 million in 1996] on media advertising. [The] cost of television advertising makes fundraising an enormous entry barrier for candidates seeking public office, an oppressive burden for incumbents seeking reelection, a continuous threat to the integrity of our political institutions, and a principal cause of the erosion of public respect for public service. [To address this problem,] broadcasters should be required, [as] a condition of their licenses, to provide free airtime for political candidates. . . .
>
> [This could be accomplished by requiring] broadcasters [to] donate [$500 million worth of] airtime to [a time] bank and [authorizing] candidates [to] draw airtime from the bank during their campaigns. [How] would we divide the time contributed to a time bank? One approach would be to grant each eligible candidate a right to a specific dollar amount of free time. Candidates would then negotiate with broadcasters for advertising time, just as they currently do, but would pay with time bank credits rather than actual dollars. Why would broadcasters accept credits? Because they would be required to provide free time worth, say, 2 percent of their annual advertising revenues as a condition of using the public airwaves for free. Indeed, it would be important for broadcasters to provide time to candidates lest they lose their licenses.

3. *Repeal of the fairness doctrine.* In 1987, the FCC repealed the fairness doctrine, asserting that the doctrine was unconstitutional because it "chilled" the first amendment rights of broadcasters.

4. *Regulating the media to achieve a "more advanced democratic society."* Consider L. Bollinger, Images of a Free Press 133–145 (1991):

> [Under the image of freedom of the press established in New York Times v. Sullivan], the goal of press freedom [was] viewed as the creation of a vast space for "uninhibited, robust, and wide-open" public discussion [and it was] assumed that the role of the Supreme Court is to stand guard against government intervention. [This approach is] insensitive to problems affecting the quality of public discussion that are posed by a laissez-faire system of modern mass media. [What is needed is a] more fundamental understanding [of press freedom].
>
> [To achieve this more fundamental understanding, we] must address the nature of our own behavior in the discussion of public questions. [A] democratic society, like an individual, should strive to remain conscious of the biases that skew, distort, and corrupt its own thinking about public issues. [Even] in a world in which the press is entirely free and open to all voices, with a perfect market in that sense, human nature would still see to it that quality public debate and decisionmaking would not rise naturally to the surface but would [need] the buoyant support of some form of collective action [involving] public institutions.

[Although the mass media may] give viewers and readers what they "want" [through] the expression of their preferences in the marketplace, [it is nonetheless imaginable] that we — the same "we" that issue our marketplace votes for what we get — might be very concerned about [what] choices we are making in that system. [Accordingly, we may] decide together, through public regulation, that we would like to alter [the] demands we find ourselves making in that market context, [for we may] recognize that if we are left to choose on our own whether and how to inform ourselves, too many will neglect to undertake the burdens of self-education, choosing instead to pursue more pleasant things. [It] would be a more [advanced] democratic society that could act to correct deficiencies arising out of [the] citizens themselves.

TURNER BROADCASTING SYSTEM, INC. v. FCC, 512 U.S. 622 (1994). The "must carry" provisions of the Cable Television Consumer Protection and Competition Act of 1992 require cable television systems to devote a portion of their channels, free of charge, to the transmission of local broadcast television stations. The rationale of these provisions was explained by the Court:

"Cable technology affords two principal benefits over broadcast. First, it eliminates the signal interference sometimes encountered in over-the-air [broadcasting]. Second, it is capable of transmitting many more channels than are available through broadcasting. [Congress] enacted the 1992 Cable Act after conducting three years of [hearings]. Congress concluded that [the] overwhelming majority of cable operators exercise a monopoly over cable service [and that] this market position gives cable operators the power and the incentive to harm broadcast competitors. The power derives from the cable operator's ability [to refuse to transmit broadcast signals]. The incentive derives from the economic reality that '[c]able television systems and broadcast systems increasingly compete for television advertising revenues.' By refusing carriage of broadcasters' signals, cable operators [can] reduce the number of households that have access to the broadcasters' programming, and thereby capture advertising dollars that would otherwise go to broadcast stations. [In such circumstances], Congress concluded that unless cable operators are required to carry local broadcast stations, '[t]here is a substantial likelihood [that] the economic viability of free local broadcast television [will] be seriously jeopardized.' [Congress] sought to avoid the elimination of broadcast television [because] '[s]uch programming is . . . free to those who own television sets and does not require cable transmission to receive broadcast signals.' [The] provisions are designed to [ensure] that every individual with a television set can obtain access to free television programming."

Although the Court divided sharply on the constitutionality of the "must carry" provisions, it was unanimous in holding that the regulation of cable television should not be governed by the same constitutional standards as broadcast regulation. Justice Kennedy delivered the opinion of the Court:

"[The] rationale for applying a less rigorous standard of First Amendment scrutiny to broadcast regulation [does] not apply in the context of cable regulation. The justification for our distinct approach to broadcast regulation rests upon the unique physical limitations of the broadcast medium. As a general matter, there are more would-be broadcasters than frequencies available in the electromagnetic spectrum. And if two broadcasters were to attempt to transmit over the same frequency in the same locale, they would interfere with one another's signals, so that neither could be heard at all. The scarcity of broadcast frequencies thus required the establishment of some regulatory mechanism to divide the electromagnetic spectrum and assign specific frequencies to particular broadcasters. [The] broadcast cases are inapposite in the present context because cable television does not suffer from the inherent limitations that characterize the broadcast medium. Indeed, given the rapid advances in fiber optics and digital compression technology, soon there may be no practical limitation on the number of speakers who may use the cable medium. Nor is there any danger of physical interference between two cable speakers attempting to share the same channel. In light of these fundamental technological differences between broadcast and cable transmission, application of the more relaxed standard of scrutiny adopted in *Red Lion* [is] inapt when determining the First Amendment validity of cable regulation. . . .

"Although the Government acknowledges the substantial technological differences between broadcast and cable, it advances a second argument for application of the *Red Lion* framework to cable regulation. It asserts that the foundation of our broadcast jurisprudence is not the physical limitations of the electromagnetic spectrum, but rather the 'market dysfunction' that characterizes the broadcast market. Because the cable market is beset by a similar dysfunction, the Government maintains, the *Red Lion* standard of review should also apply to cable. While we agree that the cable market suffers certain structural impediments, the Government's argument is flawed in two respects. First, as discussed above, the special physical characteristics of broadcast transmission, not the economic characteristics of the broadcast market, are what underlies our broadcast jurisprudence. Second, the mere assertion of a dysfunction or failure in a speech market, without more, is not enough to shield a speech regulation from the First Amendment standards applicable to nonbroadcast media."

In his opinion for the Court, Justice Kennedy conceded that the "must carry" "provisions interfere with cable operators' editorial discretion by compelling them to offer carriage [to] broadcast stations," but emphasized that "the extent of the interference does not depend upon the content of the cable operators' programming." Justice Kennedy therefore concluded that "the appropriate standard by which to evaluate the constitutionality of [the 'must carry' provisions] is [not 'the most exacting level' of first amendment scrutiny, but] the intermediate level of scrutiny applicable to content-neutral restrictions that impose an incidental burden on speech," invoking the standard set forth in United States v. O'Brien, section E3, supra.

Applying this standard, Justice Kennedy, writing at this point only for himself and three other justices, remanded for further fact-finding on whether the "must carry" rules are in fact "necessary to protect the viability of broadcast television." Justice Kennedy explained that the government "must demonstrate that the recited harms are real, not merely conjectural, and that the regulation will in fact alleviate these harms in a direct and material way. . . ."

In a concurring opinion, Justice Stevens agreed "with most of Justice Kennedy's reasoning," but concluded that the "must carry" provisions should be upheld without a remand."

Justice O'Connor, joined by Justices Scalia, Thomas, and Ginsburg, dissented in part. At the outset, Justice O'Connor observed that the act "implicates the First Amendment rights of two classes of speakers": "First, it tells cable operators which programmers they must [carry]. Second, [it] deprives [cable programmers] of access to over one-third of an entire medium. Cable programmers may compete only for those channels that are not set aside by the must carry provisions. [It] is as if the government ordered all movie theaters to reserve at least one-third of their screening for films made by American production companies, or required all bookstores to devote one-third of their shelf space to nonprofit publishers."

Justice O'Connor argued further that the "must carry" provisions are content-based, rather than content-neutral, because various congressional findings supporting the legislation expressed "[preferences] for diversity of viewpoints, for localism, for educational programming, and for news and public affairs." Although the Court concluded that such findings showed "nothing more than the recognition that the services provided by broadcast television have some intrinsic value and, thus, are worth preserving against the threats posed by cable," Justice O'Connor argued that the "controversial judgment at the heart of the statute is not that broadcast television has some value, [but] that broadcasters should be preferred over cable programmers" because of the content of broadcast programming. In Justice O'Connor's view, the government's "interest in ensuring access to a multiplicity of diverse and antagonistic sources of information [is] directly tied to the content of what the speakers will likely say." Justice O'Connor therefore reasoned that the "must carry" provisions must be tested by "exacting" standards of content-based analysis and must be "narrowly tailored to a compelling state interest." Applying this standard, Justice O'Connor concluded that the provisions could not withstand constitutional scrutiny.

Note: Turner *and the Regulation of Cable*

1. Turner *and the problem of content.* Consider Justice O'Connor's argument that the "must carry" regulations are content-based because they were designed in part to promote "access to a multiplicity of diverse and antagonistic sources of information." Is a city council's decision to permit individuals to display messages in the interior of city-owned buses "content-based" because the city council's goal is to promote "access to a multiplicity of diverse and antagonistic sources of information"? Should it make a difference whether the challenged provision attempts to achieve this goal (a) by expanding opportunities for free expression in a facially content-neutral manner or (b) by providing expanded speech opportunities for particular, otherwise underrepresented, viewpoints in an explicitly content-based manner?

2. Turner *revisited.* In Turner Broadcasting System Inc. v. FCC, 520 U.S. 180 (1997) (*Turner II*), the Court, in a five-to-four decision, upheld under "intermediate scrutiny" the constitutionality of the must-carry provisions at issue in *Turner I*, affirming the district court's decision that the expanded record presented to it on remand from *Turner I* contained substantial evidence supporting Congress's predictive judgment that the must-carry provisions further important governmental interests in preserving cable carriage of local broadcast stations, and that the provisions are narrowly tailored to promote those interests. In reaching this conclusion, the Court, in an opinion by Justice Kennedy, emphasized that "we owe Congress' findings deference [because Congress] 'is far better equipped than the judiciary to "amass and evaluate the vast amounts of data" bearing upon' legislative questions." Thus, "we need not put our imprimatur on Congress' economic theory in order to validate the reasonableness of its judgment," nor should we "re-weigh the evidence de novo" or "replace Congress' factual predictions with our own."

Justice O'Connor, joined by Justices Scalia, Thomas, and Ginsburg, dissented. Justice O'Connor maintained that "the principal opinion" exhibits "an extraordinary and unwarranted deference for congressional judgments, a profound fear of delving into complex economic matters, and a willingness to substitute untested assumptions for evidence." As a consequence, the principal opinion "trivializes the First Amendment issue at stake in this case."

The bottom line seems to be that, in at least most respects, the Court will treat cable television as more analogous to the traditional print media for first amendment purposes than to the broadcast media. Is that a sensible conclusion?

Note: The First Amendment in Cyberspace

1. *New technologies and the first amendment.* As new technologies revolutionize communication, questions inevitably arise about how the first amendment should apply. *Red Lion* struggled with the novel challenges posed by broadcasting, and *Denver Area* wrestled with how to assess the special issues posed by cable. The Court encountered similar difficulties when it first considered motion pictures and sound trucks. Recall Kovacs v. Cooper, section E1 supra. What, then, of cyberspace? Consider the following views:

a. Fiss, In Search of a New Paradigm, 104 Yale L.J. 1613, 1614–1615 (1995):

[Much of current First Amendment analysis is premised] on an outmoded paradigm: the street corner speaker. [A] body of doctrine that did no more than protect the street corner speaker from the menacing reach of the police would leave the values served by the First Amendment vulnerable [and] largely unfulfilled. [But we are now in the midst] of a new technological revolution. [What] is happening is nothing less than a redefinition of the way we read and write, the way we talk to and correspond with one another [and] how we perform our roles as citizens. [We must begin the process of thinking] through the implications for the First Amendment of the technological revolution through which we are now living.

b. Krattenmaker and Powe, Converging First Amendment Principles for Converging Communications Media, 104 Yale L.J. 1719, 1721, 1725, 1726, 1740 (1995):

No matter how often one repeats the statement, it cannot be true that "[d]ifferent communications media [should be] treated differently for First Amendment purposes." Should everything we knew about regulation of books have been discarded once talking motion pictures were invented? Did discovery of the personal computer [render] obsolete everything the courts said about the First Amendment and broadcasting, or cable, or telephones? [Past] complaints will be prologue for future complaints about what creators place on, and users receive from, [cyberspace]. Some will complain that an insufficient amount of the appropriate type or quality of information is available. Others [will] complain that users may be accessing information they ought not have. [In responding to these familiar issues,] only a unitary First Amendment for all media will do. [The] general principles underlying regulation of the [traditional print] media should apply fully to the new as well as the old electronic communications media.

2. *The first amendment in cyberspace — some specific issues.*
a. Lessig, The Path of Cyberlaw, 104 Yale L.J. 1743, 1750, 1752 (1995):

[We] can see many good reasons why someone would want to remain anonymous. [One] wants to contribute to a political discussion without suffering the costs of unpopular views; one wants to find information without revealing that one needs that information; one wants to assume a role in certain discussion groups to explore an alternative identity. [Not] all anonymity, however, is so benign. Perfect anonymity makes perfect crime possible. The ability to appear invisibly on the network [certainly] will increase the incidence of those on the network who slander, or harass or assault. [A careful] balance will have to be drawn. [Already] the extremes are well staked, with some arguing that no regulation [of anonymity] should be permitted, and others arguing that only with regulation should [anonymity] be allowed.

b. Kreimer, Technologies of Protest: Insurgent Social Movements and the First Amendment in the Era of the Internet, 150 U. Penn. L. Rev. 119, 122–124 (2001):

Given the structure of twentieth-century communications media, established or well-financed contenders in the public arena [had] a built-in advantage: the cost of disseminating arguments or information to a broad audience threatened effectively to exclude outsiders from public debate. [The internet] has changed this dynamic, for [almost] any social movement can put up a website. [From] neo-Nazism and Christian Identity to gay liberation and disability rights, [the internet] facilitates challenges to the status quo. . . .

c. C. Sunstein, republic.com 8–9, 16, 54, 65, 71, 86 (2001):

[A] well-functioning system of free expression must meet two distinctive require-ments. First, people should be exposed to materials that they would not have chosen in advance. Unplanned [encounters] are central to democracy [and people should] often come across views and topics that they have not specifically selected. Second, [citizens] should have a range of common experiences. Without shared experi-ences, [people may] find it hard to understand one another. [There] are serious dangers in a system in which individuals [restrict] themselves to opinions and topics of their own choosing. . . .

The specialization of Websites [and discussion groups] is obviously important here. [For example], there are hundreds of Websites created [by] hate groups and extremist organizations [which] provide links to one another. [Such websites] are being used [to] reinforce existing convictions. [They are] permitting people [to] spread rumors, many of them paranoid and hateful. [This is an example of group polarization, which] refers to something very simple: After deliberation, people are likely to move toward a more extreme point in the direction to which the group's members were originally inclined. . . .

With respect to the Internet, [the] implication is that groups of like-minded people, engaged in discussion with one another, will end up thinking the same thing that they thought before — but in more extreme form. [Group] polarization is unquestionably occurring on the Internet, [which] is serving as a breeding ground for extremism. [For] citizens of a heterogeneous democracy, a fragmented com-munications market creates considerable dangers.

Would it be constitutional for government to require websites like Facebook to make "opposing viewpoint buttons" available to users? Such buttons would auto-matically allow a user, with the mere push of a button, to access viewpoints that oppose the ones she has just read. See C. Sunstein, #republic 232 (2017).

d. Leiter, Cleaning Cyber-Cesspools: Google and Free Speech, in S. Levmore and M. Nussbaum, eds., The Offensive Internet 155 (2010):

I shall use the term "cyber-cesspool" to refer to those places in cyberspace — chat rooms, websites, blogs, and often the comment sections of blogs — which are devoted in whole or in part to demeaning, harassing, and humiliating individuals.

[The] Internet is currently full of cyber-cesspools. [Since] cyber-cesspools are in large part beyond the reach of regulation [because] of constitutional protections, a number of commentators have suggested enhancing private remedies by, for example, making intermediaries — those who host blogs or perhaps even service providers — liable for tortious harms on their sites. This would require repeal of Section 250 of the Communications Decency Act (47 U.S.C §230), which provides that "No providers or user of an interactive computer service shall be treated as the publisher or speaker of any information provided by another information content provider." The effect of that simple provision has been to treat cyber-cesspools wholly differently from, for example, newspapers that decide to publish similar material. Whereas publishers of the latter are liable for the tortious letters or advertisements they publish [recall New York Times v. Sullivan, section D1 supra], owners of cyber-cesspools are held legally unaccountable for even the most noxious material on their sites, even when put on notice as to its potentially tortious nature. But why should blogs, whose circulation sometimes dwarfs that of many newspapers, be insulated from liability for actionable material they permit on their site?

3. *Indecency on the Internet.* In Reno v. American Civil Liberties Union, section D7, supra, the Court invalidated provisions of the Communications Decency Act of 1996 (CDA) that prohibited any person from sending over the Internet in a way that would be available to a person under eighteen years of age any "indecent" material or any material that "depicts or describes, in terms patently offensive as measured by contemporary community standards, sexual or excretory activities or organs." In distinguishing the Internet from broadcasting, the Court explained:

> [We have] observed that "[e]ach medium of expression . . . may present its own problems." Thus, some of our cases have recognized special justifications for regulation of the broadcast media that are not applicable to other speakers [citing, e.g., *Red Lion*; *Pacifica*]. In these cases, the Court relied on the history of extensive government regulation of the broadcast medium, the scarcity of available frequencies at its inception, and its "invasive" nature.
>
> Those factors are not present in cyberspace. Neither before nor after the enactment of the CDA have the vast democratic fora of the Internet been subject to the type of government supervision and regulation that has attended the broadcast industry. Moreover, the Internet is not as "invasive" as radio or television. The District Court specifically found that "[c]ommunications over the Internet do not 'invade' an individual's home or appear on one's computer screen unbidden. Users seldom encounter content 'by accident.'" [Finally], unlike the conditions that prevailed when Congress first authorized regulation of the broadcast spectrum, the Internet can hardly be considered a "scarce" expressive commodity. It provides relatively unlimited, low cost capacity for communication of all kinds. [Our] cases provide no basis for qualifying the level of First Amendment scrutiny that should be applied to this medium.

Should local community standards apply in deciding whether sexually explicit material posted on the internet is "obscene"? See Ashcroft v. American Civil Liberties Union, section D6, supra.

4. *Registered sex offenders and the internet.* Can a state constitutionally make it a crime for registered sex offenders to access any "commercial social networking Web site where the sex offender knows that the site permits minor children to become members or to create or maintain personal Web pages"? In *Packingham v. North Carolina*, 582 U.S. ___ (2017), the Court, in an opinion by Justice Kennedy, held such a law unconstitutional because it forbids registered sex

offenders from accessing even such websites as Facebook, LinkedIn, and Twitter. Noting that cyberspace is "the most important" venue today "for the exchange of views," the Court held that even though the challenged statute was "content neutral," it was not "narrowly tailored to serve a significant government interest." Although recognizing that the state "may pass valid laws to protect children [from] abuse," and although assuming that "the First Amendment permits a State to enact specific, narrowly tailored laws that prohibit a sex offender from engaging in conduct that often presages sexual crime, like contacting a minor or using a website to gather information about a minor," the Court held that the statute at issue in this case was far too "sweeping" to meet the demands of the first amendment. Indeed, this statute, the Court observed "enacts a prohibition unprecedented in the scope of First Amendment speech it burdens" because "with one broad scope" it "bars access to what for many are the principal sources for knowing current events, checking ads for employment, speaking and listening in the modern public square, and otherwise exploring the vast realms of human thought and knowledge."

In a separate concurring opinion, Justice Alito, joined by Chief Justice Roberts and Justice Thomas, agreed that the North Carolina law swept too broadly, but suggested that, because the internet is "a powerful tool for the would-be-child abuser," the state should have broader leeway to address this problem than implied in the majority opinion.

5. *The liability of cable and internet carriers for the speech of users.* In what circumstances, if any, should cable or internet carriers be liable for the libelous, obscene, or otherwise actionable speech they carry? Consider the liability of (a) a store that sells typewriters for the messages typed by purchasers; (b) a telephone company for the speech of callers; (c) a bookstore for the contents of the books it sells; (d) a news vendor for the contents of the newspapers it sells; (e) a newspaper or magazine for the statements made by guest columnists; (f) a cable operator for the programs it carries; and (g) a computer network, such as CompuServe, for the messages it transmits. Should the standards of liability differ across these different situations? Should it matter whether the defendant exercises "editorial" control? Should the defendants in all or some of these cases be liable only "if they have actual notice that the speech has previously been adjudicated illegal or unprotected"? Myerson, Authors, Editors, and Uncommon Carriers: Identifying the "Speaker" within the New Media, 71 Notre Dame L. Rev. 79, 122 (1995).

Section 230(c)(1) of the Communications Decency Act of 1996 provides immunity from liability for providers and users of an "interactive computer service" who publish information provided by others. Facebook, for example, unlike the *New York Times*, is not liable for otherwise actionable threats, libels, or invasions of privacy posted on its site by users. Does this make sense? Consider Tushnet, Internet Exceptionalism: An Overview from General Constitutional Law, 56 Wm. & M. L. Rev. 1637, 1665 (2015): "Suppose [that] §230 were replaced by a regime requiring that intermediaries do something to limit the distribution of harmful material — that they adopt a different business model. The question is whether such business-model regulation would be constitutionally permissible, even though the regime might be described as one in which the regulation was adopted for the purpose of restricting the dissemination of harmful information."

6. *Freedom of the press in a global society.* Consider L. Bollinger, Uninhibited, Robust, and Wide-Open: A Free Press for a New Century 105–106, 116–117 (2010):

[We] are facing the emergence of a global society, with the technological capacity to provide a free and independent press to a world in desperate need of such an institution, but there is also a myriad of laws, policies, practices, and conditions that inhibit and impede that from happening. Without a central, overriding system of constitutional protections, there is a risk of a collapse to the bottom, where jurisdictions that have the least degree of freedom will undermine the freedom of those that value it the most. . . .

This situation poses a significant challenge to the United States and the world. For a society uniquely committed to unconstrained public debate and for which knowledge of the entire world is increasingly vital, we must now see how we can achieve this goal — to make it a shared principle as well as a working reality — in a world that is not in full agreement with the American conception of a free press. [To help achieve this, the Supreme Court must] begin the process of making the shift from the constitutional paradigm of a national public forum to a global one.

Note: Free Expression — Final Thoughts

Consider Post, Recuperating First Amendment Doctrine, 47 Stan. L. Rev. 1249, 1249–1250 (1995):

Contemporary First Amendment doctrine [is] striking chiefly for its superficiality, its internal incoherence, its distressing failure to facilitate constructive judicial engagement with significant contemporary social issues connected with freedom of speech. . . . [It] has become increasingly a doctrine of words merely, and not of things.

On the other hand, consider S. Shiffrin, The First Amendment, Democracy, and Romance 159 (1990):

American citizens not only feel a deep emotional attachment to the country, but also [a] sense of pride about the first amendment. The first amendment speaks to the kind of people we are and the kind of people we aspire to be. [It] plays an important role in the construction of an appealing story, a story about a nation that promotes independent people, a nation that affords a place of refuge for peoples all over the globe, a nation that welcomes the iconoclast, a nation that respects, tolerates, and even sponsors dissent. [The] image called up by this national picture [encourages] us to picture Walt Whitman's citizenry — vibrant, diverse, vital, stubborn, and independent. It encourages us to believe with Emerson that "America is the idea of emancipation."

A quarter-century later, Shiffrin offered a rather different assessment: "The main problem with the First Amendment [is] that it overprotects speech. [Free] speech doctrine downplays the harm that speech can cause. Indeed, its most problematic assumption is that free speech is considered to be so valuable that it almost always outweighs other values with which it comes into conflict. Of course, free speech is ordinarily valuable, but there is no good reason to assume that it invariably should outweigh other values. Nor is that assumption harmless."

Shiffrin goes on to note that first amendment doctrine unjustifiably runs roughshod over important competing values by protecting "privacy-invading speech," "racist speech," "violent video games," "commercial advertising that encourages a materialistic and hedonistic culture," and political contributions and expenditures that enable "corporations and wealthy individuals" to undermine democracy and thwart "the will of the people and the common good." S. Shiffrin, What's Wrong With the First Amendment 1–2 (2016).

On the other hand, consider Abrams, The Soul of the First Amendment xvi–xvii, xxiii (2017):

> The uniquely high level of American protection for free expression does not necessarily mean that American society is better served in all respects. [Nevertheless,] adopting a legal system that defends speech in a less exuberant manner than the United States has consequences. [There] is no doubt that a price is paid, sometimes a serious one, for [America's uniquely robust protection of free speech]; the American approach is not oblivious to that price but insists (as other countries do not) that the dangers of permitting the government to decide what may and may not be said, far more often than not, outweigh any benefits that may result from suppressing or punishing [such] speech. [Indeed, the] First Amendment is the rock star of the American Constitution.

On how the Court worked out the meaning of the first amendment over time, consider Kozel, Precedent and Speech, 102 Iowa L. Rev. 1187 (2017):

> [The] question is why deference to precedent — a feature the Court has described as foundational to the rule of law — is so readily overcome in the First Amendment context. [If] the purpose of stare decisis is to promote the law's stability, predictability, and impersonality, the doctrine cannot wilt at the mention of free speech. Sometimes it is better for the law to remain settled despite its failure to protect expressive liberty as vigorously as today's Court may deem appropriate.
>
> [Indeed, without] meaningful deference to precedent, judicial interpretations of the First Amendment will fluctuate [with changes in the makeup of the Court, as illustrated perhaps most dramatically by the Court's campaign finance decisions.] Stare decisis reflects [a] conception of the law [in] which constitutional rules survive changes in judicial personnel. [Sometimes] it is better for the law to remain settled despite its failure to protect expressive liberty as vigorously as today's Court may deem appropriate.

Finally, consider D. Strauss, The Living Constitution 52–53 (2010):

> [The] First Amendment — that is, the principles protecting free speech — has been a tremendous success story in American constitutional law. But where did these successful principles come from? They did not come from the text of the Constitution. The First Amendment was part of the Constitution for a century and a half before the central principles of the American regime of free speech [became] established in the law. Nor did those principles come from the original understandings. [To] the extent that we can determine the views of [the Framers], they did not think they were establishing a system of freedom of expression resembling what we have today.
>
> The central principles of the American system of freedom of expression, in other words, are not the product of a moment of inspired constitutional genius 200-plus years ago. We owe those principles, instead, to the living, common law Constitution. The central features of First Amendment law were hammered out in fits and starts, in a series of judicial decisions and extrajudicial developments, over the course of the twentieth century. The story of the emergence of the American constitutional law of free speech is a story of evolution and precedent, trial and error — a demonstration of how the living Constitution works.

VIII

The Constitution and Religion

The first amendment bars Congress from making laws "respecting an establishment of religion, or prohibiting the free exercise thereof." In addition to discussing doctrinal approaches to church/state issues, this chapter examines whether the relative clarity of the constitutional text, or its history, eases the task of constitutional adjudication or reduces the necessity for other theoretical underpinnings to the constitutional law of religion.

This chapter has four sections. The first provides historical background and outlines the general approaches that courts and commentators have taken to the religion clauses. The second examines problems of establishment, highlighting the tension between the idea that the establishment clause requires some degree of separation between church and state and a history that includes substantial state support of religious activities. The third section deals with problems of free exercise, focusing on the degree to which government must or may adjust its programs to claims that the programs burden the free exercise of religion. The fourth deals with the constitutional status of legislative efforts to accommodate religion through laws that arguably relieve burdens on the free exercise of religion.

A. INTRODUCTION: HISTORICAL AND ANALYTICAL OVERVIEW

EVERSON v. BOARD OF EDUCATION, 330 U.S. 1 (1947). New Jersey authorized its local school boards to repay parents with children in private schools for the cost of bus transportation to the schools. Most of the private schools were Roman Catholic parochial institutions. By a five-to-four vote, the Court upheld the statute against an establishment clause challenge, concluding that the state could pay the fares "as part of a general program under which it pays the fares of pupils attending public and other schools." This satisfied the first amendment's requirement that "the state [be] neutral in its relations with groups of religious believers and non-believers." Justice Black's opinion for the Court "[reviewed] the background and environment of" the first amendment: "A large

1431

proportion of the early settlers of this country came here from Europe to escape the bondage of laws which compelled them to support and attend government-favored churches. The centuries immediately before and contemporaneous with the colonization of America had been filled with turmoil, civil strife, and persecutions, generated in large part by established sects determined to maintain their absolute political and religious supremacy. With the power of government supporting them, at various times and places, Catholics had persecuted Protestants, Protestants had persecuted Catholics, Protestant sects had persecuted other Protestant sects, Catholics of one shade of belief had persecuted Catholics of another shade of belief, and all of these had from time to time persecuted Jews. In efforts to force loyalty to whatever group happened to be on top and in league with the government of a particular time and place, men and women had been fined, cast in jail, cruelly tortured, and killed. . . .

"These practices of the old world were transplanted to and began to thrive in the soil of the new America. The very charters granted by the English Crown to the individuals and companies designated to make the laws which would control the destinies of the colonials authorized these individuals and companies to erect religious establishments which all, whether believers or non-believers, would be required to support and attend. An exercise of this authority was accompanied by a repetition of many of the old-world practices and persecutions. Catholics found themselves hounded and proscribed because of their faith; Quakers who followed their conscience went to jail; Baptists were peculiarly obnoxious to certain dominant Protestant sects; men and women of varied faiths who happened to be in a minority in a particular locality were persecuted because they steadfastly persisted in worshipping God only as their own consciences dictated. And all of these dissenters were compelled to pay tithes and taxes to support government-sponsored churches whose ministers preached inflammatory sermons designed to strengthen and consolidate the established faith by generating a burning hatred against dissenters.

"These practices became so commonplace as to shock the freedom-loving colonials into a feeling of abhorrence. The imposition of taxes to pay ministers' salaries and to build and maintain churches and church property aroused their indignation. It was these feelings which found expression in the First Amendment. [Virginia,] where the established church had achieved a dominant influence in political affairs and where many excesses attracted wide public attention, provided a great stimulus and able leadership for the movement. The people there, as elsewhere, reached the conviction that individual religious liberty could be achieved best under a government which was stripped of all power to tax, to support, or otherwise to assist any or all religions, or to interfere with the beliefs of any religious individual or group.

"The movement toward this end reached its dramatic climax in Virginia in 1785–86 when the Virginia legislative body was about to renew Virginia's tax levy for the support of the established church. Thomas Jefferson and James Madison led the fight against this tax. Madison wrote his great Memorial and Remonstrance against the law. In it, he eloquently argued that a true religion did not need the support of law; that no person, either believer or non-believer, should be taxed to support a religious institution of any kind; that the best interest of a society required that the minds of men always be wholly free; and that cruel persecutions were the inevitable result of government-established religions. Madison's Remonstrance received stronger support throughout Virginia, and [when] the proposed tax measure [came] up for consideration [it] not only died in committee, but the Assembly enacted the famous 'Virginia Bill for Religious Liberty' originally written by Thomas Jefferson. The preamble to that Bill stated among other things that

> Almighty God hath created the mind free; that all attempts to influence it by temporal punishments or burthens, or by civil incapacitations, tend only to beget habits of hypocrisy and meanness, and are a departure from the plan of the Holy author of our religion, who being Lord both of body and mind, yet chose not to propagate it by coercions on either . . . ; that to compel a man to furnish contributions of money for the propagation of opinions which he disbelieves, is sinful and tyrannical; that even the forcing him to support this or that teacher of his own religious persuasion, is depriving him of the comfortable liberty of giving his contributions to the particular pastor, whose morals he would make his pattern. . . .

And the statute itself enacted

> That no man shall be compelled to frequent or support any religious worship, place, or ministry whatsoever, nor shall be enforced, restrained, molested, or burthened in his body or goods, nor shall otherwise suffer on account of his religious opinions or belief. . . .

"[The] provisions of the First Amendment, in the drafting and adoption of which Madison and Jefferson played such leading roles, had the same objective and were intended to provide the same protection against governmental intrusion on religious liberty as the Virginia statute. . . ."

The opinion summarized the meaning of the establishment clause: "[It] means at least this: Neither a state nor the Federal Government can set up a church. Neither can pass laws which aid one religion, aid all religions, or prefer one religion over another. Neither can force nor influence a person to go to or to remain away from church against his will or force him to profess a belief or disbelief in any religion. No person can be punished for entertaining or professing religious beliefs or disbeliefs, for church attendance or non-attendance. No tax in any amount, large or small, can be levied to support any religious activities or institutions, whatever they may be called, or whatever form they may adopt to teach or practice religion. Neither a state nor the Federal Government can, openly or secretly, participate in the affairs of any religious organizations or groups and vice versa. In the words of Jefferson, the clause was intended to erect 'a wall of separation between Church and State.' Reynolds v. United States [98 U.S. at 164]."

The dissenters agreed with Justice Black's description of the relevant history, but argued that the New Jersey statute breached the "wall" of separation. Questions regarding state aid to nonpublic education are discussed in more detail in section B4 infra.

Note: The History of the Religion Clauses

1. *Two views of the Memorial and Remonstrance.* In Rosenberger v. Rectors & Visitors of the University of Virginia, 515 U.S. 819 (1995), Justices Thomas (concurring) and Souter (in dissent) offered competing interpretations of the establishment clause's history.

Summarizing the view of legal commentators, Justice Thomas wrote, "For some, the experience in Virginia is consistent with the view that the Framers saw the Establishment Clause simply as a prohibition on governmental preferences for some religious faiths over others. Other commentators have rejected this view, concluding that the Establishment Clause forbids not only government preferences for some religious sects over others, but also government preferences for religion over irreligion." Justice Thomas found "much to commend the former view. [The] funding provided by the Virginia assessment was to be extended only to Christian sects, and the Remonstrance seized on this defect: 'Who does not see that the same authority which can establish Christianity, in exclusion of all other Religions, may establish with the same ease any particular sect of Christians, in exclusion of all other Sects.'" He continued:

> [Even] if Madison believed that the principle of non-establishment of religion precluded government financial support for religion per se (in the sense of government benefits specifically targeting religion), there is no indication that at the time of the framing he took the [extreme] view that the government must discriminate against religious adherents by excluding them from more generally available financial subsidies.

Justice Thomas pointed to "historical examples of funding that date back to the time of the founding. [Both] Houses of the First Congress elected chaplains." There were "other, less familiar examples of what amount to direct funding [in] early Acts of Congress. See, e.g., Act of Feb. 20, 1833 (authorizing the State of Ohio to sell 'all or any part of the lands heretofore reserved and appropriated by Congress for the support of religion within the Ohio Company's . . . purchases . . . and to invest the money arising from the sale thereof, in some productive fund; the proceeds of which shall be for ever annually applied . . . for the support of religion within the several townships for which said lands were originally reserved and set apart, and for no other use or purpose whatsoever')."

Justice Souter offered a different interpretation of Madison's position. "[The] bill [to which the Remonstrance was directed would] have allowed a taxpayer to refuse to appropriate his levy to any religious society, in which case the legislature was to use these unappropriated sums to fund 'seminaries of learning.' While some of these seminaries undoubtedly would have been religious in character, others would not have been, as a seminary was generally understood at the time to be 'any school, academy, college or [university].' N. Webster, An American Dictionary of the English Language (1st ed. 1828). [The] fact that the bill, if passed, would have funded secular as well as religious instruction did nothing to soften Madison's opposition to it."

Justice Souter continued, "Nor is it fair to argue that Madison opposed the bill only because it treated religious groups unequally. [Madison] strongly inveighed against the proposed aid for religion for a host of reasons [and] many of those reasons would have applied whether or not the state aid was being distributed equally among sects, and whether or not the aid was going to those sects in the context of an evenhanded government program. See, e.g., ¶ 1 ('In matters of Religion, no man's right is abridged by the institution of Civil Society, and . . . Religion is wholly exempt from its cognizance'); ¶ 7 ('Experience witnesseth that ecclesiastical establishments, instead of maintaining the purity and efficacy of Religion, have had a contrary operation').

[Madison's] Remonstrance did not argue for a bill distributing aid to all sects and religions on an equal basis, and the outgrowth of the Remonstrance and the defeat of the Virginia assessment was not such a bill; rather, it was the Virginia Bill for Establishing Religious Freedom, which [proscribed] the use of tax dollars for religious purposes."

2. *Some historical detail.* Justice Souter's concurring opinion in Lee v. Weisman, 505 U.S. 577 (1992), offered this view of the first amendment's background and early history:

> When James Madison arrived at the First Congress with a series of proposals to amend the National Constitution, one of the provisions read that "the civil rights of none shall be abridged on account of religious belief or worship, nor shall any national religion be established, nor shall the full and equal rights of conscience be in any manner, or on any pretext, infringed." Madison's language [was] sent to a Select Committee of the House, which, without explanation, changed it to read that "no religion shall be established by law, nor shall the equal rights of conscience be infringed." Thence the proposal went to the Committee of the Whole, which was in turn dissatisfied with the Select Committee's language and adopted an alternative proposed by Samuel Livermore of New Hampshire: "Congress shall make no laws touching religion, or infringing the rights of conscience." . . .
>
> The House rewrote the amendment once more before sending it to the Senate, this time adopting, without recorded debate, language derived from a proposal by Fisher Ames of Massachusetts: "Congress shall make no law establishing Religion, or prohibiting the free exercise thereof, nor shall the rights of conscience be infringed." [The] House rejected the Select Committee's version, which arguably ensured only that "no religion" enjoyed an official preference over others, and deliberately chose instead a prohibition extending to laws establishing "religion" in general. . . .
>
> [In] September 1789, the Senate [briefly] entertained this language: "Congress shall make no law establishing One Religious Sect or Society in preference to others, nor shall the rights of conscience be infringed." After rejecting two minor amendments to that proposal, the Senate dropped it altogether. [Six] days later, the Senate went half circle and adopted its narrowest language yet: "Congress shall make no law establishing articles of faith or a mode of worship, or prohibiting the free exercise of religion." The Senate sent this proposal to the House. . . .
>
> [The] House rejected the Senate's version of the Establishment Clause. [The] House conferees ultimately won out, persuading the Senate to accept [the] final text of the Religion Clauses. [Unlike] the earliest House drafts or the final Senate proposal, the prevailing language is not limited to laws respecting an establishment of "a religion," "a national religion," "one religious sect," or specific "articles of faith."[2]
>
> What we thus know of the Framers' experience underscores the observation [that] confining the Establishment Clause to a prohibition on preferential aid "requires a premise that the Framers were extraordinarily bad drafters — that they believed one thing but adopted language that said something substantially

---

2. Some commentators have suggested that by targeting laws respecting "an" establishment of religion, the Framers adopted the very nonpreferentialist position whose much clearer articulation they repeatedly rejected. See, e.g., R. Cord, Separation of Church and State 11–12. Yet the indefinite article before the word "establishment" is better seen as evidence that the Clause forbids any kind of establishment, including a nonpreferential one. If the Framers had wished, for some reason, to use the indefinite term to achieve a narrow meaning for the Clause, they could far more aptly have placed it before the word "religion." See Laycock, "Nonpreferential" Aid to Religion: A False Claim About Original Intent, 27 Wm. & Mary L. Rev. 875, 884–885 (1986).

different, and that they did so after repeatedly attending to the choice of language." Laycock, "Nonpreferential" Aid. . . .[3]

While some argue that the Framers added the word "respecting" simply to foreclose federal interference with State establishments of religion, the language sweeps more broadly than that. In Madison's words, the Clause in its final form forbids "everything like" a national religious establishment, and after incorporation, it forbids "everything like" a State religious establishment. The sweep is broad enough that Madison himself characterized congressional provisions for legislative and military chaplains as unconstitutional "establishments." . . .

The Framers adopted the Religion Clauses in response to a long tradition of coercive state support for religion, particularly in the form of tax assessments, but their special antipathy to religious coercion did not exhaust their hostility to the features and incidents of establishment. Indeed, Jefferson and Madison opposed any political appropriation of religion, and [they] did not always temper their rhetoric with distinctions between coercive and noncoercive state action. When, for example, Madison criticized Virginia's general assessment bill, he invoked principles antithetical to all state efforts to promote religion. An assessment, he wrote, is improper not simply because it forces people to donate "three pence" to religion, but, more broadly, because "it is itself a signal of persecution. It degrades from the equal rank of Citizens all those whose opinions in Religion do not bend to those of the Legislative authority." J. Madison, Memorial and Remonstrance. . . .

[Early] Presidents included religious messages in their inaugural and Thanksgiving Day addresses. [However, Americans] today find such proclamations less controversial than did the founding generation. President Jefferson [steadfastly] refused to issue Thanksgiving proclamations of any kind, in part because he thought they violated the Religion Clauses. Letter from Thomas Jefferson to Rev. S. Miller (Jan. 23, 1808) . . . :

> It is only proposed that I should recommend, not prescribe a day of fasting & prayer. That is, that I should indirectly assume to the U.S. an authority over religious exercises which the Constitution has directly precluded from them. It must be meant too that this recommendation is to carry some authority, and to be sanctioned by some penalty on those who disregard it; not indeed of fine and imprisonment, but of some degree of proscription perhaps in public opinion.

By condemning such non-coercive state practices that, in "recommending" the majority faith, demean religious dissenters "in public opinion," Jefferson necessarily condemned what, in modern terms, we call official endorsement of religion. He accordingly construed the Establishment Clause to forbid not simply state coercion, but also state endorsement, of religious belief and observance.[5] And if he

---

3. In his dissent in Wallace v. Jaffree, 472 U.S. 38 (1985), the Chief Justice rested his non-preferentialist interpretation partly on the post-ratification actions of the early national government. Aside from the willingness of some (but not all) early presidents to issue ceremonial religious proclamations, which were at worst trivial breaches of the establishment clause, he cited such seemingly preferential aid as a treaty provision, signed by Jefferson, authorizing federal subsidization of a Roman Catholic priest and church for the Kaskaskia Indians. But this proves too much, for if the establishment clause permits a special appropriation of tax money for the religious activities of a particular sect, it forbids virtually nothing. See Laycock, "Nonpreferential" Aid 915. Although evidence of historical practice can indeed furnish valuable aid in the interpretation of contemporary language, acts like the one in question prove only that public officials [can] turn a blind eye to constitutional principle.

5. [The] "proscription" to which Jefferson referred was [by] the public and not the government, whose only action was a noncoercive recommendation. And one can call any act of endorsement a form of coercion, but only if one is willing to dilute the meaning of "coercion" until there is no meaning left. Jefferson's position straightforwardly contradicts the claim that a showing of "coercion," under any normal definition, is a prerequisite to a successful establishment clause claim. At the same time, Jefferson's practice, like Madison's, sometimes diverged from principle, for he did include religious references in his inaugural speeches. Homer nodded. . . .

opposed impersonal presidential addresses for inflicting "proscription in public opinion," all the more would he have condemned less diffuse expressions of official endorsement.

During his first three years in office, James Madison also refused to call for days of thanksgiving and prayer, though later, amid the political turmoil of the War of 1812, he did so on four separate occasions. Upon retirement, in an essay condemning as an unconstitutional "establishment" the use of public money to support congressional and military chaplains, he concluded that "religious proclamations by the Executive recommending thanksgivings & fasts are shoots from the same root with the legislative acts reviewed. Altho' recommendations only, they imply a religious agency, making no part of the trust delegated to political rulers." . . .

Madison's failure to keep pace with his principles in the face of congressional pressure cannot erase the principles. He admitted to backsliding, and explained that he had made the content of his wartime proclamations inconsequential enough to mitigate much of their impropriety. . . .

To be sure, the leaders of the young Republic engaged in some of the practices that separationists like Jefferson and Madison criticized. The First Congress did hire institutional chaplains, and Presidents Washington and Adams unapologetically marked days of "public thanksgiving and prayer." Yet in the face of the separationist dissent, those practices prove, at best, that the Framers simply did not share a common understanding of the Establishment Clause, and, at worst, that they, like other politicians, could raise constitutional ideals one day and turn their backs on them the next. . . .

3. *A challenge to originalist approaches.* What are the implications of the observation (if correct) that the historical materials "prove [that] the Framers [did] not share a common understanding"? Consider these observations by Justice Brennan, concurring in Abington School District v. Schempp, 374 U.S. 203 (1963), which held unconstitutional the practice of devotional Bible-reading in public schools:

[An] awareness of history and an appreciation of the aims of the Founding Fathers do not always resolve concrete problems. [A] more fruitful inquiry [is] whether the practices [threaten] those consequences which the Framers deeply feared; whether, in short, they tend to promote that type of interdependence between religion and state which the First Amendment was designed to prevent. . . .

[Our] religious composition makes us a vastly more diverse people than were our forefathers. They knew differences chiefly among Protestant sects. Today the Nation is far more heterogeneous religiously. [In] the face of such profound changes, practices which may have been objectionable to no one in the time of Jefferson and Madison may today be highly offensive to many persons, the deeply devout and the nonbelievers alike.

Consider the proposition that social change, such as the expansion of government, ought to affect the interpretation of both religion clauses: When government was confined to the enforcement of the common law and relatively little else, its potential for adversely affecting religious exercises was small, and a regime of government neutrality with respect to religion might have allowed religious liberty to flourish; an expansive government means that neutral government rules may interfere substantially with religious liberty. To what extent do current controversies arise in circumstances threatening the kinds of public disorder with which the framers were familiar? Consider as well the general arguments originalists make against interpretation predicated on the (imputed) general purposes of constitutional provisions.

4. *Other traditions.* L. Tribe, American Constitutional Law 1158–1160 (2d ed. 1988), describes another tradition:

> [The] evangelical view (associated primarily with Roger Williams) [was] that "worldly corruptions [might] consume the churches if sturdy fences against the wilderness were not maintained." . . . Roger Williams saw separation largely as a vehicle for protecting churches against the state. To the extent that it was possible to accept state aid without state control, he urged cooperation; indeed, he argued that the state must "countenance, encourage, and supply" those in religious service. Thus, his view has been called one of positive toleration, imposing on the state the burden of fostering a climate conducive to all religion.
>
> Thomas Jefferson, in contrast, saw separation as a means of protecting the state from the church. [It] was Jefferson's conviction that only the complete separation of religion from politics would eliminate the formal influence of religious institutions and provide for a free choice among political views; he therefore urged the strictest "wall of separation between church and state."
>
> James Madison believed that both religion and government could best achieve their high purposes if each were left free from the other within its respective sphere; he thus urged that the "tendency to a usurpation on one side or the other, or to a corrupting coalition or alliance between them, will be best guarded against by an entire abstinence [*sic*] of the Government from interference in any way whatever, beyond the necessity of preserving public order, & protecting each sect against trespass on its legal rights by others."

For an analysis of Williams's views, see Hall, Roger Williams and the Foundations of Religious Liberty, 71 B.U. L. Rev. 455 (1991).

In Zelman v. Simmons-Harris, 536 U.S. 639 (2002), criticizing the Court's decision upholding a school voucher program that allowed vouchers to be used at religiously affiliated schools, Justice Souter discussed how, in his view, the risk that religion would be corrupted by government aid was "already being realized." He pointed to statutory provisions meaning that "the school may not give admission preferences to children who are members of the patron faith," suggesting that "a participating religious school may [be] forbidden to choose a member of its own clergy to serve as teacher or principal over a layperson of a different religion claiming equal qualification for the job," and suggesting that participating schools might not be allowed to "[teach] traditionally legitimate articles of faith as to the error, sinfulness, or ignorance of others, if they want government money for their schools." What basis is there for a constitutional rule that protects religious institutions from making decisions that judges believe to be contrary to the institutions' long-term interests?

For a discussion of the anticorruption approach to the nonestablishment principle, see Koppelman, Corruption of Religion and the Establishment Clause, 50 Wm. & Mary L. Rev. 1831, 1896–1898 (2009), describing the anticorruption approach's claims:

> Religious behavior, without sincerity, is devoid of religious value. [Establishment] exaggerates the importance of doctrinal divisions. [The] state is an unreliable source of religious authority. [Religious] teachings are likely to be altered, in a pernicious way, if the teachers are agents of the state. [Establishment] tends to produce undeserved contempt toward religion. [The] legitimate authority of the state does not extend to religious questions.

With respect to the claim about altering religious teachings, why should religious leaders be precluded from considering or reconsidering their faith commitments in light of government policies? Should the fact that the anticorruption argument is founded on a contestable theological view rule it out as a general approach to the religion clauses? Do other general approaches have analogous religious foundations?

5. *Federalism and incorporation.* Recall that the bill of rights was adopted to allay fears that the Constitution's grants of power might authorize Congress to act in matters that should be left to the states. When the first amendment was adopted, several states had churches established by law. See W. Katz, Religion and American Constitutions 8–10 (1964) (arguing that the religion clauses were designed to bar Congress from interfering with existing establishments in the states).

The framers' concern for federalism and the language of the fourteenth amendment pose some problems for the use of the amendment to make the religion clauses applicable to the states. Consider Justice Brennan's argument in *Schempp:*

> It has been suggested [that] absorption of the First Amendment's ban against congressional legislation "respecting an establishment of religion" is conceptually impossible because the Framers meant the Establishment Clause also to foreclose any attempt by Congress to disestablish the existing official state churches. [But] the last of the formal state establishments was dissolved more than three decades before the Fourteenth Amendment was ratified, and thus the problem of protecting official state churches from federal encroachments could hardly have been any concern of those who framed the post-Civil War Amendments. [The] Fourteenth Amendment created a panoply of new federal rights from the protection of citizens of the various States. And among those rights was freedom from such state governmental involvement in the affairs of religion as the Establishment Clause had originally foreclosed on the part of Congress.
>
> It has also been suggested that the "liberty" guaranteed by the Fourteenth Amendment logically cannot absorb the Establishment Clause because that clause is not one of the provisions of the Bill of Rights which in terms protects a "freedom" of the individual. [This] contention [underestimates] the role of the Establishment Clause as a co-guarantor, with the Free Exercise Clause, of religious liberty. The Framers did not entrust the liberty of religious beliefs to either clause alone. . . .
>
> Finally, it has been contended that absorption of the Establishment Clause is precluded by the absence of any intention on the part of the Framers of the Fourteenth Amendment to circumscribe the residual powers of the States to aid religious activities and institutions in ways which fell short of formal establishments. That argument relies in part upon the express terms of the abortive Blaine Amendment — proposed several years after the adoption of the Fourteenth Amendment — which would have added to the First Amendment a provision that "[n]o State shall make any law respecting an establishment of religion. . . ." Such a restriction would have been superfluous, it is said, if the Fourteenth Amendment had already made the Establishment Clause binding upon the States.
>
> The argument proves too much, for the Fourteenth Amendment's protection of the free exercise of religion can hardly be questioned; yet the Blaine Amendment would also have added an explicit protection against state laws abridging that liberty. [Further,] the religious liberty embodied in the Fourteenth Amendment would not be viable if the Constitution were interpreted to forbid only establishments ordained by Congress.

Justice Thomas discussed the federalism interpretation and its relationship to incorporation in his opinion concurring in the judgment in Elk Grove Unified

School District v. Newdow, 542 U.S. 1 (2004). He would interpret the fourteenth amendment to protect a "liberty interest of being free from coercive state establishments," and observed that such an interpretation might imply that "anything that would violate the incorporated establishment clause would actually violate the free exercise clause, further calling into doubt the utility of incorporating the establishment clause."

Note: General Approaches to the Religion Clauses

The preceding material indicates that the religion clauses deal with the general area of religious liberty, though in differing ways. Is it useful to develop an overall approach to their interpretation? In considering the following efforts at synthesis, it may help to keep in mind the following questions about each approach: Would the approach permit Congress to exempt from the Social Security or income tax those who base their objections to payment on religious grounds? Would it require Congress to do so? Would the approach permit Congress to subsidize the operation of social services by church-related institutions? Would it require Congress to do so?

1. *Strict separation*. The clauses could be read to erect an absolute barrier to formal interdependence of religion and the state. Religious institutions could receive no aid whatever, direct or indirect, from the state. Nor could the state adjust its secular programs to alleviate burdens the programs placed on believers.

Strict separation has been questioned under both clauses. As to establishment, the Court in *Everson* argued that

> state-paid policemen, detailed to protect children going to and from church schools from the very real hazards of traffic, would serve much the same purpose and accomplish much the same result as state provisions intended to guarantee free transportation of a kind which the state deems to be best for the school children's welfare. And parents might refuse to risk their children to the danger of traffic accidents going to and from parochial schools, the approaches to which were not protected by policemen. Similarly, parents might be reluctant to permit their children to attend schools which the state had cut off from such general government services as ordinary police and fire protection, connections for sewage disposal, public highways and sidewalks. Of course, cutting off church schools from these services, so separate and so indisputably marked off from the religious function, would make it far more difficult for the schools to operate. But [the] First Amendment [requires] the state to be a neutral in its relations with groups of religious believers and non-believers; it does not require the state to be their adversary. State power is no more to be used so as to handicap religions than it is to favor them.

What is the relevance, if any, of the fact that "church schools" could hire private security guards and obtain other services from private providers, at the cost of increasing their tuition or subsidies from donations to the church?

2. *Strict neutrality*. Consider Kurland, Of Church and State and the Supreme Court, 29 U. Chi. L. Rev. 1, 5 (1961): "[Religion] may not be used as a basis for classification for purposes of governmental action, whether that action be the conferring of rights or privileges or the imposition of duties or obligations." Thus, states must use purely secular criteria as the basis for their actions. Strict neutrality does not permit, much less require, accommodation of secular programs to

religious belief. It does permit aid to religious institutions that satisfy the purely secular criteria for participation in the program, at least if the courts are unwilling to conclude that the criteria were not concealed methods of using religion as a basis for the program.

3. *Noncoercion and anti-indoctrination.* Consider Schwarz, No Imposition of Religion: The Establishment Clause Value, 77 Yale L.J. 692, 693 (1968): The establishment clause prohibits "only aid which has as its motive or substantial effect the imposition of religious belief or practice." More broadly, the religion clauses prohibit the government from influencing religious choice. See Gianella, Religious Liberty, Nonestablishment, and Doctrinal Development, 80 Harv. L. Rev. 1381 (1967), 81 Harv. L. Rev. 513 (1968). Consider Gianella's argument that a society's institutions provide the structure within which choice is made, that different structures produce different choices, and that, in a society in which much is done in collective institutions, voluntarism requires aid to religion. 81 Harv. L. Rev. at 522–526. For example, the system of public education might be said to affect the values students come to acquire and might therefore influence their choices among religions or between religion and non-religion. Is that an "imposition of religious belief"? If so, does it follow that state aid to religious schools, or a voucher system in which parents receive a specified sum from the state to use for the education of their children in public or private schools, is required by the Constitution? Alternatively, consider whether the use of taxes to provide aid to religious institutions is coercive or influences religious choice.

4. *Nonpreferentialism.* According to nonpreferentialist views, government may not favor one religion over another, nor may it disfavor any particular religious view (including antireligious views), but it may support religion in general. In a religiously pluralist society, what forms of aid are nondiscriminatory? Consider the observation by Justice Souter, in Lee v. Weisman, supra, that "a nonpreferentialist who would condemn subjecting public school graduates to, say, the Anglican liturgy would still need to explain why the government's preference for Theistic over non-Theistic religion is constitutional."

Should the religion clauses protect the interests of nonbelievers? Can they do so without creating a regime of hostility to religion? In a society with wide government involvement in subsidizing social activities, are refusals to subsidize religious institutions discriminatory against religion?

Dissenting in McCreary County v. ACLU of Kentucky, 545 U.S. 844 (2005), Justice Scalia, joined on this point by Chief Justice Rehnquist and Justice Thomas, argued:

> With respect to public acknowledgment of religious belief, [the] Establishment Clause permits [disregard] of polytheists and believers in unconcerned deities, just as it permits the disregard of devout atheists. [Historical] practices [demonstrate] that there is a distance between the acknowledgment of a single Creator and the establishment of a religion. [The] three most popular religions in the United States, Christianity, Judaism, and Islam — which combined account for 97.7% of all believers — are monotheistic. All of them [believe] that the Ten Commandments were given by God to Moses, and are divine prescriptions for a virtuous life. Publicly honoring the Ten Commandments is thus indistinguishable, insofar as discriminating against other religions is concerned, from publicly honoring God. Both practices are recognized across such a broad and diverse range of the population [that] they cannot be reasonably understood as a government endorsement of a particular religious viewpoint.

Justice Stevens responded to this argument in dissenting in Van Orden v. Perry, 545 U.S. 677 (2005): "[M]any of the Framers understood the word 'religion' in the Establishment Clause to encompass only the various sects of Christianity," citing, among other sources, Justice Joseph Story's Commentaries on the Constitution. "The original understanding of the type of 'religion' that qualified for constitutional protection under the Establishment Clause likely did not include [followers] of Judaism and Islam. . . . The inclusion of Jews and Muslims inside the category of constitutionally favored religions surely would have shocked [Justice] Story. [The] history of the Establishment Clause's original meaning just as strongly supports a preference for Christianity as it does a preference for monotheism."

In his opinion in *McCreary County*, Justice Scalia replied, "Since most thought the Clause permitted government invocation of monotheism, and some others thought it permitted government invocation of Christianity, [Justice Stevens] proposes that it be construed not to permit any government invocation of religion at all. [Those] narrower views of the Establishment Clause were as clearly rejected as the more expansive ones."

The majority opinion written by Justice Souter in *McCreary County* took the position that Justice Scalia's argument "[failed] to consider the full range of evidence showing what the Framers believed."

> The dissent is certainly correct in putting forward evidence that some of the Framers thought some endorsement of religion was compatible with the establishment ban. [But there] is also evidence supporting the proposition that the Framers intended the Establishment Clause to require government neutrality in matters of religion. . . . [The] fair inference is that there was no common understanding about the limits of the establishment prohibition. . . . What the evidence does show is a group of statesmen [who] proposed a guarantee with contours not wholly worked out, leaving the Establishment Clause with edges still to be determined. And none the worse for that.
>
> [Historical] evidence thus supports no solid argument for changing course. . . . [The] divisiveness of religion in current public life is inescapable. This is no time to deny the prudence of understanding the Establishment Clause to require the Government to stay neutral on religious belief, which is reserved for the conscience of the individual.

5. *Voluntarism and separatism.* L. Tribe, supra, at 1160–1161, argues that the religion clauses rest on "a pair of fundamental [principles:] voluntarism and separatism." As to voluntarism,

> [the] free exercise clause was at the very least designed to guarantee freedom of conscience by preventing any degree of compulsion in matters of belief. It prohibited not only direct compulsion but also any indirect coercion which might result from subtle discrimination; hence it was offended by any burden based specifically on one's religion. So viewed, the free exercise clause is a mandate of religious voluntarism. The establishment clause [can] be understood as designed in part to assure that the advancement of a church would come only from the voluntary support of its followers and not from the political support of the state. Religious groups, it was believed, should prosper or perish on the intrinsic merit of their beliefs and practices. . . .
>
> Separatism [calls] for much more than the institutional separation of church and state; it means that the state should not become involved in religious affairs or derive its claim to authority from religious sources, that religious bodies should

not be granted governmental powers, and — perhaps — that sectarian differences should not be allowed unduly to fragment the body politic. Implicit in this ideal of mutual abstinence was the principle that under no circumstance should religion be financially supported by public taxation: "for the men who wrote the Religion Clauses [the] 'establishment' of a religion connoted sponsorship, financial support, and active involvement of the sovereign in religious activity."

Is the result in *Everson* consistent with these principles? When might the principles conflict with each other? Consider whether nondiscriminatory aid involves "indirect coercion" or "political support" of "a church" that might displace voluntary support by its members.

6. *"Equal Liberty."* Eisgruber and Sager, Religious Freedom and the Constitution (2007), offer a general theory they call Equal Liberty, which contains two principles: "In the name of equality [no one] ought to be devalued on account of the spiritual foundations of their important commitments and projects." Aside from attention to discrimination and "hostility and neglect," religion should not be treated "as deserving special benefits or as subject to special disabilities." In addition, a broad understanding of general constitutional liberties, such as rights of free speech and association "will allow religious practice to flourish." Id. at 52–53. For a collection of commentaries (raising questions about how to identify "hostility and neglect," and about the difference between this approach and others), see Book Review Colloquium, 85 Tex. L. Rev. 1185–1287 (2007).

7. *Religious pluralism and the political process.* Consider whether a justification for allowing governments some leeway in dealing with religion lies in the contemporary political process: The United States is a religiously pluralist society in which most religious groups are tolerant of views that diverge from their own. As proposals work their way through the political process, religiously based interest groups will affect their contours. It might be unlikely that programs threatening the values with which the religion clauses are concerned will emerge from that process. Is this pluralist sketch of the political process accurate? Are there programs on which substantial majorities can agree that disregard intense views of religious minorities, and that have substantial religious components?

In Zelman v. Simmons-Harris, 536 U.S. 639 (2002), Justice Souter's dissenting opinion argued that "[religious] teaching at taxpayer expense simply cannot be cordoned from taxpayer politics, and every major religion currently espouses social positions that provoke intense opposition. Not all taxpaying Protestant citizens [will] be content to underwrite the teaching of the Roman Catholic Church condemning the death penalty. Nor will all of America's Muslims acquiesce in paying for the endorsement of the religious Zionism taught in many religious Jewish schools, which combines 'a nationalistic sentiment' in support of Israel with a 'deeply religious' element. Nor will every secular taxpayer be content to support Muslim views on differential treatment of the sexes, or, for that matter, to fund the espousal of a wife's obligation of obedience to her husband, presumably taught in any schools adopting the articles of faith of the Southern Baptist Convention. Views like these, and innumerable others, have been safe in the sectarian pulpits and classrooms of this Nation not only because the Free Exercise Clause protects them directly, but because the ban on supporting religious establishment has protected free exercise, by keeping it relatively private. With the arrival of vouchers in religious schools, that privacy will go, and along with it will go confidence that religious disagreement will stay moderate."

In connection with those observations, consider whether religious and political pluralism might combine to moderate disagreement, either through compromises that allow each religious institution to receive public assistance while maintaining its own views or through compromises that restrict all religious institutions. (Would the latter compromises violate the free speech clause?)

For a recent discussion of how pluralism should affect constitutional doctrine, see Inazu, Confident Pluralism (2016).

8. *Baselines.* Douglas Laycock, The Underlying Unity of Separation and Neutrality, 46 Emory L.J. 43, 49, 69–71 (1997), discusses the "no aid" and "equal access" theories, similar to strict separation and nonpreferentialism:

> In the no-aid theory, the baseline is government inactivity, because doing nothing neither helps nor hurts religion. Any government aid to a religion is a departure from that baseline, and thus a departure from neutrality. In the nondiscrimination theory, the baseline is the government's treatment of analogous secular activities; a government that pays for medical care should pay equally whether the care is provided in a religious or a secular hospital.

Laycock argues for a standard of "minimizing government influence":

> [The] underlying criterion for choosing among baselines depends on the incentives that government creates. If government says that it will pay for your soup kitchen if and only if you secularize it, that is a powerful incentive to secularize. [In] this context, the baseline of analogous secular activity is substantively neutral: if government will pay both religious and secular providers, it creates no incentive for either to change. [In] the regulatory context, substantive neutrality generally requires the baseline of government inactivity. If government says it will send you to jail if you consume peyote in a worship service, that is a powerful disincentive to religious behavior. But an exemption for religious behavior rarely encourages people to join the exempted church. [When] the claim to religious exemption is not contaminated by secular self-interest, exemption minimizes government influence on religion. [If] government were free to praise or condemn religion, celebrate religious holidays, or lead prayers or worship services, government could potentially have enormous influence on religious belief and liturgy. Government is large and highly visible; for better or worse, it would model one form of religious speech or observance as compared to others.

Is Justice Souter's concern in *Zelman-Harris* that the availability of a subsidy — or exemption? — might subtly influence religious doctrine relevant to Laycock's argument?

9. *Why protect religion?* Is the constitutional text alone sufficient to justify giving religion special protection? Must we also have reasons for thinking that religion ought to be specially protected? Consider these observations: (a) Laycock, Religious Liberty as Liberty, 7 J. Contemp. Legal Issues 313, 317 (1996): "First, in history that was recent to the American founders, government attempts to suppress disapproved religious views had caused vast human suffering. [Second], beliefs about religion are often of extraordinary importance to the individual — important enough to die for, to suffer for, to rebel for, to emigrate for, to fight to control the government for. [Third], beliefs at the heart of religion [are] of little importance to the civil government." Are the first and second reasons distinctive to religion? Is the third reason true? (b) Garvey, An

Anti-Liberal Argument for Religious Freedom, 7 J. Contemp. Legal Issues 275 (1996): "We protect it because religion is important."

For recent discussions of this question, see Leiter, Why Tolerate Religion? (2012), offering a perspective from moral and political theory, and Koppelman, Defending American Religious Neutrality (2013), offering a perspective from political theory and law. For a review of these works, see Greene, Religion and Theistic Faith: On Koppelman, Leiter, Secular Purpose, and Accommodations, 49 Tulsa L. Rev. 441 (2013). See also Schwartzman, What If Religion Is Not Special?, 79 U. Chi. L. Rev. 1351 (2012):

> [Many] of the most widely held normative justifications for favoring (or disfavoring) religion are prone to predictable forms of internal incoherence [and] accounts [that] manage to avoid such incoherence succeed only at the cost of committing other serious errors, especially in allowing various types of unfairness toward religious believers, nonbelievers, or both. The upshot of all this is that principles of disestablishment and free exercise ought to be conceived in terms that go beyond the category of religion. Instead of disabling or protecting only religious beliefs and practices, the law ought to provide similar treatment for comparable secular ethical, moral, and philosophical views.

Note: Defining Religion

The religion clauses require the courts to determine whether a form of belief is a "religion" within their meaning. If the free exercise clause requires the state to accommodate its secular programs to religious, but not to nonreligious (e.g., political), belief, courts must decide whether an objector's belief is religious. The courts may be asked to decide whether the teaching of evolution or of creationism is an establishment of religion. What general considerations might guide the definitional effort?

1. *Unitary or variable definitions?* Justice Rutledge, dissenting in *Everson*, supra:

> "Religion" appears only once in the [First] Amendment. But the word governs two prohibitions and governs them alike. It does not have two meanings, one narrow to forbid "an establishment" and another, much broader, for securing "the free exercise thereof." "Thereof" brings down "religion" with its entire and exact content, no more and no less, from the first into the second guaranty, so that Congress and now the states are as broadly restricted concerning the one as they are regarding the other.

L. Tribe, American Constitutional Law 826–828 (1st ed. 1978):

> At least through the nineteenth century, religion was given the same fairly narrow reading in the two clauses: "religion" referred to theistic notions respecting divinity, morality, and worship, and was recognized as legitimate and protected only insofar as it was generally accepted as "civilized" by Western standards. . . .
>
> [But religion] in America, always pluralistic, has become radically so in the latter part of the twentieth century. [There] are, of course, many traditionally theistic American theologians, but for many others there has been a shift in religious thought from a theocentric, transcendental perspective to forms of religious consciousness that stress the immanence of meaning in the natural order. . . .
>
> [Clearly,] the notion of religion in the free exercise clause must be expanded beyond the closely bounded limits of theism to account for the multiplying forms of

recognizably legitimate religious exercise. It is equally clear, however, that in the age of the affirmative and increasingly pervasive state, a less expansive notion of religion was required for establishment clause purposes lest all "humane" programs of government be deemed constitutionally suspect. Such a twofold definition of religion — expansive for the free exercise clause, less so for the establishment clause — may be necessary to avoid confronting the state with increasingly difficult choices that the theory of permissible accommodations [could] not indefinitely resolve. . . .

Is Tribe's approach consistent with the language of the Constitution? In the second edition of his treatise, Tribe calls this proposal "a dubious solution to a problem that [may] not exist at all" because courts can and should focus on the more important ideas of tolerance and establishment. L. Tribe, American Constitutional Law 1186–1187 (2d ed. 1988).

2. *An expansive definition by the Supreme Court: the conscientious objector cases.* The Court's most extended consideration of the definition of religion occurred in a series of cases interpreting a federal statute granting an exemption from compulsory military service to any person "who, by reason of religious training and belief, is conscientiously opposed to participation in war in any form" and defining "religious training and belief" as "an individual's belief in relation to a Supreme Being involving duties superior to those arising from any human relation, but [not] any essentially political, sociological, or philosophical views or a merely personal moral code." (The reference to a "Supreme Being" was deleted in 1967.)

The Court interpreted these provisions in United States v. Seeger, 380 U.S. 163 (1965). Seeger stated on his draft form that he "preferred to leave the question as to his belief in a Supreme Being open," and that he had a "belief in and devotion to goodness and virtue for their own sakes, and a religious faith in a purely ethical creed [without] belief in God, except in the remotest sense." The Court unanimously found that Seeger qualified for the statutory exemption. The test was "whether a given belief that is sincere and meaningful occupies a place in the life of its possessor parallel to that filled by the orthodox belief in God of one who clearly qualifies for the exemption. Where such beliefs have parallel positions in the lives of their respective holders we cannot say that one is 'in relation to a Supreme Being' and the other is not." The Court mentioned "the richness and variety of spiritual life in our country."

Justice Douglas, concurring in *Seeger,* thought that a broadly defined exemption was required by the free exercise clause and by concepts of equal protection. The plurality in Welsh v. United States, 398 U.S. 333 (1970), applied the *Seeger* test to grant an exemption to someone who crossed off the word "religious" on the draft form. Justice Harlan concurred only in the result. He argued that *Seeger* had stretched the statutory language to its limit. "Congress [could eliminate] all exemptions for conscientious objectors. Such a course would be wholly 'neutral.' [However,] having chosen to exempt, it cannot draw the line between theistic or nontheistic religious beliefs on the one hand and secular beliefs on the other." To do so would violate the establishment clause.

In Gillette v. United States, 401 U.S. 437 (1971), the Court held that the statutory exemption was unavailable to those who had religious objections "relating to a particular conflict." It rejected the claim that the free exercise clause required that the exemption be available to such "selective" objectors and concluded that an exemption limited to objectors to all wars was sufficiently neutral to avoid establishment clause problems. The "de facto discrimination among religions" was not an establishment of religion because the discrimination "serves a number of purposes having nothing to do with a design to foster or favor any sect, religion, or cluster of religions [such] as the hopelessness of converting a sincere conscientious objector into an effective fighting man." The "interest in maintaining a fair system" might be defeated by requiring the draft system to inquire into the "enormous number of variables" that make selective objection "ultimately subjective." "There is a danger that as between two would-be objectors, both having the same complaint against a war, that objector would succeed who is more articulate, better educated, or better counseled." This danger was greater "the more discriminating and complicated the basis of classification." Justice Douglas dissented.

For an argument that protection should be extended to claims based on conscience as well as religion, see Smith, Converting the Religious Equality Amendment into a Statute with a Little "Conscience," 1996 BYU L. Rev. 645.

3. *The futility of definition?* Commentators, drawing on modern theology, have suggested that religion must involve "ultimate concern" or belief in "extratemporal consequences" or in a "transcendent reality." See, e.g., Note, Toward a Constitutional Definition of Religion, 91 Harv. L. Rev. 1056 (1978); Choper, Defining "Religion" in the First Amendment, 1982 U. Ill. L. Rev. 579. Are the following belief systems religions? Does it matter whether the issue is free exercise or establishment? (a) Transcendental meditation (see Malnak v. Yogi, 592 F.2d 197 (3d Cir. 1979), finding that a school board established religion when it authorized the teaching of TM in the public schools); (b) pantheism (see Africa v. Pennsylvania, 662 F.2d 1025 (3d Cir. 1981), finding a system strongly resembling pantheism not a religion when its adherent sought to require prison officials to provide him with a diet of raw foods only); (c) secular humanism (see Grove v. Mead School District, 753 F.2d 1528 (9th Cir. 1985), finding no establishment clause violation in allowing public school students to satisfy requirements by reading a book said to advance secular humanism).

Consider Freeman, The Misguided Search for the Constitutional Definition of "Religion," 71 Geo. L.J. 1519, 1553, 1556 (1983): A "religious belief system" has some of the following "relevant features": belief in a supreme being, belief in a transcendent reality, a moral code, a worldview accounting for people's role in the universe, sacred rituals, worship and prayer, a sacred text, membership in a social organization. But "there is no single feature or set of features that constitutes the essence of religion." Rather, "a belief system [may] be more or less religious depending on how closely it resembles [the] paradigm" having all eight features.

How can the religion clauses be interpreted unless there is a definition of religion? Consider whether it would be possible to develop doctrines by accepting all sincerely proffered claims that a belief is religious and then determining whether the state's secular goals justify imposing a burden on that belief or whether the state's secular goals justify its adopting the program at issue. Freeman suggests that such doctrines might be unacceptable because the courts would be unable to distinguish between belief systems at the core of the concept of religion and those at its periphery; distaste for granting a free exercise exemption to the peripheral religion might distort the doctrines dealing with the balance between secular goals and burdens on religion.

4. *Determining sincerity.* In United States v. Ballard, 322 U.S. 78 (1944), the leaders of the "I Am" religion were indicted for mail fraud. The religion, an

offshoot of the theosophy movement, was centered in the western states. Its founder, Guy Ballard, was said to have met a Master Saint Germain, who used Ballard as a messenger. Ballard's widow and son were charged with making representations that they knew were false regarding their power to cure diseases. The Supreme Court held that the jury could not be allowed to determine the truth or falsity of the representations about the Ballards' ability to cure. It could determine only whether the Ballards believed the representations they made. "Men may believe what they cannot prove. [Religious] experiences which are as real as life to some may be incomprehensible to others. [If] one could be sent to jail because a jury in a hostile environment found [his] teachings false, little indeed would be left of religious freedom." Justice Jackson would have gone further:

> I do not see how we can separate an issue as to what is believed from considerations as to what is believable. [Any] inquiry into intellectual honesty in religion raises profound psychological problems. [It] seems to me an impossible task for juries to separate fancied [religious experiences] from real ones, dreams from happenings, and hallucinations from true clairvoyance. [Further,] I do not know what degree of skepticism or disbelief in a religious representation amounts to an actionable fraud. [Religious] symbolism is even used by some with the same mental reservations one has in teaching of Santa Claus or Uncle Sam or Easter bunnies or dispassionate judges.

Chief Justice Stone, whose dissent was joined by Justices Roberts and Frankfurter, countered, "[If] it were shown that a defendant [had] asserted [that] he had physically shaken hands with St. Germain in San Francisco on a day named, or that [by] the exertion of his spiritual power he 'had in fact cured [hundreds] of persons . . . ,' it would be open to the Government to submit to the jury proof that he had never been in San Francisco and that no such cures had ever been effected." Justice Jackson agreed that a church leader could be prosecuted for fraud if he or she "represents that funds are being used to build a church when in fact they are being used for personal purposes." How does that differ from what the Ballards were charged with?

Note that inquiries into sincerity may be a disguised attempt to question whether the underlying belief is religious at all. Would that justify or cast doubt on the propriety of inquiries into sincerity?

B.   THE ESTABLISHMENT CLAUSE

In Lemon v. Kurtzman, 403 U.S. 602 (1971), the Court identified three "tests" for determining whether a statute violates the establishment clause: "First, the statute must have a secular legislative purpose; second, its principal or primary effect must be one that neither advances nor inhibits religion; finally, the statute must not foster 'an excessive government entanglement with religion.'" The so-called *Lemon* test has not been formally repudiated by the Supreme Court. A majority of the justices sitting in 2011 have criticized it, and it has not been relied on by a majority to invalidate any practice since 1985. For an overview of developments, see Lupu, The Lingering Death of Separationism, 62 Geo. Wash. L. Rev. 230 (1994). In a concurring opinion in Lamb's Chapel v. Center Moriches Union Free School District, 508 U.S. 384 (1993), Justice Scalia criticized the *Lemon* test by analogizing it to "a ghoul in a late-night horror movie that repeatedly sits up in its grave and shuffles abroad, after being repeatedly killed and buried. [It] is there to scare us [when] we wish it to do so, but we can command it to return to the tomb at will. When we wish to strike down a practice it forbids, we invoke it; when we wish to uphold a practice it forbids, we ignore it entirely. [Such] a docile and useful monster is worth keeping around, at least in a somnolent state; one never knows when one might need him."

The materials that follow are organized around some more particularized themes that can be connected to the components of the *Lemon* test. Sections B1 and B2 deal with two ways — coercion and endorsement — in which government practices might be said to "advance" (or inhibit) religion. Section B3 deals with issues that arise in connection with identifying whether a government practice has a religious or a secular purpose. Section B4 discusses cases and problems in which the effects, principal or otherwise, of a government program might be said to advance (or inhibit) religion.

1.   The Anticoercion Principle

Lee v. Weisman

505 U.S. 577 (1992)

JUSTICE KENNEDY delivered the opinion of the Court.

School principals in the public school system of the city of Providence, Rhode Island, are permitted to invite members of the clergy to offer invocation and benediction prayers as part of the formal graduation ceremonies for middle schools and for high schools. The question before us is whether including clerical members who offer prayers as part of the official school graduation ceremony is consistent with the Religion Clauses of the First Amendment, provisions the Fourteenth Amendment makes applicable with full force to the States and their school districts. . . .

[Following the school district's custom, a middle school principal invited a member of the clergy, Rabbi Leslie Gutterman, to deliver prayers at the school's graduation exercises. The principal gave Rabbi Gutterman a pamphlet, "Guidelines for Civic Occasions," prepared by the National Conference of Christians and Jews. The pamphlet recommended that prayers at civic ceremonies be composed with "inclusiveness and sensitivity." Rabbi Gutterman's invocation was:

God of the Free, Hope of the Brave. For the legacy of America where diversity is celebrated and the rights of minorities are protected, we thank You. May these young men and women grow up to enrich it. For the liberty of America, we thank You. May these new graduates grow up to guard it. For the political process of America in which all its citizens may participate, for its court system where all may seek justice we thank You. May those we honor this morning always turn to it in trust. For the destiny of America we thank You. May the graduates of Nathan Bishop Middle School so live that they might help to share it. May our aspirations for our country and for these young people, who are our hope for the future, be richly fulfilled.

[The benediction was similar in content.

[Deborah Weisman, a student at the school, challenged the practice of having prayers at public school graduations.]

These dominant facts mark and control the confines of our decision: State officials direct the performance of a formal religious exercise at promotional and graduation ceremonies for secondary schools. Even for those students who object to the religious exercise, their attendance and participation in the state-sponsored religious activity are in a fair and real sense obligatory, though the school district does not require attendance as a condition for receipt of the diploma. . . .

[It] is beyond dispute that, at a minimum, the Constitution guarantees that government may not coerce anyone to support or participate in religion or its exercise, or otherwise act in a way which "establishes a [state] religion or religious faith, or tends to do so."[Lynch v. Donnelly, infra.] The State's involvement in the school prayers challenged today violates these central principles.

That involvement is as troubling as it is undenied. A school official, the principal, decided that an invocation and a benediction should be given; this is a choice attributable to the State, and from a constitutional perspective it is as if a state statute decreed that the prayers must occur. The principal chose the religious participant, here a rabbi, and that choice is also attributable to the State. The reason for the choice of a rabbi is not disclosed by the record, but the potential for divisiveness over the choice of a particular member of the clergy to conduct the ceremony is apparent.

Divisiveness, of course, can attend any state decision respecting religions, and neither its existence nor its potential necessarily invalidates the State's attempts to accommodate religion in all cases. The potential for divisiveness is of particular relevance here though, because it centers around an overt religious exercise in a secondary school environment where [subtle] coercive pressures exist and where the student had no real alternative which would have allowed her to avoid the fact or appearance of participation.

The State's role did not end with the decision to include a prayer and with the choice of clergyman. Principal Lee provided Rabbi Gutterman with a copy of the "Guidelines for Civic Occasions," and advised him that his prayers should be nonsectarian. Through these means the principal directed and controlled the content of the prayer. "[It] is a cornerstone principle of our Establishment Clause jurisprudence that it is no part of the business of government to compose official prayers for any group of the American people to recite as a part of a religious program carried on by government," Engel v. Vitale, 370 U.S. 421, 425 (1962), and that is what the school officials attempted to do.

Petitioners argue [that] the directions for the content of the prayers were a good-faith attempt by the school to ensure that the sectarianism which is so often the flashpoint for religious animosity be removed from the graduation ceremony. The concern is understandable, as a prayer which uses ideas or images identified with a particular religion may foster a different sort of sectarian rivalry than an invocation or benediction in terms more neutral. [The] question is not the good faith of the school in attempting to make the prayer acceptable to most persons, but the legitimacy of its undertaking that enterprise at all when the object is to produce a prayer to be used in a formal religious exercise which students, for all practical purposes, are obliged to attend. . . .

The First Amendment's Religion Clauses mean that religious beliefs and religious expression are too precious to be either proscribed or prescribed by the State. The design of the Constitution is that preservation and transmission of religious beliefs and worship is a responsibility and a choice committed to the private sphere, which itself is promised freedom to pursue that mission. It must not be forgotten then, that while concern must be given to define the protection granted to an objector or a dissenting non-believer, these same Clauses exist to protect religion from government interference. . . .

These concerns have particular application in the case of school officials, whose effort to monitor prayer will be perceived by the students as inducing a participation they might otherwise reject. [Our precedents] caution us to measure the idea of a civic religion against the central meaning of the Religion Clauses of the First Amendment, which is that all creeds must be tolerated and none favored. The suggestion that government may establish an official or civic religion as a means of avoiding the establishment of a religion with more specific creeds strikes us as a contradiction that cannot be accepted.

The degree of school involvement here made it clear that the graduation prayers bore the imprint of the State and thus put school-age children who objected in an untenable position. . . .

[It] is argued that [high] school students no doubt have been required to attend classes and assemblies and to complete assignments exposing them to ideas they find distasteful or immoral or absurd or all of these. Against this background, students may consider it an odd measure of justice to be subjected during the course of their educations to ideas deemed offensive and irreligious, but to be denied a brief, formal prayer ceremony that the school offers in return. This argument [overlooks] a fundamental dynamic of the Constitution.

The First Amendment protects speech and religion by quite different mechanisms. Speech is protected by insuring its full expression even when the government participates, for the very object of some of our most important speech is to persuade the government to adopt an idea as its own. The method for protecting freedom of worship and freedom of conscience in religious matters is quite the reverse. In religious debate or expression the government is not a prime participant, for the Framers deemed religious establishment antithetical to the freedom of all. The Free Exercise Clause embraces a freedom of conscience and worship that has close parallels in the speech provisions of the First Amendment, but the Establishment Clause is a specific prohibition on forms of state intervention in religious affairs with no precise counterpart in the speech provisions. The explanation lies in the lesson of history that was and is the inspiration for the Establishment Clause, the lesson that in the hands of government what might begin as a tolerant expression of religious views may end in a policy to indoctrinate and coerce. A state-created orthodoxy puts at grave risk that freedom of belief and conscience which are the sole assurance that religious faith is real, not imposed. . . .

The lessons of the First Amendment are as urgent in the modern world as in the 18th Century when it was written. One timeless lesson is that if citizens are subjected to state-sponsored religious exercises, the State disavows its own duty to guard and respect that sphere of inviolable conscience and belief which is the mark of a free people. To compromise that principle today would be to deny our own tradition and forfeit our standing to urge others to secure the protections of that tradition for themselves.

[There] are heightened concerns with protecting freedom of conscience from subtle coercive pressure in the elementary and secondary public schools. [What] to most believers may seem nothing more than a reasonable request that the nonbeliever respect their religious practices, in a school context may appear to the nonbeliever or dissenter to be an attempt to employ the machinery of the State to enforce a religious orthodoxy.

[The] school district's supervision and control of a high school graduation ceremony places public pressure, as well as peer pressure, on attending students to stand as a group or, at least, maintain respectful silence during the Invocation and Benediction. This pressure, though subtle and indirect, can be as real as any overt compulsion. Of course, in our culture standing or remaining silent can signify adherence to a view or simple respect for the views of others. And no doubt some persons who have no desire to join a prayer have little objection to standing as a sign of respect for those who do. But for the dissenter of high school age, who has a reasonable perception that she is being forced by the State to pray in a manner her conscience will not allow, the injury is no less real. [For] many, if not most, of the students at the graduation, the act of standing or remaining silent was an expression of participation in the Rabbi's prayer. That was the very point of the religious exercise. It is of little comfort to a dissenter, then, to be told that for her the act of standing or remaining in silence signifies mere respect, rather than participation. What matters is that given our social conventions, a reasonable dissenter in this milieu could believe that the group exercise signified her own participation or approval of it.

Finding no violation under these circumstances would place objectors in the dilemma of participating, with all that implies, or protesting. [We] think the State may not, consistent with the Establishment Clause, place primary and secondary school children in this position. Research in psychology supports the common assumption that adolescents are often susceptible to pressure from their peers towards conformity, and that the influence is strongest in matters of social convention. To recognize that the choice imposed by the State constitutes an unacceptable constraint only acknowledges that the government may no more use social pressure to enforce orthodoxy than it may use more direct means. . . .

There was a stipulation in the District Court that attendance at graduation and promotional ceremonies is voluntary. [Law] reaches past formalism. And to say a teenage student has a real choice not to attend her high school graduation is formalistic in the extreme. [Everyone] knows that in our society and in our culture high school graduation is one of life's most significant occasions. A school rule which excuses attendance is beside the point. [A] student is not free to absent herself from the graduation exercise in any real sense of the term "voluntary," for absence would require forfeiture of those intangible benefits which have motivated the student through youth and all her high school years. . . .

The importance of the event is the point the school district and the United States rely upon to argue that a formal prayer ought to be permitted, but it becomes one of the principal reasons why their argument must fail. Their contention [is] that the prayers are an essential part of these ceremonies because for many persons an occasion of this significance lacks meaning if there is no recognition, however brief, that human achievements cannot be understood apart from their spiritual essence. We think the Government's position [fails] to acknowledge that what for many of Deborah's classmates and their parents was a spiritual imperative was for [Deborah] Weisman religious conformance compelled by the State. While in some societies the wishes of the majority might prevail, the Establishment Clause of the First Amendment is addressed to this contingency and rejects the balance urged upon us. The Constitution forbids the State to exact religious conformity from a student as the price of attending her own high school graduation. This is the calculus the Constitution commands.

The Government's argument gives insufficient recognition to the real conflict of conscience faced by the young student. The essence of the Government's position is that with regard to a civic, social occasion of this importance it is the objector, not the majority, who must take unilateral and private action to avoid compromising religious scruples, here by electing to miss the graduation exercise. This turns conventional First Amendment analysis on its head. It is a tenet of the First Amendment that the State cannot require one of its citizens to forfeit his or her rights and benefits as the price of resisting conformance to state-sponsored religious practice. To say that a student must remain apart from the ceremony at the opening invocation and closing benediction is to risk compelling conformity in an environment analogous to the classroom setting, where we have said the risk of compulsion is especially high. . . .

We do not hold that every state action implicating religion is invalid if one or a few citizens find it offensive. People may take offense at all manner of religious as well as nonreligious messages, but offense alone does not in every case show a violation. We know too that sometimes to endure social isolation or even anger may be the price of conscience or nonconformity. But, [the] conformity required of the student in this case was too high an exaction to withstand the test of the Establishment Clause. The prayer exercises in this case are especially improper because the State has in every practical sense compelled attendance and partic-ipation in an explicit religious exercise at an event of singular importance to every student, one the objecting student had no real alternative to avoid. . . .

[Our] society would be less than true to its heritage if it lacked abiding concern for the values of its young people, and we acknowledge the profound belief of adherents to many faiths that there must be a place in the student's life for precepts of a morality higher even than the law we today enforce. [A] relentless and all-pervasive attempt to exclude religion from every aspect of public life could itself become inconsistent with the Constitution. We recognize that, at graduation time and throughout the course of the educational process, there will be instances when religious values, religious practices, and religious persons will have some interaction with the public schools and their students. But these matters, often questions of accommodation of religion, are not before us. The sole question presented is whether a religious exercise may be conducted at a graduation ceremony in circumstances where [young] graduates who object are induced to conform. No holding by this Court suggests that a school can per-suade or compel a student to participate in a religious exercise. That is being done here, and it is forbidden by the Establishment Clause of the First Amendment.

For the reasons we have stated, the judgment of the Court of Appeals is affirmed.

JUSTICE BLACKMUN, with whom JUSTICE STEVENS and JUSTICE O'CONNOR join, concurring. . . .

[It] is not enough that the government restrain from compelling religious practices: it must not engage in them either. . . . [6]

Our decisions have gone beyond prohibiting coercion, [because] the Court has recognized that "the fullest possible scope of religious liberty," *Schempp* (Goldberg, J., concurring) [section A supra], entails more than freedom from

---

6. As a practical matter, of course, anytime the government endorses a religious belief there will almost always be some pressure to conform. "When the power, prestige and financial support of government is placed behind a particular religious belief, the indirect coercive pressure upon religious minorities to conform to the prevailing officially approved religion is plain." Engel v. Vitale, 370 U.S. 421, 431 (1962). [Relocated footnote. — EDS.]

coercion. The Establishment Clause protects religious liberty on a grand scale; it is a social compact that guarantees for generations a democracy and a strong religious community — both essential to safeguarding religious liberty. "Our fathers seem to have been perfectly sincere in their belief that the members of the Church would be more patriotic, and the citizens of the State more religious, by keeping their respective functions entirely separate." Religious Liberty, in Essays and Speeches of Jeremiah S. Black 53 (C. Black ed. 1885) (Chief Justice of the Commonwealth of Pennsylvania). . . .

[A concurring opinion by Justice Souter, joined by Justices Stevens and O'Connor, is omitted.]

JUSTICE SCALIA, with whom THE CHIEF JUSTICE, JUSTICE WHITE, and JUSTICE THOMAS join, dissenting. . . .

[In] holding that the Establishment Clause prohibits invocations and benedictions at public-school graduation ceremonies, the Court [lays] waste a tradition [that] is a component of an even more longstanding American tradition of nonsectarian prayer to God at public celebrations generally. . . .

I . . .

From our Nation's origin, prayer has been a prominent part of governmental ceremonies and proclamations. The Declaration of Independence "[appealed] to the Supreme Judge of the world for the rectitude of our intentions" and avowed "a firm reliance on the protection of divine Providence." In his first inaugural address, after swearing his oath of office on a Bible, George Washington deliberately made a prayer a part of his first official act as President:

> it would be peculiarly improper to omit in this first official act my fervent supplications to that Almighty Being who rules over the universe, who presides in the councils of nations, and whose providential aids can supply every human defect, that His benediction may consecrate to the liberties and happiness of the people of the United States a Government instituted by themselves for these essential purposes.

Such supplications have been a characteristic feature of inaugural addresses ever since. . . .

Our national celebration of Thanksgiving likewise dates back to President Washington. [This] tradition of Thanksgiving Proclamations — with their religious theme of prayerful gratitude to God — has been adhered to by almost every President. . . .

II

The Court presumably would separate graduation invocations and benedictions from other instances of public "preservation and transmission of religious beliefs" on the ground that they involve "psychological coercion." [A] few citations of "research in psychology" that have no particular bearing upon the precise issue here cannot disguise the fact that the Court has gone beyond the realm where judges know what they are doing. The Court's argument that state officials have "coerced" students to take part in the invocation and benediction at graduation ceremonies is, not to put too fine a point on it, incoherent.

A

[According] to the Court, students at graduation who want "to avoid the fact or appearance of participation," in the invocation and benediction are psychologically obligated "[to] stand as a group or, at least, maintain respectful silence" during those prayers. This assertion [does] not say [that] students are psychologically coerced to bow their heads, place their hands in a Dürer-like prayer position, pay attention to the prayers, utter "Amen," or in fact pray. [It] claims only that students are psychologically coerced "to stand . . . or, at least, maintain respectful silence." Both halves of this disjunctive [merit] particular attention.

[The] Court's notion that a student who simply sits in "respectful silence" during the invocation and benediction [has] somehow joined — or would somehow be perceived as having joined — in the prayers is nothing short of ludicrous. We indeed live in a vulgar age. But surely "our social conventions" have not coarsened to the point that anyone who does not stand on his chair and shout obscenities can reasonably be deemed to have assented to everything said in his presence. Since the Court does not dispute that students exposed to prayer at graduation ceremonies retain [the] free will to sit, there is absolutely no basis for the Court's decision. . . .

But let us assume the very worst, that the nonparticipating graduate is "subtly coerced" . . . to stand! Even that half of the disjunctive does not remotely establish a "participation" (or an "appearance of participation") in a religious exercise. [If] it is a permissible inference that one who is standing is doing so simply out of respect for the prayers of others that are in progress, then how can it possibly be said that a "reasonable dissenter . . . could believe that the group exercise signified her own participation or approval"? [Maintaining] respect for the religious observances of others is a fundamental civic virtue that government [can] and should cultivate — so that even if [the] displaying of such respect might be mistaken for taking part in the prayer, I would deny that the dissenter's interest in avoiding even the false appearance of participation constitutionally trumps the government's interest in fostering respect for religion generally.

[The] Court itself has not given careful consideration to its test of psychological coercion. For if it had, how could it observe [that] students stood for the Pledge of Allegiance, which immediately preceded Rabbi Gutterman's invocation? [Recital] of the Pledge would appear to raise the same Establishment Clause issue as the invocation and benediction.

III . . .

[The] coercion that was a hallmark of historical establishments of religion was coercion of religious orthodoxy and of financial support by force of law and threat of penalty. Typically, attendance at the state church was required; only clergy of the official church could lawfully perform sacraments; and dissenters, if tolerated, faced an array of civil disabilities. . . .

The Establishment Clause was adopted to prohibit such an establishment of religion at the federal level (and to protect state establishments of religion from federal interference). I will further acknowledge for the sake of argument that, as some scholars have argued, by 1790 the term "establishment" had acquired an additional meaning — "financial support of religion generally, by public taxation" — that reflected the development of "general or multiple" establishments, not limited to a single church. But that would still be an establishment coerced by force of law. And I will further concede that our constitutional tradition [has], with a few aberrations, ruled out of order government-sponsored endorsement of religion — even when no legal coercion is present, and indeed even when no ersatz, "peer-pressure" psycho-coercion is present — where the endorsement is sectarian, in the sense of specifying details upon which men and women who believe in a benevolent, omnipotent Creator and Ruler of the world, are known to differ (for example, the divinity of Christ). But there is simply no support for the proposition that the officially sponsored nondenominational invocation and benediction read by Rabbi Gutterman — with no one legally coerced to recite them — violated the Constitution of the United States. To the contrary, they are so characteristically American they could have come from the pen of George Washington or Abraham Lincoln himself. . . .

IV . . .

The reader has been told much in this case about the personal interest of Mr. Weisman and his daughter, and very little about the personal interests on the other side. They are not inconsequential. Church and state would not be such a difficult subject if religion were, as the Court apparently thinks it to be, some purely personal avocation that can be indulged entirely in secret, like pornography, in the privacy of one's room. For most believers it is not that, and has never been. Religious men and women of almost all denominations have felt it necessary to acknowledge and beseech the blessing of God as a people, and not just as individuals, because they believe in the "protection of divine Providence," as the Declaration of Independence put it, not just for individuals but for societies; because they believe God to be, as Washington's first Thanksgiving Proclamation put it, the "Great Lord and Ruler of Nations." One can believe in the effectiveness of such public worship, or one can deprecate and deride it. But the longstanding American tradition of prayer at official ceremonies displays with unmistakable clarity that the Establishment Clause does not forbid the government to accommodate it. . . .

I must add one final observation: The founders of our Republic knew the fearsome potential of sectarian religious belief to generate civil dissension and civil strife. And they also knew that nothing, absolutely nothing, is so inclined to foster among religious believers of various faiths a toleration — no, an affection — for one another than voluntarily joining in prayer together, to the God whom they all worship and seek. Needless to say, no one should be compelled to do that, but it is a shame to deprive our public culture of the opportunity, and indeed the encouragement, for people to do it voluntarily. The Baptist or Catholic who heard and joined in the simple and inspiring prayers of Rabbi Gutterman on this official and patriotic occasion was inoculated from religious bigotry and prejudice in a manner that can not be replicated. To deprive our society of that important unifying mechanism, in order to spare the nonbeliever what seems to me the minimal inconvenience of standing or even sitting in respectful nonparticipation, is as senseless in policy as it is unsupported in law.

For the foregoing reasons, I dissent.

Note: The Anticoercion Principle

1. *Defining coercion.* Does treating the psychological impact of a practice on dissenters as coercive create a "dissenter's veto"? Is it more accurate to describe the problem in *Lee* as one of government endorsement of religion, which on the margin induces someone to engage in prayer, rather than one of government coercion? Should there be a parallel concern (under the free exercise clause?) for the "coercion" of some religious students when presented with material — about evolution, for example — inconsistent with their religious beliefs?

Consider this perspective on *Lee*:

> [The] harm inflicted by government-sponsored religious exercises is two-fold. First, civic religious exercises force religious minorities to sever civil communion to avoid spiritual pollution. [The] second harm is that civic religious exercises wound the civil community by compelling the severance of religious minorities and thus fracturing community. [In] contrast with Justice Scalia's proposed inoculation against bigotry, [a] very different view of toleration [does] not necessarily engender affection among believers of different stripes, but simply civil cooperation. [Roger Williams] and the Separatists [remind] us that we must deny to ecumenical impulses any right to a smug place of preeminence in the history of religious freedom in America.

T. Hall, Separating Church and State: Roger Williams and Religious Liberty 158, 159–160 (1998).

2. *The scope of the principle.* In Engel v. Vitale, 370 U.S. 421 (1962), a public school allowed those who objected to state-written prayers recited at the beginning of classes to remain silent or be excused from attendance. The Court said, "When the power, prestige and financial support of government is placed behind a particular religious belief, the indirect coercive pressure upon religious minorities to conform to the prevailing officially approved religion is plain." Justice Stewart would have remanded a similar case for development of the facts involving coercion:

> [The] duty laid upon government in connection with religious exercises in the public schools is that of refraining from so structuring the school environment as to put any kind of pressure on a child to participate in those exercises; it is not that of providing an atmosphere in which children are kept scrupulously insulated from any awareness that some of their fellows may want to open the school day with prayer, or of the fact that there exist in our pluralistic society differences of religious belief. [Certain] types of exercises would present situations in which no possibility of coercion on the part of secular officials could be claimed to exist. Thus, if such exercises were held either before or after the official school day, or if the school schedule were such that participation were merely one among a number of desirable alternatives, it could hardly be contended that the exercises did anything more than to provide an opportunity for the voluntary expression of religious belief. [If] the exercises were held during the school day, and no equally desirable alternative were provided by the school authorities, the likelihood that children might be under at least some psychological compulsion to participate would be great. In such a case as the latter, however, I think we would err if we assumed such coercion in the absence of any evidence.

School District of Abington Township v. Schempp, 374 U.S. 203, 316–318 (1963).

Consider the argument of Carter, Parents, Religion, and Schools: Reflections on *Pierce*, 70 Years Later, 27 Seton Hall L. Rev. 1194, 1214 (1997):

[If] beginning the school day with a prayer is unconstitutional because it prefers religion over nonreligion, then why is not a curriculum devoid of any religious observance unconstitutional because it prefers non-religion over religion? [By] compelling school attendance, [the] state as much as announces that what occurs in its schools is of vital importance. So if none of the material is religious, children will receive the message that the state deems religion unimportant. [The] ban on prayer must be intended to help individuals to make up their own minds [about] what religions to follow. But prayer and other formal religious instruction are hardly the only things that can do that. [If] our concern is for state interference with religious choice, we would surely want to take a hard look at the curriculum and rid it of other topics of instruction that make it difficult for individuals to make up their own minds about what religions to follow.

3. *Coercion, free exercise, and free speech.* The free exercise and free speech clauses protect against coercion *away from* a person's beliefs. Would it violate a student's free exercise right to compel her to stand respectfully during the benediction? Her free speech right? If neither right would be violated, the anticoercion principle might guard against direct violations that are difficult to identify on a case-by-case basis. Should such a principle be regarded as an establishment clause or a free exercise/free speech principle? If free exercise and free speech rights are not implicated, the establishment clause might deal with structural relations between religion and government rather than with individual rights. How could the Court identify impermissible structural relations except by referring to individual rights?

N. Feldman, The Intellectual Origins of the Establishment Clause, 77 N.Y.U. L. Rev. 346, 351, 424 (2002), argues that "[liberty] of conscience [was] the central value invoked by the states that proposed constitutional amendments on the question of religion, and the purpose that underlay the Establishment Clause when it was enacted," and that "the Constitution [protects] liberty of conscience [only] in the sphere of government action that relates *specifically to religion.*" What does the establishment clause understood in this way add to the free exercise and free speech clauses?

4. *Prayers at football games.* Santa Fe Independent School District v. Doe, 530 U.S. 290 (2000), held unconstitutional a district's policy that authorized students to vote, first, whether to allow "invocations" at high school football games, and then to choose a person to deliver them. Relying on Board of Regents v. Southworth, Chapter 7, section E5, supra, Justice Stevens, writing for six justices, concluded that the speech the selected student gave would not be private speech because of the policy authorizing an election in which a majority would determine whether to have invocations. The Court then held that an invocation at a high school football game violated the principle established in *Lee*. The establishment clause was designed "to remove debate over this kind of issue from governmental supervision or control." Some students, such as cheerleaders and team members, were compelled to attend the games, and other students would feel "immense social pressure" and "truly genuine desire" to attend the games. The delivery of a religious invocation would therefore coerce them in the way condemned in *Lee*. Chief Justice Rehnquist and Justices Scalia and Thomas dissented.

Does the distinction between permissible private speech and arguably impermissible government speech make sense in the contexts of *Lee* and *Santa Fe*? Consider the suggestion in Brady, The Push to Private Religious Expression: Are We Missing Something?, 70 Fordham L. Rev. 1147, 1199 (2002), that "the most promising approach is for students of all perspectives to 'opt in' to the educational process by voicing and defending differing views" in these contexts. Would school authorities have to develop guidelines setting out the limits beyond which student speech could not go in these contexts? If so, would those guidelines convert private into government speech? Would school authorities be barred from developing such guidelines by free speech principles?

2.   The Nonendorsement Principle and De Facto Establishments

Lynch v. Donnelly

465 U.S. 668 (1984)

THE CHIEF JUSTICE [BURGER] delivered the opinion of the Court. . . .

Each year, in cooperation with the downtown retail merchants' association, the City of Pawtucket, Rhode Island, erects a Christmas display as part of its observance of the Christmas holiday season. The display is situated in a park owned by a nonprofit organization and located in the heart of the shopping district. The display is essentially like those to be found in hundreds of towns or cities across the Nation — often on public grounds — during the Christmas season. The Pawtucket display comprises many of the figures and decorations traditionally associated with Christmas, including, among other things, a Santa Claus house, reindeer pulling Santa's sleigh, candy-striped poles, a Christmas tree, carolers, cutout figures representing such characters as a clown, an elephant, and a teddy bear, hundreds of colored lights, a large banner that reads "SEASONS GREETINGS," and the crèche at issue here. All components of this display are owned by the City. . . .

[The court of appeals held that maintaining the crèche violated the establishment clause.] [Rather] than mechanically invalidating all governmental conduct or statutes that confer benefits or give special recognition to religion in general or to one faith — as an absolutist approach would dictate — the Court has scrutinized challenged legislation or official conduct to determine whether, in reality, it establishes a religion or religious faith, or tends to do so. . . .

In each case, the inquiry calls for line drawing; no fixed, per se rule can be framed. . . .

In the line-drawing process we have often found it useful to inquire whether the challenged law or conduct has a secular purpose, whether its principal or primary effect is to advance or inhibit religion, and whether it creates an excessive entanglement of government with religion. [*Lemon.*] But, we have repeatedly emphasized our unwillingness to be confined to any single test or criterion in this sensitive area. . . .

[In] this case, the focus of our inquiry must be on the crèche in the context of the Christmas season. . . . [12]

---

12. Justice Brennan states that "by focusing on the holiday 'context' in which the crèche appear[s]," the Court seeks to "explain away the clear religious import of the crèche," and that it has equated the crèche with a Santa's house or a talking wishing well. Of course this is not true. [Relocated footnote. — EDS.]

[When] viewed in the proper context of the Christmas Holiday season, it is apparent that, on this record, there is insufficient evidence to establish that the inclusion of the crèche is a purposeful or surreptitious effort to express some kind of subtle governmental advocacy of a particular religious message. In a pluralistic society a variety of motives and purposes are implicated. The City, like the Congresses and Presidents, however, has principally taken note of a significant historical religious event long celebrated in the Western World. . . .

The narrow question is whether there is a secular purpose for Pawtucket's display of the crèche. The display is sponsored by the City to celebrate the Holiday and to depict the origins of that Holiday. These are legitimate secular purposes. . . .

The dissent asserts some observers may perceive that the City has aligned itself with the Christian faith by including a Christian symbol in its display and that this serves to advance religion. We can assume, *arguendo*, that the display advances religion in a sense; but our precedents plainly contemplate that on occasion some advancement of religion will result from governmental action. [Here,] whatever benefit to one faith or religion or to all religions, is indirect, remote and incidental; display of the crèche is no more an advancement or endorsement of religion than the Congressional and Executive recognition of the origins of the Holiday itself as "Christ's Mass," or the exhibition of literally hundreds of religious paintings in governmentally supported museums. . . .

The Court has acknowledged that the "fears and political problems" that gave rise to the Religion Clauses in the 18th century are of far less concern today. [*Everson.*] We are unable to perceive the Archbishop of Canterbury, the Vicar of Rome, or other powerful religious leaders behind every public acknowledgment of the religious heritage long officially recognized by the three constitutional branches of government. Any notion that these symbols pose a real danger of establishment of a state church is far-fetched indeed. . . .

[Reversed.]

JUSTICE O'CONNOR, concurring. . . .

I

The Establishment Clause prohibits government from making adherence to a religion relevant in any way to a person's standing in the political community. Government can run afoul of that prohibition in two principal ways. One is excessive entanglement with religious institutions, which may interfere with the independence of the institutions, give the institutions access to government or governmental powers not fully shared by nonadherents of the religion, and foster the creation of political constituencies defined along religious lines. The second and more direct infringement is government endorsement or disapproval of religion. Endorsement sends a message to nonadherents that they are outsiders, not full members of the political community, and an accompanying message to adherents that they are insiders, favored members of the political community. Disapproval sends the opposite message. . . .

III

The central issue in this case is whether Pawtucket has endorsed Christianity by its display of the crèche. To answer that question, we must examine both what

Pawtucket intended to communicate in displaying the crèche and what message the City's display actually conveyed. The purpose and effect prongs of the *Lemon* test represent these two aspects of the meaning of the City's action.

The meaning of a statement to its audience depends both on the intention of the speaker and on the "objective" meaning of the statement in the community. Some listeners need not rely solely on the words themselves in discerning the speaker's intent: they can judge the intent by, for example, examining the context of the statement or asking questions of the speaker. Other listeners do not have or will not seek access to such evidence of intent. They will rely instead on the words themselves; for them the message actually conveyed may be something not actually intended. [Examination] of both the subjective and the objective components of the message communicated by a government action is therefore necessary to determine whether the action carries a forbidden meaning.

The purpose prong of the *Lemon* test asks whether government's actual purpose is to endorse or disapprove of religion. The effect prong asks whether, irrespective of government's actual purpose, the practice under review in fact conveys a message of endorsement or disapproval. An affirmative answer to either question should render the challenged practice invalid.

A

The purpose prong of the *Lemon* test requires that a government activity have a secular purpose. That requirement is not satisfied [by] the mere existence of some secular purpose, however dominated by religious purposes. The proper inquiry under the purpose prong of *Lemon* [is] whether the government intends to convey a message of endorsement or disapproval of religion.

Applying that formulation to this case, I would find that Pawtucket did not intend to convey any message of endorsement of Christianity or disapproval of non-Christian religions. The evident purpose of including the crèche in the larger display was not promotion of the religious content of the crèche but celebration of the public holiday through its traditional symbols. Celebration of public holidays, which have cultural significance even if they also have religious aspects, is a legitimate secular purpose. . . .

B

[Under the effect prong, what] is crucial is that a government practice not have the effect of communicating a message of government endorsement or disapproval of religion. It is only practices having that effect, whether intentionally or unintentionally, that make religion relevant, in reality or public perception, to status in the political community.

Pawtucket's display of its crèche, I believe, does not communicate a message that the government intends to endorse the Christian beliefs represented by the crèche. Although the religious and indeed sectarian significance of the crèche [is] not neutralized by the setting, the overall holiday setting changes what viewers may fairly understand to be the purpose of the display — as a typical museum setting, though not neutralizing the religious content of a religious painting, negates any message of endorsement of that content. The display celebrates a public holiday. [The] holiday itself has very strong secular components and traditions. Government celebration of the holiday [generally] is not understood to endorse the religious content of the holiday, just as government celebration of

Thanksgiving is not so understood. The crèche is a traditional symbol of the holiday that is very commonly displayed along with purely secular symbols, as it was in Pawtucket.

These features combine to make the government's display of the crèche in this particular physical setting no more an endorsement of religion than such governmental "acknowledgments" of religion as [printing] of "In God We Trust" on coins, and opening court sessions with "God save the United States and this honorable court." Those government acknowledgments of religion serve, in the only ways reasonably possible in our culture, the legitimate secular purposes of solemnizing public occasions, expressing confidence in the future, and encouraging the recognition of what is worthy of appreciation in society. For that reason, and because of their history and ubiquity, those practices are not understood as conveying government approval of particular religious beliefs. The display of the crèche likewise serves a secular purpose — celebration of a public holiday with traditional symbols. It cannot fairly be understood to convey a message of government endorsement of religion. It is significant in this regard that the crèche display apparently caused no political divisiveness prior to the filing of this lawsuit, although Pawtucket had incorporated the crèche in its annual Christmas display for some years. For these reasons, I conclude that Pawtucket's display of the crèche does not have the effect of communicating endorsement of Christianity.

JUSTICE BRENNAN, with whom JUSTICE MARSHALL, JUSTICE BLACKMUN, and JUSTICE STEVENS join, dissenting. . . .

I . . .

[The] nativity scene, unlike every other element of the Hodgson Park display, reflects a sectarian exclusivity that the avowed purposes of celebrating the holiday season and promoting retail commerce simply do not encompass. [The] inclusion of a distinctively religious element like the crèche [demonstrates] that a narrower sectarian purpose lay behind the decision to include a nativity scene.

The "primary effect" of including a nativity scene in the City's display is [to] place the government's imprimatur of approval on the particular religious beliefs exemplified by the crèche.. . . .

[The] Court, by focusing on the holiday "context" in which the nativity scene appeared, seeks to explain away the clear religious import of the crèche. [It] blinks reality to claim [that] by including such a distinctively religious object as the crèche in its Christmas display, Pawtucket has done no more than make use of a "traditional" symbol of the holiday, and has thereby purged the crèche of its religious content and conferred only an "incidental and direct" benefit on religion. . . .

[The] City has done nothing to disclaim government approval of the religious significance of the crèche, to suggest that the crèche represents only one religious symbol among many others that might be included in a seasonal display truly aimed at providing a wide catalogue of ethnic and religious celebrations, or to disassociate itself from the religious content of the crèche. . . .

Finally, [even] in the context of Pawtucket's seasonal celebration, the crèche retains a specifically Christian religious meaning. I refuse to accept the notion implicit in today's decision that non-Christians would find that the religious content of the crèche is eliminated by the fact that it appears as part of the City's otherwise secular celebration of the Christmas holiday. The nativity scene [is] the chief symbol of the characteristically Christian belief that a divine Savior was brought into the world and that the purpose of this miraculous birth was to illuminate a path toward salvation and redemption. For Christians, that path is exclusive, precious and holy. But for those who do not share these beliefs, the symbolic re-enactment of the birth of a divine being who has been miraculously incarnated as a man stands as a dramatic reminder of their differences with Christian faith. [To] be so excluded on religious grounds by one's elected government is an insult and an injury that, until today, could not be countenanced by the Establishment Clause. . . .

When government decides to recognize Christmas day as a public holiday, it does no more than accommodate the calendar of public activities to the plain fact that many Americans will expect on that day to spend time visiting with their families, attending religious services, and perhaps enjoying some respite from pre-holiday activities. [When public] officials participate in or appear to endorse the distinctively religious elements of this otherwise secular event, they encroach upon First Amendment freedoms. For it is at that point that the government brings to the forefront the theological content of the holiday, and places the prestige, power and financial support of a civil authority in the service of a particular faith.

[Unlike] such secular figures as Santa Claus, reindeer and carolers, a nativity scene represents far more than a mere "traditional" symbol of Christmas. The essence of the crèche's symbolic purpose and effect is to prompt the observer to experience a sense of simple awe and wonder appropriate to the contemplation of one of the central elements of Christian dogma — that God sent His son into the world to be a Messiah. [The] crèche is far from a mere representation of a "particular historic religious event." It is, instead, best understood as a mystical re-creation of an event that lies at the heart of Christian faith. To suggest, as the Court does, that such a symbol is merely "traditional" and therefore no different from Santa's house or reindeer is not only offensive to those for whom the crèche has profound significance, but insulting to those who insist for religious or personal reasons that the story of Christ is in no sense a part of "history" nor an unavoidable element of our national "heritage." . . .

II . . .

Intuition tells us that some official "acknowledgment" is inevitable in a religious society if government is not to adopt a stilted indifference to the religious life of the people. It is equally true, however, that if government is to remain scrupulously neutral in matters of religious conscience, as our Constitution requires, then it must avoid those overly broad acknowledgments of religious practices that may imply governmental favoritism toward one set of religious beliefs. . . .

[At] least three principles — tracing the narrow channels which government acknowledgments must follow to satisfy the Establishment Clause — may be identified. First, although the government may not be compelled to do so by the Free Exercise Clause, it may, consistently with the Establishment Clause, act to accommodate to some extent the opportunities of individuals to practice their religion. [That] principle would justify government's decision to declare December 25th a public holiday.

Second, [while] a particular governmental practice may have derived from religious motivations and retain certain religious connotations, it is nonetheless permissible for the government to pursue the practice when it is continued today solely for secular reasons. [The] mere fact that a governmental practice coincides to some extent with certain religious beliefs does not render it unconstitutional. Thanksgiving Day, in my view, fits easily within this principle, for despite its religious antecedents, the current practice of celebrating Thanksgiving is unquestionably secular and patriotic. . . .

Finally, we have noted that government cannot be completely prohibited from recognizing in its public actions the religious beliefs and practices of the American people as an aspect of our national history and culture. While I remain uncertain about these questions, I would suggest that such practices as the designation of "In God We Trust" as our national motto, or the references to God contained in the Pledge of Allegiance can best be understood [as] a form of "ceremonial deism," protected from Establishment Clause scrutiny chiefly because they have lost through rote repetition any significant religious content. Moreover, these references are uniquely suited to serve such wholly secular purposes as solemnizing public occasions, or inspiring commitment to meet some national challenge in a manner that simply could not be fully served in our culture if government were limited to purely non-religious phrases. . . .

The crèche fits none of these categories. . . .

III . . .

The intent of the Framers with respect to the public display of nativity scenes is virtually impossible to discern primarily because the widespread celebration of Christmas did not emerge in its present form until well into the nineteenth century. Carrying a well-defined Puritan hostility to the celebration of Christ's birth with them to the New World, the founders of the Massachusetts Bay Colony pursued a vigilant policy of opposition to any public celebration of the holiday. To the Puritans, the celebration of Christmas represented a "Popish" practice lacking any foundation in Scripture. . . .

During the eighteenth century, sectarian division over the celebration of the holiday continued. [D]enominational differences continued to dictate differences in attitude toward the holiday. [Many] nonconforming Protestant groups, including the Presbyterians, Congregationalists, Baptists, and Methodists, continued to regard the holiday with suspicion and antagonism well into the nineteenth century. This pattern of sectarian division concerning the holiday suggests that for the Framers of the Establishment Clause, who were acutely sensitive to such sectarian controversies, no single view of how government should approach the celebration of Christmas would be possible. . . .

Furthermore [the] public display of nativity scenes as part of governmental celebrations of Christmas does not come to us supported by an unbroken history of widespread acceptance. It was not until 1836 that a State first granted legal recognition to Christmas as a public holiday. [Congress] did not follow the States' lead until 1870 when it established December 25th, along with the Fourth of July, New Year's Day, and Thanksgiving, as a legal holiday in the District of Columbia. . . .

[The] City's action should be recognized for what it is: a coercive, though perhaps small, step toward establishing the sectarian preferences of the majority at the expense of the minority, accomplished by placing public facilities and funds in support of the religious symbolism and theological tidings that the crèche conveys. . . .

I dissent.

JUSTICE BLACKMUN, with whom JUSTICE STEVENS joins, dissenting. . . .

The crèche has been relegated to the role of a neutral harbinger of the holiday season, useful for commercial purposes, but devoid of any inherent meaning and incapable of enhancing the religious tenor of a display of which it is an integral part. The city has its victory — but it is a Pyrrhic one indeed.

The import of the Court's decision is to encourage use of the crèche in a municipally sponsored display, a setting where Christians feel constrained in acknowledging its symbolic meaning and non-Christians feel alienated by its presence. Surely, this is a misuse of a sacred symbol. . . .

Note: The Nonendorsement Principle

1. *Applying the nonendorsement principle.* In County of Allegheny v. American Civil Liberties Union, 492 U.S. 573 (1989), a majority of the Court joined Justice Blackmun's opinion adopting Justice O'Connor's "no endorsement" analysis as a general guide in establishment clause cases. Shifting majorities on the Court held unconstitutional a freestanding display of a nativity scene on the main staircase of a county courthouse, but upheld the display of a Jewish menorah placed next to the city's Christmas tree and a statement declaring the city's "salute to liberty." One majority concluded that the "setting" of the nativity scene, which was the "single element" in the display, "celebrate[d] Christmas in a way that has the effect of endorsing a patently Christian message."

Justice Blackmun, writing for himself, concluded that the display of the menorah was permissible. "The menorah's message is not exclusively religious," and it stood next to a Christmas tree and a sign saluting liberty, with the effect of "creat[ing] an 'overall holiday setting' that represents both Christmas and Chanukah — two holidays, not one." Justice O'Connor agreed that the display of the menorah was permissible. Although the menorah had religious content, she said, the overall display "sends a message of pluralism and freedom to choose one's own beliefs." Justices Brennan, Marshall, and Stevens dissented as to the menorah. Justice Brennan argued that the Christmas tree was a religious symbol, and that Chanukah was not a holiday with secular dimensions. The government's message in the "salute to liberty" was not religious, but "patriotic," and "the government's use of religion to promote its own cause is undoubtedly offensive to those whose religious beliefs are not bound up with their attitude toward the Nation."

Justice Kennedy, joined by Chief Justice Rehnquist and Justices White and Scalia, rejected the majority's adoption of the "no endorsement" test, saying that it "reflects an unjustified hostility toward religion." He argued that the establishment clause "permits government some latitude in recognizing and accommodating the central role religion plays in our society." To him, the Court's decisions

> disclose two limiting principles: government may not coerce anyone to support or participate in any religion or its exercise; and it may not, in the guise of avoiding

hostility or callous indifference, give direct benefits to religion in such a degree that it in fact "establishes a [state] religion or religious faith, or tends to do so." [*Lynch.*] [Symbolic] recognition or accommodation of religious faith may violate the Clause in an extreme case, [such as] the permanent erection of a large Latin cross on the roof of city hall [because] such an obtrusive year-round religious display would place the government's weight behind an obvious effort to proselytize on behalf of a particular religion. [Absent] coercion, the risk of infringement of religious liberty by passive or symbolic accommodation is minimal.

Are the ceremonial or symbolic endorsements of religion at issue in these cases more or less important for the principle of nonestablishment than monetary subsidies to church-related education? Than the practice of prayer in the public schools?

2. *Is the nonendorsement principle justifiable?* Consider the argument in N. Feldman, From Liberty to Equality: The Transformation of the Establishment Clause, 90 Cal. L. Rev. 673, 677, 718 (2002), that the nonendorsement principle rests on a mistaken reduction of the establishment clause to a principle of equality: "Religious minorities are not uniquely vulnerable to political inequality, and religious discrimination in the United States has not been noticeably worse than discrimination on the basis of political ideology, immigrant status, or language. [The] political-equality approach [cannot] provide a compelling answer to the question 'what is special about religion?' [The] harms associated with [exclusion] are no worse than the harms associated with other sorts of second-class citizenship and identity exclusion."

3. *The appropriate perspective.* Justice O'Connor would prohibit actions reasonably perceived as endorsement or disapproval. Perceived by whom? If by religious minorities, is she correct in concluding that reasonable Jews would not perceive the crèche as endorsement of Christianity? Consider the observation of S. Feldman, Principle, History, and Power: The Limits of the First Amendment Religion Clauses, 81 Iowa L. Rev. 833, 863 (1996): "In *Lynch*, the Court supported its conclusion by noting that [nobody] had complained about the crèche even though it had been publicly displayed for forty years. To the Court, this silence meant that the crèche had not generated dissension. [The] Court overlooked the possibility [that] Christian cultural imperialism had produced the silence of religious outgroup members. Silence often demonstrates domination, not consensus."

Suppose the government does not intend to endorse religion, but an observer might infer endorsement from the government's actions. How much must that person know about the government's real position?

In Capitol Square Review & Advisory Board v. Pinette, 515 U.S. 753 (1995), the Court divided over whether, and under what circumstances, an unattended display of a privately owned cross on public property could constitute an unconstitutional endorsement of religion. The Ku Klux Klan applied for a permit to display a cross in Capitol Square, the plaza surrounding Ohio's Statehouse. The square is a public forum that has been used for speeches and demonstrations. Before the Klan's application, unattended displays owned by private parties had been placed on the square three times: a "thermometer" showing the progress of a United Way fund drive, some booths during an arts festival, and a menorah.

Justice Scalia, writing for a plurality of four justices, concluded that the Constitution prohibited government endorsement of religion, but not "the government's neutral treatment of *private* religious expression." The plurality agreed that "giving sectarian religious speech preferential access to a forum close to the seat of government (or anywhere else for that matter) would violate the Establishment Clause." It "could conceive of a case in which a governmental entity manipulates its administration of a public forum [in] such a manner that only certain religious groups take advantage of it, creating an impression of endorsement *that is in fact accurate*." But "private religious speech cannot be subject to veto by those who see favoritism where there is none."

Justices O'Connor, Souter, and Breyer concurred in the judgment. Justices O'Connor and Souter both stressed the importance of having "a sign disclaiming government sponsorship or endorsement" on the cross, which would "[help] remove doubt about State approval of [the] religious message." According to Justice O'Connor, "[when] the reasonable observer would view a government practice as endorsing religion, [it] is our *duty* to hold the practice invalid. [The Establishment] Clause is more than a negative prohibition against certain narrowly defined forms of government favoritism; it also imposes affirmative obligations that may require a State [to] take steps to avoid being perceived as supporting or endorsing a private religious message. [The Clause] forbids a State from [remaining] studiously oblivious to the effects of its actions." To determine whether "the State's own actions *[actually] convey* a message of endorsement," courts must conduct the inquiry "from the perspective of a hypothetical observer who is presumed to possess a certain level of information that all citizens might not share." The reasonable observer "must be deemed aware of the history and context of the community and forum in which the religious display occurs [and] the general history of the place in which the cross is displayed. [An] informed member of the community will know how the public space in question has been used in the past."

Justice Souter argued that "[given] the domination of the square by the government's own displays, one would not be a dimwit as a matter of law to think that an unattended religious display here was endorsed by the government." He found the permit denial unconstitutional only because the board had failed to grant the application "subject to the condition that the Klan attach a disclaimer sufficiently clear and large to preclude any reasonable inference that the cross was there to 'demonstrat[e]' the government's allegiance to, or endorsement of, Christian faith.'"

Justice Stevens dissented. He argued, "If a reasonable person could perceive a government endorsement of religion from a private display, then the State may not allow its property to be used as a forum for that display. [So] it is with signs and symbols left to speak for themselves on public property. The very fact that a sign is installed on public property implies official recognition and reinforcement of its message. That implication is especially strong when the sign stands in front of the seat of the government itself. The reasonable observer of any symbol placed unattended in front of any capital in the world will normally assume that the sovereign which is not only the owner of that parcel of real estate but also the lawgiver for the surrounding territory has sponsored and facilitated its message."

Justice Ginsburg also dissented, arguing that the display at issue in the case had an inadequate disclaimer. She reserved judgment on whether "a sturdier disclaimer" would have been sufficient.

4. *Divisiveness as a criterion.* In McCreary County v. ACLU of Kentucky, 545 U.S. 844 (2005), the Court defended the principle of neutrality between religion and irreligion as "respond[ing] to one of the major concerns that prompted adoption of the Religion Clauses. The Framers and the citizens of their time

intended [to] guard against the civic divisiveness that follows when the Government weighs in on one side of religious debate." Is the question of the divisiveness occasioned by an enactment, or the potential that a proposed enactment would be divisive, an empirical question? What is the baseline against which divisiveness is to be measured? Consider the possibility that a judicial decision prohibiting a practice as an establishment of religion might be as divisive as, or more divisive than, the legislature's adoption of that practice. If divisiveness or its potential therefor is not an empirical but a conceptual matter, what are the components of the concept?

For a full discussion of the cases discussing divisiveness, see Garnett, Religion, Division, and the First Amendment, 94 Geo. L.J. 1667 (2006). Garnett concludes that the "divisiveness" argument "has rarely been outcome-determinative or done much real work," and that none of the versions of the argument he describes are convincing: "That concerns about 'political division along religious lines' are real and reasonable does not mean that they can or should supply the enforceable content of the First Amendment's prohibition on establishments of religion." Id. at 1670.

5. *De facto establishments.* Consider M. Howe, The Garden and the Wilderness 11–12 (1965):

> [Roger Williams's] principle of separation endorsed a host of favoring tributes to faith [so] substantial that they have produced in the aggregate what may fairly be described as a de facto establishment of religion [in which] the religious institution as a whole is maintained and activated by forces not kindled directly by government. [Some] elements of our religious establishment are, of course, reinforced by law. Whenever that situation prevails, as it does, for instance, when the law secures the sanctity of Sunday, the courts are apt to seek out a secular justification for the favoring enactment and, by this evasive tactic, meet the charge that an establishment de jure exists. [Yet] the Supreme Court, by pretending that the American principle of separation is predominantly Jeffersonian and by purporting to outlaw even those aids in religion which do not affect religious liberties, seems to have endorsed a governmental policy aimed at the elimination of de facto establishments.

For an argument that most aspects of "ceremonial deism" violate the Court's establishment clause doctrine, see Epstein, Rethinking the Constitutionality of Ceremonial Deism, 96 Colum. L. Rev. 2083 (1996). In McGowan v. Maryland, 366 U.S. 420 (1961), the Court rejected an establishment clause challenge to laws requiring that most large-scale commercial enterprises remain closed on Sundays. The Court's review of history demonstrated that Sunday closing laws were originally efforts to promote church attendance. "But, despite the strongly religious origin of these laws, nonreligious arguments for Sunday closing began to be heard more distinctly." The Court said that the Constitution "does not ban federal or state regulation of conduct whose reason or effect merely happens to coincide with the tenets of some or all religions." It concluded that, "as presently written and administered, most [Sunday closing laws] are of a secular rather than of a religious character." They "provide a uniform day of rest for all citizens. [To] say that the States cannot prescribe Sunday as a day of rest for these purposes solely because centuries ago such laws had their genesis in religion would give a constitutional interpretation of hostility to the public welfare rather than one of mere separation of church and State." As of 1961, was Howe's characterization of Sunday closing laws more accurate than the Court's? As of the present?

6. *History as a guide.* In Walz v. Tax Commission, 397 U.S. 664 (1970), the Court noted that every state had a property tax exemption for churches, and that the federal income tax has since its inception exempted religious organizations. It found "significant" that Congress exempted churches from real estate taxes in 1802. "[An] unbroken practice of according the exemption to churches, openly and by affirmative state action, not covertly or by state inaction, is not something to be lightly cast aside." Justice Brennan, concurring, agreed that "the existence from the beginning of the Nation's life of a practice [is] a fact of considerable import in the interpretation of abstract constitutional language. [The] more long-standing and widely accepted a practice, the greater its impact upon constitutional interpretation." He found two "secular purposes" for the exemption: Churches, like other exempt groups, "contribute to the well-being of the community in a variety of nonreligious ways," and they "uniquely contribute to the pluralism of American society."

Marsh v. Chambers, 463 U.S. 783 (1983), relied on a "unique history" to uphold the constitutionality of opening legislative sessions with prayers led by a state-employed chaplain. The history ran from colonial times to the present and included the first Congress's hiring a chaplain in 1789, only three days before it reached final agreement on the language of the first amendment:

> [Historical] evidence sheds light not only on what the draftsmen intended the Establishment Clause to mean, but also on how they thought that Clause applied to the practice authorized by the First Congress — their actions reveal their intent. [In] light of the unambiguous and unbroken history of more than 200 years, there can be no doubt that the practice of opening legislative sessions with prayer has become part of the fabric of our society.

Did *Lynch* rely on history in an appropriate way? Did *Walz* and *Marsh*? Is Justice Brennan correct in distinguishing *Lynch* from *Walz* and *Marsh*? In *Walz*, the Court stated that tax exemptions had not "given the remotest sign of leading to an established church," and in *Marsh*, it said that the fear that "prayer in this context risks the beginning of the establishment the founding Fathers feared [was] not well-founded." Is that the "lesson of history" with respect to de facto establishments?

7. *The Pledge of Allegiance, history, and ceremonial deism.* In Elk Grove Unified School District v. Newdow, 542 U.S. 1 (2004), the Court refused, on standing grounds, to consider the merits of a challenge to the constitutionality of the inclusion of the words "under God" in the Pledge of Allegiance. Chief Justice Rehnquist and Justices O'Connor and Thomas disagreed with that holding and wrote opinions explaining why they believed that the constitutional challenge should be rejected on the merits. Chief Justice Rehnquist relied on history to show that "our national culture allows public recognition of our Nation's religious history and character." He wrote, "I do not believe that the phrase 'under God' in the Pledge converts its recital into a 'religious exercise.' . . . Instead, it is a declaration of belief in allegiance and loyalty to the United States flag and the Republic. . . . The phrase [is] in no sense a prayer, nor an endorsement of any religion. . . . Reciting the Pledge, or listening to others recite it, is a patriotic exercise, not a religious one; participants promise fidelity to our flag and our Nation, not to any particular God, faith, or church."

Justice Thomas wrote, "It is difficult to see how [the phrase] does not entail an affirmation that God exists." For him, "as a matter of our precedent, the Pledge policy is unconstitutional." He would overrule Lee v. Weisman and eliminate its test of "coercion," replacing it with a test of "legal compulsion."

Justice O'Connor relied on the endorsement test, and characterized the phrase in the Pledge as an example of permissible "ceremonial deism," although she called it a "close question." Ceremonial deism, which involved "solemnizing an event and recognizing a shared religious history," included expressions that had "legitimate nonreligious purposes." Those purposes were revealed "when a given practice has been in place for a significant portion of the Nation's history, and when it is observed by enough persons that it can fairly be called ubiquitous." Further, ceremonial deism was characterized by the "absence of worship or prayer" and by a "highly circumscribed reference to God." Brief references tend "to confirm that the reference is being used to acknowledge religion or to solemnize an event rather than to endorse religion in any way," and "it makes it easier for those participants who wish to 'opt out' [to] do so without having to reject the ceremony entirely [and] tends to limit the ability of government to express a preference for one religious sect over another." Also, "no religious acknowledgement could claim to be an instance of ceremonial deism if it explicitly favored one particular religious belief system over another." She also observed that "[a]ny coercion that persuades an onlooker to participate in an act of ceremonial deism is inconsequential, as an Establishment Clause matter, because such acts are simply not religious in character."

TOWN OF GREECE v. GALLOWAY, 134 S. Ct. 1811 (2014). Town of Greece v. Galloway involved the prayer practices of the town board of Greece, a suburb of Rochester, New York. Starting in 1999, the board opened its meetings with, among other matters, a prayer given by guest chaplains chosen from a list of congregations in the town directory, nearly all of which are Christian. Some of the ministers "spoke in a distinctly Christian idiom," including invoking "the saving sacrifice of Jesus Christ on the cross."

Justice Kennedy wrote an opinion that was in part for the Court, and in part only for himself and Chief Justice Roberts and Justice Alito. The Court upheld the town's practices. It relied heavily on *Marsh*, which "[must] not be understood as permitting a practice that would amount to a constitutional violation if not for its historical foundation. The case teaches instead that the Establishment Clause must be interpreted 'by reference to historical practices and understandings.' [The] Court's inquiry [must] be to determine whether the prayer practice in the town of Greece fits within the tradition long followed in Congress and the state legislatures." But "[an] insistence on nonsectarian or ecumenical prayer as a single, fixed, standard is not consistent with the tradition of legislative [prayer]. [To] hold that invocations must be nonsectarian would force the legislatures [and] the courts [to] act as supervisors and censors of religious speech, [which] would involve government in religious matters to a far greater degree [than] is the case under the town's current practice." Justice Kennedy also wrote, "If the course and practice over time shows that the invocations denigrate nonbelievers or religious minorities, threaten damnation, or preach conversion, many present may consider the prayer to fall short of the desire to elevate the purpose of the occasion and to unite lawmakers in their common effort. That circumstance would present a different [case]." Noting that "two remarks" by guest chaplains "strayed from the rationale set out in *Marsh*," he wrote that "they do not despoil a practice that on the whole reflects and embraces our tradition. Absent a pattern of prayers that over time denigrate, proselytize, or betray an impermissible government purpose, a challenge based solely on the content of a prayer will not likely establish a constitutional violation." The town's efforts to locate guest chaplains were "reasonable," and did "not reflect an aversion or bias on the part of town leaders against minority faiths. So long as the town maintains a policy of nondiscrimination, the Constitution does not require it to search beyond its borders for non-Christian prayer givers in an effort to achieve religious balancing."

In the part of the opinion joined only by the Chief Justice and Justice Alito, Justice Kennedy addressed and rejected the argument that the prayer practice coerced participation. As to coercion, "The inquiry remains a fact-sensitive one that considers both the setting in which the prayer arises and the audience to whom it is directed," again "valuated against the backdrop of historical practice." "It is presumed that the reasonable observer is acquainted with this tradition and understands that its purposes are to lend gravity to public proceedings and to acknowledge the place religion holds in the lives of many private citizens, not to afford government an opportunity to proselytize or force truant constituents into the pews. That many appreciate these acknowledgments of the divine in our public institutions does not suggest that those who disagree are compelled to join the expression or approve its content." But "[t]he analysis would be different if town board members directed the public to participate in the prayers, singled out dissidents for opprobrium, or indicated that their decisions might be influenced by a person's acquiescence in the prayer opportunity." Addressing the respondents' claim that "the prayers gave them offense and made them feel excluded and disrespected," Justice Kennedy wrote, "Offense [does] not equate to coercion."

Justice Thomas, joined in part by Justice Scalia, wrote separately. Justice Thomas repeated his argument that the Establishment Clause was not made applicable to the states by the Fourteenth Amendment. In addition, he argued that "the municipal prayers [bear] no resemblance to the coercive state establishments that existed at the founding." The coercion relevant to Establishment Clause analysis "is actual legal coercion, [not] the 'subtle coercive pressures' allegedly felt by [respondents]."

Justice Kagan, joined by Justices Ginsburg, Breyer, and Sotomayor, dissented. Justice Breyer also dissented in a separate opinion. For Justice Kagan, "[t]he practice [here] differs from the one sustained in [*Marsh*] because Greece's town meetings involve participation by ordinary citizens, and the invocations given — directly to those citizens — were predominantly sectarian. [Greece's] Board did nothing to recognize religious diversity. [The] Town never sought (except briefly when this suit was filed) to involve, accommodate, or in any way reach out to adherents of non-Christian religions." She agreed that "Greece's Board [has] legislative functions," but its "meetings are also occasions for ordinary citizens to engage with and petition their government, often on highly individualized matters. That feature calls for Board members to exercise special care to ensure that the prayers offered [respect] each and every member of the community as an equal citizen." The sessions in *Marsh* at which prayers were offered were "floor sessions [for] elected lawyers. Members of the public take no part. [Greece's] town meetings [revolve] around ordinary members of the community," who "urge [changes] in the Board's policies [and] then, in which are essentially adjudicatory hearings, they request the Board to grant [applications] for various permits."

Let's say that a Muslim citizen of Greece goes before the Board to [request] some permit. [Just] before she gets to speak her piece, a minister deputized by the Town asks her to pray "in the name of God's only son Jesus Christ." She must think [that] Christian worship has become entwined with local governance. And now she faces a choice — to pray alongside the majority [or] somehow to register her deeply felt difference. [That] is no easy call — especially given that the room is small and her every action [will] be noticed. She does not wish to be rude to her neighbors, nor does she wish to aggravate the Board members whom she will soon be trying to persuade. And yet she does not want to acknowledge Christ's divinity. [So] assume she declines to participate with the others in the first act of the meeting — or even [stands] up and leaves the room. [She] becomes a different kind of citizen. [And] she thus stands at a remove, based solely on religion, from her fellow citizens and her elected representatives. Everything about that situation [infringes] the First Amendment.

Justice Kagan would allow some prayer activities. "What the circumstances here demand is the recognition that we are a pluralistic people. [If] the Town Board had let its chaplains know that they should speak in nonsectarian terms, [then] no one would have valid grounds for complaint. [Or] it might have invited clergy of many faiths to serve as chaplains. [But] Greece could not do what it did: infuse a participatory government body with one (and only one) faith." For her, "[when] a citizen stands before her government, [her] religious beliefs do not enter into the picture. The government she faces favors no particular religion, either by word or by deed. And that government [imposes] no religious tests on its citizens, sorts none of them by faith, and permits no exclusion based on belief. When a person goes to court, a polling place, or an immigration proceeding, [government] officials do not engage in sectarian worship, nor do they ask her to do likewise. They all participate in the business of government not as Christians, Jews, Muslims (and more), but only as Americans — none of them different from any other for that civic purpose."

Justice Alito, joined by Justice Scalia, responded to Justice Kagan in a concurring opinion, calling "the narrow aspect" of her dissent's objections to the holding "really quite niggling." He argued that "there [is] no historical support for the proposition that only generic prayer is allowed" and observed that "as our country has become more diverse, composing a prayer that is acceptable to all members of the community who hold religious beliefs has become [harder.]" Further, "if a town attempts to go beyond simply recommending that a guest chaplain deliver a prayer that is broadly acceptable, [the] town will [encounter] sensitive problems," including possible prescreening or reviewing prayers. The alternative of compiling a list of clergy from numerous traditions to serve as guest chaplains meant that Justice Kagan's objection was only the "[the] town's clerical employees did a bad job in compiling the list" they used.

Note: The Significance of Religious Pluralism

1. *Religious pluralism and the political process.* What does the Court mean in *Lynch* by saying that the crèche must be considered "in the proper context"? Is Justice Blackmun correct in his claim that religion's victory is Pyrrhic? Consider Kurland, The Religion Clauses and the Burger Court, 34 Cath. U. L. Rev. 1, 13–14 (1984): "The crèche opinion was sleazy. [I] would think that devout

Christians might take umbrage at the government, in the form of the judiciary, for labeling a depiction of the birth of the Christ child as a nonreligious symbol, like a Christmas tree or a banner proclaiming 'Seasons Greetings.'"

Does the emphasis on context suggest that there is no religious content to the use of the crèche? Or that the undeniable religious content is relatively modest? Should the Court insist that permissible de facto establishments have a low level of religious content? Consider the following argument: Contemporary society is pluralist in religion and in politics. Some religious groups oppose all governmental support of religion; others would support sectarian aid but oppose nondenominational aid; and others would support nondenominational aid. As some of these groups seek to secure legislation, they will have to adjust their programs to obtain majority support. The likely outcome of pluralist political bargaining in contemporary society on matters relating to religion is legislation having relatively modest religious content. The political process is therefore sufficient to guard against the evils at which the establishment clause is directed. Does this argument underestimate the degree to which a "least common denominator" religion may raise serious concern about establishment?

Does the crèche in *Lynch* demonstrate less governmental support for religion than nondenominational voluntary school prayer? Than student-led prayer groups held in school buildings before or after school hours? Is it sufficient to say that the Court regarded the school prayer cases as involving statutes that had no secular purposes?

2. *A cross as a war memorial?* Salazar v. Buono, 559 U.S. 700 (2010), considered but did not definitively resolve an establishment clause challenge to the 2004 transfer to private ownership of federal land on which a Latin cross had been erected in 1934. The cross was located in a remote area of the Mojave National Preserve, accessible via a blacktop road. Justice Kennedy, in an opinion joined by Chief Justice Roberts and Justice Alito, wrote, "Although certainly a religious symbol, the cross was not emplaced [to] promote a Christian message. [Time] also has played a role. The cross had stood [for] nearly seven decades before the [transfer]. By then, the cross and the cause it commemorated had become entwined in the public consciousness. Members of the public gathered regularly [to] pay their respects. [Congress] ultimately designated the cross as a national memorial. [It] is reasonable to interpret the congressional designation as giving recognition to the historical meaning that the cross had attained. [The] goal of avoiding governmental endorsement does not require eradication of all religious symbols in the public realm. [The] Constitution does not oblige government to avoid any public acknowledgement of religion's role in society. Rather, it leaves room to accommodate divergent values within a constitutionally permissible framework. [A] Latin cross is not merely a reaffirmation of Christian beliefs. It is a symbol often used to honor and respect those whose heroic acts, noble contributions, and patient striving help secure an honored place in history for this Nation and its people. Here, one Latin cross in the desert evokes far more than religion. It evokes thousands of small crosses in foreign fields marking the graves of Americans who fell in battles [whose] tragedies are compounded if the fallen are forgotten."

Concurring, Justice Alito observed that "Congress' consistent goal [has] been to commemorate our Nation's war dead and to avoid the disturbing symbolism that would have been created by the destruction of the monument." Justices Scalia and Thomas concurred in the judgment, finding that the challenger lacked standing.

Justice Stevens, joined by Justices Ginsburg and Sotomayor, dissented. "[After] the transfer it would continue to appear to any reasonable observer that the Government has endorsed the cross, [particularly because] the Government has designated the cross as a national memorial. [After] the transfer, a well-informed observer would know that the cross was no longer on public land, but would additionally be aware [that the] cross was once on public land, [Congress] transferred it to a specific purchaser in order to preserve its [display], and the Government maintained a reversionary interest in the land. [Even] though Congress recognized this cross for its military associations, the solitary cross conveys an inescapable sectarian message. [Making] a plain, unadorned Latin cross a war memorial does not make the cross secular. It makes the war memorial sectarian." In a footnote, Justice Stevens observed, "The cross is not a universal symbol of sacrifice. It is a symbol of one particular sacrifice, and that sacrifice carries deeply significant meaning for those who adhere to the Christian faith." Justice Breyer also dissented.

3. *Nondiscrimination.* In *Walz*, Justice Harlan's concurring opinion stated that "[the] Court must survey meticulously the circumstances of governmental categories to eliminate [religious] gerrymanders. [The] critical question is whether the circumference of legislation encircles a class [sufficiently] broad." What is the basis for choosing between defining the class in *Lynch* as the crèche alone or defining it as the entire holiday display?

3.   Impermissible Purposes: The School Prayer Cases

Note: Problems with a Purpose Test

1. *Determining impermissible legislative purposes.* Stone v. Graham, 449 U.S. 39 (1980), held unconstitutional a Kentucky statute requiring that a copy of the Ten Commandments be posted on the walls of each public classroom. The Court found that this requirement had "no secular legislative purpose": The commandments were "undeniably a sacred text in the Jewish and Christian faiths," and "if the posted copies [are] to have any effect at all, it will be to induce the school children to read, meditate upon, perhaps to venerate and obey, the Commandments. However desirable this might be as a matter of private devotion, it is not a permissible state objective under the Establishment Clause." Justice Rehnquist's dissent relied on a statement in the statute that its purpose was secular and argued that the requirement had a secular purpose because "the Ten Commandments have had a significant secular impact on the development of secular legal codes of the Western World."

Stone relied heavily on the school prayer cases. In Engel v. Vitale, 370 U.S. 421 (1962), the New York Board of Regents drafted and recommended that school districts have classes recite aloud the following prayer: "Almighty God, we acknowledge our dependence upon Thee, and beg Thy blessings upon us, our parents, our teachers and our Country." Justice Black, writing for the Court, stated that "in this country it is no part of the business of government to compose official prayers for any group of the American people to recite as a part of a religious program carried on by government."

In Abington School District v. Schempp, 374 U.S. 203 (1963), the Court held unconstitutional a state law requiring that ten verses from the Bible be read aloud at the opening of each day of public school. Justice Clark's opinion for the Court stated that Bible-reading had a religious character and found the state's policy of permitting nonattendance was not "consistent with the contention that the Bible is here used either as an instrument for nonreligious moral inspiration or as a reference for the teaching of secular subjects." Justice Stewart dissented, finding "a substantial free exercise claim" that "a compulsory state educational system so structures a child's life that if religious exercises are held to be an impermissible activity in schools, religion is placed at an artificial and state-created disadvantage."

Wallace v. Jaffree, 472 U.S. 38 (1985), held unconstitutional an Alabama statute authorizing schools to set aside one minute at the start of the school day "for meditation or voluntary prayer." The statute amended an earlier one authorizing a moment of silence "for meditation." The Court drew on Madison and *Everson* to conclude that "the individual freedom of conscience [embraces] the right to select any religious faith or none at all" because "religious beliefs worthy of respect are the product of free and voluntary choice by the faithful." The bill's sponsor stated that it was "an 'effort to return voluntary prayer' to the public schools." The Court said that the statute served "no secular purpose" not already served by the "meditation" statute. It noted that the statute could not be a permissible accommodation of religion because, prior to its enactment, "there was no governmental practice impeding students from silently praying for one minute at the beginning of the school day. [What] was missing [was] the State's endorsement and promotion of religion and a particular religious practice."

Justice O'Connor concurred in the judgment on the ground that the statute's "purpose and likely effect [were] to endorse and sponsor voluntary prayer in the public schools." She argued that simple "moment of silence" statutes were constitutional because "a moment of silence is not inherently religious [and because] a pupil who participates in a moment of silence need not compromise his or her belief." Thus, the "State does not necessarily endorse any activity that might occur during the period. Even if a statute specifies that a student may choose to pray silently during a quiet moment, the State has not thereby encouraged prayer over other specified alternatives. [The] crucial question is whether the state has conveyed or attempted to convey the message that children should use the moment of silence for prayer." She also wrote, "[A] legislature [might] enunciate a sham secular [purpose, but] our courts are capable of distinguishing a sham secular purpose from a real one."

Chief Justice Burger dissented, noting that the bill's sponsor testified that "one of his purposes [was] to clear up a widespread misunderstanding that a school-child is legally prohibited from [praying] once he steps inside a public school building."

Is it accurate to say that each of these statutes had no purpose other than the promotion of religion? Alternatively, do the statutes have no *substantial* secular purposes? Consider whether the purposes discussed in Lynch v. Donnelly are substantial.

2. *Determining legislative purpose: nondiscrimination and gerrymandering.* Larson v. Valente, 456 U.S. 228 (1982), involved a Minnesota statute imposing reporting requirements on religious organizations that solicit more than 50 percent of their funds from nonmembers. The legislative history included one legislator's statement that "what you're trying to get at here is the people who are running around streets and soliciting people" and another's that he was "not sure why we're so hot to regulate the Moonies anyway." Five members of the Court, in an opinion by Justice Brennan, held that the statute violated "the clearest

command of the Establishment Clause [— that] one religious denomination cannot be officially preferred over another." Such "denominational preferences" must be "justified by a compelling governmental interest, and [be] closely fitted to further that interest." The state's "interest in protecting its citizens from abusive practices" might be compelling, but the 50 percent rule was not closely fitted to preventing abuse. The distinctions in the statute "engender a risk of politicizing religion" and "led the Minnesota legislature to discuss the characteristics of various sects with a view towards 'religious gerrymandering.'" Justice White, joined by Justice Rehnquist, dissented on the ground that the statute was not "a deliberate and explicit preference for some religious denominations over others" because it "names no churches or denominations. [Some] religions will qualify and some will not, but this depends on the source of their contributions, not on their brand of religion."

McCreary County v. ACLU of Kentucky, 545 U.S. 844 (2005), revisited the issue of government posting of the Ten Commandments, and applied the "impermissible purpose" test. Noting that "[examination] of purpose is a staple of statutory interpretation [and] governmental purpose is a key element of a good deal of constitutional doctrine," the Court, in an opinion by Justice Souter, adhered to the proposition that "scrutinizing purpose does make practical sense [where] an understanding of official objective emerges from readily discoverable fact, without any judicial psychoanalysis of a drafter's heart of hearts. The eyes that look to purpose belong to an '"objective observer,"' one who takes account of the traditional external signs that show up in the '"text, legislative history, and implementation of the statute."' . . ." Justice Souter's opinion described prior cases invoking the "purpose" test as holding government action unconstitutional "only because openly available data supported a commonsense conclusion that a religious objective permeated the government's action." Government action does not violate the establishment clause, the Court continued, where it has a secular purpose that is "genuine, not a sham, and not merely secondary to a religious objective."

On the same day, the Court upheld the display of the Ten Commandments on the statehouse grounds in Austin, Texas. Van Orden v. Perry, 545 U.S. 677 (2005). The dispositive vote was cast by Justice Breyer, who wrote, "If the relation between government and religion is one of separation, but not of mutual hostility and suspicion, one will inevitably find difficult borderline cases. And in such cases, I see no test-related substitute for the exercise of legal judgment. That judgment is not a personal judgment. Rather, [it] must take account of context and consequences measured in light of those purposes. [No] exact formula can dictate a resolution to such fact-intensive cases."

Justice Breyer's opinion in Van Orden found "determinative" the fact that "40 years passed in which the presence of this monument, legally speaking, went unchallenged. . . . And I am not aware of any evidence suggesting that this was due to a climate of intimidation. [Those] 40 years suggest more strongly than can any set of formulaic tests that few individuals [are] likely to have understood the monument as amounting [to] a government effort to favor a particular religious sect, primarily to promote religion over nonreligion, [or] to 'work deterrence' of any 'religious belief.'" In light of McCreary County and Van Orden, can a government body hereafter, without violating the establishment clause, develop a program in which the Ten Commandments are posted with public support? Consider these observations, from Koppelman, The New American Civil Religion: Lessons for Italy, 41 Geo. Wash. Int'l L. Rev. 861, 866 (2010):

Douglas Laycock thinks that a lesson [is] that "separationist groups should sue immediately when they encounter any religious practice newly sponsored by the government." That is precisely the right lesson. [New] sponsorship of religious practices is far more likely to represent a contemporaneous effort to intervene in a live religious controversy than the perpetuation of old forms.

3. *A critique of the search for impermissible purposes.* In his dissenting opinion in Edwards v. Aguillard, 482 U.S. 578 (1987), Justice Scalia offered this critique of the "purpose" test:

[While] it is possible to discern the objective "purpose" of a statute (i.e., the public good at which its provisions appear to be directed), or even the formal motivation for a statute where that is explicitly set forth, [discerning] the subjective motivation of those enacting the statute is, to be honest, almost always an impossible task. The number of possible motivations, to begin with, is not binary, or indeed even finite. In the present case, for example, a particular legislator [may] have thought the bill would provide jobs for his district, or may have wanted to make amends with a faction of his party he had alienated on another vote, or he may have been a close friend of the bill's sponsor, or he may have hoped the Governor would appreciate his vote and make a fund-raising appearance for him, or he may have been pressured to vote for a bill he disliked by a wealthy contributor or by a flood of constituent mail, or he may have been seeking favorable publicity, or he may have been reluctant to hurt the feelings of a loyal staff member who worked on the bill, or he may have been settling an old score with a legislator who opposed the bill, or he may have been mad at his wife who opposed the bill, or he may have been intoxicated and utterly unmotivated when the vote was called, or he may have accidentally voted "yes" instead of "no," or, of course, he may have had (and very likely did have) a combination of some of the above and many other considerations. To look for *the sole purpose* of even a single legislator is probably to look for something that does not exist.

Putting that problem aside, however, where ought we to look for the individual legislator's purpose? We cannot of course assume that every member present [agreed] with the motivation expressed in a particular legislator's pre-enactment floor or committee statement. [Can] we assume, then, that they all agree with the motivation expressed in the staff-prepared committee reports they might have [read]? Should we consider post-enactment floor statements? Or post-enactment testimony from legislators, obtained expressly for the lawsuit? Should we consider media reports on the realities of the legislative bargaining? [Legislative] histories can be contrived and sanitized, favorable media coverage orchestrated, and postenactment recollections conveniently distorted. Perhaps most valuable of all would be more objective indications — for example, evidence regarding the individual legislators' religious affiliations. And if that, why not evidence regarding the fervor or tepidity of their beliefs?

Having achieved, through these simple means, an assessment of what individual legislators intended, we must still confront the question [how] *many* of them must have the invalidating intent. If a state senate approves a bill by vote of 26 to 25, and only one of the 26 intended solely to advance religion, is the law unconstitutional? What if 13 of the 26 had that intent? What if 3 of the 26 had the impermissible intent, but 3 of the 25 were simply attempting to "balance" the votes of their impermissibly motivated colleagues? Or is it possible that the intent of the bill's sponsor is alone enough to invalidate it — on a theory, perhaps, that even though everyone else's intent was pure, what they produced was the fruit of a forbidden tree?

Does this critique cast doubt on *all* doctrines relying on locating legislative purposes? Are inquiries into legislative purposes easier or more difficult in this context than in the equal protection setting, for example?

4. *A critique of the "ban" on impermissible purposes.* Does the ban on impermissible purposes imply that a legislator may not rely on religious convictions as a reason for supporting or opposing legislation?

In Harris v. McRae, 448 U.S. 297 (1980), the Court rejected an establishment clause attack on a statute restricting public financing of abortions. The challengers argued that the statute "incorporates into law the doctrines of the Roman Catholic Church." The Court responded that "the fact that the funding restrictions [may] coincide with the religious tenets of the Roman Catholic Church does not, without more, contravene the Establishment Clause." It mentioned that many statutory prohibitions, such as those against larceny, similarly coincided with religious tenets. Are such prohibitions distinguishable on the ground that more religious traditions converge in condemning them than condemn abortion? What more would be needed to establish a first amendment violation? Suppose the challengers showed that religious motivations not broadly shared among many religions played a substantial part in the enactment. Should the burden shift to the state to show a substantial secular purpose?

Consider these observations:

> Legislation must be justified in terms of secular objectives, but when people reasonably think that shared premises of justice and criteria for determining truth cannot resolve critical questions of fact, fundamental questions of value, or the weighing of competing benefits and harms, they do appropriately rely on religious convictions that help them answer these questions. Not only is such reliance appropriate for ordinary citizens, legislators in similar instances may also rely on their own religious convictions and those of their constituents, and occasionally such reliance is warranted even for judges. Though reliance on religious convictions may be appropriate in these settings, argument in religious terms is often an inapt form of public dialogue.

K. Greenawalt, Religious Convictions and Political Choice 12 (1988).

On the use of "argument in religious terms," S. Carter, The Culture of Disbelief 23 (1993), observes, "One good way to end a conversation — or start an argument — is to tell a group of well-educated professionals that you hold a political position (preferably a controversial one, such as being against abortion or pornography) because it is required by your understanding of God's will." How might the conversation continue? Magarian, Religious Argument, Free Speech Theory, and Democratic Dynamism, 86 Notre Dame L. Rev. 119, 138, 140 (2011), argues that "[political] arguments grounded solely in what the believer views as divinely inspired insight can destabilize public political debate [because] such arguments foreclose dialogue with nonbelievers," as do arguments that "[replicate] the position of an authoritative religion, based on the believer's submission to the leader's authority," but that the risk of introducing instability is outweighed by the contribution such arguments make to dynamism in public policy.

5. *Course selection: the creationism controversy.* Consider Epperson v. Arkansas, 393 U.S. 97 (1968). In 1928, Arkansas enacted a statute prohibiting "the teaching in its public schools and universities of the theory that man evolved from other species of life." The Court held the statute, "a product of the upsurge of 'fundamentalist' religious fervor of the twenties," unconstitutional. The law "selects from a body of knowledge a particular segment which it proscribes for the sole reason that it is deemed to conflict with a particular religious doctrine. [The] First

Amendment does not permit the State to require that teaching and learning must be tailored to the principles or prohibitions of any religious sect or dogma," despite the "State's undoubted right to prescribe the curriculum for its public schools." The Court said that "[no] suggestion has been made that [the statute] may be justified by considerations of state policy other than the religious views of some of its citizens." Justice Black, concurring, would distinguish *Epperson* from the case of "a state law prohibiting all teaching of human development." Suppose such a prohibition was motivated (a) by a new upsurge of fundamentalism that viewed the subject as inculcating antireligious values or (b) by a judgment that, as Justice Black put it, "it would be best to remove this controversial subject from its schools."

In Edwards v. Aguillard, 482 U.S. 578 (1987), the Court, in an opinion by Justice Brennan, held unconstitutional a Louisiana statute requiring public schools to teach "creation science" whenever they taught the theory of evolution. Examining the structure of the statute and statements made in the course of its adoption, the Court concluded that the statute had no secular purpose despite the statement in the statute's text that it was designed to promote "academic freedom." The Court stated that the statute would not promote academic freedom in the sense of "enhancing the freedom of teachers to teach what they will" or even "teaching all the evidence" in part because it required that curriculum guides be developed for creation science but not for evolution. The Court also stressed that the case presented "[the] same historic and contemporaneous antagonisms between the teachings of certain religious denominations and the teaching of evolution" that it had found in *Epperson*. "The preeminent purpose of the Louisiana legislature was clearly to advance the religious viewpoint that a supernatural being created humankind."

The Court's analysis concluded:

> We do not imply that a legislature could never require that scientific critiques of prevailing scientific theories be taught. [Teaching] a variant of scientific theories about the origins of humankind to school children might be validly done with the clear secular intent of enhancing the effectiveness of science instruction. But because the primary purpose of the [Louisiana] Act is to endorse a particular religious doctrine, the Act furthers religion in violation of the Establishment Clause.

Justice Powell's concurring opinion, in which Justice O'Connor joined, agreed that the statute had no secular purpose. Justice Scalia wrote a long dissent, in which Chief Justice Rehnquist joined. His examination of the legislative history led him to conclude that one purpose of the statute was to advance academic freedom, as it stated, in the sense of enhancing "*students'* freedom from *indoctrination*," which the legislature believed was occurring in biology courses that presented only the theory of evolution.

Could a legislature prohibit the teaching of evolution because it was a scientifically questionable theory whose acceptance by many scientists resulted from their antireligious biases? What sort of legislative hearings or findings would be required? Could a judge reassess the legislature's evaluation of the scientific status of the theory of evolution? In the absence of an illicit motivation of the sort found in *Aguillard*, does the Constitution require states to teach only the truth in matters of science? Political theory?

4. Facially Neutral Statutes That Incidentally Aid Religion: Permissible and Impermissible Effects

Note: The Problem and Its Background

1. *The basic problem.* The school prayer cases indicate that, de facto establishments aside, legislation with the sole (or predominant?) purpose of aiding religion is unconstitutional. Sometimes the Court will treat legislation that does not use religion as a basis for classification as a religious gerrymander, inferring an impermissible purpose from the statute's structure and history. More complex problems arise when the Court is unwilling to infer an impermissible purpose for a statute that does not use religion as a basis for classification, yet the legislation substantially aids religious institutions.

The Court has examined this problem most extensively in cases questioning legislative efforts to support nonpublic education. Below the college level, nearly all such education occurs in schools affiliated with churches, so that usually 75 percent or more of the aid goes to church-related schools. The Court's first substantial decision was *Everson.* The Court said that the first amendment "requires the state to be a neutral in its relations with groups of religious believers and non-believers; it does not require the state to be their adversary." It should not be interpreted "to prohibit [the state] from extending its general state law benefits to all its citizens without regard to their religious belief." The bus transportation statute "does no more than provide a general program to help parents get their children, regardless of their religion, safely and expeditiously to and from accredited schools."

Justice Rutledge's dissent was joined by Justices Frankfurter, Jackson, and Burton. He contended that the first amendment "broadly forbids state support, financial or other, of religion in any guise, form or degree. It outlaws all use of public funds for religious purposes." In this case, "parents pay money to send their children to parochial schools and funds raised by taxation are used to reimburse them. This not only helps the children to get to school and the parents to send them. It aids them in a substantial way to get [religious] training and teaching" in part because "transportation [is] as essential to education as any other element." He argued that it was impossible to apportion the expenditures between the parochial schools' religious instruction and their instruction in secular subjects.

The transportation subsidy makes it less expensive for parents to provide their children with a comprehensive religious education. In this sense, the subsidy "supports" or "aids" religion. But if the legislation is truly neutral, should this kind of support violate the Constitution? Is it distinguishable from the provision of general police and fire protection to churches and parochial schools, which could purchase private security services to provide those protections? In Rosenberger v. Rector & Visitors of the University of Virginia, 515 U.S. 819 (1995), Justice Souter, for four dissenters, argued that these forms of aid should be limited to "essential public benefits." Justice Thomas, in a separate concurring opinion, responded that to do so would be inconsistent with "[our] Nation's tradition of allowing religious adherents to participate in evenhanded government programs."

2. *Subsequent developments.* Laycock, A Survey of Religious Liberty in the United States, 47 Ohio St. L.J. 409, 443–446 (1986), describes six theories that "have been endorsed by one or more justices." They are (a) the "no-aid

theory: that any state money paid to a religious school or its students expands the school's budget and thereby aids religion"; (b) the "purchase-of-services theory: that state money paid to a religious school is simply a purchase of educational services"; (c) the "equal-treatment theory[, which] holds that government is obligated to pay for the secular aspects of education in religious schools [or] that government is free to make such payments if it wishes"; (d) the "child-benefit theory: that the state can provide educational benefits directly to children or their parents, even if the benefits are used at or in connection with a religious school [but] cannot provide the same aid directly to the school"; (e) the "tracing theory, [which] tries to trace each dollar of government money to see what the school spent it on"; and (f) the "little-bit theory[: that] a little bit of aid to religious schools is permissible, but it must be structured in a way that keeps it from becoming too much." Which of these theories explains which of the cases? Which, if any, makes sense of the Constitution?

Mueller v. Allen

463 U.S. 388 (1983)

[Minnesota's income tax statute permitted taxpayers to deduct from their gross income actual expenses incurred for "tuition, textbooks and transportation" for the education of their children in elementary and secondary schools. The deduction, available for expenses incurred in sending children to public as well as nonpublic schools, was limited to $500 per child in elementary school and $700 per child in secondary school. About 820,000 children attended public schools in Minnesota, while about 91,000 attended nonpublic schools, 95 percent of them in religiously affiliated schools. The court of appeals held that the statute did not violate the establishment clause.]

JUSTICE REHNQUIST delivered the opinion of the Court. . . .

One fixed principle in this field is our consistent rejection of the argument that "any program which in some manner aids an institution with a religious affiliation" violates the Establishment Clause. Hunt v. McNair, 413 U.S. 734, 742 (1973). For example, [a] state may reimburse parents for expenses incurred in transporting their children to school [Everson], and [it] may loan secular textbooks to all schoolchildren within the state [Board of Education v. Allen, 392 U.S. 236 (1968)]. . . .

A state's decision to defray the cost of educational expenses incurred by parents — regardless of the type of schools their children attend — evidences a purpose that is both secular and understandable. An educated populace is essential to the political and economic health of any community, and a state's efforts to assist parents in meeting the rising cost of educational expenses plainly serves this secular purpose of ensuring that the state's citizenry is well educated. Similarly, Minnesota, like other states, could conclude that there is a strong public interest in assuring the continued financial health of private schools, both sectarian and nonsectarian. By educating a substantial number of students such schools relieve public schools of a correspondingly great burden — to the benefit of all taxpayers. In addition, private schools may serve as a benchmark for public schools, in a manner analogous to the "TVA yardstick" for private power companies. . . .

We turn therefore to the more difficult but related question whether the Minnesota statute has "the primary effect of advancing the sectarian aims of the nonpublic schools." [*Lemon.*] In concluding that it does not, we find several features of the Minnesota tax deduction particularly significant. First, an essential feature of Minnesota's arrangement is the fact that §290.09, subd. 22, is only one among many deductions [available] under the Minnesota tax laws. [The] Minnesota legislature's judgment that a deduction for educational expenses fairly equalizes the tax burden of its citizens and encourages desirable expenditures for educational purposes is entitled to substantial deference.

Other characteristics of §290.09, subd. 22, argue equally strongly for the provision's constitutionality. Most importantly, the deduction is available for educational expenses incurred by all parents, including those whose children attend public schools and those whose children attend nonsectarian private schools or sectarian private [schools:] "the provision of benefits to so broad a spectrum of groups is an important index of secular effect."

We also agree [that,] by channeling whatever assistance it may provide to parochial schools through individual parents, Minnesota has reduced the Establishment Clause objections to which its action is subject. It is true, of course, that financial assistance provided to parents ultimately has an economic effect comparable to that of aid given directly to the schools attended by their children. It is also true, however, that under Minnesota's arrangement public funds become available only as a result of numerous, private choices of individual parents of school-age children. [It] is noteworthy that . . . our recent cases invalidating state aid to parochial schools have involved the direct transmission of assistance from the state to the schools themselves. . . . Where, as here, aid to parochial schools is available only as a result of decisions of individual parents no "imprimatur of State approval" [*Widmar*, Chapter 7, section E2, supra] can be deemed to have been conferred on any particular religion, or on religion generally.

We find it useful [to] compare the attenuated financial benefits flowing to parochial schools from the section to the evils against which the Establishment Clause was designed to protect. These dangers are well-described by our statement that "[w]hat is at stake as a matter of policy [in Establishment Clause cases] is preventing that kind and degree of government involvement in religious life that, as history teaches us, is apt to lead to strife and frequently strain a political system to the breaking point." It is important, however, to "keep these issues in perspective":

> At this point in the 20th century we are quite far removed from the dangers that prompted the Framers to include the Establishment Clause in the Bill of Rights. The risk of significant religious or denominational control over our democratic processes — or even a deep political division along religious lines — is remote, and when viewed against the positive contributions of sectarian schools, any such risk seems entirely tolerable in light of the continuing oversight of this Court.

[Wolman v. Walter, 443 U.S. 229 (1977)] (Powell, J., concurring in part, concurring in the judgment in part, and dissenting in part). The Establishment Clause of course extends beyond prohibition of a state church or payment of state funds to one or more churches. We do not think, however, that its prohibition extends to the type of tax deduction established by Minnesota. The historic purposes of the clause simply do not encompass the sort of attenuated financial benefit, ultimately controlled by the private choices of individual parents, that eventually flows to parochial schools from the neutrally available tax benefit at issue in this case.

Petitioners argue that, notwithstanding the facial neutrality of §290.09, subd. 22, in application the statute primarily benefits religious institutions. Petitioners rely [on] a statistical analysis of the type of persons claiming the tax deduction. They contend that most parents of public school children incur no tuition expenses and that other expenses deductible under §290.09, subd. 22, are negligible in value; moreover, they claim that 96% of the children in private schools in 1978–1979 attended religiously-affiliated institutions. Because of all this, they reason, the bulk of deductions taken under §290.09, subd. 22, will be claimed by parents of children in sectarian schools. . . .

[We] would be loath to adopt a rule grounding the constitutionality of a facially neutral law on annual reports reciting the extent to which various classes of private citizens claimed benefits under the law. [The] fact that private persons fail in a particular year to claim the tax relief to which they are entitled — under a facially neutral statute — should be of little importance in determining the constitutionality of the statute permitting such relief.

Finally, [if] parents of children in private schools choose to take especial advantage of the relief provided by §290.09, subd. 22, it is no doubt due to the fact that they bear a particularly great financial burden in educating their children. More fundamentally, whatever unequal effect may be attributed to the statutory classification can fairly be regarded as a rough return for the benefits [provided] to the state and all taxpayers by parents sending their children to parochial schools. In the light of all this, we believe it wiser to decline to engage in the type of empirical inquiry into those persons benefited by state law which petitioners urge. . . .

Turning to the third part of the *Lemon* inquiry, we have no difficulty in concluding that the Minnesota statute does not "excessively entangle" the state in religion. The only plausible source of the "comprehensive, discriminating, and continuing state surveillance" necessary to run afoul of this standard would lie in the fact that state officials must determine whether particular textbooks qualify for a deduction. In making this decision, state officials must disallow deductions taken [for] "instructional books and materials used in the teaching of religious tenets, doctrines or worship, the purpose of which is to inculcate such tenets, doctrines or worship." Making decisions such as this does not differ substantially from making the types of decisions approved in earlier opinions of this Court. In [Board of Education v. Allen], for example, the Court upheld the loan of secular textbooks to parents or children attending nonpublic schools; though state officials were required to determine whether particular books were or were not secular, the system was held not to violate the Establishment Clause. The same result follows in this case. . . .

[Affirmed.]

JUSTICE MARSHALL, with whom JUSTICE BRENNAN, JUSTICE BLACKMUN, and JUSTICE STEVENS join, dissenting.

I . . .

A

[Direct] government subsidization of parochial school tuition is impermissible because "the effect of the aid is unmistakably to provide desired financial support for nonpublic, sectarian institutions." "[A]id to the educational function of [parochial] schools . . . necessarily results in aid to the sectarian enterprise as a whole" because "[t]he very purpose of those schools is to provide an integrated secular and religious education." [Meek v. Pittenger, 421 U.S. 349 (1973).] . . .

Indirect assistance in the form of financial aid to parents for tuition payments is similarly impermissible. [By] ensuring that parents will be reimbursed for tuition payments they make, the Minnesota statute requires that taxpayers in general pay for the cost of parochial education and extends a financial "incentive to parents to send their children to sectarian schools." . . .

B . . .

1

. . . [The] bulk of the tax benefits afforded by the Minnesota scheme are enjoyed by parents of parochial school children not because parents of public school children fail to claim deductions to which they are entitled, but because the latter are simply *unable* to claim the largest tax deduction that Minnesota authorizes. [Parents] who send their children to free public schools are simply ineligible to obtain the full benefit of the deduction except in the unlikely event that they buy $700 worth of pencils, notebooks, and bus rides for their school-age children. Yet parents who pay at least $700 in tuition to nonpublic, sectarian schools can claim the full deduction even if they incur no other educational expenses. . . .

2

The majority also asserts that the Minnesota statute is distinguishable from the statute struck down in *Nyquist* in another respect: the tax benefit available under Minnesota law is a "genuine tax deduction," whereas the New York law provided a benefit which, while nominally a deduction, also had features of a "tax credit." . . .

This is a distinction without a difference. [The] deduction afforded by Minnesota law was "designed to yield a [tax benefit] in exchange for performing a specific act which the State desires to encourage." [*Nyquist.*] . . .

ZELMAN v. SIMMONS-HARRIS, 536 U.S. 639 (2002). In an opinion by Chief Justice Rehnquist, the Court upheld a school voucher program with the following characteristics, as described in the syllabus to the Court's opinion. The program "gives educational choices to families in any Ohio school district that is under state control pursuant to a federal-court order. The program provides tuition aid for certain students in the Cleveland City School District, the only covered district, to attend participating public or private schools of their parent's choosing and tutorial aid for students who choose to remain enrolled in public school. Both religious and nonreligious schools in the district may participate, as may public schools in adjacent school districts. Tuition aid is distributed to parents according to financial need, and where the aid is spent depends solely upon where parents choose to enroll their children. The number of tutorial assistance grants provided to students remaining in public school must equal the number of tuition aid scholarships. In the 1999–2000 school year, 82% of the participating private schools had a religious affiliation, none of the adjacent public schools participated, and 96% of the students participating in the scholarship program were enrolled in religiously affiliated schools. [Cleveland] schoolchildren also have the option of enrolling in community schools, which are funded under state law but run by their own school boards and receive twice the per-student funding as participating private schools, or magnet schools, which are public schools emphasizing a particular subject area, teaching method, or service, and for which the school district receives the same amount per student as it does for a student enrolled at a traditional public school."

Finding "no dispute that the program [was] enacted for the valid secular purpose of providing educational assistance to poor children in a demonstrably failing public school system," the Court said that "[the] question presented is whether the Ohio program [has] the forbidden 'effect' of advancing or inhibiting religion." The Court concluded that the program did not have such an effect. "[W]here a government aid program is neutral with respect to religion, and provides assistance directly to a broad class of citizens who, in turn, direct government aid to religious schools wholly as a result of their own genuine and independent private choice, the program is not readily subject to challenge under the Establishment Clause. A program that shares these features permits government aid to reach religious institutions only by way of the deliberate choices of numerous individual recipients. The incidental advancement of a religious mission, or the perceived endorsement of a religious message, is reasonably attributable to the individual recipient, not to the government, whose role ends with the disbursement of benefits."

It continued, "[the] Ohio program is neutral in all respects toward religion. It is part of a general and multifaceted undertaking by the State of Ohio to provide educational opportunities to the children of a failed school district. It confers educational assistance directly to a broad class of individuals defined without reference to religion, *i.e.*, any parent of a school-age child who resides in the Cleveland City School District. The program permits the participation of *all* schools within the district, religious or nonreligious. Adjacent public schools also may participate and have a financial incentive to do so. Program benefits are available to participating families on neutral terms, with no reference to religion. The only preference stated anywhere in the program is a preference for low-income families, who receive greater assistance and are given priority for admission at participating schools.

"There are no 'financial incentives' that 'skew' the program toward religious schools. Such incentives '[are] not present . . . where the aid is allocated on the basis of neutral, secular criteria that neither favor nor disfavor religion, and is made available to both religious and secular beneficiaries on a nondiscriminatory basis.' The program here in fact creates financial disincentives for religious schools, with private schools receiving only half the government assistance given to community schools and one-third the assistance given to magnet schools. Adjacent public schools, should any choose to accept program students, are also eligible to receive two to three times the state funding of a private religious school. Families too have a financial disincentive to choose a private religious school over other schools. Parents that choose to participate in the scholarship program and then to enroll their children in a private school (religious or nonreligious) must copay a portion of the school's tuition. Families that choose a community school, magnet school, or traditional public school pay nothing. Although such features of the program are not necessary to its constitutionality, they clearly dispel the claim that the program 'creates . . . financial incentives for parents to choose a sectarian school.'"

On whether the program gave "genuine opportunities for Cleveland parents to select secular educational options for their school-age children," the Court argued that "Cleveland schoolchildren enjoy a range of educational choices: They may remain in public school as before, remain in public school with publicly funded tutoring aid, obtain a scholarship and choose a religious school, obtain a scholarship and choose a nonreligious private school, enroll in a community school, or enroll in a magnet school. That 46 of the 56 private schools now participating in the program are religious schools does not condemn it as a violation of the Establishment Clause. The Establishment Clause question is whether Ohio is coercing parents into sending their children to religious schools, and that question must be answered by evaluating *all* options Ohio provides Cleveland schoolchildren, only one of which is to obtain a program scholarship and then choose a religious school."

Relying on *Mueller*, the Court rejected the argument that "we should attach constitutional significance to the fact that 96% of scholarship recipients have enrolled in religious schools. They claim that this alone proves parents lack genuine choice, even if no parent has ever said so. We need not consider this argument in detail, since it was flatly rejected in *Mueller*, where we found it irrelevant that 96% of parents taking deductions for tuition expenses paid tuition at religious schools." Explaining why it rejected the argument, the Court pointed out that "[the] 96% figure [discounts] entirely (1) the more than 1,900 Cleveland children enrolled in alternative community schools, (2) the more than 13,000 children enrolled in alternative magnet schools, and (3) the more than 1,400 children enrolled in traditional public schools with tutorial assistance. Including some or all of these children in the denominator of children enrolled in nontraditional schools during the 1999–2000 school year drops the percentage enrolled in religious schools from 96% to under 20%. The 96% figure also represents but a snapshot of one particular school year. In the 1997–1998 school year, by contrast, only 78% of scholarship recipients attended religious schools."

Justices O'Connor and Thomas wrote concurring opinions. Justices Stevens, Souter, Ginsburg, and Breyer dissented. Justice Souter's dissent asserted that "the espoused criteria of neutrality in offering aid, and private choice in directing it, [are] nothing but examples of verbal formalism." To apply the neutrality test, he argued, "it makes sense to focus on a category of aid that may be directed to religious as well as secular schools, and ask whether the scheme favors a religious direction. Here, one would ask whether the voucher provisions [were] written in a way that skewed the scheme toward benefiting religious schools. [The] majority looks not to the provisions for tuition vouchers, but to every provision for educational [opportunity]. The majority then finds confirmation that 'participation of *all* schools' satisfies neutrality by noting that the better part of total state educational expenditure goes to public schools, thus showing there is no favor of religion. The illogic is patent. If regular, public schools (which can get no voucher payments) 'participate' in a voucher scheme with schools that can, and public expenditure is still predominantly on public schools, then the majority's reasoning would find neutrality in a scheme of vouchers available for private tuition in districts with no secular private schools at all. 'Neutrality' as the majority employs the term is, literally, verbal and nothing more." Justice Souter also criticized the Court for what he described as its abandonment of the previously enforced limitation on provision of "substantial" aid to religious institutions.

Note: Purpose and Effect in Aid to Nonpublic Education — Benevolent Neutrality?

1. *A forerunner: Mitchell.* Justice Thomas, writing for a plurality in Mitchell v. Helms, 530 U.S. 793 (2000), proposed that statutes providing aid to "religious, irreligious, and areligious" institutions should generally be constitutional because "no one would conclude that any indoctrination that any particular recipient conducts has been done at the behest of the government. [If] the government is offering assistance to recipients who provide [a] broad range of indoctrination, the government itself is not thought responsible for any particular indoctrination." *Mitchell* upheld a statute that provided funds for state education agencies to lend computers, including software, and library books, to nonpublic schools. The amount available to a school was determined by that school's enrollment. Justice Thomas's opinion rejected as "arbitrary" the distinction between direct and indirect aid to the religious missions of religious schools. It also found irrelevant the possibility that some forms of aid might be diverted to religious uses: "[A] concern for divertibility, as opposed to improper content, is misplaced [because] it is boundless [and] thus has only the most attenuated [link] to any realistic concern for preventing an 'establishment of religion.'"

Justice O'Connor, joined by Justice Breyer, concurred in the judgment. She criticized the plurality's "near-absolute position with respect to neutrality." She also believed "significant" the "distinction between a per-capita school-aid program and a true private-choice program. [In] terms of public perception, a government program of direct aid to religious schools based on the number of students attending each school differs meaningfully from the government distributing aid directly to individual students who, in turn, decide to use the aid at the same religious schools. In the former example, if the religious school uses the aid to inculcate religion in its students, it is reasonable to say that the government has communicated a message of endorsement." She found the program in *Mitchell* constitutional because it provided sufficient guarantees that the aid would not be diverted to religious uses and because the evidence of actual diversion was de minimis. Justices Souter, Stevens, and Ginsburg dissented.

2. *Vouchers.* What, if any, limits does the establishment clause place on voucher programs? What are the criteria for determining whether a program allows participants to exercise "genuine choice" among secular and religious options? Justice O'Connor's concurring opinion in *Zelman* argued that choice should be determined by "consider[ing] all reasonable educational alternatives to religious schools that are available to parents," and pointed out that "[when] one considers the option to attend community schools, the percentage of students enrolled in religious schools falls to 62.1 percent. If magnet schools are included, [this] percentage falls to 16.5 percent."

Justice Souter's dissent criticized this focus as "confused" because it "ignores the reason for having a private choice criterion in the first place. [It] is a criterion for deciding whether indirect aid to a religious school is legitimate because it passes through private hands that can spend or use the aid in a secular school. The question is whether the private hand is genuinely free to send the money in either a secular direction or a religious one. The majority now has transformed this question [into] a question about selecting from examples of state spending (on education) including direct spending on magnet and community public schools that goes through no private hands and could never reach a religious school under any circumstance. When the choice test is transformed from where to spend the money to where to go to school, it is cut loose from its very purpose." He concluded, "If 'choice' is present whenever there is any educational alternative to the religious school to which vouchers can be endorsed, then there will always be a choice and the voucher can always be constitutional, even in a system in which there is not a single private secular school as an alternative to the religious school." For an analysis of the fiscal and political limits on voucher programs, see Ryan and Heise, The Political Economy of School Choice, 111 Yale L.J. 2043 (2002).

3. *Express discrimination?* Locke v. Davey, 540 U.S. 712 (2004), upheld against a free exercise challenge a Washington State program that awarded merit scholarships to college students, but excluded students pursuing degrees in devotional theology. Chief Justice Rehnquist noted that the religion clauses allowed some "play in the joints," and that the Washington program involved that consideration. "[We] can think of few areas in which a State's antiestablishment interests come more into play. [Given] the historic and substantial state interest at issue, we [cannot] conclude that the denial of funding for vocational religious instruction alone is inherently constitutionally suspect." Justice Scalia, joined by Justice Thomas, dissented, arguing that "[when] the State makes a public benefit generally available, that benefit becomes part of the baseline against which burdens on religion are measured; and when the State withholds that benefit from some individuals solely on the basis of religion, it violates the Free Exercise Clause no less than if it had imposed a special tax." Here, "[no] field of study but religion is singled out for disfavor. [The student] seeks only *equal* treatment. . . ." The majority responded, "[Training] for religious professions and training for secular professions are not fungible. [The] subject of religion is one in which [the Constitution] embod[ies] distinct views [that] find no counterpart with respect to other callings or professions."

Trinity Lutheran Church v. Comer, 137 S. Ct. 2012 (2017), dealt with a state program providing funding for replacing playground surfaces with materials made from recycled tires. The state excluded churches from eligibility for the grants. Trinity Lutheran ran a child- and day-care center, with a playground, located on church property. Chief Justice Roberts, writing for the Court, held that the exclusion violated the Free Exercise Clause but "put[ting] Trinity Lutheran to a choice: It may participate in an otherwise available benefit program or remain a religious institution. [The] express discrimination here is not the denial of a grant, but rather the refusal to allow the Church — solely because it is a church — to compete with secular organizations for a grant." Such an exclusion "must withstand the strictest scrutiny." The state's reasons for the exclusion, "a policy preference for skating as far as possible from religious establishment concerns," "cannot qualify as compelling."

A footnote, joined only by four Justices, stated, "We do not address religious uses of funding or other forms of discrimination." Would it be constitutionally permissible for a state to exclude from a program for reconstructing buildings damaged in a hurricane applications from churches to restore to their original condition windows depicting religious scenes? To exclude church buildings from a program to restore historic buildings? Zelman v. Simmons-Harris, above, held that it was constitutionally permissible to include religiously affiliated schools in programs providing vouchers to parents who send their children to non-public schools. Does *Trinity Lutheran Church* imply that religiously affiliated schools must be included in such programs?

4. *Further questions about vouchers.* The Court in *Locke* rejected in a footnote the argument that the exclusion was an unconstitutional viewpoint restriction, saying that the scholarship program "is not a forum for speech." Its "purpose [is] to assist students [with] the cost of postsecondary education, not to 'encourage a diversity of views from private speakers.'"

Many proposed voucher programs bar the use of vouchers at schools that discriminate in admissions or employment on the basis of race, gender, religion, or sexual orientation, or at schools that do not offer particular subjects. As applied to schools that discriminate because of religious belief (for example, the belief that women with children should not be employed outside the home) or refuse to teach some subject (for example, evolutionary theory) because of religious belief, are such provisions violations of the first amendment right of expressive association, or the free exercise clause? For discussions, see Tushnet, Vouchers after *Zelman*, 2002 Sup. Ct. Rev. 1; Berg, Vouchers and Religious Schools: The New Constitutional Questions, 72 U. Cin. L. Rev. 151 (2003).

5. *The meaning of neutrality.* Will a requirement of neutrality increase the cost of providing aid to nonpublic schools and thereby alter the political dimensions of the issue? Consider this justification for upholding direct appropriations to private schools: Public schools are subsidized through ordinary appropriations; neutrality is achieved by the separate appropriations to private schools. Finding the latter to violate neutrality artificially divides a unitary system of state-supported education that, taken as a whole, is neutral. Consider the proposal in Choper, The Establishment Clause and Aid to Parochial Schools, 56 Cal. L. Rev. 260, 266 (1968), that aid should be allowed "so long as such aid does not exceed the value of the secular educational service rendered by the school." How likely is it that a legislature, constrained by pluralist politics and tax limitations, would enact a program that violated this test? Does it simply restate the requirement of neutrality?

Berg, Religion Clause Anti-Theories, 72 Notre Dame L. Rev. 693, 703–704 (1997), argues that "[government] should, as much as possible, minimize the effect it has on the voluntary, independent religious decisions of the people as individuals and in voluntary groups. The baseline against which effects on religion should be compared is a situation in which religious beliefs and practices succeed or fail solely on their merits — as those merits are presented and judged by individuals and groups, not by government." Consider the assumptions implicit in the term "the merits" in this formulation.

For a discussion of the problem of identifying an appropriate baseline, see Gedicks, The Rhetoric of Church and State: A Critical Analysis of Religion Clause Jurisprudence 57–58, 60 (1995): "How does one identify the baseline measure of religious neutrality? [In] the modern welfare state, [government] aid to both individuals and organizations is widespread and pervasive. Since in the United States most persons and entities are entitled to some kind of government aid, religious neutrality would generally seem to require that this aid not be denied to otherwise qualified recipients simply because they are religious. Indeed, to deny aid to such persons and entities constitutes a tax on religious exercise which skews private choice away from religion. [If] one were to imagine a world of minimalist government in which secular public schools did not exist, then government action mandating religious instruction [would] violate neutrality." Berg discusses some implications of Gedicks's position: "[If] a system of subsidized secular public schools does, in fact, discourage religiously informed education, why can't government include religious teaching in the public school curriculum? [Any] statement the government makes is bound to favor one faith over another." Berg, supra, at 743.

Consider the implications of the argument that voucher and similar programs have a disparate impact on different religious denominations because of their positions on the propriety of accepting government aid even in the form of vouchers. Should the fact that the disparate impact results from religiously motivated choices be sufficient to dispel concerns about sect preference? Consider these observations:

> All institutions [have] an intense interest in their own survival. Programs distributing aid under the neutrality principle offer financial inducements for religious groups to participate in certain programs that "government" desires for the nation and that may [conflict] with certain tenets of the nation's faith communities. These programs easily can [tempt] religious groups to go against their basic principles in order to secure government funding and receive the same benefits [as] other faith traditions. [It] will be those programs that center on social issues more "in the gray" respecting a faith community's belief system that will begin the [assimilation] of our nation's religious traditions. [If a group] buckles to [the] government-supplied financial incentive and chooses to participate, after many years [will] the members of the community even remember the original position of their [tradition?] [One] might easily predict the homogenization of America's diverse faith traditions into a form of civil religion that encourages a malleability of doctrine shaped by the designs of government programs.

Davis, A Commentary on the Supreme Court's "Equal Treatment" Doctrine as the New Constitutional Paradigm for Protecting Religious Liberty, 46 J. Church & St. 717, 733–734 (2004).

6. *Indirect versus direct aid.* Do the cases support a distinction between direct aid — payments or donations of goods and services made to religiously affiliated schools — and indirect aid — payments made to parents who then use the funds to pay such schools? Would it be constitutional for a state to pay a portion of the salary of mathematics teachers in nonpublic schools as part of a "general program" of paying the salaries of all mathematics teachers? In Rosenberger v. Rector & Visitors of the University of Virginia, 515 U.S. 819 (1995), Justice Souter argued that the Court's approach "would permit a State to pay all the bills of any religious institution." Justice Kennedy's opinion for the Court responded that the student publication involved was "not a religious institution, at least in the usual sense of that term." After *Rosenberger*, must a state include religiously affiliated schools in any voucher program it adopts? What is the basis for the proposition that direct aid to religious institutions is impermissible?

7. *Monetary versus nonmonetary aid.* Justice Thomas's opinion in *Mitchell* noted that prior cases had found "'special Establishment Clause dangers' when money is given to religious schools or entities directly rather than [indirectly]. But [we] refuse to allow a 'special' case to create a rule for all cases." Justice O'Connor wrote, "If [a] per-capita-aid program is identical in relevant constitutional respects to a true private-choice program, then there is no reason that [the] government should be precluded from providing direct money payments to religious organizations [based] on the number of persons belonging to each organization." If the distinction between direct and indirect aid is "arbitrary" when nonmonetary resources are involved, is it less arbitrary when money is involved?

8. *Administrative and political entanglement.* Administrative entanglement occurs when public officials are required to scrutinize the use of public funds to ensure that they are not used for sectarian purposes. *Lemon* also discussed political entanglement. Public funds completely devoted to secular purposes result in an equal amount of nonpublic funds becoming available for sectarian purposes. Are direct and unrestricted grants to nonpublic schools therefore constitutional? *Lemon* argued that such grants had a "divisive political potential," as partisans would force candidates "to declare" on issues that will lead people to "find their votes aligned with their faith." Although political division is "normal and healthy," division "along religious lines was one of the principal evils against which the First Amendment was intended to protect. [To] have States [divide] on [these] [would] tend to confuse and obscure other issues of great urgency." Political fragmentation is "likely to be intensified" where "successive and very likely permanent annual appropriations that benefit relatively few religious groups" are involved.

Is the idea of political entanglement misconceived? *Mueller* stated that the language in *Lemon* about political entanglement must be "confined to cases where direct financial subsidies are paid." Is the distinction between direct subsidies and indirect tax benefits consistent with the realities of the legislative process? Note that legislatures must determine annual levels of direct subsidies. Would the use of some formula — for example, a stated proportion of the appropriations for public schools — avoid the political entanglement problems raised in *Lemon*?

Is there any reason to regard interest groups organized around religion as different, and more suspect, actors in the political process than interest groups organized around economic interests?

9. *Aid to "pervasively sectarian" institutions.* In Bowen v. Kendrick, 487 U.S. 589 (1988), the Court considered the constitutionality of the Adolescent Family Life Act, which authorizes federal grants to public and private organizations, including organizations with institutional ties to religious denominations, for counseling services and research in the area of premarital adolescent sexual relations and pregnancy. Applying the *Lemon* standard, the Court held that the act on its face did not violate the establishment clause. "[It] is clear from the face of the statute that the [act] was motivated primarily, if not entirely, by a legitimate secular purpose — the elimination or reduction of social and economic problems caused by teenage sexuality, pregnancy, and parenthood." Further, the "services to be provided under the [act] are not religious in character." Moreover, although the act "takes a particular approach toward dealing with adolescent sexuality and pregnancy — for example, two of its stated purposes are to 'promote self-discipline' [and] to 'promote adoption as an alternative' [to abortion] — [that] approach is not inherently religious. . . ." Although conceding that "the Establishment Clause '[prohibits] government-financed [indoctrination] into the beliefs of a particular religious faith,'" the Court reasoned that, when the aid flows to religiously affiliated institutions that are not pervasively sectarian, "we [will not] presume that it [will] be used in a way that would have the primary effect of advancing religion." The Court remanded for a determination whether the act was unconstitutional "as applied," which would turn on such determinations as whether any of the grantees under the act were "pervasively sectarian" and whether any of the "aid has been used to fund 'specifically religious activit[ies] in an otherwise substantially secular setting.'"

Justice Thomas's plurality opinion in *Mitchell* concluded that the doctrine barring pervasively sectarian institutions from receiving aid that was otherwise permissible should be rejected. "The pervasively sectarian recipient has not received any special favor, and it is most bizarre that the Court would [reserve] special hostility for those who take their religion seriously, who think that their religion should affect the whole of their lives, or who make the mistake of being effective in transmitting their views to children." In addition, "the inquiry into the recipient's religious views [is offensive]." Finally, "hostility to aid to pervasively sectarian schools has a shameful pedigree that we do not hesitate to disavow." That pedigree involved hostility to Catholic parochial schools. Justice O'Connor's opinion concurring in the judgment did not address the doctrine; the dissent treated the question of the degree of an institution's sectarianism as relevant to constitutional analysis.

10. *Neutrality, steering, and "real choice."* What considerations are relevant in determining whether a neutral program offers participants a real choice or steers them toward religious institutions? Lupu and Tuttle, Sites of Redemption: A Wide-Angle Look at Government Vouchers and Sectarian Service Providers, 18 J.L. & Pol. 537, 561, 565 (2002), suggest the following considerations: the extent to which participants are constrained in choosing the religious provider rather than not participating at all; the extent to which there are nonreligious institutions providing the services and able to accept the vouchers; the ease with which new providers can start up, making the market more or less dynamic in response to demand; and the degree to which the government's purpose is connected to a character change itself tied to religious transformation. How might these factors bear on voucher programs for the provision of child care services? For the provision of drug treatment programs offered as alternatives to incarceration?

11. *Facially neutral statutes that incidentally burden religion.* To what extent may government officials take religion into account in seeking to deter crime? May police officials direct special attention to religious institutions whose doctrine — as interpreted by the officials — suggests that church members are more likely to commit crime than members of other religious institutions? Huq, The Signaling Function of Religious Speech in Domestic Counterterrorism, 89 Tex. L. Rev. 833 (2011), argues that such actions pose threats to the "epistemic authority" of religious institutions in defining their doctrine (by deterring the development of definitions that public officials might misinterpret as signaling a greater propensity to commit crime), but that current doctrine does not afford robust protection to epistemic authority. Should it?

Note: Concluding Observations

Consider these observations from K. Karst, Law's Promise, Law's Expression 149 (1994): "Today the risk of religious polarization does seem to have lessened in the resource-allocation context, where the issues can be seen as part of the everyday grist of the political mill. [Issues] concerning governmental deployments of the symbols of religion [have] a greater capacity to polarize [because] they are not the subject of multilateral negotiation and they do not invite compromise [and because] any such symbol has a diffuse meaning, and so serves as a handy referent for a whole world view." To similar effect, consider Lupu, Government Messages and Government Money: *Santa Fe*, Mitchell v. Helms, and the Arc of the Establishment Clause, 42 Wm. & Mary L. Rev. 771, 801 (2001):

> [Issues] involving government resources in support of religion quite frequently [are] truly about "church." [When] the state provides resources to such entities, it typically does so on the theory that churches may effectively assist in the state's secular work. [Government] message cases [are] very different in their character: [They] involve officials of the state doing the work of faith institutions — that is, preaching, proselytizing, [and] generally spreading the Word or respect for the Word. [Government] message cases are not about institutional connection between agencies of government and agencies. [They are] about the political misappropriation of religious themes.

Do these observations reconcile *Mueller* with *Lynch* and *Lee*? Do they justify the Court's decisions?

C. THE FREE EXERCISE CLAUSE: REQUIRED ACCOMMODATIONS

Religious beliefs and expression are forms of speech and, as such, are protected by the free speech clause of the first amendment. Some early free speech decisions involving religious expression relied on the free exercise clause as well. See, e.g., Cantwell v. Connecticut, Chapter 7, section B2, supra; Lovell v. Griffin, Chapter 7, section C2, supra. What, if anything, does the free exercise clause add to the free speech clause?

Note: *From* Reynolds *to* Smith

The Court's discussions of required accommodations of religion have tended to ignore examination of the intentions of the drafters of the first amendment, except by referring in general terms to their interest in religious liberty. McConnell, The Origins and Historical Understanding of Free Exercise of Religion, 103 Harv. L. Rev. 1409, 1512 (1990), concludes on the basis of an examination of pre-1787 practice, the debates over the Constitution and the bill of rights, and contemporaneous political theory that "exemptions were not common enough to compel the inference that the term 'free exercise of religion' necessarily included an enforceable right to exemption. [Without] overstating the force of the evidence, however, it is possible to say that the [doctrine] of free exercise exemptions is more consistent with the original understanding than is a position that leads only to the facial neutrality of legislation." How do legislative practices of exemption support a constitutional requirement of exemption? For a study of the same materials coming equally cautiously to the opposite conclusion, see Hamburger, A Constitutional Right of Religious Exemption: An Historical Perspective, 60 Geo. Wash. L. Rev. 915 (1992).

Until 1963, the Supreme Court had not squarely held that the free exercise clause protects religious beliefs differently, or more extensively, than the free speech clause protects political beliefs. Reynolds v. United States, 98 U.S. 145 (1879), upheld a conviction of a Mormon for bigamy, rejecting a free exercise defense. The Court said that under the first amendment "Congress was deprived of all legislative power over mere opinion, but was left free to reach actions which were in violation of social duties or subversive of good order. [Laws] are made for the government of actions, and while they cannot interfere with mere religious belief and actions, they may with practices." In Cantwell v. Connecticut, 310 U.S. 296 (1940), the Court said that the free exercise clause "embraces two concepts, — freedom to believe and freedom to act. The first is absolute, but in the nature of things, the second cannot be. Conduct remains subject to regulation for the protection of society. [*Reynolds.*] [In] every case the power to regulate must be so exercised as not [unduly] to infringe the protected freedom."

BRAUNFELD v. BROWN, 366 U.S. 599 (1961). Pennsylvania's law requiring that businesses be closed on Sundays was challenged on free exercise grounds by Orthodox Jews, whose religion required that they close their stores on Saturdays. They alleged that the Sunday closing laws placed them at a competitive disadvantage so severe as to force them out of business. Chief Justice Warren's plurality opinion rejected the free exercise claim. Citing *Reynolds*, it said, "[The] statute [does] not make criminal the holding of any religious belief or opinion, nor does it force anyone to embrace any religious belief. [It simply] make[s] the practice of their religious beliefs more expensive. [To] strike down [legislation] which imposes only an indirect burden on the exercise of religion [would] radically restrict the operating latitude of the legislature. [We] are a cosmopolitan nation made up of people of almost every conceivable religious preference. [Consequently,] it cannot be expected, much less required, that legislators enact no law regulating conduct that may in some way result in an economic disadvantage to some religious sects and not to others because of the special practices of the various religions. [If] the State regulates conduct by enacting a general law within its power, the purpose and effect of which is to advance the State's secular goals, the statute is valid despite its indirect burden on religious observance unless the State may accomplish its purposes by means which do not impose such a burden." An exemption for Saturday-observers was not required because it "might well undermine the State's goal of providing a day that, as best possible, eliminates the atmosphere of commercial noise and activity. [Enforcement] problems would be more difficult [and Saturday-observers] might well [receive] an economic advantage over their competitors who must close on that day."

Justice Brennan, in dissent, described the state's interest as "the mere convenience of having everyone rest on the same day" and called the plurality's concern about a system allowing exemptions "fanciful." This "[exalts] administrative convenience to a constitutional level high enough to justify making one religion economically disadvantageous." Justice Stewart's dissent said that the law "compels an Orthodox Jew to choose between his religious faith and his economic survival. That is a cruel choice. It is a choice which I think no State can constitutionally demand. For me this is not something that can be swept under the rug and forgotten in the interest of enforced Sunday togetherness."

SHERBERT v. VERNER, 374 U.S. 398 (1963). Mrs. Sherbert, a Seventh-Day Adventist, was fired by her employer because she would not work on Saturday, her church's Sabbath. She was unable to find other employment in her town that would allow her to observe her Sabbath. She sought unemployment compensation, which was denied because she had lacked good cause to refuse suitable work. (The unemployment systems in most states, but not Sherbert's, treated inability to find work that would allow observance of the worker's Sabbath to be "good cause" for refusing to accept job offers.)

The Supreme Court, in an opinion by Justice Brennan, held that the denial of unemployment compensation violated the free exercise clause. The denial "imposes [a] burden on the free exercise" of religion. "Here not only is it apparent that appellant's declared ineligibility for benefits derives solely from the practice of her religion, but the pressure upon her to forego that practice is unmistakable. The ruling forces her to choose between following the precepts of her religion and forfeiting benefits, on the one hand, and abandoning one of the precepts of her religion in order to accept work, on the other hand. Governmental imposition of such a choice puts the same kind of burden upon the free exercise of religion as would a fine imposed against appellant for her Saturday worship."

The Court then considered "whether some compelling state interest [justifies] the substantial infringement of appellant's First Amendment right." The only interest asserted was prevention of the filing of fraudulent claims, but, according to the Court, the Constitution required that the state demonstrate that "no alternative forms of regulations would combat such abuses without infringing First Amendment rights." Unlike *Braunfeld*, where allowing exemptions would necessarily impair the interest in preserving a uniform day of rest, here exemptions could be administered without undermining the unemployment compensation system.

Justice Stewart concurred in the result. "The guarantee of religious liberty embodied in the Free Exercise Clause affirmatively requires government to create an atmosphere of hospitality and accommodation to individual belief or disbelief. [Our] Constitution commands the positive protection by government of religious freedom [for] each of us."

Justice Harlan, joined by Justice White, dissented. The Court's holding, he said, meant that "the State [must] *single out* for financial assistance those whose behavior is religiously motivated, even though it denies such assistance to others whose identical behavior [is] not religiously motivated." Justice Harlan believed that the state could choose "to create an exception to its eligibility requirements for persons like the appellant," but he could not "subscribe to the conclusion that the State is constitutionally *compelled* to carve out an exception to its general rule of eligibility in the present case. Those situations in which the Constitution may require special treatment on account of religion are, in my view, few and far between. [Such] compulsion in the present case is particularly inappropriate in light of the indirect, remote, and insubstantial effect of the decision below on the exercise of appellant's religion and in light of the direct financial assistance to religion that today's decision requires."

WISCONSIN v. YODER, 406 U.S. 205 (1972). Yoder, a member of the Old Order Amish, was fined five dollars for refusing to send his children to school after they had completed the eighth grade. His children were ages fourteen and fifteen; Wisconsin required school attendance until age sixteen. The Amish object to high school education because of their desire to live in a "church community separate and apart from the world." They believe that high schools expose children to worldly matters and emphasize "intellectual and scientific accomplishments, self-distinction, competitiveness, worldly success, and social life with other students," in contrast to the Amish desire for "informal learning-through-doing [and] wisdom, rather than technical knowledge; community welfare, rather than competition." Basic education is acceptable to them because it prepares children "to read the Bible [and] to be good farmers and citizens." The state supreme court held that the conviction violated the free exercise clause, and the Supreme Court affirmed.

Chief Justice Burger's opinion for the Court acknowledged the state's "interest in universal education," but required that it be balanced "when it impinges on fundamental rights and interests" to assure that "there is a state interest of sufficient magnitude to override the [free exercise] interest." "[Only] those interests of the highest order and those not otherwise served can overbalance legitimate claims of free exercise of religion." The Court first asked whether the Amish claim was "rooted in religious belief. [If] the Amish asserted their claims because of their subjective evaluation and rejection of the contemporary secular values accepted by the majority, much as Thoreau rejected the social values of his time and isolated himself at Walden Pond, their claims would not rest on a religious basis. Thoreau's choice was philosophical and personal rather than religious, and such belief does not rise to the demands of the Religion Clauses." But the Amish way of life was "one of deep religious conviction, shared by an organized group and intimately related to daily living." Compulsory high school education required the Amish "to perform acts undeniably at odds with fundamental tenets of their religious beliefs" and "[carried] with it a very real threat of undermining the Amish community."

The Court rejected the state's effort to rely on the distinction between belief and action; "in this context belief and action cannot be neatly confined in logic-tight compartments." Nor was it dispositive that the requirement was facially neutral, for even such a regulation "may offend the constitutional requirement for governmental neutrality if it unduly burdens the free exercise of religion [Sherbert]." The Court accepted the state's argument that "some degree of education is necessary to prepare citizens to participate effectively and intelligently in our open political system [and] to be self-reliant and self-sufficient participants in society." But the additional one or two years of formal high school education "would do little to serve those interests." The state also argued that the Amish fostered ignorance, but the Court said that the record showed "that the Amish community has been a highly successful social unit within our society, even if apart from the conventional 'mainstream.' Its members are productive and very law-abiding members of society; they reject public welfare in its usual modern forms." The Court also rejected as "highly speculative" the state's claim that its requirement served the interest in providing those Amish children who eventually leave the community with an adequate basis for "making their way in the world." It said that "there is nothing in this record to suggest that the Amish qualities of reliability, self-reliance, and dedication to work would fail to find ready markets in today's society." The Court emphasized that it was "not dealing with a way of life and mode of education by a group claiming to have recently discovered some 'progressive' or more enlightened process for rearing children for modern life." In light of the Amish's "long history as a successful and self-sufficient segment of American society," and their showing of "the adequacy of their alternative mode of continuing informal vocational education in terms of precisely those overall interests that the State advances," a showing "that probably few other religious groups or sects could make, and weighing the minimal difference between what the State would require and what the Amish already accept, it was incumbent on the State to show with more particularity how its admittedly strong interest in compulsory education would be adversely affected by granting an exemption to the Amish."

Justice Douglas's dissent focused on the potential conflict of interest between Amish parents and their children, some of whom might wish to attend high school in order to be in a position to choose whether to adhere to or "to break from the Amish tradition." The Court replied that, in the absence of evidence of actual conflicts, allowing the state to compel high school attendance because of "the potential" that some parents might "act contrary to the best interests of their children by foreclosing their opportunity to make an intelligent choice between the Amish way of life and that of the outside world" would create "such an intrusion by a State into family decisions in the area of religious training" as itself to raise "grave questions of religious freedom."

Note: Problems of Mandatory Accommodation

1. *Unemployment cases.* The Court followed *Sherbert* in three later unemployment compensation cases, which presented minor variations on the basic claim. In Hobbie v. Unemployment Appeals Commission, 480 U.S. 136 (1987), the claimant's beliefs had changed during the course of her employment, but the Court held that "the timing of [the] conversion is immaterial." Frazee v. Illinois Department of Employment Security, 489 U.S. 829 (1989), applied *Sherbert* to a person who was not a member of an established religious sect or church, one of whose tenets was a prohibition on Sunday work, but who sincerely believed that "as a Christian, he could not work on 'the Lord's Day.'" See also Thomas v. Review Board, 450 U.S. 707 (1981).

2. *Taxation.* United States v. Lee, 455 U.S. 252 (1982), rejected a claim for a constitutionally required exemption from paying the Social Security tax. Lee, a member of the Old Order Amish, was a self-employed farmer and carpenter, who did not pay the Social Security tax for his Amish employees because "the Amish believe it sinful not to provide for their own elderly and therefore are religiously opposed to the national social security system." The Court found that the limitation on religious liberty was "essential to accomplish an overriding governmental interest." Mandatory participation in the Social Security system was "indispensable to [its] fiscal vitality." Chief Justice Burger's opinion for the Court said, "Unlike [*Yoder*], it would be difficult to accommodate the comprehensive social security system with myriad exceptions flowing from a wide variety of religious beliefs. [There] is no principled way [to] distinguish between general taxes and those imposed under the Social Security Act. If, for example, a religious adherent believes war is a sin, and if a certain percentage of the federal budget can be identified as devoted to war-related activities, such individuals would have a similarly valid claim to be exempt from paying that percentage of the income tax. The tax system could not function if denominations were allowed to challenge the tax system because tax payments were spent in a manner that violates their religious belief."

Justice Stevens concurred in the judgment but criticized the Court for overstating the risk that "a myriad of other claims" would occur. He noted that "in the typical case [of general taxes], the taxpayer is not in any position to supply the government with an equivalent substitute for the objectionable use of his money." Justice Stevens noted that, "if tax exemptions were dispensed on religious grounds, every citizen would have an economic motivation to join the favored sects [while no] comparable economic motivation could explain the conduct of the [employee] in *Sherbert*," where employer-dictated changes in work arrangements forced Sherbert out of a job.

3. *Restricted environments.*

a. *The military.* Goldman v. Weinberger, 475 U.S. 503 (1986), rejected a free exercise challenge to an Air Force regulation prohibiting the wearing of headgear while indoors as applied to an orthodox Jewish officer who was disciplined for wearing a yarmulke. Writing for the Court, Justice Rehnquist emphasized the deference owed to military judgments concerning the need to "foster instinctive obedience, unity, commitment, and esprit de corps. [The] desirability of dress regulations in the military is decided by the appropriate military officials, and they are under no constitutional mandate to abandon their considered professional judgment."

Justice Stevens, joined by Justices White and Powell, wrote a concurring opinion. Although acknowledging that petitioner presented "an especially attractive case for an exception" from the regulations, Justice Stevens worried about the application of such an exemption to members of other religious groups, wishing to wear turbans, saffron robes, and dreadlocks:

> The very strength of [petitioner's] claim creates the danger that a similar claim on behalf of a Sikh or a Rastafarian might readily be dismissed as "so extreme, so unusual, or so faddish an image that public confidence in his ability to perform his duties will be destroyed" [quoting from Justice Brennan's dissenting opinion]. If exceptions from dress code regulations are to be granted on the basis of a multi-factored test[, inevitably] the decisionmaker's evaluation of the character and the sincerity of the requestor's faith — as well as the probable reaction of the majority to the favored treatment of a member of that faith — will play a critical part in the decision. [The] Air Force has no business drawing distinctions between such persons when it is enforcing commands of universal application.

In a dissenting opinion joined by Justice Marshall, Justice Brennan found "totally implausible" the claim that the group identity of the Air Force would be threatened by the wearing of yarmulkes. "To the contrary, a yarmulke worn with a United States military uniform is an eloquent reminder that the shared and proud identity of United States servicemen embraces and unites religious and ethnic pluralism." Although turbans, saffron robes, and dreadlocks were not before the Court, Justice Brennan noted that "a reviewing court could legitimately give deference to dress and grooming rules that have a *reasoned* basis in, for example, functional utility, health and safety considerations, and the goal of a polished, professional appearance. It is the lack of any reasoned basis for prohibiting yarmulkes that is so striking here."

In a separate dissenting opinion, Justice Blackmun acknowledged that the Air Force could consider not only the costs of allowing petitioner to wear a yarmulke but also the cumulative costs of accommodating other requests for religious exemptions. He also acknowledged that "to allow noncombat personnel to wear yarmulkes but not turbans or dreadlocks because the latter seem more obtrusive [would] be to discriminate in favor of this country's more established, mainstream religions." Nevertheless, he rejected the Air Force's argument because it "simply has not shown any reason to fear that a significant number of enlisted personnel and officers would request religious exemptions that could not be denied on neutral grounds such as safety, let alone that granting these requests would noticeably impair the overall image of the service."

b. *Prisons.* O'Lone v. Estate of Shabazz, 482 U.S. 342 (1987), concerned a challenge by Muslim prisoners to a prison policy that prevented them from attending Jumu'ah, a weekly Muslim congregational service mandated by the Koran. Prison regulations, adopted for security reasons, prevented prisoners with respondents' classification from being inside the building where the service was held. The Court held that in a prison context alleged infringements on free exercise interests "are judged under a 'reasonableness' test less restrictive than that ordinarily applied to [infringements] of fundamental constitutional rights." Applying this reasonableness test to the facts before it, the Court concluded that the restriction was justified by security concerns.

4. *The concept of burdens: internal government operations.* Is there a constitutionally cognizable burden in the following cases?

Bowen v. Roy, 476 U.S. 693 (1986), rejected religion-based objections to a federal statute requiring applicants for certain welfare benefits to provide the states with their Social Security numbers and requiring the states to use the numbers in administering the program. Appellees had applied for such benefits, including food stamps. They contended that providing a Social Security number for their two-year-old daughter and use of that number by the government would violate their religious beliefs.

Writing for eight justices, Chief Justice Burger rejected appellees' claim that the free exercise clause was infringed when the government used the number. "Never to our knowledge has the Court interpreted the First Amendment to require the Government *itself* to behave in ways that the individual believes will further his or her spiritual development. [The] Free Exercise Clause affords an individual protection from certain forms of governmental compulsion; it does not afford an individual a right to dictate the conduct of the Government's internal procedures." The Court did not definitively rule on the claim that appellees could not be required to apply for Social Security numbers, although a majority of the justices indicated that, were the Court to reach the issue, they would hold that free exercise required that appellees could not be so required.

Lyng v. Northwest Indian Cemetery Protective Association, 485 U.S. 439 (1988), rejected a free exercise challenge to the Forest Service's plan to permit timber harvesting and road construction in part of a national forest that was traditionally used by various Indian tribes as sacred areas for religious rituals. The Court held, in an opinion by Justice O'Connor, that the government did not have to show a compelling need to engage in the relevant projects:

In both [*Roy* and *Lyng*] the challenged governmental action would interfere significantly with private persons' ability to pursue spiritual fulfillment according to their own religious beliefs. In neither case, however, could the affected individuals be coerced by the Government's action into violating their religious beliefs; nor would either governmental action penalize religious activity by denying any person an equal share of the rights, benefits, and privileges enjoyed by other citizens.

The Court acknowledged that

indirect coercion or penalties on the free exercise of religion, not just outright prohibitions, are subject to scrutiny under the First Amendment. [But] this [cannot] imply that incidental effects of government programs, which may make it more difficult to practice certain religions but which have no tendency to coerce individuals into acting contrary to their religious beliefs, require government to bring forward a compelling justification for its otherwise lawful actions. The crucial word in the constitutional text is "prohibit."

The Court noted that the projects at issue "could have devastating effects on traditional Indian religious practices . . . intimately and inextricably bound up with the unique features" of the area, but it concluded that "government simply could not operate if it were required to satisfy every citizen's religious needs and desires."

In a dissenting opinion joined by Justices Marshall and Blackmun, Justice Brennan criticized the Court's conception of "coercion":

> Ultimately, the Court's coercion test turns on a distinction between governmental actions that compel affirmative conduct inconsistent with religious belief, and those governmental actions that prevent conduct consistent with religious belief. [The] crucial word in the constitutional text, as the Court itself acknowledges, is "prohibit," a comprehensive term that in no way suggests that the intended protection is aimed only at governmental actions that coerce affirmative conduct. [Religious] freedom is threatened no less by governmental action that makes the practice of one's chosen faith impossible than by governmental programs that pressure one to engage in conduct inconsistent with religious belief.

In what sense is the land in *Lyng* more "the government's" than was the money in *Sherbert*? Note that in *Lyng* there was even greater coercion than in *Sherbert* — an across-the-board foreclosure rather than a financial inducement to abandon religious practice.

Employment Division, Department of Human Resources v. Smith

494 U.S. 872 (1990)

JUSTICE SCALIA delivered the opinion of the Court.

This case requires us to decide whether the Free Exercise Clause of the First Amendment permits the State of Oregon to include religiously inspired peyote use within the reach of its general criminal prohibition on use of that drug, and thus permits the State to deny unemployment benefits to persons dismissed from their jobs because of such religiously inspired use. . . .

[Smith was a member of the Native American Church, which has as part of its religious ritual the supervised consumption of peyote. Peyote is a "controlled substance" under Oregon law, possession of which is a criminal offense. Smith was fired from his job at a private drug rehabilitation clinic because he ingested peyote as part of his church's ritual. He sought unemployment benefits, which were denied because he had been discharged for work-related misconduct. On his appeal from the denial of benefits, the Oregon Supreme Court held that state law did not contain an exemption from its criminal statute for religious consumption of peyote, that the criminal ban was unconstitutional as applied to the consumption of peyote in this setting, and that Smith was therefore entitled to unemployment compensation.]

II

Respondents' claim for relief rests on our decisions [which held] that a State could not condition the availability of unemployment insurance on an individual's willingness to forgo conduct required by his religion. [However,] the conduct at issue in those cases was not prohibited by law. . . .

A

[The] free exercise of religion means, first and foremost, the right to believe and profess whatever religious doctrine one desires. . . .

[The] "exercise of religion" often involves not only belief and profession but the performance of (or abstention from) physical acts: assembling with others for a worship service, participating in sacramental use of bread and wine, proselytizing, abstaining from certain foods or certain modes of transportation. [A] state would be "prohibiting the free exercise [of religion]" if it sought to ban such acts or abstentions only when they are engaged in for religious reasons, or only because of the religious belief that they display. It would doubtless be unconstitutional [to] prohibit bowing down before a golden calf.

Respondents in the present case, however, seek to carry the meaning of "prohibiting the free exercise [of religion]" one large step further. They contend that their religious motivation for using peyote places them beyond the reach of a criminal law that is not specifically directed at their religious practice, and that is concededly constitutional as applied to those who use the drug for other reasons. They assert, in other words, that "prohibiting the free exercise [of religion]" includes requiring any individual to observe a generally applicable law that requires (or forbids) the performance of an act that his religious belief forbids (or requires). As a textual matter, we do not think the words must be given that meaning. It is no more necessary to regard the collection of a general tax, for example, as "prohibiting the free exercise [of religion]" by those citizens who believe support of organized government to be sinful, than it is to regard the same tax as "abridging the freedom . . . of the press" of those publishing companies that must pay the tax as a condition of staying in business. It is a permissible reading of the text [to] say that if prohibiting the exercise of religion [is] not the object of the tax but merely the incidental effect of a generally applicable and otherwise valid provision, the First Amendment has not been offended.

[That] reading is the correct one. We have never held that an individual's religious beliefs excuse him from compliance with an otherwise valid law prohibiting conduct that the State is free to regulate. On the contrary, the record of more than a century of our free exercise jurisprudence contradicts that proposition. [We] first had occasion to assert that principle in [Reynolds]. . . .

Subsequent decisions have consistently held that the right of free exercise does not relieve an individual of the obligation to comply with a "valid and neutral law of general applicability on the ground that the law proscribes (or prescribes) conduct that his religion prescribes (or proscribes)." United States v. Lee (Stevens, J., concurring in judgment). . . .

The only decisions in which we have held that the First Amendment bars application of a neutral, generally applicable law to religiously motivated action have involved not the Free Exercise Clause alone, but the Free Exercise Clause in conjunction with other constitutional protections, such as freedom of speech and of the press, see [Cantwell], or the right of parents, acknowledged in Pierce v.

Society of Sisters, 268 U.S. 510 (1925), to direct the education of their children, see Wisconsin v. Yoder. . . . [1]

The present case does not present such a hybrid situation, but a free exercise claim unconnected with any communicative activity or parental right. Respondents urge us to hold [that] when otherwise prohibitable conduct is accompanied by religious convictions, not only the convictions but the conduct itself must be free from governmental regulation. We have never held that, and decline to do so now. "[Our] cases do not at their farthest reach support the proposition that a stance of conscientious opposition relieves an objector from any colliding duty fixed by a democratic government." Gillette v. United States.

B

Respondents argue that even though exemption from generally applicable criminal laws need not automatically be extended to religiously motivated actors, at least the claim for a religious exemption must be evaluated under the balancing test set forth in Sherbert v. Verner. [We] have never invalidated any governmental action on the basis of the *Sherbert* test except the denial of unemployment compensation. Although we have sometimes purported to apply the *Sherbert* test in contexts other than that, we have always found the test satisfied. In recent years we have abstained from applying the *Sherbert* test (outside the unemployment compensation field) at all [citing *Roy*, *Lyng*, *Goldman*, and *O'Lone*].

Even if we were inclined to breathe into *Sherbert* some life beyond the unemployment compensation field, we would not apply it to require exemptions from a generally applicable criminal law. The *Sherbert* test [was] developed in a context that lent itself to individualized governmental assessment of the reasons for the relevant conduct. [Our] decisions in the unemployment cases stand for the proposition that where the State has in place a system of individual exemptions, it may not refuse to extend that system to cases of "religious hardship" without compelling reason.

Whether or not the decisions are that limited, they at least have nothing to do with an across-the-board criminal prohibition on a particular form of conduct. [The] government's ability to enforce generally applicable prohibitions of socially harmful conduct, like its ability to carry out other aspects of public policy, "cannot depend on measuring the effects of a governmental action on a religious objector's spiritual development." [*Lyng*.] To make an individual's obligation to obey such a law contingent upon the law's coincidence with his religious beliefs, except where the State's interest is "compelling" — permitting him, by virtue of his beliefs, "to become a law unto himself" [*Reynolds*] — contradicts both constitutional tradition and common sense.[2]

The "compelling interest" requirement seems benign, because it is familiar from other fields. But using it as the standard that must be met before the government may accord different treatment on the basis of race, or before the

---

1. Both lines of cases have specifically adverted to the non-free exercise principle involved. . . .

2. Justice O'Connor seeks to distinguish *Lyng* [and]*Roy*, on the ground that those cases involved the government's conduct of "its own internal affairs," which is different because, as Justice Douglas said in *Sherbert*, "the Free Exercise Clause is written in terms of what the government cannot do to the individual, not in terms of what the individual can exact from the government." [It] is hard to see any reason in principle or practicality why the government should have to tailor its health and safety laws to conform to the diversity of religious belief, but should not have to tailor its management of public lands, or its administration of welfare programs.

government may regulate the content of speech, is not remotely comparable to using it for the purpose asserted here. What it produces in those other fields — equality of treatment, and an unrestricted flow of contending speech — are constitutional norms; what it would produce here — a private right to ignore generally applicable laws — is a constitutional anomaly.[3]

Nor is it possible to limit the impact of respondents' proposal by requiring a "compelling state interest" only when the conduct prohibited is "central" to the individual's religion. It is no more appropriate for judges to determine the "centrality" of religious beliefs before applying a "compelling interest" test in the free exercise field, than it would be for them to determine the "importance" of ideas before applying the "compelling interest" test in the free speech field. What principle of law or logic can be brought to bear to contradict a believer's assertion that a particular act is "central" to his personal faith? Judging the centrality of different religious practices is akin to the unacceptable "business of evaluating the relative merits of differing religious claims." United States v. Lee (Stevens, J., concurring).[4]

If the "compelling interest" test is to be applied at all, then, it must be applied across the board, to all actions thought to be religiously commanded. Moreover, if "compelling interest" really means what it says (and watering it down here would subvert its rigor in the other fields where it is applied), many laws will not meet the test. Any society adopting such a system would be courting anarchy, but that danger increases in direct proportion to the society's diversity of religious beliefs, and its determination to coerce or suppress none of them. Precisely because "we are a cosmopolitan nation made up of people of almost every conceivable religious preference," Braunfeld v. Brown, and precisely because we value and protect that religious divergence, we cannot afford the luxury of deeming presumptively invalid, as applied to the religious objector, every regulation of conduct that does not protect an interest of the highest order. The rule respondents favor would open the prospect of constitutionally required religious exemptions from civic obligations of almost every conceivable kind — ranging from compulsory military service, to the payment of taxes, to health and safety regulation such as manslaughter and child neglect laws, compulsory vaccination laws, drug laws, and traffic laws, to social welfare legislation such as minimum wage laws, child labor laws, animal cruelty laws, environmental protection laws, and laws providing for equality of opportunity for the races. The First Amendment's protection of religious liberty does not require this.

Values that are protected against government interference through enshrinement in the Bill of Rights are not thereby banished from the political process. Just as a society that believes in the negative protection accorded to the press by the

---

3. [Just] as we subject to the most exacting scrutiny laws that make classifications based on race, or on the content of speech, so too we strictly scrutinize governmental classifications based on religion, see McDaniel v. Paty, 435 U.S. 618 (1978). But we have held that race-neutral laws that have the effect of disproportionately disadvantaging a particular racial group do not thereby become subject to compelling-interest analysis under the Equal Protection Clause, see Washington v. Davis, and we have held that generally applicable laws unconcerned with regulating speech that have the effect of interfering with speech do not thereby become subject to compelling interest analysis under the First Amendment. . . .

4. [Dispensing] with a "centrality" inquiry is utterly unworkable. [There] is no way out of the difficulty that, if general laws are to be subjected to a "religious practice" exception, both the importance of the law at issue and the centrality of the practice at issue must reasonably be considered. [Relocated footnote. — EDS.]

First Amendment is likely to enact laws that affirmatively foster the dissemination of the printed word, so also a society that believes in the negative protection accorded to religious belief can be expected to be solicitous of that value in its legislation as well. It is therefore not surprising that a number of States have made an exception to their drug laws for sacramental peyote use. But to say that a nondiscriminatory religious-practice exemption is permitted, or even that it is desirable, is not to say that it is constitutionally required, and that the appropriate occasions for its creation can be discerned by the courts. It may fairly be said that leaving accommodation to the political process will place at a relative disadvantage those religious practices that are not widely engaged in; but that unavoidable consequence of democratic government must be preferred to a system in which each conscience is a law unto itself or in which judges weight the social importance of all laws against the centrality of all religious beliefs.
[Reversed.]

JUSTICE O'CONNOR, with whom JUSTICE BRENNAN, JUSTICE MARSHALL, and JUSTICE BLACKMUN join as to [Part] II, concurring in the judgment. . . .

II . . .

A

[Because] the First Amendment does not distinguish between religious belief and religious conduct, conduct motivated by sincere religious belief, like the belief itself, must therefore be at least presumptively protected by the Free Exercise Clause.

[A] law that prohibits [conduct] that happens to be an act of worship for someone [manifestly] does prohibit that person's free exercise of his religion. A person who is barred from engaging in religiously motivated conduct is barred from freely exercising his religion. Moreover, that person is barred from freely exercising his religion regardless of whether the law prohibits the conduct only when engaged in for religious reasons, only by members of that religion, or by all persons. It is difficult to deny that a law that prohibits religiously motivated conduct, even if the law is generally applicable, does not at least implicate First Amendment concerns.

The Court responds that generally applicable laws are "one large step" removed from laws aimed at specific religious practices. The First Amendment, however, does not distinguish between laws that are generally applicable and laws that target particular religious practices. Indeed, few States would be so naive as to enact a law directly prohibiting or burdening a religious practice as such. Our free exercise cases have all concerned generally applicable laws that had the effect of significantly burdening a religious practice. If the First Amendment is to have any vitality, it ought not be construed to cover only the extreme and hypothetical situation in which a State directly targets a religious practice. . . .

To say that a person's right to free exercise has been burdened, of course, does not mean that he has an absolute right to engage in the conduct. Under our established First Amendment jurisprudence, we have recognized that the freedom to act, unlike the freedom to believe, cannot be absolute. Instead, we have respected both the First Amendment's express textual mandate and the governmental interest in regulation of conduct by requiring the Government to justify any substantial burden on religiously motivated conduct by a compelling state interest and by means narrowly tailored to achieve that interest. The compelling interest test effectuates the First Amendment's command that religious liberty is an independent liberty, that it occupies a preferred position, and that the Court will not permit encroachments upon this liberty, whether direct or indirect, unless required by clear and compelling governmental interests "of the highest order" [*Yoder*]. . . .

[In] each of the [cases] cited by the Court to support its categorical rule, we rejected the particular constitutional claims before us only after carefully weighing the competing interests. That we rejected the free exercise claims in those cases hardly calls into question the applicability of First Amendment doctrine in the first place. Indeed, it is surely unusual to judge the vitality of a constitutional doctrine by looking to the win-loss record of the plaintiffs who happen to come before us.

B . . .

[The] essence of a free exercise claim is relief from a burden imposed by government on religious practices or beliefs, whether the burden is imposed directly through laws that prohibit or compel specific religious practices, or indirectly through laws that, in effect, make abandonment of one's own religion or conformity to the religious beliefs of others the price of an equal place in the civil community. . . .

Legislatures, of course, have always been "left free to reach actions which were in violation of social duties or subversive of good order." [*Reynolds.*] Yet because of the close relationship between conduct and religious belief, "[i]n every case the power to regulate must be so exercised as not, in attaining a permissible end, unduly to infringe the protected freedom." [*Cantwell.*] Once it has been shown that a government regulation or criminal prohibition burdens the free exercise of religion, we have consistently asked the Government to demonstrate that unbending application of its regulation to the religious objector "is essential to accomplish an overriding governmental interest" [*Lee*], or represents "the least restrictive means of achieving some compelling state interest" [*Thomas*]. To me, [the] approach more consistent with our role as judges to decide each case on its individual merits [is] to apply this test in each case to determine whether the burden on the specific plaintiffs before us is constitutionally significant and whether the particular criminal interest asserted by the State before us is compelling. Even if, as an empirical matter, a government's criminal laws might usually serve a compelling interest in health, safety, or public order, the First Amendment at least requires a case-by-case determination of the question, sensitive to the facts of each particular claim. Given the range of conduct that a State might legitimately make criminal, we cannot assume, merely because a law carries criminal sanctions and is generally applicable, that the First Amendment never requires the State to grant a limited exemption for religiously motivated conduct. . . .

[The cases] cited by the Court for the proposition that we have rejected application of the *Sherbert* test outside the unemployment compensation field are distinguishable because they arose in [narrow], specialized contexts. . . .

[There] is nothing talismanic about neutral laws of general applicability or general criminal prohibitions, for laws neutral toward religion can coerce a person to violate his religious conscience or intrude upon his religious duties just as effectively as laws aimed at religion. Although the Court suggests that the compelling interest test, as applied to generally applicable laws, would result in a "constitutional anomaly," the First Amendment unequivocally makes freedom of religion, like freedom from race discrimination and freedom of speech, a "constitutional nor[m]," not an "anomaly." [As] the language of the Clause itself makes clear, an individual's free exercise of religion is a preferred constitutional activity. See, e.g., McConnell, Accommodation of Religion, 1985 Sup. Ct. Rev. 1, 9 ("[T]he text of the First Amendment itself 'singles out' religion for special protections."). A law that makes criminal such an activity therefore triggers constitutional concern — and heightened judicial scrutiny — even if it does not target the particular religious conduct at issue. Our free speech cases similarly recognize that neutral regulations that affect free speech values are subject to a balancing, rather than categorical, approach. The Court's parade of horribles not only fails as a reason for discarding the compelling interest test, it instead demonstrates just the opposite; that courts have been quite capable of applying our free exercise jurisprudence to strike sensible balances between religious liberty and competing state interest.

Finally, the Court today suggests that the disfavoring of minority religions is an "unavoidable consequence" under our system of government and that accommodation of such religions must be left to the political process. In my view, however, the First Amendment was enacted precisely to protect the rights of those whose religious practices are not shared by the majority and may be viewed with hostility. The history of our free exercise doctrine amply demonstrates the harsh impact majoritarian rule has had on unpopular or emerging religious groups such as the Jehovah's Witnesses and the Amish. [The] compelling interest test reflects the First Amendment's mandate of preserving religious liberty to the fullest extent possible in a pluralistic society. For the Court to deem this command a "luxury" [is] to denigrate "[t]he very purpose of a Bill of Rights."

[Part III of Justice O'Connor's opinion concluded that Oregon's prohibition satisfied the compelling state interest test. She agreed that the prohibition placed a "severe burden" on the free exercise of religion, but said that the state had a "significant interest" in controlling drug use. Finding the question close, she concluded that "uniform application" of the prohibition is "essential to accomplish" the overriding purpose of preventing physical harm caused by drug use. Selective exemptions for religious believers would "seriously impair" the state's interest.]

JUSTICE BLACKMUN, with whom JUSTICE BRENNAN and JUSTICE MARSHALL join, dissenting. . . .

I

In weighing respondents' clear interest in the free exercise of their religion against Oregon's asserted interest in enforcing its drug laws, it is important to articulate in precise terms the state interest involved. It is not the State's broad interest in fighting the critical "war on drugs" [but] the State's narrow interest in refusing to make an exception for the religious, ceremonial use of peyote. [Failure] to reduce the competing interests to the same plane of generality tends to distort the weighing process in the State's favor. . . .

The carefully circumscribed ritual context in which respondents used peyote is far removed from the irresponsible and unrestricted recreational use of unlawful drugs.[6] The Native American Church's internal restrictions on, and supervision of, its members' use of peyote substantially obviate the State's health and safety concerns. . . .[7]

The State's apprehension of a flood of other religious claims is purely speculative. Almost half the States and the Federal Government have maintained an exemption for religious peyote use for many years, and apparently have not found themselves overwhelmed by claims to other religious exemptions.[8] Allowing an exemption for religious peyote use would not necessarily oblige the State to grant a similar exemption to other religious groups. The unusual circumstances that make the religious use of peyote compatible with the State's interests in health and safety and in preventing drug trafficking would not apply to other religious claims. Some religions, for example, might not restrict drug use to a limited ceremonial context, as does the Native American Church. Some religious claims involve drugs such as marijuana and heroin, in which there is significant illegal traffic, with its attendant greed and violence, so that it would be difficult to grant a religious exemption without seriously compromising law enforcement efforts. . . .

Note: Should Accommodation Be Required?

1. *Free exercise and free speech.* United States v. O'Brien, Chapter 7, section E3, supra, held that facially neutral statutes serving important purposes unrelated to suppression of speech are constitutional if the incidental impact on speech is no greater than necessary. Is the Court correct in stating that *Smith* transfers the *O'Brien* approach to the free exercise area? Gedicks, The Normalized Free Exercise Clause, 75 Ind. L.J. 77 (2000), argues that *Smith* adopts a "rational basis" standard of review and thereby "contradicts the Court's Speech Clause doctrine governing [incidental] burdens on speech occurring as the result of otherwise legitimate government regulations of conduct or the time, place, or manner of expression," which requires that such regulations satisfy an intermediate standard of review. Is Gedicks's description of free speech doctrine accurate?

2. *The scope of* Smith. How broadly does *Smith* undermine a doctrine of mandatory accommodation?

a. *Individualized determinations.* Was the unemployment commission in *Sherbert* in a position to balance the impairment of free exercise against the prevention of fraudulent claims? Consider Brownstein, Protecting Religious Liberty: The False Messiahs of Free Speech Doctrine and Formal Neutrality, 18 J.L. & Pol. 119, 191–192 (2002): Under the "individualized determination"

---

6. [Respondents'] use of peyote seems closely analogous to the sacramental use of wine by the Roman Catholic Church. During Prohibition, the Federal Government exempted such use of wine from its general ban on possession and use of alcohol. However compelling the Government's then general interest in prohibiting the use of alcohol may have been, it could not plausibly have asserted an interest sufficiently compelling to outweigh Catholics' right to take communion.

7. The use of peyote is, to some degree, self-limiting. The peyote plant is extremely bitter, and eating it is an unpleasant experience, which would tend to discourage casual or recreational use.

8. Over the past years, various sects have raised free exercise claims regarding drug use. In no reported case, except those involving claims of religious peyote use, has the claimant prevailed.

exception, "[religion] is granted something like most favored nation status. If any secular interest can justify an exemption from a law, then the state must recognize that religious interests also deserve to be exempt from the law. [But an] extraordinary range of laws contain exemptions to their application, including most civil rights laws [and] even homicide statutes. [This] militates against such an understanding." See also Duncan, Free Exercise Is Dead, Long Live Free Exercise: *Smith*, *Lukumi*, and the General Applicability Requirement, 3 U. Pa. J. Const. L. 850, 868 (2001): "[A] law burdening religious conduct is under-inclusive, with respect to any particular government interest, if the law fails to pursue that interest uniformly against other conduct that causes similar damage to that government interest." Does this meet Brownstein's concerns?

b. *Hybrid claims.* Is the Court's explanation of *Yoder* persuasive? Consider the proposition that, because there is no substantive due process right, independent of a religious claim, to keep children out of school, and there is no religious claim, independent of a due process claim, to do so, the two inadequate arguments taken together cannot add up to a valid claim. Consider Brownstein, Protecting Religious Liberty: The False Messiahs of Free Speech Doctrine and Formal Neutrality, 18 J.L. & Pol. 119, 191-192 (2002): "A hybrid rights situation involves a neutral law of general applicability that substantially burdens the exercise of religion and sufficiently burdens some other constitutionally protected interest to invoke the application of the requisite standard of review [short] of strict scrutiny." Brownstein argues that this idea is coherent but inconsistent with "basic constitutional intuitions." "Hybrid rights analysis suggests that religious people should be treated preferentially with regard to the exercise of fundamental rights when their religious beliefs influence the way they exercise their rights. [That] cannot be right. There is an equality dimension to liberty rights. [Religious] people do not get special treatment with respect to these basic freedoms. No one does."

c. *Expressive association rights.* Suppose a state adopts an antidiscrimination statute, creating civil liability and prohibiting discrimination on the basis of gender. Must a church-related school comply with that statute by hiring a teacher with a one-year-old child if the church's tenets demand that women with small children raise them at home and not participate in the paid workforce? Does the Court's discussion of cases in which free exercise claims are joined with other claims, such as freedom of association, adequately deal with this problem?

d. *The political process.* Although the political process protected the sacramental use of wine during Prohibition, it has not fully protected the sacramental use of peyote. What limitations does this suggest on reliance on the political process to protect religious liberty interests? (Congress responded to *Smith* with the Religious Freedom Restoration Act, found unconstitutional on federalism grounds in City of Boerne v. Flores, 521 U.S. 507 (1997).)

e. *Invidious motivation.* Church of the Lukumi Babalu Aye v. City of Hialeah, 508 U.S. 520 (1993), invalidated a city's ban on "ritual slaughter" as applied to animal sacrifices conducted by the church as part of its practice of the Santeria religion. The Court found that the background of the ban, and its specific language and exemptions, demonstrated that "suppression of the central element of the Santeria worship service was the object of the ordinances." The background "demonstrates animosity to Santeria adherents and their religious practices; the ordinances by their own terms target this religious exercise; the texts of the ordinances were gerrymandered with care to proscribe religious killings of animals but to exclude almost all secular killings; and the ordinances suppress much more religious conduct than is necessary to achieve the legitimate ends asserted in their defense." The ordinances did not satisfy the "rigorous scrutiny" required of regulations that are not neutral or of general application because they were "not drawn in narrow terms to accomplish" the objectives of protecting animals from inhumane slaughter or avoiding unhealthy methods of disposing of animal carcasses. Justice Blackmun, joined by Justice O'Connor, concurred in the judgment, saying that, "when a law discriminates against religion as such, [it] automatically will fail strict scrutiny [because] by definition, [it] is not precisely tailored to a compelling governmental interest."

Is *Hialeah* best understood as involving an impermissibly motivated antireligious gerrymander, that is, a statute that, though neutral on its face, actually reaches only religious activities? For the suggestion that the Court's approach, following *Smith*'s "focus[] on persecutory motivation, [elicits] the same kind of ad hominem argumentation that is reflected in 'purpose' cases under the Establishment Clause," see Smith, Free Exercise Doctrine and the Discourse of Disrespect, 65 U. Colo. L. Rev. 519, 558 (1994).

3. *(Implicit) denominational preferences?* Williams and Williams, Volitionalism and Religious Liberty, 76 Cornell L. Rev. 769, 772, 777, 908 (1991), argue that *Smith* resulted from "the Court's profound discomfort with nonvolitionalist beliefs" that "acknowledge the possibility that some religious consequences for individuals may be caused by activities or events over which they had no free choice or control," as in *Lyng* and Bowen v. Roy. On their analysis, free exercise claims lie along a spectrum ranging from "exemption" claims to "ordering" claims, "the remedy for which consists primarily of reordering some aspect of the government's program not limited in application to the individual claimant." They suggest that under a pre-*Smith* analysis, "ordering" claims, which typify those made by people with nonvolitionalist beliefs, "are, as a practical matter, likely to impose greater burdens on the government than will exemption claims." Does this raise questions about denominational preference? Note that, on some views, neither religious belief in general nor commitment to Christianity in particular results from volitional choices. See Garvey, An Anti-Liberal Argument for Religious Freedom, 7 J. Contemp. Legal Issues 275, 278 (1996): "The individual does not have complete control over choosing the religious option. It is God who makes the choice."

Greene, The Political Balance of the Religion Clauses, 102 Yale L.J. 1611 (1993), argues that the establishment clause bars "enacting legislation for the express purpose of advancing the values believed to be commanded by religion," and that "precisely because religion should be excluded from politics in this way, [the] Free Exercise Clause requires the recognition of religious faith as a ground for exemption from legal obligation. [These] exemptions are merely the appropriate remedy for the damage that precluding religious values from grounding law causes religious people." The establishment clause ban arises because, when legislation is enacted for the express purpose of advancing religious values, "a nonbeliever is effectively denied participation in the political process because the nonbeliever cannot discuss the matter on the terms that the religious believers have set." According to Greene, because one type of argument is thereby excluded from political negotiations, those who would make it are entitled to a compensatory offset.

D.   PERMISSIBLE ACCOMMODATION

Statutes that attempt to accommodate the concerns of adherents of religion lie at the borderland of the free exercise and establishment clauses. They promote "free exercise values," in the sense that they allow believers to pursue their religious beliefs without hindrance, but legislatures are rarely compelled by the free exercise clause to adopt statutory accommodations. Such statutes are in tension with some formulations of the requirements of the establishment clause because they have the purpose of advancing religion in the sense just specified. Are such accommodations constitutional? If so, why?

Consider these positions:

1. There is no tension. No regulation promoting free exercise values can violate nonestablishment values, and no statute promoting nonestablishment values impairs free exercise ones. But consider Estate of Thornton v. Caldor, infra.
2. There is no tension. Only statutory accommodations required by the free exercise clause are constitutional, and all other efforts to serve "free exercise values" are unconstitutional. Why should a legislature ever enact a statutory accommodation if this is the test? If the free exercise clause requires some accommodation, what reasons are there to think that court-devised accommodations will be more appropriate than legislative ones?
3. The tension should be resolved by preferring free exercise values to nonestablishment ones. The expansive role of the modern state creates many opportunities for facially neutral statutes to burden religious belief and reduces the role previously played by many religious institutions. Religious intolerance poses serious threats in a religiously diverse society, so that when legislation advances free exercise values, it should be encouraged. Consider the extent to which the problems discussed in Chapter 9, section B, infra, as well as the issue of state aid to religious schools, could be recast as efforts by the state to advance free exercise values.
4. The tension should be resolved by preferring nonestablishment values to free exercise ones. Mainstream religions have a powerful advantage in the political process over marginal religions and over nonreligion. Legislation is likely to enhance the positions of mainstream religions. In the long run, religious minorities will be better off under a regime of strict separation, even though the application of neutral regulations may sometimes affect them adversely.
5. There need be no tension. If states are barred from using religion as a basis for either conferring benefits or imposing burdens, legislators will be required to use neutral rules to accomplish their goals, and the legislation resulting from a political process constrained by a requirement of neutrality will threaten neither free exercise nor nonestablishment values.

Corporation of Presiding Bishop of the Church of Jesus Christ of Latter-Day Saints v. Amos

483 U.S. 327 (1987)

JUSTICE WHITE delivered the opinion of the Court.

Section 702 of the Civil Rights Act of 1964 exempts religious organizations from Title VII's prohibition against discrimination in employment on the basis of religion. The question presented is whether applying the §702 exemption to the secular nonprofit activities of religious organizations violates the Establishment Clause of the First Amendment. The District Court held that it does. . . .

[The appellee was a janitor at the Deseret Gymnasium, a nonprofit facility, open to the public, run by the Mormon church. He was fired after he failed to qualify for a certificate stating that he was a member of the church eligible to attend its temples because he observed the church's standards involving church attendance, tithing, and abstinence from coffee, tea, alcohol, and tobacco.]

"This Court has long recognized that the government may (and sometimes must) accommodate religious practices and that it may do so without violating the Establishment Clause." [*Hobbie*, section C1, supra.] It is well established, too, that "[t]he limits of permissible state accommodation to religion are by no means co-extensive with the noninterference mandated by the Free Exercise Clause." [*Walz*, section B1, supra.] There is ample room under the Establishment Clause for "benevolent neutrality which will permit religious exercise to exist without sponsorship and without interference." At some point, accommodation may devolve into "an unlawful fostering of religion" [*Hobbie*], but these are not such cases, in our view. . . .

Lemon requires first that the law at issue serve a "secular legislative purpose." This does not mean that the law's purpose must be unrelated to religion — that would amount to a requirement "that the government show a callous indifference to religious groups," Zorach v. Clauson, 343 U.S. 306, 314 (1952), and the Establishment Clause has never been so interpreted. Rather, *Lemon*'s "purpose" requirement aims at preventing the relevant governmental decisionmaker — in this case, Congress — from abandoning neutrality and acting with the intent of promoting a particular point of view in religious matters.

Under the *Lemon* analysis, it is a permissible legislative purpose to alleviate significant governmental interference with the ability of religious organizations to define and carry out their religious missions. Appellees argue that there is no such purpose here because §702 provided adequate protection for religious employers [when] it exempted only the religious activities of such employers from the statutory ban on religious discrimination. We may assume for the sake of argument that [that] exemption was adequate in the sense that the Free Exercise Clause required no more. Nonetheless, it is a significant burden on a religious organization to require it, on pain of substantial liability, to predict which of its activities a secular court will consider religious. The line is hardly a bright one, and an organization might understandably be concerned that a judge would not understand its religious tenets and sense of mission. Fear of potential liability might affect the way an organization carried out what it understood to be its religious mission. [Congress's] purpose was to minimize governmental "interfer[ence] with the decision-making process in religions." [This] purpose does not violate the Establishment Clause.

The second requirement under *Lemon* is that the law in question have "a principal or primary effect . . . that neither advances nor inhibits religion." Undoubtedly, religious organizations are better able now to advance their purposes than they were prior to the 1972 amendment to §702. [A] law is not unconstitutional simply because it allows churches to advance religion, which is their very purpose. For a law to have forbidden "effects" under *Lemon*, it must be fair to say that the government itself has advanced religion through its own activities and influence. . . .

The District Court appeared to fear that sustaining the exemption would permit churches with financial resources impermissibly to extend their influence and propagate their faith by entering the commercial, profit-making world. The cases before us [involve] a nonprofit activity instituted over 75 years ago. [Moreover], we find no persuasive evidence in the record before us that the Church's ability to propagate its religious doctrine through the Gymnasium is any greater now than it was prior to the passage of the Civil Rights Act in 1964. In such circumstances, we do not see how any advancement of religion achieved by the Gymnasium can be fairly attributed to the Government, as opposed to the Church.[15]

We find unpersuasive the District Court's reliance on the fact that §702 singles out religious entities for a benefit. Although the Court has given weight to this consideration in its past decisions, it has never indicated that statutes that give special consideration to religious groups are per se invalid. [Where], as here, government acts with the proper purpose of lifting a regulation that burdens the exercise of religion, we see no reason to require that the exemption come packaged with benefits to secular entities. . . .

[In] a case such as this, where a statute is neutral on its face and motivated by a permissible purpose of limiting governmental interference with the exercise of religion, we see no justification for applying strict scrutiny to a statute that passes the *Lemon* test. The proper inquiry is whether Congress has chosen a rational classification to further a legitimate end. [As] applied to the nonprofit activities of religious employers, §702 is rationally related to the legitimate purpose of alleviating significant governmental interference with the ability of religious organizations to define and carry out their religious missions.

[Reversed.]

JUSTICE BRENNAN, with whom JUSTICE MARSHALL joins, concurring in the judgment.

I write separately to emphasize that my concurrence in the judgment rests on the fact that these cases involve a challenge to the application of §702's categorical exemption to the activities of a nonprofit organization. I believe that the particular character of nonprofit activity makes inappropriate a case-by-case determination whether its nature is religious or secular.

[Any] exemption from Title VII's proscription on religious discrimination necessarily has the effect of burdening the religious liberty of prospective and current employees. An exemption says that a person may be put to the choice of either conforming to certain religious tenets or losing a job opportunity, a promotion, or, as in this case, employment itself. The potential for coercion created by such a provision is in serious tension with our commitment to individual freedom of conscience in matters of religious belief.

---

15. Undoubtedly, [appellee's] freedom of choice in religious matters was impinged upon, but it was the Church[, and] not the Government, who put him to the choice of changing his religious practices or losing his job. This is a very different case than Estate of Thornton v. Caldor, Inc., 472 U.S. 703 (1985). In *Caldor*, the Court struck down a Connecticut statute prohibiting an employer from requiring an employee to work on a day designated by the employee as his Sabbath. In effect, Connecticut had given the force of law to the employee's designation of a Sabbath day and required accommodation by the employer regardless of the burden which that constituted for the employer or other employees. . . .

At the same time, religious organizations have an interest in autonomy in ordering their internal affairs, so that they may be free to "select their own leaders, define their own doctrines, resolve their own disputes, and run their own institutions. Religion includes important communal elements for most believers. They exercise their religion through religious organizations, and these organizations must be protected by the [free exercise clause]." Laycock, Towards a General Theory of the Religion Clauses: The Case of Church Labor Relations and the Right to Church Autonomy, 81 Colum. L. Rev. 1373, 1389 (1981). For many individuals, religious activity derives meaning in large measure from participation in a larger religious community. Such a community represents an ongoing tradition of shared beliefs, an organic entity not reducible to a mere aggregation of individuals. Determining that certain activities are in furtherance of an organization's religious mission, and that only those committed to that mission should conduct them, is thus a means by which a religious community defines itself. Solicitude for a church's ability to do so reflects the idea that furtherance of the autonomy of religious organizations often furthers individual religious freedom as well.

The authority to engage in this process of self-definition inevitably involves what we normally regard as infringement on free exercise rights, since a religious organization is able to condition employment in certain activities on subscription to particular religious tenets. We are willing to countenance the imposition of such a condition because we deem it vital that, if certain activities constitute part of a religious community's practice, then a religious organization should be able to require that only members of its community perform those activities.

This rationale suggests that, ideally, religious organizations should be able to discriminate on the basis of religion only with respect to religious activities, so that a determination should be made in each case whether an activity is religious or secular. This is because the infringement on religious liberty that results from conditioning performance of secular activity upon religious belief cannot be defended as necessary for the community's self-definition. Furthermore, the authorization of discrimination in such circumstances [puts] at the disposal of religion the added advantages of economic leverage in the secular realm. As a result, the authorization of religious discrimination with respect to nonreligious activities [has] the effect of furthering religion in violation of the Establishment Clause.

What makes the application of a religious-secular distinction difficult is that the character of an activity is not self-evident. As a result, determining whether an activity is religious or secular requires a searching case-by-case analysis. This results in considerable ongoing government entanglement in religious affairs. Furthermore, this prospect of government intrusion raises concern that a religious organization may be chilled in its free exercise activity. While a church may regard the conduct of certain functions as integral to its mission, a court may disagree. A religious organization therefore would have an incentive to characterize as religious only those activities about which there likely would be no dispute, even if it genuinely believed that religious commitment was important in performing other tasks as well. As a result, the community's process of self-definition would be shaped in part by the prospects of litigation. A case-by-case analysis for all activities therefore would both produce excessive government entanglement with religion and create the danger of chilling religious activity.

The risk of chilling religious organizations is most likely to arise with respect to nonprofit activities. [Nonprofits] historically have been organized specifically to provide certain community services, not simply to engage in commerce. Churches often regard the provision of such services as a means of fulfilling religious duty and of providing an example of the way of life a church seeks to foster.

Nonprofit activities therefore are most likely to present cases in which characterization of the activity as religious or secular will be a close question. [This] substantial potential for chilling religious activity makes inappropriate a case-by-case determination of the character of a nonprofit organization, and justifies a categorical exemption for nonprofit activities. Such an exemption demarcates a sphere of deference with respect to those activities most likely to be religious. It permits infringement on employee free exercise rights in those instances in which discrimination is most likely to reflect a religious community's self-definition. While not every nonprofit activity may be operated for religious purposes, the likelihood that many are makes a categorical rule a suitable means to avoid chilling the exercise of religion. . . .

JUSTICE O'CONNOR, concurring in the judgment. . . .

In Wallace v. Jaffree, I noted a tension in the Court's use of the *Lemon* test to evaluate an Establishment Clause challenge to government efforts to accommodate the free exercise of religion: "On the one hand, a rigid application of the *Lemon* test would invalidate legislation exempting religious observers from generally applicable government obligations. By definition, such legislation has a religious purpose and effect in promoting the free exercise of religion. On the other hand, judicial deference to all legislation that purports to facilitate the free exercise of religion would completely vitiate the Establishment Clause. Any statute pertaining to religion can be viewed as an 'accommodation' of free exercise rights."

In my view, the opinion for the Court leans toward the second of the two unacceptable options described above. [The] Court seems to suggest that the "effects" prong of the *Lemon* test is not at all implicated as long as the government action can be characterized as "allowing" religious organizations to advance religion, in contrast to government action directly advancing religion.

This distinction seems to me to obscure far more than to enlighten. Almost any government benefit to religion could be recharacterized as simply "allowing" a religion to better advance itself, unless perhaps it involved actual proselytization by government agents. . . .

The necessary first step in evaluating an Establishment Clause challenge to a government action lifting from religious organizations a generally applicable regulatory burden is to recognize that such government action does have the effect of advancing religion. The necessary second step is to separate those benefits to religion that constitutionally accommodate the free exercise of religion from those that provide unjustifiable awards of assistance to religious organizations. [The] inquiry [should] be "whether government's purpose is to endorse religion and whether the statute actually conveys a message of endorsement." . . .

[These] cases involve a government decision to lift from a nonprofit activity of a religious organization the burden of demonstrating that the particular nonprofit activity is religious as well as the burden of refraining from discriminating on the basis of religion. Because there is a probability that a nonprofit activity of a religious organization will itself be involved in the organization's religious mission, in my view the objective observer should perceive the government action as an accommodation of the exercise of religion rather than as a government endorsement of religion.

It is not clear, however, that activities conducted by religious organizations solely as profit-making enterprises will be as likely to be directly involved in the religious mission of the organization. . . .

[An opinion by Justice Blackmun, concurring in the judgment, is omitted.]

TEXAS MONTHLY v. BULLOCK, 489 U.S. 1 (1989). A sharply divided Court held unconstitutional a statute that exempted religious publications from a state sales tax. Justice Brennan's opinion, joined by Justices Marshall and Stevens, said that "government policies with secular objectives [may] incidentally benefit religion. The nonsectarian aims of government and religious groups often overlap, and this Court has never required that public authorities refrain from implementing reasonable measures to advance legitimate secular goals merely because they would thereby relieve religious groups of costs they would otherwise incur [citing Widmar v. Vincent, 454 U.S. 263 (1981), and *Walz*, below]." However, in such cases, "the benefits derived by religious organizations flowed to a large number of nonreligious groups as well. Indeed, were those benefits confined to religious organizations, they could not have appeared other than as state sponsorship of religion." The exemption for religious publications "lacks sufficient breadth to pass scrutiny under the Establishment Clause. [Insofar] as [the] subsidy is conferred upon a wide array of nonsectarian groups as well as religious groups in pursuit of some legitimate secular end, the fact that religious groups benefit incidentally does not deprive the subsidy of the secular purpose and primary effect mandated by the Establishment Clause. However, when government directs a subsidy exclusively to religious organizations that is not required by the Free Exercise Clause and that either burdens nonbeneficiaries markedly or cannot reasonably be seen as removing a significant state-imposed deterrent to the free exercise of religion, [it] 'provide[s] unjustifiable awards of assistance to religious organizations' and cannot but 'conve[y] a message of endorsement' to slighted members of the community [*Amos*]. This is particularly true where, as here, the subsidy is targeted at writings that promulgate the teachings of religious faiths." If the state subsidized groups contributing to the community's "cultural, intellectual, and moral betterment," the exemption for religious publications would be permitted, but "if Texas sought to promote reflection and discussion about questions of ultimate value and the contours of a good and meaningful life, then a tax exemption would have to be available to an extended range of associations whose publications were substantially devoted to such matters."

Justice Scalia's dissent, joined by Chief Justice Rehnquist and Justice Kennedy, argued that the tax exemption was a permissible accommodation of religion. For him, breadth of coverage is relevant only where the state justifies its legislation on entirely secular grounds, but "where accommodation of religion is the justification, by definition religion is being singled out." Although "it is not always easy to determine when accommodation slides over into promotion, and neutrality into favoritism," the tax exemption was an easy case because imposing a general sales tax on the sale of religious publications was at least arguably unconstitutional as a burden on religion. (Does this argument survive *Smith*, section C, supra?) Justice Brennan's opinion rejected this argument on the ground that it was obviously not unconstitutional to impose a general sales tax on religious publications. For Justice Brennan, accommodations must not "impose substantial burdens on nonbeneficiaries [or must be] designed to alleviate government intrusions that might significantly deter adherents of a particular faith from conduct protected by the Free Exercise Clause." The tax exemption did burden nonbeneficiaries by increasing their tax bills and did not alleviate a "demonstrated and possibly grave imposition on religious activity sheltered by the Free Exercise Clause."

Justice Blackmun, whose opinion concurring in the result was joined by Justice O'Connor, expressed more sympathy with the accommodation argument. He argued that the tax exemption was unconstitutional because it was "limited to the sale of religious literature by a religious organization." (Justice White also concurred in the result, relying on Arkansas Writers' Project v. Ragland, Chapter 7, section F3, supra.)

BOARD OF EDUCATION OF KIRYAS JOEL VILLAGE SCHOOL DISTRICT v. GRUMET, 512 U.S. 687 (1994). The village of Kiryas Joel in New York is a religious enclave of Satmar Hasidim, a group of Orthodox Jews "who make few concessions to the modern world and go to great lengths to avoid assimilation." Most children in the village are educated in private religious schools. Educating handicapped children in such schools is quite expensive, and the village residents arranged to have a public school system provide education for their handicapped children in an annex to one of the religious schools. That arrangement ended when the Court held a similar arrangement unconstitutional in Aguilar v. Felton, 473 U.S. 402 (1985). The children were then sent to schools in the neighboring public school system. The village residents found the education there unsatisfactory in part because the children suffered "panic, fear and trauma" from "leaving their own community and being with people whose ways were so different." In 1989, the New York legislature enacted a statute designating the village of Kiryas Joel as a separate school district. The Supreme Court held the statute unconstitutional.

Justice Souter's opinion for the Court stated, "The fact that this school district was created by a special and unusual Act of the legislature [gives] reason for concern whether the benefit received by the Satmar community is one that the legislature will provide equally to other religious (and nonreligious) groups." For the Court, "[the] fundamental source of constitutional concern [is] that the legislature itself may fail to exercise governmental authority in a religiously neutral way. The anomalously case-specific nature of the legislature's exercise of state authority in creating this district for a religious community leaves the Court without any direct way to review such state action for the purpose of safeguarding a principle at the heart of the Establishment Clause, that government should not prefer one religion to another, or religion to irreligion." The difficulty was that Kiryas Joel had not received its authority "simply as one of many communities eligible for equal treatment under a general law," so the Court could not be sure "that the next similarly situated group seeking a school district of its own will receive one; [a] legislature's failure to enact a special law is itself unreviewable." The Court agreed that the state could "accommodate religious needs by alleviating special burdens," but creating a separate district "singles out a particular religious sect for special treatment" and thereby violated the principle that "neutrality as among religions must be honored."

Justice Stevens, joined by Justices Blackmun and Ginsburg, added that, to meet the concerns about "panic, fear and trauma," the state "could have taken steps to alleviate the children's fear by teaching their schoolmates to be tolerant and respectful of Satmar customs. Action of that kind would raise no constitutional concerns and would further the strong public interest in promoting diversity and understanding in the public schools." But the state's response, "a solution that affirmatively supports a religious sect's interest in segregating itself and preventing its children from associating with their neighbors," was unconstitutional. It "increased the likelihood that they would remain within the fold, faithful adherents of their parents' religious faith," and thereby "provided official support to cement the attachment of young adherents to a particular faith."

Justice Kennedy, concurring, argued that "[the] real vice of the school district [is] that New York created it by drawing political boundaries on the basis of religion." He criticized the Court's broader analysis. "[By] creating the district, New York did not impose or increase any burden on non-Satmars, compared to the burden it lifted from the Satmars, that might disqualify the District as a genuine accommodation." There was no evidence "that the legislature has denied another religious community like the Satmars its own school district under analogous circumstances. The legislature, like the judiciary, is sworn to uphold the Constitution, and we have no reason to presume that the New York Legislature would not grant the same accommodation in a similar future case. The fact that New York singled out the Satmars for this special treatment indicates nothing other than the uniqueness of the handicapped Satmar children's plight. It is normal for legislatures to respond to problems as they arise — no less so when the issue is religious accommodation."

Justice O'Connor argued that "[the] Satmars' living arrangements were accommodated by their right — a right shared with all other communities, religious or not, throughout New York — to incorporate themselves as a village." In her view, "one's religion ought not affect one's legal rights or duties or benefits," even when the government was "acting to accommodate religion." Permissible accommodations could not involve "discriminations based on sect. [A] draft law may exempt conscientious objectors, but it may not exempt conscientious objectors whose objections are based on theistic belief (such as Quakers) as opposed to nontheistic belief (such as Buddhists) or atheistic belief." The New York statute "benefits one group" and should be treated "as a legislatively drawn religious classification." It was, for Justice O'Connor, "a close question, because the Satmars may be the only group who currently need this particular accommodation. The legislature may well be acting without any favoritism, so that if another group came to ask for a similar district, the group might get it on the same terms as the Satmars. But the nature of the legislative process makes it impossible to be sure of this. [A] group petitioning for a law may never get a definite response, or may get a 'no' based not on the merits but on the press of other business or the lack of an influential sponsor. Such a legislative refusal to act would not normally be reviewable by a court. Under these circumstances, it seems dangerous to validate what appears to me a clear religious preference." According to Justice O'Connor, "A district created under a generally applicable scheme would be acceptable even though it coincides with a village which was consciously created by its voters as an enclave for their religious group."

Justice Scalia's dissent was joined by Chief Justice Rehnquist and Justice Thomas. "[The] Founding Fathers would be astonished to find that the Establishment Clause [has] been employed to prohibit characteristically and admirably American accommodation of the religious practices (or more precisely, cultural peculiarities) of a tiny minority sect." As he saw it, "[T]he Court's 'no guarantee of neutrality' argument is an assertion of this Court's inability to control the New York Legislature's future denial of comparable accommodation.

[Most] efforts at accommodation seek to solve a problem that applies to members of only one or a few religions. Not every religion uses wine in its sacraments, but that does not [require] the State granting such an exemption to explain in advance how it will treat every other claim for dispensation from its controlled-substances laws." The Court should not require "some 'up front' legislative guarantee of equal treatment for [other] sects."

Note: When — If Ever — Should Accommodations of Religion Be Permitted?

1. *The attractions of a doctrine of permissible accommodation.* Consider McConnell, Accommodation of Religion, 1985 Sup. Ct. Rev. 1, 1–3:

> The much-discussed "tension" between the two Religion Clauses largely arises from the Court's substitution of a misleading formula (the three-part *Lemon* [test]) and subsidiary, instrumental, values (especially the separation of church and state) in place of the central value of religious liberty. [Between] the accommodations compelled by the Free Exercise Clause and the benefits to religion prohibited by the Establishment Clause there exists a class of permissible government actions toward religion, which have as their purpose and effects the facilitation of religious liberty. [Only] an interpretation of the Religion Clauses based on religious liberty [satisfactorily] distinguishes permissible accommodations from impermissible establishments.

See also McConnell, Accommodation of Religion: An Update and a Response to the Critics, 60 Geo. Wash. L. Rev. 685 (1992).

2. *The scope of the principle.* Walz v. Tax Commission, 397 U.S. 664 (1970), held constitutional the practice of granting churches exemptions from the property tax. Chief Justice Burger's opinion for the Court said that the "purpose of a property tax exemption is neither the advancement nor the inhibition of religion. [The state] has not singled out one particular church [or] even churches as such; rather, it has granted exemption to all houses of worship within a broad class of property owned by nonprofit, quasi-public corporations [which the state considers] beneficial and stabilizing influences in community life." After describing the ways in which denial of tax exemption would "expand the involvement of government" with religion, the Court said, "The exemption creates only a minimal and remote involvement between church and state. [It] restricts the fiscal relationship between [them], and tends to complement and reinforce the desired separation insulating each from the other." Fiscal support of religion through the tax system is thus not the imposition of religion on nonbelievers.

3. *Permissible accommodations and antidiscrimination legislation.* Estate of Thornton v. Caldor, 472 U.S. 703 (1985), held unconstitutional a Connecticut statute providing, "No person who states that a particular day of the week is observed as his Sabbath may be required by his employer to work on that day." Chief Justice Burger's opinion for the Court said that the statute imposes "an absolute duty to conform [business] practices to the particular religious practices of the employee. [The] State thus commands that Sabbath religious concerns automatically control over all secular interests at the workplace; the statute takes no account of the convenience or interests of the employer or those of other employees who do not observe a Sabbath." Justice O'Connor, joined by

Justice Marshall, concurred, objecting to the "special and [absolute] protection" given to Sabbath observers over those with other "ethical and religious beliefs and practices." "The message conveyed is one of endorsement of a particular religious belief, to the detriment of those who do not share it."

Why are the statute's absolute nature and targeting on a particular religious practice impermissible? Consider the implications of Justice Brennan's emphasis in *Texas Monthly* that permissible accommodations must be sufficiently broad: The broader the accommodation, the more significantly it impairs the majority's ability to accomplish the substantive aims it seeks — raising revenue, for example. A requirement of breadth therefore makes permissible accommodations self-limiting, reducing the possibility that serious erosions of the nonestablishment value will occur.

Consider 42 U.S.C. §§2000e-2(a), 2000e(j):

> It shall be an unlawful employment practice for an employer to [discriminate] against any individual with respect to his compensation, terms, conditions, or privileges of employment [because] of such individual's [religion; the] term "religion" includes all aspects of religious observance and practice, as well as belief, unless an employer demonstrates that he is unable to reasonably accommodate an employee's [religious] observance or practice without undue hardship on the conduct of the employer's business.

These provisions were construed in Trans World Airlines v. Hardison, 432 U.S. 63 (1977), as not requiring an employer to adjust its seniority system to allow junior employees to avoid work on their Sabbaths by displacing senior employees entitled by the system to work on the other days. "To require TWA to bear more than a de minimis cost in order to give Hardison Saturdays off is an undue hardship." In *Thornton*, Justice O'Connor's opinion distinguished title VII because it required reasonable, not absolute, accommodation of all religious beliefs and practices. "[An] objective observer would perceive it as an anti-discrimination law rather than an endorsement of religion or a particular religious practice."

The opinions suggest that the more a statutory accommodation places a burden on nonbeneficiaries, the less likely it is a permissible accommodation. Consider the argument that, to the contrary, the greater the burden, the more permissible the accommodation because those feeling the burden will have more political influence in striking an appropriate balance.

How should the following problems be analyzed: (a) A state's antidiscrimination laws do not prohibit discrimination against LGBTQ individuals by places of public accommodation. The state enacts a statute providing that no one operating a place of public accommodation may be required to provide goods or services to any person if the operator has a religion-based objection to providing the goods or services. (b) A state's antidiscrimination laws prohibit discrimination against LGBTQ individuals. The state enacts a statute providing that no one covered by the antidiscrimination law shall be held liable for failure to provide goods or services to anyone if the person has a religion-based objection to doing so. What burdens are relevant to determining the constitutionality of this accommodation? As to burdens on the business operator, must the government accept the operator's assessment of the substantiality of the burden, or may it assess that burden independently? As to burdens on customers, consider that some burdens are material, such as the need to procure the goods or services elsewhere, and some are dignitary. How should the latter be assessed?

4. *Permissible accommodations and sect preference.* Lupu, The Lingering Death of Separationism, 62 Geo. Wash. L. Rev. 230, 270 (1994), says that New York in *Kiryas Joel* "predictably responded to the circumstances and political strength of the affected sect. [Is] it imaginable that New York State would create a new public school district at the behest of an insular group of Branch Davidians or members of the Unification Church?" If the presumption is that the legislature would not do so, how can the courts ever learn whether the legislature is in fact willing to act in a sect-neutral manner?

Does *Kiryas Joel* raise serious questions about state laws protecting the practice of labeling certain foods kosher (i.e., satisfying certain religious requirements) by making it a fraudulent practice to label a food as kosher when it has not received the approval of a specific religious institution? For a discussion, see Greenawalt, Religious Law and Civil Law: Using Secular Law to Assure Observance of Practices with Religious Significance, 71 S. Cal. L. Rev. 781, 793–796 (1998).

5. *The doctrine's justification.* On what theory of the establishment clause are statutory accommodations of religious practices permissible? Note that statutory accommodations have the purpose of benefiting religious belief as against non-belief. Consider these possibilities:

a. Justice Souter's concurring opinion in Lee v. Weisman section B1, supra, observed, "[Accommodation] must lift a discernible burden on the free exercise of religion. Concern for the position of religious individuals in the modern regulatory state cannot justify official solicitude for a religious practice unburdened by general rules. [Religious] students cannot complain that omitting prayers from their graduation ceremony would, in any realistic sense, 'burden' their spiritual callings." Note that the Court in *Amos* concedes that the church's free exercise rights would not be violated by requiring it to comply with the ban on religious discrimination as to the employees there. "Burden," thus, means some impairment of free exercise values short of a violation of free exercise rights.

b. Statutory accommodations are permissible solely to alleviate burdens that violate the free exercise clause, but legislatures have some leeway to determine what an appropriate balance is, or to devise accommodations that differ from judicially devised ones because of institutional differences between courts and legislatures.

c. Legislatures have substantial discretion to promote "free exercise values" by enacting statutory accommodations. Why is not voluntary devotional prayer in public schools a permissible accommodation? Consider also Chief Justice Burger's argument in dissent in *Jaffree*, section B3, supra, that Alabama's moment of silence statute "accommodates the purely private, voluntary religious choices of the individual pupils who wish to pray while at the same time creating a time for nonreligious reflection for those who do not choose to pray." Are such practices insufficiently broad to satisfy the doctrine's requirements?

Can any of these theories support the accommodation in *Kiryas Joel*?

Gedicks, The Normalized Free Exercise Clause, 75 Ind. L.J. 77 (2000), argues that the doctrine of permissible accommodations is inconsistent with equal protection doctrine dealing with affirmative action, which subjects assertedly benign legislation based on suspect traits to strict scrutiny. With which account of the doctrine of permissible accommodations is equal protection doctrine inconsistent?

6. *The Religious Freedom Restoration Act (RFRA) and the Religious Land Use and Institutionalized Persons Act (RLUIPA).* The Religious Freedom Restoration Act was held unconstitutional with respect to state legislation, but remains

applicable to federal legislation. See Gonzales v. O'Centro Espirita Beneficiente Unidão, 546 U.S. 418 (2005). For a controversial application of the Act, see Burwell v. Hobby Lobby Stores, Inc., __ U.S. __ (2014) (rejecting the argument that, with respect to those entitled to raise RFRA claims, the statute "did no more than codify this Court's pre-*Smith* precedents" and holding that a closely held, for-profit corporation with religious objections to certain forms of birth control was entitled to a statutory exemption from a requirement that any insurance policy it provided to its workers cover contraception).

The RLUIPA, enacted in 2000, provides, "No government shall impose a substantial burden on the religious exercise of a person residing in or confined to an institution," unless the burden furthers "a compelling governmental interest" by "the least restrictive means." Cutter v. Wilkinson, 544 U.S. 709 (2005), rejected a facial establishment clause challenge to this provision of the RLUIPA, finding it to be a permissible accommodation of religion "because it alleviates exceptional government-created burdens on private religious exercise." The provision "covers state-run institutions [in] which the government exerts a degree of control unparalleled in civilian society and severely disabling to private religious exercise." Institutionalized persons are "dependent on the government's permission and accommodation for exercise of their religion." The Court interpreted the statutory standards to conform to prior constitutional decisions indicating that "an accommodation must be measured so that it does not override other significant interests. [We] have no cause to believe that RLUIPA would not be applied in an appropriately balanced way, with particular sensitivity to security concerns." Citing Grutter v. Bollinger, 539 U.S. 306 (2003), the Court observed that "'[c]ontext matters'" in applying the statutory "'compelling government interest'" standard, and quoted legislative history indicating that "[l]awmakers supporting [the act] were mindful of the urgency of discipline, order, safety, and security in penal institutions" and "anticipated that courts would apply the Act's standard with 'due deference'" to the judgment of prison administrators. "Should inmate requests for religious accommodations become excessive, impose unjustified burdens on other institutionalized persons, or jeopardize the effective functioning of an institution, the facility would be free to resist the imposition. In that event, adjudication in as-applied challenges would be in order."

E.   FREE EXERCISE, FREE SPEECH, AND THE RIGHT OF EXPRESSIVE ASSOCIATION

HOSANNA-TABOR EVANGELICAL LUTHERAN CHURCH & SCHOOL v. EEOC, 565 U.S. 171 (2012). Cheryl Perich was a "called" teacher at a school operated by the Lutheran Church. "Called" teachers completed special training, including theological study. Most of Perich's classes were in secular subjects, but she did teach a religion class. After Perich took disability leave for narcolepsy, her employer asked that she resign. She refused and informed the school that she had consulted a lawyer. The school then fired her, citing among other things her threats to take legal action. Perich filed a complaint with the Equal Employment Opportunity Commission, which after an investigation sued the school for retaliating against Perich for threatening to file her lawsuit under the Americans with Disabilities Act. The school sought dismissal of the EEOC lawsuit, invoking the "ministerial exemption." That exemption, written into some nondiscrimination statutes but not the ADA's antiretaliation provision, is available to religious institutions in connection with the employment of "ministers."

Chief Justice Roberts, writing for a unanimous Court, held that both the establishment and free exercise clauses required that religious institutions be able to invoke a ministerial exemption, and that Perich was a minister within the constitutionally required exemption. "The members of a religious group put their faith in the hands of their ministers. Requiring a church to accept or retain an unwanted minister, or punishing a church for failing to do so, intrudes upon more than a mere employment decision. Such action interferes with the internal governance of the church, depriving the church of control over the selection of those who will personify its beliefs. [This] infringes the Free Exercise Clause, which protects a religious group's right to shape its own faith and mission through its appointments. According the state the power to determine which individuals will minister to the faithful also violates the Establishment Clause, which prohibits government involvement in such ecclesiastical decisions."

The Court found "untenable" the position that church interests were adequately protected by the right of expressive association implicit in the first amendment. That position would lead to the conclusion that "the First Amendment analysis should be the same, whether the association in question is the Lutheran Church, a labor union, or a social club. That result is hard to square with the text of the First Amendment itself, which gives special solicitude to the rights of religious organizations." Although the ADA's antiretaliation provision was "a valid and neutral law of general applicability," Employment Division v. Smith was inapposite because it "involved government regulation of only outward physical acts. The present case [concerns] government interference with an internal church decision that affects the faith and mission of the church itself."

The Court refused "to adopt a rigid formula for deciding when an employee qualifies as a minister. It is enough for us to conclude [that] the exception covers Perich. [Hosanna-Tabor] held Perich out as a minister, with a role distinct from that of most of its members. [Her] title as a minister reflected a significant degree of religious training followed by a formal process of commissioning. [Her] job duties reflected a role in conveying the Church's message and carrying out its mission." Concurring, Justice Thomas wrote that "the Religion Clauses require civil courts [to] defer to a religious organization's good-faith understanding of who qualifies as a minister. [The] question of whether an employee is a minister is itself religious in nature, and the answer will vary widely. Judicial attempts to fashion a civil definition of 'minister' through a bright-line test or multi-factor analysis risk disadvantaging those religious groups whose beliefs, practices, and membership are outside of the 'mainstream' or unpalatable to some." Also concurring, Justice Alito, joined by Justice Kagan, wrote that defining who was a minister "should focus on the function performed by persons who work for religious bodies," and "[should] apply to any 'employee' who leads a religious organization, conducts worship services or important religious ceremonies or rituals, or serves as a messenger or teacher of its faith."

Note: The Relation between the Religion Clauses and Other Protections of Expression

1. *The scope of exemption.* The justices discussed how to determine who was a minister for purposes of the constitutionally required exemption. What are the criteria for determining whether an entity is a church entitled to the exemption?

2. *Free exercise versus other protected first amendment rights?* Many activities associated with religion are forms of expression, either expressly (prayer) or as action that can be described as symbolic speech (some or all religious rituals). Would the analysis of the restriction on the use of peyote in *Smith* differ were that use characterized as symbolic speech? Conversely, why is a decision to hire or fire an employee not an "outward physical act"? Could the restriction on ritual sacrifice invalidated in *Hialeah* be characterized as discrimination against expressive activity based on its content? Epps, What We Talk about When We Talk about Free Exercise, 30 Ariz. St. L.J. 563, 577–578 (1998), argues that distinctive free exercise issues arise only in connection with "rituals that are of a concededly religious nature with symbolic content but for which there is an empirical basis to believe that [the] ritual action may also have permanent consequences in the physical world."

3. *The right of expressive association.* Had Congress not exempted it from regulation, would the right to expressive association of the church employer in *Amos* be violated by applying the antidiscrimination law to its workers in the nonprofit gymnasium? In a profit-making activity associated with the church? What accommodations, permissible under the Court's doctrine, would be required not by the free exercise clause as interpreted in *Smith* but by the right of expressive association? Is there a principled reason for distinguishing churches as expressive associations from other expressive associations such as labor unions? Is the textual basis for such a distinction strong enough to outweigh legislative judgments that all expressive associations should be required to conform to neutral laws of generally applicability, subject to a balancing test responsive to the concern that invoking such a law would interfere with the organization's ability to disseminate its message? See Magarian, Justice Stevens, Religion, and Civil Society, 2011 Wis. L. Rev 733. For a discussion of the right of expressive association, see Chapter 7, section E5, supra.

Observing that "[to] say that the Establishment Clause requires the [ministerial] exemption is to say that regulation of a religious institution violates the Establishment Clause[, which] is very odd," and that "[interference] with religious practice naturally raises Free Exercise concerns, but it is unclear how such regulation *establishes* a religion," Bhagwat, Religious Associations: *Hosanna-Tabor* and the Instrumental Value of Religious Groups, 92 Wash. U. L. Rev. 73, 84 (2014), argues that the decision, while correct, should have rested on a more vigorous application of the right of expressive association.

4. *Content- or viewpoint-based discrimination.* Widmar v. Vincent, 454 U.S. 263 (1981), invoked the free speech clause to require a state university to make its facilities available to a student prayer group, just as it would make them available to other groups seeking to use the public forum it created. The Court held that a policy of "nondiscrimination against religious speech" would not violate the establishment clause. See also Lamb's Chapel v. Center Moriches Union Free School District, 508 U.S. 384 (1993), invalidating a school district's restriction on the after-hours use of its facilities by religious groups, finding the restriction

viewpoint-based; Rosenberger v. Rector & Visitors of the University of Virginia, 515 U.S. 819 (1995), invalidating a university policy authorizing payment from the Student Activities Fund for the printing costs of a variety of student publications, but prohibiting payment for any student publication that "primarily promotes or manifests a particular belief in or about a deity or an ultimate reality." These cases find no establishment clause problem because, according to Lamb's Chapel, "There would have been no realistic danger that the community would think that the District was endorsing religion or any particular creed." See also Capitol Square Review & Advisory Board v. Pinette, 515 U.S. 753 (1995), finding no establishment clause violation in allowing a private group to display a Latin cross on public property and therefore requiring the board to permit the display.

Consider these comments on Rosenberger and related cases:

> The student Christian group won the funding of printing for its publication but at the price of having its religious message reduced to the commonality of every other form of human speech. [The] petitioners were willing to give up the special status that religion is otherwise granted. [By] wishing not to deny religion its place in a marketplace of ideas, the Court denied the special place held by religion in our constitutional framework. [If] "preaching the word" [is] only speech, it is outside the restraints of the Establishment Clause. But "preaching the word" is not mere speech; it is religion and must, therefore, suffer the inconvenience of full protection only when disassociated from the power of government. . . .
>
> The concept of equal treatment [sounds] alluringly democratic, pluralistic, and fair. [But] in fact it may signal the triumph of the postmodern relativist mind in which every statement is of equal value to any other. One's religious beliefs would be protected equally and at the same level as one's right to [live] in a certain [neighborhood]. [One's] religious faith will become on par with every other worldview and life belief. [Equality] is a hallmark of American democracy, but it should not rule in every case.

Davis, A Commentary on the Supreme Court's "Equal Treatment" Doctrine as the New Constitutional Paradigm for Protecting Religious Liberty, 46 J. Church & St. 717, 720-721, 736-737 (2004). For a related view, see Gellman and Looper-Friedman, Thou Shalt Use the Equal Protection Clause for Religion Cases (Not Just the Establishment Clause), 10 U. Pa. J. Const. L. 666 (2008). Justice White, the only dissenter in Widmar, criticized the Court for arguing that "religious worship qua speech is not different from any other variety of protected speech. [This] proposition is plainly wrong. Were it right, the Religion Clauses would be emptied of any independent meaning in which religious practice took the form of speech." He would have distinguished between "verbal acts of worship and other verbal acts," saying that "the line may be difficult to draw in many cases," but that doing so was necessary in order to avoid the result that the university could "offer a class entitled 'Sunday Mass,' [indistinguishable] from a class entitled 'The History of the Catholic Church.'" The Court responded by noting that the distinction between worship and speech about religion had no "intelligible content" because "there is no indication when 'singing hymns, reading scripture, and teaching biblical principles' cease to be ['speech,'] despite their religious subject matter [and] become 'worship.'"

The Equal Access Act, 20 U.S.C. §4071 (1984), provides, "It shall be unlawful for any public secondary school which receives Federal financial assistance and which has a limited open forum to deny equal access [to] any students who wish to conduct a meeting within that limited open forum on the basis of the religious, political, philosophical, or other content of the speech at such meetings." A limited open forum is created when the school allows "noncurriculum related student groups to meet on school premises during noninstructional time." The Court upheld the constitutionality of the Equal Access Act in Board of Education of Westside Community Schools v. Mergens, 496 U.S. 226 (1990). Justice O'Connor's plurality opinion on the constitutional question concluded that "the logic of *Widmar* applies" to the Equal Access Act. Prohibiting discrimination on the basis of political as well as religious speech was a secular purpose under *Lemon*. Equal access would not have the effect of conveying a message of government endorsement of religion. "We think that secondary school students are mature enough and are likely to understand that a school does not endorse or support student speech that it merely permits on a nondiscriminatory basis." Congress had made a similar determination, and Justice O'Connor said that the Court should not "lightly second-guess [legislative] judgments, particularly where the judgments are based in part on empirical determinations," as this one was. She noted that "the broad spectrum of officially recognized student groups [counteracts] any possible message of official endorsement of or preference for religion or a particular religion. [To] the extent that a religious club is merely one of many different student-initiated voluntary clubs, students should perceive no message of government endorsement of religion."

5. *Religion in politics.*

a. *Church members as political actors.* Torcaso v. Watkins, 367 U.S. 488 (1961), invalidated a provision in the Maryland Constitution requiring state officials to declare their belief in the existence of God. "[Neither] a State nor the Federal Government can constitutionally force a person 'to profess a belief or disbelief in any religion' [and] neither can aid those religions based on a belief in the existence of God as against those religions founded on different beliefs."

In McDaniel v. Paty, 435 U.S. 618 (1978), the Court invalidated, without dissent, a provision of the Tennessee Constitution barring ministers from serving as legislators or as delegates to the state's constitutional convention. Chief Justice Burger's plurality opinion reviewed the history of such disqualifications, which were in effect in seven of the original states and which were adopted by six states later admitted to the Union. Disqualification was designed "to assure the success of a new political experiment, the separation of church and state." But "as the value of the disestablishment experiment was perceived, 11 of the 13 States [gradually] abandoned that limitation," until by 1900 only Maryland and Tennessee retained it. The opinion continued, "[The] right to the free exercise of religion unquestionably encompasses the right to preach [and] to be a minister." If the disqualification "were viewed as depriving the clergy of a civil right solely because of their religious beliefs," *Torcaso* would control. But the disqualification was triggered by the minister's status, defined "in terms of conduct and activity rather than in terms of belief." Thus, the relevant precedent was *Yoder*, which required an "interest of the highest order." But the state had "failed to demonstrate that [the] dangers of clergy participation in the political process have not lost whatever validity they may once have enjoyed. [The] American experience provides no persuasive support for the fear that clergymen in public office will be less careful of anti-establishment interests or less faithful to their oaths of civil office than their unordained counterparts."

Justice Brennan, joined by Justice Marshall and Justice Stewart, submitted separate concurring opinions arguing that *Torcaso* controlled. Justice Brennan wrote, "[Freedom] of belief [embraces] freedom to profess or practice that belief, even including doing so to earn a livelihood." Tennessee's rule was therefore "absolutely prohibited," and no balancing of interests was required. Justice Brennan argued that

> public debate of religious ideas [may] arouse emotion, [but] the mere fact that a purpose of the Establishment Clause is to reduce or eliminate religious divisiveness or strife, does not place religious discussion, association, or political participation in a status less preferred than rights of [political] participation generally. [Religionists] no less than members of any other group enjoy the full measure of protection afforded speech. [The] antidote which the Constitution provides against zealots who would inject sectarianism into the political process is to subject their ideas to refutation in the market-place of ideas and their platforms to rejection at the polls. With these safeguards [and] with judicial enforcement of the Establishment Clause, any measure of success they achieve must be short-lived, at best.

Justice White concurred in the judgment, relying on the equal protection clause rather than the free exercise clause, because he did not see how the minister "has been deterred in the observance of his religious beliefs."

What result in *McDaniel* under the free speech clause? Is the confidence expressed by Chief Justice Burger and Justice Brennan in the political process warranted? Should a state be precluded from taking a more jaundiced view of the efficacy of the political process in matters of religion?

b. *Churches as political actors.* Larkin v. Grendel's Den, 459 U.S. 116 (1982), held unconstitutional a statute granting churches and schools the power to veto the issuance of liquor licenses to restaurants within five hundred feet of the church or school buildings. The Court acknowledged the "interest in being insulated from certain kinds of commercial establishments," but found that delegating the veto power to churches had the effect of advancing religion and "provides a significant symbolic benefit to religion in the minds of some." Further, the statute "enmeshes churches in the exercise of substantial governmental powers." Note that delegation of similar authority to other private organizations is unlikely to raise federal constitutional questions.

Justice Souter, writing only for a plurality in *Kiryas Joel*, regarded the New York statute as a delegation of state power to a religious institution, barred by *Larkin*. Justice Scalia's dissent called "breathtaking" this "steamrolling of the difference between civil authority held by a church, and civil authority held by members of a church." It "boils down to the quite novel proposition that any group of citizens (say, the residents of Kiryas Joel) can be invested with political power, but not if they all belong to the same religion. Of course such disfavoring of religion is positively antagonistic to the purposes of the Religion Clauses."

Note: Concluding Observations

Do the preceding materials demonstrate that contemporary religion clause doctrine is hostile to religion in the name of neutrality? In a religiously pluralist nation with an expansive government, is neutrality toward religion possible? Are the two religion clauses incompatible in such a nation? The establishment clause requires (some sort of) neutrality, while the free exercise clause requires (some sort of) preference to religion and may permit other preferences. Does the concept of benevolent neutrality reconcile the clauses? When does a permissible benevolence become a prohibited encouragement? Consider whether the religion clauses are incompatible because of religious pluralism: Any purported benevolent encouragement of some or many religions will discourage others; given the range of actions required by some religions and prohibited by others, no regulation can be neutral in its effects as between some religions and others or between religion and nonreligion.

IX

State Action

It is a commonplace that the commands of the Constitution are directed to governmental entities, not to private parties. This observation leads to the "state action" requirement: When private individuals or companies act, they are generally free from constitutional restrictions. The text of the Constitution seems to support this conclusion; it generally applies to governments, not to private actors.

Is there a good reason for this limitation on the Constitution's reach? On a standard view, the limitation is based on the judgment that government is generally uniquely powerful and dangerous — far more so than private entities. Government is what we have most to fear. One reason (it is often said) is that it has a monopoly on the legitimate use of force. In any case, the limitation of constitutional requirements to state actors is unquestionably important. Every day, it affects the reach of the Constitution.

Note, however, that for at least two reasons the state action limitation, standing by itself, may tell us less than we might think. First, there is a sense in which the state action requirement is merely a truism. The Constitution must be directed to state actors, because if it were directed solely to private parties, there would be no enforceable means to make those parties obey constitutional commands. For example, the thirteenth amendment prohibition against slavery is sometimes said to be an exception to the state action doctrine; even private acts of enslavement are unconstitutional. But the thirteenth amendment must be read as a directive to government officials to punish enslavement; otherwise, the right not to be enslaved would be meaningless.

Second, and more fundamentally, the statement that the Constitution controls only government conduct *tells us nothing about what the Constitution requires the government to do.* Perhaps some constitutional provisions require government to control private conduct. Even if a private person's denial of equal treatment to African Americans does not itself violate the fourteenth amendment, it remains possible that the state's decision to permit private persons to deny equal treatment to African Americans violates that amendment. Whether it does so depends on what the fourteenth amendment means. The state action doctrine says that the government and not some private person must be the defendant. But it does not say that the government is under no obligation to stop private people from injuring other people. In fact, it is generally agreed that states violate the equal protection clause if they protect whites against murder and assault but fail to protect African Americans against murder and assault.

To have meaning, then, the state action doctrine must be supplemented by some substantive ideas about the meaning of relevant constitutional provisions. This chapter examines the Court's efforts to develop these ideas.

A.   STATE ACTION, FEDERALISM, AND INDIVIDUAL AUTONOMY

A state action requirement might be thought to define an area that must remain beyond the reach of national power — at least national judicial power. Consider, for example, Lugar v. Edmondson Oil Co., 457 U.S. 922, 936 (1982):

> Careful adherence to the "state action" requirement preserves an area of individual freedom by limiting the reach of federal law and federal judicial power. [A] major consequence is to require the courts to respect the limits of their own power as directed against state governments and private interests. Whether this is good or bad policy, it is a fundamental fact of our political order.

The notion that "limiting the reach of federal law" serves to "preserve individual freedom" has considerable appeal, but it is not an uncontroversial one. The fourteenth amendment, for example, was premised to some degree on the opposite assumption — that an extension of federal law was essential to the preservation of individual rights. See Chapter 5, section A, supra. Nonetheless, the Court's analysis of the state action issue has long been influenced by the assumed link among individual freedom, state action requirements, and restrictions on federal power. Indeed, this "fundamental fact of our political order" was central to the Court's earliest effort to articulate a state action doctrine.

1.   State Action and Federalism

The modern Court has held that state action is a prerequisite to the assertion of rights contained in both the first eight amendments (originally applicable only to the federal government) and the fourteenth amendment (applicable to the states). But historically the requirement attracted little attention until passage of the Reconstruction amendments after the Civil War.

After the ratification of these amendments, the Court was required to decide the extent to which they changed the traditional balance between state and federal authority. One view was that the new amendments gave the federal government plenary authority to protect individual rights — against both public and private actors. A second view was that the amendments left untouched the states' traditional functions and authorized federal intervention only when the states defaulted in their primary obligations. See Chapter 5, section A2, supra.

The Court's earliest state action decision looked to principles of federalism to give content to the doctrine.

THE CIVIL RIGHTS CASES, 109 U.S. 3 (1883). The Civil Rights Act of 1875 provided that all persons were "entitled to the full and equal enjoyment of the accommodations, advantages, facilities, and privileges of inns, public conveyances, on land or water, theatres, and other places of public amusement; subject only to the conditions and limitations established by law, and applicable alike to citizens of every race and color, regardless of any previous condition of servitude." Private persons violating these rights were subject to civil damages and criminal penalties. The constitutionality of the act was challenged on the ground that it was not authorized by any substantive grant of power to the federal government. In an eight-to-one decision, the Court agreed and invalidated the act.

Justice Bradley delivered the Court's opinion: "Has Congress constitutional power to make such a law? Of course, no one will contend that the power to pass it was contained in the Constitution before the adoption of the [thirteenth, fourteenth, and fifteenth] amendments. . . .

"[The] fourteenth amendment is prohibitory in its character, and prohibitory upon the states. [Individual] invasion of individual rights is not the subject matter of the amendment. . . .

"[The Civil Rights Act, in contrast,] proceeds ex directo to declare that certain acts committed by individuals shall be deemed offences, and shall be prosecuted and punished by proceedings in the courts of the United States. It does not profess to be corrective of any constitutional wrong committed by the states. [It] applies equally to cases arising in States which have the justest laws respecting the personal rights of citizens, and whose authorities are ever ready to enforce such laws, as to those which arise in States that may have violated the prohibition of the amendment. In other words, it steps into the domain of local jurisprudence and lays down rules for the conduct of individuals in society towards each other, and imposes sanctions for the enforcement of those rules, without referring in any manner to any supposed action of the State or its authorities. . . .

"The wrongful act of an individual, unsupported by any [State] authority, is simply a private wrong, or a crime of that individual; an invasion of the rights of the injured party, it is true, whether they affect his person, his property, or his reputation; but if not sanctioned in some way by the State, or not done under State authority, his rights remain in full force, and may presumably be vindicated by resort to the laws of the State for redress. An individual cannot deprive a man of his right to vote, to hold property, to buy and sell, to sue in the courts, or to be a witness or a juror; he may, by force or fraud, interfere with the enjoyment of the right in a particular case; [but] unless protected in these wrongful acts by some shield of State law or State authority, he cannot destroy or injure the right; he will only render himself amenable to satisfaction or punishment; and amenable therefor to the laws of the State where the wrongful acts are committed."

Defenders of the act also relied on Congress's power to enforce the thirteenth amendment, which abolished slavery. The Court agreed that the thirteenth amendment, unlike the fourteenth, authorized legislation that was "primary and direct in its character; for the amendment is not a mere prohibition of State laws establishing or upholding slavery, but an absolute declaration that slavery or involuntary servitude shall not exist in any part of the United States."

Nonetheless, the Court concluded that the statute was not authorized under the thirteenth amendment because the refusal to serve a person in a public accommodation was no more than an ordinary civil injury and not a badge of slavery. "[Such] an act of refusal has nothing to do with slavery or involuntary servitude, and [if] it is violative of any right of the party, his redress is to be sought under the laws of the State; or if those laws are adverse to his rights and do not protect him, his remedy will be found in the corrective legislation which Congress has adopted, or may adopt, for counteracting the effect of State laws, or State action, prohibited by the Fourteenth Amendment. It would be running the slavery argument into the ground to make it apply to every act of discrimination which a person may see fit to make as to the guests he will entertain, or as to the people he will take into his coach or cab or car, or admit to his concert or theatre, or deal with in other matters of intercourse or business. . . .

"When a man has emerged from slavery, and by the aid of beneficent legislation has shaken off the inseparable concomitants of that state, there must be some stage in the progress of his elevation when he takes the rank of a mere citizen, and ceases to be the special favorite of the law, and when his rights as a citizen, or a man, are to be protected in the ordinary modes by which other men's rights are protected."

Only Justice Harlan dissented from the Court's opinion: "The [majority] opinion in these cases proceeds, it seems to me, upon grounds entirely too narrow and artificial. I cannot resist the conclusion that the substance and spirit of the recent amendments of the Constitution have been sacrificed by a subtle and ingenious verbal criticism. . . .

"[Since] slavery [was] the moving or principal cause of the adoption of [the thirteenth] amendment, and since that institution rested wholly upon the inferiority, as a race, of those held in bondage, their freedom necessarily involved immunity from, and protection against, all discrimination against them, because of their race, in respect of such civil rights as belong to freemen of other races. Congress, therefore, under its express power to enforce that amendment, by appropriate legislation, may enact laws to protect that people against the deprivation, *because of their race,* of any civil rights granted to other freemen in the same State; and such legislation may be of a direct and primary character, operating upon States, their officers and agents, and, also upon, at least, such individuals and corporations as exercise public functions and wield power and authority under the State. . . .

"The assumption that [the fourteenth] amendment consists wholly of prohibitions upon State laws and State proceedings in hostility to its provisions, is unauthorized by its language. The first clause of the first section — 'All persons born or naturalized in the United States, and subject to the jurisdiction thereof, are citizens of the United States, and of the State wherein they reside' — is of a distinctly affirmative character. . . .

"The citizenship thus acquired by [the black] race, in virtue of an affirmative grant from the nation, may be protected, not alone by the judicial branch of the government, but by congressional legislation of a primary direct character; this, because the power of Congress is not restricted to the enforcement of prohibitions upon State law or State action. It is, in terms distinct and positive, to enforce 'the *provisions of this article*' of the amendment; not simply those of a prohibitive character, but the provisions — *all* of the provisions — affirmative and prohibitive, of the amendment. . . .

"It is, I submit, scarcely just to say that the colored race has been the special favorite of the laws. The statute of 1875, now adjudged to be unconstitutional, is for the benefit of citizens of every race and color. What the nation, through Congress, has sought to accomplish in reference to that race is, — what had already been done in every State of the Union for the white race — to secure and protect rights belonging to them as freemen and citizens; nothing more.

"[Today] it is the colored race which is denied, by corporations and individuals wielding public authority, rights fundamental in their freedom and citizenship. At some future time, it may be that some other race will fall under the ban of race discrimination. If the constitutional amendments be enforced, according to the intent with which, as I conceive, they were adopted, there can not be, in this republic any class of human beings in practical subjection to another class, with power in the latter to dole out to the former just such privileges as they may choose to grant."

Note: Federalism and the Substantive Content of the State Action Doctrine

The Court has long read The Civil Rights Cases to establish "the essential dichotomy [between] deprivation by the State, subject to scrutiny under [the fourteenth amendment,] and private conduct [against] which the Fourteenth Amendment offers no shield." Jackson v. Metropolitan Edison Co., 419 U.S. 345, 349 (1974). And the Court in The Civil Rights Cases did assert that "[individual] invasion of individual rights is not the subject matter of the [fourteenth] amendment." But by itself this proposition tells us little about what should count as a *state* invasion of individual rights.

Perhaps it counts as a state invasion of individual rights for a state to *fail to remedy* acts of racial discrimination undertaken by owners of public accommodations who are required by state law to serve the public. Consider in this regard the Court's argument in The Civil Rights Cases that a wrongful act, unsupported by state authority, cannot by itself violate legal rights so long as the victim can look to state law for redress; consider especially its complaint that the 1875 act "applies equally to cases arising in States which have the justest laws respecting the personal rights of citizens, and whose authorities are ever ready to enforce such laws, as to those which arise in States that may have violated the prohibition of the amendment." Is the Court suggesting that the national government might control private discrimination if the states are failing to do so?

Consider also Justice Bradley's comments on the fourteenth amendment in correspondence with Circuit Judge (later Justice) Wood, written twelve years before he authored the majority opinion in The Civil Rights Cases: "[The fourteenth amendment] not only prohibits the making or enforcing of laws which shall abridge the privileges of the citizen; but prohibits the states from denying to all persons within its jurisdiction the equal protection of the laws. [Denying] includes inaction as well as action. And denying the equal protection of the laws includes the omission to protect, as well as the omission to pass laws for protection." (The correspondence is quoted in Bell v. Maryland, 378 U.S. 226, 309–310 (1964) (Goldberg, J., concurring).)

Under this view of the matter, The Civil Rights Cases may stand for the proposition that the states are the primary guarantors of the rights of their citizens, and that the federal government may protect those rights if — but only if — the states fail to do so. Note that this position suggests both a broad and a narrow conception of federal power. It is broad in the sense that it treats state failures to act as state action for purposes of the fourteenth amendment; it is narrow in the sense that it incorporates a federalism-based limit on the federal government's power to act.

This view was, however, severely qualified, and perhaps even rejected, in United States v. Morrison, 529 U.S. 598 (2000), where the Court held that the Violence against Women Act was beyond congressional power under the fourteenth amendment. Congress defended the act, which created a federal cause of action by victims against perpetrators of "a crime of violence motivated by gender," in part on the ground that states had not provided sufficient "protection" against such crimes, and hence a federal cause of action was necessary to ensure equal protection of the laws. The Court acknowledged legislative findings of bias in state criminal justice systems, but emphasized that Congress could not reach private conduct, which the act purported to do, by making ordinary people defendants. This appears to be an authoritative ruling that Congress cannot reach private conduct under section 5 of the fourteenth amendment even when states are failing to provide protection.

To the claim that the civil action was necessary to counteract state discrimination, the Court said that the remedy did not have a "congruence and proportionality" to the injury sought to be prevented. The act "visits no consequence whatever on any [state official] involved in investigating or prosecuting" sex-related crimes. Because it did not punish state officials, and because it "applies uniformly throughout the nation," it was different from other cases in which Congress was allowed, under section 5 of the fourteenth amendment, to proceed prophylactically.

If states in fact fail to provide "equal protection" to women who are subject to violence, why isn't a federal civil rights action against private actors a perfectly reasonable response, not to private action, but to violations of "equal protection" on the part of the states?

2.   *State Action and Individual Autonomy*

Morrison makes clear that the state action limitation cannot be reduced to the federalism idea that the national government can protect rights only when the states fail to do so. Might we look instead to principles about the scope of individual autonomy to give substantive content to the limitation?

According to this view, the Constitution is designed primarily to protect individual freedom. Without some sort of state action doctrine, private autonomy would be subject to the same limitations as government autonomy. Instead of *protecting* individual rights from *legislative* interference, the Constitution might *subject* them to *judicial* interference.

It is easy to imagine the extreme consequences that might follow. Newspapers, radio stations, websites, and social media pages might be prohibited from promoting their preferred point of view. Social clubs and private homeowners might be precluded from choosing their guests on political or racial grounds. Is that troublesome? If so, might these consequences be avoided by a different interpretation of the relevant constitutional provision? Consider in this regard Columbia Broadcasting System (CBS) v. Democratic National Committee, 412 U.S. 94 (1973). Respondents claimed that the refusal of broadcasters to accept their editorial advertisements violated the first amendment. The Federal Communications Commission rejected this contention and refused to require that broadcasters accept such advertisements. The Court agreed with the commission.

In a portion of his plurality opinion joined by only two other justices, Chief Justice Burger argued that the first amendment claim failed because the broadcasters' decision could not be attributed to the government:

> Were we to read the First Amendment to spell out governmental action in the circumstances presented here, few licensee decisions on the content of broadcasts or the processes of editorial evaluation would escape constitutional scrutiny. . . .
>
> [It] would be anomalous for us to hold, in the name of promoting the constitutional guarantees of free expression, that the day-to-day editorial decisions of broadcast licensees are subject to the kind of restraints urged by respondents. To do so in the name of the First Amendment would be a contradiction. Journalistic discretion would in many ways be lost to the rigid limitations that the First Amendment imposes on Government. Application of such standards to broadcast licensees would be antithetical to the very ideal of vigorous, challenging debate on issues of public interest.

The result in *CBS* maximizes the journalistic freedom of broadcasters, who need not account to a court or government agency for their editorial decisions. But it arguably does so at the expense of the freedom of those wishing to present editorial advertisements, who may be prevented from securing a forum. Can the state action requirement be understood as the Court's technique for balancing the conflicting rights of private individuals in cases such as *CBS*? For an argument along these lines, see Glennon and Nowak, A Functional Analysis of the Fourteenth Amendment "State Action" Requirement, 1976 Sup. Ct. Rev. 221.

How should a court go about striking this balance? In cases where some substantive constitutional provision limits the government's power to act, the answer may appear to be easy. For example, it would almost certainly be unconstitutional for the government to dictate editorial policies to newspapers. Similarly, Justice Bradley believed that the federal government lacked the constitutional power to regulate the "private" conduct in question in the Civil Rights Cases. If it is unconstitutional for the government to act in these cases, it must be constitutional for it not to act.

"Easy" cases may be atypical, however. More often, a finding of no state action means only that the Constitution does not of its own force regulate the private activity. It does not follow from such a finding that the private actor is constitutionally immune from legislative regulation.

For example, in *CBS*, Chief Justice Burger suggested elsewhere in his opinion that Congress could require networks to accept editorial advertising. Similarly, in Hudgens v. NLRB, 424 U.S. 507 (1976), the Court held that the decision of a privately owned shopping center to exclude peaceful picketers could not be attributed to the government and, therefore, did not violate the first amendment. But in PruneYard Shopping Center v. Robins, 447 U.S. 74 (1980), the Court rejected a shopping center owner's first amendment objection when a state chose to outlaw such exclusions.

Is there a coherent theory of individual autonomy that explains these results? Such a theory would have to explain why the government should not be held accountable for outcomes that it could, but chooses not to, change. It would have to distinguish between state "action" that impermissibly interferes with private autonomy and state "inaction" that allows such interference to go uncorrected.

The next section explores the Court's attempt to formulate such a theory.

B. PURE INACTION AND THE THEORY OF GOVERNMENTAL NEUTRALITY

In Jackson v. Metropolitan Edison Co., 419 U.S. 345 (1974), Justice Rehnquist, writing for the Court, summarized state action jurisprudence as follows:

> [The state action] inquiry must be whether there is a sufficiently close nexus between the State and the challenged action of the [private] entity so that the action of the latter may be fairly treated as that of the State itself. The true nature of the State's involvement may not be immediately obvious, and detailed inquiry may be required to determine whether the test is met.

Typically, the Court has organized this "detailed inquiry" under two rubrics. (1) Sometimes (though rarely!) the Court finds that a private actor must be subject to constitutional requirements because the state has delegated a traditional state (or "public") function to a private entity. (2) Sometimes the Court finds that a private actor must be subject to constitutional requirements (a) because the state has become entangled with a private entity or (b) because the state has approved, encouraged, or facilitated private conduct. Cases decided under these rubrics are considered below. Note, however, that the nexus inquiry is relevant only if one is attempting to make the state responsible for what is otherwise private conduct. When the state itself is acting — when, in other words, the state's involvement *is* "immediately obvious" — no further inquiry is necessary.

Unfortunately, though, this formulation involves some oversimplification. In virtually every "state action" case, it is possible to find *some* "immediately obvious" conduct of the state that contributes in some way to the alleged constitutional violation. For example, state officials stand ready to enforce background tort and criminal rules that inevitably will favor one party to a dispute rather than the other. If this state involvement "counted" as state action, the state would always be responsible for private conduct. Consequently, before exploring ways in which private conduct is attributed to the state, it is necessary to explore in more detail the concept of state inaction.

1. Pure Inaction

DESHANEY v. WINNEBAGO COUNTY DEPARTMENT OF SOCIAL SERVICES, 489 U.S. 189 (1989). When petitioner Joshua DeShaney was one year old, a Wyoming court granted his parents a divorce and awarded custody to his father. Shortly thereafter the father moved to Winnebago County, Wisconsin. Two years later respondent social workers working for Winnebago County began receiving reports that the father was physically abusing Joshua. The caseworkers carefully noted each of these reports, as well as Joshua's suspicious injuries, but took no action to remove him from his father's custody. Eventually, when Joshua was four years old, his father beat him so severely that he suffered permanent brain injuries that left him profoundly retarded and confined to an institution for life. This was an action brought by Joshua and his mother claiming that the state's conduct deprived him of his liberty in violation of the due process clause of the fourteenth amendment.

Justice Rehnquist delivered the Court's opinion: "[Nothing] in the language of the Due Process Clause itself requires the State to protect the life, liberty, and property of its citizens against invasion by private actors. The Clause is phrased as a limitation on the State's power to act, not as a guarantee of certain minimal levels of safety and security. [Nor] does history support such an expansive reading of the constitutional text. [Its] purpose was to protect the people from the State, not to ensure that the State protected them from each other. The Framers were content to leave the extent of governmental obligation in the latter area to the democratic political processes. . . .

"Petitioners contend, however, that even if the Due Process Clause imposes no affirmative obligation on the State to provide the general public with adequate protective services, such a duty may arise out of certain 'special relationships' created or assumed by the State with respect to particular individuals. . . .

"We reject this argument. It is true that in certain limited circumstances the Constitution imposes upon the State affirmative duties of care and protection with respect to particular individuals. . . .

"[But these cases] stand only for the proposition that when the State takes a person into its custody and holds him there against his will, the Constitution imposes upon it a corresponding duty to assume some responsibility for his safety and general well-being. [The] affirmative duty to protect arises not from the State's knowledge of the individual's predicament or from its expressions of intent to help him, but from the limitation which it has imposed on his freedom to act on his own behalf.

"Judges and lawyers, like other humans, are moved by natural sympathy in a case like this to find a way for Joshua and his mother to receive adequate compensation for the grievous harm inflicted upon them. But before yielding to that impulse, it is well to remember once again that the harm was inflicted not by the state of Wisconsin, but by Joshua's father. [In] defense of [the state officials] it must also be said that had they moved too soon to take custody of the son away from the father, they would likely have been met with charges of improperly intruding into the parent-child relationship, charges based on the same Due Process Clause that forms the basis for the present charge of failure to provide adequate protection."

Justice Brennan, joined by Justices Marshall and Blackmun, dissented: "It may well be, as the Court decides, that the Due Process Clause as construed by our prior cases creates no general right to basic governmental services. That, however, is not the question presented here. . . .

"In a constitutional setting that distinguishes sharply between action and inaction, one's characterization of the misconduct alleged [may] effectively decide the case. Thus, by leading off with a discussion (and rejection) of the idea that the Constitution imposes on the States an affirmative duty to take basic care of their citizens, the Court foreshadows — perhaps even preordains — its conclusion that no duty existed even on the specific facts before us. . . .

"The Court's baseline is the absence of positive rights in the Constitution and a concomitant suspicion of any claim that seems to depend on such rights. From this perspective, the DeShaneys' claim is first and foremost about inaction (the failure, here, of respondents to take steps to protect Joshua), and only tangentially about action (the establishment of a state program specifically designed to help children like Joshua). And from this perspective, holding these Wisconsin officials liable — where the only difference between this case and one involving a general claim to protective services is Wisconsin's establishment and operation of a program to protect children — would seem to punish an effort that we should seek to promote.

"I would begin from the opposite direction. I would focus first on the action that Wisconsin *has* taken with respect to Joshua and children like him, rather than on the actions that the State failed to take. . . .

"Wisconsin law invites — indeed, directs — citizens and other governmental entities to depend on local departments of social services such as respondent to protect children from abuse. . . .

"In these circumstances, a private citizen, or even a person working in a government agency other than [the Department of Social Services] would doubtless feel that her job was done as soon as she had reported her suspicions of child abuse to [the department]. If [the department] ignores or dismisses these suspicions, no one will step in to fill the gap. [Conceivably], then, children like Joshua are made worse off by the existence of this program when the persons and entities charged with carrying it out fail to do their jobs."

Justice Blackmun also filed a dissenting opinion.

Flagg Brothers v. Brooks

436 U.S. 149 (1978)

MR. JUSTICE REHNQUIST delivered the opinion of the Court.

The question presented by this litigation is whether a warehouseman's proposed sale of goods entrusted to him for storage, as permitted by New York Uniform Commercial Code §7-210, is an action properly attributable to the State of New York. [Section 7-210 provides that after proper notification, a warehouseman may satisfy a lien on goods in his possession by selling the goods.]

I

[When respondent Brooks was evicted from her apartment, the city marshal arranged for storage of her possessions in petitioner's warehouse. After a series of disputes over the validity of petitioner's charges for moving and storage, petitioner sent Brooks a letter threatening sale of the possessions. Brooks thereupon initiated this action, claiming, inter alia, that the sale pursuant to section 7-210 without a prior judicial hearing would violate the due process clause. She relied on a series of decisions in which the Court had held that due process requires that debtors be afforded a hearing before a creditor can utilize remedies involving the deprivation of property. See North Georgia Finishing, Inc. v. Di-Chem, Inc., 419 U.S. 601 (1975); Fuentes v. Shevin, 407 U.S. 67 (1972); Sniadach v. Family Finance Corp., 395 U.S. 337 (1969). Brooks was later joined in her action by respondent Jones, whose goods had also been stored by petitioner following her eviction.]

II

[It] must be noted that respondents have named no public officials as defendants in this action. The city marshal, who supervised their evictions, was dismissed from the case by the consent of all the parties. This total absence of overt official involvement plainly distinguishes this case from earlier decisions imposing procedural restrictions on creditors' remedies such as [*North Georgia Finishing; Fuentes*; and *Sniadach*]. In those cases, the Court was careful to point out that the dictates of the Due Process Clause "attac[h] only to the deprivation of an interest encompassed within the Fourteenth Amendment's protection." [*Fuentes.*] While as a factual matter any person with sufficient physical power may deprive a person of his property, only a State or a private person whose action "may be fairly treated as that of the State itself," [Jackson v. Metropolitan Edison Co., 419 U.S. 345 (1974)], may deprive him of "an interest encompassed within the Fourteenth Amendment's protection" [*Fuentes*]. Thus, the only issue presented by this case is whether Flagg Brothers' action may fairly be attributed to the State of New York. We conclude that it may not.

III

Respondents' primary contention is that New York has delegated to Flagg Brothers a power "traditionally exclusively reserved to the State." [*Jackson.*] They argue that the resolution of private disputes is a traditional function of civil government, and that the State in §7-210 has delegated this function to Flagg Brothers. Respondents, however, have read too much into the language of our previous cases. While many functions have been traditionally performed by governments, very few have been "exclusively reserved to the State." . . .

[The] proposed sale by Flagg Brothers under §7-210 is not the only means of resolving this purely private dispute. Respondent Brooks has never alleged that state law barred her from seeking a waiver of Flagg Brothers' right to sell her goods at the time she authorized their storage. Presumably, respondent Jones, who alleges that she never authorized the storage of her goods, could have sought to replevy her goods at any time under state law. The challenged statute itself provides a damages remedy against the warehouseman for violations of its provisions. This system of rights and remedies, recognizing the traditional place of private arrangements in ordering relationships in the commercial world, can hardly be said to have delegated to Flagg Brothers an exclusive prerogative of the sovereign.[10]

---

10. It is undoubtedly true, as our Brother Stevens says in dissent, that "respondents have a property interest in the possessions that the warehouseman proposes to sell." But that property interest is not a monolithic, abstract concept hovering in the legal stratosphere. It is a bundle of rights in personalty, the metes and bounds of which are determined by the decisional and statutory law of the State of New York. The validity of the property interest in these possessions which respondents previously acquired from some other private person depends on New York law. It would intolerably broaden, beyond the scope of any of our previous cases, the notion of state action under the Fourteenth Amendment to hold that the more existence of a body of property law in a State, whether decisional or statutory, itself amounted to "state action" even though no state process or state officials were ever involved in enforcing that body of law.

This situation is clearly distinguishable from cases such as [*North Georgia Finishing; Fuentes*; and *Sniadach*]. In each of those cases a government official participated in the physical deprivation of what had concededly been the constitutional plaintiff's property under state law before the deprivation occurred. The constitutional protection attaches not because, as in *North Georgia Finishing*, a clerk issued a ministerial writ out of the court, but because as a result of that writ the property of the debtor was seized and impounded by the affirmative command of the law of Georgia. The creditor in *North Georgia Finishing* had not simply sought to pursue the collection of his debt by

Whatever the particular remedies available under New York law, we do not consider a more detailed description of them necessary to our conclusion that the settlement of disputes between debtors and creditors is not traditionally an exclusive public function.[11] . . .

IV

Respondents further urge that Flagg Brothers' proposed action is properly attributable to the State because the State has authorized and encouraged it in enacting §7-210. [This] Court, however, has never held that a State's mere acquiescence in a private action converts that action into that of the State.

[It] is quite immaterial that the State has embodied its decision not to act in statutory form. If New York had no commercial statutes at all, its courts would still be faced with the decision whether to prohibit or to permit the sort of sale threatened here the first time an aggrieved bailor came before them for relief. [If] the mere denial of judicial relief is considered sufficient encouragement to make the State responsible for those private acts, all private deprivations of property would be converted into public acts whenever the State, for whatever reason, denies relief sought by the putative property owner.

[Here,] the State of New York has not compelled the sale of a bailor's goods, but has merely announced the circumstances under which its courts will not interfere with a private sale. Indeed, the crux of respondents' complaint is not that the State *has* acted, but that it has *refused* to act. This statutory refusal to act is no different in principle from an ordinary statute of limitations whereby the State declines to provide a remedy for private deprivations of property after the passage of a given period of time.

[Reversed.]

MR. JUSTICE BRENNAN took no part in the consideration or decision in these cases.

[Justice Marshall's dissenting opinion is omitted.]

MR. JUSTICE STEVENS, with whom MR. JUSTICE WHITE and MR. JUSTICE MARSHALL join, dissenting. . . .

[The] question is whether a state statute which authorizes a private party to deprive a person of his property without his consent must meet the requirements

---

private means permissible under Georgia law; he had invoked the authority of the Georgia court, which in turn had ordered the garnishee not to pay over money which previously had been the property of the debtor. See Virginia v. Rives, 100 U.S. 313, 318 (1880); Shelley v. Kraemer, 343 U.S. 1 (1948). . . .

11. It may well be, as my Brother Stevens' dissent contends, that "[t]he power to order legally binding surrenders of property and the constitutional restrictions on that power are not necessary correlatives in our system." But here New York, unlike Florida in *Fuentes*, Georgia in *North Georgia Finishing*, and Wisconsin in *Sniadach*, has not ordered respondents to surrender any property whatever. It has merely enacted a statute which provides that a warehouseman conforming to the provisions of the statute may convert his traditional lien into good title. There is no reason whatever to believe that either Flagg Brothers or respondents could not, if they wished, seek resort to the New York courts in order to either compel or prevent the "surrenders of property" to which that dissent refers, and that the compliance of Flagg Brothers with applicable New York property law would be reviewed after customary notice and hearing in such a proceeding.

of the Due Process Clause of the Fourteenth Amendment. This question must be answered in the affirmative unless the State has virtually unlimited power to transfer interests in private property without any procedural protections. . . .

In determining that New York's statute cannot be scrutinized under the Due Process Clause, the Court reasons that the warehouseman's proposed sale is solely private action because the state statute "*permits* but does not compel" the sale (emphasis added), and because the warehouseman has not been delegated a power "*exclusively* reserved to the State" (emphasis added). Under this approach a State could enact laws authorizing private citizens to use self-help in countless situations without any possibility of federal challenge. A state statute could authorize the warehouseman to retain all proceeds of the lien sale, even if they far exceeded the amount of the alleged debt; it could authorize finance companies to enter private homes to repossess merchandise; or indeed, it could authorize "any person with sufficient physical power," to acquire and sell the property of his weaker neighbor. An attempt to challenge the validity of any such outrageous statute would be defeated by the reasoning the Court uses today: The Court's rationale would characterize action pursuant to such a statute as purely private action, which the State permits but does not compel, in an area not exclusively reserved to the State.

As these examples suggest, the distinctions between "permission" and "compulsion" on the one hand, and "exclusive" and "nonexclusive," on the other, cannot be determinative factors in state-action analysis. There is no great chasm between "permission" and "compulsion" requiring particular state action to fall within one or the other definitional camp. [In] this case, the State of New York, by enacting §7-210 of the Uniform Commercial Code, has acted in the most effective and unambiguous way a State can act. This section specifically authorizes petitioner Flagg Brothers to sell respondents' possessions; it details the procedures that petitioner must follow; and it grants petitioner the power to convey good title to goods that are now owned by respondents to a third party.

[Cases] such as *North Georgia Finishing* must be viewed as reflecting this Court's recognition of the significance of the State's role in defining *and controlling* the debtor-creditor relationship. The Court's language to this effect in the various debtor-creditor cases has been unequivocal. In Fuentes v. Shevin the Court stressed that the statutes in question "abdicated effective state control over state power." And it is clear that what was of concern in *Shevin* was the *private* use of state power to achieve a nonconsensual resolution of a commercial dispute.

[It] is important to emphasize that, contrary to the Court's apparent fears, this conclusion does not even remotely suggest that "all private deprivations of property [will] be converted into public acts whenever the State, for whatever reason, denies relief sought by the putative property owner." The focus is not on the private deprivation but on the state authorization. "[W]hat is always vital to remember is that it is the *state's* conduct, whether action or inaction, not the *private* conduct, that gives rise to constitutional attack." Friendly, The Dartmouth College Case and The Public-Private Penumbra, 12 Texas Quarterly, No. 2, p. 17 (1969) (Supp.) (emphasis in original). The State's conduct in this case takes the concrete form of a statutory enactment, and it is that statute that may be challenged. . . .

Finally, it is obviously true that the overwhelming majority of disputes in our society are resolved in the private sphere. But it is no longer possible, if it ever was, to believe that a sharp line can be drawn between private and public actions.

[In] the broadest sense, we expect government "to provide a reasonable and fair framework of rules which facilitate commercial transactions. . . ." This "framework of rules" is premised on the assumption that the State will control non-consensual deprivations of property and that the State's control will, in turn, be subject to the restrictions of the Due Process Clause. The power to order legally binding surrenders of property and the constitutional restrictions on that power are necessary correlatives in our system. In effect, today's decision allows the State to divorce these two elements by the simple expedient of transferring the implementation of its policy to private parties. Because the Fourteenth Amendment does not countenance such a division of power and responsibility, I respectfully dissent.

LUGAR v. EDMONDSON OIL CO., 457 U.S. 922 (1982). Lugar was indebted to Edmondson Oil, a company that sued him in state court. Ancillary to that action, and pursuant to state law, Edmondson Oil filed an ex parte petition for prejudgment attachment of certain of Lugar's property. Acting on the petition, the clerk of the state court issued a writ of attachment, which was executed by the county sheriff. This effectively sequestered Lugar's property, although he remained in possession of it. The state court subsequently held a hearing on the propriety of the attachment and ordered it dismissed because Edmondson had failed to establish the statutory grounds for it. Lugar thereupon brought this federal action, alleging that Edmondson had acted jointly with the state to deprive him of his property without due process of law. In a five-to-four decision, the Court distinguished *Flagg Brothers* and held that Lugar had alleged sufficient state involvement to make out a due process violation.

Justice White delivered the Court's opinion: "Beginning with [*Sniadach*], the Court has consistently held that constitutional requirements of due process apply to garnishment and prejudgment attachment procedures whenever officers of the State act jointly with a creditor in securing the property in dispute. [In] each of these cases state agents aided the creditor in securing the disputed property; but in each case the federal issue arose in litigation between creditor and debtor in the state courts and no state official was named as a party. Nevertheless, in each case the Court entertained and adjudicated the defendant-debtor's claim that the procedure under which the private creditor secured the disputed property violated federal constitutional standards of due process. Necessary to that conclusion is the holding that private use of the challenged state procedures with the help of state officials constitutes state action for purposes of the Fourteenth Amendment. . . .

"Our cases have [insisted] that the conduct allegedly causing the deprivation of a federal right be fairly attributable to the State. These cases reflect a two-part approach to this question of 'fair attribution.' First, the deprivation must be caused by the exercise of some right or privilege created by the State or by a rule of conduct imposed by the State or by a person for whom the State is responsible. [Second], the party charged with the deprivation must be a person who may fairly be said to be a state actor. This may be because he is a state official, because he has acted together with or has obtained significant aid from state officials, or because his conduct is otherwise chargeable to the State. Without a limit such as this, private parties could face constitutional litigation whenever they seek to rely on some state rule governing their interactions with the community surrounding them. . . .

"*Flagg Brothers* focused on the [second] component of the state-action principle. [Undoubtedly] the State was responsible for the statute [authorizing Flagg Brothers' conduct]. The response of the Court, however, focused not on the terms of the statute but on the character of the defendant: [Action] by a private party pursuant to this statute, without something more, was not sufficient to justify a characterization of that party as a 'state actor.' . . .

"While private misuse of a state statute does not describe conduct that can be attributed to the State, the procedural scheme created by the statute obviously is the product of state action. . . .

"[We] have consistently held that a private party's joint participation with state officials in the seizure of disputed property is sufficient to characterize that party as a 'state actor' for purposes of the Fourteenth Amendment."

Justice Powell, joined by Justices Rehnquist and O'Connor, dissented: "[The Court] holds that respondent, a private citizen who did no more than commence a legal action of a kind traditionally initiated by private parties, thereby engaged in 'state action.' This decision is as unprecedented as it is implausible. It is plainly unjust to the respondent, and the Court makes no argument to the contrary. Respondent, who was represented by counsel, could have had no notion that his filing of a petition in state court, in the effort to secure payment of a private debt, made him a 'state actor' liable in damages for allegedly unconstitutional action by the Commonwealth of Virginia. . . .

"[It] is not disputed that the Virginia Sheriff and Clerk of Court, the state officials who sequestered petitioner's property in the manner provided by Virginia law, engaged in state action. Yet petitioner, while alleging constitutional injury from this action by state officials, did not sue the State or its agents. . . .

"From the occurrence of state action taken by the Sheriff who sequestered petitioner's property, it does not follow that respondent became a 'state actor' simply because the Sheriff was. This Court, until today, has never endorsed this non sequitur."

Chief Justice Burger filed a separate dissenting opinion.

Note: *The Problem of the Passive State*

1. *"Pure" inaction.* At the beginning of his opinion for the Court in *DeShaney*, Justice Rehnquist characterizes the due process clause as "a limitation on the State's power to act, [rather than] a guarantee of certain minimal levels of safety and security." Similarly, in *Flagg Brothers* he observes that "the crux of respondents' complaint is not that the State *has* acted, but that it has *refused* to act." Even if we assume that the state's involvement in these disputes can be fairly characterized as a "mere" refusal to act, why should that fact make a constitutional difference? Does the Constitution always permit the government to acquiesce passively in an existing situation? Consider the view that whether the Constitution permits government to do this is a question about the meaning of the relevant constitutional provision, and that any "state action" doctrine is unhelpful in answering that question.

Many equal protection cases can be characterized as involving state inaction. For example, in Plyler v. Doe, Chapter 6, section E5, supra, the Court held that the state's failure to provide public education for "undocumented" immigrant children violated the equal protection clause. Although the Court was narrowly divided on the substantive equal protection issue, not even the dissenters claimed that the challenge should fail because of the absence of state action. Of course, the state's failure to act in these situations is embedded in a context where the state is also acting; discrimination claims involve selective inaction. But is it fair to characterize New York and Wisconsin as wholly passive with regard to the disputes in *DeShaney* and *Flagg Brothers*? Didn't the state take some affirmative steps?

2. *Natural law and "invisible" state action.* None of the *DeShaney* opinions focused on the most direct way in which state action "positively" contributed to Joshua DeShaney's injury: the network of statutes and common law rules that grant custody and control of minor children to their biological parents. (State responsibility for this outcome is particularly obvious on the facts of *DeShaney*, where a state court, albeit in Wyoming rather than in Wisconsin, had adjudicated a custody dispute regarding the boy in connection with his parents' divorce.) Consider whether the state action doctrine has embedded within it unarticulated baselines formed by natural law assumptions about the "rightness" of certain initial allocations — such as the allocation of children to their biological parents — and whether these assumptions blind the court to state action that creates or maintains this "natural" state of affairs. Consider the possibility that the state action doctrine thus depends not at all on whether there has been state action, but on whether the state has deviated from a course of action that seems natural or desirable.

Compare *DeShaney* to Baltimore City Department of Social Services v. Bouknight, 493 U.S. 549 (1990), where the Court rejected the argument that a parent of a child under court supervision could invoke the fifth amendment privilege against compelled incrimination to refuse to produce the child. *Bouknight*, like *DeShaney*, involved a parent who had previously abused her biological child and who was under court supervision. But whereas in *DeShaney* the Court deemed irrelevant the governmental conduct relating to child custody decisions, that conduct was crucial to the result in *Bouknight*. The Court analogized childrearing to heavily regulated industries, where the fifth amendment privilege has generally been available in only diluted form:

> When a person assumes control over items that are the legitimate object of the government's non-criminal regulatory powers, the ability to invoke the privilege is reduced. . . . Once Maurice was adjudicated a child in need of assistance, his care and safety became the particular object of the States' regulatory interests. . . . The government demands production of the very public charge entrusted to a custodian, and makes the demand for compelling reasons unrelated to criminal law enforcement and as part of a broadly applied regulatory regime.

The *Bouknight* Court did not cite *DeShaney* — a case decided a year earlier. Are the two cases consistent?

3. *Statutes as state action.* In *Flagg Brothers*, the legislature had enacted a statute granting Flagg Brothers the right to sell the furniture. Why isn't this state action? Is the Court correct that the existence of the statute is "quite immaterial" because it merely "embodie[s the state's] decision not to act"? *Sniadach* and *Lugar* make clear that sometimes, judicial enforcement of statutory mandates at the behest of private parties does amount to state action. So long as courts stand ready to enforce the statutory mandate, why should it matter whether the parties actually resort to judicial enforcement?

Compare Reitman v. Mulkey, 387 U.S. 369 (1967). Between 1959 and 1963, California enacted various fair housing acts that prohibited racial discrimination in the sale or rental of private dwellings. In 1964, through the initiative process, California voters enacted Proposition 14, which amended the state's constitution to prohibit the state from denying the "right of any person [to] decline to sell, lease or rent [property] to such person or persons as he, in his absolute discretion, chooses." Respondents, alleging that petitioners had refused to rent them an apartment because of their race, brought an action in state court based on the fair housing acts. They contended that Proposition 14, which had the effect of repealing the acts, violated the equal protection clause. The California Supreme Court ruled in their favor, and in a five-to-four decision, the U.S. Supreme Court affirmed.

The Court, in an opinion by Justice White, agreed with petitioners that the mere repeal of a statute prohibiting racial discrimination was not unconstitutional. (The Court did not make entirely clear whether this would be because the repeal would not implicate sufficient state action or whether it would be because it would not violate the equal protection clause.) But the California Supreme Court had not

> read either our cases or the Fourteenth Amendment as establishing an automatic constitutional barrier to the repeal of an existing law prohibiting racial discrimination in housing. [The state court] held the intent of [Proposition 14] was to authorize private racial discrimination in the housing market, to repeal the [fair housing acts] and to create a constitutional right to [discriminate]. . . .
>
> [Private] discriminations in housing were now not only free from [the antidiscrimination statutes] but they also enjoyed far different status than was true before the passage of those statutes. The right to discriminate, including the right to discriminate on racial grounds, was now embodied in the State's basic charter, immune from legislative, executive, or judicial regulation at any level of the state government. Those practicing racial discriminations need no longer rely solely on their personal choice. They could now invoke express constitutional authority, free from censure or interference of any kind from official sources.

Justice Harlan, joined by Justices Black, Clark, and Stewart, dissented:

> [A]ll that has happened is that California has effected a pro tanto repeal of its prior statutes forbidding private discrimination. This runs no more afoul of the Fourteenth Amendment than would have California's failure to pass any such antidiscrimination statutes in the first instance. The fact that such repeal was also accompanied by a constitutional prohibition against future enactment of such laws by the California Legislature cannot well be thought to affect, from a federal constitutional standpoint, the validity of what California has done. The Fourteenth Amendment does not reach such state constitutional action any more than it does a simple legislative repeal of legislation forbidding private discrimination.

Can *Reitman* and *Flagg Brothers* be reconciled?

4. Flagg Brothers *and* Lugar. Does *Lugar* provide an adequate explanation for the result in *Flagg Brothers*? The Court's opinion in *Lugar* at least has the virtue of recognizing the obvious — that is, that the conduct of the state legislature in enacting a statute is "state action" for purposes of the Constitution. But according to *Lugar*, the state action problem in *Flagg Brothers* was created by the fact that

the actual defendant before the Court was a private actor who was merely invoking his statutory rights. In *Lugar*, of course, the defendant was also a private party. But, there, the defendant had relied on state assistance to assert his rights, and this joint conduct was sufficient to make the private party a state actor for constitutional purposes.

Does this distinction make sense? How did the private petitioners in *Reitman* rely on state assistance in asserting their rights? Recall that the state activity in *Lugar* did not involve any actual shift in possession of the property in question. The sheriff merely served on Lugar a piece of paper announcing Lugar's legal obligations. Would the situation be functionally different if these obligations were embodied in a statute and Lugar read of them in a codification printed by the state?

5. Tarkanian *and* Brentwood Academy. Compare *Flagg Brothers* and *Lugar* with National Collegiate Athletic Association v. Tarkanian, 488 U.S. 179 (1988), and Brentwood Academy v. Tennessee Secondary School Athletic Association, 531 U.S. 288 (2001). *Tarkanian* arose out of a National Collegiate Athletic Association (NCAA) investigation of the University of Nevada, Las Vegas (a state university) and its highly successful basketball coach, Tarkanian, for violations of NCAA rules.

Under pressure from the NCAA, the university removed Tarkanian, who thereupon sued both the NCAA and the university, claiming that their conduct violated his rights to substantive and procedural due process. The lower courts found that the NCAA's conduct constituted state action subject to constitutional restraint, and that both the NCAA and the university had violated Tarkanian's constitutional rights. In a five-to-four opinion written by Justice Stevens, the U.S. Supreme Court reversed the lower court insofar as it had held the NCAA constitutionally liable.

The Court began its analysis by noting that the situation "uniquely mirrors the traditional state action case," and that it required the court "to step through an analytical looking glass to resolve it." In more typical cases, such as *Lugar* and *Flagg Brothers*, a private party has taken steps that cause harm to the plaintiff, and the issue is whether the state was sufficiently involved to treat this private conduct as state action. Here, in contrast, the university — concededly a state actor — had suspended Tarkanian. "Thus, the question is not whether [the university] participated to a critical extent in the NCAA's activities, but whether [the university's] actions in compliance with the NCAA rules and recommendations turned the NCAA's conduct into state action."

The Court concluded that university compliance did not transform the NCAA into a state actor. "It would be ironic indeed to conclude that the NCAA's imposition of sanctions against [the university] — sanctions that [the university] and its counsel steadfastly opposed during protracted adversary proceedings — is fairly attributable to the State of Nevada. It would be more appropriate to conclude that [the university] had conducted its athletic program under the color of policies adopted by the NCAA, rather than that those policies were developed and enforced under color of Nevada law."

The Court distinguished *Tarkanian* in *Brentwood Academy*, a five-to-four decision written by Justice Souter. The case involved a statewide association incorporated to regulate interscholastic athletic competition among public and private secondary schools. On this occasion, the Court held that the association was a state actor. It distinguished *Tarkanian* as follows:

> [The] NCAA's policies were shaped not by the University of Nevada alone, but by several hundred member institutions, most of them having no connection with Nevada, and exhibiting no color of Nevada law. Since it was difficult to see the NCAA, not as a collective membership, but as surrogate for the one State, we held the organization's connection with Nevada too insubstantial to ground a state action claim.
>
> But dictum in *Tarkanian* pointed to a contrary result on facts like ours, with an organization whose member public schools are all within a single State. "The situation would, of course, be different if the [Association's] membership consisted entirely of institutions located within the same State, many of them public institutions created by the same sovereign." . . .
>
> Just as we foresaw in *Tarkanian*, the "necessarily fact-bound inquiry" [*Lugar*] leads to the conclusion of state action here. The nominally private character of the Association is overborne by the pervasive entwinement of public institutions and public officials in its composition and workings.

6. *Pope.* Consider also the Court's reading of *Lugar* and *Flagg Brothers* in Tulsa Professional Collection Services v. Pope, 485 U.S. 478 (1988). Oklahoma's probate laws require that claims arising under a contract be presented to the executor of the estate within two months of the publication of a notice advising creditors of the commencement of probate proceedings. A creditor who had not received actual notice and failed to file a claim within two months argued that the constructive notice provision violated due process. In an opinion by Justice O'Connor, the Court held that the creditor had a property interest that was protected by the due process clause. It went on to note, however, that the fourteenth amendment protected this interest only from deprivation by state action. On the state action question, it summarized the holdings *of Lugar* and *Flagg Brothers* as follows:

> Private use of state sanctioned private remedies and procedures does not rise to the level of state action, see, e.g., [*Flagg Brothers*]. Nor is the state's involvement in the mere running of a general statute of limitation generally sufficient to implicate due process. [But] when private parties make use of state procedures with the overt, significant assistance of state officials, state action may be found. See, e.g., [*Lugar*].

The Court went on to hold that, although the mere state promulgation of the limitation period would not constitute state action (what does this mean?), the probate court's "pervasive and substantial" involvement with the probate proceedings was sufficient.

It may appear that *Pope*'s "pervasive and substantial" involvement test is inconsistent with *Lugar*. Consider the possibility that *Pope* is distinguishable because the creditor was invoking the Constitution to secure the affirmative assistance of the state in *Pope*, while the debtor was invoking the Constitution to ward off state interference in *Lugar*. Taken together, do *Pope* and *Lugar* mean Ms. Brooks could have broken into Flagg Brothers' warehouse, stolen the furniture, and then successfully asserted the unconstitutionality of section 7-210 as a defense to a criminal prosecution?

2.   *Judicial Action and the Theory of Government Neutrality*

Shelley v. Kraemer

334 U.S. 1 (1948)

MR. CHIEF JUSTICE VINSON delivered the opinion of the Court.

These cases present for our consideration questions relating to the validity of court enforcement of private agreements, generally described as restrictive covenants, which have as their purpose the exclusion of persons of designated race or color from the ownership or occupancy of real property. Basic constitutional issues of obvious importance have been raised. . . .

[In each of the two cases before the Court, black families had purchased homes burdened by restrictive covenants, signed by property owners in the neighborhood, that prohibited occupancy by nonwhites. Respondents brought these actions in state court seeking to specifically enforce the covenant provisions. In each case, the state court upheld the provision and ruled that respondents were entitled to an injunction prohibiting petitioners from occupying the property.]

It cannot be doubted that among the civil rights intended to be protected from discriminatory state action by the Fourteenth Amendment are the rights to acquire, enjoy, own and dispose of property. Equality in the enjoyment of property rights was regarded by the framers of that Amendment as an essential precondition to the realization of other basic civil rights and liberties which the Amendment was intended to guarantee. Thus, [42 U.S.C. §1982], derived from §1 of the Civil Rights Act of 1866 which was enacted by Congress while the Fourteenth Amendment was also under consideration, provides:

> All citizens of the United States shall have the same right, in every State and Territory, as is enjoyed by white citizens thereof to inherit, purchase, lease, sell, hold, and convey real and personal property. . . .

It is likewise clear that restrictions on the right of occupancy of the sort sought to be created by the private agreements in these cases could not be squared with the requirements of the Fourteenth Amendment if imposed by state statute or local ordinance. We do not understand respondents to urge the contrary. . . .

But the present cases [do] not involve action by state legislatures or city councils. Here the particular patterns of discrimination and the areas in which the restrictions are to operate, are determined, in the first instance, by the terms of agreements among private individuals. Participation of the State consists in the enforcement of the restrictions so defined. The crucial issue with which we are here confronted is whether this distinction removes these cases from the operation of the prohibitory provisions of the Fourteenth Amendment.

Since the decision of this Court in the Civil Rights Cases, the principle has become firmly embedded in our constitutional law that the action inhibited by the first section of the Fourteenth Amendment is only such action as may fairly be said to be that of the States. That Amendment erects no shield against merely private conduct, however discriminatory or wrongful.

We conclude, therefore, that the restrictive agreements standing alone cannot be regarded as violative of any rights guaranteed to petitioners by the Fourteenth

Amendment. So long as the purposes of those agreements are effectuated by voluntary adherence to their terms, it would appear clear that there has been no action by the State and the provisions of the Amendment have not been violated.

But here there was more. These are cases in which the purposes of the agreements were secured only by judicial enforcement by state courts of the restrictive terms of the agreements.

[That] the action of state courts and judicial officers in their official capacities is to be regarded as action of the State within the meaning of the Fourteenth Amendment, is a proposition which has long been established by decisions of this Court. . . .

One of the earliest applications of the prohibitions contained in the Fourteenth Amendment to action of state judicial officials occurred in cases in which Negroes had been excluded from jury service in criminal prosecutions by reason of their race or color. These cases demonstrate, also, the early recognition by this Court that state action in violation of the Amendment's provisions is equally repugnant to the constitutional commands whether directed by state statute or taken by a judicial official in the absence of statute. Thus, in Strauder v. West Virginia, 100 U.S. 303 (1880), this Court declared invalid a state statute restricting jury service to white persons as amounting to a denial of the equal protection of the laws to the colored defendant in that case. In the same volume of the reports, the Court in Ex parte Virginia, [100 U.S. 339 (1880)], held that a similar discrimination imposed by the action of a state judge denied rights protected by the Amendment, despite the fact that the language of the state statute relating to jury service contained no such restrictions.

The action of state courts in imposing penalties or depriving parties of other substantive rights without providing adequate notice and opportunity to defend, has, of course, long been regarded as a denial of the due process of law guaranteed by the Fourteenth Amendment.

In numerous cases, this Court has reversed criminal convictions in state courts for failure of those courts to provide the essential ingredients of a fair hearing. . . .

But the examples of state judicial action which have been held by this Court to violate the Amendment's commands are not restricted to situations in which the judicial proceedings were found in some manner to be procedurally unfair. It has been recognized that the action of state courts in enforcing a substantive common-law rule formulated by those courts, may result in the denial of rights guaranteed by the Fourteenth Amendment, even though the judicial proceedings in such cases may have been in complete accord with the most rigorous conceptions of procedural due process. . . .

Against this background of judicial construction, extending over a period of some three-quarters of a century, we are called upon to consider whether enforcement by state courts of the restrictive agreements in these cases may be deemed to be the acts of those States; and, if so, whether that action has denied these petitioners the equal protection of the laws which the Amendment was intended to insure.

We have no doubt that there has been state action in these cases in the full and complete sense of the phrase. The undisputed facts disclose that petitioners were willing purchasers of properties upon which they desired to establish homes. The owners of the properties were willing sellers; and contracts of sale were accordingly consummated. It is clear that but for the active intervention of the state courts, supported by the full panoply of state power, petitioners would have been free to occupy the properties in question without restraint.

These are not cases, as has been suggested, in which the States have merely abstained from action, leaving private individuals free to impose such discriminations as they see fit. Rather, these are cases in which the States have made available to such individuals the full coercive power of government to deny to petitioners, on the grounds of race or color, the enjoyment of property rights in premises which petitioners are willing and financially able to acquire and which the grantors are willing to sell. The difference between judicial enforcement and nonenforcement of the restrictive covenants is the difference to petitioners between being denied rights of property available to other members of the community and being accorded full enjoyment of those rights on an equal footing.

Respondents urge, however, that since the state courts stand ready to enforce restrictive covenants excluding white persons from the ownership or occupancy of property covered by such agreements, enforcement of covenants excluding colored persons may not be deemed a denial of equal protection of the laws to the colored persons who are thereby affected. This contention does not bear scrutiny. The parties have directed our attention to no case in which a court, state or federal, has been called upon to enforce a covenant excluding members of the white majority from ownership or occupancy of real property on grounds of race or color. But there are more fundamental considerations. The rights created by the first section of the Fourteenth Amendment are, by its terms, guaranteed to the individual. The rights established are personal rights. It is, therefore, no answer to these petitioners to say that the courts may also be induced to deny white persons rights of ownership and occupancy on grounds of race or color. Equal protection of the laws is not achieved through indiscriminate imposition of inequalities.

Nor do we find merit in the suggestion that property owners who are parties to these agreements are denied equal protection of the laws if denied access to the courts to enforce the terms of restrictive covenants and to assert property rights which the state courts have held to be created by such agreements. The Constitution confers upon no individual the right to demand action by the State which results in the denial of equal protection of the laws to other individuals. And it would appear beyond question that the power of the State to create and enforce property interests must be exercised within the boundaries defined by the Fourteenth Amendment. Cf. Marsh v. Alabama, 326 U.S. 501 (1946). . . .

For the reasons stated, the judgment of the Supreme Court of Missouri and the judgment of the Supreme Court of Michigan must be reversed.

Reversed.

MR. JUSTICE REED, MR. JUSTICE JACKSON, and MR. JUSTICE RUTLEDGE took no part in the consideration or decision of these cases.

Note: Shelley v. Kraemer, State Inaction, and the Theory of Government Neutrality

1. *State action as a nonissue.* Chief Justice Vinson devotes virtually all of his opinion to a demonstration that judicial action is "state action" within the meaning of the fourteenth amendment. Why is this question hard? Suppose it is true that private agreements, taken simply as such, are not state action. How could anyone doubt that there is nonetheless state action when a state judge

issues an injunction enforceable by the state marshal and ultimately supported by the threat of contempt and incarceration in a state institution? Compare Shelley v. Kraemer with New York Times v. Sullivan, Chapter 1, section D, supra, where the Court held that the first amendment required proof of "actual malice" to support libel judgments in favor of public officials. *Sullivan*, like *Shelley*, concerned the constitutionality of a state common law rule invoked in the course of private litigation. Yet in *Sullivan* the Court devoted only a cursory paragraph to the state action problem and focused almost all its attention on the substantive constitutional question.

2. *The real issue in* Shelley? *Shelley* is the mirror image of *Sullivan*. After completing his lengthy discussion of the state action question, Chief Justice Vinson devoted only a single paragraph to petitioner's substantive contention about the meaning of the equal protection clause. But surely this is a hard question — and perhaps it is the real issue in the case. On this view, the state action question was simple; of course judicial enforcement of contracts is state action. The difficult issue was one of equal protection law. On what theory does a rule requiring uniform enforcement of any privately made covenant deny equality? Why does Chief Justice Vinson think that it is relevant that only whites have chosen to use the rule? What does he mean when he says that the equal protection clause bars the "indiscriminate imposition of inequalities"?

3. *State action and the Washington v. Davis problem.* Consider the following argument: As *Shelley* itself illustrates, it will always be possible to find some state actor implicated, in some way and at some point, in the alleged constitutional violation. The appropriate question to ask is whether, as a substantive matter, this governmental action is unconstitutional. When one asks this question in *Shelley*, the reason for the intense controversy over the Court's holding becomes clearer. Recall that in Washington v. Davis, Chapter 5, section C2, supra, the Court held that a statute neutral on its face should not be subject to heightened scrutiny simply because of its disproportionate racial impact. Such statutes need satisfy only low-level review unless they were enacted for a discriminatory purpose. See Chapter 5, section C2, supra.

If this is so, the question becomes: Was Missouri law regarding restrictive covenants neutral on its face in the Washington v. Davis sense? That question — the equal protection question — was the difficult one in *Shelley*. Consider L. Tribe, Constitutional Choices 260 (1985):

> Like other states, Missouri treats most restraints on alienability of real estate as judicially unenforceable: to enforce any such restraint, a state court must first find that the *substance* of the restraining covenant is reasonable and consistent with public policy. Therefore, the issue is not whether any judicial enforcement of racially invidious private arrangements constitutes racially invidious state action, but whether a state may *choose* automatically to enforce restrictive covenants that discriminate against blacks *while generally regarding alienability restraints as anathema*. The real "state action" in *Shelley* was Missouri's facially discriminatory body of common and statutory law — the quintessence of a racist state policy.

Compare Strauss, Discriminatory Intent and the Taming of *Brown*, 56 U. Chi. L. Rev. 935, 968 (1989):

> [This] selective enforcement argument is not a satisfactory theoretical justification of *Shelley*. The argument makes *Shelley* contingent: it implicitly concedes that

Shelley would not be correct in any state that happened to enforce all, or most, restrictive covenants. The holding of *Shelley* is not limited in this way, and the moral appeal of the result in *Shelley* [would] be very strong even in a state that enforced all restrictive covenants.

Is *Shelley* nonetheless consistent with Washington v. Davis because in *Shelley*, but not *Washington*, the state itself would be required to base a decision on the race of one of the litigants?

As you read the remaining material, consider the extent to which the controversy over "state action" in the equal protection context is really a controversy concerning the meaning and scope of Washington v. Davis and the principle of governmental neutrality that it embodies. When the Court says that there is no "state action," is it really saying that the state action is facially neutral and therefore not subject to heightened review?

4. *The reach of* Shelley. It would be a mistake to read some of the more sweeping language in *Shelley* literally. There are certainly situations in which an individual can invoke judicial processes to effectuate a discriminatory intent. It is safe to assume that no court would inquire into the racist motives of an individual invoking state trespass laws against uninvited dinner guests at a private home.

Is there something about restrictive covenants that makes the invocation of judicial processes especially troublesome in that context? Is it relevant that a network of restrictive covenants operates as the functional equivalent of zoning laws and therefore serves an essentially "governmental" function? (The "public function" strand of state action jurisprudence is discussed in section D infra.) That the state's enforcement of the covenant prevented a willing buyer and seller from dealing with each other?

a. *Governmental neutrality and the problem of money damages.* Consider the award of money damages for violation of restrictive covenants. Does *Shelley* apply if a court imposes damages on a white seller but does not prevent the African American purchaser from securing possession? In Barrows v. Jackson, 346 U.S. 249 (1953), respondent entered a restrictive covenant prohibiting the use or occupancy of his property by nonwhites. He then violated the covenant by permitting nonwhites to move into the premises. Petitioners, property owners in the same neighborhood who were also parties to the covenant, sued for damages. The Court held that *Shelley* barred the suit:

> To compel respondent to respond in damages would be for the State to punish her for her failure to perform her covenant to continue to discriminate against non-Caucasians in the use of her property. [If] the State may thus punish respondent for her failure to carry out her covenant, she is coerced to continue to use her property in a discriminatory manner, which in essence is the purpose of the covenant. Thus, it becomes not respondent's voluntary choice but the State's choice that she observe her covenant or suffer damages. The action of a state court at law to sanction the validity of the restrictive covenant here involved would constitute state action as surely as it was state action to enforce such covenants in [equity].

Chief Justice Vinson, the author *of Shelley*, was the sole dissenter:

> The *Shelley* case, resting on the express determination that restrictive covenants are valid between the parties, dealt only with a state court's attempt to enforce them directly against innocent third parties whose right to enjoy their property would

suffer immediate harm. [In] this case, the plaintiffs have not sought such relief. The suit is directed against the very person whose solemn promise helped to bring the covenant into existence. The plaintiffs ask only that respondent do what she in turn had a right to ask of plaintiffs — indemnify plaintiffs for the bringing about of an event which she recognized would cause injury to the plaintiffs.

b. *State enforcement of discriminatory testamentary and inter vivos dispositions of property.* Consider Pennsylvania v. Board of Directors of City Trusts, 353 U.S. 230 (1957). In a will probated in 1831, Stephen Girard left a fund to be held in trust for erection and operation of a school for "poor white male orphans." The will named the city of Philadelphia as the trustee, and the school was administered by a state agency. When petitioners were denied admission to the school because of their race, they brought this action. The state court denied relief, but the Supreme Court, in a brief per curiam opinion, reversed: "The Board which operates Girard College is an agency of the State of Pennsylvania. Therefore, even though the Board was acting as a trustee, its refusal to admit [petitioners] to the college because they were Negroes was discrimination by the State."

On remand in *City Trusts,* the state court appointed private trustees in order to comply with the terms of Girard's will. In Pennsylvania v. Brown, 392 F.2d 120 (3d Cir.), cert. denied, 391 U.S. 921 (1968), the court of appeals held that the substitution was unconstitutional.

Compare *City Trusts* with Evans v. Newton, 382 U.S. 296 (1966). In 1911, U.S. Senator Augustus O. Bacon executed a will that devised to the mayor and city council of Macon, Georgia, a tract of land to be used as a park. The will provided that the park should be used by white people only and was to be under the control of a board of managers, all of whom were to be white. At first, the city ran the park on a segregated basis, but when it began to admit blacks, members of the board of managers brought this suit asking that the city be removed as trustee. The city thereupon resigned as trustee, and the state court appointed new, private trustees to run the park. Black intervenors challenged this decision. The Supreme Court held that the park could not be run on a racially segregated basis. The Court, in an opinion by Justice Douglas, stated:

> If a testator wanted to leave a school or center for the use of one race only and in no way implicated the State in the supervision, control, or management of that facility, we assume arguendo that no constitutional difficulty would be encountered. [This] park, however, is in a different posture. For years it was an integral part of the City of Macon's activities. [The] momentum it acquired as a public facility is certainly not dissipated ipso facto by the appointment of "private" trustees. So far as this record shows, there has been no change in municipal maintenance and concern over this facility. [If] the municipality remains entwined in the management or control of the park, it remains subject to the restraints of the Fourteenth Amendment.

The Court went on to suggest that the park should be treated as a public institution because it was serving a "public function" and was "municipal" in character. (The "public function" strand of the state action doctrine is considered in section D infra.) Justice White concurred in the result on the ground that the trust was tainted by state legislation that validated racially discriminatory conditions. Justices Black, Harlan, and Stewart dissented.

On remand, the state court held that Senator Bacon's intention to provide a park for whites only had become impossible to fulfill. Since this limitation was, in the court's view, central to Bacon's intention, it declined to reform the trust and held instead that the trust had failed, and that the parkland reverted to the testator's heirs. In Evans v. Abney, 396 U.S. 435 (1970), the Court affirmed in a six-to-two decision. Justice Black, a dissenter in *Newton*, wrote for the Court: "We are of the opinion that in ruling as they did the Georgia courts did no more than apply well-settled general principles of Georgia law to determine the meaning and effect of a Georgia will." Justices Douglas and Brennan dissented.

The Court maintained that *Shelley* was "easily distinguishable" because "[here] the effect of the Georgia decision eliminated all discrimination against Negroes in the park by eliminating the park itself, and the termination of the park was a loss shared equally by the white and Negro citizens of Macon since both races would have enjoyed a constitutional right of equal access to the park's facilities had it continued." Compare Justice Brennan's dissenting opinion:

> Shelley v. Kraemer stands at least for the proposition that where parties of different races are willing to deal with one another a state court cannot keep them from doing so by enforcing a privately devised racial restriction. . . .
>
> [So] far as the record shows, this is a case of a state court's enforcement of a racial restriction to prevent willing parties from dealing with one another. The decision of the Georgia courts thus, under Shelley v. Kraemer, constitutes state action denying equal protection.

The Court in *Abney* rejected petitioners' argument that

> the action of the Georgia court violates the United States Constitution in that it imposes a drastic "penalty," the "forfeiture" of the park, merely because of the city's compliance with the constitutional mandate expressed by this Court in Evans v. Newton. [We] think [that] the will of Senator Bacon and Georgia law provide all the justification necessary for imposing such a "penalty." . . .
>
> [The] Georgia Supreme Court [interpreted] Senator Bacon's will as embodying a preference for termination of the park rather than its integration. Given this, the Georgia court had no alternative under its relevant trust laws, which are long standing and neutral with regard to race, but to end the Baconsfield trust and return the property to the Senator's heirs.

Compare Justice Brennan's views: "When it is as starkly clear as it is in this case that a public facility would remain open but for the constitutional command that it be operated on a nonsegregated basis, the closing of that facility conveys an unambiguous message of community involvement in racial discrimination."

Recall Palmer v. Thompson, Chapter 5, section C2, supra, decided only a year after *Abney*. In *Palmer*, Justice Black, again writing for the Court, held that a municipality's decision to close a swimming pool, rather than comply with court-ordered integration, was constitutionally permissible. Given *Palmer*, does anything turn on the state action analysis in *Abney*, or is the *Abney* decision, once again, fully explicable in terms of substantive equal protection doctrine?

c. *State enforcement of trespass laws.* Does *Shelley* prohibit judicial enforcement of facially neutral trespass laws at the behest of a property owner who attempts to exclude the defendants for racial reasons? This issue was posed in a series of cases involving sit-in demonstrations in racially segregated restaurants in the early 1960s. Although the Court managed to reverse all the resulting convictions, it never reached the *Shelley* issue. See, e.g., Bell v. Maryland, 378 U.S. 226 (1964) (convictions reversed and remanded for consideration of the effect of an intervening change in state law); Peterson v. Greenville, 373 U.S. 244

(1963) (conviction reversed because official state policy encouraged segregation). But although no majority opinion reached the issue, individual justices engaged in spirited debate about the relevance of *Shelley*. Consider, for example, the views of Justice Black in Bell v. Maryland, supra. Justice Black argued that

> [the] [Fourteenth] Amendment does not forbid a State to prosecute for crimes committed against a person or his property, however prejudiced or narrow the victim's views may be. [Such] a doctrine would [severely] handicap a State's efforts to maintain a peaceful and orderly society. Our society has put its trust in a system of criminal laws to punish lawless conduct. [Instead] of attempting to take the law into their own hands, people have been taught to call for police protection to protect their rights wherever possible. It would betray our whole plan for a tranquil and orderly society to say that a citizen, because of his personal prejudices, habits, attitudes, or beliefs, is cast outside the law's protection and cannot call for the aid of officers sworn to uphold the law and preserve the peace.

Justice Black distinguished *Shelley*:

> It seems pretty clear that the reason judicial enforcement of the restrictive covenants in *Shelley* was deemed state action was not merely the fact that a state court had acted, but rather that it had acted "to deny to petitioners, on the grounds of race or color, the enjoyment of property rights in premises which petitioners are willing and financially able to acquire and which the grantors are willing to sell." [Quoting from *Shelley*.] [This] means that the property owner may, in the absence of a valid statute forbidding it, sell his property to whom he pleases and admit to that property whom he will; so long as *both* parties are willing [parties]. [But] equally, when one party is unwilling, as when the property owner chooses *not* to sell to a particular person or *not* to admit that person, then [he] is entitled to rely on the guarantee or due process of law, that is, "law of the land," to protect his free use and enjoyment of property and to know that only by valid legislation, passed pursuant to some constitutional grant of power, can anyone disturb this free use.

Shortly after *Bell* the public accommodations controversy was mooted when Congress enacted the 1964 Civil Rights Act, which, inter alia, prohibited racial discrimination in most places of public accommodation. In Heart of Atlanta Motel v. United States, 379 U.S. 241 (1964), and Katzenbach v. McClung, 379 U.S. 294 (1964), the Court unanimously upheld the constitutionality of the act. See Chapter 2, section C, supra.

5. *The state action issue in comparative constitutional law.* Many of the world's constitutional systems have confronted the state action problem. Outside the United States, the problem is usually described as one involving the horizontal effect of constitutional norms such as procedural fairness, free expression, and nondiscrimination: In the absence of applicable statutes, to what extent do such norms apply to the actions of nongovernmental actors? (Consider why the reference to statutes is important, and note in the U.S. cases in this chapter those in which the state-action problem arises because of seeming "gaps" in statutory regulation.) Other constitutional systems deal with the problem in two ways.

a. *Direct horizontal effect.* The Constitution of South Africa, §8(2), provides: "A provision of the Bill of Rights binds a natural or a juristic person if, and to the extent that, it is applicable, taking into account the nature of the right and the nature of any duty imposed by the right." Consider why this provision is so awkward in its formulation, and so apparently limited in its application.

b. *Indirect horizontal effect.* More commonly, constitutional courts give constitutional norms "indirect" horizontal effect. This approach originated with the German Constitutional Court, in the case of Erich Lüth, 7 BverfGE 198 (1958). Under this approach, constitutional norms do not apply of their own force to a nongovernmental actor's actions, but they must be taken into account when the courts apply nonconstitutional statutory or common law rules to those actions. Constitutional norms, that is, must shape the interpretation of statutes and the common law. The U.S. system of federalism makes this approach unavailable to the federal courts when dealing with state law (why?). It raises questions of the extent to which interpretation influenced by constitutional norms can override the conclusions a court would reach by applying "ordinary" methods of statutory interpretation or common law development. Note in the U.S. cases in this chapter those in which the Court might have dealt with the state action problem, as it arose in connection with federal statutes, by interpreting the statutes in light of constitutional norms, and consider why the Court did not do so.

For additional discussion, see M. Tushnet, Weak Courts, Strong Rights: Judicial Review and Social Welfare Rights in Comparative Constitutional Law (2008).

C.   CONSTITUTIONALLY IMPERMISSIBLE DEPARTURES FROM NEUTRALITY: STATE SUBSIDIZATION, APPROVAL, AND ENCOURAGEMENT

1.   *State Subsidization of Private Conduct*

Burton v. Wilmington Parking Authority
365 U.S. 715 (1961)

Mr. Justice Clark delivered the opinion of the Court.

In this action for declaratory and injunctive relief it is admitted that the Eagle Coffee Shoppe, Inc., a restaurant located within an off-street automobile parking building in Wilmington, Delaware, has refused to serve appellant food or drink solely because he is a Negro. The parking building is owned and operated by the Wilmington Parking Authority, an agency of the State of Delaware, and the restaurant is the Authority's lessee. Appellant claims that such refusal abridges his rights under the Equal Protection Clause of the Fourteenth Amendment to the United States Constitution. [We conclude] that the exclusion of appellant under the circumstances shown to be present here was discriminatory state action in violation of the Equal Protection Clause of the Fourteenth Amendment. . . .

[The City of Wilmington created the Wilmington Parking Authority for the purpose of constructing parking facilities. Before beginning construction of the facility at issue here, the parking authority entered into a series of long-term leases with commercial tenants in order to provide needed capital for its debt service requirements. One such lease was made with Eagle for a period of twenty years, renewable for another ten years. The space leased to Eagle was directly accessible from the street and had no marked public entrance leading from the parking portion of the facility into the restaurant. The parking authority agreed to complete construction expeditiously, including decorative finishing of the leased premises and necessary utility connections. Eagle, in turn, spent some $220,000 to make the space suitable for its operation, and to the extent such improvements were attached to the realty, it enjoyed the parking authority's tax exemption. The lease contained no requirement that restaurant services be made available to the general public on a nondiscriminatory basis, although the parking authority had statutory authority to adopt rules respecting the use of its facilities so long as they would not impair the security of its bondholders. When the building was completed, the parking authority placed official signs in appropriate places indicating the public character of the building and flew from mastheads on the roof both the state and national flags.

[On being refused service by Eagle because of his race, appellant filed this lawsuit. The trial court granted his motion for summary judgment, but the Delaware Supreme Court reversed.]

[To] fashion and apply a precise formula for recognition of state responsibility under the Equal Protection Clause is an "impossible task" which "This Court has never attempted." Kotch v. Pilot Commrs., 330 U.S. 552, 556. Only by sifting facts and weighing circumstances can the nonobvious involvement of the State in private conduct be attributed its true significance. . . .

[The] Delaware Supreme Court seems to have placed controlling emphasis on its conclusion [that] only some 15% of the total cost of the facility was "advanced" from public funds; that the cost of the entire facility was allocated three-fifths to the space for commercial leasing and two-fifths to parking space; that anticipated revenue from parking was only some 30.5% of the total income, the balance of which was expected to be earned by the leasing; that the Authority had no original intent to place a restaurant in the building, it being only a happenstance resulting from the bidding; that Eagle expended considerable moneys on furnishings; that the restaurant's main and marked public entrance is on Ninth Street without any public entrance direct from the parking area; and that "the only connection Eagle has with the public facility . . . is the furnishing of the sum of $28,700 annually in the form of rent which is used by the Authority to defray a portion of the operating expense of an otherwise unprofitable enterprise." While these factual considerations are indeed validly accountable aspects of the enterprise upon which the State has embarked, we cannot say that they lead inescapably to the conclusion that state action is not present. Their persuasiveness is diminished when evaluated in the context of other factors which must be acknowledged.

The land and building were publicly owned. As an entity, the building was dedicated to "public uses" in performance of the Authority's "essential governmental functions." 22 Del. Code, §§501, 514. The costs of land acquisition, construction, and maintenance are defrayed entirely from donations by the City of Wilmington, from loans and revenue bonds and from the proceeds of rentals and parking services out of which the loans and bonds were payable. Assuming that the distinction would be significant, the commercially leased areas were not surplus state property, but constituted a physically and financially integral and, indeed, indispensable part of the State's plan to operate its project as a self-sustaining unit. Upkeep and maintenance of the building, including necessary repairs, were responsibilities of the Authority and were payable out of public funds. It cannot be doubted that the peculiar relationship of the restaurant to the parking facility in which it is located confers on each an incidental variety of mutual benefits. Guests of the restaurant are afforded a convenient place to park their automobiles, even if they cannot enter the restaurant directly from the parking area. Similarly, its convenience for diners may well provide additional demand for the Authority's parking facilities. Should any improvements effected in the leasehold by Eagle become part of the realty, there is no possibility of increased taxes being passed on to it since the fee is held by a tax-exempt government agency. Neither can it be ignored, especially in view of Eagle's affirmative allegation that for it to serve Negroes would injure its business, that profits earned by discrimination not only contribute to, but also are indispensable elements in, the financial success of a governmental agency.

Addition of all these activities, obligations and responsibilities of the Authority, the benefits mutually conferred, together with the obvious fact that the restaurant is operated as an integral part of a public building devoted to a public parking service, indicates that degree of state participation and involvement in discriminatory action which it was the design of the Fourteenth Amendment to condemn. It is irony amounting to grave injustice that in one part of a single building, erected and maintained with public funds by an agency of the State to serve a public purpose, all persons have equal rights, while in another portion, also serving the public, a Negro is a second-class citizen, offensive because of his race, without rights and unentitled to service, but at the same time fully enjoys equal access to nearby restaurants in wholly privately owned buildings. [In] its lease with Eagle the Authority could have affirmatively required Eagle to discharge the responsibilities under the Fourteenth Amendment imposed upon the private enterprise as a consequence of state participation. But no State may effectively abdicate its responsibilities by either ignoring them or by merely failing to discharge them whatever the motive may be. It is of no consolation to an individual denied the equal protection of the laws that it was done in good faith. [By] its inaction, the Authority, and through it the State, has not only made itself a party to the refusal of service, but has elected to place its power, property and prestige behind the admitted discrimination. The State has so far insinuated itself into a position of interdependence with Eagle that it must be recognized as a joint participant in the challenged activity, which, on that account, cannot be considered to have been so "purely private" as to fall without the scope of the Fourteenth Amendment.

Because readily applicable formulae may not be fashioned, the conclusions drawn from the facts and circumstances of this record are by no means declared as universal truths on the basis of which every state leasing agreement is to be tested. Owing to the very "largeness" of government, a multitude of relationships might appear to some to fall within the Amendment's embrace, but that, it must be remembered, can be determined only in the framework of the peculiar facts or circumstances present. [Specifically] defining the limits of our inquiry, what we hold today is that when a State leases public property in the manner and for the purpose shown to have been the case here, the proscriptions of the Fourteenth Amendment must be complied with by the lessee as certainly as though they were binding covenants written into the agreement itself. . . .

Reversed and remanded.

[A concurring opinion by Justice Stewart and dissents by Justice Frankfurter and Justice Harlan (joined by Justice Whittaker) have been omitted.]

Note: Subsidies, Penalties, and the Search for a Baseline

1. *State subsidization.* Does *Burton* stand for the general proposition that state subsidization of discriminatory conduct is unconstitutional? On this view, the state is not obligated to prohibit or penalize such conduct, but neither is it permitted to accord benefits to those who engage in it. But surely it is not unconstitutional, for example, for the state to provide police and fire protection to establishments that discriminate. Some subsidies or benefits are acceptable. Moreover, any theory that makes "subsidies" of discriminatory conduct unconstitutional, but does not require government to impose "penalties" on such conduct, ultimately rests on our ability to distinguish between the withholding of a benefit, on the one hand, and the imposition of a burden, on the other.

Consider, for example, Norwood v. Harrison, 413 U.S. 455 (1973), in which the Court confronted a constitutional challenge to a Mississippi statutory program under which textbooks were purchased by the state and lent to students in both public and private schools, without reference to whether any participating private school had racially discriminatory policies. The Court unanimously struck down the program as applied to discriminatory schools. Defenders of the program relied on Pierce v. Society of Sisters, 268 U.S. 510 (1925), which had established the constitutional right of parents to provide private education for their children. They argued that *Pierce* rights would be infringed by lending free textbooks to public school children but withholding them from certain private school children. The Court rejected this argument:

> In *Pierce*, the Court affirmed the right of private schools to exist and to operate; it said nothing of any supposed right of private or parochial schools to share with public schools in state largesse, on an equal basis or otherwise. [It] is one thing to say that a State may not prohibit the maintenance of private schools and quite another to say that such schools must, as a matter of equal protection, receive state aids.

Having disposed of appellees' argument that the textbook aid was constitutionally required, the Court went on to hold that it was constitutionally impermissible: "A State may not grant the type of tangible financial aid here involved if that aid has a significant tendency to facilitate, reinforce, and support private discrimination." The Court was careful to note, however, that its holding did not extend to all types of state assistance:

> Textbooks are a basic educational tool and, like tuition grants, they are provided only in connection with schools; they are to be distinguished from generalized services government might provide to schools in common with others. Moreover, the textbooks provided to private school students by the State in this case are a form of assistance readily available from sources entirely independent of the State. [The] State has neither an absolute nor operating monopoly on the procurement of school textbooks; anyone can purchase them on the open market.

After *Norwood*, would it be unconstitutional for the state to grant the same tax-exempt status to discriminatory private schools that it grants to other charitable and nonprofit institutions? See McGlotten v. Connally, 338 F. Supp. 448 (D.D.C. 1972) (tax-exempt status of discriminatory fraternal orders unconstitutional). Compare Bob Jones University v. United States, 461 U.S. 574 (1983) (Internal Revenue Service decision to deny tax-exempt status to private schools engaging in racial discrimination permissible as matter of statutory construction). Is there a constitutionally relevant distinction between tax exemptions for discriminatory institutions and direct monetary subsidies to them? (For a more detailed discussion of these issues in connection with the establishment and free exercise clauses of the first amendment, see Chapter 8, section B4, supra.)

One year after *Norwood* the Court again considered whether the provision of "generalized" government services to private discriminatory groups constituted an impermissible departure from neutrality. Gilmore v. City of Montgomery, 417 U.S. 556 (1974), arose out of the fifteen-year struggle by African Americans in Montgomery, Alabama, to desegregate the city's public parks. After protracted litigation involving repeated efforts by the city to avoid the original desegregation order, the district court enjoined the city from allowing use of city-owned recreational facilities by any private group that was racially segregated or had a racially discriminatory admissions policy. The court of appeals sustained this order insofar as it restrained the use of city facilities by private schools when the use was "exclusive" and not in common with other citizens. With respect to "nonexclusive" use by private school children and use by nonschool groups, however, the court of appeals reversed.

The Supreme Court, in an opinion by Justice Blackmun, affirmed that portion of the court of appeals decision prohibiting exclusive use of city facilities by segregated private schools. Emphasizing the city's affirmative duty to desegregate its public schools, the Court argued that "the city's actions significantly enhanced the attractiveness of segregated private schools, formed in reaction against the federal court school order, by enabling them to offer complete athletic programs. [We] are persuaded [that] this assistance significantly tended to undermine the federal court order mandating the establishment and maintenance of a unitary school system in Montgomery."

With regard to nonexclusive use by school groups and use by nonschool groups, however, the Court found that the record was insufficiently developed to render a decision. To guide the district court on remand, the Court noted that nonexclusive access by segregated school groups might well undermine outstanding school desegregation orders. "For example, all-white private school basketball teams might be invited to participate in a tournament conducted on public recreational facilities with desegregated private and public school teams. [Such] assistance, although proffered in common with fully desegregated groups, might so directly impede the progress of court-ordered school desegregation within the city that it would be appropriate to fashion equitable relief."

Use by segregated nonschool groups might also undermine the outstanding decree to desegregate park facilities:

> For example, the record contains indications that there are all-white private and all-Negro public Dixie Youth and Babe Ruth baseball leagues for children, all of which use city-provided ballfields. [Were] the District Court to determine that this dual system came about as a means of evading the parks decree, or of serving to perpetuate the separate-but-equal use of city facilities on the basis of race, through the aid and assistance of the city, further relief would be appropriate.

The Court cautioned, however, that

> [traditional] state monopolies, such as electricity, water, and police and fire protection — all generalized governmental services — do not by their mere provision

constitute a showing of state involvement in invidious discrimination. The same is true of a broad spectrum of municipal recreational facilities: parks, playgrounds, athletic facilities, amphitheaters, museums, zoos, and the like. It follows, therefore, that the portion of the District Court's order prohibiting the mere use of such facilities by any segregated "private group, club, or organization" is invalid because it was not predicated upon a proper finding of state action.

If, however, the city or other governmental entity rations otherwise freely accessible recreational facilities, the case for state action will naturally be stronger than if the facilities are simply available to all comers without condition or reservation. Here, for example, petitioners allege that the city engages in scheduling softball games for an all-white church league and provides balls, equipment, fields, and lighting. The city's role in that situation would be dangerously close to what was found to exist in *Burton*, where the city "elected to place its power, property and prestige behind the admitted discrimination." We are reminded, however, that the Court has never attempted to formulate "an infallible test for determining whether the State . . . has become significantly involved in private discriminations" so as to constitute state action [quoting *Reitman*, section B1, *supra*].

2. *State dependence on discriminatory conduct.* In *Burton*, the Court pointed out that "profits earned by discrimination not only contribute to, but also are indispensable elements in, the financial success of a governmental agency." Should the result in *Burton* have been different if Eagle were able to show that its refusal to serve blacks resulted in reduced profits? If the parking authority had charged it a lower rent so as not to capture any of the profits earned from Eagle's discriminatory conduct? Justice Clark's opinion relies on the "mutual benefits" conferred by Eagle and the parking authority on each other. Note that there is a tension between the need to avoid conferring benefits on the private actor and the need to avoid public capture of the benefits from discrimination. For example, the state could avoid benefiting from the discriminatory conduct by not taxing the profits attributable to the discrimination. But by pursuing this policy, the state would in effect subsidize the discriminatory conduct. Does the need to avoid this dilemma explain the constitutional requirement that the state divorce itself entirely from discriminatory private entities when the benefits conferred are "mutual"?

3. *State action as symbolism.* Does the result in *Burton* depend on the "message" sent to the general public when a discriminatory private entity rents space in a public building? Notice Justice Clark's emphasis on the state and federal flags that flew over the parking facility. In these circumstances, is there a risk that the public would interpret Eagle's presence in the building as connoting state approval of its policies? That it would perceive Eagle as a state entity? Should the result in the case be different if the parking authority prominently posted signs stating that it did not approve of the racial policies of its tenants?

RENDELL-BAKER v. KOHN, 457 U.S. 830 (1982). Petitioners were employees of the New Perspectives School, a privately owned institution specializing in "problem" students. Nearly all of the school's students were referred to it by public institutions. It was heavily regulated by public authorities, and between 90 and 99 percent of its operating budget came from public funds. Petitioners were discharged after disagreeing with certain school policies. They claimed that their discharge violated their constitutional rights to free speech and procedural due process. Chief Justice Burger wrote the Court's opinion:

"[The] Court of Appeals concluded that the fact that virtually all of the school's income was derived from government funding was the strongest factor to support a claim of state action. But [we] conclude that the school's receipt of public funds does not make the discharge decisions acts of the State.

"The school [is] not fundamentally different from many private corporations whose business depends primarily on contracts to build roads, bridges, dams, ships, or submarines for the government. Acts of such private contractors do not become acts of the government by reason of their significant or even total engagement in performing public contracts. . . .

"[The] decisions to discharge the petitioners were not compelled or even influenced by any state regulation. Indeed, in contrast to the extensive regulation of the school generally, the various regulators showed relatively little interest in the school's personnel matters. . . .

"[Petitioners] argue that there is a 'symbiotic relationship' between the school and the State similar to the relationship involved in [Burton]. [But] in Burton, the Court [stressed] that the restaurant was located on public property and that the rent from the restaurant contributed to the support of the garage. In response to the argument that the restaurant's profits, and hence the State's financial position, would suffer if it did not discriminate, the Court concluded that this showed that the State profited from the restaurant's discriminatory conduct. The Court viewed this as support for the conclusion that the State should be charged with the discriminatory actions. Here the school's fiscal relationship with the State is not different from that of many contractors performing services for the government. No symbiotic relationship such as existed in Burton exists here."

Justice White wrote a separate opinion concurring in the judgment.

Justice Marshall, with whom Justice Brennan joined, dissented: "The State has delegated to the New Perspectives School its statutory duty to educate children with special needs. The school receives almost all of its funds from the State, and is heavily regulated. This nexus between the school and the State is so substantial that the school's action must be considered state action. I therefore dissent."

SAN FRANCISCO ARTS & ATHLETICS, INC. v. UNITED STATES OLYMPIC COMMITTEE, 483 U.S. 522 (1987). The Amateur Sports Act of 1978 gave the United States Olympic Committee the exclusive right to use the term "Olympic." When petitioner organized and began to promote the "Gay Olympic Games," the committee brought suit under the statute to enjoin petitioner from using the word "Olympic." Petitioner responded by pointing out that the committee had allowed other groups to use the word "Olympic." It argued that the committee's discriminatory selection of such groups violated the equal protection component of the fifth amendment due process clause.

In a five-to-four decision, the Supreme Court held that the committee's selection of groups permitted to use the term was not state action. Justice Powell delivered the Court's opinion: "The fact that Congress granted [the committee] a corporate charter does not render [it] a government agent. All corporations act under charters granted by a [government]. [Nor] is the fact that Congress has granted the [committee] exclusive use of the word 'Olympic' dispositive. All enforceable rights in trademarks are created by some governmental [act]. . . .

"The [Committee's] choice of how to enforce its exclusive right [simply] is not a governmental decision. There is no evidence that the Federal Government coerced or encouraged the [Committee] in the exercise of its rights. At most, the Federal Government, by failing to supervise the [Committee's] use of its rights, can be said to exercise '[m]ere approval of or acquiescence in the initiatives' of the [Committee]. [This] is not enough to make the [Committee's] actions those of the Government."

Justice Brennan, joined by Justice Marshall, dissented: "The [Committee] and the Federal Government exist in a symbiotic relationship sufficient to provide a nexus between the [Committee's] challenged action and the Government. First, as in *Burton*, the relationship here confers a variety of mutual benefits. [The] Act gave the [Committee] authority and responsibilities that no private organization in this country had ever held. . . .

"Second, in the eye of the public, [the] connection between the decisions of the United States Government and those of the United States Olympic Committee is profound. . . .

"Even more importantly, there is a close financial and legislative link between the [Committee's] alleged discriminatory exercise of its word-use authority and the financial success of both the [Committee] and the Government. It would certainly be 'irony amounting to grave injustice' if, to finance the team that is to represent the virtues of our political system, the [Committee] were free to employ government-created economic leverage to prohibit political speech. [*Burton*.]"

Justice O'Connor, joined by Justice Blackmun, also dissented from the Court's state action determination.

Note: *State Action as Coercion or Significant Encouragement*

1. United States Olympic Committee *and* Burton. Does *United States Olympic Committee* help explain what factors triggered the finding of state action in *Burton*? Justice Powell's opinion relies on an earlier decision, Blum v. Yaretsky, 457 U.S. 991 (1982), where the Court rejected a procedural due process challenge to the decisions, made without hearings by state-subsidized nursing homes, to downgrade the level of treatment for patients receiving Medicaid payments. Although Medicaid regulations required the nursing home to maintain different levels of care for patients and to transfer patients when necessary, and although the state responded to the transfers by reducing Medicaid payments, the Court held that no state action was present because the state was not responsible for the individual transfer decisions. The Court summarized the law as follows:

> [Although] the factual setting of each case will be significant, our precedents indicate that a State normally can be held responsible for a private decision only when it has exercised coercive power or has provided such significant encouragement, either overt or covert, that the choice must in law be deemed to be that of the State. Mere approval of or acquiescence in the initiatives of a private party is not sufficient to justify holding the State responsible for those initiatives under the terms of the Fourteenth Amendment.

2. Rendell-Baker *and* Burton. According to *Rendell-Baker*, *Burton* stands for the proposition that the state may not profit from discriminatory conduct. Is that a fair reading of *Burton*? Assuming that it is, might not the school in *Rendell-Baker* pass on to the state some of the savings it realizes from avoiding the cost of due process hearings just as the restaurant in *Burton* passed on some of the profits derived from racial discrimination?

3. Rendell-Baker *and the recognition of public actors.* The Court begins its analysis in *Rendell-Baker* with the assumption that the New Perspectives School is "private." If the school itself were a "public" institution, there would be no doubt that its decision to discharge petitioners would be "state action." But given the fact that the school received virtually all of its funds from public sources, why does the Court begin with the assumption that it is "private"?

Presumably what makes the New Perspectives School private is the fact that the state exercises less pervasive control over it than it would over a state instrumentality; thus, the state did not produce the objectionable conduct at issue. But the very issue in dispute in *Rendell-Baker* was the degree of control the state was obligated to exercise. Surely the acts of state police officers would be attributable to the state even if state law left them largely unconstrained in exercising their discretion.

Compare *Rendell-Baker* with Ex parte Virginia, 100 U.S. 339 (1880), where a state judge discriminated against blacks in the selection of juries in violation of state law. The Court rejected the defendant's argument that he was not a state actor because the state had prohibited the conduct in question. "[As] he acts in the name and for the State, and is clothed with the State's power, his act is that of the State. This must be so, or the constitutional prohibition has no meaning." See also Screws v. United States, 325 U.S. 91 (1945) (state police officer who exceeds his authority under state law is nonetheless a state actor acting under color of law). Is the *Rendell-Baker* "coercion or significant encouragement" test consistent with Ex parte Virginia and *Screws*?

Compare *Rendell-Baker* to West v. Atkins, 487 U.S. 42 (1988), where the Court held that a private physician, under contract with the state to provide medical services for inmates at a state prison, was a state actor for constitutional purposes. Writing for eight justices, Justice Blackmun rejected the argument that the doctor's actions were not attributable to the state because he was exercising independent medical judgment. In a footnote, the Court distinguished *Rendell-Baker* and *Blum* as follows:

> Where the issue is whether a *private* party is engaged in activity that constitutes state action, it may be relevant that the challenged activity turned on judgments controlled by professional standards, where those standards are not established by the State. The Court has held that "a State normally can be held responsible for a private decision only when it has exercised coercive power or has provided such significant encouragement, either overt or covert, that the choice must in law be deemed to be that of the State." [*Blum; Rendell-Baker.*] In both *Blum* and *Rendell-Baker*, the fact that the private entities received state funding and were subject to state regulation did not, without more, convert their conduct into state action. . . .
>
> This determination cannot be transformed into the proposition that no person acts under color of state law where he is exercising independent professional judgment. [*Blum*] and *Rendell-Baker* provide no support for respondent's argument that a physician, employed by the State to fulfill the State's constitutional obligations, does not act under color of state law merely because he renders medical care in accordance with professional obligations.

Why wasn't the New Perspectives School "employed by the State to fulfill the State's constitutional obligations"?

4. Lebron *and* Brentwood Academy. For an extended discussion of the distinction between private and government actors, see Lebron v. National Railroad Passenger Corp., 513 U.S. 374 (1995). The controversy arose when Lebron

sought to rent a huge, illuminated billboard known as the "Spectacular" in New York's Pennsylvania Station. Lebron wished to use the space to display a photo montage parodying Coors beer commercials and attacking the brewery for its alleged support of right-wing causes. Pennsylvania Station was owned by Amtrak, a corporation created by Congress to avert the threatened extinction of passenger train service. The United States owned all of Amtrak's preferred stock, and the President appointed a majority of its board of directors. When Amtrak refused to rent the space to Lebron, he sued, claiming that his first amendment rights had been violated. The court of appeals held that Amtrak was not a government actor and therefore rejected Lebron's claim. In an eight-to-one decision, the Supreme Court reversed.

Writing for the majority, Justice Scalia began by noting that, although the Court had "held once [see *Burton*] and said many times that actions of private entities can sometimes be regarded as governmental action for constitutional purposes," it was unnecessary "to traverse this difficult terrain in the present case, since [Amtrak] is not a private entity but the Government itself."

In reaching this conclusion, the Court found irrelevant Congress's own declaration that Amtrak was not a government actor. Nor was Amtrak's corporate form determinative.

> It surely cannot be that government [is] able to evade the most solemn obligations imposed in the Constitution by simply resorting to the corporate form. On that thesis, Plessy v. Ferguson can be resurrected by the simple device of having the State of Louisiana operate segregated trains through a state-owned Amtrak. [Amtrak was a government actor because it was] established and organized under federal law for the very purpose of pursuing federal governmental objectives, under the direction and control of federal governmental appointees.

The Court reaffirmed the public status of Amtrak in Department of Transportation v. Association of American Railroads, 135 S. Ct. 1225 (2015), but this time in a context that expanded, rather than reduced Amtrak's power. Federal law granted Amtrak and the Federal Railroad Administration joint authority to issue "metrics and standards" that address the performance and scheduling of passenger railroad services. Respondents challenged this authority as an unconstitutional delegation of lawmaking authority to a private entity. In an opinion written by Justice Kennedy, that largely tracked the reasoning of *Lebron*, the Court rejected the challenge on the ground that Amtrak was a government actor.

The Court reached a similar conclusion in a different factual setting in Brentwood Academy v. Tennessee Secondary School Athletic Association, 531 U.S. 288 (2001). The issue in the case was whether a statewide association incorporated to regulate athletic competition among public and private secondary schools was a state actor when it enforced a rule against a private member school. In a five-to-four decision written by Justice Souter, the Court held that it was.

The Court relied upon the fact that "84% of [the Association's] membership [consisted of] public schools, represented by officials acting in their official capacity to provide an integral element of secondary public schooling."

> There would be no recognizable Association, legal or tangible, without the public school officials, who do not merely control but overwhelmingly perform all but the purely ministerial acts by which the Association exists and functions in practical terms. Only the 16% minority of private school memberships prevents this

entwinement of the Association and the public school system from being total and their identities totally indistinguishable.

The Court distinguished *Rendell-Baker* as follows:

Facts that address ["coercion" and "encouragement"] are significant, but no one criterion must necessarily be applied. When [the] relevant facts show pervasive entwinement to the point of largely overlapping identity, the implication of state action is not affected by pointing out that the facts might not loom large under a different test.

5. Edmonson. In Edmonson v. Leesville Concrete Co., 500 U.S. 614 (1991), the Court, in an opinion by Justice Kennedy, held that a private civil litigant who used peremptory challenges to exclude jurors on account of race was a state actor for constitutional purposes. The Court based this conclusion in part on the "overt, significant assistance of state officials" in the discriminatory conduct:

[A] private party could not exercise its peremptory challenges absent the overt, significant assistance of the court. The government summons jurors, constrains their freedom of movement, and subjects them to public scrutiny and examination. [Without] the direct and indispensable participation of the judge, who beyond all question is a state actor, the peremptory challenge system would serve no purpose. By enforcing a discriminatory peremptory challenge, the court "has not only made itself a party to the [biased act], but has elected to place its power, property and prestige behind the [alleged] discrimination." [*Burton.*]

2.   *State Licensing and Authorization*

PUBLIC UTILITIES COMMISSION v. POLLAK, 343 U.S. 451 **(1952).** Capital Transit Company was a privately owned corporation providing bus and streetcar service in the District of Columbia under a franchise from Congress. In 1948, it began experimenting with a "music as you ride" program under which radio programs were amplified through loudspeakers in the street-cars and buses. In 1949, the Public Utilities Commission, which regulated Capital, ordered an investigation of the program to determine whether it was "consistent with public convenience, comfort and safety." The commission concluded that the use of radios was not inconsistent with the public interest and dismissed its investigation. Some of Capital's passengers thereupon appealed the commission's decision, and the court of appeals reversed, holding that the broadcasts deprived passengers of liberty without due process of law. Justice Burton delivered the Court's opinion:

"It was held by the court below that the action of Capital Transit in installing and operating the radio receivers, coupled with the action of the Public Utilities Commission in dismissing its own investigation of the practice, sufficiently involved the Federal Government in responsibility for the radio programs to make the First and Fifth Amendments [applicable] to this radio service. . . .

"[We agree. In reaching this result,] we do not rely on the mere fact that Capital Transit operates a public utility on the streets of the District of Columbia under authority of Congress. Nor do we rely upon the fact that, by reason of such federal authorization, Capital Transit now enjoys a substantial monopoly of street railway and bus transportation in the District of Columbia. We do, however, recognize that Capital Transit operates its service under the regulatory supervision of the Public Utilities Commission of the District of Columbia which is an agency authorized by Congress. We rely particularly upon the fact that that agency, pursuant to protests against the radio program, ordered an investigation of it and, after formal public hearings, ordered its investigation dismissed on the ground that the public safety, comfort and convenience were not impaired thereby."

The Court then reached the merits and held that the broadcasts were not unconstitutional.

Moose Lodge No. 107 v. Irvis

407 U.S. 163 (1972)

MR. JUSTICE REHNQUIST delivered the opinion of the Court.

[Appellant Moose Lodge is a local branch of a national fraternal organization. Lodge policy restricts membership to whites and prohibits members from bringing black guests to the lodge dining room and bar. When appellee, a black man, was refused service because of his race, he filed this action, naming as defendants both Moose Lodge and the Pennsylvania Liquor Authority. He claimed that, because the liquor authority had issued Moose Lodge a license that authorized the sale of alcoholic beverages on its premises, the refusal of service was "state action." He sought an injunction requiring the liquor authority to revoke Moose Lodge's license so long as it continued its discriminatory practices. The court below ruled in his favor.]

The Court has never held, of course, that discrimination by an otherwise private entity would be violative of the Equal Protection Clause if the private entity receives any sort of benefit or service at all from the State, or if it is subject to state regulation in any degree whatever. Since state-furnished services include such necessities of life as electricity, water, and police and fire protection, such a holding would utterly emasculate the distinction between private as distinguished from state conduct set forth in The Civil Rights Cases and adhered to in subsequent decisions. Our holdings indicate that where the impetus for the discrimination is private, the State must have "significantly involved itself with invidious discriminations," [*Reitman*], in order for the discriminatory action to fall within the ambit of the constitutional prohibition. . . .

Here there is nothing approaching the symbiotic relationship between lessor and lessee that was present in [*Burton*]. Unlike *Burton*, the Moose Lodge building is located on land owned by it, not by any public authority. Far from apparently holding itself out as a place of public accommodation, Moose Lodge quite ostentatiously proclaims the fact that it is not open to the public at large. Nor is it located and operated in such surroundings that although private in name, it discharges a function or performs a service that would otherwise in all likelihood be performed by the State. In short, while Eagle was a public restaurant in a public building, Moose Lodge is a private social club in a private building.

With the exception hereafter noted, the Pennsylvania Liquor Control Board plays absolutely no part in establishing or enforcing the membership or guest policies of the club that it licenses to serve liquor. There is no suggestion in this record that Pennsylvania law, either as written or as applied, discriminates against minority groups either in their right to apply for club licenses themselves or in their right to purchase and be served liquor in places of public accommodation. The only effect that the state licensing of Moose Lodge to serve liquor can be said to have on the right of any other Pennsylvanian to buy or be served liquor on premises other than those of Moose Lodge is that for some purposes club licenses are counted in the maximum number of licenses that may be issued in a given municipality. . . .

The District Court was at pains to point out in its opinion what it considered to be the "pervasive" nature of the regulation of private clubs by the Pennsylvania Liquor Control Board. . . .

However detailed this type of regulation may be in some particulars, it cannot be said to in any way foster or encourage racial discrimination. Nor can it be said to make the State in any realistic sense a partner or even a joint venturer in the club's enterprise. The limited effect of the prohibition against obtaining additional club licenses when the maximum number of retail licenses allotted to a municipality has been issued, when considered together with the availability of liquor from hotel, restaurant, and retail licensees, falls far short of conferring upon club licensees a monopoly in the dispensing of liquor in any given municipality or in the State as a whole. We therefore hold that, with the exception hereafter noted, the operation of the regulatory scheme enforced by the Pennsylvania Liquor Control Board does not sufficiently implicate the State in the discriminatory guest policies of Moose Lodge to make the latter "state action" within the ambit of the Equal Protection Clause of the Fourteenth Amendment.

The District Court found that the regulations of the Liquor Control Board adopted pursuant to statute affirmatively require that "[e]very club licensee shall adhere to all of the provisions of its Constitution and By-Laws." . . .

The effect of this particular regulation on Moose Lodge under the provisions of the Constitution placed in the record in the court below would be to place state sanctions behind its discriminatory membership rules. . . .

Even though the Liquor Control Board regulation in question is neutral in its terms, the result of its application in a case where the constitution and bylaws of a club required racial discrimination would be to invoke the sanctions of the State to enforce a concededly discriminatory private rule. State action, for purposes of the Equal Protection Clause, may emanate from rulings of administrative and regulatory agencies as well as from legislative or judicial action. [*Shelley*] makes it clear that the application of state sanctions to enforce such a rule would violate the Fourteenth Amendment. . . .

[Appellee] was entitled to a decree enjoining the enforcement of [the] regulations promulgated by the Pennsylvania Liquor Control Board insofar as [they require] compliance by Moose Lodge with provisions of its constitution and bylaws containing racially discriminatory provisions. He was entitled to no more. . . .

Reversed and remanded.

MR. JUSTICE DOUGLAS, with whom MR. JUSTICE MARSHALL joins, dissenting.

[The] fact that a private club gets some kind of permit from the State or municipality does not make it *ipso facto* a public [enterprise]. . . .

[Liquor] licenses in Pennsylvania, unlike driver's licenses, or marriage licenses, are not freely available to those who meet racially neutral qualifications. There is a complex quota system. [What] the majority neglects to say is that the quota for Harrisburg, where Moose Lodge No. 107 is located, has been full for many years. No more club licenses may be issued in that city.

This state-enforced scarcity of licenses restricts the ability of blacks to obtain liquor, for liquor is commercially available only at private clubs for a significant portion of each week. . . .

[A dissenting opinion by Justice Brennan, joined by Justice Marshall, is omitted.]

Jackson v. Metropolitan Edison Co.

419 U.S. 345 (1974)

Mr. Justice Rehnquist delivered the opinion of the Court. . . .

[Metropolitan Edison, a privately owned utility, holds a certificate of public convenience issued by a state utility commission authorizing it to provide electricity to its customers. As a condition for holding this certificate, it is subject to extensive state regulation. Under a provision of its general tariff filed with the state commission, it has the right to discontinue service to a customer on reasonable notice of nonpayment of bills. After a lengthy dispute, Metropolitan Edison terminated Jackson's service for alleged nonpayment. Jackson thereupon brought this action, claiming that the termination constituted state action depriving her of property in violation of the due process clause of the fourteenth amendment.]

[The] mere fact that a business is subject to state regulation does not by itself convert its action into that of the State for purposes of the Fourteenth Amendment. Nor does the fact that the regulation is extensive and detailed, as in the case of most public utilities, do so. [*Pollak.*] It may well be that acts of a heavily regulated utility with at least something of a governmentally protected monopoly will more readily be found to be "state" acts than will the acts of an entity lacking these characteristics. But the inquiry must be whether there is a sufficiently close nexus between the State and the challenged action of the regulated entity so that the action of the latter may be fairly treated as that of the State itself. [*Moose Lodge.*] The true nature of the State's involvement may not be immediately obvious, and detailed inquiry may be required in order to determine whether the test is met. [*Burton*]. . . .

[Petitioner] first argues that "state action" is present because of the monopoly status allegedly conferred upon Metropolitan by the State of Pennsylvania. As a factual matter, it may well be doubted that the State ever granted or guaranteed Metropolitan a monopoly.[8] But assuming that it had, this fact is not determinative in considering whether Metropolitan's termination of service to petitioner was "state action" for purposes of the Fourteenth Amendment. In *Pollak*, [we] expressly disclaimed reliance on the monopoly status of the transit authority. Similarly, although certain monopoly aspects were presented in *Moose Lodge No. 107*, we found that the Lodge's action was not subject to the provisions of the Fourteenth Amendment. In each of those cases, there was insufficient relationship between the challenged actions of the entities involved and their monopoly status. There is no indication of any greater connection here.

---

8. [As] petitioner admits, such public utility companies are natural monopolies created by the economic forces of high threshold capital requirements and virtually unlimited economy of scale. Regulation was superimposed on such natural monopolies as a substitute for competition and not to eliminate it. . . .

We also reject the notion that Metropolitan's termination is state action because the State "has specifically authorized and approved" the termination practice. In the instant case, Metropolitan filed with the Public Utility Commission a general tariff — a provision of which states Metropolitan's right to terminate service for nonpayment. This provision has appeared in Metropolitan's previously filed tariffs for many years and has never been the subject of a hearing or other scrutiny by the Commission. Although the Commission did hold hearings on portions of Metropolitan's general tariff relating to the general rate increase, it never even considered the reinsertion of this provision in the newly filed general tariff. The provision became effective 60 days after filing when not disapproved by the Commission. . . .

The case most heavily relied on by petitioner is [*Pollak*]. [It] is not entirely clear whether the Court alternatively held that Capital Transit's action was action of the "state" for First Amendment purposes, or whether it merely assumed, arguendo, that it was and went on to resolve the First Amendment question adversely to the bus riders.[16] In either event, the nature of the state involvement there was quite different than it is here. The District of Columbia Public Utilities Commission, on its own motion, commenced an investigation of the effects of the piped music, and after a full hearing concluded not only that Capital Transit's practices were "not inconsistent with public convenience, comfort, and safety," but also that the practice "in fact, through the creation of better will among passengers, . . . tends to improve the conditions under which the public ride." Here, on the other hand, there was no such imprimatur placed on the practice of Metropolitan about which petitioner complains. The nature of governmental regulation of private utilities is such that a utility may frequently be required by the state regulatory scheme to obtain approval for practices a business regulated in less detail would be free to institute without any approval from a regulatory body. Approval by a state utility commission of such a request from a regulated utility, where the commission has not put its own weight on the side of the proposed practice by ordering it, does not transmute a practice initiated by the utility and approved by the Commission into "state action." At most, the Commission's failure to overturn this practice amounted to no more than a determination that a Pennsylvania utility was authorized to employ such a practice if it so desired. Respondent's exercise of the choice allowed by state law where the initiative comes from it and not from the State, does not make its action in doing so "state action" for purposes of the Fourteenth Amendment.

[Affirmed.]

[Dissenting opinions by Justices Douglas, Brennan, and Marshall are omitted.]

16. At one point the Court states: "We find in the reasoning of the court below a sufficiently close relation between the Federal Government and the radio service to make it necessary for us to consider those Amendments." Later, the opinion states: "We, therefore, find it appropriate to examine into what restriction, if any, the First and Fifth Amendments place upon the Federal Government . . . *assuming* that the action of Capital Transit . . . amounts to sufficient Federal Government action to make the First and Fifth Amendments applicable thereto." (Emphasis added.)

*Note: Licensing, Authorization, and Entwinement as
         State Action*

1. Pollak *and the failure to regulate.* If Congress had chosen not to regulate bus and railway service at all, the Court presumably would have held that the decision of a private company to install radio service was not "state action." Why does the government's refusal to prohibit this practice become state action when it is part of a pervasive pattern of regulation? (a) Perhaps licensing justifies a state action finding because it eliminates competitive pressures that otherwise might prevent the private entity from engaging in the challenged conduct. (b) Perhaps the absence of an alternative source for the service increases the costs of the challenged conduct to those objecting to it. Note that *Pollak* rejects Capital Transit's monopoly status as a basis for finding state action.

Is the symbolic significance of the state's affirmative imprimatur on the activity dispositive? Recall that in *Flagg Brothers*, the Court treats a statute authorizing Flagg Brothers' sale as "immaterial" because it merely "embodied [the state's] decision not to act in statutory form."

2. *Licensing and government neutrality.* Is the requirement of government neutrality relevant to the *Pollak* problem? Was the action of the Public Utilities Commission a departure from neutrality? Does it matter that its statutory mandate required it to prohibit the radio broadcast if it found that the practice was not in the public interest?

In Columbia Broadcasting System v. Democratic National Committee, 412 U.S. 94 (1973), the Federal Communications Commission refused to require broadcast licensees to accept editorial advertising. The Court rejected a first amendment attack on the broadcasters' practice. In a portion of his opinion joined by only two other justices, Chief Justice Burger argued that the Federal Communications Commission's decision did not make the actions of the broadcasters "state action." He distinguished *Pollak* as follows:

> [In *Pollak*] Congress had expressly authorized the agency to undertake plenary intervention into the affairs of the carrier and it was pursuant to that authorization that the agency investigated the challenged policy and approved it on public interest standards. [Here], Congress has not established a regulatory scheme for broadcast licensees as pervasive as the regulation of public transportation in *Pollak*. More important, [Congress] has affirmatively indicated in the Communications Act that certain journalistic decisions are for the licensee, subject only to the restrictions imposed by evaluation of its overall performance under the public interest standard. In *Pollak* there was no suggestion that Congress had considered worthy of protection the carrier's interest in exercising discretion over the content of communications forced on passengers.

Did the regulatory schemes in *Moose Lodge* and *Jackson* depart from the requirement of governmental neutrality? Both schemes are facially neutral in the Washington v. Davis sense. Do government-enforced monopolies in these contexts nonetheless constitute subsidies for conduct that threatens constitutional values? Answering this question presumably involves a comparison between the status quo and the situation that would exist if the government were completely passive. Is such a comparison meaningful?

D.   CONSTITUTIONALLY REQUIRED DEPARTURES FROM NEUTRALITY: THE PUBLIC FUNCTION DOCTRINE

Marsh v. Alabama

326 U.S. 501 (1946)

MR. JUSTICE BLACK delivered the opinion of the Court.

In this case we are asked to decide whether a State, consistently with the First and Fourteenth Amendments, can impose criminal punishment on a person who undertakes to distribute religious literature on the premises of a company-owned town contrary to the wishes of the town's management. The town, a suburb of Mobile, Alabama, known as Chickasaw, is owned by the Gulf Shipbuilding Corporation. Except for that it has all the characteristics of any other American town. The property consists of residential buildings, streets, a system of sewers, a sewage disposal plant and a "business block" on which business places are situated. A deputy of the Mobile County Sheriff, paid by the company, serves as the town's policeman. Merchants and service establishments have rented the stores and business places on the business block and the United States uses one of the places as a post office [and] according to all indications the residents use the business block as their regular shopping center. To do so, they now, as they have for many years, make use of a company-owned paved street and sidewalk located alongside the store fronts in order to enter and leave the stores and the post office. Intersecting company-owned roads at each end of the business block lead into a four-lane public highway which runs parallel to the business block at a distance of thirty feet. There is nothing to stop highway traffic from coming onto the business block and upon arrival a traveler may make free use of the facilities available there. In short the town and its shopping district are accessible to and freely used by the public in general and there is nothing to distinguish them from any other town and shopping center except the fact that the title to the property belongs to a private corporation.

Appellant, a Jehovah's Witness, came onto the sidewalk [and] undertook to distribute religious literature. In the stores the corporation had posted a notice which read as follows: "This Is Private Property, and Without Written Permission, No Street, or House Vendor, Agent or Solicitation of Any Kind Will Be Permitted." [The] deputy sheriff arrested her and she was charged in the state court with violating [a state statute] which makes it a crime to enter or remain on the premises of another after having been warned not to do so. Appellant contended that to construe the state statute as applicable to her activities would abridge her right to freedom of press and religion contrary to the First and Fourteenth Amendments to the Constitution. This contention was rejected and she was convicted. . . .

Had the title to Chickasaw belonged not to a private but to a municipal corporation and had appellant been arrested for violating a municipal ordinance rather than a ruling by those appointed by the corporation to manage a company town it would have been clear that appellant's conviction must be reversed. [Our] question then narrows down to this: Can those people who live in or come to Chickasaw be denied freedom of press and religion simply because a single company has legal title to all the town?

[We] do not agree that the corporation's property interests settle the question. [Ownership] does not always mean absolute dominion. The more an owner, for his advantage, opens up his property for use by the public in general, the more do his rights become circumscribed by the statutory and constitutional rights of those who use it. Thus, the owners of privately held bridges, ferries, turnpikes and railroads may not operate them as freely as a farmer does his farm. Since these facilities are built and operated primarily to benefit the public and since their operation is essentially a public function, it is subject to state regulation. . . .

Whether a corporation or a municipality owns or possesses the town the public in either case has an identical interest in the functioning of the community in such manner that the channels of communication remain free. [The] managers appointed by the corporation cannot curtail the liberty of press and religion of these people consistently with the purposes of the Constitutional guarantees, and a state statute, as the one here involved, which enforces such action by criminally punishing those who attempt to distribute religious literature clearly violates the First and Fourteenth Amendments to the Constitution.

Many people in the United States live in company-owned towns. These people, just as residents of municipalities, are free citizens of their State and country. Just as all other citizens they must make decisions which affect the welfare of community and nation. To act as good citizens they must be informed. In order to enable them to be properly informed their information must be uncensored. There is no more reason for depriving these people of the liberties guaranteed by the First and Fourteenth Amendments than there is for curtailing these freedoms with respect to any other citizen.

When we balance the Constitutional rights of owners of property against those of the people to enjoy freedom of press and religion, as we must here, we remain mindful of the fact that the latter occupy a preferred position. [In] our view the circumstance that the property rights to the premises where the deprivation of liberty, here involved, took place, were held by others than the public, is not sufficient to justify the State's permitting a corporation to govern a community of citizens so as to restrict their fundamental liberties and the enforcement of such restraint by the application of a state statute.

[Reversed and remanded.]

MR. JUSTICE JACKSON took no part in the consideration or decision of this case. [Justice Frankfurter's concurring opinion is omitted.]

MR. JUSTICE REED, dissenting. . . .

What the present decision establishes as a principle is that one may remain on private property against the will of the owner and contrary to the law of the state so long as the only objection to his presence is that he is exercising an asserted right to spread there his religious views. This is the first case to extend by law the privilege of religious exercises beyond public places or to private places without the assent of the owner. . . .

[CHIEF JUSTICE VINSON] and MR. JUSTICE BURTON join in this dissent.

Note: The "Public Function" Theory and the Passive State

1. Marsh *and* Shelley. Note that Justice Black might have written an opinion in *Marsh* that paralleled the Court's analysis two years later in *Shelley*. He might

have focused attention on state court enforcement of Alabama's trespass statute and held that this judicial conduct violated the first amendment. But although Justice Black makes brief reference to the state prosecution, his analysis focuses on the conduct of the company town rather than on the conduct of the state court. Why should decisions of this "private" entity be treated as if they were state decisions? Would the town's actions have been unconstitutional if its owners had physically ejected Marsh without resorting to the state's legal processes?

2. *"Public functions" and private power.* Some language in *Marsh* supports the view that the town was subject to constitutional constraint because it was acting "like" a state. Thus, Justice Black points out that, except for its private ownership, Chickasaw had "all the characteristics of any other American town." Why is this relevant?

To the extent that the opinion rests on this premise, it seems to stand for the proposition that there are limits on the extent to which the state may escape constitutional restraints by "delegating" to private parties functions traditionally performed by the state. Does the opinion make clear what those limits are or why they were exceeded in this case?

Some passages in *Marsh* suggest that the difficulty was not with the state's delegation of public functions to a private entity, but with its failure to act in the face of widespread violation of constitutional values. Viewed in this light, the opinion is a rare acknowledgment that individual freedom may on occasion be threatened as much by private as by public action. From this perspective, Gulf Shipbuilding's status was "public" because its power rivaled that of the state rather than because of any particular function it had assumed. Whereas constitutional liberty is normally associated with limits on governmental author-ity, in *Marsh* the Court arguably thought that the Constitution required the government to intervene actively to control exercises of private power.

3. *The reach of the public function doctrine.* In what other circumstances should the state's delegation of governmental power to private entities — or fail-ure to control exercises of private power — be subject to constitutional con-straint? Consider the following applications of the public function doctrine:

a. *The "white primary" cases.* In a series of cases involving the effective exclu-sion of blacks from Texas elections, the Court held that the discriminatory policies of "private" political organizations could be attributed to the state. Nixon v. Herndon, 273 U.S. 536 (1927), held that the fourteenth amendment had been violated when blacks were denied ballots in the state Democratic Party primary pursuant to a Texas statute that stated, "[In] no event shall a Negro be eligible to participate in a Democratic Party primary election held in the State of Texas." Texas thereupon rewrote the statute to provide that the State Executive Committee of the party in power could prescribe the qualifications of its mem-bers for voting. In Nixon v. Condon, 286 U.S. 73 (1932), the Court once again found that the denial of the franchise to blacks was unconstitutional. Since the committee was acting under authority expressly delegated by the state, the Court reasoned that its decisions could be attributed to the state.

In Grovey v. Townsend, 295 U.S. 45 (1935), however, where the policy of racial exclusion had been adopted by the state party convention without specific statutory authorization, the Court held that there was no state action and there-fore no constitutional violation. In the Court's view, the exclusionary policy was voluntarily adopted by the Democratic Party, which was not an organ of the state. The policy was no more than a refusal of party membership with which "the State need have no concern."

Grovey was overruled in Smith v. Allwright, 321 U.S. 649 (1944). The Court stated that "[the] privilege of membership in a party may be, as this Court said in [*Grovey*,] no concern of a State. But when, as here, that privilege is also the essential qualification for voting in a primary to select nominees for a general election, the State makes the action of the party the action of the State."

Although the Court was unambiguous in holding that the Democratic Party's exclusionary policy could be attributed to the state, the exact basis for the attribution was less clear. In part, the state action finding seemed to rest on the "public function" performed by party officials. Thus, the Court wrote that "the place of the primary in the electoral scheme makes clear that state delegation to a party of the power to fix the qualifications of primary elections is delegation of a state function that may make the party's action the action of the State."

But the state action finding seemed to rest as well on actual state involvement in the primary election process:

> When primaries become a part of the machinery for choosing officials, state and national, as they have here, the same tests to determine the character of discrimination or abridgement should be applied to the primary as are applied to the general election. If the State requires a certain electoral procedure, prescribes a general election ballot made up of party nominees so chosen and limits the choice of the electorate in general elections for state offices, practically speaking, to those whose names appear on such a ballot, it endorses, adopts and enforces the discrimination against Negroes, practiced by a party entrusted by Texas law with the determination of the qualifications of participants in the primary.

Finally, another passage in the opinion suggested that the state had an affirmative constitutional obligation to prevent private organizations from abridging electoral rights:

> The United States is a constitutional democracy. Its organic law grants to all citizens a right to participate in the choice of elected officials without restriction by any State because of race. This grant to the people of the opportunity for choice is not to be nullified by a State through casting its electoral process in a form which permits a private organization to practice racial discrimination in the election. Constitutional rights would be of little value if they could be thus indirectly denied.

Although the Court maintained virtual unanimity in *Smith*, controversy over which strand of the opinion was determinative erupted nine years later in Terry v. Adams, 345 U.S. 461 (1953), the last in this series of cases. *Terry* concerned the exclusion of blacks from "pre-primaries" held by the Jaybird Democratic Association, a Texas political organization. The Jaybirds maintained that they were not a political party at all but rather a self-governing voluntary club. Their election was not regulated by the state, and there was no legal connection between victory in that election and nomination by the Democratic Party to run in the subsequent general election. As a practical matter, however, white voters generally abided by the "recommendations" of the Jaybirds, and the Jaybird president testified that a purpose of his organization was to exclude blacks from the voting process. The Jaybirds were so successful in this endeavor that victors in the Jaybird primary had almost without exception run and won without opposition in the Democratic primaries and the general election that followed.

Although eight justices agreed that exclusion of blacks from the Jaybird primary violated the fifteenth amendment, no opinion attracted a majority.

Writing for three justices, Justice Black focused on the state's failure to control private conduct that effectively deprived blacks of political power:

> The only election that has counted in this Texas county for more than fifty years has been that held by the Jaybirds from which Negroes were excluded. The Democratic primary and the general election have become no more than the perfunctory ratifiers of the choice that has already been made in Jaybird elections from which Negroes have been excluded. It is immaterial that the state does not control that part of this elective process which it leaves for the Jaybirds to manage. [The] effect of the whole procedure, Jaybird primary plus Democratic primary plus general election, is to do precisely that which the Fifteenth Amendment forbids — strip Negroes of every vestige of influence in selecting the officials who control the local county matters that intimately touch the daily lives of citizens.

Writing only for himself, Justice Frankfurter found state involvement because state election officials had participated as voters in the Jaybird primary. The four other justices who found the requisite state action joined an opinion by Justice Clark. In his view, the record established that the Jaybirds operated, "as part and parcel of the Democratic Party, an organization existing under the auspices of Texas law." It followed that the result was dictated by Smith v. Allwright. "[When] a state structures its electoral apparatus in a form which devolves upon a political organization the uncontested choice of public officials, that organization itself, in whatever disguise, takes on those attributes of government which draw the Constitution's safeguards into play." Justice Minton cast the sole dissenting vote.

If the state had attempted to control participation in the Jaybird primary, might not the Jaybirds have had a plausible first amendment complaint?

Compare *Terry* to Tashjian v. Republican Party, 479 U.S. 208 (1986). In *Tashjian*, the Court upheld the Republican Party's constitutional challenge to a state law that prohibited nonparty members from participating in party primaries. (The Republicans had adopted a party rule permitting independents to vote in its primaries.) The Court held that

> [the] Party's attempt to broaden the base of public participation in and support for its activities is conduct undeniably central to the exercise of the right of association. [The] freedom to join together in furtherance of common political beliefs "necessarily presupposes the freedom to identify the people who constitute the association."

Why wasn't the Jaybirds' "freedom to identify the people who constitute the association" constitutionally protected?

When private groups effectively secure the power normally associated with the state, why shouldn't they be subject to the same restrictions? Is it relevant that the Jaybirds were able to wield this power only because of the voluntary decision by most white voters to adhere to the result of the Jaybird primary? Recall that on one theory, this sort of "voluntary" exclusion of discrete and insular minorities from private coalitions is precisely why laws discriminating against such minorities are subject to heightened scrutiny. See Chapter 5, section C1, supra. If the results of such exclusionary coalitions are constitutionally suspect, might the Constitution be thought to establish limits on the ability to form the coalitions in the first place?

For the Court's most recent treatment of the issue of state action and political parties, see Morse v. Republican Party of Virginia, 517 U.S. 186 (1996). The case presented the Court with a question of statutory construction — whether the Virginia Republican Party was obligated under the 1965 Voting Rights Act to obtain preclearance before changing the qualifications for participation in a state nominating convention. In the course of answering this question (in the affirmative), the Court had occasion to distinguish its prior state action precedents:

> In [*Flagg Brothers*] this Court concluded that the [defendants were] not acting under authority explicitly or implicitly delegated by the State when they carried out the challenged actions. In this case, however, [the] Party acted under the authority conferred by the Virginia election code. It was the Commonwealth of Virginia — indeed only Virginia — that had exclusive power to reserve one of the two special ballot provisions for the Party.

Compare Justice Thomas's dissent:

> The Party's selection of a candidate at a convention does not satisfy [the exclusive public function] test. [We] have carefully distinguished the "conduct" of an election by the State from the exercise of private political rights within that State-created framework. Providing an orderly and fair process for the selection of public officers is a classic exclusive state function. . . .
>   [By] contrast, convening the members of a political association in order to select the person who can best represent and advance the group's goals is not, and historically has never been, the province of the State — much less its exclusive province.
>   To be sure, the Party takes advantage of favorable State law when it certifies its candidate for automatic placement on the ballot. Nevertheless, according to our state action cases, that is no basis for treating the Party as the State. The State's conferral of benefits upon an entity — even so great a benefit as monopoly status — is insufficient to convert the entity into a State actor.

b. *Private property and public functions.* Does the public function doctrine help to explain other cases where the Court has placed constitutional limits on the owners of private property? Does it explain *Shelley?*

In Evans v. Newton, section B2, supra, the Court's opinion invalidating the exclusion of blacks from the park created by Senator Bacon's will rested in part on the public character of the facility:

> The service rendered even by a private park of this character is municipal in nature. It is open to every white person, there being no selective element other than race. Golf clubs, social centers, luncheon clubs, schools such as Tuskegee was at least in origin, and other like organizations in the private sector are often racially oriented. A park, on the other hand, is more like a fire department or police department that traditionally serves the community. Mass recreation through the use of parks is plainly in the public domain; and state courts that aid private parties to perform that public function on a segregated basis implicate the State in conduct proscribed by the Fourteenth Amendment.

The public function doctrine also played a role for at least some of the justices in analyzing state responsibility for the racial exclusions at issue in the sit-in cases. See section B2, supra. For example, in a long concurring opinion in Bell v. Maryland, section B2, supra, Justice Goldberg argued that restaurants were places of "public accommodation" that the framers of the fourteenth amendment assumed would be subject to governmental control:

> Prejudice and bigotry in any form are regrettable, but it is the constitutional right of every person to close his home or club to any person or to choose his social intimates and business partners solely on the basis of personal prejudice including race. These and other rights pertaining to privacy and private association are themselves constitutionally protected liberties. [But the] broad acceptance of the public in this and in other restaurants clearly demonstrates that the proprietor's interest in private or unrestricted association is slight. The relationship between the modern innkeeper or restaurateur and the customer is relatively impersonal and evanescent. [As] the history of the common law and, indeed, of our own times graphically illustrates, the interests of proprietors of places of public accommodation have always been adapted to the citizen's felt need for public accommodations, a need which is basic and deep-rooted.

Note that the opinion for the Court in *Evans* and Justice Goldberg's concurrence in *Bell* both emphasize the strand in *Marsh* that focused on the "inherently" public or private character of the activity involved. Both opinions tend to underplay the strand that focused on the degree to which private entities exercise the kind of coercive power normally associated with the state. Which version of the public function doctrine is more persuasive?

4. *Retreat from* Marsh? The modern Court has demonstrated considerable reluctance to burden private entities with constitutional requirements through the public function doctrine. Very few functions are now "public" for purposes of the state action doctrine. In the Court's current formulation, a function must be traditionally an exclusive state function in order to be subject to the Constitution. Thus, although shopping centers are generally as open to the public as parks, the Court has held that their owners are not bound by the first amendment. See Hudgens v. NLRB, infra, this section. Although major utilities arguably exercise coercive power rivaling that of the state, the Court has refused to impose the requirements of procedural due process on them. See Jackson v. Metropolitan Edison Co., section C2, supra, and infra this section. And in *Flagg Brothers*, section B1, supra, the Court rejected respondents' argument that "dispute resolution" was a public function. But it did find it necessary to warn that

> there are a number of state and municipal functions not covered by our election cases or governed by the reasoning of *Marsh* which have been administered with a greater degree of exclusivity by States and [municipalities]. Among these are such functions as education, fire and police protection, and tax collection. We express no view as to the extent, if any, to which a city or State might be free to delegate to private parties the performance of such functions and thereby avoid the strictures of the Fourteenth Amendment.

As you read the material below, consider whether the Court has embraced either the view of the public function doctrine emphasizing the "inherently public" character of the activity or the version emphasizing private coercion. In its current form, does the doctrine take sufficient account of the need to leave "private space" free from government control? Is it sufficiently attentive to the risk that constitutional values will be undermined by private power?

JACKSON v. METROPOLITAN EDISON CO., 419 U.S. 345 (1974). This case, which is summarized in more detail at section C2 supra, arose when Metropolitan, a privately owned utility holding a certificate of public convenience issued by the Pennsylvania Public Utility Commission, terminated Jackson's electrical service for alleged nonpayment of bills. Jackson claimed that her due process rights were violated because she was not accorded a hearing prior to the termination. Justice Rehnquist delivered the Court's opinion:

"Petitioner [urges] that state action is present because respondent provides an essential public service required to be supplied on a reasonably continuous basis by [state law], and hence performs a 'public function.' We have, of course, found state action present in the exercise by a private entity of powers traditionally exclusively reserved to the State. [Nixon v. Condon; *Marsh*; Evans v. Newton.] If we were dealing with the exercise by Metropolitan of some power delegated to it by the State which is traditionally associated with sovereignty, such as eminent domain, our case would be quite a different one. But while the Pennsylvania statute imposes an obligation to furnish service on regulated utilities, it imposes no such obligation on the State. The Pennsylvania courts have rejected the contention that the furnishing of utility services is either a state function or a municipal duty.

"Perhaps in recognition of the fact that the supplying of utility service is not traditionally the exclusive prerogative of the State, petitioner invites the expansion of the doctrine of this limited line of cases into a broad principle that all businesses 'affected with the public interest' are state actors in all their actions.

"We decline the invitation for reasons stated long ago in Nebbia v. New York, 291 U.S. 502 (1934), in the course of rejecting a substantive due process attack on state legislation:

> It is clear that there is no closed class or category of businesses affected with a public interest. . . . The phrase "affected with a public interest" can, in the nature of things, mean no more than that an industry, for adequate reason, is subject to control for the public good. In several of the decisions of this court wherein the expressions "affected with a public interest," and "clothed with a public use," have been brought forward as the criteria . . . it has been admitted that they are not susceptible of definition and form an unsatisfactory test. . . .

"Doctors, optometrists, lawyers, Metropolitan, and Nebbia's upstate New York grocery selling a quart of milk are all in regulated businesses, providing arguably essential goods and services, 'affected with a public interest.' We do not believe that such a status converts their every action, absent more, into that of the State."

Justice Douglas filed a dissenting opinion: "I agree that doctors, lawyers, and grocers are not transformed into state actors simply because they provide arguably essential goods and services and are regulated by the State. In the present case, however, respondent is not just one person among many; it is the only public utility furnishing electric power in the city. When power is denied a householder, the home, under modern conditions, is likely to become unlivable."

Justice Marshall also filed a dissenting opinion: "Private parties performing functions affecting the public interest can often make a persuasive claim to be free of the constitutional requirements applicable to governmental institutions because of the value of preserving a private sector in which the opportunity for individual choice is maximized. Maintaining the private status of parochial schools [advances] just this value. In the due process area, a similar value of diversity may often be furthered by allowing various private institutions the flexibility to select procedures that fit their particular needs. But it is hard to imagine any such interests that are furthered by protecting privately owned public utility companies from meeting the constitutional standards that would apply if the companies were state owned. The values of pluralism and diversity are simply not relevant when the private company is the only electric company in town."

Note: Public Functions as "Exclusive Prerogatives" of the State

1. *Post*-Jackson *developments.* In a series of decisions since *Jackson*, the Court has rejected "public function" arguments in many contexts:

a. *Shopping centers.* The Court overruled a prior decision and held that *Marsh* did not apply to picketing on the grounds of a private shopping center in Hudgens v. NLRB, 424 U.S. 507 (1976). It distinguished *Marsh* on the ground that shopping centers invited the public onto their property for only a limited purpose. Justice Marshall, joined by Justice Brennan, dissented.

b. *Dispute resolution.* As noted above, in *Flagg Brothers*, section B1, supra, the Court held that resolution of disputes between creditors and debtors is not a "public function." The Court focused primarily on the "exclusivity" requirement. "Creditors and debtors have had available to them historically a far wider number of choices than has one who would be an elected public official, or a member of Jehovah's Witnesses who wished to distribute literature in Chickasaw, Ala., at the time *Marsh* was decided."

c. *Schools.* In *Rendell-Baker*, section C1, supra, the Court held that a private school for "maladjusted" high school students was not subject to constitutional constraints. The Court reached this conclusion even though students were placed in the program by public officials and virtually all of the school's funding came from public sources. With regard to petitioners' public function argument, the Court conceded that "[there] can be no doubt that the education of maladjusted high school students is a public function." But in the Court's view, that was "only the beginning of the inquiry." It must further be shown that the function has been "traditionally the exclusive prerogative of the State. [Quoting from *Jackson*.]" Here, the state had elected to provide services for these students at public expense, but "[that] legislative policy choice in no way makes these services the exclusive province of the State. [That] a private entity performs a function which serves the public does not make its acts state action." Justice Marshall, joined by Justice Brennan, dissented.

d. *Nursing homes.* In Blum v. Yaretsky, section C1, supra, a case decided on the same day as *Rendell-Baker*, the Court announced that nursing homes in receipt of federal Medicaid payments were not performing a public function when they decided on the level of care for their patients. The Court rejected respondents' argument that the Medicaid statute and state law made the state responsible for providing every Medicaid patient with nursing home services. Moreover, "[even] if respondents' characterization of the State's duties were correct, [it] would not follow that decisions made in the day-to-day administration of a nursing home are the kind of decisions traditionally and exclusively made by the sovereign for and on behalf of the public." Justice Brennan, joined by Justice Marshall, dissented.

e. *Amateur sports.* In San Francisco Arts & Athletics, Inc. v. United States Olympic Committee, section C1, supra, the Court, in an opinion by Justice Powell, held that the United States Olympic Committee was not a state actor.

The Amateur Sports Act of 1978 created the committee as a "private [corpora-tion] established under Federal law." The act imposed certain requirements on the committee, provided for some funding for it, and granted it exclusive use of the word "Olympic." The Court held that

[the act] merely authorized the [committee] to coordinate activities that always have been performed by private entities. Neither the conduct nor the coordination of amateur sports has been a traditional governmental function.

Compare Justice Brennan's dissenting opinion:

In the Amateur Sports Act of 1978, Congress placed the power and prestige of the United States Government behind a single, central sports organization. Congress delegated to the [committee] functions that Government actors traditionally per-form — the representation of the Nation abroad and the administration of all private organizations in a particular economic sector. The representation function is of particular significance here [because] an organization that need not adhere to the Constitution cannot meaningfully represent this Nation. The Government is free, of course, to "privatize" some functions it would otherwise perform. But such privatization ought not automatically release those who perform government func-tions from constitutional obligations.

f. *Peremptory challenges.* Edmonson v. Leesville Concrete Co., 500 U.S. 614 (1991), is a rare exception to the modern Court's hostility to the public function doctrine. The Court relied in part on the doctrine to hold that private litigants in civil cases were state actors for constitutional purposes when they utilized peremptory challenges to eliminate jurors on the basis of race. Writing for six justices, Justice Kennedy argued that

[the] peremptory challenge is used in selecting an entity that is a quintessential governmental body, having no attributes of a private actor. . . .
    If a government confers on a private body the power to choose the government's employees or officials, the private body will be bound by the constitutional mandate of race-neutrality. [At] least a plurality of the Court recognized this principle in [Terry v. Adams]. There we found state action in a scheme in which a private organization known as the Jaybird Democratic Association conducted whites-only elections to select candidates to run in a Democratic primary [election]. . . .
    The principle that the selection of state officials, other than through election of all qualified voters, may constitute state action applies with even greater force in the context of jury selection through peremptory challenges. Though the motive of a peremptory challenge may be to protect a private interest, the objective of jury selection proceedings is to determine representation on a governmental body.

Justice O'Connor, joined by Chief Justice Rehnquist and Justice Scalia, wrote a dissenting opinion.
    See also Georgia v. McCollum, 505 U.S. 42 (1992) (holding that a defense attorney in a criminal trial who utilizes peremptory strikes on a racially discrim-inatory basis is a government actor for constitutional purposes).
    2. Jackson *and the legacy of* Marsh. Recall that the public function doctrine, as first stated in *Marsh*, seemed to rest on two interlocking rationales. First, constitutional restraints were appropriate because company towns had the power to undermine freedom as effectively as the state. Second, state intervention

to control this power was not itself subversive of individual liberty because company towns were already open to the public and serving public functions. Much of the debate in the post-*Marsh* cases stems from disagreement about which of these rationales is dominant. Does either of the original *Marsh* rationales survive *Jackson*? The emphasis on alternative means of dispute resolution in *Flagg Brothers* arguably relates to the degree of coercive power possessed by creditors. The argument that shopping centers extend an invitation to the public for only limited purposes seems responsive to the "open to the public" rationale. More generally, however, the Court now appears ready to exempt "private" entities from constitutional responsibilities even in situations in which both *Marsh* requirements are satisfied.

Instead of inquiring into the power of the private entity and its claim to individual autonomy, the *Jackson* Court asked whether its function has "traditionally" been performed by the state and whether it is the "exclusive" prerogative of the state. Even if this test is workable (see infra this Note), why should the "state action" question turn on these factors? Note, for example, that even the municipal functions at stake in *Marsh* were hardly the "exclusive" prerogatives of the state. Indeed, Justice Black argued that constitutional constraints were necessary precisely because "[many] people in the United States live in company-owned towns." Would it have made an important difference if such towns were a new development or had existed for a long time?

3. *Public functions, baselines, and natural law.* What does it mean for a function to be traditionally the exclusive prerogative of the state? Whether a function is "exclusively" the state's may depend on how the function is characterized. In *Flagg Brothers*, for example, it may make an important difference whether one thinks of the function as "dispute resolution" (nonexclusive) or as the compelled transfer of property interests (arguably exclusive). Does the *Jackson* test ultimately depend on a "natural law" view of the functions appropriately attributable to state and individual? Consider in this connection the *Jackson* Court's reliance on Nebbia v. New York, 291 U.S. 502 (1934). In *Nebbia*, which marked the beginning of the end of the "*Lochner* era," the Court upheld the constitutionality of state legislation fixing the price of milk. See Chapter 6, section D, supra. Before the demise of *Lochner*, the Court treated the private sphere as a preconstitutional given that neither legislature nor court had the power to alter. In more recent years, the Court has generally followed *Nebbia* and, at least in the area of "social and economic legislation," treated the division between public and private as a matter of legislative discretion. Is the use of *Nebbia* ironic in light of the fact that something like *Lochner* is plausibly at work in Justice Rehnquist's opinion itself? Does a version of *Lochner* survive as a "natural" barrier to judicial, as opposed to legislative, invasions of the private sphere? Is there good reason to treat legislative and judicial invasions differently?

Consider L. Seidman and M. Tushnet, Remnants of Belief: Contemporary Constitutional Issues 67–68 (1996):

[The] New Deal constitutional revolution left the public/private distinction in tatters. But although the story of its demise has been told many times, most renditions have ignored a remarkable paradox. At the moment when the distinction collapsed as a limitation on governmental power, it replicated itself as a limitation on federal judicial power. For the very reason that *Lochner*-like reasoning was rejected as a restraint on government intervention, it had to be accepted as a restraint on judicial intervention.

[The new empowerment of government meant that] in the absence of a state action doctrine courts would have been free to order a comprehensive allocation of resources on their own initiative. Since the government was now empowered to distribute goods in any way it chose, its failure to do so had to be treated as a governmental decision that was subject to constitutional review. . . .

Restraint on the judiciary was therefore necessary to make the space for the newly unrestrained political branches to engage in the vigorous government intervention at the heart of the New Deal. . . .

We are now [in] a position to understand why [state action opinions] are [unsatisfactory]. The critique of the public-private distinction that made a reformulated state action doctrine necessary also made it impossible. [State] action cases are hard because the New Deal revolution necessitated a newly formulated state action requirement to curb judicial power and simultaneously demolished the analytic tools that could have been used to articulate the requirement convincingly.

E.   UNCONSTITUTIONAL CONDITIONS AND THE BENEFIT/BURDEN DISTINCTION

At many places in this book, we have seen the problem of "unconstitutional conditions" — the problem that arises when government attaches constitutionally troublesome "strings" to government benefits, such as housing, employment, money, or licenses. Suppose, for example, the government says that only Democrats may work in the State Department, or that members of the Central Intelligence Agency must agree not to write about their activities, or that welfare beneficiaries must allow searches of their homes, or that medical facilities receiving federal funds must agree not to perform certain medical procedures. The question raised by the problem of unconstitutional conditions is how, and whether, these sorts of cases should be treated differently from "ordinary" constitutional cases.

The general problem is ubiquitous. It has clear connections to the state action doctrine because it might be said that when a state "merely" conditions a benefit, it has done nothing with respect to the person who does not receive the benefit. Moreover, as we shall see, the burden/benefit distinction raises questions about appropriate baselines for deciding whether government has behaved neutrally — questions similar to those raised in the state action context.

The following cases have been considered in other parts of this book. We offer excerpts from the majority opinions (notably, all four produced divided Courts) in order to give a sense of why they all involved arguably unconstitutional conditions.

RUST v. SULLIVAN, 500 U.S. 173 (1991). In this case, the Court upheld a new administrative interpretation of a statute. The statute said that federal funds for family services shall not "be used in programs where abortion is a method of family planning." The new administrative interpretation was that federal funds could not be used not only for abortion itself but also for all activities that "encourage, promote or advocate abortion as a method of family planning." In an opinion by Chief Justice Rehnquist, the Court said:

"The Government can, without violating the Constitution, selectively fund a program to encourage certain activities it believes to be in the public interest, without at the same time funding an alternate program which seeks to deal with the problem in another way. In so doing, the Government has not discriminated on the basis of viewpoint; it has merely chosen to fund one activity to the exclusion of the other. . . .

"[Petitioners'] assertions ultimately boil down to the position that if the government chooses to subsidize one protected right, it must subsidize analogous counterpart rights. But the Court has soundly rejected that proposition. Within far broader limits than petitioners are willing to concede, when the government appropriates public funds to establish a program it is entitled to define the limits of that program. . . .

"Petitioners also contend that the restrictions on the subsidization of abortion-related speech contained in the regulations are impermissible because they condition the receipt of a benefit . . . on the relinquishment of a constitutional right, the right to engage in abortion advocacy and counseling. [Petitioners] argue that 'even though the government may deny [a] . . . benefit for any number of reasons, there are some reasons upon which the government may not rely. It may not deny a benefit to a person on a basis that infringes his constitutionally protected interests — especially, his interest in freedom of speech.'

"Petitioners' reliance on these cases is unavailing, however, because here the government is not denying a benefit to anyone, but is instead simply insisting that public funds be spent for the purposes for which they were authorized. The Secretary's regulations do not force the Title X grantee to give up abortion-related speech; they merely require that the grantee keep such activities separate and distinct from Title X activities. . . .

"In contrast, our 'unconstitutional conditions' cases involve situations in which the government has placed a condition on the recipient of the subsidy rather than on a particular program or service, thus effectively prohibiting the recipient from engaging in the protected conduct outside the scope of the federally funded program. In [FCC v. League of Women Voters, infra, this section,] we invalidated a federal law providing that noncommercial television and radio stations that receive federal grants may not 'engage in editorializing.' Under the law, a recipient of federal funds was 'barred absolutely from all editorializing' because it 'is not able to segregate its activities according to the source of its funding' and thus 'has no way of limiting the use of its federal funds to all non-editorializing activities.' . . .

"Similarly, in [Regan v. Taxation with Representation of Washington, infra, this section,] we held that Congress could [reasonably] refuse to subsidize the lobbying activities of tax-exempt charitable organizations by prohibiting such organizations from using tax-deductible contributions to support their lobbying efforts. In so holding, we explained that such organizations remained free 'to receive deductible contributions to support . . . nonlobbying activit[ies].' . . .

"The condition that federal funds will be used only to further the purposes of a grant does not violate constitutional rights. . . .

"The same principles apply to petitioners' claim that the regulations abridge the free speech rights of the grantee's staff. [The] regulations, which govern solely the scope of the Title X project's activities, do not in any way restrict the activities of those persons acting as private individuals. The employees' freedom of expression is limited during the time that they actually work for the project; but this limitation is a consequence of their decision to accept employment in a project, the scope of which is permissibly restricted by the funding authority."

MAHER v. ROE, 432 U.S. 464 (1977). The Court upheld a state regulation granting Medicaid benefits for childbirth, but denying such benefits for nontherapeutic abortions (i.e., abortions that are not "medically necessary"). Justice Powell delivered the opinion of the Court:

"The Constitution imposes no obligation on the States to pay the pregnancy-related medical expenses of indigent women, or indeed to pay any of the medical expenses of indigents. But when a State decides to alleviate some of the hardships of poverty by providing medical care, the manner in which it dispenses benefits is subject to constitutional limitations. Appellees' claim is that [the State] must accord equal treatment to both abortion and childbirth, and may not evidence a policy preference by funding only the medical expenses incident to childbirth. This [presents] a question [under] the Equal Protection Clause. . . .

"This case involves no discrimination against a suspect class. An indigent woman desiring an abortion does not come within the limited category of [suspect classes]. Nor does the fact that the impact of the regulation falls upon those who cannot pay lead to a different conclusion.

"The [regulation] before us is different in kind from the laws invalidated in our previous [decisions. It] places no obstacles — absolute or otherwise — in the pregnant woman's path to an abortion. An indigent woman who desires an abortion suffers no disadvantage as a consequence of [the State's] decision to fund childbirth; she continues as before to be dependent on private sources for the service she desires. The State may have made childbirth a more attractive alternative, thereby influencing the woman's decision, but it has imposed no restriction on access to abortions that was not already there. The indigency that may make it difficult — and in some cases, perhaps, impossible — for some women to have abortions is neither created nor in any way affected by [the] regulation. [The challenged] regulation does not impinge upon the fundamental right recognized in *Roe*.

"[Appellees] rely on [Shapiro v. Thompson, infra, this section, and Memorial Hospital v. Maricopa County, 415 U.S. 250 (1974)]. Appellees' reliance on the penalty analysis of [those decisions] is misplaced. [*Shapiro*] and *Maricopa County* recognized that denial of welfare to one who had recently exercised the right to travel [was] sufficiently analogous to a criminal fine to justify strict judicial scrutiny. If [the State] denied general welfare benefits to all women who had obtained abortions and who were otherwise entitled to the benefits, we would have a close analogy [to] *Shapiro*, and strict scrutiny might be [appropriate]. But the claim here is that the State 'penalizes' the woman's decision to have an abortion by refusing to pay for it. *Shapiro* and *Maricopa County* did not hold that States would penalize the right to travel [by] refusing to pay the bus fares of the indigent [travelers]. Sherbert v. Verner [see Chapter 8, section C, supra] similarly is inapplicable here. . . .

"Our conclusion signals no retreat from [*Roe*]. There is a basic difference between direct state interference with a protected activity and state encouragement of an alternative [activity]. Constitutional concerns are greatest when the State attempts to impose its will by force of law; the State's power to encourage actions deemed to be in the public interest is necessarily far broader. . . .'"

NATIONAL FEDERATION OF INDEPENDENT BUSINESS v. SEBELIUS, 567 U.S. 519 (2012). Under the Medicaid program, Congress provides grants to the states to pay for the health care of poor people. To receive the grants, states must contribute to the program, cover certain specified individuals, and meet other conditions. In the Affordable Care Act, as part of an effort to provide insurance to all Americans, Congress expanded the Medicaid program to provide coverage to all individuals above the age of 65 and below 133 percent of the poverty level. For the first few years, the federal government would bear the full cost of the expansion, but then its share would decline gradually to 90 percent. States that decline to accept the expansion would lose all Medicaid funding.

Twenty-six states challenged Congress's authority to enact the expansion under the so-called "spending clause" of the Constitution, article I, section 8, clause 1. They maintained that the withdrawal of all Medicaid funding if they did not participate in the expansion was a threat rather than an offer and, therefore, exceeded Congress's spending clause power.

Although no opinion garnered majority support, the Court upheld the expansion but held that the threatened withdrawal of all Medicaid funding was unconstitutional. In an opinion joined by Justices Breyer and Kagan, Chief Justice Roberts stated that "[we] have long recognized that Congress may use [the spending] power to grant federal funds to the States, and may condition such a grant upon the States' 'taking certain actions that Congress could not require them to take. . . .'

"But when 'pressure turns into compulsion,' legislation runs contrary to our system of federalism. . . .

"We have upheld Congress's authority to condition the receipt of funds on the States' complying with restrictions on the use of those funds, because that is the means by which Congress ensures that the funds are spent according to its view of the 'general Welfare.' Conditions that do not here govern the use of the funds, however, cannot be justified on that basis. When, for example, such conditions take the form of threats to terminate other significant independent grants, the conditions are properly viewed as a means of pressuring the States to accept policy changes. . . .

"Medicaid spending accounts for over 20 percent of the average State's total budget, with federal funds covering 50 to 83 percent of those costs. The threatened loss of over 10 percent of a State's overall budget [is] economic dragooning that leaves the States with no real option but to acquiesce in the Medicaid expansion.

"Here, the Government claims that the Medicaid expansion is properly viewed merely as a modification of the existing program because the States agreed that Congress could change the terms of Medicaid when they signed on in the first place. The Government observes that the Social Security Act, which includes the original Medicaid provisions, contains a clause expressly reserving '[t]he right to alter, amend, or repeal any provision' of that statute.

"The Medicaid expansion, however, accomplishes a shift in kind, not merely degree. The original program was designed to cover medical services for four particular categories of the needy: the disabled, the blind, the elderly, and needy families with dependent children. Previous amendments to Medicaid eligibility merely altered and expanded the boundaries of these categories. Under the Affordable Care Act, Medicaid is transformed into a program to meet the health care needs of the entire nonelderly population with income below 133 percent of the poverty level. It is no longer a program to care for the neediest among us, but rather an element of a comprehensive national plan to provide universal health insurance coverage. . . ."

A joint opinion written by Justices Scalia, Thomas, Kennedy, and Alito, agreed that the Medicaid expansion was unconstitutionally coercive, but would have invalidated the expansion itself, not just the threat of withdrawal of funds.

"[The] legitimacy of attaching conditions to federal grants to the States depends on the voluntariness of the States' choice to accept or decline the offered package. Therefore, if States really have no choice other than to accept the package, the offer is coercive, and the conditions cannot be sustained under the spending power. . . .

"When a heavy federal tax is levied to support a federal program that offers large grants to the States, States may, as a practical matter, be unable to refuse to participate in the federal program and to substitute a state alternative. Even if a State believes that the federal program is ineffective and inefficient, withdrawal would likely force the State to impose a huge tax increase on its residents, and this new state tax would come on top of the federal taxes already paid by residents to support subsidies to participating States. . . ."

Justice Ginsburg, joined by Justice Sotomayor, disagreed. "Medicaid, as amended by the ACA [is] not two spending programs; it is a single program with a constant aim — to enable poor persons to receive basic health care when they need it. Given past expansions, plus express statutory warning that Congress may change the requirements participating States must meet, there can be no tenable claim that the ACA fails for lack of notice. . . .

"At bottom, my colleagues' position is that the States' reliance on federal funds limits Congress' authority to alter its spending programs. This gets things backwards: Congress, not the States, is tasked with spending federal money in service of the general welfare. And each successive Congress is empowered to appropriate funds as it sees fit. When the 110th Congress reached a conclusion about Medicaid funds that differed from its predecessors' view, it abridged no State's right to 'existing,' or 'pre-existing,' funds. [For] in fact, there are no such funds. There is only money States *anticipate* receiving from future Congresses."

NOLLAN v. CALIFORNIA COASTAL COMMISSION, 483 U.S. 825 (1987). In this case, the California Coastal Commission conditioned the grant of a permit to rebuild appellants' house on their transfer to the public of an easement across their beachfront property. The Court held that the attempt to impose this condition was a taking in the form of an unconstitutional condition. Justice Scalia wrote for the Court:

"Justice Brennan [suggests] that the Commission's public announcement of its intention to condition the rebuilding of houses on the transfer of easements of access caused the Nollans to have 'no reasonable claim to any expectation of being able to exclude members of the public' from walking across their beach.

"[But] the right to build on one's own property — even though its exercise can be subjected to legitimate permitting requirements — cannot remotely be described as a 'government benefit.' [Nor] are the Nollans' rights altered because they acquired the land well after the Commission had begun to implement its policy. So long as the Commission could not have deprived the prior owners of the easement without compensating them, the prior owners must be understood to have transferred their full property rights in conveying the lot.

"Given, then, that requiring uncompensated conveyance of the easement outright would violate the Fourteenth Amendment, the question becomes whether requiring it to be conveyed as a condition for issuing a land use permit alters the outcome. . . .

"[If] the Commission attached to the permit some condition that would have protected the public's ability to see the beach notwithstanding construction of the new house — for example, a height limitation, a width restriction, or a ban on fences — so long as the Commission could have exercised its police power (as we [assume] it could) to forbid construction of the house altogether, imposition of the condition would also be constitutional. Moreover, [the] condition would be constitutional even if it consisted of the requirement that the [appellants] provide a viewing spot on their property for passersby with whose sighting of the ocean their new house would interfere. Although such a requirement [would] have to be considered a taking if it were not attached to a development permit, the Commission's assumed power to forbid construction of the house in order to protect the public's view of the beach must surely include the power to condition construction upon some concession by the owner, even a concession of property rights, that serves the same end. . . .

"The evident constitutional propriety disappears, however, if the condition substituted for the prohibition utterly fails to further the end advanced as the justification for the prohibition. When that essential nexus is eliminated, the situation becomes the same as if California law forbade shouting fire in a crowded theater, but granted dispensations to those willing to contribute $100 to the state treasury. [In] short, unless the permit condition serves the same governmental purpose as the development ban, the building restriction is not a valid regulation of land use but 'an out-and-out plan of extortion.' . . ."

The Court elaborated on its *Nollan* holding in Koontz v. St. Johns River Water Management District, 570 U.S. ___ 133 S. Ct. 2586 (2013), where it held that the same principle was applicable when, instead of accepting the condition, as the landowner had in *Nollan*, the landholder rejected the condition leading to the denial of a permit. Writing for five justices, Justice Alito stated:

"Our decisions [reflect] two realities of the permitting process. The first is that land-use permit applicants are especially vulnerable to the type of coercion that the unconstitutional conditions doctrine prohibits because the government often has broad discretion to deny a permit that is worth far more than property it would like to take. By conditioning a building permit on the owner's deeding over a public right-of-way, for example, the government can pressure an owner into voluntarily giving up property for which the Fifth Amendment would otherwise require just compensation. So long as the building permit is more valuable than any just compensation the owner could hope to receive for the right-of-way, the owner is likely to accede to the government's demand no matter how unreasonable. Extortionate demands of this sort frustrate the Fifth Amendment right to just compensation, and the unconstitutional conditions doctrine prohibits them.

"The second reality of the permitting process is that many proposed land uses threaten to impose costs on the public that dedications of property can offset. [Insisting] that landowners internalize the negative externalities of their conduct is a hallmark of responsible land-use policy, and we have long sustained such regulations against constitutional attack.

"*Nollan* [accommodates] both realities by allowing the government to condition approval of a permit on the dedication of property to the public so long as there is a 'nexus' and 'rough proportionality' between the property the government demands and the social costs of the applicant's proposal. Our precedents thus enable permitting authorities to insist that applicants bear the full costs of their proposals while still forbidding the government from engaging in 'out-and-out . . . extortion' that would thwart the Fifth Amendment right to just compensation."

Note: Benefits, Burdens, and Coercion

1. *Origins of the unconstitutional conditions doctrine.* The cases suggest that some, but not at all, conditions on government benefits are constitutionally troublesome. But this is a relatively new development. For a long time, courts concluded that the government could accompany benefits with whatever conditions it chose. This position was reflected in many opinions by Justice Holmes, who, in a case involving a discharge of a police officer for his political views, responded: "The petitioner may have a constitutional right to talk politics, but he has no constitutional right to be a policeman. . . . The servant cannot complain, as he takes the employment on the terms that are offered him." McAuliffe v. Mayor of New Bedford, 155 Mass. 216, 220, 29 N.E. 517, 518 (1892). Eventually the Court concluded that this position was too broad. Suppose, for example, access to federally funded Medicaid was limited to people with a certain political view; surely this could not be acceptable. Before the New Deal, the Court invalidated a state's effort to allow companies to use public highways only after receiving a permit certifying that the business was for the "public convenience and necessity." Frost & Frost Trucking Co. v. Railroad Commission, 271 U.S. 583 (1926). Thus, the Court started to give birth to the idea — recognized in Rust v. Sullivan — that government may not use its "greater power" to deny a benefit altogether as a justification for exercising the "lesser power" to grant the benefit on such terms as it chooses. See Van Alstyne, The Demise of the Right-Privilege Distinction in Constitutional Law, 81 Harv. L. Rev. 1439 (1968).

2. *The "greater power" and the question of waiver.* The Court's general repudiation of Holmes's position raises many questions, especially because that position seems quite logical. Exactly why is government prohibited from exercising "the lesser power"? And how can someone who has voluntarily waived her constitutional rights be heard to complain about the waiver? Consider, for example, the practice of plea bargaining. In over 90 percent of criminal cases, defendants give up their constitutional right to a jury trial in exchange for a reduced sentence. Should we be troubled by this practice? Suppose, for example, that a judge offered a convicted sex offender the option of serving a shorter prison sentence if he agreed to undergo chemical castration? If the defendant remains free to reject the offer, does the offer make him worse off? Suppose that the shorter sentence were conditioned on regular church attendance? For a qualified defense of Holmes's position, see Easterbrook, Insider Trading, Secret Agents, Evidentiary Privileges, and the Production of Information, 1981 Sup. Ct. Rev. 309.

Consider these responses to the Holmes position:

a. The Constitution limits the reasons for government action. If the government says that welfare recipients must vote for the President, it has acted for an illegitimate reason. The illegitimacy of the reason dooms the law. Hence, both the "greater power" and the "waiver" arguments are unconvincing.

b. The government may not do indirectly what it may not do directly. It may not bring about what is in the end a constitutionally forbidden result by using its power over dollars, jobs, and licenses. See Sullivan, Unconstitutional Conditions, 102 Harv. L. Rev. 1413 (1989), for general discussion of this argument and argument a above.

c. "[The waiver argument] ignores monopoly and collective action problems, which also induce individuals to take actions that benefit their private, but not the social interest. . . . The reasons that lead us not to enforce some private bargains can thus explain why certain bargains between the government and the individual are not enforced. . . . [Limits] on the types of gains that the state can hope to extract by bargaining with its citizens can limit the social loss associated with strategic behavior. . . . The imposition of a condition on a grant is often an attempt to shift some portion of [the general social surplus] from some persons or interest groups to others. . . . The bargain that is made with one citizen may have the effect of freezing other citizens out of the market or setting them at a competitive disadvantage." Epstein, Foreword: Unconstitutional Conditions, State Power, and the Limits of Consent, 102 Harv. L. Rev. 4, 14, 102–103 (1988).

d. The problem with the waiver argument is that in many cases, a seemingly individual waiver has serious systemic effects, extending far beyond the single case. Individual citizens may often find it in their interest to give up the right of free speech in return for government benefits. But if government is permitted to obtain a number of individual waivers of the free speech right, the aggregate effect on free speech could be substantial, and the deliberative processes of the community could be skewed. See Cole, Beyond Unconstitutional Conditions: Charting Spheres of Neutrality in Government-Funded Speech, 67 N.Y.U. L. Rev. 675 (1992). See generally R. Epstein, Bargaining with the State (1994), for general discussion of this and related points.

3. *The shape of the doctrine.* The cases suggest three points that seem to organize much of current law:

a. Government is under no obligation to subsidize activity, including, for example, speech, voting, or abortion. Refusals to subsidize are by themselves acceptable, even if people have a constitutional right to do the relevant activity and to be free from coercion in so doing. See, e.g., Harris v. McRae, 448 U.S. 297 (1980); *Rust*; Regan v. Taxation with Representation of Washington, 461 U.S. 540 (1983) (upholding a federal statute saying that contributions to an otherwise tax-exempt organization, other than a tax-exempt veterans' organization, are not tax deductible if a substantial part of the organization's activities consists of attempts to influence legislation).

b. In the first amendment context, government may speak however it wishes. Public officials may say whatever they want. See *Rust*.

c. Government may not use its power over funds or other benefits to pressure people (or states) to relinquish rights that they "otherwise have," or to "penalize" the exercise of constitutional rights, at least when the limitation on exercise of the rights is unrelated to the purpose of the funding. Government cannot say that, as a condition for receiving welfare, poor people must agree to vote for a certain political party. It cannot tell you that if you want a driver's license, you must agree not to criticize the President or not to have an abortion. See FCC v. League of Women Voters, 468 U.S. 364 (1983); Shapiro v. Thompson, 394 U.S. 618 (1969) (holding that government may not limit welfare benefits to people who have not recently exercised their constitutional right to interstate travel); Sherbert v. Verner, 374 U.S. 398 (1963) (holding that government may not condition receipt of unemployment benefits on recipient's willingness to work on the Sabbath).

4. *"Mere" subsidies.* These propositions raise several questions. For one thing, it may be hard to know in which of the three categories a certain case falls. When do we have a mere failure to subsidize, and when do we have an impermissible penalty? A useful guide comes from FCC v. League of Women Voters, supra, and Regan v. Taxation with Representation, supra. In the first case, the Court said that government could not prohibit noncommercial education stations receiving

funding from the Corporation for Public Broadcasting from engaging in editorializing. In the second case, the Court said that it was permissible for the government not to subsidize — through a tax deduction — attempts to influence legislation. The cases were different because *Taxation with Representation* involved a ban on the use of taxpayer funds, whereas *League of Women Voters* involved a ban on the use of private as well as taxpayer funds. This is the basic point on which the Court is insisting in Rust v. Sullivan.

But sometimes this distinction is not so clear. The majority in Rust v. Sullivan thought that the case fell into category a; the dissenters thought that it fell into category c. But it might even be urged that the relevant category was b. Government consists, after all, of its employees, and perhaps anyone who accepts money is to that extent a government employee. Can you respond to the argument that *Rust* was an easy case because it involved government speech?

5. *Baselines*. The trickiest category may well be c. How do we know when the restriction is unrelated to the purpose of the funding? Compare, for example, Chief Justice Roberts's opinion in *Sebelius* where he treats the Medicaid expansion as a new, unrelated program, with Justice Ginsburg's dissent, where she treats it as merely an extension of the existing program. When Congress first enacted Medicaid, could it have required coverage of all individuals whose income was below 133 percent of the federal poverty line? If so, would the Medicaid expansion in the Affordable Care Act have been constitutional if, in the first section of the Act, Congress repealed Medicaid and, in the second section, reenacted it together with the expansion? Compare *Sebelius* (Ginsburg, J.) ("A ritualistic requirement that Congress repeal and reenact spending legislation in order to enlarge the population served by a federally funded program would advance no constitutional principle and would scarcely serve the interests of federalism.") with id. (Roberts, C.J.) ("[It] would certainly not be that easy. Practical constraints would plainly inhibit, if not preclude, the Federal Government from repealing the existing program and putting every feature of Medicaid on the table for political reconsideration. Such a massive undertaking would hardly be 'ritualistic.'").

Consider in this regard Harris v. McRae, 448 U.S. 297 (1980), involving a prohibition on the use of federal Medicaid funds for the performance of medically necessary abortions. See Chapter 6, section F2, supra. In *Harris*, the Court, following *Maher*, said that it was dealing with a mere failure to subsidize: "[A] woman's freedom of choice [does not carry] with it a constitutional entitlement to the financial resources to avail herself of the full range of protected choices." In a dissenting opinion, Justice Marshall argued that poor women would "otherwise" receive Medicaid payments: "Appellees have met the statutory requirements for eligibility, but they are excluded because the treatment that is medically necessary involves the exercise of a fundamental right." In a footnote, the Court responded: "A substantial constitutional question would arise if Congress had attempted to withhold all Medicaid benefits from an otherwise eligible candidate because that candidate had exercised her constitutionally protected freedom to terminate her pregnancy by abortion. . . . [But a] mere refusal to fund protected activity, without more, cannot be equated with the imposition of a 'penalty' on that activity." In short, Justice Marshall thought the case involved a penalty, whereas the Court thought it was dealing with a mere refusal to subsidize.

Who gets the better of the argument? And how does the Court tell whether there is a subsidy or a penalty? The answer must depend on the identification of the normal or natural state of affairs — just as in the distinction between a "threat" and an "offer." Thus, the problem "lies in the challenge to specify an appropriate normal course of events from which to judge deviations." See Kreimer, Allocational Sanctions, 132 U. Pa. L. Rev. 1293, 1359 (1984); see also Nozick, Coercion, in Philosophy, Science, and Method 440, 447 (S. Morgenbesser et al. eds., 1969), suggesting that threats involve a departure from a baseline of the "normal course of events." Should the "normal course" be determined by asking what has been done historically? By asking what would in fact be done if the condition were invalidated? See Kreimer, supra, for discussion. Here, there is a question about government neutrality that runs parallel to the questions in the state action area. For a suggestion that the subsidy/penalty distinction is impossible to administer and constitutionally irrelevant, see C. Sunstein, The Partial Constitution 298–301 (1993).

Consider in this regard whether the baseline problem may be different depending on whether one is dealing with a substantive right or a right to equality (embedded, for example, in the equal protection clause). When dealing with a substantive right, the baseline is often thought to be a world without government action. Thus, it might be said, government funding of live child births, but not abortions, does not coerce women into not having abortions because they are no worse off than they would have been if there were no funding at all. (Put differently, the financial pressure not to have an abortion is the product of private markets, rather than state action.) Compare this case to a hypothetical law that funded abortions for white people but not for people of color. Here, the baseline might be taken to be the treatment that white people receive. Even if people of color are no less able to obtain an abortion than they would have been if there were no funding, they are denied equality; this denial might be treated as an independent injury, apart from deprivation of the substantive benefit. How far does the equality argument extend? Consider the extent to which "baseline shifting" in the equality context provides an escape from state action limitations on constitutional obligation.

6. *The search for legitimate motivations.* Perhaps one can make sense of the cases not by asking about baselines, but by asking whether the government has a legitimate motivation for the condition that is said to be unconstitutional. If, for example, government said that companies that operate nuclear power plants must agree to allow inspections — and thus to waive their fourth amendment rights — in return for a license, the condition would almost certainly be constitutional. It would be seen as a legitimate effort to ensure safety. See in this regard Snepp v. United States, 444 U.S. 507 (1980), discussed in Chapter 7, section B3, supra, which upholds the CIA secrecy agreement on the ground that it is a legitimate effort to promote national security interests. By contrast, if government says that welfare beneficiaries must agree to vote for the President, no legitimate motivation is apparent. Instead the government is trying to regulate political behavior.

If the cases are explored in this way, there is no unitary unconstitutional conditions doctrine but instead a set of results that depend on the particular constitutional provision at issue — on what sorts of motivations it allows government to have. And if the issue is explored in this way, the question involves the meaning of the relevant provision, as (arguably) in the state action context. See, for pertinent discussion, Sullivan, supra; Epstein, Foreword, supra; Sunstein, Why the Unconstitutional Conditions Doctrine Is an Anachronism, 70 B.U. L. Rev. 593 (1990); McConnell, The Selective Funding Problem: Abortions and Religious Schools, 104 Harv. L. Rev. 989 (1991). And consider the suggestion that this line of thought leads to the conclusion that "[in] a crucial sense, all constitutional cases are unconstitutional conditions cases. Ordinary property rights are created by a government. . . . When the government says that it will take your property if you do something, it is, in essence, imposing a condition on a right that it has conferred." Sunstein, The Partial Constitution, supra, at 293.

7. *Selective subsidies and the limits of Rust v. Sullivan.* Should *Rust* be read for all that it is worth? Suppose the government decides to fund the Democratic convention but not the Republican convention or to subsidize broadcasters only to the extent that they are praising the current government. Wouldn't this be acceptable in light of *Rust*? If such selective subsidies would be unconstitutional, how can they be distinguished from funding speech opposing the use of illegal drugs but not speech favoring the use of illegal drugs? Does it matter that the speech in *Rust* was ancillary to conduct that government sought not to fund?

The Court has shed some light on these questions in subsequent cases. In Rosenberger v. Rector and Visitors of the University of Virginia, 515 U.S. 819 (1995), the Court struck down a University of Virginia policy authorizing university subsidies of some student publications but forbidding subsidies for student publications that "primarily promotes or manifests a particular belief in or about a deity or an ultimate reality." The University cited *Rust,* which appears strongly supportive of the selective subsidy. But the Court distinguished and narrowed its prior decision in such a way as to leave unsettled the status of viewpoint discrimination in government funding.

The Court explained that government can "regulate the content of what is or is not expressed when it is the speaker or when it enlists private entities to convey its own message." Thus, *Rust* was merely a case in which the government "used private speakers to transmit specific information pertaining to its own program." This means that a government appropriation of "public funds to promote a particular policy of its own" can legitimately be accompanied by appropriate "steps to ensure that its message is neither garbled nor distorted by the grantee." But it does not follow that government may impose "viewpoint-based restrictions" when the government "does not itself speak or subsidize transmittal of a message it favors but instead expends funds to encourage a diversity of views from private speakers." In this case, the University of Virginia did not contend that those who were eligible for university support are the university's agents; student organizations "are not subject to its control and are not its responsibility." Thus, when the university has decided to pay private speakers "who convey their own messages," it "may not silence the expression of selected viewpoints."

There is obvious tension between *Rust* and *Rosenberger,* and the implications of the two cases, taken together, are far from clear. The distinction seems to be that in *Rosenberger* the university did not contend that it was attempting to "convey its own message" or implement "its own program." But what if the university said that its funding policies involved "its own program," broadly speaking? What if the university denied that its purpose was "to encourage a diversity of views from private speakers"? What if the university said that it sought to encourage diversity, but subject to certain restrictions, on the ground that some funding decisions would create too much entanglement between the state and religion? In any case, *Rosenberger* could be understood broadly or very narrowly, and as the opinion is written, it is not clear that it stands as a barrier to a government decision to refuse to fund art that it deems offensive, even on the basis of viewpoint.

Compare in this regard the Court's most sustained encounter with the question of government funding of the arts, National Endowment for the Arts v. Finley, 524 U.S. 569 (1998). There, the Court was asked to assess a statute asking the NEA, in establishing procedures to assess the artistic merit of applicants, to "take into consideration general standards of decency and respect for the diverse beliefs and values of the American public." The Court upheld the statute against facial attack; but what is especially important here is what the Court did not say. The Court did not conclude that government could give out taxpayer funds however it chose. It did not accept a "strong" reading of Rust v. Sullivan, which would allow government to choose, in its discretion, its preferred candidates for public subsidization. Instead, the Court found it necessary to emphasize that the statute at issue was not, in fact, a form of viewpoint discrimination. Thus, the Court said that the considerations listed in the statute are "susceptible to multiple interpretation," and nothing in the law was introduced that "in practice, would effectively preclude or punish the expression of particular views." Both the "decency" and the "respect" criteria could be understood in a constitutional fashion, as, for example, attempting to give special consideration to "projects and productions . . . that reach, or reflect the culture of, a minority, inner city, rural, or tribal community." Because artistic funding was necessarily based on content discrimination, this case was not covered by Rosenberger, which was (in the Court's view) an indiscriminate effort to encourage a diversity of views from the private sphere. And the Court left open the possibility that in particular cases, "the denial of a grant may be shown to be the product of invidious viewpoint discrimination." Thus, any "penalty on disfavored viewpoints" would present "a different case." Justice Souter dissented on the ground that this was in fact a form of viewpoint discrimination; Justice Scalia, joined by Justice Thomas, concurred in the result, invoking a strong reading of Rust and suggesting that government may "earmark NEA funds for projects it deems to be in the public interest without thereby abridging speech."

It is not so easy to reconstruct the law as constituted by Rust, Rosenberger, and Finley. The strong version of Rust appears to have been rejected by the Court; unambiguous viewpoint discrimination appears to be impermissible, even with respect to the allocation of government funds for art. On the other hand, government may itself speak as it wishes, and if government wants to create a "program" for a proposed point of view, and to enlist private speakers in the endeavor, it is permitted to do exactly that. Thus, for example, government might have a project for democracy, or a project for the reduction of smoking among teenagers, and it might pay private speakers to help. It might even be possible for government to have a special artistic project whose purpose is to encourage (for example) celebration of the nation's natural beauty. In such cases, Rust would probably govern. (But what about a program to promote a sitting President's reelection?) Where the government is engaged in a general funding process for art, however, it is unlikely to be permitted to discriminate on the basis of viewpoint. Of course, the distinction between a specific program and a general funding process is very far from transparent.

8. *Examples.* Test your understanding of unconstitutional conditions by exploring the following cases.

(a) Government funds public schools but not private schools. Are parents of children attending private schools being subjected to an unconstitutional condition? See *McConnell,* supra, for discussion. Compare Locke v. Davey,

540 U.S. 712 (2004) (upholding state statute prohibiting state aid to post-secondary students pursuing degrees in theology).

(b) Suppose there is a great deal of criminal activity in a public housing project. The government asks all tenants to sign — as a condition for subsidized housing — an agreement that random searches will be allowed in homes. Is this an unconstitutional condition? What if 90 percent, or 60 percent, or 10 percent of the tenants are in favor of this proposal?

(c) The government decides not to fund artistic activity containing nudity. May an artist complain if his work has not been funded because it contains nudity? Compare Southeastern Promotions v. Conrad, 420 U.S. 546 (1975) (holding that a municipal board's refusal to lease a public auditorium for a production of the musical "Hair" on the ground that nudity was not in the best interests of the community was unconstitutional).

(d) May the government say that Medicaid benefits will be unavailable for any medical expense related to reproduction?

(e) May the government say that, as a condition for receiving a permit to build an expansion of your house near the National Seashore, you will allow access to the beach? See Dolan v. City of Tigard, 512 U.S. 374 (1994), and *Nollan*, supra.

(f) For an interesting unconstitutional conditions decision, see Agency for International Development v. Alliance for Open Society International, 133 S. Ct. 2321 (2013). By statute, Congress authorized the appropriation of billions of dollars to fund efforts by nongovernmental organizations to combat HIV/AIDS worldwide. Congress also imposed two conditions on the receipt of funds: (1) no funds "may be used to promote or advocate the legalization or practice of prostitution"; and (2) no funds may be used by an organization "that does not have a policy explicitly opposing prostitution."

The Court struck down the second condition. It emphasized a distinction between two kinds of conditions: (1) those that define the limits of the government spending program (specifying the activities Congress wants to subsidize) and (2) those that seek to leverage funding to regulate speech outside the contours of the federal program itself. While Congress may limit its own spending, so that cases that fall within category (1) are permissible, Congress faces constitutional limits when it restricts speech in category (2).

The Court held that the restriction at issue fell into the second category: "By demanding that funding recipients adopt — as their own — the Government's view on an issue of public concern, the condition by its very nature affects 'protected conduct outside the scope of the federally funded program.' By requiring recipients to profess a specific belief, the [requirement] goes beyond defining the limits of the federally funded program to defining the recipient." In the Court's view, the requirement "goes beyond preventing recipients from using private funds in a way that would undermine the federal program. It requires them to pledge allegiance to the Government's policy of eradicating prostitution."

Justice Scalia, joined by Justice Thomas, dissented. He contended that the requirement at issue "is nothing more than a means of selecting suitable agents to implement the Government's chosen strategy to eradicate HIV/AIDS. That is perfectly permissible under the Constitution." In his view, "the government may enlist the assistance of those who believe in its ideas to carry them to fruition; and it need not enlist for that purpose those who oppose or do not support the ideas. That seems to me a matter of the most common sense. For example: One of the purposes of America's foreign-aid programs is the fostering of goodwill towards this country. If the organization Hamas — reputed to have an efficient system for delivering welfare — were excluded from a program for the distribution of U.S. food assistance, no one could reasonably object. And that would remain true if Hamas were an organization of United States citizens entitled to the protection of the Constitution. [And] the same is true when the rejected organization is not affirmatively opposed to, but merely unsupportive of, the object of the federal program, which appears to be the case here. (Respondents do not promote prostitution, but neither do they wish to oppose it.) A federal program to encourage healthy eating habits need not be administered by the American Gourmet Society, which has nothing against healthy food but does not insist upon it."

F.   SOME FINAL THOUGHTS

Some commentators have argued that the state action requirement need never prevent a litigant from securing a decision on the merits of a constitutional claim. On this view, it will always be possible to find some government actor whose decisions are responsible for the conduct to which the plaintiff objects — and good lawyers can always structure litigation that will challenge the constitutionality of that official's conduct.

Is this so? Maybe not. Consider the difference between the conduct of large companies, such as Google and Facebook, and the conduct of state governments, such as New York and California. The former need not worry about the Constitution. The same is true of innumerable small companies, which can do their business without thinking about the due process clause, free speech, or the equal protection clause.

There is a good argument that most of American constitutional doctrine is premised on the assumption that personal freedom is linked to the absence of government power. This assumption is built into the very language of constitutional rights: speech is said to be "free" when the government passes no laws abridging it; no process is said to be "due" unless the government changes the status quo by depriving individuals of life, liberty, or property.

Is this assumption justified? Does it embody the right conception of freedom? Does it entail undue respect for baselines formed by current distributions of wealth and power? Could one imagine a system of constitutional law that functioned without it?

Table of Cases

Table of Authorities

_____, Standing to Sue in Public Actions: Is It a Constitutional Requirement?, 78 Yale L.J. 816 (1969), 128

Berger, R., Congress vs. the Supreme Court (1969), 82

_____, Government by Judiciary: The Transformation of the Fourteenth Amendment (1977), 490, 540, 720, 728, 735, 776

_____, Impeachment (1970), 77

_____, Impeachment: The Constitutional Problems (1973), 431, 432

Berman, Originalism Is Bunk, 84 N.Y.U. L. Rev. 1 (2009), 722

Berns, W., The First Amendment and the Future of American Democracy (1976), 1199

Bernstein, D, Lochner's Legacy's Legacy, 82 Tex. L. Rev. 1 (2003), 759, 760

_____, Roots of the "Underclass": The Decline of Laissez-Faire Jurisprudence and the Rise of Racist Labor Legislation, 43 Am. U. L. Rev. 85 (1993), 769

_____, Rehabilitating Lochner: Defending Individual Rights against Progressive Reform (2011), 758

Bessette, W., The Mild Voice of Reason (1994), 20

BeVier, An Informed Public, An Informing Press: The Search for a Constitutional Principle, 68 Cal. L. Rev. 482 (1980), 1408

Bezanson, Art and the Constitution, 93 Iowa L. Rev. 1593 (2008), 1167

_____, Political Agnosticism, Editorial Freedom, and Government Neutrality toward the Press, 72 Iowa L. Rev. 1359 (1987), 1415

Bhagwat, Associational Speech, 120 Yale L.J. 978 (2011), 1044

_____, Details: Specific Facts and the First Amendment, 86 S. Cal. L. Rev. 1 (2012), 1095

_____, Purpose Scrutiny in Constitutional Analysis, 85 Cal. L. Rev. 297 (1997), 1399

_____, Religious Associations: Hosanna-Tabor and the Instrumental Value of Religious Groups, 92 Wash. U. L. Rev. 73 (2014), 1523

_____, The Test That Ate Everything: Intermediate Scrutiny in First Amendment Jurisprudence, 2007 U. Ill. L. Rev. 783, 1249

Bickel, The Original Understanding and the Segregation Decision, 69 Harv. L. Rev. 1 (1955), 490

_____, 22 Pub. Interest 25 (Winter 1971), 1176

Bickel, A., The Least Dangerous Branch: The Supreme Court at the Bar of Politics (1962), 36, 37, 71, 79, 87, 164, 165, 172, 539, 723

_____, The Morality of Consent (1975), 1111, 1200

_____, The Supreme Court and the Idea of Progress (1970), 491, 783

Bikle, Judicial Determination of Questions of Fact Affecting the Constitutional Validity of Legislative Action, 38 Harv. L. Rev. 6 (1924), 756

_____, The Silence of Congress, 41 Harv. L. Rev. 200 (1927), 259

Black, C., The Bill of Rights, 35 N.Y.U. L. Rev. 865 (1960), 1009

_____, Decision According to Law (1981), 81

_____, The Lawfulness of the Segregation Decisions, 69 Yale L.J. 421 (1960), 491, 492, 852

_____, Perspectives in Constitutional Law (1963), 363

_____, Structure and Relationship in Constitutional Law (1969), 67

_____, The Unfinished Business of the Warren Court, 46 Wash. L. Rev. 3 (1970), 496

Black, J., Religious Liberty in Essays and Speeches of Jeremiah S. Black (C. Black ed., 1885), 1454

Blacksher, Majority Black Districts, Kiryas Joel, and Other Challenges to American Nationalism, 26 Cumb. L. Rev. 407 (1996), 615

Blackstone, W., Commentaries on the Law of England (1765), 901

_____, Commentaries on the Law of England (1769), 562, 1011, 1103

Blasi, The Checking Value in First Amendment Theory, 1977 Am B. Found. Res. J. 521, 1018, 1325

_____, The First Amendment and the Ideal of Civic Courage: The Brandeis Opinion in Whitney v. California, 29 Wm. & Mary L. Rev. 653 (1988), 1040, 1043

_____, Free Speech and Good Character: From Milton to Brandeis to the Present, in L. Bellinger and G. Stone, Eternal Vigilance: Free Speech in the Modern Era (2002), 1018

_____, The Pathological Perspective and the First Amendment, 85 Colum. L. Rev. 449 (1985), 1058, 1153

_____, Prior Restraints on Demonstrations, 68 Mich. L. Rev. 1481 (1970), 1107

_____, Toward a Theory of Prior Restraint: The Central Linkage, 66 Minn. L. Rev. 11 (1981), 1110

Blasi, V, ed., The Burger Court: The Counterrevolution That Wasn't (1983), 75

_____, Press Subpoenas: An Empirical and Legal Analysis, Study Report of the Reporters' Committee on Freedom of the Press, 1403

Blasi and Shiffrin, The Real Story of West Virginia Board of Education v. Barnette, in Dorf, ed., Constitutional Law Stories 433 (2004), 1077

Bloch, S., V. Jackson, and T. Krattenmaker, Inside the Supreme Court: The Institution and Its Procedures (2d ed. 2008), 174

Bloustein, The First Amendment and Privacy: The Supreme Court Justice and the Philosopher, 28 Rutgers L. Rev. 41 (1974), 1137, 1138

_____, The Origin, Validity, and Interrelationships of the Political Values Served by Freedom of Expression, 33 Rutgers L. Rev. 372 (1981), 1019

Bobbitt, P., Constitutional Fate (1982), 232

Fiss, O., The Civil Rights Injunction (1978), 1110

Flack, H., The Adoption of the Fourteenth Amendment (1908), 728

Fleming, The Balkanization of Originalism, 67 Md. L. Rev. 10 (2007), 720

Fletcher, The Structure of Standing, 98 Yale L.J. 221 (1988), 137

Flexner, E., Century of Struggle (1975), 651

Flynn, Transforming the Debate: Why We Need to Include Transgender Rights in the Struggles for Sex and Sexual Orientation Equality, 101 Colum. L. Rev. 392 (2001), 670

Foley, Equal-Dollars-Per-Voter: A Constitutional Principle of Campaign Finance, 94 Colum. L. Rev. (1994), 1365

Foner, E., Free Soil, Free Labor, Free Men: The Ideology of the Republican Party before the Civil War (1970), 470

Frank and Munro, The Original Understanding of "Equal Protection of the Laws," 1972 Wash. U. L.Q. 421, 490, 728

Frankenberg, E., G. Hawley, J. Ee, and G. Orfield, Southern Schools: More Than a Half Century After the Civil Rights Revolution (May 2017), 507

Frankfurter, John Marshall and the Judicial Function, 69 Harv. L. Rev. 217 (1955), 66

Franklin, The Anti-Stereotyping Principle in Constitutional Law, 85 N.Y.U. L. Rev. 83 (2010), 674

Frazier, E.F., The Negro in the United States (1949), 489

Freedman, The Misguided Search for the Constitutional Definition of "Religion," 71 Geo. L.J. 1519 (1983), 1447

Freund, Political Libel and Obscenity, 42 F.R.D. 491 (1966), 1126

_____, The Supreme Court and Civil Liberties, 4 Vand. L. Rev. 533 (1951), 1103, 1112

Freund, P., On Understanding the Supreme Court (1949), 756

Friedman and Lakier, "To Regulate," Not "To Prohibit": Limiting the Commerce Power, 2012 Sup. Ct. Rev. 255 (2013), 216

Friendly, The Dartmouth College Case and the Public-Private Penumbra, 12 Tex. Q. No. 2, at 17 (1969), 1541

Froomkin, The Imperial Presidency's New Vestments, 88 Nw. U. L. Rev. 1346 (1994), 445

Galanter, M., Competing Equalities (1985), 616

_____, Law and Society in Modern India (1989), 616

Gard, Fighting Words as Free Speech, 58 Wash. U. L.Q. 531 (1980), 1079

Garfield, Protecting Children from Speech, 57 Fla. L. Rev. 565 (2005), 1169

Garnett, Religion, Division, and the First Amendment, 94 Geo. L.J. 1667 (2006), 1468

Garrett, Institutional Lessons from the 2000 Presidential Election, 29 Fla. St. U. L. Rev. 975 (2001), 167

Garrison, W., Witness to America (S. Ambrose & D. Brinkley eds., 1999), 467

Garvey, An Anti-Liberal Argument for Religious Freedom, 7 J. Contemp. Legal Issues 275 (1996), 1444–1445, 1509

Gedicks, The Normalized Free Exercise Clause, 75 Ind. L.J. 77 (2000), 1507, 1520

_____, The Rhetoric of Church and State: A Critical Analysis of Religion Clause Jurisprudence (1995), 1489

Gellman and Looper-Friedman, Thou Shall Use the Equal Protection Clause for Religion Cases (Not Just the Establishment Clause), 10 U. Pa. J. Const. L. 666 (2008), 1524

Gerhardt, M., The Federal Impeachment Process: A Constitutional and Historic Analysis (1996), 432

Gerken, Justice Kennedy and the Domains of Equal Protection, 121 Harv. L. Rev. 104 (2007), 632

Gewirtz, Privacy and Speech, 2001 Sup. Ct. Rev. 139, 1138

_____, Remedies and Resistance, 92 Yale L.J. 585 (1983), 496, 504

Gey, The Apologetics of Suppression: The Regulation of Pornography as Act and Idea, 86 Mich. L. Rev. 1564 (1988), 1168

_____, A Few Questions about Cross Burning, Intimidation, and Free Speech, 80 Notre Dame L. Rev. 1287 (2005), 1238

_____, The Nuremberg Files and the First Amendment Value of Threats, 78 Tex. L. Rev. 541 (2000), 1141

Gianella, Religious Liberty, Nonestablishment, and Doctrinal Development, 80 Harv. L. Rev. 1381 (1967), 81 Harv. L. Rev. 513 (1968), 1441

Gibson, W., Aliens and the Law (1940), 700

Gill, The Shaping of Race Relations by the Federal Judiciary in Court Decisions, 11 Negro Educ. Rev. 15 (1960), 506

Ginsburg, Sexual Equality under the Fourteenth and Equal Rights Amendments, 1979 Wash. U. L.Q. 161, 651

_____, Some Thoughts on Autonomy and Equality in Relation to Roe v. Wade, 63 N.C. L. Rev. 375 (1985), 843, 912

Glaeser and Sunstein, Does More Speech Correct Falsehoods?, 43 J. Legal Stud. 65 (2014), 1044

Glennon, R., and J. Nowak, A Functional Analysis of the Fourteenth Amendment "State Action" Requirement, 1976 Sup. Ct. Rev. 221, 1535

Goldberg, Equality without Tiers, 77 S. Cal. L. Rev. 481 (2004), 637, 718

Lincoln, A., First Inaugural Address, Mar. 4, 1861, in 6 Messages and Papers of the Presidents (J. Richardson ed., 1900), 48

_____, Special Session Message (July 4, 1861), in 7 A Compilation of the Messages and Papers of the Presidents (1917), 23

Liu, "History Will Be Heard": An Appraisal of the *Seattle/Louisville* Decision, 2 Harv. L. & Poly. Rev. 53 (2008), 632

_____, Rethinking Constitutional Welfare Rights, 61 Stan. L. Rev. 203 (2008), 713

Locke, J., The Second Treatise of Civil Government, 989

Lockhart, Escape from the Chill of Uncertainty: Explicit Sex and the First Amendment, 9 Ga. L. Rev. 533 (1975), 1181

Lockhart and McClure, Literature, the Law of Obscenity, and the Constitution, 38 Minn. L. Rev. 295 (1954), 1169

Lopez, Undocumented Mexican Migration: In Search of a Just Immigration Law and Policy, 28 UCLA L. Rev. 615 (1981), 696

Lowi, T., The End of Liberalism (2d ed. 1980), 378

_____, The Personal President (1985), 21

Lund, The Unbearable Rightness of Bush v. Gore, 23 Cardozo L. Rev. 1219 (2002), 169

Lupu, Government Messages and Government Money: *Santa Fe, Mitchell v. Helms*, and the Arc of the Establishment Clause, 42 Wm. & Mary L. Rev. 771 (2001), 1492–1493

_____, The Lingering Death of Separationism, 62 Geo. Wash. L. Rev. 230 (1994), 1448, 1520

Lupu and Tuttle, Sites of Redemption: A Wide-Angle Look at Government Vouchers and Sectarian Service Providers, 18 J.L. & Pol. 539 (2002), 1492

Lusky, Footnote 4 Redux: A *Carolene Products* Reminiscence, 82 Colum. L. Rev. 1087 (1982), 542, 701, 769

Maass, A., Congress and the Common Good (1983), 71

MacKinnon, Not a Moral Issue, 2 Yale L. & Soc. Poly. Rev. 321 (1984), 1238

_____, Pornography, Civil Rights, and Speech, 20 Harv. C.R.-C.L. L. Rev. 1 (1985), 1239

_____, Roe v. Wade: A Study in Male Ideology in Abortion — Moral and Legal Perspectives (J. Garfield ed., 1985), 843

MacKinnon, C., Feminism Unmodified: Discourses on Life and Law (1987), 670

Madison, J., Memorial and Remonstrance, 1436

_____, Letter to Thomas Jefferson, Feb. 4, 1790, in The Mind of the Founder 232 (M. Meyers ed., 1969), 74

Magarian, Justice Stevens, Religion, and Civil Society, 2011 Wis. L. Rev. 733, 1523

_____, The Marrow of Tradition: The Roberts Court and Categorical First Amendment Speech Exclusions, 56 Wm. & Mary L. Rev. 1339 (2015), 1195

_____, Religious Argument, Free Speech Theory, and Democratic Dynamism, 86 Notre Dame L. Rev. 119 (2011), 1478

Magleby, D., Direct Legislation (1991), 21

Maier, Ratification: The People Debate the Constitution, 1787–1788 (2010), 22

Maine, H., Popular Government (1885), 953

Maltz, Some New Thoughts on an Old Problem — The Role of the Intent of the Framers in Constitutional Theory, 63 B.U. L. Rev. 353 (1981), 720

Manning, Separation of Powers as Ordinary Interpretation, 124 Harv. L. Rev. 1939 (2011), 433

Mansbridge, J., Why We Lost the ERA (1986), 74

Marcus, M., Truman and the Steel Seizure Case: The Limits of Presidential Power (1977), 389

Marshall, T., Commentary: Reflections on the Bicentennial of the United States Constitution, 101 Harv. L. Rev. 1 (1987), 23, 467

Marshall, W., False Campaign Speech and the First Amendment, 53 U. Pa. L. Rev. 285 (2004), 1127

Mashaw, The Supreme Court's Due Process Calculus for Administrative Adjudication in Mathews v. Eldridge: Three Factors in Search of a Theory of Value, 44 U. Chi. L. Rev. 28 (1976), 943, 944

Mashaw, J., Due Process in the Administrative State (1985), 944

Masur, Probability Thresholds, 92 Iowa L. Rev. 1293 (2007), 1058

Matsuda, Public Response to Racist Speech: Considering the Victim's Story, 87 Mich. L. Rev. 2320 (1989), 1220

Mayton, From a Legacy of Suppression to the "Metaphor of the Fourth Estate," 39 Stan. L. Rev. 139 (1986), 1012

McAllister, Funeral Picketing Laws and Free Speech, 55 U. Kan. L. Rev. 575 (2007), 1261

McCloskey, Economic Due Process and the Supreme Court: An Exhumation and Reburial, 1962 Sup. Ct. Rev. 34, 767

McCloskey, R., The American Supreme Court (1960), 34

McConnell, Accommodation of Religion, 1985 Sup. Ct. Rev. 1, 1506, 1518

_____, Accommodation of Religion: An Update and a Response to the Critics, 60 Geo. Wash. L. Rev. 685 (1992), 1518

_____, Comment, Institutions and Interpretation: A Critique of City of Boerne v. Flores, 111 Harv. L. Rev. 153 (1997), 342, 352, 476, 479

Index